GOOD BEER GUIDE 2009

Edited by
Roger Protz

Project Co-ordinator
Emma Haines

Assistant Editors
Ione Brown and Joanna Bradshaw

Managing Editor
Simon Hall

Campaign for Real Ale
230 Hatfield Road, St Albans,
Hertfordshire AL1 4LW

Contents

Editorial Assistance: Katie Hunt

Special thanks to 92,000 CAMRA members who carried out research for the pubs; Rick Pickup and Steve Westby for advising on new breweries; the Campaign's Regional Directors, who coordinated the pub entries; Paul Moorhouse for assembling the beer tasting notes; Michael Slaughter for checking pubs on the National Inventory; Marc Holmes for compiling the list of beer festivals; and CAMRA's National Executive for their support.

Thanks also to the following at CAMRA head office: Chief Executive Mike Benner; Campaigns, Marketing and Public Affairs: Louise Ashworth, Tom Blakemore, Kim Carvey, Jon Howard, Tony Jerome, Iain Loe, Jonathan Mail, Stuart South; What's Brewing: Claire-Michelle Pearson, Tom Stainer; Administration: Caroline Clerembeaux, Gillian Dale, Cressida Feiler, Robert Ferguson, Gary Ranson, Nicky Shipp; Membership Services: Debbie Campion, John Cottrell, Gary Fowler; Finance and Branch Support: Anita Gibson, Liz McGlynn, Malcolm Harding; Warehouse: Andy Camroux, Kate Camroux, Steve Powell, Ron Stocks.

Photo credits: Geoff Brandwood: p28 (t, bl, brc, br), p29 (bl, br); Michael Slaughter: p28 (blc), p29 (t, bc). All other photographs credited where they appear.

Production: Cover design: James hall; colour section design and origination of the Guide: Keith Holmes, Thames Street Studio; database, typesetting and beers index: AMA Dataset, Preston, Lancs; maps by David and Morag Perrott, PerroCarto, Machnylleth, Wales; Printed by William Clowes, Beccles, Suffolk.

Published by the Campaign for Real Ale Ltd, 230 Hatfield Road, St Albans, Herts, AL1 4LW. Tel 01727 867201. Email: camra@camra.org.uk Website: www.camra.org.uk

ISBN 978-1-85249-249-6

Real ale – the beer with bite

Craft brewers' sales are booming and choice never been greater, while CAMRA membership stands at an all-time high of 92,000

In June 2007, membership of the Campaign for Real Ale reached 92,000. During the lifetime of this edition of the *Good Beer Guide*, it's likely that CAMRA will arrive at the magic milestone of 100,000, making it the biggest single-issue consumer movement in the world. This is not idle back-slapping on our part. The continued growth of the Campaign stands as testimony to the fact that an increasing number of pub-goers prefer craft-brewed beers made with wholesome barley malt and whole hops. They reject the bland offerings of global brewers who pack their computer-controlled vessels with rice, maize, hop oils and other cheap ingredients that are often flown great distances. The demand for 'local beer for local people' takes on an added dimension as we carefully count our air miles and carbon footprints.

The number of CAMRA beer festivals, both national and local, grows year by year. Beer is also emerging from the shadow cast by wine at many other events, including the BBC's food and drink shows, A Taste of London, Beers of the World Live and the Cheltenham Food & Drink Festival. Increasingly, experts from CAMRA, the British Guild of Beer Writers and the Beer Academy are called upon to lecture and run beer tastings. Even television, which has largely ignored beer since the late Michael Jackson's seminal Beer Hunter series 18 years ago, is now showing some welcome interest in the subject, albeit on minority channels.

Graham Trott, of Triple fff brewery in Hampshire, has gone from a five-barrel plant to new fifty-barrel one

Alongside CAMRA, the Society of Independent Brewers (SIBA) is also a vigorous flag-waver for cask beer. When it was launched in 1980, SIBA was laughed to scorn by most other brewers. "It won't last... they don't know what they're doing... and they don't know how to brew" were some of the kinder remarks made at the time. Today, SIBA has some 450 members. As the Breweries section of this Guide proves, they are a power in the land. The SIBA annual conference is not only packed with enthusiastic brewers but also by the manufacturers of brewing equipment and casks, who clearly see where their bread is being buttered. SIBA runs its own beer festivals and competitions, and its relentless campaigning achieved a major breakthrough when the government agreed in 2002 to introduce Progressive Beer Duty that enables smaller brewers to pay less tax than bigger producers.

Not all small brewers are members of SIBA: some are so tiny, just pub-breweries serving one outlet, that they don't see the need to join the club. The total number of micros is estimated to stand at around 550. This means that Britain has more small craft breweries per head of population than any other country. Even the term 'micro' has little meaning when many SIBA members can boast sizeable volumes of beer produced each year. Many long-standing regional and family-owned brewers, who feel unloved and unwanted in the British Beer and Pub Association that is dominated by global brewers and national pub companies, have joined SIBA. When the likes of Fuller's and Marston's apply for membership it's clear the beer worm has turned and has created a deal of upturned earth in the process.

The global brewers can scoff and claim they spill more beer than the totality of small brewers make. But that's not the point. Size is not everything and quality is now in the ascendancy. In 2007, sales of Stella Artois, Britain's biggest-selling premium [sic] lager fell by 10 per cent while the average increase in sales for SIBA members in the same year was 11 per cent. The beer revolution is about more than just sales, however. CAMRA and SIBA have jointly created an interest in beer that has broken for ever the cosy world in which cask ale meant no more than Mild, Bitter and a stronger brew for Christmas. Walk into any beer festival run by either organisation and you will find that Mild and Bitter have been joined by a profusion of old and new styles: golden ales, harvest ales, old ales, barley wines, true IPAs, Porters and Stouts. Sometimes the pace of change is breath-taking as brewers, starting in Scotland but now spreading to England, produce oak-aged beers matured in whisky casks.

Jaclyn and Stuart Bateman

Booming from Lancs to Lincs to London

Bateman's Brewery in Wainfleet in Lincolnshire proves that increased production of cask beer is not confined merely to the new breed of craft brewers. It's a family-owned company founded in 1874 to mainly serve a small farming community but it now has 64 pubs and national free trade sales. It reported its most successful year ever in 2007. Managing director Stuart Bateman says that beer volumes were up, turnover was up, profits were up and the number of visitors to the brewery museum were also up. Sales of cask beer grew by 10 per cent and all the major brands – including XXXB, CAMRA Champion Beer of Britain – are in growth. Twenty-one of Bateman's pubs are showing 'significant growth' in spite of the smoking ban and the increase in beer duty announced in the 2008 Budget.

Artist's impression of Moorhouse's new brewery

Bateman's only struggle is keeping pace with demand. A new brewhouse called the Theatre of Beer opened in 2002 and can produce 30,000 barrels a year. The company needs to increase this output to 40,000 but will have to find space for additional fermenting vessels. Following the death of chairman George Bateman and his wife and fellow director Patricia, the brewery is now in the hands of their son and daughter, MD Stuart and marketing director Jaclyn. They have enormous passion for the brewery and its beers. They dispel the notion that family companies eventually run out of descendants with the commitment to keep them going. Bateman's is a brewery with a sound future as well as proud past.

Moorhouse's of Burnley, Lancashire, also plans to produce 40,000 barrels a year by 2010. The new volumes will mark an astonishing move from failed micro to sizeable regional brewer. The company was founded in 1865 but, for most of its life, it produced soft drinks and non-alcoholic 'hop bitters'. It started to brew proper beer in 1978 but went through a series of owners who couldn't make a success of the venture. It was saved in 1987 by Bill Parkinson, who made his fortune from Lifting Gear Hire, a firm most famous for raising the stricken Russian submarine *Kursk* with its crew from the seabed in 2000. Bill enjoyed drinking Moorhouse's Pendle Witches Brew in his local pub. One evening he was told it might be the last pint he would drink as the brewery was about to fold. Bill, following in the footsteps of the man who liked Remington razors so much he bought the company, became the owner of the Burnley brewery. The transaction took one week. Bill hired David Grant from Marston's and they have combined to move the brewery from the edge of the abyss to an expansion that will cost £3 million. Along the way they picked up CAMRA's Champion Beer of Britain award in 2000 for Black Cat Mild, which created enormous interest in all the brewery's beers in the national free trade. The company now has six pubs of its own and is a major supplier to Wetherspoons, Marston's and Scottish & Newcastle outlets. The four-percent Pride of Pendle is the company's biggest brand but the addition of a golden ale, Blond Witch, has been a remarkable success. "Lager drinkers are moving over to it in droves," David Grant says. Echoing CAMRA and the Guide, he adds: "We brew local beer for local people in local pubs. Consumers are concerned about carbon footprints, so why is beer brewed millions of miles away and trunked all round the world?"

In London, the Meantime Brewery is determined to fill the void left by Young's of Wandsworth. Meantime, run by master brewer Alastair Hook, who trained at both Heriot-Watt in Edinburgh and the world-famous brewing faculty of Munich University, has carved out a unique path for a British craft brewery. He concentrates on recreating great European beer styles, such as Bavarian wheat, Pilsener, Kölsch and Vienna Red. But based close to the original homes of both London Porter and India Pale Ale in the East End, he has added two brilliant interpretations of these styles in bottle-conditioned format. He now plans to move from his cramped site near Charlton Athletic football ground to a bigger one in the Greenwich area, where he will be able to double annual production to 15,000 barrels.

But, he is not content with one new brewery. In a dramatic development, Alastair has reached agreement with the Greenwich Foundation to excavate and renovate a small brewery that once supplied beer to the Royal Naval College between 1717 and 1860. Beers were brewed for retired or injured sailors and in that period would almost certainly have included a London Porter. Alastair plans to recreate an 18th-century Porter and will include Brettanomyces yeast. That is a wild strain that inoculated maturing Porter when it was stored for long periods in wooden vats. The wild yeast adds a sour and lactic flavour. Further recreations of old London beer styles will follow.

No longer Tiny Tim

July 2008 marked the 150th anniversary of Timothy Taylor's brewery in Keighley. This iconic Yorkshire company was born at a time when the small West Yorkshire mill town had an abundance of small breweries. Taylor's has survived as a result of an abiding belief in quality plus the good fortune to win CAMRA's Champion Beer of Britain award for Landlord Bitter three times. It has a small tied estate of around 30 pubs but has built up substantial free trade throughout the country.

In sharp distinction from giant brewers who compromise over ingredients, Taylor's never deviates from using pure water from the local Knowle Spring – so pure that former chairman John Taylor (Lord Ingrow) kept a supply at home to blend with his whisky – Golden Promise barley from Scotland, English Fuggles and Goldings whole hops, and Styrian Goldings from Slovenia. Each batch of Landlord circulates over a deep bed of Styrians, which gives the beer its distinctive floral and citrus character.

Charles Dent, Taylor's managing director

In the past 10 years a total of £10 million has been invested in expanding the brewing capacity. New fermenting vessels were installed in 2000 but still demand outstripped supply. Four additional fermenters were added in 2003 along with a temperature-controlled store house and automated cask-filling lines. Since 1990, annual production has risen from 30,000 barrels to 60,000. The singer Madonna has named Landlord her favourite beer, which she drinks in the Dog & Duck in London's Soho. Taylor's has resisted the temptation to market Landlord as 'a material beer'.

Marston's on the march

It is a sad reflection on the state of the modern brewing industry that success all too often leads to takeover and the snuffing out of independent ownership. This has been the case with two breweries in the south of England. Ringwood in Hampshire was an exemplar, the tiniest of micros set up in an old baker's shop in 1978 that moved to a former brewery site and grew to an impressive 35,000 barrels a year. The excellence of the beers, including the award-winning Old Thumper, plus a genuine abundance of free trade in the area attracted the attention of Marston's.

Not content, Marston's turned its sights on Refresh UK, based in Witney, Oxfordshire. The company owns two breweries that share the same site, Wychwood and Brakspear. Refresh won a legion of admirers for rescuing the brewing kit from Brakspear's historic brewery in Henley-on-Thames. Brakspear uses a now-unique 'double drop' fermentation system built around two-storey vessels: fermentation starts in the top storey and the liquid is then dropped to the vessels below, leaving behind dead yeast cells and unwanted protein. The result is a clean and fast second fermentation that produces a beer with another unique characteristic: a delicious hint of butterscotch. When Henley closed, the beer was briefly brewed at Burtonwood in Cheshire and the singular flavour of the beer disappeared. Refresh, under Rupert Thompson, not only bought the brands but also the Henley equipment and patiently re-assembled it at Witney. Using the original recipe and with a water supply almost identical to Henley's, Brakspear Bitter was restored to its former glory.

It's likely, however, that Marston's desire to buy Refresh was based more on the success of Wychwood's Hobgoblin than Brakspear. Hobgoblin is a

ALISTAIR IS NOBODY'S DARLING

The government seems determined to drive nails into the brewing industry's and pub trade's coffins. Alistair Darling's increase in excise duty in his 2008 Budget meant, by the time beer reached the pub bar, around 20 pence on the price of a pint. This came at a time when many pubs were already reeling from the impact of the smoking ban.

Darling's ham-fisted decision handed more power to supermarkets and encourages binge drinking, which is mainly fuelled by cheap supermarket booze. The supermarket attitude to the duty increase was simple: they told brewers not to pass it on. The Bargain Booze chain of specialist stores wrote to all its suppliers with a simple message: absorb the duty increase or don't bother to supply us.

To prove its responsible attitude to alcohol retailing, Tesco now offers cheap booze on-line. This means the group has no control over who buys its products. But, hey, watch the profits soar as young, possibly under-age drinkers soak themselves in cheap vodka and then go on the rampage in town centres at weekends.

The Morning Advertiser, a weekly trade paper for pubs and brewers, ran a campaign to ban Alistair Darling from every pub in the country. It has never had such a massive a response to a campaign in its history.

beer that defies the 'logic' of modern beer marketing. It's a dark beer and, as any global brewer will tell you, nobody wants to drink dark beer these days – apart that is from the growing number of drinkers who helped boost sales of Hobgoblin by 24 per cent in 2007. It's a brand that adds gloss as well as substantial income to Marston's burgeoning portfolio.

Marston's has a good track record of not closing the breweries it has bought – Jenning's of Cumbria being a case in point. But history proves that big companies have an inevitable desire to concentrate brewing in one major centre and to weed out less successful brands. The *Good Beer Guide* prefers breweries to remain in their original – and local – hands, the best promise of continuing independence.

Caledonian... now owned by Dutch lager brewer Heineken

Turbulence at the top

Seasoned users of the Guide will be shocked to find that the Caledonian Brewing Co in Edinburgh, producer of the award-winning Deuchars IPA, is no longer listed under Independents in the Breweries section. That's because – take a deep breath – it is now owned by Heineken, the global Dutch brewer. Early in 2008, Carlsberg and Heineken combined to buy Britain's biggest brewer, Scottish & Newcastle. Carlsberg now controls S&N's interests in Russia, the Baltic and France. Heineken owns S&N's British interests, which includes Caledonian. As Heineken's knowledge of the ale market could be written on the back of a small beer mat, the future for S&N's ale brands is a cause for concern. Fortunately, Deuchar's is a pale, golden colour and the Dutch may mistake it for lager. At the time of going to press, Heineken had not decided whether to continue to call the group S&N or adopt the ubiquitous global image. But, make no mistake, the bosses wear clogs.

Harviestoun brewery, previously a subsidiary of Caledonian, is now a stand-alone independent.

Keeping it local

Nottingham initiative is a boost for craft brewers

A quiet campaign called LocAle that started in Nottingham to boost local brewers and save on 'beer miles' has been taken up with enthusiasm in other parts of the country. Steve Westby, a tireless worker in the Nottingham branch of CAMRA, masterminded LocAle and was granted national recognition for his work with the first-ever Campaigner of the Year award at CAMRA's annual general meeting in 2008.

The inspiration for LocAle was the takeover in 2007 of Hardys & Hansons, the much-loved family brewery in Kimberley, by Greene King. Suddenly, drinkers in Nottinghamshire and surrounding counties found that not only did 'Kimberley' beers no longer taste the same but they were being trucked hundreds of miles to the Midlands from Suffolk, where Greene King is based. Steve Westby and his colleagues thought this was misleading for drinkers and damaging to the environment, with diesel fumes pumped into the atmosphere as Greene King lorries made their long journeys.

Research by CAMRA shows that foods and drink transport accounts for 25 per cent of all HGV vehicle miles in Britain. Taking into account the miles ingredients have travelled on top of distribution journeys, an imported lager produced by a multi-national brewery could have notched up more than 24,000 'beer miles'.

In Nottingham, Steve Westby's LocAle scheme asked pubs to stock at least one cask-conditioned beer that comes from a local brewery no further than 20 miles away. It further encouraged publicans to use the Direct Delivery Scheme run by SIBA, the Society of Independent Brewers, which means craft breweries can deliver direct to their local pubs instead of going through the central warehouses of pub-owning companies.

Supporters of LocAle point out that £10 spent on locally-supplied goods generates £25 for the local economy. Keeping trade local helps local enterprises, creates more economic activity and local jobs and makes other local services more viable. The scheme will also generate consumer support for local breweries.

To help publicans, branches that support LocAle – which has spread to Sheffield and York – supply lists of local breweries and the beers they produce. The Sheffield branch of CAMRA has identified seven craft breweries that fall within a radius of 20 miles of the city.

Pubs that sign up to LocAle will be given window stickers, posters and leaflets in order that pub-goers can learn more about the scheme. One of the key aims of LocAle is to give greater prominence to local craft-brewed ales that are often overlooked by pub companies. The 'pubcos' promote heavily-discounted national brands that endure long journeys, with further damage to the environment.

LocAle, on the other hand, promotes local beers and makes an important contribution to cutting down on greenhouse gases. See **www.camra.org.uk** for links to participating CAMRA branches.

Fine locals that won't lie down

In town and country, drinkers are rising up to save pubs threatened with the axe and loss of good ale

The Live and Let Live is a special pub: perched high on the bracken-clad expanse of Bringsty Common in Herefordshire, with views across woodlands towards the distant Malvern Hills, the 17th-century, Grade II-listed ex-cider house lies at the heart of a dispersed community of only 90 houses. Today, it seems inconceivable that someone would wish to convert it into a private house, but back in the late summer of 1996 the locals were shocked to the core when the owner announced that a planning application had been made to do exactly that.

The locals were quickly galvanised and, with the help of CAMRA, established the Bringsty Action Group to fight to save their pub. They also decided to attempt to raise the money to buy it themselves. With the help of individual CAMRA members, following publicity in *What's Brewing*, £158,000 was raised in less than six months – more than enough to buy and refurbish the pub, and a sum equivalent to more than £200,000 today.

But that wasn't the end of the story. The owner declined to sell the pub to the locals' co-operative, despite their matching the £125,000 asking price. And so four bitter planning battles followed, including a failed appeal, before common sense prevailed in 2002, when the pub was sold to Sue Dovey and her family. The Live would now live on.

The pub finally re-opened after 11 long years in November 2007. Unfortunately, its fabric had been neglected and much remedial work needed to be undertaken by the new owners. Sue has been meticulous in respecting the pub's special history during this project: old timbers have been recycled where possible, and by using old photographs and speaking to older Bringsty Common residents, it was possible carefully to recreate the original Live. The crowning glory is the reinstatement of its thatched roof, something it had lost back in the 1920s.

The Live... back in business

Today, the Live & Let Live stands out as Herefordshire's only thatched pub. But more importantly it's a beacon of what can be achieved by active campaigning. For Herefordshire CAMRA it highlighted issues about claims made of 'non-viability' by pub owners in support of planning applications for conversion. Questions started to be asked. Since the Live & Let Live closed back in 1996, many battles in Herefordshire have been successfully fought and pubs saved – many of which are trading well today. It's fitting that the pub that started the fightback is back with us. **Mark Haslam**

Stoking up anger

A campaign swung into action in Stoke-on-Trent in the spring and summer of 2008 in a bid to save the GBG-listed Coachmakers Arms in Hanley. The pub is threatened with closure not by its owners or a result of lack of success but because the city council wants to demolish it to build a multi-storey car park.

The best description of the pub can be found in a local publication called *City Centre*: "The Coachmakers is a treasure that preserves the best of the past without being afraid of the future... this really is a little gem for Stoke-on-Trent to be proud of." *City Centre* is published by the self-same Stoke Council that wants to knock it down.

Coachmakers... under threat from a car park

The Coachmakers is a now rare example of a 'corridor pub', with several small rooms that radiate off the corridor where drinkers can stand and drink. As well as fine ales – the Coachmakers serves a constantly changing range of beers from small craft brewers – it offers bar skittles, crib, dominoes, open fires and, to prove the council guide's point about looking to the future, a Wi-Fi connection. Sue Grocott, who runs the pub with her partner Jason Barlow, says: "It was dying on its feet when we took over four-and-a-half years ago. All the other pubs in the area have been turned into young people's bars."

Plaques on the wall show how popular the Coachmakers is. It has won CAMRA Potteries Pub of the Year, Staffordshire Pub of the Year and the Pub Preservation Group's Community Pub of the Year. The last award was presented to Jason and Sue by the Lord Mayor of Stoke... who now wants to knock it down.

The pub won't go without a fight. A campaign group is leading the battle to save it and has won repeated coverage from the local press and BBC East Midlands. By July, an on-line petition had gained 5,500 signatures. "Hopes are high we can save it," Jason says. The Coachmakers started life as a simple beer house in the 1850s, serving a coachmaker's across the road and workers from the local potteries. It was a Bass house for many decades and is now owned by Admiral Taverns.

While Jason scours the country for new beers, his best-selling ale is Draught Bass. On Fridays, retired servicemen and Potteries workers down a few gallons of Bass.

"Nobody cares about ordinary working people any more" Jason says sadly. "Our older customers wouldn't feel comfortable in the other pubs in the area and they couldn't afford the prices."

It's not too late to sign the petition: a final decision by the council won't be taken until December 2008 see: **www.thecoachmakers.co.uk**.

Putting beer on the Spot

CAMRA's National Pub of the Year celebrates real ale – and pigs – and doesn't let food dominate beer sales

Ric Sainty looks like an Old Testament prophet with a prodigious white beard and a rubicund face. He doesn't save sinners but he did turn a "smelly and dirty pub that served more cider than beer" into a busy and successful one that now proudly proclaims the title of National Pub of the Year in the annual competition staged by CAMRA.

Old Spot's Steve Herbert

The Old Spot in Dursley, Gloucestershire, has beams, open log fires, flagstone floors, old enamel brewery signs on ceilings and walls, and a plethora of ornamental pigs on every available shelf and cubby hole, for the pub is named in honour of Gloucestershire's Old Spot breed. It has a warren of small, comfortable rooms fashioned out of a farm worker's cottage that dates from 1776. Since Ric took over, the pub has been extended into a school that stood next door.

Ric Sainty and his wife Ellie accepted the challenge in 1993 of resurrecting a failed Whitbread pub called the Fox & Hounds. It became the Old Spot and Ric joined forces with Chas Wright, founder of the Uley Brewery a couple of miles away, to sell Uley beers, including a house beer called Old Ric. "We've sold thousands of cask beers over the past 15 years," Ric says, "and we have beer festivals four times a year."

Ric is now in his 70s and is officially retired, though he still owns the pub. The Old Spot is now run by Steve and Belinda Herbert and they have built on Ric's success. Steve says a belief in traditional beer and traditional values has been tweaked to make the Old Spot a pub for the 21st century. "We've let cider back in but this is essentially an ale house. 84 per cent of our sales are ale and real ale accounts for 76 per cent of that. The smoking ban has had no impact on sales. We installed a heated garden but we did that before the ban came in."

Ric and Ellie Sainty with Steve and Berlinda Herbert and Jack the pub dog

The big change at the Old Spot is that food is now available until 9pm – in Ric's day food was restricted to lunchtime. "But it's still a pub," he insists, "a pub for beer drinkers."

Gloucestershire had a remarkably successful year in 2008. As well as the Old Spot winning CAMRA's national pub award, the Wickwar Brewery won CAMRA's Champion Winter Beer of Britain Award with its Station Porter in January while the Severn Vale Brewery at Cam won the title of Supreme Champion in March with Severn Sins in the competition run by the Society of Independent Brewers.

As the Guide went to press, we heard the sad news that Ric Sainty had died.

Great ale by the silvery Tay

The Fisherman's Tavern at Broughty Ferry has featured in 35 editions of the Guide. **Forbes Brown** reports

The Fisherman's Tavern is a pub of great antiquity. It dates from 1827 and is part of a row of two-storey cottages in Broughty Ferry near the River Tay. For beer enthusiasts it has always been a byword for quality and choice in an area where cask ale is still not common.

Before the advent of CAMRA, the owner, Dick Brodie, fought a stubborn rearguard action against the onslaught of keg beer. His family had owned the pub since the 1940's, selling Drybrough's, Lorimer & Clark's and finally McEwan's ales on handpump – unusual in Scotland where air pressure dispense was the norm.

When Dick retired in 1977, the pub was bought by Michael and Graeme Lorimer. They introduced Belhaven and Maclay's beer and built an extension to the bar. Later, the Fisherman's was run by Robert Paterson, who refurbished the pub and introduced a greater range of ales. All recognised that the customers wanted real ale: a rare attitude in Dundee in the 1980s.

In 1992, Jonathan Stewart, well-known for his enthusiasm for real ale, took over the pub. He increased the size of the staff and trained them to look after the beer. Not surprisingly, the Fisherman's went on to become joint winner of CAMRA's Pub of The Year award.

Jonathan extended the pub into a small hotel. He bought neighbouring properties, added a beer garden, where an annual beer festival is held in aid of the RNLI – lifeboat crews were among the regulars – and put tables on the street outside in summer.

In 2007, Belhaven, whose beer had always been prominent, bought the Fisherman's. Belhaven had been taken over by Greene King, which has meant an increase in the latter's beers. Otherwise, little has changed and most of the staff has been kept on.

This is a special pub because it has always sold good cask-conditioned beer despite several changes in ownership, which was seldom the case in Scotland in the early days of the real ale revival. Older drinkers remember the legendary Dick Brodie and the pioneering spirit of Jon Stewart; others just enjoy a good pint and the greatest choice of ales in the Dundee area.

Forbes Browne is a member of the Tayside branch of CAMRA

The secret's in the cellar

Real ale – a bit of fuss but no fizz

Real ale stands out from the beery crowd as a perfectly natural product. Where other types of beer, including lager, are filtered, pasteurised and pumped full of gas, real ale, or cask-conditioned beer, is allowed to ferment and mature uninterrupted, and is then served without applied gas.

All beer is the result of turning malt starch into fermentable sugar, boiling the sweet extract with hops and then fermenting the liquid into alcohol. Where cask beer is concerned, brewing begins with mashing, where barley malt and – according to recipe – other grains such as wheat, are mixed with pure hot water. Enzymes in the grain convert starch to sugar. The extract, known as wort, is boiled in a copper with hops. Hops add aroma and bitterness to beer and also keep the liquid free from infection.

The hopped wort is cooled and run into fermenting vessels. The house yeast culture is thoroughly mixed, or pitched, with the liquid. Yeast converts the sugars in the liquid to alcohol and at the same time creates natural carbon dioxide. Out of concern for the environment, brewers trap the gas for re-use and don't allow it to be released into the atmosphere.

Fermentation usually last for seven days. The unfinished, or green, beer is then held in a conditioning tank for a few days to purge itself of rough, unwanted alcohols and finally is racked into casks. According to the beer style and recipe, a handful of hops may be added to each cask – known as dry hopping – for additional aroma and bitterness, while a dosage of malt sugar may be injected to encourage a strong second fermentation in cask.

This is the major dividing line between real ale and other types of beer. Keg beers, including lager, are filtered, usually pasteurised and injected with CO_2, nitrogen or both before leaving the brewery in sealed containers. Real ale, on the other hand, arrives in the pub in unfinished form. Its cask has two openings, a bung hole at one end into which a serving tap is inserted and a shive on the top. A peg, or spile, made of porous wood is driven into the shive: as the beer continues to ferment, excess carbon dioxide escapes through the spile. It's replaced after a day by a hard spile, which stops the escape of gas in order to give the beer a natural sparkle, or condition.

Either in the brewery or pub cellar, finings made from isinglass are injected into the beer to slowly drag dead yeast cells and protein to the floor of the cask. After a day or so, the beer will drop bright, or clear, and is [illegible]wn through lines or plastic tubes by a beer engine below the bar, [illegible]at[illegible]d by a handpump. Served at a temperature of 10-11 degrees C, the [illegible] w[illegible]ool, refreshing... and natural.

Beers of the Year

The beers listed below are CAMRA's Beers of the Year 2008/2009. They were short-listed for the Champion Beer of Britain competition in August 2008, and the Champion Winter Beer of Britain competition in January 2008. The August competition judged Light and Dark Milds; Bitters; Best Bitters; Strong Bitters; Golden Ales; Speciality Beers; and Real Ale in a Bottle. The winter competition judged Old Ales and Strong Milds; Porters and Stouts; and Barley Wines. Each beer was found by a panel of trained CAMRA judges to be consistently outstanding in its category and they all receive a 'full tankard' symbol in the Breweries section.

DARK AND LIGHT MILDS

Beckstones Black Freddy
Cannon Royall Fruiterers Mild
Earl Soham Gannet
Highland Dark Munro
Rhymney Dark
Rudgate Ruby Mild
St Austell Black Prince
Vale Black Swan

BITTERS

Acorn Barnsley Bitter
Elgoods Cambridge Bitter
Evan Evans BB
Fyne Piper's Gold
Hobsons Best Bitter
Humpty Dumpty Little Sharpie
Jarrow Rivet Catcher
Lees Bitter
Matthews Brass Knocker
Purity Pure Gold
St Austell Dartmoor Best
Spire Overture
Surrey Hills Ranmore Ale
Townes Speedwell Bitter
Triple fff Alton's Pride
Yates Fever Pitch

BEST BITTERS

Cairngorm Nessies Monster Mash
Great Gable Burnmoor Pale
Hawkshead Lakeland Gold
High House Farm Nel's Best
Highland Scapa Special
Malvern Hills Black Pear
Peak Ales Bakewell Best Bitter
St Austell Proper Job
Shalford Stonely Bitter
Skinners Betty Stogs
Surrey Hills Shere Drop
Thornbridge Blackthorn Ale
Timothy Taylor Landlord
Tomos Watkin OSB
Vale VPA
Woodforde's Nelson's Revenge
Wye Valley HPA

STRONG BITTERS

Bath Ales Barnstormer
Elgoods Greyhound Strong Bitter
Fuller's ESB
Highland Orkney Blast
Kelham Island Pale Rider
Otley OG
Phoenix Wobbly Bob
Thornbridge Jaipur
Wood Wonderful

GOLDEN ALES

Highland Orkney Best
Loddon Ferryman's Gold
Otley O1
Pictish Alchemist's Ale
Salopian Golden Thread
Skinners Cornish Knocker Ale
Spire Land of Hop & Glory
Wolf Golden Jackal
Wylam Gold Tankard

OLD ALES AND STRONG MILDS

Highland Dark Munro
Purple Moose Dark Side of the Moose
Spectrum Old Stoat Wobbler
West Berkshire Maggs Magnificent Mild

PORTERS AND STOUTS

Acorn Old Moor Porter
Bazen Knoll Street Porter
Butts Blackguard
Caythorpe Stout Fellow
Elland 1872 Porter
Hop Back Entire Stout
Spitting Feathers Old Wavertonian
Spire Sgt Pepper Stout
Tomos Watkin Merlin Stout
Wickwar Station Porter
Woodforde's Norfolk Nog

BARLEY WINES

Durham Benedictus
Mighty Oak Saxon Strong
Orkney Skullsplitter
Otley O8
Robinson's Old Tom

SPECIALITY BEERS

Enville Ginger
Isle of Skye Hebridean Gold
Nethergate Umbel Magna
Otley Ogarden
Salopian Lemon Dream
Wentworth Bumble Beer

REAL ALE IN A BOTTLE

Coors Worthington's White Shield
Fuller's 1845
Shalford Stonely Bitter
Traditional Scottish Ales Ginger Explosion
Vale Black Beauty Porter
Wells & Young's Special London Ale
Wye Valley Dorothy Goodbody's Wholesome Stout

CHAMPION WINTER BEER OF BRITAIN

Wickwar Station Porter

CHAMPION BEER OF BRITAIN 2008

Triple fff Alton's Pride (Bitter, 3.8% abv)

Britain's classic beer styles

You can deepen your appreciation of cask ale and get to grips with the beers listed in the Breweries section with this run-down on the main styles available

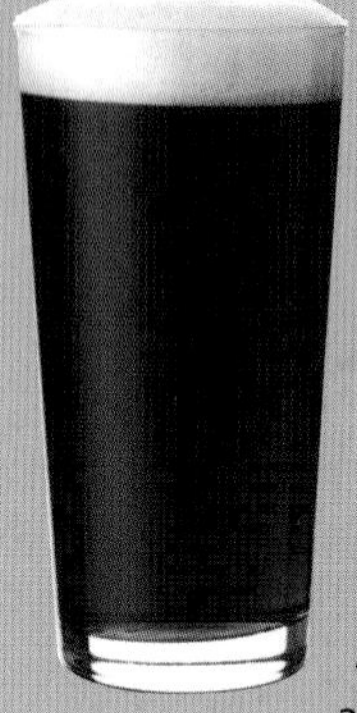

Mild

Mild was once the most popular style of beer but was overtaken by Bitter from the 1950s. It was developed in the 18th and 19th centuries as a less aggressively Bitter style of beer than Porter and Stout. Early Milds were much stronger that modern interpretations, which tend to fall in the 3% to 3.5% category, though there are stronger versions, such as Sarah Hughes' Dark Ruby. Mild ale is usually dark brown in colour, due to the use of well-roasted malts or roasted barley, but there are paler versions, such as Banks's Original, Timothy Taylor's Golden Best and McMullen's AK. Look for rich malty aromas and flavours with hints of dark fruit, chocolate, coffee and caramel and a gentle underpinning of hop bitterness.

Old Ale

Old Ale recalls the type of beer brewed before the Industrial Revolution, stored for months or even years in unlined wooden vessels known as tuns. The beer would pick up some lactic sourness as a result of wild yeasts and tannins in the wood. The result was a beer dubbed 'stale' by drinkers: it was one of the components of the early, blended Porters. The style has re-emerged in recent years, due primarily to the fame of Theakston's Old Peculier, Gale's Prize Old Ale and Thomas Hardy's Ale, the last saved from oblivion by O'Hanlon's Brewery in Devon. Old Ales, contrary to expectation, do not have to be especially strong: they can be no more than 4% alcohol, though the Gale's and O'Hanlon's versions are considerably stronger. Neither do they have to be dark: Old Ale can be pale and burst with lush sappy malt, tart fruit and spicy hop notes. Darker versions will have a more profound malt character with powerful hints of roasted grain, dark fruit, polished leather and fresh tobacco. The hallmark of the style remains a lengthy period of maturation, often in bottle rather than bulk vessels.

Bitter

Towards the end of the 19th century, brewers built large estates of tied pubs. They moved away from vatted beers stored for many months and developed 'running beers' that could be served after a few days' storage in pub cellars. Draught Mild was a 'running beer' along with a new type that was dubbed Bitter by drinkers. Bitter grew out of Pale Ale but was generally deep bronze to copper in colour due to the use of slightly darker malts such as crystal that give the beer fullness of palate. Best is a stronger version of Bitter but there is considerable crossover. Bitter falls into the 3.4% to 3.9% band, with Best Bitter 4% upwards but a number of brewers label their ordinary Bitters 'Best'. A further development of Bitter comes in the shape of Extra or Special Strong Bitters of 5% or more: familiar examples of this style include Fuller's ESB and Greene King Abbot. With ordinary Bitter, look for a spicy, peppery and grassy hop character, a powerful bitterness, tangy fruit and juicy and nutty malt. With Best and Strong Bitters, malt and fruit character will tend to dominate but hop aroma and bitterness are still crucial to the style, often achieved by 'late hopping' in the brewery or adding hops to casks as they leave for pubs.

Golden Ales

This new style of pale, well-hopped and quenching beer developed in the 1980s as independent brewers attempted to win younger drinkers from heavily-promoted lager brands. The first in the field were Exmoor Gold and Hop Back Summer Lightning, though many micros and regionals now make their versions of the style. Strengths will range from 3.5% to 5%. The hallmark will be the biscuity and juicy malt character derived from pale malts, underscored by tart citrus fruit and peppery hops, often with the addition of hints of vanilla and sweetcorn. Above all, such beers are quenching and served cool.

IPA and Pale Ale

India Pale Ale changed the face of brewing early in the 19th century. The new technologies of the Industrial Revolution enabled brewers to use pale malts to fashion beers that were genuinely golden or pale bronze in colour. First brewed in London and Burton-on-Trent for the colonial market, IPAs were strong in alcohol and high in hops: the preservative character of the hops helped keep the beers in good condition during long sea journeys. Beers with less alcohol and hops were developed for the domestic market and were known as Pale Ale. Today, Pale Ale is usually a bottled version of Bitter, though historically the styles are different. Marston's Pedigree is an example of Burton Pale Ale, not Bitter, while the same brewery's Old Empire is a fascinating interpretation of a Victorian IPA. So-called IPAs with strengths of around 3.5% are not true to style. Look for juicy malt, citrus fruit and a big spicy, peppery, bitter hop character, with strengths of 4% upwards.

Porter and Stout

Porter was a London style that turned the brewing industry upside down early in the 18th century. It was a dark brown beer – 19th-century versions became jet black – that was originally a blend of brown ale, pale ale and 'stale' or well-matured ale. It acquired the name Porter as a result of its popularity among London's street-market workers. The strongest versions of Porter were known as Stout Porter, reduced over the years to simply Stout. Such vast quantities of Porter and Stout flooded into Ireland from London and Bristol that a Dublin brewer named Arthur Guinness decided to fashion his own interpretation of the style. Guinness in Dublin blended some unmalted roasted barley and in so doing produced a style known as Dry Irish Stout. Restrictions on making roasted malts in Britain during World War One led to the demise of Porter and Stout and left the market to the Irish. In recent years, smaller craft brewers in Britain have rekindled an interest in the style, though in keeping with modern drinking habits, strengths have been reduced. Look for profound dark and roasted malt character with raisin and sultana fruit, espresso or cappuccino coffee, liquorice and molasses.

Barley Wine

Barley Wine is a style that dates from the 18th and 19th centuries when England was often at war with France and it was the duty of patriots, usually from the upper classes, to drink ale rather than Claret. Barley Wine had to be strong – often between 10% and 12% – and was stored for prodigious periods of as long as 18 months or two years. When country houses had their own small breweries, it was often the task of the butler to brew ale that was drunk from cut-glass goblets at the dining table. The biggest-selling Barley Wine for years was Whitbread's 10.9% Gold Label, now available only in cans. Bass's No 1 Barley Wine (10.5%) is occasionally brewed in Burton-on-Trent, stored in cask for 12 months and made available to CAMRA beer festivals. Fuller's Vintage Ale (8.5%) is a bottle-conditioned version of its Golden Pride and is brewed with different varieties of malts and hops every year. Expect massive sweet malt and ripe fruit of the pear drop, orange and lemon type, with darker fruits, chocolate and coffee if darker malts are used. Hop rates are generous and produce bitterness and peppery, grassy and floral notes.

Scottish Beers

Historically, Scottish beers tend to be darker, sweeter and less heavily hopped than English and Welsh ales: a colder climate demands warming beers. But many of the new craft breweries produce beers lighter in colour and with generous hop rates. The traditional, classic styles are: Light, low in strength and so-called even when dark in colour, also known as 60/-; Heavy or 70/-; Export or 80/-; and a strong Wee Heavy, similar to a barley wine and also labeled 90/-. In the 19th century, beers were invoiced according to strength, using the now defunct currency of the shilling.

Find Good Beer Guide pubs on the move – anytime, anywhere!

CAMRA is pleased to announce the launch of two hi-tech services for beer lovers – the *Good Beer Guide Mobile Edition* and *Good Beer Guide POI* sat-nav file. Together, these offer the perfect solution to pub finding on the move

Good Beer Guide goes mobile!

The *Good Beer Guide Mobile Edition* makes the ideal companion to the printed *Good Beer Guide*. Wherever you are, or wherever you are going, get information on local *Good Beer Guide* pubs, breweries and beers sent direct to your mobile phone.

Compatible with most mobile phones with Internet access, this unique service allows you to search by postcode or place name – or it will even find your current location automatically. Search results contain full information and descriptions for local pubs and breweries and tasting notes for their regular beers. Interactive maps help you navigate to your destination.

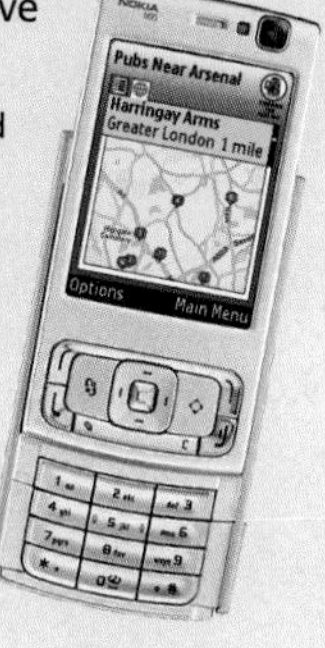

To use the service, simply text **'camra'** to **88080** (your standard network charges apply). You will then receive a text message with a web link to download the application, which will automatically install on your phone. Screen prompts help you set up and use the application, there is a clear breakdown of chrages, and full instructions are provided. Depending on the tariff, this indispensible service costs from as little as **5.5 pence per day!** (plus your standard network charges.)

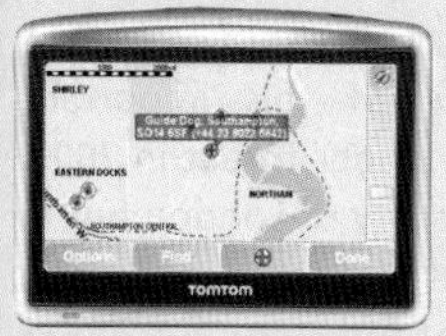

Find *Good Beer Guide* pubs using satellite navigation!

The *Good Beer Guide POI* (Points of Interest) file allows users of TomTom sat-nav systems to see the locations of all the 4,500-plus current *Good Beer Guide* pubs and plan routes to them. So, now, wherever you are, there is no excuse for not finding your nearest *Good Beer Guide* pub!

The file is simple to install and use and full instructions are provided. **Priced at just £5.00**, it is the perfect tool for any serious pub explorer. No more wasting time thumbing through road atlases or getting lost down country lanes. Navigate your way easily, every time, and make the most of Britain's best pubs.

- To download the file vist: **www.camra.org.uk/gbgpoi**

Green shoots

Hop farmers and maltsters are defending and reviving traditional varieties and are also reducing carbon footprints

Is it conceivable that a British government would seek to destroy an important element of English agriculture – the hop industry? English hops, grown mainly in Kent, Herefordshire and Worcestershire, are different to varieties grown in any other country. They are fertilised: most other hop-growing nations produce unfertilised female hops. As a result, English hops give unique aromas and flavours – piny, spicy, peppery, resinous – to British beer.

But, just as the craft brewing sector is recovering and growing, the government delivered a body blow to the future of our indigenous hops. Wye College in Kent is one of the country's oldest seats of learning. Its Department of Agricultural Sciences included a hop breeding section where new varieties of hops were developed. Wye College's work on hops was world-famous. Led by Dr Peter Darby, the hop team developed the world's first 'hedgerow hops' that grow to half the height of conventional hops – 2.5 metres (8 ft) rather than 5 metres (16 ft). This makes growing and harvesting them less labour-intensive and they also require fewer pesticides and fertilisers.

Dr Peter Darby

In addition, Dr Darby introduced a new hop variety called Boadicea that needs low levels of chemical sprays. It was the first step to developing organic hops that need no chemical sprays at all.

In spite of this important work, Wye College's future came under threat in 2000. The college was part of the University of London but in 2000 it was merged with Imperial College. In 2004, Imperial closed the Department of Agricultural Sciences while Defra, the government's Department for the Environment, Food and Rural Affairs, pulled the remaining planks away when it announced it would stop funding the hop breeding programme.

Defra's argument for removing funding was risible. It said its funds for research should not go to Wye College as its work was connected to production while Defra wants to support research that combats global

warming. But growing hops in England is closely related to tackling threats to the environment. Hops raised in Kent and the Midlands don't have to make long journeys to British breweries. An increasing volume of hops used in Britain are imported from not only mainland Europe but also as far afield as China and the United States. The bulk of organic hops used in Britain are imported from New Zealand. As Defra is worried about global warming, it might consider it beneficial to support English farmers rather than encouraging hops to be flown from the far side of the world.

Peter Darby checks his hops at Queen Court

Shorn of government backing, the hop industry has rallied round Dr Darby. He is now funded by the National Hop Association while Tony Redsell, a leading hop farmer in Kent, has provided a building at his China Farm to allow vital breeding work to continue. Shepherd Neame, the major regional brewer in Kent, has donated land at its Queen Court Farm where Dr Darby now grows traditional hop varieties. The brewery gets 20,000 visitors a year to the brewery and they will be encouraged to also visit Queen Court. A viewing platform will be built to give visitors the ability to see at close hand such historic hop varieties as Bramling Cross, East Kent Goldings and Fuggles as well as the hedgerow variety, First Gold. The hops are not intended for commercial use but as a collection – a treasure trove – of English varieties, some of which date from the 18th century.

Peter Darby, thanks to the generosity of hop farmers, is now able to continue his hop breeding programme at China Farm. He hopes that organic hops will be available within a few years – hops that will have to travel short distances within Britain rather than from New Zealand. His work marks an important contribution to the campaign to combat global warming but it's a contribution that will be lost on Defra and Imperial College. The college planned to make £100 million by building homes and commercial properties at Wye on protected countryside designated an Area of Outstanding Natural Beauty. The plan caused such local outrage that Imperial was forced to abandon it.

Turning the grain at Warminster

Barley from a farm near you

Maris Otter, a variety of malting barley that seemed destined for the scrapheap, has not only been rescued but also offers brewers the opportunity to buy direct from farms of their choice. Malt is now recognised as being as important to flavour in beer as grape varieties are to wine.

For more than 25 years, Maris Otter was the preferred malt of the brewing industry. But seed merchants developed new high yielding varieties of barley that appealed to bigger farmers and large brewers on the grounds of cost rather than flavour and character. As a result, Maris Otter was de-listed and brewers could obtain it only if it were contract-grown at a punitive price.

The loss of Maris Otter was a blow to cask beer brewers, who preferred it for its harmonious relationship with yeast and the rich biscuity character it gave to beer. Then, in the early 1990s, two seed merchants, Banhams and Robin Appel Associates, purchased the rights to market Maris Otter. Subsequently, Robin Appel bought Warminster Maltings in Wiltshire, formerly owned by Guinness, and turned it into a working shrine for Maris Otter.

Robin Appel and his team have launched a major campaign to promote the advantages of using Maris Otter. He was determined to dispel the myth, widespread in the brewing industry, that the flavour of malt does not differ from one variety to another and is used only to deliver fermentable sugar for the brewer.

The Warminster team. Below, some of the beers made with Maris Otter

He arranged with Brewing Research International to brew eight samples of beer, each one made with a different variety of malt. At the same time, he made 'beer porridge' from the eight malts and offered brewers and beer writers the opportunity to taste beer and porridge blind-fold. All those who took

part in the tastings remarked on the powerful differences they detected. Two malt varieties stood out in the tastings: Maris Otter and Optic.

Warminter Maltings has now developed a system that gives Maris Otter malt the equivalent of a French *appellation* for wine. Since 2006, brewers have been able to choose their malt from the farmer of their choice. Warminster approves farms on the basis of domain, soil type and husbandry and then supplies seeds. Each batch of barley following the harvest is tested for quality before it is turned into malt, using the slow floor-malting method. In most modern maltings, grain is packed into rotating drums and heated to convert barley into malt. In a floor maltings, the grain is spread on floors and allowed to slowly germinate before it is loaded into kilns where heat converts grain to malt. Cask beer brewers believe floor-malted grain has a juicier and more biscuity flavour as a result of the process.

Traditional rake at Warmininster

Checking Temperature

Each delivery from Warminster carries a Warranty of Origin. This enables brewers to monitor the behaviour of the malt during all the brewing and fermenting processes and to either re-order from the same farm or to seek alternatives. The end result is local beer made from local ingredients: brewers can now promote their cask ales as, for example, "Hampshire beer made from Hampshire malt".

There has been only one known objection to the work of Warminster Maltings. A writer in the journal of the Brewery History Society said he was a retired brewer and from his long experience he believed it was nonsense to claim there were any differences between one variety of malt and the next. The writer was the former head brewer at the Carlsberg lager factory in Northampton...

Roger Protz

Steaming ahead – without steam

More and more craft breweries are aiding the environment with new equipment that cuts down on wasted energy and makes better beer

"We're living in the Stone Age," Mark Woodhouse says of his family brewery in Blandford Forum, Dorset. Hall & Woodhouse dates from 1777 and much of the equipment has seen service for more than 100 years. Mash tuns and coppers are creaking at the seams, which is why the company will move to a new site by the end of the decade.

The new brewery will be fully automated and energy efficient, Mark Woodhouse says. He adds that the current plant is 93–94 per cent energy efficient but the aim will be for 98-per cent efficiency in the new site. "There will be better use of raw materials, such as malt and hops – it will mean savings of around £10 per hectolitre."

Even before the brewery moves, Hall & Woodhouse, which has a 10-per cent share of the bottled beer sector, has switched to lighter glass. With the amount of glass bottles the company handles, Mark Woodhouse says the benifit of the move "is like taking 360 cars off the the road for a year".

The St Austell Brewery in Cornwall made the headlines in 2007 when its move towards energy efficiency included managing director James Staughton swapping his executive Mercedes for a Smart Car. But head brewer Roger Ryman says the company's plans go much further and they are aided by its success in the cask beer market. "Ten years ago we were producing 15,000 barrels a year but we've grown that to 45,000 barrels. The more beer we brew, the better the utilisation of the plant."

A new steam boiler has been installed and the result is more energy and less steam pumped into the atmosphere. A malt mill dating from 1916 was only 55 per cent efficient and has been replaced by one with 85 per cent efficiency. Two new compressors in the refrigeration plant have increased efficiency by a third. Improved water management and heat recovery mean less water is used for each brew.

Employees have been heavily involved in the brewery's schemes. Focus groups have been set up in every department to consider ways to save

Look, no steam… Ian Dixon at Shepherd Neame

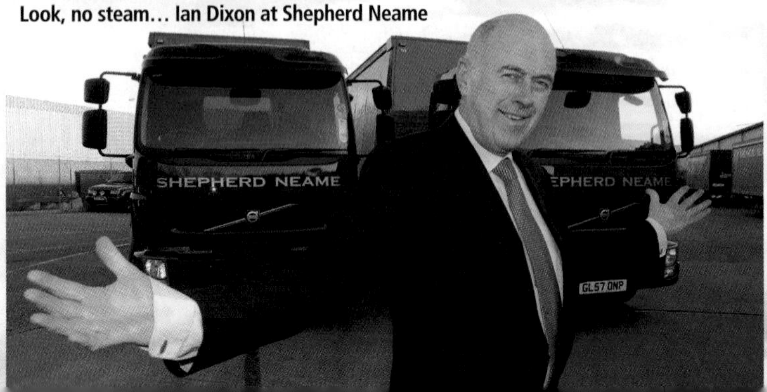

energy in brewing, distribution and the company's large estate of pubs. One important element of the policy is to source barley locally. "A quarter of our grain is grown in Cornwall and it's malted at Tucker's of Newton Abbot and Warminster," Roger Ryman says. "We will install our own bottling line in 2009. Fifteen per cent of our production is now in bottle and packaging is currently done for us by Robinson's in Stockport and Thwaites in Blackburn – both at the other end of the country. So there will be a drastic reduction in our use of diesel when we bring bottling in house. We will also move to lightweight bottles."

Adnams…
new brewhouse,
old brewery (below)

Many brewers concerned about reducing damage to the environment have been inspired by the ground-breaking work carried out by Adnams in Southwold, Suffolk. The company has invested £5.8 million in an new warehouse in the neighbouring village of Reydon, which removes delivery trucks from the narrow streets of Southwold. The warehouse complex uses solar power and collects rainwater on the roof for cleaning and even staff showers.

In Southwold, £3.7 million has been invested in a third update to the brewery in 10 years. New vessels include a mashing regime and boiling coppers that are energy efficient and environmentally friendly. The Adnams' experience has so impressed Wadworth's in Devizes that this family-owned company will follow in Southwold's footsteps with new, energy-saving equipment.

Ian Dixon, production director at Shepherd Neame, the Faversham-based family-owned brewery, welcomes visitors by pointing to the absence of steam. Steam and the smell of malt and hops were once the hallmarks of breweries but now Shepherd Neame is determined to stop both steam and carbon dioxide escaping in to the atmosphere. CO_2, a natural bi-product of fermentation, is trapped in modern fermenting vessels while steam is injected into the coppers – where the sugary extract that results from mashing is boiled with hops.

"We don't boil out the contents of the copper," Ian Dixon says. "So there's no steam leaving the brewery. We save £45,000 a year for each copper."

It's not only good news for the environment. Drinkers will get better-tasting beers as a result. Ian Dixon, named Brewer of the Year in 2008 by the Parliamentary Beer Club, explains that the new boiling regime means less caramelisation of the malt sugars. This leads to a cleaner, more flavourful beer without toffee notes.

Flying the flag for real ale...

Cask Marque's crusade for all pubs to serve the perfect pint

As cask ale grows its share of the beer market, more and more pubs are looking to use it as part of their sales proposition. This decision brings with it the responsibility of serving cask beer in great condition.

The Cask Marque Scheme

The Cask Marque accreditation scheme recognises pubs and licensees that consistently serve great beer to their customers. More than 5,000 licensees now hold the award and proudly display the Cask Marque plaque and a dated framed certificate. A list of these outlets can be found on the Cask Marque website **www.caskmarque.co.uk** or by using a unique text messaging service that will identify the two nearest outlets to your postcode (see below). You can also download a free regional guide showing the Cask Marque pubs in your area.

To gain accreditation a licensee has to pass two unannounced inspections by a qualified assessor, who is normally a brewer. The assessor will test up to six cask ales on sale for temperature, appearance, aroma and taste and each beer must pass, otherwise the inspection is failed. In subsequent years the licensee has two further visits each year, one in the summer and one in the winter. All pubs are subject to random visits at any time.

Working in the industry Cask Marque champions cask ale by:

- Along with CAMRA, helping produce the annual cask ale report 'The Intelligent Choice'
- On average delivering 30 one-day cellar management training courses per month
- Promoting cask ale to retailers through trade shows and conferences
- Advising on stocking policy and dispense equipment
- Through our Distributor Charter, which lays down best practice in the supply chain, helping to ensure that beer arrives to a licensee in the best possible condition
- Undertaking 'mystery drinker' work and cellar audits to ensure standards are being maintained

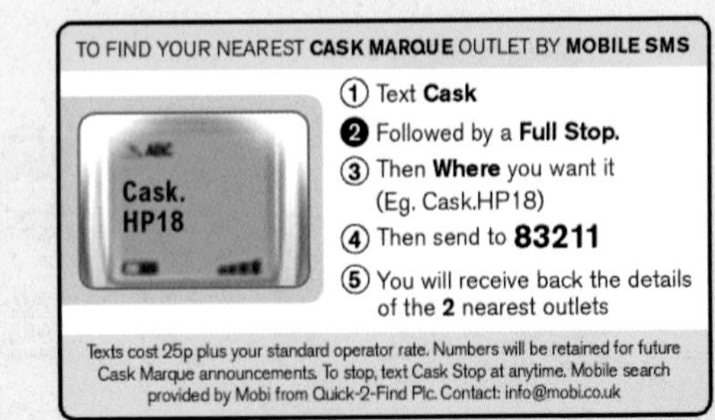

Cask Marque plaque being presented to Dominic Marriott, manager of The Warrington, by Paul Nunny and Annabel Smith in Maida Vale, London.

Cask Ale Week

Last year we ran a successful promotion with the *Daily Telegraph* encouraging consumers with a money-off voucher to visit Cask Marque outlets and vote for their favourite beer. We wish to turn this initiative into an annual event to be held each Easter and have set up a steering group which includes representation from CAMRA to maximise participation both from licensees and potential new cask ale drinkers. Do look out for the publicity on Cask Ale Week and join in the celebration.

The Cask Marque Trust is pleased to sponsor the *Good Beer Guide* for the second year in succession and you will note that our 'tick' logo now appears by the side of each pub listed in the *Good Beer Guide* that holds the Cask Marque accreditation. Always congratulate licensees on the quality of their beer and, if it is not up to expectation, do talk to the landlord. Cask Marque is happy to receive comments from cask ale drinkers either by phone, e-mail or letter.

Do help us to promote cask ale to new drinkers by raising the awareness of the Cask Marque award.

Cask Marque Trust, The Seedbed Centre, Severalls Park,
Colchester, Essex, CO4 9HT. Tel: 01206 752212.
Email: info@cask-marque.co.uk. Web: www.cask-marque.co.uk

Pubs for posterity

CAMRA detectives scour the land to save historic pubs from the planner and wreckers

Inter-war chairs and table at the Fox & Pheasant, West Brompton, London

The National Trust has announced radical plans to modernise its estate of antiquated buildings. Spokesperson Dee Stroy said, "Most of our properties are structurally sound but the interiors are, frankly, hopelessly out of date – we're going to bring them into the 21st century. As an example, many have unnecessarily small rooms. Removing a few walls will create a great contemporary open-plan feel. And as for the furniture – much of it's fit only for the antique shop."

Utterly preposterous, of course, but the actions of this fictitious NT aren't very far removed from those of our brewers and other pub owners over the past 40 years or so when it comes to their pub stock. Interiors lovingly designed and constructed to reflect the tastes of their times have been trashed in the pursuit of the fleetingly fashionable and the quick buck. Thankfully, all is not lost, though it's a pretty close call. Research by CAMRA has uncovered just 273 pubs whose interiors are sufficiently intact or which retain features exceptional enough to merit inclusion on our *National Inventory of Pub Interiors of Outstanding Historic Importance,* or NI.

Work on compiling the NI began as long ago as 1991. Since then, many pubs identified as worthy of inclusion have fallen victim either to the hand of 'improvers' or the relentless tide of pub closures. On a more positive note, even now new entries are being discovered in back streets and remote villages, having escaped the clutches of the modernisers, usually through benign neglect. CAMRA's 'pub detectives' are its Pub Heritage Group who both administer the Inventory and its regional counterparts and scour the country for possible candidates. The group also tries to raise awareness of just what fantastic places many of these pubs are to drink in as well as finding ways to protect them from spoliation. It has been successful in getting many NI pubs 'listed' under the planning laws, making it much more difficult for owners to do as they please with them.

The NI is in two parts. Part One contains pubs whose interiors have remained wholly or largely intact since World War Two or, in a few exceptional cases, up

The vast inglenook fireplace of the Philharmonic, Liverpool.

to 30 years ago. Part Two covers interiors which, though altered to a degree, retain exceptional rooms or features which are of national historic importance.

If you have access to the web, then you can enjoy virtual visits to our NI pubs at your convenience. Our site at **www.heritagepubs .org.uk** showcases all the current entries, with detailed descriptions and sumptuous photography. You can browse on maps to find NI pubs near you or where you're visiting. You can also view lists, both regional and national, which can be printed off as quick reference guides.

Should you drop into the site, or better still, the pubs themselves, what will strike you is the sheer variety of these time-capsules. They range from simple, one-room rural pubs lacking even a bar counter to late-Victorian city-centre extravaganzas; symphonies in mahogany, mirrors, stained glass and decorative tiling. Every architectural style is represented, be it Art Nouveau or Art Deco, high Gothic or post-war Brutalism. Urban back-street boozers jostle with suburban estate pubs and picture-postcard rural idylls. Most, though sadly not all, sell real ale too.

The Pub Heritage Group is currently working hard to complete the Regional Inventories (RIs). These list, in addition to NI pubs in each region, those interiors which, while too much altered for the NI, still have significant historic or architectural value. Five RIs have so far been published – for London, East Anglia, the North East, Scotland and Northern Ireland – and you can buy them from the CAMRA bookshop (**www.camra.org.uk/books**), except for the Northern Ireland guide, which is viewable only on the heritage pubs website (as are some of the other RIs). The Yorkshire RI will be the next to emerge, it is hoped by early 2009.

If you would like to help Pub Heritage Group in its efforts to save our last remaining historic pub interiors and keep yourself informed about the project, then please request our monthly e-mail update. Just send your name and e-mail address to **chairman.pubheritage@camra.org.uk**. We'd also like to hear from you if you feel that a particular pub interior deserves to be considered for either the NI or an RI, or if you know of any threat to an existing entry so that we can take what action we can. **Paul Ainsworth**

From left to right: Unique, decorative interior of the Black Friar, Blackfriars, London; magnificent late-Victorian interior of the Crown, Belfast; opulent Art Nouveau interior of the Queen's Hotel, Crouch End, London; Art Nouveau tiling at Inn 1888, Marylebone, London; snob screens at the Travellers Friend, Woodford Green, London; the tiny Oxford Bar, Edinburgh – one of the city's oldest pub interiors; curved, Art Deco bar at the Doctor Johnson, Barkingside, London.

Beer Festival Calendar 2009

THE CAMPAIGN FOR REAL ALE'S BEER FESTIVALS are magnificent shop windows for cask ale and they give drinkers the opportunity to sample beers from independent brewers rare to particular localities. Beer festivals are enormous fun: many offer good food and live entertainment, and – where possible – facilities for families. Some seasonal festivals specialise in spring, autumn and winter ales. Festivals range in size from small local events to large regional ones. CAMRA holds two national festivals, the National Winter Ales Festival in January, and the Great British Beer Festival in August; the latter features around 500 beers. The festivals listed are those planned for 2009. For up-to-date information, contact the CAMRA website: **www.camra.org.uk** and click on 'CAMRA Near You'. By joining CAMRA – there's a form at the back of the Guide – you will receive 12 editions of the campaign's monthly newspaper *What's Brewing*, which lists every festival on a month-by-month basis. Dates listed are liable to change: check with the website or *What's Brewing*.

JANUARY

National Winter Ales (Manchester)
Atherton Bent & Bongs Beer Bash
Cambridge Winter
Colchester Winter
Derby Winter
Exeter Winter
Redditch
Salisbury Winter

FEBRUARY

Battersea
Chelmsford Winter
Chesterfield
Dorchester
Dover White Cliffs Winter
Fleetwood
Gosport/Portsmouth Winter
Liverpool
Luton
Pendle
Stockton Ale & Arty
Tewkesbury Winter

MARCH

Bradford
Bristol
Burton Spring
Darlington Spring
Ely Elysian
Hitchin
Hove Sussex
Leeds
Leicester
London Drinker
Loughborough
Oldham
Overton (Hampshire)
St Neots
Walsall
Wigan

APRIL

Bexley
Bury St Edmunds East Anglian
Chippenham
Coventry
Doncaster
Farnham
Hull
Maldon
Mansfield
Newcastle-on-Tyne
Paisley
Thanet

MAY

Alloa
Banbury
Barrow Hill Rail Ale
Cambridge
Colchester
Bolsover Derbyshire Food & Drink

Halifax
Ilkeston
Glenrothes Kingdom of Fife
Lincoln
Macclesfield
Newark
Newark & Notts Show
Newport (Gwent)
Northampton Delapre Abbey
Reading
Rugby
Stockport
Stourbridge
Stratford-upon-Avon
Wolverhampton
Yapton

JUNE

Aberdeen
Braintree
Cardiff Great Welsh
Edinburgh Scottish
Kingston
Lewes South Downs
Southampton
St Ives (Cornwall)
Stafford
Thurrock
Woodchurch Rare Breeds

JULY

Ardingly
Boxmoor
Bromsgrove
Canterbury Kent
Chelmsford
Ealing
Derby
Devizes
Hereford Beer on the Wye
Plymouth
Winchcombe Cotswold
Woodcote Steam Fair

AUGUST

Great British Beer Festival (London)
Barnstaple
Clacton
Harbury
Peterborough
South Shields
Swansea
Watnall Moorgreen
Worcester

SEPTEMBER

Ascot
Birmingham
Bridgnorth Severn Valley
Burton
Chappel
Darlington Rhythm 'N' Brews
Faversham Hop
Grantham Autumn
Ipswich
Jersey
Keighley
Letchworth
Lytham
Melton Mowbray
Minehead Somerset
Nantwich
Newton Abbot South Devon
Northwich
Redcar
Rochford Cider
Saltaire
Shrewsbury
Southport
St Albans
St Ives (Cambs) Booze on the Ouse
Tamworth
Ulverston

OCTOBER

Alloa
Barnsley
Basingstoke
Bedford
Birkenhead
Chester
Eastbourne
Heathrow
Huddersfield Oktoberfest
Kendal Westmorland
Louth
Norwich
Nottingham
Poole
Redhill
Richmond (N Yorks)
Sawbridgeworth
Sheffield
Solihull
Stoke-on-Trent Potteries
Troon Ayrshire
Twickenham
Wallington
Weymouth
Worthing

NOVEMBER

Dudley
Northern Ireland
Rochford
Wakefield
Wantage
Watford
Whitchurch (Hampshire)
Woking
York

DECEMBER

Harwich
London Pig's Ear

Beer quality is the key...

How we choose pubs for the Guide

Local pubs for local people: that is the watchword of the *Good Beer Guide*. Unlike most pub guides where entries are hand-picked by a small team of full-time professionals, our Guide's strength is CAMRA's 90,000-plus members. They survey the pubs in their areas not once a year but on a regular – sometimes weekly – basis. When the Campaign's branches meet to choose their entries, democracy rules. Lists are drawn up, votes are taken and the numbers are reduced to meet the allocations for each part of the country.

It's a system that has worked well for 36 editions and singles the *Good Beer Guide* out from pub guides with fewer full entries and a low turnover from one edition to the next. The *Good Beer Guide* is unique in its methods of selection and the ability to de-list pubs between editions as a result of monthly updates in the Campaign's newspaper *What's Brewing* and on the CAMRA website.

The Guide is unique in another important way. We begin with the beer. Not thatched roofs, Turkey carpets, ciabatta sandwiches with sun-dried tomatoes, or the number of horse brasses on the stone walls. The Guide is committed to pub architecture, history, food and creature comforts, but, for us, the beer comes first. It has always been our belief that if a publican looks after his or her cask beer well then everything else in the pub – from welcome, through food, to the state of the toilets – will likely receive the same care. CAMRA branches will de-list pubs if, during the lifetime of the Guide, beer quality falls below an acceptable standard.

All CAMRA members can vote for the quality of beer in pubs throughout the country using the National Beer Scoring Scheme. The scheme uses a 0-5 scale for beer quality that can be submitted online. For more information about the scheme, go to: **www.beerscoring.org.uk**.

We are especially proud of one key aspect of the Guide: its coverage. The *Good Beer Guide* does not confine its entries to rural pubs or smart suburbs. We cover towns and cities, with pubs in abundance. But that doesn't mean we neglect rural pubs. On the contrary, CAMRA has long campaigned to save village pubs, which are often the centre of life in isolated communities. Village pubs form a vital element of the Guide, along with the many others in town, cities and suburbs. We are wedded to choice and hope to offer good pubs serving good beer in all parts of the country. We are also keen to hear from you with recommendations for possible new entries or if you feel an existing entry has fallen below expectations. See Readers' Recommendations on p887.

- You can keep your copy of the Guide up to date by visiting the CAMRA website: **www.camra.org.uk**. Click on '*Good Beer Guide*' then 'Updates to the GBG 2009' where you will find information on changes to pubs and breweries.

England

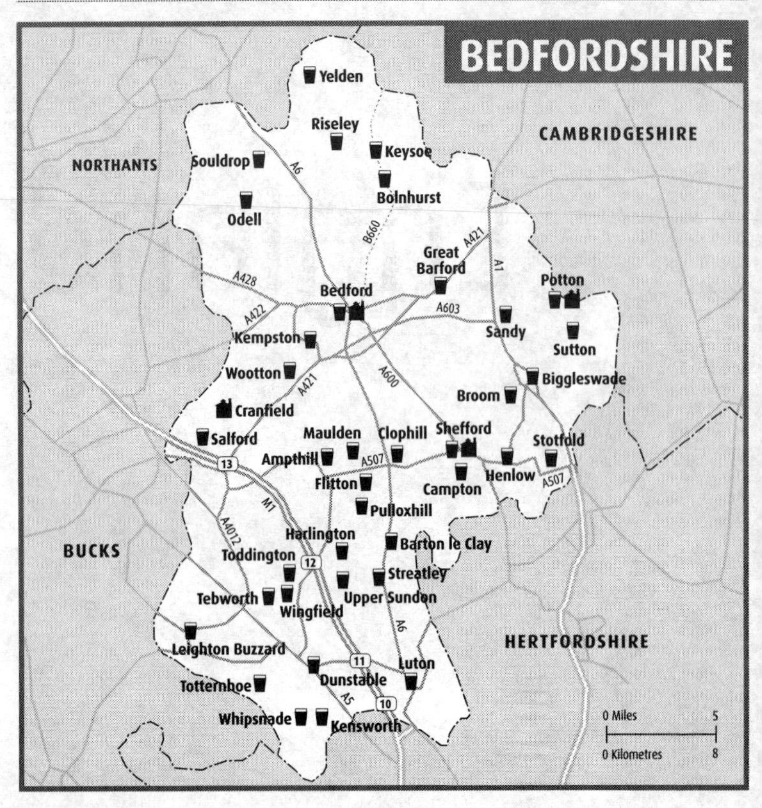

Ampthill

Old Sun

87 Dunstable Road, MK45 2NQ

12-11.30 (midnight Fri & Sat)

(01525) 405466

Adnams Bitter, Broadside; St. Austell Tribute; guest beers H

Busy and cosy establishment on Ampthill's main street with two bars plus a games room. There is a good selection of regular ales plus two guests, generally from the local Potton and B&T breweries. The walls inside feature pictures of stars of screen and stage and a real fire adds a cosy feel in winter. There are ample decked and lawned areas to the rear and tables to the front. Food is served at lunchtime. P

Barton-le-Clay

Bull

77 Bedford Road, MK45 4LL

12-2, 6-1am (2am Fri & Sat); 12-midnight Sun

(01582) 705070

Greene King IPA; St. Austell Tribute; guest beers H

Old, oak-beamed pub in the centre of the village popular with a varied clientele. Two constantly changing guest beers from the Enterprise Inns list are always on offer. Food is served on Wednesdays and Sunday afternoon. The pub has dominoes and darts teams and a pool table. A large function room is available to hire where the Barton Folk Club plays on Wednesday, with spectators welcome. Acoustic music is live in the bar every Thursday. P

Bedford

Bedford Arms

2 Bromham Road, MK40 2QA (on A428 opp Bedford Prison)

12-11 (midnight Fri & Sat); 12-10.30 Sun

(01234) 311798 bedford-arms.co.uk

Wells Eagle IPA, Bombardier; Young's Bitter, Special; guest beers H

This Charles Wells Speciality Ale House reopened in May 2007 following an extensive rebuild. Twelve handpumps dispense four regular beers alongside a changing mix of Wells & Young's and guest beers. A varied selection of English and foreign bottled beers is also available. Live music features on some weekday evenings. There is a large outside courtyard for drinking and smoking. Street parking is difficult during the day but the bus station is two minutes' walk away.

Cricketers Arms

35 Goldington Road, MK40 3LH (on A428 E of town centre)

INDEPENDENT BREWERIES

B&T Shefford
Potton Potton
Wells & Young's Bedford
White Park Cranfield (NEW)

5 (12 Sat)-11; 7-10.30 Sun
(01234) 303958 cricketersarms.co.uk
Adnams Bitter; guest beers
Small one-bar pub opposite the Bedford Blues rugby union ground, popular with fans of the game and very busy on match days. Live rugby internationals are shown on plasma screens in the wood-panelled bar and there is early opening on Sundays for live Six Nations games. The rotating guest beers are from Punch Taverns' finest cask selection so micros are rarely represented. There is a public car park almost opposite and a covered courtyard for smokers and drinkers.

Devonshire Arms

32 Dudley Street, PE28 4RA (1 mile E of town centre off A428)
5.30 (2 Fri)-11; 12-11 Sat; 12-11 Sun
(01234) 359329
Wells Eagle IPA, Bombardier; guest beers
Pleasant two-bar local in a quiet residential area east of the town centre near Russell Park and The Embankment. The landlady worked for the Charles Wells brewery for 24 years before taking over this pub so knows the trade well and hosts an annual beer festival in May. Good wine is served by the jug. The garden has a smoking area and a covered space for non smokers. Hanging baskets adorn the exterior in summer.

Three Cups

45 Newnham Street, MK40 2JR (200m S of A428 just before rugby ground)
12-11 (10.30 Sun)
(01234) 352153
Greene King XX Mild, IPA, Abbot, seasonal; guest beers
Though just five minutes from the town centre and close to Bedford rugby ground, this 1770s pub with old-style wood panelling has a village local feel and a welcoming atmosphere. A popular lunchtime menu is available with a wide range of food served in generous portions. Roast dinners feature on Sunday. The pleasant garden has a heated smoking shelter. Dogs are welcome in the public bar and garden. Quiz night is a highlight on Tuesday.

Wellington Arms

40-42 Wellington Street, MK40 2JX (off A428)
12-11 (10.30 Sun)
(01234) 308033 wellingtonarms.co.uk
Adnams Bitter; B&T Two Brewers; guest beers
Large suburban pub offering a wide range of regional and microbrewery beers, plus real cider and perry from 14 handpumps. A range of draught and bottled Belgian and imported beers is also available. Breweriana abounds throughout. Filled rolls are available. The courtyard is partly covered for drinkers and smokers. Street parking is limited bit there is a multi-storey car park adjacent. A superb mixed clientele makes this a very friendly pub to visit.

White Horse

84 Newnham Avenue, MK41 9PX (off A428)
11 (12 Sun)-11
(01234) 409306 whitehorsebedford.co.uk
Wells Eagle IPA, Bombardier; guest beers
Large suburban pub with a central bar just off the main A428, a mile east of the town centre. Good value food is on offer, with a Sunday roast and occasional themed evenings. Quiz nights are Tuesday and Sunday, and live music plays on Monday evening. The licensees and staff have won several brewery and local business awards. A May Day weekend local beer and food festival is hosted annually.

Biggleswade

Golden Pheasant

71 High Street, SG18 0JH
11-11 (midnight Fri & Sat); 12-11 Sun
(01767) 313653
Wells Eagle IPA, Bombardier; guest beers
Easy to find on the edge of the marketplace, the Pheasant has recently been refurbished to a high standard and the low oak-beamed bar is very welcoming. This Charles Wells Speciality Ale House serves a range of guest ales sourced by the landlord alongside the Wells and Young's staples. Local and not so local small independents are regularly featured, especially those from the nearby Buntingford brewery.

Stratton House Hotel

London Road, SG18 8ED
11-11 (midnight Fri & Sat)
(01767) 312442
Wells Eagle IPA, Bombardier; guest beers
Situated at the top of the High Street, this welcoming 17th-century hotel bar attracts a mixed clientele of all ages. The cosy interior features armchairs and comfortable settees. The regular beers are complemented by two guests that change every three weeks. Sparklers are fitted but cheerfully removed on request. Bar meals are served and the large restaurant is open seven days a week. The privately-run hotel has 32 letting rooms.

Bolnhurst

Plough

Kimbolton Road, MK44 2EX (on B660 at S end of village)
12-3, 6.30-11; closed Mon; 12-3 Sun
(01234) 376274 bolnhurst.com
Potton Village Bike; guest beers
Full of character, this award-winning pub restaurant offering excellent food and good service. The main bar features a modern open fireplace with a view through to the kitchen. A second room is set aside for diners. Outside is a large drinking area alongside the car park.

Broom

White Horse

30 Southill Road, SG18 9NN
12-3, 5.30 (6 Sat)-11; 12-3, 7.30-10.30 Sun
(01767) 313425 whitehorsebroom.co.uk
Greene King IPA, Abbot; guest beers
Traditional country pub looking out over the green with an open fire and exposed beams creating the feel of a real village local. The

Greene King staples are supplemented by two regularly-changing guest beers. An excellent menu of home-cooked food features local produce and the ever-popular Sunday lunch is a highlight. Camping & caravanning facilities are available at the rear of the car park.

Campton

White Hart

Mill Lane, SG17 5NX

7 (5 Fri & winter Sat)-11; 12-midnight Sat; 12-4, 7-11 Sun

(01462) 812657

Theakston Traditional Mild, Black Bull Bitter; guest beer

A Guide regular since 1976, this pub has been run by the same family for more than 38 years and offers a range of beers from Theakston and John Smith's. The 300-year-old Grade II listed free house has three bar areas with exposed brickwork, wooden beams, quarry tiled floors, inglenooks and bygone artefacts featuring throughout. The pub hosts a monthly quiz and runs several teams including darts, crib, petanque and dominoes as well as a golf society. The garden has a well-equipped play area.

Clophill

Stone Jug

10 Back Street, MK45 4BY (off A6 at N end of village)

12-3, 6-11; 12-11 Fri & Sat; 12-10.30 Sun

(01525) 860526

B&T Shefford Bitter; Fuller's London Pride; Young's Bitter; guest beers

Originally three 17th-century stone cottages, this popular village local has an L-shaped bar that serves two drinking areas and a family/function room. Excellent home-made lunches are served Tuesday to Saturday. There are picnic benches at the front and a rear patio garden for outdoor drinking in fine weather. Parking can be difficult at busy times. Bedfordshire CAMRA Pub of the Year 2006.

Dunstable

Globe

43 Winfield Street, LU6 1LS

12-11 (midnight Fri & Sat); 12-10.30 Sun

(01582) 512300 globe-pub.co.uk

B&T Two Brewers, Shefford Bitter, Black Dragon Dark Mild, Dragonslayer, Edwin Taylor's Extra Stout; guest beers

A no-frills pub with a friendly welcome, B&T's third tied pub opened in October 2005. Decorated with breweriana and without juke box or fruit machines, it is a good place to meet and chat or play darts, dominoes or cards. With 13 handpumps dispensing the regular ales plus a choice of ever-changing guest beers, why not try the third-of-a-pint option. Two beer festivals are held here annually. Winner of local CAMRA Pub of the Year in 2007 and 2008.

Victoria

69 West Street, LU6 1ST

11-12.30am (1am Fri & Sat)

(01582) 662682

Beer range varies;

A frequent CAMRA local Pub of the Year, this town centre pub usually offers four ales including a house beer, Victoria Bitter, from Tring Brewery. The ever-changing guest ales are from micro and regional breweries. Good value food is available until early evening Monday-Friday, and Saturday and Sunday lunchtimes. Darts and dominoes are popular and televised sport features in the bar. Quarterly beer festivals are held. There is no admittance after 11pm.

Flitton

Jolly Coopers

Wardhedges, MK45 5ED

12-3 (not Mon), 5.30-11.30; 12 to midnight Sat; 12-11 Sun

(01525) 860626

Wells Eagle IPA; guest beers

Charming Charles Wells two-bar pub with a traditional flag-stone floored bar and a restaurant to the rear. Two varying guest beers are sourced from a variety of brewers. The pub is the hub of the little community of Wardhedges and is home to various local interest groups and games teams. The restaurant is closed on Monday evening but meals are available in the bar.

Great Barford

Anchor Inn

High Street, MK44 3LF

12-3, 6 (5.30 Fri)-11; 12-11 Sat; 12-4, 6.30-10.30 Sun

(01234) 870364

Wells Eagle IPA; guest beers

Busy local pub situated next to the church overlooking the River Ouse. At least two guest beers are usually on handpump. Good home-cooked food is available in the bar and restaurant as well as a fine selection of wines.

Harlington

Old Sun

34 Sundon Road, LU5 6LS

12-11 summer; 12-2, 5-11 winter

(01525) 872417 theoldsunharlington.co.uk

Adnams Bitter; St. Austell Tribute; guest beers

Situated in the heart of this pretty commuter village, the Old Sun is just a short stroll from Harlington Station. The attractive, half-timbered building with two bar areas dates back to the 1640s and has been a pub since 1785. Outside there is seating and a children's play area. A wide range of food is served daily except Sunday evening and Monday.

Henlow

Engineers Arms

68 High Street, SG16 6AA

12-midnight (1am Fri & Sat)
(01462) 812284
Beer range varies
Winner of Bedfordshire Pub of the Year five out of the last six years, this two-bar free house is a mecca for the real ale enthusiast with up to 20 beers dispensed weekly from its 10 handpumps, plus six real ciders and perries, as well as a range of bottled foreign beers. Tastefully decorated rooms are adorned with sporting memorabilia and breweriana. The hub of the local community, the pub runs regular beer festivals and many brewery and cultural visits. Well-behaved children are welcome in the back room and garden.

Kempston

Half Moon

108 High Street, MK42 7BN
12-3 (4 Sat), 6 (5 Fri, 7 Sat)-11; 12-4, 7-11 Sun
(01234) 852464
Wells Eagle IPA, Bombardier
This locals' pub, situated near the Great River Ouse, has been attractively refurbished over the last 12 months and retains its comfortable lounge bar and public bar with skittles table and other games. Well supported by the community, it runs a number of teams in local leagues playing various pub games. There is a large garden with a children's play area which is popular in good weather.

Kensworth

Farmers Boy

216 Common Road, LU6 2PJ
12-11 summer; 12-2.30, 5-11 Mon & winter; 12-midnight Fri & Sat; 12-11 Sun
(01582) 872207
Fuller's London Pride, ESB; guest beers
Pretty village pub dating from the 1800s serving good food with a garden to the rear and seating out front. Children are welcome if dining and there is a play area in the garden. The licensee has a Fuller's Master Cellarman certificate and the pub was runner up in the outstanding achievement category of the Fuller's 2006/07 Pub Awards. Local community sports and events are hosted here and dogs are welcome.

Keysoe

White Horse

Kimbolton Road, MK44 2JA (on B660 at Keysoe Row crossroads)
11.30-2.30 (not winter Mon), 6-11; 11.30-11 Sat; 12-10.30 Sun
(01234) 376363
Wells Eagle IPA; guest beers
One of the oldest pubs in the Charles Wells estate, this single-bar village local has a thatched roof and low beams. Backing on to the bar area is a conservatory with a pool table and dartboard. Outside is a large garden with a children's play area. There is usually one guest beer from the Charles Wells list available. No food is served on Monday or on Sunday evening.

Leighton Buzzard

Hare

10 Southcott Village, Linslade, LU7 2PR
12-midnight
(01525) 373941
Courage Directors; Fuller's London Pride; Tring Brock Bitter; guest beers
Over the years the village of Linslade has expanded and it is now part of the town of Leighton Buzzard. This popular local overlooks the village green, attracting a good mix of drinkers. Two regularly changing guest beers are usually on offer. Old village photographs feature on the walls. An annual St George's Day beer fest is held in a marquee in the large rear garden. There is a heated external smoking area.

White Horse

9 New Road, Linslade, LU7 2LS
12-midnight (11 Sun)
(01525) 635739
Greene King IPA; Fuller's London Pride; guest beers
Genuine back-street free house, close to the Grand Union Canal and railway station. Five handpumps are a welcome sight at this friendly traditional local. Up to three guest ales are available, usually including a Tring beer. The owners are building up a good regular trade and run crib, darts and dominoes teams.

Luton

Bricklayers Arms

16-18 High Town Road, LU2 0DD
12-3, 5-11; 12-midnight Fri & Sat; 12-10.30 Sun
(01582) 611017
Everards Beacon, Tiger; guest beers
Somewhat quirky town centre pub run by the same landlady for more than 21 years. Five handpumps serve three guest beers, displayed on a notice board —on average 10 a week — sourced mainly from micro-breweries. Popular with Hatters fans, the pub's two TVs show football. Monday is quiz night. There are three draught Belgian beers and a modest selection of foreign bottled beers. Pub lunches are served Monday to Friday.

English Rose

46 Old Bedford Road, LU2 7PA
12-11
(01582) 723889 englishroseluton.co.uk
Brakspear Bitter; guest beers
Friendly town pub with a village local atmosphere. Three frequently changing guest beers are chosen from a range of breweries nationwide. Food is served Tuesday to Friday lunchtime and until early evening on Saturday, with a takeaway service. The quiz on Tuesday evening is a highlight. The garden accommodates both smokers and non-smokers in four specially designed heated huts. An annual beer festival is held.

Globe

26 Union Street, LU1 3AN
11-11; 12-10.30 Sun
(01582) 728681

Caledonian Deuchars IPA; Greene King IPA; guest beers Ⓗ
Popular one-room street corner local, just out of the town centre. Recently refurbished, it now has access from the bar to the large enclosed patio and heated smoking shelter outside. The pub offers a frequently changing guest ale from a micro or regional brewery and stages occasional beer festivals. Sport is shown on TV. Good value food is served Monday to Saturday lunchtime. ❀◐♣P⊱

Maulden

George Inn
George Street, MK45 2DF
✪ 12 (11 Wed)-3, 6-11; 12-11 Sun
☎ (01525) 751330
Adnams Bitter; Taylor Landlord; Young's Bitter; guest beers Ⓗ
Well-kept two-bar village local with a separate back room and a large garden overlooking the church. Four real ales are available with the guest sourced from a local brewery (typically B&T, Potton or Buntingford). The landlord takes great care of his ales and is proud to sell more cask beer than lager. The food served from the varied menu is of exceptional quality. The pub runs pool and darts teams and hosts a quiz every other Sunday evening.
❀◐◑⊟♿⊟♣P

Odell

Bell
Horsefair Lane, MK43 7AU
✪ 11.30-3 (12-4 Sat), 6-11.30; 12-4, 7-10.30 Sun
☎ (01234) 720254
Greene King IPA, Abbot; guest beers Ⓗ
Handsome, thatched village pub with a large garden near the River Great Ouse. With the Harrold Odell Country Park just down the lane, this is a popular stop for walkers. Sympathetic refurbishment and a series of linked but distinct seating areas help retain a traditional pub atmosphere. A good food menu offers small portions at lunchtime. ♨Q❀◐◑⊟P⊱

Potton

Rising Sun ✔
11 Everton Road, SG19 2PA
✪ 12-2.30, 6-11 (midnight Fri); 12-midnight Sat; 12-11 Sun
☎ (01767) 260231
Wells Eagle IPA, Bombardier; Hydes Jekyll Gold; St Austell Tribute Ⓗ
Originally a Phillips of Royston house, this is now a Wells pub but also offers three or four guest beers mainly from independent family brewers. The main bar area is divided by low walls and wooden beams and contains a covered well. There is also a games area and upstairs function room. Good value pub meals are available all day at the weekend and until 9.30pm in the evening during the week. Outdoor seating includes covered smoking, patio and roof-top areas. ❀◐◑⊟(E1,E2)♣P⊱

Pulloxhill

Cross Keys ✔
13 High Street, MK45 5HB
✪ 12-3, 6-11; 12-3, 7-10.30 Sun
☎ (01525) 712442
Adnams Broadside; Wells Eagle IPA, Bombardier Ⓗ
Old, oak-beamed inn in the middle of the village of Pulloxhill – a popular venue for dining due to the good home-made specials. The large restaurant area can also be used for private functions. The pub is well known locally for its jazz offering on a Sunday night. Extensive grounds include a children's play area next to the car park and another area where the local archery group practise.
Q❀◐◑♿▲⊟♣P⊱

Riseley

Fox & Hounds ✔
High Street, MK44 1DT
✪ 11.30-2.30, 6.30-11; 12-3, 7-10.30 Sun
☎ (01234) 708240
Wells Eagle IPA, Bombardier; guest beers Ⓗ
Old village inn, originally two 16th-century cottages complete with a priest's hiding hole and resident ghosts. It has a reputation for good food, with charcoal-grilled steak, sold by weight and served with salad, a speciality. The dining room can be reserved for parties, but booking is unnecessary for bar meals – relax over a pint while your food is cooked. The large lawned garden includes a covered patio with heaters. Q❀◐◑⊟P⊱

Salford

Red Lion Country Hotel
Wavendon Road, MK17 8AZ
✪ 11-2.30, 6.30-11
☎ (01908) 583117
Wells Eagle IPA, Bombardier Ⓗ
Traditional country hotel serving a fine selection of home-cooked food in the bar and restaurant. The bar, warmed by an open fire in winter, offers a selection of board games. The large garden has a covered area and secure children's play area. Accommodation is in six rooms, some with four-poster beds.
♨Q❀⊭◐◑⊟♿⇌♣P⊱

Sandy

Queen's Head
244 Cambridge Road, SG19 1JE
✪ 11.30-11 (11.30 Fri & Sat); 12-11 Sun
☎ (01767) 681115
Greene King IPA, Abbot; guest beers Ⓗ
Built by William Randall in 1750 and originally called the Maidenhead, the Queens Head retains much of the original structure and character. This friendly, unspoilt and traditional small town pub just off the market square welcomes visitors with a roaring log fire. A guest beer is always on offer alongside the IPA and Abbot, all in excellent condition. Meals are served every lunchtime with the ever-popular roast on Sunday a highlight.
♨Q❀◐♿⇌⊟P

Sir William Peel

39 High Street, SG19 1AG (opp church)
12 (11 Sat)-11; 12-10.30 Sun
☎ (01767) 680607
Everards Beacon; Nethergate Augustinian; Taylor Landlord; Tring Jack O'Legs; guest beers ⊞
Sandy's only true free house offers three ever-changing guest beers, usually sourced from small independent breweries. Catering for a more mature drinker, the single-bar interior divides into public and saloon-style areas. Acoustic open mike nights, monthly quizzes and occasional discos all feature. No food is available, but the pub is flanked by a fish and chip shop and an Indian restaurant.
❀♿⇌⊟(178)P⅟

Shefford

Brewery Tap

14 North Bridge Street, SG17 5DH
11.30-11; 12-10.30 Sun
☎ (01462) 628448
B&T Shefford Bitter, Shefford Dark Mild, Dragonslayer; Everards Tiger; guest beers ⊞
A short walk from the brewery, the Tap was rescued and renamed by B&T in 1996. Primarily a drinkers' pub, it offers four regular and one guest beer. The open plan interior is divided into two distinct areas plus a family room, all served by a single bar. Like all B&T pubs the interior features a display of breweriana. Pies and filled rolls are available at lunchtime. Outside is a patio garden with heaters for cooler evenings. The car park is through an archway next to the pub.
❀⊟♣P⅟

Souldrop

Bedford Arms

High Street, MK44 1EY
12-3, 6-11 (closed Mon); 12-3, 6-midnight Fri; 12-midnight Sat; 12-11 Sun
☎ (01234) 781384
Black Sheep Best Bitter; Young's Bitter; guest beers ⊞
Large village pub, dating in parts back to the 17th century when it was a hop house and ale house. The welcoming restaurant has a central, open fireplace and serves traditional pub favourites prepared to order, with daily specials and a roast lunch on Sunday. A large games room with skittles runs off the main bar. The spacious garden and play area are popular with families in summer.
⌂❀◑⊟♣P⅟

Stotfold

Stag

35 Brook Street, SG5 4LA
4 (1 Fri; 12 Sat)-11; 12-10.30 Sun
☎ (01462) 730261
Adnams Bitter; guest beers ⊞
Friendly village local now leased from Punch Taverns serving well-kept Adnams Bitter as well as two changing guests, often from local breweries. The main drinking area, decorated with breweriana and other interesting memorabilia, has a horseshoe-shaped bar and two real fires. The pub now serves food and has a separate dining area. Regular activities include a Sunday quiz and Friday meat raffle. Outside are two small patios with awnings and a large car park. ❀⊟(97)♣P⅟

Streatley

Chequers

Sharpenhoe Road, LU3 3PS
12-11.30 (12.30am Fri & Sat); 12-11 Sun
☎ (01582) 882072
Greene King IPA, Morland Original, Abbot, Old Speckled Hen; guest beers ⊞
Village inn of Georgian origin on the green next to the church. It usually has five real ales on handpump and is one of the few hostelries in the region to use oversized, lined pint glasses. Attracting locals and visitors alike, the pub is popular in good weather due to the large patio area. Quiz night is Tuesday and traditional jazz plays on the first Sunday afternoon of the month. ⌂❀⇔◑♿♣P⅟

Sutton

John O' Gaunt Inn

30 High Street, SG19 2NE
12-2.30, 7-11; 12-10.30 Sun
☎ (01767) 260377
Beer range varies ⊞
A 20-year veteran of the Guide, this pub is active in all aspects of the village's life. Beamed bars and a welcoming atmosphere give a timeless feel. The three handpumps are kept busy dispensing a variety of real ales in excellent condition, and a good range of home-cooked food is always available. The petanque court and the Northamptonshire skittles table are well used by local teams. Live folk music is a regular feature.
⌂Q❀◑⊟⊟♣P

Tebworth

Queen's Head

The Lane, LU7 9QB
12-3 (not Mon-Wed), 6 (7 Sat)-11
☎ (01525) 874101
Adnams Broadside; Ⓖ **Wells Eagle IPA;** ⊞ **Young's Special** Ⓖ
Traditional two-bar village local with a public bar, popular for darts and dominoes, and a lounge where live music plays on Friday. A large garden is at the rear. No food is served but customers are welcome to bring their own. The pub has featured in the Guide for more than 25 years under the present landlord who also has a career as an actor with appearances on stage, radio and TV.
⌂❀⊟♣P⅟

Toddington

Oddfellows Arms

2 Conger Lane, LU5 6BP
5-11 (midnight Fri); 12-midnight Sat; 12-11 Sun
☎ (01525) 872021
Adnams Broadside; Fuller's London Pride; guest beers ⊞
Attractive 15th-century pub facing the village green with a heavily-beamed and brassed bar and restaurant. It keeps a wide selection of

Belgian beers and Weston's Old Rosie cider, and often a guest cider or perry too, as well as a good range of bottled ciders. The varied menu offers good food (Tue-Sat eves and Sun lunch). Beer festivals are held in the spring and autumn. The patio garden is popular in summer, and has shelter for smokers.

Sow & Pigs

14 Church Square, LU5 6AA

11 (12 Sun)-midnight

(01525) 873089 sowandpigs.co.uk

Greene King IPA, Abbot; guest beers H

This 19th-century inn has featured in every edition of the Guide. Heated by open fires, the long, narrow bar is decorated with pigs, golf memorabilia and paintings of the pub by local artists. Excellent home-made food is offered daily. Restaurant meals (rare-breed pork is a speciality) and banquets are available (book in advance). The patio garden at the rear is pleasant in summer and has a shelter for smokers. Comfortable and reasonably-priced accommodation is available.

Q P

Totternhoe

Cross Keys

201 Castle Hill Road, LU6 2DA

11.30-3, 5-11; 11.30-11 Fri-Sun

(01525) 220434

Adnams Broadside; Greene King IPA; guest beers H

Attractive, thatched Grade II listed building dating from 1433 set in a glorious damson orchard with extensive views over Ivinghoe Beacon and the Vale of Aylesbury. The guest beers rotate weekly from a list chosen by the locals. Food is served daily (except Sun eve). In the warmer months barbecues are hosted and basket meals served in the garden. Dogs are welcome in the public bar. Q P

Upper Sundon

White Hart ✓

56 Streatley Road, LU3 3PQ

11-11; 12-10.30 Sun

(01525) 872493

Wells Eagle IPA; guest beer H

Attractive, mock-Tudor, two-bar Charles Wells pub with leaded windows, tucked away from the village centre on the old village green. The walls of the main bar are adorned with football memorabilia, while the second bar houses a pool table. The guest beer comes from the Charles Wells list and a large selection of malt whiskies is also stocked. A gazebo is provided for smokers. P

Whipsnade

Old Hunters Lodge

The Crossroads, LU6 2LN

11.30-2.30 (3 Sat), 6-11; 12-11 Sun

(01582) 672228 old-hunters.com

Greene King IPA, Abbot; guest beers H

Old Hunters Lodge is a 15th-century thatched inn set on the outskirts of Whipsnade village. Guest beers are normally sourced from micro-breweries. A large dining area provides food throughout the week until 7pm on Sunday. Six guest rooms are available including a bridal suite. Nearby is Whipsnade Zoo, a world-renowned centre for the breeding of endangered species of wild animals.

Q P

Wingfield

Plough ✓

Tebworth Road, LU7 9QH

12-midnight

(01525) 873077

Fuller's London Pride, ESB, Gale's HSB, seasonal beers; guest beers H

Attractive, thatched village inn dating from the 17th century, decorated with paintings of rural scenes and ploughs. Good food is available daily except Sunday evening. There are tables outside at the front; to the rear is a conservatory and prize-winning garden illuminated at night with a heated gazebo for smokers. P

Wootton

Chequers

Hall End Road, MK43 9HP TL002457

11.30-2.30, 5.30-11; 12-2.30, 6-10.30 Sun

(01234) 768394

Wells Eagle IPA; Young's Bitter H

Originally a farmhouse, the building retains a wealth of heavy wooden beams and period features. The narrow lounge has dining tables at one end. An interesting range of food is served Wednesday to Sunday lunchtime and Tuesday to Saturday evening. A skittles table features in the public bar. The large garden is popular in summer. P

Yelden

Chequers

High Street, MK44 1AW

12-2 (not Mon & Tue), 5-11 (midnight Fri & Sat); 12-10.30 Sun

(01933) 356383

Adnams Bitter; Black Sheep Best Bitter; Fuller's London Pride; Greene King Abbot; G **Taylor Landlord; guest beers** H

Traditional village pub offering five real ales and two ciders. Good, home-cooked pub meals are served daily, with occasional ticket-only guest chef days. The extensive rear garden hosts an annual beer and cider festival in July. Petanque is played and hood skittles is available by arrangement. Yelden lies on the Three Shires Way walkers' route and boasts the impressive earthworks of an abandoned Norman castle. P

> I never drink water. I'm afraid it will become habit-forming.
> **W C Fields**

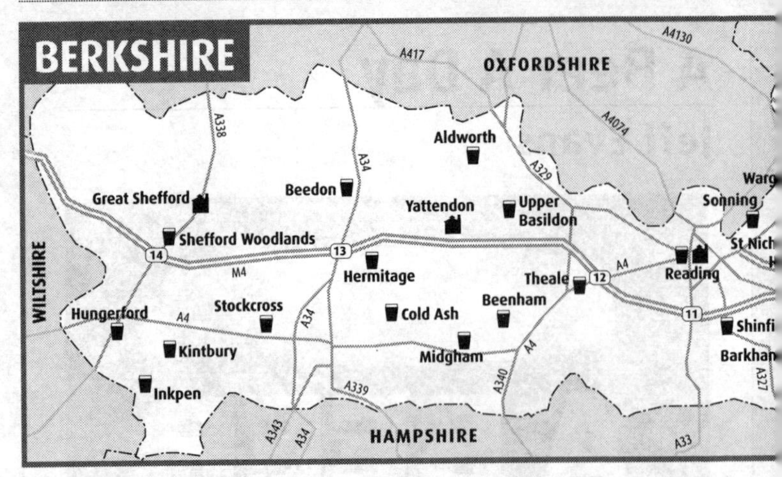

Aldworth

Bell ☆

Bell Lane, RG8 9SE (off B4009)
11-3, 6-11; closed Mon; 12-3, 7-10.30 Sun
(01635) 578272
Arkell's 3B, Kingsdown; West Berkshire Good Old Boy, Maggs Mild, seasonal beers H
The Bell is an institution, family owned by the Macaulays for more than 50 years, with an interior that features in CAMRA's National Inventory. It is popular with locals, walkers and everyone who likes a traditional inn, with no music, no games machines, no electronic till and no mobile phones. The grandfather clock has only one hand, summing up the timelessness of the place. Good Old Boy is sold as Old Tyler here. Q P

Barkham

Bull at Barkham ✓

Barkham Road, RG41 4TL (on B3349)
11.30-3; 5.30-11; 12-4 Sun
(0118) 976 0324 thebullatbarkham.com
Adnams Bitter, Broadside; Courage Best Bitter; Theakston Old Peculier; guest beers H
Named after the Bullock family who were Lords of the Manor until 1589, this Grade II listed building dates back in parts to the mid 1700s. A large village bar leads through to the restaurant in the converted old forge barn. The bar menu includes favourites such as steak and ale pie, fish and chips and bangers 'n' mash made with locally-produced sausages and renowned Barkham Blue cheese. Low-volume background music does not detract from the friendly babble of conversation at the bar. (144)P

Beedon

Langley Hall Inn

Oxford Road, World's End, RG20 8SA (on old Oxford Road from Chieveley)
11-3, 5.30-11; 11.30-7 Sun
(01635) 248332
West Berkshire Good Old Boy; guest beers H
Single-bar pub offering a warm welcome from an affable landlord who has built up a good reputation for imaginative food made with high-quality local produce. Fresh fish is a speciality. The guest ale is often a second West Berkshire Brewery beer. Divided into areas for drinking and dining, the decor is minimal. Children are welcome at weekends and there is a large garden with a petanque court built to international standards. Dogs are permitted. Three bedrooms provide overnight accommodation. (6, 9)P

Beenham

Six Bells

The Green, RG7 5NX
12-2.30 (not Mon & Tue), 6-11; 12-3, 6-11 Sat; 12-3, 6.30-10.30 Sun
(0118) 971 3368 thesixbells.net
Fuller's London Pride; guest beers H
Comfortable village pub with two bar areas, conservatory and well-appointed restaurant which doubles as a function room. Open fires create a cosy feel and the bars are adorned with interesting artefacts from around the world. Local beers are always available, usually from the West Berkshire, Butler's or Ringwood breweries. The pub also offers high-quality home-cooked food and has four en-suite letting rooms. A range of board games is on offer. The garden overlooks open fields. Q P

Binfield

Jack o' Newbury

Terrace Road North, RG42 5PH (NE of village, towards church)
11-3, 5.30-11; 12-3, 7-10.30 Sun
(01344) 454881 jackofnewbury.co.uk
Loddon Hoppit; Rebellion IPA; guest beers H
Named after a wealthy cloth merchant who assisted Henry VIII at Flodden Field in 1513, the Jack is everything you could hope for in a family-run village free house – pleasant

INDEPENDENT BREWERIES

Butts Great Shefford
West Berkshire Yattendon
Zerodegrees Reading

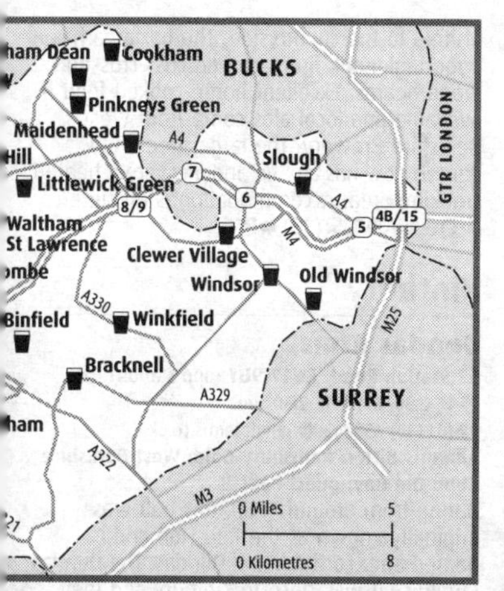

landlord, attractive garden, separate skittles alley and a choice of five beers, mostly from local micro-breweries. Guns, copper pots, brass keys, pewter and china mugs cover every surface – spot the unusual wall clock. No food is served on Sunday and Monday evening. Local CAMRA Pub of the Year in 2007 and in 2008. ♨Q❀◐🚌P

Victoria Arms ✔

Terrace Road North, RG42 5JA

⏲ 11.30-11 (midnight Fri & Sat); 12-11 Sun

☎ (01344) 483856

Fuller's Discovery, London Pride, ESB, seasonal beers Ⓗ

The longest-standing Guide entry pub in the area, this cosy, friendly Victorian inn is popular with locals and welcoming to visitors. Good honest home-cooked food is available daily. The garden has recently been redesigned and is now on two levels with a covered smoking area on the higher patio. Disabled access to the pub is good, but there are steps to the toilets. ♨❀◐🚌(53A)P🚬

Bracknell

Old Manor ✔

Church Road, Grenville Place, RG12 1BP (on inner ring road)

⏲ 9am-midnight

☎ (01344) 304490

Greene King Abbot; Marston's Pedigree; guest beers Ⓗ

This former Tudor manor house was caringly refurbished by Wetherspoon to become its first pub outside the M25. The Monks Room, which can be booked for private functions, features an original priest hole. The main bar offers four competitively-priced changing guest beers, often including an ale from the local Loddon brewery. There is plenty of seating on the patio and in the garden, plus a covered and heated smoking area.
❀◐♿≢🚌P🚬

Clewer Village

Swan

9 Mill Lane, SL4 5JQ

⏲ 5.30-11 (midnight Fri); 12-midnight Sat; 12-10.30 Sun

☎ (01753) 862069 🌐 theswan-windsor.co.uk

Theakston Best Bitter, XB Ⓗ

This 18th-century back-street pub is a rare outlet for Theakston beers in the area. The 15-minute walk from the town centre means that it is usually frequented by locals rather than tourists. Its close proximity to Windsor Racecourse makes it popular on race days. In winter the pub is warmed by a wood-burning fire. Quiz night is Tuesday. Addlestones cider is usually stocked. ♨❀🛏≢●🚬

Cold Ash

Castle Inn ✔

Cold Ash Hill, RG18 9PS

⏲ 11.30-3, 5.30-11.30; 11.30-midnight Fri & Sat; 12-11 Sun

☎ (01635) 863232

Courage Best Bitter; Fuller's London Pride; guest beers Ⓗ

Welcoming community pub with a tradition of long-serving landlords – the last hundred years have seen only four and the current tenants are in their 14th year. The interior of this 19th-century building was much altered many years ago and is now open plan with a central bar. One of the two changing guest beers always comes from the nearby West Berkshire Brewery. No evening meals are served on Monday. There is a patio out front.
♨❀◐🚌(101)♣P

Cookham

Bounty

Riverside, SL8 5RG (footpath from station car park, across bridge, along towpath) SU 907880

⏲ 12-10.30 (winter 12-dusk Sat; closed Mon-Fri)

☎ (01628) 520056

Rebellion IPA, Mutiny; guest beers Ⓗ

Quirky riverside pub that can only be reached on foot (the beer is delivered by boat). Popular with walkers and boaters, it can get very busy at weekends, especially in summer. Dogs, muddy boots and children are all welcome. The boat-shaped bar is decorated with flags and assorted nautical knick-knacks and there is a rack selling children's clothes in aid of charity in the back room. A backboard gives details of forthcoming events. Note the winter opening times.
♨⛴❀◐⛺≢(Bourne End)♣

Cookham Dean

Jolly Farmer

Church Road, SL6 9PD

⏲ 11.30-11 (11.45 Fri); 12-10.30 Sun

☎ (01628) 482905 🌐 jollyfarmercookhamdean.co.uk

Brakspear Bitter; Courage Best Bitter; Young's Bitter; guest beers Ⓗ

Situated opposite the church, this pub is owned by the village. The low-beamed Jolly Bar (adults only) is cosy with a real fire. In the larger Dean Bar, families, diners and drinkers are all welcome. There is also a more formal small dining-room used for St George's and Halloween weekend beer festivals. The large garden includes a children's play area. No evening meals are served Sunday or Monday. ♨Q❀◑◐▣P

Hermitage

Fox Inn ✪

High Street, RG18 9RB (on B4009)
✪ 12-3, 5-11; 12-11 Fri & Sat; 12-10.30 Sun
☎ (01635) 201545 ⊕ thefoxathermitage.co.uk
Fuller's London Pride; Shepherd Neame Master Brew Bitter, Spitfire; guest beers 🄷
Converted in the 19th century, this main-road pub was originally three artisan cottages dating back to the 16th century. From the outside you can still see the three doors. Up to three guest ales are served, with beer festivals held throughout the year. One of the handpumps usually dispenses a cider during the summer months. The food is home made, wholesome fare using local produce when available. No meals are served on Sunday evening. ♨❀⌸◑⊞▲▣(9)♣P⍁

Hungerford

Downgate

13 Down View, Park Street, RG17 0ED (edge of Hungerford Common)
✪ 11-11
☎ (01488) 682708 ⊕ the-downgate.co.uk
Arkell's 2B, 3B; guest beer 🄷
Friendly local on the eastern side of town, on the edge of Hungerford Common. The bar is divided into three areas, one with a TV, and a cosy sunken space with a real fire. Bank notes and photographs of old Hungerford decorate the walls. The tables outside offer pleasant views across the common and the Kennet Valley. The guest beer is a seasonal from Arkell's. Good-value, traditional pub meals are available seven days a week.
♨❀◑◐⇌▣(13)♣P⍁

Hurley

Dew Drop Inn

Batts Green, Honey Lane, SL6 6RB (1 mile S of A4130)
✪ 11.30-3, 5.30-11 (midnight Fri & Sat); 12-11 Sun
☎ (01628) 824327 ⊕ thedewdropinn.co.uk
Brakspear Bitter, Oxford Gold, seasonal beers 🄷
Off the beaten track between Hurley and Burchetts Green, this 17th-century pub attracts walkers and horse riders. Dick Turpin is reputed to have drunk here once upon a time. Good food is served daily (not Sun eve). The large outside seating area is popular in the warmer weather and ideal for families. Hitching posts, fresh hay and water are available for equine visitors. ♨Q❀◑◐♣P⍁

Inkpen

Crown & Garter

Inkpen Common, RG17 9QR
✪ 12-3 (not Mon & Tue), 5.30-11; 12-5, 7-10.30 Sun
☎ (01488) 668325 ⊕ crownandgarter.co.uk
Arkell's Moonlight; Taylor Landlord; West Berkshire Mr Chubb's Lunchtime Bitter, Good Old Boy 🄷
Set in an area of outstanding natural beauty, this 17th-century inn is ideally situated for visitors to the countryside. The bar area has a huge inglenook fireplace and criss-crossed wood beams. Excellent home-cooked food is available and local ales come from West Berkshire Brewery. The large, tree-lined garden now has a patio and a covered, heated smoking area. Accommodation is en-suite.
♨Q❀⌸◑◐⊞▣(13)♣P⍁

Kintbury

Dundas Arms

53 Station Road, RG17 9UT (opp station)
✪ 11-2.30, 6-11; 12-2.30 Sun
☎ (01488) 658263 ⊕ dundasarms.co.uk
Adnams Bitter; Ramsbury Gold; West Berkshire Good Old Boy; guest beer 🄷
Dating from around 1760, this pub was originally known as the Red Lion and renamed after Lord Admiral Dundas. The Dundas family seat was close to Kintbury and they were instrumental in building the Kennet & Avon canal, which runs alongside the pub. Known for its quality food, the pub sources ingredients from local free-range organic farms where possible. No meals are served on Sunday. The guest beer is usually a West Berkshire special. Note the bar top, covered in old pennies. Q❀⌸◑◐⇌▣(13)P⍁

Knowl Hill

Bird in Hand

Bath Road, RG10 9UP (on A4 between Reading and Maidenhead)
✪ 11-3, 5-11; 11-11 Sat; 12-10.30 Sun
☎ (01628) 826622 ⊕ birdinhand.co.uk
Brakspear Bitter; guest beers 🄷
Large, welcoming free house hotel, much modernised but with a 600-year history, with a large wood-panelled bar and warming log fire. Four regularly-changing guests are on handpump, usually including a dark beer. Bar food is served, and there is a separate, more upmarket restaurant. A function room is also available. Occasional barbecues are hosted in the pleasant garden. CAMRA Berkshire Pub of the Year 2008. ♨❀⌸◑◐⊞▣(239, 127)♣P⍁

Seven Stars

Bath Road, RG10 9UR (in lay-by on N side of A4)
✪ 11-3, 5-midnight; 11-1am Fri & Sat; 12-10.30 Sun
☎ (01628) 822967
Brakspear Bitter, seasonal beers; Wychwood Hobgoblin 🄷
Attractive, half-timbered pub set back in a lay-by off the main A4 road, popular with locals and passing trade, and with horse riders and walkers on the Knowl Hill Bridleway Circuit. The spacious garden makes for pleasant summer afternoon drinking. A real community pub, it hosts a folk night on Thursday and occasional barbecues, and has a skittles alley. Various motoring clubs also meet here, making use of the ample parking.
♨❀◑◐♿▣(239, 127)♣P⍁

Littlewick Green

Cricketers

Coronation Road, SL6 3RA
✪ 12-3, 5-11; 12-11 Fri & Sat; 12-10.30 Sun

☎ (01628) 822888
Badger K&B Sussex, First Gold, Tanglefoot, seasonal beers Ⓗ
Overlooking the village green, this three-bar pub has a cricketing theme, naturally, and a good crowd gathers to watch matches. Check out the splendid old clock inside, and walnut tree outside. An enclosed rear garden and covered smoking area at the side are recent additions. No food is served on Sunday evening. Children are welcome and accommodation includes two double and one family room. Buses run along the A4, 200 metres away. (127)P

Maidenhead

Maidenhead Conservative Club ✔
32 York Road, SL6 1SF
12 10.30-2.30, 5.30-11; 10.30-11.30 Fri & Sat; 12-3, 7-11 Sun
☎ (01628) 620579 maidenheadconclub.org.uk
Fuller's Chiswick, London Pride, seasonal beers; guest beers Ⓗ
Friendly real ale outlet close to the station. The club steward is a CAMRA member and this is reflected in the beer quality. Two guest brews are usually available, as well as bottle-conditioned beers. Monday is crib night, Tuesday and Wednesday darts. Quiz night is Sunday. Parking is limited but there is a public car park just 100 metres away. A minimal guest fee will be charged to gain entry using this Guide or your CAMRA membership card. (7A, 7B)P

Midgham

Berkshire Arms ✔
Bath Road, RG7 5UX (on A4 2 miles E of Thatcham)
11-11; 11.30-10.30 Sun
☎ (0118) 971 1802
Beer range varies Ⓗ
Originally a farmhouse, this establishment set back from the main road has been a hostelry for nearly 20 years and is now a Chef & Brewer with a Premier Inn alongside. The traditional-style interior is warm, spacious and intimately divided into a number of small rooms and alcoves served by a central bar. Food leads the way but the ever-changing range of three beers, many from distant regional breweries, makes this place much sought out. You can be sure of a warm welcome and good service. (102)P

Old Windsor

Jolly Gardeners
92-94 St Luke's Road, SL4 2QJ
12-11 (midnight Thu-Sat); 12-10.30 Sun
☎ (01753) 830215 thejollygardeners.org.uk
Courage Best Bitter; guest beers Ⓗ
Friendly locals' pub close to the village shops, with a U-shaped bar serving three areas including a lounge for diners. Good-value home-made food is available including takeaway deli-style sandwiches at lunchtime (no food all day Saturday or Sunday evening). The landlord hosts a quiz on Monday night and there is a large TV and dartboard. Reasonably-priced B&B is available. P

Pinkneys Green

Stag & Hounds
1 Lee Lane, SL6 6NU
12-10.30 (12-4, 7-10.30 winter); 12-11 (12-3, 6-11 winter) Sat; 12-10.30 Sun
☎ (01628) 630268
Rebellion seasonal beer; Sharp's Doom Bar; guest beers Ⓗ
This pub gets better every year —the landlord has recently introduced improvements to the garden and barbecue area plus a purpose-built shelter for the smoking fraternity. It offers five real ales, usually including the monthly offering from Rebellion. The public bar is cosy; the lounge has a real fire and tables for dining. The large garden is popular in summer and the function room has been converted to a carvery. Regular beer festivals are held throughout the year. Q P

Reading

Eldon Arms
19 Eldon Terrace, RG1 4DX
11-3, 5.30-11.30 (midnight Fri); 11-3, 7-midnight Sat; 12-3, 7-11.30 Sun
☎ (0118) 957 3857
Wadworth IPA, Horizon, 6X, Bishop's Tipple, seasonal beers Ⓗ
Backstreet gem located in the Eldon Square conservation area and winner of various local CAMRA awards including Pub of the Year runner-up in 2007. Licensees Brian and Anne have run the Eldon for more than 30 years. Choose from the old-fashioned public bar with dartboard or the cosy lounge with its fascinating collection of knick-knacks. Quiz night is Wednesday with the winners writing the following week's questions. The pub may close earlier in the afternoon if quiet.
Q

Foresters Arms
79-81 Brunswick Street, RG1 6NY
4-11; 3-midnight Fri; 12-midnight Sat; 12-11 Sun
☎ (0118) 959 0316
Brakspear Bitter; Harvey's Sussex Best Bitter Ⓗ
An impressive mock Tudor mid-terrace back-street local and the only corridor pub in Reading. At the front is the small, comfortable Friday's Bar (the split door opening onto the corridor was once used for off-sales) and at the back the larger Garden Bar. A keen supporter of Reading FC, the pub has football paraphernalia around the bar —and you can always follow the match on one of the screens, even in the small patio garden at the rear. (Reading West)

Hobgoblin
2 Broad Street, RG1 2BH
11-11; 12-10.30 Sun
☎ (0118) 950 8119
Beer range varies Ⓗ
A Georgian building that's bigger than it looks from the street. The front bar, with its spooky decor, is all banter and watching the world go by; the offset back room is divided into

intimate booths. Up to three beers from West Berkshire Brewery are usually available, plus five guests from micros all over the UK. Over 5,500 different brews have been served here since 1992; return in the evening after a lunchtime session and you'll normally find something new to try. ❀⇌⊟●⁵–

Nag's Head

5 Russell Street, RG1 7XD

12-11 (midnight Fri & Sat)

☎ (0118) 957 4649 nagsheadreading.com

Beer range varies Ⓗ

Refurbished and reopened in February 2007, the Nag's is now a thriving real ale haven attracting a wide variety of customers. Twelve locally-sourced ales always include a mild and a stout. Board games, darts and a selection of books and newspapers are available. The TV is used sparingly for sports. The pub runs a bus (in conjunction with the Foresters Arms) to all Reading FC home games. Basic meals are served weekday evenings and weekend lunchtimes. There is a rudimentary garden for smokers. ₼❀◗⇌(Reading West)⊟♣●P⁵–

Retreat

8 St John's Street, RG1 4EH

4.30-11; 12-11.30 Fri & Sat; 12-11 Sun

☎ (0118) 957 1593 retreatpub.co.uk

Loddon Ferryman's Gold; Ringwood Best Bitter; guest beers Ⓗ

Traditional two-room mid-terrace pub — conversation is the norm in the quiet front bar while the livelier back room has a pool table, darts and jukebox. A good selection of continental bottled beer is available and an unusual range of snacks. Thursday evening is live music night, with folk, swing, jazz or bluegrass. The pub's community feel is enhanced by a well-used notice board. A small covered area for smokers is now available at the front entrance. CAMRA's Central Southern Cider Pub of the Year 2007. ⊟♣●⁵–

Three Guineas

Station Approach, RG1 1LY

10-11; 12-10.30

☎ (0118) 957 2743

Greene King IPA; Thwaites Lancaster Bomber; Youngs Bitter; guest beers Ⓗ

Located in the Victorian railway station's former ticket hall, this is the ideal place to start or end your visit to Reading. The spacious bar area features high ceilings and dozens of rugby shirts from all over the world. Expect crowds (and plastic glasses) when London Irish or Reading FC play at home, or for major televised sporting events. Food is served until 9pm and eight real ales are always available. Train departure times are displayed on monitors. ❀◗♿⇌⊟

Ruscombe

Royal Oak

Ruscombe Lane, RG10 9JN

12-3; 6 (5 Fri)-11; closed Mon eve; 12-4 Sun

☎ (0118) 934 5190 burattas.co.uk

Brakspear Bitter; Fuller's London Pride; guest beers Ⓗ

Set away from the bustling heart of Twyford town, yet less than 15 minutes' walk from the railway station, this is a comfortable, spacious pub and restaurant. Popular with local diners, it also offers a warm welcome to those just wishing to drink. Overseen by a CAMRA-friendly landlord, the food and ale are of a high standard. The conservatory and large garden (watch out for the chickens!) are delightful in summer. Q❀◗⊟P⁵–

St Nicholas Hurst

Wheelwrights Arms ✔

Davis Way, RG10 0TR

11.30-2.30, 5.30-11; 11-3, 5-11 Fri; 11.30-11 Sat; 12-10.30 Sun

☎ (0118) 934 4100

Wadworth IPA, 6X, JCB; Ⓗ **guest beers** Ⓗ/Ⓖ

This 18th-century wheelwright's shop started selling beer when the railways arrived in the early 1850s. The pub retains the stone floors, wood beams and real fire. A friendly local, it attracts both visitors and residents, and runs bridge, gun and golf clubs, as well as a quiz night on Monday. Good food is available (not Sat or Sun eve). The manager is a real ale enthusiast and often keeps a mild on handpump. There are heated umbrellas in the smoking area.

₼Q❀◗♿⇌(Winnersh)⊟●P⁵–

Shefford Woodlands

Pheasant Inn

Ermin Street, RG17 7AA (on B4000 just N of M4 jct 14)

11-12.30am (1am Fri & Sat); 11-midnight Sun

☎ (01488) 648284 thepheasantinnlambourn.co.uk

Butts Jester; Loddon Hoppit; Wadworth 6X Ⓗ

Former drovers' inn, once known as The Boarden House due to its wooden construction, now owned by members of the horse-racing fraternity and attractively refurbished with the rare bottle-glass screen above the bar retained. A sociable haunt for drinkers, diners, too, are attracted by the highly-recommended food. Ring-the-bull can be played. A new extension grafted onto the back adds a restaurant, meeting rooms and accommodation. ₼❀⇆◗♿♣P⁵–

Shinfield

Magpie & Parrot

Arborfield Road, RG2 9EA (on A327 east of village)

12-7 (3 Sun)

☎ (0118) 988 4130

Fuller's London Pride; guest beer Ⓗ

Built circa 1756, the pub's small bar features oak beams and a chair reserved for Aitch, the pub dog, and is crammed full of odd knick-knacks. The sitting room is larger and very 'English', with comfy armchairs and sofas. No music or machines here —just conversation in the old tradition. The marquee in the huge garden is used for various events including two annual beer festivals. Note the early closing time. ₼Q❀⊟(144)♣P⁵–

Slough

Rose & Crown

312 High Street, SL1 1NB

✪ 11 (12 Sun)-11
☎ (01753) 521114
Beer range varies ⊞
Situated at the eastern end of the High Street, this Grade II listed building dates back to the late 16th century. A proper pub with two small bars, it serves up to three different beers, often including one from Rebellion. A beer festival is held in early July. Real cider is sometimes available, often in summer. Entertainment includes karaoke on alternate Friday nights and occasional live music. The recently-renovated paved rear garden has a TV. ❀⇌⊟♣⊱

Sonning

Bull Inn ✔
High Street, RG4 6UP
✪ 11-11 (11.30 Fri & Sat); 12-10.30 Sun
☎ (0118) 969 3901
Fuller's Chiswick, Discovery, London Pride; Gale's HSB; guest beers ⊞
A gem tucked away in a quaint side street next to the village church and the Thames footpath, notable for its mention in the 1889 book Three Men in a Boat. Oak beams abound, plus a real fire in the main bar, where the emphasis is on food. There is also an up-market restaurant, a separate bar for drinkers and a pleasant garden. The exterior is adorned with an award-winning display of hanging baskets in summer. ♨Q❀⊨◐⊞⊟P⊱

Stockcross

Rising Sun
Ermin Street, RG20 8LG (on B4000)
✪ 11 (12 winter)-2.30, 5.30 (6 winter)-11; 12-2.30 (11-3 winter), 5.30-11 Fri; 11 (12 winter)-11 Sat; 12-3, 7-10.30 Sun
☎ (01488) 608131 ⊕ therisingsun-stockcross.co.uk
West Berkshire Mr Chubb's Lunchtime Bitter, Maggs Mild, Good Old Boy, seasonal beers ⊞
West Berkshire Brewery's first tied house is set in the countryside in a village two miles from Newbury. The skilful refurbishment, mostly carried out by brewer Dave Maggs himself, has created three drinking areas including a snug, with a new central passageway dividing the premises. Live music is a regular feature, with folk very popular. Meals are now available during all sessions. A friendly little pub that concentrates on doing simple things well. Local CAMRA Pub of the Year 2007.
♨Q❀◐⊟(4)P

Theale

Crown
2 Church Street, RG7 5BT
✪ 11-11; 12-10.30 Sun
☎ (0118) 930 22310
Adnams Broadside; Greene King IPA; West Berkshire Good Old Boy ⊞
Theale is an old coaching stop on the London to Bath run, West of Reading. The Crown has existed in this location since 1810 although only the pub and outbuilding remain from the original old inn, which used to be owned by Strange's of Aldermaston. These days the pub has a friendly feel, offering pool, darts, cribbage (on Mondays) and Poker (Thursday nights, chips only) to amuse the traveller.
❀⇌⊟♣P⊱

Upper Basildon

Beehive
Beckfords, RG8 8LS
✪ 12-2.30, 5.30-11; 12-11 Fri & Sat; 12-10.30 Sun
☎ (01491) 671269 ⊕ thebeehiveinn.com
Beer range varies ⊞
Recent proposals for conversion of this pub to a private house were thwarted by vigorous campaigning by locals and CAMRA, and the pub's future now seems assured under a keen manager and staff. A Grade II listed building dating back to the 16th century, it has been much extended over the years and now incorporates a large dining area. The original front bar can still be recognised. Timothy Taylor Landlord often features among the beers. The pleasant front garden overlooks the classic village green. ♨❀◐⊟(132)♣P

Red Lion
Aldworth Road, RG8 8NG
✪ 11-3, 5-11; 12-10.30 Sun
☎ (01491) 671234
Brakspear Bitter; West Berkshire Good Old Boy; Fuller's London Pride; guest beers ⊞
Originally a small country beer house, set back in a dip adjacent to the Yattendon Road crossroads, the building has been extended to incorporate a popular restaurant. It remains essentially a pub, however, with live music on Thursday night. The large rear garden provides the setting for weekend barbecues on fine days, plus an annual charity music and beer festival. An interesting feature is a rather risqué mural visible to ladies only!
♨❀◐⊟(132)♣P

Waltham St Lawrence

Bell
The Street, RG10 0JJ (next to church)
✪ 12-3, 5-11; 12-11 Sat; 12-10.30 Sun
☎ (0118) 934 1788 ⊕ thebellinn.biz
Beer range varies ⊞
Traditional 14th-century pub with two cosy beamed bars and a newly refurbished light and airy dining area up a few steps (check out the view down the well from here). Courtyard tables are out front and an extensive garden to the rear. Five real ales are stocked. A varied menu includes snacks and more interesting main dishes. Children, dogs and walkers are all welcome in this pub owned by a local charity for the 'poor of the parish'. Sunday lunchtimes are busy. ♨Q♉❀◐⊟(52A)♣●

Star
Broadmoor Road, RG10 0HY (E end of village)
✪ 12-2.30, 6-11; 12-10.30 Sun
☎ (0118) 934 3486 ⊕ thestar-inn.co.uk
Wadworth IPA, 6X ⊞
Friendly and welcoming, this popular community pub is on the edge of a sprawling village. Sympathetically extended, the traditional interior features beamed ceilings and there is now a dining area to complement the comfortable main bar. The pub is

renowned for award-winning pizzas, served lunchtime and evening, as well as its full range of good meals (no food Sunday eve). Horizon is only served on draught in summer but bottles are available all year round.

Wargrave

Wargrave & District Snooker Club

Woodclyffe Hostel, Church Street, RG10 8EP

7-11 Mon-Fri

(0118) 940 3537/3184

Beer range varies

The real ale on handpump here is chosen from a range of breweries, often local, served alongside a good variety of other drinks in cans and bottles. There are no fancy lager fonts to clutter the bar. The staff are friendly and efficient and card-carrying CAMRA members are warmly welcomed. No meals are served but snacks are available including a range of pickles. Snooker tables may only be used by club members (new members always welcome).

Windsor

Carpenters Arms

4 Market Street, SL4 1PB

11-11 (midnight Fri & Sat)

(01753) 755961

Beer range varies

Popular with locals and tourists alike, this pub is situated on a cobbled street between the castle and Guildhall. Evidence of a series of tunnels originally linking it to the castle can be seen in the lower drinking area. Traditional carpenter's tools are etched into the windows at the front and rear. Five handpumps serve an ever-changing selection of ales from across Britain. Local CAMRA Pub of the Year 2008.

(Windsor & Eton Central)

Duke of Connaught

165 Arthur Road, SL4 1RZ

12-11 (1am Fri & Sat); 12-11.30 Sun

(01753) 840748 theduekofconnaught.co.uk

Greene King IPA, Abbot; guest beers

Originally No.1 Connaught Cottages, this pub was the home of Mr Charles Wilkins who was a beer retailer in 1895. Later on it was owned by the now defunct Victoria Brewing Company, Windsor. Today it is a friendly, stylish street corner tavern with a good atmosphere serving good food. It shows sport on TV and hosts live music and occasional quiz evenings. The interior has bare floorboards and the walls are decorated with old film photos. The smoking area outside is covered.

(Windsor & Eton Central)

King & Castle

15-16 Thames Street, SL4 1PL

9am-midnight (1am Fri & Sat)

(01753) 625120

Greene King Abbot; Marston's Pedigree; guest beers

Situated opposite Windsor Castle, this very large pub set on three floors was refurbished to a high standard in 2006. The wide open main bar leads to a variety of more intimate areas, some with bar stools, others with comfy sofas. Jazz plays on Wednesday night. A small dance floor gives the pub a nightclub feel later in the evening when a dress code applies. The large patio is partly heated during cooler weather. Definitely not a typical Wetherspoon's.

Two Brewers

34 Park Street, SL4 1LB

11.30-11 (11.30 Fri & Sat); 12-10.30 Sun

(01753) 855426

Courage Best Bitter; Fuller's London Pride; Wadworth 6X

This Grade II listed building was once part of the Crown Estate and is the ideal place to rest up after completing the Long Walk through Windsor Great Park. Built in the 17th century, it was reputedly a brothel and drinking house on what was then the main London-Windsor road. The frontage was replaced after a fire in the 19th century. Food is very popular here, served daily except Sunday evening (booking advisable).

(Windsor & Eton Central)

Vansittart Arms

105 Vansittart Road, SL4 5DD

12-11 (11.30 Thu; midnight Fri & Sat)

(01753) 865988

Fuller's Discovery, London Pride, ESB, seasonal beers

Originally the site of cottages housing workers from the castle, this friendly and welcoming local is situated to the west of the town centre. The two main bar areas have recesses and real fires. Barbecues and special events are hosted in the large garden in summer and there is a covered and heated area for smokers. Sport is keenly followed here with rugby taking priority on the TV screens. Live music plays occasionally.

(Windsor & Eton Central)

Winkfield

Old Hatchet

Hatchet Lane, SL4 2EE (on A330 NW of Ascot)

11-11; 12-10.30 Sun

(01344) 899911

Fuller's Chiswick, London Pride, ESB; Gale's HSB

Friendly and welcoming traditional, centuries-old country pub that dates back to the 16th century with four open fires and a covered, heated smoking area with comfortable club seats. Built over several levels, this beamed Fuller's house is full of character and serves excellent food with an ever-changing specials board. Children are welcome when dining.

Q

Wokingham

Broad Street Tavern

29 Broad Street, RG40 1AU

12-11 (midnight Thu-Sat); 12-10.30 Sun

(0118) 9773706 broadstreettavern.co.uk

Wadworth IPA, Horizon, 6X, JCB, seasonal beers; guest beers

Atmospheric town centre local with two quiet rooms at the front. The main bar leads to the tropical garden which has heaters and is partially covered. Food is available daily. Live music is held every third Thursday of the month. Real ale festivals are regular events. Three times local CAMRA Pub of the Year and winner of the Colin Lanham Award for Excellence in commemoration of the landlord's services to the promotion of real ale. ❀◑♿⇌⊟♣⚘⚡

Queen's Head ✔

23 The Terrace, RG40 1BP
✪ 12-11 (10.30 Sun)
☎ (0118) 978 1221
Greene King IPA, Morland Original, Abbot; guest beers Ⓗ
Town centre terrace pub in one of the oldest parts of Wokingham. Originally a barn in the 15th century, the earliest reference to it as the Queen's Head can be found dating back to 1777. Much of the original structure can still be seen in the traditional single bar with low ceilings and wood beams. Meat, cheese and vegetarian platters are served. There are tables outside at the front and a garden with more seating at the rear. The pub supports various sports teams and their trophies adorn the walls. ♨❀⇌⚡

Rifle Volunteer ✔

141 Reading Rd, RG41 1HD
✪ 11-11; 12-5.30, 7-11 Sun
☎ (0118) 978 4484
Courage Best Bitter; Fuller's London Pride; Sharp's Doom Bar; guest beers Ⓗ
Traditional community pub a mile from the town centre and railway station, with a spacious bar and small family room. The guest handpump serves a changing beer, often from a local micro. Snacks are available at lunchtime. Flat-screen TVs show sporting events but are switched off at other times. The enclosed and well-equipped garden is popular with families in summer. ☋❀♿⊟(190)♣P

Victoria Arms

1 Easthampstead Road, RG40 2EH
✪ 12-11 (midnight Fri & Sat); 12-10.30 Sun
☎ (0118) 978 3023
Taylor Landlord; guest beers Ⓗ
Single-bar pub with a timber-boarded floor comfortably furnished with leather chairs and sofas, pleasantly quiet during the day. However the football memorabilia proudly displayed on the walls and the five TV screens is an indication that the pub will burst into life during an evening match and at the weekends when a younger, livelier crowd can be found downing pints of locally-produced beer from Loddon Brewery. Food orders finish at 6pm at the weekend. A pay and display car park is close by. ◑⇌⊟

White Horse

Easthampstead Road, RG40 3AF
✪ 11.30-2.30, 5-11; 11-11 Fri-Sun
☎ (0118) 978 1025
Greene King IPA, Ruddles County, Abbot Ⓗ
This pub serves the best-kept Greene King beers in the area. Two miles south of town and with views over open fields, it has a distinctly rural feel. There is comfortable seating for drinkers and an area for diners. Food, including a children's menu, is available at all sessions. Unobtrusive background music plays and a TV shows major sports fixtures. Live music is hosted occasionally. Outside, there is an enclosed seating area beside the road and a beer garden at the rear where barbecues are held in summer. ❀◑♿♣P⚡

Langley Hall Inn, Beedon (Photo: Eileen Caster).

BUCKINGHAMSHIRE

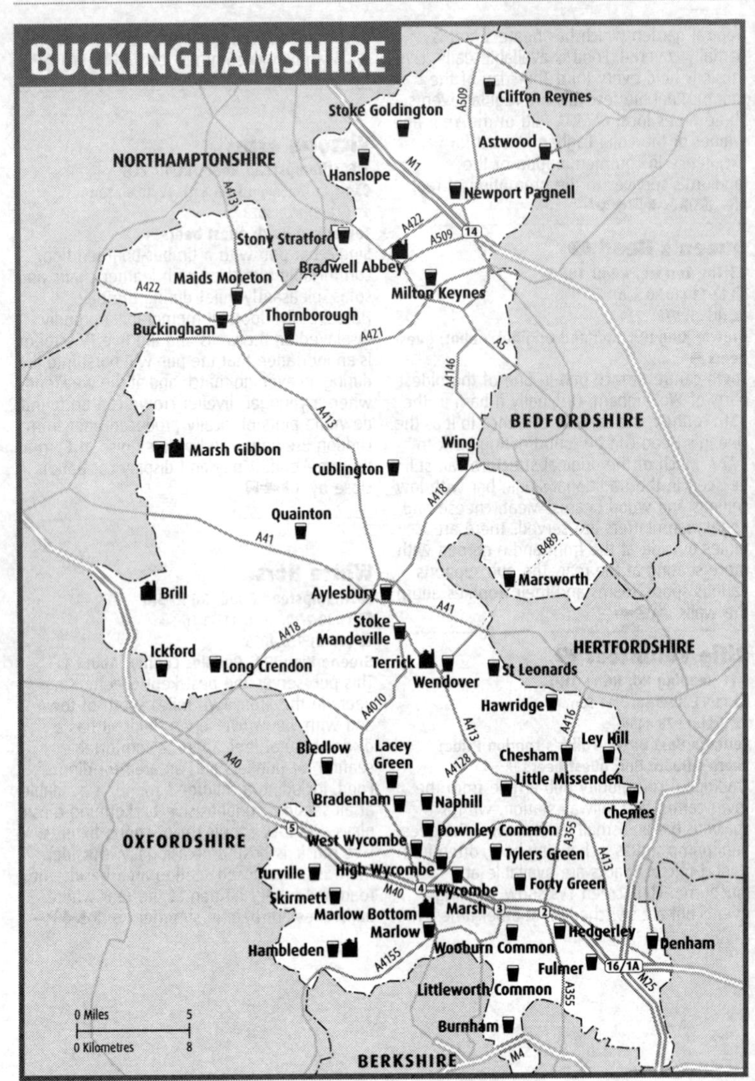

Astwood

Old Swan

8 Main Road, MK16 9JS (off A422)
11-3, 6-11; closed Mon; 12-3 Sun
☎ (01234) 391351
Adnams Bitter; guest beers Ⓗ
17th-century free house in a village just off the northern Milton Keynes-Bedford road. The pub has a superb reputation for high-quality food with fresh fish a speciality on the menu — booking is a must. A large blue china collection and an impressive display of water jugs adorns the walls and ceiling. The pub usually has two guest beers on offer in the colder months rising to three in summer. More than 100 different ales were dispensed last year. ⌂Q❀◑♿P⁻

What care I how time advances: I am drinking ale today. **Edgar Allan Poe**

Aylesbury

Hop Pole

83 Bicester Road, HP19 9AZ
12-11 (midnight Fri & Sat)
☎ (01296) 482129
Vale Best Bitter, VPA; guest beers Ⓗ
The Hop Pole boasts that it is 'Aylesbury's Permanent Beer Festival' and with 10 handpumps it easily lives up to the claim. Vale Brewery's sole outlet in the town, it also features a myriad selection of micro-brewery beers. A large function room hosts two beer

INDEPENDENT BREWERIES

Chiltern Terrick
Concrete Cow Milton Keynes (NEW)
Old Luxters Hambleden
Oxfordshire Ales Marsh Gibbon
Rebellion Marlow Bottom
Vale Brill

festivals when the range of ales on offer is more than doubled. Live music plays at the weekend. Good food is an added attraction at this friendly pub. CAMRA Aylesbury Vale & Wycombe Pub of the Year 2008.
❀🛏◑◗🚌(2,16)●

King's Head

Market Square, HP20 2RW
⏲ 11-11; 12-10.30 Sun
☎ (01296) 718812
Chiltern Ale, Beechwood, seasonal beers; guest beers Ⓗ
The oldest courtyard inn in England, situated at the top of Market Square, very close to bus and rail stations. It offers a quiet, comfortable, relaxed environment in which to enjoy beers from Buckinghamshire's oldest micro-brewery. The food is freshly sourced from local suppliers and often incorporates local ales; the menu also recommends ales to drink with many of the dishes. Publican magazine's Beer with Food Pub of the Year in 2007.
Q❀◗♿⇌🚌⅟

Bledlow

Lions of Bledlow

Church End, HP27 9PE (off B4009)
⏲ 11.30-3, 6-11; 12-10.30 (12-4, 7-10.30 winter) Sun
☎ (01844) 343345
Wadworth 6X; guest beers Ⓗ
Rambling, unspoilt, Grade II listed 16th-century free house complete with beams, inglenooks and a large log fire. Originally three shepherds' cottages. There is a restaurant and large bar with wide-ranging blackboard menus. The extensive garden is busy in summer with walkers and families. The pub has featured in many TV series including Midsomer Murders and Miss Marple.
♨Q❀◑◗P⅟

Bradenham

Red Lion

Bradenham, HP14 4HF (on A4010)
⏲ 11.30-2.30 (not Mon), 5.30-11; 11.30-10 (6 winter) Sun
☎ (01494) 562212
Brakspear Bitter; Young's Bitter; guest beers Ⓗ
Part of a National Trust-owned hamlet, the pub comprises a snug bar with wood-burning stove and lounge bar/restaurant. Top quality real ales are on offer including guest beers from breweries near and far. The bar meals are excellent with specialities including delicious hand-made pies ranging from Aberdeen Angus to chicken tikka. It is reputed that Disraeli, born in the village, and Bomber Harris, when stationed at nearby Bomber Command, imbibed here. Jazz and food nights feature on alternate Sundays.
♨Q❀◑◗⊟⇌(Saunderton)P

Buckingham

Mitre

2 Mitre Street, MK18 1DW
⏲ 5-11.30 (midnight Sat); 12-10.30 Sun
☎ (01280) 813080
Beer range varies Ⓗ
Located to the south of the town, near the route of the old railway line, this old inn looks small from the outside but is surprisingly spacious inside. New landlords have breathed fresh life into the Mitre, which was threatened with closure in 2007. Cider is from the Weston's range. Parking is challenging but the pub is accessible by public transport. The Oxford-Cambridge X5 stops at Tesco about 15 minutes' walk away. ♨❀◑🚌♣●⅟

Burnham

George

18 High Street, SL1 7JH
⏲ 12-11 (1am Fri & Sat); 12-10.30 Sun
☎ (01628) 605047
Courage Best Bitter, Directors; guest beers Ⓗ
Grade II listed 16th-century coaching inn, once a magistrates' court and believed to be the oldest pub in the High Street. The publican has built up a reputation for excellent guest beers, offering as many as 30 a month, sourced from breweries from all over the country. Two beer festivals are held annually. Karaoke, disco and live music are occasional attractions. Well-behaved dogs and children welcome before 7pm; well-behaved over-21s welcome at any time. ♨❀🚌♣P⅟

Chenies

Red Lion

Latimer Road, WD3 6ED (off A404 between Chorleywood and Little Chalfont) TQ021980
⏲ 11-2.30, 5.30-11; 12-3, 6.30-10.30 Sun
☎ (01923) 282722 🌐 redlionchenies.co.uk
Vale Best Bitter; Wadworth 6X; guest beer Ⓗ
Long-standing Guide entry with a long-standing landlord. This is a real village gem in idyllic surroundings. A cosy and comfortable place with a relaxing atmosphere, it has a main bar and small back dining room. Local micro-breweries are a mainstay with Vale and Rebellion providing specials alongside the 6X and a guest beer. This is a beer pub that also serves excellent food. Well worth a visit. Chenies Manor is nearby, along with excellent walks. ♨Q❀◑◗♿🚌(336)P⅟

Chesham

Queens Head ✔

Church Street, HP5 1JD
⏲ 12-11 (midnight Thu & Fri); 11-midnight Sat; 11-10.30 Sun
☎ (01494) 778690
Brakspear Bitter; Fuller's London Pride, ESB; guest beers Ⓗ
The river Chess runs around this street-corner pub in the old part of town. A central bar serves the public and saloon bars and there is a back room with a sporting theme. The cask selection is accompanied by a range of bottled beers. Thai food cooked in the upstairs restaurant is also available at the bar. Dogs are welcome in the public bar. Under-18s are permitted until 8.30pm. Parking is limited but there is a public car park nearby.
♨Q❀◑◗⊟♿⊖🚌♣P⅟

Clifton Reynes

Robin Hood

Church Road, MK46 5DR (off A509 Milton Keynes-Olney road) SP903512

12-3, 6.30-11; closed Mon; 12-3, 7-10.30 Sun

(01234) 711574 therobinhoodpub.co.uk

Greene King IPA, Abbot; guest beer Ⓗ

Winner of local CAMRA Pub of the Year in 2007, this village inn offers all you could wish for in a country pub. Food is a feature here, with a good range of dishes that includes traditional pub fare as well as more unusual meals. Mobile phone owners beware —a ringing phone will cost you a £1 donation to charity. Look out for details of the pub's history in the saloon, including landlords going back to 1577. Northants skittles is available. The Three Shires Way passes the door, popular with walkers and horse riders.

(42)P

Cublington

Unicorn

High Street, LU7 0LQ

12-3, 5-11; 12-midnight Fri & Sat; 12-10.30 Sun

(01296) 681261

Brakspear Bitter; Greene King IPA; Shepherd Neame Spitfire; guest beers Ⓗ

Picturesque village free house voted Community Pub of the Year in 2007 by Aylesbury Vale Council. The long, low ceilinged bar has open fires at both ends. Food is available every day from an extensive menu and served either in the bar or a small dining area. The large, attractive garden has a covered and heated smoking area. Occasional beer festivals are hosted from the first weekend in May. Live local bands entertain on Friday nights.

Denham

Falcon

Village Road, UB9 5BE

11-3, 5-11; 11-11 summer Sat; 12-10.30 Sun

(01895) 832125 falconinn.biz

Brakspear Bitter; Wells Bombardier; guest beers Ⓗ

In the heart of Denham, this small 16th-century pub has changed over the years but retains its traditional charm, especially in the cosy bar area. The lower back room leads to a delightful garden where there is a covered, heated smoking area. Parking can be difficult in the village but there is easy access to the railway station via a footpath. A community bus service operates Monday-Saturday from Uxbridge, and will drop you right outside.

QP

Downley Common

De Spencer Arms

The Common, HP13 5YQ SU849958

12-3, 6-11; 12-11 Fri & Sat; 12-10.30 Sun

(01494) 535317

Fuller's Chiswick, London Pride, ESB, seasonal beers; guest beers Ⓗ

Family oriented and much frequented by ramblers, this brick and flint building is in a remote location off Downley common. The interior divides into numerous intimate areas as well as a separate small room off the bar. In summer the pub hosts barbecues and two mini beer festivals under canvas. Good quality food is served every lunchtime and Friday and Saturday evenings. Sunday roasts are always popular. Live music is performed monthly on a Saturday, and a quiz is held weekly on Wednesday night. Dogs are welcome.

Q(31)P

Forty Green

Royal Standard of England

HP9 1XT (off Penn Road from Knotty Green) SU924918

11-11; 12-10.30 Sun

(01494) 673382 rsoe.co.uk

Brakspear Bitter; Marston's Pedigree; Rebellion Mild, IPA; guest beer Ⓗ

Reputedly 'the oldest freehouse in England', with an ale house on this site since Saxon times, this ancient, rambling and historic pub oozes mystique and quaint charm. Rustic flooring, original low beams and period bare-board furniture add to the hostelry's authenticity. Popular at all times, the pub is a must-see for tourists. Renowned for its award-winning country cooking, the menu offers traditional favourites and classics. A little tricky to find, although well signposted, the car park is huge. QP

Fulmer

Black Horse

Windmill Road, SL1 6HD (next to church)

11-midnight (1am Fri & Sat)

(01753) 663183

Greene King IPA, Abbot, seasonal beers; guest beers Ⓗ

Friendly three-bar pub in the centre of Fulmer alongside the church. Active in village life, it hosts charity events and supports local sporting activities. Popular with diners as well as drinkers, the restaurant overlooks a well-tended garden. The central bar's frontage is constructed from wood salvaged from a hut used by the ARP during WW2. QP

Hambleden

Stag & Huntsman

RG9 6RP (opp churchyard)

11-2.30 (3 Sat), 6-11; 12-3, 7-10.30 Sun

(01491) 571227 stagandhuntsman.co.uk

Rebellion IPA; Wadworth 6X; guest beers Ⓗ

Rhapsodic, traditional, unspoilt inn at the hub of a sleepy, photogenic brick and flint National Trust village. Hugely popular at all times, locals, cyclists and hikers all make a pilgrimage to this rural gem. Food is served throughout the three bars and dining room. The guest ale usually honours both local and south-west independents and micro-breweries. Thatchers dry cider is a permanent fixture on handpump. An annual beer festival is staged on the first weekend in September.

P

Hanslope

Globe

50 Hartwell Road, MK19 7BZ (N of village)
⏲ 12-3.30, 6-11; 12-4, 7-10.30 Sun
☎ (01908) 510336
Banks's Bitter; guest beers Ⓗ
Visitors can be sure of a warm welcome at this award-winning village pub located just through the main, rambling village. The interior comprises two bars including a public bar with a 'local' feel, a small and cosy lounge and a restaurant area well away from drinkers. The garden has a play area for children. Guest beers are usually from the Marston's estate. Q✿◐◑⊟⊡(33)P⁼

Hawridge

Full Moon

HP5 2UH SP936069
⏲ 12-11; 12-10.30 Sun
☎ (01494) 758959 🌐 thefullmoonpub.co.uk
Adnams Bitter; Draught Bass; Fullers London Pride; Taylor Landlord; guest beers Ⓗ
A 16th-century pub that entices visitors with an array of six ales. It has a brick-built bar and three distinct low-beamed, flagstoned drinking areas, one set around a large open fireplace. Part of the pub is set aside for diners but meals are also served in the bar. A pergola-covered patio is delightful in summer. Children and dogs are welcome; well-behaved dogs get a biscuit. Q✿◐◑♿⛺♣P⁼

Hedgerley

White Horse

Village Lane, SL2 3UY
⏲ 11-2.30, 5-11; 11-11 Sat; 12-10.30
☎ (01753) 643225
Greene King IPA; Rebellion IPA; guest beers Ⓖ
Family-run village free house, usually stocking seven real ales including five constantly-changing guests from small breweries all over the country. The annual beer festival held over the Whitsun bank holiday offers well over a hundred real ales. A draught Belgian beer as well as real cider are also always available. Good food is served at lunchtime. The garden is an added attraction. Local CAMRA Pub of the Year many times over. ⛰Q✿◐⊟⛺♣●P

High Wycombe

Belle Vue

45 Gordon Road, HP13 6EQ (100m from train station, platform 3 exit)
⏲ 12-2.30, 5-11; 12-midnight Sat; 12-10.30 Sun
☎ (01494) 524728
St Austell Dartmoor Best Bitter; guest beers Ⓗ
Purpose-built street-corner community local, just a short walk from the town centre. The U-shaped interior boasts bare boards and traditional pub values. Renowned in the town for dedication to real ale, four beers are on offer from the Punch Taverns portfolio. Busy when London Wasps are at home, the pub is also handy for city commuters due to its proximity to the train station. The rear beer garden proves popular during the summer months. An established live music venue. ⛰✿⇌⊡♣

Ickford

Rising Sun

36 Worminghall Road, HP18 9JD
⏲ 12-2.30, 5-11; 12-11 Sat; 12-10.30 Sun
☎ (01844) 339238
Adnams Bitter, Broadside; Black Sheep Best Bitter; Flowers IPA Ⓗ
Following a disastrous fire early in 2006, the pub was rebuilt, re-thatched, refurbished and reopened in April 2007. Dating originally from the 15th century, this classic local has become the hub of the village, hosting local events and games including crib, darts, quizzes and Aunt Sally. Four ales are always available and basic pub food is served at most sessions. Close to the Oxford Way, it attracts many ramblers and cyclists. Families and dogs on leads are welcome. ⛰Q✿◐◑⊡(261)♣P⁼

Lacey Green

Pink & Lily

Pink Road, HP27 0RJ SP826019
⏲ 11-11; 12-10 (4 winter) Sun
☎ (01494) 488308 🌐 pinkandlily.co.uk
Brakspear Bitter; Fuller's London Pride, seasonal beers; guest beers Ⓗ
The curious name dates back to a scandal some two hundred years ago —Mr Pink and Miss Lillie were employed at the local Hampden House but were forced to leave due to an illicit affair and set up their own hostelry. This large pub has an extensive conservatory-style seating area leading to a pleasant garden. The famous Brooke Bar snug was a favourite of WWI poet Rupert Brooke and has been preserved in keeping with that period. As well as the regular beers, two guest ales, three at Christmas, are on handpump, mainly from local breweries. ⛰✿◐◑♿♣P

Whip

Pink Road, HP27 0PG
⏲ 11-11; 12-10.30 Sun
☎ (01844) 344060 🌐 whipinn.co.uk
Beer range varies Ⓗ
A real ale cornucopia, over the last year the Whip has dispensed more than 700 different ales from its five handpumps. The beer variety is exceptional, with regulars often balloted for their own favourites. Two beer festivals are held annually including the 'Alternative Oktoberfest'. Perched on top of the Chiltern hills with an attractive enclosed garden, the pub enjoys splendid views and is popular with ramblers. Good food is served here including fish freshly landed from Devon.
⛰Q✿◐◑⊡(300)♣●⁼

Ley Hill

Swan

Ley Hill Common, HP5 1UT (opp cricket pitch) SP990018
⏲ 12-3.30, 5.30-11; 12-4, 6-10.30 Sun
☎ (01494) 783075 🌐 swanleyhill.com
Adnams Bitter; Brakspear Bitter; Fuller's London Pride; Taylor Landlord; guest beers Ⓗ

An amalgamation of separate cottages dating from the 1520s, this country pub claims to be the oldest in Buckinghamshire and was previously a last stop-off for condemned prisoners. It later became the watering hole for Hollywood actors Clark Gable, James Stewart and jazz legend Glenn Miller. Regulars still come over from the local cricket and golf clubs to sample the wide range of beers and enjoy jazz and food evenings. Good food is prepared by an experienced chef. Families are welcome. ♨Q❀◑🚌(373)P⌐

Little Missenden

Crown

HP7 0RD (off A413, between Amersham and Gt Missenden) SU924989

⏲ 11-2.30, 6-11; 12-3, 7-11 Sun

☎ (01494) 862571

Adnams Bitter; Woodforde's Wherry Best Bitter; St Austell Tribute; guest beer 🄷

Run by the same family for almost a century, this village pub has recently been refurbished to include bed and breakfast accommodation and a bigger bar, but retains its cosy, friendly atmosphere. Good pub food, served at lunchtime, is simple and generous. Popular with walkers, the large and attractive garden is a great place to relax and enjoy a peaceful pint. A regular in the Guide for more than 25 years. ♨Q❀🛏◐♣●P

Littleworth Common

Blackwood Arms

Common Lane, SL1 8PP SU937862

⏲ 11.30-3, 5-midnight; 11.30-midnight Sat; 11-9 Sun

☎ (01753) 642169

Brakspear Bitter, Oxford Gold; Hook Norton Hooky Dark, seasonal beers 🄷

Secluded country pub to the north of Burnham Beeches popular with walkers. It is the only pub in the area that regularly has cask mild available. The large outside seating area is deservedly popular in warmer weather and is suitable for families. Good food is available lunchtime and evening during the week and all day at the weekend. ♨Q❀◑♿▲P⌐

Jolly Woodman

Littleworth Road, SL1 8PF

⏲ 11-11 (midnight Fri & Sat); 12-10.30 Sun

☎ (01753) 644350 🌐 thejollywoodman.co.uk

Brakspear Bitter; Fuller's London Pride; Hop Back Summer Lightning; St Austell Tribute; Tring Sidepocket for a Toad; guest beers 🄷

Homely 19th-century country pub, close to the northern edge of Burnham Beeches. It is popular for its range of beers and good home-cooked food, as well as its live Monday night jazz sessions. The bar area contains a large collection of old beer bottles as well a rowing boat in the rafters. There is a garden seating area available. ♨❀◑▲●P⌐

Long Crendon

Eight Bells ✔

51 High Street, HP18 9AL

⏲ 12-3 (not Mon), 5.30-11 (midnight Fri); 12-midnight Sat; 12-10.30 Sun

☎ (01844) 208244

Wadworth Henry's Original, IPA; guest beers 🄷

Time-honoured, charming, hub of the village local, popular with both diners and drinkers. A fairly recent knock-through, linking the snug and lounge bars, hasn't influenced the cosy ambience too much. Part-original tiled floors, beams and an alcove dedicated to the pub's morris dancers enhance the quaint pub interior. Two ever-changing guest ales and the annual Easter beer festival are eagerly supported by the pub's real ale fraternity. ♨❀◑🚌♣P

Maids Moreton

Wheatsheaf

Main Street, MK18 1QR (off A413, Buckingham-Towcester road)

⏲ 12-3, 6-11 (not Mon eve); 12-10.30 Sun

☎ (01280) 815433

Hook Norton Hooky Bitter; Tring Side Pocket for a Toad; guest beers 🄷

Old village pub retaining much character within the older parts and sympathetically extended elsewhere. Visitors should take care with the nooks, crannies and sloping floors. Three real fires add warmth in winter. Traditional pub food is served; it is advisable to book ahead. Children are welcome in the conservatory. The location is handy for Stowe Park (NT) and the Silverstone motor racing circuit. Staff will remove sparklers on request. ♨Q❀◑🚌(32A)P

Marlow

Duke of Cambridge

19 Queens Road, SL7 2PS

⏲ 11-11.30 (12.30am Fri & Sat); 10-11 Sun

☎ (01628) 488555

Harveys Sussex Best Bitter; guest beers 🄷

Quintessential, urban, one-bar back-street local, renowned as Marlow's most adventurous real ale pub. Guest beers come from far and wide, from nationwide independents to the latest micro. The landlord even sporadically sources real ale direct from brewery visits and more than 200 ales have already been showcased. Steak night is the first Saturday of the month and popular Sunday roasts are a feature. Darts and cribbage are encouraged and there is a pool table in the large alfresco smoking area. ♨❀◐♿⇄🚌♣⌐

Three Horseshoes

Burroughs Grove Hill, SL7 3RA (on High Wycombe-Marlow road)

⏲ 11.30-3, 5-11; 11.30-11 Fri & Sat; 12-5, 7-10.30 Sun

☎ (01628) 483109

Rebellion Mild, IPA, Smuggler, Mutiny, seasonal beers 🄷

Brewery tap for the nearby Rebellion Beer Co, showcasing six of its award-winning real ales. From the town centre it's a five minute bus ride here, and well worth it. The interior comprises three distinctive areas and outside the enclosed family friendly beer garden is a summer essential. The pub is popular at all times with diners deliberating over an extensive food menu (no meals Sun eve).

Former local CAMRA Pub of the Year.
ᗑQ❀ᗡ◗🚌P

Marsh Gibbon

Plough

Church Street, OX27 0HQ
⏲ 12-midnight
☎ (01869) 278759
Greene King IPA; Oxfordshire Ales Ploughmans Pride ⊞
Situated in a quiet Domesday village near Bicester, this 16th-century pub has two bars serving pub food and a more formal dining area offering restaurant-style meals. Pool, darts, dominoes and Aunt Sally are all played here and Wii is a 21st-century newcomer. The main bar has sports TV and a juke box and hosts live music on Saturday evening. An excellent children's playground is next to the beer garden and car park. ᗑ☺❀ᗡ◗⊟🚌♣P🚬

Marsworth

Anglers Retreat ✔

Startops End, HP23 4LJ (on B489, opp Startops Reservoir car park) SP919141
⏲ 11-11; 12-10.30 Sun
☎ (01442) 822250 🌐 anglersretreatpub.co.uk
Fuller's London Pride; Tring Side Pocket for a Toad; guest beers ⊞
Traditional country pub with a fishing theme near to two reservoirs (famous for wild birds) and the Grand Union Canal. Dark beers including milds, porters and stouts all feature on the frequently-changing guest beer list. Beer festivals are regular events in April and October. Home-cooked food is served daily. A garden and small aviary attract families. Dogs and walkers are welcome.
ᗑ❀ᗡ◗🚌(61)♣P🚬

Red Lion ✔

90 Vicarage Road, HP23 4LU (off B489, by canal bridge)
⏲ 11-3, 5 (6 Sat)-11; 12-3, 7-10.30 Sun
☎ (01296) 668366
Fuller's London Pride; Vale Best Bitter; guest beers ⊞
Genuine village inn by the Grand Union Canal. Dating from the 17th-century, this three-room pub is served by a central bar. Each room has its own atmosphere —the saloon bar has sofas and a dining area, there is a small snug, and the popular, low-beamed public bar has an open fire and games area where supervised children are permitted. Darts, bar billiards, shove-ha'penny and skittles (by prior arrangement) are all played. Dogs are welcome. The rear door permits wheelchair access. A regular in the Guide for many years.
ᗑQ❀ᗡ◗⊟🚌♣●P🚬

Milton Keynes

Victoria Inn

Vicarage Road, Bradwell Village, MK13 9AQ
⏲ 11.30-midnight; 12-11 Sun
☎ (01908) 316355
Beer range varies ⊞
The popularity of its quality ales has seen this pub go from strength to strength. Four ever-changing guests are now served from a newly-installed set of water-cooled handpumps. The closest pub to the new Concrete Cow brewery, its beers often feature on the guest ale list. Other popular micros are Tring and Bank Top, although anything from anywhere in the UK may be on offer. An annual beer festival is hosted on the August bank holiday weekend. The weekday lunchtime sandwiches are huge.
❀ᗡ🚌(2)♣●P🚬

Wetherspoons ✔

201 Midsummer Boulevard, MK9 1EA
⏲ 9-midnight (1am Fri & Sat)
☎ (01908) 606074
Courage Best Bitter, Directors; Greene King Abbot; Marston's Pedigree; guest beers ⊞
Last year's return to GBG status has been fully vindicated by an unblemished record in beer quality over the last 12 months. Guest beers are now sourced direct from Concrete Cow, Great Oakley and Oldershaw. Participation in company beer festivals is wholehearted. Staff will remove sparklers if asked. The pub can get busy on food promotional nights and Friday evenings. Most buses from the station go to the city centre stop outside. There is a covered, heated patio for smokers.
❀ᗡ◗♿⇌🚌●🚬

Naphill

Wheel

100 Main Road, HP14 4QA
⏲ 12.30-2.30 (not Mon), 4.30-11; 12-midnight Fri & Sat; 12-10.30 Sun
☎ (01494) 562210 🌐 thewheelnaphill.com
Greene King IPA; guest beers ⊞
Situated in the heart of Chiltern's walking country, the Wheel is popular with locals, ramblers and bird spotters alike. Even their muddy boots are welcome. The pub sponsors High Wycombe Rugby Club and hosts regular events including quiz nights and live music. The multi-roomed local has two extensive, enclosed gardens that are popular with families and are also used to hold regular beer festivals throughout the year.
ᗑ❀ᗡ◗⊟🚌(300)♣P🚬

Newport Pagnell

Cannon

50 High Street, MK16 8AQ
⏲ 12-11 (midnight Fri & Sat)
☎ (01908) 211495
Banks's Bitter; Marston's Pedigree; guest beers ⊞
A true free house, the Cannon retains the feel of an old town centre local despite a recent refurbishment. Guest beers are often from the Marston's list but can also be local. No food is sold. Look out for the military memorabilia and various awards adorning the walls. 'Real ale' is written in four languages behind the bar and the landlord speaks them all.
ᗑ❀🚌(2, 9, 23)P🚬

Green Man

92 Silver Street, MK16 0EG
⏲ 12-11 (10.30 Sun)

☎ (01908) 611914
Banks's Bitter; guest beers Ⓗ
A welcome return to the Guide for this pub, with new proprietors bringing the focus back on the beer. The two bars have swapped roles: the door marked Lounge now leads to the livelier of the bars where there is a pool table. The old public bar is now the quieter bar, and is where you will find the three handpumps. Guest beers are from the Enterprise list.
(2)

Quainton

George & Dragon ✔
The Green, HP22 4AR
12-11 (midnight Fri & Sat); 12-11 (12-2.30, 5-11 winter) Sun
☎ (01296) 655436
Black Sheep Best Bitter; Fuller's London Pride; Hook Norton Hooky Bitter; guest beers Ⓗ
Two-bar local on the village green overlooked by a restored windmill which now provides flour for the pub. An extensive menu of value-for-money food includes vegetarian and children's options. Special price lunches for older people are available on Tuesday and steak specials on Tuesday evening (no food Sun eve or Mon lunchtime). Traditional cider is stocked in summer. The bar offers Post Office facilities on Monday and Wednesday, 9.30-11.30am. The Buckinghamshire Railway Centre is close by. Q(16)P

St Leonards

White Lion
Jenkins Lane, HP23 6NN (4 miles from Chesham on Wendover road)
11.30-midnight; 12-11.30 Sun
☎ (01494) 758387
Greene King IPA; guest beers Ⓗ
The highest pub in the Chilterns, this welcoming, friendly, classic country hostelry is situated close to the Ridgeway and Chiltern paths. The interior comprises three drinking areas and a small meeting room served by a single bar. Popular with walkers and their dogs, a real fire adds a cosy warmth in winter. The rambling garden hosts an annual beer festival. Home-cooked food is excellent and the pub can be busy at Sunday lunchtimes.
QP

Skirmett

Frog
RG9 6TG (off M40 Jct 5, through Ibstone to Skirmett)
11.30-3, 6-11; 12-10.30 (12-4 winter) Sun
☎ (01491) 638996 thefrogatskirmett.co.uk
Loddon Hoppit; Rebellion IPA; guest beers Ⓗ
With fine views across the countryside, this 300-year-old free house lies in the beautiful Hambleden Valley. The Frog is a family-owned pub exuding warmth and tranquillity. It offers a fine restaurant and high-quality accommodation. Guest beers often come from local breweries. Snacks are available in the bar where an inviting log fire burns in winter. Food is cooked to order and specials are available daily. Themed nights are a regular feature. QP

Stoke Goldington

Lamb
16-20 High Street, MK16 8NR
12-3, 5-11; 12-11 Sat; 12-8 Sun
☎ (01908) 551233
thelambstokegoldington.moonfruit.com
Nethergate IPA; guest beers Ⓗ
Run by the same owners for many years, this excellent village free house is very much the hub of the local community. Northamptonshire skittles and darts teams are based here. Good food is available and the popular Sunday lunches are excellent value. A Guide regular, the Lamb was local CAMRA Pub of the Year runner-up in 2008.
(1B)P

Stoke Mandeville

Bull
5 Risborough Road, HP22 5UP
12-3, 5.30-11; 12-11 Fri & Sat; 12-10.30 Sun
☎ (01296) 613632
Fuller's London Pride; Shepherd Neame Spitfire; Tetley Bitter Ⓗ
Small two-bar pub situated on a main road, well served by public transport. The public bar at the front is where the locals gather, with football and horse racing on TV. The comfortable lounge bar at the back tends to be quieter. Behind the pub is a large, secure garden which is popular with families, especially in summer. Q(300)P

Stony Stratford

Bull (Vaults Bar)
64 High Street, MK11 1AQ
12-11 (midnight Fri); 12-10.30 Sun
☎ (01908) 567104
Adnams Bitter, Broadside; Black Sheep Best Bitter; Draught Bass; Everards Tiger; Fuller's London Pride; guest beer Ⓗ
The Vaults Bar is to the left of the main Bull hotel. This historic hostelry is the Bull referred to as one half of the famous 'cock and bull' story. Items of bric-a-brac and some brewing-related material adorn the interior. The original handpumps are of a type that is increasingly rare. The guest beer comes from the Punch list. Impromptu folk sessions are sometimes held on Sundays. P

Fox & Hounds
87 High Street, MK11 1AT
12-3, 5.30-11; 12-11 Fri & Sat; 12-10.30 Sun
☎ (01908) 563307 foxandhounds.info
Beer range varies Ⓗ
Much changed from its previous guise, the pub now has a modern feel to it. The lounge is almost 'wine bar' in its atmosphere and decor. The range of guest ales has become more limited due to the installation of technology to measure total beer sales down to the pint. Northamptonshire skittles can still be played.
(4, 5)P

Thornborough

Two Brewers

Bridge Street, MK18 2DN (off A421, turn by Lone Tree pub)
12-2 Wed & Sat only, 6-midnight; 12-3, 7-11 Sun
(01280) 812020
Frog Island Best Bitter; guest beers H
Run by the same landlord for more than 25 years, this welcoming drinkers' pub is in the centre of the village. Play darts in the traditional public bar or relax with a pint in the lounge. During the week the pub is closed at lunchtime except on Wednesday when it offers half-price drinks to pensioners.

Turville

Bull & Butcher

RG9 6QU (off M40 jct 5 through Ibstone to Turville)
11-11; 12-10.30 Sun
(01491) 638283
Brakspear Bitter, Oxford Gold, seasonal beers; Hook Norton Hooky Dark H
Set in an unspoilt village in a beautiful Chiltern valley, this charming 16th-century timbered pub has open log fires and a bar extension that incorporates a table above a 50-foot well. The excellent à la carte menu is reasonably priced —booking is recommended. No meals are served on Sunday evenings in winter. A function room is available for meetings. Pleasant garden. QP

Tylers Green

Horse & Jockey

Church Road, HP10 8EG
12-3, 5-11; 12-11 Fri & Sat; 12-10.30 Sun
(01494) 815963 horseandjockeytylersgreen.co.uk
Adnams Bitter, Broadside; Brakspear Bitter; Fuller's London Pride; Greene King Abbot; guest beer H
Converted to a pub in 1821, this popular, cosy, traditional local is sited in a dip, canopied by Tylers Green church. A regular in the Guide, it is the hub of the village and visitors can be sure of a warm welcome. The single-room horseshoe-shaped bar attracts both diners and drinkers with its homely, congenial ambience. All six handpumped ales have their tasting notes on the bar blackboard. P

Wendover

Pack Horse

29 Tring Road, HP22 6NR
12-11 (midnight Fri & Sat); 12-10.30 Sun
(01296) 622075
Fuller's London Pride, seasonal beers; Gale's Butser Bitter; guest beers H
Small, friendly village free house dating from 1769 and situated at the end of a thatched terrace known as the Anne Boleyn cottages, on the Ridgeway path. It has been owned by the same family for 45 years. The wall above the bar is decorated with RAF squadron badges denoting connections with nearby RAF Halton. The pub runs men's and women's darts teams, dominoes and cribbage.
(54)

West Wycombe

George & Dragon

High Street, HP14 3AB (On A40)
11-3, 5.30-11; 12-3, 7-10.30 Sun
(01494) 464414
Courage Best Bitter; Taylor Landlord; Wells Bombardier; guest beers H
This rustic, oak-beamed 18th-century inn is owned by the National Trust. Two bedrooms have four-poster beds and the garden has children's play equipment. West Wycombe Park and House (NT) stand behind the village, close to the famous Hell-fire caves (home of the notorious Hell-fire Club). Dogs are welcome. Q(40)P

Wing

Queen's Head

9 High Street, LU7 0NS
11-3, 5.30-11; closed Tue; 11.30-11 Fri & Sat; 12-10.30 Sun
(01296) 688268
Adnams Bitter; Fuller's London Pride; guest beers H
A village local offering an increasing number of real ales. The 16th-century building features open log fires in the restaurant and main bar and comfortable sofas in the snug. The food here is excellent and sensibly priced. Fish dishes are a speciality. Board games are available in both bars. Outside is a large, attractive garden and patio. Aylesbury Vale Council's Village Pub of the Year 2007.
(150)P

Wooburn Common

Royal Standard

Wooburn Common Road, HP10 0JS (follow signs to Odds Farm) SU924873
12-11 (10.30 Sun)
(01628) 521121
Caledonian Deuchars IPA; Hop Back Summer Lightning; St Austell Tribute; guest beers H/G
Semi-rural roadside country pub that hosts an amazing 10 real ales, five on handpump, five on gravity dispense. Hop Back and Downton seasonal ales are often among the infinite number of beers on parade. Dark beer and an over-5% brew are also usually available. This popular pub attracts a lively crowd, particularly on warm summer evenings. Local CAMRA Pub of the Year 2007. QP

Wycombe Marsh

General Havelock

114 Kingsmead Road, HP11 1HZ (S of M40)
12-2.30, 5.30-11; 1-11 Fri & Sat; 12-10.30 Sun
(01494) 520391
Fuller's Chiswick, London Pride, ESB, seasonal beers; guest beers H
A regular entry in the Guide, this imposing pub was converted from a farmhouse and sits between playing fields and a ski slope. It welcomes a mixed clientele of all ages. The garden is a peaceful haven in summer. Food is served every lunchtime except Saturday and on Friday evening only. P

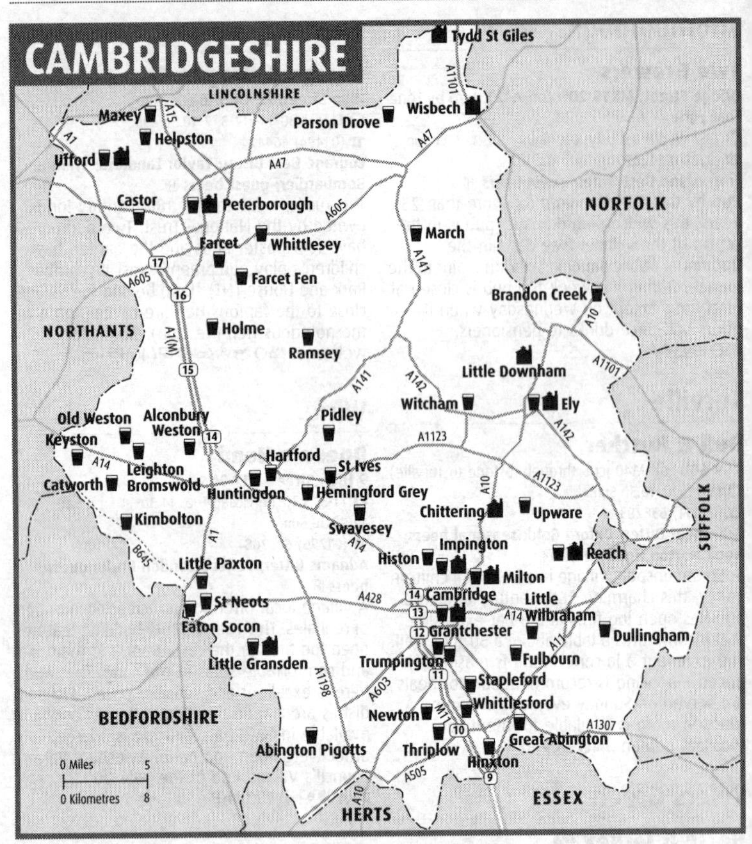

Abington Pigotts

Pig & Abbot

High Street, SG8 0SD (off A505 through Litlington)
TL307444
✪ 12-3, 6-11; 12-11 Sat; 12-10.30 Sun
☎ (01763) 853515 🌐 pigandabbot.co.uk
Adnams Bitter; Fuller's London Pride; guest beers Ⓗ
Located in a surprisingly remote part of the south Cambridgeshire countryside, this Queen Anne period pub offers a warm welcome. The bar has exposed oak beams and a large inglenook featuring a wood-burning stove. A comfortable restaurant offers a range of cuisine from home-made traditional pub food to Thai curry made with fresh herbs and spices. Guest beers are often from Woodforde's or Timothy Taylor. ⛰Q❀◑P

Alconbury Weston

White Hart

2 Vinegar Hill, PE28 4JA
✪ 12-2.30, 5.30-11; 12-4, 6.30-11 Sat; 12-5.30 Sun
☎ (01480) 890331
Adnams Bitter; Courage Directors; guest beers Ⓗ
Welcoming 16th-century coaching inn on the old Great North Road with an open-plan two-tier layout providing different drinking spaces and a darts area. Home-cooked food is served including popular Sunday lunches. International dining nights are a feature and there is occasional live music. This community pub raises funds for local amenities and is supported by villagers, local businesses and passing trade. ❀◑♿⊟♣P⊬

Brandon Creek

Ship

Brandon Creek Bridge, PE38 0PP (just off A10)
✪ 12-3, 6-midnight (closed winter Mon); 12-11 (12-4, 6-10.30 winter) Sun
☎ (01353) 676228
Adnams Bitter; guest beers Ⓗ
Large, welcoming free house on the Cambridgeshire/Norfolk border offering up to three guest beers. Varied lunchtime and evening menus featuring home-cooked food can be enjoyed in a choice of dining areas. A

INDEPENDENT BREWERIES

Cambridge Moonshine Cambridge
City of Cambridge Chittering
Devil's Dyke Reach
Elgood's Wisbech
Fenland Little Downham
Hereward Ely
Kilderkin Impington (NEW)
Milton Milton
Oakham Peterborough
Son of Sid Little Gransden (NEW)
Tydd Steam Tydd Saint Giles
Ufford Ufford

popular spot in summer, especially with boaters, the pub can become busy. Mark Twain is said to have once stayed here. There is a patio outside for drinking, with pleasing views of the river. Moorings are available. ⌂❀◐P⚐

Cambridge

Cambridge Blue

85-87 Gwydir Street, CB1 2LG (off Mill Road)
⌚ 12-2.30, 5.30-11; 12-11 Thu-Sat; 12-10.30 Sun
☎ (01223) 361382 🌐 the-cambridgeblue.co.uk
Elgood's Black Dog; Woodforde's Wherry Best Bitter; H guest beers H/G
Quiet, traditional community pub with a conservatory and large garden. Around a dozen ever-changing beers are available, some served direct from barrels in the tap room. There is also a large selection of bottled beers from all over the world and several real ciders and perries. Occasional beer festivals are held. Wholesome, home-cooked food is available at every session. ⌂Q❀◐◑⇌♣●

Castle Inn

38 Castle Street, CB3 0AJ
⌚ 11.30-3, 5-11; 11.30-3.30, 6-11 Sat; 11.30-3.30, 7-10.30 Sun
☎ (01223) 353194
Adnams Bitter, Explorer, Broadside; Fuller's London Pride; guest beers H
In the shadow of the mound of the long-gone Cambridge Castle, this Adnams house (its most westerly tied pub) offers a great range of Adnams beers plus changing guests from all over the country. There is a wide choice of drinking areas over the two floors and the sun-trap garden is a delight on warm days. Excellent food is served every session. The landlord was once one of The Rutles. ⌂❀◐◑

Champion of the Thames

68 King Street, CB1 1LN
⌚ 11-11 (midnight Fri & Sat) (hours may vary in winter); 11-10.30 Sun
☎ (01223) 352043
Greene King IPA, Abbot; guest beers H
This tiny, deeply traditional pub is an oasis of calm in the city centre. Both wood-panelled bars have low ceilings, leather upholstered benches, sturdy tables and interesting nooks and crannies. The pub name commemorates a famous oarsman, depicted in action on the fine etched windows (not original – the pub lies on the notorious King Street Run and the windows have been broken many times). A truly convivial atmosphere is enjoyed by a wide cross-section of customers including many devoted regulars who come from all over the city. The tiniest of patios is provided for smokers. ⌂Q❀⊟⊡♣⚐

Empress

72 Thoday Street, CB1 3AX (off Mill Road, E of railway line)
⌚ 4-11.30 (1.30am Fri); 12-1.30am Sat; 12-11.30 Sun
☎ (01223) 247236 🌐 theempresspub.com
Adnams Bitter; Marston's Pedigree; Taylor Landlord; Woodforde's Wherry Best Bitter; guest beers H
Back-street local popular with the town's residents and students alike. The three main drinking areas form a U-shape with the public bar on one side and lounge on the other. There is a large heated gazebo for smokers and a sun-trap patio garden beyond. Pizza is always available and there are regular barbecue and curry nights. Traditional pub games including pool are augmented by a growing collection of board games. The cider is Weston's Old Rosie. ❀◐◑⊟⇌⊡♣●⚐

Free Press ✔

Prospect Row, CB1 1DU
⌚ 12-2.30, 6-11; 12-11 Sat; 12-10.30 Sun
☎ (01223) 368337 🌐 freepresspub.com
Greene King XX Mild, IPA, Abbot, seasonal beers; guest beers H
Delightful gem of a back-street pub —this is a place for quiet conversation and no mobile phones are permitted. The two main rooms are simply furnished and there is a sheltered garden. A good menu offers plenty of choice — soup and pasta are always popular. There is a smoking area but it is not heated. ⌂Q❀◐◑⊡♣⚐▯

Kingston Arms ✔

33 Kingston Street, CB1 2NU (off Mill Rd)
⌚ 12-2.30, 5-11; 12-midnight Fri & Sat; 12-11 Sun
☎ (01223) 319414 🌐 kingston-arms.co.uk
Crouch Vale Brewers Gold; Elgood's Black Dog; Hop Back Entire Stout, Summer Lightning; Oakham JHB; Taylor Landlord; guest beers H
A classic pub, free of any keg products. The stunning blue exterior adorned with hanging baskets makes it easy to find. Simply furnished with table space often at a premium, award-winning food is served lunchtimes and evenings. There is free WiFi and Internet access for customers and a newspaper rack. The walled garden has canopies and heaters and is popular all year round. ⌂Q❀⊭◑⇌⊡●⚐

Live & Let Live

40 Mawson Road, CB1 2EA
⌚ 11.30-2.30, 5.30 (6 Sat)-11; 12-3, 7-11 Sun
☎ (01223) 460261
Adnams Bitter; Everards Tiger; Nethergate Umbel Ale; guest beer H
Friendly back-street community pub with wooden floors and railway memorabilia. A dark beer and Cassels cider are always among the seven handpumps and there is also a selection of draught and bottled Belgian beers. Several beer festivals are held throughout the year. Q◑⇌⊡(2)♣●

Regal ✔

38-39 Regent Street, CB2 3AR
⌚ 9-midnight (2am Fri & Sat)
☎ (01223) 366459
Greene King Abbot; Marston's Pedigree; Theakston Best Bitter; guest beers H
Wetherspoon's reckon this to be the biggest pub in the UK and it is certainly a whopper, filling two floors of a former cinema (the Picturehouse cinema occupies the rest of the building). Although essentially a barn, there are a few more intimate areas on the edges. Excellent value beer and food, but it does get hugely busy in the evening, when service can become an issue. Usually five guest beers.

Weston's Old Rosie cider is served.
❀◐♿🚌🍎⊱

Salisbury Arms ✔
76 Tenison Road, CB1 2DW (off Mill Road)
✪ 12-2, 5-11 (midnight Fri); 6-midnight Sat (closed lunchtime); 12-2, 7-10.30 Sun
☎ (01223) 576363
Adnams Broadside; St Austell Tribute; Wells Eagle IPA, Bombardier; guest beers Ⓗ
A short walk from the railway station, this long end-of-terrace Victorian pub was recently sensitively refurbished by Wells & Young's, maintaining its essential character and impressive collection of old folk festival and beer festival posters and other decoration. Eight handpumps dispense the regular beers plus four changing guests. The local organic cider is from Crones. No food is served on Saturday and Sunday evenings. ❀◐⇌🚌⊱

St Radegund
129 King Street, CB1 1LD
✪ 5 (12 Sat)-11; 12-2, 6.30-10.30 Sun
☎ (01223) 311794
Fuller's London Pride; guest beers Ⓗ
A new pub sign belatedly represents the correct St Radegund, a 5th-century Frankish Queen of local significance. A true free house, Cambridge's smallest pub is a regular outlet for local Milton Brewery beers. The interior is packed with mementos from steam railway photos to local sporting memorabilia. The pub is also the base of the infamous Hash House Harriers. You may want to join the Vera Lynn Appreciation Club but please avoid the Wall of Shame noticeboard. Background jazz adds to the enjoyable atmosphere. Q🚌

Castor

Prince of Wales Feathers
38 Peterborough Road, PE5 7AL
✪ 12-midnight (1am Sat)
☎ (01733) 380222 🌐 princeofwalesfeathers.co.uk
Adnams Bitter; John Smith's Bitter; Woodforde's Wherry Best Bitter; guest beers Ⓗ
Refurbished single-room village local retaining the original stained glass windows, cleverly divided into different areas to cater for a mixed clientele. Run by friendly and welcoming hosts, food is served lunchtimes only Monday to Saturday. Live music plays every other Saturday evening and there is a quiz on Sunday evening. Lined glasses are available on request. The pleasant patio to the side of the pub is popular in summer.
⛼Q❀◑♿🚌⊱Ū

Catworth

Fox
Fox Road, PE28 0PW (off A14)
✪ 11-11; closed Mon; 12-10.30 Sun
☎ (01832) 710363 🌐 thefoxcatworth.co.uk
Greene King IPA; guest beers Ⓗ
Perched above the A14 and reached via a slip road to the B660, the pub has a patio outside with a garden and children's play area. The interior is open plan with a bar in the centre and paintings associated with nearby WWII airfields on the walls. Typically three guest ales are on offer, along with an extensive blackboard food menu. A beer festival is held during June and July. Rare for the area, Weston's Old Rosie cider is available.
⛼❀◐🍎P

Dullingham

Boot
18 Brinkley Road, CB8 9UW
✪ 11-2, 5-11; 11-11 Sat; 12-3.30, 7-10.30 Sun
☎ (01638) 507327
Adnams Bitter, Broadside; guest beers Ⓗ
Basic village inn brought to life by the friendly atmosphere generated by the locals. Saved from closure a few years ago, since then it has gone from strength to strength to become Cambridge CAMRA Pub of the Year in 2005. Sport is high on the agenda, especially horseracing, and many community events are based around the pub. Children are permitted until 8pm. No meals served on Sunday lunchtime. ⛼❀◑⇌♣P⊱

Eaton Socon

Rivermill Tavern
School Lane, PE19 8GW
✪ 12-11 (midnight Fri)
☎ (01480) 219612 🌐 rivermilltavern.co.uk
Adnams Broadside; Greene King IPA, Abbot; guest beers Ⓗ
Converted from a flour mill, this popular riverside pub at Eaton Socon lock on the River Great Ouse has a galleried area above the bar. It offers an extensive and varied food menu. Live music is hosted on Tuesday, Wednesday and Friday evenings, and there is a quiz on Sunday evening. Up to two guest beers are on handpump from independent breweries. The patio has splendid views of the river and marina and moorings are available.
❀◐🚌(5)♣P⊱

Ely

Prince Albert
62 Silver Street, CB7 4JF (opp cathedral car park)
✪ 11-3.30, 6.30 (6 Fri)-11 (11.30 Fri & Sat); 12-3.30, 7-10.30 Sun
☎ (01353) 663494
Greene King XX Mild, IPA, Abbot; guest beers Ⓗ
Great little back-street local pub with a lovely sun-trap garden. A rare outlet for XX Mild, it was winner of local CAMRA Pub of the Year in 2008. Two guest beers are usually available, mainly from Greene King. No music or gaming machines disturb the pleasant bar-room banter. Secondhand books and regular events help fundraise for local good causes. Food is served Monday-Saturday lunchtime. Children are permitted in the garden only but dogs are welcome. Q❀◑⇌♣⊱

West End House ✔
16 West End, CB6 3AY
✪ 12-3, 6-11; 12-1am Fri & Sat; 12-4, 7-11 Sun
☎ (01353) 662907 🌐 westendhouseely.co.uk
Adnams Bitter; Greene King IPA; Shepherd Neame Spitfire; guest beers Ⓗ
Very much a drinkers' pub, this cosy inn is located away from the city centre and a short

distance from Oliver Cromwell's house. A cosy inn with low beamed ceilings, the interior is split into four distinct areas and a pleasant snug. Two guest beers are always available, often from local breweries. Light snacks are served at lunchtime. The enclosed patio area has a marquee and heating. Well-behaved children are welcome until 8pm. ⛫♉❀◖⚡

Farcet

Black Swan

77 Main Street, PE7 3DF (off B1091)

⏲ 12-2 (not Mon or winter), 5-11; 12-11 Fri & Sat; 12-10.30 Sun

☎ (01733) 240387

John Smith's Bitter; guest beers Ⓗ

Traditional village pub next to the river at the bottom of the village and a short walk from Farcet church bus stop. The lounge and public bars both have log fires and settles. Food is served Friday to Sunday lunchtimes and Tuesday to Saturday evenings. An annual charity beer festival is held in September. Camping is available in the extensive garden. ⛫❀◖◗⊟♿⛺🚌(3)♣P⚡

Farcet Fen

Plough

Milk & Water Drove, Ramsey Road, PE7 3DR (on B1095 S of A605)

⏲ 12-11.30 (10.30 Sun)

☎ (01733) 844307

Elgood's Black Dog; Fuller's London Pride; Oakham JHB; guest beers Ⓗ

Isolated Fenland pub with a reputation for good food and ale, always offering two guest beers. The somewhat unusual beamed bar has leather settees, a large tropical aquarium and bar billiards. Families are welcome and there is an outdoor play area for children. ❀◖◗⊟♿⛺♣P⚡

Fulbourn

Six Bells

9 High Street, CB21 5DH

⏲ 11.30-3, 6-11.30; 12-11.30 Fri & Sat; 12-11 Sun

☎ (01223) 880244

Adnams Bitter; Young's Bitter; guest beers Ⓗ

Former coaching inn with a thatched roof and low ceilings in the centre of the village. An archetypal two-bar village pub with a welcoming log fire, it serves home-cooked, locally-sourced food in the bar and dining room (not Sun or Mon evenings). In summer the comfortable patio and sprawling garden to the rear are popular. Trad jazz features in the function room on the first and third Wednesday of the month and the place is packed every Thursday for the popular quiz night. The real cider is Weston's Old Rosie. ⛫Q❀◖◗⊟♿🚌(1)♣🍏P

Grantchester

Blue Ball

57 Broadway, CB3 9NQ

⏲ 12-3, 6-11 (midnight Thu-Sat); 12-10.30 Sun

☎ (01223) 840679

Adnams Bitter; guest beers Ⓗ

Small, authentic, traditional and relaxing pub full of interesting and friendly regulars. It holds the oldest licence in Grantchester and displays a list of landlords back to 1767. Good beer, good conversation and old pub games are the order of the day. The piano is still played and there is live music every Thursday. No lager, children or food. At the back is a small walled garden with a heated gazebo for smokers. A past local CAMRA Pub of the Year. ⛫Q❀⛟♣

Great Abington

Three Tuns

75 High Street, CB21 6AB

⏲ 12-2.30, 6-11; 12-11 Sat; 12-10.30 Sun

☎ (01223) 891467 🌐 thethreetuns-greatabington.co.uk

Greene King IPA; Nethergate seasonal beers; guest beers Ⓗ

Compact two-bar free house opposite the village cricket green. There is a small dining room and slightly larger main bar with a number of sporting trophies on display. Both bars feature wood floors and panelling. An excellent Thai menu is offered from Monday to Saturday (booking advisable —no food Sun). The changing beer range often includes ales from Adnams and Woodforde's. Folk musicians visit on some Sunday evenings. ⛫Q❀◖◗⛺🚌(13)P⚡

Hartford

King of the Belgians

27 Main Street, PE29 1XU

⏲ 10-2.30, 5-11; 10-11 Fri-Sun

☎ (01480) 452030

Beer range varies Ⓗ

Sixteenth-century pub in a picturesque village setting, once called the King of the Prussians but the name was changed during WWI. It is believed that Oliver Cromwell used to frequent the establishment. The pub comprises a public bar and restaurant and offers a constantly-changing range of up to three real ales, mainly from regional breweries, and good value pub food (not served Mon eve). Q❀◖◗⊟🚌P⚡

Helpston

Blue Bell

10 Woodgate, PE6 7ED

⏲ 11.30-2.30, 5-11 (midnight Fri & Sat); 12-10.30 (6 winter) Sun

☎ (01733) 252394

Grainstore Cooking Bitter, Ten Fifty; guest beers Ⓗ

Stone-built, 17th-century village pub with traditional values. The wood-panelled bar is popular with locals and an extension into the old cellar has provided a dining area and cosy snug. The 18th-century English poet John Clare, known as the peasant poet, was a pot boy here. Three guest beers usually include a mild, and a traditional cider is added in summer. The pub runs a crib team and has a pool table. Q♉❀⛟◗⊟♿⛺🚌♣🍏P⚡

Hemingford Grey

Cock

47 High Street, PE28 9BJ (off A14, SE of Huntingdon)
⊛ 11.30-3, 6-11; 12-4, 6.30-10.30 Sun
☎ (01480) 463609 ⊕ cambscuisine.com
Buntingford Highwayman; Elgood's Black Dog; Wolf Golden Jackal; guest beers ⊞
Featuring beers brewed within an hour's drive of the pub, this is an award-winning village local and restaurant. A solid fuel stove and exposed wood beams make the pub a cosy place to enjoy the well-presented beers. Accessed via a separate door, the restaurant has won many accolades (booking essential at all times). The menu includes an extensive fish board, meat, game and excellent home-made sausages. During the summer, occasional beer festivals are held in the beer garden. ⌂Q✿◑▲⊟(5, 151)P⅟

Hinxton

Red Lion

32 High Street, CB10 1QY
⊛ 11-3 (3.30 Fri & Sat), 6-11; 12-4, 7-10.30 Sun
☎ (01799) 530601 ⊕ redlionhinxton.co.uk
Adnams Bitter; Greene King IPA; Woodforde's Wherry Best Bitter; guest beers ⊞
Sixteenth-century coaching inn with an L-shaped bar and busy, award-winning dining room in an extension that blends sympathetically with the original interior. Fine old clocks, horse brasses and stuffed animals add character, as do the unusual polished copper doorsteps. The pub offers a food menu featuring a range of classic dishes and hosts a pudding club. Winner of The Publican's Dessert Pub of the Year award in 2007. ⌂Q✿◑♣P

Histon

Red Lion

68 High Street, CB24 9JD
⊛ 10.30-3, 4-11 (midnight Fri); 10.30-11 Sat; 12-11 Sun
☎ (01223) 564437
Elgood's Black Dog; Everards Beacon; Oakham Bishops Farewell; Everards Tiger; Tring Blonde; guest beers ⊞
Both bars of this free house are filled with a magnificent collection of breweriana – bottles, water jugs, signs, mirrors, pumpclips, even a brightly lit Watneys Red Barrel. Two rapidly-changing guest beers are supplemented by three Belgian beers on draught and a large range of bottled Belgians and Germans. Food is available every lunchtime and monthly themed food nights are popular. Two beer festivals are held a year —an Easter aperitif then the main event in September with a marquee in the garden and entertainment. ⌂✿◑⊟⊟♣●P

Holme

Admiral Wells

41 Station Road, PE7 3PH (jct of B660 & Yaxley Road)
⊛ 12-2.30, 5-11; 12-11 Sat; 12-10.30 Sun
☎ (01487) 831214
Nethergate Augustinian Ale; Shepherd Neame Spitfire; Woodforde's Wherry Best Bitter; guest beers ⊞
Victorian inn that claims to be the lowest in England. It is sited next to the East Coast main line but there is no longer a station here. The pub was named after a pallbearer at Nelson's funeral. Six real ales and a traditional cider are usually available. There is a popular restaurant and function room complete with a skittle alley. The large, shady garden is pleasant in summer. ⌂✿◑♣●P⅟

Huntingdon

Market Inn

Market Hill, PE29 3NG
⊛ 11-11 (midnight Sat); 12-7 Sun
☎ (01480) 453332
Greene King Ruddles Best; Potbelly Beijing Black; guest beer ⊞
Situated down a side alley off the market square, this 400-year-old traditional town centre pub was once a series of tied cottages serving the former Fountain Hotel Brewery. The building still has the original roof and three listed fireplaces. Live music on Saturday and a quiz on Wednesday are regular features. The front bar has an attractive unspoilt wood-panelled decor and stained glass windows. Handy for the bus station. ⌂◑⊟⇌⊟♣⅟

Old Bridge Hotel ✔

1 High Street, PE29 3TQ
⊛ 11-11; 12-10.30 Sun
☎ (01480) 424300 ⊕ huntsbridge.com/theoldbridgehotel.php
Adnams Bitter; City of Cambridge Hobson's Choice; guest beers ⊞
This handsome hotel provides peace and quiet in a relaxing and welcoming environment. Residents, diners and beer drinkers alike can enjoy the main bar, more formal dining room or covered terrace where imaginative and high-quality food and wine are served. The 18th-century building was once a private bank and enjoys a prominent position alongside the River Great Ouse in the birthplace of Oliver Cromwell. The bus station is nearby.
⌂Q✿⊭◑⇌P

Impington

Railway Vue

163 Station Road, CB24 9NP
⊛ 11.30-3, 5-11; 11.30-11 Thu & Fri; 12-3, 7-11 Sat; 12-3, 7.30-10.30 Sun
☎ (01223) 232426 ⊕ railwayvue.com
Adnams Broadside; Black Sheep Best Bitter; Greene King IPA; guest beers ⊞
Large and thriving pub popular with a wide cross-section of the community. A fairly traditional public bar is adjacent to the road, while the larger and quieter lounge bar on the other side is more food-oriented and has a modern look. Home-cooked food is served on weekdays. Thanks to Beeching, the railway closed long ago, though a new guided busway is due to open this year on the track bed (Histon/Impington stop).
Q✿◑⊟♿⊖⊟♣P⅟

Keyston

Pheasant

Village Loop, PE28 0RE (on B663, 1 mile S of A14)
12-11; closed Mon; 12-2.30 Sun
☎ (01832) 710241 thepheasant-keyston.co.uk
Adnams Bitter; guest beers Ⓗ
The village is named after Ketil's Stone, probably an Anglo-Saxon boundary marker. Created from a row of thatched cottages in an idyllic setting, the pub offers high-quality food, fine wines and well-kept cask ales. There is a splendid lounge bar and three dining areas including the Garden Room, a rear extension overlooking a herb garden. Beers from local micro-breweries usually feature. ♨Q❀◑P

Kimbolton

New Sun

20 High Street, PE28 0HA
11.30-2.30, 6 (6.30 Sat)-11; 12-10.30 Sun
☎ (01480) 860052 newsuninn.co.uk
Wells Eagle IPA, Bombardier; guest beers Ⓗ
Impressive Georgian fronted building with a comfortable lounge and two dining areas. The lounge has oak beams, sofas and an open fire. The tile-floored dining area leads to an outdoor patio with a variety of potted plants. Good home-made food ranges from a constantly-changing blackboard of traditional pub food to an à la carte restaurant menu with an extensive wine list. ♨❀◑

Leighton Bromswold

Green Man

37 The Avenue, PE28 5AW (1 mile N of A14, W of Huntingdon)
12-2, 7-11; closed Mon; 12-3, 7-10.30 Sun
☎ (01480) 890238 greenmanpub.org
Nethergate IPA; Young's Special; guest beers Ⓗ
Delightful local in charming village on a ridge (the 'Bromswold') not far from the Northamptonshire border. The pub provides a congenial focus for the small village community and attracts visitors from a wide area for good food and ale. An interesting, frequently-changing beer range typically includes three guest ales and British bottled beers. Hood skittles is popular here. A real fire adds atmosphere in winter. No food is served on Sunday evening. ♨❀◑♣P

Little Gransden

Chequers

71 Main Road, SG19 3DW
12-2, 7-11; 11-11 Fri & Sat; 12-6, 7-10.30 Sun
☎ (01767) 677348
Nethergate IPA; guest beers Ⓗ
A true village local with three distinct drinking areas, run by the same family for the last 58 years. The unspoilt middle bar, with its wooden bench seating and roaring fire, is a favourite spot to pick up on the local gossip. The new Son of Sid brewhouse can be viewed from the lounge and brews for the pub and occasional beer festivals. Fish and chips night is Friday (booking essential).
♨Q❀(18A)♣P

Little Paxton

Anchor

High Street, PE19 6HA (off A1)
12-11 (midnight Fri & Sat); 12-10.30 Sun
☎ (01480) 473199 theanchorlittlepaxton.co.uk
Theakston Black Bull Bitter; guest beers Ⓗ
Built in the early 1800s, the Anchor is a friendly village pub that was extensively refurbished in 2006 to create a new dining area and large L-shaped bar. Four real ales are served. The pub is popular with locals of all age groups and attracts visitors from the nearby renowned Paxton Pits nature reserve; it is also just off the Ouse Valley Way walk. There is a large car park, beer garden and patio area. Live music plays on Saturday night.
♨❀◑♿♣P

Little Wilbraham

Hole in the Wall

2 High Street, CB21 5JY
11.30-3, 6.30-11; closed Mon; 12-3 Sun
☎ (01223) 812282 the-holeinthewall.com
Woodforde's Wherry Best Bitter; guest beers Ⓗ
Quiet, friendly village pub dating from the 16th-century featuring the original hole in the wall through which the farm labourers collected their pots of ale on their way to work in the fields. The heavily timbered bar room with a large open fireplace is simply furnished and uncluttered. Typically two guest beers from East Anglian breweries are on offer. Meals, cooked to order from locally-sourced free-range produce, are served in the bar and snug dining room. The more formal restaurant is open subject to demand (no meals all day Mon or Sun eve). ♨Q❀◑♿P

March

Oliver Cromwell Hotel

High Street, PE15 9LH
11-11; 11-4, 7-10 Sun
☎ (01354) 602890 olivercromwellhotel.co.uk
Oakham JHB; guest beers Ⓗ
Relatively new to the real ale scene, this friendly, inviting hotel with well-informed staff boasts six real ales —one permanent and five from a choice of micro-breweries. Up to four traditional ciders and perries are dispensed direct from the cellar. Meals are available in the bar and dining room. Nearby, on the outskirts of the town, is the Iron Age Stonea Camp, the lowest hill fort in Britain.
Q❀◑♿P

Maxey

Blue Bell ✔

37-39 High Street, PE6 9EE
5.30 (12 Sat)-midnight; 12-4.30, 7.30-11 Sun
☎ (01778) 348182
Abbeydale Absolution; Fuller's London Pride; Oakham JHB; guest beers Ⓗ
Superb pub at the hub of the village dating back to 1645 and well supported by locals. Built of local limestone, the building has been sympathetically modernised, retaining low beams and flagstones. Six real ales are usually available and a free buffet served on Sunday

lunchtime. Friday is Hawaiian shirt night during the summer. Dominoes and crib are played and a golf society and birdwatchers group meet here. Local CAMRA Pub of the Year 2006 and Community Pub of the Year 2007. Q♉❀⊟♿⇌♣●P⁵–⊓

Milton

Waggon & Horses

39 High Street, CB24 6DF

☺ 12-2.30, 5-11 (midnight Fri); 12-3, 6-11.30 Sat; 12-3, 7-10.30 Sun

☎ (01223) 860313

Elgood's Black Dog, Cambridge Bitter, Golden Newt; guest beers ⊞

Imposing mock Tudor, one-room pub featuring an impressive collection of hats. Elgood's most southerly house, the beers are dispensed by new cylinderless pumps. The large child-friendly garden has a slide and swings plus a petanque terrain. A challenging quiz is held on Wednesday and bar billiards remains popular. Meals are good value and recommended – baltis are the speciality on Thursday's menu. The real cider is from local producer Cassels. Dogs on a lead are welcome. Cambridgeshire County Pub of the Year 2007.
⋒❀◑⊟(9, C2)♣●⁵–

Newton

Queen's Head

Fowlmere Road, CB22 7PG

☺ 11.30-2.30, 6-11; 12-2.30, 7-10.30 Sun

☎ (01223) 870436

Adnams Bitter, Broadside, seasonal beers Ⓖ

One of ten pubs to have appeared in every edition of the Guide, this two-room village local run by the same family for many years has had just 18 landlords since 1729. Beer is served from casks behind the bar. The public bar is simply furnished with an eclectic range of fixtures including a stuffed goose that formerly patrolled the car park. The cosy lounge has a welcoming fire.
⋒Q◑⊟▲⊟♣●P

Old Weston

Swan

Main Street, PE28 5LL (on B660, N of A14)

☺ 12-2.30 Sat only, 6.30 (7 Sat)-11; 12-3.30, 7-10.30 Sun

☎ (01832) 293400

Adnams Bitter; Greene King Abbot; Taylor Landlord; guest beers ⊞

Dating from the 16th century, this oak-beamed village inn started life as two private houses which were merged, and has continued to evolve and expand over the years. At the end of the 19th century the pub had its own brewery. There is a central bar with a large inglenook, dining area and games section offering hood skittles, darts and pool. On Saturday and Sunday a varied menu of traditional pub food is available including home-made puddings. ⋒Q♉◑♣P

Parson Drove

Swan

Station Road, PE13 4HA

☺ 12-2.30 (Fri only in winter), 5-11; 12-11 Sat & Sun

☎ (01945) 700291

Elgood's Black Dog, Cambridge Bitter, Golden Newt; guest beers ⊞

Popular locals' pub dating from 1541 in a large Fenland village. Samuel Pepys stayed here in 1663, describing the village as a heathen place'. The beamed single-room L-shaped bar has bar billiards and wide range of pub games. Food is served in the separate dining room. Occasional live music plays on Saturday evenings. ⋒❀◑▲⊟P

Peterborough

Brewery Tap

80 Westgate, PE1 2AA

☺ 12-11 (late Fri & Sat)

☎ (01733) 358500

Oakham JHB, White Dwarf, Bishops Farewell; guest beers ⊞

Former 1930s labour exchange converted and sympathetically extended to produce a large airy pub with a mezzanine floor and brewery visible through large glass panels. A mix of leather settees, low tables and more traditional wooden tables and chairs creates different areas within a single room. Excellent good-value Thai food is cooked by Thai chefs. Twelve real ales always include a mild and Belgian bottled beers are also available. Live music is hosted twice a month. The Tap is under threat of closure when the North Westgate area of Peterborough is redeveloped in 2009. ◑⇌⊟

Charters

Town Bridge, PE1 1EH

☺ 12-11 (late Fri & Sat)

☎ (01733) 315700 ⊕ bluesontheboat.co.uk

Oakham JHB, White Dwarf, Bishops Farewell; guest beers ⊞/Ⓖ

Probably the largest Dutch barge in the country, moored on the Nene at Town Bridge. Twelve real ales always include a mild, and the latest beers from micros are a speciality. Beers can be dispensed by gravity on request. Traditional cider and Belgian bottled beers are also available. The largest beer garden in the city features a permanent marquee where beer festivals are hosted at Easter and in May and September. Monthly Pint and a Poem' poetry readings are held. See the website for details of regular live music. ❀◑⇌⊟♣●⁵–

Coalheavers Arms

5 Park Street, Woodston, PE2 9BH

☺ 12-2 Thu only, 5-11; 12-11 Fri & Sat; 12-10.30 Sun

☎ (01733) 565664 ⊕ individualpubs.co.uk/coalheavers

Beer range varies; ⊞

Small single-room back-street local where eight handpumps serve a mix of Milton Brewery beers plus guests, always including a mild. Belgian bottled beers and a traditional cider are also stocked. The large garden has a marquee that acts as a smoking shelter and also hosts two annual beer festivals, each with 40 to 50 beers, around the early May bank holiday and three weeks after the Peterborough CAMRA beer festival. Q❀🚌(3)⁂▭

Drapers Arms ✔

29-31 Cowgate, PE1 1LZ

☼ 9am-midnight (1am Fri & Sat)

☎ (01733) 847570

Courage Directors; Greene King Abbot; Marston's Pedigree; Theakston Old Peculier; guest beers Ⓗ

Popular city centre Wetherspoon's and local CAMRA Pub of the Year 2007. The interior is divided into intimate enclosed spaces by wood-panelled walls displaying pictures of bygone days in the city. Food is served all day. Entertainment includes food theme nights, quiz nights and Jazz on Sunday lunch. The 10 handpumps serve the regular beers plus a constantly-changing range of guest ales often from local breweries. Traditional cider is stocked. Handy for the bus and rail stations. ◑♿⇌🚌♣⁂

Goodbarns Yard

64 St Johns Street, PE1 5DD (near market)

☼ 11-11 (midnight Sat & Sun)

☎ (01733) 551830

Adnams Broadside; Caledonian Deuchars IPA; guest beers Ⓖ

Set back from the main road on the outskirts of the city centre, this modern pub is a little uninviting from the outside but quite the opposite inside. Warm and welcoming, the interior has two bar areas and a good sized conservatory. Tin advertisement signs, red painted walls and friendly locals add character. Beers are dispensed straight from the cask in the above ground cellar. Access to the car park is via Wellington Street and Pipe Lane. Q❀◑⊡♿🚌♣P

Hand & Heart ★

12 Highbury Street, Millfield, PE1 3BE

☼ 11-11

☎ (01733) 564653

John Smith's Bitter; guest beers Ⓗ

Unspoilt terraced 1930s community local. The bar and back room are accessed via an impressive black and white tiled corridor with an ornate servery. The back room has no bar, just a serving hatch. Pub games are important and the pub fields darts, dominoes and cribbage teams. A cheese club meets monthly. The pub features in CAMRA's National Inventory. ♨Q❀⊡🚌♣⁂

Palmerston Arms

82 Oundle Road, PE2 9PA

☼ 12 (4 Mon)-11 (midnight Fri & Sat); 12-11 Sun

☎ (01733) 565865 🌐 palmerston-arms.co.uk

Beer range varies Ⓖ

Stone-built 17th-century pub owned by Batemans offering up to 15 real ales including three or four from Batemans and the rest from micros, all served by gravity from the ground floor cellar behind the bar. Traditional cider is also stocked as well as Belgian and German bottled beers. Recently refurbished, this is now a one-room pub but divides into three quite distinct areas: a carpeted lounge, tiled bar and wooden-floored area in front of the new bar. Breweriana adorns the walls and a large collection of jugs hangs from the beams in the old bar. Q❀⊡🚌♣♣⁂

Wortley Almshouses

Westgate, PE1 1QA

☼ 12-11 (5 Sun)

☎ (01733) 348839

Samuel Smith OBB Ⓗ

This gem of a former workhouse is said to have inspired Dickens to write Oliver Twist. During a sympathetic refurbishment the original fireplace and floor were discovered. Pictures of the Wortley-Montague family adorn the walls. ♨Q◐🚌⁂

Pidley

Mad Cat

High Street, PE28 3BX

☼ 12-11.30 (10.30 Sun)

☎ (01487) 842245 🌐 madcatinn.co.uk

Elgood's Cambridge Bitter; guest beers Ⓗ

Community local on the edge of the fens. The village is the home of the Pidley Mountain Rescue Team, a charity supporting local disabled people. A sociable bar has a welcoming open fire, and crib and dominoes are played. The dining room attracts villagers and visitors, especially for the Sunday lunch carvery. There is a large garden with a decked patio. Cask beers are sourced from local brewers. ♨Q❀◑▲🚌(15)♣P⁂

Ramsey

Jolly Sailor

43 Great Whyte, PE26 1HH

☼ 12-2 (3 Sat), 5.30 (6 Sat)-11; 12-3, 7-11 Sun

☎ (01487) 813388

Adnams Bitter, Broadside; Black Sheep Best Bitter; Wells Bombardier; guest beers Ⓗ

A pub for 400 years, this Grade II listed building is a genuine drinkers' pub. No food or background music means that the three rooms buzz with the friendly chatter of locals enjoying good beer and good conversation. The weekly guest beer changes on Friday. A monthly quiz is hosted. ♨❀🚌♣P

Reach

Dykes End

8 Fair Green, CB25 0JD

☼ 12-3 (not Mon), 6-11; 12-3, 7-10.30 Sun

☎ (01638) 743816

Adnams Bitter; Dykes End Bitter, Mild, Pale, Victorian; Woodforde's Wherry Best Bitter; guest beers Ⓗ

Quintessential country pub saved from closure by a group of locals. It is now privately owned by a villager with a passion for good beer and real food. A family-run micro-brewery to the rear produces the Dykes End beer range. The interior comprises a food-free tap-room, bar and attractive, cosy restaurant serving freshly-prepared, home-cooked meals (no food Mon lunchtime). The idyllic garden overlooks the village green. ♨Q❀◐♿▲♣P

St Ives

Oliver Cromwell

13 Wellington Street, PE27 5AZ
☼ 11-11 (11.30 Thu; 12.30am Fri & Sat); 12-11 Sun
☎ (01480) 465601
Adnams Bitter, Broadside, seasonal beers; Oakham JHB; guest beers Ⓗ
Cosy wood-panelled bar with a warm, lively atmosphere near the old St Ives river quay. An old well can be viewed through the floor of one of the drinking areas. There are three guest beers and an imaginative lunch menu. Entertainment includes a monthly quiz and live music on the first and last Thursday evenings of the month as well as occasional Sunday afternoons. There is a smoking patio at the rear. ❀◐🚌⚐

St Neots

Lord John Russell

25 Russell Street, PE19 1BA
☼ 12-11; 9am-midnight Sat; 11-11 Sun
☎ (01480) 406330
Bateman Dark Mild, XB; Salem Porter; guest beers Ⓗ/Ⓖ
Traditional small back-street hostelry with a strong local following. The pub centres around the bar, with the main room a mix of pine panelling and brick. At the rear is a small dining area and a large conservatory leading to a patio and smoking area. The food focuses on home-made, good-value meals and snacks, with lunchtime specials. There is plenty for drinkers to choose from with three guest beers and a cider available.
Q❀◐♣●P⚐▯

Stapleford

Longbow

2 Church Street, CB22 5DS
☼ 11-3, 5-11; 11-midnight Fri; 11-3, 6-midnight Sat; 12-3, 7-11 Sun
☎ (01223) 566855
Adnams Bitter; guest beers Ⓗ
Busy community pub in a large Victorian building, offering a variety of entertainment from bar games to regular live music at weekends. The Adnams Bitter is supplemented by four guests, often from East Anglian breweries. Home-cooked food is available every session except Sunday evening; Thai food is the house speciality. The cider is from local producer Cassels and there is a wide selection of wines.
❀◐⇌(Shelford)🚌♣●P⚐

Swavesey

White Horse

Market Street, CB24 4QG
☼ 12-2.30, 6-11 (12.30am Fri); 11.30-12.30am Sat; 12-11 Sun
☎ (01954) 232470
Caledonian Deuchars IPA; guest beers Ⓗ
Fine old inn in the former market area of the village. The public bar is the oldest room and looks the part with polished floor tiles, wood-panelling and an elevated fireplace. In later years the pub expanded into adjoining buildings, adding a lounge bar with restaurant area, pool room and function room. The pub hosts an annual regional pinball meet and boasts its own fine machine in the public. A beer festival is held over the May bank holiday weekend. No meals are served on Sunday evening. ⌂Q❀◐♿🚌(15/15A)♣⚐

Thriplow

Green Man

2 Lower Street, SG8 7RJ
☼ 12-3, 6-11; closed Mon; 12-3 Sun
☎ (01763) 208855 🌐 greenmanthriplow.co.uk
Beer range varies Ⓗ
A friendly village local which, despite the name, is entirely blue on the outside. The welcoming interior is furnished and decorated to create a light and airy feel. The beer range varies widely but often includes ales from the Buntingford and Nethergate breweries. The emphasis here is on high quality food, although drinking customers are made very welcome. There is outside seating, both on the green in front of the pub and in a pleasant garden. ⌂Q❀◐⛺🚌P⚐

Trumpington

Unicorn

22 Church Lane, CB2 9LA
☼ 12-11
☎ (01223) 845102 🌐 the-unicorninn.co.uk
Shepherd Neame Spitfire; Woodforde's Wherry Best Bitter; guest beers Ⓗ
Heavily timbered, partly wood-panelled main bar divided into areas, some suitable for families. Back bar doubles as a comfortable lounge, meeting room and diners pre-dinner drinks area. Good value meals and snacks generally available except late afternoon, as bar meals or in the restaurant. Regular musical evenings and garden events. Sympathetically-styled accommodation block helps to reflect the old village inn in the heart of the village.
⌂❀🛏◐♿♣●P⚐

Ufford

White Hart

Main Street, PE9 3BH
☼ 12-11; 12-9.30 (6 winter) Sun
☎ (01780) 740250 🌐 whitehartufford.co.uk
Adnams Bitter; Ufford Idle Hour; guest beer Ⓗ
Old stone farmhouse offering ales from the on-site brewery, Ufford Ales. The guest beer may be one of its seasonal ales. Visits to the brewhouse can be arranged. The main bar has some interesting artefacts and high quality food is served. At the back of the pub is a patio overlooking large gardens. En-suite accommodation is available.
Q🛏◐♿⛺🚌●P⚐

Upware

Five Miles Inn

Old School Lane, CB7 5ZR (signed from A1123)
☼ 12-11 (12-3, 6-11 Jan & Feb)
☎ (01353) 721654 🌐 fivemilesinn.co.uk

Elgood's Black Dog Mild; Greene King Old Speckled Hen; Woodforde's Wherry Best Bitter; guest beers Ⓗ
Riverside pub on the Cam adjacent to the Fen River with moorings for up to 25 boats. It was once known as the Lord Nelson Five Miles From Anywhere No Hurry Inn, claimed to be the longest name ever for a public house. Separate spacious bar areas lead to an even larger restaurant. The pub garden is within grounds of four and a half acres and includes a children's play area. Popular for Sunday lunches. ⌂❀◐⊞⋀♣P⁄–

Whittlesey

Boat
2 Ramsey Road, PE7 1DR
✪ 7.30 (12 Sat-Mon)-11
☎ (01733) 202488
Elgood's Black Dog, Cambridge Bitter, Golden Newt, seasonal beers; guest beers Ⓖ
Popular and traditional local where visitors are made to feel at home. The lounge features an unusual boat-shaped bar. Five real ciders and a perry are available in addition to the real ales, as well as an extensive range of single malts. Live music sessions are held on Saturday evening when all musicians are welcome to play. There is a large-screen TV for sports and the pub is popular with anglers. The Boat gets a mention in the Domesday Book. Accommodation here is good value for money. ⚯⊟◑♿⊟♣●P⁄–

Bricklayers Arms
9 Station Road, PE7 1UA
✪ 11-5, 7-11; 11-11 Fri & Sat
☎ (01733) 202593
John Smith's Bitter; guest beers Ⓗ
Local drinkers' pub, popular with all ages, with a cosy lounge and a long simply-furnished bar. Conveniently close to the railway station, buses and boat moorings, the pub has a large garden that attracts visitors in summer. This is the official HQ for the Whittlesey Straw Bear Festival. Guest beers always include a mild. ⊟♿⋀⇌⊖⊟♣P⁄–▯

Letter B
53-57 Church Street, PE7 1DE
✪ 5 (12 Fri-Sun)-11
☎ (01733) 206975
Adnams Bitter; Fox Heacham Gold; guest beers Ⓗ
Traditional local run by welcoming owners and staff offering six or more real ales. An annual beer festival is held in the spring, although every weekend is a mini beer festival – more than 100 ales from micro-breweries have been dispensed in just one year. Winner of a CAMRA Gold Award for its good range of top quality ales, beers may come from Adnams, Fox, Woodforde's and Elgood's. The pub runs dominoes, ladies darts and netball teams. Q❀⊞⊟♣●

Whittlesford

Bees in the Wall
36 North Road, CB22 4NZ
✪ 12-2.30, 6-11; 12-3, 7-10.30 Sun
☎ (01223) 834289
Batemans XB; Taylor Landlord; guest beers Ⓗ
Situated on the village's northern edge, this pub really does have bees in the wall. The public bar oozes atmosphere, especially with the fire blazing, and tends to be the place where locals gather. The long split-level lounge is generally favoured by diners, opening onto a patio and huge paddock-style garden with plenty of seating. The guest beer changes weekly. No evening meals are served Sunday or Monday. The Imperial War Museum at Duxford is nearby. Closing time may vary. ⌂Q❀◑◐⊞⊟(7)♣P⁄–

Witcham

White Horse
7 Silver Street, CB6 2LF (off A142)
✪ 12.30-3 (Wed & Sat only), 6.30-11 (midnight Fri & Sat); 12-3, 7-midnight Sun
☎ (01353) 778298
Beer range varies Ⓗ
The only pub in the village, with three handpumps offering a changing range of guest beers. The interior comprises a fairly basic public bar area, relaxing split-level lounge and dining area. During WWII the pub was frequented by New Zealanders from the local airfield at Mepal and many veterans continue to come back to this day. From 1905 to 1955 it had just one licensee. Q❀◑◐⊞P

Waggon & Horses, Milton (Photo: Warren Wordsworth).

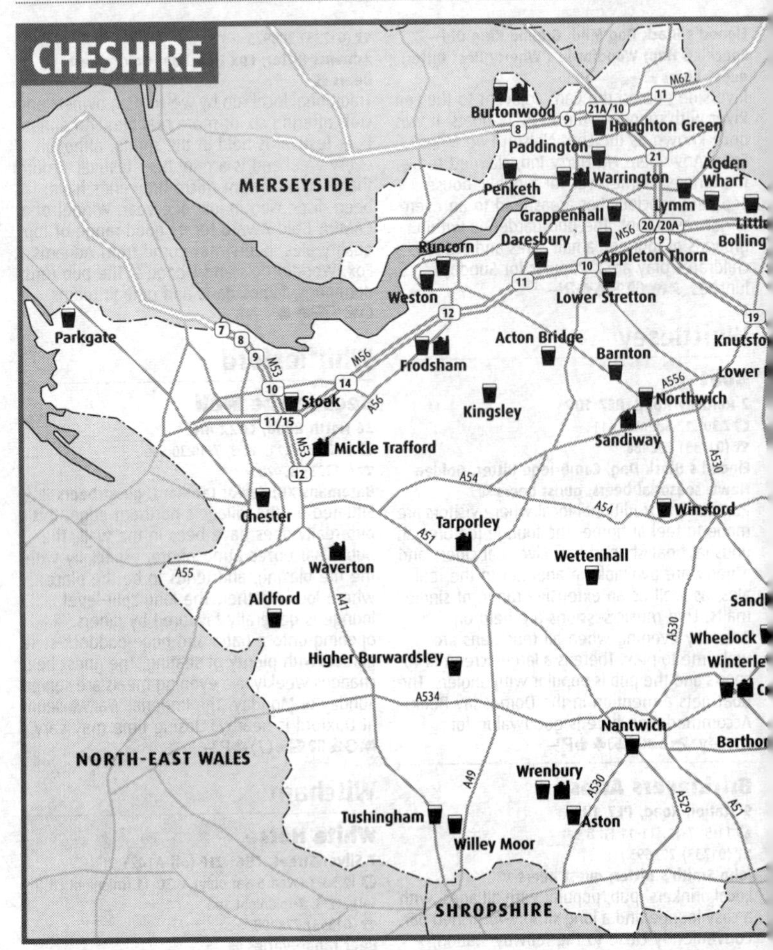

Acton Bridge

Hazel Pear Inn

1 Hill Top Road, CW8 3RA (opp railway station)
9-midnight (1am Fri & Sat)
(01606) 853195
Marston's Pedigree; Taylor Landlord; Tetley Bitter; guest beers
Named after the hazel pear trees found in the grounds. The inn has a comfortable lounge and a public bar with TV, pool and darts, plus a separate dining room and upstairs function room. Children are well provided for with a play area and mini farm with chickens, goats and ducks. There is also a dog run and bowling green outside. Guest beers come from the Punch list. (48) P

Agden Wharf

Barn Owl

Warrington Lane, WA13 0SW (off A56) SJ707872
11-11; 12-10.30 Sun
(01925) 752020 thebarnowlinn.co.uk
Jennings Cumberland Ale; Marston's Burton Bitter, Pedigree; guest beers
The boating fraternity mixes with walkers, cyclists and locals at this welcoming single bar pub nestling on the bank of the Bridgewater Canal. Six handpumps dispense beers from carefully selected breweries (mainly micros) from around the country. Excellent food with daily specials is available throughout the week. The conservatory attached to the large bar/restaurant room can be used for club activities. For tired walkers there is a free cross-canal trip in the Little Owl. A former CAMRA branch Pub of the Year. P

Aldford

Grosvenor Arms

Chester Road, CH3 6HJ (on B5130)
12-11 (10.30 Sun)
(01244) 620228 grosvenorarms-aldford.co.uk
Caledonian Deuchars IPA; Thwaites Original; Weetwood Eastgate; guest beers
Stylish Victorian free house with a large, lively open-plan bar, several well-furnished quieter areas and a pleasant conservatory with an attractive terracotta floor. As well as the regularly-changing ales there is an extensive wine list and a good range of whiskies. Families are welcome and outside there is a large neat lawn with picnic tables. Renowned for well-prepared imaginative food, the pub is

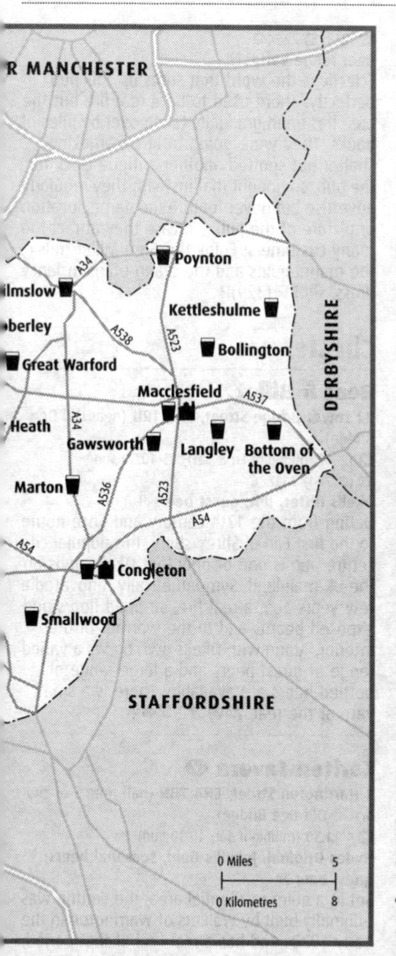

popular for dining. Dogs on leads are welcome away from dining areas. ⛰Q❀◑⊟♿P

Appleton Thorn

Appleton Thorn Village Hall

Stretton Road, WA4 4RT

7.30-11; closed Mon-Wed; 1-4, 7.30-10.30 Sun

☎ (01925) 261187 atvh.org

Beer range varies Ⓗ

Popular, award-winning club offering seven ever-changing beers from regional and micro-breweries as well as three ciders and a perry (try before you buy). Converted from the old village school, the club is the hub of the village community with regular events including live music, quizzes and a beer festival in October. Food is served Sunday lunchtime 1-3pm. Dogs are welcome. CAMRA National Club of the Year 2008.

Q❀⊭♿⊟♣●P⊱⊟

Aston

Bhurtpore Inn

Wrenbury Road, CW5 8DQ (¼ mile from the A530 Nantwich-Whitchurch road) SJ610469

12-2.30, 6.30-11.30 (midnight Fri); 12-3, 6.30-midnight Sat; 12-11 Sun

☎ (01270) 780917 bhurtpore.co.uk

Beer range varies Ⓗ

A real gem, this family-run free house in south Cheshire is a winner of many awards for beer and food including CAMRA regional Pub of the Year. Eleven regularly-changing real ales are sourced mainly from micros, with local brewers well supported. The real cider is frequently from a smaller producer too. A fine range of bottled Belgian beers and Highland malts is an added attraction. The pub is rightfully renowned for its home-made, locally-sourced food, with curries a speciality. The July beer festival is a must for all discerning beer lovers.

⛰Q❀◑◑♿▲⇌(Wrenbury)●P

Barnton

Barnton Cricket Club

Broomsedge, Townfield Lane, CW8 4LH (200m from A533 via Stoneheyes Lane)

6.30-midnight (12.30am Thu & Fri); 12 (4 Oct-Apr)-12.30am Sat; 12-midnight Sun

☎ (01606) 77702 barntoncc.co.uk

Boddingtons Bitter; Hydes Mild, 1863; Tetley Bitter; guest beers Ⓗ

Set on the edge of Barnton, this popular club is home to thriving cricket, golf, bowls, quizzes, dominoes and darts. A CAMRA membership card allows entry and the opportunity to sample beers from four regular and three guest offerings. The popular November beer festival attracts coach loads from as far away as the Wirral and Southport. Excellent value food is served Thursday to Saturday evenings and Sunday lunchtime. A former CAMRA Regional Club of the Year.

❀◑♿⊟(1,1A)♣P⊱

Barthomley

White Lion ★ ✔

Audley Road, CW2 5PG (jct Audley Road & Radway Green Road)

11.30-11; 12-10.30 Sun

☎ (01270) 882242

Jennings Cocker Hoop; Marston's Pedigree; guest beers Ⓗ

Popular, traditional, family-run three-room inn with two real fires and a dog-friendly bar. The black and white timbered pub has leaded windows, a red tiled floor and low beams in dark wood inside to maintain the cosy ambience. Fresh local food is served at lunchtime. The pub is home to a number of regular motor sport, motorbike and cycling groups. Children are welcome. ⛰Q❀◑P⊱

Bollington

Cock & Pheasant ✔

15 Bollington Road, Bollington Cross, SK10 5EJ

11.30-11 (midnight Fri & Sat); 12-11 Sun

☎ (01625) 573289

Boddingtons Bitter; Copper Dragon Golden Pippen; Theakston Best Bitter; guest beer Ⓗ

Large, popular pub on the main road entering Bollington from Macclesfield, more than 250 years old. Low ceilings and a stone-flagged floor make for a cosy bar with ample dining areas. A good pub to enjoy both beer and food, local brewer Storm Brewing often features and a well-balanced menu is served daily. A conservatory, patio and children's play area cater for all. The pub is home to an active golf society, league darts and dominoes. The bus stops right outside the front door.

Poachers Inn ✔

95 Ingersley Road, SK10 5RE (edge of Bollington heading towards Rainow)

12-2 (not Mon), 5.30 (7 Mon)-11 (midnight Fri); 12-2, 7-midnight Sat; 12-10.30 Sun

☎ (01625) 572086 thepoachers.org

Copper Dragon Best Bitter; Taylor Landlord; guest beers

Family-run free house with a friendly atmosphere converted from five stone-built terraced cottages. There is a lovely sun-trap garden for the summer and a coal fire warms in winter. Three guest beers often come from local breweries, especially Storm. Home-prepared food is available in the bar or à la carte restaurant daily. Regular quiz nights and golf days are organised. Popular with ramblers and cyclists.

Vale Inn

29-31 Adlington Road, SK10 5JT

12-2.30, 5.30-11; 12-11 Sat; 12-10.30 Sun

☎ (01625) 575147 valeinn.co.uk

Beer range varies

Originating from the 1860s, this single room, stone-built free house was closed for some years but revived by an enthusiastic new landlord. An adventurous selection of five guest beers usually includes a dark brew. Real cider is added in summer. Regular beer festivals with live music add to the attraction of this real ale gem with a garden overlooking the cricket ground near to canal and footpaths. The home-cooked food is excellent – chips are highly recommended. CAMRA branch Pub of the Year 2008.

Bottom Of The Oven

Stanley Arms

Bottom Of The Oven, Macclesfield Forest, SK11 0AR (Situated off the A537 Buxton to Macclesfield Road)

12-3, 5.30-11; 12-11 Sat; 12-10.30 Sun

☎ (01260) 252414 stanleyarms.com

Jennings Bitter; Marston's Burton Bitter, Pedigree

Comfortable and welcoming country pub close to Macclesfield Forest with tremendous views towards Shutlingsloe and the hills of the Peak District. Popular with walkers, it can get quite busy at weekends with those in search of good food. The pub's address gives its name to a signature dish, Bottom of the Oven Lamb. A recent barn conversion now provides B&B accommodation.

Burtonwood

Fiddle i' th Bag

Alder Lane, WA5 4BJ SJ584929

12-3, 4.45-11; 12-11 Sat & Sun

☎ (01925) 225442

Beer range varies

Eclectic is the word that sums up this pub perfectly. There used to be a real fire but the area has been gradually taken over by piles of books. They were going to buy a smoking shelter but spotted another antique clock for the pub, so bought that instead. They regularly advertise but never feature the name, location or picture of the pub – in case they attract too many customers! Enjoy the Glen Miller music, the mannequins and the orang-utans in fancy dress. (329)P

Chester

Bear & Billet

94 Lower Bridge Street, CH1 1RU (near Old Dee Bridge)

12-11 (midnight Fri & Sat); 12-10.30 Sun

☎ (01244) 311886

Okells Bitter, IPA; guest beers

Dating from the 17th century and once home to the first Earl of Shrewsbury, this popular city centre pub is one of only four Okells pubs on the UK mainland. Sympathetically renovated a few years ago, a real fire, stripped floors and exposed beams add to the warmth of the interior. Along with Okells own brews a varied range of guest beers and a large range of bottled beers are available. There is a small yard at the rear.

Carlton Tavern ✔

1 Hartington Street, CH4 7BN (half mile S of city across Old Dee Bridge)

4-11.30 (midnight Sat; 10.30 Sun)

Hydes Original, Jekyll's Gold, seasonal beers; guest beer

Set in a quiet residential area, the Carlton was originally built by Walkers of Warrington in the early 1920s and has a real feel of that period, retaining most of the original features. Two large, high-ceilinged rooms are separated by the bar —one a quiet lounge and the other a sports bar with pool table, darts area, plasma TV and pub games. There are usually three well-kept cask ales available from owners Hydes of Manchester, plus a guest. Q

Mill Hotel

Milton Street, CH1 3NF (by canal E of inner ring road/A51/A56 jct)

11-midnight (11.30 Sun)

☎ (01244) 350035 millhotel.com

Beer range varies

INDEPENDENT BREWERIES

Beartown Congleton
Betwixt Sandiway
Borough Arms BREWING SUSPENDED
Burtonwood Burtonwood
Coach House Warrington
Northern Sandiway
Spitting Feathers Waverton
Stationhouse Frodsham
Storm Macclesfield
WC Mickle Trafford
Weetwood Tarporley
Woodlands Wrenbury

City centre hotel in a former cornmill dating from 1830. It's a beer festival every day here with up to 16 real ales including a guest mild and a real cider. Three plasma screens show sports. Five dining areas serve a range of food from bar snacks to full restaurant fare. The hotel offers real ale cruises on the adjacent Shropshire Union Canal. Alternatively, you can simply sit on the patio and watch the narrowboats pass by. ❀⇌◐◑⊟♿⇌●P⊢

Old Harkers Arms

1 Russell Street, CH3 5AL (down steps off City Road to canal towpath)

11.30-11; 12-10.30 Sun

☎ (01244) 344525 harkersarms-chester.co.uk

Thwaites Original; Weetwood Cheshire Cat; guest beers Ⓗ

Upmarket pub converted from the derelict basement of a Victorian warehouse alongside the Shropshire Union Canal. Bookcases, prints and mirrors adorn the walls and wooden flooring features throughout the light and airy interior. Imaginative tasting notes help you to choose one of the nine or so ales on offer, mostly from independent micros. Food is available all day, with booking recommended at busy periods. A door policy is in place on Friday and Saturday evenings. Q◑♿⇌⊟●⊢

Ship Victory

47 George Street, CH1 3EQ (by St Oswald's Way, end of Frodsham Street)

12-midnight

☎ (01244) 3765453 shipvictory.com

Tetley Bitter; guest beers Ⓗ

Once a back-street pub, the Ship now stands alone beside Gorse Stacks car park, but it has lost none of its community spirit. Friendly and comfortable, it is always busy with frequent and varied live music sessions and charity fund-raising events. The guest beer is usually an interesting choice from an independent brewery. ⇌⊟♣

Telford's Warehouse ✔

Tower Wharf, CH1 4EZ (turn into Canal Street from the top of Northgate Street)

12-11 (1am Wed; 12.30am Thu; 2am Fri & Sat); 12-1am Sun

☎ (01244) 390090 telfordswarehouse.com

Taylor Landlord; Thwaites Original; Weetwood Cheshire Cat; guest beers Ⓗ

Converted warehouse with large picture windows overlooking the Shropshire Union Canal basin, popular with boaters. An industrial crane dominates the bar area and an interesting variety of artworks and memorabilia adorns the walls. A further downstairs bar is open on live music evenings and there is a restaurant on the first floor. Outside is a canal-side drinking area. A popular live music venue, admission charges apply after 10pm at weekends and during some live events. ❀◐◑P⊢

Union Vaults

44 Egerton Street, CH1 3ND

10-11 (11.30 Fri; midnight Sat); 10-10.30 Sun

☎ (01244) 405566

Caledonian Deuchars IPA; Everards Tiger; guest beers Ⓗ

Traditional street corner local near the canal and midway between the railway station and city centre, with a public bar and lounge. One of the few pubs where bagatelle –similar to bar billiards – is still played. Folk music plays regularly on Wednesday and Saturday evenings. The pub is close to both Harkers and the Mill, part of a popular circuit for beer drinkers. Q⊟⇌♣⊢

Congleton

Beartown Tap

18 Willow Street, CW12 1RL

12-2, 4-11; 12-11 Fri & Sat; 12-10.30 Sun

☎ (01260) 270990 beartownbrewery.co.uk/tap.htm

Beartown Kodiak Gold, Bearskinful, Polar Eclipse, Black Bear; guest beers Ⓗ

Just yards from Beartown Brewery, this popular local opened in 1999, quickly building a strong reputation for beer quality. It has won CAMRA's regional Pub of the Year award on two occasions. Guest beers are likely to include an ale sourced from another micro and an ever-changing selection from the Beartown range. The cider changes regularly and there is also a good selection of Belgian bottled beers. Parking is on the street outside the pub. ⛰Q❀⇌⊟♣●⊢

Congleton Leisure Centre

Worrall Street, CW12 1DT (off A54 Mountbatten Way)

7-10.30; closed Sat; 8-10.30 Sun

☎ (01260) 271552

Beer range varies Ⓗ

Municipal leisure centre bar that doesn't require membership or use of the sporting facilities. Beers usually include a rotating Copper Dragon ale and two ever-changing micro-brews (just one in the summer months), including seasonal beers unlikely to be found elsewhere in the area. At least one 20-beer real ale festival is held every year. Posters and pump clips decorate the walls, creating a real pub atmosphere. Five minutes' walk from Congleton bus station. ♿⇌⊟P

Queen's Head

Park Lane, CW12 3DE (on A527)

11-midnight (2am Fri & Sat); 12-midnight Sun

☎ (01260) 272546 queensheadhotel.org.uk

Courage Directors; Draught Bass; Greene King Abbot; Wells Bombardier; guest beers Ⓗ

Canal-side pub with its own moorings, popular with locals and canal users. It has twice earned a local CAMRA Pub of the Season award in recent years and generally offers seven or eight real ales. Guest beers change regularly and are often sourced from local micro-brewers including Woodlands and Titanic. Real cider is available in the summer. Bar meals are inexpensive and include vegetarian options. The large garden includes a children's play area. ❀⇌◐◑⇌⊟●

Crewe

Angel

2 Victoria Centre, CW1 2PU (below street level in Victoria Centre)

10-7 (10 Sat); closed Sun

☎ (01270) 212003
Oakwell Barnsley Bitter ⊞
Hidden away from sight beneath the shops, this friendly pub offers a range of home-cooked lunches at reasonable prices. One large bar covers the entire premises, with plenty of comfortable seating and a pool table. The beer is competitively priced for a town centre venue, rivalling the well-known chain outlet nearby. ◖⇌⊟♣

Borough Arms

33 Earle Street, CW1 2BG
✪ 7 (3 Fri; 12 Sat)-11; 12-10.30 Sun
☎ (01270) 254999
Beer range varies ⊞
Popular and successful town centre pub offering a constantly-changing range of small brewery beers accompanied by a fine selection of Belgians and real cider on draught. A micro-brewery on site produces occasional brews. The friendly landlord and landlady contribute to an excellent pub atmosphere with no jukebox or pool table. The refurbished garden (and downstairs room you go through to get to it) are family friendly. Q❀♿⇌⊟(14, 16)●⌐⊓

British Lion

58 Nantwich Road, CW2 6AL
✪ 5-11; 12-midnight Fri & Sat; 12-10.30 Sun
☎ (01270) 214379
Tetley Mild, Bitter; guest beer ⊞
Affectionately known locally as the 'Pig', this is a country inn in the town. One of the oldest pubs in Crewe, it has a unique bay front. The single-room interior has a cosy snug area, an unusual mural of the British lion over the coal fireplace, lead glazed windows and an internal glass partition. Outside is a heated smoking area. A very friendly pub, it has a mixed clientele including darts and dominoes teams and a golf society. The landlord and landlady endeavour to supply ales from independent breweries all over the UK. ♨Q❀♿⇌⊟♣⌐

Crown

25 Earle Street, CW1 2BH
✪ 11 (12 Sun)-11
☎ (01270) 257295
Robinson's Hatters, Unicorn, seasonal beers ⊞
Typical red-bricked Robbies pub opposite Library Square and the newly relocated war memorial. An old building in a much-redeveloped area, it retains the traditional decor in the dark wood-panelled bars. Live music plays on special occasions. A highlight is the Old Tom (March-October) with its dedicated handpump. ⊟♣⌐

Crowton

Hare & Hounds

Station Road, CW8 2RN
✪ 12-3 (not Tue), 5-11; 12-3, 7-10.30 Sun
☎ (01928) 788851
Greene King IPA; guest beers ⊞
Local CAMRA Community Pub of the Year 2007, this is a village hub that gives a warm welcome to all comers. A charity plastic duck race is held on Easter Monday each year on the stream at the rear of the pub. The parlour features a display of winning ducks over the years. Food is of excellent quality, attracting customers from near and far – booking is recommended for restaurant meals.
♨❀◖◗⊟(48)P⌐

Daresbury

Ring O' Bells ✔

Chester Road, WA4 4AJ
✪ 11-midnight (11 winter); 12-10.30 Sun
☎ (01925) 740256
Courage Directors; Theakston Best Bitter; Wells Bombardier; guest beers ⊞
Multi-roomed pub in the heart of Daresbury dating back to the 18th century. One of the rooms was the location for the local parish court in days gone by. Extensive beer gardens offer a view of the local church across the way, where Lewis Carroll's father was the vicar; related memorabilia is prominently displayed, including photographs of the commemorative stained window. Food, including daily specials, is served all day.
♨❀◖◗♿⊟P

Frodsham

Bears Paw ✔

127 Main Street, WA6 7AF
✪ 11-11; 11.30-11.30 Thu-Sat; 12-11 Sun
☎ (01928) 731502
Cains Bitter; Caledonian Deuchars IPA; Wells Bombardier; guest beers ⊞
Sandstone fronted, multi-room, popular pub dating back to the 17th century, welcoming guests with a bank of six gleaming hand-pull beer engines. Many of the original features remain; a lintel still hangs above the main entrance inscribed with the date 1632. There is even a cut-through in a wall displaying a piece of wattle and daub. Outside is a cobbled area with an all-weather seating area. Meals are served daily, noon till 6pm.
♨❀◖◗⇌⊟♣P⌐

Gawsworth

Harrington Arms ★

Church Lane, SK11 9RR (off A536)
✪ 12-3, 5-11; 12-4, 6-11 Sun
☎ (01260) 223325
Robinson's Hatters, Unicorn; guest beer ⊞
Formerly a farmhouse and inn dating from Queen Anne, this traditional country pub has had a recent makeover in keeping with its age. The original single-bar interior is partitioned into small rooms retaining the original numbered doors for quiet reflection or private conversation. Music is limited to a Friday night local fiddlers get-together. Food is basic pub grub made with locally-sourced ingredients. The Harrington features in CAMRA's National Inventory. ♨Q❀◖◗⊟⊟♣

Grappenhall

Grappenhall Community Centre

Bellhouse Farm, Bellhouse Lane, WA4 2SG (200m off A50) SJ642862
✪ 5-11.30; 4-midnight Fri; 12-midnight Sat; 12-11.30 Sun
☎ (01925) 268633 ⊕ grappenhall.com

Beer range varies Ⓗ
Founded in 1972, the Bellhouse Club is a lively private club with a comfortable lounge bar and games room, both served by a central bar. Guest beers change regularly. The games room offers darts, dominoes, pool, a Wednesday quiz and large-screen live sports including Sky and Setanta. The function room in the Olde Barn hosts a beer festival in May. There is a garden for summer drinking and the Bridgewater Canal is nearby. CAMRA members are most welcome. Q❀♿⊟♣P⊬⊡

Great Warford

Stag's Head

Mill Lane, SK9 7TY (near Mary Denby Hospital, off A535)
✪ 12-2.30, 5-11; 12-11 Sat; 12-4, 7-10.30 Sun
☎ (01565) 872350
Black Sheep Best Bitter; Boddingtons Bitter; Taylor Landlord Ⓗ
A rather stark exterior contrasts with the warm, friendly atmosphere and comfortable interior of this pub. The bar, with its stuffed stag's head, serves two adjacent areas, often used for dining, both with real fires blazing on cold nights. Busy at lunchtime and early evening with diners, locals tend to gather in the music-free bar. No food is served Sunday evening. The pleasant outdoor smoking and seating area overlooks fields. ⛫Q❀◐◑P⊬

Higher Burwardsley

Pheasant Inn

CH3 9PF (follow signs on A41 and A49 for Cheshire Workshops)
✪ 12-midnight (11.30 Sun)
☎ (01829) 770434 ⊕ thepheasantinn.co.uk
Weetwood Best, Eastgate; guest beers Ⓗ
Nestling in the Peckforton Hills, half-way along the sandstone trail, the Pheasant is a delightful collection of 300-year-old sandstone buildings popular with walkers, diners and visitors to the nearby Candle Workshops. Inside are oak-beamed ceilings, wood-panelling and real fires that warm the pub in the winter. The flower-filled courtyard with panoramic views across the Cheshire plain is delightful in summer. Excellent quality food is served and accommodation is available in 12 en-suite rooms. ⛫❀⇌◐◑♿P⊬

Houghton Green

Millhouse

Ballater Drive, WA2 0LX
✪ 12-midnight (10.30 Sun)
☎ (01925) 811405
Holts Mild, Bitter, seasonal beers Ⓗ
Built to cater for the new estates of North Warrington in the 1980s, this large two-roomed pub saw a change in style in early 2008. The spacious bar/games room remains but the large lounge has been converted to give more of a café-bar feel while retaining its local appeal. The pub hosts quizzes on Tuesday and Thursday nights and live music on Saturday. The monthly guest beer is from Holts. Runner-up local CAMRA branch Community Pub of the Year 2008.
❀◐⊟♿⊟♣P⊬

Plough

Mill Lane, WA2 0SU
✪ 11.30-11 (11.30 Thu & Sat; midnight Fri); 12-11 Sun
☎ (01925) 815409
Moorhouses Pride of Pendle; Wells Bombardier; guest beers Ⓗ
Although situated between the M62 and the sprawling estates of North Warrington, this pub manages to retain a rural feel, with its own bowling green. The modern open plan interior belies its 1774 origins. The emphasis here is on food – served seven days a week – but ale is not an afterthought, with up to five guests available throughout the year and two popular beer festivals. A quiz is held on Thursday evening. ❀◐◑♿⊟

Kettleshulme

Swan

Macclesfield Road, SK23 7QU (on B5470)
✪ 12 (5.30 Mon)-11; 12-10.30 Sun
☎ (01663) 732943 ⊕ the-swan-inn-kettleshulme.co.uk
Marston's Burton Bitter; guest beers Ⓗ
Bought by locals in 2005 to save it from closure, this small 15th-century whitewashed stone building has a small, quaint interior with timber beams, stone fireplaces and a real fire. Two or three frequently-changing guest beers, usually from micros, are always available and a small beer festival takes place in September. Food is of high quality with an interesting ever-changing menu (booking advisable). Situated in the Peak District National Park surrounded by good walking country, families and walkers are welcome. There are two outdoor patio areas and a covered, heated smoking area. ⛫❀◐◑⊟(60, 64)P⊬

Kingsley

Red Bull

The Brow, WA6 8AN (50m from B5153)
✪ 12-3 (not Mon & Tue winter), 5.30-midnight; 12-3, 5.30-11.30 Sun
☎ (01928) 788097 ⊕ redbullpub.co.uk
Copper Dragon Scotts 1816; Hornbeam Bitter; guest beers Ⓗ
Located off the main road through the village, the pub specialises in beers from micro-breweries near and far with up to three guest ales available. Home-cooked food featuring 'real' chips is available every session except Sunday evening. The pub is home to a local golf society and holds a regular quiz on Tuesday evening. Saturday nights feature occasional live music along with other entertainment such as murder mystery and close up magic. ⛫Q❀◐◑⊟(48)♣P

Knutsford

Lord Eldon

27 Tatton Street, WA16 6AD
✪ 11-11.30 (midnight Thu-Sat); 12-10.30 Sun
☎ (01565) 652261
Tetley Bitter; guest beers Ⓗ
Historic 300-year-old pub with a lovely exterior with sundial and hanging baskets. The

cosy, rambling and attractive interior has three rooms plus a bar. Roaring fires, low beams and a riot of brass and pictures provide the background to this friendly local pub. Live entertainment features regularly throughout the year, usually on a Thursday or Saturday. Outside is a pleasant but little known beer garden, well worth a visit on a sunny day.

Langley

St Dunstan Inn

Main Road, SK11 0BU

11-midnight (1am Fri); 12-1am Sat & Sun

(07801) 818868

Banks's Bitter; guest beer

Thought to be the only pub with this name in the country, this two-room, traditional terraced inn was built in 1825. A real community pub, the landlord supplies nine ales for the village fete and gets involved in local activities. Food is not available but customers may bring their own or order a takeaway. The regulars choose the guest beer. There is a pool room with a free table. Recent CAMRA branch Pub of the Season.

Little Bollington

Swan with Two Nicks

Park Lane, WA14 4TJ (off A56) SJ730871

12-11 (10.30 Sun)

(0161) 928 2914

Dunham Massey Big Tree Bitter; Taylor Landlord; guest beers

Country pub tucked away at the end of a road leading to the river Bollin. The cosy front rooms are decorated with horse brasses and pictures of local scenes. The restaurant at the back serves meals all day. The house beer Swan with Two Nicks is brewed by Coachhouse, and there are four guest beers. A pub for conversation, there is no TV or games machines and background music is kept to a low volume. Children and dogs are welcome.

(37, 37A)P

Lower Peover

Crown Inn

Crown Lane, WA16 9QB SJ737737

11.30-3, 5.30-11; 12-10.30 Sun

(01565) 722074

Caledonian Deuchars IPA; Flowers IPA; Taylor Landlord; Tetley Bitter

Traditional country pub with an L-shaped bar dividing the stone-flagged bar from the comfortable lounge. Good home-cooked food using local ingredients is available and there is a separate small restaurant (no food served Sun eve). The pub has one changing guest beer to complement the six regulars, often a mild. Darts and dominoes are played. There is a cobbled area for outdoor drinking.

Q P

Lower Stretton

Ring o' Bells

Northwich Road, WA4 4NZ (on A559 just off jct 10 M56)

12-2.30 (not Mon), 5.30-11; 12-11 Thu; 12-3, 5.30-midnight Fri; 12-3, 7-11 Sat; 12-10.30 Sun

(01925) 815409

Fuller's London Pride; Tetley Bitter; guest beer

This popular, traditional local is a welcome change from the array of food-oriented pubs that dominate the area. On the edge of the countryside, yet handy for the motorway, the main bar is a focus for locals and visitors. There are also two cosy side rooms. Lively conversation flourishes with the absence of jukebox or fruit machines. Locally-made pies are usually available. A quiz is held twice a month and dominoes is played, plus boules in summer. Q (45, 46)P

Lymm

Spread Eagle

47 Eagle Brow, WA13 0AG

11-11 (midnight Fri & Sat); 12-10.30 Sun

(01925) 757467

Lees Bitter, seasonal beers

Large, traditional inn situated in the village centre, near the lower dam and Bridgewater Canal. The interior includes a lounge and restaurant area, with a small public bar and even smaller snug boasting a real fire. An upstairs function room is also available. The pub is popular with locals as well as passing trade including walkers and boaters, and the drinking area outside gets busy in summer.

Q

Macclesfield

British Flag

42 Coare Street, SK10 1DW

5.30 (4.30 Sat)-11; 12-3; 8-10.30 Sun

(01625) 425500

Robinson's Hatters, Unicorn

Originally a ginger beer brewery in the 1860s, this old-fashioned and friendly town local is 10 minutes' walk from the railway station. Four rooms surround a central bar with one dedicated to pool and the tap room housing the landlord's trophy cabinet of Macclesfield Town football memorabilia. Pub games are popular including darts, dominoes and table skittles. A large-screen TV shows sport. Old Tom is only available in winter.

Dolphin

76 Windmill Street, SK11 7HS (side street off main London Road)

12-2.30, 5-11; 12-11 Sat; 12-10.30 Sun

(01625) 616179

Robinson's Hatters, Unicorn, seasonal beers

An original glass door leads into this welcoming and traditional local pub with brass and mirrors on the walls of the main drinking area and a separate public bar. Award-winning Old Tom is always available during the winter and there is an impressive selection of malt whiskies. Home-cooked food is served Monday-Saturday lunchtime. A previous CAMRA Pub of the Season winner.

Q

Railway View

1 Byrons Lane, SK11 7JW (off the main London Road)

7 (6 Wed & Thu; 5 Fri)-11; 12-11 Sat & Sun
(01625) 423657
Beer range varies
Free house with four to eight ales from independent or micro-breweries, usually including some local to Cheshire, Manchester or Derbyshire such as Storm, Weetwood, Hornbeam, Phoenix and Howard Town, as well as others from further afield. Originally two rooms, now knocked into one with a chimney breast dividing the two areas, the bar is along the back wall. The garden overlooks the main rail line from Manchester to the south. Regular beer festivals and music evenings are held. Beer prices are reduced on Monday.

Waters Green Tavern

96 Waters Green, SK11 6LH
12-3, 5.30-11; 11-3, 7-11 Sat; 12-3, 7-10.30 Sun
(01625) 422653
Caledonian Deuchars IPA; guest beers
A winner of numerous local CAMRA awards, this is a very popular pub in the town centre. The range of up to seven beers, frequently from Roosters, Oakham and Phoenix as well as many micro-breweries, often includes a dark beer at weekends. A friendly, traditional pub catering for all tastes, it has three distinct drinking areas including a pool room at the rear. Good value home-cooked pub food is served at lunchtime. Handy for both train and bus stations.

Marton

Davenport

Congleton Road, SK11 9HF (on A34)
11:45-3 (not Mon), 6-11; 12-11 Fri-Sun
(01260) 224269
Courage Directors; Websters Yorkshire Bitter; guest beers
Originally a farmhouse, now a popular pub and restaurant, the Davenport has taken on a new lease of life under the current owners. Guest beer often, but not always, come from Cheshire micro-brewers such as Weetwood or Storm. The restaurant is hugely popular with booking advisable at weekends – all meals contain only fresh ingredients. Bar meals are also available (no food Mon). There is a large garden and the pub hosts an annual gooseberry show (and is listed in the Guinness Book of Records for the largest gooseberry on record).

Mobberley

Bull's Head

Mill Lane, WA16 7HX on B5085
12-11 (10.30 Sun)
(01565) 880105
Black Sheep Best Bitter; guest beer
Once a row of individual cottages, this traditional inn has been freshly refurbished but retains its appeal as a popular public house. The interior is divided by a two-sided fireplace, a reminder of the original multi-room layout. A quiz is held on Sunday and folk nights on the first and third Wednesday of the month. The bowling green is nearby.

Nantwich

Black Lion

29 Welsh Row, CW5 5ED
4 (3 Fri; 1 Sat)-11; 1-10.30 Sun
(01270) 628711
Titanic White Star; Weetwood Best Bitter, Old Dog, Oasthouse Gold
This 350-year old building is full of character, with stairs adjacent to the bar leading to an upstairs lounge complete with sofas, as well as a heated conservatory. A hub of social activity, quizzes and pub games including chess are played and live music features throughout the week. Dogs are welcome as long as they can get along with the resident greyhounds.

Globe

100 Audlem Road, CW5 7EA (on A529)
11.30-2.30, 5-11; closed Mon; 11-11 Sat; 12-11 Sun
Woodlands Light Oak, Oak Beauty, Midnight Stout, Bitter, Bees Knees, Redwood
Café/bar-style pub tied to and owned by Woodlands Brewery serving local real ales. Light and airy, the two-bar interior is furnished in pine with mock beams and subtle lighting, with plenty of nooks and crannies providing more private areas for couples or families. The dining area has a blackboard menu offering good food and a range of coffees. The pub supports a range of events from an in-house beer festival to its own football team.

Northwich

Penny Black

110 Witton Street, CW9 5AB
9-midnight (1am Fri & Sat)
(01606) 42029
Greene King Abbot; Marston's Pedigree; Tetley Bitter; guest beers
Situated in the former post office of Northwich, hence the name, this pub is a fine example of a successful Wetherspoon's conversion. The Grade II listed building dates from 1914 and was the town's largest liftable building —'liftable' or timber framed structures were built in Northwich so they could be jacked back into position when subsidence occurred. The pub offers up to seven guest beers promoting local breweries in the area. The high roof and numerous skylights create a bright, pleasant atmosphere.

Paddington

Dog & Partridge

Manchester Road, WA1 3TZ
12-11 (10.30 Sun)
(01925) 813915
Black Sheep Best Bitter; Wells Bombardier; guest beers
Large, welcoming 1930s pub renowned for its good-value food based on local produce. Particularly popular with families, the extensive grounds have a children's playground and drinking areas, while sports enthusiasts can view the large screen satellite TV. Pool and darts teams compete in local leagues and the landlord organises special

events throughout the year.
❀◑🚌(3,100)P

Parkgate

Red Lion ✔
The Parade, CH64 6SB
⏲ 10.30-11 (midnight Fri & Sat); 12-11 Sun
☎ (0151) 336 1548
Greene King IPA; Jennings Cumberland Ale; Tetley Bitter; guest beers Ⓗ
A warm welcome back to the Guide for this excellent multi-roomed traditional inn. The oldest unchanged pub in Parkgate, dating from 1822, it is decorated throughout with beams and bric-a-brac. One central bar serves both the public bar and cosy lounge where panoramic views can be enjoyed towards Wales and the Dee Estuary. There is a large, attractive beer garden at the rear, unusually with waiter service. Dogs are welcome.
⛼Q❀◑🚌(487,22)♣⊱

Ship Hotel
The Parade, CH64 6SA
⏲ 11-11; 12-10.30 Sun
☎ (0151) 336 3931
Tetley Bitter; guest beers Ⓗ
Large whitewashed hotel on the front at Parkgate with dramatic views over the River Dee marshes towards the Welsh hills. The hotel dates from 1787 when it was known as the Princess Royal after a locally-built ship. Cask ales are sold in the lounge which features historic photos of old Parkgate. A roaring fire can often be found in winter. The hotel enthusiastically promotes local micro-breweries such as Brimstage and Spitting Feathers. A dog-friendly pub.
⛼Q❀⇌◐🚌(487, 22)P⊱

Penketh

Ferry Tavern
Station Road, WA5 2UJ
⏲ 12-3, 5.30-11; 12-11.30 Sat; 12-10.30 Sun
☎ (01925) 791117 🌐 theferrytavern.com
Boddingtons Bitter; Greene King Ruddles County, Abbot; guest beers Ⓗ
Opened in 1762, the Ferry Tavern sits between the St Helens Canal and picturesque Mersey, and attracts users of the Trans-Pennine Way. It offers a range of beers, ciders and Scottish and Irish whiskies. Home-cooked lunches are served Monday to Friday. Locals and visitors are treated to a wide range of events throughout the year including the Classic Car Show. There is a large garden outside and dogs are welcome. ⛼❀◐●P

Peover Heath

Dog Inn
Well Bank Lane, WA16 8UP (off A50) SJ793735
⏲ 11.30-3, 4.30-11; 11.30-11 Sat; 12-10.30 Sun
☎ (01625) 861421 🌐 doginn-overpeover.co.uk
Copper Dragon Scotts 1816; Hydes Mild, Bitter; Weetwood Best Bitter Ⓗ
Picturesque pub with a tap room for pool and darts, a comfortable lounge bar with a real fire and an extensive restaurant. There is an attractive heated patio at the front that provides cover for smokers and a small beer garden adjacent to the car park. Quizzes on Thursday and Sunday are popular, and live music is hosted once a month on a Friday. A beer festival is held at the end of July.
⛼❀⇌◑🚌♣P⊱

Poynton

Royal British Legion
Georges Road West, SK12 1JY
⏲ 12-11 (10.30 Sun)
☎ (01625) 873120
Beer range varies Ⓗ
This extensive, welcoming and comfortable club brings a refreshing variety of real ale to Poynton. The frequently-changing guest beers are invariably from micros. Beer festivals are held twice a year in spring and autumn. The club hosts regular social evenings including live music – folk nights are a highlight. Regular live sport is screened on a large TV in one room. Non-members can be signed in. Within walking distance of the railway station.
Q❀🚌≥🚌♣P⊱

Runcorn

Ferry Boat ✔
10 Church Street, WA7 1LR
⏲ 9-midnight (1am Fri & Sat)
☎ (01928) 583380
Greene King IPA, Abbot; Marston's Pedigree; guest beers Ⓗ
Located in the centre of the old town, this Wetherspoon shop conversion takes its name from the 12th-century ferry service that once linked Runcorn with Widnes. An attractive, spacious, open-plan pub, it is a welcome find in the real ale desert that is the old town. The interior is divided into several distinct seating areas and food is served all day. Q◑♿🚌⊱

Sandbach

Cricketers
54 Crewe Road, CW11 4NN
⏲ 4.30 (4 Fri, 12 Sat)-1am; 12-1am Sun
☎ (01270) 766960
Hydes Owd Oak, Original Bitter; Moorhouses Blond Witch; guest beers Ⓗ
Bright, lively town pub with a good selection of five real ales on handpump including two revolving guests from micros. A comfortably furnished house with two distinct areas separated by a corridor, it features a real fire, and has a well-used dartboard. It can get busy when big sporting fixtures are screened on TV. There is an outside decked smoking area to the rear. ⛼❀🚌(38)♣▯

Smallwood

Blue Bell
Spen Green, CW11 2XA (between A50, A534 & A34 W of Congleton)
⏲ 12-3 (not Mon), 5-11; 12-11 Fri & Sat; 12-10.30 Sun
☎ (01477) 500262
Black Sheep Best Bitter; Caledonian Deuchars IPA; Wells Bombardier; guest beers Ⓗ
This former farmstead and ale house, built in 1727, has three small rooms round the bar

and a fourth which is used as a family room. Free of piped music or fruit machines, conversation is the main entertainment. Food is available at lunchtime and Wednesday evening, and there is live music on Monday once a month. The large garden has a covered and heated gazebo for smokers. An annual beer festival is held in July.
⚓Q☺❀◐⊟♣P⌐

Stoak

Bunbury Arms

Little Stanney Lane, CH2 4HW (signed from A5117)
✪ 12-11 (10.30 Sun)
☎ (01244) 301665
Beer range varies Ⓗ
Built in the 16th century, this appealing red-brick pub has moorings on the Shropshire Union Canal 400 metres away. The interior comprises a small bar and stylish open plan lounge, and there is a heated patio outside. Four handpumps serve a wide range of guest ales, some from local breweries. The pub is popular with cyclists and walkers who fill the tranquil gardens in the summer months. Unusual pub games such as Nine Mens Morris are on offer. ⚓Q❀◐⊟♿⊡(4)♣P⌐⊓

Tushingham

Blue Bell Inn

SY13 4QS (Signed Bell' o' t' Hill from A41)
✪ 12-3 (not Mon), 6-11 (midnight Fri & Sat); 12-3, 7-11 Sun
☎ (01948) 662172
Oakham JHB; Salopian Shropshire Gold; guest beers Ⓗ
Wonderful old black and white timber framed 17th-century Cheshire pub with plenty of atmosphere, just off the A41. A cobbled front leads to an ancient heavy front door. The main bar is popular with regulars who are more than happy to bring visitors into the conversation. One of the walls in the dining room reveals part of the pub's original wattle and daub. Well-behaved dogs are welcome.
⚓Q☺❀◐⊟⛺♣●P⌐

Warrington

Albion

94 Battersby Lane, WA2 7EG (200m N of A57/A49 jct) SJ611889
✪ 12-midnight (1am Fri & Sat); 12-11 Sun
☎ (01925) 231820
Beer range varies Ⓗ
Large, friendly community pub on the edge of the town centre with a multi-room interior. Three beers from micros usually include one or two from Wapping (where the landlord occasionally brews beers under the Connoisseur label) and there is often a mild available. The range is set to expand as trade grows. Snacks and light meals are available every lunchtime except Monday, and in the evening Tuesday to Saturday. The pub supports a variety of sports teams and community activities.
Q☺❀◐⊟♿⇌⊡♣●⌐⊓

Tavern

25 Church Street, WA1 2SS
✪ 2-11; 12-11.30 Fri & Sat; 12-11 Sun
☎ (01925) 577990
Beer range varies Ⓗ
Now Warrington town centre's oldest true free house, the Tavern features an ever-changing range of six beers, mostly sourced from micros. The single room pub is popular for televised sport and attracts a crowd when rugby league is showing or Wolves are playing at home. Smokers use the covered rear courtyard which is heated and also has TV. A range of Scotch and Irish whiskies is available. Ten minutes' walk from railway and bus stations. ❀⇌⊡

Weston

Royal Oak

187 Heath Road South, WA7 4RP
✪ 12-11.30 (11 Sun)
☎ (01928) 580908
Wells Bombardier; guest beers Ⓗ
Friendly family-run pub, open plan but small and cosy, at the south end of the village. Sport is screened on TV in an alcove so if you are not a fan you can still enjoy a quiet drink. Regular activities include dominoes and darts matches and karaoke. Live music plays on Saturday night and bingo on Sunday. Food is available mainly at lunchtime. There is a large enclosed patio and smoking area outside. Parking is difficult, especially in the evening, although there is a small communal car park close by.
Q❀◐⊡♣⌐

Wettenhall

Little Man

Winsford Road, CW7 4DL SJ625605
✪ 12.30-4 (not Tue), 7 (7.30 Tue)-11; 12.30-4, 7.30-10.30 Sun
☎ (01270) 528203
Beer range varies Ⓗ
Believed to be named after a 19th-century local character, this rural inn serves the farming communities. One side of the pub has a public bar feel, with televised sport, the other opens out into a comfortable lounge/dining area, traditionally decorated, with a welcoming open fire. Five real ales are usually available, sourced from the length and breadth of the country. Local brews are often included. The management is passionately devoted to real ale and good value food.
⚓❀◐⊟♿♣P⌐⊓

Wheelock

Nags Head

504 Crewe Road, CW11 3RL (at A534/Mill Lane jct)
✪ 12-midnight
☎ (01270) 762457
Beer range varies Ⓗ
Set back from the main road, this black and white fronted pub has a lounge at the front with a beamed ceiling, leading to a small, snug dining room with a real fire. There is a public bar at the rear, and an outside covered smoking area. Good, home-cooked food is available and three ales are on handpump,

often from local micros such as Storm and Titanic. Live music plays monthly at weekends. (38)

Willey Moor

Willey Moor Lock Tavern

Tarporley Road, SY13 4HF (300m from A49)
12-2.30 (3 summer), 6-11; 12-2.30 (3 summer), 7 (6 summer)-10.30 Sun
(01948) 663274
Theakston Best Bitter; guest beers

Accessed by a footbridge over the Llangollen Canal, the Willey Moor was a former toll keeper's cottage. It is popular with canal boaters and walkers on the nearby Sandstone Trail. This genuine free house always keeps an excellent range of up to five guest beers. The interior is comfortably furnished with padded wall seats, local watercolour paintings and an unusual collection of teapots. Real fires warm in winter and an outside terrace plus enclosed beer garden are pleasant in summer. QP

Wilmslow

Coach & Four

69-71 Alderley Road, SK9 1PA (on old A34)
11.30-11 (midnight Thu & Fri); 12-midnight Sat; 12-11 Sun
(01625) 525046
Hydes Original Bitter, Jekyll's Gold, seasonal beers; guest beer

This large and comfortable old coaching house is signed as a Hydes Heritage Inn and caters for a mixed clientele of all ages. The large single room is subdivided by decorative screens to give a measure of intimacy and prevent the dominance of dining areas. Food is served all day and the bar gets very busy on Friday and Saturday evenings. There is a covered, heated patio for smokers, and the pub offers its own lodge-style accommodation. P

Riflemans Arms

113 Moor Lane, SK9 6BY
12-11 (10.30 Sun)
(01625) 537235 riflemansarms.co.uk
Boddingtons Bitter; Theakston Mild, Best Bitter; guest beers

This spacious pre-war roadhouse about a mile from the town centre has now become a popular locals' pub. A central bar serves the lounge, public bar and pool room. Darts and dominoes are played in the public bar. The landlady encourages customers to participate in the selection of guest beers. The garden and patio area are fully enclosed, ideal for families with young children. Dogs are welcome in the public bar. QP

Winsford

Queens Arms

Dene Drive, CW7 1AT
9-midnight (1am Fri & Sat)
(01606) 595350
Greene King IPA, Abbot; Marston's Pedigree; guest beers

Welcoming pub located close to the Winsford Cross shopping centre and ASDA store. A classic Wetherspoon's, it has TV screens at both ends of the bar room with the sound usually muted. There are comfortable seating and dining areas, a patio to the front and a roof terrace providing fresh air in the summer and, for the more hardy, winter. It can get very lively here, especially at the weekend. P

Winterley

Foresters Arms

473 Crewe Road, CW11 4RF (opp Winterley pool)
12-11 (10.30 Sun)
(01270) 762642
Greene King Abbot; Tetley Bitter; Theakston Mild; Weetwood Eastgate

Cosy country local in a pleasant village, run by a new, friendly landlord for the past two years. The interior has low beams and a long narrow bar with a real fire at both ends. It is decorated with wood carvings by local craftsmen. Traditional pub lunches are served and a weekly quiz night hosted. (37, 38)P

Wrenbury

Wrenbury Sports & Social Club

Nantwich Road, CW5 8EN
7 (12 Sat & Sun)-midnight
(01270) 781026
Beer range varies

Community club owned by a trust, run by tenants who took over two years ago and introduced real ale, earning a Conversion to Cask award. CAMRA members are welcome on production of a valid membership card. Beers from Spitting Feathers are often featured, along with other interesting ales from micro-breweries, and two annual beer festivals are held. CAMRA South Cheshire Club of the Year 2008. P

Your shout

We would like to hear from you. If you think a pub not listed in the Guide is worthy of consideration, please let us know. Send us the name, full address and phone number (if known). If a pub in the Guide has given poor service, we would also like to know.
Write to Good Beer Guide, CAMRA, 230 Hatfield Road, St Albans, Herts, AL1 4LW or email **gbgeditor@camra.org.uk**

Pubs Transport – 2009

HOP ON A BUS, TRAIN OR TRAM

Using public transport is an excellent way to get to the pub, but many people use it irregularly, and systems can be slightly different from place to place. This guide is designed to help you.

Information

First, you need to know the route and time. You should find information at the bus stop timetable case, which usually gives contact telephone numbers and text messaging services. You can also get information from Information Centres run nationally, regionally or locally. Remember that many operators will not tell you about other operators' services.

Information by phone

The national Traveline system (0871 200 22 23) gives information on all bus and local rail services throughout England, Scotland and Wales. Calls are put through to a local call centre and if necessary your call will be switched through to a more relevant centre. Mobile phone users will be given a series of menu options to locate the relevant centre. In London use Traveline or the Transport for London information line (020 7222 1234). For National Rail Enquiries telephone 08457 48 49 50.

On the net

Try Transport Direct, **www.transportdirect.info**, or Traveline, **www.traveline.org.uk**. For London try **www.tfl.gov.uk**. National Rail Enquiries are at **www.nationalrail.co.uk/times_fares**. Scotland has its own planner at **www.travelinescotland.com**, with a link from Traveline. Just a tip – it can help to know the post code of the pub(s) you want to visit.

Coach

The two main UK coach sites are:

National Express – telephone 08717 818181 – website **www.nationalexpress.com**

Scottish Citylink – telephone 08705 505050 – website **www.citylink.co.uk**

Using the bus

Bus stops in towns and villages are clearly marked. If there are a number of stops in an area, make sure the service you want is listed on the bus stop plate or timetable case. If no services are listed then all buses should stop there, apart perhaps from some 'express' buses. Give a clear signal to the driver to stop the bus. Some routes operate on a 'Hail and Ride' principle where the bus will stop anywhere it is safe to do so. Ask the enquiry service or operator, or, if you use a stop on the outward journey, ask the driver. If you don't know where to get off, ask the driver to let you know. It's often worth asking the driver where your return stop is, as sometimes it's not too obvious. Some buses run 'on demand' so you'll have to telephone in advance. The information centre should know, and give you the contact number.

Special fares

Where available, return tickets are often cheaper than two singles. Many operators, and some local authorities, offer 'network' tickets for a number of journeys. If buying an operator's multi-journey ticket check that you can use it on other operators' services – important if more than one company operates the route.

On trains, standard and 'saver' return tickets allow you to break your journey, so if you are visiting a number of pubs by train, book to the furthest station. This may not apply to other types of rail ticket – ask in advance.

Concessionary fares

There are concessionary fares schemes for people aged over 60 or with certain disabilities. The English national concessionary fares scheme provides free travel for pass-holders on buses anywhere in England between 9.30am and 11pm, and at any time at weekends or on bank holidays. It does not provide free bus travel outside England, nor is it generally valid on trains, trams or ferries. However, there are local exceptions where the scheme is enhanced, either for local residents or for everyone. It is worth checking locally.

The Scottish, Welsh and Northern Irish schemes are slightly different. Eligible people should enquire locally. As in England, there are local enhancements.

National Express offer half-fare discounts for people over 60 or with certain disabilities on most of their services throughout the United Kingdom. If you think you are eligible, ask before you book. If you have a concessionary fares card, this will generally give proof of entitlement. Scottish passes are valid on long distance coaches within Scotland, such as those operated by Scottish CityLink. This entitlement is only for Scottish residents.

National Rail sell a range of rail cards, including ones for people over 60, with certain disabilities, or between the ages of 16 and 25. These give a discount of 34% on most tickets, and there can be other advantages. Either ask at your nearest staffed station, telephone National Rail Enquiries, or look on the National Rail web site

Outside mainland UK, but within the area of this Guide, information services are:

NORTHERN IRELAND

Translink, 02890 666630, www.translink.co.uk or www.traveline.org.uk

ISLE OF MAN

Isle of Man Transport, 01624 662525, www.iombusandrail.info

JERSEY

Telephone 01534 877772, www.thisisjersey.com

GUERNSEY

Island Coachways 01481 720210, www.buses.gg

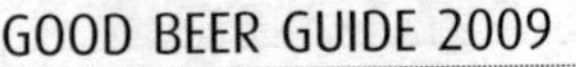

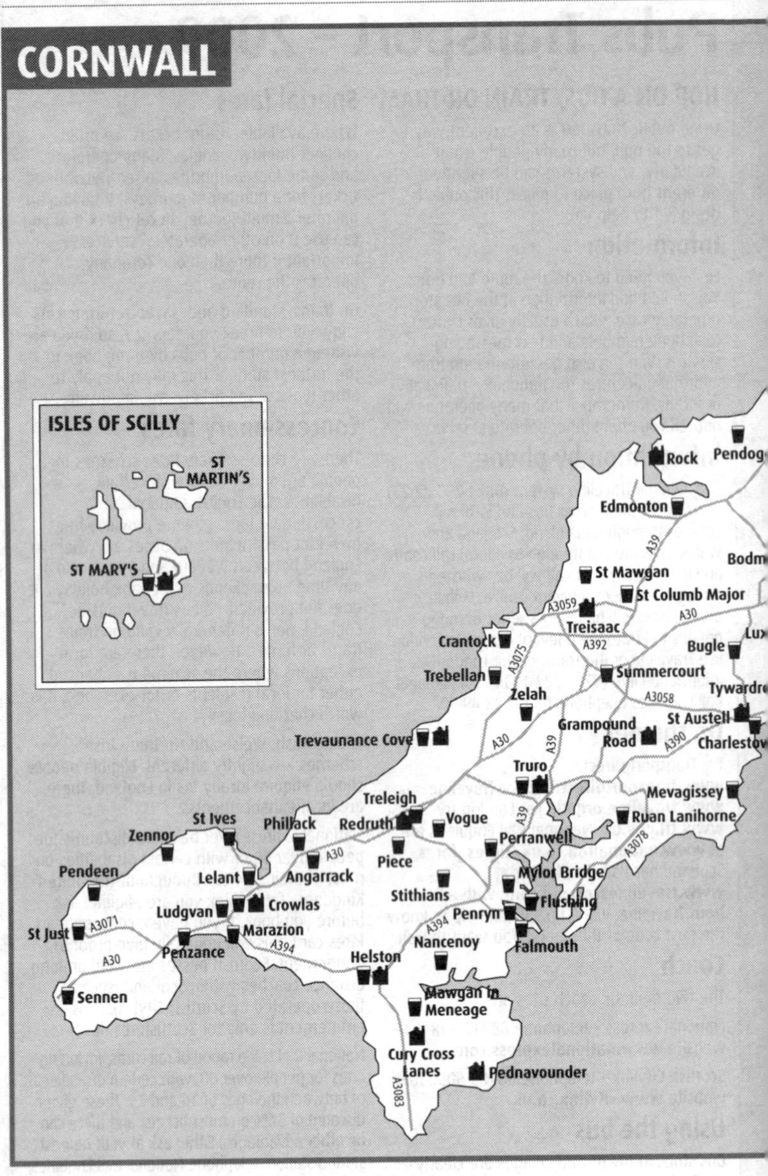

Angarrack

Angarrack Inn ✪

12 Steamers Hill, TR27 5JB (off A30)

12-2.30 (not winter), 6-11; 12-3, 7-11 Sun

☎ (01736) 752380

St Austell Tinners, Tribute, HSD Ⓗ

Comfortable and friendly village pub, close to the railway viaduct. The single-room L-shaped interior has drinkers by the fire at one end and dining tables at the other. It is decorated throughout with memorabilia and is presided over by a pair of cockatiels. Tables outside and a garden across the car park allow for alfresco drinking, while there is a heated smokers' area at the back. Folk music evenings are held on alternate Thursdays as well as occasional fundraising events for a children's hospice. Children and dogs are welcome.

⌂Q✿◐♿▲P⊱

Blisland

Blisland Inn

The Green, PL30 4JF (off A30)

11.30-11; 12-10.30 Sun

☎ (01208) 850739 ⊕ bodminmoor.co.uk/blislandinn

Beer range varies Ⓗ/Ⓖ

Winner of a number of CAMRA awards including National Pub of the Year in 2001, the Blisland sits beside the only village green in Cornwall. A friendly community pub with a plain granite exterior and a warm, welcoming atmosphere inside, it is famous for the range and quality of around six ever-varying beers, at least two from Cornish breweries. The cider

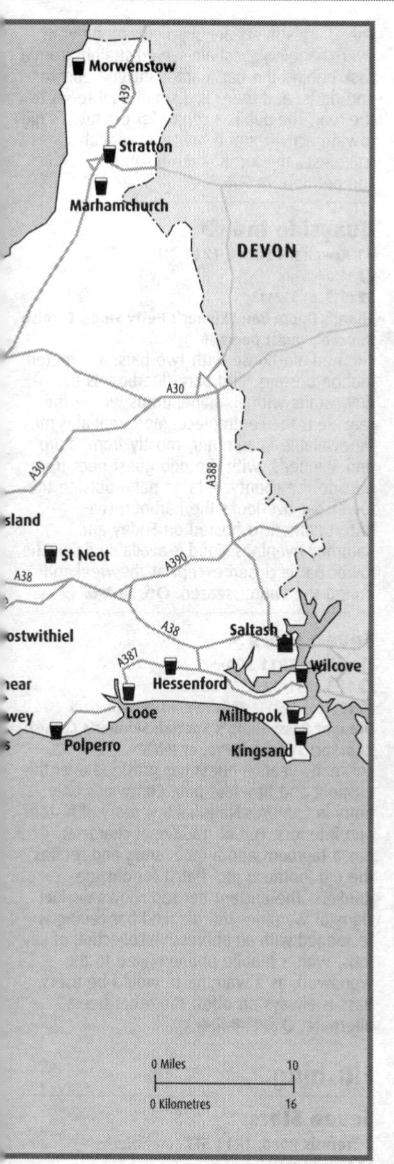

also varies and often includes a lesser-known concoction or two. Eclectic decor includes barometers, toby jugs, beer mats and pump clips. Well worth seeking out.
⛼Q☎❀◐♣●P⅃

Bodmin

Bodmin Jail

Berrycoombe Road, PL31 2NR (bottom of town near Camel Trail) SX066673
✪ 11-11 (midnight Sat); 12-11 Sun
☎ (01208) 76292
Brains SA, Rev James; Princetown Jail Ale ⊞
Bodmin Jail is an integral part of the former prison and its museum, and a tour of this impressive site while here is a must. On one side is a long room and bar, comfortably furnished and used mainly for dining; on the other, a smaller but equally comfortable lounge used for drinking, watching sports TV or for group functions. The restaurant offers freshly-cooked, locally-sourced food. Popular with cyclists and walkers —children and dogs are also welcome. Q☎❀◐ÅP

Bugle

Bugle Inn ✔

57 Fore Street, PL26 8PB (on A391)
✪ 11-midnight
☎ (01726) 850307 🌐 bugleinn.co.uk
St Austell IPA, Tribute, Dartmoor Best ⊞
Situated in the heart of the china clay district, this lively, welcoming village-centre local is named after the sound of the horn of passing stagecoaches. This comfortable pub has a large Z-shaped bar displaying an interesting collection of carved coconuts and witches' effigies. The pub is family-friendly and has five en-suite B&B rooms, making it an ideal base for touring the county or visiting the nearby Eden Project. Meals are served all day. Live music plays most Sunday evenings.
⛼❀⊏◐Å⇌⊟(529)♣P

Charlestown

Harbourside Inn ✔

Charlestown Road, PL25 3NJ (on harbour front)
✪ 11-11 (midnight Fri & Sat)
☎ (01726) 67955 🌐 pierhousehotel.com/harbourside_inn_in_cornwall.htm
St Austell Tribute; Sharp's Own; Skinner's Cornish Knocker; guest beer ⊞
Former harbourside warehouse, tastefully converted to a modern pub. Attached to the Pier House Hotel, it has an attractive single bar interior featuring exposed stonework and wooden flooring, with wood furnishing throughout. Up to seven real ales may be on offer, with guest ales changing regularly, and food is served all day. There is entertainment on Saturday evening. The glass frontage provides views over Charlestown's historic harbour and the tall ships moored there. The harbour has featured in numerous film and TV productions. ❀◐⊟(25)●

INDEPENDENT BREWERIES

Ales of Scilly St Mary's
Atlantic Treisaac
Blackawton Saltash
Blue Anchor Helston
Castle Lostwithiel (NEW)
Coastal Redruth
Driftwood Trevaunance Cove
Keltek Redruth
Lizard Pednavounder
Organic Cury Cross Lanes
Penzance Crowlas (NEW)
Sharp's Rock
Skinner's Truro
St Austell St Austell
Wooden Hand Grampound Road

Crantock

Old Albion

Langurroc Road, TR8 5RB
12-midnight (2-11 Mon-Thu, winter); 12-11 Sun
☎ (01637) 830243
Courage Best Bitter; Skinner's Betty Stogs; guest beer Ⓗ
Partly thatched picture postcard inn by the church gate. The pub has a history of smuggling, with secret tunnels to the sandy beach and church tower. Up to two guest beers are available in the summer months when holiday visitors arrive to occupy their caravans, camping sites or second homes. Mid-week meals are available during the summer only. There is a pleasant outdoor drinking area and the pub is dog friendly. ⛰❀◑⛺🚌(585,587)P⁻

Crowlas

Star Inn

TR20 8DX (on A30)
11.30-11; 12-10.30 Sun
☎ (01736) 740375
Beer range varies Ⓗ
Easily accessible by bus, this friendly free house with its own micro-brewery is an ale-drinker's paradise. House brews supplement an ever-changing beer menu with ales from micros from across the UK. The attractive single bar interior features wood and slate furnishings. Voted Cornwall CAMRA Pub of the Year in 2007, this is a real pub where the entertainment is conversation and the emphasis is on beer quality and presentation. Food, therefore, is of limited availability – phone first. Q❀⛺🚌(17,18)P

Edmonton

Quarryman Inn

PL27 7JA (just off A39 near Royal Cornwall Showground)
12-10.30 (11 Fri & Sat)
☎ (01208) 816444
Beer range varies Ⓗ
Convivial free house where conversation thrives but mobile phones are banned. This gem of a pub offers a first-class beer menu, with brews from the Skinner's range and guest ales usually from micro-breweries. Full of character, the interior divides into a public bar and a lounge with dining area – the eclectic decor creating a cosy ambience. Excellent food is made with local produce. Ever-popular and well worth a visit, the pub welcomes dogs and children (in that order!). ⛰❀🛏◑⊟⛺🚌(555)♣P⁻

Falmouth

Oddfellows Arms

Quay Hill, TR11 3HG (off Arwenack Street, near Quayside Inn)
12-11 (10.30 Sun)
☎ (01326) 318530
Sharp's Eden Ale, Special; Ⓗ **guest beers** Ⓖ
A real locals' local, this small, basic, unpretentious single-bar free house is hidden up a steep lane off the main shopping street. The Sharp's beers are supplemented by an ever-changing guest ale served straight from a cask behind the bar. Games include euchre and darts, and there is a small pool room to the rear. The pub is a centre for the town's gig rowing activities and holds an annual 'cakefest', the locals' cake-baking competition. ⇌🚌♣

Quayside Inn ✔

41 Arwenack Street, TR11 3LH
11-midnight
☎ (01326) 312113
Sharp's Doom Bar; Skinner's Betty Stogs, Cornish Knocker; guest beers Ⓗ
Themed ale-house with two bars: a carpeted lounge upstairs, and bare-floorboards bar downstairs with six handpumps where the real ale is the centrepiece. More real ales may be available in summer, mostly from Sharp's and Skinner's, with the odd guest beer from outside the county. A large patio outside the lower bar overlooks the harbour. Live entertainment is hosted on Friday and Saturday evenings. Food is available daily. The lower bar is closed except at the weekend during the winter season. Q❀◑⇌🚌

Seven Stars ★

The Moor, TR11 3QA
11-3, 6-11; 12-3, 7-10.30 Sun
☎ (01326) 312111 🌐 sevenstarsfalmouth.co.uk
Draught Bass; Sharp's Special; Skinner's Cornish Knocker; St Austell Proper Job Ⓖ
For many years a priest has presided over this unspoilt and timeless pub, Cornwall's only entry in CAMRA's National Inventory of historic pub interiors. Full of traditional character, it has a taproom and a quiet snug and retains the old 'bottle & jug' hatch for outside drinkers. The ancient bar top shows distinct signs of warping. The planked bar ceiling is festooned with an impressive collection of key fobs, with a mobile phone nailed to the woodwork as a warning to would-be users. Bass is always on offer, the other beers alternate. Q❀⊟⇌🚌🍎

Flushing

Seven Stars

3 Trefusis Road, TR11 5TY (on waterfront)
11 (12 Sun)-11
☎ (01326) 374373
Sharp's Doom Bar; Skinner's Betty Stogs, Cornish Knocker, seasonal beer Ⓗ
Central village pub with tables outside on a narrow patio overlooking the Penryn River, popular with locals and visitors alike. Inside is a large, well-furnished L-shaped bar and restaurant serving good, reasonably-priced food – fish is a speciality. Parking is difficult – easiest access to the pub during the daytime is via a short trip on the regular foot passenger ferry from Falmouth. ⛰Q❀◑🚌(400)♣⁻

Fowey

Galleon Inn

12 Fore Street, PL23 1AQ
11 (12 Sun)-midnight (11 winter)
☎ (01726) 833014 🌐 galleon-inn.co.uk

Sharp's Cornish Coaster, Doom Bar; guest beer Ⓗ
Riverside pub in the town centre dating back 400 years. It is the only untied pub in Fowey featuring Cornish real ales, as well as two weekly-changing guest beers. Delightful river views can be enjoyed from most of the modernised, wood-panelled main bar and conservatory. Outside tables are placed on the quay wall and in a sheltered, heated courtyard. A wide range of meals is offered daily. The pub has seven letting rooms, all en-suite and most with river views.
⌂Q❀⇌◐◑♿⅄⊟(25)●⁻

Safe Harbour ✔

58 Lostwithiel Street, PL23 1BQ
✪ 12-midnight (1am Fri & Sat)
☎ (01726) 833379
St Austell Tinners, Tribute, seasonal beers Ⓗ
This 300-year-old split-level pub retains separate lounge and public bars. The lower bar once housed horse-drawn wagons but is now home to a pool table, juke box and TV. The quieter upper lounge, with its polished copper bar top, has been refurbished and brightened with overstuffed sofas and chairs. There is a dining room on the first floor offering an excellent selection of meals available daily. The seasonal brew appears at busy times, when available. Q⇌◐◑⅄⊟(25)P

Helston

Blue Anchor

50 Coinagehall Street, TR13 8EU
✪ 10.30-midnight (11 Sun)
☎ (01326) 562821 ⊕ spingoales.com
Blue Anchor Jubilee IPA, Middle, Special, seasonal beer Ⓗ/Ⓖ
Rambling, unspoilt 15th-century granite building with thatched roof and its own brewery at the rear. The Blue Anchor has appeared in every Guide since 1973. There are no distracting games machines nor juke box; conversation flourishes in the two small bars. An indoor skittle alley with its own bar can be booked for group functions and is also a live music venue. The occasional seasonal beer may be a winter warmer or other commemorative brew – a 'bragget' or honey and herb based beer appears in summer.
⌂Q♉❀⇌◐⊟♣

Hessenford

Copley Arms

PL11 3HJ (On A387)
✪ 12-3, 6-11 (12-11 Fri, Sat & summer); 12-10.30 Sun
☎ (01503) 240209
St Austell Tinners, Tribute, HSD Ⓗ
Roomy old low-beamed pub in a picturesque valley setting with the River Seaton running through the grounds. The pub was originally a coaching house in the 17th century and has several comfortable rooms including extensive dining areas offering a wide-ranging food menu. Bare walls of local stonework are decorated with brass and copper ornaments. A riverside beer terrace includes a children's play space. The name comes from the arms of local gentry. ⌂Q❀⇌◐◑⊟(81,572)P

Kingsand

Rising Sun Inn

The Green, PL10 1NH
✪ 12-11 (closed winter Mon); 12-10.30 Sun
☎ (01752) 822840
Sharp's Atlantic IPA; Skinner's Heligan Honey; Wells Eagle IPA Ⓗ
Welcoming 18th-century inn, once the customs & excise house in this coastal village of narrow streets. Although popular the pub remains peaceful with a single, spacious bar room carpeted throughout, and wood-panelled walls decorated with nautical prints and photos of old Kingsand. The beers from Sharp's and Skinner's breweries may vary. Access by car is difficult, especially in summer, with parking limited to four cars. Live entertainment is hosted on Saturday evening, quiz night is Wednesday. ⌂Q⇌◐◑P

Lelant

Watermill Inn

Lelant Downs, TR27 6LQ (off A3074, on secondary St Ives road)
✪ 11-11; 12-10.30 Sun
☎ (01736) 757912
Sharp's Doom Bar; guest beer Ⓗ
Set in beautiful surroundings, this former 18th-century mill house is now a family-friendly, two storey free house. Downstairs, the traditionally-styled single room interior features the original working waterwheel, complete with millstones. The bar is separated into drinking and dining areas. Upstairs, the former mill loft functions as an evening-only restaurant specialising in seafood. An extensive beer garden straddles the mill stream. Families with children are welcome. An annual beer festival is hosted in late June.
⌂Q❀◐◑⅄⇌(Lelant Saltings)⊟(17)P

Looe

Globe Inn

Station Road, PL13 1HN (opp railway station)
✪ 11-midnight
☎ (01503) 262495
Skinner's Keel Over, Cornish Knocker Ⓗ
Friendly and comfortable local on the edge of town, convenient for a trip on the scenic Looe Valley branch railway line or as a starting point on the Rail Ale Trail. The comfortable open-plan interior has a separate dining area, and is decorated with old photos of the pub and town. The small outside patio has rustic seating with a view across the river estuary. A haven from the crowds in the summer season.
❀◐◑⅄⇌⊟♣

Lostwithiel

Globe Inn

3 North Street, PL22 0EG (Off A390)
✪ 12-11 (midnight Fri & Sat)
☎ (01208) 872501 ⊕ globeinn.com
Sharp's Doom Bar; Skinner's Betty Stogs; guest beers Ⓗ
Cosy 13th-century pub in the narrow streets of this old stannary town, close to the medieval river bridge and station. The rambling old

building has a single bar with several drinking and dining spaces, opening on to an intimate restaurant towards the rear, and a sheltered sun-trap patio. The extensive menu offers good quality home-cooked food. Live music is staged on Wednesday evening. The pub is named after the ship on which a member of a former owner's family was killed in a sea battle in 1813. ⌂Q❀⇄◑◐▭Å⇌⚡

Ludgvan

White Hart

Churchtown, TR20 8EY (on B3309)
✪ 11-2.30, 6-11; 12-3, 7-11 Sun
☎ (01736) 740574
Flowers IPA; Greene King Abbot; Sharp's Doom Bar Ⓖ
Unspoilt 14th-century inn by the village church. The uneven floorboards, wooden partitions and panelling reflect the pub's age. Two large wood-burning stoves, interesting furniture and period photographs create an authentic atmosphere, and conversation is the main entertainment. Beer is dispensed direct from casks behind the bar. The food menu offers generous helpings of good quality and value food made using local produce (no food Mon). The car park is shared with the church. ⌂Q❀◑◐▭(516)P

Luxulyan

King's Arms ✔

Bridges, PL30 5EF
✪ 12-midnight (11 Sun)
☎ (01726) 850202
St Austell Tinners, Tribute, HSD Ⓗ
This granite village pub, locally known as 'Bridges', offers a friendly, no-nonsense welcome to all, including children and dogs. Tastefully refurbished, the spacious L-shaped room is still partially divided into its original sections by an archway. The bar area houses a pool table, while the lounge is the main drinking and dining area. The pub can be reached via the beautiful Luxulyan Valley, where many remnants of an industrial past remain. Close to the station, it is on the Atlantic Coast Line Rail Ale Trail.
Q❀◑◐Å⇌▭(T24)P

Marazion

King's Arms ✔

The Square, TR17 0AP
✪ 11-11; 12-10.30 Sun
☎ (01736) 710291
St Austell Tribute, HSD Ⓗ
Situated opposite the ferry quay for St Michael's Mount, this old market-corner pub is a true locals' local, although it is also popular with tourists in the season. It has one small but comfortable family-friendly bar; additional seating is available on the pavement. Local produce features on an imaginative menu. An extra ale from the St Austell range may appear in summer. Quiz night is Tuesday.
⌂Q❀◑◐Å▭♣

Marhamchurch

Buller's Arms Hotel ✔

EX23 0HB (off A39 south of Bude) **SS225036**
✪ 11-3, 5-11; 11-midnight Sat & summer; 12-10.30 Sun
☎ (01288) 361277 🌐 bullersarms.co.uk
Greene King Abbot; St Austell Tribute; Skinner's Betty Stogs; guest beer Ⓗ
Large but cosy village pub with an L-shaped bar that separates the quiet area with its roaring log fire from the livelier area with pool table and other games. First opened as an inn around 1856, it is very popular with locals, and runs two skittles teams and a quiz team. A huge private function room, authorised for weddings, has its own bar with casks on racks. The food is excellent. Accommodation is in eight en-suite rooms.
⌂Q❀⇄◑◐♿Å▭(518)♣P⚡

Mawgan-in-Meneage

Ship Inn

Mawgan, TR12 6AD (Off B3293) **SW709250**
✪ 11-3, 6-11 (midnight Sat); 12-6 Sun
☎ (01326) 221240
Beer range varies Ⓗ
Down a steep, leafy lane off the Helston-St Keverne road, this friendly country pub is well worth seeking out. Recent refurbishment has preserved its character and charm. The welcoming interior features a single bar, snug and raised-level dining area, attractively furnished throughout. The decor is distinctly rural, open fires adding to the ambience. Local micro-breweries, particularly Organic and Skinner's, feature on the beer menu. Excellent food, made with local produce, includes home-reared pork. The bus stop is up the hill.
⌂Q❀◐Å▭P

Mevagissey

Fountain Inn ✔

3 Cliff Street, PL26 6QH
✪ 11 (12 Sun)-midnight
☎ (01726) 842320
St Austell Tinners, HSD Ⓗ
Friendly, two-bar 15th-century inn with slate floors, stone walls, historic photographs and low beams —the tunnel to the side door is particularly low. The Smugglers' Bar features signs of the pilchard press that was once housed here, a glass plate in the floor covering the pit where the fish oil was caught, which doubled as a store for contraband. The meat was compressed to feed Nelson's navy. Buses run to St Austell and the Lost Gardens of Heligan. ⌂Q⇄◑◐▭(26,526)

Millbrook

Devon & Cornwall Hotel ✔

West Street, PL10 1AA (near B3247) **SX422520**
✪ 12-midnight (11 Sun)
☎ (01752) 822320
Butcombe Bitter; Courage Best Bitter; Skinner's Betty Stogs Ⓗ
The village of Millbrook is in Cornwall's 'forgotten corner' and was once part of Devon, hence the pub name. This convivial L-shaped single-room local has an open-plan bar with

one end furnished comfortably with sofas and wing chairs, and the other end partially screened providing a more private dining and drinking area. Live music plays on Monday evenings, although conversation tends to be the main entertainment here. The Butcombe Bitter may be replaced by another ale from time to time. ❀⇌◑ ⅄⊟(81)♣

Morwenstow

Bush Inn

Cross Town, EX23 9SR (5km off A39 N of Kilkhampton) SS209150

⏱ 11-midnight

☎ (01288) 331242 🌐 bushinn-morwenstow.co.uk

St Austell HSD; Skinner's Betty Stogs; guest beers Ⓗ

Welcoming and cosy stone-built country inn dating from the 13th century with log fires in several of the small, quaint rooms. Hearty bar meals featuring local produce are served throughout the day, with an additional restaurant area available in the evening and on Sunday. The ancient courtyard at the front of the pub has a covered smokers' area; the large garden at the back, with children's play area, affords superb views over the valley and out to sea. The guest ale is Cornish. ♨Q❀⇌◑♿⅄⊟(319)♣P⊱

Mylor Bridge

Lemon Arms ✔

Lemon Hill, TR11 5NA (off A393 at Penryn) SW804362

⏱ 11-3, 6.30-11; 12-3, 7-11 Sun

☎ (01326) 373666

St Austell Tinners, Tribute, HSD Ⓗ

There has been an inn on this site since 1765. This friendly, one-bar pub in the village centre is popular with local sports teams. Good home-cooked food is available and families with children are made most welcome; it is advisable to book for Sunday lunch. Buses run from Falmouth and Truro during the week. ♨❀◑⊟(400)♣P⊱

Nancenoy

Trengilly Wartha Inn

TR11 5RP (off B329) SW732283

⏱ 11-3, 6.30-11; 12-3, 7-10.30 Sun

☎ (01326) 340332 🌐 trengilly.co.uk

Sharp's Cornish Coaster, Doom Bar; Skinner's Cornish Knocker; Ⓗ **guest beer** Ⓖ

Well-run, versatile inn in extensive grounds with a lake and boules piste in an isolated and steeply-wooded valley near the village of Constantine. Converted from a large farmhouse, the interior retains a number of rooms with a recent conservatory extension serving as the family room. The guest ale is added in summer and is usually Cornish. Famous for good food, the wide-ranging menu is prepared with Cornish produce. Quiz night is Tuesday, steak & kidney pudding night Wednesday. ♨Q⛭❀⇌◑♣●P

Pendeen

North Inn

TR19 7DN (on B3306)

⏱ 11-midnight (1am Fri & Sat); 12-11 Sun

☎ (01736) 788417

St Austell IPA, Tinners, Tribute Ⓗ

A former Cornwall CAMRA Pub of the Year, this welcoming village inn serves an area rich in the tin mining tradition, reflected in the pictures and artefacts decorating the walls of the large single-room bar. The inn is in an area of outstanding natural beauty, with nearby cliffs and good walking, and Geevor, the last working tin mine in the area and now a museum. A small upstairs restaurant affords outstanding views over the sea, and there are two double rooms available for B&B, as well as a campsite round the back.
♨Q❀⇌◑⅄⊟(17A,17B)P

Pendoggett

Cornish Arms

PL30 3HH (on B3314) SX024794

⏱ 11-11

☎ (01208) 880263 🌐 cornisharms.com

Sharp's Doom Bar; guest beer Ⓗ

Originally a brewpub, this warm, welcoming coaching inn dates from the 16th century. It is rumoured that a past landlord's daughter drowned in the vat. The quiet, charming interior has a main bar, snug, two drinking/dining areas and a restaurant. Flagstone floors, wood-panelled walls, partitions and furnishings reflect the pub's age, with open fires adding to the ambience. Caricatures of locals and a collection of handbells decorate the bar. Quality food is available and speciality themed nights are popular. The house beer is brewed by Sharp's. ♨Q❀⇌◑♿⅄♣P⊱

Penryn

Seven Stars

73 The Terrace, TR10 8EL

⏱ 11 (12 Sun)-11

☎ (01326) 373573

Blue Anchor Spingo Middle; Skinner's Betty Stogs, Heligan Honey, Cornish Knocker, Figgy's Brew Ⓗ

The nearest thing in Penryn to an ale house, this single-bar town pub is run by a jovial Dutchman. Festooned with foreign cash, postcards and beer-related clippings, the spacious interior has a raised and comfortably-furnished drinking annexe at the rear, dominated by a huge ship's wheel. The pub is home to Penryn Community Theatre, who entertain here with plays and pantos. A piano is available for competent pianists and occasional live music is performed. The Skinner's beer selection may vary. ♨❀⇄⊟⊱

Penzance

Crown Inn

Victoria Square, TR18 2EP

⏱ 12-midnight (12.30am Fri & Sat)

☎ (01736) 351070

Otter Ale; Skinner's Heligan Honey; guest beer Ⓗ

Situated on the corner of a Victorian residential square, just off the main shopping street, this small local has a comfortable, relaxed feel. The single-bar interior includes a cosy snug with settees and an open fire. The guest beer regularly changes, while good quality food, sourced locally, is available daily in summer but Thursday to Sunday only in winter. The pub is a short distance from bus and railway stations. ⚐Q⚐⚐⚐♿⚐⚐⚐♣⚐

Perranwell

Royal Oak

TR3 7PX
⚐ 11-3, 6-11; 12-3, 7-10.30 Sun
☎ (01872) 863175
Skinner's Betty Stogs; guest beer ⚐
Small, friendly and attractive 18th-century cottage-style village pub on the Maritime Line Rail Ale Trail. The focus here is on good food and most of the tables are set for diners but if you just want a drink you will still be made welcome. Booking ahead for food is recommended as the pub often gets busy with diners. The Skinner's beer may vary. A good bus service stops outside; the railway station is 10 minutes' walk away. Q⚐⚐⚐⚐P

Phillack

Bucket of Blood ✔

14 Churchtown Road, TR27 5AE SW563383
⚐ 12-2.30 Tue (not winter)-Fri, 11.30-3, 6-11 Sat; 12-4, 7-10.30 Sun
☎ (01736) 752378
St Austell Dartmoor Best, Proper Job IPA, HSD ⚐
Friendly old local that gets its name from a gory legend involving a customs officer and the pub's well. Note that the sign on the beams 'Familiarity breeds contempt' serves as a warning rather than a proverb —they are very low. The single bar room houses a pool table at one end and a cosy drinking or dining area at the other with settles and a recently-exposed old fireplace. A painted mural depicting St Ives Bay overlooks the pool table. The beers may occasionally vary. The kitchen is closed in winter. ⚐⚐⚐⚐⚐♣⚐P

Piece

Countryman Inn

TR16 6SG (on Four Lanes-Pool road) SW679398
⚐ 11-11 (midnight Sat); 12-11 Sun
☎ (01209) 215960
Courage Best Bitter; Greene King Old Speckled Hen; Sharp's Doom Bar; Skinner's Betty Stogs, Heligan Honey; guest beer ⚐
This large and lively country pub set high among the old copper mines near Carn Brea was once a grocery shop for the miners. There are two bars, the larger one hosting some form of live entertainment every night, as well as a Sunday lunchtime raffle in support of local charities. The range of up to 10 ales includes a regularly-changing Skinner's beer, which may be one of its seasonal brews, while guest ales are sourced from a range of breweries. Good value food is available all day. ⚐⚐⚐⚐⚐⚐(T14)♣P

Polkerris

Rashleigh Inn

PL24 2TL (off A3082, near Par) SX094522
⚐ 11-11; 12-10.30 Sun
☎ (01726) 813991
Taylor Landlord; guest beer ⚐
Near the Saints' Way footpath and popular with walkers, this 18th-century free house is next to a secluded beach. Formerly a pilchard boathouse, the atmospheric main bar and adjacent terrace enjoy panoramic views over St Austell Bay and the setting sun. Exposed stonework, beamed ceilings, open fires and attractive furnishings provide character and comfort. Up to four guest beers may be available. An excellent food selection ranges from bar snacks to an Á la carte menu in the split-level restaurant. ⚐Q⚐⚐⚐♣P

Polmear

Ship Inn

Polmear Hill, PL24 2AR (on A3082)
⚐ 11.30-12; 12-11.30 Sun
☎ (01726) 812540 ⚐ theshipinnpar.co.uk
Fuller's London Pride; Sharp's Doom Bar; Skinner's Cornish Knocker; guest beer ⚐
Cosy free house, popular with locals and summer visitors, next to Par beach and the coastal footpath. The spacious single-room interior was originally three separate rooms. There are numerous seating areas, with wooden wagon wheels forming one unusual partition. Fires, including a Cornish range, add to the homely atmosphere. Food is available all day and there is an upstairs restaurant. The pub has a self-catering log cabin available to rent on a weekly basis in summer. ⚐Q⚐⚐⚐⚐⚐(Par)P⚐

Polperro

Blue Peter Inn

Quay Road, PL13 2QZ
⚐ 11-11; 12-10.30 Sun
☎ (01503) 272743 ⚐ thebluepeterinn.co.uk
St Austell Tribute; guest beer ⚐
Reached by a flight of steps near the outer quay, this friendly family-run inn is the only pub in town with a sea view. Named after the naval signal flag, it offers up to four guest ales in summer and cider from Cornish Orchards. On two levels, it has atmospheric wooden floors, low beams and hidden corners, while the eclectic decor includes foreign breweriana, unusual souvenirs and work by local artists. The pub is popular with visitors, locals, fishermen and dogs – ask for a biscuit. ⚐⚐⚐⚐⚐(573)♣⚐⚐

Crumplehorn Inn

The Old Mill, PL13 2RJ (on A387)
⚐ 11-11; 12-10.30 Sun
☎ (01503) 272348 ⚐ crumplehorn-inn.co.uk
St Austell Tribute; Sharp's Doom Bar; Skinner's Betty Stogs; guest beers ⚐
Once a mill noted in the Domesday Book, this 600-year-old inn features a working waterwheel. The split-level interior is divided into three comfortable areas. Guest beers are usually Cornish, while a comprehensive food menu includes locally-caught fish. A smart

outside patio caters for alfresco drinkers, diners and smokers. Accommodation is B&B or self-catering. Buses turn round opposite – in summer, catch a horse tram down to the harbour. ♛Q❀🛏◑⛺🚌(573)♣

Ruan Lanihorne

King's Head Inn

TR2 5NX SW895420
⏲ 12-2.30, 6-11 (closed Mon)
☎ (01872) 501263 🌐 kingsheadruan.co.uk
Skinner's Betty Stogs, Cornish Knocker 🄷
On the Fal estuary within the Roseland peninsula nestles this delightful family-run free house. Its quiet, homely interior accommodates a single bar and two dining areas, and interesting decor reflects village history. A sun terrace and quaint sunken garden provide space for alfresco drinking and dining. The pub is renowned for quality ales and superb food, with local fish a speciality. The house beer is King's Ruan, and a fourth Skinner's ale may be available at times. ♛Q❀◑⛺P

St Columb Major

Ring O' Bells

3 Bank Street, TR9 6AT
⏲ 12-2 (not Wed & winter), 5-11; 12-3, 7-10.30 Sun
☎ (01637) 880259
Sharp's Doom Bar, Eden Ale; 🄷 **guest beers** 🄶
The narrow frontage of this charming 15th-century free house belies the capacious interior, with its three bars, open beams and slate floors. Each bar has its own character and is favoured by a different clientele. The rustic decor, wooden furnishings and wood-burning stoves give a traditional feel. Built to commemorate the parish church tower, this former brewhouse is the oldest pub in town, and the converted brewery is now a cosy restaurant offering a cosmopolitan menu. A guest ale is available in summer only. Q❀◑🍺⛺🚌♣🚭

St Ives

Golden Lion ✔

High Street, TR26 1RS
⏲ 11 (12 Sun)-midnight
☎ (01736) 793679
Courage Best Bitter; Sharp's Eden Ale; guest beers 🄷
A popular locals' venue, this former coaching inn is in the town centre near the church. It has two bar rooms: the small horseshoe-shaped front lounge attracting drinkers who enjoy convivial conversation, and the larger, livelier 'public' at the rear favoured by younger drinkers with the pool table. Good quality and value food is home cooked using local produce. Up to two guest ales change frequently but are usually Cornish or from Scilly. Q❀◑🍺♿⛺🚆🚌♣🚭

St Just

Star Inn ✔

1 Fore Street, TR19 7LL
⏲ 11-midnight
☎ (01736) 788767
St Austell Tinners, Dartmoor Best Bitter, Tribute, HSD 🄷
Near the square, this popular 18th-century granite inn is reputedly the oldest in town. A timeless place with a warm welcome for all, this is a proper drinkers' pub where the locals can be found spinning a yarn or two. The atmospheric bar interior bears witness to a long association with mining and the sea, while the low beams are draped with Celtic flags. A separate snug functions as a family room. Monday is 'Fiddly-Dee' night, a sort of Irish/folk jam session – and Thursday is open mic night. ♛Q👪❀♿⛺🚌♣

St Mary's: Isles of Scilly

Atlantic Inn ✔

The Bank, TR21 0HY
⏲ 11-11; 12-10.30 Sun
☎ (01720) 422323
St Austell IPA, Tinners, Tribute, Proper Job, HSD 🄷
Originally part of the Atlantic Hotel, this roomy open-plan granite pub sports five handpumps dispensing most of the St Austell range, although not all may be available, especially in winter, and the choice may vary. Prices are much the same as on the mainland, unusual for Scilly. A small patio overlooks St Mary's harbour at the rear, and there is a dining area offering a good range of food. Arguably the best pub in town for beer and conversation, and family-friendly too. 👪❀◑⛺

St Mawgan

Falcon Inn

TR8 4EP SW873658
⏲ 11-11.30 (11-3, 6-11.30 winter); 12-3, 7-10.30 Sun
☎ (01637) 860225 🌐 thefalconinn-newquay.co.uk
St Austell Tinners, Tribute, HSD 🄷
Close to Newquay and the airport in the idyllic setting of the unspoilt Lanherne valley, this 16th-century inn is the hub of village activities. The single bar interior has a cosy, relaxed atmosphere, with decor reflecting country life. Meals are served in a separate dining room where local artists display their work. The pub is family-friendly with B&B accommodation available. The large award-winning garden includes children's play equipment and a games room. ♛Q❀🛏◑⛺🚌(556)♣P🚭

St Neot

London Inn

PL14 6NG
⏲ 12-3, 6-midnight; 12-midnight Sat & summer; 12-midnight Sun
☎ (01579) 320263
Sharp's Doom Bar; John Smith's Bitter; guest beers 🄷
Dating from the 16th-century, this former coaching inn is now a lively village local – a welcoming, family-friendly, no-frills pub where beer quality is the prime concern. The open, beamed and flagstoned interior comprises a single bar, restaurant and traditional skittles alley. Real fires and wooden

furnishings add to the cosy atmosphere. Good pub grub and an evening Á la carte menu are available. A focal point for village activities, the pub supports darts, skittles and euchre teams. ⋒Q❀⇌◐P

Sennen

First and Last Inn

TR19 7AD (on A30 near Land's End)
⊙ 11.30-11 (midnight Sat)
☎ (01736) 871680 ⊕ firstandlastinn.co.uk
Beer range varies ⊞
Established in 1620 as a churchmason's dwelling, this is now a traditional granite-walled country pub. The beamed interior is decorated with a nautical theme, and a glass panel in the floor covers an old well leading to a smugglers' tunnel. Six Cornish ales and a local cider are usually available including a house beer from Skinner's. Legend has it that the ghost of a former landlady inhabits the pub – she was staked out on the beach and drowned after turning king's evidence and her body laid to rest in the pub.
⋒≿❀◐♿⅄⊟(1,504)♣♠P⺊

Stithians

Seven Stars Inn

Church Road, TR3 7DH
⊙ 12-2.30, 5.30 (5 Fri)-11; 12-midnight Sat; 12-10.30 Sun
☎ (01209) 860003
St Austell IPA, Tribute, Proper Job, ⊞
Lively and friendly single-bar village local popular with a good cross-section of the community including local rugby and football teams. A typical Cornish granite cottage-style pub, it was originally built as an extension to a farmhouse to serve the drinking needs of local tin miners at the end of the 19th century. The St Austell beers may vary and occasionally include a special brew. Bus services to Truro and Helston stop nearby.
⋒Q❀◐⊟(T1,T2,T14)♣⺊

Stratton

King's Arms ✔

Howells Road, EX23 9BX
⊙ 12-11
☎ (01288) 352396
Exmoor Ale; Sharp's Doom Bar; Shepherd Neame Spitfire; guest beer ⊞
Popular locals' local in the heart of an ancient market town. The name of this 17th-century coaching inn reflects the town's political loyalties after the Civil War. A two-bar pub, it has many original features including well-worn Delabole slate flagstone and wood floors and a large open fireplace. A small bread oven was exposed in recent years. Draught cider and an extra guest beer may appear in summer. Accommodation is in four rooms, one en-suite. ⋒Q❀⇌◐♿⊟♣♠P

Summercourt

London Inn

1 School Road, TR8 5EA (off A30)
⊙ 5 (6 Sat)-11; 12-2.30, 7-10.30 Sun
☎ (01872) 510281
Beer range varies ⊞
Once a coaching inn on the old London road, this lively, welcoming and family-friendly freehouse is central to the annual village fair celebrations in September. The spacious interior is divided by wooden screens to create distinct drinking and dining areas. An eclectic decor features Laurel and Hardy figurines among the wooden furnishings and coach lamp lighting. The two beers vary constantly, although quality does not. Traditional home-cooked food is also served. Good bus services stop nearby. ⋒Q❀◐⅄⊟♣

Trebellan

Smugglers Den Inn

TR8 5PY (off Cubert road from A3075) SW783574
⊙ 11-11 (12-3, 6-11 winter); 12-11 Sun
☎ (01637) 830209 ⊕ thesmugglersden.co.uk
Beer range varies ⊞
Approached down narrow country lanes, this idyllic thatched former farmhouse was once a hangout for smugglers. Oak beams, paved yards and curio-filled corners add to the olde-worlde charm. Four ales are on handpump, all Cornish brewed. Popular throughout the year for meals (book ahead for a table), the pub's Ale & Pie Festival in May grows bigger each year. Occasional jazz or folk evenings are hosted. Convenient for camping and caravan sites nearby. Truro-Newquay buses stop at the top of the hill. ⋒Q❀◐⅄⊟(585,587)♣P

Treleigh

Treleigh Arms

TR16 4AY (beside old Redruth bypass) SW704435
⊙ 11-11 (11-3, 6-11; 11-11 Fri & Sat winter); 11-11 Sun
☎ (01209) 315095
Draught Bass; Sharp's Doom Bar; Skinner's Betty Stogs; guest beer ⊞
Situated beside the church in a historic mining district, this traditional whitewashed cottage-style pub has a comfortable stone-walled bar and separate dining room. The friendly freehouse offers beer, cider and good food, and conversation flourishes in the absence of games machines, jukebox or TV. Beers from three Cornish breweries are usually available and may vary. Tuesday is quiz night, and there is a petanque pitch. Dogs are welcome.
⋒Q❀◐⅄⊟(T20,T21)♣♠P⺊

Trevaunance Cove

Driftwood Spars ✔

Quay Road, TR5 0RT SW721513
⊙ 11-11 (1am Fri & Sat)
☎ (01872) 552428 ⊕ driftwoodspars.com
St Austell Tinner's, Tribute; Sharp's Doom Bar; Skinner's Betty Stogs ⊞
Outstanding free house by the sea with its own micro-brewery. New brews are planned for 2009 —a popular house ginger beer is already available. Built from granite and enormous ships' spars, this former mine warehouse and sail loft harbours three comfortable bars featuring beamed ceilings, leaded windows and granite fireplaces. Steps or a lift provide access to the sun terrace and

restaurant specialising in fish and game. Weekly live music and occasional live theatre are staged. ♨Q❀⇌◑⊟♿⛺🚌(T1)●P

Truro

City Inn Hotel

Pydar Street, TR1 3SP (N side of city centre, through railway arch)
✪ 12-11.30; 11-12.30 Fri & Sat; 12-11.30 Sun
☎ (01872) 272623
Courage Best Bitter; Sharp's Doom Bar; Skinner's Betty Stogs; guest beer Ⓗ
Community-focused 19th-century pub with the feel of a village local close to the city centre near the railway viaduct. The two-bar interior has a comfortable lounge featuring several drinking areas, while the more functional back bar is sports-oriented. Up to two guest beers change regularly, the beer menu divided into 'home' (Cornish) and 'away' teams. The garden is a real suntrap. Q❀⇌◑⊟♿⇌🚌♣●

Try Dowr ✔

Lemon Quay, TR1 2LW (Near bus station)
✪ 9-midnight (1am Fri & Sat)
☎ (01872) 265840
Beer range varies Ⓗ
Occupying a former local newspaper HQ, the Try Dowr (Three Rivers in Cornish) follows the usual Wetherspoon's format, although it offers an imaginative selection of brews including up to four local ales as well as the usual national fare, and up to three real ciders. A Lloyds No 1 bar, it is hugely popular day and night – expect to wait a few minutes when the coffee-seeking shoppers are about. It tends to be noisy most evenings when the music comes on. ❀◑♿⇌🚌●

Tywardreath

New Inn

Fore Street, PL24 2QP
✪ 12-11 (10.30 Sun)
☎ (01726) 813901
Draught Bass; Ⓖ **St Austell Dartmoor Best Bitter, Tribute, Proper Job** Ⓗ
Built in 1752 by local copper mine owners, this classic local is the hub of village life, and many functions are held in the large, secluded garden. A slotted brass plate remains in the bar where miners inserted their beer tokens. Good conversation is the entertainment here, and sometimes singing in the bar. The games room houses the jukebox so the noise is confined to the rear of the pub.
♨Q♉❀⇌⛺⇌🚌(25)

Vogue

Star Inn

TR16 5NP SW724424
✪ 12-midnight (1am Fri & Sat); 12-11 Sun
☎ (01209) 820242
Draught Bass; Greene King IPA; guest beers Ⓗ
Community-orientated locals' local at the centre of activities in this former metal-mining village. The interior includes a main bar, snug, dining room and pool room, while outside there is a seating area and regularly used boules pitch. Entertainment includes live music, karaoke, quiz nights and big-screen sports. The guest beers always include a Skinner's brew plus a second, usually from another Cornish micro-brewery. Good value basic meals and Sunday lunches are a speciality. ♨❀◑♿⛺🚌(T7)♣●P⚡

Wilcove

Wilcove Inn

PL11 2PG (Off A374, 2km from Torpoint ferry) SX430563
✪ 12-2.30, 6.30-midnight; 12-midnight Sun
☎ (01752) 812381
Draught Bass; Sharp's Doom Bar; guest beer Ⓗ
Friendly, traditional village pub beside a secluded creek off the river Tamar. The guest beer is a summer migrant and usually Cornish. Children and dogs on leads are welcome. Community-oriented, the pub hosts an annual regatta with a canoe race as the main event. On fine days, enjoy the palm trees in the garden and views across the river, or woodland walks around nearby Anthony House. Beware, though, spring tides may flood the road and car park. ♨♉❀◑P

Zelah

Hawkins Arms

High Road, TR4 9HU (off A30)
✪ 11.30-3, 6-11; 12-3, 6-10.30 Sun
☎ (01872) 540339
Otter Bitter; guest beers Ⓗ
Easily found off the main A30 (follow the brown signs), this traditional village free house offers a warm welcome to locals and travellers alike and plenty of nooks and crannies to retire to with your pint. The house beer, Zelah Mist, is specially blended for the pub by Skinner's, and there are up to two guest beers. Excellent home-cooked meals promote local produce. Newquay-Truro daytime bus services stop close by.
♨Q❀◑♿⛺🚌(585,586)P

Zennor

Tinners Arms

TR26 3BY (Off B3306) SW454385
✪ 11.30-3.30, 6.30-11 (11.30-11 Sat & summer); 12-10.30 Sun
☎ (01736) 796927 🌐 tinnersarms.com
St Austell Tinners; Sharp's Doom Bar, Special Ⓗ
A popular pit-stop for walkers, this ancient granite village pub dating from 1271 is near the windswept northern cliffs and granite moors of the Penwith peninsula and on the Cornish coastal path. The Sharp's Special appears as Zennor Mermaid, and farmhouse cider is also available. In winter, food availability is variable – phone first. The south-facing sheltered garden is a superb place to enjoy a pint on sunny days. Children and dogs are welcome. ♨Q♉❀⇌◑⛺🚌(508)P

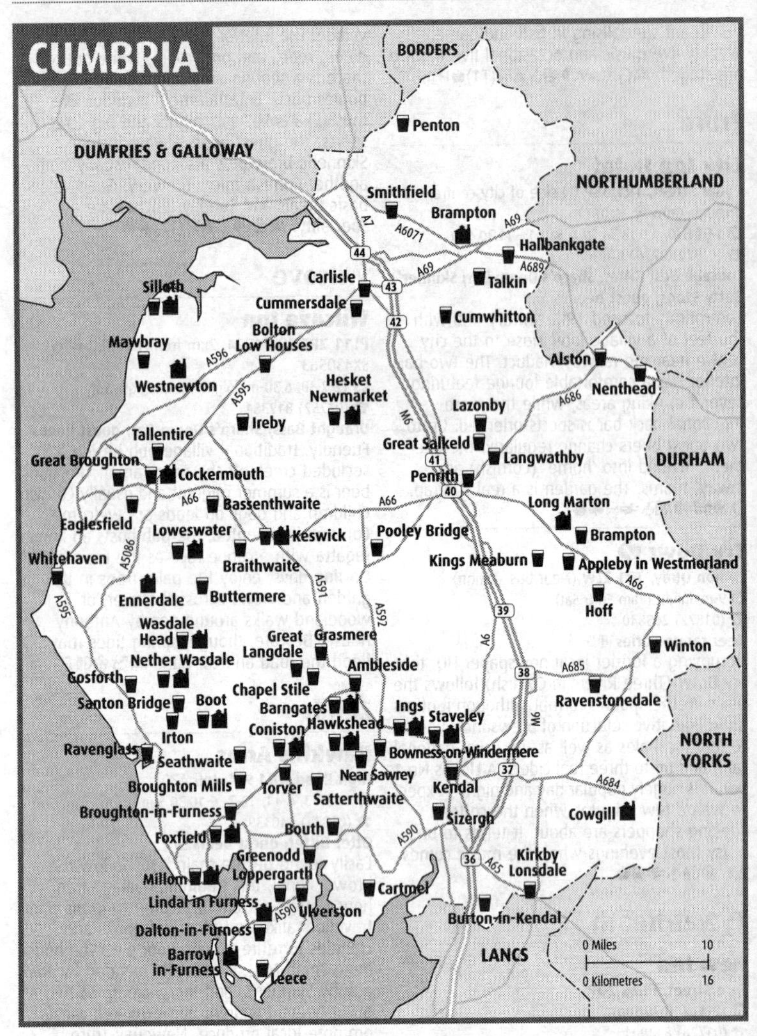

Alston

Cumberland Hotel

Townfoot, CA9 3HX

12-11 daily

(01434) 381875 alstoncumberlandhotel.co.uk

Yates Bitter; guest beers

Owned by CAMRA members, this family-run 19th-century five bedroom hotel overlooks the South Tyne River. Situated on the Coast-to-Coast cycle route and the Pennine Way, it is an ideal base to explore England's highest market town with its steep cobbled main street, South Tynedale Railway and the North Pennines. At least two Cumbrian beers are on handpump. Known as Alston's real cider venue, it serves Weston's Old Rosie, occasional Cumbrian ciders and perry. There is a separate restaurant for dining.

Keep your Good Beer Guide up to date by consulting the CAMRA website **www.camra.org.uk**

INDEPENDENT BREWERIES

Abraham Thompson Barrow-in-Furness
Barngates Barngates
Beckstones Millom
Bitter End Cockermouth
Coniston Coniston
Cumbrian Hawkshead
Dent Cowgill
Derwent Silloth
Foxfield Foxfield
Geltsdale Brampton
Great Gable Wasdale Head
Hardknott Boot
Hawkshead Staveley
Hesket Newmarket Hesket Newmarket
Keswick Keswick
Loweswater Loweswater
Strands Nether Wasdale
Tirril Long Marton
Ulverston Lindal in Furness
Watermill Ings
Whitehaven Ennerdale (NEW)
Yates Westnewton

Ambleside

Golden Rule

Smithy Brow, LA22 9AS (100m off A591 towards Kirkstone)
✪ 11 (12 Sun)-midnight
☎ (01539) 432257
Robinson's Hatters, Hartleys XB, Cumbria Way, Unicorn, Double Hop, seasonal beers ⊞
A traditional pub that has only missed one edition of the Guide, the major thrust here is the beer – no meals, piped sound, plasma TV or pool. The seasonal beer varies from the Robinson's range. A mixed clientele includes mature as well as younger locals, visitors and students attending the nearby Ambleside campus of the University of Cumbria. The rear patio and smokers' shelter catch the best of any sunshine. Owners with dogs are welcome. ♨Q❀♿⊟(555,599)♣⚟

White Lion Hotel ✔

Market Place, LA22 9DB
✪ 11-11; 12-10.30 Sun
☎ (01539) 433140
Cains Bitter; Hawkshead Bitter; guest beers ⊞
Originally a coaching inn, the former stables and grooms' staff quarters are now garages and staff accommodation. Drinks here are served promptly because food orders are taken at the tables in the dining areas. Guest beers are selected from the wide-ranging monthly Cask Fresh list. There is no jukebox or pool. The patio area with large umbrellas is an ideal spot for watching the busy passing scene. ♨❀⇔◑♿⊟(555,599)⚟

Appleby-in-Westmorland

Golden Ball

High Wiend, CA16 6RD (off Boroughgate)
✪ 11 (12 Sun)-midnight
☎ (01768) 351493
Jennings Cumberland Ale; Marston's Burton Bitter; guest beers ⊞
This traditional side-street pub has changed little over recent decades. It has a strong local following and is also popular with railway buffs using the Settle to Carlisle line – especially on steam days. The simply-furnished lounge to the left of the entrance and the bar to the right with TV and games are served from a central back-to-back bar counter. The small, walled patio has a large, covered smokers' area. Q❀⇔◑⊟⇌♣⚟

Barngates

Drunken Duck ✔

LA12 0NG NY351013
✪ 11.30-11 (10.30 Sun)
☎ (01539) 436347 🌐 drunkenduckinn.co.uk
Beer range varies ⊞
Home of the Barngates brewery, the Duck always serves four of the nine beers brewed here and brewery tours can be arranged. The bar has been extensively renovated to create a pleasing mix of local and modern styles. Bar meals served at lunchtime and the à la carte menu available in the dining room in the evening are of an exceptionally high standard. The outside seating area at the front offers magnificent views of the fells to the north east. ♨Q❀⇔◑⛺●P⚟

Bassenthwaite

Sun

CA12 4QP (From A591 head for village centre)
✪ 12 (4.30 Mon)-11
☎ (017687) 76439
Jennings Bitter, Cumberland Ale; Black Sheep Best Bitter ⊞
Built as a farmhouse, this two-roomed pub was converted to a coaching inn in the 19th century and retains the original low ceilings, exposed beams and old stone floor. There is a games room with a pool table and TV, and a selection of board games is on offer. Popular with tourists and locals alike, food is served lunchtimes (not Mon) and evenings. Four beers are usually on handpump from the Marston's list. ♨Q❀◑♿⛺⊟♣P

Bassenthwaite Lake

Pheasant Inn ☆

CA13 9YE (off A66, W end of lake)
✪ 11.30-2.30, 5.30-10.30 (11 Fri & Sat); 12-2.30, 6-10.30 (Sun)
☎ (01768) 776234 🌐 the-pheasant.co.uk
Draught Bass; Jennings Cumberland Ale; Theakston Best Bitter ⊞
Nestling on the edge of the forest below Sale Fell, this characterful 500-year-old coaching inn is now an up-market hotel where non-residents are welcome. The walls of the comfortable bar are dark and varnished and the bar is furnished with antique chairs and settles. Ales are dispensed in heavy mugs. The lounge, with its open fire, is available to drinkers at lunchtime only. The restaurant offers superb cuisine and an excellent wine list. In the summer, a family of ospreys nests nearby and can be seen fishing on the lake. ♨Q❀⇔◑⛺⊟P

Bolton Low Houses

Oddfellows Arms

New Street, CA7 8PA (off A595, 12 miles W of Carlisle)
✪ 12-3(not Mon-Thu), 7 (6 Fri & Sat)-11; 12-10.30 Sun
☎ (016973) 44452
Thwaites Original, Wainwright; guest beers ⊞
Situated between Carlisle and Cockermouth on a quiet village street now bypassed by the busy A595. On the edge of the Lake District National Park, the pub is popular with the locals and welcoming to visitors. Two drinking areas are served from a single L-shaped bar. Guest beers in summer alternate between ales from the Thwaites range and local micro-breweries. Good food, available Thursday to Sunday, is freshly prepared to order using the best of local ingredients. ♨❀◑⛺⊟♣P⚟

Boot

Brook House Inn

CA19 1TG
✪ 10-midnight
☎ (01946) 723288 🌐 brookhouseinn.co.uk

Hawkshead Bitter; Jennings Cumberland Ale; Taylor Landlord; guest beers Ⓗ
A haven of quality food and uncommon beers set in delightful Eskdale, close to Dalegarth station on the La'al Ratty tourist railway. Owned and run by a dedicated family, the pub offers three real ales throughout the year and up to six in summer. An imaginative menu of home-made food is always available in the bar, snug and restaurant. Boot's pubs collaborate in a popular June beer festival.
Q (Dalegarth)♣P

Woolpack Inn

CA19 1TH (a mile E of Boot) SD102999
11-11; 6 (11 Sat)-11 winter (closed Dec & Jan); 12-10.30 Sun
☎ (01946) 723230 woolpack.co.uk
Beer range varies Ⓗ
A lovely 25-minute walk from the La'al Ratty terminus at Dalegarth and surrounded by magnificent scenery, this pretty, rambling inn sits at the foot of the dramatic, twisting Hardknott Pass. Its friendly owners are passionate about good Cumbrian cask ales and innovative quality food sourced from fresh local ingredients. They offer their own Hardknott beers and those from other Cumbrian micros, up to six in summer. On some evenings live music is performed.
Q♣P

Bouth

White Hart

LA12 8JB (off A590, 6 miles NE of Ulverston)
12-2 (Wed-Fri), 6-11 (Mon-Fri); 12-11 Sat,; 12-10.30 sun
☎ (01229) 861229
Black Sheep Best Bitter; Coniston Bluebird; guest beers Ⓗ
Quaint old country inn festooned with old farming and hunting implements and stuffed animals. Exposed beams, a slate flagged floor and real fires give the place a welcoming, traditional atmosphere. There is a separate games room with pool tables. The food is of a high standard and uses locally-sourced ingredients. A large patio area adjoins the car park at the rear. B&B accommodation makes this an ideal base for climbers, fell walkers and cyclists. P

Bowness-on-Windermere

Royal Oak

Brantfell Road, LA23 3EG
11-11 (midnight Fri-Sat)
☎ (01539) 443970 royaloak-windermere.co.uk
Coniston Bluebird; Taylor Landlord; Tetley Bitter; guest beers Ⓗ
Just off the tourist route through the village centre, this friendly pub is well worth seeking out. A popular meeting place for local sports club members, good value meals are served in the small family room and in the main bar. There is also a raised games area with darts and pool. The Dales Way, which meanders to Ilkley in Yorkshire, passes the pub. It is also the start of the Lake to Lake walk from Windermere to Kielder Water in Northumberland.
(599,618)♣P

Braithwaite

Coledale Inn

CA12 5TN
11-11; 12-10.30 Sunday
☎ (01768) 778272 coledale-inn.co.uk
Jennings Bitter; Yates Best Bitter; guest beers Ⓗ
Situated at the top of Braithwaite village, in a peaceful hillside position with a good view of Skiddaw, this building dates from 1824 when it started life as a woollen mill, then a pencil mill. With two separate bars and a restaurant, the inn is a venue for Yates Bitter backed up by Jennings and guest ales in the summer. Paths lead to the mountains immediately outside the hotel gardens.
QP

Middle Ruddings Hotel

CA12 5RY (just off A66 at Braithwaite)
10.30-11
☎ (01768) 778436 middle-ruddings.co.uk
Beer range varies Ⓗ
Comfortable country hotel, stone built in 1903 with later extensions, with an impressive view of the Skiddaw mountain range. The restaurant serves good food with an emphasis on local produce. Three real ales are available in the bar chosen from a range of Cumbrian breweries —the landlord always checks out the brewery in person before offering its beers. Family run and family friendly, children and pets are always welcome.
QP

Brampton

New Inn

Near Appleby, CA16 6JS
12-11.30 (10.30 Sun)
☎ (01768) 351231 newinnbrampton.co.uk
Tirril Bewsher's Best Bitter, Brougham Ale, Old Faithful Ⓗ
Former farmhouse dating from 1730 with magnificent views to the Pennines. Now the tap to the nearby Tirril Brewery, it offers a varying range of Tirril beers. The interior successfully combines a minimalist modern decor with traditional furniture and fittings. The bar area has a wood floor and exposed ceiling beams. To the rear is a games area with pool. There is no jukebox, machines or TV. The dining room features a functioning kitchen range. Q♣P

Broughton Mills

Blacksmiths Arms ☆

LA20 6AX (1 mile off A593 Broughton-in-Furness-Coniston road) SD221904
12 (5 Mon)-11 summer; 12-2.30 (not Mon), 5-11; 12-11 Sat winter; 12-10.30 Sun
☎ (01229) 716824 theblacksmithsarms.com
Jennings Cumberland Ale; guest beers Ⓗ
One of only five pubs in Cumbria on CAMRA's National Inventory of Heritage Pubs. Dating back to 1577, the building was originally a farmhouse then listed as an inn, working farm of 34 acres and blacksmiths in 1748. Before this it would have been a beer house with the farmer serving ale in the kitchen to travellers and local workers. The interior remains unchanged, with three small dining rooms and

a small bar featuring an original farmhouse range, slate floors from local quarries and oak beamed ceilings. The food is justifiably popular but locals enjoy the cosy bar which is kept for drinking only. Weston's Old Rosie cider is available. ⛼Q✿◐◑●P

Broughton-in-Furness

Black Cock

Princes Street, LA20 6HQ
⏲ 11-11
☎ (01229) 716529 🌐 blackcockinncumbria.com
Marston's Pedigree; Theakston Best Bitter; guest beers ⊞
Sixteenth-century multi-roomed inn serving up to five real ales – take care with the genuine low beams. Food is served in the bars and restaurant lunchtimes and evenings. Children are welcome and have their own menu. There is a small but pleasant sheltered patio garden at the rear. The pub is a Broughton Festival of Beer venue, held on the second weekend in November. Regular themed food evenings and occasional live music make for a good all round local. ⛼✿⇌◐◑🚌(511, X7)⚐

Manor Arms

The Square, LA20 6HY
⏲ 12-11.30 (midnight Fri & Sat); 12-11 Sun
☎ (01229) 716286
Copper Dragon Golden Pippin; Yates Bitter; guest beers ⊞
Friendly, family run traditional pub overlooking the village square. Six regularly-changing guest ales come from far and wide, usually from micros, often local. Hot snacks are available until 10pm. The bar area is covered in numerous certificates awarded over the years, including CAMRA regional Pub of the Year. This is another of the magnificent seven pubs of the Broughton parish taking part in the Festival of Beer in November. Great pub, good craic, not to be missed. ⛼Q⇌🚌(X7, 511)♣●⊓

Burton-in-Kendal

Kings Arms

Main Street, LA6 1LR
⏲ 12-2, 6-11; 12-11 Sat & Sun
☎ (01524) 781409 🌐 kingsarmsburton.co.uk
Everards Beacon Bitter; Hawkshead Bitter; Jennings Dark Mild; guest beers ⊞
Close to the southern boundary of the county, this former coaching inn is a prominent feature on the high street in an attractive village, now relieved of much of its former traffic by the nearby M6. Off a central entrance vestibule is a games room to the left and a dining room to the right, with the bar area straight ahead. Beers are selected from the wide range offered via Mitchells of Lancaster. ⛼Q✿⇌◐◑♿🚌(555)♣P⚐

Buttermere

Fish Hotel

CA13 9XA (off B5289 from Keswick)
⏲ 11-3, 6-11; 11-11 Sat & Sun; winter hours vary; 11-11 Sun
☎ (01768) 770253 🌐 fish-hotel.co.uk
Jennings Bitter, Sneck Lifter; guest beers ⊞
Large, welcoming bar at the side of a historic family-owned hotel in a village situated between Buttermere and Crummock Water. This is ideal fell walking and climbing country with fishing readily available. The pub achieved notoriety in the early 19th century as the home of the Maid of Buttermere. In summer there may be seven beers on sale – guests are usually from Hesket Newmarket and Keswick breweries. Opening hours are restricted out of season. Q✿⇌◐◑⛺🚌P

Carlisle

Carlisle Rugby Club

Warwick Road, CA1 1LW (off A69, by Carlisle United FC ground)
⏲ 7 (5.30 Fri & Sat; 6 match nights)-11; 12-11 Sat in rugby season; 12-3, 7-10.30 Sun
☎ (01228) 521300
Theakston Best Bitter; Yates Bitter; guest beer ⊞
A previous winner of CAMRA Cumbria Club of the Year, this popular venue can get very busy when neighbours Carlisle United are playing at home. The building has been extended and refurbished following major floods in the city. A large TV screen shows sport and there is a function room available for hire. The Carlisle Jazz Club meets here weekly on Thursday evening. ✿🚌P⚐

Griffin ✔

Court Square, CA1 1QX (next to train station)
⏲ 9-11 (midnight Fri & Sat); 10-10.30 Sun
☎ (01228) 598941
Jennings Cumberland Ale; guest beers ⊞
Part of the John Barras chain, this former Midland Bank building features decor typical of the chain with many old photographs on the walls. The large interior of this imposing building has allowed for the construction of a second floor. A large-screen TV shows music videos and sports, and there is a separate area available for private hire. Up to three rotating guest beers are normally available. Good value meals served but please note children are not allowed. ✿◐◑♿⇌🚌⚐

King's Head

Fisher Street, CA3 8RF (behind Old Town Hall)
⏲ 10 (11 Sat; 12 Sun)-11
☎ (01228) 540100
Yates Bitter; guest beers ⊞
One of the oldest pubs in the city centre, with the castle and cathedral and Lanes Shopping Centre nearby. Pictures of Carlisle through the ages are displayed inside and a plaque outside explains why Carlisle is not in the Domesday Book. A covered all-weather yard has a large-screen TV and barbecue area. Good value lunches are served but please note that children are not allowed. A local CAMRA award winner. ✿◐⇌🚌♣⚐

Linton Holme Hotel

86 Lindisfarne Street, CA1 2NB
⏲ 5 (3 Fri; 12 Sat)-11; 12-10.30 Sun
☎ (01228) 532637
Yates Bitter; guest beer ⊞

Former hotel retaining many original features including tiled mosaic floors, etched windows and a wonderful marble pillar outside. Situated in a quiet residential area, it is well worth making the effort to seek out. Inside, a variety of rooms all open out to a bar area where there is a large pool table suitable for use by wheelchair users. The guest ale is frequently from a micro-brewery. TVs show sporting events and regular darts, pool and quiz nights are held.

Woodrow Wilson

48 Botchergate, CA1 1QS
9-midnight (1am Fri & Sat); 12-midnight Sun
(01228) 819942
Greene King Abbot; Jennings Cumberland Ale; Marston's Pedigree; guest beers
Wetherspoon's pub in a former Co-op building, offering the largest range of real ales in Carlisle and a regular outlet for Geltsdale beers. Food is available all day and large screen TVs show sporting events. Outside there is a spacious heated patio for smokers at the back and seating in the main street. Children are welcome in some areas until 8pm. Five minutes' walk from the railway station, local buses stop outside the front door. QP

Cartmel

King's Arms

The Square, LA11 6QB
11-11 (10.30 Sun); 12-10.30 Sun
(01539) 536220 kingsarmscartmel.co.uk
Moorhouses Blond Witch; Hawkshead Bitter; guest beers
A few yards from the famous Cartmel Priory beside the little River Eea, this pub has a good mix of small rooms and an open plan dining area. It sits on a site where there has been a drinking establishment for more than 900 years. Good value food is on offer made with local produce. An outdoor area at the front overlooking the square is very popular with visitors in the summer and the pub can get very busy on race days at the local racecourse. Q(532)

Chapel Stile

Wainwrights Inn

LA22 9JH (on B5343 from Skelwith Bridge)
11.30 (12 Sun)-11
(01539) 438088 langdale.co.uk/wainwrights
Thwaites Original, Lancaster Bomber; guest beers
With stunning views of Megs Gill and Raven Crag, this former farmhouse was converted into the Elterwater gunpowder works manager's house then became a pub. Refurbished following a serious fire, it maintains a wide-ranging guest beer policy but does not neglect the local brewing scene. Meals are served in the stone-floored bar area and the dining room. A glass-fronted case at the end of the bar displays various explosive samples. (516)P

Cockermouth

1761

1 Market Place, CA13 9NH
4.30-11.30;12-11.30 Sat
(01900) 829282 bar1761.co.uk
Yates Bitter; Jennings Cumberland Ale; guest beers
Records for this pub date back to 1761, hence its name. It has an original tiled entrance and stone flooring and was re-opened as a bar at the beginning of 2007. It retains original features such as a stone fireplace with stove, but is contemporary in feel. Of the two guest beers, one is always from a Cumbrian brewery. Live music is played fortnightly on a Wednesday night. A range of board games is available. Coffee is served.

Swan Inn

55 Kirkgate, CA13 9PH
6-11.30 (midnight Fri); 10-midnight Sat; 12-11 Sun
(01900) 822425
Jennings Dark Mild, Bitter, Cumberland Ale
One of the oldest pubs in town, this traditional inn with stone-flagged floors and low beams is situated on Cockermouth's cobbled Georgian square. A friendly clientele adds to the welcoming atmosphere. A variety of games is played here including darts, chess and backgammon. The pub hosts two quiz teams and supports many community events. Dogs are permitted.

Coniston

Black Bull

LA21 8DU
10-11 (10.30 Sun)
(01539) 441335 conistonbrewery.com
Coniston Bluebird, Old Man Ale, Bluebird XB
Sixteenth-century coaching inn serving excellent food and drink in traditional yet comfortable surroundings. The tap house for the on-site Coniston Brewing Company, this is an excellent place to sample its wares. Large and spacious, the bar and lounge with beamed ceilings and tasteful decor are always popular, and seating outside is perfect for the summer months. Winner of numerous awards and accolades, this family-run business at the foot of the Old Man is not to be missed. QP

Sun Hotel

LA21 8HQ
12-11
(01539) 441248 thesunconiston.com
Coniston Bluebird; Hawkshead Bitter; guest beers
Pub and hotel dating back to the 16th century, built on the old Walna Scar packhorse trail, situated up the hill and overlooking the village. A typical Lakeland bar, it has a slate floor and an open fire housed in a well-preserved iron range, making for a welcoming atmosphere after a walk on the fells nearby. There is more seating in the conservatory and outside on the sunny side overlooking the garden. Q(X12,505)P

Cummersdale

Spinners Arms

Cummersdale Road, CA2 6BD (1 mile S of Carlisle off B5299)

✪ 6 (12 Sat & Sun)-midnight

☎ (01228) 532928

Beer range varies ⊞

Refurbished and cosy family-friendly Redfern pub with unique animal- decorated gutters and a welcoming real fire. Situated at the heart of the village near the Cumbrian Way and a national cycle path, it is close to an original cloth factory on the River Caldew. The landlord and locals ensure there is a good variety of guest ales, often from Geltsdale and Hesket Newmarket. Food is served on Sunday lunchtime only. Open mike sessions are the first Saturday of the month. There is a large TV in the bar area. Well-behaved dogs are welcome. ⌂✿◑♿⛺⊟♣⁻

Cumwhitton

Pheasant Inn ✔

CA8 9EX (4 miles SE of A69 at Warwick Bridge)

✪ 6-11 (midnight Sat); closed Mon; 12-3, 6-11 Sun

☎ (01228) 560102

🌐 thepheasantinncumwhitton.co.uk

Black Sheep Bitter; guest beers ⊞

Local CAMRA Pub of the Year 2007 and 2008, this inn has taken on a new lease of life since it was taken over by the mother and daughter team now running it. The bar has a flagged floor and exposed stone walls adorned with paintings mainly by local artists, and a collection of water jugs hangs from the beams. Excellent food is served in the bar and adjacent dining room. Twice-monthly quiz nights and regular special events are always well attended by locals and visitors. ⌂✿⇌◑◗⛺♣P

Dalton-in-Furness

Black Dog Inn

Broughton Rd, LA15 8JP SD233761

✪ 4 (11 Wed-Sat)-11; closed Mon; 12-10.30 Sun

☎ (01229) 462561

Beer range varies ⊞

A quiet, unassuming country pub that is just a 20-minute walk from the town centre. The single-room interior has a quarry-tiled floor, beams and two real fires. The snug area in front of the bar provides a focal point for the locals but visitors will invariably be drawn into the conversation. Popular with diners as well as drinkers, regular beer festivals are hosted throughout the year and up to nine beers are always available. ⌂Q✿⇌◑◗P⁻⊓

Brown Cow

The Green, LA15 8LQ (just off A590)

✪ 11.30-midnight

☎ (01229) 462553 🌐 browncowinndalton.co.uk

Beer range varies ⊞

A warm and friendly atmosphere greets visitors to this 400-year-old coaching house which has retained many original features including original beams, brasses, local prints and an open fire. A winner of many awards for its five real ales, the pub also serves excellent food from a full and varied menu. Meals can be enjoyed in the large dining room or on warmer days on the charming patio with heating and lighting. Well worth a visit. ⌂Q✿⇌◑◗⇄⊟P⁻

Eaglesfield

Black Cock

CA13 0SD (off A5086, 2 miles S of Cockermouth)

✪ 8-11; 12.30-10.30 Sun

☎ (01900) 822989

Jennings Bitter; guest beers ⊞

This 17th-century village pub has changed little over the past 30 years, retaining original low beams, a traditional open fireplace and wood panelling. Although no longer part of the Marston's estate, Jennings Bitter is usually available, alongside guest beers such as Abbot, IPA and Ruddles Bitter. The pub hosts a folk night on the third Wednesday of the month and a quiz on alternate Mondays. ⌂Q⊟P

Foxfield

Prince of Wales

LA20 6BX (opp station)

✪ 12.45 (12 Fri & Sat)-11; closed Mon & Tue; 12-10.30 Sun

☎ (01229) 716238 🌐 princeofwalesfoxfield.co.uk

Beer range varies ⊞

The Prince has won so many awards they have to shrink the certificates to get them all on the wall. Beers are from all over the country including the pub's two house breweries, Foxfield and Tigertops, and there is always a mild on offer. As well as cask ales there is a fine selection of malt whiskies and continental beers. The home-made curries and pasties are justifiably famous. An eclectic mix of comfy furniture and two open fires gives the bar and side room (which houses a bar billiard table) the feel of a favourite aunt's house. ⌂Q✿⇌⇄⊟(X7,511)♣●P⁻⊓

Gosforth

Gosforth Hall Hotel

CA20 1AZ

✪ 5 (12 Fri-Sun)-midnight

☎ (01946) 725322 🌐 gosforthhallhotel.co.uk

Beer range varies ⊞

Built on the site of a 10th-century Norse hall, this historic, Grade II listed former 17th-century Pele tower and fortified farmhouse is adjacent to St Mary's Church with its famous 15ft high Viking cross. West Cumbria CAMRA Pub of the Season in spring 2007, there are always three interesting beers on offer, often a Yates and a Hawkshead. Live music plays on summer Sundays and occasional medieval themed evenings are hosted. There is a boules pitch in the large landscaped garden. Archaeological digs are offered. ⌂☕✿⇌◑◗⊟♿♣P

Grasmere

Dale Lodge Hotel (Tweedies Bar)

Langdale Road, LA22 9SW

✪ 12-11 (midnight Thu-Sun)

☎ (01539) 435300 🌐 dalelodgehotel.co.uk

Caledonian Deuchars IPA; Theakston Old Peculier; guest beers Ⓗ
Stone-flagged bar with solid furniture and a winter stove occupying the site of a former woollen mill shop. An adjoining room, equally solidly furnished, is set for dining and has views over the extensive lawned grounds. Good quality meals are served throughout. There is a separate games room to the rear. Guest beers include one from the Yates range and one from Taylor, the others come from far and wide. ⌂❀⇌◑♿▭(555,599)♣●P⌐

Great Broughton

Punchbowl Inn

19 Main Street, CA13 0YJ
⏲ 7 (11 Fri-Sun)-11
☎ (01900) 824708
Jennings Bitter; guest beers Ⓗ
Traditional village pub that is full of characters and character. Built in the 17th century with beams and an open fire, it now boasts a classic jukebox. The walls are covered in tokens of local esteem and other memorabilia, all creating a welcoming atmosphere. Two well-kept ales include Jennings and a guest from anywhere in Britain, changing two or three times a week. ⌂Q▭♣P

Great Langdale

Old Dungeon Ghyll Hotel

LA22 9JY (Over bridge at end of B5343)
⏲ 11-11; 11-10.30 Sun
☎ (01539) 437272 🌐 odg.co.uk
Black Sheep Best Bitter, Ale; Jennings Cumberland Ale; Theakston XB, Old Peculier; Yates Bitter; guest beers Ⓗ
One of the best-known climbers' and hikers' bars in the Lake District, converted from a former cowshed in the late 1940s. Wet and muddy waterproofs and boots are almost de rigueur in bad weather and the guard in front of the kitchen range often doubles as a drying rail. An extensive range of home-made meals is served in the bar and there is also a dining room in the hotel for which pre-booking is required. CAMRA Westmorland Pub of the Year 2008. ⌂Q❀⇌◑⊟▲▭(516)●P⌐

Great Salkeld

Highland Drove

CA11 9NA (off B6412 between A686 and Lazonby)
⏲ 12-3 (not Mon), 6-midnight; 12-midnight Sat & Sun
☎ (01768) 898349 🌐 highland-drove.co.uk
John Smith's Bitter; Theakston Black Bull Bitter; guest beer Ⓗ
A pub for all tastes – whether it is the well-stocked bar with three real ales, comfortable lounge with its Downstairs at the Drove' menu, the games room with pool and darts or the upstairs award-winning restaurant named 'Kyloes' after the highland cattle from the Kyles which in olden days were driven down from Scotland. Sympathetically extended, refurbished and decorated to reflect past history, a warm welcome and friendly atmosphere are assured.
⌂❀⇌◑⊟♿▲♣P⌐

Greenodd

Ship Inn

Main Street, LA12 7QZ
⏲ 6-midnight; 12-10.30 Sun
☎ (07782) 655294
Lancaster Amber; guest beers Ⓗ
Traditional village pub blending the old and the new. Beamed ceilings contrast with leather suites, and real fires enhance the ambience of the relaxed lounge and bar areas. A separate games room houses a pool table, dartboard and jukebox. Guest beers often come from local breweries and there is usually a good selection of ciders and perries available. ⌂♣●P▱

Hallbankgate

Belted Will

CA8 2NJ (on A689 Alston road 4 miles E of Brampton)
⏲ 12-2 (summer only), 5-midnight; 12-midnight Sat & Sun
☎ (01697) 746236 🌐 beltedwill.co.uk
Beer range varies Ⓗ
The pub's unusual name refers to William Howard of nearby Naworth Castle whose nickname was mentioned in a poem by Sir Walter Scott. Three real ales are on offer, at least one from a local brewery, and the pub has a reputation for good food. Its location at the foot of the Northern Pennines makes it an ideal base for fans of outdoor pursuits including walking and hiking, mountain biking and cycling, fishing, golfing, bird watching and pony trekking. According to local legend one bedroom is reputed to be haunted.
⌂❀⇌◑⊟♿▭♣⌐

Hawkshead

King's Arms Hotel

The Square, LA22 0NZ
⏲ 11-midnight
☎ (01539) 436372 🌐 kingsarmshawkshead.co.uk
Coniston Bluebird; Hawkshead Bitter; guest beers Ⓗ
Owned by the same family for more than 26 years, this busy pub dates back to Elizabethan times. Popular with locals and visitors, it has a cosy interior with an open fire and traditional oak-beamed ceilings. A spacious dining room ensures that diners can usually find a table if the bar area is busy. The outside seating area overlooks the village square. Guest beers are usually from local breweries.
⌂⇌◑▲▭(505)♣

Hesket Newmarket

Old Crown

Main Street, CA7 8JG
⏲ 12-2.30 (Fr-Sat) 5.30-11.00; 12-2.30 5.30-10.30 Sun
☎ (01697) 478288 🌐 theoldcrownpub.co.uk
Hesket Newmarket Great Cockup Porter, Blencathra Bitter, Hellvellyn Gold, Doris's 90th Birthday Ale, Old Carrock Strong Ale Ⓗ
On the edge of the northern Lakeland fells, this pub is at the centre of village life. It is owned as a co-operative by the local community, who are dedicated to maintaining

its original character. It offers the full range of Hesket Newmarket beers from the brewery situated in the barn at the rear of the pub. The kitchen offers good food made with fresh local produce. Free Internet connection is available for customers. A folk session is held on the first Sunday of the month. ⩕Q❀◑◗⊟Ⲁ⊱

Hoff

New Inn

CA16 6TA (on B6260)
✪ 12 (7.30 Mon, except Bank Hols)-midnight
☎ (01768) 351317
Tirril Bewsher's Best Bitter; guest beers Ⓗ
Originally an inn in 1823, the building was briefly converted to residential use at the end of last century but made a welcome return as a village local in 2001. The cosy stone-flagged bar features plenty of oak furniture and a raised fireplace. Exposed ceiling beams are adorned with myriad pump clips—a testament to the enthusiasm with which guest beers are sourced by the owner. Home-cooked meals are served Wednesday to Sunday and there is a live folk and blues session on Friday evening. Guest accommodation is planned. ⩕Q❀◑◗Ⲁ♣P

Ings

Watermill Inn

LA8 9PY (turn off A591 by Church)
✪ 12-11 (10.30 Sun)
☎ (01539) 821309 🌐 watermillinn.co.uk
Hawkshead Bitter; Moorhouses Black Cat; Theakston Best Bitter, Old Peculier; Watermill Collie Wobbles, Wruff Night, A Bit'er Ruff; guest beers Ⓗ
This multi award-winning free house constructed from Lakeland stone was converted from a modest guest house in 1990. Now much enlarged it has a brewery of its own which, along with the beer cellar, can be seen through viewing windows. Ales are dispensed from the two banks of eight handpumps, one in each bar. A wide range of meals is served all day except between 4.30-5pm. Dogs are warmly welcomed in the bar by the river and families in the side rooms. ⩕Q♉❀⊭◑◗♿⊟(555)♣●P⊱⊽

Ireby

Lion

CA7 1EA
✪ 6-11 (midnight Fri & Sat); 12-3, 7-11 Sun
☎ (01697) 371460 🌐 irebythelion.co.uk
Derwent Carlisle State Bitter; Jennings Bitter; guest beers Ⓗ
The pub is the focal point of the quiet rural town of Ireby, situated high above the river Ellen as it emerges from the Lakeland fells. The main bar features a wooden floor and wood panelling from local chapels and churches, but the bar itself came from a pub in Leeds. The publican is dedicated to local real ales with four usually available as well as occasional beers from further afield. Food is locally sourced and home cooked (no meals on Sun and Mon eves). ⩕Q❀◑◗♣⊱

Irton

Bower House

CA19 1TD NY131002
✪ 11-11 (10.30 Sun)
☎ (01946) 723244 🌐 bowerhouseinn.co.uk
Theakston Best Bitter; guest beers Ⓗ
Seventeenth-century inn next to the village cricket ground and almost surrounded by gardens. The unspoilt bar where 'the electronic age has no place, nor will it' is an ideal place for quiet conversation. There is a separate dining room offering many local delicacies. Live music plays once a month on a Friday night and an annual music festival is held in August. Home to the local cricket club. Food is served lunchtimes and evenings, all day during the summer and on bank holidays. ⩕Q♉❀⊭◑◗Ⲁ⥂♣P⊱

Kendal

Burgundy's Wine Bar

19 Lowther Street, LA9 4DH
✪ 11.30-3 (not Tue & Wed), 6.30-midnight; closed Mon; 7-11 Sun
☎ (01539) 733803 🌐 burgundyswinebar.co.uk
Yates Fever Pitch; guest beers Ⓗ
Friendly, family-run town centre bar on three levels: the main bar area has its entrance from Lowther street, an upper level has a large part-covered terrace through a doorway, and the lower level, with an entrance from Tanners Yard, has a small bar, games area and large adjoining lounge/function room. An above average selection of draught continental lagers as well as bottled beers from home and abroad are offered. Live jazz plays on Thursday evening. ⥂⊟(41,555)●⊱

Castle Inn

Castle Street, LA9 7AA
✪ 11.30-midnight (1am Sat); 12-11.30 Sun
☎ (01539) 729983
Black Sheep Best Bitter; Jennings Bitter; Tetley Bitter; guest beers Ⓗ
A real community pub, the central bar serves several areas: the lounge to the left with a fine fish tank in the side wall, and the bar area with an internal window from the former Duttons Brewery. Up a step is the adjoining games area. Good value, quick service lunches, especially the Sunday roast, are a popular feature. The beer range includes an ale from the local Dent brewery. The ruins of Kendal Castle are nearby. ◑⥂♣⊱

Riflemans Inn

4 Greenside, LA9 4LD
✪ 6 (12 Sat & Sun)-midnight
☎ (015397) 23224
Tetley Bitter; guest beers Ⓗ
It is well worth the steep climb up from the town centre to this 'town pub on the village green'. The single room interior is partly divided into two areas, served from a single counter offering three guest beers chosen from the Cellarman's Reserve list. Knowledgeable staff offer helpful advice to customers unsure which ale to choose. There is a separate games room and, upstairs, a room for meetings. Live music, mainly folk, plays on Thursday evening. Families are

welcome until 9pm, owners with dogs any time. Q🚌(44,48)♣

Keswick

Bank Tavern ✔

47 Main Street, CA12 5DS
11-11 (11.30 Fri & Sat); 12-10.30 Sun
☎ (017687) 72663
Jennings Bitter, Cumberland Ale, Sneck Lifter; Marston's Pedigree; guest beers H
Refurbished town centre pub with a busy food trade. A range of Jennings beers is on offer plus ales from Marston's list. Outside is a covered and heated seating area for drinkers and smokers. No children under five are permitted. ❀◐♿🚌

Kings Meaburn

White Horse ✔

CA10 3BU NY620211
7 (6 Thu & Fri)-11; 12-2am Sat; 12-3, 6-11 Sun
☎ (01931) 714256
Beer range varies H
Friendly, cosy, one-room village inn well supported by locals and very welcoming to visitors. The beers, often collected from the brewery by the owner, come from near and far. The pub hosts the Eden Valley beer festival in a marquee pitched on an adjoining field in July, with transport provided from nearby Appleby. Meals are excellent but not a high priority so it is best to enquire ahead of a visit. Weekday hours may extend in summer. Q❀◐♿♣P

Kirkby Lonsdale

Sun Inn

7 Market Street, LA6 2AU
11-11
☎ (01524) 271965 🌐 sun-inn.info
Jennings Bitter; Taylor Landlord; guest beers H
This 17th-century building is of considerable architectural interest with its wooden floors, bare stone walls and beamed bar area. Beyond a raised fireplace is a small comfortably-furnished lounge area which leads to a well-appointed dining room. Guest beers are mainly from local micro-breweries. High quality meals are served made with fresh local produce from local suppliers. The nearby Devils Bridge over the river Lune is a popular gathering place for bikers.
Q◐♿Å🚌(567)♣

Langwathby

Shepherds Inn

Village Green, CA10 1LW (on A686)
12-3 (2.30 winter), 6 (6.30 winter)-11; 12-midnight Sat; 12-11 Sun
☎ (01768) 881335
Beer range varies H
Situated on the A686 – a popular route for tourists and travellers between the north east and the Lake District – as well as on the scenic Carlisle-Settle railway line. Two ever-changing real ales and good food are available. The split-level interior has the entrance, lounge and games area on the upper level and the bar down a few steps. Close to various walks in the Eden valley, local attractions include an ostrich farm and an ancient stone circle.
❀◐⇌♣P

Lazonby

Joiners Arms

Townfoot, CA10 1BL
12-3 (not winter Mon-Fri), 6-11
☎ (01768) 898728
Hesket Newmarket Doris's 90th Birthday Ale; guest beer H
Small but welcoming hostelry reopened in 2004 by the current owner who reintroduced real ale and re-established the inn as a popular venue for locals and visitors to enjoy excellent food and beer (no meals served Mon and Tue). Entry from the road is direct into the bar which has a dining area to the rear and a games room at a lower level. Lazonby is a thriving village on the scenic Carlisle-Settle railway line —the pub is a short walk downhill from the station. ❀◐Å⇌♣

Leece

Copper Dog

LA12 0QP (3 miles E of Barrow) SD244695
11.30-3, 5.30-11 (midnight Fri); 11.30-midnight Sat; 12-10.30 Sun
☎ (01229) 877088
Beer range varies H
Spacious pub on the outskirts of the village with a large bar warmed by an open fire. The beautiful dining conservatory enjoys superb views over the surrounding countryside (available to hire for private functions). Reasonably-priced food is freshly prepared to a high standard. An annual charity beer festival is held in summer. The Castle House Hotel on Walney Island and White House Hotel in Barrow are now all under the same management. The No 10 bus stops in village.
❀◐🚌(10)P

Loppergarth

Wellington

Main Street, LA12 0JL (1 mile from A590 between Lindal and Pennington) SD260772
6-midnight (1am Fri & Sat)
☎ (01229) 582388
Beer range varies H
A real family-run local in this small hamlet. The central three-sided bar is surrounded by four distinct drinking areas, with a TV in one corner. A games and family room at the side offers pool, darts, fruit machine, jukebox and books, but the noise level is well controlled. Both rooms have cosy open fires. Handpumps feature mainly local beers, particularly from Ulverston and Foxfield, with Dark Mild usually available. Gents and ladies darts and pool teams play here, with a popular quiz on alternate Saturdays. ♣

Loweswater

Kirkstile Inn

CA13 0RU (signed off B5289) NY140210
11-11 (10.30 Sun)

☎ (01900) 85219 ⊕ kirkstile.com
Loweswater Melbreak Bitter, Kirkstile Gold, Grasmoor Dark Ale; Yates Bitter; guest beer ⊞
This 16th-century Lakeland inn sits below Melbreak between Loweswater and Crummock Water —with stunning views from the beer garden. Inside, low ceilings and stone walls add character. A deservedly popular pub serving good food all day, it can be very busy at peak times. However the service remains consistently welcoming and efficient. Home of Loweswater Brewery, three regular award-winning beers are on offer plus two seasonal beers —two available in bottles. Local CAMRA Pub of the Year 2003-2005 and 2008.
⌂Q☎❀⊭◐♿P▯

Mawbray

Lowther Arms

CA15 6QT (off B5300, through village for ½ mile)
✪ 12-midnight
☎ (01900) 881337
Beer range varies ⊞
Traditional country pub built in 1790 catering for both holidaymakers and locals. The bar area, with a stone floor and open fire, has been extended to create more space for drinkers. A local brewery usually provides one of the ales dispensed from the two handpumps, either Yates or Derwent. Dogs are permitted only after 9pm when food service stops for the evening. There is a caravan park attached to the pub. ⌂❀◐⋀⊟P

Millom

Punch Bowl

The Green, LA18 5HJ (half mile from Green Road station) SD178846
✪ 6-11 (10.30 Sun)
☎ (01229) 772605
Beckstones range; guest beers ⊞
This village pub has a family connection with the nearby Beckstones Brewery, and is effectively its tap house. Guest beers usually come from other local breweries. There is a large open plan bar area and separate games/TV room with real fires, making for a very convivial atmosphere.
⌂Q❀⇌⊟(511,X7)♣⊱▯

Near Sawrey

Tower Bank Arms

LA22 0LF (on B5285 6 miles S of Ambleside) SD370956
✪ 11-11 (closed 2.30-5.30 Mon-Fri winter)
☎ (01539) 436334 ⊕ towerbankarms.co.uk
Beer range varies ⊞
All the features of a traditional 17th-century Lakeland inn are to be found here —slate floors, oak beams and a cooking range with an open fire. Set in a beautiful rural location next to Hill Top, the former home of Beatrix Potter which is open to the public, it can be very busy at holiday times. The pub features in The Tales Of Jemima Puddleduck. Food is served in the bar and restaurant. Beers are sourced locally, mainly from Barngates and Keswick. Dogs and children are most welcome. ⌂Q❀⊭◐♣P

Nenthead

Miners Arms

CA9 3PF (5 miles SE of Alston on A689)
✪ 4-11 (not Mon), 12-11 Sat; 12-10.30 Sun
☎ (01434) 381427 ⊕ nenthead.com
Allendale Best Bitter; Black Sheep Best Bitter; guest beer ⊞
Situated high up in the Pennines at 1500 feet above sea level, this friendly, traditional 1700s-built sandstone pub is the highest village pub in England. The publican has recently celebrated 20 years' tenure. Award-winning food is made from fresh locally-sourced produce. Located close to the Nenthead Lead Mine visitor centre and a Coast-to-Coast cycle route official stamping post, the pub is an ideal base for visitors to the High Pennines. En-suite accommodation is available. Dogs are welcome in the bar.
⌂❀⊭◐♿⋀⊟P

Nether Wasdale

Screes Inn

Near Gosforth, CA20 1ET (E off A595 5 miles NE of Ravenglass) NY125040
✪ 11-11
☎ (019467) 26262 ⊕ thescreesinnwasdale.com
Derwent seasonal beers; Jennings Cumberland Ale; Whitehaven Ennerdale; Yates Bitter ⊞
One of two excellent real ale pubs in this tiny hamlet, this is a multi-level, multi-roomed country inn with a separate dining room. Situated in the Lake District National Park close to Wastwater and Scafell Pike, it is ideal for walkers. Home-cooked food is made with local produce and includes a vegetarian option. A major refurbishment is planned which will include full disabled facilities.
⌂❀⊭◐⊡♣P⊱

Penrith

Agricultural Hotel

Castlegate, CA11 7JE
✪ 11-11 (midnight Sat); 11-10.30 Sun
☎ (01768) 862622
Jennings Bitter, Cumberland Ale, Sneck Lifter; guest beers ⊞
Old, well-established pub on the edge of the Lake District a short walk from the town centre near Penrith railway station. It is overlooked by the ruins of Penrith Castle – a throwback to the Border disputes with the Reivers of old. Warm and welcoming, the Aggie, as it is known locally, serves food all day.
⌂Q❀⊭◐♿⇌⊟P⊱

Lowther Arms

3 Queen Street, CA11 7XD
✪ 11-3, 6-11 (midnight Sat); 12-3, 6-10.30 Sun
☎ (01768) 862792
Caledonian Deuchars IPA; Fuller's London Pride; guest beers ⊞
Visitors are assured of a warm welcome at this coaching inn next to the A6 in this busy market town. A sympathetic extension has added more space without losing the character of the old building. Drinkers are spoiled for choice with a range of up to eight real ales usually available. Good food is served and the pub can get busy at meal times. A

past winner of awards from CAMRA and Britain in Bloom. ♨Q◑⇌🚌

Penton

Bridge Inn

CA6 5QB NY438764

⏲ 7-11

☎ (01228) 577041

Marston's Pedigree; guest beers ⊞

The closest real ale pub to Scotland in the area, this quiet countryside drinking establishment is spread over three rooms. It is frequented by locals with several teams competing in darts and pool leagues. The regulars choose the guest ale from the list provided. ♨Q⚘♣P⊬

Pooley Bridge

Sun Inn ✔

CA10 2NN

⏲ 12-11 (10.30 Sun)

☎ (01768) 486205 🌐 suninnpooleybridge.co.uk

Jennings Cocker Hoop, Cumberland Ale, Sneck Lifter, seasonal beers ⊞

Situated in the less frequented north east corner of the Lake District, the pub is a short distance from the pier for summer cruises on Ullswater. At street level there is a wood-panelled bar and a separate dining room. Down a flight of steps is a large bar area with sports TV and access to the extensive, safe garden. Beers are from the Marston's range. Dogs are welcome throughout.
♨Q⚘🛏◑⊟⛺🚌(108)♣⊬

Ravenglass

Ratty Arms

CA18 1SN (through mainline station)

⏲ 11-11; 11-2.30, 5.30-11 winter; 12-10.30 Sun

☎ (01229) 717676

Greene King Ruddles Best; Jennings Cumberland Ale; Theakston Best Bitter; guest beers ⊞

This railway themed pub occupies the former station building at the junction of the mainline coast line and the popular La'al Ratty. The narrow gauge steam train runs deep into striking historic upper Eskdale, with more good real ale pubs, the high fells and Roman remains to explore. Local attractions are Muncaster Castle, a Roman bathhouse and the impressive estuary, rich in wildlife. Excellent, good value food is served all day and two guest beers are stocked in the summer season. ♨Q⚘◑♿⛺⇌🚌♣P⊬

Ravenstonedale

Black Swan Inn ✔

CA17 4NG (village signed off A685)

⏲ 11-midnight (1am Fri & Sat); 12-midnight Sun

☎ (015396) 23204 🌐 blackswanhotel.com

Black Sheep Best Bitter, Ale; John Smith's Bitter; guest beers ⊞

This picturesque village lies in an area of outstanding natural beauty and the family owners are proud of their comfortable, community inn. A village shop was opened recently providing essentials and fresh produce from local suppliers. The locals' bar has an archway that leads to a lounge bar and adjoining dining areas. The pub is free of tie and guest beers are usually supplied by Cumbrian micros. There is a large, beck-side garden across the road. A local music festival is hosted in September. The bar has free Internet access.
♨Q⚘🛏◑⊟♿🚌(564,569)♣P

Santon Bridge

Bridge Inn ✔

CA19 1UX (off A595 at Holmrook) NY110016

⏲ 11-midnight

☎ (019467) 26221 🌐 santonbridgeinn.com

Jennings Bitter, Cumberland Ale, Cocker Hoop, Sneck Lifter; guest beers ⊞

Once a modest mail coach halt, this is now an award-winning country inn with creaking floors, low beams and warming fires. A comprehensive range of Jennings beers and home-cooked food make this a pub not to be missed. In summer relax outside by the river and take in the magnificent mountain views. The pub hosts the immensely popular World's Biggest Liar competition in November.
♨Q⚘🛏◑♿⛺♣P

Satterthwaite

Eagles Head

LA12 8LN (4 miles S of Ambleside)

⏲ 12-2.30 (not Mon), 7 (6.30 Fri & Sat)-11; 12-2.30, 7-10.30 Sun

☎ (01229) 860237

Theakston Best Bitter; guest beers ⊞

Situated in the Grizedale Forest, this building dates from the 15th century and was originally a farmhouse – it has been a watering hole since the 16th century. A warm, welcoming classic Lakeland inn, it attracts locals, walkers and holidaymakers for excellent dining and good ale. No food is available on Monday evening. ♨Q⚘◑♿⛺P⊬

Seathwaite

Newfield Inn

LA20 6ED SD178846

⏲ 11-11

☎ (01229) 716208

Jennings Cumberland Ale; guest beer ⊞

This 17th-century free house in the Duddon Valley, Wordworth's favourite valley, is an oasis for fell walkers and travellers passing through. The inn prides itself on its quality ales from Cumbrian and other northern breweries. Good food is available daily. The spacious beer garden has excellent views over the fells. Note the unique, locally quarried banded slate floor in the bar. The pub is a venue for the Broughton Festival of Beer held each November. ♨Q☕⚘◑⊟⛺♣P

Silloth

Albion

Eden Street, CA7 4AS

⏲ 3 (7 Mon; 4.30 winter)-midnight; 2-midnight Fri; 11-midnight Sat & Sun

☎ (016973) 31321

Tetley Mild; guest beer ⊞

Traditional two-room locals' pub well supported by many visitors in summer. Pictures of old Silloth decorate the walls along with two superb models of whaling trawlers. There are also numerous photos celebrating the Isle of Man TT races alongside old motoring memorabilia. One room has a TV and pool table. The pub is very much at the heart of the community, serving as a meeting place for local groups. An ale from Derwent Brewery frequently appears on the guest handpump. ⩩Q♨❀⅄⊟♣P⅟–

Sizergh

Strickland Arms

LA8 8DZ (follow signs to Sizergh Castle off A590)
✪ 11.30-3, 5.30-11; 11.30-11 (Sat, Sun & Summer)
☎ (01539) 561010
Thwaites Original; guest beers Ⓗ
Situated close to the gates of Sizergh Castle and on the Walney to Wear cycle route, this fine listed building has been licensed since its construction in 1897. Guest beers are usually from Cumbrian micro-breweries. The diverse menu features local produce with fish dishes a speciality on Thursday evening. A pleasant garden and front patio can be enjoyed in summer, with log fires in winter. There are function/meeting rooms available upstairs. ⩩Q❀◑♿⅄⊟(555,X35)♣P⅟–

Smithfield

Robin Hood

CA6 6BP (on A6071 between Brampton & Longtown)
✪ 12 (7 Mon)-midnight; 12-1am Sat
☎ (01228) 675957
Fuller's London Pride; Geltsdale Black Dub, Kings Forest, Tarnmonath; guest beers Ⓗ
This pub sits at a crossroads that was once a meeting place for farmers from far and wide who met to trade their cattle and the area became known as Little Smithfield. The busy inn is frequented by many locals and continues to be popular with the farming community, hosting several darts teams. In 2007 it discarded the pool table and started catering and is now steadily building a reputation for good food. Up to six real ales are stocked. ❀◑♿⅄♣P⅟–

Staveley

Beer Hall ✔

Mill Yard, LA8 9LR
✪ 12-5 (6 Wed-Sun)
☎ (01539) 822644 🌐 hawksheadbrewery.co.uk
Hawkshead Bitter, Red, Lakeland Gold, Brodie's Prime; guest beers Ⓗ
The Beer Hall was purpose built as the brewery tap for Hawkshead beers and as a showcase for real ale. Situated above the beer conditioning room, large internal viewing windows give a bird's eye view of the brewing process. Tours are held at lunchtime on Saturday or by prior arrangement. Occasional beer festivals offer a choice of SIBA award-winning ales. Snacks are always available and meals can be ordered from Wilf's café next door. ◑♿⇌⊟(555)●P

Eagle & Child

Kendal Road, LA8 9LP
✪ 11-11; 12-10.30 Sun
☎ (01539) 821320 🌐 eaglechildinn.co.uk
Hawkshead Bitter; guest beers Ⓗ
Very popular village local, voted Westmorland CAMRA Pub of the Year in 2007. it is well worth seeking out for its commitment to local Cumbrian beers – only occasionally will you find a beer that is not from the north of the country. Good value lunchtime meals are always popular. An upstairs function/meeting room is available. The garden across the road overlooks the river Kent and holds tented beer festivals in May and September. ⩩❀⇔◑⇌⊟(555)●P⅟–

Talkin

Blacksmith's Arms

CA8 1LE
✪ 12-3, 6-11
☎ (01697) 73452 🌐 blacksmithstalkin.co.uk
Copper Dragon Golden Pippin; Geltsdale Brampton Bitter; Yates Bitter; guest beer Ⓗ
With a long standing reputation for great beer, good food and friendly and efficient bar staff, the Blackies is one of the busiest rural pubs in the area. Amenities include a well stocked bar, comfortable lounge, garden room and dining room. Ideally situated on the edge of an area of outstanding beauty, it has a range of outdoor recreational attractions nearby including a golf course, country park and Hadrian's Wall. ⩩Q❀⇔◑⊕♿⅄♣P⅟–

Tallentire

Bush Inn

CA13 0PT
✪ 6-midnight; closed Mon; 12-2.30, 7-11 Sun
☎ (01900) 823707
Jennings Bitter; guest beers Ⓗ
Traditional country inn with a simple uncluttered atmosphere, stone flagged floors and original fireplaces. The pub, a past winner of CAMRA branch Pub of the Season and a Pub of the Year runner up, is at the heart of many community activities. There are always two changing guest beers on offer, often from northern and Scottish breweries, and cider is available in summer. The restaurant serves high quality meals Thursday to Saturday evenings and Sunday lunchtime. Q❀⊟♣●P⅟–

Torver

Church House Inn

LA12 8AZ (2 miles SW of Coniston near jct of A593/A5084) SD285942
✪ 11-11; 12-3, 6-11 winter
☎ (015394) 41282
Barngates Tag Lag; Hawkshead Bitter; guest beers Ⓗ
Offering good food and a friendly welcome, this 14th-century inn has low beams, flagged floors and a warm fire —a welcome sight whether you have just walked up Coniston Old Man or simply come in search of a fine pint. The garden at the rear is a lovely place to sit in warmer weather. ⩩Q❀◑⅄⊟♣P

Ulverston

Stan Laurel Inn

The Ellers, LA12 0AB
12-2, 6-midnight; 12-3, 5-midnight Sun
(01229) 582814
Thwaites Original; guest beers H
Renamed in 1976 after the town's most famous son who lived only a few yards away, this bright and spacious local just outside the town centre generally sources its guest beers from local breweries. Good quality, reasonably priced meals are served every day except Monday. There is a separate room for pool and darts and an outside seating area. CAMRA Pub of the Season in summer 2007.

Swan Inn

Swan Street, LA12 7JX
3.30-11; 12-midnight Fri & Sat; 12-11 Sun
(01229) 582510
Hawkshead Bitter, Lakeland Gold, Brodie's Prime; Yates Bitter; guest beers H
Genuine free house offering up to nine beers with guest ales coming from far and wide. A good mix of regulars ensures the craic is always lively. Although open plan, the interior divides into three distinct areas: the bar with feature picture window, a seating area with an open fire and a darts area off to the side. Two TVs screen sporting fixtures. The elevated beer garden at the rear can catch the sun all day, should it appear. Dogs and well-behaved children are welcome.

Wasdale Head

Wasdale Head Inn

CA20 1EX (E off A595 at Gosforth) NY187085
11-11; 12-10.30 Sun
(01946) 726229 wasdaleheadinn.co.uk
Great Gable Burnmoor Pale, Wasd'ale, Illgill IPA, Yewbarrow H
Majestic among England's highest mountains, the pub lies deep in the Wasdale Valley — officially 'Britain's favourite view' and the birthplace of British climbing. The Ritson bar, commemorating a former landlord who was the original 'world's biggest liar', offers nine real ales and the pub is also home of the Great Gable Brewery. Take your beer outdoors on the beck-side patio in summer or by the cosy log burning stove in winter. Hearty home-cooked food is based on local produce. Voted local, Cumbrian and regional CAMRA Pub of the Year in 2006.

Whitehaven

Bransty Arch

Bransty Row, CA28 7XE
9am-midnight
(01946) 517640
Greene King Abbot; Marston's Pedigree; guest beers H
Lively town centre pub with a varied mix of customers. In addition to the two regular beers there are up to eight guests including a Jennings ale and usually another Cumbrian beer, as well as a draught cider. Beer festivals are held throughout the year. Close to the attractive harbour and station, it can get noisy in the evenings and at weekends. Food is served until 11pm. Children are welcome in the family area. CAMRA members receive a discount on presentation of a membership card.

Winton

Bay Horse Inn

CA17 4HS (off A685)
12-3 (not Mon), 6-midnight (11.30 Sun)
(01768) 371451
Beer range varies H
A fine example of a traditional, privately-owned local, overlooking the village green. Farmhouse style doors lead to a stone-flagged bar area, with a step up to the games room. An adjoining room with a small bar counter has tables set for dining while a further room, featuring an unusual fireplace, provides additional space. Beers often come from Hawkshead and Fuller's. Dogs are welcome in the bar.

Drunken Duck Inn, Barngates (Photo: Andrew Haines).

Good Beer Guide West Coast USA

Ben McFarland & Tom Sandham

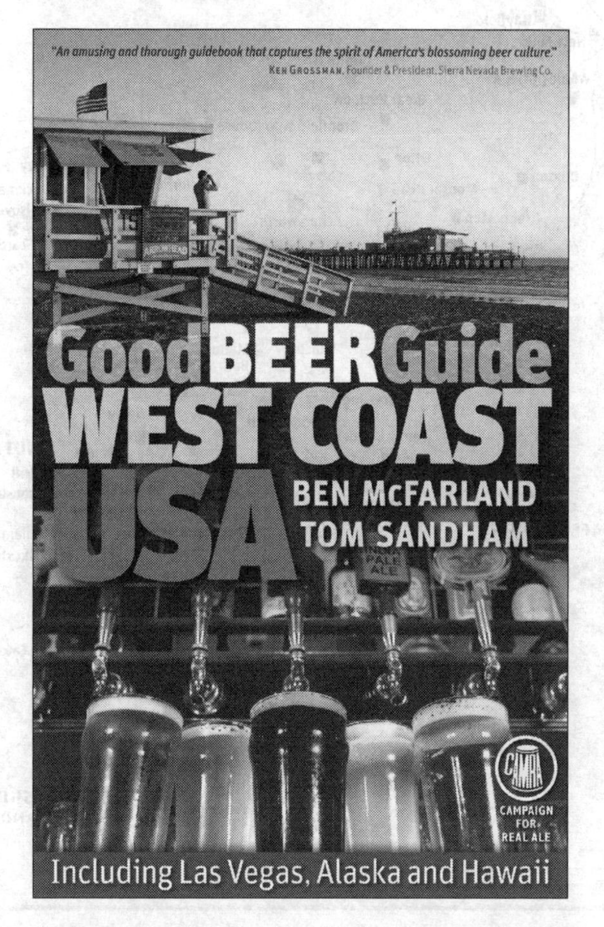

Taking in the whole western seaboard of the USA, as well as Las Vegas, Alaska and Hawaii, this is a lively, comprehensive and entertaining tour that unveils some of the most exhilarating beers, breweries and bars on the planet. It is the definitive, totally independent guide to understanding and discovering the heart of America's thriving craft beer scene, and an essential companion for any beer drinker visiting West Coast America or seeking out American beer in the UK. Written with verve and insight by two respected young beer journalists, *Good Beer Guide West Coast USA* is a must – not just for those who find themselves on the West Coast, but for all discerning beer enthusiasts and barflies everywhere.

£14.99 ISBN 978 1 85249 244 1

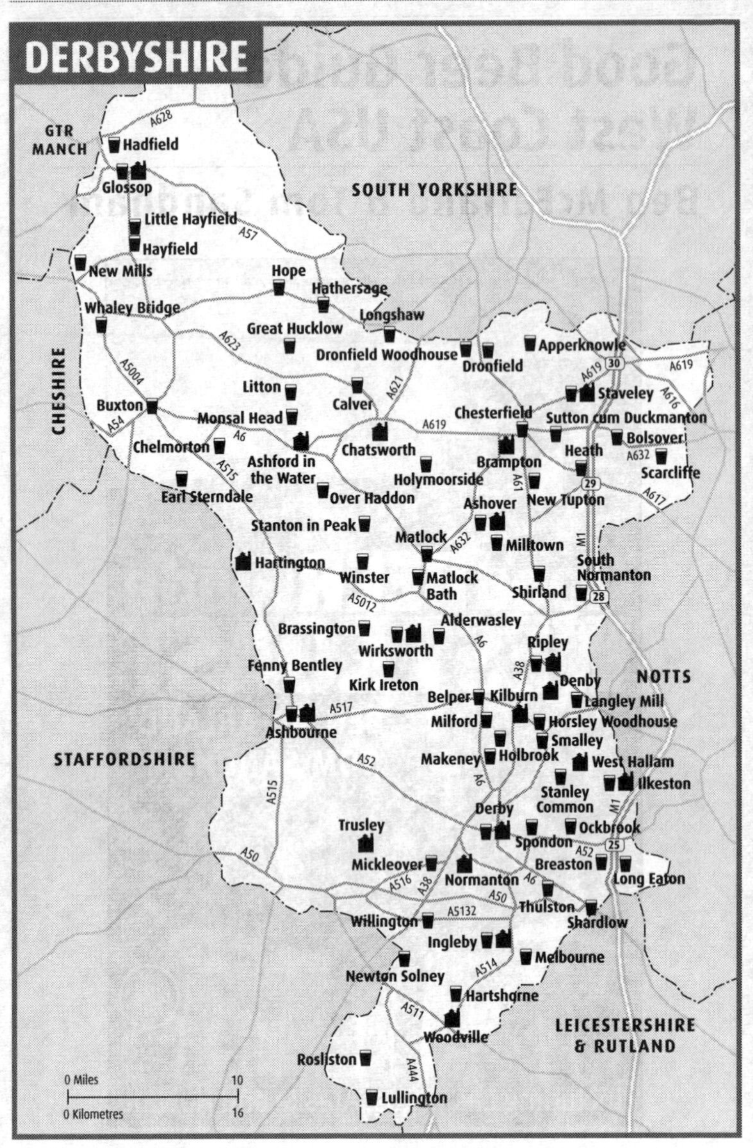

Alderwasley

Bear Inn & Hotel

DE56 2RD SK314527

⏲ 11.30-midnight

☎ (01629) 822585 🌐 thebearinnandhotel.com

Black Sheep Best Bitter; Draught Bass; Greene King Old Speckled Hen; Taylor Landlord; Whim Hartington Bitter Ⓗ

Originally a farmhouse, this pub first opened as the Brown Bear Inn in 1735. Customers are greeted by parakeets before entering the bar with its wood-burning stove and three stone-framed hatchways that form the bar, backed by paintings of bears. Rooms subdivided by settles lead off from the bar, filled with old curios. Bear Hall occupies the other end of the inn, where a carvery is served on Sunday lunchtime. The garden offers panoramic views of Derbyshire countryside towards Crich Stand.
⛫Q❀🛏◐◑P

Apperknowle

Barrack Hotel

Barrack Road, S18 4AU (turn left off New Road approaching from Unstone) SK381782

⏲ 6-midnight; 7-1am Sat; 12-5, 7 (8 winter)-midnight Sun

☎ (01246) 416555

Abbeydale Moonshine; Kelham Island Pale Rider; Tetley Bitter; guest beers Ⓗ

This stone-built pub has a terrace in front with extensive views over the surrounding countryside. The main room has an L-shaped bar with ornamental glass screen and fittings. To the rear is a separate dining room and a small games room with pool table. Home-

cooked bar meals are served Tuesday to Friday, plus Sunday lunches. Two guest beers are usually available, often from local breweries. No dogs are allowed inside.
♨🛏✿◑🚌P

Ashbourne

Green Man & Black's Head Royal Hotel

St John's Street, DE6 1GH
⏲ 11-11 (midnight Thu-Sat)
☎ (01335) 345783 🌐 gmrh.com
Greene King Abbot; Leatherbritches seasonal beers; guest beers ⊞
Warmly praised by Boswell in his famous biography of Samuel Johnson, the Green Man still has its old gallows sign across Ashbourne's main street. A rambling 300-year-old coaching inn approached by stone steps from a cobbled yard, it has welcoming fires in winter. It is close to where the ball is 'turned up' for the start of the Royal Shrovetide football game and mementos feature throughout the pub. Leatherbritches Brewery and shop are situated in outbuildings and an August bank holiday beer festival is held. ♨Q✿🛏◑⊟🚌⚋

Ashover

Black Swan

Church Street, S45 0AB (200m uphill from church)
⏲ 4 (7 Mon)-11.30; 12-12.30am Fri & Sat; 12-midnight Sun
☎ (01246) 591648
Greene King Abbot; Thornbridge Wild Swan, Kipling; guest beers ⊞
Consisting of a long, narrow bar and dining area, atmosphere is provided by exposed beams, with a real fire at one end and patio doors leading outside at the other. The inviting bar is full of pumps and dispensers, giving the visitor plenty to choose from. In the landlord's first year at the Black Swan the pub won local CAMRA Winter Pub of the Season 2007, and the food is recommended.
♨Q✿◑♿▲🚌(63,64)♣P⚋

Old Poets' Corner

Butts Road, S45 0EW (downhill from church)
⏲ 12-11
☎ (01246) 590888 🌐 oldpoets.co.uk
Ashover Light Rale, Poets Tipple; Bateman XXXB; Greene King Abbot; Taylor Landlord; guest beers ⊞
Award-winning pub also known for its traditional cider and food. The three and a half-barrel Ashover Brewery is located in the car park – ask for a look round. A warm welcome awaits you from landlord Kim and his array of up to five constantly-changing guest beers (the local Thornbridge Brewery often features). Open fires give this large pub a cosy feel, and in summer the pub is well sited for local walking. Well-behaved dogs and children are welcome.
♨Q✿🛏◑♿▲🚌(63,64)♣●P⚋

Belper

Cross Keys

35 Market Place, DE56 1FZ
⏲ 1 (12 Sun)-11
☎ (01773) 599191
Bateman XB, XXB, seasonal beers; Draught Bass; guest beers ⊞
This early 19th-century pub was formerly used as accommodation for visiting theatre troupes, and as a meeting place for Druids and Oddfellows; it has also witnessed at least one murder in its time. Two-roomed, with a central bar, the pub has enjoyed a renaissance since it was bought by Bateman's, whose beers have proved popular locally; regular beer festivals are held. A real fire warms the lounge. Bar billiards and shove-ha'penny are played and there is occasional live music in the lounge. ♨⊟♿⇌🚌♣●⚋

George & Dragon

117 Bridge Street, DE56 1BA
⏲ 11 (3 Mon)-11.30; 12-10.30 Sun
☎ (01773) 880210
Greene King Abbot; Tetley Bitter; guest beers ⊞
A fine Georgian roadside pub on the town's main thoroughfare featuring a prominent bay window and unusual covered pillared entrance. Formerly a coaching inn, it has an archway that now provides access to the car park. A deep open-plan pub, it has unusual airline style seating in the back area that comes from the old Derby Rugby Club. Outside is a skittle alley. Belper Town Football Club, River Gardens and Derwent Valley Mills World Heritage Site visitors centre are all nearby.
♨⇌🚌♣●P⚋

Bolsover

Blue Bell

57 High Street, S44 6HF
⏲ 12-3.30 (3 Sun), 6.30 (7 Sun)-midnight
☎ (01246) 823508 🌐 bolsover.uk.com
Jennings Dark Mild; Banks's Original; guest beers ⊞
A traditional, family-run two-room pub, the characterful Bell was built in the mid 1700s

INDEPENDENT BREWERIES

Amber Ripley
Ashover Ashover
Bottle Brook Kilburn
Brampton Chesterfield (NEW)
Brunswick Derby
Derby Derby
Derventio Trusley
Falstaff Normanton
Funfair Ilkeston
Globe Glossop
Haywood Bad Ram Ashbourne
Headless Derby
Howard Town Glossop
John Thompson Ingleby
Leadmill Denby
Leatherbritches Ashbourne
Nutbrook West Hallam
Peak Ales Chatsworth
Spire Staveley
Thornbridge Ashford in the Water
Tollgate Woodville
Townes Staveley
Whim Hartington
Wirksworth Wirksworth (NEW)

and retains its 300-year-old oak beams and original ceilings. The lounge is well furnished with a well-stocked bar of six real ales from the Marston's portfolio. The beer garden has a spectacular panoramic hilltop view of Derbyshire. In May, the annual 'neglected shed' beer festival is held and the pub has won a number of local CAMRA awards. No evening meals are served Wednesday or Sunday. Q❀◑▢♿⊟♣P⊬

Brassington

Olde Gate Inne

Well Street, DE4 4HJ (near church)
12-2.30 (3 Sat), 6-11 (not Mon); 12-4, 7-10.30 Sun
☎ (01629) 540448
Marston's Pedigree; guest beers Ⓗ
This Grade II-listed ivy-clad gem built in 1616 is reputedly haunted. Oak beams feature throughout, with gleaming copper utensils hanging around three open fireplaces. The main bar boasts pewter jugs and a black-leaded range, while a pipe rack in the snug dates from the 17th century. An extensive menu of home-cooked dishes is available (no food on Sunday evening). Boules is played here, no children under 10 are admitted and the tourist attraction of Carsington Water is nearby. ⛰Q❀◑♿ΔP⊬

Breaston

Navigation

Risley Lane, DE72 3BP (600m from A6005)
11.30-3, 5.30-11; 11.30-11 Sat; 12-10.30 Sun
☎ (01332) 872880
Draught Bass; Greene King Abbot; Marston's Pedigree; guest beers Ⓗ
Situated on the edge of the village, this late 18th-century inn served the Sandiacre-Derby canal that has sadly slipped into history. Extensively altered internally, the two rooms are serviced from a central bar and the pleasant ambience is enhanced by the absence of loud music. Excellent, home-cooked food using locally sourced, fresh ingredients is served daily lunchtimes and evenings Monday to Friday only.
Q❀◑♿♣P⊬

Buxton

Beltane

8A Hall Bank, SK17 6EW
11-11 (midnight Thu & Sun); closed Mon; 11-1am Fri & Sat
☎ (01298) 86010
Beer range varies Ⓗ
This café bar in converted shop premises proves you can serve good quality beer alongside wonderful locally-sourced food and coffee in a relaxed family-friendly atmosphere. During the day the emphasis is on food, but at night the bar becomes a popular local venue with three ever-changing beers on at all times, usually from micro-breweries. There is live music on Thursday evening when the bar becomes packed.
◑Δ⇌

Ramsey's Bar

Buckingham Hotel, 1 Burlington Road, SK17 9AS
6-midnight; 12-2.30, 6-midnight Sun
☎ (01298) 70481 🌐 buckinghamhotel.co.uk
Peak Ales Bakewell Best; Howard Town Wren's Nest; Whim Ales Hartington Bitter; guest beers Ⓗ
This large public bar and adjoining restaurant are part of the Buckingham Hotel. The name originates from No 1 Burlington Road, home and studio to local artist George Ramsey in the early part of the last century. With up to eight regular beers including one from Storm Brewery, the bar is very popular despite prices that are high for the area. A wide choice of food includes simple bar meals and a full restaurant menu. There is a small outdoor patio area. ❀⇔◑♿Δ⇌P

Swan

40 High Street, SK17 6HB
11-1am
☎ (01298) 23278
Black Sheep Best Bitter; Tetley Bitter; guest beers Ⓗ
This is a hostelry that prides itself on being a drinkers' pub, not a restaurant, and has a friendly, welcoming atmosphere. Three rooms surround a central bar and major sports matches are shown on the TVs, otherwise background music plays. There is always a Storm beer from nearby Macclesfield on handpump and the pub has thriving darts and dominoes teams. Quiz night is Thursday and a small outdoor patio area is available.
❀▢⇌♣P

Calver

Bridge Inn

Calver Bridge, Hope Valley, S32 3XA (on A623)
11.30-3 (3.30 Sat), 5.30-11; 12-3.30, 7-10.30 Sun
☎ (01433) 630415
Greene King Abbot, H&H Bitter Ⓗ
Sturdy, stone-built and traditionally designed pub with a central bar area separating two rooms. These are both comfortably furnished and include a collection of local guide books, some antique fire-fighting equipment and an array of hats. There is a pleasant garden overlooking the River Derwent and Arkwright's Calver Mill, now apartments. The landlord has been here since Bass owned the pub in the 1980s. Meals are not served on Monday or winter Sunday. A third beer from Greene King is often available.
⛰Q❀◑♿ΔP▽

Chelmorton

Church Inn ✔

Main Street, SK17 9SL
12-3.30, 6.30 (7 winter)-11; 12-11 (12-3.30, 7-11 winter) Sun
☎ (01298) 85319
Adnams Bitter; Marston's Burton Bitter, Pedigree; guest beers Ⓗ
Set in beautiful surroundings opposite the local church, this traditional village pub caters for both locals and walkers. Even though the main room is laid out for dining and good home-cooked food is on offer, a cosy

atmosphere is maintained with a low ceiling and real fire. The pub is run primarily as a local, serving good quality beer. Parking is available on the dead end road in front of the pub and there is a patio area outside. Monday is quiz night. ⛫Q❀⇄◐▲♣

Chesterfield

Brampton Manor

107 Old Road, Brampton, S40 3QR

10-midnight (10.30 Sun)

☎ (01246) 277760 🌐 brampton-manor.com

Peak Ales Bakewell Best Bitter, DPA; Wells Bombardier; guest beers Ⓗ

Possibly home to the fittest real ale drinkers in the land, thanks to the private leisure club attached. The bar has a go-ahead management with a real commitment to local ales. An impressive white building houses the cosy, fire-lit stone interior, which has a welcoming atmosphere. Regular local bands play here with extended opening hours to suit. Well worth the trek along the drive, especially if you also like your food.
⛫Q❀◐♿🚌P⚟

Derby Tup

387 Sheffield Road, Whittington Moor, S41 8LS

SK382735

11.30-3, 5-11; 11.30-11 Wed; 11.30-midnight Fri & Sat; 12-11 Sun

☎ (01246) 454316

Castle Rock Harvest Pale; guest beers Ⓗ

Still offering the widest range of guest beers in the area (up to 10 including a stout or porter) plus continental beers and traditional cider, it is easy to see why the 'Tup' is an award winner. On the way into the main room with its roaring fire, you pass a proper little snug on the left. At the rear is a secluded, quieter area. A true drinkers' pub with no music or other distractions, conversation and camaraderie rule here. ⛫Q◐🚌♣●

Peacock ✔

412 Chatsworth Road, Brampton, S40 3BQ (on A619)

12 (1 Sat)-11

☎ (01246) 275115

Adnams Broadside; Black Sheep Best Bitter; Caledonian Deuchars IPA; Tetley Bitter; guest beers Ⓗ

A warm welcome and some good beer reward customers at this two-roomed pub on the outskirts of Chesterfield. The beer garden is a delight in dry weather, while those unconcerned about traffic noise may sit outside at the front. An eclectic mix of customers enjoys dominoes in one side of the pub and weekly folk singing in the other. A winner of many awards including Derbyshire CAMRA Pub of the Year, the Peacock is well worth seeking out. ⛫Q❀◐♿🚌♣⚟

Portland Hotel ✔

West Bars, S40 1AY

9-midnight (1am Fri & Sat)

☎ (01246) 245410

Greene King IPA, Abbot; Marston's Pedigree; guest beers Ⓗ

This J D Wetherspoon's outlet originally opened in 1899 as the station hotel for the Lancashire, Derbyshire & East Coast Railway. A big, mock-Tudor hotel with an ornate exterior, its prime position is handy for Chesterfield's busy market. The bar is a welcome source of local beers, with offerings from Townes and Wentworth often among the choice of up to four guest ales. Nearby pubs that complement the Portland include the Market Hotel, Royal Oak (Shambles), Rutland Arms and Spa Lane Vaults. ❀⇄◐⇌🚌⚟

Red Lion

570 Sheffield Road, Whittington Moor, S41 8LX

SK381737

12-11 (10.30 Sun)

☎ (01246) 450770

Old Mill Mild, Bitter, Bullion, seasonal beers Ⓗ

Low ceilings and subdued lighting make you feel comfortable and at home in the lounge where a large-screen TV shows all the big sporting events. The bar room is brighter and home to Friday-night brain-box stumping quizzes. At the bar, Mild is available all year round, which is very rare these days. The landlady runs an annual trip for the locals to the Old Mill Brewery. Among many activities, the pub strongly supports fund-raising events for local charities. ◐🚌♣P⚟

Rutland Arms ✔

23 Stephenson Place, S40 1XL

11-11 (midnight Thu-Sat)

☎ (01246) 205857

Boddingtons Bitter; Brampton Best Bitter; Caledonian Deuchars IPA; Greene King Abbot; Taylor Landlord; guest beers Ⓗ/Ⓖ

Popular, friendly, family-run town centre pub. Up to 12 real ales are available with regular mini beer festivals staged. Guest ales come from far and wide. Good food, served all day, includes vegetarian options (try the giant filled Yorkshire puddings). The main bar area has a jukebox, TV and electronic games. A beer token pub quiz is held on Tuesday night. There is seating outside for smokers.
❀◐⇌🚌●⚟

Derby

Alexandra Hotel

203 Siddals Road, DE1 2QE

11-11; 12-3, 7-10.30 Sun

☎ (01332) 293993

Castle Rock Harvest Pale; guest beers Ⓗ

Named after the Danish Princess who married the Prince of Wales (later Edward VII) in 1863, the Alex was originally called the Midland Coffee House. The end wall once advertised Zacharia Smith's Shardlow Ales, but both sign and brewer have long gone. Originally a Shipstone's house, then a Bateman's pub, it has latterly gone to Tynemill and become a strong champion of small breweries. Two-roomed with a central bar, the pub was the birthplace of Derby CAMRA in 1974.
⛫Q❀⇄◐♿⇌🚌♣●P⚟

Babington Arms ✔

11-13 Babington Lane, DE1 1TA

9-midnight (1am Fri & Sat)

☎ (01332) 383647

Derby Penny's Porter; Greene King Abbot; Marston's Burton Bitter, Pedigree; Wyre Piddle Marcoe's King of the Watusi; guest beers Ⓗ
Probably the best Wetherspoon's house in the country, winning the company's prestigious Cask Ale Pub of the Year and also local CAMRA City Pub of the Year in 2008. It showcases an amazing range of 18 beers on handpump, with permanent guest beers from Derby and Falstaff Breweries, and regular themed brewery weekends. Originally a furniture store, the pub stands in the former grounds of Babington House. The first performance of Bram Stoker's Dracula was given in the neighbouring Grand Theatre in 1924. Q◑◗♿●

Brunswick Inn

1 Railway Terrace, DE1 2RU
⌚ 11-11; 12-10.30 Sun
☎ (01332) 290677
Brunswick White Feather, Triple Hop, Second Brew, Station Approach, Railway Porter, Father Mike's; Ⓗ/Ⓖ **Everards Beacon; Marston's Pedigree** Ⓗ
Originally built as the centrepiece of a railway village, the pub was closed in 1974 and fell into disrepair. Eventually rescued and restored, it opened as Derby's first multiple real ale house some 14 years later. A purpose-built brewery was added and it rapidly became one of the best-known free houses in the country, before being sold to Everards in 2002. High standards remain unchanged however and the pub was crowned local CAMRA City Pub of the Year in 2004. Q❀◑♿⇌♣●⚊

Crompton Tavern

46 Crompton Street, DE1 1NX
⌚ 12-11 (midnight Thu-Sat)
☎ (01332) 733629
Marston's Pedigree; Taylor Landlord; guest beers Ⓗ
Back-street city centre pub with strong, loyal community of regulars and a warm welcome for all. The long-serving licensee often features beers from the likes of Kelham Island and Durham breweries. Two U-shaped areas with lower-level wings are situated either side of a central bar where the walls frequently double as a gallery for local artists. The pub has the most distinctive and eclectic jukebox in the city, while a pleasant rear garden provides a fair-weather haven and sanctuary for smokers. ❀♣⚊

Falstaff

74 Silverhill Road, DE23 6UJ
⌚ 12-11 (midnight Fri & Sat)
☎ (01332) 342902 🌐 falstaffbrewery.co.uk
Falstaff Phoenix, Smiling Assassin, seasonal beers; guest beers Ⓗ
Known locally as The Folly and reputedly haunted, this former Allied pub was originally a latter-day coaching inn before the surrounding area was built up, closing it in. Now a free house, its on-site brewery has made it the best real ale house in Normanton. The curved bar is flanked on one side by a small lounge with a real fire where Offilers Brewery memorabilia is on display. Other collectables can be viewed throughout the games room and second bar room. ♨Q❀⚊

Flowerpot

23-25 King Street, DE1 3DZ
⌚ 11 (12 Sun)-11 (midnight Fri & Sat)
☎ (01332) 204955
Headless seasonal beers; Oakham Bishop's Farewell; Whim Hartington IPA; guest beers Ⓗ/Ⓖ
Dating from around 1800 but much expanded from its original premises, this pub reaches far back from the small, roadside frontage and divides into several interlinking rooms. One room provides the stage for a lively ongoing gig scene and another a glass cellar wall, revealing row upon row of stillaged firkins. The new Headless Brewery is at the rear. A virtual real ale showcase with up to 25 beers on offer every weekend, this was local CAMRA Pub of the Year 2007. Q❀◑◗♿●⚊

Mr Grundy's Tavern

32-34 Ashbourne Road, DE22 3AD
⌚ 11 (12 Sat)-11; 12-10.30 Sun
☎ (01332) 340279 🌐 mrgrundystavern.info
Burton Bridge Golden Delicious; Greene King Olde Trip; Hop Back Summer Lightning; Marston's Pedigree; Taylor Landlord; guest beers Ⓗ
Long two-roomed pub within the Grade II-listed Georgian House Hotel that serves up to eight real ales. The interior is wood panelled throughout with open fires, low lighting, wooden bench seating and paved, tiled and wooden floors. In the bar area are hanging hops, breweriania, film memorabilia and an unusual collection of hats. An old red telephone box, saxophone and Laurel & Hardy sign add to its charm. Outdoors is a large covered area and beer garden. No evening meals are available on Sunday.
♨❀⇌◑◗♿P⚊

Olde Dolphin Inne ★

5A Queen Street, DE1 3DL
⌚ 10.30-midnight; 12-11 Sun
☎ (01332) 267711
Adnams Bitter; Black Sheep Best Bitter; Caledonian Deuchars IPA; Draught Bass; Greene King Abbot; Marston's Pedigree; Taylor Landlord; guest beers Ⓗ
Standing below the great Gothic tower of the cathedral, the timber-framed Dolphin is Derby's most picturesque and oldest surviving pub, although much restored latterly. Reputed to be haunted, the beamed interior divides into bar, upper and lower lounges, snug and an upstairs steak bar, each with its own character. Regular themed evenings are supplemented by a beer festival in July, which spreads out on to a splendid, raised rear patio. A real gem that is not to be missed.
♨Q❀◑◗♿P⚊

Rowditch Inn

246 Uttoxeter New Road, DE22 3LL
⌚ 12-2 (not Mon-Fri), 7-11
☎ (01332) 343123
Marston's Pedigree; guest beers Ⓗ
No-frills pub with first-class beer; winner of local CAMRA City Pub of the Year in 2001 and 2006. A plain-fronted but warmly welcoming roadside hostelry, its unexpectedly deep interior divides into two drinking areas and a small snug. The long rear garden is a positive

haven in warmer weather. A large collection of pump clips adorning the walls of the bar area is evidence of the ever-changing range of guest ales. A cheese evening is held each Monday. ⛰❀⊟♣⊱

Smithfield

Meadow Road, DE1 2BH (from Market Place head over Exeter bridge, along river)

11-11; 12-10.30 Sun

☎ (01332) 370429 thesmithfield.co.uk

Draught Bass; Headless seasonal beers; Oakham Bishop's Farewell; Whim Arbor Light, Hartington IPA; guest beers Ⓗ

Bow-fronted riverside pub built to serve the cattle market, which has since moved to a new site, leaving the Smithy in a bit of a backwater. A long, basic bar is flanked on one side by a games room with dartboard and on the other by a cosy lounge with stone fireplace and old settles, overlooking a pleasant riverside patio. Exceptional beer has helped earn the pub a local CAMRA Pub of the Year award in the past. ❀◐⊟♣P⊱

Station Inn

12 Midland Road, DE1 2SN

11.30-2.30, 4 (6 Sat)-11; 11.30-11 Fri; 12-3, 7-10.30 Sun

☎ (01332) 608014

Draught Bass; Ⓖ **Black Sheep Best Bitter; Caledonian Deuchars IPA; guest beers** Ⓗ

This modest pub, but for its elaborate frontage and stained glass, was named after the Midland Railway's classical station nearby, needlessly swept away in 1983 to be replaced by the present uninspiring edifice. A traditional bar with panelled counter, cast iron foot rail and quarry-tiled floor is flanked by a games area to the right and a large lounge to the rear that acts as dining area and function room. Many cellar awards attest to the skills of the licensee. ⇌⊟♣

Dronfield

Coach & Horses

Sheffield Road, S18 2GD

5-10 Mon; 12-11 (midnight Fri & Sat); 12-10.30 Sun

☎ (01246) 413269

Thornbridge Jaipur, Ⓗ

Roadside pub north of the town centre, with one comfortably furnished open-plan room. It is owned by Sheffield FC, the world's oldest football club founded in 1857, whose ground is adjacent. The pub is operated by Thornbridge Hall Brewery, and there are usually up to five Thornbridge beers available. Good home-cooked food is made with locally sourced ingredients where possible, served in a friendly, relaxed atmosphere. Evening meals are available until 8.30pm. Q❀◐⇌⊟♣P⊱

Dronfield Woodhouse

Jolly Farmer

Pentland Road, S18 8ZQ

12-midnight (1am Fri & Sat)

☎ (01246) 418018

Black Sheep Best Bitter; Caledonian XPA; John Smith Magnet; Tetley Bitter; guest beers Ⓗ

Community pub built in 1976 by former Nottingham brewers Shipstones on a large housing estate and turned into a themed ale house in the 1990s. The cask beers are stillaged in a glass-fronted cellar behind the bar, which is free of the usual ostentatious lager pumps. The pub is open plan but has distinct areas including a tap room with pool table and a raised dining area. The beer range includes two guest beers, usually from small independents. A beer festival is held in November. Q❀◐⊟♿⊟♣P⊱

Earl Sterndale

Quiet Woman

SK17 0BU (off B5053)

12-3 (4 Sat), 7-11.30; 12-5.30, 7-11.30 Sun

☎ (01298) 83211

Jennings Dark Mild; Marston's Burton Bitter, Pedigree; guest beers Ⓗ

This unspoilt local set in the heart of the Peak District National Park is opposite the village church and green. Inside, a low-beamed room with a real fire is on the left and a small bar to the right. On one of the beams is a collection of original Marston's pump clips from long-lost beers. Traditional pub games are played with domino tables in the main bar and a separate games room. Local fresh eggs and traditional pork pies can be purchased from the bar. The pub offers its own selection of naturally conditioned bottled beers brewed by the Leek Brewery. There is a patio outside and a caravan/camping site next to the pub. ⛰Q☋❀▲♣P

Fenny Bentley

Coach & Horses

DE6 1LB (on A515)

11-11; 12-10.30 Sun

☎ (01335) 350246

Marston's Pedigree; guest beers Ⓗ

This traditional 16th-century coaching inn has kept many original features such as old flagged floors and very low beams. Coal- and log- burning stoves set in brick and stonework together with comfortable wooden chairs and settles help create a cosy atmosphere in the bar. The dining room and garden room cater for fabulous home-cooked food made from local produce. The outside drinking areas are a positive haven in summer when guest beers increase. Derbyshire's major tourist attractions are nearby. ⛰Q❀◐▲P

Glossop

Crown Inn

142 Victoria Street, SK13 8HY (on Hayfield Road out of town)

5 (11.30 Fri & Sat)-11; 12-10.30 Sun

☎ (01457) 862824

Samuel Smith OBB Ⓗ

This end of terrace local, a few minutes from the town centre and Glossop station, was built in 1846 and has been the Smith's house in the High Peak area since 1977. An attractive curved bar serves two side snugs, each with real fires in winter, and a pool/games room. Old pictures of Glossop's past add to the traditional character. A good selection of Smith's bottled beers is available at very keen prices and an outdoor drinking area is in the rear yard. ♨Q❀♿⇌⊟♣⅃

Globe

144 High Street West, SK13 8HJ
⌚ 5-2am (closed Tue); 1-1am Sun
☎ (01457) 852417 ⊕ globemusic.org
Globe Amber, Comet, seasonal beers; guest beers ⊞
The Globe Brewery at the rear of the pub was opened in 2006 by the landlord/brewer Ron Brookes who brews solely for the pub and occasional beer festivals. Seven handpumps dispense Globe and guest beers, with real cider and some British bottled beers also available. Live music features strongly with a regular folk night on Monday; quiz night is Wednesday. Excellent vegan food is on the menu and an outdoor garden area to the rear includes a covered and heated smoking area. ❀⇌⊟⅃

Star Inn

2 Howard Street, SK13 7DD (next to railway station)
⌚ 2 (4 Mon & Tue)-11 (midnight Fri & Sat); 12-10.30 Sun
☎ (01457) 853072
Black Sheep Best Bitter; guest beers ⊞
Often the first and last stop-off for visitors by public transport, as Glossop train station and bus stops are very close by. This highly-regarded local is currently run by long-standing CAMRA members. Six handpumps offer a range of ales along with real cider, served from the cellar. Pictures of bygone Glossop, wood floors and a rear tap room served by a hatch add to the traditional atmosphere. A covered and heated outdoor smoking area is available. ⇔⇌⊟♣P⅃

Great Hucklow

Queen Anne

Main Road, SK17 8RF
⌚ 12-2.30, 5-11; closed Mon; 12-11 Fri & Sat; 12-10.30 Sun
☎ (01298) 871246 ⊕ queenanneinn.co.uk
Tetley Bitter; guest beers ⊞
Recently refurbished, this pub was first granted a licence in 1704, although it was functioning as an ale house as early as 1577. The village thrived on lead mining in the 18th century and there is a Unitarian chapel dating from this period. Inside the pub, the rooms have low ceilings, beams and brasses, and there is a high-backed settle. Walkers are welcome and good value lunches are available. The pub is closed all day Monday. ♨♉❀⇔◐◑♿⛺♣P

Hadfield

New Lamp

12 Bankbottom, SK13 1BY
⌚ 12-11.30 (10.30 Sun)
☎ (01457) 860490
Beer range varies ⊞
This early Victorian pub was originally called the Commercial but earned the nickname 'The Red Lamp' when it was used as a place where navvies working on the Longdendale Reservoirs met women of easy virtue. Today the pub is extensively refurbished and provides walkers on the Longdendale Trail with a comfortable, convenient resting spot in which to enjoy a range of beers (including some from micro-breweries) and an extensive menu. The pub is home to darts, dominoes and pool teams and live music is played at weekends. ♨♉❀◐⇌⊟(237,397)♣P⅃

Hartshorne

Admiral Rodney Inn

65 Main Street, DE11 7ES (on A514)
⌚ 6-11.30; 5-midnight Fri; 12-midnight Sat; 12-3, 7-midnight Sun
☎ (01283) 216482
Marston's Pedigree; guest beers ⊞
This traditional village pub dates back to the early 19th century, but was substantially rebuilt in 1959 and more recently refurbished to provide an open-plan L-shaped drinking area, retaining original oak beams in the former snug. A small raised area behind the bar is served through a hatch. Three guest beers are usually available. Meals are limited to Wednesday themed food evenings and traditional Sunday lunches. The grounds include a cricket pitch, and the pub remains open during Sunday afternoon matches. ♨❀◐◑♿⊟(68)♣P

Hathersage

Millstone Inn ✔

Sheffield Road, S32 1DA (on A6187 E of village)
⌚ 11.30-11; 12-10.30 Sun
☎ (01433) 650258 ⊕ millstoneinn.co.uk
Abbeydale Moonshine; Black Sheep Best Bitter; Taylor Landlord; guest beers ⊞
This pub originally served the nearby millstone quarry and is now popular with walkers and climbers. It is smartly decorated with a large bar, a ballroom and an extensive outdoor area partly under cover. Guest beers are from local breweries. There are quizzes on Friday evenings, and live music on the last Sunday of the month. The landlord runs his own taxi service to the nearby station. ♨❀⇔◐◑♿⊟♣♣P

Hayfield

Royal Hotel

Market Street, SK22 2EP
⌚ 12-11
☎ (01663) 742721 ⊕ theroyalhayfield.co.uk
Hyde's Bitter; guest beers ⊞
A former vicarage, this imposing stone pub stands near the church and cricket ground alongside the River Sett. The interior boasts original oak panels and pews that create a relaxing atmosphere, with real fires in winter. A restaurant and function room complete the facilities and an annual beer festival is hosted in October. The village is the base for many leisure activities in the Dark Peak area and was also the birthplace of Arthur Lowe, the immortal Captain Mainwaring in Dad's Army. ♨Q❀⇔◐◑♿⛺⊟P⅃

Heath

Elm Tree

Mansfield Road, S44 5SE (on main road off jct 29 M1) SK446672
11.30-3, 5-midnight; 11.30-midnight Sat; 12-10.30 Sun
(01246) 850490 theelmtreeheath.co.uk
Jennings Sneck Lifter; guest beers
A community pub success story. Once threatened with closure, seven villagers took on the lease of the pub, carried out tasteful renovations and brought in a top husband-and-wife team to run it. The quality and range of up to five ales improved hugely and there is now excellent modern food cooked to order, using fresh ingredients. Fish dishes include less well-known species such as barracuda. On a sunny day, the view across to Bolsover Castle is breathtaking.

Holbrook

Dead Poets Inn

38 Chapel Street, DE56 0TQ
12-2.30, 5-11; 12-11 Fri & Sat; 12-10.30 Sun
(01332) 780301
Greene King Abbot; Marston's Pedigree; guest beers
Built in 1800 and formerly known as the Cross Keys, the pub has undergone a remarkable transformation to create an inn with a real medieval feel within. Its two rooms contain high-backed pews, stone-flagged floors, low lighting, a real fire and an inglenook. Once a free house but now owned by Everards, it was so named because its former owner believed that many of our famous poets gained inspiration from atmospheric taverns such as this one. (71,71A)

Holymoorside

Lamb

16 Loads Road, S42 7EU SK339694
5 (4 Fri)-11; 12-3, 7-11 Sat & Sun
(01246) 566167
Daleside Blonde; Theakston Black Bull; guest beers
Cosy local in a village on the edge of the Peak District National Park where everyone is made welcome including dogs and walkers (after removing their muddy boots). Winner of many CAMRA awards, the pub boasts up to six ales on the bar, four ever-changing. A roaring fire provides a focal point in winter, while the pleasant outdoor drinking area is ideal for summer evenings. Note lunchtime opening is restricted to weekends and bank holidays.
(25,50)

Hope

Cheshire Cheese

Edale Road, S33 6ZF
12-3, 6.30-11; 12-11 Sat; 12-10.30 Sun
(01433) 620381
Black Sheep Best Bitter; Peak Ales Swift Nick; Whim Hartington Bitter; guest beers
This cosy pub dating from 1578 has three small rooms, one at a lower level that was probably originally used to house animals; nowadays it is used as a dining area (no evening meals served on Sunday). The pub is situated in walking country but parking is limited and the road outside narrow. There is a strong regular trade from nearby villages, and a sloe gin-making competition is among activities centred on the pub. At the rear is a refurbished beer garden.

Horsley Woodhouse

Old Oak Inn

176 Main Street, DE7 6AW (on A609)
5 (3 Thu & Fri; 12 Sat)-11; 12-10.30 Sun
(01332) 881299
Leadmill seasonal beers; Bottle Brook seasonal beers; guest beers
Once a farmhouse, the Old Oak was under threat of demolition when it was acquired and renovated by the Denby-based Leadmill Brewery in 2003. Four interconnecting rooms, a courtyard and new rear extension provide a variety of drinking spaces with real fires and hanging hops giving the pub a genuine homely atmosphere. Eight handpumps, occasional beer festivals and live music help to make it a successful village pub. The Amberline bus from Derby stops right outside the pub during the day.

Ilkeston

Dewdrop

24 Station Street, DE7 5TE (50m from A6096)
12-11 (10.30 Sun)
(0115) 9329684
Oakham Bishops Farewell; Taylor Best Bitter; guest beers
Victorian street-corner local with traditional-style rooms. The lounge and snug are warmed by open fires, while the bar has a free jukebox and pool table. A plaque in the original lobby commemorates the wartime stay of Barnes Wallis, the inventor of the 'bouncing bomb' who was born in nearby Ripley. A haven for beer aficionados, the pub is a member of the LocAle scheme and winner of local CAMRA Pub of the Year in 2008. Interesting guest beers frequently include a locally-sourced dark ale.
(27)

Ilford

93 Station Road, DE7 5LJ (on A6096)
7.30-midnight; 7-1am Fri; 2-1am Sat; 11.30-midnight Sun
(0115) 9305789
Beer range varies
Situated by the Erewash canal, with boat moorings nearby, this former local Club of the Year champions the cause of real ale by stocking micro-brewery beers sourced from near and far, often showcasing new brewers. Traditional pub games include snooker, and live music often features on Saturday evening. Given sufficient notice, the friendly landlord will open outside stated hours for visiting groups. (27)

Poacher

69 South Street, DE7 5QQ
11 (12 Mon-Wed)-11 (midnight Fri & Sat); 12-10.30 Sun

☎ (0115) 9325452

Nottingham EPA; Taylor Landlord; guest beers 🅷

A shining example of pub refurbishment that successfully marries tasteful, contemporary style with a traditional, three-roomed layout. This former Shipstone's house boasts a modern public bar with an attractive, curved bar as its focal point. To one side is a lounge with comfortable banquettes. Another lounge to the rear has welcoming sofas. The pub promotes real ale by constantly changing its guest beers, sourced from Scottish & Newcastle's Cellarmans' Choice. A member of the LocAle scheme, it is handily positioned for local bus services. ⊟🚌♣⅃

Ingleby

John Thompson Inn

DE73 7HW (off A514)

✪ 11-2.30 (not Mon), 6-11; 12-10.30 Sun

☎ (01332) 862469

John Thompson seasonal beers; guest beers 🅷

John Thompson is the former fruit grower who revived Derbyshire's brewing industry in 1977, having turned his family home into a highly individual pub eight years earlier. Comprising a large, comfortable lounge with smaller rooms opening off it, the pub is rich in local interest, displaying many prints and watercolours. Close to the banks of the River Trent, in open country just outside the village, it also has a spacious patio and large garden, with the brewery housed in outbuildings. ❀◑♿♣P⅃

Kirk Ireton

Barley Mow ★

Main Street, DE6 3JP (off B5023)

✪ 12-2, 7-11 (10.30 Sun)

☎ (01335) 370306

Whim Hartington IPA; 🅷 **guest beers** 🅶

Set in an olde-worlde village overlooking the Ecclesbourne Valley, this gabled Jacobean building features a sundial dated 1683. Several interconnecting rooms of different size and character have low, beamed ceilings, mullioned windows, slate-topped tables, well-worn woodwork and open fires set in stone fireplaces. A small serving hatch reveals a stillage with up to six beers dispensed straight from the cask. This pub is well worth a visit – there are not many rural gems like this left. Local CAMRA Pub of the Year 2008. ⛰Q❀⇌⊟⛺♣●

Langley Mill

Railway Tavern

188 Station Road, NG16 4AE

✪ 12 (11 Sat & Sun)-midnight

☎ (01773) 764711

Alcazar Sheriff's Gold, Ale, Foxtale 🅷

This white stuccoed, Inter-War building, once a Home Brewery pub, is enjoying a renaissance following a skilful refurbishment. The multi-roomed interior is largely intact and some original fittings, including the settles in the bar area, have been retained. The Tavern is an active participant in traditional pub games, which remain popular in this area. It has the added attraction of Alcazar bottle-conditioned ales and is well served by bus and rail. Dogs are welcome. ❀⊟♿⇌(Langley Mill)🚌♣⅃

Little Hayfield

Lantern Pike

45 Glossop Road, SK22 2NG

✪ 12 (5 Mon winter)-11

☎ (01663) 747590 🌐 lanternpikeinn.co.uk

Black Sheep Best Bitter; Howard Town Wren's Nest; Taylor Landlord 🅷

Picturesque ivy-clad stone pub nestling in a hollow in this small hamlet within the Dark Peak area of the High Peak. The comfortable traditional lounge bar, with its real fire in winter, connects to separate dining areas. Coronation Street originator Tony Warren lived nearby and wrote some of the first episodes of the soap while sitting in the bar, hence the display of photographs of original characters and a letter from Warren in the lounge. The rear patio area has superb views across nearby Lantern Pike Hill. ⛰❀⇌◑🚌(61)P⅃

Litton

Red Lion ✔

Church Lane, SK17 8QU

✪ 12-11 (midnight Fri & Sat; 10.30 Sun)

☎ (01298) 871458

Abbeydale Absolution; Oakwell Barnsley Bitter; guest beers 🅷

The only pub in the village, the Red Lion is a focus of local activity and a welcome refuge for visitors. The village green opposite is complete with punishing stocks and resplendent with daffodils in spring. There is an enormous fireplace serving three cosy rooms and a fourth room has recently been opened up to create extra space. The pub keeps a collection of local guide books. A monthly quiz is held on Monday and food is available all day Thursday to Sunday. ⛰Q❀◑♣⅃

Long Eaton

Hole in the Wall

6 Regent Street, NG10 1JX

✪ 10 (11 Sun)-midnight (1am Fri & Sat)

☎ (0115) 9734920

Draught Bass; Nottingham EPA; guest beers 🅷

Attractive 19th-century Dutch-gabled freehouse conveniently situated for public transport and close to the Erewash Canal. A fine example of a back-street local, it offers two distinct drinking areas: a lively bar and a quiet lounge, both adorned with breweriana and featuring an old-style serving hatch. In summer you can enjoy your drink on the patio. Many local CAMRA awards have been bestowed upon the Hole, which serves an ever-changing range of mainly micro-brewery beers. A member of the LocAle scheme. ❀⊟🚌(5,15)♣●⅃

Royal Oak

349 Tamworth Road, NG10 3LU

✪ 11-11; 12-10.30 Sun

☎ (0115) 9835801

Beer range varies 🅷

This large, friendly Enterprise Inn built in 1913 has taken advantage of the SIBA trading arrangement to supply a guest beer to complement the regular cask ale, which is often from a national brewer. The pub features a skittle alley, children's play area and a large car park, while moorings on the Erewash at the rear attract boaters. Home-cooked food includes a vegetarian option and children's menu (no food on Saturday or Sunday evenings). Q❀◐▶⊟♿⇌⊟♣P⚟

Longshaw

Grouse Inn

S11 7TZ (on A625)
✪ 12-3, 6-11; 12-11 Sat; 12-10.30 Sun
☎ (01433) 630423
Banks's Bitter; Caledonian Deuchars IPA; Marston's Pedigree; guest beer Ⓗ
This free house, which has been in the same family since 1965, stands in isolation on bleak moorland south west of Sheffield, and is deservedly popular with walkers and climbers. There are some fine photographs of nearby gritstone edges, as well as collections of banknotes and cigarette cards on display, with a lounge at the front and a smaller bar area at the rear. No meals served on Monday evening. ♨Q☕❀◐▶♣P⊟

Lullington

Colvile Arms

Main Street, DE12 8EG
✪ 6-11; 12-3, 7-10.30 Sun
☎ (01827) 373212
Draught Bass; Marston's Pedigree; guest beers Ⓗ
Popular 18th-century free house, leased from the Lullington Estate, at the heart of an attractive hamlet at the southern tip of the county. The public bar comprises an adjoining hallway and snug, each featuring high-backed settles with wood panelling. The bar and a comfortable lounge are situated on opposite sides of a central serving area. A second lounge/function room overlooks the garden and a bowling green. Two quiz teams and the local cricket and football teams meet here. ❀⊟♣P

Makeney

Holly Bush Inn ☆

Holly Bush Lane, DE56 0RX
✪ 12-3, 4.30-11; 12-11 Sat (10.30 Sun)
☎ (01332) 841729
Greene King Abbot; Ⓗ **Marston's Pedigree;** Ⓖ **Taylor Landlord; guest beers** Ⓗ
Grade II-listed, and once a farmhouse with a brewery on the Strutt Estate, this late 17th-century, former Offilers house positively oozes character. It stood on the Derby turnpike before the Strutts opened the valley route in 1818; Dick Turpin is known to have drunk here. The enclosed wooden snug is sandwiched between two bars with real fires. Regular beer festivals are held here, a short 10-minute walk from the King William, Milford. Local CAMRA Country Pub of the Year 2007. ♨Q☕❀◐⊟⊟♣●P⚟

Matlock

Thorn Tree

48 Jackson Road, DE4 3JQ (off Bank Rd) SK300608
✪ 12-2 (not Mno), 6-11; 12-midnight Fri & Sat; 12-11 Sun
☎ (01629) 580295
Draught Bass; Black Sheep Best Bitter; Greene King Ruddles Best Bitter; guest beers Ⓗ
Situated on the hill above Matlock, the Thorn Tree is well worth seeking out. Its beer garden provides the best view over Bonsall Moor of any pub in Derbyshire. This compact two-roomed pub is popular with workers from nearby County Hall at lunchtime, and then becomes busy with local people at night when it is often bursting at the seams. Take a look at the interesting outside gents' toilet. Lunches are available Tuesday to Friday, evening meals Wednesday and Thursday. Q❀◐▶⊟⊟♣

Matlock Bath

Temple Hotel

Temple Walk, DE4 3PG (off A6)
✪ 6-10.30; 12-11 Sat; 12-10 Sun
☎ (01629) 583911 🌐 templehotel.co.uk
Beer range varies Ⓗ
Historic Georgian hotel with a public bar situated above the hustle and bustle of the Matlock Bath riverside promenade, with good views across the Derwent Valley. Nearby are the popular cable car rides and the Peak District Mining Museum. Past visitors include Lord Byron, who etched a poem on a window. The landlord focuses on beers from Derbyshire micro-breweries and up to three beers from Thornbridge, Whim and Leatherbritches often feature. ♨❀⊯◐▶♿⇌⊟(6.1)♣P

Melbourne

Alma Inn

59 Derby Road, DE73 8FE
✪ 4 (2 Fri; 12 Sat)-11 (12.30am Fri & Sat); 12-10.30 Sun
☎ (01332) 695200
Marston's Pedigree; guest beers Ⓗ
The delightful small town of Melbourne is best known for its Antipodean cousin, which actually took its name from William Lamb, 2nd Viscount Melbourne, whose family still live here. The pub gets its name from a winning overseas fixture, as did the former offices of CAMRA HQ, so it is only to be expected that beers from Marston's and its guest list are in winning form. The pub is usually lively, often catering for a younger clientele, and holds occasional beer festivals. Lunches are served Sunday only. ◐♿▲⊟(68)♣P⚟

Mickleover

Nag's Head ✔

25 Uttoxeter Road, DE3 9GF
✪ 11-11 (midnight Fri & Sat); 12-11 Sun
☎ (01332) 513104
Marston's Pedigree; guest beers Ⓗ
Recently refurbished, the open-plan interior has a number of different levels with a variety of seating including tall bar stools and tables, settees and low coffee tables. It attracts a wide clientele and specialises in charcoal-

grilled food, available all day. Quiz nights are Tuesday, Wednesday and Sunday. Regular real ales are supplemented by up to four guests. Outside seating is provided on a raised decking area and small grassed area.
❀◑♿🚌P⊱

Milford

King William IV

The Bridge, DE56 0RR (on A6)
⏲ 5 (12 Sat)-11.30; 12.30-11 Sun
☎ (01332) 840842
Taylor Landlord; guest beers Ⓗ
Fronted by the River Derwent, the pub is next to the bridge in the centre of an historic mill village which is backed by sandstone cliffs. A small, narrow, single-roomed local, it has exposed interior stone walls, a welcoming fireplace, low-beamed ceiling, quarry tiled floor and wooden settles. Bass and Pedigree rotate, with two other guests, usually one from a local micro-brewery. This is an ideal base for exploring the Derwent Valley, a world heritage site. The pub sign says just King William. ♨🛏🚌♣♠

Milltown

Nettle Inn

Hard Meadow Lane, S45 0ES (1 mile E of Ashover on B6036) SK358622
⏲ 12-2.30, 5.30-11; 12-10.30 Sun
☎ (01246) 590462
Bradfield Farmers Bitter, Farmers Blonde; guest beers Ⓗ
Cosy 17th-century inn, named after a famous local greyhound. Beamed ceilings and log fires predominate, adding to the traditional feel of the pub. The usual pub games are available, and there is also space for boules. An inspiring menu includes traditional food sourced from local farms and butchers, with ingredients such as hare and wild garlic. Children are welcome. ♨Q❀🛏◑🚃♿🚌(63,64)♣P⊱

Monsal Head

Monsal Head Hotel

DE45 1NL (on B6465)
⏲ 11.30-11; 12-10.30 Sun
☎ (01629) 640250 🌐 monsalhead.com
Theakston Best Bitter; guest beers Ⓗ
The present hotel dates from the 19th century when the new railway dived over a viaduct into a tunnel underneath, but the Stables Bar with its real ale dates from an earlier inn. It is decorated with the original stalls for horses, and gets crowded at weekends, when the large patio is used if weather permits. The hotel is noted for its food and wine. Guest beers are from local breweries such as Abbeydale, Kelham Island and Thornbridge; the house beer is from Lloyds.
♨Q❀🛏◑⛺♣P

New Mills

Pack Horse Inn

Mellor Road, SK22 4QQ
⏲ 12-3, 5-11; 12-11 Sat; 12-10.30 Sun
☎ (01663) 742365 🌐 packhorseinn.co.uk
Tetley Bitter; guest beers Ⓗ
A much extended pub built from local stone, with a recent matching extension incorporating an elegant dining room and accommodation block. However, the bar room interior remains largely unaltered with its traditional style and open fire plus stove for the winter. The guest beers are imaginatively chosen so there is always the chance of a surprise. Outside there are two stone patio areas. Be prepared for a brisk uphill walk from New Mills to reach the pub. ♨Q❀🛏◑P

New Tupton

Britannia Inn

Ward Street, S42 6XP SK397661
⏲ 4-11; 3 (11 Sat)-midnight; 11-10.30 Sun
☎ (01246) 861438 🌐 spirebrewery.co.uk/britannia.html
Beer range varies Ⓗ
Within easy reach of Chesterfield, this busy community pub is the brewery tap for the nearby Spire Brewery and features eight cask ales – four Spire Brewery beers and four from guest micro-breweries. A mild and stout or porter are always available, along with a selection of bottled beers and two quality lagers including locally-produced Czech-style lager Morovka. A big supporter of local CAMRA events and campaigns, 'The Brit' has regular quizzes and an outdoor skittles alley. It maintains strong local links with events for the community. ♨❀🚃🚌(51,98)♣P⊱🗑

Newton Solney

Unicorn Inn

Repton Road, DE15 0SG (on B5008) SK283257
⏲ 12-midnight (1am Fri & Sat)
☎ (01283) 703324 🌐 unicorn-inn.co.uk
Draught Bass; Marston's Pedigree; guest beers Ⓗ
This popular local was originally a farmhouse on the Ratcliff family estate (of Bass, Ratcliff & Gretton brewery fame), but became a pub in the late 19th century. The attractive bar area, featuring a wooden bar counter and bar stools, is linked to a small cosy lounge on one side and a dining room on the other. An August beer festival is held in a marquee erected in the car park. The garden includes a children's play area. ❀🛏◑🚃🚌(V3)♣P⊱

Ockbrook

Royal Oak

55 Green Lane, DE72 3SE
⏲ 11.30-2.30 (3 Sat), 6-11; 12-3, 7-10.30 Sun
☎ (01332) 662378
Draught Bass; guest beers Ⓗ
Set back from the road across a cobbled courtyard, this fine pub was a former CAMRA regional Pub of the Year award winner. The pub has been in the same family since Coronation year and is little changed, with each of the five rooms preserving its own distinctive character and clientele. Three ever-changing guest beers are supplemented by an annual beer festival in October. Excellent home-cooked food is served every lunchtime, and evenings Monday to Friday (except

Tuesday). The garden is family friendly.
Q❀◑♿🚌(9)♣🍎P⚐

Over Haddon

Lathkil Hotel

DE45 1JE (signed in village) SK206665
🕐 11.30-3, 6-11; 11.30-11 Sat; 12-10.30 Sun
☎ (01629) 812501 🌐 lathkil.co.uk
Whim Hartington Bitter; Everards Tiger; guest beers Ⓗ
The pub overlooks a masterpiece of Peak District scenery, marvellous in any weather (see website pictures). Walking in, one side is an old-fashioned bar room with real fire and oak beams, while superb home-cooked meals are served in the larger room opposite. A covered beer garden is the perfect place to while away summer evenings with a pint. Well-equipped rooms are available for staying over; dogs are welcome in the bar and walkers should take off their boots at the door.
⛰Q🐌❀🛏◑🍽⛺🚌P⚐▢

Ripley

George Inn

20 Lowes Hill, DE5 3DW (fork left on Butterley Hill at Talbot)
🕐 1-1am (6-midnight Mon-Thu winter); 1-1am (11-midnight winter) Sun
☎ (01773) 512041
Amber seasonal beers; guest beers Ⓗ
Forget the lager houses for the young that populate Ripley and seek out this real ale gem that is just a 10-minute walk from the town centre. This is a smartish looking pub from the outside but when you go inside do not let the plain open-plan interior put you off. The landlord certainly knows how to keep his beer, specialising in ales from the Amber Ales brewery, which is just a short trip away down the road. Amber Pale is the locals' favourite.
🚌(9.2)♣P

Rosliston

Bull's Head

Burton Road, DE12 8JU (north-western edge of village)
🕐 12-3, 7-11
☎ (01283) 761705
Draught Bass; Marston's Pedigree; guest beers Ⓗ
Late 19th-century brick-built free house with a comfortable public bar and smart, cosy lounge, both featuring open fires and beamed ceilings, plus a large function room in a converted stable block. A collection of china bulls is displayed behind the bar and interesting models of a Burton Union brewing system can be found in the public bar and the function room. The National Forest Forestry Centre is situated about half-a-mile away.
⛰◑🍽⛺🚌(22)♣P

Scarcliffe

Horse & Groom

Rotherham Road, S44 6SU (on B6417) SK490687
🕐 12-midnight
☎ (01246) 823152
Black Sheep Best Bitter; Greene King Abbot; Stones Bitter; Tetley Bitter; guest beers Ⓗ
This rural free house is a real gem with a history going back 150 years. The present stone-built inn is a past Derbyshire CAMRA Pub of the Year and has won many seasonal branch awards. Free from music and games, it serves some excellent real ales, complemented by an ever-changing list of guest beers and an impressive range of fine malts. No hot food is available. Accommodation is in three purpose-built cottages. Q🐌❀🛏🍽⛺🚌(53,81)P

Shardlow

Shakespeare Inn

117 London Road, DE72 2GP
🕐 11.30-midnight
☎ (01332) 792728
Marston's Pedigree; guest beers Ⓗ
Formerly one of England's largest inland ports, the village of Shardlow is surrounded by water and now has a large and busy marina. Shardlow's numerous pubs (all with real ale), and its restaurants are well able to serve its many visitors. The Shakespeare is a traditional pub on the main road near the church. It offers up to 12 guest beers from the Scottish & Newcastle list every month. The pub also has a separate purpose-built restaurant (no evening meals are served Sunday and Monday). ⛰❀◑🍽♿⛺🚌(ALS)♣P⚐

Shirland

Shoulder of Mutton

Hallfieldgate Lane, DE55 6AA (on B6013, Wessington-Shirland crossroad) SK393582
🕐 12 (7 Tue)-11; 12-10.30 Sun
☎ (01773) 834992
John Smith's Bitter; guest beers Ⓗ
A hidden gem with a charismatic owner and interactive regulars, this homely pub has a lounge with three distinct seating areas that overlook the garden. A small pool room with jukebox is to the roadside end. In summer the view from the garden is spectacular and well worth contemplation over a few pints. Two guest beers, usually from local micro-breweries, are served, with up to a dozen being scuttled through each week – reward enough for the half mile walk from the A61.
Q❀🍽⛺🚌♣P⚐

Smalley

Bell Inn ✔

35 Main Road, DE7 6EF (on A608)
🕐 11.30-3, 5-11; 11-11 Sat; 12-11 Sun
☎ (01332) 880635
Adnams Broadside; Mallard Duckling; Marston's Pedigree; Oakham JHB; Whim Hartington IPA; guest beers Ⓗ
This mid 19th-century inn has three rooms and a large, attractive child-friendly garden. Accommodation is offered in three flats in a converted stable adjoining the pub, where brewing and other memorabilia adorn the walls. Top quality beer and food helped earn the Bell the Derbyshire CAMRA Pub of the Year award in 2006. Situated near Shipley Country

Park, it can be reached via the Derby-Heanor H1 bus service, which stops right outside the pub. ⌂Q❀⇌☾◑⊟♿⊟(H1)P

South Normanton

Clock Inn

107 Market Street, DE55 2AA (from M1 jct 28 take B6019 towards Alfreton)
⊙ 4-11; 12-midnight Sat & Sun
☎ (01773) 811396 ⊕ theclockinn.co.uk
Bateman XXXB; Everards Tiger; Jennings Cumberland Ale Ⓗ
Free house with two rooms served by a central bar, with an outdoor covered smoking area. The pub is a local CAMRA Pub of the Season and winner of numerous Cask Marque awards that are displayed above the bar. Weston's Old Rosie Traditional Cider is available. Please note there is no entry after 11pm. Q❀⊟♣P⁻

Devonshire Arms

137 Market Street, DE55 2AA (from M1 jct 28 take B6019 towards Alfreton)
⊙ 12-midnight
☎ (01773) 810748 ⊕ the-devonshire-arms.co.uk/index.htm
Sarah Hughes Dark Ruby; guest beers Ⓗ
This award-winning family-run free house has a restaurant, games room and adjoining bar area. Live sports are shown on three large-screen TVs in the main bar area and games room. Home-cooked meals are available daily (except Sunday evening), with vegetarians, vegans and coeliacs all catered for. Three changing guest beers are stocked, at least one sourced locally, along with a wide range of bottled beers. Weston's Old Rosie cider is always available. Live entertainment plays on Friday evening. Outside is a covered and heated smoking area. No entry/re-entry after 11pm. ☎❀☾◑♿⊟♣●P⁻

Spondon

Malt Shovel

Potter Street, DE21 7LH (near church)
⊙ 11.30-2.30, 6-11.30; 11.30-midnight Fri & Sat; 12-11 Sun
☎ (01332) 674203
⊕ themaltshovelspondon.wanadoo.co.uk
Marston's Burton Bitter, Pedigree; Ⓗ **guest beers** Ⓗ/Ⓖ
Characterful, multi-roomed village local dating from 1680 which has resisted modernisation, despite 19th-century extensions. The Tudor Room has a full-sized snooker table and dartboard. Prints of old Spondon adorn the walls, while the garden area is popular in summer. Excellent value bar meals are served, with four guest beers selected from the Marston's list. Spondon itself has an unusual beery pedigree – in 1340 fire broke out in the malthouse, destroying the village, so Edward III kindly exempted the village from taxes until it was rebuilt. ⌂❀☾⊟♿⇌⊟♣P⁻

Stanley Common

White Post Inn

237 Belper Road, DE7 6FT (on A609)
⊙ 12-3, 6-11.30 (1am Fri); 12-1am Sat; 12-11.30 Sun
☎ (0115) 9300194
Greene King Old Speckled Hen; Ⓗ/Ⓖ **Marston's Pedigree; guest beers** Ⓗ
This large, white-painted roadside inn on the main thoroughfare is surrounded by some fine countryside away from the built-up sprawl. Three interlinking rooms are served by a central bar with one used as a dining area, where good food is available. An interesting range of at least two ever-changing local guest beers is supplemented by four beer festivals a year. The summer festival spills out on to the pleasant rear garden. For access catch the daytime Derby-Ilkeston 59 bus. ⌂Q☎❀☾◑♿⊟(59)♣P⁻

Stanton in Peak

Flying Childers

Main Road, DE4 2LW (off B6056 Bakewell-Ashbourne Rd) SK240643
⊙ 12-2 (not Mon & Tue), 7-11; 12-3, 7-11 Sat & Sun
☎ (01629) 636333
Black Sheep Best Bitter; Wells Bombardier; guest beers Ⓗ
Created from four cottages during the 18th century, this is an unspoilt village pub named after a famous 18th-century racehorse owned by the Duke of Devonshire. It is located near the historic Stanton Moor and is popular with walkers, tourists and locals alike. Both rooms are welcoming with real fires, and there is a pleasant beer garden to the rear of the pub. Home-made soups and snacks are available at lunchtime and the guest beer changes regularly. Dogs are welcome. ⌂Q❀⊟▲⊟♣P

Staveley

Speedwell Inn

Lowgates, S43 3TT
⊙ 6-11 (10.30 Sun)
☎ (01246) 474665
Townes IPA, Speedwell Bitter, Staveley Cross, Pynot Porter, guest beer (occasional) Ⓗ
Twice winner of Chesterfield CAMRA Pub of the Year, this is the main outlet for Townes beers, which have been brewed here for the last 10 years. The regular brews and additional specials are supplemented by a small range of bottled Belgian beers. Those who like the opportunity to join in (sometimes) lively conversation while propping up the bar enjoying a pint or two will appreciate this modest pub. Dogs are welcome. Q⊟♣⁻

Sutton Cum Duckmanton

Arkwright Arms

Chesterfield Road, S44 5JG (A632 between Chesterfield and Bolsover)
⊙ 11-11 (midnight Fri); 11-10.30 Sun
☎ (01246) 232053 ⊕ arkwrightarms.co.uk
Greene King Abbot; Taylor Landlord; guest beers Ⓗ
A warm welcome is assured at this mock Tudor-fronted free house. The public bar is separated from the lounge by a horseshoe bar, with a separate dining room. All three rooms have cosy open fires and there is an excellent range of up to 10 ever-changing

guest ales, three ciders and two perries. Beer festivals run during the Easter and August bank holidays, supplemented by mini events throughout the year. Quality food is served lunchtimes and evenings. Local CAMRA Pub of the Year 2008. (81,84)

Thulston

Harrington Arms

4 Grove Close, DE72 3EY (off B5010)

11.30-3 (not Mon), 5-11; 11.30-11 Sat; 12-10.30 Sun

(01332) 571798

Draught Bass; guest beers H

Two former cottages, refronted to stand out and brightly lit after dark, have been smartly modernised without losing a cottagey feel. The pub has low, beamed ceilings, wooden-clad interior walls and open fires in winter. Regular beer festivals are held and an adjoining restaurant serves good food. Elvaston Castle Country Park, former estate of the Earls of Harrington (hence the house beer's name), is close by; its magnificent iron entrance gates were brought back from Spain during the Napoleonic Wars.

Whaley Bridge

Shepherd's Arms

7 Old Road, SK23 7HR

3-11 (1am Fri); 12-1am Sat; 12-11 Sun

(01663) 732384

Marston's Burton Bitter, Pedigree; guest beers H

This attractive, whitewashed stone-built pub has been preserved unspoilt, conveying the feel of the farmhouse it once was. The unchanged tap room, the best for miles around, is a delight, with open fire, flagged floor and scrubbed-top tables. Additionally there is a comfortable lounge and a small drinking area in the garden, which also houses the covered smoking area. A short walk from Whaley Bridge station, the pub is also on the 199 bus route. (199)

Willington

Green Man

1 Canal Bridge, DE65 6BQ (by railway station)

11.30-3, 5-11 (11.30 Wed & Thu); 11.30-midnight Fri & Sat; 12-11 Sun

(01283) 702377

Draught Bass; Marston's Pedigree; guest beers H

A large, attractive, white-painted, two-roomed roadside pub at the heart of the village, and not far from the canal. Dating back some 150 years, the pub features oak beams throughout, along with traditional bench seating. A picture gallery of local landmarks can be found in the lounge, while a large child-friendly rear garden is complemented by tables and chairs at the front during the summer months. Live music is held regularly and good home-cooked food is served daily. (V3)

Winster

Old Bowling Green

East Bank, DE4 2DS (25m from Market Hall)

6-11 (midnight Fri & Sat); closed Mon & Tue; 12-3, 6-11 Sun

(01629) 650219 peakparkpub.co.uk

Beer range varies H

Thriving 15th-century pub, located close to the National Trust-owned market hall at the heart of this attractive Peak District village. A central bar serves an elongated room, with a cosy log fire and two smaller rooms to the rear. The walls are adorned with paintings of local scenes and posters of past wakes weeks. Up to four ever-changing beers sourced from micro-breweries within a 25-mile radius are available. Good wholesome food is served evenings and all day Sunday.
Q (172)

Wirksworth

Hope & Anchor

Market Place, DE4 4ET

12 (4 Mon & Wed)-11.30; 12-11 Sun

(01629) 823340 hopenanchor.co.uk

St Austell Tribute; guest beers H

This Grade II-listed building was once described as the governor's residence and retains some interesting original features. The corner lounge overlooking the market place towards the Black's Head has a magnificent carved wooden fireplace and a curious bow-fronted floor-to-ceiling cabinet that contains a bureau. The bar is split between pool and seating, and a gravel courtyard provides seating outside. Wirksworth Market day is Tuesday and the National Stone Centre is situated just outside the town. A guest beer is usually sourced from a Derbyshire micro-brewery. Q (6.1)

Royal Oak

North End, DE4 4FG (off B5035)

8-11.30 (midnight Fri & Sat); 12-3, 7.30-11 Sun

(01629) 823000

Draught Bass; Taylor Landlord; Whim Hartington IPA; guest beers H

Excellent, small, ultra-traditional local in a stone terrace near the market place, highlighted at night by rows of fairy lights. The bar features old pictures of local interest and there is also a pool room and smoking grotto. The Oak combines a long-standing reputation for Bass with a choice of guest beers. Wirksworth (or Wuzzer, as it is affectionately known) is well populated with pubs and the others are all worthy of a visit if staying nearby. The Ecclesbourne Valley railway line visitor attraction is not far away. (6.1)

> But there used to be in the country districts a sort of light porter which was one of the most refreshing liquids conceivable for hot weather. I have drunk it in Yorkshire at the foot of Gorseberry Topping, out of big stone bottles like Champagne magnums. But that was nearly sixty years ago.
>
> **George Saintsbury**, 1920

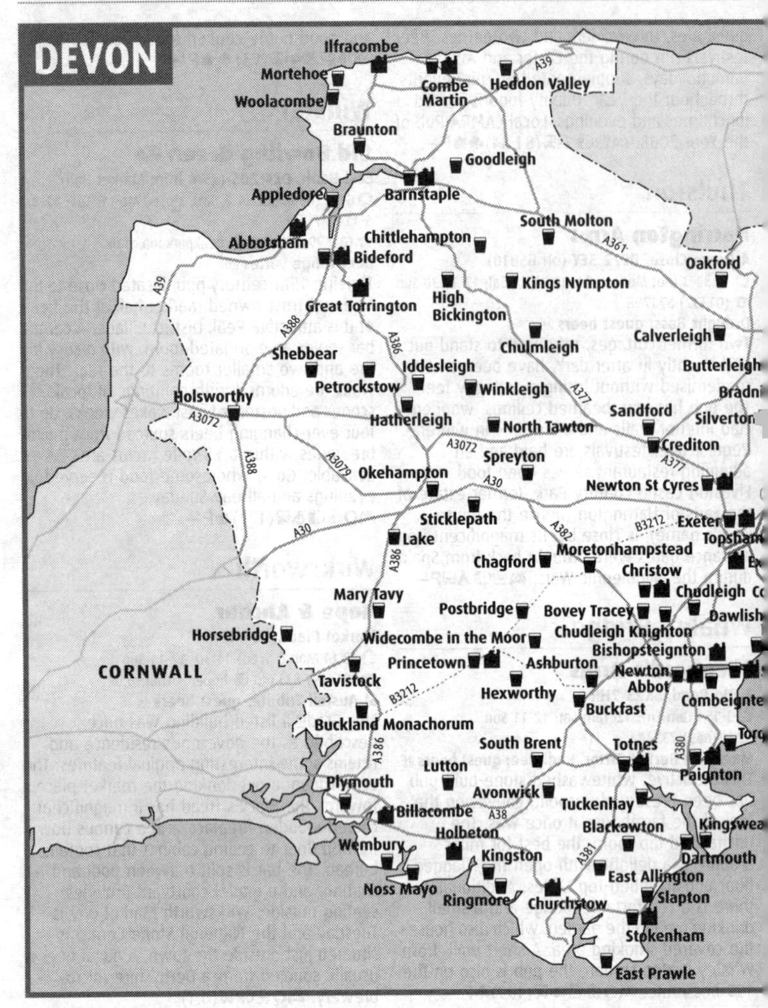

Appledore

Beaver Inn

2 Irsha Street, EX39 1RY

⌚ 11-midnight; 11.30-11 Sun

☎ (01237) 474822 🌐 beaverinn.co.uk

Sharp's Doom Bar; guest beers ⊞

Superbly located with views of the Taw and Torridge estuaries, the Beaver has a single bar where the friendly staff serve from three handpumps. The cider is from Winkleigh. Well-behaved children and dogs are welcome (dogs have their own biscuit barrel) and excellent value food is available from the bar or restaurant menus. The pub is home to the North Devon Jazz Club which meets monthly, and there is live music every Saturday plus local folk/fiddle groups play on Mondays.

❀◑⊟♣●

Ashburton

Exeter Inn

26 West Street, TQ13 7DU

⌚ 11-2.30, 5-11 (midnight Fri & Sat); 12-3, 7-10.30 Sun

☎ (01364) 652013

Badger First Gold; Greene King IPA ⊞

This friendly local, built in 1131, is the oldest pub in Ashburton, with additions in the 17th century. It was built to house the workers that constructed the nearby church and the inn was used by Sir Francis Drake on his journeys to London. The main bar is L-shaped, rustic and wood panelled, with a canopy. There are two main drinking areas either side of the entrance hallway and a further bar at the back, served via a small hatch and counter.

♨Q❀◑⊟♣⌐

Avonwick

Turtley Corn Mill

TQ10 9ES (off A38)

⌚ 11.30-11; 12-10.30 Sun

☎ (01364) 646100 🌐 avonwick.net

Bays Gold; Dartmoor Jail Ale; St Austell Tribute; Summerskills Tamar ⊞

This former roadside restaurant standing in its own river and lakeside grounds of ten acres is now a prize-winning pub. Reverting to its former name to reflect its origins, it encompasses the ethos of its owners by

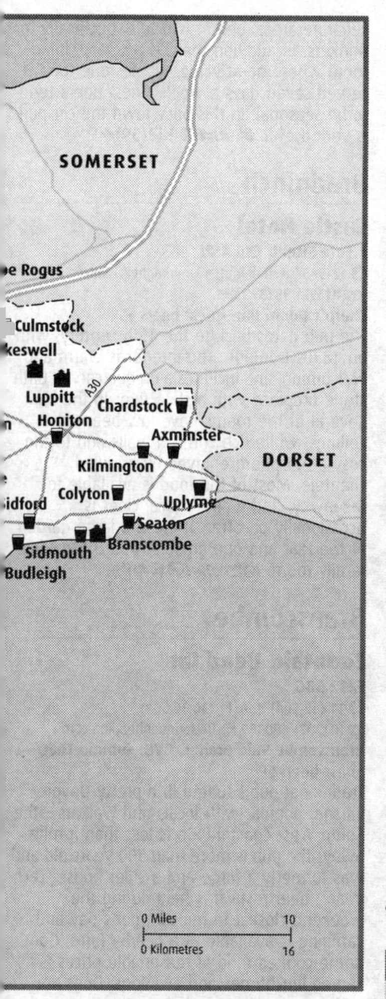

supplying local beers and locally-sourced food. Old photos of the area adorn the walls, including a very rare print of a Plymouth Brewery, now demolished. Children are welcome inside but away from the bar areas until 7pm. Well-behaved dogs are also welcome. ♔Q❀⇌◑♿P⅄

Axminster

Lamb Inn

Lyme Road, EX13 5BE
⌚ 11.30-midnight (1am Fri; 2am Sat)
☎ (01297) 33922
Branscombe Vale Branoc; guest beers ⊞
A traditional pub run by a traditional landlady. Half a mile from the town centre, it consists of a single large room with a comfortable bar, dining areas and a pool table. A large-screen TV often shows sport. In the spacious garden are two boules pistes and a heated smokers' shelter. Check before taking in a dog as there is a pub dog in residence. Food is of good quality, quantity and value. The loos are suitable for disabled users, and are worth a visit just for the pictures on the walls.
❀◑⊟P⅄

Barnstaple

Panniers ✔

33-34 Boutport Street, EX31 1RX
⌚ 9-midnight (1am Fri & Sat)
☎ (01271) 329720
Greene King Abbot; Marston's Burton Bitter, Pedigree; Shepherd Neame Spitfire; guest beers ⊞
Pleasant, efficient Wetherspoon's outlet converted from an arcade of shops. Conveniently situated in the centre of town, it is opposite the Queen's Theatre and close to the historic Pannier Market from which it takes its name. The split-level interior offers distinct seating areas where the real ale range is unrivalled, with cider from Weston's. The garden is a suntrap and offers covered seating for less clement weather. Food from the extensive menu is served all day.
♉❀◑♿⇌⊟●⅄

Reform Inn

Reform Street, Pilton, EX31 1PD
⌚ 12-11 (10.30 Sun)
☎ (01271) 323164
Barum Original, Breakfast, Firing Squad ⊞
Well-established, popular back-street community local and the brewery tap for Barum Brewery, whose beers dominate here. From the main road, look above roof level for the pub sign to locate it. The skittle alley is the place to be for the annual Green Man festival in July, while pool and music are played in the large public bar. The lounge bar is quieter. Other regular beer festivals are held and there is live music twice-monthly on Fridays.
❀⊟⇌⊟(6)♣⅄

INDEPENDENT BREWERIES

Barum Barnstaple
Bays Paignton (NEW)
Beer Engine Newton St Cyres
Blackdown Dunkeswell
Branscombe Vale Branscombe
Bridgetown Totnes (NEW)
Clearwater Great Torrington
Combe Martin Combe Martin
Country Life Abbotsham
Dartmoor Princetown
Dartmouth Newton Abbot (NEW)
Devon Earth Paignton (NEW)
Exe Valley Silverton
Exeter Exeter
Gargoyles Dawlish
Jollyboat Bideford
O'Hanlon's Whimple
Otter Luppitt
Quercus Churchstow (NEW)
Red Rock Bishopsteignton
Ringmore Shaldon (NEW)
Scattor Rock Christow
South Hams Stokenham
Summerskills Billacombe
Teignworthy Newton Abbot
Union Holbeton
Warrior Exeter
Wizard Ilfracombe

Rolle Quay Inn ✔
Rolle Quay, EX31 1JE
✪ 11 (12 Sun)-midnight (1am Fri & Sat)
☎ (01271) 345182
St Austell IPA, Dartmoor Best, HSD; guest beers Ⓗ
One minute from Barnstaple's High Street, yet also close to the River Yeo and with quick access to the Tarka Trail and its cycle-hire facility. The landlord, a previous local CAMRA award winner, is passionate about real ale. A good quality menu, including children's portions, is available. On Friday afternoons tapas are a popular feature with locals, while Sunday lunch also has an excellent reputation. Super-league darts, skittles and euchre are played here. ♨❀⇌◐⚌⊟(3,303)♣⊬

Bideford

King's Arms ✔
7 The Quay, EX39 2HW
✪ 11-11
☎ (01237) 475196 ⊕ kingsarmsbideford.co.uk
Adnams Broadside; Butcombe Bitter; Jollyboat Grenville's Renown; Sharp's Doom Bar; Shepherd Neame Spitfire Ⓗ
Sixteenth-century inn, some of which is unaltered, overlooking the River Torridge and the old Long Bridge. A convivial, low-beamed bar features a snug at one end and a dining area at the other. Visitors will find a wide selection of real ales mixed between local brews and national favourites. Old photographs of the waterfront decorate the walls and the pub makes a convenient stopover for visitors to Lundy Island, whose ferry departs close by. It can get busy on Friday and Saturday evenings. ♨❀⇌◐⊟

Blackawton

George Inn
Main Street, TQ9 7BG
✪ 12-3, 6 (7 Sun)-11 (10.30 Sun), closed Mon winter
☎ (01803) 712342
Dartmoor Jail Ale; Teignworth Spring Tide; guest beers Ⓗ
A comfortable two-bar pub with a wood-burning stove, this little gem is very much the village local and the centre of the community. A beer festival is held during the May Day bank holiday when the villagers takes part in their annual worm-charming event. The pub is reputedly haunted by resident ghosts. Another separate room is available for meetings or family dining. Three cask ales are generally available, together with Taunton Traditional cider. ♨Q⊱❀◐♠P

Bovey Tracey

Cromwell Arms
Fore Street, TQ13 9AE
✪ 11-11; 12-10.30 Sun
☎ (01626) 833473 ⊕ thecromwellarms.co.uk
Greene King IPA; St Austell IPA, Tribute; guest beers Ⓗ
A roomy, comfortable 17th-century town centre pub with character, a ghost and beams throughout. Popular with locals and visitors alike it has one large room with three separate areas, one of which is specifically for drinkers. In addition there is a smart dining room where good value, wholesome food is served seven days a week. Guest beers tend to be seasonal. In this busy town the car park is very useful. ♨❀⇌◐♿⊟(39)♣P⊬

Bradninch

Castle Hotel
1 Fore Street, EX5 4NN
✪ 12-3, 5.30-midnight; 12-midnight Fri-Sun
☎ (01392) 881378
Sharp's Doom Bar; guest beers Ⓗ
The pub dates back to the 15th century, with an 1830s frontage. The interior is warm and welcoming, and includes a unique carved Bath stone fireplace with a slate floor in the bar. Several of the rooms have low-beamed ceilings, while rich crimson walls add to the cosy atmosphere enjoyed by a mixed clientele. Most of the food is available for takeaway, and a pin of local cider is occasionally on offer. There is a large garden at the rear and one en-suite bed & breakfast family room. ♨⊱❀⇌◐⊟♣P⊬

Branscombe

Fountain Head Inn
EX12 3BG
✪ 11 (12 Sun)-3, 6-11 (10.30 Sun)
☎ (01297) 680359 ⊕ thefountainheadinn.com
Branscombe Vale Branoc, BVB, Summa That; guest beers Ⓗ
Traditional pub situated in a pretty Devon village, popular with locals and walkers – the South West Coastal Path is less than a mile away. The pub is more than 500 years old and was formerly a forge and a cider house. Each year a beer festival is held during the weekend closest to midsummer's day and camping is available at a nearby farm. Good home-cooked food at reasonable prices is served lunchtimes and evenings. Dogs are welcome in the main bar.
♨Q⊱❀◐⛺⊟♠P⊬

Braunton

Black Horse
34 Church Street, EX33 2EL
✪ 11.30-2, 5.30-11; 11.30-midnight Fri & Sat; 12-10.30 Sun
☎ (01271) 812386
Shepherd Neame Spitfire; guest beers Ⓖ
A friendly welcome greets visitors to this 400-year-old traditional pub where all ales are served on gravity from behind the bar. It is very much a village local with a community focus and has its own skittles, pool and shove ha'penny teams, plus an unobtrusive flat-screen TV and a separate dining area. Food is served every evening in summer, but weekends only in winter. Three small but popular beer festivals take place here each year. ⊱❀◐⛺⊟♣P⊬

Buckfast

Abbey Inn
TQ11 0EA (off A38)

🕘 11(12 Sun)-11
☎ (01364) 642343
St Austell Dartmoor Best, Tribute, HSD [H]
Large inn within Dartmoor National Park, close to the famous Buckfast Abbey. Inside, the warm and welcoming oak-panelled bar is spacious, with traditional furniture. The pub is situated in a beautiful setting next to the River Dart and has an outside terrace with seating and views overlooking the river, including glimpses of the abbey. The large dining room serves an excellent range of food and there any many visitor attractions within close vicinity of the pub. ⌂Q❀⇌◑⛺⊟P

Buckland Monachorum

Drake Manor Inn

The Village, PL20 7NA
🕘 11.30-2.30, 6.30-11 (11.30 Fri & Sat); 12-10.30 Sun
☎ (01822) 853892 🌐 drakemanorinn.co.uk
Courage Best Bitter; Greene King Abbot; Sharp's Doom Bar [H]
With some parts dating from the 15th century, this quintessential country pub is a friendly and cosy hostelry, located in a small Dartmoor village. The manager believes in the importance of consistency and certainly the Drake maintains a regular following, with the beers turning over frequently. Euchre, cribbage and shove ha'penny are played here. A recent development is a luxury apartment upstairs (sleeping 5-6), available all year round, while a pleasant beer garden with a stream completes the scene.
⌂Q☋❀⇌◑⊟♣P

Butterleigh

Butterleigh Inn

EX15 1PN (opp church)
🕘 12-3, 6-11 (midnight Fri & Sat); 7-10.30 Sun
☎ (01884) 855407
Cotleigh Tawny; O'Hanlon's Yellowhammer; guest beers [H]
An excellent country pub in a charming location, this splendid 17th-century Devon cob building is full of character. It has a main bar and lounge with a modern, sympathetically styled dining room. The wood-burning stoves make this a warm, welcoming place in winter. In summer, guests can drink outside, either under the new veranda or in the attractive secluded garden, enjoying the views of the surrounding rolling hills. This fine establishment has become the focus for a vibrant community. ⌂Q❀⇌◑♿♣P⊬

Calverleigh

Rose & Crown Inn

EX16 8BA (on the old Rackenford Road)
🕘 11.30-midnight; 12-11.30 Sun
☎ (01884) 256301
Butcombe Bitter; guest beers [H]
Traditional 17th-century country pub not far from the town of Tiverton, with a restaurant, beer garden and skittle alley that doubles as a function room and library with more than six hundred books. Excellent home-cooked food, made with local produce where possible, is available, together with local cider from Palmershayes across the road. Q❀◑♣●P

Chagford

Sandy Park Inn ✔

Sandy Park, TQ13 8JW (on A382 Moretonhampstead-Whiddon Down road)
🕘 12-11
☎ (01647) 433267 🌐 sandyparkinn.co.uk
Otter Bitter; St Austell Tribute; [H] guest beers [H]/[G]
Thatched free house, thought to be 17th century, in a small hamlet within Dartmoor National Park. The main bar has a large open fire, ancient beams, a stone floor and pews at the tables, while a small snug is set around a large table. Another bar becomes an intimate restaurant serving excellent home-cooked food at weekends. Castle Drogo (National Trust) and the village of Chagford are nearby. At the front of the pub is parking for five to six cars. ⌂Q☋❀⇌◑⛺⊟♣●P⊬

Chardstock

George Inn

Chard Street, EX13 7BX
🕘 11.30-2.30 (3 Sat), 6-11; 12-3, 7-10.30 Sun
☎ (01460) 220241 🌐 george-inn.co.uk
Branscombe Vale Branoc; Skinner's Betty Stogs; guest beers [H]
Attractive Grade II-listed 15th-century thatched church house in the heart of a rural village. The layout provides three bar areas, a dining room, and a pool table up some stairs. Look out for the superb linenfold panelled screen and centuries-old graffiti. A varied menu, including Sunday roasts, caters for all tastes and is sourced locally. Overnight accommodation is available in four en-suite rooms. Q❀⇌◑P⊬

Chittlehampton

Bell Inn

The Square, EX37 9QL (opp church)
🕘 11-3, 6-midnight; 11-midnight Sat; 12-11 Sun
☎ (01769) 540368 🌐 thebellatchittlehampton.co.uk
Beer range varies [H]/[G]
North Devon CAMRA pub of the year 2007, this 18th-century village-centre inn is the base for many local sports teams, as is obvous from several photos and trophies around the bar. Additional West Country ales are always available on gravity from the cellar, listed on a separate board, but only when the landlord is present. The cider is Thatcher's and good food is provided using local produce. On Tuesday a cheap lunch is available for the over 50s.
❀⇌◑♿⛺♣●⊬

Christow

Teign House Inn

Teign Valley Road, EX6 7PL (on B3193)
🕘 12-3, 5-11.30; 12-11.30 Sat & Sun
☎ (01647) 252286 🌐 teignhouseinn.co.uk
Cotleigh 25; Dartmoor Jail Ale; Sharp's Doom Bar; guest beers [H]
This welcoming, atmospheric country pub, with lots of beams and a warming log fire, has

strong local community support. The sizeable garden attracts the families of locals and visitors alike, while an adjoining large field has space for four caravans as well as campers. An annual beer festival (with up to 30 beers) is held on the second weekend in July. Great pub food, all home-cooked and with a good vegetarian choice, includes a separate gluten-free menu.
⩩❀◑◐♿⛺🚌(360)P⚡

Chudleigh

Bishop Lacy

52-53 Fore Street, TQ13 0HY
⏲ 12-midnight (1am Fri & Sat)
☎ (01626) 854585
Dartmoor Jail Ale; O'Hanlon's Yellowhammer; Sharp's Doom Bar; guest beers 🄷
Very friendly, Grade II-listed, two-bar pub opposite the church and named after a Bishop of Exeter who reputedly introduced the town's water supply in the 14th century. There is a strong emphasis on West Country breweries here, and excellent quality home-cooked food is available in both bars. The public bar is dominated by a magnificent fireplace, incredibly only half its original size, which still incorporates traditional hooks for hanging ham. The cider is Weston's Old Rosie. Dogs and children are welcome.
⩩Q◑◐⊏🚌(39,182)●⚡

Chudleigh Knighton

Anchor Inn

Plymouth Road, TQ13 0EN
⏲ 12-11 (10.30 Sun)
☎ (01626) 853123
St Austell Tribute; Wells Bombardier 🄶
This 15th-century building was once a coaching inn with stables at the rear. Despite a small exterior the pub stretches back via a delightful and largely unspoilt public bar with low oak beams and a separate games area to a smoker's gazebo, skittle alley and garden with pet rabbits. Curries are the landlord's speciality and may be custom-ordered by strength all day long. The friendly licensees are avid collectors and display a cornucopia of items ranging from small cream jugs to reclaimed machinery and equipment.
⩩Q❀◑◐⊏🚌(39,182)♣⚡

Chulmleigh

Old Court House

South Molton Street, EX18 7BW
⏲ 11.30-midnight
☎ (01769) 580045 🌐 oldcourthouseinn.co.uk
St Austell Tribute; guest beers 🄷
This friendly, cosy local is a Grade II-listed thatched inn where Charles I held court in 1634. An original coat of arms commemorating the event can be found in one of the bedrooms. Three real ales plus Thatcher's dry cider are served in the single L-shaped bar and guest beers change regularly, some at the customers' request, but at least one will always be from the South West area. Good food is served all day up until 9.30pm. Thursday quiz night supports local charities.
⩩❀⛟◑◐🚌(377)♣●⚡

Cockwood

Anchor Inn

EX6 8RA (on A379, next to small harbour)
⏲ 11-11 (10.30 Sun)
☎ (01626) 890203 🌐 anchorinncockwood.com
Adnams Broadside; Draught Bass; Fuller's London Pride; Greene King Abbot; Otter Ale; Taylor Landlord 🄷
Opposite a picturesque harbour, this inn is reputed to be more than 460 years old. It has been tastefully extended into the old village hall, to cater for larger numbers, while retaining all its former charm. Award-winning seafood is served amid rich original wood panelling and beamed ceilings. There are traditional pub games such as euchre and cribbage, a small facility for live entertainment, a covered smoker's area and a free mini-bus service for parties of eight or more. ⩩Q⛼◑◐🚌P⚡

Colyton

Kingfisher

Dolphin Street, EX24 6NA
⏲ 11-3, 6-11 (midnight Fri & Sat); 12-3, 7-10.30 Sun
☎ (01297) 552476 🌐 kingfisherinn.co.uk
Sharp's Doom Bar; guest beers 🄷
A traditional 16th-century stone and timber pub close to the centre of this delightful small town with easy parking and a nearby tram that connects to the seaside town of Seaton. A single bar is very cosy and popular with locals and visitors. The separate restaurant at the rear serves good-value food, which is locally sourced wherever possible. Quiz nights are a regular event and themed evenings take place once a month, for which booking is essential.
Q❀◑◐🚌⚡

Combe Martin

Castle Inn

High Street, EX34 0HS (opp church)
⏲ 12-1am (midnight Sun)
☎ (01271) 883706 🌐 castleinn.info
Beer range varies 🄷/🄶
Traditional English pub with an attractive elm bar, wood-panelled walls and a huge fireplace with a log fire in winter. The pool room leads into a large purpose-built function room which holds a fortnightly folk club and hosts live music to suit other tastes in between. Excellent pub food is served daily, a large rear garden holds summer barbecues and a small annual beer festival takes place during carnival week in August. A large-screen TV is available for sports lovers.
⩩⛼❀◑◐♿⛺🚌(3)♣●P⚡

Combeinteignhead

Wild Goose

TQ12 4RA
⏲ 11-2.30 (3 Fri & Sat), 5.30-11 (midnight Fri & Sat); 12-3, 7-11 Sun
☎ (01626) 872241
Skinner's Betty Stogs; guest beers 🄷

A traditional village pub since 1840, this is a genuine free house and is well supported by locals. A single long bar has two open fires and seating at both ends, with a dining room at the rear. The six beers are ever changing and usually come from South West breweries, plus two locally sourced Devon ciders (Martin Jenny & Suicider). An extensive menu includes vegetarian options and uses local produce, especially fish, wherever possible. Friday night is live music night. ♣P

Crediton

Crediton Inn

28A Mill Street, EX17 1EZ

11-11; 12-2, 7-10.30 Sun

☎ (01363) 772882 crediton-inn.co.uk

Fuller's London Pride; Sharp's Doom Bar; guest beers H

Local CAMRA Pub of the Year 2005, this well-established free house has maintained high standards. Four ales are always available, plus guest beers sourced mostly from local independent brewers. The warm, friendly atmosphere that greets visitors has been further enhanced by attractive refurbishment work, while the skittle alley doubles as a function room, and a beer festival is held every November. Good home-cooked food is served at weekends, with snacks available at other times. ♣P

Culmstock

Culm Valley Inn

EX15 3JJ

12-4, 6-11; 11-11 (Sat); 12-10.30 Sun

☎ (01884) 840354

Beer range varies G

Three hundred-year-old village inn situated by the river Culm, near to where it emerges from the Blackdown Hills. The car park was formerly the railway sidings of the Tiverton Light Railway, and the pub was previously called the Railway Inn. Local produce, often organic and free range, features on the menu, while Bollhayes and Tricky ciders are served from the cask. There is a beer festival every bank holiday weekend at the end of May.

Q♣P

Dartmouth

Cherub Inn

13 Higher Street, TQ6 9RB

11-11; 11-2.30, 5-11 winter

☎ (01803) 832571 the-cherub.co.uk

Summerskills Cherub Bitter; guest beers H

This Grade II-listed building has a small but quaint beamed bar and a cosy atmosphere. It is probably the oldest building in Dartmouth, was a merchant's house in the 12th century and underwent a variety of uses before opening as a pub in the middle of the 20th century. It retains many of its original features including some ship's timbers. The first-floor restaurant is reached via a tight steep staircase and has an enviable reputation for locally-sourced fish and seafood dishes. Three cask ales are available. Q

East Allington

Fortescue Arms

TQ9 7RA

12-2.30 (not Mon), 6-11

☎ (01548) 521215 fortescue-arms.co.uk

Butcombe Bitter; Dartmoor Dartmoor IPA; guest beers H

Divided into two distinct parts with a welcoming, traditional bar on one side and a restaurant on the other, both with real fires, this attractive village pub is well supported by residents and local organisations. Guest beers are from the south west, in particular the new Quercus Brewery. The garden has an abundance of flowers in summer and an alfresco dining area. The bar menu includes highly recommended stews, while the restaurant has a deserved reputation for fine dining. QP

East Budleigh

Sir Walter Raleigh

22 High Street, EX9 7ED (on B3170)

11.45-2.30, 6-11.30 (7-10.50 Sun)

☎ (01395) 442510

Adnams Broadside; Otter Bitter; St Austell Tribute H

A pleasant 16th-century pub located at the top of the village just after Hayes Lane, close to the birthplace of Sir Walter Raleigh at Hayes Barton. A varied selection of good food is on offer in this quiet, friendly pub that does without gaming machines or piped music. Dogs are welcome in the main bar and there is a free car park nearby on Hayes Lane.

Q♣

East Prawle

Pig's Nose Inn

TQ7 2BY

12-2.30, 7-11 (closed all day Mon and Sun eve winter)

☎ (01548) 511209 pigsnoseinn.co.uk

Bays Gold; South Hams Devon Pride, G **Eddystone** H

An old three-roomed smugglers' inn on the village green in an area that attracts birdwatchers and coastal walkers. Gravity beers are stored on a specially made rack in an alcove behind the bar and wholesome home-cooked food made with local ingredients is available. Children and dogs are welcome in the cluttered interior with its maritime theme. Occasional live music is performed at weekends in a hall adjoining the pub.

♣

Exeter

Brook Green Tavern

31 Well Street, EX4 6QL

4-12.30am (1.30am Thu & Fri); 12-1.30am Sat; 11-12.30am Sun

☎ (01392) 495699

Fuller's London Pride; Sharp's Doom Bar; Shepherd Neame Spitfire H

Traditional town pub situated close to St James Park football ground, St James Station and a five-minute walk from the town centre. The friendly landlady always offers six different ales, with guest beers usually from local breweries. Popular with students, the pub also hosts meetings of the Victorian Cricket Team and has two resident football teams. There is a small garden and limited parking.

City Gate Hotel

Iron Bridge, North Street, EX4 3RB

11 (12 Sun)-11 (midnight Fri & Sat)

(01392) 495811 citygatehotel.co.uk

Wells Bombardier; Young's Bitter, Special; guest beers [H]

Now Wells and Young's, this well-refurbished city centre hotel has attractive and well-furnished outdoor courtyard areas beneath the ancient city wall with ample covered space for smokers. Beers are restricted to the Wells and Young's range, including Courage, with a good selection of bottled beers to take home. Food is served throughout the day, a function room is available and a cellar bar provides occasional live music.

Double Locks Hotel

Canal Banks, EX2 6LT (road access from Marsh Barton Trading Estate)

11-11 (midnight Fri & Sat); 11-10.30 Sun

(01392) 256947 doublelocks.co.uk

Branscombe Vale Branoc; O'Hanlon's Royal Oak; [H] **Otter Ale;** [G] **Wells Bombardier; Young's Bitter;** [H] **guest beers** [G]

By the banks of the historic Exeter Ship Canal, this pub is popular with families, walkers, canoeists and cyclists. There are warming log fires in winter, an extensive outdoor area for summer drinking and a covered smoking area. The excellent range of ales includes up to nine guests in summer, and a beer festival takes place in May. A volleyball tournament is also staged and live music is performed on Saturday nights in summer. Food is available all day during summer months.

First & Last

90 Cowick Street, St. Thomas, EX4 1HL

11-11; 12-10.30 Sun

(01392) 439403

Hop Back GFB, Crop Circle, Summer Lightning; guest beers [H]

Genuine community pub acquired by Hop Back in 2007. It has a diverse clientele, lies about a quarter of a mile from Exeter St Thomas rail station and is well served by several bus routes. It has darts and pool teams, and features old photos of the area on the walls. Acoustic music sessions are held fortnightly and guest beers come from the Hop Back and Downton range.

Great Western Hotel

St Davids Station Approach, EX4 4NU

10-midnight

(01392) 274039 greatwesternhotel.co.uk

Branscombe Vale Branoc; Fuller's London Pride; Dartmoor Jail Ale; O'Hanlon's Yellowhammer, Port Stout; guest beers [H]

For many years this traditional railway hotel has enjoyed a well-established reputation for its extensive and varied range of ales, with up to 14 or more available at any one time. An excellent local trade is bolstered by CAMRA members travelling from afar, together with popular and regular beer festivals. Reasonably priced meals are served all day in the bar and Brunel Restaurant. There are newly installed disabled facilities. Children and dogs are welcome.

Imperial

New North Road, EX4 4AH

9-midnight (1am Fri & Sat)

(01392) 434050

Greene King Abbot; Marston's Pedigree; guest beers [H]

This popular, large Wetherspoon's pub, converted from the Imperial Hotel in 1996, and situated close to Exeter University, attracts a diverse clientele, not just students. A wide range of local and other ales is available. The Imperial has a large beer garden sloping down towards Exeter St Davids Railway Station, and hosts regular beer festivals. One bar is situated in the Orangery, but there are other drinking areas, including one with TV screens. Meals are available all day.

Mill On The Exe

Bonhay Road, EX4 3AB

11-11; 12-10.30 Sun

(01392) 214464 staustellbrewery.co.uk

St Austell Tribute, Proper Job; guest beers [H]

A short walk from the city centre, this popular riverside pub is a converted mill with outside terraces that overlook the higher weir and Millennium Footbridge. Inside it has tastefully exposed beams and wood panelling plus an extensive menu for meals and snacks. A family-friendly pub, the pub is very busy in summer with outside tables much in demand. The management's pride in its cellar ensures the beer is of consistently good quality.

Old Firehouse

50 New North Road, EX4 4EP

12-3, 5-2am (3am Sat); 12-1am Sun

(01392) 277279

Sharp's Doom Bar; Wychwood Hobgoblin; guest beers [H]

Situated close to the bus and Exeter Central rail stations, this popular city centre pub serves good value food sourced from local ingredients every lunchtime and evening, plus roasts on Sunday. Two regular beers plus two ever-changing guests from a variety of South West breweries are available, with live music on Saturday and Sunday evenings. This gem is well worth seeking out.

Well House Tavern

16-17 Cathedral Yard, EX1 1HD

11-11 (midnight Fri & Sat); 12-10.30 Sun

(01392) 223611 michaelcaines.com/taverns

Otter Bitter; Sharp's Doom Bar; guest beers [H]

This 35-year-old pub, converted from two shops, lies on the haunted Exeter Red Coat Walks route (its cellar well was found to contain skeletal remains which are now on display). The pub is part of the Royal Clarence Hotel, owned by two-star Michelin chef Michael Caines. Three guest ales change continually and Otter Bitter is the house ale. Mini beer and cider festivals are held occasionally and a live band plays on the last Sunday of the month. Quiz night is on alternate Sundays. ◑♿⇌🚌♣●

Goodleigh

New Inn

EX32 7LX (On main road through village) SS599341
⏲ 12-2.30, 6-11; 12-3, 7-10.30 Sun
☎ (01271) 342488
Sharp's Cornish Jack, Special; guest beer 🄷
Traditional old village inn with a welcoming atmosphere. There is one large bar on two levels boasting an eclectic range of decor and furnishings with a wood burning fire and old beams. The cider is Thatcher's Gold. High quality, home-cooked, locally-sourced food is served with the emphasis on meat, game and fish. Skittles and darts are played and the large beer garden has stunning country views. ♨Q❀◑♣●

Hatherleigh

Tally Ho!

14 Market Street, EX20 3JN (opp church)
⏲ 12 (11 Tue)-11; 12-1am Fri & Sat
☎ (01837) 810306 🌐 tallyhohatherleigh.co.uk
Clearwater Cavalier; St Austell Tribute; guest beers 🄷
Comfortable, traditional 15th-century inn with exposed beams and log fires. The single bar has up to three real ales, with cider from Winkleigh. Good value food made with local produce (some of it from the pub's garden) is served in the pub and garden, which also has a barbecue area and a thatched circular gazebo. Nearby, the Tarka Trail and River Torridge provide walking and fishing. Tuesday is market day, when selected real ales are reduced in price between 11am-3pm. ♨Q❀🛏◑🚌(86)●⚐

Heddon Valley

Hunters Inn

EX31 4PY (signed from A399) SS655483
⏲ 10-11
☎ (01598) 763230 🌐 thehuntersinn.net
Exmoor Ale, Fox, Gold, Stag, Beast; guest beers 🄷
Situated among landscaped gardens and a very deep valley with the sea nearby at Heddon's Mouth, this is a country inn for everyone and especially popular with walkers. Sample the complete range of Exmoor ales in a friendly, welcoming atmosphere with a huge open fire in winter. The varied menu, including local produce, also caters for children and vegetarians. Well-behaved dogs are welcome within the bars and rooms, but not the restaurant. Catch the local mummers one evening in winter. ♨Q❀🛏◑♿♣P

Hexworthy

Forest Inn

PL20 6SD
⏲ 11-2.30, 6-11
☎ (01364) 631211 🌐 theforestinn.co.uk
Teignworthy Reel Ale, Spring Tide, Beachcomber 🄷
A country inn situated in the Dartmoor Forest that welcomes walkers, horse riders, anglers, canoeists, dogs and children. Two Teignworthy beers and also Heron Valley cider are offered along with a wide range of home-cooked food, using local produce wherever possible. Accommodation comprises en-suite guest rooms and a bunkhouse. The bars are furnished with Chesterfield sofas, and there are separate dining areas. Horses can be stabled by prior arrangement. Duchy of Cornwall fishing permits are available for holders of a current NRA licence. ♨Q☕❀🛏◑●P⚐

High Bickington

Golden Lion

North Road, EX37 9BB (on B3217)
⏲ 12-3 (not Sept-Mar), 4.30-11 (closed Tue); 12-11 Sat; 12-10.30 Sun
☎ (01769) 560213
Cotleigh Barn Owl; guest beers 🄷
This 19th-century free house is an inviting place in which to meet the friendly owners and locals. The bar area includes local pictures, books and agricultural tools hanging from the ceiling. Many successful village sports teams are based here, with rows of trophies for darts, skittles and football as evidence. The cider is Sam's Dry from Winkleigh and freshly-prepared food using local produce is served, but there are no lunches in winter and the pub is closed on Tuesday. Q☕◑🚌(377)♣●P

Holcombe

Smugglers Inn

27 Teignmouth Road, EX7 0LA (on A379)
⏲ 11-11; 12-10.30 Sun
☎ (01626) 862301 🌐 thesmugglersinn.net
Draught Bass; Teignworthy Reel Ale; guest beers 🄷
With splendid coastal views, this large roadside free house is run by its owners, has an excellent reputation for food and is popular with all age groups. The bar area has a winter-warming wood-burning stove and the beer policy is to rotate West Country ales with one national brew. An outside area is popular in summer, and has a new smokers' canopy. Families are welcome in a dedicated area, and disabled facilities are excellent. There is a large car park. ♨❀◑♿⛺⇌🚌P⚐

Holcombe Rogus

Prince of Wales

TA21 0PN
⏲ 12-3, 6-11; 12-11 Sat (10.30 Sun)
☎ (01823) 672070
Courage Best Bitter; guest beers 🄷
Seventeenth-century country pub lying close to the Grand Western Canal and the Somerset border, an area popular with walkers and cyclists. Inside, the bar features unusual cash register handpumps. The dining area offers home-cooked meals (not Mon lunchtime), including vegetarian options. A large log-burning stove warms the pub in winter. The pool table and darts area are well used by local teams and a beer festival is held the first

weekend of September. The attractive walled garden is popular in summer. ♨Q◐◑⊞♣P

Holsworthy

Old Market Inn ✔

Chapel Street, EX22 6AY

11-midnight (1am Fri & Sat); 12-11 Sun

☎ (01409) 253941 🌐 oldmarketinn.co.uk

Bays Gold; Skinner's Betty Stogs; guest beers Ⓗ

Friendly, family-run free house that has been completely renovated during the past year. Situated in an historic market town that is mentioned in the Domesday Book, there are normally two guest ales from West Country brewers available all year round and the favoured cider is Autumn Scrumpy from Winkleigh. The restaurant has a relaxed, informal atmosphere where the emphasis is on good-quality locally sourced food. The Sunday carvery is very popular.
❀⊭◐◑♿⊟♣●P⚡–

Rydon Inn

Rydon Road, EX22 7HU (½ mile W of Holsworthy on A3072 Bude road) SS335041

11.30-3, 6-11 (closed Mon winter); 12-3, 6-10.30 Sun (not winter eve)

☎ (01409) 259444 🌐 rydon-inn.com

Sharp's Doom Bar, Own; guest beers Ⓗ

This welcoming gastro pub is housed in an original Devon longhouse just outside the market town of Holsworthy, on the road to Bude. The bar area has a high vaulted-pine beamed ceiling, making it light and airy, with a cosy fire for winter months. It also has a large conservatory restaurant. The food is excellent and families with well-behaved children are welcome – the pub recently won a local 'Best for Families' award.
♨Q❀◐◑♿Å⊟(X9,X90)P⚡–

Honiton

Holt

178 High Street, EX14 1LA

11-3, 5.30-11; 12-4 Sun

☎ (01404) 47707 🌐 theholt-honiton.com

Otter Bitter, Bright, Ale, Head Ⓗ

Otter Brewery's first pub is converted from a former wine bar. A good cosy bar at street level is supplemented with a dining area upstairs; both are smartly decorated, with plenty of exposed wood that adds character. The kitchen is in full view of the clientele and in addition to the regular restaurant food, tapas-style snacks are usually available. Evening meals are not served on Sunday.
⊭◐⇌⊟

Horsebridge

Royal Inn

PL19 8PJ (off A388 Tavistock-Launceston road)

12-3, 7-11 (10.30 Sun)

☎ (01822) 870214 🌐 royalinn.co.uk

Draught Bass; Sharp's Doom Bar; Ⓗ **guest beers** Ⓗ/Ⓖ

Originally built as a nunnery in 1437 by French Benedictine monks, the pub overlooks an old bridge on the River Tamar, connecting Devon to Cornwall. It now features half-panelling and stone floors in the bar and lounge, both traditional in style, with a larger room off the lounge. The terraced gardens are suitable for children, who are welcome until 9pm. The guest beers are usually served on gravity, the food is recommended and bar billiards is played here. ♨Q❀◐◑♣P

Iddesleigh

Duke of York

EX19 8BG (off B3217 next to church) SS570083

11-11 (midnight Fri & Sat); 12-10.30 Sun

☎ (01837) 810253

Adnams Broadside; Cotleigh Tawny; guest beers Ⓖ

You will receive a very warm welcome at this small village pub converted from four builders' cottages and retaining many traditional charms, including a rocking chair by the log fire. It is one of the few remaining pubs where you will find stillage behind the bar and beer straight from the tap. Good food is always available as is the local Sam's Dry cider from Winkleigh. It may seem a little remote but it is well worth seeking out. ♨❀⊭◐◑♣●

Kilmington

New Inn

The Hill, EX13 7SF

11-2.30, 7-11; 11.30-3, 6-11 Sat; 12-4, 7-10.30 Sun

☎ (01297) 33376

Palmer Copper, IPA, seasonal beers Ⓗ

Cosy, thatched Devon longhouse that has appeared in every Guide since 1974 and was sympathetically rebuilt after a major fire in 2004. It retains a warm atmosphere and now boasts excellent toilet facilities. A secluded large garden housing the landlord's aviaries provides interesting outdoor features. The well-used skittle alley (home to 11 local teams), regular quizzes and other events maintain this pub's position at the heart of village life. Good value food is popular with locals. ❀◐◑♣P⚡–

Old Inn ✔

EX13 7RB

11-3, 6-11; 11-11 Fri & Sat summer; 12-3, 7-10.30 Sun

☎ (01297) 32096 🌐 oldinnkilmington.co.uk

Branscombe Vale Branoc; Otter Bitter, Ale; guest beers Ⓗ

Thatched 16th-century inn on the A35 with a cosy bar, lounge with a good log fire and a restaurant area complemented by a sun-trap patio and raised lawn. Food is sourced locally, and the blackboard menu is changed daily. A skittle alley is available to hire for children's parties or other functions when not in use. The new landlord has introduced themed nights, so check the website for information.
♨Q❀◐◑⊞Å⊟P⚡–

Kings Nympton

Grove Inn

EX37 9ST

12-3 (not Mon), 6-11; 12-3, 7-10.30 Sun

☎ (01769) 580406 🌐 thegroveinn.co.uk

Exmoor Ale; guest beers Ⓗ

Seventeenth-century, Grade II-listed thatched pub situated within a picturesque village. The single bar has low beams, bookmarks hanging from the ceiling and an open fire in winter. The locally-sourced food has won various North Devon food and drink awards with Tuesday's fish and chips in Exmoor Ale batter being a particular favourite. The cider is Sam's Dry from Winkleigh. Quiz nights are held on the last Monday of each month. Well-behaved children and dogs are welcome.
♨Q❀◐♣●⁻

Kingston

Dolphin Inn

TQ7 4QE (next to church)
⌚ 12-3, 6-11; 12-3, 7-10 (10.30 summer) Sun
☎ (01548) 810314
Courage Best Bitter; Sharp's Doom Bar; guest beers Ⓗ
A focal point for the local community, this hostelry is popular with tourists during the summer. The main part of the pub was converted from three cottages dating from the 16th century on one side of the road, with further buildings on the other. Open fires in winter blend well with the pleasant low lighting. The food is home cooked with the emphasis on locally-sourced ingredients. The gents' toilet and family room are across the road, as is the garden. ♨☕❀⇌◐♣●P⁻

Kingswear

Ship Inn

Higher Street, TQ6 0AG
⌚ 12-midnight (closed 3.30-6 Mon-Thu winter)
☎ (01803) 752348 🌐 theshipinnkingswear.co.uk
Adnams Bitter; Greene King IPA; Otter Ale; guest beers Ⓗ
This stunning 15th-century village pub remains very much at the heart of the village. Local CAMRA Pub of the Year in 2006, it has a busy, welcoming atmosphere. There are log fires in winter and wonderful views down the River Dart from the outside patio. Quiz nights and live music nights are a regular feature and the restaurant, just two minutes from the quayside, is noted for its fish dishes and steaks. ♨Q❀◐⇌▭⁻

Lake

Bearslake Inn

EX20 4HQ (on A386 between Okehampton and Tavistock) SS528888
⌚ 11-3, 6-11; 12-4 Sun
☎ (01837) 861334 🌐 bearslakeinn.com
Otter Bitter; Teignworthy Old Moggie; guest beers Ⓗ/Ⓖ
This picturesque, Grade II-listed, family-run inn on the edge of Dartmoor is a 13th-century Devon longhouse that was originally a working farm. The bar area is very comfortable, with a flagstone floor and exposed beams. It also has an excellent restaurant offering a menu that changes daily and includes local produce. The pub is situated by the Granite Way, making it ideal for walkers and cyclists, with stunning views of Dartmoor from its delightful garden.
♨Q☕❀⇌◐♿⛺▭(86)♣P⁻

Lutton

Mountain Inn ✔

Old Chapel Road, PL21 9SA
⌚ 12 (6 Tue)-11 Mon, Wed-Sun
☎ (01752) 837247
Dartmoor Jail Ale; guest beers Ⓗ
Two-roomed village pub on the edge of Dartmoor with simple cob walls and real fires in each room. At the bar, the Jail Ale is accompanied by three wide-ranging guest ales and occasional ciders. Additionally, up to eight bottled ciders are also available and 2007 saw the introduction of an annual beer festival. The pub's name is a corruption of a local landowner's family name, Montain. Simple pub food is available daily except Tuesday. ♨Q❀◐●P

Mary Tavy

Elephant's Nest

Horndon, PL19 9LQ
⌚ 12-3, 6.30-11 (10.30 Sun)
☎ (01822) 810273 🌐 elephantsnest.co.uk
Palmer Copper Ale, IPA; guest beers Ⓗ
Formerly the New Inn, this 16th-century pub was intriguingly renamed by a previous landlord and affords magnificent views over Dartmoor. The bar remains traditional despite featuring many elephantine items that include a mural, decorative figures and curios; note the word 'elephant' spelt in many languages on the beams. Two further rooms off the bar are suitable for children. The pub has its own cricket ground and club, with regular fixtures throughout the season. Newly completed overnight accommodation is now available.
♨Q☕❀⇌◐●P

Moretonhampstead

Union Inn

10 Ford Street, TQ13 8LN
⌚ 11 (12 Sun)-11
☎ (01647) 440199 🌐 theunioninn.co.uk
Fuller's London Pride; Wickwar IKB; guest beers Ⓗ
16th-century town-centre free house named after the 1801 Act of Union. Inside, the bar is clad in 19th-century tongue-and-groove panelling and has an adjoining pool room as well as a new air-conditioned function room reached via a corridor displaying many historic artefacts. Food is home cooked, keenly priced and is served all day on Sundays. The outside seating area is next to the small, rear car park.
♨❀◐♿▭♣●P⁻⊓

Mortehoe

Chichester Arms

Chapel Hill, EX34 7DU (next to church)
⌚ 12-3, 6.30-11; 12-11 Sat and summer; 12-10.30 Sun
☎ (01271) 870411
Barum Original; Cottage Somerset & Dorset; Courage Directors; guest beers Ⓗ
Once the old vicarage, this unique 16th-century pub still has gas lighting in the bar. A

popular village free house, it is in a picturesque location with views of Lundy Island and the expansive beaches of Woolacombe Bay nearby. Busy during holiday times, quality food is served daily in summer, Wednesday to Sunday at other times of the year. There is a separate skittle alley and seating at the front of the pub for dining and drinking alfresco. ᗜ❀◑⅄⊟♣P⁓

Newton Abbot

Richard Hopkins ✔

34-42 Queen Street, TQ12 2EW (400m from railway station)
⊙ 9-midnight
☎ (01626) 323930
Greene King Abbot; Marston's Pedigree; guest beers ⊞
Wetherspoon's pub named after a local landowner who sold land to Brunel for the building of the railway. Formerly a linen store, it has a single, rectangular bar divided into separate drinking areas, with prints on the walls depicting local history and Devon heroes. Ten handpumps concentrate on South West breweries including Bays, Cottage and Cotleigh. Children are welcome until 9pm. An unusual covered verandah at the front is for alfresco drinkers and smokers. The cider is Old Rosie. Q❀◑♿⇌⊟●

Union Inn ✔

6 East Street, TQ12 1AF (opp magistrates court)
⊙ 10-11 (midnight Fri & Sat)
☎ (01626) 354775
Draught Bass; Greene King IPA; Sharp's Doom Bar; guest beers ⊞
Named after the final Act of Union with Ireland in 1801, this is a popular town-centre meeting place for both shoppers and regulars, providing a base for local darts, euchre and football teams. Two entrances feed into a horseshoe-shaped bar with two guest beers, one local and one from further afield, plus high quality, good value food made with local produce where possible. Breakfast is served daily from 8.30am. A small outside drinking area on the side pavement is handy for the bus station. ❀⇋◐⇌⊟♣⁓

Wolborough Inn

55 Wolborough Street, TQ12 1JQ
⊙ 12-midnight (11.30 Sun)
☎ (01626) 334511
Teignworthy Reel Ale; guest beers ⊞/⊡
A traditional frontage with etched windows gives way to a modernised interior that retains a relaxed, homely feel where conversation predominates. The emphasis is on comfortable simplicity and most of the original features, including wooden flooring, survive around the L-shaped bar. A recent extension includes an additional drinking area that leads to a split-level outdoor terraced space, covered for smokers. Beers are often from the Teignworthy range, plus other West Country brewers. This pub is well worth seeking out. Q❀⇌⊟♣⁓

Newton St Cyres

Beer Engine

EX5 5AX (N of A377, next to station)
⊙ 11 (12 Sun)-11
☎ (01392) 851282 🌐 thebeerengine.co.uk
Beer Engine Rail Ale, Piston Bitter, Sleeper Heavy, seasonal beers ⊞
Popular village pub and brewery, overlooking the Exeter to Barnstaple Tarka line. The ales on offer reflect the railway theme, as do the pub signs and pictures. The open-plan bar and restaurant have polished wood floors, a roaring fire and ceiling beams adorned with hops, all helping to create a friendly, welcoming atmosphere. Beneath is the brewery with a viewing gallery. Outside, an attractive, secluded patio and barbecue area provides heated shelter for smokers. ⩕Q❀◑♿⇌⊟♣P⁓⊽

North Tawton

Railway Inn

Whiddon Down Road, EX20 2BE (1 mile S of town)
SS666001
⊙ 12-3 (Fri-Sun only), 6 (7 Sun)-11
☎ (01837) 82789
Teignworthy Reel Ale; guest beers ⊞
Friendly, single-bar local that is part of a working farm. The pub stands next to the former North Tawton Station (closed 1971) and the bar decor includes railway memorabilia and old photos of the station. The beer range, although changing regularly, is generally West Country based, as is the cider stocked in summer. The dining room is popular in the evening (no food Thu eve), with light meals served at lunchtime. ⩕◐◑♣●P

Noss Mayo

Ship Inn

PL8 1EW (from Bridgend take Stoke road)
⊙ 11-11; 12-10.30 Sun
☎ (01752) 872387 🌐 nossmayo.com
Dartmoor IPA, Jail Ale; Summerskills Tamar ⊞
If you wish to sail to the pub, ring first to ascertain the tide table and moorings. Otherwise use dry land to visit this charming pub on the bank of the River Yealm, where comfortable seating allows you to savour both the local beers and locally-sourced food (served all day). This former Plymouth CAMRA Pub of the Year is a good start and finish point for walks around the coast and estuary. A daytime bus service operates Monday to Saturday. ⩕Q❀◑♿⊟(94)P⁓

Oakford

Red Lion

Rookery Hill, EX16 9ES
⊙ 12-2.30 (closed Mon & Tue winter), 6-11; 12-3, 6-10.30 Sun
☎ (01398) 351219 🌐 theredlionhoteloakford.co.uk
Dartmoor IPA; Otter Ale ⊞
Welcoming free house set in a quiet village in undulating countryside on the fringes of Exmoor. The main bar features a large inglenook fireplace, and excellent value food is served in a separate dining room. Two real

ales are complemented by Weston's cider. A small car park and garden area can be found across the road. Overnight accommodation comprises four comfortable en-suite rooms, including one with a four-poster bed.
⛼☕❀⊏◑⛺♣●P

Okehampton

Plymouth Inn

26 West Street, EX20 1HH SX586951

❂ 11-midnight

☎ (01837) 53633

Beer range varies 🄶

Old market town inn situated at the west end of town by the West Okement river bridge, with the welcoming atmosphere of a village local. It is friendly and simply furnished with two beer festivals held anually, usually in May and November. The latter coincides with the Ten Tors challenge on Dartmoor. Good food and bar snacks are always available and the cider is Sam's from Winkleigh. The beer range is mainly West Country and straight from the tap. ☕❀◑⊟♣●⁻

Paignton

Isaac Merritt

54-58 Torquay Road, TQ3 3AA

❂ 9-midnight

☎ (01803) 556066

Bays Gold; Courage Directors; Greene King Abbot; Marston's Pedigree; guest beers 🄷

Busy and popular town-centre Wetherspoon's pub with a splendid reputation for its ever-changing guest beers, augmented by mini beer festivals on Sunday and Monday. All ages enjoy the cosy alcove seating that helps to create comfortable, friendly surroundings. Good value meals are available all day in this former local Camra Pub of the Year and Wetherspoon's award winner. There is easy access for wheelchair users who have a designated ground-floor toilet. ◑♿⇌⊟●

Petrockstowe

Laurels Inn

EX20 3HJ (1 mile W of A386) SS512091

❂ 11 (12 Sun)-midnight; 12-3, 6-midnight (closed Mon) winter

☎ (01837) 810578 🌐 petrockstowe.co.uk/laurels.html

St Austell Tribute; Sharp's Doom Bar; guest beers 🄷

Seventeenth-century coaching house set in an historic village with links to the Civil War. Over time it has been a magistrates court and a home for fallen women of the parish, but new occupiers have undertaken a complete renovation. The large single bar with pool table takes up most of the pub with a cosy restaurant area to one side. Up to three real ales are available and the cider is Autumn Scrumpy from Winkleigh. ❀◑●P

Plymouth

Artillery Arms

6 Pound Street, Stonehouse, PL1 3RH

❂ 11 (10 Sat)-11; 12-10.30 Sun

☎ (01752) 262515

Draught Bass; guest beers 🄷

This corner pub at the rear of the Brittany Ferries terminal has a single bar plus a dining area where good value, home-cooked food is served (except on Sunday). It is very much a community pub, sponsoring charity fundraising events including monkey races and an annual Beach Party in February. Although not the easiest pub to locate in the back streets of Stonehouse, the effort is well rewarded by a warm and friendly welcome.
⛼Q◑⊟●

Blue Peter

68 Pomphlett Road, Plymstock, PL9 7BN

❂ 11-11; 12.30-10.30 Sun

☎ (01752) 402255

Beer range varies 🄷/🄶

In a part of Plymouth where real ale is scarce, this pub has twice been voted local CAMRA Pub of the Year. The public bar has a large-screen TV for sports events, and a games area which is also used for live entertainment. In the lounge, alcove seating is next to the main dining area (no food served Monday or Tuesday); Sunday roasts are a speciality and beer festivals are held occasionally. A patio garden is at the rear. ⛼Q❀◑⊟⊟♣P⁻

Boringdon Arms

13 Boringdon Terrace, Turnchapel, PL9 9TQ

❂ 11 (12 Sun)-midnight

☎ (01752) 402053 🌐 bori.co.uk

Draught Bass; Butcombe Bitter; RCH Pitchfork; Sharp's Doom Bar; South Hams Plymouth Pride; Summerskills Devon Dew; guest beers 🄷

This is a light, airy, waterside pub, popular with locals and walkers using the South West Coastal Path. The Bori, local CAMRA Pub of the Year 2007, is well served by road as well as water taxis from the Barbican to Mountbatten Pier. Beer festivals are held on the last weekend of odd-numbered months. The pub has a good reputation for home-cooked food which may be enjoyed alfresco in the garden planted up in the former quarry.
⛼Q☕❀⊏◑⊟⊟♣⁻

Britannia ✔

1 Wolseley Road, Milehouse, PL2 3AA

❂ 9am-midnight (1am Fri & Sat)

☎ (01752) 607596

Greene King Abbot; Marston's Burton Bitter, Pedigree; Shepherd Neame Spitfire; guest beers 🄷

A popular, busy local created by Wetherspoon from a rundown Edwardian pub, which serves its community well. The closest pub to Home Park, football supporters supplement a mixed clientele on match days. However, there is a friendly atmosphere at all times. The pub is situated on a busy crossroads within walking distance of Stoke village. Guest beers include selections from local brewery Summerskills and other south west brewers, plus cider from Weston's. ⛼Q❀◑♿⇌⊟●⁻

China House

Sutton Wharf, Sutton Harbour, PL4 0DW

❂ 11-11 (10.30 Sun)

☎ (01752) 661592

Butcombe Bitter; Marston's Pedigree; St Austell Tribute 🄷

Formerly a china clay warehouse, this large stone buildilng is situated on the edge of Sutton Harbour, with views of the Barbican and marina. The vast interior has been subdivided by large wooden posts and beams into smaller, more intimate areas. Two balconies overlook the harbour, the lower one serving as a smoking area. There is also a large patio area. Food is available all day.

Clifton

35 Clifton Street, Greenbank, PL4 8JB
11-11.30 (12.30am Fri); 12-12.30am Sat; 12-11.30 Sun
(01752) 266563 cliftonpub.com
Dartmoor Jail Ale; Sharp's Doom Bar; Summerskills Clifton Classic; guest beers H
Clifton Classic is the house beer prepared by local brewer Summerskills for this spacious back-street local not far from the city centre. The warm and friendly pub plays host to many competitive teams including darts, euchre and pool. The Clifton was once considered to be the luckiest pub in Britain, as it numbered no fewer than three National Lottery millionaires among its regulars. Two large-screen TVs provide entertainment, especially for major rugby matches. A large heated patio area is also provided.

Clovelly Bay Inn

11 Boringdon Terrace, Turnchapel, PL9 9TB
11-3, 6-11 Mon-Sat; 12-4, 7-10:30 Sun
(01752) 402765 clovellybayinn.co.uk
Beer range varies H
Family-run free house situated on the waterfront of the historic fishing village of Turnchapel. It offers a mother and baby room, free jukebox and use of a piano. The pub is renowned for many special events taking place throughout the year, together with a diverse menu including traditional Eastern dishes and Sunday roasts. The Clovelly relishes the opportunity to offer more uncommon beers upon request, as well as stocking over 30 varieties of whisky. Only very limited parking is available.

Dolphin Hotel

14 The Barbican, PL1 2LS
10-11 (midnight Fri & Sat); 11-11 Sun
(01752) 660876
Draught Bass G
No visit to the Barbican is complete without visiting the Dolphin Hotel. This unpretentious hostelry is where the Tolpuddle Martyrs stayed on their return to England. The interior is minimalist, but you are assured of a wealth of conversation with some of the colourful regulars. The Bass is served from very large barrels behind the bar. Well-behaved dogs are welcome and an attractive fireplace completes the scene. Look out for the old Octagon Brewery logos on the front windows.

Fawn Private Members Club

39 Prospect Street, Greenbank, PL4 8NY
2 (12 Sat)-11; 12-10.30 Sun
(01752) 660540 thefawnclub.co.uk
Courage Best Bitter; Sharp's Fawn Ale; guest beers H
Named after the now-scrapped HMS Fawn, the club welcomes CAMRA members with a current valid membership card, although regular visitors will be required to join. Many of the members live locally and are keen followers of rugby and other televised sports, are members of darts, pool and euchre teams, or simply enjoy the friendly ambience and reasonable prices. Two guest ales are usually available as well as Sam's real cider from Winkleigh. The covered smoking area is on the patio.

Fishermans Arms

31 Lambhay Street, PL1 2NN
12 (5 Mon winter)-11; 12-10.30 Sun
(01752) 661457
St Austell Tinners, Tribute, HSD; guest beers H
Reputed to be the second oldest pub in Plymouth, hidden away behind the famous Barbican, the Fishermans Arms has a warm and friendly atmosphere. It is popular with locals who head for the lively public bar with its dartboard and pool table. Visitors generally settle in the lounge, which has a raised seating area at the rear. The three St Austell beers are occasionally supplemented by another from the same brewery. Home-cooked Sunday roasts are a speciality.

Fortescue

37 Mutley Plain, Mutley, PL4 6JQ
11-11; 12-10.30 Sun
(01752) 660673 fortescueonline.co.uk
Butcombe Bitter; Greene King Abbot; guest beers H
This lively local where conversation flourishes is frequented by a broad section of the community. On Thursday the popular cellar bar hosts an acoustic evening, and at weekends various alternative DJs play anything but chart music. The patio beer garden draws crowds in the summer and is heated in winter. Look out for the interesting cricket memorabilia which adorns the walls. Up to three guest beers are available, as well as a real cider from Thatchers.

Lounge

7 Stopford Place, Devonport, PL1 4QT
11.30-3 (not Mon), 6-11 (midnight Fri); 11.30-11 Sat; 12-11 Sun
(01752) 561330
Draught Bass; guest beers H
A stone's throw from Devonport Park, this street-corner local is a haven in a part of the city where real ale is increasingly scarce. Good food is served at lunchtime and attracts local workers during the week. The pub can be particularly busy on Saturday, with Plymouth Albion RFC's Brickfields ground nearby. The two guest beers typically vary in strength: one higher and one lower ABV. Children are welcome for lunch. Q (Devonport)

Prince Maurice

3 Church Hill, Eggbuckland, PL6 5RJ
11-3, 7-11; 11-11 Fri & Sat; 12-10.30 Sun
(01752) 771515
Adnams Broadside; Courage Best Bitter; O'Hanlon's Royal Oak; St Austell HSD; Sharp's Doom Bar; Summerskills Best Bitter; guest beers H

This four-times winner of local CAMRA Pub of the Year sits between the church and village green in what was once a village but is now a suburb of Plymouth. It still maintains a village pub atmosphere in both bars and continues to offer eight beers plus Thatchers Cheddar Valley cider. The pub is named after the Royalist General, the King's nephew, who had his headquarters nearby during the Civil War siege of Plymouth. Food is not available at weekends.

Thistle Park Brewhouse

32 Commercial Road, Coxside, PL4 0LE

11-2am; 12-12.30am Sun

(01752) 204890

South Hams Devon Pride, XSB, Sutton Comfort, Eddystone, seasonal beers H

Friendly, convenient pub, recently refurbished to a high standard, which can be reached via the swing bridge from the Barbican. A new restaurant on the first floor features authentic Thai cuisine. All real ales are from South Hams Brewery, which was the former Sutton Brewery located adjacent to the pub. A good alternative to the branded outlets in the nearby Barbican Leisure Park, the pub is also close to the National Marine Aquarium.

Yard Arm

159 Citadel Road, The Hoe, PL1 2HU

12-midnight

(01752) 202405 yardarmplymouth.co.uk

Beer range varies H

Busy street corner pub just behind the famous Plymouth Hoe and within easy walking distance of the Barbican and city centre. Home-cooked food is served alongside up to four real ales from national and local breweries. Accommodation is supplemented by nearby guest houses and hotels. The decor features marine memorabilia and wood panelling, while the raised naturally-lit seating and lower deck add to the nautical ambience. A large-screen TV for live sports is an added bonus.

Postbridge

Warren House Inn

PL20 6TA (on B3212, 2 miles NE of Postbridge)

11-11 (5 Mon & Tue winter); 11 (12 winter)-10.30 Sun

(01822) 880208 warrenhouseinn.co.uk

Otter Ale; Summerskills Tamar; guest beers H

Isolated and exposed at 1425ft above sea level, this pub is indeed a welcome sight. The interior features exposed beams, wood panelling, rustic benches and tables, and the famous fire. Lunch and evening menus offer home-cooked dishes made with locally sourced ingredients including Dartmoor beef, plus vegetarian options. There is a large family room and tables outside with breathtaking views over the moors. Countryman cider is available, with carryouts; guest beers vary with the seasons and usually include one strong ale. QP

Princetown

Plume of Feathers

The Square, PL20 6QG

10.30-midnight (11 Sun)

(01822) 890240 smoothhound.co.uk/hotels/plume.html

Dartmoor Dartmoor IPA, Jail Ale; St Austell Tribute, HSD H

Princetown's oldest building (built in 1785), this pub features granite walls, slate floors and slate-topped tables. A later addition is the large family/function room with its own bar. Food is served here all day, with a carvery at weekend lunchtimes. There is a spacious patio and children's play area, large car park, campsite and camping barn. Breakfast is available from 7.30am.

QP

Prince of Wales

Tavistock Road, PL20 6QF (opp Dartmoor Prison)

11 (10.30 Sun)-11

(01822) 890219

Dartmoor Dartmoor IPA, Jail Ale; guest beers H

Just down the road from the main square, this pub is regarded as the brewery tap for Princetown Brewery, which has relocated from the pub to premises nearby. There is a main bar with a small pool and darts area leading off it. The function room provides additional dining space at busy times and also doubles as a skittle alley. Children are welcome and the food is recommended. The terminus of the Yelverton-Princetown cycle route is situated behind the pub. P

Ringmore

Journey's End

Near Kingsbridge, TQ7 4HL SX650460

12-3, 6-11, closed Mon; 12-3, 6-10.30 Sun

(01548) 810205

Sharp's Doom Bar; H **guest beers** G

This 13th-century Inn takes its name from Sherriff's famous play 'Journey's End', which he started writing while staying here. Up to five beers are available on gravity behind the bar in summer, three in winter, and bottled Belgian beers are always available. In addition there is cottage accommodation, a separate lounge and dining room, and a menu that changes daily and caters for children. Dogs are always welcome at this cosy village pub and a car park is 200m away opposite All Hallows Church. P

Sandford

Lamb Inn

The Square, EX17 4LW

9-midnight; 11-11 Sun

(01363) 773676 lambinnsandford.co.uk

Palmer Copper Ale; Roosters Yankee; H **guest beers** G

This 16th-century genuine free house is in the centre of the village and enjoys a traditional, inviting atmosphere. It is popular for both its beer and food and is well supported by both local and city folk. Although food does not dominate, the menu is varied and comprises local and organic produce wherever possible. Skittles is played four nights a week in the alley and there are regular themed nights, including live music and open mic comedy evenings. Sandford Orchard Farmhouse cider is available. ♨❀◑🚌♣●

Seaton

King's Arms

55 Fore Street, EX12 2AN
⏲ 11-3, 6-midnight; 11-midnight Sat; 12-10.30 Sun
☎ (01297) 23431
Branscombe Vale Branoc, Best Bitter [H]
Busy local out of the touristy town centre, located in what was the original fishing village of Seaton. The bar is one big room where very popular reasonably-priced food is available every lunchtime and evening except Sunday. There is a separate restaurant where children are welcome, and a big garden is hidden from the road, with good views over the Axe estuary. ❀◑🚌⌐

Shaldon

Clifford Arms

34 Fore Street, TQ14 0DE
⏲ 11-2.30, 5-11.30; 12-3, 6-11 Sun
☎ (01626) 872311
Dartmoor Dartmoor IPA; Greene King Abbot; Ringmore Craft Oarsome; guest beers [H]
Village centre pub with an attractive, modern interior and a warming log fire in winter. This is the only draught outlet for the local Ringmore Craft Brewery, with guest and seasonal beers sourced mainly from West Country breweries. The low-level restaurant area at the rear serves good quality food every day and leads out onto a sunny, decked patio. Special menus are available on modern jazz evenings on Monday, monthly trad jazz sessions on Sunday lunchtime, and Thursday charity quiz nights. ♨❀◑⌐

Shebbear

Devil's Stone Inn

EX21 5RU
⏲ 12-3, 6-11; 12-11 Fri & Sat; 12-10.30 Sun
☎ (01409) 281210 🌐 devilsstoneinn.com
Sharp's Special; guest beers [H]
A warm welcome awaits at this 17th-century coaching inn situated at the heart of the village square. In the church opposite, you will find the Devil's Stone that is turned every year on 5th November to ward off evil spirits. The single bar has a flagstone floor, open fire and comfortable armchairs for a cosy atmosphere. Sam's Cider from Winkleigh is available in summer, there is a games room and a separate dining room.
♨❀🛏◑♿🚌(72)♣●P⌐

Sidford

Blue Ball Inn

Trow Hill, EX10 9QL
⏲ 8-11
☎ (01395) 514062 🌐 blueballinn.net
Draught Bass; Greene King Abbot; Otter Bitter; St Austell Tribute; guest beers [H]
This pub dates back to 1385 and has been in same family since 1912. The original cob and flint building was totally destroyed by fire in 2006. It was sympathetically rebuilt in 2007 and given a new thatched roof. The main bar has a large fireplace, there is a food bar and extensive dining areas where good value, locally-sourced food is served. Overnight accommodation comprises eight en-suite rooms and outside is a large car park and colourful gardens. ♨Q🛏◑🚌P

Sidmouth

Swan Inn

37 York Street, EX10 8BY
⏲ 11-2.30 (3 Sat), 5.30-11; 12-3, 7-10.30 Sun
☎ (01395) 512849
Young's Bitter, Special; guest beers [H]
This traditional and quiet back-street inn, established around 1770, lies just off the centre of this quaint town, a short walk from the seafront and bus terminus. A cosy, old-style wood-panelled bar with an open fire attracts a strong local trade and leads to a dedicated dining area. Three beers, all from the Wells & Young's range, are normally available and various sports teams are supported. Dogs, but not children, are welcome indoors. ♨Q❀◑♿🚌♣⌐

Silverton

Lamb Inn

Fore Street, EX5 4HZ
⏲ 11.30-2.30, 6-11 (1am Thu; 2am Fri); 11.30-2am Sat; 12-11 Sun
☎ (01392) 860272
Exe Valley Dob's Best Bitter; guest beers [G]
Family-run village pub with stone floors, stripped timber and old pine furniture inside, plus a few covered tables outside. Three or more ales are served by gravity from a temperature-controlled stillage behind the bar. A multi-purpose function room plus skittle alley and bar is well used by local teams. Good value home-cooked food is served, together with popular Sunday roasts and a specials board which changes weekly. ♨❀◑🚌♣⌐

Slapton

Queen's Arms

TQ7 2PN
⏲ 12-3, 6-11 (7-10.30 Sun)
☎ (01548) 580800 🌐 slapton.org/queensarms
Otter Bitter; Teignworthy Reel Ale; guest beers [H]
Although Sandra and Kevin have run this free house for years they only became the owners in 2007. A large open fire welcomes you in the bar, with old photographs on the walls depicting the wartime evacuation. A beer festival is held every March and a full food menu includes a take-away service. Sunday lunchtime roasts and fish and chips specials on Friday are worth booking up for. There is a large flower-filled garden and children are made very welcome. ♨❀◑⛺🚌♣P

South Brent

Royal Oak

Station Road, TQ10 9BE

12-11 (11.45 Fri & Sat)
(01364) 72133 royaloaksouthbrent.co.uk
Teignworthy Reel Ale, Beachcomber; guest beers H
Busy village-centre pub on the edge of Dartmoor. The main L-shaped bar is surrounded by a large open plan area with comfortable, relaxing leather settees, while the wood-panelled bar is the place for an excellent range of real ales. At the rear a restaurant serves good quality food and a new function room can be found upstairs. There is a no-smoking courtyard outside and accommodation has recently been added. Occasional beer festivals are held at this 2007 local CAMRA Pub of the Year.

South Molton

Town Arms Hotel
124 East Street, EX36 3BU (100m E of main square)
11-midnight (1am Fri & Sat); 12-midnight Sun
(01769) 572531
Draught Bass; Sharp's Doom Bar; guest beers H
Main street local near the centre of this small, historic market town which is ideally situated for exploring Exmoor and North Devon. There is one main bar containing a pool table, an open fire and a back room. The pub can get very lively on occasions with friendly locals, particularly on Thursday which is market day. Up to three real ales are available, with the ever-changing guest beer a West Country one. Skittles and shove ha'penny are also played here.

Spreyton

Tom Cobley Tavern
EX17 5AL (on A3124)
12-3, 6-midnight (6.30-11 Mon); 12-3, 6-1am Fri & Sat; 12-3, 7-11 Sun
(01647) 231314
Clearwater Cavalier; Cotleigh Tawny; Otter Ale; St Austell Tribute, Proper Job; H **guest beers** H/G
Still riding high on the success of winning National CAMRA Pub of the Year in 2006, the pub attracts visitors from all over the country who come to witness the remarkable turnover of up to 22 ales at any one time, mainly on gravity. This 16th-century village inn always gives a warm welcome in the homely bar and spacious dining room. The beers are great, but so is the wonderful home-cooked food and extensive menu. Booking is advisable, especially for Sunday lunch.

Sticklepath

Taw River Inn
EX20 2NW (SX641941)
12-midnight (11 Sun)
(01837) 840377 tawriver.co.uk
Draught Bass; Greene King Abbot; Sharp's Doom Bar; St Austell Tribute; guest beers H
A lively pub in an active village, this is a past winner of North Devon CAMRA Pub of the Year 2005 and 2006. It has a relaxed, friendly atmosphere where families and pets are more than welcome. Good food is served and the real ales are available at attractive prices. Well situated with access to Dartmoor and the nearby Tarka Trail and Dartmoor Way, it is a convenient watering hole for walkers.
(X9,X30)

Stokenham

Tradesman's Arms
TQ7 2SZ (250m from A379)
11-11 (11.30-3, 6-11 winter); 11.30-11 Sun
(01548) 580313 thetradesmansarms.com
Brakspear Bitter; Sharp's Doom Bar; South Hams Eddystone, Knickadroppa Glory; guest beers H
Popular with locals, this pleasant free house in the South Hams is reputed to be 600 years old and features beamed ceilings and a real fire. This quiet pub is the perfect place to savour beers from the nearby South Hams Brewery; inter-connecting rooms off the bar provide ample seating and tables. The landlord previously ran a pub in the Chilterns, hence the Brakspear connection. An extensive choice of good pub food is available.

Talaton

Talaton Inn
EX5 2RQ
12-3, 7-11 (10.30 Sun)
(01404) 822214
Otter Bitter; guest beers H
This family-run free house is an excellent example of a traditional village country pub. The 16th-century building has a good-sized bar frequented by locals and a separate lounge with dining area (booking recommended). Meals are good value (not served Sun or Mon eve), with lunchtime specials and offers for senior citizens. The large skittle alley adjoining the bars is very popular. At least two guest beers are available, generally from local breweries.

Tavistock

Trout & Tipple
Parkwood Road, PL19 0JS
12-2.30 (not Tue), 6-11; 12-2.30, 6-10.30 (7-10.30 winter) Sun
(01822) 618886 troutandtipple.co.uk
Dartmoor Jail Ale; guest beers H
Just a mile north of Tavistock, close to a trout fishery, this friendly hostelry features a traditional hop-draped bar plus a large conservatory, games room and patio. Seasonal beers from Teignworthy and two changing ciders are served and the ceiling features a plethora of pump clips from past guest ales. Beer festivals are staged in February and October, with frequent single-brewery events in between. CAMRA Branch Pub of the Year 2008.

Topsham

Bridge Inn ★
Bridge Hill, EX3 0QQ (by River Clyst)
12-2, 6-10.30 (11 Fri & Sat); 12-2, 7-10.30 Sun
(01392) 873862 cheffers.co.uk

Beer range varies Ⓖ
Typical 16th-century ale house trading on traditional ideals and a true gem, run by 50 generations of family owners celebrating 111 years in residence. Up to nine gravity-fed ales are served direct from the cellar, in third pints on request. It was here 10 years ago that the Queen paid her only official UK pub visit. Limited bar snacks are available lunchtimes only. Sit in the cosy snug or outside overlooking the quiet tidal reaches of the River Clyst and pastureland beyond.
⩕Q❀⇌⊟P

Exeter Inn

68 High Street, EX3 0DY
⏲ 11.30-11, 11-midnight Fri & Sat; 12-10.30 Sun
☎ (01392) 873131
Teignworthy Beachcomber; guest beers Ⓗ
Popular 17th-century former coaching house, well supported by the rugby club and locals alike. The landlord is a keen real ale enthusiast and sources his guest beers from all over the UK; Thatchers cider is also on offer. A large-screen TV shows major sporting events. Note that sparklers on all three handpumps can be removed on request. ⩕♨⊭♿⩘⇌⊟♣●⚟

Globe Hotel

Fore Street, EX3 0HR
⏲ 11-11 (midnight Fri & Sat); 12-11 Sun
☎ (01392) 873471 ⊕ globehotel.com
Butcombe Bitter; Fuller's London Pride; Otter Ale; Sharp's Doom Bar; St Austell IPA; guest beers Ⓗ
Originally a 17th-century coaching house, this atmospheric, genuine free house retains its historic feel, situated in the centre of town not far from the quay. The interior of wooden beams and panelling is warm and welcoming, with a good range of five ales available, plus guests. The restaurant offers good traditional English food made with locally-sourced produce. The popular Topsham folk club is held on Sunday evening, while the malt house is available for functions and skittles.
Q♨❀⊭◐◑⊞⇌⊟⚟

Torquay

Buccaneer Inn ✔

43 Babbacombe Downs Road, TQ1 3LN
⏲ 12 (11 Sat)-11 (midnight Fri & Sat summer); 11-11 Sun
☎ (01803) 312661
St Austell Tribute, HSD Ⓗ
Busy, popular St Austell pub with sea views overlooking clifftop gardens. The single, spacious bar is wood panelled with a separate area for pool and darts. The forecourt provides extra space outside and an upstairs function room is available. Home-cooked food is served all year. It is a short walk from the cliff railway and the model village to the pub, while the steep descent to Babbacombe beach is nearby. ❀◐◑♿♣⚟

Crown & Sceptre ✔

2 Petitor Road, St Marychurch, TQ1 4QA
⏲ 12-4, 5.30-11; 12-midnight Fri; 12-4, 6.30-midnight Sat; 12-4, 7-11.30 Sun
☎ (01803) 328290
Badger Tanglefoot; Courage Best Bitter; Fuller's London Pride; Greene King Old Speckled Hen; St Austell Tribute; Young's Special; guest beers Ⓗ
A 200-year-old coaching house with over 30 years of unbroken entries in this Guide while under the stewardship of the same landlord. A collection of chamberpots and pennants plus a real fire lend character inside, while outside there are two small enclosed gardens. This well-supported community pub, with six regular beers and three guests, supports live music, with jazz on Tuesday evening and folk on Friday. Food is served lunchtimes, Monday to Saturday. ⩕Q❀◐⊞♣P

Hesketh Arms ✔

31-33 Meadfoot Lane, TQ1 2BW
⏲ 4 (12 Sat & Sun)-11
☎ (01803) 393478
Beer range varies Ⓗ
This 170-year-old pub reopened in 2006 after a refurbishment which gave it a smart, modern and comfortable interior but retained its traditional welcome and ambience in the single bar. Formerly known as the Stumble Inn, it usually serves four real ales, mainly from south west breweries. A separate room at the rear has a dartboard and pool table.
⊟♣

Hole in the Wall

6 Park Lane, TQ1 2AU
⏲ 12-midnight
☎ (01803) 200755 ⊕ hole-in-the-wall.co.uk
Greene King IPA; Sharp's Doom Bar; Shepherd Neame Spitfire; Theakston Mild; guest beers Ⓗ
Close to, but tucked away from the harbour, this is Torquay's oldest inn (circa 1540). A real ale haven in the town centre with beamed ceilings and cobbled floors, it is popular with seafarers, businessmen, holidaymakers and locals. The busy and roomy restaurant serves highly regarded food. The narrow passageway outside, adorned with floral displays, makes a pleasant alfresco drinking area. Dogs on leads are welcome. Q❀◐◑⊟⚟

Totnes

Bay Horse Inn

8 Cistern Street, TQ9 5SP
⏲ 12-2 (summer only), 6-11.30; 12-2, 5-11.30 Fri & Sat; 12-3, 7-11.30 Sun
☎ (01803) 862088 ⊕ bayhorsetotnes.com
Dartmoor Jail Ale; Otter Bitter; Sharp's Doom Bar; guest beers Ⓗ
Originally a 15th-century coaching inn, complete with ghosts, then a 19th-century smugglers' haunt; now a traditional, roomy town pub with an old-fashioned snug and a surprisingly large garden with a heated patio. It is popular with locals and visitors alike and hosts Irish folk music on Tuesday night, jazz on the last Sunday of the month and regular quiz nights. Good home-cooked food and quality B&B are available at this local CAMRA Pub of the Year 2008. Q♨❀⊭◐◑⊟⚟

Tuckenhay

Maltsters Arms

Bow Creek, TQ9 7EQ

11-11
(01803) 732350 tuckenhay.com
Dartmoor Dartmoor IPA; guest beers H
Overlooking the peaceful Bow Creek, this lovely old pub comprises two snug rooms, linked by a long, narrow bar. The pub holds barbecues on the quay in summer and has a good reputation for innovative pub grub. Boats can moor on the tidal River Dart, and there is occasional live music on Friday evenings. Beers are sourced mainly from West Country breweries and a mini beer is festival held in June. Accommodation is discounted for CAMRA members. Q P

Uplyme

Talbot Arms

Lyme Road, DT7 3TF
11-2.30 (not Mon & Tue), 6-11; 11-11 Sat & Sun
(01297) 443136 talbotarms.com
Beer range varies H
A friendly pub just inside the county border named after Admiral Sir John Talbot. It has a cosy lounge area and separate dining space, with a games/family room downstairs leading to the large garden. Food is popular but not always available on weekday lunchtimes out of season – ring to check. Sunday lunch is a carvery and Tuesday night is fish and chips, with take-out too. A beer festival is held in July. Q P

Wembury

Wembury Club ✔

99 Southland Park Road, PL9 0HH
7.30 (12 Sun)-midnight
(01752) 862159 wemburyclub.co.uk
Beer range varies H
CAMRA members and their families are very welcome at the Wembury. As a Cask Club of Great Britain finalist, it offers constantly-changing guest beers and cider rarely available elsewhere in the region. The management relishes the opportunity to obtain more unusual beers on request, while the walls display a vast collection of pump clips indicating the popularity of the proprietor's choice.
Q P

Westcott

Merry Harriers

EX15 1SA (on B3181, 2 miles S of Cullompton)
12-3, 6-11.30 (12.30am Fri & Sat)
(01392) 881254
Exmoor Ale; O'Hanlon's Yellowhammer; guest beers H
Traditional Devon hostelry with a friendly and welcoming atmosphere. The lounge bar is cosy with a log fire, beamed ceiling and an archway leading to the dining area where children are welcome. The pub is a winner of one of only two silver medals in the Taste of the West pub-dining category. There is seating outside, a skittle alley, spacious car park, and accommodation at the rear of the pub.
Q P

Whimple

New Fountain Inn

Church Road, EX5 2TA
12-3, 6.30-11 (7-10.30 Sun)
(01404) 822350
O'Hanlon's Firefly; Teignworthy Reel Ale; guest beer G
Small, friendly two-bar local in a lovely village, converted from cottages around 1890. A genuine free house, this pub has been owned by the current licensees for 18 years. The handpumps are not in use; ale is fetched from the cellar and there is usually one guest beer from a local brewery. Good value home-cooked food is served daily. A village heritage centre is in the car park. Q P

Widecombe in the Moor

Rugglestone Inn

TQ13 7TF (¼ mile from village centre) SX721760
11.30-3, 6-12.30; 11.30-12.30 Sat; 12-11.30 Sun
(01364) 621327
Butcombe Bitter; St Austell Dartmoor Best; guest beer G
Unspoilt, cosy pub in a splendid Dartmoor setting. The small bar area has seating and a stone floor with beer served through a hatch in the passageway. An open fire warms the lounge. Across the stream is a large grassed seating area with a shelter for bad weather. A wide selection of home-cooked food is available and children are welcome.
Q P

Winkleigh

Seven Stars

High Street, EX19 8HX
4-11; 12-midnight Mon, Fri & Sat; 12-11 Sun
(01837) 83344
Otter Bitter; guest beers H
Community-oriented local in a picturesque village – darts, skittles and pool teams are all based here. The single bar has an open fire, seating area, TV, dartboard and raised area with a pool table that is removed for regular entertainment events. The rear terraced patio includes a skittle alley and barbecue for summer use. A beer festival is held in October. Bar snacks are available. (315)

Woolacombe

Red Barn ✔

Barton Road, EX34 7DF (opp beach car park)
11-11
(01271) 870264
St Austell Tribute, HSD; guest beers H
This used to be a café and from the outside it still looks like one. But inside is a welcoming establishment serving superb food in good-sized portions. Four real ales are available, with one pump devoted solely to Devon beers that change weekly. A small beer festival is held in December. Inside there is a fine display of surf boards and local live music is regularly supported. (3B,303)

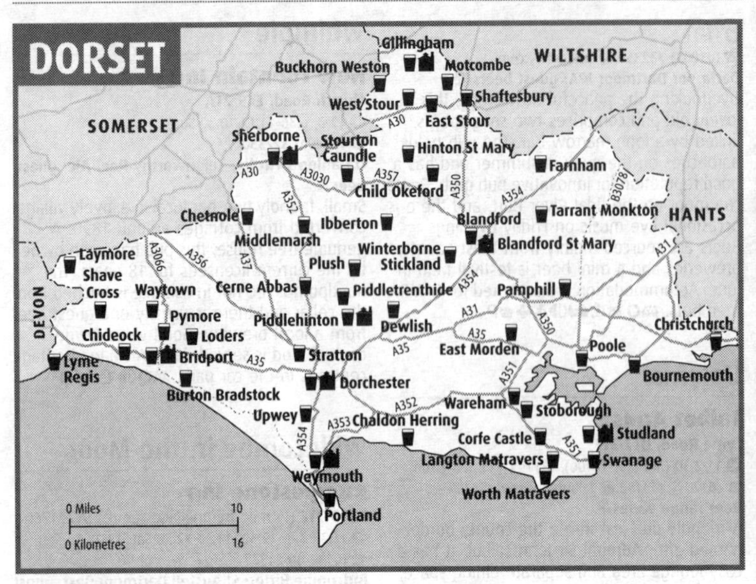

Blandford

Dolphin

42 East Street, DT11 7DR
⌚ 11.30-3, 5.15-11; 11.30-11 Wed; 11.30-midnight Thu-Sat; 12-11 Sun
☎ (01258) 456813
Caledonian Deuchars IPA; Fuller's London Pride; Ringwood Best Bitter; St Austell Tribute; Sharp's Doom Bar; John Smith's Bitter; Taylor Landlord; Theakston Old Peculier Ⓗ
Cosy, split level local pub with an authentic, old-fashioned character. Six ales are always on handpump. The quiet bar hosts games nights and is very popular with locals and visitors alike. An extensive range of good quality, value-for-money pub meals and chef's specials are served Monday-Thursday, and the traditional roast lunch is a highlight on Sunday. An extensive range of single malt whiskies is an added attraction.

Railway ✔

Oakfield Street, DT11 7EX (off B3082)
⌚ 11-3am
☎ (01258) 456374
Badger First Gold; Ringwood Best Bitter; guest beer Ⓗ
Lively community back-street local in the heart of Blandford. The Railway hosts numerous darts, pool and shove ha'penny teams and even has its own Facebook fan group. Good food is served well into the evening, four local ales are always available and there is a beer festival every May bank holiday. Games machines and TVs dominate — this is a pub for watching sport, enjoying regular live bands or taking part in karaoke accompanied by a good pint.

Bournemouth

Cricketers Arms

41 Windham Road, BH1 4RN
⌚ 11-11; 12-10.30 Sun
☎ (01202) 551589
Fuller's London Pride; guest beer Ⓗ
Traditional Victorian community pub dating from 1847. This is the oldest pub in Bournemouth and retains some impressive original features. The lounge bar, a vaulted stable, was once the boxing gym for the legendary Freddie Mills. Two guest beers are on offer and shove ha'penny is played. The 'Cricks' is dog friendly, offers live entertainment and hosts a Tuesday quiz night.

Goat & Tricycle ✔

27-29 West Hill Road, BH2 5PF
⌚ 12-11 (11.30 Fri & Sat)
☎ (01202) 314220
Wadworth IPA, 6X, JCB, seasonal beers; guest beers Ⓗ
Recently refurbished, the Goat has an impressive line of handpumps serving the full Wadworth range, complemented by seven ever-changing guest beers. An interesting selection of walking sticks adorns the ceiling of the main bar in this split-level pub. Good value, hearty food is served every day, and roasts on Sunday.

Porterhouse ✔

113 Poole Road, Westbourne, BH4 8BY
⌚ 10.30-11 (midnight Fri & Sat); 12-11 Sun
☎ (01202) 768586
Ringwood Best Bitter, Fortyniner, Old Thumper, seasonal beers; guest beers Ⓗ
Ringwood Brewery tied house selling the full range of award-winning ales. East Dorset CAMRA Pub of the Year seven times, and Winter Pub of the Season 2007, it offers an ever-changing choice of guests, from the Marston's catalogue. The cosy pub is welcoming, conversation dominates and card and board games are regularly played by the diverse clientele. Q ≠(Branksome)

Royal Oak

Wimborne Road, Kinson, BH10 7BB
⌚ 10.30-11; 12-6 Sun

☎ (01202) 572305
Isle of Purbeck IPA; guest beers Ⓗ
Traditional two bar locals' pub in the centre of the north Bournemouth district of Kinson. The basic public bar has a dartboard and is decorated with a range of curios; the comfortable lounge bar features motor racing prints on the walls. Both bars have open log fires. Occasional live entertainment is hosted. Three changing guest beers come from the Enterprise Inns list. East Dorset CAMRA Spring Pub of the Season 2007. ⌂❀⊟⊟P

Shoulder of Mutton

1010 Ringwood Road, Bear Cross, BH11 9LA
⏲ 5-11; 12-3, 5-midnight Fri; 12-midnight Sat; 12-4, 7-11.30 Sun
☎ (01202) 573344
Ringwood Fortyniner; guest beer Ⓗ
One of the oldest pubs in Bournemouth, this is a traditional local with a public and lounge bar. The public bar contains original flagstones from the 18th century, the lounge is carpeted and decorated with photographs of the Bear Cross area. Note the sheep theme throughout. There is a large garden area, with plans to develop it further during 2008. A community pub with football and darts teams, its location on the dual carriageway makes it an ideal place to stop off for visitors travelling into town. Q❀⊟⊟(6B,11)♣P⊱

Bridport

George Hotel

4 South Street, DT6 3NQ
⏲ 10 (12 Sun)-midnight
☎ (01308) 423187
Palmers Copper, IPA, 200, Tally Ho! Ⓗ
Fine, traditional and cheerful Palmers pub at the centre of this busy market town. The long main bar has a warm, comfortable feel and there is a peaceful family room across the passageway with service through a hatch to the corridor. With the thatched Palmers Brewery less than a mile away, the real ales have few beer miles on the clock. There is no parking but several public car parks nearby. ⌂Q♨◑⊟

Tiger Inn

14-16 Barrack Street, DT6 3LY
⏲ 12-11; 11-midnight Sat; 12-9 Sun
☎ (01308) 427543
Beer range varies Ⓗ
This bright and cheerful Victorian ale house offers a frequently-changing beer list from across the UK, featuring breweries from Cornwall to the Orkney Isles. The large single bar, with TV for major sports events and table skittles, is complemented by a small, attractive restaurant, a pretty garden and a full-sized skittle alley. Close to the town centre and shops, the Tiger is well worth seeking out if you like a traditional public house. Thatchers cider is available. ⌂❀◑⊟(31)♣●⊱

Woodman Inn

61 South Street, DT6 3NZ
⏲ 11 (12 Sun)-11
☎ (01308) 456455
Branscombe Vale BVB; guest beers Ⓗ
Just a short stroll from the town centre, this small but bright and attractive pub offers all the features a real ale enthusiast could want. The single bar makes space for drinkers and diners enjoying unfussy food. A full-sized skittle alley leads to the refurbished garden – an oasis for a pint in the sun. Regular live music and a pub quiz on Sunday night are added attractions at this happy little pub. ⌂Q❀◑⊟(X53)♣⊱

Buckhorn Weston

Stapleton Arms

Church Hill, SP8 5HS (between A303 and A30) ST757247
⏲ 11-3, 6-11; 11-11 Sat & Sun
☎ (01963) 370396 🌐 thestapletonarms.com
Butcombe Bitter; Taylor Landlord; guest beers Ⓗ
Imposing, recently modernised village pub. Stylish and spacious, it has a friendly, relaxed atmosphere. At least four and occasionally five beers are available, guests usually sourced from local micros. Four imported draught and many bottled foreign beers are stocked, as well as real ciders and interesting apple juices. A refined and excellent food menu is on offer throughout the pub – the hand-made pork pies and home-made chutney are particularly good. Children, dogs and muddy boots are welcome. Modern en-suite accommodation is available. ⌂Q❀⇌◑♿●P

Burton Bradstock

Three Horseshoes ✔

Mill Street, DT6 4QZ
⏲ 11 (12 Sun)-11
☎ (01308) 897259 🌐 three-horseshoes.com
Palmers Copper, IPA, Tally Ho! Ⓗ
Old thatched cottage style stone pub in an attractive village a mile from the sea. The L-shaped bar has a large inglenook and welcoming log fire in winter, with beams, lots of pictures and local photos, and rustic furniture including a large table with bench seats that was originally a double bed. Good value traditional pub food with friendly service is available in the attractive dining room. There is a small rear garden and dogs are welcome. A popular hostelry for locals, walkers and tourists. ⌂❀◑P

Cerne Abbas

Giant Inn

24 Long Street, DT2 7JF
⏲ 12-3 (not Tue), 6–11; 12-11 Sat; 12-10.30 Sun
☎ (01300) 341441 🌐 thegiantinncerneabbas.co.uk
St Austell Tribute; Wadworth IPA Ⓗ

INDEPENDENT BREWERIES

Dorset Weymouth
Dorset Piddle Piddlehinton (NEW)
Goldfinch Dorchester
Hall & Woodhouse/Badger Blandford St Mary
Isle of Purbeck Studland
Palmer Bridport
Sherborne Sherborne
Small Paul's Gillingham (NEW)

Lively village inn —the only free house in Cerne Abbas —formerly known as the Red Lion and rebuilt after a fire in 1898. The 16th-century stone fireplace remains, making it cosy in winter. Home to darts and skittles teams, this is a popular meeting place for all and regularly welcomes local Morris sides. The open-plan bar has a dining area where good pub food is on offer (telephone for times). Cream teas are also served. All major football, rugby and F1 fixtures are screened. Outside is a patio with awning and garden.

Chaldon Herring

Sailor's Return

DT2 8DN
11.30-3, 6-11; 11.30-11 Sat & Sun
(01305) 853847
Hampshire Strong's Best Bitter; Ringwood Best Bitter; guest beer
Large country pub with good views —it was once part of two thatched cottages but was later greatly extended without losing any of its rustic charm. Past visitors include Thomas Hardy and Lawrence of Arabia. The pub offers a wide selection of meals to suit all tastes including roast lunch on Sunday. The board game Uckers is played and Weston's scrumpy cider is available. In summer a beer festival is held in the large garden and marquee.
P

Chetnole

Chetnole Inn

DT9 6NU
11.30-2.30, 6.30-11.30; 12-2.30 Sun
(01935) 872337 thechetnoleinn.co.uk
Branscombe Vale Branoc; Sharp's Doom Bar; guest beer
This pub in an unspoilt village has the bonus of a bus stop outside and Chetnole station nearby. It retains an interesting Victorian tiled floor in the bar and flagstones throughout. West country micros are well supported and at Easter there is a beer festival. Excellent food is available seven days a week and the accommodation is of a high standard, with offers available for short breaks.
Q P

Chideock

Clockhouse Inn

Main Street, DT6 6JW
12-3, 6-11; 12-11 July-Sept
(01297) 489423
Otter Ale, Bitter
Spacious family-owned free house, popular with locals and visitors to the Jurassic Coast. The long bar is complemented by the restaurant on a raised floor and impressive games area with six dartboards, a skittle alley and other pub favourites. A sensibly-priced menu caters for all tastes. Weekend highlights are live music on Saturday and the fun and friendly Sunday night quiz. The pub has a 24-hour licence and stays open late when busy. Drivers beware of the speed cameras on the main road. (X53) P

Child Okeford

Saxon Inn

Gold Hill, DT11 8HD
12-3, 7-11; 12-11 Sun
(01258) 860310 saxoninn.co.uk
Butcombe Bitter; guest beer
Quaint pub set back from the main road at the north end of the village. A popular local, it draws in walkers and horse riders, as well as overnight visitors to this picturesque part of rural Dorset. The welcoming small bar has an open fire and witty brass plaques adorn the walls. A large extension with a seating area has been added to keep up with demand. A good range of wholesome food is cooked to order, with fish a speciality. This superb inn is East Dorset CAMRA Rural Pub of the Year 2007.
Q P

Christchurch

Olde George Inn

2A Castle Street, BH23 1DT
11-11.30 (midnight Fri & Sat)
(01202) 479383
Dorset Piddle Piddle; Ringwood Fortyniner; guest beers
Brewery tap for the newly founded Dorset Piddle Brewery, this historic pub, in the heart of Christchurch, dates back to the 15th century. A former coaching inn with plenty of history, tunnels remain under the pub that ran to the nearby priory and castle. Two rooms are served from the main bar and excellent food is available all day with a carvery on Sunday. Outside is a courtyard with patio heaters, leading to the former barn where there is a skittle alley and private functions are hosted.

Corfe Castle

Greyhound Inn

The Square, BH20 5EZ
11-12.30am
(01929) 480205 greyhoundcorfe.co.uk
Ringwood Best Bitter; Sharp's Doom Bar; guest beers
Situated at the gateway to the Purbecks, this 17th-century coaching inn claims to be the most photographed pub in Britain. Sitting beneath Corfe Castle's imposing ruins, the gardens provide views of the Swanage Steam Railway. The pub hosts regular live music with beer festivals in May and August as well as a sausage and cider festival in October. There is an extensive menu of food with fresh fish a speciality. Q (142,143)

Royal British Legion Club

East Street, BH20 5EQ (on A351)
12-3, 6-11; 12-midnight Sat; 12-10.30 Sun
(01929) 430591
Ringwood Best Bitter, seasonal beers; guest beers
This Purbeck stone building alongside the A351 has a small bar and a comfortable raised seating area. The guest beer is often Taylor's Landlord and Thatchers cider is available. Occasional entertainment plays on Saturday evening and a TV screen shows major events. The outside drinking area includes a boules

court. Beer is reasonably priced for an area popular with tourists. Sandwiches are available but no hot meals. Entry is with a valid CAMRA membership card or a copy of this Guide. ❀≹🚌(142,143)♣🍎P

Dewlish

Oak

DT2 7ND

⏲ 11.30-2.30, 6-11.30; 12-3, 7-10.30 Sun

☎ (01258) 837352

Beer range varies Ⓗ

Unpretentious village local with a public bar where you can enjoy a game of darts or pool while sampling one of the ever-changing local ales. There is a small dining area off the main bar and a separate dining room opening onto the patio and large garden. Food is available with Sunday roasts and home-made puds recommended. Dogs are allowed in the bar. Dewlish has been of much interest to archaeologists and some of the sites are within walking distance of the Oak.
🔥Q◑🚌♣

Dorchester

Blue Raddle

9 Church Street, DT1 1JN

⏲ 11.30-3 (not Mon), 6.30-11; 12-3, 7-10.30 Sun

☎ (01305) 267762

Otter Ale; Sharp's Doom Bar; guest beers Ⓗ

Genuine and popular town-centre free house with friendly and helpful staff. The pub has a long narrow bar with plush seating at polished tables, where home-cooked food sourced from local ingredients and real ales complement each other. Guest beers come from far and wide and local breweries are not forgotten. The landlord will take customer requests for guest ales. The pub is involved in local events and hosts regular live music with local musicians, including Irish nights. CAMRA West Dorset Pub of the Year 2007.
◑♿≹(South)🚌♣🍎

Colliton Club ✔

Colliton House, Colliton Park, DT1 1XJ (opp County Hall & Crown Court)

⏲ 9-2.30, 7-11.30; closed Sun and Bank Holidays

☎ (01305) 224503

Greene King Old Speckled Hen, Abbot; Hop Back Odyssey; Palmers IPA, Copper Ale; guest beers Ⓗ

Thriving club with a reputation for good service and real ales. Formed in 1950, the club is housed in the mainly 17th-century Grade II listed Colliton House and welcomes CAMRA members —show your membership card to gain entry. Busy in and out of office hours, this is a popular meeting place for a number of local associations. CAMRA Wessex Regional Club of the Year in 2007. Q◑≹(South, West)🚌

East Morden

Cock & Bottle

BH20 7DL (on B3075, off A35 between Poole and Bere Regis)

⏲ 11-2.30, 6-11; 12-3, 7-10.30 Sun

☎ (01929) 459238

Badger First Gold, Tanglefoot, seasonal beers Ⓗ

Delightful village pub set in lovely countryside. The Happy Chatter public bar is an unspoilt room ideal for drinkers with a large open log fire and a variety of seats, benches and settles. Award-winning food is served in the dining area, offering traditional and a la carte cuisine. The garden is perfect for a summer pint. Disabled facilities are good, with easy wheelchair access. 🔥Q❀◑🀫♿♣P⅟

East Stour

King's Arms

East Stour Common, SP8 5NB (on A30, W of Shaftesbury)

⏲ 12-3, 5.30-11; 12-midnight Sat; 12-10.30 Sun

☎ (01747) 838325 🌐 thekingsarmsdorset.co.uk

Fuller's London Pride; Palmers Copper Ale; guest beer Ⓗ

Imposing, multi-roomed, single-bar country pub alongside the A30. Beers from Palmers feature regularly, plus occasional guests chosen by the regulars. Food is excellent — made with locally sourced ingredients where possible. To ensure quality and ever-changing menus the three chefs, an Englishman, Scotsman and Frenchman, compete for a monthly prize. The garden room leads to an enclosed garden and patio. Dogs and muddy boots welcome in the bar. Q❀🛏◑♿P⅟

Farnham

Museum Inn

DT11 8DE (off A354)

⏲ 12-3, 7-11 (10.30 Sun)

☎ (01725) 516261 🌐 museuminn.co.uk

Ringwood Best bitter; guest beer Ⓗ

Originally built for visitors to the local museum, this part-thatched inn retains its flagstone floors and large inglenook despite a recent extensive refurbishment. It is always worth a visit for the changing guest beer and well kept regulars. Taylor Landlord is a popular choice and Thatchers cider is available. An extensive menu of high-quality food is served. Situated in excellent walking country, Larmer Tree Gardens and Cranborne Chase are nearby. Children are permitted. 🔥Q🚸❀🛏◑♿🍎P⅟

Gillingham

Phoenix Inn ✔

The Square, SP8 4AY

⏲ 10-2.30 (3 Sat), 7-11 (not Mon eve); 12-3, 7-10.30 Sun

☎ (01747) 823277

Badger K&B Sussex, First Gold, seasonal beers Ⓗ

Popular town centre pub built in the 15th century, originally a coaching inn complete with its own brewery. A cosy, one-bar inn, it has no games machines, just occasional background music. It is justifiably renowned for good value home-cooked food served in the bar and a separate dining area. A small courtyard for drinking alfresco is next to the quaint town square. 🔥Q❀◑♿⛺≹♣

Hinton St Mary

White Horse

DT10 1NA (off B3092)

☉ 12-3, 6 (7 Sun)-11; closed Mon
☎ (01258) 472723
Beer range varies Ⓗ
This 16th-century stone building is a genuine old-fashioned public house and at the heart of the village community. With wooden beams throughout, the public bar features stone flooring and an open fire, while the lounge is comfortable, cosy and home to the resident ghost. A warm, friendly welcome is extended to all including families and pets. No music, games machines or TV spoil the atmosphere. Excellent home-prepared food is served throughout and there is a small but pretty garden. ⌂Q❀◐♿🚌♣P⁻

Ibberton

Crown

Church Lane, DT11 0EN
☉ 12-3, 6-11; closed Mon; 12-3, 7-10.30 Sun
☎ (01258) 817448
Butcombe Bitter; Palmers IPA; guest beer Ⓗ
Dating from the 16th century, this rural hideaway retains the original flagstone floor, oak doors and a huge inglenook fireplace. In summer the lawned garden with babbling brook is a delight. Excellent food and a range of local ales attract regulars and visitors. Off the beaten track, the pub is an ideal stop off for walkers on the Wessex Ridgeway. The village of Ibberton, mentioned in the Domesday book, has one of only three churches in the country dedicated to St Eustace. ⌂Q❀❀◐P

Langton Matravers

King's Arms Hotel ✔

27 High Street, BH19 3HA
☉ 12-3, 6-11; 12-3, 7-10.30 Sun
☎ (01929) 422979
Ringwood Best Bitter, Fortyniner; guest beer Ⓗ
Dating back to 1743, this lovely four-room pub is adorned with paintings and photographs of the local area. Always the centre of the community, in the early days the front room served as the village morgue and the rest of the building was the inn. Outside is a large garden with a shed housing a pool table. The pub offers excellent food and is ideally situated for exploring the Purbecks.
⌂Q❀❀◐🚂🚌(142,143)♣⁻

Laymore

Squirrel Inn

TA20 4NT (on B3162 between Winsham & Drimpton)
☉ 11-2.30 (3 Sat), 6.30-11; 12-10.30 Sun
☎ (01460) 30298 🌐 squirrelinn.co.uk
Branscombe Vale Best Bitter; Otter Bitter; Sharp's Doom Bar Ⓗ
This is a 1952 brick reincarnation of an earlier stone pub in this rural hamlet. The pleasantly decorated interior has one long carpeted bar divided into nooks with deep pink walls and plenty of beams. At one end a brick fireplace with a copper canopy has a large log fire in winter. The furnishings are olde-worlde cottage-style. Well-cooked traditional pub food is served with a smile. There is a skittle alley and the garden has a children's play area. The local Ashen Faggot festival is held here in January. Dogs are welcome.
⌂❀🛏◐♿♣P

Loders

Loders Arms

DT6 3SA
☉ 11.30-3, 5.30-11; 12-3, 7-10.30 Sun
☎ (01308) 422431 🌐 lodersarms.com
Palmers Copper Ale, IPA, 200 Ⓗ
Seventeenth century hamstone thatched pub in an attractive village with a long pine-panelled bar with log fire, rustic furniture, brasses and old prints. A pretty dining room offers well-cooked traditional pub food with friendly service. The pub benefits from a garden and skittle alley. Popular with locals, walkers and tourists alike, dogs are welcome.
⌂❀◐⛺●P

Lyme Regis

Nag's Head

32 Silver Street, DT7 3HS
☉ 11-midnight
☎ (01297) 442312
Otter Ale; guest beers Ⓗ
Old coaching inn with magnificent views along the Jurassic Coast offering an ever-changing choice of ales in two linked bar areas warmed by a wood burner, plus a games room. The house beer Sark Lark is brewed by Otter. Live music plays on Saturday and most Wednesdays. No meals are available but regular barbecues are held in summer. The garden has a covered terrace heated by a wood burner where smoking is allowed. Good quality en-suite B&B accommodation is provided upstairs. ⌂❀🛏⛺🚌P⁻

Volunteer Inn

31 Broad Street, DT7 3QE (on A3052)
☉ 11-11; 12-10.30 Sun
☎ (01297) 442214
Fuller's London Pride; guest beers Ⓗ
Historic two-room pub in the heart of town a few steps from the seafront, with a lovely olde-worlde atmosphere. Popular with locals, the main bar buzzes with jolly banter and conversation. The house beer, Donegal, is stillaged behind the bar and named by long-serving landlord Joe after his homeland. A rotating choice of west country ales is on offer plus cask-conditioned Addlestones cloudy cider. The pub is renowned for freshly-cooked meals including fish, served in the bar and dining room, where families are welcome. No food is served on Monday. ❀◐⛺🚌●

Middlemarsh

Hunters Moon

DT9 5QN (on A352, Dorchester-Sherborne road)
☉ 10-midnight
☎ (01963) 210966 🌐 huntersmoon.co.uk
Butcombe Bitter; guest beers Ⓗ
Visitors are welcome any time from breakfast onwards at this 400-year-old country pub, now under dynamic new management. A supporter of real ales, guest beers are usually

from local brewers. There is a carvery on Friday night and Sunday lunchtime. A grassed area to the front of the pub has seating for an outdoor pint on a sunny day. Coaches are welcome (there is a spacious car park) and large groups can be catered for with advance warning. Good wheelchair access.

Motcombe

Coppleridge Inn

SP7 9HW (follow signs from village)

12-3, 6-11; 12-11 Sun

(01747) 851980 coppleridge.com

Butcombe Bitter; Greene King IPA; guest beer H

A family run country inn and restaurant, the main building is a converted farmhouse set in 15 acres of woodland, meadow and gardens. There is a cosy wood-panelled bar and a number of separate, discrete dining areas. A continually rotating guest beer is offered, often quite unusual to the area. Local produce is sourced for the excellent meals and there are occasional theme nights. The accommodation is provided in separate chalet-style rooms around a courtyard. Function and conference facilities are available and the pub is licensed for weddings.

Pamphill

Vine Inn ★

Vine Hill, BH21 4EE (off B3082) ST994003

11-3, 7-10.30 (11 Thu-Sat); 12-3, 7-10.30 Sun

(01202) 882259

Fuller's London Pride; H **guest beers** G

Built as a bakehouse over 200 years ago, the building became an inn in 1900 and the current landlady is granddaughter of the first licensee. Popular with ramblers, dog-walkers and cyclists, this superb, small pub has an intimate public bar where the locals chat and slightly larger lounge area plus an additional upstairs games and family room. The sun-trap garden has heaters for the winter. Guest beers are sourced from small regional breweries and Weston's local cider and perries are available. Sandwiches and a hearty ploughman's lunch are offered at lunchtime.

Piddlehinton

Thimble Inn

14 High Street, DT2 7TD

12-2.30, 7-11

(01300) 348270

Badger Tanglefoot; Palmers Copper Ale, IPA; Ringwood Best, Fortyniner H

Large, partly thatched village pub on the River Piddle with cheery, welcoming staff. Five well-kept ales from three local breweries are stocked, plus fruit wines and malt whiskies. The spacious low-beamed bar has two attractive brick fireplaces and plenty of nooks and crannies for cosy twosomes and larger groups. The large garden is floodlit at night with a river running alongside. Coach parties are welcome with plenty of parking. Dogs are permitted.

Piddletrenthide

European Inn

DT2 7QT

11.30-3, 6-11; closed Mon except Bank Holidays; 11.30-10.30 Sun

(01300) 348308 european-inn.co.uk

Palmers Copper Ale; guest beer H

Recently refurbished small country inn with a cosy open bar room and snug area with a fire in winter. The pub provides a friendly welcome and a positive approach to great ales, good food and the local community. The house ale is Palmers Copper, with two regularly rotating local guests coming from St Austell, Hopback, Otter, Dorset Brewing Co and others. Superb food is available lunchtimes and evenings (not Sun eve). Outside there is a garden and patio areas for alfresco drinking. B&B accommodation is delightful.

Plush

Brace of Pheasants

DT2 7RQ

12-3, 7-11; closed Mon; 12-3 Sun

(01300) 348357 braceofpheasants.co.uk

Beer range varies G

Cosy village pub with a friendly welcome for all (including dogs). Regularly changing ales are dispensed from casks behind the bar. The main bar area has a real fire with a restaurant area offering superb food. A large sloping cottage garden to the rear has tables and a heated, covered area for smokers. Widely renowned for well-kept ales and good food, the pub can get busy and booking is a must for meals.

Poole

Angel

28 Market Street, BH15 1NF

11-11.30; 12-10.30 Sun

(01202) 666431 theangeldartsteam.webs.com

Ringwood Best Bitter, Fortyniner, Old Thumper, seasonal beers; guest beers H

Ringwood Brewery's only tied house in Poole, sitting in the shadow of the historic Guildhall where an inn has stood since 1789. This is a large friendly pub, served by a central bar and offering a good range of entertainment including a quiz night on Tuesday, music quiz on Wednesday and live music evenings. Home-made food is served all week. There are views into the cask ale cellar and an attractive drinking terrace which is a sun trap.

Bermuda Triangle

10 Parr Street, Lower Parkstone, BH14 0JY

12-2.30, 5-11; 12-midnight Fri & Sat; 12-11 Sun

(01202) 748087

Beer range varies H

Crammed with maritime paraphernalia, this single bar local and Guide regular attracts real ale lovers from far and wide. Themed around the mystery of the Bermuda Triangle, one of the many drinking areas resembles a timber boat, while a section of an aircraft wing is suspended from the ceiling in the main bar. The ever-changing selection of four real ales is

cellared separately from the keg beers, assuring consistent quality and temperature. Beer aficionados will also find a variety of German lagers and Black Budvar on draft. Sadly, disabled access is impossible.
❀⇌(Parkstone)🚌(M1)

Branksome Railway Hotel

429 Poole Road, Branksome, BH12 1DQ (opp station)
⏲ 11 (12 Sun)-11
☎ (01202) 769555
Fuller's London Pride; Hop Back Summer Lightning 🄷
Typical Victorian pub with high ceilings built in 1894 to service the rail network and still benefiting from excellent links with public transport. Although essentially open plan in layout, the bar is partitioned into three distinct drinking areas —the largest of these providing an excellent vantage point for viewing passing intercity and local trains.
⇌(Branksome)🚌(M1,M2)♣P⊱

Brewhouse

68 High Street, BH15 1DA
⏲ 11-11; 12-10.30 Sun
☎ (01202) 685288
Milk Street Mermaid, Beer, seasonal beers 🄷
Owned by Milk Street Brewery, this popular local is situated in the heart of the town centre. The split level interior is served by a single bar - hops and a cartwheel hang from the ceiling in the front bar; two pool tables, a dartboard and jukebox are the main features of the rear. An outside seating area to the front and a decked area out back are perfect for sunny days and offer a haven from the shops. Guest beers are occasionally available.
❀⇌♣⊱

Portland

Royal Portland Arms

40 Fortuneswell, DT5 1LZ
⏲ 11-11.50 (12.50am Fri & Sat); 12-11.30 Sun
☎ (01305) 862255
Beer range varies 🄶
Portland stone-built pub alongside the main road with public car parks opposite and adjacent. More than 200 years old, inside you will find basic homely furnishings and a friendly welcome for all. King George III is noted to have stopped here for a drink on a visit to the island. An ever-changing range of mainly west country ales and ciders is on gravity dispense. Live music is a regular feature and the pub hosts many locally-attended social events. Q🚌●⊓

Pymore

Pymore Inn

DT6 5PN
⏲ 12-3, 6 (7 Sun)-11
☎ (01308) 422625
Otter Ale; St Austell Dartmoor Best, Tribute 🄷
Attractive ivy-clad free house a mile west of Bridport town centre providing a social hub for the village and a warm welcome to visitors. The sensibly-priced menu features locally-sourced ingredients. The large grassy garden surrounded by open fields is ideal for small people to let off steam on a sunny day and they are welcome indoors if dining accompanied by an adult. ♨Q❀◐◑♿P

Shaftesbury

Mitre

23 High Street, SP7 8JE
⏲ 10.30-midnight; 12-11 Sun
☎ (01747) 853002
Wells Bombardier; Young's Bitter, Special, seasonal beers 🄷
Historic pub close to the town hall at the top of Gold Hill, with grand views overlooking the beautiful Blackmore Vale. Popular with younger drinkers but catering for all, an extensive food menu ranges from morning coffee to cream teas to good pub food. The Mitre runs crib and darts teams and hosts charity quizzes as well as occasional live music nights. ♨❀◐◑♿♣⊱

Shave Cross

Shave Cross Inn ✔

DT6 6HW (W of B3162 Bridport-Broad Windsor road) SY416980
⏲ 11-3, 6-11; closed Mon; 12-3, 7-10.30 Sun
☎ (01308) 868358 🌐 theshavecrossinn.co.uk
Beer range varies 🄷
Classic rural pub, stone-built with a thatched roof —this award-winning free house was rescued from oblivion by the local owners who have now added impressive accommodation. A small flagstoned bar leads to the restaurant where Caribbean and world-influenced dishes feature. A remote rural idyll well worth the extra mileage.
♨Q❀◐◑●P⊱

Sherborne

Digby Tap ✔

Cooks Lane, DT9 3NS
⏲ 11-11; 12-3, 7-11 Sun
☎ (01935) 813148 🌐 digbytap.co.uk
Beer range varies 🄷
Sherborne's only free house —an oasis in a desert and worth seeking out for the building alone. Dating back to the 16th century, it was once the parish workhouse and many features of the original building remain. A strong supporter of west country ales, beers come from Teignworthy, Sharp's and Dorset Brewing Co. There are benches on a paved area outside for summer drinking. Food is served at lunchtime, Monday to Saturday.
♨Q❀◐♿⇌🚌⊱

Stoborough

King's Arms

3 Corfe Road, BH20 5AB (adjacent to B3075)
⏲ 11-3, 5-11; 11-11 Fri-Sun
☎ (01929) 552705
Black Sheep Best Bitter; Dorset Steam Beer; guest beers 🄷
This 400-year-old listed building played host to Cromwell's troops in 1642 at the time of the siege of Corfe Castle. The pub is renowned for its food, and holds popular themed evenings.

A long, slim pub with a split-level bar, its riverside dining area is always busy in summer. Up to four real ales and a cider from Cheddar Valley are available.
Q (142,143) P

Stourton Caundle

Trooper Inn

Golden Hill, DT10 2JW ST715149
12-2.30 (not Mon), 7 (6 Wed & Thu)-midnight; 12-3.30, 7-midnight Sun
(01963) 362405
Otter Bitter; guest beers
Stone-built, single-room village centre pub with a separate function room featuring a bar and skittle alley. Two large inglenook fireplaces have been converted to seating areas and there is a children's area next to the beer garden. A popular fish & chips (in paper) night is held each Friday. The pub hosts an annual beer festival and real cider is served in summer. Dogs are welcome. Q P

Stratton

Saxon Arms

The Square, DT2 9WG
11-3, 5.30-11; 11-11 Sat; 12-10.30 Sun
(01305) 260020
Ringwood Best Bitter; Taylor Landlord; guest beer
Built in recent years, this flint and thatch pub has the feel of an old country inn. Renowned for food, it is also popular with those looking for an excellent pint. Outside a patio area overlooks the village green. Inside, the bar divides into three areas —one a dining space where good locally sourced produce is served. This attractive pub is especially busy in the summer months. P

Studland

Bankes Arms

Watery Lane, BH19 3AU
11-11
(01929) 450225 bankesarms.com
Isle of Purbeck Best, Fossil Fuel, Solar Power, Studland Bay Wrecked, IPA; guest beers
This country inn, more than 200 years old, is home to the Isle of Purbeck Brewery. Nine handpumps dispense most of the beer range, along with guests from other micro-breweries and Weston's cider. Run by the same family for 25 years, the pub is owned by the National Trust. A four-day beer festival is held in August. There are magnificent views over Studland Bay from the large beer garden.
Q (150)

Swanage

Red Lion

63 High Street, BH19 2LY
11 (12 Sun)-11.30
(01929) 423533 redlionswanage.co.uk
Caledonian Deuchars IPA; Ringwood Best Bitter; Taylor Landlord; guest beers
This 17th-century hostelry has risen phoenix-like from the ashes of indifference over the last few years thanks to the current landlord. Up to six beers are served in summer, including ales from Isle of Purbeck and Palmers. The full range of Weston's ciders is complemented by bottled Aspall's, Inch's and Sheppey's. CAMRA local Pub of the Year in 2005. P

White Swan

31 High Street, The Square, BH19 2LJ
11-11
(01929) 423804 whiteswanswanage.co.uk
Ringwood Best Bitter; guest beers
Situated close to the sea but among the shops, the pub is set on four levels, offering something for everyone. The food includes a vegetarian option and children's menu at good prices. There is plenty of seating, a pool table, TV and a computer for customers' use. Occasional live music, pool nights and other entertainment are hosted. Guest beers come from local breweries.
P

Tarrant Monkton

Langton Arms

DT11 8RX
11-midnight; 12-11.30 Sun
(01258) 830225 thelangtonarms.co.uk
Ringwood Best Bitter; guest beers
Attractive 17th-century thatched inn set in a peaceful village nestling in the Tarrant Valley. The pub offers excellent food, real ales including a house beer from The Hidden Brewery and quality accommodation. There are two bars, one with a real fire, both serving food from an extensive menu. To the rear is a large function/dining room with a skittle alley and restaurant. P

Upwey

Royal Standard

700 Dorchester Road, DT3 5LA (on A354)
12-3, 6-midnight; 12-midnight Sat; 12-11 Sun
(01305) 812558
Butcombe Bitter; Hop Back GFB; Ringwood Fortyniner
Comfortable two-roomed local on the outskirts of Weymouth. The interior is dominated by a GWR railway theme. The wood-panelled public bar is complemented by a comfortable lounge with a homely feel. Although customers are welcome to use the Internet facilities here, it is a mobile phone-free zone. Look for the magnificent eagle owl in the aviary. Q P

Wareham

Duke of Wellington

7 East Street, BH20 4NN
11-11 (11.30 Fri & Sat); 12-11 Sun
(01929) 553015
Hop Back Summer Lightning; Isle of Purbeck Fossil Fuel; Ringwood Best Bitter; guest beers
Atmospheric 400-year-old town centre pub with six handpumps dispensing a range of beers, some from local breweries. Photographs of Wareham of yesteryear adorn the wood-panelled walls and copper ornaments surround the open fire. An

extensive menu is served in the bar and restaurant. East Dorset CAMRA Summer Pub of the Season and Pub of the Year 2007.
⛫Q❀⇌◑⇌⊟(142,143)♣⊬

Waytown

Hare & Hounds ✔

DT6 5LQ SY470978
11-3, 6.30 (6 summer)-11 Sat; 12-3, 7-11 Sun
☎ (01308) 488203
Palmers Copper Ale, IPA, Dorset Gold Ⓗ
Tucked away, this rural gem of an unspoilt village local is well worth seeking out. The garden, with its stunning views across the Brit Valley, is a major attraction in summer, with seating, a play area and grassy expanse for small folk to let off steam. Taunton cider is a regular and an attractive food menu features home-cooked meals and fresh local produce.
⛫Q❀◑♣●P

West Stour

Ship Inn

SP8 5RP (on A30)
12-3, 6-11; 12-11 Sun
☎ (01747) 838640 🌐 shipinn-dorset.com
Palmers Dorset Gold; Ringwood Best Bitter; guest beer Ⓗ
Built in 1750 as a coaching inn, this popular roadside pub has fine views across the Blackmore Vale. The public bar features a flagstone floor and low ceiling; the lounge and restaurant area is light and airy with stripped oak floorboards and farmhouse furniture. There is a pretty patio and large garden to the rear. This family-friendly pub is renowned for superb home-cooked food and comfortable accommodation. Dogs are welcome in the bar.
⛫Q❀⇌◑♣P

Weymouth

Boot Inn

High Street, DT4 8JH
11-11; 12-10.30 Sun
☎ (01305) 770327
Ringwood Best Bitter, Fortyniner, Old Thumper, seasonal beers; guest beers Ⓗ
Weymouth's oldest inn is tucked away behind the fire station. An old-fashioned pub where conversation dominates, the single wood-floored bar area leads to small rooms at both ends, with comfortable seating and warming coal fires. The full Ringwood range is supplemented by the landlord's choice of guest beer and Cheddar Valley cider. Local CAMRA Pub of the Year 2008.
⛫Q❀♿⇌⊟♣●

Red Lion ✔

33 Hope Street, DT4 8TU
11-11 (midnight Fri & Sat); 12-11 Sun
☎ (01305) 786940
Courage Directors; Dorset Durdle Door; Marston's Pedigree; Wells Bombardier Ⓗ
Historic red-brick friendly town local in the heart of Brewers Quay. Up to five well-kept ales include beers from the Dorset Brewing Company sited opposite. Outside is a large heated patio and seating facing the visitors centre. The atmospheric interior has scrubbed boards, candles and nautical memorabilia. TV screens show sport and traditional games include darts and dominoes. Food served daily until 8pm. ❀◑⇌⊟♣⊬

Weatherbury

7 Carlton Road North, DT4 7PX
12-midnight
☎ (01305) 786040
Fuller's London Pride; guest beers Ⓗ
Down-to-earth free house in a residential part of the town. The single bar interior is divided into different areas with a TV screen in each one. The London Pride is accompanied by frequently changing guest beers. Outside there is a patio with a covered, heated area for smokers. Well-behaved children are welcome. Q☺❀⇌⇌⊟P⊬

Wellington Arms

13 St Albans Street, DT4 8PY
11-11
☎ (01305) 786963
Marston's Burton Bitter; Ringwood Best Bitter; guest beers Ⓗ
Cosy, traditional town local, run by the same family for many years. Top quality ales come from the Marston's range. A quiet back room serves as a family room and the pub hosts regular live music sessions. Good value food is served daily. ⛫☺◑⇌⊟♣

Winterborne Stickland

Crown

North Street, DT11 0NJ (2 miles N of A354)
12-3, 6-11; 12-11 Sat & Sun
☎ (01258) 880838
Ringwood Best Bitter, Fortyniner, seasonal beers; guest beers Ⓗ
Eighteenth-century, Grade II listed, thatched village inn, popular with locals and walkers. The main bar has low beams and an inglenook fireplace with brick, flint and plaster walls. At the rear is a courtyard with original well, a games room, a terraced beer garden and a play area. ⛫☺❀◑♿Å♣P⊬

Worth Matravers

Square & Compass ★

BH19 3LF (Off the B3069) SY974777
12-2.30, 6.30-11; 12-3, 7-10.30 Sun
☎ (01258) 880838
Hop Back Summer Lightning; Ringwood Best Bitter; guest beers Ⓖ
Featuring in every edition of the Guide and runner up National Cider Pub of the Year 2007, this pub is a hidden gem on the Jurassic Coast with stunning views over the bay. Much of the pub furniture is made from driftwood, giving the pub its unique character. Owned by the Newman family for several generations.
⛫Q❀◑Å●P

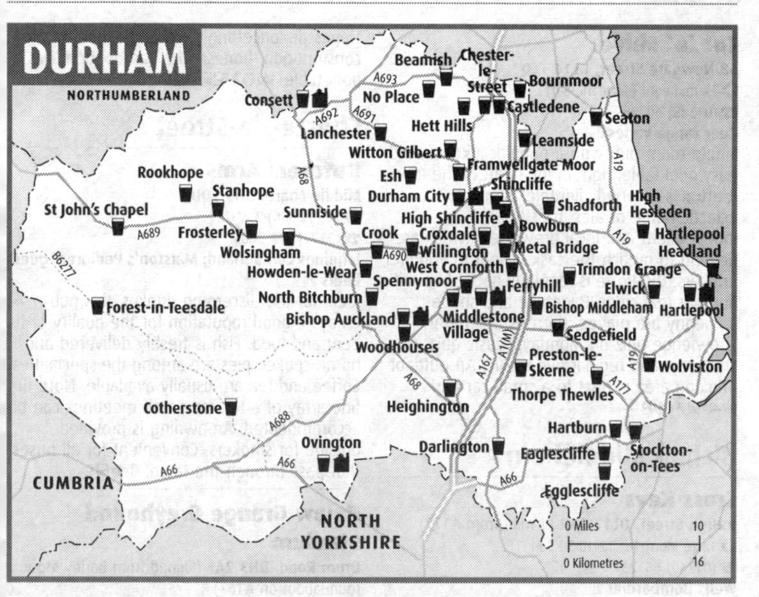

Beamish

Shepherd & Shepherdess

DH9 0RS (follow signs for Beamish Museum)
⏲ 11.30-11.30 (11 Sun)
☎ (0191) 370 0349
Black Sheep Best Bitter; Wells Eagle IPA; guest beer Ⓗ
Friendly village pub with interesting photos adorning the walls, old and new, and taxidermic animals in cases. Note the outside sign depicting a shepherd and shepherdess. A mural in oil behind the bar depicts old Durham County. Wednesday is quiz night. The guest ale is available in summer only alongside the regular ales and there is an extensive wine selection. Outside is a play area for children and baby changing facilities are available. Buses to Newcastle and Sunderland pass close to the pub. ❀◐🚌(78,28)P⊱

Bishop Auckland

Grand Hotel

Holdforth Crest, DL14 6DU (A6072, near ASDA car park)
⏲ 6 (12 Fri & Sat)-11; 12-10.30 Sun
☎ (07810) 751425 🌐 the-grand-hotel.co.uk
Beer range varies Ⓗ
The home of the Wear Valley Brewery, the pub is a showcase for its extensive range of beers as well as selected guests and a Weston's cider. Well regarded throughout the region for its live music on Saturday nights, the pub now also enthusiastically promotes local young talent on Thursday and Friday nights (see website for details). A big screen shows football. Lunches are served on Sunday only. The smoking area in the yard is covered and heated. A five-minute walk from the railway station, past Asda. ❀◐⇌♣●P⊱

Pollards

104 Etherley Lane, DL14 6TW
⏲ 11-11; 12-10.30 Sun
☎ (01388) 603539
Beer range varies Ⓗ
Now well established as a comfortable community pub with a good ambience, this is a fine example of a hostelry whose values mirror CAMRA's, with a good choice of beers, two fires, pub games and four distinct drinking areas served from a central bar. A large dining area offers good food lunchtimes and evenings, including a Sunday carvery. There are picnic tables outside the front door and large heated patio to the rear. The beer range usually includes an offering from Marston's and Jennings. ♨Q❀◐◑⊟⇌🚌(94)♣P▯

Stanley Jefferson ✔

5 Market Place, DL14 7NJ
⏲ 9am-midnight (1am Fri & Sat)
☎ (01388) 542836
Greene King IPA, Abbot; Marston's Pedigree; guest beers Ⓗ
This interesting conversion of a former solicitors' office offers the typical range of Wetherspoon's facilities. Several comfortable drinking areas are served from one long bar, with an impressive glass roof above and a large heated patio outside. The eponymous Mr Jefferson lived in the town, was schooled nearby and was better known as Stan Laurel. Ciders are Weston's Old Rosie and Organic. Food is served all day, and children are welcome with diners until 9pm. The Bishop of Durham's palace and adjacent park are nearby. ❀◐◑♿⇌🚌●⊱

INDEPENDENT BREWERIES

Camerons Hartlepool
Consett Ale Works Consett
Durham Bowburn
Four Alls Ovington
Hill Island Durham City
Wear Valley Bishop Auckland
Yard of Ale Ferryhill (NEW)

Tut 'n' Shive

68 Newgate Street, DL14 7EQ
✪ 11-midnight (1am Thu-Sat)
☎ (01388) 603252
Beer range varies Ⓗ
Single-room pub with a popular jukebox and busy pool table, right in the heart of the town. It attracts a varied clientele thanks to its eclectic range of ales, mostly from independent and local breweries, which are helping to preach the cask gospel to younger drinkers. Old Rosie is regularly backed up with another real cider. Bagatelle and shove-ha'penny are played, there is a general knowledge quiz on Monday, music quiz on Thursday, and regular live music. An outdoor drinking area is next to a small car park.
❀⇌🚌♣●P⚐

Bishop Middleham

Cross Keys

9 High Street, DL17 9AR (1 mile from A177)
✪ 12 (5 Mon)-11; 12-10.30 Sun
☎ (01740) 651231
Wells Bombardier Ⓗ
Busy family-run village pub with a warm, friendly atmosphere and a good reputation for excellent meals (booking advised). The spacious open-plan lounge/bar is complemented by a large restaurant/function room serving an extensive menu of freshly-prepared meals. Situated in excellent wildlife and walking country, a three-mile circular walk starts opposite. Quiz night is Tuesday, Teesside Tornadoes Bike Club meets on Wednesday and the pub has its own football team. ♨❀◐◑🚌

Bournmoor

Dun Cow ✔

Primrose Hill, DH4 6DY
✪ 12-11 (midnight Fri & Sat)
☎ (0191) 385 2631
Jarrow Rivet Catcher; guest beers Ⓗ
Traditional northern country pub dating from the 18th century with extensive lawns to the rear. The pub is reputed to be haunted by the 'grey lady' with sightings as recent as 2006. Home-cooked food is available in the lounge and bar and à la carte in the restaurant. A marquee can be hired for special functions. Family friendly, there is a bouncy castle in the garden. Beer festivals are held in March and October. Live rock bands appear occasionally.
❀◐◑♿🚌P

Castledene

Smiths Arms

Brecon Hill, DH3 4HE NZ299507
✪ 4-11 (12-11 Sat); 12-10.30 Sun
☎ (0191) 385 6915
Black Sheep Best Bitter; Courage Directors; Jarrow Rivet Catcher; guest beers Ⓗ
Despite being well tucked away, this country pub is very popular with drinkers and diners, particularly at the weekend. Regulars gather in the snug public bar with its real fire in winter, where two guest ales are available. There is a comfortable lounge with a floor that slopes disconcertingly – no reflection on ale consumption, honest. The games room has a pool table. ♨Q◑⊟🚌♣P

Chester-le-Street

Butchers Arms

Middle Chare, DH3 3QD
✪ 11 (12 Sun)-3, 7-11
☎ (0191) 386 3605
Jennings Cumberland; Marston's Pedigree; guest beers Ⓗ
Ideal for the discerning drinker, this pub enjoys a good reputation for the quality of its beer and food. Fish is freshly delivered and home-cooked pies are among the specialities. Coffee and tea are usually available. Note the fine array of artefacts. Small meetings can be accommodated. An awning is provided outside for smokers. Convenient for all buses that pass through the town. ◐⇌🚌⚐

Pelaw Grange Greyhound Stadium

Drum Road, DH3 2AF (Signed from Barley Mow roundabout on A167)
✪ 6.30-11 (closed Tue & Wed); 12-4 Sun
☎ (0191) 410 2141 🌐 pelawgrange.co.uk
Black Sheep Best Bitter; guest beers Ⓗ
The Grange Club at the greyhound stadium has a large open bar where children are welcome, a panoramic restaurant and a concert room all overlooking the track. The club has a lively atmosphere on race nights (Monday, Thursday and Saturday) when CAMRA members are admitted free. Managed by a CAMRA member, this is the only greyhound stadium in Britain with real ales, an annual beer festival and trips to local micro-breweries. The trackside terrace is available for smokers. Twice CAMRA Durham Branch Club of the Year. ❀◑♿🚌P⚐

Consett

Grey Horse

115 Sherburn Terrace, DH8 6NE
✪ 12-midnight
☎ (01207) 502585
Consett Ale Works Steel Town Bitter, White Hot, Cast Iron, Red Dust; Wells Bombardier; guest beers Ⓗ
An oasis in a cask beer desert, this traditional pub dates back to 1848. With Consett Aleworks Brewery at the rear, the inn is one of a chain of four including the White Swan in Stokesley that brews Captain Cook ales. The interior comprises a lounge and L-shaped bar, with a wood-beamed ceiling. Beer festivals are held twice a year and live entertainment hosted on Thursday plus a quiz on Wednesday. Cider is Weston's Old Rosie. The coast-to-coast cycle route is close by. ♨Q❀⊟♣●⚐

Cotherstone

Red Lion

Main Street, DL12 9QE
✪ 12-3 Sat only, 7-11; 12-4, 7-10.30 Sun
☎ (01833) 650236
Jennings Cumberland Ale; guest beers Ⓗ
Nestling in a terrace of stone buildings dating from around 1738, this traditional local has

changed little since the 1960s. It has a long main room with a serving hatch style bar and a further room for dining (meals served Fri-Sun), and still has outside toilets. There is no TV or jukebox, just good beer and conversation. Children and dogs are welcome and there is a small beer garden. Guest beers are from local micros. ⌂Q☺❀▲🚌♣P

Crook

Colliery

High Jobs Hill, DL15 0UL (on A690 at E edge of town) NZ177351
⌚ 12-2 (not Tue & Wed), 6.30-midnight; closed Mon; 12-3, 7-midnight Sun
☎ (01388) 762511
Camerons Strongarm; Wells Bombardier Ⓗ
Situated on the Durham road out of the town, with panoramic views over Wear Valley, this is a popular pub offering good quality, inexpensive food from a varied menu. The traditional interior features interesting ceramics and pottery. It serves as a meeting place for the local riding club and as a convenient location for nearby allotment holders to slake their thirst. The smoking area outside is covered. Q❀⇄◐♿🚌(46)P⁻

Croxdale

Daleside Arms

Front Street, DH6 5HY (On B6288, 3 miles S of Durham, off A167)
⌚ 3 (7 Tue; 12 Sat)-11 (midnight Thu-Sat); 11-8 Sun
☎ (01388) 814165
Beer range varies Ⓗ
A regular in the Guide and a previous Pub of the Year winner, this is a popular watering hole in a rural setting. An avid supporter of cask ales and local micros, it offers up to two quality ales and serves excellent home-made food on Wednesday and Friday. No nonsense and no frills, it simply gets the basics right. Check out the sporting memorabilia in the cosy main bar, and award-winning floral displays that adorn the exterior.
Q☺❀⇄◐⊟♿🚌P⁻

Darlington

Ale Cellar

24 Woodland Terrace, DL3 6NU (W of town centre, off A68)
⌚ 12 (10.30 Sat)-8; closed Sun
☎ (01325) 252022 🌐 alecellar.com
Beer range varies Ⓟ
This off licence is a real beer lover's Tardis. Stocking a range of more than 600 bottled beers including 200 bottle conditioned, it specialises in beers from local and countrywide micro-breweries. Also available is an excellent selection of European ales plus a smaller worldwide selection. Beers are competitively priced and a mail order and home delivery service is available. Well worth a visit or purchase direct from the website. 🚌

Britannia ✔

1 Archer Street, DL3 6LR (Next to ring road W of town centre)
⌚ 11.30-3, 5.30-11; 11.30-11 Thu-Sat; 12-10.30 Sun
☎ (01325) 463787
Camerons Strongarm; John Smith's Bitter; guest beers Ⓗ
Warm, friendly, popular local CAMRA award-winning pub – a bastion of cask beer for over 150 years. The pub retains much of the appearance and layout of the private house it once was – a modestly enlarged bar and small parlour (used for meetings) sit either side of a central corridor. Listed for its historical associations, it was the birthplace of teetotal 19th-century publisher JM Dent. Up to four guest beers are available. ❀🚌♣P⁻

Darlington Snooker Club

1 Corporation Road, DL3 6AE (corner of Northgate)
⌚ 11-midnight (late Fri & Sat); 12-midnight Sun
☎ (01325) 241388
Beer range varies Ⓗ
This first floor family-run and family-oriented private snooker club offers a warm, friendly welcome. Up to four guest beers from micros countrywide are available. A small, comfortable TV lounge is available for those who are not playing on one of the 10 top quality snooker tables. Twice yearly the club plays host to a professional celebrity and two beer festivals are held annually. Winner of CAMRA regional Club of the Year 2004-2007, it welcomes CAMRA members on production of a current membership card or this Guide.
☺⇌(North Rd)🚌♣

Number Twenty-2 ✔

22 Coniscliffe Road, DL3 7RG
⌚ 12-11; closed Sun
☎ (01325) 354590 🌐 villagebrewer.co.uk
Burton Bridge Bitter; Village Brewer White Boar, Zetland, Old Raby; guest beers Ⓗ
Town centre ale house with a passion for real ale and winner of many CAMRA awards. Up to 13 beers, including a stout, are always available along with nine European bottled beers. Huge curved windows, stained glass panels and a high ceiling give the interior an airy, spacious feel. This is the home of Village Brewer beers, commissioned from Hambleton by the licensee. Burton Bridge Festival Ale is sold here as Classic Burton Ale. Q◐♿⇌🚌▯

Old Yard Tapas Bar

98 Bondgate, DL3 7JY
⌚ 10-11; 12-10.30 Sun
☎ (01325) 467385 🌐 tapasbar.co.uk
John Smith's Magnet; Theakston Old Peculier; guest beers Ⓗ
Interesting mixture of a town centre bar and Mediterranean-style taverna offering a range of real ales alongside a fascinating blend of international wines and spirits. Up to four guest beers from micros countrywide are stocked. Although this is a thriving restaurant, you are more than welcome to simply pop in for a pint. The excellent pavement café is popular in good weather. TV is for sport only.
❀◐🚌

Quakerhouse

1-3 Mechanics Yard, DL3 7QF (off High Row)
⌚ 11 (12 Sun)-midnight
☎ (07845) 666643 🌐 quakerhouse.net
Jarrow Rivet Catcher; guest beers Ⓗ

Often the first point of call for CAMRA members visiting Darlington, this lively award-winning free house is situated in one of the old yards just off the pedestrianised town centre. Up to nine guests are available from micro-breweries countrywide including many rare and unusual ales. The cider is Old Rosie. Live music features on Wednesday (there is a door charge after 7.30pm). An upstairs function room is available for hire. ♿⇌🚌●

Tap & Spile

99 Bondgate, DL3 7JY
⏲ 12-11 (2am Fri & Sat); 12-midnight Sun
☎ (01325) 381679
Johns Smith's Magnet; guest beers ⊞
Recently refurbished, this friendly pub stocks four ever-changing guest ales from Northern micros including Daleside, Goose Eye and Wylam. It attracts a mixed clientele of all ages from young pool players to CAMRA members. There is a DJ on Friday, live music on Saturday and a quiz on Monday. Customers enjoy the large pavement drinking area in summer. ❀⇌🚌♣●⁻

William Stead ✔

8 Crown Street, DL1 1LU
⏲ 9am-midnight (1am Fri & Sat)
☎ (01325) 341440
Greene King IPA, Abbot; Marston's Pedigree; guest beers ⊞
This Wetherspoon's Lloyds No 1 bar is named after a celebrated 19th-century editor of the local newspaper who became one of the most influential writers of his age but drowned on the ill-fated Titanic. Popular with a mixed clientele, it offers up to three guest beers sold at value for money prices, mainly from local breweries. ◑♿⇌🚌⁻

Durham

Colpitts Hotel

Colpitts Terrace, DH1 4EL
⏲ 2 (12 Thu-Sat)-11; 12-10.30 Sun
☎ (0191) 386 9913
Samuel Smith OBB ⊞
An unspoilt gem, this late Victorian pub has changed little since it was first built. Occupying a corner site, the building has an unusual 'A' shape with three rooms: a small lounge, a snug used as a pool room and the comfortable main bar partially divided by a fireplace. Like all Sam Smith's, the noise comes from conversation not jukebox or games machines. A must-visit hostelry for anyone who appreciates pubs as they used to be. ♨Q❀⊟⇌🚌⁻

Dun Cow ✔

37 Old Elvet, DH1 3HN
⏲ 11-11; 12-10.30 Sun
☎ (0191) 386 9219
Black Sheep Best Bitter; Caledonian Deuchars IPA; Camerons Castle Eden Ale ⊞
In 995AD Lindisfarne monks were searching for a resting place for the body of St Cuthbert when they came across a milkmaid looking for her lost cow. She directed them to Dun Holm (Durham). This pub, dating back to the 16th century, is named after the historic animal. At the front of the building is a friendly snug and a larger lounge to the rear. The story of the monks' legendary journey is told on the wall of the corridor alongside the two rooms. Q⊟⇌🚌⁻

Half Moon ✔

86 New Elvet, DH1 3AQ (opp Royal County Hotel)
⏲ 11-11 (midnight Fri & Sat); 12-11 Sun
☎ (0191) 383 6981
Black Sheep Best Bitter; Draught Bass; Taylor Landlord; guest beer ⊞
A long-term regular in the Guide, this city centre pub is named after the crescent-shaped bar that runs from the front room through to the lounge area. Run by the same landlord for 23 years, the interior is largely unchanged with traditional decor throughout and interesting photos of the pub at the beginning of the 20th century on the walls. Attracting a lively crowd on Friday and Saturday evenings, it has a large backyard outdoor area next to the river which is popular in summer. The guest beer is from Durham Brewery. Q❀⊟⇌🚌⁻

Market Tavern

27 Market Place, DH1 3NJ
⏲ 11-11 (midnight Thu; 1am Fri & Sat); 12-11 Sun
☎ (0191) 3862069
Black Sheep Best Bitter; Mordue Workie Ticket; Theakston Old Peculier; guest beers ⊞
This bare-boarded ale house has undergone recent refurbishment. It features up to six cask ales from breweries all over the UK, with Houston beers often guesting. The emphasis here is on real ale with forthcoming beers advertised on a large board as you enter the pub. Meals are served until 9pm, a regular quiz hosted on Tuesday night. Handy for the Gala Theatre and the historical Norman cathedral. ◑⇌

Olde Elm Tree

12 Crossgate, DH1 4PS
⏲ 12-11; 11-midnight Fri & Sat; 12-10.30 Sun
☎ (0191) 3864621
Adnams Bitter; Camerons Strongarm; guest beers ⊞
One of Durham's oldest pubs, dating back to at least 1600. As befits its age it is reputed to have two ghosts. The interior comprises an L-shaped bar room and a 'top' room linked by a set of stairs. A popular pub, it attracts a good mix including students, locals and bikers. Arrive early for the quiz on Wednesday or folk group on Monday and Tuesday. Ask the landlord for details of the scenic walk to the river banks and cathedral. The bus station in North Road is just 200m away. ❀⇌🚌P⁻

Victoria Inn ★

86 Hallgarth Street, DH1 3AS
⏲ 11.45-3, 6-11; 12-2, 7-10.20 Sun
☎ (0191) 386 5629 🌐 victoriainn-durhamcity.co.uk
Big Lamp Bitter; guest beers ⊞
This warmly welcoming and friendly authentic Victorian pub remains almost unaltered since it was built in 1899. The quaint decor, coal fires, tiny snug and a genuine Victorian cash drawer help create an olde-worlde feel. Five superb real ales, mainly from local breweries, are on sale alongside a wide selection of whiskies. There is no food menu but toasties

are available. The excellent en-suite accommodation is renowned. Voted Durham CAMRA Pub of the Year for the fifth time in 2007. ⌂Q⊭⊟⇌⊟♣

Water House ✔

65 North Road, DH1 4SQ

⊙ 9-midnight (1am Fri & Sat)

☎ (0191) 370 6540

Greene King IPA, Abbot; Marston's Pedigree; guest beers ⊞

Situated in former water board offices and a short distance from the bus station, this pub is popular with young and old alike and extremely busy at weekends. A selection of beers from regional and micro-brewers awaits with single brewery weekends now a feature. The modern decor is complemented by coal-effect open fires. Good value food is served. An excellent place to pass the time while waiting for your bus. ⊕♿⇌⊖⊟

Eaglescliffe

Cleveland Bay

718 Yarm Road, TS16 0JE (jct of A67 and A135)

⊙ 11-12.30am

☎ (01642) 780275

Taylor Landlord; guest beer ⊞

Dating from the arrival of the world's first public railway, the Stockton & Darlington, the gate pillars from the goods yard now adorn the entrance to the car park. An ever popular pub, you can be sure of a friendly and genuine welcome from the landlord and regulars here. A recent CAMRA Pub of the Season winner, its reputation for fine cask beers continues to grow. With a separate bar, lounge and large function room, it is bustling on big sports occasions. ❀⊟⊟(7)P⊱⊓

Egglescliffe

Pot & Glass

Church Road, TS16 9DQ (400m from A135, opp church)

⊙ 12-2 (not Mon), 6-11 (5.30-midnight Fri; 6-midnight Sat); 12-11 Sun

☎ (01642) 651009

Caledonian Deuchars IPA; Draught Bass; Taylor Golden Best; guest beers ⊞

A previous CAMRA Pub of the Season winner, this classic and popular village pub is situated in a quiet cul-de-sac opposite the village church. Former licensee and cabinet maker Charlie Abbey, whose last resting place overlooks the pub, left his legacy in the form of the ornate bar fronts fashioned from old country furniture. The interior comprises a front room, back room and function room, outside is a large south-facing garden. Occasional themed food evenings support the good value home-cooked menu.
Q⊱❀⊕⊟⊟(7)P⊱⊓

Elwick

McOrville Inn

34 The Green, TS27 3EF

⊙ 12-2.30 (10-3 Sat), 5-11; 12-3, 7-10.30 Sun

☎ (01429) 273344

Camerons seasonal beers, McOrville Ale; guest beers ⊞

Ancient village inn named after a local horse who won the 1802 St Leger. Real fires and old village photos add to the traditonal ambience. Deep, damp cellars ensure the beers are kept in excellent condition. One of the guest beers is usually sourced from Camerons' micro-brewery. A superb food menu, made with local produce wherever possible, represents good value. The pub opens early on Saturday for a full English breakfast. A 2007 CAMRA Pub of the Season winner. ⌂Q❀⊕⊟(516,518)P

Esh

Cross Keys

Front Street, DH7 9QR (3 miles from A691) NZ197440

⊙ 12-3, 5.30-11; 12-10 Sun

☎ (0191) 373 1279

Black Sheep Best Bitter; Tetley Bitter ⊞

Pleasant 18th-century pub in a picturesque village offering a varied food menu including vegetarian and children's choices. A comfortable locals' bar is complemented by a lounge overlooking the Browney Valley. Delft racks display porcelain artefacts, some of which portray the old village. The village is commonly known as Old Esh to distinguish it from nearby Esh Winning. ⊕⊟P

Ferryhill

Surtees Arms ✔

Chilton Lane, DL17 0DH

⊙ 4-11; 12-midnight Fri & Sat; 12-11 Sun

☎ (01740) 655724 ⊕ thesurteesarms.co.uk

Shepherd Neame Spitfire; John Smith's Bitter; guest beers ⊞

Large multi-roomed traditional pub owned by CAMRA members —a rare nitrokeg free cask ale outlet in the town. Guest beers are sourced from wholesalers and local breweries. The now permanent real cider also changes regularly. An annual beer festival is held in the spring. Charity, live music and psychic nights are regular events. A function room is available for private gatherings. Lunches are served on Sundays only.
⌂Q⊱❀⊕⊟⊟♣●⊱

Forest in Teesdale

Langdon Beck Hotel

DL12 0XP (on B6277, 8 miles NW of Middleton in Teesdale) NY853312

⊙ 11-11; 12-10.30 Sun

☎ (01833) 622267 ⊕ langdonbeckhotel.com

Black Sheep Best Bitter; Jarrow Rivet Catcher; guest beers ⊞

Situated high in the Pennines, in some of the finest countryside in England, this inn has long been a destination for walkers, fishermen and those seeking tranquillity. Attracting visitors not only for the scenery, this gem offers excellent food plus beers that include a guest from a local micro. A beer festival is held in May. The spectacular High Force and Cauldron Snout waterfalls are not too far away and the Pennine Way passes close by.
⌂Q⊱❀⊭⊕⊟♿⚠♣P

Framwellgate Moor

Tap & Spile ✔

Front Street, DH1 5EE

12-3 (Fri & Sat only), 6 (5 Fri)-11.30; 12-3, 7-10.30 Sun

☎ (0191) 386 5451

Beer range varies Ⓗ

Offering one of the best selections of ales in Durham, this ever-popular CAMRA award-winning pub continues to fly the flag for local micros. A typical ale house divided into four rooms with wooden flooring, it offers a warm welcome and good conversation. With its display of old pump clips, some bearing testament to breweries long departed, this is a must visit for any real ale fan. Why not try you luck at the Wednesday night quiz.
Q🚌(21,1A)♣

Frosterley

Black Bull

Bridge End, DL13 2SL (100m S of A689 at W end of village)

10.30-11 (closed Mon); 10.30-5.30 Sun

☎ (01388) 527784

Beer range varies Ⓗ

Once upon a time, all pubs were like this. No lager, no keg beer, just four ales from north-eastern independent breweries, plus up to four ciders and perries. Stone and bare wooden floors throughout, plus a kitchen range and piano in the bar, add to the rustic decor and real old-fashioned pub ambience. High-quality food is made from locally-sourced ingredients. There are tables outside the front door and a covered yard to the side. The only pub in the country to have its own peal of bells. Q❀🚌(101)

Hartburn

Masham Hotel ✔

87 Hartburn Village, TS18 5DR

11-11 (11.30 Fri & Sat); 12-4, 7-10.30 Sun

☎ (01642) 645526

Black Sheep Best Bitter, Ale; Draught Bass; Greene King IPA Ⓗ

The Masham still retains the appearance of the residential house it once was. Step inside and it is like walking into somebody's front room. The multi-room interior has a central bar serving the range of real ales, some of which may change from time to time. Food is all home made, good value and deservedly popular. Outdoor facilities are impressive and extensive, with shelter for smokers.
Q❀🚌(20)P

Parkwood ✔

64-66 Darlington Road, TS18 5ER

12-11

☎ (01642) 587933 theparkwoodhotel.com

Adnams Broadside; Camerons Strongarm; Greene King Abbot; guest beers Ⓗ

This magnificent red brick Victorian building, with its imposing porch, staircase and public rooms, is the former home of the Ropner family —local shipbuilders, ship owners and civic benefactors. The licensee has been a real ale enthusiast for many years and is determined to keep the bar for drinkers, though there is a strong emphasis on food in the busy restaurant. The guest beer is usually a rarity for the area. Accommodation is in high-quality en-suite rooms.
Q❀🚌(20)P

Hartlepool

Brewery Tap

Stockton Street, TS24 7QS (on A689 in front of Camerons Brewery)

11-4 (closed Sun)

☎ (01429) 868686 cameronsbrewery.com

Camerons Strongarm, seasonal beers Ⓗ

When Camerons Brewery discovered that it owned the derelict Stranton Inn, its future was secured by turning it into a visitor centre. Visitors to this award-winning development can sample Strongarm, the brewery's flagship brand, together with monthly specials from the main brewery and Camerons' own Lion's Den micro-brewery. It also acts as the brewery shop and museum and the starting point for brewery tours. Conference facilities and evening opening for groups and social events can be arranged. Q♿🚌P

Causeway

Vicarage Gardens, Stranton, TS24 7QT (beside Camerons Brewery)

3-11 (11.30 Thu); 11-midnight Fri & Sat; 12-10.30 Sun

☎ (01429) 273954 myspace.com/thecausewaypubhartlepool

Banks's Bitter; Camerons Strongarm; Marston's Old Empire; guest beers Ⓗ

This marvellous red brick Victorian building has been Camerons' unofficial' brewery tap for decades. Though owned by Marston's, the sales of Strongarm are huge. The licensee is a keen musician so it is no surprise to find an eclectic mix of live music most evenings. A CAMRA multi-award winning pub, it even gets a mention in Hansard, where the quality of the Strongarm was praised by the local MP. Two guest beers are always available. The walled beer garden has a covered and heated area for smokers. Q❀♿🚌

Jackson's Arms

Tower Street, TS24 7HH (100m S of railway station)

12-midnight (2am Fri & Sat)

☎ (01429) 862413

Beer range varies Ⓗ

At one time a Matthew Brown tied house, this pub was also once offered as the prize in a raffle. However, at £100 a ticket there weren't many takers and the raffle was cancelled. First impressions on entering are of a warm and friendly welcome. There are two busy bars, one for convivial conversation and one for pool and darts. The function room is newly refurbished. At least three, generally four guest beers are on offer, sourced from throughout the country. 🚌

Hartlepool Headland

Fishermans Arms

Southgate, TS24 0JJ

11-11.30; 12-11 Sun

☎ (01429) 266029

Camerons Strongarm Ⓗ
Family-run pub with a licensee celebrating 21 years of service, situated close to the Fish Quay, town wall and the site of the Anglo Saxon monastery founded by St Aidan in 640AD. Pictures that adorn the walls of this one-room local remind us that the port was once bustling with fishing boats, coal staithes, pit props and ship building. The area is best known nowadays for the legend of the hanging of the monkey – but be careful who you ask. ❀🚌(7)

Heighington

Bay Horse
28 West Green, DL5 6PE
✪ 11-midnight; 12-10.30 Sun
☎ (01325) 312312
Black Sheep Best Bitter; John Smith's Magnet; guest beers Ⓗ
Picturesque, historic, 300-year-old pub overlooking the village's largest green. Its exposed beams and stone walls offer traditional surroundings, partitioned into distinct drinking and dining areas, with a large restaurant extending from the lounge. Food plays a prominent role, with home-cooked meals available as well as bar snacks. The bar area gives drinkers the chance to enjoy the beer range in the evening, which includes up to three guest beers from breweries countrywide. ❀◐◑🍴♿🚌P

Locomotion No. One
Heighington Station, Heighington Lane, DL5 6QG
✪ 11-midnight (11 Sat & Sun); 12-10.30
☎ (01325) 320132 🌐 thelocomotion1.co.uk
Beer range varies Ⓗ
This family-run pub occupies the former stationmaster's house at Heighington Station, next to the level crossing where the first ever locomotive to haul a passenger train was hoisted onto the track in 1825. The excellent range of ales and friendly atmosphere are enjoyed by locals and visitors alike. A terrace occupies the original platform with an additional courtyard for outdoor drinking. An extensive menu is served in the pub or upstairs restaurant (no food Sun or Mon eve). Beware, the last train leaves early.
⛰❀◐◑⇌♣P⁄–

Hett Hills

Moorings
DH2 3JU (from Chester-le-Street take B6313 under viaduct) NZ240513
✪ 12-11.30 (10.30 Sun)
☎ (0191) 370 1597 🌐 themooringsdurham.co.uk
Black Sheep Best Bitter; guest beers Ⓗ
Impressive pub on two levels, with a nautical theme. The bar and bistro serve food all day, offering a wide choice of traditional home-cooked English dishes. Upstairs, with views over the West Durham Hills, the Prime Rib restaurant offers quality food including fine cuts of local meats and seafood – ideal for a special occasion. A smoking cabin is available outside. ❀🛏◐◑♿🚌(28)⁄–

High Hesleden

Ship Inn
TS27 4QD NZ453381
✪ 6-11.30; closed Mon; 12-11.30 Sat; 12-9 Sun
☎ (01429) 836453 🌐 theshipinn.net
Beer range varies Ⓗ
Remote gem of a country free house in the south east of the county. Seven ales, mainly from micro-breweries, are on handpump in the comfortable bar. An award-winning selection of superb food is served in the lounge and restaurant. A nautical theme runs through the pub with models and pictures of warships on display. Adjacent to the large rear garden are six chalets plus a family room. There is ample parking and a good view of the North Sea on clear days. ⛰Q❀🛏◐◑P⁄–

High Shincliffe

Avenue Inn
Avenue Street, DH1 2PT (off A177)
✪ 12-11
☎ (0191) 386 5954 🌐 theavenue.biz
Caledonian Deuchars IPA; Camerons Strongarm Ⓗ
This friendly out of town pub is a good base for walkers enjoying the attractive countryside nearby. The Monday night quiz and dominoes knock-out competition on Thursday evening are popular with locals and visitors. Regular buses to Durham City a mile and a half away pass close by. NEEDS SYMBOLS

Howden le Wear

Plantation
40 High Street, DL15 8EZ (close to A689, between Bishop Auckland and Crook)
✪ 6 (7 Tue & Thu; 5 Fri; 2 Sat)-11; 12-3, 6-10.30 Sun
☎ (01388) 766450
John Smith's Bitter; Camerons Strongarm; guest beers Ⓗ
Very much a community pub, this roadside inn has a large drinking area with plenty of seating and a narrower bar area, providing two distinct drinking spaces. Darts and dominoes teams play on Monday, a quiz and bingo are hosted on Thursday. Other events take place by popular demand, including a conker championship. Guest beers often come from Adnams. There is a patio at the side of building and a small car park at the front.
⛰❀🚌(1)♣P⁄–

Lanchester

Queens Head
17, Front Street, DH7 0LA (off A691 Consett road)
✪ 11-11 (midnight Fri & Sat); 12-11 Sun
☎ (01207) 529990
Brakspear Oxford Gold; Wells Bombardier; guest beers Ⓗ
Attractively refurbished by pubco McKenna Inns in Sept 2007, the pub's new landlord is enthusiastic about ale and food. The interior comprises a lounge, small bar and spacious restaurant, decorated in contrasting shades of brown and cream, with stylish leather seating. Set meals and specials are served in the smart dining area. Q♉❀◐◑🍴🚌P⁄–

Leamside

Three Horse Shoes

Pit House Lane, DH4 6QQ

11-midnight; 12-11.30 Sun

(0191) 584 2394

Beer range varies

During the last year this pub has undergone extensive changes and building work. The result is well worth coming to see for yourself. With the landlord building on his experience as manager of regular winners of Sunderland and North-East CAMRA pub awards, the range of nine beers is of high quality and tends to include some ales that are rare for the area. The traditional front bar has an open fire and the back of the pub is now devoted to high quality food (booking essential).

Metal Bridge

Old Mill Hotel

Thinford Road, DH6 5NX (off A177) NZ303351

12-11 (10.30 Sun)

(01740) 652928 theoldmill.uk.com

Beer range varies

The venue of choice for discerning locals and visitors alike, this spacious inn offers good-quality food and well-kept ales. Three handpumps serve an ever-changing range, with the nearby Durham Brewery often supplying one of the beers. The food menu is extensive with daily specials written up on a board above the bar. Larger groups are welcome in the conservatory room. Accommodation is of a high standard, with all rooms are en-suite. P

Middlestone Village

Ship Inn

Low Road, DL14 8AB (on B6287)

4 (12 Fri-Sun)-11

(01388) 810904 shipinnmiddlestone.co.uk

Beer range varies

The epitome of a village pub, this bustling local is very much at the heart of the community, though regulars come from miles around. Entertainment includes darts and dominoes on Monday, a quiz on Thursday, plus regular themed nights and twice-yearly beer festivals. The open plan bar has three drinking areas and there is an upstairs function room with two rooftop patios —from here you can enjoy spectacular views south to the North Yorkshire Moors. Food is available lunchtime and evening Friday to Sunday, evening only Monday-Thursday. (2, 3)

No Place

Beamish Mary

DH9 0QH (off A693 Chester-le-Street-Consett road)

12-11 (10.30 Sun)

(0191) 370 0237

Big Lamp Lamplight, No Place Bitter; guest beers

Family-run pub in a former pit village with open fires and a collection of memorabilia dating from the 1920s and 30s. A folk club is hosted on the last Wednesday of the month in the stables. Tuesday is quiz night and a beer festival is hold on the last weekend in January. Winner of many CAMRA awards, the house beer is No Place Bitter brewed by Big Lamp. Old Rosie is the real cider.

(7B)P

North Bitchburn

Red Lion

North Bitchburn Terrace, DL15 8AL (just off A689)

12-3 (not Mon), 6.30-11 (sometimes midnight); 12-4, 6.30-midnight

(01388) 763561 theredlionbitchburn.co.uk

Black Sheep Best Bitter; Taylor Landlord; guest beers

Popular 250-year-old village pub with fine south-easterly views over the Wear Valley from the dining room. Originally a farm, it then became a way station for drovers on the way to Bishop Auckland market. The cheerful, refurbished interior is light and bright, with a comfortable bar room, small pool room and larger restaurant with a second dining area down a couple of steps. The pub has a well-deserved reputation for good food, available lunchtime and evening. Guest beers tend to come from smaller north eastern breweries, with a monthly feature brewery' such as Mordue or Jarrow. (1C)P

Ovington

Four Alls

The Green, DL11 7BP (2 miles S of Winston & A67)

7 (6 Fri; 3 Sat)-11; 12-10.30 Sun

(01833) 627302 thefouralls-teesdale.co.uk

Tetley Bitter; guest beers

Friendly 18th-century inn opposite the village green in what is known as the maypole village'. A Victorian sign denotes the four alls: I govern all (queen), I fight for all (soldier), I pray for all (parson), I pay for all (farmer)'. The pub has a bar, games room and restaurant serving excellent value food. Home of the Four Alls Brewery, it is advisable to phone first if you want to try the beers as they alternate with guests from micros countrywide.

QP

Preston-le-Skerne

Blacksmiths Arms

Preston Lane, DL5 6JH (off A167 at Gretna Green)

11.30-2; 6-11; closed Mon; 12-10.30 Sun

(01325) 314873

Beer range varies

Welcoming freehouse known locally as the Hammers, situated in a rural location. A long corridor separates the bar, lounge and restaurant. The beamed lounge is furnished in a farmhouse style. It has an excellent reputation for home-cooked food and up to three guest beers are available from micros countrywide. A former local CAMRA Rural Pub of the Year, it even has a helicopter landing pad. QP

Rookhope

Rookhope Inn

Rear Hogarth Terrace, DL13 2BG

⏲ 12-midnight
☎ (01388) 517215
Black Sheep Best Bitter; Greene King Abbot Ⓗ
Off the beaten track in the North Pennines, this Grade II listed building dating from 1680 retains the original open fires and wood beams. A welcome rest stop on the Coast to Coast cycle route, this friendly two-roomed community pub also offers accommodation. Spectacular views of upper Weardale can be enjoyed from the garden. Situated in a pretty former lead-mining village, the surrounding area provides ample opportunity for exploration. ⛼⇄◑⊟♣

St John's Chapel

Blue Bell
12 Hood Street, DL13 1QJ
⏲ 5 (12 Sat & Sun)-1am
☎ (01388) 537256
Caledonian Deuchars IPA; guest beers Ⓗ
A major hub of the community, this small, homely village local is situated in beautiful Upper Weardale. The pub hosts ladies and gents darts and pool teams and runs a quiz on Sunday night. It also has a leek club which holds an annual show, and there is a small library for patrons' use. The local angling club is based here and fishing licences are on sale at the bar. The guest beer often comes from the local Allendale Brewery. There is a covered and heated outdoor area.
⛼❀Ⲁ⊟(101)♣●P⅟

Seaton

Seaton Lane Inn
SR7 0LP (on B1404 W of A19)
⏲ 11.30-midnight (1am Fri & Sat)
☎ (0191) 581 2038 🌐 seatonlaneinn.co.uk
Taylor Landlord; Black Sheep Best Bitter; Wells Bombardier; guest beers Ⓗ
This roadside inn can trace its origins to an 18th-century blacksmith's – the basic stone-walled bar was the original building and a pictorial history is displayed on the walls. Behind this room is a small lounge next to a popular restaurant area. Quiz nights are Wednesday and Thursday. The large decked garden is licensed for live outdoor acoustic entertainment four times a year, weather permitting. ⛼Q❀◑⊟P⅟

Sedgefield

Ceddesfeld Hall
Sedgefield Community Association, Rectory Row, TS21 2AE
⏲ 7.30-10.30; 8-11 Fri & Sun; 9-11 Sat
☎ (01740) 620341
Beer range varies Ⓗ
Built in 1791 as the local parsonage, the hall comes complete with resident ghost 'the Pickled Parson'. Set in extensive grounds, ideal for a summer evening, this is a private club but CAMRA members are most welcome. There is a bar, comfortable lounge and large function room. Run by volunteers from the Sedgefield Community Association, it is used by wide variety of groups. An annual beer festival is held on the first weekend in July with very reasonably-priced ale.
Q❀⊟♿⊟P⅟

Nag's Head
8 West End, TS21 2BS
⏲ 6 (5 Wed-Fri; 12 Sat)-midnight; 12-11 Sun
☎ (01740) 620234
Taylor Landlord; guest beers Ⓗ
Situated at the centre of the village, close to Sedgefield Racecourse, this free house is a traditional local attracting all age groups – families with well-behaved children are very welcome. There is a comfortable bar and a smaller lounge as well as a restaurant serving local and international dishes prepared with fresh local produce. Meals are also served in the bar (no food Sun & Mon eve). The landlord and landlady both come from the village.
❀◑⊟♿⊟♣P⅟

Shadforth

Plough
Southside, DH6 1LL (1 mile off A181)
⏲ 12-3, 6-11; 12-11 Sat; 12-10.30 Sun
☎ (0191) 372 0375
Double Maxim Double Maxim; Marston's Pedigree Ⓗ
Situated in a small, quiet village some five miles to the east of Durham city, this pub re-opened in 2005 after extensive refurbishment. The warm and welcoming stone-tiled bar room leads through to a carpeted lounge and restaurant serving excellent quality fare, which is also available at the bar. Sunday is quiz night and the Plough football team meets here. ♨❀◑⊟♿⊟(244)♣P

Shincliffe

Seven Stars Inn
High Street North, DH1 2NU (on A177, S of Durham)
⏲ 11-11 Mon to Sat (10.30 Sun)
☎ (0191) 384 8454 🌐 sevenstarsinn.co.uk
Black Sheep Best Bitter; Caledonian Deuchars IPA; Taylor Landlord; guest beers Ⓗ
Dating from 1724, this small, cosy, beamed pub is situated on the edge of a pleasant village. Local country walks and the long Weardale Way pass nearby. Walkers are welcome in the bar – just make sure your boots are clean. Well-behaved dogs are also permitted. Meals are served in the bar and traditional restaurant. Comfortable accommodation makes the pub a great base for visiting the city and other attractions in the area. See the pubs website for details.
❀⇄◑⊟

Spennymoor

Frog & Ferret
Coulson Street, DL16 7RS
⏲ 12-midnight (11.30 Sun)
☎ (01388) 818312
Beer range varies Ⓗ
This family-run pub is now is only freehouse in Spennymoor to stock real ale. A welcoming atmosphere greets you on arrival at the central bar in the comfortably furnished lounge. The four real ales are sourced from far

and wide with local and northern micro-breweries well represented. Sunday lunches with fresh home-cooked food are now a popular feature (booking is advisable). Well-behaved children are permitted until 4pm. A quiz is held on Sunday evening. ⌂❀☾♿♣P⁻

Stanhope

Grey Bull

17 West Terrace, DL13 2PB (On A689 at W end of village)
⏲ 12-midnight Sat, Sun & summer; 2-midnight Winter
☎ (01388) 528177
Banks's Bitter; guest beers Ⓗ
Congenial pub on the edge of the largest village in Weardale. Well used by the local community, it is a meeting point for the cricket and leek clubs as well as pool and darts teams. Ideal for holidaymakers using the adjacent camping and caravan sites, it is conveniently close to the river and open air swimming pool. The 101 bus passes the door on its way up and down the Dale.
⌂ბ❀⊟♿▲⊟(101)♣⁻

Stockton-on-Tees

Georgia Browns

20 Dovecot Street, TS18 1LN
⏲ 11-midnight
☎ (01642) 676006
Milestone Colonial Reserve, Olde Home Wrecker; guest beers Ⓗ
If your passion is for stronger ales, this contemporary cafe-bar is the place for you. Reopened in 2006 following years of closure during development of the adjacent precinct, it has quickly developed a well-deserved reputation for its fine beers. Reasonably-priced food is served until 4pm daily. Happy hour is 5-7.30pm, with the already low prices discounted by a further 10 per cent – a discount that is available at all times to CAMRA members. A south-facing verandah is pleasant in warm weather. ❀☾♿⇌⊟

Sun Inn ✔

Knowles Street, TS18 1SU
⏲ 11-11; 12-10.30 Sun
☎ (01642) 611461
Draught Bass Ⓗ
Popular town centre drinkers' pub reputed to sell more Draught Bass than any other pub in the county. It was rescued from an uncertain future five years ago by a regular drinker who became the licensee and soon increased sales of Bass to 12 kils a week. The pub supports darts teams, a football team and charitable causes. On Monday evening the large back room is home to the famous Stockton Folk Club. ⇌⊟♣⁻

Thomas Sheraton ✔

4 Bridge Road, TS18 1BH
⏲ 9-midnight (1am Fri & Sat)
☎ (01642) 606134
Greene King IPA, Abbot; Marston's Pedigree; guest beers Ⓗ
This popular pub is a fine Wetherspoon conversion of the former law courts, named after one of the country's great Georgian cabinet makers and furniture designers who was born in the town in 1751. It has six drinking areas including a balcony and a sheltered patio area upstairs, both accessed by palatial staircases. High sales volumes lead to an ever-varying selection of up to 12 beers, with guests usually sourced from north east craft breweries. Weston's Old Rosie is the house cider. ბ❀☾◗♿⇌⊟●⁻

Sunniside

Moss Inn

78 Front Street, DL13 4LX (W end of village on B6299)
⏲ 6-11; 12-10.30 Sun
☎ (01388) 730447
Black Sheep Best Bitter; guest beer Ⓗ
Homely freehouse situated closed to Tow Law serving good food and ale. As well as the beers an extensive selection of malt whiskies is available to the connoisseur, perfect for enjoying in front of the open fire on a winter's night. Friday is domino night and visitors are welcome to join the friendly locals. Food is served on Sunday lunchtime and Thursday evening. ⌂☾◗⊟⊟(1B)♣P⁻

Thorpe Thewles

Hamilton Russell Arms

Bank Terrace, TS21 3JW (100m off A177)
⏲ 12-11 (10.30 Sun)
☎ (01740) 630757 🌐 hamiltonrussell.com
Marston's Pedigree; guest beers Ⓗ
Named in celebration of the marriage of Gustavson Hamilton and Emma Marie Russell in 1928, this impressive pub was formerly part of the Marchioness of Londonderry's estate. The emphasis here is on good-value top-quality food, served all day every day, attracting customers from far and wide. However real ale remains the licensee's passion and drinkers are made most welcome. Two guest beers, usually premium/strong bitters, are always available. The extensive south-facing patio areas have fine views. ⌂❀☾◗♿⊟(69)P⁻

Trimdon Grange

Dovecote Inn

Salters Lane, TS29 6EP (on B1278)
⏲ 7 (midnight Fri)-11; 12-11 Sun
☎ (01429) 880967
Beer range varies Ⓗ
The landlord of this free house hails from Charles Wells country —his twin passions are Rugby Union and real ale. Situated on the outskirts of a former mining village, the pub dates back to at least 1820, growing an extra storey in 1927, resulting in the building's distinctive tall but narrow appearance. There used to be a dovecote on one corner, hence the name. Inside, the single large room houses a popular pool table and dartboard. Quiz night is Tuesday. ⌂⊟

West Cornforth

Hare & Hounds Inn

Garmondsway, DL17 9DT

12-3, 6-11; closed Mon; 12-11 Sat & Sun
☎ (01740) 654661
Beer range varies
Formerly called the Fox Inn, the pub's origins go back to 1771 when it was part of a farm and coaching inn. Now owned by Enterprise Inns and run by tenants who appreciate real ale, it comprises a large L-shaped bar and a restaurant that doubles as a lounge, with exposed beams throughout. It specialises in meals based on locally-sourced produce, especially beef (booking is advised) and can cater for parties. P

Willington

Burn Inn

14 West End Terrace, DL15 0HW (jct B6286 & A690 at W end of village)
5.30 (12 Fri-Sun)-midnight
☎ (01388) 746291
Beer range varies
This cosy establishment has become a first class community pub, serving three ales from the Punch taverns Finest Cask range. Various pub games are played here throughout the week and a quiz is held on Wednesday. It also has its own golf society, provides a meeting point for village junior football teams and acts as a venue for local Labour Party meetings. There is a heated outdoor area for smokers. P

Witton Gilbert

Glendenning Arms

Front Street, DH7 6SY (off A691 bypass, 3 miles from city centre)
4 (3 Fri; 12 Sat & Sun)-midnight
☎ (0191) 371 0316
Black Sheep Best Bitter; guest beer
Typical village community local and Guide regular with a small, comfortable lounge and a lively and welcoming bar with the original Vaux 1970s red and white handpulls. The bar is attractively decorated in a contemporary style while the lounge remains more traditional. The pub runs darts, dominoes and football teams. Situated on the village's main road, there is ample car parking.
QP

Travellers Rest

Front Street, DH7 6TQ (off A691 bypass 3 miles from city centre)
11-11; 12-10.30 Sun
☎ (0191) 371 0458
Theakston Best Bitter; guest beers
Open-plan country-style pub, popular with diners. The bar area is split into three sections with a conservatory off to the side where families are welcome. There is also a more private dining room. Part of the Fox chain of restaurants, an extensive food menu suits all tastes with dining taking place throughout the pub. Quiz nights are Tuesday and Sunday.
QP

Wolsingham

Bay Horse Hotel

59 Uppertown, DL13 3EX (on B6296 to Tow Law)
NZ078378
11-midnight (11-3, 5-midnight Mon-Fri winter)
☎ (01388) 527220
Camerons Strongarm, Castle Eden Ale; guest beer
Large Camerons house on the north edge of the village. Excellent quality, good value food is served in the bar and à la carte restaurant. The guest beer is usually from the Camerons range. Quiz night is Sunday. There is a covered outdoor area for smokers. Good quality bed & breakfast accommodation is available, providing an ideal base for exploring Weardale. (101)P

Black Bull

27 Market Place, DL13 3AB
11-11; 12-11.30 Sun
☎ (01388) 527332
Caledonian Deuchars IPA; guest beer
Imposing hotel in the centre of the village, providing excellent food and accommodation. The pub runs various games nights and local Weight Watchers members enjoy the facilities after their meetings in the town hall opposite. It serves as headquarters of the village cricket team in the summer and hosts its social events. A good base for walkers and cyclists, it is also convenient for the Weardale Railway, which has a station in the village.
Q(101)

Wolviston

Ship Inn

50 High Street, TS22 5JX
12-3, 5-11; 12-3.30, 7-11 Sun
☎ (01740) 644420 theshipinnwolviston.co.uk
Beer range varies
In a picturesque village now completely surround by bypasses, this castle-like building was rebuilt during the 19th century on the site of an old coaching inn. The licensee follows a vigorous real ale policy, with three handpulls providing a constantly-changing range of beers. No microwave oven 'pings' here —only freshly-cooked, good value, traditional pub food is served (not Sun eve), including the Captain's Whopper Cod. There is a large south-facing beer garden and a function room available free of charge. QP

Woodhouses

Bay Horse

DL14 0LL
12-2am (last entry 11.30)
☎ (01388) 603422
John Smith's Bitter, Magnet; guest beers
A few minutes away from housing estates on the edge of Bishop Auckland, this popular single-room terraced pub with a homely ambience remains just in open country. A roaring fire greets winter visitors, while a large-screen TV sits at the other end of the bar, with a house keyboard, darts and dominoes. Guest beer is from Wear Valley. Meals served Sun lunchtime plus Fri and Sat evenings.
P

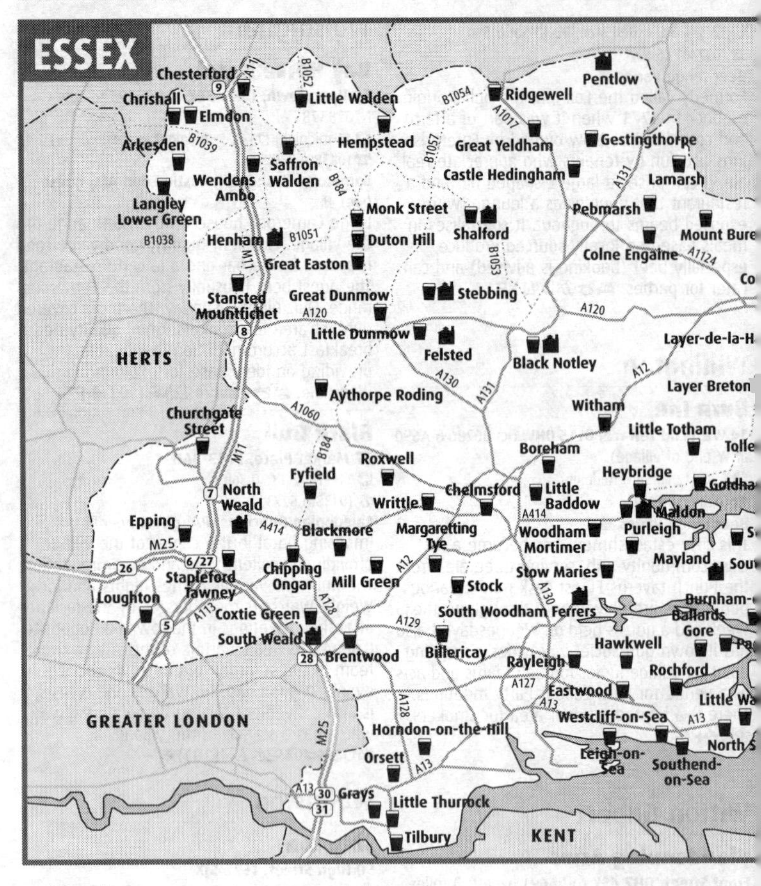

Arkesden

Axe & Compasses

Wicken Road, CB11 4EX (2 miles N of B1038) TL483344

11.30-2.30, 6-11 (11.30 Sat); 12-3, 7-10.30 Sun

☎ (01799) 550272 axeandcompasses.co.uk

Greene King IPA, Abbot, Old Speckled Hen Ⓗ

Partly-thatched, 17th-century village inn with a public bar and an award-winning restaurant. This friendly community pub is the centre of village life and the locals tend to be interested in, and talk to, strangers. The hostelry is frequented by walkers on the extensive footpath network in this pleasant area where three counties meet – the Harcamlow Way long-distance path passes nearby.

⌂Q❀◑⊕P⁻

Aythorpe Roding

Axe & Compasses

Dunmow Road, CM6 1PP (on B1845 5 miles SW of Dunmow) TL594154

11.30-11; 12-10.30 Sun

☎ (01279) 876648 theaxeandcompasses.co.uk

Nethergate IPA; Ⓗ **guest beers** Ⓖ

This isolated thatched pub was closed for some time before the current owners refurbished and reopened it in 2007. It has quickly become a favourite for good beer and good food. The three or four guest beers are all from local independent breweries and there is plenty of space for the drinkers who patronise the pub as well as diners. A pleasant beer garden at the back has views over farmland to the windmill. Q❀◑♣⁻

Ballards Gore (Stambridge)

Shepherd & Dog

Gore Road, SS4 2DA (between Rochford and Paglesham)

12-3, 6-11; 12-4, 6-10.30 Sun

INDEPENDENT BREWERIES

Brentwood South Weald
Crouch Vale South Woodham Ferrers
Famous Railway Tavern Brightlingsea
Farmer's Ales Maldon
Felstar Felsted
Hart of Stebbing Stebbing (NEW)
Harwich Town Harwich
Mersea Island East Mersea
Mighty Oak Maldon
Nethergate Pentlow
Packfield Black Notley (NEW)
Pitfield North Weald
Saffron Henham
Shalford Shalford
Wibblers Mayland (NEW)
Wonky Dog Brightlingsea (NEW)

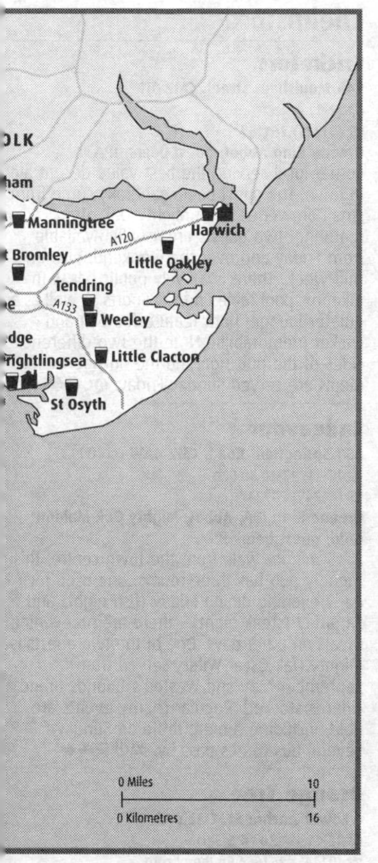

☎ (01702) 258279 🌐 shepherdanddog.piczo.com

Beer range varies Ⓗ

This excellent, comfortable cottage-style pub was voted local CAMRA Pub of the Year 2004 and Rural Pub of the Year (again) in 2008. The four changing real ales generally come from micro-breweries and are often unusual for the area. Cider is stocked in summer. The comfortable restaurant serves excellent meals together with bar snacks. Traditional pub games including Shut the Box are available on request. Walkers, cyclists and coach groups are welcome. ❀◐◑♿♣●P

Billericay

Coach & Horses

36 Chapel Street, CM12 9LU

⏲ 10-11; 12-10.30 Sun

☎ (01277) 622873

Adnams Bitter; Greene King IPA, Abbot; guest beers Ⓗ

A popular one-bar pub with a cosy, welcoming feel. Good quality food is served lunchtime and evenings, plus breakfast from 10-11.30am (not Sun). The menu features home-made pies and a varied specials board. Guest beers are from the Gray's list. The bar and food service is quick, efficient and friendly, enhancing the feel-good factor. The walls are adorned with prints and decorative plates, and a fine collection of ceramic and copper jugs hang from the ceiling. Note the CAMRA award for 10 consecutive years in the Guide.
❀◐◑⇌🚌P

Black Notley

Vine Inn

105 Witham Road, CM77 8LQ OS767208

⏲ 12-2.30 (4 Sun), 6.30-11

☎ (01376) 324269

Adnams Bitter; guest beers Ⓗ

Sixteenth-century open-plan free house with a central bar, a drinking/lounge area to the left, a restaurant area to the right and log-burning stoves at both ends. An unusual feature is the six-person mezzanine above the lounge, accessible via a steep staircase. The two guest beers are usually of East Anglian origin and one is often from Mighty Oak. Cressing railway station is a 15-minute walk away down country lanes. A heated, covered smoking area is provided outside. ⌂Q❀◐◑🚌(21)P⁻

Blackmore

Leather Bottle

Horsefayre Green, CM4 0RL

⏲ 11 (12 Sun)-11 (midnight Fri & Sat)

☎ (01277) 821891 🌐 theleatherbottle.net

Adnams Bitter, Broadside; Ⓗ **guest beers** Ⓗ/Ⓖ

Large village pub with a smallish flagstone-floored bar area. Most of the pub is taken up by a good quality restaurant. Two guest beers are generally available on handpump with a third on gravity at weekends; a beer of around 5% or higher is usually on offer. The cider is Weston's Old Rosie. An annexe to the bar has a pool table, dartboard and silent fruit machine. ⌂❀◐◑🚂🚌(32)♣●P

Boreham

Queen's Head

Church Road, CM3 3EG

⏲ 11.30-2.30, 5-11; 11.30-11 Fri-Sun

☎ (01245) 467298

Adnams Bitter; Crouch Vale Brewers Gold; Greene King IPA; guest beer Ⓗ

Tucked behind the church, this traditional village local dates from the 16th century. It has two contrasting bars, one with bench seating where darts, dominoes and cribs are played, and the other where dining takes place (no evening meals Sun). The guest beer comes from the Gray's list. Parking is limited. Q◐◑♣P⁻

Brentwood

Rising Sun

144 Ongar Road, CM15 9DJ (on A128, Western Rd jct)

⏲ 3 (12 Sat)-11.30 (midnight Fri & Sat); 12-11 Sun

☎ (01277) 213749

Brakspear Bitter; Taylor Landlord; guest beers Ⓗ

This much-improved local brings a good selection of real ales to an area where beer choice can be limited. The pub is a rare but regular outlet for Brakspear's Bitter and Taylor's Landlord as well as one or two ever-changing guest beers (including a Brentwood ale). This is a community-focused pub that hosts a charity quiz on Monday evening, cribbage on Sunday evening and frequent darts matches. Framed black and white local prints decorate the walls. Outside is a covered, heated area for smokers plus a shellfish stall at weekends. ♨❀⊟🚌♣P⌐

Brightlingsea

Railway Tavern

58 Station Road, CO7 0DT (on B1029)
⏲ 5 (3 Fri)-11; 12-11 Sat; 12-3, 7-10.30 Sun
☎ (01206) 302581
Railway Tavern Crab & Winkle Mild, Bladderwrack; guest beers 🄷
This unique town corner pub displays paintings by local artists that change monthly. There are now two drinking areas as a consequence of refurbishment over the past year. The pub has a bohemian feel with its open-plan layout; a new 15-barrel brewery can be found in the function room. This year's major win was the champion pump clip design award of East Anglia, created by local artist and regular Barry Woodcock. As ever there is a cider festival in May. ♨Q❀🚌(78)♣🍏

Burnham-on-Crouch

Queen's Head

26 Providence, CM0 8JU (opp clock tower)
⏲ 11-3 (12-4 Sat), 6-11; 12-4, 7-10.30 Sun
☎ (01621) 784825
Mighty Oak IPA; guest beers 🄷
Hidden back-street gem close to the picturesque Quayside, popular with locals and visitors. This charming pub, run by an enthusiastic landlord, has three ever-changing guest beers from the Gray's list and hosts an annual beer festival in the pretty enclosed courtyard garden. Indoors, the walls and ceiling are covered with a variety of prints. The cosy time-warp bar hosts darts and pool teams; folk nights are held monthly. Traditional home-cooked food can be enjoyed in a friendly, welcoming atmosphere.
Q❀◐◑⇌🚌(31X)♣🍏▯

Castle Hedingham

Bell

10 St James Street, CO9 3EJ (off A1017 signposted Castle Hedingham)
⏲ 11.45-3, 6-11; 11.45-12.30am Fri; 12-11.30 Sat; 12-11 Sun
☎ (01787) 460350
Adnams Bitter; guest beers 🄶
This 15th-century coaching inn is well worth a visit. It has small rooms for drinking and dining beside the two main bars, both of which have open fires. Beers are served direct from the casks, which are all on view in the public bar. An annual July beer festival is planned. Live jazz is played on the last Sunday of every month; folk and pop every Friday evening, with quizzes on a Sunday night. There is an ample car park and garden.
♨Q♉❀◐◑⊟♿🚌♣🍏P⌐

Chelmsford

Cricketers

143 Moulsham Street, CM2 0JT
⏲ 11-11
☎ (01245) 261157
Greene King Abbot; guest beers, IPA 🄷
Corner local serving the best value decent ale in town. The guest beers generally come from small breweries, with Mighty Oak often featuring; two guests are usually available from Friday and over the weekend, plus one mid-week. There is a lively public bar with jukebox, pool table and Sky Sports as well as a quieter lounge; both feature football and cricket memorabilia. Note the two different sides of the pub sign and the outside mural. Meals are served Sunday-Friday. Q◐⊟♣⌐

Endeavour

351 Springfield Road, CM2 6AW (on B1137)
⏲ 11-11; 12-10.30 Sun
☎ (01245) 257717
Greene King IPA, Abbot; Mighty Oak Maldon Gold; guest beers 🄷
A 15-minute walk from the town centre, this friendly pub has three rooms, one used for early evening dining Friday (fish night) and Saturday (steak night) – there are no evening meals on other days. One of the two guests is Mighty Oak Oscar Wilde, served from September-May and Weston's Bounds Brand cider is stocked. Regular charity events are held, including a meat raffle on Sunday. Several bus routes pass by. ♨◐◑🚌♣🍏⌐

Orange Tree

6 Lower Anchor St, CM2 0AS
⏲ 12-11 (11.30 Fri & Sat)
☎ (01245) 262664 🌐 the-ot.com
Farmer's Drop of Nelson's Blood; Mighty Oak Oscar Wilde, Maldon Gold; 🄷 **guest beers** 🄷/🄶
The Orange Tree has been reinvigorated by the arrival of the ex-landlord of the multi-award-winning Queen's Head, just 200m down the road. One of his first actions was to remove Greene King beers – one of only three Gray's pubs to do so. The range of ales has been greatly increased with four guest beers, two on handpump and two on gravity from casks behind the bar. The cider is from the Weston's range. Q❀◐⊟♿♣🍏P⌐

Original Plough ✔

28 Duke Street, CM1 1HY
⏲ 11-11 (midnight Fri & Sat)
☎ (01245) 250145
Greene King IPA; guest beers 🄷
This spacious open-plan pub opposite the bus station and next to Chelmsford railway station attracts a varied clientele and can be noisy in the evenings. The landlord is a keen rugby fan and the pub is home to a local rugby team so this is the preferred sport shown on the TV. Mild and other dark beers are often available among the nine regular guest ales. Evening meals are available until 8pm Mon-Thu. There is an outdoor patio drinking area. ❀◐◑⊖🚌P⌐

Royal Steamer

1 Townfield Street, CM1 1QJ
⏲ 11-11
☎ (01245) 258800 🌐 the-royal-steamer.co.uk

Ansells Mild; Caledonian Deuchars IPA; Greene King IPA; Wells Bombardier; Young's Bitter Ⓗ
This small family-run back-street corner pub around the back of Chelmsford station is believed to be the only pub of this name in the country. It is situated on an unusual triangular corner and has two bar areas. A games-oriented pub, with darts and pool played regularly, there is also a golf society and sport shown on a large-screen TV. A function room is available for hire. ❀◖≠♣⚡

White Horse

25 Townfield Street, CM1 1QJ
✪ 12-11 (midnight Fri & Sat); 12-10.30 Sun
☎ (01245) 269556
Adnams Bitter; Fuller's London Pride; Greene King IPA; Theakston Traditional Mild; guest beers Ⓗ
A welcome return to the Guide for the White Horse which is now under a new landlord. This games-oriented pub has one long narrow bar with a bar billiards table at one end, darts at the other and several TV screens showing sport. The three guest beers generally come from regional or larger brewers but the landlord hopes to dedicate one pump to a changing Cornish beer this year. Lunches are served Monday to Friday. ◖≠♣

Woolpack ✔

23 Mildmay Road, CM2 0DN
✪ 12-11 (midnight Fri-Sun)
☎ (01245) 259295
Greene King IPA, H&H Bitter, Abbot; guest beers Ⓗ
The Woolpack usually has six ales on handpump, generally two that are not brewed by Greene King. A public bar has darts and pool, while the larger lounge leads to a third room with leather furniture and a large-screen TV. The menu includes a weekly-changing range of local speciality sausages and evening meals are served Monday-Friday. A heated outdoor patio area is provided for smokers. ❀◖◗⊟⊡♣P⚡

Chipping Ongar

Cock

218 High Street, CM5 9AB
✪ 11-midnight (2am Sat)
☎ (01277) 362615 ⊕ thecocktavernongar.co.uk
Greene King IPA; guest beers Ⓗ
A typical 400 year-old Gray's house frequented by loyal locals of all ages, with guest beers usually from local brewers. Darts and cribbage teams meet here and the food is home-cooked. A function room can be hired and live music is staged most weekends. A public pay car park is next door and there is a good bus service to Brentwood and Epping, daytimes only. ◖◗⊡♣●⚡

Chrishall

Red Cow

11 High Street, SG8 8RN (2 miles N of B1039)
TL445394
✪ 12-3 (not Mon), 6-11; 12-10.30 Sun
☎ (01763) 838792
Adnams Bitter; guest beers Ⓗ
Thatched 14th-century pub, close to an 11th-century tithe barn in a small village very close to Cambridge and Hertfordshire borders. Guest beers are usually from East Anglia. The enthusiastic owners welcome visitors and many local groups including the cricket club (who run regular quizzes), the village book group, stall holders from the farmers' market and the WI. Special occasions can be celebrated with meals from the extensive and intelligent menu, either in the tiled bar or restaurant separated by original open timbering. ⚶❀◖◗P

Churchgate Street

Queen's Head

26 Churchgate Street, near Old Harlow, CM17 0JT
TL 483114
✪ 11.45-3, 5 (6 Sat)-11; Sun 12-4, 7-10.30
☎ (01279) 427266
Adnams Bitter, Broadside; Nethergate IPA; guest beers Ⓗ
The new town of Harlow seems a long way from this traditional village pub. It was originally built as two cottages in 1530, then joined together and converted into a pub in 1750. Wooden beams feature throughout and there is a welcoming open fire during the winter months. Guest beers are from Crouch Vale or other East Anglian breweries. A full range of food is served (not Sun eve). ⚶Q❀◖◗⊟⊡(7,59)P⚡

Colchester

Bricklayers

27 Bergholt Road, CO4 5AA (jct A134/B1508 nr North Station)
✪ 11-3, 5.30-11; 11-midnight Fri; 11-11 Sat; 12-11 (6.30 winter) Sun
☎ (01206) 852008
Adnams Bitter, Explorer, Broadside, seasonal beers; guest beers Ⓗ
This award-winning pub is a great place for a pint before catching the train, but also worth visiting any time. A traditional local with two distinct bars, pool and darts are on offer in the public bar, while the lounge has a suntrap conservatory. The full Adnams range is complemented by varied guests and Crones cider is always available. Excellent food is served at lunchtime (not Sat). The friendly, long-serving publicans organise golf and cricket matches for locals.
❀◖⊟≠(Colchester North)⊡♣●P⚡

Fat Cat

65 Butt Road, CO3 3BZ (on B1026, nr police station)
✪ 12-11 (midnight Fri); 11-midnight Sat
☎ (01206) 577990 ⊕ fatcatcolchester.co.uk
Crouch Vale Brewers Gold; Ⓖ **Fat Cat Bitter, Honey Ale; Hop Back Summer Lightning;** Ⓗ **Mighty Oak Oscar Wilde;** Ⓖ **Woodforde's Wherry;** Ⓗ **guest beers** Ⓖ
The Fat Cat is now established as a haven for ale drinkers, with up to 20 beers available on gravity. Local brewers and micros are well represented, along with a draught and bottled continental selection plus organic bottle-conditioned beers from Pitfield. Pub grub and Sunday roasts are complemented by regular

themed food evenings; the bar staff will deliver takeaways, provide plates and even wash up! Live music including open-mic sessions are held most Sunday evenings. The smoking area is covered.
Q⊙◑⇌(Colchester Town)🚌⁴–

Forester's Arms

1-2 Castle Road, CO1 1UW
⏲12-11 (12.30am Fri & Sat; 10.30 Sun)
☎(01206) 224059
Beer range varies Ⓗ
Welcoming back-street local, just two minutes from the High Street and Castle Park. Although open plan, the pub maintains a cosy two-bar atmosphere. Three to four real ales are on handpump, always including Nethergate beers. The good selection of home-cooked food offers value for money. Frequented by many local musicians, there is live music occasionally at weekends, but conversation is generally king. In summer, alfresco dining and drinking is offered on the quiet street front.
⇌(Colchester Town)🚌♣⁴–

Fox & Fiddler

1 St John's Street, CO2 7AA (jct of Head Street)
⏲11-11 (midnight Fri & Sat); 12-10.30 Sun
☎(01206) 560520
Mighty Oak IPA, Burntwood Bitter, English Oak; guest beers Ⓗ
Friendly town-centre pub with a deceptively small frontage disguising a long single bar with three separate drinking and dining areas. The pub is steeped in history and heavily timbered, with a relaxing atmosphere and comfortable seating inside. Mighty Oak beers are always available, with regularly changing guests from micro-breweries. Excellent home-cooked food using local produce is served Wednesday to Sunday lunchtime; Sunday roasts offer particularly good value. Weekend evenings can be lively, with regular music on Saturday night. The smoking area is heated and covered. ❀⊙⇌(Colchester Town)🚌P⁴–

Hole in the Wall

Balkerne Passage, CO1 1PT (opp Mercury Theatre)
⏲12-11 (midnight Fri & Sat); 12-10.30 Sun
☎(01206) 579897
Caledonian Deuchars IPA; St Austell Tribute; guest beers Ⓗ
A welcome addition to the Colchester ale scene with up to six beers on offer. The pub gets its name from the town's Roman wall — part of which was demolished by a Victorian owner to allow views of the railway. A maze of small split-level drinking areas surrounds the central bar, with two covered outdoor areas, one giving great views of the north town. Live music plays on Wednesday. Ideally placed for visitors to the Arts Centre and Mercury Theatre.
❀⊙◑⇌(Colchester Town)🚌⁴–

Hospital Arms

123-125 Crouch Street, CO3 3HA (opp hospital)
⏲12-11 (midnight Fri & Sat); 12-10.30 Sun
☎(01206) 542398 🌐 colchester-hospitalarms.co.uk
Adnams Bitter, Explorer, Broadside, seasonal beers; Fuller's London Pride; guest beers Ⓗ
A welcome return for this Guide regular, with new tenants keeping up this pub's reputation for good beer, food and conversation. Open plan with four distinct split-level bars, up to seven beers are usually on offer. Quality lunchtime home-cooked food is available, but booking for Sunday roasts is recommended. The walled patio at the rear features an unusual covered area copying the beach huts from Adnams' advertising. Well worth the 10-minute walk from the High Street. The smoking area is covered and heated.
Q❀⊙🚌⁴–

Odd One Out

28 Mersea Road, CO2 7ET (on B1025)
⏲4.30-11; 12 (11 Sat)-11 Fri & Sat; 12-10.30 Sun
☎(01206) 578140
Archers Best Bitter; guest beers Ⓗ
Classic traditional pub and a genuine, good-value free house. Five ever-changing guest ales, mainly from micros, with at least one dark beer and a strong ale are always available. Up to four real ciders are served from casks on the bar, and a large range of malt and Irish whiskies is stocked. The Oddy is home to a successful cricket team, and card schools take place in the back room, which is available for functions and meetings. Good value cheese rolls are sold.
⚜Q❀⇌(Colchester Town)🚌(8A,67)♣●⁴–

Colne Engaine

Five Bells

Mill Lane, CO6 2HY (2 miles E of Halstead) TL851303
⏲12-3, 6-midnight; 12-1am Fri & Sat; 12-11.30 Sun
☎(01787) 224166 🌐 fivebells.net
Greene King IPA; guest beers Ⓗ
This 16th-century free house with original beams is set in a peaceful village where the enthusiastic landlord has transformed the pub. Selling more than 400 different ales, local breweries and micros are well represented. Several small dining and drinking areas plus a separate restaurant serve locally-sourced quality food. The community is well represented, with pool and football teams, regular live music including jazz, plus a November beer festival. The smoking area is covered and heated. ⚜Q❀⊙◑♿🚌♣P⁴–

Coxtie Green

White Horse

173 Coxtie Green Road, CM14 5PX (1 mile W of A128, jct with Mores Lane) TQ564959
⏲11.30-11 (midnight Fri & Sat); 12-11 Sun
☎(01277) 372410 🌐 whitehorsecoxtiegreen.co.uk
Fuller's London Pride; guest beers Ⓗ
There is always a relaxed, friendly atmosphere at this excellent, small country two-bar local, CAMRA branch Pub of the Year 2004 and 2006. A varied clientele will find a well-appointed saloon bar and a public bar with dartboard and TV. Six handpumps are in constant use, featuring beers from all over, plus draught cider and perry. A beer festival is held each July in the large rear garden with its children's play area. ❀⊙♿🚌♣●P

ENGLAND

Dedham

Sun Inn

High Street, CO7 6DF (on B1029, opp Church)
12-11 (6 Sun)
(01206) 323351 thesuninndedham.com
Adnams Broadside; guest beers H
This 15th-century inn comprises a bar area, side lounge, restaurant and garden. The lounge, open to non-residents, has a range of comfortable furniture, and board games are available. Guest ales change frequently, featuring micros and local brewers. The restaurant serves an award-winning range of food and fine wines, with regular culinary lectures and tasting sessions (booking advised). One of the four well-appointed guest bedrooms has a four poster bed for that romantic weekend.

Duton Hill

Three Horseshoes

CM6 2DX (½ mile W of B184 Dunmow-Thaxted road)
12-2.30 (not Mon-Wed; 3 Sat), 6-11; 12-3, 7-10.30 Sun
(01371) 870681
Mighty Oak IPA; guest beers H
Cosy village local with a large garden, wildife pond and terrace overlooking the Chelmer Valley and open farmland. The landlord is a former pantomime dame, and the pub hosts an open-air theatre in July. A millennium beacon in the garden, breweriana and a remarkable collection of Butlins memorabilia are features of this unpretentious pub. A beer festival is held on the late Spring bank holiday in the Duton Hill Den. Look for the pub sign depicting a famous painting, The Blacksmith, by local resident Sir George Clausen.
(313)P

Eastwood

Oakwood

564 Rayleigh Road, SS9 5HX (on A1015)
11-11 (midnight Fri & Sat)
(01702) 429000
Beer range varies H
Popular two-room pub with outside patio area. One bar has pool tables, a dartboard and shows sport on TV; a smaller bar is quieter with a piano and comfortable seating. Note the pub's original stained glass windows preserved in the ceiling of the larger bar. Live entertainment is held on Saturday evening. No evening meals are served on a Sunday. The pub is on a well served bus route between Southend and Rayleigh.

Elmdon

Elmdon Dial

Heydon Lane, CB11 4NH
12-3, 6-11 (closed Mon); 12-4, 6-10.30 Sun
(01763) 837386 theelmdondial.co.uk
Adnams Bitter, Broadside; Taylor Landlord; guest beers H
CAMRA local Pub of the Year 2008, this friendly, welcoming pub dating from 1450 is owned by a real ale enthusiast. Previously called the Kings Head, the pub was closed in 1998 and became a private house. After a seven-year planning battle and support from villagers and CAMRA, it was reopened with a new name and pub sign to reflect a window sundial in the village church. The building was carefully extended in 2006 to provide a modern kitchen and restaurant in addition to a tasteful bar.

Epping

Black Lion

293 High Street, CM16 4DA
10 (12 Sun)-11.30 (12.30am Fri & Sat)
(01992) 578670
Greene King IPA; guest beers H
A 14th-century town-centre inn which has remained unchanged for many years, with low beams and a wonderful fire. Some old slogans are painted on the walls including: 'When you have lost your inns drown your empty selves, for you have lost the last of England.' The new owners hope to reopen the kitchen and beer garden shortly.

Forest Gate

Bell Common, CM16 4DZ (opp Bell Hotel) TL450011
10-2.30, 5-11; 12-3, 7-10.30 Sun
(01992) 572312
Adnams Bitter, Broadside; Nethergate IPA; H **guest beers** G
A 17th-century pub which is a genuine free house and specialises in traditional ales. On the edge of Epping Forest, it is popular with walkers, and dogs are welcome if friendly. Locals also enjoy the short walk here from the town centre. Food is usually available, with the longstanding house speciality being turkey broth. A large lawn at the front is used for summer drinking. Indoors, there are comfortable corners in which to sit.

Fyfield

Queen's Head

Queen Street, CM5 0RY (off B184)
11-3.30, 6-11; 11-11 Sat; 12-10.30 Sun
(01277) 899231 queensheadfyfield.co.uk
Adnams Bitter, Broadside; guest beers H
The emphasis here is on dining, though with only nine tables to chose from, reservations are recommended at this friendly pub. The beer is reasonably priced and customers popping in just for a drink are made very welcome. The garden goes down to the River Roding, and outside tables are popular in summer. Children and dogs are not allowed inside.

Gestingthorpe

Pheasant

Church Street, CO9 3AU (off B1058 Castle Hedingham-Sudbury road) TL813375
12-3, 6-11 (not Mon); 12-3 Sun
(01787) 461196
Beer range varies H
Set in a tiny village, this traditional pub enjoys good local trade and a reputation for good

food, ale and cider. Recently refurbished, it has three separate rooms with two bars and a large garden. Occasional quiz nights and music evenings make this pub an ideal venue for summer evenings and long winter nights.
♨Q❀◐⊟●P⅃

Goldhanger

Chequers ✔

The Square, CM9 8AS (500m from B1026)
TL904088
⏲ 11-11; 12-10.30 Sun
☎ (01621) 788203 🌐 thechequersgoldhanger.co.uk
Caledonian Deuchars IPA; Flowers IPA; Everards Tiger; guest beers Ⓗ
Classic country pub in a 15th-century building serving up to six real ales. It was a deserving winning of the local CAMRA Pub of the Year 2006 and 2008 rural award. The multi-roomed interior includes a child-free public bar, comfortable lounge, snug and games room with bar billiards. A wide range of quality food is served every day. Thursday is quiz night. Beer festivals are held in March and September, plus a sloe gin competition. There is an enclosed patio area to the rear.
♨Q☋❀◐⊟Å♣P⅃

Grays

Theobald Arms

141 Argent Street, RM17 6HR
⏲ 11-3, 5-11; 11-midnight Fri & Sat; 12-11 Sun
☎ (01375) 372253 🌐 theobaldarms.com
Courage Best Bitter; guest beers Ⓗ
Genuine, traditional pub with a public bar featuring an unusual hexagonal pool table. The changing selection of three guest beers includes local independents and a range of British bottled beers is also stocked. Regular Easter and summer beer festivals are held in the old stables and on the rear enclosed patio; the summer festival has been running for more than 10 years. Lunchtime meals are served weekdays. Darts and cards are played. A former local CAMRA Branch Pub of the Year.
❀◐⊟♿≷⊟(55)♣P⅃

White Hart ✔

Kings Walk, Argent Street, RM17 6HR
⏲ 12-11.30 (midnight Fri & Sat); 12-11 Sun
☎ (01375) 373319 🌐 whitehartgrays.co.uk
Crouch Vale Brewers Gold; guest beers Ⓗ
Since being taken over in 2006, this traditional local just outside the town centre has been transformed and rejuvenated. The two or three guest ales usually include a mild or other dark beer. Pool is played and a meeting/function room is available. Live blues bands play every other Thursday and a large beer garden enjoys views of the Thames. An annual beer festival is usually held in February or March. Local CAMRA Branch Pub of the Year 2007 and 2008. ♨❀⛟⊟≷⊟(55)♣P⅃

Great Bromley

Cross Inn

Ardleigh Road, CO7 7TL (on B1029 between Great Bromley and Ardleigh)
⏲ 12-2 (not Mon), 6.30-11; 12-3, 7-10.30 Sun
☎ (01206) 230282
Wadworth Henry's IPA; Woodforde's Wherry; guest beers Ⓖ
Quiet, cosy and warm free house featuring a single bar that feels like a private front room, with a wood burner and comfortable seating, as well as fresh flowers. The landlord has run previous pubs listed in the Guide and hosts an annual beer and folk festival, usually in May. Booking is advised for meals (served Wed to Sat). Outside is a large car park, enclosed beer garden and a heated and covered smoking area. The landlady welcomes dogs.
♨Q❀⛟◐♣P⅃

Snooty Fox

Frating Road, CO7 7JN (on B1029, 500m from A133)
⏲ 12-3, 6-11; 12-3, 5.30-midnight Sat; 12-midnight Sun
☎ (01206) 251065
Beer range varies Ⓗ
This village inn is a beer lover's paradise, with a constantly-changing range of real ales on offer from micro-breweries around the country. A warm welcome is always provided by the staff. The public bar includes a real fire which enhances the ambience of the wood-beamed interior. Excellent value for money food, ranging from the traditional to the exotic, is served in the bar and large dining room. A monthly quiz brings in customers from far and wide. ♨Q❀◐♣●P⅃

Great Chesterford

Crown & Thistle

High Street, CB10 1PL (near B1383, close to M11/A11 jct)
⏲ 12-3, 6-midnight; 12-3, 7-11 (not winter eve) Sun
☎ (01799) 530278
Greene King IPA; Woodforde's Wherry; guest beers Ⓗ
Popular inn in an interesting village, frequented by locals, including the cricket team. The pub, built in 1528 and called The Chequers, was extended in 1603 to serve as a coaching inn and renamed at that point. According to legend, James I stopped here on his way to London for his coronation. The magnificent inglenook in the bar is the earliest example of its type in Essex. A patio has seating for outdoor drinking and eating, with a heated and covered smoking area.
♨Q❀⛟◐Å≷⊟P⅃

Great Dunmow

Boars Head

37 High Street, CM6 1AB
⏲ 11-midnight (1am Fri & Sat); 12-11 Sun
☎ (01371) 873630
Adnams Bitter; Greene King IPA; guest beers Ⓗ
Four hundred-year-old traditional town centre pub on the corner of the main public car park. This timber-framed lathe and plaster building tends to 'give' a little when lorries 'bump it' while negotiating the tight bend outside. Inside are beamed low ceilings and three large-screen TVs for sport. Live music is performed on Saturday evenings. A large decking area at the rear includes covered seating for smokers. Traditional Sunday roasts

use locally-sourced meat and a fresh fish van visits on Thursday. ❀◑🚌(33,133)P⊱

Great Easton

Swan

The Endway, CM6 2HG (3 miles N of Dunmow, off B184) TL606255

⏲ 12-3, 6-11; 12-3, 7-10.30 Sun

☎ (01371) 870359 🌐 swangreateaston.co.uk

Adnams Bitter; guest beers Ⓗ

A warm welcome is assured at this 15th-century free house in an attractive village. A log-burning stove, exposed beams and comfortable sofas feature in the lounge, while pool and darts are played in the public bar. Occasional French classes are held here. All meals are freshly prepared to order from fresh local produce (including the chips). The chef looks after the beers, chosen to complement the food. Accommodation is now available in four superb double rooms.

♨Q❀🛏◑⊟▲🚌(313)♣P

Great Yeldham

Waggon & Horses

High Street, CO9 4EX (on A1017)

⏲ 11-11 (10.30 Sun)

☎ (01787) 237936 🌐 waggonandhorses.net

Greene King IPA, Abbot; guest beers Ⓗ

This 16th-century inn is a busy village hostelry and everyone is made welcome. Guest beers are only sourced from local brewers and the local Storm cider from Delvin End is always available. Food, served every day, is especially popular at weekends. Sixteen rooms in an annexe overlooking the garden provide overnight accommodation. The friendly landlord is a long-term supporter of real ale.

♨❀🛏◑♣●P

Harwich

New Bell Inn

Outpart Eastward, CO12 3EN (200m from E end of A120)

⏲ 11-3, 7-11 (midnight Sat); 12-4, 7-11 (12-11 summer) Sun

☎ (01255) 503545

Greene King IPA; guest beers Ⓗ

Tucked away at the back of the former Naval Dockyard in Harwich, this buzzing community pub is a great start/end point for a tour of the historic Old Town. The pub boasts a walled garden, three separate drinking areas and an impressive snow globe collection. The pub always has a mild on handpump in the back bar along with a good selection of ales, including one from nearby Harwich Town Brewery. Hearty home-cooked food is available at lunchtime, including delicious soups. ❀◑⊟⇌(Harwich Town)🚌P

Hawkwell

White Hart

274 Main Road, SS5 4NS

⏲ 11-11; 12-10.30 Sun

☎ (01702) 203438

Beer range varies Ⓗ

A well established friendly local dating from the 18th century facing the village green. The management has recently taken on one half of the partnership that ran The Cork & Cheese in Southend. Two well-kept guest ales have been introduced in place of the regular beers that used to be served. Lunchtime food is available Monday to Saturday. There is a large rear garden with seating and a patio area, plus picnic tables at the front of the pub.

Q❀◑⇌(Hockley)🚌P

Hempstead

Bluebell Inn

High Street, CB10 2PD (on B1054, between Saffron Walden and Haverhill)

⏲ 12-3, 6-11; 12-11 Fri & Sat; 12-10.30 Sun

☎ (01799) 599199

Adnams Bitter, Broadside; Woodforde's Wherry; guest beers Ⓗ

Late 16th-century village pub with 18th-century additions, reputed to be the birthplace of Dick Turpin – the bar displays posters about his life. Six real ales often include a guest from Fenland or Saffron breweries. The restaurant serves excellent meals from an extensive menu and the large bar has a log fire. Ample seating is provided outside, plus a children's play area. This local CAMRA Pub of the Year 2005 hosts a folk evening on Tuesday.

♨Q❀◑🚌♣P⊱

Heybridge

Maltsters Arms

Hall Road, CM9 4NJ (nr B1022)

⏲ 12-midnight (1am Fri & Sat); 12-10.30 Sun

☎ (01621) 853880

Greene King IPA, Abbot; guest beers Ⓖ

This traditional Gray's house is a single-bar local, where a warm welcome is extended to drinkers and their dogs. The pub can be busy at lunchtimes with locals and ramblers. The pleasant atmosphere is enhanced by a collection of mirrors and copper bric-a-brac. Two guest beers are usually available, one from Mighty Oak. No meals are served, but a selection of rolls is usually available. A rear patio overlooks the old course of the tidal river. Occasional mini beer festivals are held.

Q❀🚌♣⊱

Horndon-on-the-Hill

Bell Inn

High Road, SS17 8LD (nr B1007 opp Woolmarket)

⏲ 11-2.30 (3 Sat), 5.30 (6 Sat)-11; 12-4, 7-10.30 Sun

☎ (01375) 642463 🌐 bell-inn.co.uk

Draught Bass; Ⓖ **Greene King IPA; guest beers** Ⓗ

Busy, 15th-century coaching inn, where the beamed bars feature wood panelling and carvings. Note the unusual hot cross bun collection – a bun is added every Good Friday. The hilltop village, much more peaceful since the by-pass was completed, has a restored Woolmarket. Up to five guest ales are stocked, including beers from Essex breweries. The award-winning restaurant is open daily, lunchtime and evening. Accommodation includes five honeymoon suites.

♨Q❀🛏◑⊟🚌(11,374)P⊱

Lamarsh

Lamarsh Lion

Bures Road, CO8 5EP (1¼ miles NW of Bures) TL892355
12-11 (10.30 Sun)
(01787) 227918
Beer range varies H

Hard to find, but well worth visiting, this 14th-century free house has stunning views over the Stour Valley and is an ideal stopping point for those walking the Valley. The large, single drinking area has plenty of oak beams and a real fire, and an adjoining restaurant area presents a varied menu. Nethergate beers always feature on an ever-changing guest list, with micros well represented.

Langley Lower Green

Bull

CB11 4SB (off B1038 at Clavering) TL436345
12-2 (3 Sat), 6-11; 12-3, 7-10.30 Sun
(01799) 777307
Greene King IPA, Abbot, seasonal beers H

Classic Victorian village local with original cast iron lattice windows and fireplaces. It sits in a tiny isolated hamlet less than a mile from the Hertfordshire border and just a bit further from Cambridgeshire. The pub has a devoted band of local regulars including cricket and football teams. This friendly pub in beautiful rolling countryside, two miles from the highest point in Essex, is worth seeking out. A long distance footpath passes within a mile. Meals can be arranged with advance notice. Q P

Layer Breton

Hare & Hounds

Crayes Green, CO2 0PN TL944188
11.30-11; 12-10.30 Sun
(01206) 330459
Greene King IPA, Abbot; Woodforde's Wherry; guest beers H

A change of management has breathed new life into this welcoming village local. Thoughtfully refurbished, the single bar has a wood burning stove, and the separate restaurant area features a glass-topped 'well table'. The guest ale changes regularly. Quality food is served lunchtimes and evenings (not Mon), with a popular carvery from 12-6pm on Sunday. Two B&B rooms are available and the smoking area is heated and covered.

Layer-de-la-Haye

Donkey & Buskins

Layer Road, CO2 0HU (on B1026 S of Colchester) TL974208
11.30-3, 6-11; 11.30-11.30 Sat; 12-11 Sun
(01206) 734774
Greene King IPA; guest beers H

This welcoming village free house has an excellent reputation for good beer, wines and food. Guest beers are regularly available and local micro-breweries are well supported. A wide range of dishes from the grill, fish menu or traditional home-cooked board can be enjoyed in the front or rear bars. The pub organises a popular Sunday pub quiz and a variety of local societies and clubs regularly meets here. A large, secluded garden is available for relaxed summer-time drinking.
Q P

Leigh-on-Sea

Broker

213-217 Leigh Road, SS9 1JA
11-11 (midnight Fri & Sat); 12-11 Sun
(01702) 471932 brokerfreehouse.co.uk
Everards Tiger; Fuller's London Pride; St Austell Tribute; Shepherd Neame Spitfire; Young's Bitter; guest beers H

Friendly, family-run free house that has featured in every edition of this Guide since 1996, now completely refurbished following the smoking ban. This sporty, community pub organises local charity events including quizzes or live music on Sunday evening. Two guest beers are stocked, normally from small East Anglian breweries. Bar and restaurant meals are served at lunchtime (children welcome until 6.30pm). It has a garden with a covered and heated area for smokers and a pavement seating area.
(Chalkwell) (5,24)

Elms

1060 London Road, SS9 3ND (on A13)
9-midnight (1am Fri & Sat)
(01702) 474687
Courage Best Bitter, Directors; Greene King Abbot, Old Speckled Hen; Marston's Pedigree; Shepherd Neame Spitfire; guest beers H

Old coaching inn converted by J D Wetherspoon into a large, traditional-style pub decorated with old photos of the local area. Breakfast is available until noon plus main meals and snacks until 11pm. Children are admitted until 9pm. Up to four constantly-changing guest ales and two Weston's real ciders are served. There is no music but there are TVs and fruit machines. Outside is a paved, heated and covered area for smokers and a large, hedged front garden. P

Little Baddow

Rodney

North Hill, CM3 4TQ TL778080
12-3 (not Mon), 6-11; 12-8 Sun
(01245) 222385
Greene King IPA; guest beers H

The Rodney was built as a farmhouse around 1650 and has been a pub since the early 1800s, also serving as a grocer's and a bakery until the early 20th century. It has a public bar with a pool table, a small snug and a compact drinking/dining area decorated with seafaring items. One of the guest beers is sometimes Rodney's Revenge which is rebadged Morland Original; other beers come from smaller breweries. The food is all home-cooked, including daily specials. Q P

Little Clacton

Apple Tree

The Street, CO16 9LF

12-midnight
(01255) 861026
Greene King IPA; guest beers G
Strong community pub that attracts all ages, running darts and pool teams. There is a well-supported real ale club that meets on the first Tuesday of the month and includes a large number of local CAMRA members. The landlord and his wife support the local Essex and Suffolk micro-breweries, with up to three real ales available, all served on gravity. Live music can be heard at weekends with karaoke events. On Sunday night the TV screens Sky Sports. P

Little Dunmow

Flitch of Bacon

The Street, CM6 3HT (850m S of B1256)
12-3 (not Mon), 5.30 (6 Sat)-11; 12-4, 7-10.30 Sun
(01371) 820323
Fuller's London Pride; Greene King IPA; guest beers H
Traditional country inn and focal point of the village. The pub sign depicts a side, or 'flitch' of bacon, the prize awarded to a happily-married couple in an ancient contest still held every four years. Inside, there are exposed timbers and an open fire in winter. Note the old signs advertising Bass and Worthington in bottles. A menu of locally-sourced food is available in the bar or the rear restaurant area (not Sun eve). (133)

Little Oakley

Olde Cherry Tree

Clacton Road, CO12 5JH (by B1414)
12-3, 5-midnight; 12-midnight Sat & Sun
(01255) 886290
Adnams Bitter; guest beers H
Dating from the 17th century, this friendly village local is in a rural setting with extensive North Sea views yet close to Harwich. Owned by a real ale enthusiast, the bar has four handpumps, three serving constantly-changing guest ales, often from local micro-breweries. Delicious home-cooked food is served in the bar or restaurant. In winter there is a large open fire and every June a beer festival and hog roast is held in the spacious garden. P

Little Thurrock

Traitor's Gate

40-42 Broadway, RM17 6EW (on A126)
12-11 (10.30 Sun)
(01375) 372628
Beer range varies H
This friendly hostelry with a mixed clientele, mostly local, shows how a good pub attracts good trade. Two changing guest beers are served and forthcoming beers displayed on a blackboard above the bar. An amazing collection of more than 1500 pump clips shows beers that have featured over the last few years. Sport is shown most nights on a large-screen TV. The beer garden has won Thurrock in Bloom awards in recent years. Local CAMRA Branch Pub of the Year 2005.
(66)

Little Totham

Swan

School Road, CM9 8LB (1 mile SE of B1022)
TL889117
11-11; 12-10.30 Sun
(01621) 892689 theswanpublichouse.co.uk
Adnams Bitter; Crouch Vale Brewers Gold; Farmer's Pucks Folly; Mighty Oak Oscar Wilde Mild, Maldon Gold; Woodforde's Wherry; guest beers G
Twice winner of CAMRA's national Pub of the Year, this is a centuries-old 'chocolate box' village pub. The classic public bar and saloon, with beamed ceiling and walls, provide a timeless experience often missing from rural pubs these days. The extensive range of beer styles is unrivalled, and Weston's cider and perry are usually available. Mighty Oak brew the house beer Totham Parva. A June beer festival is held, plus live music and Morris dancing throughout the year. The smoking area is covered. Q P

Little Wakering

Castle Inn

181 Little Wakering Road, SS3 0JW
12-11.30 (midnight Fri & Sat); 12-10.30 Sun
(01702) 219295
Beer range varies H
The Castle has been refurbished and now offers comfortable seating, a jukebox, garden, food, pool table and large-screen TVs. More importantly, there are now four handpumps offering a good range of real ales, served by enthusiastic staff. Entertainment includes live music and a quiz, with regular themed nights adding to the lively atmosphere. The pub has the same management as the White Hart in Grays. (14,4A)P

Little Walden

Crown

High Street, CB10 1XA (on B1052)
11.30-2.30 (3 Sat), 6-11; 12-10.30 Sun
(01799) 522475
Adnams Broadside; City of Cambridge Boathouse Bitter; Greene King IPA; guest beers G
This charming, recently extended 18th-century pub in a quiet hamlet attracts customers from Saffron Walden. It features a beamed ceiling and a large walk-through fireplace, with racked cask stillage used for dispensing an excellent range of beers. An extensive food menu is on offer with evening meals served Tuesday to Saturday. The pub is used for club meetings and hosts traditional jazz on Wednesday evening. Q P

Loughton

Victoria Tavern

165 Smarts Lane, IG10 4BP (off A121 at edge of forest)
11-3, 5-11; 12-11 Sun
(020) 85081779
Adnams Bitter; Greene King IPA; guest beers H
The Victoria is a large, friendly regulars' pub where glasses and surfaces gleam with constant polishing. It has a single horseshoe

shaped bar with a raised area for dining, offering a wide selection of snacks and full meals. Visitors who drop in for a drink are made very welcome in the bar, or in the large garden with a shady tree. The pub does not accept credit cards. The smoking area is covered. ❀◐⊖⊟P⁵—

Maldon

Blue Boar Hotel

Silver Street, CM9 4QE (opp church)
11 (12 Sun)-11
☎ (01621) 855888 🌐 blueboarmaldon.co.uk
Adnams Bitter, Broadside; Crouch Vale Brewers Gold; Farmer's Drop of Nelson's Blood, Golden Boar, Puck's Folly, seasonal beers G
Fifteenth-century coaching inn in the historic heart of town. Farmer's Ales are brewed in the stable block across the yard with seasonal beers often available. This fine medieval hotel building has two bars and a meeting room upstairs. A range of meals and bar snacks is served. Folk music and jazz evenings are held on a regular basis. The church next door has a unique triangular tower and a memorial window to a local ancestor of George Washington. ♨Q❀⇌◐⊟(31X)P⁵—

Queen's Head

The Hythe, CM9 5HN
10-11 (midnight Fri & Sat); 12-10.30 Sun
☎ (01621) 854112 🌐 thequeensheadmaldon.co.uk
Adnams Broadside; Mighty Oak Maldon Gold; Greene King Abbot; Taylor Landlord; Woodforde's Wherry; guest beers H
Situated on the quay where many sailing barges are moored, this pleasant pub overlooks the River Blackwater, famed for the Mud Race. A spacious outdoor seating area, outside bar and barbecue operate in the summer, while a log fire warms the cosy front bar in winter. Food is served in the restaurant or bars in this multi-roomed pub, with seafood naturally a speciality on the extensive menu. Children are allowed in the restaurant. Good disabled access and WC facilities are provided. ♨❀◐⊟♿⁵—

Swan Hotel

71/73 High Street, CM9 5EP
10.30-11; 12-10.30 Sun
☎ (01621) 853170
Fuller's London Pride; Greene King Abbot; Woodforde's Wherry; guest beers H
This historic inn has a dominant position on the High Street, serving a mixed clientele of shoppers, visitors and locals. A variety of beers, typical of a Gray's house, is served, as well as a regularly updated food menu. There is a dining room is at the rear, and an outbuilding that hosts live music and other events. Quiz nights are held and games include pool and dominoes. ❀⇌◐⊟♣P

Manningtree

Red Lion ✔

44 South Street, CO11 1BG
11.30-3, 7-11; 12-10.30 Sun
☎ (01206) 395052
Adnams Bitter; Caledonian Deuchars IPA; guest beers H
Cosy, community-minded pub split over two levels, with the bar on the upper level. A warm welcome awaits from the landlord and landlady, and good conversation is assured from the friendly regulars. The beer range has recently expanded both in terms of availability and variety. Food is great value, tasty pub fare —the pub is renowned for its Tuesday Tapas evenings. A function room upstairs is used by many local groups, including an acoustic music club. Q☎❀⇌◐⇌⊟♣

Margaretting Tye

White Hart Inn

Swan Lane, CM4 9JX TL684011
11.30-3, 6-midnight; 11.30-midnight Sat; 12-11 Sun
☎ (01277) 840478 🌐 thewhitehart.uk.com
Adnams Bitter, Broadside; Mighty Oak Oscar Wilde, IPA; H **guest beers** G
This Local CAMRA Pub of the Year 2007 and 2008 is a large hostelry with an L-shaped bar. The main building was built in the 16th century and a modern conservatory added more recently. There are usually at least six ales available and the pub attracts custom for its food as much as its beer. The expansive grounds include a children's play area and a pets' corner. Beer festivals are held in June and October. ♨Q☎❀◐♿P

Mill Green

Viper ★

Mill Green Road, CM4 0PT TL641018
12-3, 6-11; 12-11 Sat; 12-10.30 Sun
☎ (01277) 352010
Mighty Oak Oscar Wilde; Viper Ales VIPA; guest beers H
The only pub in the country with this name, the Viper is an isolated, unspoilt country pub with a lounge, public bar and wood-panelled snug. Viper Ales are commissioned from Mighty Oak and Nethergate, who also frequently supply some of the three guest beers, but these may come from anywhere. Good home-cooked food is served at lunchtime, and Weston's cider is sold. Beer festivals are held at Easter and in September. ♨Q❀◐⊟♣●P⁵—

Monk Street

Farmhouse Inn

CM6 2NR (off B184, 2 miles S of Thaxted) TL612287
11-midnight
☎ (01371) 830864 🌐 farmhouseinn.org
Greene King IPA; Mighty Oak Oscar Wilde, Maldon Gold; guest beers H
Built in the 16th century, this former Dunmow Brewery pub has been enlarged to incorporate a restaurant in the old cart shed and accommodation; the bar is in the original part of the building. Cider is sold in summer. The quiet hamlet of Monk Street overlooks the Chelmer Valley, two miles from historic Thaxted, and is convenient for Stansted Airport and the M11. A well in the pub garden is no longer used but it did supply the hamlet with water during WWII. ❀⇌◐⊟(313)●P⁵—

Mount Bures

Thatchers Arms ✔

Hall Road, CO8 5AT (1½m S of Bures) TL905319
12-3, 6-11; closed Mon; 12-11 Sat & Sun
(01787) 227460 thatchersarms.co.uk
Adnams Bitter; Crouch Vale Brewers Gold; guest beers H
This family-friendly pub on the Essex/Suffolk border is popular with locals and visitors alike. Its two main bar areas and extensive garden overlook the Stour Valley. Up to five real ales are available, mainly from local micro-breweries, together with an extensive selection of British, Belgian and American bottled beers. Winter and spring beer festivals are held at the pub, which is also renowned for its quality food made with locally-sourced produce. Q❀◐ΔP⁻

North Shoebury

Angel

Parsons Corner, North Shoebury Road, SS3 8UD (at A13/B1017 roundabout)
11-3, 5.30-11 Mon-Sat; 12-3, 7-11 Sun
(01702) 589600 angelinn.org
Greene King IPA, Abbot; guest beers H
This jewel of a traditional pub with its thatched roof was originally three 16th-century cottages that included the local post office. It has now been tastefully restored and renovated, as can be seen in the display of photographs in the back-bar area. Hops are displayed above the wood-panelled bar, while the main bar retains its original tiled floor. No TVs, loud music or fruit machines are to be found here, but look for the carved angel in the restaurant area. Occasional beer festivals are held. Q❀◐♿🚌(4,4A)P⁻

Orsett

Foxhound

18 High Road, RM16 3ER (on B188)
11-11.30 (midnight Fri & Sat); 12-10.30 Sun
(01375) 891295
Courage Best Bitter; Greene King IPA; guest beers H
Two-bar village local that is at the centre of social life in Orsett. It has a comfortable saloon and a basic but characterful public bar. The three guest beers are usually from the Crouch Vale portfolio or other independent breweries. Excellent bar meals are served weekday lunchtimes and the Fox's Den restaurant opens at the weekend (booking advisable). It is also available for functions and business meetings. Quiz nights are held regularly. ⋒❀◐🛏♿🚌♣P

Paglesham

Punch Bowl

Churchend, SS4 2DP
11.30-2.30, 7-11 Mon; 11.30-3, 6.30-11; 12-10.30 Sun
(01702) 258376
Adnams Bitter; guest beers H
South-facing, white painted, weatherboarded pub dating from the 16th century, situated in a one-street village. A former bakery and sailmaker's house, it has been an ale house since the mid 1800s, when notorious smuggler William Blyth (known as Hard Apple), drank here and concealed his contraband in the pub. The low-beamed bar displays a large collection of mugs, brassware and old pictures, while outside at the front are a number of picnic tables. ❀◐P

Pebmarsh

King's Head

The Street, CO9 2NH (4 miles NE of Halstead) TL853336
12-3, 6-11 (closed Mon); 12-midnight Fri & Sat; 12-8 Sun
(01787) 269306 kingshead.pebmarsh.com
Greene King IPA; Woodforde's Wherry Best Bitter; guest beers H
A welcome return to the Guide for this 500 year-old popular locals pub, now under new ownership and featuring heavy oak beams with a large central open fire in winter. This pub is a haven for walkers, with plenty of benches in front of the pub and in the rear garden, where two bouncy castles are inflated during the summer. Guest beers from micro-breweries are featured regularly and quality home-cooked food is served both in the main bar and separate restaurant area. ⋒❀◐♣P

Purleigh

Bell

The Street, CM3 6QJ
11-3, 6-11; 12-3, 7-10.30 Sun
(01621) 828348
Adnams Bitter, Broadside; Taylor Landlord H
Friendly village pub in a peaceful location with fine views over the low-lying surrounding area. The building dates from the 14th century, with 16th-century modifications. Good pub food is served (not Tue evening), made with locally-sourced produce where possible. A real fire and beams lend a cosy atmosphere and a good-sized meeting room is available. St Peter's Way footpath is close by, and the neighbouring church was where George Washington's ancestor Lawrence was a former rector. ⋒Q❀◐♣P⁻

Rayleigh

Roebuck ✔

138 High Street, SS6 7BU (opp police station)
9-midnight (1am Fri & Sat)
(01268) 748430
Greene King Abbot; Marston's Pedigree; Shepherd Neame Spitfire; guest beers H
Friendly Wetherspoon's pub in the High Street located on the site of the Reverend James Pilkington's Baptist School and close to the shops. It stocks an excellent range of guest beers. Meals are served all day until 11pm and children are welcome in a sectioned-off dining area. Outdoor drinking and smoking is permitted in a cordoned-off area at the front of the pub. A Wi-Fi connection is available. Rayleigh is served by many buses and has a rail station. Q❀◐♿⇌🚌⁻

Ridgewell

White Horse Inn

Mill Road, CO9 4SG (on A1017 between Halstead and Haverhill) TL736407
12-3 (not Mon & Tue), 6-11; 12-10.30 Sun
(01440) 785532 ridgewellwh.com
Beer range varies G
This old established pub, dating from c.1860, has an atmosphere that is second to none, and offers an ever-changing range of beers from a wide variety of local and national breweries, all dispensed by gravity. Real ciders from Biddenden and Weston's are also available. The pub's first winter beer festival for dark ales was held in 2008 as well as the regular summer event. The excellent restaurant attracts organisations such as the Royal British Legion and CAMRA, who hold their official lunches/dinners here. Luxury en-suite accommodation is available.

Rochford

Golden Lion

35 North Street, SS4 1AB
11-11 (midnight Fri & Sat); 12-10.30 Sun
(01702) 545487
Adnams Bitter; Crouch Vale Brewers Gold; Greene King Abbot; guest beers H
Classic 16th-century traditional Essex weatherboarded freehouse complete with stained glass windows. The decor includes hops above the bar area and a fireplace with traditional log burner. Local CAMRA Pub of the Year 2007 and 2008, it serves six ales including three changing guests, one a dark beer, plus real cider at all times. A large-screen TV shows major sporting events and a patio garden at the back is suitable for smokers. Bar snacks are available Monday to Friday. (7,8)

Horse & Groom

1 Southend Road, SS4 1HA
11-11 (midnight Fri & Sat); 12-10.30 Sun
(01702) 544015
Mighty Oak Maldon Gold; Sharp's Special; guest beers H
Formerly known as Blanchfield's Bar when it was local CAMRA Pub of the Year 2006, this pub reverted to its original name in January 2008. The ever-changing guest ales always include a selection from Essex breweries as well as from further afield, and real cider is always available. Occasional beer festivals are held and the pub also hosts CAMRA SE Essex branch's annual cider festival in September. A separate restaurant provides good value food.

King's Head Inn

11 West Street, SS4 1BE
12-midnight
(01702) 531741
Shepherd Neame Master Brew Bitter, Kent's Best Invicta Ale, Spitfire, Bishop's Finger, seasonal beers H
Originally a coaching inn, this is now a comfortable pub split into three bars, and features a log fire in winter. Shepherd Neame beers are always served in excellent condition by friendly staff. The pub is situated in the market square, close to good public transport links. There is no jukebox but live music plays on three evenings. This is a non-TV establishment so quiet conversation is possible on most evenings. (7,8)

Rowhedge

Olde Albion

High Street, CO5 7ES (3 miles S of Colchester)
12-3 (not Mon), 5-11; 12-11 Thu-Sat; 12-10.30 Sun
(01206) 728972
Beer range varies H/G
A warm welcome is guaranteed at this well-deserved local CAMRA Pub of the Year 2007, where more than 360 different real ales were served over the year, primarily from micro-breweries. Forthcoming beers are listed above the bar, enticing you back to this riverside pub, where smugglers once plied their trade. In summer, drink alfresco watching the foot ferry to Wivenhoe. Regular beer festivals include a St George's Day tribute and June village regatta celebration. Occasional live music is played. (66)

Roxwell

Chequers

The Street, CM1 4PD
5-11; 12-2.30, 6-11 Sat; 12-3.30, 7-10.30 Sun
(01245) 248240
Greene King IPA, Abbot; guest beers H
This 17th-century village inn retains several original beams in its single bar. The sound of conversation dominates as background music is kept low and the TV is only occasionally pressed into service. There is a pool table in a separate room. The landlord will open on weekday lunchtimes for parties by prior arrangement. Two guest beers often include another Greene King ale and a Mighty Oak beer.

Saffron Walden

Old English Gentleman

11 Gold Street, CB10 1EJ (E of B184/B1052 jct)
11-11 (2am Tue-Thu; 1am Fri & Sat)
(01799) 523595
Adnams Bitter; Woodforde's Wherry; guest beers H
This 18th-century town-centre pub has log fires and a welcoming atmosphere. It serves a selection of guest ales and an extensive menu of bar food and sandwiches which changes regularly. Traditional roasts and chef's specials are available on Sunday in the bar or the dining area, where a variety of works of art is displayed. Saffron Walden is busy on Tuesday and Saturday market days. The pub has a pleasant patio at the rear.

Railway

Station Road, CB11 3HQ (near war memorial)
12-3, 6-11 (midnight Thu-Sat)
(01799) 522208
Draught Bass; guest beers H
Typical 19th-century town-centre railway tavern, recently refurbished to a high standard, with railway memorabilia including

ENGLAND

model trains above the bar and in the garden. The single, large bar features a mix of furniture and fittings that helps to convey a relaxed, comfortable atmosphere. An extensive menu of good food is available lunchtimes and evenings. ❀◑🚌P⁄–

St Osyth

White Hart ✔

Mill Street, CO16 8EN

11-11 (midnight Fri & Sat); 12-10.30 Sun

☎ (01255) 820318 thewhitehartstosyth.co.uk

Adnams Bitter; Theakstons Old Peculier; guest beers Ⓗ

Friendly, enthusiastically-run family local located near the famous priory in an historic village. The main pub dates from the 19th century, with a separate 16th-century dining room. Food specials are available at lunchtime Monday to Saturday from 12-3pm. The pub has its own darts teams and runs occasional charity race nights. It is a good starting point for local picturesque walks. ♨❀◑🚌P⁄–

Shalford

George Inn ✔

The Street, CM7 5HH

12-3, 5-midnight; 12-midnight Sat & Sun

thegeorgeshalford.co.uk

Adnams Bitter; Greene King IPA; Woodforde's Wherry Best Bitter, Nelson's Revenge; guest beers Ⓗ

Attractively beamed 15th-century inn with a warm welcome. The pub is very much at the heart of village life. In summer it is pleasant to sit outdoors on the patio, while in winter the roaring log fire draws you in. A pub attracting both drinkers and diners, with a separate dining area, it features various clubs and social events throughout the year, including a summer beer festival. ♨Q❀◑♿🚌♣P⁄–

Southend-on-Sea

Borough Arms

10-12 Marine Parade, SS1 2EJ (on seafront)

10-midnight (2am Fri & Sat)

☎ (01702) 466936

Courage Best Bitter; Harvey's Sussex Best; Hop Back Summer Lightning; guest beers Ⓗ

Called the Liberty Belle for the last 40 years, the pub has now reverted to a previous name. A recent refit revealed the original Victorian brick facade, dated 1903. Aiming to provide a traditional ale house with 21st-century facilities, it has eight handpumps, games areas, a bar and lounge. Live music plays most weekends. The pub can get busy in the summer but it is always pleasant sitting out front on a warm evening.

❀⇄♿⇌(Southend Central)🚌♣●⁄–

Cornucopia

39 Marine Parade, SS1 2EN (on seafront)

10-11 (10.30 Sun)

☎ (01702) 460770 cornucopia.county-of-essex.com

Mighty Oak Maldon Gold; guest beers Ⓗ

A big welcome awaits from the best-dressed barman on the seafront at one of the smallest pubs in Essex. This street corner local on Southend's Golden Mile usually serves two Mighty Oak beers and is popular with punters who watch Sky TV. Music is provided from a huge CD collection and there is karaoke on Friday evening. Seats out front are available for smokers. Can you spot the Victorian three-bar layout among the lead-light windows?

❀⇌(Southend Central)🚌⁄–

Southminster

Station Arms

39 Station Road, CM0 7EW (near B1021)

12-2.30, 6 (5.30 Thu & Fri)-11; 2-11pm Sat; 12-4, 7-10.30 Sun

☎ (01621) 772225 thestationarms.co.uk

Adnams Bitter; Crouch Vale Brewers Gold; Dark Star Hophead; Mighty Oak Oscar Wilde; Nethergate IPA; guest beers Ⓗ

Local CAMRA branch Pub of the Year, it provides an excellent range of attractively priced real ales. A dozen guest beers are sold every week, with two on at any one time, together with Weston's cider. Two beer festivals are held in the pub's tastefully restored barn and the courtyard is used for barbecues at festival time. The simple, tidy interior features many railway- and brewery-themed artefacts. Regular live music is staged and a legendary weekly fine meat raffle takes place. ♨Q❀⇌🚌(31X)♣●⁄–

Stansted Mountfitchet

Rose & Crown

31 Bentfield Green, CM24 8BX (½ mile W of B1383) TL507255

12-3, 6-11 (1am Fri); 12-1am Sat; 12-midnight Sun

☎ (01279) 812107

Adnams Bitter; guest beers Ⓗ

Typical family-run Victorian pub near a duck pond on the edge of a small hamlet, now part of Stansted Mountfitchet village. This free house has been modernised to provide one large bar but retains the atmosphere of a village inn and is well used by locals. The front of the pub is brightened by floral displays. Food is traditional but always excellent and good value, and the guest beers are sourced locally. The smoking area is covered and heated. ♨❀◑🚌(7)♣P⁄–

Stapleford Tawney

Moletrap

Tawney Common, CM16 7PU (3 miles E of Epping) TL500013

11.30-2.30, 6-11; 12-4, 7-10.30 Sun

☎ (01992) 522394 themoletrap.co.uk

Fuller's London Pride; guest beers Ⓗ

Former McMullen pub, now a small free house, this old pub enjoys superb views over the surrounding countryside. There are usually three guest beers from small independent breweries on offer, and good home-cooked food is served (not Sun and Mon eves). The bar can get crowded, but the large garden is delightful in good weather. Despite being close to the M25, the pub can hard to find, but worth the effort. ♨Q❀◑P

Stebbing

White Hart

High Street, CM6 3SQ (2 miles N of old A120 Dunmow-Braintree road)
✪ 11-3, 5-11; 11-11 Sat; 12-10.30 Sun
☎ (01371) 856383
Hart of Stebbing Hart Throb, Hart Beat ⊞
Friendly 15th-century timbered inn in a picturesque village. This comfortable pub features exposed beams, an open fire, eclectic collections from chamber pots to cigarette cards, and a section of exposed lathe and plaster wall behind a glass screen. A community pub, it is used by several local teams including badminton, indoor bowls and cricket. A new brewery, Hart of Stebbing, opened in December 2007, producing two beers, available in the pub. Good value food is served daily. The smoking area is covered and heated. ⛫Q❀◑♣P⁄–

Steeple

Star

The Street, CM0 7LF (E end of Village)
✪ 12-11
☎ (01621) 772646 🌐 starinnsteeple.co.uk
Adnams Bitter; Mighty Oak Burntwood Bitter; Nethergate IPA; guest beers ⊞
A busy, lively 250-year-old pub that meets modern needs. Inside is a pool table at the front and a dining room at the back, plus a covered smoking area. Campers are welcome to stay in the field but need to pre-book. Cyclists, walkers and Young Farmers meet here too. Guest real ales rotate regularly and there is a beer festival each May. A carvery is served on Sunday, with buffet nights on Tuesday and Wednesday in summer, plus Fresh Fish Friday.
⛫❀⇌◑♿Ⓐ⛟(D1,D2)♣●P⁄–

Stock

Hoop ✔

High Street, CM4 9BD (on B1007)
✪ 11-11 (12.30am Fri; midnight Sat); 12-10.30 Sun
☎ (01277) 841137 🌐 thehoop.co.uk
Adnams Bitter; Brentwood Hoop, Stock & Barrel; ⊞ **guest beers** Ⓖ
This recently refurbished 15th-century weatherboarded pub has a rustic theme in its large bar area, with an upstairs oak room restaurant offering a la carte dining. Bar meals are also served and all the food is home-cooked. At least four guest beers are on gravity dispense. The large garden is the setting for a long-established beer festival held over the Spring bank holiday. During the summer months it has an outside bar and a barbecue. Q❀◑♿⛟(100)●⁄–

Stow Maries

Prince of Wales

Woodham Road, CM3 6SA (near B1012) TL830993
✪ 11-11 (midnight Fri & Sat)
☎ (01621) 828971 🌐 prince-stowmaries.co.uk
Beer range varies ⊞/Ⓖ
One of the county's long-standing real ale free houses, offering a varied selection of beers plus Weston's Old Rosie cider and an extensive bottled and draught range from Belgium, where the pub has many friends. This 17th-century inn was once a bakery and has three open-plan drinking areas, all with real fires. The annual November fireworks display is renowned internationally. Fine meals are available, featuring local fish or seafood specialities to complement the ales on offer. Stylish farmhouse accommodation is a recent addition. ⛫Q☕❀⇌◑Ⓐ⛟♣●P

Tendring

Cherry Tree Inn

Crow Lane, CO16 9AD (on B1035/Crow Lane jct)
✪ 11-2, 6-11; closed Mon; 12-4 Sun
☎ (01255) 830340
Adnams Bitter; Greene King IPA; guest beers ⊞
A true rural gem, the Cherry Tree is tranquil and cosy. It has recently expanded its restaurant to serve enthusiastic local customers. Join regulars at the bar for lively conversation or take your seat outside in the summer to relax and enjoy the country views. At the heart of the Tendring Peninsula, this pub is a long-standing entry in the Guide and has a superb reputation for its well-kept beer and excellent food. ❀◑⛟P

Tilbury

Worlds End

Fort Road, RM18 7NR (near A1089, by river between Tilbury Ferry and Tilbury Fort)
✪ 11-11; 12-10.30 Sun
☎ (01375) 840827
Greene King Abbot; Mighty Oak IPA; guest beers ⊞
Close to Tilbury Ferry and the Fort, this riverside pub was extensively restored as a free house in 1998 following serious fire damage. The guest beer is usually from Mighty Oak. Low ceiling beams feature in one bar area, and food is available every day in the restaurant area. Monthly charity events are held to support the pub's favoured charities, Essex Air Ambulance and the RNLI.
❀◑♿⛟(99)P⁄–

Tollesbury

King's Head

1 High Street, CM9 8RG (on B1023, 5 miles SE of Tiptree)
✪ 12-11 (midnight Fri & Sat); 12-10.30 Sun
☎ (01621) 869203
Adnams Bitter; Woodforde's Wherry; guest beers ⊞
Situated in the village square, this 17th-century free house is popular with locals and visitors alike. The L-shaped saloon bar features prints and photos of marine memorabilia, and a large-screen TV does not intrude. This community pub hosts weekly motorcycle club meetings, and monthly folk and open mic sessions. Up to three guest ales are available, usually including a dark ale and at least one local brew. The smoking area is heated and covered. ⛫❀⊟⛟♣

Weeley

White Hart

Clacton Road, Weeley Heath, CO16 9ED (on B1441)
12-2.30, 4-11; 12-11 Fri-Sun
(01255) 830384
Beer range varies
A beer drinker's delight, this pub is a hit with the locals, with its stock of ever-changing real ales. It is now an outlet for ales from the Harwich Town Brewery, with three to four pumps in regular use. The friendly landlord is a regular sponsor of the Clacton Beer Festival and the pub has an active real ale club. Although out in the sticks, the pub is one mile from Weeley station and served by regular buses. (76)P

Wendens Ambo

Bell

Royston Road, CB11 4JY (on B1039, 1 mile W of B1383/old A11 jct)
11.30-3, 6-11; 11.30-12.30am Fri & Sat; 12-11.30 Sun
(01799) 540382
Adnams Bitter; Woodforde's Wherry; guest beers
Classic country pub at the centre of a picturesque village near Saffron Walden. A past winner of local CAMRA Pub of the Year, it boasts an enormous garden which hosts a beer festival in summer. Audley End station on the Liverpool Street to Cambridge line is five minutes' walk away and buses from Saffron Walden bring you close to this welcoming hostelry. Q(Audley End)P

Westcliff-on-Sea

Cricketers

225 London Road, SS0 7JG (on A13)
11-midnight (2am Fri & Sat); 12-midnight Sun
(01702) 343168
Greene King IPA, Abbot; guest beers
This large street corner pub on the edge of Southend is very popular and with its late licence gets especially busy at weekends. A Gray & Sons pub, it serves up to five constantly changing ales, plus two regular and one guest cider. The excellent music venue Club Riga next door adds to the feel-good factor and occasional beer festivals are held. The pub is on a bus route and is also close to Southend Victoria and Westcliff rail stations.
(Southend Victoria/Westcliff)

Witham

Woolpack

7 Church Street, CM8 2JP
11.30-11 (midnight Fri & Sat); 12-10.30 Sun
(01376) 511195
Mighty Oak Maldon Gold; guest beers
Friendly two-roomed back-street pub only five minutes' walk from Witham Station if you know where you are going. Two or three guest beers are on offer, usually including one at a good price. This is a games-oriented pub and is home to pool, darts and crib teams. Live music of varying styles is usually performed on the last Saturday of each month.

Wivenhoe

Horse & Groom

55 The Cross, CO7 9QL (on B1028)
10.30-3, 5.30-11 (midnight Fri); 10.30-3, 6-11 Sat; 12-4.30, 7-10.30 Sun
(01206) 824928
Adnams Bitter, seasonal beers; guest beers
Friendly locals' pub on the outskirts of Wivenhoe with a proper two-bar layout featuring a public bar that is popular for darts. Adnams beers are on offer, with changing guests often including a mild. Very good home-cooked food is served lunchtimes Monday to Saturday —the curries are well worth sampling. At the rear is a garden with a covered and heating smoking area, plus a small car park. The pub is accessible by bus and a one-mile walk from Wivenhoe station.
P

Woodham Mortimer

Hurdlemakers Arms

Post Office Road, CM9 6ST (off A414)
12-11 summer; 12-3, 6-11 winter; 12-10.30 (12-3, 7-10.30 winter) Sun
(01245) 225169
Beer range varies
This Gray & Sons country inn has a community focus and is very popular with walkers. The tenants are CAMRA members and host special events throughout the year, while traditional pub games are played in the unspoilt public bar. The cosy lounge incorporates a dining area and overlooks the huge garden where summer barbecues take place. Traditional home-cooked food is locally sourced and always available, together with three guest beers that change regularly and often include a dark beer. Real cider is stocked.
QP

Writtle

Wheatsheaf

70 The Green, CM1 3DU (S of A1060)
11-2.30 (3 Fri), 5.30-11; 11-11 Sat; 12-10.30 Sun
(01245) 420695 wheatsheafph-writtle.co.uk
Farmer's Drop of Nelson's Blood; Greene King IPA, Abbot; Mighty Oak Oscar Wilde, Burntwood Bitter, Maldon Gold
Traditional village pub with a small public bar and an equally small lounge attracting a wide variety of customers. The atmosphere is generally quiet as Sky TV in the public bar is only switched on for occasional sporting events. A folk night is held on the third Friday of each month. The Gray & Sons sign in the public bar was rescued from the brewery when it closed in 1974. There is a small roadside patio. QP

Beer makes you feel the way you ought to feel without beer.
Henry Lawson

GLOUCESTERSHIRE & BRISTOL

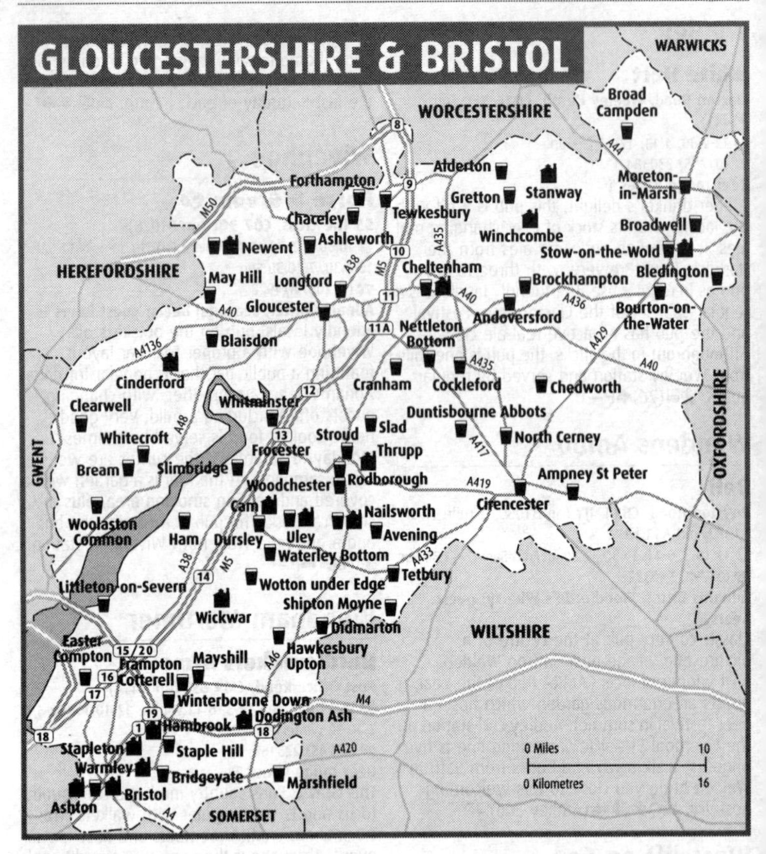

Alderton

Gardeners Arms ✓

Beckford Road, GL20 8NL

12-2.30, 6-11 (10.30 Sun)

☎ (01242) 620257

Beer range varies Ⓗ

This listed 16th-century oak-beamed free house stands at the heart of a quiet village and has an original well in the lounge; the walls are hung with local photographs and a piano is used occasionally. Regularly-changing beers are served from four handpumps and the pub holds mini beer festivals at Whitsun and Christmas, promoting local brewers. Weekly pub games, a monthly quiz and themed food nights are hosted. A range of home-cooked meals and bar snacks is served. ⋒Q❀◑▶⊟♿♣P⁻

Ampney St Peter

Red Lion ★

London Road, GL7 5SL (on A417)

12-2 (Sat only), 6-10; 12-2.30 (closed eve) Sun

☎ (01285) 851596

Hook Norton Hooky Bitter; Taylor Golden Best, Landlord Ⓗ

This wonderful pub is on CAMRA's National Inventory of Historic Pubs. It is the oldest continually licensed premises in the district and local CAMRA Pub of the Year 2007/08. For over 400 years it has had a reputation for dispensing crystal clear ale. There are two cosy rooms, some basic seating, a counter-less bar and just two handpumps in a corner. With the region's most effective log fire, this is a great place to stop for a chat. ⋒Q❀⊟⊟P

Andoversford

Royal Oak

GL54 4HR (On A436)

11-3, 5-11; 12-10.30 Sun

INDEPENDENT BREWERIES

Arbor Bristol: Stapleton
Avon Bristol (NEW)
Bath Ales Bristol: Warmley
Battledown Cheltenham
Bristol Beer Factory Bristol: Ashton
Cotswold Spring Dodington Ash
Donnington Stow-on-the-Wold
Festival Cheltenham
Freeminer Cinderford
Goff's Winchcombe
Great Western Bristol: Hambrook (NEW)
Nailsworth Nailsworth
Severn Vale Cam
Stanway Stanway
Stroud Thrupp
Uley Uley
Whittington's Newent
Wickwar Wickwar
Zerodegrees Bristol

☎ (01242) 820335
Sharp's Doom Bar; Stanway Stanney Bitter; guest beers Ⓗ
Popular, well-run local pub offering up to five quality real ales including two from local Cotswold brewers. A large open log fire creates a homely atmosphere, warming both the comfortable lounge area and a two-level restaurant with gallery. Recent refurbishment offers an attractive environment for both home-cooked meals and real ales. A patio area at the rear of the pub also provides access to the large car park. Andoversford is an expanding village between Cheltenham and the North Cotswolds.

Ashleworth

Boat Inn

The Quay, GL19 4HZ (follow sign for Quay from village) SO818250
11.30-2.30 (3 Sat; not Wed), 7-11pm; closed Mon; 12-3, 7-10.30 Sun
☎ (01452) 700272 boat-inn.co.uk
Beer range varies Ⓖ
This unspoilt, tranquil haven on the banks of the River Severn is an absolute gem. It has been owned by the same family for 400 years and serves micro-brewery beers direct from the cask, making it a frequent winner of local CAMRA awards. Several rooms are furnished with antiques and the courtyard has some tables under cover. Rolls are available at lunchtime and the pub has its own mooring for river visitors.

Avening

Bell

29 High Street, GL8 8NF (on B4014)
12-3, 5.30-11; 12-11 Sun
☎ (01453) 836422
Wickwar BOB; guest beers Ⓗ
A friendly, confidently-run old inn with exposed stone walls, adorned with myriad horse brasses and pictures. The pleasant open bar offers three beers, all from local micro-breweries, and features a wood-burning stove and a bay window seat. In the dining area you will find a competitively priced menu, providing very generous portions, particularly on Tuesday's curry night. Catch this pleasant pub on the right evening and you can try the Tudor game of shulbac.

Blaisdon

Red Hart

GL17 0AH SO702167
12-3, 6 (7 Sun)-11
☎ (01452) 830477
Hook Norton Hooky Bitter; guest beers Ⓗ
A lovely old inn with low beams, flag-stone floor and an open fire, plus friendly and helpful staff. A very welcoming pub, it offers up to five beers on the handpumps, four of which are constantly changing. There is a good choice of quality food on the menu. The permanent barbecue and outdoor seating ensure that this a summer favourite.

Bledington

Kings Head

The Green, OX7 6XQ SP243228
11-3, 6-11; 12-10.30 Sun
☎ (01608) 658365 kingsheadinn.net
Hook Norton Hooky Bitter; guest beers Ⓗ
North Cotswold CAMRA Pub of the Year 2008, this delightful 16th-century honey-coloured stone inn overlooks the village green, with its brook and ducks. The original old beams, inglenook with kettle plus military brasses, open wood fire, flagstone floors and high back settles and pews create a heart-warming atmosphere. Quality food is served in a separate dining area while 12 rooms offer charming accommodation. Guest ales are often from the local North Cotswold Brewery and the regular keg lager is also brewed nearby.

Bourton on the Water

Mousetrap Inn

Lansdowne, GL54 2AR (300 yards W of village centre)
11.30-3, 6-11; 12-3, 6-10.30 Sun
☎ (01451) 820579 mousetrap-inn.co.uk
North Cotswold Pigbrook Bitter; guest beers Ⓗ
This attractive, traditional and friendly Cotswold stone pub is a family-run free house, situated in the quieter Lansdowne part of Bourton. It is popular with the local community as well as offering 10 en-suite letting rooms for visitors. Well-kept local beers and good value home-cooked meals are served. A welcoming, cosy atmosphere is created with a feature fireplace and coal-effect fire. Out front a patio area with tables and hanging baskets provides a sheltered suntrap in summer. (801,855)

Bream

Rising Sun

High Street, GL15 6JF (opp cenotaph)
12-2.30 (3.30 Sun), 6-11
☎ (01594) 564555 therisingsunbream.co.uk
Freeminer Speculation; guest beers Ⓗ
This large 200-year-old pub has breathtaking views over the Forest of Dean. A friendly main bar overspills into two adjacent rooms, two dining rooms and a function room with its own bar. A pleasant garden to the rear is lovely in the summer. The range of beers is excellent and the food superb, while comfortable guest rooms make this a good centre from which to explore the Forest of Dean.

Bridgeyate

White Harte

111 London Road, BS30 5NA (on A420 jct wth A4175 E of Bristol)
11-2.45 (3 Sat), 5 (6 Sat)-11; 11-11 Fri; 12-10.30 Sun
☎ (0117) 9673830
Bath Ales Gem; Butcombe Bitter; Courage Best Bitter; Marston's Pedigree Ⓗ
Traditional inn dating from 1860 and extended in 1987. The large village green at the front of the pub means it is often known as the 'Inn on

the Green'. An unusual bar counter incorporates old wooden spice drawers. Reasonably priced food attracts lunchtime diners, and the pub also gets busy in the evening with people out for a drink. Pub games and sporting activities are likely conversation topics, and a quiz features on Monday evening. Black Rat cider is served.
(634,635)P

Bristol (Central)

Bag O'Nails

141 St George's Road, Hotwells, BS1 5UW (5 mins walk from Cathedral)
12-2 (Thu only), 5.30-11; 12-11 Fri & Sat; 12-10.30 Sun
(0117) 940 6776 bagonails.org.uk
Hop Back Crop Circle; O'Hanlons Port Stout; RCH Pitchfork; guest beers H
Small, friendly gas-lit terraced free house which showcases the beers of small brewers from all over. Up to six constantly-changing guest ales are served and regular beer festivals take place twice a year, usually in April and November. The basic interior features wood panelling and bare floorboards, with port holes providing a view into the cellar. A good range of British and foreign bottled beers is available. Most Bristol to North Somerset buses stop nearby. Q

Bell

Hillgrove Street, Stokes Croft, BS2 8JT (off Jamaica St)
12-2, 5-midnight (1am Thu-Sat); 1-11.30 Sun
(0117) 909 6612 bell-butcombe.com
Bath Ales Gem; Butcombe Bitter, Gold, seasonal beer H
Pleasant two-roomed pub where DJs spin their discs from 10pm nightly in the back room. Friday evenings in particular attract drinkers on their way to nearby clubs. Local workers are regular customers for the lunchtime and early evening food. Sunday lunches are popular too. A surprising feature is the pleasant rear garden with a patio which is heated in colder weather. Local art on the wood panelled walls and artistic graffiti in the toilets add character.

Bridge Inn

16 Passage St, BS2 0JF
11.30 (12 Sat)-11.30; 7-10.30 Sun
(0117) 949 9967
Bath Ales SPA, Gem, seasonal beer; guest beer H
Superbly consistent tiny pub, close to the station and surrounding hotels, yet only a short walk from the city centre. It is popular for its lunchtime food, served Monday to Saturday. Three handpumps usually feature a Bath Ales seasonal beer along with the regulars, but guests also appear. There is some seating out front in good weather. The pub underwent a major internal makeover during 2007. (Temple Meads)

Colston Yard

Colston Street, BS1 5BD
11-midnight (1am Fri & Sat)
(0117) 376 3232 colstonyard-butcombe.com
Butcombe Bitter, Gold, seasonal beers; Fuller's London Pride; guest beers H
Hugely impressive renovation of the old Smiles Brewery and Tap site, reopened by Butcombe in late 2007. Unrecognisable internally, it has a pleasant upmarket feel without being at all stuffy. In addition to the Butcombe range there are two or three guest beers, a number of interesting foreign draught beers from Europe and the USA, plus around 30 quality bottled brews from elsewhere. An extensive bar and restaurant menu features local organic produce. A very welcome addition to the Bristol pub scene.

Commercial Rooms

43-45 Corn Street, BS1 1HT
8am-midnight (1am Fri & Sat); 9am-midnight Sun
(0117) 927 9681
Butcombe Bitter, Gold; Courage Best Bitter; Greene King Abbot; Marston's Pedigree; guest beers H
Originally opened as the Bristol Rooms in 1811, this pub became Wetherspoon's first Bristol outlet in 1995. It is a palatial building with lavish Greek revival-style decor, numerous paintings, and items commemorating famous local people. There is a smaller galleried room which is quieter. Up to seven guest beers feature in this deserving winner of several Wetherspoon awards, including its 2008 Real Ale Pub of the Year. Disabled access is via the side entrance in Small Street. Q

Cornubia

142 Temple Street, BS1 6EN (opp fire station by former Courage brewery)
11-11; 12-11.30 Sat; 12-6 Sun
(0117) 925 4415
Hidden Pint, Potential, Depths, seasonal beers; guest beers H
Long-time local favourite now under new management and with much extended weekend opening hours. Three Hidden beers, three guests from other micro-breweries and changing real cider or perry are what you can expect. The pub was originally a pair of Georgian houses built in 1773 then went on to operate as the Courage tasting rooms for many years. The front is Grade II listed and can be admired from the outdoor seating in summer. Food is served all day until 9pm.
Q(Temple Meads)P

Eldon House

6 Lower Clifton Hill, BS8 1BT (off Jacobs Wells Rd)
12-3, 5-11; 12-midnight Fri; 12-11 Sat & Sun
(0117) 922 1271 theeldonhouse.co.uk
Bath Ales SPA, Gem, seasonal beers H
This pub has the same owners as the Bridge in Passage Street and the beer policy is much the same, but with more emphasis on food, which has gained a good reputation. This end of terrace pub has three small rooms, the walls are tastefully painted in pastel shades of green and cream, and the floorboards are bare in the main bar but carpeted at the rear. A real fire is located in the smallest back bar. Live music plays every Sunday evening. Q

Grain Barge

Hotwells Road, Hotwells, BS8 4RU (moored on the opposite bank to the SS Great Britain)
11.30-11 (11.30 Fri); 10.30-11.30 Sat; 11-11.30 Sun

☎ (0117) 929 9347

Bristol Beer Factory Red, No 7, Sunrise, seasonal beers Ⓗ

Another hugely welcome addition to the local scene, this boat, built in 1936 and until recently a restaurant, was purchased by the Beer Factory and converted into a floating pub offering good food. Great views of the floating harbour and passing boats are available from the top two decks. Live music plays on Friday, and popular themed food nights are held on Tuesday and Wednesday. No food is available Sunday evening or all day Monday. Thatchers cider is served. ❀◑▶🚌♠⚡

Hare on the Hill

41 Thomas Street North, Kingsdown, BS2 8LX

⏲ 12-2.30, 5-11; 12-11.30 Fri & Sat; 12-11 Sun

☎ (0117) 908 1982

Bath Ales SPA, Gem, Barnstormer, seasonal beers; guest beers Ⓗ

The original Bath Ales pub is still a class act and there is something for everyone to enjoy here. It stocks the full Bath range plus more than 30 malt whiskies. Good food includes bar snacks, curries on Tuesday, Italian on Thursday and roasts on Sunday. Large-screen TVs show major sports events. Entertainment includes live acoustic music most Sunday evenings from October to June, classic concerts in July and August, and silent comedy on Monday night. ◑▶⇌(Montpelier)🚌♣

Highbury Vaults

164 St Michaels Hill, Kingsdown, BS2 8DE (top of steep hill next to Bristol Royal Infirmary)

⏲ 12-midnight (11 Sun)

☎ (0117) 973 3203

Bath Ales Gem; Brains SA; St Austell Tribute; Wells Bombardier; Young's Bitter, Special, seasonal beers; guest beers Ⓗ

A long-standing Guide entry that has survived the closure of Smiles and merger of Young's and Wells, with the same management for more than 15 years. This is a popular haunt of university students and hospital staff. Dating from the mid-19th century, its interior is dark and dingy, and features a small front snug bar, a main drinking area and a bar billiards table. Outside is a large heated patio and garden. Good quality, great value food is served lunchtimes and weekday evenings.
Q❀◑▶⇌(Clifton Down)🚌(9)♣⚡

Hillgrove Porter Stores

53 Hillgrove Street North, Kingsdown, BS2 8LT

⏲ 4-midnight (1am Fri & Sat)

☎ (0117) 944 4780 🌐 myspace.com/thehillgrove

Goff's Tournament; Cheddar Best; Matthews Brassknocker; guest beers Ⓗ

A stone's throw from its great friendly rival the Hare on the Hill (above), this was the first of the Dawkins Taverns, the brainchild of a local entrepreneur. An excellent community pub, it is free of tie and making the most of it, usually dispensing five guest ales including dark beers and rare styles. The interior is horseshoe shaped with a wonderfully comfy lounge area hidden behind the bar. Outside is a small patio. Sunday night is quiz night. Frequent themed mini beer festivals are held in conjunction with the other Dawkins pubs. Local CAMRA Pub of the Year 2007.
❀⇌(Montpelier)🚌♣♠⚡

Hope & Anchor

38 Jacobs Well Rd, Clifton, BS8 1DR (between Anchor Rd and top of Park St)

⏲ 12-11 (10.30 Sun)

☎ (0117) 929 2987

Beer range varies Ⓗ

Popular and friendly city local frequented by students, diners and drinkers – all enjoying the chance to choose from up to six changing real ales, mostly from West Country micro-breweries. The pub has achieved a happy balance between those who come to eat the high quality food, served all day, and those who just want a pint. Subdued lighting, candles on the tables and hanging hop bines over the bar create atmosphere. On summer days the terraced garden at the rear is very pleasant. Street parking is limited but buses pass nearby. ❀◑▶🚌⚡

Kings Head ★

60 Victoria Street, BS1 6DE

⏲ 11-11; 7.30-11 Sat; 12-3, 7-11 Sun

☎ (0117) 927 7860

Bath Ales Gem; Sharp's IPA, Doom Bar; Wadworth 6X Ⓗ

Classic small pub, dating from pre-1660 and listed on CAMRA's National Inventory. A narrow area around the bar leads to the 'tramcar snug' to the rear. Multiple historical pictures of Bristol as it was long ago make fascinating viewing. A resident ghost, said to be an earlier landlady, is reputed to haunt the pub. Popular food is served weekday lunchtimes only. A few minutes' walk from Temple Meads station on the way to town, the pub is also well served by buses. There are tables for outside drinking in summer.
Q❀◑⇌(Temple Meads)🚌

Old Fishmarket ✔

59-63 Baldwin Street, BS1 1QZ

⏲ 12-11 (midnight Fri & Sat)

☎ (0117) 921 1515

Butcombe Bitter; Fuller's Discovery, London Pride, ESB, seasonal beers Ⓗ

Cracking Fuller's pub that has gone from strength to strength in recent years. It has also become the main venue for those who enjoy a great pint with their TV sport —all main events are screened. As the name suggests, this was once a fish market. It has a large front bar and a side indoor patio, as well as several discrete seating booths behind the bar for those wishing to avoid the sport. Thai and English meals are served at lunchtimes and evenings. Situated just off the centre by Bristol Bridge, the pub is 10 minutes' walk from the station with many buses passing close by.
◑▶♿⇌(Temple Meads)🚌

Orchard Inn

12 Hanover Place, Spike Island, BS1 6XT (off Cumberland Rd near SS Great Britain)

⏲ 12-11; 12-3, 7-10.30 Sun

☎ (0117) 926 2678

Bath Ales Gem; guest beers Ⓗ

One-bar street corner local tucked in behind the SS Great Britain and a 10-minute walk from the centre along the harbourside. The ferry service stops fairly close by. Renowned for its range and quality of real cider, it offers Thatchers, Black Rat and a guest, plus mulled cider in winter. The pub has also become more adventurous in its real ales, with two changing guests. Food is served Monday to Friday lunchtimes and is excellent value, as are the bar prices. Quiz night is Tuesday. An excellent community pub, it attracts a real mix of customers. Q❀◐▲🚌●⅃

Seven Stars

1 Thomas Lane, Redcliffe, BS1 6JG (just off Victoria St nr Bristol Bridge)
☉ 12-11 (10.30 Sun)
☎ (0117) 376 3970
Beer range varies Ⓗ
Small one-bar pub with poignant links to the abolition of the slave trade in Bristol. It has been rejuvenated by an enthusiastic management team, with a warm welcome and very competitive prices. Beers from Bath Ales and Sharp's feature heavily among the range of up to seven ales on handpump. The eclectic clientele often includes drinkers enjoying a few pre-gig pints before moving next door to the well known Fleece & Firkin music venue. An excellent rock jukebox is supplemented by live music on weekend afternoons. Real cider is sold occasionally. Pool is played in one corner of the pub.
⇌(Temple Meads)🚌♣

White Lion

Quay Head, Colston Avenue, BS1 1EB
☉ 11 (12 Sat)-11; 12-6 Sun
☎ (0117) 925 4819
Draught Bass; Ⓟ **Wickwar Coopers, BOB, Cotswold Way, seasonal beers; guest beers** Ⓗ
This small city-centre pub is Wickwar's only tied house in Bristol; it changed hands in 2007 but is still going strong. One room curls around the central bar and the dizzying spiral staircase to the Gents is not for the faint-hearted. Five handpumps feature a selection of Wickwar beers, often accompanied by guests from far and wide. 'Bristol's smallest beer festival' is held here twice yearly when barrels on stillage appear by the bar. Hearty sandwiches are served weekday lunchtimes. ❀🚌⅃

Zerodegrees

53 Colston Street, BS1 5BA (opp Bristol Royal Infirmary)
☉ 12-midnight (11 Sun)
☎ (0117) 925 2706 🌐 zerodegrees.co.uk
Zerodegrees Wheat Beer, Pale Ale, Pilsner, Black Lager, seasonal beers Ⓗ
This brewpub won the 2005 CAMRA National New Build Pub award and has proved hugely popular with a good mixed local clientele. The high-tech brewery is on full view. All beers are served at continental-style temperatures – much lower than the norm for pubs in this Guide. Mango Beer is usually available as well as other seasonal beers. A large restaurant serving all day is spread over two floors and features an open kitchen (booking advisable at peak times). Flat-screen TVs with the sound turned down show sport. Two balconies and a terraced patio provide an escape from the ever-present music. ❀◐◑🚌⅃

Bristol (East)

Cross Hands

1 Staple Hill Road, Fishponds, BS16 5AA (jct of A432 and B4465)
☉ 12-11
☎ (0117) 965 4684 🌐 crosshands.co.uk
Beer range varies Ⓗ
Transformed in 2006, this is a large, imposing building in the Queen Anne style, beautifully fitted out with many comfortable nooks and crannies, furnished with settees and armchairs. Up to 12 beers, mainly from local brewers, dominate the bar, and a changing cider features too. An upstairs function room can be booked and trips to local breweries are arranged. A change of management in 2007 has resulted in extended opening hours and the introduction of a new, more affordable, food menu. ❀◐◑♿🚌(48,49)●⅃

Bristol (North)

Annexe

Seymour Road, Bishopston, BS7 9EQ (behind Sportsman pub)
☉ 11.30-11.30; 12-11 Sun
☎ (0117) 9493931
Courage Best Bitter; Draught Bass; Greene King Abbot; Shepherd Neame Spitfire; Wye Valley HPA; guest beers Ⓗ
A welcome return for this community pub tucked away in a residential street close to the County Cricket Ground and a short walk from the Memorial football and rugby stadium. Inside is a converted skittle alley with a large conservatory/family room on one side and a partially covered patio on the other. Large-screen TVs show sport at both ends of the bar and out on the patio, while good simple food, including quality pizzas, is served. Quiz night is Monday and pool and darts are played.
Q🚸❀◐◑♿🚌●⅃

Duke of York

2 Jubilee Road, St Werburghs, BS2 9RS (behind Mina Road Park close to M32 jct 3)
☉ 5 (4 Sat)-11 (midnight Thu-Sat); 3.30-11 Sun
☎ (0117) 941 3677
Beer range varies Ⓗ
This well-hidden genuine free house is a traditional community local serving an eclectic clientele. The exterior features an enchanted forest mural which continues inside. Visit in daylight for the mural, then at night experience the warm glow of the grotto-like interior. Expect many fairy lights, odd memorabilia, wooden floors, 1940s newspapers, a rare skittle alley and much more. Check out the two rooms and extra bar upstairs. Three handpumps offer unusual beers, plus Weston's cider and a good range of bottled ales. Local CAMRA Pub of the Year 2008. ❀⊟⇌(Montpelier)🚌(5,25)♣●⅃

Inn on the Green

2 Filton Road, Horfield, BS7 0PA (on A38 opp sports centre)
☉ 12-11
☎ (0117) 952 1391
Butcombe Bitter, Gold; Draught Bass; Sharp's Doom Bar; guest beers Ⓗ

Local CAMRA Pub of the Year 2006, offering an amazing 11 guest beers plus four ciders and a perry. The open-plan interior is divided into three main sections, catering for the local community as well as rugby and football fans from the nearby Memorial stadium. Note that the pub closes before home football games. Good value pub food is served and a one-day beer festival is held to coincide with Bristol Rugby Club's last home game. The disabled facilities have been improved.
Q❀◑◗♿🚌♣🍎P⅟

Miners Arms

136 Mina Road, St Werburghs, BS2 9YQ (400m from M32 jct 3)
4 (2 Sat)-11 (midnight Thu-Sat); 12-11 Sun
☎ (0117) 955 6718
Fuller's London Pride; St Austell Tribute; guest beers Ⓗ
Located close to St Werburghs City Farm and Bristol Climbing Centre, this is an excellent two-roomed street corner local, part of the local Dawkins chain. The split level interior houses a hop-adorned bar where three or four guest beers, including a beer of the month, join the regulars. Another small quiet bar lies to the side. The pub dogs are called Nelson and Morris and they welcome other well-behaved canines. Parking nearby can be tricky but buses 5 and 25 stop nearby.
⛼❀⇌(Montpelier)🚌(5,25)♣

Robin Hood's Retreat

197 Gloucester Road, Bishopston, BS7 8BG (on A38)
12-11
☎ (0117) 9248639
Beer range varies Ⓗ
Elegant Victorian pub that has been transformed into a sophisticated food and drink venue, and a welcoming refuge from the bustling city. Eight handpumps offer a changing range of brews from independent outfits, and there is a regular Brewery of the Week feature. Award-winning food is produced by the chef/co-owner every day except Sunday. The pub can get very busy, especially at weekends. An outside decked area to the rear is open until 10.30pm. Children are welcome during the daytime.
Q❀◑◗♿⇌(Montpelier)🚌

Bristol (South)

Coronation

18 Dean Lane, Southville, BS3 1DD
3 (12 Sat)-11; 12-10.30 Sun
☎ (0117) 940 9044
Hop Back GFB, Odyssey, Crop Circle, Summer Lightning, seasonal beer; guest beer Ⓗ
Hop Back's only Bristol pub, this busy street corner local is a stone's throw from the River Avon, a 10-minute walk from the centre. It usually serves five Hop Back beers plus a guest from the associated Downton Brewery. The full range of Hop Back bottle-conditioned beers and a guest cider are also sold. Low-volume background music is played and a small TV is switched on for major sports events only. Quiz night is Monday. Pizzas are served every evening 6-9pm. ◗🚌🍎

Shakespeare

1 Henry Street, Totterdown, BS3 4UD (100m from A37 Wells Rd by 3 Lamps jct)
4.30 (12 Sat)-11 (midnight Fri & Sat); 12-10.30 Sun
☎ (0117) 907 8818 🌐 theshakey.co.uk
Bath Ales Gem; Bristol Beer Factory Trail Ale; Sharp's Cornish Coaster; guest beers Ⓗ
This friendly street-corner pub is a short walk from Temple Meads station. Two guest beers and a real cider complement the permanent range, which includes Falstaff – a Bristol Beer Factory exclusive. Weekly quizzes, a pool table and other pub games feature. Beer festivals with around 12 beers often coincide with bank holidays, and occasional summer barbecues are held. This social heart of Totterdown has a nightly DJ, poker on Tuesday, live bands every second Saturday and Sunday lunch with vegan options. ⛼❀⇌(Temple Meads)🚌♣🍎⅟

Windmill

14 Windmill Hill, Bedminster, BS3 4LU (next to railway station)
11(12 Sat)-11 (midnight Fri & Sat); 12-10.30 Sun
☎ (0117) 963 5440 🌐 thewindmillbristol.com
Bristol Beer Factory Red, No. 7, Sunrise Ⓗ
Completely refurbished in 2006, with pastel colours and wooden flooring throughout. Three beers from the nearby Bristol Beer Factory are always on offer, with the range changing occasionally. Weston's cider and a few foreign bottled beers are also stocked. The pub is on two levels, with a family room on the lower one. There is also a small outside patio area to the front. Good quality tasty food is served all day, and board games are available. Many buses pass nearby.
⛼❀◑◗⇌(Bedminster)🚌🍎⅟

Bristol (West)

Merchants Arms

5 Merchants Road, Hotwells, BS8 4PZ
10.30-2, 5-11; 10.30-11.30 Sat; 11-11 Sun
☎ (0117) 9040037
Bath Ales SPA, Gem, Barnstormer, seasonal beer Ⓗ
Traditional local located just before the Cumberland Basin, on all the main Bristol to North Somerset bus routes. It won a national CAMRA award for its refurbishment a few years ago, when Bath Ales first took it on. Conversation dominates in the two drinking areas, although live music is held on some Tuesdays and a quiz night on Thursday. The concealed TV is brought out occasionally to show football. Food is limited to bar snacks. Well-behaved dogs are welcome. Q🚌P

Prince of Wales

84 Stoke Lane, Westbury on Trym, BS9 3SP (off A4018, 5 mins walk from Westbury centre)
11-midnight (1am Fri & Sat); 12-11.30 Sun
☎ (0117) 962 3715
Bath Ales Gem; Butcombe Bitter, Gold, seasonal beers; Draught Bass; Fuller's London Pride; guest beers Ⓗ
Attractive, characterful and busy suburban pub owned by Butcombe and offering up to eight beers, usually from regional or better-known breweries. Brunel IPA is available winter only. The pub offers a range of seating areas and an

attractive sun-trap garden at the rear, which includes a children's play area and petanque piste. Interesting prints and sporting memorabilia adorn the walls, and foldaway TVs show major sporting events, especially rugby. Good value lunchtime meals are popular (not Sunday). Children are welcome until 8pm. Q❀◐⊟⊱

Royal Oak

50 The Mall, Clifton, BS8 4JG

12-11 (4 Sun)

☎ (0117) 973 8846

Butcombe Bitter; Courage Best Bitter; Fuller's London Pride; Sharp's Doom Bar ⊞

A short walk from the Downs in the heart of Clifton village, this is a busy split-level pub. Crowds tend to gather around the bar on one level, while quiet seats can be found in the rear area. The pub is popular with local sports clubs and the TV shows major sports, especially rugby. Lunchtime food and a Sunday roast are offered. Count how many puffer fish you can spot among the dried hops around the bar and walls. Thatchers Heritage cider is sold. ◐⊟(8,9)●⊱

Victoria ✔

20 Chock Lane, Westbury on Trym, BS9 3EX (in small lane behind churchyard)

12-2.30 (3 Sun), 6 (7 Sun)-11

☎ (0117) 950 0441 thevictoriapub.co.uk

Butcombe Bitter; Draught Bass; Wadworth Henrys IPA, 6X, seasonal beers; guest beers ⊞

Quiet, relaxed and welcoming Wadworth-owned traditional pub that has been run by the same family for more than 10 years. The beer quality is excellent; even the friendly pub dog, Bertie the beerhound, enjoys a drop. A raised garden to the rear is a suntrap in summer. Pictures of Westbury as a village adorn the walls and popular home-cooked food is available daily. Entertainment includes quizzes, themed meals and live blues featuring the landlord, on Sunday evening. Various societies meet here. Q❀◐⊟⊱

Victoria

2 Southleigh Road, Clifton, BS8 2BH (off St Pauls Rd)

4 (12 Sat & Sun)-11

☎ (0117) 974 5675

Goffs Jouster; Matthews Brassknocker; guest beers ⊞

The third Dawkins Tavern to open, this is something of a secret pub, tucked away in a side street by an old reservoir and swimming baths, yet only 100 metres from the bustling Whiteladies road. Up to eight handpumps offer a changing selection of beers and ciders from local and regional micro-brewers. An unobtrusive TV shows sport, but this is really a place for conversation. Mini beer festivals are held frequently, plus a cider festival in the Autumn. ⋔Q⇌(Clifton Down)⊟●

Broad Campden

Bakers Arms

GL55 6UR (signed from B4081)

11.30-2.30, 4.45-11; 11.30-11 Fri, Sat & summer; 12-10.30 Sun

☎ (01386) 840515

Donnington BB; Stanway Stanney Bitter; Wells Bombardier; guest beers ⊞

This genuine free house, where the owners are celebrating their 10th year, is characterised by Cotswold stone walls, exposed beams, an inglenook fireplace and an attractive oak bar counter where the local Stanney Bitter is a popular choice. Home-cooked meals prepared by the landlady can be tried in the bar or in the dining room. A framed handwoven rug is a feature of this county Pub of the Year 2005. This is a traditional Cotswold pub at its very best. ⋔Q❀◐♣●P

Broadwell

Fox Inn

The Green, GL56 0UF (off A429)

11-2.30, 6-11; 12-2.30, 7-10.30 Sun

☎ (01451) 870909

Donnington BB, SBA ⊞

This attractive stone-built pub overlooking the large village green was deservedly North Cotswold CAMRA Pub of the Year 2007. Donnington Beers are popular with visitors. The pub is a true local where good home-cooked food is enjoyed. Features include original flagstone flooring in the main bar area, jugs hanging from beams and the Aunt Sally game played in the garden. Behind the garden is a camping and caravan site. A special experience is assured at this family-run pub. ⋔Q❀◐▲♣P⊱

Brockhampton

Craven Arms

GL54 5XQ (off A436) SP035223

12-3, 6-11; 12-11 Sat; 12-10.30 (4 winter) Sun

☎ (01242) 820410

Hook Norton Hooky Bitter; Sharp's Doom Bar; guest beers ⊞

This spacious 17th-century pub is a proper free house, with guest beer usually coming from a Gloucestershire brewery. Set in an attractive hillside village with stunning views and walks, it has areas for drinking and dining separated by church-style stone windows. Bank notes from numerous countries adorn the low beams. A beer festival is held annually in August in the sizeable garden, with live music in a marquee. Handy for nearby Sudeley Castle. This is a well-managed gem, worth seeking out. ⋔Q❀⇆◐♣P

Chaceley

Yew Tree Inn

Stock Lane, GL19 4EQ SO856298

12-2.30 (3 Sat), 6-11.30 (midnight Fri & Sat); 12-3, 7-11 Sun

☎ (01452) 780333

Wickwar Coopers WPA; Wye Valley Butty Bach; guest beers ⊞

This riverside pub set on the west bank of the Severn has reverted back from the Old Ferry inn to its former name. It has been altered and extended over 200 years and now has a large public bar, comfortable lounge and a restaurant serving good value food. Both the river in the summer and real fire in the winter draw customers to this friendly pub with its own visitor moorings. ⚲☕❀◐◑⊟♿⅄P⅟

Chedworth

Seven Tuns

Queen Street, GL54 4AE (NE of village below the church) SP053121
⌚ 12-3.30, 6-11(Mon to Fri); 11-11 (Sat & Summer); 12-10.30 Sun
☎ (01285) 720242
Wells Bombardier, seasonal beers; Young's Bitter, seasonal beers Ⓗ
Unspoilt and atmospheric pub, attractively located in one of England's longest villages and a rare outlet for Young's beers. The various rooms and dining areas are tastefully furnished and display local photographs and artefacts. Upstairs the skittle alley doubles as a function room and is available for hire. On a summer's day sit outside to watch water cascading from the stream opposite into a stone reservoir. This pub is a fine stop-off close to the Roman Villa at Chedworth and beautiful walks. ⚲Q❀◐◑♣P⅟

Cheltenham

Adam & Eve

8 Townsend Street, GL51 9HD
⌚ 10-2 (not Thu), 4-11; 10-11 Sat; 12-2, 4-10.30 Sun
☎ (01242) 690030
Arkell 2B, 3B, seasonal beers Ⓗ
Run by the same landlady for 31 years, this friendly and unpretentious terraced local is home to skittles, darts and quiz teams. Parking is very limited but it is a 15-minute walk from the town centre and readily accessible by public transport: Stagecoach services C, H and 41 stop at the end of the street. The public bar forms a strong community focus and there is a separate lounge. Charity events are often hosted. Q⊟♣⅟

Bath Tavern

68 Bath Road, GL53 7JT
⌚ 11-11; 12-10.30 Sun
☎ (01242) 256122
Sharp's Doom Bar; guest beers Ⓗ
Located close to the town hall and nearby Cheltenham College with its Cricket Festival, there is always a warm welcome in this friendly and busy single bar free house. Run for more than 100 years by the Cheshire family, it now has young owners. Local produce is freshly cooked on the premises and Sunday Lunch is especially popular (booking is advisable). Music is played at a background level, but the volume may rise on weekend evenings. ◑

Cheltenham Motor Club

Upper Park Street, GL52 6SA (access from A40 London Road via Crown Passage)
⌚ 7 (12 Sat)-midnight; 12-2, 7-midnight Sun
☎ (01242) 522590 🌐 cheltmc.com
Donnington SBA; guest beers Ⓗ
Card-carrying CAMRA members are welcome at this friendly club, just outside the town centre in the former Crown pub. A finalist in the CAMRA National Club of the Year 2007, the club offers three regularly changing and interesting ales, mainly from micro-breweries, alongside Donnington SBA and Thatchers cider. There is also a range of bottled porters and foreign beers, and often a perry. The variety of beer is a huge draw. Local league quiz, darts and pool teams are based here. Q⊟⊟●P⅟

Jolly Brewmaster

39 Painswick Road, GL50 2EZ
⌚ 12-11 (10.30 Sun)
☎ (01242) 772261
Beer range varies Ⓗ
Cheltenham CAMRA 2008 Pub of the Year is also a CAMRA Good Cider Guide regular. The six handpumps regularly feature beers from local brewers, alongside Black Rat and Thatchers Heritage ciders. Booking is advised for the excellent value Sunday lunch. This busy pub is friendly and relaxed, featuring original etched windows and open fires. An attractive beer garden serves as an extra room in the summer and offers winter warmth for smokers. ⚲Q❀⊟(10)●⅟

Kemble Brewery Inn

27 Fairview Street, GL52 2JF
⌚ 11-11 (midnight Fri & Sat)
☎ (01242) 243446
Beer range varies Ⓗ
This small, popular back-street local is hard to find but well worth the effort. It can get very busy on race days or if nearby neighbours Cheltenham Town FC are at home. Six real ales are usually available, often including ones from local brewers, with traditional ciders available between March and August. Booking is necessary for the excellent Sunday lunch (12-4pm) and a special is served 11-2pm daily. Smoking is permitted in the attractive walled drinking area. Q❀◑●⅟

Royal Oak

43 The Burgage, Prestbury, GL52 3DL
⌚ 11-2.30, 5.30 (6 Sat)-11; 12-10.30 Sun
☎ (01242) 522344 🌐 royal-oak-prestbury.co.uk
Taylor Landlord; guest beers Ⓗ
Cotswold stone-built local in Prestbury village with limited parking, but handy for the racecourse. The quiet public bar features oak beams, parquet flooring, equine prints and a log fire. Good quality food is served in the lounge bar with daily specials (booking advised). The Pavilion, a skittle alley and function room in the garden, hosts an annual beer festival in May and a cider festival in August. Beers are listed on the website. Thatchers Heritage cider is available. ⚲Q❀◐◑⊟●P

Cirencester

Corinium Hotel

12 Gloucester Street, GL7 2DG (off A435 N of town centre)
⌚ 11-11 (10.30 Sun)
☎ (01285) 659711 🌐 coriniumhotel.co.uk
Uley Laurie Lee's Bitter; guest beers Ⓗ
This agreeable two-star hotel has a discreet frontage that is easy to miss. A long, narrow courtyard leads through into a comfortable lounge area with a small, flagstoned bar and an attractive restaurant. The building was

originally an Elizabethan wool merchant's house, with walls of varying thickness that can make the layout confusing on a first visit. A quiet garden at the rear of the premises is ideal for summer drinking. ⌂❀⇌◑♿P

Twelve Bells

Lewis Lane, GL7 1EA (head for town centre from A435 roundabout and straight across traffic lights)
✪ 11-3, 5-11; 12-3.30, 6.30-10.30 Sun
☎ (01285) 644549
Beer range varies Ⓗ
This old-fashioned back-street boozer has three rooms, all with real fires. The landlord has a low opinion of the big breweries, so proudly offers over 300 guest beers per annum from micro-breweries. Very much his own man, he is considered to be a 'punk landlord' by his regular customers. His son runs the constantly improving kitchen, with local produce sold in generous portions. The front bar is lively and the rear rooms much quieter. ⌂♉❀◑♿

Clearwell

Lamb

High Street, GL16 8JU SO570081
✪ closed Mon & Tue; 12-3 (not Wed & Thu), 6-11 Fri & Sat; 12-3, 7-10.30 Sun
☎ (01594) 835441
Wye Valley Bitter; Butcombe Bitter Ⓖ
This charming two-bar pub has a cosy atmosphere, with open fires and a snug with two large settles. The excellent ale is served straight from the barrels in the rear cellar. This friendly village pub has been a long-time favourite with local CAMRA members, and plays an important part in village life. Well worth a visit. Open bank holidays.
⌂Q❀⊟♣●P

Cockleford

Green Dragon

GL53 9NW (take Elkstone turn off A435)
✪ 11-11; 12-10.30 Sun
☎ (01242) 870271
Butcombe Bitter; Courage Directors; Hook Norton Hooky Bitter Ⓗ
This delightful Cotswold stone inn dating from the 17th century features two bars with log fires, a restaurant and a function room/skittle alley as well as nine en-suite rooms. The bar and furniture are all hand-crafted by Robert Thompson, the 'Mouse Man of Kilburn' – look for his trademark mice carved into the furniture. Good food is available lunchtimes and evenings. The pub can get very busy at weekends. There is a large car park across the road. ⌂Q♉❀⇌◑●P⊱

Cranham

Black Horse

GL4 8HP (off A46 or B4070) SO896129
✪ 12-3, 6.30-11; closed Mon; 12-3, 8-10.30 Sun
☎ (01452) 812217
Butcombe Bitter; Hancock's HB; Sharp's Doom Bar; guest beer Ⓗ
The rustic charm of this 17th-century free house is enhanced by its open log fire surmounted by a stag's head. Lively chat predominates, aided by the landlord's extensive fund of corny puns and the meticulous care that he shows for the ales. A blackboard lists country-style dishes designed to satisfy hearty appetites. There is a small lounge and two extra rooms upstairs for dining. Quoits and shove ha'penny may be played. No food is served Sunday evening.
⌂Q❀◑♣P⊱

Didmarton

King's Arms

The Street, GL9 1DT (on A433)
✪ 11-11; 12-10.30 Sun
☎ (01454) 238245 🌐 kingsarmsdidmarton.co.uk
Uley Bitter; Otter Ale; guest beer Ⓗ
This 17th-century coaching inn has a smart, low-key frontage that only hints at the stylish refurbishment contained within. Copious amounts of reclaimed wood give the public bar, games area and central counter a warmth and comfort that are easily matched by the smart furnishings of the popular restaurant. Friendly staff and locals ensure that you will stay for another drink, even if you choose only to admire the tidy, walled garden at the rear.
⌂❀⇌◑⊟♣P⊱

Duntisbourne Abbots

Five Mile House ☆

Old Gloucester Road, GL7 7JR (off A417 at services sign and S of petrol station)
✪ 12-3, 6 (7 Sun)-11
☎ (01285) 821432
Donnington BB; Taylor Landlord; Young's Bitter Ⓗ
The Five Mile, a Grade II-listed building, is on CAMRA's National Inventory of Historic Pubs and has been lovingly modernised to exploit the whole ground floor, snug and extended cellar. The great, award-winning restaurant has been added, while the original bar remains almost untouched. The low entrance opens into the tap room with its two settles, which leads to the small, wooden floored bar with a welcoming log fire. ⌂Q❀◑♣P⊱

Dursley

Old Spot

Hill Road, GL11 4JQ (next to bus station)
✪ 11 (12 Sun)-11
☎ (01453) 542870 🌐 oldspotinn.co.uk
Severn Vale Session; Uley Old Ric; guest beers Ⓗ
This Cotswold Way free house dates from 1776. It was named after the Gloucestershire Old Spot Pig and a porcine theme is discernible among brewery memorabilia. Low ceilings and log fires provide a cosy atmosphere and friendly staff offer a warm welcome. It serves an extensive range of independent ales and Weston's cider, and holds regular beer festivals. The pretty garden is perfect for summer and has a heated, covered area. Wholesome, freshly prepared dishes complement the real ale. CAMRA National Pub of the Year 2007.
⌂Q❀◑♿⊟♣⊱

Easter Compton

Fox

Main Road, BS35 5RA (1 mile from M5 jct 17 towards Pilning on B4055)
11-3 6-11; 11-11 Sat summer; 12-10.30 (5.30 winter) Sun
☎ (01454) 632220
Bath Ales Gem; Exmoor Fox; guest beer Ⓗ
Run by the same family for over 20 years, this pub has two distinct rooms. The comfortable, quiet lounge is popular for food, much of it home-cooked, and offers a children's menu. The more lively public bar attracts locals and darts players. The skittle alley has three regular teams and can also be hired for functions. The one guest beer changes monthly but may not be available at quieter times of year. A large garden at the rear incorporates a safe children's play area.
♨Q❀◑⊟⊡(624)♣P⊱

Forthampton

Lower Lode Inn

GL19 4RE (follow sign to Forthampton from A438 Tewkesbury-Ledbury road) SO878317
12-midnight (2am Fri & Sat)
☎ (01684) 293224 🌐 lowerlodeinn.co.uk
Donnington BB; Hook Norton Old Hooky; Sharp's Doom Bar; guest beers Ⓗ
This brick-built pub has been licensed since 1590. Standing in three acres of lawned river frontage it looks across the River Severn to Tewkesbury Abbey. It has its own moorings and a private slipway. Day-fishing permits are available and the pub is also a licensed touring park site. The regular ales are complemented by two changing guests (three in summer). There is en-suite accommodation, lunch and evening meals are served and the Sunday lunch carvery is popular.
♨Q♉❀⇌◑♿⛺♣P⊱

Frampton Cotterell

Rising Sun

43 Ryecroft Road, BS36 2HN
11.30-3, 5.30-11; 11.30-11 Fri & Sat; 12-11 Sun
☎ (01454) 772330
Brakspear Bitter; Butcombe Bitter; Cotswold Spring Old Codger; Draught Bass; Wadworth 6X; guest beer Ⓗ
Superb, family-run free house – a mainstay of this Guide for as long as most can remember. The family has recently started the Great Western Brewery at nearby Hambrook and the beers are expected soon. The three-room interior comprises the main flagstoned bar, a small raised snug, and the conservatory which acts as a restaurant during food hours. A large skittle alley is available for functions. Children are welcome until 8.30pm. A former local CAMRA Pub of the Year, conversation and conviviality rule. Q❀◑⊡(581)♣P

Frocester

George Inn ✔

Peter Street, GL10 3TQ
11.30-2.30, 5-11; 11-11 Fri & Sat; 12-10.30 Sun
☎ (01453) 822302 🌐 georgeinn.co.uk
Caledonian Deuchars IPA; Fuller's London Pride; Otter Bitter; Stroud Budding; Wychwood Hobgoblin; guest beers Ⓗ
This warm and friendly village inn is situated at the foot of Frocester Hill where it has been offering hospitality since the early 18th century when it was a coaching inn serving travellers between Gloucester and Bath. At one time renamed the Royal Gloucestershire Hussars, it reverted to its original name in 1998. It serves two regular beers with at least three changing guests, usually from small local breweries, plus Weston's Old Rosie cider on draught. Occasional mini beer festivals are held. The home-cooked food is made with local produce and there are six en-suite bedrooms. ♨Q❀⇌◑⊟♣●P⊱

Gloucester

Dick Whittington

100 Westgate Street, GL1 2PE
11-11; 12-10.30 Sun
☎ (01452) 502039
Butcombe Gold; St Austell Tribute; Wells Bombardier; guest beers Ⓗ
Behind an imposing Georgian frontage is a 14th-century building that was the town house of the Whittingtons from 1311 till 1546. The mix of furnishings creates a contemporary feel and conversation prevails in Gloucester CAMRA's City Pub of the Year 2005-2008. There is a large function room and a garden that hosts occasional beer festivals. Five guest ales are sourced from local and distant craft brewers: the draught cider varies. Excellent home-cooked food is served until 9pm (3pm Sun). Q❀◑⇌♣●⊱

Linden Tree ✔

73-75 Bristol Road, GL1 5SN (on A430 S of docks)
11.30-2.30, 6-11; 11.30-midnight Sat; 12-11 Sun
☎ (01452) 527869
Wadworth IPA, Horizon, 6X, JCB, seasonal beers; guest beers Ⓗ
The plain Georgian frontage of this popular community pub gives no indication of the smart, homely interior. Beamed ceilings, partially stone-lined walls and an open log fire, together with a carriage wheel which acts as a room divider, add to a cosy atmosphere. A skittle alley opens up to provide extra space when required. Eight ales are usually available, with guests coming mainly from Marston's. Substantial home-cooked meals are offered except Saturday and Sunday evening. The accommodation is reasonably priced.
♨Q❀⇌◑⊡♣⊱

New Inn

16 Northgate Street, GL1 1SF
11-11 (1am Fri & Sat); 12-10.30 Sun
☎ (01452) 522177
Butcombe Gold; Wychwood Hobgoblin; guest beers Ⓗ
Built in 1455 to accommodate pilgrims to the tomb of Edward II, this Grade I-listed building is the finest medieval galleried inn in the country. Travellers today are accommodated in 35 recently refurbished rooms. There is a restaurant, coffee shop, Regency function room, Outback Bar with small dance floor, wine bar and an ale bar that offers up to 10

guests mainly from local craft brewers. Plays are occasionally staged in the courtyard, and Morris dancers perform at Christmas.
❀⇌◐≢♣⌐

Pig Inn The City

121 Westgate Street, GL1 2PG
⌚ 11-midnight; 12-11.30 Sun
☎ (01452) 421960
Brakspear Bitter; Wychwood Hobgoblin; guest beers Ⓗ
A prim 19th-century listed façade belies the warm, and at times vibrant, welcome that awaits the visitor to this pub. The hosts are proud of their Black Country origins: West Midlands ales feature among the guests and provide the theme for occasional festivals. Excellent traditional home-cooked food is available daily except Monday lunchtime and on evenings when there is entertainment (Tue, Fri & Sun). There is a large function room upstairs and a small garden to the rear.
❀◐♿≢♣⌐

Water Poet

61-63 Eastgate Street, GL1 1PN
⌚ 9-11
☎ (01452) 783530
Greene King IPA, Abbot; Marston's Pedigree; guest beers Ⓗ
Opened in 2007, this has quickly become a successful second venue for Wetherspoon in the city. An abundant use of wood, a warm colour scheme, potted palms and attractive lighting give a quality feel to the pub. A large paved and bricked garden, surrounded by mature trees and shrubs, contains a spacious heated outdoor shelter for smokers. There is no music, and the silent TV shows only news. Up to four craft brewery guests are sourced locally. Q❀◐♿≢⌐

Gretton

Royal Oak

GL54 5EP (At E end of village, 1.5 miles from Winchcombe)
⌚ 12-3 (4 Sun), 6-11 (10.30 Sun)
☎ (01242) 604999
Donnington BB; Goff's Jouster; Stanway Stanney Bitter; guest beers Ⓗ
A popular Cotswold pub where a warm welcome is assured from the family owners. All the regular beers are from Gloucestershire breweries and home-cooked food can be taken in the conservatory, with outstanding views across the vale. Bar areas have a mix of wood and flagstone floors while the large garden hosts an annual beer and music festival in July. There is a tennis court for hire and the Gloucestershire Warwickshire Railway is nearby and can be seen from the garden.
♨❀◐♣P⌐

Ham

Salutation

Ham Green, GL13 9QH (from Berkeley take road signed to Jenner Museum) ST681984
⌚ 12-2.30 (not Mon), 5-11; 11-11 Sat; 12-10.30 Sun
☎ (01453) 810284
Cotswold Spring Old English Rose; Severn Vale Dursley Steam Bitter; guest beers Ⓗ
Rural free house situated in the Severn Valley within walking distance of the Jenner Museum, Berkeley Castle and Deer Park. This friendly local is popular with walkers. The pub has two cosy bars with a log fire and a skittle alley/function room. Food is served lunchtimes and early evening. There is a child-friendly garden at the front of the pub.
♨Q❀◐⊟♣P

Hawkesbury Upton

Beaufort Arms

High Street, GL9 1AU (off A46, 6 miles N of M4 jct 18)
⌚ 12-11 (10.30 Sun)
☎ (01454) 238217 ⊕ beaufortarms.com
Wickwar BOB; guest beers Ⓗ
This 17th-century Grade II-listed Cotswold stone free house has recently been restored. It includes separate public and lounge bars, a dining room and skittle alley/function room. Inside it contains an enormous amount of ancient breweriana and local memorabilia. Four ales and Wickwar Screech cider are served. The pub raised £16,000 for charity in 2007 and is home to the Long John Silver Trust. A local CAMRA award winner, it has an attractive garden. ♨Q❀◐⊟♿♣♠P

Fox Inn

High Street, GL9 1AU (off A46, 6 miles N of M4 jct 18)
⌚ 12-11
☎ (01454) 238219
⊕ thefoxinnhawkesburyupton.co.uk
Greene King Old Speckled Hen; Uley Bitter; guest beers Ⓗ
The Fox is situated in an 18th-century building in the centre of this historic village. Originally a coaching inn, today it is a typical village pub with a warm and friendly atmosphere, enhanced by a real fire in winter. Food is served every lunchtime and evening. There is a large enclosed garden and a covered smoking area. The pub has five tastefully decorated en-suite bedrooms. It stands close to the Cotswold Way in ideal walking country.
♨Q❀⇌◐♣P⌐

Littleton on Severn

White Hart

BS35 1NR (signed from B4461 at Elberton)
⌚ 12-midnight (11 Sun)
☎ (01454) 412275
Wells Bombardier; Young's Bitter, Special, seasonal beers Ⓗ
Superlative Young's pub with many rooms and much to explore. In its free house days it was a frequent winner of CAMRA Local Pub of the Year awards. Occasional guest beers appear and real cider is served. Food is mainly sourced from fresh local ingredients and cooked to order, while flagstone floors, two real fires, low wooden beams, bar billiards and board games, plus a family room, provide diversity. A large, pleasant beer garden offers views of the old Severn Bridge.
♨Q☋❀◐♣♠P⌐

Longford

Queen's Head

84 Tewkesbury Road, GL2 9EJ (on A38, N of A40 jct)

11-3 (2.30 Mon & Tue), 5.30 (6 Sat)-11; 12-3, 7-10.30 Sun

☎ (01452) 301882

Otter Bitter; Severn Vale Dursley Steam Bitter; Taylor Landlord; Wye Valley Butty Bach; guest beer Ⓗ

This partly timber-framed free house dating from the 1730s became a pub just over a century ago. In summer its exterior is transformed by a mass of colourful flower baskets, while a smart array of pictures in the public bar reveals the landlord's passion for vintage motorcycles. The pub is very popular for its sensibly priced, award-winning food, including the famed Longford Lamb (evening booking essential). No children are permitted. Moles Black Rat cider is available in summer. ◐⊟⊟P

Marshfield

Catherine Wheel

High Street, SN14 8LR (off A420 between Chippenham and Bristol)

12-3, 6-11 (midnight Sat); 12-11 Sun

☎ (01225) 892220 🌐 thecatherinewheel.co.uk

Courage Best Bitter; guest beers Ⓗ

Beautifully restored Georgian-fronted pub on the village High Street with a pretty dining room. An extensive main bar leads down from the original wood-panelled area, via stone-walled rooms, to the patio area at the rear. A superb open fire warms in winter. There are up to two local guest ales available and imaginative and well presented food is served in the bar or garden (no meals Sun evening). Children are allowed and free wireless Internet access is available.

⌂Q❀⊭◐⊟(635)P⅃

May Hill

Glasshouse

GL17 0NN (off A40 W of Huntley) SO710213

11.30-3, 6.30-11; 12-3 Sun

☎ (01452) 830529

Butcombe Bitter; Fuller's London Pride Ⓖ

This once small Forest pub has been sympathetically extended using reclaimed building materials to blend in with the surroundings. It has three areas, with an old black range in one and a log fire in another. With its flagstone floor, nooks and crannies, and beer straight from the cask, it is an interesting pub. An historic yew hedge with its own seat cut into it, a safe, fenced children's play area and very good food make this pub well worth finding. ⌂Q❀◐P

Mayshill

New Inn ✔

Badminton Road, BS36 2NT (on A432 between Coalpit Heath and Nibley)

11.45-2.30, 6-10.30 (11 Wed-Sat); 12-10 Sun

☎ (01454) 773161

Beer range varies Ⓗ

This 17th-century inn is hugely popular for its food, so booking is advised. Expect one beer from the nearby Cotswold Spring Brewery and three changing guests from far and wide. One of the guests is likely to be dark, since it is the genial Scottish landlord's favourite; expect sudden outbreaks of Scottish beer, too. The main bar is warmed by a real fire in winter, and the rear area is more of a restaurant. Children are welcome until 8.45pm. The garden is pleasant in summer. ⌂Q❀◐⊟P⅃

Moreton-in-Marsh

Inn on the Marsh

Stow Road, GL56 0DW (on A429 at S end of town)

12-2.30, 7-11; 11-3, 6-11 Thu-Sat & summer; 12-3, 7-11 Sun

☎ (01608) 650709

Banks's Original; Marston's Burton Bitter, Pedigree; guest beer Ⓗ

This charming pub, a former bakery next to a duck pond, is a rare outlet in the area for Marston's brewery. A reminder of Moreton's basket-weaving past can be seen in the baskets hanging from the rafters, while the main bar area has comfortable armchairs, old photos and hanging hops. The landlady chef offers food with a Dutch East Indies influence, served in the conservatory. The landlord, who has been in residence for over 10 years, provides a warm welcome.

Q❀◐♿⅄⇌⊟♣●P

Nailsworth

George Inn

Newmarket, GL6 0RF

11-3, 6.30-11; 12-3, 7-11 Sun

☎ (01453) 833228

Moles Tap Bitter; Taylor Landlord; Uley Old Spot Ⓗ

This outstanding village local looks south over the valley above Nailsworth and is a 15-minute walk from Forest Green Rovers football ground. Three chimneys confirm that the building was formerly three cottages; it became a pub in 1820. It was renamed in 1910 in honour of the incoming King George V. The food is renowned and can be eaten in the small restaurant or in the bar (booking is advisable). Q❀◐P

Village Inn

The Cross, Fountain Street, GL6 0HH

11-11 (midnight Thu-Sat); 12-10.30 Sun

☎ (01453) 835715

Nailsworth Artist's Ale, Mayor's Bitter, Vicar's Stout, Town Crier, seasonal beers; guest beers Ⓗ

The Village Inn, which reopened in late 2006 as the Nailsworth Brewery brewpub, is unrecognisable from the inn that closed in the mid 1990s – truly an ugly duckling reborn as a swan. An intricate warren of rooms and spaces has been created with care and flair, where salvaged furniture and fittings combine with new joinery. All it lacks is the patina of age. Do not miss the superb poster of the former Nailsworth Brewery on the stairs down to the toilets and brewhouse. ⌂Q◐●

Nettleton Bottom

Golden Heart

GL4 8LA (on A417)
❂ 11-3, 5.30-11; 11-11 Fri & Sat; 12-10.30 Sun
☎ (01242) 870261
Festival Gold; Otter Bitter; guest beers 🄷
This 300-year-old inn is a haven of peaceful idyllic charm beside the busy single carriageway section of the Swindon-Gloucester road. The small bar is hidden beyond a huge open fireplace and overlooks a patio and garden leading to cow pastures. Highest quality meats contribute to reasonably priced prize-winning meals (available all day Sunday). Guest beers come from local craft brewers, as do the genuine 'German-style' Cotswold lagers and wheat beer.
ᗰQ✿⇔◑●P⁑–

Newent

George

Church Street, GL18 1PU (off B4215 & B4216)
❂ 11-11 (midnight Fri & Sat); 12-10.30 Sun
☎ (01531) 820203 🌐 georgehotel.uk.com
Cottage Somerset & Dorset, Western Glory; Freeminer Bitter; Hancock's HB; guest beers 🄷
This mid-17th century hotel has a quiet bar at the front with a central serving area. A dartboard, fruit machines and TV screens are located at the rear. The former coach house is now the restaurant, with a games room above with a snooker table. A beer festival is held in September to coincide with Newent Onion Fair. Accommodation comprises en-suite bedrooms and a two-bedroom mews flat. Local attractions include the National Birds of Prey Centre and the Shambles Museum.
ᗰ☎✿⇔◑♿⊟♣●P⁑–

North Cerney

Bathurst Arms

GL7 7BZ (on A435)
❂ 12-3, 6-11 (7-10.30 Sun)
☎ (01285) 831281 🌐 bathurstarms.co.uk
Hook Norton Hooky Bitter; Wickwar Cotswold Way; guest beers 🄷
The ancient flagstone floors and inglenook fireplace of this pretty pub are testimony that it has served the village well since the 17th century. Half the building is now given over to the award-winning restaurant (which also cooks lunches for the local primary school). Meals are also served in the spacious, two-roomed bar. The mature garden at the front straddles the burbling River Churn. The owners are proud to source all their beers and food locally wherever possible. ᗰ✿⇔◑⊟P

Rodborough

Prince Albert

GL5 3SS (corner of Rodborough Hill & Walkley Hill)
❂ 5-11.30 (12.30am Fri & Sat); 12-10.30 Sun
☎ (01453) 755600 🌐 theprincealbertstroud.co.uk
Otter Bitter; Stroud Budding, Tom Long; guest beers 🄷
This lively, cosmopolitan, stone-built pub near Rodborough Common manages to be simultaneously bohemian, homely and welcoming. It has an imaginative colour scheme and an eclectic mix of furniture and fittings, with chandeliers from a French chateau and a Dutch brothel. Art exhibitions and themed nights are held, including a pub quiz, backgammon, crib and scrabble, folk music and live bands. Children and dogs are welcome. Bar meals are served Thursday to Saturday. Sunday lunch is followed by a film matinée. There is free Internet access and Wi-Fi. ᗰ◑⇌⁑–

Shipton Moyne

Cat & Custard Pot

The Street, GL8 8PN (on Tetbury rd)
❂ 11-3, 6-11.30; 11.30-3, 6-11 Sun
☎ (01666) 880249
Flowers Original; Taylor Landlord; Wadworth Henry's IPA, 6X; guest beer 🄷
This popular village local gets busy when the equestrian community descends upon it to sample the good, varied menu. The interior tends towards the functional, owing to the sheer numbers wanting to eat here; the pleasant bar where dog walkers converge for a pint is always lively. To the rear of the bar is a quiet snug – popular with families if the weather drives them in from the attractive front garden. The unusual pub sign is noteworthy. ᗰQ✿◑♣P

Slad

Woolpack

GL6 7QA (on B4070)
❂ 12-3, 5-11.30; 12-10.30 Sun
☎ (01452) 813429
Uley Bitter, Laurie Lee's Bitter, Old Spot, Pig's Ear; guest beer 🄷
This popular 16th-century village inn affords superb views over the Slad Valley. It achieved fame through the late Laurie Lee, author of Cider With Rosie, who was a regular customer. The building has been thoughtfully restored with wooden settles in the end room of three, where children are welcome. The bar extends to each of the four rooms and cider and perry are available. The guest beer is usually from a local small brewery. ᗰQ✿◑⊟♣●P

Slimbridge

Tudor Arms

Shepherd's Patch, GL2 7BP (from A38 1 mile beyond Slimbridge village)
❂ 11-11; 12-10.30 Sun
☎ (01453) 890306
Uley Pig's Ear; Wadworth 6X; guest beers 🄷
Large family-owned free house reached by a winding road that leads to the famous Wildfowl and Wetlands Trust site. It incorporates two bars and a number of dining areas, with a modern lodge alongside. A separately owned caravan and camping site is adjacent. Four guest ales come from craft or family brewers: the cider is Moles Black Rat. Excellent home-cooked food is available all day and children are welcome. Gloucester CAMRA Country Pub of the Year 2007 and 2008. ✿⇔◑⊟♿⛺♣●P⁑–

Staple Hill

Humpers Off Licence

26 Soundwell Road, BS16 4QW

12-2, 5-10.30; 12-10.30 Sat & Sun summer

(0117) 956 5525

Cottage Champflower; guest beers Ⓖ

Bristol's only specialist real ale off-licence is long established and sells up to four guest beers at very reasonable prices. A large range of bottled beers includes many bottle-conditioned options. Cider drinkers can select from three or more varying choices. Bring your own containers or buy them here, then you will have no excuse for hosting parties or barbecues without any real beer. A big variety of polypins can be ordered at Christmas, when opening hours may be extended. ⊟●

Stow-on-the-Wold

Queen's Head

GL54 1AB

11-11; 12-10.30 Sun

(01451) 830563

Donnington BB, SBA Ⓗ

This 17th-century Cotswold town pub stands in the heart of the square and attracts tourists and locals alike. Excellent Donnington ales can be enjoyed in both bar areas, with fascinating pictures and artefacts throughout. Flowers on the tables create a cosy atmosphere for dining. With its low beamed ceilings and flagstone floors, this pub takes you back in time and makes you want to linger. There is plenty of room for parking in the square. Dogs are welcome. Q❀◑⊟P⁻

Stroud

Queen Victoria

5 Gloucester Street, GL5 1QG

11-11 (later Fri & Sat); 12-10.30 Sun

(01453) 762396

Beer range varies Ⓗ

This imposing building formerly housed the Gloucester Street forge and records show that it was owned by the Nailsworth Brewery in 1891. The large single bar offers a constantly changing range of at least four beers from micro-breweries. This community pub fields quiz, darts and pool teams in local leagues. Across the courtyard with its tables, the spacious function room holds a beer festival at least once a year and provides live music on Thursday, Friday and Saturday evenings. ♨❀⇌♣

Tetbury

Priory Inn Hotel

London Road, GL8 8JJ

11-11 (midnight Fri & Sat) theprioryinn.co.uk

Uley Bitter; guest beers Ⓗ

From transport café to modern motel and pub, this former stable block is now a flourishing pizzeria with a great real ale bar at the rear. The owner proudly sources all his ingredients as locally as possible (the flour for the pizza travels just two miles). The main room has exposed stonework, with a large central hearth supplying the warmth. A series of arches separates the bar from the dining area. Live acoustic music plays on Sunday evening. ♨❀⇌◑♿⊟P

Tewkesbury

Tudor House Hotel

51 High Street, GL20 5BH

11.30-11 (midnight Fri & Sat)

(01684) 297755 tudorhousetewkesbury.co.uk

Greene King Old Speckled Hen; guest beers Ⓗ

Situated on the High Street, this delightful Tudor building oozes charm and dignity. Cromwell's Bar offers a selection of four real ales, three constantly changing, with Speckled Hen a favourite with locals. Pub meals are served in the bar; more upmarket cuisine is available either in the Mayor's Parlour or the Court Room. Two outdoor areas provide a relaxing place to watch the boats on the river behind the pub or enjoy a quiet drink in the Secret Garden. A coffee shop serves light refreshments. ♨❀⇌◑⊟♿⊟♣●P⁻

White Bear

Bredon Road, GL20 5BU (N of High St)

11-midnight; 12-10.30 Sun

(01684) 296614

Beer range varies Ⓗ

Family-run free house on the edge of the town centre, close to the river and marina. An L-shaped bar provides four handpumps plus local ciders. Crib, darts, skittles and local league pool all feature here. There is a separate skittle alley which can double as a function room. Live music is performed most Sunday afternoons. ❀♿⊟♣●P⁻

Uley

Old Crown

The Green, GL11 5SN

12-11

(01453) 860502

Uley Bitter, Pig's Ear; guest beers Ⓗ

This attractive 17th-century whitewashed coaching inn with a pleasant walled garden is situated in the pretty village of Uley on the edge of the Cotswold Way. The village local, it is also popular with passing walkers. The low-beamed single bar has a welcoming open fire, with beers sourced mainly from micro-breweries. The pub offers four en-suite double bedrooms and food is served lunchtimes and evenings. There is a covered smoking area. ♨Q❀⇌◑♣P⁻

Waterley Bottom

New Inn

GL11 6EF (signed from North Nibley) ST758964

12-2.30 (not Mon), 6-11; 12-11 Sat; 12-10.30 Sun

(01453) 543659

Wye Valley Butty Bach, HPA; guest beers Ⓗ

This welcoming free house, once a 19th-century cider house frequented by mill workers, nestles in a tiny hamlet in a scenic valley. It has a cosy lounge/dining area and a smaller public bar where darts and cards are played. A child-friendly, attractive garden includes a large decked area with a heated and covered pool table. Draught cider and perry are from Weston's. There is an imaginative menu (no food available on Monday) plus en-suite accommodation. Gloucestershire CAMRA Cider Pub of the Year 2007. ⌂Q❀⇌◐◑⊟♣●P⁄

Whitecroft

Miners Arms

The Bay, GL15 4PE (on B4234 near railway crossing) SO619062

✪ 12-12.30 (midnight Sun)

☎ (01594) 562483 ⊕ minersarmswhitecroft.com

Banks's Original; guest beer ⊞

A classic free house offering good value and high quality food including Sunday lunches. Voted CAMRA Cider & Perry Pub of the Year in 2005, it dispenses a range of draught ciders as well as five ever-changing guest beers. The skittle alley doubles as a blues music venue once a month, and quoits is played in the bar. The garden has a boules piste, the back garden is safe for children and steam trains from the Dean Forest Railway stop behind the pub. ⌂Q❀⇌◐◑Å⇌⊟♣●P

Whitminster

Old Forge Inn

GL2 7NP (on A38, close to M5 jct 13)

✪ 12-11 (10.30 Sun)

☎ (01452) 741306

Butcombe Bitter; Greene King IPA; Shepherd Neame Spitfire; guest beer ⊞

This mainly timber-framed building, bearing a strange mix of window styles, dates from the 16th century and was a forge during the last century. The smartly furnished interior with an aquarium, horse brasses and a collection of commemorative spoons (437 at the last count) reflects the landlady's character and interests. Excellent home-cooked food is served lunchtimes (not Mon in winter) and evenings. A large patio offers outdoor games including chess, and heated cover for smokers. Q❀◐◑Å⊟♣P⁄

Winterbourne Down

Cross Hands

85 Down Road, BS36 1BZ

✪ 12 (11 Fri & Sat)-10.30 (11 Wed-Sat); 12-10.30 Sun

☎ (01454) 850077

Courage Best Bitter; guest beers ⊞

Friendly 17th-century village free house with a spacious main bar, snug area and an alcove used by local darts players. Old sewing machines feature as decoration, together with an interesting selection of old pump clips on a dummy beer engine near the entrance. A large rear garden includes a children's play area and a smoking shelter. Parking can be tricky outside but a daytime bus service operates to nearby Hicks Common. The guest beers include Taylor Landlord. ⌂❀⊟♣●P⁄

Woodchester

Ram Inn

Station Road, GL5 5EQ (signed from A46) SO840023

✪ 11-11; 12-10.30 Sun

☎ (01453) 873329

Butcombe Bitter; Nailsworth Artist's Ale; Otter Ale; Stroud Tom Long; Uley Old Spot; guest beers ⊞

The Ram is more than 400 years old and stands in superb walking country near Woodchester Mansion. A recently completed extension has provided new toilet facilities and wheelchair access. This is a dog-friendly village pub which stocks an excellent range of ales, including at least one beer from the nearby Nailsworth and Stroud breweries. The food is highly recommended. The pub is a regular venue for the Stroud Morris Men. ⌂Q❀◐◑♿♣P⁄

Woolaston Common

Rising Sun

GL15 6NU (1 mile off A48 at Woolaston) SO590009

✪ 12-2.30 (not Tue or Wed), 6.30-11; 12-3, 7-11 Sun

☎ (01594) 529282

Wye Valley Bitter; Fuller's London Pride ⊞

This 350-year-old stone-built pub with a cosy snug and main bar area has had the same landlord for the last 30 years. Situated on the circular pub walks of the Forest of Dean, it has become a favourite watering hole for many a rambler. Good home-cooked food is available except Tuesday and Wednesday lunchtimes; well worth a detour to find. ⌂Q❀◐◑⊟P

Wotton-under-Edge

Swan Hotel

16 Market Street, GL12 7AS

✪ 10-11 (midnight Fri & Sat); 12-11 Sun

☎ (01453) 843004

Uley Pig's Ear; Young's Bitter; guest beers ⊞

This 16th-century coaching inn with an imposing exterior is situated at the top of the town, close to a free public car park. The public bar has TV and gaming machines, while the comfortable lounge and restaurant both have open fires. It is a genuine free house and sources the majority of its beers from local micro-breweries. It also offers a large selection of unusual malt whiskies. This local pub is popular with walkers using the Cotswold Way. ⌂Q◐◑⊟♣

Hold the beef

Beer has come to be acknowledged as the national beverage of England. At a recent conference, Lord Burton claimed that this country owed its high and proud position among the nations of the earth simply on account of its characteristic diet, beef and beer. Whereupon someone made the waggish comment, Why drag in the beef? **F W Hackwood, 1910**

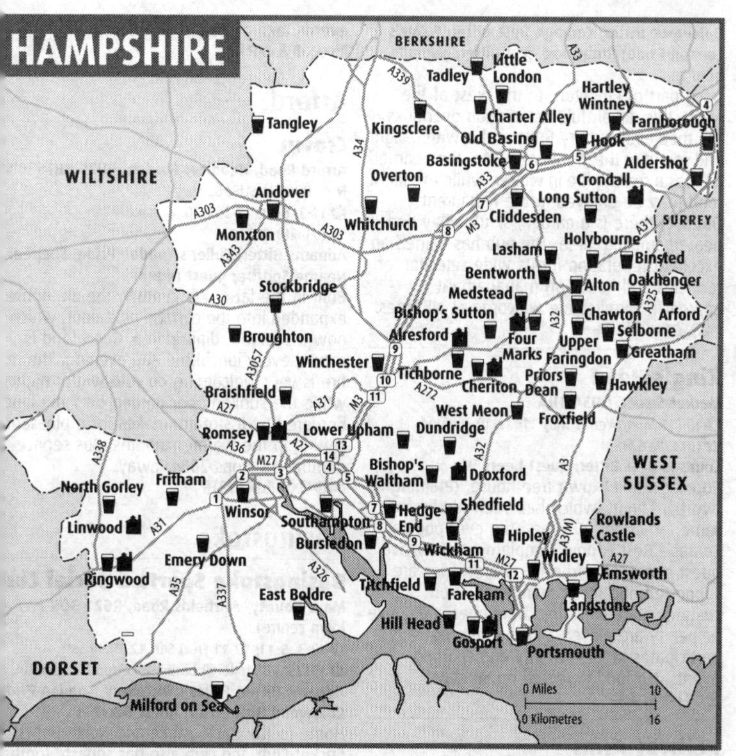

Gale's Brewery has been bought and closed by Fuller's. The beers are now brewed in London at Fuller's Chiswick brewery. When a Guide entry serves only Gale's beer we list the beers as shown on pumpclips i.e. Gale's HSB, rather than Fuller's Gale's HSB. Please see Fuller's entry in the Independent Breweries section. Please note that Ringwood is now owned by Marston's – see New Nationals section.

Aldershot

White Lion

20 Lower Farnham Road, GU12 4EA (400m from A331/A323 jct)

12-11 (midnight Fri & Sat); 12-10.30 Sun

☎ (01252) 323832

Triple fff Alton's Pride, Pressed Rat & Warthog, Moondance, seasonal beers; guest beers 🄷

Genuine two-bar pub, east of the town, with little or no TV, taken over by the Triple fff Brewery two years ago. It is so traditional you can even close the door behind you in the side room. The landlord's enthusiasm for scooters is evident in the display of items behind the bar, while substantial bar stools complement the no-nonsense plain wooden tables and church pews throughout. Open mic night is every other Thursday, quiz night is Monday and live music plays on Saturday.

Alton

Eight Bells

33 Church Street, GU34 2DA

11-11; 12-10.30 Sun

☎ (01420) 82417

Ballard's Best Bitter; Ringwood Best Bitter; guest beers 🄷

Excellent free house just outside the town centre on the old Odiham turnpike. The building dates from 1640 and is steeped in history. Opposite stands the ancient St Lawrence Church, around which the Battle of Alton was fought during the Civil War. The pub has one small, oak-beamed bar with a further drinking area at the rear and a bijou garden housing a well. Hearty filled rolls will keep hunger pangs at bay. CAMRA local Pub of the Year 2008.

French Horn ✓

The Butts, GU34 1RT

12-11 (10.30 Sun)

☎ (01420) 83269 frenchhorn.co.uk

INDEPENDENT BREWERIES

Bowman Droxford
Crondall Crondall
Flowerpots Cheriton
Hampshire Romsey
Irving Portsmouth (NEW)
Itchen Valley Alresford
Oakleaf Gosport
Red Shoot Linwood
Ringwood Ringwood
Triple fff Four Marks

Butcombe Bitter; Courage Best Bitter; Fuller's London Pride; Ringwood Best Bitter; guest beer H
Once part of Chawton, to the west of the town, this delightful, historic pub overlooks the medieval archery Butts and is within sight and sound of the Watercress Line. The beamed bar has a roaring fire in winter, while excellent food may be enjoyed in the restaurant. Outside, there is a garden, skittle alley and heated smoking area. The pub has gained an excellent reputation for its wide selection of real ales and hands-on management approach. Families are welcome at all times.
Q P

King's Head

Market Street, GU34 1HA
10 (11 Mon, Wed & Thu)-11; 12-10.30 Sun
(01420) 82313
Courage Best Bitter; guest beers H
Popular market-town free house, retaining its two-bar layout, which has been run by the same family for 20 years. The ever popular Courage Best is now complemented by two guest beers. Ales from local breweries are supported and recommendations from customers are welcome. Dominoes and shove ha'penny are played and the pub regularly participates in local charity and sporting events. No food is served on Sunday.

Railway Arms

26 Anstey Road, GU34 2RB (400m from station)
12-11; 11-midnight Fri & Sat
(01420) 82218
Triple fff Alton's Pride, Pressed Rat & Warthog, Moondance, Stairway, seasonal beers; guest beers H
Friendly pub close to the Watercress Line. Owned by Triple fff Brewery, whose own beers are supplemented by ales from a host of micros. The extension at the rear has its own bar which is available for hire. A new patio area, designed using a traditional railway theme, is at the rear, ideal for barbecues and incorporating a covered, heated smoking area. There are tables outside the front of the pub, under a striking sculpture of a steam locomotive.

Andover

Wyke Down Country Pub & Restaurant ✓

Picket Piece, SP11 6LX (follow signs for Wyke from A303)
11-2.30, 6-11 (10.30 Sun)
(01264) 352048 wykedown.co.uk
Shepherd Neame Spitfire; Taylor Landlord; guest beer H
This spacious country pub is based around an extended barn with exposed beams, in which many old agricultural implements are displayed. The large restaurant draws customers from afar and is also used for functions. A comfortable conservatory and adjacent games room complete the facilities in the main building. Outside there is a campsite, children's play area, golf driving range and a swimming pool. Various annual events take place in the grounds.
P

Arford

Crown

Arford Road, Headley, Borden, GU35 8BT (200m N of B3002) SU826365
11-3, 6-11; 12-3, 7-10.30 Sun
(01428) 712150
Adnams Bitter; Fuller's London Pride; Shepherd Neame Spitfire; guest beer H
Built in the late 17th century, the ale house expanded into the cottage next door, which is now a separate dining area. Good food is served every lunchtime and evening. The real fire is very welcoming on cold winter nights, while the sunken beer garden over the lane bordered by a stream, makes for a pleasant setting in the warmer months. Bus service number 18 stops 200m away.
Q (18)P

Basingstoke

Basingstoke Sports & Social Club

Mays Bounty, Fairfields Road, RG21 3DR (SW of town centre)
12-3, 5-11; 12-11 Fri & Sat; 12-10.30 Sun
(01256) 331646 basingstoke-sports-club.co.uk
Adnams Bitter; Fuller's Discovery, London Pride; Ringwood Best Bitter; guest beers H
Home to the Basingstoke and North Hants Cricket Club, the club also has squash, football and other sports facilities. Opening hours may vary when there are major cricket matches outside. Two or more guest beers from smaller breweries are usually available, and lunchtime snacks are served Monday to Friday. As you would expect, the TV usually shows cricket or football. Although a private members' club, CAMRA members are welcome on production of a membership card. P

Maidenhead Inn

17 Winchester Street, RG21 7ED (top of town)
9-midnight (1am Fri & Sat)
(01256) 316030
Greene King Abbot; Marston's Pedigree; guest beers H
This attractive Wetherspoon pub is situated in the historic 'Top of Town' area, with five pumps to dispense local and guest ales, including European ones. Local beers from Loddon, Hampshire and Triple fff breweries regularly feature. A large dining area leads to the compact bar with further seating to the rear over two levels, complemented by an outdoor heated beer garden.
Q

Queens Arms ✓

Bunnian Place, RG21 7JE (150m from rail station)
11-11 (10.30 Sun)
(01256) 465488
Courage Best Bitter; Fuller's London Pride; Wadworth 6X; guest beers H
A beacon of excellence in a town infamous for youth-oriented bars, the Queens attracts lovers of good fare from all walks of life. The licensees source a wide range of guest ales from the region, some of which disappear

very quickly. With no loud music, first-time visitors could find themselves quickly engaged in conversation with the gregarious locals. There is an attractive shady courtyard garden at the rear. All food is home-cooked on the premises. Q❀◐◑⇌🚌♣⅍

Royal Oak

414 Worting Road, Worting, RG22 5EA (on B3400 at Worting before railway bridge)

⏲ 10-midnight; 12-10.30 Sun

☎ (01256) 335951

Courage Best Bitter; Hogs Back TEA; guest beer 🄷

Roadside pub, set back from the main road, on the outskirts of town with a lounge and public areas plus two pool rooms at the rear. The front lounge has a small bar with handpumps and a dining area. The public bar is family friendly, with an open-plan layout, wooden floor and seats at the bar. Food is served 10-9pm daily. Live music is played some Saturday evenings, with a Rock Club held on the first Saturday of each month. There is parking front and rear. ☋❀◐◑⊟🚌(8,76)♣P⅍

Soldier's Return

80 Upper Sherborne Road, Oakridge, RG21 5RP (opp playing field)

⏲ 11-11; 12-10.30 Sun

☎ (01256) 322449

Courage Best Bitter; guest beers 🄷

Some 160 years old, the pub is on the north side of town near the A339 ring road. It is well used by the local community, as well as football teams wanting a beer after their match. The local motorcycle action group also use it as a meeting place. The public bar can get lively at times. There is outside seating in front of the pub which overlooks the playing fields opposite. Food is served 12-5pm Monday to Friday and 12-3pm Saturday. Q❀◐⊟🚌(5)♣P⅍

Way Inn

Chapel Hill, RG21 5TB (near station)

⏲ 12-11 (10.30 Sun)

☎ (01256) 321520 🌐 thewayinn.org.uk

Caledonian Deuchars IPA; Greene King Abbot; Taylor Landlord; guest beers 🄷

This extensively refurbished pub featuring a welcoming log fire in winter provides a comfortable environment for the 20+ age group. There is a spacious room at the rear where families are welcome and an outside drinking area with seating and tables in a large sun-drenched garden. Guest beers are obtained from SIBA's direct delivery scheme. There is no TV. Home-cooked traditional food, with a good vegetarian range, is available. There is a large rear car park and several buses stop outside. ⛼☋❀◐◑♿⇌🚌P

Bentworth

Star Inn

GU34 5RB

⏲ 12-3, 5-11.30; 12-11.30 Fri-Sun

☎ (01420) 561224 🌐 star-inn.com

Fuller's London Pride; Ringwood Best Bitter; guest beers 🄷

Dating back to 1841, this friendly free house has a bar warmed by open fires and an adjacent, quiet restaurant offering freshly cooked meals. A social hub for the village community, its enthusiastic staff provide an active social calendar, including Tuesday curry evening, live music on Friday and a blues jam session on Sunday evening. Visitors, especially walkers, are always made welcome. Local bottled cider is available. A bus stops outside the door. ⛼❀◐◑🚌(28)♣P⅍

Binsted

Cedars

The Street, GU34 4PB

⏲ 11.30-3, 6 (4.30 Fri)-11.30; 11.30-11.30 Sat; 12-11 Sun

☎ (01420) 22112

Courage Best Bitter; guest beers 🄷

This rural pub has a quiet and cosy bar area where customers can enjoy pub games, with many teams in local leagues. Occasional musical events are held as well as an annual beer festival. A warm welcome is extended to walkers, cyclists and campers at this convivial, friendly community pub. Caravans are also allowed. ⛼Q❀◐◑⛺♣P⅍

Bishop's Sutton

Ship Inn

Main Road, SO24 0AQ (on B3047)

⏲ 12-2.30 (not Mon), 6-11.30; 12-3, 7-11 Sun

☎ (01962) 732863

Ringwood Best Bitter; guest beers 🄷

Cosy, genuine free house with a split-level bar and a real log fire providing a quiet, comfortable, relaxing atmosphere. An adjoining room acts as a restaurant and games area while the Crow's Nest bar doubles as a family/dining room. Home-cooked food features on the daily specials board and Sunday roasts (with vegetarian option) are popular with the locals (no food Monday lunchtime). Frequent Winchester-Alton buses stop outside and the Watercress Line steam railway is just over a mile away at Alresford. ⛼Q☋❀◐◑🚌♣P

Bishop's Waltham

Bunch of Grapes

St Peter's Street, SO32 1AD (follow signs to church)

⏲ 12-2, 6-11; 12-2 Sun

☎ (01489) 892935

Courage Best Bitter; guest beer 🄶

Tiny, ancient pub, part of a row of cottages in a narrow street. This listed building has been redecorated, leaving it even more comfortable and attractive than before. Beers are gravity-dispensed from casks neatly arranged behind the bar. The guest beer is often from Goddards. This is a useful watering hole for those touring the area, with a central location close to the ruins of the bishop's palace and car parking. A pub golf society flourishes. Q❀♣

Braishfield

Newport Inn

Newport Lane, SO51 0PL (take lane opp phone box) SU373249
❂ 12-2.30 (not Mon), 6-11; 12-2.30, 7-10.30 Sun
☎ (01794) 368225
Gale's Butser Bitter, HSB, seasonal beers Ⓗ
A true time-warp pub where the world has stood still for so long you could expect to be charged in pounds, shillings and pence. This two-bar local, tucked away down a narrow lane, has a fiercely loyal, cosmopolitan clientele drawn from miles around. The landlady presides over the Saturday evening singalong on the piano, and Thursday often features an ad hoc folk session. There are no lunchtime or evening meals but you cannot go hungry here – the fabulous sandwiches and ploughmans are legendary. ⋔Q❀⊟♣P

Wheatsheaf

Braishfield Road, SO51 0QE
❂ 11 (12 Sun)-midnight
☎ (01794) 368372 🌐 wheatsheafbraishfield.co.uk
Bowman Swift One; Hampshire Pride of Romsey; Ringwood Best Bitter; guest beers Ⓗ
Rare-breed pigs, free-range hens and even quails are raised here, contributing to the award-winning kitchen's extensive menu on offer at this charming village local. Low light levels, wood panelling and gentle music also all add to the charm of this rustic, dog-friendly pub. The beer selection varies somewhat; the aim is to always offer beers from two or three local breweries. The large, child-friendly patio and garden leads down to a smallholding where the livestock can be viewed.
⋔❀◐♿●P⁄–

Broughton

Tally Ho!

High Street, SO20 8AA
❂ 12-2.30 (not Tue), 6-11; 12-3.30, 6-midnight Fri; 12-11 Sat; 12-10.30 Sun
☎ (01794) 301280
Ringwood Best Bitter; guest beers Ⓗ
Friendly pub in an appealing village on the Clarendon Way long-distance path. The simple square bar serves a large, well-appointed public bar and homely lounge, both with real fires. Outside is a neat garden with covered patio. The pub welcomes children, is popular with walkers and cyclists and supports cribbage and darts teams. Home-cooked food is served daily except Tuesday and Sunday evening. Changing guest beers usually come from local brewers. There is extra parking at the village hall. ⋔Q❀◐⊟⊞(68)♣⁄–

Bursledon

Jolly Sailor

Land's End Road, SO31 8DN (steep, signed path from station car park)
❂ 11-11; 12-10.30 Sun
☎ (023) 8040 5557
Badger K&B Sussex, First Gold, Tanglefoot, seasonal beer Ⓗ
Picturesque 16th-century pub, famous from the BBC's Howards' Way series, filmed on the River Hamble in the 1980s. This Hall & Woodhouse inn is only accessible from land by a long flight of steps; it is much easier to arrive by boat at the covered, heated pontoon. An extensive food menu is available in the bar and the restaurant, which has marine memorabilia adding to its river views. The staff are very friendly and helpful. Roadside parking is difficult – the steep path from Bursledon station is recommended.
⋔Q❀◐⇌⊞⁄–

Vine Inn

High Street, SO31 8DJ (½ mile SW of station)
❂ 5.30-11; 12-2, 5.30-11 Fri; 12-4, 7.30-10.30 Sun
☎ (023) 8040 3836
Greene King IPA, Abbot Ⓖ
Unspoilt, traditional village pub, owned by Admiral Taverns. A rare outlet serving Greene King beers by gravity, the Abbot is often brought up from the cellar. The bar is oak-beamed, with hanging copper artefacts and interesting collections of old beer bottles and local prints. Tuesday is quiz night, a meat draw is held on Sunday and the piano is available for aspiring musicians and occasional music sessions. There are river views from the garden. The car park is small, the station car park is a 10-minute walk. Dogs are allowed.
⋔❀⇔⇌⊞♣P

Charter Alley

White Hart

White Hart Lane, RG26 5QA (1 mile W of A340) SU593577
❂ 12-2.30 (3 Sat), 7-11; 12-3, 7-10.30 Sun
☎ (01256) 850048 🌐 whitehartcharteralley.com
Palmer Best Bitter; Triple fff Alton's Pride; West Berkshire Maggs Magnificent Mild; guest beers Ⓗ
The oldest building in the village, this was the place where folk used to natter, hence 'chatter alley' (Charter Alley). Oak beams and log fires enhance the welcoming atmosphere of the pub.The bar now houses six pumps and the range of beers is forever changing. Good-quality food is served in a very pleasant restaurant converted from the original skittle alley. There is also a lovely terraced garden where water features make for a peaceful drink. En-suite guest rooms are available.
⋔Q❀⇔◐⊟♣P⊡

Chawton

Greyfriar ✔

Winchester Road, GU34 1SB (opp Jane Austen's house)
❂ 12-11 (10.30 Sun)
☎ (01420) 83841 🌐 thegreyfriar.co.uk
Fuller's London Pride, ESB; Gale's HSB, seasonal beers Ⓗ
This country village pub, converted from three cottages, attracts locals and visitors due to its proximity to Jane Austen's house, which is opposite. Inside, this welcoming hostelry features designated bar areas and a cosy restaurant that has gained a good reputation for its excellent daily-changing menu. A function room is also available. The pub benefits from a pleasant garden and a separate covered smoking area. Bus route 72 passes the door. Q❀◐⊞(72)P⁄–

Cheriton

Flower Pots

SO24 0QQ (½ mile N of A272 between Winchester and Petersfield) SU581283
12-2.30 (3 Sat), 6-11; 12-3, 7-10.30
☎ (01962) 771318 flowerpots-inn.co.uk
Flowerpots Bitter, Gooden's Gold, seasonal beers G
Four-square, warm, red-brick pub with two separate bars, dating from 1820; popular with walkers and cyclists. A large rear marquee provides welcome overflow space on busy days. Two outbuildings house the pub's famous 10-barrel brewery (qv) and the four comfortable B&B rooms. All the brewery's current beers (usually at least three) are served directly from their casks. Good, home-cooked food is available daily (except Sunday evening) with Wednesday evening featuring curries from a Punjabi chef. Weston's Old Rosie cider is available. ⋒Q❀⇌◑◑⊟♣P

Cliddesden

Jolly Farmer

Farleigh Road, RG25 2JL (on B3046)
12-11 (midnight Thu-Sat); 12-10.30 Sun
☎ (01256) 473073
Beer range varies H
Busy, listed village pub close to Basingstoke offering an interesting selection of beers from the Punch Taverns list. A cider such as Weston's Old Rosie is usually available from the cellar. The quieter second bar may be used by families when not reserved for functions. At the rear, a large garden provides a secluded area for a peaceful drink, with several heated, covered areas for cooler evenings.
❀◑◑♣♣P⊁

Dundridge

Hampshire Bowman

Dundridge Lane, Bishop's Waltham, SO32 1GD (1½ miles east of B3035) SU578184
12-11 (midnight Fri & Sat); 12-10.30 Sun
☎ (01489) 892940 hampshirebowman.com
Bowman Swift One, Quiver; Ringwood Fortyniner; guest beers G
A recent refurbishment has provided an extra, larger bar where families are welcome until 9pm. This new space has comfortable tables at which to eat the excellent food and gives access to the garden – a pleasant place to pass, or lose, an afternoon. The old front bar retains its charm with a warm winter fire and beers still directly dispensed from their casks – this is the sort of place people think no longer exists. Cider is available in summer only. Camping is by prior arrangement.
⋒Q❀◑◑Ⅹ♣♣P

East Boldre

Turfcutters' Arms ✔

Main Road, SO42 7WL (1½m SW of Beaulieu, off B3054 at Hatchet Pond) SU324004
11-3, 6-11; 11-11 Fri & Sat; 12-10.30 Sun
☎ (01590) 612331 theturfcutters.co.uk
Ringwood Best Bitter, Fortyniner; guest beers H
Named from the 'right of turbary' once enjoyed by tenants, the pub stands at the edge of Bagshot Moor, close to Beaulieu's Abbey, Palace and Motor Museum and to Buckler's Hard, the 18th-century shipbuilding village. Drinkers, diners and their well-behaved dogs and children are warmly welcomed in the choice of three rustic rooms. Home-cooked food (not served Sunday evening) includes game, and snacks include local biltong. More than 70 whiskies are available, together with a demanding library and New Forest cider during summer months.
⋒Q❀⇌◑◑⊟(112)♣♣P⊁

Emery Down

New Forest Inn

SO43 7DY (½m NW of A35 at Swan Green, W of Lyndhurst) SU285084
11.30-2.30, 6-11 (11.30-11 June-Sept); 11.30-11 Sat; 12-10.30 Sun
☎ (023) 8028 4690 thenewforestinn.co.uk
Ringwood Best Bitter; guest beers H
The public area of this part 18th-century building has three levels, with a function room and weekend overflow area at the top. Heat sources include two real fires; furniture includes armchairs and milk churns. A bosky garden slopes beyond the covered drinking area abutting the rear of the bar. The menu features fresh fish (no meals available on winter Sunday evenings) and a beer festival is held in July. Clean dogs are welcome.
⋒❀◑◑⊟(X35,56)♣P⊁

Emsworth

Coal Exchange

21 South Street, PO10 7EG
10.30-3, 5.30-11; 10.30-11 Fri & Sat; 11-10.30 Sun
☎ (01243) 375866 thecoalexchange.co.uk
Fuller's London Pride, seasonal beers; Gale's Butser Bitter, HSB; guest beers H
Originally a pork butchery and ale house, this pub was used to trade local produce with coal delivered to the local harbour. Trade has now given way to leisure, with many yachts visiting the sheltered harbour. The single bar is decorated with local photographs and nautical paraphernalia and the building has an unusual green tiled front. In addition to serving award-winning food at lunchtimes, the pub also holds curry evenings on Tuesdays and international evenings on Thursdays.
⋒❀◑⇌⊟♣⊁

Lord Raglan

35 Queen Street, PO10 7BJ
11-3, 6-11; 11-11 Sat; 12-11 Sun
☎ (01243) 372587 thelordraglan.com
Fuller's London Pride; Gale's Butser Bitter, HSB H
A flint-built pub alongside Slipper Mill Pond where the River Ems meets the harbour. The garden offers views of both pond and harbour. One bar has been converted into a small restaurant and the other hosts genuine live music from local bands every Sunday evening (see the pub's website for details). Combined with excellent home-cooked food and enthusiastic staff, this pub offers something for everyone. The cider is Bulmers Traditional.
⋒Q❀◑◑⇌⊟♣♣

Fareham

Gordon Arms

107-109 Gordon Road, PO16 7TG
✪ 12-11 (10.30 Sun)
☎ (01329) 315523
Ringwood Best Bitter; guest beers Ⓗ
This pub is one of the few genuine locals' pubs in the town, especially convenient for the railway station. In addition to the main bar, there is a back room that doubles as a function room, and a large garden with a children's play area. There are normally two guest beers, with local breweries often represented. Good value food is served up to 6pm weekdays and 3pm Sunday. Regular crib evenings are held in the function room. ❀◐⇌♣⚡

Lord Arthur Lee ✔

100-108 West Street, PO16 0EP
✪ 9am-midnight (1am Fri & Sat)
☎ (01329) 280447
Beer range varies Ⓗ
Popular with office workers and shoppers, this Wetherspoon pub was built on the site of a former Co-op and is especially convenient for the town centre and bus station. Up to 10 different real ales are available at any one time, mostly from small breweries, with Ringwood beers appearing regularly. Although flat-screen TVs abound, the sound is usually turned down, except during major football matches. Wetherspoon's standard food menu is served all day. ❀◐◑♿⇌🚌⚡

Farnborough

Prince of Wales ✔

184 Rectory Road, GU14 8AL (near North station)
✪ 11.30-2.30, 5.30-11; 11.30-11 Fri & Sat; 12-10.30 Sun
☎ (01252) 545578
Fuller's London Pride; Hogs Back TEA; Hop Back Summer Lightning; Ringwood Fortyniner; Young's Bitter; guest beers Ⓗ
Popular free house close to Farnborough North station, which continues to set a very high standard for choice and quality. A single bar is flanked by separate drinking areas, with tables under cover outside at the rear. Up to five guest beers are served with a good representation of south eastern breweries, including a keenly priced session beer. Milds feature in May, strong beers around Christmas, and a very popular beer festival is held in October. Lunches are available Monday to Saturday. ❀◐⇌(Farnborough North)🚌P

Four Marks

Four Marks Golf Club

Headmore Lane, GU34 3ES (off A31 via Telegraph Lane)
✪ 10-11 (midnight Fri & Sat)
☎ (01420) 587214
Gale's HSB; Triple fff Moondance; guest beers Ⓗ
Open to the public throughout the year, this friendly and comfortable bar features beers from local breweries around Hampshire. From the patio area, views across the golf course and Hampshire countryside may be enjoyed while sampling the excellent food and ales. The varied menu is a treat for all tastes and palates. Families are welcome to enjoy a quiet time away from the hurly burly of town and traffic. Q❀◐◑♿P⚡

Fritham

Royal Oak ✔

SO43 7HJ (1 mile S of B3078) SU232141
✪ 11.30-2.30 (3 summer), 6-11; 11-11 Sat; 12-10.30 Sun
☎ (023) 8081 2606
Hop Back Summer Lightning; Ringwood Best Bitter, Fortyniner; guest beers Ⓖ
Thatched gem at the end of a New Forest track. The main bar leads into several interconnected areas featuring low beams and doors, colour-washed walls, log fires and wooden floors, and served via a hatchway. Guest beers are always from small local brewers, usually including Bowman. Simple but excellent food includes local cheeses and home-smoked sausage. The vast garden with tables hosts barbecues, hog-roasts and a mid-September beer festival. A perfect welcome awaits walkers, cyclists and equestrians (facilities provided); dogs abound. ⛰Q❀◐⛺

Froxfield

Trooper

Alton Road, GU32 1BD SU727278
✪ 12-3 (not Mon), 6-11 (not Sun)
☎ (01730) 827293 🌐 trooperinn.com
Ringwood Best Bitter; guest beer Ⓗ
Dating from the 17th century, this old inn is set high in Hampshire's rolling countryside. Although opened up inside, the single bar serves several distinct areas. Walls are adorned with photographs of film stars while classical music is played quietly in the background and the atmosphere is enhanced by candlelight at the bar and on the tables. Three beers are usually on offer, mainly from local breweries, and the extensive food menu attracts country folk. ⛰Q❀🛏◐◑P

Gosport

Clarence Tavern

1 Clarence Road, PO12 1BB
✪ 11-11; 12-3, 7-10.30 Sun
☎ (023) 9252 9726 🌐 clarencetavern.co.uk
Oakleaf Bitter, Hole Hearted, Blake's Gosport Bitter Ⓗ
Situated a short walk from the Gosport ferry and local buses, this pub is the brewery tap for the nearby Oakleaf Brewery. Seasonal beers from Oakleaf also appear occasionally, and beers from other small breweries feature at the well-established beer festivals held over the Easter and August bank holiday weekends. Adjoining the main bar area is a room whose roof came from an old chapel on the Isle of Wight. Food is available all week except Sunday evening. The pub sometimes closes on winter weekday afternoons.
⛰❀🛏◐◑♿🚌♣P⚡

Five Alls

75 Forton Road, PO12 4TD
✪ 10-11; 12-10.30 Sun
Draught Bass Ⓗ

The name of this street-corner local refers to five aldermen. The open-plan interior is divided into three distinct areas: a main bar where the walls are lined with nautical memorabilia, a games area and a small dining area. The garden has a covered and heated smoking zone. Traditional pub food is served until 7pm on weekdays and 4pm on Sunday. Probably the most interesting feature of the pub is the original urinals in the Gents' toilet.
❀◑🚌♣⚡

Queen's Hotel
143 Queen's Road, PO12 1LG
✪ 11.30-2.30 (not Mon-Thu), 5-11; 11.30-11 Sat; 12-3, 7-10.30 Sun
☎ (023) 9258 2645
Ringwood Fortyniner; Rooster's Yankee; Young's Bitter; guest beers Ⓗ
This award-winning locals' pub is hidden away in the back streets, yet it enjoys a nationwide reputation. In 2008, Sue Lampon, the licensee, celebrates 25 years here. Up to three guest beers are available from small breweries and Weston's Old Rosie cider appears all year round. A regular beer festival takes place in October. Snacks are served Friday lunchtime. Weekend opening hours are often extended by up to half an hour. ♨🚌♣🍏⚡

Greatham

Greatham Inn
Petersfield Road, GU33 6AD SU778310
✪ 12-3, 5-11; 12-11 Sat; 12-10.30 Sun
☎ (01420) 538016 🌐 thegreathaminn.co.uk
Ringwood Best Bitter, Fortyniner; guest beers Ⓗ
A delightful pub in the centre of the village where dogs are always welcome. Alongside the regular beers, there are two guests, predominantly from the south of England. You may dine in the restaurant or bar, where fresh fish dishes are available Thursday to Sunday evenings. As you enter the pub you will see a decorative coat of arms from Lady Carol, who is buried in the nearby churchyard.
♨Q❀◑▶🚌(72)P⚡

Hartley Wintney

Waggon & Horses
High Street, RG27 8NY
✪ 11-11 (midnight Fri & Sat); 12-11 Sun
☎ (01256) 842110
Courage Best Bitter; Ⓗ **Gale's HSB;** Ⓖ **guest beer** Ⓗ
A village pub whose landlord of 28 years has won several local CAMRA awards. HSB is served from a cask in the cellar and the guest beer changes constantly. The lively public bar contrasts with a quieter lounge, and tables outside on the pavement enable guests to enjoy the atmosphere of the village, renowned for its antique shops. At the rear of the pub is a pleasant courtyard garden and a heated, covered smokers' area. Food is served lunchtimes only, not Sunday.
♨Q❀◑🚂🚌(200,72)⚡

Hawkley

Hawkley Inn
Pococks Lane, GU33 6NE SU747291
✪ 12-3, 5.30-11; 12-11 Sat; 12-10.30 Sun
☎ (01730) 827205
Beer range varies Ⓗ
Set among beautiful Hampshire walking country, this is a true free house of immense character, stocking up to 10 ales from a wide range of southern independent breweries. Ciders and perry from the local Mr Whitehead's range are also available. Superb home-cooked food is served, there is a large sun-trap garden, and high-quality accommodation rounds off this superb and unique pub. Meals are not available on Sunday evening. ❀🛏◑▶🍏

Hedge End

Barleycorn ✔
Lower Northam Road, SO30 4FQ
✪ 11-11 (midnight Fri & Sat)
☎ (01489) 784171
Greene King IPA, Abbot; guest beer Ⓗ
Friendly, traditional village local close to the shops in the centre of Hedge End — a true village, despite its proximity to Southampton. Its spacious bar is popular with locals of all age groups and there are resident darts teams. Good value lunchtime food is available from Monday to Thursday. The rear garden has a covered, heated smoking area equipped with a TV for sporting events; further outdoor seating is at the front of the pub. ❀◑🚌♣P⚡

Hill Head

Crofton
48 Crofton Lane, PO14 3QF
✪ 11-11; 12-10.30 Sun
☎ (01329) 314222
Adnams Broadside; Caledonian Deuchars IPA; Hop Back Summer Lightning; guest beers Ⓗ
This award-winning estate pub is in an area that was once strawberry fields. Up to six real ales are available, including beers from SIBA breweries. Oakleaf Hole Hearted appears regularly. The building is divided into three areas: a public bar, large lounge and dining area, and a skittle alley where special events are held including a beer festival in October. Food is available all day at weekends. A covered and heated smoking area is planned.
♨Q❀◑🚂♿🚌♣P⚡

Hipley

Horse & Jockey
PO7 4QY (on Hambledon to Fareham road) SU623119
✪ 11.30-11; 12-midnight Sat; 12-10.30 Sun
☎ (023) 9263 2778
Gale's HSB; Ringwood Best Bitter; guest beers Ⓗ
This large two-bar pub set in the pleasant Hampshire countryside has several military connections. During WW II, a German aircraft crashed in a nearby field and over the years the pub has been used by many Royal Navy personnel based at the now-closed training establishment HMS Dryad. Horse racing

enthusiasts will be interested to know that the first horse to win two consecutive Grand Nationals was trained nearby. The house beer is Gale's Butser.

Holybourne

Queen's Head

20 London Road, GU34 4EG (opp Grange Hotel)
12-11 (11.30 Thu; 12.30am Fri & Sat); 12-10.30 Sun
(01420) 86331
Greene King IPA; guest beers H
This traditional pub highlights the best of Greene King, featuring a flexible and interesting guest beer list. The Queen's comprises two rooms plus a new extension and covered smoking area. The food is hearty (served evenings Wed to Sat) and features local produce. Regular live music events take place throughout the year. The extensive garden features a children's play area.
Q (Alton) (64,65) P

Hook

Crooked Billet

London Road, RG27 9EH (on A30 approx 1 mile E of Hook)
11.30-3, 6-11; 11.30-11 Sat; 12-10.30 Sun
(01256) 762118 thecrookedbillethook.co.uk
Courage Best Bitter, Directors; guest beer H
Recently extended, air-conditioned, spacious pub beside the river Whitewater, run by the same landlord for the last 20 years. The hostelry is renowned for its good food as well as its beer. An open log fire is welcoming in winter and there is plenty of space for both drinkers and diners, especially in summer when the riverside garden is at its best. Thatchers is stocked for cider drinkers and a covered area is available for smokers. Families are welcome. Q (200)P

Kingsclere

Swan Hotel

Swan Street, RG20 5PP
11-3, 5.30-11.30; 12-3.30, 7-11 Sun
(01635) 298314 swankingsclere.co.uk
Theakston XB; Young's Bitter; guest beers H
Traditional inn frequented by an eclectic mix of customers, serving four beers including two frequently changing local guests. The 400-year-old pub is one of the county's oldest coaching inns, dating from 1449 and associated with the Bishop of Winchester for 300 years. The Grade II-listed building, close to the Watership Down beauty spot, retains original oak beams and fireplaces and offers nine en-suite bedrooms. Good food is served in both the dining room and the bar.
Q

Langstone

Ship Inn

Langstone Road, PO9 1RD
11-11; 12-10.30 Sun
(023) 9247 1719
Fuller's Discovery, London Pride; Gale's Butser Bitter, HSB H
An imposing building located next to the only surviving crossing to Hayling Island, this pub is an ideal base from which to explore the paths along the coast and inland via the course of the old railway line. The nearby harbour and pond are a draw for nature enthusiasts and more intrepid explorers may find traces of the old railway bridge and Roman wade way to the island. (30,31)P

Lasham

Gliding Club

Lasham Airfield, GU34 5SS (signed from A339)
12-2, 5.30-11 (12-11 Sat summer); 12-11 Sun
(01256) 384900
Triple fff Moondance; guest beer H
This club has a friendly, comfortable lounge bar and an excellent restaurant with a resident chef. Check in advance for availability of evening meals. The establishment is open to the public at all times and children are welcome. An extensive patio area is a good place to enjoy your pint while watching the aircraft. It was voted local CAMRA Club of the Year in 2007 and 2008. P

Royal Oak

GU34 5SJ (off A339 between Alton and Basingstoke)
12-11 (10.30 Sun)
(01256) 381213 royaloak.uk.com
Gale's HSB; Ringwood Best Bitter; Triple fff Moondance; guest beers H
Situated in the centre of a quiet village next to Lasham Airfield, well known for its gliding club, the pub is more than 200 years old and has two bars. Food is served daily at lunchtime and in the evening (not Monday), plus all day on Sunday. A large car park, beautiful garden and picturesque surroundings make this pub popular with ramblers and cyclists. Children are welcome. Q (28) P

Little London

Plough Inn

Silchester Road, RG26 5EP (1 mile off A340, S of Tadley)
12-2.30 (3 Sat), 5.30 (6 Sat)-11; 12-3, 7-10.30 Sun
(01256) 850628
Ringwood Best Bitter, seasonal beers; H **guest beers** G
Wonderful, popular and informal village pub in a sympathetically restored cottage. In winter, you can enjoy a glass of porter in front of a cheery log fire, while enjoying a good range of baguettes (not Sun evening). Live music is hosted on the second Tuesday of the month. Bar billiards is played and a secluded garden at the side of the pub is an added attraction. The pub is ideally located for ramblers and cyclists visiting Silchester's Roman ruins. It was Wessex CAMRA Pub of the Year 2007 and local branch Pub of the Year 2008. Q (44) P

Long Sutton

Four Horseshoes

RG29 1TA (1 mile E of village centre) SU748471
12-2.30 (not Mon & Tue), 6.30-11; 12-2.30 Sun
(01256) 862488 fourhorseshoes.com

Beer range varies 🄷
Next to Lord Wandsworth College, this friendly local has a single bar divided by a fireplace. A small enclosed veranda at the front offers fine views over the surrounding countryside. The car park is on the opposite side of the road, where there is also a grassed area for camping. Home-cooked meals are tasty and reasonably priced. Up to three beers are available, usually under 4% ABV, with Fuller's and Archers well represented, plus an occasional mild.

Lower Upham

Woodman

Winchester Road, SO32 1HA (on B2177, by B3037 jct)
12-2.30 (6.15 Sat & Sun), 7.15-11
☎ (01489) 860270
Greene King IPA; guest beers 🄷
Members of the same family have provided a welcome at the Woodman for five decades. It has two bars: one a cosy lounge, the other a more basic public bar. As well as well-kept ales, including guests from Greene King's list, there is also a choice of 180 whiskies. Events include a Sausage Saturday in March, a mini beer festival on the nearest Saturday to St George's Day, and live blues on the first Wednesday of the month.
(69)

Medstead

Castle of Comfort

Castle Street, GU34 5LU
11.30-2.30 (3 Sat), 6-11; 12-3, 6-11 Sun
☎ (01420) 562112
Courage Best Bitter; Greene King IPA; Hook Norton Hooky Best; guest beer 🄷
Tucked behind the church, this 17th-century village local has a public bar and a small lounge which feels more like a family living room, with a wood-burning stove set in a large fireplace. The pub has a large garden and a sun-trap drinking area outside at the front. Fine floral displays decorate the establishment and bar food is available at lunchtimes. The Castle is a perfect stopping-off place for ramblers. (28)

Milford on Sea

Red Lion

32 High Street, SO41 0QD (on B3058, off A337 at Everton)
11.30-2.30, 6-11; 12-3, 7-10.30 Sun
☎ (01590) 642236
Fuller's London Pride; Ringwood Best Bitter; guest beers 🄷
Imposing 18th-century inn, comfortable, friendly and relaxing, with a notable feature fireplace. The single bar area is split up and arranged on several levels to give a multi-roomed feel. Carpeting throughout plus the absence of any mechanical music or gaming engenders peace. One area is reserved for pool and darts and the dining area can be used by drinkers when food service finishes. Real cider is served during summer months. Overnight accommodation consists en-suite rooms.

Monxton

Black Swan

The High Street, SP11 8AW
12-11 (10.30 Sun)
☎ (01264) 710260 theblackswanmonxton.co.uk
Fuller's London Pride; Ringwood Best Bitter; Taylor Landlord; guest beer 🄷
Classic English country pub in a quaint village that boasts the highest number of thatch roofs per resident in England. The pub dates from 1662 and was once a travellers' rest run by the Monxton Brewery. It is cosy and clean with low ceilings and a separate restaurant area. Dogs are allowed in the bar and the garden, but not in the restaurant area. Car parking is by the village green.

North Gorley

Royal Oak

Ringwood Road, SP6 2PB (1½m S of Fordingbridge, ½m E of A338) SU161119
12-11
☎ (01425) 652244 royaloakgorley.co.uk
Ringwood Best Bitter; guest beers 🄷
First time in the Guide for this imposing, thatched, New Forest Inn, originally a royal hunting lodge that became a pub in 1820. It is a quiet haven in winter (no food Sunday and Monday evenings) while during the summer it caters for many visitors and families. Guest beers often include a second Ringwood beer, with a wider range available in the summer. Music is important here, as the landlord was a professional musician; check the website for details. (X3)

Oakhanger

Red Lion

GU35 9JQ
12-3, 6-11 (not Sun eve)
☎ (01420) 472232
Courage Best Bitter; Ringwood Fortyniner; guest beer 🄷
Dating from the 16th century and once known as the Rising Sun, the pub is run by Nick (chef) and Gail (beer) who provide quality food and ale; the latter is regularly sourced from SIBA. Separate entrances open into the public bar and lounge, with a huge fireplace, which has been extended into the original publican's accommodation. At the rear is a large private garden and the pub is handy for walkers on the Hangers Way. Dogs are welcome.

Old Basing

Crown Inn

The Street, RG24 7BW (next to Old Basing House)
11-3, 5-11; 11-11.30 Fri & Sat; 11.30-10.30 Sun
☎ (01256) 321424 thecrownoldbasing.co.uk
Fuller's London Pride; guest beers 🄷
A Grade II-listed building dating from the Civil War when Oliver Cromwell's Roundheads laid siege to Basing House. The inn is home to the Hawkins Regiment of the re-enactment

society and a microlight club. There are two bars, one a cosy snug and one with wheelchair access. Food is available every day and includes tapas, which are very popular. Two of the three guest beers are always from local micro-breweries. Glasses are oversized, except branded ones, and smokers have a covered area. At the rear is a garden with a children's play area.
(12)P

Overton

Red Lion

37 High Street, RG25 3HQ (300m W of village centre on B3400)
11.30-3, 6-11; 12-4, 6-10.30 (closed eves Nov-Mar) Sun
(01256) 773363
Flowerpots Bitter; Triple fff Moondance; guest beer
Just a short walk from the centre of the village, the Red Lion is gaining a good reputation for high quality food at reasonable prices. As well as the main menu, which includes a vegetarian dish, there are daily specials. Three tastefully decorated separate areas include a restaurant (bookings advisable) and a cosy snug, with the main bar sandwiched between the two. A good-sized garden with a covered wooden patio overlooks the car park. The staff are friendly, extremely efficient and attentive. P

Portsmouth

Artillery Arms

Hester Road, Southsea, PO4 8HB
12-3, 6-11.30; 12-11.30 Fri-Sun
(023) 9273 3610
Bowman Swift One; Fuller's London Pride; Ringwood Fortyniner; guest beers
Typical back-street drinkers' local, with a lively public bar and a much quieter lounge bar, situated just a 15-minute walk away from Fratton Park. Up to four ever-changing guest beers are sourced mainly from southern breweries. The pub gets very busy when Portsmouth FC plays at home. A variety of filled rolls are available all week and well recommended lunches served on a Sunday. A heated and covered area for smokers has been provided. P

Barley Mow

39 Castle Road, Southsea, PO5 3DE
12 (11 Sat)-midnight; 12-11 Sun
(023) 9282 3492
Fuller's London Pride; Gale's HSB; guest beers
Traditional Victorian local corner pub. The public bar has a pool table and dartboard, with games available across the bar. The lounge bar is wood panelled with pictures and information about the area and the Battle of Southsea in 1874 on display. There are four changing beers, one usually a mild, plus two standard beers. Bar snacks are served throughout the day. This lively community pub hosts regular events that include quizzes, darts, pool, live music and a meat raffle.

Eastfield Hotel

124 Prince Albert Road, Southsea, PO4 9HT
11-11 (midnight Fri & Sat); 12-11 Sun
(023) 9275 0102
Fuller's London Pride; Hogs Back TEA; guest beers
Built in 1906 by the famous pub architect A E Cogswell, this large, imposing Edwardian pub hidden away in the backstreets of Eastney still proudly displays its original windows and tiled exterior. A large, boisterous public bar shows TV sport and supports both darts and pool teams, while a quieter, more select lounge sports original wood panelling. The guest beers are sourced from a wide range of independent breweries. Q

Fifth Hants Volunteer Arms

74 Albert Road, Southsea, PO5 2SL
3-midnight; 12-1am Fri-Sun
(023) 9282 7161
Fuller's London Pride; Gale's Butser Bitter, HSB
A solidly traditional two-bar street-corner local, the Fifth Hants retains its atmosphere following a sensitive redecoration of both bars. A plaque on the front wall commemorates the founding of the local CAMRA branch and certificates in the lounge bar show the number of years that the pub has featured in this Guide. The public bar has one of the best jukeboxes in town and the lounge displays military memorabilia relating to the pub's name.

Florence Arms

18-20 Florence Road, Southsea, PO5 2NE
12-midnight (11 Sun)
(023) 9287 5700
Adnams Bitter, Broadside; Shepherd Neame Spitfire; guest beers
One of Southsea's hidden gems, the 'Flo' has a genuine public bar, a quieter, more select lounge and a dining room serving excellent home-cooked food. Guest beers come from local independent breweries, each featuring for a month at a time. One of the main attractions is the excellent range of cider and perry, with at least 12 real ciders and perries on draught, and more than 40 in bottles. Food is not served on Saturday or Sunday evenings.
Q

Golden Eagle

1 Delamere Road, Southsea, PO4 0JA
3-11.30; 12-midnight Fri & Sat; 12-10.30 Sun
(023) 9282 1658
Fuller's Chiswick Bitter, Discovery, London Pride; Gale's HSB
Situated on the strangely routed Fawcett Road from Fratton Station to Albert Road, this back-street local has the reverse of a normal pub layout, with the pool table in the lounge. The outside smoking area has heating and a TV to prevent smokers from missing the action. The Eagle and its customers regularly raise money for charity. Live music is played most weekends and there are active darts and pool teams, so this can be a lively pub.
(Fratton)

Hole in the Wall

36 Great Southsea Street, Southsea, PO5 3BY
4-11; 12-2, 4-midnight Fri; 4-midnight Sat

☎ (023) 9229 8085 🌐 theholeinthewallpub.co.uk
Oakleaf Hole Hearted; guest beers 🄷/🄶
CAMRA branch Pub of the Year 2007 and popular with both locals and visitors, the 'Hole' is a small one-bar free house with an ever-changing range of ales from near and far, as the display of pump clips from the last three years testifies. Hole Hearted beer, named after the pub, is always on sale, while up to seven guest beers change constantly. Real cider is served. There is no admittance after 11pm. ◗⇌🚌♠▢

Leopold Tavern

154 Albert Road, Southsea, PO4 0JT
🕘 10-11 (midnight Fri & Sat); 12-11 Sun
☎ (023) 9282 9748
Bowman Swift One; Greene King Abbot; Hop Back Summer Lightning; Oakleaf Hole Hearted; guest beer 🄷
This traditional Victorian street-corner pub with a green-tiled exterior has recently undergone a tasteful internal refurbishment. It retains the island bar and original drinking areas, but at the rear a heated beer garden has been added for the use of smoking and non-smoking patrons alike. Myriad diversions are offered to customers in this much-improved gem, whose rationale is the purveyance of the highest quality real ale. It can be extremely busy during weekend evenings. ❀🚌(17,18)♣⚊

Pembroke

20 Pembroke Road, Old Portsmouth, PO1 2NR
🕘 10-midnight (11 Mon); 12-4, 7-11 Sun
☎ (023) 9282 3961
Draught Bass; Fuller's London Pride; Greene King Abbot 🄷
Built as a pub in 1711, this corner-sited, horseshoe-shaped bar was originally called the Little Blue Line, but became the Pembroke in 1900. This unchanging haven for discerning drinkers attracts a varied clientele. Efficient and friendly staff dispense excellent quality real ale from an L-shaped servery that offers the best pint of Pride in Portsmouth.
♨◖♿🚌(6)

Phoenix

13 Duncan Road, Southsea, PO5 2QU
🕘 10-midnight (1am Fri & Sat); 12-midnight Sun
☎ (023) 9278 1055
Beer range varies 🄷
A typical street-corner local with two bars and a separate games room. The excellent walled garden that separates the bars from the games room incorporates a covered area for smokers. One wall of the games room used to be part of the defunct Dock Mill brewery which burnt down and was rebuilt as the appropriately named Phoenix brewery, now also closed. The beers are mainly sourced from small local breweries such as Hampshire, Hogs Back, Irving and Ringwood. ❀🚂🚌♣⚊

Taswell Arms

42 Taswell Road, Southsea, PO5 2RG
🕘 12-midnight (11 Sun)
☎ (023) 9285 1301
Gale's HSB; Shepherd Neame Spitfire; Taylor Landlord 🄷
Following several previous uses, this Victorian building has now settled into its present incarnation as a comfortable community pub. It has just one bar but the customer area is on two levels with a basic bar area plus a quieter zone with plenty of comfortable seating. Offering two outside seating areas, excellent service and fine beer quality, this pub is well worth searching out. Disabled entry is via a street-level double door (ask for access).
❀◖◗♿🚌(17,18)♣♠

Winchester Arms

99 Winchester Road, Buckland, PO2 7PS
🕘 12 (4 Mon)-11
☎ (023) 9266 2443
Oakleaf Hole Hearted; Shepherd Neame Spitfire; guest beers 🄷
Friendly two-bar local, hidden among the terraced backs treets of Portsmouth. Quiz night is Monday and live music plays on Sunday evening. The pub has its own darts and football teams and hosts the local science fiction group on the second Tuesday of the month.There is a covered smoking area in the garden. The pub may stay open until midnight at weekends if busy. ♨Q❀🚂♣⚊

Priors Dean

White Horse (Pub With No Name)

★ ✔
GU32 1DA (¼ mile from A32 to Petersfield road)
SU715290
🕘 12-3, 6-11; 12-11 Fri-Sun
☎ (01420) 588387 🌐 stuartinns.com
Fuller's London Pride; Ringwood Fortyniner; guest beer 🄷
A well-known but lonely hostelry which is hard to find because its pub sign blew down many years ago. Surrounded by fields, this 'pub with no name' has a large garden with a pond. Two separate bars are supplemented by a restaurant, and 10 beers are served, generally from independent brewers. The two house beers are from Fuller's and Ringwood. A longest-day beer festival, with up to 100 beers, is held on the weekend nearest to 21st June. ♨Q❀◖◗🚂♿⛺♠P

Ringwood

Inn on the Furlong ✔

12 Meeting House Lane, BH24 1EY
🕘 11-11 (midnight Fri & Sat); 12-11 Sun
☎ (01425) 475139
Ringwood Best Bitter, Fortyniner, Old Thumper, seasonal beers 🄷
As a private house, this cream-painted Victorian building escaped demolition in 1985 to become Ringwood's first pub. Situated in the heart of a fine market town, by the main car park and bus terminus, it has a single, large, flag stoned bar that serves several linked areas including a sunny conservatory and a family area. Although generally a quiet pub, it can be a busy and lively meeting place for more mature customers. No meals are available on Sunday and Tuesday evenings when there may be live music.
♨Q🚼❀◖◗♿⛺🚌♣⚊

Romsey

Abbey Hotel

11 Church Street, SO51 8BT
11-3, 6-11; 12-3, 7-10.30 Sun
(01794) 513360 abbeyhotelromsey.co.uk
Courage Best Bitter, Directors; Young's Bitter H
Located directly east of the Abbey, the Abbey Hotel is a peaceful, civilised place. Entering beneath the Courage-inscribed lintel, a dining room and a large, comfortable lounge are just right for conversation. The hidden garden, with small stream and view of the 13th-century King John's Lodge, is delightful, as are the hanging flower basket displays in summer. Food is available every day except Sunday evening when a quiz takes precedence. The hotel has seven bedrooms.
Q P

Old House at Home

62 Love Lane, SO51 8DE
11-3, 5-11 (11.30 Sat); 12-4, 7-10.30 Sun
(01794) 513175
Fuller's London Pride, Discovery; Gale's Butser Bitter, HSB H
Spacious and busy gastro-pub with a traditional interior and, unusually for the town, a thatched roof, popular with locals during their lunch breaks. Interesting period pieces decorate the walls and Toby jugs hang above the bar. A separate side room is used mainly for diners and there are two other seating areas. Food is modestly priced and made with local ingredients where possible (no meals Sun eve). At the rear is a large walled garden. Q

Tudor Rose

3 The Cornmarket, SO51 8GB
10-11; 11-midnight Fri & Sat; 12-11 Sun
(01794) 512126
Courage Best Bitter; Hampshire Ironside; Shepherd Neame Spitfire; guest beer H
A small, modest pub, open long hours for the benefit of local shoppers and workers, facing the central Cornmarket, close to the bus station.The building's history is long and chequered – at times it has served as a workhouse, a brothel and a guildhall. A single, square bar has a fine ceiling and a 15th-century fireplace. Various musical entertainments take place at weekends. The cider is Thatchers and the Ironside is often re-badged as Totally Tudor. Outside is a covered and heated courtyard.

Rowlands Castle

Castle Inn

1 Finchdean Road, PO9 6DA
11-midnight
(023) 9241 2494
Fuller's London Pride, seasonal beers; Gale's Butser Bitter, HSB; guest beer H
A cosy two-bar pub on the eastern edge of the village behind the railway bridge. The floors are bare wood or stone and the open fires provide a welcoming atmosphere, especially after enjoying a walk across the nearby South Downs or Forest of Bere. The pub is also handy for both Stanstead House and Staunton Park. Good quality home-cooked food complements the beer range, making this a pub well worth seeking out. P

Selborne

Selborne Arms

High Street, GU34 3JR
11-3, 6 (5.30 Fri)-11; 11-11 Sat summer; 12-11 Sun
(01420) 511247
Courage Best Bitter; Oakleaf Suthwyck Bloomfield Bitter; Ringwood Fortyniner; guest beers H
Traditional village pub in a building that dates back to the 1600s, retaining original features including a log fire. It can be found at the bottom of Selborne Hanger and the famous zigzag path carved by naturalist Gilbert White. The guest beers showcase local micro-breweries, while the award-winning menu also features local produce. Extensive outside facilities include a covered patio heated with wood-burning fires, a play area for children and a fantastic barbecue.
Q (72,X72)P

Shedfield

Wheatsheaf Inn

Botley Road, SO32 2JG (on A334)
12-11 (10.30 Sun)
(01329) 833024
Flowerpots Bitter, Gooden's Gold, seasonal beer; guest beers G
Old-fashioned village inn, under the same ownership as the Flower Pots at Cheriton. Five or six beers are served directly from a two-level stillage behind the bar. Apart from Flowerpots, other local breweries are favoured, including Oakleaf, Ringwood and Stonehenge. Cheddar Valley cider is stocked. Blues or jazz groups play on Saturdays and a beer festival is held during the late Spring bank holiday. Evening meals are only available on Tuesday and Wednesday. Parking is across a busy road. Q P

Southampton

Bitter Virtue (off-licence)

70 Cambridge Road, SO14 6US (take Alma Rd from The Avenue, by church, 250m)
10.30-8.30 (not Mon); 10.30-2 Sun
(023) 8055 4881 bittervirtue.co.uk
Beer range varies G
Going strong since 1997, this off-licence sells beers from Belgium, Germany, Czech Republic, USA micros, Netherlands plus British bottled beers (some 350 in total). This may be why Bitter Virtue was voted one of the top three independent beer retailers at the Drinks Retailing Awards ceremony in 2005. In 2006 it was second. Two draught beers are always on sale, as are polypins. Bottled ciders (and draught in summer) are also sold. There is an extensive selection of books, T-shirts and glasses.

Cricketers Arms

34 Carlton Place, SO15 2DX (50m W of London Road)
12-midnight (1am Thu-Sat)
(023) 8022 6448

Beer range varies Ⓗ
Town pub situated in a conservation area of many fine Regency buildings, popular with the student community. It has a single horseshoe-shaped bar and an outdoor courtyard for smokers and drinkers. Three handpumps serve an ever-changing range of beers, favouring small breweries and frequently including ales from Oakleaf or Goddards. Lunches are served daily and on Sundays roasts are available lunchtimes and evenings. There is live jazz, a DJ on Sunday evening, a Monday quiz night and an annual beer festival.

Dolphin

30 Osborne Road South, St Denys, SO17 2EZ (over footbridge from St Denys station)
4-10.30 Mon; 4-11 Tue; 12-11 Wed-Thu; 12-midnight Fri & Sat; 12-10.30 Sun
☎ (023) 8039 9369 southampton-pubs.co.uk/dolphin
Adnams Broadside; Bowman Swift One; Gale's HSB; Ringwood Best Bitter; Taylor Landlord; guest beers Ⓗ
A single-bar, cosy pub with original features, once owned by the Cooper's Brewery. There is something for everyone here – many drinking areas, a garden and a covered heated area for smokers – making it a great pub in which to catch up with old friends. Changes to the pub over time are clear – the beer cellar door is in the middle of the bar. Live music is performed on Tuesday and Wednesday and families are welcome until 6pm. Old Rosie cider is served.
(St Denys) P

Fleming Arms

Wide Lane, Swaythling, SO18 2QN
11-11; 12-10.30 Sun
☎ (023) 8058 4358
Fuller's London Pride; Gale's HSB Ⓗ
Close to Southampton airport and the M27 (junction 5), this handsome, three-storey, Georgian building has dormer windows and two pillared porches, with a relief of the eponymous heraldry above one of them. The split-level interior has been extended and modernised over the years and is divided into several discrete, uncluttered areas, with much bare brickwork. The patio has a covered and heated area that may be enjoyed by smokers. Food is available all day on Sunday.
(Swaythling) P

Giddy Bridge

10-16 London Road, SO15 2AE
9-11.30
☎ (023) 8033 6346
Courage Directors; Greene King Abbot; Marston's Pedigree; Ringwood Best Bitter, Fortyniner, Old Thumper; guest beers Ⓗ
This converted furniture shop in a large, glass-fronted building has two levels with easy access to bar seating in booths or at tables. A patio smoking area is at roof level, with further seating outside. The pub is well worth the short walk from the city centre and is popular with students. Guest ales from all over the UK are available, with a 'try before you buy' policy. Beer festivals are held twice yearly; Weston's Organic Vintage and Old Rosie ciders are served.

Guide Dog

38 Earl's Road, Bevois Valley, SO14 6SF (100m W of Bevois Valley Rd, opp Aldi)
3 (12 Sat)-11; 12-10.30 Sun
☎ (023) 8022 5642
Bowman Swift One; Fuller's ESB; guest beers Ⓗ
Genuine free house with seven handpumped beers including guests mostly from local brewers, plus a selection of foreign bottled brews. The pub is welcoming at all times and situated a convenient walk from St Mary's football ground – the Saints' result may affect the normally relaxed atmosphere. The landlady's previous life as a junior teacher sometimes shows —check out the Friday meat draw. Occasional quizzes, darts competitions and other events provide a steady charity income. The October beer festival is well supported. Local CAMRA Pub of the Year 2008.
(St Denys)

Humble Plumb ✔

Commercial Street, Bitterne, SO18 6LY
11.30 (12.30 Mon)-2.30, 5-11; 11.30-11 Fri & Sat; 12-10.30 Sun
☎ (023) 8043 7577
Jennings Sneck Lifter; Wadworth IPA, Ⓗ **6X,** Ⓖ **Horizon, Bishop's Tipple; guest beers** Ⓗ
Cask Marque accredited, friendly local in Southampton's quiet suburb of Bitterne. An excellent range of ales changes regularly and this is a rare outlet for 6X dispensed by gravity from wooden casks. All beers are on a 'try before you buy' basis. Quality home-cooked food is available lunchtimes and evenings daily except Sunday evening. Outside is a colourful garden and covered, heated patio for smokers. A meat draw is held on Sunday and quiz night is Monday. Car parking is behind the pub. P

Kolebka

42-44 Bevois Valley Road, Bevois Valley, SO14 0JR (at the bottom of Bevois Valley, look for purple lights at night)
3-midnight (2am Fri & Sat)
☎ (023) 8021 1115
Young's Bitter; guest beers Ⓗ
A relaxed bar catering for a variety of tastes. Two guest beers usually supplement the regular brew, in addition to an impressive range of cocktails, wines and whiskies. Some of the original pub features including fireplaces and ledges have been retained, and a mix of seating, including sofas, makes for comfortable drinking. In summer barbecues are held on the large patio to the rear. Live jazz acts perform most Fridays, acoustic sets are on Sunday and the jukebox steps in at other times.

Park Inn

37 Carlisle Road, Shirley, SO16 4FN (at jct of Shirley Park Road)
11.30-midnight
☎ (023) 8078 7835
Wadworth IPA, 6X, Bishop's Tipple, seasonal beers; guest beer Ⓗ
Dating from the 1860s, this friendly, community local became a Wadworth hostelry in the 1980s. A single bar pub, it still retains a 'two-bar' feeling. A collection of mirrors adorns the walls and a paved, tabled area

outside is used for summer drinking, with a canopied spot for smokers. Darts and cribbage are played regularly by the locals. Six handpumps serve the Wadworth range together with a guest beer. Sunday has a popular lunchtime meat draw and an evening quiz. ❀🚌♣⚟

Richmond Inn ✔

108 Portswood Road, Portswood, SO17 2FW

⏲ 11-11 (midnight Fri & Sat)

☎ (023) 8055 4523

Greene King IPA, Abbot; guest beer Ⓗ

A traditional two-bar town pub with a magnificent brass LSD till still in use. There is a public bar featuring both TV and jukebox, and a lounge bar, decorated with pictures of ocean liners, that is quieter and more peaceful. Efforts have been made to make smokers comfortable with a covered, heated area equipped with solid garden furniture; beyond is a pleasant secluded garden. The recently redecorated meeting room is an unusual and welcome feature in a town pub.
❀⊟≋(St Denys)🚌♣⚟

South Western Arms

38-40 Adelaide Road, St Denys, SO17 2HW
(adjoins E side of St Denys Station)

⏲ 12-11 (midnight Fri & Sat)

☎ (023) 8032 4542

Butcombe Bitter; Caledonian Deuchars IPA; Sharp's Cornish Coaster; guest beers Ⓗ

Popular community pub and a regular local CAMRA Pub of the Year award winner, boasting a large selection of real ales and draught cider. Pump clips of upcoming beers are displayed together with old inn paraphernalia on the walls. The large main bar has a mezzanine level with pool, darts and table football. A pleasant, secluded garden includes a covered and heated smoking area. A meat draw takes place on Thursday and there is an annual beer festival.
❀≋(St Denys)🚌♣●P⚟

Waterloo Arms

101 Waterloo Road, Freemantle, SO15 3BS (next to church)

⏲ 12-11

☎ (023) 8022 0022

Hop Back GFB, Crop Circle, Entire Stout, Summer Lightning, seasonal beers; guest beer Ⓗ

Dating from the 1860s, this pub became a Hop Back tied house in 1991. It has a single L-shaped bar, a rear conservatory and beyond that a paved garden for outside drinkers and smokers. Eight handpumps serve the full Hop Back range plus a guest beer, and there are two annual beer festivals. Families are welcome until 9pm. Food is served every lunchtime and evening, while Tuesday evening features a popular quiz. Both Southampton Central and Milbrook stations are within reach.
❀❀◐≋(Millbrook/Central)🚌⚟

Wellington Arms

56 Park Road, Freemantle, SO15 3DE (jct of Mansion Road)

⏲ 12-11.30 (12.30am Fri & Sat)

☎ (023) 8022 0356

Adnams Bitter; Fuller's London Pride; Greene King Abbot; Ringwood Best Bitter; Wychwood Hobgoblin; guest beers Ⓗ

Dating from the 1860s, this friendly, two-bar local is now a Punch Tavern. Two guest beers complement the five regular offerings, with Hoegaarden and Leffe Blonde also featuring. The unique bars are set with hundreds of old coins and there is much Iron Duke memorabilia. The main bar has a number of boxed settles allowing for privacy. A paved garden, reached through a third room with more seating, caters for outside drinking and smoking. Thursday night has a popular quiz.
❀⊟≋(Millbrook/Central)🚌

Stockbridge

White Hart ✔

High Street, SO20 6HF (opp A30 roundabout)

⏲ 11-11; 12-10.30 Sun

☎ (01264) 810663

Fuller's London Pride; Gale's HSB; guest beer Ⓗ

This 12th-century building is just a small part of the beautiful town of Stockbridge and an ideal base from which to explore the Test Valley on foot. It has two large car parks with a large garden. A good selection of real ales is offered, plus fresh food made to order using only British meat. Thirteen different wines are sold by the glass. Shove ha'penny is among the traditional games played here. the accommodation has been awarded four diamonds by Quality in Tourism.
Q❀🛏◐♿🚌♣P⚟▯

Tadley

Bishopswood Golf Club

Bishopswood Lane, RG26 4AT (6 miles N of Basingstoke, off A340) SU591617

⏲ 11-11 (9 Mon) summer; 11-11 (6.30 Mon, 9.30 Tue & Thu) winter; 11 (12 winter)-7 Sun

☎ (0118) 981 2200 🌐 bishopswoodgc.co.uk

Beer range varies Ⓗ

The comfortable lounge requires a dress code at this club but the public bar does not. Outside, a raised terrace overlooks the golf course which can be also be seen from the lounge. A frequent winner of local CAMRA branch awards, it has two handpumps, one for beers of 4.2% ABV and above, and one below. A constantly changing selection of ales is provided, from both local and distant breweries. Food is served 12-3pm and 7-9pm (not Monday, or Tuesday and Sunday evenings). A restaurant is available on the upper floor. ❀◐⊟♿🚌♣P⚟

Tangley

Cricketers Arms

SP11 0SH (in village, towards Lower Chute) SU327528

⏲ 11-3 (not Mon), 6-11; 12-3, 7-10.30 Sun

☎ (01264) 730283 🌐 thecricketers.eu

Bowman Swift One, Wallops Wood Ⓖ

Situated in attractive countryside, this dog-friendly, 16th-century drovers' inn sits below the Berkshire downs, on the border with Wiltshire. The two Bowman ales, served from stillage behind the bar, are often supplemented in summer months by one or two local guests. The front bar, with its huge inglenook fireplace, is used mainly for drinking, while traditional home-cooked food is served in the flag stoned dining area at the rear. Behind the pub is a large Scandinavian-style wooden chalet with 10 en-suite bedrooms. ⌂Q❀⊭◐♿P⁻

Tichborne

Tichborne Arms

SO24 0NA SU571304

✪ 11.30-3 (may close earlier in winter), 6.30-11.30; 12-3, 7-11 Sun

☎ (01962) 733760

Ringwood Best Bitter; guest beers Ⓖ

This two-bar village inn includes a small, wood-panelled public bar with traditional games such as darts and shove ha'penny, plus a larger, wainscoted lounge with dining tables. Beers are served directly from their casks (jacketed and cooled) behind the bar, with guest ales usually coming from local brewers such as Bowman, Flowerpots and Hampshire. An extensive menu is served daily except Sunday evening, with many specials including local products. Thatchers cider is stocked. A large garden includes a covered, heated patio. Q❀◐⊟♣●P⁻

Titchfield

Wheatsheaf

1 East Street, PO14 4AD

✪ 12-3, 6-11; 12-11 Fri & Sat; 12-10.30 Sun

☎ (01329) 842965

Flowerpots Bitter; guest beers Ⓗ

The Wheatsheaf is a 17th-century free house situated near the centre of this picturesque village. The premises comprise a large main bar full of jocular locals, a tiny snug, a family dining room and a large garden. The two guest beers sometimes also come from the Flowerpots' range. The licensee is a qualified chef who has established a reputation for his cuisine. No food is served on Sunday night or all day Monday. ⌂❀◐⊟P

Upper Farringdon

Rose & Crown Inn

Crows Lane, GU34 3ED (signed off A32 at Farringdon Crossroads)

✪ 12-3, 6-11; 12-11 Sat; 12-10.30 Sun

☎ (01420) 588231

Adnams Bitter; Greene King IPA; guest beers Ⓗ

Off the beaten track, enter this friendly pub to find an L-shaped bar where games can be played in a cosy seating area warmed by a log fire. Deeper inside is a formal dining area leading to a modern restaurant (no food Mon eve). An imaginative menu is supplemented with lunchtime bar snacks. Families, walkers and dogs are always welcome and there is a spacious garden. Guest beers often come from the Triple fff Brewery. A monthly traditional jazz evening is held. ⌂Q❀⊭◐⊟♣P⁻

West Meon

Thomas Lord

High Street, GU32 1LN (300m E of A32)

✪ 11-3, 6-11.30 (6.30-midnight Fri); 11-midnight Sat; 12-11 Sun

☎ (01730) 829244

Ringwood Best Bitter; Ⓗ **guest beers** Ⓗ/Ⓖ

At the centre of village life, this homely pub has no music to disturb conversation. Three beers are served by handpump, with up to six further beers on gravity, all from Hampshire breweries. The superb food is sourced as locally as possible, with much of it coming from the pub's own garden, a large area that is safe for children. Meals are not served on Sunday evening. ⌂Q❀◐⊟(67)P

Whitchurch

Bell Inn

Bell Street, RG28 7DD

✪ 11 (12 Sun)-11

☎ (01256) 893120

Courage Best Bitter; Gale's HSB; Goddards Fuggle-Dee-Dum, Special Bitter Ⓗ

Whitchurch is renowned for its community pubs and the half-timbered, family-run Bell is one of the town's oldest and most traditional. Two bars and a separate higher area off the lounge provide exposed beams and space for enjoying a quiet pint in this rare outlet for Goddards beers (from the Isle of Wight). Conversation and local gossip rule here. There is a small, pleasant patio at the rear and a pool table in the public bar. You can view other Whitchurch pubs online at whitchurchpubguide.org.uk. Q❀◑⊟⊟(76,86)

Whitchurch Sports & Social Club

Longmeadow Sports Centre, Winchester Road, RG28 7RB (S edge of town, by football ground)

✪ 7-11; 12-10.30 Sun

☎ (01256) 892493

Beer range varies Ⓗ

Tucked away opposite the tranquil Millennium Meadow, this excellent club features two large bars which are open in the evening and at the weekend. As well as being home to Whitchurch United Football Club, the venue is shared by the indoor Bowling Club whose impressive green can be viewed from the comfortable lounge bar. It also has two squash courts. Regular events include parties, discos and the annual Whitchurch Beer Festival, which focuses on beers from Hampshire breweries. CAMRA members are welcome on production of a membership card. Check opening hours as they can vary. ⊟♿P⁻

White Hart Hotel ✔

The Square, RG28 7DN

✪ 11 (12 Sun)-11

☎ (01256) 892900

Arkell's Moonlight Ale, Kingsdown Ale, 3B Ⓗ

Impressive, comfortable 15th-century historic coaching inn owned by Arkell's Brewery, with several separate areas. The popular public bar is lively at weekends, and occasional live music/discos are held. To the rear is a restaurant and quiet dining area. Breakfast is available from 8am, and cream teas are served in summer. Local artists' work adorns

the walls. There is a small outside patio. The Square outside is where the 'right to demonstrate' was won for the country – the event marked by a plaque.
Q❀⇌◐ ⊟♿⊟P⊱

Wickham

Greens

The Square, PO17 5JQ
✪ 11-3, 6-11; closed Mon; 12-4 Sun
☎ (01329) 833197 ⊕ greensrestaurant.co.uk
Bowman Swift One; guest beer ⊞
The building is around 100 years old, with a restaurant and bar overlooking the square and a modern interior divided into several areas including a function room. An emphasis on food means that the real ale is served in oversized glasses, rare for this area. The garden overlooks Wickham Water Meadows and hosts special events in the summer. The gourmet menu uses fresh locally-sourced ingredients and the Local Produce Lunch Menu, served Tuesday to Saturday, is good value. Q❀◐♿⊟

Wickham Wine Bar

The Square, PO17 5JN
✪ 11.30-2, 5.30-11; closed Sun
☎ (01329) 832732 ⊕ wickhamwinebar.com
Bowman Swift One ⊞
This wine bar and restaurant are in a listed 15th-century building featuring original oak beams and a warming open log fire. Sometimes a different Bowman ale may be substituted for Swift One. The two-storey upstairs restaurant features an original 16th-century wall painting, and the garden has its own vine. Food includes fresh fish and game, and other locally sourced produce. On Wednesday evenings the ground-floor bar is cleared to make way for live jazz. ⩕Q❀◐⊟

Widley

George Inn

Portsdown Hill Road, PO6 1BE
✪ 11-11.30 (11 Sun)
☎ (023) 9222 1079
Adnams Broadside; Flowers Original; Fuller's London Pride; Greene King Old Speckled Hen, Abbot; Ringwood Best Bitter; guest beer ⊞
Set on the site of a coaching inn on the hill north of Portsmouth, this one-room pub with an island bar serves six regular beers and one guest that changes monthly, with an emphasis on local or unusual micro-brewed beers. Regular quizzes, charity events and club meetings are all on the calendar. Main meals and lighter bites are served at lunchtime only, while traditional pub games include skittles and shove ha'penny. An outdoor patio area with benches has views over Portsmouth.
❀◐⊟♣P

Winchester

Albion

2 Stockbridge Road, SO23 7BZ (200m from station, towards city)
✪ 12-11 (midnight Fri & Sat); 12-10.30 Sun
☎ (01962) 840660
Fuller's London Pride; Taylor Landlord; guest beers ⊞
This corner pub on a busy intersection below the station is a great place for watching the world go by. An assorted clientele includes commuters who step off their trains then forget to go home. No food is served, but you may bring in excellent fare from the sandwich bar next door or there is a superb Indian restaurant nearby. Local artists' work is displayed for sale. Background music is sometimes free-form jazz. The single L-shaped bar can be busy at weekends. ⩕⇌⊟

Bell Inn

83 St Cross Road, St Cross, SO23 9RE (on B3335 at edge of city)
✪ 11-11; 12-10.30 Sun
☎ (01962) 865284
Greene King IPA, Abbot; guest beers ⊞
Solid, comfortable pub retaining two separate bars: a large public bar with a pronounced cricketing theme (the St Cross ground is just metres away), and a small conversational lounge at the rear. Glazed doors lead through to a sheltered, walled garden with several gazebos and a play area. Home-cooked food is served every day. The Bell adjoins the Hospital of St Cross, Britain's oldest almshouse, dating from 1132, and is on a lovely riverside walk from the city centre. ⩕Q❀◐⊟⊟P⊱

Black Boy

1 Wharf Hill, SO23 9NQ (just off Chesil St, B3330)
✪ 12-11 (midnight Fri & Sat); 12-10.30 Sun
☎ (01962) 861754 ⊕ theblackboypub.com
Flowerpots Bitter; Hop Back Summer Lightning; Ringwood Best Bitter; guest beers ⊞
A centuries-old set of rambling buildings comprising many interconnected rooms that resemble a Dali-esque folk museum, surrounding a central bar. One room is themed as a country kitchen complete with working Aga (although the alarming stuffed donkey is a little incongruous), another simulates a butcher's, complete with papier-mâché joints of meat, while other areas look like tradesmen's workshops. Food is pub-grub style but not served on Sunday evening, Monday or Tuesday lunchtime. Two or more guest beers come from small local breweries. Dogs are welcome. ⩕Q❀◐⊱

Eclipse

25 The Square, SO23 9EX (just off pedestrianised High Street)
✪ 11-11 (1am Fri & Sat); 12-10.30 Sun
☎ (01962) 865676 ⊕ eclipseinn.co.uk
Flowers Original; Fuller's London Pride; Ringwood Best Bitter, Old Thumper, seasonal beers ⊞
Tiny, ancient building dating from 1540, which has been an inn since the 1800s. Many of the interior oak beams are original but the Tudor front, although convincing, is from the 1920s. The pub name probably commemorates a fabulous 18th-century racehorse. Its place in history is secured by being the last resting place of Lady Alice Lisle before her execution outside in 1685. An extensive lunchtime menu is available, with Sunday roasts a speciality. A quiz league is held on Wednesday night.
Q❀◐⊟

Hyde Tavern

57 Hyde Street, SO23 7DY (on B3047)

12-3, 5-11.30 (12.30am Fri); 12-12.30am Sat; 12-4, 7-11.30 Sun

☎ (01962) 862592

Beer range varies Ⓗ

Since passing from Greene King to Admiral Taverns, this pub, a conversationalist's haven, is blossoming. A small, medieval, timber-framed building, the exterior is dominated by a fine double-gable frontage. Inside, steps lead down from the street to a bar with low, beamed ceilings and undulating floors and walls. Beers are mostly from local small breweries. Plans are being developed for some internal alterations during 2008 to add more bar space and to allow for improvements to food provision.
⛬Q❀◑⇌🚌⌐

St James' Tavern

3 Romsey Road, SO22 5BE

11.30-2.30, 5.30-11; 11.30-11.30 Sat; 12-3, 6.30-10.30 Sun

☎ (01962) 890018

Butcombe Bitter; Wadworth IPA, 6X, Horizon, seasonal beer Ⓗ

Acutely-angled, end-of-terrace pub on the steep Romsey Road hill with a single split-level L-shaped bar. It is a rare outlet for Butcombe's beer. Much woodwork, including light oak panelling and bare floorboards, gives a generally warm, comfortable ambience. The raised carpeted area right of the entrance with settles and tables is ideal for small group functions. The food menu, available at all sessions, includes locally-made sausages and a good range of vegetarian dishes. Monday nights belong to the quiz league.
Q❀◑⇌🚌⌐

Wykeham Arms ✔

75 Kingsgate Street, SO23 9PE (by entrances to Cathedral Close and college)

11-11; 12-10.30 Sun

☎ (01962) 853834

Fuller's Chiswick, Discovery, London Pride; Gale's Butser, HSB Ⓗ

Rambling, Georgian inn with many interlinked rooms, immediately outside the City's ancient Kingsgate. A vast array of memorabilia, much of it Nelsonian, fills every available wall space. The Wykeham features in virtually every good inn guide as well as this one, and is frequently busy but always utterly civilised – a conversational haven away from 21st-century pressures. Booking is advised for the award-winning food (not served Sun eve). More than 20 wines are available by the glass. Accommodation is top notch. ⛬Q⛿◐◑

Winsor

Compass Inn

Winsor Road, SO40 2HE (½ mile S of A3090)

11-11 (midnight Fri); 12-10.30 Sun

☎ (023) 8081 2237

Fuller's London Pride; Gale's HSB; Greene King Abbot; Ringwood Best Bitter; guest beer Ⓗ

The Compass is a small, neat pub that feels bigger once you get inside. Three rooms include a welcoming lounge with polished wood furniture and a log-burning stove, a sombre, panelled public bar with pool table, and a rustic dining room. Food is served daily. Unusually, there is an artist in residence, with New Forest murals featuring in the Ladies' toilet. Beer festivals are held on May and August bank holidays. Dogs are most welcome. ⛬Q❀◐◑⊟▲🚌(31)♣P

The language of beer

Nose: the aroma. Gently swirl the beer to release the aroma. You will detect malt: grainy and biscuity, often likened to crackers or Ovaltine. When darker malts are used, the nose will have powerful hints of chocolate, coffee, nuts, vanilla, liquorice, molasses and such dried fruits as raisins and sultanas. Hops add superb aromas of resins, herbs, spices, fresh-mown grass and tart citrus fruit – lemon and orange are typical, with intense grapefruit notes from some American varieties. Sulphur may also be present when waters are 'Burtonised': i.e. gypsum and magnesium salts have been added to replicate the famous spring waters of Burton-on-Trent.

Palate: the appeal in the mouth. The tongue can detect sweetness, bitterness and saltiness as the beer passes over it. The rich flavours of malt will come to the fore but hop bitterness will also make a substantial impact. The tongue will also pick out the natural saltiness from the brewing water and fruit from darker malts, yeast and hops. Citrus notes often have a major impact on the palate.

Finish: the aftertaste, as the beer goes over the tongue and down the throat. The finish is often radically different to the nose. The aroma may be dominated by malt whereas hop flavours and bitterness can govern the finish. Darker malts will make their presence felt with roast, chocolate or coffee notes; fruit character may linger. Strong beers may end on a sweet or biscuity note but in mainstream bitters, bitterness and dryness come to the fore.

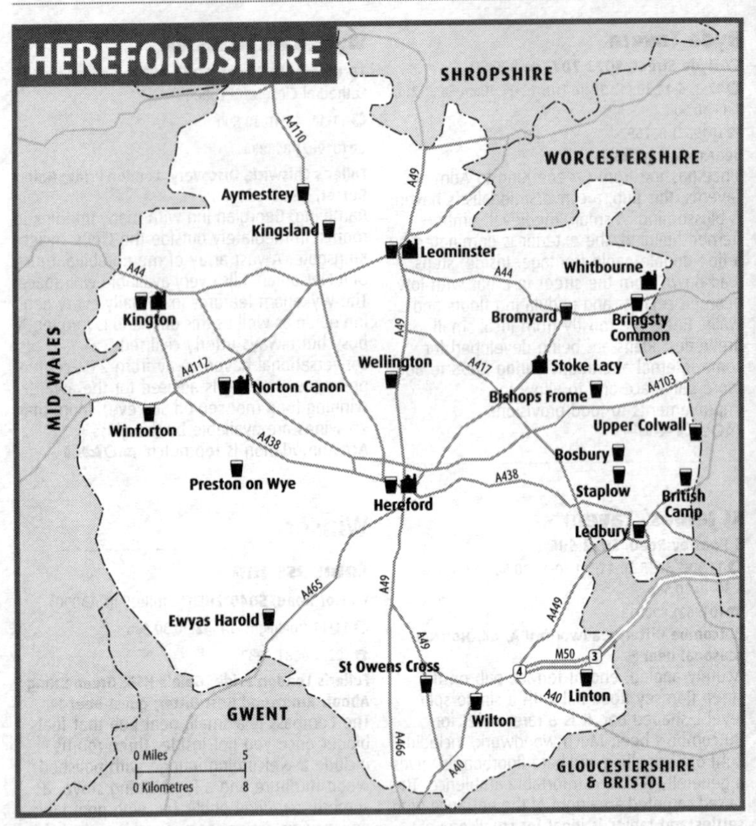

Aymestrey

Riverside Inn

HR6 9ST (on A4110)
⚙ 11-3, 6-11 (closed Mon winter); 12-3, 6-10.30 (not winter eve) Sun
☎ (01568) 708440 🌐 theriversideinn.org
Wye Valley HPA; guest beer ⊞
Always a popular venue for evening and weekend diners, the Riverside does not neglect drinkers with its stylishly-furnished bar areas. An interesting menu of well-presented dishes is available using local meat and home-grown produce, with an accent on traditional English cuisine. The guest beer is from a local brewery. Delightfully situated on the River Lugg, with its own mile of fishing rights, the pub is close to the Mortimer Trail footpath and a number of circular walks. ⌂❀⇌◐P⅟–

Bishops Frome

Green Dragon Inn

WR6 5BP (just off B4214)
⚙ 5 (4 Fri; 12 Sat)-11.15; 12-4, 7-10.45 Sun
☎ (01885) 490607
Taylor Golden Best, Landlord; Theakston Best Bitter; Wye Valley Butty Bach, house beer; guest beer ⊞
The quintessential English village inn – run with total dedication and real enthusiasm. A warm welcome and a bank of six handpumps greet visitors to this unspoilt 17th-century building. The interior features a warren of flagstone-floored rooms, low beams and a real fire in every room. A function room/restaurant has a pull-down TV which screens major sporting events. A limited menu is served until 8.30pm (not Sun), with steaks a speciality. Herefordshire CAMRA Country Pub of the Year 2006 and 2007.
⌂Q❀◐⇌♣♠P⅟–

Bosbury

Bell Inn ✔

HR8 1PS (on B4220)
⚙ 12-2.30 (not Mon), 6-11 (midnight Fri & Sat); 12-2.30, 7-10.30 Sun
☎ (01531) 640285 🌐 thebellatbosbury.co.uk
Adnams Broadside; Hancocks HB; Taylor Landlord ⊞
Two-bar black and white timbered terraced inn opposite the imposing village church. Friendly and welcoming, the pub lies at the heart of the community. A restaurant area serving good food (not Mon or Sun eve)

INDEPENDENT BREWERIES

Arrow Kington
Dunn Plowman Kington
Marches Leominster
Mayfields Leominster
Shoes Norton Canon
Spinning Dog Hereford
Willoughby Whitbourne (NEW)
Wye Valley Stoke Lacy

complements a basic yet comfortable public bar, with grand fireplace, alcoves, books and newspapers. There is a large garden at the rear. Plenty of on-street parking is available.

Bringsty Common

Live & Let Live

WR6 5UW (off A44) SO699547
12-2.30 (not Mon), 5-11; 12-11 Fri & Sat; 12-10.30 Sun
(01886) 821462 liveandletlive-bringsty.co.uk
Malvern Hills Black Pear; guest beer

Isolated on the scenic expanses of Bringsty Common, with views towards the Malvern Hills, this 17th-century thatched Grade-II listed ex-cider house reopened in November 2007 after 11 years of closure. A survivor of four planning applications for conversion to a house and a rejected community buy-out, the new owners have renovated the building to an extraordinarily high standard. Downstairs are flagstone floors, original timbers, settles and a spectacular fireplace with oak overmantle. Upstairs, the Thatch restaurant serves locally-sourced food (not Mon). P

British Camp

Malvern Hills Hotel

Jubilee Drive, WR13 6DW (jct of A449 and B4232)
10-11; 12-10.30 Sun
(01684) 540690 malvernhillshotel.co.uk
Malvern Hills Black Pear; Wye Valley Bitter, HPA; guest beers

Vibrant and welcoming landmark hotel located high on the Malvern Hills, near the Herefordshire Beacon. Run with real passion, it prides itself on offering up to five local beers. The wood-panelled bar is popular with locals and walkers alike (dry dogs and well-behaved children welcome, the latter until 4pm). Bar meals and two restaurants – one with superb views – provide good, affordable dining. Plenty of outside seating makes this an ideal venue for a fine day. P

Bromyard

Rose & Lion

5 New Road, HR7 4AJ
11-3, 5-11; 11-midnight Fri & Sat; 12-10.30 Sun
(01885) 482381
Wye Valley Bitter, HPA, Butty Bach; guest beer

Totally refurbished in late 2007, this three-roomed pub is considered to be a village pub in the town, despite its modern furniture and fittings. Friendly with a lively buzz, it hosts live folk music on Sunday night. Run by Wye Valley Brewery, it enjoys a loyal following among locals, while visitors are warmly welcomed. A large garden is the venue for the annual digging of the parsnips ceremony held in December. P

Ewyas Harold

Dog Inn

HR2 0EX (just off B4347)
10-midnight (1am Fri & Sat); 10-11 Sun
(01981) 240598 thedoginn.org.uk
Beer range varies

Stone-built village inn dating from the early 16th century, with a main bar, games room and restaurant. Three ever-changing beers are drawn from micro-breweries, mainly local. Home-prepared and locally-sourced meals are served in the restaurant and in the bar at lunchtimes. Live music features from time to time, and a beer festival is held annually in the autumn. Two cricket teams and a football team are based here.

Hereford

Barrels

69 St Owen Street, HR1 2JQ
11-11.30 (midnight Fri & Sat)
(01432) 274968
Wye Valley Bitter, HPA, Dorothy Goodbody's Golden Ale, Butty Bach; guest beers

This Hereford landmark enjoys a near cult following. Four times CAMRA Herefordshire Pub of the Year, it has four basic and distinct bars appealing to a wide clientele. A pool table occupies one bar, another has a pull-down TV (strictly for major sports events only), otherwise lively banter dominates. The building that was once home to the Wye Valley Brewery is now a new courtyard bar, and the adjacent yard is the venue for a charity beer and music festival held on the August bank holiday weekend.

Kings Fee

49-53 Commercial Road, HR1 2BJ
9-midnight
(01432) 373240
Greene King IPA; Marston's Pedigree; guest beers

Award-winning Wetherspoon's conversion of an old supermarket. A large, light and airy open-plan main bar with numerous alcoves leads to an elevated family seating area (children welcome up to 7pm) and a courtyard. Decor is contemporary in style and features local history panels and woodcut prints by a local artist. Good value food is served all day. Draught Weston's Old Rosie and Organic Vintage Cider are sold.

Three Elms

1 Canon Pyon Road, HR4 9QQ (On A4110)
11-11 (11.30 Thu, 12 Fri & Sat); 12-11 Sun
(01432) 273338
Greene King Ruddles County, Old Speckled Hen; guest beers

A large, bustling, open-plan pub which holds a quiz each Thursday and Sunday, and live comedy on the last Saturday of each month. Some sporting events are shown on a large TV in a corner of the bar. Modern pub food – both snacks and main meals, are served all day. Abbot somtimes replaces Speckled Hen. The guest beers may be from regional or micro-breweries, while beer festivals are held in April and October. P

Victory

88 St Owen Street, HR1 2QD
3 (11summer)-11 (midnight Fri & Sat); 12-11 Sun

☎ (01432) 274998
Spinning Dog Hereford Organic Bitter, Herefordshire Owd Bull, Celtic Gold, Mutley's Revenge; guest beers Ⓗ
The main bar servery built in the shape of a galleon, complete with portholes, poopdeck and cannons, which resulted from a 1990's makeover, has mellowed with age. At the rear is a skittle alley, pool table and quieter seating. The Victory is home to Spinning Dog Brewery, selling most of its range, plus an extensive selection of real cider and perry including Weston's, Gwatkins and Black Pig. A key venue for local bands, it holds mini beer and sausage festivals from time to time.
⛫❀◐♿⇌▭♣●⁄

Kingsland

Angel Inn

HR6 9QS
⏲ 12-3 (not Mon), 6-midnight; 12-3, 6-11.30 Sun
☎ (01568) 708355 🌐 theangelkingsland.co.uk
Hobsons Best Bitter; Wye Valley Butty Bach; guest beer Ⓗ
Located opposite the church, this interesting 17th-century pub has an exquisite timber-framed interior which now comprises a lounge with large stone fireplace, restaurant and games area. A panel of the original wattle wall is on display in the lounge. The Angel has a good reputation for its food, ranging from bar snacks to full meals (not Mon eve). Booking is advised for the traditional Sunday roasts. Live entertainment is hosted on most Fridays. ⛫Q❀◐▭♣P⁄

Kington

Olde Tavern

22 Victoria Road, HR5 3BX
⏲ 7-midnight Mon; 6.30-midnight Tue-Thu; 6.30-1am Fri; 12-3, 6-1am Sat; 12-3, 7-10.30 Sun
☎ (01544) 230122
Dunn Plowman Tavern Bitter, Early Riser, Shirehorse Ale, Railway Porter Ⓗ
Part of Kington's history – this award-winner is one for the connoisseur. A small, unspoiled two-room time warp, it has a small public bar full of fascinating curios, including the 1920 refurbishment plans that never came to fruition. The tap for the nearby Dunn Plowman Brewery, it offers a warm welcome from staff and locals alike. At the rear is the diminutive Jake's Bistro, serving exceptional value English cuisine made with locally-sourced ingredients (Wed-Sat eves and Sun lunch; booking essential). Q❀◐◑▭♣⁄

Ledbury

Prince of Wales ✔

Church Lane, HR8 1DL
⏲ 11-11 (10.30 Sun)
☎ (01531) 632250
Banks's Bitter; Brains Rev James; Sharp's Doom Bar; guest beer Ⓗ
Sixteenth-century terraced and timbered pub set in a chocolate-box cobbled thoroughfare approaching the imposing parish church. It comprises front and back bars and a cosy side alcove, plus an enclosed smokers' courtyard. Always bustling with locals and visitors, a popular folk jam session is hosted on Wednesday evening. Run with real passion, this is the pub in Ledbury for beer, especially foreign beers. Good value bar meals are served, with Sunday roasts especially popular. Weston's perry is available in the summer.
❀◐⇌▭♣●⁄

Talbot Hotel

14 New Street, HR8 2DX
⏲ 11-3, 5-11 (midnight Fri); 11-midnight Sat; 11.30-11 Sun
☎ (01531) 632963 🌐 visitledbury.co.uk/talbot
Wadworth IPA, 6X; Wye Valley Butty Bach; guest beer Ⓗ
Black and white half-timbered hotel, popular with drinkers, dating back to around 1596. The attractive timbered main bar and drinking areas to the side are set around an island servery. The oak-panelled dining room, with its fine carved overmantle, was once the scene of fighting between Cavaliers and Roundheads. Traditional bar snacks are available and English and continental dishes are served in the pleasant Panels restaurant – all using local ingredients. Occasional live music plays. ⛫◐◑⇌▭♣⁄

Leominster

Bell Inn ✔

39 Etnam Street, HR6 8AE
⏲ 12-11.30
☎ (01568) 612818
Wye Valley Bitter, HPA, Butty Bach; guest beer Ⓗ
A friendly pub with a single U-shaped bar and light and modern decor, plus a pleasant garden to the rear. Live music features with folk on Tuesday evening and a band on Thursday evening. Reasonably priced, home-made pub food is served at lunchtime. Run by a young and enthusiastic licensee who enjoys his beer, the guest ale is from a national brewery. On-street parking outside is free and there is a large car park nearby.
⛫❀◐⇌▭♣⁄

Chequers

63 Etnam Street, HR6 8AE
⏲ 11-11 (10.30 Sun)
☎ (01568) 612473
Banks's Bitter; Wye Valley Butty Bach; guest beers Ⓗ
Probably the oldest pub in Leominster, this timber-framed terraced building with protruding gables has a wonderful unspoiled front bar with many original features including floor tiles, timbers and a splendid off-set fireplace. A comfortable rear lounge and outside drinking area are complemented by a marvellous two-floor barn restaurant. CAMRA Herefordshire Pub of the Year 2007, adventurous guest beers along with a good atmosphere make this pub a must visit.
⛫❀◐⇌▭♣●P⁄

Linton

Alma Inn

HR9 7RY (Off B4221, W of M50 J3) SO701548

12-3 (not Mon-Fri), 6.30 (6 Fri & Sat)-11; 12-3, 7-10.30 Sun
☎ (01989) 720355 lintonfestival.org
Butcombe Bitter; Oakham JHB; guest beer ⊞
A frequent CAMRA Herefordshire Pub of the Year winner, this pub is testimony that a successful village inn does not have to sell food. Behind a plain exterior is a thriving enterprise run with real devotion. The cosy lounge with real fire complements a more basic pool room and a less-used 'other room'. The Alma champions smaller and local breweries —extensive hillside grounds are the venue for an ambitious annual Blues & Ale Festival held each June solstice weekend.
⛰Q❀Å♣P

Norton Canon

Three Horseshoes

HR4 7BH (on A480)
12-3 (Wed & Sat only), 6-11; 12-3, 7-10.30 Sun
☎ (01544) 318375
Shoes Canon Bitter, Lin's Lager, Norton Ale, Peploe's Tipple, Farriers Beer ⊞
Home of the Shoes Brewery, this isolated Herefordshire red-brick pub has a timeless and unspoilt interior that shows little evidence of the fire that ravaged the upper floors in March 2006. A welcoming public bar leads through to a larger pool room, and a small, cosy lounge furnished with an ad hoc collection of comfortable sofas and chairs. Farriers Beer, at 15.4% ABV, is now available on draught as well as in bottles. The bus stop is half mile from the pub, alight at the Weobley Turn.
⛰Q❀(461, 462)♣P

Preston on Wye

Yew Tree

HR2 9JT SO385414
7-midnight (1am Fri & Sat); 12-3, 7-11 Sun
☎ (01981) 500359
Beer range varies Ⓖ
A basic and pleasantly eccentric traditional village pub, very much a drinkers' establishment. Comfortable and welcoming, it is popular with fishermen and canoeists from the nearby River Wye as well as supporting boules, pool and quiz teams. The beer, from local or regional breweries, is served direct from the cask behind the small bar, and draught Thatchers Heritage Cider is also available. Evening meals are available in summer if ordered in advance. Live music plays monthly on Saturday. ⛰Q❀Å♣P

St Owens Cross

New Inn ✔

HR2 8LQ (jct of A4137/B4521)
11-11 (midnight Fri); 12-11 Sun
☎ (01989) 730274 newinn.biz
Marston's Burton Bitter; guest beers ⊞
Black and white-timbered 16th-century dining pub, set on a country crossroads. The split-level main bar features an inviting inglenook fireplace and plenty of cosy nooks and crannies – popular with diners at busy times. Beers are served from a pewter beer engine rescued from a long defunct pub in Ross-on-Wye. Traditional English bar snacks and meals are served in the bar, dining room and child-friendly garden. Weston's draught cider and perry is available, supplemented by Broome Farm or Gwatkins cider in Summer.
⛰❀♣P

Staplow

Oak Inn

HR8 1NP (on B4214)
12-3, 6 (5.30 Sat; 7 Sun)-11
☎ (01531) 640954
Brains Rev James; Taylor Landlord; Wye Valley Bitter; guest beer ⊞
A superb renovation has transformed an 'also-ran' roadside pub into a fine country venue for dining and drinking run with real verve. The main bar has a sofa, tables and a real fire to accommodate drinkers, and on the other side is a stylish restaurant area complete with chandelier and an open kitchen. Good food is made with local ingredients. Off to one side is a secluded snug with wood burner, and to the rear is a simple back room.
⛰Q❀P

Upper Colwall

Chase Inn

Chase Road, WR13 6DJ (Off B4218, signed British Camp) SO766430
11.30-3, 5-11; 11.30-11 Sat; 12-10.30 Sun
☎ (01684) 540276
Batham Best Bitter; Hobsons Best Bitter; Wood Shropshire Lad; guest beers ⊞
Two-bar free house located in a wooded backwater on the western slopes of the Malvern Hills, comprising a lounge bar for diners and an informal bar for drinkers crammed full of random bric-a-brac, where conversation rules. The sun-trap garden commands fine views across Herefordshire towards the Welsh Hills. Booking is essential for the popular Sunday roast (no food Mon & Tue eves). The pub is under the same ownership as the St George's Brewery and Nag's Head in Malvern. Q❀♣P

Wellington

Wellington Inn

HR4 8AT (half mile W of A49)
12-3 (not Mon), 6-11; 12-3, 7-10.30 (not Winter eve) Sun
☎ (01432) 830367 wellingtonpub.co.uk
Hobsons Best Bitter; Wye Valley HPA; Shepherd Neame Spitfire; guest beer ⊞
A fine example of a thriving traditional village hostelry serving top class food. The welcoming public bar is complemented by a separate barn-style restaurant. The chef here is winner of Pub Chef of the Year 2008 and food is a real speciality, with bar snacks, an elaborate lunchtime and evening menu, and carvery on Sunday. The bar has interesting local photographs, board games and newspapers. Guest beers are mainly from micro-breweries, and Weston's Scrumpy Cider is served.
⛰❀(492)♣P

Wilton

White Lion ✔

Wilton Lane, HR9 6AQ (just off B4260)

12-11; 12-10.30 Sun

☎ (01989) 562785 whitelionross.co.uk

Wadworth 6X; Wye Valley Bitter; guest beers Ⓗ

Sixteenth-century inn delightfully situated on the banks of the Wye next to the old Ross Bridge, with views to the town opposite. The bar is open plan with exposed beams and stonework, a large fireplace and a separate games room. Originally part of a prison house adjoining the pub, the restaurant features more bare stonework. English cuisine, freshly prepared using local ingredients, is served here and in the bar. The attractive garden leads down to the river.

Winforton

Sun Inn

HR3 6EA (on A438)

12-3, 6.30-11 (not Mon; not Mon & Tue winter); 12-4 Sun

☎ (01544) 327677

Wye Valley Butty Bach, Bitter Ⓗ

A roadside pub in a small village, the interior has a single bar with white painted walls and bare stone – one end mainly for drinkers and the other catering for diners. The food ranges from sandwiches and snacks to an enterprising menu of home-prepared dishes, highly commended in the Flavours of Herefordshire food festival in 2007. The Wye Valley Bitter may alternate with other Wye Valley beers and Taylor Landlord appears in summer.

Dog Inn, Ewyas Harold.

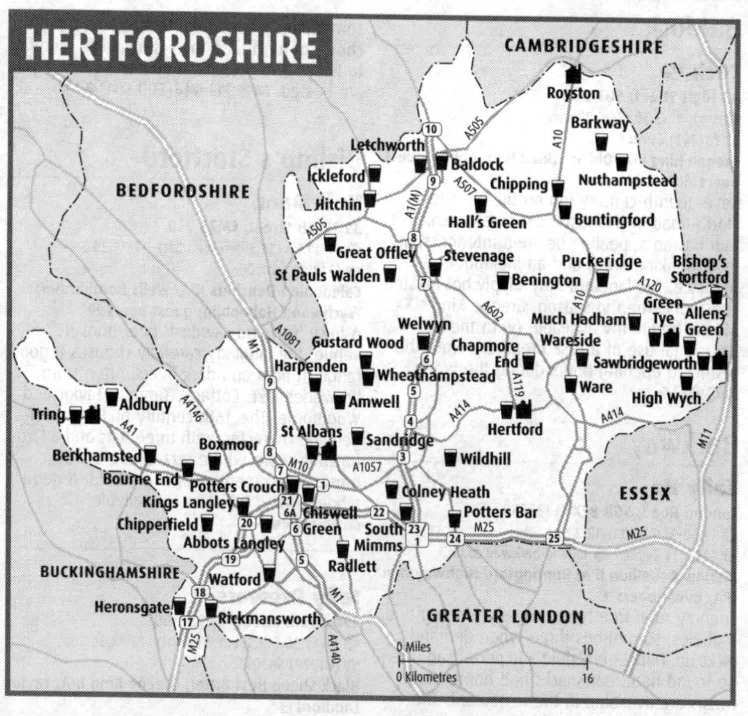

Abbots Langley

Compasses

95 Tibbs Hill Road, WD5 0LJ

11-11; 12-10.30 Sun

☎ (01923) 262870

Courage Best Bitter; Fuller's London Pride; Greene King Abbot; Shepherd Neame Spitfire Ⓗ

Deceptively large suburban local run by the same family for 24 years, with two distinct bar areas and a dining room. There is a covered decking area for smokers and a garden with a children's play house. The pub holds regular charity quizzes and has occasional live music on Saturday nights.

Aldbury

Valiant Trooper

Trooper Road, HP23 5RW (2 miles E of Tring)

11.30-11; 12-10.30 Sun

☎ (01442) 851203 valianttrooper.co.uk

Fuller's London Pride; Oakham JHB; Tring Jack O' Legs; guest beers Ⓗ

Ancient, rambling free house with many exposed beams situated in the much-filmed village of Aldbury and owned by the same family since 1980. The atmosphere is relaxing and the welcome warm. A converted stables seats 40 diners, serving excellent food. Three regular and two guest beers are kept in fine condition; bar snacks are offered throughout the two main drinking areas. No meals are served on Sunday and Monday evening. Dogs are welcome. Q P

Allens Green

Queens Head

CM21 0LS TL455170

12-2.30 (not Mon & Tue), 5-11, 12-11 Sat (10.30 Sun)

☎ (01279) 723393 shirevillageinns.co.uk

Fuller's London Pride; Mighty Oak Oscar Wilde, Maldon Gold; Ⓗ **guest beers** Ⓗ/Ⓖ

Small, traditional village inn with a large garden, popular with locals, cyclists, walkers and dogs. Although the location is deeply rural, the pub is well worth seeking out. Hot snacks are always available unless the bar is very busy. Every third weekend of the month is for 'beer lovers', with up to 15 local and unusual ales on offer. Beer festivals take place on most bank holidays. Local CAMRA BranchPub of the Year 2004, 2006 and 2008. Q

Amwell

Elephant & Castle ✔

Amwell Lane, AL4 8EA TL167131

12-2.30, 5.30-11; 12-11 Sat; 12-10.30 Sun

☎ (01582) 832175

Greene King IPA, Morland Original, Abbot; guest beer Ⓗ

Deservedly popular pub in a beautiful, peaceful setting. The back bar houses a 200ft deep well and two real fires warm the pub in winter. With the added asset of two large gardens (one for adults only), this is an excellent example of a successful country pub. The landlord, currently celebrating 40 years in the trade, is a staunch supporter of real ale. Lunches are served daily, evening meals Tues to Sat. (304,357)P

Baldock

Cock ✔

43 High Street, SG7 6BG
☼ 5-11; 12-3.30, 7-10.30 Sun
☎ (01462) 892366
Greene King IPA, Old Speckled Hen, Abbot; guest beers Ⓗ
Seventeenth-century inn on the old Great North Road in this historic market town. This pub has an appealing beamed interior, split level drinking areas and an inglenook fireplace. The landlord may supply hot roasted chestnuts when in season. Greene King's XX Mild is frequently available (with the occasional use of a cask breather). Note the restricted opening hours during the week.
♨Q✿⊟♣

Barkway

Tally Ho

London Road, SG8 8EX TL383350
☼ 11.30-3, 5.30-11; 12-3 Sun
☎ (01763) 848389 ⊕ tallyho-barkway.co.uk
Marlow Rebellion IPA; Buntingford Highwayman IPA; guest beers Ⓟ
Friendly rural free house usually offering two real ales, sometimes three when demand picks up. Dark beers, mild and porter can often be found here. Bar snacks and home-made meals are available in the restaurant. The spirits menu offers 58 whiskies, 11 gins and nine rums. Look out for the large collection of cartoons, newspaper clippings and apocryphal stories. ♨✿◐◑P

Benington

Lordship Arms

42 Whempstead Road, SG2 7BX
☼ 12-3, 6-11; 12-3, 7-10.30 Sun
☎ (01438) 869665
Black Sheep Best Bitter; Crouch Vale Brewers Gold; guest beers Ⓗ
A repeat winner of local and county CAMRA Pub of the Year awards. The single bar is decorated with telephone memorabilia; even some of the handpumps are modelled on telephones. Wednesday evening curries and Sunday roasts are always popular. The excellent garden features superb floral displays in the summer. Bar snacks are served at lunchtime and oversized glasses are used.
♨Q✿◐⊟(384)●P⊽

Berkhamsted

Lamb

277 High Street, HP4 1AJ (Northchurch end of High Street)
☼ 11-11; 12-10.30 Sun
☎ (01442) 862615
Adnams Bitter; Fuller's London Pride; Greene King IPA; Tring Ridgeway Ⓗ
Rare example of a traditional high street pub with separate doors for its two bars, though once inside you can move easily between the rooms. This is a pub for all ages, where the welcome is warm and the locals always good for a chat. There is a dartboard in the public bar and the TV is turned on only when there is something 'worthwhile' to watch. A good choice of lunchtime food is available Monday to Friday and occasional quiz and curry nights are hosted. ♨✿◐⊏≋⊟(500,501)♣⁴–

Bishop's Stortford

Half Moon

31 North Street, CM23 2LD
☼ 11-11.30 (12.30am Wed-Sat); 12-11.30 Sun
☎ (01279) 834500
Caledonian Deuchars IPA; Wells Bombardier; Wychwood Hobgoblin; guest beers Ⓗ
A busy 'spit and sawdust' beer drinkers' venue; the landlady carefully chooses a good range of light and dark beers, often from breweries B&T, Cottage, Timothy Taylor and Woodforde. The 16th-century building is of genuine character, with three bars and a large function room where jazz, blues, acoustic music and comedy events are held. A good range of malt whiskies is available.
♨✿◐≋⊟●⁴–

Jolly Brewers

170 South Street, CM23 3BQ
☼ 11-11.30 (12.30am Wed-Sat); 12-11.30 Sun
☎ (01279) 863055
Black Sheep Best Bitter; Greene King IPA; Taylor Landlord Ⓗ
The 'Jollies' usually offers a guest ale or porter in addition to the regular beers. It has two contrasting bars —a quiet lounge and a lively sports room with a pool table and TV. In summer the enclosed rear garden and front patio are popular. B&B accommodation benefits from a 24-hour connection to nearby Stansted Airport via the 510 bus.
✿⊏◐◑♿≋⊟(510,333)P⁴–

Bourne End

White Horse

London Road, HP1 2RH (½ mile from A41 jct) TL022063
☼ 11-11; 12-10.30 Sun
☎ (01442) 863888
McMullen AK, Country Ⓗ
Bought and extended by McMullen in the 1980s, this comfortable pub has developed real character over the years, catering for drinkers and diners alike. As you enter, the restaurant area is to the right and the bar, decorated with many hunting prints, to the left. Bar meals are available with a daily specials board supplementing the regular menu. Two real fires warm up the winter months while the garden at the rear is ideal for the summer. ♨✿◐◑♿⊟(500)P⁴–

INDEPENDENT BREWERIES

Alehouse St Albans
Buntingford Royston
Green Tye Green Tye
McMullen Hertford
Red Squirrel Hertford
Sawbridgeworth Sawbridgeworth
Tring Tring

Boxmoor

Post Office Arms

46 Puller Road, HP1 1QN (off St John's Rd)
3-11.30; 12-12.30am Sat; 12-11 Sun
(01442) 261235
Fuller's London Pride; Gale's HSB; guest beers H
Known locally as The Patch', this is a community local catering for all ages situated in a terraced residential street. For sports fans, the public bar has darts and a large screen TV. In contrast, the more peaceful saloon has a real fire and is decorated with local prints. The landlord, whose family has a long tradition of running pubs, has been here for more than 10 years. Sunday lunches are served and Wednesday is curry-and-a-pint night.
(Hemel Hempstead)

Buntingford

Brambles

117 High Street, SG9 9AF
12-11 (10.30 Sun)
(01763) 273158
Buntingford Highwayman IPA; Fuller's London Pride; Gale's HSB; guest beers H
Originally the Chequers, this pub has reopened after many years of closure. Situated at the north end of the High Street, you will find two bars both warmed by real fires with eight handpumps dispensing the ales. Buntingford and Red Squirrel beers are usually available. The clientele is very varied, and can get exuberant at weekends.
(700,331)P

Crown

17 High Street, SG9 9AB
12.30-3, 6-11; 12-3 Sun
(01763) 271442
Everards Tiger; Young's Bitter; guest beers H
This town centre pub has a large front bar, cosy back bar and function room. Outside is a covered patio and a secluded garden. Although the emphasis is on drinking, there are regular themed speciality food nights as well as traditional fish and chips on Thursday and Friday. Bookings are required for food. Crossword fans find the large collection of dictionaries and reference books useful, and every six weeks gents' haircuts are available!
Q(700,331)

Chapmore End

Woodman

30 Chapmore End, SG12 0HF (off B158) TL328164
12-2.30 (not Mon), 5.30-11; 12-11 Sat & Sun
(01920) 463143
Greene King IPA, Abbot; guest beers G
Classic two bar country pub in a quiet hamlet. This small unspoilt gem dispenses beer straight from cooled casks in the cellar behind the public bar. A local favourite is mix': half IPA and half Abbot. Winter Sunday lunchtimes feature traditional roasts while summer Sundays have hog roasts. Evening meals (served up to 7.30pm) include a themed set menu on alternate Thursdays. The large garden has a safe children's play area and petanque piste. QP

Chipperfield

Royal Oak

1 The Street, WD4 9BH
12-3, 6-11; 12-3, 7-10.30 Sun
(01923) 266537
Adnams Broadside; Fuller's London Pride; Young's Bitter; guest beer H
Genuine street corner local with public and saloon areas served by a central bar. The public bar has a real fire, local photographs, historic car pictures and a collection of matches and foreign currency. Some of the seating is upholstered beer casks, the tables are covered with beaten copper. The larger saloon is furnished with dark wood and brasses. Home-made lunches are served daily except Sunday. Children are welcome for meals; dogs at the landlord's discretion. Outside is a patio and there is a meeting room available by arrangement.
Q(352,R9)P

Chipping

Countryman

Ermine Street, SG9 0PG TL356319
12-11 Fri & Sat; 12-10.30 Sun
(01763) 272721
Beer range varies H
Built in 1663 and a pub since 1760, the Countryman has one split-level bar room. The interior features some well executed carvings on the bar front, an impressive fireplace and obscure agricultural implements. Usually there is just one real ale – the beer itself will vary but will usually be brown and around 4-4.5%. A second may be available during the summer months. Note the restricted opening hours.
QP

Chiswell Green

Three Hammers

210 Watford Road, AL2 3EA (on B4630)
12-11 (midnight Fri & Sat)
(01727) 846218
Fuller's London Pride; guest beers H
Well maintained 18th-century inn, orginally a blacksmith's, with a contemporary interior and large garden, situated on the main Watford Road near the National Gardens of the Rose. Six real ales include five ever-changing guests. Meals are served until 9pm every day. The pub hosts regular beer festivals and quiz nights on Sunday and Tuesday for a small cash prize. There is a bus stop outside and the pub is well placed for access to the M25, M1 and M10.
QP

Colney Heath

Crooked Billet

88 High Street, AL4 0NP
11-2.30, 4.30-11; 11-11 Sat summer; 12-10.30 Sun
(01727) 822128
Tring Side Pocket for a Toad; guest beers H
Popular and friendly cottage-style village pub dating back more than 200 years with a lively public bar. A genuine free house, it stocks three to five guest beers from national, regional and micro-breweries. A wide

selection of good value home-made food is served; booking is advisable for Sunday lunch. Summer barbecues and Saturday events are held occasionally. This is a favourite stop-off for walkers on the many local footpaths. Families are welcome in the large garden where there is play equipment.
(304)♣P

Great Offley

Red Lion

Kings Walden Road, SG5 3DZ TL145266
12-midnight (10.30 Sun)
(01462) 768281 redlionofflley.com
Fuller's London Pride; Young's Bitter; guest beers
Set in idyllic countryside, this traditional pub has a good reputation for food. Fresh fish on Wednesday, exceptional chips made from locally-grown potatoes and the speciality Red Lion pancake are highlights of the varied menu, served in the bar and conservatory restaurant. There is a large fire in the cosy main bar and delightful views can be enjoyed from the garden. ♣P

Green Tye

Prince of Wales

SG10 6JP
12-3, 5.30-11; 12-11 Sat; 11.15-10.30 Sun
(01279) 842517
Greene Tye Union Jack; Wadworth IPA; guest beers
Traditional 200-year-old village pub with a quarry tiled floor. Popular with locals, walkers and cyclists, dogs are welcome. The Green Tye Brewery is located across the car park and its beers regularly appear in the pub. Beer festivals are held on the May Day weekend and in early autumn. There is always a good collection of old and rare malt whiskies.
♣

Gustard Wood

Cross Keys

Ballslough Hill, AL4 8LA (off B651) TL174164
11-3.30 (4.30 Sat), 5.30-11; 12-4, 7-11 Sun
(01582) 832165
Adnams Bitter, Broadside; Fuller's London Pride; Greene King IPA; guest beers
Attractive 17th-century quiet and rustic country pub in a woodland setting with a wood-burning inglenook fire and a collection of model cars. Food is reasonably priced and recommended. Try the desserts at lunchtime and home-made pizzas in the evening. A large outside drinking area has plenty of tables and benches and children's play equipment. Accommodation is in three en-suite rooms with antique furniture. Q(304)P

Hall's Green

Rising Sun

SG4 7DR TL275287
11-2.30, 6-11; 11-11 Sat; 12-10.30 Sun
(01462) 790487
McMullen AK, Cask Ale, Country, seasonal beers
Traditional country inn in a small hamlet set in beautiful countryside. A real fire blazing in winter and a large garden for the summer make it an ideal location for a pint of ale all year round. The pub plays host to the local petanque league and classic car club. Good pub food is served in the conservatory and bar lunchtimes and evenings Monday to Saturday and all day Sunday. Q♣P

Harpenden

Carpenters Arms

14 Cravells Road, AL5 1BD
11-3, 5.30-11; 12-3, 7-10.30
(01582) 460311
Adnams Bitter; Courage Best Bitter; Greene King Abbot; guest beers
Harpenden's smallest hostelry is cosy and comfortable without jukebox or fruit machines. The pub has been attractively refurbished throughout and continues to uphold its real ale traditions—a fifth handpump was added in 2008. Occasional food nights (booking necessary) and barbecues (weather permitting) are hosted. Delightful in summer, the attractive outdoor area has stylish parasols and gazebos. During the winter months an open fire warms the bar. (320,321)♣P

Heronsgate

Land of Liberty, Peace & Plenty

Long Lane, WD3 5BS (close to M25 jct 17) TQ023949
11-11 (midnight Fri & Sat); 12-11 Sun
(01923) 282226 landoflibertypub.com
Red Squirrel Conservation Bitter; guest beers
A finalist in CAMRA's 2007 National Pub of the Year awards, this welcoming, single-bar country pub is becoming increasingly popular with walkers and cyclists. Gradual improvements continue: there is now a large covered, heated outdoor area next to the large garden where families are welcome (no under-14s allowed in the pub) and there is a boules piste. Six beers from a variety of family and micro-breweries are served alongside real cider and perry, plus a range of Belgian bottled beers. Regular events include food nights, beer tastings, quizzes, darts, pub games and live music. Beer festivals are held on most bank holidays. Tring Brock Bitter is badged as Liberty Ale. ♣P

Hertford

Old Barge

2 The Folly, SG14 1QD TL326128
11-11 (midnight Fri & Sat); 12-11 Sun
(01992) 581871 theoldbarge.co.uk
Black Sheep Best Bitter; Shepherd Neame Spitfire; Wells Bombardier; Young's Bitter; guest beers
In a pleasant location on Folly Island at the head of the Lee Navigation you can watch the narrowboats pass by as you enjoy your pint. The pub is renowned for its jazz nights – held on every second and last Thursday of the month. Food is available at lunchtime, including the popular Sunday roast, and

evening until 9pm (not Sun). There are twice-yearly beer festivals and a well-attended quiz on Sunday night. Children are welcome until 7pm in the bar and 9pm outdoors.
♔✿◑Å⊟♣●P⅟

Old Cross Tavern

8 St Andrew Street, SG14 1JA
12 (4 Mon)-11; 12-10.30 Sun
☎ (01992) 583133
Fuller's London Pride; Red Squirrel RSB; Pitfield Hophead; Taylor Landlord; guest beers [H]
Superb town free house offering a friendly welcome. Eight real ales, including one brewed at the pub brewery and a dark brew of some description, come from brewers large and small. There is a good selection of Belgian bottle-conditioned beers. Beer festivals are held on the patio over the Spring Bank Holiday and in October. There is no TV or music here, just good old-fashioned conversation. Filled rolls and home-made pies are served.
♔Q✿Å⊟♣●

White Horse

33 Castle Street, SG14 1HH
12-2.30, 5.30-11; 12-11 Fri & Sat; 12-10.30 Sun
☎ (01992) 501950 castlestreetparty.org.uk
Adnams Bitter; Fuller's Chiswick, Discovery, London Pride, ESB; guest beers [H]
Charming old timber-framed building with two downstairs bars and additional rooms upstairs, one with bar billiards where children are welcome until 9pm. Guest beers come from a wide range of craft brewers. Beer festivals are held over Bank Holiday weekends, with a street party in August. Home-made lunches are served daily. On Monday night is the renowned Gastronomic Tour, with a set menu of dishes from around the world. ♔Q✿◑⊟Å⊟♣⅟

High Wych

Rising Sun

CM21 0HZ (2 miles SW of Sawbridgeworth) TL465142
12-2.30, 5.30-11; 12-3, 6-11 Sat; 12-3, 7-10.30 Sun
☎ (01279) 724099
Courage Best Bitter; Mighty Oak Maldon Gold, Oscar Wilde; guest beers [G]
Recently refurbished, this small village pub has a large stone-floored bar. It is still known as 'Sid's' after a previous landlord who served all the beers on gravity. Handpumps have never been used here. Popular with walkers and regulars, entertainment includes regular quizzes and an annual vegetable competition.
Q✿⅟

Hitchin

Half Moon

57 Queen Street, SG4 9TZ
12-2.30, 5-midnight; 12-11 Sun
☎ (01462) 452448
Adnams Bitter; Young's Special; guest beers [H]
Split-level one-bar pub dating back to 1748, once owned by Hitchin brewer W&S Lucas. Up to four guest beers are on offer alongside the two regulars, often from local breweries. Two ciders and a perry are also stocked plus a good choice of wines. Twice-yearly beer festivals are hosted, one with a Nelson theme. Home-prepared food is served daily (not Tue eve). Monthly quiz and curry nights are popular. Winner of CAMRA North Hertfordshire Community Pub of the Year 2007.
♔✿◑◐⊟♣●P⅟

Nightingale

Nightingale Road, SG5 1RL
12-midnight (10.30 Sun)
☎ (01462) 457448
Nethergate Old Growler, Umbel Magna; Tring Colley's Dog; guest beers [H]
This friendly pub is around 150 years old and reputed to have three ghosts. The interior is open plan but retains the layout of the original rooms, with distinct seating areas. Five beers from Nethergate, Tring and Wychwood usually include a porter or a mild. Traditional entertainment includes darts, pool and board games. Sport is occasionally shown on the four TV screens. ✿◑≠⊟♣●P⅟

Sunrunner

24 Bancroft, SG5 1JW
12-3, 5-11; 12-midnight Fri-Sun
☎ (01462) 440717 sunrunner.co.uk
Draught Bass; Potton Shannon IPA; guest beers [H]
The Sunrunner, housed in an 18th-century building, is a mini beer festival in its own right. Two regular and six ever-changing guest beers, mainly from small or new micro-breweries, include stouts, porters and milds plus foreign beers, cider and fruit wines. Home-made lunches are served daily.
◑⊟♣●⅟

Ickleford

Old George

Arlesey Road, SG5 3UX (400m from A600 down Turnpike Lane) TL182316
11-midnight (1am Fri & Sat); 11-10 Sun
☎ (01462) 432269
Greene King IPA, Abbot, seasonal beers [H]
A very old country inn in the centre of the village with a tunnel running from the pub to St Katharine's church nearby. There is an attractive lounge bar with an inglenook fireplace and plenty of beams. The public bar is very basic but you will always be made to feel most welcome. Home-made food is cooked to order. ♔✿◑◐⊟⊟♣P

Plume of Feathers

Upper Green, SG5 3YD TL182317
11.30-3, 6-11.30; 11.30-midnight Fri-Sun
☎ (01462) 432729
Adnams Bitter; Flowers IPA; Wadworth 6X; guest beers [H]
Welcoming pub run by two sisters for the last 13 years. A lively establishment and popular with enthusiastic rugby union fans. The excellent food is prepared to order (not Sun eve) and served in the restaurant. There is a pleasant secluded garden where you can enjoy a pint on a summer's day. ♔✿◑◐⊟♣P

Kings Langley

Saracens Head

47 High Street, WD4 9HU
11-2.30, 5-11.30; 12-4, 7-10.30 Sun
(01923) 400144
Fuller's London Pride, ESB; Tring Ridgeway; guest beer H
Early 17th-century community-oriented pub popular with a mixed clientele, with ale drinkers usually in the majority. The landlord regularly wins 'In Bloom' prizes for his hanging baskets. The single-room interior has a collection of Saracens' heads, beer bottles, old bottles and jugs on display. Food is served lunchtime only (not Sun). No facilities for children. (500,501)P

Letchworth

Three Magnets

18-20 Leys Avenue, SG6 3EW
9-midnight (1am Fri & Sat); 9-11 Sun
(01462) 681093
Greene King IPA, Abbot; Marston's Pedigree; guest beers H
Wetherspoon's pub in a converted 1924 furniture shop. During the day and early evening it is popular for family dining and later on it becomes a social club. Mostly the pub is quiet except when screening national and international sports events. Food is available at competitive prices throughout the day. Interesting old photographs of early Letchworth are displayed on the walls.
Q

Much Hadham

Bull

High Street, SG10 6BU (On B1004 at N end of village)
12-3, 6-11; 12-3, 7-10.30 Sun
(01279) 842668
Brakspear Bitter; guest beers H
Food tends to dominate at this village inn, but there is space for drinkers who are always warmly welcomed. A split-level pub with low beams, it usually offers two guest beers. Popular with locals, the bar tends to get very busy, especially on Sunday lunchtime.
Q(351)P

Nuthampstead

Woodman

Stocking Lane, SG8 8NB
11-11; 12-4, 7-10.30 Sun
(01763) 848328 thewoodman-inn.co.uk
Adnams Bitter; McMullen Cask Ale; Nethergate IPA; guest beer H
Seventeenth-century free house with an L-shaped bar and wonderful open fires. The restaurant offers Á la carte meals as well as house specials and snacks (no food Sun eve). The location is ideal for visiting local attractions such as Duxford Imperial War Museum. During WWII the USAF 398th Bomber Group was based nearby and much memorabilia is displayed here.
QP

Potters Bar

Old Manor

Wyllyotts Place, Darkes Lane, EN6 2JD
11-11; 12-10.30 Sun
(01707) 650674 heritageinns.co.uk
Brakspear Bitter; Courage Directors; Young's Bitter H
Close to the railway station, this popular pub attracts a varied clientele. Dating back to the 13th century and featuring three real fires, the building is the surviving part of the Manor House of Wyllyotts and opened in its present form in 2000. The large adjoining galleried restaurant is always busy and offers a wide menu. An ideal place for a drink before or after an event at the theatre/leisure complex opposite. P

Potters Crouch

Hollybush ✓

Bedmond Lane, AL2 3NN (off A4147) TL116052
12-2.30, 6-11; 12-2.30, 7-10.30 Sun
(01727) 851792 thehollybushpub.co.uk
Fuller's Chiswick, London Pride, ESB, seasonal beers H
Attractive early 18th-century pub in rural surroundings beautifully furnished throughout to a high standard with large oak tables and period chairs. Spotless throughout, there is no jukebox, slot machine or TV to disturb visitors. The garden is delightful in summer. Food menus are interesting, specialising in traditional English pub fare. Children welcome in garden only. Q(300,301)P

Puckeridge

Crown & Falcon

33 High Street, SG11 1RN TL386233
11.30-2,30, 5.30 (6.30 Sat)-11; 12-4.30, 7-10.30 Sun
(01920) 821561 crown-falcon.demon.co.uk
Adnams Bitter; McMullen AK; guest beers H
A public house since 1530, with the Crown part of the name adopted much later from an ex-pub in the village. Changes to the interior layout can be traced on plans displayed in the bar. It is now one large open-plan room with a separate restaurant. A collection of Allied Breweries memorabilia is on display. Darts is popular. P

Radlett

Red Lion Hotel

78-80 Watling Street, WD7 7NP (on A5183)
11-midnight; 12-11.30 Sun
(01923) 855341 redlionradlett.co.uk
Courage Directors; Young's Bitter, Special, seasonal beers H
This Edwardian hotel, opposite the railway station and dating from 1906 was once a temperance house. It now has a large split-level bar plus a 60-seater restaurant, 14 guest rooms and a function room. Home-made meals are served in the bar and restaurant. The patio at the front of the hotel overlooks Watling Street. (602,632)P

Rickmansworth

Rose & Crown

Woodcock Hill, Harefield Road, WD3 1PP
✪ 11-11; 11.30-10.30 Sun
☎ (01923) 897680 ⊕ morethanjustapub.co.uk/theroseandcrown
Caledonian Deuchars IPA; Fuller's London Pride; guest beer ⊞
The focus is on quality dining at this quaint country inn but a comfortable bar has been retained to complement the spacious modern restaurant area. The hostelry maintains the feel of a genuine pub with a quiz on Thursday, board games for customers and two real fires. The farmhouse building dates from the 17th century and there are extensive gardens with a permanent marquee for functions.
⛫❀◑⊟♣P

St Albans

Boot

4 Market Place, AL3 5DG (opp Clock Tower)
✪ 12-midnight (1am Fri & Sat); 12-11.30 Sun
☎ (01727) 857533
Black Sheep Best Bitter; Caledonian Deuchars IPA; Young's Special; guest beers ⊞
Dating back to the 1400s, the Boot has been restored to a typical market town pub with low ceilings, exposed beams, log fire and wood flooring. On Wednesday and Saturday it bustles with market traders and shoppers. Live music and jam sessions feature on Tuesday evening. The landlord, a Chelsea football supporter, organises Saracens rugby club tickets and coaches to matches for customers. The ever-changing food menu is popular (booking advisable, no food Mon). ⛫◑⊟♣●

Farriers Arms

32-34 Lower Dagnall Street, AL3 4PT
✪ 12-2.30, 5.00-11; 12-11 Sat; 12-10.30 Sun
☎ (01727) 851025
McMullen AK, Cask Ale, Country; guest beers ⊞
Originally a grocer's and butcher's, the Farriers became a pub in the 1920s and is now a classic back-street local, the only pub in the city never to have forsaken real ale. A plaque on the wall outside marks the first meeting of the Hertfordshire branch of CAMRA and on 20th November 2007 it hosted the 35th anniversary of the branch. Both bars are free of gaming machines but there is a TV for sports. Parking can be difficult. ◑⊟♣

Goat

37 Sopwell Lane, AL1 1RN (off Holywell Hill)
✪ 12-11;12-3, 5-11 Mon;12-11.30 Fri & Sat (11 Sun)
☎ (01727) 833934 ⊕ goatinn.co.uk
Caledonian Deuchars IPA; St Austell Tribute; Shepherd Neame Spitfire; guest beers ⊞
Welcoming, traditional 15th-century pub, a short walk from the cathedral. Situated on the old coaching route from London, it still retains the old carriage arch. Food is served in a dining area at the rear of the pub. Weston's Old Rosie cider and a wide selection of wines and whiskies are also available. Quiz night is Sunday. Dominoes, shove ha'penny and board games are popular, and bar billiards is played. Children permitted until 9pm. ❀⇔◑⇌♣●

Mermaid

98 Hatfield Road, AL1 3RL
✪ 12-11 (midnight Fri & Sat); 12-10.30 Sun
☎ (01727) 837758
Adnams Bitter; Everards Tiger; guest beers ⊞
Friendly cottage-style pub, a short walk from the city centre, with a mixed clientele of all ages and a community focus. Backgammon, darts and three football teams are based here. Occasional live music is hosted and the second Wednesday of the month is comedy night. Well presented, interesting guest beers are sourced from micro and small regional breweries and occasional beer festivals are held. Good wheelchair access. ❀◑⇌⊟♣P

Six Bells

16-18 St Michaels Street, AL3 4SH
✪ 12-2.30, 5-11; 12-11 Fri & Sat; 12-10.30 Sun
☎ (01727) 856945
Black Sheep Best Bitter; Caledonian Deuchars IPA; Fuller's London Pride; Greene King Abbot; guest beers ⊞
Traditional , cosy 16th-century pub with an enormous fireplace situated in St Michael's parish, within walking distance of the town centre and cathedral. The only licensed premises to lie within the walls of Roman Verulamium, it is adjacent to Verulamium Park and Museum. Four regular ales and one guest are served. Food is available lunchtimes and evenings (not Sun). Quiz nights are held twice a month on Sunday and occasional live music features at this popular, friendly pub.
⛫❀◑⊟(300,301)♣●P⌐

White Hart Tap

4 Keyfield Terrace, AL1 1QJ
✪ 12-11
☎ (01727) 860974 ⊕ whiteharttap.co.uk
Caledonian Deuchars IPA; Fuller's London Pride; Taylor Landlord; guest beers ⊞
Welcoming single-bar, back-street local featuring guest beers from the Punch Taverns' range. Good value, home-made food is served every lunchtime and Tuesday to Friday evenings, with fish and chips on Friday and roasts on Sunday. Quiz night is Wednesday. Occasional live music on Saturday night. Barbecues are held in summer.
⛫❀◑⇌♣●⌐

White Lion

91 Sopwell Lane, AL1 1RN (off Holywell Hill)
✪ 12-11
☎ (01727) 850540 ⊕ thewhitelionph.co.uk
Black Sheep Best Bitter; Young's Special; guest beers ⊞
Traditional two-bar pub close to St Albans Abbey with six handpumps dispensing two regular and four guest beers from the Punch Tavern's range. The beer garden has a smokers' area, barbecue, children's play area and petanque piste. High quality, home-made food is served daily. There is live music on Tuesday and a beer festival in August. CAMRA South Herts Pub of the Year in 2006.
⛫Q❀◑⇌⊟♣●⌐

St Pauls Walden

Strathmore Arms
London Road, SG4 8BT TL193222
⏲ 12-2.30 (not Mon), 5 (6 Mon)-11; 12-11 Fri & Sat; 12-10.30 Sun
☎ (01438) 871654
Fuller's London Pride; Woodforde's Wherry Best Bitter; guest beers Ⓗ
Situated on the Bowes-Lyon estate, this pub is divided into drinking, dining and games areas. The pub does a lot of fundraising and was North Hertfordshire CAMRA Community Pub of the Year in 2006 as well as a past winner of Hertfordshire Pub of the Year. It offers a constantly changing range of beers and holds regular beer festivals.
Q❀◑⊟⅄⊟(304)♣●P

Sandridge

Green Man
31 High Street, AL4 9DD
⏲ 11-3, 5.30-11; 11-midnight Fri & Sat; 12-11 Sun
☎ (01727) 854845
Caledonian Deuchars IPA; Greene King IPA, Abbot; guest beers Ⓖ
Now a regular Guide entry, this classic Victorian red-brick pub is located in the middle of the High Street. This is a locals' pub extending a warm welcome to all discerning ale drinkers, with the landlord now in his 21st year of residence. Up to five real ales are available, four of them dispensed straight from the cask from a separate cellar area located nearby at floor level, so don't be surprised if your server disappears briefly.
⛫Q☋❀◑⊟⊟(304,320)♣P

Sawbridgeworth

Gate
81 London Road, CM21 9JJ
⏲ 11.30-2.30, 5.30-11; 11.30-11 Fri & Sat; 12-11 Sun
☎ (01279) 722313
Rebellion IPA; guest beers Ⓗ
A huge collection of pump clips adorns the beams in the front bar, while the smaller back bar is home to several sports teams. Large beer festivals are held at Easter and the August bank holiday, with smaller ones on other holidays. Home of the Sawbridgeworth Brewery, which now has a small bottling plant. Local CAMRA Pub of the Year 2007.
❀◐♿⇌⊟(510,333)♣●P

South Mimms

White Hart
St Albans Road, EN6 3PJ (on B556)
⏲ 11-11; 12-10.30 Sun
☎ (01707) 642122
McMullen AK, Country Ⓗ
Originally a coaching inn on the Great North Road, this 400-year-old building still has the stables at the rear. A traditional pub with a post-war interior, the lounge has been opened out to extend the dining facilities (no food Sun eve). The public bar is lively with darts and crib teams and many trophies are on display. The raised garden overlooks farmland.
⛫❀◑⊟♿⊟♣P

Stevenage

Our Mutual Friend
Broadwater Crescent, SG2 8EH
⏲ 12-11; 12-3, 8-11 Sun
☎ (01438) 312282
Beer range varies Ⓗ
Thriving community pub brought back from the cask ale graveyard in 2002. Since then it has appeared in every issue of the Guide and now sports seven real ales, real cider and perry plus a small range of Belgian bottled beers. A regular beer festival brightens up January. Locals drink alongside visitors who come for the good beer and regular pool and darts matches. CAMRA local Branch Pub of the Year in 2006, 2007 and 2008.
Q❀◐⊟⊟♣●P⌷

Tring

King's Arms
King Street, HP23 6BE
⏲ 12-2.30 (3 Fri), 7-11; 11.30-3, 7-11 Sat; 12-4, 7-10.30 Sun
☎ (01442) 823318
Wadworth 6X; guest beers Ⓗ
This 1830s back-street, fuchsia pink building is a frequent local CAMRA Pub of the Year and a Guide regular, having been run by the same licensees for 27 years. It offers an ever-changing array of five ales, two real fires in winter and a secluded, heated patio with canopies for outdoor drinking. Home-cooked food is based on an imaginative international menu. Children welcome lunchtime only.
⛫Q❀◑⊟●⚊

Robin Hood ✔
1 Brook Street, HP23 5ED (jct B4635/B486)
⏲ 11.30-3, 5.30-11 (11.30 Fri); 12-4, 6-11.30 Sat; 12-4, 7-10.30 Sun
☎ (01442) 824912
Fuller's Chiswick, Discovery, London Pride, ESB; guest beer Ⓗ
Warm, friendly pub situated on the edge of town and catering for all ages. The cosy bar area opens out into a welcoming conservatory, complete with wood-burning stove, which leads to the heated patio and garden. Paintings on the walls are supplied by a local gallery and are for sale. Freshly-prepared food is available all week with fish a speciality. ⛫Q☋◑⊟⚊

Ware

Crooked Billet
140 Musley Hill, SG12 7NL TL362151
⏲ 12-2.30 (Tue & Fri), 5.30-11.30 (midnight Fri); 12-midnight Sat; 12-11.30 Sun
☎ (01920) 462516
Beer range varies Ⓗ
A ppular local, well worth tracking down. There are two bars, one cosy and relaxed, the other more lively with pool and sport on TV. The landlord is a staunch Carlisle United supporter so stray fans can expect red carpet treatment. With an ever-changing range of cask ales, this is a rare outlet for dark mild during the cooler months. Additional beers are sometimes drawn direct from the cellar. Bar snacks at weekends. ⛫❀⊟(395)♣⚊

Worppell ✓

35 Watton Road, SG12 0AD TL353147
12-2.30, 5-11; 12-midnight Fri & Sat; 12-10 Sun
☎ (01920) 411666
Greene King IPA, Abbot; guest beers Ⓗ
One of Hertfordshire's longest serving landlords are now in their 26th year at the Worppell – named after the man who built the pub in the 19th century. A much-loved and comfortable single bar local, conversation and banter dominate among regulars who truly appreciate the beer quality. An occasional guest ale comes from the Greene King stable. Food available Monday to Friday lunchtime. Sunday is often busy with live TV football.
❀◐♣

Wareside

Chequers

SG12 7QY (on B1004) TL394157
12-3, 6-11; 12-4, 6-10.30 Sun
☎ (01920) 467010
Adnams Bitter; Taylor Landlord; guest beers Ⓗ
Old, traditional and spacious coaching inn run by the same owners for 13 years. It has a cosy feel with roaring fires in winter, comfortable sofas, three bars and a restaurant. Local Red Squirrel beers are often among the guests. Situated in lovely countryside and serving excellent home-cooked food with vegetarian options, the pub is often busy with walkers and cyclists. Book ahead for B&B accommodation. ♨Q❀🛏◐◑♿🚌P⊱

Watford

One Crown

156 High Street, WD17 2EN
12-11 (9 Sun)
☎ (01923) 222626
Tring Jack O' Legs, seasonal beers Ⓗ
The oldest licensed pub in Watford, dating from the 16th century. The single bar interior divides into several areas, one with a pool table and dartboard. The clientele is a mixture of locals and visitors to the town centre. A guest beer is often available, usually the current Tring seasonal ale. Sandwiches are available on weekday lunchtimes. Popular monthly events include a quiz, karaoke and a 50/60s music evening. ◐🚌♣⊱

Southern Cross ✓

41-43 Langley Road, WD17 4PP
11-11 (11.30 Thu-Sat); 12-10.30 Sun
☎ (01923) 256033
Adnams Broadside; Caledonian Deuchars IPA; Wells Bombardier; guest beers Ⓗ
Thriving, large, open-plan bar with a central serving area. Converted from two houses, it was the home of American intelligence during WWII. Three guest beers from the Beer Seller list are usually available. A regular entertainment-themed quiz is held on Tuesday and general knowledge quizzes on Thursday and Sunday. Food is served until 9pm. Board games are available. No children under 14 are allowed in the bar.
❀🛏◐♿🚌♣P⊱

West Herts Sports and Social Club

Park Avenue, WD18 7HP
12-2 summer, 4-11; 12-11 Fri & Sat; 12-10.30 Sun
☎ (01923) 229239 🌐 westhertssports.co.uk
Fuller's London Pride; Young's Bitter; guest beers Ⓗ
Former CAMRA Club of the Year on the site of Watford FC's original ground. The clubhouse features a comfortable, modern bar serving up to three guest beers. A function room, home of the CAMRA Watford Beer Festival for the past 13 years, can be hired. Darts, dominoes and cribbage are played. Rolls and pies are usually available, with oversized glasses reserved for real ale. Open to non-members with a current CAMRA membership card or a copy of this Guide. ❀♿♣P⊱🗑

Welwyn

White Horse

30 Mill Lane, AL6 9ET TL232161
12-3, 5.30-11; 12-11 Fri & Sat; 12-10.30 Sun
☎ (01438) 714366
Adnams Bitter; Caledonian Deuchars IPA; Courage Directors Bitter; Fuller's London Pride; guest beers Ⓗ
Grade II-listed, symnpathetically preserved, 17th-century coaching inn. Proud of its selection of beers, wines and whiskies, there is also an extensive menu of freshly prepared food, including a popular Sunday carvery (two sittings, booking advisable). A restaurant was added in 2007. A beer festival is staged in June. Large secluded garden. ♨❀◐◑P

Wheathampstead

Nelson

135 Marford Road, AL4 8NH
11-11; 12-10.30 Sun
☎ (01582) 831577
Greene King IPA; McMullen AK; guest beers Ⓗ
Two-hundred-year-old village local with an interior divided into several distinct areas around a central real fire.This friendly community pub hosts many social activities including a meat raffle on Sunday afternoon. Darts, cribbage and dominoes are played and a quiz held on Wednesday. Annual September beer festival. Good value lunches. Children are welcome daytime. ♨❀◐🚌♣●P⊱

Wildhill

Woodman

45 Wildhill Road, AL9 6EA TL264068
11.30-2.30, 5.30-11; 12-2.30, 7-10.30 Sun
☎ (01707) 642618
Greene King IPA, Abbot; McMullen AK; guest beers Ⓗ
Small, friendly village pub offering reasonably priced guest beers from regional and micro-breweries. All real ales are available by request in lined glasses. Popular for its excellent lunchtime food. The landlord is a keen Saracens rugby supporter. A regular entry in the Guide, the pub has won numerous awards including local CAMRA Pub of the Year a record seven times. Q❀◐♣●P⊱

ISLE OF WIGHT

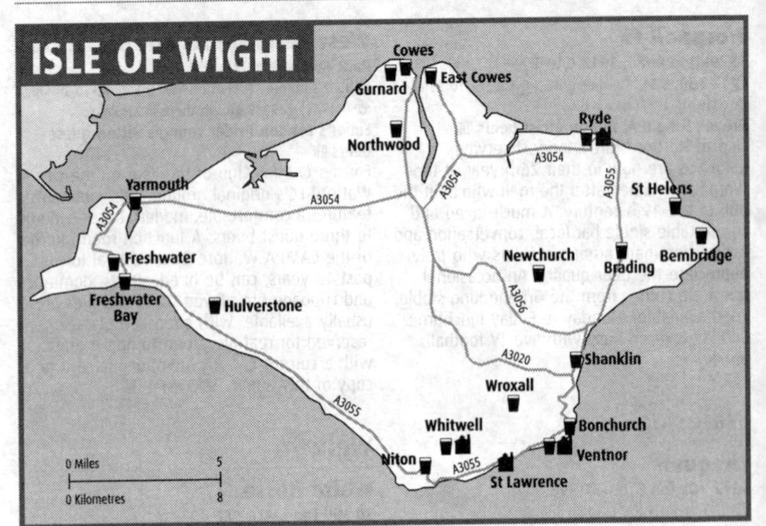

Bembridge

Olde Village Inn

61 High Street, PO35 5SF

11 (12 Sun)-11

(01983) 872616

Greene King IPA, Abbot; guest beer

Comfortable village local with a warm and friendly atmosphere. The one-bar interior is expansive but cosy. Older people are catered for Monday to Friday with lunchtime meals at reduced prices. Live music plays on occasional Fridays.

Bonchurch

Bonchurch Inn

The Chute, PO38 1NU (off Shanklin-Ventnor road)

11-3, 6.30-11; 12-3, 7-10.30 Sun

(01983) 852611 bonchurch-inn.co.uk

Courage Best Bitter, Directors; Greene King Ruddles Best, Ruddles County

Superbly preserved stone pub in a Dickensian courtyard, formerly the stables of the adjacent manor house. Little has changed since it gained its licence in the 1840s, making this one of the most unspoilt pubs on the Island. As well as featuring in an episode of The Detectives, the pub displays mementoes and keepsakes from many famous names who have popped in when visiting the Island. The Courage ales are on offer all year supplemented by Ruddles beers occasionally in summer.

Brading

Yarbridge Inn

Yarbridge, PO36 0AA

11-11.30; 12-11 (12-5, 5-11 winter) Sun

(01983) 406212 yarbridgeinn.co.uk

Beer range varies

Previously known as the Anglers, this is a pleasant single-bar pub with a changing range of nine beers on handpump. The dining area offers a fixed menu plus specials board and a choice of roasts on Sunday. Outside is a safe area for children and a paved area with parasols. Filled with railway memorabilia, the pub has its own model train and the Brading to Sandown line at the bottom of the garden. CAMRA Isle of Wight Pub of the Year in 2006 and 2007, it was also runner up in the Wessex Region in 2007. Live music is hosted occasionally.

Cowes

Anchor Inn

1 High Street, PO31 7SA

11-11; 12-10.30 Sun

(01983) 292823 theanchorcowes.com

Fuller's London Pride; Goddards Fuggle-Dee-Dum; Wadworth 6X; guest beers

Originally the Trumpeters back in 1704, this high-street pub is next to the marina, tempting visiting yachtsmen after a hard day at sea. Hugely popular during the summer months, it has a covered area outside with tables for smokers. An extensive food menu available all day caters for all tastes with families welcome. Live music plays outside in summer and in the stable bar in winter. Room-only accommodation comprises seven comfortable rooms.

Union Inn

Watchouse Lane, PO31 7QH

11-11 (closed 3-6 Mon-Wed winter); 12-10.30 Sun

(01983) 293163

Fuller's Chiswick, London Pride; Gale's HSB

One three-sided bar serves the lounge, snug, dining area and airy conservatory which was originally the yard. A roaring fire in winter adds to the cosy atmosphere and an interesting collection of maritime photographs decorates the walls. Meals are served all day in summer and the specials board has some

INDEPENDENT BREWERIES

Goddards Ryde
Stumpy's Whitwell
Ventnor Ventnor
Yates' St Lawrence

tasty offerings. A gem of a pub with four letting rooms.

East Cowes

Ship & Castle

21 Castle Street, PO32 6RB (opp the Red Funnel Car Park)

11 (12 Sun)-late

(01983) 290522

St Austell Dartmoor Best; guest beer

Adorned with seafaring memorabilia, the Ship & Castle is just how street corner pubs used to be – and very cosy in the winter when the wind whistles across the Red Funnel car park. Easy to find – turn left off the floating bridge or once around the block if arriving from Southampton. Despite the small bar there are always at least three beers on offer. Bustling on games nights, four darts teams and Sky TV keeps the locals happy.

Freshwater

Prince of Wales

Princes Road, PO40 9ED

3 (11 Fri & Sat)-11; 12-11 Sun

(01983) 753535

Flowers IPA; Greene King XX Mild, Abbot; Hampshire King Alfred's; Wadworth 6X; Yates' Undercliff Experience

Fine, unspoilt town pub run by possibly the longest serving landlord on the Isle of Wight. Situated just off the main Freshwater shopping centre, it has a large garden to relax in and pleasant public and lounge bars to sample the well-kept ales. A popular games area adds to the lively atmosphere. Should you have one too many during the evening, no need to phone for a taxi home —the landlord has one.

Freshwater Bay

Fat Cat

Sandpipers, Coastguard Lane, PO40 9QX

10.30-midnight

(01983) 758500 sandpipershotel.com

Beer range varies

A real gem within the Sandpipers Hotel, situated between Freshwater Bay and the Afton Nature Reserve. An ever-changing range of ales is on offer with many from smaller and more unusual breweries. This unique pub is well worth a visit, especially for the biggest real ale festival on the Island in early May. For children there is an adventure playground and cosy playroom with games and amusements. The hotel is well appointed with a popular restaurant.

Gurnard

Portland Inn

2 Worsley Road, PO31 8JN (opp church)

11-11 (11.30 Fri & Sat); 12-10.30 Sun

(01983) 292948

Beer range varies

This multi-tasking building has been a bakery, grocer's, hardware store and finally a pub. The landlady has injected new life into the pub by introducing real food made with locally-sourced ingredients selected personally by the resident chef. An extension into the depths of the building has created a new restaurant. Three changing beers are from the Punch list. Sky Sports screens major fixtures. Families and well-behaved children are welcome. The Gurnard Firework Charity was formed here to raise funds and support local charities.

Hulverstone

Sun Inn

Main Road, PO30 4EH

11-11; 12-10.30 Sun

(01983) 852611 sun-hulverstone.com

Draught Bass; Taylor Landlord; Wychwood Hobgoblin; Young's Special

Six-hundred-year-old hostelry in the heart of rural west Wight with a charming garden and uninterrupted views to the sea. It has a strong following for food with an extensive menu and daily specials served all day, plus a weekly curry night. There is a large restaurant and the pub caters for wedding parties in a stunning extension. Weekly music nights feature local musicians. Well-behaved children are welcome.

Newchurch

Pointer Inn

High Street, PO36 0NN

11.30-3, 6-11; 12-11 Sun

(01983) 865202

Fuller's London Pride, seasonal beers; Gale's HSB

Ancient village local with a warm, cosy atmosphere where families are welcome. The single-room interior comprises the old public bar, lounge and dining area. The restaurant has a fine reputation for nothing but home-cooked food prepared by a chef with 35 years experience (booking is essential). There is a large garden with a petanque terrain. For smokers there is a covered area. Awarded Dining Pub of the Year by the Island Magazine.

Niton

White Lion

High Street, PO38 2AT

11-midnight (11 Sun)

(01983) 730293

Beer range varies

Picturesque pub, full of character, in the centre of the village. The landlord has made a great impression since his arrival with a complete overhaul of the premises. The pub has a fine reputation for food and the Sunday roast is a sell-out. From the cellar comes a succession of four-ever changing ales – at least one is from an Island brewery and Ringwood and Bass appear regularly. There is a covered, decked area outside for smokers. Live music plays once a month.

Northwood

Travellers Joy

85 Pallance Road, PO31 8LS (on A3020 Yarmouth Road out of Cowes)

✪ 11-2.30, 5-11; 11-midnight Fri & Sat; 12-3, 7-midnight Sun

☎ (01983) 298024 🌐 tjoy.co.uk

Goddards Special Bitter; guest beers Ⓗ

Offering one of the best choices of cask ale on the Isle of Wight, this well renovated and extended old country inn was the Island's first beer exhibition house. It has been voted CAMRA branch Pub of the Year on five occasions. Seven carefully chosen ales supplement the ever faithful GSB and seasonal beers from the Island brewers are always popular – if you have mastered the 'Northwood nod' you may even get a special from the cellar. A good range of home-cooked food is available lunchtime and evening. ⛫☕❀◐▲♣P⅃

Ryde

High Park Tavern

84 High Park Road, PO33 1BX (on Ryde-Brading road)

✪ 10-midnight; 12-10.30 Sun

☎ (01983) 562841

Beer range varies Ⓗ

This free house has come alive since the arrival of Sharon and Denzil. What was once a fairly ordinary pub on a main road location has been transformed by a lick of paint, a change of decor and by recognising the needs of the community. Occasional live music is hosted with musicians gathering in the large back room for jam sessions prompted by musician Denzil. Three real ales always include one from an Island brewer. A real town pub as they ought to be, families are welcome with a fine Sunday roast to end the week. ⛫❀◐▲⊟♣⅃

Simeon Arms

21 Simeon Street, PO33 1JG (opp canoe lake)

✪ 11-midnight (11 Tue & Wed); 12-11.30 Sun

☎ (01983) 614954

Courage Directors; Goddards Special Bitter; guest beers Ⓗ

Thriving yet unlikely gem tucked away in a Ryde back street with a Tardis-like interior and annexed function hall. The pub is immensely popular with the local community who come to participate in various leagues including darts, crib and pool, and petanque on the enormous floodlit terrain in summer. Food is available weekend evenings and lunchtime. Live music plays on Saturday night. The smoking area outside is heated and covered. ❀◐⇌⊟♣⅃

Solent Inn ✔

7 Monkton Street, PO33 1JW

✪ 11-11 (12.30am Thu-Sat); closed 3-5 Mon-Thu winter; 12-10.30 Sun

☎ (01983) 563546

Banks's Bitter; Oakleaf Blake's Gosport Bitter; guest beers Ⓗ

Excellent street-corner local with a warm, welcoming atmosphere. There is live music at least three times a week and a very friendly weekly quiz. New tenants have made a splendid impression with the locals and added to the appeal of the interior with recent improvements. An interesting range of ales, including five guests, comes from the Punch portfolio. Good home-cooked food is served at lunchtime and barbecues are hosted in summer. Themed and karaoke nights are always popular. The pub has Cask Marque accreditation. ⛫❀◐⊟⇌⊟♣⅃☐

St Helens

Vine Inn

Upper Green Road, PO33 1UJ

✪ 11-11 (12.30 Fri & Sat); 11-11.30 Sun

☎ (01983) 872337 🌐 the-vine-inn.co.uk

Fuller's London Pride; guest beers Ⓗ

The front of the pub overlooks what is possibly the biggest village green in the kingdom and known locally as Goose Island. A major refurbishment has changed the emphasis to food, served lunchtime and evening. Although now a single bar, there is definitely a feel of saloon and public about the interior of this enormously successful enterprise. An eclectic selection of memorabilia reflecting local history, from railways to hunting to breweries to maritime, decorates the walls. Three guest beers include one from an Island brewery. ◐♿▲⊟♣⅃

Shanklin

Chine Inn

Chine Hill, PO37 6BW

✪ 12-4, 7-11; 12-10.30 Sun

☎ (01983) 865880

Shepherd Neame Spitfire; Taylor Landlord; guest beer Ⓗ

This inn is a classic. The pub, which has stood since 1621, must have some claim to being one of the oldest buildings with a licence on the Island. Completely refurbished, it has retained plenty of the original charm for which it was well known. On a summer's day when the sky is blue and the sun's rays are dancing on Sandown Bay, there is no finer view in England than from here. ⛫Q❀◐⊟▲⇌♣

Ventnor

Volunteer

30 Victoria Street, PO38 1ES

✪ 11-11 (midnight Fri & Sat); 12-11 Sun

☎ (01983) 853537 🌐 volunteer-inn.co.uk

Courage Best Bitter; Greene King Abbot; Ventnor Golden; guest beers Ⓗ

Built in 1866, the Volunteer is probably the smallest pub on the Isle of Wight. It operated as a beer house between 1869 and 1871 and retains many original features of a traditional drinkers' pub. A past winner of local CAMRA Pub of the Year, between four and six guest beers are usually available. No chips, no children, no fruit machines, no video games – just a pure adult drinking house and one of the few places where you can still play rings and enjoy a traditional games night. ⛫Q⊟♣♣⅃

ENGLAND

Whitwell

White Horse

High Street, PO38 2PY

11-3, 6-11; 12-3, 6-10.30 Sun

☎ (01983) 730375

Beer range varies Ⓗ

Built in 1454, this old stone building is considered to be the oldest established inn on the Isle of Wight. Fire destroyed the original thatch roof which has now been replaced with the more traditional slate. An extension to the side adds a family area and additional dining space. The remainder of the building is traditional with intimate areas to the rear. Five handpumps serve a changing range of beers and the excellent food menu is extensive. A large garden is fine for warmer days.

Q❀◑♿P

Wroxall

Four Seasons

2 Clarence Road, PO38 3BY

10.30-midnight; 11-11.30 Sun

☎ (01983) 854701

Gale's HSB; Ringwood Best Bitter; Wells Bombardier Ⓗ

Formerly known as the Star, this pub was brought back to life after a disastrous fire when it could easily have been lost to housing. Now a successful village pub, it has an Island-wide reputation for good food and has been recognised by the Tourist Board with an award for local produce quality. There is a covered, heated smokers' area.

Q❀◑♿P

Yarmouth

Wheatsheaf Inn

Bridge Road, PO41 0PH (opp George Hotel)

11-11; 12-10.30 Sun

☎ (01983) 760456

Fuller's Londons Pride; Goddards Fuggle Dee Dum; Ringwood Best Bitter Ⓗ

Spacious and comfortable old coaching house. A recent refurbishment has added more rooms and done away with much of the clutter, giving a light and airy feel to the interior. The large traditional public bar attracts locals and visiting yachtsmen. All the popular pub games are played here and pub teams compete in the local leagues. An interesting and extensive menu is served all day and families are most welcome. Accommodation is in three rooms.

❀◑♿

Pointer Inn, Newchurch.

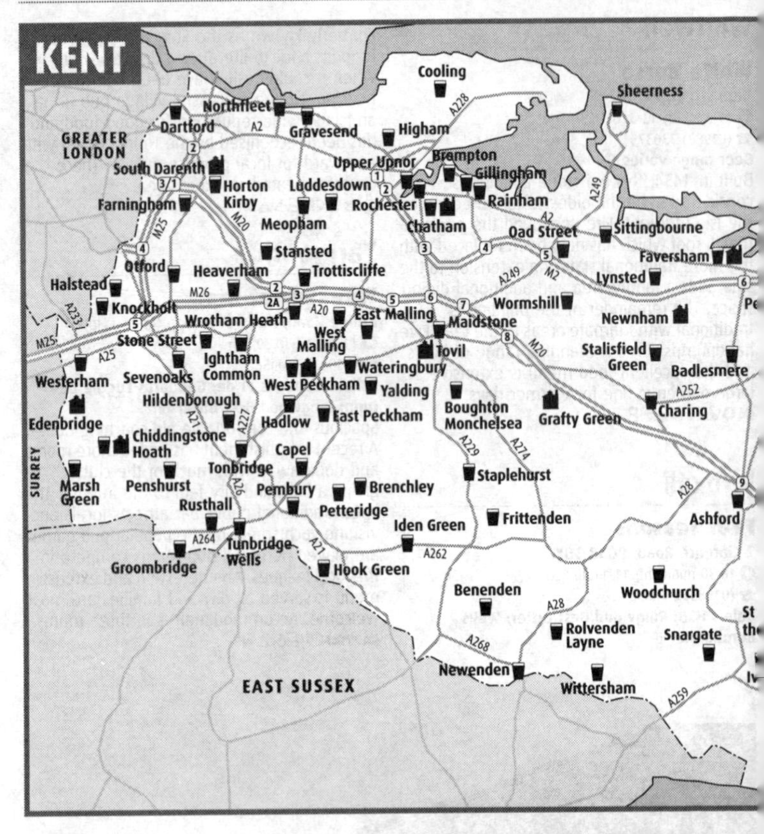

Ashford

County Hotel ✔

10 High Street, TN24 8TD

✪ 9-midnight (1am Fri & Sat)

☎ (01233) 646891

Courage Best Bitter, Directors; Greene King Abbot; Shepherd Neame Spitfire; guest beers Ⓗ

This pub was probably built circa 1710, when it was a doctor's home and medical practice. It became an inn around 1890, and was named the County Hotel in 1926. There are two bars in a split-level layout with three distinct seating areas. An interesting and varied selection of real ales is usually available. The food is good value and children are welcome in the family area providing food is ordered. This Wetherspoon pub is well worth a visit. Q❀◑♿⇌🚌P⁝

Badlesmere

Red Lion

Ashford Road, ME13 0NX (on A251)

✪ 12-3 (not Mon), 5-11; 12-midnight Fri; 12-11 Sat; 12-10.30 Sun

☎ (01233) 740320

Shepherd Neame Master Brew Bitter; Taylor Landlord; guest beers Ⓗ

A friendly free house, five miles south of Faversham, with many exposed beams and low ceilings. Beer festivals are held over the Easter and August bank holiday weekends when on-site camping is available. A range of good home-cooked food is served (no meals Fri and Sun eve). Varied live music is performed every Friday night when the pub gets very busy. The large garden is popular with families in summer. ⛰❀◑⛺🚌♣P⁝

Benenden

Bull

The Street, TN17 4DE

✪ 12 (4 Mon & Tue)-midnight

☎ (01580) 240054 🌐 thebullatbenenden.co.uk

Dark Star Hophead; Harveys Sussex Best Bitter; Larkins Traditional; guest beers Ⓗ

A 17th-century pub in the village centre whose comfortable interior features wooden floors, exposed beams and a large inglenook fireplace. Meals are served in the bar and conservatory, where booking is essential for the Sunday lunchtime carvery. Live music is staged on most Sunday afternoons and some Saturday evenings. There are two darts teams. A secluded garden has wooden decking which leads to a children's play area. Biddenden Bushells cider is available. Local CAMRA Pub of the Year 2007. ⛰❀🛏◑⛺🚌(297)♣🍏P⁝

Bishopsbourne

Mermaid Inn

The Street, CT4 5HX (1000m from A2)

✪ 12-3.30, 6 (7 Sun)-11; 12-11.30 Sat

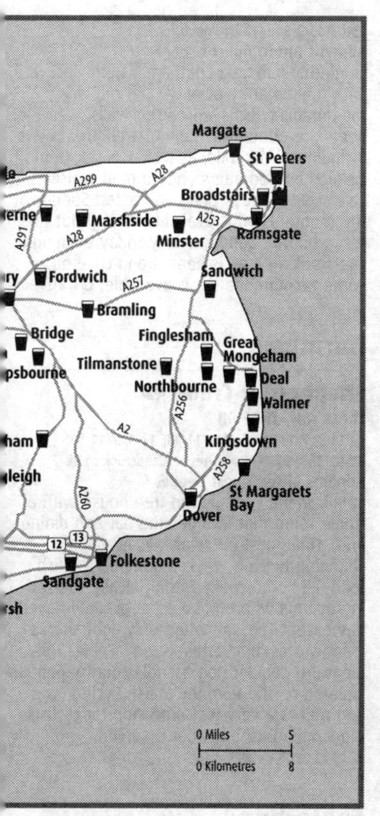

☎ (01227) 830581

Shepherd Neame Master Brew Bitter, seasonal beers 🄷

Built in 1865, this red-brick pub nestles in a pretty village in glorious Kentish countryside. Workers from Sir John Prestige's nearby estate used to frequent the pub, and the mermaid insignia is from the Prestige coat of arms. The light and airy bar areas are always busy with regulars enjoying a chat. Excellent home-cooked lunches are available in the small dining area (no meals Sun). Walkers and dogs are welcome, but check at the bar before bringing in children. The smoking area is covered and heated. ⛼Q❀◐♿♣⊱

Boughton Monchelsea

Cock Inn

Heath Road, ME17 4JD

⚙ 11-11; 12-10.30 Sun

☎ (01622) 743166

Young's Bitter, Special, seasonal beers 🄷

This excellent, dog-friendly, Young's country pub was built in 1658. It features low beams in spacious, welcoming surroundings and offers good ale and food. Meals are served in the bar and restaurant, lunchtimes and evenings (not Sun eve). There is no pool table or Sky TV, but darts and a selection of board games are available. A large patio is provided for smokers. ⛼❀◐🚌(59)♣P⊱

Bramling

Haywain

Canterbury Road, CT3 1NB

⚙ 7-11 Mon; 12-3, 6-11 (midnight Fri & Sat); 12-4 Sun

☎ (01227) 720676 🌐 thehaywainpubbramling.co.uk

Fuller's London Pride; Wells Bombardier; guest beers 🄷

The welcoming main bar features hanging hop bines and assorted curios, while the tiny snug is mainly used for diners and meetings. Traditional games include darts plus bat and trap, and there are frequent Monday night quizzes. Guest beers usually come from Shepherd Neame or small regional breweries, and two annual beer festivals are hosted in marquees in the attractive garden, on the spring bank holiday and the last week in September. Excellent home-cooked food, using local produce, is served (not Mon). ⛼Q❀◐🚌♣P

Brenchley

Halfway House ✔

Horsmonden Road, TN12 7AX (½ mile SE of village) TQ682413

⚙ 12-11.30 (11 Sun)

☎ (01892) 722526

Goacher's Fine Light Ale; Harveys Sussex Best Bitter; Larkins Chiddingstone; Rother Valley Mild; 🄷 **guest beers** 🄶

Coaching inn built in 1790, once used as a morgue and reputed to be haunted. Situated in Kent's own Isle of Wight, as proclaimed by the sign fronting the building and confirmed by the OS map. Six or more ales are served by gravity, with beer festivals on Whitsun and August bank holiday weekends featuring up to 50 beers. A large garden includes a children's play area and a separate adults-only area. Kent Regional CAMRA Pub of the Year 2007 and runner up 2008.
⛼Q⛺❀🛏◐🚌(297)♣●P⊱

Bridge

Plough & Harrow

86 High Street, CT4 5LA (1000m from A2)

⚙ 11-11; 12-10.30 Sun

☎ (01227) 830455

Shepherd Neame Master Brew Bitter, seasonal beers 🄷

Set in a large village, this pub was once a brewery but became a pub in 1832. Its history is documented with photographs on the walls of the three traditionally furnished bars. The

INDEPENDENT BREWERIES

Goacher's Tovil
Hopdaemon Newnham
Larkins Chiddingstone
Millis South Darenth
Nelson Chatham
Ramsgate Broadstairs
Shepherd Neame Faversham
Swan on the Green West Peckham
Westerham Edenbridge
Whitstable Grafty Green

back room houses a display of Shepherd Neame's famous advertising posters, while a function room hosts many local clubs. Dogs and walkers are welcome and often buy a snack at the nearby bakery to enjoy in the pub. There is a sheltered, heated smoking area and bar billiards. ♨Q❀🚌(16,17)♣P⁵—

Broadstairs

Neptune's Hall

1-3 Harbour Street, CT10 1ET

12-11 (midnight Fri & Sat); 12-10.30 Sun

☎ (01843) 861400

Shepherd Neame Master Brew Bitter, Spitfire, seasonal beers Ⓗ

Lively old fishermen's pub, close to the picturesque harbour and beach. The listed interior, built in 1815, is on CAMRA's National Inventory. Note the fine panelling behind the bar and the large collection of beer bottles on display. Regular live music is performed on Sunday evenings and this is a popular venue during the annual Folk Week. A New Year's Day swim is organised by the landlord each year for charity. A dog friendly pub, it has a large courtyard with a heated and covered smoking area. ❀◑🚌♿⁵—

Tartar Frigate

37-39 Harbour Street, CT10 1EU

11-11 (10.30 Sun)

☎ (01843) 601636

Flowers IPA; Shepherd Neame Master Brew Bitter; guest beer Ⓗ

A former Cobb's house dating from the 18th century, it is named after HMS Tartar, a frigate built in a local shipyard. Both Charles Dickens and former Prime Minister Lord Heath frequented this picturesque harbourside inn with its knapped flint façade and low-beamed interior which is reputedly haunted by the top half of a woman in black. Poker nights are held on Mondays and Thursdays and there is a folk music session every Wednesday. A top class fish restaurant is above the pub. ♨◑●♣

Wrotham Arms

9 Ramsgate Road, CT10 1QQ

11-11 (midnight Fri & Sat); 1 (12 Sat & Sun)-11 (midnight Fri & Sat) winter; 11 (12 winter)-11 Sun

☎ (01843) 861788

Shepherd Neame Master Brew Bitter, Spitfire, seasonal beers Ⓗ

Comfortable, atmospheric pub with a recently refurbished bar and upstairs accommodation. Live music covering a variety of genres is performed every Saturday and most Friday evenings – this is a popular venue during the annual Folk Week. The food is mainly traditional, using local high-street ingredients, and includes a vegetarian option and children's menu. Meals are served daily. A dog-friendly pub, outside is a heated and covered smoking area. ♨❀🛏◑●♿🚌♣⁵—

Brompton

King George V ✔

1 Prospect Row, ME7 5AL

11.45-11; 12-10.30 Sun

☎ (01634) 842418 🌐 kgpub.com

Adnams Bitter; guest beers Ⓗ

Single-bar pub near Chatham historic dockyard with a good array of naval and military memorabilia displayed on the walls. Four beers are offered of varying strength, always including a dark mild, as well as a selection of Belgian bottled beers and 40 malt whiskies. Live acoustic music plays on the last Sunday of the month. Food is available throughout the week but not Sunday and Monday evenings. The smoking area is heated and covered. Some accommodation is available. Q🛏◑⁵—

Burmarsh

Shepherd & Crook ✔

Shear Way, TN29 0JJ

11-3, 7-11 Tue & Thu; 11-11; 12-5, 7-11 Sun

☎ (01303) 872336 🌐 shepherdandcrook.co.uk

Adnams Bitter; guest beer Ⓗ

Small, friendly family-run free house with a single room that includes the bar and dining area. One guest ale is always available, changing twice a week. Traditional English food, all home cooked using locally sourced ingredients where possible, is available every day except Tuesday when only light snacks (sandwiches/baguettes) are available. This pleasant, popular dog-friendly country pub is situated on the Romney Marsh Cycle Route and makes a very welcome stop for cyclists. Biddenden Bushells cider is served.

♨Q🐎❀◑●♣●P

Canterbury

Eight Bells

34 London Road, CT2 8LN

3 (12 Sat)-11 (midnight Thu-Sat); 12-10.30 Sun

☎ (01227) 454794

Fuller's London Pride; Greene King IPA; Young's Bitter Ⓗ

Dating from 1708, this cosy, traditional local was rebuilt in 1902. It has original embossed windows and walls decorated with memorabilia, including some from WWI. Live music night is Friday, when country and western and karaoke alternate. Five darts teams play every week and many of their trophies are displayed. An online quiz is held on the first Sunday of every month. At the back is a covered patio for smokers, and an attractive, small walled garden. Dogs and children are welcome.

❀⇌(Canterbury West)🚌♣⁵—

King's Head

204 Wincheap, CT1 3RY

12-2.30, 4.45-midnight; 12-midnight Fri & Sat; 12-11.30 Sun

☎ (01227) 462885 🌐 smoothhound.co.uk/hotels/thekingshead.html

Greene King IPA; Harveys Sussex Best Bitter; guest beer Ⓗ

Traditional and friendly Grade-II listed 15th-century local a 15-minute walk from the city centre. Exposed beams, hanging hops and bric-a-brac add to its charm. Bar billiards and darts are played indoors, while bat & trap league matches are held in the garden in summer. There is a fortnightly Sunday quiz in winter, September to April. No food is served on Tuesday evening. Guest beers are normally sourced from micro-breweries. Three-star B&B is available, with parking for residents only. There is a heated and covered smoking shelter. ❀⇆◑ ⇌(Canterbury East)🚌♣P⅃

Phoenix

67 Old Dover Road, CT1 3DB
✪ 5-1am
☎ (01227) 464220
Young's Bitter; guest beers Ⓗ
Cosy corner pub full of cricket memorabilia and handy for the cricket ground. A changing range of five guest beers comes from all over Britain and includes a mild. A well-attended beer festival is held in December, showcasing a wide range of seasonal beers. Monday night is devoted to board games, while live music is performed monthly on a Saturday night. Good value food is served in generous portions (not Thu). An outdoor patio includes a covered smoking area.
⛰❀◑♿⇌(Canterbury East)🚌P⅃

Unicorn Inn

61 St Dunstan's Street, CT2 8BS
✪ 11.30-11 (midnight Fri & Sat)
☎ (01227) 463187 🌐 unicorninn.com
Caledonian Deuchars IPA; Shepherd Neame Master Brew Bitter; guest beers Ⓗ
This comfortable 1604 pub stands near the historic Westgate and boasts an attractive sun-trap garden. Bar billiards can be played, and a quiz, set by regular customers, is held weekly on Sunday evening. The two guest beers often feature a Kent micro-brewery ale. Imaginative food, available lunchtimes and evenings, ranges from pub favourites to exotic specials, and is excellent value (no food Sun). There is a covered and heated area for smoking.
⛰❀◑⇌(Canterbury West)🚌🚌(4,6)♣⅃

Capel

Dovecote Inn

Alders Road, TN12 6NU (½ mile W of A228)
TQ643441
✪ 12-3, 5.30-11.30; 12-11 Sun
☎ (01892) 835966
Gale's HSB; Harveys Sussex Best Bitter; Ⓗ **guest beers** Ⓖ
Welcoming traditional pub, popular with walkers, situated in a rural hamlet. The attractive one-bar interior features exposed red brick and wood with a real fire. Six cask ales are served by gravity from a cooled room through a mock-barrel frontage. Food is served every day except Monday, with a quiz night every other Wednesday. A large garden includes a children's climbing area and a patio for dining. All Saints church in nearby Tudeley features world-famous stained glass windows by artist Marc Chagall. ⛰Q❀◑P⅃

Charing

Bowl

Egg Hill Road, TN27 0HG (at jct of 5 Lanes)
TQ950514
✪ 12-midnight (11 Sun)
☎ (01233) 712256 🌐 bowlinn.co.uk
Fuller's London Pride; guest beers Ⓗ
Remote historic pub on the crest of the North Downs, signposted from the A20 and A251. Guest beers are often from Adnams and Harveys in addition to Kentish ales. A beer festival is held annually in mid-July. Snacks are available until 9.30pm. In winter the pub is warmed by a huge old inglenook fire. An extensive garden can be used for camping (booking essential) while five letting rooms are newly available. Note the unusual hexagonal pool table. ⛰Q❀⇆⛺♣P

Chartham

Artichoke

Rattington Street, CT4 7JE (by paper mill)
✪ 11-2.30, 7-11; 11-4, 7-1am Sat; 12-5, 7-11 Sun
☎ (01227) 738316
Shepherd Neame Master Brew Bitter, seasonal beers Ⓗ
A quaint, half-timbered exterior hints at the age of this pub, built in the 14th century as a Hall House. There is a cosy beamed bar with a large fireplace and in the dining room, one table is the glass-topped well. Evening food is only available on Friday and Saturday. Bat and trap is played in summer, and there are three dartboards and four darts teams. Quiz and race nights are held, dogs are allowed and there is a covered and heated smoking shelter.
⛰❀◑⇌🚌P⅃

Chatham

Alexandra

43 Railway Street, ME4 4RJ
✪ 11-midnight (1am Fri & Sat); 12-11 Sun
☎ (01634) 830545 🌐 alexandrachatham.co.uk
Shepherd Neame Master Brew Bitter, Spitfire, seasonal beers Ⓗ
This Victorian pub is close to the railway station. It has a large U-shaped bar and its walls are adorned with pictures of historical Chatham. Lunches are served daily. Live music is hosted every Sunday between 5-7pm and quiz night is Tuesday. Home to darts teams, there is a function room and covered outdoor smoking area. The pub is well served by local buses. ❀◑⇌🚌♣⅃

Chiddingstone Hoath

Rock

Near Edenbridge, TN8 7BS (1½ miles S of Chiddingstone, via Wellers Town)
✪ 11.30-3, 6-11; closed Mon; 12-4 Sun
☎ (01892) 870296
Larkins Traditional, Chiddingstone, Best, seasonal beer Ⓗ
Set on high ground to the West of Penshurst, the Rock is an attractive old tile-hung pub with low-beamed ceilings. It is named after one of the nearby rocky outcrops and has the distinction of belonging to the nearby Larkins Brewery. The full range of beers is available, along with good home-cooked food. The main bar has a floor of well-worn brick, with a

smaller and cosier saloon bar to the right. The unusual game of 'ringing the bull' can be played. ♨Q❀◑◐⊞♣P

Cooling

Horseshoe & Castle

The Street, ME3 8DJ

✪ 11.30 (5.30 Mon)-11 (12.30am Fri & Sat); 12-11.30 Sun

☎ (01634) 221691 ⊕ horseshoeandcastle.co.uk

Shepherd Neame Master Brew Bitter; guest beer Ⓗ

Situated in a quiet village, this pub is near a ruined castle once owned by Sir John Oldcastle, on whom Shakespeare modelled his Falstaff character, while the local graveyard was used in the film version of Great Expectations, where young Pip met the convict Magwich. Pool, darts, petanque and bat and trap can be played here. Seafood is a speciality, served in the separate dining area (no food Mon). Draught Addlestones cider is available. The pub has a Quality in Tourism four-star Inn Award for its accommodation. ♨❀⇔◑◐●P⁐

Dartford

Wat Tyler

80 High Street, DA1 1DE

✪ 9am-11 (midnight Fri & Sat); 10.30-11 Sun

☎ (01322) 272546 ⊕ wattylerinn.co.uk

Courage Best Bitter; John Smith's Bitter; guest beers Ⓗ

Dating from the early 15th century, this historic town-centre pub next to the parish church is a popular meeting place. Three constantly changing guest beers from local and micro-breweries place an emphasis on mid-brown to dark beers, as favoured by the regular patrons. A secluded mezzanine-level seating area is at the far end while high-backed wooden settles surround the bar. Handy for the railway station and the new Fastrack bus service to Bluewater Shopping Centre and Ebbsfleet International station. Q⇔♿⇌⊟♣⁐

Deal

Bohemian

47 Beach Street, CT14 6HY

✪ 11-midnight; closed Mon; 9am-midnight (7 winter) Sun

☎ (01304) 374843

Beer range varies Ⓗ

Located on Deal sea front with great sea views, this pub has a modern but very welcoming interior. The landlord travels Europe selecting the finest bottled and draught beers, together with beers from Japan and America. Up to six real ales, often from local breweries, plus perry and cider from Biddendens and Weston's, are on offer. Friday and Saturday nights are busy, the food is superb and unusual, and a sunny beer garden completes the scene. The smokers' area is heated. ❀◑◐⇌⊟●⁐

Deal Hoy

16 Duke Street, CT14 6DU

✪ 12-11 (8 Sun)

☎ (01304) 363972 ⊕ dealhoy.co.uk

Shepherd Neame Master Brew Bitter, Spitfire, seasonal beers Ⓗ

The pub's name recalls the town's maritime past, with the inn sign depicting a fine specimen of a hoy, or coastal sailing boat. Well worth seeking out towards the north end of town, this congenial drinkers' house manages to retain the best features of a good pub, unfortunately fast disappearing these days. The Victorian exterior contrasts with a relaxing, modern interior. There is a heated area for smokers, and an attractive patio area beckons in summer. Free Internet access. ❀⇌⊟(85)⁐

Prince Albert

187-189 Middle Street, CT14 6LW

✪ 6 (12 Sun)-11

☎ (01304) 375425

Beer range varies Ⓗ

Victorian pub situated in Deal's conservation area 100 metres from the sea front. A small, cosy bar offers a constantly changing range of three real ales from the smaller breweries, often local ones. The compact restaurant serves meals Wednesday to Saturday evenings and a roast lunch on Sunday. Outside, a small sheltered garden makes a pleasant refuge in summer. The pub is 10 minutes' walk to the north of the town centre, bus and railway stations. ♨Q❀⇔⇌⊟(85)⁐

Ship

141 Middle Street, CT14 6JZ

✪ 11-11.30

☎ (01304) 372222

Caledonian Deuchars IPA; Ramsgate Gadds' No 7, Gadds' Seasider; guest beers Ⓗ

Cosy, traditional local pub just off the sea front, 10 minutes' walk north of Deal's town centre, bus and railway stations. The larger, dark wood-floored front bar boasts five handpumps, featuring beers from the local Ramsgate Brewery. There is a small lounge area for reading and conversation. The smaller back room has a bar servery and steps leading down to the sheltered garden with a covered area. Both bars contain fine displays of nautical memorabilia. Live music plays on Thursday evening. Dogs are welcome. ♨Q❀⇌⊟(85)⁐

Dover

Blakes of Dover

52 Castle Street, CT16 1PJ

✪ 11.30-11; closed Sun

☎ (01304) 202194 ⊕ blakesofdover.com

Beer range varies Ⓗ/Ⓖ

A cellar bar that provides an oasis of calm near the town centre, where you can socialise and converse without shouting. The house bitter is brewed by Goacher's, whose stout is often available on draught. Guest beers come from all over the country, with an emphasis on Kent and Sussex cask ales, and occasional continental beers. Three ciders and two perries, from Double Vision, Thatchers and

Weston's, and an excellent range of malt whiskies, are also available. CAMRA Local Pub of the Year 2006.
Q❀⇄◐≠(Dover Priory)🚌●⁻

Eagle Inn

324 London Road, CT17 0SX
12-1am (2am Fri & Sat)
☎ (01304) 212929
Beer range varies H
A no-frills, popular and boisterous town local, situated on Dover's ring road. A spacious, bright open-plan room surrounds the central bar, with a large games room at the rear becoming the venue for live music on Saturday and karaoke on Friday. The pub specialises in beers from the Nelson Brewery. Meat raffles are run in aid of charity. Children are welcome until 6pm. The pub is a short walk from Dover Priory railway station and bus station. Dog friendly. ≠(Dover Priory)🚌♣

Golden Lion

11 Priory Street, CT17 9AA
10-11.30; 12-10 Sun
☎ (01304) 202919
Beer range varies H
Honest, no-frills pub close to Dover's town centre and public transport. Priory Street bus stop is just outside the door. There is invariably a lively atmosphere here with a welcome buzz of conversation. It is purely a drinkers' pub, although good value filled rolls are usually available. Karaoke evenings are sometimes staged. A good tradition of charitable donations through the Winkle Club has built up over the past 10 years, with regulars contributing in excess of £50,000.
≠(Dover Priory)🚌♣

Louis Armstrong

58 Maison Dieu Road, CT16 1RA
12-1am; 12-2, 7-1am Sun
☎ (01304) 204759
Hopdaemon Skrimshander IPA; guest beers H
Home to live music for over 40 years, the pub has an L-shaped bar with a stage to the rear. Pictures and posters of bands and musicians adorn the walls. Regular live music plays at weekends, jazz on Sunday, and occasionally on other days. The guest ale is usually from another Kent micro-brewery. Situated on Dover's one-way system, the pub is on most local bus routes. It has a fine garden to the rear plus a large car park and shops opposite.
❀🚌⁻

White Horse

Saint James Street, CT16 1QF
4-11; 1-10.30
☎ (01304) 242974
Taylor Landlord; guest beers H
A 14th-century pub adjoining the ruins of the old St James Church, this is a convenient stop for visitors to Dover Castle and cross-Channel travellers. It also has a strong local following, good conversation and up to four real ales, mainly from micro-breweries. Note the details of channel swimmers on the walls. A main bar and servery at the front has a raised rear bar area, while at the back, steps lead to a first-floor garden. Cider is from Biddendens, Thatchers and Moles. ❀🚌●⁻

East Malling

Rising Sun

125 Mill Street, ME19 6BX
12-11 (10.30 Sun)
☎ (01732) 843284
Goacher's Light; guest beer H
A terraced, family-run village local, popular with sports clubs, where thriving darts league teams play in the back room, with trophies proudly displayed. The front lounge is popular for live football matches, and a compact horseshoe-shaped central bar serves all areas. This is a genuine free house, with a keen pricing policy that ensures regular custom from local clientele and real ale connoisseurs. Simple but tasty food is available Monday to Friday lunchtimes and an extensive rear garden is ideal for summer visits.
❀◐≠🚌(58)♣⁻

East Peckham

Bush, Blackbird & Thrush

194 Bush Road, Peckham Bush, TN12 5LW (1 mile NE of East Peckham, via Pond Rd)
11-3, 6-11 (not Mon); 12-3, 6-10.30 Sun
☎ (01622) 871349
Shepherd Neame Master Brew Bitter, Spitfire, H **seasonal beers** G
A fine 15th-century tile-hung Kentish building on the edge of the village with a large garden and car park. The pub has two rooms: one is a dining room, the other is the bar, which includes tables and chairs for extra dining. There is a large open fire in both rooms and tasty home-cooked food is served lunchtimes and evenings daily. ⋒Q❀◐◑♿P

Elham

Kings Arms

The Square, CT4 6TJ (in village square near church)
11 (12 Sun)-midnight
☎ (01303) 840242
Flowers Original; Greene King IPA; Harveys Sussex Best Bitter H
Dating back to the 15th century, records show that the current saloon bar was used for brewing. This is a split-level pub where the front bar is for beer and conversation, the lower bar mainly for diners. You are assured of a warm welcome, and the place is popular with walkers. The pub acts as a centre for many community activities. Harveys Sussex Bitter heads a fine beer range and discounted meals for senior citizens are available Tuesday, Wednesday and Thursday lunchtimes. ⋒❀◐◑🚌♣

Farningham

Chequers

87 High Street, DA4 0DT
12-11 (10.30 Sun)
☎ (01322) 865222
Fuller's London Pride, ESB; Taylor Landlord; guest beers H

Bustling one-bar corner local in an attractive riverside village. Ten handpumps offer three regular beers and up to seven guests. Inside, the decor includes murals depicting local scenes plus decorative candelabra. Food is served Monday to Saturday lunchtimes and Sunday to Wednesday evenings. Parking is difficult but the village is close to the A20 and junction 3 of the M25. (421)

Faversham

Anchor

52 Abbey Street, ME13 7BP

12-11 (midnight Fri & Sat)

(01795) 536471 theanchorinnfaversham.com

Shepherd Neame Master Brew Bitter, Kent's Best, Spitfire, seasonal beers H

A 17th-century pub on the creek by the historic Standard Quay with its collection of sailing craft. The exterior is of local brick and inside the beams are old ships' timbers. The bar has a wood-burning stove for winter months and the dining room also has a large fireplace. Food is offered daily, lunchtimes and evenings, except for Sunday and Monday evenings in October, January and February. For the summer there are tables at the front and a large garden at the back.

Bear Inn

3 Market Place, ME13 7AG

10.30-3, 5.30-11 (11.30 Thu); 10.30-midnight Fri & Sat; 11.30-10.30 Sun

(01795) 532668

Shepherd Neame Master Brew Bitter, Kent's Best, Spitfire, seasonal beers H

In the historic market place, the Bear retains its three distinct bars with a long corridor at the side. The front bar, small middle bar and larger rear bar all have wood panelling and their own distinct character. The back bar has an unusual clock – instead of numbers it uses the pub's name spelt out around the dial. Wholesome home-cooked lunches are served. The pub is also popular with local folk musicians. There are tables on the pavement opposite the Guildhall.

Chimney Boy

59 Preston Street, ME13 8PG (one minute walk from station)

11 (12 Sun)-11 (midnight Fri & Sat)

(01795) 532007

Shepherd Neame Master Brew Bitter, Kent's Best H

This mid 18th-century building is said to have started life as a convent but became a hotel called the Limes around 1885. Shepherd Neame bought it in the 1930s and in the early 1970s steps leading up to a chimney were discovered and the pub was renamed the Chimney Boy. Situated by the railway station, the upstairs function room hosts many clubs and societies including the Faversham Folk Club, which meets every Wednesday evening. There is a rear patio. P

Elephant

31 The Mall, ME13 8JN

3-11.30; closed Mon; 12-midnight Sat; 12-10.30 (7 winter) Sun

(01795) 590157

Beer range varies H

Friendly, traditional ale house, which aims to provide the best choice of real ales in town. There are normally five ever-changing beers, usually including a mild, from local micro-breweries. Local Redskins cider is available in bottles. The single bar has an open fireplace and some of the seating area has wooden partitions. A function room caters for meetings and parties. The well-tended walled garden is good for the summer. Swale CAMRA Pub of the Year 2007 and 2008.

Railway Hotel

Preston Street, ME13 8PE (opp station)

12-11 (10.30 Sun)

(01795) 533173 railwayhotelfaversham.co.uk

Shepherd Neame Master Brew Bitter H

Opposite the railway station main entrance, the Railway is a true hotel with letting rooms. In the bar, the original imposing Victorian bar back dominates the spacious room, where dividing screens have been reinstated by the caring landlord. Patio tables are set outside in summer. Restaurant critics from national newspapers have heaped praise on the acclaimed dining room where meals are available Wednesday to Saturday and Sunday lunchtime. Breakfast for residents includes the proprietor's own marmalade and jams. Q P

Shipwright's Arms

Ham Road, Hollowshore, ME13 7TU (1½ miles N of Faversham) TR017636

11-3, 6-11; closed Mon winter; 12-3, 6-10.30 Sun

(01795) 590088

Goacher's Real Mild, Best Dark; guest beers G

An historic pub full of beams, character and many CAMRA awards, set in a remote location by the sea wall at the confluence of Faversham and Oare creeks. Yacht moorings are nearby and the interior has much nautical ephemera. The public bar is warmed by a log fire in winter. There is an extensive rear garden, as well as seating at the front. Beers are sourced from local micro-breweries with the house beer, Shipwrecked, brewed by Goacher's. Q P

Windmill Inn

Canterbury Road, Preston, ME13 8LT (on A2, opp Football Club)

12-midnight (1am Fri & Sat); 12-6 Sun

(01795) 536505

Shepherd Neame Master Brew Bitter, seasonal beers H

This classic two-bar pub, still with many original features, lies on Watling Street, the old Roman road from London to Dover, which is now the A2. It get its name from Preston Windmill which stood opposite until it was demolished in the early 1940s. A door leading into one of the bars has a windmill etched into the glass. Meals are available lunchtimes and evenings. The inn keeps four letting rooms, with dogs welcome. Faversham Football Club is opposite. P

Finglesham

Crown

The Street, CT14 0ND

11-3, 6-11.30; 11-11.30 Fri & Sat; 12-11.30 Sun

☎ (01304) 612555 thecrownatfinglesham.co.uk

Shepherd Neame Master Brew Bitter; guest beers H

Situated in a quiet rural hamlet, this welcoming village pub and 16th-century restaurant specialises in beers from Kentish brewers. The restaurant is proud of its home-cooked food and regularly changing specials board. Throughout the year, themed food nights and quizzes are held, and a beer festival is hosted in August. Bat & trap is played. Well-behaved dogs are welcome outside meal times. Caravan Club certified. Local CAMRA Pub of the Year 2007.
⚇❀◐◑🚌(13,14)P⌐

Folkestone

British Lion

10 The Bayle, CT20 1SQ

12-4, 7-11; 12-11 Sat

☎ (01303) 251478

Greene King IPA, Abbot; guest beers H

This town centre pub next to the church dates from 1460 and is the oldest pub in Folkestone. A former Hanbury, Mackenson and Whitbread house, it was visited by Charles Dickens when he was writing Little Dorrit. The room he used is now the Dickens Room. A comfortable, relaxed atmosphere prevails and two guest beers are always available, usually from the finest cask selection. Good pub food is served in generous portions. ⚇❀◐◑♣⌐

Chambers

Radnor Chambers, Cheriton Place, CT20 2BB (off the Hythe end of Sandgate Rd)

12-11 (midnight Fri & Sat); 7-10.30 Sun

☎ (01303) 223333

Adnams Bitter; Hopdaemon Skrimshander IPA; Ramsgate Gadd's No 5; Ringwood Old Thumper; guest beers H

Surprisingly spacious cellar bar with a café upstairs that is under the same ownership. Three guest ales normally come from Kentish breweries, as well as some from further afield, supplemented by Biddenden and Cheddar Valley ciders. Beer festivals are held over Easter and August bank holiday weekends. The food, which includes Mexican and European choices plus daily specials, is served every lunchtime, and Sunday to Thursday evenings. ◐◑⇌(Central)🚌♣●

East Cliff Tavern

13-15 East Cliff, CT19 6BU

5-11 (midnight Fri); 12-midnight Sat; 12-11 Sun

☎ (01303) 251132

Beer range varies H

Friendly terraced back-street pub near a footpath across the railway line. The main bar is to the right of the entrance and there are usually two beers, often from Kent or Sussex micro-breweries, with Biddenden cider on gravity behind the bar. Old photographs of Folkestone decorate the walls and community events include weekly raffles. The entrance to the Little Switzerland camp site overlooking the sea is about a mile north east. Q❀⛺♣●

Guildhall ✔

42 The Bayle, CT20 1SQ (close to the church)

12-11 (midnight Fri & Sat); 12-10.30 Sun

☎ (01303) 251393

Greene King IPA; guest beers H

A welcoming Cask Marque-accredited traditional pub with a single bar, situated close to the town centre in The Bayle, an attractive old area of town where Charles Dickens once lived. This is a pleasant place to enjoy good ale and to seek a break from the usual hustle and bustle of the town-centre shops. ❀◐♣P⌐

Lifeboat

42 North Street, CT19 6AF

2-10 (9 Mon); 1-midnight Fri & Sat

☎ (01303) 252877

Harveys Sussex Best Bitter; Taylor Landlord; Wells Bombardier; guest beers H

This friendly corner pub, opened in 1861, is the last example of a timber-framed pub in this part of Folkestone. The building itself dates back to 1750. This is a fine back-street pub, offering a wide range of guest beers, and decorated with photographs of lifeboats and crews over the years. An RNLI gift shop is incorporated in the pub and the clientele supports the local inshore lifeboat. Q❀♣⌐

Fordwich

Fordwich Arms

King Street, CT2 0DB

11-midnight (1am Fri & Sat)

☎ (01227) 710444

Flowers Original; Shepherd Neame Master Brew Bitter; Wadworth 6X; guest beers H

Classic 1930s building listed in Kent CAMRA's Regional Inventory. It has a large bar with a superb fireplace, a woodblock floor and a dining room with wood panelling; excellent meals are served in both areas (not Sun eve). The garden and terrace overlook the River Stour, close to the popular Stour Valley Walk. The pub hosts regular themed evenings including a popular monthly pudding night, plus folk music every first, second and fourth Sunday night. There is a heated and sheltered smoking area. ⚇Q❀◐◑⇌(Sturry)🚌(4,6)P⌐

Frittenden

Bell & Jorrocks ✔

Biddenden Road, TN17 2EJ

11-11; 12-10.30 Sun

☎ (01580) 852415 thebellandjorrocks.co.uk

Adnams Bitter; Black Sheep Best Bitter; Harveys Sussex Best Bitter; guest beer H

Fine community village pub which incorporates a Post Office. The strange name is an amalgamation of the two village pubs: the John Jorrocks (named after a fictional fox-hunting Cockney created by RS Surtees in the 19th century), which closed in 1969, and the present pub, the former Bell. This old coaching inn has an L-shaped main bar and a small back room. Ask about the Heinkel propellor hanging over the fireplace. An annual beer festival is held in April. Food is not served on Wednesday.

Gillingham

Barge

63 Layfield Road, ME7 2QY
7 (4 Fri)-11; 12-11 Sat & Sun
(01634) 850485
Daleside Gravesend Shrimpers; Wadworth 6X; guest beers
Candle-lit single bar overlooking the River Medway with superb views from the decked patio and garden. Up to five handpumps dispense two regular and three ever-changing guest beers. It is noted as a music venue, hosting regular monthly jazz, blues and folk music nights, plus an open mic night entitled Bards at the Barge, with musical instruments provided. A covered, heated area is available for smokers in the garden.

Frog & Toad

Burnt Oak Terrace, ME7 2DR
12-11 (10.30 Sun)
(01634) 852231 thefrogandtoad.com
Fuller's London Pride; guest beers
Typical back-street pub, located half a mile from the station. Four ever-changing beers are served on handpump, plus Biddenden Bushels cider and 25-30 bottled Belgian beers. The pub hosts up to four themed beer festivals on bank holidays each year. Food is served from Tuesday to Saturday until 7pm, with a traditional roast on Sunday. The pub sponsors a golf society among its sports teams. The patio outside has heaters for smokers.

Upper Gillingham Conservative Club

541 Canterbury Street, ME7 5LF (160m from traffic lights at A2 jct)
11-2.30, 7-11; 11-11 Sat; 12-10.30 Sun
(01634) 851403
Shepherd Neame Master Brew Bitter; guest beers
Expect a warm and friendly welcome at this former army storehouse which is handy for Gillingham football stadium. A club since 1922, it was runner up in the CAMRA National Club of the Year awards in 2001. To gain entry, take along a copy of this Guide or a CAMRA membership card. The U-shaped bar stocks three reasonably priced real ales at up to 4.5% ABV. There is a snooker room with two tables and a large-screen TV to watch sport.

Will Adams

73 Saxton Street, ME7 5EG
7-11; 12.30-4, 7-11 Sat; 12-4, 8-11 Sun
(01634) 575902
Hop Back Summer Lightning; guest beers
The quality of real ale is assured at this street corner, single-bar pub. Winner of Medway CAMRA Pub of the Year in 2006, a good choice of micro-brewery beers is the norm. Opening hours alter when the local football team are playing at home (11.30am Sat; 5.30pm midweek). Some unusual pub games are available to enjoy while soaking up the friendly atmosphere. The pub is named in honour of a famous local navigator.

Gravesend

Crown & Thistle

44 The Terrace, DA12 2BJ
12-11 (10.30 Sun)
(01474) 326049 crownandthistle.org.uk
Loddon Shrimpers; guest beers
Narrow terraced pub situated between the town centre and the river promenade, home to four rowing teams. A former CAMRA National Pub of the Year, it offers four frequently-changing guest beers. Pub food is limited to filled rolls but your Chinese or Indian takeaway orders can be phoned through from the bar and consumed on the premises. The pub is close to Gravesend Station and central bus services. Weston's First Quality cider is on handpump. (480,499)

Jolly Drayman

1 Love Lane, Wellington Street, DA12 1JA
12-midnight (1am Thu-Sat); 12-11 Sun
(01474) 352355 jollydrayman.com
Caledonian Deuchars IPA; guest beers
Low-ceilinged town-centre pub and small hotel on the site of the former Walker's Brewery. Children are welcome before 7pm and the restaurant has been revived, serving meals and bar snacks lunchtimes and evenings (not Sun or Mon). Spitfire and Bombardier beers alternate, plus two guests. The pub hosts two darts teams, a football team and two rowing teams. Occasional live music can be heard on Saturday evenings. Dadlums (Kentish skittles) is played on alternate Sunday evenings. A smoking area is covered and heated.
(490,499) P

Somerset Arms

9-10 Darnley Road, DA11 0RA
11-11 (2am Thu-Sat); 12-11 Sun
(01474) 533837
Greene King IPA; Young's Bitter; guest beers
Town-centre corner pub which is very close to the station. This single bar has nooks and crannies, with wooden seats which were formerly church pews. Film posters and photographs of film stars adorn the walls, together with sporting and music memorabilia. Four constantly rotating guest beers often come from Archers and Hop Back. There is a diverse clientele and the pub has a late licence for discos Thursday to Saturday. No food Sunday lunchtime. (498)

Great Mongeham

Three Horseshoes

139 Mongeham Road, CT14 9LL
12-midnight (11 Sun)
(01304) 375812
Beer range varies
Small and welcoming community pub which offers two regularly changing beers, often from local breweries. The pub supports local charities throughout the year and holds a charity fun day and beer festival in August.

Food is available Wednesday-Saturday lunchtimes and evenings, specialising in hot-rock cooking, plus a roast on Sunday. The pub has men and women's darts and pool teams, a large, secure, child-friendly garden and is dog friendly. Camping is available at Solley's Farms. ❀◐⛺🚌(14,82)♣♠P⊱

Groombridge

Crown Inn

TN3 9QH (A264 from Tunbridge Wells, then B2110)
☉ 11-3, 6-11; 11-11 Sat; 12-10.30 (5 winter) Sun
☎ (01892) 864742 ⊕ thecrowninn.co.uk
Greene King IPA; Larkins Traditional, seasonal beers Ⓗ
According to English Heritage this is one of Britain's oldest pubs, dating back to 1585. It looks onto the village green and the view is beautiful at any time of the year. Inside, an inglenook fire is very welcoming, along with generous helpings of real home-cooked food. This gem of a pub has been well worth preserving and is popular with walkers and lovers of good real ale. ♨Q❀◐⇌🚌(291)

Hadlow

Two Brewers

Maidstone Road, TN11 0DN (on A26)
☉ 12-midnight (1am Fri & Sat); 12-11.30 Sun
Harveys Hadlow, Sussex Best Bitter, Ⓗ **seasonal beers** Ⓗ/Ⓖ
Friendly two-bar local, recently refurbished by Harveys, where stripped pine and old photos of the village, including Harveys Brewery, abound. Attractive etched-glass screens separate the bar areas, where Hadlow Bitter made with local hops is served, together with regular seasonal beers. Cable TV shows sports fixtures and good pub food at reasonable prices is served regularly. Local buses stop nearby and run late evenings. ❀◐♿🚌P⊱

Halstead

Rose & Crown

Otford Lane, TN14 7EA
☉ 12-11
☎ (01959) 533120
Larkins Traditional; Whitstable East India Pale Ale; guest beers Ⓗ
Featuring in this Guide for 14 consecutive years, this two-bar flint-faced free house from the 1860s was once part of the Fox & Sons Brewery Estate and later Style & Winch. The bars display pictures of the pub and village and serves four regularly changing guest ales, including a mild, from smaller breweries. A menu of home-cooked food is offered with a takeaway option. Booking for Sunday lunch is advisable. Local CAMRA Pub of the Year runner-up in 2007 and winner 2008.
♨Q♉❀◐♿🚌(402)♣P⊱

Hastingleigh

Bowl

The Street, TN25 5HU TR095449
☉ 5 (12 Sat)-midnight; closed Mon; 12-10.30 Sun
☎ (01233) 750354 ⊕ thebowlonline.co.uk
Adnams Bitter; Fuller's London Pride; Harveys Sussex Best Bitter; guest beer Ⓗ
Lovingly restored village pub, this listed building retains many period features including a tap room that is now used for playing pool and is free from jukebox and games machines. Quiz night is Tuesday. The lovely garden has a cricket pitch to the rear where matches are played most Sundays in summer. A beer festival is held during the August bank holiday weekend. Excellent sandwiches are available at weekends.
♨Q❀◐🚌♣♠P

Heaverham

Chequers

Watery Lane, TN15 6NP (1½ miles N of A25, follow signs to Chaucer Business Park) TQ571586
☉ 12-2.30, 5-11; 12-11 Sat; 12-9 Sun
☎ (01722) 763968
Shepherd Neame Master Brew Bitter, Kent's Best, seasonal beers Ⓗ
Picturesque Kentish weatherboarded country pub in a small hamlet near Kemsing. The traditional public bar has a piano and dartboard, while a pleasant, spacious saloon bar caters for diners (no food Sun eve). Outside, a very large beer garden hosts three league bat & trap teams on Tuesday summer evenings. A league quiz is held on Tuesday and a traditional pub games evening on Wednesday features cribbage, shove-ha'penny and dominoes. Opening hours are often extended during the summer months.
♨Q❀◐🅓⇌(Kemsing)♣P

Herne

Butcher's Arms

29A Herne Street, CT6 7HL (opp church)
☉ 12-1.30, 6-9 (or later); closed Sun & Mon
☎ (01227) 371000 ⊕ micropub.co.uk
Dark Star Hophead; Fuller's London Pride, ESB; guest beers Ⓖ
The smallest pub in Kent, with space for about 12 customers ensuring that lively chat abounds. It contains the original butcher's chopping tables, plus hooks and other implements. At least four beers are cask-dispensed, alongside an ever-changing variety of guest beers and a takeaway service. A real ale drinker's delight, the landlord consults customers about which beers he should stock. There is a car park nearby. Local CAMRA branch Pub of the Year 2008. Q🚌(4,6)

First & Last

Canterbury Road, Herne Common, CT6 7JU (A291, 1km outside village)
☉ 12-11 (12.30am Fri; midnight Sat)
☎ (01227) 364465 ⊕ firstandlastfreehouse.co.uk
Fuller's London Pride; Harveys Sussex Best Bitter Ⓗ
Comfortable village pub partly dating from 1690. First licensed as an ale house in 1835, it has always been known as First & Last, due to its proximity to the area boundary. Inside is a large single bar, a restaurant area (not serving

food on Sun eve), and a large, popular function room. The wood-panelled interior is decorated with pictures and heated with two cast iron wood-burning stoves. An outdoor smoking area is planned. (4,6)P

Smugglers Inn
1 School Lane, CT6 7AN (opp church)
11-11 (1am Fri & Sat)
(01227) 741395
Shepherd Neame Master Brew Bitter, Spitfire, seasonal beers H
Quaint village local with a smuggling history, situated just inland from Herne Bay. Parts of the pub date back 400 years. The saloon bar has a low ceiling which is covered in hanging hops, plus wood panelling and a ship's binnacle. The public bar is more modern, with a pool table and dartboard. The garden has a bat & trap pitch which is used in summer months. Q

Hernhill

Three Horseshoes
46 Staple Street, ME13 9UA TR060601
12-3, 6-11; 11-11 Fri & Sat; 12-3, 7-10.30 Sun
(01227) 750842 3shoes.co.uk
Shepherd Neame Master Brew Bitter, G **Kent's Best, seasonal beers** H
Small, traditional and very much a locals' pub, this hospitable inn is set in a hamlet amid orchards and hop gardens, where it has been run by the same husband and wife team for the past 10 years. It has a well deserved reputation for good home-cooked food – meals are not available on Sunday evening or Monday. Live music, mainly blues, is played on alternate Saturday nights. A wheelie-bin grand prix race is held in mid July.
Q(638)P

Higham

Stonehorse
Dillywood Lane, ME3 8EN (off B2000 Cliffe Road)
12-11 (10.30 Sun)
(01634) 722046
Courage Best Bitter, Directors; guest beers H
A country pub with a large garden on the edge of Strood, surrounded by fields and handy for walkers. The unspoilt public bar sports a wood-burning range, darts and a rare bar billiard table. Good value food is served. The pub is dog-friendly but no children are allowed in the bar. Two guest beers are usually available. QP

Hildenborough

Cock Horse
London Road, TN11 8NH (on B245 between Sevenoaks and Tonbridge)
11-11.30; 12-11 Sun
(01732) 833232
Shepherd Neame Master Brew Bitter, Spitfire H
A family-run 16th-century coaching inn with a very comfortable bar and an inglenook fireplace to make you feel warm and welcome. Home-cooked food is available including Sunday lunches (booking recommended). An ideal location for walkers, outside this hospitable pub is a split-level decked area in which to sit and enjoy your food and drink. There is also a lawn area and ample parking space.
Q(402)P

Hook Green

Elephant's Head
Furnace Lane, TN3 8LJ
12-3, 4.30-11; 12-1am Sat; 12-midnight Sun
(01892) 890279
Harveys Hadlow Bitter, Sussex Best Bitter, Armada Ale, seasonal beers H
Built in 1489 and a pub since 1768, an interesting history of the building is framed on one wall. The well-preserved interior includes an inglenook fireplace, oak beams hung with hop bines, and a conservatory. A Harveys pub, it serves four real ales and a variety of food (not Mon or Sun eve), including traditional English fish dishes and a children's menu. A darts team plays here regularly. There is a play area for children outside.
Q(256)P

Horton Kirby

Bull
3 Lombard Street, DA4 9DF
12 (4 Mon)-11; 12-midnight Fri & Sat; 12-10.30 Sun
(01322) 862274 thebullpub.co.uk
Beer range varies H/G
Comfortable and friendly one-bar village pub with a large landscaped garden affording views across Darent Valley. One beer is on gravity stillage and three guests on handpump usually come from Dark Star and Oakham plus local micro-breweries. Good quality food is served at lunchtime (not Mon) and in the evening (Tue-Sat). League quiz nights are held on Monday and league cribbage on Tuesday. Local CAMRA branch Pub of the Year 2008.
(414)

Iden Green (Goudhurst)

Peacock Inn
Goudhurst Road, TN17 2PB (1½ miles E of Goudhurst at A262/B2085 jct)
12-11 (6 Sun)
(01580) 211233
Shepherd Neame Master Brew Bitter, Kent's Best, Bishop's Finger, seasonal beers H
This attractive country inn was built in the 17th century as a hunting lodge for the nearby Glassenbury estate, but became a pub about 150 years ago. There are two simply-furnished bars, one in the original building, the other in a 1960s extension which has been sympathetically refurbished to match the original. The old bar has an inglenook fireplace, low beams and a dining room. Excellent food with varying specials is served throughout. P

ENGLAND

Ightham Common

Old House ★

Redwell Lane, TN15 9EE (½ mile SW of Ightham Village, between A25 & A227) TQ591558
12-3 Sat & Sun only, 7-11 (9 Tue); closed Mon
☎ (01722) 822383
Flowers IPA; Ⓗ Loddon Shrimpers; Oakham JHB; guest beers Ⓖ
Kentish red-brick and tile-hung cottage dating from the 17th-century, tucked away down a steep, narrow lane. The pub is hard to spot as it has no sign. The larger room to the left features a Victorian wood-panelled bar and a large inglenook fireplace. The smaller room is an old fashioned parlour. Beers are served from a gravity stillage in a room behind the bar. ⌂Q♣P

Ivychurch

Bell Inn ✔

TN29 0AL (signed from A2070 between Brenzett and Hamstreet) TR028275
12-2 (Fri only), 4-11; 12-11 Sat; 12-10.30 Sun
☎ (01797) 344355
Black Sheep Best Bitter; Fuller's London Pride; Wadworth Henry's IPA; guest beer Ⓗ
Picturesque 16th-century inn situated in the shadow of the village church. The large bar has a dining area to the left and a games room to the right, with a serving area. This is a welcoming pub in which to relax and enjoy the four well-kept real ales on offer. There are many options for walking and cycling in the surrounding Romney Marsh area. Convenient for the Brenzett Aeronautical Museum.
⌂Q♣P

Kingsdown

King's Head

Upper Street, CT14 8BJ
5-11; 12-3, 6-11 Sat; 12-10.30 Sun
☎ (01304) 373915
Fuller's London Pride; Greene King IPA; guest beer Ⓗ
On the sloping village street leading down to the sea, this welcoming 18th-century pub has several rooms at different levels set around a central bar. There are displays of pump clips and old firearms. Note the fine, frosted glass front door bearing the name of the defunct local brewery, Thompsons of Walmer. The secluded patio at the back houses the skittle alley and covered smoking area. Good home-cooked food is served. Children and dogs are welcome. (84)♣

Knockholt

Three Horseshoes

The Pound, TN14 7LD
11.30-3, 6-11; 12-4, 7-11 Sun
☎ (01959) 532102
Adnams Bitter; Harveys Sussex Best Bitter; guest beer Ⓗ
This strong community pub offers great hospitality on every visit. An interesting selection of brass band pictures decorates the walls as the landlord was once a playing member. Home-cooked food is available, plus a takeaway and senior citizen menu. A good selection of real ales is always available. There is a large garden to the rear of the pub and dogs are welcome.
⌂Q(402)♣P

Luddesdown

Cock Inn ✔

Henley Street, DA13 0XB (1 mile SE of Sole Street Stn) TQ667671
12-11 (10.30 Sun)
☎ (01474) 814208 cockluddesdowne.com
Adnams Bitter; Goacher's Mild; guest beers Ⓗ
Superb, traditional English free house dating from 1713 and located in a pleasant rural setting, under the same ownership since 1984. There are two separate bars and a conservatory, with the pub playing host to many local clubs and societies. Petanque is played in the garden, which includes a specially designed undercover heated smoking area. The landlord hosts a devious open quiz every Tuesday. No food Sunday evenings. Local CAMRA Pub of the Year 2005-2007. ⌂Q♣P

Lynsted

Black Lion

Lynsted Lane, ME9 0RJ
11-3, 6-11; 12-3, 7-10.30 Sun
☎ (01795) 521229
Goacher's Mild, Light, Dark, Crown Imperial Stout Ⓗ
Friendly pub sought out by drinkers with three or four beers from Goacher's of Maidstone always on offer. The main bar room includes real fires, while a second bar is home to a bar billiards table and dartboard. Wooden floors throughout the pub add to its character. Food is available daily. There is a large garden at the side. The 645 bus runs every two hours or so from Sittingbourne via Teynham (not eve or Sun). ⌂Q(645)♣P

Maidstone

Druid's Arms ✔

24 Earl Street, ME14 1PP (opp Hazlitt Theatre)
11-11 (midnight Thu-Sat); 12-11 Sun
☎ (01622) 758516
Greene King IPA, Abbot, Old Speckled Hen; guest beers Ⓗ
This town centre pub, situated next to the new Fremlin Walk shopping centre, was the original Hogshead and is within easy reach of all three Maidstone stations. Monday is quiz night, and there is live music on Thursday and Saturday in the covered, heated courtyard. Popular piped music is played in the split-level bar. Also on offer is a wide variety of guest beers and regular beer festivals. Meals are served daily and Black Rat cider is available.
⌂

Flower Pot

96 Sandling Road, ME14 2RJ (off A229 N of town centre)
✪ 11-11; 12-10.30 Sun
☎ (01622) 757705
Young's Bitter; guest beers Ⓗ
Situated at the blocked-off end of what was once part of the main road to the Medway Towns. This is an end-of-terrace pub, with two split-level bars, a short walk from County Hall and the shopping area. The landlord holds an electro-acoustic jam night on Tuesday for aficionados of country, blues, soul and folk – bring your own instrument.
⛰❀⇌🚌(101,155)●

Pilot ✔

23-25 Upper Stone Street, ME15 6EU (on A229 towards Hastings)
✪ 12-3 (not Mon), 6-11 (midnight Sat); 12-midnight Fri; 12-11.30 Sun
☎ (01622) 691162
Harveys Mild, Sussex Best Bitter, Armada Ale, seasonal beers Ⓗ
Grade II-listed, 17th-century pub on a busy road heading south from the town centre. Despite its location, the interior feels like a country pub. There is live, open-mic music on alternate Thursday evenings, Saturday evening and Sunday afternoon, and a petanque pitch behind the pub. Log fires add ambience in winter, but a warm welcome is assured all year round in this friendly pub. Lunches are served Tuesday to Friday and a mild is always available. CAMRA branch Pub of the Year 2008. ⛰❀◖⇌♣

Rifle Volunteer

28 Wyatt Street, ME14 1EU
✪ 11-3 (may vary), 6 (7 Sat)-11; 12-3 (may vary), 7-10.30 Sun
☎ (01622) 758891
Goacher's Mild, Light, Crown Imperial Stout Ⓗ
A single-bar Goacher's tied house near East Station retaining most of its original features and a regular in this Guide for several years. It provides respite from the hustle of the nearby shopping area and there are no noisy machines to distract customers from quiet conversation. Note the display of interesting old bottled beers on the back bar and the unusual toy soldiers used to indicate a beer 'in the wood'. Home to two quiz league teams. Simple, good value lunches are available.
Q◖⇌(Maidstone East)♣

Swan

2 County Road, ME14 1UY (opp prison, nr County Hall)
✪ 12-3, 5-11; 12-11 Fri-Sun
☎ (01622) 751264
Shepherd Neame Master Brew Bitter, Kent's Best, seasonal beers Ⓗ
Not far from East Station, this town-centre pub is close to County Hall. The main prison entrance, as featured in Birds of a Feather on TV, is opposite. Two regular Shepherd Neame beers are sold, plus a seasonal special. Home-made sandwiches are available at lunchtime, along with tea and coffee, plus special themed food nights. There are regular quiz nights, jam nights and karaoke, plus a wide-screen TV. ❀◖♿⇌🚌♣⊢

Margate

Northern Belle

4 Mansion Street, CT9 1HE
✪ 11-11; 12-10.30 Sun
☎ (07810) 088347
Shepherd Neame Master Brew Bitter Ⓗ
This small, down-to-earth seafarers' tavern, up a tiny lane opposite the stone pier, is the town's oldest standing pub. It resulted from combining two fishermen's cottages, built around 1680, and stands right on the water's edge. It was first known as the Aurora Borealis; its present name derives from a merchant ship that ran aground in 1857. Live music is performed on some Sunday afternoons. A second Shepherd Neame beer rotates alongside the Master Brew. ⇌♣

Marsh Green

Wheatsheaf Inn

Main Road, TN8 5QL
✪ 11-11; 12-10.30 Sun
☎ (01732) 864091 🌐 thewheatsheaf.net
Harveys Sussex Best Bitter; guest beers Ⓗ
Set in a picturesque village, this spacious pub with several drinking and dining areas has been an ale house for some 100 years. Up to eight real ales change frequently and include a mild, Biddenden cider and local brews. The landlord reckons to have served 2,500 different beers during his 15 years at the pub. A beer festival is held in summer, usually coinciding with the village fete, and offering up to 30 real ales and a hog roast. Home-cooked food is served daily.
⛰Q🐴❀◖◗🚂🚌♣●P

Marshside

Gate Inn

Boyden Gate, CT3 4EB (off A28 at Upstreet)
✪ 11-2.30 (4 Sat), 6-11; 12-4, 7-10.30 Sun
☎ (01227) 860498
Shepherd Neame Master Brew Bitter, Spitfire, seasonal beers Ⓖ
Traditional village pub that has been run by the same landlord and appeared in this Guide for 33 years. A focal point for the community, the pub's fund-raising events and traditional entertainment include mummers' plays, hoodeners and morris dancing. The bars have tiled floors, a log fire and hanging hops, while the garden includes a stream, apple trees and ducks. The excellent, good value food includes black pudding and mango chutney sandwiches (not Mon eve or winter Tue).
⛰Q🐴❀◖◗⛺♣P

Meopham

George

Wrotham Road, DA13 0AH (on A227 nr church)
✪ 11-11; 12-10.30 Sun
☎ (01474) 814198
Shepherd Neame Master Brew Bitter, Spitfire, Bishops Finger, seasonal beers Ⓗ

Former coaching inn dating partly from the 15th century with an attractive Kentish weatherboard exterior. The two bars have been pleasantly restored in traditional and modern styles, with a separate restaurant serving good food until 9pm every day. The pub has a large car park and a floodlit petanque piste. A passageway under the road links the inn with the parish church. (306,308)P

Minster

New Inn

2 Tothill Street, CT12 4AG

11.30-11 (midnight Fri & Sat); 12-10.30 Sun

(01843) 821294

Greene King IPA, Abbot; guest beer H

Not far from Minster station, this friendly village local was built in 1837 as a replacement for an 18th-century enterprise which included a landscaped garden and pleasure complex. The old Cobbs brewery windows are retained and a sympathetic extension has provided a dining area and space for live music. The garden has probably the most luxurious smoking area in Thanet. No food Sunday evening. P

Newenden

White Hart

Rye Road, TN18 5PN TQ834273

11-11; 12-10.30 Sun

(01797) 252166

Fuller's London Pride; Harveys Sussex Best Bitter; Rother Valley Level Best; guest beers H

This lovely 500-year-old oak-beamed inn is reputedly haunted and stands just within Kent's boundary with East Sussex. Regular customers mark two guest ales for quality. Seasonal cider is sometimes available. The pub has six guest rooms and is a short walk from Northiam station on the Kent and East Sussex Railway. QP

Northbourne

Hare & Hounds

The Street, CT14 0LG

12-3, 6-11 (midnight Fri & Sat); 12-3, 7-10.30

(01304) 365429 thehareandhounds.net

Adnams Bitter; Greene King IPA; Hancock's HB; Harveys Sussex Best Bitter; guest beer H

This friendly local, situated in a pleasant village location, has a carpeted main bar and restaurant with a raised, smaller seating area. The food menu specialises in local and free-range produce with innovative vegetarian dishes. Events are held throughout the year, including themed dinners and live music, a beer festival in July and quizzes in winter in aid of local charities. A large, enclosed garden includes children's play equipment. Dogs are welcome and disabled access is planned for 2008. (14)P

Northfleet

Campbell Arms

1 Campbell Road, DA11 0JZ

12-11 (10.30 Sun)

(01474) 320488

Courage Best Bitter; Loddon Shrimpers; guest beers H

Friendly one-bar back-street corner local, serving four real ales, often including a mild. The two guest beers are sourced locally and are reasonably priced. This community pub hosts darts, football and pool teams. Note the Mann, Crossman & Paulin mirror behind the bar and framed photographs of old Gravesend pubs and bygone scenes above the bar counter. A foldaway screen is used to show live sport. (498,499)

Earl Grey

177 Vale Road, DA11 8BP (off Perry St)

12-11 (10.30 Sun)

(01474) 365240

Shepherd Neame Master Brew Bitter, Spitfire, seasonal beers H

Distinctive late 18th-century cottage-style building with a Kentish brick and flint exterior that is rarely seen in this area. The interior consists of an L-shaped bar, with a raised seating area at one end, and exudes a homely, convivial atmosphere. It is located near the Cygnet Leisure Centre in Perry Street. (498,499)P

Oad Street

Plough & Harrow

Oad Street, Borden, ME9 8LB (opp craft centre) TQ870620

11-11.30 (midnight Sat); 12-11 Sun

(01795) 843351 theploughandharrowpub.co.uk

Goacher's Real Mild, Best Dark; Shepherd Neame Master Brew Bitter; guest beer H

A genuine free house in a semi-rural setting in a small North Downs village. The craft centre opposite is well signposted from several directions. A large main bar and a small public bar feature breweriana and other ephemera on the walls. A rare outlet in this part of Kent for Goacher's beers, it also offers at least one guest beer. This is an ideal location to start or finish a walk in the surprisingly pretty countryside. P

Otford

Crown

10 High Street, TN14 5PQ

12-11 (11.30 Fri); 11-11.30 Sat

(01959) 522847 crownpubandrestaurant.co.uk

Harveys Sussex Best Bitter; St Austell Dartmoor Best; guest beers H

Attractive whitewashed cottage-style pub dating from the 16th century, part of which was an old bakery. Two distinct bars include one that houses a suit of armour under a bygone stairwell. Many banknotes and hotel keys adorn the beams. The landlord is a trained chef and home-cooked food is available (not Mon & Tue eves). Steak and

kidney puddings and home-made desserts are the specialities. Two regular beers are supplemented by an interesting changing range of two guests.
⌂✿◑⇌⊟(431,432)♣●⊁

Pembury

Black Horse

12 High Street, TN2 4NY (on main street next to green)
⊙ 11-11; 12-10.30 Sun
☎ (01892) 822141 ⊕ bhorse.co.uk
Adnams Broadside; Courage Best Bitter; Fuller's London Pride; Greene King Old Speckled Hen ⊞
This warm and welcoming 16th-century pub has been subject to several extensions and is now linked to its own restaurant. A centrally placed serving bar is surrounded by the oldest part of the pub to the left as you enter, with original beams and a huge inglenook. A smaller carpeted bar is on the right, with a larger lounge area behind. The restaurant offers an extensive food menu and is so popular that booking is advisable.
⌂Q✿◑♿⊟♣⊁

Penshurst

Spotted Dog

TN11 8EE (turn off B2188 S of Penshurst and follow signs)
⊙ 11-11 (10.30 Sun)
☎ (01892) 870253
Harveys Sussex Best Bitter; Larkins Traditional, Porter ⊞
On high ground overlooking the Medway Valley, the Spotted Dog has been a pub since 1520. Inside are low-beamed ceilings and quarry-tiled floors, with a restaurant leading off from the main bar. Open log fires contribute towards the cosy atmosphere in winter, while in summer a small terrace to the rear affords spectacular views over the surrounding countryside. The pub is convenient for visiting nearby Penshurst Place, which has been a stately home for 670 years.
⌂Q✿◑P

Perry Wood

Rose & Crown

ME13 9RY (1½ miles from Selling Station, signed to Perry Wood) TR042552
⊙ 11.30-3, 6.30-11 (closed Mon eve); 12-3, 7-10.30 Sun (later in summer)
☎ (01227) 752214 ⊕ roseandcrownperrywood.co.uk
Adnams Bitter; Goacher's Mild; Harveys Sussex Best Bitter; guest beers ⊞
Historic free house located in the middle of Perry Wood near East Kent's highest point. Popular with walkers and cyclists, it is well regarded for its excellent food and, of course, beer. No food is available Sunday evening and Monday. The bar area is dominated by a large fireplace and the interior is decorated with old wood-cutting tools and corn dollies. A large garden contains a bat and trap pitch and a children's play area. ⌂Q✿◑▲♣P⊁

Petteridge

Hopbine

Petteridge Lane, TN12 7NE (½ mile down lane to E of Brenchley)
⊙ 12-2.30, 6-11; 12-3, 7-10.30 Sun
☎ (01892) 722561
Badger K&B Sussex Bitter, First Gold, seasonal beer ⊞
Set in a Kentish hamlet, this CAMRA Pub of the Year runner-up is appearing in the Guide for its 20th consecutive year. It boasts a tile-hung and white weatherboarded exterior, while inside is an L-shaped bar with beams, plenty of wood panelling, a smaller dining area and a good selection of genuine home-cooked food (not available Wed). A small garden is at the rear, with tables to the side and front, where Morris dancers visit. There is a covered area for smokers. ⌂Q✿◑♿♣●P⊁

Rainham

Angel

Station Road, ME8 7UH
⊙ 12.30 (12 Sat)-11; 12-10.30 Sun
☎ (01634) 360219 ⊕ theangelrainham.com
Adnams Bitter; guest beers ⊞
The Angel is a traditional drinkers' pub situated at the bottom of Station Road, where Buster the pub dog will greet you on arrival. A fine pint of Adnams awaits, plus two changing guest beers, making this a little gem, and well worth seeking out. The Angel has been CAMRA Medway branch Pub of the Year in 2004, 2005 and again in 2007. Smokers are catered for in the large garden. ⌂✿⇌♣P⊁

Ramsgate

Artillery Arms

36 Westcliff Road, CT11 9JS
⊙ 12-11
☎ (01843) 853282
Wells Bombardier; guest beers ⊞
A small, deservedly popular, corner ale house on the road leading out of town beyond Waitrose. The pub enjoys a reputation for serving a wide selection of five beers at reasonable prices. It is a popular rendezvous for the town's many real ale enthusiasts and has several times been voted Thanet CAMRA Pub of the Year. Wednesday nights feature good value authentic curries or noodles and on Sunday the lively atmosphere is augmented by a free (if occasionally obtrusive) jukebox. ♉⊟(9)⊁

Comfort Inn (San Clu)

Victoria Parade, CT11 8DT
⊙ 11-11; 12-10.30 Sun
☎ (01843) 592345
Greene King Abbot; Wells Bombardier; guest beer ⊞
A Victorian listed building on the town's East Cliff, with stunning views across the sea. The hotel's public area has recently been revamped in a startlingly modern style, with the bar immediately adjacent to the hotel restaurant where food is served daily. The

enthusiastic bar manager presents a mixture of national real ale brands and a varying guest beer from the local Ramsgate Brewery. The garden is always busy in good weather with an uninterrupted panorama of the French coast. ❀⇄◑⊟P⁄–

Foy Boat

8 Sion Hill, CT11 9HZ

11-11; 12-10.30 Sun

☎ (01843) 591198

Fuller's London Pride; Young's Bitter; guest beers Ⓗ

Overlooking the only Royal Harbour in England, the Foy Boat is reputedly the model for the Channel Packet Inn referred to by Ian Fleming in his book Goldfinger. The current building is a post-war replacement for the old Foy Boat Tavern, a Tomson & Wotton house which fell victim to WWII bombing in 1941. The three guest beers always include one from Ramsgate Brewery. Good value food is available, including the popular Sunday roast served until 6pm. ⌂⇄◑⁄–

Montefiore Arms

1 Trinity Place, CT11 7HJ

12-2.30 (not Wed), 7-11; 12-3, 7-10.30 Sun

☎ (01843) 593265

Ramsgate Gadds' No 7; guest beers Ⓗ

Situated just off the main road to Broadstairs, this traditional, cosy back-street local enjoys a loyal following. Its unique name celebrates a 19th-century philanthropist who lived nearby. The ever-present, welcoming landlord serves a variety of beers in a friendly atmosphere, with the Sunday raffle especially well supported. Quiz, darts and cribbage teams during the week create an interesting mix of customers. The recent introduction of Biddenden's cider on draught has proved to be very popular. Q♿⇌(Dumpton Park)⊟♣●

Sir Stanley Gray

Pegwell Bay Hotel, 81 Pegwell Road, CT11 0NJ

11-midnight; 12-10.30 Sun

☎ (01843) 599590 🌐 pegwellbayhotel.co.uk

Courage Directors; guest beers Ⓗ

Located in picturesque Pegwell Bay and boasting spectacular views across the English Channel, the Sir Stanley Gray is part of the Thorley Taverns chain. Low beams and reclaimed panelling evoke an atmosphere redolent of the time when Pegwell was a hotbed of smuggling. Four real ales are usually on offer from both regionals and independents. A selection of home-cooked specials augment the bar menu. A tunnel links the pub to the Pegwell Bay Hotel, a former convalescent home, which has recently been refurbished. ⌂⇄◑▲♣P⁄–

Rochester

Britannia Bar Café

376 High Street, ME1 1DJ

10-11 (2am Sat); 12-11 Sun

☎ (01634) 815204 🌐 britannia-bar-cafe.co.uk

Beer range varies Ⓗ

Situated between Rochester and Chatham railway stations, this bar can be busy at lunchtimes, attracting a mainly business clientele. The bar offers an extensive and popular daily menu, including breakfast (10am-noon). Evening meals are served Monday to Thursday and there is a traditional Sunday lunchtime roast. A stylish bar leads out into a small walled garden that is a sun trap in summer. Occasional live music and quizzes are held. Q❀◑⇌⊟⁄–

Good Intent

83 John Street, ME1 1YL

12-midnight (11 Sun)

☎ (01634) 843118

Beer range varies Ⓖ

This two-bar ale house is for real beer enthusiasts. An invaluable local asset, it caters for traditional and contemporary drinkers, with eight beers sourced from regional and national micro-breweries. A fine range of fruit wines is also kept. Amenities include bar billiards, large-screen sport, live music and a south-facing garden. Good beer, good people, good fun – that is the Good Intent. Regular beer festivals are held and the pub is Medway CAMRA Pub of the Year 2008.
Q❀⊡♿⇌⊟♣P⁄–

Man of Kent

6-8 John Street, ME1 1YN (200m off A2 from bottom of Star Hill)

1-11 (midnight Fri); 12-midnight Sat; 12-11 Sun

☎ (01634) 818771 🌐 manofkent.org.uk

Goacher's Fine Light, Gold Star; Whitstable East India Pale Ale; guest beers Ⓗ

This back-street pub with a single L-shaped bar has an exterior of fine hung tiling, advertising the long-gone Style & Winch brewery of Maidstone. Eight handpumps showcase beers from Kent micro-breweries, while Goacher's Old is available on gravity in winter. Bushells cider is served on top pressure, plus three German beers, three Belgian fruit beers, Meantime Wheat on draught and assorted bottled beers. Live music is hosted on Wednesday and Thursday nights (see website for performers) plus a jam session on Sunday. ⌂❀⇌⊟●⁄–

Rolvenden Layne

Ewe & Lamb

26 Maytham Road, TN17 4NP TQ853302

11-1am; 12-7 Sun

☎ (01580) 241837

Adnams Bitter; Fuller's London Pride; Harveys Sussex Best Bitter Ⓗ

Situated one mile east of Rolvenden on the High Weald Landscape Trail, this is a friendly pub in which to relax and enjoy real ale. The restored interior is warmed by a log fire and high quality food is served in the dining area. At the front is a patio for drinking and there is a small courtyard at the back. Dogs are welcome and there are some beautiful local walks in the area. ⌂Q❀◑⊟P⁄–

Rusthall

Beacon

Tea Garden Lane, TN3 9JH (400m off A264 opp Rusthall cricket pitch)

🕑 11-11; 12-10.30 Sun
☎ (01892) 524252 🌐 the-beacon.co.uk
Harveys Sussex Best Bitter; Larkins Traditional; Taylor Landlord ⊞
Set in 17 acres of grounds on a sandstone outcrop, the view from the Beacon's decked seating area is magnificent. The main bar is arranged like a comfortable front room, with two large sofas in front of a fireplace surrounded by a collection of old wirelesses. The varied menu of locally sourced produce specialises in seafood and can be enjoyed in one of four dining rooms. The downstairs bar caters for functions and is licensed for weddings. Fishing and camping are possible.
Q❀⇌◐▲⊟(231)♣P⅟–

St Margaret's Bay

Coastguard

The Bay, CT15 6DY
🕑 11-11
☎ (01304) 853176 🌐 thecoastguard.co.uk
Beer range varies ⊞
This pub's superb location at the foot of the White Cliffs merits the descent of the cliff path, and even the climb afterwards. Lounge on the terrace and watch the shipping on the Strait of Dover while enjoying the view and good ale too. A changing beer selection is always on offer, with the smaller breweries of Kent and Scotland featuring in particular. Weston's cider is served alongside a wide range of continental bottled beers, and the pub has won several food awards. ❀◐●P⅟–

St Mary in the Marsh

Star Inn

TN29 0BX (opp church) TR065279
🕑 12-11 (10.30 Sun)
☎ (01797) 362139 🌐 thestarinnthemarsh.co.uk
Shepherd Neame Master Brew Bitter; guest beers ⊞
Situated in the heart of Romney Marsh, this Grade II-listed building was constructed in 1476 and became an ale house in 1711. A cosy, pretty village inn, where a warm and friendly welcome always awaits, it offers real ale from four handpumps, home-cooked food and en-suite accommodation. Opposite is St Mary the Virgin church where author Edith Nesbit is buried. Noel Coward lodged in the adjacent cottages while writing his first play.
❀⇌◐♣P

St Peters

White Swan

17 Reading Street, CT10 3AZ
🕑 11.30-2.30, 6-11; 11.30-11 Sat; 12-3, 7-10.30 Sun
☎ (01843) 863051
Adnams Best; guest beers ⊞
Situated in an historic part of Broadstairs, steeped in smuggling tradition, this popular, welcoming local offers an ever-changing roster of six real ales. Formerly tied to Tomson & Wotton, the present building dates from the early 1900s, rebuilt after the original 17th-century structure burned down. The separate public and lounge bars are maintained, as is the price differential. Good quality food is served lunchtimes and evenings, Monday to Saturday. CAMRA Branch Pub of the Year 2008.
Q◐⊟

Sandgate

Ship Inn

65 Sandgate High Street, CT20 3AH (on A259)
🕑 11.30-11.30 (1am Fri & Sat); 12-11.30 Sun
☎ (01303) 248525 🌐 shipinn-sandgate.co.uk
Greene King IPA, Abbot; Hop Back Summer Lightning; Hopdaemon Incubus; ⊞ **guest beers** ⊞/⊡
The long-established landlord provides a good selection of ales here. The beer range increases considerably during holiday periods and a real ale festival takes place over the August bank holiday. The choice of real ciders has grown, with two from Biddenden. This community pub also offers overnight accommodation in rooms with sea views.
❀⇌◐⊟⊟♣●⅟–

Sandwich

Fleur de Lis

6-8 Delf Street, CT13 9BZ
🕑 10-11; 11-10.30 Sun
☎ (01304) 611131 🌐 verinitaverns.co.uk
Greene King IPA; Wadworth 6X; guest beer ⊞
A popular and friendly pub, situated in the middle of this Cinque Port, catering for all types of customer. Each of the three areas that make up the pub has its own character, and there is a separate restaurant space with an unusual painted cupola ceiling. Good pub food is supported by a specials board. Live bands play every Friday, pictures painted by local artists are displayed for sale and dogs are welcome. ⇌◐♿▲⇌⊟

Sevenoaks

Anchor

32 London Road, TN13 1AS
🕑 11-3, 6-11.30; 10-4, 6-midnight Fri; 10-4, 7-midnight Sat; 12-5, 7-11 Sun
☎ (01732) 454898
Harveys Sussex Best Bitter; guest beer ⊞
On entering this very friendly town-centre pub, popular with all ages, observe the unusual circular lobby and the signs on the walls that reflect the long-serving landlord's sense of humour. Harveys is the regular beer, while guest ales may be kept on for a long period if they prove popular. Live blues music is played, usually on the first Wednesday of the month. Excellent food is served Monday-Friday lunchtimes and the Christmas lunch is a highlight. ◐⊟♣⅟–

Sheerness

Red Lion

61 High Street, Blue Town, ME12 1RW
🕑 11-11; 12-10.30 Sun
☎ (01795) 664354

Beer range varies Ⓗ
Facing the former naval dockyard wall, this is the only real ale outlet remaining in the old Blue Town area of Sheerness, with a cobbled High Street. Inside is a list of all the former public houses in Blue Town (over 40) and a host of maritime ephemera. Two or three beers from regional and micro-breweries are served. No meals, but there is a free buffet all day on Sunday. Outside are tables and a covered and heated smoking area next to the pub. ⛰❀⇌🚌♣⊱

Sittingbourne

Long Hop

80 Key Street, ME10 1YU (on A2)
⏲ 11.30-11; 12-10.30 Sun
☎ (01795) 425957
Greene King Old Speckled Hen; Shepherd Neame Master Brew Bitter Ⓗ
A rustic looking local on the busy A2, almost two miles west of the centre. Inside, however, you would hardly know there was a main road outside. Parts of the pub date back 200 years and it was once known as the British Queen. Its new name was chosen in a competition about 20 years ago, as a reference to the Gore Court cricket ground opposite. There is a covered smoking area.
⛰❀◑🚌(333,334)♣P⊱

Snargate

Red Lion ★

TN29 9UQ (on A2080, 1 mile W of Brenzett) TQ990285
⏲ 12-3, 7-10.30 daily
☎ (01797) 344648
Beer range varies Ⓖ
Beautiful, unspoilt, award-winning pub on the remote Welland Marsh. The interior is decorated with WWII and Women's Land Army posters and features in CAMRA's National Inventory of pubs with interiors of outstanding historical interest. A haven for good conversation, it is also a friendly place to play one of the traditional games available. Several beer festivals are hosted annually; the main festival is in June. ⛰Q❀🚌♣●P

Stalisfield Green

Plough Inn

ME13 0HY TQ955529
⏲ 12-3, 6-11 (12.30 Fri); 12-midnight Sat; 12-11 Sun
☎ (01795) 890256 🌐 stalisfieldgreen.com
Beer range varies Ⓗ
An historic multi-room pub set in attractive rural surroundings. Beers from most Kent micro-breweries are featured on a rotating basis, together with Biddenden cider. There is an extensive menu, although no food is served Sunday evening or Monday lunchtime. Varied live music is played on some Fridays (phone for details). The pub has a large enclosed garden and is a popular starting/finishing point for walks on the North Downs.
⛰❀◑♣●P

Stansted

Black Horse

Tumblefield Road, TN15 7PR (1 mile N of A20 jct 2) TQ606618
⏲ 11-11; 12-10.30 Sun
☎ (01732) 822355
Larkins Traditional; guest beers Ⓗ
Nestling in a secluded downland village, this plain Victorian building is the centre of the local community and also popular with visiting walkers and cyclists. A large natural garden with a children's play area is well used by families in summer. Biddenden cider is available and local breweries are supported. A Thai restaurant operates in the evenings (Tue to Sat) and Sunday lunches are recommended.
⛰Q☺❀⇔◑♿Ă●P⊱

Staplehurst

Bell Inn ✔

High Street, TN12 0AY
⏲ 12-11 (10.30 Sun)
☎ (01580) 893366 🌐 bellinn-staplehurst.co.uk
Westerham Finchcocks Original; guest beers Ⓗ
This late-Victorian pub was fully refurbished in 2006 and includes half-timber panelling and wooden floors throughout. The bar area has a log fire and comfortable seating, while a second room on a raised level provides additional seating. A split-level restaurant serves bar snacks and meals every day. Guest beers are from local SIBA brewers and Biddenden Bushells cider is available. The large garden includes a children's play area.
⛰Q☺❀◑Ă⇌🚌(5)♣●P⊱

Lord Raglan

Chart Hill Road, TN12 0DE (½ mile N of A229) TQ786472
⏲ 12-3, 6.30-11.30; closed Sun
☎ (01622) 843747
Goacher's Light; Harveys Sussex Best Bitter; guest beer Ⓗ
Popular and unspoilt free house with the atmosphere of a country pub from bygone days. The bar is hung with hops and warmed by two log fires and a stove, and the large orchard garden catches the evening sun. Excellent snacks and full meals are always available. The guest beer changes frequently and local Double Vision cider is sold. Well-behaved children and dogs are welcome. This pub has no distractions, thus restoring the art of lively conversation. ⛰Q❀◑🚌(5)●P

Stone Street

Padwell Arms

TN15 0LQ (1½ miles S of A25)
⏲ 12-3, 6-11.30; 12-3, 7-10.30 Sun
☎ (01732) 761532
Badger First Gold; Harveys Sussex Best Bitter; Larkins Traditional; guest beer Ⓗ
A welcoming pub in a lovely setting. Located on a walkers' route, it makes an excellent rest for the foot-weary – a good pint and home-cooked food are what this pub does best. Three local ales are always on handpump.

Acoustic jazz sessions are held every Monday and various live entertainment is hosted once a month. Sunday lunch is recommended but booking is essential. Dogs are welcome.
⛰❀◑⊟♿♣♣P⊟

Tilmanstone

Plough & Harrow

Dover Road, CT14 0HX (signed off A256 between Dover & Sandwich)
✪ 11-11; 12-10.30
☎ (01304) 617582
🌐 ploughandharrowtilmanstone.co.uk
Shepherd Neame Master Brew Bitter, Spitfire, seasonal beers Ⓗ
The bar of this rural pub has a traditional feel to it, with wooden floors, sofas, a bar billiards table and an interesting collection of Kent coalfield memorabilia on the walls. Traditional home-cooked food is served in the conservatory restaurant overlooking the garden (no food Sun eve; booking recommended). The pub is popular with ramblers and walkers, families are also welcome, as are dogs. Traditional folk music is performed monthly. ⛰❀⇌◑⊟(88)♣P⊱

Tonbridge

Vauxhall Inn ✔

TN11 0NA (next to A21 Tonbridge S exit)
✪ 11-11; 11.30-10.30 Sun
Fuller's London Pride; guest beers Ⓗ
Former 17th-century coaching inn on the southern fringe of Tonbridge which was originally part of the Sommerhill Estate. Sympathetically enlarged in recent years to incorporate the adjacent stable block, the pub is divided into a series of cosy low-lit areas. The Vauxhall offers a warm welcome to drinkers and diners alike, with the adjacent Premier Inn making it a good base for exploring this attractive corner of Kent.
⛰☕❀⇌◑♿P⊱

Trottiscliffe

Plough

Taylor's Lane, ME19 5DR TQ640602
✪ 11.30-3, 6 (6.30 Sat)-11; 12-3 Sun
☎ (01732) 822233
Adnams Bitter, Broadside; Harveys Sussex Best Bitter Ⓗ
Weatherboarded pub situated just below the Pilgrims Way on the North Downs, providing a welcome stop for all, including walkers, families and dogs. The village, pronounced locally as 'Trosley', is noted for the Coldrum Stones, a Neolithic burial chamber. Beams with horse brasses reflect the 1483 origin of this pub and there are rumours of a friendly ghost called Alice. Several drinking areas are available, as well as a small patio. The restaurant offers good quality home-cooked food. ⛰Q❀◑⊟(58)♣P

Tunbridge Wells

Grove Tavern

19 Berkley Road, TN1 1YR
✪ 12-11
☎ (01892) 526549
Harveys Sussex Best Bitter; Taylor Landlord; guest beer Ⓗ
Possibly the friendliest Pub in Tunbridge Wells, it is certainly one of the oldest. Visitors are made very welcome and often stay for just another hour to enjoy the excellent ales and partake of snooker, crosswords, or just friendly chatter. The Grove is a locals' pub in the older part of town with free wireless Internet access for laptops. Dogs are always welcome and there is a lovely park nearby with swings and slides for children. ⛰⇌♣

Rose & Crown

47 Grosvenor Road, TN1 2AY
✪ 10-11; 12-10.30 Sun
☎ (01892) 522427
Greene King IPA; Harveys Sussex Best Bitter; guest beers Ⓗ
This friendly Victorian town pub is popular with locals, and offers a good choice of real ales in a setting that is the perfect place for a quiet drink. Now under new management, the pub has benefited from recent refurbishment work. Food at lunchtime is good quality, home-cooked and served in generous helpings. A large function room upstairs is for hire. ⛰Q⇌⊟♣⊱

Sankeys

39 Mount Ephraim, TN4 8AA
✪ 10.30-11 (midnight Fri & Sat); 12-midnight Sun
☎ (01892) 511422 🌐 sankeys.co.uk
Harveys Sussex Best Bitter; Larkins Traditional Ⓗ
Busy most nights, this interesting bar, two minutes' walk from the town centre, offers a good selection of local ales plus the best selection of continental beers in west Kent, some on draught. A good collection of retro metal advertisments on the walls makes for an interesting read. An excellent restaurant downstairs specialises in fish dishes (booking recommended). The outside patio is very popular, especially in the summer.
⛰❀◑♿⇌⊟

Upper Upnor

King's Arms

2 High Street, ME2 4XG
✪ 11 (12 Sun)-11
☎ (01634) 717490
Beer range varies Ⓗ
Situated at the top of the enchanting cobbled High Street, this village local has two bars. One is for drinking and the other a restaurant, with food ranging from pub staples to a la carte. Meals are available at all times but the kitchen closes at 5.30pm on Sunday. There is a large terraced garden where regular beer festivals take place, which is very lively in summer. Bushells cider is available on draught.
Q❀◑⊟♣⊱

Tudor Rose

29 High Street, ME2 4XG

11 (12 Sun)-11

(01634) 715035

Shepherd Neame Master Brew Bitter, Kent's Best, Spitfire, Bishops Finger, seasonal beers H

This multi-roomed pub is situated at the bottom of the cobbled High Street next door to Upnor Castle, overlooking the river Medway and the former dockyard. The garden is partly surrounded by the castle's 17th-century wall. Meals are served at all times except Monday evening. This pub occasionally features beers from Shepherd Neame's micro-brewery. A convenient car park is at the top of the village.

Walmer

Berry

23 Canada Road, CT14 7EQ

11.30-2.30 (not Tue or Thu), 5.30-11.30; 11-11.30 Sat; 11.30-11 Sun

(01304) 362411

Harveys Sussex Best Bitter; guest beers H

Well worth visiting for its great atmosphere and 'no frills' approach to real ale. A full range of pub games is played here, including the more unusual game of euchre. On Thursday night there is a jam session with the Deal, Walmer & Sandwich Guitar and Musicians Club. An interesting range of beers is always on offer from regional breweries and the pub's first beer festival has been held. CAMRA local branch Pub of the Year 2008.

(13,84)

Wateringbury

North Pole Inn

434 Red Hill, ME18 5BJ (¾ mile N of village/A26) TQ696547

11-11; 12-10.30 Sun

(01622) 812392 northpolepub.com

Fuller's London Pride; Greene King IPA; Taylor Landlord; Wells Bombardier; guest beer H

Built in 1826 as a private venture, together with adjacent cottages and stabling, it was later acquired by Whitbread, as can be seen from the etched bay windows. The large enclosed garden can be reached via a staircase. The restaurant features subdued lighting and displays pictures for sale by a local artist. Traditional pub food, using fresh local produce wherever possible, is available all week except Sunday evening. There is a weekly quiz, and shut the box can be played.

P

West Malling

Bull

1 High Street, ME19 6QH (towards A20 by railway bridge)

12-2.30, 5-11; 12-11 Fri & Sat; 12-10.30 Sun

(01732) 842753

Goacher's Dark, Gold Star; Young's Bitter; guest beer H

There has been an ale house on this railway-side site since 1426. The Bull has a friendly landlord who knows his beer. The room on the left is quiet and unadorned, furnished only with tables and chairs and a serving hatch. The large saloon bar on the right extends to the back of the pub where there is access to the beer garden. At weekends, parking is free at the long-stay car park opposite.

(72,151)

West Peckham

Swan on the Green

The Green, ME18 5JW (1 mile W of B2016 at Mereworth)

11-3 (4 Sat), 6-11 (8 Mon); 12-9 (5 winter) Sun

(01622) 812271 swan-on-the-green.co.uk

Swan Fuggles, Trumpeter, Cygnet, Bewick, seasonal beers; guest beer H

Facing the quiet village green at the end of a no-through road, this pub is close to the church. It was first licensed in 1685, but refurbished at the end of the last century to create an interior with a modern feel, featuring a wooden floor and hop-adorned brick and wood-panelled walls. A varied food menu featuring locally-sourced ingredients is available (not Sun & Mon eves), amply washed down with distinctive ales from the micro-brewery behind the pub. Q P

Westerham

General Wolfe

High Street, TN16 1RQ

12-11 (midnight Fri & Sat); 12-10.30 Sun

(01959) 562104

Greene King IPA, Old Speckled Hen, Abbot H

Traditional weatherboarded pub named after a famous resident of the town, General Wolfe of Quebec. The garden wall is part of the Old Black Eagle Brewery; note the blocked up doorway that the workers used when entering the pub. The interior comprises a long slim room divided into a number of areas, with a log fire in winter. The pub serves reasonably priced meals (no food Sun eve) and a good range of malt whiskies. Quiz night is Wednesday. Q (401)P

Whitstable

Four Horseshoes

62 Borstal Hill, CT5 4NA (A290 on edge of town)

12 (11 Sat)-11; 12-10.30 Sun

(01227) 273876

Shepherd Neame Master Brew Bitter, Kent's Best H

Small, traditional local pub originally built as a forge in 1636. An unusual three-bar layout is built stepwise up the hillside. Bat & trap, darts and board games are played, while amenities include poker nights, a quiz league and occasional fun quizzes. Takeaway meals can be delivered to the pub, and the landlady will supply plates and cutlery after 6pm. By arrangement, you can have your own barbecue in the beer garden. Dogs are welcome, but children only in the garden.

Q (4,6) P

Ship Centurion ✔

111 High Street, CT5 1AY

⌚ 11-11 (11.30 Fri & Sat); 12-7 Sun

☎ (01227) 264740

Adnams Bitter; Elgood's Black Dog; guest beers Ⓗ

Kent CAMRA Pub of the Year 2007 is the only pub in town always serving mild, along with ever-changing guest beers. This busy, centrally located free house is festooned with colourful hanging baskets in summer. Fascinating photographs of old Whitstable hang in the comfortable bar. Live entertainment is hosted on Thursday evening (except January). Home-cooked bar food often features authentic German produce – the only food on Saturday is schnitzel. A public car park is close by in Middle Wall. ◑⇌⊟⊢

Whitstable Brewery Bar

East Quay, CT5 2BP

⌚ 11-11 (hours may vary)

☎ (01227) 772157 🌐 hotelcontinental.co.uk

Whitstable Brewery IPA, seasonal beers; guest beers Ⓖ

Situated on Whitstable Harbour's East Quay, right on the shingle beach, this large, modern one-room bar has slate floors and huge windows for enjoying the sea views. Plastic glasses are compulsory as many drinkers venture outside to the plentiful beach seating. The adjacent restaurant serves mostly seafood. Access to the pub is along an unmade road, and there is an admission charge on Friday evening for live music. Opening hours vary – a phone call to check is recommended. A beer festival is held in July. ₼❀♿⇌⊟(4,6)P

Wittersham

Swan Inn

1 Swan Street, TN30 7PH (on B2080 between Rye & Tenterden) TQ897275

⌚ 11-midnight (2am Fri & Sat); 12-midnight Sun

☎ (01797) 270913 🌐 swan-wittersham.co.uk

Goacher's Light; Harveys Sussex Best Bitter; Rother Valley Smild; Ⓗ **guest beers** Ⓖ

A regular local CAMRA Pub of the Year, extensively altered in 2007. It has retained its two bar character but added extra comfort for its varied clientele. Seven beers are on offer including a mild and two ciders. There are summer and winter beer festivals plus regular live music and a cider festival in May. Good value food is available and a superb welcome is assured. ₼Q❀◑⊟♿⊟●P

Woodchurch

Six Bells

Bethersden Road, TN26 3QQ (close to village green opp church) TQ942349

⌚ 11 (12 Sun)-midnight

☎ (01233) 860246

Fuller's London Pride; Harveys Sussex Best Bitter; Woodforde's Wherry; guest beers Ⓗ

A popular village local, welcoming and unspoilt, with a public bar, saloon bar and dining area, with plenty of space for drinkers. A good range of freshly-prepared meals is available, with food served all day Friday to Sunday (no food Mon and Tue). A large enclosed beer garden at the rear is ideal for families. Dogs are welcome and Weston's Old Rosie cider is served.

₼Q❀◑⊟⊟(297)♣●P

Wormshill

Blacksmiths Arms

The Street, ME9 0TU

⌚ 7-11; closed Mon; 12-4 Sun

☎ (01622) 884386 🌐 blacksmiths-arms.com

Beer range varies Ⓗ

A small 17th-century village pub with a brick floor and an open log fire in the winter. It offers frequently-changing beers from across the country, and the cosy bar is popular with locals. A candlelit restaurant serves excellent home-cooked food for Sunday lunch and evening meals, with speciality fish dishes. There are benches outside at the front. The rural location is popular with walkers and cyclists. Note the restricted opening hours.

₼❀◑P⊢

Wrotham Heath

Moat

London Road, TN15 7RR (on A20 near M26 jct)

⌚ 12-11 (midnight Fri & Sat); 12-10.30 Sun

☎ (01732) 882263

Badger First Gold, Tanglefoot, seasonal beers Ⓗ

An extensively modernised roadhouse on the A20 comprising a pub and restaurant. The new interior is bright and airy, although some original features have been retained, including four log-burning fireplaces. Food is served every day and an open quiz is hosted on Thursday. The outdoor seating area has heated lamps and umbrellas.

₼Q❀◑♿♣P⊢

Yalding

Walnut Tree

Yalding Hill, ME18 6JB (on B2010)

⌚ 11.45-11; 12-10.30 Sun

☎ (01622) 814266 🌐 walnuttreeyalding.co.uk

Fuller's London Pride; Harveys Sussex Best Bitter; Taylor Landlord; guest beer Ⓗ

Originally an oak-beamed Kentish yeoman's house built around 1492, its red-brick walls were added later, as was the extension that is now the restaurant. The bar has an inglenook fireplace in the small upper area, with steps down to a lower bar. Hops, brassware and pictures create a cosy atmosphere. Good food features local produce. ₼◑⊟(23,26)P

It was my Uncle George who discovered that alcohol was a food well in advance of modern medical thought. **P G Wodehouse**, The Inimitable Jeeves

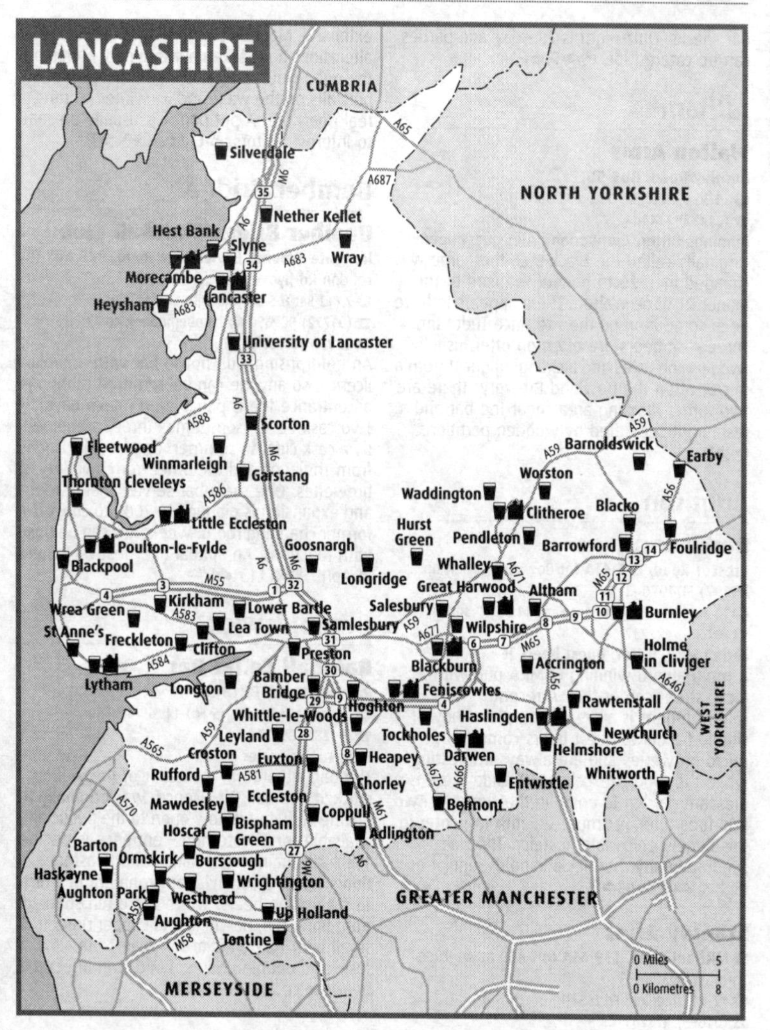

Accrington

Park Inn

68 Manchester Road, BB5 2BN (on A680 to Haslingden)

✪ 2-midnight; 1-2am Fri; 12-2am Sat; 12-midnight Sun

☎ (01254) 237043

John Smith's Bitter; guest beers Ⓗ

A local community pub that features a narrow bar area with a pool room to the side, a seating section and a separate back room. The pub is very popular with locals and can be busy at times. There is one guest beer alongside the regular John Smith's. Outside is a covered and heated smoking area. ❀🚌♣⁻

Peel Park ✔

Turkey Street, BB5 6EW (200m from A679, adj to Peel Park school)

✪ 12-11.30

☎ (01254) 235830

Tetley Bitter; guest beers Ⓗ

A genuine free house opposite the site of the old Stanley football ground. Eight beers are sold mainly from micros. The main bar is a large open front room which is divided into two sections. There is a separate little pool room, and a rear room used for dining or meetings. Two beer festivals a year are held, at spring bank holiday and in November. Outside is a covered smoking area. ❀◐🚌(23,263)♣●P⁻

Adlington

Spinners Arms

23 Church Street, PR7 4EX

✪ 12-11 (midnight Fri & Sat)

☎ (01257) 483331

Coniston Bluebird; Taylor Landlord; guest beers Ⓗ

Known as the Bottom Spinners to differentiate it from the other Spinners Arms pub in the village. A single bar serves three seating areas and there is a pleasant outdoor drinking area to the front of the pub. The guest beers, which are often sourced from local breweries, always include a mild. Pump clips from previous guest beers are displayed behind the bar. A kitchen is planned this year to provide bar snacks. Quiz night is Tuesday and parties can be catered for. ❀≈⊟♣P⁄–

Altham

Walton Arms

Burnley Road, BB5 5UL
11.30-3, 5.30-11; 11.30-11 Sun
☎ (01282) 774444
Jennings Bitter, Cumberland Ale; guest beer Ⓗ
Originally called the Black Bull, the name was changed in 1820 to honour the Lord of the Manor RT Wroe Walton. There appears to have been something on the site since Tudor times. Three cask beers are often on offer, usually two Jennings ales and a changing guest from a micro, often the Bowland Brewery. There are two futher drinking areas near the bar and a restaurant separated by wooden partitions. Q◑P

Aughton

Derby Arms

Prescot Road, L39 6TA (at Bowker's Green on B5197) SD407043
11.30-11 (midnight Fri & Sat); 11.30-10.30 Sun
☎ (01695) 422237
Tetley Mild, Bitter; guest beers Ⓗ
A multi-award winning CAMRA pub with a local, street-corner feel. A recent refurbishment is a great example of how it should be done. Guest beers come from micro-breweries and are always interesting, while the food is excellent. Outside there is a pleasant garden to enjoy in the summer. Two real fires offer yet more warmth in winter in this hugely enjoyable hostelry. The pub supports many charities and holds regular quiz nights. ⌂❀◑⊟♣P

Stanley Arms

St Michael Road, L39 6SA (off A59 at Aughton Springs) SD391055
12-11 (midnight Fri & Sat)
☎ (01695) 423241
Tetley Dark Mild, Bitter; guest beers Ⓗ
The pub is in a village setting beside an historic church but close to the A59. The exterior is in the classic village style with distinctive architecture and rambling out-buildings. Inside there are two lower rooms, one with a single table for 'private' discussions and the other with books on early brewing history. Up a few steps is the bar with other rooms off it. The walls are adorned with prints, patterned plates and Tudor-style woodwork. ⌂❀◑⊟(311,351)P⁄–

Aughton Park

Dog & Gun

233 Long Lane, L39 5BU (near railway station) SD413064
12 (4 Mon & Tue)-midnight
☎ (01695) 423303
Banks's Bitter; Jennings Bitter; Marston's Pedigree; guest beers Ⓗ
The Dog & Gun has been serving the residents of Aughton with top class ales for many years. With the demise of Burtonwood beers, the pub is now serving ales from the more extensive Marston's range. Although some alterations have taken place to partly open out the pub layout, it retains an intimacy, with old portraits on the walls and, in winter months, a real open fire. A pet parrot is usually present to interest visitors. ⌂Q☺❀◑♿≈P⁄–

Bamber Bridge

Bamber Bridge Football Club

Irongate Ground, Brownedge Road, PR5 6UX (by London Rd flyover)
7 (12 Sat & Sun)-midnight
☎ (01772) 909690 🌐 bamberbridgefc.co.uk
Beer range varies Ⓗ
An enterprising club-house bar with a public licence, so anyone can be admitted (although an entrance fee is payable on match days). Two cask beers, sometimes three, are joined by a cask cider in summer. One beer is usually from Thwaites and the other from a variety of breweries. One main bar serves a large room and expansion is planned in 2008 to convert a former changing room. Weekends can be busy with functions. An annual beer festival is held in April. ❀⊟(113)♣P⁄–

Barnoldswick

Rainhall Cellar Bar

Rainhall Road, BB18 5AF
closed Mon-Wed; 6 (5 Fri)-11; 6-10.30 Sun
☎ (01282) 813374
Beer range varies Ⓗ
The bar, situated in the cellar of the well-stocked Rainhall Off-Licence, was originally a private club, but is now open to the public and available for private hire – entrance is via the shop. Its quaint low ceilings and flagstone floors create a convivial environment in which to savour the beers, which are often sourced from Bank Top, Bowland and Copper Dragon. A small beer garden is at the rear. Note restricted opening hours, which can affect the beer choice on Sunday. ❀

Barrowford

George & Dragon ✔

217 Gisburn Road, BB9 6JD (on A682)
3 (12 Thu)-midnight; 12-1am Fri & Sat; 12-midnight Sun
☎ (01282) 612929
Moorhouse's Premier; guest beers Ⓗ

INDEPENDENT BREWERIES

Bowland Clitheroe
Bryson's Morecambe
Fallons Darwen (NEW)
Fuzzy Duck Poulton-le-Fylde
Grindleton Clitheroe
Hart Little Eccleston
Hopstar Darwen
Lancaster Lancaster
Lytham Lytham (NEW)
Moonstone Burnley
Moorhouse's Burnley
Pennine Haslingden (NEW)
Red Rose Great Harwood
Three B's Feniscowles
Thwaites Blackburn

A community village pub supporting several sports teams, situated near the Pendle Heritage Centre, Barrowford Park and a short walk from Barrowford Locks on the Leeds-Liverpool Canal. The pub is often busy at weekends and live music is played on the last Saturday of the month. The guest beers always include one from Bowland Brewery, plus another sourced from a local micro.
❀🚌(109)♣⁄

Barton

Blue Bell

Southport Road, L39 7JU (on A5147 S of Halsall) SD362088
✪ 12-11 (10.30 Sun)
☎ (01704) 841406 🌐 thebluebellhotel.co.uk
Beer range varies ⊞
A friendly pub in the heart of the countryside which caters for the needs of locals and passing visitors. Many of the rural walks in the area should include a stop here, as good value food is available along with traditional games and occasional live music in the evening. An unusual feature is the animal farm at the rear of the car park where you will find an assortment of sheep, goats, rabbits and hens.
♨❀◑🚌(300)♣P⁄

Belmont

Black Dog

2-6 Church Street, BL7 8AB SD676164
✪ 12-11 (11.30 Fri & Sat); 12-10.30 Sun
☎ (01204) 811218
Holt Mild, Bitter, seasonal beers ⊞
A Holt's estate house, this is an old, traditional village inn with a cobbled area at the front plus a modern extension. Part of the main bar in this former farmhouse has been used in the past as a court, and the seating remains. Meals are available at lunchtime and in the evening (not Tuesday), and all day Friday to Sunday. A separate dining area is used when busy. Accommodation is available, plus a new flagged and heated smokers' area.
Q❀⊭◑P⁄

Bispham Green

Eagle & Child

Maltkiln Lane, L40 3SG (off B5246)
✪ 12-3, 5.30-11; 12-10.30 Sun
☎ (01257) 462297
Thwaites Original; guest beers ⊞
Outstanding 16th-century local that overlooks the village green, with antique furniture and stone-flagged floors. The pub is renowned for its food and features occasional themed menu evenings (booking advised). An annual beer festival is held on the first May bank holiday in a marquee on the lawn behind the pub. Tables around the bowling green offer wonderful views of the surrounding countryside.
♨Q❀◑♿●P

Blackburn

Adelphi Hotel

33 Railway Road, BB1 1EZ
✪ 11-11; 12-10.30 Sun
☎ (01254) 681128
Black Sheep Best Bitter; guest beers ⊞
A friendly town-centre pub, open-plan and split-level, with up to five real ales on handpump. Other attractions include large-screen TV sports and music channels, with a Saturday night disco playing music from the 1960s to the 1990s. A favourite with visiting football supporters (as it is very convenient for trains and buses), the pub hosts pub league pool, darts and dominoes and is an ideal spot for a quick pint while waiting for travel connections. ⇌🚌♣⁄

St John's Tavern

Ainsworth Street, BB1 6AD (adj to Blackburn market)
✪ 9am-8 (10 Fri & Sat); closed Sun
☎ (01254) 51528
Thwaites Nutty Black, Original, seasonal beers ⊞
A friendly town centre pub, not far from the brewery, offering Thwaites Nutty Black and Original alongside seasonal ales. The pub has gone from strength to strength over the past few years, providing live entertainment three evenings a week (Wed, Fri & Sat). The Friday Club offers free food and discounted beer while other facilities include pool, darts and dominoes, and occasional Friday quizzes. Note the early opening and closing times – ideal for post shopping or an after-work pick-me-up.
⊟♿⇌🚌

Blacko

Cross Gaits

Beverley Road, BB9 6RF (off A682) SD867414
✪ 12-3 (not Mon & Tue), 5-midnight; 12-midnight Sat; 12-10.30 Sun
☎ (01282) 616312
Jennings Cumberland Ale; Marston's Burton Bitter; guest beers ⊞
A pleasant country pub, formerly part of the Burtonwood estate, serving good food. There is a large, comfortable garden area to the rear. Do not be misled by the inscription (dating from 1730) over the front door: 'Good ale tomorrow for nothing'. There are extensive views from the pub and a network of footpaths pass close by. The guest beer comes from the Marston's list. ♨Q❀◑P⁄

Blackpool

Churchills ✔

83-85 Topping Street, FY1 3AF (nr Winter Gardens)
✪ 10-11 (midnight Fri & Sat); 11-11 Sun
☎ (01253) 622036
Bateman XXXB; Greene King Old Speckled Hen; Shepherd Neame Spitfire; Wells Bombardier ⊞
Handy for the Winter Gardens, this characterful, traditional town centre local is popular with locals and visitors alike. A wide variety of live entertainment is provided, even including a psychic evening on Sunday. An advertisement for nude dancers ('must be modest') has had no recent takers though. Substantial fresh rolls and baguettes are available. A small terraced area to the front caters for smokers and reveals the origins of the building as the Criterion Hotel.
❀◐⇌(Blackpool North)🚌(2,15)♣⁄

Dunes Hotel

561 Lytham Road, FY4 1SA (500m from airport on B5262)
☉ 11 (12 Sun)-11 (midnight Thu-Sat)
☎ (01253) 403854
Greene King IPA; Wells Bombardier; Young's Bitter; guest beers ⊞
A regular in the Guide, this local community pub still has a separate vault. It hosts quiz nights on Thursday and Sunday. At the front of the pub, a heated, flower-decked patio allows for outdoor summer drinking. Smokers are catered for too. The meals served here are basic pub fare and finish at 7.30pm. Several buses pass nearby. ❀◑⊟♿⇌⊟♣P⚟

New Road Inn ✔

244 Talbot Road, FY1 3HL
☉ 11-midnight; 12-11.30 Sun
☎ (01253) 628872
Jennings Dark Mild, Cumberland Ale, Sneck Lifter; guest beers ⊞
This cosy street-corner local, handy for the station, retains many of its original Art Deco features. The friendly welcome attracts a mixed clientele, while entertainment includes regular Sunday and Monday karaoke. The darts, dominoes and pool teams play on Wednesday, with other games or quizzes also on offer. Traditional games are kept behind the bar. Freshly made baguettes and hot dogs are available. The pub is Cask Marque approved, with a heated and covered smoking area. ♿⇌(Blackpool North)⊟♣⚟

Pump & Truncheon

Bonny Street, FY1 5AR (behind Louis Tussaud's waxworks)
☉ 11-11 (10-midnight Fri & Sat summer)
☎ (01253) 624099
Boddingtons Bitter; guest beers ⊞
A former Hogshead Alehouse, this intimate one-room pub retains the trademark bare brick walls and floorboards of its history. The decor follows a law-enforcement theme, with badges of various police forces (belonging to the police station opposite) proudly displayed over the bar. Regular beer festivals are held. Food is served from opening until 7pm and is home cooked, generous and good value. Children are welcome if dining with adults. ⛰◑♿⊖(Central Pier)⊟

Saddle Inn ✔

286 Whitegate Drive, FY3 9PH (at Preston Old Road jct)
☉ 12-11 (midnight Fri & Sat)
☎ (01253) 767827
Draught Bass; Thwaites Original; guest beers ⊞
Blackpool's oldest pub, established in 1770, and CAMRA local Pub of the Year 2007 and 2008. The Saddle comprises a main bar and two side rooms, plus a large patio for outside drinking during the summer. This excellent, friendly pub usually has six guest beers on offer. A good menu of food is served every lunchtime and Monday to Thursday evenings. ⛰❀◑♿⊟P⚟

Shovels ✔

260 Common Edge Road, FY1 5DH (on B5261, ½ mile from A 5230 jct)
☉ 12-11 (midnight Thu-Sun)
☎ (01253) 762702
Beer range varies ⊞
Large, award-winning and recently refurbished pub, twice local CAMRA Pub of the Year. The beers are usually from micro-breweries and dispensed from six handpumps. The pub holds a week-long beer festival every October and a number of sports teams are based here. Food is served daily, with an excellent two-for-one option. ⛰❀◑♿⊟♣P⚟

Burnley

Bridge Bier Huis

2 Bank Parade, BB11 1UH (behind shoppping centre)
☉ 12-midnight (2am Fri & Sat); closed Mon & Tue
☎ (01282) 411304 🌐 thebridgebierhuis.co.uk
Hydes Bitter; guest beers ⊞
The Bridge has a large, open bar area with an adjacent small, cosy room and an optional mosaic-covered entrance. Up to five guest beers are available, usually from micro-breweries. There is an emphasis on Belgian and other foreign beers, plus a large bottled beer selection. This CAMRA Regional Pub of the Year 2007 is one of the venues for the annual Easter Burnley Blues Festival. Occasional bands appear at the weekend and Wednesday is quiz night. ◑⇌(Burnley Central)⊟

Coal Clough

41 Coal Clough Lane, BB11 4PG (200m E of M65 jct 10)
☉ 1-11; 12-midnight Fri & Sat; 12-11 Sun
☎ (01282) 423226 🌐 coalcloughpub.co.uk
Cains Bitter; Masseys Bitter; Worthington Bitter; guest beers ⊞
An end-of-terrace community local, which is always busy and friendly, includes a games room that features the popular card game Don. The Masseys beer is brewed by Tower Brewery at Burton, in an attempt to replicate a defunct Burnley brew. Usually two guest beers are available. Live music entertainment is provided on Tuesday and Thursday evenings. There is a very cosy smoking area in the back yard. ⇌(Barracks)⊟(111,112)♣⚟

Gannow Wharf

Gannow Lane, BB12 6QH
☉ 7 (5 Fri)-midnight; 12-midnight Sat & Sun
☎ (07855) 315498
Beer range varies ⊞
Next to the Leeds-Liverpool canal at Gannow Bridge, this pub offers a very friendly welcome plus at least four real ales, with regulars including Courage Directors and Wychwood Hobgoblin. This is a popular venue for the biker fraternity, and Saturday nights often include live rock music. There is a well-appointed outdoor smoking area. ⇌(Rosegrove)⊟P

Ministry of Ale

9 Trafalgar Street, BB11 1TQ
☉ 5-11 Wed & Thu; 12.30 (11 Sat)-midnight Fri; 12-11 Sun
☎ (01282) 830909
Beer range varies ⊞

The home of the Moonstone Brewery, where the 2½ barrel plant is on view in the front room. This small local with a friendly welcome places an emphasis on good beer and conversation. Two Moonstone beers are sold, alongside two rotating guests from micro-breweries. The Ministry holds regular alternative art exhibitions. A popular quiz is held on Thursday night.
❀≋(Manchester Road)🚌

Burscough

Slipway

48 Crabtree Lane, L40 0RN (off A59, by canal)
SD428126
11-11
☎ (01704) 897767
Thwaites Original; guest beers Ⓗ
The Slipway is a delightfully attractive canalside pub with a large garden and outside dining area, a children's play area, and the chance to watch narrow boats passing through the nearby swingbridge. The interior continues the nautical theme, with photographs and waterway bric-a-brac. The pub has won well-deserved CAMRA certificates over the years which are displayed near the bar, and is an excellent summertime venue. A separate function room is available, plus a covered and heated smoking area.
Q❀♿≋(New Lane)♣P⁻

Chorley

Malt 'n' Hops

50-52 Friday Street, PR6 0AH (behind railway station)
12-11 (10.30 Sun)
☎ (01257) 260967
Beartown Kodiak Gold, Bearskinful, seasonal beers; guest beers Ⓗ
Situated close to Chorley railway station and bus station, this pub has a long-standing reputation in the local area for fine cask ales. Originally converted from an old shop in 1989, it became a haven for local drinkers due to a fine selection of guest beers. Now owned by Beartown Brewery of Congleton, it still has up to seven guest beers plus permanent beers from Beartown. It keeps to traditional licensing hours and is a short walk from the town centre. ❀≋🚌♣⁻

Potters Arms

42 Brooke Street, PR7 3BY (next to Morrisons)
3-11.30 (midnight Fri); 12-4, 7-midnight Sat; 12-5, 7-11 Sun
☎ (01257) 267954
Black Sheep Best Bitter; Taylor Golden Best; Three B's Doff Cocker Ⓗ
Small, friendly free house named after the owners, Mr & Mrs Potter, and situated at the bottom of Brooke Street alongside the railway bridge. The central bar serves two games areas, while two comfortable lounges are popular with locals and visitors alike. The pub displays a fine selection of photographs from the world of music, as well as vintage local scenes. Regular darts and dominoes nights are well attended and the chip butties go down a treat. The smoking area is covered. ≋🚌♣P⁻

Prince of Wales ✔

9-11 Cowling Brow, PR6 0QE (off B6228)
12-11 (11.30 Fri-Sun)
☎ (01257) 413239
Jennings Bitter, Cumberland Ale, seasonal beers; guest beers Ⓗ
Stone terraced pub in the south-eastern part of town, not far from the Leeds-Liverpool Canal. An unspoilt interior incorporates a traditional tap room, games room, large lounge and a comfortable snug with real fire. There is photographic evidence of the licensee's love of jazz, and collections of brewery artefacts and saucy seaside postcards are also on display. A large selection of malt whiskies is behind the bar and sandwiches are served on request. ⋒❀⊟🚌(10,11)♣⁻▯

Clifton

Windmill Tavern

Station Road, PR4 0YE (off A583)
11-3, 5-11; 11-11 Sat & Sun
☎ (01772) 687203 🌐 mitchellshotels.co.uk
Thwaites Lancaster Bomber; guest beers Ⓗ
Based in one of the rural Fylde's old windmills, this building is over 300 years old and is one of the tallest windmills in Lancashire. It has only been a pub since 1974. The lounge was once the grain store and the side room is part of the original mill. A quiz night is held on Tuesday. ❀◐≋(Salwick)P

Clitheroe

New Inn

Parson Lane, BB7 2JN (just below castle)
11-11 (10.30 Sun)
☎ (01200) 443653
Coach House Gunpowder Mild; Moorhouse's Premier; guest beers Ⓗ
A true community pub, never empty, serving beers from all over Britain from up to ten handpumps. Alongside the regulars from Coachhouse and Moorhouse's, you may find beers from breweries such as Goose Eye, Oakham, Phoenix, Robinsons and Barnsley. The pub retains an original multi-roomed layout, with a TV in just one room. It is frequently used by local groups and societies for meetings, plus regular live music. A pool table is tucked away in one corner.
⋒Q❀≋🚌P

Coppull

Red Herring

Mill Lane, PR7 5AN (off B5251 next to Coppull Mill)
12-11 (11.30 Fri & Sat)
☎ (01257) 470130
Beer range varies Ⓗ
This oasis of real ale is situated in the former offices of the imposing next-door mill. It was converted to a pub some years ago and the bar is a large single room plus an extension, usually offering three micro-brewed beers. TV sports fans are catered for, as are anglers who use the mill pond opposite. The pub hosts regular music nights and barbecues and has a large first-floor function room. Trainspotters will enjoy close proximity to the West Coast Main Line. ⋒❀🚌♣P⁻

Croston

Grapes
67 Town Road, PR26 9RA
✪ 12-11 (midnight Fri & Sat)
☎ (01772) 600225
Greene King IPA; guest beers Ⓗ
Old whitewashed pub situated close to the historic parish church in the heart of this picturesque village. The Grapes has been an inn since at least 1799 and the building has also seen use as a custom house and a magistrates' court in the past. A small bar serves a compact lounge and there are two rooms at the front, plus a restaurant at the back. Five guest beers from national and regional brewers are stocked, including occasional ales from local micro-breweries.
ఠ❀◐▶♿⇌🚌(7,112)P⅟

Wheatsheaf
Town Road, PR26 9RA
✪ 12-11 (11.30 Fri)
☎ (01772) 600370
Beer range varies Ⓗ
Situated next to the village green, this former barn specialises in gastro food, especially fish dishes. However, the ale is certainly not neglected, with three beers served regularly from a pool of eight or so, plus one handpump devoted to a guest ale. Candles adorn each table to give a cosy feel. There is an outdoor drinking area to the front and live music on alternate Fridays. ⅏❀◐♿⇌🚌(7)●P⅟

Darwen

Black Horse
72 Redearth Road, BB3 2AF
✪ 12-11
☎ (01254) 873040 🌐 theblackun.co.uk
Three B's Stoker's Slake; guest beers Ⓗ
This lively, popular community local runs four major beer festivals per year. In addition, themed mini beer festivals on the last weekend of every month feature new and rare ales, drawing visitors from far and wide. Real cider is available from the cellar, and meal deals are offered at weekends. At the rear of the pub is a large paved and part-tented area with seating and a heated smoking area. Regular entertainment includes games nights, large-screen TV sport and jam music on the last Thursday of each month.
❀◐♿⇌🚌♣●⅟

Earby

Red Lion
70 Red Lion Street, BB18 6RD (follow signs to youth hostel from Earby centre)
✪ 12-2, 5-11; 12-11 Fri & Sat; 12-10.30 Sun
☎ (01282) 843395
Black Sheep Best Bitter; Copper Dragon Best Bitter; Taylor Landlord; Tetley Bitter; guest beers Ⓗ
Village pub situated close to a youth hostel and popular with walkers. Inside is a main lounge with a dining area, plus a small separate and cosy public bar. Home-cooked pies are a speciality and children are welcome in the lounge area. Beers are found at both bars and usually include a guest mild, but ask which ones are available before ordering.
Q❀◐▶⊟⅄P⅟

Eccleston

Original Farmers Arms
Towngate, PR7 5QS (on B5250)
✪ 11.30-midnight (1am Sat)
☎ (01257) 451594
Boddingtons Bitter; Phoenix Arizona; Taylor Landlord; Tetley Bitter; guest beers Ⓗ
This white-painted village pub has expanded over the years into the cottage next door, adding a substantial dining area. However, the original part of the pub is still used mainly for drinking. There are two or three frequently-changing guest ales. Meals are available throughout the day seven days a week, and there is accommodation in four good-value guest rooms. ❀⛌◐▶🚌(113,347)P⅟

Entwistle

Strawbury Duck
Overshores Road, BL7 0LU (at side of Entwistle railway station) SD727177
✪ 12-11 (10.30 Sun)
☎ (01204) 852013
Cains Dark Mild, Bitter, seasonal beers; guest beers Ⓗ
A well-established old public house, now part of the Cains Group. Inside are flagstoned floors and dark beams adorned with brasses, plus pew seats and several small rooms. The beers include a good selection of Cain's bottled beers plus one guest ale alongside the handpumps. The Strawbury Duck is close to the Wahow and Entwistle reservoirs, and next to Entwistle railway station (a request stop) so is ideal for walkers. It can be busy at meal times. Dogs are welcome. ❀◐▶⊟⇌P

Euxton

Euxton Mills
Wigan Road, PR7 6JD (at A581 jct)
✪ 11.30-10.30 (11.30 Wed-Sat); 12-10.30 Sun
☎ (01257) 264002
Jennings Bitter, Cumberland Ale; guest beers Ⓗ
A village inn that has won several Best Kept Pub awards, as well as the local CAMRA branch Pub of the Season. Outside, a large collection of hanging baskets and flowerpots are particularly attractive during summer months. The pub is renowned for the quality of its food and always serves two or three guest beers. Two beer festivals are held each year, featuring around eight ales.
❀◐▶⇌(Balshaw Lane)🚌P⅟

Feniscowles

Feildens Arms
673 Preston Old Road, BB2 5ER (at A674/A6062 jct)
✪ 12-midnight (1am Fri & Sat)
☎ (01254) 200988
Black Sheep Best Bitter; Flowers IPA; guest beers Ⓗ
Welcoming, largely stone-built pub at a busy road junction about three miles west of Blackburn and not far from junction 3 of the

M65. The guest beers come from small breweries and there is always a mild available. Brews from local breweries Moorhouse's or Anglo-Dutch often appear. The Leeds-Liverpool canal is a short stroll away and bus services stop outside. Live football is screened regularly.
(Pleasington)(124,152)P

Fleetwood

Steamer

1-2 Queens Terrace, FY7 6BT (opp market)
10-midnight (1am Fri & Sat); 12-midnight Sun
(01253) 771756
Caledonian Deuchars IPA; Wells Bombardier; guest beers H
This former Matthew Brown outlet was built opposite the terminal for the London-Scotland ferry which sailed from Fleetwood to Ardrossan. There is an old blacksmith's workshop at the rear, dating from the time when the yard was used to stable police horses. Winner of a local CAMRA Pub of the Season award, the pub features snooker, pool, darts and dominoes. Children are welcome until 7pm. (Ferry Terminal)

Thomas Drummond

London Street, FY7 6JY (between Lord St and Dock St)
9-midnight (1am Fri & Sat)
(01253) 775020
Greene King Abbot; Marston's Pedigree; guest beers H
Situated in a former church hall and furniture warehouse, this town centre pub is named after a builder who helped construct the town. A past winner of the local CAMRA silver award and Pub of the Season, it has on display details of the founder of the town, Sir Peter Hesketh Fleetwood, and architect Decimus Burton. Children are welcome until 6pm. Food is served until 11pm daily (last orders for children's food is 5pm). There is a covered and heated area for smokers.
(London Street)

Wyre Lounge Bar

Marine Hall, The Esplanade, FY7 6HF
12-4, 7-11 Fri-Sun only
(01253) 771141 marinehall.co.uk
Beer range varies H
This bar is usually open weekends only. During the week it opens only when there is a function in the hall, so it is advisable for weekday visitors to contact the box office and check opening times. The bar has been extensively modernised – some would say not for the best. It offers an excellent panoramic view of Morecambe Bay. The Fleetwood Beer Festival is held here in February.
(16)P

Foulridge

Hare & Hounds

Skipton Old Road, BB8 7PD (on A56)
12-2.30 (not Mon), 6-11; 12-11 Sun
(01282) 864235
Jennings Cumberland Ale; Marston's Burton Bitter; guest beers H

A roadside pub that was bought by Jennings before it too was acquired by the Marston's group. Jennings beers still dominate, with guests from the Marston's range. The main bar area leads to two smaller rooms that are used mostly for dining. The pub is very close to the Leeds-Liverpool canal and popular with walkers. A beer garden is at the rear, with a main car park to the front. Accommodation comprises five letting rooms. P

Freckleton

Coach & Horses

PR4 1PD
11 (12 Sun)-midnight (1am Fri & Sat)
(01772) 632284
Boddingtons Bitter; guest beers H
This community village local has retained its cosy atmosphere. It is home to Freckleton's award-winning brass band and a cabinet displays its impressive collection of trophies. A special place is reserved for mementoes of the US Eighth Air Force who served locally in WWII. The pub also has a golfing society and lunchtime meals are served on weekdays.
(2,68)P

Garstang

Wheatsheaf

Park Hill Road, PR3 1EL
10-midnight (1am Fri & Sat); 11.30-11.30 Sun
(01995) 603398
Courage Directors; Jennings Cumberland Ale; Theakston Best Bitter; guest beers H
Built as a farmhouse in the late 18th century, this is now a Grade II-listed building and was greatly extended in 2002. A disco is held every Sunday, and live music is staged monthly on a Monday. The pub serves breakfast, lunch and supper and there is a covered outdoor smoking area. A Moorhouse's brew often features among the four guest beers.
P

Goosnargh

Grapes

Church Lane, PR3 2BH (off B5269 at post office)
12 (3 Mon)-midnight
(01772) 865234
Black Sheep Best Bitter; Tetley Dark Mild; guest beers H
Situated next to the historic church, this village inn has a country pub atmosphere and is popular with locals and diners. Food is served six days a week (not Mon), with two-course lunchtime specials, and themed nights — curries on Wednesday, pizza on Friday. There is a separate drinkers' area and a games room. Three beers come from the Punch Taverns list. Outside there is a paved beer patio and a large enclosed garden and children's play area.
(4)P

Stag's Head

990 Whittingham Lane, PR3 2AU
12-11 (10.30 Sun)
(01772) 864071 thestagshead.co.uk
Theakston Best Bitter; guest beers H

Large roadside pub and restaurant situated close to the haunted Chingle Hall. Inside there are four drinking areas served by a central bar, outside is a huge garden plus a heated area for smokers. All food is sourced from local producers and home-made pickles and chutneys are available to take away. Up to three guest beers are taken from the Scottish & Newcastle Cellarman's Reserve list. There is monthly live music and an annual beer festival. ♨❀◑♿🚌(4)P⁄–

Great Harwood

Royal Hotel ✔

2 Station Road, BB6 7BE (opp jct of Queen St and Park Rd)

⏲ 4-11; 12-midnight Fri & Sat; 12-10.30 Sun

☎ (01254) 883541

Beer range varies ⊞

The pub is the brewery tap for the nearby Red Rose Brewery. Eight beers are on offer including ales from the brewery and guests from near and far. There are also always at least two dark ales as well as a good selection of bottled beers. A beer festival is held over the May bank holiday. The pub is well served by public transport from Accrington, Blackburn and Manchester. ❀⇄⛺🚌♣🍺

Victoria ★ ✔

St John's Street, BB6 7EP

⏲ 4-midnight; 3-1am Fri; 12-1am Sat; 12-midnight Sun

☎ (01254) 885210

Beer range varies ⊞

Built in 1905 by Alfred Nuttall and known locally as Butcher Brig, the pub features a wealth of original features. The lobby has floor-to-ceiling glazed tiling and there is dark wood throughout the five rooms. On the horseshoe-shaped bar are eight handpumps dispensing beers sourced from small breweries throughout Northern England and Scotland. There is an annual beer festival. The pub sits on a cycle way. Q❀⛺♣⁄–

Haskayne

Kings Arms

Delf Lane, L39 7JJ (on A5147 at bridge, between Lydiate and Halsall) SD361081

⏲ 12-midnight (1am Fri & Sat)

☎ (01704) 840245

Tetley Mild, Bitter; guest beers ⊞

A traditional, picturesque country pub with a separate tile-floored public bar. Several coal fires warm the rooms and provide a classic atmosphere on cold, draughty evenings. Meals are generous and extremely good value. Ramblers and boatmen from the nearby canal are drawn in to sample beers from the smaller breweries, including George Wright from Rainford. The smoking area is covered and heated.

♨Q❀◑♿🚌(300)♣P⁄–

Haslingden

Griffin Inn

84 Hud Rake, BB4 5AF (off A680 signposted for Rossendale Ski Slope)

⏲ 12-midnight (11.30 Sun)

☎ (01706) 214021

Pennine Ales range; guest beers ⊞

A good-sized pub which is popular with locals. Once home to the Porter Brewing Company, the pub retains its own cellar-based micro-brewery which is now owned and run by Pennine Ales. An open fire is very welcome in winter. There is always a pleasant, friendly atmosphere and good independent beers.

♨Q♣

Heapey

Top Lock

Copthurst Lane, PR6 8LS (alongside canal at Johnson's Hillock)

⏲ 11-11; 12-10.30 Sun

☎ (01257) 263376

Beer range varies ⊞

Excellent canal-side pub with an upstairs dining room and up to nine real ales which always include a mild and either a porter or stout, together with a Timothy Taylor and a Coniston beer. Up to three real ciders are also on offer. There is an annual beer festival in October with approximately 100 ales available in the pub and a marquee. Live music is played on Thursday and there is a covered smoking area. ❀◑♣P⁄–🍺

Helmshore

Robin Hood Inn

280 Holcombe Road, BB4 4NP (follow signs to Helmshore Textile Museum)

⏲ 4 (12 Sat & Sun)-11

☎ (01706) 213180

Copper Dragon Black Gold, Golden Pippin, Scotts 1816; guest beers ⊞

This is a small, rustic pub that retains a lot of character, with the original Glen Top ale brewery windows intact. They are some of the only ones still in existence locally. Behind the bar is a good selection of beer and a wide choice of spirits, while a real fire adds great atmosphere. The pub is situated close to the Helmshore Textile Museum. ♨♣🍺

Hest Bank

Hest Bank

2 Hest Bank Lane, LA2 6DN

⏲ 11.30-11 (10.30 Sun)

☎ (01524) 824339

Black Sheep Best Bitter; Boddingtons Bitter; Taylor Landlord; guest beers ⊞

An historic canalside pub dating from 1554, formerly a coaching inn for travellers crossing Morecambe Bay to Grange-over-Sands. One of the older rooms in the pub functions as a locals' bar, while another smaller bar plus other rooms on differing levels are mostly used by diners. The oldest room, with low beams and an uneven floor, was recently redecorated in a 21st-century style. Food is served from an award-winning menu daily until 9pm. Wednesday is quiz night.

♨Q❀◑🚌♣

Heysham

Royal Hotel

7 Main Street, LA3 2RN
12-11 (midnight Fri & Sat); 12-10.30 Sun
☎ (01524) 859298 heyshamonline.co.uk/royal/royal.html
Beer range varies H
A 15th-century inn in the heart of the village. As you enter the pub, a tiny locals' bar is on the right and a restaurant is on the left – the main bar is accessed via a winding passage and opens onto a large landscaped garden. Six handpumps provide an Everards beer (choose from Beacon, Tiger or Sunchaser) and there is often a beer from Moorhouse's, Dent or Bowland. Forthcoming guest beers are usually listed on the website. Outside is a covered smoking area. ⌂Q❀◐⊟⊟(4)♠⁄

Hoghton

Royal Oak

Blackburn Old Road, Riley Green, PR5 0SL (at A675/A674 jct)
11.30-11; 12-10.30 Sun
☎ (01254) 201445
Thwaites Nutty Black, Original, Wainwright, Lancaster Bomber, seasonal beers H
Stone-built pub on the old road between Preston and Blackburn, near the Riley Green basin on the Leeds-Liverpool Canal. The Royal Oak is popular with diners and drinkers. Rooms, including a dining room, and alcoves radiate from the central bar. Low-beamed ceilings and horse brasses give the pub a rustic feel. This Thwaites tied house is a regular award winner and acts as an outlet for its seasonal beers. Hoghton Towers is nearby, steeped in history and worth visiting.
⌂Q❀◐⊟(152)P

Sirloin

Station Road, PR5 0DD (off A675 near level crossing)
4 (12 Sun)-11; 12-midnight Fri & Sat
☎ (01254) 852293
Beer range varies H
Even the ghosts are friendly in this small, 250-year-old, family-run country inn. It stands near Hoghton Tower, where King James I knighted a loin of beef, and his coat of arms hangs over one of the fireplaces. Sirloin steak is, of course, a speciality on the menu served in the pub (weekend lunches only) and adjoining restaurant. Three handpumps dispense a varied range of beers. There is a heated outdoor smoking area. ⌂❀◐♿⊟(152)♣P⁄

Holme in Cliviger

Queen

412 Burnley Road, BB10 4SU (on A671 between Burnley and Todmorden)
1-11
☎ (01282) 436712
Beer range varies H
A small, friendly two-roomed village local where good beer and conversation can be expected. The rooms are cosy and convivial, with roaring fires in winter. Local historic photos clutter the walls and three beers are offered, usually from micro-breweries. The Queen is situated amid the spectacular scenery of the glacial Cliviger Gorge and is an excellent starting and finishing point for many worthwhile walks. If walking, you are welcome to bring your own food. ⌂Q⊟⊟

Hoscar

Railway Tavern

Hoscar Moss Road, L40 4BQ (1 mile from A5209) SD468116
summer: 12-2, 5.30-11; 12-11 Sat; 12-10.30 Sun; winter: 12-2 (not Mon), 5.30-11; 12-10.30 Sun; 12-10.30am
☎ (01704) 897503
Black Sheep Best Bitter; Tetley Bitter; Wells Bombardier; guest beers H
The pub is immediately adjacent to the tiny Hoscar station on the Southport-Manchester line and dates back to the same time as the railway was built. There are few reasons for alighting here, other than to enjoy the ales and food the tavern provides. Cyclists and rural road users also enjoy the premises that include a quiet garden at the back, ideal for summer drinking or trainspotting. Please note that no trains stop on Sunday at present.
⌂Q❀◐⊟♿≠P⁄

Hurst Green

Shireburn Arms ✔

Whalley Road, BB7 9QJ
12-11
☎ (01254) 826518 shireburnarmshotel.com
Bowland Chipping Steamer; Theakston Best Bitter; guest beers H
One of the few hotels in the Ribble Valley that serves real ale. Two handpumps feature one beer from nearby Bowland Brewery, while the other rotates from Theakston to another local beer, often from Moorhouse's. Beer tasting notes are provided on a chalkboard above the bar. The hotel is multi-roomed, comfortable and popular for weekend breaks, when the emphasis is on dining. Food may include dishes such as pan-fried scallops, or pheasant in black cherry sauce. The Lancashire cheese platter is well worth tasting. Q⇌◐P

Kirkham

Black Horse

29 Preston Street, PR4 2YA
12-midnight
☎ (01772) 671209
Greene King Old Speckled Hen; guest beers H
First opened in the 13th century, this friendly, traditional, two-roomed local on the main street attracts a wide range of customers. The public bar boasts a pool table, while a large-screen TV shows all major sporting events. Three guest beers are usually on sale. The pub is built above ancient monastic tunnels, and is said to be haunted by a family who died when a roof collapsed; strange noises are often heard. There is a covered smoking area outside. ❀⊟♿≠(Kirkham & Wesham)⊟♣⁄

Lancaster

Borough ✔

3 Dalton Square, LA1 1PP

12-12.30am theboroughlancaster.co.uk

Black Sheep Best Bitter; Bowland Hen Harrier; Thwaites range; guest beers

An upmarket town house built in 1824 but with a Victorian frontage. It is now a pub that succeeds in appealing to both food lovers and ale aficionados. The front area resembles a gentlemen's club with deep-buttoned chairs and chandeliers; the large back room is a restaurant and the bar is in a passage between them. Outside is a sheltered patio. Guest beers come from Barngates, Lancaster and Bryson's. CAMRA members get a 30p discount on a pint. Poker night is Monday.

Golden Lion

31 Moor Lane, LA1 1QD (next to Duke's Theatre)

12-12.30am (midnight Sun)

(01524) 842198

Caledonian Deuchars IPA; Theakston Best Bitter; guest beers

The pub is reputed to have been the last drinking place of the Pendle Witches in 1612. The present building is a mere 200 years old, and is included in the Pendle Trail. Also known as the Whittle, it is a popular pub with a friendly and relaxed atmosphere. Live music takes place every Thursday and Saturday evening, and an open mic session is held every Tuesday. Locally made pie and peas are available daily.

Sun ✔

63 Church Street, LA1 1ET

10-midnight

(01524) 66006 thesunhotelandbar.co.uk

Lancaster Amber, Red, Blonde, Black; guest beers

The decor here combines a mixture of exposed stonework, wood panelling and solid furniture with ambient candlelight in the evenings. Various original features remain including stone fireplaces and a well. The pub is the primary outlet for Lancaster Brewery in the city, as well as offering up to four guest beers. Brewery nights are held regularly, featuring numerous national independent breweries. Wi-Fi Internet access is available. Outside is a heated and covered smoking area.

Three Mariners

Bridge Lane, LA1 1EE (near Parksafe car park)

12-midnight

(01524) 388957

Black Sheep Best Bitter; Jennings Cumberland Ale; Everards Beacon Bitter; guest beers

Considered to be the oldest pub in Lancaster, the Three Mariners has been renovated and reconstructed, but retains low beams and stone mullions. It is built into the side of a hill and the narrow strip of cobbles at the front, now occupied by tables for drinkers, is Bridge Lane, which once connected the town centre to the quayside. The pub has a thriving local clientele that can enjoy six cask ales. Home-made lunchtime and evening meals are available (not Mon eve).

White Cross

White Cross Ind Est, Quarry Road, LA1 4XQ (up hill behind town hall)

11.30-11 (12.30am Fri & Sat); 12-11 Sun

(01524) 33999

Boddingtons Bitter; Caledonian Deuchars IPA; Tirril Old Faithful; guest beers

A modern conversion of an old canalside warehouse, with an open-plan interior and a light, airy feel. French windows open out onto extensive canalside seating, which makes this a popular venue on summer evenings. The ten guest beers regularly come from Bowland, Dent and other local breweries, plus Weston's Old Rosie cider. There is a quiz every Tuesday and an annual beer festival in April.

Yorkshire House

2 Parliament Street, LA1 1DB (S end of Greyhound Bridge)

7-midnight (1am Thu & Fri); 2-1am Sat; 2-11.30 Sun

(01524) 64679 yorkshirehouse.enta.net

Everards Tiger; Moorhouse's Premier; guest beers

This is known as a regulars' music pub, with possibly the best jukebox in town and bands playing most evenings in the big room upstairs. It offers a warm welcome not just to the young at heart. The mix of ages, friendly service and intimate drinking spaces, including a cosy corner with a wood-burning stove, help to explain this pub's appeal. It is one of the rare venues in the city to serve a guest cider on handpump. Table football is a further attraction. A popular quiz is held on the first Sunday of the month. The recently refurbished courtyard garden is recomended for summer drinking.

Lancaster University

Graduate College Bar

Barker House Village, Ellel, LA2 0PF

7 (6 Fri)-11; 8-11 outside term time; 8-11 Sun

(01524) 592824 gradbar.co.uk

Beer range varies

The Graduate College can be found in the complex of buildings at Alexandra Park, south-west of the main campus. The 'Gradbar', on Barker Square, attracts an age-range that is slightly higher than an average student bar, as its name suggests. The choice of beer is good, with eight handpumps often offering Lancaster, Copper Dragon, Acorn and Barngates. The place is open only to university members, staff, guests and people carrying a copy of the Guide. Weston's cider and perry are also served.

Lea Town

Smith's Arms

Lea Lane, PR4 0RP

12-midnight

(01772) 760555

Thwaites Nutty Black, Original, Lancaster Bomber, seasonal beers

Open-plan country pub situated near the Preston-Lancaster canal and adjacent to an atomic fuel factory. It is also known as the Slip Inn from a time when the Fylde farmers would

walk their cattle past on the way to Preston market and slip in for a drink. The five handpumps see plenty of use in this Thwaites house, which regularly wins awards for its quality food so it can get busy, especially on Sunday. It is home to darts and dominoes teams, and has a covered smoking area.
❀◑♿⊟♣P⚟

Leyland

Eagle & Child

30 Church Road, PR25 3AA
⏲ 11.45-11 (11.30 Thu-Sat); 12-11 Sun
☎ (01772) 433531
Banks's Bitter; Marston's Pedigree; guest beers Ⓗ
Attractive, ancient inn which is justifiably popular with drinkers aged 18 to 80. This prominent pub is something of a cask ale oasis on the fringe of the town centre. Two guest ales drawn from the Marston's list are offered, plus the two regular brews. A large beer garden to the side of the pub is popular in summer and a crown bowling green lies adjacent to the car park across the road.
❀◐♣⚟⊓

Little Eccleston

Cartford Inn

Cartford Lane, PR3 0YP (½ mile from A586)
⏲ 11-11 (midnight Fri & Sat); 11-10 Sun
☎ (01995) 670166
Theakston Old Peculier, XB; guest beers Ⓗ
The Cartford Inn is a 17th-century coaching inn nestling on the banks of the River Wyre on Lancashire's Fylde Coast. Refurbished in 2007, the Cartford combines traditional features with contemporary style, plus seven stunning bedrooms, all unique and en-suite. The restaurant is closed on Monday but is open lunchtimes and evenings the rest of the week. Guest beers include various ales from the Hart Brewery, which is based next door.
♨❀⛟◑⅄⊟(42,80)P

Longridge

Corporation Arms

Lower Road, PR3 2YJ (near jct B6243/B6245)
⏲ 11-11 (midnight Fri & Sat); 12-10.30 Sun
☎ (01772) 782644 🌐 corporationarms.co.uk
Beer range varies Ⓗ
Eighteenth-century country inn close to the Longridge reservoirs and handy as a base for local walks. A free house, it has a deserved reputation for excellent ale, food, service and accommodation. Beers are sourced from local breweries, with Moorhouse's, Bowland and Three B's some of the favourites. Luxurious overnight rooms are popular, so booking is advised. Note the old horse trough outside, now used as a planter, which was reputably used by Oliver Cromwell on his way to the Battle of Preston. ♨❀⛟◑♿⊟P⚟

Forrest Arms

1 Derby Road, PR3 3NP
⏲ 4-midnight; 12-1am Fri & Sat; 12-11.30 Sun
☎ (01772) 786210
Beer range varies Ⓗ

Situated in the centre of this market town, behind the pub's stone exterior lies an interior that is bright and modern yet retains traditional character. Light coloured walls display examples of both modern art and football memorabilia. Three handpumps on the central island bar, an unusual feature for Lancashire, dispense cask ale. The house beer, Thyme, is brewed for the pub by Bank Top. Beer festivals are held twice a year. Good quality food, often using locally sourced ingredients, is available. ❀◑♿⊟♣⚟

Old Oak

111 Preston Road, PR3 3BA
⏲ 3-11 Mon; 12-11.30 Tue-Sat; 12-11 Sun
☎ (01772) 783648
Theakston Best Bitter; guest beers Ⓗ
Situated at a road junction on the B6243 from Preston, the Old Oak is returning to the Guide after a change of licensee. It is a large, multi-area family-run community pub with a friendly, welcoming and traditional feel. There are old photographs of the area on the walls. Regular theme nights are held, and a number of local organisations, including the Old Oak Beer Appreciation Society, make it their home. Up to four guest ales are usually available, together with good local food.
♨❀◑♿⊟♣P⚟

Longton

Dolphin

Marsh Lane, PR4 5SJ (down Marsh Lane 1 mile, take right fork)
⏲ 12 (10.30 Sun)-midnight
☎ (01772) 612032
Beer range varies Ⓗ
An isolated former farmhouse, this local CAMRA award-winning marshland pub lies at the start of the Ribble Way. Inside comprises a main bar (no children), a family room, a conservatory and a function room. The four or five ales on offer always include a mild and beer from local breweries. An annual beer festival takes place in August. Food is served daily until 8pm. Outside there is a children's play area and a covered smoking area. A free minibus service is provided from local villages.
♨☕❀◑⊟●P⚟

Lower Bartle

Sitting Goose

Lea Lane, PR4 0RU
⏲ 12-midnight
☎ (01772) 690344
Thwaites Original, Wainwright, Lancaster Bomber Ⓗ
Set in open countryside, this inn comprises a pub and a restaurant that share equal billing. A long main lounge bar is divided by a prominent chimney breast and there is a large outdoor drinking area suitable for smokers. Curry night is held on Monday, quiz night is Wednesday and grill night is Thursday. There is a caravan site nearby. ♨❀◑♿⅄⊟(80)♣P⚟

Lytham

County Hotel ✔

Church Road, FY8 5LH

12-11 (midnight Fri & Sat)

☎ (01253) 795128

Boddingtons Bitter; Phoenix Pale Moonlight; guest beers Ⓗ

An imposing, attractive hotel that dates back to the 1800s and is a popular venue on Lytham's real ale scene. The large lounge is split into small, intimate areas on two levels with a large-screen plasma TV for sports lovers. An ever-changing range of up to four guest beers is complemented by good value food served in the bar all day until 9pm, with a weekend carvery restaurant open Fri-Sun. Accommodation comprises 22 en-suite rooms. Children are welcome until 9pm.

Hastings

26 Hastings Place, FY8 5LZ (close to station)

12-midnight

☎ (01253) 732839

Lytham Amber, Gold, Dark; guest beers Ⓗ

This elegant and modern club has been CAMRA National Club of the Year and now has its own brewery on site. Up to nine guest beers are usually available, together with a good selection of bottled beers from around the world. An annual beer festival is held each November and excellent home-cooked food is served. There is a patio at the front. The Hastings is a members-only club but card-carrying CAMRA members are welcome, or show a copy of this Guide to gain entry.

Taps ✔

Henry Street, FY8 5LE

11-11 (midnight Fri & Sat); 12-11 Sun

☎ (01253) 736226

Titanic Taps Best, Taps Mild; guest beers Ⓗ

This multi award-winning pub is one of the area's gems, run by legendary landlord Ian Rigg. There is always something happening here, from 'meet the brewer' evenings to turf laid throughout the pub during the golf open. This ex-Hogshead house retains the trademark bare floorboards and brickwork. There are eight beers on offer, always including a cask mild. Children are admitted until 7pm and a rear covered patio incorporates a heated smoking area. Q

Mawdesley

Black Bull ✔

Hall Lane, L40 2QY (off B5246)

12-11 (midnight Fri & Sat); 12-10.30 Sun

☎ (01704) 822202

Black Sheep Best Bitter; Jennings Cumberland Ale; Robinsons Unicorn; Taylor Landlord; guest beers Ⓗ

A pub since 1610, this low-ceilinged stone building boasts some magnificent oak beams. Older village residents know the pub as 'Ell 'Ob, a reference to a coal-fired cooking range. Certificates on display record the pub's success in Lancashire's Best Kept Village competition, and it has also earned awards for its numerous hanging baskets. During summer months the well-kept beer garden is popular with both drinkers and diners. (347)P

Robin Hood

Bluestone Lane, L40 2QY (off B5252)

11.30-11; 12-10.30 Sun

☎ (01704) 822275 robinhoodinn.co.uk

Black Sheep Best Bitter; Caledonian Deuchars IPA; Jennings Cumberland Ale; Taylor Landlord; guest beers Ⓗ

Charming, white painted inn, at the crossroads between the three old villages of Mawdesley, Croston and Eccleston. The 15th-century building was substantially altered in the 19th century. Run by the same family for 40 years, it enjoys a reputation for good food. The recently renovated Wilsons restaurant upstairs is open Tuesday to Sunday evenings. Bar food is served all day at the weekend. It still finds room for those who have come for a drink only, offering three guest ales.

(347)P

Morecambe

Owl's Nest

Bare Lane, LA4 6DD

12-midnight (11 Mon & Tue); 12-11.30 Sun

☎ (01524) 405019

Moorhouse's Black Cat; Thwaites Lancaster Bomber; guest beers Ⓗ

Situated in a village location, close to both shops and the seafront, this single-storey mock-Georgian rural pub is a former lodge house. It sits in the grounds of a large hotel, but is run as a separate entity. There is a games room at one end of the main bar, which has bare stone walls and many cosy corners. A covered smoking area is available outdoors. (Bare Lane)P

Ranch House

Marine Road West, LA4 4DG

11-midnight

☎ (01524) 851531

Beer range varies Ⓗ

Large, open-plan seaside pub with adjoining amusement arcade, built in 1930 as part of what later became the Frontierland amusement park – now largely demolished. Its facade still features a Wild West theme, but inside it is hardly noticeable. The Ranch House faces the promenade and is close to the major 1930s landmark Midland Hotel which reopened in 2008. It is popular with locals, day-trippers and holidaymakers alike. Four ever-changing brews and sandwiches are always available. Outside is a covered and heated smoking area.

Nether Kellet

Limeburner's Arms

32 Main Road, LA6 1EP

7.30-midnight; 12-2 Sun

☎ (01524) 732916

Beer range varies Ⓗ

There was once a time when most country pubs were like this – plain, simple furnishings, no food and no jukebox – the sort of pub where even shy strangers get drawn into conversation. Unsurprisingly, most of the

regulars are locals and the landlord himself is a local farmer. The old photos in the bar are a rewarding study of the area. If the bar gets too busy, there is a side room to escape to. Regional beer is always available.
Q🚌(55A,49)♣P

Newchurch

Boars Head

69 Church Street, BB4 9EH
4-midnight; 12-1am Fri & Sat; 12-midnight Sun
☎ (01706) 214687
Black Sheep Best Bitter; guest beers Ⓗ
A proud pub that has been on the site since 1674. Good atmosphere and a good selection of guest beers. Q🚌♣⁻

Ormskirk

Hayfield

22 County Road, L39 1NN SD412089
12-midnight (1am Fri & Sat); 12-11.30 Sun
☎ (01695) 571157
Holts Mild, Bitter, seasonal beers; guest beers Ⓗ
Large, modern pub on the northern outskirts of town, alongside the A59 Liverpool-Preston road. Although open-plan, the interior is divided up by attractively-designed rails and screens, creating spacious drinking areas that are comfortably furnished and relaxing. Formerly a hotel, then a free house, the pub is now part of the Joseph Holt estate. Each month the brewery provides a new seasonal beer plus guest beers from local and regional micro-breweries. Outside is a covered smoking area. ❀(ID♿⇌🚌(375,385)P⁻

Pendleton

Swan With Two Necks

Main Street, BB7 1PT (just off A59)
12-3 (not Mon), 7-11; closed Tue; 1-3, 6-11 Fri; 12-2.30, 6-11 Sat; 12-10.30 Sun
☎ (01200) 423112
Beer range varies Ⓗ
Four different beers are served in this friendly village local, usually from micro-breweries such as Marble, Grindleton, Barngates or Phoenix. The pub is run by two CAMRA members and is deservedly popular, especially at weekends. Meals are very good value but visitors should check in advance that food will be available. Pies are a speciality of the house – try the lamb and leek, or beef and Guinness. Check out the collection of tea pots – and do not sit on the white cat. ₼Q❀(IDP

Poulton-le-Fylde

Golden Ball ✔

1 Ball Street, FY6 7BA
10.30-11 (11.30 Fri & Sat); 12-10.30 Sun
☎ (01253) 882196
Tetley Bitter; guest beers Ⓗ
Much modernised former coaching inn, where only the old Golden Ball sign outside the pub hints at its age. It served as the town's reading room at the time of the Battle of Trafalgar and the petty sessions court was held here. The open area behind the pub was used for cattle auctions until the 1960s. It is now a busy town-centre drinkers' pub, serving food during the day. Irish bands play on bank holidays. There is a smoking area with umbrellas and heaters on the patio. ₼❀(I♿⇌⊖🚌⁻

Old Town Hall

5 Church Street, FY6 7AP
11-11 (11.30 Fri & Sat); 12-11 Sun
☎ (01253) 890601
Theakston Best Bitter; guest beers Ⓗ
Formerly known as The Bay Horse, this building was used as council offices for much of the 20th century but is now a pub once more. Inside, its numerous TV screens are favoured by football and racing followers. Guest beers frequently come from Thwaites, Moorhouse's, JW Lees and Hart Ales. The games area features a frieze depicting old flora and fauna, while a quieter upstairs bar serves two cask ales and opens up on Friday and Saturday to cope with the weekend crowd. ♿⇌🚌

Thatched House

12 Ball Street, FY6 7BG
11 (12 Sun)-11 (midnight Fri & Sat)
☎ (01253) 891063
Black Sheep Best Bitter; Boddingtons Bitter; Wells Bombardier; guest beers Ⓗ
The present pub stands in the grounds of a Norman church, built on the site at the beginning of the 20th century. It also has the honour of being the oldest continuously licensed premises in the Fylde. In the bar, various sporting heroes of the past are on display on the walls. Beers from the local Hart Brewery feature regularly and the pub can get busy at weekends. Local CAMRA Pub of the Season, winter 2007/2008. ₼Q⊞Å⇌🚌⁻

Preston

Bitter Suite

53 Fylde Road, PR1 2XQ
12-3, 6-11 (midnight Fri); 12-midnight Sat; 7-11 Sun
☎ (01772) 827007 bittersuitepreston.co.uk
Goose Eye Bronte Bitter; guest beers Ⓗ
Single-room bar converted from a keg-only club less than three years ago, and run by landladies with 17 years' experience at another Guide entry in the town. A genuine free house, it serves five guest beers from micro-breweries that change almost hourly. Bronte beer is badged as Bitter Suite. There are at least four regular beer festivals each year and home-cooked lunches are served Monday to Friday. Although surrounded by university buildings, it is not primarily a student bar. ❀(I🚌

Fox & Grapes

15 Fox Street, PR1 2AB
12-11 (midnight Fri & Sat); 12-10.30 Sun
☎ (01772) 561149
Beer range varies Ⓗ
The Fox & Grapes is a small, friendly and deservedly popular oasis near the bustling shopping centre, with three handpumps dispensing a changing range of ales. An impressive collection of beer mats adorns the walls and bar ceiling. Also on display are motorcycle memorabilia together with framed articles on old Preston pubs, many now long

gone. It hosts monthly comedy nights, occasional live music; chess is available for those who enjoy quieter pursuits. ⇌🚌♣

Market Tavern

33-35 Market Street, PR1 2ES

⏲ 10.30-9 (midnight Fri & Sat); 12-9 Sun

☎ (01772) 254425

Beer range varies Ⓗ

Popular city-centre local overlooking the Victorian outdoor market. Three handpumps serve an ever-changing range of guest beers, usually from micros from all over the UK. A suberb selection of imported bottled beers is also on offer, plus German weisse and French blonde on draught. Outside seating is available in summer. Conversation rules in this former local CAMRA Pub of the Year. No food is served, but you are welcome to bring your own. ❀⇌

Old Black Bull ✔

35 Friargate, PR1 2AT

⏲ 10.30-11 (midnight Fri & Sat); 12-10.30 Sun

☎ (01772) 823397

Boddingtons Bitter; Cains Traditional Bitter; guest beers Ⓗ

Mock-Tudor city-centre pub. A small front vault, a main bar with distinctive black and white floor tiles, two comfortable lounge areas and a pool table combine to make this a popular venue. There is also a patio to the rear. Live music is played on Saturday evenings and all TV sport is shown. Up to seven guest beers come from micros or small independents. Good food is served in this pub which is twice winner of local CAMRA Pub of the Year. ❀◐⊟⇌♣⁺⁄–

Old Vic

78 Fishergate, PR1 2UH

⏲ 11.30-11 (midnight Fri; 1am Sat); 12-midnight Sun

☎ (01772) 254690

Caledonian Deuchars IPA; Courage Directors; Marston's Pedigree; Theakston Best Bitter; guest beers Ⓗ

Situated opposite the railway station and on bus routes into the city, the Old Vic can be rather busy at times. The seven handpumps are to the right on the bar as you enter, together with up to three guest beers, one of which is usually from a local micro. Big screens show sports events and there is a large pool table plus pinball. The pub hosts a keen darts team. Meals are served 12-5pm (4pm Sun). A rear car park is available weekends and evenings. ❀◐⇌🚌♣⁺⁄–

Olde Dog & Partridge

44 Friargate, PR1 2AT

⏲ 11-3, 6-11.30; 11-2am Sat; 12-5, 7-11.30 Sun

☎ (01772) 252217

Fuller's London Pride; Taylor Landlord; Tetley Dark Mild; guest beers Ⓗ

Down-to-earth city centre pub that specialises in rock music. The student union rocsoc meets here. Five real ales often include one from the Museum Brewery. The landlord has been at the pub for over 30 years and there is a monthly live music night, a weekly quiz on Thursday and a rock DJ on Sunday evening. Excellent value pub lunches are served (not Sun) and a covered 'Smokey-O Joes' smoking area is provided at the rear. ❀◐⇌🚌♣⁺⁄–

Preston Grasshoppers Rugby Club

Lightfoot Green, Lightfoot Lane, PR4 0AP

⏲ 4-11 (midnight Fri); 12-midnight Sat; 12-10.30 Sun

☎ (01772) 863546

Thwaites Original, Wainwrights, Lancaster Bomber, seasonal beers Ⓗ

You do not have to be rugby-oriented to enjoy the friendly atmosphere in the Clubhouse Bar. Its premises licence means it is also a family-friendly local for the immediate area. The bar is part of a multi-roomed complex, used for a variety of activities from dancing and bridge to shooting. There is an admission charge up until 3.30pm on First XV matchday Saturdays, but this is waived for people only wanting to use the bar. ❀♿🚌(4)P⁺⁄–

Waterfront

Navigation Way, PR2 2YP (on Marina)

⏲ 11-11 (12.30am Thu; 1am Fri & Sat)

☎ (01772) 721108

Boddingtons Bitter; Taylor Landlord; guest beers Ⓗ

Popular pub situated on Preston Marina, close to the steam railway. It serves good value, freshly cooked meals until 9pm (7pm Sunday), including home-made pizzas and a Sunday carvery. The garden overlooks the marina and gets busy in summer. Thursday is quiz night and TV sports fans are well catered for. Occasional live music is played on Friday. Both guest beers tend to come from local micro-breweries or small independents, with Bowland and Salamander making regular appearances. ❀◐◑♿🚌P⁺⁄–

Rawtenstall

White Lion

72 Burnley Road, BB4 8EW

⏲ 4.30 (2 Sat)-midnight; 12-midnight Sun

☎ (01706) 213117

Black Sheep Best Bitter; Boddingtons Bitter; Copper Dragon Golden Pippin; Wells Bombardier; guest beers Ⓗ

Just out of the town centre, this pub features a wide selection of beers, with guest ales sourced from all around the UK. Loyal regulars enjoy a good atmosphere and food is served Fridays and weekends, with sandwiches often available from behind the bar. Weston's Old Rosie cider is served. Q◐◑🚌♣●

Rufford

Hesketh Arms

81 Liverpool Road, L40 1SB (on A59)

⏲ 12-11 (midnight Fri & Sat)

☎ (01704) 821002

Jennings Cumberland Ale; Moorhouse's Pride of Pendle; guest beers Ⓗ

When this former Greenalls inn, a 250-year-old listed building, closed in 1998, it left Rufford without a pub until it reopened under private ownership seven years later after extensive and time-consuming restoration. Originally built by the Hesketh family for the use of forestry workers – the forest has all but vanished – the Georgian frontage was altered and added to during the 19th and 20th centuries. Drinkers and diners are both catered for, with up to four guest beers, especially at weekends. ❀◑⇌▣P⁻

St Anne's-on-the-Sea

Trawl Boat ✔

Wood Street, FY8 1QR

✪ 9-midnight (1am Fri & Sat)

☎ (01253) 783080

Greene King IPA, Abbot; Marston's Pedigree; Moorhouse's Blonde Witch Ⓗ

The Trawl Boat is a Wetherspoon's bar located just off the main square inside converted solicitors' offices. The ambience is very much in the coffee bar mould; the interior is decorated in pale colours to offset the lack of natural light. The bar offers four permanent beers with up to five guests, as well as two real ciders. There is a large patio at the front of the building. ⛰Q❀◑♿⇌●⁻

Salesbury

Bonny Inn

68 Ribchester Road, BB1 9HQ

✪ 12-3, 6-11; 12-11 Sun

☎ (01254) 248467

Thwaites Nutty Black, Original, Lancaster Bomber, seasonal beers Ⓗ

Village local with excellent views north across the Ribble Valley – a long, narrow pub, with modern decor. Nutty Black is always available, which is a rare occurence for a Thwaites house anywhere near Blackburn, while Thwaites seasonal beers are sometimes available. Food is served all day Sunday (12-8pm), but the kitchen is closed on Monday. The varied specials board includes pan-fried snapper, but also makes use of local ingredients such as Bury black pudding. Quiz night is Tuesday. ❀◑♿P

Samlesbury

New Hall Tavern

Cuerdale Lane, PR5 0XA

✪ 12-11 (midnight Thu-Sat); 12-10.30 Sun

☎ (01772) 877217

Shepherd Neame Spitfire; guest beers Ⓗ

This pub is at a rural crossroads near to InBev's 'mega-keggery'. It is an attractive pub with a large car park and an outdoor heated smoking area. Inside, the bar's wood and glass dividers provide separate areas for dining. The excellent range of up to six real ales complements the good home-cooked food, often prepared with local ingredients. Old photographs and other items on the walls give insight into the history of the area, which includes Samlesbury Hall nearby. ⛰❀◑♿P⁻

Scorton

Priory

The Square, PR3 1AU

✪ 11-11.30 (midnight Fri); 9-midnight Sat & Sun

☎ (01524) 791255 🌐 theprioryscorton.co.uk

Bowland Nicky Nook; Thwaites Lancaster Bomber; guest beers Ⓗ

Scorton is not a tourist destination as such, yet trippers, coach parties and cycle club runs regularly converge on the place, many ending up in the Priory. This is first and foremost a restaurant, but the former blacksmith's shop at one end of the rambling range of buildings houses a fully-licensed bar, where the furniture is mostly dining-room style. In the evenings a fair number of locals gather. There is generally no music or amusements, so nothing interrupts the flow of conversation. ⛰❀⇌◑P

Silverdale

Woodlands

Woodlands Drive, LA5 0RU

✪ 7-11; 12-11.30 Sat & Sun

☎ (01524) 701655

Beer range varies Ⓗ

Large country house, circa 1878, which was converted to a pub with only minimal alterations. Most of the trade is provided by locals. The bar has a large fireplace, as big as the counter, and great views across Morecambe Bay. Beer pumps are in another room, with a list of the four available ales – they come from near and far – on the wall facing the bar. Home-made sandwiches are served at weekends. The smoking area is covered and sheltered. The pub is serviced by the Silverdale Shuttle Bus at weekends. ⛰Q♨❀▣♣P⁻▯

Thornton-Cleveleys

Victoria Hotel

183 Victoria Road, FY5 3PZ

✪ 11-11; 12-10.30 Sun

☎ (01253) 853306

Samuel Smith OBB Ⓗ

This 1930s pub is situated in a residential area close to the town centre and handy for the Blackpool-Fleetwood tramway. It is a very popular local, well known in the area for its low-priced beer, with a spacious lounge and a dining area with two real fires. There is also a meeting room available. Good value meals are served each day except Monday and Tuesday. Quiz nights are held on Sunday and Thursday. ⛰❀◑⊟⊖(Cleveleys)▣(11,16)P

Tockholes

Royal Arms

Tockholes Road, BB3 0PA SD665215

✪ 12 (6 Mon; 3 Tue)-11; 12-10.30 Sun

☎ (01254) 705373 🌐 theroyalarms.co.uk

Moorhouse's Tockholes, Treacle; Three B's Bobbin's Bitter; guest beers Ⓗ

An old, traditional free house formed from two cottages knocked together. It is small but has a great atmosphere within its four back-to-back rooms, where the original stone walls have been retained, along with flagged and wooden floors and three real fires. Guest beers are from local micro-breweries, while Moorhouse's supplies house beers. Situated on the edge of the West Pennine Moors, close to Darwen Tower and overlooking Roddlesworth woods, the pub welcomes walkers and dogs. Award-winning cuisine is available Wednesday to Sunday. ⌂❀◑P

Tontine

Delph

Sefton Road, WN5 8JU (off B5206)
11.30-midnight (1am Fri & Sat); 12-11.30 Sun
☎ (01695) 622239
Beer range varies Ⓗ
There is always a warm welcome and friendly atmosphere in this pub that retains a separate vault with a pool table. Good value meals complement the real ales in a relaxed environment. Children are welcome although not in the vault area. Darts and dominoes are played in the local league and a quiz night is held on Wednesday. The beers are normally pale ones. Wigan CAMRA Pub of the Season Autumn 2006. ❀◑♿⇌(Orrell)♣P

Up Holland

Old Dog

6 Alma Hill, WN8 0NW (off A557, near parish church)
5-midnight (1am Fri & Sat); 5-11.30 Sun
☎ (01695) 632487
Banks's Bitter; guest beers Ⓗ
This stone pub has historic connections with the local highwayman George Lyon. Unusually, the pub's four heavily-beamed rooms are on different levels, with the rear rooms affording superb views towards the Pennines. Sensitive refurbishment has retained many original features, including etched windows and a small bar area. The pub only serves cask ales, and pump clips from many past guest beers are on display. It also possesses a fine collection of ornamental dogs, and has a wine-tasting group and quiz team. Q❀

White Lion

10 Church Street, WN8 0ND (just off A577, M6 jct 26)
6 (5 Fri)-11 (midnight Fri); 1-midnight Sat; 1-10.30 Sun
☎ (01695) 622727 whitelionupholland.co.uk
Thwaites Original, seasonal beers; guest beers Ⓗ
A traditional multi-roomed, multi-level pub with many original features, built into the hillside opposite the church. Inside, there is an open fire, traditional pub games and a large-screen TV for sporting events. The pub is reputedly haunted and is rumoured to have tunnels connecting to the 700 year-old church, abbey and Old Dog pub (where the notorious highwayman George Lyon was laid out after being hanged, before burial in the church opposite). Outside is a beer garden with a covered and heated smoking area.
⌂❀(385,395)♣P

Waddington

Waddington Arms

West View, BB7 3HU
11-midnight (1am Fri & Sat); 1-11 Sun
☎ (01200) 423262 waddingtonarms.co.uk
Bowland Sawley Tempted; Moorhouse's Premier; Taylor Landlord; Theakston Best Bitter; guest beers Ⓗ
Set in one of Lancashire's most picturesque villages, this stone-built inn usually serves five real ales; the guest beer is often another beer from Bowland or Moorhouse's. A chalkboard above the bar displays the strengths and prices of beers, while a huge fireplace dominates one end of the room, which is slightly at odds with the contemporary decor in the rest of the pub. Regular menu items include Lancashire hot pot and coq au vin, plus an extensive specials board. ❀◑♿P

Westhead

Halton Castle

Crosshall Brow, L40 6JF (on A577 between Ormskirk & Skelmersdale) SD438078
12-11.30 (midnight Fri & Sat); 12-11 Sun
☎ (01695) 573596
Banks's Bitter; Jennings Cocker Hoop; guest beers Ⓗ
A recent refurbishment has combined the traditional features of wooden ceilings and an old fireplace with modern furniture and decor to create an interesting and comfortable environment. The building retains its black and white half-timbered 'brewer's Tudor' exterior but nevertheless gives a characterful impression. ❀◑♿(375,385)P

Prince Albert ✓

109 Wigan Road, L40 6HY (on A577 between Ormskirk & Skelmersdale) SD444076
12-11.30 (10.30 Sun)
☎ (01695) 573656
Tetley Mild, Bitter; guest beers Ⓗ
A small, traditional well-kept pub on the Wigan Road from Ormskirk to Skelmersdale, the Prince Albert has a small central bar that serves three snug rooms around it. Excellent home-cooked meals can be enjoyed in these restful surroundings where, on cold days, real fires blaze. ⌂❀◑♿Å(375,385)♣P

Whalley

Dog Inn

55 King Street, BB7 9SB
11-11; 12-10.30 Sun
☎ (01254) 823009
Beer range varies Ⓗ
One of four pubs serving real ale in Whalley, the Dog Inn is centrally located and opens onto the main street. The ever-changing selection of up to six ales often focuses on a single brewery, such as Grindleton, Moorhouse's or Little Valley. The central bar provides a convivial drinking area, while cosy seating areas are partly screened off. At the back of the pub is a pool table and access to an outdoor drinking area. Bar meals and snacks are available at lunchtime. ⌂❀◑⇌

Whittle-le-Woods

Royal Oak

216 Chorley Old Road, PR6 7NA (off A6)
3-11 (midnight Fri); 1.30-midnight Sat; 1-10.30 Sun
☎ (01257) 276485

Black Sheep Best Bitter; Caledonian Deuchars IPA; guest beers ⊞
Small terraced village local built in 1820 to serve workers and shippers on the adjacent branch of the Leeds-Liverpool Canal extension (now filled in). A regular local CAMRA award winner, it has been in this Guide for more than 30 years. Long and narrow, the interior comprises a small bar/lounge and a games room. Very much a community pub, it caters for a mixed clientele including TV sports enthusiasts. Note the etched windows from the long-gone Nuttalls Brewery from nearby Blackburn. ⩩❀♿🚌♣

Whitworth

Birches
145 Market Street, OL12 8RU
⌚ 12-11.30 (1am Fri & Sat)
☎ (01706) 344119 🌐 thebirchesshotel.co.uk
Moorhouse's Black Cat, Pride of Pendle; guest beers ⊞
A good pub, popular with locals, that serves excellent food all year round. The main beers are from a local brewery, while the guest is fairly well sourced from around the area. A large-screen TV is provided for sports enthusiasts, while food can also be eaten in the pleasant beer garden. ⩩❀◐◗🚌♣⌐

Wilpshire

Rising Sun
797 Whalley New Road, BB1 9BE (on A666)
⌚ 1.30 (12 Sat & Sun)-11.30
☎ (01254) 247379
Three B's Doff Cocker; guest beers ⊞
This traditional pub was once a Matthew Brown house, and the brewery's name can still seen on the windows. There is a separate bar where you can play cards and dominoes. The lounge has a coal fire and a piano that sees use on Saturday nights. Smokers can enjoy a covered, heated shelter. ⩩Q⊟≷⌐

Winmarleigh

Patten Arms
Park Lane, PR3 0JU
⌚ 4 (12 Sun)-10.30
☎ (01995) 791484
Boddingtons Bitter; Jennings Cumberland Ale; Tetley Bitter; guest beers ⊞
A genuine, isolated freehouse situated away from villages on a B-road, yet enjoying regular local custom. This early 19th-century Grade II-listed building includes a single bar with a country pub feel, high-backed bench seats, cream-painted walls and open fires. Bowland beers are a feature. There is a separate restaurant and terraced seating overlooking a bowling green. ⩩Q❀⇆◗♣⌐🝖

Worston

Calf's Head
West Lane, BB7 1QA (off A59)
⌚ 11-11
☎ (01200) 441218 🌐 calfshead.co.uk
Jennings Bitter, Cumberland Ale; guest beers ⊞
Large, rambling, stone-built pub-hotel that dates mostly from the late Victorian period, although there has been an inn on the site for longer than that. The guest beers are often from Jennings' seasonal range, but there is usually a beer from Marston's or one of the other larger breweries. The pub is handy for walkers and cyclists and often very busy on Sunday – book in advance for the good value carvery. Check out the enormous portions of fish and chips. ⩩❀⇆◐◗P

Wray

George & Dragon
Main Street, LA2 8QG
⌚ 6-11 Mon; 12-2.30, 5-11; 12-11 Sat; 12-10.30 Sun
☎ (01524) 221403
Everards Beacon; Jennings Bitter; guest beers ⊞
A genuine village local that also has an excellent reputation for its food. Inside there are two bar rooms of quite different sizes and a restaurant. Unusual pub games are available, as is Wi-Fi broadband. Home of the famous annual maggot race in March, there is also a Wednesday night quiz. The extensive beer garden has an aviary.
⩩❀◐◗🚌(80,81B)♣

Wrea Green

Villa
Moss Side Lane, PR4 2PE (¼ mile outside village on B5259)
⌚ 11-11 (10.30 Sun)
☎ (01772) 684347
Copper Dragon Scotts 1816; Jennings Cumberland Ale; guest beers ⊞
A 23-room hotel in the extensive grounds of a former 19th-century gentleman's residence. The original house features an a la carte restaurant and a large bar. In winter the best seats are the leather sofas by the real fire in the oak-panelled area. For summer there is an outside drinking and dining area. Jazz nights are monthly on a Friday, when the pub stays open until midnight. Curry night is Thursday and Sunday is very popular with families, as under 10s eat free. ⩩❀⇆◐◗♿🚌(76)P⌐

Wrightington

White Lion
117 Mossy Lea Road, WN6 9RE
⌚ 12-midnight (11 Mon & Wed); 12-10.30 Sun
☎ (01257) 425977
Banks's Bitter; Jennings Cumberland Ale; guest beers ⊞
Extremely popular country pub that has undergone extensive but sympathetic refurbishment. It attracts many locals, with a good mix of drinkers and diners. Four handpumps are in constant use, serving beers from the Marston's range. A weekly quiz takes place on Tuesday and a poker league on Thursday. Occasional themed evenings are held in the restaurant and booking is recommended for weekends. The pub is family-friendly with a large outside garden area. ❀◐◗⊟♿🚌P⌐

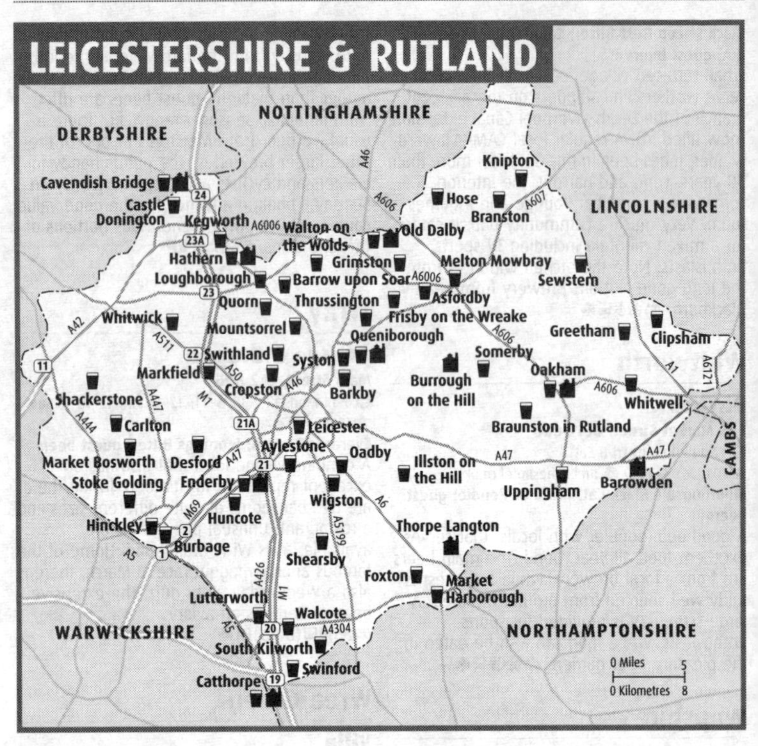

LEICESTERSHIRE

Asfordby

Horseshoes

128 Main Street, LE14 3SA
12-4, 7-11; 11.30-midnight Sat; 12-11 Sun
☎ (01664) 813392
Bateman XB; Tetley Bitter; guest beers
Friendly locals' pub in the centre of the village. A Bateman's house, it offers at least one of the brewery's ales plus seasonal beers and occasional guests. Buses from Leicester and Melton Mowbray stop outside the front door with a frequent daytime weekday service.

Aylestone

Black Horse

65 Narrow Lane, LE2 8NA
12-2.30 (not Mon), 5-11; 12-midnight Fri & Sat; 12-11 Sun
☎ (0116) 2832811 philspub.co.uk
Everards Beacon, Sunchaser, Tiger, Original, seasonal beers; guest beers
Welcoming, traditional, three-room Victorian pub with a distinctive bar servery in Aylestone village conservation area, three miles from the city centre. Home-cooked food is served lunchtimes Tuesday to Thursday and all day Friday. Outside is a large beer garden with a play area for children. The skittle alley and upstairs function room are available for hire. A popular quiz night is hosted on Sunday plus a monthly acoustic music session. Regular beer festivals are held. Dogs and horses are welcome.

Barkby

Brookside

35 Brookside, LE7 3QD (off Barkby Holt Lane)
12-2 (not Tue), 5.30 (6pm Tue & Thu)-11 (midnight Fri & Sat); 12-4, 7-10.30 Sun
☎ (0116) 260 0092
Jennings Bitter; Marston's Pedigree; guest beers
Cheery and welcoming pub with the air of a country local. Two-roomed with a traditional bar and comfy lounge, log fires blaze on cold winter nights. A restaurant leads from the lounge (no meals Sat lunch, Tue and Sun eve). The pub has a picturesque setting with a brook at the front and plenty of ducks. Dogs and horses are welcome. Guest beers come from the Marston's list. P

Barrow upon Soar

Soar Bridge Inn

29 Bridge Street, LE12 8PN
12 (3 Mon)-11; 12-10.30
☎ (01509) 412686
Everards Beacon, Tiger, Original; guest beer
Situated next to the bridge that gave it its name, this pub is popular with drinkers and diners (no food Sun and Mon). The large single room interior divides into distinct areas with a separate room for meetings or skittles. Children are welcome and there is a beer garden. (K2,CB27)P

Branston

Wheel

Main St, NG32 1RU

⏲ 11-11; closed Mon; 12-10.30 Sun
☎ (01476) 870376 🌐 thewheelinnbranston.co.uk
Bateman XB; guest beers Ⓗ
Like most of the buildings in the village, this attractive 18th-century pub is built using local stone. There is a small bar with some seating and a larger restaurant area that was originally two small rooms, now sympathetically renovated. The extensive food menu uses locally-sourced ingredients where possible, including produce from the nearby Belvoir Estate. ⌂❀◑♿P⍁

Burbage

Anchor

63 Church Street, LE10 2DA (nr church)
⏲ 12-11 (midnight Fri; 11.30 Sat)
☎ (01455) 636107
Marston's Bitter, Pedigree; guest beers Ⓗ
Typical two-roomed local in the centre of the village – no food, no jukebox, no pool. There is a dartboard and bar billiards table. One or two guest beers come from the Marston's range. Dogs are welcome, children tolerated. Note the centre pillar adorned with photographs of locals under the heading: 'Where's your Anchor lighter been?' Q❀♿🚌♣P⍁

Carlton

Gate Hangs Well

Barton Road, CV13 0DB (1 mile N of Market Bosworth)
⏲ 12-3, 6-11 (midnight Fri & Sat); 7-10.30 Sun
☎ (01455) 291845
Draught Bass; Greene King Abbot; Marston's Bitter, Pedigree Ⓗ
Welcoming, award-winning traditional village inn with seating areas served by a central bar. Popular with walkers and cyclists, there is a pleasant garden and conservatory where families with children are welcome until mid-evening. Sandwiches and rolls are made to order. Dominoes is played and live music hosted on Wednesday and Saturday. Convenient for Bosworth Battlefield, Water Trust, Ashby Canal, the Leicestershire Round and The Battlefield Line at Shackerstone. ⌂Q❀🚌(153)♣P⍁

Castle Donington

Jolly Potters

36 Hillside, DE74 2NH
⏲ 11-11; 12-10.30 Sun
☎ (01332) 811912
Draught Bass; Marston's Pedigree; guest beers Ⓗ
The landlord and locals are always happy to chat to visitors at this friendly pub, built at the turn of the 20th century. The open plan front room divides into bar and lounge areas —the basic stone-floored bar has traditional wooden pews and there is a back room with TV, jukebox and dartboard. A collection of framed beermats and cards decorates the walls, and cups, jugs and tankards hang from the ceiling. ⌂❀♿🚌♣

Catthorpe

Cherry Tree ✔

Main Street, LE17 6DB
⏲ 12-2.30, 5-11; 12-11 Sat; 12-10.30 Sun
☎ (01788) 860430
Adnams Bitter; guest beers Ⓗ
Welcoming two-roomed free house, often busy with locals who tend to congregate around the bar. A choice of four beers is available – three are ever changing and are likely to include a mild and something from Catthorpe's own Dow Bridge Brewery. Good food including Sunday roasts is made with ingredients sourced from local suppliers where possible. At the rear of the pub is a south facing patio area with a railway station theme. A beer festival is held twice a year. ⌂❀◑⛺🚌♣P⍁

Cavendish Bridge

Old Crown

DE72 2HL
⏲ 11-midnight (1am Fri & Sat); 12-midnight Sun
☎ (01332) 792392
Jennings Cocker Hoop; Marston's Pedigree, Old Empire; guest beers Ⓗ
Coaching inn dating from the 17th century with the original oak-beamed ceiling displaying an extensive collection of old jugs. The walls are covered with pub mirrors, brewery signs and railway memorabilia which even extend into the toilets. The cosy open plan interior is divided into two areas with a large inglenook on the right. ⌂❀🛏◑🚌P⍁

Cropston

Bradgate Arms

15 Station Road, LE7 7HG
⏲ 11.30-11; 12-10.30 Sun
☎ (0116) 234 0336
Banks's Bitter; Marston's Pedigree Ⓗ
Comfortable village pub popular with locals and tourists. Though extended to the rear in the early 1990s it retains many original features, with five drinking areas and a dining room on two levels. Food is served all day. Darts and long alley skittles are played. The pub is handy for the Great Central Railway at Rothley and Bradgate Country Park. 👶❀◑🚌♣P

Desford

Blue Bell Inn

39 High Street, LE9 9JF
⏲ 11-11 (midnight Fri & Sat); 12-11 Sun

INDEPENDENT BREWERIES

Barrowden Barrowden
Bees Queniborough (NEW)
Belvoir Old Dalby
Dow Bridge Catthorpe
Everards Narborough
Grainstore Oakham
Langton Thorpe Langton
Parish Burrough on the Hill
Shardlow Cavendish Bridge
Wicked Hathern Hathern

☎ (01455) 822901
Everards Beacon, Tiger; guest beers Ⓗ
Welcoming pub in the centre of the village with two rooms and a restaurant area with a central servery. A general knowledge quiz is held on Tuesday night. Food is available lunchtimes and evenings throughout the week including the traditional Sunday lunch. Dominoes, darts and pool are played. Outside, the garden has a children's play area and there is a heated and covered space for smokers. Close to Mallory Park, B&B accommodation is provided.
Q❀⇔◐▤♿🚌(152, 153)♣P⁵—

Enderby

New Inn

51 High Street, LE19 4AG
🕐 12-2.30 (3 Sat; not Mon); 7(5.30 Fri)-11; 12-3, 7-10.30 Sun
☎ (0116) 286 3126
Everards Beacon, Tiger, Original, seasonal beers; guest beers Ⓗ
Friendly, thatched village local dating from 1549 tucked away at the top of the High Street. Everards' first tied house, the pub is well know locally for the quality of its beer and often frequented by Everards brewery staff. Three rooms are served by a central bar, with long alley skittles and a snooker room to the rear. Outside is a patio area and garden. Plentiful and imaginative lunches are served Tuesday to Saturday. ♨Q❀◐♿🚌♣P⁵—

Foxton

Bridge 61 ✔

Bottom Lock, LE16 7RA
🕐 10-11
☎ (0116) 279 2285 🌐 foxtonboats.co.uk
Adnams Bitter; Banks's Original; guest beers Ⓗ
Canal-side pub situated at the bottom of the famous flight of 10 staircase locks at Foxton. The two-roomed interior has a small bar in the snug area and a larger conservatory with wide doors that open out onto the water in summer. The patio area is an ideal spot for watching the canal boats pass by. Meals are available all day. Nearby is a boatyard and canal shop with passenger trips and boats to hire; book in advance. ♨Q👶❀◐♿🚌●⁵—

Foxton Locks Inn ✔

Bottom Lock, Gumley Road, LE16 7RA
🕐 11-11 (10.30 Sun)
☎ (0116) 279 1515
Caledonian Deuchars IPA; Greene King Old Speckled Hen; Theakston Black Bull, Old Peculier; guest beers Ⓗ
Refurbished canal-side inn situated at the foot of Foxton Locks, a major attraction on the Grand Union Canal. The canal director's office, once upstairs, has been recreated at the rear of the pub, complete with a collection of original share certificates on display. Outdoor seating runs down to the canal bank where boats may be moored. Families are welcome inside the pub and blankets are available for outdoor drinkers. Q👶❀◐♿🚌♣P⁵—

Frisby on the Wreake

Bell Inn

2 Main Street, LE14 2NJ
🕐 12-2.30 (not Mon), 6 -11; 12-3, 6-10.30 (not winter) Sun
☎ (01664) 434237
Black Sheep Best Bitter; guest beers Ⓗ
Welcoming village local dating back to 1759, situated in a small village to the south of the river Wreake. The comfortable lounge bar features oak beams, flagstone floors and an open fire. There is a family room and restaurant with meals prepared using locally-sourced fresh produce wherever possible. Two ever-changing guest ales scome from near and far. The weekday daytime bus from Melton Mowbray and Leicester stops in the village. ♨Q👶❀◐🚌(128)P⁵—

Grimston

Black Horse

Main Street, LE14 3BZ
🕐 12-3, 6-11; 12-6 Sun
☎ (01664) 812358
Adnams Bitter; Belvoir Star Mild; Marston's Pedigree; guest beer Ⓗ
Overlooking the village green, this pub is very popular and busy at lunchtimes. It has a large open plan bar on two levels where a wide range of good food is available. Real cider usually replaces one of the ales in summer. A petanque court hosts several local teams. The weekday daytime bus from Melton Mowbray stops outside the pub. ♨Q❀◐🚌(23)♣●⁵—

Hathern

Dew Drop ✔

49 Loughborough Road, LE12 5HY
🕐 12-3, 6-midnight; 12-3, 7-1am Fri-Sun
☎ (01509) 842438
Greene King XX Mild, H&H Bitter; guest beers Ⓗ
Traditional two roomed local with a large bar and comfortable small lounge with real fires. Don't miss a visit to the totally unspoilt toilets with their tiled walls and original features. A large range of malt whiskies is stocked and cobs are available at lunchtime.
♨Q❀▤🚌♣P

Hinckley

Ashby Road Sports Club

Hangmans Lane, LE10 3DA
🕐 7 (5 Fri)-11; 12-11.30 Sat; 12-10.30 Sun
☎ (01455) 615159
Worthington Bitter; guest beers Ⓗ
CAMRA members are always most welcome at this private sports and social club. The club house was built in 1957 in six acres of grounds, with a good assortment of facilities for various team activities. A family-friendly bar area hosts traditional pub games. Guest beers change weekly, available from Thursday, sourced from micros, local and large breweries. Activites range from cricket, football, dominoes, darts, chess, rifle shooting and table tennis to line, modern, jive and sequence dancing. 👶❀♿⛺🚌♣P⁵—

New Plough Inn

24 Leicester Road, LE10 1LS (opp fire station)
12-2.30 Sat only, 5-11; 12-2.30, 6-10.30 Sun
(01455) 615037
Marston's Burton Bitter, Pedigree H
Built in 1900, this traditional roadside pub has a comfortable lounge with original wooden settles. The walls are adorned with local rugby memorabilia and the exterior features shields of local rugby clubs. Table skittles is played and the pub runs its own team. There is an outdoor area for drinking in summer. Dogs are welcome.

Hose

Black Horse

21 Bolton Lane, LE14 4JE
12-2 Fri & Sat only, 7-midnight; 12-4, 7-10.30 Sun
(01949) 860336
Adnams Bitter; Castle Rock Harvest Pale; Fuller's London Pride; guest beers H
Traditional pub with a lounge featuring wooden beams and a brass-ornamented brick fireplace. Blackboard menus for food and drink surround a wooden corner bar. The unspoilt public bar, decorated with pictures and mirrors, has a tiled floor, wooden furniture and a brick fireplace. The rustic, wood-panelled restaurant serves good food using local produce. Q P

Huncote

Red Lion

Main Street, LE9 3AU
12-2.30 (not Mon & Sat), 5 (4 Sat)-11; 12-10.30 Sun
(0116) 286 2233 red-lion.biz
Everards Beacon, Tiger; guest beers H
Built in 1892, the Red Lion is a friendly local offering a warm welcome. With beamed ceilings throughout, it has a cosy lounge with a wooden fireplace and log fire. The bar has an adjoining dining area and a separate pool room. The sizeable garden has picnic tables and a children's play area. Good value home-cooked lunches are served and evening meals on Tuesday and Wednesday. Skittles can by played by prior arrangement. P

Illston on the Hill

Fox & Goose

Main Street, LE7 9EG
12-2 (not Mon & Tue), 5.30 (7 Mon)-11; 12-3, 7-11 Sun
(0116) 259 6430
Everards Beacon, Tiger, Original; guest beers H
Cosy, unspoilt pub with a timeless feel, tucked away in the village and well worth seeking out. A fascinating collection of local mementos and hunting memorabilia is on display including original Mclaughlan cartoons. Popular annual events include conkers, an onion-growing championship and a fund-raising auction for local charities. Q

Kegworth

Red Lion

24 High St, DE74 2DA
11.30-11; 12-10.30 Sun
(01509) 672466
Adnams Bitter; Banks's Original; Courage Directors; Greene King Abbot; guest beers H
Georgian building standing on the 19th-century route of the London to Glasgow road (A6). It has three small bars and a separate restaurant, plus a skittle alley and petanque courts. Up to four guest beers are available as well as various flavoured Polish and Ukrainian vodkas and a good selection of malt whiskies. Outside there is a large, secure children's play area. Q P

Knipton

Manners Arms

Croxton Road, NG32 1RH
11-11; 12-10.30 Sun
(01476) 879222 mannersarms.com
Belvoir Beaver Bitter; guest beers H
Impressive Georgian hunting lodge beautifully renovated by the Duke and Duchess of Rutland with furniture and prints taken from Belvoir Castle. Served by one long bar, the lounge, with tall bookshelves and comfortable seating, and bar room are warmed by a huge open fireplace. Light bar dishes are available plus a wide range of interesting food made with local produce in the restaurant. There is a live music programme every Thursday evening. A wonderful patio and garden area, overlooked by the conservatory, is ideal for lazing on a hot summer's day. Q P

Leicester

Ale Wagon

27 Rutland Street, LE1 1RE
11-11; 12-3, 7-10.30 Sun
(0116) 2623330 alewagon.co.uk
Hoskins Hob, Best Mild, Brigadier, Bitter, EXS; guest beers H
Run by the Hoskins family, this city centre pub with 1930s interior, including an original oak staircase, has two rooms with tiled and parquet floors and a central bar. There is always a selection of Hoskins Brothers ales and guests available. The pub is popular with visiting rugby fans and real ale drinkers. It has a function room available with catering and is handy for the Leicester Theatre.

Barley Mow

149 Granby Street, LE1 6FE (200 yds from station)
11-11; 12-6 Sun
(0116) 2544663
Everards Beacon, Sunchaser, Tiger, Original; guest beers H
This spacious open-plan pub has one long bar and an open staircase up to a coffee loft which also serves excellent breakfasts. It has all the welcome of a country pub, with the convenience of the city centre, offering warm greetings to both regular customers and passing drinkers alike. Very popular on match days, when the pub can be quite busy.The ghost scenes investigators have recently declared the pub is haunted, but the only spirits you will see are in the optics.

Black Horse

1 Foxon Street, LE3 5LT (On Braunstone Gate)
3 (7 Sun)-midnight
(0116) 254 0030
Everards Beacon, Tiger, seasonal beers; guest beers Ⓗ
Small, cosy, street-corner hostelry, the only traditional pub left on Braunstone Gate, now surrounded by wine and café bars. With all the character of a lively local, it has two rooms and a central servery. The general knowledge quiz on Wednesday and Sunday is the longest-running in Leicester. Acoustic sessions are hosted on Monday and Thursday evening, live music on Friday and Saturday. Up to five guest beers come from Everards Old English Ale Club. Many malt whiskies and fruit wines are also available.

Criterion

44 Millstone Lane, LE1 5JN
12-11
(0116) 262 5418
Oakham Inferno, Bishops Farewell; guest beers Ⓗ
Two-roomed 1960s city centre pub offering up to 10 guest ales from micro and regional breweries at weekends. Beer festivals are held regularly with up to 24 beers available, many on gravity from the cellar, and more than 100 international bottled beers are stocked. Darts and dominoes are played in the bar, a pop quiz held on Tuesday, general knowledge quiz on Wednesday and live music on Thursday and Saturday. Pub food is served on Sunday and Monday and Italian style pizzas Tuesday to Saturday. Leicester CAMRA Pub of the Year 2006, 2007 and 2008, and regional Runner Up 2007.

Globe

43 Silver Street, LE1 5EU
11-11 (1am Fri); 12-10.30 Sun
(0116) 262 9819
Everards Beacon, Sunchaser, Tiger, Original, seasonal beers; guest beers Ⓗ
More than 30 years ago this city centre pub was hailed as Everards' first pub to return to a full real ale range after seven years as keg only. Major renovations in 2000 moved the bar to the centre of the pub interior. There is a snug and gas lighting throughout (electric too). An upstairs room is available for meetings. Leicester CAMRA held its first meeting here in 1974 as well as its 25th anniversary bash. Bar meals and snacks are served until 7pm. A warm welcome awaits from the landlady and her staff.

Marquis of Wellington

139 London Road, LE2 1EF
12-11 (1am Fri & Sat)
(0116) 254 0542
Everards Beacon, Sunchaser, Tiger, Original, seasonal beers; guest beers Ⓗ
The pub stands out from neighbouring buildings by virtue of its ornate frontage, large leaded windows, black and white walls and coloured highlights. The interior is a mix of open plan areas and secluded booths. On the walls are quotations by, and about, the Duke of Wellington. Nine handpumps dispense regular beers and cider alongside guests supplied by Everards to quench the thirst of students and locals. Sport is shown on a large screen. Thursday is open mike night.

Out of the Vaults

24 King Street, LE1 6RL
12-11 (2am Fri & Sat); 12-10.30 Sun
outofthevaults.com
Oakham JHB, Bishops Farewell; Ⓗ **guest beers** Ⓗ/Ⓖ
Friendly city centre free house showcasing real ales from micro-breweries. Frequent beer festivals keep both an eclectic mix of locals and visitors happy. Popular with football and rugby fans, away supporters are especially welcome. Food is served at lunchtime. Occasional live music plays on Saturday night and there are weekly Sunday afternoon acoustic sessions. Traditional pub games are available from the bar. A regular haunt of Leicester Morris dancers.

Shakespeare's Head

Southgates, LE1 5SH
12-midnight (1am Fri & Sat); 12-11 Sun
(0116) 262 4378
Oakwell Old Tom Mild, Barnsley Bitter Ⓗ
This two-roomed local was built alongside the underpass in the 1960s and has changed little since then, retaining all the charm of a typical town pub of its era. Two large glass doors lead to an off-sales area with a bar to the left and lounge to the right. Formerly a Shipstones pub, it now sells Oakwell beers at very reasonable prices. A selection of hot food is served daily (breakfast, jacket potatoes, baguettes) and Sunday lunch is popular.

Swan & Rushes

19 Infirmary Square, LE1 5WR
12-2.45, 5-11(midnight Thu); 12-midnight Fri & Sat; 12-11.30 Sun
(0116) 233 9167 swanandrushes.co.uk
Bateman XB; Oakham JHB, Bishops Farewell, seasonal beers; guest beers Ⓗ
Comfortable, triangular, two-roomed pub in the city centre with a relaxed atmosphere, filled with breweriana and framed photos on the wall. Up to nine real ales (no nationals) are available or you can choose from the bottled beer menu featuring more than 100 international classics including loads of lambics. Several food-linked beer festivals are held each year plus a cider and cheese event. The Thursday night quiz and Saturday night live gigs are well supported. Good value home-cooked food is served.

Western

70 Western Road, LE3 0GA
12-3, 5-11; 12-midnight Fri & Sat
(0116) 2545287
Beer range varies Ⓗ/Ⓖ
Popular Everards pub run by the Steamin' Billy Brewing Company. A traditional two-roomed local in a residential location, it attracts a good, mixed clientele of all ages. Old pub signs decorate the walls. Food is served lunchtimes and evenings and is cooked on the

premises. Quiz night is Sunday and the pub gets busy on match days.

Loughborough

Albion Inn

Canal Bank, LE11 1QA

11-3 (4 Sat), 6-11; 12-3, 7-10.30 Sun

(01509) 213952

Sharp's Doom Bar; Wicked Hathern Dobel's Dog Mild; guest beers

Canal-side pub built in the late 18th century at the same time as the Loughborough Canal. It has a bar, darts room and quiet lounge, and outside the patio has an aviary. The house beer, Albion Special, is brewed especially for the pub by the local Wicked Hathern Brewery. Care should be taken if driving to the pub along the tow path.

Paget Arms

41 Oxford Street, LE11 5DP

12-3, 5-11; 12-midnight Fri-Sun

(01509) 266216 myspace.com/thepaget

Steamin' Billy Bitter, Skydiver; guest beers

Located on a corner at the end of a row of terraced houses, this former Everards pub has been refurbished and is now one of Steamin Billy's locals. It offers six real ales with some served by gravity, direct from the cellar. Home-cooked food includes pizzas and doorstep sandwiches. There are two attractive rooms with ample seating and a large enclosed garden with a heated, covered area for smokers. Regular beer festivals are held.

Swan in the Rushes

21 The Rushes, LE11 5BE

11-11 (midnight Fri & Sat); 12-11 Sun

(01509) 217014 castlerockbrewery.co.uk/pub-swanintherushes.html

Adnams Bitter; Castle Rock Harvest Pale, Hemlock; Hop Back Summer Lightning; guest beers

Traditional three room Castle Rock pub comprising two quiet, comfortable bars and the Charnwood Vaults, a lively room with a jukebox and wooden bench seating. There is a constantly changing range of up to six guest beers, always including a mild, as well as real cider and perry, a limited range of continental bottled and draught beers and a good range of malt whiskies and country wines. Upstairs is a skittle alley and function room which hosts live music and twice yearly beer festivals.

Tap & Mallet

36 Nottingham Road, LE11 1EU

5 (11.30 Sat & Sun)-2am

(01509) 210028

Jennings Mild; Marston's Burton Bitter; guest beers

Genuine free house conveniently situated on a direct route from the railway station to the town centre. The five guest beers are from micro-breweries, often from the east or north-east midlands area, but usually beers not commonly found in the Loughborough area. The interior has a single room split into two distinct drinking areas, one with a pool table. The lounge can be partitioned off for private functions. Outside there is a secluded walled garden with children's play equipment and a pet's corner. Cobs are available all day. Note that the pub closes early if quiet.

Lutterworth

Unicorn Inn

27 Church Street, LE17 4AE

10.30-11 (midnight Fri & Sat); 12-11.30 Sun

(01455) 552486

Draught Bass; Greene King IPA; M&B Brew XI; Robinson's Unicorn

The Cherry Tree's large public bar is home to local teams playing traditional pub games including darts and skittles, and large-screen TVs show sporting events, particularly football and rugby matches. The quieter lounge has its own bar decorated with many photographs of old Lutterworth. Good value lunchtime snacks and meals are served throughout the week.

Market Bosworth

Olde Red Lion Hotel

1 Park Street, CV13 0LL

11(10.30 Wed)-2.30, 5.30-11; 11-11 Fri & Sat; 11-10.30 Sun

(01455) 291713

Banks's Bitter; Jennings Bitter; Marston's Pedigree; guest beers

The Olde Red Lion Hotel prides itself on providing a wide range of real ales, home-cooked food and en-suite B&B accommodation. The hotel is more than 400 years old and remains very traditional with a cosy atmosphere, original oak beams and an open fireplace. Excellent food is from local suppliers and home cooked. The first Sunday of the month is quiz night. Smokers have a heated area outside.

Market Harborough

Cherry Tree

Church Walk, Kettering Road, LE16 8AE

12.30-2.30, 5.30-11; 12-11.30 Fri & Sat; 12-11 Sun

(01858) 463525

Everards Beacon, Sunchaser, Tiger, Original; guest beers

Although this pub is situated in Little Bowden it is very much part of the Market Harborough community. A spacious building with low beams and a thatched roof, there are many alcoves and seating areas for drinkers and diners to choose from. A beer festival is held over the August bank holiday. Guest beers come from Everards Old English Ale Club.

(Market Harborough)

Markfield

Bulls Head

23 Forest Road, LE67 9UN

3 (11 Sat)-11.30 (2am Fri); 12-10.30 Sun

(01530) 242541

Marston's Burton Bitter, Pedigree

A typical country inn full of character, this long established two-roomed local is tucked away in the corner of the village with a friendly welcome for all. Darts and dominoes are played here. Q❀🛏♿🚌♣P⁼

Melton Mowbray

Anne of Cleves

12 Burton Street, LE13 1AE (Just S of St Mary's Church)
⏲ 11-11; 12-4, 7-10.30 Sun
☎ (01664) 481336
Everards Tiger, Original, seasonal beers; guest beers ⊞
One of Everards' most historic pubs and an icon for the town. Part of the property dates back to 1327 when was it was home to monks. The house was gifted to Anne of Cleves by Henry VIII as part of her divorce settlement. It is now a popular and busy hostelry following a sympathetic conversion and restoration of the building, with stone flagged floors, exposed timber roof beams and wall tapestries. The building is said to be haunted and psychic research evenings feature regularly. Up to three guest ales may be available. ♨Q❀◖◗⇌🚌P⁼

Crown Inn

10 Burton Street, LE13 1AE (next to St Mary's Church)
⏲ 11-3, 6.30-11; 11-11 Fri & Sat; 12-4, 7-10.30 Sun
☎ (01664) 564682
Everards Beacon, Tiger, seasonal beers; guest beers ⊞
Sociable two bar pub run by a long serving landlord. Situated in the centre of town, it is popular with shoppers and workers at lunchtime. Owned by Everards, the pub offers two guests or seasonal ales at most times. Access by bus from Leicester is easy, and there are hourly weekday buses from Grantham, Loughborough and Nottingham. ♨Q◖◗🛏⇌🚌

Harboro' Hotel

49 Burton Street, LE13 1AF (opp station)
⏲ 11-11 (midnight Fri & Sat); 12-11 Sun
☎ (01664) 560121 🌐 harborohotel.co.uk
Tetley Bitter; Taylor Landlord; Wychwood Hobgoblin; guest beers ⊞
Eighteenth-century coaching inn conveniently located between the town centre and railway station. The hotel is often very busy and can be a little noisy. The open plan bar has comfortable seating and bar snacks and meals are served. Guest beers vary, cider is usually available and a wide range of draught and bottled Belgian and German beers is always on offer. An Easter beer festival is held. There is a petanque court in the rear car park. ☕❀🛌◖◗♿⇌🚌♣●P⁼

Mountsorrel

Swan Inn

10 Loughborough Rd, LE12 7AT
⏲ 12-2.30, 5.30-11; 12-11 Sat; 12-3, 7-10.30 Sun
☎ (0116) 2302340 🌐 the-swan-inn.eu
Black Sheep Best Bitter; Greene King Ruddles County; Theakston Best Bitter, XB, Old Peculier; guest beers ⊞
Traditional 17th-century, Grade II listed coaching inn, formerly called the Nags Head, under the present ownership since 1990. The split level bar has stone floors and low ceilings and there is a small dining area with a polished wood floor. Good quality, interesting food is cooked to order with the menu changing every two weeks. Monthly, themed nights are popular. Outside is a secluded riverside garden with moorings. Weston's bottled cider is available. ♨❀🛌◖◗🚌P

Waterside Inn

Sileby Rd, LE12 7BB
⏲ 12-2.30, 6-11; 12-11 Sat; 12-10.30 Sun
☎ (0116) 2302758 🌐 thewatersideinn.co.uk
Everards Beacon, Tiger, Original; guest beers ⊞
Formerly called the Duke of York, this 18th-century inn is in a prime location next to Mountsorrel lock, making it a popular mooring point for narrowboats. There is a basic wood-panelled bar with bench seating and a larger, comfortable lounge and restaurant overlooking the River Soar. Food is served all day at weekends. Q❀◖◗♿🚌♣P

Oadby

Cow & Plough

Stoughton Farm Park, Gartree Road, LE2 2FB
⏲ 12-3, 5-11; 12-11 summer
☎ (0116) 2720852 🌐 steamin-billy.co.uk
Fuller's London Pride; Steamin' Billy Scrum Down, Bitter, Skydiver; guest beers ⊞
Situated in a converted farm building with a conservatory, this pub is decked out with breweriana. It is home to Steamin' Billy beers, named after the owner's now departed Jack Russell who features on the logo and pump clips. All beers are brewed at Tower Brewery. A mild and Weston's cider are always available. A large restaurant has been added in the former Farmworld buildings. Twice CAMRA East Midlands Pub of the Year and Leicester CAMRA County Pub of the Year 2007 and 2008. Q☕❀◖◗🛏♿♣●P⁼

Wheel Inn

99 London Road, LE2 5DP
⏲ 12-midnight; 12-10.30 Sun
☎ (0116) 271 2231 🌐 wheelinn.biz
Draught Bass; Marston's Pedigree; guest beers ⊞
Sports-oriented community pub where there is always something going on. As well as darts, dominoes and skittles teams there are football, cricket, golf and fishing matches, casino nights, jazz evenings, train trips, cycle rides and anything else the landlord and customers can think of. Tasty home-cooked food and an extensive selection of wines and spirits add to the appeal. The Leicester bus stops outside. ❀◖🛏🚌(31)♣P⁼

Old Dalby

Sample Cellar

Belvoir Brewery, Station Road, LE14 3NQ
⏲ 12-11 (10 Sun)
☎ (01664) 823455
Belvoir Star Mild, Beaver Bitter, seasonal beers ⊞
The brick-fronted Sample Cellar on the outskirts of the village incorporates a bar, visitors centre and function room. The comfortable, spacious interior, filled with

brewing artefacts, has a traditional bar area and there is even room for long alley skittles and a bar billiard table. Two large internal windows provide views into the brewery. A full menu is served daily with the focus on good wholesome food made with local produce. ❀◑♿♣●P⁄–

Queniborough

Britannia

47 Main Street, LE7 3DB
12-2.30, 6-11; 12-11 Sun
☎ (0116) 260 5675
M&B Brew XI; Taylor Landlord; guest beers ⊞
Two roomed comfortable village local with a traditional bar and restaurant leading off the lounge. Both rooms have an open fire providing welcome warmth on cold winter evenings. Food is available seven days a week. Old pictures of the village are on the lounge wall. Guest beers come from the Punch list. ⛰❀◑⊟⊟♣P⁄–

Quorn

Blacksmith's Arms

29 Meeting Street, LE12 8EU
12-2.30, 5.30-11; 12-3, 7-10.30 Sun
☎ (01509) 412751 🌐 geocities.com/blacksmithsatquorn
Banks's Bitter; Marston's Pedigree; guest beers ⊞
Quiet, friendly, three roomed, traditional village local with beamed ceilings. Real coal fires add warmth in winter and there is a comfortable patio for the summer. Well-behaved dogs are welcome. Thursday is quiz night. ⛰Q❀⊟⊟♣P⁄–

White Hart ✔

High Street, LE12 8DT
12-2, 5-11; 12-11 Fri & Sat; 12-10.30 Sun
☎ (01509) 412704
Caledonian Deuchars IPA; Greene King IPA; Taylor Landlord; Wadworth 6X; guest beers ⊞
The oldest pub in Quorn, the White Hart dates from 1690 and once had its own brewhouse. However, over the years it has been modernised and little evidence remains of its true age. The L-shaped bar and central chimney divide the pub into three drinking areas, each with a real fire. Outside there is an illuminated, sheltered seating area and a petanque court. Regular buses pass by from Loughborough and Leicester. ⛰❀◑Å⊟♣P⁄–

Sewstern

Blue Dog

Main Street, NG33 5RQ
11-11; 12-10.30 Sun
☎ (01476) 860097
Greene King IPA; guest beers ⊞
Friendly and welcoming pub at the west end of the village, handy for walkers at the southern end of the Viking Way. The unusual name reflects the tradition of local farm workers on the Tollemache estate being paid partly in blue tokens. The 300-year-old building was once a war hospital and has a ghost – a boy drummer called Albert. Guest ales often come from local breweries and a beer festival is held in late May. A popular fish and chip menu is available on Wednesday evening. ⛰Q❀❀◑Å⊟(55)♣P⁄–

Shackerstone

Rising Sun

Church Road, CV13 6NN (3 miles E of Twycross, 3 miles SW of Ibstock)
12-2.30, 6-midnight; 12-midnight Sat & Sun
☎ (01827) 880215 🌐 risingsunpub.com
Marston's Pedigree; Taylor Landlord; guest beers ⊞
This family-run free house since 1987 has a large wood-panelled bar area with a traditional feel. The separate sports room has pool and Sky TV. Children are welcome in the conservatory and attractive beer garden. Meals are served daily in the bar and barn-conversion restaurant, with Sunday lunches always popular. The pub is handy for the Battlefield Railway and Ashby Canal. Walkers are welcome. Regular charity fund-raising walks support Guide Dogs for the Blind. ⛰❀❀◑⊟♿⊟♣P⁄–

Shearsby

Chandlers Arms

Fenny Lane, LE17 6PL (close to A5199)
12-3 (not Mon), 7-11 (6 Fri & Sat); 12-4 Sat; 12-4, 7-10.30 (all day summer) Sun
☎ (0116) 2478384 🌐 chandlersatshearsby.co.uk
Black Sheep Ale; Dow Bridge Acris; guest beers ⊞
Classic, quaint old country pub overlooking the village green. Popular with walkers, cyclists, diners and visitors from the city, it also has strong local support. Micro-brewery beers are always on the bar. No food is served on Sunday evening in winter. ❀◑⊟♣

Somerby

Stilton Cheese

Main Street, LE14 2PZ
12-3, 6-11; 12-3, 7-10.30 Sun
☎ (01664) 454394
Grainstore Ten Fifty; Marston's Pedigree; Tetley Bitter; guest beers ⊞
Late 16th-century pub built in local ironstone, like most of the buildings in the village. The interior comprises two bars and a function room. Tall customers will note the wide range of pump clips on the low beams as they bang their heads on them. A popular pub, booking is advised for food. ⛰Q❀❀◑⊟(113)●P

South Kilworth

White Hart

Rugby Road, LE17 6DN
12-2.30 (not Wed) , 5.30-11; 12-4, 6-11 Sat; 12-4, 7-11 Sun
☎ (01858) 575416
Banks's Bitter; Jennings Cumberland Ale; guest beers ⊞
Friendly 200-year-old village local offering three real ales including a regular guest. Good home-cooked food is served in the small restaurant, including daily specials with

ingredients sourced from local farms and an excellent village butcher. The pub is home to skittles, darts and pool teams. There is a garden for summer drinking and a large real fire for winter nights. Nearby is a reservoir with a nature reserve and Stamford Hall. Bridge 27 on the Grand Union Canal is also close by. ⛫Q❀◑◐🚌♣P

Stoke Golding

White Swan

High Street, CV13 6HE
⏲ 6.30-midnight; 12-4, 7-midnight Sun
☎ (01455) 212313
Adnams Bitter, Broadside; Everards Tiger, Original; guest beers Ⓗ
Situated close to the site where Henry VII was crowned after the battle of Bosworth, the Swan was originally built for the navvies employed on the construction of the nearby Ashby canal more than 200 years ago. A relatively unspoilt two-room village local, it is known for raising money for village charities. Food is good-value and home-made where possible (no meals Sunday evening).
Q❀◑◐🀫♣P⁄

Swinford

Chequers ✔

High Street, LE17 6BL
⏲ 12-2.30, 6 (7 Mon)-11; 12-3, 7-11.30 Sun
☎ (01788) 860318 🌐 chequersswinford.co.uk
Adnams Bitter; Ansells Mild; guest beers Ⓗ
Traditional family-run village inn with a large open-plan interior catering for all ages. Bar meals and weekly specials including vegetarian options are served in a separate dining area. Mild is usually available as well as a guest beer. During the summer regular events are held in a marquee behind the pub, including a well-supported beer festival in July (see website). The large garden has a children's play area. The pub is also handy for visitors to nearby Stanford Hall.
❀◑◐⛺🚌♣P⁄

Swithland

Griffin Inn

174 Main Street, LE12 8TJ
⏲ 11-11; 11-10.30 Sun
☎ (01509) 890535
Everards Beacon, Tiger, Original; guest beers Ⓗ
Friendly and welcoming local with three comfortable rooms. Set in the heart of Charnwood Forest, there are many walking and cycling routes nearby. Swithland Reservoir, Bradgate Park and the preserved Great Central Railway are also close. As well as the regular food menu, light snacks are available every afternoon including Melton Mowbray pork pies. Guest ales are chosen from Everards Old English Ale Club, with three regularly stocked in addition to the Everards regulars. ⛫Q❀◑◐♿⛺🚌♣P⁄

Syston

Queen Victoria

76 High Street, LE7 1GQ
⏲ 2-11; 12-midnight Wed-Sat; 12-10.30 Sun
☎ (0116) 2605750
Everards Sunchaser, Beacon, Tiger, Original; guest beers Ⓗ
Large bar which has benefited from the recent addition of a very cosy snug, plus a separate restaurant to the side of the pub. The large patio and garden area are popular with families in summer. Guest beers come from the Everards Old English Ale Club, very often including a Brunswick Brewery beer. There is plenty of street parking nearby. ❀◑◐🚌♣P⁄

Thrussington

Blue Lion

5 Rearsby Road, LE7 4UD
⏲ 12-2.30 (not Wed), 5.30-11; 12-3, 6-11 Sat; 12-3, 7-10.30 Sun
☎ (01664) 424266
Marston's Burton Bitter, Pedigree, seasonal beers; guest beers Ⓗ
Late 18th-century rural inn, once two cottages. Good value pub grub, using meat supplied by the local butcher, is served in the comfortable lounge. However, the bar is the heart of the pub, where locals meet for high-pressure darts and dominoes matches, kept under control by licensees Mandy and Bob.
⛫Q❀◑◐🀫⛺🚌(128)♣P

Walcote

Black Horse

25 Lutterworth Road, LE17 4JU
⏲ 12-2.30, 5-midnight; 12-midnight Fri-Sun
☎ (01455) 552684
Beer range varies Ⓗ/Ⓖ
In 2006 this long-standing Guide entry was demolished and rebuilt six feet back from the road with a similar floor plan. The range of real ales was increased to nine on handpump and up to eight served on gravity from a glass-fronted cool room, sourced from regional and micro-breweries. Traditional food is served at lunchtimes, plus Thai dishes on Fri lunchtime and every evening. ⛫❀◑◐♿🚌♣●P⁄

Walton on the Wolds

Anchor Inn

2 Loughborough Road, LE12 8HT
⏲ 12-3 (not Mon), 7-11 (10.30 Sun)
☎ (01509) 880018
Adnams Bitter; Marston's Pedigree; Taylor Landlord; guest beer Ⓗ
Situated in an elevated position in the centre of the village, the pub has an open plan, comfortable L-shaped lounge with a real fire. Prints and photographs of classic cars and village scenes adorn the walls. Good quality food is served Tue to Sat and roasts on Sun lunchtime. Self-catering or B&B accommodation is available in four self-contained units. ⛫Q❀🛏🚌P⁄

Whitwick

Three Horseshoes ★

11 Leicester Road, LE67 5GN
⏲ 11-3, 6.30-11; 12-2, 7-10.30 Sun
☎ (01530) 83731

Draught Bass; M&B Mild; Marston's Pedigree ⊞
Listed on CAMRA's National Inventory of unspoilt pubs, the nickname 'Polly's' is thought to come from a former landlady, Polly Burton. The pub was originally two separate buildings. To the left is a long bar with quarry-tiled floor and open fires, wooden bench seating and pre-war fittings. To the right is a similarly furnished small snug. ♨Q⊟⊟♣

Wigston

Star & Garter

114 Leicester Road, LE18 1DS
11-3, 5-11; 11-11 (midnight Fri & Sat); 12-11 Sun
☎ (0116) 288 2450
Everards Beacon, Tiger; guest beers ⊞
This pub has two rooms and a central bar. Very much a locals' pub, skittles can be played by prior arrangement. Lunchtime meals served 7.30-3.30, evening meals served on a Thursday only (curry night). ❀◐⊟♣P⁼

Woodhouse Eaves

Wheatsheaf

Brand Hill, LE12 8SS
12-2.30 (3 Sat), 6-11; 12-3, 7-10.30 Sun
☎ (01509) 890320
Adnams Broadside; Draught Bass; Greene King Abbot; Taylor Landlord; guest beers ⊞
Built c. 1800 as a meeting place for miners from the Swithland quarry. This popular pub, on the outskirts of the village, is traditionally furnished with wood-beamed ceilings, open fires and a mixture of wooden pews and comfortable seating. Upstairs is an award-winning restaurant (closed Sun eve). Bar snacks and meals served at lunchtime.
♨Q❀◐⊟P

RUTLAND

Braunston in Rutland

Old Plough Inn

2 Church Street, LE15 8QY
11-11 (midnight Sat); 12-10.30 Sun
☎ (01572) 722714
Grainstore Cooking, Ten Fifty; guest beers ⊞
One of just a few pubs owned by the Grainstore Brewery. This popular inn has a bar and comfortable low beamed lounge area, conservatory/ restaurant and patio garden. Two guest beers or Grainstore seasonal beers are usually on the handpumps alongside the regular beers. ♨Q❀◐⊟♣P⁼

Clipsham

Olive Branch ✓

Main Street, LE15 7SH
12-3, 6-11; 12-11 Sat; 12-10.30 Sun
☎ (01780) 410355 🌐 theolivebranchpub.com
Beer range varies ⊞
Beautiful cottage-style Michelin-starred pub hidden just two minutes' walk from Clipsham's famous Yew Tree Lane, a line of sculptured Yew trees depicting historic events. The pub is both walker and dog friendly. Excellent food is served daily. Home-made pickles, chutneys and local honey are on sale, together with Olive Oil, a beer brewed by the Grainstore Brewery. ♨Q❀⊟◐♿⊟P

Greetham

Plough ✓

23 Main Street, LE15 7NJ (1 mile off A1 on B668)
11-3, 5-11; 11-11 Thu-Sat winter; 11-11 summer; 12-10.30 Sun
☎ (01572) 813613
Taylor Golden Best; guest beers ⊞
Genuine village pub with welcoming staff and a warm atmosphere. Excellent beer, always including a mild, is served alongside traditional cider. Good pub food is available lunchtimes and evenings. Table skittles and dominoes are played.
Q❀◐⊟Å⊟♣●P⁼

Oakham

Grainstore

Station Approach, LE15 6RE (next to station)
11-11
☎ (01572) 770065
Grainstore Rutland Panther, Cooking Bitter, Triple B, Ten Fifty, Nip, seasonal beers ⊞
This pub has been cleverly converted into a brewery over four floors, while retaining some original features. Mild ale is always available and a range of bottle-conditioned Belgian beers. Dog and walker friendly, good pub food is served at lunchtime. Live jazz or blues plays twice monthly. ❀◐♿⇌⊟♣●

Uppingham

Crown Hotel

14 High Street East, LE15 9PY
11-11; 12-10.30 Sun
☎ (01572) 822302
Everards Tiger, Original, seasonal beers; guest beers ⊞
A warm welcome is assured at this traditional market town pub, with its good, reasonably priced quality home-cooked food. The licensee has been accredited with the Everards' Gold Master of Beer status. Regular beer festivals are held each April and October. Live music hosted monthly. En-suite bedrooms available.
♨Q❀⊟◐♿⊟♣⁼

Whitwell

Noel

Main Road, LE15 8BW
12-3, 6-11; closed Mon; 12-4, 8-10.30 Sun
☎ (01780) 460374 🌐 thenoel.co.uk
Grainstore Cooking Bitter; guest beers ⊞
Just a short walk from the beautiful shores of Rutland Water, walkers, cyclists and dogs are all welcome. This pleasant and friendly family-run pub offers excellent home-made food. Local and seasonal ales are always available. Live music plays on the last Friday of the month. ♨Q❀◐♿⊟(9)P⁼

ENGLAND

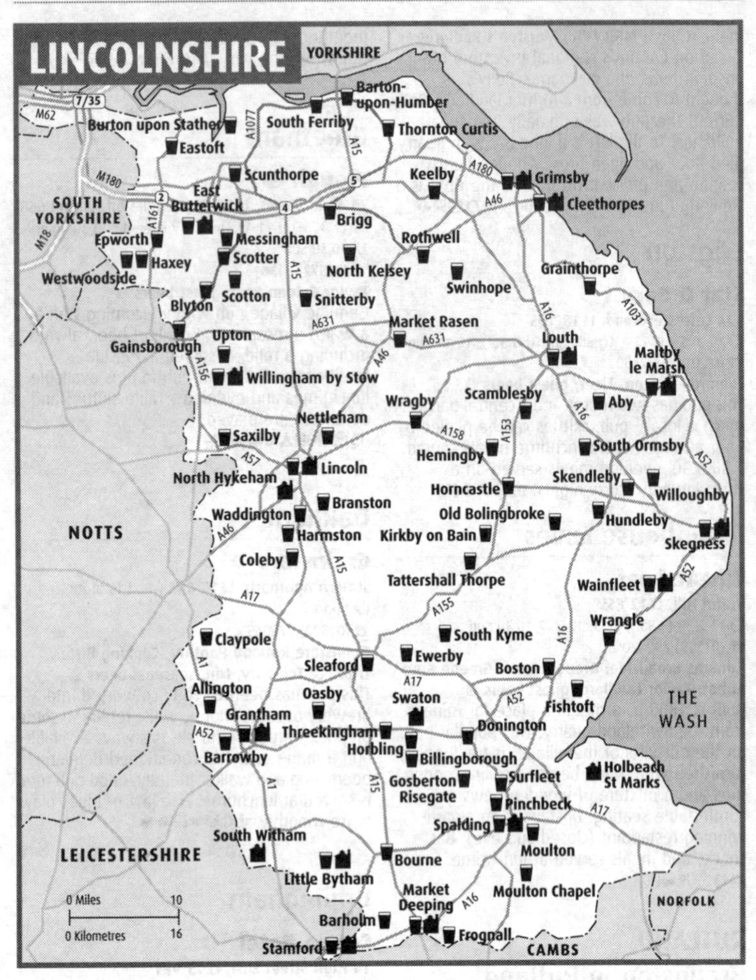

Aby

Railway Tavern

Main Road, LN13 0DR (off A16 via S Thoresby)

12-12.30am; closed Tue winter

☎ (01507) 480676

Bateman XB; Everards Tiger; guest beers Ⓗ

This cosy village pub is worth searching out for its ever-changing beer list and excellent food. Plenty of railway memorabilia includes the original Aby platform sign, and even the lighting is railway oriented. A real community pub with a warm welcome for all, an open fire and a Wednesday quiz night. Dogs are permitted and there are plenty of good walks close by. ₼Q❀◐♿⋏♣P⊬

Allington

Welby Arms ✔

The Green, NG32 2EA (1 mile from A1 Gonerby Moor Junction)

12-2, 6-11; 12-10.30 Sun

☎ (01400) 281361

John Smith's Bitter; Taylor Landlord; Wells Bombardier; guest beers Ⓗ

An attractive village pub just off the A1 in the Vale of Belvoir, within easy reach of Belton House, Belvoir Castle and Sir Isaac Newton's home in Woolsthorpe Manor. In addition to the three regular beers, an interesting range of guest ales is usually available. On the third Monday of each month is a challenging quiz night. Local Morris dancers perform throughout the year, outside the pub. Wheelchair access is by the rear door. ₼Q❀⇄♿P⊬

Barholm

Five Horseshoes

Main Street, PE9 4RA

5 (12 Sat)-11; 12-10.30 Sun

☎ (01778) 560238

Adnams Bitter; Oakham JHB; guest beers Ⓗ

Pleasant, friendly, 18th-century, multi-roomed inn situated in a quiet hamlet. This rustic pub is constructed from locally quarried Barnack stone, with a creeper-covered patio, large attractive gardens and open fires to greet visitors on chilly evenings. The inn concentrates on its real ales and always has four guests on offer. It actively supports micro-breweries, with a strong beer often available. ♔☺❀⇌♿▲⇶♣●P⊱

Barrowby

White Swan ✔

High Road, NG32 1BH

✪ 12-midnight (1am Fri & Sat)

☎ (01476) 562375

Adnams Bitter, Broadside; guest beers ⊞

There is something to please everyone at this no-nonsense village pub which is just a few hundred metres from the A52 and A1. In a traditional two-bar layout, the public bar is always busy with darts and cribbage teams, plus a pool table and TV. The lounge is very different – with no distracting music it is a peaceful room where comfortable seating around the walls makes it a good place to relax. The friendly landlord is a CAMRA member. Q❀◐⊟♣P⊱

Barton-upon-Humber

Sloop Inn

81 Waterside Road, DN18 5BA (follow Humber Bridge viewing signs)

✪ 11-11; 12-10.30 Sun

☎ (01652) 637287 ⊕ sloopinn.net

Tom Wood Shepherd's Delight, Bomber County; guest beers ⊞

This welcoming pub has nautical-themed decoration with areas named after parts of a ship. The central bar serves a games section with a pool table and darts, plus a drinking/dining area and two further rooms. Real ales from the local Tom Wood Highwood Brewery are on offer plus rotating guests. Good value home-cooked food, with many specials such as the pub's own sausages, is popular with locals and walkers. The Far Ings Nature Reserve, Waterside Visitor Centre and Humber Bridge are nearby. ❀◐♿▲⇶♣

Billingborough

Fortescue Arms

27 High Street, NG34 0QB

✪ 12-3, 5.30-11; 12-11 Sat & Sun

☎ (01529) 240228

Fuller's London Pride; Greene King Abbot, IPA; Taylor Landlord ⊞

Fine, Grade II-listed inn with an interesting multi-roomed interior and a rustic feel. The pub is also popular with diners, with a large patio to the rear providing a pleasant outdoor drinking area. Nearby is the site of Sempringham Abbey and its monument to Gwenllian, daughter of the Prince of Wales, who was confined to the priory in the 12th century. Stone from the abbey was used to build part of the inn. ♔Q❀◐⊟⊞P⊱

Blyton

Black Horse

93 High Street, DN21 3JX

✪ 12-2.30, 5-midnight; closed Mon; 12-midnight Fri-Sun

☎ (01427) 628277

Greene King IPA; guest beers ⊞

Recently reopened after a period of closure caused by floods, the pub has taken advantage of this time to extend further and update. It is now a very well-appointed and comfortable locals' pub but with a clean, fresh twist. Good, home-cooked food features, and guest beers often come from Lincolnshire's micro-breweries. Darts and quiz nights are regular events and the pub has a real community feel while remaining very welcoming to visitors. ♔Q❀◐⊟♿⊞♣P⊱

Boston

Ball House ✔

Wainfleet Road, PE21 9RL (on A52, 2 miles from town)

✪ 11.30-3, 6.30-11,; 12-3, 7-10.30 Sun

☎ (01205) 364478 ⊕ theballhouse.co.uk

Bateman XB, XXXB; Draught Bass; Greene King Abbot ⊞

A cheery welcome greets customers old and new in this early 13th-century, mock-Tudor pub that stands on the site of an old cannonball store. A varied menu features excellent home-cooked meals and bar snacks made with locally-grown produce; children's portions are available. Monthly themed nights are hosted from January to July. Award-winning floral displays can be enjoyed in the summer and there is a children's play area plus plenty of seating and a covered smoking area in the pleasant gardens.
♔Q☺❀◐♿⊞P⊱

Cowbridge

Horncastle Road, PE22 7AX (on B1183, N of Boston)

✪ 12-3, 6-11; 12-4, 7-10.30 Sun

☎ (01205) 362597

Greene King Old Speckled Hen; Theakston Mild, Black Bull Bitter; guest beers ⊞

Just out of town, this pub is popular with drinkers as well as diners. It divides into three main areas: the public bar is a no-nonsense drinking and darts environment with a large array of football scarves; the smaller lounge is cosy with an open fire, opening out into a restaurant that serves excellent freshly-

INDEPENDENT BREWERIES

Bateman Wainfleet
Blue Bell Holbeach St Marks
Blue Cow South Witham
Brewsters Grantham
Cathedral Lincoln (NEW)
DarkTribe East Butterwick
Fen Spalding
Fugelestou Louth
Grafters Willingham-by-Stow (NEW)
Highwood/Tom Wood Grimsby
Hopshackle Market Deeping
Leila Cottage Skegness (NEW)
Malt B Maltby le Marsh (NEW)
Melbourn Stamford
Newby Wyke Little Bytham
Oldershaw Grantham
Poachers North Hykeham
Riverside Wainfleet
Swaton Swaton (NEW)
Willy's Cleethorpes

cooked food. The pub is frequented by members of Boston Golf Club which is just up the road. ⩩Q♨❀◑⊟♿♣P⚋

Eagle

144 West Street, PE21 8RE (300m from railway station)
✪ 11 (11.30 Thu)-11 (midnight Fri & Sat); 12-3, 6-10.30 Sun
☎ (01205) 361116
Banks's Bitter; Castle Rock Harvest Pale; Taylor Landlord; guest beer ⊞
Part of the Tynemill chain, the Eagle is known as the real ale pub of Boston. This two-roomed, friendly pub has an L-shaped bar with a large TV screen for big sports events. The small, cosy lounge has an open fire. The pub stocks an ever-changing range of guest ales, usually including one or more from Castle Rock, and at least one cider. A function room upstairs is home to Boston Folk Club on Monday. Thursday is quiz night – allegedly the hardest in town. ⩩❀⊟♿⇌⊟♣⚋

Moon Under Water ✔

6 High Street, PE21 8SH
✪ 9-midnight (1am Fri & Sat)
☎ (01205) 311911
Greene King IPA, Abbot, Old Speckled Hen; Marston's Pedigree; guest beers ⊞
This busy town centre pub close to the tidal section of the River Witham has the usual Wetherspoon's mix of drinking and dining areas. Formerly a government building, an imposing spiral staircase leads from the central lounge area to the toilets. There are usually four guest ales alongside the regular beers. Local history dominates the wall and highlights characters associated with Boston. ⩩❀◑♿⚋

Ship Tavern

Custom House Lane, PE21 6HH
✪ 11-11; 12-10.30 Sun
☎ (01205) 358156
Bateman Dark Mild, XB; Greene King IPA; guest beers ⊞
Town centre pub conveniently placed opposite the quayside, behind the Old Custom House and near the Guildhall and theatre. A traditional hostelry, it has one large L-shaped room, with plenty of brewery memorabilia on display including some good photos of now demolished local pubs. The pub is popular with students and also gets busy on match days with football supporters. In the summer a small patio is used for outside drinking. ❀♿⇌⊟♣

Bourne

Smith's

25 North Street, PE10 9AE
✪ 10-11 (midnight Fri & Sat); 12-11 Sun
☎ (01778) 426819
Fuller's London Pride; Oakham JHB; Ufford Ales White Hart; guest beers ⊞
A winner of the national CAMRA/English Heritage Conversion to Pub Use award, this former grocer's, situated in a three-storey building, is now a popular contemporary pub. The two ground-floor bars serve a variety of comfortable seating areas throughout the building. Outside is a well-equipped patio and garden with a covered and heated area for smokers. If you miss the popular lunchtime food, a cheeseboard is available until 7pm. Q❀⊭◑♿Ă⊟

Branston

Waggon & Horses

1 Rectory Lane, LN4 1NB
✪ 12-2, 5-midnight; 12-1am Fri & Sat; 12-midnight Sun
☎ (01522) 791356
Draught Bass; John Smith's Bitter; Taylor Landlord; guest beers ⊞
This community pub recently celebrated its 50th birthday. Spot the moose head in the public bar, which is also home to darts and pool teams. The comfortable lounge hosts Monday quiz night, Tuesday jam night and live entertainment on Saturday, plus a didgeridoo workshop held on the first Wednesday of the month. Charity fundraising for LIVES is held monthly. Excellent food is available until 8pm weekdays and 6pm at weekends. Outside is a covered smoking area. ♨◑⊟⊟(2)♣P⚋

Brigg

Black Bull

3 Wrawby Street, DN20 8JH
✪ 11-3 (4 Thu), 7-11.30 (11 Wed); 11-midnight Fri & Sat; 12-3, 7-11 Sun
☎ (01652) 62153
John Smith's Bitter; Tom Wood Harvest Bitter; guest beer ⊞
Popular, friendly pub with a homely feel that gets busy on market days (Thursday and Saturday). The guest beer changes frequently. Horse racing is a regular feature on TV on Saturday. Lunches are available until 2pm throughout the week. Quiz night is Tuesday. The smoking area is covered. Brigg can be reached by bus from Scunthorpe and Barton and by train on Saturday only on the Cleethorpes to Sheffield line. ❀◑⇌⊟♣P⚋

White Hart

57 Bridge Street, DN20 8NS
✪ 11 (12 Sun)-11
☎ (01652) 654887
Banks's Bitter; Jennings Cumberland Ale; guest beers ⊞
The pub is in the centre of Brigg, located next to the old River Ancholme, with its beer garden running alongside the riverbank. The interior is traditionally decorated with photographs on the walls depicting old Brigg. The lounge bar is at the front of the pub, with the bar area towards the rear featuring a pool table. Food is served 12-2pm daily and 5-7pm weekdays only. The regular beers are quite unusual for the area. Quiz night is Thursday. ⩩❀◑⇌⊟P⚋

Yarborough Hunt

49 Bridge Street, DN20 8NS (across bridge from market place)
✪ 11 (10 Thu & Sat)-11 (midnight Thu-Sat)
☎ (01652) 658333
Greene King IPA; Tom Wood Best Bitter; guest beers ⊞

This former Sergeants Brewery tap, built in the 1700s, is now in its fifth year since reopening after restoration. Retaining original features, it is simply furnished with warming open fires lit in winter. The four guest beers are supplemented by draught Weston's Old Rosie. It also offers a good selection of bottled continental and British beers and ciders and a wide selection of malt whiskies and wines. A free WiFi service has recently been made available to customers. Trains to Brigg only run on Saturday. The smoking area is covered and heated. ♔Q❀♿⇌⊟♣●⌐

Burton-upon-Stather

Ferry House

Stather Road, DN15 9DJ (follow campsite signs)

⌚ 7 (5 summer)-11; 12-midnight Sat & Sun

☎ (01724) 721504

Beer range varies Ⓗ

Riverside village local nestling at the bottom of a steep hill adjacent to the River Trent. Decorated with a nautical theme, the large open-plan room contains a brick-fronted bar, and there is a separate lounge overlooking the riverbank. One or two real ales are offered together with a selection of draught foreign beers and lagers and Weston's Old Rosie cider. Holder of the Cask Marque Beautiful Beer award, it stages beer festivals and wine tasting evenings throughout the year. Popular for good value Sunday lunches.

❀⛟♿⛺⊟●P

Claypole

Five Bells

95 Main Street, NG23 5BJ

⌚ 11 (4 Mon)-11; 12-10.30 Sun

☎ (01636) 626561

Tetley Bitter; guest beers Ⓗ

Pleasant Victorian village free house and Newark CAMRA Pub of the Year 2007. The narrow-beamed main bar with a pool table at the far end is complemented by a second room, usually occupied by diners. A central bar serves both rooms. The pub is host to pool and dominoes teams and is often busy. Guest beers are from the Greene King portfolio plus local micro-breweries. Comfortable accommodation is available.

❀⛟◑◗⊟(602)♣P⌐

Cleethorpes

No. 2 Refreshment Room

Station Approach, DN35 8AX (on station)

⌚ 9am-1am (midnight Sun)

☎ (07905) 375587

Greene King H&H Olde Trip; Hancock's HB; M&B Mild; Worthington's Bitter; guest beers Ⓗ

Small, friendly local situated beneath the last wooden railway clock tower in Britain. What more is there to say about this free house? In the five years since it reopened after a period of closure, it has been voted local CAMRA Pub of the Year four years running and Best Station Buffet/Railway Pub 2006 in the Community Rail Awards. Smokers can use a fenced and covered area on the platform. ❀⇌⊟⌐

Nottingham House

7 Sea View Street, DN35 8EU

⌚ 12-midnight (1am Fri & Sat); 12-11 Sun

☎ (01472) 505152

Tetley Mild, Bitter; guest beers Ⓗ

This pub is a rarity in this area, still retaining three separate rooms, with an island bar serving all of them. A recent addition has been the opening of a bistro on the first floor, but meals can be eaten in any of the bars. A welcome return to the Guide for this no-frills hostelry. Q◑◗⇌⊟

Willy's

17 Highcliff Road, DN35 8RQ (on sea front)

⌚ 11-11 (2am Fri & Sat); 12-10.30 Sun

☎ (01472) 602145

Willy's Original; guest beers Ⓗ

A long-time regular in the Guide, Willy's is an institution on the local drinking scene. The publican and the brewer are long-time CAMRA members and the pub has won many awards. The attached brewery can be seen from the bar and an upstairs function room is available for hire. Home-cooked food is available lunchtimes and evenings, while guest beers include micro-brewery offerings as well as old favourites. The cider range varies. A covered area is provided front and rear for smokers.

❀◑◗⇌⊟●⌐

Coleby

Bell Inn

3 Far Lane, LN5 0AH

⌚ 11.30-3, 5.30-11; 12-10.30 Sun

☎ (01522) 810240 🌐 thebellinncoleby.co.uk

Beer range varies Ⓗ

Situated behind the church in a small village that sits on a limestone ridge of the Lincoln cliff, the pub is an ideal resting place for walkers on the nearby Viking Way. A choice of three ever-changing real ales awaits the drinker, while the food is undoubtedly of restaurant quality and includes a reasonably priced early bird menu. Dating from 1759, the pub has a separate restaurant and cosy bar, with a real fire for winter evenings.

♔Q☋❀⛟◑◗⊟(1)P⌐

Donington

Black Bull ✔

Marketplace, PE11 4ST

⌚ 11-11; 12-10.30 Sun

☎ (01775) 822228

John Smith's Bitter; Greene King Abbot; guest beers Ⓗ

Busy village local just off the A52. Two handpumps feature a constantly changing selection of guest beers from small brewers as well as larger regionals. Weston's cider is on handpump in the comfortable bar, which has low, beamed ceilings, wooden settles and a cosy fire in winter. The restaurant serves a good choice of reasonably priced evening meals; lunches are served in the bar. Tables in the car park are used for outdoor drinking. Buses run from Boston and Spalding (not Sun).

♔❀⛟◑◗P

East Butterwick

Dog & Gun

High Street, DN17 3AJ (off A18 at Keadby Bridge)
5 (12 Sat)-11; 12-11 Sun
☎ (01724) 782324
DarkTribe Full Ahead, Old Gaffer; John Smith's Bitter Ⓗ
This traditional riverside pub is the home of the DarkTribe Brewery and attracts both locals and visitors from outlying villages. There are three rooms in which to have either a quiet chat or take part in traditional pub games. In the winter you can keep warm by the real fires and in summer take a seat on the riverbank and enjoy your pint. Two DarkTribe beers are generally featured from the brewery's own range plus an occasional guest beer. Q❀♣P

Eastoft

River Don Tavern

Sampson Street, DN17 2QF (on A161 Goole-Gainsborough road)
7.30 (5 Wed-Fri; 12 Sat & Sun)-midnight
☎ (01724) 798040
Beer range varies Ⓗ
Traditional village local with country inn style decor, featuring dark wood beams, old agricultural implements plus black-and-white photographs of rural life. The interior is open plan with discrete areas for drinking and dining. In spring and summer, drinks can be enjoyed in the large orchard garden. Three rotating guest beers (two in winter) come from Yorkshire micro-breweries. Tasty, good value food is deservedly popular, and includes a weekend carvery and themed meal nights. An annual beer festival is held in summer.
❀P

Epworth

Queen's Head

19 Queen Street, DN9 1HG (off A161, near town centre)
12 (11.30 Sat)-midnight
☎ (01427) 872306
John Smith's Bitter; Rudgate Ruby Mild; guest beers Ⓗ
A locals' local catering for a mixed-age clientele in a popular tourist destination. Two years ago the long-serving licensee decided to introduce rotating guest beers, which proved a popular move and resulted in the Queen's being named local CAMRA Pub of the Season for Winter 2008. Quizzes and pub games are a regular feature of this community inn, which is a meeting place for local societies. Outdoors is a covered, heated smoking area, plus a patio and children's play area. ❀♣P

Ewerby

Finch Hatton Arms

43 Main Street, NG34 9PH
12-3, 6-11
☎ (01529) 460363 thefinchhattonarms.co.uk
Everards Tiger; guest beers Ⓗ
Substantial country inn built in the 1870s and later owned by the Finch Hatton family, hence the family crest and motto Nil Consire Sibi. The pub retains its comfortable charm and has in recent years introduced accommodation, with en-suite hotel rooms. New and changing menus have been introduced in the popular and extended dining facilities. Q❀P

Fishtoft

Red Cow Inn

Gaysfield Road, PE21 0SF
5.30 (11 Sat & Sun)-11
☎ (01205) 367552
Bateman Dark Mild, XB; Greene King IPA Ⓗ
A warm welcome is always assured at the Red Cow, run by long-serving Batemans tenants. A small, thriving, atmospheric inn, it fields many pub teams including darts, pool and dominoes. The Pilgrim Fathers Memorial is nearby. There are angling and birdwatching sites on the Wash and the RSPB site is at Freiston Shore. Q❀▲♣P

Frognall

Goat

155 Spalding Road, PE6 8SA
11.30-3, 6-11; 12-10.30 Sun
☎ (01778) 347629 thegoatfrognall.co.uk
Beer range varies Ⓗ
Cosy and comfortable pub with a friendly welcome and a real fire on chilly days. Good quality food is served in two dining areas and the bar offers a fine range of beers, usually featuring local micro-breweries. There is always a strong beer of 6% or more on handpump, plus a small but well chosen range of Belgian beers. Real draught cider is also available, and more than 50 single malt whiskies. An annual beer festival is held in summer. Q❀P

Gainsborough

Eight Jolly Brewers

Ship Court, Silver Street, DN21 2DW (behind market place)
11 (12 Sun)-midnight
☎ (07767) 638806
Beer range varies Ⓗ
Award-winning real ale venue based in a former carpenter's yard overlooking the River Trent and gardens. This Grade II-listed town-centre building houses a country pub with a patio area, main downstairs bar and two drinking areas upstairs. An ever-changing beer range features Glentworth, Castle Rock and Abbeydale breweries, with one beer usually heavily discounted. Leffe Blonde, real cider on draught and a wide selection of continental bottled beers are also available. Quality live music can be heard on Thursday nights.
Q❀P

Elm Cottage

139 Church Street, DN21 2JU (100m W of Trinity football ground)
11.30-3, 6-midnight; 11.30-midnight Fri-Sun
☎ (01427) 615474
Jennings Cumberland Ale; guest beers Ⓗ
This former CAMRA local Pub of the Season has a central bar featuring two bay windows with

seating, and a separate dining area where good value food is served daily at lunchtime. The walls are decorated with pictures of the local area past and present. There is a cabinet of trophies won by the darts, football and cricket teams based at the pub. A charity quiz is held every other Tuesday and live music on the first Saturday of the month.

Gosberton Risegate

Duke of York

105 Risegate Road, PE11 4EY

12 (6.30 Mon)-11; 12-3.30, 7-10.30 Sun

(01775) 840193

Bateman XB; Black Sheep Best Bitter; guest beers

An excellent pub with an established and well-deserved reputation for value-for-money beers and food. As well as the regular beers, guests generally come from independent brewers. The pub is a centre for the local community, supporting a range of charities, sports teams and other social events. A large fenced-in garden with amusements for children makes it popular for families. The arch above the bar shows this is a former Batemans house, modernised during the 1950s.

Grainthorpe

Black Horse Inn

Mill Lane, LN11 7HH (off A1031, signed to pub)

7-11.30 Mon & Tue; 1-3, 7-midnight Wed- Fri; 12-midnight Sat & Sun

(01472) 388229

Beer range varies

Two-roomed pub in a rural village with decor featuring pictures and brasses reflecting its country location. Teams compete in local darts, pool and dominoes leagues. Close by are good areas for walking, both countryside and coastal, with the latter offering both beach and salt marsh, and a large variety of birdlife. In winter the nearby Donna Nook hosts a colony of grey seals which come to have their pups.

Grantham

Avenue Hotel

Avenue Road, NG31 6TH (100m from town hall)

11-midnight (1am Fri & Sat); 12-midnight Sun

(01476) 561876

Taylor Landlord; guest beers

A family-run hotel and bar where Taylor Landlord is always available alongside local micro-brewery guest beers. A 'happy hour' runs from 5-8pm Monday to Friday. The bar also serves excellent home-cooked meals, with children's portions available on request. Live sport is screened regularly in the bar and there is a patio area to the front of the hotel and a beer garden to the rear.

Blue Pig

9 Vine Street, NG31 6RQ (near St Wulfram's Church)

11-11; closed Fri; 10.30-1.30am Sat; 12-11 Sun

(01476) 563704

Caledonian Deuchars IPA; Taylor Landlord; guest beers

This lovely old Tudor building, originally constructed for the stonemasons who created the nearby St Wulframs Church, is a gem that is not to be missed. A good atmosphere prevails and a wide range of well-priced bar meals makes this pub a must for locals and visitors. The roaring log fire provides a welcome on cold evenings, while the heated outdoor area for smokers contains an ever increasing collection of pigs.

Chequers

25 Market Place, NG31 6LR (on narrow side street between High St and Market Place)

12-midnight (1am Fri & Sat)

(01476) 570149

Beer range varies

A true free house tucked away in a narrow side street at the east end of the Market Place, with a range of beers sourced from micro-breweries all over the UK. The contemporary single room bar is divided into smaller drinking areas furnished with leather sofas. This pub is popular with all ages – it is quiet in the week but more lively at the weekend.

Goose at the Bank

354 – 356 High Street, NG31 6NE

11-11; 12-10.30 Sun

(01476) 574920

Draught Bass; Tetley Bitter; guest beers

This friendly, town-centre, contemporary pub was created in a converted building that was once a bank. Catering for all tastes, cask beer is competitively priced and good food is served until late. Up-to-date features include the modern technology option of Wi-Fi Internet access and large-screen TVs that show live football when appropiate.

Lord Harrowby

65 Dudley Road, NG31 9AB

4 (12 Sat & Sun)-11

Tom Wood Best Bitter; Wells Bombardier; guest beers

A back street gem, this small, friendly two-roomed traditional pub is five minutes' walk from the town centre. The lounge is decorated with aeroplane pictures, highlighting the presence of the nearby HQ of Bomber Command during World War II. Darts, cribbage and pool are played here. Live jazz is hosted on the third Friday of the month.

Nobody Inn

9 North Street, NG31 6NU (on corner, opp Asda car park)

12-11 (10.30 Sun)

(01476) 565288 nobodyinn.com

Greene King IPA; Newby Wyke Bear Island, White Squall; guest beers

Vibrant, friendly, down-to-earth and popular with all ages, this independent pub regularly features local Newby Wyke beers. Projector screens and TVs are dotted around the U-shaped room, making this an ideal pub for the discerning sports fan. Table football and a pool table are available. Watch out for the door to the toilets, which is disguised as a bookcase.

Grimsby

County Hotel

Brighowgate, DN32 0QU
12-11 (midnight Thu-Sun)
☎ (01472) 354422
Beer range varies Ⓗ
One-room pub near the Salvation Army Hostel that attracts a mixed clientele. It was once known as the Old Musician before reverting to its original title. The experienced bar manager has reintroduced cask ale on three handpumps, featuring carefully selected beers and a changing real cider, mainly from local micro-breweries such as Fugelestou. It can get pleasantly busy on weekend nights when live music features, but there is a lower alcove which is quieter. Food is served daily at lunchtimes.

Millfields Hotel

53 Bargate, DN34 5AD
11-midnight (11.30 Sun)
☎ (01472) 356068 millfieldshotel.co.uk
Black Sheep Best Bitter; Fuller's London Pride; Tom Wood Bomber County Ⓗ
A listed building, Millfields is a recently refurbished hotel with bar and leisure facilities open to the public. Inside, it has a contemporary style, with the excellent food and wide selection of handpulled ales taking centre stage. From bar snacks to fine dining, the menu includes prime steaks, fresh fish, and a healthy home-cooked Dish of the Day. The hotel is well served by several bus routes and is ten minutes' walk from Grimsby Town railway station, midway between the town centre and university campus. P

Rutland Arms

26-30 Rutland Street, DN31 3AF (behind Ramsden's Superstore)
11-11 (midnight Fri & Sat); 12-10.30 Sun
☎ (01472) 268732
Old Mill Mild, Bitter, Bullion, seasonal beers Ⓗ
Celebrating its 20-year anniversary during 2008, this once run-down social club is now a well-appointed, one-roomed local, catering mainly for the immediate vicinity. It is the only pub for miles around serving real ale and the only Old Mill tied house in the region. There are resident pool and soccer teams, while Grimsby Town FC performs its regular shenanigans at Blundell Park, a 10-minute walk from here. (New Clee)(9,13)♣

Swigs

21 Osbourne Street, DN31 1EY
9am-11 (midnight Fri & Sat); 12-10.30 Sun
☎ (01472) 354773
Willy's Original; guest beers Ⓗ
An uncompromising town-centre bar, located just away from the hustle and bustle of the local circuit. This is the second pub owned by Willy's Brewery, the first is in neighbouring Cleethorpes. A popular myth that the name is an acronym of Second Willy's In Grimsby is untrue. A varied bar snack and meal menu is available every day but not in the evening. Guest beers tend to be premium or strong ABV. Close to the bus and Grimsby Town railway stations.

Wheatsheaf ✔

47 Bargate, DN34 5AD
12-11
☎ (01472) 246821
Bateman XXXB; Caledonian Deuchars IPA; Taylor Landlord; Tetley Bitter; guest beers Ⓗ
If you are looking for good food and a selection of real ales in a friendly, relaxing atmosphere, then this Ember Inn is your place. In this well maintained pub there are two bars and a split-level layout, encompassing various seating areas. Twice-yearly beer festivals feature ales from small breweries. Outside is a seated patio area. The pub is close to the town and on the Grimsby-Louth bus route.
P

Yarborough Hotel ✔

29 Bethlehem Street, DN31 1JN (opp Grimsby Town rail station)
9am-midnight (1am Fri & Sat)
☎ (01472) 268283
Bateman Dark Mild; Greene King Abbot, IPA; Marston's Pedigree; guest beers Ⓗ
Twice local CAMRA Pub of the Year, this spacious Wetherspoon pub on the ground floor of an imposing Victorian hotel has two large bar areas and a rear snug. It is well patronised by all age groups during its long opening hours and is particularly busy at weekends. Up to seven guest beers plus Addlestone's Cloudy cider are regularly available, and good value meals are served all day until late. A patio with seating at the rear is suitable for smokers.

Harmston

Thorold Arms

High Street, LN5 9SN
12-3 (not Mon & Tue), 6-11; 12-11 Sun
☎ (01522) 720358 thoroldarms.co.uk
Beer range varies Ⓗ
Winner of CAMRA East Midlands Pub of the Year for the last two years, this is a true community pub specialising in beers from micro-breweries, with four handpumps offering a constantly-changing range. The 17th-century building has a small bar area with a mixture of tables and comfortable settees. Numerous regular events are hosted, ranging from a Burns Night celebration to a women's reading group. Harmstock, the August bank holiday festival, has to be experienced. Q(1)♣P

Haxey

Loco

31-33 Church Street, DN9 2HY (from A161 follow B1396 into village)
4-midnight (1am Fri & Sat); 12-midnight
☎ (01427) 752879 thelocohaxey.co.uk
John Smith's Bitter; guest beers Ⓗ
Converted from the village Co-op during the 1980s, this was originally decorated with railway memorabilia, but following extensive refurbishment only a locomotive smoke box remains of the original design. The Loco now offers four-star accommodation and a restaurant specialising in English and Indian cuisine, with lunch served on Sunday only. At

least one guest beer is always available. Access and facilities for wheelchair users are good. The pub participates in the annual Haxey Hood game on 6th January. 🛏◐♿🚌

Hemingby

Coach & Horses

Church Lane, LN9 5QF (1 mile from A158)
⏲ 12-2 (not Mon & Tue), 7 (6 Wed-Fri)-11; 12-3, 7-10.30 Sun
☎ (01507) 578280
🌐 coachandhorses.mysite.wanadoo-members.co.uk
Bateman Dark Mild; Riverside Dixon's Major; guest beers ⊞
This will be the landlord's 15th year at the helm of this vital community pub at the centre of village life. A quaint, family- friendly local, the pub is also a strong supporter of local brewers such as Batemans and Riverside (Wainfleet). Food, too, is sourced locally. A games room has recently been added and is ideal for children. Wi-Fi Internet access is provided throughout. Camping and caravan facilities are available. ⛫Q❀◐⛺🚌♣P⚟

Horbling

Plough Inn

Spring Lane, NG34 0PF
⏲ 12-3, 5-11; 12-11 Fri & Sat; 12-10.30 Sun
☎ (01529) 240263 🌐 theploughinnhorbling.co.uk
Beer range varies ⊞
Low-beamed pub, built in 1832 in a quiet village and owned by the parish council. In addition to the lounge and bar, it has a snug that is surely one of the smallest and most intimate of its kind. Beers are usually from local micro-breweries and change regularly. Home-cooked meals are available in the bar and restaurant. Spring wells are a feature just a few yards down the lane.
Q❀◐⊟♿🚌♣P⚟

Horncastle

Crown Inn

28 West Street, LN9 5JF
⏲ 4-11; 2 (12 Sat)-2am Fri & Sat; 12-10.30 Sun
☎ (01507) 526006
Bateman XB; Greene King IPA; guest beers ⊞
This town local has an L-shaped bar/lounge with a large brick fireplace and interesting hearth, piled high with logs in winter. The substantial wood bar itself has unusual carvings and there are two large engraved mirrors behind the bar that feature the pub crown emblem. The pub is owned by Thimbleby Lakes, a local camping and fishing enterprise. ⛫❀♿⛺🚌♣⚟▯

Red Lion

Bull Ring, LN9 5HT
⏲ 11-midnight; 12-10.30 Sun
☎ (01507) 523338
Oakwell Barnsley Bitter ⊞
Large bar/lounge with old bay windows overlooking the Bullring town centre. Above the bar a collection of 800 assorted keyrings hang on display, while framed photographs of the Lion Theatre productions from 1988 adorn the walls. The theatre is part of the pub premises, located at the rear, and run by the Horncastle Theatre Co. Productions sometimes star the landlord. A small snug-like room and a dining room also feature. The pub has three rooms for overnight accommodation.
♉❀🛏◐⊟♿🚌♣P⚟

Hundleby

Hundleby Inn ✔

73 Main Road, PE23 5LZ
⏲ 12-11 (midnight Fri & Sat)
☎ (01790) 752577 🌐 thehundlebyinn.co.uk
Bateman XB; Black Sheep Best Bitter; guest beers ⊞
This welcoming and cosy free house features a wood-panelled bar/lounge decorated with pictures of aeroplanes and sport. The dining room provides excellent, good value home-cooked food. A large outdoor space includes a children's play area, camping and caravanning, a patio and seating. The pub is located on the edge of the Wolds and has excellent walks. It is also in easy striking distance of the nearest town, Spilsby.
⛫❀◐♿⛺🚌♣P⚟

Keelby

Nag's Head

8 Manor Street, DN41 8EF
⏲ 2 (12 Fri-Sun)-midnight
☎ (01469) 560660
John Smith's Bitter; Theakston Mild; Tom Wood Best Bitter; guest beer ⊞
Firmly established village local run with a warm, personal touch. The building dates back to 1749, with a wood-beamed lounge and a busy bar offering a guest beer often from a micro-brewery. Tuesday is quiz night and live music plays at weekends three times a month. No regular food is served but a local butcher regularly hosts spring and summer weekend barbecues. A small beer garden includes a children's play area and a covered, lit and heated smoking area. ❀⊟🚌⚟

Kirkby on Bain

Ebrington Arms

Main Street, LN10 6YT
⏲ 12-3, 6-midnight; 12-11 Sun
☎ (01526) 354560
Bateman XB; Greene King Abbot; Woodforde's Wherry Best Bitter ⊞
Attractive country pub dating from 1610, close to the River Bain, with a low-beamed bar/lounge that was used by aircrew during World War II. Coins are still slotted into the ceiling beams where they were kept for when the men returned from missions. The popular restaurant offers good food made with local produce (booking advised). The garden has an awning to protect outside drinkers if the weather turns cool. There is a Caravan Club site within a mile of the pub.
⛫Q❀◐♿⛺♣P⚟

Lincoln

Dog & Bone

10 John Street, LN2 5BH (off Monks Rd)

12-3 (not Mon), 7-11
(01522) 522403
Bateman XB, Valiant, seasonal beers
A real community pub, loyally supported by its regulars, and welcoming to visitors. The U-shaped bar has two separate areas: one is lined with bookshelves for the pub's book exchange scheme. Two open fires add to the cosiness in winter. Crib and darts are regularly played and week-long beer festivals occur in summer and winter. An occasional guest beer is served at other times. The pub stays open all day on the first Sunday of the month for an open-mic music session. There is a heated, covered smokers' area.

Forum

13-14 Silver Street, LN2 1DY
9am-midnight (1am Fri & Sat)
(01522) 518630
Greene King IPA, Abbot; Marston's Pedigree; Theakston Old Peculier; guest beers
Not the most characterful of Wetherspoon conversions, the Forum occupies part of the former Lincoln Co-Op building and is comfortably furnished in contemporary style. The name reflects the city's Roman heritage, and the pub is conveniently situated for the Lincoln Drill Hall, Theatre Royal and main shopping area. Guest beers are sourced predominantly from local micro-breweries. Children's competitions are held on Sunday lunchtimes. The pub is close to Lincoln railway station. Q

Golden Eagle

21 High Street, LN5 8BD
11-11 (11.30 Fri & Sat); 12-11 Sun
(01522) 521058 goldeneagle.org.uk
Castle Rock Harvest Pale; Everards Beacon; guest beers
This friendly, traditional pub is popular with both home and visiting football supporters travelling to nearby Lincoln City ground. Up to seven guest beers, often including those from local breweries, are available as well as Weston's Old Rosie cider. A well kept garden boasts a heated marquee, floodlit petanque pitch and barbecue. Live open mic music plays on alternate Tuesdays, with a Wednesday lunchtime session once a month. Quiz night is Friday, and walks are often organised for a Saturday. Q

Jolly Brewer

27 Broadgate, LN2 5AQ
12-11 (midnight Wed & Thu; 1am Fri & Sat); 12-10.30 Sun
(01522) 528583 thejollybrewer.co.uk
Taylor Landlord; Young's Bitter; guest beers
A city-centre pub close to the Drill Hall and Usher Art Gallery. The single long bar is decorated in Art Deco style, with a dartboard, table football and jukebox at the rear. To the right a separate drinking area leads to a corridor, which opens out on to a large, partially covered and heated patio. The two guest beers are often from Lincolnshire breweries. Weston's perry and a guest cider are also on draught. Live music plays on Saturday night and open mic night is Wednesday.

Lincoln Post Office Sport & Social Club

Dunkirk Road, LN1 3JU
11-3, 6.30-11.30; 11-midnight Fri & Sat; 11-11.30 Sun
(01522) 524050
Tetley Bitter; guest beers
A modern club building provided by housing developers to replace the original building that was once next door. The main bar area is at the front and there is a large, comfortable function room at the rear where live entertainment features on the first Saturday of the month. Outside is a patio area. Entry to non-members is on presentation of a CAMRA membership card or this Guide.

Morning Star

11 Greetwell Gate, LN2 4AW
11-midnight; 12-11 Sun
(01522) 527079
Caledonian Deuchars IPA; Draught Bass; Greene King Ruddles Best Bitter, Abbot; Tetley Bitter; Wells Bombardier
Conversation is the main entertainment at this busy pub, situated uphill close to the cathedral. The front bar opens into a larger room to the left, originally an adjacent cottage, with a small additional room to the rear. The garden has a covered, heated area and hosts occasional live music in summer. Acoustic jam sessions are held on the third Wednesday of the month. Q

Tap & Spile

21 Hungate, LN1 1ES
4-midnight; 12-1am Fri & Sat
(01522) 534015 tapandspilelincoln.co.uk
Wychwood Hobgoblin; guest beers
Formerly the White Horse, this attractive red-brick pub just off the High Street has a diverse clientele that enjoys real music, ale and conversation in a convivial atmosphere. The central bar serves three drinking areas, with bare-brick walls displaying pictures of blues artistes and old advertising signs. On Friday, live music suits blues aficionados, while quizzes, acoustic jam sessions and circular chess are also hosted. Eight handpumps feature a variety of SIBA local and regional ales plus Weston's Old Rosie cider. The patio area is heated.

Tower Hotel

38 Westgate, LN1 3BD
11-11 (midnight Fri & Sat)
(01522) 529999 lincolntowerhotel.com
Caledonian Deuchars IPA; Fuller's London Pride; guest beers
A stylish and contemporary interior makes this a popular and lively bar situated in the Bail near the castle and cathedral. It is particularly busy when major soccer and rugby fixtures are showing on TV. The bar benefits from heated and lit patio areas to the front and rear, with exceptional views of the cathedral and water tower. Modern and seasonal food is served in the restaurant (no food Sun eve). The preferred guest beer is from the Batemans range.

Victoria
6 Union Road, LN1 3BJ
11-midnight (1am Fri & Sat); 12-midnight Sun
☎ (01522) 541000 victoriapub.net
Bateman XB; Castle Rock Harvest Pale; Taylor Landlord; guest beers Ⓗ
Built in 1843, the pub nestles under the West Gate of the castle. Eight handpumps usually dispense additional ales from the Batemans range as well as guest beers plus Weston's scrumpy cider. The pub has a long, narrow public bar with a smaller second room, while outside is a heated seating space and children's play area. Under new management, changes have been made to the style of the pub and the pricing policy. Q❀◑⊟●⚡

Little Bytham

Willoughby Arms
Station Road, NG33 4RA
12-11
☎ (01780) 410276 willoughbyarms.co.uk
Bateman XB; guest beers Ⓗ
Set in the heart of rural Lincolnshire, this 150-year-old gem is well worth seeking out. Formerly the waiting room and booking office for a private railway, it has been tastefully refurbished. The five guest beers are sourced from local micro-breweries, one of which is always a stout or porter. Traditional cider is also available here. Beer festivals are held in May and October. Good home-cooked food is served daily. ⛫❀⇋◑⊟●P

Louth

Boars Head
12 Newmarket, LN11 9HH (next to cattle market)
5 (9.30am Thu; 12 Fri-Sun)-11
☎ (01507) 603561
Bateman XB, Valiant; guest beers Ⓗ
A Batemans pub situated next to the cattle market, a short walk from the town centre, it has an ever-changing guest beer list. The interior includes two main rooms plus the old snug, which is now the games room. Warmed by real fires in the winter, it always provides a friendly welcome. Pub games include darts and dominoes. Thursday is cattle market day, which is why the pub opens earlier. A council-controlled car park is next door.
⛫Q⇋◑⊞♣⚡

Masons Arms
Cornmarket, LN11 9PY
10-11 (midnight Fri & Sat); 12-11 Sun
☎ (01507) 609525 themasons.co.uk
Abbeydale Moonshine; Bateman XB, XXXB; Marston's Pedigree; guest beers Ⓗ
The Masons Arms is a well-liked pub in the centre of a busy market town. A Grade II-listed building, in the 18th century it was a posting inn and staging house, and was home to the town's Masonic Lodge. Today the Masons is a thriving family-run hotel serving excellent home-cooked meals made with local produce, and ever-changing guest beers. Local CAMRA Pub of the Year 2006 and 2007, it hosts the Louth beer festival. Quiz night is Thursday and it is now home to the Louth Folk Club.
Q⇋◑⊞♿⊟♣●

Wheatsheaf
62 Westgate, LN11 9YD (close to St James' Church)
12-midnight
☎ (01507) 606262
Black Sheep Best Bitter; Daleside Old Legover; Exmoor Gold; Flowers Original; guest beers Ⓗ
A traditional style inn situated in a Georgian terrace, it is close to St James' Church which boasts the tallest spire of any parish church in England. All three rooms are warmed by coal fires in winter. Daily home-cooked specials are offered on the menu and the pub holds a beer and bangers festival at the end of May. Quiz night is Sunday. Well-behaved dogs are welcome outside. ⛫❀◑P

Maltby le Marsh

Crown Inn
Beesby Road, LN13 0JJ (jct of A157 and A1104)
12-11.30 (11 Sun)
☎ (01507) 450100
Bateman XB; guest beers Ⓗ
Following a long period of closure, this pub has been turned into an ale drinker's haven. Up to five beers are on offer, as well as ciders including Weston's Old Rosie. A small micro-brewery has been installed to supply the Crown only and its first beers have been well received. The inn and its outdoor tables are well situated for the nearby coastal strip with its many visitors, especially in summer. Bar skittles and shove ha'penny are played. Caravans allowed. ❀◑▲⊟(10)♣●P⚡

Market Deeping

Vine
19 Church Street, PE6 8AN
12-3, 5-11; 12-11 Thu-Sat; 12-10.30 Sun
☎ (01778) 344699 inn-the-vine.co.uk
Wells Eagle IPA, Bombardier; guest beers Ⓗ
Friendly town centre local, this attractive building of local limestone was originally a Victorian preparatory school. Inside, a low-ceilinged full-length front bar leads to a cosy snug at the rear. The pub has a courtyard plus a garden with a children's play area, with barbecue facilities available for public use. Guest beers are mostly from local breweries. Food is served at lunchtime. Disabled access is via the rear of the pub, and there is a large canopy outside for smokers.
Q☋❀⇋◑⊞♿▲⊟♣⚡▯

Market Rasen

Aston Arms
18 Market Place, LN8 3HL
11-11 (11.30 Fri & Sat); 12-11 Sun
☎ (01673) 842313
John Smith's Bitter; Wells Bombardier; guest beers Ⓗ
A large, popular 1930s mock-Tudor family pub in the town centre. Inside, dark wood panelling and beams feature, with an open-plan table and seating area wrapped around a central bar. Food is served every day (service ends 6.30pm Fri-Sun). Rugby events are shown on the large-screen TV and pub games include shove ha'penny. The guest beer changes frequently during the week. The

outside courtyard includes a heated and covered area. ❀◑♿⇌⊟(3)♣P⅃

Messingham

Bird in the Barley

Northfield Road, DN17 3SQ (½ mile from Messingham on A159)

⏲ 11.30-3.30, 5.30-11; closed Mon; 11.30-4, 5.30-10.30 Sun

☎ (01724) 764744

Jennings Sneck Lifter; Marston's Pedigree; guest beers Ⓗ

A mix of traditional and modern design, the interior features oak beams and wooden flooring, with a purpose-built conservatory at the rear mainly for diners (booking advisable). A seating area at one end of the pub includes leather sofas and armchairs, and low tables specifically for drinkers. There are two beer gardens, one with a large umbrella-type canopy and heater. CAMRA Cyclops tasting notes are on the handpumps. ♨❀◑♿P⅃

Horn Inn

61 High Street, DN17 3NU

⏲ 11-11 (midnight Fri & Sat)

☎ (01724) 762426

John Smith's Bitter; guest beers Ⓗ

Friendly, family-run village pub on the A159. Locals and visitors alike enjoy two guest beers drawn from the excellent SIBA list, and can choose from three distinctive drinking areas. Real fires warm the pub in the winter and a small patio is popular in spring and summer. Excellent home-made food is available at lunchtime. Entertainment includes a Monday quiz night and live music on Wednesday and some Saturdays. A large-screen TV is used selectively. ♨Q❀◑♿⊟♣P

Moulton

Swan ✔

13 High Street, PE12 6QB

⏲ 11 (12 Sun)-2.00am

☎ (01406) 370349

Tetley Bitter; Wells Bombardier; guest beers Ⓗ

A church, windmill and pub form a handsome trinity in this Fenland village. This family-run pub continues to thrive with a proven formula of good home-cooked food (Saturday breakfast is recommended), a range of ales plus a local guest and Weston's Old Rosie in polypins, and a warm and comfortable atmosphere. A pub for everyone, youngsters are catered for both in the garden and in a new family room. The pub stays open late but last entry is 11pm. The smoking area is heated and covered. ♨☕❀🛏◑⊟⊟(505)♣●P⅃

Moulton Chapel

Wheatsheaf

4 Fengate, PE12 0XL

⏲ 12-3 (not Mon), 5.30 (7 Sat)-11; 12-3, 7-10.30 Sun

☎ (01406) 380525

Beer range varies Ⓗ

The heart of this unspoilt Fenland pub is the quarry-tiled bar with its original range and stack of logs. Real life prevails here with no TV, muzak or machines. A reliable pint, often of something unexpected, and quality home-cooked food (not served Mon or Sat lunch, Mon and Tue eve) reflect the landlord and landlady's care and enthusiasm. Diners have a choice of two very pleasant rooms, both warmed by real fires in winter. Weston's cider is from polypins. ♨Q❀◑⅄⊟♣●P

Nettleham

Plough

1 The Green, LN2 2NR

⏲ 12-11

☎ (01522) 750275

Bateman XB, seasonal beers; guest beers Ⓗ

Stone-built traditional village local situated on the green. This Batemans pub has a single bar with low ceilings and exposed beams. Brass and copper artefacts are displayed around the room. Established in 1690, the inn had a period of life as a manorial court house in the 18th century. A speciality of the bar menu is traditional fish and chips (Friday only), with generous portions of fresh Grimsby Haddock. Upstairs is a mock-Tudor long-gallery style dining room. ◑⊟♣

North Kelsey

Butcher's Arms

Middle Street, LN7 6EH

⏲ 4-midnight (1.30am Fri); 12-1.30am Sat; 12-midnight Sun

☎ (01652) 678002

Tom Wood Best Bitter, Harvest Bitter; guest beers Ⓗ

Pubs do not come much more traditional than this gem, tucked away in an attractive village setting. An open-plan design features simple rustic furnishings and a large hop bine suspended above the bar. Photos of village life are displayed, along with beer memorabilia. Two Tom Wood beers are permanently stocked, plus a guest beer, the latter sourced from far and wide. A third Tom Wood beer may be added at busy times. Table skittles is played. The building is fronted by an attractive garden drinking area containing mature trees. ♨❀♿♣P⅃

Oasby

Houblon Arms ✔

Village Street, NG32 3NB

⏲ 12-2, 6.30-11; closed Tue; 12-2.30, 7-10 Sun

☎ (01529) 455215

Everards Tiger; guest beers Ⓗ

This local CAMRA Pub of the Year 2008 is not to be missed. A traditional English village pub, it nestles at the village centre and its traditional flagstone floor, open real fire and large inglenook are notable features. Excellent home-cooked food is served every day except Sunday. B&B accommodation is provided in four cottages. The pub is named after the first governor of the Bank of England – John Houblon. Local micro-breweries are featured, including Newby Wyke and Oldershaws. ♨Q❀🛏◑♿●P

Old Bolingbroke

Black Horse Inn

Moat Lane, PE23 4HH

✪ 12.30 (3.30 winter)-11; 12.30-10.30 Sun

☎ (01790) 763388

Bateman Dark Mild; Wold Top Wold Gold; Young's Bitter; guest beers ⊞

This fine old country inn, with its origins in the 17th century and extended in 1930, has history on its doorstep, with castle remains and the roses of Henry IV and the Duke of Lancaster. Guest beers are usually from micro-breweries and change regularly. Weston's Old Rosie cider is always available too. Excellent food is sourced locally, with fresh fish direct from Grimsby docks. Booking for meals is advisable, especially for the many themed celebratory meals. No food served Monday or Tuesday. ♨Q❀♿Å♣●P⍀

Pinchbeck

Bull Inn ✔

1 Knight Street, PE11 3RA (on B1356)

✪ 12-2.30, 5.30-midnight; 12-midnight Sat & Sun

☎ (01775) 723022

John Smith's Bitter; guest beers ⊞

Situated on the main junction in the village, opposite the green which still has the old stocks. The Bull has two comfortable bars: the public bar with a log fire, and the lounge used mainly for dining. A carved bull's head features on the long bar front, with the bar rail representing its horns. The pub has a reputation for good food, from bar snacks to meals in the upstairs restaurant. Guest beers change regularly, often coming from local micros. ♨Q❀◐◑⊟♿⊋P⍀

Rothwell

Blacksmith's Arms

Wold View, Hill Rise, LN7 6AZ

✪ 12-3, 5-midnight; 12-midnight Fri & Sat; 12-11 Sun

☎ (01472) 371300

Black Sheep Best Bitter; Tom Wood Shepherd's Delight; guest beers ⊞

Popular with walkers, with the Viking Way close by, the pub has drinking areas outside at the front and at the rear. The interior is pleasantly decorated, with a coal fire creating a warm atmosphere during the winter months. There is a separate restaurant but food is also served in the bars. The local Tom Wood beer from Highwood is a regular here. Local CAMRA Country Pub of the Year 2007. ♨Q❀◐◑♿♣P⍀

Saxilby

Anglers

65 High Street, LN1 2HA

✪ 11.30-2.30, 6-11; 11.30-11 Fri & Sat; 12-10.30 Sun

☎ (01522) 702200

Greene King IPA; Theakston Best Bitter; guest beers ⊞

A village pub, home to crib, darts, dominoes, pool and football teams. The landlord and many regulars are loyal Lincoln City supporters – ask about the gnome. A large TV screen is used for major sporting events. Local societies meet in the lounge bar, which has many photos of old Saxilby. Originally known as the Railway Hotel during the 1840s, the name changed because many anglers came to fish the nearby Fossdyke, England's oldest canal. Guest beers are from the Scottish & Newcastle list. ❀⊟⇌⊋♣P⍀

Scamblesby

Green Man

Old Main Road, LN11 9XG (off A153 Louth to Horncastle road)

✪ 12-2.30, 5-midnight; 12-midnight Thu-Sun

☎ (01507) 343282

Black Sheep Best Bitter; Young's Bitter; guest beers ⊞

Welcoming village pub in picturesque Wolds countryside, popular with walkers and visitors to Cadwell Park race circuit just a mile away. Accommodation is available, together with traditional good value meals, served until 8.30pm. A spacious main bar and a quiet lounge are both patrolled by Harry the pub dog. Lots of motorcycle memorabilia is on display. The guest beer usually changes every month. ♨Q♉❀⇌◐◑⊟♿Å♣P⍀

Scotter

White Swan

9 The Green, DN21 3UD (off A159 into village)

✪ 5-midnight; 11.30-1am Fri & Sat; 11.30-midnight Sun

☎ (01724) 762342 🌐 whiteswanscotter.co.uk

Black Sheep Best Bitter; John Smith's Bitter; Tom Wood Bomber County; guest beers ⊞

Olde-worlde beamed inn with later extensions for dining and functions. It has two bars on different levels: a traditional lounge and a more modern extension with a bar and cocktail lounge. The raised dining area has views over the river and beer garden, with picnic tables. Three regular real ales are served plus two guest beers, the latter generally from independent brewers. Accommodation is available. Q❀⇌◐◑P

Scotton

Three Horseshoes

Westgate, DN21 3QX

✪ 12-3 Wed, Sat & Sun only, 6-11

☎ (01724) 761129

Greene King IPA; Tetley Bitter; guest beers ⊞

Unspoilt rural village pub popular with locals and visitors owing to its unique Black Rock Grill on Wednesday, Thursday and Saturday evenings when you can cook your own meat or fish on a slab of volcanic rock. Traditional meals are also available – pie and peas night is Friday. The pub is cosy, with tiled floors, cast iron stoves, low ceilings and two public bars, plus a dining room and outdoor covered patio. Pub games are played and there are regular quiz nights. Q❀⊟♣P⍀

Scunthorpe

Berkeley

Doncaster Road, DN15 7DS (½ mile from end of M181)

✪ 11.30-2.30, 5-11; 11.30-11 Fri & Sat; 12-10.30 Sun

Samuel Smith OBB Ⓗ
Large 1930s Samuel Smith's hotel decorated in period style, 30 minutes' walk from the town centre. The interior comprises four rooms: a dining room, function room, lounge and public bar at the rear of the building with a separate entrance. Landscaped at the front, it has a beer garden at the rear. Lunchtime meals are available Thursday to Sunday, evening meals Thursday to Saturday. The pub may close on some football match days. ♔Q❀⇔◐◑⊟♿🚌P⚡

Blue Bell ✔
1-7 Oswald Road, DN15 7PU (at town centre crossroads)
⏲ 9am-midnight (1am Fri-Sun)
☎ (01724) 863921
Greene King IPA, Abbot; Marston's Pedigree; guest beers Ⓗ
Popular Wetherspoon pub with an open-plan layout on two levels. The upper level is a designated family area, with guarded fires and tables for dining. The lower level has wooden flooring and a mix of high and low tables and seating. The pub holds regular beer festivals and theme nights such as Hallowe'en and Burns Night. Food is served daily lunchtimes and evenings. A patio area at the rear has year-round picnic tables with overhead heating and can be used for smoking. Q❀◐◑⇌🚌⚡

Malt Shovel
219 Ashby High Street, Ashby, DN16 2JP (in Ashby Broadway shopping area)
⏲ 10-11 (midnight Fri & Sat)
☎ (01724) 843318
Exmoor Gold; John Smith's Bitter; guest beers Ⓗ
This thriving town pub situated in a busy shopping area is decorated in traditional style, with timber beams and country-style furnishings. It goes from strength to strength thanks to enlightened, enthusiastic licensees, and is popular for its good value, home-cooked meals, available lunchtime and evenings. Four constantly changing guest beers are featured, plus a real cider or perry on draught. Week-long beer festivals are staged in autumn and winter. Quiz nights are held on Tuesday and Thursday. Snooker facilities are available in the adjoining members-only social club. ❀◐◑🚌●

Skegness

Red Lion
Lumley Road, PE25 2DU
⏲ 9-midnight (1am Fri & Sat)
☎ (01754) 612567
Bateman XXXB; Greene King Abbot; Marston's Pedigree; guest beers Ⓗ
Large open plan pub with friendly staff, catering for all ages. It has a homely decor with wood panelling and local memorabilia adorning the walls. Both food and beer are well priced, with a regularly changing range of guest ales on offer. A separate dining area leads off the main bar. Several comfy sofas are grouped around the fire. ❀◐◑♿⇌🚌⚡

Skendleby

Blacksmith Arms
Main Road, PE23 4QE
⏲ 12-midnight; 12-3, 5.30-midnight winter; 12-2, 7-11 Sun
☎ (01754) 890662
Bateman XB; guest beers Ⓗ
Built in the 1750s, this cosy country pub set in an attractive Wolds village has a low-beamed ceiling in its snug bar, which also contains settles and a roaring fire in a period fireplace. The cellar can be viewed through a glass panel behind the bar. One of the two dining rooms has an old well and fine views. A cottage is available for overnight accommodation. ♔Q❀◐◑🚌♣P⚡

Sleaford

Marquis of Granby ✔
Westgate, NG34 7PU
⏲ 11-midnight; 12-11.30 Sun
☎ (01529) 303223
Greene King Abbot; guest beers Ⓗ
A small, no-frills pub located a short distance from the market place. Originally a private house, it was converted to a pub under the Beer House Act of 1830. Its history is described on a display above the fireplace.The pub holds occasional themed evenings, and for musicians there is an acoustic jam session on the third Sunday of the month. ♔❀◐⇌🚌⚡

Snitterby

Royal Oak
High Street, DN21 4TE (off A15)
⏲ 5 (12 Sat)-11; 12-10.30 Sun
☎ (01673) 818273
Wold Top Bitter, Wold Gold; guest beers Ⓗ
Good old-fashioned community village pub, offering up to six real ales and a friendly, warm welcome. A recent renovation has created a traditional but light and airy interior with wooden floors and real fires. Outside, a seating area overlooks the stream. High-quality food, sourced locally, is served and B&B is available in three en-suite double rooms. This pub was in the first edition of the Guide in 1973 and has won CAMRA Local Pub of the Season within six months of new ownership. ♔Q❀⇔◐◑⊟▲♣●P

South Ferriby

Nelthorpe Arms
School Lane, DN18 6HW (off A1077 Scunthorpe to Barton road)
⏲ 12 (3 Mon)-midnight
☎ (01652) 635235
Tetley Bitter; guest beers Ⓗ
A two-roomed village pub at the centre of the community, featuring a public bar with pool, darts and dominoes, plus a dining room serving home-cooked meals. The basic but welcoming bar always has Tetley Bitter, complemented by a variety of guest beers including those from Naylor's Brewery of Keighley. Live bands feature on Saturday evenings, with an open mic night on the first Thursday of every month. Accommodation is

available in four en-suite rooms.

South Kyme

Hume
High Street, LN4 4AD
11.30-2.30, 6-11; 12-3, 6-11 Sun
(01526) 869143
Greene King IPA, Abbot; guest beers
Situated in a quiet village, this country inn stands opposite the Kyme Eau where narrow boats often visit, especially for the May bank holiday gatherings. The pub was previously known as the Hume Arms and before that the Simon de Kyme. The Hume underwent tasteful interior refurbishment in 2006 and now offers excellent food menus. Two en-suite rooms are also available. A bus service stops near the pub twice per day.

South Ormsby

Massingberd Arms
Brinkhill Road, LN11 8QS (1½ miles from A16)
12-2.30, 6-11; 12-11 Wed-Sat; 12-10.30 Sun
(01507) 480492
Beer range varies
This pub, named after the local lord of the manor, is not on a main thoroughfare, but has a well-beaten track to its door by lovers of good food and beer. The ale range is constantly changing. The pub is a great stopping-off point for walkers and cyclists in a beautiful area of the country, on the edge of the Lincolnshire Wolds. Guide dogs only are admitted.

Spalding

Lincoln Arms
4 Bridge Street, PE11 1XA
11-3, 7-12.30am; 11-12.30am Sat; 11-4, 7-midnight Sun
(01775) 710017
Marston's Mansfield Cask Ale; guest beers
A welcome return to the Guide for this traditional 18th-century local, popular with drinkers of all ages. Located by the town bridge overlooking the River Welland, this welcoming pub has an open-plan layout and a serving hatch to the pool area. Pub games are popular, with teams in the local darts, cribbage and pool leagues. Spalding Folk Club meets informally on the second Thursday of the month for a jamming session.

Red Lion Hotel
Market Place, PE11 1SU
10 (12 Sun)-midnight
(01775) 722869 redlionhotel-spalding.co.uk
Draught Bass; Fuller's London Pride; Greene King Abbot; Marston's Pedigree
This 18th-century family-run town centre hotel is popular with locals as well as with visitors to Spalding and the many attractions in the area. It offers well-kept cask ales and tasty snacks and bar meals. There is a separate dining room open every evening except Sunday. The Spalding Blues Club meets here (check the website for dates).

Stamford

Green Man
29 Scotgate, PE9 2YQ
11 (12 Sun)-midnight
(01780) 753598
Caledonian Deuchars IPA; guest beers
This stone-built former coaching inn dates from 1796 and features a split-level L-shaped bar serving guest beers mainly from micro-breweries together with a good range of European bottled beers and up to seven traditional ciders. The secluded patio includes a covered area for smokers and hosts beer festivals at Easter and during September.

Jolly Brewer
1 Foundry Road, PE9 2PP
12-midnight (11.30 Sun)
(01780) 755141
Black Sheep Best Bitter; Oakham JHB; guest beers
Three hundred-year-old stone-built pub with an L-shaped room around the bar and a small dining area. The pub has a strong community spirit and fields teams in darts, dominoes, cribbage and pool. Push penny is also played. Traditional pub grub and Sunday lunches are popular. A good range of single malt whiskies is on offer. B&B accommodation is planned for Summer 2008. The pub has Wi-Fi Internet access.

Tobie Norris
12 St Paul's Street, PE9 2BE
12-11 (10.30 Sun)
(01780) 753800
Beer range varies
Parts of this stone building date back to circa 1280 and in 1617 it was bought by Tobias Norris and used as a bell foundry. Purchased by the RAFA in 1952, it remained as its club until Mick Thurlby purchased it, refurbished it and turned it into the superb pub it is today. Nooks and crannies are everywhere, with an unmissable arched ceiling upstairs. Four handpumps serve beers from regionals, micro-breweries and Ufford Ales. Pizzas with unusual toppings are the speciality of the house, as is the friendly welcome. Local CAMRA Pub of the Year 2008.

Surfleet

Ship Inn
154 Reservoir Road, PE11 4DH (off A16, S of A152 jct, follow brown signs)
11.30-3, 6-11 (midnight Fri & Sat); 12-3, 7-10.30 Sun
(01775) 680547 shipinnsurfleet.com
Adnams Broadside; guest beers
Rebuilt in 2004, all that remains of the original pub are some flagstones in the entrance and a model on the bar. The McMillan Way footpath passes the pub which is on the banks of the River Glen, a popular area for dinghy sailors and walkers. Lunchtime meals are served in a comfortable bar with a wood-burning stove, while an upstairs restaurant has views over the river (no food Sun eve or Mon). Four guest bedrooms are available and tables on the terrace are used for outdoor drinking.

Swinhope

Click'em Inn

LN8 6BS (2 miles N of Binbrook on B1203)
12-3 (not Mon), 7-11 (11.30 Fri); 12-11.30 Sat; 12-3, 7-10.30 Sun
(01472) 398253
Bateman XXXB; Shepherd Neame Spitfire; Tom Wood Shepherd's Delight; guest beers ⊞
Country pub set in the picturesque Lincolnshire Wolds. The unusual name originates from the counting of sheep through a nearby clicking gate. Its location makes it a popular stopping point for walkers and cyclists. Good home-cooked food served in the bar and conservatory attracts both locals and diners. The pub stocks two guest beers at any one time, as well as real cider. A covered but unheated area outside is provided for smokers. Q❀◐♣●P⁻

Tattershall Thorpe

Blue Bell Inn

Thorpe Road, LN4 4PE
12-3, 7-11 (10.30 Sun)
(01526) 342206
Greene King IPA; Tom Wood Bomber County, Dambuster; guest beers ⊞
A gem of a pub in a delightful location. You step back in time when you enter this lovely 13th-century inn, one of Lincolnshire's oldest. There is a large open fire with beamed ceilings covered in signed photos from World War II RAF squadrons who used the pub, including the famous Dambusters. Food is served in the bar and dining room. Three ales are usually on offer plus ever-changing guest beers. Tom Wood brews Dambuster exclusively for the pub. There is a camp site close by.
⌂Q❀◐♿▲♣P⁻

Thornton Curtis

Thornton Hunt Inn

DN39 6XW (on A1077 between Wooton and Barton)
12-3, 6.30-11
(01469) 531252 thornton-inn.co.uk
Taylor Landlord; Tom Wood Shepherd's Delight ⊞
One mile from the ruins of Thornton Abbey, this Grade II-listed village local dates from the 1850s – its rustic charm enhanced by wood panelling, beams, brasses and prints of rural life. A traditional bar menu concentrates on fresh home-cooked food made with local produce, also served in a separate dining room in the evening. Two real ales are always on offer, with a third added frequently. The garden area includes a children's fun trail. Accommodation is available in six en-suite rooms. ❀⇌◐♿⊟P⁻

Threekingham

Three Kings Inn

Saltersway, NG34 0AU
12-3, 6-11; closed Mon; 12-3, 6-10.30 Sun
(01529) 240249 threekingsinn.co.uk
Draught Bass; Taylor Landlord; guest beers ⊞
A traditional country inn that manages to be progressive without losing its character. A comfortable lounge/bar contains attractive rural prints and a panelled dining room serving locally-sourced food is deservedly popular with locals and visitors.The pub name refers to the slaying of three Danish chieftains in a battle at nearby Stow in 870; look for the effigies above the entrance. The village was established at the crossroads of the Roman Mareham Lane and Salter's Way, the trade route linking Droitwich's salt production to the Wash. ⌂❀◐▲P⁻

Upton

Rose & Crown

30 High Street, DN21 5NQ (opp church)
5 (12 Sat & Sun)-11
(01427) 838216
Beer range varies ⊞
Busy village pub originally built by the local (now defunct) Hewitts Brewery to serve American servicemen during the 1950s. There is a large bar with a lounge and adjoining function room that caters for weddings and parties. Outside is a covered patio and beer garden. The pub is home to football, cricket and darts teams, and regular themed nights are hosted. Charity quizzes are held most Thursdays. Dogs are allowed in the bar.
❀⊟♣P⁻⊡

Waddington

Three Horseshoes

Old High Street, LN5 9RF
3-11; 12-midnight Fri; 11-midnight Sat; 12-11 Sun
(01522) 720448
John Smith's Bitter; guest beers ⊞
This two-bar pub, family run for the last 19 years, is a splendid example of a proper English local. The ever-changing guest beers come from many micro-brewers. Home to football, cricket, darts and fishing teams, the pub also hosts adult learning classes. Recent charity quiz nights have provided goats for Africa. The shove ha'penny board is regularly used. Thursday night features bingo. Outside is a heated, covered area for smokers. Dogs are welcome. ⌂❀⊟⊟(1,13)♣P⁻

Wainfleet

Batemans Visitor Centre ✓

Salem Bridge Brewery, Mill Lane, PE24 4JE
11.30-3.30 (not winter Mon or Tue); evenings by appointment
(01754) 880317 bateman.co.uk
Bateman Dark Mild, XB, Salem Porter, XXXB, seasonal beers ⊞
Could there be a more appropriate place to sample those Good Honest Ales than at source in the Mill Bar at the base of the iconic windmill? Bateman's core range is generally always available plus its seasonal beers. A range of Lincolnshire food specialities is also offered. The bar adjoins the Brewery Experience exhibition with its interesting and idiosyncratic displays. Outside is a large outdoor games area. Wainfleet's proximity to

golden beaches and other attractions makes this an ideal day out. Q❀◑⊟♿Å⇌⊟♣P⁵–⊡

Westwoodside

Carpenters Arms

Newbigg, DN9 2AT
⏲ 2 (12 Sun)-midnight
☎ (01427) 752416 🌐 thecarps.co.uk
John Smith's Bitter; Taylor Landlord; Wells Bombardier; guest beers Ⓗ
A popular village local, there has been an inn on this site since 1861. The lounge is spread over two levels, and there are ambitious plans to extend the pub further. Increasing the range of beers on offer has proved a popular move with locals and real ale enthusiasts from a wider area. A second guest beer has recently been introduced. There is a covered and heated smokers' area. Winner of Doncaster CAMRA Pub of the Season award for summer 2007. ❀⊟⊟P⁵–

Willingham by Stow

Fox & Hounds

Gainsborough Road, DN21 5JX (on B1241, half a mile N of village) SK863877
⏲ 12-midnight
☎ (01427) 788274
John Smith's Bitter; guest beers Ⓗ
A friendly pub with a good, reasonably priced menu. Although a limited selection of real ale is available, the beer is well-kept, the pub is spotless, and the landlord is always welcoming. Meals are served in the pub's dining rooms. A new B&B annex has five rooms. ❀⊟◑⊟P⁵–

Half Moon

23 High Street, DN21 5JZ (200m from B1241 jct)
⏲ 12-3 (not Mon & Tue), 6-11; 12-11 Fri & Sat; 12-10.30 Sun
☎ (01427) 788340
Grafters Original, Over the Moon, Brewers Troop; guest beers Ⓗ
Home to the Grafters Brewery, this popular village inn goes from strength to strength. Long established regular ales now compete for space alongside the new Grafters range. Home-cooked meals are a must, especially the renowned fish and chip suppers (food served Thu-Sat eves; Fri & Sat lunchtime). The pub is home to the local football team and is involved in many local fundraising events. It also hosts a beer festival in summer.
⛫Q◑⊟⊟♣●⁵–

Willoughby

Willougby Arms

Church Lane, LN13 9SU (on Alford to Skegness road)
⏲ 12-2 (not Mon; 3 Sat & Sun), 7-11
☎ (01507) 462387
Bateman XB; guest beers Ⓗ
This village inn has a proud 300-year connection with Captain John Smith of Pocahontas fame – the bell from his ship hangs above the coal fire in the lounge. The pub celebrates St Patrick's Day and other events throughout the year. The bar has an L-shaped drinking area, dispensing guest beers that often reflect seasonal or calendar events. The restaurant menu changes on a weekly basis and booking is essential. Well-behaved dogs are welcome. ⛫❀◑♣P

Wragby

Turnor Arms

Market Place, LN8 5QU
⏲ 12-11 (midnight Fri & Sat)
☎ (01673) 858205
Tom Wood Best Bitter, Shepherd's Delight, seasonal beers; guest beers Ⓗ
Tom Wood's Highwood Brewery leases the ground floor of this imposing building, originally a coaching inn. A recent refurbishment gives the pub a modern feel. The plain public bar has darts and TV, while the comfortably furnished lounge opens into a large dining area. Hearty home-cooked meals made with locally produced ingredients are served. Acoustic music nights are held each month and the local branch of the Harley Davidson Riders Club holds its bi-monthly meeting here. Weston's traditional scrumpy cider is available. Q◑⊟⊟(6,10)●P⁵–

Wrangle

Angel Inn

Church End, PE22 9EW (opp church)
⏲ 12-midnight
☎ (01205) 870315
Bateman XB; Everards Tiger Ⓗ
A welcoming village local, this free house has separate public and lounge bars plus a restaurant. Pool and darts teams play in the public bar and football is screened on TV. The walls of the quiet lounge bar are covered with photographs of old Wrangle and the surrounding area. Excellent value home-cooked food can be served in the bars if requested, with full meals available in the restaurant. Sunday lunch is a carvery (booking advised) and there is a senior citizens' lunch on Friday. The outdoor smoking area is heated.
Q❀⊟◑⊟♿⊟(7)♣P⁵–

Sailors arms

Up the street, in the Sailors Arms, Sinbad Sailors, grandson of Mary Ann Sailors, drew a pint in the sunlit bar. The ship's clock in the bar says half past eleven. Half past eleven is opening time. The hands of the clock have stayed still at half past eleven for fifty years. It is always opening time in the Sailors Arms.
Dylan Thomas, Under Milk Wood

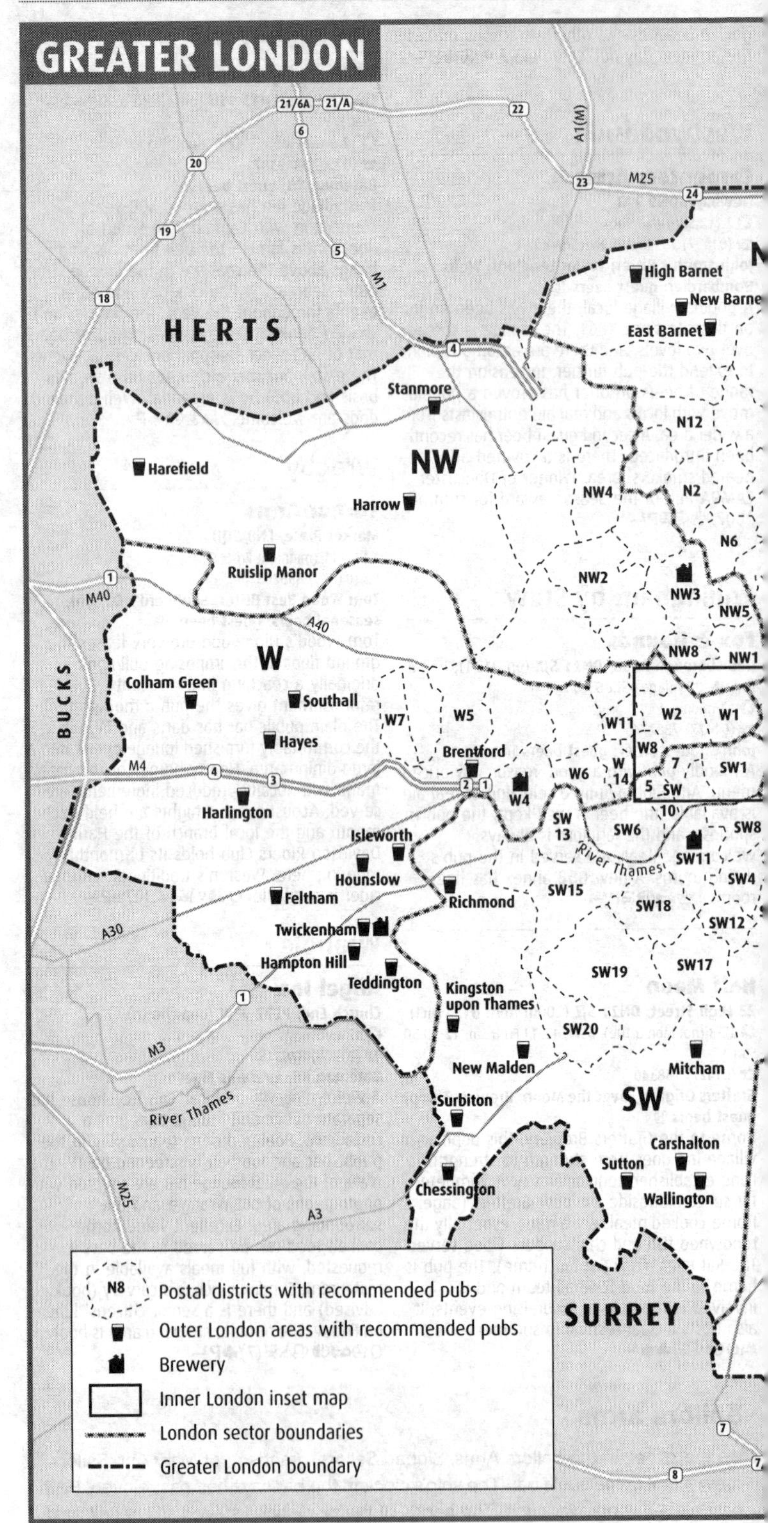
GREATER LONDON
HERTS
BUCKS
SURREY
NW
W
SW
High Barnet
New Barnet
East Barnet
Stanmore
Harefield
Harrow
Ruislip Manor
Colham Green
Southall
Hayes
Harlington
Isleworth
Hounslow
Feltham
Richmond
Brentford
Twickenham
Hampton Hill
Teddington
Kingston upon Thames
New Malden
Surbiton
Chessington
Mitcham
Carshalton
Sutton
Wallington
River Thames
N12
N2
N6
NW4
NW2
NW3
NW5
NW8
NW1
W2
W1
W8
W11
W14
W7
W5
W6
W4
SW1
SW10
SW13
SW6
SW8
SW11
SW4
SW15
SW18
SW12
SW17
SW19
SW20
M25
M1
M40
M4
M3
A1(M)
A40
A30
A3
N8
Postal districts with recommended pubs
Outer London areas with recommended pubs
Brewery
Inner London inset map
London sector boundaries
Greater London boundary

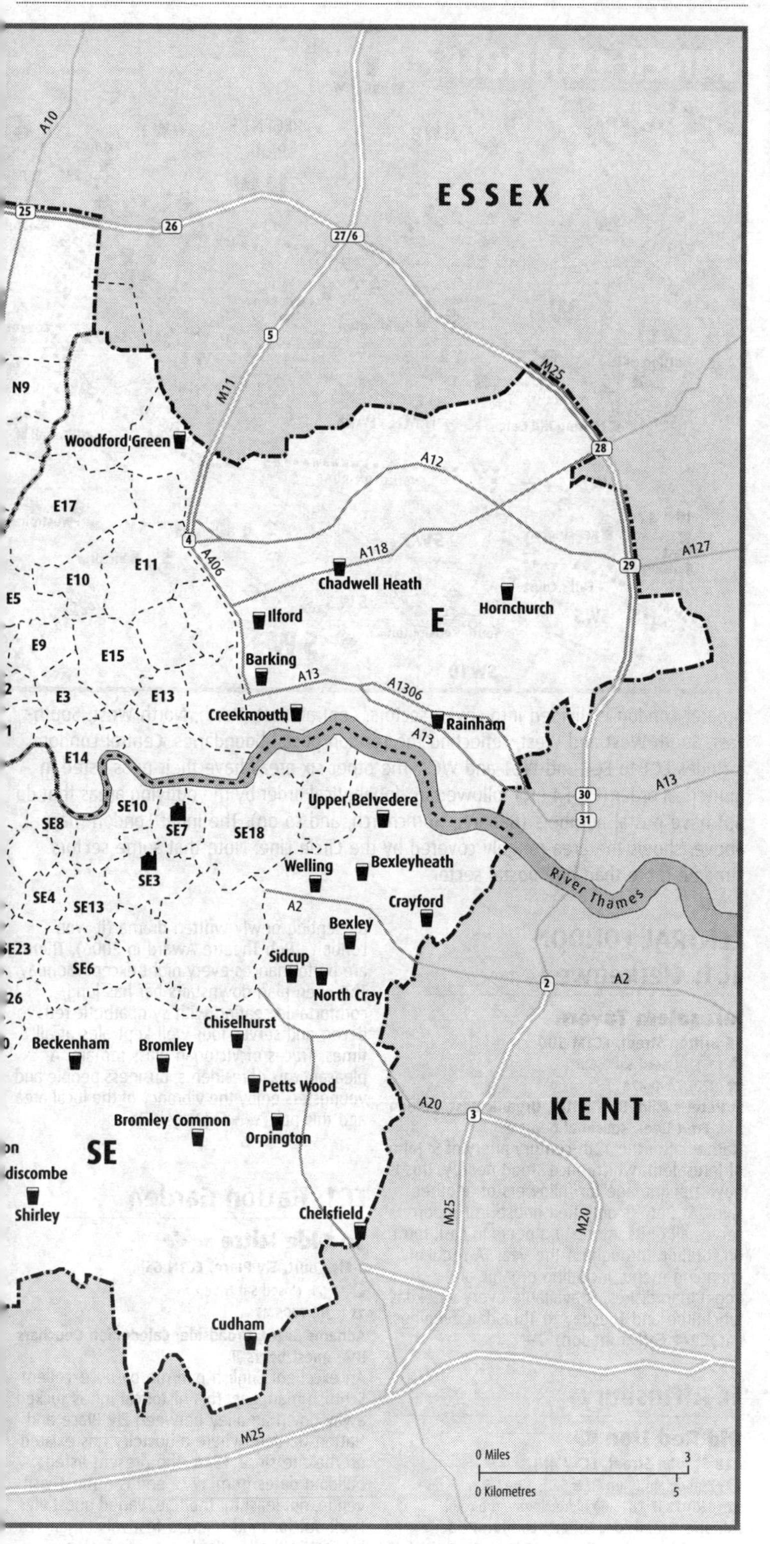

ESSEX
KENT
A10
25
26
27/6
5
M11
M25
28
A12
A127
29
4
A406
A118
Chadwell Heath
Hornchurch
Ilford
E
Barking
A13
A1306
Creekmouth
Rainham
N9
Woodford Green
E17
E11
E10
E5
E9
E15
E3
E13
E14
SE10
SE8
SE7
SE18
SE3
SE4
SE13
SE6
Upper Belvedere
Bexleyheath
Welling
Crayford
Bexley
Sidcup
North Cray
A2
2
30
31
River Thames
Chiselhurst
Beckenham
Bromley
Petts Wood
Bromley Common
Orpington
A20
3
SE
Shirley
Chelsfield
M20
Cudham
0 Miles
3
0 Kilometres
5

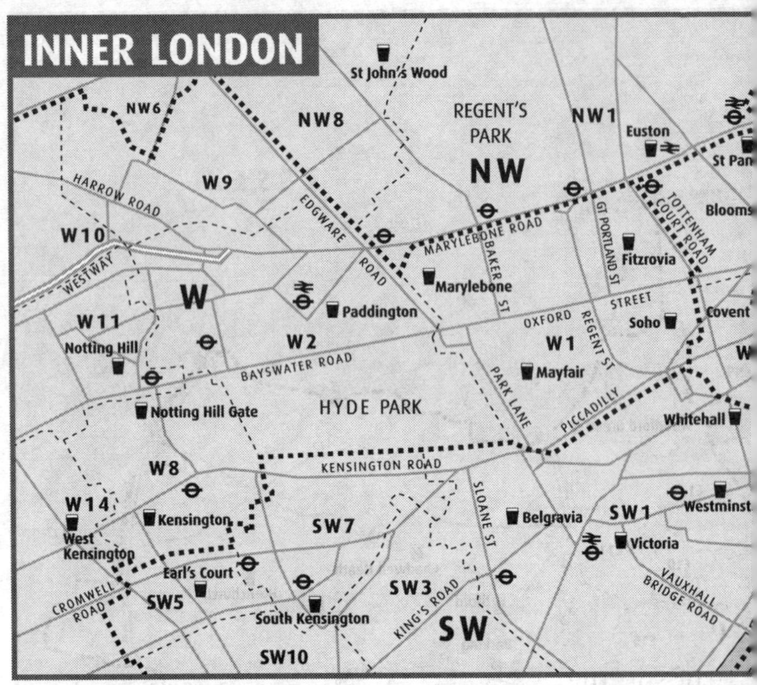

Greater London is divided into seven sectors: Central, East, North, North-West, South-East, South-West and West, reflecting the London postal boundaries. Central London includes EC1 to EC4 and WC1 and WC2. The other six areas have their pubs listed in numerical order (E1, E4 etc) followed in alphabetical order by the outlying areas that do not have postal numbers (Barking, Hornchurch, and so on). The Inner London map, above, shows the area roughly covered by the Circle Line. Note that some sectors straddle more than one postal sector.

CENTRAL LONDON

EC1: Clerkenwell

Jerusalem Tavern

55 Britton Street, EC1M 5UQ

11-11; closed Sat & Sun

(020) 7490 4281

St Peter's Mild, Best Bitter, Organic Best, Golden Ale, Fruit Beer, seasonal beers H

Named after the 12th-century priory of St John of Jerusalem, which once stood nearby, this is now a pilgrimage for followers of another saint. St Peter's only tied house in London serves all of its interesting beers in cask form, on rotation throughout the year. A regularly changing menu, including organic and vegetarian dishes, is available every weekday lunchtime and Tuesday to Thursday evenings. ⊖(Farringdon)

EC1: Finsbury

Old Red Lion ✔

418 St John Street, EC1V 4NJ

12-midnight (1am Fri & Sat); 12-11 Sun

(020) 7837 7816 oldredliontheatre.co.uk

Adnams Broadside; Fuller's London Pride; Greene King Abbot; Harveys Sussex Best Bitter H

This Victorian pub near the Angel, Islington has had a studio theatre upstairs since the 1970s, presenting newly written drama (it won London's Pub Theatre Award in 2006). There are performances every night except Monday. The open-plan downstairs bar has long, comfortable seating with sympathetic red decor, and serves four well-kept ales at all times. Traces of Victorian glass remain. A pleasant mix of residents, business people and youngsters enjoy the vibrancy of the local area and this pub. ⊖(Angel)

EC1: Hatton Garden

Ye Olde Mitre ★ ✔

1 Ely Court, Ely Place, EC1N 6SJ

11-11; closed Sat & Sun

(020) 7405 4751

Adnams Bitter, Broadside; Caledonian Deuchars IPA; guest beers H

An excellent English pub run by an excellent Scottish manager. This historical inn is tucked away down an alley between Ely Place and Hatton Garden, where a hostelry has existed on the site since 1546. The present listed building dates from 1772 and is a must-visit venue, not least for the fine, varied guest ales. Look out for mini themed festivals organised by Scottie the landlord. It opens for one weekend only during the Great British Beer Festival. A National Inventory entry and local

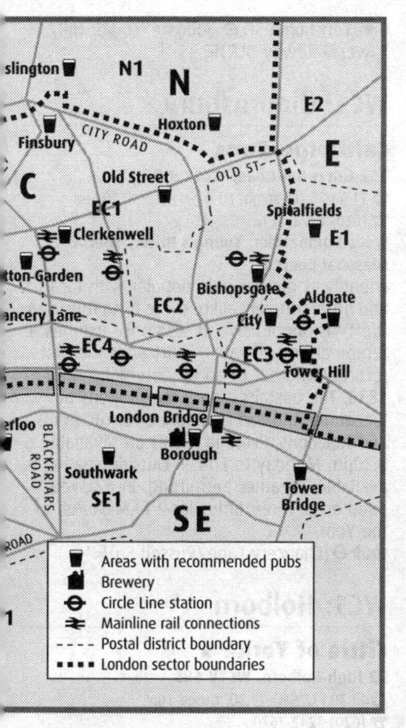

CAMRA Pub of the Year 2008.
Q❀⊟⇌(Farringdon)⊖(Chancery Lane)⊟⁻

EC1: Old Street

Masque Haunt ✔

168-172 Old Street, EC1V 9PB
9-midnight (1am Sat); 9-10.30 Sun
☎ (020) 7251 4195
Courage Directors; Greene King IPA, Abbot; guest beers Ⓗ
A light and airy Wetherspoon's corner-shop conversion on the edge of the City. The large pub is split into three areas, so you are able to avoid the TV screens if you so wish. It is a regular outlet for Hamsphire's Itchen Valley beers. Situated 200 metres west of Old Street roundabout, the short walk gives you just enough time to build up a thirst. ◐⊟♿⇌⊖⊟

Old Fountain

3 Baldwin Street, EC1V 9NU
11-11; closed Sat & Sun
☎ (020) 7253 2970
Fuller's London Pride; guest beers Ⓗ
This friendly local, just off City Road with entrances in Baldwin Street and Peerless Street, has a very good policy on guest ales, seeking out new brews and unusual seasonal ales as well as some old favourites. The Old Fountain takes its name from local medieval springs. The upper bar has a large aquarium in the corner, which makes a change from the telly. Lunchtime food includes special salt-beef sandwiches and pizza is available 5-9pm. A winter darts team plays on Wednesday.
❀◐⊟♿⇌⊖⊟

EC2: Bishopsgate

Magpie ✔

12 New Street, EC2M 4TP
11-11; closed Sat & Sun
☎ (020) 7929 3889
Fuller's London Pride; Harveys Sussex Best Bitter; Taylor Landlord; guest beer Ⓗ
Part of Mitchell & Butler's Nicholson chain, the Magpie is situated in a narrow street off Bishopsgate. Food is served in the open plan, bare-boarded bar and in the upstairs restaurant. Pies are a feature of the menu. In common with most pubs in the area, it is very busy with office workers in the early evening, but much quieter later on. The guest beer changes weekly and is usually from a well-known regional brewery.
◐⇌⊖(Liverpool St)⊟

EC3: City

Crosse Keys ✔

9 Gracechurch Street, EC3V 0DR
9-midnight (1am Fri; 7pm Sat); closed Sun
☎ (020) 7623 4824
Greene King IPA, Abbot; Shepherd Neame Spitfire; guest beers Ⓗ
Converted from the 1912 banking hall of the Hong Kong & Shanghai Bank, this large single bar displays its origins, with marble walls and columns. A Chinaman supports the clock at the rear. Several smaller rooms on the ground floor and first floor are available to customers and may be hired for meetings. Drinks are the usual Wetherspoon's staples and weekly guest beers, a recent innovation, concentrate on single breweries. A large-screen TV shows most major sports events.
◐⇌(Cannon St)⊖(Monument)⊟

East India Arms

67 Fenchurch Street, EC3M 4BR
11.30-11; closed Sat & Sun
☎ (020) 7265 5121
Shepherd Neame Master Brew Bitter, Kent's Best, Spitfire, Bishop's Finger Ⓗ
A comfortable, friendly pub just around the corner from Fenchurch Street station, serving the full range of beers from Shepherd Neame. The single open bar has wooden floors and half-panelled walls, while a shelf bar and stalls around the outside walls provide seating. Toilets are downstairs. Tables and chairs outside provide overspill from the bar, as it can get very busy at lunchtime and early evening. Smoking is allowed outside, where heaters are available.
⇌(Fenchurch St)⊖(Aldgate/Tower Hill)⊟⁻

Elephant

119 Fenchurch Street, EC3M 5BA
11-9; closed Sat & Sun
☎ (020) 7623 8970
Wells Bombardier; Young's Bitter, Special, seasonal beer Ⓗ
William Hogarth lived above this Young's pub, which dates from before the Great Fire and was originally called the Elephant & Castle. A reproduction of Hogarth's Marriage a la Mode is in the smaller upstairs bar, which can be entered from Fenchurch Street. The lower bar, accessed from Hogarth Alley, comprises

partitioned seating and wall panels in red and cream, with ample standing room. An extensive food menu is served.
◐≷(Fenchurch St)⊖(Monument)⊟

Jamaica Wine House

St Michael's Alley (off Cornhill), EC3V 9DS
11-11; closed Sat & Sun
☎ (020) 7929 6972
Caledonian Deuchars IPA; Greene King IPA; Wells Bombardier Ⓗ
Hard to find but worth the effort, this pub is tucked away in an alley off Cornhill. Reopened in 2002 and also known as the Jampot, there are three wood and glass partitions that split the bar and drinking area into smaller, more cosy sections. It was originally London's first coffee house and began trading as the Jamaica Wine House in 1869. Along with the church, the alley was destroyed by the Great Fire of London. Q◐≷⊖⊟

Swan ✔

Ship Tavern Passage, 78-80 Gracechurch Street, EC3V 1LY
11-10; closed Sat & Sun
☎ (020) 7283 7712
Fuller's Chiswick Bitter, Discovery, London Pride; guest beer Ⓗ
Small two-bar pub on two floors. The downstairs bar is narrow, with a covered walkway outside that is popular with customers in good weather. The downstairs bar closes at 9pm, with last orders upstairs at 9.30pm, so it is advisable to ring if your visit will be close to these times.
◐≷(Fenchurch St)⊖(Monument)⊟

Wine Lodge

143 Fenchurch Street, EC3M 6BL
11-11 (10 Mon & Tue); closed Sat & Sun
☎ (020) 7283 6114 thewinelodge.com
Wells Bombardier; Young's Bitter, Special; guest beer Ⓗ
Once a privately owned house known as Chapman's, then owned by Young's, now reopened as a free house. It still sells Wells & Young's beers with an occasional guest, often Harveys. During the 1930s it was rebuilt as part of an office development. Two bars are upstairs and one downstairs. The latest owners have replaced the panelling with purple paint, a wooden floor and a skylight.
◐≷(Fenchurch St)⊖(Monument)⊟

EC3: Tower Hill

Peacock

41 Minories, EC3N 1DT
12-midnight; closed Sat & Sun
☎ (020) 7488 3630
Black Sheep Ale; Butcombe Bitter; Harveys Sussex Best Bitter Ⓗ
This busy City pub is situated in the north-west corner of Ibex House, an impressive Grade I-listed building. Today, it is split into two areas: the bar and main seating downstairs, and a pool table along with darts upstairs. Table-top games are kept behind the bar for customers to play. A large-screen TV shows major sports events. The pub is closed at weekends, but can be hired out.
◐≷(Fenchurch St)⊖(Aldgate/Tower Hill/Tower Gateway DLR)⊟

WC1: Bloomsbury

Calthorpe Arms

252 Grays Inn Road, WC1X 8JR
11-11.30 (midnight Fri & Sat); 12-10.30 Sun
☎ (020) 7278 4732
Wells Bombardier; Young's Bitter, Special, seasonal beers Ⓗ
Friendly single-bar pub, popular with locals and office workers alike. There is no music and the TV is unobtrusive. It was once used as a temporary magistrates' court after the first recorded murder of an on-duty policeman in 1830. The upstairs dining room opens at lunchtime and can be booked for meetings and functions. Evening meals are available 6-9.30pm Monday to Friday. Outside seating is available, weather permitting, in a paved patio area. Three times local CAMRA Pub of the Year.
❀◐⊖(Chancery Lane/Russell Sq)⊟

WC1: Holborn

Cittie of Yorke ★

22 High Holborn, WC1V 6BS
11.30 (12 Sat)-11.30; closed Sun
☎ (020) 7242 7670
Samuel Smith OBB Ⓗ
A pub has stood on this site since 1430. In 1695 it was rebuilt as Gray's Inn Coffee House. Now an extensive three-bar pub and Grade II-listed building, the huge main bar includes small wooden drinking booths, a high beamed ceiling and large disused oak barrels over the bar. The front bar is more intimate, with wood panelling and an original chandelier, and the cellar bar is the former cellarage of the original 17th-century coffee house.
⚔Q◐♿≷(Farringdon)⊖(Chancery Lane)⊟♣

Penderel's Oak

283-288 High Holborn, WC1V 7HJ
9-1am
☎ (020) 7242 5669
Fuller's London Pride; Greene King IPA, Abbot; Marston's Pedigree; Shepherd Neame Spitfire; guest beers Ⓗ
Occupying the ground floor and basement of a modern office building, this large, L-shaped Wetherspoon's pub is unusual in that its downstairs bar (available for hire) screens sport with sound or noisy music videos. Often four guest beers are on handpump. French windows face out on to the street, where benches are available for both the hardy and

INDEPENDENT BREWERIES

Battersea SW11
Brew Wharf SE1
Bunker WC2
Florence Herne Hill, SE24 (NEW)
Fuller's W4
Horseshoe NW3
Meantime SE7
Twickenham Twickenham
Zerodegrees SE3

the smoker. A family area at the back of the main bar opens until 9pm, with last food orders at 8.30pm.
Q⚘◑♿⊖(Chancery Lane)🚌⚡

WC1: St Pancras

Mabel's Tavern

9 Mabledon Place, WC1H 9AZ
11-11 (midnight Thu-Sat); 12-10.30 Sun
☎ (020) 7387 7739
Shepherd Neame Master Brew Bitter, Kent's Best, Spitfire, Bishop's Finger, seasonal beers H
Situated off Euston Road, midway between Euston and St Pancras rail stations, this long, narrow single bar with raised sections at each end is busy throughout the day – with local office workers at lunchtime and early evening, and locals and tourists later. Major football and rugby matches are shown on TV screens. There is pavement seating for smokers or alfresco diners in summer. Good value food is available until 9.30pm Monday to Thursday (8.30pm Friday-Sunday). Local CAMRA Pub of the Year 2006. ⚘◑≠⊖🚌⚡

Skinners Arms

114 Judd Street, WC1H 9NT
12-11; closed Sat & Sun
☎ (020) 7837 6521
Greene King IPA, Abbot; Taylor Landlord; guest beer H
Named after the City Livery Company, the pub is located on a street named after a Past Master of the Company and Lord Mayor. It sports a mock Victorian decor in a long room, with a smaller, more private room to the rear and pavement seating outside. It is popular with local office workers at lunchtime and after work. Good food is available lunchtimes and evenings (not Fri eve). There are plans to hold three or four beer festivals annually.
⚘◑≠⊖🚌⚡

WC2: Chancery Lane

Knights Templar ✔

95 Chancery Lane, WC2A 1DT
9-11.30; 11-5 Sat; closed Sun
☎ (020) 7831 2660
Fuller's London Pride; Greene King Abbot; Marston's Pedigree; Shepherd Neame Spitfire; guest beers H
Spacious Wetherspoon conversion of a former bank. A mixed clientele includes the Inns of Court, the London School of Economics and the local building site. A black metal crusader on his charger sits behind the bar to ensure peace is kept. There are 12 handpumps but three or four can be duplicates. The cider is Weston's Old Rosie cider. Free Wi-Fi Internet access.
◑⊖🍎

Seven Stars

53 Carey Street, WC2A 2JB
10.30-11; 11-10.30 Sun
☎ (020) 7242 8521
Adnams Bitter, Broadside; Harveys Sussex Best Bitter; guest beers H
Heaving with law-courts trade during the week, the pub remains comfortably busy at the weekend. A central drinking area in front of the bar leads to separate rooms on either side. Black and white photographs and posters from films with a legal theme provide decor, while a little cat food betrays the presence of Tom, the resident moggy who sports a barrister's white collar. The top quality menu consists of premium cut steaks and inventive dishes such as chorizo omelettes and bruschettas. ⛰Q◑⊖🚌

WC2: Covent Garden

Freemasons Arms

81-82 Long Acre, WC2E 9NG
11-11 (midnight Fri & Sat); 12-5 Sun
☎ (020) 7836 3115 🌐 shepherdneame.co.uk/pubs/pubs.php/freemasons_arms
Shepherd Neame Master Brew Bitter, Spitfire, seasonal beers H
Large, smartly furnished bar with a raised seating area at the back that can be hired out, as can two function rooms upstairs. It is a popular, crowded hostelry with five TV screens. The present pub dates from 1896; the Royal Geological Society was founded in a previous one. An oil painting of a past president and a large landscape given to the Society hang in the bar, where there are also several good Shepherd Neame mirrors. Food is served lunchtimes and evenings. ◑⊖🚌

Harp ✔

47 Chandos Place, WC2N 4HS
10.30-11; 12-10.30 Sun
☎ (020) 7836 0291 🌐 harpbarcoventgarden.com
Black Sheep Best Bitter; Harveys Sussex Best Bitter; Taylor Landlord; guest beers H
No loud music, no fruit machines, no TV – just good beer, good food and good company. A long, narrow downstairs bar is decorated with large mirrors, numerous portraits and an intriguing framed satin programme from an 1899 production of Kipling's The Absent-Minded Beggar. The recently refurbished upstairs bar is as homey and cosy as your own living room. Winner of multiple awards, including West London CAMRA Pub of the Year in 2006 and 2008.
⛰◑≠(Charing Cross)⊖(Charing Cross/Leicester Sq)🚌

Nell of Old Drury

29 Catherine Street, WC2B 5JS
12-3, 5-11.30; 5 (12 Sat)-midnight Fri & Sat; closed Sun
☎ (020) 7836 5328 🌐 nellofolddrury.com
Adnams Bitter; Badger Tanglefoot H
Busy bar near theatres and the Royal Opera House, decorated with lots of theatre posters. The staff are friendly with positive attitudes (just don't ask a lot of questions when the theatres are emptying out). There is a wonderful bow window and some seating and bar stools, but it is mainly standing room only here. A traditional bar and upstairs room is available for private hire for parties and gatherings. ⊖🚌

WC2: Strand

Edgar Wallace ✔

40 Essex Street, WC2R 3JF

11-11; closed Sat & Sun
(020) 7353 3120 edgarwallacepub.com
Adnams Bitter; Nethergate Edgar's Pale Ale; guest beers
Near the law courts and named after a famous writer, this pub is popular with legal customers. The eclectic range of guest beers is a refreshing change from the nearby wine bars of Fleet Street. The upstairs bar can be booked for private functions and food is available all day. The pub holds occasional beer festivals, so check the website for details.
Q(Temple)

Ship & Shovell
1-3 Craven Passage, WC2N 5PH
11-11; closed Sun
(020) 7839 1311
Badger K&B Sussex Bitter, Tanglefoot, seasonal beers
Named after Admiral Sir Cloudesley Shovell who, together with some 2000 of his sailors, died when his fleet ran into the Scilly Isles in 1707. The pub is in two parts on either side of Craven Passage, where smokers can mingle with folk more intent on the nearby nightclub. The smaller southside bar has a snug and upstairs room that can be hired for private functions. The northside bar has some wonderful etched mirrors. Both bars feature some good marine prints.
(Charing Cross)(Charing Cross/ Embankment)

EAST LONDON
E1: Aldgate

Dispensary
19A Leman Street, E1 8EN
12-11; closed Sat & Sun
(020) 7977 0486 thedispensarylondon.co.uk
Adnams Broadside; Caledonian Deuchars IPA; Dark Star Original; guest beers
The large, imposing cream frontage of this former hospital building leads to an opulent, smart interior. The double-height bar has a mezzanine floor and a function room which is available for hire. The emphasis is on fine dining with a full menu and an extensive wine list, but there is also a bar menu for a more traditional alternative. Meals are served lunchtimes and evenings daily. The friendly landlady will bring you up to date on the activities of the pub's resident ghost.
(Aldgate East)

E1: Spitalfields

Pride of Spitalfields
3 Heneage Street, E1 5LJ
11-midnight (1am Thu; 2am Fri & Sat)
(020) 7247 8933
Crouch Vale Brewers Gold; Fuller's London Pride, ESB; guest beer
A small, intimate East End pub in the heart of London's Bangla Town. It nestles discreetly along Heneage Street, just a few yards off Brick Lane. Run by the same licensee for the last 20 years, it is a favourite of many for its atmosphere, the quality of its cask beers and food – which is home-cooked and served on weekday lunchtimes, plus a Sunday roast.
(Liverpool St)(Aldgate E)

E1: Whitechapel

Bar Nakoda
199 Whitechapel Road, E1 1DE
11-1am; 12-midnight
(020) 7247 6707
Nethergate Suffolk County, seasonal beers
Formerly known as the Black Bull, the pub's mock-Tudor frontage serves as a landmark at the corner of Vallance Road. A genuine free house, it offers a varying range of Nethergate ales, including its seasonal brews. The spacious open-plan area is served by a single bar at the rear, while football and other sporting events can be watched on several large-screen TVs. The pub may close early if quiet, so ring to check.
(Bethnal Green)

E2: Bethnal Green

Camel
277 Globe Road, E2 0JD
4 (1 Thu & Fri; 12 Sat)-11; 12-10.30 Sun
(020) 8983 9888 thecamele2.co.uk
Adnams Broadside; Crouch Vale Brewers Gold
Small corner pub with a tiled exterior. The interior is dimly lit and decorated with striking floral print wallpaper. An absence of TVs and gaming machines makes for a pleasant atmosphere. This is a genuine free house and the landlord is keen to increase the beer range and to introduce real cider. The Crouch Vale beer may vary.

E3: Bow

Coborn Arms
8 Coborn Road, E3 2DA
11-11 (11.30 Wed & Thu; midnight Fri & Sat); 12-11 Sun
(020) 8980 3793
Young's Bitter, Special, seasonal beers
Friendly East London pub, originally bought by Young's in 1984 and extended into the next-door house. The bar is split into three areas, although the pub started out with just one small bar in the front. It now includes a separate room with darts. Football is shown on TV (both Sky and Setanta). The licensee is a previous CAMRA North London Pub of the Year landlord.
(Mile End/Bow Road)

Palm Tree
127 Grove Road, E3 5RP
12.30-midnight (12.30am Sat); 12-midnight
Beer range varies
This well hidden gem of a pub was once on a street corner but surrounding buildings were knocked down by the GLC and it now stands alone in a small park by the Grand Union Canal. The two guest ales on offer are ever changing. Local CAMRA Pub of the Year 2007, the Palm Tree features on the London Regional Inventory of historic pub interiors for its two bars and their distinctive wallpaper.
(Mile End)P

E5: Clapton

Anchor & Hope
15 High Hill Ferry, E5 9HG (800m N of Lea Bridge Rd, along river path)
11 (12 Sat)-11; 12-10.30 Sun
(020) 8806 1730
Fuller's London Pride, ESB; guest beers Ⓗ
Overlooking the River Lea and Walthamstow Marshes, this popular, traditional Fuller's pub is a regular destination for walkers and cyclists alike. A small one-bar pub, it has three drinking areas, two inside the pub and the third outside, by the river, ideal for watching life go by. This relaxing pub gives you plenty of time to recharge your batteries. The guest ales come from Fuller's list.
(393)

Elderfield
57 Elderfield Road, E5 0LF
4 (1 Sat)-11 (midnight Thu-Sat); 1-11 Sun
(020) 8986 1591
Adnams Broadside; Fuller's London Pride; Harveys Sussex Best Bitter; Taylor Landlord Ⓗ
Since the last edition of this Guide, the Eclipse has regained its original name and is an oasis in the back streets of a somewhat notorious area. The interior has wooden furniture and sparse decor, a friendly atmosphere and various board games to entertain customers. A limited but good value snack menu (pizzas, paninis and toasties) is available all day.
(242,308)

E8: Hackney

Pembury Tavern
90 Amhurst Road, E8 1JH
12-11
(020) 8986 8597 individualpubs.co.uk/pembury
Milton Minotaur, Dionysus, Pegasus, Sparta, Nero; guest beers Ⓗ
The beers here come from Milton and other micro-breweries and usually include a mild and a stout, plus real cider or perry. A good selection of continental bottled beers, Czech Budvar on tap and a range of malt whiskies complete the drinks menu. Excellent locally-sourced food is served (all day on Sunday), while pool, bar billiards, cards, board games and wireless Internet access will keep you occupied. Check the website for beer festival details.
Q(Hackney Downs/Central)

E8: South Hackney

Dove
24-28 Broadway Market, E8 4QJ
12-11 (midnight Fri & Sat)
(020) 7275 7617
Crouch Vale Brewers Gold; Flowers IPA; Taylor Landlord; guest beers Ⓗ
Two Gods clinking together glasses of Leffe are the subject of a huge ceiling mural here. They look down on a mainly young clientele enjoying a traditional pub with a twist. Specialising in Belgian beer, there are 101 different examples on offer, including a draught guest from a Belgian micro-brewery. These are accompanied by six British real ales. Food is served all day in both the bar and 'kitchen' next door. For the Gods' sake, raise a glass to the Dove. (London Fields)

E9: Homerton

Globe in Morning Lane
20 Morning Lane, E9 6NA
11-midnight (3am Thu-Sat); 11-8.30 Sun
(020) 8985 6455
Fuller's London Pride; Young's Bitter Ⓗ
Built in 1960 on the site of a glass-blowing factory, there have been two previous pubs of the same name here. Originally two bars with an off-licence, the interior became open plan in the 1970s. This traditional pub now specialises in live music on Monday, Thursday, Friday and Saturday evenings, plus Sunday lunchtime jazz. The Monday blues jam occasionally features well-known guests.
(Hackney Central)

E10: Leyton

Leyton Orient Supporters Club
Matchroom Stadium, Oliver Road, E10 5NF
match days, 2 hrs before kick off; closing varies
(020) 8988 8288
Mighty Oak Oscar Wilde; guest beers Ⓗ
The club started serving real ale in 1992 and now has five changing guest beers from small breweries, plus a regular mild. Now in its fourth season in new premises, it holds two annual beer festivals. In addition to match days, the club also opens for internationals and cup finals on TV and some reserve games. Local CAMRA Club of the Year winner seven times and 2007 national CAMRA Club of the Year.

E11: Wanstead

Nightingale
51 Nightingale Lane, E11 3EY
10.30-midnight
(020) 8530 4540
Courage Best Bitter; guest beers Ⓗ
A mural of Dick Turpin and the inscription 'Mob's Hole' (which was the name of this area around 1700) adorn the smart exterior of this Grade II-listed building. Turpin would meet other highwaymen at this site to drink, gamble and plan raids on wealthy travellers passing through nearby Epping Forest. Today it is the bar staff who stand and deliver good beer. Fish and chip night is Monday when there is also a quiz from 8pm. Wednesday is curry night. (Snaresbrook)

E13: Plaistow

Black Lion
59-61 High Street, E13 0AD
11-11; 12-10.30 Sun
(020) 8472 2351
Courage Best Bitter; guest beers Ⓗ
Historic coaching inn that was rebuilt over 300 years ago. The former stables are now used as a function room and a quiet saloon bar is decorated with a guest beer board and historical prints on the walls. The public bar shows major sports events on TV. Three guest beers change often, with Adnams, Mighty Oak

and Archers served by an enthusiastic landlord. A large garden provides ample seating through the cobbled courtyard. Fresh home-cooked food is served Monday to Friday. ❀◐⊖🚌P⚡

E14: Isle of Dogs

North Pole

74 Manilla Street, E14 8LG
⚙ 11-3.30, 5-11; closed Sat & Sun
☎ (020) 7987 5443
Fuller's London Pride; Greene King Old Speckled Hen; Marston's Pedigree; Taylor Landlord ⊞
This pub is easier to find than the name suggests: from South Quay DLR station, head west down Marsh Wall and descend some steps to Manilla Street. Excellent pub food means it is very busy during lunchtimes and early evenings. The dartboard is only used for team matches, so it is safe to stand near it most of the time. Friendly staff and comfortable furnishings make this a cosy pub. Rarely for London these days, the pub closes in the afternoon. ❀◐⇌(South Quay DLR)🚌♣

E15: Stratford

King Edward VII

47 Broadway, E15 4BQ
⚙ 12-11 (midnight Thu-Sat); 12-11.30 Sun
☎ (020) 8534 2313 🌐 kingeddie.co.uk
Beer range varies ⊞
Busy, historic pub opposite the church. The low-ceilinged front bar has a part-flagstone floor and pew seats, while the saloon bar has a separate restaurant area. The beer range changes on a regular basis and bottle-conditioned beers are also available. Outside drinking areas are at the front and rear of the pub. Delicious home-cooked food is available from a changing menu. Live music is played on Thursday evening and Sunday lunchtime, with a quiz on Sunday evening.
❀◐◑⊟⇌⊖🚌⚡

E17: Walthamstow

Nags Head

9 Orford Road, E17 9LP
⚙ 4 (2 Fri; 12 Sat)-11; 12-10.30 Sun
☎ (020) 8520 9709
Adnams Broadside; Fuller's London Pride; Mighty Oak Oscar Wilde; Taylor Landlord; guest beers ⊞
Located in Walthamstow village, this former coaching inn, built in 1857, is a great pub. Nowadays it has a more modern feel (cosy and friendly) with a style that mixes wine bar, tavern and comfy living room. There is plenty of seating outside, with bench and tables out front to watch the world go by, plus a covered area with heaters out back. There is normally a mild on offer. Jazz and music feature on some nights – ring for details.
❀⇌⊖(Walthamstow Central)🚌⚡

Barking

Britannia

1 Church Road, IG11 8PR
⚙ 11-3, 5-11; 12-11 Fri-Sun
☎ (020) 8594 1305
Wells Bombardier; Young's Bitter, Special, seasonal beers ⊞
When you approach this friendly local you can see evidence of Barking's nautical past; it once boasted England's largest fishing fleet. The area has been extensively rebuilt with white Spanish-style low-level housing. The saloon bar offers a friendly home from home and is normally quiet, while the public bar has bare boards, darts, pool and a jukebox. Hearty, good value food is offered each lunchtime, and roasts on Sunday (booking advisable). Local CAMRA Pub of the Year 2006 and 2007.
Q❀◐⊟⇌⊖🚌♣P

Chadwell Heath

Eva Hart

1128 High Road, RM6 4AH
⚙ 9-midnight
☎ (020) 8597 1069
Courage Best Bitter, Directors; Greene King Abbot; Marston's Pedigree; guest beers ⊞
Large, comfortable Wetherspoon pub, previously the local police station but now a real ale haven. Four guest ales are usually on handpump together with Weston's Old Rosie or Vintage Cider. Children are welcome in the balcony seating area until 9pm. The pub is named after a local singer and music teacher who was one of the oldest survivors of the Titanic. Breakfast and wholesome, good value meals and snacks are served. There is a patio at the front and side of the pub.
❀◐◑♿⇌🚌●P⚡

Creekmouth

Crooked Billet

113 River Road, IG11 0EG (1½ miles S of A13)
⚙ 11-midnight; 12-11 Sun
☎ (020) 8507 0126
Fuller's London Pride ⊞
Pleasant, traditional pub in an industrial area, featuring three bars: a public bar with pool table, a saloon bar where food is served at lunchtime Monday to Friday, and a small wood-panelled bar known as the 'middle bar'. The garden is open during the summer. The pub is the base for the Creekmouth Preservation Society. Bus route 387 terminates about half a mile from the pub but extends to pass the pub four times during peak periods Monday-Friday. ♛❀◐⊟🚌(387)P

Hornchurch

JJ Moons

Unit 3, 46-62 High Street, RM12 4UN
⚙ 9-midnight (12.30am Fri & Sat); 9-11.30 Sun
☎ (01708) 478410
Greene King IPA, Morland Original, Old Speckled Hen, Abbot; guest beers ⊞
An impressive range of guest beers greets you in this busy Wetherspoon pub, near the end of the High Street. In addition to the ales, there are up to three real ciders served by gravity on the bar. The usual collection of local historical photographs and information includes a feature on John Cornwall, the boy hero of the Battle of Jutland. Breakfast is served until

midday and food up to 11pm. A family area is available until 6pm. Outside is a covered smoking area. Q◐♿⇌(Emerson Pk)🚌♣⊱

Ilford

Prince of Wales

63 Green Lane, IG1 1XJ

12-11.30

☎ (020) 8478 1326

Fuller's London Pride; Greene King IPA, Abbot; Young's Bitter; guest beers Ⓗ

A welcome return for a pub that used to appear regularly in the Guide. This very pleasant local has a small, cosy saloon bar and a larger L-shaped public bar. Regular beers are supplemented by three guests. The public bar houses a dartboard and pool table, and regular quiz nights are held. The rear garden is comfortable and well maintained, with a fairly large car park. The pub is a welcome addition to an area dominated by 'keg' pubs.

❀◐⇌🚌P⊱

Rainham

Phoenix

Broadway, RM13 9YW

11-11; 12-3, 7-10.30 Sun

☎ (01708) 553700

Courage Directors; Greene King IPA; John Smith's Bitter; Wadworth 6X; guest beer Ⓗ

Busy, spacious town pub, close to Rainham station and convenient for the RSPB Rainham Marshes nature reserve. It has two bars: a public bar with dartboard and a saloon for dining (no food Sun). Quizzes and live entertainment/music alternate on Thursday; entertainment also features on Saturday. The large garden has five aviaries and a barbecue area. Family fun days are held every bank holiday Monday. Accommodation comprises seven twin rooms and one single room.

❀◐⇌🚌♣P⊱

Woodford Green

Cricketers

299-301 High Road, IG8 9HQ

11-11 (midnight Fri); 12-11 Sun

☎ (020) 8504 2734

McMullen AK, Cask Ale, Country Bitter Ⓗ

Pleasant, friendly local with a warm and comfortable saloon bar and a slightly more basic public bar with dartboard. In the saloon there are insignia plaques for all 18 first-class cricket counties, together with a number of photographs of Sir Winston Churchill, who was for many years the local MP – and whose statue stands on the green almost opposite. Lunchtime meals served Monday to Saturday are hearty and good value for money. The patio garden includes a petanque pitch.

❀◐♿🚌(179,W13)P

Traveller's Friend

496-498 High Road, IG8 0PN

12-11; 12-4.30, 7-11 Sun

☎ (020) 8504 2435

Adnams Broadside; Courage Best Bitter; Wells Bombardier; Young's Bitter; guest beer Ⓗ

An absolute gem of a local situated on a slip road off the busy main road. This friendly, comfortable pub features oak-panelled walls and rare original snob screens. The Welsh couple who have run the pub superbly for many years are most welcoming and serve their beer in tip-top condition. At least one guest beer is always available and beer festivals are held in April and September. Lunches are served Monday to Saturday. Several buses pass the door. Local CAMRA Pub of the Year 2008. Q❀◐♿🚌P

NORTH LONDON

N1: De Beauvoir Town

Northgate

113 Southgate Road, N1 3JS

12 (5 Mon)-11 (midnight Fri & Sat); 12-10.30 Sun

☎ (020) 7359 7392

Caledonian Deuchars IPA; Fuller's London Pride; guest beer Ⓗ

Solid Victorian building, now re-styled as a gastro-pub. The single room interior, decorated in modern style, has plain glass windows and art prints; there is piped music but no TV. A restaurant with an open kitchen occupies a back corner, while the rest of the space is intended for drinkers. Modern international food is served daily. There is a large patio to the front and side with a dozen tables plus a heated, covered smoking area.

❀◐🚌(76,141)⊱

Scolt Head

107A Culford Road, N1 4HJ

12-midnight (10.30 Sun)

☎ (020) 7254 3965 🌐 thescolthead.com

Caledonian Deuchars IPA; Fuller's London Pride; guest beers Ⓗ

Large Victorian locals' pub on a triangular site, with a patio garden in front. The main bar includes an original bar back and eclectic decorations ranging from pressure gauges to a large china dog. A separate function room houses a huge TV, pool table and jukebox. Live blues music is performed on alternate Thursdays and a popular quiz held on Monday evening. An alcove has tables for dining, with pub food served lunchtimes and evenings. The smoking area is heated and covered.

⛰❀◐♿🚌(76,141)♣⊱

N1: Hoxton

Prince Arthur

49 Brunswick Place, N1 6EB

11-midnight; 12-6.30 Sun

☎ (020) 7253 3187

Shepherd Neame Master Brew Bitter, Kent's Best, Spitfire Ⓗ

A cosy, friendly single-bar back-street local situated close to Pitfield Street. The pub consists of two distinct areas, with glass-panelled windows and table seating to the front, and a dartboard in the sunken area to the rear. Decorated with pictures of racehorses throughout, there are also photographs of the landlord's days as a boxer. Background music plays, and there is a TV for the occasional sporting event, but neither intrudes on the convivial atmosphere. Outside seating is available. ❀≠⊖(Old St)🚌♣

Wenlock Arms

26 Wenlock Road, N1 7TA
12-midnight (1am Thu-Sat)
☎ (020) 7608 3406 🌐 wenlock-arms.co.uk
Adnams Bitter; guest beers 🄷
Thirteen years in the Guide and four times local CAMRA Pub of the Year, the pub stands near the site of the former Wenlock Brewery. It offers an ever-changing range of eight ales including a mild, together with a choice of cider or perry and a selection of continental bottled beers. The pub has a strong community focus. It has its own cricket team and also hosts regular jazz sessions. Substantial snacks are served, including the legendary salt beef sandwiches.
⛰≠⊖(Old St)🚌♣🍎

N1: Islington

Charles Lamb

16 Elia Street, N1 8DE
4-11 (midnight Thu-Sat); 12-10.30 Sun
☎ (020) 7837 5040 🌐 thecharleslambpub.com
Fuller's Chiswick Bitter; Taylor Landlord; guest beers 🄷
The Charles Lamb goes from strength to strength after being saved from closure in 2005. A relatively small, two-bar pub with a central island bar, this traditional, friendly back-street pub sits in a quiet residential area close to the Regent's Canal off Upper Street. It is the centre of its community and has its own wine club, a good website, a mailing list and a philosophers' debating night. Food features mainly French and English dishes. Traditional Sunday roast is available. Q◐◑⊖(Angel)🚌

Compton Arms

4 Compton Avenue, N1 2XD
12-11 (10.30 Sun)
☎ (020) 7359 6883
Greene King IPA, Abbot; guest beers 🄷
Smallish local pub with two indoor seating areas. TV screens cater for Arsenal fans on match days. The smaller back room is quieter and can be hired for functions. The decor includes wooden beams and bottle-glass windows. The pub opens at 11am for all weekend Arsenal home matches. Lunches are served 12-4pm at weekends. Children are welcome in the back room when dining and in the garden until 8pm. Wheelchair access is limited to the front bar. The garden has a smoking shelter with heating and lighting.
❀◐♿≠(Highbury & Islington/Essex Rd)
⊖(Highbury & Islington)🚌⚡

Narrow Boat ✔

119 St Peters Street, N1 8PZ
11 (12 Sun)-midnight
☎ (020) 7288 0572 🌐 narrowboat.org.uk
Adnams Bitter; Fuller's London Pride; guest beer 🄷
Long, narrow Victorian pub alongside the Regent's Canal, with a modern interior. Entry from road level is into the main bar, with balconies overlooking the canal. A large-screen TV shows sport. The downstairs bistro has an open kitchen and opens on to the canal tow path. The food is mainly modern English cooking, with fish as a speciality, served daily. The pub is popular with tourists and there is barge mooring available.
⛰❀◐♿⊖(Angel)🚌⚡

N2: East Finchley

Old White Lion ✔

121 Great North Road, N2 0NW
12-11 (midnight Tue-Thu; 1am Fri & Sat)
☎ (020) 8365 4861
Adnams Broadside; Caledonian Deuchars IPA; Taylor Landlord; Young's Bitter 🄷
This large hostelry next to East Finchley tube station mainly attracts a young clientele. The interior is styled with open brick walls and a wooden floor, and walls are decorated with paintings of rock stars; there are photos of films on display that are for sale. Weston's Old Rosie cider is served, together with a wide range of continental draught and bottled beers in addition to the cask ales. Prices are similar to central London. There is canopy cover for smokers. ❀◐⊖🚌🍎P⚡

N4: Harringay

Salisbury Hotel ★

1 Grand Parade, Green Lanes, N4 1JX
5-midnight (1am Thu; 2am Fri); 12-2am Sat; 12-11.30 Sun
☎ (020) 8800 9617
Fuller's Chiswick, Discovery, London Pride, ESB, Gales HSB, seasonal beers 🄷
Worth visiting just for the architectural feast alone, this Grade II-listed and CAMRA National Inventory pub has a glorious interior and was used as a location for the 1992 film Chaplin. The tiled walls, mosaic floors, stained glass windows, wonderful skylight in the restaurant area (an old billiards room) and two snugs ensure an interesting visit. Apart from Fuller's draught ales, there is unusual Czech lager, continental bottled beer and a good range of malt whiskies. Food is served at reasonable prices. ◐≠⊖(Turnpike Lane)🚌

N6: Highgate

Flask ✔

77 Highgate West Hill, N6 6BU
11 (12 Sat)-11; 12-10.30 Sun
☎ (020) 8348 7346
Adnams Broadside; Fuller's London Pride; Greene King IPA; Taylor Landlord; guest beers 🄷
Busy former coaching inn incorporating a variety of nooks and crannies on different levels, with low ceilings, wood panelling and roaring log fires in winter. The lower bar (now disused) has an interesting Georgian counter, with pull-down glass shutters. There is a large outside seating area which is popular in summer months with tourists as well as Bohemian locals. A varied menu with an exotic flavour is served throughout the day, with a traditional roast on Sunday.
⛰Q❀◐⊖🚌⚡

Gatehouse ✔

1 North Road, N6 4BD
9-midnight (12.30 Fri & Sat); 12-10.30 Sun

☎ (020) 8340 8054
Courage Best Bitter; Fuller's London Pride; Greene King Abbot; Marston's Pedigree; Shepherd Neame Spitfire; guest beers Ⓗ
Imposing Tudor-style pub at the heart of the village. A spacious bar and separate dining area lead to an enclosed garden, with ramped access for disabled users and heating provided. A former toll house, this is one of Highgate's oldest pubs and was once the court house for St Pancras and Hampstead boroughs, whose boundary it straddles. There is a thriving theatre upstairs and the actors often join the audience after the show.
Q❀◐⊖🚌♣⅃

Prince of Wales

53 Highgate High Street, N6 5JX
🕒 12-11 (midnight Fri & Sat); 12-10.30 Sun
☎ (020) 8340 0445
Bateman XB; Butcombe Bitter; guest beers Ⓗ
Dating back to the 17th century, this quiet, unassuming pub is set amid the hustle and bustle of the High Street. A single horseshoe bar serves a surprisingly spacious wood-panelled room with a number of prints of local dignitaries, past and present. It has a a cosy, welcoming feel. Thai food is served lunchtimes and evenings and there is a small patio favoured by smokers backing onto the open space of Pond Square. Q❀◐⊖🚌⅃

N7: Holloway

Coronet ✔

338-346 Holloway Road, N7 6NJ
🕒 9-11.30 (10.30 Sun)
☎ (020) 7609 5014
Courage Directors; Greene King Abbot; Marston's Pedigree; Theakston Best Bitter; guest beers Ⓗ
A sensitive conversion of an Art Deco cinema, this popular pub serves up to 10 real ales in superb condition at value prices, plus Weston's Old Rosie cider. Its origins as a cinema are still obvious. The pub holds two Oakham Ales beer festivals a year, plus the normal 'spoonfests. The standard Wetherspoon food range is served. There is a heated, semi-covered patio for smokers at the rear of the pub.
Q❀◐♿⇌(Drayton Pk)⊖(Holloway Rd)
🚌♣⅃

N8: Crouch End

Harringay Arms

153 Crouch Hill, N8 9QH
🕒 12-11.30 (midnight Fri & Sat)
☎ (020) 8340 4243
Adnams Broadside; Caledonian Deuchars IPA; Courage Best Bitter; Wells Bombardier Ⓗ
Small, cosy, narrow pub at the foot of Crouch Hill. Walls adorned with old photos and maps of the area during its growing years add to the quiet, friendly, conversational atmosphere, undisturbed by a small-screen TV for sports events at one end. Three of the four listed beers are available at any time. A small outside rear yard gives smokers an outlet. Darts is possible midway through the day and chess boards are available on request. Quiz night is Tuesday. ❀⇌(Crouch Hill)🚌♣⅃

N8: Hornsey

Three Compasses ✔

62 High Street, N8 7NX
🕒 11-11 (midnight Fri & Sat); 12-11 Sun
☎ (020) 8340 2729
Caledonian Deuchars IPA; Fuller's London Pride; Taylor Landlord; guest beers Ⓗ
Astute management has transformed the Three Compasses in recent years, leading to CAMRA National Community Pub of the Year and the local branch Pub of the Season awards. The pub has something for everyone – diners and big-screen football fans as well as real ale drinkers. There are usually three guest beers to back up the regular ales. A range of pub games is available and there is a quiz on Monday. Food is served until 10pm Monday to Saturday and 9.30pm Sunday.
⚠◐♿⇌🚌♣⅃☐

N9: Edmonton

Beehive

24 Little Bury Street, N9 9JZ
🕒 12-midnight (1am Fri & Sat); 12-11 Sun
☎ (020) 8360 4358
Draught Bass; Fuller's London Pride; Greene King IPA, Old Speckled Hen; guest beer Ⓗ
A one-bar pub where the licensee, who used to be a barman at the pub, has turned the trade around in the last year – the Bass now has two pumps on separate lines. Two large-screen TVs show local football team matches. Home-cooked meals include specials of pie & mash on Monday, steak on Tuesday, curry on Wednesday and fish on Friday. Live music is performed on Saturday evening, with occasional acoustic sets on Sunday evening. There is a heated, covered smoking area outside.
❀◐⇌(Bush Hill Pk)🚌(192,W8)♣P⅃

N12: North Finchley

Elephant Inn

283 Ballards Lane, N12 8NR
🕒 11-11 (midnight Fri & Sat); 12-10.30 Sun
☎ (020) 8343 6110
Fuller's Discovery, London Pride, ESB, seasonal beer Ⓗ
Comfortable three-bar pub with a front patio and its own Thai restaurant upstairs, though food is also available in the main bar. The service is friendly and efficient, with a landlady who promotes real ale, with seasonal beer from Fuller's changing every three months. Quiz night is Monday, poker night Thursday; fundraising for local charities takes place, as does occasional live music. The pub adheres to the Fuller's policy of serving the Discovery through a chiller, which may not appeal to everyone. ⚠❀◐🚌⅃

N16: Stoke Newington

Daniel Defoe ✔

102 Stoke Newington Church Street, N16 0LA
🕒 11.30-midnight; 12-10.30 Sun
☎ (020) 7254 2906 🌐 thedanieldefoe.com
Courage Directors; St Austell Tribute; Wells Bombardier; Young's Bitter Ⓗ

Busy single-bar Victorian corner local with a reputation for convivial drinking and dining. Its name acknowledges the area's literary heritage. The garden area and seating have been modernised and updated. The Michelin-star trained chef has made this a popular destination for locals as well as visitors to this fashionable area. ❀⇌◐⇌🚌

Rose & Crown

199 Stoke Newington Church Street, N16 9ES

11.30-midnight; 12-10.30 Sun

☎ (020) 7254 7497

Adnams Bitter; Marston's Pedigree; guest beer Ⓗ

A genuine locals' pub with a superb inter-war original interior, probably the work of AE Sewell – the ceiling is decorated with white vitriolite squares edged in varnished wood and there are many bevelled mirrors and wood panels proudly engraved with past Truman's beers. Note too the curved bottle-end windows. The Tuesday quiz is the highlight of the week. Situated close to Clissold Park and its controversial leisure centre, the pub is a great Sunday lunchtime retreat. ⇌◐🚌

N21: Winchmore Hill

Dog & Duck

74 Hoppers Road, N21 3LH

12-11 (10.30 Sun)

☎ (020) 8886 1987

Greene King IPA; Taylor Landlord; Wadworth 6X; guest beer Ⓗ

Situated in a predominantly residential area on a 'hail and ride' bus route, this is a small and cosy pub featuring pictures of local scenes and personalities of yesteryear. A warm welcome is assured from the friendly landlord and staff. A discreet TV caters for sports fans, while the courtyard garden contains a covered and electrically heated area – as good as it gets for smokers. ❀⇌🚌(W9)♣

Orange Tree ✔

18 Highfield Road, N21 3HA

12-midnight (1am Fri & Sat)

☎ (020) 8360 4853

Greene King IPA, Ruddles County; guest beer Ⓗ

Traditional local near the New River with varied and interesting guest beers that change regularly. A large garden incorporates a covered and heated patio, a children's play area and award-winning Enfield in Bloom floral displays. The friendly, long-standing hosts have won many local CAMRA pub awards too. Sports fans are catered for with a large-screen TV, with pool and darts also played. No admission after 11pm.
❀◐⇌🚌(329)♣P

Winchmore Hill Cricket Club

The Paulin Ground, Fords Grove, N21 3ER

7 (12 Sat)-11; 12 (6 winter)-10.30 Sun

☎ (020) 8360 1271 🌐 winchmorehill.org

Greene King IPA; guest beers Ⓗ

A cricket club yes, but much more as well: football, tennis and hockey for all ages, plus a strong social calendar. For the less active there are darts, table football and a large- screen TV for sports events. Many times winner of the local CAMRA branch Club of the Year and deservedly so: the work of the bar stewards puts many a pub to shame. Non-members are admitted on production of this Guide or a valid CAMRA membership card. Food is available at weekends only. ❀◐⇌🚌(125,329)

East Barnet

Prince of Wales

2 Church Hill Road, EN4 8TB

11-11; 12-midnight Fri & Sat; 12-11 Sun

☎ (020) 8440 5392

Adnams Bitter; Fuller's London Pride; guest beer Ⓗ

Located in the centre of East Barnet village, this is one of the most competitively priced pubs in the area. The guest beer changes on a regular basis. The pub plays host to four football teams, two at alternate weekends, so Sunday lunchtimes may be busy. Food is served daily until 8pm. Disabled access is at the rear through the car park.
❀◐♿⇌(Oakleigh Pk)🚌(184,307)

Enfield

King & Tinker

Whitewebbs Lane, EN2 9HJ (¾ mile W from A10/A1055 jct) TQ331998

12-11 (10.30 Sun)

☎ (020) 8363 6411

Adnams Broadside; Greene King IPA; Wells Bombardier Ⓗ

This idyllic rural pub dates back to the 16th century. In a quiet moment, ask the staff how it obtained its name. The White Webbs Country Park is adjacent, and a bridleway passes the side of the pub, so this is a good spot for ramblers to enjoy a walk: there is even a hitching rail. The garden has a separate children's play area and a heated and covered smoking area. A campsite within half a mile allows caravans. Weston's cider is served on gravity. ⌂❀◐⛺●P

Moon Under Water ✔

115-117 Chase Side, EN2 6NN

9-11 (10.30 Sun)

☎ (020) 8366 9855

Caledonian Deuchars IPA; Courage Best Bitter; Greene King IPA, Abbot; Marston's Pedigree; guest beers Ⓗ

This has been a Wetherspoon pub for 20 years now, located on the site of a former dairy, with a U-shaped bar and three banks of handpumps. It has a considerable window area so during the day there is a lot of natural light. The pub features Wi-Fi, large TV screens (but mainly with the sound off), breakfasts served until noon, meals until 10pm and a patio at the rear. Weston's Old Rosie cider is served on gravity.
❀◐♿⇌(Gordon Hill)🚌(191)●P

Old Wheatsheaf ✔

3 Windmill Hill, EN2 6SE

12-11.30; 11.30-midnight Fri & Sat; 11.30-10.30 Sun

☎ (020) 8363 0516

Adnams Bitter, Broadside; Black Sheep Best Bitter; Greene King IPA Ⓗ

A two-bar local, where the right-hand bar has TV screens while the left-hand one is generally quieter. Although the pub is allegedly haunted, you are assured of a warm welcome from friendly staff. There are award-winning floral displays and frosted windows. Occasional quiz nights take place and board games are also popular. The current licensee has turned around the sales of real ale, with meticulous cleaning of the pipes. Outside is a heated and covered smoking area.
❀≠(Enfield Chase)♣P

Wonder

1 Batley Road, EN2 0JG (nr jct of Chase Side and Lancaster Road)
11-11 (midnight Fri & Sat); 12-11 Sun
☎ (020) 8363 0202
McMullen AK, Cask Ale, Country Bitter, seasonal beers H
This hidden gem, local CAMRA Pub of the Year for two consecutive years, is a traditional two-bar pub with benches outside, offering a friendly service. It is a football-free pub with no TV screens, but there are regular music evenings (mainly at weekends) in one bar where it can be reminiscent of old times, with a sing-along around the piano. The other bar is always quiet.
Q❀≠(Gordon Hill)(191,W8)P

High Barnet

Lord Nelson

14 West End Lane, EN5 2SA
12-11 (10.30 Sun)
☎ (020) 8449 7249
Wells Bombardier; Young's Bitter, Special H
A well-kept pub with a regular local clientele and a friendly welcome for the visitor. The landlord takes a real pride in the quality of the real ales – evident from the number of certificates awarded by the Wells & Young's Mystery Shopper scheme. The landlady runs a quiz night on Thursday. Outside there are front and rear patios. Q❀

Sebright Arms

9 Alston Road, EN5 4ET
12-11 (11.30 Sat); 12-10.30 Sun
☎ (020) 8449 6869
McMullen AK, Country Bitter, seasonal beer; guest beer H
A true back-street local. Although only a short walk away from the bustle of the High Street, the atmosphere here is more like that of a village pub. The licensee, a CAMRA member, was for many years a regular customer of the pub, so was an ideal candidate to take over. The local CAMRA branch is made very welcome for meetings. Fish and chips are available on Friday evening and there is an outside patio. Q❀(384)♣

New Barnet

Builders Arms

3 Albert Road, EN4 9SH
12-11.30 (midnight Fri & Sat; 11 Sun)
☎ (020) 8216 5678
Greene King IPA, Abbot, seasonal beer; guest beer H
A wonderful old-fashioned back-street local, where most of the clientele drinks real ale. Originally a converted two-room cottage, the pub now has a separate back public bar with a TV and pool table. The garden is popular in the summer and often hosts barbecues. Dogs are allowed in the bar. Q❀≠

NORTH-WEST LONDON

NW1: Euston

Bree Louise

69 Cobourg Street, NW1 2HH
11.30-midnight
☎ (020) 7681 4930
Harveys Sussex Best Bitter; Sharp's Doom Bar; Taylor Landlord; H **guest beers** H/G
One-room pub where the bar is split by a pillar, with handpumps on one side, gravity dispense on the other. White walls with a large mirror above what was, at one time, a fireplace, lighten the feel of the pub. Close to Euston station, the pub is popular with commuters as well as CAMRA members (who get 40p off any pint of real ale on presention of a valid membership card). The pub is renowned for its pies. No meals are served after 5pm on Sunday.
❀≠⊖(Euston Sq)

Doric Arch

1 Eversholt Street, NW1 1DN
11-11; 12-10.30 Sun
☎ (020) 7383 3359
Fuller's Chiswick Bitter, Discovery, London Pride, ESB, seasonal beers; Hop Back Summer Lightning; guest beers H
Located east of the bus station and in front of the railway station, the pub's single bar on the first floor is reached by two entrances. Following a 2006 refurbishment, Fuller's continues to promote a range of guest beers from the likes of Archers, Castle Rock, Cottage and Dark Star, with a mild often available as well as two Weston's ciders. There is an impressive display of railway artefacts. The pub is investigating earlier opening.
Q≠⊖

NW1: Primrose Hill

Princess of Wales

22 Chalcot Road, NW1 8LL
11-11.30 (midnight Thu-Sat); 12-10.30 Sun
☎ (020) 7722 0354
Adnams Bitter; Fuller's London Pride; guest beer H
Delightful, traditional corner pub in an inner suburban backwater, close to Camden Market, the Regent's Canal and the Roundhouse. It has the feel of a pub that has cheerfully ignored all passing fads and resolved to stick to tradition. A comfortable mishmash of seating, bric-a-brac and old prints is set in cheerful decor around an island bar. A basement room leads to a 'secret' garden. Food is not served Monday evening or after 5pm on Sunday, when there are regular jazz sessions.
Q❀⊖(Chalk Farm)

NW1: St Pancras

Euston Flyer ✔

83-87 Euston Road, NW1 2RA
⏲ 11-11.30 (midnight Tue-Sat); 12-11 Sun
☎ (020) 7383 0856
Fuller's Discovery, London Pride, ESB, seasonal beers; guest beers Ⓗ
Situated across the road from the British Library, this is a popular spot for office workers and commuters, more so since the opening of the St Pancras Eurostar terminal. A large open-plan pub divided into different sections and levels, it can be boisterous in the evenings and during occasional beer festivals. Two large-screen TVs are always on for major sporting events. There is limited pavement seating outside. The pub closes some Saturday evenings during the football season. Meals are served daily until 9pm (7pm Sat).
❀◑♿⇌⊖🚌⌐

NW2: Cricklewood

Beaten Docket ✔

50-56 Cricklewood Broadway, NW2 3ET
⏲ 9-11 (12.30am Fri & Sat)
☎ (020) 8450 2972
Courage Directors; Greene King IPA, Abbot; Marston's Pedigree; guest beers Ⓗ
Thanks to a long period under the same management, this typical Wetherspoon conversion of retail premises is a local beacon for real ale. A series of well-defined drinking areas disguises the pub's vastness. The name refers to a losing betting slip; prints and paraphernalia reinforce the theme. There are benches outside all year. A local CAMRA Pub of the Season, it offers a family dining area until 7pm (last orders 6pm). Cider is served on draught from a poly-cask in the fridge.
Q❀◑⇌🚌●⌐

NW3: Hampstead

Duke of Hamilton

23-25 New End, NW3 1JD
⏲ 11 (12 Sun)-11
☎ (020) 7794 0258
Fuller's London Pride, ESB; guest beers Ⓗ
The Duke was a high-profile figure during the English Civil War and this pub was built in 1721. Though Fuller's beers are prominent, this is a free house; guests usually come from Home Counties-based brewers and the pub stages its own festival. The cider is Weston's Old Rosie. Popular with sports fans, the pub shows televised football and rugby, and runs a cricket team – a bat signed by England's 1985 Ashes-winning team hangs in the bar. The New End Theatre is next door. Lunches are served Monday to Friday.
❀◐♿⇌(Hampstead Heath)⊖🚌♣●⌐

Holly Bush ✔

22 Holly Mount, NW3 6SG
⏲ 12-11
☎ (020) 7435 2892 🌐 hollybushpub.com
Adnams Bitter, Broadside; Bateman XXXB; Fuller's London Pride; Harveys Sussex Best Bitter; guest beer Ⓗ
An attractive multi-roomed Grade II-listed building in a charming location, the Holly Bush started life as the stables of the artist George Romney's house. It has been a pub for 200 years and many original features are still evident. Traditional British food is served in the pub and in the upstairs restaurant, which opens Tuesday to Sunday and is available for private hire. The licensee is Mexican, the pub quintessentially English. Well worth seeking out. ⩕❀◑⊖🚌♣⌐

Olde White Bear

1 Well Road, NW3 1LT
⏲ 11.30-11 (11.30 Thu & Fri); 11-11.30 Sat; 12-11 Sun
☎ (020) 7435 3758
Beer range varies Ⓗ
Community pub in an historic area: Well Road takes its name from a tributary of London's famous River Fleet. The pub itself stands opposite the former site of the New End Hospital, where Karl Marx died in 1883. More recently, it has been a popular haunt for local actors. Today, it serves a constantly changing range of up to six beers, and good food seven days a week. Outdoor drinking is available both front and rear.
⩕❀◑⇌(Hampstead Heath)⊖🚌♣⌐▯

Spaniards Inn ✔

Spaniards Road, NW3 7JJ
⏲ 11 (10 Sat)-11; 10-11 Sun
☎ (020) 8731 6571
Adnams Bitter; Fuller's London Pride; Harveys Sussex Best Bitter; Marston's Old Empire; Rooster's Special; guest beer Ⓗ
Few north London pubs can match the Spaniards' history – it dates from 1585 – or its location among the acres of Hampstead Heath. Close to Kenwood House, it is invariably packed in summer, but the range of beers draws the crowds all year round, as do four beer festivals. Draught cider and perry are supplied by Weston's. The traditional British menu (served 12-10pm) is ever popular, while the large, heated garden means the pub is able to cope with the smoking ban.
⩕Q❀◑🚌(210,H3)♣●P⌐

NW4: Hendon

Greyhound

52 Church End, NW4 4JT
⏲ 12-midnight (1am Fri & Sat); 12-11 Sun
☎ (020) 8457 9730
Courage Best Bitter; Wells Bombardier; Young's Bitter, Special, seasonal beer Ⓗ
A large Young's hostelry in the picturesque old-village part of Hendon. Located between the Church Farmhouse Museum and the church itself, the Greyhound is convenient for the library and Middlesex University. This pub attracts a loyal, mixed clientele and offers board games. The interior features wooden panels with old photos of Hendon and interesting prints. There is an area for sports fans with a TV. A range of home-cooked food is available. ⩕❀◑🚌♣⌐

NW5: Dartmouth Park

Dartmouth Arms

35 York Rise, NW5 1SP
⏲ 11-11 (10.30 Sat); 10.30-10.30 Sun

☎ (020) 7485 3267 🌐 dartmoutharms.co.uk
Adnams Bitter, Broadside; Caledonian Deuchars IPA; guest beers Ⓗ
A two-room pub in a residential area, it can get very noisy when Arsenal are playing, as fans flock to the TV screens. The pub's entertainment schedule includes many themed nights: quizzes and comedy nights are staged on a rota basis. Food specials include steak and mussels. The pub offers a wide range of bottled ciders and perries.
♨Q⛱◑⇌(Gospel Oak)⊖(Tufnell Pk) 🚌♣🍎⚟🍺

Lord Palmerston

33 Dartmouth Park Hill, NW5 1HU
⏲ 12-11 (10.30 Sun)
☎ (020) 7485 1578
Adnams Bitter, Broadside; Sharp's Doom Bar; guest beers Ⓗ
A pub divided into three separate rooms: a front bar facing the road with clear windows; a side bar for diners with shelves of books, nicknamed the chapel; and a conservatory leading to a sheltered walled garden. The bar is lined with shelves containing a selection of jugs. Food is served lunchtimes and evenings daily. A heated courtyard at the front caters for smokers.
♨❀◑⇌(Gospel Oak)⊖(Tufnell Pk)🚌⚟

NW5: Kentish Town

Junction Tavern

101 Fortess Road, NW5 1AG
⏲ 12-11 (10.30 Sun)
☎ (020) 7485 9400 🌐 junctiontavern.co.uk
Caledonian Deuchars IPA; guest beers Ⓗ
With up to four guest beers, this well-established venue is local CAMRA Pub of the Year 2008. Its beer festivals in May and August feature a wide range of cask beers. The side door leads into a wood-panelled and mirrored bar, all part of the classic Victorian design. Overlooking the main road, the restaurant serves gastro-style food. Behind the bar room is a beautiful conservatory and a flourishing garden with seating. Dogs are welcome.
Q❀◑♿⇌⊖🚌⚟

Oxford

256 Kentish Town Road, NW5 2AA
⏲ 12-11.30 (midnight Sat); 12-10.30 Sun
☎ (020) 7485 3521
Beer range varies Ⓗ
Large corner pub with a busy, welcoming interior. Some period features remain, but essentially the interior has been stripped back to include a large open-plan kitchen and a dining area. A selection of regularly-changing real ales is always available. Upstairs a function room hosts live jazz and weekly comedy nights. Tables outside are used by smokers. Q❀◑♿⇌⊖🚌♣⚟

NW8: St Johns Wood

Star

38 St Johns Wood Terrace, NW8 6LS
⏲ 11-11; 12-10.30 Sun
☎ (020) 7722 1051
Fuller's London Pride; Worthington Bitter Ⓗ
A pleasant corner pub in an inner London suburban enclave. The walls of the traditional English bar are adorned with photos of cricketers (Lord's ground is close by), while original Charrington's windows have been retained on the outside. An unused fireplace has a mantelpiece with an antique clock and candlesticks for decoration. The small snug has a cabinet full of traditional glassware. There are shelves of books and traditional features such as gaslights. At the front is a heated smoking area. ❀⊖🚌⚟

Harefield

Harefield

41 High Street, UB9 6BY
⏲ 12-11 (10.30 Sun)
☎ (01895) 850003
Greene King Abbot; Hop Back GFB; guest beers Ⓗ
Previously known as the Pickle Jar, this pub was refurbished and renamed as the Harefield in spring 2007. It has quickly become known for both the quality of its beer and its food. Local produce is used for all of the freshly prepared meals, including full Sunday roasts. A beer club runs on Wednesday evening, with reduced prices for real ales. There is a patio outside. ♨❀◑♿🚌(331, U9)P

Harrow

Moon on the Hill ✔

373-375 Station Road, HA1 2AW
⏲ 9-midnight (12.30am Fri & Sat)
☎ (020) 8863 3670
Courage Best Bitter; Greene King Abbot; Marston's Pedigree; guest beers Ⓗ
Small, busy Wetherspoon pub close to the tube and served by numerous bus routes. It is popular with price-conscious regulars, office workers and students from the nearby University of Westminster campus. The usual range of meals is served all day. Please note that the pub is always very busy before football and rugby league games at the nearby Wembley Stadium. Q◑⊖(Harrow-on-the-Hill)🚌

Ruislip Manor

JJ Moons ✔

12 Victoria Road, HA4 0AA
⏲ 9-midnight (1am Fri & Sat)
☎ (01895) 622373
Courage Best Bitter, Directors; Fuller's London Pride; Greene King Abbot; Marston's Pedigree; guest beers Ⓗ
Popular Wetherspoon shop conversion conveniently located opposite the local underground station. A fairly large, typical Wetherspoon's, it is often very busy evenings and weekends. At the rear of the pub is an elevated section set aside for diners, leading out on to a small garden patio area. Good value food and beer is served, with the usual promotions. Three guest ales are available, usually including one from a local brewery, plus Weston's Old Rosie and Organic Vintage ciders. ❀◑♿⊖🚌🍎⚟

Stanmore

Man in the Moon ✓

1 Buckingham Parade, The Broadway, HA7 4EB
9-midnight (1am Fri & Sat)
(020) 8954 6119
Fuller's London Pride; Greene King IPA, Abbot; Marston's Pedigree; guest beers H
Long, narrow L-shaped Wetherspoon's house in the middle of the shopping centre, attracting a varied clientele. Seating is provided in numerous cosy alcoves and prints of early 20th-century Stanmore decorate the walls. Food is served all day. This friendly pub has a huge cellar and Weston's Old Rosie cider is served in addition to real ale. Q

SOUTH-EAST LONDON

SE1: Borough

Market Porter

9 Stoney Street, SE1 9AA
6-8.30am, 11-11; 12-11 Sat; 12-10.30 Sun
(020) 7407 2495 markettaverns.co.uk/The-Market-Porter/
Harveys Sussex Best Bitter; guest beers H
This popular beer lover's mecca is a long-standing Guide entry. Pump clips covering the wood-panelled interior provide testimony to the great range of real ales sold here. Nine handpumps offer constantly-changing beers and a wide range of guests plus Weston's cider. Beers from local brewer Meantime are available on gas dispense. A mixed clientele includes office workers, market traders and shoppers, so it can get busy, with drinkers spilling out into the street. There is a dining room upstairs.
(London Bridge) (London Bridge)

Rake

14 Winchester Walk, SE1 9AG
12 (10 Sat)-11; closed Sun
(020) 7407 0557 utobeer.co.uk
Beer range varies H
Probably the smallest pub in London, opened in August 2006, it has already won several prizes. It is owned by Utobeer, the beer distributor and retailer, and is its showcase on tap. In addition to two ever-changing real ales from small British breweries, a wide range of imported bottled beers is on offer, around a third of which are bottled conditioned. The helpful staff have a good knowledge of their stock. Third of a pint glasses are available.
Q (London Bridge) (London Bridge)

Royal Oak ✓

44 Tabard Street, SE1 4JU
11 (6 Sat)-11; 12-6 Sun
(020) 7357 7173
Harveys Pale, Sussex XX Mild, Sussex Best Bitter, seasonal beers H
A fine two-bar Victorian pub with a great range of Harveys ales on draught and in bottles. Tucked away close to Borough tube, this pub is a gem, with no music or gambling machines to intrude on the enjoyment. Home-cooked food is excellent value and served in good portions. There is a meeting room upstairs. A welcome recent addition is Thatcher's Heritage cider on draught.
Q (London Bridge)

SE1: London Bridge

Barrowboy & Banker ✓

6-8 Borough High Street, SE1 9QQ
11-11; 12-4 Sat; closed Sun
(020) 7403 5415
Fuller's Chiswick, Discovery, London Pride, ESB, seasonal beer H
A traditional-style pub in a grand former bank building on the south west end of London Bridge. The bar area is blessed with an authentic curved staircase which leads to the upper bar, and there are impressive chandeliers and a cavalry painting. The pub is busy with business people. Q

Horniman at Hays ✓

Unit 26, Hay's Galleria, Counter Street, SE1 2HD
11-11 (midnight Thu-Sat); 12-10.30 Sun
(020) 7407 1991
Adnams Broadside; Taylor Landlord; guest beers H
Large riverside pub next to the Belfast museum ship and the popular and stylish Hay's Galleria shopping area. The main bar is long, with plenty of raised ground seating and the main area at one end; in addition there is an upper galleried bar and outside seating. The pub is busy, and has excellent views of Tower Bridge and the City.

SE1: Southwark

Charles Dickens ✓

160 Union Street, SE1 0LH
11.30-11; 12-6 Sat & Sun
(020) 7401 3744 thecharlesdickens.co.uk
Adnams Bitter; guest beers H
Popular one-bar, wooden-floored, traditionally-furnished free house with a large rear patio, majoring on real ales from independent breweries. Charles Dickens lived in neighbouring Lant Street as a boy while his father was in Marshalsea Prison for debt. The lower walls are wood-panelled; upper walls carry framed illustrations from Dickens' stories. The house beer Charles Dickens Best is brewed by Nethergate and the four guests always include a mild. Above average, reasonably-priced meals are served lunchtimes and evenings. Quiz night is Wednesday.
Q (Waterloo East) (Southwark/Borough)

SE1: Tower Bridge

Bridge House ✓

218 Tower Bridge Road, SE1 2UP
11.30-11.30 (12.30am Fri & Sat)
(020) 7407 5818
Adnams Bitter, Explorer, Broadside, seasonal beer H
This flagship Adnams pub is superbly located on the approach to Tower Bridge. The main café-style bar has mixed seating with dining tables and sofas. Local Meantime beers are available, but sadly they are served by gas dispense. In the basement there is a cosy bar

serving two ales, with an entrance on Horselydown Lane, and on the first floor is a function room and bar available for hire, with superb views of the River Thames and the City. (London Bridge) (Tower Hill/ London Bridge)

SE1: Waterloo

Kings Arms

25 Roupell Street, SE1 8TB
11-11; 12-10.30 Sun
(020) 7207 0784
Adnams Bitter; Fuller's London Pride; Greene King IPA; Wells Bombardier
Excellent street-corner local in a quiet residential street of Victorian terraced cottages behind Waterloo East station. Attracting a good mix of local residents and commuters, it can get very busy early evening, but the welcoming, friendly and efficient staff can cope. The narrow public bar and bigger saloon carry historic photographs of the pub and the street. A large rear conservatory with more pictures and historic artefacts provides additional drinking space. The dining area serves reasonable Thai food in the evening. Deservedly popular.
Q (Waterloo East) (Waterloo/ Southwark)

SE4: Brockley

Brockley Barge

184 Brockley Road, SE4 2RR
9-midnight (1am Fri & Sat)
(020) 8694 7690
Courage Best Bitter; Greene King Abbot; Marston's Pedigree; guest beers
A purpose-built Victorian pub given a Wetherspoon makeover which disappointingly included painting the old wood panelling an odd pale mauve. The island bar has been moved to one wall, creating a large, spacious area which thankfully still has a few large pillars that create a bit of cosiness, as well as some areas with comfortable banquette seating. The clientele is lively, mixed and friendly, and there is a pleasant courtyard outside.

SE5: Camberwell

Hoopers

28 Ivanhoe Road, SE5 8DH
5.30 (5 Fri; 2 Sat)-11; 3-11 Sun
(020) 7733 4797 hoopersbar.co.uk
Beer range varies
Hidden in back streets close to the Dog Kennel Hill thoroughfare, this pub was reopened in 2007. A rare example of a London free house, ales from micro-breweries predominate, with beers from Harveys, Dark Star and Mighty Oak as frequent visitors. Draught cider is available on gravity, alongside several foreign bottled beers. Historic breweriana from London and the south east is on display. Every Thursday an intellectually stimulating quiz is hosted, plus occasional beer festivals. A meeting room is available. Meals are served Wednesday-Friday 6-10pm and 12-10pm at weekends.
(Denmark Hill/East Dulwich) (P13)

SE6: Catford

Catford Ram

9 Winslade Way, SE6 4JU
11-11 (midnight Fri & Sat); 12-10.30 Sun
(020) 8690 6206
Young's Bitter, Special, seasonal beer
This well-established pub is a stone's throw from the Broadway Theatre and Broadway Market. It has a comfortable raised seating area and a spacious standing area. Lunches are available Monday to Saturday. Sporting events are shown on large-screen TVs.

SE8: Deptford

Dog & Bell

116 Prince Street, SE8 3JD
12-11.30 (10.30 Sun)
(020) 8692 5664 thedogandbell.com
Fuller's London Pride, ESB; guest beers
A London gem, this small, clean, back-street local has been a popular free house since its owners bought it in 1988. Traditional and well-lit, it has modern touches such as wall-mounted art from local colleges. A mixed clientele enjoys rotating beers from diverse micro-breweries, together with bottled ciders, perries and imported beers. The bar billiards is decades old, quiz night is Sunday and a small courtyard is used in the summer and by smokers. Wi-Fi Internet access is available.
Q

SE10: Greenwich

Ashburnham Arms

25 Ashburnham Grove, SE10 8UH
12-11 (midnight Thu-Sat)
(020) 8692 2007
Shepherd Neame Master Brew Bitter, Kent's Best, Spitfire, seasonal beers
Tidy back-street local with a relaxed atmosphere, background music and daily papers to peruse. A small function room at the rear, with access to the garden, is available for private parties. Immaculate loos with shared wash basins can be found behind a large modern art map of the area. Quizzes are held on Tuesday nights. Food is served lunchtimes and evenings (not Mon, 12-6pm Sun). Wi-Fi is available. Q (DLR)

Cutty Sark

4-6 Ballast Quay, SE10 9PD
11-11; 12-10.30 Sun
(020) 8858 3146
Adnams Broadside; Fuller's London Pride; Greene King Abbot; St Austell Tribute
Lovely Georgian public house building with a friendly atmosphere in a conservation area of Greenwich. It has a superb riverside setting with an outside patio and excellent views of the river from its upstairs rooms. The tourist mecca of Greenwich is a 10-minute stroll away along the riverside path. Well worth seeking out to escape the crowds.
Q (Maze Hill)

Richard I (Tolly's)
52-54 Royal Hill, SE10 8RT
11-11 (midnight Fri & Sat); 12-10.30 Sun
(020) 8692 2996
Wells Bombardier; Young's Bitter, Special, seasonal beers H
A popular, unpretentious local. Its appearance has changed little over the years, with unusual bowed windows at the front and some wood panelling inside. Food is served every lunchtime and evening (all day on Sunday) with lunchtime meal deals available Monday-Thursday. Chess club is on Tuesday and a quiz night on Sunday. A wide range of hot drinks is also available. (DLR)

SE13: Lewisham

Jolly Farmers
354 Lewisham High Street, SE13 6LE
11-11.30; 12-11 Sun
(020) 8690 8402
Beer range varies H/G
This unique pub has constantly changing beers and generally includes at least one Cornish ale. Delicious home-cooked food is served lunchtimes and evenings Tuesday-Friday and Sunday afternoons, with a loyalty card scheme operating for meals. A small TV shows major sporting events but does not dominate. Occasional live music is performed on Friday night and there is an outside patio.
(Ladywell)

SE15: Nunhead

Old Nun's Head
15 Nunhead Green, SE15 3QQ
12-midnight (1am Fri & Sat); 12-10.30 Sun
(020) 7639 4007 oldnunshead.com
Caledonian Deuchars IPA; guest beers H
Built in 1934 on the site of a much older pub which was formerly a nunnery. The Mother Superior was beheaded on the order of Henry VIII, giving the name to the pub and the area. Four real ales are on sale and the manager takes great pride in the beer quality. Food is gastro-pub style, but the pub retains an unpretentious feel. (78,P12)

SE15: Peckham

Gowlett
62 Gowlett Road, SE15 4HY
12-midnight (1am Fri & Sat); 12-10.30 Sun
(020) 7635 7048 thegowlett.com
Beer range varies H
Once described as the jewel in Peckham's crown, this 2005 SE London CAMRA Pub of the Year keeps going from strength to strength. Very light and airy, this back-street pub with four guest beers and marvellous pizzas is a haven for all. Quiz and music nights add a special feel to this very friendly oasis. Check it out at the weekend for a laid-back relaxing treat. There is a patio outside. Wi-Fi is available.
(E Dulwich/Peckham Rye)

SE18: Plumstead Common

Old Mill
1 Old Mill Road, SE18 1QG
11.30-11.30 (12.30am Fri); 12-10.30 Sun
(020) 8244 8592
Beer range varies H
Popular, friendly local pub built around a windmill that dates back to the 17th century. Beer has been served here since 1848. Today it offers six ever-changing ales, and food is served lunchtimes Monday-Saturday. Occasionally the pub stages live music. It also celebrates many calendar dates, including St George's Day and Hallowe'en. The large garden has an aviary. No entry after 11pm on a Friday night.

SE18: Woolwich

Prince Albert (Rose's Free House)
49 Hare Street, SE18 6NE
11-11.30; 12-10.30 Sun
(020) 8854 1538
Beer range varies H
This great little local is well loved by regulars and the stream of visitors who seek it out. An ale haven, barely changed since the 1960s, it features six handpumps, with three ever-changing guests from micro-breweries. Murals of dockyard scenes by local artists adorn the wall and it hosts league darts and crib teams. 'Rose's' as it is known by all who love it, may look imposing, but it is one of the friendliest pubs around – just ask the locals.
Q(Woolwich Arsenal)

SE20: Penge

Moon & Stars
164-166 High Street, SE20 7QS
9-11 (10.30 Sun)
(020) 8776 5680
Courage Directors; Greene King Abbot; Marston's Pedigree; guest beers H
Spacious Wetherspoon house in a town centre location, well served by public transport. The venue is stylish inside and out, with good architecture, creating shades of the Victorian era. Seventeen comfortable booths add to the friendly, cosy atmosphere. A zealous real ale management ensures a choice of numerous well kept ales as well as Weston's Old Rosie cider. The usual Wetherspoon fare is served efficiently all day. At the rear is a pleasant, quiet patio area with heating for smokers.
Q(Kent House)(Beckenham Rd Tramlink)P

SE22: East Dulwich

Herne Tavern
2 Forest Hill Road, SE22 0RR
12-11 (1am Sat); 12-10.30 Sun
(020) 8299 9521 theherne.net
Fuller's London Pride; Ringwood Bitter; Taylor Landlord; guest beers H
A Regional Inventory pub with, among other features, some eye-catching ornate leaded windows. The former public bar now has tables set for dining, but the right-hand bar

retains much of its pub atmosphere. Dark half-height wood panelling throughout is a cosy link with the past. The excellent large garden has a children's play area and function room. ❀◐▶🚌(63,363)

SE23: Forest Hill

Blythe Hill Tavern

319 Stanstead Road, SE23 1JB

🕐 11-midnight

☎ (020) 8690 5176

Courage Best Bitter; Fuller's London Pride; Westerham Black Eagle; guest beers Ⓗ

A must see! Local CAMRA Pub of the Year 2008, this ex-Courage local is in a convenient location on the main road yet at the foot of beautiful Blythe Hill which boasts wonderful London views. It is a three-bar traditional wood-panelled boozer manned the old way, by friendly staff in smart attire. The banter here is second to none, especially on Thursday evening – Irish music night. The beer is kept in tip-top condition at all times and the old tiled hearth makes a great centrepiece. Q❀⊟⇌(Catford/Catford Bridge)🚌(171,185) ♣P⊱

Capitol ✔

11-21 London Road, SE23 3TW

🕐 9-midnight (1am Fri & Sat)

☎ (020) 8291 8920

Courage Best Bitter; Greene King IPA, Abbot, Old Speckled Hen; Marston's Pedigree; guest beers Ⓗ

This Wetherspoon's conversion of a Grade II-listed former cinema and bingo hall retains many of the original features and includes a small coffee bar at the front. A spacious pub set on a number of levels, it has several large-screen TVs showing sporting events. The patio at the side of the building provides an outdoor drinking and smoking area. Q❀◐▶♿⇌🚌⊱

SE25: South Norwood

Albert Tavern

65 Harrington Road, SE25 4LX

🕐 12-11 (midnight Fri & Sat); 12-10.30 Sun

☎ (020) 8654 0452

Greene King IPA, Ruddles County, Old Speckled Hen, Abbot, seasonal beers Ⓗ

Modern 1960s pub replacing the original Albert which suffered a direct hit from a V-1 in 1944. A friendly local, it has a pool table, large-screen TV, quiz nights and other regular events to entertain a wide customer base. Its commitment to quality real ale has recently earned it Cask Marque status. There is a heated and covered smoking area. ❀◐▶♿⇌(Norwood Jct)⊖(Harrington Rd Tramlink)🚌⊱

SE26: Sydenham

Dolphin ✔

121 Sydenham Road, SE26 5HB

🕐 12-11 (11.30 Wed & Thu; midnight Fri & Sat); 12-10.30 Sun

☎ (020) 8778 8101 🌐 thedolphinsydenham.com

Adnams Broadside; Fuller's London Pride; Taylor Landlord Ⓗ

A detached 1935 brewers' Tudor pub given the gastro treatment in late 2006. Inside, the spacious U-shaped room still has dark 1930s wood panelling that creates a cosy atmosphere, albeit dissipated by large, clear-glass windows that look out on to busy Sydenham Road. A pleasant garden is at the rear. Real ale was absent for many years but reintroduced in 2006. ❀◐▶🚌⊱

Dulwich Wood House

39 Sydenham Hill, SE26 6RS

🕐 11-11; 12-10.30 Sun

☎ (020) 8693 5666

Wells Bombardier; Young's Bitter, Special, seasonal beer Ⓗ

This large and somewhat curious house was originally built as a private dwelling in the mid-19th century on land sold off by Dulwich College. It was designed by Crystal Palace architect Joseph Paxton, and inside there are photographs of the fire that brought down this masterpiece. Take a walk through Sydenham Woods then reward yourself with a glass of great ale and the barbecue held in the pub's large beer garden. Very child-friendly, especially during the summer months. Q🛋❀◐▶⇌(Sydenham Hill)🚌P

Windmill

125-131 Kirkdale, SE26 4DJ

🕐 11-11; 12-10.30 Sun

☎ (020) 8291 9281

Courage Best Bitter; guest beers Ⓗ

Do not be put off by the fact that this spacious, modern pub, converted from a furniture shop in 2001, does not look like a traditional pub. It ticks most of the right boxes – friendly staff, a likeable crowd of regular customers and Sydenham's best selection of real ales. Customers sometimes get to choose the next guest ale from a long list. A former Wetherspoon's, it is now a proper food-free boozer, and free of any ties. There is a small courtyard at the rear for smokers. ♿⇌🚌⊱

Addiscombe

Claret Free House

5A Bingham Corner, Lower Addiscombe Road, CR0 7AA

🕐 11.30-11 (11.30 Thu; 11.45 Fri); 12-11 Sun

☎ (020) 8656 7452

Palmers IPA; guest beers Ⓗ

One-time wine bar which long ago moved from grape to grain. It is now a successful beer shop which dispenses an ever-changing range of guest ales from five of its six handpumps. A board on the wall lists names, strengths and prices of up to 48 current and forthcoming ales. Two TVs are on hand for major sporting events. A convenient tram stop is just around the corner. ♿⊖🚌

Cricketers

47 Shirley Road, CR0 7ER

🕐 12-11 (10.30 Sun)

☎ (020) 8655 3507

Dark Star Hophead; Harveys Sussex Best Bitter; guest beers Ⓗ

Robust local with a mock-Tudor exterior. The keen landlord promotes brewery nights and runs mini beer festivals when additional beers

to those usually available on six handpumps are supplied on gravity. Guest ales are often from micro-breweries. The pub can get very crowded when major sports events are shown on TV.
❀◐◑⊖(Addiscombe/Blackhorse Lane Tramlink)🚌(130,367)♣P⊱

Beckenham

Jolly Woodman

9 Chancery Lane, BR3 6NR
✪ 12 (4 Mon)-11 (midnight Fri & Sat); 12-11 Sun
☎ (020) 8663 1031
Harveys Sussex Best Bitter; Taylor Landlord; H guest beers H/G
Friendly, quiet back-street local tucked away behind the Beckenham to Bromley main road. It benefits from strong local support and discerning visitor drinkers. It opened at the beginning of the Victorian era and operated a beer licence only for many years. It now serves beverages across the board and is particularly strong on malt whiskies. The pub has one bar, two simply appointed rooms and a rear patio for smokers. Darts and shove-ha'penny are played and weekday lunches are served. There is no entry after 11pm on Friday and Saturday.
Q❀◐⇌(Beckenham Jct)⊖(Beckenham Jct Tramlink)🚌♣⊱

Bexley

Black Horse

63 Albert Road, DA5 1NJ
✪ 11.30-11 (midnight Fri); 12-11.30 Sat; 12-11 Sun
☎ (01322) 523371
Courage Best Bitter; guest beers H
Four bus routes stop within five minutes' walk of this friendly back-street local which offers good value lunches on weekdays. The open-plan bar is split into two: to the left is an open space with a dartboard while to the right is a smaller, more intimate area and bar. The pub supports a local golf society. The publican aims to put on a different beer every time one of his two guest ales runs out. ❀◐⇌🚌♣⊱

Old Wick

9 Vicarage Road, DA5 2AL
✪ 12-11.30 (12.30am Fri & Sat)
☎ (01322) 524185
Shepherd Neame Master Brew Bitter, Kent's Best, Spitfire, seasonal beers H
This excellent pub on the road from Bexley to Dartford Heath changed its name from the Rising Sun in 1996. The welcoming, cosy interior is enhanced by subdued lighting and friendly staff make everyone feel welcome. Shepherd Neame porter is served, along with other seasonal beers. Food is served lunchtimes and evenings on weekdays plus Sunday lunch. Accommodation and on-site camping are available.
♨❀🛏◐◑⛺⇌🚌(492,B15)♣P⊱

Bexleyheath

Furze Wren

6 Market Place, DA6 7DY
✪ 9-11
☎ (020) 8298 2590
Courage Best Bitter; Greene King Abbot; Marston's Pedigree; Shepherd Neame Spitfire; guest beers H
This Wetherspoon establishment was originally meant to be called the Imperial Eagle, then opened as a Lloyds No 1 before being converted and becoming the Furze Wren (Dartford Warbler) in 2007. Its location in the heart of the shopping centre ensures the pub has a broad clientele. Everything is on the ground floor, including the award-winning toilets. This is a great place to sit and watch buses and people go by. ◐◑♿🚌●

Robin Hood & Little John

78 Lion Road, DA6 8PF
✪ 11-3, 5.30 (7 Sat)-11; 12-4, 7-10.30 Sun
☎ (020) 8303 1128
Adnams Bitter, Broadside; Brains Rev James; Brakspear Bitter; Fuller's London Pride; Harveys Sussex Best Bitter; guest beers H
Dating from the 1830s when it sat amidst fields and farms, this delightful little back-street pub is well worth a visit. It offers eight real ales with guest beers from small independent breweries. It has a well deserved reputation for its home-cooked food at lunchtimes (not Sunday), with themed specials and regular Italian dishes. Dining tables are made from old Singer sewing machines. Voted local CAMRA Pub of the Year 2000-2008 and London winner three times. Over 21s only. ❀◐🚌(B13)

Royal Oak (Polly Clean Stairs)

Mount Road, DA6 8JS
✪ 12-3, 6-11; 12-3, 7-10.30 Sun
☎ (020) 8303 4454
Courage Best Bitter; Fuller's London Pride; guest beer H
Once the village store, this attractive brick and weatherboarded pub manages to keep its rural character despite being engulfed by 1930s suburbia. Inside, the country charm continues with plates and tankards adorning the walls and ceiling. The nickname derives from a house-proud landlady who used to object when people stood their beer on the stairs in the pub. It has been run by the same licensee since 1958. Kentish Daddlums is played on alternate Sunday evenings. There is a heated canopy in the garden for smokers.
Q❀🚌(B13)♣P⊱

Wrong 'Un

234-236 Broadway, DA6 8AS
✪ 9-midnight
☎ (020) 8298 0439
Greene King Abbot; Marston's Pedigree; Shepherd Neame Spitfire; guest beers H
Single storey Wetherspoon's pub in a building converted from a furniture store. Regularly changing guest ales are served here and there are Monday Club and Ale Wednesday offers each week. Several CAMRA members are among the staff. Many bus routes pass by and there is a stop right outside. ☕◐◑🚌⊱

Bromley

Anglesea Arms

90 Palace Road, BR1 3JX

⏲ 11-11 (11.30 Fri & Sat); 12-11 Sun
☎ (020) 8460 1985
Shepherd Neame Master Brew Bitter, Spitfire, seasonal beers Ⓗ
This back-street local in a well-pubbed area is only five minutes' walk from Bromley North station and many bus routes. It was renovated fairly recently but has kept its traditional feel and atmosphere. Local workers and residents are well catered for, with lunches on Wednesday to Saturday. There is a well-maintained patio garden at the rear incorporating a covered area for smokers, plus a couple of tables at the front.
✿◐♿⇌(Bromley North)🚌⚡

Bitter End Off Licence

139 Masons Hill, BR2 9HW
⏲ 5-9 Mon; 12-3, 5-10 Tue-Fri; 11-10 Sat; 12-2, 7-9 Sun
☎ (020) 8466 6083 🌐 thebitterend.biz
Beer range varies Ⓖ
A well-established independent off-licence selling an ever-changing range of real ales and ciders in four-and-a-half and nine-pint containers to take away. Real ales regularly include Oakham and Harveys. Minipins, polypins and firkins are available to order. In addition to cask ales, Biddenden and Weston's ciders are usually available, together with a selection of bottled Belgian beers and a full range of Sam Smith's bottled beers.
⇌(Bromley South)🚌🍎

Bricklayers Arms

141-143 Masons Hill, BR2 9HW
⏲ 11-3, 5-11.30; 12-3.30, 7-11 Sat; 12-3.30, 7-10.30 Sun
☎ (020) 8460 4552
Shepherd Neame Master Brew Bitter, Spitfire, Bishops Finger, seasonal beers Ⓗ
This locals' pub has been run by George and Pam Pearson for the last 38 years and they have picked up Shepherd Neame Pub of the Year and Lifetime Achievement awards. Pam's Sunday lunches are a highlight. The Wurlitzer jukebox with its 50s hits is only a decorative feature in the light and airy interior. Outdoors is a unique heated drinking and smoking area on two levels, with seating, table football, a dartboard and a small TV.
Q✿◐⇌(Bromley South)🚌⚡

Bromley Labour Club

HG Wells Centre, St Marks Road, BR2 9HG (behind police station)
⏲ 11-11 (midnight Fri & Sat); 12-11 Sun
☎ (020) 8460 7409
Shepherd Neame Master Brew Bitter; guest beer Ⓗ
This small, friendly club shows all major sporting events on a large-screen TV. There is a function room for hire and other facilities include a pool room, darts, dominoes and draughts behind the bar. Outdoors is a patio area with seating. The club is open to card-carrying CAMRA members.
✿♿⇌(Bromley South)🚌♣P⚡

Partridge

194 High Street, BR1 1HE
⏲ 12-11 (midnight Fri & Sat); 12-10.30 Sun
☎ (020) 8464 7656
Fuller's Discovery, London Pride, ESB, seasonal beers; Gale's HSB Ⓗ
An excellent conversion of a grand traditional National Westminster Bank, the pub retains many features from its banking days. The manager's office is now a nice little snug, while the bar is where the original service counter stood. There is a dining area where delicious meals can be enjoyed in peace and quiet. A good range of Fuller's bottled beers is stocked. Sky Sports is shown on large-screen TVs and there is an outdoor patio.
✿◐◑♿⇌(Bromley North)🚌⚡

Prince Frederick

31 Nichol Lane, BR1 4DE
⏲ 11-11 (11.30 Fri & Sat); 12-11 Sun
☎ (020) 8466 6741
Greene King IPA, Ruddles County, Abbot Ⓗ
Superb traditional back-street pub which retains a public bar and some very impressive bar ceilings. A large-screen TV shows sport and there is an excellent covered and heated smoking area outside. The pub is situated on the Green Chain Walk and is only five minutes' walk from Sundridge Park station.
✿⊟♿⇌(Sundridge Park)🚌♣⚡

Red Lion

10 North Road, BR1 3LG
⏲ 11 (12 Sun)-11
☎ (020) 8460 2691
Greene King IPA, Abbot; Harveys Sussex Best Bitter; guest beers Ⓗ
The husband and wife licensee team share the credit for the popularity of this local CAMRA Pub of the Year 2007. Situated in the back streets near Bromley North station, this charismatic pub with its single bar, original tiling, shelves of books and newspapers is an asset to the community. It was a Beard's Brewery pub prior to acquisition by Greene King a few years ago. Forthcoming guest ales are announced on a blackboard behind the bar. Q✿◐⇌(Bromley North)🚌⚡

Richmal Crompton

23 Westmoreland Place, BR1 1DS
⏲ 9-11.30
☎ (020) 8464 1586
Courage Best Bitter; Greene King Old Speckled Hen, Abbot; Marston's Pedigree; Shepherd Neame Spitfire; guest beers Ⓗ
Originally a large supermarket on the ground floor of an office block, this Wetherspoon/ Lloyds No 1 Bar has a large raised seating area and a spacious standing area. Several large-screen TVs show sports or news. This is a handy pub to relax in after shopping in Bromley High Street, or when waiting for a train. In the evenings and at weekends it is very popular. Children are welcome until 9pm. Outside is a heated patio .
✿◐◑⇌(Bromley South)🚌⚡

Tom Foolery

204-206 High Street, BR1 1PW
⏲ 11-11 (11.30 Fri & Sat); 12-10.30 Sun
☎ (020) 8290 2039
Fuller's Discovery, London Pride, ESB, seasonal beers; guest beers Ⓗ
Modern town-centre pub with a relaxed atmosphere serving good quality, award-

winning food. Sky Sports is shown on a large-screen TV and there is monthly live entertainment. Piped music is often played and there is a heated outdoor smoking area. Fuller's Pub of the Year 2005.
❀◐♿⇌(Bromley North)🚌⚡

Bromley Common

Two Doves

37 Oakley Road, BR2 8HD

12-3, 5.30 (5 Mon)-11; 12-11.30 Fri & Sat; 12-11 Sun

☎ (020) 8462 1627

St Austell Tribute; Wells Bombardier; Young's Bitter, Special, seasonal beer Ⓗ

Discerning drinkers across the age range frequent this friendly Young's house. An attractive bar displays a collection of beer steins plus pewter and ceramic tankards. This quiet pub boasts a relaxing rear conservatory with a delightful and carefully attended rear garden, with a covered, heated section for smokers. Occasional quiz nights are hosted and terrestrial TV coverage is limited to major sporting events. Q❀◐🚌(320)⚡

Chelsfield

Five Bells

Church Road, BR6 7RE

12-11 (10.30 Sun)

☎ (01689) 821044

Courage Best Bitter; Harvey's Sussex Best Bitter; Sharp's Cornish Coaster, Doom Bar Ⓗ

A delightful weatherboarded country pub with a traditional public bar and dining room that have remained unchanged for decades. A beamed saloon bar is a separate room, while outside is a very large garden. The pub is only two miles from Orpington and the bus stops right outside. ♨Q❀◐◑🚌(R3)♣P

Chislehurst

Bulls Head

Royal Parade, BR7 6NR

11-11 (midnight Fri & Sat); 12-11 Sun

☎ (020) 8467 1727 🌐 thebullsheadhotel.co.uk

Wells Bombardier; Young's Bitter, Special, seasonal beers; guest beers Ⓗ

Early 19th-century red-brick pub and hotel with three bars. It is locally listed and comfortably furnished, with wood-panelled walls creating a cosy atmosphere. The restaurant provides meals lunchtimes and evenings, with a Sunday carvery each week. Barbecues are held in the summer and children are welcome until 6.30pm. A function room caters for weddings, salsa and singles nights. The large garden incorporates a covered smoking area.
Q♨❀🛏◐◑🚌(61,273)P⚡

Ramblers Rest

Mill Place, BR7 5ND (off Old Hill)

12-11 (10.30 Sun)

☎ (020) 8467 1734

Brakspear Bitter; Courage Best Bitter; Fuller's London Pride; Wells Bombardier; guest beer Ⓗ

This locally listed timber-fronted pub, on the fringe of the common, was originally a squatters' cottage dating back to the early 18th century. The public bar has wood-panelled walls, with stairs leading to the lower lounge bar. A garden to the rear incorporates a covered area for smokers. Food is served Monday-Saturday, with free bar snacks on Sunday. Quiz nights are monthly on Wednesday, cribbage is often played and the pub is well-known for its charity fundraising. Children are allowed.
Q❀◐◑⇌🚌(269,162)♣P⚡

Crayford

Crayford Arms

37 Crayford High Street, DA1 4HH

12-11.30 (midnight Fri & Sat)

Shepherd Neame Kent's Best, Spitfire Ⓗ

This friendly corner local retains a traditional atmosphere, enhanced by many original features. The small entrance lobby was once used for off-sales. To the right is a cosy public bar and to the left a wood-panelled saloon bar. Note the original doors leading to both bars. In the saloon bar an attractive oak staircase leads up to a large function room. Occasional live music is performed and a covered smoking area is outside.
❀◑⇌🚌♣P⚡

Croydon

Dog & Bull

24 Surrey Street, CR0 1RG

11-11 (midnight Thu-Sat); 12-10.30 Sun

☎ (020) 8667 9718

Wells Bombardier; Young's Bitter, Special, seasonal beers Ⓗ

One of Croydon's oldest inns, a pub has stood here in the market for hundreds of years. Parts of the present building date back to the 18th century and the involvement of Young's dates from the late 19th century. The island bar has two rooms leading off, with a TV in the rear room. There are bare wood floors and wood-panelled walls throughout. An excellent pub garden has a covered area where summer barbecues are held. No children or dogs allowed.
❀◐⇌(East/West Croydon)⊖(George St Tramlink)🚌♣⚡

Green Dragon ✔

60 High Street, CR0 1NA

10-midnight (1am Fri & Sat); 12-10.30 Sun

☎ (020) 8667 0684 🌐 myspace.com/greendragonpub

Fuller's London Pride; Shepherd Neame Spitfire; Ⓗ **guest beers** Ⓗ/Ⓖ

Originally created as a Hogshead pub from former bank premises and, after the demise of Hogshead, now revitalised by an enthusiastic landlady. Two of the guest beers are dispensed by gravity from an eye-level stillage. Spacious accommodation on two floors hosts almost daily events, including darts and pool competitions, quiz nights and jazz, acoustic and alternative music sessions, plus a twice-yearly beer festival. Food is available all day until 9pm. Local CAMRA Pub of the Year 2008.
◐◑⇌(East/West Croydon)⊖(George Street Tramlink)🚌

Royal Standard ✔
1 Sheldon Street, CR0 1SS
12-midnight (11 Sun)
☎ (020) 8688 9749
Fuller's Chiswick, London Pride, ESB, seasonal beers Ⓗ
This long-standing Guide entry is situated not far off the High Street but hidden away behind the Wandle Road multi-storey car park. A small street-corner pub, it now has three distinct drinking areas – the third was added by expansion work during the 1990s. The garden lies across the road beneath the Croydon flyover and is surprisingly quiet considering its location. Lunchtime food is served weekdays only.
Q❀◐⇌(East/West Croydon)⊖(George St Tramlink)🚌

Ship of Fools ✔
9-11 London Road, CR0 2RE
9-11 (midnight Fri & Sat)
☎ (020) 8681 2835
Courage Best Bitter, Directors; Greene King Abbot; Marston's Pedigree; Shepherd Neame Spitfire; guest beers Ⓗ
Situated at the north end of the town centre, opposite West Croydon station, this Wetherspoon pub was formerly a Sainsburys. An extensive ground-floor bar has pale-coloured café-style decor, with matching tables and chairs. Food is served all day until 11pm and Weston's Old Rosie cider is available. Mini beer festivals are held occasionally.
◐♿⇌(West Croydon)⊖(West Croydon Tramlink)🚌🍎

Skylark ✔
34-36 South End, CR0 1DP
9-midnight
☎ (020) 8649 9909
Courage Best Bitter, Directors; Greene King Abbot; Marston's Pedigree; Shepherd Neame Spitfire; guest beers Ⓗ
Spacious Wetherspoon's pub located in a former gym and health club. It is laid out on two floors, with a mezzanine area adjoining the ground floor. The Skylark promotes micro-brewery guest beers and runs Meet the Brewer evenings; Westerham Brewery has participated in these and its beers are now regularly on offer. Occasional mini beer festivals are held.
Q❀◐♿⇌(South Croydon)🚌⚡

Spreadeagle ✔
39 High Street, CR0 1NX
11-11 (midnight Fri & Sat); 12-10.30 Sun
☎ (020) 8781 1134
Fuller's Chiswick, Discovery, London Pride, ESB, seasonal beers; Gale's HSB; guest beers Ⓗ
Large two-floor conversion of former bank premises in the town centre beside Croydon's old town hall. The interior features lots of dark wood and mirrors and is an impressive showcase for the complete Fuller's range of ales. An outdoor canopied area caters for smokers.
◐⇌(East/West Croydon)⊖(George St Tramlink)🚌⚡

Cudham

Blacksmiths Arms
Cudham Lane South, TN14 7QB (opp New Barn Lane) TQ446598
11-11 (11.30 Fri & Sat); 12-10.30 Sun
☎ (01959) 572678
Adnams Bitter; Courage Best Bitter; Sharp's Doom Bar; guest beer Ⓗ
This friendly, spacious country pub with a large garden and paved, heated patio area is perched above the steep Cudham Valley. A blue plaque declares it as the birthplace of Harry Relph 'Little Tich' Music Hall Comedian 21/07/1867. The licensee is strongly committed to real ale and serves four well kept beers. Evening meals are available Tuesday-Saturday. Dogs are allowed in the bar area near the main entrance.
🔥Q❀◐🚌(R5)P⚡

North Cray

White Cross
146 North Cray Road, DA14 5EL
11-11; 12-10.30 Sun
☎ (020) 8300 2590
Courage Best Bitter, Directors; guest beers Ⓗ
This pub retains a rural setting despite its location by a dual carriageway. One side of the building is principally for drinking and to the left is a large extension set aside for meals at busy times. The pub is renowned for its fine food, served daily until closing time. Guest beers are normally from micro-breweries all over the UK. Q❀◐🚌(492)♣P⚡

Orpington

Cricketers
93 Chislehurst Road, BR6 0DQ
12-3, 5-11.30; 12-11.30 Sat; 12-10.30 Sun
☎ (01689) 812648
Adnams Bitter, Broadside; Wadworth 6X Ⓗ
This traditional pub is in a quiet residential area, about five minutes' walk from the town centre. Before you enter, be sure to look out for the horse's head on the stable door by the car parking area. The pub has been run by the same family for over 30 years and your dog will be made as welcome as you are by the friendly bar staff. Framed displays of cigarette cards featuring cricketers add a historic touch. Lunches are served weekdays only.
Q🛏❀◐🚌(61)P

Petts Wood

Sovereign of the Seas
109-111 Queensway, BR5 1DG
10-11 (11.30 Fri & Sat)
☎ (01689) 891606
Greene King Abbot; Marston's Pedigree; Shepherd Neame Spitfire; Theakston Best Bitter; guest beers Ⓗ
This long Wetherspoon's pub has varied seating areas including sofas, cosy alcoves and high tables. Mixed decor includes painted wooden panels, local history information, bookshelves and modern art. Originally a furniture shop, the pub takes its name from a Navy warship built by local shipbuilder Peter

Pett in 1638. The local area also takes its name from the Pett family. Wi-Fi is available.
Q❀◐◑♿≋🚌

Shirley

Orchard
116 Orchard Way, CR0 7NN
✪ 12-11
☎ (020) 8777 9011
Fuller's London Pride; Harveys Sussex Best Bitter Ⓗ
Dating from the 1960s, this community pub is at the end of a shopping parade in the Monks Orchard area of Shirley. Despite its name, it is partly obscured by a prominent cedar tree at the front. Two connected drinking areas can be entered by the front or side door. Furnishings include fixed alcove seats along the walls. 🚌(367)♣P

Sidcup

Alma
10 Alma Road, DA14 4EA
✪ 11-3, 5.30-11; 11-midnight Fri; 11-4, 6-midnight Sat; 12-3, 7-11 Sun
☎ (020) 8300 3208
Courage Best Bitter; Fuller's London Pride Ⓗ
Back-street local near Sidcup station that is popular with commuters. The pub dates from 1868 when it was called the Railway Tavern. It has a traditional pub atmosphere indoors, while outside is a grassed garden that is popular in summer. Lunches are served on weekdays only and limited parking is available. Q❀◐≋🚌♣P

Upper Belvedere

Victoria
2 Victoria Street, DA17 5LN
✪ 12-11 (midnight Fri & Sat); 12-10.30 Sun
☎ (01322) 433773
Adnams Bitter; Shepherd Neame Spitfire Ⓗ
Traditional back-street local with a cosy atmosphere. The horseshoe-shaped bar contains sporting photos and memorabilia as well as photos of the local area in bygone days. TVs showing live football and darts are not obtrusive. An attractive drinking area outside is ideal for warm weather drinking. ♨❀🚌(99,401)♣⌐

Welling

New Cross Turnpike
55 Bellgrove Road, DA16 3PB
✪ 9-midnight
☎ (020) 8304 1660
Courage Best Bitter; Greene King Abbot; Marston's Pedigree; Shepherd Neame Spitfire; guest beers Ⓗ
A typical Wetherspoon pub with an attractive layout on four levels including a gallery and two patios. Disabled access includes a wheelchair lift. Varied guest ales are served by helpful staff. Note Monday Club and Ale Wednesday special offers. The smoking area is heated and covered. Q❀◐◑♿≋🚌⌐

SOUTH-WEST LONDON

SW1: Belgravia

Antelope
22 Eaton Terrace, SW1W 8EZ
✪ 12-11; closed Sun
☎ (020) 7824 8512
Fuller's Chiswick, Discovery, London Pride, ESB, seasonal beers Ⓗ
Constructed in 1827 as a mews pub, the Antelope was designed to meet the needs of household staff and tradespeople providing for local properties. These days, it attracts a more diverse clientele. A large island bar is the outstanding feature inside. The rear area has a relaxing atmosphere with leather seating and a fireplace, while the impressive upstairs room has its own bar and may be booked for functions. Meals are available daily except Saturday. ◐◑⊖(Sloane Square)🚌

Horse & Groom
7 Groom Place, SW1X 7BA
✪ 11-11 (midnight Thu & Fri); closed Sat & Sun
☎ (020) 7235 6980
Shepherd Neame Master Brew Bitter, Spitfire Ⓗ
Friendly and welcoming traditional mews pub. It has a small, cosy bar and an upstairs room that can be hired for functions; the whole pub can be booked at the weekend. You can order a pizza from a takeaway and eat it in the pub. You may meet a piper from the nearby Caledonian Club who will play for you. ☕◐⊖(Hyde Pk Corner)🚌⌐

Nag's Head
53 Kinnerton Street, SW1X 8ED
✪ 11-11; 12-10.30 Sun
☎ (020) 7235 1135
Adnams Bitter, Broadside Ⓗ
Yes, this is the Nag's Head. You could be forgiven for thinking it is the Kevin Moran, as the landlord's name is on the pub sign. You are entering a time warp. This pub looks as though it has been preserved from the 1950s, with a penny arcade machine and a 'What the Butler Saw'. An old penny from the bar will take you back to a time when even pornography was quaint. No mobiles allowed. ♨Q❀◐⊖(Hyde Pk Corner/Knightsbridge)🚌

Star Tavern ✔
6 Belgrave Mews West, SW1X 8HT
✪ 11-11; 12-10.30 Sun
☎ (020) 7235 3019
Fuller's Chiswick, Discovery, London Pride, ESB, seasonal beers Ⓗ
A Grade II-listed pub dating from 1848, the Star underwent a refurbishment in early 2008. No glass and chrome here – the ambience takes you back to when a pub looked like a pub. In recent years the pub has organised a posse of regulars to take part in fundraising events to raise money for cancer research. Winner of numerous awards for many years and resident in the Guide since its first edition. Q◐◑🛏♿⊖(Hyde Pk Corner/Knightsbridge)🚌

SW1: Victoria

Cask & Glass

39-41 Palace Street, SW1E 5HN

11-11; 12-9 Sat; closed Sun

(020) 7834 7630

Shepherd Neame Master Brew Bitter, Kent's Best, Spitfire, Bishops Finger, seasonal beers H

This corner pub, originally named the Duke of Cambridge, was first licensed in 1862. An attractive bar back features the name of the brewery on mirrors. The walls also include decorative mirrors, caricatures of politicians and photographs of brewery activities. Outside is an attractive display of flowering plants, with tables and seating. The street behind the pub has a house used in the opening shot of the cult 1960s TV series The Prisoner.

Q

Jugged Hare

172 Vauxhall Bridge Road, SW1V 1DX

11-11 (11.30 Fri); 12-10.30 Sun

(020) 7828 1543 juggedhare.co.uk

Fuller's Chiswick, Discovery, London Pride, ESB, seasonal beers H

Converted from a former bank and located in a residential and business area close to Tachbrook Street Market. It has many impressive features including tall windows, a large chandelier, a tiled floor and a prominent upstairs balcony. An attractive refuge from the busy streets during quiet periods, the pub attracts a varied clientele comprising local residents, workers and business people. A good food menu is offered both lunchtimes and evenings. The balcony and rear room can be booked for functions.

Willow Walk

25 Wilton Road, SW1V 1LW

9-midnight; 10-11.30 Sun

(020) 7828 2953

Greene King Abbot; Marston's Pedigree; guest beers H

Wetherspoon conversion of ex-retail premises decked out in 1990s style with historical references to Pimlico and Ranelagh Gardens. It is popular with locals enjoying the reasonable prices and, situated near to Victoria Station, a favourite watering hole for commuters. The guest beer range is better than the average Wetherspoon's, with two banks of handpumps and regular beer festivals and promotions.

SW1: Westminster

Buckingham Arms

62 Petty France, SW1H 9EU

11-11; 12-10.30 Sun

(020) 7222 3386

Young's Bitter, Special, seasonal beers H

Large main bar with a corridor to the side, once used by servants to drink in secrecy from their masters, now more likely to be occupied by MPs avoiding the prying eyes of journalists. A traditional Victorian pub with a devoted following – some of whom have been popping in every week for more than 30 years. This is one of two London pubs listed in every issue of the Guide since it was first published in 1974. Due for extensive refurbishment during 2008. Q (St James's Pk)

Royal Oak

2 Regency Street, SW1P 4BZ

11-11; closed Sat; 12-4 Sun

(020) 7834 7046

Wells Bombardier; Young's Bitter, seasonal beers H

This busy corner pub is packed with office workers in the early evening. With windows on three sides there is not much room for pictures, but two good marine paintings and several interesting prints adorn the remaining wall. Established in 1831 and rebuilt in 1872, the pub was saved from demolition following a campaign by local people, with the help of CAMRA. Lunches are served Monday-Friday.

(Victoria) (St James's Pk)

Sanctuary House Hotel

33 Tothill Street, SW1H 9LA

11-11; 12-10.30 Sun

(020) 7799 4044 sanctuaryhousehotel.com

Fuller's Chiswick, London Pride, ESB, seasonal beers H

Situated on the site of a monastery and formerly MI5 HQ during WWII, this is now a 34-bedroom hotel, recently refurbished to provide modern hotel facilities in one of London's oldest and most fashionable areas. There is an Ale & Pie House on the ground floor which is classic Fuller's: smart and modern in execution.

(St James's Park)

Speaker

46 Great Peter Street, SW1P 2HA

12-11; closed Sat & Sun

(020) 7222 1749

Shepherd Neame Spitfire; Young's Bitter; guest beers H

Located near the heart of Westminster, this pub is popular with civil servants and MPs and, like most bars in the area, has its own division bell. There are caricatures of MPs and clay pipes throughout the wood-panelled interior. Regular themed beer festivals are held, utilising two handpumps.

Q (St James's Pk)

St Stephen's Tavern

10 Bridge Street, SW1A 2JR

10-11.30 (midnight Fri); 10.30-10.30 Sun

(020) 7925 2286

Badger Tanglefoot, seasonal beers H

Established in 1875, the inn is popular with workers, members of parliament (division bell installed, but no tunnel under the road) and tourists. It reopened in December 2003 with some old fittings and fixtures – oak panelling, high ceilings, Pugin wallpaper, engraved mirrors, windows (a view of Big Ben) and hanging pendant lights. Churchill drank here and Disraeli founded St Stephen's Gentlemen's Club. It is slightly below street level, with two bars, button-leather couch seating and an upstairs balcony room. Proper English puddings are promoted. Q

SW1: Whitehall

Lord Moon of the Mall ✔

16-18 Whitehall, SW1A 2DY

9-11.30 (midnight Fri & Sat); 9-11 Sun

(020) 7839 7701

Fuller's London Pride; Greene King Abbot; Marston's Pedigree; Wells Bombardier; guest beers

Formerly a Barclays Bank, this is an early Wetherspoon pub conversion decked out in mock open-plan Victoriana that was all the rage in the 1990s. Located on Whitehall, this pub is popular with tourists who frequent the rear of the pub with their families enjoying the food, as well as civil servants and MPs. Regular beer festivals and promotions are held.

Q≠(Charing Cross)⊖(Charing Cross/ Westminster)

SW2: Streatham Hill

Crown & Sceptre ✔

2A Streatham Hill, SW2 4AH

9-11 (midnight Fri & Sat)

(020) 8671 0843

Courage Best Bitter; Greene King Abbot; Marston's Pedigree; guest beers

The new management has revitalised this large Wetherspoon pub with its cosy, split-level interior. The first such conversion in south west London, it retains its Truman fascia, thanks to the local history society. Cask beer is very important here and mini festivals are often held. The pub tries to maintain four guest beers, usually including one from Westerham, and sells Weston's Old Rosie cider. Q≠P

SW4: Clapham

Bread & Roses

68 Clapham Manor Street, SW4 6DZ

12 (5 Mon & Tue)-11 (midnight Fri & Sat); 12-10.30 Sun

(020) 7498 1779 breadandrosespub.com

Sharp's Doom Bar; guest beers

An award-winning design on the site of a once closed pub, funded by a local trades council that still retains an interest. The name of the pub is explained above the bar. High quality food and drinks are available, with tasting notes on the pumps. Cask beer festivals are popular and as well as the draught beers there are interesting foreign beers to try. At the rear is a family room and a sheltered garden. There is also a front patio.

≠(Clapham High St)⊖(Clapham Common/North)

Manor Arms

128 Clapham Manor Street, SW4 6ED

1-11; 12-midnight Fri & Sat; 12-11 Sun

(020) 7622 2894

Black Sheep Best Bitter; Hop Back Summer Lightning; Taylor Landlord; guest beer

Just off the bustle of Clapham High Street, the Manor has a continental feel and is very lively when big sporting events are shown on the three TV screens. The front area is a good place to watch the world go by. A marquee at the back is used for private functions and fundraising events, often in support of London Hibs football club.

≠(Clapham High St)⊖(Clapham Common/ North)

Rose & Crown

2 The Polygon, Clapham Old Town, SW4 0JG

2 (12 Fri & Sat)-midnight (1am Thu-Sat); 12-midnight Sun

(020) 7627 5369

Greene King IPA, Morland Original, Ruddles County, Abbot, seasonal beer; guest beer

Uncompromising, traditional pub – no food at all – showcasing the range of Greene King cask ales and a changing guest beer, all kept in excellent condition. The small, half wood-panelled single bar is screened into different areas by structural pillars, creating an intimate atmosphere. There is a pavement drinking area in front of the attractive, tiled frontage; a heated, part-covered yard at the back now accommodates smokers. This is a pub for drinkers, cared for with pride and attitude.

⊖(Clapham Common)

Windmill on the Common

Clapham Common South Side, SW4 9DE

11-11; 12-10.30 Sun

(020) 8673 4578 windmillclapham.co.uk

Wells Bombardier; Young's Bitter, Special, seasonal beer

A large, historic pub on Clapham Common with modern, restrained decor and several distinct areas. Interesting glasswork in the main bar area, panelling in the eponymous panel room, the dome room and the restaurant all contribute to the stylish interior. There has been a pub on this site since 1665, although the current building dates mostly from the 18th and 19th centuries. Quiz night is Sunday. Parts of the pub are available for hire. Outside is a heated, covered smoking area.

Q⊖(Clapham Common)P

SW5: Earls Court

Blackbird ✔

209 Earls Court Road, SW5 9AN

11-11; 12-10.30 Sun

(020) 7835 1855

Fuller's Chiswick, Discovery, London Pride, ESB

This pub was converted from a bank premises in 1993 and has retained some features from its early days – the toilets are in the old vault. One of Fuller's Ale & Pie pubs, it has a seated area for diners. Handy for Earls Court exhibition centre. ⊖

SW6: Fulham

Temperance ✔

90 Fulham High Street, SW6 3LF

12-11

(020) 7384 3573 myspace.com/ temperancefulham

Caledonian Deuchars IPA; Taylor Landlord; guest beers

Built in 1909 as a billiards hall on the corner of Fulham High Street and Church Gate, the building was transformed into a Firkin brewpub before becoming an Irish theme bar. It was given its current name when real ale was restored after refurbishment in late 2006. The building's amazing high ceilings and stained glass have been highlighted, together with new decor, lighting and furniture, in comfortable airy lounge areas and formal dining areas. Weston's real cider or perry is served. (Putney Bridge)

SW6: Parsons Green

White Horse

1-3 Parsons Green, SW6 4UL

11-11.30 (midnight Thu-Sat); 11-11 Sun

(020) 7736 2115 whitehorsesw6.com

Adnams Broadside; Harveys Sussex Best Bitter; guest beers

Large, light and airy pub in a very well-heeled area offering up to seven cask ales and several continental beers on handpump. An impressive rosewood horseshoe bar fits the pub's name very well. The interior is comfortably furnished with wooden benches and leather sofas. An extensive menu includes gastronomic delights such as Calvados pot roast pheasant with a recommendation of accompanying ales. The spacious area outside fronting Parsons Green gets very busy in the summertime.

SW7: South Kensington

Anglesea Arms

15 Selwood Terrace, SW7 3QG

11-11; 12-10.30 Sun

(020) 7373 7960

Fuller's London Pride; guest beers

Attractive rustic local, popular with the area's residents and visiting diners. A large room at the front conceals the restaurant at the rear that you might not know was there without a trip to the loo. Artwork is a study in contrasts, with an oil painting of a pretty young girl sharing wall space with one of an older, rugged-looking man. Q

SW8: Stockwell

Priory Arms

83 Lansdowne Way, SW8 2PB

12-11 (10.30 Sun)

(020) 7622 1884

Harveys Sussex Best; Hop Back Summer Lightning; guest beers

Award-winning free house that continues to be a bastion of quality beers and good food, attracting a wide range of customers who chat, read the free newspapers or watch big match sport. The vast number of pump clips indicates the range of guest beers sold over the years. Foreign beers and a choice of 25 malt whiskies are popular. There is an upstairs function room. The listed frontage is a riot of colourful hanging baskets in summer.
(Vauxhall/Wandsworth Rd)

SW9: Brixton

Trinity Arms

45 Trinity Gardens, SW9 8DR

11-11 (midnight Fri & Sat); 12-11 Sun

(020) 7274 4544

Wells Bombardier; Young's Bitter, Special, seasonal beer

Named after the ancient asylum in Acre Lane. The pub is a well-deserved regular entry in the Guide, thanks to the management team of the last 10 years. A glorious retreat from the noise of Brixton High Street, it is becoming increasingly popular as more people discover the excellent beers and the opportunity to talk in a quiet and relaxed atmosphere. There are no lunches on Saturday but Sunday roasts are excellent value. The rear garden is well used. Not to be missed.

SW10: Chelsea

Chelsea Ram

32 Burnaby Street, SW10 0PL

11-11; 12-10.30 Sun

(020) 7351 4008

Wells Bombardier; Young's Bitter, Special, seasonal beers

Located near the former Lots Road Power Station and Auction Rooms. Refurbished by Young's with a light and spacious gastro-pub ambience, it has not lost its original community atmosphere. There are distinctive arched windows with the Ram symbol etched in the glass. The staff show commitment to beer quality plus an emphasis on good food availability, including daily specials.
Q(C3)

SW11: Battersea

Beehive

197 St John's Hill, SW11 1TH

11-11 (midnight Fri & Sat); 12-11 Sun

(020) 7564 1897

Fuller's London Pride, ESB; guest beer

Fuller's only tied house in SW11 or Wandsworth, this small, friendly, one-room local has a public bar feel to it. The guest beer changes every week and the quality of the ales meant the Beehive was a SW London CAMRA Pub of the Year finalist in 2007. There is unobtrusive background music and live performances on Thursday evening. Wholesome lunches are served Monday to Friday. Everyone is welcome, including well-behaved children. Ten minutes' walk from Clapham Junction, it has six Wandsworth-bound bus routes passing close by.
(Clapham Jct)

Eagle Ale House

104 Chatham Road, SW11 6HG

12-11 (10.30 Sun)

(020) 7228 2328

Sharp's Doom Bar; Westerham IPA; guest beers

A real ale haven hidden away from the trendy bars and affluent young family establishments of Northcote Road. The Eagle has seven ever-changing real ales from micro-breweries and one real cider. An unspoilt, dog-friendly local, the somewhat chaotic interior features big leather sofas, old bottles and dusty books. A loyal, mixed clientele is welcoming to all. The large-screen TV shows major sporting events. Curry night is Thursday and on Sunday there are roasts plus a quiz in the evening. There is a

heated marquee in garden.
(319,G1)

Falcon ☆ ✔

2 St John's Hill, SW11 1RU
10-11 (midnight Thu-Sat); 10-10.30 Sun
(020) 7924 8041
Adnams Broadside; Fuller's London Pride; Shepherd Neame Spitfire; Taylor Landlord; Wadworth 6X; Wells Bombardier; guest beers
This local landmark, now part of the Nicholson's chain, has recently been refurbished. There is a stronger emphasis on food and real ale, but the Victorian splendours of this National Inventory pub remain. The island bar is reputed to have one of the longest continuous counters in the country, and there is some fine panelling at the rear. The Falcon was once run by Mr Robert Death, hence the stained glass depiction of undertakers frolicking at his door.
(Clapham Jct)

SW12: Balham

Nightingale

97 Nightingale Lane, SW12 8NY
11 (12 Sun)-midnight
(020) 8673 1637
Wells Bombardier; Young's Bitter, Special, seasonal beer
The 'Bird' is an utterly traditional Young's house where the customer is the main focus. A warm welcome is guaranteed and the draught beer is always a big seller. This pub is regularly shortlisted for the local Pub of the Year ballot. The legendary charitable walk in April has raised huge sums over the years and its exploits are chronicled on the walls. Food is served all day, every day. Altogether a wonderful community pub.
Q(Wandsworth Common)
(Clapham South)(G1)

SW13: Barnes

Red Lion ✔

2 Castelnau, SW13 9RU
11-11; 12-10.30 Sun
(020) 8748 2984
Fuller's Discovery, London Pride, ESB, seasonal beers
A large Georgian landmark pub, situated at the entrance to the Wetland Centre. It has been opened out in recent years, although the rear room still has a more exclusive feel. From here guests reach a decked patio area and the spacious garden. Excellent food is always available from a varied, modern menu, and children are welcome during the day.
P

SW15: Putney

Bricklayers Arms

32 Waterman Street, SW15 1DD
12-11 (10.30 Sun)
(020) 8789 0222 bricklayers-arms.co.uk
Taylor Dark Mild, Golden Best, Best Bitter, Landlord, Ram Tam; guest beers
Off the Lower Richmond Road, this delightful pub, dating from 1826 and rescued from closure in 2005, has gone from strength to strength, winning CAMRA branch Pub of the Year award in 2006 and the 2007 London regional title. Four guest ales from micro-breweries plus Weston's cider are served and occasional beer festivals are held. Modestly furnished, and decorated with old photos and Putney-related cartoons, this locals' pub is busy when Fulham FC are at home. Shove ha'penny and bar skittles are played.
(Putney Bridge)

Half Moon

93 Lower Richmond Road, SW15 1EU
12 (4 Mon)-midnight; 12-11 Sun
(020) 8780 9383 halfmoon.co.uk
Wells Bombardier; Young's Bitter, Special, seasonal beer
Imposing corner pub, rebuilt in 1903 and well known as a venue for live rock music. The uncarpeted bar is decorated with photos and posters of bands who have played here, including, in their early days, the Rolling Stones and U2. There is live music every night: the music room is entered through swing doors at the rear. The pub is frequented by drinkers and rock fans of all ages. No food is served on Monday.

SW17: Summerstown

Leather Bottle

538 Garratt Lane, SW17 0NY
11-11 (11.30 Thu-Sat); 12-10.30 Sun
(020) 8946 2309
Courage Directors; Young's Bitter, Special
Mock elections for Mayor of Garratt were once held on a green opposite this pub, a 260-year-old listed building and a Young's pub for at least 175 years. Refurbished in 2004, it has a large, paved, partly covered and heated beer garden at the back. Inside facilities on two levels include a restaurant with an extensive menu. A regular hog roast and specialised food nights are held. Tuesday is poker league night. Boules is played outside in summer.
(Earlsfield)P

SW18: Battersea

Freemasons

2 Wandsworth Common North Side, SW18 2SS
11-11; 12-10.30 Sun
(020) 7326 8580 freemasonspub.com
Everards Tiger; Taylor Landlord
A Victorian corner building with an ornate entrance lobby that includes a mosaic floor featuring the pub's name. Tables and chairs are on one side of the bar, a restaurant area on the other, with sofas and armchairs at the front. There is patio seating outside at the front. Excellent food includes up to seven main courses, changing daily. Cask ale is served from unusual glass canisters. Quiz night is Monday at 8pm (booking essential). Close to the 1988 Clapham rail disaster memorial.
(77,219)

SW18: Wandsworth

Alma

499 Old York Road, SW18 1TF

11-midnight; 12-11 Sun
(020) 8870 2537 almawandsworth.com
Wells Bombardier; Young's Bitter, Special, seasonal beer
This lively upmarket inn retains its attractive, green tiled façade and some remarkable painted mirrors, hence its inclusion on CAMRA's London Regional Inventory. Directly opposite Wandsworth Town station, the pub is generally very busy and even more so when rugby matches are shown on two big screens. It is very popular for its excellent food and booking is advisable for the restaurant, although the same menu is available in the bar. (Wandsworth Town)

Earl Spencer
260-262 Merton Road, SW18 5JL
11-11 (midnight Fri); 12-10.30 Sun
(020) 8870 9244 theearlspencer.co.uk
Fuller's London Pride; Hook Norton Hooky Bitter; guest beers
A quiet music and TV-free venue with a smart, mixed clientele, this award-winning gastro-pub makes drinkers welcome. It has a no reservations policy and does not serve food all day. Cream painted walls with dark blue woodwork and a ceiling with gilt mouldings make for an attractive, airy interior. Two guest beers come from the Spatchcock Inns list, usually from smaller brewers. The function room upstairs can be hired. There is pavement patio seating at the front.
Q (Southfields) (156)

Gardeners Arms
268 Merton Road, SW18 5JL
11-11 (midnight Fri & Sat); 12-11.30 Sun
(020) 8874 7624
Young's Bitter, Special, seasonal beer
A corner house community pub built in the 1930s with fine green exterior tiling. A U-shaped bar divides the interior into a public bar area with dartboard and a lounge area which has been extended into the former shop next door, where sport is shown on TV. A quiz and buffet is held on Tuesday. There is no food on Saturday and lunch only on Sunday. There has been a Young's pub on the site since 1875. (Southfields) (156)

Grapes
39 Fairfield Street, SW18 1DX
12-11 (midnight Fri & Sat); 12-10.30 Sun
(020) 8874 3414
Young's Bitter, Special
This friendly, traditional local pub is a stone's throw from the now defunct Ram Brewery. In the summer customers can enjoy the delightful garden, a true oasis often difficult to find in London. Smokers can enjoy the heated patio all year round. This lively establishment welcomes well-behaved children and shows major sporting events on several TV screens. Excellent lunches are served Monday to Friday. South West London CAMRA Pub of the Year 2005, this is definitely not one to miss.
(Wandsworth Town)

Spread Eagle
71 Wandsworth High Street, SW18 4LB
11-11 (midnight Fri & Sat); 12-11 Sun
(020) 8877 9809
Wells Bombardier; Young's Bitter, Special
A large pub in the centre of Wandsworth with an outstanding Victorian etched glass interior and an external canopy (watch out for the smokers gathered underneath in inclement weather), worth visiting as much for the architecture as for the beer. Three distinct drinking areas include a public bar with pool table and large TV screen. A quieter room at the back is available for meetings and functions. Food is served weekdays and Sunday roasts are a welcome addition.
Q (Wandsworth Town)

Wheatsheaf
30 Putney Bridge Road, SW18 1HS
11-midnight; 12-11 Sun
(020) 8874 5753
Young's Bitter, Special, seasonal beer
A fantastic unspoilt pub making its second appearance in the Guide and deservedly so. Dispensing well kept ales, this little gem is welcoming to both families and dogs, and shows Sky Sports on TV. Customers can buy their own food from local takeaways and eat it in the pub. This is one definitely worth seeking out. (Wandsworth Town)

SW19: South Wimbledon

Princess of Wales
98 Morden Road, SW19 3BP
11-11 (midnight Fri); 12-11 Sun
(020) 8542 0573
Young's Bitter, Special, seasonal beer
A cosy, medium-sized, one-bar community pub. The main bar leads to a quieter area and to the side is the former public bar, with a dartboard. The pub dates from the mid 19th century and has evolved over time, but retains its Victorian frontage. It is twinned with the Horse Brass Pub, Portland, Oregon, whose regulars presented the portrait of Princess Diana by American artist James Macko. No evening meals are available at weekends. The rear patio is heated, part covered and well furnished, including a sofa.
Q (Morden Rd Tramlink) (93,470) P

Sultan
78 Norman Road, SW19 1BT
12-11 (midnight Fri & Sat)
(020) 8544 9323
Hop Back GFB, Entire Stout, Summer Lightning; guest beer
Well-run, traditional, two-bar corner local with a cheerful welcome for both its regulars and those seeking out London's only Hop Back tied house. A guest beer is also normally available from the Hop Back seasonal or Downton range. It has a dartboard in the small bar (only open evenings). The Beer Club offers reduced beer prices between 6-9pm on Wednesday and there is a quiz on Tuesday. The pub holds a weekend beer festival in the autumn.
(Colliers Wood)

Trafalgar
23 High Path, SW19 2JY
12 (11 Wed-Fri)-11
(020) 8542 5342 thetraf.com
Beer range varies

CAMRA SW London Pub of the Year 2007, the Traf is a homely, one-bar community corner pub – the smallest and oldest free house in Merton. A real ale haven, it provides six handpumps dispensing an ever-changing range of beers, often milds, from small micro-breweries. The beer festivals are unmissable. Nelson-related prints decorate the walls; a wooden spoked wheel from an old Thames barge divides the bar area. There is live music on Saturday evening, jazz on Sunday afternoon. Monday is quiz night. No food at weekends.

SW19: Wimbledon

Crooked Billet

14-15 Crooked Billet, SW19 4RQ
10-11 (midnight Fri & Sat); 12-10.30 Sun
(020) 8946 4942
thecrookedbilletwimbledon.co.uk
Wells Bombardier; Young's Bitter, Special, seasonal beers

A late 18th-century pub on the edge of Wimbledon Common, bought by Young's in 1888 and extended in 1969 into an adjoining cottage. Real fires and exposed beams add to the warm welcome at this busy, friendly pub. It has an intimate restaurant room at the rear and food is also served in the bar – Sunday lunches are very popular. The Crooked Billet specialises in German beers, holding an Octoberfest festival each October. (200)

Hand in Hand

6 Crooked Billet, SW19 4RQ
10-11 (midnight Fri & Sat); 12-10.30 Sun
(020) 8946 5720
Wells Bombardier; Young's Bitter, Special, seasonal beers

Originally a bakehouse in buildings owned by Daniel Watney, whose grandson founded that brewery, this award-winning pub was a beer house belonging to the Holland family until Young's bought it in 1974. Much altered and extended, it retains an intimate atmosphere in the drinking areas around the central bar, a separate family room and a suntrap patio. Opposite, the grass triangle provides a summer drinking, picnic and play area well used by customers of this pub and the Crooked Billet. (200)

SW20: Raynes Park

Edward Rayne

8-12 Coombe Lane, SW20 8ND
9-11.30
(020) 8971 0420
Greene King IPA, Abbot; Marston's Pedigree; guest beers

Opened in 2006 on the site of a Co-operative supermarket, this spacious Wetherspoon pub commemorates the 19th-century farmer whose lands became Raynes Park. A tastefully designed, single-room establishment with wood panelling and half mirrored pillars, pastel shades and soft lighting, it attracts local families. TV news is shown with subtitles but no sound and fruit machines are also mute. Weston's Old Rosie and Organic Vintage ciders are served on gravity from fridges behind the bar. Q

Carshalton

Greyhound Hotel

2 High Street, SM5 3PE
11 (12 Sun)-midnight
(020) 8647 1511 greyhoundhotel.net
Wells Bombardier; Young's Bitter, Special, seasonal beers

Large pub with restaurant and hotel overlooking Carshalton Ponds. The front Swan Bar (restricted opening hours) overlooks the ponds and this, along with its wood-panelled walls and furnishings, makes it one of the area's most atmospheric drinking places. Some parts of the building date from 1706; look out for the old mosaic floor at the front entrance depicting a greyhound. There is a small front forecourt. Q P

Racehorse

17 West Street, SM5 2PT
11-11; 12-10.30 Sun
(020) 8647 6818 racehorseinns.co.uk
Courage Best Bitter; Greene King IPA, Old Speckled Hen; guest beers

Established in the 1870s, the Racehorse caters for both diners and drinkers in traditional English pub/restaurant surroundings. This two-bar hostelry serves bar food as well as a restaurant menu in the formal dining area in the lounge. Guest beers are selected in consultation with regular customers in this local CAMRA Pub of the Year 2007. Q P

Railway Tavern

47 North Street, SM5 2HG
12-2.30, 5-11; 12-11 Sat; 12-10.30 Sun
(020) 8669 8016
Fuller's London Pride, ESB, seasonal beers

This small Victorian corner local lies just north of the railway bridge. A U-shaped bar has walls adorned with railway memorabilia, together with certificates awarded for its beer quality and outdoor floral displays. A small patio garden is at the rear. Sporting events are screened on the TV. Lunches are served weekdays only.

Windsor Castle

378 Carshalton Road, SM5 3PT
11-11 (11.30 Fri & Sat); 12-11 Sun
(020) 8669 1191
Hancock's HB; Fuller's London Pride; guest beers

Large one-bar pub on a crossroads at the west side of Carshalton. A restaurant area adjoins the bar, where the walls are adorned with pump clips for the vast range of guest beers dispensed over the years. A courtyard at the rear (covered for smokers) leads to a function room and enclosed garden. Quiz night is Thursday and live music is played on Saturday evening. An annual beer festival is held in May. Local CAMRA Pub of the Year 2008. (Carshalton Beeches) P

ENGLAND

Chessington

North Star ✔

271 Hook Road, KT9 1EQ

❂ 12-11 (midnight Fri & Sat)

☎ (020) 8391 9811

Adnams Bitter; Caledonian Deuchars IPA; Fuller's London Pride; guest beers Ⓗ

This Ember Inn dates back some 150 years and is the oldest pub in the area. A varied clientele uses the different drinking areas; some eastern decor is echoed by the Thursday curry night when the set price menu includes a pint of real ale. This community pub hosts a golf society and a Sunday football league; pub quizzes take place twice a week. A shelter has been built in the garden for smokers. The annual autumn beer festival is a popular event. ✿◑♿🚌P⊱

Kingston upon Thames

Canbury Arms

49 Canbury Park Road, KT2 6LQ

❂ 9-11; 12-10.30 Sun

☎ (020) 8255 9129 🌐 thecanburyarms.com

Gale's HSB; Harveys Sussex Best Bitter; Taylor Landlord; guest beers Ⓗ

This modernised pub is strongly food-and-wine oriented, but is also keen on real ale. The single-bar interior with two fires and a piano is supplemented by a large, heated marquee. Pictures of Cuban life, along with a Morecambe and Wise canvas, adorn the walls. Backgammon and chess are available and the local five-a-side teams meet here. Occasional guest beers are served. Excellent food, including brunch, is served daily except Sunday. Q◐◑♿⇌🚌P

Park Tavern

19 New Road, KT2 6AP

❂ 11-11; 12-10.30 Sun

Fuller's London Pride; Taylor Landlord; Young's Bitter; guest beers Ⓗ

A 19th-century pub converted from two houses, situated on a quiet side street near the Kingston Gate of Richmond Park, half a mile from Norbiton station. Inside you will find a real log fire for winter, dominoes, cards, and a changing range of three, often rare, guest beers. Dogs are welcome, as are well-behaved children, until 7pm. The small patio at the front is covered by a trellis. Filled rolls are available lunchtimes Monday to Saturday. ♨✿🚌(371)♣

Queens Head ✔

144 Richmond Road, KT2 5HA

❂ 12-11 (midnight Thu-Sat); 12-10.30 Sun

☎ (020) 8546 9162

Adnams Bitter; guest beers Ⓗ

Large, welcoming, family-friendly Victorian corner pub, which has recently reverted from the Owl & Pussycat to its original name. Up to five beers are available alongside a Victorian-inspired food menu plus Kobe steak burgers. An open-plan layout incorporates two semi-secluded rooms, one with a real fire, suitable for meetings. A strange mix of pictures adorns the walls. The glass-covered terrace out front is heated for smokers, and there is a garden at the rear. Board games are available. Accommodation comprises five rooms. ♨👶✿🛏◐◑♿⇌🚌(65)♣P⊱

Willoughby Arms

47 Willoughby Road, KT2 6LN

❂ 10.30 (12 Sun)-midnight

☎ (020) 8546 4236 🌐 thewilloughbyarms.com

Fuller's London Pride; Twickenham Naked Ladies; Wells Bombardier; guest beers Ⓗ

Victorian back-street pub, divided into a sports bar with games and large-screen TV, and a quieter lounge area. An upstairs function room hosts occasional live music. Beer festivals are held twice a year, on St George's Day and Hallowe'en. One of the three guest beers is usually a second beer from Twickenham Brewery. Barbecues are held in the large garden at weekends during the summer. The garden has its own TV screen and a covered, heated smoking area. ✿⊟♿🚌(371,K5)♣⊱

Wych Elm ✔

93 Elm Road, KT2 6HT

❂ 11-3, 5-midnight; 11-midnight Sat; 12-11

☎ (020) 8546 3271

Fuller's Chiswick, London Pride, ESB, seasonal beer Ⓗ

Welcoming and friendly back-street local, run by its Spanish landlord for 25 years. It has a smart saloon with a glass partition and a basic but tidy public bar with dartboard. Local CAMRA Pub of the Year in 2005, it has also won prizes for its garden and floral displays out front. Good quality home-cooked lunches are served daily except Sunday. Jazz sessions are held on the last Saturday of the month, performed by a band of 50 years' standing. The smoking area is heated and covered. Q✿◐⊟⇌🚌(K5)♣⊱

Mitcham

Queen's Head

70 Cricket Green, CR4 4LA

❂ 11-midnight (1am Fri & Sat); 11-11 Sun

☎ (020) 8648 3382

Shepherd Neame Master Brew Bitter, Spitfire, seasonal beer Ⓗ

On the edge of Mitcham's historic cricket green, this early 20th-century pub has two rooms. The comfortable lounge bar has some interesting pictures with connections to the pub's name, while the smaller public bar has TV sports, games machines and a dartboard. Excellent food is served at lunchtime, plus wonderful fish and chips to eat in or take away on Friday. The pub hosts several darts teams and holds charity events, plus a Sunday quiz night. There is a heated, covered smoking area. ✿◐⊖(Mitcham Tramlink)🚌(127)♣P⊱

New Malden

Woodies

Thetford Road, KT3 5DX

❂ 11-11; 12-10.30 Sun

☎ (020) 8949 5824 🌐 woodiesfreehouse.co.uk

Adnams Broadside; Fuller's London Pride, ESB; Young's Bitter; guest beers Ⓗ

Open-plan former sports pavilion and local CAMRA Pub of the Year 2006-2008. Sporting and showbusiness artefacts cover the ceiling and walls. Three guest beers are sourced from small local breweries, with forthcoming ales listed on the website and an annual beer festival in August. Families are welcome in the raised bar area. A Sunday carvery and summer weekend barbecues are held. The large outdoor patio incorporates a heated and covered smoking area. Live music plays on alternate Saturdays, quiz night is alternate Sundays. (265)P

Richmond

Red Cow

59 Sheen Road, TW9 1YJ

11-11.30 (midnight Fri & Sat); 11-11 Sun

☎ (020) 8940 2511 redcowpub.com

Wells Bombardier; Young's Bitter, Special, seasonal beers H

Sympathetically restored, this popular local is a few minutes' walk from Richmond's shops and station. There are three distinct drinking areas, with rugs on bare floorboards and period furniture creating a traditional atmosphere. Good lunches are served every day, evening meals Monday to Thursday until 9pm. Tuesday is quiz night and live music is performed regularly. The first floor has four en-suite bedrooms.

Roebuck

130 Richmond Hill, TW10 6RN

12-11; 11-midnight Fri & Sat; 12-10.30 Sun

☎ (020) 8948 2329

Beer range varies H

Overlooking the World Heritage view of Petersham Meadows and the Thames, this 200-year-old, reputedly haunted pub is close to Richmond Park Gate. Patrons are welcome on the terrace opposite to enjoy the view cherished by their forbears and highwaymen for 500 years. A recent refurbishment has opened up three drinking areas on the first floor. Four handpumps dispense regularly changing beers, and an updated food menu offers great choice. Local CAMRA Pub of the Year for 2007. (371)

Waterman's Arms

12 Water Lane, TW9 1TJ

11 (12 Sun)-11

☎ (020) 8940 2893

Wells Bombardier; Young's Bitter, Special, seasonal beers H

Historic pub, one of the oldest in Richmond (rebuilt in 1898), retaining its Victorian two-bar layout. Situated in a lane leading to the river, generations of watermen have drunk here and some, along with others in riparian occupations, still do. In the 1950s it was a lunchtime stop for the Swan Uppers en-route from Blackfriars to Henley. Full of character, it has a truly local feel – good food is served until late. The pub hosts a Monday music club upstairs. Q

White Cross

Riverside, Water Lane, TW9 1TJ

11-11; 12-10.30

☎ (020) 8940 6844

Wells Bombardier; Young's Bitter, Special, seasonal beers H

A prominent feature on Richmond's waterfront, this pub dates from 1835 and a stained-glass panel is a reminder that it stands on the site of a former convent of the Observant Friars, whose insignia was a white cross. It is reached by steps for good reason: the river often floods here. An island bar serves two side rooms (one a mezzanine); an unusual feature is a working fireplace beneath a window. The ground-level patio bar opens at busy times. Q

Surbiton

Cap in Hand

174 Hook Rise North, KT6 5DE (on A3/A243 jct)

9-midnight

☎ (020) 8397 3790

Greene King IPA; Marston's Pedigree; guest beers H

There are surprisingly agreeable views along the A3 towards the North Downs from this spacious 1930s roadhouse. Originally the Southborough Arms, this strategically located Wetherspoon's has an airy conservatory that is designated a family area until 9pm. A good beer range from local micro-breweries is always available: Itchen Valley, Pilgrim and King often feature, as does Weston's cider. Food is served all day until 11pm. An area with patio heaters is provided for smokers.

Q P

Coronation Hall

St Marks Hill, KT6 4LQ

9-midnight

☎ (020) 8390 6164

Courage Best Bitter; Greene King Old Speckled Hen, Abbot; Marston's Pedigree; Shepherd Neame Spitfire; guest beers H

This is a splendid conversion of a former music hall that has also seen life as a cinema, bingo hall and nudist health club. Inside there is a movie theme with pictures of film stars and artefacts from yesteryear along with pictures of George V's coronation. Guest beers change regularly with a preference for locally brewed beers from Twickenham and Hogs Back among others. Weston's Old Rosie and Organic Vintage ciders are served from polypins.

New Prince

117 Ewell Road, KT6 6AL

11-11 (midnight Fri & Sat)

☎ (020) 8296 0265

Fuller's London Pride; Gale's Butser Bitter, HSB H

Locals' pub, formerly known as the Prince of Wales, which caters for all ages. A pleasant beamed interior includes horse brasses, historical prints of the local area and a piano. The carpeted single bar leads to a dining area and a large garden with a heated and covered space for smokers. Typical pub food is served promptly. The pub supports men and women's darts teams and two football teams. Sport is shown regularly on TV.

Sutton

Little Windsor

13 Greyhound Road, SM1 4BY

12-11.30 (midnight Fri & Sat)
(020) 8643 2574
Fuller's Discovery, London Pride, ESB, seasonal beers; guest beers
Cosy street-corner local in the New Town area east of Sutton town centre. The small L-shaped bar leads to a covered terrace which is heated for smokers, and a garden. There are also two tables and chairs outside the front door. Discounts are offered on ales 12-5pm Monday-Thursday.

Robin Hood
52 West Street, SM1 1SH
11-11; 12-10.30 Sun
(020) 8643 7584 robinhoodsutton.co.uk
Young's Bitter, Special, seasonal beers
One the few established traditional pubs in Sutton. Located west of the town centre, it comprises a large L-shaped bar with a small rear courtyard and seats outside on the pavement, plus a large upstairs function room. Discounts are available on four-pint jugs of beer and takeaways of Young's bottled beers. Quiz night is Monday.
(Sutton/West Sutton)

Wallington

Whispering Moon
25 Ross Parade, Woodcote Road, SM6 8QF
9am-midnight (1am Fri & Sat)
(020) 8647 7020
Courage Best Bitter, Directors; Greene King Abbot; Marston's Pedigree; guest beers
The Wetherspoon formula has been applied on a modest scale to this small former cinema premises, situated across the road from the railway station and backing on to the tracks. A split level L-shaped drinking area offers a continually changing range of micro-brewery guest beers plus Weston's Old Rosie cider. Occasional mini beer festivals are also hosted. Food is served all day until 11pm. Handy for Wallington Hall – home of the local CAMRA branch's annual October Beer & Cider festival.
Q

WEST LONDON

W1: Fitzrovia

King & Queen
1-2 Foley Street, W1W 6DL
11 (7 Sun)-11
(020) 7636 5619
Adnams Bitter; St Austell Tribute; guest beers
Gilbert's major general would have loved this pub with all its kings and queens gazing down from the walls – you would probably have to go to the National Portrait Gallery to see any better. Royalty competes with sporting photographs and prints for wall space. There is also a display of 55 playing cards (three jokers, one of which is Edward VIII) with some imaginative images of kings prior to 1066. In the upstairs function room there is a good display of brewery mirrors. (Goodge St)

W1: Marylebone

Carpenters Arms
12 Seymour Place, W1H 7NE
11-11; 12-10.30 Sun
(020) 7723 1050
Adnams Broadside; Black Sheep Best Bitter; Harveys Sussex Best Bitter; guest beers
A local pub within walking distance of Oxford Street. There are six handpumps with a varied choice of beers. Three TV screens show most sporting events and the bar can get crowded. There is a dartboard at the back for those who prefer to make their own entertainment. A function room upstairs can be hired out.
(Marble Arch)

Wargrave Arms
40-42 Brendon Street, W1H 5HE
11-11; 12-10.30 Sun
(020) 7723 0559
Young's Bitter, Special, seasonal beers; guest beers
Built in 1866, this is an ex-Finch's pub that has changed little since it was acquired by Young's. The Wargrave is a warm and welcoming local, serving traditional home-cooked food and a good selection of beers. The local chess club meets every Tuesday evening and a quiz night runs on Wednesday evening. Rugby is popular – note the Munster flag and signed Wallaby shirt – and most major rugby tournaments are shown on TV. Board games are available.
(Edgware Rd)

W1: Mayfair

Coach & Horses
5 Bruton Street, W1J 6PT
11-11; 12-8 Sat; closed Sun
(020) 7629 4123
Fuller's London Pride; Taylor Landlord; guest beers
Popular pub dating from 1933 with a mock-Tudor exterior in the midst of West End shops, galleries and offices. Features include stained glass windows and an interesting collection of prints, including several Vanity Fair portraits that are rarely seen in pubs. A marvellous display of pump clips and beer mats around the bar is evidence of beers previously featured. Good food is served in large helpings. An upstairs room provides additional seating for drinkers and diners and can be hired with the use of its own bar.
(Oxford Circus)(8)

Coach & Horses
5 Hill Street, W1J 5LD
12-11; closed Sat & Sun
(020) 7355 1055
Shepherd Neame Kent's Best, Spitfire
A popular one-bar pub, busy at lunchtime and early evening, attracting nearby office staff. It is the oldest surviving pub in Mayfair, dating from 1744, with leaded windows. Prints and photos show the history of the area and of a famous former landlady. It has an imposing bar and probably the smallest gents' loo in London. (Green Park)

W1: Soho

Dog & Duck ☆
18 Bateman Street, W1D 3AJ

⊙ 11-11 (11.30 Fri & Sat); 12-10.30 Sun
☎ (020) 7494 0697
Fuller's London Pride; Taylor Landlord; guest beers Ⓗ
In the bustling heart of Soho, this CAMRA National Inventory pub was built in 1897. Elaborate mosaic tiles depict dogs and ducks, and wonderful advertising mirrors adorn the walls. The upstairs Orwell Bar is a great place to watch over the frenetic streets of West One.
◑≠(Charing Cross)⊖(Leicester Sq/ Tottenham Ct Rd)🚌

Pillars of Hercules
7 Greek Street, W1D 4DF
⊙ 11-11; 12-10.30 Sun
☎ (020) 7437 1179
Adnams Bitter, Broadside; Caledonian Deuchars IPA; Theakston Old Peculier; Wells Bombardier; guest beers Ⓗ
A traditional mock-Tudor pub which has been on this site for centuries. There are six handpumps offering a range of beers from the the usual suspects to the more adventurous. Pictures and photos on the wall depict London, from the debauchery of Hogarth to the primness of Victoria. Monday is quiz night.
◑⊖(Tottenham Ct Rd)🚌

Ship ✔
116 Wardour Street, W1F 0TT
⊙ 11-11; closed Sun
☎ (020) 7437 8446
Fuller's Discovery, London Pride, ESB, seasonal beers Ⓗ
Frosted and etched glass windows conceal a pub that has been the rendezvous of many a rock star from the 1960s and 1970s. Today, it is the staff who look as though they are auditioning for a punk rock group. Subdued at lunchtime, the music can be loud in the evenings. Victorian photos line the walls. If you look closely, you will see Johnny Rotten in a bow tie and a top hat. Over 21s only.
◑⊖(Tottenham Ct Rd)🚌

W2: Paddington

Mad Bishop & Bear ✔
Upper Level, Paddington Station, W2 1HB
⊙ 8-11 (11.30 Fri); 10-10.30 Sun
☎ (020) 7402 2441
Fuller's Chiswick, Discovery, London Pride, ESB, seasonal beers; guest beers Ⓗ
No ordinary station waiting room this – it is difficult to imagine a Brief Encounter here. Accessed by escalator, the traditional pub interior features a long bar, mirrors, good prints and a rather grand chandelier. Even in the rush hour it is not too crowded and you can watch as your train departs on the CCTV screens. TV sport is shown. When football crowds are expected, the police may order the pub to be closed for a few hours.
Q❀◑≠⊖🚌⁻

Victoria ☆ ✔
10A Strathearn Place, W2 2NH
⊙ 11-11 (10.30 Sun)
☎ (020) 7724 1191
Fuller's Discovery, London Pride, ESB, seasonal beers Ⓗ
The Victoria is special amongst historic pubs with its listed mid-Victorian interior. The impressive bar back includes a clock, large decorated mirrors and columns. The two distinct bar areas both have fireplaces, one with a print of Queen Victoria, Albert and family above it. Upstairs are the Library, with comfortable furnishings, and the Theatre Bar with fittings from the former Gaiety Theatre. The pub's first beer festival was held in 2007 and another is planned.
Q❀◑≠⊖(Lancaster Gate/Paddington)🚌⁻

W4: Chiswick

Fox & Hounds and Mawson Arms ✔
110 Chiswick Lane South, W4 2QA
⊙ 11-8; closed Sat & Sun
☎ (020) 8994 2936
Fuller's Chiswick, Discovery, London Pride, ESB, seasonal beers Ⓗ
A haven for beer drinkers with wooden floors, panelling, tables and chairs and a well polished bar also made of wood. The tap for the Griffin Brewery, the exterior of the pub unusually displays different names on the front and side. Along with the Fuller's range it stocks a good supply of bottled beers, including Vintage. Walls are decorated with portraits of the three founders of Fuller, Smith & Turner, vintage beer adverts and photographs of employees from the turn of the 19th century posing with the tools of their trade. ◑🚌(190)

George & Devonshire ✔
8 Burlington Lane, W4 2QE
⊙ 12-11 (10.30 Sun)
☎ (020) 8994 1859 🌐 georgeanddevonshire.co.uk
Fuller's Chiswick Bitter, London Pride, ESB, seasonal beers Ⓗ
Situated on a roundabout a stone's throw from the Griffin Brewery of Fuller, Smith & Turner, the interior has standing room at the bar bracketed by two fairly large rooms either side. Warm wooden floors and furnishings and a comfy padded bench alongside the bay window feature. Facilities for the sports-minded include a pool table and large-screen TV. ❀◑⊟🚌(190)P⁻

W5: Ealing

Questors (Grapevine Bar) ✔
12 Mattock Lane, W5 5BQ
⊙ 7-11; 12-2.30, 7-10.30 Sun
☎ (020) 8567 0071 🌐 questors.org.uk/grapevine
Fuller's London Pride, seasonal beers; guest beers Ⓗ
The Grapevine is the club bar for visitors to the Questors Theatre. Run by volunteers, the Club is very popular for pre-show drinks and welcomes CAMRA members at all times. Alongside London Pride, two other regularly changing guest ales are available, always including a session bitter. Check the website to see what is currently available. Beer festivals are held several times a year and the Club stocks Belgian ales and a wide range of whiskies. There is a patio outside.
Q❀♿≠⊖(Ealing Broadway)🚌P

ENGLAND

Red Lion ✓
13 St Mary's Road, W5 5RA
11-11 (midnight Thu-Sat); 12-11 Sun
☎ (020) 8567 2547
Fuller's Chiswick, London Pride, ESB, seasonal beer; guest beer H
The pub is situated opposite Ealing Studios and affectionately known as Stage 6. Many photographs of TV programmes and films produced at the studios adorn the walls. With the refurbishment several years ago, the licensee was able to add facilities for preparing home-made food while retaining the feel of the original building. At the front the decor is traditional, with a more modern extension at the rear, and a covered patio.
Q❀◑◐♿⇌(Ealing Broadway)⊖(Ealing Broadway/South Ealing)🚌(65)

Rose & Crown ✓
Church Place, W5 4HN
12-11.30 (midnight Fri & Sat); 12-11 Sun
Fuller's Chiswick, London Pride, ESB, seasonal beers H
A large pub with three distinct drinking areas. Fuller's recently refurbished the pub, making sure it kept the Grade II-listed area intact, retaining the feeling of a small public bar at the front. There is a large dining area leading into the garden. ❀◑◐♿⊖(South Ealing)🚌(65)

W6: Hammersmith

Andover Arms ✓
57 Aldensley Road, W6 0DL
12-11 (11.30 Fri & Sat); 12-3.30, 7-10.30 Sun
☎ (020) 8741 9794
Fuller's Chiswick, London Pride, ESB, seasonal beers H
Stylish haven in the back streets of Hammersmith – an oasis of calm not far from the bustle of King Street. This pub appears often in the Guide, with a high quality British and European menu. The late Michael Jackson was a regular here. Well worth a visit.
Q◑◐⊖(Ravenscourt Pk)🚌

Brook Green Hotel
170 Shepherds Bush Road, W6 7PB
11-midnight (11 Mon); 11-11 Sun
☎ (020) 7603 2516 🌐 brookgreenhotel.co.uk
Wells Bombardier; Young's Bitter, seasonal beers H
Large corner pub overlooking Brook Green. It has a modern interior with seating areas in different styles, but retains some original ornate features around the back of the bar, fireplace surrounds and lighting. At the rear is a paved seating area for smokers which also provides wheelchair access to the pub. A cellar bar is used for live music and has different opening hours from the main bar.
❀⇌◑◐♿⊖🚌

Dove ✓
19 Upper Mall, W6 9TA
11-11; 12-10.30 Sun
☎ (020) 8748 9474
Fuller's Discovery, London Pride, ESB, seasonal beers H
Legendary and ancient Thames-side pub with two main drinking areas, one of the smallest snugs in the country and a wonderful riverside terrace that gets very lively in the summer. Arts and crafts pioneer William Morris lived just down the road.
⛼Q❀◑◐⊖(Ravenscourt Pk)🚌♣

Plough & Harrow ✓
120-124 King Street, W6 0QU
9-11.30
☎ (020) 8735 6020
Courage Best Bitter, Directors; Fuller's London Pride; Greene King Abbot; Marston's Pedigree; guest beers H
Opened in 2002 in the former car showroom that had occupied the site since the demise of the original Plough & Harrow in 1959. This Wetherspoon pub has a spacious, modern interior with an Art Deco touch. It has tiled floors, a carpeted rear area reserved for families and diners, and a small enclosed back lounge. A Holiday Inn hotel occupies the upper floors.
⏰◑◐⊖(Hammersmith/Ravenscourt Pk)🚌

Salutation ✓
154 King Street, W6 0QU
11-11 (12.30am Sat); 12-10.30 Sun
☎ (020) 8748 3668
Fuller's Discovery, London Pride, ESB, seasonal beers H
A good mixture of Hammersmith local and sporty mecca for football fans, this pub has many attributes including a classic tile frontage, large skylight, leather sofas and a daily pizza menu. There is a conservatory that leads to a spacious paved garden.
❀⊖(Ravenscourt Pk)🚌⌐

W7: Hanwell

Fox
Green Lane, W7 2PJ
11-11; 12-10.30 Sun
☎ (020) 8567 3912 🌐 thefoxpub.co.uk
Black Sheep Best Bitter; Fuller's London Pride; Taylor Landlord; guest beers H
A previous Courage pub that is now a free house, the Fox is a short walk from the Grand Union Canal at the end of Green Lane and is popular with walkers and boaters alike. The pub has a strong link with the community and takes part in the annual Hanwell carnival and other events. Beer festivals are held at Easter and in October. Lunches are served every day, evening meals Wednesday-Saturday and excellent Sunday roasts. Local CAMRA Pub of the Year 2007. ⏰❀◑◐🚌(E8)⌐

W8: Kensington

Britannia
1 Allen Street, W8 6UX
10-midnight; 10.30-11.30 Sun
☎ (020) 7937 6905 🌐 britanniakensington.co.uk
Young's Bitter, seasonal beers H
This Young's tied house was extensively refurbished a couple of years ago and is immaculately presented. The interior is modern and stylish, with different seating areas by the bar. There is a 50-seat restaurant at the rear and outside seating along the side

of the pub, where smoking is allowed.
❀◐◑⊖(High Street Kensington)🚌

Scarsdale Tavern ✔
23a Edwardes Square, W8 6HE
✪ 12-10 (10.30 Sun)
☎ (020) 7937 1811
Fuller's London Pride; guest beers Ⓗ
Tucked away on a leafy square off busy Kensington High Street, four handpumps at the bar and a shelf full of empty champagne bottles lining the walls show that the pub caters for all tastes. Behind the half-frosted windows lies an L-shaped dark wood bar with an ornate etched mirrored back. Walls are decorated with elegantly framed paintings, the most striking of which is David's Napoleon Crossing the Alps. The patio out front has tables and heating.
◐◑⊖(High Street Kensington)🚌⚐

W8: Notting Hill Gate

Churchill Arms ✔
119 Kensington Church Street, W8 7LN
✪ 11-11 (midnight Thu-Sat); 12-10.30 Sun
☎ (020) 7727 4242
Fuller's Chiswick, Discovery, London Pride, ESB, seasonal beers Ⓗ
Built in 1924, this must surely be one of the most atmospheric pubs in London. Inside, it is easy to be overwhelmed by the bric-a-brac collection hanging from the ceiling. The Churchill theme is prominent with memorabilia, photographs and a framed butterfly collection. The popular licensee has maintained a welcoming presence since 1984. Thai food is served in the rear conservatory area where diners are surrounded by an amazing display of numerous pot plants. Evening Standard Pub of the Year 1999.
Q◐◑⊖🚌

Uxbridge Arms
13 Uxbridge Street, W8 7TQ
✪ 12-11 (10.30 Sun)
☎ (020) 7277 7326
Fuller's London Pride; St Austell Tribute; Wells Bombardier Ⓗ
The Uxbridge Arms is a back-street local dating from 1836. Wood-panelled and carpeted throughout, with three small drinking areas, it has a welcoming bar with a warm feel about it. A collection of photographs and china plates adorns the walls. Also on display and framed is an officer's dress tunic in the rank of Lieutenant Colonel. This pub was threatened with closure a few years ago but a petition organised by its devoted locals managed to save it. Q❀⊖🚌⚐

W11: Notting Hill

Cock & Bottle
17 Needham Road, W11 2RP
✪ 11-11; 12-10.30 Sun
☎ (020) 7229 1550
Hogs Back TEA; St Austell Tribute Ⓗ
A friendly backstreet oasis, this CAMRA Regional Inventory pub has a particularly ornate bar back, Corinthian columns and stained glass panels depicting swans – the former name of the pub. With two separate rooms, this pub is a good starting point for a Notting Hill pub crawl.
♨Q❀⊖(Notting Hill Gate/Bayswater)🚌⚐

W14: West Kensington

Crown & Sceptre ✔
34 Holland Road, W14 8BA
✪ 11-11 (midnight Fri & Sat); 12-11 Sun
☎ (020) 7602 1866
Hog's Back TEA; Itchen Valley Winchester Ale; Oakham JHB; guest beers Ⓗ
A corner establishment with a split level layout, the Crown & Sceptre was CAMRA's West London Pub of the Year in 2007. The pub dates from 1856 and spent its first year as the Napoleon III. Close to the Olympia Exhibition Centre, it offers an ever-changing guest beer line-up. As well as the beer, the interior is also of interest. Refurbished some years ago, the existing traditional bar has been retained, as has an inscription of the pub's name carved into the wood. Cribbage is played and a regular quiz night held on Tuesday.
Q◐◑♿⇌(Kensington Olympia)⊖(Olympia)🚌♣⚐

Brentford

Express Tavern ✔
56 Kew Bridge Road, TW8 0EW
✪ 11.30-3, 5.30 (6.30 Sat)-11 (midnight Thu-Sat); 12-10.30 Sun
☎ (020) 8560 8484
Draught Bass; Young's Bitter; guest beers Ⓗ
This historic and friendly local is a welcome sight as you come north over Kew Bridge. More than 200 years old, it played a part in the beginnings of Brentford FC, the old Brentford market, Norway's 100 Best Pubs in London guide, and even CAMRA. The regular beers are usually supplemented by two guests. Home-cooked food is served lunchtimes and most evenings. It has two cosy bars, a mock-manorial lounge and a beer garden with a smoking area.
Q❀◐⊟♿⇌(Kew Bridge)🚌⚐

Magpie & Crown
128 High Street, TW8 8EW
✪ 11 (12 Sun)-midnight (1am Thu-Sat)
☎ (020) 8560 5658
Beer range varies Ⓗ
This mock-Tudor pub, stepped back from the road, is very popular with beer lovers. There are usually four real ales on offer – some 2000 ales have been served during the last 12 years – at least one cider, draught Budvar, Paulaner and Stiegel, a guest white beer and a range of continental and British bottled beers. Thai food is available most evenings (not Mon) and some lunchtimes. Bar billiards and other games are played. There are tables and a cycle rack outside at the front, plus a rear patio.
❀◑⇌🚌♣●

O'Brien's
11 London Road, TW8 8JB (near canal bridge at W end of High St)
✪ 11-11; 12-10.30 Sun
☎ (020) 8560 0506 🌐 obrienspub.co.uk

Fuller's London Pride; guest beers Ⓗ
Formerly the Northumberland Arms, this compact pub on the main road through Brentford features an ever-changing range of beers, frequently from the local Twickenham Brewery, as well as some Belgian specialities. Acoustic music sessions are held on Tuesday evening and a quiz night on Wednesday. TV coverage of sporting events provides regular entertainment. ❀◑≥⊟⊱

Colham Green

Crown

Colham Green Road, Uxbridge, UB8 3QH
12-11 (10.30 Sun)
☎ (01895) 442303
Fuller's London Pride, ESB; guest beers Ⓗ
Pleasant one-bar locals' pub which has pictures of celebrities adorning the walls and a separate dining area away from the bar. A large Spanish-style garden with a covered area allows for good outdoor drinking, whatever the weather. Food is available all day, with roast lunches served on Sunday. This is a decent pub and well worth a visit.
Q❀◑♿⊟(U3,U5)P⊱

Feltham

Moon on the Square ✔

30 The Centre, High Street, TW13 4AU
9-midnight (1am Fri & Sat)
☎ (020) 8893 1293
Courage Best Bitter, Directors; Greene King Abbot; Shepherd Neame Spitfire; guest beers Ⓗ
This real ale oasis continues to flourish in a changing Feltham. The interior is early Wetherspoon: wood panels and glass-partitioned booths, with pictures and history panels depicting how Feltham has altered over the years. The welcome is warm and genuine and the pub always offers eight ales, often including a Scottish beer (reflecting the manager's origins) and Weston's cider. Families and children are welcome until early evening. ◑♿≥⊟●

Hampton Hill

Roebuck

72 Hampton Road, TW12 1JN
11-11 (11.30 Fri & Sat); 12-4, 7-10.30 Sun
☎ (020) 8255 8133
Sharp's Doom Bar, Special; Young's Bitter; guest beers Ⓗ
And still the collection of bric-a-brac grows here, with fishing rods (and of course a Harley-Davidson) hanging from the ceiling, bank notes of the world in frames (white fivers are behind the bar), a life-sized carved wooden Red Indian chief, and every table with pages from old newspapers under the glass. Otherwise the pub is simply furnished. The award-winning garden has a new gazebo for smokers and a summer house. No food is available at weekends.
⌂❀⊏◐≥(Fulwell)⊟♣⊱

Harlington

White Hart ✔

158 High Street, UB3 5DP
11-11 (11.30 Thu; midnight Fri & Sat); 12-11 Sun
☎ (020) 8759 9608
Fuller's Discovery, London Pride, ESB, seasonal beer; guest beer Ⓗ
A large roadside pub near Heathrow Airport. Six handpumps dispense both the Fuller's regulars and seasonal and guest ales. One side of the pub has a dartboard and a large TV for sports, while the other end is quieter and favoured by diners. Food is all home-cooked and the menu covers a wide variety of dishes. Quiz night is Thursday and live music is a regular feature. ❀◑♿⊟P⊱

Hayes

Botwell Inn ✔

25-29 Coldharbour Lane, UB3 3EB
9-midnight (1am Fri & Sat)
☎ (020) 8848 3112
Courage Best Bitter, Directors; Greene King Abbot; Marston's Pedigree; guest beers Ⓗ
A large Wetherspoon shop conversion that has recently been refurbished. It has several areas for drinking and dining, one of them with large, comfortable settees. Outdoor facilities include a pavement area to the front and a small patio at the back, with large market parasols and heaters to cater for smokers. The area is associated with George Orwell, who taught in a local school. Food is served all day and Weston's Old Rosie and Organic Vintage ciders are stocked. Q❀◑♿▲≥⊟●⊱

Hounslow

Moon Under Water ✔

84-88 Staines Road, TW3 3LF (W end of High St)
10 (12 Sun)-11
☎ (020) 8572 7506
Courage Best Bitter; Greene King Old Speckled Hen, Abbot; Marston's Pedigree; guest beers Ⓗ
Early Wetherspoon shop conversion, enlarged more recently, in typical original style and still displaying a few local history panels and photos. Very popular, it has a diverse customer base. There are normally three guest ales – far more at festival times, when all 12 handpumps offer different beers. Children are welcome until 8.30pm; the rear is considered the family area, with an outside patio.
Q❀◑♿⊖(Hounslow Central)⊟⊱

Isleworth

Red Lion

92-94 Linkfield Road, TW7 6QJ
11-11.30 (midnight Fri & Sat); 12-10.30 Sun
☎ (020) 8560 1457 🌐 red-lion.info
Fuller's London Pride; Hogs Back TEA; Young's Bitter; guest beers Ⓗ
Spacious two-bar free house with a strong community focus. There is often something going on: a production on stage or in the garden performed by its own theatre group, live music (Saturday evening, Sunday afternoon), a quiz (Thursday), or darts and pool competitions. Up to six beers

complement the three regulars, and twice-yearly beer festivals feature champion beers. Lunches are offered daily, and evening meals Monday-Saturday, at local CAMRA's Pub of the Year 2003 & 2004. ❀◑⊟♿⇌⊟♠⅟

Southall

Conservative & Unionist Club

Fairlawn, High Street, UB1 3HB

⊙ 11.30-2.30 (3 Fri & Sat), 7 (6 Fri & Sat)-11; 12-3, 7-10.30 Sun

☎ (020) 8574 0261

Rebellion IPA, seasonal beers; guest beers Ⓗ

Almost the last place in Southall to sell real ale, this gem is hidden down an alley between the Town Hall and Habib Bank. Weekday lunches are reasonably priced (no food at weekends). There are four snooker tables and live music is played on the last Saturday of each month. Monday is quiz night. Visit Southall for a curry. ❀◐⇌⊟♣P⅟

Teddington

Kings Head

123 High Street, TW11 8HG

⊙ 11 (12 Sun)-11

☎ (020) 8943 2259

Harveys Sussex Best Bitter; St Austell Tribute; Sharp's Doom Bar; guest beers Ⓗ

The smart bar is behind an upmarket restaurant (L'Auberge) which rather monopolises the signage. The bar is decorated predominantly in crimson – its style is somewhere between a hotel lounge and a gentlemen's club, with several leather sofas. There is also a meeting room for hire (with a French film club – details at the bar). One of the guest beers usually comes from the local Twickenham Brewery. Teddington Lock is about five minutes' walk away to the south. ❀◑⇌⊟P⅟

Twickenham

Ailsa Tavern

263 St Margarets Road, TW1 1NJ

⊙ 11-11 (11.30 Fri & Sat); 12-10.30 Sun

☎ (020) 8892 1633 ⊕ ailsatavern.com

Black Sheep Best Bitter; Fuller's London Pride; Taylor Landlord; guest beers Ⓗ

A traditional community pub named after a landlady from Victorian times. This listed building is in a residential area within sight of the Twickenham rugby ground. Outside, wisteria vines decorate the walls to the front and the beer garden is a favourite haunt, as there are not many in this area. Regular beer festivals are held. There are three separate drinking areas, offering fine ales and food from around the world, prepared by an award-winning cellarman and chef. The smoking area is heated.

♨Q❀◑⇌(St Margarets)⊟(H37)⅟

Fox ✔

39 Church Street, TW1 3NR

⊙ 11-11 (12.30am Thu-Sat); 12-10.30 Sun

☎ (020) 8892 1535

Caledonian Deuchars IPA; Fuller's London Pride; guest beers Ⓗ

Twickenham's oldest pub, dating from around 1670, was originally known as the Bell but changed its name to the Fox in the early 1700s. It is a local favourite in this attractive area. The street outside is now some 18 inches higher than when the pub was first built, so visitors must step down into the small bar, where a good selection of real ales awaits including beers from the Twickenham Brewery. Its function room was built as the Assembly Rooms around 1900. Outside is a heated smoking area. ♨❀◑⇌⊟⅟

Prince Blucher ✔

124 The Green, TW2 5AG

⊙ 11-11 (midnight Fri & Sat); 12-11 Sun

☎ (020) 8894 1824

Fuller's Chiswick, Discovery, London Pride, ESB, seasonal beers Ⓗ

Historic 1815 inn, the first to be built on the newly enclosed Twickenham Green and reputedly the only pub remaining in the UK still to pay homage to the Duke of Wellington's left flanker at Waterloo. Four separate bar areas suit most tastes. The enthusiastic landlord of 11 years' standing offers home-cooked food all day and in summer hosts hog roasts and barbecues in the ample child-friendly garden. Food and real ale festivals are also regular features. Outside is a heated smoking area.

♨Q❀◑⇌(Strawberry Hill)⊟P⅟

Prince of Wales

136 Hampton Road, TW2 5QR

⊙ 12 (4 Mon)-11

☎ (020) 8894 5054

Adnams Bitter; St Austell Tribute; Twickenham Crane Sundancer, seasonal beers; guest beers Ⓗ

An inn has existed on this site for over 150 years, once serving as the final staging post on the Windsor-London stagecoach route. The original stables survive and are listed. Now an unspoilt community pub with an attractive garden, this is the unofficial tap for the Twickenham Fine Ales brewery nearby. A bi-annual beer festival features ales from micro-breweries. Acoustic music plays on Tuesday and quiz night is Thursday. The cuisine is French (no food Mon/Tue). Outside is a heated smoking area.

♨Q❀◑⇌(Fulwell/Strawberry Hill)⊟⅟

Turk's Head ✔

28 Winchester Road, TW1 1LF

⊙ 12-11 (11.30 Thu; midnight Fri & Sat); 12-10.30 Sun

☎ (020) 8892 1972

Fuller's Discovery, London Pride, ESB, seasonal beers Ⓗ

Built in 1902, this is a genuine local corner pub offering fine beers and food, and hosting live music on Friday. Beatles fans used to flock here to see the pub location for a scene from A Hard Days Night, and the Bearcat Comedy Club has been inviting top comedians to the function room every Saturday night for more than 20 years. Rugby fans form human pyramids on match days and try to stick their tickets on the high ceiling. The smoking area outside is heated.

♨Q❀◑♿⇌(St Margaret's)⊟(H37)⅟

GREATER MANCHESTER

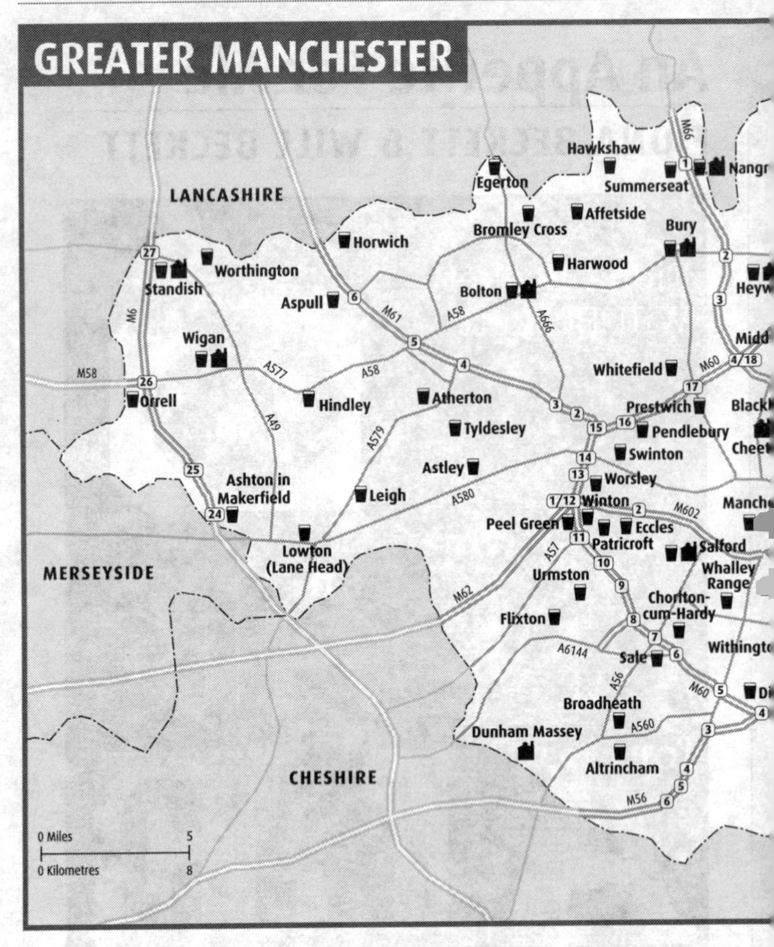

Affetside

Pack Horse

52 Watling Street, BL8 3QW (approx 2 miles NW of Walshaw) SD755136

12-3, 6-11; 12-midnight Sat & Sun

☎ (01204) 883802

Hydes Owd Oak, Original Bitter, seasonal beers Ⓗ

This country pub benefits from superb panoramic views thanks to its situation high up on a Roman road. The bar areas and cosy lounge with real fire are part of the original pub, dating from the 15th century. It has a function and a pool room, while the Hightop bar is used as a family room. Many a tale is told about the ghost of a local man whose skull is on view behind the bar. Good quality food is served. ⛰Q☕❀◑▲P⚡–

Altrincham

Old Market Tavern

Old Market Place, WA14 4DN (on A56)

12-11 (midnight Wed-Sat)

☎ (0161) 927 7062 🌐 oldmarkettavern.com

Caledonian Deuchars IPA; Phoenix Arizona; Bank Top Volunteer; guest beers Ⓗ

Black and white former coaching inn. A plaque on the wall describes how George Massey manufactured gas for the first time in Altrincham in 1844 to illuminate the pub. Up to eight guest beers are sourced mainly from micro-breweries including the local Dunham Massey Brewery. Meals are served until 8pm (6pm at weekends), live heavy rock/blues is performed every Saturday and Sunday night, while Wednesday is quiz night, with a free buffet. Children are welcome until 8.30pm. Local CAMRA Pub of the Year 2008.

⛰Q❀◑⇌⊖🚌♣

Orange Tree

15 Old Market Place, WA14 4DE (On A56)

12-midnight (1am Fri & Sat)

☎ (0161) 928 2935

Caledonian Deuchars IPA; guest beers Ⓗ

Standing in front of the stocks at the Old Market Place, legend has it that a man sold his wife here for a shilling and sixpence in 1823. Meals are served lunchtimes and evenings daily. Sky Sports is shown, karaoke takes place monthly and poker is played. The pub is dog friendly, children are welcome until 8.30pm and there is a heated smoking shelter to the rear. Q❀◑⇌⊖🚌♣⚡–

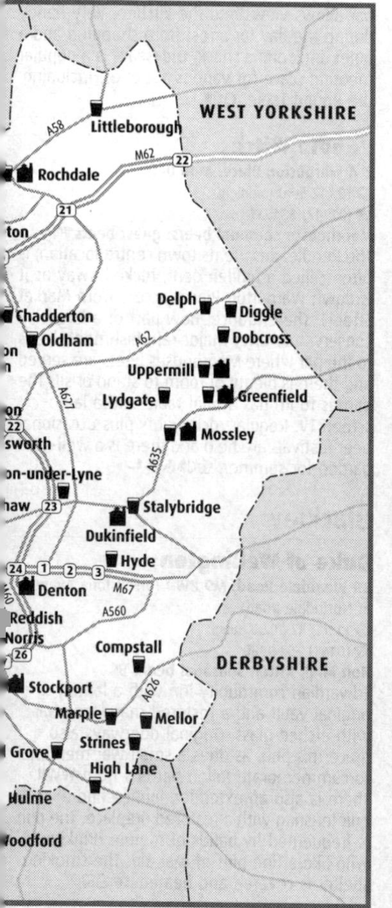

Ashton-in-Makerfield

Jubilee Club

167-169 Wigan Road, WN4 9ST (near Bryn station heading towards Ashton)
⏲ 8 (7.30 Fri & Sat)-midnight
☎ (01942) 202703 🌐 jubileeclubashton.co.uk
Beer range varies Ⓗ
A warm, friendly social club with a welcoming atmosphere. It has a small games room and lobby bar area, a main lounge bar available for functions, plus a small function room upstairs. At least one ever changing cask ale, often from a local micro-brewery, is served at a competitive price. The Jubilee Club actively raises money for charity. Non-members are welcome subject to constraints on frequency of visits and payment of a nominal admission charge. Outside is a covered smoking area.
⇌(Bryn)🚌♣P⊬⊓

Sir Thomas Gerrard ✔

2 Gerrard Street, WN4 9AN (on A58)
⏲ 9-midnight (1am Fri & Sat)
☎ (01942) 713519
Greene King IPA, Abbot; Marston's Pedigree; guest beers Ⓗ
Known locally as the Tom & Jerry, this Wetherspoon pub is a former supermarket. It has a number of interesting features including a tiled mural depicting aspects of Ashton-in-Makerfield's history. There are two raised areas away from the busy main floor and small booths to the rear which are good for a cosy drink. Guest beers are often sourced from local micro-breweries. The pub gets busy at weekends and on race days as it is within walking distance of Haydock Park Racecourse.
✿◑♿🚌P⊬

Ashton-under-Lyne

Dog & Pheasant

528 Oldham Road, OL7 9PQ
⏲ 12-11 (11.30 Fri & Sat); 12-10.30 Sun
☎ (0161) 330 4849
Banks's Original; Marston's Burton Bitter, Pedigree; guest beers Ⓗ
Nicknamed the Top Dog, this popular, friendly local near the Medlock Valley Country Park has a large bar serving three areas, plus another room at the front. The menu of good value food includes vegetarian options. On Tuesday and Thursday evenings a quiz is hosted. Up to three guest beers from the Banks/Marston's portfolio are available at all times. A regular Guide entry over the years, this pub is well worth a visit. ⛰✿◑🚌P⊬

Junction Inn

Mossley Road, OL6 9BX
⏲ 12-3 (not Mon), 5-midnight; 12-midnight Sat & Sun
☎ (0161) 343 1611
Robinson's Hatters, Unicorn Ⓗ
Small pub of great character that has remained little changed since the 19th century. Built of local stone, close to Ashton golf course and open country, it is the first building out of town that is not of brick construction. The small, cosy rooms make it welcoming, and the unpretentious tap room is traditional in every respect. The famous home-made rag pudding, a Lancashire speciality, is served alongside other pub food

INDEPENDENT BREWERIES

3 Rivers Reddish
All Gates Wigan
Bank Top Bolton
Bazens' Salford
Boggart Hole Clough Moston
Dane Town Denton (NEW)
Dunham Massey Dunham Massey (NEW)
Green Mill Rochdale (NEW)
Greenfield Greenfield
Holt Cheetham
Hornbeam Denton
Hydes Manchester: Moss Side
Lees Middleton Junction
Leyden Nangreaves
Marble Manchester
Mayflower Wigan
Millstone Mossley
Outstanding Bury (NEW)
Phoenix Heywood
Pictish Rochdale
Prospect Standish (NEW)
Robinson's Stockport
Saddleworth Uppermill
Shaws Dukinfield

lunchtimes and evenings Tuesday to Friday. Traditional Sunday lunch is also available.
Q✿◗⊟⊟♣P⚐

Oddfellows Arms

1-7 Alderley Street, Hurst, OL6 9LJ

☉ 12-1am

☎ (0161) 330 6356

Robinson's Hatters, Unicorn ⊞

Within a terrace of former cottages, the 'Oddies' has been in the same family since 1914 and is the longest serving Guide entry in the east of Greater Manchester. A small hatch and screen leads to the polished bar with its stained glass and nooks and crannies. Two cosy vestibules are to the left. Adjoining the lounge is Tom's Room, named after the late landlord. In the walled garden there is a newly refitted patio for smokers and a fish pond.
Q✿⇌⊟(38,39)⚐

Aspull

Victoria

50 Haigh Road, WN2 1YA (on B5239)

☉ 1-midnight

☎ (01942) 830869

Beer range varies ⊞

This traditional two-room local has enjoyed a new lease of life after becoming Wigan's Allgates Brewery's first pub. The smart yet intimate lounge displays photographs depicting the history of Aspull and Haigh. Two large-screen TVs cater for sports fans, although the one in the lounge is usually switched off. The pub is well located for Haigh Hall Country Park and is halfway between Bolton Wanderers and Wigan Athletic football grounds. Guest beers come from Allgates or other micro-breweries. The smoking area is covered. ⊟⊟♣P⚐

Astley

Cart & Horses

221 Manchester Road, M29 7SD

☉ 12-11 (1am Fri & Sat); 12-10.30 Sun

☎ (01942) 870751

Holt Mild, Bitter ⊞

Popular, friendly local with an open-plan lounge that was formerly two rooms and still retains a divided feel. There is also a busy tap room to the side of the bar, and a raised seating area that leads to the patio, large walled garden and rear car park. The pub's front door is interesting, with etched windows either side and a Holt's roof sign. Regular quiz nights are held; the local golf society and the Leigh Premier Cycling Club meet here.
✿◗⊟♣P⚐

Atherton

Old Isaacs

48 Market Street, M46 0DG

☉ 11-midnight; 12-11 Sun

☎ (01942) 882885

Phoenix seasonal beers ⊞

Large, popular town centre pub with two rooms at the front for dining or chatting. The main lounge has several comfortable seating areas, while the standing area in front of the bar allows views into the kitchen. Very handy during the day for a rest from shopping and a quiet drink and a snack, Old Isaacs is a popular meeting place for various societies, including the Round Table. Q◑

Pendle Witch

2-4 Warburton Place, M46 0EQ

☉ 10 (12 Sun)-midnight

☎ (01942) 884537

Moorhouses seasonal beers; guest beers ⊞

The Pendle, despite its town centre location, is often called a hidden gem, tucked away as it is down Warburton Place (access from Market Street). The entrance, now part of a large conservatory after major refurbishment, leads to the bar where Moorhouses beers are served and there is plenty of room to stand or sit. The games room has a pool table and a large-screen TV. Regular rock nights plus occasional beer festivals are held and there is a well-kept garden for summer. ✿◑♿♣⚐

Blackley

Duke of Wellington

39 Weardale Road, M9 8WR (off Victoria Avenue at Northdale Road)

☉ 11-11; 12-10.30 Sun

☎ (0161) 702 1380

Holt Mild, Bitter, seasonal beers ⊞

Edwardian community inn with a largely original vault and a restored mahogany bar with etched glass. Original doorways also grace this pub, as does a small war memorial to commemorate fallen patrons from WWII. There is also an extended lounge and a quieter snug with a restored fireplace. The pub is frequented by bands of mature drinkers who like a fine pint of real ale. The smoking shelter is covered and heated. ✿⊟⊟

Golden Lion

47 Old Market Street, M9 8DX (off Rochdale Road)

☉ 11-11 (midnight Fri & Sat)

☎ (0161) 740 1941

Holt Mild, Bitter ⊞

A friendly community pub that offers fine ales and good service in a vault, as well as a lively lounge and a quieter side room. A rare, well-used crown bowling green has had an outside verandah added to accommodate a covered and heated smoking shelter. Folk music and live bands are planned for Saturday evenings. An exceptional event is the occasional 1920s-themed Murder Mystery Quiz, for which teams come in fancy dress. ✿⊟⊟(51,112)P⚐

Bolton

Ainsworth Arms ✔

606 Halliwell Road, BL1 8BY (Jct A58/A6099)

☉ 11.30-2 (not Tue-Thu), 5-11 (midnight Fri); 11.30-10.30 Sun

☎ (01204) 840671

Taylor Landlord; Tetley Mild, Bitter; guest beers ⊞

Near Smithills Hall, a Grade I listed building, this dog-friendly local comprises several areas. There is a raised space with alcoves and a basic tap room, complete with bell pushes that were in use until 1981. The pub has a long association with football and is the meeting place for many local sports teams. The jukebox is only switched on by request. Lunches are served Friday to Sunday, and breakfasts are excellent. Guest beers come from small, independent breweries. Q❀◐♣

Barristers Bar

7 Bradshawgate, BL1 1HJ (on A575, near Market Cross)

12-1am (2am Fri & Sat)

☎ (01204) 365174

Black Sheep Best Bitter; Tetley Bitter; Wychwood Hobgoblin; guest beers Ⓗ

The Barristers Bar is part of the Swan Hotel, a listed building dating from 1845. Formerly the Malt & Hops, it was closed for many years until a change of ownership in 2004. The wood-panelled interior has been retained and tastefully decorated to create the atmosphere of a traditional pub. The regular range of real ales is supplemented by guest beers primarily from small local independent brewers. A courtyard with tables is well used in warmer weather and heated for smokers. ❀≹⁻

Bob's Smithy Inn

1448 Chorley Old Road, BL1 7PX (on B6226 uphill from A58 ring road)

4.30 (12 Sat)-11 (midnight Fri & Sat); 12-11 Sun

☎ (01204) 842622

Bank Top Flat Cap; Taylor Best Bitter; Tetley Bitter; guest beers Ⓗ

An intimate stone-built hostelry on the edge of the moors, handy for walkers and visitors to the Reebok Stadium. The inn is about 200 years old and is named after a blacksmith who allegedly spent more time here than he did at his smithy across the road. This is a genuine free house, offering guest beers from small independent breweries. Dogs are welcome and there is a covered smoking area at the side of the pub. ❀🚌(125,126)P⁻

Doffcocker

780 Chorley Old Road, BL1 5QE (on B6226)

11-11 (midnight Fri & Sat)

☎ (01204) 843656

Holt Mild, Bitter, seasonal beers Ⓗ

This splendid listed building is a rare example of a calendar pub, with a strong community spirit. The upstairs function room is home to seven clubs, including one that devotes itself to old English pub games. Live football on TV is well patronised, and there are many Bolton Wanderers photographs adorning the walls. Every Wednesday lunchtime there is a fun quiz in the comfortable lounge. Food is served daily 12-5.30pm. ❀◐⊟🚌♣P⁻

Dog & Partridge

22 Manor Street, BL1 1TU

7-midnight (3am Fri); 1-3am Sat

☎ (01204) 388596

Thwaites Original, Lancaster Bomber Ⓗ

This unspoilt three-room local is situated on the edge of the town centre. The pub dates from the 18th century and features a traditional vault with a curved bar, a small back room with a fine example of an acid-etched Cornbrook Ales window and a larger side room. Here live bands play regularly at weekends and popular acoustic music sessions take place on Sundays. There may be an admission charge for live bands, but go into the vault if you just want a drink. ⊟≹

Hen & Chickens ✔

143 Deansgate, BL1 1EX (opp post office)

11.30 (7 Sun)-11 (extended hours on request)

☎ (01204) 389836

Tetley Dark Mild, Bitter; guest beers Ⓗ

The landlord is an enthusiastic promoter of cask beer and supplies three regularly changing real ales from the Punch Taverns portfolio. The pub is renowned for its excellent home-cooked lunchtime food and friendly atmosphere. A popular quiz night is held on Wednesday evening and the pub is also HQ for a local quiz league. The pub is available for private hire during the day on Sunday, and is handy for the adjacent bus station. ◐≹⁻

Hope & Anchor

147 Chorley Old Road, BL1 5QH (on B6226)

12-midnight (1am Fri & Sat)

☎ (01204) 842650

Lees Bitter; Taylor Landlord; Tetley Bitter Ⓗ

Situated less than two miles from Bolton town centre, just near Doffcocker Lodge, a well-known nature reserve, this traditional local dating from the late Victorian era attracts walkers and bird watchers. A central bar serves two distinct snugs used for different functions (quiz nights, etc). Locals call the pub the Little Cocker, to distinguish it from the big Doffcocker Inn across the road. A new extension with disabled access and pool room does not affect the original pub layout. TV sports are shown. Sandwiches are always available. Q🍼❀🚌♣P⁻

Lodge Bank Tavern

260 Bridgeman Street, BL3 6SA

2-midnight; 12-2am Fri & Sat; 12-midnight Sun

☎ (01204) 531946

Lees Bitter Ⓗ

Welcoming local near Bobby Heywood's Park (with free use of the floodlit pitches). The main room is divided into three smaller areas, and there is a pool room at the back of the bar. Karaoke sessions take place on Friday and Saturday evenings – these are well attended and quite noisy. The only Lees house in town, it was the last pub to change its ale house status to a full licence. Children are welcome until 7pm. Outside is a covered, heated smoking shelter. ❀≹♣P⁻

Spinning Mule ✔

Unit 2, Nelson Square, BL1 1JT

9-midnight (1am Fri & Sat)

☎ (01204) 533339

Greene King IPA; Marston's Pedigree; guest beers Ⓗ

Newly built in 1998, this town-centre pub, just off Bradshawgate, is an open-plan split-level building with a comfortable dining area in a modern Wetherspoon style. It is named after Samuel Crompton's Mule, a revolutionary invention in cotton spinning that made Bolton famous throughout the world. The original device may be seen in the town's museum and Crompton himself is immortalised by the statue in the square. The Mule supports Bank

Top, Moorhouses and other local breweries.
Q◑♿⇌

Sweet Green Tavern

127 Crook Street, BL3 6DD (opp Sainsbury's, off A579)
⌚ 11-11; 12-10.30 Sun
☎ (01204) 392758 🌐 sweetgreentavern.com
Beer range varies ⊞
This dog-friendly, genuine free house is on the edge of the town centre and close to the rail/bus interchange, comprising four small rooms served by a central bar. The enterprising landlord offers up to 11 cask beers sourced from independent breweries, including the local Bank Top. Room-only accommodation is available and visitors are welcome to consume their own food on the premises. The pub featured on the Al Murray Happy Hour due to its alleged resident ghosts. Pub games include free use of a Wii console.
⛫Q☕❀⛽⇌♣P⁻

Broadheath

Railway ★

153 Manchester Road, WA14 5NT (on A56 adjacent to business park)
⌚ 11-11 (midnight Fri & Sat); 11-10.30 Sun
☎ (0161) 941 3383
Holt Mild, Bitter ⊞
A small and often boisterous three-room pub built in the angle of a long-gone railway viaduct. The Railway was saved from demolition in the 1990s by a campaign involving CAMRA and local people. The surrounding area has been extensively redeveloped. The car park behind does not belong to the pub and is locked up outside shopping hours. The snug little rooms are named after Manchester's railway stations (and the toilets after one of London's). Children are welcome until 6pm. Outside is a covered smoking area. ⛫❀⊡⇌⊖⊟♣⁻

Bromley Cross

Flag Inn ✔

Arnold Road, Egerton, BL7 9HL (off B6472 Darwen Road)
⌚ 12-11 (midnight Fri & Sat)
☎ (01204) 598267
Greene King IPA; Taylor Landlord; guest beers ⊞
Close to the Last Drop village, walkers are attracted to this pub for its proximity to good walking country. A minimum of eight handpumps include four changing beers from the local Bank Top Brewery, plus three regularly rotating guest beers. The tasty, extensive menu is competitively priced (not served Fri-Sun eves). The pub often gets busy at weekends. Live TV sport is shown. Note the unusual viewing cellar.
⛫❀◑⇌⊟(533,563)⁻

Bury

Dusty Miller

87 Crostons Road, BL8 1AL (jct B1263 & B1264)
⌚ 1 (12 Sat & Sun)-midnight
☎ (0161) 764 1124
Moorhouses Black Cat, Premier Bitter, Blond Witch, Pendle Witches Brew; guest beers ⊞
Unpretentious, traditional tied Moorhouses pub which is set back from a busy road junction, thus making parking difficult. A central bar serves two rooms: one a comfortable lounge, the other a more basic vault. To the rear a covered courtyard provides additional drinking space. The vault is host to pool and darts teams, while a Thursday quiz with free supper is held is the lounge. Sky Sports is screened in both rooms. The guest beer often comes from a local micro-brewery.
❀⊡⊟⁻

Two Tubs

19 The Wylde, BL9 0LA (opp central parish church)
⌚ 12 (11.30 Wed)-11 (1am Thu; 2am Fri & Sat); 5-midnight Sun
☎ (0161) 764 2206 🌐 caseleisure.com
Thwaites Original, Lancaster Bomber, seasonal beer ⊞
This historic pub, centrally located in the culture quarter, is a 400-year-old Grade II listed building. The rear part of the pub is a modern extension, with a separate bar that is only open at peak times. The rest of the pub features lath and plaster panels, with a bar in the vault to the left as you enter the front door. It is a popular food venue on weekday lunchtimes and gets very busy at weekends.
❀◑⊡♿⇌⊖⁻

Wyldes

4 Bolton Street, BL9 0LQ
⌚ 11.30-11 (1am Fri & Sat); 12-11 Sun
☎ (0161) 797 2000 🌐 joseph-holt.com
Holt Mild, Bitter, seasonal beers ⊞
Large modern pub converted from a bank and situated in the culture quarter close to the Metro-link/bus station and the East Lancs Railway. The impressive interior consists of two floors with a mezzanine. A top bar opens during busy periods and is a quiet getaway during the day. The main lounge and bar provide a comfortable mix of tables, chairs and sofas. Beer prices are lower up to 8pm. An extensive menu includes child portions and vegetarian options. Wednesday is Curry Club night. ◑♿⇌⊖

Castleton

New Inn

818 Manchester Road, OL11 3AW (200m from railway station)
⌚ 3 (12 Sat & Sun)-1am
☎ (01706) 667533 🌐 thenewinncastleton.co.uk
Robinson's Hatters, seasonal beers ⊞
Traditional Robinson's pub on a main street where two standard beers plus a changing seasonal are always available. The young, enthusiastic landlady has developed this pub into a busy, friendly and comfortable venue where all are made welcome. The pleasant interior is well decorated, with plenty of wood panelling. Toilet facilities are immaculate, having been completely rebuilt with disabled access. Quiz and darts nights are held, along with Irish folk or Lancastrian nights. Children are welcome until 8pm. ⛫Q♿⇌⊟(17)♣⁻

Chadderton

Horton Arms

19 Streetbridge Road, OL1 2SZ (on B6195)
12 (11.30 Fri & Sat)-midnight; 12-10.30 Sun
(0161) 624 7793
Lees Brewer's Dark, Bitter
Well appointed open-plan pub divided into discrete drinking areas plus a small side room for sport fans with a TV. The buzz of conversation dominates and there is an enthusiastic following for the cask mild (Brewer's Dark). Good value food is served every day and until 6pm on Friday and at weekends. Winner of Lees Best Kept Cellar Competition 2007. (412)P

Rifle Range Inn

372 Burnley Lane, OL1 2QP
2 (12 Sat & Sun)-11
(0161) 678 6417
Lees Brewer's Dark, Bitter
This pub was originally a farmstead, first licensed around 1860. It has a friendly family atmosphere with an open-plan lounge and a separate vault. Sports fans visiting nearby Boundary Park are welcome at all times and TV sports are shown. The pub runs football, darts and pool teams, plus a quiz night on Tuesday. It hosts live entertainment on Saturday evening and barbecues on the heated patio in summer. (24,181)♣P

Cheadle Hulme

Cheadle Hulme

47 Station Road, SK8 7AA (on A5149)
11.30-11 (midnight Fri & Sat); 12-10.30 Sun
(0161) 485 4706
Holt Mild, Bitter, seasonal beers
Despite losing its traditional Holt's weatherboarding during a stylish 2004 makeover, this remains a fine community pub. All age groups congregate here, whether to enjoy the music (alternate Tuesdays), the quiz (Thursday) or simply for a good natter. Office workers and locals appreciate the extensive lunchtime and evening food menu. Adjacent to the station, and once known as the Junction, this is a pub worth missing the train for. (157,313)♣P

Church

90 Ravenoak Road, SK8 7EG (jct A5149/B5095)
11-11 (midnight Fri & Sat); 12-10.30 Sun
(0161) 485 1897
Robinson's Hatters, Unicorn, seasonal beers
Once known as the Knapsack Inn, this friendly, family-run pub is the oldest in Cheadle Hulme. Its cottage-like appearance reflects a cosy interior with low ceilings, wood panelling and brass plates. The busy Edwardo's Restaurant serves excellent, freshly prepared food evenings and weekends (booking recommended). Darts is played in the snug, while the lounge boasts a real fire and quiet conversation. Q(157,313)♣P

Chorlton-cum-Hardy

Bar

531-533 Wilbraham Road, M21 0UE
12 (12 Thu)-11.30; 12-12.30 Fri & Sat; 12-11.30 Sun
(0161) 861 7576
Marble Janine's One, Manchester Bitter, JP Best, Ginger Marble; Pictish Alchemist; guest beers
Laid back but modern, this expanded pub attracts a regular professional crowd. An always welcoming open fire draws you in to the environs, while the leather sofas and wooden church pews of the main area house a lively, sociable community. The varied menu, served daily until 8pm, offers a selection for all tastes, with ingredients sourced locally, just like the beers that come from nearby micro-breweries. Foreign draught and bottled beers are also available. The smoking area is heated and covered. (55)

Marble Beer House

57 Manchester Road, M21 9PW
12-11 (midnight Thu-Sun)
(0161) 881 9206 marblebeers.co.uk
Marble Janine's One, Manchester Bitter, JP Best, Ginger Marble, Lagonda, Stouter Stout; guest beers
The Marble Beer House has been the out-of-town showcase for Marble beers for many years and the range continues to grow. Its traditional cafe-bar style attracts a mixed crowd and it is invariably busy. Guest beers are sourced from regional brewers, with Pictish and Phoenix among the favourites. A range of continental beers and draught cider is also available. Food is limited to a range of interesting nibbles. Pub games include dominoes, scrabble and backgammon. Q♣

Compstall

Andrew Arms

George Street, SK6 5JD
11-11; 12-10.30 Sun
(0161) 484 5392
Robinson's Hatters, Unicorn
Detached stone-built pub in a quiet village off the main road and close to Etherow Country Park, which has wildlife and river valley walks. The pub features a comfortable lounge and a small traditional games room in addition to a separate dining room. A genuine local, popular with all ages, it is the centre for many social activities. A good kitchen serves traditional food and holds themed nights. Q♣P

Delph

Royal Oak (Th' Heights)

Broad Lane, Heights, OL3 5TX SD982090
7-11 (closed winter Mon); 12-5, 7-10.30 Sun
(01457) 874460
Black Sheep Best Bitter; guest beers
Isolated, 250-year-old stone-built pub on a packhorse route overlooking the Tame Valley. In a popular walking area, it benefits from outstanding views. The pub comprises a cosy bar and three rooms, each with an open fire. The refurbished side room boasts a hand-carved stone fireplace, while the comfortable snug has exposed beams and old photos of the inn. Good home-cooked food is served Friday and Saturday evenings. The house beer

is brewed by Moorhouses and guests include a beer from Millstone. ⛫Q❀◗P

Didsbury

Fletcher Moss

1 William Street, M20 6RQ (off Wilmslow Rd, A5145)
12-11 (midnight Fri & Sat); 12-10.30 Sun
☎ (0161) 438 0073 🌐 hydesbrewery.co.uk
Hydes Owd Oak, Original Bitter, Jekyll's Gold, seasonal ales Ⓗ
Once known as the Albert, the pub was acquired by Hydes who enlarged it to the rear and renamed it in memory of Alderman Fletcher Moss, the former owner of a nearby park and gardens. Two comfortable, well-appointed rooms at the front lead to an island bar then on to a spacious conservatory. Good furnishings add an historic air. An eclectic clientele enjoys the relaxed atmosphere created by licensees who have been here since the Albert days. Q❀♿⇌🚌(42,142)P⌐

Nelson

3 Barlow Moor Road, M20 6TN (jct A5145/B5093)
12-midnight (11 Sun)
☎ (0161) 434 5118
Jennings Cumberland Ale; guest beer Ⓗ
A single-bar pub with traditional decor and a regular clientele, which sets it apart from most other pubs in Didsbury village. Much TV sport is shown, so the place is often bustling with life. Other entertainment is provided by a DJ spinning folk or Motown discs a couple of nights a week. The Nelson is part of a local darts league. The guest beer is usually from Moorhouses. ⇌🚌(42,142)♣

Diggle

Diggle Hotel

Station Houses, OL3 5JZ (Half mile off A670)
SE007081
12-3, 5-midnight (1am Fri); 12-1am Sat; 12-midnight Sun
☎ (01457) 872741
Black Sheep Best Bitter; Copper Dragon Black Gold; Taylor Landlord; guest beers Ⓗ
Stone pub in a pleasant hamlet close to the Standedge Canal Tunnel under the Pennines. Built as a merchant's house in 1789, it became an ale house and general store on the construction of the nearby railway tunnel in 1834. Affording fine views of the Saddleworth countryside, this makes a convenient base in a popular walking area. Comprising a bar area and two rooms, the accent is on home-cooked food (served all day Sat and Sun). Brass bands play on alternate summer Sundays and the pub holds occasional mini beer festivals. ❀◑◗🚌(184)P

Dobcross

Navigation Inn

21-23 Wool Road, OL3 5NS (on A670)
12-2.30, 5-11 (midnight Fri); 12-11 Sat; 12-10.30 Sun
☎ (01457) 872418
Lees Bitter; Moorhouses Black Cat, Pendle Witches Brew; Wells Bombardier; guest beers Ⓗ
Next to the Huddersfield Narrow Canal, this stone pub was built in 1806 to slake the thirst of the navvies cutting the Standedge Tunnel. It comprises an open-plan bar and L-shaped interior. Live brass band concerts are staged on alternate Sundays in summer. The pub is the venue for annual events such as the Beer Walk in spring and the Rushcart Festival in August. The guest ale often comes from a local micro-brewery. Home-cooked meals including special offer weekday lunches are popular (no food Sun eve). Q❀◑◗🚌(184,350)P⌐

Swan Inn (Top House)

The Square, OL3 5AA
12-3, 5-11 (midnight Thu-Sat); 12-11 Sun
☎ (01457) 873451
Jennings Bitter, Cumberland Ale, Cocker Hoop; guest beers Ⓗ
Built in 1765 for the Wrigley family of chewing gum fame, part of the building was later used as a police court and cells. Overlooking the attractive village square, the pub has been well renovated, with flagged floors and three rooms, plus a fine function room that caters for 50 people. It gets busy during the Whit Friday brass band contest and the August Rushcart Festival. Imaginative home-cooked food features dishes from around the world (served all day Sun). ⛫Q❀◑◗🚌(184,353)⌐

Eccles

Eccles Cross ✔

13 Regent Street, M30 0BP (opp Metrolink station)
9-midnight (1am Fri & Sat)
☎ (0161) 788 0414
Greene King IPA, Abbot; Marston's Pedigree; guest beers Ⓗ
The pub opened in 1920 as the New Regent Picture House and converted to a Wetherspoon pub in 1999. An open-plan layout is split into four levels to create distinct drinking areas including three sunken snugs, each displaying local historic information. The ceiling formation reflects its original use and can be seen to good effect from the rear of the pub. A large Celtic cross mural dominating the back wall relates to the pub's namesake opposite. Outside is a covered smoking area. ❀◑◗♿⇌⊖🚌P⌐

Lamb Hotel ★

33 Regent Street, M30 0BP (opp tram terminus)
11.30-11 (11.30 Fri & Sat); 12-11 Sun
☎ (0161) 787 7297
Holt Mild, Bitter Ⓗ
A fine example of an Edwardian heritage pub, both inside and out. An original vault, billiard room with full-size table and two lounges are served from a carved wood and etched glass bar. An unusual incorporated display cabinet is full of trophies and a collection of ornamental lamb figures brought in by customers. By the bar lobby is a fine oak staircase graced with green wall tiles, which can be clearly seen as customers walk in. Q⊟⇌⊖🚌♣P

Egerton

Masons Arms

156-158 Blackburn Road, BL7 9SB (on A666)

4 (3 Fri)-11 (midnight Thu & Fri); 12-midnight Sat; 12-11 Sun
☎ (01204) 303517
Greene King Ruddles Best Bitter; Theakston Bitter; guest beers Ⓗ
Situated about three miles from Bolton, this inviting pub dates from the late Victorian era. Good value beers are dispensed from four handpumps on an imposing bar, which is the main interior feature. There is a small beer garden at the back, and in summer hanging baskets and window boxes enhance the attractive brick and stone facade. This is a pub for those who like a genuine local. It is always packed on Tuesday quiz night. ❀🚌♣⅋

Failsworth

Willow Tavern

278 Ashton Road East, M35 9HD
12-3, 7-midnight; 12-3, 5-12.30am Fri; 12-12.30am Sat; 12-midnight Sun
☎ (0161) 681 1698
Black Sheep Best Bitter; Greenfield Dobcross Bitter; guest beers Ⓗ
Originally built as an ale house in 1870, paintings of the former building can be seen over the fireplace. The pub is a community hub that serves as a home for local football and cricket teams, plus the Failsworth branch of the Manchester City Supporters' Club. There is a separate tap room, beer garden and family room. The lounge has a large engraved glass window featuring a willow tree. Good value food is available weekday lunchtimes. ❀(52,74)♣P⅋

Flixton

Church Inn

34 Church Road, M41 6HS
11-11 (11.30 Tue & Thu); 11-midnight Fri & Sat; 12-11 Sun
☎ (0161) 748 2158
Taylor Landlord; Theakston Black Bull; guest beers Ⓗ
A short walk from Flixton railway station on the Manchester/Warrington line, this comfortable village style pub is next to the Norman/Georgian church. The bar serves three seating areas including a section on the left of the main entrance used for traditional games such as darts and cribbage. Popular for its ales and food, it offers reasonably priced meals from the Spirit Group menu all day, every day. The outside seating area overlooks the churchyard. Quiz nights are held on Sunday and Tuesday. ❀◐≠🚌(247)♣P⅋

Gorton

Vale Cottage

Kirk Street, M18 8UE (off Hyde Rd A57, east of jct with Chapman St)
12-3 (4 Sun), 5 (7 Sat & Sun)-11
☎ (0161) 223 2477
Taylor Landlord; Theakston Black Bull; guest beers Ⓗ
Tucked away in the Gore Brook conservation area, the Vale Cottage has the feel of a country pub. Parts of the building date from the 17th century, hence the low-beamed ceilings, multiple drinking areas and reputed ghost. A relaxed, friendly atmosphere, where conversation predominates, is disturbed only by the ever popular lively quizzes on Tuesday (general knowledge) and Thursday (music). Excellent home-cooked meals are available lunchtimes and early evenings. Do not miss this hidden gem. Q❀◐≠🚌(201,203)P⅋

Greenfield

King William IV

134 Chew Valley Road, OL3 7DD
12-midnight
☎ (01457) 873933
Caledonian Deuchars IPA; Lees Bitter; Tetley Bitter; guest beers Ⓗ
Detached stone pub at the village centre, comprising a central bar area and two rooms. A cobbled forecourt with benches allows for outdoor drinking. It offers two or three changing guest beers, often including a mild. Food is served Wednesday to Sunday until 7.30pm. Handy for walks over the moors, the pub is the centre of village life, participating in annual beer walks and the Rushcart Festival in August, and hosting a Whit Friday brass band contest. ❀◐≠🚌♣P⅋

Railway

11 Shaw Hall Bank Road, OL3 7JZ (opp station)
12-12 (1am Thu-Sat)
☎ (01457) 872307 🌐 railway-greenfield.co.uk
Caledonian Deuchars IPA; Taylor Landlord; Theakston Mild; Wells Bombardier; guest beer Ⓗ
Unspoilt pub where the central bar and games area draw a good mix of old and young. The tap room has a log fire and old Saddleworth photos. In a picturesque area, the pub provides a good base for various outdoor pursuits and affords beautiful views across Chew Valley. The venue for live Cajun, R&B, jazz and pop music on Thursday, Friday (unplugged night) and Sunday, it also hosts top class entertainment every month in the large function room. Weston's and Thatchers cider are served on gravity.
⅏❀⇌Ⓓ⅄≠🚌♣●P

Harwood

House Without A Name

75-77 Lea Gate, BL2 3ET (on B6196, near A676 jct)
12-11 (11.30 Thu; midnight Fri & Sat)
☎ (01204) 304750
Holt Bitter; guest beers Ⓗ
A cosy stone-built local dating from 1810. Known as the No Name, it was historically an un-named drinking den. When a licence was applied for, no one knew what to call it, so the magistrate declared it a House Without A Name. The pub is the HQ of the local Trafalgar Society, hence the display of memorabilia in the lounge. Guest beers are chosen by the enthusiastic landlady from the Punch Taverns portfolio. ❀◐Ⓓ🚌(506,507)♣⅋

Hawkshaw

Red Lion

81 Ramsbottom Road, BL8 4JS (on A676 Burnley Road)

12-3, 6-11; 12-11 Sat; 12-10.30 Sun
(01204) 856600 redlionhawkshaw.com
Jennings Bitter, Cumberland Ale; guest beers H
Attractive stone pub nestling in a picturesque village. Inside you will find a single, large room that is a favourite with locals. The excellent menu of freshly prepared dishes has made the inn popular with diners, too, who can opt to eat in the pub or the adjacent restaurant. Meals are served all day Saturday and Sunday. Guest beers often come from Bank Top or Phoenix. P

Hazel Grove

Grapes

196 London Road, SK7 4DQ (on A6, jct with Hatherlow Lane)
11.30-11 (midnight Fri & Sat); 12-10.30 Sun
(0161) 4834479 frederic-robinson.com
Robinson's Hatters, Unicorn H
This very old building retains its classic urban pub layout. The central bar separates a large vault on the left from the comfortable three-roomed lounge, which features some original woodwork. The back room has images of old Hazel Grove, while pictures of local sports teams dominate the remainder of the pub. To the rear is a small beer garden with well-tended floral tubs, courtesy of the landlady.
(192,199)P

Heaton Norris

Nursery ★

258 Green Lane, SK4 2NA (off A6, jct with Heaton Road)
11.30-11 (11.30 Fri; midnight Sat); 12-11.30 Sun
(0161) 432 2044 hydesbrewery.co.uk
Hydes Mild, Owd Oak, Original Bitter, Jekyll's Gold, seasonal beers; guest beers H
CAMRA's National Pub of the Year 2001 and a Guide regular, the Nursery is a classic unspoilt 1930s pub, hidden away in a pleasant suburb. The multi-roomed interior includes a traditional vault with its own entrance and a spacious wood-panelled lounge, used by diners at lunchtime. The home-cooked food draws customers from miles around – children are welcome if dining. The pub's immaculate bowling green – an increasingly rare feature – is well used by local league teams.
QP

Heywood

Edwin Waugh

10-12 Market Street, OL10 4LY
9-12.30 (1am Fri & Sat)
(01706) 621480
Beer range varies H
Spacious single-floor Wetherspoon emporium with easy chairs as well as various heights of tables and seats. There is a small patio area at the rear entrance. The pub is named after the dialect poet Edwin Waugh, who died in 1890 and was described as the 'Burns of Lancashire'. The beer range changes often and quite regularly supports local family and micro-breweries such as Phoenix. An extensive menu featuring vegetarian and child options is served all day, every day.
Q(471)

High Lane

Royal Oak

Buxton Road, SK6 8AY
12-3, 5-11; 12-10.30 Sun
(01663) 762380
Jennings Bitter, Cocker Hoop; Marston's Burton Bitter; guest beers H
A well-appointed pub with a pleasing exterior. Although it has an open-plan layout, there are three distinct drinking areas, one used for games. Live entertainment is hosted most Fridays and an innovative food menu is served all sessions. The garden and outdoor play area make this a good summer and family pub. Beer is sourced from the Banks/Marston's range. QP

Hindley

Edington Arms

186 Ladies Lane, WN2 2QJ (off A58)
12-11.30 (12.30am Fri & Sat)
(01942) 259229
Holt Mild, Bitter, seasonal beers H
Also known as the Top Ale House, the Edington is a cosy, welcoming pub. The single bar is centrally situated in the front lounge. There is also a games room with pool table that leads to the beer garden at the rear. Standing next to the Liverpool-Manchester rail line it is ideally situated for any 'rail ale crawl' into Wigan or Manchester. P

Horwich

Crown

1 Chorley New Road, BL6 7QJ (jct A673/B6226)
12-11 (midnight Fri & Sat)
(01204) 690926
Holt Mild, Bitter, seasonal beers H
Spacious pub on the edge of town handy for the Reebok Stadium (visiting away fans welcome), Rivington Pike and the West Pennine Moors. Lever Park across the road was gifted by Lord Leverhulme, the soap magnate, and a great benefactor to his home town. The pub has a vault and games room at the rear in which dogs are allowed. Wednesday is quiz night and on Sunday evening the locals enjoy singalongs with the organ. Children are welcome at lunchtime when dining. P

Hyde

Cheshire Ring

72 Manchester Road, SK14 2BJ
4 (2 Tue & Wed; 1 Thu-Fri)-11; 12-11 Sat; 12-10.30 Sun
(07917) 055629 thecheshirering.co.uk
Beartown Kodiak Gold, Bearskinful, seasonal beers; guest beers H
A warm welcome is assured at this friendly pub, one of the oldest in Hyde and comprehensively overhauled by Beartown. Seven handpumps offer a range of Beartown beers and other brews in addition to three ciders/perries (only one will be on display)

and continental beers. A range of bottled beers is also stocked and beer festivals periodically offer additional drinking choice. Gentle background music plays and outside is a covered smoking area. ❀⊟≠⊟●P⊬

Queens Inn

23 Clarendon Place, SK14 2ND

11-11; 12-10.30 Sun

☎ (0161) 368 2230

Holt Mild, Bitter, seasonal beers Ⓗ

A real town centre community pub with a warm welcome. Home to several sports teams, the interior is divided into four distinct areas and rooms to cater for all needs, including a large function room that is a favourite for wedding receptions. Situated close to Hyde bus station and the market, the Queens is popular with shoppers during the day. A late licence is used for special events throughout the year. Rail travellers can use either Newton for Hyde or Hyde Central stations. ⊟♿≠⊟♣

Sportsman

57 Mottram Road, SK14 2NN

11-11; 12-10.30 Sun

☎ (0161) 368 5000

Moorhouses Black Cat; Pennine Sunshine; Phoenix Bantam; Pictish Brewers Gold; Plassey Bitter; Taylor Landlord; guest beers Ⓗ

True free house serving six regular beers and two guests in addition to a range of continental beers. This pub is a former local CAMRA Pub of the Region and hosts a full-size snooker table. A loyal and mixed group of regulars enjoys live entertainment every second Friday in the month. The rear patio features a covered and heated smoking area. The pub is within walking distance of both Hyde Central & Newton for Hyde railway stations. ⚘❀⊟≠⊟P⊬

Leigh

Boars Head

2 Market Place, WN7 1EG

11-11 (1am Thu-Sat)

☎ (01942) 673036

Boddingtons Bitter; Moorhouses Pride of Pendle; guest beers Ⓗ

Opposite Leigh's parish church, this is the second free house to open in the last year. The imposing red brick exterior contains clues to its history, from the Bedford Brewing Company to Walkers Warrington Ales. Behind the pub are unusual two-storey listed stables. The large pool room houses a collection of Rugby League team photographs from various eras, while the lounge contains a collection of Lancashire colliery plates. The main room is divided by a fireplace and live music sessions are held most Saturdays. Food is served. ❀◐⊟♣⊬

Bowling Green

Manchester Road, WN7 2LD

11-midnight (1am Fri & Sat); 12-11 Sun

☎ (01942) 882885

Holt Bitter; guest beers Ⓗ

Handy for Butts Bridge Marina on the Bridgewater Canal, the pub is 10 minutes' walk from the centre of Leigh. A large, friendly community pub, it has an open-plan layout in the lounge with various seating areas. The dining room is also available for drinkers, while the tap room can be busy with the pub's teams either practising or competing in various local leagues. The local golf society and share club meet here and regular quizzes are held on Sunday and Thursday. Q❀◐⊟♿♣P⊬

Thomas Burke ✔

20A Leigh Road, WN7 1QR

9-midnight (1am Fri & Sat)

☎ (01942) 685640

Greene King IPA, Abbot; Marston's Pedigree; guest beers Ⓗ

Wetherspoon spent a fortune developing this pub from the original Leigh Hippodrome. It is named after a renowned tenor, known as the Lancashire Caruso, who was born in Leigh and performed at the theatre. The pub splits into three areas: the main long bar, a raised dining area and, in what was once the cinema foyer, lounge-style seating. Ten handpumps offer a changing range of beers plus local brews. The arrival of the Thomas Burke was the best thing to happen to beer choice in Leigh since the pub swaps of the early 1970s. ◐♿⊬

Waggon & Horses

68 Wigan Road, WN7 5AY

7 (4 Fri)-midnight; 12-1am Sat; 12-11 Sun

☎ (01942) 673069

Hydes Light, Mild, Original Bitter Ⓗ

Friendly community pub that attracts all ages. The main lounge is hidden behind a large hearth and includes a large-screen TV for sporting events. It can get lively when certain Rugby League teams are playing. The bar, hub of the pub, is a good spot for conversation, while a snug leads off to one side. A large games room includes a pool table, darts and dominoes and is host to the pub's various teams. Regular theme nights are held throughout the year. Children are welcome until 8pm. ❀♣⊬

Littleborough

Moorcock

Halifax Road, OL15 0LD (A58 from Littleborough Centre to Halifax)

11.30-midnight (11.30 Sun)

☎ (01706) 378156

Taylor Landlord; guest beers Ⓗ

Built as a farmhouse in 1681 and first licensed in 1840, this traditional pub in the Pennine foothills features an 80-seat restaurant with separate pub space. Families, ramblers and equestrians are all welcome in the pub which also caters for football fans via large-screen TVs. Outside there are fantastic panoramic views while inside there are always one or two guest beers, usually from local micro-brewers such as Pictish, plus six rooms offering overnight accommodation. ⚘Q❀⊟◐⛺⊟(528)P⊬

White House

Halifax Road, OL15 0LG (on A58 towards Halifax)

12-3, 6.30-midnight; 12.30-10.30 Sun

☎ (01706) 378456 🌐 thewhitehousepub.co.uk

Theakston Best Bitter; guest beers Ⓗ

The Pennine Way passes this 17th-century coaching house, situated 1300 feet above sea level. It is a landmark that benefits from panoramic views of the surrounding hills and as far away as Cheshire and Wales. A family-run inn extending a warm, friendly welcome, it has two bars, both with log fires. Local guest ales, continental bottled beers and a good range of wines complement the excellent menu and daily specials board. Meals are served all day Sunday. ⋒Q❀◑▲⊟P⌐

Lowton

Travellers Rest

443 Newton Road, WA3 1NX

12-11 (midnight Fri & Sat)

☎ (01925) 224391

Marston's Pedigree; guest beers ⊞

Comfortable, friendly roadside local with a separate restaurant that leans towards the Greek style. Meals are available throughout the pub, with the low-ceilinged lounge containing various discrete seating areas. The bar is the social focal point of the hostelry, while a large patio and garden to the rear provide plenty of seating. Q❀◑♣P⌐

Lydgate

White Hart

51 Stockport Road, OL4 4JJ (close to A669/A6050 jct)

12-midnight

☎ (01457) 872566 thewhitehart.co.uk

Lees Bitter; Taylor Golden Best, Landlord; Tetley Bitter; guest beers ⊞

Detached stone free house dating from 1788, commanding impressive views over the hills above Oldham. Adjoining the village church and school, the pub has four rooms, two used for dining. The snug has its own servery and the main bar has eight handpumps. An extension, with bar, is used for weddings and gourmet meals prepared by the award-winning chef. Guest beers are usually from local micro-breweries. The pub makes an excellent base for visiting Saddleworth's villages and moors. Eighteen en-suite rooms are available. ⋒Q❀⊭◑♿⊟(180,184)P

Manchester City Centre

Ape & Apple

28-30 John Dalton Street, M2 6HQ (off Cross St corner of Albert Sq)

12-11 (midnight Fri & Sat); 12-9 Sun

☎ (0161) 839 9624

Holts Mild, Bitter, seasonal beers ⊞

This old building has seen many incarnations but has been a pub for 10 years. It boasts a fabulous upstairs dining/function room. Quiz night is Thursday, curry night is Wednesday and there is a free comedy club. The decor is a mixture of old and new reclaimed materials, creating an unusual feeling of opulence for a Holts house. The pub retains many regulars and has a friendly atmosphere. There is a partially heated and covered smoking area on the roof terrace. Food is served 12-3pm. ❀◑♿⇌⊖⊟⌐

Bar Fringe

8 Swan Street, M4 5JN (30m from A665/A62 jct)

11-11; 12-12.30am Fri & Sat; 12-11 Sun

☎ (0161) 835 3815

Beer range varies ⊞

A one-room Belgian-style bar which offers an ever-changing range of up to five real ales and regularly featured local micros, as well as others from all over the country. It also stocks a large selection of draught and bottled continental beers and draught Thatchers cider. The walls are adorned with framed posters, cartoons and numerous other items to provide interesting viewing, including a fish tank. Hot and cold food is served until 8pm. ⋒◑⇌(Shudehill)⊖(Victoria)⊟●⌐

Castle Hotel

66 Oldham Street, M4 1LE (near Warwick St)

11-midnight; 12-8 Sun

☎ (07969) 618357 castlepub.co.uk

Robinson's range ⊞

Robinson's only Manchester city-centre outlet attracts an eclectic clientele, young and old, and sells up to nine beers from the rare Dark Mild to Old Tom. The bar dominates the front room; the middle room houses a piano, TV and library. The back room hosts daily live music of all styles. A mosaic of the late, popular and redoubtable landlady, containing her ashes, watches over proceedings from the end of the bar. ⇌(Piccadilly)⊖(Market St)⊟♣

City Arms ✔

46-48 Kennedy Street, M2 4BQ (near town hall)

11 (12 Sat)-11; 12-8 Sun

☎ (0161) 236 4610

Tetley Dark Mild, Bitter; guest beers ⊞

Busy little two-roomed pub situated behind the Waterhouse which has received a local CAMRA award for appearing in this Guide for 12 consecutive years. It can be busy with local office workers at lunchtime when good food is served. Early evening is often hectic, too, but it settles down and gives way to a quieter period with a 'local' mood. Five guest beers are served and a 'guess the mystery ale' competition takes place on Friday. ◑⇌(Oxford Rd)⊖(St Peters Sq)⊟

Crown & Kettle

2 Oldham Road, Ancoats, M4 5FE (Corner of Oldham St & Great Ancoats)

11-11 (midnight Fri & Sat); 12-10.30 Sun

☎ (0161) 236 2923 crownandkettle.com

Beer range varies ⊞

Grade II listed building comprising a main bar, vault and modern snug. There is an original ornate ceiling and on a wall inside is the original pub sign from the long-defunct local brewer Wilsons. Four to six real ales are available from a constantly changing range, with Greenfield Brewery providing the house beer. Various real ciders, Belgian beers and single malts complement the ales. Food, both hot and cold, is available on weekdays until 6pm. ◑♿⇌(Victoria)⊖(Shudehill)⊟●⌐

Dutton Hotel

37 Park Street, Strangeways, M3 1EU (near MEN Arena)

11.30-11; 12-11 Sun

☎ (0161) 834 4508

Hydes Original Bitter Ⓗ
Virtually triangular in shape with an imposing gable end, this back-street pub is a hidden gem, but very handy for the MEN Arena, as it is situated on the far side, right by Strangeways prison. There are three distinct drinking areas with a cosy back room giving more seclusion and leading to a covered smoking area. The clientele includes loyal regulars and passing trade from the Arena. The publican can extend his hours until 2am at his discretion when trade allows.
❀≠(Victoria)⊖🚌♣⁵—

Font Bar
7-9 New Wakefield Street, M1 5NP (off Oxford Rd by railway viaduct)
☺ 12-1am (12.30am Sun)
☎ (0161) 236 0944
Beer range varies Ⓗ
The antithesis of a traditional pub, the Font is a café-bar during the day and a thriving student venue by night, with loud music and dim lighting. The main bar is up a few stairs, with a secondary bar downstairs. Two cask beers are on offer, usually from local micros. Bottled beers include interesting examples of German, Belgian and British brewing. Home-cooked food at bargain prices is available every day until 8pm. Bands play monthly on Sunday night, with computer games available on a big screen. ◐♿≠⊖🚌

Jolly Angler ✔
47 Ducie Street, M1 2JW (corner of Pigeon St)
☺ 12-3, 5.30-11; 12-11 Sat; 12-6, 8-10.30 Sun
☎ (0161) 236 5307
Hydes Original Bitter Ⓗ
Small, basic and friendly street corner local with a bar serving two rooms. The smaller room in front of the bar has a real fire. Traditional music is played by local musicians on Thursday and Saturday nights. The pub received a local branch CAMRA award last year for being a Guide regular and for being run by the same family for over 20 years. Entrance is restricted before and after Manchester City home games, as the pub lies on the route between the ground and the city centre.
⛫≠(Piccadilly)⊖🚌

Knott
374 Deansgate, M3 4LY
☺ 12-11.30 (midnight Thu; 12.30 am Fri & Sat)
☎ (0161) 839 9229
Beer range varies Ⓗ
A well-established pub with a great mix of customers, it offers a selection of local and national beers that always provides the chance to try something new and keeps the locals happy. Excellent transport links make this a great pub to start and finish a crawl. The partly-covered upstairs balcony is now the designated smoking area. Food is served daily 12-8pm with interesting vegetarian and vegan options. Addlestones cider is available on draught, together with a fine selection of Belgian bottled beers.
❀◐≠(Deansgate)⊖(G-Mex)🚌⁵—

Lass O' Gowrie
36 Charles Street, M1 7DB
☺ 12-11 (midnight Thu-Sat); 12-10.30 Sun
☎ (0161) 273 6932 🌐 thelass.co.uk
Caledonian Deuchars IPA; Lass Ale; Shepherd Neame Spitfire; Taylor Landlord; Wells Bombardier; guest beers Ⓗ
A splendid tiled exterior is just one of the many attractions at this famous Manchester pub. The in-house brewery has long gone but its memory lives on in the form of Lass Ale, brewed by an unknown micro. This is accompanied by a changing range of guest beers, some from the Greene King list and some sourced independently (and often from North Wales micros). The food, served lunchtimes and evenings, is imaginative and good value. Live music on Friday and Sunday adds to the appeal. ◐≠⊖🚌⁵—

Marble Arch ☆ ✔
73 Rochdale Road, M4 4HY (on A664 200m from A665 junction)
☺ 11.30-11 (midnight Fri & Sat); 12-10.30 Sun
☎ (0161) 832 5914 🌐 marblebeers.co.uk
Marble GSB, Manchester Bitter, JP Best Bitter, Ginger Marble, Lagonda IPA, seasonal beers; guest beers Ⓗ
Listed brew pub on a corner site now surrounded by new luxury apartments. The Marble Arch's impressive main room has a green-tiled sloping floor with a decorative drinks frieze, which the brave can attempt to 'drink their way round'. A smaller back room beyond the bar enjoys views of the Soil Association-accredited Marble Brewery. A selection of the brewery's organic beers is served, complemented by varied guests and a changing cider. Excellent food is available until 8pm (6pm Sun).
⛫❀◐≠(Victoria)⊖(Shudehill)🚌●P⁵—

Paramount ✔
33-35 Oxford Street, M1 4BH
☺ 9-midnight (1am Fri & Sat)
☎ (0161) 233 1820
Greene King Abbot; Marston's Pedigree; Moorhouses Pendle Witches Brew; guest beers Ⓗ
This large, comfortable Wetherspoon house gets its name because of its location in Manchester's old theatreland (handy for both Library and Palace theatres). On the walls are pictures of nearby historic buildings and landmarks. What really distinguishes the pub, however, is the management and staff who are very customer- and cask beer-oriented. As a result, real ale sales have almost tripled, with four or five guest beers available, mostly from local micros. Food is served 9-11pm daily.
◐≠(Oxford Rd)⊖(St Peter's Sq)🚌(1,3)⁵—

Sand Bar
120-122 Grosvenor Street, All Saints, M1 7HL (off Oxford Rd A34/B5117 jct)
☺ 12 (4 Sat)-11 (midnight Thu & Sat; 2am Fri); closed Sun
☎ (0161) 273 8449 🌐 sandbaronline.co.uk
Moorhouses Black Cat; Phoenix All Saints; Taylor Landlord; guest beers Ⓗ
This successful conversion of two Georgian town houses continues to be one of the real ale highlights of the bustling university area. Customers range from university staff and students to all those who appreciate good ale in friendly and bohemian surroundings. The

guest beers are usually sourced from local micros and are complemented by a range of foreign beers plus a rare unfiltered Pilsner from the local Phoenix Brewery. A changing guest cider and inventive lunchtime food with interesting vegetarian options add to the winning formula.
◐⇌(Oxford Rd)🚌(42,43)♣⁴–

Smithfield Hotel & Bar

37 Swan Street, M4 5JZ (20m from A665/A62 jct)
✪ 12-11; 12-10.30 Sun
☎ (0161) 839 4424
Robinson's Dark Mild; guest beers Ⓗ
Long-established hotel and bar in the heart of Manchester's Northern Quarter. One long single room is dominated by a pool table at the front, with more seating and a TV at the rear. Six out of eight handpumps dispense beers from all around the country to supplement the house bitter from Phoenix. Occasional beer festivals at which numerous new and rare beers are served have achieved near legendary status. Accommodation is good value. ⇌⇌(Victoria)⊖(Shudehill)♣P

Unicorn

26 Church Street, M4 1PW
✪ 11.30-11; 12-5.30 Sun
☎ (0161) 834 8854
Boddingtons Bitter; Copper Dragon IPA; Draught Bass Ⓗ
Classic multi-roomed Edwardian pub with an interior featuring waxed oak panelling. The central bar serves a vault on one side and a narrow lobby on the other, revealing two more rooms offering a measure of seclusion plus a small snug. Upstairs there is a large function room where 'The Honourable Order of Bass Drinkers' used to have its HQ. This is one of the few ex-Bass pubs still serving Draught Bass in Manchester.
⇌(Victoria)⊖(Shudehill)🚌(59,135)

Marple

Hare & Hounds ✔

Dooley Lane, Otterspool, SK6 7EJ
✪ 11.30-11; 12-10.30 Sun
☎ (0161) 427 0293
Hydes Bitter, Jekyll's Gold Ⓗ
This is an attractive pub by the River Goyt on the Marple to Romiley road. It is difficult to imagine that when this pub was first built it was at the end of a row of terraced cottages – they were demolished long ago when the road was realigned. The pub's Hyde's beers now provide some welcome variety in the area. An open-plan interior has a separate dining area and conservatory, plus an improved and pleasant outdoor area. The pub now caters for all tastes and good value, popular food is served. Q❀◐▶P⁴–

Hatters Arms

81 Church Lane, SK6 7AW
✪ 12-midnight
☎ (0161) 427 1529 🌐 hattersmarple.co.uk
Robinson's Hatters Mild, Unicorn, Ⓗ **Old Tom,** Ⓖ **seasonal beers** Ⓗ
At a time when pubs struggle for custom, this little gem thrives. Parking close by is difficult, therefore the trade is mainly local and the landlord tries to make sure there is some form of entertainment for visitors. The pub is tiny and cosy, at the end of a row of hatters' cottages. Inside there are three small rooms and an attractive panelled bar. It is within walking distance of Rose Hill station.
❀◐♿⇌(Rose Hill)🚌⁴–

Railway

223 Stockport Road, SK6 3EN
✪ 12-11 (11.30 Fri & Sat)
☎ (0161) 427 2146
Robinson's Hatters, Unicorn, seasonal beers Ⓗ
This impressive pub first opened in 1878 alongside Rose Hill Station and many rail commuters still number among its customers. The pub is little changed externally, and is handy for walkers and cyclists on the nearby Middlewood Way. Two open-plan airy and relaxing rooms are complemented by an outside verandah and drinking area in this deservedly popular pub.
❀◐♿⇌(Rose Hill)🚌P⁴–

Mellor

Oddfellows Arms

73 Moorend Road, SK6 5PT
✪ 12-3, 5.30-11; 12-11 Sat & Sun
☎ (0161) 449 7826 🌐 theoddfellowsarms.com
Adnams Bitter; Black Sheep Best Bitter; Caledonian Deuchars IPA; Marston's Burton Bitter; Taylor Landlord Ⓗ
Lovely three-storey stone building at the foot of a steep hill leading to the edge of the Peak District. The emphasis has always been on food, as local buses are non-existent and local trade limited. Flagged floors, open fires and low beams make this a most attractive and relaxing haven. In front of the building is a small flagged patio. ⌂Q❀◐▶▲🚌(375)P⁴–

Middleton

Old Boar's Head

111 Long Street, M24 6UE
✪ 12-11 (10.30 Sun)
☎ (0161) 643 3520
Lees Brewer's Dark, Bitter Ⓗ
Ancient half timbered, multi-roomed pub dating back to at least 1632. Flagged floors and multiple discrete drinking areas add to the charm. The large session room is ideal for meetings and once served as a court for local magistrates. This room is also used for occasional brass band concerts. The pub runs a Customer of the Month award and displays winners on a noticeboard in the bar. Excellent hot lunches are a popular attraction (not Sun).
❀◐♿🚌(17)P⁴–

Tandle Hill Tavern

14 Thornham Lane, M24 2HB (1 mile along unmetalled road off A664 and A627) SD907094
✪ 5 (12 Sat)-midnight
☎ (01706) 345297
Lees Brewer's Dark, Bitter, seasonal beers Ⓗ
Popular with local farmers, a host of regulars and walkers from the nearby country park, this delightful two-roomed hidden gem, nestling amid farms and rolling hills, is reached by a pot-holed lane from Middleton (A664) or

Royton (A627). Inside, decoration includes local photographs and, unusually, witch paraphernalia. Dogs are welcome, with water and dog biscuits provided. Good value fresh food, sourced locally where possible, is available until 8pm. The pub was Manchester Food and Drink Pub of the Year 2007. ⌂❀◐

Mossley

Britannia Inn

217 Manchester Road, OL5 9AJ

☉ 3 (11 Sat)-11; 12-11 Sun

☎ (01457) 832799

Marston's Burton Bitter; guest beers Ⓗ

This imposing gritstone building is yards from Mossley Station. Marston's acquired it in 1961 when they bought Rothwell's (who had in turn bought it from Shaw & Bentley's in 1902). The Brit is now owned by Admiral Taverns. The pub offers a range of beers that rivals many free houses. Smokers and drinkers may use the compact, partially covered area in front of the pub. Food is served from opening time until 7.30pm (5pm Sun).
❀◐⇌🚌(343,350)♣

Dysarts Arms

Huddersfield Road, OL5 9BT (on B6175 half a mile S of A635)

☉ 12-midnight (1am Sat)

☎ (01457) 832103

Robinson's Old Stockport, Unicorn Ⓗ

Robinson's obtained this pub when it took over Schofield's Brewery of Ashton-under-Lyne in 1926. The Dysarts used to have three floors, but under Robinson's tenure it has lost the top floor and gained its current Bavarian-style roof. The interior has a spacious, comfortable bar area and a cosy lounge, with a real fire in winter. Outside, a partially covered patio to the side is used for drinking and smoking. No food Saturday or Sunday.
⌂❀◖⛺🚌(350)♣P

Rising Sun

235 Stockport Road, OL5 0RQ

☉ 6 (2 Sun)-midnight

☎ (01457) 834436 🌐 risingsunmossley.co.uk

Black Sheep Best Bitter; guest beers Ⓗ

This pub is well named – situated high out on Mossley's northern fringes, and nearly a mile from the station, it has splendid views east over the Tame Valley and towards Saddleworth Moor. The interior is semi open plan with a games room (used by the local Blue Grass Boys on Tuesday and a folk club every other Wednesday). There is a pavement patio for outdoor drinking and smokers have a sheltered courtyard. Note the range of vodkas and malts. ⌂❀🚌(353)♣P

Tollemache Arms

415 Manchester Road, OL5 9BG

☉ 12-midnight (1am Fri & Sat)

☎ (01457) 834555

Robinson's Old Stockport, Unicorn, Ⓗ **Old Tom** Ⓖ

Locals call this pub the Tolley. It is a good example of an end of terrace Northern pub, where much of the original timber and glasswork can still be seen. The pub is tucked between the Huddersfield Narrow Canal and Manchester Road (A635) about a mile north of the station, where road and canal cross. The patio has direct access to the towpath. While the canal was being restored, it was the haunt of the Huddersfield Canal Society.
❀⛺🚌(354)♣P

Nangreaves

Lord Raglan

Mount Pleasant, BL9 6SP

☉ 12-2.30, 7 (5 Fri)-11; 12-11 Sat; 12-10.30 Sun

☎ (0161) 764 6680

Leyden Nanny Flyer, Light Brigade, Raglan Sleeve, seasonal beers; guest beers Ⓗ

A country inn at the end of a cobbled lane with open views of the surrounding hills, this is the home of the Leyden Brewery and an impressive selection of its beers always features on the bar. The Leyden family has run this friendly pub for half a century. Good food is served in both restaurant and bar, prepared by the chef who is also the head brewer. The interior is decorated with antique glass and pottery, and old photographs. Q❀◐🚌P

Oldham

Ashton Arms ✔

28-30 Clegg Street, OL1 1PL

☉ 11.30-11 (11.30 Fri & Sat)

☎ (0161) 630 9709

Beer range varies Ⓗ

This friendly free house is situated opposite the old town hall, within the conservation area of Oldham. Seven superb constantly changing real ales are served. The pub specialises in local micros and seasonal ales, and welcomes new and established breweries. Traditional cider and a selection of interesting continental bottled beers are served. Note the 200-year-old stone fireplace. The food is good value and highly recommended. Quiz night is Tuesday and annual themed beer festivals are held regularly. ⌂◖⇌🚌♣●

Royal Oak

172 Manchester Road, Werneth, OL9 7BN (on A62 opposite Werneth Park)

☉ 2-midnight; 12-1am Sat; 12-11.30 Sun

☎ (0161) 284 3797

Robinson's Hatters, Unicorn Ⓗ

Traditional local pub with four rooms around a central bar. This popular community local features wood panelling, old-fashioned cast-iron radiators and an antique Gledhill cash register which is still in use as a till. A folk group meets here on Sunday and other groups meet in the separate room available for hire. The pub is in a restricted parking zone, but a small public car park is nearby. Regular bus services stop close by. Q♿⇌🚌(82,83)♣

Openshaw

Legh Arms

741 Ashton Old Road, M11 2HD (on A635, opp college)

☉ 11 (12 Sun)-11

☎ (0161) 223 4317

Moorhouses Black Cat, Pendle Witches Brew; guest beers Ⓗ

An oasis in a real ale desert, this pub is run by a licensee who is as passionate about his beer as he is about nearby Manchester City FC – the house beer brewed by Moorhouses is called, fittingly, Blue. An eclectic local clientele extends a warm welcome in this once multi-roomed pub, which still retains quiet nooks and crannies. With pool and darts (on an unusual log-end board) plus an enclosed beer garden at the rear, complete with barbecue and bouncy castle, the Legh Arms has something for everyone.
❀≷⊟(53,219)♣●⁵⁻

Orrell

Robin Hood

117 Sandy Lane, WN5 7AZ (near rail station)
⊙ 2-midnight; 12-1am Fri & Sat; 12-11 Sun
☎ (01695) 627429
Beer range varies ⊞
Well worth finding, this small sandstone pub tucked away in a residential area has a reputation for serving good home-cooked food (Thu-Sun, booking advisable). The lounge is used for dining at meal times. Three handpumps provide semi-regular beers include Deuchars IPA, Old Speckled Hen and Taylor Landlord. Not surprisingly, the decor has a Robin Hood theme. ❀◐≷♣P

Running Horses

St James Road, WN5 7AA
⊙ 4 (12 Fri & Sat)-midnight; 1-11.30 Sun
☎ (01942) 512604
Banks's Bitter; guest beers ⊞
Dating back to the 1800s, with a large extension added in 1920 and further modernisation in 2004, the pub offers a warm, cosy interior, with sofas arranged around a fireplace. There is a separate pool and darts room. Sports events are shown on large-screen TVs. Lunches are served on Sunday only (booking advisable). A regular Sunday night quiz and charity events are organised. Quality guest ales cover all tastes. The smoking area is heated and covered. ❀◐♿≷P⁵⁻

Patricroft

Stanley Arms ★

895 Liverpool Road, M30 0QN (opp fire station on A57)
⊙ 12-11 (10.30 Sun)
☎ (0161) 788 8801
Holt Mild, Bitter ⊞
Classic street-corner local which has remained virtually unchanged for over 100 years. There is a vault at the front, while at the rear of the bar is a comfortable lounge. The green-tiled lobby and corridor lead to a back room that features an old kitchen range fireplace. Old photographs of Eccles adorn the walls. In 2008 the pub was the first recipient of the local CAMRA branch's Neil Richardson Trophy for a traditional unspoilt pub.The smoking area is covered and heated. Q❀⊟≷⊟⁵⁻

Peel Green

Grapes Hotel ★

439 Liverpool Road, M30 7HD (A57 near M60 jct 11)
⊙ 11-11 (midnight Fri & Sat); 12-11 Sun
☎ (0161) 789 6971
Holt Mild, Bitter ⊞
Originally known as the Bowling Green, this monumental Edwardian red-brick inn was bought by Holt's in 1889, then demolished and rebuilt in 1906, in splendid Edwardian style. This often lively heritage pub has a billiard room which is today used as a pool room. Four other rooms include a large vault. The pub is adorned with mosaic floors, tiled walls, etched glass and polished mahogany. ⊟≷(Patricroft)⊟(10,67)P⁵⁻

Pendlebury

Lord Nelson

653 Bolton Road, M27 4EJ (A666/B5231 jct)
⊙ 11-11 (11.30 Fri); 12-11 Sun
☎ (0161) 794 3648
Holt Mild, Bitter ⊞
The first pub on this site dated back to 1824, was purchased by Holt's in 1875, and stood until the 1970s when it was rebuilt. The 1970s building comprises a large lounge with a raised curtained stage and a snug-like corner plus a spacious separate vault. A back-to-back double bar serves both rooms. Seafaring pictures reinforce the Nelson theme, as do numerous concrete bollards. The smoking area is covered and heated. ❀⊟≷⊟♣P⁵⁻

Windmill Hotel

690 Bolton Road, M27 8FH (jct A666 & B5231)
⊙ 11-11; 12-10.30 Sun
☎ (0161) 794 1609
Samuel Smith OBB ⊞
The pub is named after a windmill that once stood at nearby Clifton Green. The building was rebuilt in 1876 after a fire at an adjoining mill caused the original 1828 building to be crushed by collapsing masonry. A long, large pub, it has a large central lounge served by a long bar. To the left is a snug and to the right another distinct drinking area. A vault is at the rear, with its own bar. ⋔Q⊟≷⊟♣P

Prestwich

Friendship

Scholes Lane, M25 0PD (on A6044 near Heaton Park)
⊙ 12-11 (11.30 Fri & Sat)
☎ (0161) 773 2645
Holt Mild, Bitter, seasonal beers ⊞
Large, recently renovated red-brick roadside pub with a drinking and smoking area out front. Inside there is a traditional, separate small public bar and a pleasant wooden-surround servery and hatches. These dispense beer to the bar and the rest of the pub, which comprises a corridor with a standing area and a large comfortable lounge, plus a separate dining area. The standard Holt's menu is supplemented by home-cooked daily specials. Food is available until 8pm. ❀◐⊟♿P⁵⁻

Rochdale

Baum

33-37 Toad Lane, OL12 0NU (follow signs for Co-op Museum)
✪ 11.30-11 (midnight Fri & Sat)
☎ (01706) 352186 🌐 thebaum.co.uk
Boddingtons Bitter; Flowers IPA; guest beers Ⓗ
Just outside the town centre in a conservation area next to the world's first Co-op store and facing the splendid St Mary's Church stands this delightful, traditional pub. The Baum, a split-level inn, stocks three guest ales and a good selection of continental beers. Excellent food including vegetarian options is served daily, with a tapas menu available at weekends. To the rear of the inn is a large outside area with tables at which to eat and drink. ❀◐◑≉⁼

Cemetery Hotel ★

470 Bury Road, OL11 5EY (on B622, a mile from centre)
✪ 12-2am (1am Sat); 12-10.30 Sun
☎ (01706) 645635
Beer range varies Ⓗ
Rochdale's original free house from the early 1970s, this pub's interior is listed in CAMRA's National Inventory because of the many original features it retains – especially the tile work. Upstairs is a well appointed restaurant specialising in traditional Lancashire dishes. Downstairs there is a multi-roomed layout, with two lovely snugs. The pub can get very busy with Rochdale AFC fans on match days. Q⛵◐◑🚌P⁼

Flying Horse Hotel

37 Packer Street, OL16 1NJ (opp town hall)
✪ 11 (12 Sun)-midnight
☎ (01706) 646412 🌐 theflyinghorsehotel.co.uk
Lees Bitter; Taylor Best Bitter, Landlord; guest beers Ⓗ
Impressive stone building by the side of an even more impressive town hall, the Flying Horse was built as a hotel in the early 20th century. The well decorated open-plan lounge attracts a mixed clientele and gets very busy at weekends. The pub is centrally located, close to all amenities and easy to find. Food is served upstairs in the restaurant. One of the guest beers is usually from Phoenix. Rochdale station is nearby. 🛏◐◑≉🚌⁼

Merry Monk ✔

234 College Road, OL12 6AF (at A6060/B6222 jct)
✪ 12-11; 12-5, 7-10.30 Sun
☎ (01706) 646919
Hydes Owd Oak, Original Bitter, Jekyll's Gold Premium, seasonal beer; guest beers Ⓗ
This detached Victorian brick local was first licensed in 1850. Its history can be glimpsed in the fine pair of Phoenix of Heywood tile sets in the entrance. The pub passed to Bass via Cornbrook and was sold as a free house in 1984. The open-plan pub is home to strong darts and quiz teams, while Ring the Bull and other games are played. Outside are two full-sized petanque pistes. The wide range of Hydes beers is served, alongside one or two guests. ❀🚌♣⁼

Regal Moon ✔

The Butts, OL16 1HB (next to bus station)
✪ 9-midnight (1am Fri & Sat); 11-11 Sun
☎ (01706) 657434
Beer range varies Ⓗ
Right in the middle of the town, this Wetherspoon pub has been converted from an Art Deco Regal cinema. Now a large, single-storey split-level affair with a raised area used for families, many original features survived the change, including a mannequin seated at an organ over the bar. The walls are adorned with pictures of old film stars and old Rochdale. The bar dispenses up to 10 constantly changing real ales. Food is served all day every day with breakfast until noon. ❀◐◑♿≉🚌⁼

Sale

Railway

35 Chapel Road, M33 7FD (behind town hall)
✪ 12-1am
☎ (0161) 973 8177
Robinson's Unicorn, Double Hop, seasonal beers Ⓗ
This small Robinson's hostelry is located just off the town centre – look for the unusual white cladding. The interior has benefited from a recent refit, making it more attractive to the local clientele and to those visiting the newly built Sale Waterside theatre complex. The pub is also a meeting place for local quiz teams, jazz enthusiasts and a ramblers' club. A DJ plays on Friday and Sunday, and there is karaoke on Thursday. Wheelchair access is via the rear door. ⛱♿⊖🚌P⁼

Volunteer Hotel

81 Cross Street, M33 7HH
✪ 12-midnight (11 Sun)
☎ (0161) 973 5503
Holts Mild, Bitter, seasonal beers Ⓗ
Dating back to the late 19th century, this once multi-roomed pub has been opened up into one large room served by a single bar. The interior is warm and welcoming, with friendly, helpful staff. Meals are served from a traditional menu Tuesday to Saturday 12-8pm (12-4pm Sun). Three darts teams are based here, which makes for some lively evenings, while karaoke takes place most Thursdays. There is a fine oak-panelled room upstairs which is available for meetings. 🛏♿⊖🚌♣P⁼

Salford

Crescent

20 The Crescent, M5 4PF
✪ 11 (12 Sun)-midnight (1am Fri & Sat)
☎ (0161) 736 5600
Bazens' Black Pig Mild; Hydes Original Bitter; Phoenix Wobbly Bob; Rooster's Special; guest beers Ⓗ
Saved from threatened closure by new owners, this famous pub – where Karl Marx allegedly drank – now stocks four regular ales and up to eight guests, all served in oversized glasses. Two real ciders and foreign beers are also sold. One bar serves three drinking areas, plus an overspill room. A recent refurbishment

has seen it spruced up throughout but unchanged in character. A varied mix of customers includes staff and students from nearby Salford University. Wednesday is curry night. No entry after 11pm. ⌂◐⇌▭●P⁴─▯

King's Arms

11 Bloom Street, M3 6AN (near Central station)
⌚ 12-11 (midnight Fri & Sat); 12-6 Sun
☎ (0161) 839 8726 ⊕ kingsarmssalford.com
Bazens' Pacific; Moorhouses Blond Witch; guest beers ⊞
The pub has a large oval lounge, corridor and a comfortable side snug, with a large collection of mirrors. Up to six real ales are available, with guests from Facers, All Gates, Wells & Young's and Copper Dragon among others. The rear bohemian-style smoking shelter is heated by an outdoor coal fire and contains more mirrors. The pub is well known for its Studio Salford Arts For All (live bands, theatre, comedy and poetry) and the Monday evening knitting circle. Good hot and cold food is served daily. Q◐◑⇌▭P⁴─

New Oxford

11 Bexley Square, M3 6DB
⌚ 12-midnight
☎ (0161) 832 7082 ⊕ thenewoxford.co.uk
Bazens' Flatbac; guest beers ⊞
Nestling almost within the shadow of Salford Cathedral, this well-appointed two-room bar is dedicated to the worship of quality beer. Rescued from an unpromising past by the committed management team, it was crowned CAMRA Greater Manchester Pub of the Year in 2007. Up to 15 guest beers, often from local micro-breweries, are complemented by a superlative range of Belgian beers, with several on draught. Czech and German beers also feature. Regular beer festivals are hosted. Food is served until 6pm. ❀◐⇌▭●─

Racecourse Hotel

Littleton Road, Lower Kersal, M7 3SE (next to River Irwell)
⌚ 12-midnight (1am Fri & Sat); 12-11 Sun
☎ (0161) 792 1420
Oakwell Barnsley Bitter ⊞
This imposing pub dates from 1930. It was built to cater for visitors to the nearby Manchester racecourse which ran its last race in 1963. Racing mementoes and historic information adorn the walls. The large central bar serves several distinct drinking areas, and you can only imagine how busy it would have been in its racing heyday. Wooden panelling and flooring, along with the revolving entrance door, add to the character of this splendid building. Food is served daily. ❀◐◑⊟▭(93,95)♣P⁴─

Star Inn

2 Back Hope Street, Higher Broughton, M7 2FR (off Great Clowes St)
⌚ 1.30-11.30 (11.45 Sat); 1.30-10.30 Sun
☎ (0161) 792 4184
Robinson's Unicorn ⊞
Tucked away, but still in the heart of the community and in a conservation area, the regulars here are loyal, but all are welcomed. First-timers are easily spotted as they enter and walk straight into the long saloon, as it is easy to miss the tiny bar and vault that seats nine. The pub dates back to the middle of the 19th century with a front yard, which partially serves as a covered smoking area. The quieter back room has a pool table. ❀▭(98)♣P

Union Tavern

105 Liverpool Street, M5 4LG (between A6 and A7, near A6066)
⌚ 12-midnight
☎ (0161) 736 2885
Holt Mild, Bitter ⊞
Traditional, basic Holt's outlet set in an area that has seen considerable change and development during the last two decades. The pub comprises a lounge and a vault, plus a games room at the rear, all served from a central bar. Several darts teams are active and many of their trophies are on display behind the bar. The pub is run by one of Salford's longest serving licensees, with more than 35 years in the trade. ⊟♿⇌▭♣P⁴─

Stalybridge

Stalybridge Station Refreshment Rooms (Buffet Bar) ☆

Rassbottom Street, SK15 1RF (Platform 1)
⌚ 9.30 (alcohol from 11)-11; 11-10.30 Sun
☎ (0161) 303 0007 ⊕ buffetbar.freewebspace.com
Boddingtons Bitter; Flowers IPA; guest beers ⊞
Nobody minds delayed or missed trains at Stalybridge. This institution for educated drinkers serves an ever-changing range of up to nine cask beers, usually from micros, plus often rare brews. These can be enjoyed in convivial Victorian splendour by the roaring fire while enjoying black peas or a good value, simple, traditionally cooked meal; or perched outside watching the world and the trains go by. Foreign bottled beers are also available and a folk club plays on Saturday. Regular beer festivals are held. ⌂Q❀◐◑⊟♿⇌▭●P⁴─

Stamford Arms

815 Huddersfield Road, Heyheads, SK15 3PY
⌚ 12-midnight (1am Fri & Sat)
☎ (01457) 832133 ⊕ stamfordarms.co.uk
Thwaites Original, Lancaster Bomber, seasonal beers ⊞
This Grade II listed building is popular with walkers, ramblers and locals alike. It is Stalybridge's most northerly pub, standing by the pre-1974 Cheshire/Lancashire border. Mossley station is but a mile and a half away. The large beer garden to the side overlooks the fairways of Stamford Park Golf Club. There is live entertainment on Saturday evening and a quiz night on Tuesday. Food is not available on Thursday. ❀◐◑▭(234,343)♣P⁴─

Standish

Dog & Partridge

33 School Lane, WN6 0TG (off A49 towards M6)
⌚ 1-11.30 (1am Fri; midnight Sat); 12-11 Sun
☎ (01257) 401218
Tetley Bitter ⊞
Two areas around a central bar are decorated in the style of a lounge, with leather sofas and comfortable chairs. Guest beers are normally

sourced from micro-breweries. This pub has a strong focus on sports, with screens always in view from any seat. Outside, a heated patio area also has a sports screen. ❀🚌(362)P⁄

Stockport

Arden Arms ★

23 Millgate, SK1 2LX (jct of Corporation St)
⏲ 12-11
☎ (0161) 480 2185 🌐 arden-arms.com
Robinson's Hatters, Unicorn, Double Hop, Old Tom, seasonal beers Ⓗ
Grade II listed and on CAMRA's National Inventory, the Arden's distinctive curved, glazed bar, its hidden snug, chandeliers and grandfather clock conjure a Victorian ambience. Gourmet lunches (noon-4 daily), quiz nights and wine tastings, however, add a contemporary touch. Conveniently close to Stockport's historic market and the Peel Centre shops, the place is abuzz at lunchtimes, but more intimate in the evenings. The cellars retain body niches in the walls, testament to the building's former use as a mortuary.
♨❀◖🚌♣⁄

Armoury

31 Shaw Heath, SK3 8BD (on B5465)
⏲ 10.30-midnight (2am Fri & Sat); 11-midnight Sun
☎ (0161) 477 3711 🌐 frederic-robinson.com
Robinson's Hatters, Unicorn, Old Tom Ⓗ
Busy community local with three separate rooms and friendly, knowledgeable staff. Some superb original glass panels remain on the internal doors, bearing the old Bells Brewery logo, while the walls feature memorabilia from the Cheshire Regiment. Convenient for Edgeley Park football ground, the home of Sale Sharks and Stockport County, bar food is often available when the teams are at home. Darts is very much a feature here, with two leagues often playing on the same night. An upstairs room often features live folk music sessions. Q❀⇌🚌(310,369)♣⁄

Bakers Vaults

Market Place, SK1 1ES
⏲ 11-midnight (1.30am Fri & Sat); 5-midnight Sun
☎ (0161) 477 7312 🌐 frederic-robinson.com
Robinson's Hatters, Unicorn, seasonal beers Ⓗ
This excellent market pub has a unique atmosphere that is cosy and relaxed, yet lively and vibrant. Architecturally impressive, the bohemian feel is enhanced by the general decor and in particular the unusual artwork on display – look out for the medieval faces in the panels on the bar counter. Live music (Tue-Sat) is eclectic, ranging from relaxed jazz to folk rock and R&B. On Sunday a DJ plays Northern Soul classics. Food is served weekday lunchtimes. ◖🚌

Blossoms

2 Buxton Road, Heaviley, SK2 6NU (at A6/A5102 jct)
⏲ 12-3, 5-11 (11.30 Fri); 12-11.30 Sat; 12-10.30 Sun
☎ (0161) 477 2397 🌐 frederic-robinson.com
Robinson's Hatters, Unicorn, Ⓗ **Old Tom** Ⓖ
Early Victorian multi-roomed house that retains its original lobby bar and three rooms. The 'room' has an elegant carved fireplace surround as well as stained glass panels. A tunnel connects the pub to nearby St George's Church – it was built in Victorian times to ensure the choir were not seen to be going to the pub after services. Food is served weekday lunchtimes.
Q❀◖⇌(Davenport)🚌(192,199)♣P⁄

Crown

154 Heaton Lane, SK4 1AR (jct of King Street West under viaduct)
⏲ 12-11 (10.30 Sun)
☎ (0161) 480 5850 🌐 thecrowninn.uk.com
Beer range varies Ⓗ
Local CAMRA branch Pub of the Year 2008, the Crown is busy, especially in the evenings. A choice of around 16 ever-changing beers is usually available, often including Pictish and Copper Dragon plus other micros and real cider. Four rooms radiate from the bar: two compact snugs, a large lounge with feature overmantel, and a pool room. The atmosphere is friendly and the staff knowledgeable. Good food is served weekday lunchtimes and live music hosted twice weekly (Wed and Sun).
♨❀◖⇌🚌●⁄

Olde Vic

1 Chatham Street, SK3 9ED (jct of Shaw Heath)
⏲ 5 (7 Sat)-late (last entry 10.15); closed Mon; 7-10.30 Sun
☎ (0161) 480 2410 🌐 yeoldevic.com
Hydes Original Bitter; guest beers Ⓗ
One-roomed, characterful pub undergoing a slow programme of refurbishment. Beware the licensee's wicked sense of humour! A strict no-swearing rule belies the easy-going, friendly nature of the pub, which can be particularly busy when Sale Sharks are at home. Five handpumps dispense an ever-changing range of guest beers, usually from micro-breweries. One handpump is reserved for guest ciders. Supervised Internet access is available. Note the pub is only open in the evening. ♨❀⇌🚌(310,369)●⁄

Olde Woolpack

70 Brinksway, SK3 0BY (on A560, jct Hollywood Way)
⏲ 12-11 (10.30 Sun)
☎ (0161) 476 0688
Beer range varies Ⓗ
After a fallow period following the untimely death of the pub's founder, this former award-winning hostelry, now revitalised, is ticking all the right boxes once again. Two well-fitted lounges and a plainer vault-cum-dining room surround the bar. With a licensee keen on locally brewed cask beers, and food served daily (with a carvery at weekends), the pub has great appeal to locals and nearby businesses alike. Quiz night is Wednesday.
❀◖♿🚌(307,312)P⁄

Pack Horse

2 Market Place, SK1 1EW
⏲ 12-11 (10.30 Sun)
☎ (0161) 480 5686
Copper Dragon Bitter; Tetley Bitter Ⓗ
Overshadowed by St Mary's Church, behind Stockport's Victorian market hall, this cosy pub looks older that it really is – it dates from 1931. In contrast to its neighbours, there is no live music, which creates a more relaxing

atmosphere. Note the stained glass windows to your side as you enter the pub and the tiling around the fireplaces in the two lounges.

Pineapple

159 Heaton Lane, SK4 1AQ (off A6)
12-11 (10.30 Sun)
(0161) 480 3221 frederic-robinson.com
Robinson's Hatters, Cumbria Way, Unicorn, seasonal beer
This traditional former coaching house became a pub in 1820, but later became the HQ of Stockport's Botanical Society until c.1904. At the rear of the pub is a games room featuring a pool table, dartboard, and a display of trophies. Both front rooms have beamed ceilings, and the walls are decorated with plates from around the world and a brewery mirror, creating a cosy and appealing atmosphere. Very handy for the Hat Museum. Lunches are served Monday to Saturday.

Railway

1 Avenue Street, SK1 2BZ (jct of Great Portwood St/A560)
12-11 (10.30 Sun)
(0161) 429 6062
Pennine Floral Dance, Hambledon Bitter, Railway Sleeper, Porter, Sunshine, seasonal beers; guest beers
Bustling, single-room street corner pub showcasing the Pennine (formerly Porter) Brewery beers – both brewery and pub changed hands in 2007. It was recently reprieved when a threatened redevelopment of the area was postponed for four years. Eleven handpumps dispense the full range of Pennine beers, plus three guests at weekends. Real cider is stocked, plus a wide range of Belgian, German and other bottled beers. Home-made lunches are served Monday to Saturday. Local CAMRA Pub of the Year 2007.

Thatched House

74 Churchgate, SK1 1YJ (jct Wellington St)
closed Mon & Tue; 8-11 Wed; 8-1am Thu; 7-2am Fri; 3-11 Sat & Sun
(0161) 335 1910 thatched-live.co.uk
Black Sheep Best Bitter; Wychwood Hobgoblin; guest beers
One of the town's premier venues for live music, mainly rock, metal and punk bands, playing Thursday, Friday and Saturday nights. A quiet pub it is not. Remaining architectural details of note are a mosaic floor in the porch and rare windows featuring Showell's Brewery. The large, open-plan main bar leads to a pool room and beer garden. Two guest beers are usually available, along with a changing guest cider, plus a good range of bottled beers.

Three Shires

30-32 Great Underbank, SK1 1NB
11-11 (9 Mon & Tue); 12-9 Sun
(0161) 477 4579
Beer range varies
A two-minute walk from the shopping precinct, this black and white building dating from c1580 (see blue plaque) is still called a wine bar. However, with four ever-changing guest beers from smaller and micro-breweries, usually including one from Copper Dragon, it is not one to walk past. A wide selected of freshly prepared food is available lunchtimes and evenings.

Strines

Sportsman's Arms

105 Strines Road, SK6 7GE
12-3, 5-11; 12-11 Sat & Sun
(0161) 427 2888 the-sportsman-pub.co.uk
Boddingtons Bitter; Cains Bitter; guest beers
A superb picture window view of the Goyt Valley unfolds from this pub. A monumental fireplace, with log fires in winter, adorns the open-plan lounge. There is also a small separate tap room. Outside, a terrace and balcony are popular in summer and provide a year-round heated and covered facility for smokers. Three guest beers are usually available, often coming from micro-breweries. Fortunately, the bus between Stockport and Hayfield stops just outside and the last bus back runs after midnight.

Summerseat

Footballers Inn

28 Higher Summerseat, BL0 9UG SD788145
2-12.30am; 12-1am Sat; 12-11 Sun
(01204) 883363 footballersinn.co.uk
Black Sheep Best Bitter; Hydes Original Bitter; Taylor Landlord; guest beers
This friendly, family-run pub in the quiet village of Summerseat caters for all, with one large room divided into several separate drinking areas. The bar boasts six cask beers, featuring a wide selection of ales. Enjoy the excellent views from the rear garden where you can play petanque, or even practise your golf swing in the covered driving range. The pub runs numerous social events including a very popular quiz evening. It is dog friendly and also offers a Wi-Fi hot spot.
(477)

Swinton

White Horse

384 Worsley Road, M27 0FH
12-11 (midnight Fri & Sat)
(0161) 794 2404
Boddingtons Bitter; Greene King IPA; Theakston XB; Wells Bombardier; guest beers
Thriving whitewashed community pub set back from the busy Worsley Road. One bar serves several distinct drinking areas. Handpumps are scattered around the bar, while a blackboard lists the available ales, usually including two guests from independent breweries. Several TV screens show mainly sporting events. There is a large garden and smoking area at the rear. Good value food is served until 9pm.

White Swan

186 Worsley Road, M27 5BN (close to jct A572/A580 East Lancashire Road)
12-11 (10.30 Sun)
(0161) 794 1504

Holt Mild, Bitter Ⓗ
A fine example of a red-brick 1920s pub that has retained plenty of original features including fireplaces, mahogany panels in all the main rooms and an old-fashioned L-shaped vault where traditional pub games are popular. Also worthy of note are the stained glass windows. A large back room acts as a family, TV and darts room.
(12,26)P

Tyldesley

Half Moon

115-117 Elliot Street, M29 8FL
11-4, 7-midnight; 12-midnight Sat; 12-11 Sun
☎ (01942) 883481
Holt Bitter; guest beers Ⓗ
Town-centre two-room local popular with a clientele of all ages. The main lounge, with its display cabinets, has various seating and standing areas, while the second lounge is comfortable and ideal for get-togethers. In summer the patio is a good place to catch the sun and take in the views of Winter Hill.

Mort Arms

235-237 Elliot Street, M29 8DG
12-midnight (1am Fri & Sat); 12-11 Sun
☎ (01942) 883481
Holt Mild, Bitter Ⓗ
This 1930s pub has changed little over the years. From the façade to the interior it is recognisable as a Holt's hostelry. The entrance has two etched doors directing you into the tap room or the lounge. The bar serves both rooms. In the lounge, walls are wood panelled, with seating and tables all around. At the rear, behind the fireplace, is what was once part of the pub's private quarters. The tap room is a bright contrast and just how a tap room should be.

Uppermill

Cross Keys

off Running Hill Gate, OL3 6LW (off A670, up Church Road)
12-midnight (11 Sun)
☎ (01457) 874626
Lees Brewer's Dark, Bitter, Moonraker, seasonal beers Ⓗ
Overlooking Saddleworth Church, this attractive 18th-century stone building has exposed beams throughout. The public bar features a stone-flagged floor and Yorkshire range. The pub is the centre for many activities, including mountain rescue and the Saddleworth Runners. It is especially busy during annual events such as the Folk Festival in July, and the Road and Fell Race and Rushcart Festival in August. Folk nights are hosted on Wednesday in the barn. Home-cooked food features puddings, pies and real chips (not Mon but all day Sat-Sun).
QP

Waggon Inn

34 High Street, OL3 6HR
11.30-11 (12.30am Fri & Sat); 12-10.30 Sun
☎ (01457) 872376 thewaggoninn.co.uk
Robinson's Hartleys XB, Unicorn, Ⓗ **Old Tom,** Ⓖ **seasonal beers** Ⓗ
This mid-19th century stone pub stands in a picturesque village opposite Saddleworth Museum and the Huddersfield narrow canal. With a central bar, three rooms and a restaurant, it also offers high quality B&B. It is the venue for many annual events including the Whit Friday brass band contest, the July Folk Festival and in August the Yanks weekend and the Rushcart Festival. Good home-cooked food includes senior and early bird specials and themed events (no eve meals Sun or Mon). QP

Urmston

Lord Nelson

49 Stretford Road, M41 9LG SJ769944
11-11 (11.30 Fri & Sat); 12-11 Sun
Holt Mild, Bitter, seasonal beers Ⓗ
Big, friendly drinkers' pub in a building that dates back to the Battle of Trafalgar and looks incongruously like a French chateau. The interior has been opened out but retains high ceilings with decorative cornices. For a quiet drink and a degree of privacy go into the snug (or 'laying out room') to the right of the entrance; for heated debates on sport use the back room. Quiz night is Tuesday. The outside drinking area closes at 9pm. P

Whalley Range

Hillary Step

199 Upper Chorlton Road, M16 0BH
4-11.30 (12.30am Fri & Sat); 12-11.30 Sun
☎ (0161) 881 1978
Thwaites Thoroughbred; guest beers Ⓗ
Lively, modern bar – a pub for conversation, with wonderful bar snacks but no meals. Live jazz features on a Sunday night and broadsheet papers are available most of the time. Guest beers are generally from micro-breweries, and there is a good choice of wines and whiskies. A front patio houses an outside drinking area.

Whitefield

Eagle & Child

Higher Lane, M45 7EY (on A665, 300m from A56)
11-11 (midnight Fri & Sat)
☎ (0161) 796 2334
Holt Mild, Bitter, seasonal beers Ⓗ
A pub on this site dates from the 1800s. The original was bought by Holt's in 1907 but rebuilt in 1936. Set back from the road, this large building has a large lounge area and a public bar, both served by a central bar. A smaller room is ideal for meetings or private parties. At the rear a bowling green is superbly maintained and well used by the pub's 11 teams. A barbecue is held on Sunday, with live music on Friday. P

Wigan

Anderton Arms

82 Ince Green Lane, WN2 2DG
12-midnight (12.30am Fri & Sat); 12.30-midnight Sun
☎ (01942) 247576

Beer range varies 🄷
After a few years untenanted, this free house has been lovingly restored and features leather upholstery and dark wood panelling. A central bar area serves three distinct drinking spaces. There are unobtrusive TV screens in the pool area and lounge. Family oriented, the pleasant patio yard has a children's play space (children permitted until 7.30pm) as well as a decking area with a canopy for smokers. ❀🚌(630,674)🍎⚐🥛

Anvil ✔

Dorning Street, WN1 1ND (next to Wigan bus station)
⏲ 11-11 Mon-Sat; 12-10.30 Sun
☎ (01942) 239444 🌐 allgatesinns.co.uk
Hydes Mild, Bitter; guest beers 🄷
Popular town centre pub, a frequent winner of local CAMRA seasonal and Pub of the Year awards and now Premiership Pub of the Season (2006-2007 Football & Real Ale Guide). Six handpumps offer rotating beers, including those from the nearby Allgates brewery, plus six draught continental ales and a range of bottled beers. A mixed clientele enjoys excellent service from attentive bar staff. The pub can be busy on match days as it close to the JJB Stadium, home to Wigan Athletic and Wigan Warriors. ❀⇌🚌⚐

Berkeley ✔

27-29 Wallgate, WN1 1LD (opp Wallgate station)
⏲ 11.30-11 (midnight Fri & Sat); 12-10.30 Sun
☎ (01942) 242041
Theakston Mild, Old Peculier; guest beer 🄷
The Berkeley, a former coaching house, has a friendly, comfortable atmosphere, offering something for everyone. Regular sporting fixtures are shown on large-screen TVs in the open-plan bar. The pub's clever design means that the comfortable, split-level areas give the impression of distinct seating sections. Food is served daily until 8pm. A first-floor function room is available for hire. There is a dress code on Saturday night. ◐⇌🚌

Boulevard

Wallgate, WN1 1LD (near Wallgate station)
⏲ 4-2am (2.30am Fri & Sat); 4-11.30 Sun
☎ (01942) 497165 🌐 wiganboulevard.co.uk
Allgates Young Pretender; John Smith's Bitter; guest beers 🄷
This surprisingly large basement pub (look for a yellow and black sign indicating the entrance) opened in 2006. From the bar you enter a large back room that features regular entertainment. Live music is performed on Friday and Saturday. Open until very late, it is close to both Wigan Wallgate and North Western train stations. Winner of CAMRA Wigan New Cask Outlet award for 2007 and Pub of the Season Autumn 2007. ⇌🚌

Bowling Green

106 Wigan Lane, WN1 2LS
⏲ 3 (12 Sat & Sun)-11 (1am Fri & Sat); 12-11 Sun
☎ (01942) 519871
Caledonian Deuchars IPA; Greene King Old Speckled Hen; Tetley Bitter; Thwaites Lancaster Bomber; guest beers 🄷
This red-brick pub, built in 1904, was once used as a soup kitchen. The building has received some sympathetic internal alterations, creating a comfortable lounge with two distinct drinking areas. There is a separate games and pool room, and a beer garden to the rear with a covered smoking area. A function room is available for hire. In addition to the regular beers, there are changing guest ales. Daily newspapers are available in the lounge. ♨❀⊟⇌🚌♣⚐

Brocket Arms ✔

Mesnes Road, Swinley, WN1 2DD
⏲ 9-midnight (1am Fri & Sat)
☎ (01942) 403500
Greene King IPA, Abbot; Marston's Pedigree; guest beers 🄷
The Brocket is one of the few Wetherlodges in the country. The interior is spacious, light and airy. While open plan, there are intimate booths and flexible seating to accommodate groups of all sizes. The usual Wetherspoon food and conference rooms are available and a patio area to the front of the pub caters for smokers. Guest beers from local micro-breweries feature regularly. ❀◐☽♿🚌P⚐

Crooke Hall Inn

Crooke Road, Standish Lower Ground, WN6 8LR (signed off B5375)
⏲ 12-midnight
☎ (01942) 247524 🌐 allgatesinns.co.uk
Beer range varies 🄷
Multi-roomed pub owned by Allgates Brewery and featuring beers from its range. Situated in an attractive village overlooking the Leeds-Liverpool canal to the rear and close to Crooke Marina, it attracts walkers and canal traffic all year round. There is a pool table in one section, a dartboard in another, with the largest room suitable for diners. A cellar function room hosts occasional beer festivals. Food is available from 12-8pm (children welcome until 9pm). ❀◐☽♣P

Swan & Railway

80 Wallgate, WN1 1BA (Opp North Western station)
⏲ 12-11
☎ (01942) 495032
Banks's Bitter; guest beers 🄷
A magnificent mosaic floor and tiled passageway lead you into a superbly traditional urban pub where a warm welcome awaits the weary traveller. The interior features much wood and there is an impressive stained glass window above the bar depicting a swan and the railway. A separate pool room and a large lounge are to the rear. Up to five beers are available. ⇌🚌

Winton

Ellesmere

26 King William Street, M30 8HZ (off B5211 next to M602 flyover)
⏲ 11-11 (12.30am Sat); 12-11 Sun
☎ (0161) 787 9003
Holt Mild, Bitter 🄷
A well-run community hostelry in a street that was just missed by the motorway that looms overhead. This placed the pub at the back of a cul-de-sac, giving it a secluded air. There is a sizeable vault and a similar-sized lounge.

Recently a large investment has been made in upgrading the beer garden to a high standard and building a covered smoking area. Quizzes and other entertainments are a regular feature. The family room is available until 7pm.

Withington

Victoria

438 Wilmslow Road, M20 3BW (on B5093, jct Davenport Avenue)
11.30-11; 12-10.30 Sun
(0161) 434 2600 hydesbrewery.co.uk
Hydes Mild, Original Bitter, Jekyll's Gold, seasonal beers; guest beers H
This 19th-century pub has retained some of its original features, notably its high ceilings and windows, and all of its character. Although there are TVs for football (including one in the smoking area), there is always a quiet corner, even when a Manchester derby is being played. The clientele is a cross-section of Withington life, from students to OAPs. In the decade the licensees have been here, the pub has improved immeasurably, winning several awards. (42,142)

Woodford

Davenport Arms (Thief's Neck)

550 Chester Road, SK7 1PS (on A5102, jct Church Lane)
11-3.30, 5.15-11; 11-11 Sat; 12-3, 7-10.30 Sun
(0161) 439 2435 frederic-robinson.com
Robinson's Hatters, Unicorn, Old Tom, seasonal beers H
Unspoilt red-brick farmhouse-style pub where the licence has been in the same family for 75 years. The cosy rooms are warmed by real fires, and children are welcome at lunchtimes in the right-hand snug. Excellent food is mostly home made, with some adventurous specials. Outside, the spacious forecourt and attractive garden, set well away from the road, are popular in the summer months when impressive floral displays are on show. Q(157)P

Worsley

Barton Arms

2 Stablefold, M28 2ED (at side of Bridgewater canal on Barton Rd)
12-11
(0161) 728 6157
Black Sheep Best Bitter; Caledonian Deuchars IPA; Taylor Landlord H
Large, plush and comfortable pub with a number of distinct dining and drinking areas and a strong emphasis on food. Beer festivals, with regularly changing guest beers, are held occasionally. Guest beers also feature at Christmas, when customers are encouraged to vote for their favourites. The pub is in an area of immense historic value, with the Bridgewater Canal nearby – the Duke of Bridgewater's boathouse is just across the 'cut'. No children permitted under 14. (33,68)P

Worthington

Crown Hotel

Platt Lane, WN1 2XF
12-11 (10.30 Sun)
(08000) 686678 thecrownatworthington.co.uk
Beer range varies H
Local CAMRA Pub of the Year 2006, this country inn offers seven cask beers, mainly from micro-breweries. It is also a rare outlet for Mayflower beers. High quality home-cooked food is served in the bar and conservatory-restaurant, while a large decked sun terrace at the rear has patio heaters. The larger of the two function rooms hosts beer festivals in March and October. There are also regular themed evenings and 10 en-suite rooms for staying over. P

White Crow

Chorley Road, WN1 2XL (on A5106 between Standish and Coppull)
12-3, 5.30-11; 12-11 Fri & Sat; 12-10.30 Sun
(01257) 474344
Beer range varies H
Large roadside country pub on the Lancashire border with up to four guest ales on offer. It serves an extensive menu and has earned a deserved reputation for its good food. There is a large dining area and children's room, while a pool table and TV are tucked away at one end. Close to Worthington lakes, the pub benefits from a large car park and children's play area. There is also a disabled WC. QP

The soul of beer

Brewers call barley malt the soul of beer. While a great deal of attention has been rightly paid to hops in recent years, the role of malt in brewing must not be ignored. Malt contains starch that is converted to a special form of sugar known as maltose during the brewing process. It is maltose that is attacked by yeast during fermentation and turned into alcohol and carbon dioxide. Other grains can be used in brewing, notably wheat. But barley malt is the preferred grain as it gives a delightful biscuity / cracker / Ovaltine note to beer. Unlike wheat, barley has a husk that works as a natural filter during the first stage of brewing, known as the mash. Cereals such as rice and corn / maize are widely used by global producers of mass-market lagers, but craft brewers avoid them.

Barnston

Fox & Hounds ✓

107 Barnston Road, Wirral, CH61 1BW

✪ 11-11; 12-10.30 Sun

☎ (0151) 648 7685 🌐 the-fox-hounds.co.uk

Brimstage Trappers Hat, Rhode Island Red; Theakston Best Bitter, Old Peculier; Webster's Yorkshire Bitter; guest beers Ⓗ

Built in 1911 to replace an earlier ale house, the pub is situated in a picturesque village. Outside is a courtyard with an abundance of flower tubs and baskets. The original cosy snug and bar have a real fire and lots of bric-a-brac while the lounge, converted from tea rooms, is quiet with no music or games machines. A popular lunchtime venue, snacks, platters and daily specials are available plus home-made comfort food.

♛Q☎❀◑⊟♿≠⊟♣P⁻

Bebington

Rose & Crown

57 The Village, Wirral, CH63 7PL

✪ 2-11 (midnight Fri) 12-midnight Sat; 12-11 Sun

☎ (0151) 643 1312

Thwaites Original, Lancaster Bomber, seasonal beers Ⓗ

Former coaching inn built in 1732, adjacent to Mayer Park and now a thriving suburban pub with a bar and games room. Satellite TV sport is prominent. Nearby is Port Sunlight Village, founded by William Hesketh Lever in 1888 to house his soap factory workers. In the village is the Lady Lever Art Gallery, home to one of the most beautiful collections of art in the country. ⊟≠(Port Sunlight)⊟(410,487)♣P

Birkenhead

Brass Balance ✓

39-47 Argyle Street, CH41 6AB

✪ 9-midnight (1am Fri & Sat)

☎ (0151) 650 8950

Cains Bitter; Greene King IPA, Abbot; Marston's Burton Bitter, Pedigree; guest beers Ⓗ

Busy town centre Wetherspoon's with a large modern bar and outside courtyard drinking area. A strong supporter of local breweries, beers from Brimstage, Northern and Spitting Feathers regularly feature. Two draught Weston's ciders are on handpump. A popular meeting place for shoppers, office workers and local residents, good value food is served all day.

❀◑♿⊖(Conway Pk/Hamilton Sq)⊟●⁻

INDEPENDENT BREWERIES

Brimstage Brimstage
Cains Liverpool
Cambrinus Knowsley
George Wright Rainford Junction
Higson's Liverpool
Southport Southport
Wapping Liverpool

Crank

Red Cat

Red Cat Lane, WA11 8RU (B5201 off A570)
❂ 12-11 (10.30 Sun)
☎ (01744) 882422
Flowers IPA; guest beers ⊞
Situated in the hamlet of Crank, between Rainford and Billinge, the Red Cat is part of a row of traditional stone cottages, extended to the rear. A central bar serves the lounge and dining room, with additional rooms off the bar area. Note the many cat-related curios. A welcome refuge for cyclists and walkers after enduring the ascent of Crank Hill, there is seating on an outside patio. Two rotating guest beers complement the Flowers. The pub has a well-deserved reputation for good food.
Q❀◑⊟⊟(152,356)P

Crosby

Crows Nest ✔

63 Victoria Road, L23 7XY
❂ 12-11 (midnight Fri & Sat)
☎ (0151) 924 6953
Cains Bitter; Greenalls Bitter; Theakston Best Bitter; guest beers ⊞
Comfortable community local with a tiny snug and cosy lounge around a central serving area. The building retains the original Higsons etched windows. Friendly staff serve a changing range of guest beers alongside the regulars. There are outside tables and a small beer garden for fine weather. Two large screens show local football fixtures.
Q❀⊟≉⊟P⅟

Stamps Bar

4 Crown Buildings, L23 5SR
❂ 12-11 (midnight Fri & Sat)
☎ (0151) 286 2662 🌐 stampsbar.co.uk
Beer range varies ⊞
Located in the centre of Crosby village, this bar is situated in an old Post Office, hence the name. Crosby's premier real ale outlet, six beers are served, frequently from George Wright and Southport Breweries. The excellent food and quality beer, along with an occasional cask cider, attract a varied clientele of all ages. Monday is curry night. Live music of all kinds is well supported. There is free internet access and newspapers are provided.
◑♿≉⊟

Eccleston

Griffin Inn

Church Lane, St. Helens, WA10 5AD (from A570 Windle take B5201 to Prescot)
❂ 12-11 (10.30 Sun)
☎ (01744) 27907 🌐 griffininn.co.uk
Cains Bitter; Marston's Pedigree; guest beer ⊞
The Griffin has a distinctive sandstone frontage dating from 1812. Contemporary decor and hardwood and leather furnishings create a relaxing environment. The large car park to the rear has a children's play area and the garden has bench seating and a decked patio. Good food is served in the bar and popular restaurant. The guest beer changes frequently to complement the Cains and Pedigree regulars. Closing time is midnight when Saints play at the nearby rugby ground. Quiz night is Wednesday. Q❀⇄◑⊟⊟P⅟

Hoylake

Plasterers Arms

35 Back Seaview, CH47 2DJ
❂ 12-midnight
☎ (0151) 632 3023 🌐 theplasterersarms.com
Brimstage Trappers Hat; Black Sheep Best Bitter; Caledonian Deuchars IPA; Weetwood Cheshire Cat; Wells Bombardier ⊞
Cosy, friendly pub in an old fishing community, sadly long gone, 100 metres from the beach. Set back off Market Street, it is a short walk from buses and the local rail station. Lunchtime meals are served in the snug and lounge including a good Sunday roast. Local legend 'Fred the fisherman', aged 95, still frequents the pub. Popular with walkers and bird watchers, there is a children's playground opposite. Music plays on Sunday, Wednesday and the last Friday of the month. ❀◑⊟≉⊟(38,83)♣P⅟

Kings Moss

Colliers Arms

Pimbo Road, WA11 8RD (off B5201 from A570, follow Houghwood Golf Club signs)
❂ 12-11 (10.30 Sun)
☎ (01744) 892894
Beer ranges varies ⊞
Situated in the rural hamlet of Kings Moss at the foot of Billinge Hill, part of a row of traditional miners' cottages next to the former site of the Hillside Colliery. A central bar serves four distinct areas, with mining memorabilia and a selection of books for a relaxing visit. Rotating guest beers complement the regular Greenalls Bitter. Popular for food, families are welcome and there is a small enclosed children's play area to the rear.
⩕Q❀◑⊟⊟(356,152)P

Liverpool: Anfield

Strawberry

Breckfield Road South, L6 5DR (off ASDA car park)
❂ 12-11 (1am Fri & Sat); 12-10.30 Sun
☎ (0151) 261 9364
Oakwell Barnsley Bitter, Old Tom Mild ⊞
This Oakwell pub continues to serve both Oakwell beers. Lying between Breck Road and West Derby Road, the pub is a welcome oasis for thirsty fans visiting Liverpool Football Club (it may open early on match days with an early kick off). The interior is divided to create a separate games area with a pool table and dartboard. Food is served until 6pm.
❀◑♿⊟(14)♣P⅟

Liverpool: Childwall

Childwall Abbey

Score Lane, L16 5EY (off Childwall Valley Road)
❂ 11.30-11 (midnight Fri & Sat); 12-11 Sun
☎ (0151) 722 5293
Jennings Cumberland Ale; Marston's Pedigree; guest beers ⊞
This turreted Grade I listed building is more than 300 years old. A bar area caters for

drinkers and three further rooms are mainly used for dining while food is being served (last food orders 8.30pm, 6.45pm Sun). Guest beers are supplied from the Marston's range. There is a panoramic view from the lounge. Seven en-suite rooms are available for overnight stays. Q

Liverpool: City Centre

Augustus John

Peach Street, L3 5TX (off Brownlow Hill)
11-11 (midnight Fri); closed Sun
(0151) 794 5507
Greene King Abbot; Tetley Bitter; guest beers
Sixties-style open-plan pub run by the university, popular with an eclectic mix of students, lecturers and locals. The artist Augustus John was a lecturer at the university in 1901 and the pub was opened by his son. Guest beers are from local micros including Hanby and York. Ask for the real cider which is kept in a cooler. A beer festival is held once a year. Sky Sports is screened.
(Lime St) (Central) (78,79)

Baltic Fleet

33 Wapping, L1 8DQ
12-11; 11-midnight Sat
(0151) 709 3116 wappingbeers.co.uk
Wapping Bitter, Summer, seasonal beers
Located near the Albert Dock, Liverpool's only brew pub is Grade II listed —based upon the 'flat iron' principle with a nautically-themed interior. As well as the ales listed, other beers from the on-site Wapping brewery are frequently available. Brunch is served until 4pm at the weekend alongside lunches and evening meals made with locally-sourced ingredients (check in advance for serving times). A recent refurbishment has brought the upstairs rooms back into public use.
Q (James St) (500)

Belvedere Arms

8 Sugnall Street, L7 7EB (off Falkner Street)
12-11 (midnight Fri & Sat)
(0151) 709 0303
Higson's Bitter; guest beers
A few years ago permission was granted to convert this 1830s listed building into a house, but fortunately it has re-opened. Many of the original fixtures and fittings feature in the two small rooms including some interesting glasswork. Although it is close to the city centre it is very much a community pub and usually features a Copper Dragon beer as well as a choice of guests. Pizzas are served all day.
Q

Cambridge

Mulberry St, L7 7EE (on university campus)
11.30-11 (midnight Fri); 4-midnight Sat; 12-11 Sun
(0151) 708 7150
Marston's Pedigree; guest beers
Two-roomed pub on the university campus, popular with students. Now a Marston's tenancy, previously a Burtonwood pub, it has been run by the same couple for over 20 years. There is usually one guest beer and good value food is served at lunchtime. Quiz night is Sunday. Saturday opening hours may change in term time.
(Lime St) (Central) (86)

Cornmarket

Old Ropery, Fenwick Street, L2 7NT
11.30 (7.30 Sat)-11; closed Sun
(0151) 236 2131
Beer range varies
Once the watering hole of merchants from the nearby Corn Exchange, hence the name. This Victorian pub is in the business district, situated behind a block of shops on Fenwick Street. It has a large lounge and a smaller lower area, serving two real ales chosen from the Enterprise Inns range. There is a heated area in the courtyard for smokers. Closed Saturday lunchtime and Sunday.
(James St)

Cracke

13 Rice Street, L1 9BB (near Philharmonic Hall)
12-11 (midnight Fri & Sat); 12-10.30 Sun
(0151) 709 4171
Phoenix Wobbly Bob; Thwaites Original; guest beers
Typical of pubs that came into existence following the passing of the Beer Act in 1830, this was originally a one-room hostelry consisting of what is now the public bar. Originally called the Ruthin Castle, it rapidly acquired the nickname of the Cracke because of its small size. Since then it has extended into two houses next door but still remains relatively compact. Food is served until 6pm daily except Monday.
(Lime St) (Central)

Crown Hotel ☆

43 Lime Street, L1 1JQ
8-11 (midnight Fri & Sat); 10-midnight Sun
(0151) 707 6027
Cains Bitter; Tetley Bitter; guest beers
This Grade II listed building is just a few seconds' walk from Lime Street Station. It boasts an Art Nouveau-style interior, with an ornate glass dome above the curved staircase. The two downstairs rooms retain many original features and have recently been redecorated. The upstairs function room is also available for family dining. A small range of well-kept beers is available, and reasonably priced food is served from early morning until mid evening. (Lime St) (Central)

Dispensary

87 Renshaw Street, L1 2SP
12-11 (midnight Fri & Sat)
(0151) 709 2180
Cains Mild, IPA, Bitter, FA, seasonal beers; guest beers
In the shadow of St Luke's Church (known locally as the 'bombed out church'), the Grapes (as it was previously known —the old name can still be seen over the bar) was bought, converted and renamed the Dispensary by Cains. It won the CAMRA/ English Heritage refurbishment award, and has recently celebrated its 10th anniversary in 2008. A popular place for a drink before or after dining at one of the many restaurants nearby. (Lime St) (Central)

Doctor Duncan's

St John's House, St John's Lane, L1 1HF (opp St George's Gardens)
10am-11 (midnight Fri & Sat); 10-10.30 Sun
☎ (0151) 709 5100
Cains Mild, IPA, Bitter, FA, seasonal beers Ⓗ
A handsome pub, lovingly refurbished in authentic Victorian style. The name commemorates Doctor Duncan, a relentless campaigner against poor living conditions in Victorian Liverpool, and the first Chief Medical Officer of Health in the UK. As Cains' flagship pub it was the first to win Cask Marque accreditation in Liverpool, and offers the full range of Cains beers.
≹(Lime St)⊖(Central)

Everyman Bistro

5-9 Hope Street, L1 9BH (beneath Everyman Theatre)
12 (11 Sat)-midnight (2am Fri & Sat); closed Sun
☎ (0151) 708 9545 everyman.co.uk
Beer range varies Ⓗ
The Everyman Bistro is as much a Liverpool institution as the theatre above it. Much thought is given to the award-winning home-produced food and equally the ale range which concentrates on Yorkshire and north west beers, with regulars from York, Derwent, George Wright and Brimstage. The bar can be busy early evening before a performance, attracting an eclectic mix of students, professors, media types and locals.
Q≹(Lime St)⊖(Central)

Fly in the Loaf

13 Hardman Street, L1 9AS
11-11 (midnight Fri & Sat)
☎ (0151) 708 0817
Okells Bitter, seasonal beers; guest beers Ⓗ
The second Manx Cat inn to be opened on the mainland by the IoM brewer Okells. The previous Kirkland's bakery – slogan 'no flies in the loaf' – was tastefully refurbished with ecclesiastical fittings and opened in 2004. The service is good and so is the beer range — there are usually up to seven guest beers from micro-breweries alongside the Okells beers and a good selection of foreign bottled beers. Very popular and busy on weekend evenings and when Sky Sports screens football and rugby matches. There is a function room with handpumps upstairs.
≹(Lime St)⊖(Central)

Globe

17 Cases Street, L1 1HW (opp Liverpool Central Station)
11 (10 Sat)-11; 12-10.30 Sun
☎ (0151) 707 0067
Black Sheep Best Bitter; Cains Bitter; Caledonian Deuchars IPA; guest beers Ⓗ
Small two-roomed traditional local in the city centre, handy for the shops and stations. A lively, convivial pub, it is popular with regulars as well as visitors to the area. An unusual sloping floor takes you through to the small quiet back room where there is a brass plaque commemorating the inaugural meeting of the Merseyside branch of CAMRA in 1974.
≹(Lime St)⊖(Central)

Lion Tavern ☆

67 Moorfields, L2 2BP
11-11; 12-10.30 Sun
☎ (0151) 236 1734 liontavern.co.uk
Caledonian Deuchars IPA; Lees Bitter; Young's Bitter; guest beers Ⓗ
The Grade II listed Lion is named after the locomotive that worked the Liverpool to Manchester railway. In 1915 the original small building was amalgamated with the adjoining licensed premises, creating the existing corridor layout. The interior features exquisite tile work, etched and stained glass, carefully restored wooden panelling and an ornate glass dome in one of the two comfortable lounges. The pub attracts a mixed clientele throughout the day including office staff and journalists. Bar food is available, with speciality cheeses and hand-made pork pies particularly recommended.
≹(Lime St)⊖(Moorfields)

Peter Kavanagh's ★

2-6 Egerton Street, L8 7LY (off Catharine Street)
12-midnight (1am Fri & Sat)
☎ (0151) 709 3443
Cains Bitter; Greene King Abbot; guest beers Ⓗ
This back-street pub is on the edge of the city centre, in an area once occupied by rich merchants. The staff are happy to tell visitors about the pub's history and the politically incorrect Peter Kavanagh. Featuring in CAMRA's National Inventory, the original part of the building has stained-glass windows and wall paintings by Eric Robinson, commissioned to cover a debt. A number of small breweries from the region supply this delightful pub directly. Q

Philharmonic ★

36 Hope Street, L1 9BX
11-midnight (1am Fri & Sat)
☎ (0151) 707 2837
Beer range varies Ⓗ
Featuring in CAMRA's National Inventory, this Grade II listed pub was described by no less an authority than historic pub expert Geoff Brandwood as the finest pub of its kind. Adjacent to the Philharmonic Hall, the interior is divided into several discrete and highly ornate drinking areas, notably the splendidly refurbished Grand Lounge. Food is served until 10pm. While ladies are invited to visit the amazingly ornate gentlemen's toilet, it is polite to check before doing so.
Q≹(Lime St)⊖(Central)(86)

Pilgrim

34 Pilgrim Street, L1 9HB
11-11
☎ (0151) 709 2302
Beer range varies Ⓗ
Popular student pub set on two floors although usually only the basement is open. Very much a basic pub, it has a jukebox and TVs screening sport. Food is served until 4pm Monday to Saturday and 5pm on Sunday. There is usually a Phoenix beer available alongside a range of ales mostly from the north of England.
≹(Lime Street)⊖(Central)

Richard John Blackler ✔

1-2 Charlotte Row, L1 1HU

8am-midnight (1am Fri & Sat)

(0151) 709 4802

Beer range varies H

Expansive generic Wetherspoon's conversion from the former Blackler's department store famous for its rocking horse. Handily placed for shops and public transport, it can get very busy at times. The guest beers are often from local micros including George Wright. Real cider is kept in a cooler and a range of foreign bottled beers is stocked. Beer festivals are a regular feature. Local football games are shown on a big screen and families are welcome until 6pm.

≈(Lime St)⊖(Central)

Roscoe Head

24 Roscoe Street, L1 2SX

11.30-11 (midnight Fri & Sat); 12-11 Sun

(0151) 709 4365

Jennings Bitter; Marston's Burton Bitter; Tetley Mild, Bitter; guest beers H

Welcoming back-street local where conversation is king. One of only 10 pubs in the country to appear in every edition of the Guide, this traditional hostelry has been run by the same family for more than 20 years. The interior retains the original small rooms and snugs, with a sensitive re-decoration. Two guest beers usually come from micros. Quiz night is Tuesday and cribbage night Wednesday. Children are welcome until 6pm.

Q≈(Central)⊖(Lime St)(86)♣

Ship & Mitre

133 Dale Street, L2 2JH (by Birkenhead tunnel entrance)

11-11 (midnight Thu-Sat)

(0151) 236 0859 shipandmitre.com

Beer range varies H

An Art Deco building circa 1935, the Ship & Mitre has 13 handpumps for real ales and 13 fonts for Belgian, German and other continental beers as well as a large selection of foreign bottled beers, all served by a young, enthusiastic staff. Tasters of draught ales are happily provided even during the four beer festivals held here each year. Good quality food is served lunchtimes and evenings.

Q≈(Lime St)⊖(Moorfields)P

Swan Inn

86 Wood Street, L1 4DQ

12-11 (2am Thu-Sat); 12-10.30 Sun

(0151) 709 5281 myspace.com/swaninn

Hydes Original; Phoenix Wobbly Bob; guest beers H

With its blue-tiled facade and stained-glass windows, the outside of this building looks quite unimposing. Inside you will find a pub that has changed little over the years, retaining its unique atmosphere. Although known locally as a bikers and rockers pub, everyone is made welcome. Set on three levels, only the ground floor has six guest ales as well as the regular beers and bottled Belgian beers. A fairly basic pub with wooden floors, it is renowned for its famous rock jukebox, while the second floor has TV screens showing rock videos and sports.

≈(Lime St)⊖(Central)

Thomas Rigby's ✔

23-25 Dale Street,, L2 2EZ

11.30-11

(0151) 236 3269

Okells Bitter, seasonal beers; guest beers H

The Grade II listed building bearing the name of wine and spirit dealer Thomas Rigby once comprised offices and a pub called the George. Today, you will find an extensive world beer range and up to four changing guest ales. Food is highly recommended, served daily until 7pm, with one room offering a friendly and efficient table service. The pub is a Publican magazine national award winner and has won numerous other accolades for its beer and food.

≈(Lime St)⊖(Moorfields)

Welkin ✔

7 Whitechapel, L1 6DS

9am-midnight (1am Fri & Sat)

(0151) 2431080

Beer range varies H

Wetherspoon's Welkin is situated in the city centre, close to the popular Cavern Walks. Very much a café/bar rather than a traditional pub, it has two rooms: one large and L-shaped on the ground floor, and a smaller room with a dining area upstairs. An ever-changing choice of beers is on offer including seasonal options and ales from local breweries. Beer festivals are a regular feature. Good value food is available daily.

≈(Lime St)⊖(Central)

White Star ✔

2-4 Rainford Gardens, L2 6PT

11.30-11; 12-10.30 Sun

(0151) 231 6861 thewhitestar.co.uk

Draught Bass; Bowland White Star IPA, seasonal beers H

A rare traditional Victorian public house located among the trendier establishments of Mathew Street, the White Star is full of fascinating local memorabilia and pictures of White Star liners. A sporting theme is highlighted by an abundance of boxing photography and the regular broadcasting of football matches on screens in two rooms. The pub is linked with bars in the Czech Republic and Norway. Additional beers from the Bowland range are available.

≈(Lime St)⊖(Central/ Moorfields)

Liverpool: Kirkdale

Thomas Frost ✔

177-187 Walton Road, Kirkdale, L4 4AJ (opp Aldi and Iceland on A59)

12-11.30

(0151) 207 8210

Beer range varies H

This Wetherspoon's pub occupies the site of a former drapery store owned by Thomas Robert Frost, hence the name. The layout is open plan, broken only by a few supporting pillars with framed photographs showing scenes from local historic events. The pub is convenient for both Goodison Park and Anfield football grounds.

ENGLAND

Liverpool: Lydiate

Scotch Piper ★

Southport Road, L31 4HD (on A5147)
12-midnight (1am Fri & Sat)
(0151) 526 0503
Banks's Bitter; guest beers Ⓗ
Centuries-old thatched inn set back from the road overlooking farmland. This quiet pub is very cosy with a small bar area ideal for reading the papers and a roaring fire in winter. Two cask beers are always available. There is a disabled outdoor toilet but the pub itself is not wheelchair accessible. Q(300)P

Liverpool: Melling

Bootle Arms

Rock Lane, L31 1EN SD388002
11.30 (12 Sun)-11
(0151) 526 2886
Banks's Bitter; Marston's Pedigree; guest beers Ⓗ
Much extended village pub with a large garden and children's play area. Though only minutes from Liverpool and the motorway, the location is surprisingly tranquil. There is an emphasis on food here, served until 10pm daily. Although accessible by public transport, buses do not run in the evening or on Sunday. Q(133,236)P

Liverpool: Mossley Hill

Storrsdale

43-47 Storrsdale Road, L18 7JY
3-11; 2-11.30 Fri; 12-11.30 Sat; 12-11 Sun
(0151) 724 3464
Black Sheep Best Bitter; Caledonian Deuchars IPA; Taylor Landlord; Tetley Bitter Ⓗ
An oasis in the south Liverpool suburban real ale desert. This stylish two-roomed local has a comfortable, quiet wood-panelled lounge and a stone-floored bar with dartboard and jukebox. Leaded windows and attractive exterior tiling reflect the 1930s construction. A mix of locals, students and thirsty sports people from the nearby playing fields are drawn here by the friendly, relaxed atmosphere and recently expanded cask beer range. Sky Sports football is screened and live music plays at weekends. There is a covered and heated area outside for drinkers and smokers. Q(86)

Liverpool: Smithdown

Willowbank

329 Smithdown Road, L15 3JA
12-11 (11.30 Wed & Thu; midnight Fri & Sat)
(0151) 733 5782
Greene King IPA, Abbot; Taylor Landlord; Tetley Bitter; guest beers Ⓗ
Previously a Walker's Heritage Inn, this Victorian pub has retained many of its original features with the public bar largely unchanged. Up to six guest beers come from regional and small breweries, and seasonal beer festivals are held. Sky Sports is screened. Food is served until 7pm weekdays and 6pm weekends, and children are welcome until 6pm. Quiz night is Wednesday. Liverpool CAMRA Community Pub of the Year 2007. (86)P

Liverpool: Stoneycroft

Navigator

694 Queens Drive, L13 5UH
9-11.30
(0151) 220 2713
Beer range varies Ⓗ
Occupying a former showroom, this Wetherspoon's has an open-plan layout with alcoves along one side. A welcome oasis on the edge of a busy shopping area, it has a separate area set aside for families. Children are welcome until 9pm when dining. The company's national beer festivals are well supported here.

Liverpool: Toxteth

Brewery Tap

Stanhope St, L8 5XJ (by Cains Brewery)
11am-midnight; 12-10.30 Sun
(0151) 709 2129
Cains Mild, IPA, Bitter, FA, seasonal beers Ⓗ
Cains' brewery tap, set within the walls of the brewery, usually offers the full range of beers on handpump. Formerly the Grapes – the name remains in the terracotta facade – it hosts the brewery tours. An interesting collection of breweriana, especially beer labels from former Merseyside breweries, is on display. The building was returned to full Victorian splendour in 1993 and awarded Best Refurbished Pub by English Heritage/CAMRA. Food is served until 8pm. (82)P

Liverpool: Walton

Raven

72-74 Walton Vale, L9 2BU (on A59)
9-midnight (1am Fri & Sat)
(0151) 524 1255
Greene King IPA, Abbot; Marston's Pedigree; guest beers Ⓗ
This suburban Wetherspoon's on the site of a former Kwik Save supermarket was initially themed around Edgar Allen Poe. More recently it has changed the focus to Aintree which is just down the road –it is the closest pub to the racecourse serving real ale. A local pub that pays more attention to real ale than many Wetherspoon's, it gets ludicrously crowded on race days. Q(Orrell Pk)

Liverpool: Waterloo

Stamps Too

99 South Road, L22 0LR (opp Waterloo Station Merseyrail)
12-midnight (1am Fri & Sat); 12-11.30 Sun
(0151) 280 0035
Beer range varies; Ⓗ
This bar is now well established on the real ale scene in Waterloo, selling excellent well kept cask ale from six handpumps. Food is served lunchtimes and evenings with café style seating at the front of the pub and a bar at the rear. There is a carvery on Sunday and Thursday is curry night. Live bands play from Thursday to Sunday and a monthly comedy

night is hosted. Internet access is available. (53)

Touchwoods
32-36 Church Road, L22 5NB
0151; 928 5656
(4.30-11.30) 4-11 Sun
Beer range varies;
Tucked away in a quiet road off South Road, this bar occupies the building that once housed the local newspaper offices. Seating is bistro-style around small tables in a single long room. An evening menu includes tapas and steaks. Board games are available on request at the bar. Watch out for the surreal coal fire in winter. (53)

Volunteer Canteen ★
45 East Street, L22 8QR
12-11 (10.30 Sun)
(0151) 928 4676
Black Sheep Best Bitter; Tetley Bitter; guest beers
Situated in the older part of Waterloo, this community local has a central bar servery for the public bar and comfortable lounge. The public bar is home to the pub golf society and darts team and has a small TV for sports events. Table service is available in the lounge which has a warm, convivial atmosphere, friendly banter and daily newspapers. Look for the old Higson's Brewery etched windows and Higson's detailing on the outside of the building. Q(53)

Liverpool: Wavertree

Edinburgh
4 Sandown Lane, L15 8HY
12-midnight
(0151) 733 3533
Cains Mild, IPA, Bitter, FA, seasonal beers
There was a time when the Wavertree High Street, with a pub on most corners owned by a different brewery, was a good area to visit. Now this Cains tied house is the only one still serving real ale. The pub dates back to around 1860, with a bar and small snug. The landlord is keen to encourage conversation, so restricts TV and music. There is Irish music on Monday evening, a quiz on Tuesday and sometimes a cappella singing on Wednesday.
(78,79)

Liverpool: Woolton

Gardeners Arms
101 Vale Road, L25 7RW
4 (2 Fri)-11; 12-11 Sun
(0151) 428 1443
John Smith's Bitter; Black Sheep Best Bitter; Cains Bitter; Caledonian Deuchars IPA
Friendly one-room community village pub a short walk from the centre of Woolton, hidden from the main road behind high-rise flats. A locals' pub with a relaxed atmosphere, visitors are made welcome. Inside, separate drinking areas surround the central bar. The pub supports local sports and is home to golf, football and ladies' netball teams. Note the Titanic History of Events display on the back wall and the large collection of spirits. Sky TV screens major sporting events. A popular quiz is held on Tuesday evening. Q

New Brighton

Queen's Royal
Marine Promenade, CH45 2JT
10.30-11 (10.30 Sun)
(0151) 691 0101 thequeensroyal.com
Brimstage Trappers Hat, Rhode Island Red; guest beers
A welcome debut in the Guide for this large restaurant and bar in a traditional Victorian building. Airy, modern, and wood floored, the bar has a pubby feel – it is the only public bar that exclusively sells local Brimstage Brewery ales, a third Brimstage beer often appearing as a guest. The drinking area outside affords superb views over Liverpool Bay. Good value bar meals are available until 7pm, the restaurant is open until 9pm.

Telegraph Inn
25-27 Mount Pleasant Road, CH45 5EW
11.30-11.30 (11 Sun)
(0151) 639 1508
Brimstage Rhode Island Red; Wells Bombardier; Wychwood Hobgoblin; guest beers
A first time in the Guide for what is believed to be New Brighton's oldest pub. A friendly, traditional, multi-roomed local, it has a conservatory extension where good value home-cooked food is served daily. A popular outlet for local Brimstage ales, the guest beers often come from local micro-breweries and an annual beer festival is hosted. A regular live folk music venue. (410)

New Ferry

Freddies Club
36 Stanley Road, CH62 5AS
5 (12 Sat & Sun)-11
(0151) 645 3023
Beer range varies
Small, cosy club in the back streets of New Ferry, a welcome oasis in an area considered to be a beer desert. Entry is available to CAMRA members carrying either a membership card or a current copy of the Guide. A comfortable lounge bar serves two guest beers, usually from the local Brimstage or Wapping breweries. Friday features Freddies' ever-popular fun quiz. The snooker room has two full-sized tables. QP

Raby

Wheatsheaf Inn
Raby Mere Road, CH63 4JH (from M53 jct 4 take B5151)
11.30-11; 12-10.30 Sun
(0151) 336 3416
Black Sheep Best Bitter; Brimstage Trappers Hat; Greene King Old Speckled Hen; Tetley Bitter; Thwaites Original; Wells Bombardier
Ancient thatched pub of great character rebuilt after a fire in 1611. Wirral's oldest pub, the original building dates from the 13th century and it has been an inn for more than 350 years. It is reputed to be haunted by 'Charlotte' who died here. A main bar with

eight handpumps serves two rooms and the dining room in a converted cowshed. The walls are decorated with old photographs of Raby. Q🚸❀◐⊟♿🚌P⁵⁻

Rainford Junction

Junction

News Lane, WA11 7JU (from A570 follow station signs)

⏲ 12-midnight (1am Fri & Sat)

☎ (01744) 882876 🌐 thejunctionrainford.co.uk

Weetwood Old Dog Bitter; guest beers Ⓗ

Situated next to Rainford Junction Station with fine views of the rural area, this popular community local is a meeting place for a variety of clubs and social gatherings. Live music plays on Wednesday evening, blue grass on Sunday and folk on Thursday. Quiz night is Monday. A separate bar area has a dartboard and pool table. Rotating beers from Weetwood complement the guest beers. Wi-fi Internet access is available and there is a function room upstairs. ❀◐◑⊟⇌🚌♣P

St Helens

Beechams Bar ✔

Water Street, WA10 1PZ (jct of Westfield St and Water St)

⏲ 11.30-11; closed Sun

☎ (01744) 623420

Beer range varies Ⓗ

Part of St Helens college campus, this town-centre pub is a conversion from the original Beechams factory offices, with a landmark clock tower. Soft leather furnishings and attractive hardwood chairs and tables create a contemporary and relaxing environment, away from the single bar area with sport TV. There is a 10% discount on production of a CAMRA or NUS card. Six handpulls dispense a range of value-for-money rotating guest beers and Weston's cider served in oversize glasses. ◐♿⇌(Central)🚌●⊟

Royal Tavern

21-23 Westfield Street, WA10 1QF

⏲ 11.30-midnight 1.30am Fri & Sat; 12-10.30 Sun

☎ (01744) 756868

Beer range varies Ⓗ

Traditional pub in the town centre, a welcome refuge from the surrounding trendy bars of the Westfield locality. The L-shaped open-plan interior retains some of the original etched windows and has a bar and comfortable lounge areas. There is also a large bar and games room leading to the outside patio with a covered smoking area. A rotating guest beer from the Enterprise Inns range is always of interest. Good value lunchtime food is popular, especially Sunday lunch. There is a disco on Friday and Saturday and occasional live music. ❀◐⊟⇌🚌♣⁵⁻

Turks Head ✔

49-51 Morley Street, WA10 2DQ

⏲ 2 (12 Sat)-11; 12-11 Sun

☎ (01744) 751289

Beer range varies Ⓗ

Distinctive turreted half-timbered free house, a short distance from the town centre. Six handpumps dispense a range of beers that is constantly changing due to high demand. Up to five real ciders and perry are also stocked, plus draught and bottled foreign beers. This popular community local has a bar with large-screen TV, pool and darts at mezzanine level. The lounge displays a large collection of miniatures. Quiz night is Tuesday, curry is Thursday. CAMRA Regional Pub of the Year 2007. 🔥❀◐⊟🚌(32)●⁵⁻⊟

Southport

Ainsdale Conservative Club

630 Liverpool Road, Ainsdale, PR8 3BH (on main A565 road at Ainsdale roundabout)

⏲ 7 (12 Sat)-midnight; 12-11 Sun

☎ (01704) 578091

Beer range varies Ⓗ

Thanks to the dedicated bar manager, this suburban local community club offers at least one interesting guest beer from anywhere in the UK. Settle into one of the comfortable seats in the large L-shaped room or enjoy a chat with the locals at the bar. Two TV screens show sports and other major events, and live entertainment is occasionally staged. Show a copy of the current Guide or your CAMRA membership card for entry. Q❀⇌(Ainsdale)🚌(44,48,X2)♣

Baron's Bar (Scarisbrick Hotel) ✔

239 Lord Street, PR8 1NZ (main A565 road, opp Eastbank Street)

⏲ 11-11.30 (11.30 Fri & Sat); 12-11 Sun

☎ (01704) 543000 🌐 baronsbar.com

Flag & Turret; Moorhouses Pride of Pendle; Tetley Bitter; guest beers Ⓗ

This award-winning bar in the Scarisbrick Hotel provides an extensive choice of ales often from micro-breweries, plus its own house bitter, Flag & Turret. Real cider is usually stocked, a rarity for the town. Two significant beer festivals are held, one that begins on 1st May and the SIBA Northern Beer Festival in mid-January. The local community is well-served with two league quiz teams, monthly quizzes and live music. Good value barm cakes are available at lunchtime. ❀🛏♿⇌🚌●⁵⁻

Cheshire Lines

81 King Street, PR8 1LQ

⏲ 11.30-midnight (1am Thu-Sat); 12-midnight Sun

☎ (01704) 532178

Tetley Dark Mild, Bitter Ⓗ

A small half-timbered Tudor-style hostelry with attractive hanging baskets and original windows. Inside, the L-shaped bar serves a small front room and a snug opposite. A large room at the rear is used for dining, serving excellent good-value local food. Many railway locomotive prints decorate the walls. The stone hearth comes from the original Cheshire Lines railway terminus on nearby Lord Street (a grand building in front of Morrisons). 🔥Q❀◐⇌🚌♣⁵⁻

Guest House ✔

16 Union Street, PR9 0QE

⏲ 11-11 (11.30 Fri & Sat); 10.30-10.30 Sun

☎ (01704) 537660

Cains Bitter; Caledonian Deuchars IPA; Courage Directors; Theakston Best Bitter; guest beers ⊞
Superb Edwardian town centre pub festooned with flower baskets in summer, with a delightful flower-bedecked courtyard to the rear. The pub has three traditionally-styled rooms furnished with wood panelling, rustic paintings and brass ornaments. The interior retains original features including a tiled entrance lobby, glass-fronted bar and elegant fireplaces. Guest beers represent local, regional and national micro-breweries.
Q❀⊟⇌⊟⊱

London

14 Windsor Road, PR9 0SR (off A5267)
❂ 12-midnight (1am Fri & Sat); 12-11 Sun
☎ (01704) 542885
Oakwell Old Tom Mild, Barnsley Bitter ⊞
Large Victorian establishment near railway sidings on the corner of Kensington Road in an area known as Little London. The pub has a large lounge with a separate family and meeting room. There is also a little used public bar down a couple of steps behind the main bar. The locals welcome visitors and darts and pool are played – many trophies on display show the success of the pub teams in local leagues. The reasonably-priced Oakwell beers here are unique to the town. An excellent bowling green can be enjoyed while sipping your pint on a summer evening.
❀⇌⊟(43,44)♣P⊱

Mason's Arms

44 Anchor Street, PR9 0UT
❂ 11-1am
☎ (01704) 534123
Robinson's Unicorn, seasonal beers ⊞
The Mason's is a small back-street local behind the post office and next to a new development of flats. It is the only outlet for Robinson's ales in the area. A traditional snug is shoehorned into a corner of the building, ideal for couples. The main bar is where the lively regulars congregate to put the world's problems to rights. The sunny roof garden is a fine place to enjoy some peace in this town centre location. Access is by request from the bar staff. ⛫❀⇌⊟(Lord St)♣

Richmond

Scarisbrick New Road, Kew, PR8 5HL (on main A570 Ormskirk road)
❂ 12-11 (midnight Fri & Sat)
☎ (01704) 884544
Holts Mild, Bitter, seasonal beers ⊞
Recently built pub that sprung from the ashes of the original nondescript local, near the Kew Retail Park. The Richmond is attractively decorated with pine woodwork and exposed brick giving an airy and spacious feel to the interior. There are separate dining areas split by steps and handrails and a tile-floored drinking section. Now operated by the Manchester brewer Holts, and its only outlet in the Southport urban area, this hostelry is a good addition to the local ale scene.
❀◑♿⊟(42,44,375,385)P

Sir Henry Segrave ✓

93-97 Lord Street, PR8 1RH (on main A565 road)
❂ 9-midnight
☎ (01704) 530217
Greene King Abbot; Marston's Pedigree; guest beers ⊞
Town centre Wetherspoon's pub situated on Southport's famous Lord Street in an 1880s building, formerly a furniture emporium. The pub is named after a local hero who broke the world land speed record of 152mph on nearby Birkdale Sands in 1926. Segrave was also the first British driver of a British car to win the French Grand Prix in 1923. A pub that caters for all tastes, it usually features beers from local breweries such as Cains and George Wright. Real cider is occasionally available.
Q❀◑♿⇌⊟⊱

Willow Grove ✓

387 Lord Street, PR9 0AG
❂ 9-midnight (1am Fri; 2am Sat)
☎ (01704) 517830
Greene King Abbot; Marston's Burton Bitter; guest beers ⊞
Opposite the War Memorial monument, this L-shaped modern bar is a typical Lloyds No 1 with flat-screen TVs and brightly-lit fridges displaying bottles from far and wide. A 'living flame' fire is surrounded by comfortable couches and there is a dance area which is vibrant until the small hours. Upstairs another bar has a quieter feel with curved seating areas, however real ale is not available in this bar. ◑♿⇌⊟⊱

Windmill

12-14 Seabank Road, PR9 0EL (off Lord St)
❂ 11.30-11 (midnight Thu-Sat); 12-10.30 Sun
☎ (01704) 547319
Moorhouses Black Cat; Theakston Best Bitter; guest beers ⊞
A community pub situated between Lord Street and the Promenade, the Windmill boasts a league-winning ladies' darts team and a sociable men's darts team. Activities include a Wednesday quiz, live Irish music on Thursday, plus live middle-of-the-road music on Friday. Excellent value quality food is served lunchtimes and evenings except Wednesday. The only regular outlet for Black Cat Mild, the landlord claims to be the town's longest serving publican.
❀◑♿⇌⊟(Lord St)♣⊱

Wallasey Village

Cheshire Cheese

CH44 2DH
❂ 11.30-11 (midnight Fri & Sat); 12-11 Sun
☎ (0151) 638 3641
Theakston Mild, Best Bitter; guest beers ⊞
A warm welcome awaits at this friendly community local which has gone from strength to strength since it was taken over by the current landlord. The multi-roomed pub has a separate bar and snug, with a courtyard beer garden outside. The handpumps are in the lounge. Excellent home-cooked food is served until early evening (not Thu). Regular beer festivals are held. Wirral CAMRA Pub of the Year 2007. Q❀◑⊟⇌⊟♣⊱

100 Belgian Beers to Try Before You Die!

Tim Webb & Joris Pattyn

100 Belgian Beers to Try Before You Die! showcases 100 of the best Belgian beers as chosen by internationally-known beer writers Tim Webb and Joris Pattyn. Organised by brewery, each entry includes a history of the brewery, tasting notes for the beer, visitor information and the authors' verdict. Lavishly illustrated throughout with photography of the beers, the breweries, Belgian beer bars and some of the characters involved in Belgian brewing, the book encourages both connoisseurs and newcomers to Belgian beer to sample them for themselves, both in Belgium and at home.

£12.99 ISBN 978 1 85249 248 9

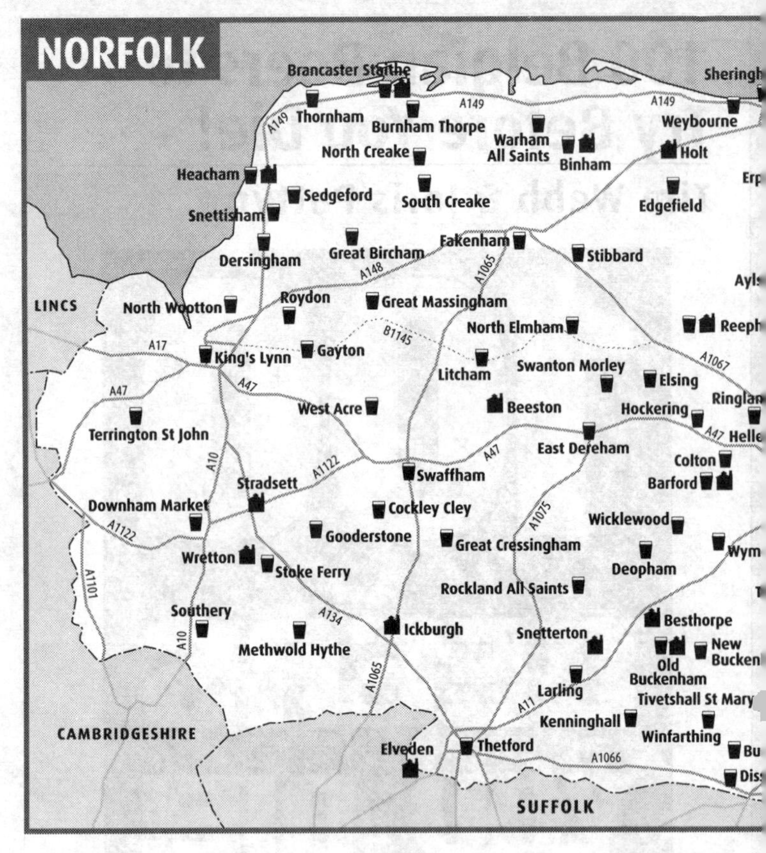

Aylsham

Feathers

54 Cawston Road, NR11 6EB
⏲ 12-11; 12-3, 7-10.30 Sun
☎ (01263) 732314
Wells Bombardier; guest beers Ⓗ
A popular and lively traditional pub, just out of the centre of town, with a low-ceilinged, comfortable front bar and a separate smaller room. Both bars are full of interesting breweriana and other intriguing items. The two guest ales are generally from regional brewers and local beers such as Humpty Dumpty Porter and Oulton Nautilus often feature in the frequently-changing range. ♨❀🚌(44)♣P⌐

Barford

Cock Inn

Watton Road, NR9 4AS (on B1108) TG111074
⏲ 12-3, 6 (7 Sun)-11
☎ (01603) 759266
Blue Moon Easy Life, Sea of Tranquillity, Dark Side, seasonal beers Ⓗ
Home to the Blue Moon Brewery tap, the pub has two rooms, one larger with a real fire in winter and a smaller one in front of the bar. The Cock is famed for its food, served in the bar or multi-roomed restaurant. The menu features fish and game in season (booking essential at weekends). There is an interesting selection of East Anglian brewerania on display. Table skittles is played and there is a bowling green in the garden. ♨Q❀◐◑♣P

Binham

Chequers Inn

Front Street, NR21 0AL (3km S of Stiffkey)
⏲ 11.30-2.30, 6-11 (11.30 Fri); 11.30-11.30 Sat; 12-11 (12-2.30, 7-11 winter) Sun
☎ (01328) 830297
Front Street Binham Cheer, Callums Ale, Unity; guest beers Ⓗ
This pub is a tremendously popular place with both locals and visitors. It has roaring fires in winter and features its own micro-brewery which produces a range of 17 quality real ales. Superb, regularly-changing meals made from local produce are prepared by the talented chef. Up to three guest beers are always available, as well as an extensive range of foreign bottled beers. September brings a three-day beer festival with live entertainment. ♨Q❀◐◑♿🚌P⌐

Brancaster Staithe

Jolly Sailors

Main Road, PE31 8BJ
⏲ 11-11; 12-10.30 Sun
☎ (01485) 210314 🌐 jollysailors.co.uk
Brancaster IPA, Old Les; guest beers Ⓗ

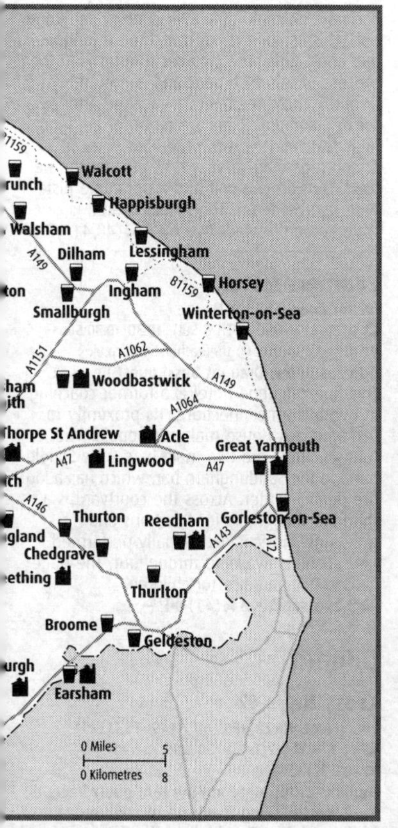

Dating from 1796, the Sailors has a very cosy interior, with three drinking areas and two restaurants. Run by real-ale enthusiasts, a five-barrel brewery set up here in 2003 and provides the regular ales. The pub hosts quizzes and other social activities. A good base for exploring this part of the north Norfolk coast, it is also just a short walk to the White Horse (see below). The smoking area is covered and heated. ⛼Q❀◐◑⊟P⸗

White Horse

Main Road, PE31 8BY

☼ 11-11; 12-10.30 Sun

☎ (01485) 210262 ⊕ whitehorsebrancaster.co.uk

Adnams Bitter; Fuller's London Pride; Woodforde's Wherry Best Bitter 🄷

This large, modern pub sits on the edge of the salt marshes on the beautiful north Norfolk coast. It bridges the gap between local and tourist pub, catering well for both types of pubgoer. Three beers are always available and the seafood is of course very, very fresh. The village is a wonderful place to explore and is home to many seafood stalls.
⛼Q❀⛿◐◑♿⊟♣P⸗

Broome

Artichoke

162 Yarmouth Road, NR35 2NZ (just off A143)

☼ 12-11 (midnight Fri & Sat); closed Mon

☎ (01986) 893325

Adnams Bitter; Elgood's Black Dog; guest beers 🄷/🄶

Mentioned in White's 1845 Directory of Norfolk with a victualler by the name of Wm. Crowfoot, this was the original home of the long-defunct Crowfoot Brewery. The copper from the brewery is now in the nearby Bungay Museum. Flagstone and wood floors, wooden settles, scrubbed tables and a real fire give a rural ambience to the bar area of this welcoming, friendly pub. Home-cooked food is available in a dining area and conservatory. Up to eight beers feature regularly, with an emphasis on local breweries. Some are served by gravity from a tap room.
⛼Q❀◐◑Ă⊟(580,588)P⸗

Burnham Thorpe

Lord Nelson

Walsingham Road, PE31 8HN (off B1355)

☼ 11-11 summer; 12-3, 6-11, closed Mon, winter; 11-11 (12-3, 6.30-10.30 winter) Sun

☎ (01328) 738241 ⊕ nelsonslocal.co.uk

Greene King Abbot; Woodforde's Wherry Best Bitter 🄶

Situated in the village of Nelson's birth and used by the Norfolk hero to throw a farewell party in 1793, this pub was the first to be named in his honour. The dispense is all gravity from a traditional tap room; the beer served in a bar that contains the original settles. Live bands perform on Thursday to bring it right up-to-date. There will soon be a Nelson memorabilia shop and Nelson historical walks. Evening meals are not served on Sunday and guest beers are available during school holidays. The smoking area is heated and covered. ⛼Q❀◐◑♣P⸗

Burston

Crown Inn

Crown Green, IP22 5TW (2 miles W of A140) TM138834

☼ 12-11.30 (10.30 Sun)

☎ (01379) 741257 ⊕ burstoncrown.com

Adnams Bitter; Greene King Abbot; guest beers 🄷/🄶

This attractive 16th-century Grade II-listed pub is a cosy haven, featuring exposed beams, deep sofas and a blazing fire in the inglenook fireplace. Three real ales are served directly from the cask. There are two bars, one with a pool table, and boules is played in the garden in summer. The two beers on gravity come from East Anglian breweries including Earl Soham and Oak. A small restaurant serves locally-sourced freshly-cooked food (no food Sun eve). ⛼❀◐◑P⸗

Chedgrave

White Horse ✔

5 Norwich Road, NR14 6ND

☼ 12-3, 6-11.30 (midnight Fri & Sat); 12-2.30, 6-11

☎ (01508) 520250

Black Sheep Best Bitter; Caledonian Deuchars IPA; Taylor Landlord; guest beers 🄷

A village pub that has separate drinking and restaurant facilities. Drinkers are well catered for with a range of four real ales sourced from all round the UK. Timothy Taylor's Landlord often features as a regular. There is a large, pleasant garden for use in summer. Although technically in Chedgrave, the pub is actually within easy walking distance of the holiday moorings in neighbouring Loddon. Beer festivals are held here in April and November. ⛰Q❀◑◐♿▲🚌(X74)♣P

Cockley Cley

Twenty Churchwardens

Swaffham Road, PE37 8AN
🕐 11-3, 7-11; 12-10.30 Sun
☎ (01760) 721439
Adnams Bitter Ⓗ
This unusually named pub in a converted village schoolhouse performs many other functions in this pretty village. The food is straightforward, reasonably priced and excellent (no food Sun eve). The atmosphere is slightly eccentric but very friendly and the pub can be very busy at weekends. Nearby is the Iceni Village tourist attraction. A covered shelter is available for smokers.
⛰Q❀◑◐♿♣P⚟

Colton

Ugly Bug Inn

High Horse Farm Lane, NR9 5DG (2 miles S of A47) TG104908
🕐 12-2.30, 5-10.30; 12-2, 5-11 Fri & Sat; 12-3, 7-10 Sun
☎ (01603) 880794 🌐 uglybuginn.co.uk
Beeston Worth the Wait; guest beer Ⓗ
Opened in 1991 in a converted barn, this large pub is situated in tranquil rural countryside just a few miles to the west of Norwich. It has a huge garden and eight en-suite bedrooms. Inside there is a large rambling single bar with numerous dining areas in which to enjoy the extensive menu of locally sourced food at very competitive prices. Real ales are supplied from local micro-brewery Beeston; the house beer is brewed by Wolf. Jazz bands play in the dining rooms on selected days. ❀🛏◑◐P

Deopham

Victoria

Church Road, NR18 9DX (1½ miles off B1108) TG050008
🕐 12 (5 Mon)-11; closed Tue; 12-4, 7-midnight Sun
☎ (01953) 850783
Beer range varies Ⓗ
Situated in the centre of the village, this old pub has three distinct areas around the bar – a pool-table space, seating area with tables and chairs, and a snug with comfortable seating around the fire. There is also a restaurant. The guest beers usually come from East Anglian micro-breweries, with a Spectrum beer often available. There is no food on Monday or Sunday evenings. ⛰❀🛏◑◐♿P⚟

Dersingham

Coach & Horses

77 Manor Road, PE31 6LN
🕐 12-midnight
☎ (01485) 540391
Woodforde's Wherry Best Bitter; guest beers Ⓗ
A classic example of a 19th-century carrstone pub, this establishment has come a long way in a short time. The two-bar interior is in the process of refurbishment and is now much brighter. The three beers are looked after by a former landlord. Plans are afoot for an annual beer festival. It is recommended you call ahead regarding serving times for lunchtime food. Outside you will find a petanque piste with its own team. The smoking area is covered and heated. ⛰❀🛏◑◐🚌(40,41A)P⚟

Feathers Hotel

Manor Road, PE31 6LN
🕐 10.30-11 (midnight Fri & Sat); 10.30-10.30 Sun
☎ (01485) 540207 🌐 thefeathershotel.co.uk
Adnams Bitter; Draught Bass; guest beers Ⓗ
This fine carrstone hotel is a former coaching inn with royal connections. Its proximity to Sandringham House makes it popular with tourists. There are two main bars – the Saddle bar and the Sandringham bar, which has a log fire during winter. Across the courtyard is a third bar that caters for functions and meetings. Music is occasionally performed here. Food is available throughout. The huge garden is a paradise for children.
⛰Q🚸❀🛏◑◐♿▲🚌(41)♣P⚟

Dilham

Cross Keys ✔

The Street, NR28 9PS (off A149) TG332251
🕐 12-3, 6-11; 12-3, 7-10.30 Sun
☎ (01692) 536398
Adnams Bitter; Greene King IPA; guest beers Ⓗ
Well worth taking the time to seek out, this traditional Broadland village local is attractively placed alongside a bowling green

INDEPENDENT BREWERIES

Beeston Beeston
Blackfriars Great Yarmouth
Blue Moon Barford
Brancaster Brancaster Staithe
Buffy's Tivetshall St Mary
Bull Box Stradsett
Chalk Hill Norwich
Elmtree Snetterton
Elveden Elveden
Fat Cat Norwich
Fox Heacham
Front Street Binham
Grain Alburgh
Humpty Dumpty Reedham
Iceni Ickburgh
Norfolk Cottage Norwich
Norfolk Square Great Yarmouth (NEW)
Reepham Reepham
Spectrum Tharston
Tindall Seething
Tipples Acle
Uncle Stuarts Lingwood
Wagtail Old Buckenham
Waveney Earsham
Why Not Thorpe St Andrew
Winter's Norwich
Wissey Valley Wretton
Wolf Besthorpe
Woodforde's Woodbastwick
Yetman's Holt

and just a short walk from quiet moorings. The pub is close to the north Norfolk coast and known locally for quality ales. It is popular for its home-cooked meals which in summer may be enjoyed alfresco on the south-facing terrace. A variety of pub games is available in the public bar. Q P

Diss

Cock Inn

63 Lower Denmark Street, IP22 4BE (off A1066) TM112795
12-11 (10.30 Sun)
(01379) 643633
Adnams Bitter; Fuller's London Pride; Taylor Landlord; guest beers H
This Grade II-listed pub dates from 1520 and faces a large green on the outskirts of the market town. One bar serves four distinct drinking areas furnished with a range of sofas plus wooden tables and chairs. On cold nights a large log fire welcomes customers. A large-screen TV provides entertainment in one room. During live music sessions the pub stays open later. The pub provides an excellent spot for watching the sun go down over Fair Green. Meals are served weekday lunchtimes and Thursday to Saturday evenings. P

Downham Market

Crown Hotel

12 Bridge Street, PE38 9DH
9.30-11; 11-11 Sun
(01366) 382322
Adnams Bitter; Greene King IPA, Abbot; guest beers H
A refurbished 17th-century coaching inn at the heart of the old town, the Crown is popular with locals and visitors alike. The single bar has a beamed ceiling, large fireplace and four handpumps. One guest ale is always available, usually from a local brewer. A new restaurant has been added recently and a separate function room caters for parties and weddings. The smoking area is located under the coaching arch. P

Earsham

Queens Head

Station Road, NR35 2TS
12-3, 5-11; 12-11 Sat; 12-10.30 Sun
(01986) 892623
Waveney East Coast Mild, Lightweight; guest beers H
The pub dates back to the 17th century and an original brick in the fireplace has the date and initials. Over the fireplace is a beam with carved upside down Ws – allegedly to ward off witches. Home to the Waveney Brewing Co, an annual beer festival takes place. The ceiling is low and decorated with pump clips of guest beers that have appeared on the bar. There is a flagstone floor and lovely old fireplace and settles. Successful darts, pool and football clubs are based here. The smoking area is unheated. (580) P

East Dereham

George Hotel

Swaffham Road, NR19 2AZ (near war memorial)
10-11 (midnight Fri & Sat)
(01362) 696801
Adnams Bitter, Broadside; Beeston Worth the Wait, On the Huh; Woodforde's Wherry Best Bitter; guest beers H
This welcoming bar is part of a market-town hotel open to non-residents. The landlord is a strong promoter of local beers. An excellent range of traditional bar meals is available as well as an a la carte menu in the restaurant. The comfortable bar features wood panelling and pictures of local historical interest. There is a fine conservatory and a heated outdoor patio for drinkers. The George is handy for the Mid-Norfolk Railway and has a secure car park. (Mid-Norfolk Railway) P

Kings Head Hotel

42 Norwich Street, NR19 1AD (near Cowper Rd car park)
10-11; 12-10.30 Sun
(01362) 693842
Greene King IPA, Abbot; Shepherd Neame Spitfire; guest beer H
Close to the town centre, this hotel has a cosy carpeted bar open to non-residents plus a small function room. The three regular beers are supplemented by a guest. There is also an adjoining dining area. An extensive garden is excellent for relaxed summer drinking. The hotel supports many activities including quizzes, themed nights and Dereham Arts Festival activities in May. (Mid-Norfolk Railway) (X1) P

Edgefield

Pigs

Norwich Road, NR24 2RL (on B1149) TG098343
11-3, 6-11; closed Mon; 12-4 Sun
(01263) 587634 thepigs.org.uk
Adnams Bitter, Broadside; Woodforde's Wherry Best Bitter; guest beers H
Dating from 1826, this is a super pub, attractively refurbished in 2007 and featuring an award-winning restaurant. Food served in the bar and restaurant is sourced locally and prepared at the pub. You can even barter local produce for pints. There is a quiz night on Wednesday plus a series of events throughout the year – see the Pig Issue newssheet for details. Ask what an 'iffit' is when you visit. P

Elsing

Mermaid Inn

Church Street, NR20 3EA TG053165
12-3, 7 (6 Fri & Sat; 6.30 Sun)-midnight
(01362) 637640
Adnams Broadside; Wolf Golden Jackal; Woodforde's Wherry Best Bitter; guest beers G
This 17th-century pub is located opposite a large 14th-century parish church in a small village in the charming upper Wensum Valley. The interior has a large bar with a log fire at one end and a pool table at the other. There is also a dining area. Cask ales sold here are

mainly from local breweries and are gravity dispensed. ⌂❀◑♿♣P⊱

Erpingham

Spread Eagle

Eagle Lane, NR11 7QA
11-11 summer; 11-3, 6.30-11 winter; 12-4 (3 winter), 7-11 Sun
☎ (01263) 761591
Adnams Bitter; Greene King IPA; Woodforde's Wherry Best Bitter, IPA; guest beers Ⓗ
This village pub dates back to 1620 and was previously home to Woodforde's Brewery which has now moved to Woodbastwick. The long, open-plan interior features a timber-beamed ceiling and wood-panelled decor, a central bar and a stove at one end, surrounded by comfortable sofas and seating. At the other end is a dining area. An extension is being built to house a restaurant and B&B accommodation. There are unsurfaced car parks at the front and rear of the building. ⌂❀◑Ʌ⊱

Fakenham

Bull

Bridge Street, NR21 9AG
10 (12 Sun)-midnight
☎ (01328) 853410 🌐 thefakenhambull.co.uk
Woodforde's Wherry Best Bitter; guest beers Ⓗ
A comfortable town-centre pub with inviting leather settees as well as chairs and tables. Four real ales are always available, some from as far away as the Isle of Man, as well as Old Rosie draught cider. Two hundred different beers were served over the course of last year. Newspapers are provided. There is an excellent lunchtime menu and meals can be home delivered in the surrounding area, plus a steak night on Wednesday. All food is sourced locally. Definitely worth a visit. ⌂❀⇔◑⊟●⊱

Star

44A Oak Street, NR21 9DY (near Tesco)
12-2.30, 5.30-11.30 (12.30am Thu-Sat); 12-4, 7-11.30 Sun
☎ (01328) 862895
Beer range varies Ⓗ
Set back slightly from the main street, this pub is a welcoming town-centre local that boasts original wooden beams and fine panelling. A rotating choice of two beers is always available. No food is served but a good chip shop is a few doors away. There is a large child-friendly garden with play equipment at the rear of the pub. Q❀⊟♣P

Gayton

Crown ✔

Lynn Road, PE32 1PA
12-11 (midnight Fri & Sat)
☎ (01553) 636252
Greene King XX Mild, IPA, Old Speckled Hen, Abbot; guest beers Ⓗ
A true gem, voted local CAMRA Pub of the Year 2004. This is a rare outlet for XX Mild and the food is excellent in both pub and dining rooms. Live music evenings and special events are well supported by locals. The pub features many wildlife pictures by a local photographer. This is an inn for all seasons, with gardens front and back and a huge log fire in winter. Dogs are welcome. ⌂Q♨❀⇔◑⊟♿Ʌ⊟(48)♣P⊱

Geldeston

Locks Inn

Locks Lane, NR34 0HW (through village to Ellingham Mill, turn left onto track across marshes) TM390908
12-midnight summer; closed Mon & Tue, 5 (12 Fri & Sat)-11 winter; 12-midnight Sun
☎ (01508) 518414
Green Jack Canary, Orange Wheat, Grasshopper, Gone Fishing, seasonal beers; guest beers Ⓗ
Reached down a long, meandering track between dykes on the marshes, the Locks fronts the River Waveney, with expansive gardens and overnight moorings. The small main bar, with low ceiling beams and clay pamment floor, retains an authentic, welcoming feel, while modern extensions allow the pub to maintain an active live music scene. With two beer festivals a year and the celebrated Friday curry night – all freshly cooked – this is a real community pub with something for everyone. Guest beers in summer come from Oakham, Tipples and Crouch Vale. There is a smoking area in the garden. ⌂Q❀◑♣●P⊱

Gooderstone

Swan Inn

The Street, PE33 9BS
12 (4 winter)-11; 12-11 Sat; 12-10.30 Sun
☎ (01366) 328365
Greene King IPA; guest beers Ⓗ
Located in the heart of a tiny village, the Swan is always popular. The low-ceilinged interior provides a warm, welcoming environment and the beer is well kept, with an excellent small beer festival held annually. A large-screen TV shows sport in the bar but there are also quiet places to sit, except perhaps on weekly live music nights. Evening meals are not served on Wednesday. The garden includes a smoking area. ⌂Q❀◑♣P⊱

Gorleston-on-Sea

New Entertainer

80 Pier Plain, NR31 6PG
12-11
☎ (01493) 441643
Greene King IPA; guest beers Ⓗ
Surrounded by road on three sides, this pub dates back to the 1800s. It has a unique rounded end, complete with Lacons windows. A pool table sits in the rounded end, while on the other side of the pub are seating, a large-screen TV and a book-lending service. The five guest beers frequently come from the local Nethergate and Iceni breweries. There is also a good selection of bottled Belgian beers. The smoking area outside is heated. ⊟♣⊱

Great Bircham

King's Head

Lynn Road, PE31 7RJ
11-11; 12-10.30 Sun
(01485) 578265 the-kings-head-bircham.co.uk
Adnams Bitter; Fuller's London Pride; Woodforde's Wherry Best Bitter; guest beers
Situated in a picturesque and peaceful village, this refurbished hotel soaks up much trade from visitors to the scenic north Norfolk coast. The comfortable bar is of a bold, distinct, modern design that works well. The award-winning and stylish restaurant serves excellent food, both lunchtimes and evenings. There are nine bedrooms with facilities that include Playstations, home-made cookies and mini bars. The owner is quite a character and the pub won local CAMRA Pub of the Year 2007.

Great Cressingham

Windmill Inn

Water End, IP25 6NN (off A1065 S of Swaffham) TF846019
11-11
(01760) 756232 oldewindmillinn.co.uk
Adnams Broadside; Greene King IPA; guest beers
Full of character, this rambling multi-roomed country inn provides a different atmosphere in each of its drinking areas, ranging from olde worlde with open fires and real beams to a modern extension. The pub makes a worthwhile detour from the Peddars Way walk. A good selection of real ales includes the house beer, Windy Miller, while guest beers are rotated weekly. Thirty different malt whiskies are also stocked alongside bottled and keg lagers. Good home-cooked food is available.

Great Massingham

Dabbling Duck

11 Abbey Road, PE32 2HN
11-11; 12-10.30 Sun
(01485) 520827 thedabblingduck.co.uk
Adnams Broadside; Beeston Worth the Wait; Greene King IPA; Woodforde's Wherry Best Bitter; guest beers
Barely recognisable from its former incarnation as the Rose & Crown, this pub owes its continued existence to the campaigning efforts of the local villagers and West Norfolk District Council. Their reward is a cosy pub with an open fire, a drinking area and a dartboard, as well as a dining area and restaurant. The decor features pale colours and wooden floors, but look out for the Norfolk mural. The food is locally sourced. The pub's name comes from The Wind in the Willows, reflecting the close proximity of the village's two duck ponds.

Great Yarmouth

Gallon Pot

Market Place, NR30 1NB (next to market place)
10 (10.30 Mon)-11; 12-10.30 Sun
(01493) 842230
Adnams Bitter; Fuller's London Pride; Woodforde's Wherry Best Bitter
The original pub was built in 1772 by William Burroughes and sadly destroyed by enemy fire in 1943 when this area of the town was heavily bombed. It was rebuilt in 1959 by the nearby Lacons Brewery and stilll retains many Lacons features including a wall frieze. The interior is dark wood with comfortable seating. Situated very close to the market place, the pub can be busy on market days (Wed and Sat). It overlooks the largest parish church in England. (Vauxhall)

Mariners Tavern

69 Howard Street South, NR30 1LN
11 (12 Sun)-11
(01493) 332299
Greene King Abbot; guest beers
Family-run local comprising a main bar and a smaller wood-panelled lounge complete with pool table. An annual beer festival is held to coincide with the Yarmouth maritime weekend in September. Many of the seven guest ales come from local micro-breweries and there is a small selection of foreign beers.

Red Herring

24-25 Havelock Road, NR30 3HQ
12-3, 6.30-midnight; 12-midnight Sat & Sun
(01493) 853384
Blackfriars Yarmouth Bitter; guest beers
Formerly the Derby Wine Vaults, this back-street corner local is very close to the award-winning Time & Tide Museum. It has a relaxed, comfortable atmosphere, with the pool table and TV tucked away in a separate function room behind folding doors. The walls are decorated with photos of Old Yarmouth from its herring fishing days when the town was host to many Scottish boats. Evidence of the old smoke house is still visible in the area. The cider is Weston's Old Rosie.

St Johns Head

53 North Quay, NR30 1JB
12-midnight
(01493) 843443
Elgood's Cambridge Bitter; guest beers
Dating from 1787, this pub originally belonged to the Lacons Brewery. It was later rendered in cement but this was removed in 1961 to reveal traditional flintstone and oval windows at the front of the pub. A single bar houses a large TV screen and sport is very popular here. Four real ales include three regularly changing guest beers. The smoking shelter is minimalist but heated. (Vauxhall)

Happisburgh

Hill House

NR12 0PW (just off B1159) TG381311
11-11 summer; 12-3, 7-11; 12-11 Thu-Sat winter; 12-11 Sun
(01692) 650004
Beer range varies
Sixteenth-century inn situated very close to the sea in an attractive north Norfolk coastal village. This rural retreat was a favourite with author Sir Arthur Conan Doyle in the late 19th century. Hot meals are available lunchtimes

and evenings. The pub usually offers a range of up to six real ales, mostly from local brewers. It hosts a mid-summer beer festival each June that offers around 40 real ales and attracts visitors from near and far.
⩕Q≿❀⇔◐♿⊟♣P

Heacham

Fox & Hounds

22 Station Road, PE31 7EX
✪ 12-11 (10.30 Sun)
☎ (01485) 570345 🌐 foxbrewery.co.uk
Adnams Broadside; guest beers Ⓗ
Home of the Fox Brewery and CAMRA's West Norfolk Branch Pub of the Year 2008, this pub always offers six beers, four from Fox, one guest and a house beer. Bottled beer is also available including the brewery's own, plus a range of foreign beers. The restaurant at the rear offers beer recommendations to match the cuisine. Live music is staged on Tuesday evening and a quiz is held on Thursday. Three beer festivals are hosted throughout the year. Check out the posh loos. Dogs on a lead are welcome. ❀◐♿⊟(40,41)♣P⁼

Hellesdon

Whiffler

Boundary Road, NR6 5JB (on northern Norwich ring road)
✪ 9-midnight (1am Fri & Sat)
☎ (01603) 427660
Greene King IPA, Abbot; Marston's Pedigree; guest beers Ⓗ
A popular Wetherspoon's pub serving both the local community and passing trade, with five regularly changing guest beers on handpump. An extensive and inexpensive menu for all the family is available all day, up to an hour before closing. Speciality evenings are regular events – grill night Tuesday, quiz night Wednesday, curry club Thursday, steak meal offers on Saturday and roasts on Sunday. A local beer festival is held each quarter. The large enclosed beer garden includes plenty of tables. Disabled access is good. ❀◐⊟♿⊟P⁼

Hockering

Victoria

The Street, NR20 3LH (just off A47) TF863355
✪ 12-3 (not Mon-Wed), 6-11; 12-3, 7-10.30 Sun
☎ (01603) 880507
Elgood's Black Dog; guest beers Ⓗ
Located in the centre of the village, this friendly local pub offers a warm welcome. A good range of six real ales is available, along with a selection of bottled Belgian and continental beers. The interior has a single bar with a dartboard and wide-screen TV at one end and a roaring real fire at the other. The walls are adorned with old photos of the village, framed beer mats and Arsenal memorabilia. ⩕❀◐♿⊟(X1)♣●P⁼

Horsey

Nelson Head

The Street, NR29 4AD (300m N of B1159 coast road) TG460228
✪ 11-11; 12-10.30 Sun
☎ (01493) 393378 🌐 nelsonheadhorsey.co.uk
Woodforde's Wherry Best Bitter, Nelson's Revenge; guest beers Ⓗ
A friendly pub close to the coast, Horsey Nature Reserve, Broad and Mill. It has a quiet, timeless atmosphere with a log fire in winter and a large collection of marshman's implements plus local pictures and Nelson memorabilia on display. A good selection of home-cooked meals made with locally sourced produce is available in the bar and dining room. The pub is popular with artists, walkers, boaters and locals alike and the large garden area welcomes children. A sloe gin festival is held on the last Saturday in January. ⩕Q≿❀◐P⁼

Horsham St Faith

Kings Head ✔

Back Street, NR10 3JP (opp parish church)
✪ 12-3, 6-11.30 (midnight Fri & Sat); 12-4, 7-11 Sun
☎ (01603) 898911 🌐 kingsheadhorshamstfaith.co.uk
Adnams Bitter; guest beers Ⓗ
Excellent, unspoilt village pub with beams and interesting old photographs. A hostelry has existed on this site uninterrupted since 1600 and the present owners are keen to retain an authentic rural atmosphere. Reasonably priced food is cooked fresh to order and the staff are happy to adjust portions/contents to individual needs (try the home-made steak & ale pie). A meeting and function room is available, plus a buffet if required. The small beer garden includes a gazebo for smokers. A popular aviation museum is a short walk away. ❀⇔◐⊟▲⊟(44)P⁼

Ingham

Swan Inn

Swan Corner, Sea Palling Road, NR12 9AB (1 mile NE of Stalham on B1151) TG390260
✪ 12-3, 6-11 (10.30 Mon & Tue winter); 12-10.30 Sun
☎ (01692) 581099
Beer range varies Ⓗ
Charming 14th-century thatched and flint-built inn in a rural setting close to the church, with the north Norfolk coast and the Broads nearby. The pub has an interesting split-level interior with a wealth of warm brick, flint and beams. The beers rotate around the full Woodforde's range. An excellent choice of freshly prepared meals made with local produce may be enjoyed in the restaurant area or, in summer, the secluded courtyard. High quality en-suite rooms in a separate block are available all year round with short break rates to include dinner, bed and breakfast. ⩕Q❀⇔◐P

Kenninghall

Red Lion

East Church Street, NR16 2EP (opp church)
✪ 12-3, 5.30-11; 12-11 Fri & Sat; 12-10.30 Sun
☎ (01953) 887849
Greene King IPA, Old Speckled Hen, Abbot; Woodforde's Wherry Best Bitter; guest beers Ⓗ/Ⓖ
The beautifully-restored interior comprises a bar with log fire, a pine-panelled snug and a

restaurant decorated in the style of a stable. Abbot is available from a cask behind the bar and there are generally two guest beers. Good quality, home-cooked food with interesting vegetarian options is served every day in the restaurant, and bar snacks are also available (except Fri and Sat evenings). ᗑ❀⇔ᑕᑐ♿P⁵–

King's Lynn

Stuart House Hotel

35 Goodwins Road, PE30 5QX
✪ 6-11; 7-10.30 Sun
☎ (01553) 772169 ⊕ stuart-house-hotel.co.uk
Beer range varies Ⓗ
Find the hotel along a gravel drive from Goodwins Road, not far from King's Lynn FC and the Walks park. The pleasant hotel bar has a roaring fire in winter, and there is a beer garden for the summer months. Three ales, often local, are available. There is regular live music on Friday evening and an annual beer festival each July. The bar is open evenings only (except by arrangement). ❀⇔ᑐ♣P

Larling

Angel Inn

NR16 2QU (off A11 between Thetford and Norwich, signed by B1111 East Harling) TL983890
✪ 10-midnight; 11-11 Sun
☎ (01953) 717963 ⊕ larlingangel.moonfruit.com
Adnams Bitter; guest beers Ⓗ
A treasure just off the A11. The Angel features a superb range of ales from micro-breweries across the country, always including a mild. An excellent range of home-cooked food is available (booking advisable) and both the lounge and bar have open fires. The bar is frequented by friendly locals and passers by. A summer beer festival features more than 70 ales and the pub also hosts a whisky week, serving a good selection of malts.
ᗑQ❀⇔ᑕᑐ⊟♿⛺⇌(Harling Rd)P⁵–□

Lessingham

Star Inn

School Road, NR12 0DN (300m off B1159 coast road) TG388283
✪ 12-3, 7-midnight
☎ (01692) 580510 ⊕ thestarlessingham.co.uk
Buffy's Bitter; Greene King IPA; guest beers Ⓗ
An excellent village pub with an easy-going feel. The wood burner in the inglenook fireplace at one end of the bar is especially welcoming on cold winter days. In summer the large beer garden is a great place to relax. Home-cooked food is available (lunches Wed-Sun only). A huge display of beer mats attached to the bar timbering is testament to the many guest beers offered in the past. The guest beer is often from Nethergate and the cider is Weston's Old Rosie. Dogs are welcome in the bar. ᗑQ❀⇔ᑕᑐ⛺⊟(34,36)♣●P

Litcham

Bull Hotel

Church Street, PE32 2NS
✪ 12 (6 winter)-midnight; 12-10.30 Sun
☎ (01328) 701340

Beeston Worth the Wait, On the Huh Ⓗ
Situated in the centre of a picturesque village, this 17th-century inn abounds with low wood ceiling beams and wooden floorboards. The cask ales sold here are from the local Beeston micro-brewery. There is a separate dining room and a small patio drinking area at the rear. The pub offers accommodation in nine rooms, all en-suite and some converted for disabled use. ᗑ❀⇔ᑕᑐ⊟♣P

Methwold Hythe

Green Man

White Plot Road, IP26 4QP
✪ 12-2.30, 6.30-midnight; 12-midnight Sun
☎ (01366) 728537
Beer range varies Ⓗ
This superb pub with a friendly welcome is slightly off the beaten track between Methwold and Feltwell, but well worth seeking out. Up to three real ales from independent breweries, local and national, mean there is always something lovely and interesting to sample. An excellent and reasonably priced food menu is also available.
ᗑ❀ᑕᑐP⁵–

New Buckenham

King's Head

Market Place, NR16 2AN (opp village green)
✪ 12-3, 7-11 (10.30 Sun)
☎ (01953) 860487
Adnams Bitter; guest beer Ⓗ
This friendly, two-room free house facing the green in a medieval village served as a coaching inn between London and Norwich in the early part of the 16th century. A wood burner in the large inglenook fireplace warms the back room. Traditional home-cooked food is available and Sunday lunch is especially popular with pubgoers. Quiz night is every second Thursday. Nearby is a 12th-century Norman church and the remains of a Norman castle. The guest beer comes mainly from a local brewery. ᗑQᑕᑐ⁵–

North Creake

Jolly Farmers

1 Burnham Road, NR21 9JW
✪ 11-2.30, 7-11; closed Mon and Tue; 12-3, 7-10.30 Sun
☎ (01328) 738185 ⊕ jollyfarmers-northcreake.co.uk
Woodforde's Nelson's Revenge, Wherry Best Bitter; guest beers Ⓖ
Above the buzz of contented conversation in this cosy pub you may just notice the strains of classical music. The small rooms with beams and tiled floors are enhanced on a cold day by a roaring log fire. The beer is on gravity and the menu features both interesting main meals and a range of lighter snacks and sandwiches, with much of the produce coming straight from local suppliers. ᗑ❀ᑕᑐP⁵–

North Elmham

Railway Hotel

Station Road, NR20 5HH
✪ 11-11

☎ (01362) 668300
Beer range varies Ⓗ/Ⓖ
Situated in central Norfolk near the ancient Anglo-Saxon North Elmham Cathedral, this is both a rural gem and a fine community pub. Most of the beers here come from local micro-breweries, with a few from further afield. Home-cooked meals using mainly locally sourced ingredients are available at lunchtime and in the evening. The pub hosts an annual beer festival during the third week of August.
⌂❀◑ΛP

North Walsham

Bluebell

Bacton Road, NR28 0RA (on B1150 Bacton Rd)
⏲ 11 (12 Sun)-11
☎ (01692) 404800
Adnams Bitter, Broadside; Greene King IPA, Abbot; Woodforde's Wherry Best Bitter Ⓗ
A pleasant suburban pub situated on the north-west side of this bustling north Norfolk market town. The interior has a comfortable bar/lounge with a separate dining area. An attractive large garden at the back of the pub includes a spacious covered beer terrace with seats and tables. A regular quiz takes place on Sunday afternoon to raise money for local charities. ❀◑▶P

North Wootton

House on the Green

Ling Common Road, PE30 3RE
⏲ 11.30 (4 Mon)-11; 11.30-11.30 Fri & Sat; 12-11.30 Sun
☎ (01553) 631323
Adnams Broadside; Greene King IPA; Shepherd Neame Spitfire Ⓗ
Friendly pub on the outskirts of the village with a large car park and close to a bus stop. A good range of beers is always on offer. Food is served in the restaurant and bars and there is a separate lounge bar with a dining room. The public bar has music and a TV. Occasional live music and charity fund-raising events are held. The large garden includes play apparatus for children and excellent seating for outdoor meals in summer. Food is not served on Monday or Sunday evening.
⌂❀◑▶⊟♿▭♣P⁻

Norwich

Alexandra Tavern

16 Stafford Street, NR2 3BB (off Dereham Road or Earlham Road)
⏲ 10.30-11 (midnight Thu-Sat); 12-11 Sun
☎ (01603) 627772
Chalk Hill Tap, Best; Grain Brewery Tamarind; Oakham JHB; Taylor Landlord; guest beers Ⓗ
A long-standing, not-to-be-missed Norwich institution. The landlord 'Tiny' Little has connections with the city's Chalk Hill Brewery and the pub features its ales. Up to six guest beers are also regularly available. The inn is old, unspoilt and comfortable, with a log burner in both the lounge and public bar. High-quality food, prepared from fresh local produce, is served 12.30-7pm every day and the specials menu is a must. There is a strong community atmosphere and children are welcome up to 8pm. 'Tiny' rowed the Atlantic to raise money for the Davenport Trust Charity.
⌂Q❀◑▶⊟♿▭⁻

Champion

101 Chapelfield Road, NR2 1SE (top of St Stephen's St)
⏲ 10.30-11 (midnight Sat); 12-10.30 Sun
☎ (01603) 765611
Bateman XB, XXB; Woodforde's Wherry Best Bitter, Nelson's Revenge; guest beers Ⓗ
Small, popular L-shaped Bateman's pub situated close to the city centre, serving six real ales. The Champion hosts occasional music evenings, and quiz nights are held most Tuesdays. Photographs of local boxing heroes adorn the walls of the larger of the two drinking areas, reminding us of a time when this was a Lacons house in the 1960s and early 1970s. There is a small outdoor area adjacent to the pub. Food is served lunchtimes only, when the pub becomes a favoured resting place for weary shoppers as well as regulars.
❀◑▭♣⁻

Coachmakers

9 St Stephen's Road, NR1 3SP
⏲ 11-11; 12-10.30 Sun
☎ (01603) 662080
Greene King Abbot; Wolf Golden Jackal; Woodforde's Wherry Best Bitter Ⓖ
Dating from the 17th century, this former coaching inn stands on the site of an old asylum which is said to be haunted. The spacious courtyard has been converted into a large drinking area and there is also a pleasant garden patio. Beer is served on gravity dispense from behind the bar. The addition of Sky TV and darts makes this a popular city-centre pub that is not to be missed.
⌂❀◑▶♣⁻

Duke of Wellington

91-93 Waterloo Road, NR3 1EG
⏲ 12-11.30 (10.30 Sun)
☎ (01603) 441182 🌐 dukeofwellingtonnorwich.co.uk
Elgood's Black Dog; Fuller's London Pride; Oakham JHB, Bishops Farewell; Wolf Golden Jackel, Straw Dog; guest beers Ⓗ/Ⓖ
One of the city's premier real ale establishments, offering a wide selection of 22 ales either on handpump or from a small tap room which can be seen from the bar. A friendly and welcoming community inn, it has many nooks and crannies. The pub holds popular folk nights and supports a bowls team which plays in the local park. An interesting feature is the red-brick, World War II air raid shelter, accessed via a trap door and down a winding staircase. There is a covered smoking area. ⌂❀▭(9A,16)♣P⁻

Eaton Cottage

75 Mount Pleasant, NR2 2DQ
⏲ 12-11 (midnight Fri & Sat)
☎ (01603) 453048
Fuller's London Pride; Wolf Golden Jackal; guest beers Ⓗ
A friendly, suburban local situated south west of the city centre. The interior comprises an open-plan U-shaped bar and a small lounge area. Two regular beers are served, plus up to

four guest beers often including Deuchars IPA and a house beer brewed by Winters. The pub hosts jazz and blues bands on Thursday nights and occasionally at the weekend. The building is reputed to be haunted by two ghosts: an elderly lady and a cat. ❀♿🚌(25)●

Fat Cat

49 West End Street, NR2 4NA

11-11 (midnight Fri & Sat); 12-10.30 Sun

☎ (01603) 624364

Adnams Bitter; Elgood's Black Dog; Hop Back Summer Lightning; Fat Cat Bitter, Top Cat, Honey Cat, Marmalade Cat; Woodforde's Wherry Best Bitter; guest beers H/G

An extremely popular public house with a staggering range of real ales that has twice won CAMRA's National Pub of the Year. The pub also serves a tremendous range of foreign beers and real ciders, with a newly introduced 'Round the World' collection of more than 80 bottled beers from countries ranging from Jamaica to Laos. The layout is compact and cosy, with many interesting pieces of brewery memorabilia adorning the walls. A back room can be used for meetings. ❀🚌♣●⁻

Gate House

391 Dereham Road, NR5 8QJ

12-11 (midnight Fri & Sat)

☎ (01603) 620340 🌐 internetpubguide.co.uk

Greene King IPA, Abbot; Woodforde's Wherry Best Bitter; guest beers H

Situated two miles west of Norwich city centre, this warm and welcoming traditional pub was built in the 19th century on the site of the old tollhouse at the entrance to the city. It has a large garden that backs on to the River Wensum. The pub fields three pool teams, a crib team and a ladies' darts team. No hot food is served. ❀♿♣P⁻

King's Arms

22 Hall Road, NR1 3HQ

11-11 (midnight Fri & Sat); 12-10.30 Sun

☎ (01603) 766361

Adnams Bitter; Bateman XB Bitter, XXXB; Hop Back Summer Lightning; Wolf Coyote Bitter; guest beers H

This busy pub is just a short distance from the football ground. A former CAMRA East Anglian Pub of the Year, it is a Batemans hostelry and hosts two beer festivals a year along with regular events for St George's Day, Burns Night and other occasions. Up to eight guest beers are usually available. Traditional, good-value pub food is served at lunchtime, plus Sunday roast dinner. At other times you are welcome to 'bring yer own' food: plates and condiments provided. There is a patio area to the rear. ❀(♿🚌♣⁻

King's Head

42 Magdalen Street, NR3 1JE

12-midnight (11 Sun)

☎ (01603) 620468

Winter's Kings Head Bitter; H **Woodforde's Nelson's Revenge; guest beers** H/G

Unique, friendly keg-free hostelry that sells only cask-conditioned ale from the local area plus a selection of guest beers from other micro-breweries around the region, including a house beer brewed by Winter's. A large range of bottled continental ales is also available. Real cider is from the Norfolk Cider Co. The interior is split into two distinct areas: at the rear, a large space houses a bar billiards table, one of only three in the city. The pub attracts a wide variety of locals, from office workers to CAMRA members. CAMRA branch Pub of the Year in 2006 and 2008.

Q🚌♣●⁻

Nelson

122 Nelson Street, NR2 4DR

12-midnight (11.30 Sun)

☎ (01603) 626362 🌐 thenelsonpubnorwich.co.uk

Caledonian Deuchars IPA; Hop Back Summer Lightning; Shepherd Neame Spitfire; Winter's Golden; Woodforde's Wherry Best Bitter; guest beers H

A friendly two-bar community local featuring seven real ales and music most evenings. Food is served between 12-2pm and 5.30-7.30pm weekdays, with traditional roast lunch on a Sunday. The pub has two beer festivals a year. It plays host to the local pigeon club in season and darts and football teams. At the back of the building a large car pack adjoins the garden area which is very popular and pleasant on a sunny summer afternoon. A small patio space is reserved for smokers. ❀()♣P⁻

Reindeer

10 Dereham Road, NR2 4AY

11-11 (midnight Fri & Sat); 12-10.30 Sun

☎ (01603) 666821

Elgood's Black Dog, Cambridge, Golden Newt, Greyhound Strong; guest beers H

An Elgood's pub that regularly serves up to nine real ales. It has an open plan dining space plus an outside decking area where smoking is permitted. Excellent food is served at lunchtimes and early evenings, with a carvery available Tuesday to Sunday. A beer festival is held each March. A large-screen TV shows major sports events, especially those involving a certain red-decked Manchester football team. Music is staged monthly, along with themed food nights which may require pre-booking. ❀()♿🚌P⁻

Rosary Tavern

95 Rosary Road, NR1 4BX

12-11.30 (11 Sun)

☎ (01603) 666287

Black Sheep Best Bitter; Caledonian Deuchars IPA; Wolf Straw Dog; guest beers H

Situated at the top of a hill near the railway station, this community-minded pub offers up to five guest ales, plus good food at lunchtime and early evening. It hosts football, darts and bar billiards teams and is home to the long-established Norfolk Pipe Smoking Club. There are occasional live music and quiz nights and a conservatory at the back of the building can be used for meetings. The garden is due to be renovated and used for summer theme nights in the future. The real cider is Kingfisher. ❀()⇌🚌♣●P

Trafford Arms ✔

61 Grove Road, NR1 3RL

11-11 (11.30 Fri & Sat); 12-10.30 Sun

☎ (01603) 628466

Adnams Bitter; Tetley Bitter; Woodforde's Wherry Best Bitter; guest beers 🄷
A popular community local famous for hosting a regular Valentine's beer festival which raises funds for charity. The pub serves up to 10 real ales as well as Kingfisher cider. It is divided into a dining area and a games room with pool table. The landlord is a Norwich City football supporter and the large-screen TV shows regular live sports events. Food is served lunchtimes and evenings. At the front of the pub is a small patio seating and smoking area. This hostelry has deservedly won many local awards including CAMRA branch Pub of the Year. ❀◑🚌(9,17)♣●P⅟–

Whalebone ✔

144 Magdalen Road, NR3 4BA
⏲ 11-11 (midnight Fri & Sat); 12-11 Sun
☎ (01603) 425482
Adnams Bitter; Fuller's London Pride; Hop Back Summer Lightning; Oakham JHB; Shepherd Neame Spitfire; Woodforde's Wherry Best Bitter 🄷
This community local is conveniently situated just to the south of Sewell Park. The pub serves eight beers and is divided into three areas: the original front and rear bar spaces plus a newly refurbished back area that leads to a covered and heated terraced patio which is very popular, especially during summer months when barbecues are held. The pub hosts an annual beer festival in July and supports three cricket teams as well as a golf society. Wine and beer tasting evenings are held occasionally. ❀🚌(10,18)♣P⅟–

Wig & Pen ✔

6 St Martin at Palace Plain, NR3 1RN
⏲ 11.30-11 (midnight Fri & Sat); 11.30-6 Sun
☎ (01603) 625891
Adnams Bitter; Buffy's Norwich Terrier; Fuller's London Pride; guest beers 🄷
A well-known, friendly local pub with a reputation for serving fine ales and award-winning quality food. Six beers are served in this compact hostelry where a small back room can be used for meetings or as a dining area. An annual beer festival is held early each spring. The spacious outside patio area is well frequented in the summer months and major sporting events are shown on a large-screen TV. 🜲❀◑🚌♣⅟–

Old Buckenham

Gamekeeper

The Green, NR17 1RE (on B1077) TM064915
⏲ 11.45-11; 12-10.30 Sun
☎ (01953) 860397
Adnams Bitter, Broadside 🄷
Seventeenth-century Grade II-listed free house overlooking the 40 acre village green – the biggest in the country. The interior is split into four distinct areas with some quarry tiled floors. There are two drinking spaces serving Adnams beers plus a house beer called Gamekeeper brewed by Wolf, together with a pool room and a restaurant. A large baronial-style hall on the left of the building is used as a carvery on Sunday lunchtime and as function room. The pub offers overnight accommodation in three rooms. 🜲❀🛏◑P

Poringland

Royal Oak

The Street, NR14 7JT (on B1332) TG267023
⏲ 12-3, 5-11; 12-midnight Fri & Sat; 12-11 Sun
☎ (01508) 493734
Beer range varies 🄷
Large village local that attracts real ale drinkers from miles around. The inn has a number of separate areas and features memorabilia from the former RAF radar station which was situated nearby. Beers are sourced from all over the UK, including many rarely found in this region. If you would like to sample a Scottish 80/- next to a West Country ale, this is the place to be. Cider is from Weston's. The pub makes no apology for concentrating on its ale, but for those in need of solid sustenance there is an excellent fish and chip shop next door. The smoking area is covered and heated. 🜲❀♿🚌♣●P⅟–▯

Reedham

Ferry Inn

Ferry Road, NR13 3HA TG407015
⏲ 10.30-3, 6-11; 11-10.30 Sun
☎ (01493) 700429 🌐 archerstouringpark.co.uk
Adnams Bitter, Broadside; Woodforde's Wherry Best Bitter; guest beers 🄷
Situated on the north bank of the River Yare next to the historic ferry – the last one remaining on the Broads – this superb 17th-century inn has beamed ceilings, stone floors, a collection of rural tools and a log fire in winter. Extensive free moorings provide easy access. High-quality ales and excellent freshly-prepared meals of local fish, game and seafood as specialities are always available, plus guest beers during the summer. Look out for themed evenings offering dishes from around the world. Note the interesting business card gallery. 🜲Q♉❀◑▲P

Reepham

King's Arms

Market Place, NR10 4JJ
⏲ 11.30-3, 5.30-11; 12-3, 7-10.30 Sun
☎ (01603) 870345
Adnams Bitter; Elgood's Cambridge Bitter; Greene King Abbot; Taylor Landlord; Woodforde's Wherry Best Bitter 🄷
This 17th-century former coaching inn is located in the picturesque market square of Reepham. Although open plan, the split-level layout includes several intimate drinking and dining areas. Charm and character have been retained with many original beams, brickwork and open fires. An original glass-topped well can be viewed in the conservatory. The comprehensive menu includes food sourced from nearby butchers and bakers. On summer Sundays live jazz plays in the rear forecourt. Dogs are welcome. There is no car park but plenty of space to park on the market square. 🜲Q❀◑♿🚌P⅟–

Ringland

Swan Inn ✔

The Street, NR8 6AB TG140138

⌚ 11-11 (1am Fri & Sat); 12-11 Sun
☎ (01603) 868214
Beer range varies Ⓗ
A real gem, this 400-year-old country pub is a traditional local. The Australian-themed restaurant adjoining the pub ensures that the bar food menu is a cut above the rest, while a full events programme includes theme nights, quiz nights, live music and even a raft race on the nearby River Wensum. The pub is Cask Marque registered and serves four real ales, including beers from Adnams and Woodforde's. Regular beer festivals featuring local ales are hosted. Disabled access is via the restaurant. ♨❀◑♿P⚐

Rockland All Saints

White Hart
The Street, NR17 1TR TL992965
⌚ 11-3, 6-11; closed Mon; 12-3, 6-11 Sun
☎ (01953) 483361
Adnams Bitter; Fuller's London Pride; guest beers Ⓗ
Village local with contemporary decor and furnishings features two small dining areas, a bar area and a family room with sport on TV. The home-cooked food is locally sourced and reasonably priced, with a children's menu. The garden has a play area and a covered patio for smokers. Directions are available for a rural walk that starts and ends at the pub.
♨⚇❀◑P⚐

Roydon

Union Jack
30 Station Road, PE32 1AW
⌚ 12 (4 Tue-Thu)-midnight
☎ (01485) 601347
Beer range varies Ⓗ
This is a rare village drinkers' pub that relies solely on its wet trade. It offers four guest beers, mostly around 4-5% ABV, with a mild often featuring. Ales change frequently and are chosen in consultation with the regulars. Occasional beer festivals are held. The pub supports many sports activities and a good quantity of trophies is on display. Live music is performed some weekends and dogs are welcome in the bar. ♨❀🚌(48)♣P

Sedgeford

King William
Heacham Road, PE36 5LU (on B1454)
⌚ 11 (6 Mon)-11; 12-10.30 Sun
☎ (01485) 571765 🌐 thekingwilliamsedgeford.co.uk
Greene King Abbot; Woodforde's Wherry Best Bitter; guest beers Ⓗ
This large village pub has a separate dining room and is deservedly popular for its food. Meals are served all day on Sunday and takeaway food is available on Friday evening. But if all you want is a drink you will be more than welcome, maybe after a walk on the nearby Peddars Way long distance footpath. The wood-burning stove will warm you and the absence of loud music allows conversation to flourish. ♨Q❀🛏◑P⚐

Sheringham

Lobster
13 High Street, NR26 8JP
⌚ 11.30-midnight (1am Sat)
☎ (01263) 822716 🌐 the-lobster.com
Adnams Bitter; Greene King Abbot; Taylor Best Bitter, Landlord; Woodforde's Wherry Best Bitter; guest beers Ⓗ
This multi-roomed pub with open fires is child and dog friendly. Fishing implements adorn the walls and nautical maps are pinned to the ceilings. It has an excellent restaurant serving food all day in the summer and at weekends, including a vegan and vegetarian selection. Beer festivals take place every bank holiday throughout the year. A large heated outdoor seating area is used for regular barbecues during the summer. There are up to five rotating guest beers available and an extensive wine selection.
♨Q⚇❀◑⊟♿⇌🚌(50)♣⚐

Windham Arms
15-17 Wyndham Street, NR26 8BA
⌚ 11 (12 Fri-Sun)-midnight
☎ (01263) 822609
Greene King Abbot; Woodforde's Wherry Best Bitter; guest beers Ⓗ
Situated on a narrow back street just behind the High Street, this cosy two-bar local has a basic but welcoming bar and a carpeted lounge, plus a separate dining room. Outside is a small drinking area. Around five cask ales are usually available, with guest beers coming mostly from local breweries. Home-cooked food is sourced locally and available lunchtimes and evenings. ♨Q⚇❀◑⇌🚌●

Skeyton

Goat Inn
Long Road, NR10 5DH (on unclassified road N of ex RAF Coltishall) TG250244
⌚ 12-2 (3 Sun), 6-11
☎ (01692) 538600 🌐 skeytongoatinn.co.uk
Adnams Bitter; Woodforde's Wherry Best Bitter; guest beers Ⓗ
An old isolated thatched inn outside the village centre but worth seeking out. A small traditional bar area in the centre of the pub links to a restaurant at one end and dining areas at the other. Home-cooked food is served (booking advisable for weekend dining). Up to four beers are available. The Goat is situated in more than seven acres of land, some used for camping and caravanning – the pub is registered with The Caravan Club.
❀◑▲♣P⚐

Smallburgh

Crown
North Walsham Road, NR12 9AD TG330245
⌚ 12-3 (not Mon), 5.30 (7 Sat)-11; 12-3 Sun
☎ (01692) 536314
Adnams Bitter; Greene King IPA, Abbot; guest beers Ⓗ
Thatched village pub, once a 15th-century coaching inn, retaining some original timbers that lend character and charm to the friendly atmosphere. A log fire makes the bar cosy in winter and a fine selection of five ales and

high-quality, home-cooked food using seasonal local produce is available. Meals may be enjoyed in the dining room, the bar or, in summer, the peaceful, tree-fringed garden. The pub is close to the Broads and the north Norfolk coast. A warm welcome awaits at this popular gem. ♨Q❀🛏◑🚌♣P⁄

Snettisham

Rose & Crown

Old Church Road, PE31 7LX
⏲ 11-11; 12-10.30 Sun
☎ (01485) 541382 🌐 roseandcrownsnettisham.co.uk
Adnams Bitter, Broadside; Woodforde's Wherry Best Bitter; guest beers Ⓗ
This well preserved village inn said to date back to the 14th century has modern hotel facilities at the rear and is well worth visiting. The front bars are small and unspoilt with old fireplaces, tiled floors, exposed beams and low ceilings. A larger back room is reached through a narrow passage. Home-cooked meals are prepared using local produce.
♨Q☊❀🛏◑⊟🚌(40,41)P⁄

South Creake

Ostrich Inn

Fakenham Road, NR21 9PB TF862355
⏲ 12-11 (10.30 Sun) summer; 12-3, 5-11 (10.30 Sun) winter
☎ (01328) 823320 🌐 ostrichinn.co.uk
Greene King IPA; Woodforde's Wherry Best Bitter; guest beers Ⓗ
Attractively modernised village inn dating from the 17th century, serving up to five beers. The Ostrich, which takes its name from the crest of the Earls of Leicester, offers excellent, freshly-prepared meals. In summer the garden is the perfect spot for relaxed dining, while in winter the bar is warm and cosy. A large restored barn is used for functions and the pub offers overnight accommodation. ♨☊❀🛏◑♿🚌P⁄

Southery

Old White Bell

20 Upgate Street, PE38 0NA
⏲ 11 (3 Wed)-11; 12-10.30 Sun
☎ (01366) 377057 🌐 oldwhitebell.co.uk
City of Cambridge Rutherford IPA; guest beers Ⓗ
Just off the A10 near Ely, the Bell is a real community pub with a warm welcome and an enthusiastic local football team. In the long single-room bar, football is usually shown on the TV. Good food is available in the small, quiet dining area and the Sunday roast is recommended. Do not miss the football shirt collection on display above the pool table.
❀◑🚌(37)♣P

Stibbard

Ordnance Arms

Guist Bottom, NR20 5PF (on A1067) TF987267
⏲ 12-3 (Sat only), 5.30-midnight; 12-10.30 Sun
☎ (01328) 829471 🌐 ordnancearms.co.uk
Adnams Bitter; Woodforde's Nelson's Revenge; guest beer Ⓗ
Situated on the main Norwich to Fakenham road, this old local gem is one of the few remaining estate-owned public houses in the county. The front area of the building is very traditional, with stone floors and wooden furniture. One room has a pool table. At the rear you may feel as though you have been transported to the Far East as there is a traditional Thai restaurant offering excellent food seven nights a week. ♨Q▶🚌P⁄

Stoke Ferry

Bluebell

Lynn Road, PE33 9SW
⏲ 12-11
☎ (01366) 502056
Adnams Bitter; guest beers Ⓗ
A rejuvenated village local in the heart of the industrial village of Stoke Ferry. The emphasis here is on good quality, home-cooked food (no food Sun eve or Mon). The long, single-room interior has a dining area on one side and a pool table and drinking space on the other. One guest beer – usually from Elgood's – is available in spring and another is added in the summer months. Outside is a large secure garden where children are welcome.
♨❀◑♿Δ♣P⁄

Swaffham

Lydney House Hotel

Norwich Road, PE37 7QS
⏲ 7-10.30; closed Sun
☎ (01760) 723355 🌐 lydney-house.demon.co.uk
Woodforde's Wherry Best Bitter, Nelson's Revenge Ⓖ
Small privately-owned hotel next to the town's medieval church and within walking distance of the market place. The hotel bar serves excellent ales on gravity and occasional guest ales from local breweries. Many traditional pub games are available. Food is served evenings only. Lydney House is a good ale oasis in an area that is a decent ale desert.
Q❀🛏▶🚌(X1)♣P

Swanton Morley

Angel Inn

Greengate, NR20 4LX TG012162
⏲ 12-11; 12-10 (8 winter) Sun
☎ (01362) 637407 🌐 theangelpub.co.uk
Hop Back Summer Lightning; Mighty Oak Oscar Wilde; Wolf Golden Jackal; guest beers Ⓗ
Parts of this old inn date back to 1610 and it was once owned by an ancestor of Abraham Lincoln. The present owners are long-standing CAMRA members. Inside, the pub has a large spacious main bar with real fire, a dining room serving food lunchtimes and evenings, and a small games room with pool and darts. Five beers are available. The extensive garden includes a bowling green. The pub now hosts two beer festivals each year at Easter and in November. ♨❀◑♣P

Terrington St John

Woolpack

Main Road, PE14 7RR

⌚ 11.30-2.30, 6.30-11.30; 12-3, 7-10.30 Sun
☎ (01945) 881097
Greene King IPA; Tom Wood's Best Bitter; guest beers Ⓗ
Positioned halfway between Kings Lynn and Wisbech, the Woolpack draws a clientele from a large area. The guest beers are varied, as is the excellent Australian-influenced food menu. The interior is decorated in a modern style and features the floral paintings of the colourful landlady (guess where the Aussie influence comes from). See what happens if you let on it is your birthday!
(X1,98)P

Thetford

Albion

93-95 Castle Street, IP24 2DN (opp Castle Hill)
⌚ 11-3, 6-11 Tue & Wed; 11-11 (11.30 Thu; midnight Fri & Sat); 12-3, 7-11 Sun
☎ (01842) 752796
Greene King IPA, Abbot Ⓗ
A small and comfortable pub situated in a row of flint cottages, in a quiet area close to the town centre. This well-established pub looks out over scenic Castle Park and the earthworks of Castle Hill. You will always find a friendly welcome here, either in the conversational main bar or the lower room which has pool and darts on offer. There is an intimate patio for relaxed drinking in warmer weather. Quiz nights are held twice a week and the pub has recently introduced a takeaway menu.
QP

Thornham

Lifeboat

Ship Lane, PE36 6LT (signed off A149 coast road)
⌚ 11-11 (10.30 Sun)
☎ (01485) 512236 🌐 lifeboatinn.co.uk
Greene King IPA, Abbot; Woodforde's Wherry Best Bitter; guest beers Ⓗ
Now part of a 14-bedroom hotel featuring fine food, the drinking part of the pub still evokes its origins as a 16th-century smugglers' haunt. The bar's dim light is provided by oil lamps and its dark wood and panelling create a cosy atmosphere in winter and a cool one in summer. A large conservatory and outdoor drinking area welcome walkers, children and dogs, even when they arrive straight from the salt marshes which start virtually at the door. Old Rosie cider is available.
QP

Thurlton

Queen's Head

Beccles Road, NR14 6RJ TM414984
⌚ 5-11; 12-midnight Sat; 12-10 Sun
☎ (01508) 548667 🌐 queensheadthurlton.co.uk
Beer range varies Ⓗ
Bustling village local with an adjoining restaurant. This large single-bar community pub was saved a few years ago when a consortium of local residents banded together to use its talents and cash to renovate and reopen it. It caters for everyone, with a warm welcome assured. Food is served Thursday to Sunday evening and Sunday lunchtime.
P

Thurton

George & Dragon

2 The Street, NR14 6AL (just off A146 Norwich-Lowestoft road) TG328009
⌚ 11.30-11.30 (midnight Fri & Sat); 12-10.30 Sun
☎ (01508) 480242
Adnams Bitter; Elgood's Black Dog, Cambridge Bitter; guest beers Ⓗ
Closed for more than two years, this pub reopened recently after a sympathetic refurbishment. A spacious, open bar area features a low and heavily-beamed ceiling and a huge inglenook fireplace with gas fire. The half-timbered panelled walls are complemented by an area of exposed brickwork. The food is good, served daily and the portions are generous. Guest beers are from local breweries and there is a small selection of foreign beers. The landlord and landlady are keen and enthusiastic CAMRA members and there are plans for regular beer festivals. (X2,570)P

Trunch

Crown

Front Street, NR28 0AH (opp church) TG287348
⌚ 12-3, 5.30-11; 12-11 Fri-Sun
☎ (01263) 722341 🌐 trunchcrown.co.uk
Bateman Dark Mild, XB Bitter, Valiant; Greene King IPA; guest beers Ⓗ
Trunch is one of north Norfolk's prettiest villages, with several very old flint cottages and larger houses. Set in the middle of the village, this is Batemans' only pub in the area, and offers an excellent choice of beers. The restaurant is open Wednesday to Sunday. Check the website for details of beer festivals and forthcoming events, such as the monthly quiz night. Dogs are welcome in the bar.
Q(5,34)P

Walcott

Lighthouse Inn ✔

Coast Road, NR12 0PE (on B1159) TG359319
⌚ 11-11
☎ (01692) 650371 🌐 lighthouseinn.co.uk
Beer range varies Ⓗ
This large family-friendly pub can be found on the coast road between Cromer and Great Yarmouth. Situated in a tourist area, the trade here is fairly seasonal, with the range of real ales very limited in winter months, so it is best to visit during the busy summer season for a wider choice of ales. There is a spacious garden with a family marquee put up for the summer season. Hot food is available all day until 10.30pm and there is an extensive children's menu. P

Warham All Saints

Three Horseshoes ★

Bridge Street, NR23 1NL (2 miles SE of Wells)
⌚ 12-2.30, 6-11 (10.30 Sun)
☎ (01328) 710547 🌐 warham.biz

Greene King IPA; Woodforde's Wherry Best Bitter; guest beers Ⓗ/Ⓖ
Stone floors, scrubbed pine furniture and gas lighting set the tone for this pub which has been serving ale for nearly 300 years. Its three connected rooms are filled with a jumble of antiques, pictures and a couple of functioning one-arm bandits from 1935 and the 1960s. The pub is renowned for good plain cooking featuring soups, pies and puddings. It is busy with diners during lunch and early evening in the summer, but perfect for a pint and a natter at other times. ⛰Q❀⇌◑♿⛺♣●P

West Acre

Stag

Low Road, PE32 1TR
⏲ 12-2.30 (3 summer), 7 (6.30 summer)-11; 11-11 Fri; closed Mon winter; 12-2.30, 7-10.30 Sun
☎ (01760) 755395 🌐 westacrestag.co.uk
Beer range varies Ⓗ
The pub is situated at the east end of the picturesque village of West Acre, which is famous for its summer theatre in the priory ruins. Voted local CAMRA Pub of the Year 2005, a choice of three ever-changing real ales is available, mostly from local micro-breweries. Regular events are staged here, including beer festivals. Camping is available by prior arrangement (no caravans). No dogs are allowed in the bar. ⛰Q❀◑♿⛺♣P

Weybourne

Ship

The Street, NR25 7SZ TG111430
⏲ 11-3, 5-11; 11-midnight Fri-Sun
☎ (01263) 588721 🌐 shipinnweybourne.co.uk
Woodforde's Wherry Best Bitter; Yetman's Red, Swallowtail; guest beers Ⓗ
Situated in the heart of this attractive north Norfolk coastal village, the pub has been under new management since July 2007. The owners provide up to six cask ales from local brewers including Woodforde's, Humpty Dumpty and Yetman's. Home-cooked food is available lunchtimes and evenings. Live jazz music is played on Sunday lunchtime. The pub is close to the Muckleburgh Military Vehicle Museum. ⛰◑⊟♿⛺🚌P⁻

Wicklewood

Cherry Tree

116 High Street, NR18 9QA TG075022
⏲ 12-3, 6-11; 12-1am Fri & Sat; 12-11 Sun
☎ (01953) 606962 🌐 thecherrytreewicklewood.co.uk
Buffy's Bitter, Polly's Folly, Hopleaf, Norwegian Blue; guest beers Ⓗ
Buffy's first tied house, with all the beers originating from the brewery. The pub is divided into three distinct areas: the bar, a lounge with sofas separated from the bar by a fireplace, and a dining room. The bar counter is formed from naturally curved planks of solid oak, so take care when putting down your glass. Home-cooked food is made using local ingredients and features a range of pies with imaginative fillings. Food is served all day Saturday and Sunday. A quiz night is held on the first Wednesday of the month. ❀◑P

Winfarthing

Fighting Cocks

The Street, IP22 2ED (on B1077) TM108858
⏲ 12-3 (not Mon), 5.30-11; 12-5 Sun
☎ (01379) 643283
Adnams Bitter; guest beers Ⓗ/Ⓖ
The large main bar has a log fire and is heavily beamed. A separate games room includes a pool table and dartboard and there is a small outside seating area at the back of the pub. Well-presented, home-cooked food is served (not Sun and Mon eves). Adnams is available from a cask behind the bar as well as on handpump and a house beer brewed by Elgood's is complemented by a regularly-changing guest beer from a Norfolk brewery. ⛰❀◑♣P

Winterton-on-Sea

Fisherman's Return

The Lane, NR29 4BN (off B1159) TG495194
⏲ 11-2.30, 6-11; 11-11 Sat; 12-10.30 Sun
☎ (01493) 393305 🌐 fishermans-return.com
Adnams Bitter, Broadside; Woodforde's Wherry Best Bitter, Norfolk Nog; guest beers Ⓗ
A friendly, traditional brick and flint 17th-century pub in the centre of this attractive north Norfolk coastal village. Inside are interesting memorabilia and log fires in winter for a cosy atmosphere. An extensive range of excellent home-cooked meals may be taken in the bar or a smaller dining room. The separate function/family room caters for all occasions and there are en-suite bedrooms available. Great Yarmouth is only eight miles away and the pub is close to the beach and the Norfolk Broads. The cider is Weston's Old Rosie. ⛰Q♉❀⇌◑⊟♿🚌♣●P⁻

Woodbastwick

Fur & Feather Inn

Slad Lane, NR13 6HQ (just off B1140) TG328151
⏲ 11.30-3, 6-11; 12-10.30 Sun
☎ (01603) 720003 🌐 thefurandfeatherinn.co.uk
Woodforde's Mardlers, Wherry Best Bitter, Sun Dew, Nelson's Revenge, Norfolk Nog, Admiral's Reserve, Headcracker Ⓗ
Adjacent to the award-winning Woodforde's brewery on the Norfolk Broads, this independently-run pub was converted from three thatched cottages. A full range of Woodforde's beers is always on tap (with four-pint takeout pitchers available). A food-oriented pub, extended in 2005 to include a large dining/function room, it has a comprehensive menu. Some dishes feature Woodforde's beers, and the steak & kidney pudding is a speciality. The absence of TV, jukebox or pool table adds to the ambience. Q❀◑♿P

Wymondham

Cross Keys

Market Place, NR18 0AX
⏲ 11-11 summer; 11-3, 5-11; 12-10.30 (12-4, 7-10.30 winter) Sun
☎ (01953) 602152

Adnams Bitter; Fuller's London Pride; Wolf Straw Dog Ⓗ
Grade II-listed town centre pub at the top end of the market place, sympathetically refurbished recently to a high standard. Bar food is served at lunchtimes only, while evening meals are available Monday to Saturday in the restaurant. For every pint of the house beer Abbey Ale sold, a donation goes to the Wymondham Abbey restoration fund. Accommodation is planned for the future. ⛼❀◐⇌🚌(X3,X4)

Feathers Inn

13 Town Green, NR18 0PN
⏲ 11-2.30, 7-11; 11-2.30, 6-midnight Fri; 12-2.30, 7-11 Sun
☎ (01953) 605675
Adnams Bitter; Greene King Abbot; Marston's Pedigree; guest beers Ⓗ
An excellent example of a cosy market town local. Records show that the Feathers existed as far back as the 18th century, although much of the present building dates from the early 19th century. The interior of the pub features cosy alcoves and walls covered with entertaining memorabilia, some old farm implements and early photographs. The real ale range includes two guest beers plus a house beer, Feathers Tickler, brewed by Elgood's. ❀◐◑♿⇌🚌♣⚐

Railway

Station Road, NR18 0JY (next to station)
⏲ 11.30-11; 12-10.30 Sun
☎ (01953) 605262 🌐 therailwaypub.com
Adnams Bitter; guest beers Ⓗ
A short walk from the town centre brings you to this pub next to the railway station. The comfortable interior includes photos, railway memorabilia and pictures. An extensive menu makes this a fairly food-oriented pub over several split levels. Four real ales are available, with most of the beer coming from local breweries. ❀◐◑♿⇌P⚐

Fur & Feathers, Woodbastwick (Photo: Warren Wordsworth).

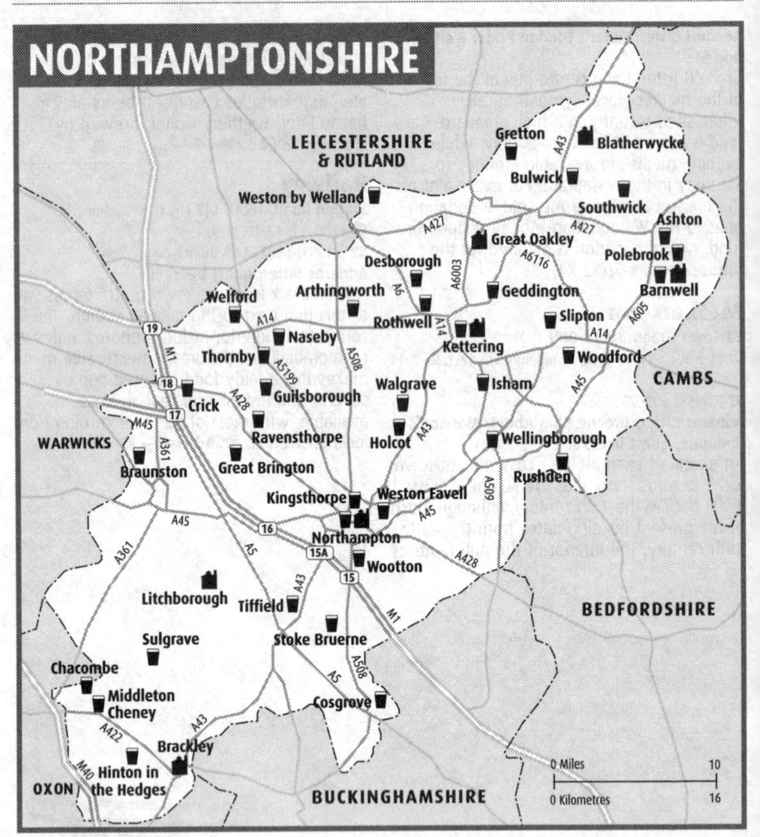

Arthingworth

Bull's Head

Kelmarsh Road, LE16 8JZ (off A508)

12-3, 6-11; 12-10.30 Sun

☎ (01858) 525637

Everards Tiger, Original; Thwaites Original; guest beers Ⓗ

Large, 19th-century village inn converted from a former farmhouse, with an L-shaped bar, log fires and secluded drinking areas. The pub was threatened with closure a few years ago but was saved by a local campaign and now goes from strength to strength. Three guest ales are usually available and a popular August Bank Holiday beer festival is held each year. A favourite with walkers and cyclists, the hostelry has a three-star rating from the English Tourist Board. ⌂Q❀⊨◑♿Ⅸ♣P

Ashton

Chequered Skipper

The Green, PE8 5LD

11.30-3, 6-midnight; 11.30-11 Sat; 12-11.30 Sun

☎ (01832) 273494

Beer range varies Ⓗ

Attractive stone and thatch pub set in the centre of the Rothschild's model village of Ashton. The white interior has a modern feel with dining areas at both ends of the single long room. There are five real ales available on the handpumps at all times, often from local brewers. The village green to the front of the pub is the scene of the annual World Conker Championship held in October. The pub also hosts beer festivals during the year and a cider festival in October. Q❀◑⊟♿♣●P

Barnwell

Montagu Arms

PE8 5PH (close to A605)

12-3, 6-11; 12-11 Sat; 12-10.30 Sun

☎ (01832) 273726

Adnams Bitter; guest beers Ⓗ

This 16th-century inn has two main rooms, with a restaurant at the rear and public bar to the front overlooking a stream and stone bridge. The bar has oak beams, a flagstone floor and open fires. Outside is a large garden with a play area for children and a petanque court. The large car park leads to the village hall. A popular pub with locals, it stocks various ales from the nearby Digfield Ales Brewery. ⌂Q❀◑⊟♿Ⅸ⊟♣●P⁻

Braunston

Wheatsheaf

10 The Green, NN11 7HW

4 (12 Fri & Sat)-11 (midnight Sat); 12-10.30 Sun

☎ (01788) 890748

Flowers IPA; Greene King Abbot; guest beers Ⓗ

Friendly, open-plan pub offering a frequently-changing guest ale to complement the regular Greene King beers. Unusually, the pub has a

ENGLAND

Chinese takeaway operating from 5pm each evening. It hosts live music on the first and third Friday of the month as well as Saturday night. An hourly bus between Rugby and Banbury passes through the village. ❀🚌♣⚲

Bulwick

Queen's Head

Main Street, NN17 3DY

⏲ 12-3, 6-11; closed Mon; 12-4.30, 7-10.30 Sun

☎ (01780) 450272

Shepherd Neame Spitfire; guest beers Ⓗ

A hidden gem, this four-roomed limestone pub dates from 1653 and retains the original wood beams. Renowned for the quality of its real ale, five beers are stocked including a wide range of guest ales from micros. Overlooked by the church, the pub has a large car park and a small enclosed patio. The main bar area is for drinking with the other rooms set for dining. Fine traditional food is served, made with locally sourced ingredients.
⛺Q❀◑⊟P

Chacombe

George & Dragon

1 Silver Street, OX17 2JR (between A361 and B4525 near Banbury)

⏲ 12-11.30

☎ (01295) 711500

Everards Beacon, Tiger; guest beers Ⓗ

Welcoming, traditional stone-built country pub situated in front of a small village green. Inside, four distinct areas have flagstone floors and Elizabethan windows, and the rear leaded glass door depicts the pub's name. One room features a large inglenook and photographs of the long-closed Chalcombe Halt. The bar itself has a glass top revealing an illuminated 26ft deep well. Home-made, locally sourced food is organic where possible. Two guest beers are from the Everards range.
⛺Q☕❀🛏◑♿⛺🚌♣P⚲

Cosgrove

Navigation

Thrupp Wharf, Station Road, MK19 7BE (off A508)

⏲ 12-3, 5.30-11; 12-11 Sat; 12-10.30 Sun

☎ (01908) 543156

Greene King IPA, Old Speckled Hen; guest beers Ⓗ

Popular canal-side pub between the rural villages of Cosgrove and Castlethorpe. Predominantly a food pub, serving good quality meals with home-made specials, drinkers and diners mix in the spacious bar, and there is a separate restaurant. The large garden, balcony and conservatory alongside the canal are all very pleasant on summer evenings. Live music plays on Friday evening. Two guest beers are usually available.
⛺❀◑P⚲

Crick

Royal Oak

22 Church Street, NN6 7TP

⏲ 2.30 (12 Sat)-11; 12-10.30 Sat & Sun

☎ (01788) 822340

Greene King IPA, Abbot; guest beers Ⓗ

Hidden from the main A428 near the village church, this friendly, welcoming wood-beamed cottage-style free house offers an ever-changing beer range with up to 12 guest ales available each week. Open fires warm the two main drinking areas, giving the pub a cosy feel. Northants skittles and darts are played in the games room and a function room can be booked with catering on request. Chinese takeaway food is available. ⛺☕❀◑🚌♣⚲

Desborough

George

79 High Street, NN14 2NB

⏲ 11-midnight (1am Fri & Sat); 12-midnight Sun

☎ (01536) 760271

Everards Beacon, Tiger; guest beers Ⓗ

Situated opposite Desborough Cross, this coaching inn built in local ironstone dates from the 17th century. The interior has been modernised with two main drinking areas and a separate lounge. Home to football, cricket, darts and pool teams, this community-oriented pub is popular with sports fans and has large TV screens. In summer the part-covered sun-trap yard comes into its own. Guest ales are from the Everards list.
❀🛏◑♿🚌(19)♣P

Geddington

Star Inn

2 Bridge Street, NN14 1AZ (follow signs for Eleanor Cross)

⏲ 12-3, 6-11.30 (12.30am Fri & Sat); 12-10.30 Sun

☎ (01536) 742386 🌐 star-inn-geddington.com

Greene King IPA; guest beers Ⓗ

The Star, close to the busy A43 trunk road, is the perfect place to stop for a break from your journey. It is situated opposite one of the finest Eleanor crosses, built by Edward I to mark the nightly resting places of Queen Eleanor's coffin on her last journey from Nottingham to London. The guest ales, including at least one local brew at all times, and home-cooked food are popular with villagers and visitors alike. ⛺❀◑⊟♿♣P⚲

Great Brington

Althorp Coaching Inn (Fox & Hounds)

Main Street, NN7 4EW

⏲ 11-11 (11.45 Fri & Sat); 12-10.30 Sun

☎ (01604) 770651

Fuller's London Pride; Greene King IPA, Old Speckled Hen, Abbot; guest beers Ⓗ

INDEPENDENT BREWERIES

Cherwell Valley Brackley (NEW)
Digfield Barnwell
Frog Island Northampton
Great Oakley Great Oakley
Hoggleys Litchborough
Nobby's Kettering/Guilsborough
Potbelly Kettering
Rockingham Blatherwycke

This wonderful stone-built and thatched pub has been serving the public since 1620. The bar is largely unspoilt with oak beams, a flagstone floor and open fireplace, and the dining area has a massive inglenook. Outside there is an enclosed courtyard with tables leading to a flower-filled garden. A good food menu is complemented by up to four guest beers. Althorp House, the former home of Princess Diana, is close by. ⌂Q❀◐◑P

Gretton

Bluebell

90 High Street, NN17 3DF (off A6003 on Corby Rd)
⏲ 5 (4 Fri, 12.30 Sat)-midnight; 12.30-midnight Sun
☎ (01536) 770404
Greene King IPA, Abbot; guest beers Ⓗ
Friendly 14th-century village local, originally a bakery in a row of mellow stone houses. Three connecting rooms on different levels have been opened out and furnished in a mix of old fashioned and modern styles. The paved drinking area outside catches the sun and comes into its own during the Welland Valley beer festival in June. Meals must be pre-booked. ⌂❀♣⊱

Guilsborough

Ward Arms

High Street, NN6 8PY
⏲ 12-2.30, 5-11; 12-midnight Fri & Sat; 12-11 Sun
☎ (01604) 740265
Nobby's Claridges Crystal; guest beers Ⓗ
Situated opposite the old Grammar School, this 17th-century pub is built from local ironstone and today has white rendering with a thatched roof. In its earlier days, it was frequented by the Duke of York who later became George VI. The late Queen Mother also put in an appearance. Handpumps take pride of place on the bar with a blackboard showing five changing guest beers from various micros, plus another beer from Nobby's. A 10-barrel plant is to be installed in the rear courtyard. Live music plays on the last Saturday of the month. Traditional home-cooked food is served. ⌂Q☋❀◐◑⊟♣●P⊡

Hinton in the Hedges

Crewe Arms

Sparrow Corner, NN13 5NF (off A43/A422)
⏲ 6-11; 12-10.30 Sun
☎ (01280) 705801
Hook Norton Hooky Bitter; guest beers Ⓗ
Tucked away down a lane in a village that can be hard to find, this is a genuine gem. Following a two year closure, the pub was a bought by two locals who refurbished and redecorated the interior. The interior is divided into four comfortable areas and retains a traditional bar. Dining is popular here and guest beers often come from local micro breweries. ⌂❀◑♿P

Holcot

White Swan

Main Street, NN6 9SP (Moulton to Walgrave Rd)
⏲ 11-3, 5.30-11; 11-11 Sat; 12-10.30 Sun
☎ (01604) 781263
Bateman XB; Black Sheep Best Bitter; guest beers Ⓗ
White-painted stone and thatched country local run by a landlord who really knows his real ale. The three-roomed pub has a cosy, welcoming bar popular with Saints' rugby supporters. A split-level restaurant hosts regular themed evenings including a curry night and quiz and skittle nights. Occasional beer festivals are planned. Handy for Pitsford Reservoir, the Holcot Hobble and Holcot Steam Rally & Country Fair. ❀◐◑♿⊟P⊱

Isham

Lilacs ✔

39 Church Street, NN14 1HD (off A509 at Church)
⏲ 12-3, 5.30-1am (1.30am Fri & Sat); 12-4, 8-12.30am Sun
☎ (01536) 723948
Greene King IPA, Ruddles Best, Abbot; guest beers Ⓗ
Named after a breed of rabbit, this hard-to-find village pub is at the heart of the community – popular with locals, diners and those who seek out a traditional unspoilt pub. The lounge and a cosy snug at the front are complemented by a large games room towards the rear with two pool tables, darts and Northants skittles. The guest beers are from the Greene King list. ⌂☋❀◐⊟⊟P⊱

Kettering

Alexandra Arms

39 Victoria Street, NN16 0BU
⏲ 2-11 (midnight Fri & Sat); 12-11 Sun
☎ (01536) 522730
Beer range varies Ⓗ
Local CAMRA Pub of the Year 2007, this back street locals' pub just gets better and better. No fewer than 3,694 different beers from 525 different breweries have passed through the 10 handpumps in just five years. Nobby's beers are brewed in the cellar and at least one is available at all times. The front bar is covered with pump clips and the larger back bar is home to Northants skittles and pool. No under 14s are permitted. If you visit just one pub in Northants, make it this one.
❀⊏⊟⇄⊟♣⊱

Piper ✔

Windmill Avenue, NN15 6PS
⏲ 11-3, 6-11; 12-10.30 Sun
☎ (01536) 513870
Hook Norton Hooky Bitter; guest beers Ⓗ
Welcoming 1950s two-roomed pub close to this county's 'Alton Towers' —Wicksteed Park. Five or six changing real ales are from the Enterprise Inns list. The interior has a lively bar/games room to complement the quiet lounge. Sunday is quiz night. Two beer festivals are held a year. Home-cooked food is served until 10pm. Q❀◐◑⊟♿♣●P

Sawyers

44 Montague Street, NN16 8RU
⏲ 4 (2 Sat & Sun)-7, 8-midnight; closed Mon
☎ (01536) 484800 🌐 sawyersvenue.co.uk
Beer range varies Ⓗ

Formerly the Swan, now named after a former landlord, this is a major music venue and bands as famous as Dr Feelgood have played here. On Wednesday night it hosts an acoustic session, Sunday is blues night. Regular festivals and all-day events are held. The pub acts as the tap for Potbelly Brewery and on music nights has two of its beers on handpull as well as casks on the bar. Opening times can vary, so please check in advance. ⇌⊟●P

Shire Horse

18 Newland Street, NN16 8JH
✪ 11-11; 12-10.30 Sun
☎ (01536) 519078
Tetley Bitter, Burton Ale; guest beers Ⓗ
Down to earth locals' pub where visitors are welcome, with frequently changing guest beers. Pool and shove ha'penny are played in the open-plan bar where motorcycle prints cover the walls and numerous pump clips are displayed. A wide selection of music plays. The bus station is next door. ❀⇌⊟♣●⌙

Kingsthorpe

Queen Adelaide

50 Manor Road, NN2 6QJ (off A519)
✪ 11.30-11; 12-10.30 Sun
☎ (01604) 714524 ⊕ queenadelaide.com
Adnams Bitter, Broadside; Woodforde's Wherry Best Bitter; guest beers Ⓗ
The Adelaide was originally a village inn until Kingsthorpe was swallowed up into Northampton. The friendly four-room pub has been opened out but retains low beams and an uneven floor plus quiet areas for intimate conversation. Four guest ales include a locally-brewed micro-brewery beer and a mild. A cider or perry is always available, often from a local producer, and a beer festival is held on the first weekend in September. Local CAMRA Pub of the Year runner-up in 2007.
❀◐⊟⊟♣●P⌙

Middleton Cheney

New Inn ✔

45 Main Road, OX17 2ND (S off A422)
✪ 12-3, 5-12.30am; 12-1am Fri & Sat; 12-11.30 Sun
☎ (01295) 710399
Fuller's London Pride; Hook Norton Hooky Bitter; guest beers Ⓗ
Once a coaching inn, this stone-built 17th-century pub has flagstone flooring in the dining area and wooden seating set into the walls. The main drinking areas are tiled with a small open hearth providing a warm and cosy environment. A live band plays on Friday night and a beer festival is held in the summer. Guest beers are from the Punch list. Now run by an Australian, the traditional themed Aussie Christmas is not to be missed. Note the unusual pub sign. ⩕Q❀◐♣P

Naseby

Royal Oak

Church Street, NN6 6DA
✪ 4.30 (12 Sat)-midnight; 12-7 Sun
☎ (07985) 408240
Beer range varies Ⓗ
This traditional brick-built village pub is close to the site where the famous battle of Naseby was fought in 1645. The L-shaped single room interior is divided to create the feel of a separate lounge and bar. Northants skittles, pool and darts are played in the games area. Adjoining barns host a popular beer festival in October and during St George's week in April. A meeting place for classic car and bike enthusiasts, five regularly-changing beers are always available, often from local micros.
⩕Q❀▲♣●P⌙

Northampton

Lamplighter

66 Overstone Road, NN1 3JS
✪ 5 (4 Fri)-11 (midnight Fri); 12-midnight Sat; 12-6 Sun
☎ (01604) 631125
Beer range varies Ⓗ
Delightful traditional town-centre street-corner local just a few minutes' walk from the bus station. The welcoming single bar/lounge is on a split level with soft furnishings. Above the bar is a coloured canopy bearing the pub's name. Quiz nights are Wednesday and Friday. Four changing guest beers are available, often including one from Timothy Taylor. Food is available until 8pm, 4pm on Sunday.
❀◐⊟♣⌙

Malt Shovel Tavern

121 Bridge Street, NN1 1QF (opp Carlsberg factory)
✪ 11.30-3, 5-11; 12-3, 7-10.30 Sun
☎ (01604) 234212
Frog Island Natterjack; Fuller's London Pride; Great Oakley Wot's Occurring, Harpers; Tetley Bitter; guest beers Ⓗ
Popular, award-winning freehouse just out of the town centre circuit. The Shovel is the tap for the Great Oakley Brewery, with up to four of its beers among the 14 handpumps. There is also a fine selection of draught and bottled Belgian beers and traditional farm cider. The interior is filled with breweriana, much of it from the Phipps Brewery which once stood opposite the pub before it was demolished to make way for the Carlsberg factory. Blues bands perform on Wednesday evening and there is a monthly quiz. Q❀◐♿⇌⊟●⌙

Moon on the Square ✔

6 The Parade, NN1 2EA
✪ 9-midnight (1am Fri & Sat)
☎ (01604) 634062
Courage Best Bitter, Directors; Greene King IPA, Abbot; Marston's Pedigree; Shepherd Neame Spitfire; guest beers Ⓗ
Situated in the town centre opposite the historic market, this large, open-plan pub is on two levels (lift provided). It offers a good selection of beers and cider, and holds beer festivals several times a year. Food is served all day, every day. There are TV screens with the volume turned down and Wi-Fi Internet is provided free. The enthusiastic manager holds regular 'meet the brewer' events. ◐♿⇌⊟●

Racehorse

15 Abington Square, NN1 4AE
✪ 12-midnight (1am Sat)
☎ (01604) 631997

Hampshire King Alfred's, Richard The Lionheart; guest beers 🄷
Relaxed and friendly pub attracting an eclectic clientele with a wide age range. The wood-panelled bar has bench seating and Dickensian-style bow windows to the front. A varied range of up to five guest beers includes many local micro ales and draught continental lagers, while cider is occasionally available on gravity. Monday is quiz night and live bands play in a remote room with a stage. The large outdoor area has a log burner. ❀🚌(2,8)●P⅟—

Romany
NN2 6JN (½ mile E of Kingsthorpe)
🕐 11.30-11.30; 12-11 Sun
☎ (01604) 714647
Beer range varies 🄷
Large 1930s pub offering a range of nine changing ales, often from local breweries, alongside Weston's cider and perry. The public bar and games room has Northants skittles and two pool tables. The lounge has live music on Thursday, Saturday and Sunday, karaoke on Friday and a quiz night on Monday. On the first Tuesday of the month an open mic literary evening is held. CAMRA members receive a discount on Tuesday and Wednesday.
❀🚌♣●P⅟—

Victoria Inn
2 Poole Street, NN1 3EX
🕐 12-midnight (1am Fri & Sat)
☎ (01604) 633660
Vale VPA; guest beers 🄷
Well worth seeking out, this friendly late-Victorian end of terrace local has been revitalised by the new landlady. It offers up to seven guest beers, often from local micros, and a choice of bottled Belgian beers. The interesting one-roomed interior has wood-panelled and mirrored walls, ornate window illuminations and vintage memorabilia. Quizzes are held on Tuesday and Wednesday, and regular live music nights hosted. Sunday lunch is popular (book ahead), otherwise it is snacks only. There is a small decked area outside for the summer. ♣⅟—

White Elephant
Kingsley Park Terrace, NN2 7HG (on A43 opp old racecourse)
🕐 11-11 (10.30 Sun)
☎ (01604) 711202
Greene King IPA; guest beers 🄷
The manager is keen to promote real ale in this community pub, with guest beers regularly coming from local micros. Opposite a sports park, it has a sporting theme and runs two football teams as well as sponsoring a cricket and rugby team. The large open-plan interior divides into different areas —bar, games area, and a small lounge and dining space where families are welcome. Italian-style pizzas are cooked in the pub's pizza oven and generous snacks are available at lunchtime. ❀◐♿🚌(2,8)♣⅟—

Wig & Pen
19 St Giles Street, NN1 1JA
🕐 12-midnight (2am Fri & Sat); 12-11 Sun
☎ (01604) 622178
Beer range varies 🄷
A second entry in the Guide for this town centre pub which was purchased by the Fenland Brewery nearly two years ago. Formerly a Mansfield pub, the Wig & Pen was called the Black Lion until 11 years ago. The frontage is over 300 years old, while the long L-shaped bar was created with an extension 150 years ago. Up to seven guest beers are stocked from micro-breweries, including a choice of Fenland beers. Regular live music plays on a small rear stage. ❀◐🚌♣●⅟—

Polebrook

Kings Arms ✔
Kings Arms Lane, PE8 5LW
🕐 12-2.30, 6-11; closed Mon; 12-11.30 Sat; 12-10.30 Sun
☎ (01832) 272363
Adnams Bitter; guest beers 🄷
Traditional thatched stone-built public house in the middle of the small village of Polebrook. The three-sided bar has four handpumps with distinctive wooden handles. An inglenook fireplace separates the drinking area from the space set aside for diners. A good sized enclosed garden is ideal for children to play. The pub is supplied with various beers from the nearby Digfield Ales Brewery. ⌂Q❀◐♿P

Ravensthorpe

Chequers
Chequers Lane, NN6 8ER (Between A428 and A5199)
🕐 12-3, 6-11; 12-11 Sat; 12-3, 7-10.30 Sun
☎ (01604) 770379
Black Sheep Best Bitter; Greene King IPA; Jennings Bitter; guest beers 🄷
Brick-built Grade II listed free house situated opposite the church in this sprawling village. Popular with locals, walkers and fishermen, you can be sure of a warm welcome from the friendly hosts. Inside, the beams display a collection of jugs and there are banknotes on the half-panelled walls. An extensive menu of good value food is served and guest beers are often local. Outside, there is an adventure play area for children and a building for Northants skittles. 🛏❀◐🚌♣

Rothwell

Woolpack Inn
Market Hill, NN14 6BW (off A14/B576, follow signs for Glendon)
🕐 11-11 (midnight Thu-Sat)
☎ (01536) 710284
Marston's Pedigree; guest beers 🄷
This pub is situated close to the centre of this small, ancient market town, which was once important for its sheep markets. The long, narrow bar area leads to three rooms – a games room, a dining room overlooking the garden, and a large, homely lounge with a wood fire, TV and tables and chairs giving it an old farmhouse feel. The changing guest beers mainly come from local micro-breweries.
⌂❀◐♿🚌(19)P

Rushden

Rushden Historic Transport Society

Station Approach, NN10 0AW
7.30 (12 Sat)-11; 12-3, 7.30-10.30 Sun
☎ (01933) 318988 rhts.co.uk
Fuller's London Pride; Oakham Bishops Farewell; guest beers Ⓗ
Many times local CAMRA Club of the Year and national winner in 2000, the Station' offers up to seven ales including a dark beer at the weekend. The bar is gas lit and enamel advertisements adorn the walls inside and out. A unique lounge has opened on the station platform in part of a former Royal Mail parcel van with a Northants skittles table. Visitors are charged £1 per person or couple. Open weekends are held during the summer and there is a steam rally in May. The museum is open on summer Sundays. Q♣

Slipton

Samuel Pepys

Slipton Lane, NN14 3AR (off A6116)
12-3, 6-11; 12-11 Sat; 12-10.30 Sun
☎ (01832) 731739 samuel-pepys.com
Greene King IPA; Hop Back Summer Lightning; Oakham JHB; Potbelly Aisling; Ⓗ **guest beers** Ⓖ
Three-roomed pub set in a small village where almost every house is built of local ironstone. Formerly know as the Red Cow, the building dates from the 1600s, with a modern conservatory added to become the main restaurant (booking advised). Meals can also be taken in the lounge or in the large garden in summer. Two guest beers are available on gravity all year round, usually from local micros. Q(16)P

Southwick

Shuckburgh Arms

Main Street, PE8 5BL
12-2, 6-11; closed Mon; 12-3, 6-9 Sun
☎ (01832) 274007
Digfield Barnwell Bitter; Fuller's London Pride; guest beers Ⓗ
Located next to the village hall and cricket pitch, this stone-built pub has two rooms — one a seating area, the other a larger room with the bar and an inglenook fireplace. The spacious enclosed garden at the rear is used by campers during the summer months. Up to three beers are available on handpump throughout the year. QP

Stoke Bruerne

Boat Inn

Shutlanger Road, NN12 7SB (opp canal museum)
11-3, 6-11; 11-11 Fri, Sat & summer; 12-10.30 Sun
☎ (01604) 862428 boatinn.co.uk
Banks's Bitter; Marston's Burton Bitter, Pedigree, Old Empire; guest beers Ⓗ
Situated alongside the Grand Union Canal opposite the canal museum, the Boat Inn has been run by the same family since 1877. Drinkers use the tap bar – a couple of cosy rooms in the original thatched stone building. A large extension houses the lounge bar, restaurant and bistro, where generous helpings of good food are served. A small shop caters for canal users (from 9am summer, 10am winter). Three guest beers are available. Q♣P

Sulgrave

Star Inn

Manor Road, OX17 2SA
11-3, 6-11; 12-5, 6-9.30 Sun
☎ (01295) 760389
Hook Norton Hooky Bitter, Old Hooky, seasonal beers Ⓗ
Lovely 300-year-old stone-built pub off the beaten track but well worth the effort to find. Set in the beautiful village of Sulgrave, it is almost opposite Sulgrave Manor, the ancestral home of the George Washington family. The traditional front bar area is relatively unchanged with a flagstone floor, beamed ceiling and inglenook fireplace, and there is also a small, intimate dining area. To the rear is the restaurant where quality home-cooked food is prepared by the French owners. QP

Thornby

Red Lion

Welford Road, NN6 8SJ (on A5199)
12-2.30, 5-11; 12-11 Sat; 12-10.30 Sun
☎ (01604) 740238
Everards Tiger; Frog Island Shoemaker; Greene King IPA; Tetley Bitter; guest beers Ⓗ
Friendly, traditional village pub dating back over 400 years. The three-room interior features wooden beams, a stone floor in the bar area and a wood-burning open fire set halfway up the chimney breast in the cosy lounge. There is also a compact restaurant. Collections of beer steins, tankards and paintings are displayed throughout. A quiz is held fortnightly on a Tuesday. Outside is a large garden with seating areas. ♣P

Tiffield

George Inn ✔

21 High Street, NN12 8AD (off A43)
12-3 (not Tue), 6-midnight; 12-midnight Sat (9.30 Sun)
☎ (01327) 350587
Greene King IPA; Wells Bombardier; guest beers Ⓗ
A new entry to the Guide, this traditional 15th-century three-roomed pub has Victorian and 20th-century extensions. Reputed to be haunted by a cattle drover, it is popular with walkers to the Gayton Marina and Blisworth Canal Tunnel. Thatcher's cider is stocked during the summer months. Recently awarded CAMRA Pub of the Season. ♣P

Walgrave

Royal Oak

Zion Hill, NN6 9PN (2 miles N of A43)
12-3, 5.30 (5 Fri & Sat)-11; 12-10.30 Sun
☎ (01604) 781248
Adnams Bitter; Greene King Abbot; guest beers Ⓗ

This old ironstone building has been a pub since 1840. The long front bar has three distinct areas, two mainly for dining. Although food is a priority here, with an extensive, reasonable menu on offer, three guest beers are usually available. Across the yard is a games room where Northants skittles is played, and the beer garden has a children's play area. ⛰❀⊄◗⊟♣

Welford

Wharf Inn

NN6 6JQ (on A5199 N of village)
12-11 (1am Thu-Sat)
☎ (01858) 575075
Banks's Bitter; Marston's Pedigree; guest beers Ⓗ
Brick-built inn situated at the end of the Welford Arm of the Grand Union Canal and popular with barge travellers, locals and tourists alike. The landscaped garden provides the starting point to five historic walks. Three rotating guest beers often include one from a local micro-brewery. Beer festivals and themed events are held throughout the year. Accommodation and wireless Internet access are available. ⛰❀⊄◗♿P

Wellingborough

Coach & Horses

17 Oxford Street, NN8 4HY (on A5128)
12-midnight (6 Sun)
☎ (01933) 441848
St Austell Tribute; guest beers Ⓗ
Recently refurbished town centre local, adult-only at all times. Nine real ales are on handpump, including one from Adnams and four from local micros. Good, traditional home-cooked British food is served lunchtimes and evenings. Old bottles, jugs, stone jars and pictures fill the bar walls and shelves. Sky TV is on for sporting events. There is a large garden to the rear with a heated smoking shelter. ⛰❀◗⊟♣●P⁄–

Locomotive

111 Finedon Road, NN8 4AL (on A510)
11 (12 Sun)-11
☎ (01933) 276600
Beer range varies Ⓗ
Originally three cottages, this steam railway themed pub is close to the railway line, with a '00' gauge line running above the bar. A good food menu complements an excellent ever-changing range of up to nine ales, including many from local breweries. Themed beer festivals are held over bank holiday weekends. ⛰❀◗⊟≠⊟(45)♣P⁄–

Old Grammarians Association

46 Oxford Street, NN8 4JH (on A5128)
12-2.30, 7-11; 11.30-11 Sat; 12-10.30 Sun
☎ (01933) 226188
Greene King IPA; Hook Norton Old Hooky; Young's Bitter; guest beers Ⓗ
Welcoming members-only club just out of the town centre with plenty of parking. Inside there is a large main bar, a smaller TV lounge and a games/function room. Three or four guest beers are on offer. The club holds a quiz night on the first Tuesday of the month and hosts regular music events. Show a CAMRA membership card or a copy of this Guide to gain entry – but regular visitors will be asked to join. ⛾◗⊟♿⊟P⁄–

Weston by Welland

Wheel & Compass

Valley Road, LE16 8HZ
12-3, 6-11; 12-11 Sat; 12-10.30 Sun
☎ (01858) 565864
Banks's Bitter; Greene King Abbot; Marston's Burton Bitter, Pedigree; guest beers Ⓗ
This multi-room village inn is always popular due to its reputation for good quality food: 'We do not serve fast food, we serve good food as fast as we can.' The large rear garden attracts families in summer with benches and seats plus swings and slides for children. The pub offers two changing guest beers as well as the regular ales. ⛰Q❀◗P

Weston Favell

Bold Dragoon

48 High Street, NN3 3JW
11.30-11.30; 12-10.30 Sun
☎ (01604) 401221
Black Sheep Best Bitter; Fuller's London Pride; Greene King IPA, Abbot; Taylor Landlord; guest beers Ⓗ
This 1930s pub has a busy food-oriented trade, offering both bar and restaurant menus, but this does not detract from the selection and quality of the ales. The bar has a pool table and sports TV, and a music quiz is held on Sunday evening. Q❀◗⊟♿⊟♣●P

Woodford

Duke's Arms

83 High Street, NN14 4HE (off A14/A510)
12-11 (10.30 Sun)
☎ (01832) 732224
Greene King IPA, Abbot; guest beers Ⓗ
Popular locals' village pub once known as the Lords Arms, but renamed in honour of the Duke of Wellington, a regular visitor to Woodford. Home-cooked food is served daily except Sun evening. Northants skittles, darts and pool are played. Entertainment is held on Sun and Thu evenings. Summer beer festival. ⛰⛾❀◗⊟♿⊟(16)♣●P

Wootton

Wootton Working Men's Club

High Street, NN4 6LW (off A508 near jct 15 of M1)
12-2 (3 Sat), 7-11 (4.30-11.30 Fri); 12-10.30 Sun
☎ (01604) 761863
Great Oakley Wot's Occurring; guest beer Ⓗ
This ironstone building was rescued from closure by the regulars. It is now an award-winning club, with drinking areas including a bar, quiet lounge, live music room and games room with Northants skittles. Up to six changing guest beers are available. Show this Guide or a CAMRA membership card for admittance. Local CAMRA Club of the Year 2008. Q⛾⊟♣P

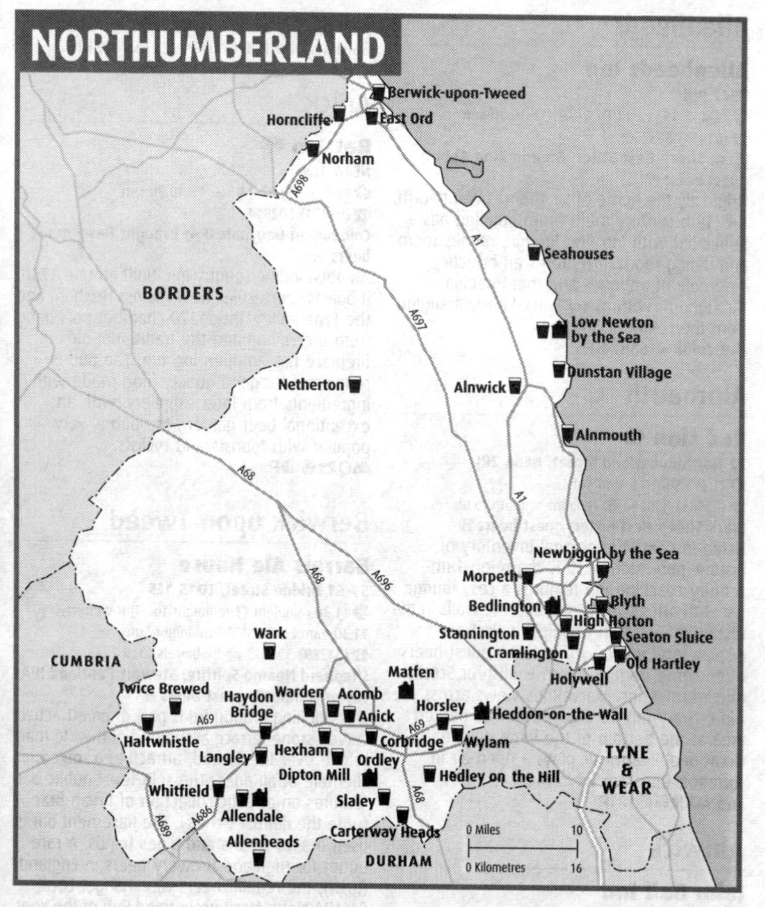

Acomb

Miners Arms

Main Street, NE46 4PW

5-12.30am (midnight Sun)

(01434) 603909 theminersacomb.com

Black Sheep Best Bitter; Yates Bitter; guest beers H

The name of this 1746 inn is a reminder of the once prominent mining industry in the area. A central staircase divides the interior into two drinking areas: a small cosy bar and a comfortable lounge with a real fire. Four real ales are always on handpull —The Miners is a rare outlet in the north east for Yates Bitter. Freshly-prepared, home-made food is served in the dining-room to the rear.

(880,882)

Allendale

Golden Lion

Market Place, NE47 9BD

12-1.30am (2.30am Fri-Sun)

(01434) 683225

Allendale Best Bitter, Golden Plover; Draught Bass; guest beers H

Pleasant 18th-century pub in the main square with an open fire, popular with ramblers and day trippers who wish to take advantage of excellent nearby countryside walks. Pictures of the annual new year tar barrel procession are displayed on the walls. The local choir practises here on Tuesday evening and there is live Irish music on the last Wednesday of the month. (688)♣

Kings Head

Market Place, NE47 9BD

12-midnight

(01434) 683681

Banks's Original; Jennings Cumberland Ale; Marston's Pedigree H

Dating from 1754, this welcoming inn in the town square is popular with day trippers, cyclists and ramblers. The refurbished bar area retains original features including an open fire. Traditional pub food is served all day. Rail and bus links are good to Allendale and it is well worth the effort to seek out this small market town. (688)

INDEPENDENT BREWERIES

Allendale Allendale
Hexhamshire Ordley
High House Matfen
Northumberland Bedlington
Ship Inn Newton-by-the-Sea (NEW)
Wylam Heddon on the Wall

Allenheads

Allenheads Inn

NE47 9HJ

12-4, 7-11; 12-11 Fri & Sat; 12-10.30 Sun

(01434) 685200

Black Sheep Best Bitter; Greene King Abbot; guest beers

Originally the home of Sir Thomas Wentworth, this 18th-century multi-room building has a public bar with log fire, lounge, games room and dining room. It features an eclectic assembly of antiques and memorabilia throughout, with many knick-knacks hanging from the ceiling in the bar.

(688)P

Alnmouth

Red Lion

22 Northumberland Street, NE66 2RJ

11 (12 Sun)-11 Mon-Sat

(01665) 830584 redlionalnmouth.co.uk

Black Sheep Best Bitter; guest beers

Listed in CAMRA's regional inventory of historic pub interiors, this charming 18th-century coaching inn features a cosy lounge bar with attractive woodwork. The walls in the restaurant are built of ships' ballast and display local artists' work. Three guest beers often come from northern English or Scottish micro-breweries. Marvellous views across the Aln estuary can be enjoyed from a decked area at the bottom of the large garden. Occasional live music plays —open air in summer. Dogs are welcome.

(518)P

Alnwick

John Bull Inn

12 Howick Street, NE66 1UY

12-3 (Sat only), 7-11; 12-3, 7-10.30

(01665) 602055 john-bull-inn.co.uk

Beer range varies

A multiple winner of local CAMRA awards, this 180-year-old inn thrives on its reputation as a 'back street boozer'. The landlord is passionate about ale and offers four cask-conditioned beers, often from local micros, and a real cider – unusual for the area. He also holds an annual beer festival and is noted for stocking the widest range of bottled Belgian beers in the county, 120 different single malt whiskies and a big selection of board games. The pub upholds the north-east tradition of an annual leek show. Q

Tanners Arms

2-4 Hotspur Place, NE66 1QF

12-midnight; 12-3 (Fri & Sat only), 5-midnight winter; 12-midnight Sun

(01665) 602553

Beer range varies

Just off the town centre, this street-corner single room pub has bare stone walls, flagstone floors and a tree-like beer shelf at its centre. Gentlemen beware – the Gents' door is sliding! Five frequently changing real ales often come from north eastern micro-breweries and occasional beer festivals are hosted. Live bands play monthly, there is a popular weekly general knowledge quiz and a well-used jukebox. The famous Alnwick Gardens and Playhouse are nearby.

Anick

Rat Inn

NE46 4LN

12-3, 6-11; 12-11 Sat; 12-10.30 Sun

(01434) 602814

Caledonian Deuchars IPA; Draught Bass; guest beers

An outstanding country inn. Built around 1750, it boasts spectacular views across Hexham and the Tyne Valley. Inside, 20 chamber pots hang from the ceiling and the traditional old fireplace has an open log fire. The pub is renowned for good quality food made with ingredients from local suppliers. With an exceptional beer garden, the pub is very popular with tourists and cyclists.

QP

Berwick upon Tweed

Barrels Ale House

59-61 Bridge Street, TD15 1ES

11.30-midnight (3-midnight Tue-Thu winter); 11.30-1am Fri & Sat; 12-midnight Sun

(01289) 308013 thebarrels.co.uk

Shepherd Neame Spitfire; Stewart Pentland IPA; Taylor Landlord; guest beers

This drinking emporium is part of an attractive curved stone terrace at the end of the old road bridge over the Tweed, attracting a mixed clientele of all ages. The split-level public bar features an eclectic collection of bric-a-brac (note the dentist's chair). The basement bar is used mainly by DJs and blues bands. A rare outlet for Highland Brewery beers in England (just!), the regular beers can change. Local CAMRA North Northumberland Pub of the Year 2008.

Foxtons

26 Hide Hill, TD15 1AB

10-11 (midnight Fri & Sat); closed Sun

(01289) 303939

Caledonian Deuchars IPA, 80

An unusual regular in the Guide, Foxtons looks more like a coffee shop or bistro than a pub. An extensive Mediterranean, British and Northumbrian food menu is offered to real ale drinkers and diners alike. Near the main shopping street, it is popular with shoppers taking a break, visitors to the nearby Maltings art centre and tourists.

Pilot

31 Low Greens, TD15 1LX

12-midnight (10.30 Sun)

(01289) 304214

Caledonian Deuchars IPA; guest beers

Stone-built end of terrace local dating from the 19th century. Listed in CAMRA's regional inventory for the north east, the original three room layout has been retained and includes a drinking corridor —an unusual feature for the region. The wood-panelled public bar features nautical artefacts that are more than 100 years old. Note the fine mosaic floor at the entrance. Guest beers are usually from Scottish and north east micros. The pub hosts music nights and runs darts and quoits teams. ⛰⇌◑⊟≷⊟

Blyth

Olivers

60 Bridge Street, NE24 2AP

⏲ 11 (2 Sat)-11; 12-10.30 Sun

☎ (01670) 540356

Black Sheep Best Bitter; Jarrow Bitter; guest beers Ⓗ

Former newsagent's converted to a real ale oasis in a town known for its football team heroics in the FA Cup run of the 70s. Note the framed menu 'ports from the wood' which hangs on the wall in the bar. Do not be surprised to find complementary food on the bar come Saturday teatime at this warm and friendly hostelry. A local ladies group meets on Monday evening. ♣

Carterway Heads

Manor House Inn

DH8 9LX (on A68 S of Corbridge)

⏲ 12-11 (10.30 Sun)

☎ (01207) 255268

Courage Directors; Theakston Best Bitter; Wells Bombardier; guest beer Ⓗ

Welcoming country inn near Derwent Reservoir enjoying splendid views over the Derwent Valley. Guest ales, usually from local micro-breweries, can be enjoyed along with excellent home-cooked food, served in the bar and restaurant. The pub has its own shop selling local produce. Excellent accommodation is available. ⛰❀⇌◑♣P

Corbridge

Angel Inn

Main Street, NE45 5LA

⏲ 10-11 (10.30 Sun)

☎ (01434) 632119

Allendale Golden Plover; Taylor Landlord; guest beers Ⓗ

Dating from 1726, this coaching inn is kept in pristine condition. The superior lounge area has comfortable sofas and traditional armchairs, and there is a pleasant outside seating area for the summer. This establishment is very popular for food and the bar has a reputation for a fine selection of malt whiskies. ⛰Q❀⇌◑♿≷⊟(685)P

Black Bull ✔

Middle Street, NE45 5LE

⏲ 11-11

☎ (01434) 632261

Greene King IPA, Ruddles County, Old Speckled Hen Ⓗ

Beautiful stone-built pub in this ancient town with strong links to the Romans. The L-shaped bar has an area for dining with a log fire. Good quality food is available all day, cooked to order by the pub's chef. This Greene King pub is popular with locals, tourists and ramblers. ⛰◑≷⊟(685)P

Cramlington

Plough

Middle Farm Buildings, NE23 1DN

⏲ 11-3, 6-11; 11-11 Thu-Sat; 12-10.30 Sun

☎ (01670) 737633

Theakston XB; guest beers Ⓗ

In the centre of the ancient village of Cramlington, this pub faces the parish church. Once a farm, the old buildings were sympathetically converted some years ago. The bar is small and busy with a door leading to an outdoor seating area. The large lounge has a round 'gin gan' making it feel even more spacious. Local micros feature among the guest breweries. Regular visitors benefit from the loyalty card system: on Tuesday and Thursday get a card stamped every time you buy a beer, six stamps entitles you to a free pint. ❀◑≷⊟♣P⊱

Dipton Mill

Dipton Mill Inn

Dipton Mill Road, NE46 1YA

⏲ 12-2.30, 6-11; 12-3 Sun

☎ (01434) 606577

Hexhamshire Devil's Elbow, Shire Bitter, Devil's Water, Whapweasel, Old Humbug Ⓗ

The tap for Hexhamshire brewery, this small inn is run by a keen landlord who brews his own excellent beers. To complement the ales there is great home-cooked food. A cosy atmosphere and warm welcome make this pub well worth seeking out. The large garden has a stream running through it and there is plenty of countryside to explore. ⛰Q❀◑P

Dunstan

Cottage Inn

Dunstan Village, NE66 3SZ

⏲ 12-11 (10.30 Sun)

☎ (01665) 576658 🌐 cottageinnhotel.co.uk

Beer range varies Ⓗ

A few minutes from the spectacular Northumbrian coastline, this inn offers something for everyone. Surprisingly spacious, it has a bar, restaurant, conservatory and covered and open patios. Good food complements the excellent beer. Craster village, famed for its kippers, is half a mile away. The inn is ideally located for birdwatchers, walkers, golfers and tourists. ⛰Q❀⇌◑♿♣

East Ord

Salmon Inn

TD15 2NS

⏲ 11-3, 5-11; 11-11 Fri & Sat; 12-10.30 Sun

☎ (01289) 305227

Caledonian Deuchars IPA, 80; Wells Bombardier Ⓗ

Situated on the main road through the village near the large green, the pub is renowned for its locally sourced food, with Sunday lunches particularly popular. The single room interior is divided into drinking and dining areas, with a real fire where the regulars congregate in winter. A tunnel-shaped marquee in the back garden accommodates the overflow at busy times. The pub runs a leek club and is home to a quoits team. It also hosts quiz nights and barbecues in summer. The Tweed Cycle Way passes nearby. ⛫❀◐◑▲⊟(67)P⊬

Haltwhistle

Black Bull

Market Square, NE49 0BL

✪ 12-11; 7-11 Mon; 12-3, 6-11 Tue & Thu winter

☎ (01434) 320463

Caledonian Deuchars IPA; Greene King Abbot; Theakston Black Bull; guest beers ⊞

Warm, friendly two-room pub down a cobbled street just off the market place. Winner of a Cask Marque Beautiful Beer award in 2008, it has six handpumps. Also noted for good food, it offers an excellent menu plus blackboard specials (no meals Sun and Mon eves). An open fire, low wood-beamed ceiling and horse brasses add to the traditional ambience. Very popular with tourists and ramblers, Hadrian's Wall is nearby. ⛫Q❀◐◑⇌⊟(685)

Haydon Bridge

General Havelock

9 Ratcliff Road, NE47 7HU

✪ 12-2.30, 7-midnight

☎ (01434) 684376

Beer range varies ⊞

This comfortable pub has a well-deserved reputation for good food and beer, with two handpumps dispensing ales from local breweries. The restaurant is in a small converted barn with fine views of the River Tyne. There is also a patio area for outdoor drinking. A popular local walk, the John Martin Trail, starts nearby – ask at the bar for a leaflet. ⛫Q⚯❀◐◑⇌⊟(685)♣

Railway Hotel

Church Street, NE47 6JG

✪ 11-midnight; 12-10.30 Sun

☎ (01434) 684254 ⊕ railwayhotel.net

Black Sheep Best Bitter; Caledonian Deuchars IPA ⊞

Homely, traditional one-room pub with an open fire and friendly customers and staff, offering reasonably-priced home-cooked food. The pub is home to two cricket teams and darts and dominoes teams. Folk and R&B evenings are hosted on the second and fourth Monday of the month. Near the railway station, an hourly bus stops just around the corner. The pub is handy for Hadrian's Wall, Vindolanda and Chesters Roman forts, and close to popular rambling areas. ⛫⛿◐⇌⊟(685)♣

Hedley on the Hill

Feathers

NE43 7SW

✪ 12-11

☎ (01661) 843607 ⊕ thefeathers.net

High House Farm Nel's Best; guest beers ⊞

A cracker of a pub, with exposed stone walls and wood beams, set in a hamlet high above the Tyne valley where you can enjoy views of three counties and one city. Thriving under relatively new management, it serves high quality home-cooked food to complement the four real ales. The pub holds a mini beer festival at Easter culminating on Monday with the famous uphill barrel race, with the winners rewarded with real ale. ⛫Q⚯❀◐◑P

Hexham

Tap & Spile ✔

1 Eastgate, NE46 1BH

✪ 11-11.30 (midnight Fri & Sat); 12-4, 7-11.30 Sun

☎ (01434) 602039

Black Sheep Best Bitter; Caledonian Deuchars IPA; guest beers ⊞

Traditional main street corner pub dating from 1862 oozing with character. The back room was once a corner shop. A shelf in the bar is overflowing with cups and trophies won by the successful darts team, while locals come here to enjoy a game of dominoes. Food is served at lunchtime (not Sunday). Folk musicians play every third Thursday of the month. Q◐⊟⇌⊟(685)♣

High Horton

Three Horseshoes

Hathery Lane, NE24 4HF (off A189 N of Cramlington, follow A192) NZ276793

✪ 11-11 (midnight Fri & Sat); 12-11

☎ (01670) 822410 ⊕ 3horseshoes.co.uk

Greene King Abbot; Tetley Bitter; guest beers ⊞

Extended former coaching inn at the highest point in the Blyth Valley, with views of the Northumberland coast. The pub is open plan with distinct bar and dining areas plus a conservatory. Dedicated to real ale, seven handpumps serve three regular beers and a constantly changing list of guests including ales from local micro-brewers. Real cider and perry is usually stocked during the pub's regular beer festivals. An extensive range of meals and snacks is available. Meals are served lunchtimes and evenings, all day Friday to Sunday. Q⚯❀◐◑P⊬

Holywell

Olde Fat Ox Inn

Holywell Village, NE26 3TW

✪ 12-11 (midnight Fri & Sat)

☎ (0191) 237 0964

Caledonian Deuchars IPA; guest beers ⊞

Traditional wood-beamed pub in the heart of the village, popular with locals and tourists. The walls of the bar feature several signed, framed photographs of film stars including Bob Hope and Bette Davis. The garden overlooking the magnificent Holywell Dene is outstanding and has won the Blyth Valley In Bloom competition five years in a row. Regular theme nights are hosted and the pub runs an over-40s football team. ❀⇌⊖⊟

Horncliffe

Fishers Arms

Main Street, TD15 2XW

✪ 12-3, 6-10.30 (11 Fri & Sat); 12-2, 6-10.30 Sun

☎ (01289) 386866

Caledonian Deuchars IPA; Camerons Strongarm ⊞

The only surviving business and employer in the village, the Fishers Arms is at the very heart of community life. Part of a terrace in the village centre, its single room interior is divided into dining and drinking areas. It is handy for Tweed Cycle Way and not far from the famous Union or Chain Bridge linking England and Scotland – built in 1820, this is the oldest suspension bridge in the country still carrying road traffic. ⛺◑🚌(67)♣

Horsley

Lion & Lamb ✔

NE15 0NS

✪ 12-11 (10.30 Sun)

☎ (01661) 832952

Caledonian Deuchars IPA; Camerons Castle Eden Ale; Flowers IPA; Jennings Cumberland Ale; guest beers Ⓗ

Originally a farmhouse in 1718, built with stone from nearby Hadrian's Wall, it was converted into a coaching inn in 1744. A warning notice to 'Mind Ya Heed' is a reminder of the age of the building, with its low beamed ceiling and doorways. Wooden tables enhance the traditional ambience. Well patronised by locals and visitors, this establishment has an excellent reputation for good food. The large garden has fine views of the Tyne Valley. ⛰Q☺❀◑🚌(685)P

Langley

Carts Bog Inn

NE47 5NW (3 miles off A69 on A686 to Alston)

✪ 12-2.30 (not Mon), 5-11; 12-11 Sat; 12-10.30 Sun

☎ (01434) 684338

Beer range varies Ⓗ

You are assured of a warm welcome at this traditional, unspoilt country pub serving a discerning local community as well as travellers on the A686. The current building dates from 1730 and is built on the site of an ancient brewery (circa 1521). The name is derived from a steeply banked corner on the old road where on wet days the horse-drawn carts were invariably bogged down. A large, unusual open fire divides the two rooms. The walls proudly display pictures of bygone days including the nearby former local railway station, closed to passengers in 1930, now a tourist attraction called the Garden Station. ⛰Q❀◑P

Low Newton by the Sea

Ship Inn

Newton Square, NE66 3EL

✪ 11-11 summer; 11-3, 6-11 winter; 11-11 Sat; 12-10.30 Sun

☎ (01665) 576262

Beer range varies Ⓗ

An oasis in a wilderness, set among a row of whitewashed cottages around the village green and virtually on the beach. Despite its remote location the Ship is very busy at most times, even in winter. It is easier to access on foot by walking along the Northumberland coastline than by road as cars must use the village car park at the entrance to Low Newton and then walk down the hill to the village itself. Excellent guest ales come from local micro-breweries. ⛰Q❀◑

Morpeth

Tap & Spile

23 Manchester Street, NE61 1BH

✪ 12-2.30, 4.30-11; 12-11 Fri & Sat; 12-10.30 Sun

☎ (01670) 513894

Black Sheep Best Bitter; Caledonian Deuchars IPA; Everards Tiger; guest beers Ⓗ

An excellent local, popular with regulars and visitors alike. It has a busy front bar and quieter lounge to the rear. Eight handpumps offer a variety of ales, with local beers from High House Farm, Mordue, Northumberland and Wylam breweries often available. The cider is Weston's Old Rosie. Northumberland pipers play on Sunday lunchtimes. The outdoor smoking area is heated and partially covered. The pub is a recent local CAMRA award winner. Q⊞🚌♣♠⚡

Netherton

Star Inn ★

NE65 7HD

✪ 7.30-10 (11 Fri; 10.30 Sat); closed Mon

☎ (01669) 630238

Camerons Castle Eden Ale Ⓖ

Entering this gem —the only pub in Northumberland to appear in every issue of the Guide —is like entering the private living room of a big house. The bar area is basic with benches round the walls and the beer is served on gravity from the cellar at a hatch in the panelled entrance hall. The walls display the many awards the pub has received. Children are not allowed in the bar. Opening hours may vary, please ring to check. **QP**

Newbiggin by the Sea

Queens Head (Porters) ✔

7 High Street, NE64 6AT

✪ 9.45-midnight

☎ (01670) 817293

John Smith's Magnet; guest beers Ⓗ

Featuring in the CAMRA North East inventory of historic pub interiors, the original Edwardian layout of the pub has been retained with a public bar area, lounge area displaying many photographs of bygone Newbiggin, and snug to the rear. Outstanding features include the curved bar counter, bench seating, fireplace, etched windows and mosaic floors. The landlord sells competitively priced real ales and displays an ever-growing collection of guest beer pump clips, many from north eastern micro-breweries. All Newbiggin buses pass the door. 🚌♣♠

Norham

Mason's Arms

17 West Street, TD15 2LB

✪ 12-3, 7-11; 12-10.30

☎ (01289) 382326 🌐 tweed-sports.co.uk

Belhaven 80/-; Caledonian Deuchars IPA; guest beers Ⓗ

Situated at the opposite end of the village to the famous 12th-century castle, this traditional public bar features an attractive screen at the entrance, two fine coloured-glass ceiling panels, and an old William Younger & Co India Pale Ale mirror above the fireplace. The pub displays an eclectic collection of water jugs, fishing tackle, carpentry tools and photographs of local scenes in bygone times. Guest beers come from Greene King. The Tweed Cycle Way passes close by. (67)

Old Hartley

Delaval Arms

NE26 4RL (jct of A193/B1325 S of Seaton Sluice)
12-11 (10.30 Sun)
(0191) 2370489
Caledonian Deuchars IPA; guest beers
Multi-roomed Grade II listed building dating from 1748, with a listed WWI water storage tower behind the beer garden and great views up and down the Northumberland coast. Good quality, affordable meals complement the beer, with guest ales coming from local micros. To the left as you enter there is a room served through a hatch from the bar and to the right a room where children are welcome.
QP

Seahouses

Olde Ship Hotel

7-9 Main Street, NE68 7RD
11-11
(01665) 720200
Black Sheep Best Bitter; Courage Directors; Draught Bass; Greene King Ruddles County; Hadrian & Border Farne Island; Theakston Best Bitter; guest beers
Featuring in CAMRA's North East regional inventory, parts of the building date back to 1745. The Olde Ship has three bars including a cosy 1950s-style cabin bar with an abundance of maritime memorabilia. Always busy, the hostelry functions as a locals' bar, hotel and restaurant, offering a range of home-produced dishes. Situated by Seahouses harbour and handy for boat trips to the Farne Islands, plenty of trade ensures that the large range of beers is in top condition. QP

Seaton Sluice

Melton Constable

Beresford Road, NE26 4DA
12-11 (10.30 Sun)
(0191) 237741
Adnams Broadside; Theakston XB; Wells Bombardier
Large roadhouse facing the sea and overlooking the small harbour with several drinking areas and a separate dining space. The pub is named after the southern seat of Lord Hastings, a member of the local Delaval family. A popular quiz is held on Wednesday evening. Guest ales come from local micros.
P

Slaley

Travellers Rest

NE46 1TT (on B6306, 1 mile N of village)
12-11 (10.30 Sun)
(01434) 673231 1travellersrest.com
Black Sheep Best Bitter; guest beers
Licensed for over 150 years, this welcoming inn started life as a farmhouse in the 16th century. Living up to its name, it offers guests an excellent choice of beers, wonderful food and accommodation. The bar has a large open fire and stone walls, flag floors and comfortable furniture. An extensive choice of good food made with local produce is served in the bar and restaurant. Children are welcome and there is a safe play area beside the pub. QP

Stannington

Ridley Arms

NE61 6EL
11.30-11; 12-10.30 Sun
(01670) 789216
Black Sheep Best Bitter; guest beers
An excellent Fitzgerald pub with a multi-room interior, dating back to the 18th century. Eight handpumps serve guests from the north east as well as breweries countrywide, with Caledonian Deuchars IPA a popular choice. Renowned for its quality food made from local produce, meals are served all day and the pub is often busy, especially Sunday lunchtime. Ramps and widened doors allow good wheelchair access. There is a covered area outside for smokers. QP

Twice Brewed

Twice Brewed Inn

Military Road, Bardon Mill, NE47 7AN (on B6318)
11-11.30; 12-11.30 winter; 12-10.30
(01434) 344534 twicebrewedinn.co.uk
Twice Brewed Bitter; guest beers
This pub in the middle of nowhere has a surprisingly long list of facilities available to visitors. The inn is a rural transport interchange with several bus routes stopping here, and offers an IT suite with Internet connection for use by locals and visitors. There is full disabled access and staff are trained in sign language. Five real ales include a house beer Twice Brewed Bitter brewed by Yates Brewery, and guest beers often come from Scottish breweries. Due to its proximity to Hadrian's Wall it can be busy in summer.
Q

Warden

Boatside Inn

NE46 4SQ (off A69)
11-11; 12-10.30 Sun
(01434) 602233 boatsideinn.co.uk
Beer range varies
Excellent riverside country pub nestling between the river South Tyne and the wooden slopes of Warden Hill, close to Hadrian's Wall, and very popular with walkers, cyclists and tourists. Scenic woodland footpaths and bridleways surround the inn. Tasty home-cooked food is served lunchtimes and early evenings, all day Sunday. B&B and self-catering cottages are available.
(804)

Wark

Battlesteads Hotel

NE48 3LS
11-11; 12-10.30
(01434) 230209 battlesteads.com
Black Sheep Best Bitter; Durham Magus; Wylam Gold Tankard; guest beers
Traditional Northumberland farmhouse inn and restaurant close to Hadrian's Wall and National Park. The cosy bar has an open fire in winter and there is a new sunny conservatory within the secret walled garden. A Temperance hotel in the early 20th century, the pub continues to provide organic lemonade, dandelion & burdock and ginger beer, delicious if you are driving. Live folk music nights are hosted and excellent accommodation includes ground floor rooms with disabled access. P

Whitfield

Elks Head

NE47 8HD (on Haydon Bridge-Alston road)
12-11.30; 12-3.30, 6-11.30 winter
(01434) 345282
Allendale Golden Plover; guest beers
Country pub in a popular walking area where visitors are made very welcome. Originally it was the Blue Black Club, a private club for the Whitfield sporting estates, and the estate office is next door. The stone-walled bar is home to darts, pool and quoits teams, and a leek club. Excellent food is made with local produce, served in the dining room.
P

Wylam

Black Bull

Main Street, NE41 8AB
4 (12 Fri-Sun)-11
(01661) 853112 blackbull-wylam.co.uk
Wylam Gold; guest beers
Cheerful pub with a friendly landlord and staff located on the main street in Wylam, very popular with the locals. Regular theme nights are hosted and local home-cooked specialities feature in the restaurant. Nearby is Wylam Waggonway, a popular walk that passes George Stephenson's cottage. Voted Best Free House in North East 2007 by the Morning Advertiser.

Boathouse

Station Road, NE41 8HR
11-11 (midnight Sat); 12-10.30 Sun
(01661) 853431
Wylam Gold Tankard; guest beers
Friendly real ale emporium boasting 12 handpumps, offering a wide variety of guest ales from a range of breweries. Situated next to Wylam railway station, this classic two-room pub is a popular stopping off point for Whistle Stop travellers (see cannybevvy.co.uk for details). The brewery tap for Wylam, you will often find the brewers in here chatting to the locals. The pub is also renowned for quality Sunday lunches. Winner of several local CAMRA Pub of the Year awards.
P

Battlesteads Hotel, Wark.

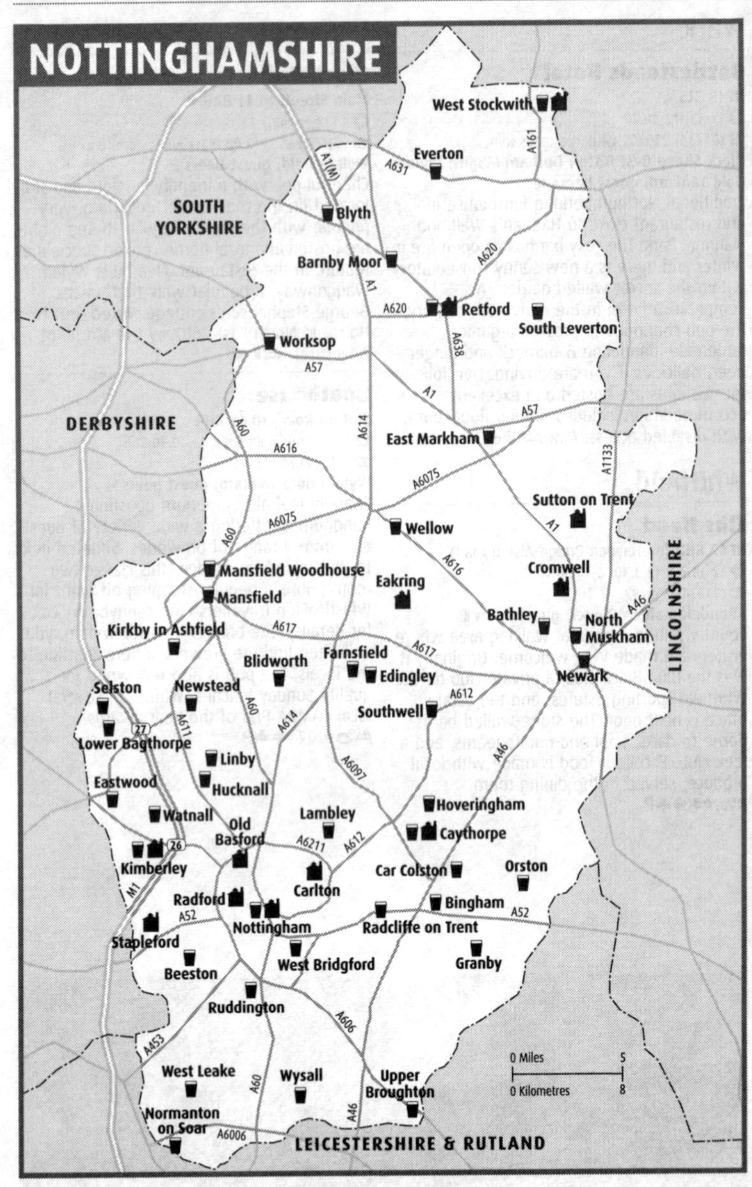

Barnby Moor

White Horse

Great North Road, DN22 8QS (on A638)
🕰 11 (12 Sun)-11
☎ (01777) 707721
Beer range varies Ⓗ
Attractive village pub at the side of the A638 with a large lounge, smaller public bar area and separate dining space. Up to six changing cask ales are available depending on the time of the year, most coming from local micro-breweries. The walls in the lounge bar are covered with paintings, some of the local Grove & Rufford Hunt which has its kennels across the road and meets at the pub every Boxing Day. ⌂Q❀◑▶⊟P

Bathley

Crown

Main Street, NG23 6DA (1 mile from A1 turn-off for Muskham)
🕰 11-3, 7-2am; 11-2am Fri-Sun
☎ (01636) 702305
Jennings Cumberland Ale; Marston's Burton Bitter; guest beer Ⓗ
Popular, unspoilt village pub at the heart of the community. Two well-kept ales are supported by a guest beer, with excellent food complementing the beer provision. Darts, dominoes and skittles are played. The pub regularly holds fund-raising events for charity. Outside, there is plenty of seating for summer drinking. Local attractions include Laxton Open Field Farming System and the Holocaust

Centre. Newark Castle and Southwell Minster and Racecourse are nearby. ⛫❀◑♣P⚟

Beeston

Malt Shovel ✔

1 Union Street, NG9 2LU
⏲ 11-11 (midnight Fri & Sat); 12-11 Sun
☎ (0115) 922 2320
Nottingham Rock Mild, Rock Bitter; guest beers ⊞
Just off the busy High Road, this one-room pub offers a friendly welcome. The modern interior uses furnishings and decor to create the feel of different drinking areas. Wooden floors, bright colours and comfortable leather sofas create a light, airy ambience with a cosy atmosphere. There is a good value food menu (no meals Sun eve), a quiz night on Wednesday and live music on Friday. A LocAle pub, committed to serving at least one beer from a local brewery. ⛫❀◑♿🚌♣●P⚟

Victoria Hotel

85 Dovecote Lane, NG9 1JG (off A6005 by station)
⏲ 10.30 (12 Sun)-11
☎ (0115) 925 4049 🌐 victoriabeeston.co.uk
Castle Rock Harvest Pale, Hemlock; Everards Tiger; guest beers ⊞
Buzzing Victorian architectural gem. This former CAMRA Nottingham Pub of the Year is popular with drinkers and diners alike. The multi-roomed layout includes a dining area, public bar and covered outside drinking space. Twelve beers are served including a local ale, mild, stout and two real ciders from regional and micro-brewers. Freshly-cooked food, with a wide vegetarian choice, is available all day. Regular music festivals are held, outside in summer. ⛫Q❀◑🛏♿⚌🚌●P

Bingham

Horse & Plough ✔

25 Long Acre, NG13 8AF
⏲ 11-11 (11.30 Fri & Sat); 12-11 Sun
☎ (01949) 839313 🌐 horseandploughbingham.com
Caledonian Deuchars IPA; Fuller's London Pride; Wells Bombardier; guest beers ⊞
Situated in the heart of a busy market town, this warm, friendly one-room free house was a former Methodist chapel and has a cottage-style interior and flagstone floor. Six cask ales are always available including three guests, with a 'try before you buy' policy. The first floor a la carte restaurant offers a seasonal menu and steak night on Tuesday. A fresh bar menu is served weekday lunchtimes and a traditional roast on Sunday. Local CAMRA Pub of the Year 2007. ◑♿⚌🚌

Blidworth

Black Bull

Main Street, NG21 0QH
⏲ 11-midnight (1am Fri & Sat); 12-midnight Sun
☎ (01623) 792291
Black Sheep Best Bitter ⊞
Three roomed beamed local, at least 400 years old. The public bar, with log-burning stove, lounge and snug, are all served from a central bar. Popular with locals, the pub has an outdoor skittles alley in frequent use, with visiting teams warmly welcomed. Parking can be difficult, but do make the effort to visit this hostelry. ⛫Q❀🛏🚌♣⚟

Blyth

Red Hart

Bawtry Road, S81 8HG
⏲ 12-midnight (11.30 Sun)
☎ (01909) 591221
Beer range varies ⊞
Attractive pub situated in the centre of the well-kept village of Blyth with separate lounge and bar areas and a reasonably-sized dining room. The walls in the lounge are decorated with photographs and paintings of the village. Regularly-changing guest ales come from several micro-breweries. Restaurant quality food is served at pub prices. ⛫Q❀◑🚌P

Car Colston

Royal Oak ✔

The Green, NG13 8JE
⏲ 11.30-3 (not Mon), 5.30-midnight; 11.30-midnight Fri; 1.30-midnight Sat; 12-10.30 Sun
☎ (01949) 20247
Jennings Cumberland Ale; Marston's Burton Bitter; Mansfield Cask; guest beer ⊞
Impressive country inn situated on England's largest village green. The two-room interior includes a lounge and restaurant on one side and bar with comfortable seating on the other. Note the bar's interesting brickwork ceiling – a legacy from the building's previous life as a hosiery factory. A good quality, traditional food menu is served lunchtimes and evenings. There is a skittle alley to the rear. The landlord is rightly proud of his 100 per cent record of appearance in the Guide. ⛫Q❀◑♿⛺♣P

Caythorpe

Black Horse

29 Main Street, NG14 7ED
⏲ 12-2.30, 5 (6 Sat)-11; closed Mon; 12-4, 7 (8 winter)-10.30 Sun
☎ (0115) 966 3520
Caythorpe Dover Beck, One Swallow; guest beers ⊞
This 18th-century free house has been in the same family for 37 years. It features a comfortable lounge, a gem of a snug bar with hatch servery, inglenook, bench seats, beams

INDEPENDENT BREWERIES

Alcazar Old Basford
Castle Rock Nottingham
Caythorpe Caythorpe
Full Mash Stapleford
Grafton Retford
Holland Kimberley
Idle West Stockwith
Magpie Nottingham
Mallard Carlton
Maypole Eakring
Milestone Cromwell
Nottingham Radford
Springhead Sutton-on-Trent

and wood panelling. A private dining room is available for dinner parties. Bar food is popular, mostly cooked to order using fresh ingredients (booking essential). The home of Caythorpe Brewery, guest beers are often from other local micros. ⌂Q❀◐◑⊟♣P

East Markham

Queen's Hotel

High Street, NG22 0RE
12-11 (10.30 Sun)
☎ (01777) 870288
Adnams Bitter; guest beer ⊞
One of two pubs in East Markham selling cask ales, this cosy house has a warm, friendly atmosphere enhanced by an open fire in winter. A single bar serves the lounge, pool room and dining area. Food, ranging from hot and cold snacks to full home-cooked meals, is available Tuesday-Sunday. There is a large garden area at the rear where you can enjoy a drink on a warm summer's day.
⌂Q❀◐◑⊟♣P

Eastwood

Three Tuns

58 Three Tuns Road, NG16 3EJ (near fire station)
11-midnight (1am Fri & Sat)
☎ (01773) 713377
Black Sheep Best Bitter; Caledonian Deuchars IPA; Everards Tiger; guest beers ⊞
This large pub has a modern feel, with a historic past. Located in the heart of DH Lawrence country, it featured as the Moon & Stars' in his novel Sons and Lovers. The central bar has six handpumps dispensing beers from larger regional brewers and occasional micros. Several large screen TVs and a pool table cater for sports fans. Visitors to the spacious gardens may sometimes spot the pub tortoise – the landlord's pride and joy. ❀◐◑♿⊟♣P⁄–

Edingley

Old Reindeer

Main Street, NG22 8BE (off A614 towards Southwell)
11 (12 Sun)-11
☎ (01623) 882253
Marston's Pedigree, Old Empire; guest beers ⊞
Traditional 18th-century village pub, modernised inside to provide a comfortable dining space and cosy bar area without losing the essence of a country pub. With six real ales in tip-top condition usually on offer and high quality food, this is a popular pub, and games and activities are organised for regulars. There is an attractive garden for families and B&B accommodation. A pub for beer connoisseurs, this is one to savour. ⌂Q❀⊨◐◑⊟♿⊟♣P⁄–

Everton

Blacksmith's Arms

Church Street, DN10 5BQ
10-midnight
☎ (01777) 817281
John Smith's Bitter; Theakston Old Peculier; guest beers ⊞
A regular winner of local CAMRA Pub of the Season awards, this 18th-century free house stands at the heart of the village. Drinking areas include the locals' bar with its original tiled floor and the games room (formerly the old smithy). The comfortable lounge area leads to a large restaurant where the emphasis is on fresh, home-cooked food (booking is advisable). Outside is a Mediterranean-style garden. En-suite accommodation is available in the converted stables. ⌂Q⊱❀◐◑⊟♿⊟P

Farnsfield

Plough Inn

Main Street, NG22 8EA (off A614 towards Southwell)
11-11
☎ (01623) 882265
Jennings Cocker Hoop; guest beers ⊞
A comfortable pub for a quiet drink, popular with locals and visitors. The interior includes a snug with comfy armchairs next to the fire, a bar and open plan lounge, and a separate dining room. A wide range of traditional pub games is available. Adequate parking is provided. ⌂Q❀◐◑⊟♿⊟♣P⁄–

Red Lion

Main Street, NG22 8EY
11-3, 6-11; 12-3, 7-11 Sun
☎ (01623) 882304
Marston's Mansfield Cask, Pedigree; guest beers ⊞
Friendly, family run local, where the landlord is often found playing dominoes with the regulars. The open plan lounge, divided by pillars, has a cosy feel, with seating around the window area and plenty of tables. Good home-cooked food is served in the restaurant. An ever-changing range of guest ales is always in first class condition.
Q❀◐◑♿⊟♣P⁄–

Granby

Marquis of Granby

Dragon Street, NG13 9PN
11.30-2.30 (not Mon), 5.30-midnight; 11.30-midnight Fri-Sun
☎ (01949) 859517
Brewster's Hophead, Marquis; guest beers ⊞
Believed to be the original Marquis of Granby, dating back to 1760 or earlier, this small, two-roomed pub is now the brewery tap for Brewster's Brewery. York stone floors complement the yew bar tops and wood-beamed rooms, period wallpaper features throughout and the lounge has a welcoming open fire in winter months. Guest beers complement the Brewster's range and come from micros, usually including a mild, stout or porter. All food is home-made and sourced locally. Local CAMRA Pub of the Year 2008.
⌂Q❀◐◑⊟♿♣

Hoveringham

Reindeer Inn

Main Street, NG14 7JR SK699469
12-2, 5-midnight; 12-midnight Sat & Sun

☎ (0115) 966 3629
Black Sheep Best Bitter; Castle Rock Harvest Pale; Caythorpe Stout Fellow; guest beers Ⓗ
Genuine free house in a pleasant country village with traditional beams and a log fire for cold winter nights. A central servery divides the bar and restaurant areas of the pub. Good home-cooked food includes vegetarian and vegan choices. The outside drinking area overlooks a cricket pitch. The local Caythorpe stout replaces Guinness on the bar. ⩕Q✿◐⇌(Thurgaton)♣P⁄

Hucknall

Green Dragon ✔
Watnall Road, NG15 7JW
✪ 12-11 (11.30 Thu-Sat)
☎ (0115) 964 0941
Beer range varies Ⓗ
Situated just out of the town centre, this traditional hostelry offers five ever-changing hand-pulled beers. The airy open plan interior comprises a lounge with raised area for dining, games area with pool and darts, and a ground floor dining room available for parties and functions. This busy pub hosts a quiz night on Wednesday, karaoke on Thursday, pool knockout on Tuesday and darts league on Monday. ✿◐♿⇌⊖🚌♣P⁄

Kimberley

Nelson & Railway ✔
12 Station Road, NG16 2NR
✪ 11-midnight; 12-11 Sun
☎ (0115) 938 2177 🌐 nelsonandrailway.co.uk
Greene King H&H Bitter, H&H Olde Trip, Ruddles County; guest beers Ⓗ
Formerly the brewery tap for Hardys & Hansons, this popular pub lies in the shadow of the defunct brewery buildings. Beers are mainly from the Greene King portfolio but guest ales also appear. Full of character, this friendly local is renowned for its good quality food and accommodation. ✿🛏◐♿🚌♣P⁄

Stag Inn ✔
67 Nottingham Road, NG16 2NB
✪ 5 (1.30 Sat)-11; 12-10.30 Sun
☎ (0115) 938 3151
Adnams Bitter; Marston's Pedigree; Taylor Landlord; guest beer Ⓗ
A regular Guide entry, this two-room inn has low wood beams adorned by old photographs of Shipstones, the former brewery that once owned the pub. Old-style mechanical slot machines feature in one room and traditional games including table skittles are played. The spacious rear garden includes a children's play area. The pub holds an annual beer festival each late-May bank holiday weekend, raising money for charity. Q✿♿🚌♣P⁄

Kirkby in Ashfield

Ashfields ✔
Sutton Road, NG17 8HX
✪ 11.30-11.30
☎ (01623) 557943
Palmer Best Bitter; Shepherd Neame Spitfire; Wells Bombardier Ⓗ
Large pub with an imposing facade. Inside, the open-plan interior includes an L-shaped bar, dedicated dining area, drinking space in front of the bar and a public bar area with games. An imaginative choice of guest beers comes from Scottish & Newcastle's list and varies frequently. TV is evident but not too intrusive, except when major sporting fixtures are shown live. ✿◐🚌♣P⁄

Lambley

Woodlark
Church Street, NG4 4QB
✪ 12-3, 5.30-11; 12-6, 7-11 Sun
☎ (0115) 931 2535
Black Sheep Best Bitter; Fuller's London Pride; Taylor Landlord; guest beers Ⓗ
This delightful red-brick village inn serves a local ale and is mercifully free of electronic machines. The bare brick and beamed bar is welcoming and dog friendly. It has a justifiable reputation for good home cooking and booking is recommended. A popular downstairs steak bar is also open on Fri and Sat evenings until 9pm. Folk music nights are held every other Mon.
⩕Q✿◐🀫🚌(7,61)♣🍎P⁄

Linby

Horse & Groom ✔
Main Street, NG15 8AE
✪ 12-11 (10.30 Sun)
☎ (0115) 963 2219
Greene King IPA, Old Speckled Hen; Theakston Mild; Wells Bombardier; guest beers Ⓗ
Charming and unspoilt village pub dating back to 1800. This multi-roomed establishment is Grade II listed and has an inglenook in the public bar, a snug and roaring open fires. The Green Room welcomes families. Fine food is available at lunchtime from an extensive and varied menu. Evening dining is on Friday and Saturday only. There is a conservatory and the extensive garden has a children's play area.
⩕Q♉✿◐🀫🚌(141)♣P⁄

Lower Bagthorpe

Dixies Arms
School Road, NG16 5HF (1½ miles from M1 jct 27)
✪ 12-11
☎ (01773) 810505
Greene King Abbot; Theakston Best Bitter; guest beer Ⓗ
Built in the late 1700s, this pub offers a friendly welcome to all. Locals and visitors alike can be found warming themselves around the real fires in the public rooms, playing darts or dominoes, or gossiping in the snug. Live music plays on Saturday, a quiz is held on Sunday. It is a haven for real ale drinkers. ⩕✿🀫⛺🚌♣P⁄

Shepherds Rest
Wansley Lane, NG16 5HF (2 miles from M1 jct 27)
✪ 12-midnight (10.30 Sun)
☎ (01773) 811337
Greene King Abbot; Wells Bombardier; guest beers Ⓗ

In an idyllic countryside setting, this traditional country pub, dating back to the 1700s, is reputed to be haunted. It has an extensive garden area with numerous benches and a children's play area. Take your freshly prepared, home-cooked food into the garden if you wish, or enjoy the ambience of the interior with exposed oak beams, flagstone floors and open fires. Home-cooked food is served every day of the week.
♨❀◑⊡🚌♣P⊱

Mansfield

Bold Forester ✔

Botany Avenue, NG18 5NF (on A38 ½ mile from town centre)
⊙ 11-11 (midnight Fri & Sat); 12-11.30 Sun
☎ (01623) 623970
Greene King IPA, Ruddles County, Old Speckled Hen, Abbot; guest beers Ⓗ
Large open plan pub with split levels including a dining area, small snug and bar area with pool table, with partitions creating an impression of privacy. Background music is not intrusive and the TV can be avoided. Weekly quizzes, run by the landlord, are popular. Live music plays on Sunday. A beer festival is held on St George's Day and another festival features some time during the year. With excellent meals served all day, this is one of Mansfield's flagship real ale pubs.
❀◑♿≋●P⊱

Court House ✔

Market Place, NG18 1HX
⊙ 9-11 (midnight Fri & Sat)
☎ (01623) 412720
Greene King Old Speckled Hen, Abbot; Marston's Burton Bitter, Pedigree; guest beers Ⓗ
A first class conversion typical of Wetherspoon's. The building was the former Town Court House and features a number of court house style rooms. A good selection of local guest beers is well kept by the current manager. Smoking is permitted on the forecourt. The pub is a former CAMRA branch Pub of the Season. Q☕◑♿≋🚌●⊱

Railway Inn

9 Station Street, NG18 1EF
⊙ 10.30-11.30 (8 Tue); 11.30-6 Sun
☎ (01623) 623086
Hop Back Special; Kelham Island Easy Rider; guest beers Ⓗ
The only traditional real ale pub in town, this is a popular community meeting place. Home-cooked food is of exceptional value, served daily at lunchtime. There is a small garden to the side and a heated smoking area in the courtyard. The real ales change constantly and there is a good selection of bottled beers available. The pub was saved from the threat of closure by the current owners, who offer a warm welcome, fine beer and good food.
◑⊡♿≋🚌♣

Widow Frost ✔

Leeming Street, NG18 1NB
⊙ 9-midnight (1am Fri & Sat)
☎ (01623) 666790
Greene King IPA, Abbot; guest beers Ⓗ
Spacious open plan lounge/bar with plenty of seating and tables. An area at the rear is used mainly for dining but food can be eaten at any of the tables. A typical Wetherspoon's menu is on offer and guest beers are from the Wetherspoon's list. Large TV screens show sporting events. Q◑♿≋🚌●

Mansfield Woodhouse

Greyhound

82 High Street, NG19 8BD
⊙ 12-11 (midnight Fri & Sat); 12-10.30 Sun
☎ (01623) 464403
Caledonian Deuchars IPA; Greene King Old Speckled Hen, Abbot; Sharp's Cornish Coaster; Theakston Mild; guest beers Ⓗ
This stone built pub, reputedly dating from the 17th century, has featured in the Guide for more than 15 years. Located near the old market square, this popular, friendly hostelry has two rooms: a lively tap room with pool table and traditional pub games, plus a quiet, comfortable lounge. Five real ales are always on offer. Quiz nights are held on Monday and Wednesday. Q❀⊡♿≋🚌♣P⊱

Newark

Castle & Falcon

10 London Road, NG24 1TW
⊙ 7-midnight (1am Thu); 12-3, 7-1am Fri & Sat; 12-3, 7-midnight Sun
☎ (01636) 703513
John Smith's Bitter; guest beers Ⓗ
Friendly local on the outskirts of the town centre. Pub games are very popular here with some combination of darts, pool, skittles and dominoes taking place most evenings both in the bar and the spacious lounge. An interesting range of sporting memorabilia is displayed alongside a comprehensive collection of Mackenzie Thorpe prints. The guest beers are ever changing from an imaginative and varied portfolio. Newark CAMRA Pub of the Year 2008.
❀⊡≋(Newark Castle)🚌♣⊱

Fox & Crown

4-6 Appletongate, NG24 1JY
⊙ 10.30-11 (midnight Fri & Sat); 12-11 Sun
☎ (01636) 605820
Bateman XB; Castle Rock Sherriff's Tipple, Harvest Pale, Hemlock; Everards Tiger; guest beers Ⓗ
A Castle Rock pub with up to five guest beers, as well as a range of flavoured vodkas, malt whiskies and Belgian bottled beers. A LocAle pub, it offers at least one beer from a local brewery. The food menu offers a decent selection of food, reasonably priced and sourced locally. The pub is mainly open plan but with several cubby holes. Live entertainment is hosted on every second Thursday plus occasional Sundays.
◑♿≋(Castle/Northgate)

Vine

117 Barnbygate, NG24 1QZ
⊙ 3 (12 Sat & Sun)-11.30
☎ (01636) 704333
Springhead Liberty, Roaring Meg; guest beers Ⓗ

No-frills traditional pub owned by the Springhead Brewery. Mention your interest in real ale and you will be assured a warm welcome from Paul, the landlord, who is a CAMRA member. To the front is the public bar, frequented by colourful characters. To the side is a small games room and at the rear, a lounge with dartboard. A heated area in the rear yard accommodates smokers.
❀⊟≹(Northgate)♣⁻

Newstead

Station Hotel

Station Road, NG15 0BZ (next to station)
✪ 11-3, 5-11.30; 11-3, 7-midnight Sat; 12-3, 7-11 Sun
☎ (01623) 753294
Oakwell Old Tom Mild, Barnsley Bitter Ⓗ
Enjoying a new lease of life with the advent of the Robin Hood Line from Nottingham to Worksop, this traditional railway station pub is steeped in atmosphere. Once part of a busy colliery village, it retains a community feel. The locals are quick to make visitors welcome and the landlady and staff greet you as old friends. Two beers are available from Oakwell Brewery, always in tip-top condition. With a small public bar and several rooms available for private functions and meetings, this is a favourite CAMRA branch meeting place.
♨Q❀⊟≹♣⁻

Normanton-on-Soar

Plough

Main Street, LE12 5HB
✪ 11.30-11; 12-10.30 Sun
☎ (01509) 842228
🌐 probablythebestpubsintheworld.co.uk
Draught Bass; Greene King Abbot; Jennings Cumberland Ale; guest beer Ⓗ
Charming, picturesque, riverside inn, tastefully renovated in a sympathetic contemporary style. Primarily a food pub, it has a snug area with a real fire to enjoy drinks away from the main dining room and open plan bar. The food menu includes a wide choice of home-cooked meals. Extensive beer gardens sweep down to the River Soar where there are moorings for boats. A function room is available for private parties. ♨❀◐♿⊟(R5)P⁻

North Muskham

Muskham Ferry

Ferry Lane, NG23 6HB (just off A1)
✪ 12-11 (10.30 Sun)
☎ (01636) 704943
Beer range varies Ⓗ
One of Nottinghamshire's hidden gems, this is a welcoming Trent riverside pub. Originally the ferryman's house, it became a pub in the 1850s. It offers a choice of three beers, one from a local micro, and excellent value food, served in the bar or restaurant. A terraced beer garden overlooks moorings for visiting river craft. A large car park, good sized function room and 30 pegs for fishing are available. The village church and nature reserve are close by. ❀◐⊟(37)♣P⁻

Nottingham: Central

Canalhouse

48-52 Canal Street, NG1 7EH
✪ 11-11 (midnight Thu; 1am Fri & Sat); 11-10.30 Sun
☎ (0115) 955 5060
Castle Rock Harvest Pale, Preservation; guest beers Ⓗ
This listed three-storey LocAle pub has a surprise. The canal basin runs through the inside, traversed by wooden walkways. The building used to house a canal museum before conversion into this attractive open-plan pub. One floor doubles as a function room. The canal-side decked patio is very popular in summer, half-covered and heated for overcast evenings. Food is available daily, ranging from simple to exotic choices.
❀◐♿≹⊖(Station St)⊟⁻

Kean's Head

46 St Mary's Gate, NG1 1QA (opp St Mary's Church)
✪ 10.30 (10 Sat)-midnight (12.30am Fri & Sat); 12-10.30 Sun
☎ (0115) 947 4052
Bateman Valiant; Castle Rock Harvest Pale, Preservation; guest beers Ⓗ
Cosy one-room pub opposite the imposing St Mary's Church in the historic Lace Market district. Named in honour of the 19th-century actor Edmund Kean, it is often busy at weekends and attracts a diverse and varied clientele. Owned by the Castle Rock group, it offers inventive, freshly prepared food from an ever-changing menu. Three guest beers are usually available, often from Castle Rock's Natural Selection series. Occasional live music and themed brewery nights are held.
◐♿≹⊖(Lace Market)⊟

King William IV

6 Eyre Street, Sneinton, NG2 4PB
✪ 12 (11 Fri & Sat)-11; 12-10.30 Sun
☎ (0115) 958 9864
Oakham Bishops Farewell, JHB; guest beers Ⓗ
Nicknamed the King Billy, this cosy Victorian gem nestling on the edge of town is just a stone's throw from the Ice Arena. A family-run free house that oozes charm and character, it is a haven for real ale drinkers, with a choice of seven micro-brewery ales from near and far. Occasional live music and unusual televised sports feature. A fine selection of rolls is available. This is one pub not to miss on a visit to Nottingham. ❀♿≹⊟♣⁻

Lincolnshire Poacher

161-163 Mansfield Road, NG1 3FR (on A60 N of city centre)
✪ 11-11 (midnight Thu-Sat); 12-11 Sun
☎ (0115) 941 1584
Bateman XB, Valiant; Castle Rock Harvest Pale, Sheriff's Tipple; guest beers Ⓗ
Atmospheric two-roomer with a conservatory and enclosed patio to the rear. This is a true drinkers' pub —an institution for the real ale fraternity. The range of beers from micro-breweries is ever changing, always including a local ale, mild, stout or porter and cider. Popular home-cooked food uses locally sourced fresh ingredients. Entertainment includes live music on Sunday night, brewery evenings and micro-brewery trips. All NCT

Brown, Purple, Yellow and Lime Line buses pass the door. ❀◑♿🚌♣🍎⁄

Newshouse

123 Canal Street, NG1 7HB

⏲ 12-11 (midnight Fri & Sat)

☎ (0115) 950 2419

Castle Rock Sheriffs Tipple; Everards Tiger; guest beers Ⓗ

Basic, friendly, two-roomed Castle Rock local. At one time the national news used to be read out to customers, hence the name. Memorabilia from BBC Radio Nottingham and the local Evening Post adorns the walls. Look for the brewery names etched into ceramic wall tiles in the public bar where sport is shown on a large screen or TV. Darts and bar billiards are played. Up to eight cask beers always include a mild and local ale.
❀◑⊟⇌⊖(Station St)🚌♣🍎⁄

Olde Trip to Jerusalem ★ ✔

1 Brewhouse Yard, NG1 6AD (below castle)

⏲ 10-11 (midnight Sat); 12-11 Sun

☎ (0115) 947 3171 🌐 triptojerusalem.com

Greene King XX Mild, IPA, H&H Olde Trip, Ruddles County, Old Speckled Hen, Abbot; guest beers Ⓗ

The world famous Olde Trip to Jerusalem is reputed to date from 1189. It has a number of rooms, some cut out of the castle rock. Upstairs the Rock lounge is home to the Cursed Galleon. A museum room houses a tapestry depicting Nottingham's history. A covered courtyard and a seated pavement drinking area with waitress service are available Easter to August. The top bar can be reserved for private functions. Cellar tours are by appointment. Children welcome until 7pm.
⛰Q❀◑⊟⇌⊖(Station St)🚌♣⁄

Salutation Inn

Houndsgate, Maid Marian Way, NG1 7AA

⏲ 11-midnight (2am Fri & Sat)

☎ (0115) 988 1948 🌐 myspace.com/thesalutationnottingham

Beer range varies Ⓗ

Steeped in history, this lively 17th-century inn with oak beams and stone floor is a favourite venue with young and old. Regular live rock music plays upstairs while downstairs there are quiet snugs for drinking and conversation. The pub sells national, local and micro-brewery beers and a Hallowe'en beer festival is an annual highlight. Good food is based on local produce cooked on the premises. The labyrinth of caves under the pub is reputed to be haunted. ⛰♉❀◑⊖(Market Sq)🚌🍎⁄

Sir John Borlase Warren

1 Ilkeston Road, Canning Circus, NG7 3GD

⏲ 11-11.30 (midnight Fri & Sat); 12-11 Sun

☎ (0115) 947 4247

Everards Sunchaser, Tiger; Greene King IPA; Taylor Landlord; guest beers Ⓗ

A short hop on the bus uphill from the city centre, this comfortable and friendly pub makes an excellent meeting place. Although open plan, it has four distinct areas plus the bar with cosy seating. The original artwork decorating the walls is for sale. Good food, usually sourced locally, is served lunchtimes and evenings. In summer, the outside seating is a real find. Q❀◑🚌⁄

Vat & Fiddle

12-14 Queen's Bridge Road, NG2 1NB

⏲ 11-11 (midnight Fri & Sat); 12-11 Sun

☎ (0115) 985 0611

Castle Rock Harvest Pale, Hemlock, Elsie Mo, Preservation; guest beers Ⓗ

Opposite the railway station, the Castle Rock brewery tap is a true drinkers' pub, offering seven guest beers, always including a local ale and a mild, mainly from micros, as well as a real cider. Home-cooked food is served at lunchtime including the popular roast dinner on Sunday and chilli on Saturday. There is a pleasant patio area at the front with attractive flower tubs. You can enjoy an afternoon folk session on the second Sunday of the month and gypsy jazz on the last.
Q❀◑♿⇌⊖(Station St)🚌🍎⁄

Nottingham: East

Bread & Bitter

153 Woodthorpe Drive, Mapperley, NG3 5JL

⏲ 10-11 (midnight Fri & Sat); 11-11 Sun

☎ (0115) 960 7641

Bateman Valiant; Castle Rock Harvest Pale, Preservation; Everards Tiger; Thornbridge Jaipur; guest beers Ⓗ

Brand new pub from Castle Rock built on the premises of the old Judge's bakery on Mapperley Top. The original baker's ovens are still embedded in an inside wall, giving the place a warm and welcoming feel. The pub's name was voted for in a competition run by the local newspaper. Food is all home cooked and varies frequently or look for the specials board. Up to 12 beers, always including a local ale and a mild, are available along with an extensive foreign bottled beer list.
Q❀◑♿🚌⁄

Nottingham: North

Bar Deux

2 Clumber Avenue, Sherwood Rise, NG5 1AP
(behind Clarendon College)

⏲ 5-11 (11.30 Fri & Sat); 4-11 Sun

☎ (0115) 985 6724 🌐 hoteldeux.com

Bateman XB; Everards Tiger; Oakham Bishops Farewell; Whim Arbor Light Ⓗ

Two venues in one, this is a friendly, popular and pleasant three-room hotel-style bar, with live music playing in the larger Guitar Lounge. Note that this bar is generally only open in the evening but opening hours may extend during the summer months when the large lawns and outside drinking area can be used. Occasional admission charges are made for entry into the live performance area. Families are welcome and the venue is available for private functions and conferences.
Q❀⊟🚌♣P⁄

Chestnut Tree

482 Mansfield Road, Sherwood, NG5 2EL

⏲ 11-11 (midnight Fri & Sat); 12-11 Sun

☎ (0115) 9856388

Nottingham Rock Bitter; guest beers Ⓗ

Recently rebuilt on the site of a former hotel on the south side of Sherwood, this open-plan community pub has a friendly and comfortable atmosphere. The pub is a supporter of the LocAle scheme, always offering at least one local brewery beer, and serves four ever-changing SIBA guest beers. A weekly quiz, regular live music and multi-screens showing Setanta and Sky Sports cater for the locals. Honest, good-value traditional pub food is served. ❀◑♿P⅟

Fox & Crown

33 Church Street, Basford, NG6 0GA

12-midnight

☎ (0115) 942 2002 alcazarbrewery.co.uk

Alcazar Ale, New Dawn, Brush, Nottingham Nog, Vixens Vice, Windjammer IPA, seasonal beers; guest beers H

The excellent Alcazar brewery tap is a pleasant, spacious pub serving at least six Alcazar beers and a range of Alcazar bottled beers, also available to buy online. The patio to the rear is a pleasant place for outdoor drinking in summer. The pub is renowned for its excellent Thai food. A large mural of Robin Hood in Sherwood Forest painted by a local artist on the wall outside makes this pub hard to miss. ❀◑♿⊖(Basford)🚌(69)♣P⅟

Gladstone ✔

45 Loscoe Road, Carrington, NG5 2AW (off A60)

5 (3 Fri, 12 Sat)-11 (11.30 Thu-Sat); 12-11 Sun

☎ (0115) 912 9994

Caledonian Deuchars IPA; Fuller's London Pride; Greene King Abbot; Taylor Landlord; guest beers H

Two-room back street pub in the middle of a Victorian terrace. Memorabilia is on display in the public bar, and the TV shows sporting events. The lounge is pleasantly decorated with a homely atmosphere: cluttered with old bottles, brass ornaments and classic pictures. A shelf of books is available for customers to peruse. The Carrington Folk Club has been meeting in a room upstairs on a Wednesday night for the last 25 years. A LocAle pub, it always stocks at least one beer from a local brewery. ❀🂠🚌♣⅟

Horse & Groom ✔

462 Radford Road, Basford, NG7 7EA

11-11 (11.30 Fri & Sat)

☎ (0115) 970 3777 horseandgroombasford.com

Caledonian Deuchars IPA; Fuller's London Pride; guest beers H

The former Shipstone's Brewery stands just a few yards south of this popular pub. Access is via steps up to the front door, with disabled access available on request. The small bar area accommodates nine handpumps serving mainly micro-brewery beers, at least one a local ale and one a mild. The split-level pub has several distinct areas and a function room. On Monday night there is a quiet quiz and backgammon club. ⋒◐⊖(Shipstone St)🚌

Nottingham: South

Globe

152 London Road, NG2 3BQ

11.30 (11 Sat)-11; 12-10.30 Sun

☎ (0115) 986 6881 theglobenottingham.com

Nottingham EPA, Legend; guest beers H

Light, airy, popular pub near Nottingham's cricket, football and rugby grounds. Cold snacks are served on match days only. Sport features regularly on several large screens. Six handpumps serve ales mainly from micro-breweries with Nottingham beers usually available. Ask about the CAMRA discount. An upstairs function room has room for up to 100 people with catering facilities available. ≹🚌P⅟

Nottingham: West

Plough

17 St Peters Street, Radford, NG7 3EN

12-11

☎ (0115) 970 2615

Nottingham Rock Mild, Extra Pale Ale, Rock Bitter, Legend, Supreme; guest beers H

This popular back street local is the brewery tap for the Nottingham Brewery, situated at the back of the pub. A quiz night with free chilli is held on Thursday evening. The TV in the bar is turned on for sporting events only. Sword dancers practise in the upstairs function room and occasionally perform in the pub itself. Wireless Internet access is available at all times. ⋒❀◑🂠🚌(28,30)♣P⅟

Orston

Durham Ox

Church Street, NG13 9NS

12-3, 6-11 (not Mon); 11.30-11 Sat; 12-3, 7-10.30 Sun

☎ (01949) 850059

Fuller's London Pride; Greene King IPA; Marston's Mansfield Cask; Wells Bombardier H

A delightful pub for locals and visitors alike, situated opposite the village church. Outside, there are hitching rails for horses and ferrets. The large but cosy bar area features many equine pictures and prints, reflecting the landlady's interest in the local area. No hot meals are served but delicious filled rolls can be made to order. Regular well-attended charity fund-raising events are held at the pub all year round. An attractive garden and outdoor drinking space are popular in summer. Q♉❀◐♿♣P⅟

Radcliffe-on-Trent

Horse Chestnut ✔

49 Main Road, NG12 2BE

11-11 (11.30 Fri & Sat); 12-11 Sun

☎ (0115) 933 1994 horsechestnutradcliffe.com

Bateman XB; Castle Rock Harvest Pale; Fuller's London Pride; guest beers H

Totally refurbished in 2006 with a smart 1920s style decor, this pub was previously called the Cliffe Inn. The impressive interior has a separate library area furnished with sumptuous leather seating —even the toilets are worth a visit. Eight real ales include a local beer and ever-changing guests. The food menu features imaginative home-cooked meals made with local ingredients. Quiz night is Thursday and on Monday there is a curry night in winter and a barbecue in summer. ❀◑♿≹🚌P⅟

Retford

Dominie Cross ✔

Grove Street, DN22 6LA

11-3, 5-11, 11-midnight Sat & Sun

☎ (01777) 704441

Greene King Abbot; Marston's Pedigree; Shepherd Neame Spitfire; guest beers H

This former car showroom, garage and Netto supermarket is another Wetherspoon's Lloyds No 1 Bar, attractively decorated with old photographs of Retford on the walls. There is a choice of seating areas, from quiet little corners to a raised area commanding a good view of the bar. Smoking is permitted in a heated area outside. The main Retford Market Square and newly refurbished bus station are close by.

Galway Arms ✔

Bridgegate, DN22 7UZ

10-1am

☎ (01777) 702446

Beer range varies H

Close to Retford Market, this is a fine example of a typical olde worlde English inn, with a pleasant atmosphere and friendly service. Divided into three areas with two bars, the public bar has two large plasma TVs showing major sporting events. The lounge area is more peaceful or there is the quaint snug with room for up to 12 people. Food is served at lunchtime and early evening. P

Rum Runner

Wharf Road, DN22 6EN (by fire station)

12-11

☎ (01777) 860788

Beer range varies H

Formerly home to the now closed Broadstone Brewery, the Rum Runner makes a welcome return to the Guide after a two-year absence. The interior includes a long room warmed by a real fire and a second room, formerly the restaurant, with its own serving hatch through to the bar. A quiz night is held on Wed as well as frequent music nights. Mini beer festivals are a regular feature. Large enclosed beer garden. Q♣P

Ruddington

Three Crowns

23 Easthorpe Street, NG11 6LB

12-3 (11 Sat), 5-11; 12-10.30 Sun

☎ (0115) 921 3226 nottinghamthai.co.uk

Adnams Bitter; Fullers London Pride; Nottingham EPA, Rock Mild; guest beers H

Smart, modern, popular single-bar village local known as the Top House because of its roof-top chimneys. Regular beer festivals are held, often in conjunction with another village local. The well-respected Luk Pra Tor Restaurant is at the rear of the pub, open Tue-Sat evenings only (booking advisable). Handy for walkers in the nearby country park.

Selston

Horse & Jockey

Church Lane, NG16 6FB SK459535

12-4, 7-11; 12-3, 7-10.30 Sun

☎ (01773) 781012

Greene King Abbot; Taylor Landlord; G **guest beers** H

Friendly village local dating back to 1664, reputed to be haunted, with a main bar, snug and lounge with iron range. Flagstone floors, open fires and low-beamed ceilings create a cosy feeling throughout. You are welcome to play pool or a selection of pub games. Up to eight real ales and a cider are available at all times. Winner of several local CAMRA awards and Nottinghamshire Pub of the Year 2004. Q(90)♣P

South Leverton

Plough

Town Street, DN22 0BT (opp village hall)

10-1am (midnight Sun)

☎ (01427) 880323

Greene King Ruddles County; guest beers H

The locals will make you feel very welcome at this small, friendly, community pub opposite the village hall, which also houses the local post office. Some of the seating appears to be old church pews. There certainly cannot be many pubs where you can have a pint and buy your stamps at the same time. A recent winner of a local CAMRA Pub of the Season award, this is a true gem. Q♣P

Southwell

Old Coach House

69 Easthorpe, NG25 0HY

5 (4 Fri; 12 Sat)-11; 12-10.30 Sun

☎ (01636) 813289

Beer range varies H

Seventeenth-century free house, close to the Southwell minster and racecourse. A traditional pub with three main drinking areas and three real fires, six handpumps serve regularly-changing beers from regional and local micros. Pub games and a large selection of board games are played. The bijou patio is a popular suntrap. Quiz night is Sunday. (101)♣

Upper Broughton

Golden Fleece

Main Street, LE14 3BG

12-11 (10.30 Sun)

☎ (01664) 822262

Taylor Landlord; guest beers H

Large, attractive pub situated just off the main Nottingham to Melton road (A606). A dining pub, the spacious interior has a small area for drinkers and a larger dining space and conservatory. The wide and varied menu receives very good reports locally. A guest ale often comes from a micro-brewery and occasional beer festivals are hosted. ♣P

Watnall

Queens Head

40 Main Road, NG16 1HT

12-11.20

☎ (0115) 938 6774

Adnams Broadside; Everards Tiger, Original; Greene King Old Speckled Hen; Wells Bombardier; guest beers Ⓗ
Reputedly haunted, this 17th-century rural gem has a lounge/dining area, a small snug hidden behind the bar and an area where locals congregate. Fittings around the bar are original and old photographs adorn the walls. Good home-cooked food is served.
Q(331)P

Wellow

Olde Red Lion

Eakring Road, NG22 0EG (opp maypole)
12-11
(01623) 861000
Wells Bombardier; guest beers Ⓗ
This 400-year-old pub opposite the village green returns to the Guide after a two year absence. The traditional wood-beamed interior includes a restaurant, lounge and bar area with photographs and maps depicting the history of the village.
QP

West Bridgford

Stratford Haven

2 Stratford Road, NG2 6BA
10.30-11 (midnight Thu-Sat); 12-11 Sun
(0115) 982 5981
Bateman XB, XXXB; Caledonian Deuchars IPA; Castle Rock Harvest Pale, Sherriff's Tipple; Everards Tiger; Hop Back Summer Lightning; guest beers Ⓗ
Busy, gimmick-free Castle Rock pub, tucked down a side street. The beer range includes a rotating mild, local ale and Castle Rock beers. A good food menu including vegetarian options is available. Monthly brewery nights are a highlight and feature live music.
Q

West Leake

Star

Melton Lane, LE12 5RQ (S edge of village)
12-midnight (12.30am Fri & Sat)
(0115) 984 2228
Caledonian Deuchars IPA; Draught Bass; Greene King Abbot; Taylor Landlord Ⓗ
Converted from an old pit house and reputed to be haunted, this roadside pub has a three-room interior including a room with a pool table and small plasma screen showing sport, plus a dining room. Children's play area and smoking tent to the rear. Two rooms are available for B&B. P

West Stockwith

White Hart

Main Street, DN10 4ET
11-1am
(01427) 890176
Beer range varies Ⓗ
Home to the newly formed Idle Brewery, this small country pub has a little garden at the side looking out onto the River Trent with the Chesterfield Canal and West Stockwith Marina close by. A single bar serves the main bar area, lounge and dining area.
QP

Worksop

Grafton Hotel

Gateford Road, S80 1UQ (close to railway station)
11-11
(01909) 500342
Beer range varies Ⓗ
New to the Guide, this single-bar pub is situated on the edge of Worksop town centre, close to the railway station. Comprising a bar, lounge area plus dedicated dining area, the pub is home to Grafton Brewery beers which are brewed in a converted stable block at the back of the Packet Inn in Retford.
QP

Mallard

Station Approach, S81 7AG (on railway platform)
5 (2 Fri, midnight Sat)-11; 12-4 Sun
(01909) 530757
Beer range varies Ⓗ
Formerly the Worksop station buffet. Two real ales are always available, plus a large selection of foreign bottled beers and fruit wines. A room downstairs is used for special events including the pub's three annual beer festivals. Local CAMRA Pub of the Year in 2004 and 2005, and a regular winner of Pub of the Season. QP

Regency Hotel

Carlton Road, S81 7AG (opp railway station)
11-2, 7-11; 12-2, 7-10.30 Sun
(01909) 474108
John Smith's Magnet; guest beers Ⓗ
Situated on the edge of the town centre opposite Worksop railway station, the Regency is a large hotel with one bar and a dining area. Two guest ales are dispensed alongside the John Smith's. Good selection of reasonably-priced food. QP

Shireoaks Inn

Westgate, S80 1LT
11.30-4, 6-11; 11.30-11 Sat; 12-4.30, 7-10.30 Sun
(01909) 472118
Beer range varies Ⓗ
Warm, friendly pub converted from cottages. The public bar has a pool table and large screen TV. There is a comfortable lounge bar and dining area where good-value, tasty, home-cooked food is served.
Q

Wysall

Plough Inn

Main Street, Keyworth Road, NG12 5QQ
11-midnight (1am Thu-Sat)
(01509) 880339
Draught Bass; Fuller's London Pride; Greene King Abbot; Taylor Landlord; guest beers Ⓗ
This pleasing, traditional village free house occupies an elevated position overlooking the road. The comfortable interior retains much of its original character with beamed ceilings and cosy alcoves.
P

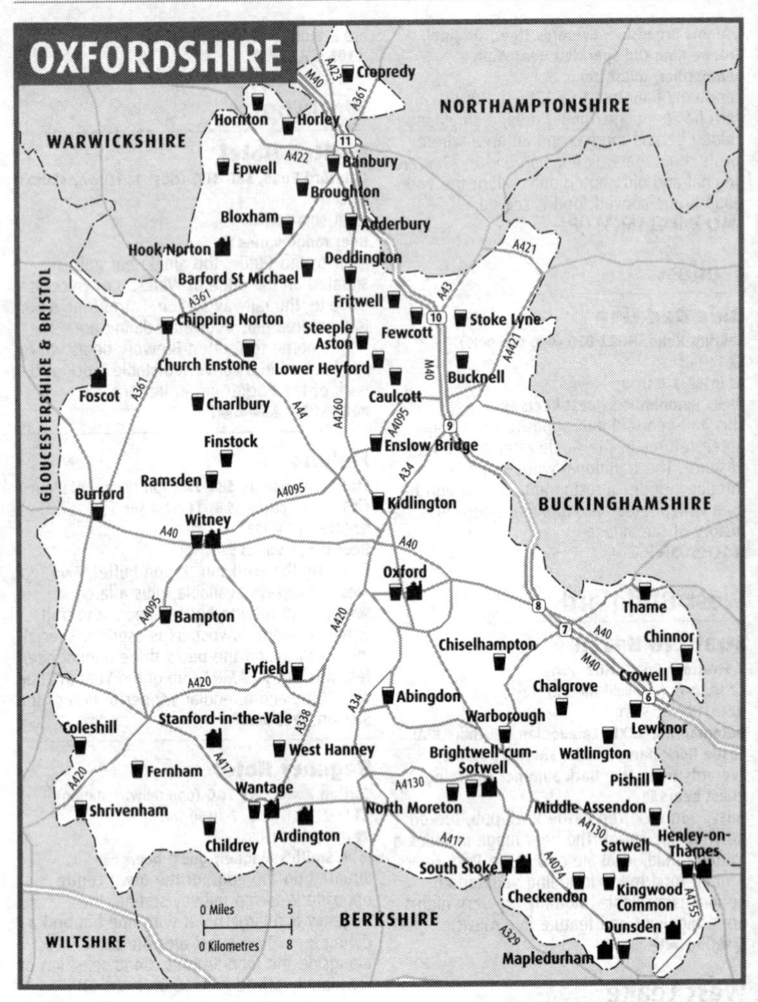

Abingdon

Brewery Tap ✔

40-42 Ock Street, OX14 5BZ

11-11.30 (1am Fri & Sat); 12-4, 7-11 Sun

☎ (01235) 521655 thebrewerytap.net

Greene King Morland Original, Old Speckled Hen; guest beers

Morland created a tap for its brewery in 1993, in an award-winning conversion of three Grade II listed town houses. The brewery was closed and its site redeveloped in 2000 following a takeover by Greene King but the pub, run by two generations of the same family since it first opened, has thrived. The attractive interior features panelled walls, stone floors and an open fire. Lunches are served daily. Although the bar stays open until 1pm on Friday and Saturday nights, last admission is midnight. Q P

Adderbury

Bell Inn

High Street, OX17 3LS

12-2.30, 6-11 (midnight Fri & Sat); 12-3, 7-11 Sun

☎ (01295) 810338 the-bell.com

Hook Norton Hooky Dark, Hooky Bitter, Hooky Gold, seasonal beers; guest beers

Located in the heart of this beautiful village, close to the famous church, this Tardis-like 18th-century ale house retains its character with oak beams, panelling and inglenook fireplace. A Beautiful Beer award-winning pub, discounts are available to CAMRA

INDEPENDENT BREWERIES

Adkin Wantage (NEW)
Appleford Brightwell-cum-Sotwell
Best Mates Ardington (NEW)
Brakspear Witney
Burford Witney
Butler's Mapledurham
Cotswold Foscot
Hook Norton Hook Norton
Loddon Dunsden
Lovibonds Henley-on-Thames
Old Bog Oxford
Ridgeway South Stoke
White Horse Stanford-in-the-Vale
Wychwood Witney

members who join the cask ale drinkers club. There are no games machines, pool table or jukebox to disturb your enjoyment of up to six real ales. Freshly-cooked quality food is served. Well-behaved dogs, children and walkers are welcome.
Q (59) ♣

Bampton

Morris Clown

High Street, OX18 2JW
5 (12 Sat)-11; 12-10.30 Sun
☎ (01993) 850217
West Berkshire Good Old Boy; guest beers
Saved from closure many years ago by the current landlord's father, this pub continues to thrive as a village local totally dependent on wet sales. The name reflects Bampton's Morris dancing traditions, celebrated on Whit Monday with a beer and dancing festival. The interior features murals depicting customers, and has a bar billiards table. A former CAMRA local Pub of the Year, guest beers come from local micro-breweries and change almost daily.
♣ P

Banbury

Olde Reindeer Inn

47 Parsons Street, OX16 5NA
11-11; 12-3 Sun
☎ (01295) 264031
Hook Norton Hooky Dark, Hooky Bitter, Old Hooky; guest beers
Historic pub dating back to 1570, retaining an olde-worlde feel with wood panelling and beams. There is a large collection of brewery memorabilia – ask to see the Globe Room, used by Oliver Cromwell during the Civil War. Good value home-cooked lunches are available. The full Hook Norton range of beers is available along with a seasonal beer or guest ale. ♣P

Woolpack at Banbury Cross

28 Horsefair, OX16 0AE (opp Banbury Cross, on A361)
11-11; 12-10.30 Sun
☎ (01295) 265646 banbury-cross.co.uk/woolpack
Purity Gold; Hook Norton Hooky Bitter; guest beers
Despite its location in the centre of town overlooking the famous Banbury Cross, the Woolpack has the atmosphere of a village inn, with two bars and a snug. Banbury's only free house, it stocks five constantly-changing real ales, predominately from micro-brewers. The landlord is a keen and knowledgeable real ale drinker, and organises a yearly beer festival. The pub enjoys an excellent reputation for home-cooked food based around an eclectic menu.

Barford St Michael

George Inn

Lower Street, OX15 0RH (off B4031)
7-1am; 12-4 Sun
☎ (01869) 838226
Beer range varies
A warm welcome awaits you from the landlord and his labrador Dillon at this delightful thatched free house dating from 1672 in the centre of the village. There are open fires in the winter and four ever-changing beers are usually available, with a beer festival held during the summer. Weddings and special events can be catered for in a marquee in the garden. Well-behaved dogs are welcome. ♣P

Bloxham

Elephant & Castle

Humber Street, OX15 4LZ (Off A361 4 miles W of Banbury)
10-3, 5-11; 10-11 Sat; 12-11 Sun
☎ (01295) 720383 bloxhampub.co.uk
Hook Norton Hooky Bitter, Old Hooky, seasonal beers
This warm, friendly 16th-century pub with its wide carriageway entrance once straddled the old turnpike from Banbury to Chipping Norton. It has open fires in winter and good food is served at lunchtimes Monday-Saturday. The old traditional bread oven can still be seen in the restaurant area. Dogs on leads are welcome. Accommodation is available in two double bedrooms. The landlord, Chas, has run this Hook Norton house for more than 36 years. ♣P

Brightwell-cum-Sotwell

Red Lion

Brightwell Street, OX10 0RT
11-3, 6-11.30; 12-3, 7-10.30 Sun
☎ (01491) 837373 redlion.biz
Loddon Hoppit; West Berkshire Good Old Boy; guest beers
Traditional half-timbered thatched inn dating from the 16th century, situated in a quiet village. The current owners took over in 2007 and their enthusiasm has revitalised this delightful pub. The comfortable bar features wood beams and exposed brick, leading to a restaurant area to one side. The beers are all from local breweries and good quality, reasonably-priced pub food is served.
Q (130)P

Broughton

Saye & Sele Arms

Main Road, OX15 5ED (3 miles W of Banbury on B4035)
11.30-2.30 (3 Sat), 7-11; 12-5 Sun
☎ (01295) 263348 sayeandselearms.co.uk
Adnams Bitter; guest beers
Welcoming and friendly village free house built in local Hornton stone at the edge of Broughton Castle grounds. The beamed and flagstoned bar always has three guest ales on offer, often from local breweries. The popular restaurant has a varied and interesting menu featuring landlord Danny's signature pies and home-made desserts. A huge collection of water jugs is on display. In summer the well-kept, colourful garden and patio are perfect for alfresco dining before visiting the castle.
Q (480)♣P

Bucknell

Trigger Pond ✔

Bicester Road, OX27 7NE

⏲ 12-3, 6-11; 12-11 Sat & Sun

☎ (01869) 252817 🌐 triggerpond.co.uk

Wadworth IPA, 6X; guest beers Ⓗ

This historic inn dates back to 1763, however the interior has a more modern feel, tastefully furnished and with separate dining and drinking areas. A recent addition is the large conservatory overlooking the extensive landscaped beer garden. The full Wadworth range of beers is stocked including its own rotating guest ales. A good range of home-cooked food is served lunchtimes and evenings. ♔❀◑◗♣P⊶

Burford

Highway Inn

117 High Street, OX18 4RG

⏲ 11-3, 6-11; 11-11 Fri & Sat; 11-10.30 Sun

☎ (01993) 823278 🌐 thehighwayinn.co.uk

Hook Norton Hooky Bitter; guest beer Ⓗ

Historic family owned hotel dating from 1480, now fully refurbished and returned to its former glory. The main bar has low beams, comfortable chairs, a log fire and plenty of space for drinkers, serving two real ales and Cotswold Lager. The attractive side bar overlooks the High Street, and there is a cellar restaurant ideal for private functions. Excellent food is available with a curry night on Thursday. Quiz night is Sunday. Outside is a patio garden. ♔Q❀⊏◑◗⅄⊟

Royal Oak

26 Witney Street, OX18 4SN (off A361)

⏲ 11-2.30 (not Tue), 6.30-11; 11-11 Sat; 11-3, 7-10.30 Sun

☎ (01993) 868333

Wadworth IPA, 6X; guest beer Ⓗ

Tucked away down a side street in this tourist town, this is a genuine local with a traditional pub atmosphere. The flagstone front bar leads to a long carpeted side bar with a bar billiards table at the far end. The walls are covered with interesting pictures and memorabilia. An ancient clock chimes melodiously and around 1,000 tankards hang from the ceiling. Excellent home-made food from local produce is served. Walkers are welcome and a boot scraper is provided. ♔Q❀⊏◑◗⅄⊟♣●P

Caulcott

Horse & Groom

Lower Heyford Road, OX25 4ND (on B4030 between Middleton Stoney and Lower Heyford)

⏲ 12-3, 6-11; 12-3, 7-10.30 Sun

☎ (01869) 343257

Hook Norton Hooky Bitter; guest beers Ⓗ

A small, cosy pub with a big welcome. The French landlord/chef offers fabulous food and the Bastille Day celebrations are not to be missed. A genuine free house, three guest ales can come from any part of the country, although local micros usually feature. Real cider is sold in summer. No under 10s are admitted and booking is advised for meals, especially Sunday lunch. The attractive garden is popular in summer. Car parking is available nearby. A gem. ♔Q❀◑◗♿●

Chalgrove

Red Lion

115 The High Street, OX44 7SS

⏲ 11.30-1am (11.30-3, 6-1am winter); 11.30-11 (11.30-4, 6.30-11 winter) Sun

☎ (01865) 890625

Adnams Bitter; Fuller's London Pride; Taylor Landlord; guest beers Ⓗ

Picturesque village local dating from the 16th century, owned by the Church of England. Enter by crossing the small brook that runs alongside the road. Inside, the comfortable bar is split into 'near', 'middle' and 'far', with plenty of exposed wood beams creating an olde-worlde feel. There is a sunny garden to the front of the pub with seating for drinkers, and a large child-friendly garden to the rear. Car parking is available opposite. ♔❀◑◗♿⊟(101)♣⊶

Charlbury

Rose & Crown ✔

Market Street, OX7 3PL

⏲ 12-11 (midnight Wed & Thu; 1am Fri) 11-1am Sat

☎ (01608) 810103 🌐 myspace.com/theroseandcrownpub

Young's Bitter; guest beers Ⓗ

Popular, traditional town-centre free house, 22 years in this Guide. Simply furnished, it has a split-level bar and a large lounge plus a patio courtyard. Situated on the Oxfordshire Way path, walkers are welcome to bring their own food. A pub for the discerning drinker, with seven real ales on handpump it offers one of the best selections in the area and strongly supports micro-breweries. Regular music nights are hosted. Three times CAMRA North Oxon Pub of the Year. ♔❀⅄⇄⊟●⊶

Checkendon

Black Horse

Burncote Lane, RG8 0TE SU666841

⏲ 12-2, 7-11 (10.30 Sun)

☎ (01491) 680418

Butler's Oxfordshire Bitter; West Berkshire Good Old Boy, Old Father Thames Ⓖ

The Black Horse has been in existence for more than 350 years and run by the same family for the last century. This unspoilt gem is hidden away up a lane, which at first glance appears to lead nowhere. Well worth seeking out, it is popular with walkers and horse riders from the adjoining stables. Locals and visitors alike are attracted by its old world charm and the promise of a good pint and conversation. There is no hot food although filled baguettes are often available at lunchtime. The alfresco toilets are worth a visit, too. ♔Q❀⅄⊟(142)P

Childrey

Hatchet Inn

Main Street, OX12 9UF (on B4001)

⏲ 12-2.30 (not Mon & Tue; 3 Sat), 7-11; 12-3.30, 7-10.30 Sun

☎ (01235) 751213

Greene King Morland Original; guest beers Ⓗ
One-room, split level pub with a small quiet area off to one side, offering a warm welcome to all. At the centre of this small village community, it is close to the historic Uffington White Horse. Thriving and well-supported pool and quiz teams represent the pub in local leagues. Well-behaved dogs are welcome. A regular entry in the Guide, the pub is a previous winner of local CAMRA branch Pub of the Year. ✿◑♿▲🚌(38,67)♣P

Chinnor

Red Lion ✔
3 High Street, OX39 4DL (on B4009)
⏲ 12-3, 5-11; 12-11 Fri-Sun
☎ (01844) 353468
Greene King IPA; Loddon Ferryman's Gold; guest beers Ⓗ
This friendly 300-year-old local was originally three cottages. Situated near the village centre, it is also within easy reach of the fine Chiltern countryside and a local steam railway. Quiz nights are held monthly. Guest ales usually change twice a week. The outside drinking area has been refurbished with wooden decking and heaters for smokers. Families are welcome and so are well-behaved dogs. No meals are served on Sunday. ♨Q✿◐◑🚌(40)♣⚑

Chipping Norton

Chequers ✔
Goddards Lane, OX7 5NP (next to theatre)
⏲ 11-11 (midnight Fri & Sat); 11-10.30 Sun
☎ (01608) 644717
Fuller's Chiswick, London Pride, ESB, seasonal beers Ⓗ
Dating back to the 1500s, this pub maintains the atmosphere of a traditional pub of yesteryear with low lighting and simple furnishing. The main bar is surrounded by four seating areas without jukebox, TV or games machines to disturb the enjoyment of the superb ales. The restaurant in the covered courtyard serves good old-fashioned pub food (not Sun eve) and is popular with theatre-goers visiting the small theatre next door. ♨Q◐◑🚌

Chiselhampton

Coach & Horses
Watlington Road, OX44 7UX
⏲ 11.30-11; 11-3.30 Sun
☎ (01865) 890255 ⊕ coachhorsesinn.co.uk
Hook Norton Hooky Bitter; guest beers Ⓗ
Dating back to the 16th century, the Coach & Horses provides good food in four dining areas and a separate bar. Plenty of beams, brickwork and open log fires create a traditional pub atmosphere. It's not all nostalgia though – the pub features a Wi-fi hotspot, free to customers. For summer drinking there is a large patio and lawn. Nine chalet-style bedrooms offer quality accommodation. ♨✿🛏◐◑♿🚌(101)P

Church Enstone

Crown
Mill Lane, OX7 4NN (off A44, on B4030)
⏲ 12-3 (not Mon winter), 6-11; 12-4 Sun
☎ (01608) 677262
Hook Norton Hooky Bitter; guest beers Ⓗ
Dating from the 17th century, this Cotswold stone pub with an inglenook and local village photographs on the walls is a gem. The restaurant features award-winning menus of fresh fish, seafood and game (in season), made with local produce (no food Mon). The pub is popular with locals and visitors who enjoy pleasant conversation without intrusive music or games machines. An ideal place to visit after a walk in the surrounding countryside. ♨Q✿◐◑🚌(20)P

Coleshill

Radnor Arms
32 Coleshill, SN6 7PR
⏲ 11.30-3, 6-11; closed Mon; 12-3, 7-10.30 Sun
☎ (01793) 861575 ⊕ theradnorarms.co.uk
Beer range varies Ⓖ
Set in a beautiful National Trust village, the 18th-century building was the former blacksmith's to the Coleshill estate. Old smithy's tools are displayed in the dining room. There is also a main bar and cosy snug. The emphasis here is on quality, reasonably-priced, locally-sourced food served in a pub atmosphere. At least two beers are available, dispensed by gravity from behind the bar. There are close links with the countryside – walkers (boots off), children and well-behaved dogs are welcome. ♨Q✿◐◑♣P⚑

Cropredy

Red Lion ✔
8 Red Lion Street, OX17 1PB (opp church)
⏲ 12-2.30 (3.30 Sat), 6 (5.30 Tue & Fri)-11 (midnight Sat); 12-3.30, 6.30-10.30 Sun
☎ (01295) 750224 ⊕ redlioncropredy.co.uk
Hook Norton Hooky Bitter; guest beers Ⓗ
A warm welcome awaits at this cosy thatched village pub. Beloved by locals, walkers and boaters from the nearby canal, its tranquillity is disturbed by the seething masses supporting the annual folk-rock festival in early August. Four rooms, two heated by log fires in winter, are served from one bar where three handpumps dispense the regular Hooky Bitter plus two changing guest ales. The popular restaurant offers a comprehensive menu. ♨☺✿◐◑♿▲P⚑

Crowell

Shepherd's Crook
The Green, OX39 4RR (Off B4009 between Chinnor and M40 Jct 6) SU744997
⏲ 11.30-3, 5-11; 11-11 Sat; 12-10.30 Sun
☎ (01844) 351431
Chiltern Ale; Taylor Golden Best; guest beers Ⓗ
In the foothills of the Chilterns, this comfortable inn is renowned for its wide selection of beers —the landlord is a real ale fanatic as well as a horse-racing and cricket enthusiast. The pub menu specialises in fish

which comes direct from the west country, while excellent steak and kidney pies and steaks come from the local butcher. Beers from local breweries are often available and a beer festival is held on the August bank holiday weekend. Dogs are welcome here. ♨Q✿◐◑🚌(40)P⌐

Deddington

Crown & Tuns

New Street, OX15 0SP (on A4260)
⌚ 12-3 (not Mon), 5.30-11; 12-11 Sun
☎ (01869) 337371 🌐 puddingface.com
Hook Norton Hooky Bitter; guest beers Ⓗ
Sixteenth-century building overlooking the main Oxford to Banbury road, originally a coaching inn. It has been sympathetically redecorated with simple wood furnishings to complement the building's original features and has a real fire in winter. The pub attracts a mixed clientele of all ages. Its speciality is good home-made pies with a variety of fillings, however if pies are not your thing, other food is available on the 'But not Pies' menu. ♨✿🛏◑🚌(59)♣⌐

Enslow Bridge

Rock of Gibraltar

OX5 3AY (on A4095/B4027 beside Oxford canal)
⌚ 11 (4 Tue)-1am; 12-10 Sun
☎ (01869) 331373
Beer range varies Ⓗ
Large canal-side free house dating from the 1780s. It offers a good range of local and national beers on two handpumps, with Wye Valley Butty Bach a regular choice. The large garden attracts visitors in good weather and during the annual Canalfest, usually late summer. Good home-cooked food is served in the restaurant, with Greek nights a speciality. No food is served Tuesday and Sunday evening. Folk music plays on Thursday night. ♨⛴✿◑P

Epwell

Chandlers Arms

Sibford Road, OX15 6LH (off B4039 Banbury to Shipston road) SP353403
⌚ 11-11 (1am Fri & Sat)
☎ (01295) 780344
Hook Norton Hooky Bitter, Old Hooky, seasonal beers; guest beers Ⓗ
Traditional country pub unspoilt by progress, dating back to the 17th century. A true drinkers' pub, open all day every day, Hooky beers are always available, often accompanied by guests. Downstairs, there are two rooms with a roaring fire in winter where pub games are played including Aunt Sally in season. Upstairs, the pool room has interesting old photographs on the walls. ♨Q✿♣P⌐

Fernham

Woodman Inn

SN7 7NX (on B4508)
⌚ 11-11; 12-10.30 Sun
☎ (01367) 820643 🌐 thewoodmaninn.net
Beer range varies Ⓖ
First licensed in 1652, this delightful and spacious inn caters for all. Most of the building's internal walls were removed years ago but it retains many original features including the huge roaring fire. Popular with visitors for its locally renowned food, there is an equally warm welcome for those who just want to sample the four ever-changing cask ales, all stored behind the bar and dispensed by gravity. Thatcher's cider is available in summer. ♨Q✿◐◑♿🚌(67)♣🍎P⌐

Fewcott

White Lion

Fritwell Road, OX27 7NZ (1 mile from jct 10 of M40)
⌚ 7 (5.30 Fri; 12 Sat)-11; 12-6.30 Sun
☎ (01869) 346639
Beer range varies Ⓗ
A true free house and the hub of the community, offering a constantly-changing choice of four ales from micros and larger brewers near and far, often including stout and porter. This popular village pub is ideal for enjoying conversation, watching sport on TV or playing pool, though it can get noisy on darts nights. The large garden is busy in summer. Former North Oxon CAMRA Pub of the Year. ♨✿♿♣P

Finstock

Plough Inn

The Bottom, OX7 3BY
⌚ 12-3, 6-11; closed Mon; 12-11 Sat; 12-6 Sun
☎ (01993) 868333 🌐 theplough-inn.co.uk
Adnams Broadside; guest beers Ⓗ
Charming thatched free house dating from mid-18th century with a simply furnished flagstone-floored public bar featuring old local photos, a piano, library and old sack weighing machine. The snug bar is filled with comfortable settees around an inglenook fireplace and the beamed dining room serves excellent food from a small but interesting menu. Walkers (with boots off), children and dogs are welcome and there is a large well-kept garden for the summer. North Oxon CAMRA Cider Pub of the Year 2006. ♨Q✿◐◑🍺🚌♣🍎P

Fritwell

Kings Head

92 East Street, OX27 7QF (2 miles West of M40 jct 10)
⌚ 12 (3 Mon)-11; 12-9 Sun
☎ (01869) 346738 🌐 thekingsheadfritwell.co.uk
Hook Norton Hooky Bitter; Wadworth 6X, Ⓗ **guest ales** Ⓗ/Ⓖ
Stone built north Oxfordshire pub with a bar room and separate dining room, with a welcoming fire to greet drinkers on colder days. The two regularly-changing guest ales come from national and micro-breweries, served on gravity if you ask. Food is served daily except Monday, with an excellent steak menu. More improvements are planned including an outside smokers' area. Disabled

access is through a back door from the car park. ♨✿◐♿♣P

Fyfield

White Hart

Main Road, OX13 5LW

⏲ 12-3, 5.30-11; closed Mon except Bank Hols & Dec; 12-11 Sat; 12-10.30 Sun

☎ (01865) 390585 🌐 whitehart-fyfield.com

Beer range varies Ⓗ

Historic 15th-century former chantry house retaining many original features including the flagstone floors, vaulted ceilings and minstrels' gallery. Renowned for its outstanding locally-sourced food, it continues to retain the role of a friendly village local, with a welcoming log fire in winter. Four ever-changing beers usually include a Hook Norton brew and Thatchers cider is available. Beer festivals are held over the May and August bank holiday weekends. ♨✿◐🚌(66)●P⅃

Henley-on-Thames

Bird in Hand

61 Greys Road, RG9 1SB SU760824

⏲ 11.30-2.30, 5-11; 11.30-11 Sat; 12-10.30 Sun

☎ (01491) 575775 🌐 henleybirdinhand.co.uk

Brakspear Bitter; Fuller's London Pride; Hook Norton Hooky Dark; guest beers Ⓗ

Henley's only genuine free house, this friendly one bar local is popular with regulars and visitors. A former Morlands pub, it has been under the same ownership since 1993 and in this Guide for the past nine years. The large secure garden, reached through the family room, has an aviary, pond and pets. Two guest beers often come from micro-breweries. Reasonably-priced lunches are served during the week. Local CAMRA Pub of the Year in 2006 and 2008. ♉✿◐▲⇌🚌(139,800)♣⅃

Horley

Red Lion

OX15 6BQ

⏲ 6-11; closed Mon; 12-6 Sun

☎ (01295) 730427

Hook Norton Hooky Bitter; Taylor Landlord Ⓗ

Traditional beer-only pub, little has changed over the years. Friendly and welcoming, it is at the heart of the village community and pub games are popular. Poker, darts and dominoes are contested Tuesday to Thursday night and Aunt Sally is played in the garden. Musical entertainment is hosted occasionally at the weekend, when a guest beer is added to the range. Beer festivals are held now and again. ♨✿♣P⅃

Hornton

Dun Cow

West End, OX15 6DA (signed from green in centre of village) SP391449

⏲ 6 (12 Sat)-11; 12-10.30 Sun

☎ (01295) 670524 🌐 drunkenmonk.co.uk

Hook Norton Hooky Bitter; Wells Bombardier; guest beers Ⓗ

Once a butcher's slaughterhouse, this thatched, low beamed and flagstone-floored pub is located in a quiet and attractive village. It is home to the Drunken Monk and Vitis Wines outlets and some of the historic ales, meads and fruit and country wines are stocked. Beer festivals are held in February and July. Freshly-cooked food is available lunchtimes (weekdays by arrangement) and evenings. North Oxfordshire CAMRA Cider and Perry Pub of the Year 2007. ♨♉✿◐♣●P

Kidlington

King's Arms

4 The Moors, OX5 2AJ

⏲ 11-3, 5.30-11.30; 11-midnight Fri & Sat; 12-11.30 Sun

☎ (01865) 373004

Greene King IPA; Wells Bombardier; guest beers Ⓗ

Picturesque, traditional two-room local where darts is popular. Guest beers are a major attraction and can be of any style from any brewery, with dark beers often putting in an appearance. The heated, covered patio is used to play Aunt Sally and also for a twice-yearly beer festival. Good value, high quality lunches are served, with a roast on Sunday. ♨✿◐◐♿🚌♣P⅃

Kingwood Common

Unicorn

Colmore Lane, RG9 5LX SU700819

⏲ 12-3 (not Mon), 6 (6.30 Sun)-11

☎ (01491) 628452 🌐 the-unicorn.co.uk

Brakspear Bitter, seasonal beers; Hook Norton Hooky Dark Ⓗ

Pleasant and welcoming country pub, a favourite among locals and popular with those simply looking for good drink and food. Deep leather chairs next to a real fire in the bar and a well-presented dining room create a modern yet heritage feel. The pub has cricket, darts and cribbage teams and holds a regular Monday night quiz. Free wireless Internet is available for customers. A one-room letting suite is an ideal weekend getaway or business stopover. ♨Q✿🛏◐🚌(137)♣P

Lewknor

Leathern Bottle

High Street, OX49 5TW SU716976

⏲ 11-2.30, 6-11; 12-3, 7-10.30 Sun

☎ (01844) 351482

Brakspear Bitter, seasonal beers Ⓗ

Classic old pub spread over three rooms separated by a large open fire and bar area. The ancient Icknield way passes close by and the area known as the Knapp above the village has revealed remains of an early Iron Age and Anglo Saxon cemetery. Consistently good ale and an extensive menu make this an ideal stop-off from the nearby M40 motorway. The pub has featured in all but one edition of this Guide. ♨Q♉✿◐♿🚌P

Lower Heyford

Bell

21 Market Square, OX25 5NY

⏲ 11.30-3, 6-11; 12-3, 6-10.30 Sun

☎ (01869) 347176

Beer range varies Ⓗ
Large multi-roomed pub at the centre of the village, a short walk from Heyford station over the canal bridge. Four guest ales always include a Titanic seasonal ale on the newly installed handpump. One guest ale rotates monthly and the other changes more frequently. A real cider is often available in summer. Food is served daily lunchtimes and evenings. A jazz night is held on the last Friday of the month and there are occasional live music nights. ⛰❀◑◗♿⇌🚌(25A)♣

Mapledurham

Pack Saddle

Chazey Heath, RG4 7UD SU696772
⏲ 11-3, 6-11; 11-11 Fri & Sat; 12-10.30 Sun
☎ (0118) 946 3000 🌐 thepacksaddleinn.co.uk
Wadworth IPA, 6X, JCB, seasonal beers Ⓗ
Located between two golf courses, a few miles from Mapledurham House, this is a genuine pub with a traditional feel. The lower bar area is the main drinking area although it is used by diners on Sunday lunchtime. High quality food is freshly made, with the emphasis on traditional English fare, and excellent value (booking advisable in busy periods). There is an enclosed garden with children's play area, and a large paddock for beer festivals and regulars who occasionally arrive by helicopter.
⛰Q❀◑◗♿🚌(39,40)♣P▯

Middle Assendon

Rainbow

RG9 6AU SU738858
⏲ 12-3, 6-11 (not Mon eve winter); 12-3, 7-10.30 Sun
☎ (01491) 574879
Brakspear Bitter, seasonal beers Ⓗ
Compact and unspoilt pub nestling in the Stonor Valley in the parish of Bix and Assendon. The cosy public bar can be packed after local field events, while the lounge serves good home-cooked food including locally sourced game. Ideally located for Chiltern walks, it is a popular stop for local horse-drawn tours of the area. Cribbage is played on Wednesday evening in winter. The pub is very much the hub of the village and visitors will often be drawn into lively conversations in the bar. Q❀◑◗⊟♣P

North Moreton

Bear at Home

High Street, OX11 9AT SU561894
⏲ 12-3, 6-11 (midnight Thu); 12-11 Sat
☎ (01235) 811311 🌐 bear-at-home.co.uk
Taylor Landlord; guest beers Ⓗ
Originally a 15th-century coaching inn, this is a friendly village local with a wide range of mostly local real ales in an old-style beamed and bricked interior. The seating arrangement in the main bar is relaxed with sofas and an open fire, a cosy space for drinkers and plenty of tables for diners. The licensees originally lived in the village and also run an antiques business, with many items on display in the pub available to buy. Oxfordshire CAMRA Pub of the Year in 2007. ⛰❀◑◗🚌(95)♣P

Oxford

Angel & Greyhound

30 St Clements Street, OX4 1AB
⏲ 11-11.30 (midnight Fri & Sat); 12-11 Sun
☎ (01865) 242660
Wells Bombardier; Young's Bitter, Special; guest beers Ⓗ
This busy conversation and games pub serves good bottled and draught beer along with excellent food. There are front and rear patios, covered and heated at the rear for smokers. Originally called the Oranges and Lemons' (note the address), this student and locals' local is now named after the nearby water meadow. Guest beers are from the Wells and Young's range. ⛰Q❀◑◗🚌♣⚊

Eagle & Child ✔

49 St Giles, OX1 3LU
⏲ 11.30-11.30 (midnight Fri & Sat); 12-11 Sun
☎ (01865) 302925
Adnams Broadside; Brakspear Bitter; guest beers Ⓗ
Known locally as the 'Bird & Baby', famous writers CS Lewis and JRR Tolkien were said to frequent this historic pub. With a narrow but surprisingly deep interior, the pub is one of the city's classics, attracting a mix of students and visitors. Guest beers come from M&B and often include a mild. ◑◗⇌

Gardener's Arms

39 Plantation Road, OX2 6JE
⏲ 12-2.30 (not Mon & Tue), 5-midnight; 12-11 Sun
☎ (01865) 559814 🌐 thegarden-oxford.co.uk
Beer range varies Ⓗ
A favourite of students and young professionals who live in the surrounding area, the pub has a large beer garden which is very popular in summer. Four frequently-changing cask beers are always available, drawn from the Marston's range and guest list. Thatchers Heritage cider is also stocked. The food is entirely vegetarian, with a number of vegan options, but the imaginative menu offers a wide choice of dishes that will appeal to meat eaters as well. Q❀◑◗🚌●

Gardener's Arms

8 North Parade Avenue, OX2 6LX (off Banbury Road ½ mile N of city centre)
⏲ 11-2.30, 5-11; 12-3, 6-11 Sun
☎ (01865) 554007
Greene King IPA, Abbot; guest beer Ⓗ
A friendly welcome is guaranteed at this small suburban pub run by long-standing licensees on a lively, narrow street just north of the city centre. The long single room is divided into two distinct areas by the bar and galley style kitchen. A guest beer complements the two regular ales from owners Greene King, and good value food is served lunchtimes and evenings. Take care not to confuse this pub with the other Gardener's Arms nearby!
Q◑◗🚌⚊

Harcourt Arms

Cranham Terrace, Jericho, OX2 6DG (off Walton Street)
⏲ 12-2, 5-11; 12-2, 5.30-midnight Fri & Sat; 12-2, 7-11 Sun
☎ (01865) 310630

Fuller's Chiswick, Discovery, London Pride, ESB; guest beers Ⓗ
Atmospheric corner pub in the quiet suburb of Jericho, just yards from the vibrant Walton Street with its shops, bars and restaurants. Subdued lighting, modern art, quiet background jazz and two real log fires give the pub a relaxed feel. Customers enjoy conversation, board games, newspapers and the excellent Fuller's ales. Toasted sandwiches are the house speciality, or try pistachio nuts by the pint to share. ⩕Q✿♣

King's Arms

40 Holywell Street, OX1 3SP
✪ 10.30 (12 Sun)-midnight
☎ (01865) 242369
St Austell Tribute; Young's Bitter, Special, seasonal beers; guest beers Ⓗ
Dating from 1607, the pub is set among the university buildings of central Oxford and owned by Wadham College, with students housed on the upper floors. Internally, a warren of rooms includes two bars and much wood panelling. Popular with students, university staff and tourists, it is often very busy but the bar service remains efficient. Food is served until 9pm daily. Outside there are pavement tables and benches. This is the only city centre pub open until midnight throughout the week. ⩕Q✿◐⇶

Lamb & Flag

12 St Giles, OX1 3JS
✪ 12-11
☎ (01865) 515787
Fuller's London Pride; Palmers IPA; Shepherd Neame Spitfire; Skinner's Betty Stoggs; Theakston Old Peculier; guest beers Ⓗ
Saved from conversion to student accommodation in a vigorous local campaign some years ago, the pub is now run as a free house by St John's College. Now a flagship for real ale in the city, it draws its clientele equally from the academic, tourist and local communities. Many of the regular beers and guests come from the west country. Q◐⇶

Masons Arms

2 Quarry School Place, Headington Quarry, OX3 8LH
✪ 5-11; 11-11 Sat; 12-4, 7-10.30 Sun
☎ (01865) 764579 🌐 masonsquarry.co.uk
Brakspear Oxford Gold; Hook Norton Old Hooky; West Berkshire Good Old Boy; guest beers Ⓗ
Family-run community pub full of character and charm, a meeting place for local darts players and Aunt Sally teams. Guest ales change weekly, and a popular annual beer festival is held in September. The pub has its own micro-brewery, Old Bog, on the premises. The Old Bog beers tend to sell out fast when a new batch goes on sale – contact the pub or consult the website to check availability. The heated decking area is popular all year round, and the function room can be booked for private events. ✿♣P⚊

Old Bookbinders

17-18 Victor Street, Jericho, OX2 6BT
✪ 12-2, 5-midnight; 12-midnight Fri & Sat; 12-11 Sun
☎ (01865) 553549 🌐 oldbookbinders.co.uk
Greene King IPA, seasonal beers; guest beers Ⓗ
Back street Jericho local furnished in ale house style with plenty of bric-a-brac and a collection of pump clips. The welcome is friendly, the food excellent and well priced, and the atmosphere often vibrant. Guest beers feature alongside Greene King brews, and occasional beer festivals are held. Well-behaved children, dogs and students are welcome, and free wireless Internet access is available. ◐⇶♣●

Rose & Crown

14 North Parade Avenue, OX2 6LX (off Banbury Road ½ mile N of city centre)
✪ 10-midnight (1am Fri & Sat)
☎ (01865) 510551 🌐 rose-n-crown.com
Adnams Bitter, Broadside; Hook Norton Old Hooky Ⓗ
Well-known Victorian pub on a busy, vibrant north Oxford street, comprising three small rooms with a heated, covered courtyard behind and a small room that can be booked for functions. It attracts a good mix of students, locals and academics, drawn here by the warm hospitality, lively conversation and excellent beer. Mobile phones are banned and there is no intrusive music – children and dogs are not admitted. Opening times can vary outside term time. Q✿◐🚌⚊

Turf Tavern ✔

7 Bath Place, OX1 3SU (off Hollywell Street)
✪ 11-11; 12-10.30 Sun
☎ (01865) 243235 🌐 theturftavern.co.uk
Beer range varies Ⓗ
Traditional 16th-century pub with two bars, popular with students and always busy during university term times. Outside there are three flagstoned courtyards, one with parts of the old city wall standing three storeys high, all with heating and umbrellas for drinkers and smokers. Up to 11 real ales are available, plus Weston's Old Rosie cider. Two beer festivals are held each year in spring and autumn. Winner of The Publican Perfect Pub Award 2007. Q✿◐⚊

White Horse

52 Broad Street, OX1 3BB
✪ 11-11 (midnight Fri & Sat); 11-10.30 Sun
☎ (01865) 204801
Brakspear Oxford Gold; Caledonian Deuchars IPA; St Austell Tribute; Taylor Landlord; White Horse Weyland Smithy; Wychwood Hobgoblin Ⓗ
Claiming to be the smallest pub in Oxford and sandwiched between the two entrances to Blackwell's famous bookshop, this classic Grade II listed 16th-century city centre pub has a single long and narrow bar and a small snug at the rear. Up to six cask ales are dispensed, usually including a guest beer from the White Horse Brewery. Popular with students and tourists, the pub regularly features in Inspector Morse and more recently the Oxford Murders. Bill Clinton is reputed to have been a frequent patron in his Oxford days. Q◐🚌

Pishill

Crown Inn

RG9 6HH SU718902
✪ 11.30-2.30, 6-11; 12-3, 7-10.30 Sun
☎ (01491) 638364 🌐 crownpishill.co.uk

Brakspear Bitter; guest beers 🄷
Fifteenth century brick and flint coaching inn with origins that may well date back to the 11th Century – the 400-year-old barn is still in use for music nights on the last Wednesday of the month. The theory behind the name of Pishill is that when horses and wagons climbed out of Henley-on-Thames past the Crown, they stopped at the inn, and while the ostlers had an ale the horses relieved themselves. Though a free house, Brakspear always features, plus one or two regularly changing guest beers. ⌂Q❀⊭◐◑⊡P

Ramsden

Royal Oak

High Street, OX7 3AU
⏲ 11.30-3, 6.30-11; 12-3, 7-10.30 Sun
☎ (01993) 868213
Hook Norton Hooky Bitter; Young's Bitter; guest beers 🄷
Popular 17th century free house run by the same owners for 22 years. It has an excellent reputation for good food and well-kept real ales. Comfortably furnished in traditional style, the main bar has an attractive inglenook fireplace and there is a small snug bar. The spacious restaurant opens onto a pleasant courtyard for summer drinking. No music, TV, fruit machines or games disturb the peace — this is a pub for relaxation and conversation. Children, dogs and walkers are welcome. ⌂Q❀⊭◐◑♿⊟●P

Satwell

Lamb

RG9 4QZ SU706834
⏲ 12-11 (midnight Sat); 12-10.30 Sun
☎ (01491) 628482 🌐 awtonline.co.uk
Fuller's London Pride; guest beers 🄷
Characterful old pub with oak beams and a log fire, tucked away off the main road and rebuilt after a serious fire in 1992. Bought from Brakspear in 2006 by TV chef Antony Worrall Thompson, the pub's aims are to serve 'real beer and real food'. Two guest beers come from local micro-breweries: one from Loddon, the other from Butler's or Rebellion. Food is bistro style with all meals less than £10. The garden has tables among tall pine trees and is convenient for those arriving on horseback. Look out for 'George', the resident ghost. ⌂❀◐◑P

Shrivenham

Prince of Wales

High Street, SN6 8AF
⏲ 12-3, 6-11 (not Sun eve)
☎ (01793) 782268 🌐 powshrivenham.co.uk
Wadworth IPA, 6X, Horizon, Bishop's Tipple, seasonal beers; guest beers 🄶
Family-friendly Grade II listed pub with a cosy atmosphere offering good home-cooked food including Sunday roasts. Board games including shuffle board, newspapers, wireless Internet access and a small meeting room are available, and the pub holds regular quiz nights. Trips are organised to breweries and beer festivals, and the pub has its own festival over the spring bank holiday. A regular entry in the Guide and a previous winner of local CAMRA branch Pub of the Year. ⌂❀◐◑⊟(66)♣●P⅃

South Stoke

Perch & Pike

The Street, RG8 0JS
⏲ 12-3, 5-11, 12-11.30 Sat; 12-10.30 Sun
☎ (01491) 872415
Brakspear Bitter, seasonal beers 🄷
Seventeenth-century brick and flint pub in the centre of the village. The adjoining barn has been converted to a restaurant and four en-suite bedrooms. The original part of the pub comprises three separate areas with low beams, a real fire, sofas and benches with plenty of cushions and newspapers to read. ⌂❀⊭◐◑♿⊟(132)P⅃

Steeple Aston

White Lion

Southside, OX25 4RR
⏲ 12-midnight
☎ (01869) 340307
Beer range varies 🄷
Single room community pub dating from the 19th century, offering a variety of ales, with Timothy Taylor and Wadworth beers often featuring. There is always something going on here, with chess by the fire, satellite TV, pool, occasional live music and free Wi-fi Internet access. Fresh food is served daily. ⌂❀◐◑⊟(59)♣⅃

Stoke Lyne

Peyton Arms ★

OX27 8SD (off B4100)
⏲ 12-2, 5-11; closed Mon; 12-11 Sat; 12-7 Sun
☎ (01869) 345285
Hook Norton Hooky Bitter, Old Hooky 🄶
This classic National Inventory listed pub featuring memorabilia from the1950s and 1960s has to be seen to be believed, with visitors coming from far and wide. The beer is served straight from the barrel with no pub furniture on the bar. The hosts are local legends, very much part of the character of this pub. Value-for-money filled rolls are always available. No children are admitted in the bar. ⌂❀♣⅃

Thame

Falcon

1 Thame Park Road, OX9 3JA
⏲ 12-11 (10.30 Sun)
☎ (01844) 212118
Hook Norton Hooky Bitter, seasonal beers; guest beers 🄷
Thriving, unspoilt community local rescued from possible oblivion by Hook Norton in 2006. A small distance from the town centre, it is run by two families of enthusiastic newcomers to the pub trade. The walls are adorned with a collection of reproduction pub signs and there is a separate dining area where light lunches are served Monday-Friday. Children are welcome in the bar until

8pm. The Thame/Risborough Phoenix Cycle Trail runs along the old railway track nearby.

Wantage

Royal Oak Inn

Newbury Street, OX12 8DF (S of market square)
5.30-11; 12-2.30, 7-11 Sat; 12-2, 7-10.30 Sun
(01235) 763129 royaloakwantage.2ya.com
Wadworth 6X; H/G West Berkshire Maggs Mild, Dr Hexter's Wedding Ale, Dr Hexter's Healer; G guest beers H/G
Photographs of ships bearing the pub's name adorn the walls of this street-corner pub. The lounge bar features a wrought-iron trellis, largely hidden by more than 300 pump clips. The smaller public bar attracts a younger crowd. It is the primary outlet for West Berks beers in the area, including two carrying the landlord's name. Wadworth beers from wooden casks and a range of cider are also available. Current local CAMRA Pub of the Year.

Shoulder of Mutton

38 Wallingford Street, OX12 8AX
12-11 (10.30 Sun)
(07788) 190822
Butts Traditional; guest beers H
Corner pub, renowned for its friendly atmosphere, with a cosy snug that accommodates half-a-dozen at a pinch plus public and lounge bars with traditional decor and furnishings. The lounge has a computer with Internet access. If you prefer to stand, you may also drink in the 'lay-by' in the corridor leading to a small outdoor patio which in summer is adorned with an abundance of hanging baskets.

Warborough

Cricketers

Thame Road, OX10 7DD SU598936
12-3, 6-midnight; closed Mon; 12-midnight Fri-Sun
(01865) 858192 thecricketersatwarborough.co.uk
Beer range varies H
Not far from the picturesque village green, this family-friendly pub welcomes drinkers as well as diners who come for the good value, home-cooked food. An open fire warms the bar in winter months and diners are catered for in the cosy restaurant. Aunt Sally is played in the pub garden. (39)P

Watlington

Carriers Arms

Hill Road, OX49 5AD SU692944
9.30-midnight; 10-11 Sun
(01491) 613470
Adnams Bitter; Butler's Oxfordshire Bitter; Fuller's London Pride; guest beers H
Lively village free house recently taken over by a real ale enthusiast. This thriving local has five darts teams and features a quiz and a curry every Thursday evening. The pub offers a late breakfast and serves food every lunchtime and evening (except Sun eve). Situated close to the Ridgeway long distance footpath, from the garden there is a good view of the White Mark, a chalk triangle on Watlington Hill. (101, 125)P

West Hanney

Plough

Church Street, OX12 0LN
12-3, 6-11; 12-10.30 Sun
(01235) 868674 ploughwesthanney.co.uk
Brakspear Bitter; Greene King Abbot; Taylor Landlord; guest beers H
Welcoming, atmospheric Grade II listed 16th-century thatched inn, with a cosy, beamed split-level bar with an open fire and dining room serving locally renowned traditional British food. A large garden plays host to Aunt Sally and outdoor skittles in summer. Two beer festivals are held annually.
Q P

Witney

Eagle Tavern

22 Corn Street, OX28 6BL
11-3, 5-12.30am (2.30am Fri); 11-2.30am Sat; 12-12.30am Sun
(01993) 700121
Hook Norton Hooky Dark, Hooky Bitter, Old Hooky, seasonal beers H
The landlord knows his beers; he was born in a pub, brought up in another, and has been with Witney Inns for 18 years. A traditional market town tavern, it offers a warm welcome to all. Winner of the Hook Norton Best Cellar Award 2008, the cellar can be viewed through a window in one of the three bar rooms. Darts and crib are played. Q

New Inn

111 Corn Street, OX28 6AU
5-midnight; 4-1am Fri; 12-11.30 Sat & Sun
(01993) 703807
Black Sheep Best Bitter; Brakspear Bitter; Taylor Landlord; Wychwood Hobgoblin; guest beers H
Transformed some years ago into a real ale pub by the landlord, who is a Maasai Elder and an aficionado of ale. The interior has three distinct areas: a cosy reading room with books and encyclopaedias, a bar area with window seats and an open log fire, and a sports bar with TV, plus live music on Sat night.
Q P

Three Horseshoes

78 Corn Street, OX28 6BS
12-3, 6.30-11; 12-4.30 Sun
(01993) 703086 thethreehorseshoes.tablesir.com
Adnams Broadside; Harveys Sussex Best Bitter; Wychwood Hobgoblin H
Run by the same landlord for 17 years, this Grade II listed building became an inn around 120 years ago. A popular food pub, serving ever-changing daily specials made with local produce, it has two candle-lit dining rooms. The atmospheric front bar is more relaxed.
Q

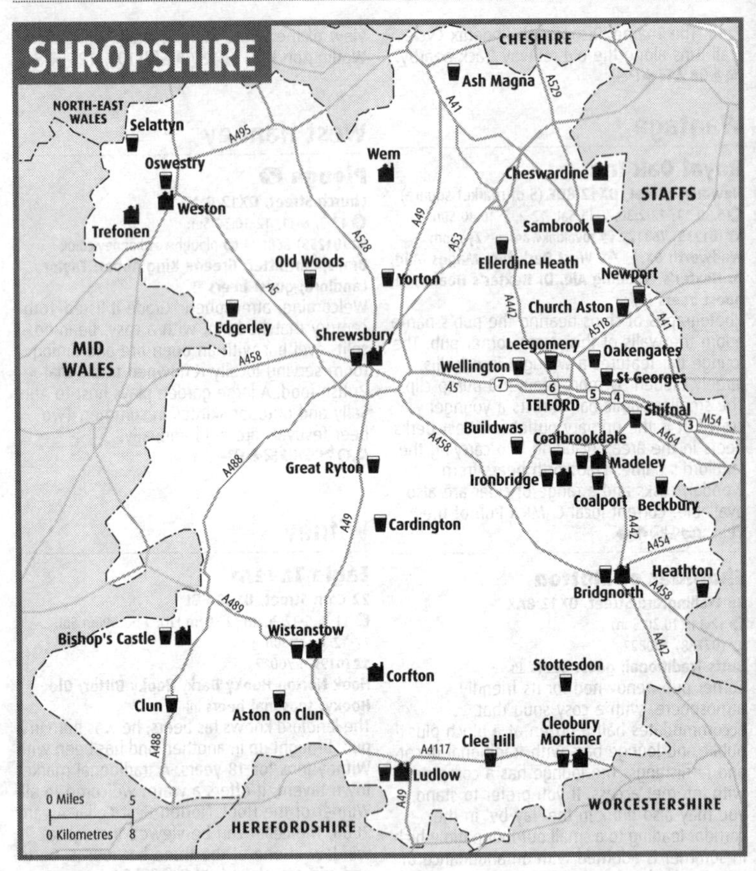

Ash Magna

White Lion

Ash Magna, SY13 4DR (just off A525)
12-2 (Sat only), 6-11; 1-4, 7-10.30 Sun
☎ (01948) 663153
Draught Bass; Taylor Landlord; Worthington's Bitter; guest beers Ⓗ
This pub is the heart of the village. The landlord and his wife have run award-winning pubs in other parts of the county and their experience shows. The busy public bar displays real ale artefacts; the welcoming lounge bar, where food is served, has golf prints. The landlady is from Germany and dishes from her native country feature on the food menu. A barbecue is held on Saturday evening in summer. Weston's cider is available in summer. No meals are served on Wednesday or Sunday. ⅏Q❀◑⊟♣●P⁵–⊓

Aston on Clun

Kangaroo

Clun Road, SY7 8EW (on B4368)
12-3 (not Mon & Tue), 6-11; 2-11 Fri; 12-11 Sat & Sun
☎ (01588) 660263 🌐 kangarooinn.co.uk
Wells Bombardier; Wye Valley HPA; guest beers Ⓗ
The only pub in Britain with this name, dating from the 19th century. This cosy village local has a small lounge, public bar, games room, dining area and a large garden and patio. Good home-cooked food is served (not Sun-Tue eves). The pub supports the nearby annual Arbour tree redressing ceremony at the end of May and the Clun Valley Beer Festival at the beginning of October, and hosts its own annual beer festival on the August Bank Holiday. The Bike-roos meet here on Sunday afternoon. Dogs are welcome.
⅏Q❀◑⇌(Broome)⊟♣●P⁵–⊓

Beckbury

Seven Stars ✔

Madeley Road, TF11 9DN (off B4176)
12-3 (not Mon), 6-11 (11.30 Thu; midnight Fri & Sat); 12-4 7-11 Sun
☎ (01952) 750229 🌐 sevenstarsbeckbury.co.uk
Banks's Original; guest beers Ⓗ
Rural pub built in the 1700s popular with locals, walkers and cyclists —and if you arrive on horseback there is a hitching post at the end of the car park. The pub is highly regarded for its food and has won awards locally — themed nights are always popular. Guest beers change frequently. Families are welcome and there is a children's play area in the garden. ⅏Q◑♣P⁵–

Bishops Castle

Castle Hotel

Market Square, SY9 5BH

⏲ 12-2.30, 6-11; 12-2.30, 7-10.30 Sun

☎ (01588) 638403

🌐 thecastlehotelbishopscastle.co.uk

Hobsons Best Bitter; Six Bells Big Nevs, Goldings; guest beers ⊞

For 19 years now Nikki and Dave, supported by their attentive staff, have lavished loving care on their 17th-century hotel. Magnificently landscaped terraced gardens benefit from fine views over the Shropshire Hills. Three comfortable bar areas retain much original woodwork and furnishings to provide the perfect setting to enjoy excellent home-cooked food and local beer. A beer festival in July is actively supported.

♔Q❀⇆◑⊟♿⛺⊟(553)♣P

Six Bells

Church Street, SY9 5AA

⏲ 12-2.30 (not Mon), 5-11; 12-11 Sat; 12-10.30 (12-2.30, 7-10.30 winter) Sun

☎ (01588) 638930

Six Bells Big Nevs, Goldings, 1859, Cloud Nine; guest beers ⊞

This is the Six Bells Brewery tap – the adjoining brewery was re-established on the site of the original one which closed in the early 1900s. You can be sure of a friendly welcome in the wooden beamed bar where four real ales are on handpump plus monthly specials and Montgomery Cider. Excellent fresh food is served in the dining/lounge bar. A local beer festival in July offers around 20 ales and real ciders plus live music in the courtyard.

♔Q❀◑⊟♿⊟(553)♣●⁄

Three Tuns

Salop Street, SY9 5BW

⏲ 12-11 (10.30 Sun)

☎ (01588) 638797

Three Tuns Stirling, Three 8, XXX, Clerics Cure; guest beer ⊞

One of the Famous Four in the county who were still brewing in the early 1970s, this historic pub, together with the adjoining but separately owned Three Tuns Brewery, has been on this site since 1642. The building has been extended and now has four rooms —a dining lounge, busy front bar, central snug and a timber-framed glass-sided dining room. As well as good food the pub offers regular music sessions including jazz in the top room. Dogs are welcome. ♔Q❀◑⊟⊟(443,745)♣●⁄

Bridgnorth

Bell & Talbot

2 Salop Street, High Town, WV16 4QU

⏲ 5-midnight; 12-2.30, 5.30-11 Sun

☎ (01746) 763233 🌐 odleyinns.co.uk

Batham Best Bitter; Hobsons Town Crier; guest beers ⊞

This 'once seen never forgotten' old coaching inn is full of quaint features. In the larger of the two bars records and musical instruments reflect the pub's long tradition of live music, hosted on Friday and Sunday. The foliage-adorned conservatory leads to an umbrella-covered smoking area. Guest beers are usually bitters selected from local Shropshire or Black Country breweries; cider is occasionally served in the summer. ♔⇆≢(SVR)⊟♣⁄

Black Horse

4 Bridge Street, Low Town, WV15 6AF

⏲ 12-midnight

☎ (01746) 762415

Banks's Original, Bitter; Batham Best Bitter; Enville Ale; Hobsons Town Crier; guest beers ⊞

A mid-1700s ale house with accommodation and food served all day until 8pm. The small front bar has antique bar fittings and a dartboard, and the large wood-panelled lounge bar leads to a dining room and conservatory. Wide screen TVs mainly show sporting events. The external smoking area leads to a long courtyard, pleasant for outdoor drinking, with access to the nearby River Severn. Guest beers include seasonal ales.

❀⇆◑⊟♿≢(SVR)⊟P⁄▯

Friars Inn

3 St Mary's Street, High Town, WV16 4DW

⏲ 11-midnight; 12-10.30 Sun

☎ (01746) 762396

Olde Swan Original, Entire; Wye Valley HPA, Dorothy Goodbody's Golden Ale; guest beer ⊞

A popular local tucked away in a quiet courtyard off the High Street, this is one of the oldest surviving inns in Bridgnorth. First licensed in 1828 as a posting house, it has been a brewery, cider house and blacksmith's. The blackboard menu offers delicious home-cooked casseroles and several varieties of locally sourced sausages with mash as well as regular pub favourites (but no chips).

Q❀⇆◑≢(SVR)⊟

Golden Lion Inn

83 High Street, High Town, WV16 4DS

⏲ 11.30-2.30, 6-11; 11-11 Fri & Sat; 12-10.30 Sun

☎ (01746) 762016 🌐 goldenlionbridgnorth.co.uk

Banks's Original, Bitter; Greene King IPA; Hobsons Town Crier; guest beers ⊞

A traditional coaching inn with accommodation, the history of this 17th-century inn is displayed on the walls of the two pleasant, quiet lounge bars. Dominoes, darts and quiz teams are based in the public bar, and quoits is also available. Outside there is a patio drinking area and a covered smoking space. Home-cooked food is served at lunchtime. Q❀⇆◐⊟≢(SVR)⊟♣P⁄

INDEPENDENT BREWERIES

Bridgnorth Bridgnorth
Corvedale Corfton
Dolphin Shrewsbury
Hanby Wem
Hobsons Cleobury Mortimer
Ironbridge Ironbridge (NEW)
Lion's Tail Cheswardine
Ludlow Ludlow
Offa's Dyke Trefonen
Salopian Shrewsbury
Six Bells Bishop's Castle
Stonehouse Weston
Three Tuns Bishop's Castle
Wood Wistanstow
Worfield Madeley

Kings Head

3 Whitburn Street, High Town, WV16 4QN
⏲ 11-11 (midnight Fri & Sat); 12-10.30 Sun
☎ (01746) 762141
Hobsons Best Bitter, Town Crier; Bridgnorth Apley Ale, Best, Northgate Gold; guest beers Ⓗ
Grade II listed 16th-century coaching inn sympathetically renovated, featuring timber beams, flagstone floor, leaded windows and roaring fires in winter. Local beers are always available and there is a constantly-changing selection of guest beers. Lunch and evening menus offer plenty of variety with char grills featuring local produce a speciality. The recently opened Stable Bar at the back of the pub, with seven handpulls, is the Bridgnorth Brewery tap. The courtyard has a pleasant seated area. ♨Q❀◐◑♿⇌(SVR)🚌P⁻🍸

Railwayman's Arms

Hollybush Road, WV16 5DT (follow signs for SVR)
⏲ 11.30-4, 6-11; 11-11 Sat; 12-10.30 Sun
☎ (01746) 764361 🌐 svr.co.uk
Batham Best Bitter; Hobsons Best Bitter; guest beers Ⓗ
A licensed refreshment room since 1900, owned by SVR, this is an exceptionally busy drinking spot, attracting beer drinkers and steam buffs from around the country. The platform drinking area is perfect for soaking up the atmosphere of the steam era, with plenty of fine railway memorabilia on display. A free house, three guest beers tend to be from smaller, often local, brewers, plus one changing Belgian beer. A large selection of local and European bottled beers is also available. Sandwiches and pies are occasionally served. A CAMRA beer festival is hosted in the car park every September. ♨Q❀⇌(SVR)🚌●P⁻🍸

Buildwas

Abbey Sports & Social Club

Much Wenlock Road, TF8 7BP
⏲ 12-2.30 (not Mon & Tue), 7-11
☎ (01952) 432437
Wye Valley Butty Bach; guest beers Ⓗ
You could write a book on the heritage of this Grade I historic abbey building. Founded in the 11th century, it was originally an abbots' meeting house for Buildwas Abbey until the Reformation of Henry VIII. In private ownership until 1963, it then became a sports and social club with the ruined abbey as a backdrop to the manicured lawns. There is a one and a half mile nature trail next to the car park with outstanding views along the River Severn. Excellent home-cooked food is available (not Sun or Mon eve). Q❀◐◑P

Cardington

Royal Oak

SY6 7JZ
⏲ 12-2.30 (3.30 Sun), 7-midnight (1am Fri & Sat); closed Mon
☎ (01694) 771266 🌐 at-the-oak.com
Hobsons Best Bitter; Wye Valley Butty Bach; guest beers Ⓗ
Ancient 15th-century free house in a conservation village. Reputedly the oldest continuously licensed pub in Shropshire, it retains the character of a traditional country pub. The low-beamed bar has a roaring fire in winter in a vast inglenook fireplace and the dining room has exposed old beams and studwork. Guest beers mostly come from local breweries. The food menu includes Fidget Pie – a Shropshire recipe that has been handed down from landlord to landlord.
♨Q❀◐◑⛺♣P⁻

Church Aston

Last Inn ✔

Wellington Road, TF10 9EJ
⏲ 12-midnight
☎ (01952) 820469 🌐 thelastinn.co.uk
Everards Tiger; Fuller's London Pride; Greene King Abbot; Salopian Shropshire Gold; Taylor Landlord; guest beer Ⓗ
A recent refurbishment has added a spacious but sociable lounge and dining area to this traditional country inn dating from 1866, attracting a mixed clientele of all ages. The garden is outstanding, especially during the summer. An excellent, family-friendly pub serving good pub food, the pub supports the local cricket club. ❀◐◑♿🚌♣P⁻

Clee Hill

Kremlin

SY8 3NB (200m off A4117) SO592755
⏲ 12 (5 Mon)-midnight (closed Mon winter); 12-1am Sat; 12-midnight (10 winter)
☎ (01584) 890950 🌐 thekremlininn.com
Hobsons Mild, Best Bitter; guest beer Ⓗ
Shropshire's highest pub at 1,400ft above sea level and an inn for more than 100 years, this is a former quarry master's house. It gained its name in the 1980s when the jukebox would pick up Radio Moscow. Good quality home-cooked food in generous portions is available at reasonable prices and well-behaved children are welcome. The quarry nearby has a peregrine falcon viewing point with spectacular views over the water. The pub attracts walkers who on a clear day can enjoy panoramic views over seven counties.
♨❀🛏◐◑🚌♣●P

Cleobury Mortimer

Kings Arms

6 Church Street, DY14 8BS
⏲ 10-11 (midnight Thu-Sat); 10-10.30 Sun
☎ (01299) 271954
Hobsons Mild, Best Bitter, Town Crier; guest beer Ⓗ
An inscription on the wall commemorates this pub as the recipient of Hobson's first beer delivery. Now the brewery tap, it has been tastefully refurbished retaining many traditional features, particularly the original wooden floors and beamed ceilings. Although open plan it has separate bar and tap room areas and lounges with comfy sofas. Food ranges from a full English breakfast to a set lunch menu with daily changing specials and home-made pies. A heated, covered terrace is provided for smokers. ♨❀🛏◑♿🚌♣⁻

Clun

White Horse Inn ✓

The Square, SY7 8JA
11 (12 Sun)-midnight
(01588) 640305 whi-clun.co.uk
Hobsons Mild, Best Bitter; Salopian Shropshire Gold; Three Tuns XXX; Wye Valley Butty Bach; guest beers H
Comfortable, 16th-century coaching inn and post house that stands in the old market square at the centre of a wonderfully timeless town, described by AE Houseman as 'one of the quietest places under the sun'. A friendly local, it has an L-shaped bar with low beams and a new adjoining dining room serving excellent, reasonably-priced home-made food. Weston's First Quality cider and interesting foreign bottled beers are stocked. Outside is a secluded garden. Jam nights are held once a month. Winner of local CAMRA Pub of the Year 2007, it boasts its own 'nano' brewery.

Edgerley

Royal Hill ☆

SY10 8ES (between Pentre and Melverley)
12-2, 5-midnight; 12-midnight Sat & Sun
(01743) 741242
Salopian Shropshire Gold; guest beer H
Set on a quiet road, with its garden bordering the River Severn, this delightful pub dating from the 18th century looks out towards the Breidden Hills. The well-preserved building comprises a number of cosy rooms and a tiny bar. Camping is permitted at the back of the pub's grounds, caravans too. Food is served lunchtime and evenings, but you may wish to phone in advance.

Ellerdine Heath

Royal Oak

TF6 6RL (2 miles off A442 towards A53) SJ604225
12-midnight (10.30 Sun)
(01939) 250300
Hobsons Best Bitter; Salopian Shropshire Gold; Wye Valley HPA; guest beers H
In a rural setting and known locally as the Tiddly, this pub has a friendly clientele – 'come in a stranger and leave as a friend', says one local. Hosts Barry and Rose provide roaring fires, good food, real cider, keen prices, a children's area and disabled access to the rear. In late July there is a cider festival that attracts a huge following. No food is available on Tuesday.

Great Ryton

Fox Inn

SY5 7LS (1 mile east of A49 Dorrington) SJ489031
12-2.30 (not Mon), 7-11 (midnight Sat); 12-3.30, 7-1am Sun
(01743) 718499
Jennings Cumberland Ale; Salopian Shropshire Gold; Stonehouse Station Bitter; guest beer H
Country pub nestling beneath the Stretton Hills. At the heart of the local community, the Fox is popular with locals and visitors from neighbouring villages. Local beers are always stocked and an annual beer festival is hosted. The lunchtime bar menu is good and an extensive high quality food menu is offered in the evening. Autographed football and sports memorabilia adorn the walls.

Heathton

Old Gate Inn

WV5 7EB (between B4176 and A458 near Halfpenny Green) SO813923
12-2.30 (not Mon), 6.30-11; 12-3, 7-10.30 Sun
(01746) 710431 oldgateinn.com
Taylor Landlord; Three Tuns XXX; guest beers H
A regular Guide entry, this busy country pub dating from the 1600s is off the beaten track but well worth seeking out. The landlord Jamie has been here since 1988. Two bars have a welcoming atmosphere with exposed timbers and open fires. Excellent meals are served including fresh fish specialities (no meals Sun eve). The children's area outside has been recently refurbished.

Ludlow

Church Inn

The Buttercross, SY8 1AW
11-11 (11.30 Fri & Sat); 12-11 Sun
(01584) 872174 thechurchinn.com
Hobsons Mild, Town Crier; Ludlow Boiling Well, Gold; Weetwood Eastgate Ale; Wye Valley Bitter; guest beers H
Situated in the centre of Ludlow, close to the castle and market square, the Church is the only free house within the town walls and now has a resident ale conner to ensure the quality of the beer. The landlord, a former mayor of Ludlow, is a strong advocate of real ale and also owns the Charlton Arms at Ludford Bridge. Guest beers usually come from the Salopian or Three Tuns breweries. The upstairs bar affords a wonderful view of the South Shropshire Hills and the church. Nine guest and family rooms with Spa Baths. Dogs are welcome.

Nelson Inn

Rocks Green, SY8 2DS (on A4117 Kidderminster road)
5 (7 Tue)-11; 1-midnight Fri & Sat; 12-midnight Sun
(01584) 872908
St Austell Tribute; guest beers H
On the outskirts of Ludlow, the Nelson Inn dates back some 300 years and is a fine example of a traditional beer house. The bar has a pool table, darts, quoits and a jukebox featuring 70s and 80s music. The lounge is decked out with musical instruments – spontaneous music events sometimes occur. The pub has its own beer festival at Easter and early September in conjunction with Ludlow's Food and Drink Fair. The tasty real chips on the menu are highly recommended. Real cider and from time to time perry are sold. Dogs are welcome.

Newport

Fox

Pave Lane, Chetwynd Aston, TF10 9LQ (half mile west of A41)
12-11 (10.30 Sun)
☎ (01952) 815940 fox-newport.co.uk
Stonehouse Fox Golden; Thwaites Original; Wood Shropshire Lad; guest beers ⊞
Popular drinking and dining establishment attracting a wide clientele of all ages, close to the National Sports Centre. Although open plan it has a mix of private corners and spacious rooms, one with the original fireplace. The large south-facing terrace enjoys views out over the rolling countryside and wooded hills beyond. ⋒Q❀◑♿P⌙

Old Woods

Romping Cat

SY4 3AX
4 (12 Sat & Sun)-midnight
☎ (01939) 290273
Hobsons Mild, Best Bitter; Three Tuns 1642; guest beers ⊞
A warm welcome awaits at this traditional roadside country pub. Six handpumps dispense a selection of ales mainly from independent breweries —Shropshire beers always feature and Moles Black Rat Cider is also stocked. Recent changes to the bar layout have added a snug, complete with open fire. Plans are in hand to create a garden at the rear with a smoking shelter. A range of rolls and baps is usually available.
⋒Q❀⊟(576)♣●P▯

Oswestry

Fox Inn

Church Street, SY11 2SU
11.30-3 (not Mon), 6-midnight; 11.30-11.30 Fri & Sat; 11.30-11.30 (12-3, 6-11 winter) Sun
☎ (01691) 679669
Jennings Dark Mild, Bitter; guest beers ⊞
Occupying a long, narrow late-medieval site, this town centre pub has timber-beamed rooms including a cosy front bar and a larger room with a log fire. The outside courtyard has a roofed stage for bands and actors —live music is hosted once a month. Barbecues are held in the summer. A small art gallery features local artwork for sale. Five cask ales are always available alongside two cask ciders —Thatchers Heritage and Traditional Scotch. Beer festivals are hosted occasionally. The pub has a strict no swearing policy.
⋒Q⊱❀◑⊟♣●⌙▯

Sambrook

Three Horseshoes

TF10 8AP (half mile E of A41)
12-2 (not Mon), 5 (4 summer)-11; 11-10.30 (11 summer) Sun
☎ (01952) 551133
Banks's Original; St Austell Tribute; Salopian Shropshire Gold; guest beers ⊞
A third consecutive year in the Guide for this welcoming country pub situated in a quiet rural village. Very popular with early doors drinkers, regulars even come from Newport five miles away. Traditional pub games are played in the cosy quarry-tiled bar and the occasional live music evening is hosted. No food is served on Sunday evening.
⋒Q❀◑⊟♿♣●P⌙

Selattyn

Cross Keys ★

Glyn Road, SY10 7DH (On B4579 Oswestry-Glyn Ceiriog road)
closed Mon & Tue; 7 (6 Fri)-11; 12-5, 7-11 Sun
☎ (01691) 650247
Stonehouse Station Bitter; guest beers ⊞
Listed in CAMRA's National Inventory, this building dates from the 17th century and has been an inn since 1840. It is situated next to the church in a small village close to the Welsh border and Offa's Dyke. The cosy, small bar has a quarry-tiled floor and a real fire. Irish music plays on Thursday evening. The pub opens at lunchtimes Monday to Saturday by prior arrangement only. Two guest beers are always available. There is a self-catering cottage attached to the pub. ⋒Q⊱❀⊟▲♣P

Shifnal

White Hart ✔

4 High Street, TF11 8BH
12-11
☎ (01952) 461161
Adnams Broadside; Exmoor Gold; Holden's Mild, Bitter; Wye Valley HPA; guest beers ⊞
Not to be missed, this popular, welcoming 16th-century inn is a frequent winner of local CAMRA Pub of the Year. The impressive listed black and white half-timbered pub is everything a traditional pub should be, with seven handpulls in two bars, a warm, friendly atmosphere and good quality home-made lunchtime food (not Sun). Outside there is a pleasant secluded patio and garden.
Q❀◑≹⊟♣P⌙

Shrewsbury

Abbey Hotel ✔

83 Monkmoor Road, SY2 5AZ
11.30-11 (midnight Fri & Sat); 12-11 Sun
☎ (01743) 236788
Fuller's London Pride; M&B Mild, Brew XI; guest beers ⊞
Gary the landlord runs what must be Ember Inns' flagship real ale house. This large, imposing pub on a suburban road offers a range of up to nine cask ales, always including a mild. A quiz is held twice a week. Children under 14 years of age are not permitted.
⋒Q❀◑⊟P⌙

Admiral Benbow

24 Swan Hill, SY1 1NF
5 (12 Sat)-11; 7-10.30 Sun
☎ (01743) 244423
Greene King IPA; Ludlow Gold; Six Bells Cloud Nine; guest beers ⊞
Situated just off the main town square, this spacious free house specialises in Shropshire and Herefordshire ales. Local ciders include Gwatkin's Foxwhelp and Yarlington Mill

together with Blakeney Red Perry. A good range of Belgian beers is also usually available. A small room off the bar can be used for private functions. Children are not permitted and under 30s are served at the management's discretion. CAMRA West Midlands Cider Pub of the Year 2007.
⛼Q❀⊟⇌♣●⌐

Coach & Horses ✔

Swan Hill, SY1 1NP (near Music Hall)
⏲ 11.30-midnight (12.30am Fri & Sat); 12-11.30 Sun
☎ (01743) 365661 ⊕ odleyinns.co.uk/coach&horses.htm
Salopian Shropshire Gold; Wye Valley HPA; guest beers Ⓗ
Set in a quiet street off the main shopping area, the Coach & Horses provides a peaceful haven, with magnificent floral displays in summer. Victorian in style, the interior includes a wood-panelled bar, small side snug area and large lounge where meals are served at lunchtime and in the evening. Cheddar Valley cider is sold alongside the real ales. Live music, mainly electro-acoustic, plays most Sunday evenings in the lounge.
Q◐⊟♿⇌●⌐

Nags Head

Wyle Cop, SY1 1XB
⏲ 11-midnight (1am Fri & Sat); 12-midnight Sun
☎ (01743) 362455
Greene King IPA; Taylor Landlord; Wells Bombardier; guest beers Ⓗ
Situated on the historic Wyle Cop, this timber-framed building is best appreciated from the outside, in particular the upper storey jettying and, to the rear, the timber remnants of a 14th-century hall house including a screened passage that provided protection from draughts (and now provides shelter for smokers). The old-fashioned interior has remained unaltered for many years. The pub attracts a mixed clientele and can be very busy at times. It is reputed to be haunted and features on the Shrewsbury Ghost Trail.
❀⊟⇌⊟♣●⌐

Prince of Wales

Bynner Street, Belle Vue, SY3 7NZ
⏲ 12-2 (not Mon), 5-midnight; 12-midnight Fri-Sun
☎ (01743) 343301 ⊕ princeofwaleshotel.co.uk
Ansells Mild; Greene King IPA; St Austell Tribute; guest beers Ⓗ
Welcoming two-roomed community pub with a large decked sun-trap and bowling green overlooked by an 18th-century maltings. Darts, dominoes and bowls teams are based here. Two beer festivals are held a year – the Winter Ales festival in February and another festival in May. Shrewsbury Town FC memorabilia adorn the building both inside and out, with some of the seating from the old Gay Meadow ground skirting the bowling green. Local CAMRA branch Pub of the Year and runner up in 2005 and 2007.
⛼❀◐⊟♿♣●⌐▯

Salopian Bar

Smithfield Road, SY1 1PW
⏲ 12-11 (midnight Fri & Sat); closed Mon
☎ (01743) 351505 ⊕ thesalopianbar.co.uk
Dark Star Hophead; Stonehouse Cambrian Gold; Thornbridge Various; Wye Valley Butty Bach; guest beers Ⓗ
Modern, comfortable pub with an attractive interior featuring work for sale by local artists displayed on the walls. The young and dedicated management continually strives to increase the beer, cider and perry range to satisfy public demand. Cider and perry come from Weston's, Gwatkins and Renshaws. A small selection of bottled real ale is also available. Live acoustic music plays on Friday. Major non-satellite sports events are screened on TV. Winner of local CAMRA Pub of the Year 2008. ♿⇌⊟♣●⌐

Three Fishes ✔

Fish Street, SY1 1UR
⏲ 11.30-3, 5-11; 11.30-11.30 Fri & Sat; 12-4, 7-10.30 Sun
☎ (01743) 344793
Hobsons Mild; Taylor Landlord; guest beers Ⓗ
Fifteenth-century building standing in the shadow of two churches, St Alkmond's and St Julian's, within a maze of streets and passageways in the medieval quarter of the town. Freshly-prepared food is available at lunchtime and early evening (not Sun eve). The pub offers a selection of up to six local and national beers, with dark ales featuring regularly, alongside a varied range of real cider and perry. Local CAMRA Pub of the Year runner up in 2007. Q◐⇌⊟●

Wheatsheaf ✔

50 High Street, SY1 1ST
⏲ 11-midnight; 12-11 Sun
☎ (01743) 272702
Banks's Bitter; Marston's Old Empire; guest beers Ⓗ
Comfortable town centre street corner pub with a view to St Julian's Church, with three distinct bar areas displaying many pictures of old Shrewsbury. Popular with regulars, visitors and shoppers, food is made using locally-sourced produce (lunches only, not Sun). Beer festivals are held in March and October. Live electro-acoustic music plays on most Thursday evenings. In fine weather seating is available out on the pavement. ◐⇌⊟

Woodman Inn

Coton Hill, SY1 2DZ
⏲ 4 (12 Sun)-11
☎ (01743) 351007
Hobsons Best Bitter; Shepherd Neame Spitfire; Weetwood Oasthouse Gold; guest beers Ⓗ
Half brick and half timbered black and white corner pub originally built in the 1800s but destroyed by a fire in 1923 and rebuilt in 1925 – the building is reputed to be haunted by the ex-landlady who died when the pub burned down. The bar retains the original stone-tiled flooring, wooden seating, log fire and listed leaded windows, and the wonderful oak-panelled lounge has two real log fires and traditional settles. Local CAMRA branch Pub of the Year runner up in 2006 and 2007.
⛼Q☕❀⊟♿⇌⊟●⌐▯

Stottesdon

Fighting Cocks

1 High Street, DY14 8TZ
6-midnight; 5-1am Fri; 12-midnight Sat; 12-11.30 Sun
(01746) 718270
Hobsons Mild, Best Bitter, Town Crier; guest beer
An alehouse since 1830, this traditional pub has beamed ceilings, a cosy bar with a log fire, two dining areas and a function room. Excellent award-winning food is served in the evening (not Sun), made only with fresh locally-sourced produce. Monday is 'Curry and Jam' night with an open mike, and live music plays on alternate Saturday nights. A beer festival is hosted in the autumn. A hub of activity for the local community, the pub has a shop and Internet access for customers.

Telford: Coalbrookdale

Coalbrookdale Inn

12 Wellington Road, TF8 7DX (opp Museum of Iron)
12-3, 5-midnight; 12-midnight Sat & Sun
(01952) 433953 coalbrookdaleinn.co.uk
Hobsons Town Crier; Three Tuns XXX; Wye Valley Butty Bach; guest beers
Situated across the road from the Museum of Iron and known locally as the Dale, the pub welcomes locals and visitors alike. Three guest beers, usually local, are available in addition to the regulars. The pub has a good reputation for food too, served in the bar and restaurant. All meats and vegetables (organic wherever possible) are sourced from the Shropshire area. Accommodation is in three double en-suite bedrooms. Extra parking is available at the community centre close by.

Telford: Coalport

Shakespeare Inn

High Street, Coalport, TF8 7HT
5-11; 12-midnight Sat & Sun
(01952) 580675 shakespeare-inn.co.uk
Enville Ale; Everards Tiger; guest beers
Warm, welcoming family run pub with wonderful views of the Severn Gorge and River, ideally situated for the Coalport China and Tar Tunnel museums. The Silkin Way leading to the Blists Hill Museum is nearby. A good selection of guest ales, often from local brewers, includes favourites Exmoor Gold and Three Tuns XXX. The tempting menu of excellent home-cooked dishes (eve meals Tue-Sat only) is always popular, and booking in advance is advised. There is a large, three-tiered beer garden with children's play equipment.

Telford: Ironbridge

Golden Ball

Newbridge Road, TF8 7BA (off B4373 Madeley Road Hill)
12-11 (10.30 Sun)
(01952) 432179
Everards Tiger; Hobsons Town Crier; guest beers
Historic inn set in the Ironbridge Gorge. Handy for the sights and museums, it is a must when visiting the area. Good food features heavily, with an extensive bar menu and separate restaurant. However the Golden Ball is much more than a dining pub, with a vibrant bar atmosphere and a strong local following. Two regular beers are supplemented by three guests, usually from local breweries. A range of Belgian bottled beers is also available.

Robin Hood Inn

33 Waterloo Street, TF8 7HQ
10-midnight
(01952) 433100 yeolderobinhoodinn.co.uk
Holden's Mild, Bitter, Golden Glow, Special; guest beers
Overlooking the River Severn opposite Jackfield Bridge, this 18th-century inn is situated in the birthplace of the Industrial Revolution. A Holden's pub since 2004, it has three rooms with oak beamed interiors and a warm atmosphere. Known for its traditional pub grub and fine beers, guest ales vary, complemented by real cider. Live folk music plays on the second Tuesday of the month. Large murals of local scenes painted by a well-known local artist decorate the walls.

Telford: Leegomery

Malt Shovel

Hadley Park Road, TF1 6QG (off A442 near Leegomery Roundabout)
12-2.30, 5-11; 12-11 Fri-Sun
(01952) 242963
Banks's Original; Marston's Burton Bitter, Pedigree; guest beers
A proper pub! There is always a buzz about this place, attracting locals as well as a regular business clientele. There are two rooms: a comfortable, spacious lounge and lively bar. Televised sport draws a crowd in the bar, and traditional pub games remain popular. Tasty, reasonably priced lunches are served at lunchtime during the week. Pies and rolls are usually available at other times.

Telford: Madeley

All Nations

20 Coalport Road, TF7 5DP (off Legges Way opp Blists Hill Museum)
12-midnight
(01952) 585747
Worfield Coalport Dodger Mild, Dabley Ale, Dabley Gold; guest beers
Historic home-brew house now with the Worfield Brewery on site. Close to the Blists Hill Museum, it attracts many visitors. However it remains very much a community local – family friendly with traditional pub games, regular quiz nights and a keen rugby following. Rolls and toasties can be made to order at any time during opening hours. Recent developments including real cider or perry on draught, camping facilities and two B&B rooms.

Telford: Oakengates

Crown Inn ✔

Market Street, TF2 6EA

12-3, 5-11 Mon & Tue; 12-11 Wed-Sun

☎ (01952) 610888 crown.oakengates.net

Hobsons Best Bitter; guest beers Ⓗ

A fine example of a town hostelry. Fourteen handpulls increase to 34 at the pub's famous beer festivals held on the first weekends of May and October, when there are upwards of 60 ales to choose from. An extensive whisky menu complements the large range of continental bottled beers. Prices are very keen even by Midlands standards, and the locals very friendly. Current refurbishments include a sun-trap courtyard. Live music features on Thursday evening and the Telford acoustic club meets each Wednesday.

Telford: St Georges

St Georges Sports & Social Club

Church Road, TF2 9LU

7-midnight (12.30am Fri); 12-12.30am Sat & Sun

☎ (01952) 612911

Banks's Original, Bitter; guest beers Ⓗ

This club is a regular winner of CAMRA awards for its enthusiastic support and promotion of real ale. Beers are mainly showcased from Shropshire and Black Country breweries, but not exclusively. The outside drinking area overlooks one of the grounds used by Shropshire Cricket Club, and many local sports teams use the club as a base. A large function room is available to hire and hosts occasional beer festivals. CAMRA members are always warmly welcomed. P

Telford: Wellington

Cock Hotel

148 Hollyhead Road, TF1 2DL

4-11.30; 12-11.30 Thu & Fri; 12-11.45 Sat; 12-4, 7-11 Sun

☎ (01952) 244954 cockhotel.co.uk

Hobsons Best Bitter; guest beers Ⓗ

A long-standing entry in the Guide, this 18th-century coaching inn has been run by a husband and wife team for many years. The imposing building on the main road (old A5) has a hop-festooned main bar with eight handpulls dispensing constantly-changing guests, one always a mild and one a stout or porter, and one a cider. A selection of foreign beers, draught and bottled, is also available. Lively conversation is the norm here, with no games machines or music. A genuine free house, it is local CAMRA Pub of the Year for 2008. Q P

Wistanstow

Plough Inn

SY7 8DG (next to Wood Brewery)

12-2.30, 5-midnight; 12-11 Sun

☎ (01588) 673251 ploughwistanstow.co.uk

Wood Parish, Shropshire Lad; guest beers Ⓗ

Traditional country pub dating from 1782 on the doorstep of the Wood Brewery. There are two main bars, with the public bar a few steps down from the entrance, and a games room. Food is home made using Shropshire produce wherever possible and served in the large lounge (not Mon and Sun eve). Handpulls are over 100 years old and have recently been renovated. The tap for Wood, presentation packs of its beers are for sale and there is a fine display of Royal Wedding commemorative bottled beers.

Q P

Yorton

Railway Inn

SY4 3EP (200m from Yorton Railway Station)

12.30-4 (not Thu), 7-11; 12-4, 7-11 Sun

☎ (01939) 220240

Salopian Hop Twister; Three Tuns 1642; Wadworth 6X; Wood Shropshire Lad; guest beers Ⓗ

Stepping inside the Railway Inn is like going back in time —little has changed since 1936 when the owners moved in. Then a Southam's pub, it became a free house when the family purchased it from Whitbread. The small bar with its settles and quarry-tiled floors is popular with locals and railway travellers. Real cider is Thatchers Medium served from the cellar. A selection of bottled ciders and perrys is also available. Q P

Beer suitable for vegetarians and vegans

A number of cask and bottle-fermented beers in the Good Beer Guide are listed as suitable for vegetarians and vegans. The main ingredients used in cask beer production are malted grain, hops, yeast and water, and these present no problems for drinkers who wish to avoid animal products. But most brewers of cask beer use isinglass as a clearing agent: isinglass is derived from the bladders of certain fish, including the sturgeon. Isinglass is added to a cask when it leaves the brewery and attracts yeast cells and protein, which fall to the bottom of the container. Other clearing agents – notably Irish moss, derived from seaweed – can be used in place of isinglass and the Guide feels that brewers should take a serious look at replacing isinglass with plant-derived finings, especially as the sturgeon is an endangered species.

Vegans avoid dairy products: lactose, a bi-product of cheese making, is used in milk stout, of which Mackeson is the best-known example.

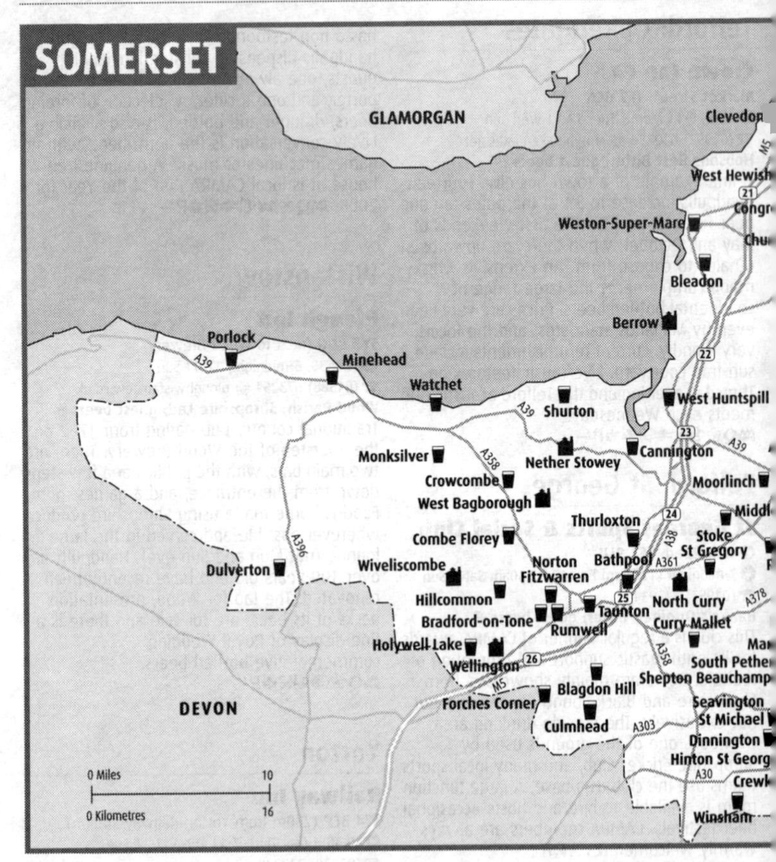

Aller

Old Pound Inn

TA10 0RA (on A372 between Langport and Othery)
⏲ 5.30 (11.30 Sat & Sun)-11
☎ (01458) 250469 🌐 oldpoundinn.co.uk
Sharp's Doom Bar; guest beers Ⓗ

A genuine free house dating from the 16th century in a rural village setting where constantly changing West Country beers are kept in a temperature-controlled cellar. A large well-maintained bar, on different levels, leads to a family room, spacious restaurant and function facilities. An extensive food and wine menu is available. Over 40 malt whiskies are stocked. Dogs are welcome. Outside is a small, secluded garden.
♨❀⊟◐♿Å⊟(16)♣P⊱

Ashcott

Ring O' Bells

High Street, TA7 9PZ
⏲ 12-2.30, 7-11 (10.30 Sun)
☎ (01458) 210232 🌐 ringobells.com
Beer range varies Ⓗ

Village pub near the church with three connected bar areas on different levels and a large function room with disabled access. Award-winning food is served throughout. Local ales from Moor and Glastonbury are often available among the constantly changing range of beers, along with local cider from Wilkins. A former Somerset CAMRA Pub of the Year, it has been run by the same family for more than 20 years.
❀◐♿⊟(29,375)♣●P

Barton St David

Barton Inn

Main Street, TA11 6BZ
⏲ 12-2.30, 4.30-11 (midnight Sat & Sun)
☎ (01458) 850451
Beer range varies Ⓖ

Dump your ferret (well-behaved ones only) on the bar and park the muddy dog next to the fire to dry out, before sampling some of the ales racked behind the counter. This real country pub is full of both character and characters, where eccentricity appears to be the norm. Sympathetic enlargement of the bar area has not destroyed the cosy feeling and, while the pub may be somewhat off the beaten track, it is worth making the effort to find. ♨❀◐♿♣●P⊱

Bath

Bell

103 Walcot Street, BA1 5BW
⏲ 11.30-11; 12-10.30 Sun
☎ (01225) 460426 🌐 walcotstreet.co.uk

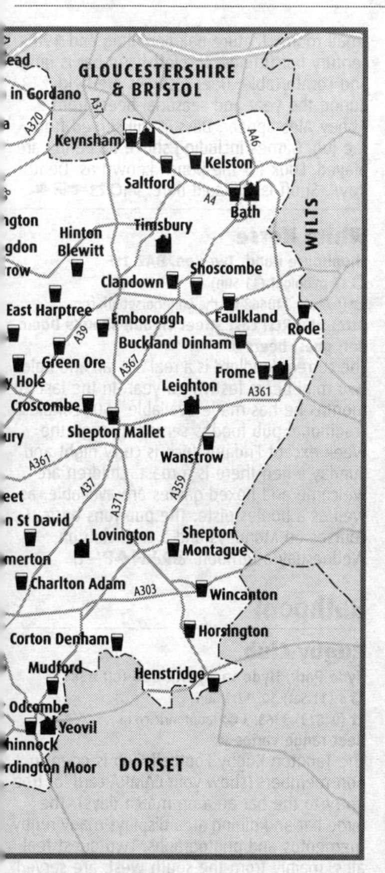

Abbey Bellringer; Bath Ales Gem; Hop Back Summer Lightning; Otter Bitter; RCH Pitchfork; Stonehenge Danish Dynamite; guest beers H
The Bell features bands performing on Monday and Wednesday evenings and Sunday lunchtimes. There is a long main bar and a number of seating areas. The wall space inside is taken up with posters for gigs and other events in the Walcot area. Redecoration has been so subtle that at least one regular did not notice. Wi-Fi facilities are available. At the back of the pub is a garden with plenty of seating. Local CAMRA Pub of the Year 2004.

Curfew

11A Cleveland Place West, BA1 5DG
5-11 (midnight Thu & Fri); 12-midnight Sat & Sun
☎ (01225) 424210
Wadworth Henry's IPA, 6X, seasonal beers H
A traditional pub located on Bath's busy London Road serving only Wadworth's beers. Downstairs has traditional wooden decor, while an unexpected comfortable upstairs room is furnished with sofas. The main bar has a number of distinct drinking areas. A small courtyard at the rear is pleasant in summer. Despite the traffic outside, all is calm inside.

Hop Pole

Albion Buildings, Upper Bristol Road, BA1 3AR
12-11 (midnight Fri & Sat)
☎ (01225) 446327
Bath Ales SPA, Gem, Barnstormer; Butcombe Gold; guest beers H
The Hop Pole is a friendly place situated between Victoria Park and the River Avon. Six real ales are normally available, including four from Bath Ales. A range of bottled foreign beers is also stocked. High quality food is available most lunchtimes and evenings until 9pm (not Sun). There is a separate restaurant which was converted from the skittle alley. An alleyway connects to the river towpath, part of the Bath-Bristol cycle path. Outside is a pleasant garden.

Old Green Tree ★

12 Green Street, BA1 2JZ
11-11; 12-10.30 Sun
☎ (01225) 448259
Blindmans Green Tree Bitter; RCH Pitchfork; Wickwar Mr Perretts Stout; guest beers H
Classic, unspoilt pub in a 300-year-old building. An atmosphere of quiet cosiness pervades all three of the small oak-panelled rooms, where the panelling dates from the 1920s. The lounge bar at the front is decorated with pictures of World War II aircraft. The pub can get very crowded, but space can sometimes be found in the comfortable back bar. The range of beers is complemented by an occasional perry and a choice of malt whiskies. Q

Pig & Fiddle

2 Saracen Street, BA1 5BR
11-11; 12-10.30 Sun
☎ (01225) 460868
Abbey Bellringer; Butcombe Bitter; guest beers H
A large and busy town centre pub with a varied clientele and friendly atmosphere. One end is an old shop front, the other an outside courtyard with drinking benches and covered heaters. The decor is an esoteric collection of sports memorabilia such as signed rugby shirts, a pair of signed Olympic skis and an Olympic oar from the Coxed Eight gold medallists. Up to three guest beers come from local breweries. Table football is available. Handy for the rugby ground.

Pulteney Arms

37 Daniel Street, BA2 6ND
12-3 (not Mon & Tue), 5-11 (midnight Fri); 12-midnight Sat; 12-10.30 Sun
☎ (01225) 463923 pulteneyarms.co.uk
Bath Ales Gem; Fuller's London Pride; Sharp's Doom Bar; Wadworth 6X; Young's Bitter; guest beers H
The building dates from 1759 and is known to have been a pub as early as 1792. There is still extensive use of gas lighting, with five lights above the bar. The decor shows an emphasis on sport, particularly rugby. The pub sponsors a number of sports teams, including a hockey team and Bath Ladies Rugby. The food menu is extensive and deservedly popular. The cat symbol on the pub sign refers to the Pulteney coat of arms. Q

Raven

6-7 Queen Street, BA1 1HE
11-11 (midnight Fri & Sat); 12-10.30 Sun

☎ (01225) 310324
Blindmans Raven, Raven Gold; guest beers H
In a cobbled street near Queen Square, the pub has been extensively refurbished and has reverted to an original Bath pub name. There is a bar and dining area upstairs; pies and sausages are a speciality, with at least nine flavours of pie available. Occasional live acoustic music is staged and the pub hosts a variety of events such as storytelling evenings and the Bath Science Café. There is a mountain bike team, and newcomers are welcome.
◑≉

Royal Oak
Lower Bristol Road, Twerton, BA2 3BW
12-midnight
☎ (01225) 481409 theroyaloak-bath.co.uk
Beer range varies H
Shut for six years, this pub opened again in 2005 and is now an established free house. An ever-changing range of up to 10 ales from micros far and wide means there should be something new for everyone to try. Irish music plays on Wednesday and other music some weekends. Beer and music festivals are held in December, February and July. A discount is available for CAMRA members. Local CAMRA Pub of the Year 2007 & 2008.
⛼Q❀◑≉⊟♣●P

Royal Oak
Summerlays Place, BA2 4HN
11-11 (summer); 12-2.30, 5-11 (winter); 11-11 Sun
☎ (01225) 335220
Bath Ales Gem; Butcombe Gold; Courage Best Bitter; Otter Ale; guest beers H
This pub has undergone a massive refurbishment in the past year and has been transformed from a rather dingy place into a more open, light, airy and modern-feeling establishment. The large garden contains a boules piste. In addition to the changing guest beer, the pub hopes to add Thatchers cider in summer. The pub is also useful for the magistrates court. ❀◑≉⊟♣⁻

Salamander
3 John Street, BA1 2JL
11.30-11 (midnight Fri & Sat); 12-10.30 Sun
☎ (01225) 428889
Bath Ales SPA, Gem, Barnstormer; guest beers H
Former 18th-century coffee house now fitted out in the familiar Bath Ales style, with wooden floorboards, wood panelling and hanging hops. The pub is subtly divided downstairs, with a separate restaurant upstairs, and can get crowded very quickly. Restaurant food includes beer-themed meals. The pub also offers a selection of bottled Belgian beers. Bath Ales merchandise and beers to take home can be purchased. There is an Irish band on Tuesday evening. ◑≉⊟

Star ★ ✔
23 The Vineyards, BA1 5NA
12-2.30, 5.30-midnight (1am Fri); 12-1am Sat; 12-midnight Sun
☎ (01225) 425072 star-inn-bath.co.uk
Abbey Bellringer; H **Draught Bass;** G **guest beers** H
This pub, licensed in 1760, is one of the oldest in Bath and is now a listed building. Its many small rooms feature oak panelling and 19th-century bar fittings. The left-hand bar is quiet and comfortable. Beer festivals are held during the year and seasonal beers from Abbey Ales appear. Bass is still served from the jug. Games including shove ha'penny are played. Look for the bench known as 'Death Row'. Snuff is still sold here. ⛼Q♉≉⊟♣

White Horse
Shophouse Road, Twerton, BA2 1EF
12-midnight (11 Sun)
☎ (01225) 340668 thewhitehorsebath.com
Otter Ale; RCH East Street Cream; Sharp's Doom Bar; guest beers H
The current landlord is a real ale fan and holds two mini beers festivals a year. In the last 20 months he has made available 150 real ales. Traditional pub food is served through the week except Friday which is curry night and Sunday when there is a roast. Children are welcome and boxed games are available, as well as a boules piste. The pub runs basic IT courses on Mondays and a craft club on Wednesday afternoon. ❀◑♿⊟♣P⁻▯

Bathpool

Rugby Club
Hyde Park, Hyde Lane, TA2 8BU (off A38)
6 (11 Sat)-10; 12-3 Sun
☎ (01823) 336363 tauntonrfc.co.uk
Beer range varies H
The Taunton Rugby Football Club is open to non-members (show your CAMRA card for free entry to the bar area on match days). The large bar and dining area displays many rugby mementos and photographs. Two guest real ales, mainly from the south west, are served on handpump. A carvery lunch is available on Sunday, otherwise lunchtime food is only served on match days. A large covered area is provided for smokers.
Q❀◐♿▲⊟(15,21)♣P⁻

Blagdon

New Inn
Church Street, BS40 7SB (100m off A368)

INDEPENDENT BREWERIES

Abbey Ales Bath
Berrow Berrow
Blindmans Leighton
Butcombe Wrington
Cheddar Ales Cheddar
Cotleigh Wiveliscombe
Cottage Lovington
Exmoor Wiveliscombe
Glastonbury Somerton
Keynsham Keynsham
Matthews Timsbury
Milk Street Frome
Moor Ashcott
North Curry North Curry (NEW)
Odcombe Lower Odcombe
Quantock Wellington (NEW)
RCH West Hewish
Stowey Nether Stowey
Taunton West Bagbrough
Yeovil Yeovil

☉ 11-3, 6-11.30; 12-3, 6-10.30 Sun
☎ (01761) 462475
Wadworth Henry's IPA, 6X, seasonal beers Ⓗ
Sixteenth-century whitewashed inn. The main entrance is at the rear and leads into two rooms furnished with exposed beams, comfy sofas and horse brasses. Two large fireplaces add warmth in winter, and generously portioned, reasonably priced meals are on offer at all sessions. The Green Room to the right of the bar is quieter, while the rear beer garden offers panoramic views of Blagdon Lake and the Mendip Hills. Dogs are admitted. A fairly limited bus service runs nearby.
⩩Q❀◑♣P

Blagdon Hill

Lamb & Flag

TA3 7SL (4 miles S of Taunton)
☉ 11-11 (midnight Fri); 12-10.30 Sun
☎ (01823) 421736
Otter Bitter; guest beers Ⓗ
Situated on the northern slopes of the Blackdown Hills, this 16th-century pub is frequented by locals and visitors. The open main bar area has the original flagstone floor and a large fireplace separating the bar and candlelit dining area. The four ales come from south-west micro-breweries. A skittle alley and function room are situated beyond the bar. The large garden has panoramic views from the Brendon to the Mendip hills. Food is locally sourced and home cooked.
⩩ఠ❀◑♣●P⍽

Bleadon

Queen's Arms

Celtic Way, BS24 0NF (off A370)
☉ 11.30-11
☎ (01934) 812080 🌐 queensarms-butcombe.com
Butcombe Bitter, Gold, seasonal beers; guest beers Ⓖ
Oldest pub of three in Bleadon, situated in the centre of the village. Three rooms converge on the bar and there is a garden/patio sales hatch. From time immemorial the ale here has only been served on gravity. Food sales are strong, but beer is a popular attraction too. Thatchers cider is also sold. The family area includes an enormous fireplace. Expect Morris men on May Day Monday.
⩩Qఠ❀◑🚌(83)●P⍽

Bradford-on-Tone

White Horse Inn

Regent Street, TA4 1HF (off A38 between Taunton and Wellington)
☉ 11.30-3, 5.30-11; 12-3, 7-10.30 Sun
☎ (01823) 461239 🌐 whitehorseinnbradford.co.uk
Cotleigh Tawny; guest beers Ⓗ
Very much a community pub at the centre of the village, there are a post office and shop in outbuildings. Guest beers are sourced primarily from south west breweries. Excellent home-cooked food is served (booking advised) and speciality evenings are a feature. Real fires warm both bars in winter, while the beautiful large garden hosts barbecues in summer. The skittle alley doubles as a function room and bar billiards can be played. Buses stop a 15-minute walk away.
⩩❀◑♿🚌(22,92)♣P⍽

Buckland Dinham

Bell

High Street, BA11 2QT
☉ 12-3 (not Mon & Tue), 6-midnight; 12-2.30, 7-11.30 Sun
☎ (01373) 462956 🌐 bellatbuckland.co.uk
Butcombe Bitter; Fuller's London Pride; Wychwood Hobgoblin; guest beers Ⓗ
This good, warm and cosy local pub is involved in community activities such as producing a village recipe book, using local beers in each dish. It also offers a facility to order and pay for beer online. A three-day summer beer festival is run with live music – very convenient for the on-site campers. Boules is also played. ⩩ఠ❀◑⊟♿⛺🚌♣●P⍽▭

Cannington

Rose & Crown

30 High Street, TA5 2HF (off A39)
☉ 12-11 (10.30 Sun)
☎ (01278) 653190
Caledonian Deuchars IPA; Greene King IPA, Old Speckled Hen, Abbot; guest beers Ⓗ
An atmospheric, friendly 17th-century pub with a loyal local following. Original beams are covered with interesting objects donated by locals and there is a collection of clocks. The single bar has a pool table, table skittles and a collection of games hand made by locals. The 'Outside Inn' is a covered, comfortable smoking area in an award-winning large garden. ⩩❀🚌(14)♣P⍽

Charlton Adam

Fox & Hounds

Broadway Road, TA11 7AU (off A37)
☉ 12-3, 6-11 (10.30 Sun)
☎ (01458) 223466
Beer range varies Ⓗ
Friendly pub on the east side of the village. The single bar has a large collection of tankards hanging from the ceiling and the walls are decorated with hunting scenes and a former pub sign. Look out for the 1970s price list – those were the days! Good food is served in the bar and conservatory, with steak on Thursday and special offers on Monday. Three handpumps serve mainly West Country beers. An accredited camping site is at the rear.
⩩❀◑♿⛺♣P⍽

Cheddar

White Hart

The Bays, BS27 3QW
☉ 11.30-2.30, 5.30-11; 11.30-11 Sun
☎ (01934) 741261 🌐 thewhitehartcheddar.co.uk
Butcombe Bitter; St Austell Tribute; guest beers Ⓗ
A delightfully welcoming local pub situated near Cheddar Gorge and licensed since 1842. A large open log fireplace is a central feature, complemented by engaging photos depicting the regulars' day trips out, organised by the

pub. Many clubs and societies meet here and dogs are welcome too. To the rear is a large beer garden and parking. Regular quiz, music and themed nights are hosted. Thatchers cider, both draught and bottled, is available. Good food is served. No jukebox or fruit machines here. ♨Q❀◖◗▲🚌(126)♣●P

Churchill

Crown Inn

The Batch, Skinners Lane, BS25 5PP (off A38, ¼ mile S of A368 jct)
⏲ 11.30-11 (midnight Fri & Sat); 12-10.30 Sun
☎ (01934) 852995
Butcombe Bitter; Cheddar Best; Cotleigh Batch; Draught Bass; Palmers IPA; RCH Hewish; guest beers Ⓖ
This long-time Guide regular and winner of many CAMRA awards has been in the same hands for 23 years. It is tucked away down a small lane yet close to the village centre. Several small rooms with stone-flagged floors are warmed by two log fires and offer an assortment of seating. Excellent food is provided at lunchtimes only and in fine weather inspiring views from the outside patio gardens add further delight. Up to nine beers are served straight from the cask, usually sourced from local breweries. ♨Q❀◖▲🚌(121)●P

Clandown

Lamb

Chapel Road, BA3 3BP
⏲ 10.30-midnight; 11-11 Sun
☎ (01761) 435777
Badger First Gold; Bath Ales Gem; St Austell Tribute; guest beers Ⓗ
A very friendly local, with an involved and enthusiastic landlord, serving an excellent variety of real ales and good bar food. The pub is home to local skittles, darts and crib teams, and table tennis. Live entertainment is also provided. This hostelry is popular with a mixed clientele of all ages. ♨❀◖🖵♿🚌♣P⁻

Clapton in Gordano

Black Horse

Clevedon Lane, BS20 7RH (2 miles from M5 jct 19)
⏲ 11-11; 12-10.30 Sun
☎ (01275) 842105 🌐 thekicker.co.uk
Butcombe Bitter; Ⓖ **Courage Best Bitter;** Ⓗ **Shepherd Neame Spitfire;** Ⓖ **Wadworth 6X; Websters Green Label;** Ⓗ **guest beers** Ⓖ
Excellent 14th-century pub hidden away down a small lane. The snug was once the village lock-up, but now feels nice and cosy. A large fireplace with a display of old rifles dominates the main bar. Beers are served from a small serving hatch. The games room doubles as a family room, and there is a children's play area in the pleasant garden. The Gordano Valley cycle route is nearby. Dogs are welcome. Thatchers Dry and Moles Black Rat cider are sold. ♨Q🐴❀◖▲♣●P⁻

Clevedon

Old Inn ✔

9 Walton Road, BS21 6AE (on Portishead road)
⏲ 11-11.30 (midnight Fri & Sat)
☎ (01275) 340440 🌐 theoldinnclevedon.co.uk
Courage Best Bitter; guest beers Ⓗ
A warm welcome is assured at this delightful 15th-century inn that once served the carriage trade from Weston to Portishead. One large room features old wooden beams and many pictures. A wonderful community feel is sometimes enhanced by piano playing or other jollity. Three guest beers are often adventurous or unusual. Excellent pub food is served at good value prices, including a children's menu. Six bed and breakfast rooms are available, together with a pleasant beer garden. The popular National Trust attraction Tynsfield is close by. ♨❀🛏◖◗▲🚌♣●P⁻

Combe Florey

Farmers Arms

TA4 3HZ (on A358 between Bishops Lydeard and Williton)
⏲ 12-11 (10.30 Sun)
☎ (01823) 432267 🌐 farmersarmsatcombeflorey.co.uk
Cotleigh Tawny; Exmoor Ale, Gold; St Austell HSD; guest beers Ⓗ
This family-owned, 16th-century thatched inn is set in picturesque countryside close to the West Somerset Railway. Comprising a bar area with inglenook fireplace and a restaurant, it is justly famous for the quality of its local ales, which are popular with regulars and tourists. Themed evenings and special events are organised. The pub featured in the Sunday Times' list of Top 10 Pubs in 2006. ♨🐴❀◖◗♿▲🚌(28)♣P⁻

Congresbury

Old Inn

St Pauls Causeway, BS49 5DH (off A370)
⏲ 11.30-11.30 (12.30am Fri & Sat); 12-11.30 Sun
☎ (01934) 832270
Wells Bombardier; Young's Bitter, Special; guest beers Ⓗ
Popular 16th-century village local, owned by Young's. This cosy pub has a wonderful inglenook fireplace that burns chunky logs during the winter. There are low ceilings throughout and a main bar area plus two smaller rooms, one with a TV and the other used for families. The main bar has leather straps hanging from the ceiling to steady yourself after one too many! No food is served. ♨Q🐴❀🚌(X1,353)♣●P

Plough

High Street, BS49 5JA (off A370)
⏲ 11.30-2.30, 4.30-11; 11.30-11 Fri & Sat; 12-3, 7.30-11 Sun
☎ (01934) 877402
Butcombe Bitter; Cheddar Potholer; St Austell Tribute; guest beers Ⓗ
Friendly, characterful village pub with flagstone floors and many original features, decorated with interesting local artefacts. Sunday is quiz night. Guest beers are always available and are sourced mainly from local breweries. No food is served on Friday or

Sunday evenings. The regular Bristol to Weston buses pass on the A370 nearby.
⛼Q❀◐⊟♣P⊱

Corton Denham

Queen's Arms

DT9 4LR (3 miles from A303)
⊙ 11-3, 6-11; 11-11 Sat; 12-10.30 Sun
☎ (01963) 220317 ⊕ thequeensarms.com
Butcombe Bitter; Taylor Landlord; guest beers Ⓗ
A gem of a village pub amid rolling countryside on the Somerset/Dorset border. The single bar has a wood and flagstone floor, wooden chairs and tables, and church pews, heated by a wood-burning stove. Real ale is a speciality – there is also a good selection of wines and malt whiskies, and mulled wine and cider in winter. Quality food is served. A selection of real ciders is offered, particularly local ones. Dogs and muddy boots are welcome. ⛼Q❀⇔◐♣P

Crewkerne

Old Stagecoach

Station Road, TA18 8AL (next to station)
⊙ 11-2 (not Sat), 6-11; 12-2, 6-11 Sun
☎ (01460) 72972 ⊕ stagecoach-inn.co.uk
Glastonbury Mystery Tor; guest beers Ⓗ
Conveniently situated near the railway station, the Stagecoach offers all you could want from a pub – good food and drink. If you want more, there is a garden with plenty of space for smokers, ample parking and a bed for the night. The Belgian owner stocks an excellent range of beers from his home country. Opening hours can be flexible if notice is given. ⛼Q❀⇔◐⇌⊟(47,61)P

Croscombe

George Inn

Long Street, BA5 3QH (on A371 between Wells and Shepton Mallet)
⊙ 12-3, 7 (6 Fri)-11; 11.45-3, 7-11 Sat
☎ (01749) 342306
Blindmans King George the Thirst; Butcombe Bitter; Cheddar Gorgeous George; guest beers Ⓗ
This 17th-century inn, sympathetically refurbished by the landlord, serves at least two guest ales and hosts two beer festivals a year at Whitsun and late October. There is a large main bar with a smaller bar attached, and a separate dining room. The food is home cooked using locally sourced ingredients. At the rear is a skittle alley and a garden with a covered terrace. The guests are from local independents. (Gorgeous George is a 3.8% late-hopped semi-regular guest.)
⛼Q❀⇔◐♿⊟♣P⊱

Crowcombe

Carew Arms

TA4 4AD (off A358)
⊙ 11-11.30 (1am Sat); 12-4, 7-11.30 Sun
☎ (01984) 618631 ⊕ carewarms.co.uk
Exmoor Ale; Otter Bright; guest beers Ⓗ
Village inn situated in a postcard village at the bottom of the Quantock Hills. The ancient flagstoned public bar includes benches and an inglenook, and is popular with locals and their dogs. A larger lounge/restaurant overlooks a spacious patio garden and the Brendon Hills. Real cider is served in summer and a music and beer festival is held in August. Food is sourced locally where possible, and the ales are mostly from the West Country.
⛼Q☋❀⇔◐⊟♿▲⊟(28)♣P

Culmhead

Holman Clavel

TA3 7EA (¼ mile off B3170)
⊙ 12-11; 12-11 (12-3, 7-11 winter) Sun
☎ (01823) 421432
Butcombe Bitter, Gold; guest beers Ⓗ
The only pub in England with this name, a clavel is a beam across the fireplace made from holm oak. Fresh fish and game when in season feature on the food menu, which has choices to suit all tastes and budgets. Guest beers come from both micro-breweries and regional brewers. The pub is allegedly haunted by the ghost of a defrocked monk – but a warm welcome is assured.
⛼Q❀◐▲♣P⊱

Curry Mallet

Bell Inn

Higher Street, TA3 6SY (near post office and village hall)
⊙ 11.30-3, 5.30-11 (midnight Fri); 11.30-11 Sat; 12-10.30 Sun
☎ (01823) 480310
Fuller's London Pride; guest beers Ⓗ
This cosy pub is off the beaten track but worth the effort to find. Although essentially one room, a large fireplace effectively divides the pub into two spaces. The pub is host to a darts team and a regular quiz night. Guest ales are from the south west and much of the food is also locally produced. The friendly landlord is dedicated to the art of running a good pub and this is reflected in the beer quality.
⛼❀⇔◐♿♣P⊱

Dinnington

Dinnington Docks

TA17 8SX
⊙ 11.30-3.30, 6-11.30; 11.30-11.30 Sat; 12-11 Sun
☎ (01460) 52397
Butcombe Bitter; Wadworth 6X; guest beers Ⓗ
A fabulous village pub which always seems to be busy with regulars enjoying the local ales and ciders, and partaking of hearty meals from the traditional home-cooked menu. It is even possible to get your hair cut on the fourth Tuesday of the month. Dogs and walkers are welcome in the L-shaped bar, which is decorated with oddments and various photographs – one depicting the old railway crossing outside is of particular interest.
❀◐♿♣P

Dulverton

Woods

4 Bank Square, TA22 9BU (near church)
⊙ 11-3, 6-11; 12-3, 7-10.30 Sun
☎ (01398) 324007

Exmoor Ale; guest beers Ⓖ
Popular and friendly bar serving both beer-loving locals and visitors wanting to dine in the adjoining open-plan restaurant, where award-winning locally-produced food is served. The rustic interior features a wood-burning stove in winter, wooden floors, breweriana and rural-themed paraphernalia, while three West Country beers are served straight from the wood. An occasional beery treat is the appearance of specially brewed beers from St Austell's micro-brewery. German Schneider Weisse is available on draught. ⩩❀◑♿⛺🚌(25,398)●⁵⁄—

East Harptree

Castle of Comfort

BS40 6DD
✪ 12-3, 6-11; 12-11 (12-3, 6-11 winter) Sun
☎ (01761) 221321 ⊕ castleofcomfort.com
Butcombe Bitter; guest beers Ⓗ
Splendid sprawling inn on the Mendip Hills, not really in East Harptree at all, but within reach of both Cheddar Gorge and Wookey Hole caves. The name is said to derive from the time when the pub housed condemned criminals on their last night before execution. A hostelry since 1684, it is popular for its locally-sourced and generously-portioned food. Guest beers come from all over the south west and sometimes further afield. The child-friendly garden is busy in summer. Dogs are allowed in the lower bar.
⩩Q❀◑♣●P⁵⁄—

Emborough

Old Down Inn

BA3 4SA ST628513
✪ 12-2 (3 Sun), 6.30-11.30
☎ (01761) 232398 ⊕ olddowninn.co.uk
Butcombe Bitter; Draught Bass; guest beers Ⓖ
A free house first licensed in 1640, this pub was once an important coaching inn. The spirit of the past lives on in the pub's wood-panelled main bar, where beer is served straight from the barrel. Guests from local breweries are generally available. Bar snacks are excellent value, likewise the main meals. The pub has recently been refurbished throughout. This friendly and popular hostelry is a classic example of a traditional Somerset inn. ❀⛟◑P

Faulkland

Tucker's Grave ★

BA3 5XF (on A366 1 mile E of village)
✪ 11.30-3, 6-11; 12-3, 7-10.30 Sun
☎ (01373) 834230
Butcombe Bitter; Draught Bass Ⓖ
This pub was built in the mid 17th century and has changed very little since then. It was named after Tucker, who hanged himself and was buried at the crossroads outside. Beers and Thatchers cider are served from an alcove rather than a bar. Shove ha'penny is played and there is a skittle alley. Camping is available in the grounds. A warm welcome is guaranteed in this traditional pub, which featured in a song by the 1970s punk band The Stranglers. ⩩Q❀⛺♣●P

Forches Corner

Merry Harriers

EX15 3TR (3 miles SE of Wellington)
✪ 12-3, 6.30-11; closed Mon; 12-3.30 Sun
☎ (01823) 421270 ⊕ merryharriers.co.uk
Cotleigh Harrier Lite; Otter Head; guest beers Ⓗ
Attractive old inn on the Somerset/Devon border, high on the Blackdown Hills, with a good reputation for food. The guest beer is normally from a micro-brewery in Somerset or Devon and occasionally a second cider is served in summer. Despite its relatively remote location, the inn has a thriving local trade. Families are welcome in all parts of the pub and there is a large, pleasant garden as well as a skittle alley. A rare Somerset outlet for Bollhayes Devon Cider.
⩩Q♉❀◑⛺♣●P⁵⁄—

Frome

Griffin Inn

Milk Street, BA11 3DB
✪ 5-11 (1am Fri & Sat); 12-3, 6.30-10.30 Sun
☎ (01373) 467766 ⊕ milkstreetbrewery.com
Milk Street Nick's, Beer; guest beers Ⓗ
Situated in the older part of Frome known as Trinity or Chinatown and owned by Milk Street Brewery, the small brewhouse out the back is based in a former adult cinema. It produces a wide range of ales, served alongside guests and seasonal beers. The single bar retains original features including open fires, etched windows and wooden floors. Live music plays on some nights. A small garden opens in summer. ⩩❀⇶🚌♣P⁵⁄—

Lamb

1 Christchuch Street East, BA11 1QA
✪ 12-11 (10.30 Sun)
☎ (01373) 472042 ⊕ thelambinnfrome.co.uk
Blindmans Lamb Gold, Buff, Lamb Ale, Mine Beer, Icarus; guest beers Ⓗ
Reopened by Blindmans Brewery after a long closure, this pub, once the brewery tap for the defunct Lamb Brewery, has been refurbished to a very high standard, including the hotel accommodation and restaurant. The pub, which is very near the town centre, is now light and spacious throughout, with a slate floor and local artwork on the walls. Cider is from Rich's and guest beers are from local breweries. ⛟◑⇶🚌●P

Glastonbury

Riflemans Arms

4 Chikwell Street, BA6 8DB (just E of Country Life Museum)
✪ 11-11 (midnight Fri & Sat); 12-10.30 Sun
☎ (01458) 831023
Butcombe Bitter; Skinner's Cornish Knocker; guest beers Ⓗ
Ancient tavern with a well-worn 16th-century facade, a wide, low doorway, a deep wooden bar and bare floors. Behind the pub is an ample patio for sun worshippers and smokers. The interior is split between the old and the

new, with customers tending to gravitate one way or the other depending on their age. The old bar is often filled with white-haired folk, while the relatively new extension features live music for the younger generation. Wilkins Cider is served. ♨✿◑🚌●P⅟

Green Ore

Ploughboy Inn

BA5 3ET (on A39/B3135 crossroads)
⊛ 11-2.30, 6.30-11; closed Mon; 12-2.30, 7-11 Sat & Sun
☎ (01761) 241375 🌐 ploughboyinn.com
Butcombe Bitter; Otter Ale; guest beers Ⓗ
In the same safe hands for over 20 years, this substantial stone free house to the north of Wells occupies a large corner plot by the traffic lights in the hamlet of Green Ore, with speed cameras right outside. The 376 Wells to Bristol bus runs very nearby and there is a large car park and pleasant beer garden to the rear. A single good-sized L-shaped bar provides reasonably priced, excellent food and the local butcher's huge, meaty sausages are recommended. ♨Q✿◑🚌P

Hardington Moor

Royal Oak

Moor Lane, BA22 9NW (turn left off A30 at Yeovil Court Hotel)
⊛ 11.30 -3.30 (not Mon), 6.30-11; 11.30-5, 6.30-10.30 Sun
☎ (01935) 862354
Beer range varies Ⓗ
Sonny's, as it is locally known, is a superb village pub providing a selection of eight to ten ales on gravity. The small dining room has scrubbed wooden tables to support a fine menu, which boasts both traditional and unusual dishes. Dogs are welcome but are expected to make way for the occasional special function. The pool table is in a separate room and skittles are played every weekday night of the winter, with a popular summer league operating too. ♨✿◑♿♣●P⅟

Henstridge

Bird in Hand

2 Ash Walk, BA8 0RA (100m S of A30/A357 jct)
⊛ 11-2.30, 5.30-11; 11-11 Sat; 12-3, 7.30-10.30 Sun
☎ (01963) 362255
Beer range varies Ⓗ
Old stone-built pub at the centre of the village. Up to three real ales are available at any one time from a continually rotating range, with favourites returning regularly. The main bar is quiet and has a well-equipped games room leading off the skittle alley at the rear. The atmosphere is warm and friendly, with lunchtime snacks particularly recommended. ♨Q✿◑♿🚌♣●P

Hillcommon

Royal Oak

TA4 1DS (on B3227 Taunton-Wiveliscombe road)
⊛ 12-3, 5-11; 12-11 Sat & Sun
☎ (01823) 400295 🌐 royaloak-taunton.co.uk
Beer range varies Ⓗ
Village pub set on the main road, frequented by drinkers and diners. The large open-plan bar is set for diners but there is always seating available for drinkers, with ales mainly from the West Country. A beautiful garden is at the rear of the pub. Food is locally sourced, with a carvery on Tuesday, Thursday and Sunday lunchtimes (booking advised). There is a skittle alley and a traditional fire in the winter. Live music is on the last Friday of the month. ♨✿◑◐♿🚌(25)♣P⅟

Hinton Blewitt

Ring O' Bells

Upper Road, BS39 5AN (2 miles W of A37 at Temple Cloud) ST594569
⊛ 12-3, 5-11; 12-midnight Sat; 12-11 Sun
☎ (01761) 452239
Butcombe Bitter, Gold, seasonal beer; Fuller's London Pride; guest beers Ⓗ
At the heart of the village and of village life, there is always a buzz about this pub. Entered via a small yard with a pleasant garden to the side, you are soon in the warmth of the intimate bar where many cricketing mementos feature – indeed the pub runs its own team. The food is popular and can be enjoyed in the smaller snug area or outside in good weather. Children and dogs are welcome. ♨Q✿◑◐P⅟

Hinton St George

Lord Poulett Arms

High Street, TA17 8SE
⊛ 12-3, 6.30-11
☎ (01460) 73149 🌐 lordpoulettarms.com
Branscombe Vale Branoc; Otter Ale; guest beers Ⓗ
A bar-mounted gravity stillage is a welcome sight on entering this 17th-century village pub with a delightful interior featuring stone-flagged floors and ancient wood furniture. The bar is well stocked with magazines and books, while outside is a Mediterranean garden for quiet enjoyment, complete with a petanque court, leading to a secluded beer garden and a pelotta wall dating from Napoleonic times. Cider is served in summer.
♨Q✿⛺◑◐⊟♿🚌♣●P

Holywell Lake

Holywell Inn

TA21 0EJ (1 mile N of A38 W of Wellington)
⊛ 12-2.30 (not Mon & Tue), 7-11 (not Mon winter); 12-3, 7-10.30 (summer only) Sun
☎ (01823) 672770 🌐 theholywell.com
Beer range varies Ⓗ
Fifteenth-century village inn retaining cob walls in the main bar but enlarged to include a restaurant and skittle alley/function room. Ales normally include one each from Cotleigh and Exmoor breweries and a guest beer, usually from a West Midlands micro. Although very near the A38 trunk road, this is a quiet, charming country pub. Well-behaved dogs are welcome, as are walkers – the pub lies on the Land's End to John O'Groats walking route. The Holy Well is opposite the pub entrance.
♨Q✿◑◐♿♣⅟

Horsington

Half Moon

BA8 0EF (200m off A357)
12-2.30 (3 Sat), 6-11; 12-3, 7-10.30 Sun
(01963) 370140 horsington.co.uk
Wadworth 6X; guest beers
Real ale is a passion for the owners with more than 1,000 different beers sold over the past 10 years. Up to six ales are on handpump with the range of guests changing continuously. As well as the well-known nationals, local micros are always represented and feature prominently in the annual beer festival held each May. Friendly staff welcome locals and visitors alike. Reasonably priced food is available and there is accommodation in chalets to the rear. P

Huish Episcopi

Rose & Crown (Eli's) ☆

Wincanton Road, TA10 9QT (on A372)
11.30-2.30, 5.30-11; 11.30-11 Fri & Sat; 12-10.30 Sun
(01458) 250494
Teignworthy Reel Ale; guest beers
This traditional thatched inn, known locally as Eli's, has been in the same family for generations. The character and unusual features remain unchanged, taking you back in time. The pub is divided into several cosy rooms and the drinks are served in a flagstoned tap room. Good traditional home-cooked food is served at lunchtime and early evening. The bus stop is about 15 minutes' walk away. Q(54)P

Kelston

Old Crown

Bath Road, BA1 9AQ (3 miles from Bath on A431)
11.30-11; 12-10.30 Sun
(01225) 423032
Bath Gem; Butcombe Bitter, Gold; Draught Bass; Wadworth 6X
This attractive multi-roomed 18th-century coaching inn is owned by Butcombe Brewery. The old beer engine in the bar, flagstone floors, open fires and settles all help to create a friendly atmosphere. A choice of quality, imaginative food is served in the restaurant and bar areas (no food Sun or Mon eves). In summer barbecues are occasionally held in the large attractive garden and the front of the pub is bedecked with colourful flowers.
Q(319,332)P

Keynsham

Ship

93 Temple Street, BS31 1ER
12-3 6-11; 12-11 Fri-Sun
(0117) 9869841
Marston's Burton Bitter, Pedigree, Mansfield Cask Ale; guest beers
Grade II-listed, this is one of the oldest buildings in Keynsham, retaining some original features from its days as a coaching inn, with a number of areas in different sizes for dining and drinking. The garden at the rear overlooks the park and the River Chew beyond. No food is available Sunday or Monday evenings. The car park is very small, but local buses pass close by. P

Lower Odcombe

Masons Arms

41 Lower Odcombe, BA22 8TX (off Yeovil to Montacute road)
12-2.30, 6-midnight
(01935) 862591 masonsarmsodcombe.co.uk
Odcombe No 1, Spring; guest beers
A picturesque thatched free house in the main street of an attractive village. A small brewhouse to the rear of the pub brews for the Masons only. Good food is served using local produce (booking advisable for the restaurant). There is also a monthly curry night. Well-behaved children and dogs are welcome. Local events are held in the rear field and at the back of the pub is a caravan site with hook-ups, showers and a laundry room. (81)P

Martock

White Hart Hotel

East Street, TA12 6JQ
12-2 (3 Sat), 5.30-midnight (2am Fri & Sat); 12-3 Sun
(01935) 822005 whitehartotelmartock.co.uk
Otter Bitter; guest beers
Pleasant town centre, family-run hamstone coaching inn dating from 1735, with a Gallic flavour. A single, L-shaped bar has Chesterfield sofas around the fireplace and a rear skittle alley can be booked for conferences. Many of the guest beers are from West Country breweries. A separate restaurant serves excellent food and the lunchtime bistro menu is exceptionally good value. Martock is a good touring centre for the Somerset countryside and coast. (52,633)P

Middlezoy

George Inn

42 Main Street, TA7 0NN (off A372, 1 mile NW of Othery)
12-3 (not Mon), 7-midnight; 12-3, 7-11.30 Sun
(01823) 698215
Butcombe Bitter; guest beers
Dating from the 17th century, little has changed at this inn with exposed beams, a huge fireplace and stone-flagged floor. Visitors are invariably warned of the step in the middle of the bar by a chorus of locals and the booming voice of the South African landlord. There is an excellent selection of guest ales, real cider and superb home-cooked food. An annual beer festival is held at Easter. It's a former local CAMRA Pub of the Year.
Q(16)P

Minehead

Queen's Head

Holloway Street, TA24 5NR (off the Parade)
12-3, 5.30-11 (midnight Fri); 12-midnight Sat; 12-3, 6.30-11 Sun
(01643) 706000
Draught Bass; Exmoor Fox, Gold; Otter Ale; St Austell Tribute; guest beers

Popular town pub situated in a side street off the Parade. Usually eight beers are sold, with guest ales coming mainly from local breweries such as Cottage. Beer festivals are held in spring and autumn. The pub has a large single bar room, one end with a raised seating area for dining and families. Good value food is served – try the delicious home-made pies. There is also a games room. The West Somerset Railway is 10 minutes' walk away. ◑♿▲⇌🚌(28,39)♣⅟

Monksilver

Notley Arms

TA4 4JB (on B3188)
⏲ 12-2.30 (not Mon), 6.30-11
☎ (01984) 656217 🌐 thenotleyarms.co.uk
Exmoor Ale; Wadworth 6X; guest beers Ⓗ
Rural pub retaining many curious features in a pretty village in walking country. The West Somerset Railway stations at Stogumber and Washford are two to three miles away. A good reputation for food is complemented with a fine selection of ales, and real cider is also available all year. The pleasant garden includes children's play equipment as well as an unusual upstairs skittle alley. Food is locally sourced and home cooked. The pub enjoys a varied clientele including locals, tourists and businessmen. ♨Q☕❀◑♿♣●P⅟

Moorlinch

Ring O' Bells

TA7 9BT (between A39 and A361 near Street)
⏲ 12-2 (not Mon), 5-midnight; 12-midnight Sat; 12-10.30 Sun
☎ (01458) 210358
Flowers IPA; guest beers Ⓗ
This traditional village pub serves two constantly changing West Country beers. Locally sourced home-cooked food is available in the public bar, big lounge bar or the separate dining room. Vegetarian meals are also available. The pub does not open on Monday lunchtime. Although a bit off the beaten track, it is well worth looking for. ♨Q❀◑♿🚌(19)♣●P⅟

Mudford

Half Moon

Main Street, BA21 5TF (on A359 between Yeovil and Sparkford)
⏲ 12-11 (10.30 Sun)
☎ (01935) 850289 🌐 thehalfmoon.co.uk
RCH Pitchfork, East Street Cream, seasonal beers Ⓖ
Large, comfortable, friendly roadside inn dating from the 17th century, restored in an authentic style. Several separate seating areas and the absence of music ensure a cosy atmosphere. Though the pub is free of tie, all ales come from RCH, served from the stillage behind the bar. Good food and bar snacks are available all day. Fourteen superior en-suite rooms are provided in the former skittle alley. The pub has good disabled facilities throughout. ♨Q❀🛏◑♿🚌(1)●P

Nailsea

Blue Flame

West End, BS48 4DE (off A370 at Chelvey)
ST448690
⏲ 12-3, 6-11; 12-10.30 Sun
☎ (01275) 856910
Fuller's London Pride; RCH East Street Cream; Ⓖ **guest beers** Ⓗ
Lovely rustic 19th-century free house, unaltered for many years, comprising two rooms, one with a bar and a snug. Coal fires help create a cosy atmosphere in winter. Simple, almost Spartan decor and outside toilets feature. Food is limited to filled rolls. Live music plays on the first and third Tuesday of the month. The large rear garden is ideal for families in summer. Camping is available but phone first. Well worth seeking out. ♨Q❀▲♣●P

Norton Fitzwarren

Cross Keys ✔

TA2 6NR (at A358/B3227 jct W of Taunton)
⏲ 11-11; 12-10.30 Sun
☎ (01823) 333062
Beer range varies Ⓗ
Large roadside pub divided into several areas with plenty of exposed beams in contemporary style. The wide-ranging menu is supplemented by daily chef's specials. Beers often come from local breweries, as well as those from other parts of the UK, including regional brewers as well as micros. There is also a small selection of bottled Belgian and German beers. The large garden is bordered by a stream. ♨❀◑🚌(25,28)P⅟

Pitney

Halfway House

Pitney Hill, TA10 9AB (on B3153)
⏲ 11.30-3.30, 5.30-11 (midnight Fri & Sat); 12-3.30, 7-11 Sun
☎ (01458) 252513 🌐 thehalfwayhouse.co.uk
Branscombe Vale Own; Butcombe Bitter; Hop Back Crop Circle, Summer Lightning; Otter Bright; guest beers Ⓖ
Thriving traditional village pub serving a wide variety of local ales all on gravity alongside a range of international bottled beers. Superb home-cooked food is based on local produce (no food Sun). No background music or fruit machines disturb the buzz of conversation in this multiple award-winning pub. It is Somerset CAMRA Pub of the Year for 2008 and was CAMRA's National Pub of the Year in 1996 and the Telegraph Pub of the Year in 2007. A real gem. ♨Q❀◑▲🚌(54)♣●P⅟

Porlock

Ship Inn ✔

High Street, TA24 8QD
⏲ 11-midnight
☎ (01643) 862507 🌐 shipinnporlock.co.uk
Exmoor Ale; Otter Ale; Palmers Traditional Best Bitter; guest beers Ⓗ
Known locally as the Top Ship, this 13th-century inn was recorded in Lorna Doone. The bar appears not to have changed much since

then, with flagstoned floors, inglenook fires and a good selection of real ales and cider. Located at the bottom of the notorious Porlock Hill, care needs to be taken when leaving the pub. A later extension has added a restaurant and en-suite bedrooms but these do not detract from the unspoilt gem of a public bar.
(39,300) P

Portishead

Poacher

106 High Street, BS20 6AJ
11-2.30, 6-11; 11-11 Fri & Sat; 12-10.30 Sun
(01275) 844002
Bath Ales Gem; Sharp's Doom Bar; guest beers H
Originally two cottages, the Poacher has been a pub since the 17th century at least. Four or five beers are served and the landlord produces a monthly Poachers Beer List newsletter inviting suggestions for guest beers. A weekly quiz is held on Monday and poker and crib are played on Tuesday. On Friday the car park becomes a market. Smokers are provided with a shelter at the front. P

Windmill Inn

58 Nore Road, BS20 6JZ (next to municipal golf course)
11-11; 12-10.30 Sun
(01275) 843677
Butcombe Gold; Courage Best Bitter; Draught Bass; RCH PG Steam; guest beers H
Large split-level free house with a spacious tiered patio to the rear. Situated on the edge of town with panoramic views over the Severn estuary, both Severn bridges can be seen on clear days. A varied menu is served all day and is enormously popular. One large area is set aside for families. The guest ales are often locally sourced and there is an Easter beer festival. Thatchers Cider is stocked.
Q (359) P

Priddy

Hunters Lodge

BA5 3AR (1 mile from A39 at Green Ore) ST549500
11.30-2.30, 6.30-11; 12-2, 7-11 Sun
(01749) 672275
Blindmans Mine Beer; Butcombe Bitter; guest beers G
Timeless, classic roadside inn near Priddy, the highest village in Somerset, popular with cavers and walkers. The landlord has been in charge for more than 40 years. Three rooms include one with a flagged floor, a good atmosphere and barrels behind the bar. Local guest beers come from brewers such as Cheddar Ales. The simple home-cooked food is excellent and exceptional value. A folk musicians' drop-in session is held on Tuesday evening in the back room. Wilkins cider is served. The garden is pleasant and secluded. Mobile phones are not welcome.
Q P

Queen Victoria Inn

Pelting Drove, BA5 3BA (on minor road to Wookey Hole, S of village centre)
12-3, 6-11; 12-11.30 Sat; 12-11 Sun
(01749) 676385
Butcombe Bitter, Gold; guest beers G
Traditional creeper-clad inn, a pub since 1851. Four rooms feature low ceilings, flagged floors and three log fires. This is a wonderfully warm and relaxing haven on cold winter nights and is popular during the Priddy Folk Festival in July and the annual fair in August. Reasonably priced, home-cooked food is a speciality. Children and dogs are allowed and there is a play area by the car park. Cheddar Valley cider is sold. Q P

Rode

Cross Keys

20 High Street, BA11 6NZ ST803537
11.30-3, 6-11.30; 11.30-11.30 Sat; 12-11.30 Sun
(01373) 830900 butcombe.com
Butcombe Bitter; guest beers H
Reopened in 2004 after 10 years of closure, this was originally the brewery tap for the long-closed Fussell's brewery, and more latterly a Bass depot. Sympathetically restored, it has succeeded in bringing back a strong village trade. A passageway featuring a deep well links the two bars. There is also a large restaurant. Though now owned by Butcombe, there are always one or two guests available, sourced from micros near and far. Regular mini beer festivals are held.
Q

Rowberrow

Swan Inn ✔

Rowberrow Lane, BS25 1QL (signed off A38)
11.30-3, 6-11; 11.30-11 Fri & Sat; 12-11 Sun
(01934) 852371
Butcombe Bitter, Gold, seasonal beer; guest beers H
Believed to date from around the late 17th century, this Butcombe Brewery-owned country pub enjoys an attractive setting, nestling beneath the nearby Dolebury Iron Age Hill Fort. A convenient refreshment stop for walkers on the Mendip Hills, the emphasis is on home-cooked food with unusual specials, but customers who just want a drink are very welcome. There is an interesting collection of artefacts around the walls and a grandfather clock. Thatchers cider is available. The large, attractive beer garden and car park are opposite. Q P

Rumwell

Rumwell Inn

TA4 1EL (on A38 between Taunton and Wellington)
11-3, 6-11; 12-3, 7-11 Sun
(01823) 461662 therumwellinn.co.uk
Otter Bitter; guest beers H
This 16th-century coaching inn is on the A38 – the old coaching road from Bristol to Exeter. An atmospheric, friendly pub, you can be sure of a warm welcome from the staff. The guest ales normally include one from the south west and one sourced nationally. A wide variety of both pub and restaurant food uses ingredients mainly from local suppliers, as well as fish from Brixham. A good stop en route to or from

the west, it is just five minutes from junction 26 of the M5. ⩎Q❀◑⊟(22,92)P⁄–

Saltford

Bird in Hand

58 High Street, BS31 3EJ (set back 400m from main A4)
✪ 11-3.30, 6-11; 11-11 Sat; 12-11 Sun
☎ (01225) 873335 ⊕ birdinhandsaltford.co.uk
Abbey Bellringer; Butcombe Bitter; Courage Best Bitter; guest beer ⊞
A pub dating back to 1869 situated at the foot of the old high street in the oldest part of the village, adjacent to the Bristol to Bath cycle path and the main railway line. This is a food-oriented pub and the dining area is in a recently built conservatory with fine views over the garden and hills beyond. There is a small family area at one end. A petanque pitch features in the spacious garden. Thatchers cider is sold. ♉❀◑♿⊟♣●P⁄–

Seavington St Michael

Volunteer ✔

New Road, TA19 0QE (on former A303, 2 miles E of Ilminster)
✪ 12-2.30, 6.30-11; 12-3, 7-11 Sun
☎ (01460) 240126 ⊕ thevolly.co.uk
St Austell Tribute; guest beers ⊞
Friendly village-centre three-room local hosting many community activities. One guest ale is from a Somerset micro, a second from the Manchester area. A range of bottled real ciders is kept and there are discount deals on bottles of wine. An excellent menu offers home-cooked meals made with local ingredients where possible – Wednesday is Pie Night and traditional roasts on Sunday are good value. Dogs and walkers are welcome. ⩎Q❀⇌◑⊟♿⛺⊟(99)♣P⁄–

Shepton Beauchamp

Duke of York

North Street, TA19 0LW
✪ 12-11 (midnight Sat)
☎ (01460) 240314
Otter Bright; Teignworthy Reel Ale; guest beers ⊞
This friendly village pub is very popular with locals and hosts numerous darts and skittles teams. Pool is in a separate room. On pleasant days, tables on the raised pavement outside enable patrons to enjoy a snapshot of rural Somerset life with the butcher's, post office, school, church and village hall all on panoramic display. Recently-built holiday accommodation makes staying the weekend here an attractive proposition.
⩎♉❀⇌◑⊟(633)♣P⁄–

Shepton Mallet

Swan Inn

27 Town Street, BA4 5BE
✪ 11-midnight
☎ (01749) 344995 ⊕ stumbles-inn.co.uk
Matthews Bob Wall; guest beers ⊞
Formerly called The Stumbles Inn until it was renamed in 2008, this pub is situated in a terrace of small shops. Inside, the front area is arranged mainly for diners (no meals Mon or Sun and Tue eves), with chairs and tables extending out onto the pavement. The bar area at the rear offers darts and shove ha'penny. Live music is played once or twice a month. Guest ales are chosen from small brewers. ⇌◑♣P

Shepton Montague

Montague Arms

BA9 8JW (signed off A359 and A371) ST675315
✪ 12-3, 6-11; closed Mon; 12-3 Sun
☎ (01749) 813213
Bath Ales Gem; Greene King Abbot; Wadworth IPA; guest beers ⊡
This attractive pub is in a sparsely populated village between Wincanton, Castle Cary and Bruton and is well known in the region for its outstanding cuisine, complemented by its real ales kept in pins in an anteroom behind the bar. Thatchers cider is usually available. The single bar is cosy and welcoming, with discrete dining areas. The patio and garden enjoy spectacular countryside views towards the famous folly Alfred's Tower.
⩎Q♉❀⇌◑♿●P⊡

Shoscombe

Apple Tree ✔

BA2 8LS ST712565
✪ 12-2.30 (not Mon & Tue), 7-11; 12-11 Sat & Sun
☎ (01761) 432263
Exmoor Stag; Greene King IPA; Matthews Bob Wall ⊞
A good community village pub with a large beer garden, real fire, superb views and a children's play area. It is not easy to find, but well worth the effort when you do. The pub is noted for its fish dishes cooked by the landlord, as well as ostrich and crocodile steaks to complement the traditional fare. This is a good place to end up after a long country walk. Parking is limited. ⩎❀◑♿●P⁄–

Shurton

Shurton Inn

TA5 1QE (3 miles N of A39 near Nether Stowey)
✪ 12-3, 6 (7 Sun)-11
☎ (01278) 732695
Exmoor Ale; Sharp's Doom Bar; guest beers ⊞
This out of the way inn, displaying pictures by local artists, is well worth finding. A 400-year-old pub, it has two bar areas, a conservatory, a restaurant, a large garden and car parking. Low wooden beams and wooden trestle seats await the walker and fisherman alike. Rumour has it that 300 years ago an unwelcome pirate had his throat cut in the bar, but the present landlord offers a much warmer welcome. Thatchers cider is served. ⩎❀⇌◑♿♣●P⁄–

South Petherton

Brewers Arms ✔

18 St James Street, TA13 5BW (½ mile off A303)
✪ 11.30-2.30, 6-11 (midnight Fri & Sat); 12-10.30 Sun
☎ (01460) 241887
Otter Bitter; guest beers ⊞

Terrific village-centre local just off the A303 with a constantly changing selection of beers from all over the UK – more than 1,000 have been served during the current landlord's 10-year tenure, each chosen to complement the pub's food. A magnificent courtyard smokers' area boasts a TV. Beer festivals are held twice a year during late May and August bank holidays. A true community pub for all (including dogs). Runner-up Somerset CAMRA Pub of the Year 2006 and 2007 and a past winner. ♨❀◑⛺🚌(81,633)♣●⊢

Stoke St Gregory

Royal Oak

TA3 6EH (opp church)

⌚ closed Mon; 7.30-11 Tue & Wed; 12-3, 7-11.30; 12-midnight Sat; 12-3, 7-11 Sun

☎ (01823) 400602

St Austell Tribute; guest beers Ⓗ

A warm, friendly pub in the centre of the village. It has become a real part of the community, with several skittles teams plus darts and pool. A family concern since 2005, in the course of a visit you will probably meet most of its members. The pub is ideally positioned for taking a break when walking the Somerset Levels or the long distance Parrett Trail. ❀◑⊟♿🚌(51)♣●P

Stoke sub Hamdon

Prince of Wales

Ham Hill, TA14 6RW

⌚ 8.30-11

☎ (01935) 822848

Beer range varies Ⓖ

It seems that most of Somerset can be viewed from the extensive outside seating areas of this truly rural pub, located on the top of Ham Hill in the Country Park west of Yeovil. Recent improvements include a stone-built outside bar for summer weekends. The flagstone interior is mud-friendly, which means that well-behaved walkers, with or without dogs, are welcome. Hot drinks are available from 8.30am and there is free Wi-Fi to encourage students and businessmen. ♨❀◑♿●P⊢

Street

Two Brewers

38 Leigh Road, BA16 0HB

⌚ 11-2.30, 6-11 (11.30 Fri & Sat)

☎ (01458) 442421 🌐 thetwobrewers.co.uk

Courage Best Bitter, Directors; Greene King Ruddles County; guest beers Ⓗ

Friendly, well-kept pub on the fringe of the town centre – described accurately as 'a country pub in the town'. A comfortable single bar with a raised dining area serves excellent ale and food, including vegetarian dishes and a children's menu. A regular pub newsletter is produced. There are no music or gaming machines. A new feature is accommodation in three en-suite rooms in a former stable block. Q❀⛌◑🚌♣P⊢

Taunton

Wings Club (RAFA)

68 Cheddon Road, TA2 7DW

⌚ 4 (12 Fri-Sun)-11

☎ (01823) 284883

Beer range varies Ⓗ

Taunton's branch of the Royal Air Force Association, this club has a comfortable lounge bar at the front and a separate bar at the back used for darts, skittles and functions, where children are welcome until 8pm. The real ales come mainly from West Country breweries, especially Otter, but occasionally from other parts of Britain. Show this Guide or a CAMRA membership card to gain admission. ⇌🚌(1,3)♣P⊢

Wyvern Club

Mountfields Road, TA1 3BJ

⌚ 7-11; 12-3, 7-10.30 Sun

☎ (01823) 284591 🌐 wyvernclub.co.uk

Exmoor Ale; guest beers Ⓗ

Large, busy sports and social club offering a variety of West Country beers, with guest ales changing frequently – beers from three different breweries are usually on offer, at club prices. Meals are available each evening until 9pm, plus Sunday lunchtime. The club premises are available for daytime meetings and evening functions. Show this Guide or your CAMRA membership card to be signed in as a guest. A real ale festival is held in October. ♨❀◑♿🚌(1A,99)♣P

Thurloxton

Maypole Inn

TA2 8RF (just off A38 between Taunton and North Petherton)

⌚ 12-3, 6-11; 12-3, 7-10.30 Sun

☎ (01823) 412286

Sharp's Doom Bar; guest beers Ⓗ

Large, cosy village pub, split into various areas – some are mainly for dining, but there is ample space for those who just want to relax with a drink. Beers are often from West Country breweries and St Austell Black Prince is regularly featured – unusual in Somerset. An extensive menu, with meals to suit all tastes, emphasises local produce. Parts of the building date back to the 18th century. There is a skittle alley/function room and a large garden. ♨❀◑🚌(15,21)♣●P⊢

Wanstrow

Pub ✔

Station Road, BA4 4SZ

⌚ 6.30-11 Mon; 12-2.30 (3 Fri & Sat), 6-11; 12-3, 7-10.30 Sun

☎ (01749) 850455

Draught Bass; Hop Back GFB; guest beers Ⓗ

An absolute gem, this friendly village local has a lounge bar with open fire and flagstone floors that leads to a small restaurant. The pub serves up to six guest ales and Cheddar Valley and Thatchers ciders are also offered. Games include skittles, bar billiards and ring the bull. A small but imaginative menu is offered and all food is home cooked. ♨Q❀◑⊟♣●P

Watchet

Esplanade Club

The Esplanade, TA23 0AJ (opp marina)
7-midnight; 12 (2 winter)-midnight Sun
(01984) 634518
Sharp's Doom Bar; St Austell Tribute; guest beers H
A warm welcome awaits at this local club with views over the marina and Bristol Channel. Built in the 1860s as a sail-making factory, it has been a club since the 1930s. The walls are full of local historic photos. Visitors showing this guide or a CAMRA membership card are welcome, and will be signed in by the staff. Any boat owner mooring in the marina is automatically an associate member.
(14,28)

Star Inn

Mill Lane, TA23 0BZ
12-3.30, 6.30-midnight (1am Fri & Sat); 12-4, 7-midnight Sun
(01984) 631367
Cotleigh Tawny; guest beers H
Situated in the centre of Watchet, this pub was created by knocking three 15th-century cottages into a single building. Four or five beers are sourced from local, regional and national breweries. The pub comprises a cosy main bar with small side rooms. Watchet marina is across the road and the West Somerset Railway is within walking distance; so too is the nearest bus stop.
Q(14,28)

West Chinnock

Muddled Man

Lower Street, TA18 7PT
11-2.30 (not Mon winter), 7-midnight; 11-midnight Fri & Sat; 12-10.30 Sun
(01935) 881235
Beer range varies H
Friendly, family-run free house of character in an attractive village. A good, ever-changing range of beers from West Country brewers is served, plus Burrow Hill cider. Many people have been converted to real ale here, with visits to breweries and beer festivals a regular feature. The food is good value (booking essential for Sunday lunch). A skittle alley doubles as a function room and accommodation is provided in two newly-converted rooms. Conversation is actively encouraged. P

West Huntspill

Crossways Inn

TA9 3RA (on A38)
11-3, 5.30-midnight; 11-midnight (11-3, 5.30-midnight winter) Sat; 12-11 Sun
(01278) 783756 crossways-inn.com
Flowers IPA; Fuller's London Pride; guest beers H
This 17th-century inn had been under the same ownership for more than 30 years until a recent change of hands. It remains a free house in private ownership however, with the new landlord running it in the same way as before. Guest beers change frequently and the food menu is enhanced by a specials board. Live music and themed meals are regular events. Four rooms are available for overnight accommodation. (21)P

Royal Artillery Arms

2 Alstone Lane, TA9 3DR (on A38)
12-11 (10.30 Sun)
(01278) 783553
Beer range varies H
This recently refurbished roadside hostelry provides a warm, cosy welcome. On the bar there are now eight handpumps with a very good selection of real ales always available, often featuring beers from the RCH Brewery. A skittle alley doubles as a function room and an annual beer festival takes place on the August bank holiday weekend. Regular theme nights are held during the year; these are listed on the blackboard behind the bar.
(21,670)P

Weston-super-Mare

Off the Rails

Station Approach, BS23 1XY (on railway station concourse)
7 (9 Sun)-11
(01934) 415109
RCH Hewish IPA; guest beers H
This genuine free house conveniently situated at the railway station doubles up as the station buffet with snacks, sandwiches and magazines available. The two guest beers usually come from West Country micro-breweries, with the occasional beer and guest cider from further afield. The landlord is happy to receive suggestions from his regulars for which beers to stock. Two-pint carry-out containers are a handy feature for train travellers. Three TVs show sporting events. Quiz night is Tuesday and there is a free jukebox.

Regency

22-24 Upper Church Road, BS23 2AG (just off sea front)
9.45-11.30 (midnight Fri & Sat); 10.45-11 Sun
(01934) 633406
Butcombe Bitter; Courage Best Bitter; Draught Bass; Flowers IPA H
Comfortable and friendly town-centre local opposite Weston College, attracting a mixed clientele. The pub has pool, skittles and crib teams, but also offers a quiet refuge for conversation. The pool room is separate from the main bar area, and children are welcome here. Home-cooked food at good value prices is served at lunchtimes.

Wincanton

Red Lion

3 Market Place, BA9 9LD
11-11; 12-10.30 Sun
(01963) 824530
Butcombe Bitter; RCH IPA; guest beers H
Multi-roomed, friendly town-centre pub with a single bar, recently renovated in a traditional style. Excellent food includes oven-baked pizzas. The pub is a regular in this Guide and has previously been awarded CAMRA Branch Pub of the Year. Two guest beers from local

micros are usually on offer. The cider is Wilkins Farmhouse. ⛫Q◑♿🚌🍎

Winsham

Bell Inn

11 Church Street, TA20 4HU (on B3162 S of Chard)
12-2.30 (3 Sat), 7-11; 12-3, 7-10.30 Sun
☎ (01460) 30677
Branscombe Vale Branoc; guest beers H
Real ales, skittles and home-cooked pies are all popular in this village local. Very much a community pub, it has a public bar, a function room with jukebox and pool table, plus a skittle alley to the rear. An area outside provides extra seating for drinkers and smokers. There is a spacious car park. ⛫❀◑🚌(99)♣P

Wookey Hole

Wookey Hole Inn

High Street, BA5 1BP (opp Wookey Hole caves)
12-11 (10.30 Sun)
☎ (01749) 676677 🌐 wookeyholeinn.com
Beer range varies H
Charismatic, picturesque pub and restaurant with a unique style, situated opposite the major tourist attraction of the famous caves. Four handpumps serve changing guest beers from small, often unusual brewers, plus a local cider and a wide choice of draught continental beers and lagers. Top quality food is served at restaurant prices, ideal for special occasions (booking recommended at weekends). The huge sculpted rear garden is superb in summer. A lurid pink function room and six highly individual bedrooms complete the picture. ⛫❀🛏◑⛺🚌🍎P

Wrington

Golden Lion

Broad Street, BS40 5LA
12-midnight
☎ (01934) 862205
Butcombe Bitter; guest beers H
Family-run village-centre local which prides itself on offering a warm welcome. It runs its own football team, golfing society and shooting syndicates, and is well frequented by the local community. No food is served, but great attention is paid to offering quality beer. Three guest ales are usually sourced from West Country brewers and the landlord will consider customers' suggestions. Events include a beer festival on the late May bank holiday weekend, a summer hog roast and live music on Saturday nights. ⛫❀🚌(121)♣⊢

Yeovil

Pall Tavern

15 Silver Street, BA20 1HW
11-11 (1am Fri & Sat); 12-11 Sun
☎ (01935) 476521 🌐 palltavern.co.uk
Greene King Old Speckled Hen; guest beers H
Friendly, comfortable oasis amid the nightclubs of Yeovil town centre, the Pall (pronounced 'pal') feels more like a country village inn. The cosy single bar serves three real ales and excellent food in generous portions – try the Sunday roast. A new feature is themed food nights. The subdued radio and mute TV encourage conversation, so everyone feels welcome here. This is a safe pub, even at weekends. Children are welcome and the pub is dog friendly. ❀🛏◑🚌♣⊢

Masons Arms, Lower Odcombe.

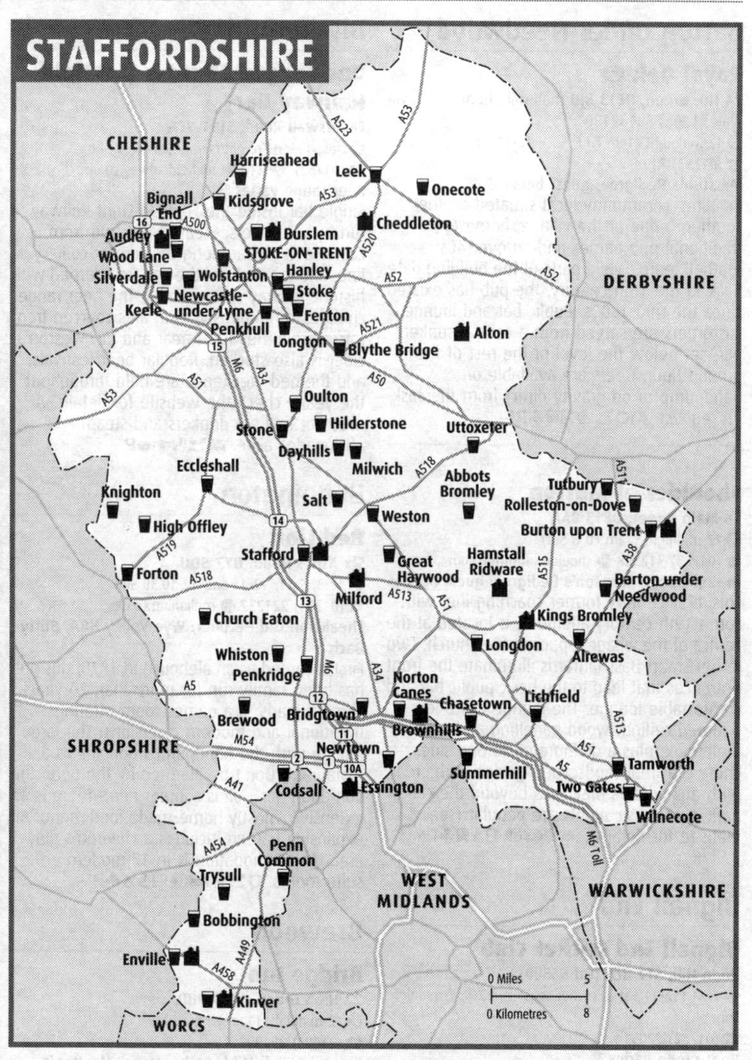

Abbots Bromley

Coach & Horses

High Street, WS15 3BN

✪ 12-2.30 (not Mon), 5.30-11; 12-10.30 Sun

☎ (01283) 840256

Greene King Abbot; Marston's Pedigree ⊞

Grade II listed coaching inn dating back to 1745, although the building is even older, with links to Burton Abbey. Inside, the long narrow lounge bar features a beamed ceiling and an assortment of memorabilia and bric-a-brac including brasses and old photographs. There are several settees for the comfort of the more laid-back drinker. The dining room is at the back of the pub. Abbots Bromley is famous for its annual Horn Dance – see abbotsbromley.com/horn_dance for information. ⌂❀⇌◐♣P⅟

Alrewas

Crown Inn

7 Post Office Road, DE13 7BS

✪ 12-2.30 (not Mon winter), 5-11; 12-11 (12-3, 5-11 winter) Sat; 12-10.30 Sun

☎ (01283) 790328

Draught Bass; Jennings Cumberland Ale; Marston's Pedigree; guest beer ⊞

This 500-year-old former coaching inn once housed the village post office. Near the Trent & Mersey Canal, families, boaters and walkers are welcome. The cosy public bar and adjacent intimate snug feature very old and low beamed ceilings. Meals are served in the larger comfortable lounge – good value home-cooked food includes a fish night on Thursday and a Sunday lunchtime carvery (no eve meals winter Sun or Mon). Live jazz plays on Monday, folk or acoustic guitar most Wednesdays. ⌂Q❀◐⊟Å⊟♣P⅟

Barton under Needwood

Royal Oak ✔

74 The Green, DE13 8JD (half mile from B5016 via Wales Lane) SK182180

12-midnight (1am Fri & Sat); 12-11 Sun

☎ (01283) 713852

Marston's Pedigree; guest beers H/G

Bustling, community local situated on the southern edge of the village, home to traditional pub games and an over-40s football team. While parts of the building date back to the 16th-century, the pub has existed since the mid-1800s. Public bar and lounge customers are served from a central sunken bar, set below the level of the rest of the ground floor. Beers are available on handpump or on gravity direct from the cask, on request. ♨Q❀♣P

Shoulder of Mutton

16 Main Street, DE13 8AA

12-midnight (1am Fri & Sat)

☎ (01283) 712568 shoulderofmutton.com

Draught Bass; Marston's Pedigree; guest beer H

This 17th-century former coaching inn, with some 19th-century additions, is located at the centre of the village, opposite the church. Two rather smart Bass lanterns illuminate the front entrances that lead to the basic public bar and comfortable lounge. The lounge has a low-beamed ceiling, wood panelling and inglenook, plus a dining area to one side. There is a small landscaped garden to the rear, with a children's play area beyond the car park. Live music nights are popular (see website for details). ♨❀♣P

Bignall End

Bignall End Cricket Club

Boon Hill, ST7 8LA (Off B5500)

7-11 (12-11 Sat in cricket season); 12-4, 7-midnight Sun

☎ (01782) 720514

Beer range varies H

Long-established cricket club in a small village outside Newcastle-under-Lyme, with a large bar, snooker room with full-size table, plus a large upstairs function room. A popular beer festival is held in November. The cricket pitch has extensive views across Cheshire. CAMRA members are admitted as guests on match days. P

Swan

Chapel Street, ST7 8QD

12-11; 12-10.30 Sun

☎ (01782) 720622

Draught Bass; guest beers H

Known to locals as The Duck', this is Potteries CAMRA Pub of the Year 2007. The traditional pub has a bar and lounge with real fires, with eight handpumps serving ever-changing guest beers, two real ciders from Weston's and Thatchers, and a perry. The Swan holds regular beer festivals and the pub's Real Ale Club organises days out and events.

♨❀(34)

Blythe Bridge

One Legged Shunter (Foxfield Railway Bar)

Caverswall Road, ST11 9EA

closed Mon-Fri; hours vary Sat; 12-9 Sun

☎ (01782) 396210 foxfieldrailway.co.uk

Beer range varies H

Single bar inside the Foxfield Light Railway, run by volunteers. Steam trains run from Easter every year along the former colliery line, and the walls of the bar are adorned with historic railway memorabilia. The beer range changes continuously, with ales sourced from micro-breweries from near and far. Weston's cider is also stocked. Regular beer festivals and themed weekends are held throughout the year – check the website for details. A must for real ale drinkers and steam aficionados alike. ♨P

Bobbington

Red Lion

Six Ashes Road, DY7 5DU

12-3, 5-11; 12-11 Sat; 12-10.30 Sun

☎ (01384) 221237 redlioninn.co.uk

Theakston Old Peculier; Wye Valley HPA, Butty Bach H

First recorded as an alehouse in 1820, this pub has been family run for more than 20 years. The bar leads to a games room offering traditional and modern diversions. The large lounge with the handpumps doubles as a restaurant. Don't be alarmed by the pouncing lion and tiger – all is content here. There is an extensive, mostly home-made food menu. An expansive garden includes a children's play area. Accommodation is in 17 modern en-suite rooms. Q❀♣P

Brewood

Bridge Inn

22 High Green, ST19 9BD

12-midnight (1am Fri & Sat)

☎ (01902) 851999

Jennings Dark Mild, Cocker Hoop; Marston's Mansfield Bitter; guest beers H

Popular with boaters and walkers, the inn stands on the Shropshire Union Canal and the Staffordshire Way. Dogs are welcome in the

INDEPENDENT BREWERIES

Beowulf Brownhills
Black Hole Burton upon Trent
Blythe Hamstall Ridware
Burton Bridge Burton upon Trent
Enville Enville
Kinver Kinver
Leek Cheddleton
Marston's Burton upon Trent
Morton Essington
Old Cottage Burton upon Trent
Peakstones Rock Alton
Quartz Kings Bromley
Shugborough Milford
Slater's Stafford
Titanic Burslem
Tower Burton upon Trent
Town House Audley

small, traditional bar which can get busy when national sporting events are shown on TV. Home-cooked food is available all day, including Sunday, in the comfortable lounge and rear restaurant (but not Monday evening which is quiz night). Note the covered smoking shelter overlooking the canal in the style of a narrow boat.
⚔Q❀◑◐⊞♿⊟(3, 76)●P⚟

Swan Hotel

15 Market Place, ST19 9BS
⏲ 11.45-11 (11.30 Thu-Sat); 12-11 Sun
☎ (01902) 850330
Courage Directors; Theakston Black Bull, XB; guest beers Ⓗ
Comfortable village centre coaching inn with low beamed ceilings and log fires, within easy walking distance of the Shropshire Union Canal. The bar is flanked by two cosy snugs displaying pictures of old Brewood, and there is a skittle alley above the entrance to the car park. Ask the landlady to explain the unusual collection of witches' figures. A CAMRA regional Pub of the Year. ⚔Q♿⊟(3, 76)♣P

Bridgtown

Stumble Inn

264 Walsall Road, WS11 0JL (just off A34/A5/M6 toll jct)
⏲ 12-2, 6-11; 5-midnight Fri & Sat; 12-11 Sun
☎ (01543) 502077
Banks's Original; Taylor Landlord; guest beer Ⓗ
Comfortable single-room venue with a split-level interior including a pool and darts area plus a small function room. A music pub, there is a lively disco on Friday, live music on Saturday and showcase nights for new local talent every other Tuesday. All rounded off with karaoke on Wednesday and Sunday nights. Weekday lunches are excellent value. There is a covered and heated smoking area.
❀◑♿⇌(Cannock)⊟♣P⚟

Burton upon Trent

Burton Bridge Inn

24 Bridge Street, DE14 1SY (on A511, at town end of Trent Bridge)
⏲ 11.30-2.15, 5-11; 12-2, 7-10.30 Sun
☎ (01283) 536596 ⊕ burtonbridgebrewery.co.uk
Burton Bridge Golden Delicious, Sovereign Gold, Bridge Bitter, Burton Porter, Festival Ale, seasonal beer; guest beer Ⓗ
This 17th-century pub is the flagship of the Burton Bridge Brewery estate and fronts the brewery itself. Sensitively renovated and extended in 2000, it has two rooms served from a central bar: a smaller front room with wooden pews displaying awards and brewery memorabilia, and a back room featuring oak beams and panels. The beer range is supplemented by a fine selection of malt whiskies and fruit wines. No meals are served Sunday. A small dining/function room and a skittle alley are upstairs. ⚔Q❀◑⊟♣⚟

Coopers Tavern

43 Cross Street, DE14 1EG (off Station Street)
⏲ 12-3, 5-11; 12-midnight Fri & Sat; 12-3, 7-10.30 Sun
☎ (01283) 532551
Castle Rock Harvest Pale; Ⓗ **Draught Bass;** Ⓖ **guest beers** Ⓗ/Ⓖ
Originally the Bass Brewery bottle store, this classic, unspoilt 19th-century ale house was once the Bass Brewery tap and is now a free house. The intimate inner tap room has barrel tables and bench seats. The beer is served from a small counter next to the cask stillage, using a mixture of gravity and handpumps. Draught cider and perry plus fruit wines are also available. The more comfortable lounge, sometimes hosting impromptu folk music, leads to a third small room.
⚔Q❀◑⊞⇌⊟●⚟

Devonshire Arms

86 Station Street, DE14 1BT
⏲ 11.30-2.30, 5.30-11; 11.30-11.30 Fri & Sat; 12-3, 7-10.30 Sun
☎ (01283) 562392
Burton Bridge Golden Delicious, Bridge Bitter, Burton Porter, Stairway to Heaven; guest beer Ⓗ
One of five Burton Bridge Brewery hostelries in the town, this popular old pub dating from the 19th-century and Grade II listed has a small public bar at the front and a larger, comfortable, split-level lounge to the rear. Note the 1853 map of Burton, old photographs and unusual arched wooden ceilings. The rear patio features a fountain. Continental bottled beers and English fruit wines are also stocked. No meals are served on Sunday. ⚔❀◑⊞⇌⊟♣P⚟

Elms Inn

36 Stapenhill Road, Stapenhill, DE15 9AE (On A444)
⏲ 2-11 (midnight Fri); 12-midnight Sat; 11-10.30 Sun
☎ (01283) 535505
Draught Bass; Marston's Pedigree; guest beers Ⓗ
Busy free house overlooking the River Trent. Built as a private house in the late 19th-century, this is one of Burton's original 'parlour pubs'. Renovated in a Victorian style with a small public bar and snug at the front and larger, comfortable lounge to the rear, it has an intimate and friendly atmosphere. Social activities include a walking club, race trips, Tuesday quiz night and summer barbecues. Guest ales usually include a Tower beer. A real cider is often available in summer.
⚔Q❀⊞⊟♣●P⚟

Oak & Ivy

119-122 Wellington Street, DE14 2DP (on A5121, near town hall)
⏲ 11-11 (10.30 Sun)
☎ (01283) 532508
Banks's Bitter; Marston's Pedigree; guest beers Ⓗ
Pleasant, friendly, mid-terrace local with a central bar serving a lively public bar and comfortable lounge. The town's brewing history is illustrated by old photographs and shelves of brewery memorabilia. Simple bar snacks are enhanced by a speciality cheese board on Sunday lunchtime. Up to three guest beers from the Marston's list are available. The enclosed garden at the rear includes a children's play area. Q❀⛟⊞⇌⊟♣⚟

Old Cottage Tavern

36 Byrkley Street, DE14 2EG (off Derby Street A5121, behind town hall)
12-11
(01283) 511615
Old Cottage Oak Ale, Stout, Pastiche, Halcyon Daze; guest beers Ⓗ
This welcoming local is now a privately owned free house but continues to operate as the Old Cottage Brewery tap, although no longer owned by the brewery. The public bar at the front and the recently renovated wood-panelled lounge to the rear are served from a central bar. There is also a cosy snug to one side of the public bar, plus a small restaurant beyond the lounge. Upstairs, the games/function room has a skittle alley.

Chasetown

Uxbridge Arms

2 Church Street, WS7 3QL
12-3, 5.30-11; 12-11 Fri & Sat; 12-10.30 Sun
(01543) 677852
Draught Bass; Courage Directors; guest beers Ⓗ
Busy corner local a short distance from Chasewater Country Park and Chasetown Football Club. A large public bar and lounge offer three guest beers usually sourced from micros along with two real ciders. There is also a wide choice of country wines and 50 malt whiskies. The Hayloft restaurant is upstairs (no food served on Sunday evening).
P

Church Eaton

Royal Oak

High Street, ST20 0AJ
5 (12 Sat)-midnight; 12-10.30 Sun
(01785) 823078 churcheaton.org.uk
Banks's Original, Bitter; guest beer Ⓗ
The only pub in the village, three years ago it was threatened with closure but was saved by a small consortium of local people and is now the hub of the community. It has a modern interior with four inter-connecting rooms – a bar, restaurant, TV room and pool room. Children are welcome until 7pm or later if eating in the restaurant. The ever-changing guest beers are mostly sourced from local micro-breweries. P

Codsall

Codsall Station

Chapel Lane, WV8 2EJ
11.30-2.30, 5-11; 11.30-11.30 Fri & Sat; 12-10.30 Sun
(01902) 847061
Holden's Mild, Bitter, Golden Glow, Special, seasonal beers; guest beers Ⓗ
Former station master's house and waiting room converted by Holden's Brewery in 1999. The interior, displaying worldwide railway memorabilia, comprises a bar, lounge, snug and conservatory. Outside a raised terrace overlooks the working platforms on the Wolverhampton-Shrewsbury line. The floodlit boules piste is the site of the early September beer festival. Good value home-cooked food is served daily (not Sun eve). QP

Dayhills

Red Lion

Uttoxeter Road, ST15 8RU (3 miles E of Stone on B5027)
6-11; 4-midnight Fri; 12-midnight Sat; 12-10.30 Sun
(01889) 505474
Draught Bass; Ⓗ/Ⓖ **Worthington's Bitter; guest beer** Ⓗ
Welcoming country pub known locally as the Romping Cat. Unspoilt and full of character, it has been in the same family since 1920, along with the adjoining farm. The main room has a timeless feel with a quarry tile floor, meat hooks in the ceiling and an inglenook fireplace. The atmosphere is undisturbed by music, gaming machines or TV. Draught Bass may be served straight from the cask during winter months. QP

Eccleshall

George Hotel

Castle Street, ST21 6DF
11-11; 12-10.30 Sun
(01785) 850300
Slater's Bitter, Original, Top Totty, Premium, Supreme, seasonal beers Ⓗ
Slater's Brewery has outgrown the extended outbuilding behind the pub, but six handpulls serving the full range of its award-winning ales are still the main attraction at the George. Originally a coaching inn in the 17th century but sadly neglected for much of the last century, the George has thrived under the Slater family's ownership. It now boasts attractive bar and lounge areas and serves excellent meals throughout the day.
QP

Star Inn

Copmere End, ST21 6EW SJ803294
12-3 (not Mon), 6-11; 12-11 Sat summer; 12-4 (11 summer) Sun
(01785) 850279 thestarinn-eccleshall.co.uk
Draught Bass; Titanic Anchor; Wells Bombardier Ⓗ
Thriving 100-year-old pub in the heart of the beautiful Staffordshire countryside next to the Cop Mere Lake and popular with walkers. The post office next door has been closed for a number of years but keeps the Victorian post box. An excellent selection of bar meals and an à la carte menu are offered.
QP

Enville

Cat

Bridgnorth Road, DY7 5HA (on A458)
12-2.30 (3 Sat), 6.30-11; closed Mon; 12-6 Sun
(01384) 872209 theenvillecat.co.uk
Enville Ale; guest beers Ⓗ
Parts of this traditional country pub date back to the 16th century. It has three oak beamed rooms, two with real fires, and a family/function room. Hanging baskets adorn the garden and courtyard during the summer months. Up to five guest ales are served including beers from local breweries. Home-made dishes and daily specials, made with local produce wherever possible, are served. A

separate menu is offered in the restaurant.
♨☕❀◑P

Forton

Swan Inn

Eccleshall Road, TF10 8BY
⌚ 12-3, 5.30-11; 12-11 Fri & Sat; 12-10.30 Sun
☎ (01952) 812169
Greene King IPA, Abbot; guest beer Ⓗ
Former free house owned by British Country Inns since October 2007. Originally the manager's house on the Aqualate Estate, this dining pub is described as 'somewhere different' and has 14 bedrooms, six luxury and eight in a barn conversion. A number of large rooms are available including a library where guests may read or borrow books. The Regency Room is available for private hire. There is a carvery on Friday, Saturday evening and all day Sunday. ♨Q❀⛿◑ΔP⅃

Great Haywood

Clifford Arms ✔

Main Road, ST18 0SR (off A51 4 miles NW of Rugeley)
⌚ 12-11.30; 12-midnight Fri & Sat; 12-11 Sun
☎ (01889) 881321
Adnams Broadside; Draught Bass; Greene King Old Speckled Hen; guest beers Ⓗ
Village-centre inn with a large bar providing plenty of seating and a restaurant adorned with old photographs of the pub. A lively local, home to cribbage, dominoes and quiz teams, it also has a tug 'o' war team. Popular with walkers, cyclists, boaters and visitors to the nearby Shugborough Estate (National Trust), The Staffordshire Way and bridge 73 of the Trent and Mersey Canal are 200 metres along Trent Lane. The pub is dog-friendly.
♨❀◑⊟♿🚌♣P⅃

Harriseahead

Royal Oak

High Steeet, ST7 4JT
⌚ 7 (5 Fri & Sat) - 11; 12-3, 7-10.30 Sun
☎ (01782) 513262 🌐 royaloak-harriseahead.com
Courage Directors; Fuller's London Pride; guest beers Ⓗ
Two-roomed free house in the village, popular with the locals, situated in a fine walking area with Mow Cop folly half a mile away. A warm welcome and a good night out await at this friendly pub, where the guest beers come from small, independent micro-brewers. An upstairs function room provides extra space for the annual beer festival held in December. A range of bottled Belgian beers is always available, plus one on draught. A quiz is held once a month. ♨Q❀⊟♣P⅃

High Offley

Anchor Inn

Peggs Lane, Old Lea, ST20 0NG (by bridge 42 of Shropshire Union Canal) SJ775256
⌚ 12-3, 7-11 (10.30 Sun); winter hours vary
☎ (01785) 284569
Wadworth 6X Ⓖ
On the Shropshire Union Canal, this Victorian inn has changed little since the days of commercial waterways and has been run by the same family since 1870. Hard to reach by road but well worth seeking out, it remains a rare example of an unspoilt country pub, with two small bars where cask ale and cider are served from jugs. Freshly-made sandwiches are always available. There is a large award-winning garden with a canalware gift shop at the rear. Opening hours vary in winter – ring to check. ♨Q❀⊟Δ●P

Hilderstone

Roebuck Inn

Sandon Road, ST15 8SF (on B5066)
⌚ 3-midnight (1am Fri); 12-1am Sat; 12-11 Sun
☎ (01889) 505255
Banks's Original; Taylor Golden Best; Wadworth 6X; guest beers Ⓗ
This friendly and comfortable pub has a cosy lounge bar with a TV showing sports and music and a games room with a dartboard. Two guest beers from the SIBA scheme are offered and Thatchers cider is usually available in summer. Entertainment includes a busker's night on Sunday and a live act or karaoke on most Saturday nights. The licensee's growing collection of ornamental pigs is displayed around the rooms. ♨❀♣P⅃

Keele

Keele Postgraduate Association (KPA)

Horwood Hall, University Campus, ST5 5BJ
⌚ 11-midnight (1am Fri); closed Mon; 5-midnight Sat; 7-11 Sun
☎ (01782) 584228 🌐 keele.ac.uk/socs/kpa
Beer range varies Ⓗ
The KPA was founded in 1967 as the Keele Research Association, but changed its name and moved to the present site in 1994. Two real ales often from local breweries are always on offer, soon to be three when renovation and an extension are completed. CAMRA members are welcome as guests. There is a quiet reading area with newspapers.
◑♿🚌(25)

Kidsgrove

Blue Bell

Hardingswood, ST7 1EG (off A50 near Tesco)
⌚ 7.30-11; closed Mon; 1-4, 7-11 Sat; 12-10.30 Sun
☎ (01782) 774052 🌐 bluebellkidsgrove.co.uk
Beer range varies Ⓗ
A regular winner of awards, this canal-side pub lies at the junction of the Trent and Mersey and Macclesfield canals. The bar offers six ever-changing guest beers from a wide range of independent and micro-breweries. Real cider and perry are available, plus German and Czech beers. Free from jukebox, gaming machine and TV, this is a convivial place to drink and chat. Dogs are welcome.
Q❀⇌🚌●P

Kinver

Constitutional Social Club

119 High Street, DY7 6HL

5-11; 4-midnight Fri; 11.30-midnight Sat; 12-10.30 Sun

(01384) 872044

Banks's Original; Greene King Abbot; Hobsons Best Bitter; Wye Valley HPA; guest beers

Built in 1902 on the site of an old pub, this converted hotel has three main areas: a smart restaurant, a large snooker room and a bar dispensing up to six guest beers from myriad breweries, at reasonable prices. The club enjoys an enviable sporting reputation and hosts regular quiz and music nights. Meals are served Sunday lunchtime and Thursday to Saturday evenings (booking advised). Card-carrying CAMRA members are welcome but must be signed in. Local CAMRA Club of the Year in 2007 and 2008.

(227, 228)

Vine

1 Dunsley Road, DY7 6LJ

12-11

(01384) 877291 vineinnkinver.co.uk

Enville Ale; Fuller's London Pride; Kinver Edge

The Vine was opened in 1863 in competition with the Lock Inn that once stood opposite. Originally two converted cottages, it extended into adjacent cottages over the years and most internal walls were removed in 1980. Now a one-roomed pub, it retains distinct areas on different levels, with the restaurant overlooking Kinver lock on the Staffs & Worcs Canal. There are extensive canal-side gardens. Food is served all day on Saturday.

(227, 228)P

Knighton

Haberdashers Arms

Knighton, ST20 0QH SJ753275

12.30 (7 Wed & Thu)-midnight; 12.30-1am Fri & Sat; 12-midnight Sun

(01785) 280650

Banks's Original, Bitter; guest beer

Traditional community pub, built about 1840, offering a warm, friendly welcome. This former local CAMRA Pub of the Year has four compact rooms all served from a small bar. The large garden is used for events including the annual Potato Club Show. It is well worth the drive through leafy country lanes to get here. QP

Leek

Den Engel

Stanley Street, ST13 5HG

5-11; 11-11.30 Wed & Thu; 11-midnight Fri & Sat; 12-11.30 Sun

(01538) 373751

Beer range varies

Walking down Stanley Street in the Moorlands town of Leek, the last thing the casual visitor expects to see is an authentic Belgian bar. So it is a treat to discover Den Engel (The Angel), offering around 10 Belgian beers on draught plus a multitude in bottles. The four handpumps dispense ever-changing beers from British micro-breweries, with a bias towards Yorkshire breweries such as Ossett and Rudgate. The front bar overlooks the street and the patio to the rear is a pleasant sun-trap in summer months. Q

Wilkes Head

St Edward Street, ST13 5DS

12 (3 Mon)-11; 12-10.30 Sun

(01538) 383616

Whim Arbor Light, Hartington Bitter, IPA, seasonal beers; guest beers

Cosy three-roomed pub, a rare Whim tied house, at the top of St Edwards Street. Named after the 18th-century politician, the bar room boasts a real fire and a plaque detailing the life of John Wilkes. The landlord is an enthusiastic musician and the quiet back room is decorated with pictures of his favourite artists. Also not to be missed is Dolly the pub dog, who sits in the window waiting for customers to make a fuss of her.

Lichfield

Acorn

12-18 Tamworth Street, WS13 6JJ

9-midnight (1am Fri & Sat)

(01543) 263261

Greene King Abbot; Marston's Burton Bitter, Pedigree; guest beers

Flanked by pubs on both sides, the Acorn is one of the better examples in the Wetherspoon's chain. A good ambassador for promoting real ale to all age groups, it offers an excellent selection of up to six guests including micro-brewery beers, and has an enthusiastic clientele to keep the ale flowing. The pub tends to get very busy in the evening, towards the weekend. The name was a suggestion from a local pub historian —the neighbouring Oak was originally the Acorn until about 15 years ago. (City)

Bowling Green

Friary Road, WS13 6QJ

11.30-11

(01543) 257344

Banks's Bitter; Marston's Pedigree; guest beer

Spacious inn situated to the west of the city centre in the middle of a large traffic island, with a comfortable interior that divides into distinct drinking areas. For the peckish, a comprehensive bar meal menu is available. The prominent clock tower on the city side of the pub was moved from its original Bore Street location in the 1920s. Nearby parking is pay and display. (City)

Duke of Wellington

Birmingham Road, WS14 9BJ

4 (12 Thu-Sun)-11

(01543) 263261

Black Sheep Best Bitter; Fuller's London Pride; Marston's Pedigree; guest beers

The reward for a 15-minute walk from the city centre is an excellent choice of real ales consistently on top form, including two ever-changing guest beers frequently sourced from micros. The interior has been opened out into three distinct drinking areas served from a single bar. The long rear garden is popular during the summer months and includes a large open fronted, wooden pavilion to

protect smokers from the weather.
♨❀◑⊟♣P⛿

George & Dragon

28 Beacon Street, WS13 7AJ
⏲ 12-11; 11-midnight Thu-Sat; 12-10.30 Sun
☎ (01543) 253667
Banks's Original, Bitter; Marston's Pedigree; guest beer Ⓗ
Compact, two room pub north of the Cathedral and close to Beacon Park. The lounge walls illustrate the story of the second siege of Lichfield in 1643 when Royalists bombarded the Cathedral from a mound above the pub garden. Bar snacks and a selection of teas and coffee are always available. A charity quiz is held on Thursday night. ❀⊟≋(City)⊟♣P⛿

Queens Head ✔

4 Queen Street, WS13 6QD
⏲ 12-11 (11.30 Fri & Sat); 12-3, 7-11 Sun
☎ (01543) 410932
Adnams Bitter; Marston's Pedigree; Taylor Landlord; guest beers Ⓗ
The Queens Head has long been a mecca for real ale fans and frequently offers local micro-ales as guests. Usually a quiet pub, it can get lively on Saturday afternoon when live rugby is televised. Good value home-cooked lunches are served Monday to Saturday, and a selection of bread, cheeses and pâtés are available during all sessions. With smokers in mind there is now an outdoor drinking area, complete with heaters. Q◑≋(City)⊟♣⛿

Longdon

Swan with Two Necks ✔

40 Brook End, WS15 4PN (250m off A51)
⏲ 12-3, 6-11; 12-11 Sat; 12-10.30 Sun
☎ (01543) 490251
Adnams Bitter; Ansells Mild; Taylor Landlord; guest beer Ⓗ
A meeting place for locals from the village and surrounding countryside, this fine pub has been in the Guide for more than 28 years. Three regular beers are supplemented by a guest, usually from a micro. Meals are of a very high quality and the restaurant area is open on Friday and Saturday evenings. The pleasant outdoor terrace is popular during the summer months. ♨Q❀◑◐P

Milwich

Green Man

Milwich, ST18 0EG (on B5027)
⏲ 12-2.30 (not Mon-Wed), 5-11; 12-11 Sat; 12-10.30 Sun
☎ (01889) 505310 🌐 greenmanmilwich.com
Adnams Bitter; Draught Bass; Wells Bombardier; guest beers Ⓗ
A pub since 1775, this free house offers guest beers from regional and micro-breweries nationwide – see website for forthcoming guests. The current licensee is in his 18th year here and a list of his predecessors dating back to 1792 is displayed. A popular pub with walkers and cyclists, there is a small restaurant area within the bar (lunch served Thu-Sun, evening meals Wed-Sat). Weston's or Thatchers cider is stocked. Local CAMRA Pub of the Year 2006 and 2007. ♨❀◑◐♣●P⛿

Newcastle-under-Lyme

Arnold Machin ✔

37 Ironmarket, ST5 1PB
⏲ 9am-midnight (12.30am Fri & Sat)
☎ (01782) 557840
Courage Directors; Draught Bass; Greene King IPA, Abbot; Marston's Pedigree; Slater's Premium; guest beers Ⓗ
This spacious Wetherspoon's pub was previously the post office and stamps are prominently displayed on the walls, including the Machin Head by local sculptor Arnold Machin. It is situated in a pleasant location opposite the library, overlooking the Jubilee Gardens. Up to a dozen regular and varied guest ales adorn the bar, coming from near and far, together with a choice of real ciders, and a varied range of continental beers, both draught and bottled. Well worth a visit.
❀◑◐♿⊟●⛿

Museum

29 George Street, ST5 1JU
⏲ 12-11
☎ (01782) 623866
Draught Bass; Everards Tiger; Marston's Pedigree; Worthington's Bitter; guest beer Ⓗ
Traditional two-room pub with an outdoor patio area. A friendly local just outside the town centre, it has a basic bar and more comfortably appointed lounge. Dominoes, crib and darts teams are in residence, and a coach is run for supporters to Stoke City home matches. Music plays on Saturday night. Lunches are served Monday to Friday. Q◑⊟

Old Brown Jug ✔

Bridge Street, ST5 2RY
⏲ 3pm-midnight (1am Wed); 12-midnight Fri-Sun
☎ (01782) 711393
Marston's Pedigree; guest beers Ⓗ
Situated down a side street at the north end of town, this Marston's pub is one of the very best in the chain, with around five beers on handpump, always including a Jennings ale, plus something from outside the usual Marston's range. Cider is also an attraction, with three on draught and more in bottles. This single-room pub is renowned for live music on Wednesday and Sunday evenings, when it can get very busy and an entrance fee may be charged. ❀⊟●⛿

Newtown

Ivy House

62 Stafford Road, WS6 6AZ (on A34)
⏲ 12-2.30, 5-11; 12-11.30 Fri & Sat; 12-11 Sun
☎ (01922) 476607
Banks's Original, Bitter; Marston's Pedigree; guest beers Ⓗ
This 200-year-old building is a traditional pub with a country feel – the restaurant and garden back on to open farm land. The interior includes three rooms on two levels plus the open plan restaurant serving excellent, high quality food. A visit is highly recommended and a warm welcome assured. Walsall CAMRA

Pub of the Year for the last three years.
Q❀◑♿⊟(1, 351)P⅃

Norton Canes

Railway Tavern ✔

63 Norton Green Lane, WS11 9PR (off Walsall Road)
✪ 12-midnight (1am Fri & Sat)
☎ (01543) 279579
Banks's Original, Bitter; Greene King IPA; guest beers ⊞
This community-focused pub has one spacious drinking area with a large open plan lounge/dining space. Outside is a fully covered patio for smokers and drinkers, an enclosed garden and children's play area. A good selection of meals is served daily. ❀◑♿⊟(63)♣●P⅃

Onecote

Jervis Arms

ST13 7RU (on B5053 N of A53 Leek-Ashbourne road)
✪ 12-3, 7 (6 Sat)-midnight; 12-midnight Sun
☎ (01538) 304206
Sharp's Doom Bar; Titanic Iceberg; Wadworth 6X; guest beers ⊞
A regular in the Guide, the pub is set within the Peak District National Park, close to Alton Towers. A stream runs between the pub entrance and a large car park, and new outdoor seating had recently been added. The landlord has a passion for real ale and the guest beers are always changing, mainly sourced from micro-breweries both near and far. Food is available from an extensive menu and a beer festival is held every July.
♉❀◑ÅP⅃

Oulton

Brushmakers Arms

8 Kibblestone Road, ST15 8UW (500 yds W of A520, 1 mile NE of Stone)
✪ 12-3, 6-midnight (1am Fri-Sat); 12-3, 7-11 Sun
☎ (01785) 812062
Thwaites Original, Lancaster Bomber; guest beers ⊞
Built in 1865 and thought to be named after a local cottage industry, the pub is a classic example of a local that has retained its traditional public bar and lounge. The unspoilt bar is decorated with old photographs and the lounge is intimate and comfortable without gaming machines or jukebox. Guest ales include favourites from Archers and Black Sheep. A small patio garden at the rear is popular in summer, especially at lunchtime.
⩕Q❀⊟♿⊟♣P⅃

Penkridge

Star Inn

Market Place, ST19 5DJ (150m from A449)
✪ 12-11 (11.30 Thu; midnight Fri & Sat)
☎ (01785) 712513
Banks's Bitter, Original; Jennings Cocker Hoop; guest beer ⊞
One-room pub with a patio and seating area outside. Situated in an old market place, the Star first traded as an inn in 1827. Early in the 20th century it became a Co-op store, then a private residence. It was restored to the licensed trade in the second half of the 20th century. Market days are Wednesday and Saturday. ⩕Q❀◑⊟P⅃⊡

Penn Common

Barley Mow

Pennwood Lane, WV4 5JN (follow signs to Penn Golf Club from A449) SO901949
✪ 12-2.30, 6-11; 12-11 Sat; 12-10.30 Sun
☎ (01902) 333510
Caledonian Deuchars IPA; Greene King Abbot; Taylor Landlord; guest beers ⊞
Small low-beamed pub dating from the 1600s, on the border of Wolverhampton and Staffordshire. A small extension was added in the 1990s. This hidden gem has a well-deserved reputation for food, with meat supplied from the landlord's own award-winning butcher's shop. Next to the local golf course, the pub is a short walk over the Seven Cornfields from Wolverhampton. Q❀◑P

Rolleston-on-Dove

Jinnie Inn

177 Station Road, DE13 9AB SK245278
✪ 11.30-11; 12-10.30 Sun
☎ (01283) 812155
Marston's Pedigree; guest beers ⊞
This popular and attractive village pub was converted from a farmhouse in 1991, although it served briefly as an alehouse in the mid 19th-century to benefit the builders of the Burton-Tutbury railway, nicknamed the 'Tutbury Jinnie', after which the pub is named. The comfortable lounge bar and plainer dining room, off to one side, feature beamed ceilings and exposed timber-framed walls. Note the unusual bar counter top, inlaid with 4,600 1p coins (plus three hidden foreign ones). No food is served Sunday evening or Monday.
⩕❀◑♿Å⊟(V1)♣P⅃

Salt

Holly Bush Inn

Salt, ST18 0BX (off A518 opp Weston Hall) SJ959277
✪ 12-11 (midnight Fri & Sat)
☎ (01889) 508234 🌐 hollybushinn.co.uk
Adnams Broadside; Marston's Pedigree; guest beer ⊞
The Holly Bush is believed to be the second English inn to be granted a licence, claiming origins as far back as 1190. The oldest part of the building is still thatched, with many extensions and alterations over the centuries. The interior has three distinct areas: a bar towards the middle of the pub, a dining room and a snug mainly occupied by diners. The pub has won many awards for its scrumptious food served at reasonable prices. ⩕Q❀◑Å⊟P⅃

Silverdale

Bush

High Street, ST5 6JZ
✪ 12-11 (midnight Fri & Sat); 12-10.30
☎ (01782) 713096 🌐 the-bush.co.uk

Wells Bombardier; guest beers Ⓗ
An imposing pub in a former mining village. Formerly called the Sneyd Arms, the Bush has three rooms and a large enclosed beer garden. Six beers are on handpump, with five ever-changing guest ales, mainly from micros and regional breweries, including Abbeydale, Oakham, Titanic, Townhouse, Whim and Woods. Good value food is available – Wednesday is steak night and Sunday lunch is especially popular. There is live entertainment on Friday and Saturday nights and the pub runs dominoes, pool and football teams.
ᗜ❀◐◑⊟♿⊞♣P⊱

Stafford

Bird in Hand

Victoria Square, ST16 2AQ
⌚ 12-11 (midnight Fri & Sat); 12-10.30 Sun
☎ (01785) 252198
Courage Best Bitter; Fuller's London Pride; Wells Bombardier; guest beer Ⓗ
The Bird' was once a Joules pub and the trademark cross can still be seen on the door frames outside. Midway between the railway station and Stafford town centre, it has four rooms – a bar, snug, lounge and function room – with live music on Saturday evening. Several sports societies are based here including a rugby team and golf club. Wireless broadband is available on request. Qᗜ❀⊟♿⇌⊞♣⊱

Greyhound

12 County Road, ST16 2PU (opp jail)
⌚ 4 (2 Fri; 12 Sat & Sun)-11
☎ (01785) 222432
Wells Bombardier; guest beers Ⓗ
A short walk from the town centre, opposite Stafford's gaol, this 1830s pub retains a separate bar and lounge following a sensitive refurbishment. The building was threatened with closure a few years ago and lost its car park to make way for a block of flats. Now a free house, it is going from strength to strength, offering eight handpulled ales, most of them from local micro-breweries and regional brewers. ♨❀⊟⊞♣⊱

Railway Inn

23 Castle Street, ST16 2EB
⌚ 5-midnight; 4-1am Fri; 12-1am Sat; 12-11 Sun
☎ (0796) 7799401
Draught Bass; Caledonian Deuchars IPA; Greene King Abbot; Wells Bombardier Ⓗ
A traditional end of terrace Victorian pub which has changed very little over the years. The landlord is a rugby player and enthusiast, and rugby may take precedence over football on Sky Sports. A variety of clubs are based here, notably a fencing club and walking club which meet on Thursday evening. Due to popular demand an extensive selection of whiskies has been reintroduced and there are currently 60 different malts on offer.
♨Qᗜ❀♿⇌⊞♣⊱

Spittal Brook

106 Lichfield Road, ST17 4LP (off A34)
⌚ 12-3, 5-11; 12-11 Sat; 12-4, 7-10.30 Sun
☎ (01785) 245268
Black Sheep Best Bitter; Everards Tiger; Fuller's London Pride; Jennings Cumberland Ale; Marston's Pedigree; guest beer Ⓗ
Thriving, traditional two-roomed alehouse supporting a variety of pub games and sporting clubs and societies including water polo, netball and golf. Live entertainment includes a folk night on Tuesday and a quiz on Wednesday. ♨Q❀⇔◐◑⊟♿⊞♣P⊱

Star & Garter

87 Wolverhampton Road, ST17 4AW (on A449 near town centre)
⌚ 12-midnight
☎ (01785) 251717
Beer range varies Ⓗ
Close to the town centre along the busy Wolverhampton Road, the Star and Garter dates back to the 1820s. Originally a doctor's surgery, it was the last pub in Stafford to admit women. Now a cheery local, two roaring fires warm the interior on cold days. Well known in the area for live music, it usually offers three hand-pulled beers.
♨❀♣P⊱

Stoke-on-Trent: Burslem

Bulls Head

St John's Square, ST6 3AJ
⌚ 3-11 (11.30 Wed & Thu); 12-11.30 Fri & Sat; 12-11 Sun
☎ (01782) 834153 🌐 titanicbrewery.co.uk/bulls.html
Titanic Steerage, Anchor, Iceberg, White Star; guest beers Ⓗ
Two-roomed pub a 10 minute' walk from Vale Park and popular with locals as well as away fans. The tap for the Titanic Brewery, guest beers are often themed to seasonal events or moments in history. Thatchers real cider is also available. The bar has bar billiards, table skittles and a jukebox. The lounge is a quieter area, often with a real fire. A limited range of good food is available. Titanic Brewery and the pub have won many awards in recent years.
♨Q⊟⊞♣●⊱

Leopard Hotel

Market Place, ST6 3AA
⌚ 11-11 (midnight Fri & Sat)
☎ (01782) 819644
Beer range varies Ⓗ
Formerly a large hotel, the Leopard is one of the oldest pubs in the area —the first meeting to arrange the cutting of the Trent and Mersey Canal was held here. Eight handpumps offer a constantly-changing selection of beers from micro-breweries and two more are soon to be added; a real cider from Weston's is also available. Food is served. Q◐◑⊞●⊱

Post Office Vaults

Market Place, ST6 3AA
⌚ 11-11 (1am Fri & Sat); 12-11 Sun
☎ (01782) 811027
Greene King Abbot; Fuller's London Pride; guest beers Ⓗ
Small, one-room pub in the centre of Burslem, popular with locals and those coming to enjoy the beer delights of the area. Sport and music feature on TVs throughout the pub, including the purpose-built covered and heated area outside. Up to three guest beers are stocked,

chosen from an increasing number of breweries.

Stoke-on-Trent: Fenton

Malt 'n' Hops
King Street, ST4 3EJ
12-4, 7-11; 12-3, 7-10.30 Sun
(01782) 313406
Beer range varies
This free house has been in the same family for almost 20 years. The single-room interior divides into separate drinking areas. A changing range of guest beers is available, many from local breweries —the house bees are produced by Tower at Burton. Some Belgian beers are stocked. The pub is popular with the horse racing fraternity.
(Longton)

Stoke-on-Trent: Hanley

Coachmakers Arms
Lichfield Street, ST1 3EA (off A5008 Potteries Way ring road)
12-11.30 (midnight Fri & Sat); 12-11 Sun
(01782) 262158
Draught Bass; guest beers
A fine and rare example of a Potteries town pub with four rooms and a central, tiled drinking corridor. The six constantly-changing guest ales always include a mild and porter or stout, and Weston's Old Rosie is also available. Just outside Hanley town centre and close to the bus station, it has a varied clientele attracted by the excellent beer quality and character. CAMRA Potteries Pub of the Year in 2006. Q

Unicorn
Piccadilly, ST1 1EG
12-1am (12.30am Sun)
(01782) 281809 myspace.com/theunicorninn
Fuller's London Pride; guest beers
Small, friendly, city centre pub in the heart of the cultural quarter across from the Regent theatre. Above the bar is a large collection of Toby jugs and there are numerous brasses decorating the cosy room and adjoining sitting area. Sandwiches are available at lunchtime. Two guest beers are served in rotation.

Wheatsheaf Stores
78 Keelings Road, Northwood, ST1 6PB (on B5049)
12-midnight
(01782) 851138
Draught Bass; guest beers
A new addition to the Guide, this friendly, two-roomed, corner local was established in the early 1900s and, despite refurbishment, retains some interesting and original features. The bar is situated in the main lounge and the former snug now contains a pool table. Two rotating guest beers sit alongside the permanent Bass. A real fire is lit during the winter months and there is a covered smoking area outside. (38,40)

Stoke-on-Trent: Longton

Congress
Sutherland Road, ST3 1HJ (opp police station)
12-8 (11 Tue-Thu; midnight Fri & Sat); 12-4, 7-11 Sun
(07790) 660845
Hydes Original; Jennings Sneck Lifter; Titanic Mild; guest beers
You can be sure of a warm Potteries welcome at this traditional pub. There is a relaxed feel to the open-plan interior, with a pool table at the rear. Wide screen TVs are switched on for major sporting events and live entertainment is hosted occasionally. Artwork from local artists is displayed throughout. The licensees pride themselves on the excellent range of real ales with up to seven handpumps in use. Beers from local brewers and ciders are available. A beer festival is held in April.

Stoke-on-Trent: Penkhull

Beehive
Honeywall, ST4 7HU
10-2.30, 4-1am; 11-4, 7-11 Sun
(01782) 846947 beehiveinn.com
Marston's Burton Bitter, Pedigree; guest beers
Deservedly popular local with a warm and friendly atmosphere, managed by a husband and wife team. The pub is popular with Stoke City supporters on match days and displays a wide range of club memorabilia. Hot food is served Mon- Fri, sandwiches and snacks at the weekend. A refurbishment is planned to increase the number of handpumps to 10.
P

Stoke-on-Trent: Stoke

Wheatsheaf
84 Church Street, ST4 1BU
9am-midnight (1am Fri & Sat)
(01782) 747462
Courage Directors; Greene King Abbot; Marston's Pedigree; guest beers
This former coaching inn is now a cosy, friendly Wetherspoon's outlet, more a traditional local than a city centre bar. Recently refurbished, it retains its original character, with plaques on the wall illustrating the local pottery industry. Guest beers can number up to six, with a local ale always available. The pub also hosts several local brewer beer festivals.

Stone

Poste of Stone
1 Granville Square, ST15 8AB
9-midnight (1am Fri & Sat)
(01785) 827920
Greene King IPA, Abbot; Marston's Pedigree; guest beer
Large open plan Wetherspoon's pub converted from the former main post office. A guest beer from Milestone, Slater's, Springhead or Titanic is usually available. Breakfast and beer are served from 9am at this busy and friendly pub where children are welcome in the large restaurant area. Food club nights include steak on Tuesday and curry on Thursday. The Trent

and Mersey Canal and boatyards are nearby.
₪❀◗♿⇌🚌●P⊱

Star Inn

21 Stafford Street, ST15 8QW
⏲ 11-11 (11.30 Thu-Sat); 12-11 Sun
☎ (01785) 813096
Banks's Bitter; Marston's Pedigree; guest beer Ⓗ
An old canal pub, popular with boaters and locals alike. The small canal bar pre-dates the opening of the Trent and Mersey Canal in 1777. There is a large lounge with a dining area and outside seating and tables next to the canal lock. An exterior plaque declares that the pub has an entry in the Guinness Book of Records for the greatest number of floor levels in a public house. Guest beers are usually from Marston's or Jennings.
₪Q❀◗⊟⇌P⊱

Swan Inn

18 Stafford Street, ST15 8QW
⏲ 11-midnight (1am Thu-Sat); 12-11 Sun
☎ (01785) 815570
Coach House Gunpowder Mild, John Joule Old Knotty, John Joule Old Priory, John Joule Victory; guest beers Ⓗ
Grade II-listed building renovated in 1999 with one large L-shaped room featuring real fires. Beers from more than 400 breweries have been served to date and six guest beers are always available. Tuesday is quiz night and live music is performed four nights a week. A free buffet is served Sun lunchtime and snacks are offered Tue-Sat. An annual beer festival is held during the second week of July. Over-18s only. ₪❀◗♿⇌🚌●⊱

Summerhill

Boat

Walsall Road, WS14 0BU
⏲ 12-3, 6-11; 12-11 Sun
☎ (01543) 361692 🌐 oddfellowsintheboat.com
Beer range varies Ⓗ
Lovers of good food and real ale flock to this free house. The Mediterranean-style reception area is the perfect place to peruse the extensive chalk board menu and watch the cooking. Excellent chefs prepare a range of delectable dishes, while an ever-changing selection of beers is sourced from local and national brewers. ₪Q❀◗♿P⊱

Tamworth

Albert Hotel

32 Albert Rd, B79 7JS
⏲ 12-11 (12.30am Thu-Sat); 12-10.30 Sun
☎ (01827) 64694 🌐 tamworthhotel.co.uk
Banks's Original, Bitter; Marston's Pedigree; guest beers Ⓗ
Close to the railway station, this friendly town centre hotel has a small side bar, popular lounge at the front and games room at the back. Outside, front and rear patio drinking areas are well used in summer. A regular in this Guide, the pub offers guest beers from the Marston's range, and is well known locally for its good quality food. Quiz night is Thursday.
❀🛏◗⇌🚌(765)♣P⊱

Globe Inn

Lower Gungate, B79 7AT
⏲ 11-11; 7-10.30 Sun
☎ (01827) 60455 🌐 theglobetamworth.com
Draught Bass; Holden's Mild; Worthington's Bitter; guest beer Ⓗ
Well-appointed single room hotel bar in the centre of town with a rear dining area and separate function room. The guest beer usually alternates between Archers and Holden's. The pub can get quite lively on function nights or when its large-screen TVs show live football or rugby matches. There is a public car park next door. 🛏◖⇌

Market Vaults

7 Market Street, B79 7LU
⏲ 12-3, 6.30-11; closed Mon; 11-midnight Fri & Sat; 12-3, 7-11 Sun
☎ (01827) 69653
Banks's Original, Bitter; guest beer Ⓗ
Located on the medieval Market Street in Tamworth and adjacent to the 18th-century former town hall, this traditional town centre pub is entered via a narrow side alley which also leads to a neat heated and covered rear beer garden and smoking area. The pub has two rooms offering quality hand-pulled Marston's beers. Good value food is served lunchtimes and evenings. Q❀◖⊟⇌⊱

Sir Robert Peel

12-13 Lower Gungate, B79 7BA
⏲ 12-11 Mon; 5-11.30 Tue; 5-11 Wed; 5-midnight Thu; 12-midnight Fri & Sat; 12-11.30 Sun
☎ (01827) 300910
Beer range varies Ⓗ
Local CAMRA Pub of the Year for 2008, this lively town centre pub is a friendly, family run business that is proud of its regularly-changing guest beers – there is an impressive display of pump clips on the back of the bar. Two guest ales and a regular real cider are almost always available, making this a regular haunt for CAMRA members. The pub has live music on Sunday and Tuesday nights. ⇌●

White Lion

1 Aldergate, B79 7DJ
⏲ 5-11; 12-midnight Fri-Sun
☎ (01827) 64630
Banks's Bitter; Wychwood Hobgoblin; guest beers Ⓗ
Three to four real ales are regularly available at this town-centre corner public house, with guest beers mainly from local micro-breweries. Sport is screened on large TVs in the main bar. Pool and darts are played in the games room and at the rear is a heated, part-covered beer garden. Good, reasonably-priced food available daily. ❀◖◗⊟♿⇌♣⊱

Trysull

Bell

Bell Lane, WV5 7JB SO852940
⏲ 11.30-3, 5-11; 11.30-11 Sat; 12-10.30 Sun
☎ (01902) 892871
Batham Best Bitter; Holden's Bitter, Golden Glow, Special, seasonal beers; guest beer Ⓗ
Eighteenth-century inn standing next to the medieval church in the centre of the village,

on the site of a much older pub. It has three rooms: a pleasant bar, comfortable lounge and newly refurbished restaurant serving good value home-made meals. The ever-changing guest beer usually comes from a micro-brewery. Q🍺❀◑♿P⊓

Tutbury

Cross Keys

39 Burton Street, DE13 9NR SK215287
10-3, 5.30 (6 Sat)-11; 12-3, 7-10.30 Sun
☎ (01283) 813677
Tetley Bitter, Burton Ale; guest beer Ⓗ
Popular late 19th-century free house with a fine view of Tutbury Castle along Burton Street and overlooking the Dove Valley. The two split-level rooms, public bar and lounge, have a homely feel, served from a similarly split-level bar. There is a separate 40-seat restaurant, Wendy's, to the rear (no meals Sun eve). One of the few pubs in the area to have remained loyal to Draught Burton Ale since its launch in Burton in 1975. ❀◑⊟♿⊟P

Two Gates

Bull's Head

446 Watling Street, B77 1HW
12-3, 5-11; 12-11 Fri-Sun
☎ (01827) 287820
Marston's Pedigree; guest beer Ⓗ
Although situated in a residential area, this community local resembles a Victorian farmhouse. The two-roomed pub has a split-level lounge leading out to the patio and a small, friendly bar. It is home to many sports and clubs. The guest beers are very popular and change regularly.
Q❀⊟⇌(Wilnecote)⊟(116, 767)♣P

Uttoxeter

Plough Inn

Stafford Road, ST14 8DW (On A518)
12-midnight (11 Sun)
☎ (01889) 562381
Black Sheep Ale; Courage Directors; Draught Bass; Greene King Ruddles County; Marston's Pedigree; Theakston Old Peculier; guest beer Ⓗ
Essentially rural in location, the Plough was once part of the Loxley Park Estate and a framed document on display gives details of the sale of the pub in 1918. Off the central bar area is a snug, dining room and small pool room. The clientele is drawn mainly from the local community, supplemented by passing trade visiting the local racecourse and nearby Alton Towers. ⌂Q❀◑⊟♣P⅃

Weston

Saracens Head

Stafford Road, ST18 0HT (on A518)
12-11 summer; 12-3, 5 (12 Fri & Sat)-11 winter; 12-10.30 Sun
☎ (01889) 270286
Marston's Pedigree; Worthington's Bitter; guest beer Ⓗ
Friendly family pub situated in a delightful village, catering for visitors en route to Alton Towers, narrowboats on the nearby Trent and Mersey Canal, and the local community. Diners can enjoy views over open countryside in the conservatory. Drinkers can make themselves at home in the public bar or more comfortable in the lounge.
⌂Q🍺❀◑⊟⋀⊟♣P⅃

Whiston

Swan Inn

ST19 5QH SJ895144
12-3 (not Mon), 5-11; 12-11 Sun
☎ (01785) 716200
Holden's Mild, Bitter, Golden Glow; guest beer Ⓗ
Although remotely situated, high quality, well kept ales and superb food make this a thriving pub. Built in 1593, burned down and rebuilt in 1711, the oldest part today is the small bar housing an inglenook fireplace. The lounge features an intriguing central double sided log fire. Six acres of grounds include a children's obstacle course, aviary and rabbits.
⌂Q🍺❀◑⊟♿⋀⊟♣P⅃

Wilnecote

Globe Inn

91 Watling Street, B77 5BA
11-3.30, 7-11; 12-3, 7-10.30 Sun
☎ (01827) 280885
Marston's Pedigree Ⓗ
A genuine community alehouse, this pub is renowned locally for the quality of its Pedigree. In Germany it is said that it takes seven minutes to pour the perfect pilsener. Well it takes the same here, but it is well worth the wait. A one-roomed, cosy pub, it is home to local sports teams including darts, dominoes and football. Q❀⊟(9)♣⅃

Wolstanton

Archer

21 Church Lane, ST5 0EH
12 (11 Sat)-11; 12-10.30 Sun
☎ (01782) 740467
Everards Tiger; Hop Back GFB, Crop Circle, Summer Lightning; Marston's Pedigree; guest beers Ⓗ
Ever popular village local formerly known as the New Smithy.Three Hop Back beers are usually available plus two ever-changing guests, often including a beer from the local Titanic brewery. Real cider is always available. This pub gets very busy at the weekend, especially in summer. ❀⊟♣●P⅃

Wood Lane

Wood Lane Cricket Club

Megacre, ST7 8PA
closed Mon; 8 (7.30 Fri; 2 Sat)-11.30
☎ (01782) 721458
Beer range varies Ⓗ
This club has developed its cellar and dispense systems specifically to serve real ale, with assistance from Woodlands Brewery. Three handpumps deliver beers from a range of more than 30 real ales drawn from regional and micro-brewers, while a fourth is dedicated to ciders from the Weston's range.
⊟(34)♣●P

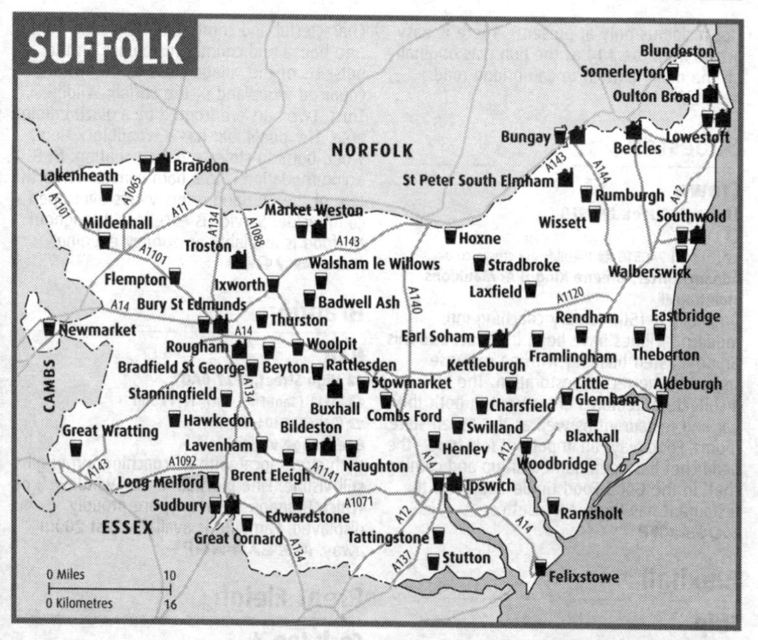

Aldeburgh

Mill Inn

Market Cross Place, IP15 5BJ (opp Moot Hall)

11-11; 11-3, 6-11 winter; 12-10.30 Sun

☎ (01728) 452563

Adnams Bitter, Broadside, seasonal beers; guest beers Ⓗ

Centrally positioned inn in an attractive coastal town, the pub has two main bars: a snug and a restaurant (no food Mon or Sun eve). Locally caught fish is a speciality and themed food evenings a highlight. The famous 'fish sheds' can be seen from the pub. A sea-front seating area close to nearby Moot Hall is busy on summer days. Folk music sessions are held monthly on Sunday afternoons.

White Hart

222 High Street, IP15 5AJ

11.30-11; 12-10.30 Sun

☎ (01728) 453205

Adnams Bitter, Explorer, Broadside; guest beers, seasonal beers Ⓗ

Lively single room bar, formerly a public reading room, adjacent to the town's renowned fish and chip shop. The pub is a popular meeting place for locals and visitors in this delightful coastal town. A diverse selection of live music plays every Saturday and Sunday evening.

Badwell Ash

White Horse

The Street, IP31 3DP

7-11 Mon; 6-midnight Tue-Thu; 12-2, 5-midnight Fri; 12-11 Sat & Sun

☎ (01359) 259909

Greene King IPA; guest beers Ⓗ

This large 16th-century village free house still displays the original tiled Lacons sign. The main L-shaped bar has a wood burner and a TV at one end and a dartboard and pool table at the other. A smaller, quieter bar and restaurant/lounge have been newly renovated. Good value curry and steak nights.

Beyton

Bear Inn

Tostock Road, IP30 9AG

12-2.30, 5-11; 12-4, 7-10.30 Sun

☎ (01359) 270249 thebearinn.net

Greene King IPA; Woodforde's Wherry Best Bitter; guest beers Ⓗ

Rebuilt in 1900 after the original thatched Bear burned down in a July thunderstorm – you can read a full account of this event in the bar. The pub has been run by the same family since 1922. The current landlord has updated the building without spoiling a very traditional inn, with two bars and a separate dining room

INDEPENDENT BREWERIES

Adnams Southwold
Bartrams Rougham
Brandon Brandon
Cox & Holbrook Buxhall
Earl Soham Earl Soham
Green Dragon Bungay
Green Jack Lowestoft
Greene King Bury St Edmunds
Hektors Beccles (NEW)
Kings Head Bildeston
Mauldons Sudbury
Old Cannon Bury St Edmunds
Old Chimneys Market Weston
Oulton Oulton Broad
Red Rat Troston (NEW)
St Judes Ipswich
St Peter's St Peter South Elmham

(for residents only at present). There is easy access from the A14 as the pub was originally on the main Ipswich to Cambridge road.
⊞⊞⊞P

Bildeston

Crown

104 High Street, IP7 7EB
11-11
(01449) 740510 thebildestoncrown.co.uk
Adnams Bitter; Greene King IPA; Mauldons Moletrap ⊞
Originally a 15th-century coaching inn, modern facilities have been introduced to this Grade II listed building with no expense spared in the recent restoration. The architectural features are a treat in both the bar and restaurant as well as the 12 en-suite rooms. Food plays an important role here – the head chef has been named an up and coming chef' in the Good Food Guide 2008 and the restaurant has three AA rosettes.
Q⊞P

Blaxhall

Ship

School Road, IP12 2DY
12-3, 6-midnight
(01728) 688316 blaxhallshipinn.co.uk
Adnams Bitter; Taylor Landlord; guest beers ⊞
On the edge of the Suffolk Sandlings and long famed as a traditional music pub, the Ship has been spruced up and offers a friendly welcome in attractive surroundings with good ale and food. The cosy, timber framed building has low ceilings, simple tiled floors, benches and scrubbed tables. The food menu is varied with many options on the chalkboards. Music plays on most nights of the week with local folk groups playing on some evenings. B&B accommodation is available for those with time to explore this pleasant rural area.
Q⊞P

Blundeston

Plough

Market Lane, NR32 5AN
12-3, 7 (6.30 Fri & Sat)-11.30; 12-3, 7-10.30 Sun
(01502) 730261
Adnams Bitter; guest beers ⊞
Charles Dickens mentioned this pub in his book David Copperfield – it was the starting point for Barkis, the carrier – and not surprisingly the contemporary pub displays a wealth of Dickensian memorabilia. Large, attractive gardens are an added attraction together with comfortable surroundings and exposed beams. The main bar has a pool room and the restaurant serves freshly-prepared meals. One of the real ales is usually from a local brewery. ⊞P

Bradfield St George

Fox & Hounds

Felsham Road, IP30 0AB
12-2.30, 6-11; closed Mon; 12-2.30, 7-10.30 Sun
(01284) 386379
Adnams Bitter; guest beers ⊞
Characterful and comfortable Victorian built free house and country restaurant on the outskirts of the village close to the historic coppiced woodland of the Suffolk Wildlife Trust. Two bars are fronted by a glazed dining area. The public bar has a woodblock floor, wood burning stove and pine seating. B&B accommodation is in a barn conversion to the rear of the pub and offers views over open countryside. Service is excellent throughout. No food is available on Sunday evening.
Q⊞P

Brandon

Bell

48 High Street, IP27 0AQ
11-11 (1am Fri & Sat); 12-11 Sun
(01842) 810465
Beer range varies ⊞
High street local with its coaching inn origins still visible. Fine blocked-in 'tax windows', of which Brandon has many, are proudly displayed. Camping is available just 200m away. ⊞P

Brent Eleigh

Cock Inn ★

Lavenham Road, CO10 9PB
11-4, 6-11; 12-11 Sat; 12-10.30 Sun
(01787) 247371
Adnams Bitter; Greene King Abbot; guest beers ⊞
An absolute gem —this pub will transport you back in time. In winter both bars are snug and warm; in summer, with the doors open, the bar is at one with its surroundings. Good conversation is guaranteed —sit and listen, you will soon become involved. The Scottish-born landlord has introduced a large range of single malts to complement the excellent ales. Close to Lavenham and the Brett Valley, comfortable accommodation is recommended. CAMROT (Campaign for Real Outside Toilets) approved! Q⊞P

Bungay

Green Dragon

29 Broad Street, NR35 1EE
11-3, 5-11; 11-midnight Fri; 12-midnight Sat; 12-3, 7-11 Sun
(01986) 892681
Green Dragon Chaucer Ale, Gold, Bridge Street, seasonal beers ⊞
Green Dragon's beers and bottle-conditioned seasonal ales are brewed in outbuildings next to the car park and brewery tours are available by appointment. This town pub has a public bar, lounge and dining area that doubles as a family room, leading through to the secluded garden. Flexible hours depend upon demand – in summer the pub may be open all day if busy. ⊞P

Bury St Edmunds

Nutshell ★

17 The Traverse, IP33 1BJ
11-11; 12-10.30 Sun
(01284) 764867

Greene King IPA, Abbot ⊞
Situated in the historic town centre of the large market town, this tiny bar has been serving beer for 135 years. At just over 15ft by 7ft (4.5m x 2.1m), it is easily Britain's smallest pub. With just 20 people needed to fill the single bar, it is no surprise that the record of 102 customers at one time remains unbroken since 1984. This unique pub is full of curiosities including a 400-year-old cat, a three-legged chicken and a human lower leg.

Old Cannon Brewery

86 Cannon Street, IP33 1JR
✪ 12-3 (not Mon), 5-11; 12-3, 7-10.30 Sun
☎ (01284) 768769 ⊕ oldcannonbrewery.co.uk
Adnams Bitter; Old Cannon Best Bitter, Blonde Bombshell, Gunner's Daughter; guest beers ⊞
Formerly the St Edmunds Head, this brew pub is on the site of the original Cannon Brewery. It is regarded as the best place in town for real ale, with beers brewed on site and a good range of guest and foreign beers. Food is served most days (not Sun eve or Mon lunch) and accommodation is available (booking essential). ⩋Q❀⇌◑♿⇋P⊬⊓

Rose & Crown ✔

48 Whiting Street, IP33 1NP
✪ 11.30-11 (11.30 Thu & Fri); 11.30-3, 7-11.30 Sat; 12-2.30, 7-11 Sun
☎ (01284) 755934
Greene King XX Mild, IPA, Abbot; guest beers ⊞
Listed red brick street corner pub with two bars and a rare off sales counter, run by the same family for more than 30 years. Good value lunches are available Monday to Saturday in this homely hostelry. The pub is in sight of Greene King's Westgate Brewery. Suffolk CAMRA Pub of the Year in 2005. Q❀◑⊟♣⊬

Spread Eagle ✔

Outwestgate, IP33 2DE
✪ 11-11 (midnight Fri & Sat); 12-11 Sun
☎ (01284) 754523
Greene King IPA; guest beers ⊞
Large split-level lounge diner just a short walk from the town centre with a separate public bar. Both rooms screen live sports on Sky TV. The food menu is supplemented by specials on chalkboards and monthly 'round the world' themed evenings. The building dates from 1833 and is adjacent to Stamford Bridge. It was reputedly the last local pub in WWI to be fined for allowing early drinking (after emergency licensing laws were introduced to protect munitions workers), when people were found 'skulking in the yard' early one morning. ❀◑⊟♿⊟P⊬

Charsfield

Three Horseshoes

The Street, IP13 7PY
✪ 11.30-2.30 (not Thu), 7-11; 12-3, 7-10.30 Sun
☎ (01473) 737330
Earl Soham Victoria; guest beers ⊞
Small two-bar pub set in a pretty village that will be forever linked with the fictional village of Akenfield. The bright and cheerful public bar with tiled floor and simple furnishings contrasts with the quieter lounge bar which is also used as a restaurant and has a piano. The food menu is traditional with specials listed on chalkboards. The landlord keeps regulars informed of forthcoming guest beers and events by e-mailing them an alemail'. ⩋☋❀◑⊟⊟♣P⊬

Combs Ford

Gladstone Arms

2 Combs Ford, IP14 2AP
✪ 11-3, 5-11 (11-11 on Fri & Sat); 12-4, 7-11 Sun
☎ (01449) 612339
Adnams Bitter, Broadside; guest beers ⊞
Adnams tied-house situated in a hamlet just 10 minutes' walk from Stowmarket. A large single bar area with tiles close to the open fire and servery and with carpeting elsewhere, provides separate areas for drinking, games and eating. A selection of good value, home-cooked food includes vegetarian options. No food on Sunday evenings. Monthly quiz nights. ⩋☋❀◑⊟♣P

Earl Soham

Victoria

The Street, IP13 7RL (on A1120)
✪ 12-3, 7-11
☎ (01728) 685758
Earl Soham Victoria, Albert, Sir Roger's Porter, seasonal beers ⊞
Abundant with old world charm, this traditional Victorian bar has bare floorboards, scrubbed tables and an open fire place. Home-made, good-value meals are served at lunchtimes and evenings, and the pub can be busy with diners at weekends. The locals are friendly and welcoming, and the rather laid-back landlord may offer golfing tips. The original Earl Soham Brewery (now derelict) was located behind the pub but today the beer is brewed just a short walk away. ⩋Q❀◑⩓♣P

Eastbridge

Eel's Foot

Leiston Road, IP16 4SN (close to entrance of Minsmere nature reserve)
✪ 12-3, 6-11; 11-midnight Sat; 12-10.30 Sun
☎ (01728) 830154 ⊕ theeelsfootinn.co.uk
Adnams Bitter, Explorer, Broadside, seasonal beers ⊞
A wonderfully cosy country pub which, despite its popularity with visitors to the area, manages to retain an air of intimacy. Excellent home-cooked, locally-sourced food is available every day. Local musicians often play on Thursday evening and a traditional folk night is hosted on the last Sunday of the month. There is a large garden and en-suite B&B accommodation is now available, with camping facilities nearby. The RSPB reserve at Minsmere is close by. ⩋Q☋❀⇌◑♿⩓♣P

Edwardstone

White Horse

Mill Green, CO10 5PX TL951426
✪ 12-11 Fri & Sat; 12-3 (Sat only), 5-11 winter; 12-3, 5-11 Sun

☎ (01787) 211211 🌐 edwardstonewhitehorse.co.uk
Adnams Bitter; Greene King IPA; guest beers ⊞
Well off the beaten track, this lovely rural free house is an ideal holiday base. Camping & Caravan Club approved, it also has two self-catering chalets. The owner has erected a windmill to supply power to the pub, chalets and a new green eco-brewery. Delicious home-made food uses locally sourced and seasonal organic ingredients when available. Regular beer festivals are popular locally and the pub has a late licence when trade demands. Award-winning ciders are stocked. ⌂Q❀⊨◐◑⊟▲♣●P⊓

Felixstowe (Walton)

Half Moon

303 Walton High Street, IP11 9QL
⏲ 12-2.30 (not Mon), 5-11; 12-11 Sat; 12-3, 7-10.30 Sun
☎ (01394) 216009 🌐 felixstowe-halfmoon.co.uk
Adnams Bitter, Broadside; guest beers ⊞
Traditional community pub that retains the feel of a bygone era, with fine ale, good company and a welcoming landlord. Quiz nights are hosted, darts is played and there is a selection of books for customers to read. The pub is also a meeting place for local groups of all kinds. Gaming machines and music do not feature here – the main entertainment is the banter in the bar between locals and landlord. Buses stop outside the door. ⌂Q❀⊟⊟♣P⁻

Flempton

Greyhound

The Green, IP28 6EL
⏲ 11.30-3, 5-midnight; 12-4, 7-midnight Sun
☎ (01284) 728400 🌐 thegreyhoundflempton.com
Greene King IPA; Woodforde's Wherry Best Bitter; guest beers ⊞
Traditional pub on an attractive green, neatly tucked away behind the church. This is a quiet village so most trade is local or passing, but folk nights and Morris dancing in the summer are popular. Pub games are played most nights. Close to local attractions at Lackford Lakes (RSPB) and West Stow Country Park with its replica Saxon village, the Greyhound is good for a post-visit pint.
⌂ᘛ❀⊨◐◑⊟▲⊟♣●P⁻

Framlingham

Station

Station Road, IP13 9EE (on B1116)
⏲ 12-3, 5-11
☎ (01728) 723455 🌐 thestationhotel.net
Earl Soham Gannett Mild, Victoria, Brandeston Gold; guest beers ⊞
Small but distinctive bar set in a former station buffet built in 1859 – sadly the branch line closed in 1963. Chalkboards offer simple but well-cooked food options and the pub can be very busy with diners during the evening. The interior is charming with wood panelling, bare floorboards, scrubbed tables and various candles, pots and jars. A small second snug leads to an enclosed patio area behind the building. All real beers are dispensed from a set of fine Edwardian German silver handpumps. Imported Veltins and Maisel's Weisse are regularly on draught. A beer festival is held on the last weekend in July. ⌂Q❀◐◑⊟P

Great Cornard

Five Bells

63 Bures Road, CO10 0HU
⏲ 11-midnight (1am Sat); 11-11.30 Sun
☎ (01787) 379016 🌐 5bells.co.uk
Greene King XX Mild, IPA, Old Speckled Hen, Abbot ⊞
Friendly community ale house situated near the Great Cornard church (home of the five bells) on the main Sudbury to Bures road. The pub fields several teams playing traditional games plus some rarer ones including petanque and uckers. Live music usually plays on a Friday. The pub is Cask Marque accredited. ⌂Qᘛ❀⊟♿⊟♣P⁻

Great Wratting

Red Lion

School Road, CB9 7HA (on B1061 2 miles N of Haverhill)
⏲ 11-2.30, 5-11; 11-1am Fri & Sat; 12-3, 7-10.30 Sun
☎ (01440) 783237
Adnams Bitter, Broadside, seasonal beers; guest beers ⊞
Good beer, food and conversation are the mainstays of this traditional village local. Ideal for families in the summer months, it has a huge back garden with plenty to keep children occupied. Take a look at the amazing collection of copper and brass while sampling the Adnams beers or perhaps an occasional guest. Good food is served in the bar and restaurant. Look out for the whale's jawbone that you pass through as you enter the front door. ⌂❀◐◑P

Hawkedon

Queen's Head

Rede Road, IP29 4NN
⏲ 5-11; 12-11 Sat; 12-10.30 Sun
☎ (01284) 789218
Adnams Bitter; Greene King IPA; guest beers ⊞
With up to six cask ales and a strong community spirit, it is no wonder this was West Suffolk CAMRA Pub of the Year in 2007. The July beer festival is not to be missed, along with other entertainment including live music, sporting events and theatre suppers. For summer there is a huge back garden and in winter the enormous fire in the bar is hard to resist. The food, served at weekends only, is imaginative and very good.
⌂Q❀◐◑▲♣●P⁻

Henley

Cross Keys

Main Road, IP6 0QP
⏲ 11-11 (midnight Thu-Sat); 12-10.30 Sun
☎ (01449) 760229 🌐 henleycrosskeys.co.uk
Adnams Bitter; Woodforde's Wherry Best Bitter; ⊞ **guest beers** ⊞/⊡
You can be sure of a warm welcome from the landlord at this friendly pub set in tranquil

countryside. Up to six cask ales are stocked, many served on gravity, and two beer festivals are hosted a year. Good food is available until 9pm every day including a popular three-course roast lunch on Sunday. Entertainment includes live music, quizzes and karaoke. P

Hoxne

Swan

Low Street, IP21 5AS
12-3, 6-11; 12-10.30 Sun
(01379) 668275 hoxneswan.co.uk
Adnams Bitter, Broadside; Woodforde's Wherry Best Bitter; guest beers [H]
Built for the Bishop of Norwich in about 1480 and used as a brothel for many years afterwards, today the fine timber framed, Grade II building offers a wealth of character in a mix of public rooms including a splendid bar with large carved beams and impressive fireplace. Fresh, seasonal home-cooked food prepared with local produce includes various game dishes. Outside there is a large garden beside the river and ample car parking. An annual beer festival is held in early June (check website for details) with music from local groups. P

Ipswich

Dales

Dales Road, IP1 4JY
11-2.30, 4.30 (6 Sat)-11; 12-2.30, 7-11 Sun
(01473) 250024 thedalespub.com
Adnams Bitter; Greene King IPA; guest beers [H]
Modern and popular two roomed estate pub serving three constantly changing guest ales – Black Sheep Best Bitter and Woodforde's Admirals Reserve often feature. Food ranges from traditional roasts, curries and omelettes to rolls and baguettes. Outside is a comfortable garden and patio areas where barbecues are hosted in summer.
Q P

Dove Street Inn

St Helens Street, IP4 2LA
12-10.45
(01473) 211270 dovestreetinn.co.uk
Adnams Broadside; Crouch Vale Brewers Gold; Fuller's London Pride; Mighty Oak Oscar Wilde Mild; Woodforde's Wherry Best Bitter; [H] **guest beers** [H]/[G]
Grade II-listed, timber framed building full of character and charm. A huge range of up to 20 beers and four ciders is available alongside quality home-made food, bar treats and snacks. Three highly popular beer festivals are held annually, each with around 66 different beers. East Anglian CAMRA Pub of Year 2006/07, and a former runner up in CAMRA's national competition. Children and dogs are welcome.

Fat Cat

288 Spring Road, IP4 5NL
12-11 (midnight Fri); 11-midnight Sat
(01473) 726524 fatcatipswich.co.uk
Crouch Vale Brewers Gold; Fuller's London Pride; [G] **Woodforde's Wherry Best Bitter;** [H] **guest beers** [G]
With no music and no games machines, this pub is always a joy to visit. Scattered around the walls are original enamel signs, posters and other interesting artefacts. Ales are dispensed from the tap room situated behind the bar. Always very popular, in the summertime you can relax in the garden or on the patio. Plates are provided for takeaway meals (but not Friday or Saturday evening). Children under 16 and dogs are not permitted.
Q (Derby Rd) (2, 75)

Greyhound

9 Henley Road, IP1 3SE
11-2.30, 5-11; 11-11 Fri & Sat; 12-10.30 Sun
(01473) 252862 thindog.co.uk
Adnams Bitter, Explorer, Broadside, seasonal beers; guest beers [H]
Welcoming traditional pub, close to the town centre and popular with workers at lunchtime and a wide clientele of all ages in the evening. It has a small and cosy public bar at the front and a larger drinking and dining area to the rear. Fresh home-made food from a blackboard menu is served daily. A regular entry in the Guide, do not miss this pub if you are visiting the town. Q P

Lord Nelson

81 Fore Street, IP4 1JZ
11-2.30, 6-11 (12.30am Fri & Sat); 11-11.30 Sun
(01473) 254072 ipswichlordnelson.com
Adnams Bitter, Explorer, Broadside, seasonal beers [G]
Located in the town's historic dock area, this nautically-themed pub is steeped in history. Dating back to the 17th century, it has a half-timbered frontage and dormer windows. An unusual gravity dispense system is used incorporating a row of old wooden casks to good effect and also guaranteeing temperature-controlled real ales. Families are welcome. No food is served on Monday or Sunday evening. P

Mannings

8 Cornhill, IP4 1DD (next to town hall)
11-11; 12-5 Sun
(01473) 254170
Adnams Bitter, Broadside; Fuller's London Pride; Woodforde's Wherry Best Bitter [H]
A gem of a pub —an oasis of calm in the town centre, especially on Friday and Saturday nights. Outdoor tables and chairs in the summer provide the ideal place to sit and watch the world go by. There is also a small enclosed patio and garden at the back.

Woolpack

1 Tuddenham Road, IP4 2SH
11.30-5, 7-midnight; 11.30-1am Fri & Sat; 12-10.30 Sun
(01473) 253059
Adnams Bitter, Broadside; Black Sheep Best Bitter; Caledonian Deuchars IPA; Young's Bitter; guest beers [H]
Close to Christchurch Park (with a museum in the famous Tudor mansion), this pub is just a short walk from the town centre. An attractive

village-style local, it retains three bars including a tiny snug, public bar and separate lounge with an inviting fire in the winter months. To the front of the building an ever-popular paved garden area has benches and umbrellas. The extensive menu of home-cooked food is served daily (except Sun eve), with fish and seafood dishes the specialities. ⌂Q❀◑⊟⊠P⁴–

Ixworth

Greyhound

High Street, IP31 2HJ

❂ 11-3, 6-11; 12-3, 7-11 Sun

☎ (01359) 230887

Greene King XX Mild, IPA, Abbot; guest beers Ⓗ

Situated on the town's pretty High Street, this traditional inn has three bars including a lovely central snug. The heart of the building dates back to Tudor times. The pub is a rare outlet for XX Mild. Good value lunches and early evening meals are served in the restaurant. Dominoes, crib, darts and pool are played in leagues and for charities. ◑⊟⊠♣P⁴–

Kettleburgh

Chequers

The Street, IP13 7JT

❂ 12-2.30, 6-11; 12-3, 7-11

☎ (01728) 723760 ⊕ thechequers.net

Elgood's Black Dog Mild; Greene King IPA; guest beers Ⓗ

Splendid single room pub with an entertaining landlord, built in 1913 to replace an earlier building destroyed by fire. An unusual arrangement of branches and lights adorns the ceiling and gives the bar a distinctive character. A large garden leads down to the River Deben, providing an excellent location to while away some time on sunny days. Accommodation is available in rooms at the bottom of the garden.
⌂♉❀◑♿⊠(118)♣P⁴–

Lakenheath

Brewer's Tap

54 High Street, IP27 0AU

❂ 12-midnight; 12-4.30, 7-12 Sun

☎ (01842) 862328

Beer range varies Ⓗ

A true free house, this village pub is full of character. Bigger than it looks from the outside, there is a patio area at the back. Three or four handpumps offer local and national beers and traditional Sunday lunches are popular. Crib, darts and poker are played. A public car park is nearby. Q❀◐⊠♣⁴–

Lavenham

Angel Hotel

Market Place, CO10 9QZ

❂ 11-11; 12-10.30 Sun

☎ (01787) 247388 ⊕ maypolehotels.com/angelhotel/index.html

Adnams Bitter, Broadside; Greene King IPA; Nethergate Suffolk County Ⓗ

The Angel was first licensed in 1420 and stands in the centre of this historic village. It is popular with both locals and visitors, however the bar area can be overtaken by diners at busy times. Seating outside overlooking the famous marketplace provides a good spot for people watching all year round. The enclosed garden to the rear is also popular in summer. Eight well-equipped en-suite bedrooms and a stunning residents' sitting room make this a comfortable place to stay. ⌂Q❀⇌◑

Laxfield

King's Head (Low House) ★

Gorams Mill Lane, IP13 8DW

❂ 12-4, 7-midnight; 12-3, 7-11 winter; 12-4, 7-11 Sun

☎ (01986) 798395 ⊕ laxfield-kingshead.co.uk

Adnams Bitter, Broadside, seasonal beer; guest beer Ⓖ

Retaining all the traditions of the beer house, this multi-roomed, thatched pub with listed high-back settles, quarry tiled floors and low ceilings dispenses its ales by gravity from the tap room. An interesting menu sourced from local ingredients is on offer in the dining room (booking essential for Sunday evening). Set in a village in the heart of the countryside, Morris dancers, plays and live music in the garden add to the magic of this hidden gem. Two en-suite rooms and a self-contained flatlet are available to let. ⌂Q♉❀⇌◑⊠♣P

Little Glemham

Lion Inn ✔

Main Road, IP13 0BA

❂ 12-2.30, 6-11; closed Mon; 12-3, 7-10.30 Sun

☎ (01728) 746505

Adnams Bitter, Broadside; guest beer Ⓗ

Recently refurbished, this popular, family-oriented pub is on the Main Road —an ideal stopping point for both locals and travellers making their way to the Suffolk heritage coast. Food is traditional, home cooked and invariably locally sourced, with vegetarian options and a special menu available for children. Themed food evenings and quiz sessions are hosted. ⌂❀◑⊠P

Long Melford

Crown

CO10 1JL

❂ 11.30-11; 12-10.30 Sun

☎ (01787) 377666 ⊕ thecrownhotelmelford.co.uk

Adnams Bitter; Nethergate seasonal beers; Taylor Landlord Ⓗ

Family run, historic inn built in 1610 retaining many interesting features including its Tudor cellars and exposed beams. In 1885 the hotel earned its place in history as the last place that the Riot Act was read in West Suffolk. The bar is arranged around a central serving area, with a variety of comfortable seating. Long Melford's high street is reputedly the longest village street in England, with a fine parish church and two impressive Tudor mansions plus a variety of antique shops. ⌂❀⇌◑

Lowestoft

Norman Warrior

Fir Lane, NR32 2RB

10.30-midnight (12.30am Fri & Sat); 12-11.30 Sun
(01502) 561982
Woodforde's Wherry Best Bitter; guest beers
Large estate pub on the north side of town with ample parking and a garden where an annual beer festival is held in August. The comfortable lounge area leads through to a spacious restaurant serving food all day at weekends (booking advisable). The public bar has Sky TV for sporting occasions. The beer range has increased and the bar now houses five handpumps serving local beers plus other guest ales. Weston's cider is available occasionally.
(Oulton Broad North) P

Oak Tavern

Crown Street West, NR32 1SQ
10.30-11; 12-10.30 Sun
(01502) 537246
Adnams Bitter; Greene King Abbot; guest beers
Lively drinkers' back street local with an open plan interior. The walls are adorned with Belgian brewery memorabilia, with four real ales always on handpump, usually including a dark beer during the winter months. An extensive range of Belgian bottled beers is served in appropriate glasses. Popular with sports fans, the pub has a large-screen TV for sporting events and fields football, pool and darts teams. P

Plough & Sail

212 London Road South, NR33 0BB
11-midnight (1am Fri & Sat); 12-11 Sun
(01502) 566695
Adnams Bitter; guest beers
Set back from the road with a small frontage, this pub is close to the beach. Inside, the long bar has wooden flooring and wood panelling throughout. A secluded courtyard with a canvas-covered smoking area leads to a private function room. Live music and quiz evenings are regular attractions. One Greene King beer is always available, alongside guests from micro-brewers. P

Triangle Tavern

29 St Peters Street, NR32 1QA
11-11 (midnight Thu; 1am Fri & Sat); 12-10.30 Sun
(01502) 582711 thetriangletavern.co.uk
Green Jack Canary, Orange Wheat, Grasshopper, Mahseer IPA, seasonal beers; guest beers
Popular town centre venue with two contrasting bars situated on the Triangle market place. The flagship inn for the attached Green Jack Brewery, the cosy front bar is adorned with many awards for its fine ales, including Ripper which was Champion Winter Beer in 2007. A corridor decorated with brewery memorabilia leads to the back bar housing a pool table, where the younger generation congregate. Customers are welcome to bring in food from nearby takeaways. Draught and bottled Belgian beers are also available together with real cider from Weston's and Banham.

Market Weston

Mill Inn

Bury Road, IP22 2PD (on B1111)
12-3 (not Mon), 5-11; 12-3, 7-11 Sun
(01359) 221018
Adnams Bitter; Greene King IPA; Old Chimneys Military Mild, Great Raft; guest beer
This striking white brick and flint faced inn stands at a crossroads and is the closest outlet to the Old Chimneys Brewery, located on the other side of the village. It has been run by same landlady for more than 12 years. An excellent choice of beers is complemented by a good menu of home-cooked meals (no food Mon eve). QP

Mildenhall

Queens Arms

42 Queensway, IP28 7JY
12-2.30, 5-11.30; 12-11.30 Fri-Sun
(01638) 713657
Woodforde's Wherry Best Bitter; guest beers
Comfortable and homely pub, used as a community centre by locals. Extremely popular with real ale drinkers since being taken over by Admiral Taverns, four handpumps are in constant use. The landlord is very keen on real ale and holds an annual beer festival on the August bank holiday to coincide with a cycle rally in the town. A range of alternating Belgian beers is stocked and real cider is occasionally available. QP

Naughton

Wheelhouse

Whatfield Road, IP7 7BS (450m off B1078 close to airbase)
5-10.30 (8 Tue; 11 Wed & Thu); 4-11 Fri; 6-11 Sat; 12-10.30 Sun
(01449) 740496
Beer range varies
Splendid, two bar rural pub, full of character and well worth seeking out. Set in an old thatched, timber-framed building, the low ceiling in the main bar remains a hazard, despite the tiled floor now being lower than it used to be. The more spacious public bar is much brighter and leads to a games room with pool table and darts. Outside there is a pleasant garden. An interesting selection of beers is always available. Opening times vary to suit local demand (check before visiting). QP

Newmarket

Five Bells

15 St Mary's Square, CB8 0HZ (behind Rookery shopping centre)
11-midnight (2am Sat); 12-midnight Sun
(01638) 602868
Courage Directors; Woodforde's Wherry Best Bitter; guest beers
Popular town local with a much improved beer range since becoming 'ex-Greene King'. Situated away from the busy high street, it has a lively atmosphere, especially when darts and petanque teams are visiting. The large garden houses the petanque terrain and holds regular barbecues in summer. Parking in front of pub is limited but there is a public car park 300 metres away.

Ramsholt

Ramsholt Arms

Dock Road, IP12 3AB (signed off B1083)
🕔 11.30-11
☎ (01394) 411229
Adnams Bitter, Broadside; guest beers 🄷
Isolated Victorian pub in a wonderful scenic location on the north bank of the River Deben. Popular with walkers, sailors and bird watchers, it can be very busy during the summer months. Food is mostly locally sourced and features fish and vegetarian options. Local photographs commemorate the crew of an aeroplane that crashed in the river while making a flight from a nearby WWII airfield. The pub is both child and dog friendly. ♨Q♿❀⇌◐P

Rattlesden

Five Bells

High Street, IP30 0RA
🕔 12-12.30am (11.30 Sun)
☎ (01449) 737373
Beer range varies 🄷
Set beside the church on the high road through the village, this is a good old Suffolk drinking house – few of its kind still survive. Three well chosen ales on the bar are usually sourced direct from the breweries. The cosy single room has a games room on a lower level. ♨Q❀●

Rendham

White Horse

Bruisyard Road, IP17 2AF
🕔 12-2.30, 6-11; 12-3, 7-10.30 Sun
☎ (01728) 663497
Earl Soham Victoria; Mauldons Suffolk Pride; Taylor Landlord; guest beers 🄷
Cosy, traditional, single bar pub with two comfortable seating areas warmed by a real fire. A regular quiz night features on the first Monday of the month and various themed evenings are hosted. A varied menu changes every five or six weeks, offering a selection of locally-sourced produce including a fish and chip takeaway on Friday evening. Live music plays occasionally. An annual beer festival is on the August bank holiday. ♨♿❀◐◑⊟♣P

Rumburgh

Buck

Mill Road, IP19 0NS
🕔 11.45-3, 6.30-11; 12-3, 7-10.30 Sun
☎ (01986) 785257
Adnams Bitter, seasonal beers; guest beers 🄷
Full of character, this pub was Suffolk CAMRA Pub of the Year in 2007. Formerly a guest house for a nearby medieval priory, refurbishments and extensions have added two dining areas, a public bar and games room around the historic original building. Booking is recommended for diners. A popular local at heart of village life, folk music evenings, quiz nights and darts matches are hosted. Guest beers are mainly local. ❀◐◑⊟▲⊟♣P

Somerleyton

Duke's Head

Slugs Lane, NR32 5QX
🕔 11-11; 11-3, 6-11 winter; 11-11 Sat; 12-10.30 Sun
☎ (01502) 730281 🌐 somerleyton.co.uk
Adnams Bitter; Greene King IPA; guest beers 🄷
Situated in a picturesque village, the Duke's Head overlooks marshes near to the River Waveney. This atmospheric pub has a public bar separated from the lounge by an open fireplace alongside a garden room restaurant. Guest beers are sourced from local micro-brewers. The large garden and play area are popular with families and the pub opens all day in summer. Somerleyton Hall with its famous maze is nearby. ♨❀◐◑⊟▲⇌⊟P

Southwold

Lord Nelson

42 East Street, IP18 6EJ
🕔 10.30-11; 12-10.30 Sun
☎ (01502) 722079
Adnams Bitter, Explorer, Broadside, seasonal beers 🄷
Situated next to the Sailor's Reading Room Museum, just a stone's throw from the sea, this pub is popular with locals and holidaymakers. It offers three drinking areas, with children welcome in the side room and partly covered patio. The main bar is flagstoned and has an open fire. Not surprisingly, there is much Nelson memorabilia. The pub is well known locally for its reasonably priced food. Dogs are welcome. ♨♿❀◐▲⊟

Sole Bay

7 East Green, IP18 6JN
🕔 11-11; 12-10.30 Sun
☎ (01502) 723736
Adnams Bitter, Explorer, Broadside, seasonal beers 🄷
Single bar pub situated in the shadow of the lighthouse and adjacent to Adnams' brewery. The full range of Adnams' beers is dispensed in fine form from a bank of handpumps. The interior retains the original wooden flooring but has been modernised into a bistro-style bar with disabled access and baby changing facilities. Meals are served at lunchtime and Thursday to Saturday evenings. ◐♿▲⊟

Stanningfield

Red House

Bury Road, IP29 4RR
🕔 12 (5 Wed)-11.30
☎ (01284) 828330 🌐 theredhouse.zoomshare.com
Greene King IPA; Woodfordes range; guest beers 🄷
Built in 1866 in Victorian red brick, the building was originally a cobbler's workshop, but licensed by 1900 and now free of tie. It was named after the red tunics of the Suffolk regiment. Neat and clean inside and out, this single-bar local has a relaxed and comfortable atmosphere. Live music features monthly and pub games and sports are well supported. No food is served on Saturday or Sunday evenings. Recently voted local CAMRA Pub of the Month. ❀◐♣P⊢

Stowmarket

Royal William

53 Union Street, IP14 1HP

11 (12 Sun)-11

☎ (01449) 674553

aledonian Deuchars IPA; Greene King IPA; guest eers [G]

riendly and lively back-street pub, efurbished throughout in 2007, just a short walk from the railway station. During the week it is popular with local darts and crib eams. At the weekend the landlord offers various special meal options. During the ummer months a second, outside bar opens n an outbuilding within the enclosed garden, with up to eight beers on gravity available on hursday and Friday evenings. Sky Sports is creened on occasion.

Stradbroke

Queens Head

Queens Street, IP21 5HG

12-midnight (1am Fri & Sat)

☎ (01379) 384384

Adnams Bitter; Greene King IPA; Woodforde's Wherry Best Bitter; guest beer [H]

Large, timber framed, community pub situated close to the centre of the village. Good food is available throughout the day, making this a favourite venue for local people and walkers. A large jazz festival (see website: festival.stradbroke.org.uk) is held in conjunction with the pub's annual beer festival on the second weekend in May with around 30 beers on offer. Sadly the annual navy day' celebrations are no longer held but maritime artefacts adorn the public bar walls.

Stutton

Gardeners Arms

Manningtree Road, IP9 2TG

12-3, 6-11 (closed Mon eve); 12-3, 6-10 Sun

☎ (01473) 328868

Adnams Bitter; guest beers [H]

This cosy two bar pub is set on the edge of a small village and very close to the River Stour, just four miles from the historic Flatford Mill. An eclectic selection of artefacts on display includes many musical instruments, framed posters, old sports equipment plus huge bellows and a crossbow. A large patio and garden feature a raised ornamental fish pond. An interesting menu is available with specials on chalkboards. Jazz plays twice a month plus occasional folk/shanty singing. Children and dogs are welcome.

Sudbury

Waggon & Horses

Church Walk, Acton Square, CO10 1HJ

11-3, 7 (5 Wed-Fri)-11

☎ (01787) 312147

Greene King IPA; guest beers [H]

Back street local behind Market Hill with several drinking areas, a games area with pool and darts, and a small dining area. Guest beers are from the Greene King list. Food is home cooked with frequent special menus (booking is advisable). The Phoenix Court flats nearby are built on the site of the defunct Phoenix Brewery, so named because the building arose from the ashes of a fire in 1890.

Swilland

Moon & Mushroom

High Road, IP6 9LR

11-2.30 (not Mon), 6-11; 12-3, 7-10.30 Sun

☎ (01473) 785320

Buffy's Norwich Terrier, Hopleaf; Crouch Vale Brewers Gold; Nethergate Suffolk County; Wolf Bitter, [G] **Golden Jackal;** [H] **Woodforde's Wherry Best Bitter, Nelson's Revenge** [G]

Comfortable and cosy single bar, attractively decorated throughout with local pictures, tiled floors and scrubbed tables. A wide range of beers on gravity from independent brewers is served from the tap room. Home-cooked food, usually including game dishes, is served in the bar and adjoining dining room (not Mon). Occasional live music and themed nights are hosted.

Tattingstone

White Horse

White Horse Hill, IP9 2NU

12-3, 6-11; 12-11 Fri & Sat; 2-10.30 Sun

☎ (01473) 328060 whitehorsetattingstone.co.uk

Adnams Bitter; Crouch Vale Brewers Gold; Woodforde's Wherry Best Bitter; guest beers [H]

Seventeenth century Grade II listed inn just north of Alton Water Reservoir. The interior includes a lounge/snug where local folk singers perform, main bar with large black beams, tiled floor and inglenook fireplace, and a small restaurant area with bare floorboards. Food is always available (booking recommended for Sun evening). Wonderfully preserved outside toilets have under-floor heating in the Ladies.

Theberton

Lion

Main Road, IP16 4RU

12-3, 6-11 (midnight Fri & Sat); 12-3, 7-10.30 Sun

☎ (01728) 830185

Adnams Bitter; Woodforde's Wherry Best Bitter; guest beers [H]

Comfortable, large single bar with an interesting collection of local photographs. An eclectic range of live music plays once a month on Sunday. Locally-sourced freshly-prepared food includes popular Sunday lunches and fresh fish on Friday, with meal deals from Monday to Thursday. The pub is served by the local Coastlink taxi/bus service.

Thurston

Fox & Hounds

Barton Road, IP31 3QT

12-2.30, 5-11; 12-midnight Fri & Sat; 12-10.30 Sun

☎ (01359) 232228 foxandhoundsthurston.co.uk

Adnams Bitter; Greene King IPA; guest beers [H]

Dating from 1800, this listed building is now a regular entry in the Guide. A busy village local, it offers a good selection of ever-changing real ales on handpump, served by the ever-cheerful landlord and staff. Good home-cooked food is available. The public bar has a pool table, darts and Sky TV while the lounge is quieter and more comfortable. West Suffolk CAMRA Pub of Year 2007 and 2008.

Walberswick

Anchor

Main Street, IP18 6AU
11-4, 6-11; 11-11 Sat; 12-11 Sun
(01502) 722112 anchoratwalberswick.com
Adnams Bitter, Broadside, seasonal beers
Situated in an idyllic coastal village, the pub caters for holidaymakers and locals alike. The interior comprises three cosy, wood-panelled rooms, with a real fire in winter and a spacious restaurant committed to serving seasonal, local produce. Every dish on the menu has a recommended real ale to accompany it. The pub is family, walker and dog friendly. Summer and winter beer festivals are held in the adjacent barn.

Walsham-le-Willows

Blue Boar

The Street, IP31 3AA
12-2.30, 5-midnight; 12-1am Fri & Sat; 12-11.30 Sun
(01359) 258533
Adnams Bitter; guest beers
An ale house most of time since 1420, this true free house offers a fine selection of beers on handpump and gravity and is a supporter of local breweries. Regular themed food nights and live music evenings are hosted. A May bank holiday beer festival is held in a marquee in the garden.

Wissett

Plough

The Street, IP19 0JE
10.30-12.30am; 11.30-11.30 Sun
(01986) 872201
Adnams Bitter; guest beers
Seventeenth century inn with a large garden where visitors can pitch their tents. Inside, there is a central bar area, wood flooring and original wood beams. To one side is a themed area called the potting shed' with garden and agricultural artefacts adorning the walls and a real fire in winter. At the centre of village life, the pub holds quiz nights, charity events and an annual beer festival in July. The house beer is brewed by Grain Brewery.

Woodbridge

Cherry Tree Inn

73 Cumberland Street, IP12 4AG
7.30am-11; 9am-11 Sat & Sun
(01394) 384627 thecherrytreepub.co.uk
Adnams Bitter, Explorer, Broadside, seasonal beers; guest beers
Although the tree no longer remains, it can still be seen in a picture on display in the inn by the famous Suffolk painter Thomas Churchyard. Child, wheelchair and dog friendly, the pub offers traditional food served all day from breakfast onwards. Informal card games and quiz nights are popular, with family games available to play. A mild is always among the eight beers on offer and a beer festival is held twice a year. Accommodation is provided in a converted barn, set back from the pub beside the pretty garden.

Old Mariner

26 New Street, IP12 1DX
11-3, 5 (6 Sat)-11; 12-10.30 Sun
(01394) 382679
Adnams Bitter; Black Sheep Best Bitter; Fuller's London Pride; Shepherd Neame Spitfire; Young's Bitter
Cosy, traditional bar offering a welcome refuge from the modern world. The front bar has a low ceiling and scrubbed tables – the only obvious link to the 21st century is a large TV used only when international rugby is broadcast, as the landlord and locals are passionate followers. Meals are served in the rear bar. Food is freshly prepared and the menu based around casserole dishes, stews and roasts.

Sekforde Tap

76 Seckford Street, IP12 4LZ
12-2.30, 6-11.30 (midnight Fri & Sat); 12-2.30, 7-10.30 Sun
(01394) 384446 thesekfordetap.com
Earl Soham Victoria; guest beers
Comfortable and well furnished multi-roomedpub where popular meal-themed evenings are hosted as well as quiz nights and occasional acoustic music sessions. The food menu changes regularly and features a range of tapas (no food Sun or Mon eve). At least eight different ales are stocked, always including something local.

Woolpit

Bull

The Street, IP30 9SA
11-3, 6-11 (midnight Fri); 12-4, 6-midnight Sat; 12-4, 7-10.30 Sun
(01359) 240393 bullinnwoolpit.co.uk
Adnams Bitter; guest beers
Large roadside inn with a traditional bar and lounge, separate pool room, comfortable restaurant and conservatory. Wholesome, home-cooked food is served (not Sun eve) and three guest beers are always stocked. A garden with a children's play area leads off the car park. One letting room is available with disabled access.

Bread is the staff of life, but beer is life itself.
Traditional

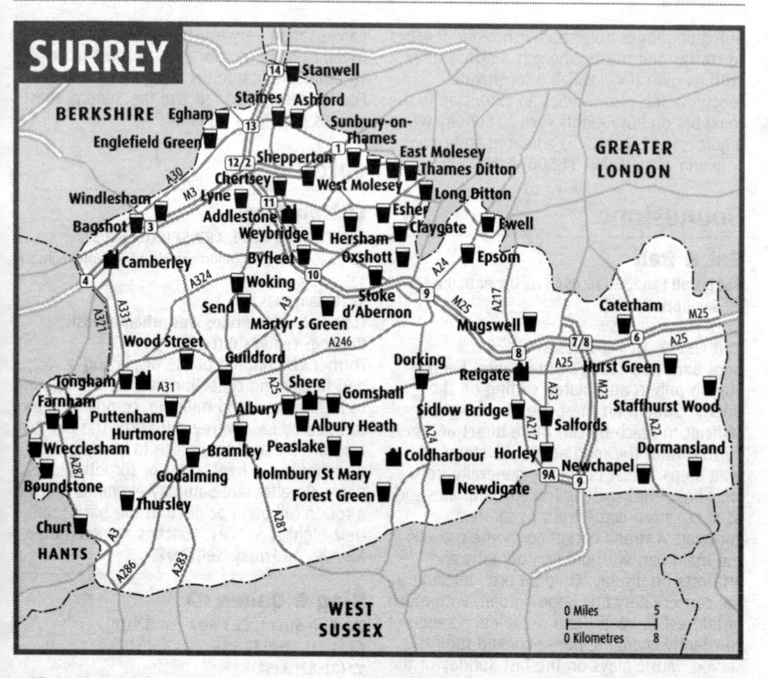

Albury

Drummond Arms

The Street, GU5 9AG (on A248)

11-11; 12-10.30 Sun

☎ (01483) 202039 thedrummondarms.co.uk

Courage Best Bitter; Surrey Hills Shere Drop; guest beers H

Small family-run 19th century hotel featuring a lovely garden in an attractive location by the banks of the Tillingbourne. The single wood-panelled bar leads to a dining conservatory and there is a function room used as a restaurant on Sunday (no food Sun eve). The guest beer changes monthly. Smokers gather outside under a heated canopy. Accommodation comprises 10 en-suite rooms.

Albury Heath

William IV

Little London, GU5 9DG TQ066467

11-3, 5.30-11; 12-3, 7-11 Sun

☎ (01483) 202685 williamivalbury.com

Flowers IPA; Hogs Back TEA; Surrey Hills Ranmore Ale, Shere Drop H

Dating from the 16th century, this secluded and unspoilt country pub offers beers from local micro-breweries. The cosy main bar has a flagstone floor and wood beams, with a magnificent wood-burning fire. Tables in the front garden are well used in summer. The restaurant has been recently extended and sells Gloucestershire Old Spot pork from the pigs kept in the field behind the pub (no food Sun eve). Real cider is sold in winter, usually replaced with another local beer in summer.

Q P

Ashford

Kings Fairway ✔

91 Fordbridge Road, TW15 2SS (on B377)

12-11 (midnight Fri & Sat)

☎ (01784) 424801

Fuller's London Pride; Young's Bitter; guest beers H

Comfortable Ember Inns establishment with attentive staff and a real ale-friendly management team. Six handpumps dispense the regular beers and four ever-changing guests and real ale, world lager and wine festivals feature through the year. Food is served daily until 9pm. Quiz nights are Wednesday and Sunday. There is patio seating outside in warmer weather.

(290)P

Bagshot

Foresters Arms

173 London Road, GU19 5DH (on A30)

12-2.30, 5-11; 12-3, 7-11 Sun

☎ (01276) 472038

Courage Best Bitter; Fuller's London Pride; Hogs Back TEA; Taylor Dark Mild; guest beers H

Cosy, traditional pub with a growing reputation locally for its cask ales since the arrival of the present landlords 11 years ago and a regular Guide entry. Good home-made

INDEPENDENT BREWERIES

Ascot Camberley (NEW)
Farnham Farnham
Hogs Back Tongham
Leith Hill Coldharbour
Pilgrim Reigate
Surrey Hills Shere
Wayland's Addlestone

pub grub ranges from sandwiches and toasties to curries and roasts. There is a skittle alley with its own bar, available for private functions. It is also used as an extension to the main bar on busy nights such as Sunday when a quiz is held. Outside is a heated and covered smoking area. ❀◐▤(34,500)♣P⁻

Boundstone

Bat & Ball

Bat & Ball Lane, GU10 4SA (via Upper Bourne Lane off Sandrock Hill Rd)

11-11; 12-10.30 Sun

☎ (01252) 792108 ⊕ thebatandball.co.uk

Hogs Back TEA; Young's Bitter; guest beers ⊞

Superb pub in an isolated setting on the Bourne Stream on the edge of suburbia. Difficult to reach by car, more direct access is by foot from the road above via steep and unlit steps. Guest beers are generally from local breweries such as Triple fff, but ales such as Sharp's can come from as far away as Cornwall. A strong cricketing theme prevails in the main bar, with old photographs and artefacts on display. Children are welcome in the conservatory and large garden, with much of interest to keep them occupied. A range of constantly changing home-cooked food is served. Music plays on the last Sunday of the month and Tuesday is quiz night.

ⴰQ❀◐♿▤(16)P

Bramley

Jolly Farmer

High Street, GU5 0HB (on A281)

11 (12 Sun)-11

☎ (01483) 893355 ⊕ jollyfarmer.co.uk

Beer range varies ⊞

An exceptional free house with eight handpumps dispensing a diverse, constantly-changing range of guest beers from all over the country. The atmospheric interior features low beams, solid furniture and a veritable cornucopia of artefacts ranging from stuffed animals, cigarette cards, plates and paintings on the walls to the ceilings with agricultural implements, bank notes and beer mats from a previous era. Excellent quality food is served in the bar and restaurant.

ⴰQ❀◐▤(53, 63)P

Byfleet

Plough ✔

104 High Road, KT14 7QT (off A245)

11-3, 5-11; 12-5, 7-10.30 Sun

☎ (01932) 353257

Courage Best Bitter; Fuller's London Pride; guest beers ⊞

Fascinating pub with bags of atmosphere. The interior features two roaring fires, solid furniture, an old cash till, exposed brickwork and a variety of adornments including plates and old agricultural equipment. Dominated by an L shaped bar with a suspended pub sign, three drinking areas include a conservatory where children are allowed. Ten handpumps dispense both local beers and imaginative choices from considerably further afield. Traditional values survive, with the art of conversation very much alive —you use a mobile phone at your peril. A must in good weather, the garden is easily overlooked. Food is recommended and the Sunday roasts always popular. ⴰQ❀◐▤P

Caterham

Clifton Arms

110 Chaldon Road, CR3 5PH (on B2031)

11.30-2.30, 4-11 (midnight Fri); 12-3, 5-midnight Sat; 12-11 Sun

☎ (01883) 343525

Fuller's London Pride; Westerham British Bulldog; Young's Bitter ⊞

Former Charrington house displaying a vast and fascinating collection of artefacts relating to local history and militaria, complementing the nearby East Surrey museum. The bar is a comfortable and cosy place to enjoy a drink, whether it is a beer, cider or sometimes a perry. On alternate Saturday evenings there is a rock'n'roll band or disco in the back room. Quiz night is Sunday. Lunches are served Monday to Friday. ❀◐▤●P

King & Queen ✔

34 High Street, CR3 5UA (on B2030)

11-11; 12-10.30 Sun

☎ (01883) 345438

Fuller's Chiswick, London Pride, ESB, seasonal beers; guest beers ⊞

A drinkers' pub, this welcoming 400-year-old red brick and flint inn has evolved since the 1840s from three former cottages. It retains three distinct areas —a front bar facing the high street, a high-ceilinged wood-beamed middle room with inglenook, and a small lower-level rear area leading to a patio garden. A side room has a dartboard. One of Caterham's early ale houses, its name refers to Britain's only joint monarchy, William and Mary. No meals are served on Sun.

ⴰ❀◐▤♣⁻

Chertsey

Coach & Horses ✔

14 St Ann's Road, KT16 9DG (on B375)

12-11; 12-3, 7-10.30 Sun

☎ (01932) 563085 ⊕ coachandhorseschertsey.co.uk

Fuller's Chiswick, London Pride, ESB ⊞

Long-standing Guide entry, near to the historic Abbey site and dedicated to Fuller's traditional cask ales. It is handy for the town's football and cricket clubs —the third stump is reputed to have been introduced at Chertsey —and also the museum. Good value English food is available during the week only. Quiz night is the first Thursday of the month. A seating area at the front has a large awning for smokers. Frequent daytime buses to Staines and Addlestone stop nearby. ⴰ❀⇔◐▤♣P⁻

Churt

Crossways

Churt Road, GU10 2JE (on A287)

11-3.30, 5-11; 11-11 Fri & Sat; 12-4, 7-10.30 Sun

☎ (01428) 714323

Courage Best Bitter; Hop Back Crop Circle; Ringwood Fortyniner; ⊞ **guest beers** ⊞/Ⓖ

This enduringly popular rural free house is a regular winner of local CAMRA Pub of the Year awards. Two main drinking areas cater for a happy mix of customers including friendly locals, passers by, ramblers and diners enjoying the traditional home-cooked lunches served Monday to Saturday. Five guest beers are drawn from casks in the cellar and, incredibly for the area, four real ciders served on stillage behind the bar. The spacious garden is well used in summer, especially during the excellent and highly popular annual beer festival. Q❀◐⊟▲⊟(19)♣●P⁵–

Claygate

Foley Arms

106 Hare Lane, KT10 0LZ

11 (12 Sun)-midnight

☎ (01372) 462021

Wells Bombardier; Young's Bitter, Special, seasonal beers Ⓗ

Traditional two-bar Victorian pub named after local landowners, with a large garden featuring a children's play area. Home-cooked food and sandwiches are available at lunchtime and early evening (not Sun eve). A selection of board games includes draughts and backgammon, and darts is also played. The popular folk club meets on Friday, with occasional comedy nights on Saturday. ⅏Q❀◐⊟⇌⊟(K3)♣P⁵–

Dorking

Cricketers ✔

81 South Street, RH4 2JU (on A25 one-way system westbound)

11-11 (midnight Fri); 12-11 Sun

☎ (01306) 889938

Fuller's Chiswick, London Pride, ESB, seasonal beers; guest beers Ⓗ

The walls of this compact one bar pub are covered with framed cricket shirts and a variety of photographs, both cricket-themed and of the local area. There is live music on alternate Saturdays and monthly quiz nights. No food is served on Saturday lunchtime. Occasional barbecues are held in summer. The attractive Georgian walled patio garden provides shelter and warmth for smokers. ❀⊟♣⁵–

Watermill ✔

Reigate Road, RH4 1NN (on A25, 1 mile E of town)

11-11; 12-10.30 Sun

☎ (01306) 883248

Courage Best Bitter, Directors; guest beers Ⓗ

Large and comfortable Chef & Brewer bar and restaurant which makes good use of the company's guest beer list – three guest ales are usually available, changing weekly. Food is served throughout the day from a regularly changing menu, with fish and other specials always available, and various themed nights. The patio garden has fine views across to Box Hill, with a heated area for smokers. ❀◐♿⊟P⁵–

Dormansland

Old House At Home

63 West Street, RH7 6QP TQ402422

11.30-3.30, 6-midnight; 12-4, 7-midnight Sun

☎ (01342) 832117

Shepherd Neame Master Brew Bitter, Ⓗ **Kent's Best,** Ⓖ **Spitfire** Ⓗ

Traditional old pub hidden on the western side of the village. The main bar dates from the 16th century, but there are later additions. The restaurant serves good quality home-made food (not Sun eve). There is a patio for outdoor drinking. Awarded Shepherd Neame Food Pub of the Year in 2007. ⅏Q❀◐⊟(409)♣P

Plough Inn

44 Plough Road, RH7 6PS (just off B2028) TQ406427

12-11 (midnight Fri & Sat; closed 3-5 Mon)

☎ (01342) 832933

Fuller's London Pride; Harveys Sussex Best Bitter Ⓗ

Large, traditional 18th-century pub with plenty of low wood beams and an inglenook. One side is set aside for diners, with a choice of Thai or traditional English pub food. The pleasant garden is popular in summer. Conveniently situated for Lingfield racecourse nearby. ⅏Q❀◐⊟(236, 409)P

East Molesey

Europa

171 Walton Road, KT8 0DX (on B369)

11-11 (midnight Wed-Sat); 12-11 Sun

☎ (020) 8979 8838

Caledonian Deuchars IPA; Courage Best Bitter; Fuller's London Pride; Greene King Abbot; Harveys Sussex Best Bitter; Youngs Bitter Ⓗ

Rather good labyrinthine three-bar locals' pub not far from East Molesey shops. The public bar has a dartboard and TV and the saloon features stained glass signs and ceiling skylights. A mural on an outside wall celebrates the jubilee of 2002. The large garden is ideal for children and has a covered patio with heaters for smokers. A popular jazz night is hosted on Sunday and a jam session on Wednesday evening. ❀◐⊟⊟(411)♣P⁵–

Egham

United Services Club

111 Spring Rise, TW20 9PE

12-2.45, 6-11; 12-midnight Fri-Sat; 12-11 Sun

☎ (01784) 435120 🌐 eusc.co.uk

Rebellion IPA; guest beers Ⓗ

This friendly social club offers real ale in tip-top form in comfortable surroundings. A big screen shows live sports fixtures and a full-sized snooker table is complemented by darts, cards, crib and dominoes. Live music plays on most Saturday evenings and occasional barbecues are held on the patio outside. Guest beers can come from local brewery Wayland. Daily Happy Hour (not Sunday). Show this Guide or CAMRA membership card for access. Local CAMRA Club of the Year 2008. ❀◐⇌⊟♣P⁵–

Englefield Green

Happy Man

12 Harvest Road, TW20 0QS (off A30)
11-11 (midnight Fri & Sat); 12-10.30 Sun
(01784) 433265
Hop Back Summer Lightning; guest beers H
Local CAMRA Pub of the Year 2008, this building was originally two Victorian cottages and converted to a pub to serve the workers building Royal Holloway College (and now a regular student haunt). The internal layout has barely changed over the years, with two rooms either side of the bar and a back room for darts. Four handpumps dispense an ever-changing range of guest beers from micro-breweries around the country, sometimes supplemented by beers on gravity from the cellar and up to three real ciders. The rear smokers' refuge is heated.

Monkeys Forehead

8 Egham Hill, TW20 0BQ (on A30)
10-11.30 (midnight Fri & Sat); 10-11 Sun
(01784) 432164 themonkeysforehead.co.uk
Beer range varies H
A second entry in the Guide for this sports bar known previously as the Pack Horse, and more recently the Royal Ascot. It tends to cater for the younger end of the market but offers two ever-changing beers from the likes of Hogs Back or Triple fff. Smooth beers are banned here! Male customers are advised to take sunglasses if visiting the Gents' toilet. Outside is a front patio and heated and covered smoking area. Breakfast is served from 10am with meals until 9pm. Handy for visiting Ascot races or the golf at Wentworth.

Epsom

Barley Mow ✔

12 Pikes Hill, KT17 4EA (off A2022)
12-11.30 (midnight Fri & Sat); 12-10.30 Sun
(01372) 721044
Fuller's Discovery, London Pride, ESB; guest beers H
Smart, traditional pub tucked away down a narrow side road. The pub has been extended over the years to occupy what was once three adjoining cottages. It has a central bar with wood floors and panelling, with seating areas at both ends, plus a conservatory and garden. The large Upper High Street public car park is nearby, with a path leading to the pub's garden entrance. Food is served all day at the weekend. The guest beer is supplied by Fuller's and may be from another family brewer.

Esher

Albert Arms

82 High Street, KT10 9QS (on A307)
10.30-11 (midnight Fri & Sat); 12-10.30 Sun
(01932) 465290 albertarms.com
Fuller's London Pride; Surrey Hills Shere Drop; guest beers H
Town centre pub with a popular drinking area and larger restaurant space. Six constantly rotating guest beers are mainly supplied by smaller breweries from the local area. Major sporting events are screened on the TV in the bar and there is an area for hire for private functions. No evening meals are available on Sunday. Local CAMRA Pub of the Year 2008.

Ewell

Wheatsheaf

34 Kingston Road, KT17 2AA (off B2200)
11 (12 Sun)-11
(020) 8393 2879
Wells Bombardier; Young's Bitter; guest beers H
Small, smart traditional local a short walk from the village centre, opposite the Hogsmill River. It has a single wood-panelled bar with an adjoining lounge area, carpeted throughout except for stone flags in front of the bar. Original etched windows remain inside and out, as well as leaded Isleworth Brewery windows behind the bar. Photographs of old Ewell decorate the walls and there are two bare brick fireplaces. No lunches are available on Saturday.

Farnham

Hop Blossom ✔

50 Long Garden Walk, GU9 7HX (down alley off Castle St)
12-3, 5-11; 11-11 Fri & Sat; 12-10.30 Sun
(01252) 710770
Fuller's Chiswick, London Pride, ESB, seasonal beers; guest beers H
Compact pub just off the town centre situated among a row of terraced cottages and mews housing. The interior comprises three drinking areas that meld into one with a roaring fire at the front, a good sized room for dining and meetings at the back, and a conservatory sandwiched in between. The walls are decorated with an eclectic collection of mementos and customer related artefacts including one man's search for his first million! All Fuller's beers make an appearance at some time during the year.

Lamb

43 Abbey Street, GU9 7RJ (off A287)
11-2.30, 5-11; 11-11 Sat; 12-10.30 Sun
(01252) 714133
Shepherd Neame Kent's Best, Spitfire, seasonal beers G
The Lamb is a bastion of real ale with beautiful beers served with quiet efficiency by a dedicated landlord and staff. Situated in a quiet residential area, an ambience of conviviality and quiet conversation generally dominates, except on Friday night when live blues/rock music plays (September to April). The food is excellent value (not available Tue eve or all day Sun).

Shepherd & Flock ✔

Moor Park Lane, GU9 9JB (centre of roundabout at A325/A31 jct E of town)
11-11.30; 12-11 Sun
(01252) 716675 shepherdandflock.com
Beer range varies H
Situated on Europe's largest inhabited roundabout, the pub retains an air of calm and tranquillity despite the din and fumes created by the constant traffic carousel. Local micros

are well represented within the constantly-changing guest beer list. A large outer garden and a safe and secluded rear drinking area make this the place to be on a summer's evening, with a covered and heated space for smokers. Well presented beers can be enjoyed with good food daily. (14, X65)P

Forest Green

Parrot Inn

Horsham Road, RH5 5RZ (just off B2127)
TQ124413
11-11; 12-10.30 Sun
(01306) 621339 theparrot.co.uk
Ringwood Best Bitter; Young's Bitter; guest beers H

The Parrot is set in a glorious position opposite the village green with fine views over the surrounding countryside. The owners farm locally, and their beef and lamb feature prominently on the excellent menu. Meals are served in the bar and restaurant (not Sun eve), situated behind the pub shop where you can buy good quality local produce including meat, bread and cheese. The large bar, with flagstones, a wood-burning stove and rustic tables, contains many hidden nooks and crannies for quiet drinking. Up to four guest beers are sold. QP

Godalming

Anchor

110 Ockford Road, GU7 1RG (on A3100)
11-midnight (1am Fri & Sat); 12-11 Sun
(01483) 424543
Hop Back Summer Lightning; Shepherd Neame Spitfire; guest beers H

Photographs of the pub at the turn of the century adorn the walls of this family-friendly local. Outside is an excellent terraced and spacious garden with heating, barbecues, giant umbrellas and chess pieces – a regular winner of Godalming in Bloom awards. Very much a community pub, many fund-raising events are held, with beer festivals planned and seasonal ciders to come. Food is good value and portions are generous, with the Sunday roast and curries highly recommended (meals served Wed-Sun lunchtime and Thu-Sat eve). Q

Jack Phillips

48-56 High Street, GU7 1DY
9-11 (midnight Thu; 1am Fri & Sat)
(01483) 521750
Courage Best Bitter, Directors; Greene King Abbot; Marston's Pedigree; guest beers H

A converted supermarket, this town centre Wetherspoon's was named after the radio operator on the Titanic. Ten handpumps feature at least three changing guests including ales from local breweries such as Pilgrim. The interior is narrow but deep, broken up by pillars and decorated in pastel shades. In the summer the front opens up with alfresco seating on the pavement. Quiz night is Monday and the cider is Weston's Old Rosie.

Star

17 Church Street, GU7 1EL
11-midnight (12.30am Thu; 2am Fri & Sat); 12-midnight Sun
(01483) 417717 thestargodalming.co.uk
Greene King IPA, H&H Olde Trip; H **guest beers** H/G

Originally a bakery, situated in a delightful and historic part of town. Despite a narrow exterior the pub is remarkably spacious inside, with a beamed, traditional area that leads to a conservatory and a heated outdoor area for smokers. Up to eight real ales are available, including four from the cellar dispensing five guests a week. Up to three real ciders are also stocked. Enormously popular themed beer festivals are held in a marquee in the garden at Easter and Halloween.

Gomshall

Compasses

50 Station Road, GU5 9LA (on A25)
11-11; 12-10.30 Sun
(01483) 202506
Surrey Hills Ranmore Ale, Shere Drop, Gilt Complex (summer), Albury Ruby (winter) H

Originally called God Encompasses, the name of this early Victorian pub has contracted over time. It has two main areas: the bar with several small seating areas and the restaurant. Beers and ingredients for the home-made food are locally sourced. There is a large garden just the other side of the Tillingbourne River. The pub is reputed to have a friendly ghost who plays with the taps. Live music plays on Friday night. Accommodation is in two en-suite twin rooms. P

Guildford

Keystone

3 Portsmouth Road, GU2 4BL (on A3100)
12-11 (midnight Fri & Sat); 12-7 Sun
(01483) 575089 thekeystone.co.uk
Black Sheep Best Bitter; Wadworth 6X; guest beers H

Originally the tap for the Cannon Brewery, the Keystone has gone from strength to strength since it reopened in 2003. A modern and comfortable over-21s town centre pub with sofas, wooden floors and large tables for groups, it hosts many events during the year including barbecues, Morris dancing and hog roasts. Excellent freshly-made food is served with themed evenings always popular (no food Fri-Sun eve). The rear patio overlooks the church, heated and lit with giant umbrellas for smokers. Live music plays occasionally.

Varsity Bar

Egerton Road, University of Surrey, GU2 7XU (off A3 near hospital)
11-11 (8.30 Sat); 12-10.30 Sun
(01483) 683226
Beer range varies H

An unlikely venue but this university sports bar offers an excellent range of three ever-changing beers from the local area (Surrey Hills, Hogs Back) and further afield (Archers and Sharp's). Open to all with the entrance via the shop below, it can be busy on match days (Wednesday and Saturday) although quiet the rest of the time. The last Friday of the month celebrates one brewery and its ales. Annual beer festival and excellent value food. ◑◗🚍P

Hersham

Royal George

130 Hersham Road, KT12 5QJ (off A244)
⏲ 11-11 (midnight Fri & Sat); 12-11 Sun
☎ (01932) 220910
Young's Bitter, Special Ⓗ
Popular local built in 1964. A Senegal parrot and the pub cat happily preside over the spacious main bar. The public bar has a dartboard and an interesting plan of a Napoleonic Wars ship-of-the-line, one of which the pub is named after. There is an extensive English and Thai lunch menu and excellent Thai food in the evening (not Sun). Quiz night is Tuesday. Outside is a heated awning for smokers. Local CAMRA Pub of the Year 2007. ⌂❀◑◗⊟♿🚍(218)♣P⚟

Holmbury St Mary

King's Head

Pitland Street, RH5 6NP (off B2126) TQ112442
⏲ 12 (4 Mon)-11; 12-10.30 Sun
☎ (01306) 730282
Greene King IPA; King Horsham Best Bitter; Surrey Hills Shere Drop; guest beers Ⓗ
Wonderful unspoilt pub hidden away on a side road. The wooden-floored bar has a bar billiards table, real fire and some interesting old shooting photos on the walls. Excellent food is served in the restaurant including daily specials and a changing fish menu in the evening (no food Sun eve or Mon). The pub is popular with ramblers and mountain bikers exploring the lovely Surrey Hills countryside. Beer festivals held Spring and August Bank Holidays. ⌂Q❀◑◗🚍(21)♣P

Horley

Farmhouse ✔

Ladbroke Road, Langshott, RH6 8PB (off A23/B2036 jct) TQ 290441
⏲ 12-11
☎ (01293) 782146 🌐 thefarmhousepub.co.uk
Courage Best Bitter; Fuller's London Pride; Shepherd Neame Spitfire; guest beers Ⓗ
A Grade II listed building, this is the original farmhouse for Hewitts farm. It dates back to the early 17th century although there have been several additions over the years. The bar is in the old farmhouse and retains many original features. The guest beer changes weekly, usually from a local brewery and is in the 4-5% range. Food is available all day until 9pm (8pm Sun). The large garden has table tennis and skittles as well as swings and a climbing frame for children. ⌂❀◑◗🚍♣P

Hurst Green

Diamond

Holland Road, RH8 9BQ
⏲ 11-11; 12-10.30 Sun
☎ (01883) 716040
Fuller's London Pride; Harveys Sussex Best Bitter; Taylor Landlord; Young's Bitter Ⓗ
This pleasant, dog friendly community pub on the edge of Hurst Green has undergone considerable refurbishment and now offers three distinctive drinking areas and a darts bar. There is a fine collection of antique handpumps and no shortage of clocks for those who find timekeeping a problem. The beer range occasionally changes. Card carrying CAMRA members receive a discount on cask beers. No food is served on Sunday evening. ⌂❀◑◗⇌🚍(594)♣P⚟

Hurtmore

Squirrel

Hurtmore Road, GU7 2RN (off A3)
⏲ 11-11; 12-10.30 Sun
☎ (01483) 860223 🌐 thesquirrelinn.co.uk
Fuller's London Pride; guest beers Ⓗ
Approached via a slip road off the busy A3, the attractive pub has a heated patio/veranda at the front and side gardens. Inside there is something for everyone with a comfortable bar, two lounge areas furnished with relaxing chairs and sofas, and a dining area. A changing range of guest beers is complemented by three real ciders (one organic), a perry and 36 bottled beers. There is a good choice of food ranging from bar snacks to full main meals served in the bar or dining area (not Sun eve). ⌂❀🛏◑◗🚍(46)♣●P⚟

Long Ditton

City Arms

5-6 Portsmouth Road, KT7 0XE (on A307)
⏲ 11-11; 12-10.30 Sun
☎ (020) 8398 3552 🌐 thecityarms.net
Caledonian Deuchars IPA; Courage Best Bitter; guest beers Ⓗ
Welcoming local on the main road between Kingston and Esher, run by a real ale friendly landlord for the last four years. The long front bar is for drinkers, with a real fire at one end that makes it cosy. A quieter back bar and side room are used for dining. Two regular ales are complemented by a weekly changing guest beer from the S&N list. Good value home-made traditional English food is served (not Sun eve). Quiz night is Wednesday and board games are available. ⌂❀◑◗🚍♣P⚟

Lyne

Royal Marine

Lyne Lane, KT16 0AN (off B386) TQ012663
⏲ 12-2.30, 5.30-11; 12-2.30 Sat; 12-3 Sun
☎ (01932) 873900
Courage Best Bitter; Hogs Back TEA; Wayland Adled Ale; guest beers Ⓗ
Converted from two cottages 160 years ago, this small, cosy country pub is located in a quiet hamlet not far from St Peter's Hospital and the M25. The name is said to commemorate Queen Victoria reviewing her troops nearby following the Crimean War. Marine bric-a-brac and drinking jugs are on display along with CAMRA awards. The landlord supports local breweries and sometimes offers a mild. All food is freshly

cooked and the portions are generous. Darts, cards, crib and dominoes played.
⌂Q❀◐⊟(P3)♣P

Martyr's Green

Black Swan

Old Lane, KT11 1NG (off A3/M25 jct) TQ089573
⊙ 11-midnight (10.30 Sun)
☎ (01932) 862364 ⊕ geronimo-inns.co.uk
Adnams Bitter; Fuller's London Pride; Surrey Hills Shere Drop; guest beers ⊞
Extensively rebuilt in 2006, this family-friendly country pub is modern, light and airy – open plan but divided into different areas. Fronting the road is the informal bar area with brick fireplaces; to the left is the lounge with comfy chairs and a central open fire. A more formal dining area is to the rear (no eve meals Sun). The guest beer is often from a local micro. Monthly beer and food matching evenings are held. There is an open mike session every Sunday evening. ⌂Q❀◐♿P⁄–

Mugswell

Well House Inn ✔

Chipstead Lane, CR5 3SQ (off A217) TQ 259552
⊙ 12-11 (10.30 Sun)
☎ (01737) 830640 ⊕ wellhouseinn.co.uk
Adnams Bitter; Cottage Golden Arrow; Fuller's London Pride; guest beers ⊞
A fine multi-roomed Grade II listed pub with two drinking areas, a conservatory and restaurant serving generous portions of good food made with local ingredients (no food Sun eve and Mon). The main bar is wooden beamed and panelled and displays an excellent collection of pewter and ceramic tankards. The Domesday Book mentions the well outside which is still monitored today for its water level. Harry the monk's ghost is a pub regular. At least one beer comes from a local micro-brewery. ⌂Q❀◐⊞P⁄–

Newchapel

Blacksmith's Head ✔

Newchapel Road, RH7 6LE (on B2028, off A22)
⊙ 11-3, 6-11 (11-11 Fri summer); 12-11 Sat; 12-6 Sun
☎ (01342) 833697 ⊕ theblacksmithshead.co.uk
Fuller's London Pride; Harveys Sussex Best Bitter; guest beers ⊞
Built in the 1920s on the site of a former forge, this one-bar country free house has a restaurant area to the side and provides quality accommodation. Food is freshly prepared with restaurant, bar and tapas menus to choose from. Portuguese influences reflect the nationality of the licensees. Occasional quizzes are held and two regularly-changing guest beers come from small independents or micros. ⌂Q❀⊭◐⛺♣P⁄–

Newdigate

Surrey Oaks

Parkgate Road, RH5 5DZ (on road to Leigh from Newdigate) TQ 205436
⊙ 11.30-2.30 (3 Sat), 5.30 (6 Sat)-11; 12-10.30 Sun
☎ (01306) 631200 ⊕ surreyoaks.co.uk
Harveys Sussex Best Bitter; Surrey Hills Ranmore Ale; guest beers ⊞
Local CAMRA Pub of the Year on many occasions, the Soaks is a strong supporter of micro-breweries. More than 300 different beers are sold each year —see the website for details. The main bar of this 16th-century building has low beams, flagstones and an inglenook with a real fire. Good home-made food is served in the bar and restaurant (not Sun or Mon eves). Outside is a lovely garden with a boules pitch. Beer festivals are held on the late spring and August bank holidays.
⌂Q❀◐♣●P

Oxshott

Bear

Leatherhead Road, KT22 0JE (on A244)
⊙ 10-11 (midnight summer Fri & Sat)
☎ (01372) 842747 ⊕ thebearoxshott.co.uk
Young's Bitter, Special, seasonal beers ⊞
Dating from at least 1816, this pub has undergone many changes. A sensitive, recent refurbishment has created a restaurant to the rear and several distinct drinking areas. There is a heated, decked area at the front, part-covered and heated for smokers and a pleasant garden at the rear with pergolas and a barbecue. Tea and coffee are available from 10am and a contemporary British menu is served from noon until 10pm. Tuesday is quiz night. ⌂❀◐♿⊟(408)P⁄–

Peaslake

Hurtwood Inn

Walking Bottom, GU5 9RR TQ086446
⊙ 12-3, 5.30-11 (midnight Fri); 12-11 Sat & Sun
☎ (01306) 730851 ⊕ hurtwoodinnhotel.com
Hogs Back TEA; Surrey Hills Shere Drop; guest beers ⊞
The Hurtwood Bar at this three-star 21-bedroom hotel serves as a local for the village as well as the bar for hotel guests and lunch stop for walkers in the beautiful surrounding countryside. Seating ranges from plush sofas to bar stools, and there is a genuine 1960s Rock-Ola jukebox. Food is served in the bar as well as the restaurant. Ramblers are welcome if they remove their muddy boots.
❀⊭◐⊟(25)P

Puttenham

Good Intent ✔

The Street, GU3 1AR (off B3000) SU931478
⊙ 11-3, 6-11; 11-11 Sat; 12-10.30 Sun
☎ (01483) 810387 ⊕ thegoodintent-puttenham.co.uk
Harveys Sussex Best Bitter; Ringwood Best Bitter; Taylor Landlord; guest beers ⊞
Welcoming 16th-century former coaching inn situated on the North Downs and Pilgrims Way and National Cycle Route 22. Popular with walkers and cyclists, families and dogs are welcome. The L-shaped bar is garlanded with a hop bine from the last field to produce the once world-renowned Farnham hop. Fish and chips night is Wednesday (no food Sun and Mon eves). Guest beers from local micros often feature and an annual beer festival is

held over the late May bank holiday weekend.
⛫Q❀◑⛺♣P⅃

Salfords

Salfords Club

Mead Avenue, RH1 5DD (off A23)
⏲ 7 (4 Fri & Sat)-11; 12-10.30 Sun
☎ (01293) 430064
Beer range varies Ⓗ
Friendly members' club which extends a warm welcome to those in possession of this Guide and to card-carrying CAMRA members. The large bar area has a pool table, darts and table football. The two beers change frequently and are often from small independents or micros. A number of events such as music nights are held. Frequent visitors would be expected to join the Club. CAMRA Regional Club of the Year 2007. ❀♿⇌🚌(100)♣P⅃

Send

New Inn

Send Road, GU23 7EN (on A247)
⏲ 11-11; 12-10.30 Sun
☎ (01483) 762736
Adnams Bitter; Fuller's London Pride; Greene King Abbot; Ringwood Best Bitter; guest beer Ⓗ
Situated on the Wey Navigation, one of Britain's oldest waterways built in the 1660s when it was a vital source of grain supplies for the growing London market. Nowadays leisure boats moor here and the waterside garden can get crowded in summer, especially when the barbecue is in service. One L-shaped bar serves three areas, but beware the step in the middle. An excellent rural pub—well worth the escape from nearby suburbia.
Q❀◑🚌(462, 463)P

Shepperton

Barley Mow

67 Watersplash Road, TW17 0EE (off B376)
⏲ 12-11 (10.30 Sun)
☎ (01932) 225326
Hogs Back TEA; Hop Back Summer Lightning; guest beers Ⓗ
The landlord of this out-of-the-way Shepperton Green pub is a keen supporter of new local micro-breweries. The horseshoe-shaped bar is adorned with pump clips and bottled beers. Jazz is performed on Wednesday, rock and roll and blues on Friday and Saturday. The menu has Caribbean influences and on Sunday lunchtime there is a traditional roast (no meals Sat, eve meals Weds only). Outside is a covered, heated space for smokers. North Surrey CAMRA Pub of the Year 2007. ❀◑🚌P⅃

Sidlow Bridge

Three Horseshoes ✔

Ironsbottom, RH2 8PT (off A217) TQ 252461
⏲ 12-11 (9 Sun)
☎ (01293) 862315 🌐 sidlow.com
Fuller's London Pride, ESB; Harveys Sussex Best Bitter; Young's Bitter; guest beers Ⓗ
Old fashioned, traditional pub, originally a coaching stop on the London to Brighton run. The bar is approached through a small ante-room which leads to an L-shaped wood-panelled room. The Shoes is popular with drinkers and diners, offering a good selection of home-cooked food made from local ingredients. Helicopters are welcome but must book in advance. Q❀◑🚌(324)♣P

Staffhurst Wood

Royal Oak ✔

Caterfield Lane, RH8 0RR TQ407485
⏲ 11-11 (closed 3-5 Mon & Tue winter); 12-10.30 Sun
☎ (01883) 722207
Adnams Bitter; Harveys Sussex Best Bitter; Ⓗ
guest beers Ⓗ/Ⓖ
Friendly rural freehouse well worth seeking out. Guest beers usually come from local micro-brewers, served alongside a selection of bottled British and Belgian beers and a variety of ciders. The landlord also runs a vintage port club. Excellent quality meals made from locally-sourced ingredients are available in the bar and restaurant (not Sun eve). Views from the garden are superb and dogs are welcome. Card-carrying CAMRA members receive a discount on cask beers and bar meals.
⛫❀◑🍎●P

Staines

Bells

124 Church Street, TW18 4ZB (off B376)
⏲ 12-3, 5-11; 12-midnight Fri; 12-11 Sat & Sun
☎ (01784) 454240
Wells Bombardier; Young's Bitter, Special, seasonal beers Ⓗ
Traditional 18th-century English pub in a quiet location opposite St Mary's Church and close to the Thames but within easy walking distance of the town centre. This community pub with friendly bar staff serves impressive beers and food, with fish dishes a speciality. The pleasant rear patio garden has a large heated smoker's canopy and is especially popular in summer with local workers and shoppers. There is an excellent function room for hire.
Q❀◑♿🚌⅃

George ✔

2-8 High Street, TW18 4EE (on A308)
⏲ 9am-midnight (1am Fri & Sat)
☎ (01784) 462181
Courage Best Bitter; Greene King Abbot; Marston's Pedigree; Shepherd Neame Spitfire; guest beers Ⓗ
Wetherspoon's pub built on the site of a former supermarket around 10 years ago, situated opposite the old town hall and war memorial close to the Thames. The large downstairs bar has several booths and is often busy but a quieter bar can be reached via a spiral staircase. Six guest ales, often from local breweries such as Itchen Valley, Twickenham and Loddon, adorn the front bank of handpumps with the usual suspects relegated to the second bank. ◑♿⇌🚌●⅃

Stanwell

Rising Sun

110 Oaks Road, TW19 7LB

11-11 (midnight Fri & Sat)
☎ (01784) 244080
Fuller's London Pride; Greene King Abbot; guest beers Ⓗ
One bar pub located close to Heathrow airport by the Duke of Northumberland's and Longford Rivers on the northern edge of the village. The inn was first opened in March 1931, replacing a pub of the same name at the opposite end of Oaks Road near the village church. Guest beers are generally from the Punch list and food is served until 8pm daily. Live sports events are shown on satellite TV. A paved area outside has a heated smokers' canopy. (441)P

Stoke D'Abernon

Old Plough ✔
2 Station Road, KT11 3BN (off A245)
11.30-11; 12-10.30 Sun
☎ (01932) 862244 theoldplough.net
Beer range varies Ⓗ
Large, open plan pub with a landlord passionate about ale. Up to five beers are on offer, often from the SIBA list and local —some chosen by the regulars. The L-shaped bar with a side room and conservatory at the rear has a cosy, country pub feel. The large garden is very popular in summer with barbecues and bouncy castle. Basket meals are served at lunchtime with a full menu in the evening and all day on Sunday. Family and dog friendly, board games are available.
(408)♣P

Sunbury-on-Thames

Grey Horse
63 Staines Road East, TW16 5AA (on A308)
11 (12 Sat)-11; 12-10.30 Sun
☎ (01932) 782981
Fuller's London Pride; Twickenham Original; guest beers Ⓗ
Friendly, comfortably furnished little local with a surprisingly rural feel although just a few yards from Sunbury Cross and close to Kempton Park racecourse. Guest beers change regularly, often from Twickenham Ales. Live sports are shown on TV. Good value freshly prepared home-cooked food is served Monday to Friday lunchtime and in the evening Monday to Thursday. The large beer garden has a covered and heated smoking area. There are rumours of a resident ghost.

Thames Ditton

George & Dragon
High Street, KT7 0RY (on B364)
11 (12 Sun)-11
☎ (020) 8398 2206
Shepherd Neame Master Brew Bitter, Kent's Best, Spitfire, seasonal beers Ⓗ
Welcoming and friendly traditional local with an open plan interior divided into various areas, often busy with rugby fans. Family and dog friendly, a local jazz band plays on Tuesday night. Home-made traditional English food is served including popular Sunday roasts (eve meals Wed-Sat). Smokers are well cared for with a heated, covered area with its own TV. Former local CAMRA Pub of the Year.
Q(514, 515)P

Thursley

Three Horseshoes
Dye House Road, GU8 6QD (off A3)
12-3, 5.30-11; 12-11 Sat; 12-10.30 Sun
☎ (01252) 703268
Fuller's London Pride; Hogs Back TEA; guest beers Ⓗ
Under threat of closure and conversion into housing in 1999, the pub was purchased by 24 local supporters and reopened in 2004. A short drive from the A3, it is set in open countryside on the Greensand Way and is ideal for walkers. High quality home-made food is served in the restaurant and bar where it can sometimes dominate. This is a welcoming pub deservedly popular with families.
QP

Tongham

Hogs Back Brewery Shop
Manor Farm, The Street, GU10 1DE (off A31)
9-6 (8.30 Wed-Fri); 10-4.30 Sun
☎ (01252) 784495 hogsback.co.uk/breweryshop.htm
Hog's Back HBB, TEA, HOP, seasonal beers Ⓖ
Situated in a barn partially overlooking the brewery, the shop sells Hogs Back draught beers and bottle-conditioned ales. It also stocks a large selection of bottled beers from Britain and all over the world and a good choice of country wines, plus some excellent Hogs Back souvenir merchandise. Either Weston's or Mr Whitehead's cider is also available. Show your CAMRA membership card to receive a 5% discount on Hogs Back products. (3, 20)P

White Hart
76 The Street, GU10 1DH (off A31)
12-11 (midnight Fri & Sat); 12-10.30 Sun
☎ (01252) 782419 whitehart tongham.co.uk
Beer range varies Ⓗ
This family-run pub usually offers up to six real ales including a mild or porter and a local brew, dispensed from an island bar serving three wood-beamed rooms. The village bar is where the locals gather for drinking and chat, leading to a more family-oriented lounge where meals are served most lunchtimes and evenings. The sports bar has pool, TV, darts and jukebox. The cider is Weston's Old Rosie. Dogs are welcome. (3, 20)♣P

West Molesey

Royal Oak
317 Walton Road, KT8 2QG (on B369)
11-3, 5-11; 11-11 Sat; 12-10.30 Sun
☎ (020) 8979 5452
Courage Best Bitter; Hogs Back TEA; Wychwood Hobgoblin Ⓗ
Situated next to the church, this community pub is comfortably furnished and carpeted throughout. The open-plan bar divides into a sports area with music, games and sport on TV, and a quiet lounge area. Wood panelling creates a traditional pub feel, along with oak

beams, horse brasses and decorative plates. Families are welcome until 8pm and there is a secure garden at the rear. A quiz is held once a month and live music plays occasionally. Games include shove ha'penny.No food Sunday.
♨Q❀◑🚌(411)♣P🚬

Weybridge

Jolly Farmer

41 Princes Road, KT13 9BN (off A317)
⏲ 11-3, 5.30-11.30; 12-3, 7-11.30 Sun
☎ (01932) 856873
Banks's Bitter; Jennings Cocker Hoop; Marston's Mansfield Cask Ale, Pedigree; guest beers 🄷
Quiet pub down a back street near the cricket green, popular with locals. A comfortable, friendly mid-Victorian inn, it has a low-beamed ceiling and L-shaped bar. Large mirrors and pictures of old Weybridge decorate the walls and there is a collection of Toby jugs on display. The spacious garden is popular in summer with a heated canopy for smokers. The guest beer changes monthly, supplied by Marston's. Q❀◑🚌(471)🚬

Old Crown ✔

83 Thames Street, KT13 8LP (off A317)
⏲ 11 (10 summer)-11 (midnight Fri & Sat)
☎ (01932) 842844 🌐 theoldcrownweybridge.co.uk
Courage Best Bitter, Directors; Young's Bitter; guest beer 🄷
Weatherboarded, Grade II listed building dating from the 16th-century. This family run pub is adjacent to the River Thames where it meets the River Wey and the garden runs down to the river with access for small boats. Three wood-panelled drinking and dining areas all have their own character. A good range of food is served (no eve meals Sun to Tue). Children are welcome in the conservatory. Q❀◑⊟♿🚌P

Windlesham

Half Moon ✔

Church Road, GU20 6BN (off B386)
⏲ 11-3, 5.30-11.30; 12-4 Sun
☎ (01276) 473329
Fuller's London Pride; Hogs Back TEA; Ringwood Fortyniner; Taylor Landlord; Theakston Old Peculier; guest beers 🄷
This is a true free house, in the hands of the Sturt family since 1909. As well as a wide range of beers the pub is renowned for its varied menu of traditional English food including game shot locally (no eve meals Sun). It has a spacious patio and garden with a Wendy house and slide for children and a covered and heated area for smokers. Disabled access is good. Q❀◑◐♿🚌(500)P🚬

Woking

Sovereigns ✔

Guildford Road, GU22 7QQ (on A320)
⏲ 12-11 (midnight Fri & Sat)
☎ (01483) 751426
Caledonian Deuchars IPA; guest beers 🄷
Six handpumps greet the drinker at this large, comfortable Ember Inn, the oldest pub in Woking, dating from 1840. Food is served daily until 9pm with a grill night on Tuesday and curry night on Thursday. Quizzes are held on Monday and Wednesday evenings. There is outside seating to the front and side with patio heaters and umbrellas. Local CAMRA Pub of the Year in 2007, it hosts occasional beer festivals. ♨❀◑◐♿⇌🚌♣P🚬

Wetherspoons ✔

51-57 Chertsey Road, GU21 5AJ
⏲ 9am-midnight (1am Fri & Sat)
☎ (01483) 722818
Courage Directors; Greene King IPA; Hogs Back TEA; Marston's Pedigree; guest beers 🄷
Difficult to believe that this vibrant town centre meeting place was once Woolworths. It is now a haven for discerning real ale drinkers enjoying the four ever-changing guest beers that come and go with remarkable speed. HG Wells is everywhere, from the time machine clock on the ceiling to the mysterious invisible metal man gazing down on drinkers. Families are welcome on Sunday from 12-4pm. Local CAMRA Pub of the Year 2008.
Q❀◑◐♿⇌🚌🍎

Wood Street

Royal Oak

89 Oak Hill, GU3 3DA
⏲ 11-3, 5-11; 12-3, 7-10.30 Sun
☎ (01483) 235137
Courage Best Bitter; Surrey Hills Shere Drop; guest beers 🄷
Superb free house and frequent winner of local CAMRA awards, attracting drinkers from far and wide with four ever-changing and imaginative guest beers, always including a mild. Lunchtime meals are popular, served Monday to Saturday, with an impressive range of vegetables, but definitely no chips. The large garden is safe for children and includes swings and a windmill. Note the Hodgson's Brewery plaque on the front wall.
Q❀◑🚌(3,17)♣P

Wrecclesham

Sandrock

Sandrock Hill, Boundstone, GU10 4NS (off B3384)
SU830444
⏲ 12-11 (10.30 Sun)
☎ (01252) 715865 🌐 thesandrock.com
Batham Best Bitter; Bowman Swift One; guest beers 🄷
Originally a quarry master's house where the miners were paid, this is now a delightful retreat famed for its emphasis on Black Country beers. Batham's is often available and you may find Holden's or Enville beers, as well as ales from local breweries, occasionaly including mild. The atmosphere is relaxing and unpretentious with a choice of drinking areas and a roaring fire. Award-winning food concentrates on traditional British classics (not Sat lunch or Sun eve). Children are welcome in the restaurant and side bar and there is occasional live music. ♨Q❀◑◐🚌(16)P

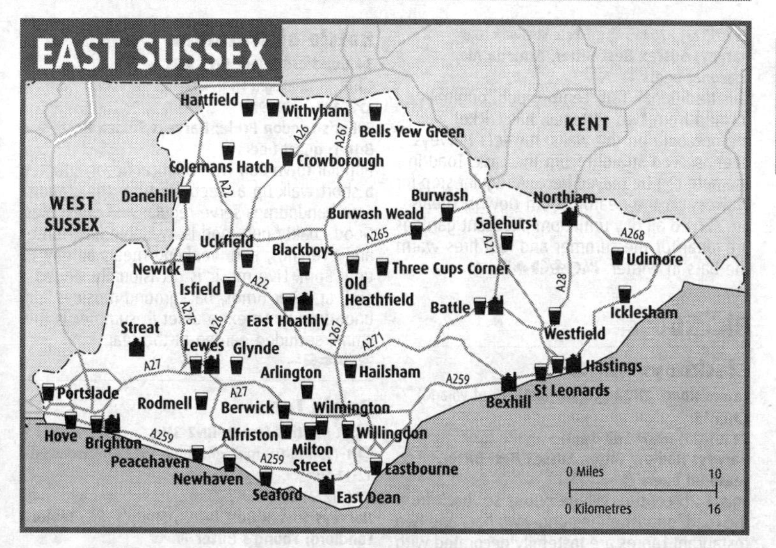

SUSSEX (EAST)

Alfriston

Smugglers Inn

Waterloo Square, BN26 5UE (by market cross)

11-11; 12-10.30 Sun

(01323) 870241 yeoldesmugglersinne.co.uk

Fuller's London Pride; Harveys Sussex Best Bitter, XXXX Old Ale; Taylor Landlord H

A traditional 14th-century village pub, originally known as the Market Cross Inn, whose name change represents its major links with 'the men of the night'. An impressive, imposing inglenook fireplace, oak beams, horse brasses and all sorts of interesting iron implements adorn the walls, helping to create atmosphere in this relaxed country inn. A varied pub food menu and an outside seating area attract many South Downs walkers and visitors to this picturesque village location.

Q(126)

Arlington

Old Oak

Caneheath, BN26 6SJ (1 mile E of village)

TV557079

11-11

(01323) 482072

Badger First Gold; Harveys Sussex Best Bitter; guest beers G

Close to Michelham Priory and the recreational areas of Abbot's Wood, this cosy, beamed free house serves a varied menu of home-cooked food. Originally four alms houses, it was first used as an ale and cider house for agricultural, brick and charcoal workers in the early 1900s. On the walls are a variety of old photographs and other memorabilia including a display of items from a brewer's sundriesman. Toad in the hole can be played here. Real cider is only available in summer. P

Battle

Chequers Inn

Lower Lake, TN33 0AT (by mini roundabout S of High Street)

11-11 (midnight Fri & Sat); 11-10.30 Sun

(01424) 772088 chequersinn.eu

Adnams Broadside; Fuller's London Pride; Harveys Sussex Best Bitter; guest beers H

This 15th-century inn features exposed beams and open fires. The dining/children's room boasts a large inglenook, while the back garden overlooks the 1066 battlefield. Award-winning floral displays adorn the pub in summer, when there is also a beer festival, usually held in August. Good pub food is served from an extensive menu. A draught cider from Biddenden is available. The smoking area is covered.

P

Bells Yew Green

Brecknock Arms

TN3 9BJ

12-3, 6-11 (closed Sun eves winter)

(01892) 750237

Harveys XX Mild, Sussex Best Bitter, seasonal beers H

Under new management, this traditional ale house dating from the 1850s is once more serving excellent beer and good quality food. A fourth handpump has recently been installed. The public and saloon bars are small and comfortable with open fires. Pictures of Harveys Brewery adorn the walls of the saloon bar. Very much the hub of the community, the pub has a number of local cricket teams visiting regularly.

Q(Frant)P

Berwick

Cricketers' Arms

Berwick Village, BN26 6SP (S of A27, W of Drusilla's roundabout)

11-3, 6-11; 11-11 Sat & summer; 12-10.30 Sun

☎ (01323) 870469 🌐 cricketersberwick.co.uk
Harveys Sussex Best Bitter, Armada Ale, seasonal beers G
This traditional 18th-century pub, originally formed from two cottages, has cricket memorabilia on the walls. It offers Harveys beers served straight from the cask. Toad in the hole can be played here. A regular stop for walkers on the nearby South Downs, meals are served all day until 9pm. Pleasant gardens are ideal for the summer and real fires warm the bars in winter.

Blackboys

Blackboys Inn ✔
Lewes Road, TN22 5LG (on B2192 S of village)
11-11
☎ (01825) 890283 🌐 theblackboysinn.co.uk
Harveys Hadlow Bitter, Sussex Best Bitter, seasonal beers H
This 14th-century village pub is set back from the road, opposite the pond. Two bars and two restaurant rooms are tastefully decorated with old prints, hop bines and interesting artefacts, to add to the relaxed atmosphere. Outside is a large terrace plus a covered smoking area, together with an intimate garden set aside just for adults. Harveys Old Ale is available in winter, and there is an extensive food menu, from bar snacks to restaurant meals.

Brighton

Barley Mow
92 St George's Road, BN2 1EE (in Kemp Town, 1 mile E of city centre)
11-11 (midnight Fri & Sat); 12-11 Sun
☎ (01273) 682259
Harveys Sussex Best Bitter; guest beers H
A single front bar with wooden tables and plenty of seats. Music is played, but at a reasonable volume. Up to six real ales are served, with a good representation from local breweries. A wide-ranging menu includes fish as a speciality and a selection of wines are available by the glass. Nostalgic sweets such as fruit salad chews and shrimps are sold. Board games are available, Thursday is quiz night and outside is a covered and enclosed smoking patio. (37,47)

Basketmakers Arms ✔
12 Gloucester Road, BN1 4AD
11-11 (midnight Fri & Sat); 12-11 Sun
☎ (01273) 689006
Fuller's Discovery, London Pride, ESB, seasonal beers; Gale's HSB; guest beers H
Street-corner local situated in the vibrant North Laine district of the city, with its bohemian shopping area. The Basketmakers is a Fuller's tied house, offering beers from the Fuller's/Gale's range plus a guest ale. Popular with shoppers and the local business community, it has a good reputation for home-cooked inexpensive pub food which is made using organic, locally sourced produce wherever possible. The walls are covered with old metal advertising signs and containers.

Battle of Trafalgar
34 Guildford Road, BN1 3LW
12-11 (midnight Fri & Sat)
☎ (01273) 327997
Fuller's London Pride; Harveys Sussex Best Bitter; guest beers H
Popular town pub with nautical decor, situated a short walk up a steep hill from the station. Four handpumps serve regular and guest ales. Good quality pub food is available lunchtimes and evenings, and weekend meals all day until 5pm. Live music is occasionally staged and, at other times, background music is unobtrusive. An extra asset in summer is the small, secluded garden at the rear.

Bugle Inn
24 St Martins Street, BN2 3HJ
4-11; 4 (3 Fri)-midnight Thu & Fri; 12-midnight Sat; 12-11 Sun
☎ (01273) 607753
Harveys Sussex Best Bitter; Sharp's IPA; Taylor Landlord; Young's Bitter H
Traditional back-street local with a friendly welcome. Customers are a good mix of students and locals. Strong Irish connections mean that the craic is mighty. Rugby is televised and leads to a packed pub, especially for internationals. Traditional Irish music plays on Sunday afternoon and Thursday evening. Children are welcome in the family room until 8.30pm and there is a lovely, sheltered garden for smokers. Real cider is available in summer.

Evening Star
55-56 Surrey Street, BN1 3PB (400m S of station)
12-11; 11.30-midnight Fri & Sat
☎ (01273) 328931 🌐 eveningstarbrighton.co.uk
Dark Star Hophead, seasonal beers; guest beers H
Excellent pub close to the main railway station with exposed brickwork and wooden bench seating, owned by the Dark Star Brewery. Conversation dominates, with no distractions from large-screen TVs, jukeboxes or fruit machines. Several guest ales complement the Dark Star beers, together with a range of mainly bottled Belgian, German and other continental beers, cider and perry. The Star hosts occasional live music and popular beer festivals. Thatchers Medium cider is served. The smoking area has a retractable awning.

Greys
105 Southover Street, BN2 9UA (500 yds E of A270 opp The Level)
4-11.30; 12-midnight Fri & Sat; 12-11 Sun

INDEPENDENT BREWERIES

1648 East Hoathly
Beachy Head East Dean
Fallen Angel Battle
FILO Hastings
Harveys Lewes
Kemptown Brighton
Rectory Streat
Rother Valley Northiam
White Bexhill-on-Sea

☎ (01273) 680734 🌐 greyspub.com
Harveys Sussex Best Bitter; Taylor Landlord Ⓗ
Single-bar street-corner Victorian pub situated in the hilly Hanover area. The L-shaped room has a wooden floor, with a mixture of benches and settles. An Á la carte menu with vegetarian options is on offer (booking essential) with a roast on Sunday. A wide selection of Belgian beers is available and an annual Belgian beer festival is held. Live music is performed by artists from the UK and the USA. Check the website for details of music and beer festivals. (37,37B)

Lion & Lobster

24 Sillwood Street, BN1 2PS (100m from seafront just W of City centre)
11-midnight; 12-11 Sun
☎ (01273) 327299
Harveys Sussex Best Bitter; guest beers Ⓗ
Popular pub close to Brighton city centre and easy to find, as it is painted pink. The interior of the single U-shaped bar and rather gloomy back room is a mix of the traditional and the quirky. Old pictures decorate the bar, while the walls of the Gents are covered in antique mirrors. There is discreet piped music and sport is often shown on multiple TVs. Up to five real ales are available, plus a selection of food, including Sunday roasts.

Lord Nelson ✓

36 Trafalgar Street, BN1 4ED (near station)
11.30-11 (midnight Fri & Sat); 12-10.30 Sun
☎ (01273) 695872 🌐 thelordnelsoninn.co.uk
Harveys XX Mild, Hadlow Bitter, Sussex Best Bitter, Armada Ale, seasonal beers Ⓗ
An unspoilt two-bar back-street local in Brighton's North Laine, near the station. It also has a back bar area for meetings and a conservatory beyond that is used as a gallery and function room. A pull-down screen is used for viewing sports. A folk club operates on the first Monday of every month, an open mic night the second Monday, and a quiz night every Tuesday. A Guide regular, the pub is part of the local Ale Trail. Food is served daily. Weston's draught cider available.

Mitre Tavern

13 Baker Street, BN1 4JN
10.30-11; 12-10.30 Sun
☎ (01273) 683173 🌐 mitretavern.co.uk
Harveys XX Mild, Sussex Best Bitter, Armada Ale, seasonal beers Ⓗ
A welcoming pub with background music, this Harveys tied house attracts a more mature customer and is situated in a side street off one of the city's main shopping areas, close to the Open Market. The pub dates back to Victorian times and is divided into a long, narrow lounge bar and a cosy snug bar. There is an outside courtyard smoking area (not on the pavement).

Prestonville Arms

64 Hamilton Road, BN1 5DN (between Preston Circus & Seven Dials)
5-11; 12-midnight Fri & Sat; 12-11 Sun
☎ (01273) 701007
Fuller's Discovery, London Pride, seasonal beers; Gale's Butser, HSB; guest beers Ⓗ
Slightly off the beaten track, this welcoming local pub with an excellent atmosphere provides great food including Sunday roasts (children's and vegetarian options available) and unmissable Wednesday curry/chilli nights. Also recommended are the two weekly quizzes: Sunday is general knowledge, Tuesday is music. The friendly staff serve a well-kept pint in relaxed surroundings among decor of old photographs, beer mats and historic advertisements lining the walls. The pub also sells local artwork from a permanent display.

Sir Charles Napier ✓

50 Southover Street, BN2 9UE
4-11; 3-midnight Fri; 12-midnight Sat; 12-11 Sun
☎ (01273) 601413
Fuller's Discovery, London Pride; Gale's HSB; guest beers Ⓗ
A convivial atmosphere is assured when you visit this traditional corner local situated in the Hanover district of the city. Inside, the walls are adorned with items relating to Admiral Sir Charles Napier, period photographs and old plans of the local area. A very popular pub quiz is held every Sunday, with occasional themed events, such as Beaujolais Nouveau day. Good value Sunday lunches are available. The secluded walled garden is popular in warmer weather. Q (37)

Burwash

Rose & Crown ✓

Ham Lane, TN19 7ER (signed from High Street)
11-3, 5-11; 11-11 Sat; 11.30-11 Sun
☎ (01435) 882600 🌐 roseandcrownburwash.co.uk
Harveys Hadlow Bitter, Sussex Best Bitter, Armada Ale, seasonal beers Ⓗ
A 15th-century village local with an exposed well at the main entrance. The single large bar has timber beams and an inglenook fireplace, and is decorated with sheet music, instruments and hop bines. Food ranges from bar snacks to à la carte meals in the bar or restaurant, and is available at all sessions except Sunday evenings between October and March. The smoking area is covered and heated. Q

Burwash Weald

Wheel Inn

Heathfield Road, TN19 7LA (on A265)
12-11 (10 Sun)
☎ (01435) 882758
Harveys Sussex Best Bitter; guest beers Ⓗ
A popular village pub with a light, airy and spacious feel inside and a large garden outside, with a climbing frame for children. The main bar features an inglenook fireplace and there is a separate games room and restaurant, the latter serving full meals and snacks, with a Sunday lunchtime carvery. Regular evening events include live music, curry, games and quiz nights. The smoking area is covered. P

Colemans Hatch

Hatch Inn

TN7 4EJ (400m S of B2110)

11.30-2.30, 5.30-11; 12-10.30 Sun

(01342) 822363 hatchinn.co.uk

Harveys Sussex Best Bitter; Larkins Traditional; guest beers

Originally three 15th-century cottages, this building has been an inn for the last 200 years. An attractive low-beamed pub, it is extremely popular with visitors to the nearby Ashdown Forest. Meals are much in demand and the dining area is frequently full, so early arrival or advanced booking is recommended. A rare outlet in Sussex for the excellent Larkins ale. No meals are served on Monday evening.

Crowborough

Coopers Arms

Coopers Lane, TN6 1SN (follow St John's Rd from Crowborough Cross)

12-2.30, 6 (5 Fri)-11; 12-10.30 Sun

(01892) 654796

Greene King IPA; guest beers

A free house well worth visiting for its ever changing range of beers, including many from Sussex breweries. Beer festivals are held at Easter, the August bank holiday and the end of November, supplemented by some themed weekends. The simply-furnished interior includes a main bar, an alcove with a dartboard and TV, and a separate dining room. Food is served lunchtimes, and Wednesday to Saturday evenings. Thursday is quiz night. Petanque is played. QP

Wheatsheaf

Mount Pleasant, Jarvis Brook, TN6 2NF

12-11 (10.30 Sun)

(01892) 663756 wheatsheafcrowborough.co.uk

Harveys XX Mild, Hadlow Bitter, Sussex Best Bitter, Armada Ale, seasonal beers

Dating from 1750, this pub has the feel of a friendly village local, with three separate drinking areas, each with open fires, served from a central bar. The full range of Harveys regular and seasonal beers is available. Beer festivals at the end of May and October concentrate mainly on ales from micro-breweries. Live music is performed twice a month. Lunches are served daily except Sunday and evenings meals Tuesday to Thursday only. P

Danehill

Coach & Horses

Coach and Horses Lane, RH17 7JF (off A275)

12-3 (4 Sat), 6-11; 12-4, 6-10.30 Sun

(01825) 740369

Harveys Sussex Best Bitter; guest beers

This rural two-bar free house boasts an award-winning restaurant. The large front garden has a children's play area, but the rear patio is for adults only. The guest beers change regularly and sometimes include some unusual ales. The pub is convenient for Ashdown Forest, Sheffield Park Gardens and the Bluebell Railway. No food is available on Sunday evening. Q(270)P

East Hoathly

Kings Head

1 High Street, BN8 6DR

11-11 (midnight Fri & Sat); 12-4, 7-11 Sun

(01825) 840238

1648 Original, Signature, seasonal beers; Harveys Sussex Best Bitter

A 17th-century pub situated in the centre of the village offering a range of beers from the 1648 Brewery next door. Good food from an extensive menu is served lunchtimes and evenings, with the U-shaped bar accommodating both diners and drinkers. A room at the side serves as a family room, while a small walled garden is available for smokers. QP

Eastbourne

Dewdrop Inn

37-39 South Street, BN21 4UP (E of town hall)

11 (12 Sun)-midnight (1am Fri & Sat)

(01323) 723313

Greene King IPA, H&H Olde Trip; guest beers

Situated in the 'Little Chelsea' area of Eastbourne, convenient for the Saffrons cricket and football grounds, the pub is popular with drinkers of all ages. One central bar serves the horseshoe-shaped drinking area which is split into two, with furnishings ranging from wooden chairs and tables to sofas. There is a small garden outside. Food is available 12-6pm and there is occasional live music.

Hurst Arms

76 Willingdon Road, BN21 1TW (on A2270)

11-11; 12-10.30 Sun

(01323) 721762

Harveys Sussex Best Bitter, Armada Ale, seasonal beers

Friendly Victorian local with two bars, a quiet homely lounge and a lively public bar; the latter has a pool table, darts, a jukebox and widescreen TV. There is a quiet rear garden and a front patio by the road. Harveys beers are served to an unfailingly high standard. Last year the pub held its first beer festival, which is to become a regular event.

Lamb

36 High Street, BN21 1HH (on A259 in Old Town)

10.30-11 (midnight Fri & Sat)

(01323) 720545

Harveys Hadlow Bitter, Sussex Best Bitter, Armada Ale, seasonal beers

This pub in the Old Town dates back to the 12th or 13th centuries – the exact date is unknown. Both the interior and exterior are wonderfully antique, although a recent fire destroyed the rear top section of the building. However, a sympathetic restoration has included the addition of a function room and B&B facilities. The three bars remain unchanged. A folk club and Sussex Story Tellers meet here on a regular basis. Q

Terminus Hotel

153 Terminus Road, BN21 3NU

10-midnight (1am Fri & Sat)

(01323) 733964

Harveys XX Mild, Hadlow Bitter, Sussex Best Bitter, Armada Ale, seasonal beers ⊞
The Terminus makes a well-deserved return to the Guide. The Victorian building is situated in a pedestrian area with tables and chairs set out in front. There is a conservatory-style extension at the side for dining and drinking. Inside, the single bar benefits from natural light from front windows and a large skylight. The restaurant area is to the rear. Upstairs is a pool lounge and function room. No meals are served in the evening. Wi-Fi Internet access is available. ❀◐♿⇌🚌⚊

Victoria Hotel ✔

27 Latimer Road, BN22 7BU (behind TAVR Centre, off A259)
⏲ 11-11 (1am Fri & Sat); 12-10.30 Sun
☎ (01323) 722673 🌐 victoriaeastbourne.co.uk
Harveys Sussex Best Bitter, Armada Ale, seasonal beers ⊞
Traditional family-run local situated close to the seafront and the Redoubt fortress. The large front bar has a homely feel, decorated with prints of old Eastbourne, while the smaller back room has pool and toad in the hole tables, a dartboard and TV. There is a secluded rear garden that hosts a beer festival over the Easter weekend. Good value pub food is served Thursday to Sunday, lunchtimes and evenings. ❀⇆◐🚌♣⚊

Glynde

Trevor Arms ✔

The Street, BN8 6SS (over bridge from station)
⏲ 11 (11.30 Sun)-11
☎ (01273) 858208
Harveys Sussex Best Bitter, seasonal beers ⊞
Popular village pub with four separate rooms located close to Glynde railway station. This establishment is a Harveys tied house and serves good quality, value food Monday to Saturday lunchtimes and evenings, plus Sunday lunch. Vintage car owners gather at the pub bi-monthly and the local area is popular with walkers. Glyndebourne is close by and it is rumoured that impromptu music performed by musicians from the Opera House may be heard in the extensive garden on Sundays during the summer.
Q❀◐⊟⇌🚌(125)♣P⚊

Hailsham

Grenadier ✔

High Street, BN27 1AS
⏲ 11-11 (11.30 Fri & Sat); 12-11 Sun
☎ (01323) 842152 🌐 thegrenny.com
Harveys XX Mild, Hadlow Bitter, Sussex Best Bitter, seasonal beers ⊞
Around 200 years old, this pub was used by the Grenadier Guards as a drinking house. Traditional pub games, darts, shove ha'penny, toad in the hole and table skittles are played in the public bar, while the comfortable lounge bar is quieter. There is a children's play area situated in the garden and at weekends the hostelry is family oriented. The pub raises money for guide dogs and there are photographs of some of them displayed in both bars. Dogs are welcome. ❀◐⊟♿🚌♣P⚊

Hartfield

Anchor

Church Street, TN7 4AG
⏲ 11-11; 12-10.30 Sun
Harveys Sussex Best Bitter; Larkins Traditional; guest beers ⊞
A basic village local dating from the 14th century with two bars and a restaurant. Situated in the centre of the historic village of Hartfield – famous for A A Milne's Pooh Bridge – it is an ideal base for exploring the attractions of Ashdown Forest. Q❀⇆◐◑🚌P

Hastings

First In Last Out

14-15 High Street, TN34 3ET (in Old Town, near Stables Theatre)
⏲ 12 (11 Sat)-11
☎ (01424) 425079 🌐 thefilo.co.uk
FILO Crofters, Cardinal, Ginger Tom; guest beers ⊞
Four beers are usually available here, the home of the FILO Brewery since 1985. Ginger Tom was awarded Best Sussex Micro Beer at the Eastbourne Beer Festival in 2007. The large bar is heated by an attractive open log fire in the centre, and has plenty of alcove seating. Organic, freshly cooked food is available Tuesday to Saturday lunchtimes. In the garden at the rear, beer festivals are held most bank holiday weekends. ♨Q❀◐🚌♣▯

White Rock Hotel

1-10 White Rock, TN34 1JU (on A259 opp pier)
⏲ 10 (12 Sun)-11
☎ (01424) 422240 🌐 thewhiterockhotel.co.uk
Beer range varies ⊞
The hotel bar, situated next door to the White Rock Theatre, serves up to four beers, all from independent Sussex breweries. A good range of freshly prepared food is available throughout the day. The large bar area has ample seating and a spacious outside terrace that overlooks the seafront. Q❀⇆◐◑⇌🚌●

Hove

Downsman

189 Hangleton Way, BN3 8ES (N of Hangleton)
⏲ 11 (11.30 Winter)-4, 6-11; 12-4, 7-11 Sun
☎ (01273) 711301
Harveys Sussex Best Bitter; guest beers ⊞
Friendly two-bar pub located at the northern edge of Hangleton, just a short walk from the South Downs via the Dyke Railway Trail. Two guest beers are normally available. The smart saloon bar is traditionally decorated with rural prints. Darts is played in the public bar. The piped music is not intrusive and there is an outdoor drinking area.
♨❀◐⊟🚌(5,16)♣P⚊

Neptune

10 Victoria Terrace, Kingsway, BN3 2WB
⏲ 12-1am (2am Fri & Sat); 12-midnight Sun
☎ (01273) 736390 🌐 theneptunelivemusicbar.co.uk
Dark Star Hophead; Greene King Abbot; Harveys Sussex Best Bitter, seasonal beers; guest beers ⊞
The Neptune is a free house offering five real ales from its handpumps. One of the oldest

pubs in Hove, it is situated about 200 metres from the seafront. The pub is a traditional local and attracts a slightly more mature customer. The interior walls of the single room are festooned with photos of blues singers and other artists. Live music is played on Friday and Saturday evenings, with blues and rock always popular. ≋⊟(20)

Icklesham

Queen's Head

Parsonage Lane, TN36 4BL (off A259, opp village hall)

⏲ 11-11; 12-10.30 Sun

☎ (01424) 814552 🌐 queenshead.com

Greene King IPA; guest beers ⊞

This award-winning Guide regular is always worth a visit. A busy pub all year round, it serves five to six beers of varied strengths and styles, combined with an interesting, affordable menu. It is host to a mini beer festival in the autumn and live music most Sundays. The interior is split into five areas, with three log fires in winter and an eclectic mix of decorations and memorabilia. A spacious garden offers great views towards Rye. ⛫❀◑⊟♣P⁵–⊽

Isfield

Laughing Fish ✔

Station Road, TN22 5XB (off A26 between Lewes and Uckfield)

⏲ 11.30-11

☎ (01825) 750349 🌐 laughingfishonline.co.uk

Greene King IPA, H&H Olde Trip, Morland Original; guest beers ⊞

Victorian village local situated next to the preserved Lavender Line Railway with a large, well-kept garden that includes a children's play area plus a heated, covered patio area for smokers. Good food is served (not Sun eve) with smaller portions available for senior citizens and children. A fish and chips takeaway service is also on offer Monday to Thursday. The pub runs numerous themed events and has popular bar games including darts and bar billiards.

⛫❀◑⊟♿⛺⊟(29)♣P⁵–

Lewes

Brewers Arms

91 High Street, BN7 1XN (near Lewes Castle)

⏲ 10-11; 12-10.30 Sun

☎ (01273) 475524 🌐 brewersarmslewes.co.uk

Harveys Sussex Best Bitter; guest beers ⊞

Family-run two-bar free house on the site of taverns that date back to the 17th century. The front bar features seven handpumps serving an ever-changing variety of ales and cider. On the walls are historic photographs of Lewes, the original 1906 building plans for the pub, and a list of licensees from 1744. The back bar features large-screen TVs for sports. Toad in the hole and darts are played. Food is available until 6.45pm every day and draught Biddenden cider is served. Free WiFi Internet access. Q❀◑⊟≋⊟(28,29)♣●⁵–

Dorset ✔

22 Malling Street, BN7 2RD

⏲ 11-11; 12-8 Sun

☎ (01273) 474823 🌐 thedorsetlewes.com

Harveys Hadlow Bitter, Sussex Best Bitter, Armada Ale, seasonal beers ⊞

Refurbished in 2006, this Harveys tied house has several drinking and dining areas, a large patio and six reasonably priced en-suite bedrooms. It serves at least four ales on handpump. An extensive menu features traditional home-cooked dishes and an ever-changing fish menu using ingredients fresh from Newhaven. It is home of the Cliffe Bonfire Society – the largest of the five Lewes bonfire societies. Closing times may vary in winter so it is advisable to check beforehand. ⛫❀⛾◑⊟♿⊟(28,29)●⁵–

Elephant & Castle

White Hill, BN7 2DJ (off Fisher St)

⏲ 11.30-11 (midnight Fri & Sat); 12-11 Sun

☎ (01273) 473797 🌐 elephantandcastlelewes.co.uk

Harveys Sussex Best Bitter; guest beers ⊞

This lively pub is popular with younger drinkers. Built in 1838 for the former Southdown and East Grinstead Brewery, the interior comprises a front area with wooden chairs and tables, a side room with a pool table, games machines and TV, and a small drinking area behind the central island bar. The walls are adorned with stuffed animal heads and other curiosities. Food is available lunchtimes and Tuesday to Thursday evenings. Weston's Old Rosie cider is served on tap.

⛫◑≋⊟(28,29)♣●⁵–

Gardener's Arms

46 Cliffe High Street, BN7 2AN

⏲ 11-11(11.30 Fri & Sat); 12-10.30 Sun

☎ (01273) 474808

Harveys Sussex Best Bitter; guest beers ⊞

A compact, genuine two-bar free house run by a football loving landlord, whose allegiances can be viewed in the Gents. Harveys Best is always stocked and guest beers come from small independent breweries. Black Rat cider is available via handpump. The pub's sporting teams include cricket, stoolball and the Sussex game of toad in the hole. Many community groups are also supported, including the Cliffe Bonfire Society. Lewes bus station is five minutes' walk away. ⊟(28,29)♣●

Lewes Arms ✔

1 Mount Place, BN7 1YH

⏲ 10 (11 Sun)-11 (midnight Fri & Sat)

☎ (01273) 473152

Greene King IPA, Abbot, seasonal beers; Harveys Sussex Best Bitter, seasonal beers ⊞

Historic, curved-fronted two-bar pub built into the castle ramparts and home of the World Pea-Throwing Championship. Greene King removed Harveys beers from the pub in 2007, but the locals mounted a successful media campaign which resulted in the reinstatement of Harveys Sussex Best and the appearance of Harveys' seasonal ales. Black Rat cider is stocked, together with Weston's. Toad in the hole can be played in the games room. Evening meals are served until 8.45pm. Mobile phones are banned.

⛫Q❀◑⊟≋⊟(28,29)♣●

Milton Street

Sussex Ox

BN26 5RL (signed off A27)
⏲ 11.30-3, 6-11; 12-3, 6-10.30 (12-5 winter) Sun
☎ (01323) 870840 🌐 thesussexox.co.uk
Dark Star range; Harveys Sussex Best Bitter; guest beers ⊞
Set in the hamlet of Milton Street at the foot of the South Downs, this pub has a small bar and intimate bar area, with the remainder of the space set for diners. There is also a separate restaurant. The large car park, often full, gives an indication of the popularity of the excellent food and ale served here.
♛Q❀◐◑P

Newhaven

Jolly Boatman

133-135 Lewes Road, BN9 9SJ (N of town centre)
⏲ 11-11 (midnight Fri & Sat); 11-10.30 Sun
☎ (01273) 510030
Fuller's London Pride; Harveys Sussex Best Bitter; guest beers ⊞
Genuine street-corner pub, a short walk from the town centre in Newhaven, the Sussex port town. The pub has a single bar on two levels, offering an ever-changing range of guest beers, focusing on local and independent brewers. Regular ales include Harveys Best and Fuller's London Pride. Real cider is available in the summer. Pub games include darts and crib. Dogs are welcome. Unusually, chocolates and sweets are sold from behind the bar. ♛⇌🚌(123)♣●⅃

Newick

Royal Oak

1 Church Road, BN8 4JU
⏲ 11-11 (10.30 Sun)
☎ (01825) 722506
Fuller's London Pride; Harveys Sussex Best Bitter ⊞
Situated on the edge of the green in the centre of the village, this weatherboarded pub has three distinct areas: a public bar, the main bar area with a lovely real fire in winter and, leading from it, a dining area. Two regular beers are occasionally supplemented by a guest beer and, in summer only, by Weston's Old Rosie cider. ♛❀◐◑⊟🚌(31,121)●P

Old Heathfield

Star

Church Street, TN21 9AH (next to church)
⏲ 11-3, 5.30-11; 11-11 Sat; 12-10.30 Sun
☎ (01435) 863570
Harveys Sussex Best Bitter; guest beers ⊞
This building dates from 1348 when it was built as a hostel for workers constructing the neighbouring church; it has been serving ale since 1388. Inside there are low beamed ceilings and an inglenook fireplace. The walls are decorated with tankards and miscellaneous country artefacts. Food is served lunchtimes and evenings Monday to Saturday, and Sunday lunchtime. There is an extensive garden. ♛Q❀◐◑⅄♣P⅃

Peacehaven

Telscombe Tavern

405 South Coast Road, BN10 7AD (on A259 between Rottingdean and Newhaven)
⏲ 11 (12 Sun)-1am
☎ (01273) 584674
Adnams Broadside; Greene King Old Speckled Hen; Harveys Sussex Best Bitter; guest beers ⊞
Gloriously situated on the cliff side of the coastal road, this two-bar pub has a restaurant at the rear which specialises in reasonably priced, fresh, locally-sourced food. Regular live music dating from the 1960s to more recent times attracts a mixed crowd of regulars. Karaoke and disco nights are also hosted. A popular quiz is held on Wednesday evening. Good, affordable accommodation makes this an excellent base for exploring the South Downs, or as a stopover for the Newhaven-Dieppe ferry. ❀⇌◐◑🚌(12,14)P⅃

Portslade

Stanley Arms

47 Wolsley Road, BN41 1SS
⏲ 3 (4 Mon)-11; 12-11 Sat; 12-10.30 Sun
☎ (01273) 430234 🌐 thestanley.com
Beer range varies ⊞
Street corner family-run local – a genuine free house serving ales from many different UK breweries on five handpumps, together with draught real cider and perry and an extensive selection of Belgian and British bottled beers. Beer festivals are held in spring, summer and autumn. Various hot and cold snacks such as pies and sausage rolls are available but no cooked meals. A large-screen TV shows sporting events and regular live music is hosted. Local CAMRA Branch Pub of the Year 1999-2003 and 2007-08. ❀⅄🚌(2,46A)●⅃▯

Rodmell

Abergavenny Arms

Newhaven Road, BN7 3EZ
⏲ 11-3, 5.30-11; 11-11 Sat; 12-11 Sun
☎ (01273) 472416 🌐 abergavennyarms.com
Beer range varies ⊞
The pub is situated in the small village of Rodmell which is famous for being the home of writer Virginia Woolf and her husband Leonard. A traditional inn, parts of which date from the Norman Conquest, it boasts an indoor well and oak beams from Spanish Armada shipwrecks. Good local food is freshly cooked to order. Located on the South Downs Way, this is an ideal stopping point for a refreshing pint of ale. There are plans to provide overnight accommodation.
♛❀◐◑⊟⅄🚌(123)P⅃

St Leonards

Bull

530 Bexhill Road, TN38 8AY (on A259, W of St Leonards)
⏲ 12-11 (10.30 Sun)
☎ (01424) 424984 🌐 the-bull-inn.com
Shepherd Neame Kent's Best, Master Brew Bitter, Spitfire, seasonal beers ⊞

Welcoming roadside pub noted for its range of Shepherd Neame Beers. Voted by the local Observer newspaper's readers as the best pub in the Hastings area in 2006 and 2007. It offers an excellent menu of home-cooked food. The large rear garden has barbecue facilities and a covered smoking area. The pub is convenient for the Glynde Gap shopping centre.
⛺Q❀◐♿⊟♣P⌐

Dripping Spring

34 Tower Road, TN37 6JE

11.30-11 (midnight Fri & Sat)

☎ (01424) 436222

Beer range varies Ⓗ

A friendly local two-bar pub tucked away in the Bohemia area of St Leonards, making a welcome return to this Guide. A choice of six beers of varying strengths and styles caters for all tastes. The Drip enjoys a loyal following and all are warmly welcomed by the new hosts. It can get very busy at times. A small garden at the back provides a smoking area and is a good suntrap in summer.
Q❀⊟⇌(Warrior Sq)⊟♣●⌐

Horse & Groom

4 Mercatoria, TN38 0EB

11-11; 12-10.30 Sun

☎ (01424) 420612 🌐 sussex200.com

Adnams Broadside; Greene King IPA; Harveys Sussex Best Bitter; guest beers Ⓗ

A first class free house, at the heart of Old St Leonards, serving a good range of beers. The unusual horseshoe-shaped bar forms two areas, with a quiet room at the rear. An adjoining restaurant is open Tuesday to Saturday evenings and Sunday lunchtime. The pub is a short walk from the sea and Warrior Square station. Q❀⇌(Warrior Sq)⌐

Salehurst

Halt

Church Lane, TN32 5PH (by church)

12-3, 6-11; 12-11 Fri-Sun; closed Mon

☎ (01580) 880620

Harveys Sussex Best Bitter; guest beers Ⓗ

Originally a steam railway stop on the Guinness hop-picking line, this historic, community-led free house was saved from redevelopment by two local families who now own and run it. The traditional single bar features an open fire, low beams, oak floors, wooden furniture and a comfortable snug, while the rear patio and beer garden afford superb views over the Rother Valley. The menu includes dishes made from locally reared meat. Live music plays on alternate Sundays from 4pm. Draught cider is often available. ⛺Q❀◐♣⌐

Seaford

Seven Sisters

Alfriston Road, BN25 3PY (N of A259 jct with Alfriston Rd)

11-11 (11.30 Fri & Sat); 12-3, 7-10.30 Sun

☎ (01323) 896548

Greene King IPA; Harveys Sussex Best Bitter; Shepherd Neame Spitfire Ⓗ

Unusual curved 1930s roadhouse pub set back from Alfriston Road, originally with a three-bar layout but since opened out. The interior features dark-stained timber-panelled walls and ceiling with Art Deco-style lampshades and panels above the bar, together with ceramic flying Guinness toucans in the lounge bar area. Lunches are served daily, evening meals Monday to Saturday. The smoking area is covered. ❀◐⊟(12)P⌐

Three Cups Corner

Three Cups Inn

TN21 9LR

12-11 (10.30 Sun)

☎ (01435) 830252

Dark Star Hophead; Harveys Sussex Best Bitter; guest beers Ⓗ

Dating from the 16th century, the pub once had connections with smugglers. It serves as a local for the village, while attracting plenty of visitors for its excellent food and beer. The ample interior with exposed beams and an inglenook fireplace is supplemented by large gardens to the front and rear. Shut the box and darts can be played, and ladies can enjoy half-price food on Mondays. ⛺❀◐♿♣P⌐

Uckfield

Alma ✔

65 Framfield Road, TN22 5AJ (on B2102)

11-3, 5-11; 12-3, 6-10.30 Sun

☎ (01825) 762232

Harveys XX Mild, Sussex Best Bitter, seasonal beers Ⓗ

Friendly two-bar pub, situated a five-minute walk from Uckfield town centre, railway station and buses. All Harveys seasonal beers are stocked, including Olympia in summer and the much-revered Old Ale in winter. Traditional pub games such as crib, darts, dominoes and shove ha'penny are played in the public bar. Live jazz sessions are hosted every third Saturday evening. Sunday roasts are very popular. No food is available on Tuesdays or Sunday and Monday evenings. Lunchtime opening hours may vary in winter. Real cider is stocked in summer.
Q❀◐⊟♿⇌⊟(318)♣●P⌐

Udimore

Kings Head

Rye Road, TN31 6BG (on B2089, W of village)

11-3.30 (not Mon), 6-11

☎ (01424) 882349

Harveys Sussex Best Bitter; guest beers Ⓗ

Built in 1535, then extended in the 17th century, this traditional village ale house features exposed beams, two open fires and a very long bar. The pub serves excellent home-cooked food (lunch Tue-Sun, eves Mon-Sat). Trevor and Anita have run this pub for 20 years and offer a warm, friendly welcome. Situated in an area of outstanding natural beauty, there are many scenic walks nearby, while pleasant views over the surrounding countryside unfold from the garden. ⛺Q⛄❀◐⊟♣P

Westfield

Old Courthouse

Main Road, TN35 4QE
⏲ 12-11 (10.30 Sun)
☎ (01424) 751603 🌐 oldcourthousepub.co.uk
Harveys Sussex Best Bitter; guest beers Ⓗ
This pub is central to the village and community focused. The main bar has an open fire and, be warned, a low ceiling. Traditional games including bar billiards are played here. There is also a second, smaller bar. Hot food is served all day, with a roast on Sunday lunchtime. The first Friday of the month is curry night. A mini beer festival is held over the August bank holiday weekend. CAMRA South East Sussex Pub of the Year 2007.
⛫Q❀◑◗⊟⊟♣P⊱

Willingdon

Red Lion ✔

99 Wish Hill, BN20 9HQ (S end of village)
⏲ 11-3, 5-11; 11-midnight Fri & Sat; 12-11 Sun
☎ (01323) 502062
Badger K&B Sussex, First Gold, Tanglefoot, seasonal beers Ⓗ
Friendly village community pub, popular with locals and walkers, situated close to Butts Brow and the South Downs. The larger front bar has wood panelling and two brick fireplaces, plus a bar billiards table and a dartboard. There is a dining area to the rear which has access to the much used split-level garden. Good quality home-cooked food is on offer. Quiz night is Wednesday and an annual beer festival takes place over the August bank holiday weekend. ❀◑◗⊟♣P

Wilmington

Giant's Rest

The Street, BN26 5SQ (off A27)
⏲ 11-3, 6-11; 11.30-11 Sat; 12-10.30 Sun
☎ (01323) 870207 🌐 giantsrest.co.uk
Harveys Sussex Best Bitter, Armada Ale; Hop Back Summer Lightning; Taylor Landlord Ⓗ
A short walk from the Long Man, a chalk figure cut into the Downs and Wilmington Priory, this Victorian building has outside seating to the front and a patio to the rear, overlooking farmland and the Downs. The interior is modern, airy and mainly of wood. A varied menu features much local produce. Morris men visit at least once a year, when they dance at the foot of the Long Man. B&B accommodation is available in two rooms.
⛫❀⊭◑◗♿⊟P

Withyham

Dorset Arms ✔

TN7 4BD (on B2110)
⏲ 11.30-3 (not Mon), 6-11; 12-3, 7-10.30 Sun
☎ (01892) 770278 🌐 dorset-arms.co.uk
Harveys Hadlow Bitter, Sussex Best Bitter, seasonal beers Ⓗ
This busy, attractive pub, set back from the B2110, is a 15th-century listed building with oak floors and a separate restaurant. A wide-ranging menu of home-cooked food is available except on Sunday and Monday evenings. Early arrival or advanced booking is advisable for those seeking meals. Extremely popular with walkers, dogs are welcome in the bar. ⛫⛟❀◑◗⊟(291)P

SUSSEX (WEST)

Arundel

King's Arms

36 Tarrant Street, BN18 9DN
⏲ 11-11; 12-10.30 Sun
☎ (01903) 882312 🌐 tinyurl.com/2axe8p
Fuller's London Pride; Young's Bitter; guest beers Ⓗ
Arundel's only remaining free house, popular with locals and visitors alike, and believed to be over 500 years old. Situated on a corner just below the cathedral, it comprises a lounge bar with handpumps, a separate public bar with jukebox offering 70's rock music, a snug and heated rear patio area with awning. Guest beers often include Summer Lightning. No food is available at any time. Fines are levied for mobile phone usage and donated to the RNLI. A dog-friendly pub. ❀⊟⛺≋♣⊱

Ashurst

Fountain Inn

Horsham Road, BN44 3AP (on B2135)
⏲ 11.30-11; 12-10.30 Sun
☎ (01403) 710219 🌐 tinyurl.com/2h9er2
Harveys Sussex Best Bitter; guest beers Ⓗ
Fine 16th-century pub and restaurant based in a former farmhouse with many period features including a classic rural tap room, three wood-burning fires, flagstone floors and thick oak beams throughout. A large garden includes an orchard and a duck pond, with seating areas and tables plus a pontoon area to the side of the pond for dining. A traditional large brick and wooden barn serves as a skittle alley and function room. Summertime classic car events are hosted in the car park.
⛫Q❀◑◗⊟♣P⊱

Bepton

Country Inn

Severals Road, GU29 0LR (1 mile SW of Midhurst)
SU870206
⏲ 11.30-3, 5-midnight; 11.30-12.30am Fri & Sat; 12-midnight Sun
☎ (01730) 813466
Ballard's Midhurst Mild; Sharp's Doom Bar; Young's Bitter; guest beers Ⓗ
Popular local in a quiet spot serving a changing guest beer from a small local

INDEPENDENT BREWERIES

Arundel Ford
Ballard's Nyewood
Dark Star Ansty
Gribble Oving
Hammerpot Poling
Hepworth Horsham
King Horsham
Langham Lodsworth
Welton's Horsham

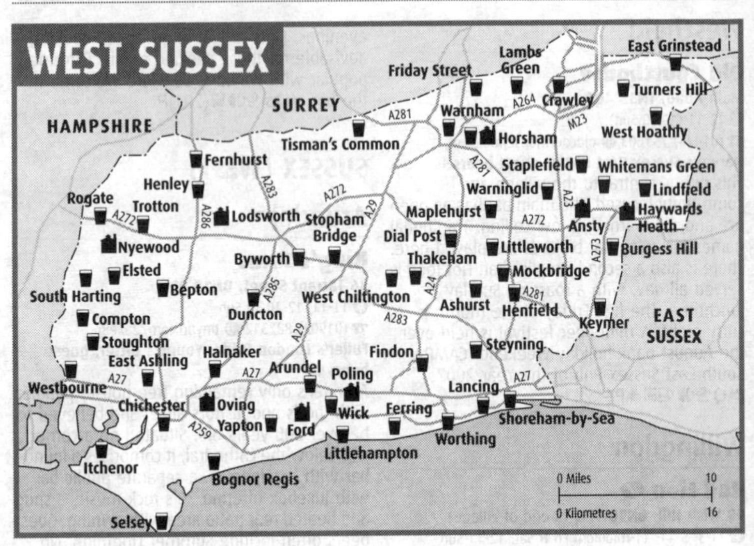

brewer, an easy walk down the lane from Midhurst and the stop for the bus from Chichester. A single bar serves two distinct drinking areas on one side, with a log fire opposite. The dining area enjoys a busy trade (not Sun eve). Outside at the front there are tables, while the extensive rear garden has children's play equipment. Closing may be later on busy nights. ⌂Q❀◐🚌(60)♣P⍀

Bognor Regis

Alex

56 London Road, PO21 1PU (150m SE of railway station)
⚙ 10-11 (midnight Fri & Sat); 12-5 Sun
☎ (01243) 863308
Courage Best Bitter; Greene King Old Speckled Hen; guest beers Ⓗ
Technically a one-bar pub, but the layout feels like two separate bars, with a small snug on the left and a main bar on the right, with a good-sized seating area and a ceiling covered with mugs and jugs. Beyond is a small, informal dining area. This traditional town local really came into its own with the smoking ban and now stocks a regularly-changing guest beer from an independent brewer. A rear patio includes a heated, covered smokers' shelter. Q❀◑≠🚌⍀

Burgess Hill

Watermill Inn

1 Leylands Road, RH15 0QF
⚙ 11(12 Sun)-11
☎ (01444) 235517
Fuller's London Pride; guest beers Ⓗ
Neighbourhood local in the World's End area of Burgess Hill, close to Wivelsfield Station. Guest beers are usually from an Isle of Wight brewer or another independent southern brewery. The pub is on the edge of some excellent countryside and pictures of rural scenes, some with a period flavour, reflect this. The hostelry also features a bar billiards table, a pleasant garden with an adjoining covered smoking area and a quiz night on Thursday. Snack meals are available.
⌂❀≠(Wivelsfield)🚌♣P⍀▯

Byworth

Black Horse

GU28 0HL (off A283, 1 mile SE of Petworth)
⚙ 11 (12 Sun)-11
☎ (01798) 342424 🌐 tinyurl.com/26ua65
Flowerpots Bitter; Fuller's London Pride; guest beers Ⓗ
Unspoilt 16th-century village pub with a friendly atmosphere. There are many cosy areas for diners, while the rustic front bar, with its enormous fireplace, is local and traditional. An old spiral staircase leads to the heavily timbered function room and games area. The distinctive large garden is steeply terraced and has good country views, while the two guest handpumps offer ever-changing beers, often from Sussex or Hampshire micro-breweries. ⌂Q❀◑◐⊟🚌(1)♣P

Chichester

Bell Inn

3 Broyle Road, PO19 6AT (opp Festival Theatre)
⚙ 11.30-3, 5-midnight; 12-3, 7-midnight Sun
☎ (01243) 783388
Adnams Bitter; guest beers Ⓗ
Cosy, comfortable city local whose ambience is enhanced by exposed brickwork, wooden panelling and beams. An extensive blackboard menu of traditional pub meals includes several vegetarian options (no food Sun eve). The two guest beers always include one from a local micro. At the back is a suntrap rear garden, with a smoking shelter heated by a coal stove. Q❀◑◐≠🚌(60)♣P⍀

Bull Inn

4-5 Market Road, PO19 1JW (opp Cattle Market car park)
⚙ 11-11; 12-10.30 Sun
☎ (01243) 839555
Beer range varies Ⓖ

Recently restored to its original name, this fine town pub is a welcome addition to the Guide. Dating back to the 18th century, the Bull was formed from two cottages and the adjoining house of the Cattle Market steward. It now comprises a single open-plan bar with beer served direct from the casks on stillage behind the counter, a small patio to the rear and a separate games room beyond that. The beers come from the Punch list, with local micros predominating. ♨❀◐◑≠⊟♣⊢

Eastgate Inn

4 The Hornet, PO19 7JG (500m E of Market Cross, off Eastgate Square)

⌚ 12 (11 Wed; 10 Sat)-11 (midnight Fri & Sat); 12-11 Sun

☎ (01243) 774877

Fuller's London Pride; Gale's Butser Bitter, HSB, seasonal beers Ⓗ

A fine town pub that featured in the first edition of this Guide in 1973. Dating from 1793, the bar is now open plan, with an area for diners. At the rear is a pool room and a patio garden. Good value traditional pub meals are served from the specials board at lunchtime and on summer evenings. Customers include locals, holidaymakers and visitors to the nearby market. A midsummer beer festival is hosted each year.
♨❀◐◑≠⊟♣⊢

Four Chesnuts

243 Oving Road, PO19 7EJ (900m E of Market Cross)

⌚ 12-11 (midnight Fri & Sat); 12-10.30 Sun

☎ (01243) 779974

Arundel Sussex Mild; Caledonian Deuchars IPA; Oakleaf Hole Hearted; guest beers Ⓗ

Traditional town hostelry and local CAMRA Pub of the Year 2007, the Chesnuts has been converted to a single bar but retains its distinct drinking areas. The skittle alley doubles as a dining room at busy times and occasionally serves as a venue for successful beer festivals. The menu of good hearty meals includes a 'pie of the moment' (no food Mon & Sun eve). The pub has a Saturday music night and hosts the local folk club on Tuesday plus a regular quiz night on Wednesday. Football and rugby matches are often shown on TV.
♨❀◐◑♿▲≠⊟♣P⊢

Compton

Coach & Horses

The Square, PO18 9HA (on B2146)

⌚ 11.30-3 (4 Sat), 6-11; 12-10.30 Sun

☎ (023) 9263 1228

Dark Star Hophead; Fuller's ESB; guest beers Ⓗ

This 16th-century pub lies in a remote but charming village, close to lovely local walks. The front bar is warm and welcoming, with two open fires and internal window shutters. The rear bar is a restaurant (reservation required) – this is the oldest part of the pub and features plenty of exposed beams and another open fire. Up to five guest beers from independent breweries are usually available. There is a bar billiards table. Food is served Tuesday to Saturday. ♨Q❀◐◑⊟(54)♣

Crawley

Swan ✔

1 Horsham Road, West Green, RH11 7AY

⌚ 12-11 (1am Fri & Sat)

☎ (01293) 527447

Flowers Original; Fuller's London Pride; guest beers Ⓗ

Welcoming local on the edge of the town centre which has appeared in this Guide many times over the years. The pub dates back to the coming of the nearby railway in 1848. The public bar has a ceiling decorated with film posters, and plays host to live music on Friday evening, while the saloon is much quieter. The owners offer a changing range of four guest ales. Evening meals are served 5-7pm. Weston's cider is available during summer months. ❀◑⊟≠⊟●

Dial Post

Crown Inn

Worthing Road, RH13 8NH (just off A24)

⌚ 11.30-3, 6-11; 12-4 Sun

☎ (01403) 710902 🌐 crowninndialpost.co.uk

Harveys Sussex Best Bitter; King Horsham Best Bitter; guest beers Ⓗ

Attractive old coaching inn set in the peaceful village of Dial Post, featuring wooden pillars and beams throughout, an open fire in the bar area and beers from local breweries, plus an organic lager from Hepworth's. There is a comfortable sun lounge at the front and a dining/function room at the lower level. The ingredients for the excellent menu are sourced locally where possible. On Sunday the pub closes at 4pm. ♨Q❀◐◑⊟♣P⊢

Duncton

Cricketers Arms

High Street, GU22 0LB

⌚ 11 (12 Sun)-11

☎ (01798) 342473 🌐 tinyurl.com/2bm4lv

King Horsham Best Bitter; Skinners Betty Stogs; guest beers Ⓗ

This listed 16th-century coaching inn, featuring a large inglenook and wooden panelling, was the last stop for the horses before Duncton Hill, on the London to Chichester route. The pub has recently been renovated by the new owner and has strong links with cricket. It was purchased by WG Grace for the famous Victorian cricketer James Dean, and features appropriate memorabilia. Guest ales and food ingredients are sourced locally, with the field mushroom stack particularly recommended. ♨Q❀◐◑●P

East Ashling

Horse & Groom

PO18 9AX (On B2178)

⌚ 12-3, 6-11; 12-6 Sun

☎ (01243) 575339

🌐 thehorseandgroomchichester.co.uk

Dark Star Hophead; Harveys Hadlow Bitter; Hop Back Summer Lightning; Young's Bitter Ⓗ

This welcoming 17th-century inn features flagstones, old settles and half-panelled walls, with heating in the bar provided by an open fire and a fine old range. The pub has been improved but not spoilt, and attracts drinkers and diners in equal measure. The beers benefit from a deep cellar under the handpumps. A comfortable restaurant offers a diverse, high-quality menu of home-cooked dishes, all sourced locally (not Sun eve). Accommodation is en-suite, some in a converted 17th-century oak-beamed flint barn. ♔Q❀⊭◐◑♿⛺⊟(54)♣P⁴–

East Grinstead

Old Mill ✔

Dunnings Road, RH19 4AT (half mile from town centre on road to West Hoathly)
⊙ 11-11 (midnight Sat)
☎ (01342) 326341 ⊕ theolddunningsmill.co.uk
Harveys Hadlow Bitter, Sussex Best Bitter, seasonal beers Ⓗ
Formerly the Dunnings Mill, the interior of the pub has been divided into several areas, with a drinking space away from the dining area. Harveys seasonal ales are usually available. A wide-ranging menu features traditional pub food. Children are welcome in the pub and dog owners may bring their dogs into the drinking area. The old 16th-century water wheel has been restored to working order. Food is served all day. ♔Q❀◐◑♿⊟P⁴–

Elsted

Three Horseshoes

GU29 0JY (E end of village)
⊙ 11-2.30, 6-11; 12-3, 7-10.30 Sun
☎ (01730) 825746
Ballard's Best Bitter; Bowman Swift One; Fuller's London Pride; Taylor Landlord; guest beers Ⓗ
Former drovers' inn, ideal for cosy winter evenings with its small, low beamed rooms and open fires, or in summer enjoy the views of the Downs from the large garden. It serves as the village local, with one room exclusively for dining, but often food is served in all four rooms because of the popularity of the meals. A good range of home-cooked traditional country food is always available, with game a speciality. ♔Q❀◐◑⊟P

Fernhurst

Red Lion ✔

The Green, GU27 3HY (N end of village green)
⊙ 11.30-3, 5-11; 11.30-11 Thu-Sat; 11.30-10.30 Sun
☎ (01428) 643112
Fuller's Chiswick, London Pride, ESB, seasonal beers Ⓗ
Idyllically set by the village green, the Red Lion has been a pub since 1592. Inside is a single bar with a low, timbered ceiling and two side rooms, plus a splendid inglenook fireplace with a large wood-burning stove. In fine weather, customers can sit overlooking the green at the front, or in the large rear garden where the covered, heated and lit smokers' shelter is situated. The pub is popular with both locals and diners.
♔Q☋❀◐◑⊟(70,71)♣P⁴–

Ferring

Henty Arms ✔

2 Ferring Lane, BN12 6QY (N of level crossing)
⊙ 11 (12 Sun)-11 (midnight Fri & Sat)
☎ (01903) 241254 ⊕ tinyurl.com/29mg64
Black Sheep Best Bitter; Caledonian Deuchars IPA; Fuller's London Pride; Young's Bitter; guest beers Ⓗ
Friendly community pub with a comfortable quiet lounge decorated with old local photographs and a collection of miniature bottles. A lower dining area serves popular good-value food (all day Sat & Sun). Breakfasts are also available. The livelier public bar with games room has a shuffleboard and shove-ha'penny is played. A beer festival is held in July, which coincides with Worthing Seafront Fair.
♔Q❀◐◑⊞⊟(700)♣P⁴–

Findon

Snooty Fox

High Street, BN14 0TA (just S of village centre)
⊙ 12-2.30, 6.30-11; 12-10.30 Sun
☎ (01903) 872733 ⊕ findonmanor.com
Fuller's London Pride; Greene King Abbot; Harveys Sussex Best Bitter; Skinner's Betty Stogs; guest beers Ⓗ
Originally a rectory, this building dates back to the 16th century and is now the public bar for the Findon Manor Hotel. The bar food is well worth trying, particularly the appetising daily specials. The pub is very child-friendly, with a log fire during winter months and an attractive area outside for summer months. An excellent base or stop-off point for walkers, with easy access to the South Downs.
♔Q❀⊭◐◑⊟(1)P⁴–

Friday Street

Royal Oak

RH12 4QA (on Rusper to Capel road, signed down side road) TQ183367
⊙ 11-3, 5-11; 11-11 Sat; 12-9 Sun
☎ (01293) 871393
Dark Star Best; Oakleaf I Can't Believe It's Not Bitter; Surrey Hill Ranmore Ale; guest beers Ⓗ
Free house gem attracting locals and visitors from further afield who are in the know. Seven handpumps dispense an ever-changing range of guest ales, mainly from local micro-breweries, together with Thatchers Medium Cheddar Valley cider, plus another in summer. Community events include a pantomime horse race and special food nights featuring home-cooked food made with local ingredients. The 'shed' at the end of the pub has been refurbished to provide additional space for drinkers and diners. WiFi available. CAMRA Sussex Pub of the Year 2008.
♔◐◑♣●P

Halnaker

Anglesey Arms

Stane Street, PO18 0NQ (on A285)
⊙ 11-3, 5.30-11.30; 11-11 Sat; 12-10.30 Sun
☎ (01243) 773474 ⊕ angleseyarms.co.uk
Adnams Bitter; Young's Bitter; guest beers Ⓗ

Family-run listed Georgian pub with a wooden and flagstone-floored public bar, complete with roaring fire, plus a comfortable restaurant renowned for good food using local seasonal produce (reservations essential). Steak and fresh fish are specialities. Two hoppy CIBA guest beers and Old Rosie cider are usually available, along with several Belgian beers. Cribbage, darts and cricket are played by pub teams. A two-acre rear garden and numerous flowering baskets make this a pub not to be missed. Camping is on-site (book ahead). ⛫Q❀◑♿⛺🚌(55,99)♣●P⚟

Henfield

Plough Inn

High Street, BN5 9HP
⏲ 11-11 (midnight Fri & Sat); 12-11 Sun
☎ (01273) 492280
Fuller's London Pride; Greene King Old Speckled Hen; Harveys Sussex Best Bitter; guest beers Ⓗ
A busy pub in the centre of the village, the Plough was extensively refurbished in the 1970s and has a comfortable single-bar layout with a separate restaurant area leading to a patio at the rear. An old photograph shows the pub as a Tamplins house, serving beer from the wood. The restaurant menu offers a good selection of food with home-made tapas a speciality. Occasional live music is hosted. ⛫❀◑🚌(17,100)♣⚟

Henley

Duke of Cumberland Arms

Henley Village, GU27 3HQ (off A286, 3 miles N of Midhurst) SU894258
⏲ 12-3 (11 Fri & Sat); 12-10.30 Sun
☎ (01428) 652280
Adnams Broadside; Harveys Sussex Best Bitter; guest beers Ⓖ
Stunning 15th-century inn nestling against the hillside and set in three and a half acres of terraced gardens with extensive views. Often threatened with redevelopment, it was rescued in 2007 by a band of locals who have vowed it will not be spoilt. The single bar has scrubbed-top tables and benches plus a log fire at both ends. You can find your own dinner swimming in the trout ponds at the front. Real outside toilets and a smokers' shelter with its own woodburner are features of this rural gem. Up to two guest beers come from local micros, notably Langham. ⛫Q❀◑🚌(70)♣P⚟

Horsham

Beer Essentials

30A East Street, RH12 1HL
⏲ 10-6 (7 Fri & Sat); closed Sun & Mon
☎ (01403) 218890 🌐 thebeeressentials.co.uk
Arundel Gold; Dark Star Festival; guest beers Ⓖ
Specialist beer shop with an extensive range of more than 150 ever-changing bottled beers, plus a constantly changing selection of six locally sourced beers drawn straight from the barrel. Bottles include fruit beers, porters and stouts from around the UK, as well as a range of foreign beers. JB Medium cider is always stocked, along with a range of bottled ciders and lagers. Minipins and polypins are available. The proprietor runs a popular autumn beer festival in a local hall. ●

Black Jug

31 North Street, RH12 1RJ
⏲ 12-11 (midnight Fri & Sat); 12-10.30 Sun
☎ (01403) 253526 🌐 blackjug-horsham.co.uk
Greene King IPA; Harveys Sussex Best Bitter; guest beers Ⓗ
Bustling town-centre pub with friendly and efficient staff. A large conservatory leads to an outdoor seating area, while in winter real fires and book-lined walls impart a cosy feel. The pub has an excellent reputation for its food, much of it locally sourced. Meals are served all day until 9.30pm. The house beer is brewed by Welton, who are based in the town. Cask-conditioned cider is available. The Jug is a good meeting place for the nearby arts centre. ⛫Q❀◑⇌🚌●⚟

Foresters Arms

43 St Leonards Road, RH13 6EH
⏲ 12-3 (not Mon), 6-11; 12-11.30 Fri & Sat; 12-10.30 Sun
☎ (01403) 254458
Harveys Sussex Best Bitter; Wells Bombardier; Young's Bitter Ⓗ
Welcoming pub in a residential side street with a good community feel and the emphasis firmly placed on conversation and beer. A real fire adds a cosy touch during winter months. The pub is handily placed for the local recreation ground and its garden incorporates a boules court. No food is available on Monday or Sunday evening. A little way from the town centre, this genuine local is well worth seeking out. ⛫Q❀◑♿⚟

Malt Shovel

15 Springfield Road, RH12 2PG
⏲ 11-11 (midnight Fri & Sat); 12-11 Sun
☎ (01403) 254543 🌐 maltshovel.com
Harveys Sussex Best Bitter; Taylor Landlord; Ⓗ **guest beers** Ⓗ/Ⓖ
This town-centre pub stocks up to 13 real ales at a time, some on gravity. These comprise an ever-changing range of guest ales, often including at least one from Hepworth. Live sport is shown on wide-screen TVs and the pub hosts regular live music evenings. Dogs are welcome. ⛫❀◑♿⇌🚌♣P⚟

Itchenor

Ship Inn

The Street, PO20 7AH (100m from harbour)
⏲ 11-11; 12-10.30 Sun
☎ (01243) 512284 🌐 theshipinn.biz
Ballard's Best Bitter; Itchen Valley Godfathers; King Horsham Best Bitter; Ringwood Fortyniner Ⓗ
Attractive 1930s-built pub in the main street of the village, leading down to the picturesque Chichester Harbour. The homely wood-panelled bars decorated with yachting memorabilia add to its character, and the wide front patio is a sun-trap in summer. Two rooms are dedicated to dining, offering a wide range of traditional meals, often including locally-landed fish. Up to four beers from the smaller local breweries are normally available,

with session beers competitively priced.
Q❀⊕♣P

Keymer

Greyhound Inn

Keymer Road, BN6 8QT (1 mile E of Hassocks station on B2116)
11-midnight; 12-10.30 Sun
☎ (01273) 842645
Adnams Bitter; Fuller's London Pride; Harveys Sussex Best Bitter; guest beers Ⓗ
Situated opposite the village church, this is a comfortably furnished old pub with laid-back service and wood-panelled decor. Bar billiards can be played in the small public bar. A large collection of ceramic beer and beverage mugs hangs from the low beams in the saloon and dining area – the latter is tucked away behind the inglenook. Guest beers tend to come from regional breweries. No food is served Monday evening. Q❀⊕(33,C2)♣P

Lamb's Green

Lamb Inn

RH12 4RG (2 miles N of A264)
11.30-3, 7-10.30
☎ (01293) 871336 thelambinn.info
Beer range varies Ⓗ
Until autumn 2007 this was WJ King's only tied house. Now a free house, rotating guest ales abound, though King's beers are normally present, along with other Sussex brewers. This is a delightful country pub where visitors are surrounded by oak beams and cosy nooks, and a real log fire adds to the timeless atmosphere in winter. Home-cooked food is available daily, and a large conservatory provides an extension to the dining area. ❀●P

Lancing

Crabtree Inn

140 Crabtree Lane, BN15 9NQ (W end of lane)
12-11 (11.30 Fri & Sat)
☎ (01903) 755514
Fuller's London Pride; guest beers Ⓗ
A 1930s red-brick community local of traditional Kemptown House design, offering three rotating guest beers. The large public bar hosts darts and pool teams; sporting prints are displayed on the part-panelled walls, while comfortable Chesterfield sofas are placed near the window. The smaller lounge bar has an attractive cupola and framed prints adorn the walls. A traditional Sunday carvery is popular (no food Mon). The garden is child and dog friendly with a heated and covered smoking area. Q❀⇌♣P

Lindfield

Red Lion ✔

High Street, RH16 2HL
11-11 (midnight Thu-Sat); 12-11 Sun
☎ (01444) 487000
Fuller's London Pride; Harveys Sussex Best Bitter; guest beers Ⓗ
Situated in the historic High Street, the pub has a wealth of interesting features including mathematical tiles on the bay windows, an unusual raised bench facing the bar, panelled rooms and a reconstructed Horse Gin House in the large garden. The pub started life as a coaching inn in 1720; the original Red Lion stands next door. An extensive, value for money food menu is on offer lunchtimes and 12-8pm Sunday. A family room is available and the toilets have disabled facilities. The smoking area is covered.
Q❀♿(82)♣

Stand Up Inn

47 High Street, RH16 2HN
11.30-11.30 (midnight Fri & Sat); 12-11.30 Sun
☎ (01444) 482995
Dark Star Hophead, Best, seasonal beers; guest beers Ⓗ
Situated at the heart of this picturesque village, the inn was originally the brewery tap for the long-gone Durrents Brewery, whose original buildings still stand at the rear of the pub. In the early days there were no seats here – hence the name. Thankfully, times have changed. An extensive range of Dark Star and guest beers are on offer, together with ciders, a perry and continental beers. Pasties are available at lunchtime.
Q❀(82)♣●

Littlehampton

New Inn

5 Norfolk Road, BN17 5PL (E end of esplanade)
11 (12 Sun)-11
☎ (01903) 713112
Arundel Gold; Courage Best Bitter; guest beers Ⓗ
Fifty yards from the eastern end of the esplanade, this two-bar corner pub is a popular local. A busy public bar features a large fireplace, pool table, dartboard and jukebox. The comfortable lounge has a real log fire and is the venue for live bands on Saturday evening and the popular open mic night, held on the second and fourth Tuesday of every month. Guest beers are often sourced locally. There is a covered and heated patio for smokers. ❀♿⇌(12)

Littleworth

Windmill

Littleworth Lane, RH13 8EJ (off A272 W of Cowfold)
11.30-3, 5.30 (6 Sat)-11; 12-3, 7-10.30 Sun
☎ (01403) 710308
Badger K&B Sussex, Tanglefoot, seasonal beers Ⓗ
Pleasant unspoilt village local where the landlord extends a warm welcome to one and all. The comfortable lounge has a large open fireplace and is adorned with an unusual collection of brass and china windmills, while the locals' bar has a very friendly feel. The building is of classic Sussex style, with a sun-trap garden area for hot summer days offering views of Sussex farmland. A wide choice of home-cooked food is served (no meals Sun eve). The smoking area is to the front.
Q❀♿♣P

Maplehurst

White Horse

Park Lane, RH13 6LL
12-2.30, 6-11; 12-3, 7-10.30 Sun
(01403) 891208
Harveys Sussex Best Bitter; Hogs Back HBB; Welton's Pride and Joy; guest beers H
Now in its 22nd year in the Guide, this delightful country pub never fails to impress. The roomy interior oozes character, with its imposing timber bar and many different drinking areas including a large conservatory opening onto an attractive garden. Food is served, but the emphasis is firmly on conversation. Numerous ales and real cider are on offer, often guests sourced from small independents. The landlord is a classic car enthusiast. Many times local CAMRA branch Pub of the Year, most recently in 2007.
Q P

Mockbridge

Bull Inn

London Road, BN5 9AD (on A281 1½ miles N of Henfield)
12-3 (3.30 Sat), 6-11; 12-10.30 Sun
(01273) 492232 thebullinnhenfield.co.uk
Fuller's London Pride; Harveys Sussex Best Bitter; guest beers H
The Bull is a pleasant, welcoming country pub with exposed brickwork in one bar and panelling throughout the remainder. The restaurant/bar area features a collection of hanging baskets. A separate function room with its own skittle alley is available for hire. Good food is served, with home-baked pizzas a speciality. The guest beer comes from the WJ King seasonal range. The large garden has a children's play area during the summer months and a baby-changing room is available. Q (17)P

Rogate

White Horse Inn

East Street, GU31 5EA (on A272)
11-3, 6-11.30 (midnight Fri); 11-midnight Sat; 12-10.30 Sun
(01730) 821333
Harveys Hadlow Bitter, Sussex Best Bitter, Armada Ale, seasonal beers H
Dating from the 16th century, this old coaching inn has oak beams, flagstone floors and a huge log fire. As a Harveys tied house, you can expect up to five of its beers, including seasonal brews. Half the pub is used for dining – a large range of meals includes steaks and vegetarian choices, plus specials on the blackboard (no food Sun eve). The car park overlooks the village sports field behind the pub. Q (91)P

Selsey

Seal

6 Hillfield Road, PO20 0JX (on B2145)
10.30-midnight (1am Sat); 12-midnight Sun
(01243) 602461 the-seal.com
Badger First Gold; Dark Star Hophead; Hop Back Summer Lightning; guest beers H
Spacious town free house with a restaurant area to the rear where home-cooked food and local fish can be enjoyed (booking required at busy times). Popular with locals and holidaymakers in summer, there are usually up to three guest beers from local micros on the pumps spread out around the central bar. Smokers have a large front patio with umbrellas and seating. Local CAMRA Pub of the Year 2008. (51)P

Shoreham-by-Sea

Buckingham Arms

35 Brunswick Road, BN43 5WA
11-11 (10.30 Sun)
(01273) 453660
Greene King XX Mild, Morland Original; Harveys Sussex Best Bitter; Hop Back Summer Lightning; Taylor Landlord; guest beers H
Smart new decking adorns the front of this real ale mecca near Shoreham station, where you can sit and watch the world – and the trains – go by. Eleven handpumps dispense the regular and ever-changing guest beers. The L-shaped bar has a loyal clientele and beer festivals are held each February and August. TV and occasional live music are offered. Keith, the landlord, is proud of his record sales of Harveys Tom Paine, which often exceed those of Harveys tied houses. (2,9)P

Duke of Wellington

368 Brighton Road, BN43 6RE (on A259)
12-11 (1am Fri & Sat)
(01273) 389818
Dark Star Hophead, seasonal beers; guest beers H
The Welly stands on the coast road and is easily recognised by the enormous Wellington boot sign hanging outside. Above the door is the mark of the defunct Kemp Town Brewery, while inside the porch is a stained glass window from the brewery, which stopped trading 50 years ago. The pub is operated by Dark Star Brewery and usually features three of its products plus a guest and a cider. Live music is often to be heard on Friday night.
(2,9)

Red Lion

Old Shoreham Road, BN43 5TE
12-11 (10.30 Sun)
(01273) 453171
Beer range varies H
This picture postcard 16th-century coaching inn is situated close to the busy A27 flyover but far enough away for traffic noise not to intrude. The main bar has a low-beamed ceiling and oozes traditional charm. Five handpumps dispense an ever-changing range of beers from family- and micro-breweries. The pub has an excellent reputation for home-cooked food, ranging from basic pub food to Á la carte. A regular beer festival is held over Easter. Q (2A)P

South Harting

Ship

North Lane, GU31 5PZ (at B2146 jct)
11 (12 Sun)-11

☎ (01730) 825302
Ballard's Nyewood Gold; Bowman Swift One; Dark Star Hophead; Palmer IPA; guest beers Ⓗ
Friendly 17th-century free house built using old ship's timbers. It has a small public bar and a larger lounge and restaurant where good-value meals are served (not Tue or Sun eves, Sept-Feb). Booking is recommended at weekends. An enclosed garden flanks the B2146. The guest beer is always from an independent or micro-brewery.
(54,91)P

Staplefield

Jolly Tanners
Handcross Road, RH17 6EF
11-3, 5.30-11; 11-11 Sat; 12-10.30 Sun
☎ (01444) 400335
Fuller's London Pride; Harveys Sussex Best Bitter; guest beers Ⓗ
Dating back to 1600, this former coaching inn and hotel is now an appealing free house opposite the village green. A good selection of home-cooked food attracts custom from far and wide. The beer range is good, with a mild available all year round. At the centre of village life, the pub is home to a number of clubs, including the Sussex Goon Preservation Society who meet here on the first Wednesday of every month. QP

Steyning

Chequer Inn ✔
41 High Street, BN44 3RE
10-11 (midnight Fri; 12.30am Sat)
☎ (01903) 814437 chequerinnsteyning.co.uk
Dark Star Best Bitter; Fuller's London Pride; Gales HSB; Taylor Landlord; guest beers Ⓗ
Historic 15th-century coaching inn with an impressive frontage. Many original interior features remain, including timber-framed architectural details. One small room contains a large painting of the High Street and local residents, who have all been identified. The pub also houses a collection of old documents and a 100-year-old snooker table. Guest ales and food ingredients are sourced locally. The famous breakfasts are served from 10am.
Q(2A)P

Stopham Bridge

White Hart
Stopham Road, RH20 1DS (off A283 1 mile W of Pulborough)
11.30-11; 12-10.30 Sun
☎ (01798) 873321 whitehartstophambridge.co.uk
Arundel Gold; Hogs Back TEA; King Horsham Best Bitter Ⓗ
This is a superb riverside pub next to the 14th-century Stopham Bridge over the River Arun. One bar with an open fire leads in each direction to a quaint and cosy room. A good selection of locally brewed beer is served. Meals are justifiably popular here, but food service does not dominate – the pub achieves the difficult balance between watering hole and eatery. The garden next to the river makes an idyllic setting on a sunny day.
QP

Stoughton

Hare & Hounds
PO18 9JQ (off B2146) SU802115
11-3, 6-11; 11-11 Fri, Sat & summer; 12-10.30 Sun
☎ (023) 9263 1433 hareandhoundspub.co.uk
Harveys Sussex Best Bitter; Itchen Valley Hampshire Rose; Taylor Landlord; guest beers Ⓗ
Traditional country pub in a beautiful downland valley – an ideal base for walking. A large dining room serves fresh local produce, while the public bar, warmed by an open fire, is the locals' choice. There are three open fires which, along with stone-flagged floors, beams and simple furniture, produce a wonderful atmosphere. Outside is a paved drinking area at the front and a garden at the back.
QP

Thakeham

White Lion Inn
The Street, RH20 3EP (500m from B2139)
11-11; 12-10.30 Sun
☎ (01798) 813141
Caledonian Deuchars IPA; Harveys Sussex Best Bitter; guest beers; Hogs Back TEA Ⓗ
Peaceful, welcoming 18th-century village pub with beams, old flooring, an ancient inn sign and distinctive areas including a dining room with a large fireplace in which joints of meat are smoked. There are historic passages below the pub, by which bootleggers came from the church. All food is home-cooked – the kitchen and ingredients can be viewed by the rear entrance. Q(74)P

Trotton

Keepers Arms
GU31 5ER (on A272, 3 miles W of Midhurst)
12-3, 6-11; 12-4.30, 7-10.30 Sun
☎ (01730) 810780 keepersarms.co.uk
Ballards Best Bitter; Dark Star Hophead; guest beers Ⓗ
Set high above the road and the River Rother, near Trotton Bridge, this 17th-century inn features low ceilings, bare wood floors and comfortable sofas surrounding an open log fire. Recent refurbishment has created smart dining areas to complement the adventurous menu, but the bar remains welcoming to drinkers. The elevated patio around two sides of the pub is popular in fine weather. The guest beer is usually from Bowman, Ringwood or King, while cider or perry is Weston's.
QP

Turners Hill

Red Lion ✔
Lion Lane, RH10 4NU (off North St, B2028)
11-3, 5-11; 11-11 Sat; 12-10.30 Sun
☎ (01342) 715416
Harveys XX Mild, Sussex Best Bitter, seasonal beers Ⓗ
Still very much the village local, a friendly welcome is assured at this split-level pub with an inglenook fireplace. Mild Ale is now available as a result of customer demand. Twice monthly quiz nights are held in aid of local charities. Occasional live music is played

in the garden during summer months. Wi-Fi Internet access is available. Children and dogs are welcome. ♕Q❀◑⊟♣P⚟

Warnham

Sussex Oak ✔

2 Church Street, RH12 3QW
✪ 11-11 (10.30 Sun)
☎ (01403) 265028 ⊕ thesussexoak.co.uk
Adnams Bitter; Fuller's London Pride; Taylor Landlord; Young's Bitter; guest beers Ⓗ
This large 16th-century pub welcomes locals and visitors alike. There is a range of rotating guest ales, often from local breweries, and a separate restaurant serves an extensive home-cooked menu which features local produce. The pub is gaining a reputation for its bank holiday beer festivals and both dogs and families are welcome. A large garden is popular with drinkers in the summer. The smoking area is heated.
♕ᘐ❀◑⊟♿⊟♣P⚟

Warninglid

Half Moon

The Street, RH17 5TR (on B2115 crossroads, 1 mile W of A23)
✪ 11.30-2.30, 5.30-11; 12-10.30 Sun
☎ (01444) 461227 ⊕ thehalfmoonwarninglid.co.uk
Harveys Sussex Best Bitter; Greene King Old Speckled Hen; Ringwood Best Bitter; Ⓗ **guest beers** Ⓗ/Ⓖ
A popular village pub, previously threatened with closure and redevelopment, but saved through public protest. The owners are developing a thriving food trade based on British menus, as well as offering a good range of well-kept cask ales; beer and food take equal billing. Once a year customers are invited to donate apples to the pub's own cider press for cider sold in aid of CHASE, the children's hospice charity. Children are not allowed inside the pub but dogs are permitted in the bar. The large garden is pleasant in summer. ♕Q❀◑⊟♿⊟P⚟

West Chiltington

Five Bells

Smock Alley, RH20 2QX (1 mile S of West Chiltington) TQ091170
✪ 12-3, 6-11; 12-3, 7-10.30 Sun
☎ (01798) 812143 ⊕ westchiltington.com/five_bells.htm
Arundel Sussex Mild; Harveys Sussex Best Bitter; Palmer Copper Ale; guest beers Ⓗ
West Chiltington's best-kept secret is this traditional, award-winning pub, serving an excellent choice of five good quality beers, including a mild, two guests and a premium, plus a local draught cider. Hearty appetites will appreciate fresh, home-cooked fare (not Sun or Mon eves). B&B accommodation is available in five double en-suite bedrooms. Dogs are warmly welcomed throughout. Local CAMRA Pub of the Year 2007 and 2008.
♕Q❀⇌◑♣●P

West Hoathly

Cat Inn

Queen's Square, RH19 4PP (opp church)
✪ 11.30-3, 6-11; closed Mon; 11-11 Sat; 11.30-3.30, 7-10.30 Sun
☎ (01342) 810369
Harveys Sussex Best Bitter; guest beers Ⓗ
This village free house attracts local trade as well as visitors from further afield. A network of cosy rooms, including one with a glass-covered well, is dominated by a real fire in the winter months. The pub is reputedly the oldest building in the village. A separate restaurant serves good quality, home-cooked food made with local produce. Harveys Old is a regular ale in winter and Hepworth's Organic Lager is supplied on keg. No children under 14 are allowed in the pub. ♕Q❀◑⊟P⚟

Westbourne

Cricketers

Commonside, PO10 8TA (N from The Square, turn E at Lashley's Garage) SU758082
✪ 5-11; 12-midnight Thu-Sat; 12-11 Sun
☎ (01243) 372647
Fuller's London Pride; Hop Back Crop Circle; Ringwood Fortyniner; 1648 Signature; Suthwyk Liberation Ⓗ
This 300-year-old pub is the only free house in a village of good pubs. Situated on the northern outskirts, it is hard to find but well worth the effort. Conversation abounds in the single L-shaped half-panelled bar. There is a sun-trap garden to the side, with a covered and heated smoking area. The beer range may vary between various Hants and Sussex micros. No food is served.
♕Q❀⊟(11,36)♣P⚟

Whitemans Green

Ship Inn

RH17 5BY (N of Cuckfield at B2115/B2036 jct)
✪ 12-2.30 (not Wed), 5.30-11; 12-11 Sat; 12-3 Sun
☎ (01444) 413219
Harveys Sussex Best Bitter; guest beers Ⓖ
Friendly single-bar village local with a separate games room and dining area. Handpumps are for decoration only – the four beers are served by gravity dispense from a cool room behind the bar. This free house is family run and has a comfortable interior with sofas next to the unusual double-sided open fire. Food is served lunchtimes (not Wed) and evenings (not Sun), with a changing range of specials in addition to the regular menu.
♕Q❀⇌◑⊟(271,272)P⚟

Wick

Dew Drop Inn

96 Wick Street, BN17 7JS (opp Wick Parade shops)
✪ 10.30-3, 5.30-11; 10.30-11 Sat; 10.30-10.30 Sun
☎ (01903) 716459 ⊕ tinyurl.com/2ea78z
Gale's Butser; Ringwood Best Bitter; guest beers Ⓗ
This unpretentious free house is situated just south of the A259, on the road into Littlehampton. The beer range changes with the seasons and local bottled beer is available.

A public bar is home to the bar billiards table and a collection of ceramic frogs, while the unspoilt comfortable lounge has possibly the shortest bar in the area, at only five foot one inch long. A warm welcome is assured at this classic pub. Q➢⇌(Littlehampton)🚌(700)♣

Worthing

George & Dragon

1 High Street, Tarring, BN14 7NN (bottom of Tarring High Street)
⏲ 11-11 (midnight Fri & Sat); 12-10.30 Sun
☎ (01903) 202497 🌐 tinyurl.com/28b8r3
Courage Directors; Greene King Abbot; Harveys Sussex Best Bitter; Hop Back Summer Lightning; Young's Bitter; guest beers Ⓗ
Busy neighbourhood pub in the centre of Tarring village. A low-beamed ceiling and warm lighting give the pub a welcoming atmosphere, while a small beer garden offers quiet refuge from the bustling bar areas. A new chef has recently taken over and the Sunday lunch menu is especially impressive and very reasonable. Sunday lunchtimes also host a weekly raffle. Two or three beer festivals are held throughout the year. The nearest station is West Worthing.
⛰☾⇌(West Worthing)🚌P

Selden Arms

41 Lyndhurst Road, BN11 2DB (near Worthing Hospital)
⏲ 11 (12 Sat)-11 (midnight Wed-Fri); 12-10.30 Sun
☎ (01903) 523361 🌐 tinyurl.com/25ozbv
Ringwood Best Bitter, Fortyniner; Dark Star Hophead; guest beers Ⓗ
This family-run free house was once a Brickwoods house and is reckoned to be one of the oldest pubs in Worthing. It is a must for real ale fans, with photos of old Worthing hostelries lining the walls. The Selden has six handpumps offering a wide choice of ales from small independent breweries, plus bottled Belgian beers. A beer festival is held during the last week in January. Dogs are welcome. Winner of CAMRA local branch Pub of the Year on numerous occasions. ⛰☾⇌🚌●

Swan Inn

79 High Street, BN11 1DN
⏲ 11-11 (midnight Fri & Sat); 12-11 Sun
☎ (01903) 232923
Greene King Abbot; Harveys Sussex Best Bitter; Shepherd Neame Spitfire; guest beers Ⓗ
This 19th-century oasis bears all the hallmarks of the archetypal village local: Sussex flint walls, beams, brasses and agricultural implements. One of its fireplaces is flanked by stained glass windows from the Kemp Town Brewery, each depicting a white swan. By day the pub attracts a blend of locals and shoppers, by night the atmosphere gets livelier. Attractions include a bar billiards table, quizzes during the week and entertainment on Friday, Saturday and Sunday nights.
⛰❀☾⇌

Yapton

Maypole Inn

Maypole Lane, BN18 0DP (off B2132, pedestrian access from Lake Lane) SU978042
⏲ 11.30-11 (midnight Fri & Sat); 12-11 Sun
☎ (01243) 551417
Arundel Sussex Mild; Bowman Swift One; Skinner's Betty Stogs; guest beers Ⓗ
This small flint-built inn is hidden well away from the village centre. Maypole Lane was cut off by the railway in 1846 and the pub has enjoyed its quiet isolation ever since. The cosy lounge boasts two open fires and an imposing row of seven handpumps, dispensing up to four constantly-changing guest beers from small breweries. The larger public bar has a jukebox, darts, pool and a TV for sports events. A skittle alley/function room can be booked. There is a covered verandah for smokers.
⛰Q❀☾◻🚌(66,66A)♣●P⁄–

Sussex Ox, Milton Street.

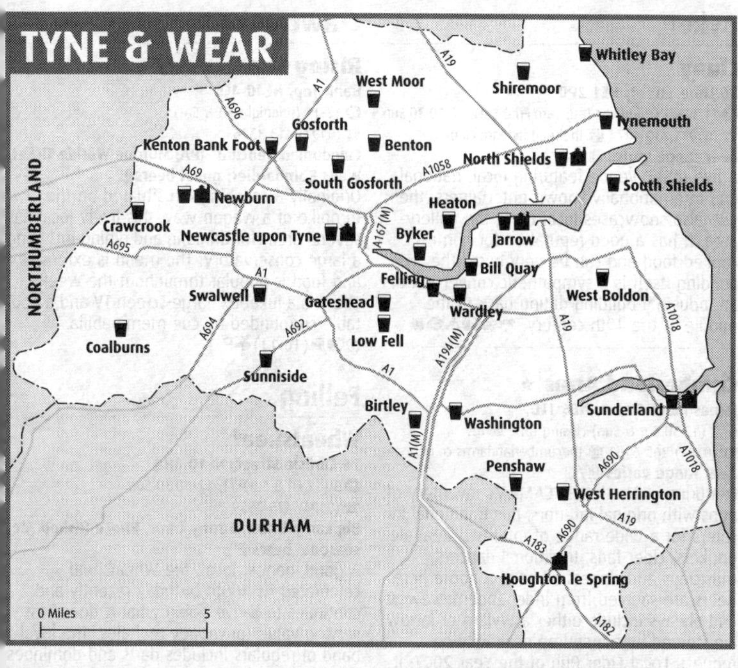

Benton

Benton Ale House

Front Street, NE7 7XE

11-11 (11.30 Wed; midnight Fri & Sat); 12-11 Sun

(0191) 266 1512 bentonalehouse.co.uk

Banks's Bitter; Jennings Cumberland Ale, Cocker Hoop; Marston's Pedigree; guest beers H

Stylish pub with a U-shaped room divided into a variety of drinking areas to suit all tastes. The range of ales is rare for the region and differs in the front and back bars so check first what is on offer. Meals are very popular, especially at weekends, so booking is advised. The nearest Metro is Four Lane Ends.

Bill Quay

Albion

10 Reay Street, NE10 0TY

4-11 (midnight Fri); 12-midnight Sat; 12-11 Sun

(0191) 469 2418

Jarrow Bitter, Rivet Catcher, Swinging Gibbet, seasonal beers; guest beers H

Six handpulls feature owner Jarrow Brewery's highly respected beers plus a guest from a handpicked micro or regional brewery from anywhere nationwide. The lively lounge bar with buskers, quiz and weekly bands is renowned for its views across the River Tyne. Darts is played and there is a pool table in the conservatory. Keelmans Way walk and Coast-to-Coast cycle routes pass the pub.

(Pelaw) P

Birtley

Barley Mow Inn

Durham Road, Barley Mow, DH3 2AH

11-midnight; 10-11.30 Sun

(0191) 410 4504

Black Sheep Best Bitter; guest beers H

This 1930s former roadhouse has a public bar with a pool table and split-level lounge leading to the dining room, which offers a takeaway service on request. Many of the six guest beers come from northern England micro-breweries. The runs runs pool, dominoes and darts teams, and hosts a weekly quiz and live music at weekends. An annual music and beer festival is held in February. P

Moulders Arms

Peareth Terrace, Birtley Lane, DH3 2LW

11-3, 5.30-11; 12-3, 7-11 Sun

(0191) 410 2949

Boddingtons Bitter; Greene King Old Speckled Hen; guest beers H

Located in a residential area close to a school, the pub is named after an ironworks' worker, reflecting the town's industrial past. It has a split-level lounge where food is served lunchtimes and evenings and a beamed public bar with friendly, chatty locals and a TV. It hosts a weekly quiz and runs a golf society. The guest beer often comes from a north eastern micro-brewery. If anything in the pub unaccountably moves then blame the poltergeist. P

INDEPENDENT BREWERIES

Big Lamp Newburn
Bull Lane Sunderland
Darwin Sunderland
Double Maxim Houghton le Spring (NEW)
Hadrian & Border Newcastle upon Tyne
Jarrow Jarrow
Mordue North Shields

Byker

Cluny

36 Lime Street, NE1 2PQ

11.30-11 (midnight Thu; 1am Fri & Sat); 12-10.30 Sun

(0191) 230 4474 theheadofsteam.co.uk

Beer range varies H

A live music venue featuring local, national and internationally known entertainers, the pub also showcases local art in the gallery area. It has a good reputation for home-cooked food and can be very busy. The building itself is a sympathetic conversion of an industrial building dating back to the middle of the 19th century.

Cumberland Arms ★

James Place Street, NE6 1LD

3 (12.30 Sat & Sun)-closing time varies

(0191) 265 6151 thecumberlandarms.co.uk

Beer range varies H/G

Featuring in North East CAMRA's inventory of pubs with original interiors, this traditional inn caters for a wide range of interests. Real ale drinkers, cider fans, traditional dancers, musicians and singers all have a home here. Beers are sourced from independent brewers and always include either a Wylam or Jarrow ale, served by handpump or gravity on request. Local Cider Pub of the Year 2007, it holds annual summer and winter beer festivals. QP

Free Trade Inn

St Lawrence Road, NE6 1AP

11-11 (midnight Fri & Sat); 12-10.30 Sun

(0191) 265 5764

Beer range varies H

Genuine, basic hostelry, renowned for one of the best views from a pub anywhere in the country. From here you can see the Winking Eye Millennium Bridge, the traditional Tyne bridges beyond and the Newcastle and Gateshead quaysides. At the right time of the year this is the ideal spot to watch the sun setting over the city's dramatic skyline. Local small independent breweries are enthusiastically supported. Well-behaved dogs are welcome. (106,Q2)

Coalburns

Fox & Hounds (Coalies)

NE40 4JN

4-11; 1-midnight Sat; 2-11 (11-11 summer) Sun

(0191) 4132549

Black Sheep Best Bitter; Caledonian Deuchars IPA; guest beers H

Welcoming, traditional pub with friendly management and bar staff on the outskirts of Greenside. Dating from 1795, the walls and ceilings are decorated with memorabilia from the local industries of centuries ago. Sheep shears, fishing rods, a traditional open fire complete with granny's oven', kettles, tankards and framed photographs of former village folk give the bar a homely feel. The original games room and snug are still in use. The pub has regular themed nights, a folk club on Sunday, quiz night on Wednesday and live music on Saturday. QP

Crawcrook

Rising Sun

Bank Top, NE40 4EE

12-11 (midnight Fri & Sat)

(0191) 413 3316

Caledonian Deuchars IPA; Mordue Workie Ticket; Wells Bombardier; guest beers H

Originally a coaching inn situated on the turnpike of a wagon-way, this lively local has several areas for drinking and dining including a large conservatory. The menu is extensive and food is popular throughout the week. There is a jukebox, large-screen TV and a pool table surrounded by cue memorabilia.

(10,11)P

Felling

Wheatsheaf

26 Carlisle Street, NE10 0HQ

5 (12 Fri & Sat)-11; 12-10.30 Sun

(0191) 420 0659

Big Lamp Bitter, Sunny Daze, Prince Bishop Ale, seasonal beers H

A good, honest local, the Wheatsheaf celebrated its 100th birthday recently and continues to thrive doing what it does best – serving value for money real ales. The loyal band of regulars includes darts and dominoes schools and members of Felling Silver Band. An impromptu folk night is a long-standing tradition on Tuesday. Well worth the short Metro journey from Newcastle city centre to Felling.

Gateshead

Borough Arms

82 Bensham Road, NE8 1PS

12-11 (midnight Fri & Sat)

(0191) 478 1323

Wells Bombardier; Wylam Gold Tankard; guest beers H

This single-room bare-boards local was formerly a tollhouse and is regarded as the oldest pub in Gateshead. The closest pub to the town centre offering real ale, its six handpulls include three guests, frequently from northern England micro-breweries. Weekly quiz and buskers' nights are hosted and local bands perform monthly. It is also home to three darts teams and a golf society. P

Gosforth

County

Gosforth High Street, NE3 1HB

12-11 (10.30 Sun)

(0191) 285 6919

Black Sheep Best Bitter; Caledonian Deuchars IPA; Fuller's London Pride; Wells Bombardier; guest beers H

Standing on a main road into Newcastle city centre, this hostelry offers up to 13 hand-pulled beers. A popular pub with a mixed clientele of all ages, the main bar is spacious enough to avoid becoming overcrowded. A small back room is an ideal spot for meetings or just to enjoy a drink in peace and quiet. Q(Regent Centre)P

Job Bulman ✔
St Nicholas Avenue, NE3 1AA
🕘 9am-11 (10.30 Sun)
☎ (0191) 223 6320
Greene King IPA, Abbot; Marston's Pedigree; guest beers Ⓗ
A tasteful conversion of a former post office, this one-room Wetherspoon's has a pleasant outdoor heated space for smokers and an area for families. A separate bar area for food orders has speeded up service for drinkers and the choice of reasonably-priced guest ales is very popular with the locals. Buses from Newcastle stop at the nearby High Street, and South Gosforth Metro is a 10-minute walk.
❀◑♿⛺⚡

Heaton

Chillingham Arms
Chillingham Road, NE6 5XN
🕘 11-11 (midnight Fri & Sat); 12-10.30 Sun
☎ (0191) 265 3992
Black Sheep Best Bitter; Jarrow Bitter; Mordue Workie Ticket, guest ales Ⓗ
Large, welcoming two-roomed pub standing on the main road through Heaton and one of very few real ale pubs in this part of Newcastle. Popular with locals as well as the many students who live nearby, good value food is served. Occasional live music events are held in the upstairs function room. There is pavement seating outside.
❀◐⊟⊖(Chillingham Rd)●P

Jarrow

Robin Hood
Primrose Hill, NE32 5UB (on A194, half mile south of A19)
🕘 12-11 (11.30 Fri & Sat; 10.30 Sun)
☎ (0191) 4285454 🌐 jarrowbrewery.co.uk
Jarrow Bitter, Rivet Catcher, Joblings Swinging Gibbet, seasonal beers; guest beers Ⓗ
Comprising two bars, a conservatory and restaurant, the Robin Hood is well worth a visit. A former winner of CAMRA local and regional Pub of the Year awards, it is also home of the award-winning Jarrow Brewery. An excellent selection of cask ales is always available. In addition to Jarrow beers, there are usually guest ales from micro-breweries.
Q⚒◑⊟♿⊖(Fellgate)🚌●P

Kenton Bank Foot

Twin Farms
22 Main Road, NE13 8AB
🕘 11-11 (11.30 Fri); 12-10.30 Sun
☎ (0191) 286 1263
Black Sheep Best Bitter; Taylor Landlord; guest beers Ⓗ
Large, imposing stone building in its own grounds near Newcastle Airport and Newcastle Falcons rugby football club. The pub offers a good selection of beers and has an excellent reputation for fine food. The single room is broken up into various comfortable alcoves and seating areas with real fires, adding to the cosy atmosphere. Outside there are a number of places for sitting and drinking or dining when the weather allows.
♨⚒❀◑♿⊖(Bank Foot)🚌(101)P⚡

Low Fell

Aletaster
706 Durham Road, NE9 6JA
🕘 12-11 (midnight Fri); 11-midnight Sat
☎ (0191) 487 0770
Durham White Amarillo; Jennings Cumberland Ale; Marston's Pedigree; Mordue Workie Ticket; Theakston Best Bitter, Old Peculier; guest beers Ⓗ
A Guide regular since the current landlord took over in 1990. With seven regular real ales, three guests often from north eastern micro-breweries plus a real cider, rare for the area, it offers by far the widest selection of hand-pulled beers in the area. The lively L-shaped public bar is complemented by the cosy snug served from the back of the bar counter. A weekly quiz is held plus occasional live music and beer festivals. ❀⊟🚌♣●P⚡

Newburn

Keelman
Grange Road, NE15 8NL
🕘 11-11; 12-10.30 Sun
☎ (0191) 267 1689
Big Lamp Bitter, Sunny Daze, Summerhill Stout, Prince Bishop Ale, seasonal beers Ⓗ
This Grade II listed building now houses the Big Lamp Brewery and brewery tap in a converted water pumping station. An extension and conservatory have made more room for the growing band of diners and drinkers who come for the good value food and the full range of Big Lamp beers. Quality accommodation is provided in the adjacent Keelman's Lodge and Salmon Cottage. Next to the Coast to Coast cycle way and Hadrian's Wall path. ❀🛏◑♿P

Newcastle upon Tyne

Bacchus
42-48 High Bridge, NE1 6BX
🕘 11.30-11 (midnight Fri & Sat); 7-10.30 Sun
☎ (0191) 261 1008
Jarrow River Catcher; guest beers Ⓗ
At first sight the bar here appears to be a cross between a hotel reception area and an ocean-going liner's first class lounge. It is in fact one of the finest ale houses in the city. Eight handpumps serve independent brewery ales alongside a range of foreign bottled beers. Situated in the city centre near the Theatre Royal, it gets busy at peak times, but there is plenty of room to sit or stand and enjoy the beers. ◐♿⇌⊖(Monument)

Bodega
125 Westgate Road, NE1 4AG
🕘 11-11 (midnight Fri & Sat); 12-10.30 Sun
☎ (0191) 221 1552
Big Lamp Prince Bishop; Durham Magus; Mordue Workie Ricket; guest beers Ⓗ
Two fine original stained glass ceiling domes feature at this impressive pub. The single-room interior is broken up into different areas with separate booths for more intimate

drinking and a number of interesting brewery mirrors on the walls. Unusual beers from various parts of the country ensure a good crowd of keen beer drinkers at all times. Because of its proximity to St James Park the pub can get very full on match days or when live football is shown on TV. ◐⇌⊖(Central)♣

Bridge Hotel

Castle Garth, NE1 1RQ

✪ 11.30-11 (midnight Fri & Sat); 12-10.30 Sun

☎ (0191) 232 6400

Black Sheep Best Bitter; Caledonian Deuchars IPA; guest beers Ⓗ

Next to the high level bridge built by Stephenson, the front windows of this single room pub look out on to the keep of the 'New' castle that gave the city its name; the rear windows have views of the beer garden and former defensive walls to the River Tyne and beyond. The main bar is divided into a number of seating areas on different levels. Among the live music events held in the upstairs function room is what claims to be the oldest folk club in the country. ❀◐⇌⊖(Central)♣

Crown Posada ★

33 Side, NE1 3JE

✪ 11 (12 Sat)-11; 7-10.30 Sun

☎ (0191) 232 1269

Black Sheep Best Bitter; Hadrian Gladiator; Jarrow Bitter; Taylor Landlord; guest beers Ⓗ

Wonderful stained glass windows and an ornate ceiling make this architecturally one of the finest, if smallest, pubs in the area. Featuring in CAMRA's National Inventory of pubs with original interiors, it is near to Newcastle's historic Quayside and an ideal base for riverside walks and visits to the Sage and Baltic in Gateshead. Electric buses passing the door provide a speedy and silent journey back to the city centre. ⇌⊖(Central)🚌⌐

Duke of Wellington

High Bridge, NE1 1EN

✪ 11-11; 12-10.30 Sun

☎ (0191) 261 8852 🌐 dukeofwellingtonpub.co.uk

Caledonian Deuchars IPA; guest beers Ⓗ

No airs and graces, simply a good little pub. Not far from Newcastle's Bigg Market area, this hostelry is a peaceful retreat in which to sample a decent selection of ales in a friendly environment. The regulars are avid followers of sport, shown on screens dotted around the walls. Pub grub is available until 5.30pm. ◐⇌⊖

Head of Steam

1 Neville Street, NE1 5EN

✪ 12-1am (midnight Sun)

☎ (0191) 232 4379 🌐 headofsteam.co.uk

Beer range varies Ⓗ

Situated in an office block facing the central railway station, the main bar upstairs has a lively atmosphere in the evening, with four cask beers and a good selection of continental draught beers on offer. Down in the basement is one of the most popular live music venues in the city centre, where the real ales on handpump are selected to match to the type of music and audience. ⇌⊖(Central)

New Bridge

2 Argyle Street, NE1 6PF

✪ 11-11 (11.30 Thu & Fri); 12-10.30 Sun

☎ (0191) 232 1020

Beer range varies Ⓗ

A little to the east of the city centre, this pub has no regular beers, instead offering a constantly changing range. In an area with a large student population, it attracts a mixed crowd with office workers at lunchtime followed by locals, real ale fans and students later in the day. Lots of local pictures and maps line the walks. A large-screen TV is popular when live sport is screened, and the bar can fill up with football fans on their way to the match if Newcastle United are at home. ◐⊖(Manors)

Newcastle Arms

57 St Andrews Street, NE1 5SE

✪ 11-11; 12-10.30 Sun

☎ (0191) 260 2490 🌐 newcastlearms.co.uk

Caledonian Deuchars IPA; guest beers Ⓗ

Traditional single room pub with a constantly changing flow of beers from all parts of the country plus interesting ciders and perries. Winner of CAMRA Pub of the Year awards from 2006 to 2008, it is renowned for summer and winter beer festivals. A popular pub situated on the edge of the thriving China Town area and near the home of Newcastle United, it can be very busy. ⇌⊖(Monument/St James)♣

Tilley's

105-109 Westgate Road, NE1 4AG

✪ 12-11 (10.30 Sun)

☎ (0191) 232 0692 🌐 theheadofsteam.co.uk

Beer range varies Ⓗ

Next door to the magnificent Tyne Theatre and facing the longest remaining section of town wall built as protection against the Scots, Tilley's offers a good selection of beers, often featuring unusual independent Irish breweries. The pub can get quite lively, but it is possible to escape from the main bar into a quieter seating area where the walls are decorated with pictures of old Havana. ◐⇌⊖(Central/St James)♣

North Shields

Oddfellows

7 Albion Road, NE30 2RJ

✪ 11 (12 Sun)-11

☎ (0191) 257 4288 🌐 oddfellowspub.co.uk

Greene King Abbot; Jarrow Bitter; guest beers Ⓗ

The walls of this small, friendly single-room lounge bar are covered with historic maps and photographs of pre-war North Shields and newspaper cuttings of former local boxing heroes. The pub has strong sporting connections and football is shown on the large flat-screen TV. Home to football and darts teams, it also fundraises for charity. A beer festival is held in the garden in early May. ❀♿⊖🚌⌐

Porthole

11 New Quay, NE29 6LQ

✪ 11-midnight; 12-12.30 Sun

☎ (0191) 257 6645

Courage Directors; guest beers Ⓗ

Dating from 1834 and rebuilt around 1900, the Porthole is next to the ferry landing for South Shields. In keeping with its location, the pub displays plenty of ship memorabilia in the two bars. Local breweries supply the guest ales. Live entertainment plays regularly throughout the week. Excellent fish and chips can be found at the nearby Fish Quay.
Q❀⊖🚌(313,R19)♣⅟

Prince of Wales
2 Liddell Street, NE30 1HE
⏲ 12 (3 Tue)-11; 12-10.30 Sun
☎ (0191) 296 2816
Samuel Smith OBB Ⓗ
There are records for this pub dating back to 1627 but the current building, faced with green glazed brick, dates from 1927. The premises lay empty for some years before a restoration in traditional style by Sam Smith's and reopened in 1992. A rare outlet for Sam Smith's this far north, it is well worth a visit. Crab sandwiches and fish and chips are served at lunchtime. ⛰Q🛏❀◐🂠⊖🚌

Tap & Spile
184 Tynemouth Road, NE30 1EG
⏲ 12-11 (10.30 Sun)
☎ (0191) 257 2523
Draught Bass; Caledonian Deuchars IPA; guest beers Ⓗ
A past winner of CAMRA Tyneside & Northumberland Pub of the Year, following a change of management and redecoration this hostelry is once again delighting beer enthusiasts. Offering two regular beers and an ever-changing guest list, this popular pub is well worth a visit again. 🂠⊖

Penshaw

Monument
Old Penshaw Village, DH4 7ER (off A183 signed Old Penshaw)
⏲ 11 (12 Sun)-11
☎ (0191) 584 1027
Jennings Cumberland Ale Ⓗ
Popular locals' pub at the foot of Penshaw Monument, a local landmark and folly, with a small bar dominated by a roaring real fire in winter and games room. The pub is decorated with old pictures tracing the history of the village. Food is limited to simple snacks and toasties. Handy for Herrington Country Park.
⛰❀🂠♿🚌(78,78A)●

Shiremoor

Shiremoor House Farm
Middle Engine Lane, NE29 8DZ
⏲ 11-11 (10.30 Sun)
☎ (0191) 257 6302
Mordue Workie Ticket; Taylor Landlord; guest beers Ⓗ
Excellent Fitzgerald's conversion of a former farmhouse retaining many original features including the interesting gin-gan. A well-deserved reputation for the quality of its real ales and good value food means it can get busy at times, especially Sunday lunchtime. Three handpulls serve two regular beers and a quest. Q🛏❀◐◑♿P⅟

South Gosforth

Victory ✔
Killingworth Road, NE3 1SY
⏲ 12-11 (midnight Fri & Sat)
☎ (0191) 285 1254
Caledonian Deuchars IPA; Courage Directors; Taylor Landlord; Theakston Best Bitter; Wells Bombardier; guest beers Ⓗ
Established on this site since 1861, the pub takes its name from Nelson's flagship and once served the local mining community. Essentially a single room, the bar has different levels and areas with wood ceilings, traditional decor and two fireplaces. A range of malt whiskies complements the quality beers. Busy at weekends with tables outside during the summer, there is a covered and heated area for smokers. ❀◐♿⊖🚌P⅟

South Shields

Alum Ale House ✔
River Drive, NE33 1JR
⏲ 11-11 (midnight Thu-Sat); 12-11 Sun
☎ (0191) 427 7745
Banks's Bitter; guest beers Ⓗ
Classic old-fashioned riverside pub, just a stone's throw from the market square. A long-standing favourite with the real ale fraternity and visitors to the local Customs House theatre, the pub comprises a main bar, side room and cellar bar/function room. Pump clips mounted on the central beam in the main bar come from just a few of the hundreds of different beers served. Wooden floors and low ceilings give the pub a comfortable, warm feel and window seats overlook the River Tyne. ❀⊖

Bamburgh ✔
175 Bamburgh Avenue, NE33 1JR (on Coast Road)
⏲ 11 (12 Sun)-11
☎ (0191) 454 1899
Greene King IPA, Abbot; guest beers Ⓗ
Spacious pub with an open plan interior served from a central bar with a dining area and games room. There are excellent views from the front terrace across the Leas of the North Sea and finishing line of the Great North Run. Guest beers come from the Greene King portfolio. ❀◐◑♿▲P⅟

Dolly Peel
137 Commercial Road, NE33 1SH
⏲ 12-11 (midnight Thu-Sat)
☎ (0191) 427 1441
Black Sheep Best Bitter; Caledonian Deuchars IPA; Courage Directors; Draught Bass; Taylor Landlord; guest beer Ⓗ
Named after a local fish wife and smuggler, this pub has featured regularly in the Guide for 19 years and is a former local CAMRA Pub of the Year. A single room on two levels, there is no loud music and the TV sets are only turned on for football games. It attracts a mature clientele but becomes more lively at weekends and on buskers' night on Wednesday. The four regular beers are complemented by two guest ales.
Q⊖(Chichester)

Maltings

Claypath Lane, NE3 4PG (off Westoe Road)
4-11.30
(0191) 427 7147 jarrowbrewery.co.uk
Jarrow Bitter, Joblings Swinging Gibbet, Rivet Catcher, Westoe IPA, seasonal beers; guest beer H
Built on the first floor of a former dairy, the Maltings is the home of Jarrow Brewery's second plant, the Westoe Brew House on the ground floor. The full range of Jarrow beers is complemented by an excellent range of imported ales. The large wood-panelled bar is reached by an imposing staircase and has a number of separate seating areas. Wednesday is quiz night when there is a free buffet. Children are welcome until 9pm.
Q

Rosie Malones

5 Market Place, NE33 1BH (E side of Market Place)
10-6.30 (11 Tue-Thu; midnight Fri & Sat); 11-10.30 Sun
(0191) 4551596
Jennings Cumberland Ale; guest beers H
Friendly Irish theme pub close to the main shopping area and very busy on market days (Mon, Fri and Sat) when home-cooked food is served. A live band plays on Sat afternoon and every other Sat evening. The Twilight World Paranormal Research Society meets in the upper function room on Wed evening. A quiz is held in the bar on Wed evening.

Stag's Head ☆

45 Fowler Street, NE33 1NS
11-11 (midnight Fri & Sat); 12-midnight Sun
(0191) 427 2911
Draught Bass; Greene King Abbot; Houston Killelan Bitter H
Traditional town centre local unchanged by the ravages of time. Well used by the folk of Shields, it enjoys strong community links. Darts and dominoes feature and an upstairs lounge is available for hire. The curry quarter is within easy walking distance. ♣

Steamboat

Coronation Street, Mill Dam, NE33 1EQ
12-11 (10.30 Sun)
(0191) 454 0134
Caledonian Deuchars IPA; Wells Bombardier; Wychwood Hobgoblin; guest beers H
One of the oldest pubs in South Shields, the Steamboat has strong nautical links. With tunnels linked to the river and a resident ghost there are rumours that it was once a smugglers' meeting place. The manager, Joe, celebrated 20 years in the pub in 2008. An extra handpull has recently been added so six real ales are now always available. Beer festivals and curry cook-offs are regular events, and a local alternative historian also makes an appearance. Dogs are welcome.

Sunderland

Clarendon

143 High Street, SR1 2BL
12-3 (11 Fri-Sun)
(0191) 510 3200 bull-lane-brewing.co.uk
Beer range varies H
Basic one-room local on the banks of the Wear offering a warm welcome and fine views across the river. Popular with a varied clientele, it hosts a buskers' night on Thursday and occasional live music on Sunday afternoon. Up to six beers are on offer from the Bull Lane Brewery located in the cellar. Just outside the city centre, it is well worth the walk. (5,5A)

Cliff

Mere Knolls Road, Roker, SR6 7LG
12-11 (midnight Fri & Sat; 10.30 Sun)
(0191) 548 6200
Courage Directors; Marston's Pedigree; guest beers H
Spacious community pub in a side street close to Roker Park and a short walk from the seafront. The large open-plan lounge is served from an L-shaped bar. Two regular beers are complemented by a rotating guest beer, usually from one of the larger regional breweries. Numerous TV screens throughout the pub show sport.

Fitzgerald's

10-12 Green Terrace, SR1 3PZ
11-11 (midnight Fri & Sat); 12-10.30 Sun
(0191) 567 0852
Beer range varies H
Part of the real ale friendly Sir John Fitzgerald's chain, this is a mecca for cask ale lovers and usually offers nine frequently-changing guest beers, many sourced from north east micro-breweries. The pub has two rooms on two levels – the smaller Chart Room downstairs is quieter than the main bar.
(University)

Harbour View

Benedict Road, Roker, SR6 0NL
10.30-11.30 (7 Fri; 12.30am Sat)
(0191) 567 1402
Caledonian Deuchars IPA; guest beers H
Modern pub overlooking Roker Marina and a short walk from Roker Beach. The ground floor bar features wood panelling and exposed brickwork with a horseshoe-shaped bar in the centre. Four handpumps offer three guest beers frequently from local independent brewers. Afternoon meals are served in the first floor Benedicts Bar, with fine views over the marina. The pub can get busy when Sunderland are at home.
(Stadium of Light)(E1)

King's Arms

Beach Street, Deptford, SR4 6BU
11-11 (midnight Fri & Sat); 12-10.30 Sun
(0191) 567 9804
Taylor Landlord; guest beers H
CAMRA Branch and Regional Pub of the Year for the last two years, the King's Arms is a privately owned old-fashioned pub with an unspoilt interior. Nine handpumps offer an ever-changing range of beers from micro-breweries from the north east and across the country, as well as a real cider. Large-screen TVs show sport and the pub can get very busy when Sunderland are at home. Live music plays in a marquee during the summer.
(University/ Millfield)(18,11)

Promenade
1 Queens Parade, SR6 8DA
🕒 11-11; 12-10.30 Sun
☎ (0191) 529 2226
Caledonian Deuchars IPA; Tetley Bitter 🄷
Relaxing lounge bar with a separate dining area and wide-ranging sea views from the windows. Good value bed and breakfast accommodation is available and children are welcome. Monday is quiz night when the pub can be busy. Buses from the city centre stop nearby. ◑🚌⁼

Rosedene ✔
Queen Alexandra Road, SR2 9BT
🕒 11-11; 12-10.30 Sun
☎ (0191) 528 4313
Greene King IPA, Old Speckled Hen, Abbot 🄷
Large, impressive pub set back from the main road. Inside, the bright, cheerful, spacious room has an island bar decorated with wood arches and rails. Seating is in a raised area at one end, with small alcoves for more intimate drinking. A comprehensive bar food menu is available with daily specials. Upstairs is a function room and there is a separate restaurant. All premier league matches are televised and a regular quiz night held on Wednesday. ❀◐◑♿🚌(10)P⁼

Saltgrass
Hanover Place, Deptford, SR4 6BY
🕒 12-11 (midnight Fri & Sat)
☎ (0191) 565 7229
Black Sheep Best Bitter; Caledonian Deuchars IPA; Draught Bass; guest beers 🄷
Situated at the bottom of a hill next to a once bustling shipyard, this welcoming two-roomed pub oozes character. The interior has open fires, polished wooden floors and beamed ceilings. The pub is named after the tough saltgrass that used to dominate the area before the shipyards. There is an outside patio for warmer weather. Monday is music night and quiz night is Tuesday.
♨❀◑⊟⊖(Millfield)🚌(11)●⁼

Wolsey
40 Millum Terrace, Roker, SR6 0ES
🕒 11-11 (midnight Fri & Sat)
☎ (0191) 567 2798
Theakston Best Bitter; guest beers 🄷
After an absence of 20 years the Wolsey makes a welcome return to the Guide. The large open plan lounge bar has two handpumps – a guest ale from the Cellarman's Reserve List is available in addition to the regular beer. Live music plays on Saturday evening and a weekly quiz is held. The pub overlooks Roker Marina and is a short walk from Roker Beach. Q❀◐♿🚌(E1)P

Sunniside

Marquis of Granby
Streetgate, NE16 5ES (on A692 between Lobley Hill and Sunniside)
🕒 11-11; 12-10.30 Sun
☎ (0191) 488 0954
Beer range varies 🄷
This stone-built open-plan pub is all that remains of a small community known as Low Streetgate.The pub was rebuilt in 1900, but there has been a public house on this site from at least the 19th century. Popular for excellent food, two ales are available on handpull, usually from local micros. Jazz plays on Thursday evening, live music on Sunday and a quiz night on Monday. Children are welcome. ♉❀◐◑♿P⁼

Swalwell

Sun Inn
Market Lane, NE16 3AL
🕒 11 (12 Sun)-11
☎ (0191) 488 7783
Beer range varies 🄷
Situated in the modern village of Swalwell just a stone's throw from the Metrocentre shopping complex, this pub has been in existence for more than 100 years. The central bar divides the interior into two rooms, with a buskers' night held on Saturday. Regular darts and quiz nights are also hosted. Bar food and snacks are available throughout the week and on Sunday free traditional fare is on offer. ❀⊟🚌♣⁼

Tynemouth

Cumberland Arms
17 Front Street, NE30 4DX
🕒 12-11 (10.30 Sun)
☎ (0191) 257 1820 🌐 cumberlandarms.co.uk
Courage Directors; Theakston Best Bitter; Wells Bombardier; guest beers 🄷
Spilt-level pub with two bars each dispensing six real ales. One of the guests is often a mild. A dining area at the rear serves good value meals. The pub can get very busy at weekends as all the major football matches are shown live on a large screen TV – the manager is a big football fan. ♨◐◑⊖

Turks Head ✔
41 Front Street, NE30 4DZ
🕒 12-11 (midnight Fri & Sat; 10.30 Sun)
☎ (0191) 257 6547
Courage Directors; Theakston Best Bitter; Wells Bombardier; guest beers 🄷
Popular pub next to the sea front and Tynemouth Priory, with eight handpumps. Locally known as the Stuffed Dog, if you look to your left from the front bar you will see why. Food is served in a dining area at the rear. Football fans can watch matches no matter where they are in the pub —TVs are everywhere. ◐◑⊖

Tynemouth Lodge
Tynemouth Road, NE30 4AA
🕒 11-11; 12-10.30 Sun
☎ (0191) 257 7565 🌐 tynemouthlodgehotel.co.uk
Draught Bass; Caledonian Deuchars IPA; Mordue Workie Ticket; guest beers 🄷
This attractive externally tiled free house built in 1799 has been in every issue of the Guide since 1984 when it was taken over by the present owner. The comfortable single room lounge is noted for its Scottish real ales on handpump and is reputed to sell the highest volume of Draught Bass on Tyneside.
♨Q❀⊖🚌P

Wardley

Green

White Mare Pool, NE10 8YB
11-11
(0191) 495 0171
Beer range varies Ⓗ
Resembling a huge bungalow from the outside, this self-styled bar and brasserie is part of the well-respected Sir John Fitzgerald group and its four real ales frequently come from local micro-breweries. Stylishly furnished throughout and decorated with black and white motor racing photographs, the public bar has a large-screen TV. A quiz is held weekly. The restaurant has a good reputation.

Washington

Courtyard

Arts Centre, Biddick Lane, Fatfield, NE38 8AB
11-11 (midnight Fri & Sat); 12-11 Sun
(0191) 417 0445
Taylor Landlord; guest beers Ⓗ
Modern café bar situated within the Washington Arts Centre, owned by Sunderland Council and home of the famous Davy Lamp Folk Club. Seven ever-changing cask beers are available, many unusual for the area, and a range of Belgian beers. Beer festivals are held over the Easter and August bank holiday weekends. QP

William de Wessyngton

2-3 Victoria Terrace, Concord, NE37 2SY (opp bus station)
9-11.30
(0191) 4180100
Greene King IPA, Abbot; Marston's Pedigree; guest beers Ⓗ
Large open plan Wetherspoon's in a former snooker hall and ice cream parlour, named after one of George Washington's earliest ancestors. Ten handpumps offer a varying range of cask ales from all over the country. The manager arranges his own beer festivals in addition to the chain's national events. The pub can get very busy when major football matches are shown. Q

West Boldon

Black Horse

Rectory Bank, NE36 0QQ (off A184)
11-11; 12-10.30 Sun
(0191) 536 1814
Black Sheep Best Bitter Ⓗ
This two-roomed pub has an L-shaped bar and restaurant. The walls are adorned with bric-a-brac and the tables are candle-lit. Live music plays on Sunday evening. The house beer comes from Darwin Brewery in Sunderland. (9,9A)

West Herrington

Stables

McLaren Way, DH4 4ND (off B1286)
12-11 (midnight Fri & Sat; 10.30 Sun)
(0191) 584 9226
Black Sheep Best Bitter; Taylor Landlord; guest beers Ⓗ
Built with natural stone, this quaint, Tardis-like country pub blends in well with the adjacent stone houses. The main feature is the large open fire in the centre of the room, but mock beams and a timber parquet floor add to the appeal of this delightful pub. Food is now available at lunchtime. Q(35)P

West Moor

George Stephenson

Great Lime Road, NE12 7NJ
12-11
(0191) 268 1073 georgestephensoninn.com
Caledonian Deuchars IPA; guest beers Ⓗ
Much altered over the last century, this pub retains two separate drinking areas which, when required, can become a single room by opening the dividing doors. A side patio outside is in the lee of the East Coast rail line. A well-established music venue, live bands play on several evenings and some Sunday afternoons —check the website for details. Several guest beers are on offer, often from smaller breweries. P

Whitley Bay

Briardene

71 The Links, NE26 1UE
11-11; 12-10.30 Sun
(0191) 252 0926
Black Sheep Ale; guest beers Ⓗ
This Fitzgerald's pub has a large, attractive lounge with sea views to the links and St Mary's lighthouse, and a more compact rear bar with widescreen TV, pool and darts. The pub is well known for its food, with local fish and chips a speciality. Guest beers change regularly. Children are welcome in a family area in the lounge. There is seating outside at the front of the pub. P

Fitzgeralds

2-4 South Parade, NE26 2RG
11-11; 12-10.30 Sun
(0191) 251 1255
Beer range varies Ⓗ
Large, friendly town centre pub near the Metro and local bus services. Three frequently-changing beers are usually available, with a wider range on offer at the weekend when the pub can be very busy. Like most of the Fitzgerald's chain, the pub offers good value and popular food.

Rockcliffe Arms

Algernon Place, NE26 2DT
11-11 (11.15 Fri & Sat); 12-11 Sun
(0191) 253 1299
Beer range varies Ⓗ
Outstanding back-street Fitzgerald's pub, a few minutes' walk from the Metro station and the mayhem of Whitley Bay weekend nightlife. Four constantly-changing guest beers are kept in tip-top condition. Regular darts and dominoes matches are held in the snug.

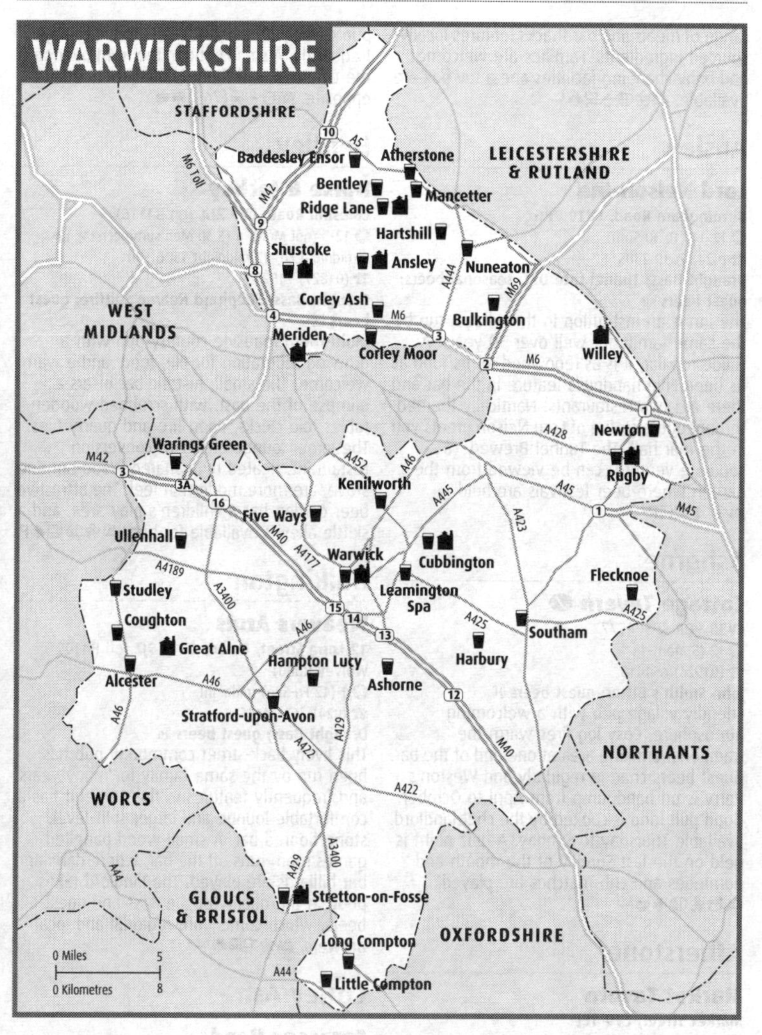

Alcester

Holly Bush

Henley Street, B49 5QX

12-midnight (1am Fri & Sat); 12-11.30 Sun

(01789) 762482

Black Sheep Best Bitter; Purity Pure Gold; Sharp's Doom Bar; Uley Bitter; guest beers H

This traditional 17th-century local in an historic market town is a frequent CAMRA branch Pub of the Year. Restoration has preserved its five rooms and many original features. There is a function room and an award-winning walled garden at the rear. Four regular ales and four guests are always available and beer festivals are held in June and October. Good traditional English food is served (not Sun eve). Regular folk sessions are held twice a month with spontaneous music at any time. White Hart Morris dncers practise here on Mon evening.

Three Tuns

34 High Street, B49 5AB (next to post office)

12-11

(01789) 762626

Hobsons Best Bitter; guest beers H

This must-visit local CAMRA award-winning pub is how a real pub used to be: no music, no pool and no food. It has a single room interior with low beams, stone flagged floor and an exposed area of wattle and daub. Up to eight ales from micros and independents provide a permanent yet ever-changing mini beer festival. Q

Turks Head

4 High Street, B49 5AD

12-3 (not Mon), 5-11; 12-11 Sat; 12-10.30 Sun

(01789) 765948 theturkshead.net

Purity Pure Gold; Taylor Landlord; Wye Valley HPA H

Converted back to a pub in 1999 after many years as an antique shop, this 17th-century town house has a rustic atmosphere with bare wooden floors, old furniture, wattle and daub walls and a brick chimney breast. The building has a narrow front but extends way back in traditional market town style to a lovely walled garden at the rear. An adventurous range of meals and bar snacks features locally-sourced ingredients. Families are welcome and baby changing facilities and a toy box are available. ♨❀◑♿⊟♣⁻

Ansley

Lord Nelson Inn

Birmingham Road, CV10 9PG
⊙ 12-11 (10.30 Sun)
☎ (024) 7639 2305
Draught Bass; Tunnel Late OTT, seasonal beers; guest beers Ⓗ
The inn is an institution in the village, run by the same family for well over 30 years. A Guide regular, it is as renowned for its food as its beer. Five handpulls feature in the bar and there are two restaurants. Nautically themed throughout, a statue of Lord Nelson greets you in the rear hall. The Tunnel Brewery (a separate venture) can be viewed from the garden where beer festivals are held.
♨❀◑⊞⊟P⁻

Ashorne

Cottage Tavern ✔

CV35 9DR SP304577
⊙ 12 (5 Mon)-11
☎ (01926) 651410
John Smith's Bitter; guest beers Ⓗ
Friendly village pub with a welcoming atmosphere. Cosy log fires warm the traditional drinking area at one end of the bar. Guest beers change regularly and Weston's Perry is on handpump from April to October. Good pub food is cooked by the chef landlord, available Thursday to Sunday. A quiz night is held on the last Sunday of the month and dominoes and crib matches are played.
♨ኔ❀◑♣●⁻

Atherstone

Market Tavern

Market Street, CV9 1ET
⊙ 12-11 (1am Fri & Sat)
Warwickshire Best Bitter, Lady Godiva, Golden Bear, Churchyard Bob, King Maker, seasonal beers; guest beer Ⓗ
A friendly inn with welcoming locals, this traditional, unspoilt ale house overlooks the pretty market square. Café-style seating at the front of the pub overlooks the square, and a rear beer garden includes a covered area for smokers. Simple, good value food is available all day. There is a free beer draw every Tuesday, and a discount on ale for card-carrying CAMRA members. ♨❀⊟(48,765)⁻

Baddesley Ensor

Red Lion

The Common, CV9 2BT (from Grendon roundabout on A5 go S up Boot Hill)
⊙ 12-3 (Sat only), 7-11; 12-3, 7-10.30 Sun
☎ (01827) 718186
Everards Tiger; Marston's Pedigree; guest beers Ⓗ
A warm welcome awaits at this friendly one-room village pub with a roaring fire in winter, decorated with a wealth of brasses. Traditional pub games are played. Guest beers change frequently. A small patio at the front overlooks the common and there is off street parking opposite. ♨Q❀⊟(765)♣●

Bentley

Horse & Jockey

Coleshill Road, CV9 2HL (on B4116)
⊙ 12-3 (not Mon), 6 (5.30 Mon summer)-11; 12-3, 5-midnight Fri; 12-midnight Sat & Sun
☎ (01827) 715236
Draught Bass; Shepherd Neame Spitfire; guest beers Ⓗ
Multi-room roadside country pub with a growing reputation for ale, food, and a warm welcome. The small, historic bar offers a glimpse of the past, with scrubbed wooden tables, old clocks, open fire and quarry tiles. The larger lounge and barn-conversion restaurant, heated by a shared wood-burning stove, are more modern in feel. The attractive beer garden has a children's play area, and a skittle alley is available for hire. ♨❀◑⊞♣P

Bulkington

Weavers Arms

12 Long Street, Ryton, CV12 9JZ (off B4109 Wolvey Road)
⊙ 1 (12 Fri-Sun)-midnight
☎ (024) 7631 4415
Draught Bass; guest beers Ⓗ
This lively back-street community pub has been run by the same family for many years and frequently features in the Guide. It has a comfortable lounge and larger split-level, stone-floored bar. A small wood-panelled games room runs off the bar, where darts and bar billiards are played. The landlord takes pride in the quality of the Bass and guest beers, which come from regional and local brewers. ♨❀⊞⊟♣⁻

Corley Ash

Saracens Head

Tamworth Road, CV7 8BP (on B4098 at jct with Highfield Lane)
⊙ 12-2.30, 5.30-11; 12-11 Fri & Sat; 12-10.30 Sun
☎ (01676) 540853
Flowers Original; Ringwood Best Bitter; Wadworth 6X; guest beer Ⓗ
You cannot miss this imposing, three storey, roadside pub with a garden and children's play area. The split-level stone and wood-floored bar runs the length of the building, decorated with horse brasses and brass plates. There are four handpulls and forthcoming guest ales are

INDEPENDENT BREWERIES

Atomic Rugby
Church End Ridge Lane
Discovery Little Packington (NEW)
Griffin Inn Shustoke (NEW)
North Cotswold Stretton-on-Fosse
Purity Great Alne
Rugby Willey
Slaughterhouse Warwick
Tunnel Ansley
Warwickshire Cubbington

displayed on a board by the bar. The pub has a good reputation for its food, served in the bar and dining room. ❀◐⊟(735)♣P⁻

Corley Moor

Bull & Butcher ✓

Common Lane, CV7 8AQ SP282850
⌚ 10-midnight (1am Fri & Sat); 10-11 Sun
☎ (01676) 540241
Draught Bass; Greene King Abbot; M&B Brew XI; guest beers Ⓗ
This traditional village inn adorned with hanging baskets is very much the focal point of community life. The public bar with a small snug never changes but the lounge has been extended to create a conservatory restaurant with decking, enjoying clear views over the countryside. Good quality food includes breakfasts served daily and the popular Sunday carvery. The garden is ideal for families and has a bouncy castle in summer. ♔Q❀◐⊟♿⚠P⁻

Coughton

Throckmorton Arms

Coughton Hill, B49 5HX (on A435 between Studley and Alcester) SP078609
⌚ 12-11 (10.30 Sun)
☎ (01789) 766366 🌐 thethrockmortonarms.co.uk
Hobsons Best Bitter; St Austell Tribute; guest beers Ⓗ
Situated opposite Coughton Court with its Gunpowder Plot connections, this large roadside hotel provides a smart and comfortable environment to enjoy a pint or a meal. A traditional coaching inn steeped in history and charm, it has an L-shaped bar serving the open plan oak-beamed interior. A separate restaurant overlooks the large patio, with commanding views of the Warwickshire countryside. The hotel itself attracts business people during the week and visitors to the area at the weekend. Two guest beers come from local breweries. ♔❀⊨◐♿⊟P⁻

Cubbington

Queen's Head

20 Queen Street, CV32 7NA
⌚ 1-11; 12-10.30 Sun
☎ (01926) 429949
Adnams Bitter; Ansells Mild; Draught Bass; Greene King IPA; guest beer Ⓗ
Traditional Victorian village pub with a public bar, pool room and comfortable lounge. A genuine drinkers' pub, the only noise is the buzz of conversation. Home to darts and crib teams, it is also the meeting place for village societies and groups – a true community local. A large TV in the bar screens major sporting events. The guest beer changes four or five times a week. Q❀⊟♿⊟(68)♣P⁻

Five Ways

Case is Altered

Case Lane, CV35 7JD (off Five Ways Road near A4141/A4177 jct) SP225701
⌚ 12-2.30, 6-11; 12-2, 7-10.30 Sun
☎ (01926) 484206
Greene King IPA; Sharp's Doom Bar; guest beers Ⓗ
Well worth seeking out, this charming 350-year-old whitewashed inn is a rural time warp and true drinking pub – no children, music or mobile phones (£1 fine to charity if yours rings!) are permitted. The tiny main bar is decorated with posters of long-gone local breweries; a Sopwith Camel aircraft propeller hangs from the ceiling. The bar billiards table in the entrance hall takes old sixpence coins. Two guest beers, one always a standard session beer, are mainly sourced form local breweries. ♔Q❀♿♣P⁻

Flecknoe

Old Olive Bush

CV23 8AT
⌚ 7-11 (closed Tue); 12-2.30, 7-11 Sat; 12-3, 8-10.30 Sun
☎ (01788) 891134
Greene King IPA, Abbot; guest beer Ⓗ
This small, friendly village local with a warm and cosy atmosphere is also a meeting place for various community groups. The tiny bar holds no more than 20 people, with an area for skittles and darts up four steps. There is also a lounge/dining area for families. The garden is adorned with plants and shrubs, providing a delightful backdrop for alfresco drinking. Men's and ladies skittles teams play in local leagues. In summer a beer festival is held with a pig roast and music. ♔Q☺❀◐⊟⚠♣P⁻

Hampton Lucy

Boar's Head

Church Street, CV35 8BE
⌚ 11.30-11; 11-11 Fri & Sat; 12-10.30 Sun
☎ (01789) 840533
Ansells Best Bitter; Fuller's London Pride; guest beers Ⓗ
Friendly, cosy village pub dating back to the 17th century when it was built as a cider house – the present kitchen was originally a mortuary. Situated on a Sustrans cycle route and close to the River Avon, it attracts cyclists, walkers and visitors to nearby Charlecote Park (NT). A sheltered rear garden is popular for Sunday afternoon barbecues in summer. The guest beers change frequently, with up to 10 served in a week, mostly from small independent brewers. ♔❀◐P

Harbury

Old New Inn

Farm Sreet, CV33 9LS
⌚ 3 (11 Fri-Sun)-12.30am
☎ (01926) 614023
Beer range varies Ⓗ
Large pub built from local Jurassic white lias limestone. Over the years several small rooms have been knocked through to create the main bar; the resulting variation in ceiling heights can catch out tall people. A large stone fireplace dominates the space. The lounge has a homely feel, often used by domino and crib teams. An attractive garden is full of colour in the summer. One Church End real ale is

available during the week, two at weekends.
⛫Q✿◐◑⊟⊡(64)♣P⊱

Hartshill

Anchor Inn

Mancetter Road, CV10 0RT (on A4131)
⏲ 12-2.30 (not Mon), 6-1am; 12-11 Sat; 12-10.30 Sun
☎ (024) 7639 8839
Everards Tiger, Original; guest beers Ⓗ
The Anchor was thought to be a trading post and mail collection point for narrowboat workers following completion of the canal in 1790. It has a cosy feel in winter with wooden beams and open fires; in summer there are plenty of outdoor areas including a children's playground. Three restaurants and a carvery are on different levels (no eve meals Sun). Up to four guest beers complement the Everards.
⛫✿◐◑♿P⊱

Kenilworth

Engine ✔

8 Mill End, CV8 2HP
⏲ 4 (12 Thu)-midnight; 11-1am Fri & Sat; 11-midnight Sun
☎ (01926) 853341
M&B Brew XI; guest beers Ⓗ
Away from the main part of town, this building became an inn in 1854. The friendly pub has a single wood-beamed room around a U-shaped bar, serving two changing guest beers from the Punch Taverns list. Meals are served on Thursday afternoon only —originally just for pensioners but now available to all, and very popular. A large-screen TV shows sports. Outside is a covered and heated area for smokers. ✿⊡(16,X17)♣⊱

Old Bakery

12 High Street, CV8 1LZ (near A429/A452 jct)
⏲ 5.30 (5 Fri & Sat)-11; 12-2, 7-10.30 Sun
☎ (01926) 864111 🌐 theoldbakeryhotel.co.uk
Hook Norton Hooky Bitter; St Austell Tribute; guest beers Ⓗ
Attractively restored former bakery in a 400-year-old building in the centre of the old town, with two rooms plus a small outside patio. Fish and chip suppers are available on Monday evening. Disabled access is via the rear car park. Abbey Fields is nearby and the castle is a 10-minute walk. Q✿⛟♿⊡(12)P

Virgins & Castle

7 High Street, CV8 1LY (A429/A452 jct)
⏲ 11-11.30 (midnight Fri & Sat); 12-11 Sun
☎ (01926) 853737
Everards Beacon, Sunchaser, Tiger, Original; Fuller's London Pride; guest beer Ⓗ
Centuries old pub full of atmosphere with an L-shaped bar in the centre and a plethora of quirky rooms alongside the main lounge. A contemporary food menu mixes English, Japanese and Filipino dishes. Outside is a heated terrace for cooler evenings. Children and pets are welcome. There is limited parking at the front but a public car park is close by. Served by buses from Coventry, Leamington Spa and Warwick University.
⛫Q☋✿◐◑♿⊡(12)⊱

Wyandotte Inn

Park Road, CV8 2GF (jct of Park Road/Stoneleigh Road)
⏲ 12-midnight (1am Fri); 11.30-1am Sat; 11.30-11 Sun
☎ (01926) 859076
Jennings Cocker Hoop; Marston's Burton Bitter; guest beers Ⓗ
Pleasant corner pub with an open-plan bar on two levels, popular with locals and students. Named after an Indian tribe, a large wooden North American Indian takes pride of place in the bar. Guest beers come from the Marston's list and Thatchers Heritage cider is sold. Several TV screens show major sporting events. There is a a large patio with heaters and umbrellas for smokers. Buses stop close by on Stoneleigh Road. ✿⊡(U2,X17)♣●P⊱

Leamington Spa

Newbold Comyn Arms

Newbold Terrace East, CV32 4EW
⏲ 12 (5 Mon-Wed)-midnight
☎ (01926) 338810 🌐 newboldcomynarms.co.uk
Beer range varies Ⓗ
Classic free house in Newbold Comyn Park, opposite the leisure centre and adjoining a 27-hole municipal golf course. Converted from farm buildings, the Stables Bar features open beamed ceilings, higgledy-piggledy brickwork and a roaring log fire. Outside is a large south-facing terrace and garden with children's play area plus miles of walks in the park. Six changing cask ales, regular beer festivals, live music, giant pub games, Sky Sports and a separate function room are all available at this CAMRA Community Pub of the Year.
⛫☋✿◐▲♣●P⊱

Red House

113 Radford Road, CV31 1JZ
⏲ 11.30-11 (midnight Thu-Sat); 12-11 Sun
☎ (01926) 881725
Adnams Broadside; Draught Bass; Hook Norton Hooky Bitter; guest beer Ⓗ
Although located on the main road near the edge of town, this small cosy, popular and very friendly Victorian pub has the atmosphere of a village community local. The single bar has two seating areas at the front and a corridor at the back for vertical drinkers. Look for the fine collection of Guinness toucans and the unusual blue and pink handpumps. Quiz night is Wednesday. The large garden at the rear is child friendly and has a barbecue area for summer evenings.
Q☋✿◑⊡⊱

Woodland Tavern

3 Regent Street, CV32 5HW
⏲ 12-midnight (1am Fri & Sat); 12-11.30 Sun
☎ (01926) 425868
Slaughterhouse Saddleback Ⓗ
Traditional 19th-century two-room street corner pub retaining a separate bar and lounge with individual entrances and original features – note the ceilings. Just a short walk from the town centre, the pub is a meeting point for the local community with darts, crib and dominoes played. Sports are shown on TV in the lounge, but conversation dominates.

The real ale is from Slaughterhouse Brewery, less than a mile away. Q❀⊟⇌⊟♣P⁄–

Little Compton

Red Lion

GL56 0RT

⌚ 12-3, 6 (7 Sun)-11

☎ (01608) 674397 ⊕ red-lion-inn.com

Donnington BB, SBA Ⓗ

This Cotswold stone pub has flagstoned floors and log fires to welcome you in winter. There are settles in the public bar on which you can relax and maybe watch a game of pool. Food is served from a substantial menu in the restaurant or bar and both Donnington beers are available on handpump. Dogs are welcome as are children (with restrictions) and in the summer Aunt Sally is played in the garden. The Rollright Stones are nearby.
⊟Q❀⇌◐⊟⅄♣P⁄–

Long Compton

Red Lion

Main Street, CV36 5JS

⌚ 10.30-2.30, 6-11; 10.30-11 Fri & Sat; 12-11 Sun

☎ (01608) 684221 ⊕ redlion-longcompton.co.uk

Hook Norton Hooky Bitter; guest beers Ⓗ

Hooky Bitter is always on handpump at this stone built pub on the edge of the Cotswolds. Two further handpumps offer changing beers such as Bass and local ales from Warwickshire micro-breweries. Food is served lunchtime and evening every day and children and dogs are most welcome inside the pub and in the large garden. In winter a log fire warms the flagstoned bar and on the first Wednesday of the month there is acoustic live music.
⊟❀⇌◐♿⅄⊟(50)P

Mancetter

Blue Boar

Watling Street, CV9 1NE

⌚ 12-11.30 (10.30 Sun)

☎ (01827) 716166

Draught Bass; guest beer Ⓗ

Spacious, multi-roomed 1940s rebuild of an earlier Blue Boar on the same site. Choose from the boisterous bar, comfy lounge, function room or elegant conservatory restaurant. Well-regarded food is served throughout the pub, and good value, high quality B&B is available. The keenly-priced guest beer is a rotating choice from Tunnel Brewery, located at sister pub the Lord Nelson in Ansley. Buses stop right outside.
⊟❀⇌◐⊟♿⊟(48, 765)P

Newton

Stag & Pheasant

27 Main Street, CV23 0DY

⌚ 12-3, 6 (7 Sun)-midnight

☎ (01788) 860326

Banks's Original; Jennings Cumberland Ale; guest beer Ⓗ

Popular thatched village local, reputed to be the second oldest A-framed building in Warwickshire. The large single room adorned with exposed beams has a bar in the middle and a comfortable seating area with tables made from wooden casks, sofas and a real fire. Pool, skittles and traditional pub games are played. Thursday evening is quiz night. Home-made food is available weekday lunchtimes and Friday evening. Dogs are welcome. ⊟❀◐⊟♣P⁄–

Nuneaton

Crown

10 Bond Street, CV11 4BX

⌚ 12-11 (midnight Fri & Sat)

☎ (024) 7637 3343 ⊕ thecrownnuneaton.com

Oakham JHB; Shardlow Golden Crown; guest beers Ⓗ

Seven ales and three ciders are on offer in this popular town centre split-level bar. A beer and music festival is held in June and other festivals throughout the year. Live rock bands perform on Saturday and quizzes are a regular feature. There is an outside drinking area and the pub has a function room for hire. Golden Crown is the house beer and a perry is usually available. ⊟❀⇌⊟●P⁄–

Hearty Goodfellow

285 Arbury Road, Stockingford, CV10 7NQ

⌚ 11-11; 12-10.30 Sun

☎ (024) 7638 8152

Marston's Burton Bitter; guest beers Ⓗ

Lively and friendly sports-oriented community pub popular with all ages where visitors are made to feel very welcome by the locals. A large one-room pub, football team pennants, shirts and sport trophies decorate the walls, with pool and darts teams flourishing. Large screen TVs keep you up to date with the day's sports. Three of the four handpulls supply the guests, usually from the Marston's group.
❀⊟♣⁄–

Rose Inn

Coton Road, CV11 5LY (opp church)

⌚ 11-11.30 (11 Sun)

☎ (024) 7674 2991

Marston's Burton Bitter, Pedigree; guest beers Ⓗ

The Rose was the venue for CAMRA's first AGM and an account of this occasion hangs on the wall. Landlord Tony is passionate about his ales and also his clock collection, on display around the L-shaped lounge. The bar at the front has a pool table and dartboard. No meals are served on Monday lunchtime.
❀◐⊟♿⊟♣P⁄–

Ridge Lane

Church End Brewery Tap

109 Ridge Lane, CV10 0RD (two miles SW of Atherstone) SP295947

⌚ 6 (12 Fri & Sat)-11; closed Mon-Wed; 12-10.30 Sun

☎ (01827) 713080 ⊕ churchendbrewery.co.uk

Beer range varies Ⓗ

Eight handpumps are constantly in use serving brewery-fresh real ales in this modern, roomy tap. Pre-booked tours of the brewery, visible from the bar, are recommended. Two large, airy rooms are decorated with brewery paraphernalia and cheeky posters. A mild is always available, plus a changing real cider and an excellent Belgian beer range.

Customers are welcome to bring their own food. Children are not allowed inside, but enjoy the large meadow-style beer garden. Q❀♿Ⓐ♣●P

Rugby

Alexandra Arms

72 James Street, CV21 2SL (next to multi-storey car park)
11-midnight; 12-10.30 Sun
☎ (01788) 578660 alexandraarms.co.uk
Alexandra Petit Blonde; Greene King Abbot; guest beers Ⓗ
Seven times winner of Rugby CAMRA Pub of the Year, the pub is home to a micro-brewery producing the Alexandra Ales and Atomic ranges. Guest beers include milds, stouts and porters. The pub has a quiet, comfortable L-shaped lounge where lively debate flourishes among the locals, and a noisier back room featuring a fabulous rock jukebox along with pool, skittles and bar billiards. The large garden has open and covered seating and hosts summer beer festivals. Q❀◐♿⇌♣

Merchants Inn

5-6 Little Church Street, CV21 3AN (behind Marks & Spencer)
12-midnight (1am Fri & Sat); 12-11 Sun
☎ (01788) 571119 merchantsinn.co.uk
B&T Shefford Bitter; Everards Tiger; Ⓗ **guest beers** Ⓗ/Ⓖ
Established ale house, reigning Rugby & Warwickshire CAMRA Pub of the Year. With a warm and cosy atmosphere inside, it has wooden seating, comfortable sofas, flagstone floors, an open fireplace and an abundance of brewery memorabilia. Up to 10 ales are on offer (one gravity dispensed) plus traditional cider and perry and a superb selection of Belgian beers. Home-cooked food is served seven days a week. Big-screen rugby internationals and live music every Tuesday evening attract a crowd. Large beer festivals are held in April and October. ♨◐♿♣●

Raglan Arms

50 Dunchurch Road, CV22 6AD (opp Rugby school)
4-11 Mon; 12-midnight Tue-Sun
☎ (01788) 544441
Ansells Mild; Fuller's London Pride; Greene King Abbot; Raglan Original Bitter; Ⓗ **guest beers** Ⓗ/Ⓖ
This traditional old favourite has been refurbished to a high standard. Closed for 15 months, the three-roomed town pub now has a comfortable, homely atmosphere. Up to 10 beers are available including the Raglan Original Bitter (brewer a secret), with two served straight from the cask. The snug is available for club meetings. Beer festivals, brewery visits, poker nights and a golf society are planned. Q❀◐♣

Seven Stars ✔

40 Albert Square, CV21 2SH
12-11; 12-10.30 Sun
☎ (01788) 561402
Wells Bombardier; guest beers Ⓗ
Genuine local community pub with a traditional bar area, lounge and conservatory. An interesting range of guest ales comes from Adnams, St Austell, Bateman and other regional brewers. The good value food menu includes specials of the day, a Saturday 'Gut buster' breakfast and Sunday lunch. The Stars holds regular quiz nights and curry days, and is home to darts, dominoes, skittles and cricket teams. ❀◐♿⇌♣

Squirrel Inn

33 Church Street, CV21 3PU
12-11 (10.30 Sun)
☎ (01788) 544154
Marston's Pedigree; guest beers Ⓗ
Traditional free house featuring ever-changing guest ales including many local brews as well as Weston's Organic vintage cider. Dating from the early 18th century, it is one of the oldest buildings in Rugby. Now a single room, the pub was originally three tiny rooms and the boundaries are still clearly evident. Entertainment includes live acoustic music every Wednesday and a wide selection of games such as table skittles, darts and chess. Rugby CAMRA's Most Improved Pub in 2006. ♨Q⇌♣●

Victoria Inn

1 Lower Hillmorton Road, CV21 3ST
4-11 (1am Fri); 12-1am Sat; 12-11.30 Sun
☎ (01788) 544374 downthevic.com
Atomic Bomb, Fission, Fusion, Strike, Half Life; guest beers Ⓗ
The Atomic Ales brewery tap is a genuine two-room street corner local. The traditional bar doubles as a games room where darts and pool are played, while the lounge has retained its original Victorian character and is a pleasure to drink in. The pub is now more spacious with two recently opened side rooms, plus a rear outside area for smokers. A selection of foreign beers is available and Sky Sports is shown on request. Beer festivals are held twice a year. Q❀⇌♣●

Shustoke

Griffin Inn

Church Road, B46 2LB (on B4116)
12-2.30, 7-11; 12-3, 7-10.30 Sun
☎ (01675) 481205
Banks's Original; Hook Norton Old Hooky; Marston's Pedigree; RCH Pitchfork; Theakston Old Peculier; guest beers Ⓗ
This deserving Guide regular has been championing cask ale for decades – some of the old beermats on the rafters must be collectors' items. Five ever-changing guests supplement the regular ales. The music and TV-free interior features low beams and inglenooks with wood-burning stoves, while outside there is patio seating and a large, grassy play area. Children are welcome in the conservatory. Food is served Monday to Saturday lunchtime; local eggs, cheese and seasonal produce are on sale at the bar. ♨Q❀◐ⒶP

Southam

Stoneythorpe Hotel

10 Warwick Road, CV47 0HN
10.30-11; 12-2.30, 7-10.30 Sun

☎ (01926) 812365 🌐 thestoneythorpehotel.co.uk
Fuller's London Pride; guest beers Ⓗ
Originally an eye-hospital founded in 1774 by Dr Henry Lilley-Smith, the building has been an independently run hotel for 46 years. In 1823 the world's first dispensary was established here, celebrated by a nearby monument and in the naming of the hotel's bar. Five guest beers are usually available in the comfortable, airy lounge. Monthly live music events are hosted and a midsummer beer festival is held in June.
Q♨❀⇌◑♿🚌(63,64)P⚟

Stratford-upon-Avon

Golden Bee ✔

42 Sheep Street, CV37 6EE
⏲ 9-midnight (1am Fri & Sat)
☎ (01789) 203860
Greene King Abbot; Marston's Pedigree; Purity Pure UBU; guest beers Ⓗ
Large town-centre Wetherspoon's within easy walking distance of the River Avon, theatres, bus routes and rail station. Opened in 2001, it takes its name from the refreshment rooms that occupied this timber-framed building in the early 20th century. The walls are adorned with pictures of Shakespeare and his plays, and free Wi-fi access is available. Three or four guest ales come from nationals and micro-breweries, and regular mini-festivals are held throughout the year. Q♨◑♿🚌⚟

Stretton-on-Fosse

Plough

GL56 9QX
⏲ 11.30-2.30, 6-11; 12-10 Sun
☎ (01608) 661053
Hook Norton Hooky Bitter; Purity Pure Gold; guest beers Ⓗ
Popular with villagers and visitors alike, this stone pub with flagstoned bar and restaurant area has four handpumps providing a choice from breweries near and far. Dominoes, cribbage, bridge, whist and Aunt Sally are played, and quizzes and folk musicians hosted on Sunday evenings. Delicious food is available from a blackboard menu.
♨Q❀◑♣P⚟

Studley

Little Lark

108 Alcester Road, B80 7NP SP075632
⏲ 12-3, 6-11; 12-midnight Sat; 12-3, 6.30-10.30 Sun
☎ (01527) 853105
Adnams Bitter; Ansells Mild; Taylor Landlord; guest beer Ⓗ
This popular village local has four areas served by a central bar, with many traditional fruit wines and single malt whiskies available. A number of themed nights are celebrated including Burns Night, St George's Day and Halloween, and a cheese festival is held in March. Home-cooked meals are served seven days a week including Sunday evening – the cow pie is the chef's speciality.
♨Q❀◑♿🚌♣🍎⚟

Ullenhall

Winged Spur

Main Street, B95 5PA
⏲ 12-midnight
☎ (01564) 792005 🌐 thewingedspur.com
Beer range varies Ⓗ
Steeped in history, this village pub offers up to four guest beers and a choice of ciders – a board above the bar shows what is coming next. An extensive range of home-made dishes is on offer lunchtimes and evenings, ranging from lambs liver and bacon to superb fresh fish to vegetarian Wellington, all with suggestions for wines and beers to accompany them. Outside is an excellent smoking area with a real log fire and settees.
♨Q❀◑♿🍎P

Warings Green

Blue Bell Cider House

Warings Green Road, B94 6BP SP127742
⏲ 11.30-11; 12-10.30 Sun
☎ (01564) 702328
Weatheroak Light Oak; guest beers Ⓗ
Friendly canal-side free house offering three real ales and five draught ciders, including a house special from Weston's. Eight temporary moorings make it a popular stop for boaters, and the area is pleasant for walking, cycling and fishing. The large lounge and cosy bar have real fires in winter, and families are welcome in the large conservatory. Reasonably-priced food, regular quiz nights and occasional live music.
♨Q♨❀◑⊟♿♣🍎P⚟

Warwick

Cape of Good Hope

66 Lower Cape, CV34 5DP (off Cape Road)
⏲ 12-11 (10.30 Sun)
☎ (01926) 498138 🌐 capeofgoodhope.co.uk
Church End Two LLocks; Greene King IPA, Abbot; Tetley Bitter; Weatheroak Keystone Hops; guest beer Ⓗ
True canal-side pub with the water a few feet from the front door. Built just after the canal opened in 1800, the Cape has given its name to the canal locks, the street and the surrounding district. It has a traditional bar at the front and a spacious lounge at the rear. Good value meals are served and live music is regularly hosted. Q❀◑⊟🚌(G1)♣P

Old Fourpenny Shop

27-29 Crompton Street, CV34 6HJ (near racecourse, between A429 and A4189)
⏲ 11-11
☎ (01926) 491360 🌐 fourpennyshophotel.co.uk
RCH Pitchfork; guest beers Ⓗ
Three times winner of CAMRA's Warwickshire Pub of the Year award, the pub has six handpumps providing a constantly changing selection of beers, focusing on small and local breweries. Popular with real ale fanatics from near and far. The contemporary, bright and airy single bar has a comfortable feel and welcoming atmosphere. A recently-opened restaurant serves good quality English food. Accommodation is in 11 bedrooms. Q⇌◑🚌P

WEST MIDLANDS

Aldridge

Lazy Hill Tavern

196 Walsall Wood Road, WS9 8HB

12-2.30 (Sat only), 6-11 Sat; 12-2.30, 7-10.30 Sun

☎ (01922) 452040

Caledonian Deuchars IPA; Courage Best Bitter; Greene King Abbot; Marston's Pedigree; Theakston Mild; guest beer H

Large, welcoming family-run free house run by the same licensee for 30 years. Originally a farmhouse, it became a country club, then finally a pub in 1986. Four separate rooms are all similarly and comfortably furnished, with original beams exposed in the middle two. The large 160-seater function room is used midweek by local sports organisations and can be booked for weddings. ⌂Q⊟(367,56)P

Amblecote

Maverick ✔

Brettell Lane, DY8 4BA (jct of A491/A461)

12-midnight (1am Wed, Fri & Sat); 12-11 Sun

☎ (01384) 824099

Jennings Cumberland Ale; guest beers H

A large street-corner pub with access from both sides leading to the main bar. Between the two entrances is a separate Mexican-style room. A Wild West room doubles as a live music venue, catering for a wide variety of tastes including folk, blues, roots and bluegrass. A corridor leads to the garden, which has a large, covered smoking area. Up to four real ales are available on handpump. Sky TV screens sport. ❀⊟♣⁻

Robin Hood ✔

196 Collis Street, DY8 4EQ (on A4102, off Brettell Lane)

12-3, 6-11; 12-midnight Fri & Sat; 12-11 Sun

☎ (01384) 821120

Bathams Best Bitter; Enville Ale, Ginger; guest beers H

In the Glass Quarter and close to the canal network, this family owned and run free house prides itself on the range and quality of its Cask Marque award-winning beer, regularly offering four guest ales. The restaurant is open every day and features good home-cooked food that has earned the pub plaudits. A lively quiz takes place on the first Tuesday of the month. En-suite accommodation is available, including a family room, and guests are served a hearty breakfast. ⌂❀⊭(1◗♿⊟(311)●P⁻

Swan

10 Brettel Lane, DY8 4BN (on A461 towards Dudley, ⅓ mile after A491)

12-11 Mon; 4-11 Tue-Thu; 12-11 Fri-Sun

☎ (01384) 76932

Beer range varies H

A friendly neighbourhood free house comprising a basic public bar with TV for popular sporting events and a homely lounge with patterned carpet and floral wallpaper. Three handpumps dispense an ever-changing

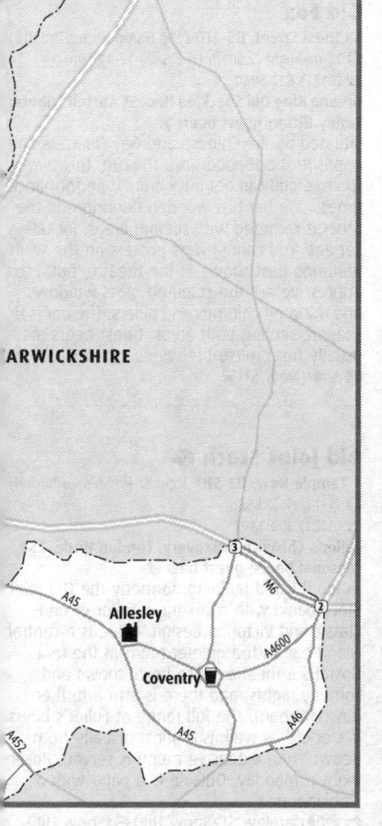

range of beers. The popular sun-trap garden is accessed through the lounge, while there is a covered smoking area beyond the toilets. The pub is experimenting with extended afternoon opening hours, but is always open all day at weekends. ❀⊞🚌♣⁵—

Barston

Bulls Head ✔

Barston Lane, B92 0JU

⏲ 11-2.30, 5-11; 11-11 Fri & Sat; 12-10.30 Sun

☎ (01675) 442830 🌐 thebullsheadbarston.co.uk

Adnams Bitter; Hook Norton Hooky Bitter; guest beers Ⓗ

A former coaching inn, this lovely, genuine village local has appeared in the Guide for 17 consecutive years. There are two bars, each with a log fire in winter, plus a separate restaurant room in the oldest part of the building. All serve both bar and restaurant food choices, the latter from a seasonally changing menu (no meals Sun eve). Outside is a secluded beer garden and a covered, heated smokers' area. Barston's annual fete takes place in adjacent fields. ♨Q❀◑♣P⁵—

Bilston

Olde White Rose

20 Lichfield Street, WV14 0AG

⏲ 12-11 (11.30 Fri & Sat)

☎ (01902) 498339

Beer range varies Ⓗ

A Grade II listed frontage leads to a long, narrow pub that offers up to 12 real ales, along with cider and perry from Weston's. In addition to the standard food menu served 12-9pm daily, a carvery operates lunchtimes and evenings (12-5pm Sun). Quiz nights are held every Tuesday and Wednesday, with live folk music down in the bierkeller on Thursday. Bus and Metro stations are nearby.
❀◑♿⊖(Bilston Central)🚌●⁵—

Trumpet

58 High Street, WV14 0EP

⏲ 11-3.30 (4 Sat & Sun), 7.30-11.30

☎ (01902) 493723 🌐 trumpetjazz.org

Holden's Mild, Bitter, Golden Glow, seasonal beers Ⓗ

Busy, compact, one-room local serving Holden's award-winning ales at reasonable prices. Plenty of musical memorabilia is on display, including concert tickets from Slade to Glenn Miller and musical instruments on the walls and ceiling. Live jazz is performed here seven nights a week and you are likely to find the landlord joining in on the drums most nights. A collection plate is passed around for the bands. Sandwiches are available. There is an outside drinking area at the back.
❀⊖(Bilston Central)🚌⁵

Birmingham: Balsall Heath

Old Moseley Arms

53 Tindal Street, B12 9QU

⏲ 12-11 (10.30 Sun)

☎ (0121) 440 1954

Black Sheep Best Bitter; Enville Ale; Greene King Abbot; guest beers Ⓗ

Lovely back-street pub where food is not generally available but a curry night is held every Tuesday and Thursday. Quiz night is Tuesday, and live music from the Chaos Acoustic Club is performed on Sunday evening. A history of the pub is displayed above the fireplace including a list of all the landlords since 1838. Sporting events are shown on big screens including one in the covered and heated outside smoking area. ❀⊞🚌(50)⁵—

Birmingham: City Centre

Briar Rose ✔

25 Bennetts Hill, B2 5RE

⏲ 7-midnight (1am Fri & Sat); 8-midnight

☎ (0121) 634 8100

Greene King Abbot; Marston's Pedigree; guest beers Ⓗ

Large, city-centre Wetherspoon pub located in the former Abbey House building, the first branch of Abbey National. This simple and comfortable pub has plenty of tables, sofas and booths. Attached is a 40-room Wetherlodge with a large function room. Children are welcome in the rear family area until 6pm. The pub offers the full Wetherspoon menu. Guest ales from a chosen local brewery often feature for up to a week at a time.
🛏◑♿⇌(New St/Snow Hill)⊖(Snow Hill)🚌●

Bull

1 Price Street, B4 6JU (off St Chads Queensway)
12-11; closed Sun
(0121) 333 6757 thebull-pricestreet.com
Adnams Broadside; Ansells Mild; Marston's Pedigree; guest beer
One of Birmingham's oldest pubs, this popular and friendly local is close to Aston University and the Children's Hospital. Two rooms are served by a central bar, and there is a quieter room at the rear, with easy chairs. Food is traditional and homely fare, served daily until 9.30pm. A vast collection of jugs and plates, along with old photos, is displayed on the shelves and walls of the bar. The windows have etched Ansells insignia.
Q (Snow Hill) (Snow Hill)
P

Craven Arms

Upper Gough Street, B1 1JG (near the Mailbox)
9-midnight (2am Fri); 12-6 Sun
(0121) 643 6756
Banks's Original, Bitter; guest beer
A true architectural gem, this superb city centre Victorian-tiled locals' pub is tucked away in a side street near the Mailbox complex. The interior is simple, in dark wood, with a large bar facing you as you enter. It has a cosy, relaxed atmosphere and is fairly small so it gets busy at certain times – particularly with BBC staff from the nearby studios. Traditional, hearty food is served.
(New St)

Figure of Eight

236-239 Broad Street, B1 2HG
9-midnight (1am Thu-Sat)
(0121) 633 0917
Greene King IPA, Abbot; Marston's Pedigree; guest beers
Huge Wetherspoon pub in the heart of Birmingham's entertainment district. It takes its name from the canal network which cuts a figure of eight shape around Birmingham. It is a welcome antidote to most of the bars in the area, featuring bookshelves and the usual Wetherspoon collection of old pictures on the walls. Very popular with after-work drinkers and busy too during the early evening at weekends. The pub has a dining area and large beer garden. Cask Marque approved.

Old Contemptibles

176 Edmund Street, B3 2HB (100m from Snow Hill Station)
10 (12 Sat)-11; closed Sun
(0121) 200 3831
Fuller's London Pride; Marston's Pedigree; Taylor Landlord; guest beer
Run down for many years, this famous pub by Snow Hill Station has benefited from an extensive £1 million refurbishment. It has a London pub feel to it, with a long bar, tasteful wooden panelling and luxurious furnishings. A separate snug at the rear is used for dining. The decor features mementos commemorating World War I military campaigns of the British Expeditionary Force, after which the pub is named. Excellent food is served until 10pm.
Q (Snow Hill/New St) (Snow Hill)

Old Fox

54 Hurst Street, B5 4TD (opp Hippodrome Theatre)
11-midnight (2.30am Fri & Sat); 12-11 Sun
(0121) 622 5080
Greene King Old Speckled Hen; St Austell Tribute; Tetley Bitter; guest beers
Situated by the Chinese and Gay Quarters and opposite the Hippodrome Theatre, this two-roomed pub can get busy around performance times. One bar has wooden flooring and the other is carpeted with seating areas, including settees. You cannot miss posters on the walls featuring past shows at the theatre, but also impressive are the coloured glass windows and mirrored columns and pillars. The bar is U-shaped, serving both areas. Guest beers are usually from micro-breweries, often local.
(New St)

Old Joint Stock

4 Temple Row, B2 5NY (opp St Philip's Cathedral)
11-11; closed Sun
(0121) 200 1892
Fuller's Chiswick, Discovery, London Pride, ESB, seasonal beers; guest beer
Grade II listed building, formerly the Old Joint Stock bank, with a striking interior of neo-Classic and Victorian design. There is a central island bar with a quieter room at the rear. Upstairs a theatre space hosts shows and comedy nights, and there is also a further function room. The full range of Fuller's beers is stocked as well as a guest, usually from Beowulf. An extensive menu is served. Poker night is Monday. Outside is a patio with a smoking area.
(New St/Snow Hill) (Snow Hill)

Old Royal

53 Church Street, B3 2DP (off Colmore Row)
8am-10; 12-11 Sat & Sun
(0121) 200 3841
Fuller's London Pride; Taylor Landlord; guest beer
Open at 8am for breakfast and the morning coffee trade, this classic Victorian pub dominates the corner of Church and Edmund streets. Popular with local office and construction workers, it can get busy at lunchtime and early evening. The pub boasts stained glass windows and original tiling on the staircase leading to the upstairs function room/restaurant area. A heated, covered smoking area is accessed from a passage to the side of the stairs.
Q (Snow Hill) (Snow Hill)

INDEPENDENT BREWERIES

Batham Brierley Hill
Black Country Lower Gornal
Highgate Walsall
Holden's Woodsetton
Olde Swan Netherton
Rainbow Allesley
Sarah Hughes Sedgley
Toll End Tipton
Windsor Castle Lye

Pennyblacks ✓

132-134 Wharfside Street, The Mailbox, B1 1XL (within Mailbox complex at canal level)
10-11 (midnight Fri & Sat); 10-10.30 Sun
(0121) 632 1460 penny-blacks.com
Church End What The Fox's Hat; Enville Ale; Hook Norton Hooky Bitter; St Austell Tribute; guest beer
Situated next to other bars and restaurants and by the canal, Pennyblacks has lovely views of the Gas Street Basin and the Mailbox. It is the only bar in the complex to serve real ale. An open, modern, simple bare-bricked interior makes it feel comfortable. Interestingly you can see the barrels on stillage through a screen behind the bar. Although renowned for quality food and extensive wines, real ale features heavily.
(New St)

Prince of Wales ✓

84 Cambridge Street, B1 2NP (behind ICC/NIA and Rep Theatre)
12-11 (10.30 Sun)
(0121) 643 9460
Adnams Broadside; Ansells Mild; Everards Tiger; Taylor Landlord; Wells Bombardier; guest beers
Small and intimate pub nestling behind the International Convention Centre, attracting a mixture of locals and real ale enthusiasts. One regular even has a plaque denoting his seat. The pub is prone to surges of customers after shows at the NIA, ICC and Repertory Theatre finish. Generous portions of good value food are available lunchtime and early afternoon. Live music plays most Sunday afternoons and there are occasional 70s/80s disco nights.
(Snow Hill) (Snow Hill)

Shakespeare

Lower Temple Street, B2 4JD
11-11 (midnight Fri & Sat); 12-10.30 Sun
(0121) 316 7841
Fuller's London Pride; Marston's Pedigree; guest beer
This city-centre pub is an oasis just off the hustle and bustle of the New Street shopping area. Some of the original M&B tiled features remain in this well-refurbished pub. A raised drinking area is located at the front, with a quieter area to the rear. A sectioned-off pavement drinking space is also used by smokers. (New St)

Wellington

37 Bennetts Hill, B2 5SN
10-midnight
(0121) 200 3115 thewellingtonrealale.co.uk
Black Country BFG, Fireside, Pig On The Wall; Wye Valley HPA; guest beers
Birmingham CAMRA Pub of the Year 2005 and 2006, the Wellington enjoys the reputation of a real city centre local. A wide range of cask ales, ciders and perries is always available, together with many foreign beers. Regular beer festivals, quiz nights and cheese tasting are popular. No food is available but you can bring your own (cutlery provided).
Q(New St/Snow Hill) (Snow Hill)

Birmingham: Digbeth

Anchor ★

308 Bradford Street, B5 6ET
10 (11 Sat)-11; 12-10.30 Sun
(0121) 622 4516 anchorinndigbeth.co.uk
Hobsons Mild; Tetley Bitter; guest beers
Birmingham CAMRA Pub of the Year 2008 has been in the Keane family for 35 years. The friendly staff offer a warm welcome in the heart of the Irish Quarter. Constantly changing guest beers (up to eight at a time) are displayed on large blackboards. Recently redecorated, the lively public bar complements the quieter rooms and lounge, while the yard provides designated smoking and no-smoking areas. Regular beer festivals and themed weekends are held. Football is shown on large-screen TVs.
Q(New St/Moor St)

White Swan ★

276 Bradford Street, B12 0QY
12-11 (1am Fri & Sat)
(0121) 622 2586
Banks's Original, Bitter; Jennings Cumberland Ale, Cocker Hoop; guest beer
This red-brick Victorian pub is situated in the developing Irish Quarter of the city, and is a reminder of times gone by. A long, narrow public bar has bench-type seating along the walls and stools at the bar, which also serves a smallish lounge; both rooms are joined by an impressive, ornately tiled hallway and have large-screen TVs. This recently redecorated pub has a welcoming feel and can get busy at popular times. The guest beer is from the Jennings/Marston's portfolio.
(New St/Moor St)

Birmingham: Harborne

Green Man ✓

2 High Street, B17 9NE
12-11 (1am Fri & Sat)
(0121) 427 0961
M&B Brew XI; Taylor Landlord; guest beers
A recently refurbished Ember Inn which is popular and lively most nights. Situated on the High Street, it boasts a good value food menu, served daily until 9pm. Seating is available outside on a patio area by the pavement, and at the rear of the pub by the large car park, where there is also a heated smoking shelter. Quiz nights are held on Sunday and Wednesday. P

Junction ✓

212 High Street, B17 9PT
12-11 (midnight Thu-Sat); 12-10.30 Sun
(0121) 427 0991
Beer range varies
Extensively and expensively refurbished former O'Neills pub which dominates the High Street. Some original tiling remains by the staircase and toilets; the large, comfortable seating area has a real fireplace. An interesting beer range is supplemented by lager and cider. You can see the chef in action in the open-plan kitchen area at the rear, where food is served until 10pm (9pm Sun). A superb large, heated and covered smoking

shelter is in the rear courtyard. Board games are available. ⛫❀◐♿🚌♣🍎⚡

White Horse ✔

2 York Street, B17 0HG (100m off High Street)
✪ 11-11 (11.30 Thu; midnight Fri & Sat); 12-10.30 Sun
☎ (0121) 427 6023
🌐 whitehorseharborne.homestead.com
Adnams Broadside; Greene King IPA, Abbot; Marston's Pedigree; Tetley Bitter; Wells Bombardier; guest beers Ⓗ
This popular suburban pub is a short bus ride from the city centre, just off the High Street. It features a central island bar with a snug at the front. Televised sporting events are shown on big screens in both front and back areas. The pub offers a good range of guest beers and a decent food menu until 6pm. There is a small, heated, covered smoking shelter at the rear. Quiz night is after the football on Tuesday. ❀◐♿🚌⚡

Birmingham: Highgate

Lamp

257 Barford Street, B5 7EP (500m from Pershore Road)
✪ 12-11
☎ (0121) 622 2599
Church End Gravediggers Mild; Everards Tiger; Stanway Stanney Bitter; guest beers Ⓗ
Small, friendly back-street pub just outside the city centre, popular with regular locals and visiting beer enthusiasts. It has been run by the same landlord for over a decade and has been honoured by Birmingham CAMRA. The only regular city outlet for Stanway beers, it also serves micro-brewery guests. The small bar area gets busy, but a large function room at the rear is well used by local societies and as a venue for live acts. A late licence is used occasionally. ♿⇌(New St)🚌🀫

Birmingham: Hockley

Black Eagle

16 Factory Road, B18 5JU (in Jewellery Quarter)
✪ 11-3, 5.30-11; 11-11 Fri; 12-3, 7-11 Sat; 12-3 Sun
☎ (0121) 523 4008 🌐 blackeaglepub.co.uk
Ansells Mild, Best Bitter; Taylor Landlord; guest beers Ⓗ
This pub is a real back street gem. Many of the original features remain, including Minton tiles and a cosy room layout. A four-times CAMRA Pub of the Year, it also enjoys an excellent reputation for food. A beer festival is held in the well-tended garden every year in July, when real cider is also offered. ⛫❀◐🍽♿⊖(Soho Benson Road)🚌⚡

Lord Clifden

34 Great Hampton Street, B18 6AA
✪ 9-1am
☎ (0121) 523 7515 🌐 thelordclifden.co.uk
Wye Valley Butty Bach, HPA; guest beers Ⓗ
Formerly a rather shabby but very friendly hostelry with a fine stained glass front window, the pub has recently undergone a substantial and eclectic refurbishment. The separate front bar has been retained at the request of regulars and now majors on sports fixtures, while the rear lounge is ideal for dining or a quieter drink. Excellent food is cooked by the landlord, a former London hotel chef. A superb sun-trap beer garden includes a smoking shelter.
❀◐🍽⊖(Jewellery Quarter)🚌♣⚡

Birmingham: Kings Heath

Kings Heath Cricket Club ✔

Charlton House, 247 Alcester Road South, B14 6DT
✪ 12-11.30
☎ (0121) 444 1913
Fuller's London Pride; Wye Valley Butty Bach, HPA; guest beers Ⓗ
Award-winning family-friendly club with multi-sports facilities. The Sports Bar features excellent coverage of Sky Sports channels and houses two full-size snooker tables, while the lounge bar has a more tranquil atmosphere. The pavilion is open at weekends in the summer. Two beer festivals are held each year in April/May and November. Various social events including quizzes and live entertainment are held throughout the year. CAMRA members are welcome on production of a valid membership card (maximum 10 visits per year). Q❀◐♿🚌(50)P⚡

Birmingham: Moseley

Prince of Wales

118 Alcester Road, B13 8EE
✪ 12-11.30 (1am Fri & Sat); 12-11 Sun
☎ (0121) 449 4198
Caledonian Deuchars IPA; Greene King Abbot; Wells Bombardier; guest beers Ⓗ
A new landlord has revitalised this busy community pub without changing its essential character. Food has been introduced and includes hearty meals, quality pub snacks and sharing platters. The extensive garden has a smoking area. A front public bar leads to two quieter rooms at the back where darts and other games are played. Regular events include curry nights, quizzes and chess nights, with live jazz and blues on Thursday.
Q🍼❀◐🍽♿🚌(50)♣⚡

Birmingham: Newtown

Bartons Arms ☆

144 High Street, B6 4UP (at A34/B4144 jct, opp Newtown Baths)
✪ 12-11; 11-10.30 Sun
☎ (0121) 333 5988 🌐 oakham-ales.co.uk
Oakham JHB, White Dwarf, Bishops Farewell; guest beers Ⓗ
Decorated throughout with ornate Minton tiles, this is Birmingham's most spectacular pub interior. A gilded staircase and snob screens around the rear of the bar demonstrate the height of Victorian pub opulence. Wonderful authentic Thai dishes are a real draw and a perfect accompaniment to the Oakham ales and constantly-changing guests from micro-breweries. An adventurous bottled beer selection plus real cider and perry are available. Two large function rooms host a range of activities. ⛫🍼◐🍽♿🚌🍎P🀫

Birmingham: Stirchley

British Oak ★

1364 Pershore Road, B30 2XS (on main A441 close to Bournville station)
11-11 (1am Fri & Sat); 12-11 Sun
☎ (0121) 458 1758
M&B Mild; guest beers Ⓗ
Large roadside pub, a fine example of a 1920s-style roadhouse and featuring in CAMRA's National Inventory of historic pub interiors. This multi-roomed hostelry displays many fine and original features. The public bar can be very lively at times but the rear rooms are quiet and peaceful. A large garden at the rear includes a bowling green, however the Bowling Club is for gentlemen only. There is a smoking area at the rear of the pub.
(Bournville)(45,47)P

Blackheath

Bell & Bear Inn ✔

71 Gorsty Hill Road, B65 0HA (on A4099)
11.30-11 (11.30 Fri & Sat); 12-11 Sun
☎ (0121) 561 2196
Taylor Landlord; guest beers Ⓗ
Despite its location in the heart of the Black Country, this 400-year-old hostelry has a rather rural look and feel to it. Its hilly setting provides interesting views of the industrial area from the rear patio, which includes a covered, unheated smoking area and leads down steps to extensive gardens. Quality food, including renowned chunky chips, is served daily until 9pm. Regular themed nights are held, plus a quiz on Thursday and Sunday. Up to seven real ales are usually on handpump. (Old Hill)(417,230)P

Britannia ✔

124 Halesowen Street, B65 0EG
9-midnight (1am Fri & Sat)
☎ (0121) 559 0010
Greene King IPA, Abbot; Marston's Pedigree; guest beers Ⓗ
Smart, open-plan Wetherspoon conversion situated in the centre of Blackheath, with a friendly, community feel. An ever-changing range of up to 10 guest ales is served, along with the usual Wetherspoon food menu. A covered smoking area is at the rear. Close to Rowley Regis train station and Blackheath town centre, where a wide range of buses stop from Dudley, Birmingham and West Bromwich.
Q(Rowley Regis)P

Malt Shovel

61 High Street, B65 0EH (5 mins' walk from Blackheath centre)
11-11 (2am Fri); 10-2am Sat; 12-11 Sun
☎ (0121) 561 2321
Enville Ale; Holden's Golden Glow; guest beer Ⓗ
This small, sports oriented locals' pub has a single L-shaped interior with four TV screens. There is a large garden at the rear. A marquee is erected six to eight times a year for special events such as live music, and a skittles alley is available. There are barbecues throughout the summer, whatever the weather. The cider is Thatchers Cheddar Valley and the guest beer is usually one of the other Enville beers.
(Rowley Regis)(404)

Waterfall

132 Waterfall Lane, B64 6RG (at top of main Blackheath-Old Hill road)
12-3, 5-11; 12-midnight Fri & Sat; 12-10.30 Sun
☎ (0121) 561 3499
Bathams Best Bitter; Holden's Bitter, Golden Glow, Special; guest beers Ⓗ
Acquired by Holden's a few years back, this characterful pub is near Blackheath town centre. It serves up to six guest beers, tending towards stronger brews. The outside drinking area affords wonderful views, although the elevated position means a steep walk uphill from Old Hill station. The lounge bar is unusually located at the front of the pub, with an elongated bar area to the rear. Basic pub meals at reasonable prices are served daily. A popular hostelry, it can get very crowded at weekends. (Old Hill)P

Bloxwich

Lamp Tavern

34 High Street, WS3 2DA (by leisure centre)
12-11
☎ (01922) 479681
Holden's Mild, Bitter; guest beers Ⓗ
Conveniently located adjacent to the leisure centre, this one-room pub split into two sections features a bar on one side and a smaller, comfortable, quieter lounge area on the other. This is a well-decorated pub with local community links. Karaoke nights are popular on Friday and Sunday evenings.
(301,372)

Turf Tavern ★

13 Wolverhampton Road, WS3 2EZ (opp Bloxwich Park)
12-3, 7-11
☎ (01922) 407745
Titanic Mild; guest beers Ⓗ
Grade II listed building, known locally as Tinkys, which has been in the same family for over 130 years. The three rooms are dominated by the bar with its splendid tiled floor. Tinkys is a haven for quiet conversation, which adds to its traditional charm. Outside, the courtyard serves as a pleasant drinking area in warmer weather. Well worth a visit.
Q(Bloxwich)(301)

Brierley Hill

Rose & Crown

161 Bank Street, DY5 3DD (on B4179)
12-2, 6-11; 12-11 Fri & Sat; 12-3.30, 7-11 Sun
☎ (01384) 77825 roseandcrownbrierleyhill.co.uk
Holden's Mild, Bitter, Special, seasonal beers; guest beer Ⓗ
This traditional pub five minutes' walk from the High Street was originally two terraced properties. The lounge has a cosy, relaxed atmosphere; one end of the bar is dominated by a dartboard. A conservatory extension adds extra space, opening onto a small garden with tables and benches. A large selection of good value quality food is served lunchtimes and evenings Monday-Saturday. The ever-

changing guest beer comes from a variety of small breweries. Q♣P

Vine (Bull & Bladder)

10 Delph Road, DY5 2TN
12-11 (10.30 Sun)
(01384) 78293
Bathams Mild, Best Bitter, XXX (winter) H
Classic, unspoilt brewery tap with an ornately decorated facade proclaiming the Shakespearian quotation: 'Blessings of your heart, you brew good ale'. Inside there is a labryrinthine feel. The rooms have contrasting characters – the front bar is small and staunchly traditional, while the larger rear bar, with its own servery and leather seating, houses the dartboard. On the other side of the central passageway is a homely lounge converted from former brewery offices. Good value Black Country lunches are served.
Q(138,139)♣P

Brownhills

Royal Oak

68 Chester Road, WS8 6DU (on A452)
12-11 (midnight Thu-Sat)
(01543) 452089 theroyaloakpub.co.uk
Banks's Original; Caledonian Deuchars IPA; Greene King Abbot; Tetley Bitter; guest beers H
Known locally as the Middle Oak, this pub has gone back to its roots and is beautifully decorated in a 1930s Art Deco style, retaining some original features. Games are played in the traditional bar, while the comfortable lounge has a more relaxed atmosphere. There is a separate dining room and a large enclosed garden with a drinking area at the rear. The smoking area is covered by umbrellas.
(394)♣P

Coseley

New Inn

Birmingham New Road, Ward Street, WV14 9LQ (on A4123)
4-11; 12-11.30 Sat; 12-10.30 Sun
(01902) 676777
Holden's Mild, Bitter, seasonal beers; guest beer H
Cosy one-roomed local, best approached from the Birmingham New Road (126 bus route). The lounge area is housed in a late 20th-century extension while the bar area is in the older 19th-century part of the building, separated by a modern bar counter which is the hub of the pub. An extensive menu is offered Tuesday-Saturday evenings with hot pork sandwiches on Saturday lunchtime. Sunday lunches are a highlight. Family parties and events can be catered for. The patio is covered and heated.
Q(Coseley)(126)♣P

Coventry

Beer Engine

35 Far Gosford Street, CV1 5DW (off A4600)
12-11 (midnight Thu-Sat)
(024) 7627 0015 thebeerengine.net
Black Sheep Best Bitter; guest beers H
A pub of contrasts, this is a friendly local on weekdays and a packed, bustling live music venue at weekends. An ever changing selection of six real ales is available, together with a choice of continental and Eastern European bottled beers. A single-room pub, the front is adorned with film posters, while the back is a gallery for the work of local artists. Sunday roasts are served – at other times you can bring your own food. The pleasant courtyard includes heated shelters for smokers. (27,32)♣

Burnt Post

Kenpas Highway, CV3 6AW (jct of A45/Wainbody Avenue)
12-11 (midnight Thu-Sun)
(024) 7669 2671
Beer range varies H
Former Bass local with an open-plan bar and lounge shared by drinkers and diners alike. An Ember Inns pub, it is well furnished and offers an extensive food menu and a wide range of changing cask beers. The hostelry attracts a diverse clientele of all ages.
(15)P

City Arms

1 Earlsdon Street, CV5 6EP
9-midnight (1am Fri & Sat)
(024) 7671 8170
Greene King IPA, Abbot; Marston's Pedigree; guest beers H
Typically busy Wetherspoon hostelry in the heart of Earlsdon. Well served by public transport, it is popular with students and locals alike. The pub offers a good choice of guest beers, with mini beer festivals featuring a range of ales from breweries such as Church End, Phoenix and RCH. Part of the lively Earlsdon weekend scene, it can be crowded on Friday and Saturday evenings. Food is served all day until 11pm; children are permitted until 9pm if dining.
(12,19)P

Craven Arms

58 Craven Street, Chapelfields, CV5 8DW (1 mile W of city centre, off Allesley Old Road)
11 (4 Tue)-11.30 (midnight Fri & Sat); 12-11 Sun
(024) 7671 5308
Flowers Original; Holden's Golden Glow; Sarah Hughes Dark Ruby; Oakham JHB; guest beers H
Traditional street-corner local with a community atmosphere, situated in a conservation area. The pub forms an integral part of the Craven Street Crawl. It is the only regular outlet in the area for beers from Sarah Hughes and Holden's, both of which were originally stocked at the request of regulars. The pub comprises a lounge and a separate room housing a pool table and a dartboard. Live music is a popular feature on Sunday evening. (10,32)♣

Gatehouse Tavern

46 Hill Street, CV1 4AN (jct 8 of ring road)
11-3, 5-11; 11-midnight Thu-Sat; 12-11 Sun
(024) 7625 6769 gatehousetavern.com
Beer range varies H
One of the few genuine free houses in the city, converted in 1995 from the gatehouse of Leigh Mills worsted and woollen factory,

which was built in 1866. It has an excellent pub garden, the only one in the city centre with a lawn, and is a mecca for Rugby Union fans. Good value home-cooked food is served (not Sun). Most buses travelling to and from the city centre pass within 150 metres. (10,32)

Greyhound Inn

Sutton Stop, Hawkesbury Junction, CV6 6DF
11-11; 12-10.30 Sun
(024) 7636 3046 thegreyhoundinn.com
Highgate Dark Mild; Marston's Pedigree; guest beers H
Winner of the 2005/06/07 Godiva Award for best pub in Coventry and Warwickshire, this canalside inn dates back to around 1830 and has retained many original features. The restaurant and bar serve an extensive menu created by an award-winning chef. Regular beer festivals are hosted in April and September. The terrace and rear garden have their own bar in summer, offering four real ales straight from the cask at weekends. Q (C37,C47) P

Hare & Hounds

Watery Lane, Keresley End, CV7 8JA (jct of Bennetts Road/Watery Lane)
11-11
(024) 7633 2716 hareandhounds.co.uk
Adnams Broadside; Draught Bass; M&B Brew XI; Shepherd Neame Spitfire; guest beer H
Situated on the northern edge of the city, this pub makes a good start, or finish, for country walks. A large, comfortable L-shaped bar area includes real fires. Good value bar meals are available and more interesting dishes are served in the restaurant, where a popular two-for-one offer on lunchtime meals is available. The garden has outdoor seating, floral displays and a children's play area. A large function room including a skittle alley may be hired. Q (36) P

Nursery Tavern

38-39 Lord Street, Chapelfields, CV5 8DA (1 mile W of city centre, off Allesley Old Road)
12-11.30; 11-midnight Fri & Sat; 12-11 Sun
(024) 7667 4530
Courage Best Bitter; Fuller's London Pride; John Smith's Bitter; Taylor Golden Best; guest beers H
Very much a community pub, situated in a terrace in the historic watchmaking area. The pub has three rooms including one at the back used for traditional games, live music and social events. Three guest beers are always on offer. The pub is home to Rugby Union and Formula One clubs, and paraphernalia from both sports is displayed. Beer festivals have been held for many years under cover on the patio. Q (10,32)

Old Windmill

22-23 Spon Street, CV1 3BA
11-11 (midnight Fri & Sat); 12-midnight Sun
(024) 7625 2183
Caledonian Deuchars IPA; Greene King Old Speckled Hen; Taylor Landlord; Theakston Old Peculier; Wychwood Hobgoblin; guest beers H
One of the few timber-framed buildings in the street that actually belongs here. This pub, known as Ma Browns, is said to be the oldest inn in Coventry. It was sympathetically extended a few years ago, using flagstones and timber. An old brewhouse, complete with brick-built copper and other vessels, can be viewed within the premises. Weston's Old Rosie cider is available. (10,32)

Rose & Woodbine

40 North Street, Stoke Heath, CV2 3FW
12-11; 12-5, 7-11 Sun
(024) 7645 1480
Banks's Original; Draught Bass; Tetley Bitter; Wells Bombardier; guest beers H
A popular venue with the locals, this unremarkable pub was built for the Northampton Brewing Company in an area where good pubs are now sparse. Apart from the usual pub games, it also hosts the Premier Homing Society and the Barras Green Homing Society (pigeon racing). Children are welcome until 7pm. The pub is well known for its good value steak meal. Lunchtimes are extended a little on Friday and Saturday. (10,36)

Town Wall Tavern

Bond Street, CV1 4AH (behind Belgrade Theatre)
12-11 (midnight Fri & Sat); 12-6 Sun
(024) 7622 0963
Adnams Bitter, Broadside; Draught Bass; Caledonian Deuchars IPA; M&B Brew XI; guest beer H
Convivial city centre pub with a diverse clientele, ideal for theatregoers. Its three rooms include a delightful snug known as the Donkey Box. Freshly cooked lunchtime meals include seasonal dishes such as spiced Moroccan mutton or rabbit, or prune and cider casserole, offered alongside goat's cheese tart and more traditional fare. Filled ciabatta rolls are also available (no meals Sun). Under-14s are admitted only if dining with adults. (10,32)

Whitefriars Olde Ale House

114-115 Gosford Street, CV1 5DL
12-midnight (1am Fri & Sat); 12-11 Sun
(024) 7625 1655 whitefriarscov.com
Beer range varies H
Originally built in the 14th century, part of this building was combined with its 17th-century neighbour in 1850 to form a butcher's shop. Many features are still discernible today and it is worth taking a look upstairs. Six frequently changing guest beers are available, with Wye Valley Brewery often represented, together with a changing selection of British bottled beers. Beer festivals are held on summer bank holidays in the semi-covered garden at the rear. Q (27,32)

Cradley Heath

Holly Bush

53 Newtown Lane, B64 5EA
4 (2 Sat)-2am
(07949) 594484 ilovethebush.com
Teme Valley T'Other; guest beers H
Two-roomed split-level corner pub just off the High Street. The lower level front bar has an open fireplace and a small raised area just inside the entrance where music and comedy performances take place (Thu-Sat, see website for details). A larger lounge at the

rear provides an alternative haven in which to enjoy the three changing guest beers.
⛼❀◐⊟≈⊞♣●⁻

Darlaston

Prince of Wales

74, Walsall Road, WS10 9JJ
✪ 3 (12 Fri & Sat)-11; 12-10.30 Sun
☎ (0121) 5266244
Holden's Bitter, Golden Glow; guest beers Ⓗ
Traditional Black Country pub with a small, comfortable, family-friendly lounge adorned with photographs of local swimming, football clubs and old town maps. The long, narrow bar is decorated with advertising mirrors and has a dartboard at one end. At the rear is a conservatory and a garden, with a play area and bench seats. Occasional quiz and live music nights are hosted and there is a covered area for smokers. ☕❀◐⊟⊞♣⁻

Dudley

Full Moon ✔

58-60 High Street, DY1 1PY
✪ 9-midnight
☎ (01384) 212294
Enville Ale; Greene King Abbot; Marston's Burton Bitter, Pedigree; guest beers Ⓗ
The Full Moon is a large, centrally located Wetherspoon pub offering good value food and drink. Originally a town-centre department store and then a pizza restaurant, it opened as a pub in August 1996. Recently refurbished, it has a friendly, comfortable atmosphere. Historic local photographs and facts adorn the walls. Food is served 9am-11pm. It is close to the main Dudley bus station, where buses from all over the region terminate. Q☕◐♿⊞●

Halesowen

Coombs Wood Sports & Social Club

Lodgefield Road, B62 8AA (off A4099 to Blackheath)
✪ 7.30 (7 Fri)-11; 12.30-11 Sat; 12-10.30 Sun
☎ (0121) 561 1932
Beer range varies Ⓗ
This former steel works' cricket club has thrived in recent years, providing a social centre for the community. The club is family friendly, with sports naturally dominating: there are large-screen TVs, pool and darts indoors and various sports are played outside in the extensive grounds. The enthusiastic manager provides five or six ever-changing ales, increasing to 12 for the annual beer festival in late January. Bar snacks are available. A CAMRA National Club of the Year finalist, CAMRA members and holders of this Guide are welcome. ❀⊞(244,242A)♣

Hawne Tavern

78 Attwood Street, B63 3UG
✪ 4.30 (12 Sat)-11; 12-10.30 Sun
☎ (0121) 602 2601
Banks's Bitter; Bank Top Dark Mild; Bathams Best Bitter; Red Lion White Lion; guest beers Ⓗ
This busy pub, now in its eleventh consecutive year in the Guide, is a fine example of a community free house, offering four regular and up to six guest beers. It has two rooms: a small cosy lounge and a more lively open bar area, with pool, darts and a sports TV. Sun worshippers and smokers enjoy the enclosed rear garden. Bar snacks are available evenings and Saturday. Children are allowed until 9pm.
Q❀⊟⊞(9)♣P⊡

Somers Sports & Social Club

The Grange, Grange Hill, B62 0JH (on bypass at A456/B4551 jct)
✪ 12-2.30 (3 Sat), 6-11; 12-2, 7-10.30 Sun
☎ (0121) 550 1645
Banks's Bitter; Bathams Mild, Best Bitter; Malvern Hills Black Pear; Olde Swan Original; guest beers Ⓗ
The club occupies a large 250-year-old house set in extensive grounds. Leading off the bar area is a comfortable lounge and a spacious patio overlooking the bowling green. To add to previous CAMRA national awards, the club won Regional Club of the Year in 2008. To gain admission, show a CAMRA membership card or a copy of the current Guide to the steward. Groups of five or more should phone ahead.
❀⊞(9)P

Waggon & Horses

21 Stourbridge Road, B63 3TU (on A458, ½ mile from bus station)
✪ 12-11.30 (12.30am Fri & Sat)
☎ (0121) 550 4989
Bathams Best Bitter; Bank Top Dark Mild; Holden's Golden Glow; Nottingham EPA; Oakham White Dwarf; Red Lion White Lion; guest beers Ⓗ
This CAMRA branch Pub of the Year 2008 has a national reputation, but a real community feel. Its regular beers, supplemented by eight guests, many from independent and micro-breweries, make this pub a must for enlightened drinkers. Quieter seating at both ends complements the traditional bar. Real cider and four Belgian beers are also on draught. Tasty home-made cobs are available 12-6.30pm Monday to Saturday, and a charity quiz is held on alternate Wednesdays.
Q⊞(9)●

Hampton in Arden

White Lion ✔

High Street, B92 0AA
✪ 12-11 (10.30 Sun)
☎ (01675) 442833 🌐 thewhitelioninn.com
Adnams Bitter; Black Sheep Best Bitter; M&B Brew XI; guest beer Ⓗ
A charming Grade II listed 17th-century timber-framed building, the White Lion has been licensed since 1838. A popular local, it has a cosy lounge and public bar, both with lovely real fires. The separate restaurant is ideal for intimate dining, while traditional bar meals are also available. The proprietor took over in 2006, increasing the quality of real ales to such an extent that the White Lion was local CAMRA's Most Improved Pub in 2007.
⛼Q⛟◐⊟♿≈⊞P⁻

Kingswinford

Bridge

110 Moss Grove, DY6 9HH (on A491)
✪ 12-3, 5-11.30; 12-11.45 Fri & Sat; 12-11.30 Sun
☎ (01384) 352356
Banks's Original, Bitter; guest beers Ⓗ
In addition to a healthy local trade, this pub is most welcoming to visitors. The bar extends across the front of the building and there is a cosy lounge behind. Outside is a well-equipped garden with a children's play area. One or two guest beers come from the brewery list. Occasional live entertainment takes place at weekends. Hot pies and pasties are available, with sandwiches made to order. Several bus routes from Dudley, Wolverhampton and Stourbridge stop nearby. ☊❀⊡🚌(256,257)♣P⚟▯

Knowle

Vaults

St Johns Close, B93 0JU (off High Street A4141)
✪ 12-2.30, 5-11.30; 12-11.30 Fri & Sat; 12-11 Sun
☎ (01564) 773656
Ansells Mild; Caledonian Deuchars IPA; Gale's HSB; Tetley Bitter; guest beers Ⓗ
Located just off the High Street, this free house was fully refurbished in June 2007 but retains the traditional ambience for which it is well known. An ever-changing selection of guest beers is offered, many from small breweries, and Weston's cider is also available. The pub holds occasional beer festivals and an annual pickled onion competition. Light meals are served lunchtimes Monday to Saturday. Local CAMRA Pub of the Year 2008. ◖🚌(40A,40C)●

Lower Gornal

Black Bear

86 Deepdale Lane, DY3 2AE
✪ 5 (4 Fri)-11; 12-11 Sat; 12-10.30 Sun
☎ (01384) 253333
Kinver Black Bear IPA; Shepherd Neame Spitfire; guest beers Ⓗ
This charming traditional pub, originally an 18th-century farmhouse, is built on the hillside with views over the south of the Black Country, and supported with massive buttresses. Inside, the L-shaped, split-level room has discrete and comfortable seating areas. Up to five guest beers are usually available, mainly from smaller breweries. Gornal Wood bus station is about 10 minutes' walk away. ❀🚌(257)♣

Five Ways

Himley Road, DY3 2PZ (jct of B4176/4175)
✪ 12-11 (midnight Fri & Sat); 12-10.30 Sun
☎ (01384) 252968
Bathams Best Bitter Ⓗ
Warm and welcoming wayside watering hole on the western edge of the West Midlands conurbation. Its one crook-shaped room is just big enough to accommodate a large TV screen for football matches at one end without interrupting the civilised social discourse at the other. There is a raised decking area overlooking the car park at the back of the pub. Good value weekday lunches are served. ❀◖🚌(257)♣●P⚟

Fountain

8 Temple Street, DY3 2PE (on B4157)
✪ 12-11 (10.30 Sun)
☎ (01384) 242777
Enville Ale; Greene King Abbot; Hook Norton Old Hooky; RCH Pitchfork; guest beers Ⓗ
Twice winner of Dudley CAMRA Pub of the Year, this excellent free house serves nine real ales accompanied by draught and bottled Belgian beers, real cider and 20 fruit wines. The busy, vibrant bar is complemented by an elevated dining area serving excellent food until 9pm Monday to Saturday and Sunday lunches until 5pm. During the summer months the rear garden is a pleasant area to while away an hour or two. ☊❀◖◗♿🚌(541)♣●

Old Bulls Head

1 Redhall Road, DY3 2NU (at Temple Street jct)
✪ 2 (1 Fri)-11; 12-11 Sat & Sun
☎ (01384) 231616 🌐 oldbullshead.co.uk
Black Country BFG, Pig on the Wall, Fireside; guest beer Ⓗ
This imposing late-Victorian pub has two rooms. The larger lounge bar is popular for pub games and has a raised area at one end serving as a stage for varied entertainment on several evenings a week. The sports lounge includes a pool table, dartboard and large-screen TV. The Black Country Ales Brewery is at the rear and there are usually at least four of its beers available, including a guest seasonal from the brewery or another small independent brewer. Cobs are available daily. ♛❀🚌(541)♣●P⚟

Lye

Windsor Castle Inn ✔

7 Stourbridge Road, DY9 7DG
✪ 11-11
☎ (01384) 897809 🌐 windsorcastlebrewery.com
Sadler's Jack's Ale, Mild, Worcester Sorcerer, Thin Ice, IPA, seasonal beers; guest beer Ⓗ
The Windsor Castle Inn is the brewery tap for Sadler's Ales (Windsor Castle Brewery), re-housed in Lye in 2004 by the descendants of the original brewery. The interior combines genuine rustic features with modern technology and the pub won local CAMRA Pub of the Year 2007 plus several awards from the licensed trade. Most of the Sadler's range of ales is available, with seasonal beers and guests from other micros when space permits. Brewery tours are held every Monday evening (telephone first). ◖◗⇌🚌(9,247)P⚟

Netherton

Olde Swan (Ma Pardoe's) ☆

89 Halesowen Road, DY2 9PY
✪ 11-11; 12-4, 7-10.30 Sun
☎ (01384) 253075
Olde Swan Original, Dark Swan, Entire, Bumblehole, Black Widow (winter), seasonal beers Ⓗ
Characterful pub on CAMRA's National Inventory of historic pub interiors and home to the Olde Swan Brewery. The pub was runner-

up CAMRA National Pub of the Year in 2004. The front bar is an unspoilt gem, with an enamelled ceiling and solid-fuel stove, and there is a cosy rear snug. The upstairs restaurant is highly regarded for its a la carte menu; Sunday lunches are also available (booking is essential). Olde Swan Entire and Bumblehole are available in bottles.
⌂Q❀◐◑⊟♿⊟P

Oldbury

Waggon & Horses ★ ✔

17A Church Street, B69 3AD
⊙ 12-11 (midnight Fri & Sat); 12-10.30 Sun
☎ (0121) 552 5467
Brains Rev James; Enville White; Oakham JHB; guest beers Ⓗ
CAMRA National Inventory listed pub, courtesy of its ornate tiled walls, Holt's Brewery etched windows and interesting panelled ceiling. This pub is popular with shoppers and office workers who enjoy its fine ales. Reasonably priced, freshly cooked food including a vegetarian selection is served at lunchtimes Monday to Saturday and evenings Tuesday to Friday. There is a large public car park behind the pub and Oldbury bus station is a two-minute walk away.
⌂Q◐◑⊟♿⇌(Sandwell & Dudley) ⊟(87,120)P

Oldswinford

Shrubbery Cottage

28 Heath Lane, DY8 1RQ
⊙ 12-11 (10.30 Sun)
☎ (01384) 377598
Holden's Bitter, Golden Glow, Special, seasonal beers; guest beer Ⓗ
Welcoming pub with a single, spacious, open room and a large U-shaped bar. There is a large-screen TV at one end which usually shows live golf or football matches. The pub provides full disabled access from the car park and has Wi-Fi Internet access. The large garden area has a purpose-built barbecue.
❀◐♿⇌(Stourbridge Jct)⊟P⁻

Pensnett

Fox & Grapes

176 High Street, DY5 4JQ (A4101)
⊙ 1 (12 Sat)-11; 12-10.30 Sun
☎ (01384) 261907 🌐 bathams.co.uk
Bathams Mild, Best Bitter, XXX (winter) Ⓗ
A former Holt, Plant & Deakin pub acquired by Bathams to replace the nearby Holly Bush that was closed in 1999. Beyond the striking brick frontage, a Bathams-tiled passageway leads to several drinking areas around a central bar. A solid-fuel stove heats two rear areas, while the front area is more akin to a public bar. There is a heated, covered patio area at the rear, with tables and benches out front.
⌂❀⊟♣P⁻

Rushall

Manor Arms ★

Park Road, off Daw End Lane, WS4 1LQ (off B4154 at Canal Bridge)
⊙ 12-midnight (11 Sun)
☎ (01922) 642333
Banks's Original, Bitter; Jennings Cocker Hoop; guest beers Ⓗ
Listed in CAMRA's National Inventory of Historic Pubs, this inn was built in 1102. It is known locally as the 'Pub With No Bar', because the beer pulls come straight out of the wall. With exposed beams and much olde world charm, it also has a reputation for being haunted. Glenn Miller is said to have frequented the pub during World War II. Reasonably priced, good food is served. The large beer garden next to the canal and local country park is extremely popular in summer months. ⌂Q❀◐◑⊟⊟(355,356)P⁻

Sedgley

Beacon Hotel ★

129 Bilston Street, DY3 1JE (A463)
⊙ 12-2.30 (3 Sat), 5.30 (6 Sat)-11; 12-3, 7-10.30 Sun
☎ (01902) 883380
Sarah Hughes Pale Amber, Sedgley Surprise, Dark Ruby, seasonal beers; guest beers Ⓗ
This classic, beautifully restored Victorian tap house and tower brewery is the home of Sarah Hughes ales. The heart of this atmospheric, popular pub is the small island servery with hatches. Off the central corridor is a traditional tap room with benches, a small cosy snug, a large main room and a family room with access to a well-equipped garden and play area. Cobs are available. Dudley CAMRA branch Pub of the Year 2008 and West Midlands County Pub of the Year.
Q❀⊟(545)P⁻

Bull's Head

27 Bilston Street, DY3 1JA (A463)
⊙ 10 (11 Sun)-11.30
☎ (01902) 661676
Holden's Mild, Ⓗ **Bitter,** Ⓗ/Ⓟ **Golden Glow, seasonal beers; guest beer** Ⓗ
The Bull's Head is a small, double-fronted, street-corner listed building. Close to the centre of Sedgley village, it has a community atmosphere. The front bar is lively with local chatter, pub games and a sports screen. To the side is a lounge which can be curtained off to provide a small function room. Children are welcome in this area. Behind the pub is a pleasant walled yard housing a well-equipped smoking shelter. Cobs are available.
⌂❀⊟(545,558)♣⁻

Mount Pleasant (Stump)

144 High Street, DY3 1RH (A459)
⊙ 7 (6.30 Wed-Sat)-11; 12-3, 7-10.30 Sun
☎ (0795) 0195652
Beer range varies Ⓗ
The mock-Tudor exterior of this sensitively refurbished free house fronts a friendly and cheerful interior. The good-sized front bar has a convivial feel, while the homely and warm rear lounge is split into two rooms on different levels, both with coal stoves. Eight handpumps provide a good range of guest beers. Dog-friendly, the pub is a five-minute walk from Sedgley centre.
⌂Q❀⊟⊟(558)♣P⁻

Shirley

Bernie's Real Ale Off-Licence

266 Cranmore Boulevard, B90 4PX

11.30-2, 5-10; 7-9 Sun

(0121) 7442827

Beer range varies H

An oasis for discerning drinkers, Bernie's has enjoyed 26 consecutive years in the Guide. Three or four guest beers are generally available, mainly from micro-breweries all around the country, but predominantly northern. Customers are encouraged to try before they buy, and can take away their favourites in a bottle, carry-keg or poly-pin. Rich's Draught cider is also available and there is an excellent selection of British and Belgian bottled beers. This is truly beer at home as it should be.

Solihull

Fieldhouse

10 Knightcote Drive, Monkspath, B91 3JU

12-11 (11.30 Thu; midnight Fri & Sat)

(0121) 711 8011

M&B Brew XI; guest beers H

Part of the Ember Inns chain, this large, modern pub is tastefully decorated and comfortably furnished, featuring four large fires (one real, three coal-effect) and pleasant patio areas. It usually serves four guest ales from across the country, often unusual ones that change frequently. Always busy, it attracts a wide age range, but children must be over 14 and dining. Regular quiz nights are held on Sunday and Tuesday.

P

Golden Acres

Rowood Drive, Damsonwood, B92 9NG

12-11 (midnight Fri & Sat)

(0121) 704 9002

Beer range varies H

Very much a community hostelry, this 1960s estate pub has an enthusiastic landlord who always offers at least three beers from small breweries. Particular favourites are Wye Valley and Cottage. Seasonal beers are also a speciality. Food is from an in-house Cantonese/Chinese operation on the basis of eat in or takeaway. The outdoor heated smoking area has a large-screen TV.

(76,966A)P

Stourbridge

Royal Exchange

75 Enville Street, DY8 1XW

1 (12 Sat)-11; 12-10.30 Sun

(01384) 396726

Bathams Mild, Best Bitter, XXX (Winter) H

Popular locals' pub in the Batham's estate with a lively bar and a small, quiet lounge, plus a large paved patio area, all accessed from a narrow passageway. There is also an upstairs meeting room available for private hire, a public car park opposite and the bus stops right outside. The absence of TV, games machines or background music makes this an ideal pub to enjoy the banter and test your wits with the 'quote' and 'word' of the week.

Q(Town)

Sutton Coldfield

Bishop Vesey

63 Boldmere Road, B73 5UY

9-11

(0121) 355 5077

Courage Directors; Greene King Abbot; Marston's Pedigree; Shepherd Neame Spitfire; guest beers H

Named after the town's Tudor benefactor, this busy and popular Wetherspoon pub provides a convenient and welcoming meeting place. It has an open-plan layout with upstairs seating and an outside patio area for smokers. Children are allowed in the family area if dining until 9pm. Themed evenings and regular beer festivals feature.

(Wylde Green)

Crown

66 Walsall Road, Four Oaks, B74 4RA

12-11 (midnight Thu-Sat)

(0121) 323 2715

M&B Brew XI; Marston's Pedigree; guest beers H

An Ember Inn pub, the Crown has a tastefully designed, spacious interior, with individual seating areas and a large, curved bar, attracting a mixed clientele. There is a large car park and outside seating areas equipped with umbrellas and heaters. The food quality ensures a busy pub, as does the varying range of well kept ales and the warm, friendly atmosphere. (Butlers Lane)P

Tipton

Port 'n' Ale

178 Horseley Heath, DY4 7DS

12-11 (midnight Fri & Sat)

(0121) 520 6572

Greene King Abbot; guest beers H

This friendly pub serves up to 10 ever-changing real ales, including at least one dark beer. It also usually stocks two traditional ciders. A large central bar area serves an open-plan interior and in addition there is a conservatory and a beer garden. Good food is served all day and children are allowed until 9pm. Regular quiz nights take place each Tuesday, plus beer festivals in spring and autumn. (74)P

Rising Sun

116 Horseley Road, DY4 7NH (off B4517)

12-2.30, 5-11; 12-11 Sat; 12-10.30 Sun

(0121) 530 2308

Banks's Original; Oakham JHB; guest beers H

Imposing Victorian hostelry comprising two distinct rooms: the bar to the right is adorned with pictures of local sporting heroes, and the comfortable lounge to the left is divided into two areas by a wooden screen and warmed by an open fire in cold weather. In summer the backyard is open for drinking and occasional functions. Up to six guest beers complement the two regulars. Great Bridge bus station is a 10-minute walk, with frequent services to Dudley, West Bromwich and Birmingham. (401,402)

Upper Gornal

Britannia (Sally's) ☆

109 Kent Street, DY3 1UX (on A459)

12-11 (10.30 Sun)

(01902) 883253

Bathams Mild, Best Bitter, XXX (winter) Ⓗ

The Britannia owes its CAMRA National Inventory listing to the cosy tap room at the rear, named after legendary former landlady Sally Perry. Its wall-mounted handpumps can be seen in action on Friday evening. At other times service is from the main front bar, itself a very comfortable place to be. There is also a family/games room with a TV. Behind the pub is the former brewhouse, a delightful backyard, a smoking shelter and garden. Local pork pies are served. (558)

Jolly Crispin

25 Clarence Street, DY3 1UL (on A459)

4-11; 12-11 Fri & Sat; 12-10.30 Sun

(01902) 672220 thejollycrispin.co.uk

Titanic Crispy Nail; guest beers Ⓗ

Dating in part from the 18th century, this vibrant pub is entered down a couple of steps from street level (take care!), leading into the front bar with two distinct cosy areas. At the rear is a comfortable lounge with a panoramic view over the north of the Black Country. The pub is deservedly popular with locals and visitors and is dog friendly. There are eight ever-changing guest beers. CAMRA West Midlands County Pub of the Year 2007.

(558)P

Walsall

Arbor Lights

127-128 Lichfield Street, WS1 1SY (off A4148 ring road)

10 (12 Sun)-11

(01922) 613361 arborlights.co.uk

Beer range varies Ⓗ

Opened in 2003, this modern open plan, town centre pub is popular with drinkers and diners alike. The award-winning restaurant offers good locally-produced food (booking recommended, especially at the weekend). The pub's name is derived from the nearby arboretum illuminations, known locally as 'The Lights', held annually in September. Three rotating guest beers are always available and Weston's Old Rosie cider is stocked in summer.

(394,997)

Butts Tavern

44 Butts Street, WS4 2BJ

12-11 (midnight Fri & Sat)

(01922) 629332 buttstavern.co.uk

Jennings Cocker Hoop; guest beers Ⓗ

A friendly, two-roomed community local with a pleasant atmosphere. The large main bar features a stage at one end, while a smaller room includes a pool table. Four handpumps offer one permanent beer and up to three changing guests. Quiz night is Tuesday and live entertainment takes place most Fridays and Saturdays. Sky Sports is screened but is not too intrusive. There is an external smoking area at the rear.

Fountain

49 Lower Forster Street, WS1 1XB (off A4148)

12-midnight

(01922) 629741

Caledonian Deuchars IPA; Fuller's London Pride; guest beer Ⓗ

Small two-roomed Victorian local in a conservation area. It has been sympathetically modernised and recently redecorated, featuring a display of photographs of old Walsall. Good pub food includes home-cooked pies and Sunday roasts (evening meals served Tue-Sat). Live entertainment is held on Friday, Saturday and Sunday evenings. Local history and leather museums are nearby. This friendly community pub on the edge of the town centre makes a welcome break from the circuit. Q(394,977)

Lyndon House Hotel

9-10 Upper Rushall Street, WS1 2HA

11-11.30 (2am Fri & Sat); 12-11 Sun

(01922) 612511 lyndonhousehotel.co.uk

Courage Directors; Greene King Abbot; Highgate Dark Mild; Theakston Best Bitter; guest beers Ⓗ

This sensitively developed pub, with an island bar and balcony drinking area, forms part of a larger hotel, formerly a Salvation Army hostel and an Italian restaurant. A warm, cheerful and comfortable venue, it is frequented by diners, drinkers, shoppers, hotel guests and the local business community. Situated so close to Walsall Market and the Parish church of St Matthews that one sees a real slice of Walsall life. Q(51,377)

New Inns (Pretty Bricks)

5 John Street, WS2 8AF (off B4210, near magistrates court)

12-11 (midnight Fri & Sat)

(01922) 637182

Copper Dragon Golden Pippin; Greene King Abbot; guest beers Ⓗ

Small, friendly back-street local with a comfortable bar, cosy lounge and corridor drinking area, plus a coal fire in winter. It is known as the Pretty Bricks thanks to its glazed-tiled frontage. This is one of the pubs where CAMRA launched nationally in 1972, and Walsall CAMRA was founded here in the same year. Eight handpumps serve up to six guest beers. Live music features weekly in the upstairs lounge bar, which is also available for private hire. (301)

Prince

239 Stafford Street, WS2 8DF

10 (10.30 Sun)-midnight

(07973) 329746

Banks's Original, Bitter; guest beers Ⓗ

Situated near the town centre and art gallery, this pub is named after the Prussian General Blucher, who fought with Wellington at Waterloo. The facade still carries the logo of former owners North Worcester Breweries. You will find a potted history of the pub in the front bar, where traditional pub games are played. The spacious lounge has a pool table and there is a benched area at the rear. Live entertainment takes place Friday to Sunday. The smoking shelter is heated. P

ENGLAND

Rose & Crown
5 Old Birchills, WS2 8QH (off A34)
12-midnight (1am Fri & Sat); 11-midnight Sun
(01922) 720533
Black Country Pig on the Wall, BFG; guest beers
Grade II listed, this three-roomed corner pub dating from 1901 once belonged to Lord's Brewery, a company noted for the quality of its buildings. Visitors enter into a central corridor that also serves as a drinking area. The long bar has a fine bar back with glazed tiling. There is live entertainment on Saturday evening and karaoke on Friday evening and Sunday afternoon. A pool table, function room and Sky Sports TV are also available.

Walsall Arms
7 Bank Street, WS1 2EP (behind Royal Hotel, off A34B)
12-2 (3 Fri & Sat), 6-11; 12-5, 7-10.30 Sun
(01922) 626660
Marston's Mansfield Dark Mild, Mansfield Cask Ale, Burton Bitter, Pedigree; guest beers
Friendly, traditional back-street locals' pub. It has an attractive saloon bar with a tiled floor and a smaller, more intimate public bar. A particular feature is the excellent and popular skittle alley. Although a little way from the shopping area, it is easily accessible on the Birmingham to Walsall main bus route.
(51,377)

Walsall Cricket Club
Gorway Road, WS1 3BE (off A34, by university campus)
8-11; 7-11.30 Fri; 12-11.30 Sat; 12-11 Sun
(01922) 622094 walsallcricketclub.com
Marston's Burton Bitter; Wye Valley HPA; guest beers
Established in 1830, the Club has occupied this site since 1907. The comfortable lounge displays cricket memorabilia and the bar is staffed by members. On match days, the cricket can be viewed through panoramic windows. In good weather the lounge is opened onto the patio area. Beer festivals are staged here. Entry to the Club for non-members is by showing this Guide or a CAMRA membership card. Q (51)P

White Lion
150 Sandwell Street, WS1 3EQ
12-11 (midnight Thu-Sat)
(01922) 628542
Adnams Bitter; Greene King IPA; Highgate Dark Mild; Jennings Cocker Hoop; guest beer
Imposing late-Victorian back-street local. The classic sloping bar, with its deep end and shallow end, is one of the best in town. A plush, comfortable lounge caters for the drinker who wants to languish. This pub is a great community melting pot, with live music on some nights. A small garden caters for smokers. Q (404)

Wednesbury

Old Blue Ball
19 Hall End, WS10 9ED (off B4200)
12-3, 5-11; 12-11 Fri; 12-4.30, 7-11 Sat; 12-3.30, 7-11 Sun
(0121) 5560197
Everards Original; Taylor Landlord; guest beers
A traditional back-street pub where cask sales are booming. The bar now boasts six handpumps dispensing four changing guest beers. The interior comprises three rooms: a small bar through a sliding door on the right, a family room where darts is keenly contested on the left and the quieter back room snug. Drinking is acceptable in the corridor which, like the snug, has a serving hatch. The large garden has plenty of seating and a children's play area.
Q (Great Western St)

Olde Leathern Bottel
40 Vicarage Road, WS10 9DW (off A461)
12-2.30 (not Mon), 6-11 (11.30 Fri); 12-11.30 Sat; 12-4, 7-11 Sun
(0121) 505 0230
Worthington's Bitter; guest beers
Set in cottages dating from 1510, the bar and snug have bench seating, while the split-level lounge features soft furnishings. Drinkers can also stand in the passage and there is additional seating out in the rear yard. The pub is decorated throughout with old photos and prints. Good value home-cooked meals include a vegetarian selection. Children are welcome to dine here. The pub hosts the local history society, and stages a Sunday night quiz.

Rosehill Tavern
80 Church Hill, WS10 9DU (off A461, near top of Church Hill)
12-11 (1am Fri & Sat)
(0121) 530 8128
Banks's Original; guest beers
Friendly, welcoming pub situated in the Church Hill area of the town. It has three rooms including a family room and a bar decorated with sporting memorabilia and offering two rotating guest beers. The pub also has a spacious garden and an upstairs function room. A novel feature is the covered smoking area with a wall-mounted large-screen TV.
(Great Western St) (311A,313) P

Wednesfield

Pyle Cock
Rookery Street, WV11 1UN (on old Wolverhampton Road)
10.30-11 (11.30 Fri & Sat); 11-11 Sun
(01902) 732125
Banks's Original, Bitter; guest beers
A friendly welcome awaits you at this traditional three-roomed pub dating back to the 1860s. The public bar offers wooden settlebacks, and the lounge and further rooms are reached via a corridor. With its wide mix of regulars, visitors are soon drawn into conversation. Darts, dominoes and crib teams play here regularly and the lounge hosts entertainment on Saturday evening. The guest beers are usually from Marston's or Jennings, plus additional beers from the Marston's list.
(559) P

Royal Tiger ✓

41-43 High Street, WV11 1ST
9am-midnight (1am Fri & Sat)
(01902) 307816
Banks's Original; Enville Ale; Greene King Abbot; Marston's Pedigree; guest beers H
A modern, purpose-built pub which opened in 2000, this Wetherspoon's outlet offers a range of real ales and cider. Standard Wetherspoon's food includes Sunday lunches and curry and steak nights. The patio at the rear, adjacent to the canal, now includes a covered, heated smoking area. The pub is next to a bookmakers – the site of the original Royal Tiger pub which closed in 1994.
(559)

Vine ★

35 Lichfield Road, WV11 1TN
11.30 (12 Sun)-11
(01902) 733529
Black Country BFG, Pig On The Wall, Fireside; guest beers H
A rare intact example of a simple inter-war working class pub. Built in 1938, this CAMRA National Inventory and Grade II listed hostelry retains its bar, lounge and snug. Revitalised since being taken over by Black Country Traditional Inns after a period of closure, it serves an ever-changing range of up to five guest beers and a cider to complement the Black Country ales. Beer festivals are held regularly in the rear snug.
Q(559)P

West Bromwich

Greets Green Sports & Bowling Club

101 Whitehall Road, B70 0HG (on B4166)
5.30-11; 12-midnight Fri & Sat; 11.30-11 Sun
(0121) 557 1388
Beer range varies H
Popular local community club, set back from the main road in the Greets Green area of West Bromwich. It has two large, comfortable lounges, one available to hire for functions. A third, more intimate room, once the local clinic, is home to an annual beer festival.
(401,402A)P

Willenhall

Falcon

77 Gomer Street West, WV13 2NR (off B4464)
12-11 (10.30 Sun)
(01902) 633378
Greene King Abbot; Oakham JHB; Olde Swan Dark Swan; RCH Pitchfork; guest beers H
Walsall CAMRA Pub of the Year 2005-2007 and boasting seven beers, the Falcon is the flagship real ale pub in Willenhall. It has been run by the same family since 1984 and this continuity has without doubt led to its ever-growing reputation and popularity. The pub was built in 1936 and has two rooms – a lively bar and a quieter lounge. Popular darts and crib teams are based here. Handy for Willenhall Lock Museum.
(525,529)

Wollaston

Forresters Arms

Bridgnorth Road, DY8 3PL (on A458 towards Bridgnorth)
12-2.30, 6-11.30; 6-midnight Fri & Sat; 12-3, 7-11 Sun
(01384) 394476
Banks's Original; Enville Ale; Marston's Pedigree H
Friendly local on the outskirts of Wollaston. The L-shaped room provides a convenient area where diners can sample good value food. Quizzes are held on the first and third Sunday of each month and a poker night is held on Monday. An event not to be missed is the annual Wollaston charity fun run which starts from outside the pub and finishes at the Unicorn, half a mile away. It is followed by a barbecue. The pub also hosts the Forresters Golf Club. P

Unicorn

145 Bridgnorth Road, DY8 3NX (on A458 towards Bridgnorth)
12-11; 12-4, 7-10.30 Sun
(01384) 394823
Bathams Mild, Best Bitter, XXX (winter) H
This former brewhouse was purchased by Bathams in the early 1990s following the death of the last member of the Billingham family. Since becoming part of the estate, it is widely regarded as the pub that serves its finest pint. The original brewhouse remains to the side, but sadly will never brew again. The pub remains a two-bar house, popular with all ages. It serves generous cobs at lunchtime and offers a free Wi-Fi service. QP

Wolverhampton

Chindit ✓

113 Merridale Road, WV3 9SE
2 (12 Sat)-11; 12-11 Sun
(01902) 425582 thechindit.co.uk
Caledonian Deuchars IPA; Enville Ale; Wye Valley HPA; guest beers H
Street-corner pub named in honour of the local men who served with the South Staffordshire regiment, taking part in the 194 Chindit campaign in Burma. The pub comprises two rooms: a comfortable lounge and a bar with a pool table, both with TV screens showing live sport. Up to three guest beers are available, usually from local micro-breweries. Live music is staged on Friday evening and an outdoor beer festival over the May Day weekend. (513,543)P

Combermere Arms

90 Chapel Ash, WV3 0TY (on A41 Tettenhall Rd)
11-3, 5.30-11; 12-midnight Fri & Sat; 12-10.30 Sun
(01902) 421880
Banks's Original, Bitter; guest beers H
Family-friendly three-room local with a bar and a snug off a corridor and a servery leading to a covered and heated courtyard, with seating for smokers. A beer garden to the rear includes seating and the outside Gents' toilets are built around a tree. Band nights are held on Saturday in the courtyard and bar meals are available weekday lunchtimes only.
P

Great Western

Sun Street, WV10 0DJ

11-11; 12-3, 7-10.30 Sun

(01902) 351090

Bathams Best Bitter; Holden's Mild, Bitter, Golden Glow, Special; guest beer H

This historic 150-year-old corner pub is a joy to behold. It is situated opposite the former Great Western low-level railway station which is being redeveloped. The original pub building was extended in the 1990s and it is now an award-winning hostelry famous for its good value food. The interior features both railway and Wolverhampton Wanderers memorabilia. (St George's)P

Hogshead

186 Stafford Street, WV1 1NA

12-midnight (2am Thu-Sun)

(01902) 717955

Caledonian Deuchars IPA; Enville White; Greene King Old Speckled Hen; Wells Bombardier; guest beers H

Built around 1894 as the Vine (the name is still evident in the brickwork), it closed in 1984 before reopening as the Hogshead in 1998. The pub is locally listed for its excellent terracotta exterior. It attracts customers of all ages and there are plenty of alcoves to sit in if you want to get away from the TV screens and pool tables. Food is served daily until 9pm (may be earlier at weekends). Live music is staged monthly. (St George's)

Moon under Water

53-55 Lichfield Street, WV1 1EQ

9am-midnight (1am Fri & Sat)

(01902) 422447

Banks's Original; Enville Ale; Greene King IPA, Abbot; Marston's Pedigree; guest beers H

Former Co-op store converted by Wetherspoon's in 1995. The decor includes pictures showing the industrial and social history of Wolverhampton. The Grand Theatre is opposite and the pub is popular with theatre patrons – it can also get busy on weekend evenings with pre-clubbers. Beers from Enville and Highgate breweries often appear as guests, along with Weston's cider. Food is served until 11pm. (St George's)

Newhampton

19 Riches Street, Whitmore Reans, WV6 0DW

11-11 (midnight Fri & Sat); 12-11 Sun

(01902) 745773

Caledonian Deuchars IPA; Courage Best Bitter, Directors; Wye Valley HPA; guest beers H

Multi-roomed local with an unexpectedly large garden where games facilities include a bowling green and a boules piste. Its upstairs function room is a thriving venue for folk and other music. It also has a pool room and bowls pavilion. Outside is a play area with a slide and climbing frame.

Posada

48 Lichfield Street, WV1 1DG

12-11 (midnight Thu-Sat); closed Sun

Adnams Broadside; Caledonian Deuchars IPA; Greene King Abbot; Wells Bombardier; guest beers H

Built in 1884 on the site of a pub called the Noah's Ark, the distinctive frontage was added in 1907. It was visited by Lawrence of Arabia in 1934. The interior layout of the pub was altered in 1983, when it was turned into one room. It retains its original tiles, together with a superb bar back, open fireplace and snob screens. CAMRA members get a discount on real ale. (St George's)

Shoulder of Mutton

62 Wood Road, Tettenhall Wood, WV6 8NF

11.30-2.30, 5-11 (midnight Fri & Sat); 12-2.30, 7-11 Sun

(01902) 756672

Banks's Original, Bitter; guest beer H

One-roomed, low-ceilinged pub with genuine oak beams, in a conservation area. This friendly, welcoming local was recently saved from demolition with the help of the local CAMRA branch, who named it Community Pub of the Year for 2008. The games room is served from a hatch and can be booked for meetings. There is a large car park and a patio area, with space for barbecues. Occasional live entertainment is held on weekday evenings. Q(510)P

Stile

3 Harrow Street, Whitmore Reans, WV1 4PB

11-11; 12-10.30 Sun

(01902) 425336

Banks's Original, Bitter P

A late-Victorian community pub with a bar and games/family room. It was built in 1900 to replace the former inn on the site – the stable block opposite the L-shaped bowling green still survives. The Stile attracts a varied mix of customers, from locals to an influx of football fans on match days as it is close to the football ground. Occasional guest beers are served. (505,507)

Swan (at Compton)

Bridgnorth Road, Compton, WV6 8AE

11-11 (11.30 Thu; midnight Fri & Sat); 12-11 Sun

(01902) 754736

Banks's Original, Bitter; guest beer H

Grade II listed inn in the Compton area of the city. This is a basic, unspoilt gem with a convivial atmosphere – the traditional bar features wooden settles, exposed beams and a faded painting of a swan dating from 1777. The bar and L-shaped lounge are both supplied from a central servery. The lounge has Sky TV for sports and doubles as a games room, with a dartboard. The patio is partially covered for smokers. Q(510,890)P

Tap & Spile

35 Princess Street, WV1 1HD

10am-11 (10.30 Sun)

(01902) 713319

Beer range varies H

City-centre pub comprising a narrow bar and two snugs. A large-screen TV and three further screens show major sporting events and music. It can get busy with Wolves fans on match days and with night-time clubbers. Darts is also popular, with four teams playing. The beer is delivered direct from local micro-breweries via the SIBA scheme. Weston's cider is also available. Handy for bus and railway stations. (St George's)

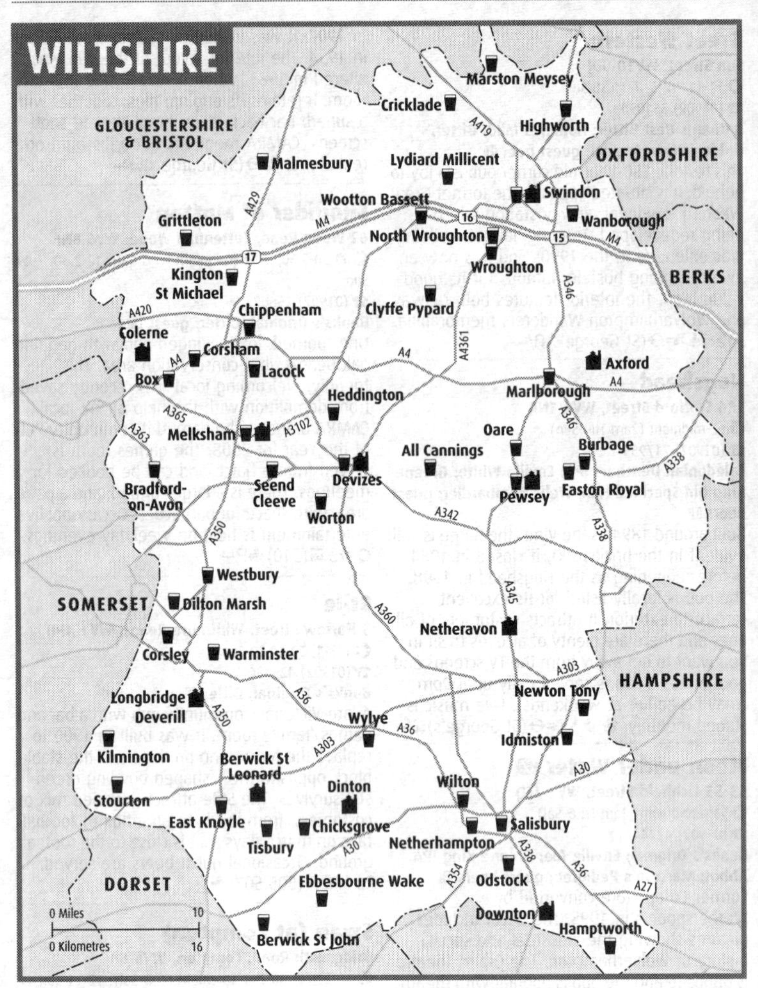

All Cannings

Kings Arms Inn ✓

The Street, SN10 3PA SU069618

12-3 (not Mon winter), 7-11 (10.30 Sun)

☎ (01380) 860328

Wadworth IPA, Horizon, 6X Ⓗ

Tucked away in the village, this friendly local is well known for its excellent Wadworth ales —the landlord is a recent winner of cellarmanship awards. Home-cooked food is also high quality, with a wide-ranging menu on offer. The large entrance bar has a raised restaurant area on one side and a games room on the other. The pub is popular with visitors who come to see the nearby crop circles and is home to the local cricket team in the summer. ❀◑⛺♣P

Berwick St John

Talbot

The Cross, SP7 0HA (S of A30, 5 miles E of Shaftesbury)

12-2.30, 6-11; 12-4 Sun

☎ (01747) 828222

Draught Bass; Ringwood Best Bitter; Wadworth 6X; guest beers Ⓗ

The Talbot opened as a beer house circa 1832 despite vehement opposition from the parson's wife. The building is predominantly stone built with a long, low bar with beams and inglenook fireplace. As well as offering three regular ales the landlord is keen to promote local micros with a choice of guest ales. The more inquisitive visitor may find the cosy dining room behind the inglenook. The pub is very popular with walkers from the local downs. ♨Q❀⇌◑♿♣P

Box

Quarryman's Arms

Box Hill, SN13 8HN (S of A4 between Corsham and Box) ST834693

11-3, 6-11.30; 11-midnight Fri & Sat; 11-11.30 Sun

☎ (01225) 743569 🌐 quarrymans-arms.co.uk

Butcombe Bitter; Moles Best Bitter; Wadworth 6X; guest beers Ⓗ

This pub can be hard to find, but is well worth the effort to seek out (phone for directions if you need to). A 300-year-old miner's pub offering a friendly welcome, it is renowned for

high quality food and ales. These can be enjoyed in the bar, restaurant or garden, which has a heated area for smokers. Quiz nights, often themed, are held every second Wednesday. Black Rat cider is occasionally on offer. Bed and breakfast accommodation is available in four rooms.
Q (231) P

Bradford-on-Avon

Barge Inn

17 Frome Road, BA15 1JY (S of canal bridge)
12-11 daily
(01225) 863403
Hidden Barge Bitter; guest beers H
A lovely canalside pub with mooring for several narrow boats. The pub boasts three ever-changing guest beers and its own 'Barge Bitter' ale, brewed for them by the Hidden Brewery. Warm and comfortable inside, there are large gardens for the warmer days including a 'hidden' area beside the canal. An extensive menu is available lunchtime and evenings. Q P

Beehive

263 Trowbridge Road, BA15 1UA
12-3, 7-11; 12-11 Fri-Sun
(01225) 863620 beehivepub.com
Butcombe Bitter; guest beers H
Next to the Kennet & Avon canal, this 19th-century inn continues to refresh the canal trade. Up to five changing guest beers are available and good pub food (not Sun eve or Mon). A popular venue, especially in summer, the large garden has a children's play area and boules piste. Entrance to the car park is a test of skill and accuracy. Q P

Bunch of Grapes

14 Silver Street, BA15 1JY
11-3, 6-11; 11-11 Wed & Thu; 11-12 Fri & Sat; 12-10.30 Sun
(01225) 863877
Young's Bitter, Special, seasonal beers; guest beers H
Town centre pub easily recognisable by the vine growing down the side. The narrow bar is divided into three distinct drinking areas and the restaurant upstairs serves good value food. A carvery is available every Sunday and a theme night is hosted once a month. This small pub can become crowded very quickly on busy nights.

Castle Inn

10 Mount Pleasant, BA15 1SJ (just off A363 at top of Masons Lane)
9-11; 10-10.30 Sun
(01225) 865657 flatcappers.co.uk
Three Castles Barbury Castle, Vale Ale, Knight's Porter; guest beers H
Acquired by pubco Flatcappers in 2006 and transformed by wholesale refurbishment, this quiet, cosy, relaxing pub caters for a wide clientele. The interior comprises a large bar with flagstone floor, lime-washed walls, open fireplace and magnificent reclaimed mahogany bar, and three smaller rooms with elm floorboards, exposed walls and worn club chairs. Food is served throughout premises. The garden with flagstone terrace has commanding views towards Salisbury Plain. The Three Castles beers are badged as Flatcapper, served alongside three guest beers sourced from local micros.
Q P

Rising Sun

231 Winsley Road, BA15 1QS
12 (4 Tue)-11; 12-10.30 Sun
(01225) 862354
therisingsunatbradfordonavon.co.uk
Courage Best Bitter; guest beers H
Popular local at the top of a hill in the town. There are two bars: a small, quiet lounge and a more spacious, livelier saloon with two large TV screens. The pub is home to darts, quiz, crib and football teams. Guest beers are usually from local breweries and the cider is Cheddar Valley. The pub's ancient spaniel is still there, ready to welcome you.

Burbage

Three Horseshoes ✔

Stibb Green, SN8 3AE (signed from the main road through the village)
12.30-2.30, 6 (7 Sun)-11
(01672) 810324
Wadworth IPA, Horizon, 6X H
The Three Horsehoes was established in the 19th century at the height of the railway construction era and much memorabilia from the three railways that operated in the area decorates the pub. The interior is divided into a dining area and public bar. Food is served every lunchtime and evening. Use of mobile phones is banned in the bar. To the rear is the garden and car parking. Q P

Chicksgrove

Compasses Inn

Lower Chicksgrove, SP3 6NB (signed from A30 at Fovant) ST974294
12-3, 6-11; 12-3, 7-10.30 Sun
(01722) 714318 thecompassesinn.com
Draught Bass; Hidden Quest, seasonal beers; Keystone Large One, seasonal beers H
In the middle of beautiful Wiltshire countryside, the bar is in the cellar of this 14th-century thatched cottage, with flagstone floors, old beams and a large inglenook fireplace. Once a resting place for smugglers between Poole and Warminster, it now offers visitors a warm welcome, good ale, excellent

INDEPENDENT BREWERIES

Archers Swindon
Arkell's Swindon
Box Steam Colerne
Downton Downton
Hidden Dinton
Hop Back Downton
Keystone Berwick St Leonard
Moles Melksham
Ramsbury Axford
Stonehenge Netheravon
Three Castles Pewsey
Wadworth Devizes
Wessex Longbridge Deverill

food, accommodation, wonderful views and some peace and quiet. ♨Q❀⇌⊄◑♣●P⁄–

Chippenham

Old Road Tavern

Old Road, SN15 1JA (200m from railway station)
11-11.30 (12.30am Fri & Sat); 11.30-11.30 Sun
☎ (01249) 652094
Black Sheep Best Bitter; Fuller's London Pride; guest beers Ⓗ
Good old back street local with an eclectic mix of regulars ensuring lively and friendly conversation. Local folk musicians and Morris dancers frequent the pub and impromptu music sessions may result, and there is regular live music on Saturday evening. Live sports are sometimes shown on TV. Two guest beers are often sourced from local micro-breweries. The large garden has plenty of seating, providing an attractive but secluded place to drink in summer. The pub is a venue for the annual Chippenham Folk Festival held over the late May bank holiday weekend. ❀◐⊟⇌⊟♣⁄–

Three Crowns

18 The Causeway, SN15 3DB
11 (12 Sun)-11 (midnight Sat)
☎ (01249) 652388
Courage Best Bitter; St Austell Tribute; Wye Valley HPA; guest beers Ⓗ
A five-minute walk from the bus station and town centre, this is a popular pub with locals. A new entry to the Guide, it was discovered by local CAMRA members during a pub crawl one evening —to their surprise. Good quality regular ales are occasionally supplemented with guest beers in the large bar (ring the bell for service in the much smaller lounge). A quiz is held every other Monday and the pub also has a Sunday League football team. ⊟⊟P

Clyffe Pypard

Goddard Arms

Wood Street, SN4 7PY (signed from Wootton Bassett to Marlborough Road) SU074769
12-2.30, 7-11; 12-11 Sat; 12-10.30 Sun
☎ (01793) 731386 🌐 clyffepypard@yha.org.uk
Beer range varies Ⓗ
This historic, friendly community pub set in a conservation area close to the Ridgeway, is ideally situated for walkers, cyclists or anyone wanting a well-kept pint. Run by the well-travelled Libby and Raymond Orchard, the pub also houses a YHA hostel, open all year round and offers excellent home-cooked food, a large garden with covered patio area and a hitching post for thirsty horses; dogs with well-behaved owners are also welcome. Beers are sourced from mainly local micro-breweries. ♨Q❀⇌◐⊟⊟♣P

Corsham

Hare & Hounds ✔

48 Pickwick, SN13 0HY
12-11 (10.30 Sun)
☎ (01249) 652388
Bath Ales Gem; Butcombe Blond; guest beers Ⓗ
Busy community pub on the old London to Bath coaching road. Charles Dickens is reputed to have stayed here and is thought to have based a number of the characters in The Pickwick Papers on people he met here, including the landlord at the time, Moses Pickwick. The pub is close to Bath, Castle Combe and the National Trust village of Lacock. There is a popular quiz on Tuesday evening, and occasional beer festivals. Two guest beers usually come from local breweries. ⊟♿⊟P

Two Pigs

38 Pickwick, SN13 9BU
7-11; 12-2.30, 7-10.30 Sun
☎ (01249) 712515 🌐 the2pigs.info
Stonehenge Pigswill, Danish Dynamite; guest beers Ⓗ
Friendly mid-18th century Grade II listed free house run in the owners' unique style, concentrating on serving real ale in a relaxed atmosphere. A pig theme dominates throughout, and the outdoor drinking area is known as the sty. The pub is known for its live music every Monday evening, from a selection of local bands and artists, with unintrusive background music playing at other times. Hop Back Summer Lightning sometimes replaces the Danish Dynamite. ❀♿⊟(231)

Corsley

Cross Keys

Lye's Green, BA12 7PB (off A362 Corsley Heath roundabout) ST821462
12-3, 6.30-11; 12-4, 7-10.30 Sun
☎ (01373) 832406
Wadworth IPA, 6X, JCB; guest beers Ⓗ
Welcoming 18th-century pub with a large open fire, serving excellent bar food and restaurant meals. A good portfolio of guest beers makes this always worth a visit, so persevere down those country lanes. The pub has a friendly and relaxing atmosphere. There is a function room and an attractive garden for outside drinking. The pub is situated close to Longleat House and Safari Park. ♨Q❀◐P

Cricklade

Red Lion

74 High Street, SN6 6DD
12-11 (10.30 Sun)
☎ (01793) 750776
Moles Best; Ramsbury Gold; Sharp's Doom Bar; Wadworth 6X; guest beers Ⓗ
Friendly 16th-century ale house serving a variety of up to nine real ales from small breweries. Food is served in what used to be the back bar and is now the restaurant (no food Mon). A past winner of CAMRA South West Regional Pub of the Year.
♨Q❀⇌◑⊟♣P

Devizes

British Lion

9 Estcourt Street, SN10 1LQ (on Swindon road out of town)
11-11 (midnight Fri & Sat); 12-11 Sun
☎ (01380) 720665
Beer range varies Ⓗ

Genuine back street pub – even if the sawdust has been replaced by laminate – serving fine hand-pulled ale. There are four pumps on the go at all times, ranging from pump one, with the weakest beer, to pump four, serving the good night' brews. The choice of ales changes continually (with almost never the same beer twice on the same pump), so if you hit it right you could manage to taste eight different beers! ⌂❀⊟♣●P

Southgate

Potterne Rd, SN10 5BY (on A360)
⊙ 11-11 (1am Thu; 4am Fri & Sat); 12-11 Sun
☎ (01380) 722872
Beer range varies Ⓗ
Small, welcoming and comfortable pub with a friendly Italian landlord. A range of ales, often from the Hop Back Brewery, together with ciders and foreign beers, is complemented by a good selection of spirits. Outside is a pleasant open drinking area and a more secluded patio. A function room occasionally hosts live music. The pub can be very busy at weekends. ❀⊟P⊬

Dilton Marsh

Prince of Wales

94 High Street, BA13 4DZ
⊙ 12-2.30 (not Mon & Tue, 3 Sat), 7 (6 Fri)-11 (midnight Thu-Sat); 12-3, 7-midnight Sun
☎ (01373) 865487
Wadworth 6X; Young's Bitter; guest beers Ⓗ
Friendly village local with a single bar serving two drinking areas plus a pool table area and skittle alley. It offers frequently changing guest ales, mostly session beers. The pub participates in local skittles, crib and pool leagues and there is a weekly Sunday evening quiz. Moles (not necessarily the beer) are something of a feature at the pub. Can you spot the error on the pub sign?
Q❀◑♿⥱⊟♣P⊬

East Knoyle

Seymour Arms

The Street, SP3 6AJ
⊙ 12-3, 7-11 (10.30 Sun); closed Mon
☎ (01747) 830374
Wadworth IPA, 6X, JCB, seasonal beers Ⓗ
Sixteenth-century ivy-covered stone inn in the village where Sir Christopher Wren was born, named after the family of Jane Seymour, third wife of Henry VIII. Very much at the heart of the local community, the pub enjoys an excellent reputation for high quality food (no meals Sun eve). The single bar features a number of discrete areas. Outside there is a pleasant garden with a children's play area.
⌂Q❀⇌◑♿P

Easton Royal

Bruce Arms ★

Easton Road, SN9 5LR
⊙ 12-2.30, 6-midnight; 11-3, 6-midnight Sat; 12-3, 7-midnight Sun
☎ (01672) 810216
Wadworth IPA, 6X Ⓗ
Built between 1848 and 1855, this CAMRA National Inventory-listed pub has a tiny snug and a small lounge that is more like a living room than a pub lounge. The small bar room has a bar that was fitted in 1934 and tables and benches going back to the 1850s. The large back room has a skittle alley and pool tables. The 'Westerners' regularly re-enact gun battles on the football pitch opposite, with fortresses erected for the fights. There are vintage vehicle gatherings and EROS (Easton Royal Onion Society) meets every Friday night. Rolls are available at lunchtime.
⌂Q☋❀⊟♿▲♣P

Ebbesbourne Wake

Horseshoe Inn

The Cross, SP5 5JF (just off A30) ST993239
⊙ 12-3 (not Mon), 6.30-11; 12-3, 6.30-11.30 Fri & Sat; 12-4 Sun
☎ (01722) 780474
Bowman Swift One; Otter Bitter; Ringwood Best Bitter; guest beer Ⓖ
Unspoilt 18th-century pub in a remote rural setting at the foot of an old ox drove. This friendly pub has two small bars and a restaurant and conservatory. Good local food is served or you can just pop in for a pint and a chat. The bars display an impressive collection of old farm implements, tools and lamps. Four beers are served direct from casks stillaged behind the bar. Service is either via the bar or the original serving hatch just inside the front door. There is a pleasant garden and bed and breakfast is offered. ⌂Q❀⇌◑⊟⊟●P

Grittleton

Neeld Arms

The Street, SN14 6AP
⊙ 12-3 (3.30 Sat), 5.30-11; 12-3.30, 7-11 Sun
☎ (01249) 782470 ⊕ neeldarms.co.uk
Wadworth IPA, 6X; guest beers Ⓗ
Cosy, comfortable 17th-century inn set in a beautiful and unspoilt south Cotswold village with old prints and photographs adorning the walls and a welcoming log fire in winter. A good selection of home-made food is offered and an ever-changing choice of guest beers means there is always something different to try. Popular with locals and visitors, the pub is central to the community. Tourist attractions including Castle Combe, Malmesbury and Bath are close by. ⌂Q☋❀⇌◑P⊬

Hamptworth

Cuckoo Inn

Hamptworth Rd, SP5 2DU (follow signs from A36 for Hamptworth Golf Club) SU244197
⊙ 11.30-2.30, 5.30-11; 11.30-11 Sat; 12-10.30 Sun
☎ (01794) 390302
Hop Back GFB, Summer Lightning; Ringwood Best Bitter; guest beers Ⓖ
Beautiful thatched pub within the New Forest National Park. Inside are four small rooms, three served from the same bar. Ales are dispensed direct from casks racked in the ground floor cellar. At least two guest ales and up to six in the summer are available alongside Frams scrumpy cider. The large

garden has a quiet adults-only space as well as a children's area with swings. An annual beer festival is held in late summer. Pasties and snacks are available. ⛼Q🚼❀♣●P⅟–

Heddington

Ivy

Stockley Road, SN11 0PL (2 miles off A4 from Calne)
✪ 12-3 (not Mon), 6.30-11; 12-4, 7-10.30 Sun
☎ (01380) 850276
Wadworth IPA, 6X, seasonal beers Ⓖ
At the foot of the Marlborough Downs, this idyllic thatched village local was originally three 15th-century cottages. The Ivy, with its cosy rustic bar and large log fire, has a reputation for excellent beer and good food (restaurant booking advisable – eve meals served Thu to Sat). The pub is a focal point for this area of outstanding natural beauty and there are a number of footpaths and cycle ways passing nearby. ⛼Q❀◐◑🚌♣P⅟–

Highworth

Cellar Bar

10 High Street, SN6 7AG (S side of Market Square) SU201924
✪ 4 (2 Sat & Sun)-11
☎ (01793) 763828
Beer range varies Ⓖ
An unusual little cellar bar, once the kitchen for the house above. The cellar extends under the road and it is said that it used to be a tunnel to the church, dating from the English Civil War. A small patio area is at ground level in the side alley next to the town council office. The beer range includes a constant supply of milds throughout May, a cider and perry festival on the second May bank holiday and a themed beer festival in October. Burford Cellarbaration is brewed exclusively for the Cellar Bar. Cheddar Valley cider is usually available and a perry in summer. ❀🚌♣●–

Idmiston

Earl of Normanton

Tidworth Road, SP4 0AG (on A338) SU195382
✪ 12-2.30, 6-11; 12-3, 7.45-10.30 Sun
☎ (01980) 610251 🌐 earlofnormanton.co.uk
Flowerpots Bitter; Hop Back Summer Lightning; guest beers Ⓗ
Popular roadside pub with a village atmosphere. Formerly the Plough Inn, the pub was renamed in honour of previous owners the Normanton estate. Two regular and three guest ales are mostly from local breweries and cider is available. Good value home-cooked food is served. There is a small, pleasant garden on the steep hill behind the pub and a heated, covered smoking area. A former Salisbury CAMRA Pub of the Year.
⛼Q❀◐◑♿🚌(63,64,66)P⅟–

Kilmington

Red Lion Inn ✔

BA12 6RP (on B3092 to Frome)
✪ 11-2.30, 6.30-11; 12-3, 7-10.30 Sun
☎ (01985) 844263
Butcombe Bitter; Butts Jester; guest beers Ⓗ
Originally a farm worker's cottage, this National Trust-owned pub is more than 400 years old. It is close to Stourhead House and Gardens, next to a coach road and the South Wiltshire Downs. The single bar is mainly stone-flagged with a real fire at each end and a smaller room to one side. Excellent, value-for-money food is served at lunchtime only. Walkers and dogs are welcome. The large garden has a superb smoking facility. CAMRA Branch Pub of the Year 2008. ⛼Q❀◐♣●P⅟–

Kington St Michael

Jolly Huntsman

80 Kington St Michael, SN14 6JB (signed from A350)
✪ 11-2.30, 6-11 (midnight Fri & Sat); 12-3, 7-10.30 Sun
☎ (01249) 750305 🌐 kingtonstmichael.com
Greene King IPA; Wadworth 6X; guest beers Ⓗ
Situated on the High Street, at the heart of the village, you will find a warm welcome at this free house offering a good variety of ales and ciders. Various entertainment is held including live music and games. An excellent range of food is served lunchtimes and evenings. Dogs are welcome. ⛼🛏◐◑♿🚌(99)●P⅟–

Lacock

Bell Inn

The Wharf, Bowden Hill, SN15 2PJ
✪ 11.30-2.30, 5-11; 11.30-11 Sat; 12-10.30 Sun
☎ (01249) 730308
Bath Ales Gem; Wadworth 6X; guest beers Ⓗ
A friendly welcome awaits you at this family run, well-established free house on the edge of the beautiful National Trust village of Lacock. Local CAMRA Pub of the Year for five consecutive years, it has an excellent reputation for its food and constantly-changing stock of real ales. An annual winter beer festival is held in late January/early February. Originally canal cottages, the pub lies beside the National Cycle Route, with excellent cycle tracks and walks between Chippenham and Melksham. ❀◐◑♿♣●P⅟–

Rising Sun

32 Bowden Hill, SN15 2PP (1 mile E of Lacock) ST9377680
✪ 12-3, 6-11 (midnight Wed-Fri); 12-midnight Fri & Sat; 12-11 Sun
☎ (01249) 704363
Moles Tap, Best Bitter, Rucking Mole, Molecatcher, seasonal beers Ⓗ
Stone built 17th-century pub near the top of Bowden Hill with flagstone floors and traditional settles. The spacious conservatory and large terraced garden enjoy spectacular views over the Avon Valley. The brewery tap for the local Melksham brewery Moles, the full range of its beers is available. A wide choice of pub food including daily specials is also on offer. A welcoming and convivial pub with live music on Wednesday evening.
⛼Q❀◐◑♣●P⅟–

Lydiard Millicent

Sun Inn
SN5 3LU SU096857
11.30-3, 5.30-11.30 (5-12.30am Fri); 11.30-3, 6-11.30 Sat; 12-4, 6.30-11 (all day summer) Sun
(01793) 770425
Sharp's Doom Bar; guest beers H
This 18th-century traditional village pub is the focal point of community life, offering a warm and friendly welcome to locals and visitors alike. Two separate dining areas, open fires and original wood beams throughout add to its charm, with a variety of artwork on sale by local artists. It has a well-deserved reputation for excellent food as well as two ever-changing guest ales from local and national breweries. A large garden with heated patio makes this a popular choice in summer. Dogs are always welcome. Q P

Malmesbury

Whole Hog
8 Market Cross, SN16 9AS
11-11; 12-10.30 Sun
(01666) 825823
Archers Best Bitter; Wadworth 6X; Young's Bitter; guest beers H
Located between the 15th-century Market Cross and Abbey, the building has at various times served as a cottage hospital, gas showroom and café/restaurant before becoming a licensed premises. With a warm, friendly atmosphere, the pub attracts locals and visitors alike. Meals can be eaten in the adjacent restaurant (no food Sun eve). Traditional cider from Weston's is available in the summer. Q

Marlborough

Green Dragon
12-13 High Street, SN8 1AA
10-11 (1am Fri & Sat); 12-10.30 Sun
(01672) 512366
Wadworth IPA, 6X; guest beers H
This large, multi-level pub is one of the oldest in Marlborough. It has a bar and front room at street level and a smaller room, pool room and dining area at a lower level at the back. The large riverside garden is very pleasant in summer. Breakfast is served Monday to Saturday. The pub is a venue for the popular Marlborough Jazz Festival in July.

Marston Meysey

Old Spotted Cow
SN6 6LQ
12-2.30, 5.30-11; closed Mon; 12-11 Sat; 12-10.30 Sun
(01285) 810264
Sharp's Doom Bar; Young's Bitter; guest beers H
Former farmhouse made of Cotswold stone. This friendly country pub has a cosy interior with log fires, beamed ceilings and a restaurant/family area, plus large gardens. Four handpumps deliver three real ales plus a cider, alternating between Black Rat and something from Stowford. The pub is popular with locals, who usually congregate around the bar, and diners. The Thames Path is about a mile away. There are infrequent bus services to Cirencester and Swindon, a fate shared by most of the surrounding rural areas.
Q P

Netherhampton

Victoria & Albert
SP2 8PU (opp church) SU108298
11-3.30, 5.30-11; 12-3, 7-10.30 Sun
(01722) 743174
Beer range varies H
Lovely thatched country pub built in 1540, with a real log fire to welcome visitors on a cold night. Outside is a large covered and heated patio area and garden. Four constantly-changing real ales are from small independent brewers. All food is prepared in the pub and the menu ranges from snacks to restaurant meals. Camping is available at the nearby racecourse. Dogs are welcome. Salisbury CAMRA Pub of the Year 2005 and 2007. Q P

Newton Tony

Malet Arms
SP4 0HP (opp village green) SU215403
11-3, 6-11; 12-3, 7-10.30 Sun
(01980) 629279
Beer range varies H
Classic country pub named after a local family who are well represented in the village churchyard. There is a spacious main bar and restaurant. The bar features a huge fireplace and a window reputed to come from an old galleon. The five real ales frequently come from Stonehenge, Hop Back and Hogs Back, with others from further afield. The cider is Weston's Old Rosie. The menu is based on locally-produced ingredients and changes daily. Q (63,64) P

North Wroughton

Check Inn
79 Woodland View, SN4 9AA
11.30-3, 6-midnight; 11.30-1am Fri & Sat; 12-midnight Sun
(01793) 845584
Fuller's Discovery, London Pride, ESB; Gale's Butser, HSB H
Attractively refurbished Fuller's pub hidden away down a residential cul de sac on the edge of rolling fields and countryside. Old Wroughton photographs decorate the walls. A weekly quiz and occasional music nights are hosted. Good food is served lunchtimes and evenings (not Sun eve). Bed and breakfast accommodation is available in three rooms above the pub. Q (49,54) P

Oare

White Hart
SN8 4JA (on A345 between Marlborough and Pewsey)
11-3, 6.30-midnight; closed Mon
(01672) 562273

Butts Bitter, Jester; Ramsbury Bitter; Wadworth 6X 🄷
Originally three cottages, the White Hart was purchased by the Wadworth brewery at the end of the 18th century and converted into a pub. Purchased by the present owner in 2000, it is now a free house selling a good range of beer and excellent home-cooked food. A popular ramblers' destination, it offers accommodation for those who wish to explore this lovely area close to the Kennet & Avon Canal. Q

Odstock

Yew Tree Inn

Whitsbury Road, SP5 4JE
11-3, 6-11; 12-3, 7-10.30 Sun
☎ (01722) 329786
Beer range varies 🄷
Picture postcard thatched 16th-century country inn with low beams and an inglenook fireplace. In summer the garden provides a tranquil dining and drinking area. The landlord is enthusiastic about his real ale and varies the two beers every week or so. The menu makes extensive use of local produce. Outside is a covered area for smokers. There is a good bus service during the day from the Pulseline buses. Q

Pewsey

Crown Inn

60 Wilcot Road, SN9 5EL
12-midnight (1am Sat & Sun)
☎ (01672) 562653
Wadworth 6X; guest beers 🄷
Popular inn away from the town centre with a small public bar with pool and darts and a large lounge with seating and more darts. A real ale drinkers' pub, there is a choice of five changing beers, often including an ale from Pewsey's own brewery Three Castles.

Salisbury

Deacons

118 Fisherton Street, SP2 7QT
5-11.30; 4-1am Fri; 12-midnight Sat & Sun
☎ (01722) 504723
Hop Back GFB, Summer Lightning; Sharp's Doom Bar 🄷
Traditional, friendly drinkers' pub, convenient for the city centre and railway station. Popular with a mixture of locals and visitors, the front bar has woodblock flooring and an open gas fire in a traditional hearth. The back bar has table football. Last entry is normally around 10.40pm.

Rai d'Or

69 Brown Street, SP1 2AS
5-11; closed Sun
☎ (01722) 327137 raidor.co.uk
Beer range varies 🄷
Historic freehouse dating from 1292 retaining its original atmosphere with an open fireplace, wooden floor and panelled benches. The name originated over 700 years ago when it was a brothel and tavern in the old red light district of Salisbury. Today you will find two beers from local micro-breweries, frequently Stonehenge or Downton, a welcoming landlord and centuries of history. The pub specialises in excellent Thai food, served at all opening times. Salisbury CAMRA Pub of the Year 2008.

Royal George ✔

17 Bedwin Street, SP1 3UT (close to Salisbury Arts Centre)
12-midnight; 12-3, 7-10.30 Sun
☎ (01722) 327782
Hop Back GFB, Summer Lightning; Ringwood Best Bitter 🄷
Originally a 15th-century inn, this Grade II listed pub is named after the sister ship of HMS Victory and has a wood beam said to be from that ship. The low beamed bar is decorated with pictures of ships and sea battles. A city pub with the feel of a country local, it is well known for its involvement in crib, darts and pool leagues. Outside is a large secluded garden.

Village Freehouse

33 Wilton Road, SP2 7EF (on A36 near St Paul's roundabout)
12-midnight
☎ (01722) 329707
Downton Quadhop; Taylor Landlord; 🄷 **guest beers** 🄷/🄶
This friendly inn serves three ever-changing guest beers and occasionally a fourth from a cask behind the bar. The beer selection focuses on local micro-breweries and beers unusual for the area. A dark ale, mild, porter or stout is always available, making it the only regular outlet for these beers in the city. Guest beer requests can be written up on a whiteboard by visitors. Close to the station, it is popular with visitors by rail, and railway memorabilia adorns the walls. Cricket, rugby and football are shown on a small TV. Salisbury CAMRA Pub of the Year 2001 and 2004.

Wyndham Arms

27 Estcourt Road, SP1 3AS
4.30-11.30; 3-midnight Fri; 12-midnight Sat; 12-11.30 Sun
☎ (01722) 331026
Downton seasonal beers; Hop Back GFB, Crop Circle, Spring Zing, Summer Lightning, seasonal beers 🄷
This is the original home of the Hop Back Brewery although brewing has long since moved to nearby Downton. A carved head of Bacchus greets you as you enter the pub. A genuine local, it caters for all – inside is a small bar and two further rooms, one where children are welcome. This pub is all about beer, with six real ales available, usually five from Hop Back and one from Downton. There is also a selection of bottled ales including Entire Stout. Salisbury CAMRA Pub of the Year 2006.

Seend Cleeve

Brewery Inn

SN12 6PX (off A361 between Trowbridge and Devizes) ST930611

❂ 12-3.30, 6.30-11; 12-midnight Fri & Sat; 12-10.30 Sun
☎ (01380) 828463
Ringwood Best; Sharp's Doom Bar; guest beers Ⓗ
Friendly village pub central to the community, popular with locals and tourists alike. The public bar, adorned with rural artefacts, has steps leading to the games room with darts, pool and cribbage. Outside is a decked area for smokers, a secure children's play area and garden. Pub food favourites featuring locally sourced produce are served, and traditional ciders are always available. Sunday barbecues are held during the summer. The Kennet & Avon Canal is within easy walking distance.
⩕Q🚸❀◑🀄♿🚌♣●P⁄

Stourton

Spread Eagle Inn

Church Lawn, BA12 6QE (600m from B3092 north of A303 Mere)
❂ 10-11; 12-10.30 Sun
☎ (01747) 840587 🌐 spreadeagleinn.com
Butcombe Bitter; Cheddar Potholer; Wessex Kilmington Best; Ⓗ **guest beers** Ⓖ
Mellow brick and slate pub owned by the National Trust within the Stourhead Estate and adjacent to the famous Stourhead House and Gardens. Spacious and comfortable, the inn offers a selection of local ales and bottled ciders. Guest beers are available in the summer and served on gravity. Excellent English cooking features dishes made with locally sourced ingredients.
⩕Q🚸❀🛏◑♿♣P⁄

Swindon

Glue Pot

5 Emlyn Square, SN1 5BP (behind railway museum on Fleet Street)
❂ 12-11; 11-midnight Fri & Sat; 11-10.30 Sun
☎ (01793) 523935
Beer range varies Ⓗ
A friendly pub with strong links to the local CAMRA branch, it is in the heart of the Great Western Railway workers' village. A range of six Hop Back beers and two guests is sold, with four real ciders alongside. Good pub grub is served at lunchtime including doorstep sandwiches and ham and chips. The pub is usually quiet but gets busy on weekend evenings. Major sporting events are screened but the TV is not obtrusive or loud.
❀◐⇌🚌(8,54)⁄

Steam Railway ✔

14 Newport Street, SN1 3DX
❂ 12-11; 12-1am Fri & Sat; 12-10.30 Sun
☎ (01793) 538048
Fuller's London Pride; Wadworth 6X; Wells Bombardier; guest beers Ⓗ
A former railway hotel, it has a traditional real ale bar with a low ceiling and wood panelling, with nine handpumps offering three regular and several guest beers, always including one from Adnams. The bar gets busy when major sporting events are screened on TV; at other times you can enjoy a quiet drink. The largest part of the pub is the roofed-over courtyard where screens show sports and discos take place. Meals are served until 8pm Monday to Friday and 4pm at weekends. ⩕❀◑🚌♣⁄

Wheatsheaf ✔

32 Newport Street, SN1 3DP
❂ 5-11; 12-midnight Fri & Sat; 12-10.30 Sun
☎ (01793) 523188
Wadworth IPA, Horizon, 6X; guest beers Ⓗ
Popular two bar town pub dating back to the 1820s. The larger back bar incorporates what was originally a large courtyard and is where the students gather, giving it a lively feel. The recently refurbished front bar is smaller and quieter with a more traditional feel, ideal for a peaceful pint. Traditional cider, or occasionally perry, is stocked. Lunches are available on Friday & Saturday only.
⩕Q❀🛏◑🀄⇌🚌♣●⁄

Tisbury

Boot Inn

High Street, SP3 6PS
❂ 12-2.30, 7-11; 12-4 Sun
☎ (01747) 870363
Beer range varies Ⓖ
Fine village pub built of Chilmark stone, licensed since 1768. Run by the same landlord since 1976, it has a relaxed, friendly atmosphere appealing to locals and visitors alike. Three beers are served direct from casks stillaged behind the bar. Ringwood Best is frequently available and the landlord makes good use of the range of beers available on the Marston's list. Excellent food is served (pizza only on Tuesday) and there is a spacious garden. Salisbury CAMRA Pub of the Year 2003. ⩕❀◑⇌🚌♣P⁄

Wanborough

Harrow ✔

High Street, SN4 0AE
❂ 12-3, 6-11 (5.30-midnight Fri & Sat); 12-3, 7-midnight Sun
☎ (01793) 790622 🌐 theharrowinnwanborough.com
Black Sheep Best Bitter; Wadworth 6X; guest beers Ⓗ
This thatched pub dates back to 1637, making it the oldest in the village. It features two enormous fire grates and many concealed cupboards in the eaves, used by smugglers to hide their illegal goods. Today's more law abiding visitors can enjoy good food and fine ale including two guest beers (no food Sun eve). Live music plays on Sunday evening. There are three attractively furnished bedrooms in the new accommodation block.
⩕Q❀🛏◑🀄🚌♣P⁄

Warminster

Fox & Hounds

6 Deverill Road, BA12 9QP
❂ 11-11
☎ (01985) 216711
Ringwood Best Bitter; Wessex Warminster Warrior; guest beers Ⓗ
Friendly two bar local just off the town centre. One of the bars is a cosy snug, the other has a pool table and TV at the back. Two real ciders from Rich's and Thatchers are a mainstay of

the pub. A regular outlet for the Wessex Brewery, the guest beer is usually sourced from another local micro. Closing time may be later than 11pm. ♨Q✿⊟♿⇌⊟♣●P⁻

Organ

49 High Street, BA12 9AQ

⏲ 4 (12 Sat)-midnight; 12-11 Sun

☎ (01985) 211777

Beer range varies Ⓗ

The Organ was converted from a fish and fruit shop in 2006. The building dates from around 1770 and was a public house up until 1913. New landlords have created a welcoming pub with a traditional feel. There are three rooms including a snug and a games room, and a skittles alley. Two ciders are always stocked and the beer range includes three ever-changing guests usually sourced from local micros. The brewer of Organ Bitter is a close secret. ♨Q✿⊟♿Ⲗ⇌⊟♣●P⁻

Westbury

Horse & Groom

Alfred Street, BA13 3DY

⏲ 12-11

☎ (01373) 822854 🌐 westburyales.co.uk

Beer range varies; Ⓗ

This pub used to boast its own brewery but its beers are now brewed by Wessex Brewery under the Westbury Ales name. A popular locals' pub, it has a separate public and lounge bar – one lively, the other more sedate. The food is honest pub grub and the welcome is genuine. Crib and quiz nights are held. The skittle alley can sometimes be used for functions. A place to recover after hiking up to the White Horse. ♨Q✿◐◑⇌⊟♣P⁻

Wilton

Bear Inn

12 West Street, SP2 0DF (by Market Square)

⏲ 11-3, 4.30-midnight; 12-3, 6-midnight Sun

☎ (01722) 742398

Badger First Gold, Tanglefoot Ⓗ

Dating back some 300 years, this is a traditional country-style town pub, homely and welcoming. A coal fire offers warmth in the winter and there is a large, quiet, walled garden offering both sun and shade, with a heated, covered smoking area. A range of Badger bottled beers is available. Darts, bar billiards and rings, a game from the Isle of Wight, are played. Parking is available nearby in the Market Square. ♨✿◐⊟(60, 61)♣⁻

Wootton Bassett

Five Bells ✔

Wood Street, SN4 7BD

⏲ 12-3, 5-11.30; 12-midnight Fri & Sat; 12-4, 6.30-11 (all day summer) Sun

☎ (01793) 849422

Black Sheep Best Bitter; Fuller's London Pride; guest beers Ⓗ

Charming thatched pub dating back to 1841, situated just off the High Street. The bar area has an open fire and low-beamed ceiling while a second room offers further seating, a dartboard and TV for major sporting events. Outside is a large patio. Three ever-changing guest ales appear alongside two regulars and an Addlestones cider. Excellent home-cooked food is available at lunchtime, with a themed food evening on Wednesday and generous roasts for Sunday lunch. Well-behaved dogs are welcome. ♨✿◐⊟♣●P⁻

Worton

Rose & Crown

108 High Street, SN10 5SE ST976575

⏲ 12-3 (not Mon), 7-11; 12-3, 7-10.30 Sun

☎ (01380) 724202

Sharp's Doom Bar; guest beers Ⓗ

Cosy, welcoming village pub with a small bar and large dining room. The pub is a focal point for the village with many activities and trips organised. A large function room at the rear is used for live music at the weekend and hosts a beer festival. Food is good value for money. The licensee is committed to real ale and offers a choice of beers that varies from time to time. Cider is also available. Table tennis is played here. ✿◐◑⊟♣●P

Wroughton

Carters Rest ✔

High Street, SN4 9JU

⏲ 5-midnight (1am Fri); 12-1am Sat; 12-11 Sun

☎ (01793) 812288

Bath Ales Gem; Cotswold Spring Old English Rose; Hop Back Crop Circle; Sharp's Doom Bar Ⓗ

Decorated with photographs of bygone Wroughton, this large two-bar traditional pub situated on the High Street is a real locals' local, but visitors are always warmly welcomed. Ten real ales are displayed on boards in both bars, including five guests sourced from local and regional breweries. Live music events are held twice a month and quiz night is Thursday. The pub welcomes children until early evening and allows well-behaved dogs. ♨Q✿⊟♿⊟♣P⁻

Wylye

Bell

High Street, BA12 0QP

⏲ 11-3, 6-11; 12-3, 6-10.30 Sun

☎ (01985) 248338 🌐 thebellatwylye.com

Hidden Pint, Quest, Pleasure, seasonal beers Ⓗ

A former coaching inn built in 1373, the building has changed little over the years and offers an authentic interior with an open fire within an inglenook, flagstone floors and a wealth of old beams. The pub was acquired by the Hidden Brewery in 2005 and is its brewery tap. A warm welcome is offered to all including children and pets. It is a few minutes' walk from the bus stop at the Deptford interchange. ♨✿⇔◐◑♿⊟(24)P⁻

Give my people plenty of beer, good beer and cheap beer, and you will have no revolution among them. **Queen Victoria**

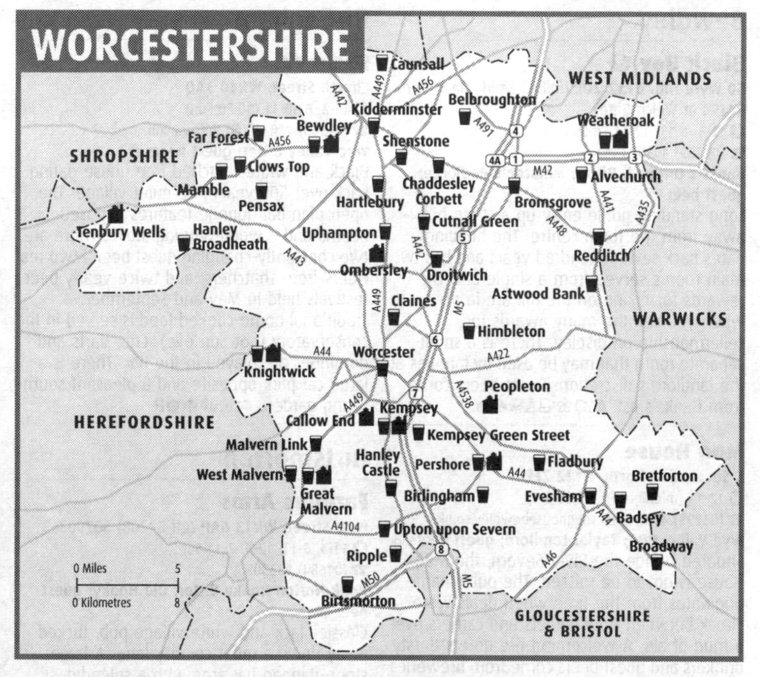

Alvechurch

Weighbridge

Scarfield Wharf, Scarfield Hill, B48 7SQ SP019720
12-3 (4 Sat summer), 7-11 (10.30 Sun)
(0121) 445 5111 the-weighbridge.co.uk
Kinver Bargee's Bitter; guest beers H
Cosy, award-winning and friendly pub at Alvechurch Marina on the Worcester and Birmingham Canal with two lounges and a public bar. Excellent, good value, home-cooked food is served every day. Two beer festivals are held, one in the summer and one in the autumn, and there is an outside marquee for private functions. The two guest beers are invariably from small breweries. Redditch & Bromsgrove CAMRA Pub of the Year in 2005 and 2007.

Astwood Bank

Oddfellows Arms

24 Foregate Street, B96 6BW
12-midnight (12.30am Fri & Sat); 12-11.30 Sun
(01527) 892806
M&B Brew XI; Wye Valley HPA H
Known locally as The Oddies', the pub has two rooms plus a function room for diners. Live matches are shown on TV in the lounge and darts is played in the bar. In the beer garden a large patio is sheltered by a huge canopy which is often heated. Food is served Wednesday and Thursday evenings, with an all-you-can eat curry buffet on Friday and roast lunch on Sunday afternoon. The pub holds an annual Oktoberfest in aid of the local carnival charity. (70)

Badsey

Round of Gras

47 Bretforton Road, WR11 7XQ (on B4035 at E end of village)
11-11
(01386) 830206 roundofgras.co.uk
Flowers IPA; Uley Pig's Ear; guest beers H
Open-plan roadside inn, on the eastern edge of the village with an attractive beer garden. It is named in honour of the asparagus that is the speciality of this part of the Vale of Evesham: the 'gras' is prominent on the menu from April to June, and other locally-sourced produce features all year round. Two guest beers, often from micros or independents, and Weston's Old Rosie cider complement the regular ales. (247, 554)

Belbroughton

Four Winds

Bromsgrove Road, Hollies Hill, DY9 9TX (on A491)
12-11 (10.30 Sun)
(01562) 730332 the-four-winds.co.uk
Beer range varies H
A comfortable, well-appointed place to enjoy a drink or meal, with a single, wood-panelled bar/lounge and separate restaurant. Up to four guest beers often come from local breweries such as Hobsons, and a Wye Valley beer always features. An extensive menu of freshly-cooked food made with locally-sourced produce is on offer. There are excellent views to the Clee and Abberley Hills from the patio. P

Bewdley

Black Boy ✔

50 Wyre Hill, DY12 2UE (follow Sandy Bank from B4194 at Welch Gate)
12-3, 6-11; 12-11 Fri-Sun
(01299) 403523
Banks's Original, Bitter; Marston's Pedigree; guest beer Ⓗ
Long-standing guide entry up a steep hill away from the town centre. The building dates back several hundred years and has two main rooms served from a single bar. The rewards for taking on the hill are in no doubt when you see the many awards for cellarmanship on display. There is a small separate room that may be used by families at the landlord's discretion. Guest beers come from Banks's list.

Mug House

5 Severnside North, DY12 2EE
12-11 (midnight Fri; 11.30 Sat)
(01299) 402543 mughousebewdley.co.uk
Wye Valley HPA; Taylor Landlord; guest beers Ⓗ
Situated beside the River Severn, the Mug House is not to be missed. The pub's name originates from the time when deals were struck between trow haulers and carriers over a mug of ale. A welcoming fire greets thirsty drinkers and guest beers come from breweries such as RCH, Titanic, Beowulf and Wye Valley. Local English wine is also stocked. The May Day weekend beer festival is a regular fixture. Fine food is available in the restaurant, including live lobster.

Waggon & Horses

91 Kidderminster Road, DY12 1DG (on Bewdley-Kidderminster road, Wribbenhall side of river)
12-3, 6-11; 12-midnight Fri & Sat; 12-11.30
(01299) 403170
Banks's Original, Bitter; Batham Best Bitter; guest beer Ⓗ
Friendly locals' pub approached through the enclosed front garden with a single bar serving two rooms and a third room used as a dining area complete with old kitchen range. The small snug has settles, tables and a dartboard, the larger room has a large roll-down screen for major sporting events. Food is available at lunchtime and evenings with a carvery on Sunday (booking advised). Guest ales come from local independents.

Woodcolliers Arms

76 Welch Gate, DY12 2AU
12-3 (not Mon), 5-midnight; 12-midnight Sat & Sun
(01299) 400589 woodcolliers.co.uk
Wye Valley HPA; guest beers Ⓗ
Just a short walk from the centre of Bewdley, this friendly local offers a constantly changing range of guest beers, often from Sadlers, Hobsons or Woods. An old-style pub dating from 1870 with real open fires and beams, it has undergone some changes under the Russian landlady and now offers speciality Russian food alongside traditional pub fare, and a bottled Russian beer, Baltika. Quiz night is Tuesday and a jazz night features on the first Wednesday of the month.

Birlingham

Swan ✔

Church Street, WR10 3AQ
12-3, 6.30-11 (10.30 Sun)
(01386) 750485 theswaninn.co.uk
Wye Valley Bitter; guest beers Ⓗ
Black and white thatched free house dating back over 500 years in a quiet village. The open plan bar/lounge features exposed beams and a wood-burning stove. There are two constantly-changing guest beers, two real ciders from Thatchers, and twice-yearly beer festivals held in May and September. Traditional home-cooked food is served in the conservatory (not Sun eve). Crib, darts and dominoes are played in the bar. There is a large car park opposite and a pleasant south-facing garden.

Birtsmorton

Farmers Arms

Birts Street, WR13 6AP (off B4208) SO790363
11-4, 6-11; 12-4, 7-11 Sun
(01684) 833308
Hook Norton Hooky Bitter, Old Hooky; guest beer Ⓗ
Classic black and white village pub, tucked away down a quiet country lane. A large stone-flagged bar area with a splendid inglenook fireplace is complemented by a cosy lounge area with very low beams. Good value, home-made, traditional food is on offer every day, lunchtimes and evenings. The guest beer usually comes from a small independent brewer, often local. The spacious, safe garden with swings provides fine views of the Malvern Hills in the distance.

Bretforton

Fleece Inn ★

The Cross, WR11 7JE
11-11 (closed 3-6 Mon-Fri winter)
(01386) 831173 thefleeceinn.co.uk
Hook Norton Hooky Bitter; Purity Pure Ubu; Uley Pig's Ear; guest beers Ⓗ
Famous old National Trust owned village pub which re-opened in 2005 following a fire which all but gutted the interior. Fortunately the public area escaped almost unscathed, including the renowned collection of 17th-century pewter-ware. The restoration has been excellent and the pub remains one of the stars of CAMRA's National Inventory. Visitors may drink inside or in the orchard, which is especially good for families in fine

INDEPENDENT BREWERIES

Bewdley Bewdley (NEW)
Blue Bear Kempsey
Brandy Cask Pershore
Cannon Royall Ombersley
Joseph Herbert Smith Hanley Broadheath (NEW)
Malvern Hills Great Malvern
St George's Callow End
Teme Valley Knightwick
Weatheroak Weatheroak
Wyre Piddle Peopleton

weather and the site of the famous asparagus auction in the (very short) season. Draught ciders are available from Weston's and Thatchers. CAMRA Worcestershire County Pub of the Year 2006. Q (554)

Broadway

Crown & Trumpet

Church Street, WR12 7AE

11-2.30 (3 summer), 5-11; 11-11 Fri & Sat; 12-10.30 Sun

(01386) 853202 cotswoldholidays.co.uk

Taylor Landlord; Stanway seasonal beers; guest beers H

Fine 17th-century Cotswold stone inn on the road to Snowshill, with oak beams and log fires alongside plenty of Flowers Brewery memorabilia. The menu offers specials made with locally grown fruit and vegetables, attracting locals, tourists and walkers alike. The pub offers an unusual range of pub games, with live music on Saturday evenings. The Stanway seasonal beers rotate throughout the year, some brewed exclusively for the pub, and many of the guest beers are local from the Gloucestershire Ale Trail initiative. P

Bromsgrove

Golden Cross Hotel

20 High Street, B61 8HH

9-midnight (1am Fri & Sat)

(01527) 870005

Enville Ale; Greene King Abbot; Marston's Pedigree; guest beers H

Opened in 1994, this Wetherspoon pub is the former Golden Cross Hotel, which was rebuilt in 1932 on the site of one of Bromsgrove's oldest coaching inns of the same name. The spacious interior has a lengthy bar serving up to 12 ales, and beer festivals are hosted throughout the year. Interesting information about Bromsgrove's local history is displayed on panels on the walls. Food is served daily from 9am-11pm. Pay and display parking is available to the rear. P

Red Lion

73 High Street, B61 8AQ

10.30-11 (11.30 Thu; midnight Fri & Sat); 11-3 Sun

(01527) 835387

Banks's Original, Bitter; Jennings Dark Mild; guest beers H

Busy one room pub in the main shopping high street with a covered, heated smoking area outside. Traditional home-cooked food is available lunchtimes and evenings. Up to seven real ales are on offer and beer festivals, beer and cider tastings and food themed events are held on a regular basis. Music plays on most Thursday evenings. A winner of many CAMRA awards including Pub of the Year 2003 and 2004. P

Caunsall

Anchor Inn

DY11 5YL (off the A449 Kidderminster-Wolverhampton road)

11-4, 7-11; 11-3, 7-10.30 Sun

(01562) 850254 theanchorinncaunsall.co.uk

Hobsons Best Bitter, Town Crier; guest beer H

Popular, friendly, traditional local run by the same family for 80 years. Little has changed inside, with two main rooms served by a long bar retaining the original 1920s tables and chairs. Renowned for its generously-filled cobs, the friendly atmosphere and delightful location attract an impressive mix of customers. Within easy reach of the nearby canal, this is a gem of a pub. Q P

Chaddesley Corbett

Fox Inn

Bromsgrove Road, DY10 4QN

11.30-2.30; 5-11; 11.30-11 Sat; 12-10.30 Sun

(01562) 777247 foxinn-chaddesleycorbett.co.uk

Beer range varies H

Smart roadside pub with a large car park to the south of an attractive village. The changing range of three beers, many from local independent breweries, is available in a large L-shaped lounge with a games area in one corner. Food is served throughout the pub and in the separate air-conditioned restaurant. A comprehensive range of main meals and snacks is on offer daily alongside a good value carvery on Tuesday to Sunday lunchtimes and Wednesday and Friday evenings. The cider is from Thatchers. P

Swan

The Village, DY10 4SD

11-3, 6-11; 11-11 Fri & Sat; 12-10.30 Sun

(01562) 777302

Bathams Mild Ale, Best Bitter, XXX (winter) H

Dating from 1606, this traditional inn is well worth seeking out. The public bar is flanked by a large lounge, a small snug and a restaurant where evening meals are served Thursday to Saturday. Lunch is available daily, however there is no hot food on Monday. Well-behaved dogs are welcome in the public bar and the pub is popular with walkers. Thursday evenings feature a varied programme of live jazz. The cider is Weston's Old Rosie. Q P

Talbot

The Village, DY10 4SA

11-3, 5-11; 11-11 Sat summer; 12-3, 6-11 Sun

(01562) 777388 talbotinn.net

Banks's Original, Bitter; guest beers H

This smart, half-timbered historic inn occupies a site where there has been an inn since 1600. Inside there is a public bar with pool table, two cosy wood-panelled lounges with hidden alcoves and an upstairs restaurant. Food from a varied and interesting menu is served daily, lunchtimes and evenings. Guest beers are from the Martson's portfolio. Outside is a large rear veranda shaded by a grape vine, a large car park and a garden with children's play area. Q P

Claines

Mug House

Claines Lane, WR3 7RN

12-2.30, 5-11; 12-11 Sat (& Fri summer); 12-11 Sun

(01905) 56649

Banks's Original, Bitter; ⓟ guest beers ⊞
One of the original Severn 'Mug Houses', uniquely situated in a picturesque churchyard. The pub dates from the 15th century and has a classic multi-room layout. Banks's beers are served from electric pumps in lined glasses and two hand-pulled guests come from the expansive Marston's range. The garden attracts early evening drinkers in summer. Occasional jazz nights are held.
⛰Q☕❀◐⊟⛺⊡⊓

Clows Top

Colliers Arms

Tenbury Road, DY14 9HA (on A456 Kidderminster-Tenbury road)
✪ 11-3, 6-11; 11-11 Sat; 11-6 Sun
☎ (01299) 832242 ⊕ colliersarms.com
Hobsons Best Bitter; guest beer ⊞
Family-owned and run free house set in Worcestershire countryside. Full of traditional atmosphere, it has cosy front and back bars with a log fire and polished wooden tables, and an airy dining room with pleasant views of the garden. Good quality, home-cooked food is made with seasonal, locally-sourced ingredients. Monthly live music events and quiz nights are hosted as well as celebratory specials. Outside, the patio and garden are in a picturesque setting. **⛰Q☕❀◐◑♿⊡P**

Cutnall Green

Live and Let Live

The Green, WR9 0PW (on A442)
✪ 12-2.30, 6-11; 12-3.30 Sun
☎ (01299) 851257
Holden's Golden Glow; guest beer ⊞
Situated halfway between Droitwich and Kidderminster, this cosy and smart pub dating from the 18th century concentrates on lunchtime and evening food. The narrow open plan interior has a bar at one end and a small seating area at the other, with a pleasantly quiet and relaxed atmosphere. A guest beer is available at weekends. **Q❀◐◑P⌐**

Droitwich

Hop Pole

40 Friar Street, WR9 8ED
✪ 12-11 (10.30 Sun)
☎ (01905) 770155 ⊕ thehoppoleatdroitwich.co.uk
Malvern Hills Black Pear; Wye Valley HPA, Butty Bach; guest beer ⊞
Close to the train station and bus routes, this traditional, welcoming 300-year-old pub offers good value food at lunchtime in a rustic interior with oak settles, exposed beams and a pool room. Darts and cards are played by quieter patrons while lively music features on some evenings, popular with youngsters. A gazebo outside for smokers has its own bar and is also used for beer festivals in the summer. **⛰☕❀◐⇌⊡♣⌐**

Evesham

Old Swanne Inne ✔

66 High Street, WR11 4HG
✪ 9-midnight (1 am Fri & Sat)
☎ (01386) 442650
Greene King Abbot; Marston's Pedigree; guest beers ⊞
Busy town centre Wetherspoon's on the High Street by the bus station, offering the widest range of beers in Evesham. Opened in late 1998, the building has undergone many changes since it first became an inn in 1586. Evesham Civic Society commended the refurbishment which, 'transformed a scruffy and derelict building into one which is an asset to the town'. Many photographs of old Evesham adorn the walls. It offers two or three guest beers, although the range may be smaller mid-week, and hosts several mini-festivals throughout the year.
Q☕❀◐◑♿⇌⊡⌐

Far Forest

Plough

Cleobury Road, DY14 9TE (half mile from A456/B4117 jct)
✪ 12-11.30; 11-11 Sat
☎ (01299) 266237
Wood Shropshire Lad, Shropshire Lass; Wye Valley HPA; guest beers ⊞
Busy, popular country pub/restaurant with open fires and rustic decor in a number of drinking and dining areas served from the main bar. The front room is mainly for drinkers and the large dining area extends into a conservatory where children are permitted. The beer range varies with ales from Wood, Purity, Wye Valley and Sadlers featuring regularly. For diners, there is a renowned carvery and extensive menu choice. Food is served all day Sunday (booking essential).
⛰☕❀◐◑♿⛺⊡♣●P⌐

Fladbury

Anchor Inn

Anchor Lane, WR10 2PY
✪ 11.30-3, 5-11; 11.30-11 Fri & Sat; 11.30-10 Sun
☎ (01386) 860391 ⊕ anchorfladbury.co.uk
Batham Best Bitter; Fuller's London Pride; M&B Brew XI; Wood Shropshire Lad ⊞
Traditional country pub, family owned and run, set on the Green at the heart of the picturesque village of Fladbury. You can be sure of a warm greeting at this welcoming local from the friendly landlord and his cat Charley. The 17th-century pub is at the centre of the local community and a variety of local groups meeting here. The cosy dining room serves home-made food and there is a function room and pool room.
⛰❀◐♿⊡(551)♣

Great Malvern

Great Malvern Hotel

Graham Road, WR14 2HN
✪ 10-11; 11-10.30 Sun
☎ (01684) 563411 ⊕ great-malvern-hotel.co.uk
Draught Bass; Malvern Hills Feelgood; guest beers ⊞
Popular hotel public bar close to the Malvern Theatres complex – an ideal venue for pre- and post- performance refreshment. At least one beer always comes from a local brewery.

Meals are served in the bar and brasserie area or you can relax in the comfortable lounge with comfortable sofas and fresh coffee, daily newspapers and free WiFi access. Parking is limited but nearby public parking is plentiful. It is a short walk down the hill to the rail station and most local buses stop nearby.
Q☎⇌◑⇌⊟P

Hanley Broadheath

Fox Inn

B4204, WR15 8QS
✪ 5-11.30; 3-1am Fri; 2-1am Sat; 12-11 Sun
☎ (01886) 853189 ⊕ foxinn-broadheath.co.uk
Batham Best Bitter; JHS Amy's Rose, Foxy Lady; guest beer Ⓗ
You can be sure of a friendly welcome from the staff and locals at this 400-year-old black and white country pub where a wood-burning stove adds warmth throughout the winter. Four real ales include at least two from the pub's own JHS brewery, plus a real cider or perry. An annual beer festival is held in the field next to the pub in August. Food is served Friday and Saturday evening and sandwiches are available throughout the day. There is a separate games room plus beer garden and outdoor play area. Dogs are welcome.
⛫❀◑⊟♣●P⍭

Hanley Castle

Three Kings ☆

Church End, WR8 0BL (signed off B4211) SO838420
✪ 12-3, 7-11 (10.30 Sun)
☎ (01684) 592686
Butcombe Bitter; Hobsons Best Bitter; guest beers Ⓗ
Unspoilt 15th-century country pub on the village green and near the church, run by the same family since 1911. A former CAMRA National Pub of the Year and on the National Inventory, the three room interior comprises a small snug with large inglenook, serving hatch and settle wall, a family room, and Nell's Lounge with another inglenook and beams. Three interesting guest ales often come from local breweries and a popular beer festival is held in November. Regular live music sessions are hosted. ⛫Q☎❀◑⊟(363)●P

Hartlebury

Hartlebury British Legion

Millridge Way, Waresley, DY11 7TJ (off A449, down a track on Waresley Court Road)
✪ 12-2 (Tue only), 8 (7 Fri)-11; 12-11 Sun
☎ (01299) 250252
Hobsons Mild; guest beers Ⓗ
Although off the beaten track, it is well worth seeking out this friendly, welcoming club on the edge of Hartlebury. Views from the patio extend over the asparagus fields to Kidderminster and Stourport and on a clear day to the Clee Hills. A large open-plan lounge-bar offers comfortable seating, a widescreen TV, pool table and dartboard. The four reasonably-priced guest beers are all bitters, usually from micro-breweries. All real ale drinkers are welcome – bring a copy of this Guide or a CAMRA membership card for admittance. Q☎❀♿⇌⊟(100)♣●P⍭

Himbleton

Galton Arms

Harrow Lane, WR9 7LQ
✪ 12-2 (closed Mon), 4.30-11; 11-11 Sun
☎ (01905) 391672
Banks's Bitter; Batham Best Bitter; Wye Valley HPA; guest beer Ⓗ
Popular village local with a welcoming atmosphere. Formerly known as the Harrow Inn, the building has been a pub since the 1800s and was renamed after a local family. The interior comprises a beamed main bar, dining room and an upstairs restaurant with an extensive menu. Guest beers are usually from local micro-breweries. No food is available on Sunday or Monday evenings.
⛫Q☎❀◑♿P

Kempsey

Walter de Cantelupe ✔

34 Main Road, WR5 3NA
✪ 12-2.30, 6-11; closed Mon; 12-2.30, 7-10.30 (12-10.30 summer) Sun
☎ (01905) 820572 ⊕ walterdecantelupeinn.com
Cannon Royall Kings Shilling; Wye Valley Dorothy Goodbody Golden Ale; Taylor Landlord; guest beer Ⓗ
Named after the 13th-century bishop of Worcester, the interior of this pub comprises a bar area with large inglenook, dining area and an attractive walled garden where dogs are welcome. A settle dating from the 1700s, which used to sit in front of the inglenook, now marks the entrance to the dining area. The high quality food menu makes use of local food where possible —ploughmans and sandwiches made with local bread and cheeses are a speciality. Regular events are held throughout the year and include a paella party in July. ⛫Q❀⇌◑P⍭⊓

Kempsey Green Street

Huntsman Inn

Green Street, WR5 3QB SO871490
✪ 12-3.30 Sat & Sun only, 5-midnight
☎ (01905) 820336
Batham Best Bitter; Greene King IPA; Wye Valley HPA Ⓗ
A cosy and friendly atmosphere greets visitors to this 300-year-old former farmhouse. A number of rooms are served by a central bar, with real fires and exposed wood beams adding character. Reasonably priced home-cooked food is served in a separate restaurant. The impressive skittle alley has its own bar and there is an attractive garden to the side. Dogs are welcome. ⛫Q☎❀◑⊟●P

Kidderminster

Boar's Head

39 Worcester Street, DY10 1EW
✪ 12-11 (12.30am Thu-Sat); 7-11.30 Sun
☎ (01562) 68776
Banks's Bitter; guest beers Ⓗ

Popular town centre Victorian pub. The cosy lounge has wood panelling and a wood burning stove. The main bar leads to a large covered and heated courtyard where live music is staged on Thursday and Sunday evenings. There is also a tented garden area for the summer. Note the Pop Art style paintings and pump clip collection dotted around the pub. An ever-widening range of guest beers comes from the Banks's list. There is a free mineral water dispenser for drivers. ⛫❀◐⊟♿⇌⊟●⁴–

King & Castle

SVR Station, Comberton Hill, DY10 1QX

✪ 11-3, 5-11; 11-11 Sat; 12-10.30 Sun

☎ (01562) 747505

Batham Best Bitter; Wyre Piddle Royal Piddle; guest beers Ⓗ

A Guide regular, popular with locals and visitors to the Severn Valley Railway, this is a replica of a GWR refreshment room and has direct access to the SVR concourse and platforms. There is plenty of seating and even the carpet features the GWR logo. A varied selection of guest beers is on offer, many from local independents, including Royal Piddle brewed especially for the pub. A wheelchair-accessible WC is available on the platform. ⛫Q♉◐◑♿⇌⊟P

Olde Seven Stars

13-14 Coventry Street, DY10 2BG

✪ 11-11; 11-3, 6-11 Sun

☎ (01562) 755777 ⊕ yeoldesevenstars.co.uk

Beer range varies Ⓗ

Kidderminster's oldest public house, close to the town centre and within walking distance of the Severn Valley Railway. The interior is wood panelled throughout with a polished wood floor and inglenook fireplace. Customers are welcome to bring in their own food from local takeaways with plates, cutlery and condiments supplied. The pub boasts the largest garden in town, with a covered smoking area. CAMRA Pub of the Season winner in winter 2008, this is a pub not to be missed. ♉❀♿⇌⊟♣⁴–⊓

Red Man ✔

92 Blackwell Street, DY10 2DZ

✪ 11.30-11 (midnight Thu-Sat); 12-10.30 Sun

☎ (01562) 67555

Adnams Broadside; Black Sheep Best Bitter; Greene King Old Speckled Hen, Abbot; Taylor Landlord; guest beer Ⓗ

Popular hostelry styling itself as a country pub in the town. The two bars have quite a different feel: the quiet front lounge is favoured by diners and the large backroom is more lively with Sky sports, pool tables and darts. Five regular beers are supplemented by one changing guest. A large room to the rear is ideal for children, and there is a garden and conservatory. Food is served daily until early evening. ♉❀◐⊟♿⇌⊟♣P⁴–

Knightwick

Talbot

WR6 5PH (on B4197, 400m from A44 junction)

✪ 11-midnight; 12-10.30 Sun

☎ (01886) 821235 ⊕ the-talbot.co.uk

Hobsons Best Bitter; Teme Valley This, That, T'Other Ⓗ

Historic pub and hotel next to the River Teme serving cask ales mostly produced by the Teme Valley Brewery situated behind the inn. It was badly flooded twice in the summer of 2007, but has been refurbished and is back to its best. The renowned restaurant serves traditional food using local ingredients. A highlight in the calendar is the Green Hop Festival held in October after hop picking. A farmer's market is held in front of the pub on the second Sunday of the month. Worcester CAMRA Pub of the Year 2007. ⛫Q❀◐◑⊟♿⊟(420)♣●P

Malvern Link

Nags Head ✔

21 Bank Street, WR14 2JG

✪ 11-11.15 (11.30 Fri & Sat); 12-11 Sun

☎ (01684) 574373

Banks's Bitter; Batham Best Bitter; St George's Maiden's Saviour, Charger, Dragons Blood; Sharp's Doom Bar; guest beers Ⓗ

Award-winning hostelry at the top of Malvern Link Common with stunning views over the hills. This very popular pub has several rooms in which to enjoy a huge range of frequently changing beers dispensed from 17 handpumps. Outside there are various covered drinking areas. The Nag's Tail restaurant, accessible by wheelchair, serves food until 9pm. ❀◑⇌⊟●⁴–

Star

59 Cowleigh Road, WR14 1QE

✪ 4.30-11 (midnight Fri & Sat); closed Mon; 12-10.30 Sun

☎ (01684) 891918

Beer range varies Ⓗ

Interesting pub with an unusual fusion of Chinese and English themes. Drinks are served in the light and airy bar with a fabulously ornate original bar back; high quality Chinese food is available in a separate restaurant (bookings essential Fri and Sat). A takeaway service operates from what was the snug. Wye Valley HPA is a regular guest ale. ❀◐◑⊟⇌⊟P⁴–

Mamble

Sun & Slipper

DY14 9JL (signed from A456)

✪ 12-3, 6.30-midnight (1am Fri & Sat); 12-4, 7-midnight Sun

☎ (01299) 832018 ⊕ thesunandslipperinn.co.uk

Banks's Original; Hobsons Best Bitter; guest beers Ⓗ

In the centre of the village on the old village green, this attractive country pub has a small, cosy bar with pool table and open fire plus a dining room with log burning stove. Old photos of village life decorate the hallway. It recently won an award for its pristine loos. The food is good with menus changing monthly. Two regularly changing guest beers often come from local independents. Look out for the large, friendly dog. ⛫Q❀◐◑⊟♣P⊓

Pensax

Bell

WR6 6AE (on B4202, Clows Top-Great Witley road)
12-2.30 (not Mon), 5-11; 12-10.30 Sun
(01299) 896677
Hobsons Best Bitter; guest beers
Current West Midlands CAMRA Pub of the Year, the Bell is well worth a visit. It offers a constantly changing range of real ales, many from local independents, as well as real cider and perry. Ales are chalked up on a board with their ABV and price. Welcoming and friendly with pew-style benches, wooden floors, real fires and hanging hops, the interior comprises a popular bar, snug and restaurant with spectacular views. Good food uses local seasonal ingredients. Q P

Pershore

Brandy Cask

25 Bridge Street, WR10 1AJ
11.30-2.30 (3 Fri & Sat), 7-10.30 (11.30 Thu-Sat); 12-3, 7-11 Sun
(01386) 552602
Brandy Cask Whistling Joe, Brandy Snapper, John Baker's Original; guest beers
Superb brew pub offering three regular house ales as well as seasonal brews and a wide range of guest beers from around the country. Real cider is also usually available. Food is good and reasonably priced (not Tue in winter). The garden runs down to the river Avon and is delightful in summer. A 'must visit' when in Pershore. Q

Redditch

Bramley Cottage

Callow Hill Lane, Walkwood, B97 5QB (B4504 Windmill Drive/Callow Hill Lane jct)
12-11 (midnight Thu-Sat)
(01527) 551911
Banks's Bitter; guest beers
Large, single room estate pub with a central L-shaped bar with three sets of handpumps. The food is excellent value for money with frequent price promotions. Children over 14 are welcome if dining with adults, otherwise they are permitted only in the patio and garden. Beer festivals supported by Ember Inns are held twice a year. Q P

Ripple

Railway Inn

Station Road, GL20 6EY
6-11 Mon; 12-3, 6-midnight Tue-Fri; 12-midnight Sat; 12-11 Sun
(01684) 592225
Sharp's Cornish, Doom Bar; guest beers
At the front of this village pub is a beamed restaurant serving genuine home-cooked food. The bar area is organised around the fireplace and next to it is a seating area with comfortable sofas. Old photos of the pub and long gone railway station decorate the walls. A games bar to the rear has a couple of pool tables and a skittle alley. An unusual choice of regular beers is complemented by guests from local breweries. (351) P

Shenstone

Plough

Shenstone Village, DY10 4DL (off A450/A448)
12-3, 6-11; 12-3, 7-10.30 Sun
(01562) 777340
Bathams Mild Ale, Best Bitter, XXX (winter)
This traditional rural pub serving excellent value Bathams beers is a regular local CAMRA award winner. There is a single servery for the public and lounge bars, each with a real fire. Many pictures of the Falklands War and other memorabilia adorn the walls. No cooked food is available but bar snacks and delicious locally-made pork pies are on offer. Children are welcome in the courtyard.
Q P

Uphampton

Fruiterers Arms

Uphampton Lane, WR9 0JW (off A449 at Reindeer Pub) SO838648
12.30-3.30, 7-midnight; 12-midnight Sat & Sun summer; 12-4.30, 7-midnight Sun
(01905) 620305
Canon Royall Fruiterer's Mild, Arrowhead, Muzzle Loader, seasonal beers
Down a narrow country lane, this pub is home to the Cannon Royal Brewery which has been brewing on site since 1993. A central dispense serves a public bar and lounge decorated with antique pictures, guns and horse brasses. Filled rolls are available Friday to Sunday. There are patio drinking areas to the front and rear of the pub. Children under 14 are welcome until 9pm. Q P

Upton upon Severn

White Lion Hotel

High Street, WR8 0HJ
10am-12.30am
(01684) 592551 whitelionhotel.biz
Greene King Abbot; guest beers
This historic inn dating from the 16th century featured in Henry Fielding's novel Tom Jones. The resident owners ensure that while the facilities and service are three-star, the welcome is unstuffy, warm and relaxed. Bar meals are available or you can spoil yourself in the high quality restaurant. Three guest ales often include one from a local brewery. The Lion & Pepperpot beer festival is held during the last bank holiday in May and events are organised around Upton's many riverside music festivals. Q P

Weatheroak

Coach & Horses

Weatheroak Hill, B48 7EA (Alvechurch-Wythall road) SP059740
11.30-11; 12-10.30 Sun
(01564) 823386
Hobsons Mild, Best Bitter; Weatheroak Light Oak, Ale, Keystone Hops; Wood Shropshire Lad; guest beers
Home of the Weatheroak Brewery, this attractive rural pub sits on the corner of Icknield Street and Weatheroak Hill. Reputedly once frequented by JRR Tolkien, it has a quarry

tiled public bar with real fire, a split level lounge/bar and a modern restaurant. The large, family-friendly garden and patio host beer festivals, barbecues and morris dancing. Children under 14 are not allowed in the bars. Winner of numerous local CAMRA awards.
⛰Q🛏❀⊄▶⊟♣●P⚋

West Malvern

Brewers Arms

Lower Dingle, WR14 4BQ

🕒 12-3, 6-midnight; 12-midnight Sat & Sun

☎ (01684) 568147 🌐 brewersarmswithaview.co.uk

Marston's Burton Bitter; guest beers Ⓗ

Following the success of its first beer festival in September, the Brewers Arms continues to go from strength to strength. At the centre of the village community, it supports many local clubs and sports teams. In a beautiful setting with stunning views across to the Black Mountains, it won an award for Best Pub View in Britain in 2005. The cosy bar can get busy at times, with good pub food served in a separate dining area. ⛰Q❀⊄▶🚌(475)

Worcester

Bell

35 St Johns, WR2 5AG

🕒 10 (11 Sun)-11.30

☎ (01905) 424570

M&B Brew XI; guest beers Ⓗ

This busy community local is currently undergoing a refurbishment which will lead to an increased range of beers. The pub has a front bar on one side of a corridor, with two small rooms on the other side where children are permitted. At the rear is a skittles alley and a second bar used only at busy times and available for functions. Occasional live music plays at weekends. ⛰❀🚌♣

Berkeley Arms

School Road, WR2 4HF

🕒 1-3.30, 5-midnight; 1-12.30am Fri; 12-12.30am Sat; 12-3.30, 7-11.30 Sun

☎ (01905) 421427

Banks's Original, Bitter; Ⓟ **Jennings Dark Mild; guest beers** Ⓗ

Two drinking areas are served by a single bar at this recently refurbished pub which now offers an enhanced beer range. Two guest beers are supplied by Marston's, usually either its seasonal brews or ales from the larger independents. Pub games are popular here, played in a room at the rear which can also be used for meetings or as a children's room. The patio is now partially enclosed for the benefit of smokers. ❀⊟🚌♣P⚋

Cricketers

6 Angel Street, WR1 3QT

🕒 11-11; 12-3, 7-10.30 Sun

☎ (01905) 23583

Beer range varies Ⓗ

A welcoming single-room pub with a central bar, described by the landlady as 'a village pub in the city centre'. Four real ales are rotated regularly and a traditional cider from Thatchers and a perry from Weston's are available. As you would expect from the name, the pub features a wealth of cricketing memorabilia. Gathered over 25 years, the collection includes signed bats, balls, photographs, paintings and cigarette cards from county and national sides. There is a function room available.
🛏⊄♿⥂(Foregate St)🚌●

Dragon Inn

51 The Tything, WR1 1JT

🕒 12-3, 4.30-11 (11.30 Fri); 12-11 Sat; 1-4.30, 7-10.30 Sun

☎ (01905) 25845 🌐 thedragoninn.com

Beer range varies Ⓗ

This real ale paradise, winner of many awards, has six handpumps serving the widest range of beers from smaller independent and local brewers in Worcester, plus a range of bottle-conditioned Belgian beers. The walls are adorned with pump clips and mementos of life in the pub. A partially covered and heated rear patio is perfect for summer evenings. Good value lunchtime meals (not Sun).
❀⊄⥂(Foregate St)🚌●⚋

Plough

23 Fish Street, WR1 2HN (next to fire station)

🕒 12-11 (midnight Fri & Sat)

☎ (01905) 21381

Hobsons Best Bitter; Malvern Hills Black Pear; guest beers Ⓗ

This friendly Grade II listed pub is a must for any visitor to the Faithful City. Four changing guest ales comes from breweries in Worcestershire and surrounding counties, and draught cider and perry are from local producers. Downstairs there are two rooms, each with a fire and original features (including the ghost!). A small outside area provides views towards the Cathedral. Good food is served Fri and Sat lunchtimes, plus Sun roast dinners. Worcester CAMRA Pub of the Year 2007. 🛏❀⊄⥂(Foregate St)♣●⚋

Postal Order ✔

18 Foregate Street, WR1 1DN

🕒 9am-midnight (1am Fri & Sat)

☎ (01905) 22373

Greene King Abbot; Marston's Pedigree; Teme Valley This; guest beers Ⓗ

Classic Wetherspoon's pub in what was once the old Worcester telephone exchange. Beers from local micros feature prominently, together with up to six guests, plus a monthly showcase of a selected brewer's beers. Traditional Weston's Old Rosie and Vintage Organic cider are also available. Good value food served daily.
Q🛏⊄▶♿⥂(Foregate St)🚌●⚋

Winning Post

Pope Iron Road, WR1 3HB

🕒 12-midnight (10.30 Sun)

☎ (01905) 21178

Canon Royall Arrowhead; guest beers Ⓗ

Cosy back-street single-room pub to the north of the city centre close to the racecourse. The only outlet in the city to stock Canon Royall beer permanently, it also has two guest beers that rotate every six to eight weeks. Sports TVs features large.
⊄♿🚌♣⚋

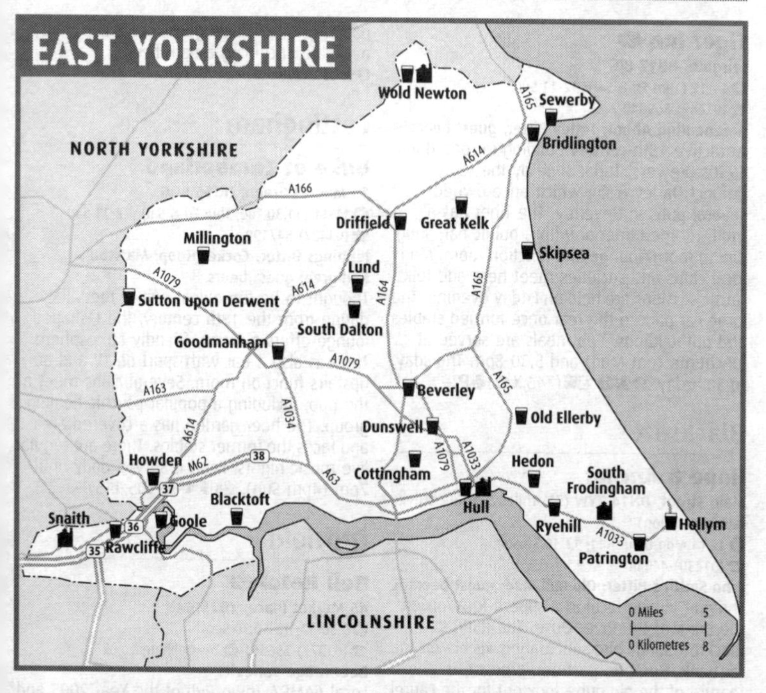

YORKSHIRE (EAST)

Beverley

Dog & Duck

33 Ladygate, HU17 8BH

11-4, 7-midnight; 11-midnight Fri & Sat; 11.30-3, 7-11 Sun

(01482) 862419

Caledonian Deuchars IPA; Copper Dragon Best Bitter; John Smith's Bitter; guest beers H

Situated just off the main Saturday Market, next to the historic Picture Playhouse building, the Dog & Duck, built in the 1930s, has been run by the same family for over 30 years. It comprises a former tap room with a period brick fireplace and bentwood seating, a lounge and a rear snug area; only the dividing walls have been removed. The good value, home-cooked lunches are popular and include pensioners' specials. Guest accommodation is in six purpose-built, self-contained rooms to the rear.

Durham Ox

48 Norwood, HU17 9HJ

10.30-11; 12-11 Sun

(01482) 679444

John Smith's Bitter; Tetley Bitter; guest beers H

Victorian local on the A1035, 200m east of the bus station. This two-roomed pub has been refurbished after consultation with CAMRA's local pub preservation officer. The lounge was extended to include a games area but retains its original etched windows; the public bar has the old wooden floor, with an off-sales hatch in the entrance lobby. The pub fields five darts and two dominoes teams. Off-street parking is possible directly opposite. Meals are served daily.

Green Dragon

51 Saturday Market, HU17 8AA

11-11 (midnight Thu-Sat); 12-11 Sun

(01482) 889801

Beer range varies H

This historic Tudor-fronted inn was renamed the Green Dragon in 1765. It dispenses ales mainly from Yorkshire micro-breweries such as Cropton, Rudgate and Wold Top. The pub was extensively refurbished and substantially extended 12 years ago; most internal fittings of note were lost, although some wood panelling remains and the bar is incredibly long. Meals are served daily until 9pm; quiz nights are Tuesday and Wednesday. Weekends are busy. CAMRA's East Yorkshire Town Pub of the Year 2007.

Molescroft Inn

75 Molescroft Road, HU17 7EG (1 mile NW of town centre)

11.30-11 (midnight Fri & Sat); 12-11 Sun

(01482) 862968

Jennings Bitter, Sneck Lifter; guest beers H

A much enlarged village local dating back to the 18th century, the Molescroft was comprehensively altered in the 1980s with the loss of some small rooms to create a large L-shaped lounge/dining room with separate bar area around a central servery. There is a dining area adjacent to the pub's large car park. Meals, including specials, are served daily. (121)P

INDEPENDENT BREWERIES

Great Newsome South Frodingham
Old Mill Snaith
Whalebone Hull
Wold Top Wold Newton

Tiger Inn ✔

Lairgate, HU17 8JG

11-11 (1am Fri & Sat); 12-11 Sun

☎ (01482) 869040

Greene King Abbot; Tetley Bitter; guest beers Ⓗ

Attractive 18th-century building refronted in a 1930s brewers' Tudor style by the sadly defunct Darley & Co, which once owned several pubs in Beverley. The Tiger has a multi-roomed interior with a public bar, snug, dining room/lounge and function room. Many local clubs and societies meet here and folk music sessions are held on Friday evening. The large car park to the rear once formed stables and outbuildings. Pub meals are served at lunchtime (not Mon) and 5.30-8pm Thursday to Saturday. Q (X46,X47)P

Blacktoft

Hope & Anchor

Main Street, DN14 7YW (3½ miles S of Gilberdyke railway station)

12 (4 Mon & Tue)-11; 12-10.30 Sun

☎ (01430) 440441

John Smith's Bitter; Old Mill Mild; guest beers Ⓗ

Thriving village local in a superb location on the bank of the River Ouse. The RSPB's Blacktoft Sands bird sanctuary is visible on the far bank. Humour, past and present, is a feature of the old pub – look out for the Laurel and Hardy memorabilia and the sharp wit of the licensee. The conservatory offers fine river views and popular home-cooked meals – the haddock is huge. Two guest beers change regularly. P

Bridlington

Marine Bar

North Marine Drive, YO15 2LS (1 mile NE of centre)

11-11 (11.30 Sat)

☎ (01262) 675347

John Smith's Bitter; Taylor Landlord; guest beers Ⓗ

Large, triangular-shaped, open-plan bar, part of the Expanse Hotel, situated on the seafront to the north east of the town. The bar attracts a good mix of regulars throughout the year and is welcoming to the influx of summer visitors. A good menu of home-cooked food (including vegetarian) is available daily. The guest beer is often from Wold Top Brewery. There is ample car parking on the promenade at the front.

Prior John ✔

34-36 The Promenade, YO15 2QD

9-midnight (1am Fri & Sat)

☎ (01262) 674256

Greene King IPA, Abbot; Marston's Pedigree; guest beers Ⓗ

Large, busy Wetherspoon's pub in the town centre and close to the bus station. Modern in appearance, the interior is basically one large half-moon shape. To the right of the serving area is a first-floor gallery, reached by a sweeping metal staircase. The downstairs room is a clever mix of metal and wood with a segmented ceiling supported by steel pillars. The decor is plain and bright using mainly pastel colours. Three guest beers are always available, including a dark beer.

Q

Cottingham

Duke of Cumberland

10 Market Green, HU16 5QG

11-11 (11.30 Tue; Thu; Fri & Sat); 12-11 Sun

☎ (01482) 847199

Jennings Bitter, Cocker Hoop; Marston's Pedigree; guest beers Ⓗ

Thought to be the oldest pub in the village, dating from the 18th century, the L-shaped lounge offers a warm, friendly atmosphere. There is also a bar with sport on TV and an upstairs function room. Several clubs meet at the pub, including a popular psychic healing group. The beer garden has a covered area and faces the former stables. There are regular live music nights. Food is served daily until 7pm (4pm Sun). (105,115)

Driffield

Bell Hotel ✔

46 Market Place, YO25 6AN

9.30-11; 12-10.30 Sun

☎ (01377) 256661 bw-bellhotel.co.uk

Beer range varies Ⓗ

Local CAMRA Town Pub of the Year 2005 and runner-up 2007, this inn has a feeling of elegance, featuring a long, wood-panelled bar and red leather seating, substantial fireplaces, antiques and prints. Two or three beers are kept, usually from Wold Top, Hambleton or Highwood breweries, but other micros are also represented. Over 300 malt whiskies are stocked. A covered courtyard functions as a bistro, and there is a splendid lunchtime carvery buffet (Mon-Sat); Sunday lunch must be booked. Children are welcome until 7.30pm. Q(121)P

Mariners Arms

47 Eastgate South, YO25 6LR (near old cattle market)

3 (12 Sat & Sun)-midnight

☎ (01377) 253708

Banks's Bitter; Jennings Bitter; guest beers Ⓗ

This street-corner local is well worth seeking out as an alternative to the John Smith's outlets that dominate the 'Capital of the Wolds'. Formerly part of the Hull Brewery estate, its four small rooms have now become two: a basic bar and a more comfortable lounge. Live sport is shown and the pub fields various sports teams. The long-standing licensees enjoy a loyal following among locals and offer a friendly welcome to all visitors.

(121)P

Rose & Crown ✔

North Street, YO25 6AS (400m N of centre)

12 (11 Sat)-midnight (11 Wed; 1am Thu-Sat); 12-11 Sun

☎ (01377) 253041

John Smith's Bitter; guest beers Ⓗ

Family-run pub opposite the town's Green Flag awarded park, comprising a main bar/lounge and a pool room. Two guest beers, usually from independents, change every few days. Table service is available Thursday-Saturday evenings, and benches are provided outside for summer drinking. Live sport is shown on TV, Thursday is quiz night and regular entertainment is staged on Saturday evening. Numerous sports teams represent the pub. The railway station is a 20-minute walk. ❀🚌(121)♣P⅟

Tiger Inn

65 Market Place, YO25 6AW

✪ 10.30-midnight; 11.30-10.30 Sun

☎ (01377) 257490

Camerons Strongarm; John Smith's Bitter; guest beers Ⓗ

This town-centre pub has been tastefully modernised and extended while retaining its traditional charm and providing the same friendly service as ever. It is a relief to see that the original tap room remains untouched. There is a large patio area in the beer garden for that relaxing summer drink. The pub is a five-minute walk from the railway station. ♨Q❀♿⇌🚌(121)♣P⅟

Dunswell

Ship Inn

Beverley Road, HU6 0AJ (on main Hull-Beverley road)

✪ 11-11 (11.30 Fri & Sat); 12-11 Sun

☎ (01482) 854458 🌐 theshipsquarters.co.uk

Black Sheep Best Bitter; John Smith's Bitter; Taylor Landlord; guest beers Ⓗ

This whitewashed inn fronting the old Hull-Beverley road once served traffic on the nearby River Hull, and this is reflected in its nautical memorabilia and decor. Two log fires warm the convivial interior which is partly divided to form a separate dining area with church pew seating. Meals are served daily until 7pm (3pm Sun) and barbecues are held occasionally in the adjoining paddock. A detached extension provides overnight accommodation, aptly named the Ship's Quarters. ♨❀🛏◐◑🚌(121,246)♣P

Goodmanham

Goodmanham Arms

Main Street, YO43 3JA

✪ 5 (12 Sat & Sun)-11

☎ (01430) 873849

Black Sheep Best Bitter; Theakston Best Bitter; guest beers Ⓗ

Village local opposite the Saxon church and close to the Wolds Way footpath. The public bar is relatively unspoilt, with a quarry-tiled floor and a warming log fire. The entrance corridor has been combined with an adjacent room and is warmed by a log burner. At the front of the building is a small beer garden, to the side a small car park, with access to the outside Gents WC. Additional parking is available nearby. Hot snacks are served Sunday lunchtime. ♨Q❀◐⊟P⅟

Goole

City & County ✔

Market Square, DN14 5DR (next to clock tower)

✪ 9-midnight

☎ (01405) 722600

Greene King IPA, Abbot; Marston's Pedigree; guest beers Ⓗ

Large, bustling town-centre pub with a welcoming sense of space, thanks to its lofty ceiling and an open-plan bar. Converted from a former bank by Wetherspoon's, the pub features real ales in abundance – the lengthy bar includes ten handpumps – and an extensive food menu. A heated rear courtyard provides a quiet sanctuary away from town centre life. The pub is a short walk away from bus and train stations. Q❀◐◑♿⇌🚌⅟

Macintosh Arms

13 Aire Street, DN14 5QE

✪ 10.30-midnight (1 am Tue & Thu; 2am Fri & Sat)

☎ (01405) 763850

Tetley Dark Mild, Bitter; Marston's Best Bitter; guest beers Ⓗ

This Grade II-listed building, originally a magistrate's court, is a gem. Left alone by town planners, it retains a traditional feel. Three rooms set around a central bar have panelled walls featuring pictures of old Goole. A glass ceiling in the pool bar allows a glimpse of the original plaster ceiling. A motorcycle club meets here; live music plays on the last Friday of the month and karaoke is hosted on Sunday night. The smokers' area outside is covered and heated. ❀♿⇌🚌♣P⅟

Great Kelk

Chestnut Horse

Main Street, YO25 8HN

✪ 6 (5.30 Fri & Sat)-11; 12-10.30 Sun

☎ (01262) 488263

Camerons Strongarm; guest beers Ⓗ

Built in 1793, this delightful Grade II-listed rural community pub is situated between the Wolds and Holderness. It has a cosy bar with a real fire and a comfortable games room that doubles as a daytime family room. Darts, dominoes and chess are played. Two guest beers are sold alongside draught Hoegaarden and Peroni beer; Belgian bottled beers are served in authentic glasses. The restaurant serves fine, home-cooked meals until 8.45pm daily (7.30pm Sun). ♨Q❀◐◑♿♣P

Hedon

Haven Arms ✔

Havenside, off Sheriff Highway, HU12 8HH (½ mile S of A1033 crossroads)

✪ 12-11 (midnight Fri & Sat); 12-10.30 Sun

☎ (01482) 897695 🌐 havenarms.co.uk

Black Sheep Best Bitter; Taylor Landlord; Tetley Bitter; guest beers Ⓗ

Situated in the historic Haven area of town, which was once the largest port on the River Humber. The popular bar is divided into a number of areas to cater for all tastes. Traditional, reasonably priced pub food, freshly prepared from local ingredients, is served all day. The concert and cabaret room serves as the focal point for the activities of a large number of community clubs and teams. Guest beers feature local micro-breweries and interesting ales. 🐻❀◐◑♿⛺🚌(76,77)♣P⅟

Hollym

Plough Inn

Northside Road, HU19 2RS
⌚ 12 (2 winter Mon & Wed)-midnight
☎ (01964) 612049 🌐 theploughinnhollym.co.uk
Tetley Bitter; guest beers Ⓗ
This family-run, 200-year-old, genuine free house of wattle and daub construction has undergone considerable refurbishment. Primarily a locals' pub, it is a haven for discerning holidaymakers in summer. Part of the pub dates from the 16th century, while photographs in the bar depict its role as a WWII ARP station. Imported bottled Coopers beers are often stocked. Accommodation comprises three en-suite letting rooms. Runner-up in CAMRA's East Yorkshire Village Pub of the Year 2007 competition.
♔❀⇌◑▲🚌(76,77)♣●P⁵–▽

Howden

Barnes Wallis

Station Road, DN14 7LF (on B1228)
⌚ 5 (12 Sat)-11; closed Mon; 12-10.30 Sun
☎ (01430) 430639 🌐 barneswallisinn.com
John Smith's Bitter; Greene King IPA; Taylor Landlord; guest beers Ⓗ
The pub is named after the designer of the bouncing bomb, R100 Airship and Wellington Bomber who lived in the area and worked at nearby Brough. The pub's single-room layout has a welcoming feel; the decor is themed around Wallis's aeronautical achievements and the walls feature a display of artefacts and pictures. The large secluded garden is ideal for children. Lunches are served weekends only, evening meals Tuesday to Sunday.
♔Q❀◑♿≥♣P⁵–

Hull

Admiral of the Humber ✔

1 Anlaby Road, HU1 2NT
⌚ 9-midnight (1am Fri & Sat)
☎ (01482) 381850
Greene King Abbot, IPA; Marston's Pedigree; guest beers Ⓗ
Wetherspoon's first outlet in the city centre and one of the few outlets in the new town selling cask ales. A short walk from the Transport Interchange, the large one-roomer has a raised area for drinks and booths on both sides with plenty of seating. Up to five guest beers are stocked alongside three regular ales. The bar shows live sport on a large screen and two wide-screen TVs. Meals are served until 11pm every day. ◑♿≥

Falcon

60 Falkland Road, HU9 5SA
⌚ 11-11.30 (midnight Thu-Sat); 12-11.30 Sun
☎ (01482) 713721
Lees Bitter; guest beers Ⓗ
Well worth seeking out, this gem lies deep in the former real ale desert of East Hull, and on a 1960s council estate, showing what can be achieved with commitment. Up to three guest beers are served in the front bar, usually including a mild, and there is a rear games room. Old Rosie cider is available. Close to Hull KR rugby ground, it gets busy on match days. Hull CAMRA Pub of the Year runner-up 2006 and 2007. ❀⊟🚌(40,42)♣●P⁵–

Gardeners Arms

35 Cottingham Road, HU5 2PP
⌚ 11 (12 Sun & Mon)-midnight
☎ (01482) 342396
Black Sheep Best Bitter; Tetley Bitter; guest beers Ⓗ
Situated just under a mile north of the city centre, the Gardeners is well worth a visit. The original front bar has seen many alterations, but retains the matchwood ceiling that blends with the current ale house style. This room is popular for its friendly feel as well as its choice of six guest beers. The large rear extension is comfortably furnished, housing seven pool tables and plasma TV screens. The pub sponsors local Rugby Union, football and ten-pin bowling teams and hosts three weekly quizzes. There is a large outdoor drinking area at the front. ❀◑⊟♿🚌♣●P⁵–

George Hotel

Land of Green Ginger, HU1 2EA
⌚ 11-11.30 (12.30am Fri & Sat)
☎ (01482) 226373
Fuller's London Pride; Hop Back Summer Lightning; Rooster's Yankee; Shepherd Neame Spitfire; guest beers Ⓗ
Situated in the old town, this traditional pub has beamed ceilings, wood-panelled walls and pictures of old Hull on the walls, with faux gas lamps providing subdued lighting. The bar offers darts and dominoes, TV and piped music. Food is served at lunchtimes daily, with a curry/steak night on Thursday evening and fish & chips on Friday night. Food is served upstairs, but disabled customers can ask to eat downstairs. ◑≥🚌♣

Hop & Vine

24 Albion Street, HU1 3TG
⌚ 11-11 (midnight Fri & Sat); closed Mon; 4-10 Sun
☎ (07787) 564264 🌐 hopandvinehull.co.uk
Beer range varies Ⓗ
A much-needed addition to the ale scene in Hull city centre, this small free house cellar bar serves a constantly changing selection of two or three real ales from micro-breweries plus ciders and perry in oversized glasses and a good range of Belgian bottled beers. This is a rare outlet for Budvar Dark and Pilsner Urquell. An interesting menu of freshly made snacks and hot drinks is served until 9pm; the innovative website displays the daily food and drinks menu. Worthy joint winner of CAMRA's Hull Pub of the Year Award 2007.
◑≥🚌●⁵–▽

Olde White Harte ★

25 Silver Street, HU1 1JG
⌚ 11-midnight (1am Fri & Sat); 12-midnight Sun
☎ (01482) 326363
Caledonian Deuchars IPA, 80; Theakston Best Bitter, Old Peculier Ⓗ
Historic, 16th-century courtyard pub at the heart of the old town's commercial centre, reputedly the residence of the governor of Hull when he resolved to deny Charles I entry to the city. An impressive staircase leads to the plotting room. The whole of the first floor is used as a restaurant on Wednesday to

Saturday evenings. The ground floor comprises two distinct areas, each with a bar. Award-winning floral displays, superb dark woodwork, stained-glass windows and inglenooks feature. Outside is a heated, covered drinking area. Q❀◐⇌▣

Three John Scotts ✔

Lowgate, HU1 1XW
9-midnight (1am Fri & Sat)
☎ (01482) 381910
Greene King Abbot; Marston's Pedigree; Theakston Old Peculier; guest beers ⊞
Converted from an Edwardian post office and situated opposite St Mary's Church in the old town, this open-plan Wetherspoon's features modern decor and original works of art. It is named after three past incumbents of the church. The clientele is mixed at lunchtime, with circuit drinkers appearing at weekends. The covered, heated rear courtyard has seating. Up to six guest beers are available, usually including one from Acorn and Rooster's, plus Weston's cider and perry. Food is served until 11pm, with a steak club on Tuesday and a curry club on Thursday.
❀◐◑♿●⅟

Walters

21 Scale Lane, HU1 1LA
12-11 (11.30 Fri & Sat)
☎ (01482) 224004
Beer range varies ⊞
Contemporary bar recently established as a free house by the former licensee of the nearby Old Black Boy and operating an over 21s door policy. It provides a welcome retreat from the fashion bars of the old town area. The bar is named after the barber who traded on the premises during the 1820s. Up to eight regularly changing guest beers are available, plus Belgian and German draught and bottled beers, fruit beers and Lindisfarne fruit wines.
♿▣

Wellington Inn

55 Russell Street, HU2 9AB (50m N of Freetown Way)
4-11; 12-midnight Fri & Sat; 12-11 Sun
☎ (01482) 329486 🌐 thewellington-hull.co.uk
Tetley Bitter; guest beers ⊞
Hidden free house gem just off Freetown Way, this former Hull Brewery pub dates from 1861 and serves up to six guest micro beers. It features a walk-in cooler stocking over 100 European bottled beers; note the impressive glass-fronted display in the back bar. Farmhouse ciders and perry can also be found, plus specialist European beers on draught and Lindisfarne fruit wines. No food is served but you can bring your own sandwiches. Joint winner of local CAMRA Pub of the Year 2005-2007. ⇌●P⅟

Whalebone

165 Wincolmlee, HU2 0PA (500m N of North Bridge on W bank of river)
11-midnight
☎ (01482) 226648
Copper Dragon Best Bitter; Taylor Landlord; Whalebone Diana Mild, Neckoil Bitter, seasonal beers; guest beers ⊞
Built in 1796 on the site of the old Lockwood's Brewery, this pub is situated on the harbour in a former industrial area – look for the illuminated M&R Ales sign. The comfortable saloon bar is adorned with photos of bygone Hull pubs, CAMRA awards and the city's sporting heritage. The adjacent Whalebone Brewery opened in 2003. Two real ciders, together with European draught and bottled beers, are also stocked. Hot snacks are available. Hull & East Yorkshire Cider Pub of the Year 2007. ♛♣●

Lund

Wellington Inn ✔

19 The Green, YO25 9TE
12-3 (not Mon), 6.30-11 (11.30 Fri & Sat); 12-11 Sun
☎ (01377) 217294
Black Sheep Best Bitter; John Smith's Bitter; Taylor Landlord; guest beers ⊞
Enjoying a prime location on the green in this award-winning Wold village, most of the pub's trade comes from the local farming community. It was totally renovated by the present licensee, and features stone-flagged floors, beamed ceilings and three real fires. The multi-roomed interior includes a games room and candle-lit restaurant serving evening meals (Tue-Sat). Good food can also be enjoyed at lunchtime from the bar menu and specials board. CAMRA East Yorkshire Village Pub of the Year 2006.
♛❀◐◑⊟♿♣P⅟

Millington

Gait Inn

Main Street, YO42 1TX SE832517
12-4 (not Mon-Thu), 7-11; 12-10.30 Sun
☎ (01759) 302045
Black Sheep Best Bitter; John Smith's Bitter; Tetley Bitter; Theakston Best Bitter; guest beers ⊞
This lovely 16th-century free house is old-fashioned in the very best sense. Genuine horse brasses adorn exposed beams and rural paraphernalia gathers on every shelf, but here it is quite authentic rather than themed. The large map of Yorkshire pasted to the ceiling is discoloured from years of smoke, probably from the open fire beneath. The pub name refers to the plot of open grazing land on Millington Pastures formerly issued to every villager. Good food is available, including on Sunday evening. ♛❀◐◑♣P⅟

Old Ellerby

Blue Bell

Crabtree Lane, HU11 5AJ
12-4 (Sat only), 7-11.30 (midnight Fri & Sat); 12-5, 7-11.30 Sun
☎ (01964) 562364
Black Sheep Best Bitter; Tetley Bitter; guest beers ⊞
This 16th-century inn has an L-shaped bar and a single room split into distinct areas, including a snug to the right and a rear pool area where children are welcome until 8.30pm. Regional CAMRA Village Pub of the Year three times and runner-up in 2006, the

inn has a strong community feel, hosting several darts and dominoes teams. Three guest beers in winter increase to four in summer. Outside is a fish pond and bowling green. Popular with walkers (wipe your shoes please). ⌂Q❀⚘Å♣P⁄—

Patrington

Station Hotel ✓

Station Road, HU12 0NE

⊙ 12-11 (midnight Sat)

☎ (01964) 630262

Tetley Bitter; guest beers ⊞

A family-owned free house on the western edge of the village, this hotel used to service passengers of the Hull-Withernsea railway which closed in the 1960s. The Anglo-German owners have completely refurbished this once run-down pub over the last three years, with a games room the most recent feature. The hotel is renowned locally for its excellent food as well as its interesting guest ales sourced from far and wide. ⚘◐♿Å⊟(76,77)♣P⁄—

Rawcliffe

Jemmy Hirst at the Rose & Crown

26 Riverside, DN14 8RN (down Chapel Lane from the village green)

⊙ 6 (5 Fri)-11; 12-11 Sat & Sun

☎ (01405) 831038

Taylor Landlord; guest beers ⊞

Much loved by visitors across the region, you can be sure of a warm welcome from the owners, locals and Bruno the dog. A constantly changing array of ales suits every taste. The rustic interior with a real fire and book-lined walls provides a welcome retreat, with lazy summer days on the patio or river bank. Weston's Traditional cider is available. A gem that is difficult to leave. CAMRA branch Pub of the Year 2004-2006 and 2008, and runner-up Yorkshire Pub of the Year 2007.
⌂Q⚘♿⊟♣●P⁄—

Ryehill

Crooked Billet ✓

Pitt Lane, HU12 9NN (400m off A1033 E of Thorngumbald)

⊙ 12-2.30 (not Mon), 5-midnight; 12-midnight Sun

☎ (01964) 622303

Jennings Dark Mild, Bitter, Cumberland Ale, seasonal beers; guest beers ⊞

This 16th-century coaching inn has stone floors, upholstered bench seats and a rear dining area. Six handpumps offer three regular beers and at least one other Jennings or Marston's beer, plus guests. High quality home-cooked food is served every day except Monday lunchtime and also Sunday night in winter. At the heart of the community, the pub features bar skittles and shove ha'penny, and hosts monthly jazz and piano evenings. Monday is themed food night. CAMRA East Yorkshire Village Pub of the Year 2007.
⌂⚘⇌◐⊟(76)♣P⁄—

Sewerby

Ship Inn ✓

Cliff Road, YO15 1EW

⊙ 11-11

☎ (01262) 672374 ⊕ shipinnsewerby.co.uk

Banks's Bitter, seasonal beers; guest beers ⊞

Village centre pub serving both locals and those holidaying to the north of Bridlington. One bar is wood panelled with a beamed ceiling and food comprises main meals and snacks. The pub is family friendly, welcoming children and dogs, and the beer garden includes a children's play area. Nearby attractions include a model village, Sewerby Hall and cliff-top walks. The pub sponsors the local cricket club that plays only 100 metres away. ⌂❀⚘◐⊡Å⊟(103,110)♣P⁄—

Skipsea

Board Inn

Back Street, YO25 8SU

⊙ 6 (7 winter)-11; 12-midnight Sat; 12-11 Sun

☎ (01262) 468342

Marston's Pedigree, seasonal beers; guest beers ⊞

Traditional village local dating from the 17th century with distinct public and lounge bars as well as a recently extended restaurant. The public bar, with its sporting focus (especially Rugby League), hosts two darts teams, two pool teams and a dominoes team. The comfortable lounge is home to the landlady's water jug collection. Home-cooked food is served daily from 6pm, and in summer attracts many holiday-makers for Sunday lunch (booking advisable). Dogs are welcome.
⌂Q⚘◐⊡Å♣P⁄—

South Dalton

Pipe & Glass

West End, HU17 7PN (follow signs off B1248)

⊙ 12-3, 6.30-11 (not Mon); 12-10.30 Sun

☎ (01430) 810246 ⊕ pipeandglass.co.uk

Black Sheep Best Bitter; guest beers ⊞

This characterful pub with exposed beams serves three regularly changing guest beers from Yorkshire breweries. Its kitchen focuses strongly on modern British food, which is served lunchtimes and evenings in both the bar and the restaurant. Ask for the separate vegetarian menu. Children are welcome throughout and there is a food menu for children available on request. ⌂⚘◐●P

Sutton upon Derwent

St Vincent Arms

Main Street, YO41 4BN (on B1228 S of Elvington)

⊙ 11.30-3, 6-11; 12-3, 7-10.30 Sun

☎ (01904) 608349

Fuller's London Pride, ESB; Old Mill Bitter; Taylor Golden Best, Landlord; Wells Bombardier; York Yorkshire Terrier; guest beers ⊞

Family owned and run for many years, this pretty white-painted building is situated on a bend in the road through the village. The L-shaped bar to the right is popular with locals; note the large Fuller, Smith & Turner mirror. Another bar to the left with a serving hatch leads to the dining rooms. Twice local CAMRA Pub of the Year. An excellent restaurant specialises in many fish dishes. Q❀◑⊟P

Wold Newton

Anvil Arms

Bridlington Road, YO25 3YL
⊙ 12-midnight
☎ (01262) 470279
Black Sheep Best Bitter; John Smith's Bitter; guest beers Ⓗ
Reputedly haunted, this Grade II-listed building stands opposite the pond in a picturesque village on the edge of the Wolds. Sympathetically restored, it comprises a bar, games room with pool table and a restaurant that opens Friday and Saturday evenings and Thursday and Sunday lunchtimes (booking essential). Snacks are sometimes on offer – ask at the bar. It fields darts and dominoes teams. The guest beer is likely to come from Great Newsome, Hambleton, Daleside or Rudgate breweries. ⌂Q⛟❀⊟⛺♣P⊬

YORKSHIRE (NORTH)

Acomb

Sun Inn

35 The Green, YO26 5LL SE571514
⊙ 11-midnight
☎ (01904) 798500 🌐 thesuninnacomb.com
John Smith's Bitter; guest beers Ⓗ
Inviting ale house pleasantly located overlooking Acomb village green, with convenient bus links east to the centre of York. A variety of bars comfortably accommodate sporting, family and lunchtime requirements, with a mixture of calm and bustle to suit every taste. Daily newspapers are available, and each week a quiz is held on Sunday and a jam session on Wednesday which reinforce the community atmosphere.
⛟❀◐⊟♿⛍(4,16)♣P

Aldbrough St John

Stanwick Inn ✔

High Green, DL11 7SZ (1 mile from B6275)
⊙ 12-2 (not Mon), 6.30-11; 12-7 Sun
☎ (01325) 374258
Daleside Bitter; guest beers Ⓗ
Set in a picturesque North Yorkshire village on the county's second largest village green, this stunning, welcoming 19th-century inn overlooks the meandering beck. It has two bars: one for drinkers and one serving two excellent restaurants. The pub demonstrates a passion for real ale, with guest beers coming from local micros. There is a quiz every third Wednesday. The pub is ideally situated for exploring the Yorkshire Dales and Teesdale.
⌂Q❀🛏◑⊟⛍(29)♣P⊬

Appletreewick

Craven Arms Inn

BD23 6DA
⊙ 11-3, 6-11 Mon & Tue; 11.30-11 Wed-Sat; 11.30-10.30 Sun
☎ (01756) 720270 🌐 craven-cruckbarn.co.uk
Taylor Golden Best; Tetley Bitter; Theakston Best Bitter; guest beers Ⓗ
Built originally in 1548 as a farm, local craftsmen have recently returned many historical features to this building including oak beams, stone flagged floors, gas lighting and open fires, to create a charming atmosphere. To the rear is a cruck barn, the first one built for 400 years in the Dales. The ever changing menu ranges from a la carte to bar meals and the public bar boasts a rare Ring The Bull pub game and a dartboard. The house beer Cruck Barn Bitter is from Moorhouses.
⌂Q❀◑⛺⛍(74)♣P

New Inn

BD23 6DA (W end of village)
⊙ 12-11
☎ (01756) 720252
Black Sheep Best Bitter; Daleside Bitter, Blonde; John Smith's Bitter; Theakston Old Peculier Ⓗ
Friendly, unspoilt village local with two rooms, both warmed by roaring fires, with a pool table in a third room to the rear. Black and white photographs of bygone Appletreewick adorn the walls. A fine range of bottled beers from around the world is always available. Walkers and cyclists enjoying the surrounding Dales countryside are very welcome, along with their well behaved dogs. A nearby cycle livery is on hand for any necessary maintenance. ⌂Q❀🛏◑⛺⛍(74)♣P

Askrigg

Crown Inn ✔

Main Street, DL8 3HQ
⊙ 12-1am (midnight Sun)
☎ (01969) 650298
John Smith's Bitter; Theakston Best Bitter, Black Bull; guest beers Ⓗ
Set at the top of the main street of this village which gained fame as the setting for the TV series All Creatures Great and Small, this busy,

INDEPENDENT BREWERIES

Abbey Bells Hirst Courtney
Black Sheep Masham
Brown Cow Barlow
Captain Cook Stokesley
Copper Dragon Skipton
Cropton Cropton
Daleside Harrogate
Dark Horse Hetton (NEW)
Great Heck Great Heck (NEW)
Hambleton Melmerby
Litton Litton
Marston Moor Tockwith
Naylor's Crosshills
North Yorkshire Pinchinthorpe
Redscar Redcar (NEW)
Richmond Richmond (NEW)
Rooster's/Outlaw Knaresborough
Rudgate Tockwith
Samuel Smith Tadcaster
Selby Selby (Brewing Suspended)
Theakston Masham
Three Peaks Settle
Wensleydale Bellerby
York York
Yorkshire Dales Askrigg

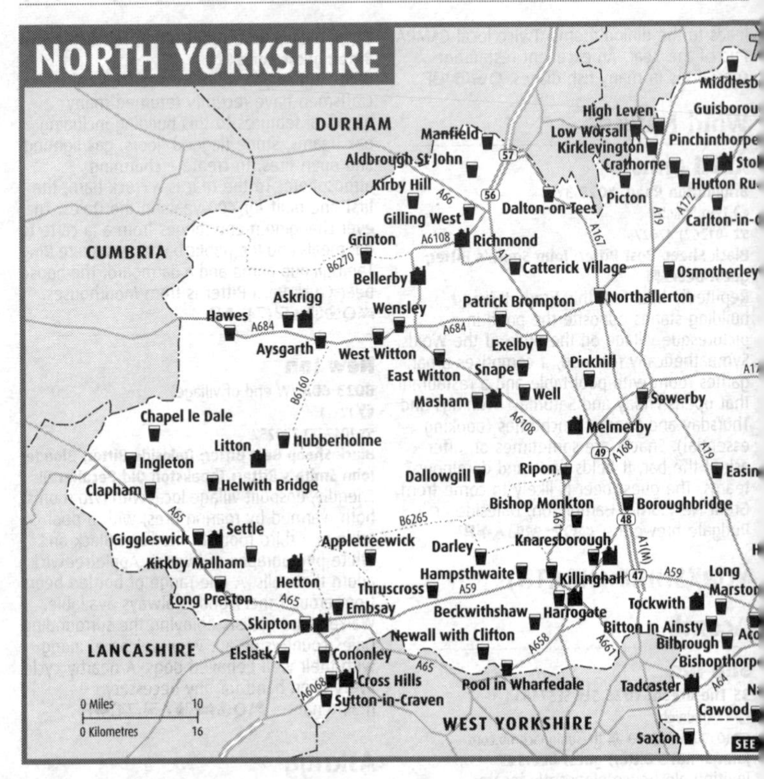

friendly Dales inn attracts a good mix of locals and visitors, and is particularly popular for its bar meals. The interior has been opened out but retains much of its traditional character, with a particularly impressive fireplace.
⛰❀◐◑⊟(157)♣P⁻

White Rose Hotel

Main Street, DL8 3HG
⏲ 12-1am (midnight Sun)
☎ (01969) 650515
Black Sheep Best Bitter; John Smith's Bitter; Theakston Best Bitter; Yorkshire Dales Askrigg Ale Ⓗ
This family run hotel offers a warm welcome to regulars and visitors to this picturesque village. The building was refurbished in 2006 and is an excellent place to unwind after a day walking in the Dales, with good value food and accommodation. The nearby Yorkshire Dales Brewery delivers by wheelbarrow.
❀⇌◐◑⊟(157)♣P⁻

Aysgarth

George & Dragon

DL8 3AD
⏲ 11.30 (12 Sun)-2am
☎ (01969) 663358 🌐 georgeanddragonaysgarth.co.uk
Black Sheep Best Bitter, Ale; Theakston Best Bitter; guest beers Ⓗ
Situated within a 15 minute walk of the tourist hot spot of Aysgarth Falls on the main route through Wensleydale, this cosy 17th-century inn serves a range of local beers always including one from the nearby Yorkshire Dales Brewery. Friendly service, good food and accommodation, and a picturesque location make this free house a perfect stop on a journey through the Dales.
⛰Q☎❀⇌◐◑⋀⊟(156)♣P⁻

Beck Hole

Birch Hall Inn ★

YO22 5LE (1½ km N of Goathland)
⏲ 11-11 summer; 11-3, 7.30-11 (closed Mon eve & Tue) winter
☎ (01947) 896245 🌐 beckhole.info
Black Sheep Best Bitter; guest beers Ⓗ
This unspoilt rural gem and CAMRA multi-award winner, including Pub of the Year 2007, comprises two bars sandwiching a sweet shop. One guest beer is served in winter, two guests and a perry in summer. The house ale Beckwater is brewed organically by North Yorkshire Brewery. An oil painting of the Murk Esk by Algernon Newton, Royal Academy, has been hanging outside the pub since 1944 – it was given to the village as a thank you for its hospitality during his seven year residency. Substantial sandwiches, pies and beer cake are served. ⛰Q❀⇌◐◑⊟♣●P

Beckwithshaw

Smiths Arms

Church Row, HG3 1QW (on B6161)
⏲ 11-11; 12-10.30 Sun
☎ (01423) 304871
Daleside Bitter, Blonde, Old Legover Ⓗ
The pub's name reflects the fact that the original tenancy required the landlord to be a

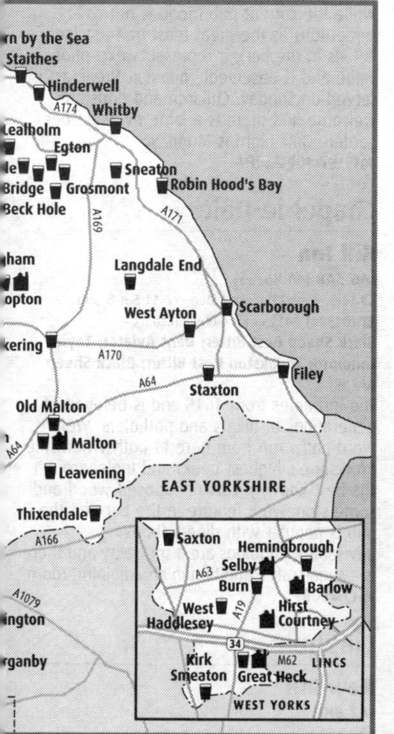

blacksmith serving the local estate owner, so part of the building was a smithy. In addition, the upper floor was used as a school room until the mid 19th century. Now extended, the pub provides a range of good food and local ales to village residents and visitors to Harrogate and the nearby Harlow Carr Gardens. ⛫Q❀◑P

Bilbrough

Three Hares

Main Street, YO23 3PH (off A64, 6 miles W of York)
⏲ 12-3, 5-midnight; closed Mon; 12-midnight Fri-Sun
☎ (01937) 832128
Black Sheep Best Bitter; Bradfield Farmers Blonde; Taylor Landlord Ⓗ
Delightful whitewashed village pub in the centre of Bilbrough (York CAMRA Pub of the Season summer 2000). The traditional exterior leads to a stylish, contemporary interior, where four rooms are each furnished differently: two of the rooms are set aside for diners while the two closest to the bar are for drinkers and serve bar meals. A large outdoor dining area includes a fountain. The pub manages a good balance between drinking and dining – a pub brunch is offered for punters on the way to York races. ⛫❀◑♿P

Bilton in Ainsty

Chequers ✔

YO26 7NN (S off B1224 Wetherby-York road) SE477498
⏲ 12-3, 6-11; closed Mon; 12-10.30 Sun
☎ (01423) 359637
Caledonian Deuchars IPA; Black Sheep Best Bitter; guest beers Ⓗ
This large, family-run, beautifully maintained pub was built in the 16th century and extended in the 1970s. A good-sized bar offers a variety of comfortable seating, a smart, panelled dining room and a smaller dining area suitable for families. High quality meals are particularly popular at weekends. There are two outside areas, one with picnic tables and another which is covered and heated. The pub offers accommodation in three en-suite bedrooms. ⛫❀◑♿♣P⊬

Bishop Monkton

Lamb & Flag

Boroughbridge Road, HG4 3QN (off A61)
⏲ 12-3 (closed Mon), 6.30-11.30
☎ (01765) 677332 🌐 lambandflagbarn.co.uk
Daleside Bitter; Tetley Bitter Ⓗ
A true village local supporting local charities and fund-raising events. The pub has two rooms, both served from a central bar and warmed by a single real fire. There are blackboards providing details of home-cooked food and the pub also has AA 4-star accommodation available – visit the website for details. A large car park is available at the rear. ⛫Q❀◑Ⓐ(56)♣P⊬

Bishopthorpe

Ebor Inn

46 Main Street, YO23 2RB
⏲ 11-11.30 (11 Sun)
☎ (01904) 706190
Samuel Smith OBB Ⓗ
Originally known as the Brown Cow, this 16th-century hotel, close to the archbishop's palace, is officially haunted (Ghost Research Foundation study, 2003). The landlord of 27 years makes customers feel very welcome. Fish from Whitby is a speciality, and vegetarian food is available too from a freshly cooked and varied menu, served lunchtimes and evenings. The large child-friendly garden to the rear hosts village fetes and a popular bonfire party. The pub features on the Dog-Friendly Britain website and also welcomes children. Q❀◑♿(11)♣

Boroughbridge

Black Bull Inn

6 St James Square, YO51 9AR
⏲ 11 (12 Sun)-midnight
☎ (01423) 322413
John Smith's Bitter; Taylor Best Bitter; guest beers Ⓗ
Situated in the main square, this 13th-century Grade II-listed inn, complete with resident ghost, is very popular. A comfortable snug and a larger distinctive bar serve good value beers and there is a wide choice of bar meals. The smart restaurant, converted from old stables, boasts an international menu. This little gem, complete with friendly locals, is well worth a visit. Free town parking nearby.
⛫Q◑Ⓐ♣P

Burn

Wheatsheaf

Main Road, YO8 8LJ
12-11
(01757) 270614 wheatsheafburn.co.uk
John Smith's Bitter; Taylor Best Bitter; guest beers
This genuine free house stocks four guest beers from local micro-breweries, with a beer from Brown Cow always available. The interior has been opened out and the pub is adorned with memorabilia of 578 Squadron, which was stationed at Burn during World War II, plus an array of antiques, knick-knacks and bottles of beer. Food is served lunchtimes and evenings Thursday to Saturday. Dogs are welcome.
P

Carlton-in-Cleveland

Blackwell Ox Inn

Main Street, TS9 7DJ
11.30-11
(01642) 712287
Black Sheep Best Bitter; Worthington's Bitter; guest beers
Located in a beautiful area on the edge of the National Park, this previous CAMRA Pub of the Season winner is an impressive and popular village inn, renowned for its first class, good value Thai cuisine. An eclectic and ever-changing beer range offers something to suit all tastes. The garden has an extensive children's play area and the pub also has its own camping and caravan site.
Q(80,89)P

Catterick Village

Bay Horse Inn

38 Low Green, DL10 7LP
12-3 (not Mon & Thu), 6-11; 12-midnight Fri & Sat; 12-11 Sun
(01748) 811383
Jennings Bitter, Cumberland Ale; guest beers
Long established village pub with a pleasant southerly aspect. The cosy L-shaped bar area is mainly open plan with a small quiet area off to one side, which has one or two well-used dartboards. The pub is conveniently situated close to the A1 and Catterick race course. Good food made with fresh produce is served in both the bar area and the modern conservatory restaurant at the rear of the building; guest ales are from the Jennings seasonal range. P

Cawood

Ferry Inn

2 King Street, YO8 3TL (S side of river, near swing bridge) SE573378
4.30-11; 12-midnight Thu-Sat; 12-11 Sun
(01757) 268515 theferryinn.com
Caledonian Deuchars IPA; Rooster's Yankee; Taylor Landlord
This welcoming 16th-century free house owes its name to the ferry service across the River Ouse prior to the erection of the current swing bridge. Cardinal Wolsey, when Archbishop of York, briefly resided nearby at Cawood Castle. While the current pub menu is not as sumptuous as the great feast of 1464 (see details in the bar), it represents exceptional value and is deservedly popular. Breakfast is served on Sunday. Children and dogs are welcome and there is a large riverside beer garden. Quiz night is Monday.
QP

Chapel-le-Dale

Hill Inn

LA6 3AR (on B6255)
12-3, 6.30-11; closed Mon; 12-11 Sat & Sun
(01524) 241256 oldhillinn.co.uk
Black Sheep Best Bitter; Dent Aviator; Taylor Landlord; Theakston Best Bitter; Black Sheep Ale
The inn dates from 1615 and is beloved of generations of hikers and potholers. Well-worn paths run from here to both Whernside (Yorkshire's highest peak) and Ingleborough (its best known). Lots of exposed wood and some stonework feature in the bar and the pub is popular with diners (booking advisable); puddings are a speciality and there is a sugarcraft exhibition in an adjoining room.
QP

Clapham

New Inn

LA2 8HH
11-11
(01524) 251203 newinn-clapham.co.uk
Black Sheep Best Bitter; Copper Dragon Best Bitter, Golden Pippin; Taylor Landlord
Spacious 18th-century coaching inn situated in a major tourist village and featuring two lounge bars. One includes oak panelling, the other has walls decorated with photos and cartoons depicting caving, and is home to pub games. Children are welcome in the restaurant. Other beers are sometimes available.The railway station is one mile away.
(581)♣P

Cononley

New Inn

Main Street, BD20 8NR
12-2.30, 5.30-midnight; 12-1am Fri & Sat; 12-10.30 Sun
(01535) 636302 newinncononley.co.uk
Taylor Dark Mild, Golden Best, Best Bitter, Landlord, Ram Tam
An historic inn situated in a Dales village between Keighley and Skipton, with mullioned windows and low, beamed ceilings. It has been a public house for 200 years and is always busy. A local community pub, it has a reputation for serving excellent good value meals alongside Taylor cask ales. Quiz night is Tuesday. Just a short walk from Cononley railway station – if catching a train south, allow time to cross the level crossing barrier.
(78A)♣

Crathorne

Crathorne Arms

TS15 0BA

✪ 11.30-3, 5-11; 11-11 Sat; 12-4, 6-11 Sun
☎ (01642) 701931
Black Sheep Best Bitter; Taylor Landlord; guest beers ⊞
The bustling A19 trunk road now bypasses this whitewashed gem of a village pub, which is locally known by the name of the farm to the rear – Free House Farm. As the focus of village life, it caters for all interests. Customers are drawn from far and wide to sample its fine ales and good value locally sourced home-cooked food. Whatever you are looking for in a pub, it is probably here.
♨Q☺❀◐♿🚌(82)♣P⁄

Cropton

New Inn

Woolcroft, YO18 8HH (5 miles off A170, Pickering-Kirkbymoorside road) SE754888
✪ 11-11 (midnight Fri & Sat); 12-11 Sun
☎ (01751) 417330 🌐 croptonbrewery.co.uk
Cropton Two Pints, Monkmans Slaughter; guest beers ⊞
This outstanding village inn with its own brewery comprises a cosy bar, a small lounge and a pool room, plus six handpumps providing a choice of Cropton Brewery beers and other guests. Its good-value accommodation makes it an excellent base for visitors to the North Yorkshire Moors and coast. Home-cooked meals are served in the bars, restaurant and conservatory overlooking the garden. Children are welcome in some areas. The North Yorkshire Moors Railway is nearby. Brewery tours are available and an annual beer festival is hosted.
Q☺❀🛏◐⊟▲♣P⁄🍺

Cross Hills

Old White Bear

6 Keighley Road, BD20 7RN (on A6068, close to jct with A629)
✪ 11.30-11; 12-10.30 Sun
☎ (01535) 632115
Naylors Pinnacle Mild, Pale Ale, Bitter, Porter ⊞
Built in 1735, the inn has had a chequered history. Before becoming the pub that is today it has been a hotel, brothel, council meeting room and dance hall. Children and dogs are welcome if well behaved. Food is served daily lunchtimes and evenings in a separate restaurant. This is a regular outlet for Naylors Brewery and is one of the few remaining places where the Ring the Bull pub game is still played. Quiz night is Thursday.
♨❀◐🚌♣P⁄

Dallowgill

Drovers Inn

HG4 3RH (2 miles W of Laverton on road to Pateley Bridge) SE213722
✪ 6.30-11.30 (7-11 winter); closed Mon; 12-3, 6.30-11 Sat & Sun
☎ (01765) 658510
Black Sheep Best Bitter; Hambleton Bitter; Old Mill Mild or Bitter ⊞
A Guide regular for more than eight years, this tiny pub continues to do what it does best, which is to serve good beer and food in a friendly, welcoming atmosphere. Situated high up near the moors, it overlooks Nidderdale. Morris dancers and shooters from the Grouse Moors all frequent the pub at various times throughout the year. Evening meals are served until 8.30pm. Although somewhat isolated, this pub is well worth the effort to find. ♨Q❀◐▲♣P⁄

Dalton-on-Tees

Chequers Inn

DL2 2NT
✪ 12-3, 5.30-11; 12-10.30 Sun
☎ (01325) 721213
Banks's Bitter; guest beers ⊞
Traditional inn dating back to the 1840s, comprising a bar, lounge and restaurant, with a warm welcome guaranteed. Formerly known as the Crown & Anchor, this was once part of the now-defunct Fryer's Brewery estate. The landlord is passionate about real ale and at least two guest beers are sourced from micros countrywide. Regular gourmet evenings take place and a quiz is held every Wednesday. Overnight accommodation comprises five rooms.
Q❀🛏◐♿🚌(72,X72)P⁄

Danby

Duke of Wellington

2 West Lane, YO21 2LY (200m N of railway station)
✪ 12-3 (not Mon), 7-11; 12-11 Fri & Sat; 12-3, 7-10.30 Sun
☎ (01287) 660351 🌐 dukeofwellingtondanby.co.uk
Copper Dragon Scotts 1816; Daleside Bitter; guest beers ⊞
This 18th-century inn, a previous local CAMRA Pub of the Season award winner, is set in idyllic countryside and was used as a recruiting post during the Napoleonic War. A cast-iron plaque of the first Duke of Wellington, unearthed during restoration work, hangs above the fireplace in the bar. Both the regular beers and the guest come from local breweries. The blackboard menu offers traditional British meals, using locally sourced meat, fish and game. The Moors Visitor Centre is nearby. ♨Q❀🛏◑⇌🚌♣

Darley

Wellington Inn

HG3 2QQ (on B6451 near Harrogate)
✪ 11.30-11; 12-10.30 Sun
☎ (01423) 780363 🌐 wellington-inn.co.uk
Caledonian Deuchars IPA; Taylor Landlord; Tetley Bitter; Theakston Best Bitter ⊞
Spacious stone roadside inn, some 200 years old, nestling in a picturesque valley with views from the beer garden across Nidderdale, an area of outstanding natural beauty. The pub has high-backed bench seating and a low, beamed ceiling, as well as an open fire. Signature dishes from the varied restaurant menu included Darley lamb and Wellington fish pie. The pub makes a good starting point for walking or cycling in the Dales. ♨Q☺❀🛏◐🚌♣P

Easingwold

George Hotel ✔

Market Place, YO61 3AD
⏲ 10-midnight
☎ (01347) 821698 🌐 the-george-hotel.co.uk
Black Sheep Best Bitter; Boddingtons Bitter; Moorhouses Pride of Pendle; guest beers Ⓗ
Overlooking Easingwold's cobbled market square opposite the market cross, this old coaching inn dates from the 18th century. Now a comfortable country inn at the hub of the local community, it offers a range of freshly cooked food and quality accommodation. Its cosy rooms are served by a central bar, where the landlord has a free choice of guest beers. There is a bench outside the front of the hotel that is used for drinking from Easter to the end of September.
⛰Q❀🛏◐◑♿🚌P⚊

East Witton

Cover Bridge Inn

DL8 4SQ (half mile N of village on A6108) SE144871
⏲ 11-11; 12-11.30 Sun
☎ (01969) 623250 🌐 thecoverbridgeinn.co.uk
Black Sheep Best Bitter; John Smith's Bitter; Taylor Landlord; Theakston Best Bitter, Old Peculier; guest beers Ⓗ
An outstanding country inn situated where the Rivers Cover and Ure meet. A CAMRA multi-award winner, the pub serves up to eight cask ales on a regular basis. Once you have fathomed out the door latch, you enter the ancient public bar, with its splendid hearth and open fire. A tiny lounge leads to a very attractive riverside garden with a play area. It has an enviable reputation for food, with lunchtime and evening meals served daily.
⛰Q👶❀🛏◐◑⊟♿🚌(159)♣P⊡

Egton

Wheatsheaf Inn

High Street, YO21 1TZ
⏲ 11.30-2.30, 5.30-11; closed Mon; 11.30-11 Sat; 12-11 Sun
☎ (01947) 895271 🌐 wheatsheafegton.com
Black Sheep Best Bitter; Caledonian Deuchars IPA; guest beer Ⓗ
Popular Grade I-listed 19th-century pub where a warm welcome awaits. You can sit on church pews in the cosy bar, where collectables bought at local auctions add to the character. In the lounge, numerous fly rods are attached to the ceiling; both bars are warmed by coal fires. The recommended upmarket menu is based on local seasonal produce (no food Sun eve). A grassy area to the front and a patio area to the rear are ideal for summer. There are three letting bedrooms.
⛰❀🛏◐◑⊟♿🚌(99)♣P⚊

Egton Bridge

Horseshoe Hotel

YO21 1XE (down hill from Egton station)
⏲ 11.30-3, 6.30-11; 11.30-11 Sat; 12-11 Sun
☎ (01947) 895245
Black Sheep Best Bitter; John Smith's Bitter; guest beers Ⓗ
Secluded gem in a natural hollow, easily accessed from the station or across the stepping stones of the River Esk. The bar is furnished with old-fashioned settles and warmed by a large fire. Five handpumps provide a wide beer selection, with guests usually from Copper Dragon and Durham. A large raised grassy area with mature trees makes outdoor drinking a pleasure. The regular menu and specials board offer good value locally-sourced food. Dogs are welcome. A former CAMRA Pub of the Year award winner. ⛰Q👶❀🛏◐◑♿⇌P⚊

Elslack

Tempest Arms ✔

BD23 3AY (off A56 Skipton-Colne road)
⏲ 11-11; 12-10.30 Sun
☎ (01282) 842450 🌐 tempestarms.co.uk
Black Sheep Best Bitter; Copper Dragon Scotts 1816; Taylor Best Bitter, Landlord; Theakston Best Bitter Ⓗ
Large, popular, upmarket country pub, just off the A56, serving good food from an extensive menu in a separate dining area/restaurant. The house beer is from Moorhouses and a good range of foreign bottled beers is also available. The decor is a tasteful mix of traditional and contemporary, while conference facilities and a function room are available for hire. There is a Puffa Hut for smokers. Pennine bus 215 Burnley to Skipton passes close by. ⛰❀🛏◐◑♿🚌(215)P⚊

Elvington

Grey Horse ✔

Main Street, YO41 4AG (on B1228 6 miles SE of York)
⏲ 5-11 (12-3 Wed & Thu summer); 12-11 Fri-Sun
☎ (01904) 608335 🌐 thegreyhorse.com
Black Sheep Best Bitter; Taylor Landlord; Theakston Best Bitter; guest beers Ⓗ
A two-roomed local served by a central bar, this village pub has been wonderfully well maintained and developed by the current licensee. The refurbished lounge boasts a feature beer wall and a collection of old radios. The guest beers change regularly and are interesting and varied. Food is served in the lounge or, when busy, in the upstairs Hayloft function room (no food Mon). Tables at the front provide a pleasant outside drinking area, while smokers are catered for at the back. ⛰👶❀🛏◐◑⊟♿♣P⚊

Embsay

Elm Tree Inn

5 Elm Tree Square, BD23 6RB
⏲ 11.30 (12 Sun winter)-3, 5.30-11; 12-11 Sat & Sun summer
☎ (01756) 790717
Copper Dragon Scotts 1816; Goose Eye No-Eye Deer; Wells Bombardier; guest beers Ⓗ
Former coaching inn situated in the village square. Inside it has an open feel with oak beams and horse brasses. As well as the large main bar there is a smaller side room, used mainly by diners. Look out for the worn mounting steps outside. Well-situated for

walking on the edge of the Yorkshire Dales National Park, Bolton Abbey Steam Railway line is nearby. Weston's cider and perry are served regularly. ❀⇄◑⊟♣P⁻

Exelby

Green Dragon

High Road, DL8 2HA

⊛ 12-2.30, 5-midnight; 12-midnight Fri & Sat; 12-11 Sun

☎ (01677) 422233 ⊕ thegreendragonexelby.co.uk

Black Sheep Best Bitter; Tetley Bitter; guest beers Ⓗ

Handy for the busy A1 trunk route, this welcoming inn has grown over the years from a small row of 19th-century cottages to a multi-roomed pub with a 60-seat restaurant and a covered patio area to the rear. In the comfortable lounge traditional decor complements the low beams and open fireplace. The pub has not lost its role as a village local, but enjoys a good reputation for its food, much of which is locally sourced. ♨❀⇄◑⊟ΔP⁻

Filey

Bonhommes Bar

Royal Crescent Court, The Crescent, YO14 9JH

⊛ 11 (12 winter)-midnight (1am Fri & Sat); 12-midnight Sun

☎ (01723) 514054

Tetley Bitter; guest beers Ⓗ

Known since the 1950s as the American Bar and situated just off the fine Victorian Royal Crescent Hotel complex, its present name celebrates John Paul Jones, father of the American Navy. His ship, the Bonhomme Richard, was involved in a battle off nearby Flamborough Head during the War of Independence. Five handpumps serve Timothy Taylor, Copper Dragon and Camerons beers plus two other rotating guests. Occasional live music is hosted. Voted by local CAMRA as runner-up rural Pub of the Year 2007. ⇌⊟

Fulford

Saddle Inn

Main Street, YO10 4PJ (A19 2 miles S of York)

⊛ 11.30-4, 5.45-midnight; 11.30-midnight Fri & Sat; 12-11 Sun

☎ (01904) 833317

Jennings Bitter; Banks's Bitter; Mansfield Bitter; Marston's Pedigree; guest beers Ⓗ

This 150-year-old roadside inn in a suburb south of York is well preserved, offering good food (not lunchtime Mon-Wed) and good-value accommodation. A comfortable L-shaped lounge includes sports TV, darts and pool, and children are welcome in the adjacent dining room. The attractive garden beyond the car park has a petanque terrain and visitors are made welcome by the pub's enthusiastic team at open sessions. ♨☋❀⇄◑♣P⁻

Giggleswick

Hart's Head Hotel ✔

Belle Hill, BD24 0BA (on B6480 ½ mile N of Settle)

⊛ 12-2.30 (not Thu), 5.30-11; 11-11 Sat; 12-10.30 Sun

☎ (01729) 822086 ⊕ hartsheadhotel.co.uk

Copper Dragon Golden Pippin, Scotts 1816; Tetley Bitter; guest beers Ⓗ

Welcoming 18th-century coaching inn, now established as a regular entry in this Guide. The open-plan bar retains a multi-room feel, with some comfortable sofa seating. An excellent range of up to six cask beers is on offer, mostly from local breweries. Food is highly featured at this hostelry: note the enormous blackboard menu displayed at the entrance to the dining area. The refurbished cellar houses a full-sized snooker table. ♨Q❀⇄◑⊟⊟♣P⁻

Gilling West

White Swan Inn

51 High Street, DL10 5JG (2 miles W of Scotch Corner, off A66)

⊛ 12-11 (10.30 Sun)

☎ (01748) 821123

Black Sheep Best Bitter; John Smith's Bitter; guest beers Ⓗ

Friendly 17th-century country inn with an open plan bar and a dining room offering an extensive menu. This free house sources guest beers from local and national micro-breweries. The bar's beams are covered in bank notes, old and new, while a notable feature in the Gents' toilet is the barbed-wire toilet seat! The pub fields darts and dominoes teams and has a clay-pigeon shooting club. There is live music on alternate Wednesdays. ♨Q❀◑Δ⊟(29)♣⁻

Glaisdale

Arncliffe Arms

1 Arncliffe Terrace, YO21 2QL (at the bottom of the village)

⊛ 12-11 summer and Sat winter; closed Mon; 12-2.30 (not Tue), 6-11 winter; 12-10.30 Sun

☎ (01947) 897555 ⊕ arncliffearms.co.uk

Black Sheep Best Bitter; guest beers Ⓗ

In a scenic location close to the River Esk and Beggars Bridge, the pub is popular with locals and visitors alike. Two guest beers from local breweries are served in the summer, while upmarket restaurant meals and substantial bar food are sourced from local produce wherever possible. Children are welcome until 9pm. An excellent pub website gives details of a number of circular walks, together with details of the NYMR train which calls at Glaisdale on summer Saturdays. Dog friendly. ♨Q❀⇄◑⇌⊟(99)♣P

Great Heck

Bay Horse

Main Street, DN14 0BE (follow signs from A19)

⊛ 5-11.30 Mon; 12-12.30am Tue-Sat; 12-11.30 Sun

☎ (01977) 661125

Old Mill Bitter, seasonal beers Ⓗ

An outlet for the local Old Mill Brewery, the pub was converted from cottages some years ago. Although open plan, it has distinct areas including a lounge bar and a dining area. An open fire, exposed beams and brasses add traditional character. Home-cooked meals are served from an extensive menu and Sunday roasts are sourced from local farmers. A rear patio is ideal for warm weather and there is a covered area for smokers. Thursday is quiz night, followed by supper. ⚲❀◑♿P⌐

Grinton

Bridge Inn

DL11 6HH (on B6270, 1 mile E of Reeth)
✪ 12-midnight (1am Fri & Sat); 12-11 Sun
☎ (01748) 884224
Jennings Dark Mild, Cumberland Ale, Cocker Hoop ⊞
On the banks of the River Swale and beneath Fremington Edge, this former coaching inn has been sensitively renovated to retain its traditional character. Inside there is a lounge with wooden panelling and beams, a restaurant to the left and games room to the right. Food prepared from seasonal produce is served daily. Families and pets are welcome but mobile phones are not, and their use incurs a fine. Thursday is musicians' night and mini beer festivals are hosted in March and October. ⚲❀◑◐Å⊟(30)♣P⌐

Grosmont

Crossing Club

Co-operative Building, Front Street, YO22 5QE (opposite NYMR car park)
✪ 8-11 (closed Mon winter)
☎ (01947) 895040
Beer range varies ⊞
Converted by volunteers from the Co-op store delivery bay, the club is decorated throughout with railway memorabilia. A single bar serves five beers, one usually from Wold Top – more than 500 different beers have been served during its eight-year existence. Access is through a glass door (ring the bell). A summer beer festival is held and beer is supplied for the Whitby Music Train that runs on Friday evenings in summer. Opening hours are extended during the NYMR steam train galas. QÅ≠⊟(99)♣

Guisborough

Tap & Spile

11-13 Westgate, TS14 6BG
✪ 12-1am (2am Fri & Sat); 12-12.30am Sun
☎ (01287) 632983
Beer range varies ⊞
One of the oldest pubs in the town, this impressive inn is a large two-roomed affair with bare boards and exposed wooden beams in the bar, while the back room is available for functions. Up to seven beers are served, alongside Weston's Old Rosie cider. The pub has a pleasant covered and heated outdoor drinking area. Live bands perform on Wednesday and Sunday evenings. No meals are available on Monday and Tuesday lunchtimes. Q❀◐Å⊟●⌐

Hampsthwaite

Joiners Arms

High Street, HG3 2EU (off A59)
✪ 11.30-2.30, 5.30-11; 11-11 Sat; 12-10.30 Sun
☎ (01423) 771673
Rudgate Viking; Tetley Bitter ⊞
On entering this popular village local one is presented with a traditional choice of tap room or lounge, but behind the bar these are linked by an unusual snug with stone floor and vaulted ceiling, which was once the cellar. The lounge features an inglenook fireplace and leads to an attractive dining room adorned with a collection of rare gravy boats. Here food is served Wednesday to Saturday evenings, although bar meals are available every lunchtime. Q◐◑⊟(24)P

Harrogate

Coach & Horses

16 West Park, HG1 1BJ (opp The Stray)
✪ 11-11; 12-10.30 Sun
☎ (01423) 568371
Taylor Landlord; Tetley Bitter; guest beers ⊞
A central bar is surrounded by snugs and alcoves, creating a cosy atmosphere. Excellent meals are served at lunchtime and there are frequent themed food evenings. Many of these, together with a Sunday night quiz, raise money for a local children's hospice. Tetley Bitter and Taylor Landlord are always available, with three other beers sourced from local breweries. A few tables and chairs are placed outside for smokers. Window boxes provide year-round colour, with a quite spectacular display in summer. ◐◑≠⊟

Empress

10 Church Square, HG1 4SP (At jct of Skipton, Wetherby and Knaresborough roads)
✪ 11.30 (12 Sun)-11.30
☎ (01423) 567629
Daleside Bitter, Blonde; John Smith's Bitter; Tetley Bitter ⊞
Situated in the oldest part of Harrogate, this pub can lay claim to standing on the site of the town's earliest inn, although the present building, with views of the Stray, dates only from the 19th century. The entrance lobby to the large single bar acts as a buffer between a games area with pool table and darts and a more relaxed lounge area, where newspapers are available for customers, along with a tropical fish tank. ◐⊟

Hales Bar

1-3 Crescent Road, HG1 2RS
✪ 11-midnight (1am Thu-Sat); 12-11 Sun
☎ (01423) 725570
Daleside Special Bitter; Draught Bass; Tetley Bitter; guest beers ⊞
This traditional town centre heritage pub is Harrogate's oldest bar, and on CAMRA's regional inventory. There are two rooms, each with its own servery. Both bars have large wooden casks set into the wall, and the lounge bar features a collection of stuffed birds and old brewery prints and mirrors. The Victorian interior retains its original gas lanterns. Guest beers are from the SIBA direct delivery scheme. ◑◐≠⊟⌐

Old Bell Tavern ✔

6 Royal Parade, HG1 2SZ (500m W of A61)
✪ 12-11 (10.30 Sun)
☎ (01423) 507930

Black Sheep Best Bitter; Theakston Best Bitter; guest beers Ⓗ
Two regular beers and two regular featured breweries are complemented by four guest ales. A mild is always available as well as a good selection of bottled beers, mainly Belgian, plus three foreign beers on draught. Top quality bar food is served and a separate upstairs restaurant opens during the evening.
Q◐⇌🚌

Tap & Spile ✔
Tower Street, HG1 1HS (100m E of A61)
⏲ 11.30-11; 12-10.30 Sun
☎ (01423) 526785
Fuller's London Pride; Rooster's Yankee; Theakston Old Peculier; guest beers Ⓗ
Well established, quality ale house with a central bar linking three dining areas. Wood panelling and bare brick walls display many photographs of old Harrogate. The pub is popular with all ages and hosts a folk music session on Tuesday and rock music on Thursday. A quiz is held on Monday evening, and darts is played on alternative Tuesdays and Wednesdays. Some outdoor seating is provided. ❀⇌🚌♣●⁄–

Winter Gardens ✔
4 Royal Baths, HG1 2WH
⏲ 9-midnight (1am Fri & Sat)
☎ (01423) 887010
Marston's Burton Bitter, Pedigree; guest beers Ⓗ
Magnificently recreated main hall of the Victorian Royal Bath Complex, with Harrogate Turkish Baths next door. At least five guest beers are always available at reasonable prices, and a comprehensive range of bottled beers is also stocked. Regular mini beer festivals are hosted. Good food is served all day. Children are welcome until 9pm on week days. ⛟❀◐◑♿⇌🚌⁄–

Hawes

Fountain Hotel
Market Place, DL8 3RD
⏲ 11-midnight
☎ (01969) 627206 🌐 fountainhawes.co.uk
Black Sheep Best Bitter, Ale, Riggwelter; John Smith's Bitter; Theakston Best Bitter Ⓗ
Run by the same family for 20 years and situated in the busy market town of Hawes in Wensleydale, this large friendly hotel serves a good array of local beers. The large single-room interior is divided into two areas, with the bar to the left and the dining area to the right. Food is served daily, lunchtimes and evenings. The pub is particularly busy on market day Tuesday and is popular with walkers on the Pennine Way and other routes.
♨❀🛏◐◑⛺🚌(156,157)♣P⁄–

Haxby

Tiger Inn
29 The Village, YO32 3HS
⏲ 11-3, 7-11 Tue; 11-11; 11-10.30 Sun
☎ (01904) 768355
Samuel Smith's OBB Ⓗ
This comfortable and welcoming pub is in the centre of the village, among shops and opposite the church. It is a fine example of Sam Smith's traditional approach with restrained decor, no distractions and low priced, well-kept ales. The two good-sized bars and large car park attract locals and passing trade. Lunchtime food is served but not on Saturday. Q❀◐🚌(1,12)♣P

Helwith Bridge

Helwith Bridge
BD24 0EH (off B6479, across the river) SD810695
⏲ 2.30 (12 Fri & Sat)-midnight
☎ (01729) 860220 🌐 helwithbridge.com
Caledonian Deuchars, 80; Greene King Old Speckled Hen; John Smith's Bitter; Webster's Bitter; Wells Bombardier; guest beers Ⓗ
The tiny hamlet of Helwith Bridge lies in the shadow of Pen-y-ghent and is a mecca for walkers, climbers and cavers. Despite its relative isolation, the pub is a welcoming, no-frills, thriving community local, run with warmth and a sense of humour. Railway artefacts and humorous material clutter the walls and ceiling. Bar snacks are on offer over and above the main menu times. Bunkhouse accommodation and limited camping facilities are available. The house beer is from Three Peaks Brewery.
♨Q❀🛏◐◑⛺🚌(581,930C)♣P⁄–

Hemingbrough

Crown
Main Street, YO8 6QE (off A63, E of Selby)
⏲ 3-11 (11.30 Thu); 12-midnight Fri-Sun
☎ (01757) 638434 🌐 thecrowninn.net
John Smith's Bitter; guest beers Ⓗ
Unpretentious community pub that caters for local people. A central bar serves two rooms: the front room is host to many sports teams including darts, and has a TV showing football and rugby. The rear room is used by families at the weekend and diners in the evening (not Mon). The kitchen makes good use of fresh local ingredients according to season, providing excellent home-cooked food. Lunches are also served at weekends. On Thursday evening the quiz draws quite a crowd. ⛟❀◐◑🚌♣P⁄–

High Leven

Fox Covert
Low Lane, TS15 9JW (on A1044, 3 km E of Yarm)
⏲ 11.30-11 (midnight Fri & Sat); 12-11 Sun
☎ (01642) 760033 🌐 thefoxcovert.com
Caledonian Deuchars IPA; Theakston Old Peculier Ⓗ
Recent local CAMRA Pub of the Season award winner, this popular, long established and uniquely named inn has been in the same family for more than 20 years. Originally a farmhouse, the pub was built in the traditional longhouse style, with whitewashed walls and a pantiled roof. Inside it is warm and cosy, with two open fires and two drinking areas with superbly kept beers. The pub is noted for its food, served all day every day. Conference facilities are available. ♨❀◐◑♿🚌(17)P

Hinderwell

Brown Cow

55 High Street, TS13 5ET (on A174)

11 (12 Sun)-1am

☎ (01947) 840694

Beer range varies Ⓗ

Situated between the moors and the coast, this family-run village pub has a strong local following, as well as attracting many holiday visitors. Two busy handpumps serve weaker beers during the week and stronger beers at weekends. The pub supports three darts teams, charity quiz nights, dominoes and whist drives. Children and dogs are welcome. Substantial snacks are available all day, in addition to daily lunchtime and evening meals. There is a separate pool room. Accommodation is in three letting bedrooms. (X56)♣P

Hubberholme

George Inn

Kirk Gill, BD23 5JE (opp church, 1 mile NW of Buckden, off B6160) SD926782

12-3, 6-11; closed Mon

☎ (01756) 760223 thegeorge-inn.co.uk

Black Sheep Special Ale; Copper Dragon Golden Pippin; guest beers Ⓗ

Dating from the 1600s, this Grade II-listed building was a one-time farmstead then a vicarage, sitting beneath the fells of Langstrothdale. Reputedly a favourite haunt of author JB Priestley, the George is a cosy pub with mullioned windows, thick stone walls, flagged floors and a coal fire. A lit candle on the bar represents the Hubberholme Parliament, a yearly land-letting auction held in aid of the poor of the parish. 2008 local CAMRA Pub of the Season. QP

Hutton Rudby

King's Head

36 North Side, TS15 0DA

12-11.30 (12.30am Fri & Sat)

☎ (01642) 700342

Camerons Strongarm; Jennings Cockerhoop, Cumberland Ale; guest beers Ⓗ

At the west end of this unspoilt picturesque village, this traditional pub comprises a main bar replete with beamed ceiling and brasses, plus a snug furnished with leather settees, where children are made welcome. Happy hour on Friday (5.30-6.30pm) has become a 20-year-old tradition for some. Tapas are served all day, while themed food nights are held regularly. Friendly locals and three real fires, together with monthly jazz/blues nights, add to the ambience. Outside is a sheltered, walled beer garden complete with TV. (82)

Ingleton

Wheatsheaf

22 High Street, LA6 3AD

12-11

☎ (01524) 241275 wheatsheaf-ingleton.co.uk

Cains IPA, Bitter, FA, seasonal beer; Tetley Bitter Ⓗ

Handy for the finish of the Waterfalls Walk, the Wheatsheaf has a good reputation for food and accommodation, as well as beer. The long, narrow bar is divided into different areas: one end has a pool table, the other leads into the restaurant which is as large as the bar. The attractive garden has an aviary with birds of prey. ♣P

Killinghall

Travellers Rest ✔

Otley Road, HG3 2AP (at A59/B6161 jct)

11-11 (1am Fri & Sat); 12-11 Sun

☎ (01423) 503518

Tetley Bitter; guest beers Ⓗ

Modest roadside pub with a homely atmosphere that has the feel of a real local. The main entrance to the stone building leads to a small public bar and an equally small lounge, both warmed by real fires in winter. The guest ale is often an unusual beer from a distant part of the country. No evening meals are served on Sunday. P

Kirby Hill

Shoulder of Mutton

DL11 7JH (2½ miles from A66, 4 miles NW of Richmond)

12-3 (Sat only), 6-11.30; 12-3, 6-11 Sun

☎ (01748) 822772 shoulderofmutton.net

Black Sheep Best Bitter; Daleside Bitter; guest beers Ⓗ

Ivy-fronted country inn in a beautiful hillside setting overlooking Lower Teesdale and the ruins of Ravensworth Castle. The pub has an opened-out front bar that links the lounge with a cosy restaurant to the rear. Three guest beers are chosen by the pub's regulars and live music is performed every Monday. A popular pub for walkers, there are five en-suite guest bedrooms available, with meals served Wednesday to Sunday, although the bar area remains for drinkers.

Q♣P

Kirk Smeaton

Shoulder of Mutton

Main Street, WF8 3JY

12-2, 6-midnight; 12-1am Fri & Sat (winter hours vary); 12-midnight Sun

☎ (01977) 620348

Black Sheep Best Bitter; Old Mill seasonal beers Ⓗ

This popular Doncaster CAMRA District Pub of the Year 2007 is a traditional village inn, comprising a large lounge with open fires and a cosy dark-panelled snug. Outside is a spacious beer garden and, for smokers, a covered and heated shelter. Convenient for walkers visiting the nearby Went Valley and Brockadale Nature Reserve, ample parking is provided. A quiz is held on Tuesday evening. The excellent beers are sourced directly from two independent breweries. P

Kirkby Malham

Victoria Inn

BD23 4BS

⌚ 7 (12 Fri-Sun)-11
☎ (01729) 830499
Bowland Sawley Tempted, Hen Harrier; Taylor Golden Best, Landlord; Tetley Bitter 🄷
Village pub built in 1840 close to a magnificent parish church, popular with both locals and visitors to the nearby tourist honeypot of Malham. The large hostelry has a lounge bar at the front, a tap room at the back and a separate dining room, with wood-burning stoves to give a cosy atmosphere in winter. Outside is a garden at the rear and a patio area by the front door. An extensive range of meals is served, except on Monday. The pub opens at weekday lunchtimes during the holiday season. ₩❀⇄◐⊟⅄⊟P

Kirklevington

Crown

Thirsk Road, TS15 9LT (on A67, close to A19 Crathorne jct)
⌚ 12-11.30 (11 Sun)
☎ (01642) 780044
Draught Bass; John Smith's Magnet 🄷
It is hard to believe that this was once a run-down Whitbread pub with few customers. Transformed by the enthusiastic licensee, this thriving village local, warmed throughout the winter by roaring fires, now features all-day opening for the first time in its history. Home-cooked food is also now served all day (not Sun eve), using locally sourced produce where possible, and often prepared by the landlady herself. Booking is essential on Sunday lunchtime to avoid disappointment.
₩Q❀◐⊟♿⊟(82)P⅟

Knaresborough

George & Dragon

9 Briggate, HG5 8BQ (next to Holy Trinity church)
⌚ 5-11 (midnight Fri); 12-midnight Sat & Sun
☎ (01423) 862792
John Smith's Bitter; guest beers 🄷
Traditional local known as the Top House because of its location at the top of a steep hill. An open-plan interior is divided by a central bar and beers from local brewers Daleside and Rooster's are always among the four guests. Dominoes, darts and pool are played, with sports matches shown on three TV screens. The backyard beer garden is overlooked by the imposing spire of Holy Trinity church. Wheelchair access is via the back door and well-behaved dogs are welcome. ❀♿⇌⊟♣P

Mitre Hotel

4 Station Road, HG5 9AA
⌚ 12-11 (12.30am Sat)
☎ (01423) 868948
Black Sheep Best Bitter; Thwaites Wainwright; guest beers 🄷
Reopened after nearly five years of closure by Ian Fozard of Market Town Taverns, this hotel is not technically part of the group, but bears all its hallmarks. A wide selection of real ales with a Yorkshire bias is served alongside a good choice of foreign beers (bottled and draught) in a modern setting. Good food is available in the bar every lunchtime and evening (all day Sunday) and a downstairs brasserie is open Wednesday and Saturday evenings.

Langdale End

Moorcock Inn

YO13 0BN SE938912
⌚ 11-2, 6.30-11; 12-3, 6.30-10.30 Sun
☎ (01723) 882268
Beer range varies 🄷/🄶
Sympathetically restored some years ago, the pub is situated in the picturesque hamlet of Langdale End, near the end of the Dalby Forest Drive. The beers are usually from York, Wold Top and Slaters breweries, and served through a hatch to both bars. The pub can get busy in summer but winter opening hours may vary, so ring to check. There is a grassy area for outdoor drinking and/or smoking. Bar meals prepared from local produce include a popular steak pie. ₩Q❀◐⅄♣P⅟

Lastingham

Blacksmith's Arms

Front Street, YO62 6TL (4 miles N of Helmsley off A170)
⌚ 12-midnight summer; 12-2.30, 6-midnight winter; 12-midnight Sat & Sun
☎ (01751) 417247
Theakston Best Bitter; guest beers 🄷
Pretty pub in a conservation village, opposite the 11th century St Mary's Church. A flagged hallway leads into a cosy front bar with low beams and a Yorkist range. There is also a snug and two dining rooms, plus a secluded rear beer garden. Excellent food, including local game, is served every day. Popular with walkers and locals, this is a pub with a warm welcome, excellent beer and food. Twice winner of local CAMRA Country Pub of the Season. ₩Q❀⇄◐

Lealholm

Board Inn

Village Green, YO21 2AJ (by River Esk)
⌚ 9-midnight (2am Fri & Sat)
☎ (01947) 897279 🌐 theboardinn.com
Black Sheep Best Bitter; Camerons Strongarm; guest beers 🄷
Superb, picturesque 17th-century free house, appealing not only to locals but also drawing visitors to this idyllic spot. It comprises a public bar with four handpumps and two ciders, a comfortable lounge, and a restaurant where food is served from 9am daily. Huge breakfasts use eggs from the pub's 45 laying hens and home-smoked meats. A daily chalkboard menu reflects the seasons. The large outdoor drinking area overlooks the Esk. An Easter beer festival is held.
₩Q♨❀⇄◐⊟♿⅄⇌⊟(99)●P⅟

Leavening

Jolly Farmer

Main Street, YO17 9SA
⌚ 7 (6 Fri)-midnight; 12-midnight Sat & Sun
☎ (01653) 658276
Black Sheep Best Bitter; Taylor Landlord; Tetley Bitter; guest beers 🄷

Situated on the edge of the Yorkshire Wolds between York and Malton, this 17th-century pub is a former York CAMRA Pub of the Year. The original multi-room layout has been extended yet retains its cosiness in two small bars plus a family room and dining rooms. Varied guest beers are sourced from independent breweries and there is an annual beer festival. The extensive menu includes locally caught game. ⌂❀◐♣P⁴–▯

Long Marston

Sun Inn

York Road, YO26 8BN (on B1224 York-Wetherby road)

12-2.30, 6-11; 12-11 Sat; 12-3.30, 7-10.30 Sun

☎ (01904) 738258

Samuel Smith's OBB Ⓗ

Oliver Cromwell is remembered as a famous visitor to this friendly pub in the village centre. Nowadays drinkers are mainly local, but customers travel from further afield for its popular home-cooked food, available every session except Sunday evening. The central bar serves a tap room and a larger drinking area, with a snug off one end and a dining area at the other. Children are welcome and there is a safe play area at the rear, next to the beer garden. ⌂Q❀◐♣P

Long Preston

Maypole Inn

Main Street, BD23 4PH

11-2.30, 6-midnight; 11-midnight Sat; 12-11 Sun

☎ (01729) 840219 maypole.co.uk

Moorhouses Premier Bitter; Taylor Landlord; guest beers Ⓗ

Situated by the village green and eponymous maypole, this friendly local pub has been run by the same welcoming licensees for 25 years. The cosy lounge displays old photographs of the village and surrounding area, plus a list of all licensees since 1695. Dogs are welcome in the tap room, which has carved Victorian bench seating. Good quality, home-cooked food may be enjoyed in the lounge or dining room.
⌂Q❀◐♣P

Low Worsall

Ship

TS15 9PH

12-11

☎ (01642) 780314

Taylor Landlord; guest beers Ⓗ

Situated beside the old Richmond to Yarm turnpike and near a disused quay that once marked the limit of navigation for commercial boats on the River Tees. Guest beers are usually from Hambleton and the pub is known for the quality of its good value food, served all day every day. Smaller portions are available for those unable to tackle the impressively large helpings. The pub is child friendly, with a small play area in the garden. Q❀◐P⁴–

Malton

Crown Hotel (Suddaby's)

12 Wheelgate, YO17 7HP

11-11 (11.30 Fri & Sat); 12-10.45 Sun

☎ (01653) 692038 suddabys.co.uk

John Smith's Bitter; Suddaby's Double Chance, seasonal beers; Theakston Best Bitter; guest beers Ⓗ

Grade II-listed market town-centre pub that has been in the same family for 138 years. No brewing now takes place on the premises; the beers are contract-brewed at Brown Cow. Beer festivals are held at Easter, summer and Christmas. The on-site shop stocks over 200 different beers, specialising in Belgian and German brews as well as British micro-breweries, wine and breweriana. A covered smoking patio is at the rear of the pub. Accommodation includes two en-suite family rooms – a discount is available for CAMRA members. ⌂Q❀♣P⁴–

Manfield

Crown Inn

Vicars Lane, DL2 2RF (500m from B6275)

5-11; 12-11.30 Sat; 12-11 Sun

☎ (01325) 374243 crowninn.villagebrewer.co.uk

Village White Boar, Zetland; guest beers Ⓗ

Yorkshire CAMRA Pub of the Year 2005 and a regular local award winner, this attractive 18th-century pub sits in a quiet village. It has two bars, a games room and a trellised heated smoking area. A mix of locals and visitors creates a friendly atmosphere. Up to six guest beers come from micro-breweries countrywide, along with up to two ciders or perries. Two beer festivals and a cider festival are held annually. Dogs are welcome in this rural gem. ⌂Q❀◐(29)♣P⁴–▯

Masham

Black Sheep Brewery Visitors Centre ✔

Wellgarth, HG4 4EN

10-4.30 (11 Thu-Sat)

☎ (01765) 680101 blacksheepbrewery.com

Black Sheep Best Bitter, Ale, Riggwelter Ⓗ

This popular tourist attraction is housed in the spacious former maltings. As well as offering the opportunity to sample the breweries products at the 'baaar', there is a high quality cafe/bistro serving snacks and full meals with an emphasis on local ingredients. A 'sheepy' shop stocks the bottled product and Black Sheep souvenirs. Visitors can book a 'shepherded' tour of the brewery. A small garden overlooks scenic lower Wensleydale and the River Ure. ❀◐P▯

White Bear ✔

12 Crosshills, HG4 4EN (follow brown tourist signs on A6108)

12-11 (10.30 Sun)

☎ (01765) 689319

Caledonian Deuchars IPA; Theakston Best Bitter, Black Bull Bitter, XB, Old Peculier; guest beers Ⓗ

A recently refurbished brewery tap that has been extended into the old brewery offices to make extra room for diners, as well as adding

14 bedrooms and conference facilities. Although the changes have cost £1.5m, the pub has not lost any of its charm as an award-winning hostelry. It is a great favourite with the locals, and directors and staff from the Theakston Brewery too.

Middlesbrough

Isaac Wilson

61 Wilson Street, TS1 1SF
9-midnight (1am Fri & Sat)
(01642) 247708
Greene King IPA, Abbot; Marston's Pedigree; guest beers
Named after a 19th-century railway industry magnate who was company director of the world's first public railway, the Stockton and Darlington, this pub is a superb Wetherspoon conversion of the former law courts. It comprises one long bar with 12 handpulls, and a large single room with walls adorned with photographs of old Middlesbrough, accompanied by a wealth of historical information. Guest beers are usually sourced from north east craft breweries, while Weston's Old Rosie is the house cider.

Star

14 Southfield Road, TS1 3BX
11-11 (1am Fri & Sat); 12-11 Sun
(01642) 245307 sjf.co.uk
Beer range varies
This popular pub opposite the university campus makes a welcome return to the Guide following its recent closure for refurbishment. With a licensee dedicated to promoting a wide variety of real ales, four beers are usually available, together with Weston's Old Rosie cider. A contemporary, relaxed atmosphere prevails, with sofas and easy chairs adding to the ambience. The pub attracts a wide-ranging clientele and it can get extremely busy at weekends. Good value pub food is on offer. The smoking area is heated and covered.

Naburn

Blacksmiths Arms

Main Street, YO19 4PN (W of A19 on S side of York)
12-11
(01904) 623464
Marston's Burton Bitter, Pedigree
Situated in the village centre, this pub is a true hub of the community, catering for all tastes and age groups and providing good wholesome food seven days a week. It is situated within easy distance of the York-Selby Cycle Path, Naburn Marina and Naburn Caravan Site. It is also close to the River Ouse, and is popular with boaters, walkers, cyclists and caravanners.

Newall with Clifton

Spite

Roebuck Terrace, LS21 2EY (1½ miles N of Otley on Newall Carr road)
12-3, 6-11; 12-11 Thu-Sun
(01943) 463063
Tetley Bitter; guest beers
Stone-built country pub situated at the end of a terraced row, one mile north of Otley. A low-beamed characterful inn, it has an open plan room divided into two distinct cosy areas and a separate dining room. A warming fire and traditional country furniture are very inviting. Meals are served daily except Monday.

Northallerton

Standard

24 High Street, DL7 8EE
12-2.30, 5-midnight; 11-midnight Fri-Sun
(01609) 772719
Caledonian Deuchars IPA; John Smith's Bitter; Marston's Pedigree; guest beers
This community pub just outside the town centre is worth seeking out, if only to admire the Jet Provost aircraft in the beer garden. Inside, the bar has been opened out but retains distinct drinking areas and offers good value food. Unofficial home to the town's Rugby League club, the pub holds regular charity nights and an annual spring bank holiday beer festival. Named after the nearby Battle of the Standard of 1138, it is more peaceful now.

Station Hotel

2 Boroughbridge Road, DL7 8AN (outside railway station)
12-2 (3 Sat), 5-11; 12-3, 7-10.30 Sun
(01609) 772053 stationhotel-northallerton.com
Caledonian Deuchars IPA; Tetley Bitter; guest beers
Splendid Edwardian building, handy for the town's railway station and County Hall. The attractively restored bar features etched windows and there are many other original fittings including an impressive mosaic-tiled hallway. The rear of the building is much older and once served the town's long-vanished racecourse. Sunday lunches are particularly popular, as are the Sunday evening quizzes and occasional live music. Ten letting rooms offer good value accommodation.

Tithe Bar & Brasserie

2 Friarage Street, DL6 1DP
12-11 (midnight Fri & Sat)
(01609) 778482 markettowntaverns.co.uk
Taylor Landlord; guest beers
Part of the small Market Town Taverns chain, this bar is utterly committed to cask beer. Winner of numerous CAMRA awards, it is located just off the town's High Street and offers a constantly changing selection of six cask ales and a good array of European beers. The three downstairs rooms have the feel of a continental beer café and offer a tranquil haven during the day, although evenings can be busy. Good value bar meals are complemented by good food in the brasserie upstairs, open Tuesday-Saturday evenings.

Old Malton

Royal Oak

47 Town Street, YO17 7HB (400m off A64 Malton bypass)
⏲ 5-midnight; 12-1am Fri & Sat; closed Mon Jan & Feb; 12-midnight Sun
☎ (01653) 699334
Copper Dragon Golden Pippin; Tetley Bitter; guest beers ⊞
Quiet pub set in a picturesque village close to the Eden Camp military museum. A welcoming and friendly atmosphere prevails in a cosy snug at the front of the pub, while a larger rear room leads to an extensive beer garden with a large covered smoking area. Guest beers are usually from Timothy Taylor, York, Moorhouses and Wold Top. Traditional meals featuring locally sourced produce are served weekend lunchtimes. Functions can be catered for. The Yorkshire Coastliner bus service stops outside the pub.
♨Q✿◖⛺≠⊟(843)♣P⊱

Osmotherley

Golden Lion

6 West End, DL6 3AA
⏲ 12-3.30, 6-11; 12-midnight Sat; 12-10.30 Sun
☎ (01609) 883526 🌐 goldenlionosmotherley.co.uk
John Smith's Magnet; Taylor Landlord; guest beers ⊞
A short distance from the A19, this small pub, with a simple but elegant interior featuring mirrors and whitewashed walls, is in the centre of a picturesque moors village, and very popular with ramblers. Excellent pub food made with local produce is available in the bar and upstairs restaurant – at times most of the bar is given over to food service. Guest ales are sourced from local Yorkshire breweries. Tables outside at the front offer a magnificent view. ♨◖◗⛺⊟(80,89)

Patrick Brompton

Green Tree

DL8 1JW
⏲ 12-3 (Sat only), 6 (5.15 Sat)-11; closed Tue; 12-3, 7-10.30 Sun
☎ (01677) 450262
Black Sheep Best Bitter; Taylor Landlord; guest beers ⊞
This attractive, traditional free house nestles beside the gates of the picturesque church at the west end of this village on the main A684 Wensleydale route. There is a small but neat public bar with open fire and a larger but still cosy restaurant serving locally-sourced produce. Guest beer is usually from one of the region's micro-breweries. Outside is a small beer garden. Take care entering the car park – it is a particularly tight squeeze. Opening times may vary out of season.
♨Q✿◖◗⊟⊟(156,157)♣P

Pickering

Rose

Bridge Street, YO18 8DT (opp Beck Isle Museum)
⏲ 12-midnight (1am Fri & Sat)
☎ (01751) 475366
Taylor Landlord; Tetley Bitter ⊞
A welcoming atmosphere greets locals and steam railway enthusiasts at this multi-roomed low-ceilinged pub, situated on the banks of the attractive Pickering Beck, opposite the Beck Isle Museum of Country Life. The terminus of the North York Moors Steam Railway is nearby. Meals are made with locally sourced produce. Children are welcome until 8pm. There is an extensive outdoor drinking area next to the beck. The pub has flooded six times in nine years in times of torrential rain.
♨✿◖◗≠⊟♣P⊱

Pickhill

Nag's Head

YO7 4JG (1 mile off A1 just N of jct with B6261 Masham-Thirsk road) SE345833
⏲ 11 (12 Sun)-11
☎ (01845) 567391 🌐 nagsheadpickhill.co.uk
Black Sheep Best Bitter; Hambleton Bitter; Theakston Black Bull; guest beers ⊞
This deservedly long-standing entry in the Guide is renowned for its quality food and locally brewed beers, finding just the right balance between a village pub and dining establishment. A warm and friendly atmosphere is backed up by brisk and efficient service, with a splendid range of food served in the restaurant, lounge and bar. There is also high class accommodation, making this an ideal base to explore the Yorkshire Moors and Dales or take in the local race meetings.
♨Q✿⇌◖◗⊟⛺♣P⊱

Picton

Station

TS15 0EA (at level crossing on Kirklevington-Picton road)
⏲ 11-2.30 (Sat only), 6-11; 11-11.30 Sun
☎ (01642) 700067
John Smith's Magnet ⊞
Situated beside the Middlesbrough to York railway, this remote pub is well worth the journey, although sadly not by train, as the adjacent station was closed in the 1960s. One superb real ale is served alongside an impressive and varied food menu, using local produce where possible. The portions are of such a size that going home hungry is not an option. Cool in the summer, warm and inviting in the winter, this is a pub for everyone.
♨Q✿◖◗P

Pool in Wharfedale

Hunters Inn

Harrogate Road, LS21 2PS (on A658 between Otley and Harrogate)
⏲ 11-11; 12-10.30 Sun
☎ (0113) 2841090
Tetley Bitter; Theakston Best Bitter; guest beers ⊞
Roadside pub with all the feel of a country lodge. A large single room incorporates a raised area on the left as you enter. Before approaching the bar with its impressive range of nine handpumps, check out the list of ales on the blackboard. Well-behaved children are allowed in the pub until 9pm and a welcome

is extended to all, with a warming real fire greeting customers during the colder months.

Ripon

Magdalens

26 Princess Road, HG4 1HW (near fire station)
12-midnight (2am Fri & Sat)
(01765) 604746
John Smith's Bitter; Theakston Best Bitter; guest beers
A recent CAMRA Pub of the Season which always has some community activity going on – darts and dominoes are played, there are golf teams and even a horse racing club. As well as the two regular beers, at least three guests are available. The landlord is a keen gardener whose hanging baskets and extensive beer garden are a riot of colour in the summer, winning awards in the Ripon in Bloom competition. An outdoor children's play area is adjacent to the garden.

One-Eyed Rat

51 Allhallowgate, HG4 1LQ (near bus station)
5 (12 Fri & Sat)-11; 12-10.30 Sun
(01765) 607704 oneeyedrat.com
Black Sheep Best Bitter; guest beers
This tiny-fronted old pub continues to maintain its policy of offering five guest beers at all times. Cask Marque accreditation was recently awarded and a large selection of continental bottled beers is stocked. The long bar serves both the cosy coal-fired front room and the large back room, complete with bar billiards table. There is a beer garden at the rear. Nearby, the Old Ripon Workhouse Museum gives a fascinating insight into times past.

Royal Oak

36 Kirkgate, HG4 1PB (off Market Square)
11-11 (midnight Fri & Sat); 12-10.30 Sun
(01765) 602284 royaloakripon.co.uk
Taylor Golden Best, Best Bitter, Landlord
The exterior of this Grade II-listed building is very traditional but the pub has had a complete internal makeover in Timothy Taylor house style with light woods and comfortable seating areas. It is situated near the cathedral and the Market Square where a market has been held every Thursday since the 12th century. Home-cooked food made from local produce is available from midday until 10pm daily. There are now six en-suite bedrooms above the pub.

Robin Hood's Bay

Victoria Hotel

Station Road, YO22 4RL (at the top of the cliff)
12-11 (10.30 Sun) summer; 12-2, 6-11 winter
(01947) 880205 thevictoriahotel.info
Banks's Bitter; Camerons Bitter, Strongarm; guest beers
A warm welcome awaits you at this impressive 19th-century hotel, set in a superb location on the edge of the cliffs and overlooking the bay of this picturesque seaside resort. The large, busy and friendly bar, popular with regulars and visitors alike, serves five beers including two guests. A good value, highly regarded menu, including daily specials, is available at lunchtimes and evenings. Stunning views are afforded from the comfortable family room and the large gardens. (X56,93)

Saltburn-by-the-Sea

Saltburn Cricket, Bowls & Tennis Club

Marske Mill Lane, TS12 1HJ (next to leisure centre)
8-midnight (1am Fri & Sat); 2-midnight Sat match days; 11.30-3, 8-midnight Sun
Beer range varies
This private sports club, well supported by the local community, fields cricket, tennis and bowls teams, and also acts as the watering hole for the local diving club. A spacious lounge can be divided for different functions and social events. The balcony, well used on sunny days, overlooks the cricket field. Two continually rotating beers are served. Casual visitors are made most welcome without having to join the club.

Saxton

Greyhound

Main Street, LS24 9PY (W of A162, 5 miles S of Tadcaster)
11.30-3, 5.30-11; 11-11 Sat; 12-10.30 Sun
(01937) 557202
Samuel Smith OBB
This picturesque, Grade II-listed 13th-century village inn nestles by the village church. It was originally a teasel barn and formerly listed in CAMRA's National Inventory for pubs with outstanding interiors. A low-ceilinged stone-flagged corridor leads to a tiny bar. Real fires blaze in two of the three rooms in winter and the extensive collection of colourful plates and paraphernalia create a cosy atmosphere. The pub is popular with locals and walkers.

Scarborough

Angel

46 North Street, YO11 1DF
11-midnight
(01723) 365504
John Smith's Bitter; Tetley Bitter; Wells Bombardier
Friendly town-centre local, close to the main shopping area, with a single-room horseshoe bar displaying an excellent collection of saucy seaside postcards. An interest in sport and games is reflected in the impressive array of trophies won by various pub teams and the large-screen TVs used for sporting events. Occasional guest beers are added in summer. Note the Tardis-like quality of the surprisingly large and well appointed patio garden at the rear.

Cellars

35-37 Valley Road, YO11 2LX
12-midnight; 4-11 Mon & Tue winter; 12-10.30 Sun
(01723) 367158 scarborough-brialene.co.uk
Beer range varies

Family-run pub converted from the cellars of an elegant Victorian house. The bar keeps six beers: ales come from Archers, Black Sheep and Durham breweries and guests mainly from Yorkshire micros. Real cider is also available. Excellent, good value, home-cooked food made with locally sourced produce is served lunchtimes and evenings. Live music night is Saturday, with an open mic night on Wednesday. Beer festivals are staged occasionally. The patio gardens are popular for alfresco drinking. Children and dogs are welcome.

Golden Ball

31 Sandside, YO11 1PG
11-11; 12-10.30 Sun
(01723) 353899
Samuel Smith OBB H
Pub with striking mock Tudor appearance situated on the seafront, with fabulous views from the Harbour Bar across the harbour to the lighthouse and South Bay. The only Sam Smith's pub in Scarborough, it is multi-roomed and features a family room and a popular summer garden. It becomes a cosy gem in winter, warmed by a real fire. Lunches are served all year round, with evening meals during the summer season. Free of music, for those who prefer a quiet drink.

Indigo Alley

4 North Marine Road, YO12 7PD
4-2am
(01723) 381900
Beer range varies H
Lively, popular one-roomed pub, offering five constantly changing real ales including a regular Rooster's brew. Belgian Leffe Blonde and Hoegaarden are on draught, while a selection of continental bottled beers is also on offer. Live music is performed several times a week. Local CAMRA Pub of the Year for three consecutive years, this is an absolute cracker and not to be missed.

North Riding Hotel

161-163 North Marine Road, YO12 7HU
12-midnight (1am Fri & Sat)
(01723) 370004 northridinghotel.co.uk
Taylor Landlord; Tetley Bitter; York Guzzler; guest beers H
Friendly, popular family-run pub voted local CAMRA Town Pub of the Year 2006 (runner-up 2007), located near the cricket ground and opposite Scarborough bowls centre on the North Bay. The pub has a public bar, a refurbished quiet lounge and an upstairs dining room serving home-cooked food. It stocks two or more guest beers from micro-breweries, continental bottled beers and occasional draught continental beers. Seasonal beer festivals are held, as well as a weekly quiz on Thursday.

Old Scalby Mills

Scalby Mills Road, YO12 6RP
11 (12 winter)-11
(01723) 500449
Wold Top Premium; guest beers H
Popular seafront local, this building was originally a watermill but has seen many uses over the years – old photographs and prints chart its history. Admire the superb views of the North Bay from the sheltered patio or lounge. The Cleveland Way reaches the seafront here and there is a Sealife Centre nearby. Children are welcome in the lounge. Premium beer from the local Wold Top Brewery is only available here; guest beers invariably include a stout, porter or mild.

Scholars

Somerset Terrace, YO11 2PW
4.30 (12 Sat)-11; 12-10.30 Sun
(01723) 360084
Copper Dragon Golden Pippin; guest beers H
A warm, friendly atmosphere prevails in this town centre pub located at the rear of the main shopping centre. It has a large front bar and a games room. Two handpumps serve rotating beers from Durham and Ossett breweries and a third provides changing beers from micro-breweries. Numerous screens show major sporting events. Monday is quiz night and a monthly music quiz is held on a Thursday.

Valley

51 Valley Road, YO11 2LX
12-midnight (1am Thu-Sat)
(01723) 372593 valleybar.co.uk
Theakston Best Bitter; Wold Top Mars Magic; guest beers H
CAMRA National Cider Pub of the Year 2007 and local CAMRA Town Pub of the Year 2005 and 2007. This family-run multi-roomed pub has a popular cellar bar. Seven handpumps feature beers mainly from micro-breweries, plus eight real ciders and perries. A hundred different bottled Belgian beers and gluten-free bottled beers and lager are also stocked. The kitchen prepares freshly cooked bar meals including fresh fish at very reasonable prices and gluten free dishes.

Skipton

Devonshire

Newmarket Street, BD23 2HR
9-midnight (1am Fri & Sat)
(01756) 692590
Greene King IPA, Abbot; Marston's Pedigree; guest beers H
Built in the 1870s, this establishment has an impressive Queen Anne-style frontage, set back from the road with an open patio area. The interior has a large main bar with several areas for drinking and dining off to the side and a Grade II listed staircase to the toilets. The beer range is Wetherspoon's usuals, plus ales from local micros.

Snape

Castle Arms

DL8 2TB (off B6268 Bedale-Masham road)
12-3, 2-midnight (2am Thu-Sat); 12-4, 6-midnight Sun
(01677) 470270
Jennings Bitter, Cumberland Ale; Marston's Pedigree; guest beers H
Historic pub with a friendly bar area featuring an open fire, with a stone-flagged floor

throughout. Named after nearby Snape Castle, once home to Catherine Parr, wife of Henry VIII, the pub is situated in the centre of this beautiful village and is handy for the Thorpe Perrow Arboretum. Its locally renowned food is served in the bar and adjacent restaurant. Nine letting rooms and a small caravan park to the rear add to a thriving local trade. ⅏Q❀⇔◑Å⊟♣P

Sneaton

Wilson Arms

Beacon Way, YO22 5HS (off B1416)
⏲ 12-2.30 (Sat only), 6.30-11; closed Mon winter; 12-3, 6.30-11 (12-4 winter) Sun
☎ (01947) 602552
Black Sheep Best Bitter; John Smith's Bitter; guest beers Ⓗ
Grade II-listed building dating from the early 18th century in a quiet village a couple of miles from Whitby and close to Sneaton Beacon and Beacon Farm, which is famous for its ice cream. A warm welcome is guaranteed in this single bar with beamed ceilings and a roaring fire. Three beers are served plus a guest which is usually Timothy Taylor Golden Best, as well as a fine selection of whiskies. Traditional home-cooked meals are available. There is a separate pool room and seven letting bedrooms. ⅏Q♉❀⇔◑Å♣P

Sowerby

Crown & Anchor

138 Front Street, YO7 1JN
⏲ 12-midnight (1am Thu-Sat)
☎ (01845) 522448 🌐 crownandanchorsowerby.co.uk
John Smith's Bitter; York Guzzler, Stonewall, Terrier; guest beers Ⓗ
Recently refurbished, this thriving village local offers at least one brew from the York Brewery, plus a guest or two from micros such as Leeds or Durham, and a range of continental beers. Good no-nonsense food menus range from sandwiches and bar snacks to Sunday lunch with all the trimmings (booking is advised). A beer garden and covered smoking area look out onto the large car park. An annual beer festival is held in September. ♉❀◐⊟♿⊟♣●P⁻

Staithes

Captain Cook Inn

60 Staithes Lane, TS13 5AD (off A174, by village car park)
⏲ 11-midnight
☎ (01947) 840200
Banks's Bitter; Rudgate Viking Bitter; guest beers Ⓗ
CAMRA multi award-winning pub, formerly known as Station Hotel, and close to the site of the Staithes railway viaduct and Boulby Cliffs, the highest in England. Five handpumps provide a mix of beer styles, including milds, porters and stouts. Beer festivals celebrate St George's Day, the Jazz Festival, Lifeboat Week and Hallowe'en, when the beer range extends to 12 ales, all handpulled. Meals are not served on Saturday or Sunday evening. Four letting bedrooms and a holiday cottage are available. ⅏Q❀⇔◑Å⊟(X56)♣P

Staxton

Hare & Hounds

Main Street, YO12 4TA
⏲ 12-11.30
☎ (01944) 710243
Black Sheep Special; Stones Bitter; Theakston Old Peculier; guest beers Ⓗ
Imposing former coaching inn on the A64 – an excellent stopping-off point when travelling to the East Coast. The bar and lounge/dining area feature low beams and real fires. Guest beers are usually sourced from the Enterprise/SIBA scheme and often come from Wold Top and Copper Dragon breweries. Home-cooked meals are available all day every day, with seafood sourced from Flamborough a speciality in summer. There are large grassed drinking areas at the front and rear of the pub. ⅏Q❀◑ÅP⁻

Stokesley

Spread Eagle

39 High Street, TS9 5BL
⏲ 11-1am; 12-12.30am Sun
☎ (01642) 710278
Camerons Strongarm; Marston's Pedigree; guest beers Ⓗ
A welcome return to the Guide for this small, unspoilt market-town pub. Friendly regulars drink at one end and an open fire welcomes diners at the other. Excellent, good value home-cooked food, sourced locally where possible, is served all day every day. Two interesting guest beers are always available. Children are welcome and an enclosed rear garden leads down to the tranquil River Leven, where over-fed ducks amuse children and adults alike. Tuesday is live music night. ⅏Q❀◑Å⊟(29,81)⁻

White Swan

1 West End, TS9 5BL
⏲ 11.30 (12 Sun)-11
☎ (01642) 710263 🌐 thecaptaincookbrewery.co.uk
Captain Cook Sunset, Slipway; Consett Red Dust, White Hot, seasonal beers; guest beers Ⓗ
Traditional 18th-century one-room pub, situated in one of the prettiest areas of this market town. It has a J-shaped bar with six handpumps and is now an outlet for the adjacent prize-winning Captain Cook Brewery as well as the Consett Ale Works. Well supported by the local community, the pub holds a quiz on Wednesday, while Thursday is live music nights. A cheese and beer festival is held at Easter. Children are not permitted in the pub. ⅏Q❀Å⊟(29,81)

Sutton-in-Craven

Dog & Gun Inn ✔

Colne Road, Malsis, BD20 8DS (on A6068)
⏲ 12-11 (10.30 Sun)
☎ (01535) 633855
Taylor Dark Mild, Golden Best, Best Bitter, Landlord, Ram Tam; guest beers Ⓗ

Formerly a farmhouse and coaching inn, this attractive roadside pub places a strong emphasis on quality food. The comfortable interior has several areas including a library corner, and a real-fire stove and fireplace make for a warm welcome, together with friendly, helpful staff. Very popular with families, booking is advisable at peak times. The full Taylor range of beers is stocked.

Thixendale

Cross Keys

YO17 9TG SE845611

12-3, 6-11; 12-3, 7-10.30 Sun

(01377) 288272

Jennings Bitter; Tetley Bitter H

Established in 1156, the sloping pastures of this village attracted monastic interest long before discovery by the modern-day hikers walking the Wolds Way. As Thixendale is the focus of 16 dry valleys, so the Cross Keys is a welcome sight for many a thirsty walker. Resting in this one-roomed pub, close to the roaring fire with a well-kept pint and a plate of tasty home-cooked food, is ample reward for any such exertion.

Thorganby

Ferryboat Inn

Ferry Lane, YO19 6DD (1 mile NE of village, signed from main road) SE697427

7-11; closed Mon; 12-midnight Sat

(01904) 448224

Acorn Barnsley Bitter; guest beers H

This haven of tranquillity, a quiet no-frills pub without gaming machines or music, is a traditional family-run pub, now in its third generation. Well worth a visit, it has a large river frontage and is popular with anglers and boaters who use the River Derwent, as well as ramblers and cyclists. A varied selection of beers from Yorkshire micros is served alongside other guests. The landlady makes beautiful home-made sandwiches. Outdoors is a delightful family-friendly lawned area and a small caravan site with full facilities.

Q P

Thruscross

Stonehouse Inn

Duck Street, HG3 4AH (2 miles N of A59 at Blubberhouses) SE160586

12-3, 6-11; closed Mon; 12-5 Sun

(01943) 880325

Black Sheep Best Bitter; guest beers H

This rural pub, built 300 years ago, reopened in 2005 after a period of closure. The family-run inn is characterised by exposed beams, a Yorkshire stone-flagged floor, settles and a stone-fronted bar. Two snug alcoves give a feeling of partial seclusion. The pub runs a darts team, with matches on alternate Tuesdays, and hosts a weekly open dominoes competition. The menu caters for vegetarians and breakfast can be served by arrangement. Popular with locals and walkers. P

Welburn

Crown & Cushion

YO60 7DZ (1 mile off A64 between York and Malton)

11.30-3, 5.30-midnight; 11.30-midnight Sat; 12-midnight Sun

(01653) 618304

Flowers IPA; Tetley Bitter; guest beers H

Situated near Castle Howard in the Howardian Hills area of natural beauty, this village inn retains its traditional layout with a wooden-floored bar and bar billiards table, plus a cosy lounge with a roaring log fire for cooler months. Additionally there is a small drinking area and a separate restaurant. Up to three regularly changing guest beers are offered and delicious meals are served, often including locally-caught game when in season. A pleasant rear garden includes a heated patio area for smokers.

(181) P

Well

Milbank Arms

Bedale Road, DL8 2PX (off B6267 2 miles E of Masham)

12-2.30 (not Mon), 5-11

(01677) 470411

Black Sheep Best Bitter; Rudgate Viking; guest beers H

Small village inn well known in the area for its classic pub food menu supplemented by a good varied specials board, with locally sourced produce used as much as possible. The recently renovated bar now has the feel of a cosy local rather than an extension of the restaurant. Weekend guest beers tend to be from nearby breweries such as Copper Dragon and Salamander. P

Wensley

Three Horseshoes

DL8 4HJ (on A684)

11-11

(01969) 622327 3horseshoeswensley.com

John Smith's Bitter; Wensleydale Rowley Mild, H **Bitter, Semer Water, Sheep Rustlers Nut Brown Ale, Coverdale Poacher IPA** H/G

Situated in the attractive village of Wensley, this traditional country pub serves as the tap for Wensleydale Brewery. Four or five beers from the Wensleydale range are available throughout the season, with the full range stocked in bottle-conditioned form. Unique in this area, four beers are also available by gravity dispense from a stillage behind the bar. Good quality, reasonably priced meals are served, including regular curry and Italian nights. Live music sessions take place most weekends. (156,157)P

West Ayton

Olde Forge Valley

5 Pickering Road, YO13 9JE

11.30-1am (2am Fri & Sat); 12-1am Sun

(01723) 862146

Black Sheep Best Bitter; Tetley Bitter; guest beers H

Roadside Tudor-style coaching inn built in the 18th century alongside John Carr's bridge over the River Derwent. Popular with locals and visitors, it has a large lounge, back bar and function room with an impressive high ceiling. Home-cooked meals include an excellent Sunday roast, served 12-2pm and 6-8pm. Folk night is Thursday and jazz night the last Wednesday of the month. Outside is a spacious beer garden and children and dogs are welcome. ⛰☺❀◑⊕▲⊟♣P⚐

West Haddlesey

George & Dragon

Main Street, YO8 8QA (1 mile W of A19, 5 miles S of Selby) SE565266

✪ 5-midnight (1am Fri); 2-1am Sat; 12-10.30 Sun

☎ (01757) 2281987

Brown Cow White Dragon; guest beers Ⓗ

There was a watering hole in this place before there was a pub – the covered well that now features in the bar. A friendly Lancastrian landlord has made this free house his Yorkshire home, with house beer from the local micro-brewery and two guest beers often from Yorkshire micros. Food is available daily including takeaways. A weekly quiz night is held, as well as folk or jazz music on alternate weeks. An annual beer festival is hosted in April close to St George's day. ⛰Q❀◑♿♣P⚐

West Witton

Fox & Hounds

Main Street, DL8 4LP

✪ 12-4, 6-midnight; 12-midnight Sat & Sun

☎ (01969) 623650 🌐 foxwitton.com

Black Sheep Best Bitter; John Smith's Bitter; guest beers Ⓗ

A CAMRA award-winning free house, run by the same family for 12 years, this Grade II-listed building dates back to 1400. It was originally a resthouse for monks from Jervaulx Abbey. The bar is separated from the pool and darts area by the fireplace. A recently renovated dining room features an inglenook fireplace and a beehive oven. Guest beers are often from the Yorkshire Dales Brewery and other local micros. Good value meals are served all week, plus a Sunday roast. A Friday quiz and Saturday piano session alternate fortnightly. ⛰❀◑▲⊟(156)♣P⚐⊡

Whitby

Black Horse ✔

91 Church Street, YO22 4BH (E side of bridge on approach to Abbey steps)

✪ 11-11; 12-10.30 Sun

☎ (01947) 602906 🌐 the-black-horse.com

Adnams Bitter; Black Dog Rhatas; Taylor Landlord; guest beers Ⓗ

Dating from the 1600s, this 2007 CAMRA Pub of the Season award winner always offers a warm welcome. The frontage, with its frosted glass windows, together with one of Europe's oldest public serving bars, were built in the 1880s and remain largely unchanged to this day. Alongside beer served from five handpumps a hot meal is available daily (weekends only in winter). Tapas, olives and Yorkshire cheeses are on offer all day every day. The cider is Weston's Old Rosie. Accommodation is in four letting bedrooms. Q⇌◑⊕♿▲⇌⊟(56,93)♣●

First In Last Out

1 York Terrace, Fishburn Park, YO21 1PT (400m S of railway station)

✪ 12-midnight (11.30 Sun)

☎ (01947) 602149 🌐 firstinlastoutpub.co.uk

Camerons Strongarm; Tetley Bitter Ⓗ

One of only three pubs with this name in the country, this street-corner local is one of Whitby's gems and is well worth seeking out. It is popular with locals and with those canny tourists who have found out about it. Tuesday is folk night, while on Friday live bands play. The pub supports darts teams and also a combined darts/dominoes team. There is no food here but one of Whitby's finest fish and chip shops, the Railway Chippy, is directly opposite. ❀⊕▲⇌⊟(56,93)♣P⚐⊡

Station Inn

New Quay Road, YO21 1DH (opp railway station)

✪ 10-midnight (11.30 Sun)

☎ (01947) 603937

Black Dog Whitby Abbey Ale; Copper Dragon Best Bitter; Courage Directors; Daleside Blonde; Jennings Cumberland Ale; Taylor Golden Best; guest beers Ⓗ

Opposite the harbour, railway station and bus station, this multi-roomed pub is popular with locals and tourists alike. Eight handpumps, Weston's cider and a dozen fruit wines offer something for everybody. Lunches are served Easter to October and live bands perform Wednesday and Friday evenings. For the discerning traveller, the pub can also double as the railway station waiting room during summer months. The NYMR steam train now connects with Whitby, while the ever popular Music Train runs on summer Friday evenings. ☺◐⊕▲⇌⊟(56,93)●

York

Blue Bell ★

53 Fossgate, YO1 9TF

✪ 11-11; 12-10.30 Sun

☎ (01904) 654904

Adnams Bitter; Black Sheep Best Bitter; Caledonian Deuchars IPA; Taylor Landlord; Tetley Dark Mild; guest beers Ⓗ

Friendly, memorable, cosy and many times an award-winner, this pub is recognised locally, regionally and nationally. A true community local in the heart of York, it has a CAMRA National Inventory interior featuring wood panelling dating from 1903, two small rooms and an unusual corridor servery. This is a cosy haunt for true pub lovers and the tapas menu is well worth a try. Watch out for the street beer festival in November. Two guest beers complement a range that has something for everyone. Q⊕⊟♣

Brigantes Bar & Brasserie ✔

114 Micklegate, YO1 6JX

✪ 12-11

☎ (01904) 675355 🌐 markettowntaverns.co.uk

Taylor Landlord; York Guzzler; guest beers Ⓗ

A Market Town Taverns pub located some 100 metres from York's famous Micklegate Bar. It serves a great range of beers from mainly Yorkshire breweries, including a beer from Leeds and other breweries such as Rudgate and E&S Elland. This listed Georgian building was the birthplace of Joseph Aloysius Hansom – a renowned architect, inventor and designer of landscape gardens. Q◑♿⇌🚌

Golden Ball ★

2 Cromwell Road, YO1 6DU
⏲ 5-11 (11.30 Thu-Sat)
☎ (01904) 652211 🌐 goldenball-york.co.uk
Caledonian Deuchars IPA; Everards Tiger; Greene King Ruddles County; John Smith's Bitter; Wells Bombardier; guest beers Ⓗ
Traditional and welcoming mid-Victorian street-corner local with an external tile and glazed brick façade. The narrow entrance hall opens out to four different rooms: a main bar, snug, billiards room and lounge, each with its own atmosphere. The large south-facing beer garden hosts barbecues in the summer. A National Inventory pub, the decor is very much in keeping with the pub's traditional feel and has changed little since an extensive refurbishment by John Smith's Tadcaster Brewery in 1929. Q❀♿⇌♣⌐

Golden Lion ✔

9 Church Street, YO1 8BG
⏲ 10-11; 12-10.30 Sun
☎ (01904) 620942
Greene King IPA; John Smith's Bitter; Taylor Landlord; Theakston Old Peculier; guest beers Ⓗ
This single-roomed city centre pub has a cosy, country feel, with stained wood floors, a large wooden bar and pictures of old York on the walls. One of the best selections of real ale and pub food in the city makes this a popular pub. There is something for everyone, with discreetly positioned TVs and games machines, as well as quiet corners in which to have a chat with friends in a convivial atmosphere. Live music plays on some evenings. ◑🚌

Last Drop Inn

27 Colliergate, YO1 8BN
⏲ 11-11 (midnight Fri & Sat); 12-11 Sun
☎ (01904) 621951 🌐 yorkbrew.demon.co.uk
York Guzzler, Stonewall, Terrier, Centurion's Ghost Ⓗ
Opened in 2000 following conversion from a solicitor's office, this single bar resembles some of the older pubs in the city with its predominantly wooden interior split over two levels. Large glass windows afford fine views of King's Square, a popular spot for street entertainers. Close to the city centre, the historic street known as The Shambles, and the town market, this is an ideal stopping-off point for shoppers and tourists. Children are not admitted. ❀◑♿🚌●

Maltings

Tanners Moat, YO1 6HU (below Lendal Bridge)
⏲ 11-11; 12-10.30 Sun
☎ (01904) 655387 🌐 maltings.co.uk
Black Sheep Best Bitter; guest beers Ⓗ
A haven for ale lovers, ideally situated near the railway station with easy access to all parts of the town centre, this pub serves six guest beers, usually including an ale from Rooster's or Outlaw, as well as a selection of real ciders. A large room with a central bar leads to a smaller room off to the side. A good menu offers home-cooked food in generous portions, including real chips and a chilli that is not for the faint hearted. ◑⇌🚌●

Minster Inn

24 Marygate, YO30 7BH
⏲ 2-11; 11-11 Fri & Sat; 12-10.30 Sun
☎ (01904) 624499
Jennings Sneckslifter; Marston's Burton Bitter; guest beers Ⓗ
A traditional multi-roomed pub built in 1903 and still intact. Located away from the busy tourist areas, this is a peaceful haven where you can always find interesting ales. The community atmosphere is evident in the warm welcome given to families and dogs. Local organisations use the rooms for meetings. Whether you want a quiet pint, a lively chat or a game of Nine Mens Morris or Shut the Box with your beer, this is the perfect place. ♨Q♨❀◑⇌🚌♣⌐

Rook & Gaskill

12 Lawrence Street, YO10 3WP (near Walmgate Bar)
⏲ 12-11 (midnight Fri & Sat)
☎ (01904) 674067
Castle Rock Harvest Pale, seasonal beers; guest beers Ⓗ
Now owned outright by Castle Rock, the Rook & Gaskill was originally developed in conjunction with York Brewery. The single room has terrazzo flooring and comfortable bench seating while the bar boasts 12 handpumps. Great care is taken to ensure that a well-balanced range of beers, including a mild and a stout or porter, is usually available. A stillage is erected in the rear conservatory during the popular twice-yearly beer festivals. The cider varies. There is no food on Sunday. ◗🚌●⌐

Tap & Spile

29 Monkgate, YO31 7PB (200m outside city walls at Monkbar)
⏲ 12-11 (midnight Thu-Sat)
☎ (01904) 656158
Rooster's Yankee; guest beers Ⓗ
Imposing Flemish-style house dating from 1897. Formerly known as the Black Horse, the pub was renamed in 1988 when it became one of the first Tap & Spiles in the chain. A spacious interior includes a raised bar area at one end and a separate library-style lounge with imposing fireplace at the other. Five guest ales come mainly from the SIBA scheme. Regular music nights are held and the annual pork pie festival is a highlight. ❀◑P⌐

Three-Legged Mare

15 High Petergate, YO1 7EN (50m from the Minster)
⏲ 11-midnight; 12-11 Sun
☎ (01904) 638246
York Guzzler, Stonewall, Wonkey Donkey, Centurion's Ghost; guest beers Ⓗ
The second York Brewery pub to open in the city, following conversion from a shop in

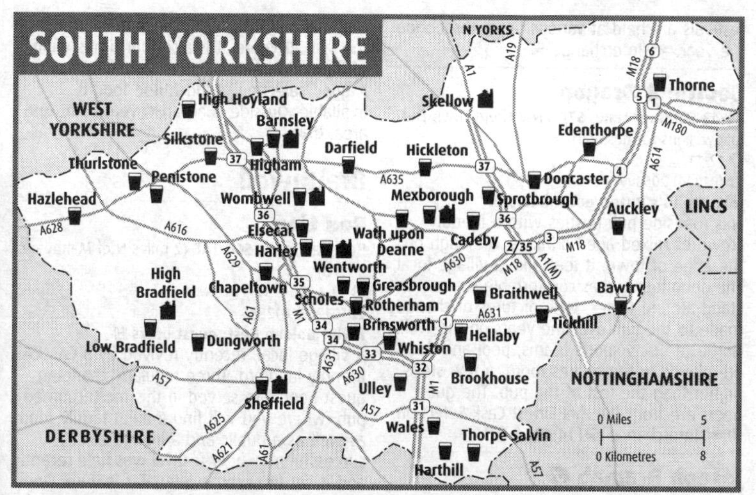

2001, it is situated just metres from the Minster in the heart of the city centre, a short walk from York railway station. Named after a triangular structure for hanging three criminals simultaneously, the pub has a single bar that leads to a pleasant conservatory, and a small beer garden which contains a replica of a three-legged mare. Q◐⇌🚌⊱

Yorkshire Terrier

10 Stonegate, YO1 8AS

11-11 (midnight Fri & Sat); 12-11.30 Sun

☎ (01904) 676722

York Guzzler, Stonewall, Yorkshire Terrier, Centurion's Ghost; guest beers Ⓗ

The frontage of the pub is the York Brewery shop, with an entrance to the bar on the left. Inside it has three areas: a main bar with nine handpumps, a space at the back and another to the side. An upstairs room overlooks Stonegate. The Yorkshire Terrier won the 2005 CAMRA Pub Design Award for best conversion to a pub, and is a recent branch Pub of the Season winner. Q◐♿⇌🚌

YORKSHIRE (SOUTH)

Auckley

Eagle & Child

24 Main Street, DN9 3HS (on B1396)

11.30-3, 5-11; 11.30-11.30 Fri & Sat; 12-11 Sun

☎ (01302) 770406

Black Sheep Best Bitter; John Smith's Bitter; Theakston XB; guest beers Ⓗ

A gem of a village pub, popular with locals, with a long tradition of ales that are of good range and quality. Five cask beers are always available, including two guest beers usually sourced from micro-breweries. The pub also offers a fine and varied range of meals at reasonable prices. Robin Hood Airport is nearby. The smoking area is covered and heated. Winner of several local CAMRA awards including Pub of the Year 2006 and 2007. ❀◐🚌P⊱

Barnsley

Dove Inn

102 Doncaster Road, S70 1TP

12-11 (midnight Fri & Sat)

☎ (01226) 288351

Old Mill Bitter, Bullion, seasonal beers Ⓗ

The comfortable interior features much pale wood panelling. A games room has pool and darts, while a large-screen TV shows non-Sky entertainment. The small back room leads to one of the best pub gardens in the area, where extensive work has produced an attractive space for summer drinkers. The first-floor decking has views of the football club and eastern Barnsley, while the courtyard with covered areas keeps the sun worshippers and smokers happy. Opens earlier on match day Saturdays. ❀⇌(Interchange)🚌♣⊱

Gatehouse

35 Eldon Street, S70 2JJ (outside transport interchange)

11-11; closed Sun

☎ (01226) 282394

Acorn Barnsley Bitter, IPA; guest beers Ⓗ

Standing on one of the main gateways into town, this is how the pub got its name. An open-plan interior has wooden floors and tasteful decor. Popular with a 30-plus crowd, a large-screen TV shows free-to-view sporting events and Thursday night has a popular karaoke. Four guest beers are sourced from independent breweries on the SIBA list: Acorn, Idle, Ossett and Wentworth are regulars. Beer

INDEPENDENT BREWERIES

Abbeydale Sheffield
Acorn Wombwell
Bradfield High Bradfield
Concertina Mexborough
Crown & Wellington Sheffield
Glentworth Skellow
Kelham Island Sheffield
Little Ale Cart Sheffield
Oakwell Barnsley
Sheffield Sheffield
Wentworth Wentworth

festivals are held at various times throughout the year. ≠(Interchange)🚌

George & Dragon

41-43 Summer Lane, S70 2NW (from Town End follow signs for hospital)

⏲ 12-11

☎ (01226) 205609

John Smith's Bitter; guest beers Ⓗ

This roadside pub bustles with a friendly crowd of mixed-aged drinkers. Although on the edge of town, it feels like a village local. The open lounge has comfortable seating and stand-around tables, with pictures of changes made to the pub over the years on the walls. Home to many sports teams, pool and darts are played in the games room, a few steps higher than the rest of the pub. The guest beers are from Punch's Finest Cask Selection. ❀≠(Interchange)🚌(14,43)♣P⊡

Joseph Bramah ✔

15 Market Hill, S70 2PX

⏲ 10-midnight (1am Wed, Fri-Sun)

☎ (01226) 320890

Greene King Abbot; Marston's Pedigree; guest beers Ⓗ

A Lloyds No.1 bar with a long, narrow T-shaped interior set over two floors, dimly lit apart from two shiny bars (one on each level). It appeals to young and old alike but can be noisy during the evening. Up to eight cask-conditioned beers are served including ales from Greene King and Marston's, as well as four beers from independent breweries, with regular beer festivals. The pub opens from 9am for food and non-alcoholic drinks. Smokers are catered for in the splendid courtyard which has patio heaters and lighting. ❀◐≠(Interchange)🚌⁄

Keel Inn

18 Canal Street, S71 1LJ (off A61 near ASDA)

⏲ 5 (7 Sat; 12 Sun)-11

☎ (01226) 284512

Beer range varies Ⓗ

Hidden just off the busy Old Mill Lane (A61) beside ASDA, this locals' free house offers two changing guest beers from nearby micro-breweries, often Ossett and Wentworth. Sited next to the now filled-in Barnsley canal, the pub's nautically themed interior reminds visitors of its history. Various drinking areas allow for pool, TV, functions and darts, with a cosy real fire. The pub is larger than it first appears and Barnsley CAMRA has successfully held beer festivals here each October since 2004.
ᗰ❀⇆≠(Interchange)🚌(11,59)♣P⁄⊡

Bawtry

Turnpike

28-30 High Street, DN10 6JE (on A638)

⏲ 11-11; 12-10.30 Sun

☎ (01302) 711960

Caledonian Deuchars IPA; Greene King Ruddles Best Bitter; John Smith's Bitter; guest beers Ⓗ

This pleasant, friendly pub is situated in the market place, ideal for parking and bus stops. The interior is divided into six areas of different sizes, divided by wood and glass partitions. The licensee has been in charge for 22 years and the pub has been in the Guide for the last 20 years. It is also four-times winner of the Local CAMRA Pub of the Season award. A good selection of lunchtime food is available. Outside is a part-covered smoking area. ◐🚌⁄

Braithwell

Red Lion

Holywell Lane, S66 7AF (2 miles N of Maltby on B6376)

⏲ 12-3, 5-11; 12-11 Fri-Mon

☎ (01709) 812886

Taylor Golden Best; guest beers Ⓗ

A village local, recently revived by a CAMRA-friendly landlord. Three regularly changing guest beers are served in this multi-roomed pub, where you will find a quiet family room as well as a public and a lounge bar. A successful mini beer festival was held recently and is set to become a regular feature. On display is a selection of old photographs of the village wheelbarrow race. A whist drive takes place on the first Wednesday of the month.
ᗰ♉❀⊟♿🚌♣⁄

Brinsworth

Phoenix Sports & Social Club ✔

Pavilion Lane, S60 5PA (off Bawtry Road)

⏲ 11-11; 12-10.30 Sun

☎ (01709) 363788

Fuller's London Pride; Stones Bitter; Wentworth seasonal beers; Worthington Bitter Ⓗ

Members of the public are very welcome at the Phoenix. A regular outlet for local Wentworth beers, the comfortable refurbished lounge now offers four cask ales, all expertly kept by the enthusiastic stewards. A family room, TV room and snooker room with two full-sized tables are also popular. Lunchtime and evening meals are available and the club boasts third place in the local CAMRA Club of the Year awards 2007. ♉❀◐♿♣P⁄

Brookhouse

Travellers' Rest

Main Street, S25 1YA (1.2 miles from Dinnington near viaduct)

⏲ 5-11 (12-11 Sat & Sun)

☎ (01909) 562661

Greene King XX Mild, H&H Bitter, Olde Trip Ⓗ

Bungalow-style pub in a farming village, originally a house built using stone from a watermill that stood on the site until the 1960s. The pub has been crowned local CAMRA Rural Pub of the Year 2008. In a handy location for walkers with access to Roche Abbey and Laughton, it has extensive gardens by the brook providing seating, an old boat, two bouncy castles and a children's ride. Duck races takes place on bank holidays. Good value food is served. ❀◐⊟♣P⁄

Cadeby

Cadeby Inn ✔

Main Street, DN5 7SW

⏲ 11-11 (midnight Fri & Sat); 12-10.30 Sun

☎ (01709) 864009 🌐 cadeby-inn.co.uk

Black Sheep Best Bitter; John Smith's Bitter; guest beers
Converted from an old farmhouse, the pub retains much of its original character with open fires, stone-flagged floors and exposed beams. With extensive outdoor drinking areas both front and back, it is a perfect place for a pint on a summer evening. A real attraction is the a la carte menu which changes monthly and is proving popular with diners, thanks to its locally sourced fresh produce. Denaby Ings Nature Reserve is nearby, making the pub handy for walkers and cyclists.

Chapeltown

Commercial

107 Station Road, S35 2XF
12-3, 5.30-11; 12-11 Fri & Sat; 12-10.30 Sun
(0114) 2469066
Wentworth Imperial, WPA, Bumble Beer; guest beers
Located on a main road near Asda, this inn was built in 1890. A former Stroutts pub, it is now a regular outlet for Wentworth beers, including seasonals, as well as five guest ales and a rotating cider. An island bar serves the lounge, public/games bar and the snug. Successful beer festivals are held in May and November. Summer outdoor drinking facilities are to the side and rear, with a stream at the bottom of the garden. Children are welcome. Hot roast pork sandwiches are available until 10pm on Saturday (no meals Sun eve).

Darfield

Darfield Cricket Club

School Street, S73 9EZ
7 (6 Fri)-11; 12-3, 7-11 Sat; 12-10.30 Sun
(01226) 752194
Beer range varies
Founded in 1857, this CAMRA award-winning club is situated in the heart of the village in idyllic surroundings. The club offers two rotating guest beers sourced from local micro-breweries. Quality, good value food is available on Friday evening and Sunday lunchtime. Quiz night is Wednesday. The club can be busy during the cricket season. Show your CAMRA membership card or a copy of this Guide to gain admittance. Children are welcome. (X19,219)

Doncaster

Corner Pin

145 St Sepulchre Gate West, DN1 3AH
12-midnight (1am Fri & Sat)
(01302) 323159
John Smith's Bitter; guest beers
CAMRA's Pub of the Season Spring 2008 and Pub of the Year 2008 for the Doncaster area, this traditional street corner hostelry comprises a smart lounge area and a public bar area. Out back is an attractive decked space. Guest beers are from small independent breweries, sourced via the SIBA scheme. The pub supports football, darts and dominoes teams, and live music is performed every Thursday.

Gatehouse

Priory Walk, DN1 3EF (pedestrian walkway close to the Mansion House)
9-midnight (1am Fri-Sun)
(01302) 554540
Beer range varies
Although not a traditional pub, this bistro-style Wetherspoon's bar goes a long way to encourage CAMRA members and real ale drinkers by giving them the opportunity to vote for beers they would like to see available. Breweries from South Yorkshire are often featured, together with those from further afield. Do not overlook the bank of handpumps at the end of the bar.

Leopard

1 West Street, DN1 3AA (W of ring road near railway station)
11-11 (midnight Fri-Sun)
(01302) 363054 myspace.com/theleoparddoncaster
John Smith's Bitter; guest beers
Lively street-corner pub with a superb tiled frontage that recalls its origins as a Warwick & Richardson's house. A long-standing regular outlet for the local Glentworth Brewery, one of its beers is always available, as well as an independent guest beer. An eclectic mix of music is on the jukebox in both the comfortable lounge and the lively bar/games room. Upstairs a function room hosts regular gigs, featuring a wide range of up-and-coming rock and pop bands.

Red Lion

37-38 Market Place, DN1 1NH (SE corner of Market Place, near fish market)
9-11 (midnight Fri-Sat)
(01302) 732120
Beer range varies
This large, historic pub has been given a new lease of life since it was taken over by Wetherspoon's. A lively front drinking area gives way to a quieter area with tables and chairs towards the rear. Although much altered over the years, it was here in 1776 that discussions took place to organize the St Leger Stakes, the oldest Classic horse race. Plaques are on display commemorating the event and listing post-war winners, including many famous jockeys.

Salutation Hotel

14 South Parade, DN1 2DR
11.30-midnight (1.30am Fri & Sat)
(01302) 340705
Tetley Bitter; guest beers
A coaching inn on the way to the racecourse, built around 1780, it has a changing choice of guest beers that can be enjoyed in the large bar area or adjacent smaller, snug-like areas. Attracting all ages, big-screen football is often shown and there is a popular Tuesday night quiz. A function room upstairs has its own bar, and there is a patio that is ideal for summer days and smokers.

Tut 'n' Shive ✔

6 West Laith Gate, DN1 1SF (next to Frenchgate shopping centre)
11-11 (1am Fri & Sat); 12-midnight
☎ (01302) 360300
Black Sheep Best Bitter; Greene King IPA, Abbot, Old Speckled Hen; guest beers 🄷
Up to six real ales are available at this busy town-centre pub with a stone floor, boarded ceiling and walls decorated with pump clips from past guest beers. Quiz nights are Wednesday and Sunday. Classic rock is well represented on the jukebox and in a lively music programme. A large-screen TV shows major sporting events. Trains, buses and town centre shopping are only metres away. A relaxed but lively atmosphere ensures that all feel welcome.

Dungworth

Royal Hotel

Main Road, S6 6HF
6 (12 Sat)-11; 12-4, 7-10.30 Sun
☎ (0114) 285 1213 royalhotel-dungworth.pwp.blueyonder.co.uk
Tetley Bitter; guest beers 🄷
A small 19th-century rural pub to the north west of Sheffield in the Vale of Bradfield, with panoramic views over the Loxley Valley. One bar serves two drinking areas, with a separate room to the left. Meals are served early evenings on weekdays, all day until 8pm Saturday and lunchtime Sunday. Do try the home-cooked pies. Sunday lunchtime carol singing from mid-November to Christmas is popular. Children, walkers and well-behaved pets are welcome. Three en-suite rooms are available in the adjoining lodge.
Q P

Edenthorpe

Beverley Inn

Thorne Road, DN3 2JE (on A18)
12-3, 5-11; 12-3, 7-10.30 Sun
☎ (01302) 882724
John Smith's Bitter; guest beers 🄷
Conveniently located, welcoming village inn, well supported by the local community. An extensive menu of home-cooked food is served by friendly staff, and the Sunday carvery is especially popular. Two constantly changing guest beers come from far and wide, chosen with the help of knowledgeable customers. A pleasant beer garden is available for outside drinking, and the pub has accommodation in 14 rooms. P

Eden Arms ✔

Edenfield Road, DN3 2QR (off A18)
12-11 (midnight Thu-Sat)
☎ (01302) 888682
Taylor Landlord; guest beers 🄷
Modern, food-based pub located in a village which is served by a frequent bus service. There are a variety of seating areas, including a heated patio outside. The pub has a large car park, good disabled access and facilities for wheelchair users. A pub quiz is held every Monday evening. P

Elsecar

Market Hotel

2-4 Wentworth Road, S74 8EP
12 (11 Sat)-11
☎ (01226) 742240
Wentworth WPA; guest beers 🄷
This pub is a beer lover's paradise, offering a changing selection of different breweries' beers. All the ales are sold at the same price, irrespective of ABV. A number of different rooms including a function room and large games room give a choice of company in this warm, friendly village local. Many clubs meet here. There is an outside drinking area to the rear. It is a short walk to unspoilt countryside including the Dove and Dearne Canal and the Trans-Pennine Trail. Next door is the Elsecar Heritage Centre. Q (227,66)P

Milton Arms

Armroyd Lane, S74 8ES
12-3, 7-11.30; closed Wed winter; 12-5, 7-11 Sun
☎ (01226) 742278
Stones Bitter; guest beers 🄷
This comfortable pub has three rooms, each with a real fire, and is home to several groups including two falconry clubs. The annual Milton Six race attracts runners from all over Yorkshire. The award-winning beer garden with aviaries makes the pub as welcoming in summer as the real fires do in winter. Food is available daily and the landlord is a class chef. Guest beers are usually from the local Wentworth Brewery. (227,66)P

Greasbrough

Prince of Wales

9 Potters Hill, S61 4NU
11-4, 7-11; 12-3, 7-10.30 Sun
☎ (01709) 551358
Beer range varies 🄷
The Prince continues to go from strength to strength as it celebrates its 14th consecutive entry in the Guide. This popular street corner pub has a spacious, well-decorated lounge and tap room. The friendly landlord is approaching his 30th year of tenancy and continues to provide cask beers from a variety of breweries. The guest beer can change up to three times in one day, ensuring its quality. In summer tables and chairs outside allow customers to watch the world go by.
Q

Harley

Horseshoe Inn

9 Harley Road, S62 7UD (off A6135)
4 (2 Sat)-11; 12-10.30 Sun
☎ (01226) 742204
John Smith's Bitter; Wentworth WPA, seasonal beers; guest beers 🄷
This street corner pub is situated close to the local Wentworth Brewery and stocks at least one Wentworth beer. The hostelry hosts regular events and is home to a pool team. The guest beer changes regularly to ensure its quality, with ales often coming from local breweries. A carvery is held on Sunday.

Harthill

Beehive

16 Union Street, S26 7YH (opp church on road from Kiveton crossroads)
12-3 (not Mon), 6-11; 11-11 Sat & Sun
☎ (01909) 770205
Caledonian Deuchars IPA; Taylor Landlord; Tetley Bitter Ⓗ
Local CAMRA Rural Pub of the Year 2007, this welcoming village inn is close to Rother Valley Country Park and on the Five Churches walk. It provides space for drinkers and diners and is home to a number of local clubs. The rear room houses a full-sized snooker table. There is a function room upstairs with stairlift access which is available to hire. Q♣◐◑ᕲ♿♣P

Hazlehead

Dog & Partridge

Bord Hill, S36 4HH (2 miles westbound on A628 Flouch roundabout)
12-11
☎ (01226) 763173 🌐 dogandpartridgeinn.co.uk
Acorn Barnsley Bitter; guest beers Ⓗ
Surrounded by the Dark Peak District's stunning views, this pub is a splendid place in which to enjoy nature in the wild. Situated on the Woodhead Pass (formerly the Psalters Brooke pack horse route), giving welcome and succor to travellers, weary or otherwise, has been a tradition here for many years. The pub serves four excellent ales from local micros. A huge fire blazes in winter and in summer there is the chance of a helicopter ride from the field at the side of the car park.
ᕲQ♣◐◑♿P

Hellaby

Stockyard

Hellaby Lane, S66 8HN (On industrial estate next to jct 1 of M18)
4 (12 Sun)-11
☎ (01709) 730083
Black Sheep Best Bitter; Taylor Landlord Ⓗ
A popular truckstop for long-haul lorry drivers, this friendly pub has a timber interior with a restaurant area that opens to serve breakfast to truckers and meals in the evening. It offers a book exchange service where you can pick up a book and return it at a later date. The Sunday carvery is very popular and the pub also has an outdoor seating area and large car park. Q♣◑♿P

Hickleton

Hickleton Village Hall

Castle Hill Lane, DN5 7BG (off A635)
6 (12 Sat & Sun)-midnight; closed Mon
☎ (01709) 898651
Beer range varies Ⓗ
Tucked away in a conservation village, this private members club owned by Lord Halifax was metamorphosed into a real ale haven in 2007, and won a local CAMRA Pub of the Season award. Up to six cask beers are available in the characterful bar, including ales from a Yorkshire micro-brewery. Lunch is served weekends only (no evening meal Sun). If you enjoy drinking great ale in a relaxed atmosphere you will love it here – the secret's out. Card-carrying CAMRA members are welcome if signed in. ᕲ◐◑♣

High Hoyland

Cherry Tree

Bank End Lane, S75 4BE
2-3, 5.30-11; 12-11 Sat & Sun
☎ (01226) 382541
Black Sheep Best Bitter; E&S Elland Best Bitter, Nettlethrasher; John Smith's Bitter; Tetley Bitter Ⓗ
Located close to Cannon Hall Country Park, this pub has fantastic far-reaching views over Barnsley and open countryside, and is popular with locals and visitors alike. As well as five real ales, the pub offers good value quality food (booking advised). The interior has a long central bar with dining areas to both sides. Outside is plenty of seating to enjoy the views. Walkers are welcome. ♣◐◑♿P⅟

Higham

Engineers Arms

Higham Common Road, S75 1PF (off A635 or A628)
12-3, 7-11
☎ (01226) 384204
Samuel Smith OBB Ⓗ
Community pub that hosts activities every night of the week. Three cricket teams play on the field outside, while inside conversation is king, with no TV or background music. The split-level bar serves the lounge from the lower level, where pictures from the TV series Last of the Summer Wine adorn the walls. The upper level is a welcoming public bar, and features a Yorkshire 'doubles' dart board. The pub serves one cask-conditioned beer, one of the most competitively priced in the area.
Q♣ᕲ(92A)♣P

Low Bradfield

Plough Inn

New Road, S6 6HW
12-3.30, 6 (7 Tue)-midnight; 12-midnight Wed-Sun
☎ (0114) 285 1280 🌐 the-plough-inn.com
Bradfield Plough; guest beers Ⓗ
Nestled in the heart of the Loxley Valley, this former farm, built in the early 18th century, celebrates 200 years as a pub during 2009. This genuine free house provides guest beers, one from Sheffield, while the other is sourced from Yorkshire or the north east. Good food is made from locally sourced produce, with the pies a speciality. A folk night is held on the last Tuesday of the month. ᕲ♣◐◑ᕲ♿♣P⅟

Mexborough

Concertina Band Club

9A Dolcliffe Road, S64 9AZ
12-4, 7-11; 12-1, 7-10.30 Sun
☎ (01709) 580841
Concertina Club Bitter, Bengal Tiger, Club Extreme; John Smith's Bitter Ⓗ
Affectionately known as the 'Tina', this long-established social club is unique, with its own

brewery in the cellar. Photographs on the wall acknowledge how the club got its name – it was the home of a bygone band. Note the many awards the club has won, including CAMRA Yorkshire Club of the Year runner-up 2007. A warm welcome awaits visitors carrying a CAMRA membership card or this Guide; however, there is no talking in the concert room during bingo! ⇌⊟♣☐

Penistone

Wentworth Arms

Sheffield Road, S36 6HG (off train station approach)

⏲ 12.30-11 (midnight Fri & Sat); 12-11 Sun

☎ (01226) 762494

Banks's Bitter; guest beers Ⓗ

A no-nonsense, no-frills community local with a cosy lounge and bar serving the best beer in Penistone. The licensee now offers a mild on a regular basis. Very conveniently sited by the rail station, with the Trans-Pennine trail running on the disused Sheffield-Manchester line alongside, this pub is a useful watering hole with an adjacent fish and chip shop. As well as the great beers, pool, darts and an old-fashioned jukebox provide the entertainment. ♔ᕳ❀⅄⇌⊟(29,23)P⌐

Rotherham

Bluecoat ✔

The Crofts, S60 2JD (behind town hall)

⏲ 9-midnight (1am Fri & Sat)

☎ (01709) 580841

Greene King Abbot; Marston's Pedigree; guest beers Ⓗ

This converted school is situated behind the town hall and is well worth seeking out. Winner of the local CAMRA branch Pub of the Year award 2006-2008, it is also Wetherspoon's Pub of the Year 2006. The Bluecoat offers a wide selection of beers from national and local breweries. Weston's Old Rosie Cider is also on handpull.
❀◑♿⇌●P⌐

Hare & Hounds

52 Wellgate, S60 2LR

⏲ 11.30 (11 Sat)-11; 11-10.30

☎ (01709) 821554

Greene King Abbot; guest beers Ⓗ

Situated in Rotherham town centre, the Hare & Hounds is back in the Guide by popular demand. The pub is split into three sections, each with a large-screen TV, and there is an upstairs function room. Greene King Abbot is always served, alongside a changing guest beer, both of which enjoy a quick turnover. There is a small garden which houses a covered smoking area and the pub is flanked by municipal car parks. ❀⇌⊟♣⌐

Scholes

Bay Horse

Scholes Lane, S61 2RQ (off A629, near M1 jct 35)

⏲ 5 (12.30 Sat & Sun)-11.30; 12-11.30 Sun

☎ (0114) 246 8085

Kelham Island Pale Rider; Taylor Landlord; guest beers Ⓗ

Traditional village pub next to the cricket club. It serves good home-cooked food including Dan's Cow Pie (earn a certificate if you finish everything on the plate), popular curries and Sunday lunches. Hog roasts feature up to four times a year. Further entertainment is provided by a choir on Thursday and two weekly quizzes. Situated on the Rotherham Round Walk and the Trans-Pennine Trail, the pub is also near the local attraction of Keppels Column. ♔Q❀◑♿P

Sheffield: Central

Bath Hotel ★

66 Victoria Street, S3 7QL

⏲ 12-11; 7-10.30 Sun

☎ (0114) 249 5151

Abbeydale Moonshine; Acorn Barnsley Bitter; Tetley Bitter; guest beers Ⓗ

The carefully restored 1930s interior gives this two-roomed pub a place on CAMRA's National Inventory of historic pubs. The drinker has a choice between the clear lines of the tiled lounge and the warmth of the well-upholstered snug. With up to three guest beers from local breweries and micros from further afield, there is also a good choice of malt whiskies. Located off Glossop Road, between West Street and Sheffield University tram stops. Q◐⊖⊟

Devonshire Cat ✔

49 Wellington Street, S1 4HG

⏲ 11.30-11 (midnight Fri & Sat); 12-10.30 Sun

☎ (0114) 279 6700 🌐 devonshirecat.co.uk

Abbeydale Moonshine, Absolution; Caledonian Deuchars IPA; Theakston Old Peculier; Thornbridge Jaipur; guest beers Ⓗ

Showcasing what is probably the best selection of beer in the county, the 'Dev Cat' is a great place for the discerning drinker. Twelve handpumps adorn the bar, with the house beer brewed by the local Kelham Island Brewery. Whatever time of day you visit, the clientele is a mix of beer enthusiasts, students and those in need of a liquid libation. A must if you are on a short visit to the city, but be warned, you may never leave. ◑♿⊖⊟●

Fagans

69 Broad Lane, S1 4BS

⏲ 12-11.30 (11 Sun)

☎ (0114) 272 8430

Abbeydale Moonshine; Tetley Bitter Ⓗ

Away from the main drinking areas, this pub is hard to categorise, and you feel it would be more at home on a side street rather than on one of the city's main arteries. Well dressed in green and red, with dark wood panelling, the pub hosts folk music every night and a fiendish quiz on Thursday. Whether just calling in for quick pint or looking for a longer session, this pub would have to be near the top of your list. ◑⊖⊟

Fat Cat

23 Alma Street, S3 8SA

⏲ 12-11 (midnight Fri & Sat)

☎ (0114) 249 4801

Kelham Island Best Bitter, Pale Rider; Taylor Landlord; guest beers Ⓗ

Opened in 1981 and still going strong, this is the pub that started the real ale revolution in the area. Beers from all over the country are served alongside those from its neighbour and sister enterprise, the Kelham Island Brewery. It is famed for its food in which vegetarian and gluten-free dishes feature heavily (no food Sun eve). Take time to browse the large number of awards for the pub and brewery which cover the walls. A curry and quiz night is held on Monday. Q✿◐◑♿⊖🚌♠P⁵⁄

Harlequin

108 Nursery Street, S3 8GG

⏲ 11-11; closed Sun

☎ (0114) 275 8195

Bradfield Farmers Blonde; John Smith's Magnet; guest beers 🄷

A more recent addition to the city's 'Valley of Beer' pub crawl, the Harlequin (formerly the Manchester) takes its name from another former Wards pub around the corner, sadly now demolished. The large open-plan interior features a central bar, with seating areas on two levels. As well as local brews, the eight handpumps serve beers from far and wide, with an emphasis on micro-breweries. There is a quiz on Wednesday and regular live music at weekends. ◑🚌♣♠

Kelham Island Tavern

62 Russell Street, S3 8RW

⏲ 12-11 (midnight Fri-Sun)

☎ (0114) 272 2482 🌐 kelhamislandtavern.co.uk

Acorn Barnsley Bitter; Bradfield Farmers Blonde; Pictish Brewers Gold; guest beers 🄷

Sheffield CAMRA Pub of the Year 2003-2007 and Yorkshire regional winner in 2004 and 2007. An impressive 10 permanent handpumps include two that always dispense a mild and a stout/porter, so you are sure to find something to quench your thirst. A visit in the warmer months enables you to sample the pub's multi-award winning subtropical beer garden – a true gem. Regular folk music plays on Sunday and quiz night is Monday. No meals Sunday or Monday. ✿◑♿⊖🚌♠⁵⁄–⊓

Red Deer ✔

18 Pitt Street, S1 4DD

⏲ 11.30 (12 Sat)-11; 7.30-10.30 Sun

☎ (0114) 2722890 🌐 red-deer-sheffield.co.uk

Adnams Broadside; Banks's Bitter; Black Sheep Best Bitter; Caledonian Deuchars IPA; Greene King Abbot; Taylor Landlord; guest beers 🄷

A genuine, traditional local in the heart of the city, hidden away behind the West Street circuit. The small frontage of the original three-roomed pub hides an open-plan interior extended to the rear with a gallery seating area. The pub mirrors and Guinness clock sit alongside prints and watercolours of local scenes, some of which are for sale. The impressive range of nine handpulled ales includes at least one rotating guest. There is also a selection of continental bottled beers. Evening meals until 7pm; no food at weekends. Q✿◑◐⊖🚌

Red Lion

109 Charles Street, S1 2ND

⏲ 11.30-11.30 (midnight Fri & Sat); 7-11 Sun

☎ (0114) 272 4997

Black Sheep Best Bitter; Caledonian Deuchars IPA; guest beers 🄷

A street corner pub now surrounded by the ever-expanding Hallam University City Campus. A corner door leads directly into a small snug, while the main entrance gives access to the lounge, with a conservatory and a raised area at the rear, which was once a separate concert room. Comfortably furnished throughout, its location in the Cultural Industries Quarter ensures a busy lunchtime and early evening crowd. Guest beers are from local breweries, especially Abbeydale, Bradfield and Sheffield, through the SIBA scheme. ✿◑⇌⊖🚌

Three Tuns ✔

39 Silver Street Head, S1 2DD

⏲ 11-11; 7-11.30 Sat

☎ (0114) 272 0646

Taylor Landlord; Tetley Bitter; guest beers 🄷

The Three Tuns is easy to miss – but make sure you don't. It was once described as having 'more character than Gerard Depardieu'. This V-shaped pub is regularly frequented by the 'suits' who work in nearby offices and has a buzzing atmosphere during early evening hours. Make sure you check out the two handpumps on the upper level of the bar. Previously used as a nuns' washroom, the building now serves a much better purpose. No weekend meals. ◑⊖🚌

Wig & Pen

44 Campo Lane, S1 2EG

⏲ 11-11 (midnight Fri & Sat); closed Sun

☎ (0114) 276 3988 🌐 wigandpensheffield.com

Abbeydale Moonshine; guest beers 🄷

At the rear of Sheffield Cathedral, this smart city centre venue unusually offers a good choice of real ales. The main bar runs along the frontage, with relaxed seating, mood lighting and music. Tapas and quality food are served in the restaurant area, while regular food and drink events feature regional and international themes. Occasional beer festivals are hosted. Guest beers are mainly from local micro-breweries. ◑◐♿⇌⊖🚌♠

Sheffield: East

Carlton

563 Attercliffe Road, S9 3RA

⏲ 11-11; 7.30-10.30 Sun

☎ (0114) 244 3287

Beer range varies 🄷

Built in 1862, this former Gilmours house lies behind a deceptively small frontage. Carefully renovated in recent years, it has been transformed from a basic workmen's pub to a thriving community local. The main room around the bar is comfortably furnished in traditional style. To the rear is a newly extended games room and a recently created garden. A strict no-swearing policy enhances the friendly atmosphere. Beers are mainly from local breweries and often include Clark's and Wentworth, with some from further afield. ✿⊖🚌♣⁵⁄–⊓

Cocked Hat ✔

75 Worksop Road, S9 3TG

⏲ 11-11; 11-3, 7-11 Sat; 12-3 Sun

☎ (0114) 244 8332
Marston's Burton Bitter, Pedigree, seasonal beers; guest beers Ⓗ
Corner pub, now standing in isolation, originally at the heart of the steel industry when it was built in the 1840s. It lies in the shadow of the Don Valley Stadium, with players and fans providing some of the custom. The open-plan layout around a central bar includes stalled seating at one end and a raised area occupied by the bar billiards table. A handy refreshment stop for walkers on the Five Weirs Walk.

Sheffield: North

Gardeners Rest

105 Neepsend Lane, S3 8AT
3 (12 Fri & Sat)-11; 12-10.30 Sun
☎ (0114) 272 4978 sheffieldbrewery.com
Sheffield Crucible Best, Five Rivers, Seven Hills, Blanco Blonde, seasonal beers; guest beers Ⓗ
The tap for the Sheffield Brewery, this pub offers up to four beers from Sheffield and up to eight beers from other local and regional breweries. Refurbished in 2008 following a flood the previous year, it has a clean, bright feel but retains its cosy lounge. A larger tap room holds art exhibitions, music, a Sunday quiz and a bar billiards table. The conservatory leads to the beer garden which backs onto the River Don. A beer festival is hosted in October. Q

Hillsborough Hotel

54-58 Langsett Road, S6 2UB
11-11 (midnight Fri & Sat); 12-11 Sun
☎ (0114) 232 2100 hillsborough-hotel.com
Crown Middlewood Mild, HPA, Primrose Pale, Loxley Gold, Stannington Stout, seasonal beers; guest beers Ⓗ
Family-run hotel, now with extended opening hours and serving home-cooked food. Ever-changing guest ales are supplemented by beers from the house brewery in the cellar which brews under the Crown name, with four of the listed beers available at all times. Brewery tours are available. The conservatory and raised terrace at the rear feature panoramic views along the upper Don Valley. Seasonal beer festivals, regular themed events, folk music and a popular quiz night on Tuesday are held. Q

New Barrack Tavern

601 Penistone Road, S6 2GA
11-11 (midnight Fri & Sat); 12-11 Sun
☎ (0114) 234 9148 tynemill.co.uk
Abbeydale Moonshine; Acorn Barnsley Bitter; Castle Rock Sheriffs Tipple, Harvest Pale, Elsie Mo; guest beers Ⓗ
An essential stop-off for football fans travelling to nearby Hillsborough, this pub offers 11 handpumps, pre-match sustenance and a warm welcome. The home-cooked food is popular at all times and available late night Friday and Saturday, with a carvery on Sunday. The small front bar has darts, the main room features live music (weekend evenings and folk Mondays). A wide choice of continental beers, single malts plus a real cider are served. Outside is an award-winning heated, covered patio garden. Q

Rawson Spring

Langsett Road, Hillsborough, S6 2LN
9-11.30 (12.30am Fri & Sat)
☎ (0114) 285 6200
Greene King IPA, Abbot; Marston's Pedigree; guest beers Ⓗ
Cavernous Wetherspoon pub in the former swimming baths at the Hillsborough tram stop. It is popular on match days and has past Wednesday team photos adorning the walls, along with other historical prints. It takes its name from the local spring that supplied fresh water to the nearby barracks. The eponymous house beer is provided by Bradfield. Six other handpumps supply a range of guest ales, with food available every day until 11pm. Family-friendly throughout, it has a beer garden and covered, heated patio area.

Wellington

1 Henry Street, S3 7EQ
12-11; 12-3.30, 7-10.30 Sun
☎ (0114) 249 2295
Beer range varies Ⓗ
Formerly the Cask & Cutler, this street-corner pub has reverted to its original name but is often referred to as the Bottom Wellie. It continues to champion an ever-changing range of beers from small independent brewers, with eight handpumps always offering a mild, a stout or porter and a real cider, plus a range of continental bottled beers. One pump is often dedicated to a Millstone Brewery beer. The house brewery, which adjoins the secluded garden at the rear, has been mothballed for the moment.
Q

Sheffield: South

Archer Road Beer Stop

57 Archer Road, S8 0JT
11 (10.30 Sat)-10; 5-10 Sun
☎ (0114) 255 1356
Beer range varies Ⓗ
Small corner-shop off-licence now well into its second decade of bringing real ale to the take-home market. Four handpumps dispense mainly local ales from micro-breweries. In addition the shelves are filled with a vast range of bottle-conditioned beers, together with continental and world classics. All products are competitively priced. The shop has won a number of local CAMRA awards and has featured in every edition of this Guide since 1997.

Cricket Inn

Penny Lane, Totley Bents, S17 3AZ
11-11
☎ (0114) 236 5256 brewkitchen.co.uk
Thornbridge Cricketers, Lord Marples, Jaipur IPA; guest beers Ⓗ
In a rural location overlooking the village cricket green, yet only five minutes' walk from suburbia. At the weekend it is possible to sit in the beer garden and watch a game of cricket or football. This is a pub of two halves, one a traditional country inn with an open fire and cosy corners, the other an open-plan dining room. The pub is run by Brewkitchen, a partnership between a local restaurateur and

Thornbridge Brewery. The guest beer is from the Thornbridge range. ⛰❀◑♿🚌P🚭

Sheaf View

25 Gleadless Road, Heeley, S2 3AA

🕐 12-11.30

☎ (0114) 249 6455

Bradfield Farmers Blonde; Kelham Island Easy Rider; Wentworth WPA; guest beers 🄷

Former John Smith's and Marston's pub, transformed in 2000 after reopening as a genuine free house. The pub is tastefully furnished with lots of breweriana and also has excellent disabled access. Five guest beers are available, together with a considerable range of draught and bottled continental beers. A large choice of malt whiskies is stocked and all drinks are competitively priced. Unsurprisingly an award-winning pub, this is arguably CAMRA's flagship in the south of the city. Q❀♿🚌♣🍎🚭

Union Hotel

1 Union Road, S11 9EF

🕐 12-2.30, 5.30-11; 12-2.30, 7-10.30 Sun

☎ (0114) 255 0689

Abbeydale Moonshine; Black Sheep Best Bitter; Taylor Landlord; Tetley Bitter; guest beer 🄷

A pub since 1845, the Union is now only on its 15th landlord, with the full list of previous incumbents on display. This warm and inviting locals' hostelry is in the heart of the Nether Edge suburb. The comfortably furnished open plan lounge has several seating areas around a central bar. Outside is a tree-lined verandah and seating. A popular quiz is held on Monday. Lunches are served weekdays only. Q❀◑🚌🚭

White Lion

615 London Road, Heeley, S2 4HT

🕐 12 (2 Mon & Tue)-11 (midnight Thu-Sat)

☎ (0114) 255 1500

Taylor Landlord; Tetley Dark Mild, Bitter; guest beers 🄷

One of Sheffield's finest pubs, possessing many original features. The small frontage with stained-glass windows belies an extensive interior which comprises a number of interesting small rooms on either side of a tiled corridor, leading to a large concert room. This is one of three award-winning pubs operated by the Just Williams group. Two guest ales complement the regulars. Jazz is featured on the first Tuesday of the month, with live rock music most Thursdays. ❀🚌♣🚭

Sheffield: West

Cobden View

40 Cobden View Road, Crookes, S10 1HQ

🕐 1-midnight (1am Fri); 12-1am Sat; 12-midnight Sun

☎ (0114) 266 1273

Black Sheep Best Bitter; Bradfield Farmers Blonde; Caledonian Deuchars IPA; Wychwood Hobgoblin; guest beers 🄷

A busy community pub that caters for a varied clientele, ranging from students to retired folk. Although opened out, the original room layout is still apparent, with the bar serving a snug at the front, a games area to the rear and a lounge to the right of the front entrance. Quizzes are held on Sunday and Tuesday evenings and there is live music most Thursdays and Saturdays. The spacious garden is used for regular summer barbecues and contains a large covered smoking area. ❀♿🚌♣🚭

Fox & Duck

227 Fulwood Road, Broomhill, S10 3BA

🕐 11-11.30 (midnight Fri & Sat); 12-11.30 Sun

☎ (0114) 263 1888

Abbeydale Moonshine; John Smith's Magnet; guest beers 🄷

Busy pub at the heart of the Broomhill shopping area. Although owned by the university Students Union, it is popular with locals as well as students. Originally a two-roomed pub, it was converted to its present open-plan format in the 1980s and extended more recently into an adjacent shop. No food is served, but drinkers may bring in their own from the numerous nearby takeaways. Four or five guest beers are sourced from local and regional brewers. ❀🚌🚭

Ranmoor Inn

330 Fulwood Road, S10 3GD

🕐 11.30-11; 12-10.30 Sun

☎ (0114) 230 1325

Abbeydale Moonshine; Bradfield Farmers Blonde; Caledonian Deuchars IPA; Taylor Landlord; guest beers 🄷

Renovated Victorian local with original etched windows, lying in the shadow of Ranmoor church in the leafy suburb of Fulwood. Now open plan, the seating areas reflect the old room layout. A friendly, old-fashioned pub, it attracts a diverse clientele that includes choirs and football teams – the piano by the bar is often played by regulars. Food is served Tuesday to Saturday. A small front garden is supplemented by the former stableyard which has been opened as a partly-covered and heated drinking area. Q❀◑🚌♣🚭

Rising Sun

471 Fulwood Road, S10 3QA

🕐 11(12 Sun)-11 🌐 abbeydalebrewery.co.uk/risingsun

Abbeydale Absolution, Brimstone, Daily Bread, Matins, Moonshine, seasonal beers; guest beers 🄷

Large suburban roadhouse in the leafy western side of the city. Operated by local brewer Abbeydale, it was Sheffield's first pub to ban smoking when it reopened early in 2006. The two rooms are comfortably furnished, with a main bar and raised area to the rear. A range of Abbeydale beers is always available, with up to five guests on the impressive bank of handpumps.

Entertainment includes live music on Monday and Wednesday and quizzes on Sunday and Tuesday. Q❀◑♿🚌♣P🚭

Walkley Cottage

46 Bole Hill Road, S6 5DD

🕐 11 (12 Sun)-11

☎ (0114) 234 4968

Black Sheep Best Bitter; Greene King Abbot; Taylor Landlord; Tetley Bitter; guest beers 🄷

Spacious roadhouse-style suburban local retaining two rooms. The tap room has a snooker table and a large-screen TV, while the comfortable L-shaped lounge has a food servery. Built for Gilmours between the wars

on a large site, the extensive garden affords panoramic views over the Rivelin Valley. A lively pub, it holds a popular quiz on Thursday. The two rotating guest beers are from a wide variety of local and regional brewers.
❀◑◐⊟🚌♣P

Silkstone

Ring O' Bells ✔

High Street, S75 4LN
✪ 12-11 (midnight Sat & Sun)
☎ (01226) 790298
Greene King H&H Bitter, H&H Olde Trip, Ruddles County, Abbot ⊞
Cosy community local with a beautiful frontage that features hanging baskets and pot plants and is a real suntrap in summer. A central bar sits between a lounge to the right and a vault, with real fire and TV, to the left. The keen landlord and landlady are persevering with the ex-Kimberley beers of Hardys & Hansons Bitter and Olde Trip, despite the Greene King takeover. A winner of numerous CAMRA awards, every village should have a pub like this.
⌂Q❀🚌(20,22)⊱

Sprotbrough

Ivanhoe Hotel

Melton Road, DN5 7NS
✪ 11-11; 12-10.30 Sun
☎ (01302) 853130
Samuel Smith OBB ⊞
In a commanding position by the village crossroads, this local CAMRA Pub of the Season Autumn 2006 attracts locals and visitors for its well-kept, competitively-priced beer. The pub comprises a spacious lounge with adjoining conservatory in which families are welcome, and a separate public bar with pool and snooker tables. Good value food is available (not Sun or Mon eve), with Sunday lunch particularly popular. Outside there is a large beer garden adjacent to the village cricket pitch. Q♉❀◑◐⊟♿🚌♣P

Thorne

Windmill Inn

19 Queen Street, DN8 5AA (near Finkle St shopping precinct)
✪ 2-11 (midnight Fri); 12-midnight Sat; 12-11 Sun
☎ (01405) 812866
Adnams Bitter; Black Sheep Best Bitter; John Smith's Bitter; Tetley Bitter ⊞
A mere stone's throw from the old Darley Brewery Tower, this extremely well-kept, efficiently-run pub is highly popular with the local community. Sports fans are catered for here, but TV sound levels are never allowed to compete with conversation. The friendly clientele includes players from the Thornensians Rugby Team, and the Windmill even has its own golf society. This is one pub you can take your Auntie Ethel to without having to cover her ears. The smokers' area outside is heated and covered.
❀⊟♿▲⇌♣P⊱

Thorpe Salvin

Parish Oven

Worksop Road, S80 3JU
✪ 12-2.30 (not Mon), 5.30-11; 12-11 Sat; 12-10.30 Sun
☎ (01909) 770685
Black Sheep Best Bitter; guest beers ⊞
The Parish Oven gets its name from its location on the site of a former communal bakery. This award-winning pub is a popular venue for Sunday lunch (booking advisable) and evening meals, offering a variety of home-cooked dishes. There is a large outside play area and well-behaved dogs are welcome in the bar area. The pub is on the Five Churches and Round Rotherham walks.
❀◑◐♿P⊱

Thurlstone

Huntsman

136 Manchester Road, S36 9QW (on A628)
✪ 6 (12 Sun)-11
☎ (01226) 764892
Black Sheep Best Bitter; Taylor Landlord; Tetley Bitter; guest beers ⊞
It would be easy to pass by this roadside pub on the busy main road through the village, but that would be a big mistake. Inside you are welcomed by six real ales and a landlord and landlady who regard every customer as a friend. Truly a locals' pub, it offers many activities from quiz nights to acoustic evenings. Though mainly open plan, it has several cosy nooks in which to enjoy a chat and a beer. ⌂Q❀🚌(23,24)

Tickhill

Carpenter's Arms

Westgate, DN11 9NE
✪ 4 (12 Tue-Thu)-11.30; 12-midnight Fri & Sat; 12-11.30 Sun
☎ (01302) 742839
Everards Tiger; Jennings Cumberland Ale; John Smith's Bitter ⊞
An appealing pub that has retained a cosy front room and adjoining bar despite the alterations that have taken place over the years. A large conservatory area doubles as a family room and leads to the garden. Decking has been installed at the front of the pub, making it ideal for warm evenings. Traditional folk music sessions are held regularly, Tuesday and Wednesday are quiz nights, while Sunday is cabaret night. Lunches are served Wednesday, Saturday and Sunday.
⌂♉❀◑⊟♿🚌♣P⊱

Scarbrough Arms

Sunderland Street, DN11 9QJ (near Buttercross local landmark)
✪ 12-11 (10.30 Sun)
☎ (01302) 742977
Courage Directors; Greene King Abbot; John Smith's Bitter; guest beers ⊞
A deserving Guide entry since 1990, this three-roomed stone pub has won several awards from CAMRA including local Pub of the Year and, more recently, Pub of the Season. Originally a farmhouse, the building dates back to the 16th century, although structural changes have inevitably taken place over the

years. The snug is a delight, with its barrel-shaped tables and real fire, while bar billiards can be played in the bar. Traditional cider is also available, with brands rotated regularly.

Ulley

Royal Oak

12 Turnshaw Road, S26 3YG (off Main Street)
12-2.30 (4 Sat), 6-11; 12-10.30 Sun
(0114) 2872464
Samuel Smith OBB
A Sam Smith's pub set in the picturesque village of Ulley. The pub's stone and timber interior is split into a restaurant area and public bar. The front of the pub boasts large gardens including a children's play area, making it family friendly. Home-cooked meals are available throughout the week.

Wales

Duke of Leeds

16 Church Street, S26 5LQ (off A618 into School Rd)
12-3 (not Sat), 5-midnight; 12-midnight Sun
(01909) 770301
John Smith's Bitter; guest beers
Once the coaching inn of the Duke of Leeds, this old-fashioned country inn is more than 300 years old. It prides itself on its home-cooked food and welcoming atmosphere. Outdoor drinking areas afford views of the village. On the Five Churches walk, ample parking space is provided behind the pub. It is handy for the railway station.

Wath upon Dearne

Church House

Montgomery Square, S63 7RZ
9-midnight (1am Fri & Sat)
(01709) 879518
Marston's Pedigree; guest beers
This impressive Wetherspoon's pub is set in a pedestrian square in the town centre with excellent access to local bus services. In a handy spot for exploring the RSPB Wetlands Centre at Wombwell, it serves a wide variety of beers from both national and local brewers, including the nearby Acorn Brewery.

Wentworth

George & Dragon

85 Main Street, S62 7TN
10-11 (10.30 Sun)
(01709) 742440
Taylor Landlord; Wentworth WPA, seasonal beers; guest beers
Situated in the picturesque village of Wentworth, the pub is just 500 metres from Rotherham's only brewery. It takes up to four ales from the brewery along with other beers from local and national brewers plus a cask cider. Set back from the road, it has generous gardens out front. Home-cooked food is very popular. Private parties can be booked in the upstairs function room.

Whiston

Golden Ball

7 Turner Lane, S60 4HY (off A618, 1½ miles from M1 jct 33)
12-11 (midnight Thu-Sat)
(01709) 726911
Taylor Landlord; Tetley Bitter; guest beers
Small cottage-style pub in the village of Whiston. The pub has returned to the Guide after a year out, during which time it has been fully refurbished and the beer range increased. The interior has several small enclaves and a comfortable snug to the rear. There are large gardens at the back and an ample car park to the front. Some parts of the building are over 500 years old and the pub is popular with both drinkers and diners.

Hind

285 East Bawtry Road, S60 4ET (on link road between M1 and M18)
12-11 (midnight Thu-Sat)
(01709) 704351
Taylor Landlord; Tetley Bitter; guest beers
This large pub was built for the Mappins Brewery in 1936. Originally known as King Edward VIII, it was renamed when the king abdicated. The pub has improved considerably under new management and won a local CAMRA Pub of the Season award for summer 2007. It is popular for its daytime and evening food. Since refurbishment the interior has opened out, creating good disabled access. There are extensive gardens to the rear and a snooker table upstairs (membership required to play).

Wombwell

Horseshoe

30 High Street, S73 0AA
9-midnight (1am Fri & Sat)
(01226) 273820
Acorn Old Moor Porter; Greene King Abbot; Marstons Pedigree; guest beers
A busy Wetherspoon pub with the usual emphasis on keenly-priced food and beer. The open-plan layout features a raised family dining area at the back and a long bar counter with 10 handpumps – although not all are used permanently. Downstairs toilets lead to an outdoor smoking and drinking walled garden, where additional benches complement those at the front. The staple beers are supported by regularly changing guest ales from a variety of breweries, including the nearby Acorn Brewery just down the road. (226,229)

YORKSHIRE (WEST)

Ackworth

Boot & Shoe

Wakefield Road, WF7 7DF (on A638 400m N of roundabout)
11.30-midnight (1am Fri & Sat); 11.30-11 Sun
(01977) 610218 theboootandshoe.co.uk
Marston's Pedigree; John Smith's Bitter; Samuel Smith OBB; guest beers

WEST YORKSHIRE

Busy, non-food pub next to the cricket field in the village of Ackworth, which once supplied the grindstones for Sheffield's cutlery industry. The building dates back to the late 16th century, retaining some original features such as a delightful semi-circular vestibule. The pub is a rare outlet for Sam Smith's in the free trade. The venue has a strong reputation for live music, with special musical events on bank holidays – it has won an award for Best Live Music Venue. ⛼❀♿🚌(35,245)♣P⚟

Allerton

Reservoir

137 Allerton Road, BD8 0AA

⌚ 4 (2 Fri)-11; 12-11 Sun

☎ (01274) 541731

Tetley Bitter; guest beers Ⓗ

Detached 18th-century village local with three drinking areas served from a central bar, all of which are TV-free apart from a small portable on a shelf in the front lounge. Now run by a well-known Bradford publican with many years' experience, the Reservoir has quickly earned a fine reputation for its beer quality and range. A single visit is just not enough, as any of the many regulars will tell you. A quiz is held on Tuesday evening. ❀🚌🍎⚟

Armitage Bridge

Armitage Bridge WMC (Monkey Club)

Dean Brook Road, HD4 7PA (off B6108 Meltham Road)

⌚ 5 (7 winter)-11; 12-11 Sun

☎ (01484) 664891 🌐 freewebs.com/the-monkey-club

Taylor Best Bitter; guest beers Ⓗ

Follow the stream running by the side of the lane to this quaint, friendly little club, in the middle of the hamlet of Armitage Bridge. Downstairs there is an L-shaped bar lounge with comfortable seating, upstairs is a games room with a pool table and dartboard. Two guest beers are usually available, often from independent micros. Outside, there is a small seating area among the surrounding cottages. Show this Guide or a CAMRA membership card to be signed in. ❀🚌(321,323,324)♣P

Baildon

Junction

1 Baildon Road, BD17 6AB (on Otley road, ¾ mile from Shipley)

⌚ 12-midnight (1am Fri & Sat)

☎ (01274) 582009

Dark Star Hophead; Fuller's ESB; Red Lion White Lion; Tetley Bitter; guest beers Ⓗ

Friendly CAMRA multi award-winning community local with three drinking areas in the main bar plus a lounge and games room off to the sides. Beers change constantly, but usually include one from the nearby Saltaire Brewery, as well as other micros. This is a rare outlet for Dark Star beers in Bradford. Home-cooked food is served weekday lunchtimes and a music jam session is hosted most Sunday evenings. ❀◐⇌(Shipley)🚌⚟

Bankfoot

Woodman ✔

1062 Manchester Road, BD5 8NN

⌚ 12-midnight

☎ (01274) 306445

John Smith's Bitter; Tetley Bitter; Taylor Golden Best; guest beers Ⓗ

This is the landlord and lady's first foray into the pub trade and in two years they have built up a regular clientele and a reputation for quality ales. Among numerous featured breweries are Copper Dragon, Ossett and Hambleton. An L-shaped single room includes a small stage at one end and a pool table at the other. Regular live music is played on Thursday evening and the pub hosts several

local pool and darts teams. A recently erected smoking area includes a wide-screen TV.
❀♿🚌♣P🚬

Batley

Cellar Bar

51 Station Road, WF17 5SU (opp Batley rail station)
⏲ 4-11; 12-1am Fri &Sat; 12-11 Sun
☎ (01924) 423419 🌐 downthecellar.com
Black Sheep Best Bitter; Copper Dragon Golden Pippin; guest beers 🄷
Single-room bar situated in the basement of a Grade II-listed former textile selling house. Recently refurbished, it has a raised, decked games area, leather Chesterfield seating, exposed brickwork and a slate floor. The exterior has many notable features including carvings – look for the stone dog guarding the building. Usually one Leeds Brewery beer is among the guest ales, alongside a rotating beer that changes in style. Quiz night is Thursday and live music plays most Saturday evenings. Lunches are served at the weekend only. ◐⇌

Bingley

Myrtle Grove ✔

141 Main Street, BD16 1AJ
⏲ 9-midnight
☎ (01274) 568637
Greene King Abbot; Marston's Pedigree; Theakston Old Peculier; guest beers 🄷
Moderately-sized Wetherspoon's pub with eight handpumps, two of which are used for cider, namely Weston's Old Rosie and Organic draught vintage. Many of the guest ales are sourced from local micros. Glass doors along the front of the pub are opened at the height of summer. The pub is often busy on Thursday and Friday nights, when service can become haphazard. Two lock complexes of the Leeds-Liverpool Canal are nearby. Q◐◑♿⇌🚌●

Birstall

Black Bull

5 Kirkgate, WF17 9PB (off A652)
⏲ 12-11 (10.30 Sun)
☎ (01274) 873039
Boddingtons Bitter; John Smith's Bitter; guest beers 🄷
Grade II-listed building dating in parts from the 17th century. The upstairs function room is a former courtroom, complete with prisoner's dock and witness box. It is thought the last trial was held in 1839. The ground floor comprises several partly opened-out areas and a small secluded snug, creating a pleasant ambience. Good value lunches and evening meals (Tue-Sat) are served. Despite the age of the building, the pub has good wheelchair access – ask for the ramps.
♨❀◐◑♿🚌(220,283)P🚬

Bradford

Castle Hotel

20 Grattan Road, BD1 2LU
⏲ 11-11; 12-9 Sun
☎ (01274) 393166
Mansfield Cask Ale; guest beers 🄷
Former Webster's house with an open-plan layout that lends a spacious feel. The building dates from the late 19th century and retains many exterior features. The beer choice varies weekly, with a regular ale from Old Spot Brewery; others change in line with the range from the Cullingworth brew plant. Occasional music nights are hosted, along with a quiz on some Tuesday nights. Bottled Belgian and other foreign beers are also available, together with ales from Copper Dragon, Ossett and Saltaire.
♿⇌(Forster Sq/Interchange)🚌🚬

Cock & Bottle ★

93 Barkerend Road, BD3 9AA (jct of Shipley Airedale Rd & Barkerend Rd)
⏲ 11-11; 12-10.30 Sun
☎ (01274) 222305
Beer range varies 🄷
Dating from the 19th century, this Grade II listed Victorian building is on CAMRA's National Inventory of pubs with historic interiors. A multi-roomed building, it retains many original features such as the mahogany back bar, etched windows and woodwork. On Bradford's heritage trail, it plays host to the local Topic folk club as well as afternoon singalongs on Thursday. Up to six guest ales, mainly from Northern micros, are usually available. 🎪⇌(Forster Sq/Interchange)🚌♣P

Corn Dolly

110 Bolton Road, BD1 4DE
⏲ 11.30-11; 12-10.30 Sun
☎ (01274) 720219
Black Sheep Best Bitter; Draught Bass; Everards Tiger; Moorhouses Dolly Bitter; guest beers 🄷

INDEPENDENT BREWERIES

Anglo Dutch Dewsbury
Atlas Mill Brighouse (NEW)
Barearts Todmorden
Bob's Ossett
Bridestones Hebden Bridge
Briscoe's Otley
Clark's Wakefield
Eastwood Elland
Elland Elland
Empire Slaithwaite
Fernandes Wakefield
Golcar Golcar
Goose Eye Keighley
Halifax Steam Hipperholme
Leeds Leeds (NEW)
Linfit Linthwaite
Little Valley Hebden Bridge
Mallinsons Huddersfield (NEW)
Old Bear Keighley
Old Spot Cullingworth
Ossett Ossett
Riverhead Marsden
Rodham's Otley
Ryburn Sowerby Bridge
Salamander Bradford
Saltaire Shipley
Summer Wine Brockholes
Tigertops Wakefield
Timothy Taylor Keighley
WF6 Altofts (Brewing suspended)

This free house has been in the same family for nearly 20 years. A single room pub, it is divided into two distinctive areas, one with a pool table and terrestrial TV. It is popular with office workers, Bradford City followers and a loyal band of drinkers. The interior is festooned with certificates reflecting its many CAMRA awards, together with pump clips from the hundreds of past ales to have graced the four guest ale handpumps. Outside there is a sturdy smoking shelter.
(Forster Sq/Interchange)P

Fighting Cock

21-23 Preston Street, BD7 1JE
11.30-11; 12-10.30 Sun
(01274) 726907
Copper Dragon Golden Pippin; Greene King Abbot; Red Lion White Lion; Taylor Best Bitter, Golden Best, Landlord; guest beers
Popular, unassuming pub, just a short walk or bus ride from the city centre. Twelve real ales are usually available including at least one dark beer. Additionally, this regular local CAMRA award winner serves ciders, foreign bottled beers and fruit wines. It attracts a wide variety of customers from loyal locals to well-travelled real ale enthusiasts. Lunches are served Monday to Saturday.

Haigy's

31 Lumb Lane, Manningham, BD8 7QU
5 (12 Fri & Sat)-2am; 12-11 Sun
(01274) 731644
Tetley Bitter; guest beers
Friendly locals' pub, a former winner of Bradford CAMRA Pub of the Year, that lies on the edge of the city centre. It offers up to four guest ales from northern micros including Phoenix, Newby Wyke and Ossett. The comfortable lounge sports a fine collection of porcelain teapots. The pub is popular with Bradford City fans on match days. Pool players excel on the unusual hexagonal revolving table.
(Forster Sq/Interchange)(620,621)
P

Shoulder of Mutton

28 Kirkgate, BD1 1QL
12-11
(01274) 726038
Samuel Smith OBB
This small multi-roomed city centre pub, a former coaching inn, dates from the early 1800s. It is a popular lunchtime venue for business people, shoppers and locals, who all appreciate the good value food. Its appeal is enhanced by a large sun-trap garden. The pub has been refurbished without ruining its traditional atmosphere – pictures, photographs and drawings of the old city abound. It is the main base for the Airedale quiz league.
(Forster Sq/Interchange)

Sir Titus Salt

Unit B, Windsor Baths, Morley Street, BD7 1AQ (behind Alhambra Theatre)
9-midnight (1am Fri & Sat)
(01274) 732853
Greene King IPA, Abbot; Marston's Pedigree; guest beers
Splendid Wetherspoon conversion of the original swimming baths, now named after a local industrialist and philanthropist. An upstairs seating area overlooks the main bar where framed pictures depict the educational heritage of the city. The pub draws a cosmopolitan clientele including students from the university and college, together with theatre-goers, clubbers and diners from nearby Indian restaurants. The location is handy for the National Media Museum.
Q(Forster Sq/Interchange)

Brighouse

Crown

6 Lightcliffe Road, Waring Green, HD6 2DR
SE141233
11-11.30 (midnight Fri & Sat); 12-11 Sun
(01484) 715436
Springhead Roaring Meg; Taylor Landlord; Tetley Bitter; guest beers
This welcoming stone-built pub has three distinct seating areas and a large pool room. It is particularly popular on Saturday night, when the resident pianist provides live music. Additional entertainment comes from the large-screen TV showing major sports events.
P

Red Rooster

123 Elland Road, Brookfoot, HD6 2QR (on A6025)
3 (12 Fri & Sat)-11; 12-10.30 Sun
(01484) 713737
Kelham Island Easy Rider; Taylor Landlord, Ram Tam; guest beers
This small stone-faced pub lies on the inside of a sharp bend. Its former four-roomed layout is still apparent, with a stone-flagged floor throughout. The six guest beers always include an ale from Moorhouses. Live blues music is performed on the last Sunday afternoon of the month. A charity week is held in mid-August and a beer festival in September. There is a small area of decking for outside drinking. It was local CAMRA Pub of the Year 2005 and 2007.

Richard Oastler

Bethell Street, HD6 1JN SE145227
9-midnight (1am Fri & Sat)
(01484) 401756
Greene King IPA, Abbot; Marston's Pedigree; Theakston Old Peculier; guest beers
A Grade II-listed former Methodist chapel converted to a successful Wetherspoon pub. Indoors the magnificent but inaccessible upper floor with original chapel pews and impressive ceiling has been retained. Up to eight guest beers are served, usually including at least one from one of the local micro-breweries.
(Brighouse)

Castleford

Glass Blower

15 Bank Street, WF10 1JD (just off town centre)
9-midnight (1am Fri & Sat)
(01977) 520390
Greene King IPA, Abbot; Marston's Pedigree; guest beers

Former post office converted in 1998 into a popular Wetherspoon establishment. The pub was to have been called The Glass House in reference to the town's history of glass bottle manufacture, but local people objected because of the link with prison. Pictures of the work of Henry Moore, the sculptor who was born in the town, adorn the walls. Three regular beers are stocked along with a selection of guest ales. Excellent value food is served all day and children are welcome. Cask Marque accredited. Q❀◐◑⇌🚌⅃

Shoulder of Mutton

18 Methley Road, WF10 1LX (off A6032)

✪ 11 (12 Sun)-4, 7-11

☎ (01977) 736039

Tetley Dark Mild, Bitter; guest beer Ⓗ

This traditional free house started life as a farmhouse in 1632. The landlord is an enthusiastic supporter of cask ale and is justifiably proud of the many awards he has won for his cellarmanship. Expect lively conversation and a warm welcome. Traditional pub games include Ringing the Bull and Nine Men's Morris, and there are wooden puzzles available. The George Formby Society meets here on the last Wednesday of each month. Live music sessions are on Sunday, when the pub stays open all day. ♨Q❀⊟♿⇌🚌(153,189)♣P⅃

Darrington

Spread Eagle

Estcourt Road, WF8 3AP

✪ 12-3, 5-11 (midnight Fri & Sat); 12-10.30 Sun

☎ (01977) 699698

Draught Bass; Tetley Bitter; guest beers Ⓗ

Pleasant, friendly pub in the heart of the village. Popular with a wide cross-section of the community, it is very lively in the evenings. Good food is served either in the bar or in a small restaurant-style area. A quiz is held on Monday evening and there is a function room for hire. There are rumours of a ghost – a boy who was shot for horse rustling in 1685. Children are allowed in the pub until 9pm. Q❀◐◑♿🚌(408,409)P⅃

Dewsbury

Huntsman

Chidswell Lane, Shaw Cross, WF12 7SW (400m from A653/B6128 jct)

✪ 12-3 (not Mon), 7 (5.30 Thu-Sat)-11

☎ (01924) 275700

Taylor Landlord; guest beers Ⓗ

At the edge of the village, this pub affords a fine view over open countryside, particularly from the picnic benches in the garden. A warm and friendly atmosphere attracts locals as well as cyclists and walkers, aided by the traditional Yorkshire range, horse brasses and real fires. Guest beers are often from local brewers. Good value, hearty lunches are served lunchtimes Tuesday to Saturday. The house beer, Chidswell Bitter, is brewed by Highwood. ♨❀◐🚌P

Leggers Inn

Calder Valley Marina, Mill Street East, WF12 9BD (off B6409, follow brown signs to Canal Basin)

✪ 11.30 (12 Sun)-11

☎ (01924) 502846

Everards Tiger; guest beers Ⓗ

Adjacent to the marina, this converted hayloft overlooks a busy boatyard. Bric-a-brac on low beams (mind your head) includes pub memorabilia and old newspaper headlines. A pool table and games machine are in one room, while the bar area has a warming fire in winter. Six handpumps dispense the beer, one of which comes from Rooster's. A rotating guest cider or perry is also stocked and light meals are served. There is a large function room. Dewsbury bus and rail stations are within a mile. ♨❀◐◑♣●P⅃

Shepherds Boy

157 Huddersfield Road, WF13 2RP (on A644 half mile from town centre)

✪ 3-11 Mon-Wed; 12-midnight Thu; 12-1am Fri & Sat; 12-11 Sun

☎ (01924) 454116 🌐 ossett-brewery.co.uk

Ossett Pale Gold, Excelsior; Taylor Landlord; guest beers Ⓗ

An excellent reconstruction of an Ossett Brewery pub with many original features including the Webster's front door. Four comfortable drinking areas are furnished with interesting Yorkshire memorabilia. Eight handpulls dispense Ossett and guest beers including a rotating mild or stout. Quality draught and bottled international beers and a range of good wines are also available. Tuesday night is quiz night, while live music is hosted on the last Wednesday of the month. The smoking area is heated and covered. ❀♿🚌♣P⅃

West Riding Licensed Refreshment Rooms ✔

Railway Station, Wellington Road, WF13 1HF (platform 2 of Dewsbury station)

✪ 11 (12 Mon)-11 (midnight Thu-Sat); 12-11 Sun

☎ (01924) 459193 🌐 imissedthetrain.com

Black Sheep Best Bitter, Riggwelter; Taylor Dark Mild, Landlord; guest beers Ⓗ

This multi-award winning pub occupies part of the Victorian Grade II-listed building. Eight handpumps include one for Dewsbury's Anglo-Dutch Brewery – others supply a good variety of guests from micro-breweries. The pub was a finalist in the 2006 CAMRA National Pub of the Year contest. Summer and winter beer festivals and live music events are held here; see the website for dates. Lunches and evening specials are renowned. Outside is a large, decked semi-covered patio. ♨❀◐♿⇌🚌⅃

Eccleshill

Royal Oak

39 Stony Lane, BD2 2HN

✪ 11-11 (11.30 Fri & Sat)

☎ (01274) 639182

Caledonian Deuchars IPA; John Smith's Bitter; Taylor Landlord; Tetley Bitter Ⓗ

Cellarmanship awards adorn the walls of this busy, traditional local – a testament to the landlord's dedication to the real ale trade, as well as to his loyal customers. The pub has two distinct drinking areas as well as a separate tap room that enhance the traditional feel of the pub. Quizzes take place Monday and Friday teatimes and also Tuesday evening. ❀⊄🚌(640,641)♣⁵–

Elland

Barge & Barrel ✔

10-20 Park Road, HX5 9HP (on A6025 over Elland Bridge)
✪ 12-midnight (1am Fri & Sat)
☎ (01422) 350169
Abbeydale Moonshine; Black Sheep Best Bitter, Riggwelter; Elland Bargee; Phoenix Wobbly Bob; Shepherd Neame Spitfire; guest beers Ⓗ
Spacious canal and roadside pub with a large bar area that retains three of the original West Riding Brewery windows. The Eastwood Brewery is to the side of the pub and five guest ales come from micro-breweries. Beer festivals are held over the spring bank holiday weekend and in late autumn. Good food is available including a Sunday curry night. There is a pleasant drinking area outside overlooking the canal. Quiz night is Wednesday.
⛼❀◑◗🚌(537,538)♣P⁵–

Golcar

Rose & Crown

132 Knowle Road, HD7 4AN (off A6)
✪ 11.30-2.30, 5-midnight (1am Thu); 11.30-2am Fri & Sat; 11.30-midnight Sun
☎ (01484) 460160
Golcar Dark Mild, Bitter; guest beers Ⓗ
It is hard to miss this imposing roadside pub on your right as you approach Golcar village. A spacious interior has two main rooms: a lounge with paintings and a real fire in winter, and a tap room with a pool table. Both have large-screen TVs. Additionally, there is a separate function room. Note the quaint miniature model of the pub in the lounge's whisky cabinet. This is very much a community pub, with its own football team. Sunday lunches are available. ⛼❀🚌♣P⁵–

Greetland

Greetland Community & Sporting Association

Rochdale Road, HX4 8JG (on B6113)
✪ 5-11; 4-midnight Fri & Sat; 12-11 Sun
☎ (01422) 370140
Coachhouse Duckworth's Delight; Taylor range; guest beers Ⓗ
Award-winning sports and social club set back from the road at the top of Greetland Village. The club is a past winner of both the CAMRA Yorkshire and National Club of the Year awards. It has a wooden decked area outside which in summer affords great views over Halifax. A very warm welcome is offered to all visitors. ❀🚌P

Guiseley

Coopers ✔

4-6 Otley Road, LS20 8AH (opp Morrisons on A65)
✪ 12-11
☎ (01943) 878835
Black Sheep Best Bitter; Taylor Landlord; guest beers Ⓗ
One of the Market Town Taverns chain, this light, airy, modern cafe-bar serves eight ales, generally from Yorkshire micros and independents. It also stocks a large selection of continental bottled beers. A diverse range of meals is available until 9pm in a separate dining area. The large upstairs function room has regular music events and also serves as a dining room. Q❀◑◗♿⇌🚌⁵–

Guiseley Factory Workers Club

6 Town Street, LS20 9DT (off A65, near St Oswald's Church)
✪ 1-5 (4 Tue-Thu), 7-11; 1-midnight Fri; 12-midnight Sat; 11-11 Sun
☎ (01943) 874793
Tetley Bitter; guest beers Ⓗ
Small, friendly working men's club, a meeting place for community groups, local clubs and societies. A traditional three-roomed layout includes a lounge, snooker room and concert room hosting Saturday night turns. Quiz night is Sunday; sports are shown on a large-screen TV on Friday and Saturday. A beer festival is held in April. There is a large walled and lawned beer garden at the rear. Show your CAMRA membership card or a copy of this Guide for entry. Leeds CAMRA Pub of the Year 2006. ❀⇌🚌♣P

Ings

45A Ings Lane, LS20 9HR (off A65, near Guiseley Town FC)
✪ 11-11 (midnight Fri & Sat); 12-11 Sun
☎ (01943) 873315
Black Sheep Best Bitter; John Smith's Bitter; Taylor Landlord; Tetley Bitter Ⓗ
From the pub's rear windows there are scenic views of the surrounding wet marshland area from which it derives its name. The interior features three tiled fireplaces and suspended tabletop canopy lighting plus a memorable collection of artefacts and pictures. A music quiz on Tuesday and a general knowledge quiz on Thursday provide entertainment.
⛼Q❀⇌🚌P

Red Lion

The Green, LS20 9BB
✪ 11-11 (midnight Fri & Sat); 12-11 Sun
☎ (01943) 878835
Tetley Mild, Bitter; guest beers Ⓗ
A traditional pub, recently refurbished, in the old Towngate area of the town and opposite the parish church of St Oswald. The main room is divided into two separate areas, plus a games room with pool table and dartboard. Sporting events are shown on one of three large screens. Thursday is quiz night and food is served 12-6pm daily except Sunday and Monday. 🚌

Halifax

Big Six

10 Horsfall Street, Saville Park, HX1 3HG (off A646, Skircoat Moor road at King Cross)
✪ 5-11; 3.30-11.30 Fri; 12-11.30 Sat; 12-11 Sun
☎ (01422) 350169

Adnams Bitter; guest beers Ⓗ
Busy, convivial mid-terraced pub close to the Free School Lane recreation ground. A through corridor divides two lounges from the bar, which has standing room and a cosy seating area, plus artefacts from the erstwhile Big Six mineral water company that operated from the premises a century ago. Guest beers on offer are chiefly from respected regional and local micro-breweries. Dog are welcome. The outside area for smokers is across Horsfall Street. ᗰQ❀🚌♣

Three Pigeons ★

1 Sun Fold, South Parade, HX1 2LX
⏲ 3 (12 Thu-Sat)-11.30; 12-11 Sun
☎ (01422) 347001
Ossett Pale Gold, Excelsior, 3 Pigs; Taylor Landlord; guest beers Ⓗ
This CAMRA National Inventory listed and award-winning pub dates from 1932. Its period features have been restored following its acquisition by Ossett Brewery and the decor is very much in keeping with the period. It has a central octagonal space with a painted ceiling and three of its four rooms radiate from this space. Usually there are four guest beers on offer including one from Ossett and a dark beer. Real cider is stocked, together with a selection of Belgian beers. ᗰQ❀⇌🚌♣●

William IV ✔

247 King Cross Road, HX1 3JL
⏲ 11-11; 11.30-10.30 Sun
☎ (01422) 354889
Tetley Bitter Ⓗ
Popular watering hole located in Kings Cross shopping street. The lounge has seating and standing space facing the bar, and to the rear there is a small public bar served by a hatch. A raised drinking area created from former shop premises provides additional seating. Guests can enjoy lunches served Monday to Saturday, or keep up to date with sporting activities on the TV screens. There are picnic benches out back for outdoor drinking and ample parking nearby. ❀⊟🚌♣

Haworth

Fleece Inn ✔

67 Main Street, BD22 8DA
⏲ 12 (10 Sat)-11.30; 10-10.30 Sun
☎ (01535) 642172 🌐 timothy-taylor.co.uk/fleeceinn
Taylor Dark Mild, Best Bitter, Golden Best, Landlord, Ram Tam Ⓗ
A three-storey former coaching inn situated halfway up the historic, pretty and steep cobbled Haworth main street. The Haworth brass band can be heard outside on some evenings rehearsing in their band room above the pub; combined with the surroundings, this provides a real traditional Yorkshire atmosphere. The pub offers good beer, food and accommodation to visitors, and is also popular with locals. A range of foreign bottled beers is stocked.
ᗰ⛟◐♿⚑⇌(KWVLR)🚌(664,665)

Haworth Old Hall Inn ✔

8 Sun Street, BD22 8BP
⏲ 11-11 (11.30 Thu; midnight Fri & Sat); 12-11 Sun
☎ (01535) 642709 🌐 hawortholdhall.co.uk
Jennings Bitter, Cumberland Ale, Cocker Hoop, Sneck Lifter, seasonal beers; guest beers Ⓗ
Magnificent Yorkshire stone Tudor manor house at the foot of the historic Haworth main street, whose impressive interior and exterior merit a visit on their own. The pub also impresses in its offerings of quality ale, food and accommodation. David's popular quiz on a Thursday night is a legend, regularly attracting more than 15 local teams competing for a cash prize. ᗰ❀⛟◐♿⚑⇌(KWVLR)🚌P⊱

Keighley & Worth Valley Railway Buffet Car

Keighley & Worth Valley Light Railway Ltd, Haworth Station, BD22 8NJ (join at any station on Worth Valley line)
⏲ 11-5.15 Sat & Sun; Mon-Fri Jul, Aug and school hols; other dates as advertised (check timetable)
☎ (01535) 645214 🌐 kwvr.co.uk
Beer range varies Ⓗ
Situated in the heart of Bronte country, this 1950s-style steam railway line has been run by volunteers for the past 40 years. Famous for the Railway Children film, the line runs every weekend and also weekdays during school holidays. The buffet car offers up to three ever-changing beers, decanted into tea urns for serving on board. Special events include a beer and music weekend in October. Please note that a ticket to travel must be purchased. Q⚑⇌🚌P

Heath

King's Arms ☆ ✔

Heath Common, WF1 5SL (off A655 Wakefield-Normanton road)
⏲ 12-3, 5-11 (11-midnight Sat) winter; 12-11 (midnight Sat) summer; 12-11 Sun
☎ (01924) 377527
Clarks Classic Blonde; Taylor Landlord; Tetley Bitter; guest beers Ⓗ
Built in the early 1700s and converted to a pub in 1841, the King's Arms is one of four pubs owned by Clarks Brewery of Wakefield. The interior consists of three oak-panelled rooms, lit by gas lamps. Bar snacks are served lunchtimes and evenings; there is also a restaurant serving evening meals. Quiz night is Tuesday. Children are welcome in the conservatory. There is disabled access to both the pub and toilets. ᗰQ☺❀◐♿🚌♣P⊱

Heaton

Kings Arms

10 Highgate, BD9 4BB (off A650 Keighley Road, opp St Bede's School)
⏲ 12-midnight
☎ (01274) 543165 🌐 kingsarmsheaton.co.uk
Copper Dragon Golden Pippin; Taylor Golden Best; guest beers Ⓗ
Situated near the top of the urban village of Heaton, this comfortable pub is thriving once again thanks to the landlord's commitment to beers from local breweries and the popular folk and blues music at weekends. Now with an open plan interior, there is a large games room on the first floor. For alfresco drinkers there is a choice of either a rear garden or a

front patio. The guest beer is often from the Saltaire brewery. ❀🚌(680)♣⚟

Hebden Bridge

Fox & Goose

9 Heptonstall Road, HX7 6AZ (on A646)
11.30 (7.30 Mon)-midnight; 12-11.30 Sun
☎ (01422) 842649 🌐 foxale.co.uk
Millstone Margery's Tiddlywink; guest beers Ⓗ
Family-owned, traditional free house and local CAMRA Pub of the Year 2004 and 2006. A hillside beer garden built by the owners using local materials provides a superb view across the Calder Valley. Two beer festivals are held each year and live music sessions are hosted including a folk club on the first Sunday of the month. The house beer is brewed exclusively for the pub and is unfined, so is suitable for vegans. The four guest beers include a good variety of ales. ♨Q❀⇌🚌♣●⚟

Moyles

4-10 New Road, HX7 8AD (on A646 opp canal marina)
7.30-11 (10.30 Sun)
☎ (01422) 845272
Pictish Brewers Gold; guest beers Ⓗ
A stylish four-room bar-restaurant with minimalist decor but comfy sofas. Food is a major attraction here, but the beer is well kept and served from handpumps below bar level. Four guest beers always come from micro-breweries. The decking area outside at the front of the pub provides a stage from which to observe life on the street and the canal. ♨Q❀🛏◑♿⇌🚌⚟

New Delight Inn ✔

Jack Bridge, Colden, HX7 7HT
5 (12 Sat)-midnight; 12-midnight (10 winter) Sun
☎ (01422) 846178
Black Sheep Best Bitter; Bridestones Bottleneck Bride; guest beers Ⓗ
This splendid rural pub was recently saved from closure. It nestles at the head of a steep Pennine valley, offering fine views. The bar links directly to two of the four rooms, with stone-flagged floors throughout. Open fires are particularly welcoming in winter. The landlord runs Bridestones Brewery, which operates from a nearby farm, and one of the guest beers is likely to be another one of his brews. The pub is gaining a good reputation for wholesome home-cooked food. ♨Q❀🛏◑⛺🚌P

Stubbing Wharf

King Street, HX7 6LU (on A646 ½ mile W of Hebden Bridge)
12-11 (midnight Fri & Sat)
☎ (01422) 844107 🌐 stubbingwharf.com
Black Sheep Best Bitter; Copper Dragon Golden Pippin; Taylor Landlord; guest beers Ⓗ
Busy, friendly pub sandwiched between the river and the canal, popular with drinkers and diners and used by various community groups. There are stone, wood and carpeted floors, a good display of hops, and pictures with a canal theme on the wall. Seating by the canal can be enjoyed in good weather. Two or three guest beers are from smaller breweries, and one or more ciders are supplemented by a summer cider festival. Gents disabled toilets are planned. ♨❀◑♿🚌(590,592)●P⚟

Heckmondwike

New Charnwood

4 Westgate, WF16 0EH (on A638 near green)
11-11; closed Mon; 12-10.30 Sun
☎ (01924) 406512
Taylor Landlord; guest beers Ⓗ
An inviting front garden leads to this attractive bay-windowed former Oddfellows Hall, now described as a pub and dining room. Guest beers are mostly from local breweries and usually include a dark mild or old ale. The 80-seat function room also has handpumps. Freshly prepared food is cooked to order at lunchtime and Wednesday to Saturday evenings. A recent Yorkshire Pudding competition winner, the pub also offers superb local ice creams including a Timothy Taylor Landlord flavour. Good bus links. ❀◑♿🚌P⚟

Hipperholme

Cock o' the North

The Conclave, South Edge Works, Brighouse Road, HX3 8EF
5 (4 Fri)-11; 12-11 Sat & Sun
☎ (07974) 544980 🌐 myspace.com/cockofthenorthbar
Cock o' the North Cock o' the North, Jamaican Ginger, Uncle Jon; guest beers Ⓗ
Situated in a red sectional building next to the imposing Vulcan works, the bar is to the rear of the Cock o' the North Brewery. A single room divided by a glass panel, with polished floors and fittings, the interior is inspired by 1930s Art Deco ocean liners. A showcase for the growing range of beers (130 to date), there are usually 10 to 12 ales on offer, with occasional guests, increasing to 25 during frequent beer festivals. The atmosphere is relaxed, with a friendly, varied clientele. ❀🚌P

Travellers Inn

53 Tanhouse Hill, HX3 8HN (on A58, back of camping centre)
12-11.30
☎ (01422) 202494
Ossett Pale Gold, Travellers Ale, Excelsior; Taylor Landlord; guest beers Ⓗ
Situated opposite the former railway station, this traditional, friendly stone-built local has taken in adjoining cottages to create a series of distinct spaces. Children are welcome until 7pm in the upper area, where a wide selection of board games is available. Dogs are also permitted during quiet periods. There is a small south-facing roadside seating area. A wide range of Belgian bottled beers, eight malt whiskies and 27 wines are stocked, plus the occasional traditional cider. A covered yard is provided for smokers. ♨❀🚌♣●⚟

Holbeck

Cross Keys

Water Lane, LS11 5WD
12-11 (10.30 Sun)

(0113) 243 3711 the-crosskeys.com
Beer range varies
Exposed beams, stone flags, tiles and bare brickwork abound in this pub which is under the same ownership as the city-centre North Bar and Reliance. Up to four guest beers are served, with one handpump reserved for a stout or porter, plus two ever-changing guest beers. Downstairs two rooms wrap around a central bar area, each with its own wood burning stove. Upstairs is another bar and function room. Sunday meals are served 12-8pm.
(Leeds)

Grove Inn

Back Row, LS11 5PL
12-11 (midnight Fri & Sat); 12-10.30 Sun
(0113) 243 9254
Caledonian Deuchars IPA, 80/-; Daleside Blonde; Moorhouses Black Cat; guest beers
Surrounded by office blocks and situated next to the tallest building in Yorkshire, the Grove is an oasis of history in a sea of modernity. A rare surviving example of a traditional West Riding corridor pub, first mentioned in a survey of Leeds in 1850, its four rooms include a concert room and a tap room. A wide variety of live music is played here. Weston's Old Rosie cider is available. Winner of many CAMRA Leeds awards in recent years.
(Leeds)

Holmfirth

Farmers Arms

2-4 Liphill Bank Road, Burnlee, HD9 2LR (off A635, below Compo's Café)
5 (12 Fri-Sun)-midnight
(01484) 683713
Adnams Bitter; Greene King IPA; John Smith's Bitter; Taylor Landlord; Wells Bombardier; guest beers
Three weavers' cottages were knocked together in the 1920s to create this delightful community pub situated in a quiet corner of 'Summer Wine' country. The pub has a warm, relaxing and welcoming atmosphere and is popular with locals. Home-cooked food is served lunchtime and evenings – Sue's Meat & Potato Pie is a must – to complement the wide range of beers from local and national brewers. Also unmissable is folk night on the last Thursday of the month. P

Rose & Crown (Nook)

7 Victoria Square, HD9 2DN (down alley off Hollowgate)
11.30 (12 Sun)-midnight
(01484) 683960 thenookholmfirth.co.uk
Kelham Island Kelham Gold; Moorhouses Black Cat Mild; Taylor Best Bitter, Landlord; Tetley Bitter; guest beers
There has been a pub on this site since 1754 and the Nook has featured over 30 times in the Guide. A deceptively spacious pub, it provides home-cooked food all day, with the speciality being the Nook Burger. In addition to the usual pub games, poker is very popular, with a monthly tournament. A further attraction is live music on the last Saturday of the month. An annual beer festival is held and a micro-brewery opens in 2009.

Horbury

Boons

6 Queen Street, WF4 6LP
11-3, 5-11; 11-11 Fri & Sat; 12-10.30 Sun
(01924) 280442
Clarks Classic Blonde; John Smith's Bitter; Taylor Landlord; guest beers
Centrally situated just off the High Street, this Clarks Brewery tied house caters for all age groups and is a real community pub. Three guest ales are always available, alongside beers from the Clarks range. At the back of the pub there is a large outdoor drinking area which is used to hold the annual beer festival in summer.

Horbury Bridge

Bingley Arms

221 Bridge Road, WF4 5NL (between River Calder and Aire & Calder Canal)
12-midnight (10.30 Sun)
(01924) 281331
Black Sheep Best Bitter; Caledonian Deuchars IPA; Tetley Bitter
This pub is bordered by the River Calder on one side and by the Aire & Calder Navigation Canal on the other. It has two rooms, both with open fires. The pub is named after the Earl of Bingley who funded the building of the nearby canal; it has its own moorings on the canal, popular in the summer months. It also has a good-sized beer garden which gets busy on summer evenings and weekends.
P

Horsforth

Town Street Tavern

16-18 Town Street, LS18 4RJ
12-11 (10.30 Sun)
(0113) 281 9996 markettowntaverns.co.uk
Black Sheep Best Bitter; Leeds Best Bitter; Taylor Best Bitter; guest beers
Once a shop on Horsforth's main street, this dog-friendly pub offers a great range of British ales and a selection of foreign beers on draught and in bottles. Many of the guest ales are sourced from local micro-breweries. The upstairs brasserie offers excellent food from 6pm while the downstairs bar serves food daily. The bar is adorned with breweriana plus reminders of the many ales previously served. A small patio area provides space for outdoor drinking. Q

Huddersfield

Cherry Tree

16-18 John William Street, HD1 1BA
9-midnight (1am Fri-Sat)
(01484) 448190
Greene King IPA, Abbot; Marston's Pedigree; guest beers
Town-centre Wetherspoon pub converted from a bed shop in part of a 1960s office block. It has one large room, with a raised area at the back and a small downstairs

lounge. There are seven guest beers, many from local micros, and two real ciders – Weston's Old Rosie and Vintage. Close to Huddersfield Station. ◑♿⇌🚌●

Grove

2 Spring Grove Street, HD1 4BP
✪ 12-11 (midnight Fri & Sat)
☎ (01484) 430113 ⊕ groveinn.co.uk
College Green Molly's Chocolate Stout; Empire Grove Grog; Fuller's Chiswick, ESB; Taylor Golden Best, Landlord; Thornbridge Jaipur IPA; guest beers ⊞
The Grove attracts beer lovers from across the region and beyond. Eleven guest ales, many rare for the region and personally selected by the landlord on his many beer expeditions, always include mild, stout and strong ale plus seasonals. This two-room corner pub also offers 180-plus bottled beers and eight foreign and European draughts, including a guest (see website). The cider is Thatcher's Cheddar Valley. Enjoy your pint in airy yet traditional surroundings featuring interesting artwork, unusual bar snacks and spontaneous folk music. Q❀⊟⇌🚌●▽

King's Head

St George's Square, HD1 1JF (in station buildings)
✪ 11.30-11; 12-10.30 Sun
☎ (01484) 511058 ⊕ the-station-tavern.co.uk
Beer range varies ⊞
Despite reverting to an earlier name and some light refurbishment, the former Station Tavern remains the same quirky place, offering a variety of 10 beers. The main mosaic-tile floored room features live bands on Sunday afternoon, a piano singalong on Monday evening and monthly folk and blues evenings. There are two smaller rooms, one with a computer. ⛼♿⇌🚌

Marsh Liberal Club

31 New Hey Road, Marsh, HD3 4AL (on A640)
✪ 12-2 (Mon & Fri only), 7-11; 12-11 Sat & Sun
☎ (01484) 420152 ⊕ marshlib.co.uk
Taylor Golden Best, Best Bitter, Landlord; guest beers ⊞
An impressive ashlar stone-faced Grade II listed building is home to this friendly club. Two guest beers are normally available, usually from independent micros. The extensive ground floor has four separate rooms, with snooker and pool tables available. Crown green bowling is popular outside in the summer. Finalist in the Club Mirror Cask Club of the Year awards two years running, the building has wheelchair access and a disabled WC. Show this Guide or a CAMRA membership card to be signed in. ❀♿🚌♣P

Rat & Ratchet

40 Chapel Hill, HD1 3EB (on A616 below ring road)
✪ 12 (3 Mon & Tue)-midnight (12.30am Fri & Sat); 12-11 Sun
☎ (01484) 542400
Ossett Pale Gold, Silver King, Excelsior; Taylor Landlord; guest beers ⊞
This award-winning traditional pub, a long standing fixture on the Huddersfield real ale scene, boasts over a dozen handpumps. A mild, a stout or porter and a real cider are always available. Brewery advertisements and music posters adorn the walls, and the rear room is heated by a welcoming stove during the winter months. In summer a beer festival is held, plus a mild festival in May. Outside at the rear is a terrace with seating.
⛼❀◑🚌●P⁵–

Star Inn

7 Albert Street, HD1 3PJ (off A616)
✪ 5 (12 Sat)-11; closed Mon; 12-10.30
☎ (01484) 545443 ⊕ thestarinn.info
Pictish Brewers Gold; Taylor Best Bitter, Landlord; guest beers ⊞
Traditional back-street local that has earned deserved success since its opening. The emphasis here is on quality ale, good conversation and a friendly atmosphere achieved without TV, pool table, jukebox or games machines. One large drinking area surrounds the bar and an open fire. A wide range of beers is on offer from seven constantly changing handpulls, with one pump dedicated to mild, stout and porter. Three regular beer festivals are held in the large garden marquee. ⛼Q❀♿🚌⁵–

White Cross Inn ✔

2 Bradley Road, Bradley, HD2 1XD (on A62)
✪ 11.45-11; 12-10.30 Sun
☎ (01484) 425728
Copper Dragon Black Gold; Taylor Golden Best; guest beers ⊞
This busy community pub, located at the busy crossroad of Leeds Road and Bradley Road, offers a warm welcome to both locals and passers-by. The large lounge extends either side of the central bar area where four guest beers are on handpump. Past landlords are recorded from 1806 until the present day. The Cross has won a number of awards for its beer quality, including Huddersfield CAMRA Pub Of The Year 2005 and Cask Marque accreditation. An annual beer festival is held in February.
❀◑♿🚌(202,203)♣P⁵–

Idle

Idle Working Mens Club

23 High Street, BD10 8NB
✪ 12-4 Mon & Fri, 7-11; 11-5, 7-11 Sat; 11-4, 7-11 Sun
☎ (01274) 613602 ⊕ idle-workingmensclub.com
Tetley Bitter, guest bitter ⊞
This club attracts members simply because of its name, and even has souvenir merchandise available to buy. The concert room hosts live entertainment on weekend evenings, while the lounge offers a quieter alternative. The games room downstairs houses two full-size snooker tables plus a large-screen TV for sports events. Parking is available at a nearby doctors' surgery, outside hours. Show this Guide or a current CAMRA membership card to gain admission. 🚌♣

Symposium Ale & Wine Bar ✔

7 Albion Road, BD10 9PY
✪ 12-2-30 (closed Mon & Tue), 5.30-11; 11-midnight Fri & Sat; 12-10.30 Sun
☎ (01274) 616587 ⊕ markettowntaverns.co.uk
Beer range varies ⊞
At the heart of Idle village, this popular bar and restaurant places equal emphasis on the quality of both food and beer. A member of

the Market Town Taverns group, it hosts occasional themed evenings and menus. The beers change consistently, with suppliers predominantly from the north of England. A wide range of foreign beers is available in bottle and on draught. The rear snug leads to a terrace which is very popular in summer.
Q❀◑⊱

Ilkley

Bar T'at ✔

LS29 9DZ
⏲ 12-11
☎ (01943) 608888 🌐 markettowntaverns.co.uk
Black Sheep Best Bitter; Copper Dragon Golden Pippin; Taylor Landlord; guest beers Ⓗ
Popular side-street pub from the Market Town Taverns group, renowned for the quality of its beer and food. Guest ales usually include a mild or porter, plus brews from Yorkshire micros. A wide choice of good foreign beers is available in bottles and on draught, including Belgian fruit beers. Home-cooked food is on the menu every day. This three-storey building has a music-free bar area. It stands next to the main town centre car park.
Q❀◐◑⇌🚌⊱

Riverside Hotel

Riverside Gardens, Bridge Lane, LS29 9EU
⏲ 10-11 (10.30 Sun)
☎ (01943) 607338 🌐 ilkley-riversidehotel.com
Copper Dragon Best Bitter; Samuel Smith OBB; Tetley Bitter Ⓗ
Family-run hotel with 10 rooms, set by the River Wharfe in a popular park. The adjacent fish and chip shop and ice cream servery, also run by the hotel, are popular in summer. Meals are served until early evening and the bar runs a happy hour on week days, 4-8pm. The open fire is a welcome sight in cold weather. The start of the Dales Way is at the old pack horse bridge close to the hotel.
♔❀🛏◐◑⇌🚌P⊱

Keighley

Boltmakers Arms ✔

117 East Parade, BD21 5HX
⏲ 11-11 (midnight Tue-Sat); 12-11 Sun
☎ (01535) 661936 🌐 timothy-taylor.co.uk/boltmakers
Taylor Dark Mild, Best Bitter, Golden Best, Landlord, Ram Tam; guest beer Ⓗ
This classic Keighley town centre pub is the unofficial Taylor Brewery tap and a recent local CAMRA Pub of the Season winner. The tiny split-level layout is unfeasibly small, but adds character to the place. The licensees take pride in the pub and it is always very welcoming. Brewery, whisky and music memorabilia adorn the walls. If you like your beer distilled, there is also a fine selection of single malts. Quiz night is Tuesday and occasional live music is hosted. ♔❀⇌🚌♣🍎⊱

Brown Cow ✔

5 Cross Leeds Street, BD21 2LQ
⏲ 4-11; 12-10.30 Sun 🌐 browncowkeighley.co.uk
Taylor Dark Mild (summer), Best Bitter, Golden Best, Landlord, Ram Tam (winter); guest beers Ⓗ
Popular, friendly open-plan local with a side room used for meetings. Now in its fifth year of real ale renaissance, 600-plus guest ales have been sold since it reopened. The pub features local breweriana, including the original sign from Bradford's Trough Brewery. Other curios include a collection of policemen's helmets. Bad language is banned. Guest beers are sourced mainly from local micros, often from the Brown Cow Brewery.
♔❀⇌🚌♣P

Cricketers Arms

Coney Lane, BD21 5JE
⏲ 11.30-midnight; 12-11.30 Sun
☎ (01535) 669912
Moorhouses Premier Bitter; guest beers Ⓗ
Back street pub revitalised by frequent live music sessions, with bands from near and far. The ground level bar is now complemented by a downstairs bar (open Thursday to Saturday evenings). Note the interesting montage of photographs taken of regulars at the top of the stairwell. Five guest beers are served from regional and micro-breweries from nationwide, and a range of foreign bottled beers is stocked. Occasional beer festivals are held. ❀⇌🚌🍎⊱

Friendly Inn ✔

2 Aireworth Street, BD21 1NS
⏲ 4 (12 Fri)-midnight; 12-1am Sat; 12-midnight Sun
☎ (01535) 665444
Taylor Dark Mild, Golden Best, Best Bitter, Landlord Ⓗ
Located just outside the town centre, this corner pub retains a slightly old-fashioned feel. A typically small Timothy Taylor hostelry, it has been reinvigorated by new tenants into a real community town centre local, and is especially busy on its frequent quiz and games nights. This is possibly the only pub that offers the oportunity to compare electric- and hand-pumped Golden Best and Best Bitter. ⇌🚌♣

Livery Rooms ✔

89-97 North Street, BD21 3AA (near jct of Cavendish St and North St)
⏲ 9-midnight (1am Fri & Sat)
☎ (01535) 682950
Greene King IPA, Abbot; Marston's Pedigree; guest beers Ⓗ
Opened in June 2004 by Wetherspoon, this pub has become very popular with beer fans and diners alike. The premises have previously been stables, a temperance hall, a bingo hall and several shops, and this varied history is displayed, using different art forms, on the walls throughout the pub. The guest beer policy gives strong support to ales from local micros. Conveniently located close to the bus station. ♔◐◑♿⇌🚌🍎⊱

Ledsham

Chequers Inn

Claypit Lane, LS25 5LP
⏲ 11-11; closed Sun
☎ (01977) 683135
Brown Cow Bitter, seasonal beers; John Smith's Bitter; Taylor Landlord; Theakston Best Bitter Ⓗ
A mile to the north of Fairburn Ings bird sanctuary, this is a quintessential old English

country pub (with well-regarded restaurant and idyllic garden) in the picturesque village of Ledsham. It has two main rooms either side of the bar, plus two smaller rooms complete with oak beams, wood fires, jugs, brasses, racing memorabilia, old photographs and beer mats from previous guest beers. An extensive range of meals and sandwiches is served at all times, and can be enjoyed outside in the summer.

Leeds: City

Mr Foley's Cask Ale House

159 The Headrow, LS1 5RG (opp town hall)
11-11; 12-10.30 Sun
(0113) 242 9674 yorkbrew.demon.co.uk
Beer range varies

Named after Patrick James Foley, founder of Pearl Assurance, in whose Grade II-listed building you will find York Brewery's first venture outside its home city. A real treasure, the well-stocked bar, with 10 handpumps, provides an extensive selection of bottled ales and ciders, plus international draught beers. The ample interior comprises four distinct split-level areas, including a bar area with stools, a raised area with tables and comfortable seating, plus a well-apportioned balcony and a large, comfortable room with Chesterfield settees.

North Bar

24 New Briggate, LS1 6NU
12-1am (2am Wed-Sat); 12-10.30 Sun
(0113) 242 4540 northbar.com
Beer range varies

Now more than 10 years old, this pioneering bar is one of just a few in Leeds serving handpumped beer. The long, thin bar is covered in fonts and includes three handpumps, one serving an ever-changing dark beer and one a Rooster's. Plain walls towards the front of the pub exhibit art, while at the rear a huge beer menu is displayed. The mix of real ale and global beer, plus the simple platter snacks, attracts a diverse and interesting clientele. Regular beer festivals are held.

Palace

Kirkgate, LS2 7DJ
11-11.30 (midnight Fri & Sat); 12-11 Sun
(0113) 244 5882
Draught Bass; Tetley Bitter; guest beers

This large one-roomed pub on two levels still bears traces of its former three-roomed layout. Up to eight regularly changing guest beers are on offer, always including a mild/stout or porter, a Rooster's/Outlaw beer and Weston's Old Rosie Cider on gravity. First recorded as an inn in 1841, the pub was once owned by Melbourne Brewery; several features of its ownership survive. Set into the parish chuchyard wall at the front of the pub is the East Bar Stone, which once marked the City boundary.

Scarbrough Hotel

Bishopsgate Street, LS1 5DY
11-midnight; 12-10.30 Sun
(0113) 243 4590
Tetley Bitter; guest beers

Historic pub, formerly the King's Arms and renamed in the late 1890s after the noted theatre impresario Henry Scarbrough. Now a vibrant city-centre pub, it has been opened out into one bar with several drinking areas. Up to seven guest beers are served, increasing to 16 when the extra bar is used during beer festivals (held jointly with the Grove) in January and August. The latter celebrates Yorkshire Day, with Yorkshire ales and produce. Cider and perry are on gravity.

Templar

2 Templar Street, LS2 7NU
11-11; 12-10.30 Sun
(0113) 245 9751
Tetley Mild, Bitter; Wells Bombardier; guest beer

The fine cream and green tiled exterior of the pub is emblazoned with Melborne Arms down the side, a reminder of a long gone Leeds brewery. Inside there is wood panelling and leaded windows with stained glass featuring heraldic shields and a stylised picture of a Knight Templar. At one end of the bar are some drinking booths and at the other an area with an attractive red tiled fireplace.

Town Hall Tavern

17 Westgate, LS1 2RA
11.30-11; closed Sun
(0113) 244 0765
Taylor Golden Best, Best Bitter, Landlord, seasonal beers

Originally three rooms, the interior has been opened out into a single room with several distinct areas – traces of the former layout can be seen in the fabric of the building. Comfortable seating areas are set aside for drinking and dining and there is space for those who prefer to stand and sup. Close to the courts and the town hall, the pub attracts a mixed clientele. The walls are adorned with cartoons and pictures of bygone Leeds.

Victoria Family & Commercial

28 Great George Street, LS1 3DL (behind town hall)
11.30-11; closed Sun
(0113) 245 1386
Black Sheep Best Bitter; Taylor Landlord; Tetley Mild, Bitter; guest beers

This astonishing red-brick Victorian façade is a fine example of the city architecture that is gradually being lost to redevelopment. Inside, the large, ornate entrance hall is a popular, busy place, yet has a cosy, entertaining feel thanks to booths with large tables separated by wood and glass partitions, and a mixed clientele. At the front a raised area contains more tables, a TV and games machine. The ales are always plentiful and of good quality. Jazz music plays every Thursday. Meals are served daily. Q

Whitelocks First City Luncheon Bar ★

Turks Head Yard, Off Briggate, LS1 6HB (down alley near Marks & Spencer)
11-11; 12-10.30 Sun
(0113) 245 3950 whitelocks.co.uk

ENGLAND

Caledonian Deuchars IPA; John Smith's Bitter; Theakston Best Bitter, Old Peculier; guest beers Ⓗ
Traditionally regarded as the finest pub interior in Leeds, concern about the future of its splendid features led to the formation of the 'Friends of Whitelocks', to safeguard the pub for future generations to enjoy. The pub dates back to the 16th century and features on CAMRA's National Inventory of historic pub interiors. The Top Bar is now open Wednesday to Saturday. No discerning drinker should miss this gem.

Leeds: North

Arcadia Ale & Wine Bar

34 Arndale Centre, Otley Road, Headingley, LS6 2UE
12-11
(0113) 274 5599 marketowntaverns.co.uk
Black Sheep Best Bitter; Elland seasonal beers; Taylor Landlord; guest beers Ⓗ
Part of the Market Town Taverns chain, this award-winning conversion of a former bank has a ground-floor bar area and an upstairs mezzanine floor overlooking the busy Otley Road. Eight beers tends to be locally sourced from Yorkshire micros, and there is an extensive range of bottled and draught beers from Europe and beyond. The pub has a small library of reference books and games. Dogs are welcome, but unfortunately children are not admitted.

Reliance

76-78 North Street, LS2 7PN
12-11 (midnight Fri & Sat); 12-10.30 Sun
(0113) 295 6060
Beer range varies Ⓗ
A light and airy three-roomed bar comprising a mezzanine restaurant, a bar and a side room, with bare boards throughout, an eclectic mix of tables, squashy sofas and chairs, as well as local art for sale on the walls. The pub is part of the North Empire group, with an impressive range of draught and bottled beers assured on the large chalk boards, as well as two regularly changing ales.

Three Hulats

13 Harrogate Road, Chapel Allerton, LS7 3NB
12-midnight (1am Fri & Sat); 9-midnight Sun
(0113) 262 0524
Greene King IPA, Abbot; Marston's Pedigree; Theakston Old Peculier; guest beers Ⓗ
This 1930s-built Tetley's house, known as the Mexborough, has been revitalised as an out-of-town Wetherspoon outlet. Eight handpumps dispense regular and changing guest beers, with Northern micros particularly popular with drinkers. Three drinking areas are separated by a long corridor. Outside tables are provided for the more hardy. The old nightclub dance floor is now the dining area, where families are welcome until 9pm. Prints of bygone Chapel Allerton adorn the walls. Thursday Curry night is always popular.
P

Linthwaite

Sair Inn

139 Lane Top, HD7 5SG (top of Hoyle Ing, off A62)
SE100143
5 (12 Fri & Sat)-11; 12-10.30 Sun
(01484) 842370
Linfit Bitter, Gold Medal, Special, Autumn Gold, English Guineas Stout, Old Eli Ⓗ
Iconic brew pub perched on a hillside overlooking the Colne Valley, much sought out by visitors and locals alike. A long-standing entry in this Guide, it has been under the same keen management for over 20 years and has won many awards. The pub's layout reflects its carefree individuality and community spirit – a cluster of small rooms radiating from a central bar, where information on local events and attractions is displayed and a real fire provides warmth in winter. Weston's 1st Quality cider is available.
P

Liversedge

Black Bull

37 Halifax Road, WF15 6JR (on A649, W of A62)
12-midnight (1am Fri & Sat)
(01924) 403779
Ossett Pale Gold, Black Bull, Excelsior; guest beers Ⓗ
The first of a maturing chain of Ossett Brewery pubs, this 300-year-old building retains much of its original shape despite having been partly opened out. As well as a bar snug there are four further rooms in various styles, one dubbed the chapel thanks to its attractive wood and stained glass. Nine handpulls include a mild or dark ale, and a good selection of wines and continental beers are also served. Children are allowed until 8pm. The rear patio has a covered, heated area.
P

Swan

380 Bradford Road, WF15 6JE (A62/A638 jct)
12 (4.30 Mon)-midnight (1am Sat); 12-11.30 Sun
(01924) 401855
Daleside Bitter; Taylor Landlord; Tetley Bitter; guest beers Ⓗ
Friendly, busy modern community pub midway between Cleckheaton and Heckmondwike with a strong darts following, pool table and Sky Sports in the snug bar. A large, versatile main bar is home to well-supported karaoke nights on Thursday, Friday and Saturday. Jazz night is Wednesday and quiz night Sunday. Food is served on weekend lunchtimes. Generous support is also given to Liversedge ARLFC. Two heated, covered smoking areas add to the attractions of this local. P

Marsden

Riverhead Brewery Tap

Argyle Street, HD7 6BR (overlooking River Colne)
12-11.30 (1am Fri); 11-1am Sat; 12-midnight Sun
(01484) 841270
Ossett Pale Gold, Silver King; Riverhead Sparth Mild, Butterley Bitter; Taylor Landlord; guest beers Ⓗ

A popular brewpub, formerly a Co-op, now part of Ossett Brewery's estate, at the centre of village life. The pub has been refurbished to a high standard, providing a relaxed atmosphere and pleasant surroundings. Great pictures of Marsden adorn the walls. Fantastic food is served in the restaurant and there is a riverside terrace for alfresco drinking. The micro-brewery is visible from the bar. Up to 10 beers are available, usually five from Riverhead, three from Ossett, Landlord and a guest. Q❀≉⊟(350,352)

Tunnel End Inn

Waters Road, HD7 6NF
8 (5 Tue-Thu)-11; 12-midnight Fri-Sun
☎ (01484) 844636 tunnelendinn.com
Black Sheep Best Bitter; Taylor Landlord; guest beers ⊞
A friendly pub set in magnificent Pennine scenery in the upper Colne Valley close to the Standedge Tunnel – the longest, deepest and highest canal tunnel in the UK. Guest beers come from local micros and are well kept. Delicious home-cooked food is served Friday-Sunday, while Wednesday night is Meat and Tatty pie night. Customers are assured of a warm, personable welcome from the proprietors. Dogs are permitted.
⌂Q❀⊭◑◗≉⊟♣

Mirfield

Navigation Tavern

6 Station Road, WF14 8NL (between rail station and canal)
11.30-11 (midnight Fri & Sat); 12-10.30 Sun
☎ (01924) 492476
John Smith's Bitter; Theakston Best Bitter, Black Bull Bitter, XB, Old Peculier ⊞
Congenial canalside free house next to a boatyard on the Calder and Hebble Navigation near the centre of Mirfield, and a stone's throw from Mirfield railway station. The pub is popular with all ages, hosting an active sports and pool team, and offering a comprehensive range from Theakston (all at the same competitive price). The pub is registered as an Ambassador for Theakston's Beer. Ring ahead to check food availability. The smokers' area is covered. ❀⊭≉⊟♣P⅟

Mytholmroyd

Shoulder of Mutton

86 New Road, HX7 5DZ (on B6138, near station)
11.30-3, 7-11; 7-11 Tue; 11.30-11 Sat; 12-11 Sun
☎ (01422) 883168
Black Sheep Best Bitter; Greene King IPA; Taylor Landlord; guest beers ⊞
Village inn with a strong community feel and a warm welcome for walkers and other visitors. The guest beers usually include two from Copper Dragon. Quality home-cooked food is excellent value and available lunchtimes and evenings (not Mon and Tue). Major sporting events are shown on Sky TV, but there is normally a quiet corner to be found. The bar displays memorabilia relating to the Cragg Vale Coiners, a gang of 18th-century forgers. The pub is close to the station. ❀◑◗≉⊟♣P⅟

Newlay

Abbey ✔

99 Pollard Lane, LS13 1EQ (vehicle access from B6157 only) SE239367
12-11 (10.30 Sun)
☎ (0113) 258 1248 theabbey-inn.co.uk
Naylors range; Tetley Bitter; guest beers ⊞
Grade II listed building with low, beamed ceilings, situated between the Leeds-Liverpool canal and the River Aire, with moorings nearby. The pub takes its name from the 12th-century Kirkstall Abbey just over a mile away, and is popular with walkers exploring the valley. The guest beers are mainly from local breweries, with some from further afield. There are jam sessions on Tuesday, live music on Saturday and a quiz night on Sunday. Two annual beer festivals are held. ❀◑◗⊟♣P⅟

Ossett

Brewer's Pride

Low Mill Road, WF5 8ND (at bottom of Healey Rd, 1½ miles from Ossett town centre)
12-11 (10.30 Sun)
☎ (01924) 273865 brewers-pride.co.uk
Bob's Brewing Co White Lion; Rudgate Ruby Mild; guest beers ⊞
Genuine free house five minutes' walk from the Calder & Hebble Canal. One of the nine handpulls is dedicated to a rotating stout or porter. Good value lunches are served – on Wednesday evening curries, pies, pasta or steaks feature on the menu. Monday is quiz night and Tuesday is bluegrass music night with 'all pickers welcome'. The local folk club meets on Thursday evening, and live music is performed on the first Sunday of the month. An annual beer festival is held each summer bank holiday. ⌂Q❀◑◗⊟(106)⅟

Tap

2 The Green, WF5 8JS
3 (12 Thu)-1am; 12-2am Fri & Sat; 12-1am Sun
☎ (01924) 272215 ossett.brewery.co.uk
Ossett Pale Gold, Silver King, Excelsior; guest beers ⊞
Recently taken over by Ossett Brewery, the Tap has been refurbished to a very high standard. Both the landlady and the regulars make you feel very welcome. It has a centrally situated bar with a room at one end and a partitioned area at the other, both with an open fire. Walls are of exposed stone and there is a flagstone floor. Children are welcome in the two end rooms at all times. In addition to the three regular beers, there is usually a special from Ossett plus four guest ales. ⌂Q❀⊟P⅟

Otley

Junction

44 Bondgate, LS21 1AD
11-11 (midnight Fri & Sat); 12-10.30 Sun
☎ (01943) 463233
Caledonian Deuchars IPA; Taylor Best Bitter, Landlord; Theakston Best Bitter, XB, Old Peculier; guest beers ⊞
Traditional one-roomed pub with a stone-flagged floor and a central fireplace. Eleven handpumps are here to satisfy,

complemented by 30 malt whiskies. Live music can be heard on Tuesday and Sunday and a quiz night takes place on Wednesday. During the day, food can be brought in from Bondgate Bakery just along the street. Dogs are welcome.

Manor House

Walkergate, LS21 1HB

11-11 (10.30 Sun)

(01943) 463807

Thwaites Dark Mild, Original, seasonal beers

Friendly local set in a row of terraced houses close to the maypole and the town hall. Three drinking areas and a real fire give the pub a cosy feel during winter months. For the summer there is an outdoor drinking area to the rear of the premises which is advertised as a south-facing sun trap. Also to the rear is a covered smoking area. Regular live music evenings are held.

Red Lion

43-45 Kirkgate, LS21 3HN (100m from bus station)

11-11; 12-10.30 Sun

(01943) 464217 theredlionotley.com

John Smith's Bitter; Taylor Landlord; guest beers

A former 18th-century coaching inn, this listed building has an open-plan front lounge with three comfortable drinking areas, one with an inglenook fireplace and log-burning fire. There is also a room to the rear of the compact bar and an upstairs room which are popular with local community groups. In addition to guest beers from local breweries, draught Leffe is available. Live music is played on alternative Sunday evenings.

Pontefract

Robin Hood

4 Wakefield Road, WF8 4HN (off A645, opp traffic lights)

1-4, 7-11.30; 2-11.30 Fri & Sat; 12-4.30, 7-11 Sun

(01977) 702231

John Smith's Bitter; Tetley Bitter; guest beers

Busy pub near the notorious Town End traffic lights which are known locally as Jenkins Folly. There are three separate drinking areas along with a public bar. Twice-weekly quizzes are held on Tuesday and Sunday evenings and darts and dominoes teams play in the local charity league. The Robin Hood stages a beer festival over the summer bank holiday weekend. Winner of many local CAMRA awards, including Pub of the Year.

(Tanshelf/Baghill)

Tap & Barrel

13 Front Street, WF8 1AN (off A639, opp court house)

11.30-11 (1am Fri & Sat); 12-10.30 Sun

(01977) 699918

John Smith's Bitter; Taylor Landlord; Theakston Old Peculier

This 200-year-old town-centre pub, formerly known as the Greyhound, is situated on the fringe of the weekend drinking circuit. The nearest pub to the racecourse, it retains a sporting theme. A large-screen TV around the central bar features horse racing, Rugby League and football. Pool, darts and dominoes are all played and a popular quiz night is hosted every Wednesday.

(Tanshelf/Baghill)

Pudsey

Fleece

100 Fartown, LS28 8LU

12-11 (10.30 Sun)

(0113) 236 2748

Taylor Landlord; Tetley Bitter; guest beers

Situated just on the edge of Pudsey, the Fleece is a grand-looking pub with a secluded beer garden and a neat and tidy two-roomed interior. A small tap room has all the accoutrements, while a larger, but still cosy, lounge has seats that can be at a premium. Flowers and famous film stars form the decor. The guest beer is usually from Brown Cow, known here as Simpson's, but can also be from other small Yorkshire breweries. P

Queensbury

Waggoners

18 Ford Hill, BD13 2BG

3 (2 Wed)-11; 11-11 Thu-Sat; 12-10.30 Sun

(01274) 814458 waggoners-queensbury.co.uk

Black Sheep Best Bitter; Wells Bombardier

This friendly community local, which for many years served only keg beers, has been transformed by the current lady licensee, with two regular beers occasionally augmented by a guest ale. Situated on the main road through the village, this stone-built pub hosts live music on alternate Thursdays, a quiz night on Wednesday, karaoke on Friday and a disco on Saturday. A function room is also available to hire. (576)P

Rastrick

Roundhill Inn

75 Clough Lane, HD6 3QL (on A6107, 400m from jct with A634)

5 (4 Fri)-midnight; 12-midnight Sat; 12-11 Sun

(01484) 713418

Black Sheep Best Bitter; Fuller's London Pride; Taylor Golden Best, Landlord; guest beers

A genuine two-room free house overlooking the hill that gives it its name, with spectacular views to Brighouse and beyond. The smaller Maddocks bar may be available for functions. Guest beers are usually from independent breweries. Monday is quiz night. Children over 14 are allowed. Q(547,549)P

Ripponden

Old Bridge Inn

Priest Lane, HX6 4DF

12-3, 5.30-11; 12-11 Sat; 12-10.30 Sun

(01422) 822595 porkpieclub.com

Taylor Golden Best, Best Bitter, Landlord; guest beers

Reputedly the oldest pub in Yorkshire, this timber-framed Grade II listed building dates back to the 14th century. It has three rooms, one featuring a fine cruck beam. The high-quality food is a great attraction, with lunchtime buffets available Monday to Friday, and snacks on Saturday and Sunday lunchtimes. Evening meals are available on Friday and Saturday. The Pork Pie Appreciation Society meets here on Saturday evening and stages a competition in March or April. Impromptu live folk group sessions are held. ⌂Q❀◑⊟P

Rodley

Owl

1 Rodley Lane, LS13 1LB (on A657, corner of Bagley Lane)

✪ 12-11.30 (midnight Fri & Sat); 12-11 Sun

☎ (0113) 256 5242 ⊕ theowlatrodley.co.uk

Beer range varies Ⓗ

This family-run pub has a traditional tap room at the front with pub games including pool and darts. A larger lounge to the rear hosts live music on Friday and Saturday, and a quiz on Thursday. The conservatory leads to a spacious beer garden and play area. The beer range is varied, with up to eight guest ales. Food is served until 8pm Monday to Saturday and 5pm on Sunday. ❀◑⊟♿⊟♣P⁻

Rodley Barge

182-184 Town Street, LS13 1HP (on A657, by Leeds-Liverpool canal)

✪ 12-3, 5-11; 12-11 Fri-Sun

☎ (0113) 257 4606 ⊕ therodleybarge.wetpaint.com

Clarks Rodley Barge Bitter; Tetley Bitter; guest beers Ⓗ

Traditional stone-built pub adjacent to the Leeds-Liverpool canal. As you enter the pub, a corridor leads to two bars on the left hand side. Both rooms are traditionally decorated and have a cosy feel. Families are welcome in the smaller back bar. A pleasant beer garden at the rear of the pub backs on to the canal. ⌂❀◑⊟♿⊟♣⁻

Saltaire

Fanny's Ale & Cider House

63 Saltaire Road, BD18 3JN (on A657 opp fire station)

✪ 12 (5 Mon)-11 (midnight Fri & Sat)

☎ (01274) 591419

Taylor Golden Best, Landlord; Theakston Old Peculier; guest beers Ⓗ

Near the historic Salt's Mill complex in the World Heritage Site of Saltaire Village, this cosy pub was originally a beer shop, but is now a fully-licensed free house. The lounge is gas lit and adorned with old brewery memorabilia. An extension in early 2008 increased the seating area and included disabled access, while an upstairs room has comfortable seating. The pub stocks an excellent range of beers and also serves a number of draught ciders including Stowford Press. ⌂≷⊟●

Victoria ✔

192 Saltaire Road, BD18 3JF

✪ 12-midnight (11 Sun)

☎ (01274) 595090

Greene King Abbot; John Smith's Bitter; guest beers Ⓗ

Traditional two-room community pub, a former Bradford CAMRA Pub of the Season. A member of the SIBA scheme, the guest ales change weekly, with 260 beers dispensed since 2006. One room has a pool table and jukebox, while the other has comfortable lounge-style seating. The pub hosts twice-weekly live entertainment and a Wednesday night quiz. The Victoria has been Cask Marque accredited for the past two years. ❀⊟♿≷⊟♣P

Shipley

Shipley Club

162 Bradford Road, BD18 3DE

✪ hours vary

☎ (01274) 201842

Beer range varies Ⓗ

For more than a century this thriving sports and social club has served its members, going from strength to strength thanks to an enthusiastic stewarding team. Up to three ales are available, often from Yorkshire micros such as Litton and Salamander. The local Saltaire Brewery now sponsors some club matters, including a handpump at the bar. Bowling is available subject to the club's commitments, while two snooker tables attract young and old alike to the green baize. A current CAMRA membership card or this Guide will gain you entry. ❀⊟♣P

Sir Norman Rae ✔

Victoria House, Market Square, BD18 3QB

✪ 9-midnight (1am Fri & Sat)

☎ (01274) 535290

Greene King IPA, Old Speckled Hen, Abbot; Marston's Pedigree; guest beers Ⓗ

Situated in the heart of Shipley town centre, this converted department store opened in 2002 as a Lloyds No. 1 bar. Recent refurbishment has seen it attract a more mainstream Wetherspoon target clientele. Beer range and quality have improved beyond measure, hence its first appearance in the Guide. The large open-plan layout provides comfortable surroundings in which to enjoy the wide-ranging food and beer menus. Many ales come from local micros to accompany the regular Greene King selection. Beer festivals and Meet the Brewer nights are held. ◑♿≷⊟●

Silsden

Kings Arms ✔

Bolton Road, BD20 0JY

✪ 12-midnight

☎ (01535) 653216 ⊕ kingsarms-silsden.co.uk

John Smith's Bitter; guest beers Ⓗ

A vibrant pub featuring regular folk sessions, quizzes and live music. Originally three cottages, the pub is now divided into three rooms, one containing a coal fire. Pub games include darts, dominoes, cards and cribbage. Two regularly changing guest beers are from the Punch Finest Cask list. Gales fruit wines are also available. Dogs and well-behaved children are welcome. ⌂❀◑⊟♣P⁻

Slaithwaite

Swan

Carr Lane, HD7 5BQ (off A62, turn right at village centre, under viaduct)
4-midnight; 12-1am Fri & Sat; 12-midnight Sun
(01484) 843225 itsourlocal.com
Taylor Landlord; guest beers
Homely roadside pub in a quiet corner of Slaithwaite village. Very community-focused, the licensees support local causes and charities, as well as eagerly promoting real ale, having had much experience within the pub trade. Beers from the nearby Empire Brewery are usually on offer – typically the beer choice is three in number – expanding considerably during the beer festivals which the pub stages occasionally. This is a good example of a village pub benefiting from enthusiastic management. Meals are served 12-6pm Friday to Sunday.

South Elmsall

Barnsley Oak

Mill Lane, WF9 2DT (on B6474)
12-11.30 (10.30 Sun)
(01977) 643427
John Smith's Bitter; guest beer
Built in 1970 and serving a former mining area, this is a fine example of a community pub which has built a loyal following for its guest beers, often sourced from Yorkshire breweries. Quiz nights are held on Tuesday and Sunday and the pub also hosts the Barnsley Oak Golf Society (BOGS). Excellent value meals are served all day until 8pm (4.30pm Sun). Children are welcome and meals can also be taken in the conservatory, which affords panoramic views of the Elm Valley.
(Moorthorpe/S Elmsall)(46,496)

Sowerby Bridge

Shepherd's Rest

125 Bolton Brow, HX6 2BD (on A58)
3-11.30; 12-midnight Thu-Sun
(01422) 831937
Ossett Pale Gold, Excelsior; Taylor Landlord; guest beers
Built in 1877, this pub was bought by Ossett Brewery in 2005 and it provides the house beer Shepherd's Rest. There is live acoustic music on the first Wednesday of each month, a quiz every Monday night and a bridge night on Thursday, where new players are warmly welcomed. Bottled beer and malt whiskies are available. The interior is open plan with an arched brick fireplace, stone-flagged floor and a large butter churn.

White Horse

Burnley Road, Friendly, HX6 2UG
12-11 (10.30 Sun)
(01422) 831173
Elland Beyond the Pale; Tetley Mild, Bitter
This white-painted pub stands just back from the busy A646, where regular buses between Halifax and Todmorden pass close by. A welcoming local, it has a tap room and a larger partially divided lounge bar. A strong local following includes members of the Friendly Brass Band and a dominoes club. Stunning prize-winning floral displays feature in summer. There is a smoking area at the rear. (590)

Works

12 Hollins Mill Lane, HX6 2QG (opp swimming pool)
12-11 (10.30 Sun)
(01422) 834821
Taylor Golden Best, Best Bitter, Landlord; guest beers
Converted from a former joinery shop, the Works features a simple, spacious open-plan interior with exposed brick walls, wooden floorboards and a partly-beamed high ceiling. It is a past winner of the CAMRA Pub Design Award for Conversion to Pub Use and of the local branch Pub of the Season. An impressive L-shaped bar includes nine handpumps. Home-cooked food is served daily, with a curry night on Wednesday. Live blues, jazz and folk music is staged, but not so loud as to prevent easy conversation.

Sowood

Dog & Partridge

Forest Hill Road, HX4 9LP (¼ mile W of B6112)
7-11; 12-4.30, 7-10.30 Sun
(01422) 374249
Black Sheep Best Bitter; Taylor Landlord; guest beers
There are few pubs like this still in existence today. A friendly two-roomed, stone-built free house, it has been run by the same family for more than 50 years and is often known as Mable's, after the present landlord's mother, who ran the pub into her 90s. This is a rural no-frills inn where the peace is disturbed only by the hum of conversation. Frank the landlord may be coaxed into playing the piano. The guest beer is often supplied by a micro-brewery. Q(537,538)P

Thornhill

Saville Arms

Church Lane, WF12 0JZ (on B6117, 2½ miles S of Dewsbury)
5(4 Fri)-11; 12-4, 7.30-11 Sat & Sun
(01924) 463738
Black Sheep Best Bitter, Ale; Theakston Best Bitter
Known as the Church House, parts of this building are 600 years old. The tap room is on consecrated ground, situated in the graveyard of the Grade I-listed church of St Michael's. A much talked about mural depicts local history, from cavemen to the present. Children are welcome in the large garden, which also accommodates smokers. Pie and peas are available on Friday evening (booking essential). (128,281)

Todmorden

Masons Arms

1 Bacup Road, OL14 7PN
12-midnight
(01706) 812180

Copper Dragon Best Bitter, Golden Pippin; Tetley Bitter; guest beers Ⓗ
A Copper Dragon Brewery pub dwarfed by a railway viaduct, and close to the Rochdale Canal. This traditional local has a corridor entrance leading to the bar. There is seating and a pool table in one area and a fireplace in another cosy room. Its tables were once used for laying out bodies. Thursday evening usually features English folk music. The canal towpath provides an interesting walk to Todmorden. ⛫Q❀◑⇌(Walsden)🚍(590)♣⁻

Top Brink ✔
Brink Top, Lumbutts, OL14 6JB (near Lumbutts Mill Activity Centre) SD956236
✪ 12-3 (not Mon & Tue), 5.30-midnight; 12-midnight Sat & Sun
☎ (01706) 812696
Boddingtons Bitter; Flowers Original; Taylor Landlord; guest beer Ⓗ
Overlooked by rugged moorland, with views over the Calder Valley, this pub is popular with diners and attracts customers from the adjacent Pennine bridleway and the nearby Pennine Way. In summer a floral display can be enjoyed from the outside seating. Inside, rooms are arranged around three sides of the bar, one with attractive brassware. Children are welcome in the games room. Guest beers are from small independent breweries.
❀◑◗♿⛺🚍(T6,T8)P⁻

Undercliffe

Milners Arms
126 Undercliffe Road, BD2 3BN (300m from Eccleshill Library)
✪ 4-11 (11-30 Fri); 12-11.30 Sat; 12-11 Sun
☎ (01274) 639938
Beer range varies Ⓗ
Pleasant and cosy two-roomed community local with a central bar serving both the tap room and the lounge. Themed nights take place on the first Saturday of each month and are very popular with a loyal and regular clientele. The landlord is enthusiastic about real ale and always keeps two on handpump, one from a Yorkshire micro-brewery such as Rudgate, Saltaire or Salamander.
❀⊟🚍(601)♣⁻

Wakefield

Alverthorpe WMC
111 Flanshaw Lane, WF2 9JG
✪ 11.30-4, 6.30-11; 11.30-11 Fri & Sat; 12-3.30, 7-11 Sun
☎ (01924) 374179
Tetley Mild, Bitter; guest beers Ⓗ
Multi-roomed CIU-affiliated club with a cosy interior featuring unusual stained glass and an extensive collection of pot horses. It stocks a wide selection of guest beers, mostly from local micros, and holds an annual beer festival in October. This regular local CAMRA award winner host live entertainment on Saturday and Sunday, while snooker and darts are among the traditional games. A large-screen TV is provided for armchair sports enthusiasts. Outside is a floodlit bowling green.
❀⊟♿🚍(104)♣P⁻

Black Rock
3 Cross Square, WF1 1PQ (top of Westgate, near Bull Ring)
✪ 11-11 (midnight Sat); 12-10.30 Sun
☎ (01924) 375550
Tetley Bitter; guest beers Ⓗ
An arched, tiled façade leads to a traditional, compact city centre locals' ale house providing a hint of the comfort and elegance of a Victorian gin palace, with photographs of Old Wakefield adorning the walls. At the centre of Wakefield's drinking and clubbing culture, the 'Rock' has recently acquired an extra handpull to double the choice of guest ales it serves. This is a real pub on the edge of the fizz-dispensing shoeboxes and blaring discos of the youth zone. ⇌(Westgate/Kirkgate)🚍⁻

Fernandes Brewery Tap & Bier Keller
5 Avison Yard, Kirkgate, WF1 1UA
✪ 4-11 (midnight Thu); 11-1am Fri & Sat; 12-midnight Sun
☎ (01924) 386348 🌐 ossett-brewery.co.uk
Beer range varies Ⓗ
This pub, a CAMRA award-winner, has recently been taken over by Ossett Brewery. The new Bier Keller is a welcome addition (open Wed-Sun, hours vary). The pub has eight handpulls, one dedicated to a mild, stout or porter, and stocks a good selection of bottled Belgian beers. The Bier Keller has 12 premier foreign beers and cider on draught, plus Ossett Silver King on handpump. Plans are in place to increase the number of cask ales on offer in the pub. ⛫◑⇌(Kirkgate/Westgate)🚍●⁻

Harry's Bar
107B Westgate, WF1 1EL (opp Westgate station)
✪ 5-11 (midnight Fri & Sat); 12-11 Sun
☎ (01924) 373773
Ossett Silver King, Excelsior; Taylor Landlord; guest beers Ⓗ
Winner of CAMRA branch Pub Of The Year for 2007, this small, one-roomed pub with an exposed brick and wood interior is hidden away down a ginnel off Westgate. Alongside the regular and guest beers is a range of bottled Belgian beers. For fine weather there is a sun deck and a shady yard. The pub is adjacent to a car park. ⛫❀⇌(Westgate)🚍

Henry Boons ✔
130 Westgate, WF2 9SR (100m below Westgate station)
✪ 11-11 (1am Fri & Sat); 12-10.30 Sun
☎ (01924) 378126
Clark's Classic Blonde, Westgate Gold, seasonal beer; Taylor Landlord Ⓗ
Quiet in the daytime, the pub gets very busy in the evenings as it is situated on the 'Westgate Run'. It is the brewery tap for Clark's, which is behind the pub. Hogsheads are in use as tables and there are many items of breweriana on display plus a thatched bar. The pub caters for drinkers of all ages and features live music on Thursday, Friday and Saturday. Two function rooms are available for hire. ⇌(Westgate/Kirkgate)🚍♣

Redoubt

28 Horbury Road, WF2 8TS (corner of Horbury Rd & Westgate)

⏲ 12 (11 Sat)-11.30; 11-11 Sun

☎ (01924) 377085

Taylor Landlord; Tetley Mild, Bitter Ⓗ

A Tetley Heritage Pub with low ceilings and four cosy rooms. The walls are adorned with a mixture of Rugby League photos and illustrations of old Wakefield. Known as a 'sporty' pub, the Redoubt has its own cricket and football teams. Disabled access is to the pub only. ♨Q✿♿≋(Westgate)🚌♣P⚡

Wakefield Labour Club (The Red Shed)

18 Vicarage Street, WF1 1QX

⏲ 12-5 (Fri only), 7-11; 11-4, 7-11 Sat; 12-4 Sun

☎ (01924) 215626 🌐 theredshed.org.uk

Ossett Pale Gold; guest beers Ⓗ

The Red Shed is a old army hut which has survived the redevelopment of the area. Home to many trade union, community and charity groups, quiz night is Wednesday and live music plays on alternate Saturdays. There are three rooms, two of which can be hired for functions. An extensive collection of Union plates and badges is displayed over the bar, together with numerous CAMRA awards adorning the walls. (The club plans to open Sun eves). ≋(Westgate/Kirkgate)🚌♣P🗑

Walton

New Inn

144 Shay Lane, WF2 6LA

⏲ 12-midnight

☎ (01924) 255447 🌐 newinnwalton.co.uk

Jennings Cumberland Ale; John Smith's Bitter; Leeds Pale Ale, seasonal beer; Taylor Landlord Ⓗ

Traditional 18th-century vernacular stone building with a flagstone roof. Inside it has several areas including a restaurant that offers exceptionally good food (not Mon). A coffee shop is also open daily from 10am (not Mon). This is a community-focused pub attracting people from all walks of life. Regular live music sessions are held – see the website for details. An ideal start or finish to rural walks along the route of the Barnsley Canal. ✿◐♿🚌P⚡

Weetwood

Stables Bar ✔

Weetwood Hall, Otley Road, LS16 5PS (just off Leeds ring road on A657, by Weetwood roundabout)

⏲ 12-11 (10.30 Sun)

☎ (0113) 230 6000 🌐 weetwood.co.uk

Black Sheep Best Bitter; Copper Dragon Golden Pippin, Challenger IPA; Taylor Landlord; guest beers Ⓗ

This pub has a rustic feel with wooden beams and exposed brickwork complemented by country artefacts such as saddles and harnesses adorning the walls. Even the carpet has a horseshoe motif. Food is served until 9pm, with a blackboard showing the daily specials. There is a large courtyard for alfresco drinking. The pub is part of the Weetwood Hall hotel and leisure complex, and holds a charity quiz on Sunday. ♘✿◐♿🚌P⚡

Wetherby

Muse Ale & Wine Bar ✔

16 Bank Street, LS22 6NQ

⏲ 12-11

☎ (01937) 580201 🌐 markettowntaverns.co.uk

Beer range varies Ⓗ

Formerly a restaurant, now part of the Market Town Taverns chain. Four handpumps offer a changing range of beers, focusing on Yorkshire micros, together with a large selection of foreign bottled and draught beers. To the left is a small comfortable bar and a feature fireplace, with a larger room to the right, used mainly as a dining area. A comprehensive menu is available lunchtime and evening. Children are admitted only if dining. Dogs are welcome. Q✿◐♿🚌P

Wintersett

Angler's Retreat

Ferrytop Lane, WF4 2EB (between Crofton & Ryhill) SE382157

⏲ 12-3, 7-11; 12-11 Sat; 12-3.30, 7-10.30 Sun

☎ (01924) 862370

Acorn Barnsley Bitter; Bateman XXXB; Samuel Smith OBB; Tetley Imperial Ⓗ

Set in the tiny hamlet of Wintersett, this is a fine example of an old-fashioned rural ale house. Its location close to the Angler's Country Park means that it attracts bird watchers as well as bikers. There is a large beer garden to the side and seats at the front for fine-weather drinking. ♨Q✿◻🚌♣P⚡

> Ah! My beloved brother of the rod, do you know the taste of beer – of bitter beer – cooled in the flowing river? Take your bottle of beer, sink it deep, deep in the shady water, where the cooling springs and fishes are. Then, the day being very hot and bright, and the sun blazing on your devoted head, consider it a matter of duty to have to fish that long, wide stream. An hour or so of good hammering will bring you to the end of it, and then – let me ask you avec impressement – how about that beer? Is it cool? Is it refreshing? Does it gurgle, gurgle and 'go down glug' as they say in Devonshire? Is it heavenly? Is it Paradise and all the Peris to boot? Ah! If you have never tasted beer under these or similar circumstance, you have, believe me, never tasted it at all.
>
> **Francis Francis**, By Lake and River, 16th century

Wales

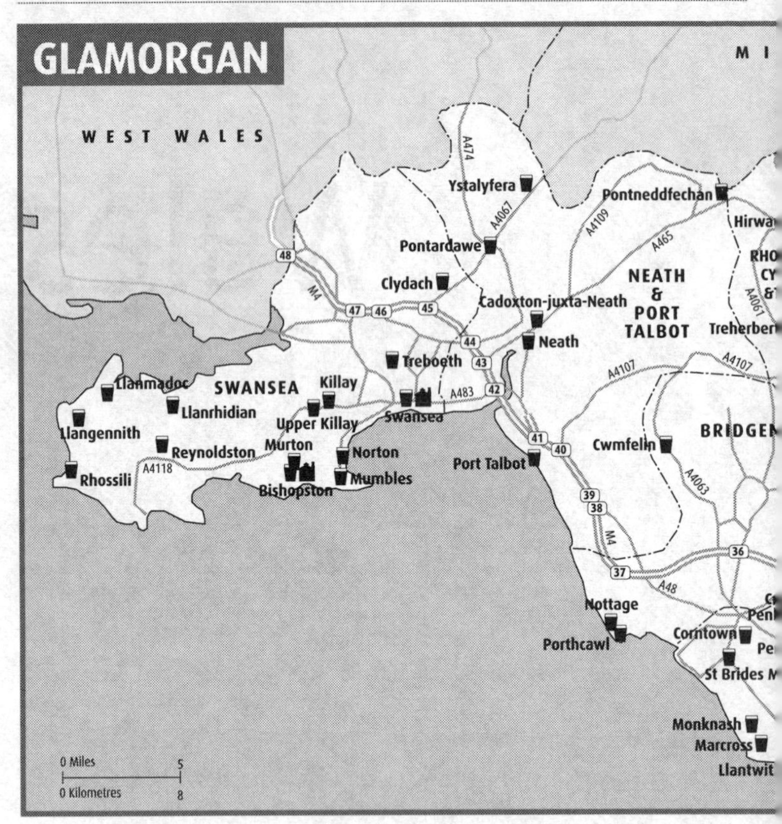

Authority areas covered: Bridgend, Caerphilly, Cardiff, Merthyr Tydfil, Neath & Port Talbot, Rhondda Cynon Taff, Swansea, Vale of Glamorgan

Aberdare

Cambrian Inn

60 Seymour Street, CF44 7DL
12 (11 Sat)-11; 12-10.30 Sun
☎ (01685) 879120
Beer range varies Ⓗ
A short walk from the shops and rail and bus stations, this welcoming town pub has a pleasant atmosphere, its comfortable interior drawing customers from all walks of life. Just one real ale is served, usually sourced from a micro-brewery, but turnover is brisk. Good-value lunches are available. A quiz is held on Wednesday night and there is live acoustic music on Thursday. The pub sign portrays the choral conductor and brewer Caradog (Griffith Rhys Jones), a famous son of Aberdare.
(≥♣

Aberthin

Hare & Hounds

Aberthin Road, Cowbridge, CF71 7LG (on A4222)
12 (4 Mon winter)-midnight; 1-1am Fri & Sat
☎ (01446) 774892
Banks's Bitter; Marston's Pedigree, Old Empire; guest beers Ⓗ/Ⓖ
At least 300 years old, this traditional two-roomed village pub is friendly and welcoming. Owned by Marston's but offering several guest beers, it makes a welcome return to the Guide this year. The traditional bar has wooden settles and a collection of historic photos. Tables and chairs are out front in summer, a roaring fire inside in winter. Q❀⚊

Barry

Barry West End Club

St Nicholas Road, CF62 6QW
2 (11 Sat)-11.30; 12-10.30 Sun
☎ (01446) 735739
Brains Dark, Bitter; guest beer Ⓗ
Voted Club of the Year by Vale of Glamorgan CAMRA for the last two years, this traditional working men's club is open to CAMRA

INDEPENDENT BREWERIES

Brains Cardiff
Bullmastiff Cardiff
Celt Experience Caerphilly (NEW)
Dare Godreaman (NEW)
Newmans Caerphilly
Otley Pontypridd
Rhymney Merthyr Tydfil
Swansea Bishopston
Tomos Watkin Swansea
Vale of Glamorgan Barry
Zerodegrees Cardiff

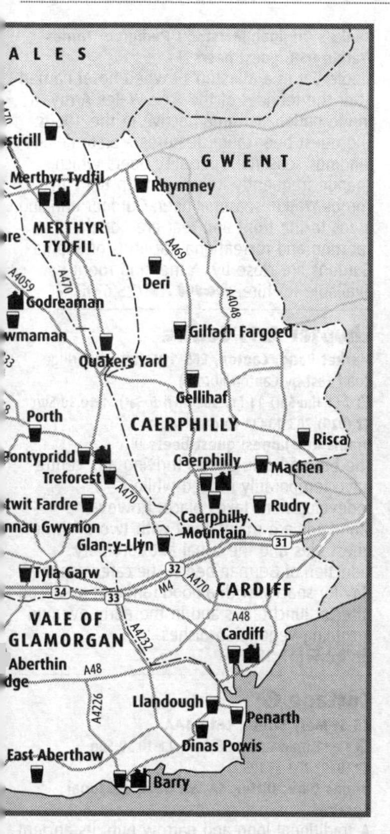

members on production of their membership card. In recent years the steward has boosted the club's reputation for providing excellent, well-kept real ales. The smoking area outside is sheltered by umbrellas.

Castle Hotel

44 Jewel Street, CF63 3NQ

12-11.30 (midnight Fri & Sat); 12-11 Sun

(01446) 408916

Brains Bitter, SA; guest beers

This multi-roomed late Victorian former hotel was voted Vale of Glamorgan CAMRA Pub of the Year 2008. A Brains tied house offering three guest ales, with live music and quizzes, it is the best outlet for real ale in Barry. The building retains many fine features as well as connections to the docks. (Docks)

Bishopston

Joiners Arms

50 Bishopston Road, SA3 3EJ

11.30-11; 12-10.30 Sun

(01792) 232658

Courage Best Bitter; Marston's Pedigree; Swansea Bishopswood, Three Cliffs Gold, Original Wood; guest beers

Home of the Swansea Brewing Company, this 1860s pub is popular with locals and is always busy in both bars. Beer festivals and music events are held occasionally, adding to the excellent ale range. Good, value-for-money food is served and social events are organised.

This is a village hub and has won several local CAMRA awards. There is a small car park – if full, try 100 metres down the hill.
Q (14) P

Brynnau Gwynion

Mountain Hare

Brynna Road, CF35 6PG (off A473 between Pencoed and Llanharan)

5-11.30; 2-midnight Fri & Sat; 12-11 Sun

(01656) 860458 mountainhare.co.uk

Bullmastiff Welsh Gold; Evan Evans BB; guest beers

Situated where the Vale of Glamorgan meets the former mining valleys, this family-owned village pub has a large, comfortable lounge and a bar full of character where two guest beers are available at all times. Car parking is ample and the surrounding area, popular in summer, hosts an annual Ales of Wales beer festival. Q P

Cadoxton-juxta-Neath

Crown & Sceptre Inn

Main Road, SA10 8AP

11-11 (10.30 Sun)

(01639) 642145

Draught Bass; Tomos Watkin OSB

Built in 1835 as a tap for the local brewery, this former coach house has a bar, lounge and restaurant. A popular local, it has a good reputation for its ale and freshly-cooked home-made meals. A wide range of à la carte and bar food is on offer, with beef and ale pie a favourite. Neath Abbey and Aberdulais Falls are nearby. Q (154,158)P

Caerphilly

Masons Arms

Mill Road, CF83 3FE

12-11.30 (midnight Fri & Sat)

(029) 208 83353

Brains Bitter; guest beers

A warm welcome is assured at this traditional local just 10 minutes' walk from Caerphilly Castle. Good value meals are served, mainly in the rear lounge which adjoins the local park. Visitors to the bar will need to ask staff which real ales are on sale, as the pumps are out of view. Q P

Caerphilly Mountain

Black Cock Inn

Waun Waelod Way, CF83 1BD

10.30 (12 Sun)-midnight

(029) 20880534 theblackcockinn.co.uk

Hancock's HB; Theakston Old Peculier; guest beers

Off the beaten track, this rural restaurant and bar nestles in the hilltop forest between Cardiff, Caerphilly and Tongwynlais – access is easiest from Caerphilly Mountain. Two guest beers are stocked, usually from small brewers, with real cider in summer. Food and drink has a Welsh focus. The bar is popular with ramblers and is dog-friendly. The outdoor smoking area is heated and lit.
P

Cardiff

Albany

105 Donald Street, CF24 4TL

12-11 (11.30 Fri); 11-11.30 Sat; 12-10.30 Sun

(029) 203 11075

Brains Dark, Bitter, SA, seasonal beers; guest beers

This award-winning street-corner local continues to maintain its customary high standards, offering a popular range of guest beers. You can enjoy a quiet drink in the lounge or in the more lively main area where there is a large screen TV. The pub is a focus for a number of leisure activities – a Sunday night poker league has recently been added to weekly quiz and karaoke nights. It has a covered and heated smoking area, skittle alley and large beer garden. Q

Beverley Hotel

75-77 Cathedral Road, CF11 9PG

10-11.30 (12.30am Fri & Sat); 10-11 Sun

(029) 203 43443

Beer range varies

Large hotel bar popular with locals and visitors, situated in the Cathedral Road conservation area less than a mile from the city centre and close to Glamorgan cricket ground. The management enthusiastically promotes real ale from the extended range available from M&B, with up to three cask ales on tap at any one time. Discounted hotel rates are available for CAMRA members – please mention on booking and show your membership card at check-in.

Birchgrove

Caerphilly Road, CF14 4AE

12 (11 Sat)-11(11.30 Thu-Sat)

(029) 20311319

Brains Dark, Bitter, SA, Reverend James, SA Gold; guest beer

Suburban community pub on a busy crossroads. Built in the Arts and Crafts style, the interior retains many heritage fittings including an oak bar in the public bar and original red brick fireplaces in both bar and large lounge, which has a number of distinct drinking areas. The two guest beers are from family brewers or larger micros. Sky Sports is available.

Butchers Arms

29 Llandaff Road, Canton, CF11 9NG

11-11 (11.30 Fri & Sat); 11.30-10.30 sun

(029) 202 27927

Brains Dark, Bitter, SA; guest beers

Friendly street corner local with a jovial public bar and more comfortable family-friendly lounge. The decor is reminiscent of the Brains pubs of yesteryear and adds to the cosy feel of the interior. The guest ale varies, always a welcome addition to the regular beers. Two small outside drinking areas cater for the bar and lounge customers. Two darts teams are based here. Dogs are welcome.

(17,18)

Cayo Arms

36 Cathedral Road, CF11 9LL

11.30-11 (midnight Fri & Sat); 11-10.30 Sun

(029) 203 91910

Banks's Original; Marston's Pedigree; Tomos Watkin OSB; guest beers

Single bar in a Marston's-owned hotel named after the founder of the Free Wales Army, a fringe nationalist group active in the 1960s. The guest beer range features Marston's and Jennings seasonal/speciality beers which change frequently, together with the current Tomos Watkin seasonal beer. Outdoor drinking areas to the front and rear are popular. The sporting and recreational facilities of Sophia Gardens are close by. A meeting room is available for hire. (25,62)P

Chapter Arts Centre

Market Road, Canton, CF5 1QE (off Cowbridge Road East by Canton library)

5 (1 Thu-Sat)-11 (12.30am Fri & Sat); 4-10.30 Sun

(029) 203 13431 chapter.org

Brains Rev James; guest beers

The bar and café of this thriving arts centre have temporarily moved while redevelopment takes place. However standards are maintained with two or three guest ales and the usual extraordinary selection of German beers. The café is open all day for snacks, with a good range of meals on offer at lunchtimes and in the early evening including vegetarian dishes.

(17,18)P

Cottage

25 St Mary Street, CF10 1AA

11-11 (midnight Fri & Sat); 11-10.30 Sun

(029) 203 37195

Brains Dark, Bitter, SA, SA Gold, seasonal beers

A traditional long and narrow pub, its ancient origins are reflected in its shape and layout, typical of the burgage system of medieval Cardiff. A classic Brains town pub serving home-cooked food and offering a warm welcome, it is a convivial retreat on a street where the nightlife can be frenetic. The interior features old photographs of Cardiff.

Fox & Hounds

Old Church Road, Whitchurch, CF14 1AD

11-11; 12-10.30 Sun

(029) 206 93377

Brains Dark, SA, Rev James, SA Gold; guest beers

Friendly community pub not to be missed if you are in the Whitchurch area. The wood-panelled interior houses one long bar with large screens for viewing sporting events, a quiet area for dining and drinking, and an extension used for beer festivals. The pleasant garden is popular in summer with a canopy and heaters for cooler days. P

Goat Major

33 High Street, CF10 1PU

11-midnight; 12-11 Sun

(029) 203 37161

Brains Dark, Bitter, SA, SA Gold

Despite recent refurbishment, this popular city-centre Brains pub is recognised for its traditional appearance and friendly atmosphere, attracting a brisk trade from both locals and visitors. It is named for the mascot of the Royal Welsh Regiment, a fact that is proudly illustrated in the many photographs that adorn the interior. Traditional Welsh food is served throughout the day.

Heathcock ✓

58 Bridge Street, Llandaff, CF5 2EN
12-11 (midnight Fri & Sat); 12-10.30 Sun
(029) 205 75005
Beer range varies H
Busy community pub with a lounge and public bar situated on the northern edge of the historic cathedral city of Llandaff. Adnams ales are always popular and the guest beer policy promotes ales from micro-breweries from South Wales and further afield. Food includes a range of curries. The beer garden and skittle alley are available for hire.

Mochyn Du

Sophia Close, CF11 9HW
12-11 (midnight Fri & Sat); 12-10.30 Sun
(029) 203 71599
Brains Bitter; guest beers H
Independent free house converted from a Gothic Victorian park-keeper's lodge, with a restaurant in the conservatory-style extension. Cwrw Mochyn is brewed exclusively for the pub by Vale of Glamorgan, and the guest ale policy promotes local breweries including Rhymney, Otley, Breconshire and Vale of Glamorgan. Cardiff CAMRA Pub of the Year 2007, the pub is handy for the Welsh Institute of Sport and Glamorgan cricket ground. A short riverside walk from Cardiff Castle, it is popular with Welsh speakers (many staff speak the language) and visitors alike.
(25,62)P

Pendragon ✓

Excalibur Drive, Thornhill, CF14 9BB
11.30-11.30 (midnight Fri & Sat); 11.30-11 Sun
(029) 206 10550
Brains Dark, Bitter, SA, Reverend James H
Situated to the north of Cardiff on the lower slopes of Caerphilly Mountain, the pub is approached via a long drive leading to the large car park. A friendly inn popular with the local community, it has extensive views across the city from the covered patio. A varied menu of good value food is served until 9pm Monday-Saturday and traditional lunch on Sunday (booking recommended at the weekend). Staff are welcoming and the atmosphere cordial.

Yard ✓

42-43 St Mary Street, CF10 1AD
10-1am; 11-12.30am Sun
(029) 20227577
Brains Dark, Bitter, SA, SA Gold H
The Yard is situated on the site of the original 1713 Brains brewery which was bought in 1882 by Samuel Arthur and Joseph Benjamin Brain, along with its brewery tap 'the Albert' and several other pubs. A modern, lively pub on two levels, it makes use of steel, copper and aluminium to reflect its past history as a brewery. Situated in the redeveloped brewery quarter with its many dining and drinking venues, it stays open late to meet demand.
Q

Clydach

Carpenters Arms

High Street, SA6 5LN
11-11; 12-10.30 Sun
(01792) 843333 carpentersarmsclydach.co.uk
Evan Evans Cwrw; Greene King Old Speckled Hen; Wye Valley Butty Bach; guest beer H
This popular stone-fronted pub has a busy public bar and a split-level lounge-restaurant which serves a wide range of high-quality meals. Live music is played most Saturdays and the pub is used by the local cycle group for meetings and events. Real ale festivals are held on Bank Holidays and the pub received an ITV community pub award in 2006.
P

Corntown

Golden Mile

Corntown Road, CF35 5BA (off A48) SS926773
11.45-3, 5-11; 12-3.30 Sun
(01656) 654884
Evan Evans BB; guest beers H
Situated below road level, this fine inn is easily overlooked. It has a bar, comfortable lounge and a restaurant. Reasonably priced, quality food can be enjoyed in the restaurant or, if preferred, in the cosy lounge with its log fire and brass adornments. Since the arrival of the current owner the pub has increased in popularity. Q P

Cowbridge

Vale of Glamorgan Inn

53 High Street, CF71 7AE
11.30-11 (midnight Fri & Sat); 12-10.30 Sun
(01446) 772252
Celt Experience Bronze; Hancock's HB; Shepherd Neame Bishops Finger; Wye Valley HPA; guest beers H
Friendly pub in a prime spot in the centre of an attractive, historic town. It has just one room with a comfortable carpeted lounge area and a bar area with wooden boards and a warming fire. A pub for convivial conversation, there is no background music or machines. Excellent home-cooked lunches are on offer (not Sun). In summer the rear courtyard garden is a delight with its display of hanging baskets and tubs of flowers. The outbuildings were once the home of the Vale of Glamorgan Brewery (no connection with the current business of that name) which was taken over by Hancock's in 1913. A beer festival is hosted in October. Q

Craig Penllyn

Barley Mow

CF71 7RT (off A48) SS977772
12-3 (not Tue), 6-11; 12-11 Sun
(01446) 772558 barleymow.net
Brains Bitter; Hancock's HB; guest beers H
Old-established inn with a strong local following and a friendly welcome for visitors. The cosy public bar area leads through a low doorway (duck!) to a larger lounge/dining room; outside a small courtyard makes a pleasant suntrap. The varied menu and early

WALES

evening food deals make this a popular dining venue – Sunday lunchtime is especially popular when young children can eat free. An interesting restored well lies to the south of the village. (V3)P

Cwmaman

Falcon Hotel

1 Incline Row, CF44 6LU SN008998

11-11 (10.30 Sun) thefalcon.co.uk

Beer range varies

Although close to the village, the pub is isolated at the end of a lane and can be difficult to find. It is popular with locals and travellers alike, especially in summer when its riverside setting adds to the appeal. Three 'outside' beers are usually on offer alongside brews from the pub's own Dare Brewery. The large bar was built using timber from a local chapel. The letting accommodation is well-appointed and touring caravans are welcome. Once visited, the Falcon will be long remembered. (7,8)P

Cwmfelin

Cross Inn

Maesteg Road, CF34 9LB (on A4063)

11.45-midnight (1am Fri & Sat); 12-11 Sun

(01656) 732476

Brains Bitter, seasonal beers; Wye Valley Butty Bach; guest beers

An oasis in an area where good real ale is hard to find, this friendly, welcoming, multi-room pub is situated on the main road from Bridgend to Maesteg, with good public transport. Children are welcome until 7pm, well-behaved dogs are permitted too (please ask first). The back room displays some interesting photographs. (Garth)

Deri

Old Club

93 Bailey Street, CF81 9HX

4-midnight (2am Fri & Sat); 12-midnight Sun

(01443) 830278

Beer range varies

Proudly independent, the Old Club stocks three guest beers of great variety. Local craft brewers are well represented alongside some of the more interesting regionals. Access is easy by bus from Bargoed, or by foot or cycle along the former railway path – pleasanter than the road. A little further on is Cwm Darran country park and hilltops popular with paragliders. The Old Club always welcomes visitors – just show this Guide for admittance. (1,4)

Dinas Powys

Star

Station Road, CF64 4DE

11.30-11 (midnight Fri & Sat); 12-10.30 Sun

(029) 205 14245

Brains Dark, Bitter, SA, SA Gold; guest beers

More state of the art than the traditional Brains tied house, this spacious pub is characterful, welcoming and cheerful. Open-plan and recently refurbished, it has cosy seating and dining areas where good home-cooked food is available. There is a large car park and patio to the rear with disabled access to the pub by wheelchair lift. P

Three Horseshoes

1 Station Road, CF64 4DE

12 (11 Sat)-midnight; 11.30-midnight

(029) 20514848

Beer range varies

This small pub on the village square is growing in reputation, featuring local beers on an ever-changing guest list. It comprises an attractive lounge and flagstone-floored bar. Snacks are available but no full meals. Serving what is now a substantial commuter community between Barry and Cardiff, the pub was originally built as a farmhouse in 1456.

East Aberthaw

Blue Anchor

CF62 3DD (on B4265)

11-11; 12-10.30 Sun

(01446) 750329 blueanchoraberthaw.com

Brains Bitter; Theakston Old Peculier; Wadworth 6X; Wye Valley HPA; guest beer

Fourteenth-century family-run pub with an adjoining restaurant, rebuilt and restored after a serious fire. Beneath the thatched roof lies a multi-room, flagstone-floored pub with thick stone walls that defeat most mobile phones. The guest beer is often from a local brewery. The car park is across the road. QP

Gellihaf

Coal Hole

Bryn Road, NP12 2QE (on A4049 S of Fleur-de-Lys)

12-3, 6.30-11; 11-11 Fri & Sat; 12-10.30 Sun

(01443) 830280

Greene King Old Speckled Hen; Shepherd Neame Spitfire; guest beers

Set back from the road, this friendly one-bar pub was converted from farm buildings during the 19th century – the bar occupies the former stables. Excellent food is available daily, served in both the bar and restaurant, with Sunday lunch a highlight. Extensive views of the Rhymney Valley can be enjoyed together with good ale and a warm welcome. P

Gilfach Fargoed

Capel Hotel

Park Place, CF81 8LW

12-11 (11.30 Fri & Sat); 12-10.30 Sun

(01443) 830272

Brains SA; John Smith's Bitter; guest beers

This impressive Edwardian hotel retains much of its original character. Guest beers and ciders are from smaller, often local, producers – real cider and perry are served on gravity from a cold cabinet, so ask the staff what is available before you order. A beer festival is held in May. Many visitors arrive by rail, but check the timetable as not all trains call at the local station. Q(X38,50)

Glan-y-Llyn

Fagins Ale & Chop House

9 Cardiff Road, CF15 7QD

11-midnight (1am Fri & Sat); 11-11 Sun

(029) 208 11800

Otley 01; guest beers

Superb independent free house specialising in craft beers, where the rare and welcoming sight of gravity dispense gives the impression of a permanent beer festival. Local beers feature alongside a wide variety from all over the UK; the cider is the powerful and characterful Black Dragon from local producer Gwynt y Ddraig. The value for money meals have to be seen to be believed (no eve meals Sun or Mon). Outside drinking is on roadside tables. Glan-y-Llyn is the northern part of the larger settlement of Taffs Well, with its railway station a not too strenuous walk away.

(26,132)

Hirwaun

Glancynon Inn

Swansea Road, CF44 9PH

11-11; 12-10.30 Sun

(01685) 811043

Greene King Abbot; guest beers

The main outlet for real ale in the area, this large country pub with its oak beams and congenial atmosphere is popular with drinkers and diners alike. Guest beers are usually from Welsh breweries and the restaurant uses local organic produce where possible. The pub features a pleasant lounge with a split-level bar leading to a beer garden. A little off the beaten track, it is nevertheless easy to find. Lunch is served on Sunday only (booking essential), no evening meals on Sunday.

P

Killay

Black Boy

444 Gower Road, SA2 7AL

11.30-11 (midnight Fri & Sat); 12-11 Sun

(01792) 299469

Brains Bitter, SA, Reverend James, seasonal beers

The single L-shaped room in this large, popular Brains pub is divided into several distinct areas, some mostly for dining – food is available all day until 9pm. The decor is traditional, with several TV screens used mainly for sporting events. Monday is quiz night. Bus routes 20 and 21 are the main routes from Swansea, others will take you on into Gower. (20,21)P

Village Inn

5-6 Swan Court, Gower Road, SA2 7BA

10.30-11.30; 12-11 Sun

(01792) 203311

Evan Evans Bitter; Fuller's London Pride; Taylor Landlord; Worthington's Bitter

Split-level L-shaped single room bar tucked away in the shopping precinct of a suburban Swansea village. The room is divided into several nooks and crannies, some with an extensive display of plates and sporting memorabilia. Quiz nights are Sunday and Tuesday. Food is served lunchtimes and Mon-Sat evenings until 8.30pm. There is free public parking within 50 metres. (20,21)P

Llandough

Merrie Harrier

117 Penlan Road, CF64 2NY

12-11; 11.30-11.30 Fri; 11-11.30 Sat

(029) 20303994

Brains Dark, Bitter, SA, SA Gold; guest beers

Situated in Cardiff's commuter belt, this large Brains roadhouse lies on a busy road junction near Llandough Hospital (which boasts the longest corridor in Europe). The large, comfortable lounge bar has live sport on TV and an extensive menu. Service may be a little slow at times, but the beer is worth the wait. (Cogan)P

Llangennith

Kings Head

SA3 1HX

11 (12 Sun)-11

(01792) 386212 kingsheadgower.co.uk

Draught Bass; Hancock's HB; guest beers

Large and historic stone-built pub and hotel extended over the years to incorporate adjoining farm buildings. Welcoming to dogs, it is popular with locals, visitors and surfers. The pub has two rooms, one for games, the other with a large display of images of local scenes and historic characters. Food is served all day from an enticing blackboard menu. There are impressive views of nearby beaches.

QP

Llanmadoc

Britannia Inn

Llanmadoc Gower, SA3 1DB

12-11

(01792) 386624 britanniainngower.co.uk

Marston's Pedigree; guest beers

Timbers from ships wrecked on the nearby coast were used in the construction of this pretty and popular 17th-century pub set in a quiet corner of Gower. There is a cosy bar at the entrance serving good food and beer; the rear bar area has been converted into a fine restaurant. Beer gardens front and rear offer stunning views over the nearby estuary, with an aviary and pet area popular with children.

QP

Llanrhidian

Dolphin Inn

SA3 1EH

5 (1 Fri, Sat & summer)-11

(01792) 391069

Fuller's London Pride; guest beer

Real ale outsells lager in this cosy village pub, reopened in March 2007 after 12 years' closure. Close to the Loughor estuary, it commands panoramic views of the water. Recently refurbished in traditional style, it has a long single room and a stone-faced bar. Local artwork and photography are on display. Light snacks such as ploughman's lunches are available. P

WALES

Greyhound Inn

Old Walls, SA3 1HA
⏲ 11-11; 12-10.30 Sun
☎ (01792) 391027
Draught Bass; guest beers Ⓗ
Welcoming to locals and visitors alike, this large and popular inn usually has up to five real ales available. Families are well catered for and there are separate games and function rooms. The pub has a reputation for good food, which is served in all its bars. The Sunday carvery is especially popular. The car park is large. ♨Q❀◑⊟⅄⊞♣P

Llantwit Fardre

Bush Inn

Main Road, CF38 2EP
⏲ 11-11; 12-10.30 Sun
☎ (01443) 203958
Tomos Watkin OSB; guest beers Ⓗ
This lively village local has something going on most nights – quiz, darts or live music. It may stay open later on music evenings (usually Thursday, some Saturdays). Three guest beers are usually on offer, one from a Welsh brewery, the other two may be well-known national brands but are often unusual for the area. ❀⊞(100,400)♣P

Llantwit Major

Kings Head

East Street, CF61 1XY
⏲ 11.30-11; 12-10.30 Sun
☎ (01446) 792697
Brains Dark, Bitter, SA; guest beers Ⓗ
Well-established local with an ever-growing reputation for the quality of its ale and excellent lunchtime meals. The large and popular bar has pool, darts, dominoes and a large-screen TV for sport. The quieter lounge is comfortably furnished and retains the character cherished by locals for many years. If drinking in the lounge, don't forget the Brains Dark (on handpump only in the bar). There is room for just two cars in the car park.
♨Q❀◐⊟⅄⇌⊞♣P⅟–

Old Swan Inn

Church Street, CF61 1SB
⏲ 12-11 (10.30 Sun)
☎ (01446) 792230 🌐 oldswaninn.com
Beer range varies Ⓗ
The oldest pub in a historic town, this excellent hostelry has won numerous awards for its fine ales and excellent food. Although ownership changed in March 2008, the management, extensive high-quality menu and beer policy remain unchanged. Two real ales are on offer during the week, four at weekends, with an emphasis on South Wales breweries alongside regular supplies from Cottage in Somerset. The lively back bar has pool and a jukebox while the traditional front lounge is quieter and attracts diners and drinkers. The smoking area is heated.
♨❀◑⊟⅄⇌⊞♣●⅟–

Machen

White Hart

Nant-y-Ceisiad, CF83 8QQ ST441005
☎ (01633) 441005
Beer range varies Ⓗ
An unusual blend of old and new, the interior of this inn is adorned with fittings from the liner Empress of France. Although close to the main road, the pub was built to serve the old Rumney Tramroad which now forms a cycle route. An independent free house, it stocks up to three guest beers, mainly from smaller breweries, and holds occasional beer festivals. Booking is advisable for Sunday lunch.
❀⇔◑⊞(50)♣P

Marcross

Horseshoe Inn

CF61 1ZG
⏲ 12-11 (10.30 Sun)
☎ (01656) 890568
Brains Bitter, Bread of Heaven, SA Gold Ⓗ
Due to its proximity to Nash Point lighthouse, this popular village pub on the heritage coast was until recently known as the Lighthouse, but was restored to its original name by the award-winning licensee. An Internet bottled-beer business operates from the pub (realbeerbox.com). The pub itself is a two-bar comfort zone attracting drinkers and diners in equal measure, and boasts a successful darts team. The bus stop is just yards away.
♨Q❀◐⊟⊞♣P⅟–

Merthyr Tydfil

Rose & Crown ✔

20 Morgan Street, The Quarr, CF47 8TP (off Brecon Rd S of Cyfarthfa Park)
⏲ 12-midnight
☎ (01695) 723743
Brains Bitter; Greene King Abbot; Wye Valley Bitter; guest beers Ⓗ
This busy, welcoming local is convenient for the Taff Trail but can be tricky to find – narrow one-way streets add to its elusiveness, and parking is limited. Sport is keenly followed, but can be easily avoided in some of the many rooms. Four beers are stocked, which may vary at times from those listed above.
♿⊞(26)♣⅟–

Monknash

Plough & Harrow

CF71 7QQ (off B4265 between Wick and Marcross)
⏲ 12-11 (10.30 Sun)
☎ (01656) 890209 🌐 theploughmonknash.com
Draught Bass; Worthington's Bitter; Wye Valley HPA; guest beers Ⓗ
Justifiably renowned throughout Wales, this superb ancient building and long-standing pub serves up the finest of foods to complement an ale range good enough for the gods. Customers in the lounge should note that the beer and cider range is displayed in the bar. The huge beer garden is perfect in summer, especially for the annual July beer festival. Proudly supporting Welsh brewers and cider makers, the pub also offers a home delivery

service. An absolute must if you are in the area. ⛰❀◑⊟⛺🚌♣●P⚡

Mumbles

Mumbles Rugby Club

588 Mumbles Road, SA3 4DL
⏲ 6.30 (4 Sat)-11; 12-5 Sun
☎ (01792) 368989 🌐 mumblesrfc.co.uk
Tomos Watkin OSB, Chwarae Teg, seasonal beers Ⓗ
This popular club, established in 1887 and located on the Mumbles seafront, welcomes non-members. The clubhouse, decorated with a wide range of rugby memorabilia, has a small but comfortable downstairs bar; the large function room upstairs gets lively on international days. The rugby club is proud to sell beer from one of Swansea's two small independent breweries – Chwarae Teg is a particularly appropriate choice, the name meaning 'fair play'. ⊟🚌♣

Park Inn

23 Park Street, SA3 4AD
⏲ 4 (12 Fri-Sun)-11
☎ (01792) 366738
Beer range varies Ⓗ
At this regular Swansea CAMRA Pub of the Year, five handpumps dispense an ever-changing range of beers with particular emphasis on independent breweries from Wales and the west of England. The convivial atmosphere in this small establishment attracts discerning drinkers of all ages, though the games room is particularly popular with younger people. Alongside a fine display of pump clips, pictures of old Mumbles and its pioneering railway adorn the walls. Q🚌♣●⚡

Victoria Inn

21 Westbourne Place, SA3 4DB
⏲ 12 (11.30 Sat)-11; 12-10.30 Sun
☎ (01792) 360111 🌐 victoriainnmumbles.co.uk
Draught Bass; Greene King Old Speckled Hen; Worthington's Bitter; guest beers Ⓗ
This traditional back-street corner local dates from the mid 19th century. Recently refurbished in comfortable style, it retains many original features of historic interest including a well in the bar area, the source of water in the days when the pub brewed its own beer. Live music alternate Fridays. ❀🚌♣⚡

Murton

Plough & Harrow ✔

88 Oldway, SA3 3DJ
⏲ 11-11; 12-10.30 Sun
☎ (01792) 234459
Courage Best Bitter, Directors; guest beers Ⓗ
One of Gower's oldest pubs, the Plough & Harrow has been enlarged and renovated in recent times, but retains its character and popularity. The pub combines a busy food trade with the traditions of a local. The bar area has TV and pool, and there is a quieter space for conversation or a meal. Tuesday is quiz night. Heaters are used to warm the large, covered and decked outdoor area, which unusually also has a pool table. ⛰Q❀◑⊟⛺🚌♣P⚡

Neath

Borough Arms

New Henry Street, SA11 1PH
⏲ 4 (12 Sat)-11; 12-3, 6-10.30 Sun
☎ (01639) 644902
Beer range varies Ⓗ
Local CAMRA Pub of the Year three years running, and South Wales winner in 2008, this traditional local, just outside the town centre, offers a warm welcome. A U-shaped bar serves two separate areas, one with pub games. The pub has strong rugby connections with Neath and the Ospreys and is busy on Six Nations match days. An interesting range of beers is always on offer, mainly from outside Wales. Slightly off the beaten track but well worth seeking out, it offers a covered area for smokers. ❀⇌🚌♣⚡

David Protheroe ✔

7 Windsor Road, SA11 1LS
⏲ 9-midnight (1am Fri & Sat)
☎ (01639) 622130
Evan Evans Welsh; Greene King Abbot; Marston's Pedigree; guest beers Ⓗ
This large, popular, open-plan Wetherspoon pub was formerly the police station and is named after Neath's first police officer. The taxi rank and rail and bus stations are nearby. There is a family area, and a beer garden with cover and heating for smokers. The pub participates in the chain's standard meal deals, beer festivals and other promotions. ❀◑♿⇌🚌⚡

Highlander

2 Lewis Road, SA11 1EQ
⏲ 12 (4 Mon)-11
☎ (01639) 633586
Beer range varies Ⓗ
Large single-room pub with a central bar and elevated dining area serving reasonably priced meals. Two or more changing guest beers are supplied from independent breweries. A list of forthcoming beers is displayed over the side door. The front seating area has a large-screen TV but conversation is the main entertainment here. ◑⇌🚌

Norton

Beaufort Arms

1 Castle Road, SA3 5TE
⏲ 11.30-11; 12-10.30 Sun
☎ (01792) 401319
Draught Bass; Greene King Abbot; Worthington's Bitter; guest beers Ⓗ
Eighteenth-century village local with a traditional bar with TV and dartboard and a small, comfortable lounge. Both rooms have real fires, and there is a small outside drinking area. A pub team usually enters the Mumbles raft race each year, recorded in many photographs on the walls. A charming pub with a friendly, welcoming atmosphere. ⛰Q❀◑⊟🚌(2,3)♣⚡

WALES

Nottage

Farmers Arms

Lougher Row, CF36 3TA
⏲ 11-11; 12-10.30 Sun
☎ (01656) 784595
Draught Bass; Greene King Old Speckled Hen, Abbot; guest beers ⊞
Traditional stone-built pub overlooking the village green with benches for outside drinking. Inside, the comfortable lounge has a long bar down one side and large-screen TV for sport. Live entertainment draws a crowd. There is a separate restaurant at the back. Nottage is now effectively part of Porthcawl, but retains a village atmosphere of its own.
⌂◑⊟P⊱

Rose & Crown Hotel

Heol y Capel, CF36 3ST
⏲ 12-11 (1am Fri & Sat)
☎ (01656) 784850
Courage Best Bitter; Greene King Ruddles County; guest beers ⊞
A welcome return to the Guide for this large, traditional pub in a small, picturesque village. Three bars including the cosy real ale bar offer up to three guest beers. Very popular with local residents, children are welcome in the pub. The restaurant provides a good selection of food throughout the week. For overnight guests, four doubles and four twin rooms are available. ✿⇌◑⊟⅄P

Penarth

Albion ✔

28 Glebe Street, CF64 1EF (N of Hilltop between town centre and marina)
⏲ 11-11 (midnight Fri & Sat); 12-11 Sun
☎ (029) 203 03992
Brains Dark, Bitter, SA, SA Gold; guest beer ⊞
Small street-corner two-room community local with a landlady who is a strong supporter of real ale. The regulars' preference accounts for the preponderance of Brains beers – this is not a tied house. Beer festivals are held twice a year. The interior comprises a comfortable lounge and a lively bar, both rooms smart and tidy. ⊟≷⊡♣

Bear's Head ✔

37-39 Windsor Road, CF64 1JD
⏲ 9-11.30
☎ (029) 20706424
Brains Bitter; Bullmastiff Welsh Gold, Son of a Bitch; Evan Evans Welsh Ale; Greene King Abbot; Marston's Burton Bitter; guest beers ⊞
This Wetherspoon pub attracts a mixed clientele of all ages, including the brewers from Bullmastiff Brewery (quality control, we're sure). Hardly an architectural gem, but the pub is a welcome change from the usual local outlets. The venue is named after a dubious English translation of the town's name – Pen Arth meaning Bear's Head.
◑♿≷⊡

Saint Fagans Castle

114 Glebe Street, CF64 1EB
⏲ 11-11; 12-10.30 Sun
☎ (029) 20704672
Caledonian Deuchars IPA; Taylor Landlord; guest beer ⊞
Typical town-centre pub with a loud public bar attracting a younger crowd and a quieter more traditional lounge bar with a real fire for older folk. Guest beers change regularly. The eponymous Castle, situated some miles away in the Cardiff suburbs, was given to the National Museum of Wales in 1947 by Penarth's leading landowner, and now houses Wales' hugely rewarding National History Museum. ⌂⊟≷⊡

Windsor

93 Windsor Road, CF64 1JF (on A4160 N of town centre)
⏲ 9 (12 Thu)-11.30 (11 Sun)
☎ (029) 207 02821
Brains Bitter, SA Gold; Greene King Abbot; Hancock's HB; Taylor Landlord; guest beers ⊞
Lively, traditional flagstone-floored pub offering an excellent choice of real ale and serving a good range of food starting with breakfast at 9am. Lunches are available daily and evening meals on Wednesday, Friday and Saturday evenings. There is a jazz club on Wednesday evening and a poker school most nights. A separate function room is available and an outdoor covered smoking area.
◑♿≷(Dingle Road)⊡♣⊱

Penllyn

Red Fox

CF71 7RQ (off A48) SS973763
⏲ 12-midnight (11 Sun)
☎ (01446) 772352
Hancock's HB; Tomos Watkin OSB; guest beers ⊞
Popular with the residents of this scattered community as well as visitors enjoying nearby walks, the pub offers quality food and drink in a friendly atmosphere. The main room, with its flagstone floor and nooks and crannies, has a large log fire, while a separate room is used as a dining area. Exposed stone walls are decorated with pictures, mostly relating to the red fox and its pursuit. An attractive patio to the front and a rear garden are pleasant for outdoor drinking. Quiz night is the last Thursday of the month. ⌂Q✿◑⊡(V3)P

Pontardawe

Pontardawe Inn ✔

123 Herbert Street, SA8 4ED
⏲ 12 (4 Mon)-midnight (1am Fri & Sat), closed Bank Hol Mon; 12-11 Sun
☎ (01792) 830791 🌐 pontardaweinn.co.uk
Banks's Original; Marston's Pedigree; guest beers ⊞
Also known as the Gwachel, this 250-year-old pub has three rooms served by a central bar, and a restaurant. Live music plays on Wednesday (folk), Friday and Saturday; beer festivals are held in March and August (the latter coinciding with Pontardawe Music Festival celebrating folk and world music). Food theme nights are always popular. An excellent focal point for the community, but also used by walkers and cyclists on Route 43, the pub provides a boules piste and a heated and covered area for smokers.
Q✿◑⊟♿⊡P⊱

Pontneddfechan

Angel Inn

Pontneathvaughan Road, SA11 5NR (on B4242 nr A465 jct)
11.30-11.30 summer; 11.30-4, 6.30-11.30 winter; 12-11.30 Sun
☎ (01639) 722013
Draught Bass; Rhymney Bitter Ⓗ
Former coaching inn on the edge of the Brecon Beacons National Park and near the area's famous waterfalls. It comprises a main dining area, restaurant and a small area beside the main bar to enjoy a quiet drink. A dining pub with the emphasis on food, it enjoys a deservedly high reputation for excellent home-cooked meals, including fresh fish and daily specials. Outside tables are in demand in the summer. Q❀◑♿🚌(X56)P⊬

Pontsticill

Red Cow ✔

CF48 2UN (follow signs for Brecon Mountain Railway)
11-midnight
☎ (01685) 384828
Wye Valley Bitter; guest beers Ⓗ
Set within the Brecon Beacons National Park, this traditional pub has flagstone floors and a landlord whose enthusiasm for real ale shines through. With strong local trade, the pub is also popular with walkers and visitors to the nearby Dolygaer outdoor pursuits centre. The Brecon Mountain Railway is within walking distance and there are two golf courses nearby. ♛♖❀◑♿🚌(24)♣P⊬

Pontypridd

Bunch of Grapes

Ynysangharad Road, CF37 4DA (off A4054 just N of A470 jct)
12-midnight
☎ (01443) 402934 🌐 bunchofgrapes.org.uk
Otley 01; guest beers Ⓗ
Just a few minutes' walk from the town centre stands this multi award-winning flagship for Otley Brewery. The eclectic range of ale on offer may include other Otley products, both draught and in a bottle. Real cider, often from leading local producer Gwynt y Ddraig, is available by jug from the cellar. This Tardis-like pub crams in a high-class restaurant – meals can also be taken in the bar, but booking is advisable. Allow plenty of time to experience the fabulous atmosphere here – this is a hostelry you will not want to leave. Note that last admission is 10.30pm. No meals Sun evening. Note that last admission is 10.30pm. ♛◑♣●P⊬

Llanover Arms

Bridge Street, CF37 4PE (opp N entrance to Ynysangharad Park)
12-midnight (11 Sun)
☎ (01443) 403215
Brains Bitter; Felinfoel Double Dragon; guest beer Ⓗ
This free house stands opposite the park and is just a short stroll from Pontypridd's historic Old Bridge and Museum. The pub's three rooms are festooned with a variety of artefacts including old mirrors, maps and clocks, but the major attraction here is the constantly changing guest beer which attracts a loyal following. There is outside drinking on the patio. ❀⊟≋🚌♣P

Port Talbot

Lord Caradoc ✔

69-73 Station Road, SA13 1NW
9-midnight (1am Thu-Sun)
☎ (01639) 896007
Brains SA, Rev James; Evan Evans Welsh; Greene King Abbot; Marston's Pedigree; guest beers Ⓗ
This L-shaped town-centre Lloyds No 1 (Wetherspoon's) pub near the rail and bus stations has a raised drinking area and welcomes children in the family area at the rear. A patio area outside has shelter and heating for smokers. The chain's standard range of all-day food, meal deals, beer festivals and other promotions applies. ❀◑♿≋🚌⊬

Porth

Rheola

Rheola Road, CF39 0LF
2-midnight; 1-1am Fri; 12-1am Sat; 12-midnight Sun
☎ (01443) 682633
Brains SA Gold; Draught Bass; guest beers Ⓗ
Comfortable and friendly pub with a lively bar and cosy lounge. A new guest beer is added every weekend to supplement the regulars. Situated at the gateway to the Rhondda and only a short distance from the Rhondda Heritage Park, this is a pub not to be missed. Note that last admission is 10.30pm. The outdoor smoking area is covered. ⊟≋🚌♣P⊬

Porthcawl

Lorelei Hotel

36-38 Esplanade Avenue, CF36 3YU
5 (12 Fri & Sat)-11; 12-10.30 Sun
☎ (01656) 788342
Draught Bass; Ⓖ **Rhymney Export;** Ⓗ **guest beers** Ⓗ/Ⓖ
This inconspicuous hotel in a terraced street is a real ale oasis. The number of pump clips on display reflects the commitment to a wide range of interesting guest ales, further enhanced by beer festivals in spring and autumn. Czech Budvar is served on draught along with other European beers. Real cider is available in summer. The hotel has two drinking areas and a dining room where children are admitted. The outside smoking area is covered. ♖❀⊏◑▲●⊬

Quakers Yard

Glantaff Inn

Cardiff Road, CF46 5AH
11-4, 6-1am; 11-1am Fri & Sat; 11-midnight Sun
☎ (01443) 410822
Courage Directors; guest beers Ⓗ
Comfortable pub featuring a large collection of water jugs, boxing memorabilia and old photographs of local interest. Guest beers are frequently from the local Otley and Rhymney

breweries, bringing in the locals as well as walkers and cyclists on the Taff Trail from Cardiff to Brecon. The village's name comes from an old Quaker burial ground. ◑▭(7,78)

Reynoldston

King Arthur Hotel

Higher Green, SA3 1AD
✪ 11-11; 12-10.30 Sun
☎ (01792) 390775 ⊕ kingarthurhotel.co.uk
Draught Bass; Felinfoel Double Dragon; guest beers Ⓗ
Set in the heart of Gower's beautiful countryside, this splendid pub, hotel and restaurant is deservedly popular with locals, walkers and tourists alike. During the summer the large outside area offers idyllic surroundings for drinking and dining, and in winter the cosy atmosphere in the bar is enhanced by a roaring fire. An excellent menu features local produce served in a choice of attractive dining areas. This a pub not to be missed if you are in the area.
⛫Q❀⇌◑ ▭Ä▭♣P

Rhossili

Worm's Head Hotel

SA3 1PP
✪ 11 (12 Sun)-11
☎ (01792) 386212 ⊕ thewormshead.co.uk
Tomos Watkin Worm's Head Ale, seasonal beers Ⓗ
Perched on the cliffs at the extreme western end of Gower and offering stunning views of Rhossili's magnificent beach and the headland that gives it its name, this friendly hotel, popular with walkers and tourists, has a spacious, comfortable public bar with a large TV often showing sport, and a separate dining area. Good food is available all day. The large outside terrace is busy during fine weather – sunsets can be spectacular from here.
⛫Q❀⇌◑ ▭Ä▭⁻

Rhymney

Farmers Arms

Old Brewery Lane, NP22 5EZ
✪ 12-11; 12-3.30, 7-11 Sun
☎ (01685) 840257
Brains Bitter; Fuller's London Pride; guest beers Ⓗ
Open-plan pub next to the site of the old Rhymney Brewery, whose memory is kept alive by old photographs and breweriana – the landlord, landlady and many customers are former brewery staff. The bar retains a traditional atmosphere enhanced by the recently-installed real fire. A function room is available for up to 40 people. Quiz night is Thursday. No food Sunday evening.
⛫Q❀◑ ⇌♣P

Risca

Commercial Inn ✔

Commercial Street, Pontymister, NP11 6AB (on B4591 at Brookland Rd jct)
✪ 11-11.30 (midnight Fri & Sat); 12-11 Sun
☎ (01633) 612608
Hop Back Summer Lightning; guest beers Ⓗ
Very popular pub with plenty of seating for drinkers and diners out on a spacious front patio, which can be covered by a retractable awning when required. Inside, the pub is comfortably furnished with an adjoining lounge and bar/games areas. A number of TVs are dotted around, mainly showing sport. The menu includes a good range of main meals plus lighter bites such as baguettes and sandwiches. Gwent CAMRA Pub of the Year 2008. ❀◑ ⇌▭♣⁻

Rudry

Maenllwyd Inn ✔

CF83 3EB
✪ 12-11 (10.30 Sun)
☎ (029) 208 82372
Beer range varies Ⓗ
Busy Chef & Brewer dining pub in a rural retreat just north east of Cardiff —a pleasant sanctuary from the bustle of the capital and nearby towns. The original Victorian inn forms the entrance to a now much extended establishment. Four guest beers are stocked, mostly from larger and regional brewers.
⛫Q❀◑▭P

St Brides Major

Farmers Arms

Wick Road, Pitcot, CF32 0SE
✪ 12-3, 6-11; 12-10.30 Sun
☎ (01656) 880224
Brains SA; Greene King IPA; Hancock's HB; Wadworth 6X; Wychwood Hobgoblin Ⓗ
Spacious, attractive roadside pub on the edge of the village opposite the pond, enjoying a good reputation for both food and beer. The lounge bar is comfortably furnished and has china jugs hanging from the wood beams; there is also a separate restaurant. Live entertainment is hosted at the weekends. The car park is large. ⛫Q❀◑ ▭▭♣P

Swansea

Brunswick

3 Duke Street, SA1 4HS
✪ 11-11; 12-10.30 Sun
☎ (01792) 465676
Theakston XB; Courage Best Bitter; Ⓗ **guest beer** Ⓖ
This well-run side street pub has the air of a country inn in the city. Wooden beams and comfortable seating create a traditional, relaxing atmosphere. The walls are adorned with an interesting, ever-changing display of artwork, with pictures for sale. A quiz is held on Monday evening and live acoustic music plays on Sunday, Tuesday and Thursday. The guest beer is sometimes from a local brewery.
◑♿

Eli Jenkins

24 Oxford Street, SA1 3AQ
✪ 8-midnight; 11-11 Sun
Badger Tanglefoot; Brains Bitter; guest beers Ⓗ
City centre pub near the bus station named after the chapel minister in Swansea-born Dylan Thomas' Under Milk Wood. The interior

features wooden alcoves with varied seating layouts and prints of local views on the walls. Popular throughout the day from the moment it opens for early breakfast, it is particularly busy at lunchtime and early evening. Two guest beers, sometimes including Fuller's ESB, are sold.

Potters Wheel

85 The Kingsway, SA1 5JE
9-midnight (1am Fri & Sat)
(01792) 465113
Brains SA; Evan Evans Welsh; Greene King Abbot; Marston's Pedigree; guest beers
This city-centre Wetherspoon's pub named after the local industry shows a greater than usual commitment to a wide range of beers from micro-breweries, and an interesting selection of guest beers has boosted sales of real ale. A long, sprawling bar area has various seating layouts and attracts customers of diverse ages and backgrounds. A real cider from Weston's is often on handpump.

Queens Hotel

Gloucester Place, SA1 1TY
11-11; 12-10.30 Sun
(01792) 521531
Brains Buckley's Best Bitter; Theakston Best Bitter, Old Peculier; guest beers
This vibrant free house, local CAMRA Pub of the Year 2008, is located near the Dylan Thomas Centre, City Museum, National Waterfront Museum (covering science and Industry) and marina. The walls display many photographs depicting Swansea's rich maritime heritage. The pub enjoys strong local support and the home-cooked lunches are popular. Evening entertainment includes a Sunday quiz and live music on Saturday. Two guest beers are sold.

Westbourne

1 Brynymor Road, SA1 4JR
11-11.30 (12pm Thu; 12.30am Fri & Sat); 12-11 Sun
(01792) 476637 westbourneswansea.com
Draught Bass; Felinfoel Double Dragon; Greene King Abbot; Marston's Pedigree; guest beers
Set on the western fringe of the city centre, this well-known, modernised street-corner pub is now predominantly purple, inside and outside. A popular venue for young and old, it hosts a quiz on Tuesday evening and Sky TV attracts sports enthusiasts. Food is served all day until 6pm (4pm Sun).

Wig

134 St Helen's Road, SA1 4BL
12-11 (midnight Fri & Sat)
(01792) 466519
Beer range varies
A short walk from the city centre near the Guildhall, the Wig is approached by a number of steps, with disabled access to the right. The L-shaped interior includes a bright, comfortable open-plan area to the front and a smaller games area with darts and pool to the rear. Outside seating is popular in summer. Four handpumps serve a rotating range of beers, often from Adnams, Cottage and Rhymney breweries. High-quality food is available until 8pm (6pm Sun).

Treboeth

King's Head

Llangyfelach Road, SA5 9EL (on B4489)
12-11 (midnight Fri-Sun)
(01792) 773727
Beer range varies
Large, popular, family-friendly pub in a Swansea suburb comprising a split-level lounge bar, restaurant and function room. Two real ales are always available from small independent breweries, mostly from Wales and south-west England. Tasty meals are served all day. Quiz nights every Sun and Tue. The patio area to the front has benches for warmer weather and smokers. P

Treforest

Otley Arms

Forest Road, CF37 1SY
11-12.30am (1.30am Fri & Sat); 12-12.30am
(01443) 402033
Otley 01, OG; guest beers
This much-extended end of terrace hostelry has a number of drinking areas, always in demand by the mixed clientele of locals and Glamorgan University students – as is the range of beers, which may include others from Otley Brewery. There is a large following for sport on multiple TV screens. A good local rail service makes the pub easily accessible from Cardiff and many valley towns. The outdoor smoking area is heated and covered.
(100,244)

Treherbert

Baglan Hotel

30 Baglan Street, CF42 5AW
12 (3 Mon)-11 (1am Sat); 11-11 Sun
(01443) 776111
Brains Rev James; Felinfoel Double Dragon; guest beers
This welcome oasis for real ale has been in the same family for more than 60 years. Photos of well-known visitors adorn the walls. Its location at the head of the Rhondda valley makes the hotel a good base for the more active visitor, particularly if interested in outdoor pursuits such as hill walking or mountain biking. (120,130)

Tyla Garw

Boar's Head

Coedcae Lane, CF72 9EZ (600m from A473 over level crossing) ST029815
12 (4 Mon)-11; 12-4, 7-11 Sun
(01443) 225400
Brains Rev James; RCH Pitchfork; guest beers
Former CAMRA regional Pub of the Year with an excellent reputation for beer and food. A very friendly hostelry, it serves up to six ales which change frequently and can include an unusual choice for the area. The restaurant is extremely popular, with Tuesday steak night and Wednesday curry evening. Booking is necessary for Sunday lunch (no meals Sun eve nor Mon lunchtime).
Q (Pontyclun) P

WALES

Upper Killay

Railway Inn

553 Gower Road, SA2 7DS

12-2, 4-11; 12-11 Sat; 12-10.30 Sun

(01792) 203946

Swansea Deep Slade Dark, Bishopswood, Three Cliffs Gold, Original Wood; guest beers

Built in 1864, this friendly pub is a popular local with a warm welcome for visitors too, hosting many social events in the summer. The old railway formation that runs alongside this former station house is now a footpath and cycleway leading to Swansea Bay. No food is served, and no children permitted inside. A former local and regional CAMRA Pub of the Year.

P

Ystalyfera

Wern Fawr Inn

47 Wern Road, SA9 2LX

7 (6.30 Fri)-11; 2-10.30 Sun

(01639) 843625 bryncelynbrewery.org.uk

Bryncelyn Buddy Marvellous, Holly Hop, Oh Boy, seasonal beers

Brewery tap for the multi award-winning Bryncelyn Brewery, whose beers, with names themed on Buddy Holly, have picked up over 15 awards since 1999 including three category winners at CAMRA's Champion Beer of Wales 2007. The bar is full of domestic and industrial artefacts including breweriana and a collection of locally-made bricks. There is also a comfortable lounge. Darwin Awards in the Gents are amusing. Outside is a covered space for smokers.

Q

Mountain Hare, Brynnau Gwynion

Authority areas covered: Blaenau Gwent, Monmouthshire, Newport, Torfaen

Abergavenny

Angel Hotel

15 Cross Street, NP7 5EN

10-3, 6-11 (11.30 Fri & Sat); 12-3, 6-10.30 Sun

(01873) 857121 angelhotelabergavenny.com

Fuller's London Pride; Wye Valley HPA; guest beer 🄷

Former town centre coaching inn, sympathetically and lovingly restored to something of its former glory, including the installation of a brand new set of handpumps in the bar. The main Foxhunter Bar is a comfortable room with large tables, leather sofas, original wood panelling and an open fire. There is also a separate quiet lounge featuring interesting old paintings of Abergavenny. Outside, the well appointed courtyard is pleasant for alfresco drinks. Excellent food is served in the bar as a less formal alternative to the restaurant.

Q P

Coliseum ✓

Lion Street, NP7 5PE

9-midnight (1am Fri & Sat)

(01873) 736960

Evan Evans Welsh Ale; Greene King Abbot; Marston's Pedigree; guest beers 🄷

This former cinema is now a spacious Wetherspoon's, retaining the original high ceilings. A curved staircase with a stair lift leads to the bar with its long serving counter. The pub attracts a diverse clientele at all times of the day, particularly young people at the weekend. As well as the staple fare of Pedigree, Abbot and Weston's cider, guest beers, both local and far flung, are almost always available.

Kings Head Hotel

60 Cross Street, NP7 5EU

10-30-11; 12-4, 7-10.30 Sun

(01873) 853575

Wells Bombardier; guest beer 🄷

Next to the town hall and market in the heart of the town centre, this pub attracts a wide range of customers. Busy during the day with shoppers, particularly for Tuesday market day, it gets livelier at night when a mainly younger crowd comes in, especially on Fridays when there is often live music. The large open-plan room has wooden beams and etched windows featuring drinks and breweries long since gone. No food Sun.

INDEPENDENT BREWERIES

Cwmbran Upper Cwmbran
Kingstone Tintern
Tudor Abergavenny (NEW)
Warcop Wentlooge

Station

37 Brecon Road, NP7 5UH

⏲ 5 (1 Wed & Thu)-midnight; 12.30-1am Fri; 12-1am Sat; 11.30-11 Sun

☎ (01873) 854759

Draught Bass; Fuller's London Pride; Wye Valley HPA; Rhymney Bitter; guest beers 🄷

An indication of this pub's past is evident in the railway pictures that adorn the walls of the cosy, traditional bar. Attractive settles make this an ideal place to while away some time in quiet conversation, particularly in the late afternoon or early evening before the atmosphere gets more lively. As you enter from the main road a small, comfortable lounge is situated to the right of the bar. There is no entry after 11pm. ❀⊟🚌♣

Bassaleg

Tredegar Arms ✔

4 Caerphilly Road, NP10 8LE (1 mile N of M4 jct 28)

⏲ 11 (12 Mon)-11; 11-midnight Fri & Sat; 12-10.30 Sun

☎ (01633) 894237

Greene King IPA, Ruddles County, Old Speckled Hen, Abbot; 🄷 **guest beers** 🄷/🄶

Large, imposing pub dominating a busy roundabout in a residential area to the west of Newport. A former Whitbread house, now Greene King, it offers one of the largest selections of real ales in the area. Guest ales come from both the Greene King stable and smaller independent breweries; the cider is Moles Black Rat. There are two separate bars, the larger one with dining and family areas. Outside is a large garden and play area with a purpose built smoking section.
❀◐⊟♿🚌●P⚟

Brynmawr

Hobby Horse Inn

30 Greenland Road, NP23 4DT (off Alma St)

⏲ 12-3, 7-midnight; 11.30-midnight Sat & Sun

☎ (01495) 310996 🌐 hobbyhorse.cjb.net

Beer range varies 🄷

Taking its name from the old Rhymney Brewery logo, with the distinctive Hobby Horse sign outside, this cosy nook is at the hub of the local community. The small servery is in an intimate snug, decorated with sporting memorabilia and a colourful array of pump clips. There is a larger room that is popular with lunchtime diners and families, and a restaurant used primarily for Sunday lunches. Good value B&B is available. ❀🛏◐🚌♣⚟

Caerleon

Bell Inn

Bulmore Road, NP18 1QQ (off New Road B4236)

⏲ 12-3 (not Mon & Tue), 6-11; 12-11 Fri & Sat; 12-10.30 Sun

☎ (01633) 420613 🌐 thebellatcaerleon.co.uk

Beer range varies 🄷

A regular CAMRA award winner, what was once an under-performing pub has been transformed with innovation and hard work into a real gem. Behind the impressive stone facade is a cosy low-beamed dining room, fireside bar and snug. Serving excellent Welsh/Breton food and an appealing drinks range, including an extensive choice of ciders and perries, its appeal extends beyond its locality. Real ale and cider events are hosted throughout the year while Celtic music plays weekly. If travelling by bus, alight at the Ship Inn. ❀◐🚌(2)♣●P⚟

Hanbury Arms

Uskside, High Street, NP18 1AA

⏲ 11.30-11 (midnight Fri & Sat); 12-10.30 Sun

☎ (01633) 420361

Brains SA, Rev James; Greene King Abbot; guest beers 🄷

Enter this old pub and you step into Caerleon's past. Its Norman tower and picturesque riverside location helped inspire Tennyson during his writing of Idylls of the King – his stay in 1856 is commemorated with a wall plaque. The large, rambling interior has various areas for comfortable drinking and dining, while the extensive gardens are hugely popular in fine weather. Outstanding local Roman remains and other attractions are nearby. ❀◐🚌♣P⚟

Caldicot

Castle Inn

64 Church Road, Monmouthshire, NP26 4HN (opp St Mary's Church)

⏲ 12-11 (midnight Fri & Sat)

☎ (01291) 420509

Flowers IPA; Greene King IPA; guest beers 🄷

Nestling in its own grounds with wooded surrounds, this popular pub attracts a good, mixed clientele including families. The central servery is in a low, beamed open plan room, with an area given over to diners. The pub is renowned locally for the quality of its food, with a choice of dishes from an extensive menu. Its large neighbour, the impressive 12th-century Caldicot Castle, draws many visitors to the area. 🔥❀◐⛺🚌P

Chepstow

Coach & Horses

Welsh Street, NP16 5LN

⏲ 12-11 (10.30 Sun)

☎ (01291) 622626 🌐 coachandhorsesinn.co.uk

Brains Dark, SA, Rev James; guest beers 🄷

Popular town-centre pub where you can enjoy well-kept beer and friendly conversation. The choice of ales includes five from Brains (four in the summer when a Weston's cider replaces the Dark) alongside one guest. The Coach's summertime beer festival celebrates more than 30 ales from independents and coincides every other year with the town's folk festival, when the pub becomes a mecca for musicians and dancers. Good-value home-prepared food is available at lunchtime and Monday to Friday evenings. ❀🛏◐⇌🚌●⚟

Clytha

Clytha Arms

NP7 9BW (on B4598 Old Road between Raglan & Abergavenny) SO366088

⏲ 12-3 (not Mon), 6-11; 12-11 Sat; 12-4, 7-10.30 Sun

☎ (01873) 840206 🌐 clytha-arms.com

Beer range varies Ⓗ
Renowned pub and restaurant, also offering high quality accommodation, set in extensive grounds in a magnificent house that was once the Dower House for the nearby Clytha Estate. Winning awards for its beer and food, including Gwent CAMRA Pub of the Year, has become almost routine. A well-chosen selection of beers is always on offer, together with draught cider and perry. The Clytha hosts separate festivals of Welsh beers and ciders every year. ⌂Q❀⇌◑⊟♣●P

Coed-y-Paen

Carpenters Arms

NP4 0TH SO334986
✪ 12-3 (not Mon), 6-11; 12-11 Sat; 12-5 Sun
☎ (01291) 672621 ⊕ thecarpenterscoedypaen.co.uk
Beer range varies Ⓗ
Located in an attractive rural setting, a degree of modernisation has not spoilt the cosy feel of this interesting village local. Convenient for Llandegveth reservoir, with facilities for boating and wind-surfing, there are also good walks and golfing in the area. There is a large beer garden with camping facilities next door. The restaurant features the produce of the local area, and the beer range usually includes a guest from Wye Valley. ⌂Q❀◑ÅP

Cwmbran

Queen Inn

Upper Cwmbran Road, NP44 5AX
✪ 12-midnight (11 Sun)
☎ (01633) 484252 ⊕ thequeeninn.co.uk
Beer range varies Ⓗ
One of just two pubs in Britain with this name, this is a pristine, whitewashed inn surrounded by trees, with a fast flowing stream at the front where ducks and chickens reside in a lovely garden setting. Originally three old miners cottages, now knocked together, it has three adjoining areas: a lounge cum dining room, a small public bar, and a restaurant with an old dresser. The beers are mainly from independent breweries. ⌂❀◑⊟⊟P⁄–

Govilon

Bridgend Inn

Church Lane, NP7 9RP
✪ 12-4 (not Mon), 7-11 (midnight Tue-Thu); 12-10.30 Sun
☎ (01873) 830177
Beer range varies Ⓗ
In the middle of the village next to a canal bridge and babbling brook, the pub is a handy refreshment stop for those venturing along the canal. The lounge is full of character with scattered musical instruments on display – the landlord is a keen musician and live music features occasionally on Friday. Up to four interesting guest ales may be on handpump depending on the time of year. The public bar and sun-trap smoking patio are at the rear. Q❀⊟⊟P⁄–

Grosmont

Angel Inn

Main Street, NP7 8EP
✪ 12-2.30 (not Mon), 6-11; 12-2, 7-10.30 Sun
☎ (01981) 240646
Beer range varies Ⓗ
This community pub was rescued from closure by a local consortium a few years ago. Now it is truly at the heart of this delightful village. Part of a row of old whitewashed cottages, it is close to the impressive castle remains and parish church that indicate the former importance of this now fairly isolated border village – definitely in Wales, though the darts team plays in a Herefordshire league. Beers usually come from Tomos Watkin and Wye Valley breweries. If dining, try the award-winning sausages made by a local butcher. ⌂❀◑P

Llangattock Lingoed

Hunter's Moon

NP7 8RR SO363201
✪ 12-3 (not Mon-Fri Oct-March), 6.30-midnight; 12-3, 6.30-11 Sun
☎ (01873) 821499 ⊕ hunters-moon-inn.co.uk
Wye Valley HPA; Ⓗ **guest beers** Ⓗ/Ⓖ
Situated on Offa's Dyke path, this 13th-century pub stands next to an equally ancient church which is also worth visiting. As well as the tasty ale, good quality food and accommodation are also on offer. In summer, raised decking overlooking the churchyard is pleasant, and there is also a grassy area surrounding a natural pool with ducks. Weston's Old Rosie cider is available on draught. ⌂❀⇌◑●P⁄–

Llanhennock

Wheatsheaf

NP18 1LT ST353928
✪ 11-11; 12-3, 7-10.30 Sun
☎ (01633) 420468 ⊕ thewheatsheafllanhennock.co.uk
Fuller's London Pride; guest beers Ⓗ
Two miles north of the ancient Roman town of Caerleon, this is a fine example of a traditional country pub. It has a cosy lounge with dining and a public bar displaying old photos and other memorabilia. The guest beer is usually from a micro brewery, often local. Gwent boules (petanque) players gather here to play in the car park. Views of the surrounding countryside are excellent, front and back. ⌂❀◑⊟♣P

Llanishen

Carpenters Arms

NP16 6QH (on B4293 between Monmouth and Devauden) SO478032
✪ 12-3 (not Tue), 5.30 (6 Tue)-11; closed Mon; 12-3, 7-10.30 Sun
☎ (01600) 860812
Wadworth 6X; guest beers Ⓗ
Locals, townies and visitors to the area are equally welcome in this cosy roadside village inn, a natural staging post for today's walkers and riders on the high old road northwards from Chepstow. Now in its fourth century and

WALES

wearing well, the Carps hosts a choice of darts and pool on one side of a central divide and tables for diners on the other. A guest beer from the local Kingstone Brewery features frequently. Q◐▣♣P

Newport

John Wallace Linton ✔
10-12 The Cambrian Centre, Cambrian Road, NP20 1GA
9-midnight (1am Fri & Sat)
☎ (01633) 251752
Brains SA; Evan Evans Original Welsh Ale; Greene King Abbot; Marston's Pedigree; guest beers H
Popular Wetherspoon's pub named after local World War II hero, submarine commander 'Tubby' Linton VC. Close to the railway station and late night venues, the pub attracts travellers in the daytime and pre-nightclub revellers in the evening. The interior is spacious with local heritage scenes and modern artwork dotted around the walls. The front has some provision for outdoor drinking under awnings. Interesting guest ales from independent breweries plus the regular beers make for a good choice. Q❀◐♿⇌▣●⅂

Old Murenger House
53 High Street, NP20 1GA
11-11; 12-10.30 Sun
☎ (01633) 263977 🌐 murenger.com
Samuel Smith OBB H
This survivor from Tudor times provides a traditional haven in the heart of the city's main drinking area. It is named after a medieval tax collector who was responsible for maintaining the city's defences. Furnished with much dark wood and decorated with pictures with a local historic theme, there is also a framed top on display donated by local rap/hip-hop band Goldie Lookin Chain. Divided into different areas, this is a pleasant pub with a relaxing environment where conversation dominates. Q◐⇌▣

Red Lion
47 Charles Street, NP20 1JH
12 (11 Wed & Thu)-midnight (1am Fri & Sat); 12-10.30 Sun
☎ (01633) 264398
Beer range varies H
One of very few traditional pubs left in a city where others have been decimated by uncaring owners. It is far enough away from the centre not to attract late night revellers but close enough to be handy for local transport links. The range of up to three guest ales varies within the restrictions of the owning pub company. Sporting events are popular on the large screen TV and this is a local hot spot for lovers of shove-ha'penny.
⋈❀⇌▣♣⅂

St Julian Inn
Caerleon Road, NP18 1QA
11.30-11.30 (midnight Thu-Sat); 12-11 Sun
☎ (01633) 243548 🌐 stjulian.co.uk/
John Smith's Bitter; Wells Bombardier; guest beers H
Established Guide regular, the 'Ju's' is renowned for the consistency of its fine ales, including a diverse guest beer sourced from anywhere in the UK. It has excellent outdoor facilities for smokers and unrivalled views of the River Usk and ancient Roman historic site at nearby Caerleon. Popular with young and old, locals and visitors to the area, it is the hub of the community and has a pool table, boules and a skittle alley. Close to the Celtic Manor Ryder Cup golf course. ❀◐▣♣P⅂

Pantygelli

Crown
Old Hereford Road, NP7 7HR SO302178
12-2.30 (3 Sat, not Mon), 6-11; 12-3, 6-10.30 Sun
☎ (01873) 853314 🌐 thecrownatpantygelli.com
Draught Bass; Rhymney Best Bitter; Wye Valley HPA; guest beers H
Rapidly establishing a name for offering quality food to rival its fine ales, this family-run free house continues to go from strength to strength. In recent years it has been upgraded and redecorated without losing any of its essential charm and character, offering a friendly welcome to visitors and locals. On warm days the delightful patio overlooking the Skirrid Mountain is a great place for alfresco dining. ⋈❀◐P

Penallt

Boat Inn
Lone Lane, NP25 4AJ SO535098
11-3, 5-11; 11-11 Sat; 12-10.30 Sun
☎ (01600) 712615
Beer range varies G
In an idyllic location on the banks of the River Wye, this stone-built pub is hugely popular in summer. Beers, often including a Wye Valley ale, are served from the cask, perfect for washing down the tasty fresh food. In fine weather drinkers and diners sit out in the raised garden area overlooking the river. As many as 12 bottled and cask ciders are on offer as well as a selection of country wines. Live music plays every Tuesday and Thursday. If travelling by bus, alight at Redbrook.
⋈Q❀◐▣●

Pontypool

John Capel Hanbury ✔
130-131 Osborne Road, NP4 6LT
9am-midnight (1am Fri & Sat)
☎ (01495) 767080
Brains SA Gold; Evan Evans Original Welsh Ale; guest beers H
This successful Wetherspoon's Lloyds No 1 shop conversion has considerably enhanced the town's real ale and entertainment scene. Named after a former Lord Lieutenant of the County and member of a great coal and steel industry dynasty, much local history is depicted on the walls, illustrating the rich industrial heritage of the area. The interior is spacious but divided into different areas with a variety of seating from comfy sofas to traditional tables and chairs. ◐♿▣●⅂

Raglan

Beaufort Arms ✔
High Street, NP15 2DY

⚙ 11-11; 12-10.30 Sun
☎ (01291) 690412 🌐 beautfortraglan.co.uk
Brains Rev James; Fuller's London Pride; guest beers Ⓗ
Large 16th-century coaching inn with a spacious rambling interior whose decor befits its great age. The traditional Stable Bar is cosy, while the lounge offers a comfortable alternative with sofas and a large fireplace. A full menu includes locally sourced produce and features weekly specials; you may eat in the lounge or brasserie. The beer range is usually selected from independent family or regional breweries, while a cider appears in summer. Q❀⇌◗⊟⊡●P⁻

Ship Inn
High Street, NP15 2DY
⚙ 11.30 (12 Mon)-11.30; 11.30-11.30 Sun
☎ (01291) 690635
Beer range varies Ⓗ
The approach to this Grade II listed building is via a small cobbled courtyard that serves as an outside drinking area. The interior comprises a small bar with a larger room to the right and a dining area to the left. The games room has now become a restaurant. There are usually three ales on offer, often from micros, and the food is freshly prepared. ⌂Q❀◗⊟⊡

Rogerstone

Tredegar Arms
157 Cefn Road, NP10 9AS
⚙ 12-3, 5.30-11; 12-11 Thu-Sat; 12-4, 7-10.30 Sun
☎ (01633) 664999
Draught Bass; Courage Best Bitter; guest beers Ⓗ
Welcoming roadside pub built on traditional lines, popular with locals and visitors alike. The pleasant interior has separate lounge and public bars and a dining room. Outside there is a patio and large garden, attracting families in summer. Renowned for its wide choice of good food, a large noticeboard in the lounge displays the menu (no meals Sun eve). The guest beer is ever changing and frequently from a micro-brewer. Q❀◗⊟P

Sebastopol

Open Hearth
Wern Road, NP4 5DR
⚙ 11.30-midnight; 12-11.30 Sun
☎ (01495) 763752
Caledonian Deuchars IPA; Greene King Abbot; guest beers Ⓗ
Formerly the Railway before being renamed with a nod towards the local steelworks, this family run multi-roomed pub adjoins the towpath of the Monmouthshire & Brecon Canal. Outside there are benches, a patio and children's play area which are popular in fine weather. Up to four guest ales are usually from regional or family brewers but occasionally a local beer appears. The lounge is a popular dining venue. Q❀◗⊟⊡P⁻

Sebastopol Social Club
Wern Road, NP4 5DU
⚙ 12-11.30 (12.30am Fri & Sat); 12-11 Sun
☎ (01495) 763808
M&B Brew XI; guest beers Ⓗ
South & Mid Wales CAMRA Club of the Year 2008, this was formerly the Comrades of the Great War Club. It is the base of the local Torfaen Jazz Society which hosts events in the upstairs bar on Wednesday and Friday. Up to seven ales, mostly from micro-breweries, are available. The enthusiastic stewardess has introduced oversized lined glasses. The club is home to several sports teams and gets extremely busy on major sporting occasions. Non members are welcome subject to normal visitor rules. ❀◗⊡♣P⊓

Skenfrith

Bell Inn
NP7 8UH (on B4521 between Abergavenny and Ross on Wye)
⚙ 11-11 (not Mon, Nov-March); 12-10.30 Sun
☎ (01600) 750235 🌐 skenfrith.co.uk
Breconshire Golden Valley; St Austell Tribute; Taylor Landlord; guest beers Ⓗ
Award-winning hotel and restaurant with a stone-flagged and oak-beamed bar next to a low bridge over the Monnow. An open log fire in winter helps to create a warming retreat while the garden is particularly attractive in summer. The cider is from Broome Farm in neighbouring Herefordshire. Nearby is an interesting Norman castle which is part of the Three Castles Walk from Grosmont to Skenfrith and Whitecastle. ⌂Q❀⇌◗⊟●P⁻

Talywain

Globe Inn
Commercial Road, NP4 7JH (off B4246 at Abersychan)
⚙ 5 (1 Sat)-11; 12-10.30 Sun
☎ (01495) 772053
Breconshire Brecon County Ale; Rhymney Bevans Bitter; guest beers Ⓗ
You cannot miss this friendly valleys' pub with a striking three-dimensional Globe sign outside. A survivor of a once familiar breed of traditional two-roomers, the cosy public bar is warmed by a real fire on colder days. Interesting pictures of former local railway stations and other industrial heritage scenes are displayed in both the bar and lounge. The lounge has a pool table at the rear and hosts occasional live entertainment at weekends. Real cider is often available in the summer months. ⌂❀⊟⊡♣●⁻

Tintern

Moon & Sixpence
NP16 6SG
⚙ 12-11 (midnight Thu; 1am Fri & Sat)
☎ (01291) 689284
Wye Valley Bitter, Butty Bach; guest beer Ⓗ
Comfortable multi-roomed pub with some parts dating from the 15th century. The fascinating interior layout is on several levels and features old oak beams, much stonework and a fountain. A games room has darts, pool and sports TV. From the terrace you can look across the River Wye towards Tintern Abbey in the heart of this area of outstanding natural beauty. There is an extensive, good value food menu. ⌂Q❀◗Å⊡♣P

WALES

Trellech

Lion Inn

NP25 4PA

🕒 12-3, 6 (7 Mon)-11 (midnight Thu); 12-midnight Fri & Sat; 12-4.30 Sun

☎ (01600) 860322

Beer range varies Ⓗ

Award-winning, massively popular village inn where drinkers and diners alike are warmly welcomed. Its 16th-century walls, originally home to a brewery, today embrace a two-part open-plan bar. Up to four cask ales are on offer, with Bath SPA a frequent guest, and Belgian beers Chimay and Duvel available in bottles. Hungarian dishes are complemented by local 'wild food' dishes in a wide range of superb home-cooked food. Each June brings a beer festival, echoed by a bottled-beer event every November. ⋒Q❀⊭◐⊟♣P

Upper Llanover

Goose & Cuckoo

NP7 9ER SO292073

🕒 11.30-3, 7-11; closed Mon; 11.30-11 Fri & Sat; 12-10.30 Sun

☎ (01873) 880277 🌐 gooseandcuckoo.co.uk

Brains Rev James; Breconshire Welsh Pale Ale; guest beers Ⓗ

Mobile phones are banned at this refreshingly untouched pub where a welcoming pint and conversation are the order of the day. The Grade II listed building can be recognised by the distinctive pub sign and provides welcome respite for walkers and cyclists alike. From the large garden where your companions may be ducks and goats there are glorious panoramic views out over the valley towards the Skirrid Mountain and beyond. Two beer festivals are held annually at Whitsun and August bank holidays. ⋒Q❀⊭◐♣P

Usk

Kings Head Hotel

18 Old Market Street, NP15 1AL

🕒 11-11; 12-10.30 Sun

☎ (01291) 672963

Fuller's London Pride; Taylor Landlord Ⓗ

Through the lobby turn left into the main bar where you will find a homely room on two levels with a dark, relaxing decor. Food is served here and in the Lionel Sweet dining room that adjoins it. Dotted around is an array of items of interest such as old books, numerous implements and artefacts, fishing pictures and trophies – compliments of the owner. A popular place for dining out, en suite and standard B&B is available. ⋒⊭◐⊟P

Nags Head Inn ✔

Twyn Square, NP15 1BH

🕒 11-3, 5.30-11; 12-3, 5.30-10.30 Sun

☎ (01291) 672820

Brains Rev James; guest beers Ⓗ

This old inn looks resplendent in season with a superb colourful floral display set against a white exterior. Take some time to look around the dark wood-beamed interior and admire the range of interesting artefacts and local memorabilia before settling down to enjoy locally-sourced cuisine washed down by the best Brains beer for miles. The lighter Tack Room has a horse-racing theme with an impressive display of equine tack on its wood panelled walls. Q◐⊟

Royal Hotel

26 New Market Street, NP15 1AT

🕒 12-3, 7-11.30; closed Mon; 12-5 Sun

☎ (01291) 672931

Draught Bass; guest beers Ⓗ

Something of a local institution, the Royal has a timeless appeal. There is a pleasant lounge and dining room on one side; on the other the traditional public bar includes a high back settle and a large wooden table. Renowned for serving top class food cooked to order, you may have to wait a little while for your meal to arrive, so make the most of the opportunity and enjoy some really tasty ale. A public car park is opposite. ⋒Q❀◐⊟⊟P⁻

Usk Conservative Club

The Grange, 16 Maryport Street, NP15 1AB

🕒 12-3, 7-11 (10.30 Sun)

☎ (01291) 672634

Beer range varies Ⓗ

Well appointed private members' club set in its own grounds. The smart servery is at the centre of a comfortably furnished lounge with a games area on one side and a dining room on the other. Pictures of Tory Party notables hang from the walls including the local real ale loving MP. Expect to see a Fuller's beer plus one or two guests from established family and regional brewers. Non-members are welcome but club entry rules may be applied. No lunches Monday; evening meals Wednesday, Friday and Saturday only. ❀◐⊟♣P

The Cherry Tree in Tintern, which appeared without a break in 35 editions of the Good Beer Guide, has closed due to objections by Monmouthshire council to the pub's road sign. The pub had a sign on the main road and the council told pub owners Steve and Jill Pocock to take it down. When they refused, the council issued a court summons and Steve Pocock was given a six-month suspended sentence.

The Pococks reluctantly took down the sign and their sales then dropped by 50 per cent between September 2007 and July 2008. They had run the pub for eight years but had to sell. They now run the nearby Anchor Inn but have already run foul of the council. Steve Pocock said he had been visited by both planners and environmental health officers and once again has been told to alter signs for the pub.

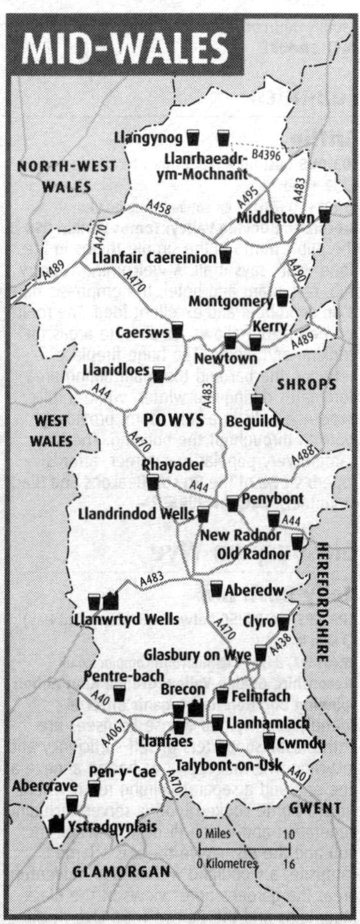

Authority area covered: Powys

Abercrave

Copper Beech Inn

133 Heol Tawe, SA9 1XS (off A4067)

11 (2 Mon & Tue winter)-midnight

☎ (01639) 730269

Beer range varies Ⓗ

Situated on the edge of the Brecon Beacons National Park, this village pub offers accommodation and lunchtime and evening meals. A central bar serves up to four changing guest beers with one handpump dedicated to Welsh micro-breweries. On the right of the bar two settles cosy up to a large inglenook fireplace with log-burning stove. A comfortable lounge area with a relaxed atmosphere attracts locals, walkers, cyclists, climbers and cavers. ⛰Q❀⇄◐♿⊟P⅟

Aberedw

Seven Stars

LD2 3UW (off B4567)

12-3, 6.30 (6 Fri & Sat)-11; 12-3.30, 6.30-10.30 Sun

☎ (01982) 560494 🌐 7-stars.co.uk

Beer range varies Ⓗ

Cosy pub with exposed beams, open stonework and flagstone floors. Legend has it that Llywelyn ap Gruffudd, the last true Prince of Wales, had his horse shod with reversed shoes here by a local smith to enable him to escape his pursuers. Tragically the ruse was unsuccessful and Llywelyn was killed at nearby Cilmeri. The smithy is now part of the inn. The pub opens around 9am most mornings for tea and coffee. Real cider, and often perry, are now available.

⛰Q❀⇄◐⊟♿⛺♣●P⅟

Beguildy

Radnorshire Arms ✔

LD7 1YE (on B4355)

7-midnight (1am Fri & Sat); closed Mon; 12-3, 7-midnight Sun

☎ (01547) 510354

Fuller's London Pride; Wye Valley Beguildy Bitter; guest beers Ⓗ

Picturesque 16th-century roadside inn very close to the English border and originally used by drovers. It has seen some change over the years – the thatched roof is no more and the interior has undergone a number of sympathetic alterations. The guest beers are sourced from a range of breweries including Breconshire, Hobsons, Six Bells and Wye Valley. No meals are served on Sunday evening. The outdoor smoking area is heated.

Q❀◐⊟♣P⅟

Brecon

Boar's Head

Ship Street, LD3 9AL

11-midnight (2am Fri & Sat); 12-1am Sun

☎ (01874) 622856

Breconshire Welsh Pale Ale, Golden Valley, Ramblers Ruin, seasonal beers; Fuller's London Pride Ⓗ

The Breconshire Brewery tap is a popular and lively town centre pub with two distinct bars – the wood-panelled front bar houses the majority of the handpumps and tends to be a little quieter than the larger back bar, which has a pool table and gets very busy on match days when Rugby internationals are shown on TV. Live music evenings and quiz nights are held throughout the year, and the pub is a favourite spot during the Jazz Festival. The riverside patio garden enjoys superb views over the river and up to the Brecon Beacons.

⛰❀◐⊟♣●P⅟

Bulls Head

86 The Street, LD3 7LS

12-midnight (may vary)

☎ (01874) 623900

Evan Evans BB, Cwrw, Warrior, seasonal beer Ⓗ

A friendly and welcoming ale house, the Bulls Head has reverted to its original name after a brief spell as the Black Bull. The central bar and large pillars create three separate drinking

INDEPENDENT BREWERIES

Breconshire Brecon
Bryncelyn Ystradgynlais
Heart of Wales Llanwrtyd Wells

and dining areas, but with plenty of wood and good lighting the interior has a spacious, airy feel. Thursday quiz night is well supported and food is served until 9pm every evening except Monday. Real cider is occasionally sold.

Clarence

25 The Watton, LD3 7ED
12-midnight (2am Fri & Sat)
(01874) 622810
Beer range varies
Two-roomed town centre community pub with a contemporary, welcoming, relaxed atmosphere. The front bar tends to be frequented by locals, while the larger back bar is more popular with diners, and the large screen draws a crowd for big sporting events. The spacious garden is a major attraction, especially during the Jazz Festival. Beers are generally sourced from local breweries.

Caersws

Red Lion

Main Street, SY17 5EL (on B4569)
3 (12 Fri, Sat & summer)-11
(01686) 688023
Beer range varies
Friendly wood-beamed village pub comprising a small cosy bar and a lounge/restaurant with a comfortable feel, attracting a varied clientele of all ages. Good home-cooked food is served and three en-suite letting rooms are available. A summer beer festival is held and there is an attractive drinking area outside for warmer weather.
(X75, X85)P

Clyro

Baskerville Arms Hotel

HR3 5RZ
10-1am (midnight Sun)
(01497) 820670 baskervillearms.co.uk
Brains Bitter; Draught Bass; Wye Valley Bitter
Historic inn in the same village as Baskerville Hall of Sherlock Holmes fame, with wood beams and panelling and an impressive fireplace at the end of the main bar. One room has a pool table, and there is a large function room used for live music and other events. Lunches are served at the weekend. The spacious beer garden has excellent views over the Wye Valley to Hay Bluff. P

Cwmdu

Farmers Arms

NP8 1RU (on A479 between Crickhowell and Talgarth)
12-3, 6-11; closed Mon
(01874) 730464
Beer range varies
Village pub boasting exposed beams and a large fireplace, complete with a cast iron wood-burning range and a hop-bedecked bar that separates the drinking and dining areas. Superb home-cooked food is served, with local produce and regional specialities alongside old favourites. Guest beers are usually sourced from local breweries.
QP

Felinfach

Griffin

LD3 0UB (just off A470 3 miles NE of Brecon)
12-11.30
(01874) 620111 eatdrinksleep.ltd.uk.
Breconshire Golden Valley; Tomos Watkin OSB
The pub's motto – 'the simple things in life — done well', says it all. A welcoming country pub, restaurant and hotel, the emphasis here is on good beer and excellent food. The multi-roomed layout allows for discrete areas for drinking and dining. The huge fireplace between the bar and the main dining area dominates during the winter, while a full-sized Aga lurks in a side room, providing warmth throughout the building. The large garden, very popular in summer, affords superb views of the Brecon Beacons and Black Mountains. QP

Glasbury on Wye

Holly Bush Inn

HR3 5PS (on B4350 between Glasbury and Hay)
8am-late
(01497) 847371 hollybushcamping.co.uk
Breconshire Golden Valley; Greene King Abbot; Spinning Dog Hereford Organic Bitter
Friendly country pub whose licensees are enthusiastic supporters of self-sufficiency and recycling. The main bar area has an annexe at one end and a separate dining room where superb home-cooked food is served including vegetarian and vegan dishes. Between the pub and the River Wye there is a large campsite, a woodland walk and an adventure area. The gardens boast views of the Black Mountains and the Begwn Hills. Live music features regularly.
QP

Kerry

Kerry Lamb

SY16 4NP (on A489)
5 (12 Fri-Sun)-midnight
(01686) 670226
Hobsons Best Bitter; guest beers
This popular village pub has two bars: the front bar mainly used for dining, and the large rear bar with a real fire creating a homely feel. The inn attracts a varied clientele of all ages. Guest beers are from independent breweries. The pub's name refers to a breed of sheep named after the village. P

Llandrindod Wells

Conservative Club

South Crescent, LD1 5DH
11-2, 5.30-11; 11-11.30 Fri & Sat; 11.30-10.30 Sun
(01597) 822126
Brains Bitter; Jennings Cumberland Ale; guest beers
A quiet, comfortable haven overlooking the Temple Gardens, the 'Con' has a large lounge, TV room, games bar, snooker and pool tables, and a small front patio. Lunches are available

Thursday to Saturday. Live entertainment is hosted occasionally in the evening. CAMRA members are welcome but non-members must be signed in. Q❀◐♿⇌🚌♣⊱

Llanfaes

Drovers Arms

Newgate Street, LD3 8SN
🕘 12-midnight
☎ (01874) 623377
Brains Bitter; guest beers 🄷
A lively local community pub with a contemporary feel. The central bar faces out into the main room, which has several TV screens showing sporting events. A small room to one end of the bar has its own servery. The secluded patio garden is behind the pub, offering alfresco drinking and relief to smokers. Guest ales are sourced from the nearby Breconshire Brewery. ❀◐🚌♣●⊱

Llanfair Caereinion

Goat Hotel

High Street, SY21 0QS (off A458)
🕘 11-11 (midnight Fri & Sat)
☎ (01938) 810428
Beer range varies 🄷
This excellent beamed inn has a welcoming atmosphere and attracts both locals and tourists. The plush lounge, dominated by a large inglenook with an open fire, has comfortable leather armchairs and sofas, complemented by a dining room serving home-cooked food and a games room at the rear. The choice of three real ales always includes one from the Wood Brewery.
⛫❀🛏◐♣P

Llangynog

Tanat Valley Hotel

SY10 0EX (on B4391)
🕘 6-midnight; 12-11 Fri-Sun
☎ (01691) 780210
Beer range varies 🄷
This popular village pub has a friendly, relaxed feel. The pleasant wood-beamed interior has a stone fireplace, tiled floor and wood-burning stove. Downstairs from the lounge is an additional drinking area with a pool table. The B4391 north-west to Bala is the only road crossing the Berwyns, most unspoilt of Wales' mountain ranges. ⛫◐P

Llanhamlach

Old Ford Inn

LD3 7YB (on A40 3 miles E of Brecon)
🕘 12-11
☎ (01874) 665220
Beer range varies 🄷
This 12th-century coaching inn has been much extended but retains its original character. The central bar features some unusual copper work and a collection of nip bottles. A larger room beyond the bar, used mainly by diners, has panoramic views of the Brecon Beacons. The excellent food includes regional dishes. Beers are usually sourced from local breweries. ⛫Q👶❀🛏◐🗔♿🚌P

Llanidloes

Crown & Anchor Inn ★

41 Long Bridge Street, SY18 6EF (off A470)
🕘 11-11; 12-10.30 Sun
☎ (01686) 412398
Brains Rev James; Worthington's Bitter 🄷
Wonderful, unspoilt town-centre gem with a relaxed and friendly atmosphere, featuring in CAMRA's National Inventory of historic pub interiors. Landlady Ruby has been in charge since 1965 and throughout that time the pub has remained unchanged, retaining its public bar, lounge, snug and two further rooms, one with a pool table and games machine. A central hallway separates the rooms.
🗔🚌(X75)♣

Red Lion Hotel

Long Bridge Street, SY18 6EE (off A470)
🕘 11-midnight (1am Fri & Sat)
☎ (01686) 412270
Beer range varies 🄷
Wood-beamed town-centre hotel with a plush lounge with red leather sofas. The public bar divides into two areas – the front area has an interesting wood-panelled fireplace, the rear space has a pool table and games machines. Three real ales are usually available. In warmer weather there is drinking outside on the patio at the rear of pub.
⛫❀◐🗔🚌(X75)♣

Llanrhaeadr-ym-Mochnant

Plough Inn

SY10 0JR (on B4580)
🕘 3 (12 Sat & Sun)-midnight
☎ (01691) 780654
Beer range varies; 🄷
This true community local was converted from a private house. The multi-roomed interior retains the timber beams and tiled floors, and the front bar has a large open fireplace. A games area at the rear features pool and table football. The range of beers usually includes Brains Rev James. Wales's highest waterfall Pistyll Rhaeadr is close to the village. ⛫❀♣

Llanwrtyd Wells

Neuadd Arms Hotel

The Square, LD5 4RB
🕘 11-midnight (2am Fri & Sat); 11-11 Sun
☎ (01591) 610236 🌐 neuaddarmshotel.co.uk
Felinfoel Double Dragon; Heart of Wales Aur Cymreig, Bitter, Noble Eden, seasonal beers 🄷
This large Victorian hotel serves as the tap for the Heart of Wales Brewery, situated behind the building in the old laundry. The Bells Bar features a large fireplace and range, and an eclectic mix of furniture. The bells formerly used to summon servants remain on one wall, along with the winners' boards from some of the town's more unusual competitions such as bog-snorkelling or man vs horse. The lounge bar is a little more formal with deep carpets, sofas and many paintings on the walls. The hotel takes part in many of the town's annual events including the beer festival in November and food festivals.
⛫Q❀🛏◐🗔⛺⇌♣●P

WALES

Stonecroft Inn

Dolecoed Road, LD5 4RA
⊙ 5-midnight; 12-1am Fri-Sun
☎ (01591) 610332 ⊕ stonecroft.co.uk
Brains Rev James; guest beers [H]
This warm and friendly community pub acts as a hub for the town's many and varied festivities – bog-snorkelling, beer and food festivals, real ale rambles and much more. The hostelry has three main areas for drinking, dining and games, plus a large riverside garden with an aviary. Excellent food complements the fine range of beers. Lodge accommodation is popular with walkers and mountain bikers. ♨❀⇔◑Δ⇌♣●P⚐

Middletown

Breidden Hotel

SY21 8EL (on A458)
⊙ 12-2.30, 5-11; 12-midnight Sat & Sun
☎ (01938) 570250
Beer range varies [H]
Wood-beamed village local with a large L-shaped bar with comfortable seating, a pool table and games machines. At one end of the bar is a small, cosy restaurant area and the pub has a good reputation for eastern cuisine. The hotel takes its name from Breidden Hill, topped by the 18th-century Admiral Rodney's Pillar, which dominates the neighbourhood.
❀◑⊟(X75)♣P

Montgomery

Dragon Hotel

Market Square, SY15 6PA
⊙ 11-3, 6-11; 12-3, 7-10.30 Sun
☎ (01686) 668359 ⊕ dragonhotel.com
Beer range varies [H]
Small, cosy bar in a 17th-century coaching inn at the centre of a tiny and charming town. The beams and masonry are reputedly from Montgomery Castle, which was destroyed by Cromwell. Assorted bric-a-brac adorns the bar walls. The hotel is well appointed and has a function room. The beer range usually includes a beer from Wood Brewery. ♨Q⇔◑♣P

New Radnor

Radnor Arms

Broad Street, LD8 2SP
⊙ 12-2.30, 5-11; 12-midnight Sat; 12-11 Sun
☎ (01544) 350232
Beer range varies [H]
Set in the Welsh Marches close to the English border, this cosy pub is an ideal base for an away-from-it-all break. The area offers excellent walking, trekking and cycling; Offa's Dyke is nearby and Hereford 25 miles away by car or bus. Food, served every day, includes a takeaway service and a popular Sunday carvery (booking advisable). Guest beers are mainly from smaller breweries including Cottage, Six Bells and Wye Valley. Real cider and perry are available.
♨Q☋❀⇔◑⊞⊟♣●P⚐

Newtown

Bell Hotel

Commercial Street, SY16 2DE (on B4568)
⊙ 4 (12 Sun)-midnight
☎ (01686) 625540
Beer range varies [H]
This edge-of-town local, popular with a mixed clientele of all ages, comprises a public bar with pool table and comfortable lounge/ dining area. Live music plays at the weekend. Three real ales are available, usually including one from the Six Bells Brewery. ⇔◑♣P

Railway Tavern

Old Kerry Road, SY16 1BH (off A483)
⊙ 12-2.30, 6-midnight Mon, Wed & Thu; 11-1am Tue, Fri & Sat; 12-10.30 Sun
☎ (01686) 626156
Draught Bass; Hancock's HB; guest beer [H]
At the edge of the town centre, this friendly one-bar local has a traditional feel and is very handy for the station. It owes its welcoming atmosphere and large following to its long-serving landlord and landlady who celebrated 25 years in the Railway in 2008. The pub has a successful darts team and match nights can get crowded. Guest beers come from a wide range of independent breweries.
❀⇌⊟(X75)♣

Old Radnor

Harp Inn

LD8 2RH
⊙ 12-3 (Sat & Sun only), 6-11; closed Mon except Bank Hols
☎ (01544) 350655 ⊕ harpinnradnor.co.uk
Beer range varies [H]
This early 15th-century Welsh longhouse commands a fine view over the Radnor Valley. The interior is a tasteful mix of old and new – slate-flagged floors, beamed ceilings, open fireplace, settles, a modern restaurant and en-suite accommodation. The beers are sourced mainly from micro-breweries both local (Hobsons, Three Tuns, Wye Valley) and far-flung (Bath, Leadmill, Millstone). There is also a good range of malt whiskies.
♨Q❀⇔◑⊞♿♣●P

Pen-y-Cae

Ancient Briton

SA9 1YY (on A4067 between Ystradgynlais and Dan-yr-Ogof caves)
⊙ 11-midnight
☎ (01639) 730273
Draught Bass; Brains Buckleys Best Bitter; Wye Valley Butty Bach; guest beers [H]
Situated in the Brecon Beacons near the Dan-yr-Ogof caves, this is a regular haunt for hikers, cavers, climbers and visitors to the area. It offers an eclectic range of up to six real ales and one cider. Home-cooked food is served in the bar and restaurant, and the letting rooms have been recently refurbished. There is a children's play area and camping ground at the rear. The annual September beer festival coincides with a festival celebrating the Welsh prince and freedom fighter Owain Glyndwr. ♨❀⇔◑♿Δ⊟●P⚐

Pentre-Bach

Tafarn y Crydd (Shoemakers Arms)

LD3 8UB (signed Country Pub from A40 in Sennybridge) SN909329
11.30-3 (not Tue), 5.30-11; 12-3, 6-11 Sun
☎ (01874) 636508
Brains Rev James; guest beers H
Community-owned country pub situated on the edge of the Epynt firing ranges. A warm welcome, excellent food and well-kept ales await you at this previous local CAMRA Pub of the Year. The garden offers superb views of the Brecon Beacons and Mynydd Epynt in an area abundant with wildlife – look out for the red kites. Well worth seeking out – but opening times may vary with the seasons, so it is a good idea to phone ahead. Q&P

Penybont

Severn Arms

LD1 5UA
11.30-3, 6-midnight (1am Fri & Sat); 12-3, 7-11 Sun
☎ (01597) 851224 severn-arms.co.uk
Beer range varies H
This 18th-century coaching inn was built to serve the route between Hereford and Aberystwyth (today's A44). The spacious bar with its large open fireplace leads to gardens overlooking the River Ithon (six miles of free fishing for residents); there is also a quiet, secluded restaurant (the Cheesments) and a games room. The guest beers are sourced from a wide range of breweries and there is an above average selection of malt whiskies on offer. Trotting races take place twice yearly on a nearby course. Q♣P

Rhayader

Cornhill Inn

West Street, LD6 5AB
1-midnight; closed Mon (except Bank Hols)
☎ (01597) 810029 cornhillpub.co.uk
Adnams Broadside; Jennings Cocker Hoop; guest beers H
Dating back to around 1540, despite alterations this pub continues to look its age with low ceilings and a large inglenook. The cottage at the rear of the pub used to house a smithy and is now used for self-catering accommodation. Guest beers are sourced from the Marston's guest beer list. Light refreshments are available. The outdoor smoking area is heated and covered. ♣

Crown Inn

North Street, LD6 5BT
11 (6 Mon Jan & Feb)-11 (midnight Fri & Sat); 12-10.30 Sun
☎ (01597) 811099 thecrownrhayader.co.uk
Brains Dark, Bitter, Rev James, seasonal beers H
This 16th-century beamed pub has an open-plan bar crammed with photographs of local inhabitants and scenes, nearly all with written descriptions – look for the item referring to the eccentric Major Stanscombe, a former owner. The linen-fold bar front was saved from a demolished house. This is a rare outlet locally for real mild (recommended), and the current Brains seasonal or one-off beer is usually available. The outdoor smoking area is covered. Q♣

Talybont on Usk

Star Inn

LD3 7YX (on B4558 between Brecon and Crickhowell) SO114226
11-3, 6-11; 12-3, 7-11 Sun
☎ (01874) 676635
Beer range varies H
Large and lively pub with an excellent reputation, situated alongside the Brecon and Monmouth Canal. The spacious garden is extremely popular in summer. The beer range is mostly drawn from local breweries, with some better-known ales added from time to time. Locally produced cider is also available. Live music evenings are held regularly, and quiz nights are popular. The excellent food makes good use of local produce.
♣

Definitions

bivvy – beer
bumclink – inferior beer
bunker – beer
cooper – half stout, half porter
gatters – beer
shant of gatter – glass of beer
half and half – mixture of ale and porter, much favoured by medical students
humming – strong (as applied to drink)
ponge or pongelow – beer, half and half
purl – mixture of hot ale and sugar, with wormwood infused
rot-gut – bad
small beer shandy – gaffs ale and gingerbeer
shant – pot or quart (shant of bivvy – quart of beer)
swipes – soup or small beer
wobble-shop – shop where beer sold without a licence
J C Hotten, The Slang Dictionary, 1887

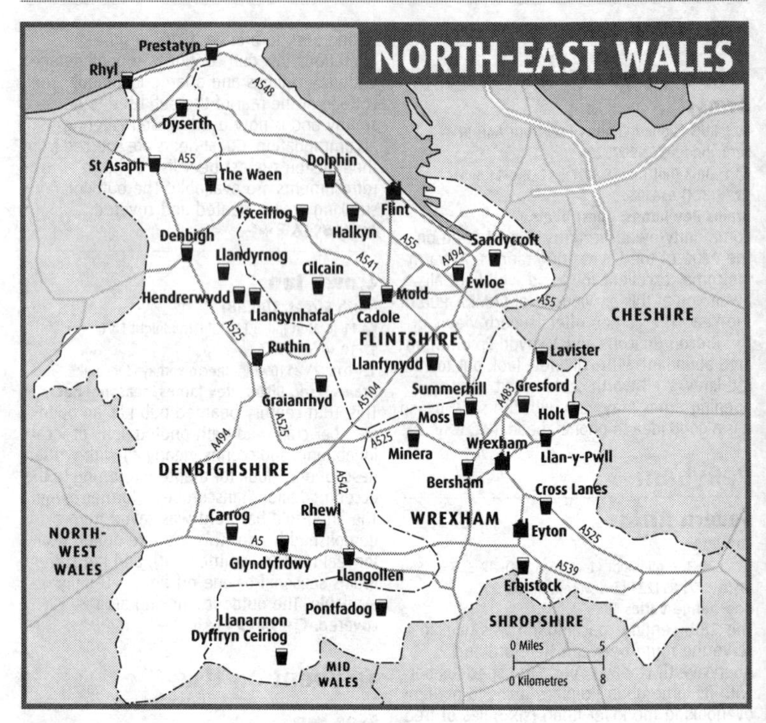

Authority areas covered: Denbighshire, Flintshire, Wrexham

Bersham

Black Lion

LL14 4HN (off B5099 near Bersham Heritage Centre)

12 (11.30 Fri & Sat)-2am; 12-1am Sun

(01978) 365588

Hydes Original Bitter, seasonal beers H

Known by locals as the Hole in the Wall, this friendly pub with a long-serving landlord is set on a hillside on the Clywedog Industrial Trail. A wood-panelled bar serves the front room and side room, both with real fires in winter, and a games room. There is a play area in the garden and a patio at the rear for summer drinking. Bar meals are available all day. Well-behaved dogs on leads are welcome. P

Cadole

Colomendy Arms

Village Road, CH7 5LL (off A494 Mold-Ruthin road)

7 (6 Thu; 4 Fri; 2 Sat)-11; 2-10.30 Sun

(01352) 810217

Beer range varies H

Delightful, traditional village local on the edge of Loggerheads Country Park. This frequent Local CAMRA Pub of the Year winner is popular with families, walkers, cavers and runners. Friendly conversation is the main entertainment. The cosy single bar has a roaring fire in winter. Five handpumps provide an ever-varying range of ales (some change more than once during a busy evening), many from local breweries. Q P

Carrog

Grouse Inn

Nr Corwen, LL21 9AT SJ114437

12-1am (3am Fri & Sat)

(01490) 430272 thegrouseinn.co.uk

Lees Bitter; guest beers H

Situated alongside the River Dee with spectacular views of the Dee Valley and Berwyn Mountains. Nearby is Carrog Station, terminus of the Llangollen Railway, with a campsite next door. The single bar leads to two separate dining rooms where food is available throughout the day until 10pm. An outbuilding has been converted to a games room and there is a covered patio area overlooking the valley. Q (X94)P

Cilcain

White Horse

CH7 5NN SJ177651

12-3, 6.30-11; 12-11 Sat; 12-10.30 Sun

(01352) 740142

Banks's Bitter; guest beers H

This welcoming village pub, located near the foot of Moel Famau, has provided refreshment for generations of locals, walkers and visitors alike. A panelled and copper topped bar,

INDEPENDENT BREWERIES

Facer's Flint
Jolly Brewer Wrexham
McGivern Wrexham (NEW)
Nant Llanrwst
Plassey Eyton

complete with coat hooks for those using the bar stools, serves several cosy lounge areas, and there is also a separate, tile-floored public bar. A handsome long clock, lantern lighting, maps, prints, historic photographs and bright-metal artefacts help to create a traditional atmosphere. ⋔Q❀◐◑⊟♣P⁵⁻

Cross Lanes

Cross Lanes Hotel (Kagan's Brasserie)

Bangor Road, Marchwiel, LL13 0TF (on A525)
11-midnight (11 Sun)
☎ (01978) 780555 crosslaneshotel.co.uk
Plassey Bitter; guest beer Ⓗ
A rare local outlet for the local Plassey Brewery, this comfortable hotel lounge bar is in a pleasant rural setting. Served by a central bar, the drinking area comprises an airy, well lit and comfortably furnished front room along with a more rustic back room. The adjoining dining area is decorated with old prints, maps and photographs of the Wrexham area. Note the magnificent 17th century oak panelling in the front hall. ⋔Q❀◐◑♿P⁵⁻

Denbigh

Hand

Lenten Pool, LL16 3PF
10am-1am (2am Fri & Sat)
☎ (01745) 814286
Jennings Bitter; guest beers Ⓗ
A pub just off the town centre serving beers from the Marston's list, the Hand has a central bar with three separate areas. The bar has a large TV and a second bar area with an 8ft screen for sporting enthusiasts; this room is used as a lounge at quieter times. There is a pool table in the games room. The 51 bus runs every 20 minutes from Rhyl and the pub is close to Denbigh Castle. ◐⊟(51)♣P⁵⁻

Railway

2 Ruthin Road, LL16 3EL
12-midnight
☎ (01745) 812376
Beer range varies Ⓗ
The Railway is a basic but cosy locals' pub on the edge of town with five rooms: bar, snug, lounge, sports room with a pool table and an entrance hall with a serving hatch. The landlord is keen to support local beers and always has two on tap. All rooms have railway-themed prints on display. Denbigh is an historic town, with the castle, built by Edward I, overlooking it. The 51 bus runs every 20 minutes to Rhyl. ⊼⊟(51)♣⁵⁻

Dolphin

Glan yr Afon Inn

Milwr, Holywell, CH8 8HE
12-11
☎ (01352) 710052 glanyrafoninn.co.uk
Tetley Bitter; guest beers Ⓗ
Situated in a quiet location with view of the Dee Estuary, this country inn offers food, drink and accommodation while claiming to be female-friendly. Function facilities are available. The interior includes a cosy fire, panelled walls, pews, a display of local interest newspaper stores and information about the nearby network of caves. An old map shows how, once, there were a large number of pubs in this locality. Walkers and dogs are welcome and gardens include a children's play area. ⋔Q❀◐◑P⁵⁻

Dyserth

New Inn

Waterfall Road, LL18 6ET
12-11
☎ (01745) 570482 thenewinndyserth.co.uk
Banks's Original, Bitter; Marston's Burton Bitter, Pedigree; guest beer Ⓗ
Roadside inn situated close to the base of the Afon Ffyddion waterfall – a popular local tourist attraction. Three main rooms divide the interior with dining throughout. The emphasis here is on food and the pub has a good reputation for its cooking. Photographs of bygone days in Dyserth adorn the walls. There is a large outdoor drinking space with a good-quality play area for children.
⋔Q❀◐◑⊟(35,36)P⁵⁻

Erbistock

Boat

LL13 0DL SJ355413
12-midnight (11 Sun)
☎ (01978) 780666
Tetley Bitter; guest beers Ⓗ
Exceptionally picturesque pub on the site of an old ferry crossing by the banks of the River Dee. The original 17th-century building, littered with oak beams, has recently been extended to house an upmarket restaurant. The bar area with a constant real coal fire gives way to a small seating area, while the restaurant is always busy and booking is recommended. The attractive outdoor area is popular with families and bikers alike during the summer months. ⋔Q❀◐◑⊟P

Ewloe

Boars Head

Holywell Road, CH5 3BS (at B5125/B5127 jct, just off A494)
12-3, 5.30-11; 12-midnight Sun
☎ (01244) 531065
Black Sheep Best Bitter; Draught Bass; guest beers Ⓗ
Intimate old-fashioned hostelry built in 1704, just off the main North Wales Expressway. Brasses and a fine fireplace feature in the tiny half-timbered bar, with more seats in the mezzanine and beer garden. Food is served in a dining room to the rear (not Sat lunch or Sun/Mon eve). Two guest ales are usually on offer. There are no buses in the evening.
⋔❀◐◑⊟(X44,111)P⁵⁻

Glyndyfrdwy

Sun

LL21 9HG (on A5) SJ150426
12-3.30 (Sat & Sun only), 6-11
☎ (01490) 430517
Beer range varies Ⓗ

WALES

Situated between Llangollen and Corwen on the A5 alongside the river Dee with views of the Berwyn Mountains, this free house has three drinking areas. There is also a games room, separate dining area and a beer garden. The enthusiastic licensee provides a range of interesting real ales —a bitter, mild and a guest premium ale are usually on offer. Nearby is Glyndyfrdwy Station on the Llangollen Railway. **Q❀◑⇌⊟(X94)P**

Graianrhyd

Rose & Crown

Llanarmon Road, CH7 4QW SJ218560
✪ 4 (12 Fri & Sat)-11; 12-10.30 Sun
☎ (01824) 780727 ⊕ theroseandcrownpub.co.uk
Flowers IPA; guest beers ⊞
Friendly, welcoming, traditional inn, winner of many CAMRA awards including local Pub of the Year 2006 and 2007. Popular with locals and walkers, the pub is split into two rooms served by a single bar: one with an open fire, the other with a wood burner. Two ever-changing guest beers are sourced from local breweries and real cider is occasionally on offer. The cheery landlord is justifiably proud of his excellent pub food and fine ales. **⛫Q❀◑⊟♣P**

Gresford

Griffin

Church Green, LL12 8RG
✪ 4-11
☎ (01978) 852231
Adnams Bitter; guest beers ⊞
Welcoming community pub adjacent to the 15th-century All Saints Church – its bells are one of the Seven Wonders of Wales. The pub is a picturesque, white building just off the road in an attractive part of the village. Pictures of the Gresford mining disaster adorn the walls, offering some historical perspective. There is a lawned area to the side of the building with seating. Children are welcome in some areas of the pub until 8pm. **Q❀⊟(1)♣P⊬**

Pant-yr-Ochain

Old Wrexham Road, LL12 8TY (off A5156, follow signs to The Flash)
✪ 12-11 (10.30 Sun)
☎ (01978) 853525 ⊕ pantyrochain-gresford.co.uk
Flowers Original; Taylor Landlord; Thwaites Original; guest beers ⊞
Overlooking a small lake, this picturesque, converted manor house is approached via a sweeping drive. The interior has been redesigned into a large open plan space with a central bar and numerous snugs and dining areas. The decor is predominantly stripped wood with an impressive 16th-century fireplace.The food is highly regarded and booking is recommended. Guest beers are often from local micros. **⛫Q❀◑♿●⊬**

Halkyn

Blue Bell ✔

Rhosesmor Road, CH8 8DL (on B5123) SO209123
✪ 5-11 (midnight Fri); 12-11 Sat & Sun
☎ (01352) 780309 ⊕ bluebell.uk.eu.org
Blue Bell Bitter; guest beers ⊞
Situated on Halkyn Mountain with spectacular views, this pub is a focal point for community activities including organised walks, games nights and Welsh classes (see website). The house beer brewed by Facer's is accompanied by two guest beers usually from small independent breweries. The pub has won several CAMRA awards including the 2007 Regional Cider Pub of the Year for Merseyside, Cheshire and North Wales, and regularly features two ciders and a perry, including its own Rosie's Blue Bell cider when in season. **⛫◑▲⊟(126)♣●P**

Hendrerwydd

White Horse

LL16 4LL SJ121634
✪ 12-3, 6-11; closed Mon; 12-3.30 Sun
☎ (01824) 790218 ⊕ white-horse-inn.co.uk
Beer range varies ⊞
Historic pub set in the beautiful Clwydian range with superb views over Dyffryn Clwyd from the rear. An extensive and imaginative food menu attracts walkers and diners. The main area is mostly for diners and has a large fireplace with comfortable seating. A smaller bar area is separate and has its own entrance at the side of the pub. **⛫❀◑⊡⊟(76)♣P**

Holt

Peal O' Bells

12 Church Street, LL13 9JP (400m S of Holt-Farndon bridge)
✪ closed Mon; 6-11 Tue; 12-11 Wed & Thu; 12-midnight Fri & Sat; 12-11 Sun
☎ (01829) 270411 ⊕ pealobells.co.uk
Adnams Bittter; Marston's Pedigree; guest beer ⊞
Popular family-friendly village pub next to St Chads Church. Good value home-cooked food is served in the restaurant Wednesday-Sunday lunchtime and Thursday-Saturday evening (booking essential at the weekend). The sizeable fully-enclosed garden has a small play area and excellent views of the Dee Valley and Peckforton Hills. Real perry is on handpump. **⛫❀◑♿⊟⊬**

Lavister

Nag's Head

Old Chester Road, LL12 8SN (on Old Chester-Wrexham road)
✪ 12-11.30 (midnight Fri & Sat); 12-11 Sun
☎ (01244) 570486
Cains Bitter; Flowers IPA; guest beers ⊞
Large roadside pub, popular with both locals and visitors, comprising a small, welcoming lounge and a public bar with pool table, darts and Sky TV. A plaque on the wall proclaims that the first CAMRA members were signed up here. Food is available Friday to Sunday and good value Sunday lunches are always in demand. The guest beers usually include at least one from a local micro. The garden has a large children's play area. **⛫❀◑⊡♿⊟♣P⊬**

Llan-y-Pwll

Gredington Arms

Holt Road, LL13 9SD (on A534)
12-2.30, 5-11 (midnight Fri); closed Mon; 12-midnight Sat & Sun
(01978) 661728 gredingtonarms.co.uk
Hydes Original Bitter, seasonal beers; guest beers H

Typical 19th-century building modernised to give a modern bistro feel. A medium-sized bar area next to an open-plan dining space creates a pleasant, relaxing atmosphere. The pub has a reputation for good, locally sourced food. The owner, Rod, is proud of his cask ale and also offers an extensive wine list. Q(C56)P

Llanarmon Dyffryn Ceiriog

Hand Hotel

LL20 7LD SJ157328
11-11 (12.30am Fri & Sat); 12-11 Sun
(01691) 600666 thehandhotel.co.uk
Weetwood Eastgate H

Welcoming and laid-back hotel set at the head of the picturesque Ceiriog Valley. A public bar/games room, lounge and restaurant cater for all tastes. Known principally for its excellent food (booking advised at weekends), the introduction of Weetwood Eastgate on handpump has been a popular move with drinkers. A second guest ale is now planned for the summer months. This popular destination for cyclists and walkers is also dog friendly. P

Llandyrnog

Golden Lion

LL16 4HG (on B5429)
12 (3 Tue-Thu)-11; 2-1am Fri & Sat; 2-11 Sun
(01824) 790373
Thwaites Original; guest beer H

Listed building at the heart of the village. A central bar serves two distinct drinking areas: a lounge area as you enter and the bar area to the rear. The guest beer is normally from Facer's Brewery. During the summer months the pleasant beer garden is popular. The pub has strong links with the local football team, Llandyrnog United, who frequent the bar after each home game. (76)

White Horse (Ceffyl Gwyn)

LL16 4HG (B5429 next to the church) SJ107650
12-3, 6-11; closed Mon
(01824) 790582
Beer range varies H

Situated next to the church in the picturesque village of Llandyrnog, this pub enjoys an excellent reputation for its home-cooked food. A single bar serves all areas, and there is a dining area to the rear. Comfortable seating is available next to the fireplace – a popular spot for the locals. The pub is linked with the Golden Lion (see above) and those looking for a quieter atmosphere normally choose the White Horse. (76)P

Llanfynydd

Cross Keys

LL11 5HH
5-midnight (1am Fri & Sat); closed Mon; 12-midnight Sun
(01978) 760333 crosskeysllanfynydd.co.uk
Greene King IPA; guest beers H

Attractive, traditional hostelry with a black and white exterior, the perfect place to end a visit up Hope Mountain. A basic quarry-tiled bar leads to the restaurant, while a small, cosy lounge, once the village blacksmith's, features carved settles and a real fire. An intimate snug is ideal for meetings. Good quality meals are served in the evening and Sunday lunchtime. Guest beers are often from a local micro. (41)P

Llangollen

Corn Mill

Dee Lane, LL20 8PN (on town side of River Dee bridge) SJ214421
12-11 (10.30 Sun)
(01978) 869555 cornmill-llangollen.co.uk
Beer range varies H

Stunning conversion of an old mill next to the River Dee retaining many original features including oak beams and a water wheel. There are two bars on separate levels with several dining and drinking areas. Up to six cask beers are available. The outdoor terrace, with a covered area for smoking, has superb river views and a grandstand view of the Llangollen terminus of the restored railway. Good quality food is served daily until about an hour before closing. Q

Sun Inn

49 Regent Street, LL20 8HN (on A5 about ½ mile E of town centre)
5-1am; 3-2am Fri & Sat; 3-1am Sun
(01978) 860079
Salopian Shropshire Gold; Thwaites Original; guest beers H

Lively pub, particularly at the weekend, offering six real ales including four changing guests, plus continental beers, more than 50 single malt whiskies and at least 10 varieties of rum. The large single room interior has a slate floor, single bar, three real fireplaces and a games area. A small snug leads to an outside covered seating area for smokers and drinkers. Live music plays Wednesday to Saturday with jazz, folk and rock on different nights.

Llangynhafal

Golden Lion Inn

LL16 4LN
closed Mon; 6 (4 Thu)-12.30am; 4-2am Fri; 12-2am Sat; 12-11.30 Sun
(01824) 790451 thegoldenlioninn.com
Holt Bitter; Coach House Gunpowder Mild; guest beer H

Nestling at the foot of the Clwydian hills, this two-roomed pub provides a rare opportunity to sample Holt's beers in North Wales with the landlord collecting the ale directly from the brewery himself to guarantee supply. Voted by CAMRA members as runner-up in the

Merseyside, Cheshire and North Wales Regional Pub of the Year for 2007, the Golden Lion ticks all the boxes with a good choice of beer and cider served in lined glasses to guarantee a full measure. B&B is available in two en-suite rooms.
⛰❀⇔◗⊟⅄⊟(76)♣●P⊓

Minera

Tyn-y-Capel

Church Road, LL11 3DA (off B5426)
✪ 12-11 (midnight Sat); closed Mon & Tue winter; 12-10.30 Sun
☎ (01978) 757502 ⊕ tyn-y-capel.co.uk
Greene King IPA; guest beers ⊞
The Tyn-y-Capel (chapel house) was first listed as an ale house in 1764. The attractive whitewashed exterior with sturdy stone-flanked windows belies a modern – but reputedly haunted – interior. Step down to the bar and marvel at the stunning views across the valley. Up to five guest beers are on offer and fine cuisine is served in a separate restaurant. **Q**❀◖◗⊟♿♣**P**

Mold

Glasfryn

Raikes Lane, CH7 6LR SJ239658
✪ 11.30-11; 12-10.30 Sun
☎ (01352) 750500 ⊕ glasfryn-mold.co.uk
Caledonian Deuchars IPA; Purple Moose Snowdonia Bitter; Taylor Landlord; Thwaites Bitter; guest beer ⊞
A spacious pub has been created within a building that was originally a residence for circuit judges attending the courts opposite. The grounds include a car park and a seating area with views of the town and surrounding hills. The interior is decorated with displays of books, prints, cartoons, artefacts and posters. Tasting notes of beers on sale – many brewed locally – are on blackboards above the bar. Food is served until 9.30pm (9pm Sun).
⛰◖◗♿P⊱

Gold Cape ✔

8-8A Wrexham Road, CH7 1ES (next to Market Square crossroads)
✪ 9-midnight (1am Fri & Sat)
☎ (01352) 705920
Facer's Gold Cape Bitter; Marston's Pedigree; guest beers ⊞
Run by staff who are interested in cask-conditioned beer, this is one of the more interesting local Wetherspoon's outlets to visit. As well as a changing range of guest beers including a house bitter brewed locally, the usual range of Wetherspoon's facilities is to be found. The pub is named after an important and local archaeological find: a replica of the Gold Cape is displayed near the entrance. Other local history artefacts are on display throughout the pub. ◖❀◖◗⊟●⊱

Moss

Clayton Arms

Moss Hill, LL11 6ES SJ306538
✪ 7 (4 Sat)-11; closed Tue & Wed; 12-10.30 Sun
☎ (01978) 756444
Beer range varies ⊞
Refurbished pub in Moss Valley, a local beauty spot and part of the Clywedog Industrial Trail. Inside, Chesterfields abound in which to relax in front of roaring log fires on a winter's night. The restaurant is a good place to enjoy an expansive Sunday lunch after a walk in Moss Valley. The single cask beer changes twice weekly and is usually an interesting choice from an independent brewery. ⛰**Q**❀◗**P**⊱

Pontfadog

Swan

LL20 7AR (on B4500)
✪ 12-2.30 (3 Sat), 5.30-11; 12-3, 5.30-10.30 Sun
☎ (01691) 718273
Beer range varies ⊞
Village pub in the picturesque Ceiriog Valley. A hub for local community activities, the main bar is popular for its character and friendly welcome. A large fireplace creates an almost separate snug at the end of the bar, and a dining room completes the layout. The real ale is usually from a regional brewer, although a house beer from local micro Jolly Brewer may also be available. Three bed and breakfast rooms will open during 2008. ⛰⇔⊟♣P⊱

Prestatyn

Royal Victoria

Sandy Lane, LL19 7SG SJ063831
✪ 11.30-11 (11.30 Fri & Sat); 12-11 Sun
☎ (01745) 854670
Marston's Burton Bitter; John Smith's Bitter; guest beers ⊞
Large, two roomed pub just north of the railway station and close to the town centre. Both rooms have interesting brass wall lamps; look for the ornamental elephants, too. The regulars are keen on darts and dominoes and the pub has the trophies on display to prove it. It is a five minute walk to the beach and the start of Offa's Dyke. Guest beers come from the Admiral Taverns portfolio. No food is served. ❀⊟⅄⇌⊟♣⊱

Rhewl

Sun

LL20 7YT (signed from B5103/A542 jct) SJ178447
✪ 12-2.30; 6-11; 12-10.30 Sun
☎ (01978) 861043
Beer range varies ⊞
Delightful whitewashed 14th-century former drovers' inn overlooking the Dee valley in the isolated hamlet of Rhewl. Close to the Horseshoe Falls, there are many scenic walks in the area. The central bar serves three small rooms – a traditional front-room public bar, dining area and small inglenook, each full of character. Children are welcome, except in the main bar. Food is served daily (all day on Sunday) and is recommended. The cask ales are usually from established regional brewers.
⛰**Q**❀◖◗⊟⅄♣●

Rhyl

Crown Bard

Rhuddlan Road, LL18 2RL (on A525)

11.30-3, 5-11.30; 11-11 Fri & Sat; 11.30-3, 5-11 winter; 12-10.30 Sun
☎ (01745) 338465
Beer range varies Ⓗ
Built in 1963 by the now defunct Bent's Brewery, this pub has changed little in the intervening years. The licensee is keen to promote micro-breweries and often offers beers from Purple Moose. The single bar serves three areas: a public bar with separate access, a larger lounge area with space for dining, and a relatively quiet snug area with a novel variation on a cuckoo clock. Meals are served lunchtime and early evening with some attractive deals available.
⾋❀◐◑⛺🚌(51)🍎P⊬

Swan
13 Russell Road, LL18 3BS
11-11 (11.30 Fri & Sat); 12-10.30 Sun
☎ (01745) 336694
Thwaites Dark Mild, Original, Lancaster Bomber; guest beer Ⓗ
Two linked bars serve two distinct areas: the public bar has wide-screen TVs mainly for sports fans (there is even a TV in the smoking area leading off the bar), the lounge has a dining space with lunches served 12 to 2.30pm. There are three Thwaites beers on offer with an occasional seasonal beer. The bar team won a national award for service in 2007. A welcome stop close to Rhyl town centre. ◐⊟⇌🚌⊬

Ruthin

Boars Head
Clwyd Street, LL15 1HW
12-11 (midnight Thu; 1am Fri & Sat); 12-11 Sun
☎ (01824) 703355
Marston's Burton Bitter; guest beer Ⓗ
Friendly black and white town centre pub with two drinking areas served from a single bar and a raised area with a pool table to the rear. The wide-screen TV shows mainly sport. Several pictures on the walls feature local views. Once a month or so there is live music on a Friday evening. 🚌⊬

St Asaph

Plough
The Roe, LL17 0LU SJ033744
12-11 (1am Fri & Sat); 12-10.30 Sun
☎ (01745) 585080
Plassey Bitter; guest beers Ⓗ
Large hostelry on the main street through the town. As well as the Plassey Bitter, this pub specialises in beers from other North Wales breweries. A central bar serves several drinking areas on the ground floor. The first floor has a popular restaurant and wine bar. Live music is hosted on Friday night, when a small entry charge may be made. Easily reached by a regular bus service from Rhyl.
⾋❀◐◑♿⛺🚌(51,52)P⊬

Sandycroft

Bridge Inn ✔
Chester Road, CH5 2QN (on B5129)
12-11 (11-30pm Fri & Sat)
☎ (01244) 538806
Caledonian Deuchars IPA; Jennings Cumberland Ale; Shepherd Neame Spitfire Ⓗ
Bright and airy real ale oasis on the edge of the Deeside beer desert. Good value home-cooked food is served and children are welcome in the family dining area. The pub is reached by a wooden footbridge from the car park and boasts a large beer garden. The open plan lounge is adorned with photographs of old Chester. ⾋❀◐◑⊟

Summerhill

Crown ✔
Top Road, LL11 4SR (1 mile from A483/A541 jct)
12-midnight
☎ (01978) 755788
Hydes Original Bitter, seasonal beers; guest beer Ⓗ
You can be sure of a warm welcome from the award-winning landlord at this large, traditional pub overlooking Alyn and Deeside Valley. Inside, to the front is a large lounge decorated in contemporary style with plenty of upholstered bench seating. At the rear the public bar has an adjoining pool and darts area. The pub runs dominoes, darts and pool teams. Reasonably-priced rotating seasonal and guest beers can be found alongside the Hydes Bitter. ⾋⊟⇌(Gwersyllt)🚌♣P⊬

The Waen

Farmers Arms
Near St Asaph, LL17 0DY SJ061730
12-2, 5.30-midnight; closed Mon
☎ (01745) 582190 🌐 the-farmers-arms.co.uk
Beer range varies Ⓗ
Dating in parts back to the 18th century when it was called the Waen Tavern; it became the Farmers Arms around 1890-1920. During WWII it was a regular haunt for American soldiers stationed nearby. A single bar serves several areas: bar, lounge and large function room/restaurant. The North Wales Jazz Society holds monthly musical evenings. Beers are from local Welsh micros including Facer's and Great Orme. Meals are served. Q❀◐⊟⛺P⊬

Ysceifiog

Fox ★
Ysceifiog Village Road, CH8 8NJ (village signposted from B5121 between Brynford and Lixwm) SJ153714
Summer – Mon-Fri 6-11(closed Wed), Sat 12 Noon -11, Sun 12 Noon -10.30; Winter – Mon-Fri 6-11(closed Wed), Sat 4-11, Sun 12 Noon -10.30
☎ (01352) 720241
Brakspear Bitter; guest beers Ⓗ
A single bar serves three drinking areas in this gem, which joined the CAMRA National Inventory in 2003. The bar itself features a novel 'bar seat'. The bar area ceiling is adorned with water jugs, some with a whisky association, and there is a display of pump clips of previous beers. The rear of the bar serves a lounge area. There is a separate family room. Dogs are welcome. ⾋Q⛄❀⊟

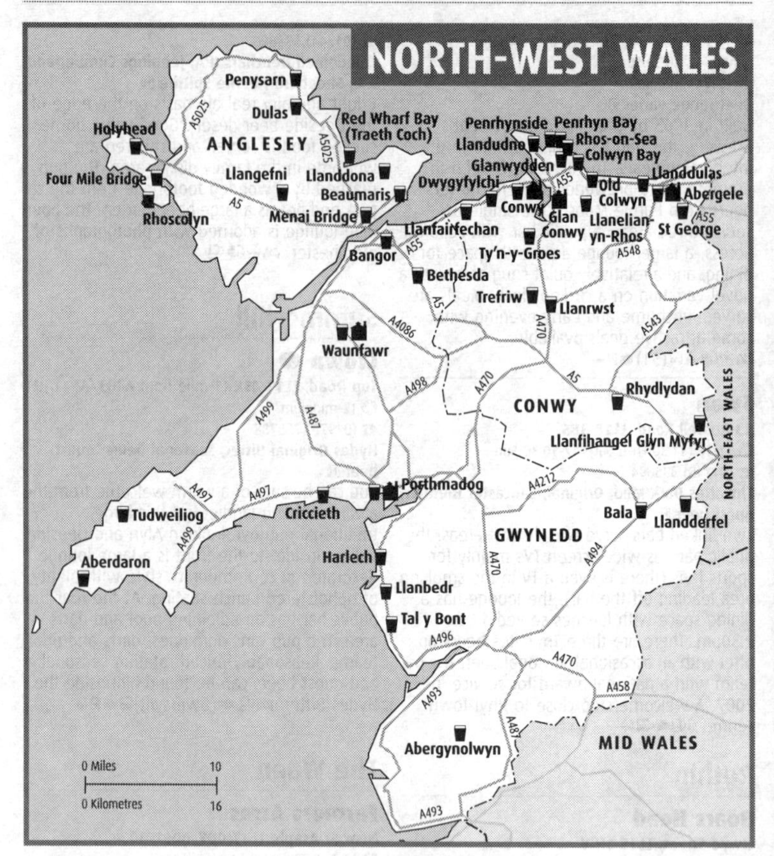

Authority areas covered: Anglesey, Conwy, Gwynedd

Aberdaron

Ship Hotel

LL53 8BE

11-11

☎ (01758) 760204 theshiphotelaberdaron.co.uk

Beer range varies Ⓗ

The Ship is situated in the centre of the village of Aberdaron at the tip of the Lleyn Peninsula. You can be sure of a friendly welcome in the two bars, one with a games area. Excellent food made with locally sourced fresh ingredients is recommended. Two handpumps in summer and one in winter dispense local Welsh beer. The village has a bus service but check times first.

Abergele

Pen-y-Bont

Bridge Street, LL22 7HA

1 (12 Fri & Sat)-11; 12-10.30 Sun

☎ (01745) 833905

Brains Dark, Rev James Ⓗ

This family owned and run genuine free house is a one-roomed pub with two areas separated by a central bar. To the left as you enter is the lounge with large screen TV showing major sporting events; to the right is a bar games area for darts, dominoes and pool. It is home to two pigeon clubs who meet three nights a week. Dogs and cyclists are always welcome. (12,15)

Abergynolwyn

Railway Inn

LL36 9YN (on B4405)

12-midnight (11 Sun)

☎ (01654) 782279

Beer range varies Ⓗ

Friendly community local in the centre of the village not far from the Talylln Railway. You can still see the remains of the old incline that brought goods traffic down from the railway to the village. Excellent food is served and, following a recent refit, the range of beers is set to increase. The pub has stunning views of the surrounding hills and there is wonderful walking nearby.

(Talyllyn Railway)

INDEPENDENT BREWERIES

Conwy Conwy
Great Orme Glan Conwy
North Wales Abergele
Purple Moose Porthmadog
Snowdonia Waunfawr

Bala

Olde Bulls Head

78 High Street, LL23 7AD
⏲ 12-11 (2am Fri & Sat)
☎ (01678) 520438
Greene King Abbot; Purple Moose Glaslyn Ⓗ
Former Allied Breweries' pub on the High Street, with a large bar and lounge with a separate pool room, which has escaped modernisation. A locals' local, conversation and banter are the main entertainment, most of it centring on sport and pub games. Bar snacks are available during the week plus lunch on Sunday. Welsh is spoken as a first language by most locals. A friendly place to visit. ⛫❀⛺⊟(X94)♣P⊡

Bangor

Black Bull/Tarw Du ✔

107 High Street, LL57 1NS
⏲ 9-midnight (1am Fri & Sat); 10-midnight Sun
☎ (01248) 387900
Greene King IPA, Abbot; Marston's Pedigree; guest beers Ⓗ
Wetherspoon's pub in a converted church and presbytery at the top of the High Street. It has spacious drinking areas and an outside patio overlooking upper Bangor and the university. Popular with students, it is very busy during term time. Draught cider is regularly available. A lift is available for disabled access.
❀◑♿≢●⊱

Boatyard

Garth Road, LL57 2SF (off old A5, follow pier signs)
⏲ 11 (12 Sun)-11
☎ (01248) 362462
Marston's Burton Bitter; guest beers Ⓗ
Formerly the Union Garth, this large multi-roomed pub is in lower Bangor near Dickies Boatyard. Recently refurbished, every room is packed with local history, horse racing pictures, brasses, wall plates and more. Part of the pub is now a well-appointed restaurant. The garden overlooks sailing boats and the sea. Bangor Pier (a third of a mile long) is well worth a visit. Guest beers can be a little expensive. ⛫Q❀⇌◑⊟P⊱

Harp Inn

80-82 High Street, LL57 1NS
⏲ 11-1am; 12-10.30 Sun
☎ (01248) 361817
Caledonian Deuchars IPA; Greene King Abbot; guest beers Ⓗ
One of the oldest pubs in Bangor, now owned by Scottish & Newcastle. Popular with students, it has a large open plan bar area with steps leading to a games room and a small snug to the side of the bar. Busy during term time, live music and karaoke nights on Thursday can be noisy. There is a covered outdoor drinking and smoking area above the pub. ⛫❀◑≢♣⊱

Tap & Spile

Garth Road, LL57 2SW (off old A5, follow pier signs)
⏲ 12-11 (11.30 Tue, Fri & Sat)
☎ (01248) 370835
Beer range varies Ⓗ
Popular split-level pub overlooking the renovated Victorian pier offering superb views of the Menai Straits. The pub has a back to basics feel with old wooden tables, chairs and several church pews, but the large screen TV and fruit machines can dominate. Food is served daily except Sunday evening. Local CAMRA Pub of the Year in 2004, 2006 and 2007. ◑♣

Beaumaris

Olde Bulls Head Inn

Castle Street, LL58 8AA
⏲ 11-11; 12-10.30 Sun
☎ (01248) 810329 🌐 bullsheadinn.co.uk
Draught Bass; Hancock's HB; guest beer Ⓗ
Grade II listed building that was the original posting house of the borough. In 1645 General Mytton, a parliamentarian, commandeered the inn while his forces lay siege to the nearby castle. The Royalists surrendered on 25th June 1646. Dr Johnson and Charles Dickens were famous guests and each bedroom is named after a Dickens character. The beamed bar has a large open fire. Parking is limited.
⛫Q⇌◑⊟P

Bethesda

Douglas Arms Hotel ★

London Road, LL57 3AY
⏲ 6-11; 3.30-midnight Sat; 1-3, 7-11 Sun
☎ (01248) 600219
Marston's Burton Bitter, Pedigree; guest beer Ⓗ
This Grade II listed building features in CAMRA's National Inventory. Built in 1820, it was an important coaching inn on the historic Telford post route from London to Holyhead. The four-room interior has not changed since the 1930s and includes a snug, lounges and a large tap room with a full sized snooker table. Bethesda, originally a town built on slate quarries, is convenient for buses to the Ogwen Valley and the surrounding mountains.
Q⊟⛺⊟♣

Colwyn Bay

Pen-y-Bryn

Pen-y-Bryn Road, Upper Colwyn Bay, LL29 6DD (top of King's Rd) SH842782
⏲ 11.30-11; 12-10.30 Sun
☎ (01492) 533360 🌐 penybryn-colwynbay.co.uk
Thwaites Original; guest beers Ⓗ
Open plan pub popular with all ages, with large bookcases, old furniture and open fires in the winter months. The walls are decorated with old photographs and memorabilia from the local area. Panoramic views of Colwyn Bay and the Great Orme can be admired from the terrace and garden. Excellent imaginative bar food is served; the menu is updated daily on the website. Six beers include five guests mainly from independent breweries. A former local CAMRA branch Pub of the Year.
⛫Q❀◑♿⊟♣P⊡

Picture House ✔

24-26 Princes Drive, LL29 8LA SH849791
⏲ 9-midnight (1am Fri & Sat)
☎ (01492) 535286

Courage Directors; Greene King Abbot; Marston's Pedigree; guest beers Ⓗ
Wetherspoon's pub in what was once the Princess Theatre, an Art Deco Grade II listed building with multiple levels and a balcony. Interesting framed old theatre programmes adorn the walls. There are eight handpumps and beer can be served in third-of-a-pint tasting glasses. Local and national beer festivals are held regularly. Quiz night is Monday. Popular with locals and holidaymakers, families are welcome. Close to Colwyn Bay railway station and bus routes 12, 14 and 15. Q◑♿⇌🚌●

Wings Social Club

Station Square, LL29 8LF (opp Colwyn Bay Station)
11-3 (4 Fri), 7-11; 11-11 Sat; 12-4, 7-10.30 Sun
☎ (01492) 530682
Lees Brewer's Dark, Bitter, seasonal beer Ⓗ
Local CAMRA Club of the Year 2008, this popular social club is across the road from the resort's mainline rail station and two minutes' walk from the main coast road bus services. A warm welcome awaits visitors and their families. The bar area serves a large L-shaped lounge which incorporates a small dance floor. The club holds a wedding licence and also hosts other functions. There are separate rooms for billiards, pool, snooker, darts and TV. A regular music night is held on Saturday. ⇌🚌♣⁵⁻

Conwy

Bridge Inn (Y Bont)

Rosehill Street, LL32 8LD SH783775
11-11 (midnight Fri & Sat); 12-11 Sun
☎ (01492) 573482 bridge-conwy.com
Banks's Bitter; Jennings Cocker Hoop; Marston's Pedigree; guest beers Ⓗ
A warm welcome awaits at this busy, traditional pub within sight of the medieval Conwy Castle. An open-plan lounge with coal fire is served by a central bar and there is a lower corner dining area. Here you can order excellent quality home-cooked meals made with locally-sourced ingredients; daily specials are written on the blackboard. Up to two guest beers are on offer and a good selection of malt whiskies. En-suite accommodation is available in a range of pleasant rooms. ⛫⛺◑⇌🚌⁵⁻

Criccieth

Castle Inn

LL52 0RW
12-11
☎ (01766) 523515
Beer range varies Ⓗ
Traditional three-roomed pub just off the A497 Porthmadog to Pwllheli road, catering for locals and tourists alike. Three handpumps dispense an ever-changing range of beers from regional and small breweries, as well as cider in summer. Well served by public transport, the Cambrian Coast railway station is less than 100 metres away. For enjoying a pint on a warm summer evening there is a small outdoor area. ⛫❀◑⊟Ⲁ⇌🚌♣●

Dulas

Pilot Boat Inn

LL70 9EX (on A5025)
11 (12 Sun)-11
☎ (01248) 410205
Robinson's Unicorn Ⓗ
Friendly, rural, family pub with a play area and converted double decker bus to keep children amused. Originally a cottage-type building, now much extended, the lounge features an unusual bar created from half a boat. The pub is much used by walkers; the coastal path passes through the car park. It is worth visiting Mynydd Bodafan for its spectacular views and Traeth Lligwy for the sands. Meals are served all day. Q❀◑Ⲁ🚌♣P⁵⁻

Dwygyfylchi

Gladstone ✔

Ysgubor Wen Road, LL34 6PS (off jct 16 A55) SH730772
12-11 (midnight Fri & Sat)
☎ (01492) 623231
Caledonian Deuchars IPA; Tetley Bitter; guest beers Ⓗ
Extensively refurbished by the owners, the pub has retained its original features. A galleried balcony with tables and booths overlooks a central bar and comfortable sofas surround a wood-burning stove. The decor features wood panelling with old photographs. Beers are served in the correct glasses. Imaginative food is sourced locally. The outdoor seating area has magnificent sea views, and there is a covered smoking area. Function rooms are also available. ⛫❀⛺◑♿Ⲁ🚌P⁵⁻

Four Mile Bridge

Anchorage Hotel

LL65 3EZ (on B4545, just past bridge to Holy Island)
11 (12 Sun)-11
☎ (01407) 740168
Draught Bass; Taylor Landlord; Theakston XB; guest beer Ⓗ
This family-run hotel is situated on Holy Island close to Trearddur Bay. There is a large, comfortable lounge bar and a dining area serving a wide selection of meals. The hotel is near some fine, sandy beaches and coastal walks. Its proximity to the A55 makes it a useful stopping off point for Holyhead Port. Q❀⛺◑Ⲁ🚌P⁵⁻

Glanwydden

Queen's Head

LL31 9JP SH817804
11-3, 6-11 (10.30 Mon & Tue); 12-10.30 Sun
☎ (01492) 546570 queensheadglanwydden.co.uk
Adnams Bitter; guest beers Ⓗ
This former wheelwright's cottage in the centre of the village welcomes locals and holidaymakers alike. Run by the same owner for more than 20 years, the olde-worlde pub has a traditional front bar with a cosy atmosphere and a rear bar with a dining area. There is a heated seating area outside. Good quality food is made with local Welsh produce.

Guest beers come from Great Orme, Weetwood and Spitting Feathers.
♨Q✿⊨◑⊟▲⊡P⸗

Harlech

Branwen Hotel

Ffordd Newydd, LL46 2UB (on A462 below Harlech Castle) SH583312
⏲ 11-11
☎ (01766) 780477 🌐 branwenhotel.co.uk
Beer range varies Ⓗ
Warm and welcoming family run hotel and bar overlooked by Harlech Castle. The hotel is named after a princess whose tales are found in a collection of Welsh myths known as Y Mabinogion. The popular and stylish bar offers a wide range of cask ales as well as foreign beers. A large selection of wines and malt whiskies is also stocked. Ask for your favourite malt —they are sure to have it.
✿⊨◑♿▲≢⊡♣P⸗

Holyhead

79

79 Market Street, LL65 1UW
⏲ 11-11; 12-10.30 Sun
☎ (01407) 763939
Young's Bitter; guest beer Ⓗ
Comfortable, refurbished town centre pub enjoying a good year round local trade. It is one of the few outlets for real ale in the town. There are two bars, a pool room, Sky TV and a split level dining area. Good food is served all day. Visit the Celtic Gateway Bridge, the Roman Wall and the ancient parish church at the start of the Anglesey Coastal Path. ◑≢♣

Llanbedr

Ty Mawr Hotel

LL45 2HH
⏲ 11-11
☎ (01341) 241440
Worthington's Bitter; guest beers Ⓗ
Small country hotel set in its own grounds. The modern lounge bar has a slate flagged floor and cosy wood-burning stove. Unusual flying memorabilia reflect connections with the local airfield. French windows lead on to a verandah and landscaped terrace with seating. A beer festival is held in a marquee on the lawn each year. Popular with locals and walkers, dogs and children are welcome. Meals are served all day. ♨✿⊨◑♿▲≢P

Llandderfel

Bryntirion Inn

LL23 7RA (on B4401, 4 miles E of Bala)
⏲ 11 (12 Sun)-11
☎ (01678) 530205
Jennings Cumberland Ale; guest beer Ⓗ
Old coaching inn in a rural setting with views to the River Dee. Off the pleasant public bar is a family room and there is a lounge where meals are served in a quiet environment. Bar snacks are also available. There is outdoor seating in the front car park; at the rear is a courtyard and larger car park. Three bedrooms offer good value accommodation.
♨Q♘✿⊨◑⊟♣P

Llanddona

Owain Glyndwr

Beaumaris, LL58 8UF (signed off B5109, Pentraeth-Beaumaris road)
⏲ 12 (5 Mon)-midnight; winter hours vary
☎ (01248) 810710
Beer range varies Ⓗ
Originally cottages and a shop, this multi-room pub opened in 1981. It has a bar area, games room, lounge and dining area, and hosts live music every other Saturday. One beer is available in winter and two in summer, all from micro-breweries. Dogs are welcome in the drinking areas. The pub is in the centre of the village, close to the beach and the Anglesey Coastal Path. ♨Q✿◑⊡♣P⸗

Llanddulas

Valentine

Mill Street, LL22 8ES SH908781
⏲ 4-11; 3-midnight Fri; 12-midnight Sat & Sun
☎ (01492) 518189
Thwaites Lancaster Bomber; guest beers Ⓗ
Traditional village pub dating from the 18th-century with a well-furnished, comfortable lounge with an open fire in winter. The separate public bar has a TV. Two beer festivals are held annually: Ales in Wales on the spring bank holiday and Celtic Ales on the August bank holiday. Brewery memorabilia and many old framed photographs relating to the Valentine decorate the walls. Quiz night is Thursday. Dogs are welcome.
♨Q✿⊟▲⊡(12, 13)♣⸗

Llandudno

King's Head

Old Road, LL30 2NB (next to Great Orme Tramway) SH778827
⏲ 12-midnight (11 Sun)
☎ (01492) 877993
Greene King IPA, Abbot; guest beers Ⓗ
The 300-year-old King's Head is the oldest pub in Llandudno; it makes an ideal stop after walking on the Great Orme or riding on Britain's only cable hauled tramway. The traditional split level bar is dominated by a large open fire. The sun-trap patio with its award-winning flower display is a great place to watch the trams pass by. There is a grill restaurant at the rear of the pub serving good quality food. ♨♘✿◑▲⊖⊡P

Llanelian-yn-Rhos

White Lion

LL29 8YA (off B583) SH863764
⏲ 11.30-3, 6-midnight; closed Mon; 12-4, 6-11 Sun
☎ (01492) 515807 🌐 whitelioninn.co.uk
Marston's Burton Bitter, Pedigree; guest beer Ⓗ
Traditional 16th-century inn next to St Elian's Church in the hills above Old Colwyn. There is a slate flagstoned bar area with a real log fire, antique settles and large comfortable chairs. Decorative stained glass is mounted above the bar of the tiny snug. The spacious restaurant

WALES

has a collection of jugs hanging from the ceiling. Two white stone lions guard the door of this attractive family run inn which has been in the Guide for 17 years.
⛫Q♂❀◗⊟⛺♣P⚋

Llanfairfechan

Virginia

Mill Road, LL33 0TH SH685746
⏲ 12-midnight; 12-3, 7-11 Sun
☎ (01248) 680584
Beer range varies Ⓗ
Situated next to the River Ddu, this is a great traditional boozer. The quarry-tiled hallway leads to a central small hatched bar surrounded by three rooms all furnished with basic period items. The old manual till and genuine Allsopps Burton Ales mirror add to the charm of this terraced gem. The licensees have been here for over 30 years. The beer is served from a vertical stillage and often comes from the local Conwy brewery. ⛫❀⊟🚌♣⚋

Llanfihangel Glyn Myfyr

Crown Inn

LL21 9UL (on B5105, 3 miles E of Cerrig-y-Drudion) SH992493
⏲ 7-11; closed Mon & Tue; 12 (4 winter)-11 Sat & Sun
☎ (01490) 420209
Beer range varies Ⓗ
Lovely old inn, a rural gem, situated beside the Afon Alwen. The unspoilt interior of the front bar with slate flooring and an open fire provides a warm welcome. The games room is across the corridor with darts, pool and TV. Children are welcome in the pub and there are terraced gardens beside the river. Camping is permitted in the grounds and permits are available for trout fishing – the licensee owns the rights. Beers, one or two, come from small independent breweries. A frequent winner of CAMRA awards. ⛫Q❀⛺♣P⚋

Llangefni

Railway Inn

48-50 High Street, LL77 7NA
⏲ 4 (3 Thu & Fri)-11; 12-midnight Sat; 12-11 Sun
☎ (01248) 722166
Lees Bitter Ⓗ
Classic, friendly, small town pub with a warm welcome, next to the old railway station, displaying photographs of the railway and old Llangefni. The main bar is hewn out of the stone wall. Near the centre of this county town, the pub is also close to Oriel Mon (museum) where you can find out about the history of Anglesey, see Tunnicliffe's bird books and pictures and view Sir Kyffin Williams' paintings. 🚌♣⚋

Llanrwst

New Inn

Denbigh Street, LL26 0LL SH798617
⏲ 11-1am (2am Fri & Sat); 12-2am
☎ (01492) 640467
Banks's Original; Marston's Burton Bitter; guest beer Ⓗ
Popular, traditional, terraced town pub. One bar serves a comfortably furnished, narrow lounge and a corner snug which has an open fire and TV. There is a separate games area with a pool table and jukebox. Outside, there are a few picnic tables at the back of the inn where smoking is allowed. This friendly pub appeals to all generations, and you are assured of a warm welcome. Last entry is 11.30pm. ⛫❀⛺⇌🚌♣

Pen-y-Bont

Bridge Street, LL26 0ET SH799615
⏲ 11-11; 12-10.30 Sun
☎ (01492) 640202
Beer range varies Ⓗ
Fourteenth-century inn overlooking the picturesque 17th-century stone bridge crossing of the nearby Conwy River. This family-run pub has plenty of character with its quaint low-beamed rooms. A central bar serving two frequently-changing real ales from independent brewers separates the congenial public bar and the cosy lounge, both with welcoming real fires. A dining area at the rear has a family section and there is a traditional games room.
⛫Q♂◗⊟⛺⇌🚌♣P⚋

Menai Bridge

Auckland Arms

Water Street, LL59 5DD
⏲ 12-3, 5-midnight (1am Fri & Sat)
☎ (01248) 712545 🌐 anglesey-hotel.co.uk
Beer range varies Ⓗ
Around 120 years old, the hotel is in a superb location, close to the pier and the Strait. The busy bar, popular with students, has two pool tables and a range of pub games including a popular Monday night quiz. Open microphone night is Thursday. Food is available lunchtimes and evenings seven days a week. Beers change constantly but often feature Greene King. There is a patio and garden and the comfortable B&B accommodation is recommended. Check opening hours out of term time. ❀🛏◗⛺♣⚋

Tafarn y Bont (Bridge Inn)

Telford Road, LL59 5DT (on right as you come off bridge)
⏲ 11-midnight; 12-10.30 Sun
☎ (01248) 716888
Banks's Bitter; Marston's Pedigree; guest beers Ⓗ
Mid 19th-century former shop and tea rooms, close to the famous bridge, now a brasserie-style pub with an excellent restaurant. A beamed interior, log fires and numerous hideaway rooms give the pub an olde-worlde feel. Snowdonia is a short drive away and the Anglesey Coastal Path is very close by.
⛫♂❀◗⛺🚌⚋

Victoria Hotel

Telford Bridge, LL59 5DR (between bridge and town centre)
⏲ 11-11; 12-10.30 Sun
☎ (01248) 712309
Draught Bass; guest beers Ⓗ
Situated 300 metres from the Menai Suspension Bridge, this 19-room hotel

overlooks the Straits and affords delightful views from the garden and patio. It is licensed for weddings and has a spacious function room with widescreen HD TV for sports. Live music is a regular added attraction. There is easy access to Snowdonia and the hotel is near the Anglesey Coastal Path.

Old Colwyn

Cuckoo

325-329 Abergele Road, LL29 9PF (on main Colwyn Bay to Abergele road) SH866784
10 (11 Sun)-11
(01492) 514083
Conwy Welsh Pride; guest beer H

Formally known as Clwb y Gornel (the Club on the Corner), the Cuckoo is aptly named with several cuckoo clocks greeting you as you walk in. The main room has wide-screen TV and a bar with three handpumps dispensing one regular ale and up to two guests. A door to the left leads to a smaller lounge and games room with a pool table and dart board. To the rear is a large covered and heated patio area.

Red Lion

385 Abergele Road, LL29 9PL (on main Colwyn Bay to Abergele road) SH868783
5-11; 4-midnight Fri; 12-midnight Sat; 12-11 Sun
(01492) 515042
Marston's Burton Bitter; guest beers H

This ever popular local serves up to six guest beers from independent and local brewers including a regular guest mild. A genuine free house, it has won many local CAMRA awards including Pub of The Year 2007. The cosy L-shaped room is warmed by a real coal fire and features antique brewery mirrors and other memorabilia. The traditional public bar has a pool table, darts and TV. To the rear is a covered and heated smoking area.

Sun Inn

383 Abergele Road, LL29 9PL (on main Colwyn Bay to Abergele road) SH868783
12-11 (midnight Fri & Sat); 12-11.30 Sun
(01492) 517007
Marston's Burton Bitter, Pedigree; Theakston Dark Mild; guest beer H

The only original pub building in Old Colwyn, dating from 1844. A typical beer drinker's local, the central bar serves a cosy lounge area with a welcoming real coal fire. CAMRA literature is displayed prominently on the top of a piano. The bar also serves a side room with TV and jukebox. There is a large games/meeting room at the back with dartboard and pool table. Outside is a heated and covered smoking area.

Penrhyn Bay

Penrhyn Old Hall

LL30 3EE SH816815
12-3, 5.30-11; 12-3, 7-10.30 Sun
(01492) 549888
Draught Bass; guest beer H

Medieval hall dating from the 12th century which has been in the Marsh family since 1963. The wood-panelled Tudor bar dating back to 1590 has a large fireplace concealing a priest hole. Good value meals are served daily in the restaurant. A jazz night is held on the first Sunday of the month and the Penrhyn Bay Players stage occasional pub theatre here.

Penrhynside

Penrhyn Arms

Pendre Road, LL30 3BY (off B5115) SH814816
5.30 (5 Thu)-midnight; 12-1am Fri & Sat; 12-11 Sun
(07780) 678927 penrhynarms.com
Banks's Bitter; Marston's Pedigree; guest beers H

A former runner-up in CAMRA's National Cider & Perry Pub of the Year and current local branch Pub of the Year 2008 winner, this welcoming local is a real gem. It has a spacious L-shaped bar where pool and darts are played and a widescreen TV. Framed pictures of notable drinkers and brewery memorabilia adorn the walls. There are real ciders and perries plus up to four guest beers including mild and winter ale on gravity at Christmas. Check the website for current beers and tasting notes.

Penysarn

Bedol

LL69 9YR
12 (2 winter Mon-Fri)-11; 12-11 Sat; 12-11 (2-10.30 winter) Sun
(01407) 832590
Robinson's Hartleys XB, seasonal beers H

The Bedol (Horseshoe) was built in 1985 to serve a small village, but the regulars now come from a much wider area. This Robinson's tied house hosts regular live entertainment. Food is available all day, except midweek lunchtime in winter. Some of Anglesey's beautiful beaches and the coastal path are nearby. Q

Porthmadog

Spooner's Bar

Harbour Station, LL49 9NF
10-11; 12-10.30 Sun
(01766) 516032 festrail.co.uk
Beer range varies H

An all year round mini beer festival – Spooner's has built its reputation on an ever-changing range from small breweries, including the local Purple Moose. Situated in the terminus of the world famous Ffestiniog Railway, steam trains are outside the door most of the year. Food is served every lunchtime, but out of season only Thursday to Saturday in the evening. Local CAMRA Pub of the Year 2005 and 2007. Q

Station Inn

LL49 9HT (on mainline station platform)
11-11 Mon-Wed; 11-midnight Thu-Sat; 12-11 Sun
(01766) 512629
Brains Rev James; Purple Moose Snowdonia; guest beer H

Situated on the Cambrian Coast railway platform, this pub is popular with locals and visitors alike. There is a large lounge and smaller public bar. It can get very busy at the weekend and on nights when live football is shown on TV. A range of pies and sandwiches is available all day. ❀⊟♿⅄⇌⊟♣P

Red Wharf Bay

Ship Inn ✔

LL75 8RJ (off A5025 between Pentraeth and Benllech)

☉ 11-11 (10.30 Sun)

☎ (01248) 852568 🌐 shipinnredwharfbay.co.uk

Adnams Bitter; Brains SA; Tetley Bitter; guest beers Ⓗ

Red Wharf Bay was once a busy port exporting coal and fertilisers in the 18th and 19th centuries. Previously known as the Quay, the Ship enjoys an excellent reputation for its bar and restaurant, with meals served lunchtimes and evenings. It gets busy with locals and visitors in the summer. The garden has panoramic views across the bay to south-east Anglesey. The resort town of Benllech is two miles away and the coastal path passes the front door. ⋔Q☋❀◑⊟P⊬

Rhos-on-Sea

Toad

West Promenade, LL28 4BU SH847795

☉ 11-11.30 (10.30 Sun)

☎ (01492) 532726

Jennings Cumberland Ale; guest beers Ⓗ

Traditional seaside pub overlooking the bay with a cosy restaurant at the rear serving quality home-made food and famous Sunday lunches. There is a downstairs pool room and a spacious front patio on the promenade with stunning sea views. This attractive and popular pub is also available for private functions. A warm welcome for locals and visitors awaits from the friendly, approachable management and staff. ⋔❀◑⊟♣P⊬

Rhoscolyn

White Eagle

LL65 2NJ (off B4545 signed Traeth Beach) SH271755

☉ 12-3, 6-11; 12-11 Sat; 12-10.30 Sun

☎ (01407) 860267 🌐 white-eagle.co.uk

Marston's Burton Bitter, Pedigree; Weetwood Eastgate; guest beers Ⓗ

Saved from closure by new owners, this pub has been renovated and rebuilt with an airy, brasserie-style atmosphere. There is a fine patio enjoying superb views over Caernarfon Bay and the Lleyn Peninsula to Bardsey Island. The nearby beach offers safe swimming with a warden on duty in the summer months. The pub is near to the coastal footpath. Excellent food is available lunchtimes and evenings, all day during the school holidays. ⋔Q❀◑⊟♿⅄P

Rhydlydan

Giler Arms

LL24 0LL SH892508

☉ 11-2.30, 6-1am summer; 12-2.30, 6.30-11 winter; 12-1am Sat; 12-10.30 (12-2.30, 6.30-10.30 winter) Sun

☎ (01690) 770612

Batham Mild, Best Bitter Ⓗ

Friendly country hotel, recently extensively refurbished, in six acres of grounds including a coarse fishing lake, small camping and touring caravan site, plus picturesque gardens beside the small River Merddwr. The comfortable lounge has a large open stove and the public bar with open fire is popular with the locals. There is also a small pool room. The dining room has lovely views over the lake. Children are welcome in this Batham's pub. Accommodation is in seven bedrooms, mainly en-suite. ⋔Q❀⇔◑⊟⅄⊟♣P⊬

St George

Kinmel Arms

LL22 9BP SH974758

☉ 12-3, 6-11; closed Mon; 11.30 Fri & Sat; 12-5 Sun

☎ (01745) 832207 🌐 thekinmelarms.co.uk

Thwaites Original; guest beers Ⓗ

Former 17th-century coaching inn set on the hillside overlooking the sea. An L-shaped bar serves a large combined dining and drinking area with a real log fire in one corner and a spacious conservatory at the rear. Up to three guest beers including a mild come from independent breweries, plus a rotating Weston's cider and a selection of Belgian beers. The pub has a reputation for good food and has received numerous awards including local CAMRA's Best Pub Food. ⋔Q❀⇔◑♿⊟●P⊬

Tal y Bont

Abbeyfield Hotel

LL57 3UR (turn right at Penrhyn Castle)

☉ 12-3, 6.30-midnight; 12-midnight Sat & Sun

☎ (01248) 352219 🌐 abbeyfieldhotel.co.uk

Great Orme Best Bitter, Three Feathers Ⓗ

Initially a converted 17th-century farmhouse, this is now a popular country hotel and pub, renowned for its restaurant and fine cuisine. The pub is a free house offering local beer from Llandudno's Great Orme Brewery as well as occasional seasonal beers. The hotel, with 11 en-suite bedrooms, is ideally located for Snowdonia and the resorts of Anglesey. ☋❀⇔◑⊟♣P

Trefriw

Old Ship/Yr Hen Long

LL27 0JH (on B5106) SH781632

☉ 12-3, 6-11; 12-11 Sat; 12-10.30 Sun

☎ (01492) 640013 🌐 the-old-ship.co.uk

Banks's Bitter; Marston's Pedigree; guest beer Ⓗ

This former 16th-century customs house is now a busy village local. The small bar serves a cosy L-shaped lounge with an open fire and pictures of historic and nautical interest. The dining room has an inglenook. This genuine free house serves a good range of guest beers and home-cooked food. A self-catering holiday cottage is available. ⋔❀⇔◑⊟P

Tudweiliog

Lion Hotel

LL53 8ND (on B4417)

🕘 11-11 (12-2, 6-11 winter); 11.30-11 Sat; 11-10.30 (12-3 winter) Sun

☎ (01758) 770244

Beer range varies Ⓗ

Village pub on the glorious, quiet north coast of the Lleyn Peninsula. The cliffs and beaches are a mile away by footpath, a little further by road. The origins of this free house go back over 300 years. Up to four beers are served depending on the season, with Purple Moose a firm favourite. The pub is accessible by No 8 bus from Pwllheli – but not in the evening. Closed Monday lunchtime in winter.

Q⛼❀🛏◑◐⊟♿🚌P

Ty'n-y-Groes

Groes Inn

LL32 8TN (2 miles from Conwy on B5106) SH777740

🕘 12-3, 6.30 (6 Sat)-11; 12-10.30 Sun

☎ (01492) 650545 🌐 groesinn.com

Great Orme Orme's Best; Tetley Burton Ale Ⓗ

The first licensed house in Wales, dating back to 1573, the Groes Inn has been in the Humphreys family for 22 years. This multi-roomed inn has retained its original architectural features and there is a function room available on the upper floor. Excellent food using local produce is available in the bar or restaurant. You can stay at the inn, a luxury cabin in the hills or a cottage in Conwy.

⛰Q❀🛏◑◐🚌(19)P

Waunfawr

Snowdonia Park

Beddgelert Road, LL55 4AQ

🕘 11-11 (10.30 Sun)

☎ (01286) 650409 🌐 snowdonia-park.co.uk

Marston's Mansfield Dark Mild, Burton Bitter, Pedigree; guest beers Ⓗ

Home of the Snowdonia Brewery. There are children's play areas inside (separate from the bars) and outside. Meals are served all day. The large campsite gives a discount to CAMRA members. The pub adjoins Waunfawr station on the Welsh Highland Railway; stop off here before going on to Rhyd Ddu (soon to be Beddgelert) on one of the most scenic sections of narrow gauge railway in Britain.

Q⛼❀◑◐⊟♿⛺⇌🚌♣P

Crown Inn, Llanfihangel Glyn Myfyr.

WEST WALES

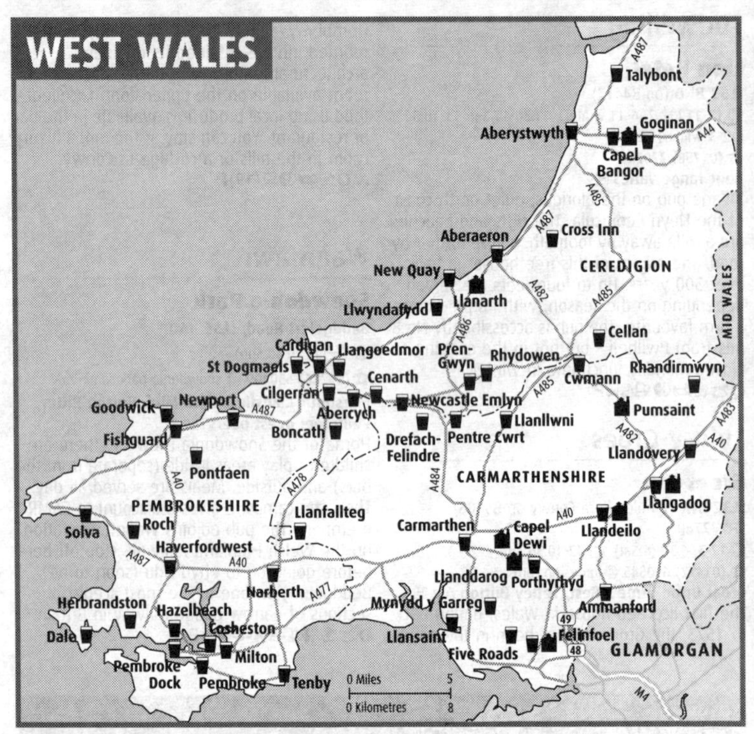

Authority areas covered: Carmarthenshire, Ceredigion, Pembrokeshire

Aberaeron

Cadwgan

10 Market Street, SA46 0AU

12 (5 Mon)-midnight (1am Fri & Sat); 12-10.30 Sun

(01545) 570149

Brains Bitter; guest beer H

Small, cosy pub opposite the inner harbour in this charming Regency town. It is very much a social centre for a more mature clientele and a meeting place for local societies. The decor is simple, but look for the fascinating photographs of bygone Aberaeron on the walls in the bar. The guest beer usually comes from a micro-brewery anywhere in the UK, though occasionally a second Brains beer may be on offer. There is outdoor drinking at pavement tables. (X40,550)

Harbourmaster

2 Quay Parade, SA46 0BT (off A487, overlooking harbour)

10-midnight

(01545) 570755 harbour-master.com

Evan Evans BB; guest beers H

The new bar, housed in a former aquarium (originally a grain warehouse), opened in 2007, but this classy hotel with bar and restaurant was already well established. The bar offers harbour views and a stylish space to enjoy a pint or a meal (served lunchtimes and evenings). With bilingual signage and staff, the ethos is confidently Welsh, as reflected in the provenance of the food and drink. One guest beer is usually from Tomos Watkin, while a second Welsh guest is added in summer. If fine, drink outside by the harbour wall. (X40,550)P

Abercych

Nags Head

SA37 0HJ (on B4332 between Cenarth and Eglwyswrw)

11-3 (not Mon), 6-11; 12-10.30 Sun

(01239) 841200

Beer range varies H

This well restored old smithy boasts a beamed bar and riverside garden. The bar area is furnished with collections of old medical instruments, railway memorabilia, and timepieces showing the time in various parts of the world. Space is also found for an extensive display of beer bottles. House beer Old Emrys is brewed for the pub. P

Aberystwyth

Glengower Hotel

Victoria Terrace, SY23 2DH (N end of promenade)

INDEPENDENT BREWERIES

Black Mountain Llangadog
Coles Llanddarog
Evan Evans Llandeilo
Felinfoel Felinfoel
Ffos y Ffin Capel Dewi
Gwynant Capel Bangor
Jacobi Pumsaint
Penlon Cottage Llanarth

⌚ 12-11
☎ (01970) 626191
Caledonian Deuchars IPA; Theakston Best Bitter, guest beer (summer) Ⓗ
The Glen is a popular meeting place for students and townsfolk, who can enjoy fine sea views from the decking at the front during the summer (and, if hardy, at other times). Televised sport draws the crowds but does not dominate the front bar, and darts, pool and fuseball are played. Evening food finishes at 8pm, available all day at the weekend until 6pm on Sun. The guest beer is usually from a large brewery – and if you fancy a nightcap, there is a very creditable selection of malt whiskies. Buses from the university campus stop nearby. ❀⇌◑◗≠⊟(501)♣⁴–

Nags Head
23 Bridge Street, SY23 1PZ
⌚ 12 (11 Sat)-midnight (1am Thu-Sat); 12-11.30 Sun
☎ (01970) 624725
Banks's Original, Bitter Ⓗ
The least altered of Aberystwyth's clutch of Banks's pubs, this town-centre house serves a varied but largely local clientele, and it can get very busy on weekend evenings. The main bar, with part quarry-tiled floor, has a TV and pool table, and there is a quieter lounge to the right. At the rear, a corridor lined with photos of bygone darts teams leads to a large games room and sun-trap outdoor drinking area.
⚇❀⊡Å≠⊟♣⁴–

Ship & Castle
1 High Street, SY23 1JG
⌚ 2-midnight
Wye Valley HPA; guest beers Ⓗ
This friendly town pub is a mecca for the area's real ale drinkers. First mentioned in 1822, it would have been a popular inn with mariners and shipbuilders from the nearby harbour. Today's customers are an interesting mix of students and townsfolk of all ages. A varied range of up to five draught beers comes mainly from micro-breweries from Wales and beyond; the real cider is usually Weston's Old Rosie. Beer festivals are held in the spring and autumn, folk music on Wednesday night, and occasional quiz nights are run by local CAMRA. A frequent Ceredigion Pub of the Year.
Å≠⊟♣●

Ammanford

Ammanford Hotel
Wernolau House, 31 Pontamman Road, SA31 2JB
⌚ 5.30 (1 Sat)-11; 12-10.30 Sun
☎ (01269) 592598
Beer range varies Ⓗ
Originally a colliery manager's house, this pleasant hotel stands on the outskirts of the town, set in five acres of landscaped grounds and woodland. It is renowned not only for the choice and quality of its beer but also for the warm welcome. Log fires burn in winter and there is a large function room catering for weddings and private events.
♨Q❀⇌◑◗Å⊟P

Boncath

Boncath Inn
SA37 0JN (on B4332 between Cenarth and Eglwyswrw)
⌚ 11-11; 12-8.30 Sun
☎ (01239) 841241
Worthington's Bitter; guest beers Ⓗ
Pembrokeshire CAMRA Pub of the Year 2006 and 2007, this pub dates back to the 18th century and is the centre of village life. The interior is divided into several seating areas creating an intimate atmosphere, and the walls display items of local historic interest. The home-cooked meals are recommended. A beer festival is held each August bank holiday weekend. ♨❀◑◗♿Å⊟♣P⁴–

Capel Bangor

Tynllidiart Arms
SY23 3LR
⌚ 11.30-3, 5-11; 11-11 Fri-Sun
☎ (01970) 880248
Gwynant Cwrw Gwynant; St Austell Tribute; Wye Valley Butty Bach; guest beers Ⓗ
More than 300 years old, this friendly village pub is the only outlet for Cwrw Gwynant, made in the world's smallest commercial brewery (Guinness Book of Records) at the front of the building. The upstairs restaurant provides excellent food, also served in the bar (no food winter Monday). Tables outside at the front are by the main road but a more peaceful pint can be enjoyed on raised decking at the rear. A guest beer is available in summer, and there is a good selection of whiskies. ♨❀◑Å⊟(525)P⁴–

Cardigan

Red Lion/Llew Coch
Pwllhai, SA43 1DB
⌚ 11-11; 12-10.30 Sun
☎ (01239) 612482
Brains Buckley's Best Bitter; Greene King Old Speckled Hen Ⓗ
Visitors are made most welcome in this homely local where Welsh is the first language. A smaller private lounge and restaurant area complement the main bar. Live music is a regular feature, and snacks are available at most times. Tucked away in a quiet corner of town, this pub is well worth seeking out. ❀◑◗⊟♣⁴–

Carmarthen

Queen's Hotel
Queen Street, SA31 1JR
⌚ 11-11
☎ (01267) 231800
Beer range varies Ⓗ
Town centre pub near Carmarthenshire County Hall with a bar, lounge and small function room. The public bar is used by locals and has TV for sporting events. Local beers are usually on sale. The patio nestles beneath the castle walls and is a suntrap during the summer months. Food is served daily with a 'two meals for the price of one' offer. ❀≠⊟⁴–

Stag & Pheasant

34 Spilman Street, SA31 1LQ
11-11; 12-10.30 Sun
(01267) 236278
Beer range varies H
Extensively refurbished in 2007, this single-bar pub serves three real ales from Marston's range. There is a new terraced area to the rear, and a covered smoking area. The pub can get very busy for food at lunchtime, with mostly local trade in the evenings. There are large TVs at both ends of the room. Ten minutes' walk from the railway and bus stations, it is near County Hall.

Cellan

Fishers Arms

SA48 8HU (on B4343)
4.30-11; 12-11 summer; 12-11 Sun
(01570) 422895
Beer range varies H
Situated close to the River Teifi, one of Wales' premier trout and salmon rivers, the pub dates from 1580 and was first licensed in 1891. The main bar has a log burner and flagstone floor. The beers change frequently and are often from Welsh micro-breweries, though the house beer is from Tetley. The pub is served by buses from Aberystwyth and Lampeter weekday daytimes. Q(585)P

Cenarth

Three Horseshoes

SA38 9JL
11 (12 Sun)-11
(01239) 710119
Brains Buckleys Best Bitter; guest beers H
Situated in the centre of a picturesque village noted for its waterfalls, this pub offers a warm welcome to visitors and locals alike, and is a haunt of Teifi Valley fishermen. The building dates from around 1800 and features an open bar with several nooks and crannies and a real fire, plus a restaurant area. There are always two real ales on offer, with a third in summer. Good value meals are served, often featuring local produce. A thatched coffee shop opens from Easter to early autumn.
(460)P

Cilgerran

Pendre Inn

High Street, SA43 2SL
12-11 (10.30 Sun)
(01239) 614223
Shepherd Neame Spitfire; guest beers H
Welcoming, traditional, unspoilt 14th-century pub standing at the heart of a large village whose attractions include a castle, wildlife centre and the Teifi Gorge. The public bar leads to a lounge area and a separate restaurant. Up to two guest beers change regularly and real cider often appears. Though bar snacks are generally available, evening meals are served Wednesday to Saturday only. Sunday lunch is popular (booking advisable).
P

Cosheston

Brewery Inn

SA72 4UD
12-3, 6-11; closed Mon; 12-4, 7-11 Sun
(01646) 686678
Courage Best Bitter; guest beers H
Set between Cosheston Pill and the Carew Estuary just north-east of Pembroke, this light and airy stone-built inn boasts a traditional slate floor and bar, roof beams and comfortable seating with old tables. Paintings and drawings by local artists adorn the walls. The outdoor smoking area is heated in winter.
QP

Cross Inn

Rhos yr Hafod Inn

SY23 5NB (at B4337/B4577 crossroads)
5-11; closed Mon winter; 12-3, 6-11 Sun
(01974) 272644 rhos-yr-hafod-inn.co.uk
Young's Bitter; guest beers H
Now under new licensees, this crossroads pub in a small village remains an oasis of good beer in the rolling uplands of mid-Ceredigion. Linked drinking areas cluster round a central bar – the back room has some fine photographs of local scenes. While quiet background music often plays, conversation is the main entertainment among a mainly local crowd (though some holidaymakers find their way up from the coast in summer). One or two guest beers are usually from regional or larger craft breweries. Sunday lunch is served in summer. P

Cwmann

Cwmann Tavern

SA48 8DR (jct of A482/A485)
4-midnight; closed Mon; 12-midnight Sun
(01570) 423861
Beer range varies H
Built in 1720 on a drovers' route, a short walk from Lampeter, the pub is popular with locals and students. Three drinking areas around the central bar feature wooden beams, posts and floors. Beers are from small breweries and Weston's Old Rosie cider is always on, backed up with a good range of bottled beers. Tuesday night is quiz night, Thursday night a folk session, Friday live band, and Saturday karaoke or DJ. Q(X40)P

Tafarn Jem

SA48 8HF (on A482 4 miles SE of Cwmann)
SN615438
12 (4.30 Tue & Wed winter)-11
(01558) 650633
Breconshire Ramblers Ruin, Brecon County H
Welcoming 19th-century pub, originally an old drovers' ale house, with stunning views over the valley from the outside area. It has excellent access for wheelchair users off the car park. Although the pub is open plan there are two distinct areas, the bar and the lounge/restaurant. Food is served every day except Tuesday and Wednesday from opening until 9.30pm. The menu changes every six weeks. P

Dale

Griffin Inn
SA73 3RB
⏲ 12-11 (12-2, 5.30-11 winter); 12.30-2.30, 5.30-10.30 Sun
☎ (01646) 636227
Brains Rev James; Fuller's London Pride; Worthington's Bitter; guest beers 🄷
In an enviable location at the water's edge and close to the slipway on the Milford Haven waterway, the Griffin is popular with both locals and visitors, including those walking the Pembrokeshire Coast Path. Some of the outside seats are right by the water. Inside you can have some fun with table skittles. The village is the centre for a thriving sailing club. ⌂Q❀◐⊟♿🚌♣⁴–

Drefach-Felindre

Tafarn John y Gwas
SA44 5XG
⏲ 12-11
☎ (01559) 370469 🌐 johnygwas.co.uk
Beer range varies 🄷
Originally a series of shops, this traditional village inn was built in the early 1800s. A locals' pub, there is always a friendly welcome for tourists – and their pets. Two real ales are on offer in winter, three in summer. Home-cooked food is available until 9pm every day, with a roast on Sunday. The food is reasonably priced with children under 12 eating for free. The beer garden has a covered area for smokers. You can play pool or darts, or take part in quiz night on the last Sunday of the month. ⌂❀◐⊟▲🚌(460)♣P⁴–

Felinfoel

Harry Watkins
2 Millfield Road, SA14 8HY (on A476)
⏲ 12-11; closed Mon
☎ (01554) 776644
Beer range varies 🄷
Renamed after a local rugby hero of yesteryear who features on the pub walls, the pub was originally called the Bear. The open-plan, split-level, family-friendly pub has defined dining areas and a function room. There are covered and open drinking areas outside. Although there is no car park there is usually ample room on the road. National cycle and walking paths to the Swiss Valley and beyond are nearby. 👶❀◐🚌⁴–

Fishguard

Pendre Inn
High Street, SA65 9AT (on A487 300m SW of market square)
⏲ 11 (4 Mon)-midnight; 12-11.30 Sun
☎ (01348) 874128
Worthington's Bitter; guest beers 🄷
This friendly, traditional pub on the outskirts of town has a good local following, with pool and darts in the big back bar and a growing reputation for its beer. Two guest beers change regularly and may come from anywhere in the UK. No food is served except packet snacks. ⌂❀⊟🚌(411,412)P⁴–

Royal Oak Inn
Market Square, SA65 9HA
⏲ 11-11; 12-10.30 Sun
☎ (01348) 872514
Beer range varies 🄷
This charming, friendly, comfortable pub has connections with the last invasion of mainland Britain, by a French force at nearby Carregwastad Point in 1797, and displays some fascinating memorabilia from the period. Full of character, it has a bustling public bar and pleasant beer garden. Home-cooked meals are served at affordable prices from a varied menu. Two changing Brains beers are served alongside one or more guests; a beer and folk festival takes place over the Spring Bank Holiday weekend with 18 real ales on offer. ❀◐♿▲🚌(411,412)♣⁴–

Five Roads

Waun Wyllt Inn
Horeb Road, SA15 5AQ (off B4329)
⏲ 11-11
☎ (01269) 860209 🌐 waunwyllt.com
Greene King Abbot; guest beers 🄷
Situated just off National Cycle Trail 47 (the Celtic trail), the Waun Wyllt is set in the heart of the Carmarthenshire countryside. It was built in the 18th century and although recently refurbished retains many original features. The inn was recently purchased by the Great Old Inns group and has become its flagship. It offers a warm welcome, good food and beer including a range of bottled real ales.
⌂Q❀🛏◐♿▲P

Goginan

Druid Inn
High Street, SY23 3NT (on A44 6 miles E of Aberystwyth)
⏲ 12-midnight (1am Fri & Sat)
☎ (01970) 880650 🌐 goginan.com/druid
Banks's Bitter; Wye Valley Butty Bach; guest beer 🄷
This popular pub has gone from strength to strength since its chef became the licensee in 2007. A true community local, it lies at the heart of village life and occasionally hosts live bands. The locally-sourced guest beer is drawn from a wide range of mainly micro-breweries. Food, served 12-9.30 daily, is excellent, the Sunday roast recently attracting plaudits from a national newspaper. The B&B next door, no longer part of the pub business, is useful for visitors wishing to stay in this glorious area. Local CAMRA Pub of the Year 2008.
👶❀◐🚌(525)♣⁴–

Goodwick

Rose & Crown
SA64 0BP
⏲ 11-12.30am; 12-midnight Sun
☎ (01348) 874449
Marston's Pedigree; guest beers 🄷
Picturesque inn close to the ferry port with good views of the harbour and beach. The dining area offers food at lunchtimes and evenings, specialising in pizzas and Mexican dishes. The local lifeboat crew uses the pub as

WALES

a meeting place. Two guest beers are served. Trains to Fishguard Harbour are infrequent and timed to connect with Irish Ferries.
⚓Q❀◐Ⓓ▲⇌(Fishguard Harbour)🚌♣P

Haverfordwest

Bristol Trader

Quay Street, SA61 1BE
11-11 (1am Sat); 12-10.30 Sun
☎ (01437) 762122
Worthington's Bitter; guest beers Ⓗ
Dating back to Haverfordwest's days as a port, this pub retains some character despite recent modernisation. A quiet venue in the daytime popular for dining, food is served in a large dining area or at outside tables overlooking the river. It gets lively in the evening. Two guest beers are served; beers can be served without tight sparkler on request. ◐Ⓓ♿🚌P

Pembroke Yeoman

11 Hill Street, SA61 1QQ
11-11
☎ (01437) 762500
Draught Bass; Flowers IPA; guest beers Ⓗ
In this local pub conversation is king, though there is a well-stocked jukebox should it flag. Two guest ales change often and come from small breweries. Food is served in large portions. Known as the Upper Three Crowns until the 1960s, the pub's name was changed to reflect the presence nearby of the local yeomanry headquarters. ⚓Q◐Ⓓ🚌♣

Hazelbeach

Ferry House Inn

SA73 1EG (signed Llanstadwell from A477 in Neyland)
12-3 (2 Sun), 6-11
☎ (01646) 600270
Brains Rev James; guest beers Ⓗ
Situated on the Milford Haven waterway, this pub is convenient for Neyland, with its marina and Brunel connections, and lies on the Pembrokeshire Coast Path. The conservatory restaurant overlooks the river, with fresh local fish featuring on the menu. Three guest beers are served. Good-quality accommodation makes this an ideal base for exploring the area. Q❀🛏◐Ⓓ⊞♿P⌐

Herbrandston

Taberna Inn

SA73 3TD (3 miles W of Milford Haven)
12-11
☎ (01646) 693498
Hop Back Summer Lightning; guest beers Ⓗ
Built in 1963 in a village dominated by a large oil refinery, this pub has a pleasant atmosphere and welcoming locals. Two guest beers are served alongside Weston's and Moles Black Rat cider, and the pub issues its own listing of all the guest beers sold throughout the year. ⚓Q❀🛏◐Ⓓ⊞♿🚌●P⌐

Llandeilo

White Horse

Rhosmaen Street, SA19 6EN
11-11; 12-10.30 Sun
☎ (01558) 822424
Evan Evans Cwrw, seasonal beers; guest beers Ⓗ
Grade II listed coaching inn dating from the 16th century, this multi-roomed pub is popular with all ages. There is a small outdoor drinking area to the front and a large council car park to the rear with access to the pub down a short flight of steps. The covered area for smokers has its own TV to watch the sport. ❀🚌♣⌐

Llandovery

Red Lion ★

2 Market Square, SA20 0AA
5.30-10.30 Fri; 12-2, 7-11 Sat; closed Sun-Thu
☎ (01550) 720813
Beer range varies Ⓖ
You are assured of a warm welcome at this superb old pub which features in CAMRA's National Inventory of historic interiors. The landlord is semi-retired, hence the short opening hours. He is a mine of information about the town and its rugby team – note that Saturday lunchtime hours may vary depending on rugby fixtures. ⚓⇌🚌

Llanfallteg

Plash

SA34 0HN (N off A40 at Llanddewi Velfrey)
5-11; 12-midnight Wed-Sun
☎ (01437) 563472
Brains Bitter; Wye Valley Butty Bach; guest beer Ⓗ
Terrace-style cottage pub with a garden. An inn for more than 180 years, it has had four different names in that time. The pub is the centre of village life with welcoming locals who will talk to anyone who wishes to join in. The attractive bar was rescued from a local outfitters' shop. Traditional home-made dishes are served in the small restaurant. The guest beer is usually from a small, independent brewery. A disabled entrance is to the rear. ⚓Q❀🛏◐Ⓓ♿♣P

Llangadog

Red Lion

Church Street, SA19 9AA
12-midnight
☎ (01550) 777357 🌐 redlionllangadog.co.uk
Evan Evans Cwrw; guest beers Ⓗ
A recent refurbishment of this Grade II listed 16th-century coaching inn has taken it back to its origins. It was reputed to be a safe house for royalist soldiers during the Civil War. Family friendly, it is full of character and atmosphere. Its excellent, fresh, locally-sourced food attracts locals and tourists alike. Guest beers include Welsh ales as well as those from across the border. Car parking is through the arch. Carmarthenshire CAMRA Pub of the Year 2008. ⚓❀🛏◐Ⓓ♿▲⇌🚌P

Telegraph Inn

Station Road, SA19 9LS
4 (12 Sat)-midnight; 12-11 Sun
☎ (01550) 777727
Black Mountain Black 5; guest beers Ⓗ

On the edge of the village, the inn is next to the railway station on the spectacular Heart of Wales line. It is home to the Black Mountain Brewery which brews weekly. Built around 1830, the welcoming pub has a basic bar area and comfortable lounge. Food is served Wednesday to Saturday including takeaways. Curry night is Wednesday. Self-catering accommodation sleeps five.
(280)P

Llangoedmor

Penllwyndu

SA43 2LY (on B4570, 4 miles E of Cardigan) SN241458
3.30 (12 Sat)-11; 12-10.30 Sun
(01239) 682533
Brains Buckleys Best Bitter; guest beers
Old-fashioned ale house standing at an isolated crossroads where Cardigan's evil-doers were once hanged; the pub sign is worthy of close inspection. The cheerful and welcoming public bar has a slate floor and inglenook with wood-burning stove. Snacks are usually available and there is a separate dining area. The guest beer is often from Cottage Brewery. A second guest beer is occasionally added in summer. P

Llanllwni

Belle Vue Inn

SA40 9SQ (on A485 2 miles N of B4336 jct)
12-2.30 (Sat only), 5-10.30 (11 Fri & Sat); closed Tue; 12-2.30, 6-10.30 Sun
(01570) 480495 bellevueinn.co.uk
Beer range varies
Set on the main road in a long and straggling village, this former 17th-century farmhouse and smithy was converted to an inn in the 1800s. Both licensees are classically trained chefs and have gained a well-deserved reputation for excellence with the emphasis on local produce; the special themed evenings are very popular. With two rotating guest ales plus bottled beers, this friendly family-run free house is a magnet for locals and visitors alike: an oasis in a desert of blandness.
Q (X40)P

Llansaint

King's Arms

13 Maes yr Eglwys, SA17 5JE
12-2.30, 6-11; closed Tue winter; 12-2.30, 6.30-10.30 Sun
(01267) 267457
Brains Buckley's Best Bitter; guest beers
This friendly village local, a former Carmarthenshire CAMRA Pub of the Year, has been a pub for more than 200 years. Situated near an 11th-century church, it is reputedly built from stone recovered from the lost village of St Ishmaels. Music and poetry nights are held on the third Friday of the month. Good value home-cooked food is served. Carmarthen Bay Holiday Park is a few miles away. Q P

Llwyndafydd

Crown Inn & Restaurant

SA44 6BU (off A487 at Gwenlli chapel, 1 mile S of A486 jct, signed Caerwedros) SN371554
12-11 (10.30 Sun)
(01545) 560396 the-crown-inn.moonfruit.com
Enville Ale; Flowers IPA; guest beers
Among the loveliest pubs in Wales, the Crown offers good food, great beer and a garden play area in an idyllic village setting. Young, energetic licensees make this Dylan Thomas Trail pub a friendly place in which to savour the expertly prepared local produce. Other Enville beers sometimes replace the Ale; guests (one in winter, two in summer) are usually from regional brewers. Quiz night is Thursday. The coastal 'Cardi Bach' bus comes this way from June to October.
Q P

Milton

Milton Brewery

SA70 8PH (on A477)
12-3, 4.30-11; 12-11 Sun
(01646) 651202 themiltonbrewery.com
Courage Directors; guest beer
Attractive and substantial ivy-covered pub set on a mill stream flowing into the Carew River. It ceased brewing in the early 1900s but there are plans to start again, using water from a capped well which can be seen inside the pub. There is a large caravan park at the rear.
Q P

WALES

Mynydd y Garreg

Prince of Wales

SA17 4RP
7 (5 Sat)-11; 12-3 Sun
(01554) 890522
Bullmastiff Brindle, Son of a Bitch; guest beers
This little gem of a pub, a former Carmarthenshire CAMRA Pub of the Year, is well worth seeking out for both its beer range and its ambience. As well as the two regular Bullmastiff beers there are up to four rotating guest beers usually from smaller breweries. The cosy single-room bar is packed with movie memorabilia and the small restaurant offers good, reasonably priced food.
Q P

Narberth

Dragon Inn

5 Water Street, SA67 7AT
9am-11 (12.30am Fri & Sat)
(01834) 861667
Marston's Pedigree; guest beers
Set in an attractive town 10 miles north of Tenby with a prominent place in Welsh mythology, this pub has a split-level bar leading to dining areas. The whitewashed walls display horseracing photographs. Narberth railway station is a mile from the town. Visit the Landsker Visitor Centre to find out more about this fascinating area.

New Quay

Seahorse Inn

Uplands Square, SA45 9QH
✪ 11-midnight (1am Fri & Sat)
☎ (01545) 560736
Beer range varies Ⓗ
A great year-round local in a holiday town, this is the place to enjoy a well-kept pint and watch the racing – and your dog is welcome too. There is one real ale in winter, two in summer, mostly from Wales or southwest England – Brains SA Gold often features, and locally made Toloja cider is sometimes seen. No cooked food is available but the generously filled crusty rolls are the talk of the town. Live music plays Friday-Sunday evenings, a quiz is set some Thursdays, and there is a sloe gin competition every Mothering Sunday. ❀▲🚌(550)♣

Newcastle Emlyn

Bunch of Grapes

Bridge Street, SA38 9DU
✪ 8am (9am Sun)-2am
☎ (01239) 711185 🌐 thebunchofgrapes.com
Courage Directors; guest beers Ⓗ
Located near the castle ruins, this 17th-century listed town pub retains its charm and appeal following new ownership. With its oak beams and cosy rustic look it is worth a visit. Live music is guaranteed on Thursday and Saturday evenings all year round. Excellent, reasonably priced food is served in the restaurant and bar area; the menu changes regularly. Recent additions to the entertainment include quiz nights, themed food nights and karaoke, all weekly.
♨❀◑◗⊟🚌(460)♣⚐

Pelican Inn

Sycamore Street, SA38 9AP
✪ 2.30 (12 Fri & Sat)-11.30
☎ (01239) 710606
Draught Bass; guest beer Ⓗ
If you want to enjoy a decent pint while you watch the rugby, this friendly local in the heart of town is the place to be. It has an inviting open fire and there are plenty of cosy nooks for a quiet chat. The bar has Sky TV, a dartboard and pool table. ♨❀🚌(460)♣⚐

Newport

Castle Hotel

Bridge Street, SA42 0TB
✪ 11-11; 12-10.30 Sun
☎ (01239) 820472
Greene King Old Speckled Hen; Theakston Best Bitter, XB; guest beer Ⓗ
This friendly, popular local in a small town full of character has an attractive bar with some impressive wood panelling. Food is served at lunchtimes and evenings in the extensive dining area. An off-street car park is situated behind the hotel. A wealth of prehistoric remains adds interest to the many local walks.
♨❀❀🛏◑◗▲🚌(412)P⚐

Golden Lion

East Street, SA42 0SY (on A487)
✪ 12-midnight (11 Sun)
☎ (01239) 820321
Brains Rev James; Draught Bass; guest beers Ⓗ
Another of Newport's sociable locals, this one is reputed to have its own resident ghost. A number of internal walls have been removed to form a spacious open-plan bar area with distinct sections, helping to retain a cosy atmosphere. Car parking space is available on the opposite side of the road.
♨Q◑◗▲🚌(412)P⚐

Pembroke

Royal George Hotel

9 Northgate, SA71 4NR
✪ 11-12.30 (1am Fri & Sat)
☎ (01646) 682751
Banks's Original; guest beers Ⓗ
Pleasant, cheery riverside local standing directly below Pembroke Castle at what used to be the town's north gate, forming part of the old town wall. The large, split-level, L-shaped room has a single bar serving two guest beers; current and future guests are listed beside the bar. 🛏⊟♿⇌🚌♣P

Pembroke Dock

Flying Boat Inn

6 Queen Street, SA72 6JL
✪ 10-12.30am; 12-10.30 Sun
☎ (01646) 682810
Beer range varies Ⓗ
Featuring exposed stone and black beams, the bar of this relaxed and friendly pub displays memorabilia from the heyday of flying boats stationed locally. Sky Sports is shown on the large screen, a beer festival is held annually, and the local folk club meets every Friday evening. Irish Ferries sails twice daily from Pembroke Dock to Rosslare.
♨Q❀❀🛏⊟♿⇌🚌♣⚐

Station Inn

Hawkestone Road, SA72 6JL (in station building)
✪ 7-11 Mon; 11-3, 6-midnight (12.30am Fri & Sat); 12-3, 7-10.30 Sun
☎ (01646) 621255
Beer range varies Ⓗ
Housed in the town's railway station where trains still depart for Carmarthen and Swansea, this town centre pub is close to the Irish Ferries terminal and Pembrokeshire Coast Path. Meals are excellent value (no lunches Mon, evening meals Wed-Sat only). Three real ales are generally on sale, drawn from an eclectic range, with Young's Bitter a frequent visitor and a new beer coming on every Tuesday. The June beer festival offers around 20 beers. Live music is performed on Saturday evening. ♨Q❀🛏◑◗⊟♿⇌🚌P⚐

Pentre Cwrt

Plas Parke

SA44 5AX (on B4335 between Llandysul and Newcastle Emlyn)
✪ 4 (3 Sat & Sun)-11
☎ (01559) 362684
Draught Bass; guest beers Ⓗ
Friendly family-run pub, popular with villagers and visitors to this tourist area. It has two cosy

bars with wood burners and another more intimate area for a quiet drink. The restaurant offers good home-made meals served in generous portions. In the summer sheltered seating is provided in the garden under gazebos, with barbecues at weekends (phone to check). Guest beers may come from anywhere in the UK. ⌂❀◗⅄P⅃

Pontfaen

Dyffryn Arms ★

SA65 9SG (off B4313)

⌚ hours vary

☎ (01348) 881305

Draught Bass; Tetley Burton Ale Ⓖ

This much-loved pub, whose landlady is in her 80s, resembles a 1920s front room where time has stood still. The beer is still served by the jug through a sliding serving hatch. Conversation is the main form of entertainment, and the pub's relaxed atmosphere is captivating. Set in the beautiful Gwaun Valley between the Preseli Hills and Fishguard, the pub is at the heart of almost all local community activity. ⌂Q❀⅄♣

Porthyrhyd

Mansel Arms

Banc y Mansel, SA32 8BS (on B4310 between Porthyrhyd and Drefach)

⌚ 5 (3 Sat)-11; 12-4 Sun

☎ (01267) 275305

Beer range varies Ⓗ

Friendly 18th-century former coaching inn with wood fires in each room. There is a games room for pool and darts to the rear which was originally used for slaughtering pigs. The original limestone flags have been broken up and used in the fireplace. Low beams have been added to create atmosphere and numerous jugs hang from beams in the bar. Food is served Friday and Saturday evenings and Sunday lunch. ⌂Q◖◗⅄⊟♣●

Pren-gwyn

Gwarcefel Arms

SA44 4LU

⌚ 12-midnight (1am Fri & Sat); closed Wed Nov-Easter; 12-11 Sun

☎ (01559) 362720 ⊕ gwarcefelarms.co.uk

Beer range varies Ⓗ

Set where five roads meet, this family-run country pub has a main bar with open fire and cosy seating, games area with pool and darts, and covered outdoor smoking area. A separate bar serves the restaurant, where functions and parties can be catered for. Guest beers come from breweries including Breconshire, Cottage, Jacobi and Tomos Watkin. ⌂❀◖◗♣P⅃

Rhandirmwyn

Royal Oak

SA20 0NY

⌚ 12-3 (2 winter), 6-11; 12-2, 7-10.30 Sun

☎ (01550) 760201 ⊕ rhandirmwyn.com

Beer range varies Ⓗ

Remote, stone-flagged inn with excellent views of the Tywi Valley and close to an RSPB bird sanctuary. Originally built as a hunting lodge for the local landowner, it is now a focal point for community activities and popular with fans of outdoor pursuits. A fine range of bottled beers and whiskies is stocked, and the good wholesome food is recommended. The pub has been voted Carmarthenshire CAMRA Pub of the Year four times. ⌂Q❀⊭◖◗⅄♣P

Rhydowen

Alltyrodyn Arms

SA44 4QB (at A475/B4459 crossroads)

⌚ 3 (12 Sat)-midnight; closed Mon; 12-8 Sun

☎ (01545) 590319

Beer range varies Ⓗ

This 400-year-old country pub serves a wide selection of real ales from across Britain (no keg beer sold), increasing the range for its August Bank Holiday Beer Festival. A games room with pool and darts complements the main bar, and home-made food is served in the dining room. The beer garden, with a covered decking area for smokers, has lovely valley views, and families and dogs are always welcome. Buses are infrequent. ⌂❀◖◗⊟(551)♣P⅃

Roch

Victoria Inn

SA62 6AW (on A487)

⌚ 12-2.30am (10.30 Sun)

☎ (01437) 710426 ⊕ the-victoriainn.co.uk

Beer range varies Ⓗ

A little gem with views across St Brides Bay, this locals' pub offers a warm welcome to all. The inn was established in 1851 although some parts of the building date back to the 18th century. It has retained much of its old-world charm with beamed ceilings and low doorways. The menu features Welsh dishes and curry night is Friday. For those in a hurry there is a beer carry-out service. Occasional live music plays. ⌂Q♁❀⊭◖◗⊞♿⊟(411)♣P

St Dogmaels

White Hart

Finch Street, SA43 3EA

⌚ 10 (11 Sun)-11 (later in summer)

☎ (01239) 612099

Felinfoel Double Dragon; Greene King IPA; guest beers Ⓗ

Set in Pembrokeshire's northernmost village, this small, cheery community pub enjoys a good local following. Guest beers (three in summer, two in winter) change regularly and are often from breweries rarely seen locally. The landlord is a rugby enthusiast. The beach at nearby Poppit Sands marks the northern terminus of the Pembrokeshire Coast Path. ⌂Q◖◗⅄⊟P⅃

Solva

Cambrian Inn

SA62 6UU (on A487 by bridge)

⌚ 11-11

☎ (01437) 721210
Tomos Watkin OSB; guest beers Ⓗ
Situated in a popular coastal village, renowned as one of the most delightful places in Pembrokeshire, this sympathetically restored local pub has a high reputation for both beer and food. The bar area has been decorated with local crafts, creating a cosy atmosphere enjoyed by village residents and visitors alike. Q◑◐🚌(411)P⚟

Harbour Inn ✔

SA62 6RF (on A487 next to harbour)
🕐 11-11
☎ (01437) 720013
Brains Dark, SA; guest beers Ⓗ
This delightful seaside inn, next to the harbour where emigrants once left for North America, remains the same from year to year. A community pub with a traditional atmosphere, it serves as a base for many village activities and is popular with locals who come to enjoy a quiet, relaxing pint. The nearby camping facilities cater for both caravans and tents. ⛼Q❀🛏◑◐♿🚌(411)P⚟

Ship

15 Main Street, SA62 6UU (on A487)
🕐 12 (11 Fri & Sat summer)-11.30 (midnight Fri & Sat)
☎ (01437) 721427
Banks's Bitter; Jennings Cocker Hoop; Marston's Pedigree; guest beer Ⓗ
Families are made particularly welcome in this traditional pub. The Sunday roast is popular; authentic Indian curries are served in the evening with a free delivery service available subject to a minimum order value. An outdoor smoking area is covered and heated, and ample parking is available nearby at the harbour. ⛼❀🛏◑◐♿⛺🚌(411)⚟

Talybont

White Lion/Llew Gwyn

SY24 5ER (7 miles N of Aberystwyth on A487)
🕐 11-1am; 12-midnight Sun
☎ (01970) 832245
Banks's Original, Bitter; guest beer Ⓗ
This welcoming community pub by the village green has recently been smartly but comfortably refurbished. The front bar retains its flagstone floor, the family/games room is now at the rear, and the dining room is to the left of the entrance. A snug area houses a fascinating display of local history. The summer guest beer is usually from a well-established brewery. Local seafood is a speciality. ⛼🐎❀🛏◑◐♿⛺🚌(28,X32)♣P⚟

Tenby

Hope & Anchor

St Julian Street, SA70 7AS
🕐 11-11; 12-10.30 Sun
☎ (01834) 842131
Brains Rev James; Worthington's Bitter; guest beers Ⓗ
Near the harbour and close to the beaches, this pub caters for locals and tourists alike. A range of bar snacks, which may be enjoyed inside or out, makes it an ideal place to take a break when exploring the area. Impressive stretches of the medieval town walls can be seen nearby. ⛼❀◑◐♿⛺⇌🚌⚟

Rhos yr Hafod Inn, Cross Inn.

Scotland

ABERDEEN & GRAMPIAN

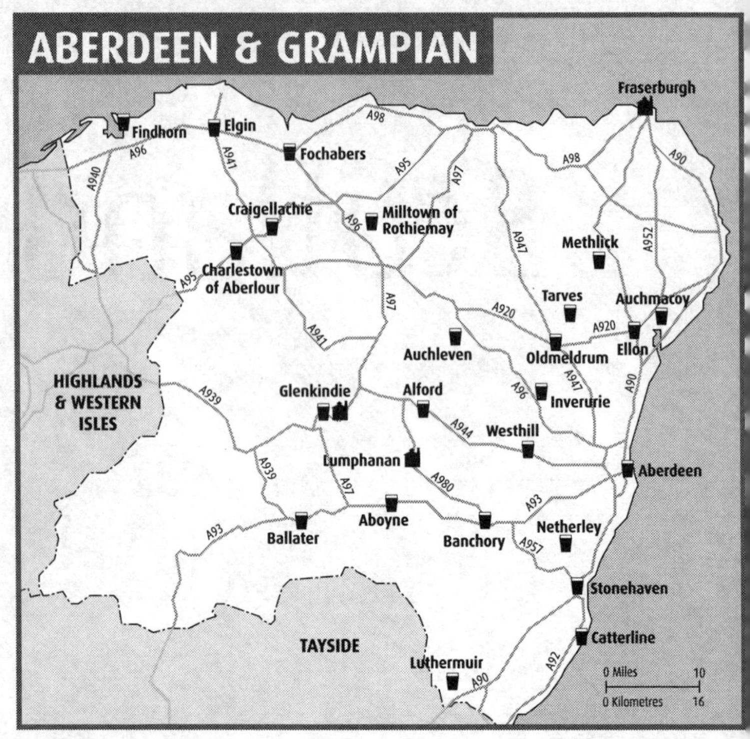

Authority areas covered: Aberdeenshire, City of Aberdeen, Moray

Aberdeen

Aitchies Ale House

10 Trinity Street, AB11 5LY
8am-10 (11 Fri & Sat); closed Sun
(01224) 575972
Orkney Dark Island H
This small corner bar is the closest real ale outlet to the city rail and bus stations, with hours to suit the early traveller. Although renovated in 1994, it retains the flavour of an old-fashioned Scottish pub. Bar food may be described as traditional Scottish pub grub, including roast beef stovies. A good selection of whiskies includes Bell's special edition decanters. The friendly service here is second to none, a reminder of how pubs used to be in the past.

Carriages

101 Crown Street, AB11 6HH (below Brentwood Hotel)
11-2.30 (not Sat), 4.30-midnight; 6-11 Sun
(01224) 595440 brentwood-hotel.co.uk
Caledonian Deuchars IPA, 80; guest beers H
Located in the basement of the Brentwood Hotel just a few minutes from the bustle of Union Street, this is a comfortable pub with an atmosphere that goes beyond the typical hotel bar. With its 10 handpumps, the bar offers the widest selection of real ales in Aberdeen, and has earned a number of awards from the local CAMRA branch over the years. Beers include a continuously changing combination of well-known national brands and local Scottish beers. The adjoining restaurant offers good food, and lunches are also available in the bar. P

Grill ★

213 Union Street, AB11 6BA
10-midnight (1am Fri & Sat); 12.30-midnight Sun
thegrillaberdeen.co.uk
Caledonian 80; guest beers H
Centrally located on Union Street with an exquisite interior dating back to a redesign in 1926, and remaining largely unchanged since then, this is the only CAMRA National Inventory pub in the Aberdeen area. A men-only bar until the Sex Discrimination Act of 1975, ladies toilets were provided in 1998. Situated across from the Music Hall, musicians often visit during concert breaks. Guest beers may include Landlord, Bitter & Twisted and Isle of Skye. An extensive collection of malt whiskies is offered and a variety of bar snacks is available. UK Whisky Bar of the Year.

Moorings

2 Trinity Quay, AB11 5AA (opp quayside at bottom of Market Street)
12-midnight (1am Fri & Sat); 12.30-midnight Sun
(01224) 587602
Beer range varies H
Hard rock meets real ale in this unique and laid-back dockside haven, CAMRA's City Pub o

INDEPENDENT BREWERIES

Brewdog Fraserburgh
Hillside Lumphanan
Old Foreigner Glenkindie

the Year 2008. The pub has a friendly welcome for all, with relatively low prices for the city centre. Five handpumps dispense an ever-changing selection of ales, usually from Scottish breweries (often BrewDog) and one cider (Thatchers). Note the unusual 'elastic band' method of quality control. Frequent live rock bands play, particularly at weekends, and the jukebox tends to be in constant use. CLose to public transport and the Maritime Museum.

Old Blackfriars

52 Castle Street, AB11 5BB
11-midnight (1am Fri & Sat); 12.30-11 Sun
(01224) 581922
Caledonian 80; Greene King Abbot; Inveralmond Ossian's Ale; guest beers H
Local CAMRA Pub of the Year 2007, located in the historic Castlegate city centre. Set on two levels, with bars on both, it is part of the Belhaven/Greene King chain and actively maintains an independent choice of ales mainly from Scottish breweries. Occasional themed beer festivals are hosted and there is a quiz night on the first Tuesday of the month. The pub has a reputation for good food, served until 8.30pm (8pm Fri-Sun). Free Wi-Fi is available.

Prince of Wales

7 St Nicholas Lane, AB10 1HF (opp Marks & Spencer)
10-midnight (1am Fri & Sat); 12-midnight Sun
(01224) 640597
Caledonian 80; Inveralmond Prince of Wales; Theakston Old Peculier; guest beers H
Listed in CAMRA's Scottish Inventory and a frequent winner of CAMRA's City Pub of the Year, this is one of the oldest pubs in Aberdeen, with possibly the longest bar in the city. It has a friendly atmosphere and traditional feel. Now part of the Belhaven/Greene King empire, at least two of the eight handpumps serve Greene King beers supplemented by a selection of Scottish and English ales. Good value food is available lunchtimes. There is a folk music session on Sunday evening and Monday is quiz night. Wi-fi available. Q

Quarter Deck Bar Diner

Salvesen Tower, Blaikies Quay, AB11 5PW (next to NorthLink ferry)
11-midnight (8 Sat); 12.30-8 Sun
(01224) 571523 quarterdeckaberdeen.com
Beer range varies H
Next to the ferry terminal for the Orkney and Shetland ferries, this dull brick building at the foot of an office tower block conceals a friendly, well-stocked bar. The two handpumps feature a range of beers, often including one from Timothy Taylor. The pub is busy at lunchtime with workers from harbour-side offices and also a popular waiting room prior to ferry departures. It has a pool table and plasma screens for sport. Good value food is served and the pub caters for functions.

Tilted Wig

55-56 Castle Street, AB11 5BA (opp Court House)
12-midnight (1am Fri & Sat); 12.30-midnight Sun
(01224) 583248
Caledonian Deuchars IPA; Courage Directors; Theakston XB; guest beers H
Located on the city's historic Castlegate, the name comes from the pub's proximity to the local Sheriff Court, and the walls are adorned with pictures of wigged gentlemen with varying degrees of tilt. This long, narrow venue was originally known as the Lang or Saloon bar, and in the 70s, the Welly Boot. With a recently extended menu, food is served until 10pm daily. There is a large-screen TV for sport, with a second screen in a seating area to the front. A quiz is held on alternate Tuesdays and live music is hosted occasionally.

Under The Hammer

11 North Silver Street, AB10 1RJ (off Golden Square)
5 (4 Fri; 2 Sat)-midnight (1am Thu-Sat); 5-11 Sun
(01224) 640253
Caledonian Deuchars IPA; Inveralmond Ossian's Ale; guest beers H
Atmospheric, comfortable and inviting basement pub, next door to an auction house – hence the name. Paintings by local artists are displayed on the walls and for sale if they take your fancy. Convenient for the Music Hall and His Majesty's Theatre, the large noticeboard has posters advertising forthcoming events in town. Guest beers tend to contrast in style from the two regulars.

Aboyne

Boat Inn

Charleston Road, AB34 5EL (N bank of River Dee next to Aboyne Bridge)
11-2.30, 5-11 (midnight Fri); 11-midnight Sat; 11-11 Sun
(01339) 886137 boatinnaboyne.co.uk
Draught Bass; guest beers H
Popular riverside inn with a food-oriented lounge featuring a log-burning stove and spiral staircase leading to an upper dining area. Junior diners (and adults) may request to see the model train, complete with sound effects, traverse the entire pub at picture-rail height upon completion of their meal. Two guest ales are usually from Scottish micros. Good food is served made with locally-sourced produce. The local Rotary Club regularly meets here. Accommodation available in a self-contained flat.
P

Alford

Forbes Arms Hotel

Bridge of Alford, AB33 8QJ (on A944 1 ½ miles W of Alford)
11-2.30, 5-11 (midnight Thu & Fri); 11-midnight Sat; closed Mon; 12-11 Sun
(01975) 562108
Beer range varies H
Small fishing-oriented hotel on the banks of the River Don. The public bar has the feel of a dark, wood-lined cave with one end dominated by a projection TV screen used for sporting events. The lounge bar has a dining area with river views and the riverside garden is popular in summer. Two beers are on

SCOTLAND

handpump, one in each bar, during busy periods, often including a Scottish micro. The Grampian Transport Museum with its own miniature railway is nearby. The Castle Trail and a dry ski slope are also close.
⩁❀⇔◑◐⊞Å♣P

Auchleven

Hunter's Moon

3 The Belts, AB52 6QB
✪ 5-11 (4-1am Fri; 12-12.30am Sat); closed Mon; 12.30-11 Sun
☎ (01464) 820380
Beer range varies Ⓗ
A friendly welcome is assured at this recently refurbished village local. An interesting, seasonal menu of freshly-cooked, locally-sourced food is available in both the restaurant and spacious bar. Children are permitted in the bar until 8pm. Pool and darts are played and there is a wide-screen TV as well as live music and karaoke sessions. The ever-changing beers are from the Cellarman's Reserve range. Run by young owners keen to promote real ale, this pub is well worth a visit.
⩁❀◑◐⊞♿♣P

Auchmacoy

Poachers Rest

Denhead, AB41 8JL (off A90 Ellon bypass)
✪ 11-2.30, 5-11 (midnight Thu & Fri); closed Mon; 11-midnight Sat; 12-11 Sun
☎ (01358) 722114
Inveralmond Thrappledouser Ⓗ
Situated in a pleasant rural location on the edge of a large country estate in what was once a general merchant's store, this is primarily a split level restaurant, with a small bar at the top end and a lounge. In addition to the regular ale, a small range of bottled beers is available. After a meal, parents can relax over a pleasant pint of ale while their children enjoy the play area outside. ❀◑◐♿P

Ballater

Prince of Wales

2 Church Square, AB35 5NE
✪ 12-11 (1am Fri & Sat)
☎ (01339) 755877
Caledonian Deuchars IPA; guest beers Ⓗ
Cosy, well-maintained bar in the centre of a tourist village. A wood-burning stove keeps the main bar and adjacent pool room warm on a cold winter's evening. Two guest ales are available in the peak summer tourist season. The pub is next to the bus terminus and the renovated Victorian railway station/museum where the Queen used to alight on her way to Balmoral – one of many nearby tourist attractions. It is also close to camping and caravanning sites and the golf club.
⩁◑◐♿Å🚌

Banchory

Douglas Arms Hotel

22 High Street, AB31 5SR
✪ 11-midnight (1am Fri & Sat)
☎ (01330) 822547 ⊕ douglasarms.co.uk
Beer range varies Ⓗ
Small hotel offering good value accommodation. The bar, pool area and snug all feature separate plasma TV systems showing different sports. The public bar is a classic Scottish long bar with etched windows and vintage mirrors, listed in CAMRA's Scottish Inventory. The lounge has recently been upgraded and is primarily used for bar suppers. A large, south-facing exterior decking area is ideal for summer afternoons and evenings. Two guest ales are on handpump, often from Scottish micros.
⩁Q☺❀⇔◑◐⊞♿Å🚌(201,202)♣P

Ravenswood Club (Royal British Legion)

25 Ramsay Road, AB31 5TS (up Mount St from High St)
✪ 11-2.30, 5-midnight (11 winter); 11-midnight Fri & Sat; 11-11 Sun
☎ (01330) 822347 ⊕ banchorylegion.com
Beer range varies Ⓗ
Large, welcoming British Legion Club with a comfortable lounge adjoining the pool and TV room, and a spacious function room used by local clubs and societies as well as members. Darts and snooker are popular and played most evenings. The two handpumps offer excellent value and the beer choice is constantly changing, with ales consistently the best quality in the village. An elevated terrace has fine views of the Deeside hills. Show your CAMRA membership card or a copy of this Guide for entry as a guest. ❀⇔◑◐♿Å♣P

Catterline

Creel Inn

AB39 2UL (on coast off A92, 5 miles S of Stonehaven) NO868782
✪ 12-3, 6-midnight (1am Fri & Sat); 12-midnight Sun
☎ (01569) 750254 ⊕ thecreelinn.co.uk
Beer range varies Ⓗ
A compact village inn in a stunning clifftop location, built in 1838, now incorporating a neighbouring row of fisherman's cottages. Locally caught seafood is a speciality and reservations are recommended if dining. Crawton Bird Sanctuary lies two miles to the north, and the St Cyrus National Nature Reserve is eight miles to the south. Kinneff Old Church two miles away was the hiding place of the Scottish crown jewels for 10 years from 1651. A selection of more than 30 mainly Belgian specialist bottled beers is available and an extensive selection of whiskies.
⩁Q❀◑◐P⊱

Charleston of Aberlour

Mash Tun

8 Broomfield Square, AB38 9QP (signed from main village square)
✪ 11-11 (11.45 Thu & Sun, 12.30am Fri & Sat)
☎ (01340) 881771 ⊕ mashtun-aberlour.com
Beer range varies Ⓗ
Built in 1896 as the Station Bar, this unusual, round ended building has a light interior featuring extensive use of timber. A pledge in the title deeds allowed a name change if the railway closed but it must revert to Station Bar

if a train ever pulls up again outside. The Speyside Way now runs past the door and patrons may drink their ales and enjoy the view on the former station platform. Two beers are served during the tourist season and one in winter, mainly from local micros, especially Cairngorm. A former CAMRA Country Pub of the Year. Q❀⛼◐🚌

Craigellachie

Highlander Inn

10 Victoria Street, AB38 9SR (on A95)

⏲ 12-11 (12.30am Fri & Sat)

☎ (01340) 881446 🌐 whiskyinn.com

Cairngorm Trade Winds; guest beers Ⓗ

Picturesque whisky and cask ale bar on Speyside's Whisky Trail, close to the Speyside Way. Visitors can enjoy the atmosphere of the small, well furnished bars offering a fine selection of malts and good-value tasting sessions. CRAC (Craigellachie Real Ale Club) meet monthly – its members help to choose the pub's guest ales with the full support of the owners and staff. The area is good for fishing and walking. Q❀⛼◐🚌(336)♣P⁄–

Elgin

Muckle Cross ✔

34 High Street, IV30 1BU

⏲ 11-midnight (1am Fri & Sat); 9am-11.45 Sun

☎ (01343) 559030

Greene King Abbot; guest beers Ⓗ

Typical small Wetherspoon's outlet converted from a bicycle shop on Elgin's High Street. A pleasant long room with ample seating, a family area and a long bar, it can get very busy, particularly at weekends. Five handpumps offer a wide range of beers from all over the nation, usually including a Scottish micro-brewery ale. The house beer, Muckle Cross Ale, is brewed by Isle of Skye Brewery. The pub also offers Weston Old Rosie cider and a wide range of malt whiskies from more than 25 local distilleries. ◐♿⇌🚌🍎

Sunninghill Hotel

Hay Street, IV30 1NH

⏲ 12-2.30, 5-11 (12.30am Fri & Sat)

☎ (01343) 547799 🌐 sunninghillhotel.com

Beer range varies Ⓗ

Family-run hotel set in its own grounds in a quiet residential area close to the town centre and the railway station. A comfortable lounge includes a dining area and there are additional tables in the conservatory, making it a popular venue for families. There are four handpumps serving a variety of beers, often from Scottish micros, and a large selection of whiskies is also on offer. Outside, there is seating on the patio. ❀⛼◐♿⇌🚌P

Ellon

Station Hotel

Station Brae, AB41 9BD (Half mile W of village centre)

⏲ 11-11 (11.45 Thu & Sat; 1am Fri)

☎ (01358) 720209

Beer range varies Ⓗ

Impressive Victorian hotel situated on the now closed Buchan railway line, but the energetic may still cycle along the old route from Dyce. A public bar, lounge bar and restaurant all serve food. The range of ale varies depending on availability, but usually features beers from larger English breweries. The hotel has excellent function facilities and a room is available for private parties. Fishing and shooting can be arranged, the golf course is adjacent and Haddo Country Park is five miles away. ☋⛼◐🀱♿P

Tolbooth

21-23 Station Road, AB41 9AE

⏲ 12-11 (midnight Thu; 12.30pm Fri & Sat); 12.30-11 Sun

☎ (01358) 721308

Greene King Abbot; guest beers Ⓗ

A large pub popular with a mature clientele close to the centre of town, with separate seating areas on split levels including a conservatory. The range of ales varies depending on availability, often including beers from larger English breweries. A small attic bar is available for meetings. ❀♿🚌(X50,260)

Findhorn

Crown & Anchor Inn

44 Findhorn, IV36 3YF

⏲ 12-11 (midnight Wed & Thu; 1am Fri & Sat); 12-11.30 Sun

☎ (01309) 690243 🌐 crownandanchorinn.co.uk

Taylor Landlord; guest beers Ⓗ

Situated in an historic village, with glorious views over Findhorn Bay, the pub is frequented by ornithologists, yachtsmen and local RAF personnel. If time permits, the shop at the nearby world famous Findhorn Foundation is worth a visit for its selection of interesting organic beers from around the planet. There is a large, open wooden shed with space heaters in the car park for smokers. ♨❀⛼◐🀱⛺🚌(336)♣P⁄–

Fochabers

Gordon Arms Hotel

80 High Street, IV32 7DH (A96 at W end of village)

⏲ 11 (12 Sun)-11

☎ (01343) 820508

Caledonian Deuchars IPA; Marston's Pedigree; guest beers Ⓗ

Traditional coaching inn with low ceilings on the main street of the village, with an up-market restaurant and accommodation. The real ale handpumps are in the public Ghillies Bar, which is decorated with a Speyside fishing theme, but beer is also served in the lounge. The venue is close to the River Spey and handy for the Speyside Way and the Malt Whisky Trail. The Baxters factory and visitor centre is close by.
Q❀⛼◐🀱♿🚌(10,305,315)P⁄–

Glenkindie

Glenkindie Arms Hotel

AB33 8SX (on A97 at E end of village)

⏲ 12 (5 Mon-Fri winter)-11 (1am Fri; 11.45 Sat)

☎ (01975) 641288 🌐 theglenkindiearmshotel.com
Old Foreigner Sentinel, Gartly Nagger, seasonal beers; guest beers H
Home to the Old Foreigner Brewery, a single barrel plant established in May 2007, this tiny 400-year-old former drovers' inn occupies a listed building known as The Lodge due to its former Masonic use. The hotel stands on the Castle Trail between Kildrummy and Corgarff Castles and is close to the Lecht Ski Centre. An extensive menu of local produce is available all day until 9pm. Local brews are complemented by a changing range of malt whiskies and Belgian beers. Check winter opening hours before travelling. P

Inverurie

Edwards

2 West High Street, AB51 3SA
10-1am; 12.30-midnight Sun
☎ (01467) 629788 🌐 edwardsinverurie.co.uk
Beer range varies H
Modern café bar converted from an old hotel several years ago, which quickly became part of the town circuit. The decor is light and modern with a hint of Art Deco about it. There is a series of comfortable snugs to relax in while enjoying a snack and browsing the newspapers. Up to three beers may be available, mainly from Scottish breweries. The upstairs function room doubles as a disco at weekends. (10,305,315)

Luthermuir

Sauchieburn Hotel

Sauchieburn, by Laurencekirk, AB30 1PX (on B974 between A90 &Fettercairn)
12-2.30, 5.30-11 (midnight Fri & Sat; 1am Sun); closed Tue
☎ (01674) 840587 🌐 sauchieburnhotel.com
Beer range varies H
Situated in the Howe of the Mearns, this is a pleasant country venue mainly for dining, where good food is available made with local, fresh ingredients. Lunches are served 12-2pm and evening meals 5.30-8.30pm (9pm Sat). Booking is advisable. Beers are from the Inveralmond range. The hotel is close to Angus Glens, Kirriemuir Camera Obscura and the Grassic Gibbon Centre. Stable Cottage is available for rent, sleeping up to four people. May close at 9pm if not busy. P

Methlick

Kingscliff Sporting Lodge

AB41 7HQ (1 mile W of village on B9005 Methlick-Fyvie)
12-11 (midnight Fri & Sat); closed Mon & Tue
☎ (01651) 806375 🌐 kingscliff.co.uk
Beer range varies H
Why not arrange to have a day clay pigeon shooting or quad biking then retreat to the bar to unwind with a pint or enjoy a meal in the recently extended restaurant? Beers usually come from Scottish micros. Transport may be arranged by the centre's own minibus. Warning – do not rely on sat-nav to get here. Q P

Ythanview Hotel

Main Street, AB41 7DT
11-2.30, 5-11 (1am Fri); 11-12.30am Sat; 11-11 Sun
☎ (01651) 806235 🌐 ythanview.com
Beer range varies H
Comfortable village local with a relaxing restaurant and a welcoming fire. Fundraising events are held here for various community teams, including the famous MCC (Methlick Cricket Club). Good quality local ingredients are used in the competitively priced food, including Jay's special curry with whole chillies —try it if you dare.
Q (290,291,294)

Milltown of Rothiemay

Forbes Arms Hotel

AB54 7LT
12-2.30 (not Mon & Tue), 5-11
☎ (01466) 711248
Beer range varies H
Small family-run hotel in a pleasant country location with a public bar and dining area. Fishing and shooting activities are nearby. Popular with the local folk club, a live session is hosted on the second Thursday of the month. Two beers are usually available from various breweries including Houston and Hebridean, alongside beers from local supplier Ardo Ales. P

Netherley

Lairhillock Inn

AB39 3QS (signed off B979, 3 miles S of B9077)
11-11 (midnight Fri & Sat)
☎ (01569) 730001 🌐 lairhillock.co.uk
Courage Directors; Greene King IPA; Taylor Landlord; guest beers H
Set in the heart of beautiful countryside, the traditional wood-panelled public bar with log fire is ideal for a convivial drink, while the lounge and conservatory are used by diners. The conservatory, with breathtaking views whatever the season, is a popular choice for families. A log fire in the lounge helps to create an intimate atmosphere. Guest beers usually include a Scottish micro ale. Look out for the 'INN' on the roof. Convenient for attractions in Stonehaven and Royal Deeside.
Q P

Oldmeldrum

Redgarth Hotel

Kirk Brae, AB51 0DJ (off A947 towards golf course)
11-2.30, 5-midnight; 12-2.30, 5-11 Sun
☎ (01651) 872353 🌐 redgarth.com
Beer range varies H/G
Winner of many local CAMRA awards, this renowned hotel has imposing views over the eastern Grampian mountains. A successful blend of popular family restaurant with a marvellous real ale pub, it is appreciated by a dedicated core of regulars who come from miles around to sample the imaginatively chosen beers on offer. During occasional Brewers in Residence evenings, three handpumped ales may be supplemented by many more on gravity.
(305,325)♣

Stonehaven

Marine Hotel

9-10 Shorehead, AB39 2JY

11-11 (1am Fri & Sat); 11-midnight (11 winter) Sun

(01569) 762155 britnett-carver.co.uk/marine

Beer range varies H

Scottish CAMRA Pub of the Year 2008, the hotel is situated on the picturesque harbour front, with an outdoor seating area for drinkers. Downstairs there is a simple wood-panelled bar, tastefully restored, and an adjacent lounge with an open fireplace. Dunottar Ale house beer brewed by Inveralmond is supplemented by an impressive range of up to five guest beers mostly from Scottish micros, with some Southern imports, often from Timothy Taylor. An impressive range of imported Belgian bottled beers and continental ales on tap add to the attraction. (107,117)

Ship Inn

5 Shorehead, AB39 2JY

11-midnight (1am Fri & Sat)

(01569) 762617 shipinnstonehaven.com

Beer range varies H

Traditional old pub facing the harbour front with an outside seating area providing a good view of the harbour. The wood-panelled bar has a maritime theme, with an original mirror from the long defunct Devanha Brewery on the wall at one end. Two handpumps serve an ever-changing range of real ales, and an extensive collection of malt whiskies is also on offer. Food is served in the restaurant and bar, all day at the weekend. Accommodation is in six guest rooms. (107,117)

Tarves

Aberdeen Arms Hotel

The Square, AB41 7GX

12-2, 5-11 (1am Fri); 12-12.30 Sat; 12.30-11 Sun

(01651) 851214 geocities.com/aberdeenarmshotel

Beer range varies H

Previously a farm, the building became a hotel around the 1860s, and is now a small, family-run community local in the middle of a conservation area. Very much a cheery regulars' establishment, it is renowned for its warm welcome to visitors. A wide range of good value, home-cooked food is available. The location is convenient for visiting Tolquhon Castle and Pitmedden Gardens which were laid out in the 17th century by Sir Alexander Seddon with elaborate flower beds, fountains and pavilions.

Q (290,291)

Westhill

Shepherds Rest

10 Straik Road, Arnhall Business Park, AB32 6HF

12-11

(01224) 740208

Beer range varies H

Situated around half a mile from the village across the busy A944, this pub was built in 2000 but recently extended. It has a large, rustic-style interior with plenty of nooks and crannies providing some privacy if preferred. Six handpumps offer a surprisingly good choice of interesting ales. Very popular with families, an extensive food menu is available all day. A Premier Inn next door provides accommodation for the traveller.

P

Douglas Arms, Banchory.

ARGYLL & THE ISLES

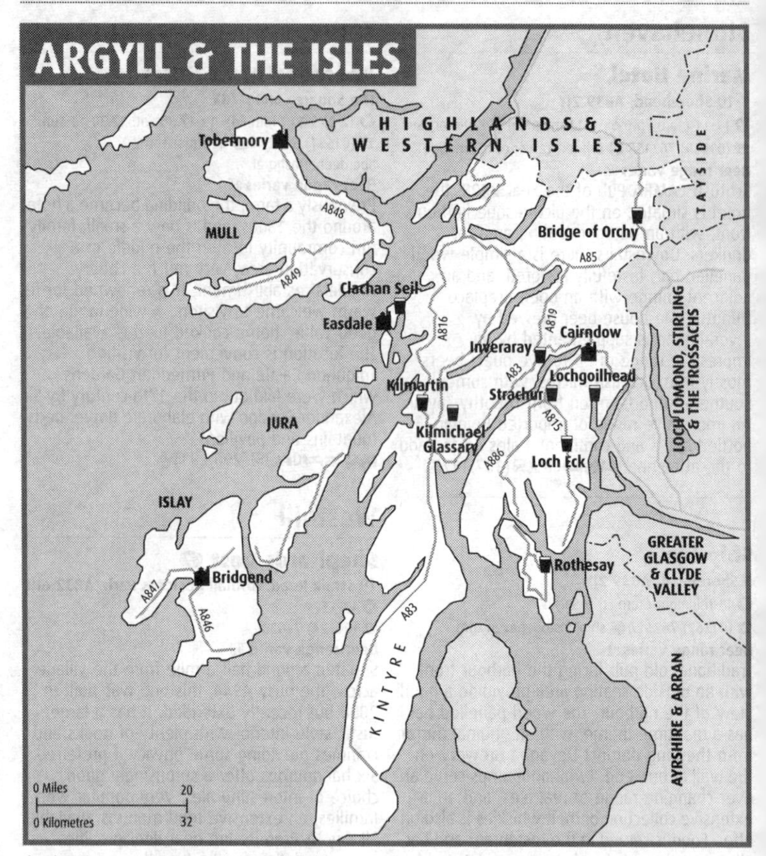

Authority area covered: Argyll & Bute

Bridge of Orchy

Bridge of Orchy Hotel

PA36 4AD (on A82 at N end of Glen Orchy) NN298395

11-11 (1am Fri & Sat); 12.30-11 Sun

(01838) 400 208 bridgeoforchy.co.uk

Caledonian Deuchars IPA, 80; guest beers H

Situated on the West Highland Way, this hotel is a magnet for walkers, climbers, canoeists and skiers. Both road and rail can deliver you with ease from the centre of Glasgow into another world with impressive scenery comprising mountains, glens, rivers and lochs. Three handpumps serve two regular ales plus a guest to complement the good quality food, designed for people who have worked up an appetite. Sometimes closes temporarily in winter so phone to check.
(914)P

Clachan Seil

Tigh an Truish

Isle of Seil by Oban, PA34 4QZ (on B844 5 miles W of A816 jct, by Clachan Bridge) NM784196

11-11 summer and Sat in winter; 11-2.30, 5-11 winter; 12-11 Sun

(01852) 300 242 tighantruish.co.uk

Beer range varies H

The exterior of this building is part covered in climbing plants and features one of the few remaining George Younger pub signs. A multi-roomed pub inside, the decor is traditional with much woodwork. The trestled bench at the bar is a rare feature, as is the unusual bar counter. There is an attractive beer garden and a small front patio with views of the famous bridge across the Atlantic. The real ales usually come from local breweries such as Atlas and Fyne. (418)P

Inveraray

George Hotel

Main Street East, PA32 8TT

11 (12 Sun)-midnight

(01499) 302 111 thegeorgehotel.co.uk

Beer range varies H

A whitewashed hotel in the centre of historic Inveraray sited in a picturesque location on the shore of Loch Fyne. Dating from 1770, it has been owned by the same family since 1860. The main entrance leads via a passage to

INDEPENDENT BREWERIES

Fyne Cairndow
Islay Bridgend
Isle of Mull Tobermory
Oyster Easdale

several atmospheric rooms full of olde-worlde charm, including a stone-walled and floored lounge. The public bar to the rear has TVs showing sports. Beers from Fyne Ales change regularly and good food is available.
(926,976)P

Kilmartin

Kilmartin Hotel

PA31 8RQ (on A816 10 miles N of Lochgilphead) NR835989
12 (5pm winter)-midnight (1am Fri & Sat); 12-1am Sat winter; 12-midnight Sun
(01546) 510 250 kilmartin-hotel.com
Caledonian 80; Fyne Highlander; guest beers H
The scenic Kilmartin Glen, dating back 5000 years, is full of standing stones, burial mounds, stone circles and carvings, and surrounded by superb views. This atmospheric family-run hotel is an ideal stopping place for visitors to the historic glen and museum and travellers exploring Argyll and the western highlands and islands. The pub serves up to two regular beers plus a guest, especially in summer. Live traditional music plays occasionally and there is a pool table. Good food is available 12-2.30pm and 6-9pm.
Q(423)P

Kilmichael Glassary

Horseshoe Inn

Bridgend, PA31 8QA (off A816 3 miles N of Lochgilphead) NR852928
5-11 (midnight Fri); 12-midnight Sat; 12-11 Sun
(01546) 606 369 horseshoeinn.biz
Beer range varies H
Tucked away in a quiet village, this conversion of a former farmhouse nestles in a glen of prehistoric significance. The pub has a games room to the rear, a cosy bar and a separate dining area. Good food is available alongside an ever-changing selection of beers from Fyne Ales. There are plenty of sights to enjoy in the area including the scenic Kilmartin Glen, the ancient hilltop Dunadd Fort and The Crinan Canal. (423)P

Loch Eck

Coylet Inn

PA23 8SG (on A815 near S end of Loch Eck) NS143885
11 (12.30 Sun)-11
(01369) 840 426 coyletinn.co.uk
Caledonian Deuchars IPA; Fyne Highlander; guest beers H
Nearly 400 years old, nestling on the shore of Lock Eck, this former coaching inn offers grand loch and mountain views. A small, cosy bar welcomes drinkers and you can enjoy good local food in the restaurant. Fishing permits and boat hire are available and there are several attractions to explore nearby including Benmore Botanical Gardens and Pucks Glen. Meals are served 12-2pm and 6-9pm and the restaurant can be busy so it is advisable to ring ahead if dining. (484)P

Lochgoilhead

Shore House Inn

PA24 8AD (at head of Loch Goil) NN198015
12-midnight; closed Tue
(01301) 703 340 theshorehouse.net
Fyne Highlander; guest beers H
Located at the head of Loch Goil, this former Church of Scotland manse dates from 1851 and has been a pub since 1990. There are superb views of the loch and mountains from the restaurant and beer garden. The bar offers a Carlsberg/Tetley guest list in addition to the regular beer. On the Cowal Way and within Loch Lomond & The Trossachs National Park, it is close to the golf course and holiday chalets and attracts locals and tourists. Free Internet access is available.
Q(484,486)P

Rothesay: Isle of Bute

Black Bull Inn

3 West Princess Street, PA20 9AF (on promenade opp marina)
11 (5pm winter)-11 (midnight Fri & Sat); 12.30-11 Sun
(01700) 502 366
Caledonian Deuchars IPA; Greene King Abbot H
Once you have admired the splendour of the Wemyss Bay Rail Station, enjoyed the ferry crossing and viewed the impressive Victorian toilets on Rothesay Pier, you can visit this characterful inn on the promenade and enjoy the ales along with a good pub meal. Refreshed, there are the colourful Mount Stuart Gardens to visit, or take in the fine views on a round-the-island bus tour. Opposite the marina, the pub is popular with yachtsmen.

Strachur

Creggans Inn

PA27 8BX (on A815 Cairndow-Dunoon road, near A886 jct) NN087024
11-11; 12.30-1am Sun
(01369) 860 279 creggans-inn.co.uk
Beer range varies H
A previous owner of this 1700s coaching inn overlooking Loch Fyne was Sir Fitzroy Maclean, the man who inspired the character of James Bond. The inn also has connections with Mary Queen of Scots. The traditional cosy bar is semi-divided from a larger drinkers' area. A single ale, usually from local Fyne Ales, increases to two in the tourist season. An oasis for locals and visitors, it has two restaurants and offers visitors free moorings and Internet access. (484,486)P

How easy can the barley-bree
Cement the quarrel.
It's aye the cheapest lawyer's fee
To taste the barrel. **Robert Burns**

SCOTLAND

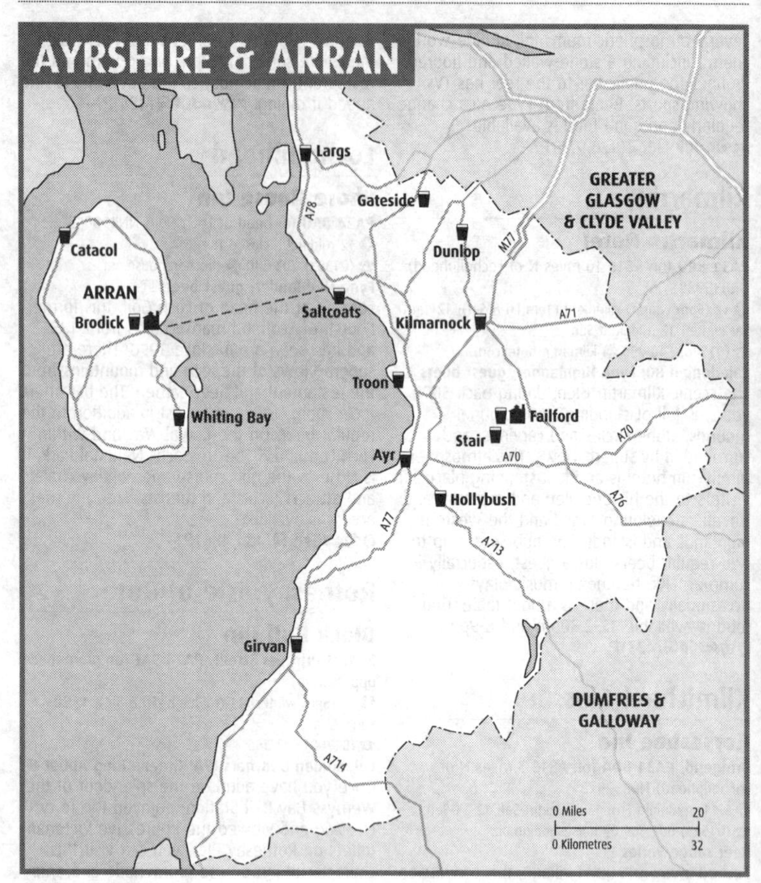

Authority areas covered: East Ayrshire, North Ayrshire, South Ayrshire

Ayr

Chestnuts Hotel

52 Racecourse Road, KA7 2UZ (A719, 1 Mile S of centre)

11 (12 Sun)-midnight

(01292) 264393 chestnutshotel.com

Beer range varies H

This hotel, once owned by the town's Jewish community and now part of a local chain, has recently been refurbished. The warm, comfortable lounge bar has a large collection of water jugs and golfing memorabilia. The two real ales are usually from the larger regional brewers, but occasionally beers are offered from local breweries. The meals are of a very high standard and served in the bar area or restaurant. (A9)P

Geordie's Byre

103 Main Street, KA8 8BU (N of centre, over river towards Prestwick)

11-11 (midnight Thu-Sat); 12.30-11 Sun

(01292) 264925

Caledonian Deuchars IPA; guest beers A

The rather ordinary exterior belies a gem of a pub where the landlord and landlady have reigned supreme for more than 30 years. Both the public bar and the lounge feature a wealth of memorabilia. Up to four guest ales are sourced from far and near; at least one is from a local micro. More than 100 malt whiskies and around 30 rums are also available. Several buses stop outside the front door. The pub is the winner of numerous CAMRA awards, including joint branch winner 2006.

Q(Newton-on-Ayr)

Old Racecourse Hotel

2 Victoria Park, KA7 2TR (A719 1 mile S of centre)

11-midnight (12.30 Fri & Sat); 12.30-11 Sun

(01292) 262873 oldracecoursehotel.co.uk

Beer range varies H

This family-run hotel has a small lounge bar dominated by a large flat-screen TV. Drinkers are also welcome to use the adjacent restaurant areas. Up to four changing guest ales are sourced from far and near. The racecourse in the name refers to a former horseracing venue nearby, now playing fields and a golf course. This hotel is an ideal base to visit the world-renowned golf courses, Burns Heritage Park and the other delights of south Ayrshire. (A9)P

INDEPENDENT BREWERIES

Arran Brodick
Windie Goat Failford

Wellingtons Bar

17 Wellington Square, KA7 1EZ

🕐 11-12.30; 12.30-midnight Sun

☎ (01292) 262794 🌐 wellingtonsayr.co.uk

Beer range varies H

A large Wellington boot advertises the location of this basement bar. Close to the seafront, bus station and local government offices, it is popular with tourists and office workers alike. The Wednesday evening quiz is very popular and weekend music features live bands or DJ (Saturday) and an acoustic session (Sunday). The two changing ales usually include at least one from either Kelburn or Strathaven breweries. Good value food is served all day until 9pm. ◑⇌🚌

West Kirk ✔

58A Sandgate, KA7 1BX

🕐 9-12.30am (midnight Sun)

☎ (01292) 880416

Beer range varies H

This Wetherspoon's conversion of a former church retains many of the original features, access to the toilets being via the pulpit. Up to six changing guest ales are offered and local micros are usually well represented. Meals are available all day with breakfast from 9am. The pub is centrally located and close to the bus station. The front patio drinking area has a shelter for smokers. ❀◑♿⇌🚌⌐

Brodick: Isle of Arran

Ormidale Hotel

Knowe Road, KA27 8BY (off A841 at W end of village)

🕐 12-2.30 (not winter), 4.30-midnight; 12-midnight Sat & Sun

☎ (01770) 302293 🌐 ormidale-hotel.co.uk

Arran Ale, Blonde; guest beers A

This large red sandstone hotel is set in seven acres of grounds, including a large wooded area. The bar serves its ales through traditional tall founts. Beer prices are rather expensive considering the proximity of Arran Brewery. The public bar has tables in the shape of Arran, the large conservatory hosts discos and live music during the summer, and there is a separate pool room. There is an attractive beer garden with views across Brodick Bay. Accommodation is only available in summer. ♨❀🛏◑🍽🚌♣P

Catacol: Isle of Arran

Catacol Bay Hotel

KA27 8HN

🕐 12-midnight (1am Thu-Sat); 11-midnight Sun

☎ (01770) 830231 🌐 catacol.co.uk

Draught Bass; guest beers H

This former manse sits in its own grounds adjacent to the Twelve Apostles, a listed terrace of former estate workers' houses. Both the garden and the bar offer superb views over Kilbrannan Sound to Kintyre. Run by the same family since 1979, this hotel is an ideal base for exploring the north and west of Arran. The guest beer in summer is usually from the local Arran Brewery. Bar meals are served all day until 10pm, with the renowned Sunday buffet lunch always popular. ♨☕❀🛏◑🍽🚌(324)♣P

Dunlop

Auld Hoose

68 Main Street, KA3 4AG

🕐 5-midnight (1am Thu-Fri); 1-1am Sat; 1-midnight Sun

☎ (01560) 484951

Beer range varies H

A cottage-style building in a conservation village, this is very much a community pub. It hosts quiz nights, occasional live music and sports dinners as well as providing a base for the village football team and a local Burns club. Two ales are available, usually including one from Strathaven Brewery. Q◑♿⇌🚌(337)♣

Failford

Failford Inn

KA5 5TF (on B743 Mauchline-Ayr road)

🕐 12-midnight (12.30am Fri & Sat); 12.30-midnight Sun

☎ (01292) 540117 🌐 failfordinn.co.uk

Beer range varies H

Country inn set on the banks of the River Ayr, with low ceilings and an old tiled range. Both restaurant and garden overlook the river. Meals are prepared by the chef/owner with an emphasis on freshly-cooked local produce. The inn is a good starting point for the River Ayr Walk which passes through a dramatic gorge. Home of the Windie Goat Brewery, one of its beers is usually on handpump. Regular beer festivals are held, and often live music on Friday. CAMRA Scottish Pub of the Year 2006. ♨Q❀◑🍽🚌(43)⌐

Gateside

Gateside Inn

39 Main Road, KA15 2LF (on B777 1 mile E of Beith)

🕐 11-11 (midnight Fri & Sat); 12.30-11 Sun

☎ (01505) 503362

Caledonian Deuchars IPA; guest beers H

Friendly village inn with a wide mix of customers from all over the Garnock Valley, which is otherwise a beer desert. The guest beer is usually from the Punch Taverns list and the pub also stocks a wide range of bottled beers and malts. Good food is served all day in the bar and dining area. The walls are adorned with old pictures of the village. Bus route 337 passes nearby and connects to Glengarnock Station. ❀◑🚌P

Girvan

Royal Hotel

36 Montgomery Street, KA26 9HE

🕐 11-12.30; 12.30-midnight Sun

☎ (01465) 714203 🌐 royalhotelgirvan.com

Beer range varies H

Small hotel in a Clyde coast town that still clings to fishing and tourist trades. The traditional public bar attracts local trade as well as fishing, cycling and walking groups. The world-renowned Turnberry golf course is five miles away and the hotel is a good stopping off point for travellers to and from

Irish ferries. The regular beer is from Houston Brewery, with a summer-only guest ale. A small but interesting range of bottled beers is also stocked. Buses pass along the main road nearby. ❀⇌◑⊟♿⛺⇌⊟♣P

Hollybush

Hollybush Inn

KA6 6EY (on A713 Ayr-Dalmellington road)
✪ 9am-midnight
☎ (01292) 560580
Beer range varies Ⓗ
A modernised country pub on the main Ayr-Galloway tourist route, about four miles from Ayr hospital. Traditional Scottish food is prepared on the premises made with fresh ingredients. There are stunning views of the Carrick Hills and the Isle of Arran from the conservatory. Winter opening hours can be shorter – phone to check. ❀◑♿⛺⊟(52)P

Kilmarnock

Brass & Granite

53 Grange Street, KA1 2DD
✪ 11-midnight (1am Thu-Sat); 12.30-midnight Sun
☎ (01563) 523431
Beer range varies Ⓗ
Modern open-plan town centre pub in a quiet street behind the post office, popular with a varied mix of customers. Belgian fruit beers are available on draught as well as a variety of bottled ales, with occasional tasting sessions held. The pub also has a good food selection and holds some speciality evenings. There are several large-screen TVs, mostly used to screen sporting events. A pub quiz is held on Sunday, Monday and Wednesday. Many bus routes pass close by. ◑⇌⊟♣

Wheatsheaf Inn

70 Portland Street, KA1 1JG
✪ 9-11 (midnight Thu; 1am Fri & Sat); 9-midnight Sun
☎ (01563) 572483
Caledonian Deuchars IPA; Greene King Abbot; guest beers Ⓗ
Large town centre Lloyd's No 1 pub situated a short walk from the bus and rail stations. It has various seating areas including booths, sofas and a raised dining space. No music plays Monday to Wednesday, but a live DJ entertains on Friday and Saturday. However the pub is large enough to find a quieter area if you want to. The food menu is standard Wetherspoon's fare. ❀◑⇌⊟

Largs

Charlie Smith's

14 Gallowgate Street, KA30 8LX (on seafront A78, close to pier)
✪ 10-midnight (1am Thu-Sat); 12.30-midnight Sun
☎ (01475) 672250
Beer range varies Ⓗ
Friendly town centre pub situated on the corner opposite the 10-pin bowling alley, pier and ferry terminal. Food is available all day. Live music plays at weekends. This is a good place for catching (or missing) the ferry to Cumbrae and, in summer, the Waverley paddle steamer. Largs is also home to two fine golf courses and the Vikingar Centre. ◑♿⇌⊟♣

Saltcoats

Salt Cot

7 Hamilton Street, KA21 5DS
✪ 10-11 (1am Thu-Sat); 12.30-11 Sun
☎ (01294) 465924
Greene King Abbot; guest beers Ⓗ
An excellent Wetherspoon's conversion of a former cinema, decorated with photos of the cinema in its heyday and old Saltcoats. Children are allowed in one area and there is a family menu. The pub's name comes from the original cottages at the salt pans. Although there are TVs in the bar area the sound is never turned on. Q◑♿⇌⊟

Stair

Stair Inn

KA5 5HW (B730, 7 miles E of Ayr, 4 miles W of Mauchline)
✪ 12-11 (1am Fri & Sat); 12.30-11 Sun
☎ (01292) 591650 ⊕ stairinn.co.uk
Beer range varies Ⓗ
Family-run inn nestling at the foot of a glen on the banks of the River Ayr. The bar, with an open log fire, has bespoke hand-made furniture and the bedrooms are furnished in similar style. Built around 1700, it serves a widespread area and is very close to the historic Stair Bridge. The food is renowned, especially the home-smoked fish platter, and Houston beers are regulars. The River Ayr Walk passes close by. ♨Q❀⇌◑♿P

Troon

Ardneil Hotel

51 St Meddans Street, KA10 6NU (next to station)
✪ 11-midnight (11 Sun)
☎ (01292) 311611 ⊕ ardneil-hotel.co.uk
Fuller's London Pride; guest beers Ⓗ
Family-run hotel next to Troon station and a three-wood drive from three municipal golf courses and the town centre. Three ales are served including two guests. The bar hosts a Wednesday night quiz, regular inter-pub pool competitions, and Tapas nights on Wednesday and Thursday. The hotel is popular with locals, tourists and golfers from across Europe who take advantage of cheap flights into Prestwick Airport, four miles away. There is a large beer garden and a heated, covered area for smokers. ❀⇌◑⇌⊟(14,110)P⁻

Bruce's Well

91 Portland Street, KA10 6QN
✪ 11 (12.30 Sun)-midnight
☎ (01292) 311429
Caledonian Deuchars IPA; guest beers Ⓗ
Friendly, spacious and comfortable lounge bar close to Troon town centre, serving two guest ales. Major sporting events are shown on three plasma TVs and the pub hosts occasional live music nights. The bar benefits from a temperature-controlled cellar, situated next door. ⇌⊟(14)

Harbour Bar

169 Templehill, KA10 6BH

11-12.30; 12.30-midnight Sun

(01292) 312668

Beer range varies H

Overlooking Troon's North Bay, the bar has lounge and public bars with a nautical theme, decorated with pictures and artefacts from the now closed Ailsa shipyard. Two real ales are on offer, mostly from local breweries and reasonably priced for the area. A good range of malt whiskies and rums is also available. The public bar has a pool table and a well-stocked jukebox; the lounge bar has a dartboard. Popular meals are served throughout the day. CAMRA Branch Pub of the Year 2007. P

Whiting Bay: Isle of Arran

Eden Lodge Hotel

KA27 8QH

12-midnight (1am Thu-Sat); 12.30-midnight Sun

(01770) 700357 edenlodgehotel.co.uk

Caledonian Deuchars IPA; guest beers H

Bar Eden is the hotel's large, bright public bar with superb views across the bay to Holy Island. Adjacent to the village's bowling green, this family-run hotel, eight miles south of Brodick's ferry terminal, is an ideal base to take advantage of many local walks, including the spectacular Glenashdale Falls. Home-cooked bar meals featuring local produce are available all day until 9pm except mid-week winter afternoons. Winter hours may be restricted. (323)P

Scottish beer

Just as monks call their Lenten beers 'liquid bread', it's tempting to call traditional Scottish ales 'liquid porridge'. They are beers brewed for a cold climate, a country in which beer vies with whisky (uisge breatha – water of life) for nourishment and sustenance.
Brewers blend not only darker malts such as black and chocolate with paler grains, but also add oats, that staple of many foodstuffs in the country. In common with the farmer-brewers of the Low Countries and French Flanders in earlier centuries, domestic brewers in Scotland tended to use whatever grains, herbs and plants were available to make beer. The intriguing use of heather in the Fraoch range of ales recalls brewing practice in Scotland from bygone times.

Different

Traditionally, Scottish ales were brewed in a different manner to English ones. Before refrigeration, beer was fermented at ambient temperatures far lower than in England. As a result, not all the sugars turned to alcohol, producing rich, full-bodied ales. As hops had to be imported from England at considerable cost, they were used sparingly. The result was a style of beer markedly different to English ones: vinous, fruity, malty and with only a gentle hop bitterness.

Many of the new breed of ales produced by micro-brewers in Scotland tend to be paler and more bitter than used to be the norm. For the true taste of traditional Scottish ales you will have to sample the products of the likes of Belhaven, Broughton, Caledonian and Traquair.

Complexities

The language of Scottish beers is different, too. The equivalent to English mild is called Light (even when it's dark in colour), standard bitter is called Heavy premium bitter Export, while strong old ales and barley wines (now rare) are called Wee Heavies.

To add to the complexities of the language differences, many traditional beers incorporate the word Shilling in their names. A Light may be dubbed 60 Shilling, a Heavy 70 Shilling, an Export 80 Shilling, and a Wee Heavy 90 Shilling. The designations stem from a pre-decimalisation method of invoicing beer in Victorian times. The stronger the beer, the higher the number of shillings.

Until recent times, cask-conditioned beer in Scotland was served by air pressure. In the pub cellar a water engine, which looks exactly the same as a lavatory cistern but works in reverse, used water to produce air pressure that drove the beer to the bar. Sadly, these wonderful Victorian devices are rarely seen, and the Sassenach handpump and beer engine dominate the pub scene.

SCOTLAND

Authority area covered: Scottish Borders

Ancrum

Cross Keys Inn

The Green, TD8 6XH (on B6400, off A68)

✪ 12-2.30 (not Mon), 6-11 (5-1am Fri); 12-midnight Sat; 12.30-11 Sun

☎ (01835) 830344 ⊕ ancrumcrosskeys.co.uk

Beer range varies Ⓗ

Friendly village local with a bar that has changed little since 1908. It has the original pine panelling through into the gantry, compact seating and tables made from old sewing machines. The spacious back lounge has been sympathetically refurbished, retaining the overhead tramlines from the former cellar. A good, varied food menu is supplemented by daily specials. Children and dogs are welcome. It has free Wi-Fi Internet access. ⋒Q❀◑◐⊟♿Ʌ⊟♣P⊬

Auchencrow

Craw Inn

TD14 5LS (signed from A1)

✪ 12-2.30, 6-11 (midnight Fri); 12-midnight Sat; 12.30-11 Sun

☎ (01890) 761253 ⊕ thecrawinn.co.uk

Beer range varies Ⓗ

Very friendly village inn, dating from 1680. The beamed bar has bench seating at one end and wooden tables, chairs and a church pew by the log burning stove at the other. The two real ales are usually from smaller breweries and change frequently. A beer festival is held in November. At the rear is the restaurant, which features special food events during the year. Children are welcome. CAMRA Borders Pub of the Year 2008. ⋒Q❀⊭◑◐♿⊟♣P

Carlops

Allan Ramsay Hotel

Main Street, EH26 9NF

✪ 12-11 (1am Fri & Sat); 12.30-midnight Sun

☎ (01968) 660258

Caledonian Deuchars IPA; guest beers Ⓗ

Hotel in a small village beside the Pentland hills, dating from 1792. Several rooms have been knocked through into a single area, retaining many original features including a fine stone fireplace. Tartan upholstery gives a Scottish feel. One end is a restaurant, the central part is a bar area, and a pool table occupies the far end. The bar is inlayed with pre-decimal pennies. Children and dogs are welcome and food is served all day on Saturday and Sunday. ⋒❀⊭◑◐⊟♣P

Coldingham

Anchor Inn

School Road, TD14 5NS

✪ 12-midnight (may be earlier in winter)

☎ (01890) 771243

Beer range varies Ⓗ

INDEPENDENT BREWERIES

Broughton Broughton
Traquair Traquair

Multi-roomed village local welcoming visitors and regulars alike. The bar is wood panelled while local photographs adorn the walls in the cosy, well appointed lounge/dining room. There is a mirror recovered from the wreck of the Glenmire, which sank off St Abbs Head in 1910. The food menu is extensive and includes a good vegetarian selection. Takeaways are available. Children are welcome in the lounge and dining room.
⩩Q❀◑⛺⊟(235,253)♣

Denholm

Auld Cross Keys Inn

Main Street, TD9 8NU (on A698)
✪ 11-11 (1am Fri & Sat); 12.30-11 Sun
☎ (01450) 870305 ⊕ crosskeysdenholm.co.uk
Beer range varies Ⓗ
Eighteenth-century inn by the village green. The cosy bar has a low ceiling, varnished pine plank walls and a lino tiled floor. At one end is a real fire, at the other is a pool table. To the rear is a more upmarket lounge and dining area which opens out into a large function room. Quizzes, folk music sessions and concerts are regular events. Good home-cooked food is served and on Sunday a carvery is available all day. Children are welcome, and dogs are permitted in the bar.
⩩❀⛟◑⊡⊟(20)♣P

Fox & Hounds Inn

Main Street, TD9 8NU
✪ 11-3, 5-midnight (1am Fri); 11-1am Sat; 12.30-midnight Sun
☎ (01450) 870247 ⊕ foxandhoundsinndenholm.co.uk
Wylam Gold Tankard; guest beers Ⓗ
Village local built in 1728 overlooking the village green. The main bar retains the original beams, with a real fire giving it a cosy feel in winter. Pictures and memorabilia decorate the walls. The rear lounge has a coffee house feel. An upstairs dining room is used in the evening. In summer a courtyard offers sheltered outdoor drinking, and is now the all-year smoking area. Children are welcome until 8pm and dogs are permitted.
⩩❀⛟◑⊡⊟(20)♣⊱

Duns

Black Bull Hotel

15 Black Bull Street, TD11 3AR
✪ 11-midnight (1am Fri & Sat); 12.30-midnight Sun
☎ (01361) 883379 ⊕ blackbullhotelduns.com
Caledonian Deuchars IPA; guest beers Ⓗ
Recently refurbished 200-year-old hotel with a bar, lounge, restaurant and function room. The cosy front bar, where local characters are often in residence, has dark wood panelling, with framed sketches produced by a local artist above the upright piano. The lounge area, with bench seating, is more suited to families and children are welcome. The refurbished letting rooms are all named after local historic figures. Dogs are permitted in the bar. ❀⛟◑⊡⊟♣P⊱

Ettrickbridge

Cross Keys Inn

TD7 5JN
✪ 12-2.30, 6.30-10.30 (11 Thu-Sat); closed Mon & Tue winter
☎ (01750) 52224 ⊕ cross-keys-inn.co.uk
Beer range varies Ⓗ
Seventeenth century inn located in the historic Ettrick valley. The cosy main bar and adjacent dining room are decorated with old photographs, water jugs and the odd stuffed animal. There is a strong emphasis on quality food and tables are set for diners. However the bar stools are always in use and there is a smaller room with TV dedicated to drinkers. The real ales are often from smaller Scottish breweries such as Broughton and Inveralmond. Children are welcome.
⩩❀⛟◑⊡♿♣P

Galashiels

Salmon Inn

54 Bank Street, TD1 1EP
✪ 11-11 (midnight Thu, 1am Fri & Sat); 12.30-midnight Sun
☎ (01896) 752577
Caledonian Deuchars IPA; guest beers Ⓗ
Comfortable, friendly pub, centrally situated by the fountain and gardens. It can be very lively when sports events are shown on the flat screen TVs. The single room, decorated with historic photographs of the Galashiels area, is divided into two areas. The guest beers, often from smaller breweries, change regularly. The pub is popular for its good home-cooked meals (no food on Sunday). Children are welcome at lunchtime. Dogs are also permitted. ❀◑⛺⊟♣⊱

Innerleithen

St Ronan's Hotel

High Street, EH44 6HF
✪ 11-midnight (12.45am Fri & Sat); 12-midnight Sun
☎ (01896) 831487
Beer range varies Ⓗ
This village hotel takes its name from the local saint who is also associated with a well. The functional public bar is long and thin and has a brick and wooden fireplace. There are two alcoves, one with seating, the other with a dartboard and a wide-angled photograph of the village on the wall. A further room has a pool table. Food is only served in the summer. A pick up service is available for Southern Upland Way walkers. Children and dogs are welcome. ⩩❀⛟◑⛺⊟(62)♣⊱

Traquair Arms Hotel

Traquair Road, EH44 6PD (B709, off A72)
✪ 11-11 (midnight Fri & Sat); 12-11.30 Sun
☎ (01896) 830229 ⊕ traquairarmshotel.co.uk
Caledonian Deuchars IPA; Taylor Landlord; Traquair Bear Ale Ⓗ
Elegant 18th-century hotel in the scenic Tweed Valley. The comfortable lounge bar features a relaxing tropical fish tank and a welcoming real fire in winter. An Italian bistro area and separate restaurant provide plenty of room for diners. Food is served all day at weekends. This is one of the few outlets for

SCOTLAND

draught ales from Traquair House. Children are welcome. ⌂❀⇌ℂ◗▲⊟(62)P

Kelso

Cobbles Inn

7 Bowmont Street, TD5 7JH (off NE side of town square)

⊙ 11-3, 5-10 (1am Fri); 11-11 summer; 11-midnight Sat; 11-10 Sun

☎ (01573) 223548 ⊕ thecobblesinn.co.uk

Beer range varies Ⓗ

Completely refurbished in 2008, this gastro pub has a lounge bar with a huge open fire that draws you in on a cold day. There is also a dining area, though dining is permitted anywhere in the pub. The bar menu features hearty favourites, while the dinner menu and daily specials board offer more adventurous choices. Food is served all day at the weekend. A third handpump is planned to expand the choice of interesting ales from both sides of the border. Private functions are catered for upstairs. Children are welcome. ⌂❀ℂ◗♿⊟(20,52)

Kirk Yetholm

Border Hotel

The Green, TD5 8PQ

⊙ 11-midnight (1am Fri & Sat); 12-midnight Sun

☎ (01573) 420237 ⊕ theborderhotel.com

Beer range varies Ⓗ

This 260-year-old coaching inn is very popular with walkers, situated at the start/finish of the Pennine Way and on the ancient St Cuthbert's Way. The building has now been fully refurbished following a serious fire in 2006. The wood-beamed bar has a roaring coal fire in winter and the walls are adorned with photographs of local worthies and friezes showing country pursuits. There are also some smaller rooms and a conservatory dining area. Dogs and children are welcome. The hotel may close early in winter. ⌂❀⇌ℂ◗⊡▲⊟♣P

Lauder

Black Bull Hotel

Market Place, TD2 6SR

⊙ 12-11 (midnight Sat); 12-2.30, 5-11 winter; 12-11 Sun

☎ (01578) 722208 ⊕ blackbull-lauder.com

Beer range varies Ⓗ

A changing range of beers supplied by Broughton Ales and an excellent choice of seasonal food and specials are on offer at this well-appointed old coaching inn. The small wood-panelled bar is adorned with artefacts and retains much of the character of yester-year. Good food is served with main courses averaging around £9 – the menu might include Guinness & mushroom pie, fillet of salmon, or breast of duck with Puy lentils and teriyaki vegetables. Dogs and children are welcome. Q❀⇌ℂ◗♿▲⊟(29)♣P

Paxton

Cross Inn

TD15 1TE (off B6460)

⊙ 11 (12.30 Sun)-3, 6.30-midnight; closed Mon

☎ (01289) 386267

Stewart Pentland IPA; guest beers Ⓗ

Friendly village pub, circa 1870s, named after the restored old cross outside. The wooden panelled bar has a bright but intimate feel, with a south-facing bay window providing plenty of light. The guest beer is often from Wylam. Popular for food, there is an appealing, extensive menu featuring home cooked dishes using locally sourced ingredients. A small dining room provides a more formal dining area. Children and dogs are welcome. ❀ℂ◗⊡♿⊟♣P

Peebles

Bridge Inn

Portbrae, EH45 8AW

⊙ 11 (12.30 Sun)-midnight

☎ (01721) 720589

Caledonian Deuchars IPA; Stewart Pentland IPA; Taylor Landlord; guest beers Ⓗ

Cheerful, welcoming single roomed town-centre local, also known as the 'Trust'. The mosaic entrance floor shows it was once named the Tweedside Inn. The bright, comfortable bar is decorated with jugs, bottles, memorabilia of outdoor pursuits and photos of old Peebles. An outdoor heated patio area overlooks the river. The gents is superb, with well-maintained original Twyford Adamant urinals. A child free zone, but dogs are welcome. ❀▲⊟(62)♣⚐

Selkirk

Heatherlie House Hotel

Heatherlie Park, TD7 5AL (half mile W of centre)

⊙ 12-11 (midnight Fri & Sat); 12.30-midnight Sun

☎ (01750) 721200 ⊕ heatherlie.freeserve.co.uk

Beer range varies Ⓗ

A family run hotel in tranquil surroundings. Once a Victorian villa, it retains a stately air of grandeur with a magnificent hand-carved fireplace depicting barn owls in the entrance and beautiful cornices. The bar, which is also a dining area, is comfortable and airy, with views through the large bay windows to the gardens. The real ale is often from Inveralmond or Stewart Brewing. Children are welcome until 8pm. ⌂❀⇌ℂ◗▲⊟♣P

West Linton

Gordon Arms Hotel

Dolphinton Road, EH46 7DR (on A702)

⊙ 11-11 (midnight Tue; 1am Fri & Sat); 12-midnight (11 winter) Sun

☎ (01968) 660208

Stewart Pentland IPA; guest beers Ⓗ

Situated in a village close to the Pentland hills. The public bar is L-shaped with stone walls and interesting cornices. A real fire and a collection of sofas and chairs create a homely feel, with a jukebox and TV providing entertainment. The attractive, comfortable restaurant has wooden floors and neatly arranged dining tables. Meals are served all day Saturday and Sunday. Children and dogs are welcome. ⌂❀⇌ℂ◗⊡⊟(100,101)♣P

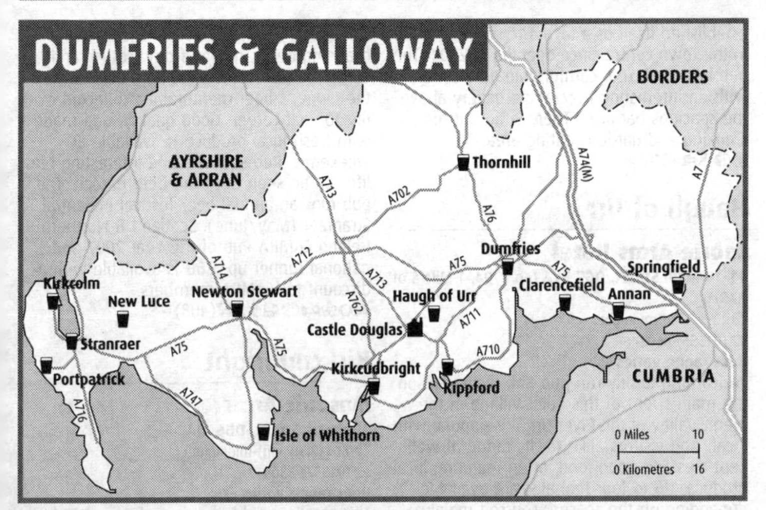

Authority area covered: Dumfries & Galloway

Annan

Bluebell Inn

10 High Street, DG12 6AG

11-11 (midnight Thu-Sat); 12.30-11 Sun

☎ (01461) 202385

Caledonian Deuchars IPA; guest beers H

Fine old coaching inn retaining original panelling and features from its time as a Gretna & District State Management Scheme house. It is adjacent to the River Annan and easily identified by the large blue bell above the main entrance. This friendly pub offers a wide selection of beers from across the UK. It also has pool, darts and large-screen TV. During the summer you can drink outside in the rear courtyard.

Clarencefield

Farmers Inn

Main Street, DG1 4NF (on B724)

11-2.30, 6-11.30 (12.30am Fri); 12-12.30am Sat; 12.30-11.30 Sun

☎ (01387) 870675 farmersinn.co.uk

Beer range varies H

Late 16th-century coaching inn with a varied history. The current building opened in 1983 with the original bar area still in use. It was the post office and also housed the village's first telephone exchange. Robert Burns was a customer when he came on a visit to the Brow Well for health reasons. Nearby tourist attractions include the world's first savings bank at Ruthwell and the 8th-century Ruthwell Cross. P

Dumfries

Cavens Arms

20 Buccleuch Street, DG1 2AH

11-11 (midnight Thu-Sat); 12.30-11 Sun

☎ (01387) 252896

Beer range varies H

Lively town centre pub with a varied selection of beers on handpump. Customers are encouraged to request ales that they would like to try and they are notified when the beers are available at the bar. A range of good value meals is served until 9pm every day except Monday. Local CAMRA Pub of the Year in 2007.

Coach & Horses

66 Whitesands, DG1 2RS

11 (12.30 Sun)-11

☎ (01387) 265224

Draught Bass H

Next door to the Tourist Information Centre on the Whitesands in the town centre, this pub was extensively renovated in 2006. It now has a very pleasant large bar area with an impressive flagstone floor. The food menu offers a variety of good freshly-cooked dishes served in the upstairs dining room. There are occasional live music sessions. The location is handy for local tourist attractions and car parking. Q

New Bazaar

39 Whitesands, DG1 2RS

11-11 (midnight Thu-Sat); 12.30-11 Sun

☎ (01387) 268776 newbazaardumfries.co.uk

Beer range varies H

Former coaching inn with a pleasing Victorian gantry in the small, welcoming bar. The pub also has a cosy, quiet lounge with a warming coal fire in winter, and a separate room available for meetings. Beside the river Nith in the town centre, it is ideally situated for car parking and local tourist attractions. It gets busy with football fans on match days. There is an outside smoking area.

Robert the Bruce

81-83 Buccleuch Street, DG1 1DJ

11-midnight (1am Fri & Sat); 12.30-midnight Sun

☎ (01387) 270320

Caledonian Deuchars IPA; guest beer H

Former 19th-century church, sympathetically converted by Wetherspoon's. It has

INDEPENDENT BREWERIES

Sulwath Castle Douglas

SCOTLAND

established itself as a favourite meeting place in the town centre since opening in 2001. The pub has a relaxed, comfortable atmosphere, with an interesting mezzanine gallery above the spacious bar area. There is an outside smoking and garden seating area.
❀◑♿⇌🚌⁴

Haugh of Urr

Laurie Arms Hotel

11-13 Main Street, DG7 3YA (on B794, 1 Mile S of A75)
✪ 12-3, 5.30-midnight
☎ (01556) 660246
Beer range varies Ⓗ
Welcoming family-run pub and restaurant on the main street of this quiet village in the scenic valley of the River Urr, it is popular with locals and visitors alike for its range of well-kept ales and good food, often featuring local produce. Up to four real ales are available depending on the season, sourced mainly from independent breweries from across Britain. Open fires set in local stone surrounds feature in both main rooms. ♨Q❀◑🚌♣P

Isle of Whithorn

Steam Packet Inn ✔

Harbour Row, DG8 8LL (A750)
✪ 11-11 (1am Fri; 12.30am Sat); 11-2.30, 6-11 Tue-Thu winter; 12-11 Sun
☎ (01988) 500334 🌐 steampacketinn.com
Theakston XB; guest beers Ⓗ
An attractive family-run hotel overlooking the harbour. The range of real ales, available in both public and lounge bars, has been increased to four, from a wide variety of breweries. The bar areas are popular with locals and tourists alike. There is an extensive food menu, served in both the lounge bar and restaurant, featuring local produce. Opening hours may be restricted in winter.
♨Q♉❀🛏◑🀆🚌(415)♣

Kippford

Anchor Hotel

DG5 4LN
✪ 11-3, 6-11 (midnight summer)
☎ (01556) 620205
Beer range varies Ⓗ
Situated on the main street in the heart of this popular sailing centre, this friendly inn has fine views over the Urr estuary. The varied menu includes meals made with local produce as well as good vegetarian options. There is usually one beer available throughout the year with more during the tourist season – the ale often comes from the local Sulwath Brewery. The village is served by an infrequent daytime bus service. 🛏◑▲🚌P

Kirkcolm

Blue Peter Hotel

23 Main Street, DG9 0NL (A718 5 miles N of Stranraer)
✪ 6-11.30; 12-midnight Sat; 12.30-11.30 Sun
☎ (01776) 853221 🌐 bluepeterhotel.co.uk
Beer range varies Ⓗ
This family-run hotel offers at least two ever-changing beers, mostly from Scottish and Cumbrian craft breweries. Both bars display the owner's beer memorabilia collected over his 30-year career. Good quality food made with fresh local produce is available at weekends. Red squirrels and interesting bird life can be seen from the beer garden. The pub runs an annual beer festival in central Stranraer (May/June). Scotland & Northern Ireland CAMRA Pub of the Year 2007 and national runner-up. B&B is available with a discount for CAMRA members.
♨Q❀🛏◑🀆♿▲🚌(408)⁴

Kirkcudbright

Masonic Arms

19 Castle Street, DG6 4JA
✪ 11 (12.30 Sun)-midnight
☎ (01557) 330517
Beer range varies Ⓗ
This small, sociable bar is welcoming to both locals and visitors. The tables and bar fronts are made from old malt whisky casks from Islay's Bowmore Distillery. One beer is available throughout the year with up to two more during the summer months. The Masonic also offers draught Budvar, a selection of 30 bottled beers from all over the world, and 100 malt whiskies. The town is very picturesque with a variety of tourist attractions. ♨Q▲🚌♣

New Luce

Kenmuir Arms Hotel

31 Main Street, DG8 0AJ (8 miles N of Glenluce along old military road)
✪ 10 (9 Sun)-midnight
☎ (01581) 600218 🌐 kenmuirarmsnewluce.com
Beer range varies Ⓗ
Situated in a picturesque village close to the Southern Upland Way, this small hotel offers camping in the well-kept gardens. It backs on to the River Luce, and fishing and various country pursuits can be arranged. The public bar serves two real ales in summer but usually just one in winter, and occasional beer festivals are held. Food is served all day, but groups should book in advance. On quiet days contact the staff using the walkie talkie on the bar. ♨Q❀🛏◑🀆▲♣P⁴

Newton Stewart

Creebridge House Hotel

Minigaff, DG8 6NP (on old main road, E of river)
✪ 12-2.30, 6-11.30 (midnight Sat); 12.30-11 Sun
☎ (01671) 402121 🌐 creebridge.co.uk
Caledonian Deuchars IPA; guest beers Ⓗ
Traditional country house hotel with three acres of idyllic gardens and woodland, next to the River Cree and close to the town centre. The bar serves up to three real ales, including a guest beer from the local Sulwath Brewery. There are 18 bedrooms and a separate restaurant, plus a large lounge area attached to the main bar. The hotel has a good reputation for freshly prepared food. It also sells very fine walking sticks.
♨Q❀🛏◑🚌♣P⁴

Portpatrick

Harbour House Hotel

53 Main Street, DG9 8JW
11 (12 Sun)-midnight
(01776) 810456 theharbourhousehotel.co.uk
Beer range varies H
This popular hotel stands close to the picturesque harbour. Its outdoor drinking area is a prime spot to sit and watch the boats coming in and going out to sea. The bars have been refurbished recently and real ale is available in the main bar. Two beers are served in summer, just one in winter, and a good range of Belgian beers is also stocked. (358,367)

Springfield

Queens Head

Main Street, DG16 5EH
5 (12 Sat)-11 (midnight Thu & Fri); 12.30-11 Sun
(01461) 337173
Caledonian Deuchars IPA H
This single-room village pub, although slightly off the beaten track, is actually little more than a stone's throw from Gretna, wedding capital of the country. It is very close to the A74(M) and about a mile from Gretna Green railway station. Just one real ale is served in this friendly, unpretentious local. Note there is no lunchtime opening on weekdays. P

Stranraer

Grapes ★

4-6 Bridge Street, DG9 7HY
11-11 (midnight Fri & Sat); 12-midnight Sun
(01776) 703386
Beer range varies H
This traditional 1940s-style town centre bar with a warm and welcoming atmosphere features in CAMRA's National Inventory of historic interiors. One real ale is sold in the bar, as well as a wide selection of malt whiskies and vodkas. A function room is available.

Thornhill

Buccleuch & Queensberry Hotel

112 Drumlanrig Street, DG3 5LU
11-midnight (1am Thu-Sat); 12.30-midnight Sun
(01848) 330215 buccleuchhotel.co.uk
Beer range varies H
Friendly hotel, situated on the A76 in the middle of Thornhill, popular with locals and visitors to the area. The solitary guest beer could be from anywhere in the UK. The food is always hearty – watch the blackboard for special dishes. The nearby Drumlanrig Castle is worth a visit and regularly hosts special events. The area is an ideal location for country pursuits. Q P

SCOTLAND

Hops: the essential flavouring

Hops are famous for adding bitterness to beer. But this remarkable perennial climbing plant – a member of the hemp family, Cannabinaceae – also contains acids, oils and resins that impart delightful aromas and flavours to beer.

These can be detected in the form of pine, spice, sap and tart, citrus fruit. Fruit is often similar to lemon and orange, while some English hop varieties give powerful hints of apricots, blackcurrants and damsons. American hop varieties, the Cascade in particular, are famous for their grapefruit aroma and flavour.

Many British brewers now use hops from mainland Europe – such as Styrian Goldings from Slovenia and Saaz from the Czech Republic – that have been developed primarily for lager brewing. They impart a more restrained aroma and flavour, with a gentle, resinous character. Lager hops used in ale brewing are usually added late in the copper boil to give a fine aroma to the finished beer.

Kent is often thought of as the main hop-growing area of Britain but in 2004 it was overtaken by Herefordshire. The main hop varieties used in cask beer production are the Fuggle and Golding, but First Gold, introduced in the 1990s, is now a major variety. First Gold was one of the first dwarf or hedgerow hops that grow to only half the height of conventional varieties. As a result they are easier to pick, are less susceptible to disease and aphid attack, and therefore use fewer agri-chemicals. In 2004, a new hop variety called Boadicea was introduced: it is the first aphid-resistant hop and therefore needs fewer pesticides. The hop industry is working on trials of new varieties that need no pesticides or fertilisers and should gain Soil Association approval as organic hops within the next few years.

EDINBURGH & THE LOTHIANS

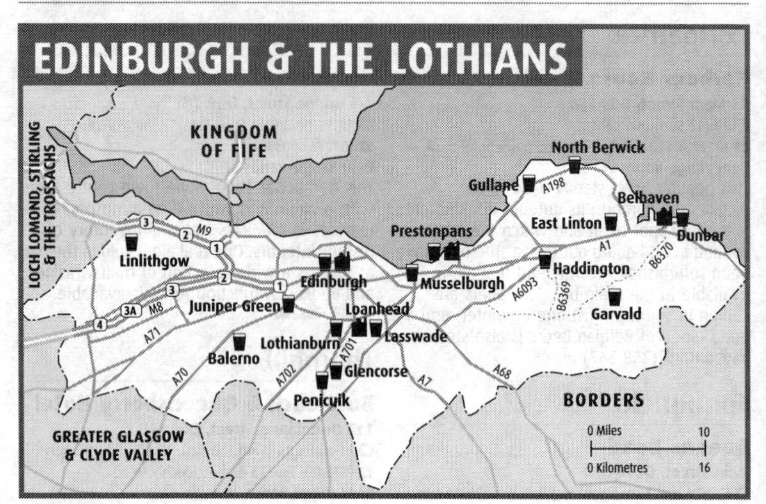

Authority areas covered: City of Edinburgh, East Lothian, Midlothian, West Lothian

Balerno

Grey Horse

20 Main Street, EH14 7EH (off A70, in pedestrian area)

10 (12.30 Sun)-1am

(0131) 449 2888

Caledonian Deuchars IPA; guest beers

Traditional stone built village centre pub dating from around 200 years ago. The public bar retains some original features with wood panelling and a fine Bernard's mirror. The lounge is pleasantly decorated and has green banquette seating. The café next door is part of the pub so you can have a beer with your meal. Children are permitted in the lounge until 8pm. Dogs are warmly welcomed with water and biscuits. An outdoor shelter for smokers is planned. Q

Belhaven

Masons Arms

8 High Street, EH42 1NP

12-3, 5-11; 12-midnight Fri & Sat; 12.30-11 Sun

(01368) 863700

Belhaven 80/-; guest beers

Friendly pub close to Belhaven Brewery with fine views to the Lammermuir Hills. The bright, comfortable public bar has banquette seating and an attractive wood laminate floor. The walls are decorated with pictures of old sailing ships. There is also a pleasant dining room where food from a quality menu is served (not Sunday evening). The guest beer is from the Belhaven or Greene King lists.

Dunbar

Rocks

Marine Road, EH42 1AR (on clifftop, W of centre)

11 (12.30 Sun)-11

(01368) 862287 experiencetherocks.co.uk

Beer range varies

Imposing 'Scottish Riviera' red stone villa, now a hotel. Set back from the cliffs, it has panoramic views across Dunbar Bay. The well-appointed bar has a high ceiling and dark wood decor, with several dining areas leading off it. The friendly staff are happy to offer advice on the adventurous seafood oriented menu. Some items are expensive, but expect excellent quality. A wide variety of real ales is dispensed from the two handpumps. Children are welcome.

Volunteer Arms

17 Victoria Street, EH42 1HP

12-11 (midnight Thu; 1am Fri & Sat); 12.30-midnight Sun

(01368) 862278

Beer range varies

Close to Dunbar harbour, this is a friendly, traditional locals' pub. The cosy panelled bar is decorated with lots of fishing and lifeboat memorabilia. Two real ales usually come from smaller breweries. Upstairs is a restaurant serving an excellent menu with an emphasis on seafood. In summer, food is served all day until 9.30pm. Children are welcome until 8pm and dogs permitted after 9pm.

East Linton

Crown

25-27 Bridge Street, EH40 3AG

11 (12 winter)-11 (1am Thu-Sat); 11-midnight Sun

(01620) 860335 thecrowneastlinton.co.uk

Adnams Broadside; Caledonian Deuchars IPA; guest beers

Small 18th-century stone-built hotel in the centre of a historic conservation village. The functional, cosy bar has a real log fire, lots of wood panelling and original Dudgeon windows. To the rear is a large lounge/restaurant that serves good quality pub food

INDEPENDENT BREWERIES

Caledonian Edinburgh
Fowler's Prestonpans (Brewing suspended)
Stewart Loanhead

from an imaginative menu. (Served all day in summer, not Sunday to Wednesday evenings in winter). One of the guest beers is usually from Stewart Brewing. Children are permitted in the lounge and family room. Dogs are also welcome.

Edinburgh

Athletic Arms (Diggers)

1-3 Angle Park Terrace, EH11 2JX (1m SW of centre)
11 (12.30 Sun)-midnight
☎ (0131) 337 3822 theathleticarms.co.uk
Caledonian Deuchars IPA, 80; Stewart Diggers 80/-; Ⓐ guest beers Ⓗ
Situated between two graveyards, the name Diggers became synonymous with this Edinburgh legend, which opened in 1897. Banquette seating lines the walls, and a compass drawing in the floor provides direction. A brass wall plaque set among the pictures and memorabilia makes for interesting reading. A smaller back room houses a dartboard and further seating. Quieter now than in its heyday, the pub continues to extend a warm welcome to local characters and visitors alike. Dogs are also admitted.

Auld Hoose

23 St Leonards Street, EH8 9QN (0.7m S of centre)
11.30 (12.30 Sun)-12.45am
☎ (0131) 668 2934 theauldhoose.co.uk
Caledonian Deuchars IPA; Greene King Old Speckled Hen; guest beers Ⓗ
Traditional hostelry dating back to the 1860s with a large central U-shaped bar and lots of pictures of old Edinburgh. Located in the student quarter, this is a friendly pub with a wide clientele. Try the alternative jukebox, enjoy a game of darts with the locals or enter the quiz on Tuesday evening. Good pub food is served all day including vegetarian and vegan options. The guest beer is usually from a Scottish micro. Dogs are welcome, and there is free Wi-Fi access.

Barony Bar ✔

81-85 Broughton Street, EH1 3RJ (E edge of New Town)
11-midnight (1am Fri & Sat); 12.30-midnight Sun
☎ (0131) 558 2874
Black Sheep Best Bitter; Caledonian Deuchars IPA, 80; Theakston Old Peculier; guest beers Ⓗ
Characterful city pub, listed on the Scottish pub inventory due to its many fine internal features. Splendid tile work and stained wood are much in evidence while the bar and gantry are also noteworthy. Detailed cornices and a wooden floor add to the atmosphere of the L-shaped bar. Magnificent whisky mirrors adorn the walls. Food is served all day until 10pm (7pm Sun). Q(Waverley)

Bennets Bar

1 Maxwell Street, Morningside, EH10 5HT (1.5m S of centre)
11-midnight; closed Sun
☎ (0131) 447 1903
Greene King IPA; Inveralmond Ossian; guest beers Ⓐ
Couthy back street boozer in the wealthy suburb of Morningside, yet only yards from one of the city's main trunk roads south. The pub has been owned by the eponymous family for generations and retains many features from the last major refurbishment some 50 years ago. The walls are adorned with photographs of old Edinburgh, including some of the long gone original Bennets next to Waverley station. The outdoor drinking area is available all year round for hardier souls.

Blue Blazer

2 Spittal Street, EH3 9DX (SW side of centre)
11 (12.30 Sun)-1am
☎ (0131) 229 5030
Cairngorm Trade Winds; Ⓗ Caledonian Deuchars IPA; Ⓐ Stewart 80/-; guest beers Ⓗ
Wood floors and panels, high ceilings and frosted glass windows give this two-room city centre pub a traditional feel, though wee candles along the bar and unobtrusive background music are nice modern touches. It is often busy, but competent staff keep things moving. Find details of the eight real ales, often from small Scottish breweries, on Facebook (I Love The Blue Blazer). Try the wide range of whiskies, or the monthly rum tasting club, for good measure. Dogs are welcome. (Haymarket)

Bow Bar

80 West Bow, EH1 2HH (old town, off Grassmarket)
12-11.30 (11 Sun)
☎ (0131) 226 7667 bowbar.com
Belhaven 80/-; Caledonian Deuchars IPA; Taylor Landlord; guest beers Ⓐ
A classic Scottish one-roomed alehouse dedicated to traditional Scottish air pressure dispense and perpendicular drinking. The five guest beers can be from anywhere in the UK. The walls are festooned with original brewery mirrors and the superb gantry does justice to an award-winning selection of single malt whisky. A map of the original 33 Scottish counties hangs above the fireplace. Bar snacks are available at lunchtime. Dogs are welcome.
Q(Waverley)

Café Royal ☆ ✔

19 West Register Street, EH2 2AA (centre off E end of Princess St)
11-11 (midnight Thu; 1am Fri & Sat); 12.30-11 Sun
☎ (0131) 556 1884
Caledonian Deuchars IPA, 80; guest beers Ⓗ
One of the finest Victorian pub interiors in Scotland, listed on CAMRA's National Inventory. It is dominated by an impressive oval island bar with ornate brass light fittings and six magnificent ceramic tiled murals of innovators made by Doulton from pictures by John Eyre. The superb sporting windows of the Oyster Bar were made by the same Edinburgh firm who supplied windows for the House of Lords. The Gents features an unusual hand basin. Meals are served all day.
(Waverley)

Cask & Barrel

115 Broughton Street, EH1 3RZ (E edge of New Town)
11-12.30am (1am Thu-Sat); 12.30-12.30am Sun

SCOTLAND

☎ (0131) 556 3132
Caledonian Deuchars IPA, 80; Draught Bass; Hadrian & Border Cowie; Harviestoun Bitter & Twisted; guest beers 🄷
Spacious and busy ale house drawing a varied clientele of all ages, ranging from business people to football fans. The interior features an imposing horseshoe bar, bare floorboards, a splendid cornice and a collection of brewery mirrors. Old barrels act as tables for those who wish to stand up, or cannot find a seat. The guest beers, often from smaller Scottish breweries, come in a range of strengths and styles. Sparklers can be removed on request. ❀◑♿≉(Waverley)🚌

Clarks Bar

142 Dundas Street, EH3 5DQ (N edge of New Town)
⏲ 11-11 (11.30 Thu-Sat); 12.30-11 Sun
☎ (0131) 556 1067
Caledonian Deuchars IPA, 80; 🄷/🄿 **guest beers** 🄷
Basic tenement bar popular with locals and workers from the many offices nearby. The internal layout is interesting with two private rooms off the bar. Several brewery mirrors and some photos from the days when trams passed by outside adorn the main room. The steep stairs make a trip to the toilets a good test of sobriety. Take a look at the mural on the way. Dogs are welcome. ◑🚌(23,27)

Cloisters Bar

26 Brougham Street, EH3 9JH (SW edge of centre)
⏲ 12-midnight (1am Fri & Sat); 12.30-midnight Sun
☎ (0131) 221 9997
Cairngorm Trade Winds; Caledonian Deuchars IPA; Stewart Holy Grail; Taylor Landlord; guest beers 🄷
A former parsonage, this bare boarded ale house is popular with a broad cross section of drinkers. Large bench seats give the pub a friendly feel. A fine selection of brewery mirrors adorns the walls and the wide range of single malt whiskies does justice to the outstanding gantry, which is built using wood from a redundant church. A spiral staircase makes visiting the loo an adventure. Food is served 12-6pm on Friday and Saturday, lunchtimes and evenings during the week. Dogs are welcome. Q◑▶🚌♣●

Dagda Bar

93-95 Buccleuch Street, EH8 9NG (0.7m S of centre)
⏲ 12 (11 Sat)-1am; 12.30-1am Sun
☎ (0131) 667 9773 🌐 dagdabar.co.uk/index.php
Beer range varies 🄷
Convivial, cosy bar in the university area attracting a wide ranging clientele. The single room has banquette seating on three sides and the bar counter on the other. The stone flagged floor is a little uneven in places. The staff are happy to let you sample the three real ales, which are usually from smaller breweries. Fresh ground coffee and quality tea are also available. Dogs are welcome.
🚌(41,42)♣

Dalriada

77 Promenade, Joppa, EH15 2EL (3m E of centre, off Joppa Rd)
⏲ 12-11 (midnight Fri & Sat); closed Mon Jan & Feb; 12-11 (10 winter) Sun
☎ (0131) 454 4500
Beer range varies 🄷
Located on the Portobello/Joppa promenade, you can enjoy a pint and watch out for seals. The imposing entrance of this stone-built villa has an original tiled floor and fireplace. There are three bar areas with wooden flooring and furniture. The bar counter has a polished Italian granite top. An extensive snack menu is available 12-3pm (not Mon). Children are welcome until 8pm. Dogs are permitted on a lead and bowls provided. Live music plays at weekends. ♨❀≉(Brunstane Rd)🚌P⁻

Foot O' T' Walk ✔

183 Constitution Street, Leith, EH6 7AA
⏲ 9-11 (midnight Thu-Sat); 12.30-11 Sun
☎ (0131) 553 0120
Caledonian Deuchars IPA, 80; Greene King Abbot; guest beers 🄷
JD Wetherspoons pub attracting a large cultural cross section of Leith's denizens. Reasonably priced food is served in a seemingly low ceilinged but spacious room, divided into discrete dining areas by the trademark dias in one corner and waist high wood panels with brass railings. Its corner location affords two main entrances, and a third door to Constitution Street. Food is served all day and children are welcome until 8pm. ◑▶♿🚌●

Halfway House

24 Fleshmarket Close, EH1 1BX (up steps opp. station's Market St entrance)
⏲ 11-midnight (1am Fri & Sat); 12.30-midnight Sun
☎ (0131) 225 7101 🌐 halfwayhouse-edinburgh.com
Beer range varies 🄷
Cosy, characterful bar hidden halfway down an old town 'close'. Railway memorabilia and current timetables adorn the interior of this small, often busy pub. Usually there are four interesting beers from smaller Scottish breweries on offer. Over the summer a different brewery is showcased each week. Card-carrying CAMRA members get a discount on their first pint. Good quality, reasonably-priced food is served all day. The pub may stay open until 1am at busy times of the year. Dogs and children are welcome.
❀◑▶≉(Waverley)🚌♣⁻

Kay's Bar

39 Jamaica Street, EH3 6HF (New Town, off India St)
⏲ 11-midnight (1am Fri & Sat); 12.30-11 Sun
☎ (0131) 225 1858
Caledonian Deuchars IPA; Theakston's Best Bitter; guest beers 🄷
Small, cosy and convivial pub, a popular haunt of lawyers in the early evening. There is an impressive range of beers for the size of the bar. One wall is decorated with whisky barrels, and there is also a good whisky selection behind the bar. An even smaller back room holds a well stocked library. The lunches consist of mainly traditional Scottish fare. The building was once used as a wine merchant's and the remains of the pipes can still be seen. Dogs are welcome after 2.30pm. ♨Q◑♣

Leslies Bar ★

45 Ratcliffe Terrace, EH9 1SU

11-11 (11.30 Thu; 12.30am Fri & Sat); 12.30-11.30 Sun

(0131) 6677205 lesliesbar.com

Caledonian Deuchars IPA, 80; Taylor Landlord; guest beers H

Outstanding Victorian pub, listed on CAMRA's National Inventory, retaining its original fine ceiling, cornice, leaded glass work and half wood panelling. The island bar has a spectacular snob screen which divides the pub. Small 'ticket window' hatches allow customers to order drinks. A plaque near the fire place gives further details of this busy, vibrant but orderly pub. The three guest beers are usually from smaller breweries. Simple bar snacks are served. Regular live jazz plays on Monday evening. Dogs are welcome. (42)

Malt & Hops

45 The Shore, Leith, EH6 6QU

12-11 (midnight Wed & Thu; 1am Fri & Sat); 12.30-11 Sun

(0131) 555 0083

Caledonian Deuchars IPA; Marston's Pedigree; guest beers H

One roomed public bar dating from 1749 and in the heart of 'new' Leith's riverside restaurant district. Wood panelling gives an intimate feel with numerous mirrors, artefacts and a large oil painting adding interest. The superb collection of pump clips, many from now defunct breweries, indicates the ever-changing interesting range of guest beers, often from Scottish breweries. No meals are served on Saturday or Sunday. Children are welcome until 6pm. Dogs are welcome at any time.

Old Dock Bar

3-5 Dock Place, Leith, EH6 6LU

12-11 (1am Fri & Sat); 12.30-11 Sun

(0131) 553 7223

Beer range varies H

Small traditional bar adjoining a large restaurant. The walls are decorated with maritime prints and photographs of old Leith. The building has been a bar since 1813, and claims to be Leith's oldest. It is now home of the original eight handpump bank from Todd's Tap. The location is handy for visitors to the Scottish Government offices and Ocean Terminal shopping centre. Good quality meals are served all day and bar snacks are also available. Children are welcome.

Ormelie Bar

44 Joppa Road, Joppa, EH15 2ET (3m of centre)

11-midnight (12.45am Fri & Sat); 12.30-11 Sun

(0131) 669 3323

Caledonian Deuchars IPA; Stewart 80/-; guest beers H

A historic tenement lounge bar, converted from a shop in the late 19th century, situated close to Portobello promenade. This welcoming locals' pub features a lovely long bar surrounded by ornate lanterns. The gantry is stocked with a huge array of malt whiskies. Historic photos and golf memorabillia adorn the walls. Bar snacks are available. Dogs are welcome. (26)

Oxford Bar ★

8 Young Street, EH2 4JB (New Town, off Charlotte Sq)

11-midnight (1am Thu-Sat); 12.30-11 Sun

(0131) 539 7119 oxfordbar.com

Caledonian Deuchars IPA; guest beers H

Small, basic, vibrant New Town drinking shop decorated with Scottishesque memorabilia. It is renowned as a favourite watering hole of Inspector Rebus and his creator Ian Rankin. It has also been the haunt of many other famous and infamous characters over the years so you never know who you might bump into. Why not visit the website and contribute a story. It is a real taste of New Town past and listed on CAMRA's National Inventory of historic pub interiors. Simple bar snacks are available. Dogs are welcome.

Regent

2 Montrose Terrace, EH7 5DL (0.7m E of centre)

11-1am; 12.30-1am Sun

(0131) 661 8198

Caledonian Deuchars IPA; guest beers H

Large tenement bar with two rooms, one music free, popular with gay and lesbian real ale drinkers. It offers an interesting range of three guest beers. The comfortable seating consists of banquettes, leather sofas and armchairs. Bar snacks and meals are served all day. A novel slant on pub games is the gymnastic pommel horse by the toilets. CAMRA Edinburgh Pub of the Year 2008. Dogs are welcome and free Wi-Fi access is available.

Stable Bar

Mortonhall Park, 30 Frogston Road East, EH16 6TJ (S edge of city)

11-11 (midnight summer); 12.30-11 Sun

(0131) 664 0773

Caledonian Deuchars IPA; Stewart Pentland IPA, Copper Cascade H

A real country pub on the edge of the city. The comfortable bar is dominated by a large stone fireplace, with a roaring log fire in winter. Food is served all day until 9pm (10pm summer), with the plainer back room mainly for diners. With real ales coming from breweries less than three miles away, this is a true local pub. Watch out for the Little Miss Muffet seat. Children and dogs are welcome. Close by, numerous footpaths are ideal for exploring the surrounding woods. (11,18) P

Starbank Inn

64 Laverockbank Road, EH5 3BZ (1.5m N of centre)

11-11 (midnight Thu-Sat); 12.30-11 Sun

(0131) 552 4141 starbankinn.co.uk

Belhaven Sandy Hunter's Traditional Ale, 80/-; Caledonian Deuchars IPA; Taylor Landlord; guest beers H

Bright, airy, bare-boarded ale house, with a U-shaped layout extending into a conservatory dining area. The walls sport several rare brewery mirrors. Enjoy the superb views across the Firth to Fife. At least four interesting guest ales, often from Scottish independent breweries, are usually available. Meals are served all day on Saturday and Sunday. Children are welcome until 8.30pm. Dogs are

SCOTLAND

also permitted if on a lead. Occasional jazz sessions on Sunday. Q❀◐◑♿🚌♣⅟

Thomson's ✓

182-184 Morrison Street, EH3 8EB (W edge of centre)

⏲ 12-11.30 (midnight Thu-Sat; 1am Fri); 4-11.30 Sun

☎ (0131) 228 5700 🌐 thomsonsbar.co.uk

Caledonian Deuchars IPA; guest beers Ⓐ

Modelled on the architectural style of Glasgow's Alexander 'Greek' Thomson, this award-winning pub is dedicated to traditional Scottish air pressure dispense. The superb, custom-built gantry features mirrors inlaid with scenes from Greek mythology. The walls are a veritable history of Scottish brewing, featuring rare mirrors from long defunct Scottish breweries. Guest beers are often from Pictish, Hop Back or Atlas. No food is served on Sunday, just pies on Saturday. Dogs are welcome. Q❀◐⇌(Haymarket)🚌

Winston's ✓

20 Kirk Loan, Corstorphine, EH12 7HD (3 miles W of centre, off St Johns Road)

⏲ 11-11.30 (midnight Thu-Sat); 12.30-11 Sun

☎ (0131) 539 7077

Caledonian Deuchars IPA; guest beers Ⓗ

This comfortable lounge bar is situated in Corstorphine, just over a mile from Murrayfield Stadium and not far from the zoo. The small, modern building houses a warm and welcoming community pub, popular with old and young alike. The one-room interior has a golf and rugby themed decor. Children are welcome until 3pm. Simple bar snacks are served all day and lunchtime meals feature wonderful homemade pies. Dogs are welcome. ❀◐🚌♣⅟

Garvald

Garvald Inn

EH41 4LN

⏲ 12-3, 5-11 (midnight Fri & Sat); closed Mon; 12.30-11 (5 winter) Sun

☎ (01620) 830311

Beer range varies Ⓗ

Family-run 18th century pub in a pretty village by the Lammermuir Hills. The bar is cosy and welcoming with half-panelled walls, a crimson colour scheme and a wall with exposed stone. The single real ale is often from Stewart Brewing or Hadrian & Border. Good food is served in both the bar and tiny dining room – the dinner menu is particularly impressive. Occasional live music plays. Well-behaved dogs are permitted but not in the dining room. Children are also welcome.
⛼Q❀◐◑♣P⅟

Glencorse

Flotterstone Inn

Milton Bridge, EH26 0PP (off A702 near Pentlands visitor centre)

⏲ 11.30 (12.30 Sun)-11

☎ (01968) 673717

Stewart Pentland IPA; guest beers Ⓗ

The large, rectangular lounge bar has church pew seating and numerous Toby jugs and plates around the walls. Two dining rooms have bare stone walls and wooden ceilings. A modern timber clad extension overlooks the enclosed garden and provides additional space. Good food is served all day. This is a pleasant place to recover from a day on the Pentland hills, and it can be busy at weekends. Children and dogs are welcome.
❀◐◑♿🚌♣P

Gullane

Old Clubhouse

East Links Road, EH31 2AF (W end of village, off A198)

⏲ 11-11 (midnight Thu-Sat); 12.30-11 Sun

☎ (01620) 842008 🌐 oldclubhouse.com

Caledonian Deuchars IPA; Taylor Landlord; guest beers Ⓐ

There's a colonial feel to this pub, which looks out over the golf links to the Lammermuir Hills. The half-panelled walls are adorned with historic memorabilia and stuffed animals. Caricature-style statuettes of the Marx Brothers and Laurel and Hardy look down from the gantry. Food features highly and is available all day. The extensive menu includes seafood, pasta, barbecue, curries, salads and burgers. Children are welcome until 8pm. Dogs are also permitted.
⛼❀◐◑♿🚌(124,X5)●⅟

Haddington

Tyneside Tavern ✓

10 Poldrate, EH41 4DA (on A6137)

⏲ 11-11 (midnight Thu; 12:45am Fri & Sat); 12.30-midnight Sun

☎ (01620) 822221 🌐 tynesidetavern.co.uk

Caledonian Deuchars IPA, 80; guest beer Ⓗ

Set close to the River Tyne near an old water mill, this community pub has a long narrow bar that attracts a mixed clientele and is popular for watching sport on TV. The lounge has been extended and now serves as a busy bistro at lunchtimes and evenings, all day on Sunday until 7pm. It has wooden floors plus wood-topped tables with cast iron legs. Children are welcome until 9pm and dogs are permitted. Guest beers are from the S&N guest list. ⛼❀◐◑🚇♿🚌♣⅟

Juniper Green

Juniper Green Inn

542 Lanark Road, EH14 5EL

⏲ 11-11 (midnight Thu-Sat); 12.30-11 Sun

☎ (0131) 458 5395

Caledonian Deuchars IPA; guest beers Ⓗ

Well-appointed, single room lounge bar in a late 1800s building. The decor is clean and attractive throughout; the bar counter is mahogany with a more modern gantry designed to match. The pub has a very strong community spirit. Pictures of the old Balerno branch line provide interest. The food is freshly cooked to a high standard. A secluded patio and garden are popular in summer. Not a pub to visit if you are wearing dirty overalls.
❀◐🚌⅟

Lasswade

Laird & Dog Hotel

5 High Street, EH18 1NA (A768, near river)
11-11.30 (11.45 Thu; 12.30am Fri & Sat); 12.30-11.30 Sun
(0131) 663 9219
Caledonian Deuchars IPA; guest beers H
Comfortable village local catering for all tastes, from those who enjoy a quiet drink or meal to music loving pool players. The guest ale is usually from a smaller brewery. Food is available all day with a good menu, daily specials and cheaper bar snacks. Pictures and horse brasses decorate the bar areas. There is also a conservatory, an unusual bottle-shaped well and a real fire surrounded by armchairs. Dogs and cats are welcome. Children are also welcome until 8pm.
(31,141)P

Linlithgow

Four Marys

65-67 High Street, EH49 7ED
11-11 (11.45 Thu-Sat); 12.30-11 Sun
(01506) 842171
Belhaven 80/-, St Andrew's Ale; Caledonian Deuchars IPA; Greene King IPA; guest beers H
Named after the four ladies-in-waiting of Mary Queen of Scots who was born in nearby Linlithgow Palace, the building dates from around 1500 when it was a dwelling house. The pub has seen several changes of use through the years; it was once a chemist's shop run by the Waldie family whose most famous member, David, established the anaesthetic properties of chloroform in 1847. Beer festivals are hosted in May and October when the handpumps are increased from eight to 18.

Platform 3

1A High Street, EH49 7AB
10.30-midnight (1am Fri & Sat); 12.30-midnight Sun
(01506) 847405
Caledonian Deuchars IPA; guest beers H
Small, friendly hostelry on the railway station approach, originally the public bar of the hotel next door. It was purchased and renovated in 1998 as a pub in its own right and stages occasional live music. Note the interesting memorabilia displayed on the walls and look out for the train running above the bar. The guest ale rotates on one pump and is from either Cairngorm or Stewart Breweries.

Lothianburn

Steading

118-120 Biggar Road, EH10 7DU (on A702)
11-midnight (earlier if quiet); 12.30-11 Sun
(0131) 445 1128
Caledonian Deuchars IPA; Orkney Dark Island; Taylor Landlord; guest beer H
The pub was converted from farm cottages and has distinct areas for drinkers and diners. The popular restaurant includes a large conservatory extension and food is served all day. A simple menu is available in the bar. The outside drinking area has excellent views of the Pentland Hills and the pub is ideally placed for a relaxing pint after walking in the hills or visiting the nearby dry ski slope. Children and dogs are welcome. (4,15)P

Musselburgh

Levenhall Arms

10 Ravensheugh Road, EH21 7PP (on B1348, 1 mile E of centre)
12-11 (midnight Thu; 1am Fri & Sat); 12.30-midnight Sun
(0131) 665 3220
Stewart Pentland IPA; guest beer H
Three roomed hostelry dating from 1830, popular with locals and race-goers. The lively, cheerfully decorated public bar is half-timber panelled and carpeted, with a smaller area leading off with a dartboard and pictures of old local industries. The quieter lounge area with vinyl banquette seating is used for dining; food is served all day until 8pm. Dogs are welcome in the bar and children permitted until 8.30pm in the lounge. Opening times and food menu may vary in winter.
Q(Wallyford)P

Volunteer Arms (Staggs)

81 North High Street, EH21 6JE (behind Brunton Hall)
12-11 (11.30 Thu, midnight Fri & Sat); 1-10 Sun
(0131) 665 9654
Caledonian Deuchars IPA; guest beers H
Superb pub run by the same family since 1858. The bar and snug are traditional with a wooden floor, wood panelling and mirrors from defunct local breweries. The superb gantry is topped with old casks. The snug has a nascent history collection featuring local breweries. The more modern lounge opens at the weekend. Three guest beers, often pale and hoppy, change very regularly. Dogs are welcome in the bar, but don't bring the kids. CAMRA Lothian Pub of the Year 2008.

North Berwick

Nether Abbey Hotel

20 Dirleton Avenue, EH39 4BQ (on A198, W of town centre)
11-11 (midnight Thu; 1am Fri & Sat)
(01620) 892802 netherabbey.co.uk
Beer range varies A
Family run hotel in a stone built villa with a bright, contemporary, open-plan interior. The room is on two levels: the lower area is a bar and the upper a restaurant. The marble topped bar counter features a row of modern chrome founts. The middle ones, with horizontally moving levers, dispense the real ales. Food is served all day in summer and at weekends. Children are welcome until 9pm. Dogs are also permitted. P

Penicuik

Navaar

23 Bog Road, EH26 9BY
12-1am (midnight Sun)
(01968) 672693
Stewart Pentland IPA H
A lively pub with a strong community spirit, situated in an old private house, circa 1870.

SCOTLAND

The large bar is open plan with a log and coal fire and TV screens. There is also a restaurant offering an extensive à la carte menu, with meals served all day. Snacks are available in the bar. A large patio and decked area is popular in summer. Dogs are welcome.
⚐❀⇌◑◐⊟♣P⁻

Prestonpans

Prestoungrange Gothenburg ☆

227 High Street, EH32 9BE
11-11 (1am Fri & Sat); 12.30-11 Sun
☎ (01875) 819922 ⊕ prestoungrange.org/gothenburg
Beer range varies Ⓗ

Superbly refurbished Gothenburg pub, winner of the 2005 English Heritage pub refurbishment award and on CAMRA's National Pub Inventory. The magnificent painted ceiling in the bar has to be seen to be appreciated. Fowler's mothballed micro-brewery can be viewed through a window. There is a bistro on the ground floor and upstairs is a lounge and function room with superb views over the Forth. The walls throughout are covered in murals and paintings depicting past local life. Meals are served all day Friday-Sunday. Children are welcome. ⚐◑◐⊟♿⅄⊟(26,129)**P**

Café Royal, Edinburgh (Photo: Chani McBain).

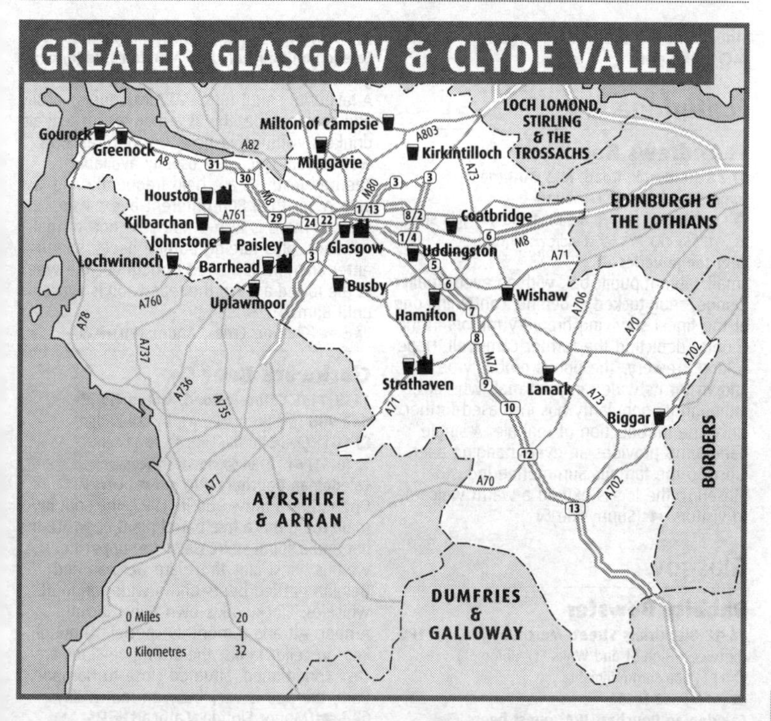

Authority areas covered: City of Glasgow, East Dunbartonshire, East Renfrewshire, Inverclyde, North Lanarkshire, Renfrewshire, South Lanarkshire

Barrhead

Cross Stobs Inn

4 Grahamston Road, G78 1NS (on B7712)
11-11 (midnight Thu; 1am Fri; 11.45pm Sat); 12.30-11 Sun
☎ (0141) 881 1581
Kelburn Misty Law; guest beers Ⓗ
Eighteenth century coaching inn on the road to Paisley. The public bar has a real coal fire and retains much of its original charm with antique furniture and service bells. The lounge is spacious and leads out to an enclosed rear garden. There is also an outside drinking area at the front of the pub. Inside there is a pool room off the public bar and a function suite that can be hired. Children are welcome at lunchtime. Occasionally a second Kelburn beer is available.

Waterside Inn

Glasgow Road, The Hurlet, G53 7TH (A736 near Hurlet)
11-11 (midnight Fri & Sat); 12.30-11 Sun
☎ (0141) 881 2822
Kelburn Misty Law; guest beers Ⓗ
Comfortable bar-restaurant near Levern Water. Although the emphasis is on food, there is a cosy area around the real fire for those who only want to drink in a relaxed manner. The restaurant holds themed nights with musical accompaniment. Local pictures adorn the walls adding to the ambience of the inn. Although the guest beer varies it nearly always comes from the Kelburn Brewery.
P

Biggar

Crown Inn ✔

109-111 High Street, ML12 6DL
11-1am; 12.30-midnight Sun
☎ (01899) 220116
Beer range varies Ⓗ
Located in the centre of the historic little town of Biggar, this 300-year-old coaching inn has a wood-panelled public bar at the front and several smaller rooms plus a beer garden at the rear. The beers constantly change, with Inveralmond's Lia Fail a favourite choice among the locals. The home-cooked meals are also a major attraction. The pub has strong links with the local rugby club so can be busy on match days. (191,100)

Busby

White Cart ✔

61 East Kilbride Road, G76 8HX (on A726 near station)
11 (12.30 Sun)-11
☎ (0141) 644 2711
Beer range varies Ⓗ
The spacious interior is divided by large oak beams into several cosy nooks. The decor is from an earlier period, featuring a grandfather clock, dressing tables and a host of bric-a-brac. Parts of the strong walls at the rear of the building are thought to be from the stables formerly on the site. Although the emphasis here is on food, especially fish, recent refurbishment has created a nook mainly intended for non-diners. Two ales are on offer, one from the local Kelburn Brewery and the

other from the Scottish & Newcastle range.
⛲Q❀◐◑♿⇌P

Coatbridge

St Andrews Bar

37-38 Sunnyside Road, ML5 3DG (near Summerlee Heritage Museum)
11-midnight (1am Fri & Sat); 12.30-midnight Sun
☎ (01236) 423 773 standrewsbar.com
Beer range varies H
Small, vibrant public bar, with an even smaller lounge/snug tucked in behind, containing one of the finest surviving brewery mirrors in the country depicting the former Campbell, Hope & King Brewery. The pub is probably best known for its wide range of malt whiskies, although its popularity has increased further since the introduction of real ale. A single handpump provides an ever-changing beer. Close to the famous Summerlee Industrial Museum, the locals extend a warm welcome to visitors. ⇌(Sunnyside)🚌

Glasgow

Babbity Bowster

16-18 Blackfriars Street, Merchant City, G1 1PE (between High St and Walls St/Albion St)
11 (12.30 Sun)-midnight
☎ (0141) 552 5055
Caledonian Deuchars IPA; guest beers P
Located in a quiet pedestrianised area between two streets, Babbity's provides a combination of features unique in central Glasgow. Good local food concentrating on fish and game and Scottish and French menus is served in the bar and upstairs restaurant. Traditional tall founts dispense two Scottish ales plus one from south of the border. There is a peat burning fire, accommodation, and a beer garden – a Glasgow rarity – where barbecues and boules can be enjoyed.
⛲Q❀🛏◐◑⇌(High Street/Argyle St/Queen St)⊖(Buchanan St)🍎P⁻

Blackfriars

36 Bell Street, Merchant City, G1 1LG (corner of Albion Street)
11 (12.30 Sun)-midnight
☎ (0141) 552 5924 blackfriarsglasgow.com
Beer range varies P
This vibrant pub in Glasgow's smart Merchant City district attracts a wide clientele. Increasingly popular, it can be hectic on Friday and Saturday nights although a refurbishment has added a quieter area to the rear. Five pumps, including a traditional tall fount, support a mixture of Scottish and English micro-brewery beers, with a rotating ale from the local Kelburn Brewery. There is also a selection of bottled and draught foreign beers and farmhouse ciders. Live jazz plays on Sunday evening, comedy on Thursday and a quiz on Monday.
❀◐◑♿⇌(High St/Argyll St/Queen St)⊖(Buchanan St)🍎⁻

Bon Accord

153 North Street, G3 7DA (between Mitchell Library and Argyle St)
11-midnight; 12.30-11 Sun
☎ (0141) 248 4427 thebonaccord.freeserve.co.uk
Caledonian Deuchars IPA; Marston's Pedigree; guest beers H
A favourite haunt for CAMRA members, locally and countrywide, this is a magnet for real ale drinkers visiting Glasgow. Up to 10 ales, as well as real cider, are usually available. Themed festivals are held frequently and last year more than 800 different beers were served. There is also a fine selection of malt whiskies, plus foreign bottled beers. Various entertainment is staged throughout the week in the raised area to the rear. Food is available until 8pm.
◐◑♿⇌(Charing Cross/Anderston)♣🍎⁻

Clockwork Beer Co.

1153-1155 Cathcart Road, Mount Florida, G42 9BH (Kings Park Rd jct, by rail bridge)
11-11 (midnight Thu-Sat); 12.30-11 Sun
☎ (0141) 649 0184 clockworkbeer.com
Caledonian Deuchars IPA; guest beers A
Opened as a brew pub in 1997, the split level main room has a five barrel plant opposite the bar and a spiral staircase to the upper floor. As well as guest ales there are German and Belgian bottled beers and a wide range of whiskies. Clockwork's own beers include Amber, Alt and a monthly special. Although kept in cellar tanks, the strong versions are cask conditioned. Situated close to Hampden Park, the pub is very busy on match days.
◐◑♿⇌(Mount Florida/Cathcart)🚌P⁻

Counting House ✔

2 St Vincent Place, G1 2DH (on George Square)
9 (12.30 Sun)-midnight
☎ (0141) 225 0160
Cairngorm Wildcat; Caledonian Deuchars IPA, 80; Greene King Abbot Ale; Marston's Pedigree; guest beers H
A large pub with several areas providing a range of seating from comfy chairs to high window seats. Some overlook George Square, others St Vincent Place. A Wetherspoon conversion of a former bank, the impressive decor includes a glazed central dome and wall statues. The bar has handpumps on all three sides providing an ever-changing range of ales. The central location means the pub can get busy with shoppers, tourists, travellers and city workers. Children are welcome until 8pm.
Q◐◑♿⇌(Queen St/Central)⊖(Buchanan St)

Crystal Palace ✔

36 Jamaica Street, G1 4QD
9 (12.30 Sun)-midnight
☎ (0141) 221 2624
Caledonian Deuchars IPA; Greene King Abbot; guest beers H
One of Glasgow's largest pubs, this Wetherspoon's conversion of a furniture store has massive windows and bars on two floors, often serving different beers. A downstairs rear area is family friendly and children are welcome until 7pm. The pub retains the

INDEPENDENT BREWERIES

Clockwork Glasgow
Houston Houston
Kelburn Barrhead
Strathaven Strathaven

original cage lift, allowing access upstairs for the disabled, where it is usually less hectic. Popular with a wide variety of people, the location is conveniently close to Central rail station and on a major bus route.
Q ≋ ◐ ♿ ⇌(Central) ⊖(St Enoch) 🚌

Drum & Monkey ✔

91 St Vincent Street, G2 5TF

11 (12.30 Sun)-midnight

☎ (0141) 221 6636

Caledonian Deuchars IPA, 80; guest beers Ⓗ

Busy corner pub a short walk from George Square with windows overlooking two streets and a large split level lounge/bar with a U-shaped counter projecting into the room. Formerly a bank, designed by Balfour to classic American style, the walls feature white marble and an ornate ceiling supported by square black marble pillars. To the rear is a quieter restaurant area with wood panelling. The varied menu attracts city workers at lunchtime and diners in the evening.
◐ ♿ ⇌(Central/Queen St) ⊖(Buchanan St) 🚌

Esquire House ✔

1487 Great Western Road, Anniesland, G12 0AU

11-11 (midnight Fri & Sat); 2.30-11 Sun

☎ (0141) 341 1130

Caledonian Deuchars IPA; Greene King Abbot; guest beers Ⓗ

Smart, modern pub with a long, split level interior. A corner space and a raised area to one side of the central counter are reserved for families. Large windows overlook the patio garden and car park which leads to a busy main road with frequent buses. Ten handpumps dispense two regular and up to six guest ales. The pub is popular with Anniesland residents and regulars from further afield, who come to enjoy the fine ales and food.
Q ✿ ◐ ♿ ⇌(Anniesland) 🚌(20,66) P

Horseshoe Bar ★

17-21 Drury Street, G2 5AE

11 (12.30 Sun)-midnight

☎ (0141) 229 5711

Caledonian Deuchars IPA, 80; guest beers Ⓗ

This CAMRA National Inventory listed pub is not to be missed. The horseshoe theme is everywhere, represented in mirrors, fireplaces and the original horseshoe-shaped counter dating from 1884, the longest in the UK. Atop the gantry is a large statue of a black horse striding through a giant golden horseshoe. Also look out for the superb stained glass windows and ceiling panel and mosaic floor squares. The four reasonably priced ales and good value food makes this pub very popular.
◐ ♿ ⇌(Central) ⊖(St Enoch/Buchanan St)

Mulberry Street

778 Pollokshaws Road, G41 2AE

11-11 (midnight Fri & Sat); 12.30-11 Sun

☎ (0141) 424 0858

Caledonian Deuchars IPA; Harviestoun Bitter & Twisted; guest beers Ⓗ

Family run café bar and restaurant strongly supported by the locals. It is situated in the Strathbungo Conservation Area associated with famed Glasgow architect Alexander 'Greek' Thompson, whose work can be viewed at nearby Moray Palace. Large windows provide views to the busy street (a major bus route) and nearby Queen's Park. The regular beers are often supplemented by a guest and there is a selection of imported ales. Food is available in the bar and restaurant. The bar can be busy at weekends.
◐ ♿ ⇌(Queen's Park/Pollokshields West) 🚌

Pot Still

154 Hope Street, G2 2TH

11-11 (midnight Thu-Sat); 6pm-11 Sun

☎ (0141) 333 0980 🌐 thepotstill.co.uk

Caledonian Deuchars IPA; guest beers Ⓗ

Cosy city pub with upholstered seating along the walls and a mezzanine corner with views over the main bar room. The decor is dark wood, creating an olde-worlde feel. The gantry displays a selection of around 400 malt whiskies including rarities. Four handpumps dispense at least three ales including two guests, usually Scottish. A retreat from the busy city, the pub is frequented by city workers, businessmen and whisky lovers. On a major bus route and near Central station.
⇌(Central/Queen St) ⊖(Buchanan St) 🚌

Samuel Dows

69-71 Nithsdale Road, G41 2PZ

11-11 (midnight Fri & Sat); 12.30-11 Sun

☎ (0141) 423 0107

Caledonian Deuchars IPA; guest beers Ⓗ

Traditional locals' pub within Glasgow's original railway suburb and conservation area Strathbungo on the city's south side. Two ales are provided with London Pride a popular guest. In addition to the narrow bar room there is a larger function room up steps to the rear, where live bands are hosted from Thursday to Saturday and occasional Sundays. There are several large, strategically placed TV screens to ensure that patrons do not miss a moment of sports action. Food is served until 6pm daily.
◐ ⇌(Pollokshields West/Queen's Pk) 🚌 ⚊

State Bar

148 Holland Street, G2 4NG

11 (12.30 Sun)-midnight

☎ (0141) 332 2159

Caledonian Deuchars IPA, 80; Houston Killellan; Stewart Edinburgh No.3 Premium Scotch Ale; guest beers Ⓗ

Current Glasgow CAMRA Pub of the Year, sited just off the city's famous Sauchiehall Street and near the Kings Theatre. A Glasgow coat of arms, historical photographs and theatrical memorabilia are much in evidence. The large island bar with brass rails and a tall gantry serves several distinct areas, some divided by screens and alcoves. Four regular beers plus three guests are on handpump. Good value food is available. Live blues plays on Tuesday night. ◐ ⇌(Charing Cross) ⊖(Cowcaddens) 🚌

Tennents ✔

191 Byres Road, G12 8TN

11-11 (midnight Thu-Sat); 12.30-11 Sun

☎ (0141) 341 1021

Cairngorm Wild Cat; Caledonian Deuchars IPA, 80; Harviestoun Bitter & Twisted; Orkney Dark Island; Taylor Landlord; guest beers Ⓗ

Situated on a busy road junction, Tennents has been at the centre of the city's West End since

SCOTLAND

its establishment in the late 19th century. The large U-shaped bar serves a constantly changing and varied clientele including locals, shoppers, students and academics, some who come to watch TV on one of the many screens, others to talk or read a newspaper. Six regular and six guest ales are on offer and good value meals are served all day.
◑⊖(Hillhead/Kelvinhall)🚌

Three Judges ✔
141 Dumbarton Road, G11 6PR
⊙ 11-11 (midnight Fri; 11.45 Sat); 12.30-11 Sun
☎ (0141) 337 3055
Beer range varies Ⓐ
Close to Kelvingrove Museum and Art Gallery, Kelvinhall and the Museum of Transport, this traditional corner tenement pub has won numerous awards. A varied clientele enjoys eight changing ales from small English and Scottish micros, plus traditional farmhouse cider. Trad jazz is played on Sunday afternoon in a raised corner area at the front, which looks out to busy Partick Cross. A rear area provides more peace and privacy. Pork pies are available, but customers may bring in their own takeaway meals.
⇌(Partick)⊖(Kelvinhall)🚌●

Toby Jug
97 Hope Street, G2 6LL
⊙ 11-11 (midnight Thu-Sat); 12.30-midnight Sun
☎ (0141) 221 4159
Beer range varies Ⓗ
Sited opposite the north entrance to Central station and a bus stop on a major bus route, this is an ideal pub for travellers, commuters and shoppers. The large room is subdivided by booths with a raised, quieter area to the rear. Window seats at the front provide views to the station forecourt. The main bar area can be busy at weekends. Four handpumps supply a constantly changing selection of ales from north and south of the border.
◐♿⇌(Central/Queen St)⊖(Buchanan St/St Enoch)🚌

Gourock

Spinnaker Hotel
121 Albert Road, PA19 1BU
⊙ 11-midnight (12.30am Thu; 1am Fri & Sat); 12.30-midnight Sun
☎ (01475) 633107 🌐 spinnakerhotel.co.uk
Belhaven 80/-; guest beers Ⓗ
Family run hotel situated in a listed sandstone Victorian building on the coast road heading west out of Gourock. Three ever changing guest ales supplement the regular beer. All food is home made with an accent on local produce. A highlight for any first time visitor to this pub is the view from the large bay windows and front patio looking out across the Firth of Clyde to Dunoon and the beginning of the Highlands. Q❀🛏◐◑

Greenock

James Watt ✔
80-92 Cathcart Road, PA15 1DD
⊙ 11-11 (midnight Thu; 1am Fri & Sat); 12.30-midnight Sun
☎ (01475) 722640
Greene King Abbot; guest beers Ⓗ
Easy to find near the Central train station, this is a roomy, town centre Wetherspoon's with typical JDW trimmings. It has good wheelchair access and a separate area for families. Food is popular and served all day. Guest beers come from local breweries as well as further afield. Outside is a heated patio. ❀◑♿⇌(Central)

Hamilton

George Bar
18 Campbell Street, ML3 6AS (off Cadzow St)
⊙ 12-11.45 (1am Fri; 11.45 Sat); 12.30-11.45 Sun
☎ (01698) 424 225 🌐 thegeorgebar.com
Beer range varies Ⓗ
Now one of Lanarkshire's longest established quality real ale pubs, situated near the bus station. The range of three constantly changing beers increases during twice-yearly beer festivals. Top class home made food is available except on Sunday when there is free soup to compensate. Over recent years the pub has been gradually renovated while retaining its character. It is popular with locals, regulars and visitors who come from near and far to this award-winning pub.
❀◐▲⇌(Central)🚌

Houston

Fox & Hounds
South Street, PA6 7EN
⊙ 11-midnight (12.30am Fri & Sat); 12.30-midnight Sun
☎ (01505) 612448 🌐 houston-brewing.co.uk/
Houston Killellan, Peter's Well, Texas, Warlock Stout, seasonal beers; guest beers Ⓗ
This 17th-century coaching inn is also the home of the Houston Brewing Co. The large and comfortable lounge bar, with a viewing window to the brewery, is decorated with hunting memorabilia and paintings. The Stables Bar has large alcoves with tables and benches, pool table, large screen TV and fruit machine. Upstairs is the Huntsman's Bar with two restaurants offering a la carte and bar menus. Food is served all day as well as a traditional roast on Sunday. ◐◑⊟♿P

Johnstone

Coanes
26-28 High Street, PA5 8AH
⊙ 11-11.30pm (midnight Fri & Sat); 12.30-11.30 Sun
☎ (01505) 322925
Caledonian Deuchars IPA, 80; guest beers Ⓗ
This town centre bar and lounge is a regular front runner for local CAMRA Pub of the Year. The lounge has a raised area that doubles as a restaurant while the bar has fake beams and a friendly atmosphere. Seven real ales are on handpump, always including one from the Kelburn range. Q◐◑♿⇌

Kilbarchan

Glen Leven Inn
25 New Street, PA10 2LN (A737 to Kilbarchan slip road)
⊙ 11-11 (midnight Thu; 1am Fri & Sat); 12.30-11 Sun
☎ (01505) 702481

Beer range varies Ⓗ
Very friendly pub in a conservation village with a restaurant and comfortable lounge. The well-stocked bar has two handpumps supplying various guest ales. Entertainment includes get-togethers by local groups and quiz nights. (35)

Trust Inn
8 Low Barholm, PA10 2ET
11.45-11.30; 11-1am Fri & Sat
(01505) 702401
Caledonian Deuchars IPA; Tetley Burton Ale; guest beers Ⓗ
Spacious and light contemporary-style village pub with a welcoming atmosphere. Although it has no family room, children are permitted. A large screen is used to show sports and there is regular entertainment including bands and quiz nights. The guest beer is usually from Houston Brewery. (36)

Kirkintilloch

Kirky Puffer
1-11 Townhead, G66 1NG next to canal
11 (12.30 Sun)-midnight
(0141) 775 4140
Caledonian Deuchars IPA; Greene King Abbot; guest beers Ⓗ
Wetherspoon conversion of a former police station, subdivided into several different areas with some rooms that were probably once cells. Six handpumps dispense two regular and four guest ales, including some from local micros. Major attractions nearby are the Forth & Clyde Canal and Roman Antonine Way making the pub a convenient watering hole for tourists. It is also popular with locals and families. Several regular bus services from Glasgow serve the town. Q

Lanark

Horse & Jockey
56 High Street, ML11 7ES
11-midnight (11.45 Sat); 12.30-11 Sun
(01555) 664 825
Beer range varies Ⓗ
This site in the centre of Lanark has been home to a pub for 300 years. The public bar at the front has a low, narrow corridor leading to the lounge/diner at the rear. The pub's name is one of the few remaining reminders that horse racing once flourished in Lanark. There is occasional live music in the small bar. Tourists visiting nearby New Lanark Village and the Falls of Clyde receive a warm welcome from locals and staff. Beers are from micro-breweries on rotation. (41)

Wallace Cave
11 Bloomgate, ML11 9ET
11-1am (11.45pm Sat); 12.30-1am Sun
(01555) 663 662
Beer range varies Ⓗ
A historic locals' pub in a historic town – the site has associations with William Wallace. The single room interior is split in such a way that half has the feel of a public bar and the other half a lounge. There is also an upstairs function room. The house beer is from Houston with a rotating guest, most commonly from Stewart. No food is usually available but there are free pies on special occasions. The pub opens at 7am during the local Lanimers Festival.

Lochwinnoch

Brown Bull
33 Main Street, PA12 4AH
12-11 (midnight Fri; 11.45 Sat); 12.30-11 Sun
(01505) 843250
Caledonian Deuchars IPA; guest beers Ⓗ
Traditional village inn popular with locals and outdoor sports enthusiasts. It has a bare stone and stained wood interior, a friendly atmosphere and helpful staff. The two guest ales change regularly, covering a wide range of beer styles and coming from many regional breweries. Food is served in the upstairs restaurant.

Milngavie

Talbot Arms
30 Main Street, G62 6BU
11-11 (midnight Thu & Sat; 1am Fri); 12.30-11 Sun
(0141) 955 0981
Caledonian Deuchars IPA, 80; guest beers Ⓗ
Corner bar, frequented by locals and visitors walking the West Highland Way. Following a refurbishment the large room is now open plan, but two original wooden dividers with frosted glass panels survive. Three distinct areas are formed by the central counter which dispenses two regular ales plus a guest. Four TV screens show sport and on match days the pub can be boisterous. Regulars can tell stories of Rob Roy MacGregor's escapades in the locality.

Milton of Campsie

Kincaid House Hotel
Birdston Road, G66 8BZ (signed on B757, just S of village at end of long, wooded drive) NS650759
11-11.30 (1am Fri); 12.30-midnight Sun
(0141) 776 2226 kincaidhouse.com
Beer range varies Ⓗ
After negotiating the long driveway to this Scottish country house, visitors must walk round to a smaller building at the rear where the real ale is served. A long counter separates the pool table and lounge areas. Two handpumps serve a rotating selection of beers, mostly from national breweries. Meals are popular with local families and tourists walking the Antonine Way and Campsie Hills. The pub is child-friendly with a safe garden. (85) P

Paisley

Gabriels
33-35 Gauze Street, PA1 1EX
11-midnight (1am Fri & Sat); 12.30-midnight Sun
(0141) 887 8204
Beer range varies Ⓗ
Popular town centre pub serving two or three real ales, and up to six at times, featuring beers from the Houston and Kelburn breweries. A large-screen TV shows all popular sports. Good food is served daily and a

separate function room is available for hire. ◐≷(Gilmour St)

Last Post ✔
2 County Square, PA1 1BN
11-midnight (1am Fri & Sat); 12.30-midnight Sun
☎ (0141) 849 6911
Greene King Old Speckled Hen, Abbot; guest beers Ⓗ
Large Wetherspoon's hostelry situated in a building that used to be the main post office. It has an open plan design, plenty of seating downstairs and more on the upstairs balcony. The standard Wetherspoon's food menu is available. Situated next to the entrance to Gilmour Street station, the pub is handy for a pint between trains. Q◑♿≷(Gilmour St)

Wee Howff
53 High Street, PA1 2AN
12-11 (1am Fri & Sat); closed Sun
☎ (0141) 889 2095
Caledonian Deuchars IPA; Houston seasonal beers; guest beers Ⓗ
Small town pub near the university, frequented by a varied clientele of all ages. The guest beer alternates between an offering from the Houston and Kelburn breweries. The Wee Howff has appeared in every issue of the Guide for the last 19 years. ≷(Gilmour St)

Strathaven

Weavers
1-3 Green Street, ML10 6LT
4.30 (11 Mon)-12.30am (1.30am Thu); 11-1.30am Fri & Sat; 7-1.30am Sun
Beer range varies Ⓗ
This family-run pub is the current CAMRA Lanarkshire Pub of the Year and was formerly the Crown Hotel. It takes its name from the traditional trade of the town. The interior is decorated with pictures of Hollywood film stars, from Laurel & Hardy to Arnold Schwarzenegger, now governor of California. There is always a beer available from the local Strathaven Brewery (its Clydesdale IPA is currently CAMRA Glasgow Beer of the Year), along with two guests. Note the restricted mid-week opening times. Q🚌(13)

Uddingston

Rowan Tree
60 Old Mill Road, G71 7PF
11-11.45pm (1am Sat); 12.30-11.45 Sun
☎ (01698) 812 678
Caledonian Deuchars IPA; Fuller's London Pride; guest beers Ⓗ
A real gem, this Grade B-listed building is one of CAMRA Scotland's True Heritage Pubs. Now sensitively refurbished, it retains many interesting features including extensive wood panelling, an impressive gantry, original cigar boxes, a wooden telephone booth and intriguing ornaments. The central bar, in a symmetrical room with two side rooms, has two handpumps. Situated in an area not well served for real ale, the pub is popular with locals and an essential visit. ⛰Q≷🚌

Uplawmoor

Uplawmoor Hotel
66 Neilston Road, G78 4AF (off A736)
12-2.30, 5-11; 12-midnight Sun
☎ (01505) 850565 🌐 uplawmoor.co.uk
Beer range varies Ⓗ
Popular village pub next to a 14-bedroom hotel. The interior is rustic and cosy with gentle lighting, red carpeting and wood panelling throughout. Bar meals are served all day and the hotel also boasts an award-winning restaurant. Weekends are particularly lively. Two beers are usually available – one from the Houston seasonal range and one from the Kelburn Brewery. ❀⇄◑⊟♿P

Wishaw

Wishaw Malt ✔
62-66 Kirk Road, ML2 7BL
11-11 (midnight Thu, 1am Fri & Sat); 12.30-midnight Sun
☎ (01698) 358 806
Beer range varies Ⓗ
Large Wetherspoon's pub with a single room interior divided into numerous sections on different levels, each with its own individual character. The decor highlights the history of the local area, especially its industrial heritage. Several interesting guest beers are served alongside two regulars. The food is above average Wetherspoons's fare. CAMRA Lanarkshire Pub of the Year 2008, it is popular with locals and convenient for travellers and visitors in an area with few real ale alternatives. ❀◑♿≷🚌(240,267)

Choosing pubs

CAMRA members and branches choose the pubs listed in the Good Beer Guide. There is no payment for entry, and pubs are inspected on a regular basis by personal visits; publicans are not sent a questionnaire once a year, as is the case with some pub guides.

CAMRA branches monitor all the pubs in their areas, and the choice of pubs for the Guide is the result of democratic voting at branch meetings. However, recommendations from readers are welcomed and will be passed on to the relevant branch: write to **Good Beer Guide, CAMRA, 230 Hatfield Road, St Albans, Hertfordshire, AL1 4LW**; or send an email to: **camra@camra.org.uk**

Authority areas covered: Highland, Western Isles

Applecross

Applecross Inn

Shore Street, IV54 8LR (on unclassified road off A896)
11-11.30 (midnight Fri); 12.30-11.30 Sun
(01520) 744262 applecross.uk.com
Beer range varies Ⓗ
Owned by the same family since 1989, the inn is spectacularly situated on the shore of the Applecross Peninsula, enjoying views of the Isles of Skye and Raasay. It is reached by a single track road over the highest vehicular ascent in Britain, or by a longer scenic route. Two handpumps dispense beer from the Isle of Skye Brewery. Comfortable accommodation is available and seafood is a speciality. Regular ceilidhs feature and the area is ideal for climbing, walking and wildlife watching.

Aviemore

Cairngorm Hotel

Grampian Road, PH22 1PE (opp train station)
11-midnight (1am Fri & Sat); 11.30-midnight Sun
(01479) 810233 cairngorm.com
Cairngorm Stag Ⓗ
The lounge bar of this 31-room privately owned hotel, though large, has a cosy feel, enhanced by two bay windows, distressed wooden furniture and a large coal effect fire. Though the trade is mainly holidaymakers, it is very popular with locals, with a large-screen TV showing only sport. There is a Scottish theme throughout the hotel with tartan wall coverings and Scottish entertainment on many afternoons and evenings.

Dalfaber Golf & Country Club

Dalfaber Drive, Dalfaber, PH22 1ST
11 (12.30 Sun)-midnight
(01479) 811244 macdonaldhotels.co.uk
Cairngorm Tradewinds; guest beers Ⓗ
Dalfaber Lounge Bar serves Tradewinds and one other guest ale from the local Cairngorm Brewery. With live entertainment most evenings and a Sunday night pub quiz, the bar has a lively, friendly and informal atmosphere where families are most welcome. It has two full size snooker tables and there is a leisure club attached with swimming pool and sports hall regularly hosting tournaments for local teams. All major sports are screened on TV.

Old Bridge Inn

Dalfaber Road, PH22 1PU
12-11 (midnight Thu-Sat); 12.30-11 Sun
(01479) 811137 oldbridgeinn.co.uk
Beer range varies Ⓗ
Busy pub, popular with outdoor enthusiasts, serving good quality food. Originally a cottage and now greatly enlarged, it lies on the road to the Strathspey Steam Railway, overlooking the River Spey. One of the three handpumps usually serves a Scottish beer. The Aviemore Beer Festival is held here in March. Children are welcome and there is a modern

bunkhouse attached accommodating 40.

Brora

Sutherland Inn

Fountain Square, KW9 6NX
11 (12.30 Sun)-midnight
(01408) 621209
Beer range varies H
Dating from 1853, this recently refurbished inn has two bars, one with a welcoming open fire. A good range of food is served including steaks and seafood, with vegetarians well catered for. In addition to beers from the Isle of Skye Brewery, a wide range of whiskies is available. The lounge bar and restaurant feature an exhibition of local photographs, which are available for purchase. There is free wireless Internet in all rooms throughout the hotel.

Carrbridge

Cairn Hotel

PH23 3AS (on B9153)
11-midnight (1am Fri & Sat); 12.30-11 Sun
(01479) 841212 cairnhotel.co.uk
Beer range varies H
In the centre of a pleasant village, just off the A9 and close to the Landmark Heritage Park, this busy pub is part of the hotel. It is popular with locals and visitors, particularly walkers and cyclists. The two handpumps dispense mainly Scottish ales including brews from Cairngorm, Isle of Skye, Caledonian, Orkney and Atlas. Bar meals, soup and toasties are available all day.

Cawdor

Cawdor Tavern ✓

The Lane, IV12 5XP
11-11; 11-3, 5-11 Oct-Apr; 11-midnight Fri & Sat; 12.30-11 Sun
(01667) 404777 cawdortavern.com
Beer range varies H
At the heart of this conservation village, the pub is a short walk from the famous castle and within easy reach of Fort George and Culloden battlefield. A pub full of character, it has a spacious lounge bar, cosy public bar and large restaurant. Both bars are wood panelled with log fires, the public bar featuring a splendid antique mahogany bar and a ceiling covered in old maps. It belongs to the same family that owns Atlas and Orkney, and features beers from these breweries.

Cladach Chireboist: North Uist

Westford Inn

HS6 5EP (5km NW of A867/865 jct) NF781655
11 (4 Oct-Mar)-midnight (1am Thu-Sat); 12.30-midnight Sun
(01876) 580653
Isle of Skye Red Cuillin H
Popular with local fishermen and tourists, this slightly eccentric and dog-friendly pub has a traditional atmosphere where a quick drink can turn into a ceilidh. A Georgian listed building on the edge of the Atlantic in a working crofting community with grazing highland cattle, it provides live music, both traditional and modern. Home-cooked pub food is available late into the evening and rea fires are fuelled by peat from the pub's own peat cutting.

Drumnadrochit

Benleva Hotel

IV63 6UH (signed, 800m from A82)
12-midnight (1am Fri); 3-11 (1am Fri) winter; 12.30-11 Sun
(01456) 450080 benleva.co.uk
Beer range varies H/G
Popular, friendly village inn catering for locals and visitors. A 400-year-old former manse, the sweet chestnut outside was once a hanging tree. Four handpumps dispense mainly Highlands beers, including Isle of Skye, with an occasional beer from the wood. Weston's cider is on handpump. Good evening meals and lunches are available (no lunches winter). The pub hosts the Loch Ness Beer Festival in September, occasional quiz nights and traditional music. A former local CAMRA Pub o the Year.

Fort Augustus

Bothy

Canalside, PH32 4AU
11-1am (12.30am Sat); 12.30-midnight Sun
(01320) 366710 lochnessrestaurant.co.uk
Caledonian Deuchars IPA; guest beers H
Situated in the centre of a busy tourist village beside the Caledonian Canal, Loch Ness and the Great Glen Way, this thick stone walled building has been put to many uses in the past, serving as a canal pay office, waiting room and exhibition centre. Two handpumps offer an Isle of Skye ale alongside the popula Deuchars IPA. A cosy, friendly bar area with an open fire leads to the conservatory where good food is served daily.

Fort William

Ben Nevis Inn

Claggan, Achintee, PH33 6TE (at start of Ben Nevi footpath) NN125729
11-midnight (1am Thu-Sat); 12-11.45 Sun
(01397) 701227 ben-nevis-inn.co.uk
Beer range varies H
Popular with walkers, mountaineers and local alike, the Ben Nevis Inn is in a unique locatio just outside Fort William, at the very foot of Ben Nevis. The characterful 200-year-old

INDEPENDENT BREWERIES

An Teallach Dundonell
Atlas Kinlochleven
Black Isle Munlochy
Cairngorm Aviemore
Cuillin Sligachan
Glenfinnan Glenfinnan
Hebridean Stornoway
Isle of Skye Uig
Plockton Plockton (NEW)

building, warmed by an attractive wood-burning stove, is famous for its informal and friendly atmosphere, an ideal setting for regular live music. A daily changing menu offers a mix of fresh local produce and exciting international dishes to accompany the choice of three real ales from local breweries.

Grog & Gruel

66 High Street, PH33 6AE

12-11 (1am Thu-Sat); 5-11 Sun

(01397) 705078 grogandgruel.co.uk

Beer range varies

In the shadow of Britain's highest mountain, this bare-floored traditional ale house keeps up to six beers in summer, fewer in winter. Owned by the same family as the Clachaig Inn in Glencoe, it holds regular live music and beer festivals. The beers are predominantly Scottish and the bar is busy with locals, outdoor enthusiasts and tourists. Home-cooked food is available in the upstairs dining room or from the limited bar menu. It has an interactive live web cam.

Nevisport Bar

Airds Crossing, High Street, PH33 6EU NN104741

11-11.30 (1am Fri & Sat)

(01397) 704921

Beer range varies

A warming open fire welcomes winter visitors to this cosy and informal lounge-style bar. The walls are adorned with a collection of classic mountaineering photographs and outdoor gear, giving an interesting insight into times gone by. The close proximity of the Ben Nevis mountain range, the end of the West Highland Way and start of the Great Glen Way, make this a favourite meeting place for outdoor enthusiasts. Mainly Scottish beers are served, often from Highlands and Islands breweries.

Fortrose

Anderson

Union Street, IV10 8TD

4 (11.30 Sat)-11.30; 12.30-11.30 Sun

(01381) 620236 theanderson.co.uk

Beer range varies

Homely bar in a quiet seaside village, part of a nine-bedroom hotel. The owners are an international beer writer and self confessed 'beer geek' and his wife, a New Orleans trained chef. Serving beers and ciders from independent breweries, this eclectic beer drinkers' mecca also offers more than 200 malts and 100 Belgian beers, earning it a prestigious UK award and the Belgian Ambassadeur d'Orval 2008. In the winter there is a barley wine festival. The food is reasonably priced, high quality international cuisine. CAMRA members are offered a discount on accommodation.

Gairloch

Old Inn

Flowerdale, IV21 2BD (opp harbour)

11-1am (11.45 Sat); 12-11.15 Sun

(0800) 542 5444 theoldinn.net

An Teallach Ale; Greene King Abbot; Isle of Skye Red Cuillin; guest beers

Traditional Highland coaching inn in a delightful riverside setting at the foot of the picturesque Flowerdale Glen. Up to eight real ales (three in winter) are served to accompany the enticing menu of home-cooked game and locally caught seafood. Convenient for Inverewe Gardens, Torridon and the Beinn Eighe Nature Reserve, this is an ideal base for outdoor activities. Spectacular paintings adorn the bar and there is a pottery, walkers' lodge and natural climbing wall in the grounds. Regular CAMRA Wester Ross Pub of the Year.

Glencoe

Clachaig Inn

PH49 4HX NN128567

11-11 (midnight Fri; 11.30 Sat); 12.30-11 Sun

(01855) 811 252 clachaig.com

Beer range varies

The Clachaig is almost as famous as the historic glen in which it is located. The main bar is the archetypal climbers' and walkers' pub with rustic wooden tables and stone floor. There is also a comfortable lounge plus a snug bar in the original beer cellar. Depending on the time of year, there are anything from five to 15 real ales on offer, mostly from Scotland's many thriving micro-breweries, as well as occasional cider.

(916)

Inverie

Old Forge

PH41 4PL (100m from ferry terminal)

11-midnight (1am Thu-Sat)

(01678) 462267 theoldforge.co.uk

Beer range varies

The most remote pub in mainland Britain can be reached only by ferry from Mallaig or a 15-mile hilly walk. In a spectacular setting on the shore of Loch Nevis, it provides an ideal location for walking the rough bounds of Knoydart. Moorings welcome waterborne visitors. The two handpumps serve mainly Isle of Skye beers. Excellent food is served all day featuring locally caught seafood specials. The pub has a relaxed atmosphere with impromptu music sessions – just pick up an instrument and play.

Inverness

Blackfriars

93-95 Academy Street, IV1 1LU

11-11 (12.30am Fri & Sat); 12.30-11 Sun

(01463) 233881 blackfriarshighlandpub.co.uk

Beer range varies

Across the road from the Ironworks music venue, this traditional town centre pub has a spacious single room interior with a large standing area by the bar and ample seating in comfortable alcoves. Guest ales are split between English and Scottish breweries with Scottish beers often from An Teallach and Highland. Good value meals feature home-cooked Scottish fare with daily specials. A

SCOTLAND

music oriented pub, it hosts ceilidh, folk, country and jazz nights, with local bands often performing at weekends. ◑▲≠⊟●

Castle Tavern

1 View Place, IV2 4SA (top of Castle Street) NH666449
✪ 11-11 (midnight Thu-Sat); 12.30-11.45 Sun
☎ (01463) 718178 ⊕ castletavern.net
Beer range varies ⊞
This 19th-century listed building, facing Inverness Castle and overlooking the River Ness at the end of the Great Glen Way, houses a buzzing city centre pub which has all the friendliness of a village local. A Victorian-style canopy covers the beer patio. Four handpumps dispense an Isle of Skye house beer plus changing guests mostly from Scottish independents. Bar meals are served all day, and there is a restaurant on the first floor. The Castle and the Clachnaharry Inn host the Inverness Beer Festival. ❀◑▲≠⊟⊱

Clachnaharry Inn

17-19 High Street, Clachnaharry, IV3 8RB (on A862 Beauly Road)
✪ 11-11 (midnight Thu-Sat); 12.30-11.45 Sun
☎ (01463) 239806 ⊕ clachnaharryinn.co.uk
Adnams Broadside; Greene King Abbot; Isle of Skye Red Cuillin; Orkney Dark Island; guest beers ⊞
A friendly welcome is guaranteed at this popular, award-winning 17th-century coaching inn, a regular local CAMRA Pub of the Year. Families are made welcome, and real log fires warm the cosy bars in winter. The lounge and large patio provide fine views over the Caledonian Canal sea lock and Beauly Firth toward the distant Ben Wyvis. Good value bar meals are served all day, every day, and beers from Highlands & Islands breweries regularly feature in the changing range of guest ales. ♨Q❀◑⊟▲⊟(19A)P⊱

Number 27

27 Castle Street, IV2 3DU
✪ 11-11 (12.30am Fri & Sat); 12.30-11 Sun
☎ (01463) 241999 ⊕ theroomandno27.co.uk
Caledonian Deuchars IPA; guest beers ⊞
Alongside the two handpumps, this popular city centre bar/restaurant stocks 17 draught keg lagers and ciders, together with a bottled range including many continental brews. Complementing the regular ale is a guest beer usually from a Scottish micro. There is also a good range of malt whiskies. Lunchtime food ranges from sandwiches to light bites; the comprehensive evening menu features more traditional main courses made with locally sourced ingredients including venison and steak. Free Wi-Fi access is provided. ◑♿▲≠⊟

Snowgoose ✔

Stoneyfield, IV2 7PA (On A96)
✪ 12 (12.30 Sun)-10.15
☎ (01463) 701921
Caledonian Deuchars IPA; Taylor Landlord ⊞
This traditional dining house supports a popular bar trade with an area reserved for customers who are not eating. Situated next to a Holiday Inn and a Travelodge, most of the custom comes from the local area. A converted 1788 coach house, the single large L-shaped room has alcoves and log fires to give it a more cosy and intimate feel. A wide variety of food is offered all day at reasonable prices. An extremely well run Mitchells and Butler's Vintage Inn. ♨Q❀◑♿⊟(1,10)P⊱

Nairn

Braeval Hotel

Crescent Road, IV12 4NB
✪ 12-midnight (12.30am Thu-Sat); 12.30-midnight Sun
☎ (01667) 452341 ⊕ braevalhotel.co.uk
Beer range varies ⊞
Real ale is served in the Bandstand Bar in this 10-bedroom hotel overlooking the Moray Firth close to Nairn beach. A comfortable, family run hotel renowned for its food, its award-winning chef uses fresh local ingredients to create a blend of imaginative dishes as well as traditional Scottish dishes and seafood specials. Three handpumps serve both Scottish and English ales, the Scottish ales usually from Orkney or Highland. ❀⊟◑▲≠⊟(10,305)P⊱

Newtonmore

Glen Hotel ✔

Main Street, PH20 1DD
✪ 11 (12.30 Sun)-midnight
☎ (01540) 673203 ⊕ theglenhotel.co.uk
Beer range varies ⊞
Small, welcoming hotel in Monarch of the Glen country in the Cairngorms National Park. It has a good local trade and is also popular with walkers and tourists. There is a large bar with separate games and dining rooms. Four handpumps dispense the house ale Glenbogle from Isle of Skye, one English beer, one Scottish beer plus a Weston's cider. An extensive menu includes a good selection of vegetarian dishes. The hotel holds the prestigious Eat Safe award and Cask Marque. ♨❀⊟◑♿▲≠⊟●P⊱

Onich

Corran Inn

Nether Lochaber, PH33 6SE (by E terminal of Corran ferry) NN022635
✪ 11-11 (1am Fri-Sat); 11-1am Sun
☎ (01855) 821235 ⊕ corraninn.co.uk
Beer range varies ⊞
Sitting on the shores of Loch Linnhe beside the Corran ferry, close to Glencoe and the Ben Nevis range of mountains, this is an ideal base for exploring a beautiful part of the Scottish Highlands. Once a temperance hotel, the bar was built on to the rear of the building, only accessible from an outside door. Food is served all day and guests planning long days on hill or glen can arrange early breakfasts and late evening meals. Real ales are usually from local brewers. ♨Q❀⊟◑▲⊟P

Plockton

Plockton Hotel ✔

Harbour Street, IV52 8TN
✪ 11-midnight; 12.30-11 Sun
☎ (01599) 544274 ⊕ plocktonhotel.co.uk

Beer range varies Ⓗ
Located in the heart of the beautiful village of Plockton, this popular hotel is set among a row of traditional waterfront buildings and boasts spectacular views over Loch Carron. Palm trees take advantage of a coastline warmed by the Gulf Stream. Locally caught fish and shellfish take pride of place on the award-winning menu. Close to the Isle of Skye and the mountains of Torridon, the village has much to offer and is a regular haunt for outdoor enthusiasts. ⩕Q☋❀⇌◑⊟♿≠♣P

Portree: Isle of Skye

Bosville Hotel

9-11 Bosville Terrace, IV51 9DG
⌚ 11 (12.30 Sun)-11
☎ (01478) 612846 🌐 bosvillehotel.co.uk
Beer range varies Ⓗ
Town centre hotel and bar, close to the bus station and picturesque harbour. The tastefully decorated bar has two handpumps, one selling the house ale, The Ditcher from the Isle of Skye Brewery, alongside an ale from the Cuillin Brewery. Relax and unwind in the friendly atmosphere after a day sightseeing, climbing or walking on the island. Excellent lunches are served in the bar and evening meals in the adjoining award-winning restaurant. ⩕⇌◑♿⊟

Rosemarkie

Plough Inn

48 High Street, IV10 8UF
⌚ 11-midnight (1am Fri; 11.45 Sat); 12.30-11 Sun
☎ (01381) 620164
Beer range varies Ⓗ
Beautiful old pub in a pretty seaside village just 100 metres from the beach. It has a cosy wood-panelled bar with an ancient marriage stone lintel (dated 1691) over the fireplace. A wide choice of beers is served from north of Scotland breweries including Orkney, Cairngorm, An Teallach and Hebridean. Food ranges from lunchtime bites to an a la carte menu featuring Black Isle produce such as lamb, beef and game. Booking is recommended. ⩕❀◑⊟▲⊟♣P

Roy Bridge

Stronlossit Hotel

PH31 4AG
⌚ 11-11.45 (1am Thu-Sat); 12.30-11.45 Sun
☎ (01397) 712253 🌐 stronlossit.co.uk
Beer range varies Ⓗ
Traditional Scottish inn situated at the foot of the Nevis mountain range, making an ideal base for outdoor activities or touring in the Highlands. Bar meals featuring local produce are available all day. The three handpumps dispense a selection of Scottish beers, often from the Highland Brewery, and an occasional cider. Opening times may vary in December and January. ⩕❀⇌◑♿▲≠⊟●P

Scourie

Scourie Hotel

IV27 4SX (on A894 between Laxford Bridge and Kylesku)
⌚ 11-2.30, 5-11; 5-9.30 (10.30 Fri) winter; 12-2.30, 5-11 Sat; 12-2.30, 6-10.30 Sun
☎ (01971) 502396 🌐 scourie-hotel.co.uk
Beer range varies Ⓗ
Popular with fishermen, this converted 1640 coaching inn overlooks Scourie Bay, handy for the bird reserve of Handa Island and the peaks of Arkle and Foinavon. The bar has a fishing theme with 1940s fishing nets as decoration. In addition to a fixed bar menu, the hotel dining room serves high quality four-course meals featuring seafood, with the menu changing daily. Four handpumps dispense mainly Scottish beer, usually from Cairngorm in winter, and one or two ciders.
Q❀⇌◑⊟▲♣●P⌐

Thurso

Central Hotel

Traill Street, KW14 8EJ
⌚ 11-11.45 (1am Fri & Sat); 12.30-11.45 Sun
☎ (01847) 893129
Beer range varies Ⓗ
Lively town centre hotel which offers something for the whole family. The downstairs sports bar (adults only), known as Top Joes, has large TV screens, a pool table and a choice of three real ales. The spacious upstairs bar and restaurant caters for all the family with a soft play area and bouncy castle. A good selection of home-cooked food including a children's menu is sold all day. An ideal base for touring Caithness, accommodation is available.
☋⇌◑⊟♿▲≠⊟♣▯

Uig: Isle of Skye

Uig Hotel

IV51 9YE
⌚ 11 (5 winter)-midnight (closed Jan); 12.30 (5 winter)-11 Sun
☎ (01470) 542205 🌐 uighotel.com
Beer range varies Ⓗ
This attractive and imposing family-run old coaching inn has spectacular views across Uig Bay to the ferry terminal for the Western Isles. The cosy lounge bar dispenses Isle of Skye beers from two handpulls in summer and one in winter. The friendly staff provide excellent service and meals are available in both the bar and adjoining restaurant. The hotel keeps its own highland cattle. Handy for a visit to the Isle of Skye Brewery. ⩕Q☋❀⇌◑♿⊟P

Ullapool

Morefield Motel

North Road, IV26 2TQ (off A835) NH125947
⌚ 12 (12.30 Sun)-11
☎ (01854) 612161 🌐 morefieldmotel.co.uk
Beer range varies Ⓗ
Locally caught seafood is the speciality on the menu at this friendly and welcoming hostelry. Three ales are predominantly from local Highland breweries. Landlord Tony organises

the annual Ullapool Beer Festival, held at the Morefield in October. Comfortable motel accommodation provides an excellent base for discovering the surrounding area. The Western Isles ferry terminal is a short distance away. Q❀⇌◑♿⛺♣P⅟

Waternish: Isle of Skye

Stein Inn ✓

IV55 8GA (N of Dunvegan, on B886) NG263564

11-midnight (1am Fri; 12.30am Sat); 4 (12 Sat)-11 (midnight Fri; 12.30am Sat) winter; 11.30 (12.30 winter)-11 Sun

☎ (01470) 592362 steininn.co.uk

Isle of Skye Red Cuillin; guest beers Ⓗ

Family-run 18th-century inn, the oldest on the Isle of Skye, located in a tiny fishing village on the shores of Loch Bay. Enjoy the warm fireside of a traditional Highland bar in winter or the loch-side beer garden in summer. Fresh seafood, landed at the nearby jetty, is served in season. Both inn and garden afford fine views over the sea loch to Rubha Maol. Facilities for seafarers include council moorings, showers, food supplies (by arrangement), and message relay services. ♨Q⛵❀⇌◑⊟♿♣P⅟

Whitebridge

Whitebridge Hotel

IV2 6UN

11-11 Apr-Oct; 11-2.30, 5-11 Nov-Mar; 12.30-11 Sun

☎ (01456) 486413 whitebridgehotel.co.uk

Caledonian 80; guest beers Ⓗ

Built in 1899, this hotel is situated on an original Military Road through the foothills of the Monadhliath mountains. There is a classic Wade Bridge nearby and the famous Falls of Foyers are close. It has fishing rights on two local lochs. The attractive pitch pine panelled main bar has an alcove with a pool table. The second handpump sells a variety of Scottish ales in summer. Most of the traditional pub food is home cooked. ♨Q❀⇌◑⊟🚌♣P

Benleva Hotel, Drumnadrochit.

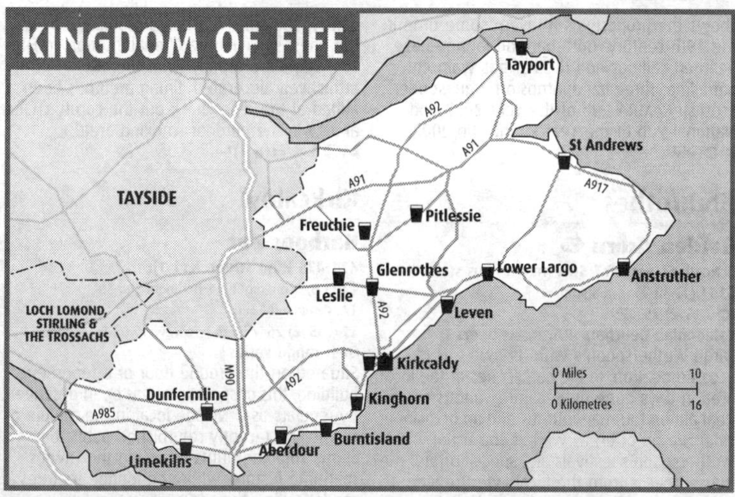

Authority area covered: Fife

Aberdour

Aberdour Hotel

38 High Street, KY3 0SW

4-11; 3-11.45 Fri; 11-11.45 Sat & Sun

(01383) 860325 aberdourhotel.co.uk

Caledonian Deuchars IPA; guest beers

Small, friendly, family run hotel in a popular town overlooking the Forth, handy for the golf course and beaches. The hotel started life as a coaching inn and the old stables are still evident to the rear. The cosy bar has one real ale during the winter, two in spring and summer. Excellent meals are available in the evening and at weekends, made with fresh local produce. (7)P

Anstruther

Dreel Tavern

16 High Street, KY10 3DL

11 (12.30 Sun)-midnight

(01334) 310727

Beer range varies

An ex Fife CAMRA Pub of the Year, the Dreel is housed in an old stone building in a fishing village on the Forth with traditional crow step gables and pantile roof. The public and lounge bars are separated by an open fire, and the conservatory to the rear provides a pleasant dining area. Local, freshly caught seafood features on the menu. Three beers are usually available. Q(X26,95)

Ship Tavern

49 Shore Street, KY10 3AQ

11-midnight (1am Fri & Sat); 12.30-midnight Sun

(01333) 310347

Caledonian Deuchars IPA; guest beers

An old traditional pub on the harbour front. The main bar has a picture window overlooking the harbour, which provides berths for around 100 boats. The bar has many pictures of working fishing boats and is the office for the Reaper, a herring drifter over 100 years old which still sails to sea festivals during the summer.

Burntisland

Crown Tavern

17 Links Place, KY3 9DY

11 (12.30 Sun)-midnight

(01592) 873697

Beer range varies

Two-roomed traditional small town pub with a lively, spacious public bar and even larger lounge with pool table. An attractive gantry, wood panelling and splendid etched glass windows create an old fashioned, traditional feel in the bar. One beer is on handpump with a second at weekends and busy times. (6,7)

Dunfermline

Commercial Inn

13 Douglas Street, KY12 7EB

11-11 (midnight Fri & Sat); 12.30-11 Sun

(01383) 733876

Caledonian Deuchars IPA, 80; Courage Directors; Theakston Old Peculier; guest beers

Well known ale house in a building dating back to the 1820s. A cosy town centre pub, it is situated opposite the main post office off the High Street. This is a pub for conversation, with quiet background music. Good quality food and friendly service assure an eclectic clientele. Eight ales are always available plus one cider. An extensive food menu includes regular specials, available lunchtimes and evenings Monday-Thursday. Fife CAMRA Pub of the Year 2005 and 2006.

Freuchie

Albert Tavern

2 High Street, KY15 7EX (half km E of A92 Kirkcaldy to Dundee rd)

11-2, 5-11; 12-1am Fri & Sat; 12.30-11 Sun

(07765) 169342

Beer range varies

Family friendly village local, reputedly a coaching inn when nearby Falkland Palace was a royal residence. An old photograph shows the property as a tavern some time in the 19th century. Both bar and lounge have beamed ceilings and the bar has wainscot panelling. Three handpumps offer guest beers. Scottish CAMRA Pub of the Year 2002 and National Pub of the Year Runner Up 2002.

Glenrothes

Golden Acorn

1 North Street, KY7 5NA (next to bus station)
11 (12.30 Sun)-midnight
(01592) 751175
Caledonian Deuchars IPA; guest beers H
Large Wetherspoon's with its own accommodation. In the bar, scenes of the local area in days gone by decorate various pillars. Real ale on four handpumps and an occasional cider are on offer, as well as the usual Wetherspoon's festivals and special offers. The house beer is from the local Fyfe Brewing Company. Families are welcome if dining until 6pm. The bus station is nearby.
P

Kinghorn

Auld Hoose

6-8 Nethergate, KY3 9SY
12 (11 Sat)-midnight; 12.30-midnight Sun
(01592) 891074
Beer range varies H
Busy village local situated on a steep side street leading off the east end of Kinghorn main street, handy for the station and Kinghorn beach. Popular with locals and visitors, the main bar has a TV and pool table to keep sports fans happy and features dominoes competitions at the weekend. The lounge is quieter and more comfortable with a relaxed atmosphere. Two regular and two guest beers are dispensed from three handpumps and one Scottish upright font on air pressure. (6,7)

Crown Tavern

55-57 High Street, KY3 9UW
11 (12.30 Sun)-11.45
(01592) 890340
Beer range varies H
Bustling two roomed local situated to the west end of the main street. Two ever-changing ales are dispensed by cheery bar staff. Beers are always from Scottish independents. Attractive stained glass panels feature on the windows and the door. Very much a football/ horseracing pub, there is a TV screen in the bar and a pool table in the rear room. A collection of signed footballs adorns the bar. (6,7)

Ship Tavern

2 Bruce Street, KY3 9TJ
12 (12.30 Sun)-midnight
(01592) 890655
Caledonian Deuchars IPA; guest beers H
One of the older buildings in Kinghorn, originally built as a house for Bible John who printed the first bibles in Scotland. The unobtrusive entrance door, which faces the main road, opens into a fine timber-panelled interior with a long bar counter and ornate gantry. The small jug bar is probably one of the finest surviving traditional interiors in Fife. Two beers are usually available. An attractively decorated dining area has been added at the rear. Check out the comfy chairs and TV in the outdoor smoking area.
(6,7)

Kirkcaldy

Harbour Bar

471-475 High Street, KY1 1JL
11-3, 5-midnight; 11-midnight Thu-Sat; 12.30-midnight Sun
(01592) 264270 fyfebrewery.co.uk
Beer range varies H
Situated on the ground floor of a tenement building, this unspoilt local has been described by regulars as a 'village local in the middle of town'. The recently refurbished public bar sports shipping prints depicting the town's maritime history, while the lounge features model sailing ships in glass cases. Six handpumps sell up to 20 beers each week from micros all over Britain, including those from the Fyfe Brewery situated to the rear of the pub. Fife CAMRA Pub of the Year several times, Scottish Pub Of The Year and national runner up in 2000.

Robert Nairn

2-6 Kirk Wynd, KY1 1EH (opp end of High St from bus station)
11 (12.30 Sun)-midnight
(01592 205049)
Beer range varies H
A Lloyds No. 1 with a split-level lounge and a separate family area. Several sections have bookcases and there are pictures of old Kirkcaldy. Six handpumps sell a variety of ales and there is one selling cider. Meals are served until 10pm.

Leslie

Burns Tavern

184 High Street, KY6 3DD
12 (11 Fri & Sat)-midnight; 12.30-midnight Sun
(01592) 741345
Taylor Landlord; guest beers H
Typical Scottish two-room main street local in a town once famous for paper making. The public bar is on two levels, the lower lively and friendly, the upper with a large-screen TV and pool table with football memorabilia on the walls. The lounge bar is quieter and more spacious. Pub quizzes are held on Wednesday and Thursday evenings and dominoes/darts/ pool competitions on Sunday afternoon. A good, honest, friendly community local. Two beers are usually available.
(X1,201)

Leven

Caledonian Hotel

81 High Street, KY8 4NG
11-11 (1am Fri & Sat); 12.30-11 Sun

INDEPENDENT BREWERIES

Fyfe Kirkaldy

☎ (01333) 424101 🌐 thecaledonianhotel-leven.co.uk
Beer range varies Ⓗ
The Caledonian Hotel is situated next to the cross on a pedestrian-only street, a five-minute walk from the beach and bus station. The hotel has been newly refurbished, now with seating on two levels, and the food oriented lounge has its own bar. A fresh, varied food menu is available, including the Big Roast on Sunday. There is a campsite 10 minutes' walk away.

Limekilns

Ship Inn
Halkett's Hall, KY11 3HJ (on the promenade)
11-11 (midnight Fri & Sat); 12.30-11 Sun
☎ (01383) 872247
Beer range varies Ⓗ
Long established village pub on the north shore of the River Forth with superb views from well placed seats outside. With its single room interior, the bar area at one end gets very congested on Friday and Saturday evenings while the seating area is quiet. Two ales from small independents throughout the year rise to three during the summer and holiday periods. Good quality home-cooked bar lunches have become more popular since the smoking ban was introduced so it is advisable to book a table for lunch.
(73,76)

Lower Largo

Railway Inn
1 Station Wynd, KY8 6BU
11 (12.30 Sun)-midnight
☎ (01333) 320239
Beer range varies Ⓗ
Small two room pub close to the picturesque harbour. The bar has a nautical theme, and also displays some photographs of the last trains to pass on the viaduct overhead before the Beeching measures of the 1960s. The beers usually rotate and include Caledonian Deuchars, Fuller's London Pride, Orkney Dark Island and Taylor Landlord. Q

Pitlessie

Village Inn
Cupar Road, KY15 7SU
11-2, 5-midnight; 11-midnight Fri & Sat; 12.30-midnight Sun
☎ (01337) 830595
Beer range varies Ⓗ
A typical Scottish village pub from the outside, the public bar is a pleasant surprise featuring bare stonework and an open fire. It has the feel of a bothy with bare wooden tables for dining. Good restaurant standard food is available at all times. Several rooms, one with an old Rayburn cooker, provide space for families, and pub games including pool. A cosy wee village local with the emphasis very much on conversation. Q

St Andrews

Aikman's Cellar Bar
32 Bell Street, KY16 9UX
6-midnight; 1-1am Thu-Sat
☎ (01334) 477425 🌐 cellarbar.co.uk
Beer range varies Ⓗ
This basement lounge bar has featured in the Guide since 1987, selling a good selection of real ales together with a variety of continental bottled beers. The rolled copper bar top was salvaged from the White Star liner Oceanic (same shipping line as the Titanic). Opening hours outside term time can vary and the bar is closed most lunchtimes but cask ales are available on request in the Bistro upstairs. Regular music and occasional beer festivals are hosted (see website for details).

Central Bar ✔
77-79 Market Street, KY16 9NU
11-11.45 (1am Fri & Sat); 12.30-11.45 Sun
☎ (01334) 478296
Caledonian Deuchars IPA; Greene King Old Speckled Hen; Theakston Best Bitter, Old Peculier; guest beers Ⓗ
Student oriented town centre pub, also popular with the locals. It has a Victorian style island bar, large windows and ornate mirrors creating a late 19th-century feel. The only pub in town that serves food until 10pm, pavement tables are available, weather permitting. A good mix of students, local business folk and tourists make this an interesting, bustling hostelry. Ten minutes' walk from the bus station.

Whey Pat Tavern
2 Argyle Street, KY16 9EX
11-11.30 (11.45 Fri & Sat); 12.30-11.30 Sun
☎ (01334) 477740
Beer range varies Ⓗ
Town centre pub on a busy road junction just outside the old town walls and three minutes from the bus station. There has been a hostelry on this site for a few centuries. It was taken over by Belhaven in 2002 but has changed little since then, with three beers on handpump. The front bar is L-shaped with a dartboard and TV, and there is an airy lounge/meeting room to the rear. A mixed clientele of all ages frequent this usually busy venue.

Tayport

Bellrock Tavern
4-6 Dalgleish Street, DD6 9BB
11-midnight (1am Thu-Sat); 12.30-midnight Sun
☎ (01382) 552388
Caledonian Deuchars IPA; guest beers Ⓗ
Friendly small town local opposite the picturesque harbour, with wonderful views across the Tay to Dundee and Broughty Ferry. The bar is on three levels, each with a mainly nautical theme, including old charts, photographs of ships and aircraft, old Dundee and the Tay Ferries. Good value home cooking is served at lunchtimes. One beer is on handpump with a second at busy times. Close to the Fife coastal path, the pub is well worth seeking out. Q

LOCH LOMOND, STIRLING & THE TROSSACHS

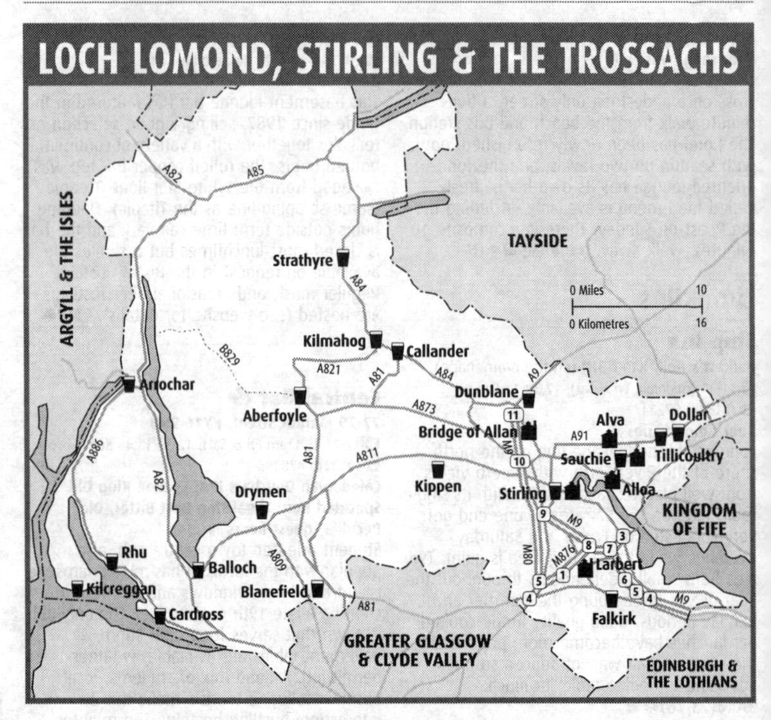

Authority areas covered: Argyll & Bute (part), Clackmannanshire, Falkirk, Stirling, West Dumbartonshire

Aberfoyle

Forth Inn Hotel

Main Street, FK8 3UQ

11-midnight (1am Fri & Sat)

☎ (01877) 382272 forthinn.com

Belhaven St Andrew's Ale; guest beers H

This 100-year-old inn is popular with locals and tourists alike. It has wood panelled walls in the bar and lounge, a restaurant and an additional function room. Situated within Scotland's first national park, there are many outdoor activities locally. This family-run inn is a must see for visitors to the Trossachs. Two beers from the Belhaven family are usually available. ⛬Q❀⇌◑◐♿Δ🚌♣P⁻

Arrochar

Village Inn

Shore Road, G83 7AX (on A814) NN293034

11-midnight (1am Fri & Sat); 12-midnight Sun

☎ (01301) 702 279 maclay.com

Caledonian Deuchars IPA; guest beers H

Situated just a mile from Arrochar/Tarbet station, the Village Inn and surrounding area provide a great day out, including a scenic journey from Glasgow. Good food and a selection of three ales, often from nearby Fyne Ales, are on offer. The garden has pines and views of Loch Long and the Arrochar Alps. This former Pub of the Year is an ideal base or stopping point for hill walkers and tourists. Friendly locals provide a warm welcome. ⛬Q❀⇌◑♿Δ🚌P⁻

Balloch

Tullie Inn

Balloch Road, G83 8SW (next to rail station)

11-midnight (1am Fri & Sat); 12-midnight Sun

☎ (01389) 752 052 maclay.com

Caledonian Deuchars IPA; Greene King Abbot; guest beers H

More than a century old, this inn has recently been refurbished in a comfortable, contemporary style, with split levels creating distinct drinking areas. The large beer garden is also on two levels, extending from front to rear. Up to four ales are stocked, with guest beers from local micro Fyne Ales. The pub is situated next to Balloch Station and Country Park on the banks of Loch Lomond and 45 minutes from Glasgow by train. Popular with locals and visitors. ❀⇌◑♿Δ≹🚌P⁻

Blanefield

Carbeth Inn

Stockiemuir Road, G63 9AY (on A809 N of Milngavie, near B821 jct) NS524791

11-11 (midnight Fri & Sat); 12.30-11 Sun

☎ (01360) 770 002

Beer range varies H

INDEPENDENT BREWERIES

Bridge of Allan Bridge of Allan
Devon Sauchie
Harviestoun Alva
Traditional Scottish Ales Stirling
Tryst Larbert
Williams Alloa

Despite the 1816 plaque, the building is older and there is evidence that Rob Roy held his stag night here. The main bar area with flagstone floor has a semi-divided quieter area and is overlooked by a stag's head near the passageway to the restaurant. A single handpump serves an ever-changing guest ale. The beer garden is a sun trap. The pub is popular with walkers exploring Mugdock Country Park and the West Highland Way, and bikers. There is live music on Thursday, a quiz on Sunday. Meals are served until 8pm.
⛰❀◑⛺🚌P⛳

Callander

Waverley Hotel

88-92 Main Street, FK17 8BD
🕔 11-midnight (1am Fri & Sat)
☎ (01877) 330245 🌐 thewaverley.co.uk
Beer range varies 🄷
Renowned for its quality and range of good ales, the Waverley also hosts two beer festivals each year in September and December. Four ales are usually available, increasing to around eight at the height of the tourist season, including some from mainland Europe. Ideally sited for tourists, it is on the whisky trail in beautiful Perthshire. The pub is also well known for its quality food made with local ingredients. Q🛏◑⛺●

Cardross

Coach House Inn

Main Road, G82 5JX NS347775
🕔 12-midnight (1am Fri & Sat)
☎ (01389) 841358 🌐 coachhousecardross.com
Caledonian Deuchars IPA; guest beers 🄷
This fine old coaching inn has been tastefully refurbished. In the smart public bar, locals enjoy playing pool and watching sport on TV. A comfortable lounge area opens into the dining room, popular with regulars who come to enjoy the good food menu for which the inn is renowned. In summer, meals may also be taken in the beer garden. A guest ale is available at the weekend. The pub is 35 minutes from Glasgow by train.
⛰❀🛏◑🖫♿⇌🚌(216)♣P⛳

Dollar

Castle Campbell Hotel

11 Bridge Street, FK14 7DE
🕔 11-11.30 (1am Fri; midnight Sat); 12.30-11 Sun
☎ (01259) 742519 🌐 castle-campbell.co.uk
Caledonian Deuchars IPA; Harviestoun Bitter & Twisted 🄷
Comfortable and well appointed hotel with a restaurant, lounge bar and two separate lounges. It is located in the centre of the historic and scenic village of Dollar on the southern side of the Ochil Hills, well placed for hill walking, golf and fishing. Castle Campbell is a pleasant walk up through Dollar Glen, with wonderful views over the Forth Valley.
⛰Q🛏◑🖫⛺🚌P⛳

Kings Seat ✔

19-23 Bridge Street, FK14 7DE
🕔 12-midnight (1am Sat); 12.30-midnight Sun
☎ (01259) 742515
Courage Directors; Harviestoun Bitter & Twisted; guest beers 🄷
A very popular inn with locals and visitors alike. The bistro-style restaurant serves quality meals at reasonable prices. Up to four ales are on handpump at any one time. An old coaching inn, the building has low ceilings and an old-fashioned feel. Located on the main street of a historic and attractive village at the southern foothills of the Ochils, the pub is well placed for rambling, golf and fishing, with Stirling just 15 miles away. ◑⛺🚌

Drymen

Winnock Hotel

The Square, G63 0BL
🕔 11-midnight (1am Sat); 12.30-11 Sun
☎ (01360) 660 245 🌐 winnockhotel.com
Caledonian Deuchars IPA, 80; guest beers 🄷
Located in the centre of a village five miles east of Loch Lomond, this hotel is convenient for those exploring Loch Lomond & Trossachs National Park and West Highland Way. The central room houses the bar and also serves the Scottish-themed Ptarmigan Bar on one side and a comfy lounge on the other. A wood fire built into the wall warms two rooms. There is also a function room, beer garden and conservatory. ⛰Q❀🛏◑♿🚌♣P⛳

Dunblane

Dunblane Hotel ✔

10 Stirling Road, FK15 9EP
🕔 11-midnight (1am Fri & Sat)
☎ (01786) 822178
Greene King Abbot; Taylor Landlord; guest beers 🄷
Situated next to the railway station, this is a popular stopping place for those on their way home from work. The bar is comfortable and decorated with old brewery mirrors. The lounge has an excellent view over the River Allan. Dunblane is well known for golfing and accommodation here is good if you like small, cosy surroundings. A range of national and micro beers is on offer, including three frequently-changing guest ales, so it is well worth a visit or two to try something new. Meals are served lunchtimes and evenings.
❀🛏◑🖫♿⇌♣P

Tappit Hen ✔

Kirk Street, FK15 0AL
🕔 11-11.45 (12.45am Fri & Sat); 12.30-11.30 Sun
☎ (01786) 825226
Caledonian Deuchars IPA; guest beers 🄷
Forth Valley's CAMRA Pub of the Year 2007, this is an excellent example of an old-fashioned pub popular with locals, with a wide range of cask ales on offer including up to three varying guest ales. A single bar room is partitioned into smaller areas by the use of screens. The pub lies next to Dunblane's famous cathedral. ♿⇌🚌♣

Falkirk

Wheatsheaf Inn

16 Baxters Wynd, FK1 1PF

SCOTLAND

11-11 (12.30am Sat); 12.30-11 Sun
☎ (01324) 623716
Caledonian Deuchars IPA; guest beers Ⓗ
A firm favourite with locals and real ale enthusiasts alike, this public house dates from the late 18th century and retains much of its original character. The bar is wood panelled and furnished in traditional style with plenty of interesting features from the past. A regular winner of local CAMRA Pub of the Year, including 2008, this is definitely one to visit. Two guest beers are usually available.
(Grahamston/Falkirk High)

Kilcreggan

Kilcreggan Hotel
Argyll Road, G84 0JP (At tip of Rosneath Peninsula approx 200m off B833) NS238805
11.30-midnight (1am Fri & Sat); 12.30-midnight Sun
☎ (01436) 842 243
Beer range varies Ⓗ
A typical Victorian mansion sited a modest walk from Kilcreggan Pier. The hotel can be approached by train from Glasgow to Helensburgh and from there by bus no. 316 around the scenic Rosneath Peninsula to Kilcreggan. It can also be reached by ferry to/from Gourock, all on a Daytripper ticket. Up to four beers are on handpump, mainly from local micro-breweries. Locals and visitors can take time to enjoy the food and great views over the Firth of Clyde. No evening meals are available at weekends. (316)P

Kilmahog

Lade Inn
FK17 8HD (A84/A821 jct, 1 mile W of Callander)
12-11 (1am Fri & Sat); 12.30-11 Sun
☎ (01877) 330152 theladeinn.com
Trossachs Waylade, Ladeback, Ladeout; guest beers Ⓗ
The Lade Inn goes from strength to strength, ever popular with locals and tourists. Its three cask ales are unique to the pub. Live entertainment is laid on most weekends. The beer garden allows you to compete with the midges for your pint in the summer. The Scottish Real Ale shop next to the pub has more than one hundred bottled beers on sale. A beer festival and tasting weekend takes place during the summer. The restaurant uses local produce as much as possible with good results. P

Kippen

Cross Keys Hotel
Main Street, FK8 3DN (on B822)
12 (12.30 Sun)-11
☎ (01786) 870293
Harviestoun Bitter & Twisted; guest beers Ⓗ
A very comfortable, traditional pub with a real olde worlde feel to the premises. It has a number of small rooms used mainly for dining, a small bar and a larger lounge/restaurant. Surrounded by lovely countryside, the location is ideal for tourists visiting Stirling and the Trossachs. QP

Rhu

Rhu Inn
49 Gareloch Road, G84 8LA
11-11.45 (12.45am Fri & Sat); 12.30-11 Sun
☎ (01436) 821048 therhuinn.co.uk
Caledonian Deuchars IPA; guest beers Ⓗ
Traditional, friendly local dating from 1648. Possibly the smallest bar in Strathclyde, but boasting mahogany features, Tiffany-style windows, real fires and a flagstone floor. The front overlooks a yachting harbour on the Firth of Clyde. There is a larger rear lounge and a small snug. The pub has a rare charm and is very popular with locals while extending a warm welcome to visitors. Live music plays at weekends. (316)P

Sauchie

Mansfield Arms ✔
7 Main Street, FK10 3JR
11-11.30 (12.30am Fri & Sat); 12.30-11.30 Sun
☎ (01259) 722020 devonales.com
Devon Original, Thick Black, Pride Ⓗ
This brew pub, manufacturing the glorious Devon ales, is the oldest operating brewery in the county. The pub is very popular with locals in this ex-mining community and families come to enjoy good value meals, served in the lounge. Situated close to the once famous brewing town of Alloa, the pub is on a frequent bus route to Stirling. Golf and fishing are available on the doorstep. P

Stirling

No. 2 Baker Street ✔
2 Baker Street, FK8 1BJ
11-midnight (1am Fri & Sat); 12.30-midnight Sun
☎ (01786) 448722
Beer range varies Ⓗ
Bustling, noisy pub, popular with local residents and students. There is live Scottish music on Wednesday, a 60/70s disco every second Friday and a live music event once a month on Saturday. The bare floorboards and paintings depicting local history create a traditional atmosphere. Greene King National Cask Ale Pub of the Year 2006.

Portcullis Hotel
Castle Wynd, FK8 1EG (close to Stirling Castle esplanade)
11.30 (12.30 Sun)-midnight
☎ (01786) 472290
Orkney Dark Island; guest beers Ⓗ
Situated close to Stirling Castle, the Portcullis is a busy pub renowned for fine food and good ale. Diners are advised to reserve a table in the evening and at weekends during the tourist season. Located in a former 18th-century grammar school, the building reflects the historic nature of its setting. It is popular with tourists and locals alike. Q

Settle Inn
91 St Mary's Wynd, FK8 1BU
3 (12 Sat)-midnight (1am Fri & Sat); 12-midnight Sun
☎ (01786) 474609
Beer range varies Ⓗ
Dating from 1733, the Settle Inn lives up to its name – settle down with a pint next to the

cosy fire and you may not want to leave, ghosts or no ghosts. Situated on one of the routes descending from the castle and attracting locals and visitors alike, the pub offers a friendly welcome. Excellent community links, a Sunday night quiz and a Thursday night open mike session all contribute to a lively yet civilised atmosphere. ⛫≹

Strathyre

Inn & Bistro

Main Street, FK18 8NA (on A84)
⏲ 12 (12.30 Sun)-11
☎ (01877) 384224 🌐 innatstrathyre.com
Orkney Northern Light Ⓗ
This pub has a main bar with an open fire and cosy atmosphere. Meals and snacks are available in both the bar and bistro. The inn is family run with the emphasis on local produce, both food and ales. It has hill walking, fishing, golf and water sports on its doorstep. Accommodation is available and families and dogs are very welcome. The beer range varies, usually including a brew from the Traditional Scottish Ales portfolio.
⛫Q❀⊭◑♿🚌♣P⁻

Tillicoultry

Woolpack

1 Glassford Square, FK13 6AU
⏲ 11-midnight (1am Fri & Sat); 12.30-midnight Sun
☎ (01259) 750332
Caledonian Deuchars IPA; Harviestoun Bitter & Twisted; guest beers Ⓗ
Originally a coaching inn, this pub retains the low ceilings and has a comfortable feel to it. Situated on the southern foothills of the Ochils on the start/finish routes on to the hills, it is very attractive to walkers. The pub is also popular with more mature locals, and you will always find someone with a tale to tell propping up the bar. Also ideal for golfing, fishing and touring, with Stirling 12 miles away on a regular bus route. **Q⊟⛺🚌**

Lade Inn, Kilmahog.

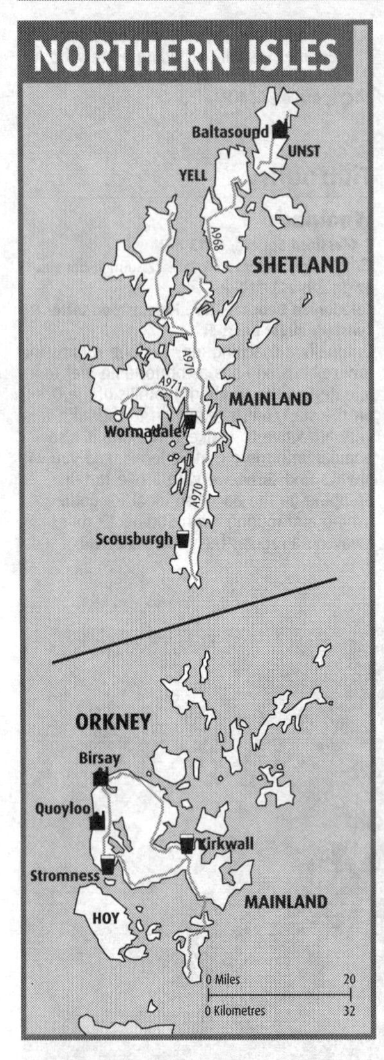

Kirkwall: Orkney

Bothy Bar (Albert Hotel)

Mounthoolie Lane, KW15 1HW
11-midnight (1am Thu-Sat); 12-midnight Sun
☎ (01856) 876000 alberthotel.co.uk
Highland Scapa Special; Orkney Red MacGregor, Dark Island, seasonal beers Ⓗ
Devastated by fire around three years ago, the bar has been rebuilt using a lot of the original timber. It is now on just one level and more spacious than before. In the centre of town, it is handy for shops, buses and ferries to the outer isles. A popular bar after work and part of the night scene at weekends. Meals are served daily.

Scousburgh: Shetland

Spiggie Hotel

ZE2 9JE (signed from A970 off B9122) HU379174
12-2, 5-11 (midnight Fri); 12-midnight Sat; 12.30-11 Sun
☎ (01950) 460409 thespiggiehotel.co.uk
Beer range varies Ⓗ
Small family-run hotel built as the original terminus of the Northern Isles ferries. It has a small stone floored bar and adjacent restaurant with views of St Ninian's Isle and the Loch of Spiggie. Birdwatching and trout fishing on the loch may be arranged. Three handpumps offer a beer from the local Valhalla Brewery and up to two summer guests. Q❀P

Stromness: Orkney

Ferry Inn

John Street, KW16 3AA (100m from ferry terminal)
9 (9.30 Sun)-midnight (1am Thu-Sat)
☎ (01856) 850280 ferryinn.com
Highland Scapa Special, seasonal beers; Orkney Red MacGregor, Dark Island, seasonal beers; guest beer Ⓗ
A former temperance hotel, this is a welcome sight after the ferry crossing from Scrabster. The hostelry is popular with locals and visitors, particularly the divers who come to Orkney to explore the wrecks of Scapa Flow. Local folk musicians meet regularly. Music features throughout the year and the pub hosts annual blues and folk festivals in conjunction with Stromness Hotel. ❀

Stromness Hotel

15 Victoria Street, KW16 3AA (opp pier head)
11-11 (1am Fri & Sat); 12-11 Sun
☎ (01856) 850298 stromnesshotel.com
Highland Scapa Special, seasonal beers; Orkney Red MacGregor, Dark Island, seasonal beers; guest beers Ⓗ
On the first floor of this imposing hotel is a large bar, the Hamnavoe Lounge, with windows and a small balcony overlooking the harbour. In winter a roaring fire and comfy settees welcome the visitor; during the season more space is given up to dining. Used as an Army HQ during WWII, the hotel is well placed for visiting world heritage sites such as Scara Brae and the Ring of Brodgar. Annual jazz, blues, folk and beer festivals are held.
❀P

Wormadale: Shetland

Westings Inn

ZE2 9LJ (8 miles N of Lerwick on A 971) HU398459
12.30-2.30, 5.30 (6.30 Sun)-10.30 (midnight if busy)
☎ (01595) 840242 westings.shetland.co.uk
Beer range varies Ⓗ
White painted inn in a stunning location near the summit of Wormadale Hill. It has marvellous views out to sea of Whiteness Voe, western Shetland and the outlying islands. Caravans are welcome and camping is available in the pub grounds. Evening meals are served by arrangement. The beer range usually includes one ale from the local Valhalla Brewery and up to two summer guests.
Q❀♣P

INDEPENDENT BREWERIES

Highland Birsay
Orkney Quoyloo
Valhalla Baltasound

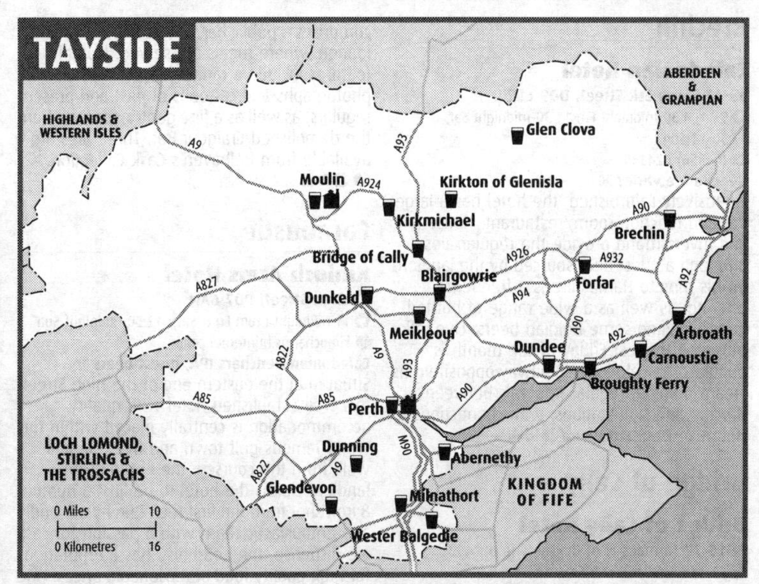

Authority areas covered: Angus, City of Dundee, Perth & Kinross

Abernethy

Crees Inn

Main Street, PH2 9LA

11-2, 5-11; 11-11 Sat & Sun

☎ (01738) 850714 creesinn.co.uk

Beer range varies H

Comfortable former farmhouse in a quiet village, lying in the shadow of one of only two Pictish watch towers in Scotland. A free house, the timber panels and beams display an impressive collection of pump clips reflecting the varied beer range. Up to six ales are available, often from English breweries. Hops adorn the beams in the lounge seating area. A good selection of meals is available lunchtimes and evenings made with fresh local produce. The village of Abernethy was once the southern Pictish capital of Scotland. Q❀⇌◑♿P

Arbroath

Corn Exchange ✓

Market Place, DD11 1HR

11-midnight (1am Fri & Sat); 12.30-midnight Sun

☎ (01241) 432430

Greene King Abbot; guest beers H

Wetherspoon's conversion of a large town-centre building that was built as a corn exchange in 1854. Good value meals are served all day and the famous Arbroath Smokies (smoked haddock) may be sampled just five minutes walk away at one of several 'fit o' the toon' cottages. The bar is equipped with eight handpumps usually offering three guest beers as well as Weston's Old Rosie cider. Beer festivals are held in spring and autumn when all handpumps are put into use. ⊄▲⊖P

Beer: A high and mighty liquor.
Julius Caesar

Blairgowrie

Ericht Alehouse

13 Wellmeadow, PH10 6ND

1-11 (11.45pm Thu; 12.30am Fri & Sat); 1-11.30 Sun

☎ (01250) 872469

Beer range varies H

Established in 1802, this friendly, traditional town centre pub has two seating areas divided by a well stocked bar. Recently refurbished, the lounge area features a log-burning open fire. The range of up to six beers varies all the time, with ales coming from Scottish and English breweries. Inveralmond is a local favourite. Liefmans Frambozen is available on tap and there is a good selection of bottled beer. Although no food is available, customers are welcome to bring their own. Weekends can be busy with occasional live music. ♨Q♿⊡

Royal Hotel

Main Street, PH10 6AB

11-3, 5-11.30 (11-midnight Sat); 12.30-midnight Sun

☎ (01250) 872226 theroyalhotel.rg.uk

Beer range varies H

Built in 1852 on the site of an earlier townhouse, the Royal Hotel commands a prominent situation directly opposite the former position of the town's Old Mercat Cross looking along Blairgowrie High Street. Outwardly it retains the charm and character of early Victorian architecture. Internally, the hotel has been renovated and tastefully refurbished to cater for the 21st century lifestyle and now offers outstanding facilities. ❀⇌◑♿🚌(57,58)P

INDEPENDENT BREWERIES

Inveralmond Perth
Moulin Moulin

Brechin

Caledonian Hotel

43-47 South Esk Street, DD9 6DZ
✪ 5-11; 4.30-midnight Fri; 11.30-midnight Sat; 12.30-11 Sun
☎ (01356) 624345
Beer range varies 🄷
Extensively refurbished, the hotel has a large bar and function room/restaurant. Houston and Inveralmond provide the regular ales although a guest beer sourced by the landlord on his trips to Hampshire is a frequent offering, as well as a wide range of bottled beer including some Belgian beers. Live folk music on the last Friday of the month is popular. The Caledonian Railway opposite runs steam trains at regular intervals between Brechin and Dun stations, with connections to House of Dun. ⛼Q❀⇌◑⊟♣⊱

Bridge of Cally

Bridge of Cally Hotel

PH10 7JJ (6 miles N of Blairgowrie on A93)
✪ 11-11 (12.30am Fri & Sat); 12-11 Sun
☎ (01250) 886232 🌐 bridgeofcallyhotel.com
Beer range varies 🄷
Situated beside the River Ardle in the heart of scenic Perthshire, at the foothills of the Cairngorms, the hotel provides a practical and unfussy base from which to enjoy the widest range of local pastimes and attractions. The 63-mile Cateran Trail, Scotland's newest long distance walk, starts and finishes at nearby Blairgowrie. Bar food is available for most of the day and evening, with the restaurant offering more formal dining surroundings. Two ever-changing ales are available, with Houston beers a regular choice.
⛼Q♘❀⇌◑⊟♿♣P

Broughty Ferry

Fisherman's Tavern Hotel

10-12 Fort Street, DD5 2AD (by lifeboat station)
✪ 11-midnight (1am Fri & Sat); 12.30-midnight Sun
☎ (01382) 775941
Beer range varies 🄷
Now owned by Belhaven, this 19th-century hostelry has developed from a small bar to a modest hotel with two bars, lounge and dining room. The public bar retains many original features including low ceilings, a wood and glass partition separating it from the snug, a corner table designed for a ship, and tongue and groove panelled walls. A former CAMRA Scottish and British Pub Of The Year, the hotel hosts an annual beer festival in its walled garden. Six ales are available from all over Britain, as well as foreign draught and bottled beers. ⛼Q❀⇌◑⊟♿⇌⊟

Royal Arch ✔

258 Queen Street, DD5 2DS
✪ 11-midnight; 12.30-11 Sun
☎ (01382) 779741 🌐 royal-arch.co.uk
Caledonian Deuchars IPA; guest beers 🄷
This strikingly refurbished street-corner bar in the centre of Broughty Ferry takes its name from a former Masonic lodge nearby, although the pub sign portrays the former Victoria Arch in Dundee's dockland. The welcoming interior comprises a public bar, where the ale is, and a lounge, where meals are served. Notable features include a range of sporting photographs and cartoons of past and present regulars, as well as a fine gantry, rescued from the demolished Craigour Bar. Three ales are available from Belhaven's Cask Collection.
◑⊟⇌⊟

Carnoustie

Kinloch Arms Hotel

27 High Street, DD7 6AN
✪ 11-midnight (1am Fri & Sat); 12.30-midnight Sun
🌐 kinlocharms.btinternet.co.uk
Caledonian Deuchars IPA; guest beers 🄷
Situated at the eastern end of the High Street, this well established hotel with quality accommodation is centrally placed within this world famous golf town and five minutes' walk from the course – the enterprising landlord claims the hotel to be 'just a number 8 iron shot from the first tee'. Run by a friendly and enthusiastic team with a passion for cask ale dispense, the hotel also has a reputation for high quality food at reasonable prices. One IPA and one guest ale are stocked.
⛼♘◑♿⇌⊟♣P⊱

Station Hotel

Station Road, DD7 6AR
✪ 11-2.30, 4-midnight; 12-1am Fri; 11-1am Sat; 12.30-midnight Sun
☎ (01241) 852447 🌐 stationhotel.uk.com
Beer range varies 🄷
In the same family hands since 1977 and part of the town's history, this hotel was formerly named the Panmure Arms after the local lord. The daily delivery of fresh fish and produce justifies the hotel's reputation for excellent quality meals, served lunchtimes and evenings. A collection of railway memorabilia and heritage photographs adorns both the lounge and busy public bar, where traditional games are played. One constantly changing guest beer is on offer. ⇌◑⊟♿⇌⊟P⊱

Dundee

Counting House ✔

67-71 Reform Street, DD1 1SP
✪ 9am-midnight; 11-midnight Sun
☎ (01382) 225251
Greene King Abbot; guest beers 🄷
This Wetherspoon's house maintains the elegant interior of a former bank, featuring a fine moulded ceiling and pictures of old Dundee. It stands on the corner of Reform Street and Albert Square near the splendid McManus Galleries and Museum. Good value meals are served from 9am and a range of four to six low-priced ales is available on handpump. ◑♿⊟

Phoenix

103 Nethergate, DD1 4DH
✪ 11 (12.30 Sun)-midnight
☎ (01382) 200014
Caledonian Deuchars IPA; Taylor Landlord; guest beers 🄷
A striking example of the kind of imaginative pub interior usually associated with Edinburgh,

the ceiling and pillars are original, but the bar and gantry reputedly came from a demolished Welsh pub. Unusual metal adverts, brewery mirrors – including a rare Ballingalls of Dundee – bric-a-brac and secluded seating alcoves all contribute to a place of great character, deservedly popular. The bar now offers an increased range of ales, mainly from Timothy Taylor, as well as several draught foreign beers.

Speedwell (Mennies) ★ ✔

165-167 Perth Road, DD2 1AS

11 (12.30 Sun)-midnight

☎ (01382) 667783 mennies.co.uk

Caledonian Deuchars IPA; guest beer

One of the finest examples of an Edwardian pub interior in the country and featuring in CAMRA's True Scottish Heritage Pubs, this bar was built for James Speed in 1903. However it is generally known as Mennie's, after the family who ran it for more than 50 years. The L-shaped bar is divided by a part-glazed screen, and has a magnificent mahogany gantry and counter, dado panelled walls and an anaglypta Jacobean ceiling. There are also two sitting rooms, separated by a glass screen. Q

Dunkeld

Taybank

Main Street, PH2 9LA

11-midnight (1am Fri & Sat); 12.30-midnight Sun

☎ (01241) 432430 thetaybank.com

Inveralmond Ossian

Known as 'Scotland's Musical Meeting Place', the Taybank is a haven for lovers of traditional Scottish and Irish music, often of a spontaneous nature. The small public bar is comfortable and full of character with an open fire and a large range of musical instruments including a piano. There is also a small music room where live events are regularly held. The garden is located on the banks of the River Tay looking across to Birnam Hill.
Q P

Dunning

Kirkstyle Inn

Kirkstyle Square, PH2 0RR

11-2.30, 5-11 (midnight Fri); 11-midnight Sat; 12.30-11 Sun

☎ (01764) 684248

Beer range varies

The Kirkstyle is a traditional village inn circa 1760, located in the centre of Dunning at the foothills of the Ochil range, dominated by the Norman steeple of St Serfs Church. It has a small public bar with a wooden floor and wood-burning stove where up to three ales are served – Harviestoun Bitter & Twisted and Greene King IPA feature regularly. There is a small snug area next to the bar, a restaurant area and a room downstairs with a pool table.
Q

Forfar

Plough Inn

48 Market Street, DD8 3EW

11-midnight (1am Fri & Sat); 12.30-midnight Sun

☎ (01307) 469288 ploughinnforfar.co.uk

Inveralmond Ossian, Thrappledouser; guest beers

This community local near the old railway station in the county town of Angus has earned a reputation for good food and cask ale since a change of landlord two years ago. It has three handpumps usually dispensing Scottish micros beers. The pub hosts many live music nights, and occasional beer festivals are held in the function hall. High teas are served at lunchtimes and evenings. Make sure to try a 'Forfar bridie'. As well as traditional pub games, foosball and backgammon are played here.

Glen Clova

Glen Clova Hotel

DD8 4QS (15 miles N of Kirriemuir)

11-11 (1am Fri & Sat); 12-11 Sun

☎ (01575) 550350 clova.com

Beer range varies

Comfortable country hotel in a magnificent setting, below the corrie of Loch Brandy. Once a drovers' inn dating from the mid 1800s, this is a popular venue for walkers, climbers, in fact anyone enjoying the great outdoors. The hotel has been upgraded and provides accommodation from bunk house to four-poster bedroom, plus two luxury lodges. Ales including Houston and Caledonian are served in the Climbers Bar. A beer festival is held every summer. Q P

Glendevon

An Lochan Tormaukin

FK14 7JY

11-11 (midnight Sun)

☎ (01259) 781252 anlochan.co.uk

Beer range varies

This former 18th-century drovers' inn is located in a peaceful setting surrounded by the Ochil Hills. The Tormaukin (meaning 'hill of the mountain hare' in old Scots) is an ideal base for outdoor activities such as walking, fishing and golf. Up to three ales are available with Harviestoun and Inveralmond beers among the favourites. Natural stone and timber, and real fires, help to create a warm and relaxing atmosphere in the two comfortable lounge bars. An extensive menu is on offer with traditional Scottish fare and international dishes. Q P

Kirkmichael

Strathardle Inn

PH10 7NS (on A924 Bridge of Cally to Pitlochry road)

12-2, 6-11 (11.30 Fri & Sat)

☎ (01250) 881224 strathardleinn.co.uk

Beer range varies

The Strathardle is an old coaching inn dating back to the late 1700s, retaining the original barn and stables. It has an attractive woodland garden along with a 700 metre beat of the River Ardle, offering salmon and trout fishing. An excellent base for exploring the Southern Highlands, the Cateran Trail passes in front of

SCOTLAND

the hotel and the Cairngorm National Park is a few miles north. Up to three ales are available depending upon the season, with a strong commitment to Scottish micros.
Q P

Kirkton of Glenisla

Glenisla Hotel

PH11 8PH (on B591 10 miles N of Alyth)
11.30-2.30, 4.30-11; closed Mon; 11.30-1.30am Sat; 12-11 Sun
(01575) 582223 glenisla-hotel.com
Beer range varies
An oasis for thirsty and hungry travellers, this 17th-century ex-coaching inn is also a centre for a large selection of outdoor activities including walking, fishing, shooting, skiing and pony trekking. Now fully refurbished, the hotel's cosy oak beamed bar with a wood-burning fire welcomes visitors and locals. Occasional traditional music sessions are held and various clubs meet in this social centre for Glen Isla. Dogs are welcome.
Q P

Meikleour

Meikleour Hotel

PH2 6EB
11-3, 6-11 (midnight Fri); 11-midnight Sat; 12-11 Sun
(01250) 883206 meikleour-inn.co.uk
Beer range varies
Warm, welcoming country village inn with a stone-flagged bar and comfortable lounge offering up to three cask ales. It is a popular venue for walkers and fishermen as well as those wanting a good meal or drink in a relaxing environment. The house beer, Lure of Meikleour, is brewed by Inveralmond. Nearby is the Meikleour Beech Hedge (100ft high and a third of a mile long), which was planted in 1745 and is recognised in the Guinness Book of Records as the tallest hedge in the world.
Q P

Milnathort

Village Inn

36 Westerloan, KY13 9YH
2-11; 11-11.30 Fri & Sat; 12.30-11 Sun
(01577) 863293
Inveralmond Thrappledouser; guest beer
Friendly village local at the heart of the village with a semi-open plan interior. There is a comfortable lounge area at one end with low ceilings, exposed joists, stone walls and log fire in the bar area. Unobtrusive pipe music adds to the relaxing atmosphere. The games room at the rear has a pool table. Nearby places of interest are the island castle on Loch Leven where Mary Queen of Scots was imprisoned and the RSPB site at Vane Farm.

Moulin

Moulin Inn

11-13 Kirkmichael Road, PH16 5EH
12-11 (11.45 Fri-Sun)
(01796) 472196 moulininn.co.uk
Moulin Light, Braveheart, Ale of Atholl, Old Remedial
First opened in 1695, the inn is the oldest part of the Moulin Hotel. It is situated within the village square of Moulin, an ancient Scottish crossroads near to Pitlochry, the 'Gateway to the Highlands'. Full of character and charm, it is furnished in traditional style with two log fires. A good choice of home-prepared local fare is available along with its own beer, brewed in the old coach house behind the hotel. An ideal base for outdoor pursuits, there are a number of marked walks passing nearby. Q P

Perth

Cherrybank Inn

210 Glasgow Road, PH2 0NA
11-11 (11.45 Sat & Sun)
(01738) 624349 cherrybankinn.co.uk
Inveralmond Independence, Ossian Ale; guest beers
Thought to be one of the oldest public houses in Perth, the Cherrybank has a well appointed lounge bar and a small public bar with two adjacent snug rooms. Up to five cask ales are available with a strong commitment to the local Inveralmond Brewery. Since its days as a drovers' inn more than 200 years ago, the pub has been a popular venue for passing travellers, situated on the western approach to Perth. The nearby Cherrybank Gardens are well worth a visit, with the UK's largest collection of heathers. Q

Greyfriars

15 South Street, PH2 8PG
11-11 (11.45 Fri & Sat); 3-11 Sun
(01738) 633036 greyfriarsbar.com
Caledonian Deuchars IPA; guest beers
Arguably the smallest lounge bar in Perth city centre, this is indeed 'aite blath agus cardeil!' – 'a warm and friendly place!', as it states over the entrance. It has a vibrant and friendly atmosphere with good value lunches served in the bar. Up to four cask ales are available, including the house ale Friars Tipple brewed by the local Inveralmond Brewery, with other Inveralmond beers regularly stocked. Ideally located on the edge of the shopping area, nearby attractions include a Victorian theatre, art gallery, museum and concert hall.

Wester Balgedie

Balgedie Toll Tavern

KY13 9HE
11-11 (11.30 Thu; 12.30 Fri & Sat); 12.30-11.30 Sun
(01592) 840212
Harviestoun Bitter & Twisted; guest beers
Welcoming and comfortable country tavern dating from 1534 which, like many others built at the time in Scotland, was situated at a road toll where travellers had to break their journey to pay tolls before travelling on. Now much extended, the oldest part of the building (the toll house) is at the southern end. It has three seating areas plus a small bar with low ceilings, oak beams, horse brasses, wooden settles and works of art by a local painter. A good selection of meals and bar snacks is available. Q P

Northern Ireland
Channel Islands
Isle of Man

NORTHERN IRELAND

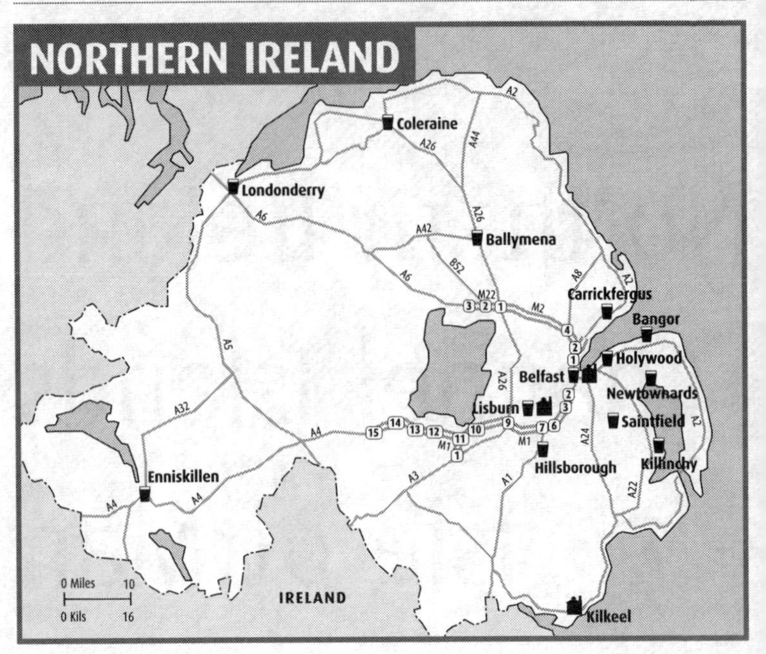

Ballymena

Spinning Mill

17-21 Broughshane Street, BT43 6EB

9-11 (1am Fri & Sat)

(028) 2563 8985

Greene King IPA, Abbot; guest beer

Spacious Wetherspoon's pub on two floors around 15 minutes' walk from Ballymena rail/bus station. There are a number of different areas to drink in and some unusual woodwork rescued from churches to admire. The upstairs bar has three handpumps and three screens showing major sporting events, while there are five pumps downstairs. Alcohol is served from 11.30am (12.30 Sunday).

Bangor

Esplanade

12 Ballyhome Esplanade, BT20 5LZ (opp Ballyholme beach)

11.30-11 (1am Fri & Sat); 12.30-10 Sun

(028) 9127 0954

Whitewater Glen Ale, Belfast Ale; guest beer

Large corner site comprising bar, lounge, off sales and upstairs restaurant, situated opposite the beach in the suburbs of town. A heated garden at the front has wonderful views of Belfast Lough and over to Scotland. The bar has two screens showing sport, and contains three handpumps. Friendly staff are willing to serve ale in the lounge or garden. The pub runs a quiz night and golfing society. A separate restaurant opens in the evening. On bus route B10 (not Sunday).

Belfast

Botanic Inn

23-27 Malone Road, BT9 6RU

11.30-1am; 12-midnight Sun

(028) 9050 9740 botanicinns.com

Whitewater Belfast Ale

Big, busy pub in the university area, not far from Queen's. Very popular with the student population, it has a number of screens showing football and rugby matches, so it can be very busy on match days. Good food is served from opening time until 8pm daily. Live bands play on Monday and Friday. There is a smaller, more traditional area of the bar where the ale is a little cheaper.

Bridge House

37-43 Bedford Street, BT2 7EJ (opp BBC building in Ormeau Avenue)

9-midnight (1am Thu-Sat)

(028) 9072 7890

Greene King IPA, Abbot; guest beer

Busy, friendly, Wetherspoon's outlet converted from a sports bar, with two bars, a large family area and an outside smoking area. It is popular with shoppers and guests at the nearby Holiday Inn, who come here for breakfast served from 9am. An excellent choice of foreign beers and a varied selection of ciders are on offer. Sky Sports and News play on screens without sound. No alcohol is

Keep your Good Beer Guide up to date by consulting the CAMRA website **www.camra.org.uk**

INDEPENDENT BREWERIES

College Green Belfast
Hilden Lisburn
Whitewater Kilkeel

served before 11.30am (12.30 Sunday). (Gt Victoria St)

Crown ★

46 Great Victoria Street, BT2 7BA (opp Europa Hotel and Great Victoria Street station)
11.30-midnight; 12.30-11 Sun
(028) 9027 9901
Whitewater Belfast Ale; guest beers H
Belfast's historic gem has been restored to its former glory during the past year. The interior has been cleaned up, real gas lights put in and the Victorian calling system made operational. The pub dates from 1885 and contains eight snugs, a unique find in the city centre. It has three handpumps, all dispensing Whitewater ales. Food is served in the bar and upstairs in the Crown Dining Rooms. Not to be missed by historic pub fans. (Gt Victoria St)

John Hewitt

51 Donegal Street, BT1 2FH (100m from St Anne's Cathedral)
11.30 (12 Sat)-1am; 7-midnight Sun
(028) 9023 3768 thejohnhewitt.com
Hilden Ale; guest beer H
Run by the Unemployed Resource Centre, the John Hewitt is a pub with a difference. It provides training and employment for unemployed people and hosts a range of art and musical events. No TV or jukebox here, just live music most nights and good food served at lunchtime. In the last year the bar has gained an extra handpump, usually dispensing Hilden and guest ales. In the centre of the Cathedral Quarter, the pub is often very busy. CAMRA Northern Ireland Pub of the Year 2008.

King's Head

829 Lisburn Road, BT9 7GY (opp Kings Hall at Balmoral)
12-1am (midnight Mon & Sun)
(028) 9050 9950
Whitewater Belfast Ale; guest beer H
Located opposite the King's Hall about three miles from the centre of Belfast, the pub is easy to get to by train or bus. The interior has three distinct sections – a dining area, public bar and very cosy lounge. The ale is on two handpumps in the public bar, usually from Whitewater Brewing. There is a restaurant upstairs which serves a variety of good food. Live music plays in the bar and in the attached Live Lounge on Saturday night.
(Balmoral)P

Kitchen Bar

1 Victoria Square, BT1 4QG (access off Ann St via Upper Church St)
11.30-11.30 (midnight Mon; 1am Fri & Sat); 12-6 Sun
(028) 9032 4901
Whitewater Belfast Ale; guest beer H
Now in its fourth year, the Kitchen is one of the newest bars in the city centre. It is easier to access now that building of the adjacent Victoria Square shopping complex is complete. Converted from a former shipping office, the Kitchen is a long, bright bar with friendly staff. There are usually two ales on handpump, mainly from Whitewater, and good food is available. Three screens show sporting events, and music plays on Friday and Saturday nights. (Central)

McHugh's

29-31 Queens Square, BT1 3FG (near Albert Clock)
12-1am (midnight Sun)
(028) 9050 9999 botanicinns.com
Whitewater Belfast Ale; guest beer H
Situated in the increasingly lively Customs House Square area, this is a modern pub built within an old building. It has a number of different drinking areas, and the bar has two handpumps serving Whitewater ales. Food can be eaten in the bar or in the upstairs restaurant. An outside terrace is pleasant for drinking on a sunny day. Sport and music feature heavily in the bar and in the basement. (Central)

Molly's Yard

1 College Green Mews, Botanic Avenue, BT1 4QB (behind Queen's University)
12-9 (9.30 Fri & Sat); closed Sun
(028) 9032 2600
College Green Molly's Chocolate Stout, Headless Dog H
Molly's Yard is a restaurant in the heart of Belfast's bustling University area, housed in the restored stables of College Green House. As Hilden Brewery's second restaurant, it won a best newcomer's award from the Restaurant Association of Ireland in 2005. College Green ales are served, but these are currently brewed at the Hilden Brewery and not on the premises. Last food orders is 9pm (9.30pm Fri & Sat). (Botanic)

Ryan's

116-118 Lisburn Road, BT9 6AH
11.30-1am; 12-midnight Sun
(028) 9050 9850
Whitewater Belfast Ale H
This corner pub situated on the Lisburn Road is modern looking inside, with several different drinking areas. The downstairs bar has one handpump and there is a restaurant upstairs. Patrons are generally students, locals or sports fans. A general knowledge and music quiz are held every week and live matches are screened. Ryan's is a popular pub and can get crowded. (Botanic)

Carrickfergus

Central Bar

13-15 High Street, BT38 7AN (opp Carrickfergus Castle)
9am-11 (midnight Wed; 1am Fri & Sat)
(028) 9335 7840
Greene King Abbot; guest beer H
Smallish but otherwise typical Wetherspoon's in the town centre with excellent views of the adjacent 12th-century castle. The lively ground floor public bar has a TV (sound usually off), and the quieter family-friendly first floor lounge, decorated in standard Wetherspoon's style, is occasionally enlivened by entertainingly fractious children. Food and real ale are available on both levels, served by an eclectic group of hard-working staff. Alcoholic refreshments are available from 11.30am (12.30pm Sun).

Coleraine

Old Courthouse

Castlerock Road, BT51 3HP

9am-11 (1am Fri & Sat)

(028) 7032 5820

Greene King Abbot; guest beer

Formerly a county courthouse, this is now an outstanding Wetherspoon's outlet. A large, bright pub with two floors, the bar is downstairs and a dining area upstairs. A range of ales is available from five handpumps, along with good value food. Drinking on the patio area is popular when the weather is good. In common with other pubs in the chain, alcohol is not served until 11.30am and 12.30 on Sunday.

Enniskillen

Linen Hall

11-13 Townhall Street, BT74 7BD

10-11 (1am Fri & Sat)

(028) 6634 0910

Greene King Abbot; guest beer

A very popular Wetherspoon's pub in the centre of town opposite the bus station. It has four distinct areas: the front entrance, bar, rear door, and a family area at the back. The bar features five handpumps and Weston's cider on gravity. In common with other Wetherspoon's in the province the screens show news and sport, usually with the sound turned off. Enniskillen is 85 miles from Belfast, and is well worth visiting. Alcohol is not served until 11.30am (12.30 Sunday).

Hillsborough

Hillside

21 Main Street, BT26 6AE

12-11.30 (1am Fri & Sat); 12-11 Sun

(028) 9268 2765

Whitewater Belfast Ale; guest beer

This former local CAMRA Pub of the Year has a public bar and a food area known as The Refectory. There are three handpumps in the public bar usually serving Whitewater ales with occasional guests. A heated beer garden at the side doubles as a smoking area. Hillsborough is about 12 miles from Belfast, and the Hillside is halfway up the steep main street that dominates the village.

Q

Holywood

Dirty Duck Ale House

3 Kinnegar Road, BT18 9JW (by railway station)

11.30-11.30 (1am Thu-Sat); 12.30-midnight Sun

(028) 9059 6666

Beer range varies

Picture windows in the bar and upstairs restaurant give superb views of Belfast Lough. Live music plays on Thursday to Saturday nights, with traditional Irish music on the last Wednesday of the month. The pub has a golfing society and runs a quiz every Tuesday. Three handpumps dispense beers from Tom Wood, Inveralmond and Hilden breweries. Extra handpumps are installed for the annual August beer festival. There is a new covered, heated area for smokers.

Killinchy

Daft Eddy's

Sketrick Island, BT23 6QH

11.30-11.30 (1am Fri); 12-10.30 Sun

(028) 9754 1615

Whitewater Belfast Ale; guest beer

This is a public bar, lounge and restaurant in a very desirable location overlooking Whiterock Bay. One handpump features Belfast and other Whitewater ales. The restaurant is highly recommended, specialising in seafood (book in advance). There is a TV and pool table in the public bar, and a piano player entertains on Sunday night. The pub is not easy to find, but is well worth seeking out for the superb views over the Bay. Q P

Lisburn

Tap Room

Hilden Brewery, Hilden, BT27 4TY (5 minutes' walk from Hilden railway halt)

11.30-2.30, 5.30-9; closed Monday; 12.30-3 Sun

(028) 9266 3863

Hilden Molly Malone; guest beer

This is Hilden Brewery's own licensed restaurant where good food is available and ales from the brewery next door are served to diners. A short walk from Hilden station, the Tap Room is in a beautiful location beside the family's Georgian mansion. An increasingly popular venue, it is often used to host business, social and music events. The highlight is the excellent beer festival held on August bank holiday.

Q (Hilden) (325H) P

Tuesday Bell

Units 1 & 2, Lisburn Square, BT28 2TU

9-11.30 (1am Fri & Sat); 9-11 Sun

(028) 9262 7390

Greene King IPA, Abbot; guest beer

Large Wetherspoon's pub in the Lisburn Square shopping area in the middle of the town. Although open for breakfast from 9am, alcohol is not served until 11.30am (12.30 Sundays). It has two floors, both with three handpumps. Screens are upstairs only and show sport, usually with the sound turned off. Food is a major attraction, making the bar very busy at lunchtimes and the weekend.

Londonderry

Diamond

23-24 The Diamond, BT48 6HP (centre of the walled city)

9-11 (midnight Wed, Thu & Sun; 1am Fri & Sat)

(028) 7127 2880

Greene King IPA, Abbot; guest beer

Located in the Diamond square, inside the walled part of the Maiden City, this is a two storey Wetherspoon's pub with good views from the upper floor. There are large bars on both floors, the upstairs with a children's room. A varied range of guest ales is usually available alongside the regulars. As with other

pubs in the chain, alcohol is served from 11.30am (12.30 Sunday).
ᗢ◑♿⇌(Waterside)●⁼

Ice Wharf

Strand Road, BT48 7AB
✪ 9-midnight (1am Thu-Sat)
☎ (028) 7127 6610
Greene King IPA, Abbot; guest beer Ⓗ
Five minutes' walk from the city's bus station, head through Guildhall Square and turn right into Strand Road to reach this hostelry. A former hotel, it was Wetherspoon's first Lloyds No 1 in Northern Ireland. Now a large single floor pub, it has a separate room for families. As well as the regular and guest ales, cider is available on gravity. In common with other Wetherspoon's, alcohol is served from 11.30am (12.30 Sunday). ᗢ◑♿●⁼

Newtownards

Spirit Merchant

54-56 Regent Street, BT23 4LP (opp bus station)
✪ 9-11 (1am Fri & Sat); 9-midnight Sun
☎ (028) 9182 4270
Greene King IPA, Abbot; guest beer Ⓗ
Friendly, welcoming Wetherspoon's with the feel of a local pub, formerly the Jolly Judge bar. TV screens show Sky Sports and news. Breakfast is served from 9am, beer after 11.30am (12.30 on Sunday). Two regular ales and up to three guests from mainland breweries are on handpump, plus an excellent range of foreign beers and ciders. The standard Wetherspoon's food menu includes daily specials. There is a smoking area at the front and a heated courtyard at the side.
❀◑♿●P⁼

Saintfield

White Horse

49 Main Street, BT24 7AB
✪ 11.30-11.30; 12-10.30 Sun
☎ (028) 9751 1143
Whitewater Mill Ale, Glen Ale, Belfast Ale, Knight Porter; guest beers Ⓗ
This very popular pub, particularly among CAMRA members, has won the province's Pub of the Year award three times. The bar has five handpumps serving Whitewater beers and guest ales. Food is available in the bar; the downstairs restaurant has been converted into a games room. The White Horse is very much a community pub, a mainstay of village life in Saintfield. The annual beer festival is an unmissable social event for CAMRA members.
♛❀◑♿⊟(15,215)⁼

Tap Room, Lisburn.

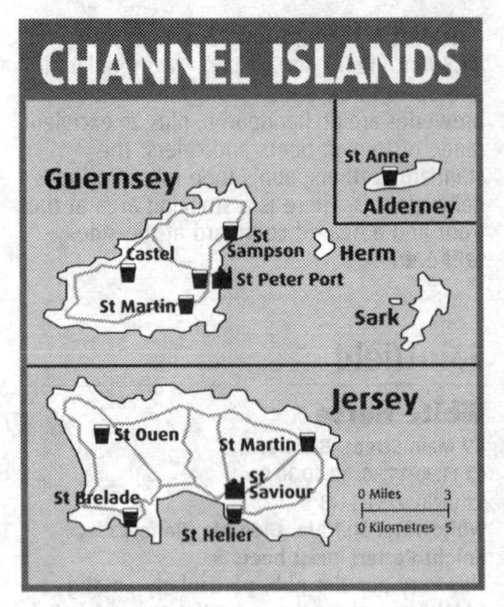

ALDERNEY

St Anne

Georgian House Hotel

Victoria Street, GY9 3UF

10-12.30am; 10.15-2.30, 6.30-midnight winter; 10.15-4 Sun

☎ (01481) 822471 georgianhousealderney.com

Ringwood Best Bitter Ⓗ

Situated just up from the town church, the hotel extends a warm welcome to all. There is a choice of areas to sit, from the left hand bar where the handpump is situated, through to the small dining room, the Orangery restaurant or out in the sheltered garden. Good food is served from a choice of menus (not Mon). A very popular venue, it can be crowded in the season. Q❀⇌◑⊟⋀

GUERNSEY

Castel

Fleur du Jardin

Kings Mills, GY5 7JT

11.30-11.45

☎ (01481) 257996 fleurdujardin.com

Fuller's London Pride; Worthington's Bitter Ⓗ

A building of unique charm with two bars: one traditional, small and cosy attached to the restaurant, the other recently renovated in a more contemporary style to create a comfortable, relaxing area to enjoy a beer. A door from this area leads to a large covered patio and out to the garden. The large bar at the rear was refurbished last year to become a dining area. Menus in both the bar and restaurant feature fresh local produce. ⛬Q❀⇌◑♿P⊱

Rockmount Hotel

Cobo, GY5 7HB

10-11.45 (12.45am Fri & Sat); 12-10.30 sun

☎ (01481) 256757

White Horse Wayland Smithy Ⓗ

A pub for all seasons, it has two bars: a public to the rear by the large car park and a newly refurbished front bar by the road. A warming fire in winter makes it a cosy retreat from the gales. The old snooker room has been opened up to create a sports-themed area to one side. A good range of food is served and the pub is just across the road from a sandy beach, providing a refreshing pint on a hot summer day. The perfect place to relax with a good pint and enjoy one of the island's best views of Guernsey's legendary sunsets. ⛬◑⊟⊞P

St Martin

Ambassador Hotel

Route de Sausmarez, GY4 6SQ

12-3, 6-11.45; 12-3.30 Sun

☎ (01481) 238356 ambassador.guernsey.net

White Horse Village Idiot Ⓗ

The hotel is situated just down from Sausmarez Manor on the main road from St Peter Port to St Martin. A delicious range of meals is available, served in the bar, the restaurant or the Old Guernsey conservatory. There is a patio area to the rear of the bar for sunny days. Accommodation is good value. The car park to the front is quite small and can be busy. ⇌◑⊞P

Captain's Hotel

La Fosse, GY4 6EF

11-11 (midnight Fri & Sat); 12-4 Sun

☎ (01481) 223890

Fuller's London Pride Ⓗ

In a secluded location down a country lane, this is a popular locals' pub with a lively, friendly atmosphere. There is a small, raised area in front of the bar furnished with a sofa to make a 'comfy zone'. Meals can be eaten in the bar or the newly refurbished bistro area at the rear. A meat draw is held on Friday. There is a car park to the rear which can fill up quickly. ⇌◑P

St Peter Port

Cock & Bull

Lower Hauteville, GY1 1LL

11.30-2.30, 4-12.45am; 11.30-12.45am Fri & Sat; occasional Sunday

☎ (01481) 722660

Beer range varies Ⓗ

Popular pub, just up the hill from the town church, with five handpumps providing a changing range of beers. Live music takes place on different nights of the week, ranging from salsa, baroque or jazz on a Monday, open microphone on Tuesday, to Irish on Thursday. There is even a poetry night. The pub opens on occasional Sundays for Six Nations and other rugby events. Seating is on three levels and there is a large screen for sporting events. Hot bar snacks are served at lunchtime. ⊱

Cornerstone Café

La Tour Beauregard, GY1 1LQ

10 (8am Thu & Fri)-midnight; occasional Sunday

☎ (01481) 713832 cornerstoneguernsey.co.uk

Badger First Gold; M&B Mild, Brew XI Ⓗ

Situated across the road from the States Archives, the café has a small bar area to the

INDEPENDENT BREWERIES

Jersey St Saviour: Jersey
Randalls St Peter Port: Guernsey

front with bar stools, and further seating to the rear. Regular quiz evenings are held. The menu offers a wide range of good quality hot and cold meals with a daily specials board. CAMRA branch Pub of the Year winner in 2006. ◑

Randy Paddle

North Esplanade, GY1 2LQ
✪ 10-11.45 (12.45am Fri & Sat); closed Sun
☎ (01481) 725610
Fuller's London Pride; Wadworth 6X Ⓗ
Across the road from the harbour and next door to the tourist board, the pub is in a perfect position for a drink before a meal at one of the varied restaurants surrounding it. The bar has a nautical theme and although small, makes good use of space, attracting a mixed crowd of regulars and visitors to the island.

Ship & Crown

North Esplanade, GY1 2NB (opp Crown Pier car park)
✪ 10-12.45am; 12-10 Sun
☎ (01481) 721368
Beer range varies Ⓗ
Now a free house, the pub has a nautical theme, with pictures of ships and a model of the Seven Seas, complete with tiny cannon balls, in a glass case. Situated across the road from Victoria Pier (known locally as Crown Pier), this busy pub attracts a varied clientele of all ages. Real cider – Weston's 1st Quality – is available on handpump. Excellent bar meals are served in generous portions throughout the day, with a daily changing range of specials. ◑♣

St Sampson

La Fontaine Inn

Vale Road, GY2 4DS
✪ 10-11.45; 12-3.30 (6 summer) Sun
☎ (01481) 247644
White Horse Wayland Smithy Ⓗ
Popular with the local community, the small public bar at the front is home to the handpumps. Go through the doorway and you are into an L-shaped lounge, with a bar at the end and a handy serving hatch halfway along. Shove-ha'penny is played in the public bar and darts in the lounge. A meat draw is held on Friday. ❀⊟♣P

JERSEY

St Brelade

Old Court House

Le Boulevard, St Aubin's Harbour, JE3 8AB
✪ 11-11
☎ (01534) 746433
Draught Bass; Wells Bombardier; Ⓗ **guest beer** Ⓗ/Ⓖ
Situated on the bulwarks of St Aubins Harbour, the Old Court House is primarily a restaurant and hotel but the Granite Bar and conservatory are popular for drinking. A real ale from Skinner's is served on gravity. There is a good bus service from St Helier and it is just a short walk over the hill to the Smugglers at Ouaisne. Q❀⊭◑⊟⊁

Old Smugglers Inn

Le Mont du Ouaisne, JE3 8AW
✪ 11-11 (winter opening hours vary)
☎ (01534) 741510 🌐 oldsmugglersinn.com
Draught Bass; Ⓗ **Greene King Abbot;** Ⓖ **Wells Bombardier; guest beers** Ⓗ
Perched on the edge of Ouaisne Bay, the Smugglers has been the jewel in the crown of the Jersey real ale scene for many years. One of just a few free houses on the island, it is set on several levels within granite-built fishermen's cottages dating back hundreds of years. Up to four real ales are usually available including one from Skinner's, and mini beer festivals are held in winter and summer. The pub is well known for its good food and fresh daily specials. ♨Q◑

St Helier

Lamplighter ✔

9 Mulcaster Street, JE2 3NJ
✪ 11-11
☎ (01534) 723119
Ringwood Best Bitter, Fortyniner, Ⓗ **Old Thumper;** Ⓖ **Wells Eagle IPA, Bombardier;** Ⓗ **guest beers** Ⓖ
A traditional pub with a modern feel. The gas lamps that gave the pub its name remain, as does the original antique pewter bar top. An excellent range of up to eight real ales is available including one from Skinner's —four are served direct from the cask. The pub was CAMRA Pub of the Year in 2006 and received a Beautiful Beer award from the BBPA. ◑⊟

St Martin

Rozel

La Vallee de Rozel, JE3 6AJ
✪ 11-11
☎ (01534) 869801
Greene King Abbot; Ringwood Best Bitter; Wells Bombardier; guest beers Ⓗ
Charming little hostelry tucked away in the north-west corner of the island. The pub has a delightful beer garden and there is an excellent restaurant upstairs. Bar meals are served in the public bar and snug, where there is a real fire in winter. A Skininer's beer is often available. The locals are very friendly if sometimes a little rumbustious! ♨Q❀◑⊟⊟P

St Ouen

Moulin de Lecq

Le Mont de la Greve de Lecq, JE3 2DT
✪ 11-11 (4-11 Mon-Fri Jan & Feb)
☎ (01534) 482818 🌐 moulindelecq.com
Greene King Old Speckled Hen, Ⓗ **Abbot,** Ⓖ **seasonal beers; Wells Bombardier; guest beers** Ⓗ
The only other free house on the island to offer a range of real ales, the Moulin is a converted 12th-century watermill situated in the valley above the beach at Greve de Lecq. The waterwheel is still in place and the turning mechanism can be seen behind the bar. A newly-built restaurant adjoins the mill. There is a children's playground.
♨Q❀◑⊟♣P⊁

ISLE OF MAN

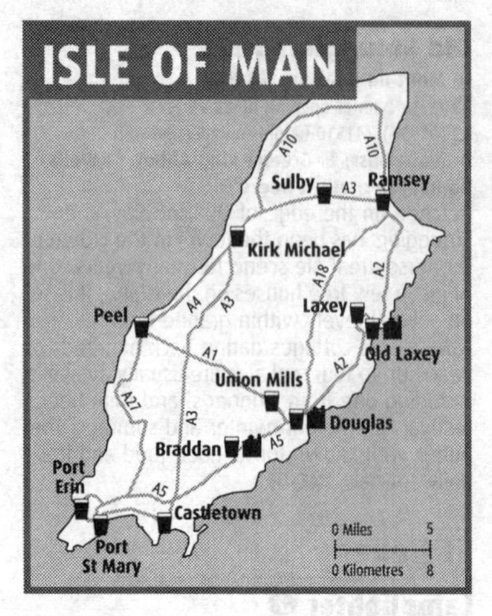

Braddan

Hop Garden

Mount Murray, Santon, IM4 1JE (on main Douglas-Castletown road)
12-11
☎ (01624) 619527 hop-garden.com
Bushy's Bitter; guest beers H
The Hop Garden is situated in front of Bushy's Brewery. Popular for food, the traditional dining area has been extended into the attractive conservatory. For drinkers there is a comfortable side lounge, with guest beers and ciders added in summer. There are beautiful gardens where you can relax, drink and dine during warmer months. Beware, however, the food is too good to share and the ducks are very persistent. (1)P

Castletown

Sidings

Victoria Road, IM9 1EF (next to railway station)
11.30-11 (midnight Fri & Sat)
☎ (01624) 823282
Bushy's Mild, Bitter, Castletown Bitter; guest beers H
The Sidings is a welcome sight as you arrive in the Island's ancient capital by train. Its impressive and ornate wooden counter dispenses the three regular ales at reasonable prices, plus an ever-changing variety of around seven cask ales from all over the British Isles. No food is served on Sunday. Local CAMRA Pub of the Year in 2003 and 2005. (IMR)

Douglas

Albert Hotel ✓

3 Chapel Row, IM1 2BJ (next to bus station)
10-11 (11.45 Fri & Sat); 12-11 Sun
☎ (01624) 673632
Okells Mild, Bitter; guest beers H
The Albert is the nearest real ale pub to the sea terminal. A busy, unspoilt local, it has a traditionally laid out central bar and dark wood panelling. Sport on TV is a constant feature but never loud enough to spoil a conversation. The three resident beers include a house beer brewed by Okells, Jough Manx Ale. Jough is Manx Gaelic for beer. Bushys Castletown Bitter is a regular guest. Q(IMR)

Cat With No Tail

Hailwood Court, Hailwood Avenue, Governors Hill, IM2 7EA
12-11 (midnight Fri & Sat)
☎ (01624) 616364
Okells Bitter; guest beers H
A modern building on a relatively new housing estate, it has two bars: a lounge and a public. The main beer is Okells Bitter and various guest beers are served, including Shepherd Neame Spitfire. Quizzes are held on Sunday and Thursday evenings and there is monthly karaoke. The public bar has a pool table and dartboard. Children are allowed in the conservatory and food is served in the lounge bar lunchtimes and evenings except Sunday evening. P

Manor Hotel

School Road, Willaston, IM2 6PQ
12-11 (midnight Fri & Sat)
☎ (01624) 676957
Okells Bitter H
A true community pub in the heart of the Willaston Estate, this popular venue is close to the TT Grandstand. There is a large lounge area with dark wood panelling. Corporation owned but on a long term lease, the pub hosts live music and has separate darts and pool rooms. Upstairs is a meeting room widely used by many local clubs and societies. Four dartboards in the upstairs area are used for local tournaments. Q(22)P

Prospect Hotel ✓

Prospect Hill, IM1 1ET
12-11 (midnight Fri); 6-midnight Sat; closed Sun
☎ (01624) 616773
Okells Bitter; guest beers H
Spacious, stylish pub in the financial centre of Douglas, popular with office workers. The single bar interior has a traditional feel, displaying old law court photographs. The Prospect is a tied house with a blackboard outside listing the guest beers available. Food is served at lunchtime only. There is a quiz night on Thursday. (IMR)

Queens Hotel

Queens Promenade, IM2 4NL (on seafront)
12-midnight (1am Fri & Sat)
☎ (01624) 674438
Okells Bitter; guest beers H
Popular with locals and holidaymakers, this is a cheery and friendly open-plan pub. The interior has three distinct areas including a games area. The lounge features a large-screen TV for sporting events. There is a very good outside space under awnings with heaters and a great view of Douglas Bay, with the steam packet ferries coming and going. Horse trams stop right outside.
Q(IMR)

INDEPENDENT BREWERIES

Bushy's Braddan
Okells Douglas
Old Laxey Old Laxey

Rovers Return

11 Church Street, IM1 2AG (behind town hall)
12-11 (midnight Fri & Sat)
☎ (01624) 676459
Bushy's Mild, Bitter, seasonal beers; guest beers
A popular back street pub offering a good range of beers on handpump, plus a wide selection of bottled ales. Well known for its room that is a shrine to Blackburn Rovers FC, there are eight further rooms, two with real fires in winter, and an outside seating area for smokers. Live music plays most weekends.
(IMR)

Woodbourne Hotel

Alexander Drive, IM2 3QF
5 (12 Fri-Sun)-midnight
☎ (01624) 676754
Okells Mild, Bitter; guest beers
This is a Victorian-built, no frills, friendly local pub, with three bars and a pool room. A tied house, it offers a good choice of local beers (including seasonal) plus two guest ales. The Woodbourne is popular with all ages. It is situated a 10-minute walk out of town, and a quarter of a mile from the Rosemount Terrace shops. Q

Kirk Michael

Mitre

IM6 1AJ
12-2.30 (not Mon), 5-11 (midnight Fri); 12-midnight Sat; 12-11 Sun
☎ (01624) 878244
Okells Bitter; guest beers
Cosy village pub with plenty of charm enhanced by a real fire in the winter months. A small room off the main lounge area has numerous photos of motorcycles and bikers of bygone eras that will impress motorbike enthusiasts and historians alike – just ask your hosts for a viewing. Quality beer, good value meals and views of the hills from the rear garden make the Mitre well worth a visit.
P

Laxey

Bridge Inn

6 New Road, IM4 7BE
11.30-11 (midnight Fri & Sat)
☎ (01624) 862414
Bushy's Mild, Bitter
Popular and lively local pub in the centre of the village. The Bridge has recently been refurbished but retains its friendly atmosphere and continues to serve an excellent pint. It offers occasional live music, wide screen TV, a function room upstairs as well as B&B accommodation. In 1897 after the Snaefell mining disaster in which 20 men perished the cellar area was used as a temporary morgue. There are rumours of a resident ghost.
(MER)(3)P

Queen's Hotel

New Road, IM4 7BP
12-11 (midnight Fri & Sat)
☎ (01624) 861195
Bushy's Mild, Bitter; guest beers
In this busy local every wall is covered with pictures, photos and memorabilia of the local area. Many feature bikes and bikers including several photos of the famous TT rider the late Joey Dunlop. Seating areas include the bar space with comfortable button back benches, a snug porch and several sturdy benches outside where you can sit and watch the world go by. But beware, you may just get too comfortable in the relaxing, friendly atmosphere and watch your bus go by.
P

Old Laxey

Shore Hotel

IM4 7DA
12-midnight
☎ (01624) 861509
Old Laxey Bosun Bitter
Friendly 18th-century village pub with an adjacent micro-brewery, the Old Laxey Brewing Company. Close to Laxey harbour and beach, the one-roomed interior features a number of nautical artefacts, pictures and chart maps. Food is served in the bar or outside by the river in the summer months. Live music plays most Saturdays. In winter the cosy atmosphere is enhanced by a real fire. This is the only place on the island where Bosun Bitter is regularly available.
P

Peel

Creek Inn

Station Place, IM5 1AT (by harbour)
10-midnight
☎ (01624) 842216
Okells Bitter; guest beers
Central for Peel Castle, House of Manannan museum and Kipper Factory, the Creek has two bars, one with a pool table, TV screens and live music at the weekend. In summer the patio is the perfect place to enjoy the excellent views. Up to four guest beers are available at any one time, and beer festivals are held in the spring and autumn. Information about the ales is available from the bar, food is served all day and there is Wi-Fi Internet access. P

White House Hotel

Tynwald Road, IM5 1LA (150m from bus station)
11-midnight
☎ (01624) 842252
Bushy's Bitter; Flowers Original; Okells Mild, Bitter; Taylor Landlord; guest beers
Popular family-run multi-roomed free house with all the rooms converging on a central bar. The additional Captain's Cabin snug has its own bar. The pub has remained largely unchanged since the 1930s and the landlord is one of the longest serving on the island. He recently passed the milestone of having supplied more than 1,000 guest ales during his tenure. Live local music plays on Friday and Saturday. QP

Port Erin

Bay Hotel

Shore Road, IM9 6HL
⏲ 12-midnight (1am Fri & Sat)
☎ (01624) 832084
Bushy's Castletown Bitter, Bitter, Old Bushy Tail, seasonal beers; guest beers [H]
Situated on the lower promenade with views of the beautiful Port Erin Bay, this large hotel has an unspoilt interior with two rooms and a separate dining area, each with its own real fire. Up to five real ales are served and at least one real cider. The pub also hosts an annual beer festival during the Manx Grand Prix in September and attracts many visitors, especially in summer. ⛰🛏◑◧⇌(IMR)♣●

Falcon's Nest Hotel

Station Road, IM9 6AF
⏲ 11-midnight daily
☎ (01624) 834077 🌐 falconsnesthotel.co.uk
Bushy's Bitter; Okells Bitter; guest beers [H]
Family run hotel with a lounge bar open to all dispensing local ales including at least one guest beer. The bar has been sympathetically extended with a full-length conservatory where you can enjoy spectacular elevated views over Port Erin Bay, Bradda Head, and on a clear day the distant hills of Northern Ireland. A wide variety of meals is available including a popular carvery served on Sunday. ⛰Q🛏◑◧⇌(IMR)🚌

Port St Mary

Albert Hotel

Athol Street, IM9 5DS (next to bus terminal)
⏲ 11.30-midnight; 12-1am Fri & Sat; 12-midnight Sun
☎ (01624) 832118
Bushy's Ruby Mild, Old Bushy Tail; Okells Bitter; guest beers [H]
This traditional pub has impressive views over the inner harbour of Port St Mary. There are three rooms including a spacious games room with a real fire and a separate entrance. The comfortable, traditional lounge area is even cosier in colder months when the fire is lit, making the Albert an ideal stop-off after a fishing trip. Dining and accommodation are usually available; however during refurbishment in 2008/09 ring to check first. ⛰❀◧🚌♣P⅟

Shore Hotel

Shore Road, Gansey, IM9 5LZ (on main Castletown-Port St Mary road)
⏲ 12-midnight (1am Fri & Sat)
☎ (01624) 832269
Bushy's Bushy Tail; Okells Bitter; guest beers [H]
Busy, friendly local which has grown in popularity in recent years, with good views of Carrick Rock and Bay. A large TV screen shows sport and there is a pool table in the main bar. The dining room offers good quality food. B&B accommodation is available in four rooms. 🛏◑🚌♣P

Ramsey

Swan

Parliament Square, IM8 2LM
⏲ 12-11.30 (12.30am Fri & Sat)
☎ (01624) 814236
Okells Mild, Bitter [H]
Friendly pub refurbished in 2007. The larger of the two bars has a dartboard and pool table plus two plasma TVs. Food is served lunchtimes and evenings including some specials. There are two outdoor heated drinking areas. Well-situated on the TT course and close to the bus station, high street and harbour, the terminus for the electric railway is a five-minute walk. Guest ales are served at Christmas, during TT fortnight and the week of the Grand Prix races. ❀◑◧♿🚌⅟

Trafalgar Hotel ✔

West Quay, IM8 1DW (on quayside)
⏲ 11-11 (midnight Fri & Sat); 12-4, 8-11 Sun
☎ (01624) 814601
Black Sheep Best Bitter; Moorhouses Black Cat; Okells Bitter; guest beers [H]
A popular free house, the Trafalgar is comfortable and friendly. Always busy, it offers a good selection of real ales. Situated just a short walk from the Parliament Square section of the TT course, it overlooks Ramsey inner harbour. Guest ales are sourced from throughout the UK and the 'Traf' has been a regular finalist for local CAMRA Pub of the Year in recent times. ⇌(MER)🚌♣⅟

Sulby

Sulby Glen Hotel ✔

Main Road, IM7 2HR
⏲ 12-midnight (1am Fri & Sat); 12-11 Sun
☎ (01624) 897240 🌐 sulbyglenhotel.net
Bushy's Bitter; Okells Bitter; guest beers [H]
Long serving hosts Eddie and Rosie offer a warm welcome to visitors to this large open-plan lounge and bar with a friendly atmosphere. Situated on the Sulby Straight, a fast section of the TT course, this is a very popular hostelry for continental TT and Manx Grand Prix motorbike fans. Excellent home-cooked food made with locally-sourced ingredients is served from a varied menu. Live bands and themed nights are hosted regularly. Accommodation is high quality in well-appointed en-suite rooms. ⛰Q🛏❀🛏◑◧♿⛺🚌♣●P⅟

Union Mills

Railway Inn

Main Road, IM4 4NE (on main A1 Douglas-Peel road)
⏲ 12-11 (midnight Fri & Sat)
☎ (01624) 853006 🌐 iomrailwayinn.com
Okells Mild, Bitter, seasonal beers; guest beers [H]
Busy village inn dating back to 1841, this historic hostelry has been in the same family for five generations. Now open plan, it has three separate seating areas, the back room providing a comfortable lounge space. Located on part of the famous TT course, the pub has an interesting display of TT photos, and is a favourite spot for viewing the races. It offers a good choice of at least two guest ales, often from Bushy's. Local CAMRA Pub of the Year twice, most recently in 2007. ❀⛺🚌♣P⅟

The Breweries

How beer is brewed

Real ale is made by taking raw ingredients from the fields, the finest malting barley and hops, along with pure water from natural springs or the public supply, and carefully cultivated strains of brewers' yeast; in this exploded drawing by Trevor Hatchett of a classic British ale brewery, it is possible to follow the process that begins with raw grain and finishes with natural, living cask beer.

1. On the top floor, in the roof, are the tanks where pure water – called liquor by brewers – is stored. Soft water is not suited to ale brewing, and brewers will add such salts as gypsum and magnesium to replicate the hard, flinty waters of Burton-on-Trent, home of pale ale.

2. In the malt store, grain is weighed and kept until needed.The malt drops down a floor to the mills, which grind it into a coarse powder suitable for brewing. From the mills, the ground malt or grist is poured into the mash tuns along with heated liquor. During the mashing period, natural enzymes in the malt convert starches into fermentable malt sugars.

3. On the same floor as the conditioning tanks are the coppers, where after mashing, the wort is boiled with hops, which add aroma, flavour and bitterness.

4. At the end of the boil, the hopped wort is clarified in a vessel called the hop back on the ground floor. The clarified wort is pumped back to the malt store level where it is passed through a heat exchange unit. See 5.

5. The heat exchange unit cools the hopped wort prior to fermentation.

6. The fermenters are on the same floor as the mash tuns.The house yeast is blended or pitched with the wort.Yeast converts the malt sugars in the wort into alcohol and carbon dioxide. Excess yeast is skimmed off by funnels called parachutes.

7. Fermentation lasts for a week and the 'green' beer is then stored for a few days in conditioning tanks.

8. Finally, the fresh beer is run into casks on the ground floor, where additional hops for aroma and sugar to encourage a secondary fermentation may be added.The casks then leave for pubs, where the beer reaches maturity in the cellars.

How to use the Breweries section

Breweries are listed in alphabetical order. The independents (regional, smaller craft brewers and brew-pubs) are listed first, followed by the nationals and the globals. Within each brewery entry, beers are listed in increasing order of strength. Beers that are available for less than three months are described as 'occasional' or 'seasonal' brews. If a brewery also produces bottle-conditioned beers, this will be mentioned in the main description: these are beers that have not been pasteurised and contain live yeast, allowing them to continue to ferment and mature in the bottle as a draught real ale does in its cask.

Symbols

A brew-pub: a pub that brews beer on the premises.

◆ CAMRA tasting notes, supplied by a trained CAMRA tasting panel. Beer descriptions that do not carry this symbol are based on more limited tastings or have been obtained from other sources.
Tasting notes are not provided for brew-pub beers that are available in fewer than five outlets, nor for other breweries' beers that are available for less than three months of the year.

A CAMRA Beer of the Year in 2007.

One of the 2008 CAMRA Beers of the Year, a finalist in the Champion Beer of Britain competition held during the Great British Beer Festival in London in August 2008, or the Champion Winter Beer of Britain competition held earlier in the year.

The brewery's beers can be acceptably served through a 'tight sparkler' attached to the nozzle of the beer pump, designed to give a thick collar of foam on the beer.

The brewery's beer should NOT be served through a tight sparkler. CAMRA is opposed to the growing tendency to serve southern-brewed beers with the aid of sparklers, which aerate the beer and tend to drive hop aroma and flavour into the head, altering the balance of the beer achieved in the brewery. When neither symbol is used it means the brewery in question has not stated a preference.

Abbreviations

OG stands for original gravity, the measure taken before fermentation of the level of 'fermentable material' (malt sugars and added sugars) in the brew. It is a rough indication of strength and is no longer used for duty purposes.

ABV stands for Alcohol by Volume, which is a more reliable measure of the percentage of alcohol in the finished beer. Many breweries now only disclose ABVs but the Guide lists OGs where available. Often the OG and the ABV of a beer are identical, ie 1035 and 3.5 per cent. If the ABV is higher than the OG, ie OG 1035, ABV 3.8, this indicates that the beer has been 'well attenuated' with most of the malt sugars turned into alcohol. If the ABV is lower than the OG, this means residual sugars have been left in the beer for fullness of body and flavour: this is rare but can apply to some milds or strong old ales, barley wines, and winter beers.

*The Breweries section was correct at the time of going to press and every effort has been made to ensure that all cask-conditioned beers are included.

The independents

*Indicates a new brewery since the last edition; SIBA indicates a member of the Society of Independent Brewers; IFBB indicates a member of the Independent Family Brewers of Britain; EAB indicates a member of the East Anglian Brewers Co-operative.

1648 SIBA

1648 Brewing Co Ltd, Old Stables Brewery, Mill Lane, East Hoathly, East Sussex, BN8 6QB
☎ (01825) 840830
✉ brewmaster@1648brewing.co.uk
🌐 1648brewing.co.uk
Tours by arrangement

⊗ The 1648 brewery, set up an the old stable block at the King's Head pub in 2003, derives its name and some of the beer names from the time of the deposition of King Charles I. One pub is owned and more than 30 outlets are supplied. Additional fermenting vessels were installed in 2007 doubling capacity to 884 barrels. Seasonal beers: Three Threads (ABV 4.3%, Apr-Jul), Bee-Head (ABV 4.6%, May-Sep), Lammas Ale (ABV 4.2%, Jul-Oct), Armistice Ale (ABV 4.2%, Oct-Nov), Ginger Nol (ABV 4.7%, Oct-Mar), Winter Warrant (ABV 4.8%, Dec-Mar), Declaration (ABV 4.1%, cricket season).

Hop Pocket (OG 1038, ABV 3.7%)

Original (OG 1040, ABV 3.9%)
Light, quaffable and easy drinking.

Signature (OG 1044, ABV 4.4%)
Light, crisp, medium hoppy clean beer with a bitter finish.

Saint George (OG 1045, ABV 4.5%)
Traditional English ale with a balanced malt and hop flavour.

Gold Angel (OG 1049, ABV 5%)

3 Rivers SIBA

3 Rivers Brewery Ltd, Delta House, Greg Street, Reddish, Stockport, Cheshire, SK5 7BS
☎ (0161) 477 3333
✉ contacts@3riversbrewing.co.uk
🌐 3riversbrewery.co.uk
Tours by arrangement

◎ 3 Rivers was launched in 2003. There is a members' club on site, a purpose-built tasting area for brewery tours and a classroom designed for brewing courses. More than 200 outlets are supplied. The brewery also contract brews 'Cellar Rat' beers for the Crown Inn in Stockport. Seasonal beers: phone for details. Bottle-conditioned beer is also available.

GMT (OG 1038, ABV 3.8%)
Golden bitter with an underlying malt character supported by moderate hop bitterness and a light floral finish.

Harry Jacks (ABV 4.1%)

Manchester IPA (OG 1041, ABV 4.2%)
Light russet/amber colour with a refreshing biscuit-like flavour, supplemented by a complex citrus finish.

Pilgrim's Progress (ABV 4.2%)

Fathers Favourite (OG 1045, ABV 4.5%)
Light amber-coloured ale with hints of coffee and caramel, complemented by a spicy hop character and a complex aroma.

Hillary Gold (OG 1044, ABV 4.5%)

Oxbow (ABV 4.5%)

Crystal Wheat (OG 1048, ABV 5%)

Julie's Pride (ABV 5%)

Old Disreputable (OG 1054, ABV 5.2%)
Dark malty brew with distinctive coffee and chocolate hints and a lasting bitter finish.

Suitably Irish (ABV 5.6%)
Full-bodied black stout.

Abbey Ales SIBA

Abbey Ales Ltd, Abbey Brewery, Camden Row, Bath, Somerset, BA1 5LB
☎ (01225) 444437
✉ enquiries@abbeyales.co.uk
🌐 abbeyales.co.uk
Tours by arrangement

⊗ Abbey Ales is the first and only brewery in Bath for nearly 50 years. It supplies more than 80 regular accounts within a 20-mile radius of Bath, while selected wholesalers deliver beer nationally. One tied house, the Star Inn, Bath, is listed on CAMRA's National Inventory of heritage pubs. Seasonal beers: Bath Star (ABV 4.5%, spring), Chorister (ABV 4.5%, autumn), White Friar (ABV 5%), Black Friar (ABV 5.3%, winter), Twelfth Night (ABV 5%, Xmas).

Bellringer (OG 1042, ABV 4.2%) ◆
A notably hoppy ale, light to medium-bodied, clean-tasting, refreshingly dry, with a balancing sweetness. Citrus, pale malt aroma and dry, bitter finish.

Abbey Bells

Abbey Bells Brewery, 5 Main Road, Hirst Courtney, Selby, North Yorkshire, YO8 8QP
☎ 07940 726658
✉ enquiries@abbeybells.co.uk
🌐 abbeybells.co.uk
Tours by arrangement (for up to 12 persons only)

⊗ The brewery was launched in 2002 and has a 2.5-barrel plant with cellar tanks from the defunct Brigg Brewery and other parts from a dairy maker in Congleton. Some 30 outlets are supplied. Seasonal beers: Santa's Stocking Filler (ABV 4.5%), Black Satin (ABV 6.2%, winter).

Monday's Child (OG 1035, ABV 3.7%)
An easy-drinking session beer, made with Maris Otter malt and Goldings hops. Pale and refreshing.

Amber Neck Tie (OG 1040, ABV 4%)

Hoppy Daze (OG 1041, ABV 4.1%)

Similar in colour to Monday's Child, the beer is hopped with Target.

Cordelia's Gift (OG 1042, ABV 4.3%)
The combination of Pearl and chocolate malts and Fuggles hops imparts a flavour reminiscent of dandelion and burdock.

Leper Squint (OG 1045, ABV 4.5%)

Grease (OG 1045, ABV 4.6%)

1911 Celebration Ale (OG 1048, ABV 4.8%)

Original Bitter (OG 1050, ABV 5.1%)
Made from Pearl malt with a dash of crystal and flavoured with Goldings hops.

Abbeydale SIBA

Abbeydale Brewery Ltd, Unit 8, Aizlewood Road, Sheffield, South Yorkshire, S8 0YX
☎ (0114) 281 2712
info@abbeydalebrewery.co.uk
abbeydalebrewery.co.uk

Since starting in 1996, Abbeydale Brewery has grown steadily; it now produces upwards of 70 barrels a week, and the gradual expansion programme is set to continue. The regular range is complemented by ever-changing seasonals, each of which is available for two months – see website for details. It also produces beers under the 'Beer Works' name.

Matins (OG 1034.9, ABV 3.6%)
Pale and full flavoured; a hoppy session beer.

Daily Bread (OG 1037, ABV 3.8%)

Brimstone (OG 1039, ABV 3.9%)
A russet-coloured bitter beer with a distinctive hop aroma.

Moonshine (OG 1041.2, ABV 4.3%)
A beautifully balanced pale ale with a full hop aroma. Pleasant grapefruit traces may be detected.

Absolution (OG 1050, ABV 5.3%)
A fruity pale ale, deceptively drinkable for its strength. Sweetish but not cloying.

Black Mass (OG 1065, ABV 6.7%)
A strong black stout with complex roast flavours and a lasting bitter finish.

Last Rites (OG 1097, ABV 11%)
A pale, strong barley wine.

Acorn SIBA

Acorn Brewery of Barnsley Ltd, Unit 3, Mitchell Road, Aldham Industrial Estate, Wombwell, Barnsley, South Yorkshire, S73 8HA
☎ (01226) 270734
acornbrewery@tiscali.co.uk
acornbrewery.net
Shop Mon-Fri 9am-5pm
Tours by arrangement

Acorn Brewery was set up in 2003 with a 10-barrel ex-Firkin plant. Expansion to a 20-barrel plant was completed in 2007 when demand outgrew capacity. All beers are produced using the original Barnsley Bitter yeast strains, dating back to the 1850s. The brewery currently has a 100-barrel a week capacity. Seasonal beers: see website.

Barnsley Bitter (OG 1038, ABV 3.8%)
A complex aroma of malt and hops. A hint of chocolate with a fresh fruit and bitter taste.

Northdown Blonde (OG 1039, ABV 4%)
A refreshing blonde ale with light bitterness and an excellent aroma from the English Northdown hops.

Barnsley Gold (OG 1041.5, ABV 4.3%)
Fruit in the aroma and taste. There is also a hoppy flavour throughout. A well-hopped, clean, dry finish.

Old Moor Porter (OG 1045, ABV 4.4%)
A rich roast malt aroma with chocolate, cherry and liquorice flavours. A creamy mouthfeel leads to a dry finish.

Sovereign (OG 1044, ABV 4.4%)
Well-balanced bitter with plenty of fruit and malt. Excellent mouthfeel.

IPA (OG 1047, ABV 5%)
Full of hoppy and fruit aroma, a hoppy dry and fresh citrus fruit and bitter flavour that leads to a crisp citrus, hoppy finish.

Gorlovka Imperial Stout (OG 1058, ABV 6%)
A deep malt and hoppy aroma with liquorice throughout. Roast, fruit and hops also carry through this full-bodied stout.

Adkin*

Adkin Brewery, Adkin Way, Wantage, Oxfordshire
☎ 07709 086149

Adkin was established in 2007 and supplies beer festivals and local pubs. No beer list is available at present.

Adnams IFBB

Adnams plc, Sole Bay Brewery, East Green, Southwold, Suffolk, IP18 6JW
☎ (01502) 727200
info@adnams.co.uk
adnams.co.uk
Shop 10am-6pm daily

The company was founded by George and Ernest Adnams in 1872, who were joined by the Loftus family in 1902; a member of each family is still a director of the company. New fermenting vessels were installed in 2001, 2003 and 2005 to cope with demand while a new eco-friendly distribution centre has been opened in neighbouring Reydon. Real ale is available in all 70 pubs and there is national distribution to the free trade. All beers are now from a new energy efficient brewery, built within the confines of the present site. Seasonal beers: see website.

Bitter (OG 1037, ABV 3.7%)
Hops dominate this classic bitter, from the almost overpowering aroma to the dry, lingering aftertaste.

Explorer (OG 1042, ABV 4.3%)
Brewed with American hops, hence the name. Citrus fruit in the mouth, with a long, sweet aftertaste.

Broadside (OG 1049, ABV 4.7%)

The aroma and initial taste boom with prunes. Malt and sultanas with a trace of pepper in the mouth. The finish is long, turning drier.

Alcazar SIBA

Sherwood Forest Brewing Co Ltd, Alcazar Brewery, Church Street, Old Basford, Nottingham, NG6 0GA
☎ (0115) 978 5155/2282
✉ alcazarbrewery@tiscali.co.uk
alcazarbrewery.co.uk
Tours by arrangement

Alcazar was established in 1999 and is located behind its brewery tap, the Fox & Crown. The brewery is full mash with a 10-barrel brew length. Production is mainly for the Fox & Crown and other freehouses within the Turnstone Taverns estate. Seasonal beers: Maple Magic (ABV 5.5%, winter), Mocha Stout (ABV 5%), Black Fox Mild (ABV 3.9%, spring), Desert Fox (ABV 4.3%, summer), Nottingham Nog (ABV 4.2%), Bowmans Bitter (ABV 3.8%, spring/summer).

Sheriffs Gold (OG 1036, ABV 3.6%)
A golden ale made with First Gold and Goldings hops.

Alcazar Ale (OG 1040, ABV 4%)
A session ale made with a blend of English and North American hops; pale, full-flavoured with a fruity aroma and finish.

New Dawn (OG 1045, ABV 4.5%)
Golden ale made with North American hops that give a unique fruity aroma and crisp, malty taste.

Foxtale Ale (OG 1050, ABV 4.9%)
A classic bitter, amber in colour with full malt flavour and a slight sweet edge.

Vixen's Vice (OG 1052, ABV 5.2%)
A pale, strong ale with a malt flavour balanced by a clean, crisp, hop taste.

Windjammer IPA (OG 1060, ABV 6%)
Traditional IPA brewed with five varieties of North American hops. Strong and hoppy.

Bombay Castle IPA (OG 1065, ABV 6.5%)
Traditional IPA brewed with English hops.

Alehouse

Alehouse Pub & Brewing Company Ltd, Verulam Brewery, Farmers Boy, 134 London Road, St Albans, Hertfordshire, AL1 1PQ
☎ 07872 985918
✉ contact@alehousebrewery.co.uk
alehousebrewery.co.uk
Tours by arrangement

Alehouse took over the Verulam Brewery in 2006. As well as brewing two of the original house beers for the Farmers Boy next door, numerous ales are produced under the Alehouse banner including many seasonal and one-off brews. Beers are supplied direct to local outlets, the West Midlands and Yorkshire.

Simplicity (OG 1039, ABV 3.6%)

I Can't Believe It's Not GBH (OG 1038, ABV 3.8%)

Commercial Mild (OG 1039, ABV 3.9%)

Sauvin So Good! (OG 1038, ABV 4%)

Robust Porter (OG 1044, ABV 4.3%)

Technician's Pale (OG 1040, ABV 4.3%)

Balance & Poise (OG 1043, ABV 4.4%)

For Farmers Boy, St Albans:

Clipper IPA (OG 1039, ABV 4%)

Farmers Joy (OG 1043, ABV 4.5%)

Ales of Scilly SIBA

Ales of Scilly Brewery, 2b Porthmellon Industrial Estate, St Mary's, Isles of Scilly, Cornwall, TR21 0JY
☎ (01720) 423233
✉ mark@alesofscilly.co.uk
Tours by arrangement

Opened in 2001 as a two-barrel plant and expanded in 2004 to five barrels, Ales of Scilly is the most south-westerly brewery in Britain. Nine local pubs are supplied, with regular exports to mainland pubs and beer festivals. The brewery moved to new premises in 2007. Seasonal beers: Firebrand (ABV 4.2%, Easter-Sep), Old Bustard (ABV 4.2%). Bottle-conditioned beer is also available.

Scuppered (ABV 4.6%) ◆
The aroma is of fruit and hops, leading to a rich, malty, creamy taste balanced by hops. An initial burst of sweetness is followed by an increasing bitterness on the tongue.

Alexandra Ales

See Atomic

All Nations

See Worfield

Allendale

Allendale Brewing Co Ltd, Allen Mills, Allendale, Hexham, Northumberland, NE47 9EQ
☎ (01434) 618686
✉ tom@allendalebrewco.co.uk
allendalebrewco.co.uk
Shop Mon-Sat 9am-5pm
Tours by arrangement

Allendale was set up in 2006 and is run by father and son team, Jim and Tom Hick. Their locally themed ales are on sale in nearby free houses and also in Newcastle, Durham and surrounding areas. Seasonal beers: Black Grouse Bitter (ABV 4%, Aug-Jan), Curlew's Return (ABV 4.2%, Feb-Jul). All beers are also available bottle-conditioned.

Best Bitter (OG 1037, ABV 3.8%)

Golden Plover (OG 1039, ABV 4%)

Wolf (OG 1053, ABV 5.5%)

All Gates

All Gates Brewery Ltd, The Old Brewery, Brewery Yard, off Wallgate, Wigan, WN1 1JQ
☎ (01942) 234976
✉ information@allgatesbrewery.com

🌐 allgatesbrewery.com
Tours by arrangement

All Gates started brewing in 2006 in a Grade II listed building at the rear of Wigan Main Post Office. The building is an old tower brewery that has been lovingly restored, but with a new five-barrel plant. Beers are distributed regionally and to an owned estate of five pubs. There are plans for a brewery shop and for a bottling plant. Seasonal beers: Randy Rudolph (ABV 4.8%, Dec-Jan), Hung, Drawn & Portered (ABV 5.2%, Nov-Dec).

Mild at Heart (OG 1037, ABV 3.8%)
Dark brown beer with a malty, fruity aroma. Creamy and malty in taste, with blackberry fruits and a satisfying aftertaste.

Young Pretender (OG 1037, ABV 3.8%)

Napoleon's Retreat (OG 1038, ABV 3.9%)

Bright Blade (OG 1039, ABV 4%)

Hops & Charity (OG 1040, ABV 4.1%)
10p per pint donated to Wigan Hospice

Hasty Knoll (OG 1041, ABV 4.2%)

Twist & Stout (OG 1044, ABV 4.5%)

Reverend Ray (OG 1044, ABV 4.6%)

Amber

Amber Ales Ltd, PO Box 7277, Ripley, Derbyshire, DE5 4AP
☎ (01773) 512864
✉ info@amberales.co.uk
🌐 amberales.co.uk
Shop Thu-Fri 2-6pm
Tours by arrangement

Amber Ales began production in 2006 on a five-barrel plant from the Firkin brewpub chain. Part-time at first, it switched to full-time ahead of plan due to strong local interest. Amber produces four core beers plus one seasonal at any one time. Around 70 outlets are supplied direct. Bottle-conditioned beers are available.

Original Stout (OG 1040, ABV 4%)

Amber Pale (OG 1042, ABV 4.4%)

Colonial IPA (OG 1048, ABV 5.1%)

Imperial IPA (OG 1060, ABV 6.5%)

Anglo Dutch SIBA

Anglo Dutch Brewery, Unit 12, Saville Bridge Mill, Mill Street East, Dewsbury, West Yorkshire, WF12 9AF
☎ (01924) 457772
✉ angdutchbrew@yahoo.co.uk
🌐 anglo-dutch-brewery.co.uk
Tours by arrangement

Paul Klos (Dutch) set up the brewery with Mike Field (Anglo), who also runs the Refreshment Rooms at Dewsbury Station. Most beers contain wheat except for Spike and Tabatha, which contain lager malt. A bottle-conditioned fruit beer range is also available. Seasonal beers: Devil's Knell (ABV 4.8%, Jan), Wild Flower (ABV 4.2%, Sep).

Best Bitter (ABV 3.8%)

Kletswater (OG 1039, ABV 4%)
Pale-coloured beer with a hoppy nose and a good hop and citrus fruit flavour.

Spike's on 't' Way (OG 1040.5, ABV 4.2%)
Pale bitter with citrus/orange flavour and dry, fruity finish.

Spikus (OG 1040.5, ABV 4.2%)
Made with organic lager malt and New Zealand hops.

Ghost on the Rim (OG 1043, ABV 4.5%)
Pale, dry and fruity.

Yorkshire Wit (ABV 4.5%)

Tabaa-tje (OG 1047.5, ABV 5%)

At 't' Ghoul and Ghost (OG 1048, ABV 5.2%)
Pale golden bitter with a strong citrus and hoppy aroma and flavour. The finish is long, dry, bitter and citrus.

Tabatha the Knackered (OG 1054, ABV 6%)
Golden Belgian-style Tripel with a strong fruity, hoppy and bitter character. Powerful and warming, slightly thinnish, with a bitter, dry finish.

Ann Street

See Jersey

An Teallach

An Teallach Ale Co Ltd, Camusnagaul, Dundonnell, Garve, Ross-shire, IV23 2QT
☎ (01854) 633306
✉ ataleco1@yahoo.co.uk
Tours by arrangement

An Teallach was formed in 2001 by husband and wife team, David and Wilma Orr, on Wilma's family croft on the shores of Little Loch Broom, Wester Ross. The business has grown steadily each year. 60 pubs are supplied. All beers are also available bottled.

Beinn Dearg Ale (OG 1038, ABV 3.8%)
This malty, sweetish beer has a distinct yeasty background.

An Teallach Ale (OG 1042, ABV 4.2%)
A sweetish pint in the Scottish 80/- tradition. Malt and blackcurrant feature in the taste, which can also have a yeasty background.

Crofters Pale Ale (OG 1042, ABV 4.2%)
A good quaffing golden ale with no strong flavours. Meaty, with yeast often to the fore.

Brew House Special (OG 1044, ABV 4.4%)
A golden ale with some hoppy bitterness and often with yeast and sulphur background.

Kildonnon (OG 1044, ABV 4.4%)
Some fruit and a good smack of bitterness.

Appleford

Appleford Brewery Co Ltd, Unit 14, Highlands Farm, High Road, Brightwell-cum-Sotwell, Wallingford, Oxfordshire, OX10 0QX
☎ (01235) 848055
✉ sales@applefordbrewery.co.uk
🌐 applefordbrewery.co.uk

⊗ Appleford Brewery opened in 2006 when two farm units were converted to house an eight-barrel plant. Deliveries are made to a number of local outlets as well as nationally, via the brewery or wholesalers. Bottle-conditioned beers are planned. Seasonal beer: Brightwell Gold (ABV 4%, May-Oct).

River Crossing (ABV 3.8%)
A dark, hoppy session beer

Power Station (ABV 4.2%)
A copper-coloured slightly malty bitter.

Arbor

Arbor Ales Ltd, The Old Tavern, Blackberry Hill, Stapleton, Bristol, BS16 1DB
☎ 07823 335392 / 07884 641597
✉ beer@arborales.co.uk
🌐 arborales.co.uk

⊗ Arbor Ales opened in 2007 in the back of the Old Tavern pub in the building that housed the original Old Tavern Brewery, which is believed to have been brewing until around 1930. A 2.5-barrel plant is used. A wide range of monthly, seasonal and occasional beers are also brewed, with strong, dark beers being a speciality. Bespoke beers are also brewed to order. Around 75 outlets are supplied direct.

Trendlewood Bitter (OG 1039, ABV 4.2%) ◆
Light, fruity and hoppy bitter.

Old Knobbley (OG 1042.5, ABV 4.5%) ◆
Brown, malty and complex best bitter.

For Watershed Café Bar:

Arbor Harbour (OG 1043, ABV 4.3%)
A light, easy-drinking bitter.

Archers

Archers the Brewers Ltd, Penzance Drive, Swindon, Wiltshire, SN5 7JL
☎ (01793) 879929
✉ sales@archersbrewery.co.uk
🌐 archersbrewery.co.uk
Shop Mon-Fri 9.30am-4.30pm
Tours by arrangement

⊗ Archers Brewery was founded in 1979 and has continued to consolidate its position as one of the leading regional breweries in the south. More than 3,000 trade outlets are supplied direct. Champion beer awards for IPA and Golden were achieved at festivals in 2006 to add to an International Brewing bronze in 2005. The company was taken over by new management in 2007. Seasonal beers: Dark Mild (ABV 3.4%), Special Bitter (ABV 4.7%) plus up to six speciality beers per month.

Pride (OG 1038, ABV 3.6%)
Blonde in colour, light and fresh.

Village (OG 1035, ABV 3.6%) ◆
A dry, well-balanced beer with a full body for its gravity. Malty and fruity in the nose, then a fresh, hoppy flavour with balancing malt and a hoppy, fruity finish.

Best Bitter (OG 1040, ABV 4%) ◆
Slightly sweeter and rounder than Village Bitter, with a malty, fruity aroma and pronounced bitter finish.

IPA (OG 1042, ABV 4.2%)
Pale golden, rich in citrus and grapefruit aroma and flavour with a crisp, bitter finish.

Golden (OG 1046, ABV 4.7%) ◆
A full-bodied, hoppy, straw-coloured brew with an underlying fruity sweetness. A gentle aroma, but a strong, distinctive bitter finish.

Crystal Clear (OG 1050, ABV 5%)
Blond, packed with hop aroma with a subtle, balanced finish.

Arkell's IFBB SIBA

Arkell's Brewery Ltd, Kingsdown, Swindon, Wiltshire, SN2 7RU
☎ (01793) 823026
✉ arkells@arkells.com
🌐 arkells.com
Brewery merchandise can be purchased at reception
Tours by arrangement

⊗ Arkells Brewery was established in 1843 and is still run by the family. The brewery owns 105 pubs in Berkshire, Gloucestershire, Oxfordshire and Wiltshire. Seasonal beers: Summer Ale (ABV 4%), JRA (ABV 3.6%), Noel Ale (ABV 5.5%). Bees Organic Beer (ABV 4.5%) is suitable for vegetarians and vegans.

2B (OG 1032, ABV 3.2%) ◆
Light brown in colour, malty but with a smack of hops and an astringent aftertaste. It has good body for its strength.

3B (OG 1040, ABV 4%) ◆
A medium brown beer with a strong, sweetish malt/caramel flavour. The hops come through strongly in the aftertaste, which is lingering and dry.

Moonlight Ale (OG 1046, ABV 4.5%)

Kingsdown Ale (OG 1051, ABV 5%) ◆
A rich, deep russet-coloured beer, a stronger version of 3B. The malty/fruity aroma continues in the taste, which has a hint of pears. Hops come through in the aftertaste.

Arran SIBA

Arran Brew Ltd t/a The Arran Brewery, Cladach, Brodick, Isle of Arran, Strathclyde, KA27 8DE
☎ (01770) 302353
✉ info@arranbrewery.co.uk
🌐 arranbrewery.com
Shop Mon-Sat 10am-5pm; Sun 12.30-5pm in summer, reduced hours in winter
Tours by arrangement

The brewery opened in 2000 with a 20-barrel plant. Production is up to 100 barrels a week with additional bottling capability. 50 outlets are supplied. Bottle-conditioned beer is available occasionally. Seasonal beers: Sunset (ABV 4.4%, Feb-Mar), Fireside (ABV 4.7%, Oct/Nov-Feb/Mar).

Ale (OG 1038, ABV 3.8%) ◆
An amber ale where the predominance of the hop produces a bitter beer with a subtle balancing sweetness of malt and an occasional hint of roast.

Dark (OG 1042, ABV 4.3%) ◆

A well-balanced malty beer with plenty of roast and hop in the taste and a dry, bitter finish.

Blonde (OG 1048, ABV 5%)
A hoppy beer with substantial fruit balance. The taste is balanced and the finish increasingly bitter. An aromatic strong bitter that drinks below its weight.

Arrow

Arrow Brewery, c/o Wine Vaults, 37 High Street, Kington, Herefordshire, HR5 3BJ
☎ (01544) 230685
✉ deanewright@yahoo.co.uk

Former Bridge Street brewer Deane Wright has built his five-barrel brewery at the rear of the Wine Vaults and re-started brewing in 2005.

Bitter (OG 1042, ABV 4%)

Arundel SIBA

Arundel Brewery Ltd, Unit C7, Ford Airfield Industrial Estate, Ford, Arundel, West Sussex, BN18 0HY
☎ (01903) 733111
✉ arundelbrewery@dsl.pipex.com
arundelbrewery.co.uk
Off-sales available Mon-Fri 9am-4pm at brewery

Founded in 1992, Arundel Brewery is the historic town's first brewery in more than 70 years. A range of occasional brands are available in selected months. Seasonal beers: Footslogger (ABV 4.4%, spring), Summer Daze (ABV 4.7%, summer), Autumn Fall (ABV 4.1%, autumn), Black Beastie (ABV 4.9%, winter).

Sussex Mild (OG 1037, ABV 3.7%)
A dark mild. Strong chocolate and roast aromas, which lead to a bitter taste. The aftertaste is not powerful but the initial flavours remain in the dry and clean finish.

Castle (OG 1038, ABV 3.8%)
A pale tawny beer with fruit and malt noticeable in the aroma. The flavour has a good balance of malt, fruit and hops, with a dry, hoppy finish.

Sussex Gold (OG 1042, ABV 4.2%)
A golden-coloured best bitter with a strong floral hop aroma. The ale is clean-tasting and bitter for its strength, with a tangy citrus flavour. The initial hop and fruit die to a dry and bitter finish.

ASB (OG 1045, ABV 4.5%)
A special bitter with a complex roast malt flavour leading to a fruity, hoppy, bittersweet finish.

Stronghold (OG 1047, ABV 4.7%)
A smooth, full-flavoured premium bitter. A good balance of malt, fruit and hops comes through in this rich, chestnut-coloured beer.

Old Knucker (OG 1055, ABV 5.5%)
A black coloured ale with a powerful bitter-sweet taste and a roasted burnt flavour coming at the end. Oily mouthfeel and a long, tangy, sweet aftertaste.

Ascot*

Ascot Ales Ltd, Unit 5, Compton Place, Surrey Avenue, Camberley, Surrey, GU15 3DX
☎ (01276) 686696
✉ info@ascot-ales.co.uk
ascot-ales.co.uk
Tours by arrangement

Ascot Ales began production in 2007 on a four-barrel plant. New owners Chris & Suzanne Gill took over the brewery in late 2007 and plan to add new beers and build on the success of the current ales. They also run the Quaffs Beer Stall at Spitalfields Fine Food Market, London, E1 6DT where the beers are available bottled and in minicasks. Seasonal beer: Santa's Reserve (ABV 5.2%, Xmas). Bottle-conditioned beers are also available.

Shagadellic Session (OG 1039, ABV 3.8%)

Posh Pooch (OG 1042, ABV 4.2%)
A well-balanced best bitter with slightly more hop bitterness than biscuity malt sweetness. The clean, hoppy aftertaste leaves you wanting more.

Alligator Ale (OG 1047, ABV 4.6%)

Anastasia's Exile Stout (OG 1049, ABV 5%)
Burnt coffee aromas lead to a roast malt flavour in this black beer. The presence of some hop feeds into the bitter aftertaste.

Ashover

Ashover Brewery, 1 Butts Road, Ashover, Chesterfield, Derbyshire, S45 0EW
☎ 07803 708526
✉ info@ashoverbrewery.co.uk
ashoverbrewery.co.uk
Tours by arrangement

Ashover Brewery was established in 2006 on a 3.5-barrel plant in the garage of the cottage next to the Old Poet's Corner pub. The brewery caters mainly for this and its sister pub, the Poet & Castle in Codnor, but other local free houses and festivals are also supplied.

Light Rale (OG 1038, ABV 3.7%)

Poets Tipple (OG 1041, ABV 4%)

Rainbows End (OG 1045, ABV 4.5%)

Coffin Lane Stout (OG 1050, ABV 5%)

Butts Pale Ale (OG 1055, ABV 5.5%)

Aston Manor

Aston Manor Brewery Co Ltd, 173 Thimble Mill Lane, Aston, Birmingham, West Midlands, B7 5HS
☎ (0121) 328 4336
✉ sales@astonmanor.co.uk
astonmanor.co.uk

Aston Manor is the former owner of the Highgate Brewery in Walsall (qv). Its own plant concentrates on cider. Beer is bottled at Highgate but is not bottle-conditioned.

Atlantic

Atlantic Brewery, Treisaac Farm, Treisaac, Newquay, Cornwall, TR8 4DX

☎ (0870) 042 1714
✉ contact@atlanticbrewery.com
⊕ atlanticbrewery.com

Atlantic started brewing in 2005. All beers are organic, Soil Association certified and suitable for vegetarians and vegans. It concentrates on bottle-conditioned beers: Gold (ABV 4.6%, summer), Blue (ABV 4.8%), Red (ABV 5%), Fistral (ABV 5.2%).

Atlas SIBA

Atlas Brewery, Sinclair Breweries Ltd, Lab Road, Kinlochleven, Argyll, PH50 4SG
☎ (01855) 831111
✉ info@sinclairbreweries.co.uk
⊕ atlasbrewery.com
Shop open office hours
Tours by arrangement

Founded in 2002, Atlas is a 20-barrel brewery in a 100 year-old listed Victorian industrial building on the banks of the River Leven. It merged in 2004 with Orkney (qv) and now forms part of Sinclair Breweries. Production remains at both sites. Around 250 outlets in Scotland are supplied direct and via wholesalers to the rest of Britain. Seasonal beers: Equinox (ABV 4.5%, spring), Wayfarer (ABV 4.4%, summer), Tempest (ABV 4.9%, autumn), Blizzard (ABV 4.7%, winter).

Latitude (OG 1036, ABV 3.6%)
This golden ale has a light citrus taste with a hint of hops in the light, bitter finish.

Three Sisters (OG 1043, ABV 4.2%)
Full of malt and summer fruits in the nose and taste, followed by a short, hoppy bitter finish.

Nimbus (OG 1050, ABV 5%)
A full-bodied golden beer using some wheat malt and three types of hops. Dry and fruity at the front, it becomes slightly astringent with lasting fruit and a pleasant, dry finish.

Atlas Mill*

Atlas Mill Brewery Ltd, Atlas Mill Road, Brighouse, West Yorkshire, HD6 1ES
☎ (01484) 720440

Atlas Mill was built in late 2006 and came on stream in 2007. The Brewery Tap, the Tipp Inn, was opened in September 2007. Seasonal Beer: Christmas Ale (ABV 6%).

Mild (ABV 3.6%)

Bitter (ABV 3.8%)

Gold (ABV 3.8%)

Premium (ABV 4.2%)

Stout (ABV 4.4%)

Herculese (ABV 4.5%)

IPA (ABV 5%)

Atomic

Atomic Brewery, c/o Sounds Expensive, 12 Regent Street, Rugby, Warwickshire, CV21 2QF
☎ (01788) 542170
✉ sales@atomicbrewery.com
⊕ atomicbrewery.com
Tours by arrangement

Atomic Brewery started production in 2006 and is run by CAMRA members Keith Abbis and Nick Pugh. They own one pub, the Victoria Inn in Rugby, which acts as the brewery tap. Future plans include new beers and the purchasing of more pubs.

Strike (OG 1039, ABV 3.7%)

Fission (OG 1040, ABV 3.9%)

Fusion (OG 1042, ABV 4.1%)

Reactor (OG 1047, ABV 4.5%)

Half-Life (OG 1051, ABV 5%)

Bomb (OG 1054, ABV 5.2%)

Avon*

Avon Brewing Company Ltd, Unit 4, Russell Town Avenue Industrial Centre, Bristol, BS5 9LT
☎ (0117) 955 3353
⊕ avonbrewing.co.uk

Avon began brewing in May 2008 on an eight-barrel plant.

Gurt Lush (OG 1046, ABV 4.5%)

AVS

See Loddon

B&T SIBA EAB

B&T Brewery Ltd, The Brewery, Shefford, Bedfordshire, SG17 5DZ
☎ (01462) 815080
✉ brewery@banksandtaylor.com
⊕ banksandtaylor.com
Tours by arrangement

Banks & Taylor – now just B&T – was founded in 1982. It produces an extensive range of beers, including monthly special brews together with occasional beers: see website for details. Four pubs are owned. Bottle-conditioned beers are available.

Two Brewers (OG 1036, ABV 3.6%)
Bronze-coloured bitter with citrus hop aroma and taste with a dry finish.

Shefford Bitter (OG 1038, ABV 3.8%)
A pale brown beer with a light hop aroma and a hoppy taste leading to a bitter finish.

Shefford Dark Mild (OG 1038, ABV 3.8%)
A dark beer with a well-balanced taste. Sweetish, roast malt aftertaste.

Golden Fox (OG 1041, ABV 4.1%)
A golden, hoppy ale, dry tasting with a fruity aroma and citrus finish.

Black Dragon Mild (OG 1043, ABV 4.3%)
Black in colour with a toffee and roast malt flavour and a smoky finish.

Dragonslayer (OG 1045, ABV 4.5%)
A golden beer with a malt and hop flavour and a bitter finish. More malty and less hoppy than is usual for a beer of this style.

Edwin Taylor's Extra Stout (OG 1045, ABV 4.5%)

A complex black beer with a bitter coffee and roast malt flavour and a dry bitter finish.

Fruit Bat (OG 1045, ABV 4.5%) ◈
A warming straw-coloured beer with a generous taste of raspberries and a bitter finish.

Shefford Pale Ale/SPA (OG 1045, ABV 4.5%) ◈
A well-balanced beer with hop, fruit and malt flavours. Dry, bitter aftertaste.

SOD (OG 1050, ABV 5%)
SOS with caramel added for colour, often sold under house names.

SOS (OG 1050, ABV 5%) ◈
A rich mixture of fruit, hops and malt is present in the taste and aftertaste of this beer. Predominantly hoppy aroma.

Badger

See Hall & Woodhouse

Ballard's SIBA

Ballard's Brewery Ltd, Unit 3, The Old Sawmill, Nyewood, Rogate, Petersfield, Hampshire, GU31 5HA
☎ (01730) 821301/821362
✉ info@ballardsbrewery.org.uk
🌐 ballardsbrewery.org.uk
Shop Mon-Fri 8am-4pm
Tours by arrangement

⊗ Launched in 1980 by Mike and Carola Brown at Cumbers Farm, Trotton, Ballard's has been trading at Nyewood since 1988 and now supplies around 60 free trade outlets. Seasonal beers: Trotton Bitter (ABV 3.6%, spring), Wheatsheaf (ABV 5%, summer), On the Hop (ABV 4.5%, autumn), Old Bounder Series (ABV over 9%, winter). Bottle-conditioned beers are also available.

Midhurst Mild (OG 1034, ABV 3.5%)
Traditional dark mild, well-balanced, refreshing, with a biscuity flavour.

Golden Bine (OG 1038, ABV 3.8%) ◈
Amber, clean-tasting bitter. A roast malt aroma leads to a fruity, slightly sweet taste and a dry finish.

Best Bitter (OG 1042, ABV 4.2%) ◈
A copper-coloured beer with a malty aroma. A good balance of fruit and malt in the flavour gives way to a dry, hoppy aftertaste.

Wild (ABV 4.7%)
A blend of Mild and Wassail.

Nyewood Gold (OG 1050, ABV 5%) ◈
Robust golden brown strong bitter, very hoppy and fruity throughout, with a tasty balanced finish.

Wassail (OG 1060, ABV 6%) ◈
A strong, full-bodied, tawny-red, fruity beer with a predominance of malt throughout, but also an underlying hoppiness.

Bank Top SIBA

Bank Top Brewery Ltd, The Pavilion, Ashworth Lane, Bolton, Lancashire, BL1 8RA
☎ (01204) 595800
✉ dave@banktopbrewery.com
🌐 banktopbrewery.com
Tours by arrangement

⊚ Bank Top was established in 1995 by John Feeney and has enjoyed gradual expansion. It relocated to the Grade II listed pavilion in 2002 and in 2004 John formed a partnership with David Sweeney. In 2007 the brewing capacity was doubled with the installation of a new 10-barrel plant and David became the sole proprietor when John retired. The beers are supplied to around 150 outlets locally and throughout the North-west and Yorkshire. Seasonal beers: Santa's Claws (ABV 5%, Xmas), Leprechaun Stout (ABV 6%, Mar). Bottle-conditioned beers are also available.

Bikes, Trikes and Beer (OG 1036, ABV 3.6%) ◈
A gold-coloured beer with a grainy mouthfeel. Hoppy, fruity aroma with citrus, hops and bitterness in taste and aftertaste.

Bowl Town Bitter (ABV 3.8%)
A straw-coloured session bitter with citrus and blackcurrant flavours and a distinctive hoppy aftertaste.

Bad to the Bone (OG 1040, ABV 4%)

Dark Mild (OG 1040, ABV 4%) ◈
Dark brown beer with a malt and roast aroma. Smooth mouthfeel, with malt, roast malt and hops prominent throughout.

Flat Cap (OG 1040, ABV 4%) ◈
Amber ale with a modest fruit aroma leading to a beer with citrus fruit, malt and hops. Good finish of fruit, malt and bitterness.

Gold Digger (OG 1040, ABV 4%) ◈
Golden coloured, with a citrus aroma, grapefruit and a touch of spiciness on the palate; a fresh, hoppy citrus finish.

Pavilion Pale Ale (OG 1045, ABV 4.5%) ◈
A yellow beer with a citrus and hop aroma. Big fruity flavour with a peppery hoppiness; dry, bitter yet fruity finish.

Volunteer Bitter (OG 1045, ABV 4.5%)

Blonde (ABV 5%)
An extremely pale ale made with New Zealand hops resulting in a pleasant woody flavour and distinct berry aroma.

Port O Call (OG 1050, ABV 5%)

Banks's

See Wolverhampton & Dudley in New Nationals section

Barearts

Barearts Brewery, Off sales, Bar & Gallery: 108-110 Rochdale Road, Todmorden, West Yorkshire, OL14 7LP
☎ (01706) 839305
🌐 barearts.com
Shop Fri 4-7pm; Sat 11am-3pm; Sun 3-7pm

A four-barrel craft brewery that began production in 2005 and is owned by Kathryn and Trevor Cook. It is named after their gallery, which is dedicated to nude art work.

They specialise in beers to drink at home – each brew is unique and a range of over a dozen beers is always available. Ciders and perries are also produced. Their real ales are available in bottles, 5 litre mini casks and 8.5 litre Party Pigs. Barearts beers are only available from their brewery shop or by mail order.

Barge & Barrel

See Eastwood

Barngates SIBA

Barngates Brewery Ltd, Barngates, Ambleside, Cumbria, LA22 0NG
☎ (015394) 36575
✉ info@barngatesbrewerytrade.co.uk
🌐 barngatesbrewerytrade.co.uk
Tours by arrangement

Barngates Brewery started brewing in 1997 and initially provided only the Drunken Duck Inn. The brewery became a limited company in 1999 upon expansion to a five-barrel plant. Further expansion in 2008 included a brand new, purpose-built 10-barrel plant enabling production to keep pace with demand. Around 60-80 outlets are supplied direct throughout Cumbria, Lancashire, Yorkshire and Northumberland.

Cat Nap (OG 1037, ABV 3.6%) ◆
A golden, hoppy beer with a hint of grapefruit. The high impact bitterness is sustained through the aftertaste.

Mothbag (ABV 3.6%)

1077 – 10th Anniversary Ale (OG 1039, ABV 3.9%)
Warm copper colour, with a vibrant, fruity aroma and taste. A full-flavoured classic bitter.

Cracker Ale (OG 1038, ABV 3.9%)
Copper-coloured with a subtle hoppy aroma, clean, smooth and refreshing, developing into a long bitter finish.

K9 Commemorative Ale (OG 1041, ABV 4%)
A light gold beer with a delicate grapefruit aroma and fresh, bitter, citrus flavour.

Pride of Westmorland (OG 1042, ABV 4.1%)
Ruby red with a berry fruit aroma and delicious malt and hop flavours. A polished, soft, bitter finish builds in the aftertaste.

Westmorland Gold (OG 1043, ABV 4.2%) ◆
A golden ale with a good balance of malt and hops, perhaps not as intense as previously.

Tag Lag (OG 1044, ABV 4.4%) ◆
A pale amber beer, smooth and sweetly malty to begin but a lasting, bitter finish.

Red Bull Terrier (OG 1048, ABV 4.8%)
A deep red tone and a complex hop nose are complemented by tangy fruit and malt flavours with a spicy aftertaste.

Chester's Strong & Ugly (OG 1052, ABV 5.2%) ◆
Complex and well-balanced, a richly satisfying dark beer with plenty of roast and hop bitterness.

Barrowden SIBA

Barrowden Brewing Co, c/o Exeter Arms, 28 Main Street, Barrowden, Rutland, LE15 8EQ
☎ (01572) 747247
🌐 exeterarms.com
Tours by arrangement

The brewery was established by Peter Blencowe in 1998. Martin Allsopp bought the pub and brewery in 2005 and has increased volume with new beers. Seasonal beers: Danny (ABV 4.5%, spring), Winter Hop (ABV 4.7%, winter), Attitude Two (ABV 6%, autumn).

Beech (OG 1038, ABV 3.8%)

Owngear (ABV 4%)

Hopgear (OG 1044, ABV 4.4%)

Bevin (OG 1045, ABV 4.5%)

Bartrams SIBA EAB

Bartrams Brewery, Rougham Estate, Ipswich Road (A14), Rougham, Suffolk, IP30 9LZ
☎ (01449) 737655
☎ 07768 062581
✉ marc@bartramsbrewery.co.uk
🌐 bartramsbrewery.co.uk
Shop Tue & Sat 12-6pm
Tours by arrangement

The brewery was set up in 1999. In 2005 the plant was moved to a building on Rougham Airfield, the site of Bartram's Brewery between 1894 and 1902 run by Captain Bill Bartram. His image graces the pump clips. Beers are available in a selection of local pubs and there is a large amount of trade through local farmers' markets. Marld, Beltane Braces and all porters and stouts are suitable for vegetarians and vegans, as are all bottled beers. Seasonal beers: see website.

Marld (ABV 3.4%)
A traditional mild. Spicy hops and malt with a hint of chocolate, slightly smoky with a light, roasted finish.

Rougham Ready (ABV 3.6%)
A light, crisp bitter, surprisingly full bodied for its strength.

Trial and Error (ABV 3.6%)
A full malty bitter, fruity with a lot of character.

Premier (ABV 3.7%)
A traditional quaffing ale, full-flavoured but light, dry and hoppy.

Little Green Man (ABV 3.8%)
A golden bitter with the peppery and delicate citrus tones of subtle coriander. Dry and bitter.

Red Queen (ABV 3.9%)
Typical IPA style, chocolate malt in the foreground while the resiny hop flavour lingers.

Cats Whiskers (ABV 4%)
A straw-coloured beer with ginger and lemons added; a unique flavour experience.

Grozet (ABV 4%)
Using Little Green Man as the base beer, gooseberries are added to give an appealing extra dimension.

Bees Knees (ABV 4.2%)
An amber beer with a floral aroma; honey softness on the palate leads to a crisp, bitter finish.

Catherine Bartram's IPA (ABV 4.3%)
A full-bodied malty IPA style; tangy hops lead the malt throughout and dominate the dry, hoppy aftertaste.

Mother McCleary's Milk Stout (ABV 4.3%)

Jester Quick One (ABV 4.4%)
A sweet reddish bitter using fruity American Ahtanum hops.

Beltane Braces (ABV 4.5%)
Smooth and dark.

Coal Porter (ABV 4.5%)
Plenty of body in this ruby beer, supported by ample hops.

Stingo (ABV 4.5%)
A sweetish, fruity bitter with a hoppy nose. Light honey softens the bitter finish.

Beer Elsie Bub (ABV 4.8%)
Originally brewed for a Pagan wedding, this strong honey ale is now brewed all year round.

Captain Bill Bartram's Best Bitter (ABV 4.8%)
Modified from a 100-year old recipe, using full malt and traditional Kentish hops.

Captain's Stout (ABV 4.8%)
Biscuity dark malt leads to a lightly smoked aroma, plenty of roasted malt character, coffee notes and a whiff of smoke.

Cherry Stout (ABV 4.8%)
Sensuous hints of chocolate lead to a subtle suggestion of cherries.

Damson Stout (ABV 4.8%)
A robust, full-bodied stout with the chocolate and smoky aroma giving way to a lingering finish.

Trafalgar Squared (ABV 4.8%)
Brewed using malt grown a few miles from Nelson's birthplace and Goldings hops.

Suffolk 'n' Strong (ABV 5%)
A light, smooth and dangerously potable strong bitter, well-balanced malt and hops with an easy finish.

Comrade Bill Bartram's Egalitarian Anti-Imperialist Soviet Stout (ABV 6.9%)
A Russian stout by any other name, a luscious easy-drinking example of the style.

Barum SIBA

Barum Brewery Ltd, c/o Reform Inn, Pilton, Barnstaple, Devon, EX31 1PD
☎ (01271) 329994
✉ info@barumbrewery.co.uk
🌐 barumbrewery.co.uk
Tours by arrangement

⊗ Barum was formed in 1996 by Tim Webster and is housed in a conversion attached to the Reform Inn which acts as the brewery tap and main outlet. Distribution is exclusively within Devon. Seasonal beers: Mild (ABV 4.2%, spring), Gold (ABV 4%, summer), Barnstablasta (ABV 6.6%, winter), Agincourt (ABV 4.5%, St Crispins Day).

Basil's Best (OG 1040, ABV 4%)

Original (OG 1044, ABV 4.4%)

Breakfast (OG 1048, ABV 5%)

Bateman IFBB SIBA

George Bateman & Son Ltd, Salem Bridge Brewery, Mill Lane, Wainfleet, Lincolnshire, PE24 4JE
☎ (01754) 880317
✉ enquiries@bateman.co.uk
🌐 bateman.co.uk
Shop 11.30am-3.30pm daily
Daily tours 2.30pm (no booking necessary); Evening tours by prior arrangement

Bateman's Brewery is one of the few remaining independent family-owned brewers. Established in 1874 they have been brewing award-winning beers for four generations of Batemans. All but one of the 67 tied houses serve cask-conditioned beer. Please see website for seasonal and speciality beers.

Dark Mild (OG 1030, ABV 3%) ◆
Characteristic orchard fruit and roasted nut nose with hops evident. One of the classic mild ales, although the lasting bitter finish may not be entirely true to type; nevertheless, a ruby-black gem.

XB Bitter (OG 1037, ABV 3.7%) ◆
A mid-brown balanced session bitter with malt most obvious in the finish. The taste is dominated by the house style apple hop, which also leads the aroma.

Valiant (OG 1042, ABV 4.2%)
A delicious golden beer, clean, crisp and zesty.

Salem Porter (OG 1048, ABV 4.7%) ◆
A black and complex mix of chocolate, liquorice and cough elixir.

XXXB (OG 1048, ABV 4.8%) ◆
A brilliant blend of malt, hops and fruit on the nose with a bitter bite over the top of a faintly banana maltiness that stays the course. A russet-tan brown classic.

Bath Ales SIBA

Bath Ales Ltd, Units 3-7, Caxton Business Park, Crown Way, Warmley, Bristol, BS30 8XJ
☎ (0117) 947 4797
✉ hare@bathales.co.uk
🌐 bathales.com
Shop Mon-Fri 9am-5pm; Sat 9am-12pm
Tours by arrangement

⊗ Bath Ales started brewing in 1995 and moved in 1999 to new premises with a 15-barrel plant. The company now has a purpose-built site on the edge of east Bristol, and can brew 250 barrels a week. Around 350 outlets are supplied direct. Ten pubs are owned, all serving cask ale. Seasonal beers: Festivity (ABV 5%), Rare Hare (ABV 5.2%). Most beers are available for purchase from the website or shop.

SPA (OG 1037, ABV 3.7%) ◆
Gold/yellow colour, this is a light-bodied dry, bitter beer with a citrus hop aroma. Long malty, dry and bitter finish with some fruit.

Gem Bitter (OG 1042, ABV 4.1%)
This well-balanced, medium-bodied bitter is malty (pale and crystal with caramel), fruity and hoppy throughout. Amber-coloured, it is dry and bitter at the end.

Barnstormer (OG 1047, ABV 4.5%)
Malt, hops and fruit aroma with a faint hint of roast, with toffee sweetness. Dark brown, well balanced and smooth with a malty, bitter, dry finish.

Wild Hare (OG 1048, ABV 5%)
Pale organic strong bitter. Toasted grapefruit aroma, hoppy/fruity taste developing into a long-lasting dry, fruity finish. Refreshing and clean on the palate.

Batham IFBB

Daniel Batham & Son Ltd, Delph Brewery, Delph Road, Brierley Hill, West Midlands, DY5 2TN
☎ (01384) 77229
info@bathams.com
bathams.com

A classic Black Country small brewery established in 1877. Tim and Matthew Batham represent the fifth generation to run the company. The Vine, one of the Black Country's most famous pubs, is also the site of the brewery. The company has 11 tied houses and supplies around 30 other outlets. Batham's Bitter is delivered in 54-gallon hogsheads to meet demand. Seasonal beer: XXX (ABV 6.3%, Dec).

Mild Ale (OG 1036.5, ABV 3.5%)
A fruity, dark brown mild with malty sweetness and a roast malt finish.

Best Bitter (OG 1043.5, ABV 4.3%)
A pale yellow, fruity, sweetish bitter, with a dry, hoppy finish. A good, light, refreshing beer.

Battersea SIBA

Battersea Brewery Co Ltd, 43 Glycena Road, Battersea, London, SW11 5TP
☎ (020) 7978 7978
enquiries@batterseabrewery.com
batterseabrewery.com

Battersea has been brewing since 2001. The beers are all sold locally and in south-east England to the free trade and pub chains. The beers are made from hops and malt sourced as close as possible to the brewery and no additives are used. Bottle-conditioned beer is available.

Pagoda (OG 1038, ABV 3.7%)
Pale amber ale with a citrus fruit and sweet malt character.

Bitter (OG 1040, ABV 4%)
A well-balanced, easy-drinking, copper-coloured bitter; malt, apple and a slightly bitter hoppiness linger through to a short finish.

Power Station Porter (OG 1049, ABV 4.9%)
Raisins and some citrus hops are present on nose, palate and finish of this ruby-black beer. The black roasted malt balances the sweetness and its bitter character lingers.

Battledown

Battledown Brewery llp, Keynsham Works, Keynsham Street, Cheltenham, Gloucestershire, GL52 6EJ
☎ (01242) 693409
☎ 07734 834104
roland@battledownbrewery.com
battledownbrewery.com
Shop open Wed/Thu/Sat am
Tours by arrangement

Established in 2005 by Roland and Stephanie Elliott-Berry, and joined in 2006 by Ben Jennison-Phillips (ex-Whittingtons), Battledown operates an eight-barrel plant from an old engineering works and supplies over 150 outlets. Visitors are always welcome.

Saxon (OG 1038, ABV 3.8%)
Fresh and crisp with a hoppy finish.

Sunbeam (OG 1039, ABV 4%)
A smooth and light gold California Common beer, using a lager yeast at ale temperatures.

Tipster (OG 1041, ABV 4.2%)
A golden beer, the malts evident but giving way to the triple hop addition to give a spicy and slightly citrus finish.

Turncoat (OG 1046, ABV 4.5%)
A deep red and smooth porter, coffee notes and a hint of bitterness.

Brigand (OG 1048, ABV 4.7%)
Rich in malt with a hint of spice from Challenger hops.

Cheltenham SPA (OG 1050, ABV 5.2%)
A traditional IPA, crisp with plenty of hops.

Four Kings (OG 1066, ABV 7.2%)
Strong ale. Rich and smooth.

Bays*

Bays Brewery Ltd, Aspen Way, Paignton, Devon, TQ4 7QR
☎ (01803) 555004
info@baysbrewery.co.uk
baysbrewery.co.uk
Shop Mon-Fri 8am-5pm
Tours by arrangement

Bays Brewery opened in early 2007 in an old steel fabrication unit in Paignton on a 20-barrel plant. Over 200 outlets are supplied direct.

Best (OG 1037, ABV 3.7%)

Gold (OG 1042, ABV 4.3%)

Breaker (OG 1046, ABV 4.7%)

Bazens' SIBA

Bazens' Brewery, Rees Bazen Brewing Co Ltd, Unit 6, Knoll Street Industrial Park, Knoll Street, Salford, Greater Manchester, M7 2BL
☎ (0161) 708 0247
bazensbrewery@mac.com
bazensbrewery.co.uk
Tours by arrangement for CAMRA groups

Run by husband and wife Richard and Jude Bazen, Bazens' Brewery was established in 2002 and moved to its present location a year later. Around 50 pubs are supplied direct.

Black Pig Mild (OG 1037, ABV 3.6%)
A dark brown beer with malt and fruit aromas. Roast, chocolate and fruit flavours, with an underlying bitterness, lead to a dry, malty and slightly smoky aftertaste.

Pacific Bitter (OG 1039, ABV 3.8%)
Gold-coloured bitter with a fruity nose. Hops and citrus fruit dominate the taste and there is a bitter, hoppy finish.

Flatbac (OG 1042, ABV 4.2%)
Well-balanced, distinctive and refreshing blonde beer. A full hop character has pronounced citrus/floral notes.

Zebra Best Bitter (OG 1043, ABV 4.3%)
A complex premium bitter, loaded with full malt flavour and crisp fruity hop character.

Blue Bullet (OG 1045, ABV 4.5%)
Yellow in colour, this golden ale has a fruity aroma. Hops, fruit and bitterness are in the taste and linger in the finish.

Knoll Street Porter (OG 1055, ABV 5.2%)
Dark brown beer with a chocolaty and malt aroma. Roast and chocolate malt, hops and fruit to taste, with a satisfying complex finish.

Beachy Head

Beachy Head Brewing Co Ltd, Seven Sisters Sheep Centre, Birling Manor Farm, Birling Gap Road, East Dean, East Sussex, BN20 0AA
(01323) 423906
charlie@beachyhead.org.uk
beachyhead.org.uk
Tours by arrangement

The 2.5-barrel brew plant was installed at the rear of the Seven Sisters Sheep Centre in October 2006. Beachy Head mainly produces bottle-conditoned beers and supplies to around eight outlets. Some cask-conditioned beer is also produced for beer festivals and one or two local pubs on an occasional basis. Bottle-conditioned beers: Beachy Original (ABV 4.5%), Legless Rambler (ABV 5%), Parson Darbys Hole (ABV 4%), Snow Drop (ABV 6.2%, Xmas).

Beartown SIBA

Beartown Brewery Ltd, Bromley House, Spindle Street, Congleton, Cheshire, CW12 1QN
(01260) 299964
headbrewer@beartownbrewery.co.uk
beartownbrewery.co.uk
Tours by arrangement

Congleton's links with brewing can be traced back to 1272. Two of its most senior officers at the time were Ale Taster and Bear Warden, hence the name of the brewery. Both the brewery's Navigation in Stockport and the Beartown Tap have been named CAMRA regional pubs of the year. There are plans are to extend the tied estate to 15 outlets over the next two years. Beartown supplies 250 outlets and owns five pubs. A new 25-barrel plant has been installed.

Bear Ass (OG 1040, ABV 4%)
Dark ruby-red, malty bitter with good hop nose and fruity flavour with dry, bitter, astringent aftertaste.

Ginger Bear (OG 1040, ABV 4%)
The flavours from the malt and hops blend with the added bite from the root ginger to produce a quenching finish.

Kodiak Gold (OG 1040, ABV 4%)
Hops and fruit dominate the taste of this crisp yellow bitter and these follow through to the dryish aftertaste. Biscuity malt also comes through on the aroma and taste.

Bearskinful (OG 1043, ABV 4.2%)
Biscuity malt dominates the flavour of this amber best bitter. There are hops and a hint of sulphur on the aroma. A balance of malt and bitterness follow through to the aftertaste.

Bearly Literate (OG 1045, ABV 4.5%)

Polar Eclipse (OG 1048, ABV 4.8%)
Classic black, dry and bitter stout, with roast flavours to the fore. Good hop on the nose following through the taste into a long dry finish.

Black Bear (OG 1050, ABV 5%)
Advertised as a strong mild, this beer is rather bitter for the style. Bitter and malt flavours are balanced and there is also a good roast character along with a hint of liquorice. Aftertaste is short and reasonably dry.

Bruins Ruin (OG 1050, ABV 5%)

Beckstones SIBA

Beckstones Brewery, Upper Beckstones Mill, The Green, Millom, Cumbria, LA18 5HL
(01229) 775294
david@beckstonesbrewery.com
beckstonesbrewery.co.uk

Beckstones started brewing in 2003 on the site of an 18th-century mill with its own water supply.

Leat (OG 1038, ABV 3.6%)
A refreshing golden bitter with tangy fruit and a rising hop finish.

Black Dog Freddy Mild (OG 1038, ABV 3.8%)
A full-bodied, beautifully balanced ruby dark mild, replete with fruit and roast malt.

Iron Town (OG 1040, ABV 3.8%)
A well-balanced, malt and hops session ale.

Beer O'Clock (OG 1040, ABV 3.9%)
A golden, hoppy beer.

Border Steeans (OG 1042, ABV 4.1%)
Scottish Borders style, bittersweet with berry fruit undertones.

Hematite (OG 1058, ABV 5.5%)
A luscious strong dark mild, mellow but punchy, full of dark fruit and a hint of liquorice.

Beer Engine SIBA

Tuttles Unique Co Ltd t/a The Beer Engine, Newton St Cyres, Devon, EX5 5AX
(01392) 851282
info@thebeerengine.co.uk
thebeerengine.co.uk
Tours by arrangement

⊗ Beer Engine was developed in 1983 and in 2008 celebrated 25 years as a fully functional micro-brewery. In 2007 the brewery underwent some much needed repairs and still employs the original 1984 brewer, Ian Sharp. The brewery is visible behind glass downstairs in the pub. Around five outlets are supplied regularly. Seasonal beer: Whistlemas (ABV varies, winter).

Rail Ale (OG 1037, ABV 3.8%) ◆
A straw-coloured beer with a fruity aroma and a sweet, fruity finish.

Piston Bitter (OG 1043, ABV 4.3%) ◆
A mid-brown, sweet-tasting beer with a pleasant, bittersweet aftertaste.

Sleeper Heavy (OG 1052, ABV 5.4%) ◆
A red-coloured beer with a fruity, sweet taste and a bitter finish.

Bees*

Bees Brewery, c/o Branstons, 1487 Melton Road, Queniborough, Leicester, LE7 3FP
☎ **(0116) 260 7715**
☎ **07971 577526**
Tours by arrangement

Brewing started in February 2008 on a 9.5-barrel plant. More beers are planned in the near future including an organic and a gluten-free beer. Both regular beers are also available bottle conditioned.

Navigator (OG 1045, ABV 4.5%)

Wobble (OG 1050, ABV 5%)

Beeston

Beeston Brewery Ltd, Fransham Road Farm, Beeston, Norfolk, PE32 2LZ
☎ **(01328) 700844**
☎ **07768 742763**
✉ **mark_riches@tesco.net**
🌐 **beestonbrewery.co.uk**
Tours by arrangement

⊗ The brewery was established in 2007 in an old farm building using a five-barrel plant. Brewing water comes from a dedicated borehole and raw ingredients are sourced locally whenever possible. Both cask beers are also available bottle conditioned.

Afternoon Delight (OG 1036, ABV 3.7%)
A blonde ale, suitable for a lunchtime refreshment or as an evening session beer.

Worth the Wait (OG 1041, ABV 4.2%) ◆
Jaunty gold-coloured bitter with a refreshingly citrus tang. An underlying hoppiness continues through to a short grapefruit finish that refreshes the palate.

On the Huh (OG 1048, ABV 5%)
An old-style traditional strong bitter, smooth, malty and full-bodied.

Belhaven

See Greene King in New Nationals section

Bell's

Bell's Brewery & Merchants Ltd, c/o Quench, 52D Main Street, Broughton Astley, Leicestershire, LE9 6RD
☎ **(01455) 289828**
✉ **jon@bellsbrewery.co.uk**
🌐 **bellsbrewery.co.uk**
Shop Tue-Sat 9am-5pm; Sun 10am-4.30pm
Tours by arrangement (Wed/Thu daytime only)

⊗ Bell's opened in 2004 and relocated from Bitteswell to Ullesthorpe in 2005. In spring 2008 the Ullesthorpe operation was closed and the main selling outlet for the beers became the brewery's shop in Broughton Astley. A new location for the brew plant was being sought at the time of going to press. All beers are also available bottle conditioned.

Wide Mouth Frog (OG 1038, ABV 3.8%)

Smalley's Stout (OG 1041, ABV 4.1%)

Mad Cow (OG 1043, ABV 4.3%)

Arapahoe (OG 1049, ABV 5.3%)

Copernicus (OG 1085, ABV 9%)

Belvoir SIBA

Belvoir Brewery Ltd, Crown Park, Station Road, Old Dalby, Leicestershire, LE14 3NQ
☎ **(01664) 823455**
✉ **colin@belvoirbrewery.co.uk**
🌐 **belvoirbrewery.co.uk**
Tours by arrangement

⊗ Belvoir (pronounced 'beaver') Brewery was set up in 1995 by former Shipstone's brewer Colin Brown. Long-term expansion has seen the introduction of a 20-barrel plant that can produce 50 barrels a week and a visitor centre. Bottle-conditioned beers are produced using in-house bottling equipment. Up to 150 outlets are supplied. Seasonal beers: Whippling Golden Bitter (ABV 3.6%, spring/summer), Peacock's Glory (ABV 4.7%, spring/summer), Old Dalby (ABV 5.1%, winter). Bottle-conditioned beers are also available.

Star Mild (OG 1034, ABV 3.4%) ◆
Reddish/black in colour, this full-bodied and well-balanced mild is both malty and hoppy with hints of fruitiness leading to a long, bittersweet finish.

Star Bitter (OG 1039, ABV 3.9%) ◆
Reminiscent of the long-extinct Shipstone's Bitter, this mid-brown bitter lives up to its name as it is bitter in taste but not unpleasantly so.

Beaver Bitter (OG 1043, ABV 4.3%) ◆
A light brown bitter that starts malty in both aroma and taste, but soon develops a hoppy bitterness. Appreciably fruity.

Melton Mowbray Oatmeal Stout (OG 1044, ABV 4.3%)

Beowulf SIBA

Beowulf Brewing Co, Chasewater Country Park, Pool Road, Brownhills, Staffordshire, WS8 7NL
☎ **(01543) 454067**
✉ **beowulfbrewing@yahoo.co.uk**

Tours by arrangement

Beowulf Brewing Company beers appear as guest ales predominantly in the central region but also across the country. The brewery's dark beers have a particular reputation for excellence. Seasonal beers: Hurricane (ABV 4%, autumn), Glutlusty (ABV 4.5%, autumn), Blizzard (ABV 5%, winter), Grendel's Winter Ale (ABV 5.8%, winter), Wergild (ABV 4.3%, spring/summer), Wuffa (ABV 4.4%, spring/summer), Gold Work (ABV 5.1%, spring/summer). Bottle-conditioned beer is also available.

Beorma (OG 1038, ABV 3.9%) ◆
A pale session ale with a malty hint of fruit giving way to a lingering bitterness.

Noble Bitter (OG 1039, ABV 4%) ◆
Golden with a sweet malty aroma. Malty start becomes very hoppy then bitter, but not an over-long finish.

Wiglaf (OG 1043, ABV 4.3%) ◆
A golden bitter, with a malty flavour married to a pleasing bitterness, with three hop varieties used.

Chasewater Bitter (OG 1043, ABV 4.4%) ◆
Golden bitter, hoppy throughout with citrus and hints of malt. Long mouth-watering, bitter finish.

Dark Raven (OG 1048, ABV 4.5%)

Swordsman (OG 1045, ABV 4.5%) ◆
Pale gold, light fruity aroma, tangy hoppy flavour. Faintly hoppy finish.

Dragon Smoke Stout (OG 1048, ABV 4.7%) ◆
Black with a light brown creamy head. Roast aromas of tobacco, charcoal, liquorice with raisins and mixed fruity tangs. Tastes of burnt and smoked fruit with hops providing a bitter edge. Smooth mouthfeel but gives continual flavours to a mouth-watering finish. Hints of a good port emerge and warm you through.

Finn's Hall Porter (OG 1049, ABV 4.7%) ◆
Mint chocolate fumes laced with liquorice. Full roast flavours with fruit and toffee. Delicious hoppy finish with liquorice stick reminders, leading to a long nutty, dry astringency.

Heroes Bitter (OG 1046, ABV 4.7%) ◆
Gold colour, malt aroma, hoppy taste but sweetish finish.

Mercian Shine (OG 1048, ABV 5%) ◆
Amber to pale gold with a good bitter and hoppy start. Plenty of caramel and hops with background malt leading to a good bitter finish with caramel and hops lingering in the aftertaste.

Berrow SIBA

Berrow Brewery, Coast Road, Berrow, Burnham-on-Sea, Somerset, TA8 2QU
☎ (01278) 751345
Tours by arrangement

⊗ The brewery opened in 1982 and production is now around five barrels a week. It celebrated its silver jubilee in 2007. All the beers have won prizes at beer festivals. 15-20 outlets are supplied. Seasonal beers: Carnivale (ABV 4.7%, Oct-Nov), Christmas Ale (ABV 4.7%, Nov-Dec), Winter Sport (ABV 4.7%).

Best Bitter/4Bs (OG 1038, ABV 3.9%) ◆
A pleasant, pale brown session beer, with a fruity aroma, a malty, fruity flavour and bitterness in the palate and finish.

Berrow Porter (OG 1046, ABV 4.6%)
A ruby-coloured porter with a pronounced hop character.

Silver Berrow (OG 1047, ABV 4.7%)
A pale ale with good hop character, created to celebrate the brewery's silver jubilee.

Topsy Turvy (OG 1055, ABV 5.9%) ◆
A gold-coloured beer with an aroma of malt and hops. Well-balanced malt and hops taste is followed by a hoppy, bitter finish with some fruit notes.

Best Mates*

Best Mates Brewery Ltd, Sheep House Farm, Ardington, Wantage, Oxfordshire, OX12 8BQ
☎ (01235) 835684
✉ **bestmatesbrewery@btconnect.com**
🌐 **bestmatesbrewery.co.uk**
Tours by arrangement

Best Mates Brewery was established in 2007 on a five-barrel plant and uses locally sourced water. Bottle-conditioned beers are available.

Vicar's Daughter (OG 1037, ABV 3.7%)

Scutchaman's Knob (OG 1037, ABV 3.8%)

Alfie's (OG 1044, ABV 4.4%)

Satan's Sister (OG 1046, ABV 4.5%)

Betwixt

Betwixt Beer Co Ltd, c/o Northern Brewing Ltd, Blakemere Brewery, Blakemere Craft Centre, Chester Road, Sandiway, Northwich, Cheshire, CW8 2EB
☎ 07792 967414
✉ **brewer@betwixtbeer.co.uk**
🌐 **betwixt.co.uk**

⊗ The company was created in 2005 and is situated on the Wirral peninsula 'Betwixt the Mersey and the Dee'. The brewery currently uses spare capacity at Northern Brewing (qv) in Cheshire but recently purchased the plant from former Grand Union Brewery in London and hopes to start brewing at the new premises soon. The beers are sold through farmers markets, festivals and in local pubs. Seasonal beers: BeWilder (ABV 4.3%, Sep-Nov), BeLotment (ABV 4.3%), Ice Breaker (ABV 6%). Bottle-conditioned beers: as for cask beer range including seasonals.

Dark Matter (OG 1040, ABV 4%)

Sunlight (OG 1043, ABV 4.3%)

Red Admiral (OG 1050, ABV 5%)

Bewdley*

Bewdley Brewery Ltd, Unit 7, Bewdley Craft Centre, Lax Lane, Bewdley, Worcestershire, DY12 2DZ
☎ (01299) 405148
✉ **bewdleybrewery@hotmail.co.uk**
🌐 **bewdleybrewery.co.uk**
Tours by arrangement

Bewdley began brewing in May 2007 on a six-barrel plant. Seasonal and bottle-conditioned beers are planned for the future.

William Mucklow's Dark Mild (ABV 3.6%)

Old School Best (ABV 3.8%)

Severnside Stout (ABV 4.2%)

Big Lamp

Big Lamp Brewers, Grange Road, Newburn, Newcastle upon Tyne, Tyne & Wear, NE15 8NL
☎ (0191) 267 1689
✉ admin@biglampbrewers.co.uk
🌐 biglampbrewers.co.uk
Tours by arrangement

Big Lamp started in 1982 and relocated in 1997 to a 55-barrel plant in a former water pumping station. It is the oldest micro-brewery in the north-east of England. Around 35 outlets are supplied and two pubs are owned. Seasonal/occasional beers: Keelman Brown (ABV 5.7%), Old Genie (ABV 7.4%), Blackout (ABV 11%).

Sunny Daze (OG 1037, ABV 3.7%)
Golden, hoppy session bitter with a clean taste and finish.

Bitter (OG 1039, ABV 3.9%)
A clean tasting bitter, full of hops and malt. A hint of fruit with a good hoppy finish.

Double M (OG 1043, ABV 4.3%)
Copper red in colour. A fruity mouth feel with slight traces of malt and a pleasant dry aftertaste.

Summerhill Stout (OG 1044, ABV 4.4%)
A rich tasty stout, dark in colour with a lasting rich roast character. Malty mouthfeel with a lingering finish.

Prince Bishop Ale (OG 1048, ABV 4.8%)
A refreshing easy drinking bitter, golden in colour, full of fruit and hops. Strong bitterness with a spicy, dry finish.

Premium (OG 1052, ABV 5.2%)
A well-balanced, flavoursome bitter with a big nose full of hops. The sweetness lasts into a mellow, dry finish.

Embers (OG 1055, ABV 5.5%)

Bitter End

Bitter End Pub & Brewery, 15 Kirkgate, Cockermouth, Cumbria, CA13 9PJ
☎ (01900) 828993
✉ info@bitterend.co.uk
🌐 bitterend.co.uk
Tours by arrangement

The brewery was established by Mike Askey in 1995, behind glass at the back of the Bitter End pub and was upgraded in 2004 to a four-barrel copper clad system imported from the US. Three regular beers are brewed with some distribution to the free trade along with a seasonal range of traditional English beer styles. One-off and festival beers are also produced.

Lakeland Bitter (ABV 3.8%)

Lakeland Pale Ale (ABV 4%)

Lakeland Best Gold (ABV 4.3%)

Blackawton SIBA

Blackawton Brewery, Unit 7, Peninsula Park, Moorlands Trading Estate, Saltash, Cornwall, PL12 6LX
☎ (01752) 848777
✉ info@blackawtonbrewery.com
🌐 blackawtonbrewery.com

Blackawton was once Devon's oldest operating brewery, but relocated to Cornwall in 2000 and ownership changed in 2004. Around 30 outlets are supplied. Seasonal beers: Saltash Sunrise (ABV 5%, summer), Winter Fuel (ABV 5%). Bottle-conditioned beers are also available.

Original Bitter (OG 1037, ABV 3.8%)
A copper-coloured bitter; an ideal session beer with a fresh floral hop aroma.

Westcountry Gold (OG 1039, ABV 4.1%)
A light, golden, fresh-tasting summer beer with sweet malt flavours and delicate vanilla and fruit hints from Styrian Goldings hops.

44 Special (OG 1044, ABV 4.5%)
A premium, full-strength bitter that is rich and sweet with the aroma of ripe hops and fruit.

Peninsula Ale (OG 1046, ABV 4.6%)
A dark amber-coloured premium bitter with a hoppy, bitter finish.

Exhibition Ale (OG 1047, ABV 4.7%)

Headstrong (OG 1048, ABV 5.2%)
A deceptively smooth beer with a bitter malt taste.

Black Country

Black Country Ales, Old Bulls Head, 1 Redhall Road, Lower Gornal, Dudley, West Midlands, DY3 2NU
☎ (01384) 480156
☎ 07946 454150
✉ info@blackcountryales.co.uk
🌐 blackcountryales.co.uk
Tours by arrangement

The brewery was set up in 2004 by director Angus McMeeking and brewer Guy Perry from nearby Sarah Hughes (qv). The brewery uses a new plant situated in part of the pub's original tower brewery, dating from 1834, which had last brewed in 1934. Oak vessels that were installed in 1900 have been refurbished and brought into production. One-off beers are produced for distributors. Seasonal beers: English Summer (ABV 4.5%), English Winter (ABV 5.5%).

Bradley's Finest Golden (OG 1040, ABV 4.2%)

Pig on the Wall (OG 1040, ABV 4.3%)

Fireside (OG 1047, ABV 5%)

Black Dog

Black Dog Brewery, Foulsyke Farm, Fylingdales, Whitby, North Yorkshire, YO22 4QL
☎ (0845) 301 2337
🌐 blackdogbrewery.co.uk

Black Dog started brewing in 1997 in the centre of Whitby, but closed in 2000. In 2006 Tony Bryars purchased the original Black Dog five-barrel plant, together with recipes, and re-established the brewery on his farm, using local spring water. The beers are now contract brewed by Hambleton Ales.

Blackdown

Blackdown Brewery Ltd, Unit C6 Dunkeswell Business Park, Dunkeswell, Honiton, Devon, EX14 4LE
☎ (01404) 890096
✉ info@blackdownbrewery.co.uk
blackdownbrewery.co.uk
Tours by arrangement

The brewery, established in 2002, is family-run and covers Devon, Dorset and Somerset. The brewery has recently been expanded to double its original brewing capacity. Some 180 outlets are supplied. Seasonal beers: Palm (ABV 4.2%), Honey (ABV 4.4%).

Devon's Pride (OG 1038, ABV 3.8%)

Gold (OG 1043, ABV 4.3%)

Dark Side (OG 1045, ABV 4.5%)

Premium (OG 1047, ABV 4.7%)

Blackfriars

Blackfriars Brewery Ltd, Unit 4, Queens Road Business Centre, Great Yarmouth, Norfolk, NR30 3HT
☎ (01493) 850578
✉ pints@blackfriars-brewery.co.uk
blackfriars-brewery.co.uk

The brewery was established in 2004 on a purpose-built five-barrel plant and was extended in 2007. Around 40 outlets are supplied. All beers are available in bottle-conditioned form.

Mild (ABV 3.4%)
Sweet and malty in true Norfolk fashion. Red-hued with a gentle roast malt aroma. Stewed prunes and caramel lurk in the background as the finish lingers long and sweet.

Yarmouth Bitter (OG 1036, ABV 3.8%)
A malt-dominated brew. Pale brown and smooth drinking with a distinctly malty nose. A bittersweet fruitiness in the taste turns to an increasing bitterness to rival the malt character.

Miter Gold (OG 1044, ABV 4%)

Whyte Angel (ABV 4.5%)
Fragrant hoppy aroma leads to a strong bitter first taste. Golden hued with honey notes softening the dryness of the bitter hops. Gentle malt background throughout.

Maritime (ABV 5%)
Copper-coloured, rich, heavy and malty brew. Vinous, fruitcake characteristics supplement the richness of taste. A muted hoppy bitterness can be detected in the long finish.

Old Habit (OG 1052, ABV 5.6%)
Old-fashioned mix of roast, malt and plummy fruitiness. Smooth and aromatic with coffee notes and a heavy mouthfeel. Finish softens to a malty character.

Black Hole

Black Hole Brewery Ltd, Unit 63, Ground Floor, Imex Business Park, Shobnall Road, Burton upon Trent, Staffordshire, DE14 2AU
☎ (01283) 534060
✉ beer@blackholebrewery.co.uk
blackholebrewery.co.uk
Tours by arrangement

The brewery was established in January 2007 on a purpose-built 10-barrel plant in the old Ind Coope bottling stores. More fermenters are planned in the near future to expand production, as is a bottling plant. Around 150 outlets are supplied.

Bitter (OG 1040, ABV 3.8%)
Gentle malt and hop aroma from this amber beer. After a grassy start the bitterness develops into a satisfying hop bite. There is a dry finish with some fruitiness with hints of mint.

Cosmic (ABV 4.2%)

Red Dwarf (OG 1044, ABV 4.5%)

Super Nova (ABV 4.8%)

No Escape (ABV 5.2%)

Milky Way (ABV 6%)

Black Isle SIBA

Black Isle Brewery Ltd, Old Allengrange, Munlochy, Ross-shire, IV8 8NZ
☎ (01463) 811871
✉ greatbeers@blackislebrewery.com
blackislebrewery.com
Shop open Mon-Sat 10am-6pm; 11am-6pm Sun (Apr-Sep)
Tours offered between 10am-5pm

Black Isle Brewery was set up in 1998 in the heart of the Scottish Highlands. The five-barrel plant is due to be upgraded to a 20-barrel plant in the near future and a move is planned to a nearby purpose-built 'eco' brewery. All beers are organic, suitable for vegetarians and vegans and have Soil Association certification. Bottled beer are available by mail order to anywhere in mainland Britain. Seasonal beers: Hibernator (ABV 7%, winter), Raspberry Wheat (ABV 5.6%), Goldeneye (ABV 5.2%), Ruby (ABV 6.4%). Bottle-conditioned beers: Wheat Beer (ABV 4.5%), Scotch Ale (ABV 4.5%), Porter (ABV 4.5%), Hibernator III (ABV 7%), Goldeneye (ABV 5.6%).

Yellowhammer (OG 1038, ABV 3.9%)
A refreshing hoppy, golden ale with light hop and passion fruit throughout. A short bitter finish with a yeasty background.

Red Kite (OG 1041, ABV 4.2%)
Tawny ale with light malt on the nose and some fruit on the palate. Slight sweetness in the taste and a short bitter finish.

Blonde (OG 1043, ABV 4.5%)

Porter (OG 1045, ABV 4.6%)

A hint of liquorice and burnt chocolate in the nose and a nice creamy mix of malt and fruit in the taste.

Black Mountain

Black Mountain Brewery Ltd, Telegraph Inn, Station Road, Llangadog, Carmarthenshire, SA19 9LS
☎ (01550) 777727
✉ khwrigley@aol.com
Tours by arrangement

Black Mountain was established in 2006 on a four-barrel plant by Dave Porter in a converted garage behind the Telegraph Inn.

Black Five (ABV 4.1%)

Black Sheep SIBA

Black Sheep Brewery plc, Wellgarth, Masham, Ripon, North Yorkshire, HG4 4EN
☎ (01765) 689227
blacksheepbrewery.com
Shop 10am-5pm daily
Tours by arrangement

Black Sheep was established 1992 by Paul Theakston, a member of Masham's famous brewing family, in the former Wellgarth Maltings. The company has enjoyed continued growth and now supplies a free trade of around 700 outlets, but owns no pubs. The brewery specialises in cask ale (70% of production). Occasional beer: Emmerdale Ale (ABV 4.2%).

Best Bitter (OG 1038, ABV 3.8%) ◆
A hoppy and fruity beer with strong bitter overtones, leading to a long, dry, bitter finish.

Ale (OG 1044, ABV 4.4%)
A premium bitter with robust fruit, malt and hops.

Riggwelter (OG 1059, ABV 5.9%) ◆
A fruity bitter, with complex underlying tastes and hints of liquorice and pear drops leading to a long, dry, bitter finish.

Blackwater

Blackwater Brewery, Brewers Wholesale, Unit 2b Gainsborough Trading Estate, Rufford Road, Stourbridge, West Midlands, DY9 7ND
☎ (01384) 374050
✉ enquiries@thebrewerswholesale.co.uk
thebrewerswholesale.co.uk
Beers contract brewed by Salopian Brewery (qv).

Blakemere

See Northern

Blencowe

See Barrowden

Blindmans SIBA

Blindmans Brewery Ltd, Talbot Farm, Leighton, Frome, Somerset, BA11 4PN
☎ (01749) 880038
✉ info@blindmansbrewery.co.uk
blindmansbrewery.co.uk
Tours by arrangement

Blindmans Brewery was established in 2002 in a converted milking parlour. In 2004 the brewery was bought by Paul Edney and Lloyd Chamberlain. The brewery has its own exclusive water spring. They opened their first pub in January 2008, the Lamb Inn in Frome, serving several exclusively brewed ales. Seasonal beers: Siberia (ABV 4.7%), Bah Humbug! (ABV 4.5%).

Buff (ABV 3.6%)
Amber-coloured, smooth session beer.

Golden Spring (ABV 4%)
Fresh and aromatic straw-coloured beer, brewed using selected lager malt.

Eclipse (ABV 4.2%)
A porter, full of chocolate flavours and subtle bitterness

Mine Beer (ABV 4.2%)
Full-bodied, copper-coloured, blended malt ale.

Icarus (ABV 4.5%)
Fruity, rich, mid-dark ruby ale.

Blorenge

See Tudor

Blue Anchor SIBA

Blue Anchor Inn Brewery, 50 Coinagehall Street, Helston, Cornwall, TR13 8EL
☎ (01326) 562821
✉ theblueanchor@btconnect.com
spingoales.com
Tours by arrangement

Dating back to the 15th century, this is the oldest brewery in Cornwall and was originally a monks' hospice. After the dissolution of the monasteries it became a tavern brewing its own uniquely flavoured beer called Spingo at the rear of the premises. Brewing has continued to this day and people travel from all over the world to sample the delights of this wonderful inn, untouched by time. Five outlets are supplied. Seasonal beers: Spingo Bragget (ABV 6.1%, Apr-Oct), Spingo Easter Special (ABV 7.6%), Spingo Christmas Special (ABV 7.6%). All draught beers are available in bottle conditioned form. Bragget is a recreation of a medieval beer style.

Spingo Jubilee/IPA (OG 1045, ABV 4.6%)

Spingo Middle (OG 1050, ABV 5.1%)
A copper-red beer with a fruity aroma, a hint of vanilla and a peppery note from the hops. The palate is nutty, with a fruit cake note. The complex bittersweet finish is fruity and dry.

Spingo Special (OG 1066, ABV 6.7%)
Darker than Middle with a pronounced earthy character on the nose balanced by rich fruit. Fruit and peppery hops dominate the mouth, followed by a finish with malt, fruit and hops.

Blue Bear

Blue Bear Brewery Ltd, Unit 1 Open Barn Farm, Kempsey, Worcestershire, WR5 3LW
☎ (01905) 828258
bluebearbrewery.co.uk
Tours by arrangement (for 12 people or more)

Blue Bear started production in 2006 in an old potato store. Bottle-conditoned beers are available. Seasonal beers: Warderlust (ABV 3.8%, Apr-Oct), Hop the Wag (ABV 4.8%).

Roar Spirit (OG 1040, ABV 4.2%)
An amber-coloured beer with a rounded, malted flavour and a spicy, blackcurrant aftertaste.

White Bear (OG 1043, ABV 4.5%)
A golden premium ale with a fruit character that leaves a smooth mouth feel of citrus on the palate.

Blue Bell

Blue Bell Brewery, Sycamore House, Lapwater Lane, Holbeach St Marks, Lincolnshire, PE12 8EX
☎ (01406) 701000
enquiries@bluebellbrewery.co.uk
bluebellbrewery.co.uk
Tours by arrangement

The Blue Bell Brewery was founded in 1998 in a former potato shed located behind the Blue Bell pub, Whaplode St Catherine, and is run by Emma Bell and Pat Sage. The brewery operates as a separate business from the Blue Bell pub but the pub does act as the brewery tap. Around 30 outlets are supplied.

Old Honesty (OG 1040, ABV 4.1%)

Old Gold (OG 1045, ABV 4.5%)

Old Fashioned (OG 1045, ABV 4.8%)

Old Comfort (OG 1050, ABV 5%)

For Blue Bell Inn, Whaplode St Catherine:

Ingle Dingle (OG 1054, ABV 5.1%)

Blue Cow

Blue Cow Inn & Brewery, High Street, South Witham, Lincolnshire, NG33 5QB
☎ (01572) 768432
enquiries@bluecowinn.co.uk
bluecowinn.co.uk
Tours by arrangement

Owned by Simon Crathorn since 2005, a traditional 13th-century pub with a brewery. The beers are only available in the pub.

Best Bitter (OG 1038, ABV 3.8%)

Witham Wobbler (OG 1045, ABV 4.5%)

Blue Moon

Blue Moon Brewery, Cock Inn, Watton Road, Barford, Norfolk, NR9 4AS
☎ (01603) 757646

The brewery supplies the Cock Inn and around 40 other free trade outlets. Seasonal beer: Moon Dance (ABV 4.7%, summer).

Easy Life (OG 1040, ABV 3.8%)
Light, refreshing bitter with hop notes in both aroma and taste. Soft fruit and a sweet toffeeness provide balance but do not detract from the crisp, hoppy finish.

Dark Side (OG 1048, ABV 4%)

Sea of Tranquility (OG 1042, ABV 4.2%)
An undemanding malty bitter with fruity undertones. A hint of bananas in the nose continues into the initial taste but is lost in the short, malty finish.

Hingham High (OG 1050, ABV 5.2%)
A complex multi-layered reddish brew. A rich, malty nose leads into a suprisingly bitter first taste. Early hints of malt and fruit subside into a long, increasingly dry finish.

Milk of Amnesia (OG 1055, ABV 5.2%)
A complex, mid-brown beer. The taste has a port-like note; cinnamon and ginger jostle with pepper and citrus as the flavours continue to hold up well.

Liquor Mortis (OG 1075, ABV 7.5%)
A heavy blackcurrant signature introduces this dark brown barley wine. A mature roast beginning counter-balances the fruity sweetness that carries through to a long, filling finish.

Total Eclipse (ABV 9%)

Blythe SIBA

Blythe Brewery, Blythe Farm House, Lichfield Road, Hamstall Ridware, Rugeley, Staffordshire, WS15 3QQ
☎ 07773 747724
info@blythebrewery.plus.com
blythebrewery.co.uk
Tours by arrangement

Robert Greenway started brewing in 2003 using a 2.5-barrel plant in a converted barn on a farm. As well as specials, seasonal beers are produced on a quarterly basis. Fifteen outlets are supplied. Seasonal beer: Old Horny (ABV 4.6%, Sep-Nov). Bottle-conditioned beers: as for cask beers listed below.

Bitter (OG 1040, ABV 4%)
Amber with a full hoppy aroma and sweet touch. Immediate full hoppy taste that develops into an intense hoppy, lingering finish.

Chase Bitter (OG 1044, ABV 4.4%)
Copper to tawny coloured, with a fruit and hop start with caramel sweetness developing; lingering bitterness with a sweet edge.

Staffie (OG 1044, ABV 4.4%)
Hoppy and grassy aroma with hints of sweetness from this amber beer. Caramel start is soon overwhelmed by hops which just get hoppier and hoppier.

Palmer's Poison (OG 1045, ABV 4.5%)
Mid brown with spicy tastes amid the fruit and hops. The hops develop but sweet caramel holds back the long hoppy taste.

Johnson's (OG 1056, ABV 5.2%)
Black with traces of ruby and a liquorice aroma with whiffs of smoke, caramel and malt; even a hint of sulphur. Full roast taste supports hops and the fruit as the caramel fades. Long dry finish with Autumn fruits, blackberry and sloe.

Winter fire finish, mouth-wateringly hoppy without the astringency.

BMG Brewing

BMG Brewing Ltd, c/o Tower Brewery, Old Water Tower, Walsitch Maltings, Glensyl Way, Burton upon Trent, Staffordshire, DE14 1LX
☎ **(01283) 561330**

Beers are contract brews by Tower Brewery for Beer My Guest distributors.

Bob's

Bob's Brewing Co Ltd, c/o Red Lion, 73 Dewsbury Road, Ossett, West Yorkshire, WF5 9NQ
☎ **07789 693597**

The brewery was founded in 2002 by Bob Hunter, formerly one of the partners in Ossett Brewery, in outbuildings behind the Red Lion pub. The beers are sold as 'Red Lion Ales'. Around 10 outlets are supplied.

Brewers Gold (OG 1039, ABV 3.9%)

White Lion (OG 1043, ABV 4.3%)
Pale, flowery, lager-style beer using American Cascade hops.

Yakima Pale Ale (OG 1045.5, ABV 4.5%)
A hoppy and bitter yellow beer that uses hops from the Yakima Valley in Washington State, U.S.

Chardonnayle (OG 1051.5, ABV 5.1%)
Complex, stylish strong pale ale with hints of lemongrass and fruits, with Willamette hops for aroma.

Boggart Hole Clough

Boggart Hole Clough Brewing Co, Unit 13, Brookside Works, Clough Road, Moston, Manchester, M9 4FP
☎ **(0161) 277 9666**
✉ **boggartoffice@btconnect.com**
🌐 **boggart-brewery.co.uk**

The brewery was set up by Mark Dade in 2001 next to Boggart Hole Clough Park. Boggart Beer Distribution was launched in 2003 and beers are now sold to more than 250 outlets throughout the country. Monthly specials are produced as are bottle-conditioned beers.

Ruby Tuesday (ABV 3.8%)
A reddish-coloured hoppy session ale.

Bog Eyed (ABV 4%)
A light-coloured session ale with pronounced hoppiness and aroma.

Dark Mild (ABV 4%)
A classic dark mild.

Natalis (ABV 4%)
Traditional bitter with extra hop flavour and bitterness.

Standard Pioneer (ABV 4%)
A light-coloured session ale with lemon citrus taste and aroma.

Angel Hill (OG 1042, ABV 4.2%)
A premium, golden pale ale with an aromatic explosion of flavour.

Boggart Brew (OG 1043, ABV 4.3%)
A quaffable ruby-red beer.

Dark Side (OG 1044, ABV 4.4%)
A classic porter with a smooth roast finish and subtle hop aftertaste.

Sun Dial (OG 1047, ABV 4.7%)
A pale beer with a refreshing, fruity hop taste and aroma.

Waterloo Sunset (ABV 5%)
Traditional porter with an oak roast finish.

Steaming Boggart (ABV 9%)

Borough Arms

Borough Arms, 33 Earle Street, Crewe, Cheshire, CW1 2BG
☎ **(01270) 254999**

A two-barrel brewery opened in 2005 at the pub. Brewing is currently suspended.

Bottle Brook

Bottle Brook Brewery, Church Street, Kilburn, Belper, Derbyshire, DE56 0LU
☎ **(01332) 880051**
☎ **07971 189915**

Bottle Brook was established in 2005 using a 2.5-barrel plant on a tower gravity system. The traditional brewery uses only rare and unusual hop varieties. There are no permanent house beers, just a series of experimental ales. A cider-making plant is planned.

Bowland SIBA

Bowland Beer Co Ltd, Bashall Town, Clitheroe, Lancashire, BB7 3LQ
☎ **(01200) 443592**
☎ **07952 639465**
✉ **richardbakerbb@btconnect.com**
🌐 **bowlandbrewery.com**
Shop Mon-Sun 10.30am-5pm
Tours by arrangement

Bowland started brewing in 2003 and has steadily expanded capacity to 50 barrels, supplying over 100 outlets in the north west. Bottle-conditioned five litre mini-casks are sold through the on-site shop and visitor centre. A new range of quirky bottled beers was launched in 2008. At least one new cask ale is brewed each month. Seasonal beers include: Golden Trough, Sorceress, Headless Peg and Sleigh Belle.

Hunters Moon (OG 1039, ABV 3.7%)
A dark mild with chocolate and coffee flavours.

Sawley Tempted (OG 1038, ABV 3.7%)
A copper-coloured fruity session bitter with toffee in the mouth and a spicy finish.

Bowland Gold (OG 1039, ABV 3.8%)
A hoppy golden bitter with intense grapefruit flavours.

Chipping Steamer (OG 1040, ABV 3.9%)
A mid-gold bitter with hints of orange and a slightly floral finish.

Hen Harrier (OG 1040, ABV 4%)

A pale gold bitter with soft citrus, peach and apricot flavours throughout.

Oak (OG 1041, ABV 4%)
A light chestnut coloured bitter with generous maltiness balanced by lime-marmalade hop flavours.

Dragon (OG 1043, ABV 4.2%)
A golden bitter with rounded fruit in the mouth and a refreshing finish.

Bowman

Bowman Ales Ltd, Wallops Wood, Sheardley Lane, Droxford, Hampshire, SO32 3QY
☎ (01489) 878110
✉ info@bowman-ales.com
bowman-ales.com
Tours by arrangement

Brewing started in 2006 on a 20-barrel brew plant in converted farm buildings. The brewery supplies more than 75 outlets. Future plans include bottling and a range of unusual celebratory and occasional brews. Seasonal beer: Nutz (ABV 5%, winter).

Elderado (OG 1035, ABV 3.5%)
Yellow-coloured beer containing elderflower. A citric aroma with a fruity, bitter taste and good hoppiness. A dry bitter finish.

Swift One (OG 1038, ABV 3.8%)
A glorious golden ale characterised by strong hoppiness throughout. Aroma of grapefruit leads to a pleasing bitterness and a long, dry finish.

Wallops Wood (OG 1040, ABV 4%)
Well-balanced bitter, with no distinctive flavour dominating this well-crafted beer. Malt flavours throughout are balanced by toffee notes and a slightly dry finish.

Quiver Bitter (OG 1045, ABV 4.5%)

Box Steam

Box Steam Brewery, Oaks Farm, Rode Hill, Colerne, Wiltshire, SN14 8AR
☎ (01225) 858383
✉ enquiries@boxsteambrewery.com
boxsteambrewery.com
Tours by arrangement

The brewery was founded in 2004 and boasts a Fulton steam-fired copper, hence the name. Under present ownership since 2006, the brewery has undergone a series of expansion work to increase production capacity. Two pubs are owned and more than 100 outlets are supplied. Seasonal beer: Figgy Pudding (ABV 5%, Xmas).

Reverend Awdry's Ale (OG 1037.5, ABV 3.8%)

Tunnel Vision (OG 1040.5, ABV 4.2%)

Blind House (OG 1044.5, ABV 4.6%)

Dark and Handsome (OG 1047.5, ABV 5%)

Bradfield

Bradfield Brewery, Watt House Farm, High Bradfield, Sheffield, South Yorkshire, S6 6LG
☎ (0114) 285 1118
✉ info@bradfieldbrewery.com
bradfieldbrewery.co.uk
Shop Mon-Fri 10am-5pm; Sat 10am-4pm; Sun 10am-2pm

Bradfield Brewery is a family-run business, based on a working farm in the Peak District. Only the finest ingredients are used, along with pure Milstone Grit spring water from a borehole. More than 200 outlets are supplied. Seasonal beer: Farmers Belgian Blue (ABV 4.9%, Xmas). Bottle-conditioned beers are also available.

Farmers Bitter (OG 1039, ABV 3.9%)
A traditional copper-coloured malt ale with a floral aroma.

Farmers Blonde (OG 1041, ABV 4%)
Pale, blonde beer with citrus and summer fruits aromas.

Farmers Brown Cow (OG 1042.5, ABV 4.2%)
Deep chestnut-coloured ale with a smooth, creamy head. A citrus taste gives way to a long, dry finish.

Farmers Stout (OG 1045, ABV 4.5%)
A dark stout with roasted malts and flaked oats and a subtle, bitter hop character.

Farmers Pale Ale (OG 1049, ABV 5%)
A full-bodied pale ale with a powerful floral bouquet leaving a predominantly dry aftertaste.

Farmers Sixer (OG 1056, ABV 6%)
A strong, lager-type ale with a fruity, pleasant finish.

Brains IFBB

S A Brain & Co Ltd, Cardiff Brewery, PO Box 53, Crawshay Street, Cardiff, CF10 1SP
☎ (029) 2040 2060
✉ brains@sabrain.com
sabrain.com

S A Brain began trading at the Old Brewery in Cardiff in 1882 when Samuel Arthur Brain and his uncle Joseph Benjamin Brain purchased a site founded in 1713. The company has remained in family ownership ever since. The full range of Brains ales is now produced at the company's Cardiff Brewery (formerly Hancock's), bought from Bass in 1999. The company owns 260 pubs, has a sizeable free trade and a wholesale estate of more than 3,000 accounts. Brains is the official sponsor of the Wales Rugby Union Team, Glamorgan County Cricket Club and the Football Association of Wales.

Dark (OG 1035.5, ABV 3.5%)
A tasty, classic dark brown mild, a mix of malt, roast, caramel with a background of hops. Bittersweet, mellow and with a lasting finish of malt and roast.

Bitter (OG 1036, ABV 3.7%)
Amber coloured with a gentle aroma of malt and hops. Malt, hops and bitterness combine in an easy-drinking beer with a bitter finish.

Bread of Heaven (OG 1040, ABV 4%)
Traditional cask ale with a distinctive reddish hue and rich hop aroma, finely balanced by a fruity finish.

SA (OG 1042, ABV 4.2%)

A mellow, full-bodied beer. Gentle malt and hop aroma leads to a malty, hop and fruit mix with a balancing bitterness.

Rev James (OG 1045.5, ABV 4.5%) ◆
A faint malt and fruit aroma with malt and fruit flavours in the taste, initially bittersweet. Bitterness balances the flavour and makes this an easy-drinking beer.

SA Gold (OG 1047, ABV 4.7%) ◆
A golden beer with a hoppy aroma. Well balanced with a zesty hop, malt, fruit and balancing bitterness; a similar satisfying finish.

Brakspear

See Marston's in New Nationals section

Brampton*

Brampton Brewery Ltd, Unit 5, Chatsworth Business Park, Chatsworth Road, Chesterfield, S40 2AR
☎ **(01246) 221680**
✉ **info@bramptonbrewery.co.uk**
🌐 **bramptonbrewery.co.uk**
Shop via website
Tours by arrangement

The old Brampton Brewery existed in the town for over 100 years before being taken over in 1955. After a lapse of 52 years the Brampton name was re-registered for a new brewery a stone's throw away from the original. The first commercial brew took place in October 2007 on the eight-barrel plant. Occasional and seasonal beers will be added to the range together with bottle-conditioned ales.

Golden Bud (OG 1037, ABV 3.8%)

Best (OG 1041, ABV 4.2%)

Impy Dark (OG 1047, ABV 4.3%)

Wasp Nest (OG 1049, ABV 5%)

Brancaster EAB

Brancaster Brewery, Jolly Sailors, Main Road, Brancaster Staithe, Norfolk, PE31 8BJ
☎ **(01485) 210314**
✉ **jayatjolly@aol.com**
🌐 **jollysailors.co.uk**

Brancaster opened in 2003 with a five-barrel plant squeezed into a converted ocean-going steel container adjacent to its own pub/restaurant. Occasional specials are produced. Both beers are also available bottle conditioned.

IPA (ABV 3.7%)

Old Les (ABV 5%)

Brandon

Brandon Brewery, 76 High Street, Brandon, Suffolk, IP27 0AU
☎ **(01842) 878496**
☎ **07876 234689**
✉ **enquiries@brandonbrewery.co.uk**
🌐 **brandonbrewery.co.uk**
Shop Mon-Sat 9am-5pm (please ring before visiting)
Tours by arrangement

Brandon started brewing in 2005 in the old dairy of a 15th-century cottage. Visitors are welcome and encouraged to sample from the beer shop. 60 outlets are supplied. The entire range of beers is also available bottle conditioned.

Breckland Gold (OG 1037, ABV 3.8%)
A combination of Goldings and Fuggles hops give a delicate, smooth, slightly spicy taste and a dry, lingering, malty finish.

Bitter (OG 1040, ABV 4%)
A full-bodied but balanced bitterness with pleasant floral and spicy notes and a gentle, hoppy, dry aftertaste.

Saxon Gold (ABV 4%)
A pale, golden beer with a subtle aroma of hops. The taste is a clean, crisp mix of spice and bitter fruits with a dry, hoppy finish.

Molly's Secret (ABV 4.1%)
A pale ale based on an old recipe.

Norfolk Poacher (ABV 4.1%)
A reddish amber beer. Full-bodied and malty with a hoppy, fruit flavour.

Royal Ginger (ABV 4.1%)
A refreshing summer ale with a distinctive mix of malt and hoppy spice, balanced with a gentle ginger flavour and finish.

Gun Flint (OG 1041, ABV 4.2%)
Roasted malts are used to produce a malty, chocolate flavour. This combines well with spicy, citrus hops to give a dry, bittersweet, roasted malt finish.

Wee Drop of Mischief (ABV 4.2%)
An amber-coloured premium bitter. Gentle malt flavours give way to a delightful hop character and a dry, increasingly bitter aftertaste.

Rusty Bucket (OG 1043, ABV 4.4%)
Based on a traditional best bitter brew, this beer is smooth on the palate with a soft and fruity flavour.

Slippery Jack (OG 1044, ABV 4.5%)
A dark brown stout. Complex but well-balanced flavours of roasted grain and hop bitterness. Dry with a lingering, pleasantly bitter finish.

Nappertandy (OG 1047, ABV 4.8%)
A reddish amber beer, full-bodied with a malty aroma. Crisp and spicy with an underlying citrus flavour and a dry, malty, bitter fruit finish.

Brandy Cask SIBA

Brandy Cask Pub & Brewery, 25 Bridge Street, Pershore, Worcestershire, WR10 1AJ
☎ **(01386) 552602**
Tours by arrangement

Brewing started in 1995 in a refurbished bottle store in the garden of the pub. Brewery and pub now operate under one umbrella, with brewing carried out by the owner/landlord.

Whistling Joe (ABV 3.6%) ◆

A sweet, fruity, copper-coloured beer that has plenty of contrast in the aroma. A malty balance lingers but the aftertaste is not dry.

Brandy Snapper (ABV 4%) ◈
Golden brew with low alpha hops. Plenty of fruit and hop aroma leads to a rich taste in the mouth and a lingering aftertaste.

Ale Mary (ABV 4.8%) ◈
A rich malt and fruit aroma leads to an equally complex taste with no one flavour dominating. A dry finish.

John Baker's Original (ABV 4.8%) ◈
A superb blend of flavours with roasted malt to the fore. The rich hoppy aroma is complemented by a complex aftertaste.

Branscombe Vale SIBA

Branscombe Vale Brewery Ltd, Branscombe, Devon, EX12 3DP
☎ **(01297) 680511**
✉ **branscombebrewery@yahoo.co.uk**

⊗ The brewery was set up in 1992 by former dairy workers Paul Dimond and Graham Luxton in cowsheds owned by the National Trust. Paul and Graham converted the sheds and dug their own well. The NT built an extension for the brewery to ensure future growth. Branscombe Vale currently supplies 80 regular outlets. Seasonal beers: Anniversary Ale (ABV 4.6%, Feb-Mar), Hells Belles (ABV 4.8%), Yo Ho Ho (ABV 6%, Xmas). Bottle-conditioned beer is also available.

Branoc (OG 1038, ABV 3.8%) ◈
Pale brown brew with a malt and fruit aroma and a hint of caramel. Malt and bitter taste with a dry, hoppy finish.

On The Rocks (OG 1041, ABV 4.1%)

Draymans Best Bitter (OG 1042, ABV 4.2%)
A mid-brown beer with hop and caramel notes and a lingering finish.

BVB Best Bitter (OG 1045, ABV 4.6%) ◈
Reddy/brown-coloured beer with a fruity aroma and taste, and bitter/astringent finish.

Summa That (OG 1049, ABV 5%)
Light golden beer with a clean and refreshing taste and a long hoppy finish.

Breconshire SIBA

Breconshire Brewery Ltd, Ffrwdgrech Industrial Estate, Brecon, Powys, LD3 8LA
☎ **(01874) 623731**
✉ **sales@breconshirebrewery.com**
🌐 **breconshirebrewery.com**
Shop Mon-Fri 8.30am-4.30pm
Tours by arrangement

⊗ Breconshire Brewery was founded by Howard Marlow in 2002 as part of C H Marlow, a wholesaler and distributor of ales, beers, wines and spirits in the south Wales area for more than 30 years. The 10-barrel plant uses British Optic malts blended with a range of British whole hops. The beers are distributed throughout mid, south and west Wales and the west of England. Seasonal beers include: Winter Beacon (ABV 5.3%, Nov-Feb). Bottle-conditioned beers are also available.

Brecon County Ale (OG 1037, ABV 3.7%) ◈
A traditional amber-coloured bitter. A clean hoppy flavour, background malt and fruit, with a good thirst-quenching bitterness.

Welsh Pale Ale (OG 1037, ABV 3.7%)
Pale golden, mildy hopped session ale. Brewed to an old Welsh style of pale ale.

Golden Valley (OG 1042, ABV 4.2%) ◈
Golden in colour with a welcoming aroma of hops, malt and fruit. A balanced mix of these flavours and moderate, building bitterness lead to a satisfying, rounded finish.

Cribyn (OG 1045, ABV 4.5%)
A very pale, straw-coloured aromatic best bitter. Brewed with Northdown, Challenger and Bramling Cross hops.

Red Dragon (OG 1047, ABV 4.7%)
A red-hued premium ale brewed with a complex grist of Optic and wheat malts and a blend of hedgerow hops.

Ramblers Ruin (OG 1050, ABV 5%) ◈
Dark amber, full-bodied with rich biscuity malt and fruit flavours; background hops and bitterness round off the beer.

Brentwood SIBA

Brentwood Brewing Co Ltd, Frieze Hall Farm, Coxtie Green Road, South Weald, Essex, CM14 5RE
☎ **(01277) 375577**
✉ **brentwoodbrewing@aol.com**
🌐 **brentwoodbrewing.co.uk**
Tours by arrangement

⊗ Since its launch in 2006 Brentwood has steadily increased its capacity and distribution, and a major expansion and relocation in 2007/08 means a new 18-barrel plant is now being used. It supplies over 30 local outlets as well as beer festivals and selected tied houses through its own distribution and the SIBA Direct Distribution Scheme. Seasonal beers: Summer Virgin (ABV 4.5%), Volcano (ABV 4.6%, winter).

Spooky Moon (OG 1040, ABV 3.8%) ◈
Well-balanced session bitter. The sweet marmalade aroma hints at the citrus bitterness to be found in the finish.

Best (OG 1042, ABV 4.2%)

Hope & Glory (OG 1046, ABV 4.5%)

Devils Dyke (OG 1048, ABV 4.8%)

Lumberjack (OG 1052, ABV 5.2%)

Brewdog

Brewdog Ltd, Unit 1, Kessock Workshops, Kessock Road, Fraserburgh, AB43 8UE
☎ **(01346) 519009**
✉ **info@brewdog.com**
🌐 **brewdog.com**
Tours by arrangement

Brewdog was established in March 2007 by James Watt and Martin Dickie. Most of the production goes into bottles but a limited amount of cask ale is available.

Physics (OG 1050, ABV 5.2%)

Hop Rocker (ABV 5.5%)

Punk IPA (OG 1058, ABV 6.2%)

Rip Tide (OG 1075, ABV 8%)

Paradox (OG 1075, ABV 10%)
Matured in whisky barrels.

Brewster's SIBA

Brewster's Brewing Co Ltd, Burnside, Turnpike Close, Grantham, Lincolnshire, NG31 7XU
☎ (01476) 566000
✉ sara@brewsters.co.uk
🌐 brewsters.co.uk
Tours by arrangement

Brewster is the old English term for a female brewer and Sara Barton is a modern example. Brewster's Brewery was set up in the heart of the Vale of Belvoir in 1998 and moved in 2006 to its current premises. Beer is supplied to some 250 outlets throughout central England and further afield via wholesalers. Seasonal beers: see website.

Hophead (OG 1036, ABV 3.6%) ◆
This amber beer has a floral/hoppy character; hops predominate throughout before finally yielding to grapefruit in a slightly astringent finish.

Marquis (OG 1038, ABV 3.8%) ◆
A well-balanced and refreshing session bitter with maltiness and a dry, hoppy finish.

Daffys Elixir (OG 1042, ABV 4.2%)
A pale golden best bitter, well-balanced with a big hop finish.

Hop A Doodle Doo (OG 1043, ABV 4.3%)
A copper-coloured ale with a rich, full-bodied feel and fruity hop character.

Rutterkin (OG 1046, ABV 4.6%) ◆
A premium bitter with a golden appearance. A zesty hop flavour from American Mount Hood hops combines with a touch of malt sweetness to give a rich, full-bodied beer.

Wicked Women Range (OG 1048, ABV 4.8%)
(Varies seasonally)

Belly Dancer (OG 1050, ABV 5.2%) ◆
Well-balanced, ruby-red ale with a full-bodied taste from crystal and roast malts, with a subtle hop finish from Bramling Cross and Fuggles.

Brew Wharf

Brew Wharf Co Ltd, Brew Wharf Yard, Stoney Street, London, SE1 9AD
☎ (020) 7378 6601
✉ brewer-brewwharf@vinopolis.co.uk
🌐 brewwharf.com

Brew Wharf opened in 2005 and has a bar plus a restaurant where dishes are matched with beer. Wharf Best is the permanent cask ale with a changing special beer brewed each month.

Wharf Best (OG 1041, ABV 4.2%)

Bricktop

Bricktop Brewery, c/o Gate Hangs Well, Woodgate Road, Stoke Prior, Worcestershire, B60 4HG
☎ (01527) 821957
✉ info@thegatehangswell.co.uk
🌐 thegatehangswell.co.uk

Beers are brewed at Weatheroak Brewery under the Bricktop Brewery name exclusively for the owner's pub, Gate Hangs Well in Stoke Prior. See Weatheroak listing for beers brewed.

Bridestones

Bridestones Brewery, The Brewery, Smithy Farm, Blackshaw Head, Hebden Bridge, West Yorkshire, HX7 7JB
☎ (01422) 847104
☎ 07921 211870
✉ dan@newdelight.freeserve.co.uk

Bridestones started brewing in 2006 and supplies around 20 outlets. There are plans to bottle beer in the near future. Seasonal beer: Pennine Stout (ABV 4.8%, Sep-Mar) plus monthly specials.

Pennine Best (OG 1041, ABV 4%)

Pennine Gold (OG 1043, ABV 4.3%)

Pennine Bier (OG 1045, ABV 4.4%)

Pennine Pale Ale (OG 1048, ABV 5%)

Bridge of Allan SIBA

Bridge of Allan Brewery, The Brewhouse, Queens Lane, Bridge of Allan, Stirlingshire, FK9 4NY
☎ (01786) 834555
✉ brewery@bridgeofallan.co.uk
Shop 12-5pm daily

Beer is now brewed by Traditional Scottish Ales at Stirling (qv). Bridge of Allan beer, however, is still available from the Brewhouse. The Brewhouse also showcases a range of Scottish bottled beers, which includes both bottle-conditioned and organic beers.

Bridgetown*

Bridgetown Brewery, Albert Inn, Bridgetown Close, Totnes, Devon, TQ9 5AD
☎ (01803) 863214

Bridgetown started brewing in April 2008 on a 2.5-barrel plant. Seasonal beers are planned.

AA (The Real Emergency Service) (ABV 3.8%)

Realaleativity (ABV 4.8%)

Bridgnorth

Bridgnorth Brewing Co Ltd, The Old Brewhouse, Kings Head Courtyard, Whitburn Street, Bridgnorth, Shropshire, WV16 4QN
☎ (01746) 762889
✉ info@bridgnorthbrewing.com
🌐 bridgnorthbrewing.com
Tours by arrangement

Brewing started in April 2007 with the original four-barrel plant expanding to 16 barrels by 2008. The King's Head Stable Bar opened next door as the brewery tap, serving real ale and fine wines. It supplies to over 30 outlets all over Shropshire and through SIBA.

Apley Ale (OG 1040, ABV 3.9%)

Best Bitter (OG 1044, ABV 4.4%)

Pale Ale (OG 1045, ABV 4.5%)

Northgate Gold (OG 1046, ABV 4.6%)

Bishop Percy (OG 1048, ABV 4.7%)

Strong Dark Mild (OG 1058, ABV 6%)
A smooth and malty strong dark mild with a good hop character.

Badger Stone Bitter (OG 1044, ABV 4.4%)
A classic English bitter, packed with the flavour of malt and hops.

Three Peaks Ale (OG 1045, ABV 4.5%)
A strong, pale premium bitter brewed with only pale malt and traditional hops.

Otley Gold (OG 1043, ABV 4.6%)
A pale, fairly full-flavoured but soft beer brewed in the style of a lager.

Victorian Velvet (OG 1049, ABV 4.9%)
A malty, fruity and smooth copper-coloured special bitter. Small amounts are available bottle conditioned from the brewery at Xmas.

Brimstage

Brimstage Brewing Co Ltd, Home Farm, Brimstage, Wirral, CH63 6HY
☎ (0151) 342 1181
☎ 07870 968323
✉ info@brimstagebrewery.com
🌐 brimstagebrewery.com
Tours by arrangement (max of 20 people)

Brewing started in 2006 on a 10-barrel plant in a redundant farm dairy in the heart of the Wirral countryside. This is Wirral's first brewery since the closure of the Birkenhead Brewery in the late 1960s. Around 60 outlets are supplied.

Sandpiper Light Ale (ABV 3.4%)

Trappers Hat Bitter (ABV 3.8%)
Gold-coloured with a complex bouquet. It provides a mouthful of fruit zest, with hints of orange and grapefruit. A refreshingly hoppy session brew.

Rhode Island Red Bitter (ABV 4%)
Red, smooth and well-balanced malty beer with a good dry aftertaste. Some fruitiness in the taste.

Scarecrow Bitter (ABV 4.2%)
Orange marmalade in colour, this well-balanced session brew has a distinct citrus fruit bouquet.

Oyster Catcher Stout (ABV 4.4%)
A smooth easy drinking stout with rich chocolate aromas leading to a mellow roasted coffee flavour and lingering bitter finish.

Briscoe's

Briscoe's Brewery, 16 Ash Grove, Otley, West Yorkshire, LS21 3EL
☎ (01943) 466515
✉ briscoe.brewery@virgin.net

The brewery was launched in 1998 by microbiologist/chemist Dr Paul Briscoe in the cellar of his house with a one-barrel brew length. Following a spell brewing on a larger scale at the back of a local pub, Dr Briscoe is currently producing occasional brews on his original plant. Seasonal beers: Rombalds Reviver (ABV 3.8%), Runner's Ruin (ABV 4.3%), Shane's Shamrock Stout (ABV 4.6%), Chevinbrau Pilsner-style lager (ABV 5.2%), Puddled and Barmy Ale (ABV 5.8%).

Burnsall Classic Bitter (OG 1040, ABV 4%)
A full-flavoured, reddish-coloured bitter with a good hop flavour.

Chevin Chaser (OG 1043, ABV 4.3%)
A refreshing, pale-coloured, all-malt bitter with a distinct hop finish.

Dalebottom Dark (OG 1043, ABV 4.3%)

Bristol Beer Factory

Bristol Brewing Co Ltd, t/a Bristol Beer Factory, Unit A The Old Brewery, Durnford Street, Ashton, Bristol, BS3 2AW
☎ (0117) 902 6317
✉ enquiries@bristolbeerfactory.co.uk
🌐 bristolbeerfactory.co.uk
Tours by arrangement

The Beer Factory is a 10-barrel micro-brewery in a part of the former Ashton Gate Brewing Co, which closed in 1933. 50 outlets are supplied.

Red (OG 1038, ABV 3.8%)
Dark ale with slight roast barley taste, fruity aroma and ruby red tint.

No. 7 (OG 1042, ABV 4.2%)
Mid-brown, old-fashioned style, malty best bitter. Good body and mouthfeel, some apple-type fruit flavours, with a drying bitter and astringent finish.

Sunrise (OG 1044.5, ABV 4.4%)
Light, gold-coloured best bitter, with a strong hoppy finish.

Milk Stout (OG 1059, ABV 4.5%)
Dark creamy stout, reviving an old Bristol recipe. Black colour with a creamy mouthfeel.

Gold (OG 1048.5, ABV 5%)
Full-bodied and strong-flavoured golden ale. Complex aroma of pineapple and unripe pale fruits with hints of butterscotch and pear drops. A dry and bitter beer.

Brothers

See Freedom

Broughton SIBA

Broughton Ales Ltd, Broughton, Biggar, Peebles-shire, ML12 6HQ
☎ (01899) 830345
✉ beer@broughtonales.co.uk
🌐 broughtonales.co.uk
Shop Mon-Fri 8am-5pm
Tours by arrangement

Founded in 1979 in the Scottish Border country, Broughton Ales has been brewing cask beers for more than 25 years but more than 60% of production goes into bottle for sale in Britain and export markets. Seasonal beers: Champion Double Ale (ABV 5%), Winter Fire (ABV 4.2%), Scottish Oatmeal Stout (ABV 4.2%), The Ghillie (ABV 4.5%), Dr Johnson's Definitive (ABV 5%). All bottled beers are suitable for vegetarians and vegans.

Coulsons EPA (OG 1034, ABV 3.5%)
A light, yellow-coloured ale with a mellow lingering flavour and tangy aftertaste.

The Reiver (OG 1038, ABV 3.8%)
A light-coloured session ale with a predominantly hoppy flavour and aroma on a background of fruity malt. The aftertaste is crisp and clean.

Bramling Cross (OG 1041, ABV 4.2%)
A golden ale with a blend of malt and hop flavours followed by a hoppy aftertaste.

Clipper IPA (OG 1042, ABV 4.2%)
A light-coloured, crisp, hoppy beer with a clean aftertaste.

Merlin's Ale (OG 1042, ABV 4.2%) ◆
A well-hopped, fruity flavour is balanced by malt in the taste. The finish is bittersweet, light but dry.

Exciseman's 80/- (OG 1045, ABV 4.6%)
A traditional 80/- cask ale. A dark, malty brew. Full drinking with a good hop aftertaste.

Old Jock (OG 1070, ABV 6.7%)
Strong, sweetish and fruity in the finish.

Brown Cow

Brown Cow Brewery, Brown Cow Road, Barlow, Selby, North Yorkshire, YO8 8EH
☎ (01757) 618947
✉ susansimpson@browncowbrewery.co.uk
🌐 browncowbrewery.co.uk

Set up in 1997 by Susan Simpson and joined by husband Keith in 2004, the brewery has steadily expanded, the five-barrel plant now brewing at its capacity of 15 barrels a week. In addition to the four regular beers, an innovative range of seasonal, occasional and one-off brews is crafted. Beers are supplied throughout Yorkshire and to outlets in southern counties.

Bitter (OG 1038, ABV 3.8%) ◆
A well-hopped traditional session bitter.

White Dragon (OG 1039, ABV 4%)
A pale, aromatic best bitter.

Captain Oates Dark Oat Mild (OG 1044, ABV 4.5%)
A satisfying dark beer with fruit and mild hop flavours throughout.

For Suddaby's Brewery:

After Dark Coffee Porter (OG 1052, ABV 5%)
Full-flavoured porter with complex mix of malts and a hint of coffee.

Brunswick SIBA

Brunswick Brewery Ltd, 1 Railway Terrace, Derby, Derbyshire, DE1 2RU
☎ (01332) 290677
🌐 brunswickinn.co.uk
Tours by arrangement

The Brunswick is a purpose-built tower brewery that started brewing in 1991. A viewing area allows pub users to watch production. Bought by Everards in 2002, it is now a tenancy supplying beers to local outlets and the Everard's estate. Seasonal beer: Rambo (ABV 7.3%, winter).

Mild (OG 1036, ABV 3.6%) ◆
A light-bodied, well-balanced Midlands dark mild with liquorice and hints of coffee on the nose and balanced fruit, caramel and roast in the taste.

White Feather (OG 1037, ABV 3.6%)
Extremely pale and full-bodied session ale. Refreshingly crisp with a citrus hop nose.

Triple Hop (OG 1038, ABV 4%) ◆
A pale gold colour and citrus hop bouquet promise sweetness but the hops deliver a firm, dry, lasting bitterness.

Second Brew (OG 1042, ABV 4.2%) ◆
This tawny best bitter, also known as The Usual, presents an aroma of sulphur and hops that continue throughout, accompanied by a striking bitterness and astringency.

Porter (OG 1045, ABV 4.3%)
Typical English porter – dark black chocolate caramel with deep bitter undertones.

Triple Gold (OG 1045, ABV 4.5%)
Straw-coloured bitter with lingering hints of citrus, with a hoppy aftertaste.

Old Accidental (OG 1050, ABV 5%)
A well-balanced, malty beer leading to a bitter finish with warming aftertaste. A light, vinous floral hop has underlying malt notes.

Father Mike's Dark Rich Ruby (OG 1055, ABV 5.8%) ◆
A smooth, near black mild with a hint of red. Well-balanced and filled with sweet roast flavours that conceal its strength.

Black Sabbath (OG 1058, ABV 6%)
A genuine mild with a voluptuous feast of coffee, chocolate and caramel flavours. High alcohol balanced with fine body.

Bryncelyn

Bryncelyn Brewery, Unit 303, Ystradgynlais Workshops, Trawsffordd Road, Ystradgynlais, SA9 1BS
☎ (01639) 841900
✉ bryncelynbrewery@hotmail.co.uk
🌐 bryncelynbrewery.org.uk

A one-quarter barrel brewery was opened in 1999 by William Hopton (owner) and Robert Scott (brewer) and capacity was increased to a three-quarter barrel plant in the same year. The brewery relocated to its present premises in 2008 with a six-barrel plant acquired from the old Webb's Brewery of Ebbw Vale. As the beer names imply, the owner is fond of Buddy Holly: Feb 59 commemorates the singer's death. Seasonal beers: Feb 59 (ABV 3.7%), Peggy's Brew (ABV 4.2%, Mar), May B Baby (ABV 4.5%, May), That Will Be the Sleigh (ABV 6.6%, Dec-Jan).

Holly Hop (ABV 3.9%) ◆
Pale amber with a hoppy aroma. A refreshing hoppy, fruity flavour with balancing bitterness; a similar lasting finish. A beer full of flavour for its gravity.

Buddy Marvellous (OG 1040, ABV 4%) ◆
Dark brown with an inviting aroma of malt, roast and fruit. A gentle bitterness mixes roast with malt, hops and fruit, giving a complex, satisfying and lasting finish.

Buddy's Delight (OG 1042, ABV 4.2%)

Cwrw Celyn (OG 1044, ABV 4.4%)

CHH (OG 1045, ABV 4.5%) ◆
A pale brown beer with hints of red malt and an inviting hop aroma, with fruit and bitterness adding to the flavour. The finish is clean and hoppy-bitter.

Oh Boy (OG 1045, ABV 4.5%) ◆
An inviting aroma of hops, fruit and malt, and a golden colour. The tasty mix of hops, fruit, bitterness and background malt ends with a long, hoppy, bitter aftertaste. Full-bodied and drinkable.

Buddy Confusing (OG 1050, ABV 5%)

Rave On (OG 1050, ABV 5%)

Brysons

Brysons Brewery, Newgate Brewery, White Lund Industrial Estate, Morecambe, Lancashire, LA3 3PT
☎ **(01524) 39481**
✉ **petermcross@msn.co.uk**
🌐 **brysonsbrews.co.uk**

Established by George Palmer who still continues to brew his cask-conditioned ales. Due to steady growth a new 20-barrel brew plant was installed in 2008. Around 20 outlets are supplied.

Westmorland Bitter (ABV 3.6%)

Lancashire Bitter (ABV 3.8%) ◆
Light-bodied, easy-drinking session ale.

Union Flag (ABV 3.9%)

Hurricane Bitter (ABV 4.1%)

John McGuinness Bitter (ABV 4.2%)

Buffy's SIBA EAB

Buffy's Brewery Ltd, Rectory Road, Tivetshall St Mary, Norfolk, NR15 2DD
☎ **(01379) 676523**
✉ **buffysbrewery@gmail.com**
🌐 **buffys.co.uk**

⊗ Buffy's was established in 1993. The brewing capacity is 45 barrels, but a move to bigger premises is in hand with plans for a bottling plant. The brewery owns two pubs, the Cherry Tree at Wicklewood and the White Hart at Foulden. Around 150 outlets are supplied. Seasonal beers: Sleigher (ABV 4.1%, Dec-Jan), Hollybeery (ABV 5.5% Dec-Jan).

Norwich Terrier (OG 1036, ABV 3.6%) ◆
A fragrant peachy aroma introduces this refreshing, gold-coloured bitter. Strong bitter notes dominate throughout as hops mingle with grapefruit to produce a long, increasingly dry finish.

Bitter (OG 1039, ABV 3.9%) ◆
The strong malty aroma contrasts totally with the dry bitterness of the taste. A pale brown beer with an increasingly hoppy finish that grows and grows.

Mild (OG 1042, ABV 4.2%) ◆
A complex brew, deep red with a smooth but grainy feel. Caramel and blackcurrant bolster the heavy malt influence that is the main characteristic of this understated, deceptively strong mild.

Polly's Folly (OG 1043, ABV 4.3%) ◆
A mixture of hoppiness, citrus fruit and malt gives this well-balanced offering a lively, satisfying feel. Grapefruit creeps into the flavour towards the end as the overall character becomes biscuity dry.

Hopleaf (OG 1044.5, ABV 4.5%) ◆
Pale brown beer with a gentle hop nose. Strawberries mingle with the hops and malt, remaining as the malt gently subsides to leave a bittersweet, dry finish.

Mucky Duck (OG 1044, ABV 4.5%)
Porter style beer. Slightly sweet but with a good bitter edge.

Norwegian Blue (OG 1049, ABV 4.9%) ◆
A gentle hoppy nose belies the rich warming character of the taste explosion. A complex, ever-changing mix of malt, hops, bitterness and fruit. A long, lingering, bittersweet ending.

Roger's Ruin (OG 1063, ABV 6.2%)
A warming, full-bodied, satisfying beer with a spicy kick. Deep copper in colour.

Bull Box

Bull Box Brewery, c/o 1 Brickyard Cottage, Fordham, Downham Market, Norfolk, PE38 0LW
☎ **(01366) 385349**
☎ **07920 163116**
✉ **bullboxinfo@msn.com**

Bull Box Brewery was launched in 2006 and operates on a two-barrel plant based in Stradsett. There are plans for bottle-conditioned ales.

Bitter (ABV 4%)

Bagge's Bitter (ABV 4.5%)

Brewers Drop (ABV 4.5%)

Mid Life Crisis (ABV 4.5%) ◆
Red-coloured with a rich coffee character. Hop notes with a background of roast and malt give some depth to a somewhat light, uncomplicated brew.

Kerb Crawler (ABV 5.2%)

Moot Point (ABV 6.5%)

Bull Lane

Bull Lane Brewing Co, The Clarendon, 143 High Street East, Sunderland, Tyne & Wear, SR1 2BL
☎ **(0191) 510 3299**
✉ **bullanebrewingco@hotmail.co.uk**
🌐 **bull-lane-brewing.co.uk**
Tours by arrangement

Sunderland's first brew-pub started production in 2005 in the cellar of the Clarendon pub on a 2.5-barrel plant. There are plans to extend the brewery on to land behind the pub. The beers are widely available throughout the north east. Seasonal and one-off brews are regularly available.

Nowtsa Matta BB (OG 1037, ABV 3.7%)

Sun Inn Light Bitter (OG 1038, ABV 3.8%)

Ryhope Tug (OG 1039, ABV 3.9%)

Terry's All Gold/TAG (OG 1042, ABV 4.2%)

Clary Brown (OG 1045, ABV 4.5%)

Jack's Flag (OG 1045, ABV 4.5%)

Nowtsa Matta XB (OG 1045, ABV 4.5%)

Sauce of the Niall (OG 1045, ABV 4.5%)

White Bull (OG 1048, ABV 4.8%)

Bull Terrier (OG 1050, ABV 5%)

Bullmastiff SIBA

Bullmastiff Brewery, 14 Bessemer Close, Leckwith, Cardiff, CF11 8DL
☎ (029) 2066 5292

An award-winning small craft brewery run by brothers Bob and Paul Jenkins since 1987. The name stems from their love of the bullmastiff breed. They have no ambitions for expansion or owning any pubs, preferring to concentrate on quality control. 30 outlets are supplied. Seasonal beers: Summer Moult (ABV 4.3%), Mogadog (ABV 10%, winter).

Welsh Gold (OG 1039, ABV 3.8%)
A hoppy and fruity aroma leads into the same juicy blend of flavours. Bittersweet initially, an easy-drinking and refreshing beer.

Jack the Lad (OG 1041, ABV 4.1%)

Thoroughbred (OG 1046, ABV 4.5%)
A good hop aroma leads to a hoppy flavour with accompanying fruit, malt and balancing bitterness. There is a quenching hoppy bitterness in the finish.

Welsh Black (OG 1050, ABV 4.8%)

Welsh Red (OG 1048, ABV 4.8%)

Brindle (OG 1050, ABV 5.1%)
A full-bodied, flavoursome pale beer. Good hop aroma with a mix of malt, hops, fruit and bitterness in the taste. A lasting and satisfying finish.

Son of a Bitch (OG 1062, ABV 6%)
A complex, warming amber ale with a tasty blend of hops, malt and fruit flavours, with increasing bitterness.

Bunker

Bunker Bar, 41 Earlham Street, Covent Garden, London, WC2H 9LD
☎ (020) 7240 0606
✉ info@bunkerbar.com
bunkerbar.com

A micro-brewery producing Freedom lager – see entry for Freedom.

Buntingford SIBA

Buntingford Brewery Co Ltd, Greys Brewhouse, Therfield Road, Royston, Hertfordshire, SG8 9NW
☎ (01763) 250749
☎ 07947 214058
✉ catherine@buntingford-brewery.co.uk
buntingford-brewery.co.uk
Tours by arrangement

Production started in 2005 using a 15-barrel plant capable of producing up to 45 barrels a week. Locally grown barley is used whenever possible, all floor malted by Warminster Maltings. The brewery is located on a conservation farm: all brewery waste liquids are treated in a reedbed and plans are in hand to make full use of green energy sources. Beers are delivered over a wide area. Occasional beers: Royston Red (ABV 4.8%), Grey Partridge (ABV 4%, autumn/winter), Night Owl Porter (ABV 4.2%).

Pargetters (ABV 3.7%)
A traditional style dark mild.

Challenger (ABV 3.8%)
Pale session beer with citrus hop flavours.

Royston Pale Ale (ABV 4.3%)
Golden best bitter.

Britannia (ABV 4.4%)
Light brown best bitter.

Oatmeal Stout (ABV 4.4%)
A quaffing stout with oats and plenty of hop flavour.

Silence (ABV 5.2%)
Lager malt and American hops combine with a strong citrus character.

Burford

Burford Brewery Ltd, Downs Road, Witney, Oxfordshire, OX28 0SY
☎ (01993) 703333
✉ burfordbrewery@yahoo.co.uk

Burford started brewing in 2005 using a five-barrel plant. Some 40 outlets in Oxfordshire and Gloucestershire are supplied, together with many beer festivals. Bottled and organic beers are planned for the near future.

Cotswold Boy (ABV 3.8%)

Cellarbaration Ale (ABV 4%)

Best (ABV 4.3%)

Burton Bridge SIBA

Burton Bridge Brewery Ltd, Bridge Street, Burton upon Trent, Staffordshire, DE14 1SY
☎ (01283) 510573
✉ bbb@burtonbridgebrewery.fsnet.co.uk
midlandspubs.co.uk
Shop at Bridge Inn 11.30am-2.15pm, 5-11pm
Tours by arrangement (Wed evenings)

A brewery established in 1982 by Bruce Wilkinson and Geoff Mumford. The brewery owns four pubs in the town, including its CAMRA award-winning brewery tap. More than 300 outlets are supplied direct. An ever-changing range of seasonal/monthly beers is available. Bottle-conditioned beers are also available.

Golden Delicious (OG 1037, ABV 3.8%)
A Burton classic with sulphurous aroma, well balanced hops and fruit, and a lingering, mouth-watering bitter finish and hint of astringency. Light, crisp and refreshing.

XL Bitter (OG 1039, ABV 4%)
Another Burton classic with sulphurous aroma. Golden with fruit and hops and characteristic aftertaste.

Bridge Bitter (OG 1041, ABV 4.2%)
Pale brown and hoppy with a hint of roast and caramel. Complex taste with hops just dominating to provide a lingering hoppy finish.

Burton Porter (OG 1044, ABV 4.5%)
Unusually malty throughout but with lots of roast and fruit and liquorice, long bitter aftertaste.

Stairway to Heaven (OG 1049, ABV 5%)
Golden bitter. A perfectly balanced beer. The malty and hoppy start leads to a hoppy body with some astringency.

Top Dog Stout (OG 1049, ABV 5%)
Black and rich with a roast and malty start. Fruity and abundant hops give a fruity, bitter finish with a mouth-watering edge. Also available as Bramble Stout.

Festival Ale (OG 1054, ABV 5.5%)
Pale brown with a fruity aroma. Fruity start reminiscent of Xmas pudding ingredients; sweet fruity finish that develops to bitterness.

Thomas Sykes (OG 1095, ABV 10%)
Rich and warming, fruity, heady and hoppy. A true barley wine to be handled with caution.

Burtonwood

Thomas Hardy Burtonwood Ltd, Bold Lane, Burtonwood, Warrington, Cheshire, WA5 4TH
☎ **(01925) 220022**
thomashardybrewery.co.uk

Following the sale of 60% of its brewing operation to Thomas Hardy in 1998, Burtonwood PLC sold the remaining 40% in 2004 to become solely a pub-owning group that was bought by Marston's (qv) in 2005. Burtonwood is now Thomas Hardy's only brewery, run by Peter Ward as a contract operation, principally for Scottish & Newcastle.

Bushy's SIBA

Mount Murray Brewing Co Ltd, Mount Murray Brewery, Mount Murray, Braddan, Isle of Man, IM4 1JE
☎ **(01624) 661244**
bushys@manx.net
bushys.com
Tours by arrangement

Set up in 1986 as a brew-pub, Bushy's moved to its present site in 1990 when demand outgrew capacity. It owns four tied houses and the beers are also supplied to 25 other outlets. Bushy's goes one step further than the Manx Pure Beer Law, which permits only malt, hops, sugar and yeast, preferring the German Reinheitsgebot (Pure Beer Law) that excludes sugar. Seasonal beers are numerous – see website.

Castletown Bitter (OG 1035, ABV 3.5%)
A light, golden beer full of floral and citrus hints. A refreshing session beer.

Ruby (1874) Mild (OG 1035, ABV 3.5%)
An authentic malt brewed Mild with a fine aroma of crystal malt and Fuggles.

Bitter (OG 1038, ABV 3.8%)
An aroma full of pale malt and hops introduces a beautifully hoppy, bitter beer. Despite the predominant hop character, malt is also evident. Fresh and clean-tasting.

Old Bushy Tail (OG 1045, ABV 4.5%)
A reddish-brown beer with a pronounced hop and malt aroma, the malt tending towards treacle. Slightly sweet and malty on the palate with distinct orangy tones. The full finish is malty and hoppy with a hint of toffee.

Piston Brew (OG 1045, ABV 4.5%)
A ruby-coloured ale, slightly sweet with subtle hop flavours coming through from the late addition of Challenger and Fuggles hops. Malty with hints of toffee.

Weiss Beer (OG 1040, ABV 4.5%)
A light, refreshing, cloudy wheat beer.

Butcombe SIBA

Butcombe Brewery Ltd, Cox's Green, Wrington, Bristol, BS40 5PA
☎ **(01934) 863963**
info@butcombe.com
butcombe.com
Shop Mon-Fri 9am-5pm; Sat 9am-12pm
Tours by arrangement

Established in 1978 by Simon Whitmore and sold to Guy Newell and friends in 2003, Butcombe moved to a new purpose-built brewery in 2004. It supplies about 500 outlets and similar numbers via wholesalers and pub companies. Butcombe has an estate of 15 freehouses. Seasonal beers: Blond (ABV 4.3%, Apr-Sep), Brunel IPA (ABV 5%, Oct-Mar).

Bitter (OG 1039, ABV 4%)
Amber-coloured, malty and notably bitter beer, with subtle citrus notes. Hoppy, malty, citrus and a slight sulphur aroma, and a long, dry, bitter finish.

Gold (OG 1044, ABV 4.4%)
Aroma of pale malt, citrus hops and fruit. Medium bodied, well-balanced, with good pale malt, hops and bitterness. It is fruity, slightly sweet, with an abiding dryness.

Butler's SIBA

Butler's Brewery Co Ltd, The Brewery, Whittles Farm, Mapledurham, Oxfordshire, RG4 7UP
☎ **(0118) 972 3201**
butlerbrew@aol.com
butlersbrewery.co.uk

The brewery was started by Mark and Sarah Butler in 2003. An old cart shed was converted into a brewery and a six-barrel plant was installed. A bottling plant is now operating and the brewery is concentrating on its bottle-conditioned range. Around 30-40 outlets are supplied in Berks, Bucks and Oxon. All beers are suitable for vegetarians.

Oxfordshire Bitter (OG 1036.6, ABV 3.6%)

Swift (OG 1040, ABV 4%)

Butts SIBA

Butts Brewery Ltd, Northfield Farm, Wantage Road, Great Shefford, Hungerford, Berkshire, RG17 7BY
☎ (01488) 648133
✉ sales@buttsbrewery.com
🌐 buttsbrewery.com

The brewery was set up in a converted Dutch barn in 1994. In 2002, the brewery took the decision to become dedicated to organic production: all the beers brewed use organic malted barley and organic hops when suitable varieties are available. All beers are certified by the Soil Association. Some 60 outlets are supplied. Seasonal beers: Mudskipper (ABV 4.5%, summer), Bit o'Posh (ABV 4.2%, autumn). Bottle-conditioned beers are also available.

Jester (OG 1036, ABV 3.5%)
A pale brown session bitter with a hoppy aroma and a hint of fruit. The taste balances malt, hops, fruit and bitterness with a hoppy aftertaste.

Traditional (OG 1040, ABV 4%)
A pale brown bitter that is quite soft on the tongue, with hoppy citrus flavours accompanying a gentle, bittersweetness. A long, dry aftertaste is dominated by fruity hops.

Blackguard (OG 1045, ABV 4.5%)
A porter with caramel, malt, roast and fruit dominating the aroma. The taste is a combination of sweet, malt and roast with caramel undertones and a hoppy finish.

Barbus Barbus (OG 1046, ABV 4.6%)
Golden ale with a hoppy aroma and a hint of malt. Hops dominate taste and aftertaste, accompanied by fruitiness and bitterness, with a hint of balancing sweetness.

Golden Brown (OG 1050, ABV 5%)
A golden brown ale with malt and caramel dominating the aroma. A malty, bittersweet taste lingers on into the subtle aftertaste.

Le Butts (OG 1050, ABV 5%)
Brewed with lager yeast and hops resulting in a crisp and refreshing European-style beer.

Coper (OG 1059, ABV 6%)

Cains SIBA

Cains Beer Company plc, Stanhope Street, Liverpool, Merseyside, L8 5XJ
☎ (0151) 709 8734
✉ info@cains.co.uk
🌐 cains.co.uk
Shop: Brewery Tap open 12-11pm daily
Tours by arrangement

The Dusanj brothers, Ajmail and Sudarghara, bought the brewery in 2002, have invested heavily and won many awards for their beers. 105 pubs are owned all serving cask beer and around 300 outlets are supplied. All of the beers are suitable for vegetarians and vegans. Seasonal beers: see website.

Dark Mild (OG 1034.5, ABV 3.2%)
Sweetish, fruity mild with roast notes throughout and a dry aftertaste.

IPA (OG 1036, ABV 3.5%)
A light, full-flavoured session beer with a subtle hop aroma.

Finest Bitter (OG 1041, ABV 4%)
Blackcurrant fruit and malt dominate the aroma. A sweetish malty bitter with hints of roast and caramel. Hops come through in the dry, bitter aftertaste.

2008 Culture Beer (OG 1049, ABV 5%)
A pale-coloured bitter with an abundance of citrus hop character. Subtle hints of malt and fruit in the aroma and on the palate.

Formidable Ale/FA (OG 1049, ABV 5%)
A bitter and hoppy beer with a good dry aftertaste. Sharp, clean and dry.

Cairngorm SIBA

Cairngorm Brewery Co Ltd, Unit 12, Dalfaber Industrial Estate, Aviemore, Highlands, PH22 1ST
☎ (01479) 812222
✉ info@cairngormbrewery.com
🌐 cairngormbrewery.com
Shop Mon-Sat 9am-5pm (online shop also available)
Tours: Mon-Fri 10.30am-2.30pm (Sat tours by arrangement)

The brewery has enjoyed much success since winning Champion Beer of Scotland in 2004 and 2005, and gold medals at GBBF in 2004 and 2005. Seven regular cask beers are produced along with a rolling programme of seasonal ales throughout the year. Expansion continued during 2008, taking weekly capacity to 100 barrels. The free trade is supplied as far as the central belt with national delivery via wholesalers. Seasonal beers: See website.

Stag (OG 1040, ABV 4.1%)
A drinkable best bitter with plenty of hop bitterness throughout. This tawny brew has some malt in the lingering bitter aftertaste.

Trade Winds (OG 1043, ABV 4.3%)
A massive citrus fruit, hop and elderflower nose leads to hints of grapefruit and apricot in the mouth. The exceptional bittersweetness in the taste lasts through the long, lingering aftertaste.

Black Gold (OG 1044, ABV 4.4%)
Worthy Championship-winning beer with many accolades. Roast malt dominates but the liquorice and blackcurrant in the taste and nose give it a background sweetness. Very long, dry, bitter finish.

Nessies Monster Mash (OG 1044, ABV 4.4%)
A good, traditional, English-type bitter with plenty of bitterness and light malt flavour. Lingering bitterness in the aftertaste with diminishing sweetness.

Cairngorm Gold (OG 1044, ABV 4.5%)

Sheepshaggers Gold (OG 1044, ABV 4.5%)
A golden amber brew with faint aromas and tastes of grapefruit and passion fruit. Some light bitterness in the otherwise sweet aftertaste.

Wildcat (OG 1049.5, ABV 5.1%)

A full-bodied strong bitter. Malt predominates but there is an underlying hop character through to the well-balanced aftertaste.

Caledonian

See S&N/Heineken in Global Giants section

Callow Top

See Haywood Bad Ram

Calvors*

Calvors Brewery Ltd, Home Farm, Coddenham, Ipswich, Suffolk, IP6 9UN
☎ (01449) 711055
✉ info@calvors.co.uk
🌐 calvors.co.uk

No real ale. Calvors Brewery was established in early 2008 and brews one bottled real lager, Calvors (ABV 5.2%). There are plans for more beers in the near future.

Cambridge Moonshine

Cambridge Moonshine Brewery, 28 Radegund Road, Cambridge, Cambridgeshire, CB1 3RS
☎ 07906 066794
✉ mark.watch@ntlworld.com

A micro-brewery established in 2004. A new 2.5-barrel plant was installed in 2006. Plans for the future are to move to larger premises. The brewery concentrates on supplying CAMRA beer festivals, with two outlets supplied direct. Bottle-conditioned beers are available.

Harvest Moon Mild (OG 1040, ABV 3.8%)

Mulberry Whale Bitter (OG 1040, ABV 4%)

Red Watch Blueberry Ale (OG 1042, ABV 4.4%)

Black Hole Stout (OG 1044, ABV 4.5%)

Pigs Ear Porter (OG 1048, ABV 4.7%)

Cambrinus SIBA

Cambrinus Craft Brewery, Home Farm, Knowsley Park, Knowsley, Merseyside, L34 4AQ
☎ (0151) 546 2226

⊗ Established in 1997, Cambrinus is housed in part of a former farm building on a private estate. It produces around 250 hectolitres a year on a five-barrel plant. Some 45 outlets are supplied on a regular basis in and around Lancashire, Cheshire and Cumbria. The brewery supplies own label beer to Knowsley Safari Park in filtered bottle form. Seasonal beers: Bootstrap (ABV 4.5%, spring), Fruit Wheat Beer (summer), St Georges Ale (ABV 4.5%, Apr), Clogdance (ABV 3.6%, May), Solstice (ABV 3.8%, Jun), Honeywheat (ABV 3.7%, Jul), Dark Harvest (ABV 4%, autumn), Hearts of Oak (ABV 5%, Oct), Parkin (ABV 3.8%, Nov), Lamp Oil (ABV 4.5%, winter), Celebrance (ABV 5.5%, Xmas).

Herald (OG 1036, ABV 3.7%)
Light summer drinking bitter, pale and refreshing.

Yardstick (OG 1040, ABV 4%)
Mild, malty and lightly hopped.

Deliverance (OG 1040, ABV 4.2%)
Pale premium bitter.

Endurance (OG 1045, ABV 4.3%)
IPA-style, smooth and hoppy, fermented in oak.

Camerons

Camerons Brewery Ltd, Lion Brewery, Stranton, Hartlepool, Co Durham, TS24 7QS
☎ (01429) 266666
✉ martindutoy@cameronsbrewery.com
🌐 cameronsbrewery.com
Shop Mon-Sat 11am-4pm
Tours by arrangement

⊛ Founded in 1865, Camerons was bought in 2002 by Castle Eden brewery, which moved production to Hartlepool. In 2003 a 10-barrel micro-brewery, the Lions Den, opened to produce and bottle small brews of guest ales and to undertake contract brewing and bottling. Around 75 pubs are owned, with five selling real ale. Seasonal beers have been dropped in favour of monthly guest beer production.

Bitter (OG 1036, ABV 3.6%) ◆
A light bitter, but well-balanced, with hops and malt.

Strongarm (OG 1041, ABV 4%) ◆
A well-rounded, ruby-red ale with a distinctive, tight creamy head; initially fruity, but with a good balance of malt, hops and moderate bitterness.

Castle Eden Ale (OG 1043, ABV 4.2%) ◆
A light, creamy, malty sweet ale with fruit notes and a mellow dry bitterness in the finish.

Nimmo's XXXX (OG 1045, ABV 4.4%) ◆
Light golden beer with a well-balanced character derived from English malt and Goldings hops.

For Scottish & Newcastle/Heineken:

John Smith's Magnet (OG 1039.8, ABV 4%)
Ruby-red ale with good balance between malt and hops

Cannon Royall SIBA

▮ Cannon Royall Brewery Ltd, Fruiterer's Arms, Uphampton Lane, Ombersley, Worcestershire, WR9 0JW
☎ (01905) 621161
✉ info@cannonroyall.co.uk
🌐 cannonroyall.co.uk
Tours by arrangment (CAMRA only)

Cannon Royall's first brew was in 1993 in a converted cider house behind the Fruiterer's Arms. It has increased capacity from five barrels to more than 16 a week. The brewery supplies a number of outlets throughout the Midlands. Seasonal beers are regularly produced. Bottle-conditioned beers are also available.

Fruiterer's Mild (OG 1037, ABV 3.7%) ▮ ◆

This black-hued brew has rich malty aromas that lead to a fruity mix of bitter hops and sweetness, and a short balanced aftertaste.

King's Shilling (OG 1038, ABV 3.8%) ◆
A golden bitter that packs a citrus hoppy punch throughout.

Arrowhead Bitter (OG 1039, ABV 3.9%) ◆
A powerful punch of hops attacks the nose before the feast of bitterness. The memory of this golden brew fades too soon.

Muzzle Loader (OG 1042, ABV 4.2%) ◆
The lingering aftertaste bears witness to this amber liquid's agreeable balance of malt and hoppy flavours that is evident in the aroma and palate.

Arrowhead Extra (OG 1045, ABV 4.3%)
An intense hop aroma with some sweetness on the palate. The finish is long and bitter.

Captain Cook SIBA

Captain Cook Brewery Ltd, White Swan, 1 West End, Stokesley, North Yorkshire, TS9 5BL
☎ (01642) 710263
✉ jeff.hind@thewynyardrooms.com
🌐 thecaptaincookbrewery.co.uk
Tours by arrangement

The Captain Cook Brewery is located within the 18th-century White Swan pub. The brewery, with a four-barrel plant, started operations in 1999. Under new ownership since September 2007, capacity is increasing to 12 barrels a week in order to supply other pubs. Seasonal beer: Easter Island (ABV 4.1%, Easter-Nov).

Sunset (OG 1040, ABV 4.1%)
An extremely smooth light ale with a good balance of malt and hops.

Slipway (OG 1042, ABV 4.2%)
A light-coloured hoppy ale with bitterness coming through from Challenger hops. A full-flavoured ale with a smooth malt aftertaste.

Black Porter (OG 1044, ABV 4.4%)

Castle Rock SIBA

Castle Rock Brewery, Queensbridge Road, Nottingham, Nottinghamshire, NG2 1NB
☎ (0115) 985 1615
✉ admin@castlerockbrewery.co.uk
🌐 castlerockbrewery.co.uk
Tours by arrangement

Castle Rock has been brewing next door to the Vat & Fiddle pub since 1998. Production now runs at around 100 barrels a week with possible further expansion in capacity under review. Beers are distributed through wholesalers on both a local and national basis. A different beer with a wildlife theme is brewed every month in conjunction with the Nottinghamshire Wildlife Trust. Seasonal beers: see website. Bottle-conditioned beers are also available.

Black Gold (OG 1038, ABV 3.8%)
Hints of caramel and fruit balanced by bitterness in this dark mild.

Harvest Pale (OG 1037, ABV 3.8%)
Assertive citrus hop bitterness with some underlying sweetness leading to a refreshing zesty finish.

Hemlock Bitter (OG 1040, ABV 4%)
Aromas of dried fruit enhance this well-rounded, bittersweet session beer.

Preservation Fine Ale (OG 1044, ABV 4.4%)
A full-flavoured beer with some residual sweetness that is well-balanced with a resinous hop character.

Elsie Mo (OG 1045.5, ABV 4.7%)
Blond beer with a subtle floral nose and lemongrass freshness delivering a clean finish.

Castle*

Castle Brewery, Unit 9a, Restormel Industrial Estate, Liddicoat Road, Lostwithiel, Cornwall, PL22 0HG
☎ 07800 635831
✉ castlebrewery@aol.com

Castle started brewing in early 2008 on a two-barrel plant. Only bottle-conditioned ales are produced; Battle Stout (ABV 4.6%), Once A Knight (ABV 5%), Lostwithiale (ABV 7%), Hung, Drawn & Slaughtered (ABV 10%).

Cathedral*

Cathedral Ales, Green Dragon Hotel, Broadgate, Lincoln, Lincolnshire, LN2 5DH
☎ (01636) 822255
✉ info@cathedralales.co.uk

Cathedral Ales opened in April 2008 on a five-barrel plant. The Milestone Brewery is also owned. Five regular ales plus seasonals are planned – no further information was available at the time of going to press.

Caythorpe SIBA

Caythorpe Brewery Ltd, c/o Black Horse, 29 Main Street, Caythorpe, Nottinghamshire, NG14 7ED
☎ (0115) 966 4933
☎ 07913 434922
✉ caythorpebrewery@btinternet.com
Tours by arrangement

Caythorpe was set up using a 2.5-barrel brewery in a building at the rear of the Black Horse pub in 1997. Ownership changed in 2005 but the brewery continues to produce its small range of beers that have a big reputation in the local area. Seasonal beers: Winter Light (ABV 3.6%, autumn/winter), One Swallow (ABV 3.6%, spring/summer).

Bitter (OG 1034.7, ABV 3.7%)

Dover Beck (OG 1037, ABV 4%)

Stout Fellow (OG 1038.6, ABV 4.2%)

Cellar Rat

See 3 Rivers

Celt Experience*

Celt Experience Brewery Ltd, Unit 2E, Former Hill Buildings, Pontygwindy Industrial Estate, Caerphilly, CF83 3HU

☎ 0870 803 3876
✉ celt@theceltexperience.co.uk
🌐 theceltexperience.co.uk

Celt Experience first brewed in late 2007. A sister brewery to Newmans, they share the 40-barrel plant.

Celt Golden (ABV 4.2%)

Celt Bronze (ABV 4.5%)

Cwrw Celt (ABV 5%)
A real lager.

Chalk Hill

Chalk Hill Brewery, Rosary Road, Norwich, Norfolk, NR1 4DA
☎ (01603) 477078
✉ chalkhillinns@ntlworld.com
Tours by arrangement

Chalk Hill began production in 1993 on a 15-barrel plant. It supplies local pubs and festivals.

Tap Bitter (OG 1036, ABV 3.6%)
A light, fruity beer with underlying hop notes. A malty bitterness and a slightly resinous feel to the initial taste. The balance of flavour remains to the end of the short, light finish.

CHB (OG 1042, ABV 4.2%)
A copper-coloured brew with a dominant bitter flavour. Hops in the bouquet continue through and give a dry, lingering aftertaste. Background maltiness gives balance.

Gold (ABV 4.3%)
A well-balanced golden ale. Malt, hops, citrus notes and bitterness can all be found in subtle amounts in both the aroma and taste. Surprisingly long finish develops a slight dryness.

Dreadnought (OG 1049, ABV 4.9%)
A rich plummy fruitiness pervades the nose and taste of this mid-brown strong bitter. Malt joins with a caramel and roast background to give depth. Sweetness outlasts a quick finish.

Flintknapper's Mild (OG 1052, ABV 5%)
Chocolate, stewed fruits, liquorice, hops and malt can all be found in this rich, red-coloured brew. The light malt nose belies the variety of flavours.

Old Tackle (OG 1056, ABV 5.6%)
Red hued with a blackcurrant bouquet, this rich malty brew slowly subsides to a long dryish end. Roast notes remain consistent.

Cheddar Ales

J.R. Ham t/a Cheddar Ales, Winchester Farm, Draycott Road, Cheddar, Somerset, BS27 3RP
☎ (01934) 744193
✉ jem@cheddarales.co.uk
🌐 cheddarales.co.uk
Shop Mon-Fri 8am-4pm; Sat-Sun 9am-2pm by appointment
Tours by arrangement

Cheddar Ales is a 20-barrel brewery set up in 2006 by former Butcombe brewer Jeremy Ham. The kit was sourced from a barn in Dublin, where it had sat unused for six years. Some 50-60 outlets are supplied regularly.

Mild Cheddar (ABV 3.6%)
A dark brown ale with a rounded blend of rich malt flavours, balanced with a light hop bitterness.

Gorge Best Bitter (OG 1040, ABV 4%)

Potholer (OG 1043.5, ABV 4.3%)
Amber malty best bitter, biscuity aroma and citrus in the mouth. Bitter fruit finish.

Totty Pot (ABV 4.5%)
A rich, dark porter with a roasted malt character and subtle hop highlights.

Cherwell Valley*

Cherwell Valley Brewery Ltd, Unit 2, St David's Court, Top Station Road, Brackley, Northamptonshire, NN13 7UG
☎ (01280) 706888
🌐 cherwellvalley.co.uk

Cherwell Valley first brewed in early 2008 using a 2.5-barrel plant. Seasonal beers: Larkrise (ABV 4%, summer), Old Noll (ABV 5%, winter). Bottle-conditioned beers are also available.

CVB (ABV 3.5%)

Cropredy Bridge (ABV 4.2%)

Chiltern SIBA

Chiltern Brewery, Nash Lee Road, Terrick, Aylesbury, Buckinghamshire, HP17 0TQ
☎ (01296) 613647
✉ info@chilternbrewery.co.uk
🌐 chilternbrewery.co.uk
Shop Mon-Sat 9am-5pm
Tours by arrangement

Founded in 1980, the brewery is one of the first dozen micro-breweries to have been established in the country and is the oldest independent brewery in the Chilterns. This second generation family brewery produces a broad range of award-winning beers with English ingredients. The brewery tap is the Farmers' Bar at the King's Head in Aylesbury. Seasonal beers: Chiltern's Nut Brown Mild (ABV 3.9%, spring), Cobblestones (ABV 3.5%, summer), Copper Beech (ABV 4.4%, autumn), Glad Tidings (ABV 4.6%, winter). Bottle-conditioned beers are also available.

Ale (OG 1037, ABV 3.7%)
An amber, refreshing beer with a slight fruit aroma, leading to a good malt/bitter balance in the mouth. The aftertaste is bitter and dry.

Beechwood Bitter (OG 1043, ABV 4.3%)
This pale brown beer has a balanced butterscotch/toffee aroma, with a slight hop note. The taste balances bitterness and sweetness, leading to a long bitter finish.

Three Hundreds Old Ale (OG 1049, ABV 4.9%)
A complex, copper-coloured old ale. The mixed fruit/caramel aroma leads to a balanced taste, with sweetness slightly dominating. The finish starts sweet and leads to a long-lasting bitterness.

Church End SIBA

Church End Brewery Ltd, Ridge Lane, Nuneaton, Warwickshire, CV10 0RD
☎ (01827) 713080
stewart@churchendbrewery.co.uk
churchendbrewery.co.uk
Shop during tap opening hours
Tours by arrangement
Stewart Elliot started brewing in 1994 in an old coffin shop in Shustoke. He moved to the present site and upgraded to a 10-barrel plant in 2001. The brewery tap was opened on the same site a year later. A portfolio of around 60 irregular beers are produced as well as many one-off specials, including fruit, herb and spice beers. Some 500 outlets are supplied.
Seasonal beers: Without-a-Bix (ABV 4.2%), Pews Porter (ABV 4.5%), Old Pal (ABV 5.5%), Arthurs Wit (ABV 6%), Rest-in-Peace (ABV 7%). Bottle-conditioned beers are also available.

Poachers Pocket (ABV 3.5%)

Pheasant Plucker (ABV 3.7%)

Cuthberts (ABV 3.8%) ◆
A refreshing, hoppy beer, with hints of malt, fruit and caramel taste. Lingering bitter aftertaste.

Goat's Milk (ABV 3.8%)

Gravediggers Ale (ABV 3.8%) ◆
A premium mild. Black and red in colour, with a complex mix of chocolate and roast flavours, it is almost a light porter.

Hop Gun (ABV 4.1%)

What the Fox's Hat (ABV 4.2%) ◆
A beer with a malty aroma, and a hoppy and malty taste with some caramel flavour.

Pooh Bear (ABV 4.3%)

Vicar's Ruin (ABV 4.4%) ◆
A straw-coloured best bitter with an initially hoppy, bitter flavour, softening to a delicate malt finish.

Stout Coffin (ABV 4.6%)

Fallen Angel (ABV 5%)

For Cape of Good Hope, Warwick:

Two Llocks (ABV 4%)

City of Cambridge EAB

City of Cambridge Brewery Co Ltd, Ely Road, Chittering, Cambridge, CB5 9BH
☎ (01223) 864864
sales@cambridge-brewery.co.uk
cambridge-brewery.co.uk
City of Cambridge opened in 1997 and moved to its present site in 2002. The brewery site is in the process of being redeveloped, with the intention of keeping the brewery on the site. At present all brewing is being done under contract by Oxfordshire Ales. In addition to prizes for its cask beers, the brewery holds a conservation award for the introduction of native reed beds at its site to treat brewery water. All beers are available bottled.

Jet Black (ABV 3.6%)
Uniquely styled black beer, mild but full in flavour and body.

Boathouse Bitter (ABV 3.7%) ◆
Copper-brown and full-bodied session bitter, starting with impressive citrus and floral hop; grassy fruit notes are present with finally a gentle bitterness.

Hobson's Choice (ABV 4.1%) ◆
This golden ale has a predominantly spicy hop aroma. Bittersweet on the palate with plenty of hops leading through to a dry, hoppy finish.

Atom Splitter (ABV 4.7%) ◆
Robust copper-coloured strong bitter with a hop aroma and taste, and a distinct sulphury edge.

Parkers Porter (ABV 5.3%) ◆
Impressive reddish brew with a defined roast character throughout, and a short, fruity, bittersweet palate.

City of Stirling

See Traditional Scottish Ales

Clark's SIBA

HB Clark & Co (Successors) Ltd, Westgate Brewery, Wakefield, West Yorkshire, WF2 9SW
☎ (01924) 373328 Ext 211
rickp@hbclark.co.uk
hbclark.co.uk
Tours by arrangement

Founded in 1906, Clark's recently celebrated its centenary. It ceased brewing during the 1960s/70s but resumed cask ale production in 1982 and now delivers to around 220 outlets. Four pubs are owned, all serving cask ale.
Seasonal beers: see website.

Classic Blonde (OG 1039, ABV 3.9%)
A light-coloured ale with a citrus and hoppy flavour, a distinctive grapefruit aroma and a dry finish.

No Angel (OG 1040, ABV 4%)
A bitter with a dry hop finish, well-balanced and full of flavour. Pale brown in colour with hints of fruit and hops.

Westgate Gold (OG 1042, ABV 4.2%)
A light-coloured, fruity beer with a full body and rich aroma.

Rams Revenge (OG 1046, ABV 4.6%) ◆
A rich, ruby-coloured premium ale, well-balanced with malt and hops, with a deep fruity taste and a dry hoppy aftertaste, with a pleasant hoppy aroma.

Clearwater SIBA

Clearwater Brewery, 2-4 Devon Units, Hatchmoor Industrial Estate, Great Torrington, Devon, EX38 7HP
☎ (01805) 625242
brian@clearwaterbrewery.co.uk
Tours by arrangement

Clearwater took on the closed St Giles in the Wood brewery in 1999 and has steadily grown since. Around 60-70 outlets are supplied.
Seasonal/occasional beers: Ebony & Ivory (ABV 4.2%, winter), 1646 (ABV 4.8% – bottled

only). Bottle-conditioned beers are also available.

Village Pride (OG 1036, ABV 3.7%)

Cavalier (OG 1041, ABV 4%)
Mid-brown, full-bodied best bitter with a burnt, rich malt aroma and taste, leading to a bitter, well-rounded finish.

High Tide (OG 1046, ABV 4.5%)

Olivers Nectar (OG 1052, ABV 5.2%)

Clockwork

The Clockwork Beer Company, Maclay Inns PLC, 1153-5 Cathcart Road, Glasgow, G42 9HB
☎ (0141) 649 0184
clockworkbeerco.com
Tours by arrangement

The brewpub, the oldest in Glasgow, was established in 1997. The beers are kept in cellar tanks where fermentation gases from the conditioning vessel blanket the beers on tap (but not under pressure). A wide range of ales, lagers and specials are produced. Most beers are naturally gassed while some, such as Lager, Gosch and Seriously Ginger, are pressurised. Since the change of ownership to Maclay Inns plans are afoot to supply other Maclay pubs and trial brews are underway of old Maclays recipes.

Amber IPA (ABV 3.8%)

Red Alt (ABV 4.4%)

Gosch (ABV 4.8%)

Original Lager (ABV 4.8%)

Hazy Daze Seriously Ginger (ABV 5%)

Oregon IPA (ABV 5.5%)

Strong Ale (ABV 6%)

Thunder & Lightning (ABV 6%)

Coach House SIBA

Coach House Brewing Co Ltd, Wharf Street, Warrington, Cheshire, WA1 2DQ
☎ (01925) 232800
info@coach-house-brewing.co.uk
coach-house-brewing.co.uk
Tours by arrangement for CAMRA groups

The brewery was founded in 1991. In 1995 Coach House increased its brewing capacity to cope with growing demand and it now delivers to around 250 outlets throughout Britain, either from the brewery or via wholesalers. The brewery also brews a large number of one-off and special beers. Its visitor centre opened in 2008. Seasonal beers: Ostlers Summer Pale Ale (ABV 4%, summer), Squires Gold (ABV 4.2%, spring), Summer Sizzler (ABV 4.2%, summer), Countdown (ABV 4.7%, 6 Dec onwards), Taverners Autumn Ale (ABV 5%), Blunderbus Old Porter (ABV 5.5%, winter).

Coachman's Best Bitter (OG 1037, ABV 3.7%)
A well-hopped, malty bitter, moderately fruity with a hint of sweetness and a peppery nose.

Gunpowder Mild (OG 1037, ABV 3.8%)
Biscuity dark mild with a blackcurrant sweetness. Bitterness and fruit dominate with some hints of caramel and a slightly stronger roast flavour.

Honeypot Bitter (OG 1037, ABV 3.8%)

Farrier's Best Bitter (OG 1038, ABV 3.9%)

Dick Turpin (OG 1042, ABV 4.2%)
Malty, hoppy pale brown beer with some initial sweetish flavours leading to a short, bitter aftertaste. Sold under other names as a pub house beer.

Flintlock Pale Ale (OG 1044, ABV 4.4%)

Innkeeper's Special Reserve (OG 1045, ABV 4.5%)
A darkish, full-flavoured bitter. Quite fruity, with a strong, bitter aftertaste.

Postlethwaite (OG 1045, ABV 4.6%)
Thin bitter with a short, dry aftertaste. Biscuity malt dominates.

Gingernut Premium (OG 1050, ABV 5%)

Posthorn Premium (OG 1050, ABV 5%)
Dry golden bitter with a blackcurrant fruitiness and good hop flavours leading to a strong, dry finish. Well-balanced but slightly thin for its gravity.

For John Joule of Stone:

Old Knotty (ABV 3.6%)

Old Priory (ABV 4.4%)

Victory (ABV 5.2%)

Coastal

Coastal Brewery, Unit 9B, Cardrew Industrial Estate, Redruth, Cornwall, TR15 1SS
☎ 07875 405407
coastalbrewery@tiscali.co.uk
coastalbrewery.co.uk

Coastal was set up in late 2006 on a five-barrel plant by Alan Hinde, former brewer and owner of the Borough Arms in Crewe, Cheshire. Two monthly seasonals are brewed. Around 30 outlets are supplied.

Hop Monster (OG 1038, ABV 3.7%)

Handliner (OG 1040, ABV 4%)

Merry Maidens Mild (OG 1040, ABV 4%)

Angelina (OG 1042, ABV 4.1%)

Golden Hinde (OG 1044, ABV 4.3%)

Engine House (OG 1052, ABV 5.1%)

Golden Sands (OG 1058, ABV 5.8%)

Erosion (OG 1080, ABV 8%)

Coles

Coles Family Brewery, White Hart Thatched Inn & Brewery, Llanddarog, Carmarthen, SA32 8NT
☎ (01267) 275395
Tours by arrangement

The brewery is based in an ancient inn built in 1371. Centuries ago beer was brewed on site, but brewing only started again in 1999 on a nine-gallon plant. A one-barrel plant was fitted in 2003.

Nettle Ale (OG 1039, ABV 3.8%)

Black Stag (OG 1042, ABV 4%)

Liquorice Stout (OG 1042, ABV 4%)

Roasted Barley Stout (OG 1042, ABV 4%)

Llanddarog Ale (OG 1043, ABV 4.1%)

Swn y Dail (ABV 4.2%)

Beetroot Ale (ABV 4.3%)

Cwrw Blasus (OG 1044, ABV 4.3%)

Golden Ale (ABV 4.3%)

To Gwellt (ABV 4.5%)

White Stag (ABV 4.5%)

College Green

College Green Brewery, 1 College Green Mews, Botanic Avenue, Belfast, BT7 1LW
☎ (02890) 322600 / (02892) 660800
✉ info@collegegreenbrewery.com
🌐 collegegreenbrewery.com
Tours by arrangement

College Green was set up in 2005 by Owen Scullion as a sister brewery to Hilden Brewery. Located in Belfast's lively university area, College Green (the city's only brewery) is housed in a tiny 19th-century coach house and brews for Molly's Yard Restaurant in the adjoining stables building.

Molly's Chocolate Stout (OG 1042, ABV 4.2%)
A dark chocolate-coloured beer with a full-bodied character due to the use of whole malted oats. A small amount of pure cocoa is added to give added credence to the name.

Headless Dog (OG 1042, ABV 4.3%)
A bright amber ale, using Munich malt. The well-hopped beer is named after the mural of a headless dog at the front of the brewery.

Belfast Blonde (OG 1047, ABV 4.7%)
A natural blonde beer with a clean and refreshing character, derived from the use of lager malt along with a small proportion of maize.

Combe Martin

Combe Martin Brewery, 4 Springfield Terrace, High Street, Combe Martin, Devon, EX34 0EE
☎ (01271) 883507

Combe Martin started by making country wine, then moved on to beer and cider. It operates from the kitchen and backyard of the owner's house on a one-barrel plant.

Past Times (OG 1036, ABV 3.9%)

Hangman's Bitter (OG 1044, ABV 4.5%)

Shammick Ale (OG 1062, ABV 6.2%)

Concertina SIBA

Concertina Brewery, 9a Dolcliffe Road, Mexborough, South Yorkshire, S64 9AZ
☎ (01709) 580841
Tours by arrangement

The brewery started in 1992 in the cellar of a club once famous as the home of a long-gone concertina band. The plant produces up to eight barrels a week for the club and other occasional outlets. Other beers are brewed on a seasonal basis, including Room at the Inn at Xmas.

Club Bitter (ABV 3.9%) ◆
A fruity session bitter with a good bitter flavour.

Old Dark Attic (OG 1038, ABV 3.9%)
A dark brown beer with a fairly sweet, fruity taste.

One Eyed Jack (OG 1039, ABV 4%)
Fairly pale in colour with plenty of hop bitterness. Brewed with the same malt and hop combination as Bengal Tiger, but more of a session beer. Also badged as Mexborough Bitter.

Bengal Tiger (OG 1043, ABV 4.6%) ◆
Light amber ale with an aromatic hoppy nose followed by a combination of fruit and bitterness.

Dictators (OG 1044, ABV 4.7%)

Ariel Square Four (OG 1046, ABV 5.2%)

Concrete Cow*

Concrete Cow Brewery, 59 Alston Drive, Bradwell Abbey, Milton Keynes, Buckinghamshire, MK13 9HB
☎ (01908) 316794
✉ dan@concretecowbrewery.co.uk
🌐 concretecowbrewery.co.uk

Concrete Cow opened in August 2007 on a 5.5-barrel plant. The beers are named after aspects of local history and all are available bottled as well as in casks. The brewery supplies pubs, farmers markets, local shops and restaurants.

Midsummer Ale (OG 1039, ABV 3.8%)

Cock 'n' Bull Story (OG 1041, ABV 4.1%)

Watling Gold (OG 1044, ABV 4.5%)

Old Bloomer (OG 1045, ABV 4.7%)

Coniston SIBA

Coniston Brewing Co Ltd, Coppermines Road, Coniston, Cumbria, LA21 8HL
☎ (01539) 441133
✉ sales@conistonbrewery.com
🌐 conistonbrewery.com
Shop (in Black Bull Inn) 10am-11pm
Tours by arrangement

A 10-barrel brewery set up in 1995 behind the Black Bull inn, Coniston. It now brews 40 barrels a week and supplies 50 local outlets while the beers are distributed nationally by wholesalers. One pub is owned. Bottle-conditioned Coniston beers are brewed by Refresh UK using Hepworth's Horsham plant: Bluebird (ABV 4.2%), Bluebird XB (ABV 4.4%), Oldman Ale (ABV 4.8%).

Olivers Light Ale (OG 1035, ABV 3.4%)
A light, straw-coloured light mild with subtle hops and Demerera sugar.

Bluebird Bitter (OG 1036, ABV 3.6%) ◆
A yellow-gold, predominantly hoppy and fruity beer, well-balanced with some sweetness and a rising bitter finish.

Bluebird XB (OG 1040.5, ABV 4.2%) ◆

Well-balanced, hoppy and fruity golden bitter. Bittersweet in the mouth with dryness building.

Oldman Ale (OG 1040.5, ABV 4.2%) ◆
Delicious fruity, winey beer with a complex, well-balanced richness.

Quicksilver (OG 1044, ABV 4.3%)
A golden amber ale, smooth and fruity with malt and hop tones.

Blacksmiths Ale (OG 1047.5, ABV 5%)
A well-balanced strong bitter with hints of Xmas pudding.

Consett Ale Works

The Consett Ale Works Ltd, Grey Horse, 115 Sherburn Terrace, Consett, Co Durham, DH8 6NE
☎ (01207) 502585
✉ jeffhind@aol.com
thegreyhorse.co.uk
Tours by arrangement

The brewery opened in 2006 in the stables of a former coaching inn, the Grey Horse, Consett's oldest pub at 160 years old. They expanded in 2007 to cope with demand. Some 60 outlets are supplied direct.

Steeltown Bitter (ABV 3.8%)

White Hot (ABV 4%)

Cast Iron (ABV 4.1%)

Last Tap (ABV 4.4%)

Red Dust (ABV 4.5%)

Conwy

Conwy Brewery Ltd, Unit 3, Morfa Conwy Enterprise Park, Parc Caer Selon, Conwy, LL32 8FA
☎ (01492) 585287
✉ enquiries@conwybrewery.co.uk
conwybrewery.co.uk
Shop Mon-Fri 9am-5pm (please ring if making special trip)
Tours by arrangement

Conwy started brewing in 2003 and was the first brewery in Conwy for at least 100 years. Due to steady growth it has recently moved premises. Around 50 outlets are supplied. Seasonal beers: Mulberry Dark (ABV 3.8%, May), Sun Dance/Dawns Haul (ABV 4%, summer), Telford Porter (ABV 5.6%, autumn), Hoppy Xmas/Nadolig Hopus (ABV 4.3%, Dec). Bottle-conditioned beers are also available.

Castle Bitter/Cwrw Castell (OG 1037, ABV 3.8%) ◆
Malty session bitter with some toffee and caramel notes in the aroma and taste. Full, smooth mouthfeel leading to a satisfying hoppy finish.

Welsh Pride/Balchder Cymru (OG 1040, ABV 4%)

Celebration Ale (OG 1041, ABV 4.2%)

Honey Fayre/Cwrw Mel (OG 1044, ABV 4.5%) ◆
Amber best bitter with hints of honey sweetness in the taste balanced by an increasingly hoppy, bitter finish. Slightly watery mouthfeel for a beer of this strength.

Special/Arbennig (OG 1043, ABV 4.5%) ◆
Rich, fruity and smooth dark bitter. Fruit dominates the aroma and leads into the flavour where malt is also prominent, as are some nuttiness and roasty hints. Dry aftertaste.

For Cobdens Hotel, Capel Curig:

Cobdens Hotel Bitter/Cwrw Gwesty Cobdens (OG 1040, ABV 4.1%)

Copper Dragon SIBA

Copper Dragon Brewery Ltd, Snaygill Industrial Estate, Keighley Road, Skipton, North Yorkshire, BD23 2QR
☎ (01756) 702130
✉ post@copperdragon.uk.com
copperdragon.uk.com
Shop Mon-Fri 11am-5pm; Sat hours TBC – please ring
Tours by arrangement

Copper Dragon began brewing in 2003 and quickly reached maximum capacity of 250 barrels a week. The new brewery, close to the original site, sports a new 'double 60' brewhouse (capable of 120 barrels a day). Beer distribution is widespread across northern England. A small number of pubs are owned.

Black Gold (OG 1036, ABV 3.7%) ◆
A dark ale with subtle fruit and dark malts on the nose. Quite bitter with roast coffee flavours throughout and a long burnt, bitter finish.

Best Bitter (OG 1036, ABV 3.8%) ◆
A gently hoppy, fruity aroma leads to an aggressively bitter and hoppy taste with a bitter finish. A very consistent brew.

Golden Pippin (OG 1037, ABV 3.9%) ◆
This golden ale has an intense citrus aroma and flavour, characteristic of American Cascade hops. The dry, bitter astringency increases in the aftertaste.

Scotts 1816 (OG 1041, ABV 4.1%) ◆
A well-balanced, full-bodied, copper-coloured premium bitter with a hoppy, tropical fruit character. Bitterness continues in the finish to leave a dry, hoppy fruitiness.

Challenger IPA (OG 1042, ABV 4.4%) ◆
Amber-coloured, this is more of a best bitter than a traditional IPA, with a fruity hoppiness in the aroma and taste and a growing dry bitter finish.

Corvedale SIBA

Corvedale Brewery, Sun Inn, Corfton, Craven Arms, Shropshire, SY7 9DF
☎ (01584) 861239
✉ normanspride@aol.com
suninncorfton.co.uk
Tours by arrangement

Brewing started in 1999 in a building behind the pub. Landlord Norman Pearce is also the brewer and he uses only British malt and hops, with water from a local borehole. One pub is owned and 100 outlets are supplied. Seasonal beer: Teresa's Pride (ABV 4.7%, Jan). All beers are on sale in the pub in bottle-conditioned form and are suitable for vegetarians and vegans.

Katie's Pride (OG 1040, ABV 4.3%)

Norman's Pride (OG 1043, ABV 4.3%)
A golden amber beer with a refreshing, slightly hoppy taste and a bitter finish.

Farmer Ray Ale (OG 1045, ABV 4.5%)
A clear, ruby bitter with a smooth malty taste. Customers are invited to guess the hop!

Dark and Delicious (OG 1045, ABV 4.6%)
A dark ruby beer with hops on the aroma and palate, and a sweet aftertaste.

Cotleigh SIBA

Cotleigh Brewery Ltd, Ford Road, Wiveliscombe, Somerset, TA4 2RE
☎ (01984) 624086
✉ sales@cotleighbrewery.com
🌐 cotleighbrewery.co.uk
Shop Mon-Fri 9am-4pm
Tours by arrangement for select CAMRA groups

⊗ Situated in the historic brewing town of Wiveliscombe, Cotleigh has become one of the most successful independent breweries in the West Country. The brewery, which started trading in 1979, is housed in specially converted premises with a modern plant capable of producing 165 barrels a week. 300 pubs and 100 retail outlets are supplied; the beers are also widely available through wholesalers. Cotleigh's charitable partner is The Hawk and Owl Trust. Seasonal beers: See website. Bottle-conditioned beers are also available.

Harrier (OG 1035, ABV 3.5%)
A delicate floral and fruity aroma with a refreshing, sweet and lightly hopped finish.

Tawny Owl (OG 1038, ABV 3.8%) ◆
Well-balanced, tawny-coloured bitter with plenty of malt and fruitiness on the nose, and malt to the fore in the taste, followed by hop fruit, developing to a satisfying bitter finish.

25 (ABV 4%)

Golden Seahawk Premium Bitter (OG 1042, ABV 4.2%) ◆
A gold, well-hopped premium bitter with a flowery hop aroma and fruity hop flavour, clean mouthfeel, leading to a dry, hoppy finish.

Peregrine Porter (ABV 4.4%)
An old-style porter – smooth and dark with a dry, well-hopped finish.

Barn Owl Premium Ale (OG 1045, ABV 4.5%) ◆
A pale to mid-brown beer with a good balance of malt and hops on the nose; a smooth, full-bodied taste where hops dominate, but balanced by malt, following through to the finish.

Buzzard Dark Ale (ABV 4.8%)
An old ale brewed with roasted malts. Dark and satisfying with a dry, hoppy finish.

Cotswold Spring

Cotswold Spring Brewery Ltd, Dodington Ash, Chipping Sodbury, Gloucestershire, BS37 6RX
☎ (01454) 323088
✉ info@cotswoldbrewery.com
🌐 cotswoldbrewery.com
Shop Mon-Fri 9am-6pm; Sat 10am-1pm
Tours by arrangement

☺ Cotswold Spring opened in 2005 with a 10-barrel refurbished plant that produces beers brewed using only the finest malted barley, subtle blends of hops and natural Cotswold spring water. All the beers are fermented in traditional vessels using specialist strains of yeast. They contain no artificial preservatives, flavourings or colourings. Seasonal beers: Christmas Old Ale (ABV 5%), Codrington Old Ale (ABV 4.8%), Codrington Winter Royal (ABV 5%).

Old English Rose (OG 1040, ABV 4%) ◆
Beautifully balanced quaffing ale with delicate floral aroma and hints of tropical fruit. Bittersweet finish.

Codrington Codger (OG 1042, ABV 4.2%) ◆
Mid-brown best bitter with the emphasis on malt. Nutty character.

Codrington Royal (OG 1045, ABV 4.5%) ◆
Ruby in colour with dark, sweet malt. Fruity with a hint of dandelion and burdock.

Cotswold

Cotswold Brewing Co Ltd, Foxholes Lane, Foscot, Oxfordshire, OX7 6RL
☎ (01608) 659631
☎ 07971 902385
✉ lager@cotswoldbrewingcompany.com
🌐 cotswoldbrewingcompany.com
Tours by arrangement

Cotswold Brewing Co is an independent producer of lager and speciality beers. The brewery was established in 2005 with the intention of supplying quality lagers to the local Cotswold market. Inspiration is drawn from continental Europe. The brewery is housed in an old Cotswold stone barn, part of a working farm estate. More than 50 outlets are supplied. Seasonal beer: Autumn Ale (ABV 4.3%), Winter Lager (ABV 5.3%). Bottle-conditioned beer is also available.

Three Point Eight Lager (OG 1035, ABV 3.8%)

Wheat Beer (OG 1040, ABV 4.2%)

Premium Lager (OG 1044, ABV 5%)

Cottage SIBA

Cottage Brewing Co Ltd, The Old Cheese Dairy, Hornblotton Road, Lovington, Somerset, BA7 7PS
☎ (01963) 240551
Tours by arrangement

⊗ The brewery was established in 1993 in West Lydford. The brewery moved to larger premises in 1996, doubling brewing capacity at the same time. In 2001, Cottage installed a 30-barrel plant. 1,500 outlets are supplied. The names of beers mostly follow a railway theme. Seasonal beers: Goldrush (ABV 5%),

Santa's Steaming Ale (ABV 5.5%, Xmas). Bottle-conditioned beer is also available.

Southern Bitter (OG 1039, ABV 3.7%) ◆
Gold-coloured beer with malt and fruity hops on the nose. Malt and hops in the mouth with a long fruity, bitter finish.

Broadgauge Bitter (OG 1040, ABV 3.9%)
A light tawny-coloured session bitter with a floral aroma and a balanced bitter finish.

Champflower Ale (OG 1041, ABV 4.2%) ◆
Amber beer with a fruity hop aroma, full hop taste and powerful bitter finish.

Somerset & Dorset Ale (OG 1044, ABV 4.4%)
A well-hopped, malty brew, with a deep red colour.

Golden Arrow (OG 1043, ABV 4.5%) ◆
A hoppy golden bitter with a powerful floral bouquet, a fruity, full-bodied taste and a lingering dry, bitter finish.

Goldrush (OG 1051, ABV 5%)
A deep golden strong ale brewed with Cascade hops.

Norman's Conquest (OG 1066, ABV 7%) ◆
A dark strong ale, with plenty of fruit in the aroma and taste; rounded vinous, hoppy finish.

Country Life SIBA

Country Life Brewery, The Big Sheep, Abbotsham, Bideford, Devon, EX39 5AP
☎ (01237) 420808
☎ 07971 267790
✉ simon@countrylifebrewery.co.uk
🌐 countrylifebrewery.co.uk
Shop 12-4pm daily
Tours by arrangement

⊗ The brewery is based at the Big Sheep tourist attraction that welcomes more than 100,000 visitors in the summer. The brewery offers a beer show and free samples in the shop during the peak season (Apr-Oct). A 15.5-barrel plant was installed in 2005, making Country Life the biggest brewery in north Devon. Bottling is now carried out on site. Around 100 outlets are supplied. All cask ales are also available in bottle-conditioned form plus Devonshire Ten-der (ABV 10%). Seasonal beer: Black Boar (ABV 5%, winter).

Old Appledore (OG 1037, ABV 3.7%)

Lacey's Ale (OG 1042, ABV 4.2%)

Pot Wallop (OG 1044, ABV 4.4%)

Golden Pig (OG 1046, ABV 4.7%)

Country Bum (OG 1058, ABV 6%)

Cox & Holbrook EAB

Cox & Holbrook, Manor Farm, Brettenham Road, Buxhall, Suffolk, IP14 3DY
☎ (01449) 736323
Tours by arrangement

⊗ First opened in 1997, the brewery concentrates on producing a range of bitters, four of which are available at any one time, along with more specialised medium strength beers and milds. There is also a strong emphasis on the preservation and resurrection of rare and traditional styles. Bottle-conditioned versions of draught beers are available at varying times of the year.

Crown Dark Mild (OG 1037, ABV 3.6%) ◆
Thin tasting at first but plenty of malt, caramel and roast flavours burst through to give a thoroughly satisfying beer.

Shelley Dark (OG 1036, ABV 3.6%)
Full-flavoured and satisfying.

Beyton Bitter (OG 1038, ABV 3.8%)
A traditional bitter, pale tawny in colour, malty with Fuggles and Goldings hops.

Old Mill Bitter (OG 1038, ABV 3.8%)
Pale, hoppy and thirst quenching.

Rattlesden Best Bitter (OG 1043, ABV 4%)
A full-bodied and malty best bitter.

Goodcock's Winner (OG 1050, ABV 5%)
An amber ale, rather malty yet not too heavy, with a sharp hop finish.

Ironoak Single Stout (OG 1051, ABV 5%)
Full-bodied with strong roast grain flavours and plenty of hop bitterness plus a distinct hint of oak.

Remus (OG 1051, ABV 5%)
An amber ale, soft on the palate with full hop flavours but subdued bitterness.

Stormwatch (OG 1052, ABV 5%)
An unusual premium pale ale with a full, slightly fruity flavour.

Stowmarket Porter (OG 1056, ABV 5%) ◆
Strong caramel flavour and lingering caramel aftertaste, balanced by full malt and roast flavours. The overall impression is of a very sweet beer.

Uncle Stan Single Brown Stout (OG 1053, ABV 5%)
Unusual soft malt and fruit flavours in a full and satisfying bit of history.

East Anglian Pale Ale (OG 1059, ABV 6%)
Well-matured, pale beer with a strong Goldings hops character.

Prentice Strong Dark Ale (OG 1083, ABV 8%)
A strong porter.

Crondall

Crondall Brewing Co Ltd, Lower Old Park Farm, Dora's Green Lane, Dora's Green, Nr Crondall, Hampshire, GU10 5DX
☎ (01252) 319000
✉ crondallbrewery@btinternet.com
🌐 crondallbrewery.co.uk
Shop Fri 3-7pm; Sat 10am-4.30pm

Crondall was established in 2005 using a 10-barrel plant in a converted granary barn. The company sells to the general public and to local free houses in the area, and supplies around 75 outlets. Seasonal beers include Easter Gold, Mr T's Wedding Ale, Ghoulies, Rocket Fuel, Crondall's Stocking Filler.

Crondall's Best (ABV 4%) ◆
A pleasant and uncomplicated golden bitter. A modest bouquet and initially bitter palate lead to a satisfying, dry, bitter aftertaste.

Sober as a Judge (ABV 4%) ◆

A brown bitter, with a noticeably malty aroma. Sharp flavour which leads to an astringent finish but remaining noticably malty throughout.

Mitchell's Dream (ABV 4.5%)
Sweet bitter with a pronounced malty nose. Roast and caramel flavours build into a rich rounded taste.

Cropton SIBA

New Inn & Cropton Brewery, Woolcroft, Cropton, North Yorkshire, YO18 8HH
☎ (01751) 417330
info@croptonbrewery.co.uk
croptonbrewery.com
Tours by arrangement

Cropton was established in the cellars of the New Inn in 1984 on a five-barrel plant. This was extended in 1988, but by 1994 it had outgrown the cellar and a purpose-built brewery was installed behind the pub. A brand new state of the art brewery was opened in 2006 that can produce 100 barrels per week. All the beers, with the exception of Haunting Hanks, are available bottle conditioned and are suitable for vegetarians and vegans. Seasonal beer: Rudolph's Revenge (ABV 4.6%, winter).

Endeavour Ale (OG 1038, ABV 3.6%)
A light session ale, made with best quality hops, providing a refreshing drink with a delicate fruity aftertaste.

Two Pints (OG 1040, ABV 4%)
A good, full-bodied bitter. Malt flavours initially dominate, with a touch of caramel, but the balancing hoppiness and residual sweetness come through.

Honey Gold (OG 1042, ABV 4.2%)
A medium-bodied beer, ideal for summer drinking. Honey is apparent in both aroma and taste but does not overwhelm. Clean finish with a hint of hops.

Scoresby Stout (OG 1042, ABV 4.2%)

Balmy Mild (OG 1044, ABV 4.4%)

Uncle Sam's (OG 1046, ABV 4.4%)

Yorkshire Moors Bitter (OG 1046, ABV 4.6%)
A fine ruby beer brewed with Fuggles and Progress hops. A hoppy beer with a fruity aftertaste.

Monkmans Slaughter (OG 1060, ABV 6%)
Rich tasting and warming; fruit and malt in the aroma and taste, with dark chocolate, caramel and autumn fruit notes. Subtle bitterness continues into the aftertaste.

Crouch Vale SIBA

Crouch Vale Brewery Ltd, 23 Haltwhistle Road, South Woodham Ferrers, Essex, CM3 5ZA
☎ (01245) 322744
info@crouchvale.co.uk
crouchvale.co.uk
Shop Mon-Fri 8.30am-5pm
Tours by arrangement

Founded in 1981 by two CAMRA enthusiasts, Crouch Vale is now well established as a major craft brewer in Essex, having moved to larger premises in 2006. The company is also a major wholesaler of cask ale from other independent breweries, which they supply to more than 100 outlets as well as beer festivals throughout the region. One tied house, the Queen's Head in Chelmsford, is owned. Seasonal beers: one beer is available each month, details on website.

Essex Boys Bitter (OG 1035, ABV 3.5%)
Light-bodied bitter with a malty, biscuity taste and an astringent finish.

Blackwater Mild (OG 1037, ABV 3.7%)
A dark bitter rather than a true mild. Roasty and very bitter towards the end.

Brewers Gold (OG 1040, ABV 4%)
Pale golden ale with a striking citrus nose. Sweet fruit and bitter hops are well matched throughout.

Crouch Best (OG 1040, ABV 4%)
Dry, fruity session bitter with biscuity malt taste and pronounced bitterness in the finish.

Amarillo (OG 1050, ABV 5%)
A strong golden ale with a spicy aroma, juicy malt mouthfeel and an extremely long and bitter hop finish.

Brewers Gold Extra (OG 1052, ABV 5.2%)

Crown

Crown Brewery, Hillsborough Hotel, 54-58 Langsett Road, Sheffield, South Yorkshire, S6 2UB
☎ (0114) 232 2100
Tours by arrangement

The brewery was set up in 2001 with a five-barrel plant in the cellar of the hotel. It was sold to Edale Brewery in 2004 and has been owned by the Walker family since 2006. Around 25 outlets are supplied direct. Seasonal beer: Wheetie-Bits (ABV 4.4%). Bottle-conditioned beers are also available.

Middlewood Mild (OG 1039, ABV 3.8%)
A dark traditional mild with flavours of chocolate and liquorice, and toffee in the aftertaste.

Hillsborough Pale Ale/HPA (OG 1038, ABV 3.9%)
A straw-coloured bitter with a citrussy nose, flowery head and petal undertones.

Traditional Bitter (OG 1039, ABV 4%)
A traditional style, amber-coloured malty bitter.

Primrose Pale Ale (OG 1042, ABV 4.2%)
Fairly bitter yellow ale with medium hoppiness and hints of grapefruit in the aftertaste.

Loxley Gold (OG 1043, ABV 4.5%)
Golden coloured premium pale ale, hoppy with a clean, dry finish.

Stannington Stout (OG 1050, ABV 5%)
Jet black, rich tasting, bitter yet smooth.

Samuel Berry's IPA (OG 1049, ABV 5.1%)
Fairly dark IPA style fruity bitter, with some sweetness in the aftertaste.

Cuillin

Cuillin Brewery Ltd, Sligachan Hotel, Sligachan, Carbost, Isle of Skye, IV47 8SW
☎ (01478) 650204
☎ 07795 250808
✉ steve@cuillinbrewery.co.uk
🌐 cuillinbrewery.co.uk
Tours by arrangement

The brewery opened in 2004 and consists of a five-barrel plant that came from a Firkin pub. Four beers are produced and are available on the island and occasionally on the mainland. All beers are suitable for vegetarians and vegans. The brewery is closed in winter. Seasonal beers: Black Face (Easter-Aug), Eagle Ale (Easter-Aug).

Skye Ale (ABV 4.1%)

Pinnacle (OG 1047, ABV 4.7%) ◆
Amber-gold sweet brew with a light nose and syrupy background.

Cumbrian SIBA

Cumbrian Legendary Ales Ltd, Old Hall Brewery, Hawkshead, Cumbria, LA22 0QF
☎ (015394) 36436
✉ info@cumbrianlegendaryales.com
🌐 cumbrianlegendaryales.com

Old Hall Brewery and its 10-barrel brewhouse were established in 2006 in a renovated Tudor farmstead on the western shores of Esthwaite Water. Characters from Cumbrian folklore and legends give their names to each beer produced by brewer David Newham. Over 70 outlets are supplied. In 2008 in addition to cask ales the brewery introduced its own range of beers from around the world, including a doppelbock, a Pilsner and an IPA. Seasonal beers: Old Hall Mild (ABV 3.2%, winter), Claife Crier (ABV 5%, winter), Old King Cole (ABV 4.6%, winter).

Wicked Jimmy (OG 1037, ABV 3.6%)
A copper-coloured, hoppy bitter with a creamy head and fresh, fruity aroma.

Dickie Doodle (OG 1040, ABV 3.9%)
A golden bitter with distinctive flavour and aroma of American Cascade hops.

King Dunmail (OG 1042, ABV 4.2%)
A rich, dark, traditional best bitter.

Buttermere Beauty (OG 1047, ABV 4.8%) ◆
A creditable English lager, full-bodied and fruity with a clean finish.

Cwmbran SIBA

Cwmbran Brewery, Gorse Cottage, Graig Road, Upper Cwmbran, Torfaen, NP44 5AS
☎ (01633) 485233
✉ cwmbran.brewery@btopenworld.com
🌐 cwmbranbrewery.co.uk

Cwmbran is a craft brewery on the slopes of Mynydd Maen in Upper Cwmbran in Gwent's eastern valley. Founded in 1994, it is sited alongside the brewer's cottage home. A mountain spring supplies the water used for brewing liquor. An extension to the brewery has increased both capacity and flexibility. Seasonal beers: See website. Bottle-conditioned beer is also available.

Blackcurrant Stout (OG 1050, ABV 4%)

Crow Valley Bitter (OG 1042, ABV 4.2%) ◆
Faint malt and hops aroma. Amber coloured with a clean taste of malt, hops and fruit flavours. Bitterness builds with a lasting bitter finish.

Crow Valley Stout (OG 1048, ABV 4.2%)

Nut Brown Premium Ale (OG 1044, ABV 4.5%)

Pure Welsh (OG 1045, ABV 4.5%)

Full Malty (OG 1048, ABV 4.8%)

Daleside

Daleside Brewery Ltd, Camwal Road, Starbeck, Harrogate, North Yorkshire, HG1 4PT
☎ (01423) 880022
✉ enquiries@dalesidebrewery.com
🌐 dalesidebrewery.com
Shop Mon-Fri 9am-4pm (Off sales only)

Opened in 1991 in Harrogate with a 20-barrel plant, beer is now supplied to around 200 local outlets, via wholesalers nationally and through SIBA's direct delivery scheme. Seasonal beers: see website.

Bitter (OG 1039, ABV 3.7%) ◆
Pale brown in colour, this well-balanced, hoppy beer is complemented by fruity bitterness and a hint of sweetness, leading to a long, bitter finish.

Blonde (OG 1040, ABV 3.9%) ◆
A pale golden beer with a predominantly hoppy aroma and taste, leading to a refreshing hoppy, bitter but short finish.

Old Leg Over (OG 1043, ABV 4.1%)
Well-balanced mid brown refreshing beer that leads to an equally well-balanced fruity bitter aftertaste.

Special Bitter (OG 1043, ABV 4.1%)
A mid-amber beer with a malty nose and a hint of fruitiness. Hops and malt carry over to leave a clean, hoppy aftertaste.

Dane Town*

Dane Town Brewery, Lowes Arms, 301 Hyde Road, Denton, Manchester, M34 3FF
☎ (0161) 336 3064
🌐 lowesarms.co.uk
Tours by arrangement

Formerly the Lowes Arms Brewery, re-opened in 2007 as the Dane Town Brewery with a new brewer – harking back to Denton's Viking roots with the beers named appropriately. Only the pub is supplied. The beers are not produced at the pub at present but at the nearby Hornbeam Brewery.

Valkyrie Bitter (ABV 4.2%)
A session beer with malty aroma and hoppy finish.

Warriors Might (ABV 4.3%)
A dark best bitter with distinct roast flavours.

Dare*

Dare Brewery Ltd, Falcon Inn, 1 Incline Row, Godreaman, Aberdare, CF44 6LU
☎ 07812 366369
✉ info@darebrewery.co.uk
🌐 darebrewery.co.uk
Tours by arrangement

Dare Brewery opened in December 2007 using a 5.5-barrel plant in a refurbished barn at the Falcon Inn (run as a separate operation from the pub). Falcon Inn keeps Dare Brewery beers on the bar whenever possible. All cask beers are also available bottle conditioned. Seasonal and occasional beers are also brewed.

Dat Dare (ABV 4.1%)
A reddish-brown beer with good malt and hop character. A rounded flavour with a bitter finish and a hint of chocolate.

Dare Too (ABV 4.7%)
A smooth copper-coloured premium beer with balanced malt and hop flavours. Dry hopped in the cask for aroma.

Falcon Flyer (ABV 5.2%)
Distinctive Sovereign variety hop finish to this full-bodied tawny ale. Strong and satisfying.

Dark Horse*

Dark Horse Brewery, Coonlands Laithe, Hetton, Skipton, North Yorkshire, BD23 6LY
☎ (01756) 730555
✉ richard@darkhorsebrewery.co.uk
🌐 darkhorsebrewery.co.uk

Formerly the Wharfedale Brewery, Dark Horse opened in late 2008 with new owners. The brewery is based in an old hay barn within the Yorkshire Dales National Park.

Best Bitter (ABV 3.8%)

Hetton Pale Ale (ABV 4.2%)

Whip Cracker (ABV 5%)

Dark Star SIBA

Dark Star Brewing Co Ltd, Moonhill Farm, Burgess Hill Road, Ansty, West Sussex, RH17 5AH
☎ (01444) 412311
✉ info@darstarbrewing.co.uk
🌐 darkstarbrewing.co.uk
Tours by arrangement

⊗ Dark Star started brewing in Brighton and moved operations to its current site in 2001. Growth has been steady over the years and 2008 saw the commissioning of a new 45-barrel brewery with an on-site shop. Three pubs are now owned. The brewery's range of beers is divided between permanent, seasonal and monthly specials. Around 80 outlets are supplied. Seasonal beers: See website. Bottle-conditioned beer is also available.

Hophead (OG 1040, ABV 3.8%) ◆
A golden-coloured bitter with a fruity/hoppy aroma and a citrus/bitter taste and aftertaste. Flavours remain strong to the end.

Best Bitter (OG 1041, ABV 4%)
A slight malty flavour is complemented by East Kent Goldings hops.

Old Ale (OG 1041, ABV 4%)
A rich bronze colour with a malty caramel taste.

Espresso (OG 1043, ABV 4.2%)

Festival (OG 1050, ABV 5%)
A chestnut, bronze-coloured bitter with a smooth mouthfeel and freshness.

Original (OG 1052, ABV 5%) ◆
Dark, full-bodied ale with a roast malt aroma and a dry, bitter, stout-like finish.

DarkTribe

DarkTribe Brewery, Dog & Gun, High Street, East Butterwick, Lincolnshire, DN17 3AJ
☎ (01724) 782324
✉ dixie@darktribe.co.uk
🌐 darktribe.co.uk
Tours by arrangement

◎A small brewery was built during the summer of 1996 in a workshop at the bottom of his garden by Dave 'Dixie' Dean. In 2005 Dixie bought the Dog & Gun pub and moved the 2.5-barrel brewing equipment there. The beers generally follow a marine theme, recalling Dixie's days as an engineer in the Merchant Navy and his enthusiasm for sailing. Local outlets are supplied. Seasonal beers: Dixie's Midnight Runner (ABV 6.5%, Dec-Jan), Dark Destroyer (ABV 9.7%, Aug onwards), Daft Bat (ABV 4.9%, Halloween), Starburst (ABV 5.1%, Bonfire Night).

Dixie's Mild (ABV 3.6%)

Honey Mild (ABV 3.6%)

Full Ahead (ABV 3.8%) ◆
A malty smoothness is backed by a slightly fruity hop that gives a good bitterness to this amber-brown bitter.

Albacore (ABV 4%)

Red Duster (ABV 4%)

Red Rock (ABV 4.2%)

Sternwheeler (ABV 4.2%)

Intelligent Whale (ABV 4.3%)

RAMP (Richard's Amazing Magical Potion) (ABV 4.3%)

Bucket Hitch (ABV 4.4%)

Dixie's Bollards (ABV 4.5%)

Dr Griffin's Mermaid (ABV 4.5%)

Old Gaffer (ABV 4.5%)

Galleon (ABV 4.7%) ◆
A tasty, golden, smooth, full-bodied ale with fruity hops and consistent malt. The thirst-quenching bitterness lingers into a well-balanced finish.

Twin Screw (ABV 5.1%) ◆
A fruity, rose-hip tasting beer, red in colour. Good malt presence with a dry, hoppy bitterness coming through in the finish.

Dartmoor SIBA

Dartmoor Brewery Ltd, The Brewery, Station Road, Princetown, Dartmoor, Devon, PL20 6QX
☎ (01822) 890789
🌐 jailale.com

Established in 1994 it is the highest brewery in England at 1,400 feet above sea level. It moved into a new purpose-built building in 2005 with equipment manufactured in Germany. The capacity is now 180 barrels a week with scope for further expansion. The brewery changed name from Princetown to Dartmoor in May 2008 with no change to the structure or ownership of the company. Bottle-conditoned ales are available.

Dartmoor IPA (OG 1039, ABV 4%) ◆
There is a flowery hop aroma and taste with a bitter aftertaste to this full-bodied, amber-coloured beer.

Jail Ale (OG 1047, ABV 4.8%) ◆
Hops and fruit predominate in the flavour of this mid-brown beer, which has a slightly sweet aftertaste.

Dartmouth*

Dartmouth Brewery, Dartmouth Inn, 63 East Street, Newton Abbot, Devon, TQ12 2JP
☎ 07969 560184
✉ kieran.aylward@ntlworld.com
Tours by arrangement

Dartmouth Brewery was established in September 2007. Around 15 outlets are supplied direct. More beers are planned.

Ranger (ABV 4.2%)

Darwin SIBA

Darwin Brewery Ltd, 63 Back Tatham Street, Sunderland, Tyne & Wear, SR1 2QE
☎ (0191) 514 4746
✉ info@darwinbrewery.com
🌐 darwinbrewery.com
Tours by arrangement (based at Brewlab)

The Darwin Brewery first brewed in 1994 and expanded with the construction of its Wearside brewery in central Sunderland in 2002 after a move from the Hodges brewhouse in Crook, Co Durham. Darwin specialises in recreations of past beers and also produces trial beers from the Brewlab training and research unit at the University of Sunderland, and experiments in the production of novel and overseas styles for occasional production. Output from the brewery grew significantly in 2005. The brewery also produces the beers of the closed High Force Brewery in Teesdale. A changing portfolio of unique brews (developed by Brewlab) is available in limited edition bottles.

Sunderland Best (OG 1041, ABV 3.9%)
A light and smooth-tasting session bitter, full of hop character and moderate bitterness. Amber malt provides a smooth body and creamy character.

Evolution Ale (OG 1041, ABV 4%)
A dark amber, full-bodied bitter with a malty flavour and a clean, bitter aftertaste.

Ghost Ale (OG 1041, ABV 4.1%)

Richmond Ale (OG 1047, ABV 4.5%)

Rolling Hitch (OG 1055, ABV 5.2%)

Killer Bee (OG 1065, ABV 6%)
A strong but light ale matured with honey.

Extinction Ale (OG 1084, ABV 8.3%)

For High Force Hotel:

Forest XB (OG 1044, ABV 4.2%)

Cauldron Snout (OG 1056, ABV 5.6%)

Dent SIBA

Dent Brewery Ltd, Hollins, Cowgill, Sedbergh, Cumbria, LA10 5TQ
☎ (015396) 25326
✉ paul@dentbrewery.co.uk
🌐 dentbrewery.co.uk

Dent was set up in 1990 in a converted barn next to a former farmhouse in the Yorkshire Dales. In 2005 the brewery was completely refurbished and capacity expanded and in 2006 it purchased the George & Dragon in Dent. Monthly specials are produced, all at ABV 4.5%.

Bitter (OG 1035, ABV 3.7%) ◆
Fruity throughout and lightly hopped. This beer has a pervading earthiness. A short, bitter finish.

Aviator (OG 1039, ABV 4%) ◆
This medium-bodied amber ale is characterised by strong citrus and hoppy flavours that develop into a long bitter finish.

Rambrau (OG 1042, ABV 4.5%)
A cask-conditioned lager.

Ramsbottom Strong Ale (OG 1042, ABV 4.5%) ◆
This complex, mid-brown beer has a warming, dry, bitter finish to follow its unusual combination of roast, bitter, fruity and sweet flavours.

Kamikaze (OG 1047, ABV 5%) ◆
Hops and fruit dominate this full-bodied, golden, strong bitter, with a dry bitterness growing in the aftertaste.

T'Owd Tup (OG 1056, ABV 6%) ◆
A rich, full-flavoured, strong stout with a coffee aroma. The dominant roast character is balanced by a warming sweetness and a raisiny, fruitcake taste that linger on into the finish.

Derby SIBA

Derby Brewing Company Ltd, Masons Place Business Park, Nottingham Road, Derby, Derbyshire, DE21 6AQ
☎ (01332) 242888
☎ 07887 556788
✉ sales@derbybrewing.co.uk
🌐 derbybrewing.co.uk
Tours by arrangement

A purpose-built brewery, established 2004, in the varnish workshop of the old Masons Paintworks by owner/brewer Trevor Harris, former brewer at the Brunswick Inn, Derby. The business has grown massively over the years and the brewery has recently purchased its first pub, the Royal Standard, Derby. Over 60 outlets are supplied. Seasonal beer: White Christmas (ABV 5.5%), Christmas Porter (ABV 5%). Two new beers are brewed each month.

Hop Till You Drop (OG 1039, ABV 3.9%)

Triple Hop (OG 1041, ABV 4.1%)

Business As Usual (OG 1044, ABV 4.4%)

Dashingly Dark (OG 1045, ABV 4.5%)

Double Mash (OG 1046, ABV 4.6%)

Old Intentional (OG 1050, ABV 5%)

Derventio

Derventio Brewery Ltd, The Brewhouse, Trusley Brook Farm, Trusley, Derbyshire, DE6 5JP
☎ (01283) 733111
✉ enquiries@derventiobrewery.co.uk
derventiobrewery.co.uk
Tours by arrangement

⊗ Derventio Brewery was formed in 2005 although commercial brewing did not begin until 2007. A bottling plant was installed to contract bottle in November 2007. It recently purchased the adjacent unit with plans to operate a shop, tasting area and management training centre. 60 outlets are supplied. Seasonal beers: Aquilifer (ABV 3.8%), Et Tu Brutus? (ABV 4.5%), Winter Solstice (ABV 5%).

Roman Pale Ale (ABV 3.6%)

Maia Mild (ABV 4%)

Cupid (ABV 4.1%)

Emperors Whim (ABV 4.2%)

Centurion (OG 1042, ABV 4.3%)

Arminius (ABV 5%)

Venus (OG 1048, ABV 5%)

Caesar (ABV 6%)

Vesuvius (ABV 6.5%)

Derwent Rose

See Consett Ale Works

Derwent

Derwent Brewery Co, Units 2a/2b, Station Road Industrial Estate, Silloth, Cumbria, CA7 4AG
☎ (016973) 31522
Tours by arrangement

Derwent was set up in 1996 in Cockermouth and moved to Silloth in 1998. Derwent supplies beers throughout the north of England, with outlets in Cheshire, Cumbria, Lancashire, Yorkshire and the North-east. It is involved with the Silloth Beer Festival every September and has supplied Carlisle State Bitter to the House of Commons, a beer that recreates one produced by the former state-owned Carlisle Brewery. Seasonal beers: Summer Rose (ABV 4.2%, Jun-Aug), Spring Time (ABV 4.3%, Mar-May), Harvester (ABV 4.3%, Sep), Winter Gold (ABV 4.1%, Oct-Dec), Auld Kendal (ABV 5.7%, Dec).

Carlisle State Bitter (OG 1037, ABV 3.7%)
Amber bitter with a fruity mouthfeeel and slightly astringent bitterness that fades in the finish.

Parsons Pledge (OG 1040, ABV 4%)

Hofbrau (OG 1040, ABV 4.2%)

W&M Pale Ale (OG 1042, ABV 4.4%)
A sweet, fruity, hoppy beer with a bitter finish.

Devil's Dyke

Devil's Dyke Brewery, Dyke's End, 8 Fair Green, Reach, Cambridgeshire, CB25 0JD
☎ (01638) 743816
Tours by arrangement

⊗ Devil's Dyke came on stream in August 2007 using a plant bought from the Red Rose Brewery. It is situated in outbuildings to the rear of the Dyke's End pub, the freehold of which was bought by the village in the late 1990s to save it from being turned back into a private house. Several outlets are supplied in the area.

Bitter (OG 1036.7, ABV 3.8%)

No. 7 Pale Ale (OG 1039.8, ABV 4.1%)

Victorian (OG 1044, ABV 4.7%)

Strong Mild (OG 1049, ABV 5%)

Devon Earth*

Devon Earth Brewery, 7 Fernham Terrace, Torquay Road, Paignton, Devon, TQ3 2AQ
☎ (01803) 525778
✉ info@devonearthbrewery.co.uk

Devon Earth was launched in early 2008 on a 2.5-barrel plant. Seasonal beers are planned as are bottle-conditoned ales.

Devon Earth (ABV 4%)

Lost in the Woods (ABV 4.7%)

Grounded (ABV 5.2%)

Devon

Devon Ales Ltd, Mansfield Arms, 7 Main Street, Sauchie, Clackmannanshire, FK10 3JR
☎ (01259) 722020
✉ info@devonales.com
devonales.com
Tours by arrangement

Established in 1992 to produce high quality cask ales for the Mansfield Arms, Sauchie, Devon is the oldest operating brewery in the county. A second pub, The Inn at Muckhart, was purchased in 1994.

Original (OG 1038, ABV 3.8%)

Thick Black (OG 1042, ABV 4.2%)

Pride (OG 1046, ABV 4.8%)

Digfield

Digfield Ales, North Lodge Farm, Barnwell, Peterborough, Cambridgeshire, PE8 5RJ
☎ (01832) 293248

With equipment from the Cannon Brewery, Digfield Ales started brewing in 2005 as part of a farm diversification scheme. Digfield operates on a 7.5-barrel plant run by three partners. It supplies the local Barnwell pub, the Montagu Arms, as well as 20 other outlets.

Fools Nook (ABV 3.8%)
The floral aroma, dominated by lavender and honey, belies the hoppy bitterness that comes through in the taste of this golden ale. A fruity balance lasts.

Barnwell Bitter (OG 1039, ABV 4%)
A fruity, sulphurous aroma introduces a beer in which sharp bitterness is balanced by dry, biscuity malt.

March Hare (OG 1043, ABV 4.4%)
A straw-coloured premium ale with a subtle fruit flavour throughout.

Shacklebush (ABV 4.5%)
Dry tawny bitter with a roasty, astringent finish.

Mad Monk (ABV 4.7%)
Fruity beer with bitter, earthy hops in evidence.

Discovery*

Discovery Ales, Brook Farm, Packington Lane, Little Packington, Warwickshire, CV7 7HW
☎ (01675) 763809

Correspondence: 52 Doris Road, Coleshill, Birmingham, 39, B46 1EJ
✉ simonamanda@btinternet.com

Discovery Ales began brewing on a part-time basis in September 2007 on a 2.5-barrel plant.

Pioneer (OG 1039.6, ABV 4.2%)

Darwin's Delight (OG 1041.1, ABV 4.4%)

Colombus (OG 1043.4, ABV 4.7%)

Newton's Cream (OG 1044.2, ABV 4.8%)

Captain Cook (OG 1045.8, ABV 5%)

Dynamite (OG 1045.8, ABV 5%)

Doghouse

See Keltek

Dolphin

Dolphin Brewery Ltd, The Dolphin, 48 St Michael Street, Shrewsbury, Shropshire, SY1 2EZ
☎ (01743) 350419
✉ oz@icom-web.com

Dolphin was launched in 2000 and upgraded to a 4.5-barrel plant in 2001. In 2006 both the pub and brewery were taken over by present owner Mark Oseland. After pub alterations the brewery was re-opened with a new range of beers.

Dizzy Lizzy (OG 1040, ABV 4%)

Ollie Dog (OG 1040, ABV 4%)

George's Best (OG 1048, ABV 4.8%)

Donnington IFBB

Donnington Brewery, Upper Swell, Stow-on-the-Wold, Gloucestershire, GL54 1EP
☎ (01451) 830603

Thomas Arkell bought a 13th-century watermill in 1827 and began brewing on the site in 1865; the waterwheel is still in use. Thomas' decendent Claude owned and ran the brewery until his death in 2007, supplying 15 tied houses and a small free trade. It has now passed to Claude's cousins, Peter and James of Arkells Brewery, Swindon (qv), who plan to continue brewing Donnington beers at this unique site.

BB (OG 1035, ABV 3.6%)
A pleasant amber bitter with a slight hop aroma, a good balance of malt and hops in the mouth and a bitter aftertaste.

SBA (OG 1045, ABV 4.4%)
Malt dominates over bitterness in the subtle flavour of this premium bitter, which has a hint of fruit and a dry malty finish.

Dorset SIBA

Dorset Brewing Co, Hope Square, Weymouth, Dorset, DT4 8TR
☎ (01305) 777515
✉ info@dbcales.com
dbcales.com

Shop at Brewers Quay 10am-5.30pm daily
Tours by arrangement via Timewalk at Brewers Quay

The Dorset Brewing Company, formerly the Quay Brewery, is the most recent in a long succession of breweries in Hope Square. Brewing first started there in 1256 but in more recent times it was famous for being the home of the Devenish and Groves breweries. Brewing stopped in 1986 but restarted in 1996, when Giles Smeath set up Quay in part of the old brewery buildings. His beers are available in local pubs and selected outlets throughout the South-west. In 2008 Dorset took over the running of Dorchester's brewpub, Tom Brown's (Goldfinch Brewery). Seasonal beers: Coastguard (ABV 4.1%, spring), Chesil (ABV 4.1%, summer), Ammonite (ABV 3.8%, autumn), Silent Knight (ABV 5.9%, winter).

Weymouth Harbour Master (OG 1036, ABV 3.6%)
Light, easy-drinking session beer. Well-balanced, with a long, bittersweet, citrus finish.

Weymouth Best Bitter (OG 1038, ABV 4%)
Complex bitter ale with strong malt and fruit flavours despite its light gravity.

Weymouth JD 1742 (OG 1040, ABV 4.2%)
Clean-tasting, easy-drinking bitter. Well balanced with lingering bitterness after moderate sweetness.

Steam Beer (OG 1043, ABV 4.5%)
Citrus fruit and roasted malt dominate this complex best bitter, from the first aroma through to the long, lingering finish.

Jurassic (OG 1045, ABV 4.7%)

An organic premium bitter, pale golden colour; smooth with suggestions of honey underlying a complex hop palate.

Durdle Door (OG 1046, ABV 5%) ◆
A tawny hue and fruity aroma with a hint of pear drops and good malty undertone, joined by hops and a little roast malt in the taste. Lingering bittersweet finish.

Dorset Piddle*

Dorset Piddle Brewery Ltd, Unit 7, Enterprise Park, Piddlehinton, Dorchester, Dorset, DT2 7UA
☎ (01305) 849336
dorsetpiddlebrewery.co.uk

Dorset Piddle began brewing in late 2007 on an eight-barrel plant. Monthly seasonals are available as are bottle-conditioned beers.

Jimmy Riddle (ABV 3.7%)

Piddle (ABV 4.1%)

Cocky Hop (ABV 4.7%)

Yogi Beer (ABV 4.9%)

Silent Slasher (ABV 5.1%)

Double Maxim*

Double Maxim Beer Company Ltd, 1 Gadwall Road, Houghton le Spring, DH4 5NL
☎ (0191) 584 8844
admin@dmbc.org.uk
dmbc.org.uk

Initially the former Vaux beer Double Maxim was contract brewed by Robinsons for this company but in summer 2007 it opened its own 20-barrel plant.

Samson (ABV 4%)

Double Maxim (ABV 4.7%)

Dow Bridge

Dow Bridge Brewery, 2-3 Rugby Road, Catthorpe, Leicestershire, LE17 6DA
☎ (01788) 869121
dowbridge.brewery@virgin.net
Tours by arrangement

Dow Bridge commenced brewing in late 2001. The brewery adheres to using English whole hops and malt with no adjuncts or additives. Over 140 outlets are supplied direct through its own distribution company. All regular beers except Bonum Mild are available bottle conditioned. Beers are also contract brewed for Morgan Ales. Seasonal beers: Summer Light (ABV 3.6%), Festivus Ale (ABV 4.6%, Xmas).

Bonum Mild (OG 1035, ABV 3.5%) ◆
Complex dark brown, full-flavoured mild, with strong malt and roast flavours to the fore and continuing into the aftertaste, leading to a long, satisfying finish.

Acris (OG 1037, ABV 3.8%)

Ratae'd (OG 1042, ABV 4.3%) ◆
Tawny-coloured, bitter beer in which bitter and hop flavours dominate, to the detriment of balance, leading to a long, bitter and astringent aftertaste.

Fosse Ale (OG 1046, ABV 4.8%)

Praetorian Porter (OG 1050, ABV 5%)

For Morgan Ales:

Chedhams Ale (OG 1039, ABV 3.8%)

Churchill's Best (OG 1042, ABV 4.2%)

Downton

Downton Brewery Co Ltd, Unit 11 Batten Road, Downton Industrial Estate, Downton, Wiltshire, SP5 3HU
☎ (01725) 513313
martins@downtonbrewery.com
downtonbrewery.com

Downton was set up in 2003 with equipment leased from the Hop Back Brewery (qv). The brewery has a 20-barrel brew length and has recently expanded its capacity by installing a third 20-barrel fermenting vessel. A different monthly special is brewed every month as well as regular and seasonal beers. Monthly specials often include fruit or spiced beers. 30 outlets are supplied direct. Bottle-conditioned beers are available.

Quadhop (OG 1038, ABV 3.9%)

Elderquad (OG 1039, ABV 4%)

Dark Delight (OG 1052, ABV 5.5%)

IPA (OG 1063, ABV 6.8%)

Driftwood

Driftwood Brewery, Driftwood Spars Hotel, Trevaunance Cove, St Agnes, Cornwall, TR5 0RT
☎ (01872) 552428
driftwoodspars.com
Tours by arrangement

Brewing commenced in 2000 in this famous Cornish pub and hotel that dates back to 1660. The brewery is based in the former Flying Dutchman café across the road. The Old Horsebridge one-barrel plant has been replaced by a customised, five-barrel kit. The brewery also produces an alcoholic ginger beer called Furnace. Beers are only available at the Driftwood Public House & Hotel.

Blue Hills Bitter (OG 1040, ABV 4.2%)

Dunham Massey*

Dunham Massey Brewing Co, 100 Oldfield Lane, Dunham Massey, WA14 4PE
☎ (0161) 929 0663
info@dunhammasseybrewing.co.uk
dunhammasseybrewing.co.uk
Shop 11am-4pm daily (Mar-Oct)
Tours by arrangement

Dunham Massey commenced in October 2007, brewing traditional North-western ales. The beer range is also available bottle conditioned. Only English ingredients are used, with no added sugars. Around 15 outlets are supplied direct. Seasonal beers: Little Bollington Bitter (ABV 3.7%, summer), Winter Warmer (ABV 6.6%).

Dark Mild (OG 1040.5, ABV 3.8%)

Light Mild (OG 1040.5, ABV 3.8%)

Big Tree Bitter (OG 1041, ABV 3.9%)

Stamford Bitter (OG 1044.5, ABV 4.2%)

Deer Beer (OG 1047, ABV 4.5%)

Dunn Plowman SIBA

Dunn Plowman Brewery, Unit 1a, Arrow Court Industrial Estate, Hergest Road, Kington, Herefordshire, HR5 3ER
☎ 07716 438288
✉ dunnplowman.brewery@talk21.com
Tours by arrangement

The brewery was established in 1987 as a brew-pub, moved to Leominster in 1992, to Kington in 1993 and to its present site in 2002. It is run by husband and wife team Steve and Gaye Dunn, who also run the Olde Tavern in Kington. The brewery also supplies several free houses within a 50-mile radius.

Brewhouse Bitter (OG 1037, ABV 3.8%)

Early Riser (OG 1039, ABV 4%)

Sting (OG 1040, ABV 4.2%)

Kingdom Bitter (OG 1043, ABV 4.5%)

Shirehorse Ale (OG 1053, ABV 5.5%)

Railway Porter (OG 1056, ABV 5.7%)

Crooked Furrow (OG 1063, ABV 6.5%)

Durham SIBA

Durham Brewery Ltd, Unit 5a, Bowburn North Industrial Estate, Bowburn, Co Durham, DH6 5PF
☎ (0191) 377 1991
✉ gibbs@durham-brewery.co.uk
🌐 durham-brewery.co.uk
Shop Mon-Fri 9am-4pm; Sat 10am-12.30pm
Tours by arrangement

Established in 1994, Durham now has a portfolio of around 20 beers. These are not all available as regular beers – please see website for full list. Bottles and five litre mini-casks can be purchased via the online shop and an own label/special message service is available. Around 60 outlets are supplied direct. Seasonal beers: Sunstroke (ABV 3.6%, summer), Frostbite (ABV 3.6%, winter). Bottle-conditioned beers are also available and suitable for vegans.

Magus (ABV 3.8%)
Pale malt gives this brew its straw colour but the hops define its character, with a fruity aroma, a clean bitter mouthfeel, and a lingering dry, citrus-like finish.

Earl Soham SIBA

Earl Soham Brewery, The Street, Earl Soham, Woodbridge, Suffolk, IP13 7RT
☎ (01728) 684097
✉ info@earlsohambrewery.co.uk
🌐 earlsohambrewery.co.uk
Shop is village store next to brewery
Tours by arrangement

Earl Soham was set up behind the Victoria pub in 1984 and continued there until 2001 when the brewery moved 200 metres down the road. The Victoria and the Station in Framlingham both sell the beers on a regular basis and, when there is spare stock, it is supplied to local free houses and as many beer festivals as possible. 30 outlets are supplied and two pubs are owned. Seasonal beer: Jolabrugg (ABV 5%, Dec). Most of the beers are bottle conditioned for the shop next door and are only available there.

Gannet Mild (OG 1034, ABV 3.3%)
A beautifully balanced mild, sweet and fruity flavour with a lingering, coffee aftertaste which will have you coming back for more.

Victoria Bitter (OG 1037, ABV 3.6%)
A light, fruity, amber session beer with a clean taste and a long, lingering hoppy aftertaste.

Sir Roger's Porter (OG 1042, ABV 4.2%)
Smooth and easy drinking porter with an initial roasty flavour which is soon replaced by a sweet, lingering aftertaste.

Albert Ale (OG 1045, ABV 4.4%)
Hops dominate every aspect of this beer, but especially the finish. A fruity, astringent beer.

Brandeston Gold (OG 1045, ABV 4.5%)
A burnished gold coloured beer, full-bodied with a bitter tang.

Eastwood

Eastwood the Brewer, Barge & Barrel, 10-12 Park Road, Elland, West Yorkshire, HX5 9HP
☎ 07949 148476
✉ taggartkeith@yahoo.co.uk
Tours by arrangement

The brewery was founded by John Eastwood at the Barge & Barrel pub. 50-70 outlets are supplied direct. Seasonal beers: Savannah (ABV 3.8%), Ginger Ale (ABV 4%), Bora Bora (ABV 4.3%), El Divino (ABV 4.6%), Jollification (ABV 4%), Old Skool (ABV 5%), Pacha (ABV 4.2%), Englands Glory (ABV 4%), Diablo (ABV 5.6%), Lilburne (ABV 5.7%), Mosquito (ABV 4.7%).

Stirling (ABV 3.8%)
An amber-coloured session beer with a pleasant, long-lasting, fruity finish.

Best Bitter (ABV 4%)
Creamy, yellow, hoppy bitter with hints of citrus fruits. Pleasantly strong bitter aftertaste.

Gold Award (ABV 4.4%)
Complex copper-coloured beer with malt, roast and caramel flavours. It has a hoppy and bitter aftertaste.

Black Prince (ABV 5%)
A distinctive strong black porter with a blend of pale and chocolate malts and roasted barley.

Eccleshall

See Slater's

Edinburgh

See Greene King in New Nationals section

Elgood's IFBB SIBA

Elgood & Sons Ltd, North Brink Brewery, Wisbech, Cambridgeshire, PE13 1LN
☎ (01945) 583160
✉ info@elgoods-brewery.co.uk
🌐 elgoods-brewery.co..uk
Shop 11.30am-4.30pm daily (May-Sep)
Tours by arrangement

⊗ The North Brink Brewery was established in 1795 and was one of the first classic Georgian breweries to be built outside London. In 1878 it came under the control of the Elgood family and is still run today as one of the few remaining independent family breweries, with the fifth generation of the family now helping to run the company. The beers go to 42 Elgood's pubs within a 50-mile radius of Wisbech and free trade outlets throughout East Anglia, while wholesalers distribute nationally. Elgood's has a visitor centre, offering a tour of the brewery and the gardens. Seasonal beers: see website.

Black Dog (OG 1036.8, ABV 3.6%) ◆
Reddish black with liquorice, rounded by hints of roast malt and a growing dry bitterness.

Cambridge Bitter (OG 1037.8, ABV 3.8%) ◆
Malt and hops dominate the aroma of this copper-coloured beer. Well-balanced malt and hops on the palate and in the aftertaste. Long, dry finish.

Golden Newt (OG 1041.5, ABV 4.1%) ◆
Malt and hops are balanced both on the nose and in the flavour of this golden ale. Dry, slightly sweet flavour leads through into a short, hoppy, somewhat chewy finish.

Greyhound Strong Bitter (OG 1052.8, ABV 5.2%) ◆
A tawny/brown beer with a malty aroma. Malt and raisin fruit on the palate balanced by pleasing dryness. Dry finish with faint malt and hops.

Elland SIBA

Elland Brewery Ltd, Units 3-5, Heathfield Industrial Estate, Heathfield Street, Elland, West Yorkshire, HX5 9AE
☎ (01422) 377677
✉ brewery@eandsbrewery.co.uk
🌐 eandsbrewery.co.uk
Tours by arrangement

The brewery was originally formed as Eastwood & Sanders in 2002 by the amalgamation of the Barge & Barrel Brewery and West Yorkshire Brewery. The company was renamed Elland in 2006 to reinforce its links with the town of Elland. The brewery has a capacity to brew 50 barrels a week and offers more than 25 seasonal specials as well as a monthly Head Brewer's Reserve range of beers. More than 150 outlets are supplied.

Bargee (OG 1038, ABV 3.8%) ◆
Amber, creamy session bitter. Fruity, hoppy aroma and taste, complemented by a bitter edge in the finish.

Best Bitter (OG 1041, ABV 4%) ◆
Creamy, yellow, hoppy bitter with hints of citrus fruits. Pleasantly strong with a bitter aftertaste.

Beyond the Pale (OG 1042, ABV 4.2%) ◆
Gold-coloured, robust, creamy beer with ripe aromas of hops and fruit. Bitterness predominates in the mouth and leads to a dry, fruity and hoppy aftertaste.

Nettlethrasher (OG 1044, ABV 4.4%) ◆
Grainy amber-coloured beer. A rounded nose with some fragrant hops notes followed by a mellow nutty and fruity taste and a dry finish.

1872 Porter (OG 1065, ABV 6.5%) ◆
Creamy, full-flavoured porter. Rich liquorice flavours with a hint of chocolate from the roast malt. A soft but satisfying aftertaste of bittersweet roast and malt.

Elmtree

Elmtree Beers, The Stables, Mill Lane, Snetterton, Norfolk, NR16 2LQ
☎ (01953) 498761
✉ sales@elmtreebeers.co.uk
🌐 elmtreebeers.co.uk

⊗ Elmtree was established in 2007 using a five-barrel plant. Its produces both cask and bottle-conditioned beers of a traditional style and character. All bottle-conditioned beers are suitable for vegetarians and vegans.

Bitter (OG 1041, ABV 4.2%)

Dark Horse (OG 1048, ABV 5%)

Golden Pale Ale (OG 1048, ABV 5%)

Hot Tub (OG 1057, ABV 5.8%)

Cooper's Tipple (OG 1059, ABV 6%)

Elveden EAB

Elveden Ales, The Courtyard, Elveden Estate, Elveden, Thetford, Norfolk, IP24 3TA
☎ (01842) 878922

Elveden is a five-barrel brewery based on the estate of Lord Iveagh, a member of the ennobled branch of the Guinness family. The brewery is run by Frances Moore, daughter of Brendan Moore at Iceni Brewery (qv) and produces three ales: Elveden Stout (ABV 5%) and Elveden Ale (ABV 5.2%), which are mainly bottled in stoneware bottles. The third is Charter Ale (ABV 10%) to mark the celebrations for the award of a Royal Charter for Harwich in 1604. The beer is available in cask and bottle-conditioned versions. The phone number listed is shared with Iceni. The majority of sales take place through the farm shop, adjacent to the brewery. During 2007 the brewery building was restored as part of the development of the outbuilding of the Elveden estate as a tourist attraction. The visitor centre re-opened in summer 2008, giving regular tours – please phone for details.

Empire

Empire Brewing, The Old Boiler House, Unit 33, Upper Mills, Slaithwaite, Huddersfield, West Yorkshire, HD7 7HA
☎ (01484) 847343

empirebrewing.com
Tours by arrangement

Empire Brewing was set up 2006 in a mill on the bank of the scenic Huddersfield Narrow Canal, close to the centre of Slaithwaite. The five-barrel plant produces 20 barrels a week. Beers are supplied to local free houses and through independent specialist beer agencies. Seasonal beers are also available.

Golden Warrior (ABV 3.8%)
Pale bitter, quite fruity with a sherbet aftertaste, moderate bitterness.

Ensign (ABV 3.9%)
Pale, straw-coloured bitter made with lager malt, quite floral on the nose with a pine/lemon flavour.

Strikes Back (ABV 4%)
Pale golden bitter with a hoppy aroma and good hop and malt balance with a citrus flavour, very light on the palate. Good session beer.

Valour (ABV 4.2%)

Longbow (ABV 4.3%)
Golden bitter with a well-balanced malt, floral citrus hop aroma. Spicy yet smooth tasting.

Crusader (ABV 5%)
Light coloured ale with distinctive pine/lemon citrus flavour, good hoppy nose with moderate bitterness.

Enville SIBA

Enville Ales Ltd, Enville Brewery, Coxgreen, Hollies Lane, Enville, Stourbridge, West Midlands, DY7 5LG
☎ (01384) 873728
info@envilleales.com
envilleales.com
Tours by arrangement for small groups only

Enville Brewery is sited on a picturesque Victorian farm complex. Using the same water source as the original Village Brewery (closed in 1919), the beers also incorporate more than three tons of honey annually, and recipes passed down from the former proprietor's great-great aunt. Seasonal beers: Gothic (ABV 5.2%, Oct-Jan), Phoenix IPA (ABV 4.8%, Apr-Sep).

Chainmaker Mild (OG 1037, ABV 3.6%)
A classic mild, dark and well-balanced with a hop aroma and underlying sweetness with a smooth, malty finish.

Nailmaker Mild (OG 1041, ABV 4%)
A well-defined hop aroma and underlying sweetness give way to a dry finish.

Saaz (OG 1042, ABV 4.2%)
Golden lager-style beer. Lager bite but with more taste and lasting bitterness. The malty aroma is late arriving but the bitter finish, balanced by fruit and hops, compensates.

White (OG 1041, ABV 4.2%)
Yellow with a malt, hops and fruit aroma. Hoppy but sweet finish.

Ale (OG 1044, ABV 4.5%)
Golden ale with a sweet, hoppy aroma. Sweet start when the honey kicks in, but a hoppy ending with a whisky and heather blend; thirst-quenching.

Porter (OG 1044, ABV 4.5%)
Black with a creamy head and sulphurous aroma. Sweet and fruity start with touches of spice. Good balance between sweet and bitter, but hops dominate the finish.

Ginger (OG 1045, ABV 4.6%)
Golden bright with gently gingered tangs. A drinkable beer with no acute flavours but a satisfying aftertaste of sweet hoppiness.

Evan Evans

Wm Evan Evans, The New Brewery, 1 Rhosmaen Street, Llandeilo, Carmarthenshire, SA14 6LU
☎ (01558) 824455
info@evan-evans.com
evan-evans.com
Shop 10am-4pm daily
Tours by arrangement

Wm Evan Evans opened in 2004 with a brand new Canadian brewing plant. Additional fermenting capacity was added in 2008, taking brewing capacity to 8,000 barrels per annum. A bottling plant was installed in May 2008, along with mini keg racking. 10 pubs are owned and around 150 outlets are supplied direct. It is Wales' first Soil Association organic approved brewery. A large range of seasonal ales is available.

BB (OG 1038, ABV 3.8%)

Cwrw (OG 1043, ABV 4.2%)

Warrior (ABV 4.6%)

Everards IFBB

Everards Brewery Ltd, Castle Acres, Narborough, Leicestershire, LE19 1BY
☎ (0116) 201 4100
mail@everards.co.uk
everards.co.uk
Shop Mon-Fri 10am-5pm; Sat 10am-4pm
Tours by arrangement for parties of 8-12

Established by William Everard in 1849, Everards brewery remains an independent family-owned brewery. Four core ales are brewed as well as a range of seasonal beers – see website for more details. Everards owns a pub estate of more than 160 tenanted houses throughout the Midlands.

Beacon Bitter (OG 1036, ABV 3.8%)
Light, refreshing, well-balanced pale amber bitter in the Burton style.

Sunchaser Blonde (ABV 4%)
A golden brew with a sweet, lightly-hopped character. Some citrus notes to the fore in a quick finish that becomes increasingly bitter.

Tiger Best Bitter (OG 1041, ABV 4.2%)
A mid-brown, well-balanced best bitter crafted for broad appeal, benefiting from a long, bittersweet finish.

Original (OG 1050, ABV 5.2%)
Full-bodied, mid-brown strong bitter with a pleasant rich, grainy mouthfeel. Well-balanced flavours, with malt slightly to the fore, merging into a long, satisfying finish.

Exe Valley SIBA

Exe Valley Brewery, Silverton, Exeter, Devon, EX5 4HF
☎ (01392) 860406
✉ exevalley@supanet.com
Tours by arrangement (for a charge)

Exe Valley was established as Barron's Brewery in 1984. Guy Sheppard, who joined the business in 1991, continues to run the company. The brewery is located in a converted barn overlooking the Exe Valley and Dartmoor hills. Locally sourced malt and English hops are used, along with the brewery's own spring water. The beers are all brewed traditionally, using spring water, Devon malt and English hops. Around 60 outlets are supplied within a 45-mile radius of the brewery. Beers are also available nationally via wholesalers. Seasonal beers: Devon Summer (ABV 3.9%, Jun-Aug), Spring Beer (ABV 4.3%, Mar-May), Autumn Glory (ABV 4.5%, Sep-Nov), Devon Dawn (ABV 4.5%, Dec-Jan), Winter Glow (ABV 6%, Dec-Feb). Bottle-conditioned beer is also available.

Bitter (OG 1036, ABV 3.7%)
Mid-brown bitter, pleasantly fruity with underlying malt through the aroma, taste and finish.

Barron's Hopsit (OG 1040, ABV 4.1%)
Straw-coloured beer with strong hop aroma, hop and fruit flavour and a bitter hop finish.

Dob's Best Bitter (OG 1040, ABV 4.1%)
Light brown bitter. Malt and fruit predominate in the aroma and taste with a dry, bitter, fruity finish.

Devon Glory (OG 1046, ABV 4.7%)
Mid-brown, fruity-tasting pint with a sweet, fruity finish.

Mr Sheppard's Crook (OG 1046, ABV 4.7%)
Smooth, full-bodied, mid-brown beer with a malty-fruit nose and a sweetish palate leading to a bitter, dry finish.

Exeter Old Bitter (OG 1046, ABV 4.8%)
Mid-brown old ale with a rich fruity taste and slightly earthy aroma and bitter finish.

Exeter

Exeter Brewery Ltd, 5 Lions Rest, Station Road, Exminster, Exeter, Devon, EX6 8DZ
☎ (01392) 823013
✉ sales@theexeterbrewery.co.uk
🌐 theexeterbrewery.co.uk

The Exeter Brewery, formerly named the Topsham & Exminster, remains on the same site amid the beautiful Exminster marshes, where it has brewed since 2003. The brewery has been completely refurbished and re-equipped, providing much greater production capacity and enabling a greater range of ales. More beers are planned in the near future.

Avocet (ABV 3.7%)

Ferryman (ABV 4.2%)

Exmoor SIBA

Exmoor Ales Ltd, Golden Hill Brewery, Wiveliscombe, Somerset, TA4 2NY
☎ (01984) 623798
✉ info@exmoorales.co.uk
🌐 exmoorales.co.uk
Tours by arrangement

Somerset's largest brewery was founded in 1980 in the old Hancock's brewery, which closed in 1959. Around 250 outlets in the South-west are supplied and others nationwide via wholesalers and pub chains. Seasonal beers: Hound Dog (ABV 4%, Mar-May), Silver Stallion (ABV 4.3%, Jun-Jul), Wild Cat (ABV 4.4%, Sep-Nov), Exmas (ABV 5%, Nov-Dec).

Ale (OG 1039, ABV 3.8%)
A pale to mid-brown, medium-bodied session bitter. A mixture of malt and hops in the aroma and taste lead to a hoppy, bitter aftertaste.

Fox (OG 1043, ABV 4.2%)
A mid-brown beer; the slight maltiness on the tongue is followed by a burst of hops with a lingering bittersweet aftertaste.

Gold (OG 1045, ABV 4.5%)
A yellow/golden best bitter with a good balance of malt and fruity hop on the nose and the palate. The sweetness follows through an ultimately more bitter finish.

Hart (OG 1049, ABV 4.8%)
A mid-to-dark brown beer with a mixture of malt and hops in the aroma. A rich, full-bodied malt and fruit flavour follows through to a clean, hoppy aftertaste.

Stag (OG 1050, ABV 5.2%)
A pale brown beer, with a malty taste and aroma, and a bitter finish.

Beast (OG 1066, ABV 6.6%)
A dark beer brewed with chocolate and crystal malts.

Facer's SIBA

Facer's Flintshire Brewery, A8-9, Ashmount Enterprise Park, Aber Road, Flint, North Wales, CH6 5YL
☎ 07713 566370
✉ dave@facers.co.uk
🌐 facers.co.uk
Tours by arrangement for CAMRA groups only

Bragdy Sir y Fflint Facer's (Facer's Flintshire Brewery) is the only brewery in Flintshire, having moved west from Salford in 2006. Ex-Boddington's head brewer Dave Facer ran the brewery single-handed from its launch in 2003 until 2007, when the first employee was recruited. The brewery was expanded to twice the floor space in early 2008. Around 70 outlets are supplied.

Clwyd Gold (OG 1034, ABV 3.5%)
Clean tasting session bitter, mid-brown in colour with a full mouthfeel. The malty flavours are accompanied by increasing hoppiness in the bitter finish.

Flintshire Bitter (OG 1036, ABV 3.7%)

Northern County (OG 1037, ABV 3.8%)
Straw-coloured light bitter with a mouthwatering floral hop nose and taste. Some astringency in the long, dry, bitter finish.

Sunny Bitter (OG 1040, ABV 4.2%)

An amber beer with a dry taste. The hop aroma continues into the taste where some faint fruit notes are also present. Lasting dry finish.

DHB (Dave's Hoppy Beer) (OG 1041, ABV 4.3%)
A dry-hopped version of Splendid Ale with some sweet flavours also coming through in the mainly hoppy, bitter taste.

This Splendid Ale (OG 1041, ABV 4.3%)
Refreshing tangy best bitter, yellow in colour with a sharp hoppy, bitter taste. Good citrus fruit undertones with hints of grapefruit throughout.

Landslide (OG 1047, ABV 4.9%)
Full-flavoured, complex premium bitter with tangy orange marmalade fruitiness in aroma and taste. Long-lasting hoppy flavours throughout.

Fallen Angel

Fallen Angel Micro-brewery, PO Box 95, Battle, East Sussex, TN33 0XF
☎ (01424) 777996
custservice@fallenangelbrewery.com
fallenangelbrewery.com

The brewery was launched in 2004 by Tony Betts and his wife, who are first-time brewers. The one-barrel brewery makes bottle-conditioned beers supplied to farmers' markets and shops. Cask ales are planned for festivals. Seasonal beers are produced. Bottle-conditioned beers: St Patricks Irish Stout (ABV 3.1%), Englishmans Nut Brown Ale (ABV 3.2%), Cowgirl Lite (ABV 3.6%), Lemon Weissbier (ABV 3.7%), Fire in the Hole Chilli Beer (ABV 3.9%), Hickory Switch Porter (ABV 4.3%), Caribbean Lime (ABV 5.3%), Angry Ox Bitter (ABV 5.3%).

Fallons*

Fallons Exquisite Ales, Unit 15, Darwen Enterprise Centre, Railway Road, Darwen, Lancashire, BB3 3EH
☎ 07905 246810
info@fallonsales.com
fallonsales.com

Fallons first brewed in May 2008 on a 10-barrel plant. Monthly specials and seasonal ales are planned.

TJ Fallon (ABV 3.7%)

Angel Tears (ABV 3.8%)

Lancastrian Gold (ABV 4%)

Red Merkin (ABV 4%)

Dark Prince (ABV 4.8%)

Falstaff

Falstaff Brewery, 24 Society Place, Normanton, Derby, Derbyshire, DE23 6UH
☎ (01332) 342902
info@falstaffbrewery.co.uk
falstaffbrewery.co.uk
Tours by arrangement

Attached to the Falstaff freehouse, the brewery dates from 1999 but was refurbished and re-opened in 2003 under new management and has since doubled capacity to 10 barrels. Since 2005 Falstaff has also brewed themed monthly specials for the Babington Arms in Derby. More than 30 outlets are supplied.

Fist Full of Hops (OG 1044, ABV 4.5%)
An amber ale with lots of hop.

Phoenix (OG 1047, ABV 4.7%)
A smooth, tawny ale with fruit and hop, joined by plenty of malt in the mouth. A subtle sweetness produces a drinkable ale.

Smiling Assassin (OG 1050, ABV 5.2%)
A copper-coloured beer with sweet malt flavours.

Good, the Bad and the Drunk (OG 1058, ABV 6.2%)
A full-bodied fruity beer.

Wilko (OG 1074, ABV 8.5%)
A copper-coloured and full-bodied ale.

Famous Railway Tavern

Famous Railway Tavern Brewing Co, 58 Station Road, Brightlingsea, Essex, CO7 0DT
☎ (01206) 302581
famousrailway@yahoo.co.uk
geocities.com/famousrailway
Tours by arrangement

The brewery started life as a kitchen-sink affair in 1998 but Crouch Vale Brewery assisted the development and increased production. At the end of 2006 the brewery and pub were expanded and it is now able to brew up to 135 gallons of beer a week for the pub, other local pubs and beer festivals. Many of the beers are also available bottle-conditioned. Seasonal beers: Frog Ale (ABV 3.7%), Fireside Porter (ABV 4.4%), Nettle Ale (ABV 4.4%). Crab & Winkle Mild, Bladderwrack Stout, Nettle Ale and Fireside Porter are suitable for vegetarians and vegans.

Crab & Winkle Mild (ABV 4%)
Thin-bodied mild with a pear drop aroma and a rather roasty taste. The aftertaste is slightly ash-like with suggestions of bitter chocolate.

Bladderwrack Stout (ABV 5%)
Full-bodied stout with an intense roast grain character that is initially underpinned by subtle sweetness, which subsides to leave a drier finish.

Farmer's Ales EAB

Farmer's Ales, Stable Brewery, Silver Street, Maldon, Essex, CM9 4QE
☎ (01621) 851000
info@maldonbrewing.co.uk
maldonbrewing.co.uk
Shop open for beer sales at the brewery
Tours by arrangement for small parties only

Situated in a restored stable block behind the historic Blue Boar Hotel, the recently expanded eight-barrel brewery started in 2002 and continues to enjoy success in local pubs and beer festivals. The beers are available at the Blue Boar, selected Gray & Sons houses as well as in a number of local pubs. Other outlets are supplied through

Crouch Vale Brewery. All cask beers are available in bottle-conditioned form from the brewery and other local shops. Eight seasonal beers are also produced.

Drop of Nelson's Blood (OG 1038, ABV 3.8%) ◆
Red-brown session bitter. Initially quite sweet and fruity, with a pleasing bite to the aftertaste.

Hotel Porter (OG 1041, ABV 4.1%) ◆
Roast grain dominates this oatmeal stout, but an unusual fresh hop character is evident.

Pucks Folly (OG 1042, ABV 4.2%) ◆
Pale golden ale with spicy notes and sweet fruit. Biscuity malt in the taste fades and the finish is dominated by bitterness.

Captain Ann (OG 1045, ABV 4.5%)
A deep ruby traditional malty best bitter.

Farmer's Golden Boar (OG 1050, ABV 5%) ◆
Powerful, deep-golden ale. The hop character is initially full and citrus, but becomes more spicy in the aftertaste.

Farnham

Farnham Brewery, Claverton Marketing Ltd, t/a The Ball & Wicket Public House, 104 Upper Hale Road, Farnham, Surrey, GU9 0PB
☎ **(01252) 735278**
✉ **ballwick@ntlworld.com**

⊗ The Farnham Brewery opened in 2006 and supplies the Ball & Wicket pub as well as around 10 other local outlets. Seasonal beers: Mango Beer (ABV 4%), Spring Ale (ABV 4.2%), Xmas Ale (ABV 4%).

Bishop Sumner (OG 1040, ABV 3.8%)

William Cobbett (OG 1045, ABV 4.5%)

Mike Hawthorn (OG 1055, ABV 5.3%)

Fat Cat

Fat Cat Brewing Co, Cider Shed, 98-100 Lawson Road, Norwich, Norfolk, NR3 4LF
☎ **(01603) 788508 / 624364**
☎ **07816 672397**
✉ **norfolkcottagebeers@tiscali.co.uk**
🌐 **fatcatbrewery.co.uk**
Tours by arrangement

Fat Cat Brewery was founded by the owner of the Fat Cat free house in Norwich. Brewing started in 2005 at the Fat Cat's sister pub, the Shed, under the supervision and management of former Woodforde's owner Ray Ashworth. Seasonal beers: Stout Cat (ABV 4.6%), Fat Cat Porter (ABV 5%), IPA (ABV 7%). Bottle-conditioned beers: Top Cat, IPA, Stout Cat.

Bitter (OG 1038, ABV 3.8%) ◆
An elegant, hoppy bitter with a long, bittersweet finish. Gold-coloured with a citrus aroma and a well-balanced hoppy beginning. Malt provides a soft but noticeable background.

Honey Cat (OG 1043, ABV 4.3%) ◆
Citrus abounds in the distinctive grapefruit nose and initial taste. An even hoppy bitterness flows through to a long, dryish finish. Honey is detectable but does not become overpowering.

Top Cat (OG 1048, ABV 4.8%) ◆
Superb balance of hops and sweet maltiness. Amber with a hop nose. Vanilla and citrus add depth to the hop and malt base. Surprisingly light on the tongue for its strength.

Marmalade Cat (OG 1055, ABV 5.5%) ◆
Amber-coloured brew with a hoppy aroma and complex bitter character. Initially a subtle, sweet maltiness softens the bitterness but fades as the long finish becomes drier.

Felinfoel SIBA

Felinfoel Brewery Co Ltd, Farmers Row, Felinfoel, Llanelli, Carmarthenshire, SA14 8LB
☎ **(01554) 773357**
✉ **info@felinfoel-brewery.com**
🌐 **felinfoel-brewery.com**
Shop 9am-4pm
Tours by arrangement

Founded in the 1830s, the company is still family-owned and is now the oldest brewery in Wales. The present buildings are Grade II* listed and were built in the 1870s. It supplies cask ale to half its 84 houses, though some use top pressure dispense, and to approximately 350 free trade outlets.

Best Bitter (OG 1038, ABV 3.8%) ◆
A balanced beer, with a low aroma. Bittersweet initially with an increasing moderate bitterness.

Cambrian Best Bitter (OG 1039, ABV 3.9%)

Stout (OG 1041, ABV 4.1%)

Double Dragon (OG 1042, ABV 4.2%) ◆
This pale brown beer has a malty, fruity aroma. The taste is also malt and fruit with a background hop presence throughout. A malty and fruity finish.

Celtic Pride (OG 1043, ABV 4.3%)

Felstar EAB

Felstar Brewery, Felsted Vineyards, Crix Green, Felsted, Essex, CM6 3JT
☎ **(01245) 361504**
☎ **07973 315503**
✉ **sales@felstarbrewery.co.uk**
🌐 **felstarbrewery.co.uk**
Shop 10am-dusk daily
Tours by arrangement

⊗ The Felstar Brewery opened in 2001 with a five-barrel plant based in the old bonded warehouse of the Felsted Vineyard. A small number of outlets are supplied. Seasonal beers: Rayne Forest (ABV 4%), Chick Chat (ABV 4.1%), Dark Wheat (ABV 5.4%), Xmas Ale (ABV 6%). All cask beers are available bottle conditioned plus Peckin' Order (ABV 5%), Lord Kulmbach (ABV 4.4%).

Felstar (OG 1036, ABV 3.4%)

Crix Gold (OG 1041, ABV 4%)

Shalford (OG 1042, ABV 4%)

Hopsin (OG 1048, ABV 4.6%)

Wheat (OG 1048, ABV 4.8%)

Good Knight (OG 1050, ABV 5%)

Lord Essex (OG 1056, ABV 5.4%)

Haunted Hen (OG 1062, ABV 6%)

Fen*

Fen Ales, 19 Swapcoat Lane, Long Sutton, Spalding, Lincolnshire, PE12 9HD
☎ 07929 538975
✉ thehargreavesfamily@btinternet.com

⊗ Fen Ales was established in 2007 on an eight-barrel brewery. 12 outlets are supplied. New beers are planned in 2008. Bottle-conditioned beer is also available.

Twitching Beaver (OG 1037, ABV 3.7%)
Red Fox (OG 1040, ABV 4%)

Fenland SIBA

Fenland Brewery Ltd, Unit 2, Fieldview, Cowbridge Hall Road, Little Downham, Cambridgeshire, CB6 2UQ
☎ (01353) 699966
✉ enquiries@elybeer.co.uk
🌐 elybeer.co.uk
Tours by arrangement

The brewery opened in 1998 in Chatteris, but moved to new premises on the Isle of Ely in 2004. Beers are supplied to more than 100 outlets. Seasonal beers: see website. Bottle-conditioned beers are also available.

Rabbit Poacher (ABV 3.8%)

St Audrey's Ale (ABV 3.9%)

Babylon Banks (ABV 4.1%)

Osier Cutter (ABV 4.2%)

Smokestack Lightning (ABV 4.2%)

Sparkling Wit (ABV 4.5%)

Raspberry Stout (ABV 4.6%)

Doctors Orders (ABV 5%)

Fernandes SIBA

Fernandes Brewery, 5 Avison Yard, Kirkgate, Wakefield, West Yorkshire, WF1 1UA
☎ (01924) 291709
🌐 fernandes-brewery.gowyld.com
Tours by arrangement

The brewery opened in 1997 and is housed in a 19th-century malthouse. Ossett Brewing Company purchased the brewery and tap in 2007, and independent brewing continues. The former home-brew shop has been turned into a Bavarian style 'Bier Keller' and sells continental beers as well as real ale. The tap, which has been local CAMRA's Pub of the Year every year since 1999, sells Fernandes and Ossett beer as well as guest ales. Fernandes beers are more widely available through Ossett's supply chain. Many occasional beers are produced.

Malt Shovel Mild (OG 1038, ABV 3.8%)
A dark, full-bodied, malty mild with roast malt and chocolate flavours, leading to a lingering, dry, malty finish.

Triple O (OG 1041, ABV 3.9%)
A light, refreshing, hoppy session beer with a lingering fruity finish.

Ale to the Tsar (OG 1042, ABV 4.1%)
A pale, smooth, well-balanced beer with some sweetness leading to a nutty, malty and satisfying aftertaste.

Great Northern (OG 1050, ABV 5.1%)
Pale, citrussy and extremely hoppy.

Double Six (OG 1062, ABV 6%)
A powerful, dark and rich strong beer with an array of malt, roast malt and chocolate flavours and a strong, lasting malty finish, with some hoppiness.

Festival*

A.Forbes Ltd t/a Festival Brewery, Unit 17, Malmesbury Road, Kingsditch Trading Estate, Cheltenham, Gloucestershire, GL51 9PL
☎ (01242) 521444
✉ info@festivalbrewery.co.uk
Shop Mon-Fri 9am-4pm
Tours by arrangement

⊗ Festival was established in March 2007 on a 10-barrel plant. The beer is available within a 50 mile radius of Cheltenham and through selected wholesalers.

Bitter (OG 1036.8, ABV 3.8%)
A copper-coloured session bitter with a malt flavour, balanced with a long-lasting dry, hoppy finish.

Gold (OG 1042.6, ABV 4.4%)
Refreshing golden ale with a clear flavour that continues right through to the finish.

Ruby (OG 1045.5, ABV 4.7%)
A strong bitter, ruby-coloured with a rich and warming character.

Ffos y Ffin

Ffos y Ffin Brewery, Capel Dewi, Carmarthenshire, SA32 8AG
☎ 07838 384868
✉ info@ffosyffinbrewery.co.uk
🌐 ffosyffinbrewery.co.uk
Tours by arrangement

⊗ Established in 2006, the brewery has its own well to provide brewing liquor. The processes used are traditional with no chemical or mechanical filtering. Around 75 outlets are supplied. All beers are also available bottle conditioned.

Cothi Gold (OG 1038, ABV 3.9%)

Cwrw Caredig (OG 1039, ABV 4.1%)

Dylans Choice (OG 1042, ABV 4.4%)

Three Arches (OG 1046, ABV 4.8%)

Towy Ale (OG 1048, ABV 5%)

Paxtons Pride (OG 1053, ABV 5.5%)

FILO SIBA

FILO Brewing Co Ltd, First In Last Out, 14-15 High Street, Hastings, East Sussex, TN34 3EY
☎ (01424) 425079
✉ office@thefilo.co.uk
🌐 thefilo.co.uk
Tours by arrangement

⊗ The FILO Brewery was first installed in 1985, using old milk tanks. The current owner,

Mike Bigg, took over in 1988 and remains in control of the pub and brewery business. In 2000 the brewery went through a complete overhaul, although it remains a small, five-barrel craft brewery with the First In Last Out pub as the only outlet apart from beer festivals.

Crofters (ABV 3.8%)

Ginger Tom (ABV 4.5%)

Cardinal (ABV 4.6%)

Gold (ABV 4.8%)

Florence*

Florence Brewhouse, The Florence, Capital Pub Company PLC, 133 Dulwich Road, Herne Hill, London, SE24 0NG
☎ (020) 7326 4987
enquiries@florencehernehill.com
florencehernehill.com

The Florence has been brewing since opening in June 2007 alongside its sister brewpub, the Cock & Hen in Fulham (now closed). Beer is supplied to three outlets, the Florence itself, the Clarence in Balham and the Merchant of Battersea in Battersea.

Bonobo (ABV 4.5%)

Weasel (ABV 4.5%)

Flowerpots

Flowerpots Brewery, Cheriton, Alresford, Hampshire, SO24 0QQ
☎ (01962) 771534
flowerpots-inn.co.uk
Tours by arrangement (small groups only)

Flowerpots began production in 2006. CAMRA members Iain McIntosh and Steve Haigh are the brewers alongside the owner, Paul Tickner. Two pubs are owned and many local outlets are supplied direct.

Pots Black (OG 1033, ABV 3.2%)
A traditional style dark mild; not too bitter and with a hint of smoky malt.

Bitter (OG 1038, ABV 3.8%) ◆
Dry, earthy hop flavours balanced by malt and fruit. Good bitterness with an enticing hoppy aroma and a sharp, refreshing finish.

Elder Ale (OG 1038, ABV 3.8%)
A dry beer, very light in colour with a hint of elderflower; refreshing and fragrant.

Stottidge Stout (OG 1048, ABV 4.5%)
A traditional stout with not too much bitterness or hop character allowing the roasted barley flavour to come through.

Goodens Gold (OG 1048, ABV 4.8%)
A modern-style strong bitter with a rich golden colour. Named after land local to the Flowerpots in the parish of Cheriton.

Four Alls

Four Alls Brewery, Ovington, Richmond, North Yorkshire, DL11 7BP
☎ (01833) 627302
john.stroud@virgin.net
thefouralls-teesdale.co.uk
Tours by arrangement

The one-barrel brewery was launched in 2003 by John Stroud, one of the founders of Ales of Kent, using that name. In 2004 it became Four Alls, named after the pub where it is based, the only outlet except for two beers supplied twice yearly to Darlington beer festivals. Phone first to check if beer is available.

Iggy Pop (OG 1036, ABV 3.6%)
A honey-coloured beer made from pale, crystal and wheat malts and hopped with First Gold and Goldings.

30 Shillings (OG 1039, ABV 3.8%)
A dark session ale made from pale, crystal and chocolate malts with First Gold and Fuggles hops.

Swift (OG 1038, ABV 3.8%)
A dark mild made with pale, crystal and chocolate malts. Hopped with Fuggles and Goldings to give a smooth, pleasant character.

Red Admiral (OG 1041, ABV 3.9%)
A deep red beer that uses pale and crystal malts and is hopped with Fuggles. A malty beer with flowery notes.

Tallyman IPA (OG 1041, ABV 4%)
A citrus bitter foretaste gives way to biscuity and malty aftertaste with further citrus notes.

Smugglers Glory (OG 1048, ABV 4.8%)
A black beer made with pale, crystal and chocolate malts and roast barley. Hopped with Fuggles and Goldings, it is a stronger and more bitter version of Swift.

Fowler's

Fowler's Ales (Prestoungrange) Ltd also t/a Prestonpans Ales, 227-229 High Street, Prestonpans, East Lothian, EH32 9BE
☎ (01875) 819922
craigallan@prestoungrange.org
prestoungrange.org/fowlers
Tours by arrangement

Fowler's opened in 2004. The adjacent pub, the Prestoungrange Gothenburg, offers all the beers and the ales are also distributed to pubs in Edinburgh and the Lothians, and throughout Britain via Flying Firkin. Fowler's also offers brewsets (brewing courses). Seasonal beers: Winter Warmer (ABV 4.8%, Nov-Feb), Hop Freak Ale (ABV 3.8%, Jun-Aug). Brewing is suspended at present.

Prestonpans IPA (OG 1040, ABV 4.1%)

Prestonpans 80/- (OG 1041, ABV 4.2%)

Gothenburg Porter (OG 1043, ABV 4.4%)

Foxfield

Foxfield Brewery, Prince of Wales, Foxfield, Broughton in Furness, Cumbria, LA20 6BX
☎ (01229) 716238
princeofwalesfoxfield.co.uk
Tours by arrangement

Foxfield is a three-barrel plant in old stables attached to the Prince of Wales inn. A few other outlets are supplied. Tigertops in Wakefield is also owned. The beer range constantly changes so the beers listed here may not necessarily be available. There are many occasional and seasonal beers. Dark Mild is suitable for vegetarians and vegans.

Sands (OG 1038, ABV 3.4%)
A pale, light, aromatic quaffing ale.

Fleur-de-Lys (OG 1038, ABV 3.6%)

Dark Mild (OG 1040, ABV 3.7%)

Brief Encounter (OG 1040, ABV 3.8%)
A fruity beer with a long, bitter finish.

Fox EAB

Fox Brewery, 22 Station Road, Heacham, Norfolk, PE31 7EX
☎ (01485) 570345
info@foxbrewery.co.uk
foxbrewery.co.uk
Tours by arrangement

Based in an old cottage adjacent to the Fox & Hounds pub, Fox brewery was established in 2002 and now supplies around 50 outlets as well as the pub. All the Branthill beers are brewed from barley grown on Branthill Farm and malted at Crisp's in Great Ryburgh. A new extension has been built, which should double capacity. All cask beers are also available bottle conditioned. Seasonal beers: Nina's Mild (ABV 3.9%), Fresh as a Daisy (ABV 4.2%), Fox's Willie (ABV 4.4%), Cerberus Stout (ABV 4.5%), Heacham Kriek (ABV 5.1%), Punt Gun (ABV 5.9%).

Branthill Best (OG 1037, ABV 3.8%)
Old-fashioned best bitter.

Heacham Gold (OG 1037, ABV 3.9%) ◆
A gentle beer with light citrus airs. A low but increasing bitterness is the major flavour as some initial sweet hoppiness quickly declines.

LJB (OG 1040, ABV 4%) ◆
A well-balanced malty brew with a hoppy, bitter background. The long finish holds up well, as a sultana-like fruitiness develops. Mid-brown with a slightly thin mouthfeel.

Red Knocker (OG 1043, ABV 4.2%)
Copper coloured and malty.

Branthill Norfolk Nectar (OG 1043, ABV 4.3%)
Slightly sweet. Brewed only with Maris Otter pale malt.

Chinook (OG 1043, ABV 4.4%)
A mid amber-coloured beer with hoppy aroma and orangey citrus fruit flavour.

Grizzly Beer (OG 1048, ABV 4.8%)
Honey wheat beer brewed from an American recipe.

Bullet (OG 1050, ABV 5.1%)
Pale golden yellow beer with resinous hop aroma and tropical fruit flavours.

Nelson's Blood (OG 1049, ABV 5.1%)
A liquor of beers. Red, full-bodied; made with Nelsons Blood Rum.

IPA (OG 1051, ABV 5.2%)
Based on a 19th-century recipe. Easy drinking for its strength.

Freedom

Freedom Brewery Ltd, Bagots Park, Abbots Bromley, Staffordshire, WS15 3ER
☎ (01283) 840721
freedom@freedombrewery.com
freedomlager.com
Tours by arrangement

No real ale. Brothers Brewery was established in 2005 by acquiring Freedom Brewery, and specialises in lagers produced to the German Reinheitsgebot purity law. In 2008 it reverted to the name Freedom Brewery Ltd. It currently produces three beers, Freedom Organic Lager (ABV 4.8%), Freedom Pilsener (ABV 5%) and Freedom Organic Dark Lager (ABV 4.7%). (See also Bunker). All are suitable for vegetarians and vegans.

Freeminer SIBA

Freeminer Ltd, Whimsey Road, Steam Mills, Cinderford, Gloucestershire, GL14 3JA
☎ (01594) 827989
don@freeminer.com
freeminer.com

Founded by Don Burgess in 1992, Freeminer – previously Freeminer Brewery – has grown to be one of the vanguard of the quality bottled beers revival. It has two major national listings and bottled Fairtrade beers are being developed. These are sometimes released on draught. The brewery changed hands in 2006 but Don Burgess remains in post. Bottle-conditioned beers are available (brewed for Morrisons and Co-op).

Bitter (OG 1038, ABV 4%) ◆
A light, hoppy session bitter with an intense hop aroma and a dry, hoppy finish.

Strip & At It (OG 1035, ABV 4%)

Speculation (OG 1047, ABV 4.8%) ◆
An aromatic, chestnut-brown, full-bodied beer with a smooth, well-balanced mix of malt and hops, and a predominately hoppy aftertaste.

Frog Island SIBA

Frog Island Brewery, The Maltings, Westbridge, St James Road, Northampton, Northamptonshire, NN5 5HS
☎ (01604) 587772
beer@frogislandbrewery.co.uk
frogislandbrewery.co.uk
Tours by arrangement to licensed trade only

Started in 1994 by home-brewer Bruce Littler and business partner Graham Cherry in a malt house built by the long-defunct Thomas Manning brewery, Frog Island expanded by doubling its brew length to 10 barrels in 1998. It specialises in beers with personalised bottle labels, available by mail order. Some 40 free trade outlets are supplied, with the beer occasionally available through other micro-brewers. Bottle-conditioned beers are available.

Best Bitter (OG 1040, ABV 3.8%) ◆
Blackcurrant and gooseberry enhance the full malty aroma with pineapple and papaya joining on the tongue. Bitterness develops in the fairly long Target/Fuggles finish.

Shoemaker (OG 1043, ABV 4.2%) ◆
An orangey aroma of fruity Cascade hops is balanced by malt. Citrus and hoppy bitterness last into a long, dry finish. Amber colour.

Natterjack (OG 1048, ABV 4.8%) ◆
Deceptively robust, golden and smooth. Fruit and hop aromas fight for dominance before the grainy astringency and floral palate give way to a long, dry aftertaste.

Fire Bellied Toad (OG 1050, ABV 5%) ◆
Amber-gold brew with an extraordinary long bitter/fruity finish. Huge malt and Phoenix hop flavours have a hint of apples.

Croak & Stagger (OG 1056, ABV 5.8%) ◆
The initial honey/fruit aroma is quickly overpowered by roast malt then bitter chocolate and pale malt sweetness on the tongue. Gentle, bittersweet finish.

Front Street

Front Street Brewery, 45 Front Street, Binham, Fakenham, Norfolk, NR21 0AL
☎ **(01328) 830297**
✉ **steve@frontstreetbrewery.co.uk**
🌐 **frontstreetbrewery.co.uk**
Tours by arrangement

The brewery is based at the Chequers Inn and is probably Britain's smallest five-barrel plant. Brewing started in 2005 and three regular beers are produced as well as seasonal and occasional brews. Both cask and bottled beers are delivered to the free trade and retail outlets throughout East Anglia. Seasonal beers: China Gold (ABV 5%, winter), The Tsar (ABV 8.5%, winter). Bottle-conditioned beers are also available.

Binham Cheer (OG 1039, ABV 3.9%)

Callums Ale (OG 1043, ABV 4.3%)

Unity Strong (OG 1051, ABV 5%)

Fugelestou

Fugelestou Ales, Fulstow Brewery, Unit 13, Thames Street Business Complex, Thames Street, Louth, Lincolnshire, LN11 7AD
☎ **(01507) 363642**

Office: 6 Northway, Fulstow, Lincolnshire, LN11 0XH
✉ **fulstow.brewery@virgin.net**
🌐 **fulstowbrewery.co.uk**
Tours by arrangement

⊗ Fugelestou operates on a 2.5-barrel plant and was the first brewery to be established in Louth for over 100 years. The beers are distributed throughout the UK and one-off brews are produced on a regular basis. Seasonal ales: Xmas Spirit (ABV 5%), White Xmas (ABV 4.6%), Fawke in Hell (ABV 4.6%, Nov). Bottle-conditioned beers are also available.

Fulstow Common (OG 1038, ABV 3.8%)

Marsh Mild (OG 1039, ABV 3.8%)

Village Life (OG 1040, ABV 4%)

Northway IPA (OG 1042, ABV 4.2%)

Pride of Fulstow (OG 1045, ABV 4.5%)

Sledge Hammer Stout (OG 1077, ABV 8%)

Fuller's IFBB SIBA

Fuller, Smith & Turner plc, Griffin Brewery, Chiswick Lane South, London, W4 2QB
☎ **(020) 8996 2000**
✉ **fuller@fullers.co.uk**
🌐 **fullers.co.uk**
Shop Mon-Fri 10am-6pm; Sat 10am-5pm
Tours by arrangement

⊗ Fuller, Smith & Turner's Griffin Brewery has stood on the same site in Chiswick for more than 350 years. The partnership from which the company now takes its name was formed in 1845 and members of the founding families are still involved in running the company today. Three different Fuller's beers have won the Champion Beer of Britain title, London Pride, Chiswick Bitter and ESB. At the end of 2005 Fuller's announced an agreed acquisition of Hampshire brewer George Gale. This added 111 tied outlets to produce a combined estate of 361. Fuller's stopped brewing at the Gale's Horndean site in 2006. The main Gale's brands are now brewed at Chiswick. Some of Gale's seasonal beers are still brewed. Seasonal beers: Please see website. Bottle-conditioned beers are also available.

Chiswick Bitter (OG 1034.5, ABV 3.5%) ◆
An easy drinking pale brown beer; light and fruity, with a touch of malty sweetness, which is also on the nose and carries into the short dry bitter finish.

Discovery (ABV 3.9%) ◆
Dark golden beer designed to be drunk cold. Honey, malt and fruit in the aroma and palate, fading quickly to leave a touch of bitterness.

London Pride (OG 1040.5, ABV 4.1%) ◆
Malt is complemented by the citrus hop character in this well-balanced best bitter with a dry, bitter aftertaste that grows on drinking. Develops pleasant caramelised peel notes as beer ages.

ESB (OG 1054, ABV 5.5%) ◆
Nose and flavour are a complex mix of orange bitter marmalade softened by a slight toffee sweetness and a rich creamy mouthfeel. Flavours linger in a wonderfully warm dry finish.

Under the Gale's brand name:

Butser Bitter (OG 1034, ABV 3.4%)

HSB (OG 1050, ABV 4.8%) ◆
Good interpretation of the flagship Gale's beer previously brewed in Horndean. A sweet, full-bodied bitter with dark fruit aromas and flavours, leading to a sweet finish with a hint of dryness.

Full Mash

Full Mash Brewery, 17 Lower Park Street, Stapleford, Nottinghamshire, NG9 8EW
☎ **(0115) 949 9262**
✉ **fullmashbrewery@yahoo.com**

☺ Full Mash started brewing in 2003 with a quarter-barrel plant. The brewery has now expanded to four barrels and, with the addition of extra fermenters, 16 barrels a week are now produced. Trade is expanding with five regular beers supplied to 45 outlets.

Ouija (OG 1043, ABV 3.7%)

ESP (OG 1039, ABV 3.8%)

Seance (OG 1041, ABV 4%)

Spiritualist (OG 1044, ABV 4.3%)

Apparition (OG 1046, ABV 4.5%)

Funfair

Funfair Brewing Co, Office: 34 Spinney Road, Ilkeston, Derbyshire, DE7 4LH
☎ 07971 540186
✉ sales@funfairbrewingcompany.co.uk
funfairbrewingcompany.co.uk
Tours by arrangement

Funfair was launched in 2004 at the Wheel Inn in Holbrook. The brewery relocated to Ilkeston and in 2006 relocated again to its present site. A bottling plant was installed in 2007. Around 40 outlets are supplied. Seasonal beers: Elfer Skelter (ABV 4.3%, Xmas), Christmas Cakewalk (ABV 6.5%), House of Horrors (ABV 4.4%, Oct), Roller Ghoster (ABV 4.7%). Bottle-conditioned beers are also available.

Gallopers (OG 1038, ABV 3.8%)

Waltzer (OG 1045, ABV 4.5%)

Dive Bomber (OG 1047, ABV 4.7%)

Dodgem (OG 1047, ABV 4.7%)

Cakewalk (OG 1060, ABV 6%)

Fuzzy Duck

Fuzzy Duck Brewery, 18 Wood Street, Poulton Industrial Estate, Poulton-le-Fylde, Lancashire, FY6 8JY
☎ 07904 343729
✉ ben@fuzzyduckbrewery.co.uk
fuzzyduckbrewery.co.uk

Fuzzy Duck was started on a half-barrel plant at the owner's home in 2006. It relocated to an industrial unit and expanded capacity to eight barrels. There are plans to introduce a bottle-conditioned range of beers.

Thumb Ducker (OG 1040, ABV 3.9%)

Feathers (OG 1040, ABV 4%)

Stout (OG 1042, ABV 4%)

Pheasant Plucker (OG 1044, ABV 4.2%)

Fyfe SIBA

Fyfe Brewing Co, 469 High Street, Kirkaldy, Fife, KY1 2SN
☎ (01592) 646211
✉ fyfebrew@tiscali.co.uk
fyfebrewery.co.uk
Tours by arrangement

Fyfe was established in an old sailmakers behind the Harbour Bar in 1995 on a 2.5-barrel plant. Most of the output is taken by the pub, the remainder being sold direct to around 20 local outlets, including a house beer for JD Wetherspoons in Glenrothes. Seasonal beer: Cauld Turkey (ABV 6%, winter but can be brewed on request all year round).

Rope of Sand (OG 1037, ABV 3.7%)
A quenching bitter. Malt and fruit throughout, with a hoppy, bitter aftertaste.

19th Hole (OG 1038, ABV 3.8%)

Greengo (OG 1038, ABV 3.8%)
Golden coloured with a hoppy aroma and a citrus/bitter taste and aftertaste. Clean and refreshing.

Auld Alliance (OG 1040, ABV 4%)
A bitter beer with a lingering, dry, hoppy finish. Malt and hop, with fruit, are present throughout, fading in the finish.

Featherie (OG 1041, ABV 4.1%)
A light, refreshing, easy-drinking pale ale with a hoppy, lingering finish.

Lion Slayer (OG 1042, ABV 4.2%)
Amber-coloured ale with malt and fruit on the nose. Fruit predominates on the palate. A slightly dry finish.

Baffie (OG 1043, ABV 4.3%)
A pale coloured beer. Hops and fruit are evident and are balanced by malt throughout. A hoppy, bitter finish.

First Lyte (OG 1043, ABV 4.3%)
Clean tasting, light in colour with a good balance of malt and hops. Dry bitter finish.

Weiss Squad (OG 1045, ABV 4.5%)
Hoppy, bitter wheat beer with bags of citrus in the taste and finish.

Fyfe Fyre (OG 1048, ABV 4.8%)
Pale golden best bitter, full-bodied and balanced with malt, hops and fruit. Hoppy bitterness grows in an increasingly dry aftertaste.

Fyne SIBA

Fyne Ales Ltd, Achadunan, Cairndow, Argyll, PA26 8BJ
☎ (01499) 600120
✉ jonny@fyneales.com
fyneales.com
Shop Mon-Sat 10am-4pm; Sun seasonal
Tours by arrangement

Fyne Ales has been brewing since 2001. The 10-barrel plant was installed in a redundant milking parlour on a farm in Argyll, set in a beautiful highland glen at the head of Loch Fyne. Around 430 outlets are supplied. The range of beers is supplemented by ale brewed for special events. Seasonal beers: Innishail (ABV 3.6%), Somerled (ABV 4%), Fyne Porter (ABV 4.5%), Holly Daze (ABV 5%).

Piper's Gold (OG 1037.5, ABV 3.8%)
Fresh, golden session ale. Well bittered but balanced with fruit and malt. Long, dry, bitter finish.

Maverick (OG 1040.5, ABV 4.2%)
Smooth, nutty session beer with a sweet, fruity finish.

Vital Spark (OG 1042.5, ABV 4.4%)
A rich, dark beer that shows glints of red. The taste is clean and slightly sharp with a hint of blackcurrant.

Avalanche (OG 1043.5, ABV 4.5%)

Highlander (OG 1045.5, ABV 4.8%) ◆
Full-bodied, bittersweet ale with a good dry hop finish. In the style of a heavy although the malt is less pronounced and the sweetness ebbs away to leave a bitter, hoppy finish.

Gale's

See Fuller's

Gargoyles

Gargoyles Brewery, Court Farm, Holcombe Village, Dawlish, Devon, EX7 0JT
☎ 07773 444501

Gargoyles Brewery was established in 2005. A honey beer is planned in the near future. Around 30 outlets are supplied. Seasonal beers: Summer Ale (ABV 3.8%), Humbug (ABV 5%, winter).

Best Bitter (ABV 4.2%)
An amber-coloured beer with a fresh, hoppy aftertaste.

Geltsdale

Geltsdale Brewery Ltd, Unit 6, Old Brewery Yard, Craw Hill, Brampton, Cumbria, CA8 1TR
☎ (016977) 41541
✉ geltsdale@mac.com
🌐 geltsdalebrewery.com
Tours by arrangement (max. 15 persons)

◎Geltsdale Brewery was established in 2006 by Fiona Deal and operates from a small unit in Brampton's Old Brewery, dating back to 1785. The beers are named after local landmarks within Geltsdale. Around 70 outlets are supplied direct.

Black Dub (OG 1036, ABV 3.6%)

King's Forest (OG 1038, ABV 3.8%)

Cold Fell (ABV 3.9%)

Bewcastle Brown Ale (ABV 4%)

Brampton Bitter (ABV 4%)

Tarnmonath (OG 1040, ABV 4%)

Hell Beck (OG 1042, ABV 4.2%)

George Wright

See under Wright

Glastonbury SIBA

Glastonbury Ales, 11 Wessex Park, Somerton Business Park, Somerton, Somerset, TA11 6SB
☎ (01458) 272244
✉ info@glastonburyales.com
Tours by arrangement

⊗ Glastonbury Ales was established in 2002 on a five-barrel plant. In 2006 the brewery changed ownership and has recently grown into a 20-barrel outfit. Organic ales are in the pipeline. Seasonal beers: Love Monkey (ABV 4.2%, Feb & Jun), Solstice (ABV 4%, Jun-Aug), Pomparles Porter (ABV 4.5%, Feb-Mar), Spring Loaded (ABV 4.2%, Mar-Apr), Pilton Pop (ABV 4.2%, May-Jun), Black as Yer 'At (ABV 4.3%, Jan-Nov), FMB (ABV 5%, Sep-Dec), Holy Thorn (ABV 4.2%, Nov-Jan).

Mystery Tor (OG 1040, ABV 3.8%) ◆
A golden bitter with plenty of floral hop and fruit on the nose and palate, the sweetness giving way to a bitter hop finish. Full-bodied for a session bitter.

Lady of the Lake (OG 1042, ABV 4.2%) ◆
A full-bodied amber best bitter with plenty of hops to the fore balanced by a fruity malt flavour and a subtle hint of vanilla, leading to a clean, bitter hop aftertaste.

Hedgemonkey (OG 1048, ABV 4.6%)
A well-rounded deep amber bitter. Malty, rich and very hoppy.

Golden Chalice (OG 1048, ABV 4.8%)
Light and golden best bitter with a robust malt character.

Glenfinnan

Glenfinnan Brewery Co Ltd, Sruth A Mhuilinn, Glenfinnan, PH37 4LT
☎ 07999 261010
✉ info@glenfinnanbrewery.co.uk
🌐 glenfinnanbrewery.co.uk

Glenfinnan officially opened in May 2007.

Light Ale (ABV 3.3%)

Gold Ale (ABV 4%)

Standard Ale (ABV 4.3%)

Glentworth SIBA

Glentworth Brewery, Glentworth House, Crossfield Lane, Skellow, Doncaster, South Yorkshire, DN6 8PL
☎ (01302) 725555

◎The brewery was founded in 1996 and is housed in former dairy buildings. The five-barrel plant supplies more than 80 pubs. Production is concentrated on mainly light-coloured, hoppy ales. Seasonal beers (brewed to order): Oasis (ABV 4.1%), Happy Hooker (ABV 4.3%), North Star (ABV 4.3%), Perle (ABV 4.4%), Dizzy Blonde (ABV 4.5%), Whispers (ABV 4.5%).

Lightyear (OG 1037, ABV 3.9%)

Globe

▮ Globe Brewpub, 144 High Street West, Glossop, Derbyshire, SK13 8HJ
☎ (01457) 852417
🌐 globemusic.org

⊗ Globe was established in 2006 on a 2.5-barrel plant in an old stable behind the Globe pub. The beers are mainly for the pub but special one-off brews are produced for beer festivals.

Amber (ABV 3.8%)

Comet (ABV 4.3%)

Eclipse (ABV 4.3%)

Sirius (ABV 5.2%)

Goacher's

P & DJ Goacher, Unit 8, Tovil Green Business Park, Burial Ground Lane, Tovil, Maidstone, Kent, ME15 6TA
☎ **(01622) 682112**
🌐 **goachers.com**
Tours by arrangement

⊗ A traditional brewery, now in its 25th year, that uses only malt and Kentish hops for all its beers. Phil and Debbie Goacher have concentrated on brewing good wholesome beers without gimmicks. Two tied houses and around 30 free trade outlets in the mid-Kent area are supplied. Special is brewed for sale under house names. Seasonal beer: Old 1066 (ABV 6.7%).

Real Mild Ale (OG 1033, ABV 3.4%)
A full-flavoured dark mild with background bitterness.

Fine Light Ale (OG 1036, ABV 3.7%) ◆
A pale, golden brown bitter with a strong, floral, hoppy aroma and aftertaste. A hoppy and moderately malty session beer.

House Ale (OG 1037, ABV 3.8%)

Best Dark Ale (OG 1040, ABV 4.1%) ◆
A bitter beer, balanced by a moderate maltiness, with a complex aftertaste.

Crown Imperial Stout (OG 1044, ABV 4.5%)
A classic Irish-style stout with a clean palate and satisfying aftertaste from Kent Fuggles hops.

Gold Star Strong Ale (OG 1050, ABV 5.1%) ◆
A strong pale ale brewed from 100% Maris Otter malt and East Kent Goldings hops.

Goddards SIBA

Goddards Brewery Ltd, Barnsley Farm, Bullen Road, Ryde, Isle of Wight, PO33 1QF
☎ **(01983) 611011**
✉ **office@goddards-brewery.co.uk**
🌐 **goddards-brewery.co.uk**

Established on the Isle of Wight in 1993 and occupying 18th-century converted barns, the brewery supplies around 100 outlets. Seasonal beers: Duck's Folly (ABV 5%, early autumn), Iron Horse (ABV 4.8%, late autumn), Inspiration (ABV 5.2%), Winter Warmer (ABV 5.2%).

Ale of Wight (OG 1037, ABV 3.7%)
An aromatic, fresh and zesty pale beer.

Special Bitter (OG 1038.5, ABV 4%) ◆
Well-balanced session beer that maintains its flavour and bite with compelling drinkability.

Fuggle-Dee-Dum (OG 1048.5, ABV 4.8%) ◆
Brown-coloured strong ale with plenty of malt and hops.

Goff's SIBA

Goff's Brewery Ltd, 9 Isbourne Way, Winchcombe, Cheltenham, Gloucestershire, GL54 5NS
☎ **(01242) 603383**
✉ **brewery@goffsbrewery.com**
🌐 **goffsbrewery.com**

⊗ Goff's is a family concern that has been brewing cask-conditioned ales since 1994. The ales are available regionally in more than 200 outlets and nationally through wholesalers. The addition of the seasonal Ales of the Round Table provides a range of 12 beers of which four or five are always available: see website for details.

Jouster (OG 1040, ABV 4%) ◆
A drinkable, tawny-coloured ale, with a light hoppiness in the aroma. It has a good balance of malt and bitterness in the mouth, underscored by fruitiness, with a clean, hoppy aftertaste.

Tournament (OG 1038, ABV 4%) ◆
Dark golden in colour, with a pleasant hop aroma. A clean, light and refreshing session bitter with a pleasant hop aftertaste.

White Knight (OG 1046, ABV 4.7%) ◆
A well-hopped bitter with a light colour and full-bodied taste. Bitterness predominates in the mouth and leads to a dry, hoppy aftertaste.

Golcar SIBA

Golcar Brewery, 60a Swallow Lane, Golcar, Huddersfield, West Yorkshire, HD7 4NB
☎ **(01484) 644241**
☎ **07970 267555**
✉ **golcarbrewrey@btconnect.com**
Tours by arrangement

Golcar started brewing in 2001 and production has increased from 2.5 barrels to five barrels a week. The brewery owns one pub, the Rose & Crown at Golcar, and supplies other outlets in the local area.

Dark Mild (OG 1034, ABV 3.4%) ◆
Dark mild with a light roasted malt and liquorice taste. Smooth and satisfying.

Bitter (OG 1039, ABV 3.9%) ◆
Amber bitter with a hoppy, citrus taste, with fruity overtones and a bitter finish.

Pennine Gold (OG 1038, ABV 4%)
A hoppy and fruity session beer.

Weavers Delight (OG 1045, ABV 4.8%)
Malty best bitter with fruity overtones.

Guthlac's Porter (OG 1047, ABV 5%)
A robust all grain and malty working man's porter.

Goldfinch

Goldfinch Brewery, 47 High Street East, Dorchester, Dorset, DT1 1HU
☎ **(01305) 264020**
✉ **info@goldfinchbrewery.com**
🌐 **goldfinchbrewery.com**
Shop 11am-11pm daily
Tours by arrangement

⊗ Goldfinch has been brewing since 1987 and is situated behind the Tom Brown public house. In 2008 the brewery and pub were purchased by Dorset Brewing Co (qv). Eight outlets are supplied. Seasonal beer: Midnight Blinder (ABV 5%, Nov-Feb).

Stormbroker (ABV 4%)

Tom Brown's (ABV 4%)

Flashman's Clout (ABV 4.5%)

Midnight Sun (ABV 4.5%)

Goose Eye SIBA

Goose Eye Brewery Ltd, Ingrow Bridge, South Street, Keighley, West Yorkshire, BD21 5AX
☎ (01535) 605807
✉ gooseeyebrewery@btconnect.com
🌐 goose-eye-brewery.co.uk

Goose Eye has been run by Jack and David Atkinson for the past 16 years. The brewery supplies 60-70 regular outlets, mainly in West and North Yorkshire, and Lancashire. The beers are also available through national wholesalers and pub chains. It produces an ever-expanding range of occasional beers, sometimes brewed to order, and is diversifying into wholesaling and bottled beers (filtered but not pasteurised). No-Eye Deer is often re-badged under house names.

Barm Pot Bitter (OG 1038, ABV 3.8%) ◆
The bitter hop and citrus flavours that dominate this amber session bitter are balanced by a malty base. The finish is increasingly dry and bitter.

Bronte Bitter (OG 1040, ABV 4%) ◆
A golden amber well-hopped best bitter with bitterness increasing to give a lingering, dry finish.

No-Eye Deer (OG 1040, ABV 4%) ◆
A faint fruity and malty aroma. Strong hoppy flavours and an intense, bitter finish characterise this pale brown bitter.

Chinook Blonde (OG 1042, ABV 4.2%)
A very pale beer with plenty of hops, giving a hoppy subtle citrus flavour.

Golden Goose (OG 1045, ABV 4.5%)
A straw-coloured beer light on the palate with a smooth and refreshing hoppy finish.

Over and Stout (OG 1052, ABV 5.2%) ◆
A full-bodied stout in which roast and caramel flavours mingle with malt and dark fruit. Look also for tart fruit on the nose and an increasingly bitter, slightly astringent finish.

Pommies Revenge (OG 1052, ABV 5.2%)
An extra strong, single malt bitter.

Grafters*

Grafters Brewery, The Half Moon, 23 High Street, Willingham-by-Stow, Lincolnshire, DN21 5JZ
☎ (01427) 788340
✉ graftersbrewery@fsmail.net

Brewing started on a 2.5-barrel plant in November 2007 in a converted garage adjacent to the owner's freehouse, the Half Moon. Several new beers are planned.

Traditional Bitter (ABV 3.8%)

Over the Moon (ABV 4%)

Brewers Troop (ABV 4.2%)

Grafton

Grafton Brewing & Pub Co, Packet Inn, Bescoby Street, Retford, Nottinghamshire, DN22 6LJ
☎ (01909) 476121
☎ 07816 443581
Head Office: 8 Oak Close, Worksop, Nottinghamshire, S80 1GH
✉ allbeers@oakclose.orangehome.co.uk
Shop open during licensing hours
Tours by arrangement

The brewery became operational in early 2007 and is housed in a converted stable block at the Packet Inn. The recipes for the re-named beers were purchased from Broadstone Brewery when that closed in 2006. Around 100 outlets are supplied. Further expansion of the brewery and distribution system is planned. Seasonal beers: Snowmans Folly (ABV 4.2%, Oct-Mar), Winters Dream (ABV 4.5%, Oct-Mar).

Two Water Grog (OG 1040, ABV 4%)

Lady Julia (OG 1042, ABV 4.3%)

Lady Catherine (OG 1044, ABV 4.5%)

Blondie (OG 1046, ABV 4.8%)

Lady Mary (OG 1050, ABV 5%)

Grain

Grain Brewery, South Farm, Tunbeck Road, Alburgh, Harleston, Norfolk, IP20 0BS
☎ (01986) 788884
✉ info@grainbrewery.co.uk
🌐 grainbrewery.co.uk
Shop Mon-Sat 10am-5pm
Tours by arrangement

Grain Brewery was launched in 2006 by friends, Geoff Wright (former Marketing Manager at Adnams) and Phil Halls. The five-barrel brewery is located in a converted dairy on a farm in the Waveney Valley. 80 local outlets are supplied. Seasonal beers: Blonde Ash Wheat Beer (ABV 4%), Winter Spice (ABV 4.6%).

Oak (OG 1038, ABV 3.8%) ◆
Amber-coloured with a swirling hop and malt aroma. A barrage of hoppy bitterness greets the drinker. Malt provides a sustained counterpoint throughout.

Redwood (ABV 4.5%)
A dark and malty traditional ale balanced with light bitterness and fruity sweetness.

Blackwood Stout (OG 1048, ABV 5%)

Ported Porter (OG 1050, ABV 5.2%)
An old-style porter. Smooth and creamy, spiked with port to give it the flavour of dark berries.

Tamarind IPA (ABV 5.5%) ◆
A classic IPA style beer with an overtly bitter signature. Hops dominate the nose and combine with the bitterness to give a clean, grapefruit dryness. Malt gives both depth and balance.

Grainstore SIBA

Davis'es Brewing Co Ltd (Grainstore), Grainstore Brewery, Station Approach, Oakham, Rutland, LE15 6RE
☎ **(01572) 770065**
✉ **grainstorebry@aol.com**
🌐 **grainstorebrewery.com**
Tours by arrangement

Grainstore, the smallest county's largest brewery, has been in production since 1995. The brewery's curious name comes from the fact that it was founded by Tony Davis and Mike Davies. After 30 years in the industry Tony decided to set up his own business after finding a derelict Victorian railway grainstore building. 80 outlets are supplied. Seasonal beers: Springtime (ABV 4.5%, Mar-May), Tupping Ale (ABV 4.5%, Sep-Oct), Three Kings (ABV 4.5%, Nov-Dec). Bottle-conditioned beer is also available.

Rutland Panther (OG 1034, ABV 3.4%)
This superb reddish-black mild punches above its weight with malt and roast flavours combining to deliver a brew that can match the average stout for intensity of flavour.

Cooking Bitter (OG 1036, ABV 3.6%)
Tawny-coloured beer with malt and hops on the nose and a pleasant grainy mouthfeel. Hops and fruit flavours combine to give a bitterness that continues into a long finish.

Triple B (OG 1042, ABV 4.2%)
Initially hops dominate over malt in both the aroma and taste, but fruit is there, too. All three linger in varying degrees in the sweetish aftertaste of this brown brew.

Gold (OG 1045, ABV 4.5%)
A refreshing, light beer with a complex blend of mellow malt and sweetness, balanced against a subtle floral aroma and smooth bitterness.

Ten Fifty (OG 1050, ABV 5%)
Full-bodied, mid-brown strong bitter with a hint of malt on the nose. Malt, hops and fruitiness coalesce in a well-balanced taste; bittersweet finish.

Rutland Beast (OG 1053, ABV 5.3%)
A strong beer, dark brown in colour. Well-balanced flavours blend together to produce a full-bodied drink.

Nip (OG 1073, ABV 7.7%)
A true barley wine. A good balance of sweetness and bitterness meld together so that neither predominates over the other. Smooth and warming.

Great Gable

Great Gable Brewing Co Ltd, Wasdale Head Inn, Gosforth, Cumbria, CA20 1EX
☎ **(019467) 26229**
✉ **wasdaleheadinn@msn.com**
🌐 **greatgablebrewing.com**
Tours by arrangement

Based at the Wasdale Head Inn, the brewery lies at the foot of England's highest mountain (Scafell Pike), near its deepest lake (Wastwater) and its smallest church (St Olaf's). Howard Christie and Giles Holiday set up the five-barrel brewery in 2002. It uses its own spring water from Yewbarrow Fell. Only the Wasdale Head Inn is supplied. Occasional and seasonal beers: Liar (ABV 3.4%), Wry'nose (ABV 4%, Easter-Oct), Lingmell (ABV 4.1%), Brown Tongue (ABV 5.2%). Bottle-conditioned beer is sometimes available.

Great Gable (OG 1035, ABV 3.7%)
Refreshing hoppy, fruity bitter with a pleasant, bitter aftertaste.

Trail (OG 1036, ABV 3.8%)

Britain's Favourite View (OG 1038, ABV 3.9%)

Burnmoor Pale Ale (OG 1040, ABV 4.2%)
A dry, hoppy bitter, refreshing and clean-tasting. Straw-coloured with with a fruity taste and grapefruit overtones. Long, bitter finish.

Wasd'ale (OG 1042, ABV 4.4%)

Scawfell (OG 1046, ABV 4.8%)

Illgill IPA (OG 1048, ABV 5%)

Yewbarrow (OG 1054, ABV 5.5%)
Strong, mild dark ale with robust roast flavours, rich and malty. Satisfying, with hints of spice and fruit. Smooth, chocolate and coffee aromas.

Great Heck*

Great Heck Brewing Company Ltd, Harwinn House, Main Street, Great Heck, North Yorkshire, DN14 0BQ
☎ **(01977) 661430**
☎ **07723 381002**
✉ **greatheckbrewery@harwinnhouse.co.uk**

Great Heck began production in May 2008 on a four-barrel plant in a converted slaughterhouse.

YPA (OG 1034, ABV 4.2%)

Special Bitter (OG 1036, ABV 4.5%)

Slaughterhouse Porter (OG 1042, ABV 5.4%)

Great Newsome

Great Newsome Brewery Ltd, Great Newsome Farm, South Frodingham, Winestead, East Yorkshire, HU12 0NR
☎ **(01964) 612201**
☎ **07808 367386**
✉ **enquiries@greatnewsomebrewery.co.uk**
🌐 **greatnewsomebrewery.co.uk**

Nestled in the Holderness countryside, Great Newsome began production in spring 2007 on a 10-barrel plant, brewing in renovated farm buildings. Beer is distributed throughout East, North and South Yorkshire as well as North Lincolnshire. Seasonal beer: Holderness Dark (ABV 3.4%, Apr-May & winter), Yule Do (ABV 4.3%, Xmas).

Sleck Dust (OG 1035, ABV 3.8%)

Stoney Binks (OG 1040, ABV 4.1%)

Pricky Back Otchan (OG 1039, ABV 4.2%)

Frothingham Best (OG 1041, ABV 4.3%)

Great Oakley

Great Oakley Brewery, Bridge Farm, 11 Brooke Road, Great Oakley, Northamptonshire, NN18 8HG
☎ (01536) 744888
✉ sales@greatoakleybrewery.co.uk
🌐 greatoakleybrewery.co.uk
Tours by arrangement

The brewery is housed in converted stables on a former working farm. Partners Mike Evans and Phil Greenway started production in 2005 and supply more than 50 outlets, including the Malt Shovel Tavern, Northampton, which is the brewery tap. Seasonal beer: Wobbly Santa (ABV 4.8%, Xmas). Bottle-conditioned beers are also available.

Welland Valley Mild (OG 1037, ABV 3.6%)
A dark, traditional mild. Full of flavour.

Wagtail (OG 1040, ABV 3.9%)
Light coloured with a unique bitterness derived from New Zealand hops.

Wot's Occurring (OG 1040, ABV 3.9%)
A mid-golden session bitter with a subtle hop finish.

Harpers (OG 1045, ABV 4.3%)
Traditional mid-brown bitter with a malty taste and slight hints of chocolate and citrus in the finish.

Gobble (OG 1046, ABV 4.5%)
Straw-coloured with a pleasant hop aftertaste.

Delapre Dark (OG 1046, ABV 4.6%)
A dark, full-bodied ale made from five different malts.

Tailshaker (OG 1051, ABV 5%)
A complex golden ale with a great depth of flavour.

Great Orme

Great Orme Brewery Ltd, Nant y Cywarch, Glan Conwy, Conwy, LL28 5PP
☎ (01492) 580548
✉ info@greatormebrewery.co.uk
🌐 greatormebrewery.co.uk

Great Orme is a five-barrel micro-brewery situated on a hillside in the Conwy Valley between Llandudno and Betws-y-Coed, with views of the Conwy Estuary and the Great Orme. Established in 2005, it is housed in a number of converted farm buildings. Around 50 outlets are supplied.

Welsh Mountain IPA (OG 1040, ABV 3.8%)
A modern IPA with a full hop flavour and dry finish.

Welsh Black (OG 1042, ABV 4%)
Rich, dark and full of malt flavours.

Orme's Best (OG 1043, ABV 4.2%)
Malty best bitter with a dry finish. Faint hop and fruit notes in aroma and taste, but malt dominates throughout.

Celtic Dragon (OG 1045, ABV 4.5%)
Yellow in colour with a zesty taste full of citrus fruit flavours. Some initial sweetness followed by peppery hops and a bitter finish.

Three Feathers (OG 1051, ABV 5%)
A strong ale with balanced hop bitterness and sweet malt.

Great Western*

Great Western Brewing Company Limited, Stream Bakery, Bristol Road, Hambrook, Bristol, BS16 1RF
☎ (0117) 957 2842
✉ greatwesternbrewing@hotmail.co.uk
🌐 greatwesternbrewingcompany.co.uk
Tours by arrangement

Great Western is a 12-barrel brewery set up in March 2008 by Kevin Stone in a former bakery. Traditional brewing techniques are used and steam power has been employed. Four more permanent beers will be available along with seasonal beers in the near future. Four outlets are supplied direct and one pub is owned.

Maiden Voyage (OG 1038, ABV 4%)

Classic Gold (OG 1042, ABV 4.6%)

Green Dragon

Green Dragon Brewery, Green Dragon, 29 Broad Street, Bungay, Suffolk, NR35 1EF
☎ (01986) 892681
Tours by arrangement

The Green Dragon pub was purchased from Brent Walker in 1991 and the buildings at the rear converted to a brewery. In 1994 the plant was expanded and moved into a converted barn across the car park. The doubling of capacity allowed the production of a larger range of ales, including seasonal and occasional brews. The beers are available at the pub and beer festivals. Seasonal beers: Mild (ABV 5%, autumn/winter), Wynnter Warmer (ABV 6.5%).

Chaucer Ale (OG 1037, ABV 3.7%)

Gold (OG 1045, ABV 4.4%)

Bridge Street Bitter (OG 1046, ABV 4.5%)

Strong Mild (ABV 5.4%)

Greene King

See under New Nationals section

Greenfield SIBA

Greenfield Real Ale Brewery, Unit 8 Waterside Mills, Greenfield, Saddleworth, Greater Manchester, OL3 7NH
☎ (01457) 879789
✉ office@greenfieldrealale.co.uk
🌐 greenfieldrealale.co.uk
Shop 9am-5pm daily
Tours by arrangement

Greenfield was launched in 2002 by Peter Percival, former brewer at Saddleworth. Tony Harratt joined Peter in 2005 as a partner. 100-120 outlets are supplied.

Black Five (OG 1040, ABV 4%)

Celebration (OG 1040, ABV 4%)

Dovestones Bitter (OG 1040, ABV 4%)

Monkey Business (OG 1041, ABV 4%) ◆
Yellow in colour with a fruit and hop aroma. Hops and grapefruit in the mouth, with a dry, astringent finish.

Bill O'Jacks (OG 1041, ABV 4.1%)

Delph Donkey (OG 1041, ABV 4.1%)

Castleshaw (OG 1041, ABV 4.2%)

Dobcross Bitter (OG 1041, ABV 4.2%)

Evening Glory (OG 1041, ABV 4.2%)

Ice Breaker (OG 1041, ABV 4.2%)

Pride of England (OG 1041, ABV 4.2%)

Uppermill Ale (OG 1041, ABV 4.2%)

Brassed Off (OG 1044, ABV 4.4%)

Friezeland Ale (OG 1044, ABV 4.4%)

Icicle (OG 1044, ABV 4.4%)

Longwood Thump (OG 1050, ABV 4.5%)

Rudolph's Tipple (OG 1050, ABV 5%)

Green Jack

Green Jack Brewing Co Ltd, 29 St Peters Street, Lowestoft, Suffolk, NR32 1QA
☎ (01502) 582711
🌐 greenjackbrewery.co.uk
Tours by arrangement

⊗ Green Jack started brewing in 2003. 20 outlets are supplied and two pubs are owned. In 2008 an old Lowestoft smoke house was purchased and will be used for extra brewing capacity on a 35-barrel plant. Seasonal ales: Honey Bunny (ABV 4%, spring), Summer Dream (ABV 4%).

Canary (OG 1038, ABV 3.8%)

Orange Wheat (OG 1042, ABV 4.2%) ◆
Beatifully balanced with a golden colour. Slightly bitter on the tongue but with a strong fruit flavour and a complex aroma and aftertaste.

Grasshopper (OG 1045, ABV 4.6%)

Lurcher Stout (OG 1047, ABV 4.8%)

Mahseer IPA (OG 1048, ABV 5%)

Gone Fishing (OG 1052, ABV 5.5%)

Ripper (OG 1074, ABV 8.5%)

Green Mill*

Green Mill Brewery, Queensway Snooker Club, Green Mill, Well'ith, Rochdale, OL11 2LS
☎ 07896 702328
✉ greenmillbrewery@msn.com
Green Mill started brewing in July 2007 on a 2.5-barrel plant. Seasonal beer are available.

Gold (ABV 3.6%)

Hop Crop (ABV 3.9%)

Chief (ABV 4.2%)

Northern Lights (ABV 4.5%)

Green Tye EAB

Green Tye Brewery, Green Tye, Much Hadham, Hertfordshire, SG10 6JP
☎ (01279) 841041
✉ info@gtbrewery.co.uk
🌐 gtbrewery.co.uk
Tours by arrangement for small groups

⊗ Established in 1999 near Much Hadham, on the edge of the Ash Valley. The local free trade and neighbouring counties are supplied, and further afield via beer agencies and swaps with other micro-breweries. Cask beers are also available bottle conditioned. Seasonal beers: Snowdrop (ABV 3.9%, winter/spring), Mad Morris (ABV 4.2%, summer), Green Tiger (ABV 4.2%, summer), Autumn Rose (ABV 4.2%), Conkerer (ABV 4.7%, autumn), Coal Porter (ABV 4.5%, winter).

Union Jack (OG 1036, ABV 3.6%)
A copper-coloured bitter, fruity with a citrus taste and a hoppy, citrus aroma, with a balanced, bitter finish.

Hertfordshire Hedgehog (OG 1042, ABV 4%)
Traditional, chestnut-coloured bitter with a deep, hoppy nose. Starts soft and full with malt fruit flavours and bitterness, developing through to a full bitter finish.

East Anglian Gold (OG 1042, ABV 4.2%)

Gribble

Gribble Brewery Ltd, Gribble Inn, Oving, West Sussex, PO20 2BP
☎ 07813 321795
✉ gribblebeers@hotmail.co.uk
🌐 gribblebrewery.co.uk

⊗ The Gribble Brewery is more than 25 years old. Until 2005 it was run as a managed house operation by Hall & Woodhouse (qv) but it is now an independent micro-brewery owned by Brian Elderfield, the previous manager. Seasonal beer: Wobbler (ABV 7.2%).

Slurping Stoat (ABV 3.8%)

Toff's Ale (ABV 4%)

Best Bitter (ABV 4.1%)

Reg's Tipple (ABV 5%)
Reg's Tipple was named after a customer from the early days of the brewery. It has a smooth nutty flavour with a pleasant afterbite.

Plucking Pheasant (ABV 5.2%)

Pig's Ear (ABV 5.8%)

Griffin Inn*

Griffin Inn Brewery, Church Road, Shustoke, Warwickshire, B46 2LB
☎ (01675) 481208

Brewing started in April 2008 in the old coffin shop premises adjacent to the pub (formerly occupied by Church End Brewery) on a 2.5-barrel plant. The brewery is a venture between Griffin licensee Mick Pugh and his son Oliver. At present the brewery only supplies the Griffin but will supply festivals and other pubs as output grows.

'Ere It Is (OG 1045, ABV 4.5%)
A light, hoppy bitter.

Grindleton*

Grindleton Brewhouse Ltd, 12 Deanfield Way, Link 59 Business Park, Clitheroe, Lancashire, BB7 1QU
☎ (01200) 444808
✉ enquiries@grindletonbrewhouse.co.uk
⊕ grindletonbrewhouse.co.uk
Tours by arrangement

Grindleton began brewing in February 2007 in Bolton-by-Bowland on a five-barrel plant and moved to larger premises in April 2007. Further purchases of brewing vessels mean that capacity now approaches 60 barrels a week. An on-site retail shop is planned selling their own ales (bottled and cask) plus other UK and Continental bottled beers. It currently supplies pubs and clubs all over the north of England, concentrating mainly on GBG entries and outlets with Cask Marque accreditation. Seasonal beer: Hairy Fairy (ABV 4%).

Ribble Bitter (OG 1038, ABV 3.7%)

Ribble Rouser (OG 1039, ABV 3.8%)

Old Fecker (OG 1040.5, ABV 4%)

Ribble Gold (OG 1041.5, ABV 4.1%)

Lancashire Pale Ale (OG 1045, ABV 4.5%)

Farleys Dusk (OG 1055, ABV 5.5%)

Man Down (OG 1060, ABV 6%)

Gwynant

Bragdy Gwynant, Tynllidiart Arms, Capel Bangor, Aberystwyth, Ceredigion, SY23 3LR
☎ (01970) 880248
Tours by arrangement

Brewing started in 2004 in a building at the front of the pub, measuring just 4ft 6ins by 4ft, with a brew length of nine gallons. Beer is only sold in the pub. The brewery has now been recognised as the smallest commercial brewery in the world by the Guinness Book of Records.

Cwrw Gwynant (OG 1044, ABV 4.2%)

Hadrian & Border SIBA

Alnwick Ales Ltd t/a Hadrian & Border Brewery, Unit 11, Hawick Crescent Industrial Estate, Newcastle upon Tyne, Tyne & Wear, NE6 1AS
☎ (0191) 276 5302
✉ hadrianborder@yahoo.co.uk
⊕ hadrian-border-brewery.co.uk
Tours by arrangement

Hadrian & Border is based at the former Four Rivers 20-barrel site in Newcastle. The company's brands are available from Glasgow to Yorkshire, and nationally through wholesalers. They are hard to find on Tyneside, though the Sir John Fitzgerald group stocks them from time to time. Approximately 100 outlets are supplied.

Gladiator (OG 1036, ABV 3.8%) ◆
Tawny-coloured bitter with plenty of malt in the aroma and palate leading to a strong, bitter finish.

Tyneside Blonde (OG 1037, ABV 3.9%)

Farne Island Pale Ale (OG 1038, ABV 4%) ◆
A copper-coloured bitter with a refreshing malt/hop balance.

Flotsam (OG 1038, ABV 4%)
Bronze coloured with a citrus bitterness and a distinctive floral aroma.

Legion Ale (OG 1040, ABV 4.2%) ◆
Well-balanced, amber-coloured beer, full bodied with good malt flavours. Well hopped with a long bitter finish.

Newcastle Pioneer (ABV 4.2%)

Secret Kingdom (OG 1042, ABV 4.3%)
Dark, rich and full-bodied, slightly roasted with a malty palate ending with a pleasant bitterness.

Reiver's IPA (OG 1042, ABV 4.4%)
Golden bitter with a clean citrus palate and aroma with subtle malt flavours breaking through at the end.

Centurion Best Bitter (OG 1043, ABV 4.5%) ◆
Smooth, clean tasting bitter with a distinct hop palate leading to a good bitter finish.

Jetsam (OG 1043, ABV 4.5%)
Light-coloured, refreshing and clean tasting. Dry hopped with Styrian Goldings.

Halifax Steam

Halifax Steam Brewing Co Ltd, The Conclave, Southedge Works, Brighouse Road, Hipperholme, West Yorkshire, HX3 8EF
☎ 07974 544980
✉ david@halifax-steam.co.uk
⊕ halifax-steam.co.uk

Halifax Steam was established in 2001 on a five-barrel plant and only supplies its brewery tap, the Cock o' the North, which is adjacent to the brewery. Approximately 100 different rotating beers are produced, three of which are permanent. The brewery also produces the only rice beers in the country. 10 Halifax Steam beers are available at any one time, plus occasional guests on a fair trade basis.

Jamaican Ginger (ABV 4%)

Uncle John (ABV 4.3%)

Cock o' the North (ABV 5%) ◆
Amber-coloured, grainy strong bitter, predominately malty nose and taste, with a dry and astringent finish.

Hall & Woodhouse IFBB

Hall & Woodhouse Ltd, Blandford St Mary, Blandford Forum, Dorset, DT11 9LS
☎ (01258) 452141
✉ info@hall-woodhouse.co.uk
⊕ hall-woodhouse.co.uk
Shop Mon-Sat 9am-6pm; Sun 11am-3pm (Easter-Oct)
Tours by arrangement (Call 01258 452141 to book)

Founded by Charles Hall in 1777, Hall & Woodhouse is an independent family brewer, today run by the fifth generation of the Woodhouse family. The Badger logo was adopted in 1875. The company moved from Ansty to its present site in 1900 and a new brewery is planned on part of the current site. Cask beer is sold in all 260 pubs. Seasonal beers: Hopping Hare (ABV 4.5%, Feb-May), Fursty Ferret (ABV 4.4%, Jun-Sep), Pickled Partridge (ABV 4.6%, Nov-Jan).

K&B Sussex Bitter (OG 1033, ABV 3.5%) ◆
Well-flavoured session bitter with hints of toffee and roast malts. It has the fruitiness common in all Badger beers, but with a drier character than the others.

First Gold (OG 1040, ABV 4%) ◆
Appetising aroma with pear fruitiness gives way to a more restrained bittersweet flavour. Hops in evidence throughout with fruit returning in the aftertaste.

Tanglefoot (OG 1047, ABV 4.9%) ◆
A complex, satisfying beer that retains an easy drinking balance. Aromas of bananas and caramel and a sweetish, malty and fruity flavour. Long, bittersweet finish with echoes of the fruit aromas.

Hambleton SIBA

Nick Stafford Hambleton Ales, Melmerby Green Road, Melmerby, North Yorkshire, HG4 5NB
☎ (01765) 640108
✉ sales@hambletonales.co.uk
🌐 hambletonales.co.uk
Shop Mon-Fri 7.30am-5pm
Tours by arrangement

Hambleton Ales was established in 1991 on the banks of the River Swale in the heart of the Vale of York. Expansion over the years has resulted in relocation to larger premises on several occasions, the last being December 2007. Brewing capacity has increased to 100 barrels a week and a bottling line caters for micros and larger brewers, handling more than 20 brands. More than 100 outlets are supplied throughout Yorkshire and the North-east. Five core brands are produced along with an additional special brew each month. The company also brew beers under contract for the Village Brewer.

Bitter (ABV 3.8%)
A golden bitter with a good balance of malty and refreshing citrus notes leading to a mellow, tangy finish.

Goldfield (OG 1041, ABV 4.2%) ◆
A light amber bitter with good hop character and increasing dryness. A fine blend of malts gives a smooth overall impression.

Stallion (OG 1041, ABV 4.2%) ◆
A premium bitter, moderately hoppy throughout and richly balanced in malt and fruit, developing a sound and robust bitterness, with earthy hops drying the aftertaste.

Stud (OG 1042.5, ABV 4.3%) ◆
A strongly bitter beer, with rich hop and fruit. It ends dry and spicy.

Nightmare (OG 1050, ABV 5%) ◆
This impressively flavoured beer satisfies all parts of the palate. Strong roast malts dominate, but hoppiness rears out of this complex blend.

For Black Dog Brewery, Whitby:

Whitby Abbey Ale (ABV 3.8%)

Schooner (ABV 4.2%)

Rhatas (ABV 4.6%)

For Village Brewer:

White Boar (OG 1037.5, ABV 3.8%) ◆
A light, flowery and fruity ale; crisp, clean and refreshing, with a dry-hopped, powerful but not aggressive bitter finish.

Bull (OG 1039, ABV 4%) ◆
A pale, full, fruity bitter, well hopped to give a lingering bitterness.

Old Raby (OG 1045, ABV 4.8%) ◆
A full-bodied, smooth, rich-tasting dark ale. A complex balance of malt, fruit character and creamy caramel sweetness offsets the bitterness.

Hammerpot

Hammerpot Brewery Ltd, Unit 30, The Vinery, Arundel Road, Poling, West Sussex, BN18 9PY
☎ (01903) 883338
✉ info@hammerpot-brewery.co.uk
🌐 hammerpot-brewery.co.uk
Tours by arrangement

Hammerpot started brewing in 2005 and the brew plant has recently been upgraded to a five-barrel brew-length. The brewery supplies a wide area between Portsmouth and Newhaven and north to the M25. All cask beers are available in bottle-conditioned form. Seasonal beers: Martlet (ABV 3.5%, Apr-Sep), Bottle Wreck Porter (ABV 4.7%, Oct-Mar).

Meteor (OG 1038, ABV 3.8%)

White Wing (OG 1039, ABV 4%)

Red Hunter (OG 1046, ABV 4.3%)

Woodcote (OG 1047, ABV 4.5%)

Madgwick Gold (OG 1050, ABV 5%)

Hampshire SIBA

Hampshire Brewery Ltd, Unit 6, Romsey Industrial Estate, Romsey, Hampshire, SO51 0HR
☎ (01794) 830529
✉ online@hampshirebrewery.com
🌐 hampshirebrewery.com
Shop Mon-Fri 9am-4pm; Sat 10am-1pm
Tours by arrangement

Hampshire was founded in 1992 and moved to its present site in 2002. All the beers are also available in bottle-conditioned form. The brewery produces five core beers, monthly specials, and other seasonal beers over longer three to four month periods: see website for full details. 150 outlets are supplied. Seasonal beers: King's Ransom (ABV 4.8%, May-Sep), Penny Black Porter (ABV 4.5%, Nov-Apr). The entire range of bottled beers is suitable for vegetarians and vegans.

King Alfred's (OG 1037, ABV 3.8%) ◆
A pale brown session beer featuring a malty aroma with some hops and fruit. Rather thin but well-balanced citrus taste with plenty of malt and a dry, bitter finish.

Strong's Best Bitter (OG 1037, ABV 3.8%) ◆

Named after the original Romsey Brewery, this tawny-coloured bitter is predominantly malty. An initially hoppy aroma gives way to an increasingly bitter finish.

Ironside (OG 1041, ABV 4.2%) ◆
A clean-tasting, flavoursome best bitter with a fruit and hops aroma. Hops are predominant but balanced by malt, fruit and a hint of sweetness. The finish is long and dry.

Lionheart (OG 1042, ABV 4.5%) ◆
This golden beer has a hoppy aroma with a sharp citrus flavour that builds into a dry, hoppy finish.

Pride of Romsey (OG 1050, ABV 5%) ◆
A strong citrus aroma leads to a beautifully-balanced mix of fruit and hops that continues to build in the aftertaste.

Hanby SIBA

Hanby Ales Ltd, Aston Park, Soulton Road, Wem, Shropshire, SY4 5SD
☎ (01939) 232432
✉ info@hanbyales.co.uk
🌐 hanbyales.co.uk
Tours by arrangement

Hanby was set up in 1988 by Jack Hanby following the closure of the Shrewsbury & Wem Brewery. The aim was to continue the 200 year-old tradition of brewing in the area. In 1990 the brewery moved to its present home and has been upgraded to 30-barrel production runs. Hanby supplies 250-300 outlets. Seasonal beer: Green Admiral (ABV 4.5%, Sep-Oct).

Pure Gold (OG 1037, ABV 3.7%)

Drawwell Bitter (OG 1039, ABV 3.9%) ◆
A hoppy beer with excellent bitterness, both in taste and aftertaste. Beautiful amber colour.

Black Magic Mild (OG 1041, ABV 4%) ◆
A dark, reddish-brown mild, which is dry and bitter with a roast malt taste.

All Seasons (OG 1042, ABV 4.2%)
A light, hoppy bitter, well balanced and thirst quenching, brewed with a fine blend of Cascade and Fuggles hops.

Harry's Beer (OG 1042, ABV 4.2%)

Rainbow Chaser (OG 1043, ABV 4.3%)
A pale beer brewed with Styrian Goldings hops.

Wem Special (OG 1044, ABV 4.4%)
A pale, straw-coloured, smooth, hoppy bitter.

Cascade (OG 1045, ABV 4.5%)
A pale beer, brewed with Cascade hops, producing a clean crisp flavour and a hoppy finish.

Golden Honey (OG 1045, ABV 4.5%)
A beer made with the addition of Australian honey. Not over sweet.

Scorpio Porter (OG 1045, ABV 4.5%)
A dark porter with a complex palate introducing hints of coffee and chocolate, contrasting and complementing the background hoppiness.

Shropshire Stout (OG 1044, ABV 4.5%)
A full-bodied, rich ruby/black coloured stout. A blend of four malts produces a distinct chocolate malt dry flavour, with a mushroom-coloured head.

Premium (OG 1046, ABV 4.6%)
An amber-coloured beer that is sweeter and fruitier than most of the beers above. Slight malt and hop taste.

Old Wemian (OG 1049, ABV 4.9%)
Golden-brown colour with an aroma of malt and hops and a soft, malty palate.

Taverners (OG 1053, ABV 5.3%)
A smooth and fruity old ale, full of body.

Cherry Bomb (OG 1060, ABV 6%)
A splendid rich and fruity beer with maraschino cherry flavour.

Joy Bringer (OG 1060, ABV 6%)
Deceptively strong beer with a distinct ginger flavour.

Nutcracker (OG 1060, ABV 6%)
Tawny beer with a fine blend of malt and hops.

Hardknott

Hardknott Brewery t/a Woolpack Inn, Boot, Cumbria, CA19 1TH
☎ (019467) 23230
✉ enquiries@woolpack.co.uk
🌐 woolpack.co.uk
Tours by arrangement

Hardknott Brewery opened in 2005 using a two-barrel plant. The beers are only available at the Woolpack. Seasonal beers are also brewed including Woolly Fusion (ABV 4.2%, Jun).

Woolpacker (ABV 3.8%)

Wooliness (ABV 4%)

Lauters Lamm (ABV 4.3%)

Tenacity (ABV 4.8%)

Hardys & Hansons

See Greene King in New Nationals section

Hart

Hart Brewery Ltd, Cartford Inn & Restaurant, Cartford Lane, Little Eccleston, Lancashire, PR3 0YP
☎ (01995) 671686
✉ johnsmith@hartbreweryltd.co.uk
🌐 hartbreweryltd.co.uk
Tours by arrangement

The brewery opened 1995 behind the Cartford Hotel on rural Lancashire's Fylde Plain. Hart supplies a number of local outlets and arranges exchanges with other micro-breweries. Monthly specials are also available.

Temptress (OG 1039, ABV 3.9%)

Dishy Debbie (OG 1040, ABV 4%)

Ice Maiden (OG 1040, ABV 4%) ◆
Hoppy, crisp, straw-coloured bitter with floral notes and a dry finish.

Squirrels Hoard (OG 1040, ABV 4%)

Nemesis (OG 1041, ABV 4.1%)

Cait-Lin Gold (OG 1042, ABV 4.2%)

Hart of Stebbing*

Hart of Stebbing Brewery Ltd, White Hart, High Street, Stebbing, Essex, CM6 3SQ
☎ (01371) 856383
✉ bobdovey@tiscali.co.uk
hartofstebbingbrewery.co.uk
Tours by arrangement

The brewery was established in summer 2007 by Bob Dovey and Nick Eldred, who is also the owner of the White Hart pub where the brewery is based. More beers are planned. At present only the White Hart and local beer festivals are supplied.

Hart Throb (OG 1036, ABV 3.8%)

Hart Beat (OG 1042, ABV 4.4%)

Harveys IFBB

Harvey & Son (Lewes) Ltd, Bridge Wharf Brewery, 6 Cliffe High Street, Lewes, East Sussex, BN7 2AH
☎ (01273) 480209
✉ maj@harveys.org.uk
harveys.org.uk
Shop Mon-Sat 9.30am-4.45pm
Tours by arrangement (currently two year waiting list)

Established in 1790, this independent family brewery operates from the banks of the River Ouse in Lewes. A major development in 1985 doubled the brewhouse capacity and subsequent additional fermenting capacity has seen production rise to more than 38,000 barrels a year. Harveys supplies real ale to all its 48 pubs and 450 free trade outlets in Sussex and Kent. Seasonal beers: see website. Bottle-conditioned beer is also available.

Sussex XX Mild Ale (OG 1030, ABV 3%)
A dark copper-brown colour. Roast malt dominates the aroma and palate leading to a sweet, caramel finish.

Hadlow Bitter (OG 1033, ABV 3.5%)
Formerly Sussex Pale Ale

Sussex Best Bitter (OG 1040, ABV 4%)
Full-bodied brown bitter. A hoppy aroma leads to a good malt and hop balance, and a dry aftertaste.

Armada Ale (OG 1045, ABV 4.5%)
Hoppy amber best bitter. Well-balanced fruit and hops dominate throughout with a fruity palate.

Harviestoun SIBA

Harviestoun Brewery Ltd, Alva Industrial Estate, Alva, Clackmannanshire, FK12 5DQ
☎ (01259) 769100
✉ info@harviestoun.com
harviestoun.com
Tours by arrangement

Harviestoun started in a barn in the village of Dollar in 1985 with a five-barrel brew plant, but now operate on a state-of-the-art 60-barrel brewery in Alva. The brewery supplies local outlets direct and nationwide via wholesalers. It was bought by Caledonian Brewing Co in 2006 but is now independent following the takeover of Caledonian by Scottish & Newcastle in April 2008. Further expansion is planned. Seasonal beers: see website.

Bitter & Twisted (OG 1036, ABV 3.8%)
Refreshingly hoppy beer with fruit throughout. A bittersweet taste with a long bitter finish. A golden session beer.

Ptarmigan (OG 1045, ABV 4.5%)
A well-balanced, bittersweet beer in which hops and malt dominate. The blend of malt, hops and fruit produces a clean, hoppy aftertaste.

Schiehallion (OG 1048, ABV 4.8%)
A Scottish cask lager, brewed using a lager yeast and Hersbrucker hops. A hoppy aroma, with fruit and malt, leads to a malty, bitter taste with floral hoppiness and a bitter finish.

Harwich Town* EAB

Harwich Town Brewing Company, Station Approach, Harwich, Essex, CO12 3NA
☎ (01255) 551155
✉ info@harwichtown.co.uk
harwichtown.co.uk
Shop – see website
Tours by arrangement

Brewing started in June 2007 on a five-barrel plant next to Harwich Town railway station. The brewer is a CAMRA member and former customs officer. All beers are named after local landmarks. 50 outlets are supplied. Seasonal beers: Mayflower (ABV 4%, summer), Electric Palace Ale/EPA (ABV 4%, summer), Harwich Old (ABV 6.7%, winter). An annual festival special is brewed for Harwich Beer Festival.

Ha'Penny Mild (ABV 3.6%)

Leading Lights (ABV 3.8%)

Misleading Lights (ABV 4%)

Lighthouse Bitter (ABV 4.2%)

Redoubt Stout (ABV 4.2%)

Parkeston Porter (ABV 4.5%)

Hawkshead SIBA

Hawkshead Brewery Ltd, Mill Yard, Staveley, Cumbria, LA8 9LR
☎ (01539) 822644
✉ info@hawksheadbrewery.co.uk
hawksheadbrewery.co.uk
Shop open 12-5pm daily

Hawkshead Brewery is based in Staveley, between Kendal and Windermere in the Lake District. The brewery complex is a showcase for real ale and contains a purpose-built 20-barrel brewery and the Beer Hall, which is a brewery tap, beer shop, visitor centre and dining room. The brewery expanded in 2006, having outgrown its original site (opened in 2002) in a barn at Hawkshead. More than 100 outlets are supplied direct.

Bitter (OG 1037, ABV 3.7%)

Well-balanced, thirst-quenching beer with fruit and hops aroma, leading to a lasting bitter finish.

UPA/Ulverston Pale Ale (OG 1041, ABV 4.1%)
A very pale ale, using three English hops.

Red (OG 1042, ABV 4.2%)
A red ale; malty and spicy, with a long dry finish.

Lakeland Gold (OG 1043, ABV 4.4%)
Fresh, well-balanced fruity, hoppy beer with a clean bitter aftertaste.

Lakeland Lager (OG 1045, ABV 4.8%)
A cask-conditioned lager.

Brodie's Prime (OG 1048, ABV 4.9%)
Complex, dark brown beer with plenty of malt, fruit and roast taste. Satisfying full body with clean finish.

Haywood Bad Ram

Haywood Bad Ram Brewery, Callow Top Holiday Park, Sandybrook, Ashbourne, Derbyshire, DE6 2AQ
☎ 07974 948427
✉ acphaywood@aol.com
callowtop.co.uk
Shop 9am-5pm (seasonal)
Tours by arrangement

The brewery is based in a converted barn. There are plans for a bottling plant to supply own label beers. One pub is owned (on site) and several other outlets are supplied. The brewery is not operational during the winter.

Dr Samuel Johnson (ABV 4.5%)

Bad Ram (ABV 5%)

Lone Soldier (ABV 5%)

Woggle Dance (ABV 5%)

Callow Top IPA (ABV 5.2%)

Headless

The Headless Brewing Co Ltd, The Flowerpot, 19-25 King Street, Derby, Derbyshire, DE1 3DZ
☎ (01332) 204955

Headless is situated at the rear of the Flowerpot pub in Derby and was established in September 2007 on a 10-barrel plant. Seasonal beer: Ebenezer (ABV 6%, Xmas).

King Street Ale (KSA) (OG 1038, ABV 3.8%)

First Bloom (OG 1040, ABV 4.3%)

Owd Reg (OG 1046, ABV 5%)

Heart of Wales

Heart of Wales Brewery, Stables Yard, Zion Street, Llanwrtyd Wells, Powys, LD5 4RD
☎ (01591) 610236
✉ Lindsay@heartofwalesbrewery.co.uk
heartofwalesbrewery.co.uk
Shop 10am-6pm daily
Tours by arrangement

The brewery was set up with a six-barrel plant in 2006 in old stables at the rear of the Neuadd Arms Hotel. Selected ales are conditioned in oak barrels prior to being casked. Seasonal brews celebrate local events such as the World Bogsnorkelling Championships and the Man v Horse Marathon. Seasonal beers: Horseplay (ABV 4.2%, Jun-Jul), Boggled (ABV 4.5%, Aug-Sep), Drop Goaled (ABV 4.8%, Feb-Mar), High as a Kite (ABV 9.5%, Nov).

Aur Cymru (ABV 3.8%)

Bitter (ABV 4.1%)

Welsh Black (ABV 4.4%)

Noble Eden Ale (ABV 4.6%)

Innstable (ABV 5.5%)

Hebridean SIBA

Hebridean Brewing Co, 18a Bells Road, Stornoway, Isle of Lewis, HS1 2RA
☎ (01851) 700123
✉ info@hebridean-brewery.co.uk
hebridean-brewery.co.uk
Shop open in summer months only
Tours by arrangement

The company was set up in 2001 on a steam powered plant with a 14-barrel brew length. A shop is attached to the brewery. Seasonal beers are produced for Mods, Gaelic festivals that are the Scottish equivalent of the Welsh Eisteddfod.

Celtic Black Ale (OG 1036, ABV 3.9%)
A dark ale full of flavour, balancing an aromatic hop combined with a subtle bite and a pleasantly smooth caramel aftertaste.

Clansman Ale (OG 1036, ABV 3.9%)
A light Hebridean beer, brewed with Scottish malts and lightly hopped to give a subtle bittering.

Seaforth Ale (ABV 4.2%)
A golden beer in the continental style.

Islander Strong Premium Ale (OG 1044, ABV 4.8%)
A malty, fruity strong bitter drinking dangerously below its ABV.

Berserker Export Pale Ale (OG 1068, ABV 7.5%)
This malty, fruity 'winter warmer' is packed full of flavour, with toffee apple and caramel notes right through to the long, satisfying aftertaste.

Hektors*

Hektors Brewery Ltd, The Office, Park Farm Barns, Henham Park, Beccles, Suffolk, NR34 8AQ
☎ 07900 553426
✉ hektor@henhampark.com
hektorsbrewery.com

Hektors Brewery was formed orginally to sate the real ale appetites of visitors to the Latitude Music Festival on Henham Park in 2007. It was developed partly as a component of farm diversification but mostly for fun. 5 outlets are supplied direct.

Pure (OG 1038, ABV 3.8%)

Hepworth SIBA

Hepworth & Co Brewers Ltd, The Beer Station, Railway Yard, Horsham, West Sussex, RH12 2NW
☎ (01403) 269696
✉ mail@hepworthbrewery.co.uk
🌐 hepworthbrewery.co.uk
Sales 9am-6pm daily

Hepworth's was established in 2001, initially bottling beer only. In 2003 draught beer brewing was started with Sussex malt and hops. In 2004 an organic lager was introduced in bottle and on draught. 274 outlets are supplied. Seasonal beers: Summer Ale (ABV 3.4%), Harvest Ale (ABV 4.5%, autumn), Old Ale (ABV 4.8%, winter), Christmas Ale (ABV 7.5%), Cloud 9 (ABV 4.5%, spring).

Traditional Sussex Bitter (OG 1035, ABV 3.6%)
A fine, clean-tasting amber session beer. A bitter beer with a pleasant fruity and hoppy aroma that leads to a crisp, tangy taste. A long, dry finish.

Pullman First Class Ale (OG 1041, ABV 4.2%)
A sweet, nutty maltiness and fruitiness are balanced by hops and bitterness in this easy-drinking, pale brown best bitter. A subtle bitter aftertaste.

Prospect Organic (ABV 4.5%)
A well-balanced and traditional brew.

Classic Old Ale (OG 1046, ABV 4.8%)
A traditional winter brew, rich with a variety of roasted malts balanced with sweetness and the bitterness of Admiral hops.

Iron Horse (OG 1048, ABV 4.8%)
There's a fruity, toffee aroma to this light brown, full-bodied bitter. A citrus flavour balanced by caramel and malt leads to a clean, dry finish.

Hereward

Hereward Brewery, 50 Fleetwood, Ely, Cambridgeshire, CB6 1BH
☎ (01353) 666441
✉ michael.czarnobaj@ntlworld.com

A small home-based brewery launched in 2003 on a 10-gallon kit. The brewery supplies mainly beer festivals and also brews festival specials (brewed to order). Seasonal beer: Uncle Joe's Winter Ale (ABV 5%).

Bitter (ABV 3.8%)

St Ethelreda's Golden Bitter (ABV 4%)

Porta Porter (ABV 4.2%)

Oatmeal Stout (ABV 4.5%)

Hesket Newmarket SIBA

Hesket Newmarket Brewery Ltd, Old Crown Barn, Back Green, Hesket Newmarket, Cumbria, CA7 8JG
☎ (01697) 478066
✉ sales@hesketbrewery.co.uk
🌐 hesketbrewery.co.uk
Tours via Old Crown Inn – (01697) 478288

The brewery was established in 1988 and was bought by a co-operative of villagers in 1999, anxious to preserve a community resource. Most of the original recipes have been retained, all named after local fells except for Doris's 90th Birthday Ale. A 10-barrel plant was installed in 2004 followed small-scale bottling. Around 30 regular outlets are supplied. Bottle-conditioned beers are available.

Great Cockup Porter (OG 1035, ABV 3%)
A refreshing, dark and chocolaty porter with a dry finish.

Blencathra Bitter (OG 1035, ABV 3.3%)
A malty, tawny ale, mild and mellow for a bitter, with a dominant caramel flavour.

Skiddaw Special Bitter (OG 1037, ABV 3.6%)
An amber session beer, malty throughout, thin with a dryish finish.

Haystacks Refreshing Ale (OG 1037, ABV 3.7%)
A light, pale, refreshing beer with a zesty hop. Hint of grapefruit on the finish.

Helvellyn Gold (OG 1039, ABV 4%)

High Pike Dark Amber Bitter (OG 1042, ABV 4.2%)

Doris's 90th Birthday Ale (OG 1045, ABV 4.3%)
A full-bodied, nicely balanced malty beer with an increasing hop finish and butterscotch in the mouth.

Scafell Blonde (OG 1043, ABV 4.3%)
Pale with fruity hop notes. A good introduction to real ale for lager drinkers.

Catbells Pale Ale (OG 1050, ABV 5%)
A powerful golden ale with a well-balanced malty bitterness, ending with a bitter and decidedly dry aftertaste.

Old Carrock Strong Ale (OG 1060, ABV 6%)
A dark red, powerful ale.

Hexhamshire SIBA

Hexhamshire Brewery, Leafields, Ordley, Hexham, Northumberland, NE46 1SX
☎ (01434) 606577
✉ ghb@hexhamshire.co.uk

Hexhamshire was founded in 1992 and is operated by one of the founding partners and his family. 40 outlets are supplied direct. A relocation to the Dipton Mill Inn is planned in the near future.

Devil's Elbow (OG 1036, ABV 3.6%)
Amber brew full of hops and fruit, leading to a bitter finish.

Shire Bitter (OG 1037, ABV 3.8%)
A good balance of hops with fruity overtones, this amber beer makes an easy-drinking session bitter.

Devil's Water (OG 1041, ABV 4.1%)
Copper-coloured best bitter, well-balanced with a slightly fruity, hoppy finish.

Whapweasel (OG 1048, ABV 4.8%)
An interesting smooth, hoppy beer with a fruity flavour. Amber in colour, the bitter finish brings out the fruit and hops.

Old Humbug (OG 1055, ABV 5.5%)

Hidden SIBA

Hidden Brewery Ltd, Unit 1, Oakley Business Park, Wylye Road, Dinton, Salisbury, Wiltshire, SP3 5EU
☎ (01722) 716440
✉ sales@thehiddenbrewery.com
🌐 thehiddenbrewery.com
Tours by arrangement

The Hidden Brewery was founded in 2003 by head brewer Gary Lumber and partner Michael Woodhouse. The brewery is named after its location, hidden away in the Wiltshire countryside. It supplies approximately 1,500 outlets and has four tied houses including the Cornubia in Bristol. Seasonal beers: Hidden Spring (ABV 4.5%), Hidden Fantasy (ABV 4.6%), Hidden Depths (ABV 4.6%), Hidden Treasure (ABV 4.8%).

Pint (OG 1039, ABV 3.8%)
A clean-tasting, tangy bitter with good hop content, and a citrus fruit and malt balance. Dry finish, mid-brown in colour; light hop aroma.

Old Sarum (OG 1042, ABV 4.1%)
A well-balanced bitter with a complex combination of malts and hops. The aroma is floral and spicy, full-flavoured with a dry bitterness.

Potential (OG 1042, ABV 4.2%)
A traditional bitter with a balanced malty flavour. Clean tasting with slight citrus tones.

Quest (OG 1042, ABV 4.2%)
An amber-coloured bitter with a malt background, fruity aroma and a dry finish.

Pleasure (OG 1049, ABV 4.9%)
A deep golden coloured, strong, dry, traditional IPA with a hoppy finish.

Highgate SIBA

Highgate Brewery Ltd, Sandymount Road, Walsall, West Midlands, WS1 3AP
☎ (01922) 644453
✉ info@highgatebrewery.com
🌐 highgatebrewery.com
Tours by arrangement

Built in 1898, Highgate was an independent brewery until 1938 when it was taken over by Mitchells & Butlers and subsequently became the smallest brewery in the Bass group. It was brought back into the independent sector in 1995 as the result of a management buy-out and was subsequently acquired by Aston Manor (qv) in 2000. Highgate has nine tied houses, six of which serve cask beer. In July 2007 Highgate was bought by Global Star, a pub group in Birmingham. Some 200 outlets are supplied. The company also has a contract to supply Mitchells & Butlers pubs as well as contract brewing for Smiles Brewery. Beer range liable to change. Seasonal beer: Old Ale (ABV 5.3%, winter).

Dark Mild (OG 1036.8, ABV 3.6%)
A dark brown Black Country mild with a good balance of malt and hops, and traces of roast flavour following a malty aroma.

Davenports IPA (OG 1040.8, ABV 4%)

Special Bitter (OG 1037.8, ABV 4%)

Davenports Premium (OG 1046.8, ABV 4.6%)

Saddlers Best Bitter (OG 1043.8, ABV 4.6%)

For Coors:

M&B Mild (OG 1034.8, ABV 3.2%)

For Smiles:

Blonde (ABV 3.8%)

Best (ABV 4.1%)

Bristol IPA (ABV 4.4%)

Heritage (ABV 5.2%)

High House SIBA

High House Farm Brewery, Matfen, Newcastle upon Tyne, Tyne & Wear, NE20 0RG
☎ (01661) 886192/886769 (Sales line)
✉ info@highhousefarmbrewery.co.uk
🌐 highhousefarmbrewery.co.uk
Shop 10.30am-5pm daily except Wed
Tours by arrangement

The brewery was founded in 2003 on a working farm with visitor centre, brewery shop and exhibition and function room. Over 350 outlets are supplied. Seasonal beers: Sundancer (ABV 3.6%, summer), Red Shep (ABV 4%, autumn/winter), Black Moss (ABV 4.3%, winter).

Auld Hemp (OG 1038, ABV 3.8%)
Tawny-coloured ale with malt and fruit flavours and good bitter finish.

Nel's Best (OG 1041, ABV 4.2%)
Golden, hoppy ale full of flavour with a clean, bitter finish.

Nettle Beer (OG 1043, ABV 4.5%)

Matfen Magic (OG 1046.5, ABV 4.8%)
Well-hopped brown ale with a fruity aroma, malt and chocolate overtones with a rich, bitter finish.

Cyril the Magnificent (OG 1051, ABV 5.5%)

Highland

Highland Brewing Co Ltd, Swannay Brewery, Swannay by Evie, Birsay, Orkney, KW17 2NP
☎ (01856) 721700
✉ info@highlandbrewingcompany.co.uk
🌐 highlandbrewingcompany.co.uk
Tours by arrangement

Brewing began in 2006 and bigger plant was installed a year later. A visitor centre and café are planned. 80 outlets are supplied.

Light Munro (OG 1034, ABV 3%)
Paler and lower in alcohol than Dark Munro with delicate roast malt and a pleasant fruitiness with a hint of hop to balance the sweet finish.

Orkney Best (OG 1038, ABV 3.6%)
A refreshing, light-bodied, low gravity golden beer bursting with hop, peach and sweet malt flavours. The long, hoppy finish leaves a dry, moreish bitterness.

Dark Munro (OG 1040, ABV 4%)

The nose presents an intense roast hit which is followed by summer fruits in the mouth. The strong roast malt continues into the aftertaste. A very drinkable strong mild.

Scapa Special (OG 1042, ABV 4.2%)
A good copy of a typical Lancashire bitter, full of bitterness and background hops, leaving your mouth tingling in the lingering aftertaste.

Saint Magnus Ale (OG 1045, ABV 4.5%)
A complex tawny bitter with a stunning balance of malt and hop, and some soft roast. Full-bodied and very drinkable.

Orkney IPA (OG 1048, ABV 4.8%)
A very drinkable traditional bitter, with light hop and fruit flavour throughout.

Strong Northerley (OG 1055, ABV 5.5%)

Orkney Blast (OG 1058, ABV 6%)
A warming strong bitter. A mushroom and woody aroma blossoms into a well-balanced smack of malt and hop in the taste.

Highlands & Islands

See Sinclair Breweries

Highwood SIBA

Highwood Brewery Ltd, Grimsby West, Birchin Way, Grimsby, Lincolnshire, DN31 2SG
☎ (01472) 255500
✉ tomwood@tom-wood.com
tom-wood.com

Highwood, best known under the Tom Wood brand name, started brewing in a converted Victorian granary on the family farm in 1995. The brew-length was increased from 10 barrels to 30 in 2001, using plant from Ash Vine brewery. In 2002, Highwood bought Conway's Licensed Trade Wholesalers. It now distributes most regional and national cask ales throughout Lincolnshire and Nottinghamshire. More than 300 outlets are supplied. Seasonal beers: see website.

Best Bitter (OG 1034, ABV 3.5%)
A good citrus, passion fruit hop dominates the nose and taste, with background malt. A lingering hoppy and bitter finish.

Dark Mild (OG 1034, ABV 3.5%)

Hop and Glory (ABV 3.6%)
Hoppy golden bitter made using English grown Cascade hops.

Shepherd's Delight (OG 1040, ABV 4%)
Malt is the dominant taste in this amber brew, although the fruity hop bitterness complements it all the way.

Harvest Bitter (OG 1042, ABV 4.3%)
A well-balanced amber beer where the hops and bitterness just about outdo the malt.

Old Timber (OG 1043, ABV 4.5%)
Hoppy on the nose, but featuring well-balanced malt and hops. A slight, lingering roast/coffee flavour develops, but this is generally a bitter, darkish brown beer.

Bomber County (OG 1046, ABV 4.8%)
An earthy malt aroma but with a complex underlying mix of coffee, hops, caramel and apple fruit. The beer starts bitter and intensifies to the end.

Higson's SIBA

Higson's Brewery, Unit 17, Maritime Enterprise Park, Atlas Road, Liverpool, Merseyside, L20 4DY
☎ (0151) 922 5640
higsonsbrewery.co.uk

Higsons's was established in 2005 based on an original brewery which was founded in 1780. Beers were initially contract brewed by Mayflower Brewery but production returned to Liverpool in late 2007. Seasonal beers: see website.

Bitter (ABV 4.1%)

Hilden

Hilden Brewing Co, Hilden House, Hilden, Lisburn, Co Antrim, BT27 4TY
☎ (02892) 660800
✉ irishbeers@hildenbrewery.co.uk
hildenbrewery.co.uk
Tours by arrangement

Hilden was established in 1981 and is Ireland's oldest independent brewery. Now well into the second generation of the family owned business, the beers are widely distributed. Around 20 outlets are supplied direct and two pubs are owned.

Ale (OG 1038, ABV 4%)
An amber-coloured beer with an aroma of malt, hops and fruit. The balanced taste is slightly slanted towards hops, and hops are also prominent in the full, malty finish.

Silver (OG 1042, ABV 4.2%)
A pale ale, light and refreshing on the palate but with a satisfying mellow hop character derived from a judicious blend of aromatic Saaz hops.

Molly Malone (OG 1045, ABV 4.6%)
Dark ruby-red porter with complex flavours of hop bitterness and chocolate malt.

Scullion's Irish (OG 1045, ABV 4.6%)
A bright amber ale, initially smooth with a slight taste of honey that is balanced by a long, dry aftertaste that lingers on the palate.

Halt (OG 1058, ABV 6.1%)
A premium traditional Irish red ale with a malty, mild hop flavour. This special reserve derives its name from the local train stop, which was used to service the local linen mill.

Hill Island

Michael Griffin t/a Hill Island Brewery, Unit 7, Fowlers Yard, Back Silver Street, Durham, County Durham, DH1 3RA
☎ 07740 932584
✉ mike@hillisland.freeserve.co.uk
Tours by arrangement for groups of 10-15 (£10 per head inc beer samples)

Hill Island is a literal translation of Dunholme from which Durham is derived. The brewery began trading in 2002 and stands by the banks of the Wear in the heart of Durham City. Many of the beers produced have names reflecting local history and heritage. Brews can also be made exclusively for individual pubs. Around 40 outlets are supplied. The brewery is open to visitors most weekdays between 10am-2pm, please phone beforehand to confirm. Seasonal beers: Priory Summer Ale (ABV 3.5%), Miner's Gala Bitter (ABV 3.7%), Festive Ale (ABV 4.2%), St Oswald's Xmas Ale (ABV 4.5%).

Peninsula Pint (OG 1036.5, ABV 3.7%)

Bitter (OG 1038, ABV 3.9%)

Dun Cow Bitter (OG 1041, ABV 4.2%)

Cathedral Ale (OG 1042, ABV 4.3%)

Griffin's Irish Stout (OG 1045, ABV 4.5%)

Hillside

Hillside Brewery Ltd, Hillside, Corse, Lumphanan, Aberdeenshire, AB31 4RY
☎ (01339) 883506
✉ info@hillside-brewery.com
hillside-brewery.com

⊗ Business consultant and home brewer Rob James established Hillside Brewery in 2005 and began selling his bottle-conditioned beers into local food outlets in early 2006. There are plans to extend the existing building and scale up the brewing operation.

Brude (OG 1035, ABV 3.5%)

Macbeth (OG 1038, ABV 4.2%)

Broichan (OG 1045, ABV 5.2%)

Hobden's

See Wessex

Hobsons SIBA

Hobsons Brewery & Co Ltd, Newhouse Farm, Tenbury Road, Cleobury Mortimer, Worcestershire, DY14 8RD
☎ (01299) 270837
✉ beer@hobsons-brewery.co.uk
hobsonsbrewery.co.uk
Tours by arrangement

Established in 1993 in a former sawmill, Hobsons relocated to a farm site with more space in 1995. A second brewery, bottling plant and a warehouse have been added along with significant expansion to the first brewery. Beers are supplied within a radius of 50 miles. Hobsons also brews and bottles for the local tourist attraction, the Severn Valley Railway (Manor Ale, ABV 4.2%). Seasonal beers: Old Henry (ABV 5.2%, Sep-Apr), Steam No. 9 (ABV 4.2%, Sep).

Mild (OG 1034, ABV 3.2%)
A classic mild. Complex layers of taste come from roasted malts that predominate and give lots of flavour.

Best Bitter (OG 1038.5, ABV 3.8%)
A pale brown to amber, medium-bodied beer with strong hop character throughout. It is consequently bitter, but with malt discernible in the taste.

Town Crier (OG 1044, ABV 4.5%)
An elegant straw-coloured bitter. The hint of sweetness is complemented by subtle hop flavours, leading to a dry finish.

Hoggleys SIBA

Hoggleys Brewery, Unit 12, Litchborough Industrial Estate, Northampton Road, Litchborough, Northamptonshire, NN12 8JB
☎ (01604) 831762
✉ hoggleys@hotmail.com
hoggleys.co.uk

⊗ Hoggleys was established in 2003 as a part-time brewery. It has now expanded to an eight-barrel plant, become full-time and moved to larger premises. 20 outlets are supplied. Solstice Stout and Mill Lane Mild are suitable for vegetarians as are all bottle-conditioned beers that are available.

Kislingbury Bitter (OG 1042, ABV 4%)

Mill Lane Mild (OG 1040, ABV 4%)
Brewed from mild, black and crystal malts and hopped with Challenger and Fuggles.

Northamptonshire Bitter (OG 1044, ABV 4%)
A straw-coloured bitter brewed with pale malt only. The hops are Fuggles and Northdown, and the beer is late hopped with Fuggles for aroma.

New Brewery Bitter (OG 1036, ABV 4.3%)
Pale gold, light and refreshing.

Reservoir Hogs (OG 1042, ABV 4.3%)
Mid golden, hoppy and refreshing.

Pump Fiction (OG 1044, ABV 4.5%)
Light copper, complex but easy drinking.

Nene Bitter (OG 1050, ABV 5%)
Pronounced 'Nen' – a strong bitter with an excellent balance of malt and hops.

Solstice Stout (OG 1050, ABV 5%)

Yuletide Ale (OG 1073, ABV 7.2%)

For J.Phipps Ales (Banbury) Ltd:

Triple XXX (ABV 3.9%)

Hogs Back SIBA

Hogs Back Brewery Ltd, Manor Farm, The Street, Tongham, Surrey, GU10 1DE
☎ (01252) 783000
✉ info@hogsback.co.uk
hogsback.co.uk
Shop – see website
Tours by arrangement

⊗ This traditionally-styled brewery, established in 1992, boasts an extensive range of award-winning ales, brewed using the finest malted barley and whole English hops. The shop sells all the brewery's beers and related merchandise plus over 400 beers and ciders from around the world. See website for more info. Around 400 outlets are supplied direct. Seasonal beers: see website. Bottle-conditioned beers also produced for home and export.

HBB/Hogs Back Bitter (OG 1039, ABV 3.7%)
An aromatic session beer. Biscuity aroma with some hops and orangey notes. Well-balanced with plenty of hoppy impact in the mouth

with a long-lasting dry, hoppy, bitter aftertaste. Moreish.

TEA/Traditional English Ale (OG 1044, ABV 4.2%)
The brewery's flagship beer. A copper-coloured best bitter, with both malt and hops prominent in the nose. These carry through into a well-rounded bitter flavour, balanced by fruit and some sweetness. Hoppy bitterness grows in the aftertaste.

Hop Garden Gold (OG 1048, ABV 4.6%)
Pale golden best bitter, full-bodied and well-balanced with an aroma of malt, hops and fruit. Delicate flowery-citrus hop flavours are balanced by malt and fruit. Hoppy bitterness grows in an increasingly dry aftertaste with a hint of sweetness. Dangerously drinkable!

A Over T/Aromas Over Tongham (OG 1094, ABV 9%)
A full-bodied, tawny-coloured barley wine that is packed with flavour. The malty aroma, with hints of vanilla, lead to a well-balanced taste, where the hops cut through the underlying sweetness and dominate in the finish.

Holden's IFBB

Holden's Brewery Ltd, George Street, Woodsetton, Dudley, West Midlands, DY1 4LW
(01902) 880051
holdens.brewery@virgin.net
holdensbrewery.co.uk
Shop Mon-Fri 9am-5pm
Tours by arrangement

A family brewery going back four generations, Holden's began life as a brew-pub in the 1920s. The company continues to grow with 22 tied pubs and supplies around 70 other outlets.

Black Country Mild (OG 1037, ABV 3.7%)
A good, red/brown mild; a refreshing, light blend of roast malt, hops and fruit, dominated by malt throughout.

Black Country Bitter (OG 1039, ABV 3.9%)
A medium-bodied, golden ale; a light, well-balanced bitter with a subtle, dry, hoppy finish.

XB (OG 1042, ABV 4.1%)
A sweeter, slightly fuller version of the Bitter. Sold in a number of outlets under different names.

Golden Glow (OG 1045, ABV 4.4%)
A pale golden beer with a subtle hop aroma plus gentle sweetness and a light hoppiness.

Special (OG 1052, ABV 5.1%)
A sweet, malty, full-bodied amber ale with hops to balance in the taste and in the good, bittersweet finish.

Holland

Holland Brewery, 5 Browns Flats, Brewery Street, Kimberley, Nottinghamshire, NG16 2JU
(0115) 938 2685
hollandbrew@btopenworld.com

Len Holland, a keen home-brewer for 30 years, went commercial in 2000, in the shadow of now closed Hardys & Hansons. Seasonal beers: Holly Hop Gold (ABV 4.7%, Xmas), Dutch Courage (ABV 5%, winter), Glamour Puss (ABV 4.2%, spring), Blonde Belter (ABV 4.5%, summer).

Chocolate Clog (OG 1038, ABV 3.8%)

Golden Blond (OG 1040, ABV 4%)

Lipsmacker (OG 1040, ABV 4%)

Cloghopper (OG 1042, ABV 4.2%)

Double Dutch (OG 1045, ABV 4.5%)

Mad Jack Stout (OG 1045, ABV 4.5%)

Holt IFBB

Joseph Holt Ltd, The Brewery, Empire Street, Cheetham, Manchester, M3 1JD
(0161) 834 3285
joseph-holt.com

The brewery was established in 1849 by Joseph Holt and his wife Catherine. It is still a family-run business in the hands of the great, great-grandson of the founder. Holt's supplies approximately 100 outlets as well as its own estate of 131 tied pubs. It still delivers beer to many of its tied houses in large 54-gallon hogsheads. A dedicated 30-barrel brew plant is used for seasonal beers: see website. Bottle-conditioned beer is also available.

Mild (OG 1033, ABV 3.2%)
A dark brown/red beer with a fruity, malty nose. Roast, malt, fruit and hops in the taste, with strong bitterness for a mild, and a dry malt and hops finish.

Bitter (OG 1040, ABV 4%)
Copper-coloured beer with malt and fruit in the aroma. Malt, hops and fruit in the taste with a very bitter and hoppy finish.

Hook Norton IFBB

Hook Norton Brewery Co Ltd, The Brewery, Hook Norton, Banbury, Oxfordshire, OX15 5NY
(01608) 737210
hooky.co.uk
Shop Mon-Fri 9am-5pm; Sat 9am-3pm
Tours by arrangement

Hook Norton was founded in 1849 by John Harris, a farmer and maltster. The current premises were built in 1900 and Hook Norton is one of the finest examples of a Victorian tower brewery, with a 25hp steam engine for most of its motive power. The brewhouse has recently been expanded. Hook Norton owns 47 pubs and supplies approximately 300 free trade accounts. Seasonal beers: Double Stout (ABV 4.8%, Jan/Feb), 303AD (ABV 4%, Mar/Apr), Cotswold Lion (ABV 4.2%, May/Jun), Haymaker (ABV 5%, Jul/Aug), Flagship (ABV 5.3%, Sep/Oct), Twelve Days (ABV 5.5%, Nov/Dec).

Hooky Dark (OG 1033, ABV 3.2%)
A chestnut brown, easy-drinking mild. A complex malt and hop aroma give way to a well-balanced taste, leading to a long, hoppy finish that is unusual for a mild.

Hooky Bitter (OG 1036, ABV 3.6%)

A classic golden session bitter. Hoppy and fruity aroma followed by a malt and hops taste and a continuing hoppy finish.

Hooky Gold (OG 1042, ABV 4.1%)
A golden, crisp beer with a citrus aroma and a fruity, rounded body.

Old Hooky (OG 1048, ABV 4.6%) ◆
A strong bitter, tawny in colour. A well-rounded fruity taste with a balanced bitter finish.

Hop Back SIBA

Hop Back Brewery plc, Units 22-24, Batten Road Industrial Estate, Downton, Salisbury, Wiltshire, SP5 3HU
☎ (01725) 510986
✉ info@hopback.co.uk
🌐 hopback.co.uk
Tours by arrangement

Started by John Gilbert in 1987 at the Wyndham Arms in Salisbury, the brewery has expanded steadily ever since. It went public via a Business Expansion Scheme in 1993 and has enjoyed rapid continued growth. Summer Lightning has won many awards. The brewery has 11 tied houses and also sells to some 500 other outlets. Seasonal beers are produced on a monthly basis. Entire Stout is suitable for vegans.

GFB/Gilbert's First Brew (OG 1035, ABV 3.5%) ◆
A golden beer, with a light, clean quality that makes it an ideal session ale. A hoppy aroma and taste lead to a good, dry finish.

Odyssey (OG 1040, ABV 4%)
A new, darker beer with a blend of four malts.

Crop Circle (OG 1041, ABV 4.2%) ◆
A refreshingly sharp and hoppy summer beer. Gold coloured with a slight citrus taste. The crisp, dry aftertaste lingers.

Spring Zing (OG 1041, ABV 4.2%)

Entire Stout (OG 1043, ABV 4.5%) ◆
A rich, dark stout with a strong roasted malt flavour and a long, sweet and malty aftertaste. A beer suitable for vegans. Also produced with ginger.

Summer Lightning (OG 1049, ABV 5%) ◆
A pleasurable pale bitter with a good, fresh, hoppy aroma and a malty, hoppy flavour. Finely balanced, it has an intense bitterness leading to a long, dry finish.

Hopdaemon

Hopdaemon Brewery Co Ltd, Unit 1, Parsonage Farm, Seed Road, Newnham, Kent, ME9 0NA
☎ (01795) 892078
✉ hopdaemon@supanet.com
🌐 hopdaemon.com

Tonie Prins opened a 12-barrel plant in 2001 in Canterbury and within six months was supplying more than 30 pubs in the area, as well as exclusive bottle-conditioned, own-label beers for London's British Museum, Southwark Cathedral, the Science Museum, and more recently for the Barbican and National Gallery. In 2005 the brewery moved to bigger premises in Newnham and some 100 outlets are now supplied.

Golden Braid (OG 1039, ABV 3.7%)

Incubus (OG 1041, ABV 4%)

Skrimshander IPA (OG 1045, ABV 4.5%)

Leviathan (OG 1057, ABV 6%)

Hopshackle

Hopshackle Brewery Ltd, Unit F, Bentley Business Park, Blenheim Way, Northfields Industrial Estate, Market Deeping, Lincolnshire, PE6 8LD
☎ (01778) 348542
✉ nigel@hopshacklebrewery.co.uk
🌐 hopshacklebrewery.co.uk
Tours by arrangement

Hopshackle was established in 2006 on a five-barrel brew plant. Monthly seasonals are brewed providing variety in styles and ABVs. Over 40 outlets are supplied direct.

Amber Smooth (OG 1035, ABV 3.6%)

Bitter (OG 1037, ABV 3.8%)

Rufus Ale (OG 1039, ABV 4.2%)

Caskadia (OG 1040, ABV 4.3%)

Special Bitter (OG 1040, ABV 4.3%)

Hop and Spicy (OG 1045, ABV 4.5%)

Extra Special Bitter (OG 1045, ABV 4.8%)

Historic Porter (OG 1053, ABV 4.8%)

Shacklers Gold (OG 1048, ABV 5.2%)

Special No. 1 Bitter (OG 1048, ABV 5.2%)

Winter Ale (OG 1048, ABV 5.2%)

Momentum (OG 1065, ABV 7%)

Shacklebock (OG 1070, ABV 7.4%)

Restoration (OG 1085, ABV 9%)

Hopstar

Hopstar Brewery, 11 Pole Lane, Darwen, Lancashire, BB3 3LD
☎ (01254) 703389
✉ hopstarbrewery@hotmail.com

Hopstar first brewed in 2005 on a 2.5-barrel kit. Two new fermenters were added in 2006 to double capacity due to demand. Bottling started in 2007. 20-50 outlets are supplied direct.

Dizzy Danny Ale (ABV 3.8%)

J.C. (ABV 4%)

Smokey Joe's Black Beer (ABV 4%)

Spinning Jenny (ABV 4%)

Hornbeam

Hornbeam Brewery, 1-1c Grey Street, Denton, Manchester, M34 3RU
☎ (0161) 320 5627
☎ 07984 443383
✉ kevin@hornbeambrewery.com
🌐 hornbeambrewery.com
Tours by arrangement

Hornbeam began brewing in July 2007 on an eight-barrel plant. Seasonal beers: Dark Domination Porter (ABV 6%), Malt Mountain Mild (ABV 3.2%), Winterlong Dark Bitter (ABV 4.7%, winter). Specials beers are also brewed.

Bitter (ABV 3.8%)
A smooth, easy-drinking beer with a rich hop flavour.

Top Hop (ABV 4.2%)
Full-bodied with malt appeal and ample bitterness.

Black Coral Stout (ABV 4.5%)
A smooth, dry roast malt. Dark and full-bodied with a rich, creamy head. Satisfying with a subtle bitterness.

Golden Wraith Pale Ale (ABV 5%)
Highly aromatic and hoppy leaving citrus and floral after tones, balanced by the finest pale malt.

Horseshoe

Horseshoe Brewery/McLaughlin Brewhouse, The Horseshoe, 28 Heath Street, Hampstead, London, NW3 6TE
☎ (020) 7431 7206
getlucky@thehorseshoehampstead.com
thehorseshoehampstead.com

A micro-brewery built in July 2006 to honour the landlord's late grandfather, who owned Mac's Brewery in Rockhampton, Australia. At present it only supplies its own pub, the Horseshoe.

McLaughlin Summer (ABV 3.6%)

McLaughlin Spring (ABV 3.9%)

McLaughlin Laurie Best Bitter (ABV 4.1%)

Hoskins

Hoskins Brothers Ales, The Ale Wagon, 27 Rutland Street, Leicester, LE1 1RE
☎ (0116) 262 3330
mail@alewagon.com
alewagon.co.uk

Hoskins brothers are not currently brewing pending the building of a new brewery at the Ale Wagon in Leicester. Their beers are currently contract brewed at Tower Brewery, Burton upon Trent. See Tower for beer list.

Houston SIBA

Houston Brewing Co, South Street, Houston, Renfrewshire, PA6 7EN
☎ (01505) 612620
ale@houston-brewing.co.uk
houston-brewing.co.uk
Shop open pub hours, daily
Tours by arrangement

Established by Carl Wengel in 1997, this brewery is attached to the Fox & Hounds pub and restaurant. Brewery tours include dinner and tastings. Houston deliver throughout Britain via a network of distributors and direct. Polypins, bottles and giftpacks are for sale via the website. Seasonal beers: see website.

Killellan Bitter (OG 1037, ABV 3.7%)
A light session ale, with a floral hop and fruity taste. The finish of this amber beer is dry and quenching.

Blonde Bombshell (OG 1040, ABV 4%)
A gold-coloured ale with a fresh hop aroma and rounded maltiness.

Black & Tan (ABV 4.2%)

Peter's Well (OG 1042, ABV 4.2%)
Well-balanced fruity taste with sweet hop, leading to an increasingly bittersweet finish.

Texas (ABV 4.3%)

Tartan Terror (ABV 4.5%)

Warlock Stout (ABV 4.7%)

Howard Town

Howard Town Brewery Ltd, Hawkshead Mill, Hope Street, Glossop, Derbyshire, SK13 7SS
☎ (01457) 869800
beer@howardtownbrewery.co.uk
howardtownbrewery.co.uk
Tours by arrangement

Howard Town was established in 2005 and is the Midlands most northerly brewery. More than 100 outlets are supplied. Seasonal beers: Hope (ABV 4.1%, spring), Snake Ale (ABV 4%, autumn), Robins Nest (ABV 5.2%, winter).

Bleaklow (OG 1040, ABV 3.8%)

Monks Gold (OG 1041.5, ABV 4%)

Wrens Nest (OG 1043, ABV 4.2%)

Dinting Arches (OG 1045, ABV 4.5%)

Glotts Hop (OG 1049, ABV 5%)

Sarah Hughes

Sarah Hughes Brewery, Beacon Hotel, 129 Bilston Street, Sedgley, Dudley, West Midlands, DY3 1JE
☎ (01902) 883381
Tours by arrangement

A traditional Black Country tower brewery, established in 1921. The original grist case and rare open-topped copper add to the ambience of the Victorian brewhouse and give a unique character to the brews. Seasonal beers: Raucous (ABV 4.8%, summer), Rampur (ABV 5.2%, summer), Pale Bock (ABV 4.7%, autumn), Imperial Stout (ABV 7.3%, winter), 1921 (ABV 5.5%, Nov-Jan), Snowflake (ABV 8%, winter).

Pale Amber (OG 1038, ABV 4%)
A well-balanced beer, initially slightly sweet but with hops close behind.

Surprise (OG 1048, ABV 5%)
A bittersweet, medium-bodied, hoppy ale with some malt.

Dark Ruby (OG 1058, ABV 6%)
A dark ruby strong ale with a good balance of fruit and hops, leading to a pleasant, lingering hops and malt finish.

Humpty Dumpty

Humpty Dumpty Brewery, Church Road, Reedham, Norfolk, NR13 3TZ
☎ (01493) 701818

✉ sales@humptydumptybrewery.co.uk
🌐 humptydumptybrewery.co.uk
Shop 12-5pm daily spring/summer, 12.30-4pm Sat-Sun autumn/winter
Tours by arrangement

⊗ Established in 1998, the 11-barrel brewery moved to its present site in 2001 and changed hands in 2006. The new owners continue to brew using local ingredients and have expanded the original range. The onsite shop sells bottled and draught beer from the brewery as well as from other East Anglian micros. Seasonal beers vary from year to year, please see website.

Little Sharpie (OG 1040, ABV 3.8%)
A well-balanced golden beer with lemon and grapefruit notes. A light, hoppy nose introduces a lively initial taste with hops again to the fore. Citrus flavours mix well with malt to give depth.

Lemon & Ginger (OG 1041, ABV 4%)
An amber, crisp ale with a ginger and lemon tang.

Swallowtail (OG 1041, ABV 4%)
A pale amber ale with a lively hop finish.

Ale (OG 1043, ABV 4.1%)
An amber-coloured bitter with a predominantly fruity nose. Initial sweetness fades to leave a long, dry finish.

Reedcutter (OG 1046, ABV 4.4%)
A sweet, malty beer, golden hued with a gentle malt background. Smooth and full-bodied with a quick, gentle finish.

The King John (OG 1046, ABV 4.5%)
A golden ale with soft, fruity undertones leading to a complex bittersweet finish.

Cheltenham Flyer (OG 1048, ABV 4.6%)
A full-flavoured golden, earthy bitter with a long, grainy finish. A strong hop bitterness dominates throughout. Little evidence of malt.

Norfolk Nectar (OG 1048, ABV 4.6%)
Amber-coloured ale infused with local Reedham honey. A refreshing hop bitterness lingers on the palate leaving a slight honey and vanilla sweetness.

Railway Sleeper (OG 1051, ABV 5%)
Full-bodied tawny brew with a rich, fruity nature. A strong plummy character where sweetness and malt counterbalance the background bitterness. A quick, spicy, bitter finish.

Golden Gorse (OG 1054, ABV 5.4%)
A full-bodied, fruity beer. Hints of banana, rhubarb, vanilla, peaches, and toffee throughout. Malt is also present and helps suppress a soft, bitter background. A surprisingly short finish.

Porter (OG 1054, ABV 5.4%)
Traditional porter giving a full roast aroma with hints of liquorice on the tongue and a dry, bitter finish.

Hurns

See Tomos Watkins

Hydes IFBB

Hydes Brewery Ltd, 46 Moss Lane West, Moss Side, Manchester, M15 5PH
☎ (0161) 226 1317
✉ mail@hydesbrewery.com
🌐 hydesbrewery.com
Tours by arrangement (Mon-Thu 7pm)

Hydes has been a family-owned regional brewer since 1863 and is currently the biggest volume producer of cask ales in the north west, thanks in part to its contract brewing for InBev and others. The brewery has been on the same site for over 120 years with the brewery building itself being Grade II listed. Hydes owns over 80 tied pubs and have over 300 free trade accounts. Six seasonal beers are also produced in addition to the main range.

Light Mild/1863 (OG 1033.5, ABV 3.5%)
Lightly hopped, pale brown session beer with some hops, malt and fruit in the taste and a short, dry finish.

Owd Oak (OG 1033.5, ABV 3.5%)
Dark brown/red in colour, with a fruit and malt nose. Taste includes biscuity malt and green fruits, with a satisfying aftertaste.

Traditional Mild (OG 1033.5, ABV 3.5%)
A mid-brown beer with malt and citrus fruits in the aroma and taste. Dry, malty aftertaste.

Original Bitter (OG 1036.5, ABV 3.8%)
Pale brown beer with a malty nose, malt and an earthy hoppiness in the taste, and a good bitterness through to the finish.

Jekyll's Gold Premium (OG 1042, ABV 4.3%)
Pale gold in colour, with a fruity nose. A well-balanced beer with hops, fruit and malt in the taste and the bitter finish.

XXXX (OG 1070, ABV 6.8%)
Auburn chestnut brown in colour with a sweet malt toffee nose. A strong robust winter ale with a rich toffee taste.

For InBev UK:

Boddingtons Bitter (OG 1038, ABV 4.1%)

Iceni SIBA EAB

Iceni Brewery, 3 Foulden Road, Ickburgh, Norfolk, IP26 5HB
☎ (01842) 878922
✉ icenibrewe@aol.com
🌐 icenibrewery.co.uk
Shop Mon-Fri 8.30am-5pm; Sat 9am-3pm
Tours by arrangement

⊗ Iceni was launched in 1995 by Brendan Moore. The brewery has its own hop garden aimed at the many visitors that flock to the shop to buy the 28 different ales, stouts and lagers bottled onsite. 30 outlets are supplied as well as local farmers' markets and a tourist shop in nearby Thetford Forest. The brewery is looking to malt its own barley. Special beers are brewed for festivals and many seasonal beers are available.

Elveden Forest Gold (OG 1040, ABV 3.9%)
Forest fruits on the nose give way to strong hop bitterness in the initial taste. Residual

maltiness provides balance at first but is swamped by a long, dry, bitter finish.

Celtic Queen (OG 1038, ABV 4%)
A golden brew with a light hoppy nose giving way to distinctly bitter characteristics throughout. A shallow mix of malt and hops adds some depth. A long, lingering finish.

Fine Soft Day (OG 1038, ABV 4%)
The jam nose contrasts with the distinctly bitter character of this quick-finishing brew. Hops and malt can be found initially but soon subside.

Fen Tiger (OG 1040, ABV 4.2%)

It's A Grand Day (OG 1044, ABV 4.5%)
An amber beer with a pronounced stem ginger character. Although some traces of malt and a little hoppiness can be detected if sought for hard enough this is a real ginger beer.

Raspberry Wheat (OG 1048, ABV 5%)

Winter Lightning (ABV 5%)

Men of Norfolk (OG 1060, ABV 6.2%)
Chocolaty stout with roast overtones from initial aroma to strong finish. Malt and vine fruits counterbalance the initial roast character while a caramel undertone remains to the end.

Idle

Idle Brewery, White Hart Inn, Main Street, West Stockwith, South Yorkshire, DN10 4EY
☎ 07949 137174
✉ theidlebrewery@btinternet.com
Tours by arrangement

The brewery began production in April 2007 and is situated in a converted stable at the back of the White Hart Inn alongside the River Idle. Seasonal beer: Idle Sack (ABV 3.8%, Xmas).

Boggins Ale (ABV 3.8%)
Tawny with a bitter finish.

Dog (ABV 4%)
A copper-coloured ale, moderately hoppy with a good balance of malt and hops leading to a bitter finish.

Sod (ABV 4%)

Chef (ABV 4.2%)
A copper-coloured session bitter with a hint of hops in the aroma. Plenty of body with a lingering touch of amber.

Black Abbot (ABV 4.6%)

Cricketers (ABV 4.6%)

Landlord (ABV 4.6%)
A dark brown ale with plenty of body, a malty flavour and a caramel/coffee finish.

Brewer (ABV 5%)
A pale, straw-coloured, hoppy ale with a fresh aroma and flavour. Deceptively strong with a sweet finish.

Innis & Gunn

Innis & Gunn Brewing Co Ltd, PO Box 17246, Edinburgh, EH11 1YR
☎ (0131) 337 4420
✉ dougal.sharp@innisandgunn.com
innisandgunn.com

Innis & Gunn does not brew but an unnamed Scottish brewer produces one regular bottled (not bottle-conditioned) beer for the company, Oak Aged Beer (ABV 6.6%).

Inveralmond SIBA

Inveralmond Brewery Ltd, 1 Inveralmond Way, Inveralmond, Perth, PH1 3UQ
☎ (01738) 449448
✉ info@inveralmond-brewery.co.uk
inveralmond-brewery.co.uk

Established in 1997, Inveralmond was the first brewery in Perth for more than 30 years. The brewery has gone from strength to strength, with around 200 outlets supplied and wholesalers taking beers nationwide. In 2005 the brewery expanded ino the next door premises, more than doubling floor space and output. The brewery has now outgrown this and is planning to build a new brewery on land nearby. Seasonal beers: see website.

Independence (OG 1040, ABV 3.8%)
A well-balanced Scottish ale with fruit and malt tones. Hop provides an increasing bitterness in the finish.

Ossian (OG 1042, ABV 4.1%)
Well-balanced best bitter with a dry finish. This full-bodied amber ale is dominated by fruit and hop with a bittersweet character although excessive caramel can distract from this.

Thrappledouser (OG 1043, ABV 4.3%)
A refreshing amber beer with reddish hues. The crisp, hoppy aroma is finely balanced with a tangy but quenching taste.

Lia Fail (OG 1048, ABV 4.7%)
The Gaelic name means Stone of Destiny. A dark, robust, full-bodied beer with a deep malty taste. Smooth texture and balanced finish.

Ironbridge*

Ironbridge Brewery Ltd, Unit 7, Merrythought, The Wharfage, Ironbridge, Telford, Shropshire, TF8 7NJ
☎ (01952) 433910
✉ david@ironbridgebrewery.co.uk
ironbridgebrewery.co.uk
Tours by arrangement

Ironbridge was established in 2008 and operates on a 12-barrel brewery in an old Victorian Foundry building. 20 outlets are supplied direct.

Coracle Bitter (OG 1039, ABV 3.9%)

1779 (ABV 4.2%)

Shankers Tipple (OG 1045, ABV 4.6%)

Irving*

Irving & Co Brewers Ltd, Unit G1, Railway Triangle, Walton Road, Portsmouth, Hampshire, PO6 1TQ
☎ (02392) 389988
✉ sales@irvingbrewers.co.uk

irvingbrewers.co.uk
Shop Thu & Fri 3-6pm
Tours by arrangement

Irving's was set up by former Gale's brewer Malcolm Irving and a small team of ex-Gales employees using a 15-barrel plant. Around 60 outlets are supplied direct. Seasonal beers: Red Plum (ABV 5%, Xmas), Pompey Glory (ABV 5%, summer).

Frigate (OG 1039, ABV 3.8%)

Type42 (OG 1042, ABV 4.2%)

Invincible (OG 1048, ABV 4.6%)

Islay

Islay Ales Company Ltd, The Brewery, Islay House Square, Bridgend, Isle of Islay, PA44 7NZ
(01496) 810014
info@islayales.com
islayales.com
Shop Mon-Sat 10.30am-5pm
Tours by arrangement

Brewing started on a four-barrel plant in a converted tractor shed in 2004. The brewery shop is next door. Paul Hathaway, Paul Capper and Walter Schobert set up the brewery on an island more famous for its whisky, but it has established itself as a must-see place for those visiting the eight working distilleries on the Island. The beers are available in many hotels, pubs and restaurants on the Island.

Finlaggan Ale (OG 1039, ABV 3.7%)

Black Rock Ale (OG 1040, ABV 4.2%)

Dun Hogs Head Ale (OG 1044, ABV 4.4%)

Saligo Ale (OG 1044, ABV 4.4%)

Angus OG Ale (OG 1045, ABV 4.5%)

Ardnave Ale (OG 1048, ABV 4.6%)

Nerabus Ale (OG 1046, ABV 4.8%)

Single Malt Ale (OG 1050, ABV 5%)

Balinaby Ale (OG 1073, ABV 7.1%)

Isle of Arran

See Arran

Isle of Mull

Isle of Mull Brewing Co Ltd, Ledaig, Tobermory, Isle of Mull, PA75 6NR
(01688) 302830
isleofmullbrewing@btinternet.com

Brewing started in 2005 using a five-barrel plant. Bottled beers are available but are not bottle conditioned.

Island Pale Ale (OG 1038, ABV 3.9%)

Galleon Gold (ABV 4.1%)

Royal Regiment of Scotland (ABV 4.1%)

McCaig's Folly (OG 1042, ABV 4.2%)

Terror of Tobermory (OG 1045, ABV 4.6%)

Isle of Purbeck

Isle of Purbeck Brewery, Manor Road, Studland, Dorset, BH19 3AU
(01929) 450227
Tours by arrangement

The 10-barrel brewing equipment from the former Poole Brewery has been installed in the grounds of the Bankes Arms Hotel that overlooks Studland Bay. There are plans to add new brews. 50 outlets are supplied. Seasonal beer: Thermal Cheer (ABV 4.8%, winter).

Best Bitter (ABV 3.8%)

Fossil Fuel (OG 1040, ABV 4.1%)

Solar Power (OG 1043, ABV 4.3%)

Studland Bay Wrecked (OG 1044, ABV 4.5%)

IPA (OG 1047, ABV 4.8%)

Isle of Skye

Isle of Skye Brewing Co (Leann an Eilein) Ltd, The Pier, Uig, Isle of Skye, IV51 9XP
(01470) 542477
info@skyebrewery.co.uk
skyebrewery.co.uk
Shop Mon-Sat 10am-6pm; Sun 12.30-4.30pm (Apr-Oct)
Tours by arrangement

The Isle of Skye Brewery was established in 1995, the first commercial brewery in the Hebrides. Originally a 10-barrel plant, it was upgraded to 20-barrels in 2004. Fermenting capacity now stands at 80 barrels, with plans to further increase this and upgrade bottling facilities. Seasonal beers: see website.

Young Pretender (OG 1039, ABV 4%)
A full-bodied golden ale, predominantly hoppy and fruity. The bitterness in the mouth is also balanced by summer fruits and hops, continuing into the lingering bitter finish.

Red Cuillin (OG 1041, ABV 4.2%)
A light, fruity nose with a hint of caramel leads to a full-bodied, malty flavour and a long, dry, bittersweet finish.

Hebridean Gold (OG 1041.5, ABV 4.3%)
Porridge oats are used to produce this delicious golden speciality beer. Nicely balanced it has a refreshingly soft, fruity, bitter flavour. Thirst quenching and very drinkable. Could be mistaken for a best bitter.

Black Cuillin (OG 1044, ABV 4.5%)
A complex, tasty brew worthy of its many awards. Full-bodied with a malty richness, malts do hold sway but there are plenty of hops and fruit to be discovered in its varied character. A truly delicious Scottish old ale.

Blaven (OG 1047, ABV 5%)
A well-balanced strong amber bitter with kiwi fruit and caramel in the nose and a lingering, sharp bitterness.

Cuillin Beast (OG 1061.5, ABV 7%)
A fruity 'winter warmer'; sweet and fruity, and much more drinkable than the strength would suggest. Plenty of caramel throughout with a variety of fruit on the nose.

Itchen Valley SIBA

Itchen Valley Brewery Ltd, Prospect Commercial Park, Prospect Road, New Alresford, Hampshire, SO24 9QF
☎ (01962) 735111/736429
✉ info@itchenvalley.com
🌐 itchenvalley.com
Shop Mon-Fri 9am-5pm
Tours by arrangement

⊗ Established in 1997, Itchen Valley moved to new premises in 2006. The brewery has a gift shop and offers brewery tours and mini conferencing facilities. 300+ pubs are supplied, with wholesalers used for futher distribution. Seasonal beers: Father Christmas (ABV 5%), Rudolph (ABV 3.8%), Watercress Line (ABV 4.2%).

Godfathers (OG 1038, ABV 3.8%) ◆
A citrus hop character with a malty taste and a light body, leading to an increasingly dry, bitter finish. Pale brown in colour.

Fagin's (OG 1041, ABV 4.1%) ◆
Enjoyable copper-coloured best bitter with a hint of crystal malt and a pleasant bitter aftertaste.

Hampshire Rose (OG 1042, ABV 4.2%)
A golden amber ale. Fruit and hops dominate the taste throughout, with a good mouth feel.

Winchester Ale (OG 1042, ABV 4.2%)

Pure Gold (OG 1046, ABV 4.6%) ◆
An aromatic, hoppy, golden bitter. Initial grapefruit flavours lead to a dry, bitter finish.

Jacobi

Jacobi Brewery of Caio, Penlanwen Farm, Pumsaint, Carmarthenshire, SA19 8RR
☎ (01558) 650605
✉ justin@jacobibrewery.co.uk
🌐 jacobibrewery.co.uk

⊗ Brewing started in 2006 on an eight-barrel plant in a converted barn. Brewer Justin Jacobi is also the owner of the Brunant Arms in Caio, which is a regular outlet for the beers. The brewery is located 50 yards from the Dolaucothi mines where the Romans dug for gold. A visitor centre and bottling line are planned.

Light Ale (OG 1040, ABV 3.8%)

Original (OG 1044, ABV 4%)

Dark Ale (OG 1052, ABV 5%)

Jarrow SIBA

Jarrow Brewery, Robin Hood, Primrose Hill, Jarrow, Tyne & Wear, NE32 5UB
☎ (0191) 483 6792
✉ jarrowbrewery@btconnect.com
🌐 jarrowbrewing.co.uk
Tours by arrangement

Real ale enthusiasts Jess and Alison McConnell commenced brewing in October 2002. Three pubs are owned and around 150 outlets are supplied. Brewing also takes place at the Maltings pub in South Shields. Seasonal beers: Westoe Crown (ABV 4.2%, May, Jul & Sep), Red Ellen (ABV 4.4%, Feb-Mar & Oct-Nov), Venerable Bede (ABV 4.5%, Apr, Jun & Aug), Old Cornelius (ABV 4.8%, Dec-Jan).

Bitter (OG 1037.5, ABV 3.8%)
A light golden session bitter with a delicate hop aroma and a lingering fruity finish.

Rivet Catcher (OG 1039, ABV 4%)
A light, smooth, satisfying gold bitter with fruity hops on the tongue and nose.

Joblings Swinging Gibbet (OG 1041, ABV 4.1%)
A copper-coloured, evenly balanced beer with a good hop aroma and a fruity finish.

McConnells Irish Stout (OG 1045, ABV 4.6%)

Westoe IPA (OG 1044.5, ABV 4.6%)

Jennings

See Marston's in the New Nationals section

Jersey SIBA

Jersey Brewery, Tregear House, Longueville Road, St Saviour, Jersey, JE2 7WF
☎ (01534) 508151
✉ paulhurley@victor-hugo-ltd.com
Tours by arrangement

Following the closure of the original brewery in Ann Street in 2004, the Jersey Brewery is now located in an old soft drinks factory using a 40-barrel plant along with the eight-barrel plant from the former Tipsy Toad Brewery. Most cask beers are produced on the smaller plant, though the bigger one, which usually produces keg beer, can also be used for cask production. Cask Special was first produced for the 2005 Jersey beer festival but, after receiving the Beer of the Festival award, is now in regular production. The other cask ale, Sunbeam, is produced for the Guernsey market following the closure of the Guernsey Brewery. Up to four seasonal beers are produced each year.

Guernsey Sunbeam (OG 1042, ABV 4.2%)

Jimmy's Bitter (OG 1042, ABV 4.2%)

Special (OG 1045, ABV 4.5%)

Jollyboat

Jollyboat Brewery (Bideford) Ltd, The Coach House, Buttgarden Street, Bideford, Devon, EX39 2AU
☎ (01237) 424343

⊗ The brewery was established in 1995 by Hugh Parry and his son, Simon and is named after a sailor's leave boat. All the beers have a nautical theme. Most outlets supplied are in Devon but a trade route to Bristol has recently been established. Seasonal beers: Buccaneers (ABV 3.7%, summer), Contraband (ABV 5.8%, winter).

Grenville's Renown (OG 1037, ABV 3.8%)

Freebooter (OG 1040, ABV 4%)

Mainbrace (OG 1042, ABV 4.2%) ◆
Pale brown brew with a rich fruity aroma and a bitter taste and aftertaste.

Plunder (OG 1047, ABV 4.8%)

Jolly Brewer

Jolly Brewer, Kingston Villa, 27 Poplar Road, Wrexham, LL13 7DG
☎ (01978) 261884
✉ pene@jollybrewer.co.uk
jollybrewery.co.uk
Tours by arrangement (small groups only)

Penelope Coles has been brewing for over 26 years. Her beers can be purchased at the Butchers Market, Henblas Street, Wrexham. Pubs are supplied in the north-west of England and north Wales. House brews are also produced for many licensed premises. The brew plant is based in her home and around 15 gallons can be produced a day.

Benno's (OG 1040, ABV 4%)

Druid's Ale (OG 1040, ABV 4%)

Taid's Garden (OG 1040, ABV 4%)

Chwerw Cymru (OG 1045, ABV 4.5%)

Lucinda's Lager (OG 1045, ABV 4.5%)

Suzanne's Stout (OG 1045, ABV 4.5%)

Taffy's Tipple (OG 1050, ABV 5%)

Y Ddraig Goch (OG 1050, ABV 5%)

Tommy's (OG 1055, ABV 5.5%)

Penelope's Secret/Porter (OG 1060, ABV 6%)

Strange Brew (OG 1060, ABV 6%) ◆
Powerful, fruity, black lager-style beer. Dry, crisp, vinous and sharp with a sweetish aftertaste.

Joseph Herbert Smith*

Joseph Herbert Smith Trad Brewers, Fox Inn, Hanley Broadheath, Nr Tenbury Wells, Worcestershire, WR15 8QS
☎ (01886) 853189
☎ 07786 220409
✉ jonathansmudge2000@yahoo.co.uk
Tours by arrangement

The brewery was established in March 2007 by Jonathan Smith on a 2.5-barrel plant from Danelaw Brewery. In 2008 it relocated from Wombourne in Staffordshire to barns adjacent to the Fox Inn in Tenbury Wells. All equipment is gas fired and ingredients are sourced locally where possible. Seasonal beer: Kinny's Port Stout (ABV 4.5%, Nov-Feb).

Elm (OG 1039, ABV 3.9%)

Amy's Rose (OG 1040, ABV 4%)

Foxy Lady (OG 1043, ABV 4.3%)

Kelburn SIBA

Kelburn Brewing Co Ltd, 10 Muriel Lane, Barrhead, East Renfrewshire, G78 1QB
☎ (0141) 881 2138
✉ info@kelburnbrewery.com
kelburnbrewery.com
Tours by arrangement

Kelburn is a family business established in 2002. In the first six years of business, the beers have won 23 awards. Beers are available bottled and in take-away polypins. Seasonal beers: Ca'Canny (ABV 5.2%, winter), Pivo Estivo (ABV 3.9%, summer).

Goldihops (OG 1038, ABV 3.8%) ◆
Well-hopped session ale with a fruity taste and a bitter finish.

Misty Law (ABV 4%)
A dry, hoppy amber ale with a long-lasting bitter finish.

Red Smiddy (OG 1040, ABV 4.1%) ◆
This bittersweet ale predominantly features an intense citrus hop character that assaults the nose and continues into the flavour, balanced perfectly with fruity malt.

Dark Moor (OG 1044, ABV 4.5%)
A dark, fruity ale with undertones of liquorice and blackcurrant.

Cart Blanche (OG 1048, ABV 5%) ◆
A golden, full-bodied ale. The assault of fruit and hop camouflages the strength of this easy-drinking, malty ale.

Kelham Island SIBA

Kelham Island Brewery Ltd, Alma Street, Sheffield, South Yorkshire, S3 8SA
☎ (0114) 249 4804
✉ sales@kelhambrewery.co.uk
kelhambrewery.co.uk
Tours by arrangement

The brewery opened in 1990 behind the Fat Cat public house. Due to its success, the brewery moved to new purpose-built premises in 1999 (adjacent to the pub), with five times the capacity of the original brewery. The old building has been converted into a visitor centre. Five regular beers are brewed as well as monthly seasonal specials and more than 200 outlets are supplied.

Kelham Best Bitter (OG 1038, ABV 3.8%) ◆
A clean, characterful, crisp, pale brown beer. The nose and palate are dominated by refreshing hoppiness and fruitiness, which, with a good bitter dryness, lasts in the aftertaste.

Kelham Gold (OG 1038, ABV 3.8%)
A light golden ale, a hoppy nose and finish, a smooth drinking bitter.

Pride of Sheffield (OG 1040.5, ABV 4%)
A full-flavoured amber coloured bitter.

Easy Rider (OG 1041.8, ABV 4.3%) ◆
A pale, straw-coloured beer with a sweetish flavour and delicate hints of citrus fruits. A beer with hints of flavour rather than full-bodied.

Pale Rider (OG 1050, ABV 5.2%) ◆
A full-bodied, straw pale ale, with a good fruity aroma and a strong fruit and hop taste. Its well-balanced sweetness and bitterness continue in the finish.

Keltek SIBA

Keltek Brewery, Candela House, Cardrew Way, Redruth, Cornwall, TR15 1SS
☎ (01209) 313620
✉ sales@keltekbrewery.co.uk
keltekbrewery.co.uk
Shop Mon-Fri 8am-6pm

Keltek Brewery moved to Lostwithiel in 1999 and in 2006 moved again to Redruth and installed a new 25-barrel plant in addition to the original two-barrel plant, which is still used for specials and development. About 20 local pubs in the Redruth area are supplied direct with ales available nationally via wholesalers. All ales are also available bottle-conditioned. 2008 saw Doghouse Brewery, which closed in 2007, start to use the smaller Keltek brewing plant, thus avoiding the loss of Doghouse Ales. Keltek welcomes CAMRA members (by arrangement) to try their hand at brewing with 'Big Stu' on the small brewery.

4K Mild (OG 1038, ABV 3.8%)

Golden Lance (OG 1038, ABV 4%)

Magik (OG 1040, ABV 4.2%) ◆
A rounded, well-balanced and complex beer.

Mr Murdoch's Golden IPA (OG 1043, ABV 4.5%)

Natural Magik (OG 1044, ABV 4.5%)

Trevithick's Revenge (OG 1043, ABV 4.5%)

King (OG 1049, ABV 5.1%)

Grim Reaper (OG 1058, ABV 6%)

Kripple Dick (ABV 6%)

Uncle Stu's Famous Steak Pie Stout (OG 1060, ABV 6.5%)

Beheaded (OG 1068, ABV 7.6%)

Beheaded '76 (OG 1068, ABV 7.6%)

For Doghouse Brewery:

Wet Nose (OG 1038, ABV 3.8%)

Seadog (OG 1046, ABV 4.6%)

Kemptown SIBA

Kemptown Brewery Co Ltd, 33 Upper St James Street, Brighton, East Sussex, BN2 1JN
☎ (01273) 699595
✉ bev@kemptownbrewery.co.uk
🌐 kemptownbrewery.co.uk
Tours by arrangement

⊗ Kemptown was established in 1989 and built in the tower tradition behind the Hand in Hand, which is possibly the smallest pub in England with its own brewery. It takes its name and logo from the former Charrington's Kemptown Brewery, 500 yards away, which closed in 1964. Three free trade outlets are supplied. Seasonal beers are available.

Bitter (OG 1040, ABV 4%)

Ye Olde Trout (OG 1045, ABV 4.5%)

Keswick

Keswick Brewing Co, The Old Brewery, Brewery Lane, Keswick, Cumbria, CA12 5BY
☎ (017687) 80700
✉ info@keswickbrewery.co.uk
🌐 keswickbrewery.co.uk
Shop – call for details
Tours by arrangement

Phil and Sue Harrison set up their 10-barrel brewery in 2006. Around 50 outlets are supplied and the beers are always available in the Dog & Gun and the Square Orange, Keswick, the Middle Ruddings Hotel, Braithwaite and the Royal Oak, Ambleside. Seasonal beers: Thirst Blossom (ABV 4.1%), Thirst Quencher (ABV 4.3%), Thirst Chestnut (ABV 4%), Thirst Winter (ABV 4.4%), Thirst Blood (ABV 6%), Thirst Noel (ABV 6%).

Thirst Pitch (OG 1037, ABV 3.8%)

Thirst Ascent (OG 1034, ABV 4%)

Thirst Run (OG 1041, ABV 4.2%)

Thirst Fall (OG 1048, ABV 5%)

Keynsham

Keynsham Brewing Co Ltd, Brookleaze, Stockwood Vale, Keynsham, Bristol, BS31 2AL
☎ (0117) 983 6373
✉ jonfirth@blueyonder.co.uk
🌐 keynshambrewery.co.uk
Tours by arrangement

⊗ Keynsham opened in 2005 on the site of a former 10-barrel brewery. The brewer is John Firth, a long-standing CAMRA member and a craft brewer for many years. A wide variety of hops and grains is used. Some 30 outlets are supplied.

Pixash (OG 1042, ABV 4.1%) ◆
Mahogany-coloured best bitter with distinct dark forest fruit flavours from Bramling Cross hops.

Chew Valley Blond (OG 1044, ABV 4.3%) ◆
Pale, refreshing best bitter with undertones of lime and green apples.

Somerdale Golden (OG 1047, ABV 4.5%) ◆
Interestingly floral best bitter with spicy aroma and flavours of peppery hops and citrus.

Stockwood Stout (OG 1053, ABV 5%) ◆
Dark and complex stout, smoky, roast and liquorice flavour with a hint of sourness and sweet dark fruits fading to bittersweet.

Keystone

Keystone Brewery, Old Carpenters Workshop, Berwick St Leonard, Salisbury, Wiltshire, SP3 5SN
☎ (01747) 820426
✉ info@keystonebrewery.co.uk
🌐 keystonebrewery.co.uk
Shop Mon-Fri 9am-5pm
Tours by arrangement

⊗ Keystone Brewery was set up in 2006 with a 10-barrel plant. The beers have low food miles to help support a sustainable local community. Around 170 outlets are supplied.

Bed Rock (OG 1035, ABV 3.6%)

Gold Spice (OG 1039, ABV 4%)

Gold Standard (OG 1039, ABV 4%)

Large One/Alasdair's 1st Brew (OG 1041, ABV 4.2%)

Cheer Up (OG 1044, ABV 4.5%)

Porter (OG 1045, ABV 4.6%)

Cornerstone (OG 1047, ABV 4.8%)

Kilderkin*

Kilderkin Brewing Company, 1 Mill Road, Impington, Cambridgeshire, CB24 9PE
✉ sales@kilderkin.co.uk
🌐 kilderkin.co.uk

Kilderkin was founded in 2006 in a village just outside Cambridge. It produces bottle-conditioned ales for sale to a handful of local outlets and cask ales, which are mainly sold on an adhoc basis to local beer festivals.

Porter (OG 1048, ABV 4.8%)

Double (OG 1065, ABV 6%)

King SIBA

W J King & Co (Brewers), 3-5 Jubilee Estate, Foundry Lane, Horsham, West Sussex, RH13 5UE
☎ (01403) 272102
✉ sales@kingbeer.co.uk
🌐 kingbeer.co.uk
Shop Sat 10am-2pm
Tours by arrangement (limited to 15)

⊗ Launched in 2001 on a 20-barrel plant, the brewery had expanded to a capacity of 50 barrels a week by mid-2004. In 2004 premises next door were added to give more cellar space and to enable room to stock more bottle-conditioned beers. Around 200 outlets are supplied. Seasonal beers: Old Ale (ABV 4.5%, winter), Summer Ale (ABV 4%), Merry Ale (ABV 6.5%, Xmas).

Horsham Best Bitter (OG 1038, ABV 3.8%) ◆
A predominantly malty best bitter, brown in colour. The nutty flavours have some sweetness with a little bitterness that grows in the aftertaste.

Red River (OG 1048, ABV 4.8%) ◆
A full-flavoured, mid-brown beer. It is malty with some berry fruitiness in the aroma and taste. The finish is reasonably balanced with a sharp bitterness coming through.

Kings Head

Kings Head Brewery, Kings Head, 132 High Street, Bildeston, Ipswich, Suffolk, IP7 7ED
☎ (01449) 741434
✉ enquiries@bildestonkingshead.co.uk
🌐 bildestonkingshead.co.uk
Tours by arrangement

Kings Head has been brewing since 1996 in the old stables at the back of the pub. The plant has approximately five barrels' capacity and brewing takes place twice a week. The brewery stages a beer festival in May (Late Spring Bank Holiday) every year. Six other pubs and many beer festivals are supplied. Seasonal beer: Dark Vader (ABV 5.4%, winter).

Not Strong Beer/NSB (OG 1030, ABV 2.8%)

Best Bitter (OG 1040, ABV 3.8%)

Blondie (OG 1041, ABV 4%)

First Gold (OG 1044, ABV 4.3%)

Apache (OG 1046, ABV 4.5%)

Crowdie (OG 1050, ABV 5%)

Kingstone

Kingstone Brewery, Meadow Farm, Tintern, Monmouthshire, NP16 7NX
☎ (01291) 680111/680101
✉ shop@meadowfarm.org.uk
🌐 kingstonebrewery.co.uk

⊗ Kingstone Brewery is located in the Wye Valley where brewing began on a four-barrel plant in 2005. It moved in late 2007 to its present location and is under new ownership. All cask ales are also available bottle conditioned.

Three Castles (OG 1040, ABV 3.8%)

Challenger (OG 1043, ABV 4%)

Gold (OG 1043, ABV 4%)

No. 1 Stout (ABV 4.4%)

Classic (OG 1042, ABV 4.5%)

1503 (OG 1048, ABV 4.8%)

Abbey Ale (OG 1053, ABV 5.1%)

Humpty Dumpty (OG 1058, ABV 5.8%)

Kinver SIBA

Kinver Brewery, Unit 2, Fairfield Drive, Kinver, Staffordshire, DY7 6EW
☎ 07715 842679/07906 146777
✉ kinverbrewery@aol.com
🌐 kinverbrewery.co.uk
Tours by arrangement

Established in 2004 by two CAMRA members, Kinver Brewery consists of a five-barrel plant, producing four regular beers, seasonals and one-off brews. Kinver brews up to three times a week and supplies more than 30 pubs and clubs throughout the Midlands, including two in Kinver. A small bottling plant was purchased to enable it to sell bottle-conditoned beers. Seasonal beers: Dudley Bug (ABV 4.8%, May-Aug), Maybug (ABV 4.8%, May-Jun), Sunarise (ABV 4%, summer), Over the Edge (ABV 7.6%, Nov-Mar). Occasional beers: Caveman (ABV 5%), Crystal (ABV 4.8%).

Edge (OG 1041, ABV 4.2%) ◆
Amber with a caramel aroma. Sweet malty start with a little fruitiness developing into a strong hop and bitter finish. A good hoppy, lingering mouthfeel.

Pail Ale (OG 1044, ABV 4.4%) ◆
Gold with a hoppy aroma and malty background. Citrus hops dominate but are tempered with fruit for a bittersweet balance. Astringent note at the end.

Half Centurion (OG 1048, ABV 5%)
Pale bitter with citrus hop flavours and a bitter finish.

Khyber (OG 1054, ABV 5.8%)
Traditional strength imperial pale ale.

Lancaster

Lancaster Brewery Ltd, Unit 19, Lansil Industrial Estate, Caton Road, Lancaster, LA1 3PQ
☎ (01524) 848537
✉ sales@lancasterbrewery.co.uk
🌐 lancasterbrewery.co.uk

Lancaster began brewing in 2005. In 2007 the brewery underwent a change in direction with new faciities installed and new brands launched.

Amber (OG 1038, ABV 3.7%)

Blonde (OG 1042, ABV 4.1%)

Black (OG 1046, ABV 4.6%)

Red (OG 1048, ABV 4.9%)

Langham

Langham Brewery, Old Granary, Langham Lane, Lodsworth, West Sussex, GU28 9BU
☎ (01798) 860861
✉ office@langhambrewery.co.uk
langhambrewery.co.uk
Shop Tue & Sat 9am-5pm
Tours by arrangement

⊗ Langham Brewery was established in 2006 in an 18th-century granary barn and is set in the heart of West Sussex with fine views to the rolling South Downs. It is owned by Steve Mansley and James Berrow who both brew and run the business. The brewery is a 10-barrel steam heated plant and over 50 outlets are supplied.

Halfway to Heaven (OG 1035, ABV 3.5%)
A chestnut-coloured beer with a balanced biscuit maltiness and citrus and fruit hop character with a hint of spice.

Hip Hop (OG 1040, ABV 4%)
A blonde beer – clean and crisp. The nose is loaded with floral hop aroma while the pale malt flavour is overtaken by a dry and bitter finish.

Best (OG 1042, ABV 4.2%)
A tawny-coloured classic best with well-balanced malt flavours and bitterness.

Sundowner (OG 1042, ABV 4.2%)
A deep golden beer. The nose has tropical fruit, pineapple and citrus notes with a smooth maltiness in the background. There is a balanced dry and bitter finish with floral hop aroma.

Langham Special Draught/LSD (OG 1049, ABV 5.2%)
An auburn beer with rich, complex flavours and a deep red glow. The sweet maltiness is balanced with spicy hop aromas and a dry finish.

Langton

Langton Brewery, Grange Farm, Welham Road, Thorpe Langton, Leicestershire, LE16 7TU
☎ 07840 532826
✉ thelangtonbrewery.co.uk

⊗ The Langton Brewery started in 1999 in buildings behind the Bell Inn, East Langton. Due to demand, the brewery relocated in 2005 to a converted barn in Thorpe Langton, where a four-barrel plant was installed. All beers are available to take away in casks, polypins or bottles. Around 20 outlets are supplied. Seasonal beers: Bankers Draught (ABV 4.2%), Boxer Heavyweight (ABV 5.2%).

Caudle Bitter (OG 1039, ABV 3.9%) ◆
Copper-coloured session bitter that is close to pale ale in style. Flavours are relatively well-balanced throughout with hops slightly to the fore.

Inclined Plane Bitter (OG 1042, ABV 4.2%)
A straw-coloured bitter with a citrus nose and long, hoppy finish.

Hop On (OG 1044, ABV 4.4%)

Bowler Strong Ale (OG 1048, ABV 4.8%)
A strong traditional ale with a deep red colour and a hoppy nose.

Larkins SIBA

Larkins Brewery Ltd, Larkins Farm, Hampkin Hill Road, Chiddingstone, Kent, TN8 7BB
☎ (01892) 870328
Tours by arrangement (Nov-Feb)

⊗ Larkins Brewery was founded in 1986 by the Dockerty family, who bought the Royal Tunbridge Wells Brewery. The company moved to Larkins Farm in 1987. Since then the production of three regular brews and Porter in the winter months has steadily increased. Larkins owns one pub, the Rock at Chiddingstone Hoath, and supplies around 70 free houses within a radius of 20 miles.

Traditional Ale (OG 1035, ABV 3.4%)
Tawny in colour, a full-tasting hoppy ale with plenty of character for its strength.

Chiddingstone (OG 1040, ABV 4%)
Named after the village where the brewery is based, Chiddingstone is a mid-strength, hoppy, fruity ale with a long, bittersweet aftertaste.

Best (OG 1045, ABV 4.5%) ◆
Full-bodied, slightly fruity and unusually bitter for its gravity.

Porter (OG 1052, ABV 5.2%) ◆
Each taste and smell of this potent black winter beer (Nov-Apr) reveals another facet of its character. An explosion of roasted malt, bitter and fruity flavours leaves a bittersweet aftertaste.

Leadmill

Leadmill Brewery Ltd, Unit 1, Park Hall Farm, Park Hall Road, Denby, Derbyshire, DE5 8PX
☎ (01332) 835609
✉ tlc@leadmill.fsnet.co.uk

⊗ Originally set up in a pig sty in Selston, the brewery moved to Denby in 2002 and now has a four-barrel plant. Its sister brewery, Bottle Brook (qv), sources rare and unusual hops to be incorporated into Leadmill recipes. Its brewery tap is the Old Oak Inn, two miles away. Seasonal beers: Jersey City (ABV 5%, autumn), Ginger Spice (ABV 5%, summer), Autumn Goddess (ABV 4.2%), Get Stuffed (ABV 6.7%, Xmas).

Mash Tun Bitter (OG 1036, ABV 3.6%)

Old Oak Bitter (OG 1037, ABV 3.7%)

Duchess (OG 1041, ABV 4.2%)

Old Mottled Cock (OG 1041, ABV 4.2%)

Dream Weaver (OG 1042, ABV 4.3%)

Frosted Hop (OG 1042, ABV 4.3%)

Strawberry Blonde (OG 1042, ABV 4.4%)

Rolling Thunder (OG 1043, ABV 4.5%)

Curly Blonde (OG 1044, ABV 4.6%)

Maple Porter (OG 1045, ABV 4.7%)

Snakeyes (OG 1045, ABV 4.8%)

Agent Orange (OG 1047, ABV 4.9%)

Born in the USA (OG 1048, ABV 5%)

Retribution (OG 1048, ABV 5%)

Rampage (OG 1050, ABV 5.1%)

B52 (OG 1050, ABV 5.2%)

Destitution (OG 1051, ABV 5.3%)

Ghostrider (OG 1052, ABV 5.4%)

Beast (OG 1053, ABV 5.7%)

Rack and Ruin (OG 1055, ABV 5.7%)

Nemesis (OG 1062, ABV 6.4%)

WMD (OG 1065, ABV 6.7%)

Leatherbritches

Leatherbritches Brewery, Green Man & Blacks Head Royal Hotel, St John Street, Ashbourne, Derbyshire, DE6 1GH
☎ (01332) 864492
☎ 07976 279253

The brewery, founded in 1993 in Fenny Bentley, moved to Ashbourne in spring 2008 with a new, bigger brewing plant. The hotel and brewery business are separate but the hotel sells beers from the brewery. Bottle-conditioned beers are available.

Goldings (OG 1036, ABV 3.6%)
A light golden beer with a flowery hoppy aroma and a bitter finish.

Ginger Spice (OG 1036, ABV 3.8%)
A light, highly-hopped bitter with the added zest of Chinese stem ginger.

Ashbourne Ale (OG 1040, ABV 4%)
A pale bitter brewed with Goldings hops for a crisp lasting taste.

Belt-n-Braces (OG 1040, ABV 4.4%)
Mid-brown, full-flavoured, dry-hopped bitter.

Belter (OG 1040, ABV 4.4%)
Maris Otter malt produces a pale but interesting beer.

Dovedale (OG 1044, ABV 4.4%)

Ginger Helmet (OG 1047, ABV 4.7%)
As for Hairy Helmet but with a hint of China's most astringent herb.

Hairy Helmet (OG 1047, ABV 4.7%)
Pale bitter, well hopped but with a sweet finish.

Bespoke (OG 1050, ABV 5%)
Full-bodied, well-rounded premium bitter.

Leeds*

Leeds Brewery Co Ltd, 3 Sydenham Road, Leeds, West Yorkshire, LS11 9RU
☎ (0113) 244 5866
✉ sales@leedsbrewery.co.uk
leedsbrewery.co.uk

Leeds Brewery began production in June 2007 using a 20-barrel plant. It is the largest independent brewer in the city and uses a unique strain of yeast originally used by another, now defunct, West Yorkshire brewery. Around 300 outlets are supplied direct. Seasonal beers: see website.

Pale (OG 1037.5, ABV 3.8%)

Best (OG 1041, ABV 4.3%)

Midnight Bell (OG 1047.5, ABV 4.8%)

Leek

Staffordshire Brewing Company t/a Leek Brewery, 12 Churnet Court, Cheddleton, Staffordshire, ST13 7EF
☎ (01538) 361919
☎ 07971 808370
✉ leekbrewery@hotmail.com
Tours by arrangement

Brewing started in 2002 with a 4.5-barrel plant located behind the owner's house, before moving to the current site in 2004. The brewery was upgraded to a six-barrel plant in 2007. Cask beer is only available to special order as 95% of their beer is now in bottle-conditioned form, suitable for vegetarians. A range of beer cheeses is also made in the dairy, next door to the brewery.

Staffordshire Gold (ABV 3.8%)
Light, straw-coloured with a pleasing hoppy aroma and a hint of malt. Bitter finish from the hops, making it easily drunk and thirst-quenching.

Danebridge IPA (ABV 4.1%)
Full fruit and hop aroma. Flowery hop start with a great bitter taste. Fabulous finish of hops and flowers.

Staffordshire Bitter (ABV 4.2%)
Amber with a fruity aroma. Malty and hoppy start with the hoppy finish diminishing quickly.

Black Grouse (ABV 4.5%)

Hen Cloud (ABV 4.5%)

St Edwards (ABV 4.7%)

Rudyard Ruby (ABV 4.8%)

Double Sunset (ABV 5.2%)

Rocheberg Blonde (ABV 5.6%)

Cheddleton Steamer (ABV 6%)

Tittesworth Tipple (ABV 6.5%)

Lees IFBB

J W Lees & Co (Brewers) Ltd, Greengate Brewery, Middleton Junction, Manchester, M24 2AX
☎ (0161) 643 2487
✉ mail@jwlees.co.uk
jwlees.co.uk
Tours by arrangement

Lees is a family-owned brewery founded in 1828 by John Lees and run by the sixth generation of the family. Brewing takes place in the 1876 brewhouse designed and built by John Willie Lees, the grandson of the founder.

The brewhouse has been completely modernised in recent years to give greater flexibility. The company has a tied estate of around 170 pubs, mostly in North Manchester, with 30 in North Wales; all serve cask beer. Seasonal beers are brewed four times a year.

Brewer's Dark (OG 1032, ABV 3.5%)
Formerly GB Mild, this is a dark brown beer with a malt and caramel aroma. Creamy mouthfeel, with malt, caramel and fruit flavours and a malty finish. Becoming rare.

Bitter (OG 1037, ABV 4%)
Copper-coloured beer with malt and fruit in aroma, taste and finish.

Scorcher (OG 1038, ABV 4.2%)
A golden, easy drinking beer with a fruity aroma and a refreshing hop finish.

John Willie's (OG 1041, ABV 4.5%)
A well-balanced, full-bodied premium bitter.

Moonraker (OG 1073, ABV 7.5%)
A reddish-brown beer with a strong, malty, fruity aroma. The flavour is rich and sweet, with roast malt, and the finish is fruity yet dry. Available only in a handful of outlets.

Leila Cottage*

Leila Cottage Brewery, The Countryman, Chapel Road, Ingoldmells, Skegness, Lincolnshire, PE25 1ND
(01754) 872268
countryman_inn@btconnect.com
Tours by arrangement

Leila Cottage started brewing in November 2007. The brewery is situated at the Countryman pub – Leila Cottage was the original name of the building before it became a licensed club and more recently a pub.

Ace Ale (OG 1040, ABV 3.8%)

Leith Hill

Leith Hill Brewery, c/o Plough Inn, Coldharbour, Surrey, RH5 6HD
(01306) 711793
theploughinn@btinternet.com
ploughinn.com
Tours by arrangement

Leith Hill was formed in 1996 using home-made equipment to produce nine-gallon brews in a room at the front of the pub. The brewery moved to converted storerooms at the rear of the Plough Inn in 2001 and increased capacity to 2.5-barrels in 2005. All beers brewed are sold only on the premises.

Hoppily Ever After (OG 1036, ABV 3.6%)
A new beer originally brewed to celebrate a wedding but now added to the regular portfolio. Initially hoppy and citrusy with a sharp, hoppy, malty taste, slightly lacking in body. A hoppy, dry finish.

Crooked Furrow (OG 1040, ABV 4%)
A tangy, bitter beer, with malt and some balancing hop flavours. Pale brown in colour with an earthy, malty aroma and a long, dry and bittersweet aftertaste.

Tallywhacker (OG 1048, ABV 4.8%)
The recipe for this dark old ale has changed with the removal of caramel and a reduction in strength from 5.6% to 4.8%.

Leyden SIBA

Leyden Brewing Ltd, Lord Raglan, Nangreaves, Bury, Greater Manchester, BL9 6SP
(0161) 764 6680
Tours by arrangement

The brewery was built by Brian Farnworth and started production in 1999. Additional fermenting vessels have been installed, allowing a maximum production of 12 barrels a week. One pub is owned and 30 outlets are supplied.

Balaclava (ABV 3.8%)

Black Pudding (ABV 3.8%)
A dark brown, creamy mild with a malty flavour, followed by a balanced finish.

Nanny Flyer (OG 1040, ABV 3.8%)
A drinkable session bitter with an initial dryness, and a hint of citrus, followed by a strong, malty finish.

Light Brigade (OG 1043, ABV 4.2%)
Copper in colour with a citrus aroma. The flavour is a balance of malt, hops and fruit, with a bitter finish.

Rammy Rocket (ABV 4.2%)

Forever Bury (ABV 4.5%)

Raglan Sleeve (OG 1047, ABV 4.6%)
Dark red/brown beer with a hoppy aroma and a dry, roasty, hoppy taste and finish.

Crowning Glory (OG 1069, ABV 6.8%)

Lichfield

Lichfield Brewery Co Ltd, Upper St John Street, Lichfield, Staffordshire
robsondavidb@hotmail.com
lichfieldbrewery.co.uk

Does not brew; beers mainly contracted by Blythe, Tower and Highgate breweries (qv).

Linfit

Linfit Brewery, Sair Inn, 139 Lane Top, Linthwaite, Huddersfield, West Yorkshire, HD7 5SG
(01484) 842370

A 19th-century brew-pub that started brewing again in 1982, producing an impressive range of ales for sale at the pub. The beer is only available at the Sair Inn. English Guineas Stout is suitable for vegetarians and vegans.

Bitter (OG 1035, ABV 3.7%)
A refreshing session beer. A dry-hopped aroma leads to a clean-tasting, hoppy bitterness, then a long, bitter finish with a hint of malt.

Gold Medal (OG 1040, ABV 4.2%)
Very pale and hoppy. Use of the new dwarf variety of English hops, First Gold, gives an aromatic and fruity character.

Special (OG 1041, ABV 4.3%)

Dry-hopping provides the aroma for this rich and mellow bitter, which has a very soft profile and character: it fills the mouth with texture rather than taste. Clean, rounded finish.

Autumn Gold (OG 1045, ABV 4.7%)
Straw-coloured best bitter with hop and fruit aromas, then the bittersweetness of autumn fruit in the taste and the finish.

English Guineas Stout (OG 1050, ABV 5.3%)
A fruity, roast aroma preludes a smooth, roasted barley, chocolaty flavour that is bitter but not too dry. Excellent appearance; good, bitter finish.

Old Eli (OG 1050, ABV 5.3%)
A well-balanced premium bitter with a dry-hop aroma and a fruity, bitter finish.

Leadboiler (OG 1060, ABV 6.6%)
Powerful malt, hop and fruit in good balance on the tongue, with a well-rounded bittersweet finish.

Lion's Tale

Lion's Tale Brewery, Red Lion, High Street, Cheswardine, Shropshire, TF9 2RS
☎ **(01630) 661234**
✉ **cheslion@btinternet.com**

The building that houses the brewery was purpose-built in 2005 and houses a 2.5-barrel plant. Jon Morris and his wife have owned the Red Lion pub since 1996. Expansion is planned in the near future. Seasonal beer: Chesmas Bells (ABV 5.2%, Xmas).

Blooming Blonde (ABV 4.1%)

Lionbru (ABV 4.1%)

Chesbrewnette (ABV 4.5%)

Little Ale Cart

Little Ale Cart Brewing Co, c/o The Wellington, 1 Henry Street, Sheffield, South Yorkshire, S3 7EQ
☎ **(0114) 249 2295**

Brewing started in 2001, as Port Mahon, in a purpose-built brewery behind the Cask & Cutler. In 2007 the brewery and pub were taken over and the names of both changed to Little Ale Cart Brewing and the Wellington. The beer range is yet to be established.

Little Valley

Little Valley Brewery Ltd, Turkey Lodge Farm, New Road, Cragg Vale, Hebden Bridge, West Yorkshire, HX7 5TT
☎ **(01422) 883888**
✉ **info@littlevalleybrewery.co.uk**
littlevalleybrewery.co.uk
Shop Mon-Fri 9am-5pm
Tours by arrangement

The brewery opened in 2005 and is based in the Upper Calder Valley. The 10-barrel plant is in a converted pig shed. All beers are organic and approved by the Soil Association. Around 100 outlets are supplied. All cask beers are also available in bottle-conditioned form and have Vegan Society approval. Several beers are also contract brewed in bottle-conditioned form for Suma Wholefoods and sold under different names on Suma labels. A range of monthly specials was introduced in 2007.

Withens IPA (OG 1037, ABV 3.9%)
Creamy, gold-coloured, refreshingly light ale. Floral, spicy hop aroma, lightly flavoured with hints of lemon and grapefruit. Clean, bitter aftertaste.

Cragg Vale Bitter (OG 1039, ABV 4.2%)
Grainy, amber-coloured session bitter, light on the the palate, with a delicate flavour of malt and fruit, and a bitter finish.

Hebden's Wheat (OG 1043, ABV 4.5%)
A pale yellow, creamy wheat beer with a good balance of bitterness and fruit. A hint of sweetness but with a lasting, dry finish.

Stoodley Stout (OG 1044, ABV 4.8%)
Dark red, creamy stout with a rich roast aroma and luscious fruity, chocolate, roast flavours. Well-balanced, with a clean, bitter finish.

Tod's Blonde (OG 1045, ABV 5%)
Bright yellow, grainy, speciality beer with a citrus hop start and a dry finish. Fruity, with a hint of spice. Similar in style to a Belgian blonde beer.

Moor Ale (OG 1051, ABV 5.5%)
Tawny in colour, with a full-bodied taste. It has a strong malty nose and palate, with hints of heather and peat-smoked malt. Well-balanced with a bitter finish.

Litton

4-Bottles Ltd t/a Litton Ale Brewery, Queens Arms, Litton, North Yorkshire, BD23 5QJ
☎ **(01756) 770208**

Brewing started in 2003 in a purpose-built stone extension at the rear of the pub. Brewing liquor is sourced from a spring that provides the pub with its own water supply. The brew length is three barrels and all production is in cask form. Around 20 outlets are supplied.

Ale (OG 1038, ABV 3.8%)
An easy-drinking, traditional bitter with a good malt/hop balance and a bitter finish.

Leading Light (OG 1038, ABV 3.8%)
A long, bitter aftertaste follows a malty flavour with tart fruit and a rising hop bitterness in this light-coloured beer. Low aroma.

Gold Crest (OG 1039, ABV 3.9%)
A very pale beer with a smooth, creamy head. Heavy, fruity hoppiness with no lingering bitterness.

Dark Star (OG 1040, ABV 4%)
A smooth, creamy dark mild, full-bodied for its strength. The taste is quite bitter with roast coffee and tart dark fruit flavours, complemented by a bitter, roast finish.

Potts Beck (OG 1043, ABV 4.2%)
Malt and hops fight for control in this copper-coloured best bitter with a fruity aroma.

Lizard

Lizard Ales Ltd, The Old Nuclear Bunker, Pednavounder, Nr Coverack, Cornwall, TR12 6SE
☎ (01326) 281135
✉ lizardales@msn.com
🌐 lizardales.co.uk
Shop Mon-Fri 9am-5pm

Launched in 2004 by partners Richard Martin and Mark and Leonora Nattrass, Lizard Ales supplies around 25 regular outlets, mainly in west Cornwall. Bottle-conditioned beers are a speciality (suitable for vegetarians and vegans). The brewery moved in spring 2008 to larger premises allowing space for expansion.

Helford River (OG 1035, ABV 3.6%)

Bitter (OG 1041, ABV 4.2%)

Frenchman's Creek (OG 1042, ABV 4.6%)

An Gof (OG 1049, ABV 5.2%)

Loddon SIBA

Loddon Brewery Ltd, Dunsden Green Farm, Church Lane, Dunsden, Oxfordshire, RG4 9QD
☎ (0118) 948 1111
✉ sales@loddonbrewery.com
🌐 loddonbrewery.com
Shop Mon-Fri 8am-5pm; Sat 9am-3pm
Tours by arrangement

Loddon was established in 2003 in a 240-year-old brick and flint barn that houses a 17-barrel brewery able to produce 70 barrels a week. Over 350 outlets are supplied. The brewery site was expanded in 2007. Seasonal beers: Forbury Lion IPA (ABV 5.5%, Mar-Apr), Flight of Fancy (ABV 4.2%, May-Aug), Russet (ABV 4.5%, Sep-Nov), Hocus Pocus (ABV 4.6%, Dec-Feb). The brewery also produce monthly specials: see website. Bottle-conditioned beers are available.

Hoppit (OG 1035.5, ABV 3.5%) ◆
Hops dominate the aroma and taste of this drinkable, light-coloured session beer. A hint of malt and fruit accompanies and a pleasant bitterness carries through to the aftertaste.

Rin Tin Tin (OG 1042.8, ABV 4.1%)

Hullabaloo (OG 1043.8, ABV 4.2%) ◆
A hint of banana in the initial taste develops into a balance of hops and malt in this well-rounded, medium-bodied tawny bitter with a bitter aftertaste.

Ferryman's Gold (OG 1044.8, ABV 4.4%) ◆
Golden coloured with a strong hoppy character throughout, accompanied by malt in the mouth.

Bamboozle (OG 1048.8, ABV 4.8%) ◆
Full-bodied and well-balanced golden ale. Distinctive bittersweet flavour with hop character to accompany.

Lovibonds

Lovibonds Brewery Ltd, Rear of 19-21 Market Place, Henley-on-Thames, Oxfordshire, RG9 2AA
☎ (01491) 576596
✉ info@lovibonds.com
🌐 lovibonds.com
Shop Sat 11am-5pm
Tours by arrangement

⊗ Lovibonds Brewery was founded by Jeff Rosenmeier in 2005 and is named after Joseph William Lovibond, who invented the Tintometer to measure beer colour. In addition to cask conditioned ales, Lovibonds brews beers inspired by the traditions of other brewing nations. Around 50 outlets are supplied. Brewing also takes place on the Old Luxters Brewery plant (qv), 5 miles from Henley-on-Thames.

Henley Amber (OG 1035, ABV 3.4%)
An amber session bitter with a blend of roasted malts that gives a complex profile with a classic hop flavour and bitterness.

Henley Gold (OG 1045, ABV 4.6%)

Henley Dark (OG 1048, ABV 4.8%)

Lowes Arms

See Dane Town

Loweswater

Loweswater Brewery, Kirkstile Inn, Loweswater, Cumbria, CA13 0RU
☎ (01900) 85219
✉ info@kirkstile.com
🌐 kirkstile.com
Tours by arrangement

Loweswater Brewery was re-established at the Kirkstile Inn in 2003 by head brewer Matt Webster. The brewery produces six barrels a week for the inn and local beer festivals. Recent refurbishment and extension has increased capacity.

Melbreak Bitter (OG 1038, ABV 3.7%)
Pale bronze with a tangy fruit and hop resins aroma, and a long, bitter finish.

Rannerdale Best (OG 1042, ABV 4%)
A fruity beer made with Styrian Goldings hops.

Grasmoor Dark (OG 1042, ABV 4.3%)
Deep ruby red beer with chocolate malt on the aroma, and hop resins, roast malt and raisin fruit on the palate.

Kirkstile Gold (OG 1042, ABV 4.3%)
Pale lager-style beer with masses of tropical fruit flavour. Brewed with German hops.

Ludlow

Ludlow Brewing Co Ltd, Kingsley Garage, 105 Corve Street, Ludlow, Shropshire, SY8 1DJ
☎ (01584) 873291
✉ gary@theludlowbrewingcompany.co.uk
🌐 theludlowbrewingcompany.co.uk

The brewery opened in 2006 in a 250-year-old building that was once a malthouse. Around 30 pubs are supplied within a 50-mile radius. The six-barrel plant has been extended with two additional fermenters to cope with increased sales. All beers also available bottle-conditioned.

Best (ABV 3.7%)

Gold (ABV 4.2%)

Boiling Well (ABV 4.7%)

Lytham*

Lytham Brewery Ltd, Unit 11, Lidun Park Industrial Estate, Boundary Road, Lytham, Lancashire, FY8 5HU
☎ (01253) 737707
✉ info@LythamBrewery.co.uk
🌐 LythamBrewery.co.uk
Tours by arrangement

Lytham started brewing in early 2008 at the Hastings Club in Lytham but moved to larger premises soon after due to demand.

Amber (OG 1037, ABV 3.6%)
A traditional malty beer using English hops.

Gold (OG 1042, ABV 4.2%)
A golden beer with a fruity aroma and lasting bitter finish.

Dark (OG 1047, ABV 5%)
Dark chocolate malt with a hint of vanilla and a smooth, dry finish.

McGivern*

McGivern Ales, 17 Salisbury Road, Wrexham, LL13 7AS
☎ (01978) 354232
☎ 07891 676614

The brewery was established in early 2008. Special brews are also available. All beers are available bottle conditioned.

Matthew's Mild (ABV 3.6%)

Amber Ale (ABV 4%)

Summer Pale (ABV 4.1%)

Pale Ale (ABV 4.2%)

Swan for the Road (ABV 4.2%)

No. 17 Pale (ABV 4.4%)

McGuinness

See Offa's Dyke

McMullen IFBB

McMullen & Sons Ltd, 26 Old Cross, Hertford, Hertfordshire, SG14 1RD
☎ (01992) 584911
✉ reception@mcmullens.co.uk
🌐 mcmullens.co.uk

⊗ McMullen is Hertfordshire's oldest independent brewery, celebrating 180 years of brewing in 2007. A new brewhouse opened in 2006, giving the company greater flexibility to produce its regular cask beers and up to eight seasonal beers a year. Cask ale is served in all 135 pubs, though many managed pubs use cask breathers on all cask beers, as do some tenanted houses.

AK (OG 1035, ABV 3.7%) ◆
A pleasant mix of malt and hops leads to a distinctive, dry aftertaste that isn't always as pronounced as it used to be.

Cask Ale (OG 1039, ABV 3.8%)
A light and refreshing beer marked by the use of Styrian Goldings and English Fuggle hops.

Country Bitter (OG 1042, ABV 4.3%) ◆
A full-bodied beer with a well-balanced mix of malt, hops and fruit throughout.

Maclay

See Belhaven

Magpie

Magpie Brewery, Unti 4, Ashling Court, Ashling Street, Nottingham, Nottinghamshire, NG2 3JA
☎ 07738 762897
✉ info@magpiebrewery.com
🌐 magpiebrewery.com

◎ Magpie is a six-barrel plant launched in 2006 by three friends. It is located a few feet from the perimeter of Meadow Lane Stadium, home of Notts County FC – the Magpies – from which the brewery name naturally derived. Seasonal and occasional beers: see website.

Fledgling (ABV 3.8%)
A golden, hoppy session beer.

Trent Bridge Special (ABV 4%)
A traditional best bitter.

Thieving Rogue (ABV 4.5%)
A deceptively drinkable golden beer made entirely with pale malt.

Full Flight (ABV 4.8%)
A full-bodied dark beer with crystal and chocolate malt flavours.

JPA (ABV 5.2%)
An IPA made with Fuggles and Goldings hops and dry-hopped with Goldings.

Maldon

See Farmers Ales

Mallard SIBA

Mallard Brewery, 15 Hartington Avenue, Carlton, Nottingham, NG4 3NR
☎ (0115) 952 1289
✉ phil@mallard-brewery.co.uk
🌐 mallard-brewery.co.uk
Tours by arrangement

⊗ Phil Mallard built and installed a two-barrel plant in a shed at his home and started brewing in 1995. The brewery is only nine square metres and contains a hot liquor tank, mash tun, copper, and three fermenters. Since 1995 production has risen from one barrel a week to between six or eight barrels, which is the plant's maximum. Around 12 outlets are supplied. Seasonal beers: Waddlers Mild (ABV 3.7%, spring), DA (ABV 5.8%, Jan-Mar), Quismas Quacker (ABV 6%, Dec), Owd Duck (ABV 4.8%, winter).

Duck 'n' Dive (OG 1039, ABV 3.7%)
A light, single-hopped beer made from the hedgerow hop, First Gold. A bitter beer with a hoppy nose, good bitterness on the palate and a dry finish.

Quacker Jack (OG 1040, ABV 4%)

Feather Light (OG 1040, ABV 4.1%)

A very pale lager-style bitter with a floral bouquet and sweetness on the palate. A light, hoppy session beer.

Duckling (OG 1041, ABV 4.2%)
A crisp refreshing bitter with a hint of honey and citrus flavour.

Webbed Wheat (OG 1043, ABV 4.3%)
A wheat beer with a fruity, hoppy nose and taste.

Spittin' Feathers (OG 1044, ABV 4.4%)
A mellow, ruby bitter with a complex malt flavour of chocolate, toffee and coffee, complemented with a full and fruity/hoppy aftertaste.

Drake (OG 1045, ABV 4.5%)
A full-bodied premium bitter, with malt and hops on the palate, and a fruity finish.

Duck 'n' Disorderly (OG 1050, ABV 5%)

Friar Duck (OG 1050, ABV 5%)
A pale, full malt beer, hoppy with a hint of blackcurrant flavour.

Mallinsons*

Mallinsons Brewing Company, Plover Road Garage, Plover Road, Huddersfield, West Yorkshire, HD3 3HS
☎ (01484) 654301
✉ info@drinkmallinsons.co.uk
drinkmallinsons.co.uk
Tours by arrangement

The brewery was set up in early 2008 on a five-barrel plant in a former garage by CAMRA member Tara Mallinson. Tara is Huddersfield's only brewster. A range of seasonal and one-off specials are planned as well as bottle-conditioned beers.

Emley Moor Mild (ABV 3.4%)
Black with a ruby hint. A full-bodied mild with a nutty taste and slightly bitter finish.

Stadium Bitter (ABV 3.8%)
Straw-coloured with a clean, bitter taste and dry, fruity finish.

At Long Last... (ABV 4.1%)

Station Best Bitter (ABV 4.2%)
An amber-coloured best bitter with a balance of malt and fruity hops.

Castle Hill Premium (ABV 4.6%)
A golden-coloured premium bitter, hoppy with citrus tones.

Malt B*

Malt B Brewery, Crown Inn, Beesby Road, Maltby le Marsh, Lincolnshire, LN13 0JJ
☎ (01507) 451634

Malt B started brewing in early 2008. The beers list was not available at time of going to press.

Malvern Hills SIBA

Malvern Hills Brewery Ltd, 15 West Malvern Road, Malvern, Worcestershire, WR14 4ND
☎ (01684) 560165
✉ beer@tiscali.co.uk
malvernhillbrewery.co.uk
Tours by arrangement

Founded in 1997 in an old quarrying dynamite store. Now an established presence in the Three Counties and Black Country, the brewery has around 40 regular outlets. Future plans include a 50% expansion of the brewing capacity. Seasonal beer: Dr Gully's Winter Ale (ABV 5.2%).

Red Earl (OG 1037, ABV 3.7%)
A very light beer that does not overpower the senses. With a hint of apple fruit, it is ideal for slaking the thirst.

Feelgood (OG 1038, ABV 3.8%)

Moel Bryn (OG 1039, ABV 3.9%)

Swedish Nightingale (OG 1040, ABV 4%)

Worcestershire Whym (OG 1042, ABV 4.2%)

Priessnitz Plzen (OG 1043, ABV 4.3%)
A mix of soft fruit and citrus give this straw-coloured brew its quaffability, making it ideal for quenching summer thirsts.

Black Pear (OG 1044, ABV 4.4%)
A sharp citrus hoppiness is the main constituent of this golden brew that has a long, dry aftertaste.

Black Country Wobble (OG 1045, ABV 4.5%)
A sharp, clean-tasting golden beer with an aroma of hops challenged by fruit and malt, which hold up well in the mouth. A bitter dryness grows as the contrasting sweetness subsides.

Mr Phoebus (OG 1047, ABV 4.7%)

Dr Gully's IPA (OG 1052, ABV 5.2%)

Mansfield

See Marston's in New Nationals section

Marble SIBA

Marble Beers Ltd, 73 Rochdale Road, Manchester, M4 4HY
☎ (0161) 819 2694
✉ thebrewers_marblebeers@msn.com
Tours by arrangement

Marble opened at the Marble Arch Inn in 1997 and produces organic and vegan beers as well as some non-organic ales. It is registered with the Soil Association and the Vegetarian Society. Marble currently owns two pubs and supplies around 10 outlets. A number of bottle-conditioned beers are available as well as regular seasonals such as Port Stout (ABV 4.7%, Xmas) and Festival (ABV 4.4%, Oct).

Pint (OG 1038.5, ABV 3.9%)

Manchester (OG 1042, ABV 4.2%)
Yellow beer with a fruity and hoppy aroma. Hops, fruit and bitterness on the palate and in the finish.

JP Best (OG 1043, ABV 4.3%)
Pale tawny in colour. Hoppy with a good malt balance, assertively bitter.

Ginger (OG 1046, ABV 4.5%)

Intense and complex. Full-bodied and fiery with a sharp, snappy bite.

Stouter Stout (OG 1048, ABV 4.7%)
Black in colour, with roast malt dominating the aroma. Roast malt and hops in the mouth, with a little fruit. Pleasant, dry, bitter aftertaste.

Lagonda IPA (OG 1047.5, ABV 5%)
A golden, dry bitter. A quadruple addition of hops gives it depth and complexity.

Chocolate (OG 1054.5, ABV 5.5%)
A strong, stout-like ale.

Marches

Marches Brewing Co, 9 Oldfield Close, Leominster, Herefordshire, HR6 8PY
☎ (01584) 878999
✉ littlebeer@totalise.co.uk
Tours by arrangement

⊗ Brewing restarted at Marches in 2004. The brewery is was housed in two converted hop kilns but moved in 2008 to its present address. Beer is mostly brewed for the owner's shop in Ludlow.

Forever Autumn (ABV 4.2%)

Ludlow Gold (ABV 4.3%)

Dormington Gold (OG 1044, ABV 4.5%)
A light golden bitter brewed using First Gold hedgerow hops. It has an intense bitterness with a citrus zest.

St Lawrence Ale (ABV 4.5%)
A ruby premium bitter brewed with Boadicea hops.

Marston Moor

Marston Moor Brewery Ltd, PO Box 9, York, North Yorkshire, YO26 7XW
☎ (01423) 359641
✉ info@marstonmoorbrewery.co.uk

Established in 1983 in Kirk Hammerton, the brewery had a re-investment programme in 2005, moving brewing operations to nearby Tockwith, where it shares the site with Rudgate Brewery (qv). Two special beers are available each month, based either on a Yorkshire Airfield theme or on rural England. Around 250 outlets are supplied.

Cromwell's Pale (OG 1036, ABV 3.8%)
A golden beer with hops and fruit in strong evidence on the nose. Bitterness as well as fruit and hops dominate the taste and long aftertaste.

Matchlock Mild (OG 1038, ABV 4%)
Traditional, full-flavoured dark mild.

Mongrel (OG 1038, ABV 4%)
A balanced bitter with plenty of fruit character.

Fairfax Special (OG 1039, ABV 4.2%)
A full-bodied premium bitter, pale in colour with a well-balanced slightly citrus aroma.

Merriemaker (OG 1042, ABV 4.5%)
A premium straw-coloured ale with a typical Yorkshire taste.

Brewers Droop (OG 1045.5, ABV 5%)
A powerful golden ale with a sweet taste.

Marston's

See Banks's, Jennings & Marston's in New Nationals section

Matthews SIBA

Matthews Brewing Co Ltd, Unit 7, Timsbury Workshop Estate, Hayeswood Road, Timsbury, Bath, BA2 0HQ
☎ (01761) 472242
✉ **brewery@matthewsbrewing.co.uk**
matthewsbrewing.co.uk
Tours by arrangement

Matthews Brewing was established in 2005 on a five-barrel plant by Stuart Matthews and Sue Appleby. The emphasis is on the use of traditional techniques and quality ingredients, such as floor-malted barley from the nearby Warminster Maltings. Around 60 outlets are supplied direct and the ales are distributed more widely by wholesalers. Seasonal beers: Midsomer Pale (ABV 4.5%, summer), 40 Yard (ABV 5%, winter), Davy Lamp (ABV 5%, spring), Pit Pony (ABV 5.5%, autumn/winter). See website for further seasonal ales.

Brassknocker (OG 1037, ABV 3.8%)
Well-flavoured pale, hoppy citrus bitter with underlying sweetness; dry, astringent finish.

Bob Wall (OG 1041, ABV 4.2%)
Fruity best bitter; roasty hint with intense forest fruit and rich malt flavour continuing to a good balanced finish.

Mauldons SIBA EAB

Mauldons Ltd, Black Adder Brewery, 13 Churchfield Road, Sudbury, Suffolk, CO10 2YA
☎ (01787) 311055
✉ sims@mauldons.co.uk
mauldons.co.uk
Shop Mon-Fri 9.30am-4pm
Tours by arrangement

⊗ The Mauldon family started brewing in Sudbury in 1795. The brewery with 26 pubs was bought by Greene King in the 1960s. The current business, established in 1982, was bought by Steve and Alison Sims – both former employees of Adnams – in 2000. They relocated to a new brewery in 2005, with a 30-barrel plant that has doubled production. Some 200 outlets are supplied. There is a rolling programme of seasonal beers: see website.

Micawber's Mild (OG 1035, ABV 3.5%)
Fruit and roast flavours dominate the nose, with vine fruit and caramel on the tongue and a short, dry, coffeeish aftertaste. Full-bodied and satisfying.

Moletrap Bitter (OG 1038, ABV 3.8%)
Very easy drinking session bitter. Crisp and refreshing, hoppy and fruity throughout.

Silver Adder (OG 1042, ABV 4.2%)
A light-coloured bitter with five hop and malt combinations giving a refreshing, crisp finish.

Suffolk Pride (OG 1048, ABV 4.8%)
A full-bodied, copper-coloured beer with a good balance of malt, hops and fruit in the taste.

Black Adder (OG 1053, ABV 5.3%)
Superbly balanced dark, sweet ale, but with rich vine fruit throughout. The brewery's flagship beer.

White Adder (OG 1053, ABV 5.3%)
A pale brown, almost golden, strong ale. A warming, fruity flavour dominates and lingers into a dry, hoppy finish.

Mayfields

Mayfields Brewery, No. 8 Croft Business Park, Leominster, Herefordshire, HR6 0QF
☎ (01568) 611197
✉ info@mayfieldsbrewery.co.uk

Established in 2005, the Mayfields Brewery is located in the heart of one of England's major hop growing regions, Herefordshire. Only Herefordshire hops are used, many of which are grown on the farm where the brewery was founded and takes its name from. 2008 saw a change of location and ownership. Around 25 outlets are supplied. Seasonal beers: Crusader (ABV 4.3%, St George's Day/ Trafalgar Day), Conqueror (AB 4.3%, winter).

Hop Picker's Gold (ABV 3.6%)
Golden-coloured ale. Sweet malty notes and powerfully hoppy length.

Pioneer (ABV 3.9%)
Straw-coloured ale with a fruity finish.

Naughty Nell's (ABV 4.2%)
Smooth, copper-coloured ale with a malty body and citrussy hop finish.

Aunty Myrtle's (ABV 5%)
Full bodied and fruity.

Mayflower

Mayflower Brewery, c/o Royal Oak Hotel, Standishgate, Wigan, WN1 1XL
☎ (01257) 400605
✉ info@mayflowerbrewery.co.uk
🌐 mayflowerbrewery.co.uk

Mayflower was established in 2001 in Standish and relocated to the Royal Oak Hotel in Wigan in 2004. The original vessels and casks are still used. The Royal Oak is supplied as well as a number of other outlets in and around Wigan. Seasonal beers: Hic Bibi (ABV 5%, winter), Yule Be Lucky (ABV 5%, Dec).

Black Diamond (OG 1033.5, ABV 3.4%)

Douglas Valley Ale (OG 1044, ABV 4%)

Wigan Bier (OG 1039.5, ABV 4.2%)

Maypole

Maypole Brewery Ltd, North Laithes Farm, Wellow Road, Eakring, Newark, Nottinghamshire, NG22 0AN
☎ 07971 277598
✉ maypolebrewery@aol.com
🌐 maypolebrewery.co.uk

The brewery opened in 1995 in a converted 18th-century farm building. After changing hands in 2001 it was bought by the former head brewer in 2005. Increased demand has seen the installation of a fourth fermenting vessel. Maypole beers are always available at the Eight Jolly Brewers, Gainsborough and at the Beehive Inn, Maplebeck. Seasonal beers can be ordered at any time for beer festivals. Seasonal beers: see website.

Mayfly Bitter (OG 1038, ABV 3.8%)

Gate Hopper (OG 1040, ABV 4%)

Mayfair (OG 1039, ABV 4.1%)

Maybee (OG 1040, ABV 4.3%)

Major Oak (OG 1042, ABV 4.4%)

Mae West/Wellow Gold (OG 1044, ABV 4.6%)

Mayhem (OG 1048, ABV 5%)

Meantime SIBA

Meantime Brewing Co Ltd, Greenwich Brewery, 2 Penhall Road, London, SE7 8RX
☎ (020) 8293 1111
✉ info@meantimebrewing.com
🌐 meantimebrewing.com

Founded in 2000, Meantime brews a wide range of continental style beer and traditional English bottle-conditioned ales. Bottle-conditioned beers: Pale Ale (ABV 4.7%), Winter Time (ABV 5.4%, seasonal), Coffee Porter (ABV 6%), Wheat Grand Cru (ABV 6.3%), Raspberry Grand Cru (ABV 6.5%), Chocolate (ABV 6.5%), London Porter (ABV 6.5%), India Pale Ale (ABV 7.5%).

Meesons

See Old Bog

Melbourn

Melbourn Bros Brewery, 22 All Saints Street, Stamford, Lincolnshire, PE9 2PA
☎ (01780) 752186
✉ info@melbournbrothers.co.uk

A famous Stamford brewery that opened in 1825 and closed in 1974. It re-opened in 1994 and is owned by Samuel Smith of Tadcaster (qv). Melbourn brews spontaneously fermented fruit beers primarily for the American market but which can be ordered by the case in Britain by mail order. The beers are Apricot, Cherry and Strawberry (all ABV 3.4%). The brewery is open for tours Wednesday to Sunday 10am-4pm and there are open evenings for brewery tours, and beer and food tastings: prior booking essential.

Mersea Island

Mersea Island Brewery, Rewsalls Lane, East Mersea, Colchester, Essex, CO5 8SX
☎ (01206) 381830
✉ beers@merseawine.com
🌐 merseawine.com
Shop 11am-4pm daily (closed Tue)

The brewery was established at Mersea Island Vineyard in 2005, producing cask and bottle-conditioned beers. The brewery supplies several local pubs on a guest beer basis as well as most local beer festivals. The brewery holds its own festival of Essex-produced ales over the four day Easter weekend.

Yo Boy Bitter (OG 1038, ABV 3.8%) ◆
Pale session beer. Peach and orange on the aroma and taste, leading to a pleasantly bitter finish.

Gold (OG 1043, ABV 4.5%)
A lager/Pilsner style of ale.

Skippers Bitter (OG 1047, ABV 4.8%) ◆
Strong bitter, whose full character is dominated by pear drops and juicy malt. A raspberry tartness follows.

Oyster (OG 1048, ABV 5%)

Monkeys (OG 1049, ABV 5.1%)
A porter with deep and lasting malt and hop flavours.

Mighty Oak SIBA

Mighty Oak Brewing Co Ltd, 14b West Station Yard, Spital Road, Maldon, Essex, CM9 6TW
☎ **(01621) 843713**
✉ **sales@mightyoakbrewing.co.uk**
Tours by arrangement

Mighty Oak was formed in 1996 and moved in 2001 to Maldon, where capacity was increased to 67.5 barrels a week, increased again in 2006 to 85.2 barrels a week. Around 200 outlets are supplied plus a small number of wholesalers are used. Twelve monthly ales are brewed based on a theme; for 2008 the theme was 'Rivers' including 'In De Nile' and 'Wye Me!'. 2009 is 'Computers' including 'Spell Checker' and 'X Mouse Ale'. The brewery also market Buffer Ale (ABV 4.2%) under the 'Goods Shed' label.

IPA (OG 1031.5, ABV 3.5%) ◆
Light-bodied, pale session bitter, Hop notes are initially suppressed by a delicate sweetness but the aftertaste is more assertive.

Oscar Wilde (OG 1039.5, ABV 3.7%) ◆
Roasty dark mild with suggestions of forest fruits and dark chocolate. A sweet taste yields to a more bitter finish.

Maldon Gold (OG 1039.5, ABV 3.8%) ◆
Pale golden ale with a sharp citrus note moderated by honey and biscuity malt.

Burntwood Bitter (OG 1041, ABV 4%) ◆
Full-bodied bitter with an unusual blend of caramel, roast grain and grapefruit.

Simply The Best (OG 1044.1, ABV 4.4%) ◆
Well-balanced, mid-strength bitter with a sweet start and a dry, bitter finish.

English Oak (OG 1047.9, ABV 4.8%) ◆
Strong tawny, fruity bitter with caramel, butterscotch and vanilla. A gentle hop character is present throughout.

Milestone

Milestone Brewing Co, Great North Road, Cromwell, Newark, Nottinghamshire, NG23 6JE
☎ **(01636) 822255**
✉ **info@milestonebrewery.co.uk**
milestonebrewery.co.uk
Shop Mon-Fri 9am-5pm; Sat 9am-3pm
Tours by arrangement

The brewery has been in production since 2005 on a 12-barrel plant. It was founded by Kenneth and Frances Munro with head brewer Dean Penney. Around 150 outlets are supplied. Seasonal beers: Cool Amber (ABV 6%, May-Aug), Donner & Blitzed/Xmas Cracker (ABV 5.4%, Nov-Dec). Bottle-conditioned beers are also available.

Lions Pride (ABV 3.8%)

Classic Dark Mild (ABV 4%)

Shine On (ABV 4%)

Loxley Ale (ABV 4.2%)

Black Pearl (ABV 4.3%)

Crusader (ABV 4.4%)

Rich Ruby (ABV 4.5%)

Deliverance (ABV 4.6%)

Imperial Pale Ale (ABV 4.8%)

Olde Home Wrecker (ABV 4.9%)

Miss Sippy (ABV 5.5%)

Raspberry Wheat Beer (ABV 5.6%)

Milk Street SIBA

Milk Street Brewery Ltd (MSB Ltd), The Griffin, 25 Milk Street, Frome, Somerset, BA11 3DB
☎ **(01373) 467766**
✉ **rjlyall@hotmail.com**
milkstreetbrewery.co.uk
Tours by arrangement

Milk Street was started in 1999 in a former porn cinema attached to the Griffin pub in Frome. In 2005 the brewery expanded and is now capable of producing 30 barrels per week. Further expansion on this site is planned. It mainly produces for its own estate of three outlets with direct delivery to pubs within a 30-mile radius. Wholesalers are used to distribute the beers further afield. Seasonal specials are brewed every other month.

Funky Monkey (OG 1040, ABV 4%)
Copper-coloured summer ale boasting fruity flavours and aromas. A dry finish with developing bitterness and an undertone of citrus fruit.

Mermaid (OG 1041, ABV 4.1%)
Amber-coloured ale with a rich hop character on the nose, plenty of citrus fruit on the palate and a lasting bitter and hoppy finish.

Amarillo (OG 1043, ABV 4.3%)
Brewed with American hops to give the beer floral and spicy notes. Initially soft on the palate, the flavour develops to that of burnt oranges and a pleasant herbal taste.

Nick's (OG 1045, ABV 4.4%)
A malty best bitter with a rich nose of toffee and nuts, while the palate delivers plenty of rich chocolaty flavours. A dry finish with a slight sweetness.

Zig-Zag Stout (OG 1046, ABV 4.5%)
A dark ruby stout with characteristic roastiness and dryness with bitter chocolate and citrus fruit in the background.

Beer (OG 1049, ABV 5%)
A blonde beer with musky hoppiness and citrus fruit on the nose, while more fruit

surges through on the palate before the bittersweet finish.

Elderfizz (OG 1049, ABV 5%)
A golden yellow wheat beer with a prominent elderflower edge.

Millis

Millis Brewing Co Ltd, St Margaret's Farm, St Margaret's Road, South Darenth, Dartford, Kent, DA4 9LB
☎ (01322) 866233

John and Miriam Millis started with a half-barrel plant at their home in Gravesend. Demand outstripped the facility and Millis moved in 2003 to a new site – a former farm cold store – with a 10-barrel plant. They now supply around 40 outlets within a 50-mile radius. Seasonal beer: Winter Witch (ABV 4.8%).

Kentish Dark (OG 1035, ABV 3.5%)
A traditional dark mild with chocolate and roasted notes.

Gravesend Guzzler (OG 1037, ABV 3.7%)

Oast Shovellers (OG 1039, ABV 3.9%)
A copper-coloured ale with a pale and crystal malt base, ending with a distinctive, clean finish.

Hopping Haze (OG 1041, ABV 4.1%)

Kentish Gold (OG 1041, ABV 4.1%)
A pale, full-hopped flavoured beer with a crisp, dry finish.

Dartford Wobbler (OG 1043, ABV 4.3%)
A tawny-coloured, full-bodied best bitter with complex malt and hop flavours and a long, clean, slightly roasted finish.

Kentish Red Ale (OG 1043, ABV 4.3%)
A traditional red ale with complex malt, hops and fruit notes.

Old Kentish Ale (OG 1048, ABV 4.8%)

Millstone SIBA

Millstone Brewery Ltd, Unit 4, Vale Mill, Micklehurt Road, Mossley, OL5 9JL
☎ (01457) 835835
✉ info@millstonebrewery.co.uk
millstonebrewery.co.uk

Established in 2003 by Nick Boughton and Jon Hunt, the brewery is located in an 18th-century textile mill. The eight-barrel plant produces a range of pale, hoppy beers including five regular and seasonal/occasional beers. Several of the beers are available in bottle-conditioned form. More than 50 outlets are supplied.

Vale Mill (OG 1039, ABV 3.9%)
A pale gold session bitter with a floral and spicy aroma building upon a crisp and refreshing taste.

Three Shires Bitter (OG 1040, ABV 4%) ◆
Yellow beer with hop and fruit aroma. Fresh citrus fruit, hops and bitterness in the taste and aftertaste.

Tiger Rut (OG 1040, ABV 4%)
A pale, hoppy ale with a distinctive citrus/grapefruit aroma.

Grain Storm (OG 1042, ABV 4.2%) ◆
Yellow/gold beer with a grainy mouthfeel and fresh fruit and hop aroma. Citrus peel and hops in the mouth, with a bitter finish.

True Grit (OG 1049, ABV 5%)
A well-hopped strong ale with a mellow bitterness and a citrus/grapefruit aroma.

Milton SIBA EAB

Milton Brewery Cambridge Ltd, 111 Cambridge Road, Milton, Cambridgeshire, CB4 6AT
☎ (01223) 226198
✉ enquiries@miltonbrewery.co.uk
miltonbrewery.co.uk
Tours by arrangement

The brewery has grown steadily since it was founded in 1999. More than 100 outlets are supplied around the Cambridge area and further afield through wholesalers. Three tied houses (Peterborough and London) are owned by an associated company, Individual Pubs Ltd. Regular seasonal beers are also brewed including Mammon (ABV 7%, Dec-Feb). Nero is suitable for vegetarians and vegans.

Minotaur (OG 1035, ABV 3.3%) ◆
Characterised by malt and roast throughout, this brown/red mild is light bodied; bittersweet on initial taste with a dry finish.

Jupiter (OG 1037, ABV 3.5%) ◆
A copper-coloured bitter with malt and hops in balance on nose and palate. Some caramel sweetness, but butterscotch lingers on in the aftertaste.

Neptune (OG 1039, ABV 3.8%) ◆
Delicious hop aromas introduce this well-balanced, nutty and refreshing copper-coloured ale. Good hoppy finish.

Pegasus (OG 1043, ABV 4.1%) ◆
Fruit and some hops on the nose lead through into a fine balance of malt, fruit and hops on a bittersweet base. Malt is also present in the long, dry finish of this brown/red beer.

Sparta (OG 1043, ABV 4.3%)

Nero (OG 1050, ABV 5%) ◆
A satisfying, full-flavoured black brew with a good balance of malt, roast and fruit. Bittersweet flavours carry through to a dry finish.

Cyclops (OG 1055, ABV 5.3%)
Deep copper-coloured ale, with a rich hoppy aroma and full body; fruit and malt notes develop in the finish.

Moles SIBA

Moles Brewery (Cascade Drinks Ltd), 5 Merlin Way, Bowerhill, Melksham, Wiltshire, SN12 6TJ
☎ (01225) 704734/708842
✉ sales@moles-cascade.co.uk
molesbrewery.com
Shop Mon-Fri 9am-5pm; Sat 9am-12pm
Tours by arrangement

Moles was established in 1982 by Roger Catte, a former Ushers brewer, using his nickname to name the brewery. 12 pubs are owned, all serving cask beer. Around 200 outlets are supplied locally. The brewery achieved Soil Association certification in 2007. Seasonal beers: see website.

Tap Bitter (OG 1035, ABV 3.5%)
A session bitter with a smooth, malty flavour and clean bitter finish.

Best Bitter (OG 1040, ABV 4%)
A well-balanced, amber-coloured bitter, clean, dry and malty with some bitterness, and delicate floral hop flavour.

Landlords Choice (OG 1045, ABV 4.5%)
A dark, strong, smooth porter, with a rich fruity palate and malty finish.

Molennium (OG 1045, ABV 4.5%)
There are fruit, caramel and malty overtones in the aroma of this deep amber-coloured ale, balanced by a pleasant bitterness in the taste.

Rucking Mole (OG 1045, ABV 4.5%)
A chestnut-coloured premium ale, fruity and malty with a smooth bitter finish.

Moleten Silver (OG 1046, ABV 4.6%)
25th Anniversary ale. Gold in colour with a good malty body, distinct bitterness and aroma.

Molecatcher (OG 1050, ABV 5%)
A copper-coloured ale with a delightfully spicy hop aroma and taste, and a long bitter finish.

Moonstone

Moonstone Brewery (Gem Taverns Ltd), Ministry of Ale, 9 Trafalgar Street, Burnley, Lancashire, BB11 1TQ
☎ (01282) 830909
meet@ministryofale.co.uk
moonstonebrewery.co.uk
Tours by arrangement

A small, 2.5-barrel brewery, based in the Ministry of Ale pub. Brewing started in 2001 and beer is only generally available in the pub. Seasonal beer: Red Jasper (ABV 6%, winter).

Black Star (OG 1037, ABV 3.4%)

Blue John (ABV 3.6%)

Tigers Eye (OG 1037, ABV 3.8%)

MPA (ABV 4%)

Darkish (OG 1042, ABV 4.2%)

Moor SIBA

Moor Beer Co Ltd, Whitley Farm, Ashcott, Somerset, TA7 9QW
☎ (01458) 210050
justin@moorbeer.co.uk
moorbeer.co.uk
Tours by arrangement

Moor Beer has been brewing since 1996 on a dairy farm. Co-owner and brewer Justin Hawke recently upgraded the 10-barrel plant. The brewery also runs a wholesaling business suppling pubs and beer festivals. Specials are brewed for rail tours. All beers are available bottle conditioned.

Revival (OG 1038, ABV 3.8%)
An immensely hoppy and refreshing pale ale.

Milly's (OG 1041, ABV 3.9%)
A dark mild with a smooth mouthfeel and a slightly roasty finish.

Merlin's Magic (OG 1045, ABV 4.3%) ◆
Dark amber-coloured, complex, full-bodied beer, with fruity notes.

Peat Porter (OG 1047, ABV 4.5%) ◆
Dark brown/black beer with an initially fruity taste leading to roast malt with a little bitterness. A slightly sweet malty finish.

Confidence (OG 1048, ABV 4.6%)
Ruby-coloured premium bitter with a spicy hoppiness and rich malt profile.

Ported Peat Porter (OG 1049, ABV 4.7%)
Peat Porter with added Reserve Port.

Somerland Gold (OG 1052, ABV 5%)
Hoppy golden ale with hints of honey.

Old Freddy Walker (OG 1075, ABV 7.3%) ◆
Rich, dark, strong ale with a fruity complex taste, leaving a fruitcake finish.

JJJ IPA (OG 1090, ABV 9%)
Copper-coloured, new world triple IPA. Immensely hoppy and malty.

Moorhouse's SIBA

Moorhouse's Brewery (Burnley) Ltd, The Brewery, Moorhouse Street, Burnley, Lancashire, BB11 5EN
☎ (01282) 422864/416004
Tours by arrangement

Established in 1865 as a drinks manufacturer, the brewery started producing cask-conditioned ale in 1978 and has achieved recognition by winning more international and CAMRA awards than any other brewery of its size. Two new additional 30-barrel fermenters were installed in 2004, taking production to 320 barrels a week maximum. A new brewhouse is planned that will increase production to 40,000 barrels a year. The company owns six pubs, all serving cask-conditioned beer, and supplies some 250 free trade outlets. There is a selection of seasonal ales throughout the year: see website.

Black Cat (OG 1036, ABV 3.4%) ◆
A dark mild-style beer with delicate chocolate and coffee roast flavours and a crisp, bitter finish.

Premier Bitter (OG 1036, ABV 3.7%) ◆
A clean and satisfying bitter aftertaste rounds off this well-balanced hoppy, amber session bitter.

Pride of Pendle (OG 1040, ABV 4.1%) ◆
Well-balanced amber best bitter with a fresh initial hoppiness and a mellow, malt-driven body.

Blond Witch (OG 1045, ABV 4.5%)
A pale coloured ale with a crisp, delicate fruit flavour. Dry and refreshing with a smooth hop finish.

Pendle Witches Brew (OG 1050, ABV 5.1%) ◆
Well-balanced, full-bodied, malty beer with a long, complex finish.

Mordue SIBA

Mordue Brewery, Units D1 & D2, Narvic Way, Tyne Tunnel Estate, North Shields, Tyne & Wear, NE29 7XJ
☎ (0191) 296 1879
✉ enquiries@morduebrewery.com
🌐 morduebrewery.com
Shop Mon-Fri 11am-3pm
Tours by arrangement

The original Mordue Brewery closed in 1879 and the name was revived in 1995. In 1998, a 20-barrel plant and a move to bigger premises allowed production to keep pace with demand. By 2005 the business had expanded to the point where another move became necessary. The beers are distributed nationally and 200 outlets are supplied direct. The company was placed in administration in April 2008 but continues to trade. Seasonal beers: see website.

Five Bridge Bitter (OG 1038, ABV 3.8%) ◆
Crisp golden beer with a good hint of hops, the bitterness carries on in the finish. A good session bitter.

Geordie Pride (OG 1042, ABV 4.2%) ◆
Well-balanced and hoppy with a long bitter finish.

Workie Ticket (OG 1045, ABV 4.5%) ◆
Complex tasty bitter with plenty of malt and hops, long satisfying bitter finish.

Radgie Gadgie (OG 1048, ABV 4.8%) ◆
Strong, easy drinking bitter with plenty of fruit and hops.

IPA (OG 1051, ABV 5.1%) ◆
Easy drinking golden ale with plenty of hops, the bitterness carries on in the finish. Very moreish!

Morrells

See Burtonwood

Morton

Morton Brewery, Unit 10, Essington Light Industrial Estate, Essington, Wolverhampton, Staffordshire, WV11 2BH
☎ 07988 069647

Office: 96 Brewood Road, Coven, Staffordshire, WV9 5EF
✉ mortonbrewery@aol.com
🌐 mortonbrewery.co.uk

Morton was established in January 2007 on a three-barrel plant by Gary and Angela Morton, both CAMRA members. Eight outlets are supplied direct plus various beer festivals. Seasonal beers: see website.

Merry Mount (OG 1037, ABV 3.8%)

Jelly Roll (OG 1041, ABV 4.2%)

Scottish Maiden (OG 1045, ABV 4.6%)

Moulin

Moulin Hotel & Brewery, 2 Baledmund Road, Moulin, Pitlochry, Perthshire, PH16 5EL
☎ (01796) 472196
✉ enquiries@moulinhotel.co.uk
🌐 moulinhotel.co.uk
Shop 12-3pm daily
Tours by arrangement

The brewery opened in 1995 to celebrate the Moulin Hotel's 300th anniversary. Two pubs are owned and four outlets are supplied. Bottle-conditioned beer is available.

Light (OG 1036, ABV 3.7%) ◆
Thirst-quenching, straw-coloured session beer, with a light, hoppy, fruity balance, ending with a gentle, hoppy sweetness.

Braveheart (OG 1039, ABV 4%) ◆
An amber bitter, with a delicate balance of malt and fruit and a Scottish-style sweetness.

Ale of Atholl (OG 1043.5, ABV 4.5%) ◆
A reddish, quaffable, malty ale, with a solid body and a mellow finish.

Old Remedial (OG 1050.5, ABV 5.2%) ◆
A distinctive and satisfying dark brown old ale, with roast malt to the fore and tannin in a robust taste.

Nailsworth

Nailsworth Brewery Ltd, The Village Inn, The Cross, Nailsworth, Gloucestershire, GL6 0HH
☎ 07878 448377
✉ jonk@nailsworth-brewery.co.uk
🌐 nailsworth-brewery.co.uk
Tours by arrangement

The original Nailsworth Brewery closed in 1908. In 2004, after a gap of 98 years, commercial brewing returned in the form of a six-barrel micro-brewery. This is the brainchild of Messrs Hawes and Kemp, whose aim is to make the town of Nailsworth once again synonymous with quality beer. Around 30 outlets are supplied direct. Seasonal beers: see website.

Artist's Ale (OG 1040, ABV 3.9%)
A light-coloured bitter full of citrus flavours.

Mayor's Bitter (OG 1042, ABV 4.2%)
A best bitter with malt textures complemented by a long-lasting taste of blackcurrant.

Town Crier (OG 1046, ABV 4.7%)
A premium ale with delicate grassy and floral overtones.

Nant*

Bragdy'r Nant, Penrhwylfa, Maenan, Llanrwst, Conwy, LL26 0UA
☎ 07723 036862
✉ postmaster@jonesgw2.demon.co.uk
🌐 cwrwnant.co.uk

Commenced brewing in late 2007 with a plant purchased from the Yorkshire Dales Brewery. Capacity is currently 10-15 firkins a week. Seasonal and one-off beers are also produced including Mwnci Nell (ABV 5.9%, Xmas).

Mochyn Hapus (ABV 3.7%)

Pen Dafad (ABV 4.2%)

Chawden Aur (ABV 4.3%)

Grans's Lamb (ABV 4.5%)

Naylor's

Naylor's Brewery, Units 1 & 2, Midland Mills, Station Road, Cross Hills, Keighley, West Yorkshire, BD20 7DT
☎ (01535) 637451
✉ info@naylorsbrewery.co.uk
naylorsbrewery.co.uk
Tours by arrangement

Naylors started brewing early in 2005, based at the Old White Bear pub in Keighley. Expansion required a move to the current site in 2006 and included a rebranding of the beers. Around 75 outlets are supplied. A wide range of seasonal and special beers are available under the Brewer's Choice banner. Bottle-conditioned ales are also produced.

Pinnacle Mild (ABV 3.4%)
This brown, malty mild has complex roast flavours with chocolate and fruity undertones and a dry bitter finish.

Pinnacle Pale Ale (ABV 3.6%)

Pinnacle Bitter (ABV 3.9%)

Pinnacle Blonde (ABV 4.3%)

Pinnacle Porter (ABV 4.8%)
An intense roast bitterness characterises this full-bodied black beer. There are also hints of chocolate and coffee against a fruity background. Roast dominates the lingering aftertaste.

Nelson SIBA

Nelson Brewing Co UK Ltd, Unit 2, Building 64, The Historic Dockyard, Chatham, Kent, ME4 4TE
☎ (01634) 832828
✉ sales@nelsonbrewingcompany.co.uk
nelsonbrewingcompany.co.uk
Shop Mon-Fri 9am-4.30pm
Tours by arrangement

Nelson started out in 1995 as the Flagship Brewery but changed its name in 2004. It was acquired by the current owner, Piers MacDonald, in 2006. The brewery is based in Chatham's preserved Georgian dockyard, where Nelson's flagship, HMS Victory, was built. 80 outlets are supplied direct. All cask beers are also available bottle conditioned. Seasonal and occasional beers: see website.

Master Mate Mild (OG 1038, ABV 3.7%)

Rochester Bitter (OG 1038, ABV 3.7%)
A refreshing pale and hoppy bitter.

Pieces of Eight (OG 1039, ABV 3.8%)

Trafalgar Bitter (OG 1039, ABV 4.1%)
A light, easy-drinking ale with balanced malt and hop flavour and hints of honey and nuts to finish.

IPA (OG 1049, ABV 4.2%)

Dogwatch Stout (OG 1044, ABV 4.5%)

Friggin' in the Riggin' (OG 1048, ABV 4.7%)
Drinkable premium bitter with smooth malt flavour and bittersweet aftertaste.

Purser's Pussy Porter (OG 1049, ABV 5.1%)

Nelson's Blood (OG 1062, ABV 6%)
Malty with mellow roast tones, slightly nutty and fruity.

Nethergate SIBA EAB

Nethergate Holdings Ltd, The Growler Brewery, The Street, Pentlow, Essex, CO10 7JJ
☎ (01787) 283220
✉ orders@nethergate.co.uk
nethergate.co.uk
Tours by arrangement

Nethergate Brewery was established in 1986 at Clare, Suffolk. Production tripled in the 1990s, but the brewery was unable to meet demand and in 2005 moved to a new site to enable production to double. Around 400 outlets are supplied direct. Seasonal beers are brewed monthly and bottle-conditoned beers are available.

IPA (OG 1036, ABV 3.5%)
Bitter-tasting session beer with some fruit and malt balance the predominate hop character. Very dry aftertaste.

Priory Mild (OG 1036, ABV 3.5%)
A 'black bitter' rather than a true mild. Strong roast and bitter tastes dominate throughout.

Umbel Ale (OG 1039, ABV 3.8%)
Pleasant, easy-drinking bitter, infused with coriander, which dominates.

Three Point Nine (OG 1040, ABV 3.9%)
Light tasting, sweetish and fruity session beer.

Suffolk County Best Bitter (OG 1041, ABV 4%)
Dark bitter with roast grain tones off-setting biscuity malt and powerful hoppy, bitter notes.

Augustinian Ale (OG 1046, ABV 4.5%)
A pale, refreshing, complex best bitter. A fruity aroma leads to a bittersweet flavour and aftertaste with a predominance of citrus tones.

Essex Border (OG 1049, ABV 4.8%)
Bland, under-powered pale bitter. Does not drink its weight.

Old Growler (OG 1052, ABV 5%)
Well-balanced porter in which roast grain is complemented by fruit and bubblegum.

Umbel Magna (OG 1052, ABV 5%)
Old Growler flavoured with coriander. The spice is less dominant than in Umbel Ale, with some of the weight and body of the beer coming through.

Stour Valley Strong/SVS (OG 1063, ABV 6.2%)
A dark ruby red porter, brewed using a blend of amber, black and chocolate malts.

Newby Wyke SIBA

Newby Wyke Brewery, Willoughby Arms Cottages, Station Road, Little Bytham, Lincolnshire, NG33 4RA
☎ (01780) 411119
✉ newbywyke.brewery@btopenworld.com
newbywyke.co.uk
Tours by arrangement

The brewery is named after a Hull trawler skippered by brewer Rob March's grandfather. After starting life in 1998 as a 2.5-barrel plant in a converted garage, growth has been steady and the brewery moved to premises behind the Willoughby Arms. Current brewing capacity is 50 barrels a week. Some 180 outlets are supplied. Seasonal beers: see website.

HMS Revenge (OG 1037, ABV 4.2%)
A single-hopped ale with floral undertones.

Kingston Topaz (OG 1037, ABV 4.2%)

Bear Island (OG 1044, ABV 4.6%)
A blonde beer with a hoppy aroma and a crisp, dry citrus finish.

White Squall (OG 1045, ABV 4.8%)
A pale blonde ale with a full hop taste and a citrus finish.

For Nobody Inn, Grantham:

Grantham Gold (OG 1037, ABV 4.2%)

Newmans SIBA

T G Newman t/a Newmans Brewery, Unit 2E, Former Hill Buildings, Pontygwindy Industrial Estate, Caerphilly, CF83 3HU
☎ 0870 803 3876
✉ sales@newmansbrewery.com
newmansbrewery.com
Tours by arrangement

Newmans opened on the day England won the Rugby World Cup in November 2003. It has since expanded from a five-barrel plant to a 20-barrel in 2005 and has re-located the brewery to a 40-barrel plant in South Wales, sharing the brewery with sister brewing company, The Celt Experience Ltd.

Red Stag Bitter (OG 1039, ABV 3.6%)
Dark red session ale, smooth, malty with soft fruit accents; dry fruit finish.

Wolvers Ale (OG 1042, ABV 4.1%)
Well-rounded best bitter with good body for its strength. Initial sweetness with a fine malt flavour is balanced by a slightly astringent, hoppy finish.

Mendip Mammoth (OG 1044, ABV 4.3%)
Fruity and fresh with a continental hop presence.

Last Lion of Britain (ABV 5%)

Nobby's

Nobby's Brewery, 3 Pagent Court, Kettering, Northamptonshire, NN15 6GR
☎ (01536) 521868

Second Brewery: Ward Arms, High Street, Guilsborough, Northants, NN6 8PY
✉ info@nobbysbrewery.co.uk
nobbysbrewery.co.uk
Tours by arrangement

Paul 'Nobby' Mulliner started commercial brewing in 2004 on a 2.5-barrel plant at the rear of the Alexandra Arms in Kettering, which also serves as the brewery tap. The plant has since been enlarged to five barrels and further growth saw an extra 10-barrel plant set up at the Ward Arms, Guilsborough in 2007. The plant at the Alex will continue brewing for the pub. Seasonal beers: see website.

Claridges Crystal (OG 1036, ABV 3.6%)

Best (OG 1039, ABV 3.8%)

Tressler XXX Mild (OG 1038, ABV 3.8%)

Wild West (OG 1046, ABV 4.6%)

Landlord Own (OG 1050, ABV 5%)

T'owd Navigation (OG 1061, ABV 6.1%)

Norfolk Cottage SIBA

Norfolk Cottage Brewing, 98-100 Lawson Road, Norwich, Norfolk, NR3 4LF
☎ (01603) 788508/270520
✉ norfolkcottagebeers@tiscali.co.uk

Launched in 2004 by Ray Ashworth, founder of Woodforde's, Norfolk Cottage undertakes consultancy brewing and pilot brews for the Fat Cat Brewing Co at the same address. One best bitter is available to the trade plus bespoke ales in small quantities to order. Three outlets are supplied direct.

Best (OG 1042, ABV 4.1%)

Norfolk Square*

Norfolk Square Brewery llp, Unit 7, Estcourt Road, Great Yarmouth, Norfolk, NR30 4JQ
☎ (01493) 854484
✉ beer@norfolksquarebrewery.co.uk
norfolksquarebrewery.co.uk

Norfolk Square began brewing in May 2008 on a 2.5-barrel plant. Bottle-conditioned beers are available and seasonals are planned.

Pi (ABV 3.8%)

Scroby (ABV 4.2%)

Stiletto (ABV 4.5%)

North Cotswold SIBA

North Cotswold Brewery (Pilling Brewing Co), Unit 3, Ditchford Farm, Campden Road, Stretton-on-Fosse, Warwickshire, GL56 9RD
☎ (01608) 663947
✉ ncb@pillingweb.co.uk
northcotswoldbrewery.co.uk
Shop – please ring first
Tours by arrangement

North Cotswold started in 1999 as a 2.5-barrel plant, which was upgraded in 2000 to 10 barrels. A shop and visitor centre are on site. The brewery produces around 25 different ales a year as well as contract brewing Medieval beers. It also owns the Happy Apple Cider Company, which produces real cider and perry from orchards on the estate of the farm. Further expansion is planned as is the purchasing of a brewery tap. Around 200 outlets are supplied. Bottle-conditioned beer is available. Seasonal beers: see website.

Pigbrook Bitter (OG 1038, ABV 3.8%)

Ditchford Farm Ale (OG 1053, ABV 5.3%)

North Curry*

North Curry Brewery Company, The Old Coach House, Gwyon House, Church Road, North Curry, Somerset, TA3 6LH
☎ 07928 815053
✉ thenorthcurrybreweryco@hotmail.co.uk
thenorthcurrybrewerycouk.com
Tours by arrangement

The brewery opened in summer 2006 and is attached to one of the oldest properties in North Curry. Brewing last took place in the village in the 1920s. Five outlets are supplied direct. Both beers are available bottle conditioned; Red Heron is organic.

Red Heron (OG 1041, ABV 4.3%)

The Witheyman (OG 1043, ABV 4.6%)

Northern SIBA

Northern Brewing Ltd, Blakemere Brewery, Blakemere Craft Centre, Chester Road, Sandiway, Northwich, Cheshire, CW8 2EB
☎ (01606) 301000
sales@norbrew.co.uk
norbrew.co.uk
Tours by arrangement

Northern first brewed in 2003 on a five-barrel plant located in Runcorn. It relocated to a larger unit at Blakemere Craft Centre in 2005. A hospitality/bar area is available for brewery tours. The beer names are Northern Soul themed and at least two specials per month are produced under both the Northern and Blakemere brand names.

All-Niter (ABV 3.8%)
Full-bodied, pale bitter beer with caramel overtones. Good hoppy nose and aftertaste.

Soul Rider (ABV 4%)

Dancer (ABV 4.2%)

Soul Master (ABV 4.4%)

'45 (ABV 4.5%)
Soft, light and malty pale brown beer. Fairly sweet with fruit to the fore on the nose and in the flavour. Hop flavour leads into the aftertaste.

One-Der-Ful Wheat (ABV 4.7%)

Soul Time (ABV 5%)

Two Tone Special Stout (ABV 5%)

Flaming Embers (ABV 6%)

Northumberland SIBA

Northumberland Brewery Ltd, Accessory House, Barrington Road, Bedlington, Northumberland, NE22 7AP
☎ (01670) 822112
dave@northumberlandbrewery.co.uk
northumberlandbrewery.co.uk
Tours by arrangement

The brewery has been in operation for 11 years using a 10-barrel brew plant. More than 400 outlets are supplied. The Legends of the Tyne and Legends of the Wear series of beers are also produced as regulars. Seasonal beers: see website.

Pit Pony (ABV 3.8%)

Bucking Fastard (ABV 4%)

Fog on the Tyne (ABV 4.1%)

Sheepdog (ABV 4.7%)
An old-fashioned tawny beer, with fruit and malt throughout and a hoppy finish.

North Wales SIBA

North Wales Brewery, Tan-y-Mynydd, Moelfre, Abergele, Conwy, LL22 9RF
☎ (0800) 083 4100
northwalesbrewery@uwclub.net
northwalesbrewery.net

North Wales started brewing in June 2007 on a plant transferred from Paradise Brewery's former home in Wrenbury. Bottle-conditioned beers are available as are occasional seasonal brews.

Moelfre Mild (ABV 3.6%)

Bodelwyddan Bitter (ABV 3.8%)

Abergele Ale (ABV 5%)

North Yorkshire

North Yorkshire Brewing Co, Pinchinthorpe Hall, Pinchinthorpe, North Yorkshire, TS14 8HG
☎ (01287) 630200
sales@nybrewery.co.uk
nybrewery.co.uk
Shop 10am-5pm daily
Tours by arrangement (inc 3 course meal)

The brewery was founded in Middlesbrough in 1989 and moved in 1998 to Pinchinthorpe Hall, a moated and listed medieval estate near Guisborough that has its own spring water. The site also includes a hotel, restaurant and bistro. More than 100 free trade outlets are supplied. A special monthly beer is produced together with four beers in the Cosmic range. All beers are organic and bottle-conditioned beers are available.

Best (OG 1036, ABV 3.6%)

Golden Ginseng (ABV 3.6%)

Prior's Ale (OG 1036, ABV 3.6%)
Light, refreshing and surprisingly full-flavoured for a pale, low gravity beer, with a complex, bittersweet mixture of malt, hops and fruit carrying through into the aftertaste.

Archbishop Lee's Ruby Ale (OG 1040, ABV 4%)

Boro Best (OG 1040, ABV 4%)

Crystal Tips (OG 1040, ABV 4%)

Love Muscle (OG 1040, ABV 4%)

Honey Bunny (OG 1042, ABV 4.2%)

Mayhem (ABV 4.3%)

Cereal Killer (OG 1045, ABV 4.5%)

Blond (ABV 4.6%)

Fools Gold (OG 1046, ABV 4.6%)

Golden Ale (OG 1046, ABV 4.6%)
A well-hopped, lightly-malted, golden premium bitter, using Styrian Goldings and Goldings hops.

Flying Herbert (OG 1047, ABV 4.7%)

Lord Lee's (OG 1047, ABV 4.7%)
A refreshing, red/brown beer with a hoppy aroma. The flavour is a pleasant balance of roast malt and sweetness that predominates

over hops. The malty, bitter finish develops slowly.

White Lady (OG 1047, ABV 4.7%)

Dizzy Duck (OG 1048, ABV 4.8%)

Rocket Fuel (OG 1050, ABV 5%)

Nottingham SIBA

Nottingham Brewing Co Ltd, Plough Inn, 17 St Peter's Street, Radford, Nottingham, NG7 3EN
☎ (0115) 942 2649
☎ 07815 073447
✉ philip.darby@nottinghambrewery.com
nottinghambrewery.com
Tours by arrangement

After selling their Castle Rock Brewery in 2000, brewers Philip Darby and Niven Balfour established a purpose-built brewhouse behind the Plough Inn. Whitbread closed the old Nottingham Brewery in 1960 and when sold to Interbrew the new Nottingham Brewery bought the rights and now owns the brands.

Rock Ale Bitter Beer (OG 1038, ABV 3.8%)

Rock Ale Mild Beer (OG 1038, ABV 3.8%)

Legend (OG 1040, ABV 4%)

Extra Pale Ale (OG 1042, ABV 4.2%)

Dreadnought (OG 1045, ABV 4.5%)

Bullion (OG 1047, ABV 4.7%)

Sooty Stout (OG 1048, ABV 4.8%)

Supreme Bitter (OG 1052, ABV 5.2%)

For Finesse Hotels Group:

Cock & Hoop (OG 1043, ABV 4.3%)

For Northern Inns:

Clayton's Original (OG 1043, ABV 4.3%)

For Wetherspoons:

Spoon & Arrow (OG 1047, ABV 4.7%)

Nutbrook

Nutbrook Brewery Ltd, 6 Hallam Way, West Hallam, Derbyshire, DE7 6LA
☎ (0800) 458 2460
✉ dean@nutbrookbrewery.com
nutbrookbrewery.com
Tours by arrangement

Nutbrook was established in January 2007 on a one-barrel brewery in the owner's garage. Beers are brewed to order for domestic and corporate clients, and customers can design their own recipes. All beers are available bottle conditioned and a range of organic beers is planned.

Squirrel Bitter (OG 1043.2, ABV 4%)

Banter Bitter (OG 1040.9, ABV 4.5%)

Moor Bitter (OG 1043.2, ABV 4.8%)

O'Hanlon's SIBA

O'Hanlon's Brewing Co Ltd, Great Barton Farm, Whimple, Devon, EX5 2NY
☎ (01404) 822412
✉ info@ohanlons.co.uk
ohanlons.co.uk

Since moving to Whimple in 2000, O'Hanlon's has continued to expand to cope with ever increasing demand for its prize-winning beers. More than 100 outlets are regularly supplied, with wholesalers providing publicans nationwide with access to the cask products. A new bottling plant has increased production and enabled O'Hanlon's to contract bottle for several other breweries. Export sales also continue to grow with Thomas Hardy's Ale available in Israel, Canada, Chile, Denmark and Japan. Bottle-conditioned ales are available.

Firefly (OG 1035, ABV 3.7%)
Malty and fruity light bitter. Hints of orange in the taste.

Golde Blade Wheat (OG 1037, ABV 4%)
1999 and 2002 SIBA Champion Wheat Beer of Britain has a fine citrus taste.

Yellowhammer (OG 1041, ABV 4%)
A well-balanced, smooth pale yellow beer with a predominant hop and fruit nose and taste, leading to a dry, bitter finish.

Dry Stout (OG 1041, ABV 4.2%)
A dark malty, well-balanced stout with a dry, bitter finish and plenty of roast and fruit flavours up front.

Original Port Stout (OG 1041, ABV 4.8%)
A black beer with roast malt in the aroma that remains in the taste but gives way to hoppy bitterness in the aftertaste.

Royal Oak (OG 1048, ABV 5%)
Well-balanced copper-coloured beer with a strong fruit and malt aroma; a malty, fruity and sweet taste; and bitter aftertaste.

Thomas Hardy Ale (OG 1120, ABV 11.7%)
A tawny brown colour. Dark malts dominate with hints of sherry, treacle, molasses, toffee and port. The finish combines red wine, sherry and plenty of rich fruit.

Oakham SIBA EAB

Oakham Ales, 2 Maxwell Road, Woodston, Peterborough, Cambridgeshire, PE2 7JB
☎ (01733) 370500
✉ info@oakhamales.com
oakhamales.com
Tours by arrangement

The brewery started in 1993 in Oakham, Rutland, and expanded to a 35-barrel plant from the original 10-barrel in 1998 after moving to Peterborough. This was the brewery's main brewhouse until 2006 when a new 70-barrel brewery was completed at Maxwell Road. The 35-barrel plant was removed from the brewery tap in 2008 and replaced by a custom-built brewhouse. This allows brewing to continue within the brewery tap on what is effectively Oakham's pilot plant, used for experimental brewing. Around 100 outlets are supplied and four pubs are owned. Seasonal beers: see website.

Jeffrey Hudson Bitter/JHB (OG 1038, ABV 3.8%)
Citrus hop character dominates this golden ale Dry on the palate with a long, dry, faintly astringent finish.

Inferno (OG 1040, ABV 4%)

White Dwarf (OG 1042, ABV 4.3%) ◆
A speciality beer with fruit and hops on the aroma and in the taste. Dry and faintly astringent on the palate, leading to a strong, dry and moderately astringent finish.

Bishops Farewell (OG 1046, ABV 4.6%) ◆
This yellow-coloured golden ale has plenty of grapefruit hop character on the aroma, which leads through to a bittersweet citrus hop in the taste. Dry finish.

Oakleaf SIBA

Oakleaf Brewing Co Ltd, Unit 7, Clarence Wharf Industrial Estate, Mumby Road, Gosport, Hampshire, PO12 1AJ
☎ **(023) 9251 3222**
✉ **info@oakleafbrewing.co.uk**
🌐 **oakleafbrewing.co.uk**
Shop Mon-Fri 9am-5pm; Sat 10am-1pm
Tours by arrangement

⊗ Ed Anderson set up Oakleaf with his father-in-law, Dave Pickersgill, in 2000. The brewery stands on the side of Portsmouth Harbour. Bottled beers are sold in the Victory Shop at the historic dockyard in Portsmouth. Some 150 outlets are supplied. Seasonal beers: see website. Bottle-conditioned beers are also available.

Bitter (OG 1038, ABV 3.8%) ◆
A copper-coloured beer with a hoppy and fruity aroma, which leads to an intensely hoppy and bitter flavour, with balancing lemon and grapefruit and some malt. A long, dry finish. Full tasting for its strength.

Maypole Mild (OG 1040, ABV 3.8%) ◆
This dark mild has a gorgeous full biscuity aroma. A lasting mix of flavours; roast, toffee leads to a slightly unexpected hoppiness and a roast, bitter finish. Not typical of the style but bags of flavour for it's strength.

Nuptu'ale (OG 1042, ABV 4.2%) ◆
A full-bodied pale ale, strongly hopped with an uncompromising bitterness. An intense hoppy, spicy, floral aroma leads to a complex, hoppy taste. Well-balanced with malts and citrus flavours making for a very refreshing bitter.

Pompey Royal (ABV 4.5%)

Hole Hearted (OG 1048, ABV 4.7%) ◆
An amber-coloured strong bitter, with strong floral hop and citric notes in the aroma. These continue to dominate the flavour and lead to a long, bittersweet finish.

I Can't Believe It's Not Bitter (OG 1048, ABV 4.9%)
Cask conditioned lager.

Blake's Gosport Bitter (OG 1053, ABV 5.2%) ◆
Packed with berry fruits and roastiness, this is a complex, strong bitter, with some hoppy bitterness. Malt, roast and caramel are prevalent as sweetness builds to an uncompromising vinous finish. Warming, spicy, well-balanced and delicious.

For Suthwyk Ales:

Bloomfields Bitter (ABV 3.8%) ◆
Pleasant, clean-tasting pale brown bitter. Easy drinking and well-balanced. Beer is brewed by Oakleaf for Suthwyk using ingredients grown on their own farm.

Liberation (ABV 4.2%)

Skew Sunshine Ale (ABV 4.6%) ◆
An amber-coloured beer. Initial hoppiness leads to a fruity taste and finish. A slightly cloying mouthfeel. The beer is brewed by Oakleaf for Suthwyk using ingredients grown on their own farm.

Oakwell SIBA

Oakwell Brewery, PO Box 87, Pontefract Road, Barnsley, South Yorkshire, S71 1EZ
☎ **(01226) 296161**
✉ **jstancill@oakwellbrewery.co.uk**

☺ Brewing started in 1997. Oakwell supplies some 30 outlets.

Old Tom Mild (OG 1033.5, ABV 3.4%) ◆
A dark brown session mild, with a fruit aroma and a subtle hint of roast. Crisp and refreshing with a sharp finish.

Barnsley Bitter (OG 1036, ABV 3.8%)

Odcombe

Odcombe Brewery, Masons Arms, 41 Lower Odcombe, Lower Odcombe, Somerset, BA22 8TX
☎ **(01935) 862591**
✉ **info@masonsarmsodcombe.co.uk**
🌐 **masonsarmsodcombe.co.uk**
Tours by arrangement

Odcombe Brewery opened in 2000 and closed a few years later. It re-opened in 2005 with assistance from Shepherd Neame. Brewing takes place once a week and beers are only available at the pub. Seasonal beer: Winter's Tale (ABV 4.3%).

No 1 (OG 1040, ABV 4%)

Spring (OG 1042, ABV 4.1%)

Offa's Dyke

Offa's Dyke Brewery Ltd, Barley Mow Inn, Chapel Lane, Trefonen, Oswestry, Shropshire, SY10 9DX
☎ **(01691) 656889**
✉ **realales@offasdykebrewery.com**
🌐 **offasdykebrewery.com**
Shop Mon-Fri 5-11pm; Sat & Sun 12-12
Tours by arrangement

☺ Offa's Dyke was established in 2006 and changed hands early in 2007. This is the second brewery on this site in the last three years, the first relocating. The brewery and adjoining pub straddle the old England/Wales border, Offa's Dyke. Thomas McGuinness' five-barrel plant was acquired and brewing commenced in August 2007. The owner grows barley locally and is experimenting with small-scale hop cultivation. Bottle-conditioned beers are planned.

Harvest Moon (OG 1038, ABV 3.6%)

Barley Gold (OG 1038, ABV 3.8%)

Barley Blonde (ABV 4%)

Thirst Brew (OG 1042, ABV 4.2%)

Grim Reaper (OG 1050, ABV 5%)

Okells SIBA

Okell & Son Ltd, Kewaigue, Douglas, Isle of Man, IM2 1QG
☎ (01624) 699400
✉ mac@okells.co.uk
🌐 okells.co.uk
Tours by arrangement

Founded in 1874 by Dr Okell and formerly trading as Isle of Man Breweries, this is the main brewery on the island, having taken over and closed the rival Castletown Brewery in 1986. The brewery moved in 1994 to a new, purpose-built plant at Kewaigue to replace the Falcon Brewery in Douglas. All the beers are produced under the Manx Brewers' Act 1874 (permitted ingredients: water, malt, sugar and hops only). 36 of the company's 48 IoM pubs and four on the mainland sell cask beer and some 70 free trade outlets are also supplied. Seasonal beers: see website.

Mild (OG 1034, ABV 3.4%)
A fine aroma of hops and crystal malt. Red-brown in colour, the beer has a full malt flavour with surprising bitter hop notes and a hint of blackcurrants and oranges.

Bitter (OG 1035, ABV 3.7%)
A golden beer, malty and hoppy in aroma, with a hint of honey. Rich and malty on the tongue, it has a dry, malt and hop finish. A complex but rewarding beer.

Maclir (OG 1042, ABV 4.4%)
Beer with resiny hops and lemon fruit on the aroma, banana and lemon in the mouth and a big, bitter finish, dominated by hops, juicy malt and citrus fruit.

Dr Okells IPA (OG 1044, ABV 4.5%)
A light-coloured beer with a full-bodied taste. The sweetness is offset by strong hopping that gives the beer an overall roundness with spicy lemon notes and a fine dry finish.

Old Bear SIBA

Old Bear Brewery, Unit 4b, Atlas Works, Pitt Street, Keighley, West Yorkshire, BD21 4YL
☎ (01535) 601222
☎ 07713 161224
✉ sales@oldbearbrewery.com
🌐 oldbearbrewery.co.uk
Tours by arrangement

The brewery was founded in 1993 as a brew-pub at the Old White Bear in Crosshills. The brewery moved to Keighley in 2005 to a purpose-built unit to cater for increased production. The original 10-barrel plant was retained and there is now a one-barrel plant for specials. Beers are supplied within a 100-mile radius of Keighley and via wholesalers. Bottle-conditioned beers are available as are specials.

Bruin (OG 1035, ABV 3.5%)
The combination of hops gives off a sharp wild blackcurrant taste with a smoothness to follow.

Estivator (OG 1037, ABV 3.8%)
A light golden ale with a smooth, creamy, sweet lemon taste followed by buttery smoothness leading to a bitter, hoppy aftertaste.

Original (OG 1039, ABV 3.9%)
A refreshing and easy-to-drink bitter. The balance of malt and hops gives way to a short, dry, bitter aftertaste.

Black Mari'a (OG 1043, ABV 4.2%)
A black stout, smooth on the palate with a strong roast malt flavour and fruity finish.

Honeypot (OG 1044, ABV 4.4%)
Straw-coloured beer enhanced with golden honey.

Goldilocks (OG 1047, ABV 4.5%)
A fruity, straw-coloured golden ale, well-hopped and assertively bitter through to the finish.

Hibernator (OG 1055, ABV 5%)
A complex rich dark ale dominated by roast and bitter flavours against a background sweetness. Look for roast coffee, hints of caramel and dark vine fruit on the nose. The finish is distinctly bitter and quite astringent.

Duke of Bronte (ABV 12.5%)

Old Bog

Old Bog Brewery, Masons Arms, 2 Quarry School Place, Oxford, OX3 8LH
☎ (01865) 764579
✉ theoldbog@hotmail.co.uk
🌐 masonsquarry.co.uk

Brewing started in 2005 on a one-barrel plant. At present Old Bog brews once a week. The beers, when available, are sold at the Masons Arms and occasionally at beer festivals. A number of one-off brews appear throughout the year.

Quarry Gold (ABV 4%)

Wheat Beer (ABV 5%)

Quarry Wrecked (ABV 5.5%)

Old Cannon

Old Cannon Brewery Ltd, 86 Cannon Street, Bury St Edmunds, Suffolk, IP33 1JR
☎ (01284) 768769
✉ drink@oldcannonbrewery.co.uk
🌐 oldcannonbrewery.co.uk
Tours by arrangement (small groups only)

The St Edmunds Head pub opened in 1845 with its own brewery. Brewing ceased in 1917, and Greene King closed the pub in 1995. It re-opened in 1999 as the Old Cannon Brewery complete with a unique state-of-the-art brewery housed in the bar area. Brewing takes place on a Monday when the pub is closed. There are plans to bottle the beers. 6 outlets are supplied. Seasonal beers: Brass Monkey (ABV 4.6%, winter), St Edmund's Head (ABV 4.6%, winter).

Best Bitter (OG 1037, ABV 3.8%)
Session bitter brewed using Styrian Goldings, giving a crisp grapefruit aroma and taste. Refreshing and full of flavour.

Blonde Bombshell (ABV 4.2%)

Gunner's Daughter (OG 1052, ABV 5.5%) ◆
A well-balanced strong ale with a complexity of hop, fruit, sweetness and bitterness in the flavour, and a lingering hoppy, bitter aftertaste.

Old Chimneys

Old Chimneys Brewery, The Street, Market Weston, Diss, Norfolk, IP22 2NZ
☎ (01359) 221411/221013
🌐 oldchimneysbrewery.com
Shop Fri 2-7pm; Sat 11am-2pm
Tours by arrangement

Old Chimneys opened in 1995 and moved to larger premises in a converted farm building in 2001. Despite the postal address, the brewery is in Suffolk. The beers produced are mostly named after endangered local species. Seasonal beers: Polecat Porter (ABV 4.2%, winter), Natterjack (ABV 5%, winter), Red Clover (ABV 6%, winter). All cask ales are available bottle conditioned and are suitable for vegetarians and vegans except Black Rat and Hairy Canary.

Military Mild (OG 1035, ABV 3.3%) ◆
A rich, dark mild with good body for its gravity. Sweetish toffee and light roast bitterness dominate, leading to a dry aftertaste.

Great Raft Bitter (OG 1040, ABV 4%)
Pale copper bitter bursting with fruit. Malt and hops add to the sweetish fruity flavour, which is rounded off with hoppy bitterness in the aftertaste.

Black Rat Stout (OG 1048, ABV 4.4%)

Golden Pheasant (ABV 4.5%)

Good King Henry (OG 1107, ABV 9%)

Old Cottage

Burton Old Cottage Beer Co Ltd, Unit 10, Eccleshall Business Park, Hawkins Lane, Burton upon Trent, Staffordshire, DE14 1PT
☎ 07909 931250
✉ jwsaville@tiscali.co.uk
🌐 oldcottagebeer.co.uk
Tours by arrangement

Old Cottage was originally installed in the old Heritage Brewery, once Everard's production plant in Burton. When the site was taken over, the brewery moved to a modern industrial unit. The brewery was sold in 2005 and 2006 saw heavy investment in new production and storage facilities by the new owners. Around 10 outlets are supplied. Seasonal beer: Snow Joke (ABV 5.2%, winter), Prancers Pride (ABV 4.7%, winter).

Pail Ale (OG 1040, ABV 3.8%)

Oak Ale (OG 1044, ABV 4%) ◆
Tawny, full-bodied bitter. A sweet start gives way to a slight roast taste with some caramel. A dry, hoppy finish.

Chestnut (ABV 4.2%)

Cottage IPA (OG 1047, ABV 4.4%)

Redwood (OG 1046, ABV 4.6%)

Cloughy's Clout (OG 1047, ABV 4.7%)

Stout (OG 1047, ABV 4.7%) ◆
Dense black but not heavy. Sweet with lots of caramel, hints of liquorice and a roast and bitter finish.

Pastiche (OG 1050, ABV 5.2%)

Halcyon Daze (OG 1050, ABV 5.3%) ◆
Tawny and creamy with touches of hop, fruit and malt aroma. Fruity taste and finish.

Oldershaw SIBA

Oldershaw Brewery, 12 Harrowby Hall Estate, Grantham, Lincolnshire, NG31 9HB
☎ (01476) 572135
✉ oldershawbrewery@btconnect.com
🌐 oldershawbrewery.com

Experienced home-brewer Gary Oldershaw and his wife Diane set up the brewery at their home in 1997. Grantham's first brewery for 30 years, Oldershaw now supplies 60 local free houses. The Oldershaws have introduced small-scale bottling and sell bottle-conditioned beer direct from the brewery. Seasonal beers: Sunnydaze (ABV 4%, May-Aug), Yuletide (ABV 5.2%, Nov-Dec), Grantham Dark (ABV 3.6%), Alma's Brew (ABV 4.1%).

Pearl (ABV 3%)

Mowbrays Mash (OG 1037, ABV 3.7%)

Harrowby Pale Ale (OG 1039, ABV 3.9%)

High Dyke (OG 1039, ABV 3.9%)
Golden and moderately bitter. A predominantly hoppy session beer.

OSB (OG 1040, ABV 4%)

Newton's Drop (OG 1041, ABV 4.1%) ◆
Balanced malt and hops but with a strong bitter, lingering taste in this mid-brown beer.

Caskade (OG 1042, ABV 4.2%)
Pale, golden beer brewed with American Cascade hops to give a distinctive floral, hoppy flavour and aroma, and a clean lasting finish.

Ahtanum Gold (OG 1043, ABV 4.3%)
A gold-coloured, fruity, hoppy beer balanced with some maltiness. Moderately bitter.

Grantham Stout (OG 1043, ABV 4.3%)
Dark brown and smooth with rich roast malt flavour, supported by some fruit and bitterness. A long, moderately dry finish.

Regal Blonde (OG 1043, ABV 4.4%) ◆
Straw-coloured, lager-style beer with a good malt/hop balance throughout; strong bitterness on the taste lingers.

Isaac's Gold (OG 1044, ABV 4.5%)

Old Boy (OG 1047, ABV 4.8%) ◆
A full-bodied amber ale, fruity and bitter with a hop/fruit aroma. The malt that backs the taste dies in the long finish.

Alchemy (OG 1052, ABV 5.3%)
A golden, premium hoppy beer brewed with First Gold hops.

Olde Swan

Olde Swan Brewery, 89 Halesowen Road, Netherton, Dudley, West Midlands, DY2 9PY
☎ (01384) 253075
Tours by arrangement

A famous brew-pub best known as 'Ma Pardoe's' after the matriarch who ruled it for years. The pub has been licensed since 1835 and the present brewery and pub were built in 1863. Brewing continued until 1988 and restarted in 2001. The plant brews primarily for the on-site pub with some beer available to the trade. Seasonal beer: Black Widow (ABV 6.7%, winter). Monthly specials are available together with various commemorative beers for sporting events as well as bottle-conditioned beers from the brewery tap.

Original (OG 1034, ABV 3.5%)
Straw-coloured light mild, smooth but tangy, and sweetly refreshing with a faint hoppiness.

Dark Swan (OG 1041, ABV 4.2%)
Smooth, sweet dark mild with late roast malt in the finish.

Entire (OG 1043, ABV 4.4%)
Faintly hoppy, amber premium bitter with sweetness persistent throughout.

Bumble Hole Bitter (OG 1052, ABV 5.2%)
Sweet, smooth amber ale with hints of astringency in the finish.

Old Foreigner

Old Foreigner Brewery, Glenkindie Arms Hotel, Glenkindie, Aberdeenshire, AB33 8SX
☎ (01975) 641288
✉ eddie@theglenkindiearmshotel.com
theglenkindiearmshotel.com
Tours by arrangement

A one-barrel brew plant was installed in April 2007.

Gartly Nagger (ABV 4.2%)

The Wicked Wickerman (OG 1042, ABV 4.2%)

Sentinel (ABV 4.4%)

Old Laxey

Old Laxey Brewing Co Ltd, Shore Hotel Brew Pub, Old Laxey, Isle of Man, IM4 7DA
☎ (01624) 863214
✉ shore@mcb.net
Tours by arrangement
Beer brewed on the Isle of Man is brewed to a strict Beer Purity Act. Additives are not permitted to extend shelf life, nor are chemicals allowed to assist with head retention. Most of Old Laxey's beer is sold through the Shore Hotel alongside the brewery.

Bosun Bitter (OG 1038, ABV 3.8%)
Crisp and fresh with a hoppy aftertaste.

Old Luxters SIBA

Old Luxters Farm Brewery, Hambleden, Henley-on-Thames, Oxfordshire, RG9 6JW
☎ (01491) 638330
✉ enquiries@chilternvalley.co.uk
chilternvalley.co.uk
Shop Mon-Fri 9am-6pm (5pm winter); Sat & Sun 11am-6pm (5pm winter)
Tours by arrangement

A traditional, full-mash, independent farm brewery established in 1990 and situated in a 17th-century barn alongside the Chiltern Valley vineyard. The brewery is in Buckinghamshire despite the postal address. The three cask ales are only available through the brewery shop. It proudly boasts the Royal Warrant of Appointment to the Queen, the first micro-brewery to achieve such an accolade. Fortnum & Mason Ale (ABV 5%) and several other bottle-conditoned beers are brewed under contract. Old Windsor Dark Ale (ABV 5%) is exclusive to the Old Windsor Royal Household farm shop. Three winter warmers are brewed for Xmas.

Barn Ale Bitter (OG 1038, ABV 4%)
A fruity, aromatic, fairly hoppy, bitter beer.

Barn Ale Special (OG 1042.5, ABV 4.5%)
Predominantly malty, fruity and hoppy in taste and nose, and tawny/amber in colour. Fairly strong in flavour: the initial, sharp, malty and fruity taste leaves a dry, bittersweet, fruity aftertaste. It can be slightly sulphurous.

Dark Roast Ale (OG 1048, ABV 5%)
The use of chocolate and crystal malts give this ale a nutty, roasty bitter flavour.

Old Mill

Old Mill Brewery, Mill Street, Snaith, East Yorkshire, DN14 9HU
☎ (01405) 861813
✉ sales@oldmillbrewery.co.uk
oldmillbrewery.co.uk
Tours by arrangement to organisations and customers only

Old Mill is a craft brewery opened in 1983 in a 200-year-old former malt kiln and corn mill. The brew-length is 60 barrels. The brewery is building a tied estate, now standing at 19 houses. Beers can be found nationwide through wholesalers and around 80 free trade outlets are supplied direct. There is a rolling programme of seasonal beers (see website) and monthly specials.

Mild (OG 1034, ABV 3.4%)
A satisfying roast malt flavour dominates this easy-drinking, quality dark mild.

Bitter (OG 1038.5, ABV 3.9%)
A malty nose is carried through to the initial flavour. Bitterness runs throughout.

Old Curiosity (OG 1044.5, ABV 4.5%)
Slightly sweet amber brew, malty to start with. Malt flavours all the way through.

Bullion (OG 1047.5, ABV 4.7%)
The malty and hoppy aroma is followed by a neat mix of hop and fruit tastes within an enveloping maltiness. Dark brown/amber in colour.

Old Poet's

See Ashover

Old Spot

Old Spot Brewery Ltd, Manor Farm, Station Road, Cullingworth, Bradford, West Yorkshire, BD13 5HN
☎ (01535) 691144
✉ sales@oldspotbrewery.co.uk

oldspotbrewery.co.uk
Tours by arrangement

Old Spot started brewing in 2005 and is named after a retired sheepdog on Manor Farm. The brewery targets the ever-changing guest ale market and creates new brews every 2-3 weeks, along with the stock beers. Around 25 outlets are supplied.

Darkside Pup (ABV 3.6%)
Full-bodied dark mild with a deep coffee taste with liquorice to finish.

Inn-Spired (ABV 4.3%)
Light-coloured bitter with a light, hoppy taste and a slight, fruity finish.

Dog's in't Barrel (ABV 4.5%)
Chestnut-coloured bitter with a malty taste and bitter finish.

Organic SIBA

Organic Brewhouse, Unit 1, Higher Bochym, Cury Cross Lanes, Helston, Cornwall, TR12 7AZ
(01326) 241555
orgbrewandy@tiscali.co.uk
theorganicbrewhouse.com
Tours by arrangement

Laid out as a mini 'tower' system, Organic's production has increased to six regular beers. It was established in 2000 and is dedicated to supplying exclusively organic beer, using its own source of natural mineral water. More than 20 local outlets are supplied regularly and the beers occasionally head north with wholesalers. Bottle-conditioned beers are available. All beers are Soil Association certified and bottled beers are suitable for vegetarians.

Halzephron Gold (OG 1033, ABV 3.6%)

Lizard Point (OG 1036, ABV 4%)

Serpentine (OG 1042, ABV 4.5%)
A big malty nose, a bittersweet palate and a finish balanced by rich malt and tangy hops.

Black Rock (OG 1043, ABV 4.7%)
Hop and apple aroma masked by complex roast overtones.

Wolf Rock (OG 1046, ABV 5%)

Charlie's Pride Lager (OG 1048, ABV 5.3%)

Orkney SIBA

Orkney Brewery, Sinclair Breweries Ltd, Quoyloo, Stromness, Orkney, KW16 3LT
(01667) 404555
info@sinclairbreweries.co.uk
orkneybrewery.co.uk

Set up in 1988 in an old school building in the remote Orkney hamlet of Quoyloo, the brewery was modernised in 1995. Capacity is now 120 barrels a week, all brewed along strict ecological lines from its own water supply. All waste water is treated through two lakes on the brewery's land, which in turn support fish and several dozen mallard ducks. The brewery increased production and added a visitor centre with shop in 2008. Along with Atlas (qv), Orkney is part of Sinclair Breweries; the combined business distributes to some 600 outlets across Scotland and via wholesalers to the rest of Britain. Seasonal beer: Clootie Dumpling (ABV 4.3%, Dec-Jan).

Raven Ale (OG 1038, ABV 3.8%)
A well-balanced, quaffable bitter. Malty fruitiness and bitter hops last through to the long, dry aftertaste.

Dragonhead Stout (OG 1040, ABV 4%)
A strong, dark malt aroma flows into the taste in this superb Scottish stout. The roast malt continues to dominate the aftertaste, and blends with chocolate to develop a strong, dry finish.

Northern Light (OG 1040, ABV 4%)
A very drinkable, well-balanced Golden Ale, with a real smack of fruit and hops in the taste and an increasing bitter aftertaste.

Red MacGregor (OG 1040, ABV 4%)
Generally a well-balanced bitter, this tawny red ale has a powerful smack of fruit and a clean, fresh mouthfeel.

Dark Island (OG 1045, ABV 4.6%)
An excellent brew receiving many awards. The roast malt and chocolate character varies, making the beer hard to categorise as a stout or old ale. Generally a sweetish roast malt taste leads to a long-lasting roasted, slightly bitter, dry finish.

Skullsplitter (OG 1080, ABV 8.5%)
An intense velvet malt nose with hints of apple, prune and plum. The hoppy taste is balanced by satiny smooth malt with fruity spicy edges, leading to a long, dry finish with a hint of nut.

Ossett SIBA

Ossett Brewing Co Ltd, Kings Yard, Low Mill Road, Ossett, West Yorkshire, WF5 8ND
(01924) 261333
brewery@ossett-brewery.co.uk
ossett-brewery.co.uk
Shop Mon-Fri 9am-4.30pm
Tours by arrangement

Brewing began in 1998 but the brewery soon outgrew the premises moving to a new site 50 metres away in 2005. Ossett delivers between Newcastle and Peterborough and beer is also available through wholesalers. The brewery owns ten pubs and two independent micro-breweries. Seasonal and special beers: see website. Ossett Brewery purchased Riverhead Brewery in 2006 and Fernandes Brewery in 2007, where brewing continues independently.

Pale Gold (OG 1038, ABV 3.8%)
A light, refreshing pale ale with a light, hoppy aroma.

Black Bull Bitter (OG 1039, ABV 3.9%)
A dark, dry bitter.

Silver King (OG 1041, ABV 4.3%)
A lager-style beer with a crisp, dry flavour and citrus fruity aroma.

Fine Fettle (OG 1048, ABV 4.8%)
A strong yet refreshing pale ale with a crisp, clean flavour and citrus aroma.

Excelsior (OG 1051, ABV 5.2%)

A strong pale ale with a full, mellow flavour and a fresh, hoppy aroma with citrus/floral characteristics.

Otley

Otley Brewing Co Ltd, Units 42 & 43, Albion Industrial Estate, Cilfynydd, Pontypridd, Mid Glamorgan, CF37 4NX
☎ (01443) 480555
✉ info@otleybrewing.co.uk
🌐 otleybrewing.co.uk
Tours by arrangement

Otley Brewing was set up during the summer of 2005. Since then the brewery has doubled in size and now supplies Mid, West and East Wales. Seasonal beers: see website. Bottle-conditioned beers are also available.

Dark O (OG 1039.3, ABV 3.8%)
A medium bodied, easy-drinking mild/stout with chocolate and roasted barley flavours.

O1 (OG 1038.8, ABV 4%)
A pale golden beer with a hoppy aroma. The taste has hops, malt, fruit and a thirst-quenching bitterness. A satisfying finish completes this beer.

O2 (OG 1040.7, ABV 4.2%)
Golden-brown in colour, fruity with heavy floral aromas.

OBB (OG 1043.6, ABV 4.5%)
A tawny-red ale.

OG (OG 1052.3, ABV 5.4%)
A golden, honey-coloured ale, extremely smooth.

O8 (OG 1077.5, ABV 8%)
A pale and strong ale, deceptively smooth.

Otter SIBA

Otter Brewery Ltd, Mathayes, Luppitt, Honiton, Devon, EX14 4SA
☎ (01404) 891285
✉ info@otterbrewery.com
🌐 otterbrewery.com
Tours by arrangement

Otter Brewery was set up in 1990 and has grown into one of the West Country's major producers of beers. The brewery is located in the Blackdown Hills, between Taunton and Honiton. 2008/09 saw the completion of Otter's 'eco cellar', partly underground and built with clay blocks and a grass roof. The beers are made from the brewery's own springs and are delivered to more than 500 pubs across the south-west including the brewery's first pub, the Holt, in Honiton.

Bitter (OG 1036, ABV 3.6%)
Well-balanced amber session bitter with a fruity nose and bitter taste and aftertaste.

Bright (OG 1039, ABV 4.3%)
Pale yellow/golden ale with a strong fruit aroma, sweet fruity taste and a bittersweet finish.

Ale (OG 1043, ABV 4.5%)
A full-bodied best bitter. A malty aroma predominates with a fruity taste and finish.

Head (OG 1054, ABV 5.8%)
Fruity aroma and taste with a pleasant bitter finish. Dark brown and full-bodied.

Oulton

Oulton Ales Ltd, Lake Lothing Brewery, Harbour Road, Oulton Broad, Lowestoft, Suffolk, NR32 3LZ
☎ (01502) 587905
🌐 oultonales.co.uk
Tours by arrangement

The brewery was expanded in 2005 to give a capacity of 30 barrels a week. 20 outlets are supplied as well as its own three pubs. Five of the brands are brewed throughout the year. Bottle-conditioned ales are also available.

Bitter (OG 1037, ABV 3.5%)

Mutford Mild (OG 1038, ABV 3.7%)

Beedazzled (OG 1040, ABV 4%)

Sunrise (OG 1040, ABV 4%)

Nautilus (OG 1042, ABV 4.2%)

Sunset (OG 1041, ABV 4.2%)

Wet and Windy (OG 1044, ABV 4.3%)

Windswept (OG 1044, ABV 4.5%)
Fairly full-bodied with an intense elderflower aroma and flavour. Quite sweet but with a hint of bitterness, particularly in the finish.

Excelsior (OG 1045, ABV 4.6%)

Gone Fishing (OG 1049, ABV 5%)
The initial taste is bitter but sweetness, tinged with roast and caramel, comes through. The aftertaste is sweet and lingers.

Cormorant Porter (OG 1050, ABV 5.2%)
An initial rich, plummy fruitiness gives way to bittersweetness and a long, sweet aftertaste.

Keelhaul (OG 1060, ABV 6.5%)

Roaring Boy (OG 1075, ABV 8.5%)
A solid, vinous brew, with sultry, soft fruit notes to lighten the brooding character. A long, deep, finish.

Outlaw

See Roosters

Outstanding*

Outstanding Brewing Co Ltd, Britannia Mill, Cobden Street, Bury, Lancashire, BL9 6AW
☎ 07505 323358
✉ info@outstandingbeers.co.uk
🌐 outstandingbeers.com

The brewery was set up as a collaboration between Paul Sandiford, Glen Woodcock and David Porter. The 15-barrel plant went into production in March 2008. Selective free trade accounts are supplied nationally. Lagers (Pilsner, Clouded Out and Amber Bock) are also available as real ale on request.

OSB (OG 1042, ABV 4.4%)
A mid range copper-coloured ale with a distinctive hop finish.

Blonde (OG 1044, ABV 4.5%)

Ginger (OG 1044, ABV 4.5%)

Light brown beer with a noticeable hint of ginger.

SOS (OG 1044, ABV 4.5%)
Light brown bitter, dry and intensely bitter.

Smoked Out (OG 1049, ABV 5%)
A brown ale brewed with traditional continental smoked lager malt.

Standing Out (OG 1053, ABV 5.5%)
A pale golden ale, dry and bitter with lots of hop aroma.

Stout (OG 1057, ABV 5.5%)
Thick, jet black and bitter with liquorice overtones.

Pushing Out (OG 1065, ABV 7.3%)
A pale golden ale with a strong, distinctive dry, bitter flavour and a hop aroma.

Oxfordshire Ales

Bicester Beers & Minerals Ltd, 12 Pear Tree Farm Industrial Units, Bicester Road, Marsh Gibbon, Bicester, Oxfordshire, OX27 0GB
☎ (01869) 278765
✉ bicesterbeers@tiscali.co.uk
🌐 oxfordshireales.co.uk
Tours by arrangement

⊗ The company first brewed in 2005. The five-barrel plant was previously at Picks Brewery but has now been upgraded to a 10-barrel plant with the purchase of a larger copper. It supplies 50-60 outlets as well as several wholesalers. There are plans to produce seasonal beers and an organic beer.

Triple B (ABV 3.7%) ◆
This pale amber beer has a huge caramel aroma. The caramel diminishes in the initial taste, which changes to a fruit/bitter balance. This in turn leads to a long, refreshing, bitter aftertaste.

Pride of Oxfordshire (ABV 4.1%) ◆
An amber beer, the aroma is butterscotch/caramel, which carries on into the initial taste. The taste then becomes bitter with sweetish/malty overtones. There is a long, dry, bitter finish.

Marshmellow (ABV 4.7%) ◆
The slightly fruity aroma in this golden-amber beer leads to a hoppy but thin taste, with slight caramel notes. The aftertaste is short and bitter.

For Plough, Marsh Gibbon:

Ploughmans Pride (ABV 4.2%)

Oyster

Oyster Brewery, Ellenabeich Harbour, Isle of Seil, Oban, PA34 4RQ
☎ (01852) 300121
✉ gascoignea@tiscali.co.uk
🌐 oysterbrewery.com
Shop 9am-5pm daily
Tours by arrangement

◎ The brewery was built in 2004 and came on stream in the spring of 2005. Head brewer Andy Gascoigne brought the state-of-the-art brewery north after first installing it in his pub in West Yorkshire. A bottling plant was installed in 2006.

Easd'ale (OG 1038, ABV 3.8%)
Golden smooth bitter with a dry aftertaste.

Thistle Tickler (OG 1040, ABV 4%)
Amber, fruity session bitter using Fuggles hops and Vienna malt.

Corryvreckan (OG 1044, ABV 4.4%)

Red Pearl (OG 1044, ABV 4.4%)
Traditional red-hued Scottish ale brewed with a blend of malts and roasted barley with First Gold hops. Toffeeish aftertaste.

Old Tosser (OG 1050, ABV 5%)
Strong dark ale brewed with roasted barley and American Cascade hops to give a rich, full-bodied character.

Grey Dogs (OG 1056, ABV 5.6%)

Packfield*

Packfield Brewery Limited, Unit 6, Lynderswood Farm, Lynderswood Lane, Black Notley, Essex, CM77 8QN
☎ (01245) 364315
✉ packfieldbrewery@btconnect.com
Tours by arrangement

⊗ Packfield was founded in 2007 by Adrian Smith on a 16-barrel plant. The beers are usually available at the Hoop in Stock but may appear futher afield courtesy of SIBA. Bottle-conditioned beers are planned. Seasonal beer: Rustic Ale (ABV 5.8%, winter).

Best Bitter (ABV 3.8%)

Real IPA (OG 1038, ABV 3.8%)

Triple Gold (OG 1044, ABV 4%)

Chicken Shack Bitter (OG 1038, ABV 4.3%)

PSB/Packfield Special Bitter (ABV 4.5%)

Palmer IFBB SIBA

JC & RH Palmer Ltd, The Old Brewery, West Bay Road, Bridport, Dorset, DT6 4JA
☎ (01308) 422396
✉ enquiries@palmersbrewery.com
🌐 palmersbrewery.com
Shop Mon-Sat 9am-6pm
Tours by arrangement (Please ring 01308 427500)

⊗ Palmers is Britain's only thatched brewery and dates from 1794. It is based on the outskirts of Bridport, next to the River Brit. The company is run by John and Cleeves Palmer, great-grandsons of Robert Henry and John Cleeves Palmer, who bought the brewery in 1896. Palmers enjoys sustained growth in real ale sales. Heavy investment is made in free trade ale dispense. 57 pubs are owned and a further 240 outlets are supplied.

Copper Ale (OG 1036, ABV 3.7%) ◆
Beautifully balanced, copper-coloured light bitter with a hoppy aroma.

Best (OG 1040, ABV 4.2%) ◆
Hop aroma and bitterness stay in the background in this predominately malty best bitter, with some fruit on the aroma.

Dorset Gold (OG 1046, ABV 4.5%) ◆

More complex than many golden ales thanks to a pleasant banana and mango fruitiness on the aroma that carries on into the taste and aftertaste.

200 (OG 1052, ABV 5%) ◆
This is a big beer with a touch of caramel sweetness adding to a complex hoppy, fruit taste that lasts from the aroma well into the aftertaste.

Tally Ho! (OG 1057, ABV 5.5%) ◆
A complex dark old ale. Roast malts and treacle toffee on the palate lead in to a long, lingering finish with more than a hint of coffee.

Parish

Parish Brewery, 6 Main Street, Burrough on the Hill, Leicestershire, LE14 2JQ
☎ (01664) 454801
Tours by arrangement

Parish began in 1983 in a 400-year-old building and former stables next to the Stag & Hounds pub. The 20-barrel brewery supplies local outlets with the regular beer range and special one-off brews are produced for beer festivals across Leicestershire, Rutland and Cambridgeshire. Bottle-conditioned beers are also available.

Mild (OG 1038, ABV 3.8%)

PSB (OG 1042, ABV 4.2%)

Farm Gold (OG 1044, ABV 4.4%)

Burrough Bitter (OG 1047, ABV 4.7%)

Poachers Ale (OG 1060, ABV 6%)

Baz's Bonce Blower (OG 1120, ABV 12%)

Peak Ales SIBA

Peak Ales, Barn Brewery, Chatsworth, Bakewell, Derbyshire, DE45 1EX
☎ (01246) 583737
✉ info@peakales.co.uk
peakales.co.uk
Tours by arrangement

Peak Ales opened in 2005 in converted, former derelict farm buildings on the Chatsworth estate, with the aid of a DEFRA Rural Enterprise Scheme grant, with support from trustees of Chatsworth Settlement. The brewery supplies around 30 local outlets and selected distributors. Seasonal beer: Noggin Filler (ABV 5%, winter).

Swift Nick (OG 1038, ABV 3.8%) ◆
Traditional English session bitter with a slight fruit and hop aroma. Balanced flavours of malt and hops lead to a dry, bitter finish.

Bakewell Best Bitter (OG 1041, ABV 4.2%) ◆
Impressive copper-coloured bitter beer. Little aroma but initial sweetness leads to a complex but balanced hop and malt flavour. Bitterness is present throughout, ending in a dry, fruity finish and aftertaste.

Chatsworth Gold (ABV 4.6%)
Golden beer made with honey from the Chatsworth Estate giving a delicate sweetness which is well balanced by the hoppy bitterness.

DPA (OG 1045, ABV 4.6%) ◆
Golden brown, easy-drinking best bitter with a slight malt and hop aroma. Initial sweetness gives way to a bitter finish and aftertaste.

Peakstones Rock

Peakstones Rock Brewery, Peakstones Farm, Cheadle Road, Alton, Staffordshire, ST10 4DH
☎ 07891 350908
✉ dfedwards@fwi.co.uk
peakstonesrockbreweryalton.co.uk
Tours by arrangement

Peakstones Rock was established in 2005 on a purpose-built, five-barrel plant in an old farm building. A new fermentation vessel was installed in 2006 to keep up with demand for the beer. Further expansion is planned. Over 60 outlets are supplied direct.

Nemesis (OG 1042, ABV 3.8%) ◆
Pale brown with a liquorice aroma; roast but not burnt. Pleasing lingering bitter finish.

Chained Oak (OG 1045, ABV 4.2%)

Alton Abbey (OG 1051, ABV 4.5%)

Black Hole (OG 1048, ABV 4.8%)

Oblivion (OG 1055, ABV 5.5%)

Penlon Cottage

Penlon Cottage Brewery, Pencae, Llanarth, Ceredigion, SA47 0QN
☎ (01545) 580022
✉ beer@penlon.biz
penlon.biz

Penlon opened in 2004 and is located on a working smallholding in the Ceredigion coastal region of West Wales. Hops and malting barley are part of a programme of self-sufficiency, with grain, yeast and beer fed to pigs, sheep and chickens on the holding. Only bottle-conditioned beers are brewed. Seasonal beers: Autumn Harvest (ABV 3.2%, Sep-Nov), Shepherds Delight Xmas Ale (ABV 5.6%). Bottle-conditioned beers: Lambs Gold Light Ale (ABV 3.2%), Tipsy Tup Pale Ale (ABV 3.8%), Heather Honey Ale (ABV 4.2%), Chocolate Stout (ABV 4.5%), Stock Ram Stout (ABV 4.6%), Twin Ram IPA (ABV 4.8%), Ewes Frolic Lager (ABV 5.2%), Premium Ale (ABV 5.2%), Ramnesia Strong Ale (ABV 5.6%). All beers are suitable for vegetarians and vegans.

Pennine*

Pennine Ale Ltd, The Rossendale Brewery, The Griffin Inn, 84-86 Hud Rake, Haslingden, Lancashire, BB4 5AF
☎ (01706) 214021
✉ pennine.ale@btconnect.com
Tours by arrangement

Pennine Ale acquired the brew plant previously used by Porter Brewing Co in November 2007. It produces six regular cask ales and supplies mainly to its own three pubs but has now started to supply the local free trade. All beers are suitable for vegetarians and vegans.

Floral Dance (OG 1035, ABV 3.6%)
A pale and fruity session beer.

Hameldon Bitter (OG 1037, ABV 3.8%)
A dark traditional bitter with a dry and assertive character that develops in the finish.

Railway Sleeper (OG 1040, ABV 4.2%)
An amber bitter.

Rossendale Ale (OG 1041, ABV 4.2%)
A malty aroma leads to a complex, malt dominated flavour, supported by a dry, increasingly bitter finish.

Pitch Porter (OG 1050, ABV 5%)
A full-bodied, rich beer with a slightly sweet, malty start, counter balanced with sharp bitterness and a roast barley dominance.

Sunshine (OG 1050, ABV 5.3%)
A hoppy and bitter golden beer with a citrus character. The lingering finish is dry and spicy.

Penzance*

Penzance Brewing Company, Star Inn, Crowlas, Penzance, Cornwall, TR20 8DX
☎ (01736) 740375

Penzance began brewing in June 2008 on a five-barrel plant. Beer is mostly produced for the pub.

Crowlas Bitter (ABV 3.8%)

Phipps*

J.Phipps Ales (Banbury) Ltd, Suite 200, 29-30 Horsefair, Banbury, Oxfordshire, OX16 0BW
☎ (01295) 252061
✉ enquiries@phippsbrewers.co.uk
phippsbrewers.co.uk

Company established in 2007. Beer is contract brewed at Hoggleys Brewery (qv) at present.

Phoenix

Oak Brewing Co Ltd t/a Phoenix Brewery, Green Lane, Heywood, Greater Manchester, OL10 2EP
☎ (01706) 627009
✉ tony@phoenixbrewery.co.uk

A company established as Oak Brewery in 1982 at Ellesmere Port, it moved in 1991 to the disused Phoenix Brewery and adopted the name. It now supplies 400-500 outlets with additional deliveries via wholesalers. Many seasonal beers are produced throughout the year. Restoration of the old brewery, built in 1897, is progressing well.

Bantam (OG 1035, ABV 3.5%) ◆
Light brown beer with a fruity aroma. Balance of malt, citrus fruit and hops in taste. Hoppy, bitter finish.

Navvy (OG 1039, ABV 3.8%) ◆
Amber beer with a citrus fruit and malt nose. Good balance of citrus fruit, malt and hops with bitterness coming through in the aftertaste.

Best Bitter (OG 1039, ABV 3.9%)

Monkeytown Mild (OG 1039, ABV 3.9%)

Arizona (OG 1040, ABV 4.1%) ◆
Yellow in colour with a fruity and hoppy aroma. A refreshing beer with citrus, hops and good bitterness, and a shortish dry aftertaste.

Spotland Gold (OG 1041, ABV 4.1%)
A pale, hoppy beer with a lingering bitter finish.

Pale Moonlight (OG 1042, ABV 4.2%)

Black Bee (OG 1045, ABV 4.5%)

White Monk (OG 1045, ABV 4.5%) ◆
Yellow beer with a citrus fruit aroma, plenty of fruit, hops and bitterness in the taste, and a hoppy, bitter finish.

Thirsty Moon (OG 1046, ABV 4.6%) ◆
Tawny beer with a fresh citrus aroma. Hoppy, fruity and malty with a dry, hoppy finish.

West Coast IPA (OG 1046, ABV 4.6%)

Double Gold (OG 1050, ABV 5%)

Wobbly Bob (OG 1060, ABV 6%) ◆
A red/brown beer with malty, fruity aroma and creamy mouthfeel. Strongly malty and fruity in flavour, with hops and a hint of herbs. Both sweetness and bitterness are evident throughout.

Pictish

Pictish Brewing Co Ltd, Unit 9, Canalside Industrial Estate, Rochdale, Greater Manchester, OL16 5LB
☎ (01706) 522227
✉ mail@pictish-brewing.co.uk
pictish-brewing.co.uk

The brewery was established in 2000 by Richard Sutton and supplies 60 free trade outlets in the north-west and west Yorkshire. Seasonal beers: see website.

Brewers Gold (OG 1038, ABV 3.8%) ◆
Yellow in colour, with a hoppy, fruity nose. Soft maltiness and a strong hop/citrus flavour lead to a dry, bitter finish.

Alchemists Ale (OG 1043, ABV 4.3%) ◆
Yellow beer with generous hop and fruit on the nose and palate. Good bitter hop finish.

For Crown Inn, Bacup:

Crown IPA (OG 1050, ABV 5%)

Pilgrim SIBA

Pilgrim Brewery, 11 West Street, Reigate, Surrey, RH2 9BL
☎ (01737) 222651
✉ pilgrimbrewery@hotmail.com
pilgrim.co.uk

Pilgrim was set up in 1982 in Woldingham, Surrey and moved to Reigate in 1985. The original owner, Dave Roberts, is still in charge. Beers are sold mostly in the Surrey area to around 30 outlets. Seasonal beers: Autumnal (ABV 4.5%), Excalibur (ABV 4.5%, Easter), Crusader (ABV 4.9%, summer), Talisman (ABV 5%, winter), Pudding (ABV 5.3%, Xmas). Other beers are also produced occasionally.

Surrey Bitter (OG 1037, ABV 3.7%) ◆
Pineapple, grapefruit and spicy aromas in this well-balanced quaffing beer. Initial biscuity

maltiness with a hint of vanilla gives way to a pronounced hoppy bitterness in a refreshing bittersweet finish.

Moild (ABV 3.8%)

Porter (OG 1040, ABV 4%) ◆
Black beer with a good balance of dark malts with hints of berry fruit. Roast character present throughout to give a bittersweet finish.

Progress (OG 1040, ABV 4%) ◆
A well-rounded, tawny-coloured bitter. Predominantly sweet and malty, with an underlying fruitiness and a hint of toffee. The flavour is well-balanced overall with a subdued bitterness. Little aroma and the aftertaste dissipates quickly.

Pitfield

Pitfield Brewery, Ashlyns Farm, Epping Road, North Weald, Epping, Essex, CM16 6RZ
☎ (0845) 833 1492
✉ sales@pitfieldbeershop.co.uk
🌐 pitfieldbeershop.co.uk
Shop – Ring for times
Tours by arrangement

⊗ After 24 years in London, Pitfield Brewery left the capital in 2006 and moved to new premises in Essex. It has since moved again to an organic farm with 25 acres of organic barley for the brewery's use. The beers are sold at farmers' and organic markets in the south-east of England. Pitfield also produces organic fruit wines, cider and perry. Seasonal beer: St George's Ale (ABV 4.3%), 1896 Stock Ale (ABV 10%, Nov). All beers are organically produced to Soil Association standards and are vegan-friendly.

Dark Mild (OG 1036, ABV 3.4%)

Bitter (OG 1036, ABV 3.7%)

Lager (OG 1036, ABV 3.7%)

Shoreditch Stout (OG 1038, ABV 4%) ◆
Chocolate and a raisin fruitiness on the nose lead to a fruity roast flavour and a sweetish finish with a little bitterness.

East Kent Goldings (OG 1040, ABV 4.2%) ◆
A dry, yellow beer with bitter notes throughout and a faint hint of honey on the palate.

Eco Warrior (OG 1043, ABV 4.5%) ◆
Golden ale with a vivid, citrus hop aroma. The hop character is balanced with a delicate sweetness in the taste, followed by an increasingly bitter finish.

Red Ale (OG 1046, ABV 4.8%) ◆
Complex beer with a full, malty body and strong hop character.

1850 London Porter (OG 1048, ABV 5%) ◆
Big-tasting dark ale dominate by coffee and forest fruits. The finish is dry but not acrid.

N1 Wheat Beer (OG 1048, ABV 5%)

1837 India Pale Ale (OG 1065, ABV 7%)

1792 Imperial Stout (OG 1085, ABV 9.3%)

For Duke of Cambridge, Islington:

SB Bitter (OG 1036, ABV 3.7%)

Plassey SIBA

Plassey Brewery, Eyton, Wrexham, LL13 0SP
☎ (01978) 781111
☎ 07050 327127
✉ plassey@globalnet.co.uk
🌐 plasseybrewery.co.uk
Shop open office hours
Tours by arrangement

The brewery was founded in 1985 on the 250-acre Plassey Estate, which also incorporates a touring caravan park, craft centres, a golf course, three licensed outlets for Plassey's ales, and a brewery shop. Some 30 free trade outlets are also supplied. Seasonal beer: Ruddy Rudolph (ABV 4.5%, Xmas).

Original Border Mild (ABV 3.6%)

Welsh Border Exhibition Ale (OG 1036, ABV 3.8%)

Bitter (OG 1041, ABV 4%) ◆
Full-bodied and distinctive best bitter. Good balance of hops and fruit flavours with a lasting dry bitter aftertaste.

Offa's Dyke Ale (OG 1043, ABV 4.3%) ◆
Sweetish and fruity refreshing best bitter with caramel undertones. Some bitterness in the finish.

Owain Glyndwr's Ale (OG 1043, ABV 4.3%)

Fusilier (OG 1046, ABV 4.5%)

Cwrw Tudno (OG 1048, ABV 5%) ◆
A mellow, sweetish premium beer with classic Plassey flavours of fruit and hops.

Dragon's Breath (OG 1060, ABV 6%)
A fruity, strong bitter, smooth and quite sweet, though not cloying, with an intense, fruity aroma.

Plockton*

Plockton Brewery, 5 Bank Street, Plockton, Ross-shire, IV52 8TP
☎ (0159) 544276
✉ andy@theplocktonbrewery.com
🌐 theplocktonbrewery.com
Tours by arrangement

The brewery started trading in April 2007. A bottling plant is planned. 2 outlets are supplied direct. Seasonal beer: Starboard! (ABV 5.1%).

Crags Ale (OG 1042, ABV 4.3%)

Dall Winter Sunshine (OG 1046, ABV 4.8%)

Poachers

Poachers Brewery, 439 Newark Road, North Hykeham, Lincolnshire, LN6 9SP
☎ (01522) 807404
☎ 07959 229638
🌐 poachersbrewery.co.uk
Tours by arrangement

Brewing started in 2001 on a five-barrel plant. In 2006 it was downsized to a 2.5-barrel plant and relocated by brewer George Batterbee at the rear of his house. Regular outlets are supplied throughout Lincolnshire and surrounding counties; outlets further afield are supplied via wholesalers. Seasonal beer:

Santas Come (ABV 6.5%, Xmas). Bottle-conditioned beers are also available.

Trembling Rabbit Mild (OG 1034, ABV 3.4%)
Rich, dark mild with a smooth malty flavour and a slightly bitter finish.

Shy Talk Bitter (OG 1037, ABV 3.7%)
Clean-tasting session beer, pale gold in colour; slightly bitter finish, dry hopped.

Poachers Pride (OG 1040, ABV 4%)
Amber bitter brewed using Cascade hops that produce a fine flavour and aroma that lingers.

Bog Trotter (OG 1042, ABV 4.2%)
A malty, earthy-tasting best bitter.

Poachers Trail (OG 1042, ABV 4.2%) ◆
A flowery hop-nosed, mid-brown beer with a well-balanced but bitter taste that stays with the malt, becoming more apparent in the drying finish.

Billy Boy (OG 1044, ABV 4.4%)
A mid-brown beer hopped with Fuggles and Mount Hood.

Black Crow Stout (OG 1045, ABV 4.5%)
Dry stout with burnt toffee and caramel flavour.

Hare Repie (OG 1045, ABV 4.5%)
A golden-coloured, sweet smelling ale; dry in flavour.

Poachers Dick (OG 1045, ABV 4.5%)
Ruby-red bitter, smooth fruity flavour balanced by the bitterness of Goldings hops.

Jock's Trap (OG 1050, ABV 5%)
A strong, pale brown bitter; hoppy and well-balanced with a slightly dry fruit finish.

Trout Tickler (OG 1055, ABV 5.5%)
Ruby bitter with intense flavour and character, sweet undertones with a hint of chocolate.

Porter

Porter

See Outstanding

Port Mahon

See Little Ale Cart

Potbelly

Potbelly Brewery Ltd, Sydney Street Entrance, Kettering, Northamptonshire, NN16 0JA
☎ (01536) 410818
☎ 07834 867825
✉ toni@potbelly-brewery.co.uk
🌐 potbelly-brewery.co.uk
Tours by arrangement

Potbelly started brewing in 2005 on a 10-barrel plant. Sawyers in Kettering acts as a brewery tap and around 200 other outlets across the country are supplied. Seasonal beers: Made in England (ABV 4.4%), Jingle Bellies (ABV 5%).

Streaky (OG 1034.6, ABV 3.6%)

Best (OG 1036.9, ABV 3.8%)

Aisling (OG 1038.4, ABV 4%)

Ambrosia (OG 1038.8, ABV 4%)

Beijing Black (OG 1043, ABV 4.4%)

Pigs Do Fly (OG 1041, ABV 4.4%)

Redwing (OG 1048, ABV 4.8%)

Crazy Daze (OG 1050, ABV 5.5%)

Potton SIBA

Potton Brewery Co Ltd, 10 Shannon Place, Potton, Bedfordshire, SG19 2SP
☎ (01767) 261042
✉ info@potton-brewery.co.uk
🌐 potton-brewery.co.uk

⊠ Set up by Clive Towner and Bob Hearson in 1998, it was Potton's first brewery since 1922. The brewery expanded from 20 barrels a week to 50 in 2004 and further expansion is now taking place. Around 150 outlets are supplied. Seasonal beers: Bunny Hops (ABV 4.1%, Mar-Apr), No-Ale (ABV 4.8%, Nov-Dec). Bottle-conditioned beers are also available.

Shannon IPA (OG 1035, ABV 3.6%)
A well-balanced session bitter with good bitterness and fruity late-hop character.

Gold (OG 1040, ABV 4.1%)
Golden-coloured, refreshing beer with a spicy/citrus late-hop character.

Shambles Bitter (OG 1043, ABV 4.3%)
A robust pale and heavily hopped beer with a subtle dry hop character imparted by Styrian Goldings.

Village Bike (OG 1042, ABV 4.3%) ◆
Classic English premium bitter, amber in colour, heavily late-hopped.

Pride of Potton (OG 1057, ABV 6%) ◆
Impressive, robust amber ale with a malty aroma, malt and ripe fruit in the mouth, and a fading sweetness.

Princetown

See Dartmoor

Prospect*

Prospect Brewery Ltd, 120 Wigan Road, Standish, Wigan, Lancashire, WN6 0AY
☎ (01257) 421329
✉ info@prospectbrewery.com
🌐 prospectbrewery.com

Brewing commenced at the end of August 2007 on a five-barrel plant from Bank Top Brewery. The brewery is situated at the top of Prospect Hill – hence the name – and the beers are named along prospecting/mining themes. Over 30 outlets are supplied direct. Seasonal beers: Clementine (ABV 5%, Xmas), Lancashire Hop Top (ABV 4.5%, Nov). Bottle-conditioned beers are also available.

Silver Tally (ABV 3.7%)

Pioneer (ABV 4%)

Gold Rush (ABV 4.5%)

Pick Axe (ABV 5%)

Purity

Purity Brewing Co Ltd, The Brewery, Upper Spernall Farm, Off Spernal Lane, Great Alne, Warwickshire, B49 6JF
☎ (01789) 488007
✉ sales@puritybrewing.com
puritybrewing.com
Shop Mon-Fri 8am-5pm; Sat 10am-1pm
Tours by arrangement

Brewing began in 2005 in a purpose-designed plant housed in converted barns in the heart of Warwickshire. The brewery incorporates an environmentally-friendly effluent treatment system. It supplies the free trade within a 50-mile radius and delivers to over 200 outlets.

Pure Gold (OG 1039.5, ABV 3.8%)

Pure Ubu (OG 1044.8, ABV 4.5%)

Purple Moose SIBA

Bragdy Mws Piws Cyf/Purple Moose Brewery Ltd, Madoc Street, Porthmadog, Gwynedd, LL49 9DB
☎ (01766) 515571
✉ beer@purplemoose.co.uk
purplemoose.co.uk
Shop Mon-Fri 9am-5pm
Tours by arrangement

A 10-barrel plant opened in 2005 by Lawrence Washington in a former saw mill and farmers' warehouse in the coastal town of Porthmadog. The names of the beers reflect local history and geography. The brewery now supplies around 100 outlets. Seasonal and monthly special beers: see website.

Cwrw Eryri/Snowdonia Ale (OG 1035.3, ABV 3.6%)
Golden, refreshing bitter with citrus fruit hoppiness in aroma and taste. The full mouthfeel leads to a long-lasting, dry, bitter finish.

Cwrw Madog/Madog's Ale (OG 1037, ABV 3.7%)
Full-bodied session bitter. Malty nose and an initial nutty flavour but bitterness dominates. Well balanced and refreshing with a dry roastiness on the taste and a good dry finish.

Cwrw Glaslyn/Glaslyn Ale (OG 1041, ABV 4.2%)
Refreshing light and malty amber-coloured ale. Plenty of hop in the aroma and taste. Good smooth mouthfeel leading to a slightly chewy finish.

Ochr Tywyll y Mws/Dark Side of the Moose (OG 1045, ABV 4.6%)
A delicious dark ale with a deep malt flavour and a fruity bitterness.

Quantock*

Quantock Brewery, Unit E, Monument View, Summerfield Avenue, Chelston Business Park, Wellington, Somerset, TA21 9ND
☎ (01823) 662669
✉ rob@quantockbrewery.co.uk
quantockbrewery.co.uk

Quantock began brewing in early 2008 on an eight-barrel plant. Bottle-conditioned beers are available.

Ale (ABV 3.8%)

Sunraker (ABV 4.2%)

White Hind (ABV 4.5%)

Quartz

Quartz Brewing Ltd, Archers, Alrewas Road, Kings Bromley, Staffordshire, DE13 7HW
☎ (01543) 473965

2nd Brewery: Unit 18, Heart of the Country Village, London Road, Swinfen, Staffordshire, WS14 9QR
✉ scott@quartzbrewing.co.uk
quartzbrewing.co.uk
Shop Tue-Sun 10am-5pm
Tours by arrangement

The brewery was set up on 2005 by Scott Barnett, a brewing engineer previously with Bass, and Julia Barnett, a master brewer from Carlsberg. The brewery produces three main brands plus seasonal specials. A licensed visitor centre has opened at Heart of the Country Craft Centre, Swinfin, and supplies draught beers, bottles and mini-casks. Around 30 outlets are supplied.

Blonde (OG 1038, ABV 3.8%)
Light amber bitter, slightly sweet and fruity with a pleasant bitter finish and an astringent hint.

Crystal (OG 1040, ABV 4.2%)
Copper with aromas of caramel and touches of hops and malt. Fruity tasting with a hedgerow bitterness and short hoppy finish.

Extra Blonde (OG 1042, ABV 4.4%)

Quay

See Dorset

Quercus*

Quercus Brewery & Beer House, Unit 2M, South Hams Business Park, Churchstow, Kingsbridge, Devon, TQ7 3QH
☎ (01548) 854888
✉ info@quercusbrewery.com
quercusbrewery.com
Shop Wed-Thu 3-6pm; Fri-Sat 10am-6pm (summer); Fri-Sat 10am-5pm (winter)

Quercus began trading in summer 2007 and is a small, family-run brewery and specialist beer shop. The brewery has an eight-barrel brew length. 20 outlets are supplied direct. Seasonal beers: Stormbrew (ABV 5%), QPA (ABV 5.8%).

Prospect (OG 1039, ABV 4%)

Shingle Bay (OG 1041, ABV 4.2%)

QB (OG 1044, ABV 4.5%)

Rainbow

Rainbow Inn & Brewery, 73 Birmingham Road, Allesley Village, Coventry, West Midlands, CV5 9GT

☎ (02476) 402888
Tours by arrangement

◎ Rainbow was launched in 1994. The current landlord, Jon Grote, took over in 2001. Output is through the pub although nine-gallon casks and polypins can be ordered for home use or beer festivals.

Rotherhams Rainbow Ale (ABV 4.5%)

Ramsbury SIBA

Ramsbury Estates Ltd, Priory Farm, Axford, Marlborough, Wiltshire, SN8 2HA
☎ (01672) 520647/541407
✉ dgolding@ramsburyestates.com
🌐 ramsburybrewery.com
Tours by arrangement

Ramsbury started brewing in 2004. Ramsbury Estates is a farming company covering approximately 5,500 acres of the Marlborough Downs in Wiltshire. It grows malting barley for the brewing industry including Optic, which the brewery also uses. Additional fermenters have been purchased and contract bottling taken on. Some 90 outlets are supplied. Seasonal beer: Deerhunter (ABV 5%, winter).

Bitter (OG 1036, ABV 3.6%)
Amber-coloured beer with a smooth, delicate aroma and flavour.

Kennet Valley (OG 1040, ABV 4.1%)
A light amber, hoppy bitter with a long, dry finish.

Flintknapper (OG 1041, ABV 4.2%)
Rich amber in colour with a malty taste.

Gold (OG 1043, ABV 4.5%)
A rich golden-coloured beer with a light hoppy aroma and taste.

Ramsgate SIBA

Ramsgate Brewery Ltd, 1 Hornet Close, Pyson's Road Industrial Estate, Broadstairs, Kent, CT10 2YD
☎ (01843) 868453
✉ info@ramsgatebrewery.co.uk
🌐 ramsgatebrewery.co.uk
Shop Mon-Fri 9am-5pm
Tours by arrangement

⊗ Ramsgate was established in 2002 in a derelict sea-front restaurant and only uses locally grown hops. In 2006 the brewery moved to its current location, allowing for increased capacity and bottling. Within the brewery is possibly the smallest pub in the world, the Ram's Head, which can only accommodate three people standing. Bottle-conditioned beers are available.

Gadds' No. 7 Bitter Ale (OG 1037, ABV 3.8%)
Satisfying session bitter using local Fuggles hops.

East Kent Pale Ale (OG 1041, ABV 4.1%)

Gadds' Seasider (OG 1042, ABV 4.3%)

Gadds' No. 5 Best Bitter Ale (OG 1043, ABV 4.4%)
Complex, easy-drinking best bitter using East Kent Goldings and Fuggles hops.

Gadds' No. 3 Kent Pale Ale (OG 1047, ABV 5%)
A light and refreshing, full-strength pale ale, brewed with locally-grown East Kent Goldings hops.

Gadds' Faithful Dogbolter Porter (OG 1054, ABV 5.6%)

Randalls SIBA

RW Randall Ltd, La Piette Brewery, St Georges Esplanade, St Peter Port, Guernsey, GY1 3JG
☎ (01481) 720134
Tours by arrangement

⊗ Randalls has been brewing since 1868 and was bought in 2006 by a group of private investors, headed by Ian Rogers, the founder of Wychwood Brewery. 18 pubs are owned, nine serving cask beer and a further 50 outlets are supplied. Further beers are planned but no information was available at time of going to press.

Patois (OG 1045, ABV 4.5%)

RCH SIBA

RCH Brewery, West Hewish, Weston-Super-Mare, Somerset, BS24 6RR
☎ (01934) 834447
✉ rchbrewery@aol.com
🌐 rchbrewery.com
Shop Mon-Fri 8.30am-4pm

⊗ The brewery was originally installed in the early 1980s behind the Royal Clarence Hotel at Burnham-on-Sea. Since 1993 brewing has taken place in a former cider mill at West Hewish. A 30-barrel plant was installed in 2000. RCH supplies 150 outlets and the award-winning beers are available nationwide through its own wholesaling company, which also distributes beers from other small independent breweries. Seasonal beers: see website. Bottle-conditioned beers are also available.

Hewish IPA (OG 1036, ABV 3.6%) ◆
Light, hoppy bitter with some malt and fruit, though slightly less fruit in the finish. Floral citrus hop aroma; pale/brown amber colour.

PG Steam (OG 1039, ABV 3.9%) ◆
Amber-coloured, medium-bodied with a floral hop aroma. Bitter citrus taste with a hint of sweetness.

Pitchfork (OG 1043, ABV 4.3%) ◆
Yellow, grapefruit-flavoured bitter bursting with citrus with underlying sweetness.

Old Slug Porter (OG 1046, ABV 4.5%) ◆
Chocolate, coffee, roast malt and hops with lots of body and dark fruits. A complex, rich beer, dark brown in colour.

East Street Cream (OG 1050, ABV 5%) ◆
Pale brown strong bitter. Flavours of roast malt and fruit with a bittersweet finish.

Double Header (OG 1053, ABV 5.3%) ◆
Light brown, full-bodied strong bitter. Beautifully balanced flavours of malt, hops and tropical fruits are followed by a long, bittersweet finish. Refreshing and easy drinking for its strength.

Firebox (OG 1060, ABV 6%) ◆
An aroma and taste of citrus hops and pale crystal malt are followed by a strong, complex, full-bodied, mid-brown beer with a well-balanced flavour of malt and hops.

Rebellion SIBA

Rebellion Beer Co, Marlow Brewery, Bencombe Farm, Marlow Bottom, Buckinghamshire, SL7 3LT
☎ (01628) 476594
✉ info@rebellionbeer.co.uk
🌐 rebellionbeer.co.uk
Shop Mon-Fri 8am-6pm; Sat 9am-6pm
Tours by arrangement (1st Tue of the month – £10)

⊗ Established in 1993, Rebellion has filled the void left when Wethereds ceased brewing in 1998 at Marlow. A steady growth in fortunes led to larger premises being sought and, following relocation in 1999, the brewery has gone from strength to strength and maximised output. Rebellion's nearby Three Horseshoes pub is the brewery tap. Rebellion Mild is exclusive to this pub. Around 200 other outlets are supplied. Seasonal beers: see website. Bottle-conditioned beer is also available.

Mild (OG 1035, ABV 3.5%)

IPA (OG 1039, ABV 3.7%) ◆
Copper-coloured bitter, sweet and malty, with resinous and red apple flavours. Caramel and fruit decline to leave a dry, bitter and malty finish.

Smuggler (OG 1042, ABV 4.1%) ◆
A red-brown beer, well-bodied and bitter with an uncompromisingly dry, bitter finish.

Mutiny (OG 1046, ABV 4.5%) ◆
Tawny in colour, this full-bodied best bitter is predominantly fruity and moderately bitter with crystal malt continuing to a dry finish.

Rectory SIBA

Rectory Ales Ltd, Streat Hill Farm, Streat Hill, Streat, Hassocks, East Sussex, BN6 8RP
☎ (01273) 890570
✉ rectoryales@hotmail.com
Tours by arrangement (Easter-Sep)

⊗ Rectory was founded in 1995 by the Rector of Plumpton, the Rev Godfrey Broster, to generate funds for the maintenance of his three parish churches. 107 parishioners are shareholders. The brewing capacity is now 20 barrels a week. All outlets are supplied from the brewery. Seasonal beer: Christmas Cheer (ABV 3.8%, Dec).

Rector's Bitter (OG 1040, ABV 4%)

Rector's Best Bitter (OG 1043, ABV 4.3%)

Rector's Strong Ale (OG 1050, ABV 5%)

Red Rat*

Red Rat Craft Brewery, Broadmere Cottages, Troston, Bury St Edmunds, Suffolk, IP31 1EH
☎ (01359) 269742
☎ 07704 817632
✉ enquiries@redratcraftbrewery.co.uk
🌐 redratcraftbrewery.co.uk

Red Rat started brewing in summer 2007 on a 2.5-barrel plant. Around 30 barrels are produced a week. All beers are also available bottle conditioned.

Hadley's (ABV 4.2%)

Rock Ape (ABV 4.5%)

Talking Bull (ABV 5%)

Woolly Pig (ABV 5%)

Crazy Dog Stout (ABV 6%)

Red Rock

Red Rock Brewery Ltd, Higher Humber Farm, Bishopsteignton, Devon, TQ14 9TD
☎ 07894 035904
✉ john@redrockbrewery.co.uk
🌐 redrockbrewery.co.uk
Shop Mon-Fri 9am-4pm (phone for weekend hours)
Tours by arrangement

⊗ Red Rock first started brewing in 2006 with a four-barrel plant. It is based in a converted barn on a working farm using locally sourced malt, English hops and the farm's own spring water. All beers are also hand bottled and labelled. Around 60 outlets are supplied.

Humber Down (OG 1034, ABV 3.6%)

Back Beach (OG 1038, ABV 3.8%)

Red Rock (OG 1041, ABV 4.2%)

Drift Wood (OG 1042, ABV 4.3%)

Dark Ness (OG 1045, ABV 4.5%)

Break Water (OG 1046, ABV 4.6%)

Red Rose SIBA

Red Rose Brewery, Unit 5, New Plough Yard, Queen Street, Great Harwood, Lancashire, BB6 7AX
☎ (01254) 877373/883541
✉ beer@redrosebrewery.co.uk
🌐 redrosebrewery.co.uk
Tours by arrangement

◎ Red Rose was launched in 2002 to supply the Royal Hotel, Great Harwood. Expansion has seen several moves, the latest being in January 2008 to the present premises and as a result the beers are now available nationwide. Seasonal beers: Pissed Over Pendle Halloween Ale (ABV 4.4%), 34th Street Miracle Beer (ABV 4.5%). Special beers are available throughout the year.

Bowley Best (ABV 3.7%)
Darkish northern bitter. Malty yet sharp with hoppy citrus finish.

Treacle Miners Tipple (ABV 3.9%)

Target (ABV 4%)

Felix (ABV 4.2%)
Dry, pale and remarkably hoppy with a keen nose, yet rounded and smooth with a lingering finish.

Old Ben (ABV 4.3%)
Pale, clean-tasting, crisp beer with a strong hop presence and no sweetness.

Lancashire & Yorkshire Aleway/ Steaming (ABV 4.5%)
Copper-coloured, strong beer. Initially sweet and malty, with a good hop aroma. Full and fruity.

Paddy O'Hackers Genuine Irish Stout Brewed In Lancashire (ABV 4.6%)

Older Empire (ABV 5.5%)

Care Taker of History (ABV 6%)
A dark, strong ale with a roast malt aroma. The taste is complex, rich and warming. Well-balanced and drinkable.

Redscar*

Redscar Brewery Ltd, c/o The Cleveland Hotel, 9-11 High Street West, Redcar, TS10 1SQ
☎ (01642) 484035
✉ enquiries@theclevelandhotel.co.uk
theclevelandhotel.co.uk

Redscar first brewed in early 2008 on a 2.5-barrel plant. The brewery supplies the hotel, local pubs and beer festivals.

Sands (ABV 4.2%)

Rocks (ABV 4.5%)

Red Shoot

Red Shoot Inn & Brewery, Toms Lane, Linwood, Ringwood, Hampshire, BH24 3QT
☎ (01425) 475792
✉ redshoot@wadworth.co.uk

⊗ The 2.5-barrel brewery, owned by Wadworth, was commissioned in 1998. In summer the brewery works to capacity, half the output going to the pub and half elsewhere locally, being distributed by Wadworth. Seasonal beer: Forest Grump (ABV 3.6%, winter).

Forest Gold (ABV 3.8%)

Muddy Boot (ABV 4.2%)

Tom's Tipple (ABV 4.8%)

Red Squirrel

Red Squirrel Brewery, 14b Mimram Road, Hertford, Hertfordshire, SG14 1NN
☎ (01992) 501100
✉ gary@redsquirrelbrewery.co.uk
redsquirrelbrewery.co.uk
Tours by arrangement

⊗ Red Squirrel started brewing in 2004 with a 10-barrel plant. Several seasonal beers are also produced including Irish, Scottish and strong American ales (produced to original recipes). 40 outlets are supplied.

Dark Ruby Mild (OG 1036, ABV 3.7%)

RSB (ABV 3.9%)

Blonde (ABV 4.1%)

Conservation Bitter (OG 1040, ABV 4.1%)

Gold (OG 1041, ABV 4.2%)

London Porter (ABV 5%)

American IPA (ABV 5.4%)

Reepham

Reepham Brewery, Unit 1, Collers Way, Reepham, Norwich, Norfolk, NR10 4SW
☎ (01603) 871091
Tours by arrangement

⊗ Reepham has completed more than 20 years of continuous brewing in the same premises. A beer in the style of Newcastle Brown Ale was introduced (Tyne Brown), to show support for the Tynesiders' brewery. S&P Best Bitter was launched in 2005 to celebrate Norwich's brewing heritage: the beer is named after Steward & Patteson, bought and closed by Watneys. Some 20 outlets are supplied. Bottle-conditioned beer is available.

Granary Bitter (OG 1038, ABV 3.5%)
A gold-coloured beer with a light hoppy aroma followed by a malty sweetish flavour with some smoke notes. A well-balanced beer with a long, moderately hoppy aftertaste.

S&P Best Bitter (OG 1038, ABV 3.7%)

Rapier Pale Ale (OG 1043, ABV 4.2%)
Complex, amber-coloured brew. Malt and hops in the aroma metamorphose into a distinctly hoppy first taste with smoky bitter overtones. Long drawn-out bitter finale.

Velvet Sweet Stout (OG 1044, ABV 4.5%)
There is a heavy roast influence in aroma and taste. A smoky malt feel produces a combination that is both creamy and well-defined. Fruit and hop indicate a subtle sweetness that soon fades to leave a growing dry bitterness.

Tyne Brown (OG 1046, ABV 4.6%)
Marzipan and fruit cake overtones dominate this rich, malty brown ale. The aroma and taste are malty although a rising bitterness gives the finish a vinous quality.

St Agnes (OG 1047, ABV 4.8%)
Smooth and creamy with bananas to the fore in aroma and taste. Smoky malt overtones subside as increasing bitterness dominates a gently receding finish.

Rhymney

Rhymney Brewery Ltd, Unit A2, Valley Enterprise Centre, Pant Industrial Estate, Dowlais, Merthyr Tydfil, CF48 2SR
☎ (01685) 722253
✉ marc@rhymneybreweryltd.com
rhymneybreweryltd.com
Shop Sat 10am-2pm
Tours by arrangement

Rhymney first brewed in 2005. The 75-hl plant, sourced from Canada, is capable of producing both cask and keg beers. Around 220 outlets are supplied.

Best (OG 1038, ABV 3.7%)

1905 Centenary Ale (OG 1040, ABV 3.9%)

Dark (OG 1044, ABV 4%)

Bevans Bitter (OG 1043, ABV 4.2%)

General Picton (OG 1044, ABV 4.3%)

Bitter (OG 1044, ABV 4.5%)

Premier Lager (OG 1046, ABV 4.5%)

Richmond*

Richmond Brewing Co Ltd, The Station Brewery, Richmond, North Yorkshire, DL10 4LD
☎ (01748) 828266
✉ andy@richmondbrewing.co.uk
🌐 richmondbrewing.co.uk

Richmond began brewing in May 2008 and is situated in a multi million pound re-development of the listed Victorian Station.

Sw'Ale (OG 1036, ABV 3.6%)

Station Ale (OG 1040, ABV 4%)

Stump Cross Ale (OG 1046, ABV 4.7%)

Ridgeway SIBA

Ridgeway Brewing, Beer Counter Ltd, South Stoke, Oxfordshire, RG8 0JW
☎ (01491) 873474
✉ peter.scholey@beercounter.co.uk

Ridgeway was set up by ex-Brakspear head brewer Peter Scholey. It specialises in bottle-conditioned beers but equivalent cask beers are also available. At present Ridgeway beers are brewed by Peter using his own ingredients on a plant at Hepworth's of Horsham (qv) and occasionally elsewhere. All beers listed are available cask and bottle-conditioned. Six strong (ABV 6-9%) bottle-conditioned Christmas beers are produced annually, principally for export to the U.S.

Bitter (OG 1040, ABV 4%)

Organic Beer/ROB (OG 1043, ABV 4.3%)

Blue (OG 1049, ABV 5%)

Ivanhoe (OG 1050, ABV 5.2%)

IPA (OG 1055, ABV 5.5%)

Foreign Export Stout (OG 1078, ABV 8%)

For Coniston Brewing:

Coniston Bluebird (ABV 4.2%)

Coniston XB (ABV 4.4%)

Coniston Old Man (ABV 4.8%)

Ridleys

See Greene King in New Nationals section

Ringmore*

Ringmore Craft Brewery Ltd, Higher Ringmore Road, Shaldon, Devon, TQ14 0HG
☎ (01626) 873114
✉ geoff@ringmorecraftbrewery.co.uk

Ringmore was established in early 2007 on a one-barrel plant and is the first brewery in Shaldon since 1920. Seasonal beer: Ringmore Rollocking Christmas (ABV 5.5%). Bottle-conditioned ales are also available, including seasonal ones.

Rollocks (OG 1044, ABV 4.5%)

Oarsome Ale (OG 1046, ABV 4.6%)

Ringwood

See Marston's in New Nationals section

Riverhead

Riverhead Brewery Ltd, Riverhead Brewery Tap & Dining Room, 2 Peel Street, Marsden, Huddersfield, West Yorkshire, HD7 6BR
☎ (01484) 841270 (Pub)
☎ (01924)
✉ brewery@ossett-brewery.co.uk
🌐 ossett-brewery.co.uk

Tours by arrangement (through Ossett Brewing Co)

Riverhead is a brew-pub that opened in 1995 after conversion from an old grocery shop. Ossett Brewing Co Ltd purchased the site in 2006 but runs it as a separate brewery. It has since opened The Dining Room on the first floor, which uses Riverhead beers in its dishes. All original recipes have been retained with new beers also being added. The core range of beers are named after local reservoirs, with the height of the reservoir relating to the strength of the beer. Rotating beers: Leggers Lite (ABV 3.6%), Deer Hill Porter (ABV 4%), Wessenden Wheat (ABV 4%), Cupwith Special (ABV 4.2%), Marsden Best (ABV 4.2%), Black Moss Stout (ABV 4.3%), Premium Mild (ABV 4.7%). Seasonal beers: Ruffled Feathers (ABV 4.6%, Cuckoo Day), Bandsman's Bitter (ABV 4.5%, for Brass Band Competition), Jazz Bitter (ABV 3.8%, for Marsden Jazz Festival), Marsden Merrymaker (ABV 6.5%, Xmas).

Sparth Mild (ABV 3.6%)
A light-bodied, dry mild with a dark ruby colour. Fruity aroma with roasted flavour and dry finish.

Butterley Bitter (OG 1038, ABV 3.8%) ◆
A dry, amber-coloured, hoppy session beer.

March Haigh (OG 1046, ABV 4.6%)
A golden-brown premium bitter. Malty and full-bodied with moderate bitterness.

Redbrook Premium (ABV 5.5%)
A red-brown strong ale. Mellow yet robust with a delicate hop aroma. Slightly sweet.

Riverside

Riverside Brewery, Unit 1, Church Lane, Wainfleet, Lincolnshire, PE24 4BY
☎ (01754) 881288
🌐 wainfleet.info/shops.brewery-riverside.htm

Riverside started brewing in 2003, almost across the road from Bateman's, using a five-barrel plant. Owner John Dixon had not previously brewed but he was assisted by his father Ken, who had been head brewer at several breweries, including Bateman's. Eight barrels a week are produced for local trade, with some 15-20 outlets supplied. Seasonal beer: Dixon's Good Swill (ABV 5.8%, Nov-Dec).

Dixon's Light Brigade (OG 1038, ABV 3.9%)

Dixon's Major Bitter (OG 1038, ABV 3.9%)

Dixon's Desert Rat (OG 1048, ABV 4.8%)

John Roberts

See Three Tuns

Robinson's IFBB

Frederic Robinson Ltd, Unicorn Brewery, Lower Hillgate, Stockport, Cheshire, SK1 1JJ
☎ (0161) 612 4061
✉ brewery@frederic-robinson.co.uk
🌐 frederic-robinson.com
Tours by arrangement

Robinson's has been brewing since 1838 and the business is still owned and run by the family (5th and 6th generations). It has an estate of more than 400 pubs. Contract beers are also brewed. Seasonal beers: see website.

Hatters (OG 1032, ABV 3.3%)
A light mild with a malty, fruity aroma. Biscuity malt with some hop and fruit in the taste and finish. (A darkened version is available in a handful of outlets and badged Dark Hatters.)

Old Stockport (OG 1034, ABV 3.5%)
A beer with a refreshing taste of malt, hops and citrus fruit, a fruity aroma, and a short, dry finish.

Hartleys XB (OG 1040, ABV 4%)
An overly sweet and malty bitter with a bitter citrus peel fruitiness and a hint of liquorice in the finish.

Cumbria Way (OG 1040, ABV 4.1%)
A pronounced malt aroma with rich fruit notes. Rounded malt and hops in the mouth, long dry finish with citrus fruit notes. Brewed for the Hartley's estate in Cumbria.

Unicorn (OG 1041, ABV 4.2%)
Amber beer with a fruity aroma. Hoppy, bitter and fruity to taste, with a bitter finish.

Double Hop (OG 1050, ABV 5%)
Pale brown beer with malt and fruit on the nose. Full hoppy taste with malt and fruit, leading to a hoppy, bitter finish.

Old Tom (OG 1079, ABV 8.5%)
A full-bodied, dark beer with malt, fruit and chocolate on the aroma. A complex range of flavours includes dark chocolate, full maltiness, port and fruits and lead to a long, bittersweet aftertaste.

Rockingham SIBA

Rockingham Ales, c/o 25 Wansford Road, Elton, Cambridgeshire, PE8 6RZ
☎ (01832) 280722
✉ brian@rockinghamales.co.uk
🌐 rockinghamales.co.uk

A part-time brewery established in 1997 that operates from a converted farm building near Blatherwycke, Northamptonshire (business address as above). The two-barrel plant produces a prolific range of beers and supplies six local outlets. The regular beers are brewed on a rota basis, with special beers brewed to order. Seasonal beers: Fineshade (ABV 3.8%, autumn), Sanity Clause (ABV 4.3%, Dec), Old Herbaceous (ABV 4.5%, winter).

Forest Gold (OG 1039, ABV 3.9%)
A hoppy blonde ale with citrus flavours. Well-balanced and clean finishing.

Hop Devil (OG 1040, ABV 3.9%)
Six hop varieties give this golden ale a bitter start and spicy finish.

A1 Amber Ale (OG 1041, ABV 4%)
A hoppy session beer with fruit and blackcurrant undertones.

Saxon Cross (OG 1041, ABV 4.1%)
A golden-red ale with nut and coffee aromas. Citrus hop flavours predominate.

Fruits of the Forest (OG 1043, ABV 4.2%)
A multi-layered beer in which summer fruits and several spices compete with a big hop presence.

Dark Forest (OG 1050, ABV 5%)
A dark and complex beer, similar to a Belgian dubbel, with malty/smoky flavours that give way to a fruity bitter finish.

Rodham's

Rodham's Brewery, 74 Albion Street, Otley, West Yorkshire, LS21 1BZ
☎ (01943) 464530

Michael Rodham began brewing in 2005 on a one-barrel plant in the cellar of his house. Capacity has gradually increased and is now 2.5 barrels. All beers produced are malt-only, using whole hops. Around 15 outlets are supplied. Occasional seasonals and bottle-conditioned beers are available.

Rubicon (OG 1039, ABV 4.1%)
Amber-coloured with a nutty, malt and light fruit taste. A dry, peppery and bitter aftertaste.

Wheat Beer (OG 1039, ABV 4.1%)
Naturally cloudy, sharp and refreshing.

Royale (OG 1042, ABV 4.4%)
A golden beer with a citrus, hoppy taste, underlying malt with a bitter finish.

Old Albion (OG 1048, ABV 5%)
Ruby black premium beer with a complex mix of roasted malt, liquorice and tart fruit with a balancing bitterness.

IPA (ABV 5.9%)

Rooster's SIBA

Rooster's Brewing Co Ltd, Unit 3, Grimbald Park, Wetherby Road, Knaresborough, North Yorkshire, HG5 8LJ
☎ (01423) 865959
✉ sean@roosters.co.uk
🌐 roosters.co.uk
Tours by arrangement

Rooster's Brewery was opened in 1993 by Sean and Alison Franklin. Its sister company, Outlaw Brewery Co, started in 1996. The brewery moved to larger premises in 2001. Both breweries have a regular range of beers. Seasonal beer: Nector (ABV 5.2%, autumn/winter – Roosters). Bottle-conditioned beers are also available.

Special (OG 1038, ABV 3.9%)

Yellow in colour, a full-bodied, floral bitter with fruit and hop notes being carried over in to the long aftertaste. Hops and bitterness tend to increase in the finish.

Yankee (OG 1042, ABV 4.3%)
A straw-coloured beer with a delicate, fruity aroma leading to a well-balanced taste of malt and hops with a slight evidence of sweetness, followed by a refreshing, fruity/bitter finish.

YPA (OG 1042, ABV 4.3%)
A pale-coloured beer with pronounced raspberry and flower aromas.

Under Outlaw Brewery name:

Wrangler (ABV 3.7%)

Wild Mule (ABV 3.9%)

Dry Irish Stout (ABV 4.7%)

Dead or Alive (ABV 5%)

Rother Valley SIBA

Rother Valley Brewing Co, Gate Court Farm, Station Road, Northiam, East Sussex, TN31 6QT
☎ (01797) 253535
Tours by arrangement

Rother Valley was established in Northiam in 1993 with the brewhouse situated between hop fields and the oast house. Hops grown on the farm and from Sandhurst Hop Farm are used. Brewing is split between cask and an ever-increasing range of filtered bottled beers. Around 50 outlets are supplied. Seasonal beers: Summertime Blues (ABV 3.7%, summer), Copper Ale (ABV 4.1%), Holly Daze (ABV 4.2%, Christmas), Blues (ABV 5%, winter).

Smild (OG 1038, ABV 3.8%)

Level Best (OG 1040, ABV 4%)
Full-bodied tawny session bitter with a malt and fruit aroma, malty taste and a dry, hoppy finish.

Hoppers Ale (OG 1044, ABV 4.4%)

Boadicea (OG 1046, ABV 4.6%)

Rudgate SIBA

Rudgate Brewery Ltd, 2 Centre Park, Marston Moor Business Park, Tockwith, York, North Yorkshire, YO26 7QF
☎ (01423) 358382
✉ sales@rudgate-beers.co.uk
rudgate-beers.co.uk

Rudgate Brewery was founded in 1992 and is located in an old armoury building on a disused World War II airfield. It has a 15-barrel plant and four open fermenting vessels, producing more than 40 barrels a week. Around 300 outlets are supplied direct. Seasonal beers: Rudolphs Ruin (ABV 4.6%, Xmas), Crimble Ale (ABV 4.2%, Xmas). Other seasonal beers are produced on a monthly basis.

Viking (OG 1036, ABV 3.8%)
An initially warming and malty, full-bodied beer, with hops and fruit lingering into the aftertaste.

Battleaxe (OG 1040, ABV 4.2%)
A well-hopped bitter with slightly sweet initial taste and light bitterness. Complex fruit character gives a memorable aftertaste.

Ruby Mild (OG 1041, ABV 4.4%)
Nutty, rich ruby ale, stronger than usual for a mild.

Special (OG 1042, ABV 4.5%)
Moderately bitter leading to a citrus, hoppy finish.

Well Blathered (OG 1046, ABV 5%)
A premium bitter, golden-coloured with distinctive lemon on the nose.

Rugby

Rugby Brewing Co Ltd, The Brewery, Wood Farm Buildings, Coal Pit Lane, Willey, Rugby, Warwickshire, CV23 0SL
☎ 0845 017 8844
rugbybrewingco.co.uk
Tours by arrangement (Max. 20 people)

Rugby started brewing in 2005 and opened its new brewery tap in 2008 with views from the bar into the brewery itself. Two pubs now operate under the brewery banner, the flagship being The Criterion in Leicester. There are plans to bottle some of the beers in the near future.

1823 (ABV 3.5%)

Twickers (ABV 3.7%)

Webb Ellis (ABV 3.8%)

Victorious (ABV 4.2%)

Sidestep (ABV 4.5%)

No. 8 (ABV 5%)

Winger IPA (ABV 5.2%)

Cement (ABV 6.8%)

Ryburn

Ryburn Brewery, Rams Head Inn, 26 Wakefield Road, Sowerby Bridge, West Yorkshire, HX6 2AZ
☎ (01422) 835413
✉ ryburnbrewery@talk21.com
Tours by arrangement

The brewery was established in 1989 at Mill House, Sowerby Bridge, but has since been relocated to the company's sole tied house, the Rams Head. Some business is done with the local free trade but the main market for the brewery's products is via wholesalers, chiefly JD Wetherspoon.

Best Mild (OG 1033, ABV 3.3%)
A traditional northern-style mild with chocolate in evidence. Smooth, bitter aftertaste.

Best Bitter (OG 1038, ABV 3.8%)
Amber-coloured, fresh, fruity session bitter. Lightly flavoured with a bitter aftertaste.

Numpty Bitter (OG 1044, ABV 4.2%)
Pale brown beer with a sweeter, vinous flavour than Best Bitter.

Luddite (OG 1048, ABV 5%)

Intensely flavoured black, creamy stout. Well balanced with strong chocolate, caramel and liquorice flavours tempered by sweetness.

Stabbers (OG 1052, ABV 5.2%)
Pale brown, creamy, fruity, sweet and vinous bitter. Its drinkability belies its strength.

Saddleworth

Church Inn & Saddleworth Brewery, Church Lane, Uppermill, Oldham, Greater Manchester, OL3 6LW
☎ (01457) 820902/872415
Tours by arrangement

Saddleworth started brewing in 1997 in a brewhouse that had been closed for around 120 years. Brewery and inn are set in a historic location at the top of a valley overlooking Saddleworth and next to St Chads Church, which dates from 1215. Seasonal beers: Bert Corner (ABV 4%, Feb), St George's Bitter (ABV 4%, Apr), Ayrton's Ale (ABV 4.1%, Apr-May), Harvest Moon (ABV 4.1%, Aug-Sep), Robyn's Bitter (ABV 4.6%, Nov-Dec), Christmas Carol (ABV 6.6%, Dec-Jan).

Clog Dancer (ABV 3.6%)

Mild (ABV 3.8%)

More (ABV 3.8%)

Honey Smacker (ABV 4.1%)

Hop Smacker (ABV 4.1%)

Indya Pale Ale (ABV 4.1%)

Shaftbender (ABV 5.4%)

Sadlers

See Windsor Castle

Saffron

Saffron Brewery, The Cartshed, Parsonage Farm, Henham, Essex, CM22 6AN
☎ (01279) 850923
☎ 07747 696901
tb@saffronbrewery.co.uk
saffronbrewery.co.uk
Tours by arrangement

Founded in 2005, Saffron is situated near the historic East Anglian town of Saffron Walden, famous for its malting industry in the 18th century. The brewery was upgraded to a 15-barrel plant in early 2008 and re-located to a converted barn with a purpose built reed bed for environmentally friendly disposal of waste products. 40 outlets are supplied direct. Seasonal beers: see website. Bottle-conditioned beers are also available.

Muntjac (OG 1036, ABV 3.7%)
A copper-coloured session bitter with floral notes in the aroma. Pleasantly bitter in taste with plenty of hop character and slight sweetness.

EPA (OG 1038, ABV 3.9%)
A golden/straw-coloured ale with a subtle floral aroma with hints of blackcurrant spice.

Pledgdon Ale (OG 1042, ABV 4.3%)
An amber ale with a soft, mellow full flavour with hints of citrus and biscuit.

St Austell IFBB SIBA

St Austell Brewery Co Ltd, 63 Trevarthian Road, St Austell, Cornwall, PL25 4BY
☎ (01726) 74444
info@staustellbrewery.co.uk
staustellbrewery.co.uk
Shop Mon-Fri 9am-5pm
Tours by arrangement

St Austell Brewery celebrated 150 years of brewing in 2001. Founded by Walter Hicks in 1851, the company is still family owned, with a powerful commitment to cask beer. Cask beer is available in all 160 licensed houses, as well as in the free trade throughout Cornwall, Devon and Somerset. A visitor centre offers guided tours and souvenirs from the brewery. Bottle-conditioned beers are available.

IPA (OG 1035, ABV 3.4%)
Copper/bronze in colour, the nose blossoms with fresh hops. The palate is clean and full-bodied with a hint of toffee caramel. The finish is short and crisp.

Tinners (OG 1038, ABV 3.7%)
Golden beer with an appetising malt aroma and a good balance of malt and hops in the flavour. Lasting finish.

Dartmoor Best Bitter (OG 1039, ABV 3.9%)
Superbly balanced copper session bitter with a fruity malt nose. Full-bodied and grainy in the mouth but with a noticeable hoppy bite. Short finish of hops and malt.

Black Prince (OG 1041, ABV 4%)
Faint malt and bubblegum aroma of this black mild leads to a complex taste of roast flavours, toffee and fruit esters balanced by bitterness. Liquorice, fudge and bitterness linger on the palate.

Tribute (OG 1043, ABV 4.2%)
Medium-bodied copper-bronze premium ale. Refreshingly bittersweet with a balance of malt and hops. Aroma of Oregon hops, malt with a trace of tangy ester, while the finish is long, bitter and moderately dry.

Proper Job IPA (ABV 4.5%)
Floral aromatic hops greet the nose and persist in the mouth but mellowed by a sweet, well rounded and full-bodied taste which quickly disappears in a bittersweet aftertaste.

Hicks Special Draught/HSD (OG 1052, ABV 5%)
An aromatic, fruity, hoppy bitter that is initially sweet with an aftertaste of pronounced bitterness, but whose flavour is fully rounded.

St George's

St George's Brewing Co Ltd, Bush Lane, Callow End, Worcestershire, WR2 4TF
☎ (01905) 831316
stgeorge.brewer@btconnect.com
Tours by arrangement

The brewery was established in 1998 in old village bakery premises. It was acquired in 2006 by Duncan Ironmonger. Andrew Sankey has been the brewer and brewery manager for a number of years. The brewery supplies local freehouses and wholesalers for a wider distribution. At least two monthly specials are usually available.

Maiden's Saviour (OG 1037, ABV 3.7%)
An amber, smooth session ale with a bitter aftertaste.

Friar Tuck (OG 1040, ABV 4%)
A light, golden beer with a citrus fruity flavour.

Blues & Royals (OG 1043, ABV 4.3%)
Deep copper in colour with a biscuity, hoppy taste.

Charger (OG 1046, ABV 4.6%)
A light, refreshing beer.

Dragons Blood (OG 1048, ABV 4.8%)
A ruby red beer with a citrus flavour.

St Judes

St Judes Brewery Ltd, 2 Cardigan Street, Ipswich, Suffolk, IP1 3PF
☎ (01473) 413334
✉ gt6xxx@yahoo.co.uk
🌐 stjudesbrewery.co.uk
Shop Mon-Sat 10am-5pm; Sun 11am-5pm (please ring first)
Tours by arrangement (for up to 15 people)

⊗ St Judes was established in 2006 on a seven-barrel plant in a converted coach house hayloft. It bottles on site and supplies around 10 outlets direct. Bottle-conditioned beers are available.

St Francis (OG 1049, ABV 4%) ◆
Pale golden. Surprisingly malty aroma but the taste is all fruit and hops. Suitable for vegetarians and vegans.

Gypeswic Bitter (OG 1048, ABV 4.4%) ◆
Beautifully balanced amber bitter with fruity aroma and pleasantly lingering aftertaste.

Ipswich Bright IPA (OG 1042, ABV 4.4%) ◆
A refreshing, golden bitter beer with a long, hoppy aftertaste that seems to last forever.

Coachmans Whip (OG 1048, ABV 5.2%)

John Orfords (OG 1064, ABV 6.2%) ◆
Strong caramel and malt aroma and taste.

St Peter's EAB SIBA

St Peter's Brewery Co Ltd, St Peter's Hall, St Peter South Elmham, Suffolk, NR35 1NQ
☎ (01986) 782322
✉ beers@stpetersbrewery.co.uk
🌐 stpetersbrewery.co.uk
Shop Mon-Fri 9am-5pm; Sat & Sun 11am-5pm

⊗ St Peter's was launched in 1996 and concentrates in the main on bottled beer (80% of capacity) but has a rapidly increasing cask market. Two pubs are owned and 75 outlets are supplied. Seasonal beers: Ruby Red (ABV 4.3%), Wheat Beer (ABV 4.7%), Summer Ale (ABV 6.5%), Winter Ale (ABV 6.5%), Cream Stout (ABV 6.5%), Strong Ale (ABV 5.1%).

Best Bitter (OG 1038, ABV 3.7%) ◆
A complex but well-balanced hoppy brew. A gentle hop nose introduces a singular hoppiness with supporting malt notes and underlying bitterness. Other flavours fade to leave a long, dry, hoppy finish.

Mild (OG 1037, ABV 3.7%)
Sweetness balanced by bitter chocolate malt to produce a rare but much sought after traditional mild.

Organic Best (OG 1041, ABV 4.1%) ◆
A very dry and bitter beer with a growing astringency. Pale brown in colour, it has a gentle hop aroma which makes the definitive bitterness surprising. One for the committed.

Organic Ale (OG 1045, ABV 4.5%)
Soil Association standard, light malted barley from Scotland, with organic Target hops create a refreshing ale with a delicate character.

Golden Ale (OG 1047, ABV 4.7%) ◆
Amber-coloured, full-bodied, robust ale. A strong hop bouquet leads to a mix of malt and hops combined with a dry, fruity hoppiness. The malt quickly subsides, leaving creamy bitterness.

Grapefruit Beer (OG 1047, ABV 4.7%) ◆
With a very strong aroma and taste of grapefruit, this refreshing beer is exactly what it says on the tin. A superb example of a fruit beer.

IPA (OG 1055, ABV 5.5%)
A full-bodied, highly hopped pale ale with a zesty character.

Salamander

Salamander Brewing Co Ltd, 22 Harry Street, Bradford, West Yorkshire, BD4 9PH
☎ (01274) 652323
✉ salamanderbrewing@fsmail.net
🌐 salamanderbrewing.com
Tours by arrangement

⊗ Salamander first brewed in 2000 in a former pork pie factory. Further expansion during 2004 took the brewery to 40-barrel capacity. There are direct deliveries to more widespread areas such as Cumbria, East Yorkshire and Lancashire in addition to the established trade of about 100 outlets throughout Lancashire, Manchester, North Yorkshire and Derbyshire.

Mudpuppy (OG 1042, ABV 4.2%) ◆
A well-balanced, copper-coloured best bitter with a fruity, hoppy nose and a bitter finish.

Golden Salamander (OG 1045, ABV 4.5%) ◆
Citrus hops characterise the aroma and taste of this golden premium bitter, which has malt undertones throughout. The aftertaste is dry, hoppy and bitter.

Stout (OG 1045, ABV 4.5%) ◆
Rich roast malts dominate the smooth coffee and chocolate flavour. Nicely balanced. A dry, roast, bitter finish develops over time.

Salopian SIBA

Salopian Brewing Co Ltd, 67 Mytton Oak Road, Shrewsbury, Shropshire, SY3 8UQ
☎ (01743) 248414

✉ enquiries@salopianbrewery.co.uk
🌐 salopianbrewery.co.uk
Tours by arrangement

The brewery was established in 1995 in an old dairy on the outskirts of Shrewsbury and, having grown steadily, now produces 60 barrels a week. Over 200 outlets are supplied.

Shropshire Gold (OG 1037, ABV 3.8%)

Abbey Gates (OG 1042, ABV 4.3%)

Hoptwister (OG 1044, ABV 4.5%)

Lemon Dream (OG 1043.5, ABV 4.5%)

Golden Thread (OG 1048, ABV 5%)

Saltaire

Saltaire Brewery Ltd, Unit 6, County Works, Dockfield Road, Shipley, West Yorkshire, BD17 7AR
☎ **(01274) 594959**
✉ **info@saltairebrewery.co.uk**
🌐 **saltairebrewery.co.uk**
Tours by arrangement

Launched in 2006, Saltaire Brewery is a 20-barrel brewery based in a Victorian industrial building that formerly generated electricity for the local tram system. A mezzanine bar gives visitors views of the brewing plant and the chance to taste the beers. More than 300 pubs are supplied across West Yorkshire and the north of England.

Yorkshire Pale Bitter (OG 1038, ABV 3.8%)
Pale bitter with citrus flavours.

Blonde (OG 1040, ABV 4%)
Straw-coloured light ale with soft malt flavours.

Cascade Pale Ale (OG 1047, ABV 4.8%)
American-style pale ale with floral aromas and strong bitterness.

Sawbridgeworth

Sawbridgeworth Brewery, 81 London Road, Sawbridgeworth, Hertfordshire, CM21 9JJ
☎ **(01279) 722313**
✉ **the.gate.pub@dial.pipex.com**
Tours by arrangement

The brewery was set up in 2000 by Tom and Gary Barnett at the back of the Gate pub. One pub is owned. Tom is a former professional footballer whose clubs included Crystal Palace. Special or one-off beers are regularly brewed. All beers are also available bottle conditioned.

Selhurst Park Flyer (ABV 3.7%)

Viking (ABV 3.8%)

RACS (ABV 4%)

Is It Yourself (ABV 4.2%)

Stout (ABV 4.3%)

Brooklands Express (ABV 4.6%)

Piledriver (ABV 5.3%)

Scattor Rock

Scattor Rock Brewery Ltd, Unit 5, Gidley's Meadow, Christow, Exeter, Devon, EX6 7QB
☎ **(01647) 252120**
🌐 **scattorrockbrewery.com**

The brewery was set up in 1998 on the edge of Dartmoor National Park and is named after a local landmark. The brewery has expanded its business and now supplies around 300 outlets on a regular basis. There is a monthly rotation of seasonal brews, with two or three available in addition to the regular beers at any one time.

Scatty Bitter (OG 1040, ABV 3.8%)

Teign Valley Tipple (OG 1042, ABV 4%)
A well-balanced, tawny-coloured beer with a hoppy aroma.

Tom Cobley (OG 1043, ABV 4.2%)
A refreshing, light brown session ale.

Devonian (OG 1045, ABV 4.5%)
A strong, fruity, light-coloured ale.

Golden Valley (OG 1046, ABV 4.6%)
A golden refreshing ale.

Valley Stomper (OG 1051, ABV 5%)
Light brown and deceptively drinkable.

Selby

Selby (Middlebrough) Brewery Ltd, 131 Millgate, Selby, North Yorkshire, YO8 3LL
☎ **(01757) 702826**

Not currently brewing but there are plans to restart.

Severn Vale

Severn Vale Brewing Co, Woodend Lane, Cam, Dursley, Gloucestershire, GL11 5HS
☎ **(01453) 547550**
☎ **07971 640244**
✉ **steve@severnvalebrewing.co.uk**
🌐 **severnvalebrewing.co.uk**
Shop: Please ring first
Tours by arrangement

Severn Vale started brewing in 2005 in an old milking parlour using a new five-barrel plant. Warminster malted barley is used and mainly Herefordshire hops. Around 50 outlets are supplied. Seasonal beers: Severn Bells (ABV 4.3%, summer), Severn Swans-a-Swimming (ABV 4.7%, Xmas).

Session (ABV 3.4%)

Vale Ale (OG 1039, ABV 3.8%)
A rich amber beer with full-bodied malt flavours and a complex nose and taste.

Dursley Steam Bitter (OG 1043, ABV 4.2%)
A sparkling summer ale full of flowery hops.

Monumentale (OG 1047, ABV 4.5%)
Designed as a porter but not dissimilar to a strong mild with a lingering, malty flavour.

Severn Sins (ABV 5.2%)
A jet-black stout with a dry roast malt flavour with hints of chocolate and liquorice.

Shalford*

Shalford Brewery, c/o 3 Broome Close Villas, Church End, Shalford, Essex, CM7 5EY
☎ (01371) 850925
☎ 07749 658512
✉ nigel@shalfordbrewery.co.uk
🌐 shalfordbrewery.co.uk

⊗ Shalford began brewing in July 2007 on a five-barrel plant at Hyde Farm in the Pant Valley in Essex. Over 20 outlets are supplied direct. Bottle-conditioned beers are available.

Barnfield Bitter (ABV 4%) ◆
Pale-coloured but full-flavoured, this is a traditional, hoppy bitter rather than a golden ale. Malt persists throughout, with bitterness becoming more dominant towards the end.

Levelly Gold (ABV 4%)

Stoneley Bitter (ABV 4.2%) ◆
Dark amber session beer whose vivid hop character is supported by a juicy, malty body. A dry finish makes this beer very drinkable.

Hyde Bitter (ABV 4.7%) ◆
Stronger version of Barnfield, with a similar but more assertive character.

Levelly Black (ABV 4.8%)

Rotten End (ABV 6.5%)

Shardlow

Shardlow Brewing Co Ltd, The Old Brewery Stables, British Waterways Yard, Cavendish Bridge, Leicestershire, DE72 2HL
☎ (01332) 799188
Tours by arrangement

On a site associated with brewing since 1819, Shardlow delivers to more than 100 outlets throughout the East Midlands. Due to increased sales, two new fermenters have been added. Reverend Eaton is named after a scion of the Eaton brewing family, Rector of Shardlow for 40 years. The brewery tap is the Blue Bell Inn at Melbourne, Derbyshire. Seasonal beers: Frostbite (ABV 5.5%), Stedmans Tipple (ABV 5.1%), Six Bells (ABV 6%). Bottle-conditioned beers are also available.

Chancellors Revenge (OG 1036, ABV 3.6%)
A light-coloured, refreshing, full-flavoured and well-hopped session bitter.

Cavendish Dark (OG 1037, ABV 3.7%)

Special Bitter (OG 1039, ABV 3.9%)
A well-balanced, amber-coloured, quaffable bitter.

Golden Hop (OG 1041, ABV 4.1%)

Kiln House (ABV 4.1%)

Narrow Boat (OG 1043, ABV 4.3%)
A pale amber bitter, with a short, crisp hoppy aftertaste.

Cavendish Bridge (ABV 4.5%)

Cavendish Gold (ABV 4.5%)

Reverend Eaton (OG 1045, ABV 4.5%)
A smooth, medium-strong bitter, full of malt and hop flavours with a sweet aftertaste.

Mayfly (ABV 4.8%)

Five Bells (OG 1050, ABV 5%)

Whistlestop (OG 1050, ABV 5%)
Maris Otter pale malt and two hops produce this smooth and surprisingly strong pale beer.

Sharp's SIBA

Sharp's Brewery Ltd, Pityme Business Centre, Rock, Cornwall, PL27 6NU
☎ (01208) 862121
✉ enquiries@sharpsbrewery.co.uk
🌐 sharpsbrewery.co.uk
Shop Mon-Fri 9am-5pm
Tours by arrangement

⊗ Sharp's Brewery was founded in 1994. Within 10 years the brewery had grown from producing 1,500 barrels annually to selling 35,000. Sharp's has no pubs and delivers beer to more than 1,000 outlets across the south of England. All beer is produced at the brewery in Rock and is delivered via temperature controlled depots in Bristol, Manchester and London. Seasonal beer: Nadelik (ABV 4.6%). Bottle-conditioned beer is also available.

Cornish Coaster (OG 1035.2, ABV 3.6%) ◆
A smooth, easy-drinking beer, golden in colour, with a fresh hop aroma and dry malt and hops in the mouth. The finish starts malty but becomes dry and hoppy.

Cornish Jack (OG 1037, ABV 3.8%)
Light candied fruit dominates the aroma, underpinned with fresh hop notes. The flavour is a delicate balance of light sweetness, fruity notes and fresh spicy hops. Subtle bitterness and dry fruit notes linger in the finish.

Doom Bar (OG 1038.5, ABV 4%) ◆
Quaffing bitter with a faint flowery aroma and a moderately fruity, malty taste, although bitterness can mask other flavours. The finish is long but pleasantly bitter with some sweetness and dryness.

Atlantic IPA (OG 1040, ABV 4.2%)

Eden Pure Ale (OG 1041, ABV 4.3%)
Hops dominate the aroma complemented by light fruit esters. In the mouth hops are again the centrepiece with a dry bitterness and a hint of malty sweetness. The finish is dry and hoppy.

Own (OG 1042.5, ABV 4.4%) ◆
A deep golden brown beer with a delicate hops and malt aroma, and dry malt and hops in the mouth. Like the other beers, its finish starts malty but turns dry and hoppy.

Will's Resolve (OG 1044, ABV 4.6%)

Special (OG 1048.5, ABV 5.2%) ◆
Deep golden brown with a fresh hop aroma. Dry malt and hops in the mouth; the finish is malty but becomes dry and hoppy.

Shaws

Shaws Brewery, The Old Stables, Park Road, Dukinfield, Greater Manchester, SK16 5LX
☎ (0161) 330 5471
✉ windfab@aol.com

The brewery is housed in the stables of William Shaws Brewery, established in 1856 and closed by John Smiths in 1941. Brewing re-started in 2002 with a five-barrel plant. Beer is supplied to more than 30 local free trade outlets and beer festivals. Monthly guest beers are produced.

Best Bitter (OG 1038, ABV 4%)

Golden Globe (OG 1040, ABV 4.3%)
Yellow beer with a modest hoppy/fruity aroma. Biscuity malt and tart fruits on the palate and in the bitter aftertaste.

IPA (OG 1044, ABV 4.8%)

Sheffield* SIBA

Sheffield Brewing Co Ltd, Unit 111, J C Albyn Complex, Burton Road, Sheffield, South Yorkshire, S3 8BT
(0114) 272 7256
sales@sheffieldbrewery.com
sheffieldbrewery.com
Tours by arrangement

Sheffield began brewing in January 2007 in the former Blanco polish works on a 10-barrel plant. Building works were completed in autumn 2007 allowing the brewing plant to be relocated on a tower principle. Over 10 outlets are supplied direct. Seasonal beers: Golden Frame (ABV 3.9%), Spring Steel (ABV 4.6%), Top Forge (ABV 4.7%). Bottle-conditioned beers are also available.

Crucible Best (OG 1038, ABV 3.8%)

Five Rivers (OG 1038, ABV 3.8%)

Blanco Blonde (OG 1041, ABV 4.1%)

Seven Hills (OG 1041, ABV 4.1%)

Shepherd Neame IFBB

Shepherd Neame Ltd, 17 Court Street, Faversham, Kent, ME13 7AX
(01795) 538907
shepherd-neame.co.uk
Shop Mon-Sat 10am-4.30pm
Tours by arrangement

Kent's major independent brewery is believed to be the oldest continuous brewer in the country (since 1698), but records show brewing began on the site as far back as the 12th century. The same water source is still used today and 1914 oak mash tuns are still operational. In 2004/2005 investment increased production to more than 200,000 barrels a year. The company has 370 tied houses in the South-east, nearly all selling cask ale. More than 2,000 other outlets are also supplied. All Shepherd Neame ales use locally sourced ingredients. The cask beers are made with Kentish hops, local malted barley and water from the brewery's own artesian well. In 2007 a new micro-plant was installed inside the main brewery to brew speciality ales in small quantities for special occasions. These brews are available for a limited time in selected pubs. In the first year over 50 beers were produced. Seasonal beers: see website. Bottle-conditioned beer is also available.

Master Brew Bitter (OG 1032, ABV 3.7%)
A distinctive bitter, mid-brown in colour, with a hoppy aroma. Well-balanced, with a nicely aggressive bitter taste from its hops, it leaves a hoppy/bitter finish, tinged with sweetness.

Kent's Best (OG 1036, ABV 4.1%)
An ambient bitter which merges the biscuity sweetness of English malt with the fruity, floral bitterness of locally grown hops.

Spitfire Premium Ale (OG 1040, ABV 4.5%)
A commemorative Battle of Britain brew for the RAF Benevolent Fund's appeal, now the brewery's flagship ale.

Bishops Finger (OG 1046, ABV 5%)
A cask-conditioned version of a famous bottled beer. A strong ale with a complex hop aroma reminiscent of lemons, oranges and bananas combined with malt, molasses and toffee. Refreshing with a good malt character tinged with a lingering bitterness.

Sherborne

Sherborne Brewery Ltd, 257 Westbury, Sherborne, Dorset, DT9 3EH
(01935) 812094
stephen@walshg82.freeserve.co.uk
sherbornebrewery.co.uk

Sherborne Brewery started in late 2005 on a 2.5-barrel plant. It moved in 2006 to new premises at the rear of the brewery's pub, Docherty's Bar. Beer is supplied to the pub and to 15-20 other local outlets as a guest beer.

257 (OG 1039, ABV 3.9%)

Cheap Street (OG 1044, ABV 4.4%)

Ship Inn*

Ship Inn Brewery, Ship Inn, The Square, Newton-by-the-Sea, Northumberland, NE66 3EW
(01665) 576262
shipinnnewton.co.uk
The Ship Inn started brewing in early 2008. Beers are only produced for the pub – ABVs may vary.

Sandcastle at Dawn (ABV 2.8%)

Sea Coal (ABV 4%)

Sea Wheat (ABV 4%)

Ship Hop (ABV 4.1%)

Dolly Daydream (ABV 4.3%)

Shoes SIBA

Shoes Brewery, Three Horseshoes Inn, Norton Canon, Hereford, HR4 7BH
(01544) 318375
Tours by arrangement

Landlord Frank Goodwin was a keen home brewer who decided in 1994 to brew on a commercial basis for his pub. The beers are brewed from malt extract and are normally only available at the Three Horseshoes. Each September Canon Bitter and Norton Ale are brewed with 'green' hops fresh from the harvest. Bottle-conditioned beers are available.

Canon Bitter (OG 1038, ABV 3.6%)

Norton Ale (OG 1040, ABV 4.1%)

Peploe's Tipple (OG 1060, ABV 6%)

Farriers Ale (OG 1114, ABV 15.5%)

Shugborough

Shugborough Brewery, Shugborough Estate, Milford, Staffordshire, ST17 0XB
☎ (01782) 823447
Tours daily Mar-Oct

Brewing in the original brewhouse at Shugborough, home of the Earls of Lichfield, restarted in 1990 but a lack of expertise led to the brewery being a static museum piece until Titanic Brewery of Stoke-on-Trent (qv) began helping in 1996. Brewing takes place every weekend during the visitor season with museum guides in period costume.

Miladys Fancy (OG 1048, ABV 4.6%)

Coachmans Tipple (OG 1049, ABV 4.7%)

Gardeners Retreat (OG 1049, ABV 4.7%)

Farmers Half (OG 1049, ABV 4.8%)

Butlers Revenge (OG 1053, ABV 4.9%)

Lordships Own (OG 1054, ABV 5%)

Sinclair

See Atlas and Orkney

Six Bells SIBA

Six Bells Brewery, Church Street, Bishop's Castle, Shropshire, SY9 5AA
☎ (01588) 638930
bishops-castle.co.uk/SixBells/brewery.htm
Tours by arrangement

Neville Richards —'Big Nev' —started brewing in 1997 with a five-barrel plant and two fermenters. Alterations in 1999 included two more fermenters, a new grain store and mashing equipment. He supplies a number of customers both within the county and over the border in Wales. A new 12-barrel plant opened in April 2007. In addition to the core beer range, 12 monthly specials are produced.

Big Nev's (OG 1037, ABV 3.8%)
A pale, fairly hoppy bitter.

Goldings BB (OG 1041, ABV 4%)
Made entirely with Goldings hops; moderately hoppy with a distinctive aroma.

Cloud Nine (OG 1043, ABV 4.2%)
Pale amber-colour with a slight citrus finish.

Skinner's SIBA

Skinner's Brewing Co Ltd, Riverside, Newham Road, Truro, Cornwall, TR1 2DP
☎ (01872) 271885
info@skinnersbrewery.com
skinnersbrewery.com
Shop Mon-Sat 10am-5pm
Tours by arrangement (ring 01872 254689)

Skinner's brewery was founded by Steve and Sarah Skinner in 1997. The brewery moved to bigger premises in 2003 and opened a brewery shop and visitor centre. Merchandise and beer is now available to purchase online. Seasonal beers: see website.

Ginger Tosser (OG 1038, ABV 3.8%)
Hoppy golden ale fused with Cornish honey. The rounded finish has a hint of ginger.

Spriggan Ale (OG 1038, ABV 3.8%)
A light golden, hoppy bitter. Well-balanced with a smooth bitter finish.

Betty Stogs (OG 1040, ABV 4%)
Light hop perfume with underlying malt. Easy-drinking copper ale with balance of citrus and apple fruit, malt and bitterness, plus a hint of sulphur. Bitter finish is slow to develop but long to fade.

Heligan Honey (OG 1040, ABV 4%)
A slightly sweet amber bitter, brewed with West Country malt and Heligan Garden honey.

Keel Over (OG 1041, ABV 4.2%)
A classic Cornish bitter, amber in colour, beautifully balanced with a smooth finish.

Cornish Knocker Ale (OG 1044, ABV 4.5%)
Refreshing, amber/gold beer full of life with hops all the way through. Spice and fruit in the mouth balanced by bitter and malt undertones, with a clean and lasting bittersweet finish.

Figgy's Brew (OG 1044, ABV 4.5%)
A classic, dark, premium-strength bitter. Full-flavoured with a smooth finish.

Cornish Blonde (OG 1048, ABV 5%)
A combination of wheat malt and English and American hops makes this light-coloured wheat beer deceptively easy to drink.

Slater's SIBA

Eccleshall Brewing Co Ltd, Slater's Brewery, St Albans Road, Common Road Industrial Estate, Stafford, ST16 3DR
☎ (01785) 257976
sales@slatersales.co.uk
slatersales.co.uk
Tours by arrangement

The brewery was opened in 1995 and in 2006 moved to new, larger premises, resulting in a tripling of capacity. It has won numerous awards from CAMRA and SIBA and supplies more than 1,100 outlets. One pub is owned, the George at Eccleshall, which serves as the brewery tap. Seasonal beers are produced bi-annually.

Bitter (OG 1036, ABV 3.6%)
Amber with a hop and malt aroma. Hoppiness develops into a long dry finish.

Owzat (ABV 3.8%)

Original (OG 1040, ABV 4%)
Amber bitter. Malty aroma with caramel notes, hoppy taste develops into a dry hoppy finish with a touch of sweetness.

Top Totty (OG 1040, ABV 4%)
Great yellow colour with a fruit and hop nose. Hop and fruit balanced taste leads to citrus hints with mouth-watering edges. Dry finish with tangs of lemon.

Queen Bee (OG 1042, ABV 4.2%)
Golden with a sweet and spicy aroma and hop background. Honey sweet taste followed by a gentle bitter finish on the tongue.

Premium (OG 1044, ABV 4.4%)
Pale brown bitter with malt and caramel aroma. Malt and caramel taste supported by hops and some fruit provide a warming descent and satisfyingly bitter mouthfeel.

Slaughterhouse SIBA

Slaughterhouse Brewery Ltd, Bridge Street, Warwick, CV34 5PD
☎ (01926) 490986
✉ enquiries@slaughterhousebrewery.com
slaughterhousebrewery.com
Tours by arrangement

Production began in 2003 on a four-barrel plant in a former slaughterhouse. Due to its success, beer production now consists mainly of Saddleback, supplemented by monthly special and seasonal beers. Around 30 outlets are supplied. The brewery premises are licensed for off-sales direct to the public. Seasonal beers: see website.

Saddleback Best Bitter (OG 1038, ABV 3.8%)
Amber-coloured session bitter with a distinctive Challenger hop flavour.

For the Waterman, Hatton:
Arkwright's Special Bitter (ABV 3.8%)

Small Paul's*

Small Paul's Brewery, 27 Briar Close, Gillingham, Dorset, SP8 4SS
☎ (01747) 823574
✉ smallbrewer@aol.com
Tours by arrangement

The brewery was launched in September 2006 by an enthusiastic home brewer on a half-barrel plant. There are usually two brews a month and half a dozen local free houses and clubs are supplied direct with beers being supplied to festivals further afield. Different beers can be designed and brewed to order.

Gylla's Gold (OG 1039, ABV 3.8%)
Golden session beer with a citrus aroma.

Wyvern (OG 1044, ABV 4.4%)
A dark brown fruity beer with chocolate undertones.

Gillingham Pale (OG 1045, ABV 4.5%)
A pale bitter with floral aroma and dry finish.

Smiles

See Highgate

Samuel Smith

Samuel Smith Old Brewery (Tadcaster), High Street, Tadcaster, North Yorkshire, LS24 9SB
☎ (01937) 832225

A fiercely independent, family-owned company. Tradition, quality and value are important, resulting in traditional brewing without any artificial additives. All real ale is supplied in wooden casks, though nitrokeg has replaced cask beer in some pubs in recent years. An unfiltered draught wheat beer is a recent addition. Around 200 pubs are owned. A bottle-conditioned beer was introduced in 2008 (Yorkshire Stingo, ABV 8%) but is only available in specialist off-licences.

Old Brewery Bitter/OBB
(OG 1040, ABV 4%)
Malt dominates the aroma, with an initial burst of malt, hops and fruit in the taste, which is sustained in the aftertaste.

Snowdonia SIBA

Snowdonia Brewery, Snowdonia Parc Brewpub & Campsite, Waunfawr, Caernarfon, Gwynedd, LL55 4AQ
☎ (01286) 650409
✉ info@snowdonia-park.co.uk
snowdonia-park.co.uk

Snowdonia started brewing in 1998 in a two-barrel brewhouse. The brewing is now carried out by the new co-owner, Carmen Pierce. The beer is brewed solely for the Snowdonia Park pub and campsite.

Station Bitter (OG 1040, ABV 4%)

Snowdonia Gold (OG 1050, ABV 5%)

Welsh Highland Bitter (OG 1048, ABV 5%)

Somerset (Electric)

See Taunton

Son of Sid*

Son of Sid Brewery, The Chequers, 71 Main Road, Little Gransden, Bedfordshire, SG19 3DW
☎ (01767) 677348
✉ chequersgransden@btinternet.com

Son of Sid was established in 2007 on a 2.5-barrel plant in a separate room of the pub. The brewery can be viewed from the lounge bar. It is named after the father of the current landlord, who ran the pub for 42 years. His son has carried the business on for the past 16 years as a family-run enterprise. Beer is only sold in the pub.

First Brew (OG 1046, ABV 4.6%)

South Hams SIBA

South Hams Brewery Ltd, Stokeley Barton, Stokenham, Kingsbridge, Devon, TQ7 2SE
☎ (01548) 581151
✉ info@southhamsbrewery.co.uk
southhamsbrewery.co.uk
Tours by arrangement

The brewery moved to its present site in 2003, with a 10-barrel plant and plenty of room to expand. It supplies more than 60 outlets in Plymouth and south Devon. Wholesalers are used to distribute to other areas. Two pubs are owned. Seasonal beers: Hopnosis (ABV 4.5%), Porter (ABV 5%), Knickadroppa Glory (ABV 5.2%). Bottle-conditioned beers are also available.

Devon Pride (OG 1039, ABV 3.8%)

XSB (OG 1043, ABV 4.2%)
Amber nectar with a fruity nose and a bitter finish.

Wild Blonde (ABV 4.4%)

Eddystone (OG 1050, ABV 4.8%)

Southport SIBA

Southport Brewery, Unit 3, Enterprise Business Park, Russell Road, Southport, Merseyside, PR9 7RF
☎ 07748 387652
✉ southportbrewery@fsmail.net

The Southport brewery opened in 2004 as a 2.5-barrel plant but moved up to a five-barrel plant due to demand. Around 30 pubs are supplied in the North-west. It also supplies the free trade via Boggart Brewery (qv). Seasonal beers: Old Shrimper (ABV 5.5%, Nov-Feb), Tower Mild (ABV 3.7%, May-Sep), National Hero (ABV 4%, Mar-Apr).

Cyclone (OG 1039.5, ABV 3.8%)
A bronze-coloured bitter with a fruity blackcurrant aftertaste.

Sandgrounder Bitter (OG 1039.5, ABV 3.8%)
Pale, hoppy session bitter with a floral character.

Carousel (OG 1041.5, ABV 4%)
A refreshing, floral, hoppy best bitter.

Golden Sands (OG 1041.5, ABV 4%)
A golden-coloured, triple hopped bitter with citrus flavour.

Natterjack (OG 1043.5, ABV 4.3%)
A premium bitter with fruit notes and a hint of coffee.

For Southport Football Club:

Grandstand Gold (OG 1039.5, ABV 3.8%)
A gold-coloured bitter, available for all home matches.

Spectrum EAB SIBA

Spectrum Brewery, Unit 11, Wellington Road, Tharston, Norwich, Norfolk, NR15 2PE
☎ 07949 254383
✉ info@spectrumbrewery.co.uk
spectrumbrewery.co.uk
Tours by arrangement

Proprietor and founder Andy Mitchell established Spectrum in 2002. The brewery moved premises in 2007 as well as increasing brew length and gaining organic certification for all beers. Seasonal beers: Spring Promise (ABV 4.5%, Jan-Feb), Autumn Beer (ABV 4.5%, Sep-Oct —names and formulations vary), Yule Fuel (ABV 7%).

Light Fantastic (OG 1035.5, ABV 3.7%)
A jolly, golden brew with a lasting hoppy signature in both bouquet and taste. A solid bitterness is apparent throughout with grapefruit and lemon giving depth. Long, dry finish.

Dark Fantastic (OG 1041, ABV 3.8%)
A very dark red, malty mild.

Bezants (OG 1038, ABV 4%)
A well-hopped, clean-tasting bitter. Some maltiness can be detected in both the aroma and taste, but hops dominate. A residual bitterness adds to a long aftertaste that ends in a lingering dryness.

42 (OG 1039.5, ABV 4.2%)
Blackcurrant fruitiness vies for dominance with a strong malty base. Undercurrents of hops, caramel and bitterness give a woody feel to this pale brown brew.

Black Buffle (OG 1047, ABV 4.5%)
Dark chocolate and liquorice hold sway in this deep red porter. The nose and taste are balanced by a noticeable hop presence although the finish attains a roasted coffee dryness.

XXXX (OG 1045.5, ABV 4.6%)
A deep copper strong bitter, first brewed for the proprietor's 40th birthday.

Wizzard (OG 1047.5, ABV 4.9%)
Pale brown, smooth, easy-drinking ale. Initial golden syrup taste is reflected in the aroma. Underlying bitterness comes to the fore as the inherent maltiness subsides in a quick finish.

Old Stoatwobbler (OG 1064.5, ABV 6%)
Complex brew with dark chocolate, morello cherry, raisin and banana vying for dominance alongside hops and malt. A black-coloured brew with a solid fruity nose, and a well-balanced finish.

Trip Hazard (OG 1061.5, ABV 6.5%)
Exceptionally malty but easy-drinking for its strength. Rich fruity flavours dominate throughout, date and sultana to the fore. A growing bitterness in the finish.

Solstice Blinder (OG 1079, ABV 8.5%)
Strong IPA. Brewed twice a year, dry-hopped and left to mature (unfined) for at least three months before release in time for the solstices.

Spinning Dog SIBA

Spinning Dog Brewery, 88 St Owen Street, Hereford, HR1 2QD
☎ (01432) 342125
✉ jfkenyon@aol.com
spinningdogbrewery.co.uk
Tours by arrangement

The brewery was built in a room of the Victory in 2000 by Jim Kenyon, following the purchase of the pub. Initially only serving the pub, it has steadily grown from a four-barrel to a 10-barrel plant. In 2005 the brewery commissioned its own bottling plant, capable of producing 80 cases a day. It now supplies some 300 other outlets as well as selling bottle-conditioned beer via the internet. Seasonal/Occasional beers: Mutleys Mongrel (ABV 3.9%), Harvest Moon (ABV 4.5%), Santa Paws (ABV 5.2%), Mutleys Springer (ABV 4.4%), Christmas Cheer (ABV 4.3%), Organic Oatmeal Stout (ABV 4.4%).

Hereford Organic Bitter (ABV 3.7%)
Light in colour with a distinctive fruitiness from start to finish.

Herefordshire Owd Bull (ABV 3.9%)
A good session beer with an abundance of hops and bitterness. Dry, with citrus aftertaste.

Hereford Cathedral Bitter (OG 1040, ABV 4%)

A crisp amber beer made with local hops, producing a well-rounded malt/hop bitterness throughout and a pleasing, lingering aftertaste.

Herefordshire Light Ale (ABV 4%)
Brewed along the lines of the award-winning Mutleys Pitstop. Light and refreshing.

Mutleys Dark (OG 1040, ABV 4%)
A dark, malty mild with a hint of bitterness and a touch of roast caramel. A smooth drinkable ale.

Top Dog (OG 1042, ABV 4.2%)
A hoppy beer with both malt and fruit flavours.

Celtic Gold (OG 1045, ABV 4.5%)
A bright gold best bitter, full of fruit and blackcurrant flavours.

Mutleys Revenge (OG 1048, ABV 4.8%)
A strong, smooth, hoppy beer, amber in colour. Full-bodied with a dry, citrus aftertaste.

Mutts Nuts (OG 1050, ABV 5%)
A dark, strong ale, full bodied with a hint of a chocolate aftertaste.

Spire SIBA

Spire Brewery, Units 2-3, Gisborne Close, Ireland Business Park, Staveley, Chesterfield, Derbyshire, S43 3JT
☎ (01246) 476005
✉ info@spirebrewery.co.uk
spirebrewery.co.uk
Tours by arrangement

The brewery was set up by ex-Scots Guards musician and music teacher David McLaren in April 2006. The brewery increased capacity to 40 barrels a week due to demand and in 2007 a brewery tap was acquired in Tupton, Chesterfield. Over 80 outlets are supplied direct. Seasonal beers: Whiter Shade of Pale (ABV 4%, Mar-Oct), 80/- Ale (BV 4.3%, Oct-Dec). Bottle-conditioned beers are also available.

Overture (OG 1038, ABV 3.9%)
Traditional amber session beer with a little malt and hop aroma. Balanced malt and roast flavours lead to a developing bitterness, ending in a long, malty finish.

Dark Side of the Moon (OG 1041, ABV 4.3%)

Chesterfield Best Bitter (OG 1044, ABV 4.5%)
Classic brown strong bitter with malt and fruit flavours and a hint of caramel and chocolate in the finish. There is a little bitterness in the aftertaste.

Land of Hop & Glory (OG 1043, ABV 4.5%)
An excellent example of a clean, crisp tasting golden ale. Easy to drink with grapefruit and lemon flavours developing. These complex citrus hop flavours lead to a bitter, dry aftertaste.

Twist & Stout (OG 1043, ABV 4.5%)

Sgt Pepper Stout (OG 1053, ABV 5.5%)
Unique full-flavoured stout brewed with ground black pepper! Liquorice and pepper flavours dominate this original, complex, dark and delicious original beer. A new classic stout!

Spitting Feathers

Spitting Feathers Brewery, Common Farm, Waverton, Chester, Cheshire, CH3 7QT
☎ (01244) 332052
✉ info@spittingfeathers.org
spittingfeathers.org
Tours by arrangement

Spitting Feathers was established in 2005 at Common Farm on the outskirts of Chester. The brewery and visitors bar are in traditional sandstone buildings around a cobbled yard. Beehives provide honey for the brewery and spent grains are fed to livestock. Around 200 outlets are supplied. Seasonal beers: see website. Bottle-conditioned beers are also available. All bottled beers are suitable for vegetarians and vegans.

Farmhouse Ale (OG 1035, ABV 3.6%)

Thirstquencher (OG 1038, ABV 3.9%)
Powerful hop aroma leads into the taste. Bitterness and a fruity citrus hop flavour fight for attention. A sharp, clean golden beer with a long, dry, bitter aftertaste.

Special Ale (OG 1041, ABV 4.2%)
Complex tawny-coloured beer with a sharp, grainy mouthfeel. Malty with good hop coming through in the aroma and taste. Hints of nuttiness and a touch of acidity. Dry, astringent finish.

Old Wavertonian (OG 1043, ABV 4.4%)
Creamy and smooth stout. Full-flavoured with coffee notes in aroma and taste. Roast and nut flavours throughout, leading to a hoppy, bitter finish.

Basket Case (OG 1046, ABV 4.8%)
Reddish, complex beer. Sweetness and fruit dominate taste, offset by hops and bitterness that follow through into the aftertaste.

Springhead SIBA

Springhead Fine Ales Ltd, Old Great North Road, Sutton-on-Trent, Newark, Nottinghamshire, NG23 6QS
☎ (01636) 821000
✉ steve@springhead.co.uk
springhead.co.uk
Tours by arrangement

Springhead Brewery opened in 1990 and moved to bigger premises three years later and, to meet increased demand, expanded to a brew length of 50 barrels. Around 500 outlets are supplied. Many of the beer names have a Civil War theme. Puritans' Porter is suitable for vegans.

Liberty (OG 1036, ABV 3.8%)
A pale, straw-coloured beer with hints of lemon and a dry, biscuity finish.

Bitter (OG 1041, ABV 4%)
A clean-tasting, easy-drinking, hoppy bitter.

Puritans' Porter (OG 1041, ABV 4%)

Roundhead's Gold (OG 1042, ABV 4.2%)

Golden beer made with wild flower honey. Refreshing but not sweet.

Rupert's Ruin (OG 1042, ABV 4.2%)

Goodrich Castle (OG 1044, ABV 4.4%)
Brewed following a 17th-century recipe using rosemary: a pale ale, light on the palate with a bitter finish and delicate flavour.

Oliver's Army (OG 1044, ABV 4.4%)

Charlie's Angel (OG 1045, ABV 4.5%)
A pale, golden beer with a deeply fruity aroma and flavour, leading to a well-rounded bitter finish.

Sweetlips (OG 1046, ABV 4.6%)

Barebones (OG 1047, ABV 4.7%)

Leveller (OG 1047, ABV 4.8%)
A dark, smoky intense flavour with a toffee finish. Brewed in the style of Belgian Trappist ale.

Newark Castle Brown (OG 1049, ABV 5%)

Willy's Wheatbeer (OG 1051, ABV 5.3%)

Roaring Meg (OG 1052, ABV 5.5%)
Smooth and sweet with a dry finish and citrus honey aroma.

Cromwell's Hat (OG 1056, ABV 6%)

Stanway

Stanway Brewery, Stanway, Cheltenham, Gloucestershire, GL54 5PQ
☎ (01386) 584320
stanwaybrewery.co.uk

Stanway is a small brewery founded in 1993 with a five-barrel plant that confines its sales to the Cotswolds area (15 to 20 outlets). The brewery is the only known plant in the country to use wood-fired coppers for all its production. Seasonal beers: Morris-a-Leaping (ABV 3.9%, spring), Cotteswold Gold (ABV 3.9%, summer), Wizard (ABV 4%, autumn), Lords-a-Leaping (ABV 4.5%, Xmas).

Stanney Bitter (OG 1042, ABV 4.5%)
A light, refreshing, amber-coloured beer, dominated by hops in the aroma, with a bitter taste and a hoppy, bitter finish.

Star

See Wibblers

Stationhouse

Stationhouse Brewery, Lady Heyes Craft Centre, Kingsley Road, Frodsham, Cheshire, WA6 6SU
☎ (01928) 787917
enquire@stationhousebrewery.co.uk
stationhousebrewery.co.uk
Shop 10am-4pm daily
Tours by arrangement

Stationhouse started trading in 2005 in Ellesmere Port. The brewery moved to Frodsham in 2007 and now has a shop attached. A 5-7 barrel electric and propane powered unit is used to produce the core range as well as seasonal and celebration brews. 75 outlets are supplied direct. Seasonal/occasional beers: see website. Bottle-conditioned beers are also available.

1st Lite (OG 1037, ABV 3.8%)
Light, hoppy bitter with clean lemon/grapefruit hop flavours and the trademark Station House bitterness and dry aftertaste. Clean and refreshing.

Mynza Mild (ABV 3.9%)
A mahogany mild with fruity aftertaste.

Buzzin' (OG 1042, ABV 4.3%)
Golden fruity bitter dominated by a honey sweetness. Good hop flavours in initital taste and a long, lasting dry finish.

3 Score (OG 1043, ABV 4.5%)
An amber bronze malt beer with a fruity tang and long aftertaste.

Nightmail (ABV 4.7%)
A dry, jet black stout. Sharp with a mellow aftertaste.

Aonach (OG 1047, ABV 4.9%)
A typical Scottish style 80/- beer. Dark amber in colour.

Lammastide (OG 1048, ABV 5%)
An amber English wheat beer with distinct elderflower aromas.

Steamin' Billy

Steamin' Billy Brewing Co Ltd, Registered Office: 5 The Oval, Oadby, Leicestershire, LE2 5JB
☎ (0116) 271 2616
enquiries@steamin-billy.co.uk
steamin-billy.co.uk

Steamin' Billy was formed in 1995 by licensee Barry Lount and brewer Bill Allingham. Bill originally brewed in Derbyshire but after outgrowing the plant the beers have since been contracted out. Bill is currently brewing at Tower Brewery (qv) in conjunction with John Mills. Four pubs are owned. The beers are named after the owners' Jack Russell dog, who is featured in cartoon form on the pump clips. Seasonal beers: see website. See Tower for regular beers.

Stewart

Stewart Brewing Ltd, 42 Dryden Road, Bilston Glen Industrial Estate, Loanhead, Midlothian, EH20 9LZ
☎ (0131) 440 2442
steve.stewart@stewartbrewing.co.uk
stewartbrewing.co.uk

Established in 2004 by Steve Stewart, a qualified master brewer and specialising in high-quality premium cask ales, all made from natural ingredients. The beers are widely available in South-east Scotland. Beer for home can be purchased direct from the brewery for collection or delivery in the Edinburgh area.

Pentland IPA (OG 1041, ABV 4.1%)
Delightfully refreshing hoppy IPA. Hops and fruit announce their presence on the nose and continue through the taste and lingering bitter aftertaste of this full-flavoured beer.

Copper Cascade (OG 1042, ABV 4.2%)

A full-bodied tawny-coloured beer with a predominantly malty character. Fruit and Cascade hops give a bittersweet note with increasing bitterness in the aftertaste.

Edinburgh No.3 Premium Scotch Ale (OG 1043, ABV 4.3%) ◆
Traditional dark Scottish heavy. The pronounced malt character is part of a complex flavour profile, including fruit and hop. Initial sweetness leads into a dry, bitter, lingering finish.

80/- (OG 1044, ABV 4.4%)
Classic full-bodied, malty, bittersweet Scottish 80/-, with plenty of character.

Edinburgh Gold (OG 1048, ABV 4.8%) ◆
Full-bodied golden ale in the continental style. Plenty of hops are enjoyed throughout the drinking experience and give the beer a bitter profile balanced by the sweetness of fruit.

Stirling

See Traditional Scottish Ales

Stonehenge SIBA

Stonehenge Ales Ltd, The Old Mill, Mill Road, Netheravon, Salisbury, Wiltshire, SP4 9QB
☎ (01980) 670631
✉ info@stonehengeales.co.uk
🌐 stonehengeales.co.uk
Tours by arrangement

⊗ The beer is brewed in a mill built in 1914 to generate electricity from the River Avon. The site was converted to a gravity-fed brewery in 1984 (Bunce's Brewery) and in 1994 the company was bought by Danish master brewer Stig Anker Andersen. More than 300 outlets in the south of England and several wholesalers are supplied. Seasonal beers: Sign of Spring (ABV 4.6%), Eye-Opener (ABV 4.5%), Old Smokey (ABV 5%), Rudolph (ABV 5%).

Spire Ale (OG 1037, ABV 3.8%)
A light, golden, hoppy bitter.

Pigswill (OG 1038, ABV 4%)
A full-bodied beer, rich in hop aroma, with a warm amber colour.

Heelstone (OG 1042, ABV 4.3%)
A crisp, clean, refreshing bitter, deep amber in colour, well balanced with a fruity blackcurrant nose.

Great Bustard (OG 1046, ABV 4.8%)
A strong, fruity, malty bitter.

Danish Dynamite (OG 1048, ABV 5%)
A strong, dry ale, slightly fruity with a well-balanced, bitter hop flavour.

Stonehouse

Stonehouse Brewery, Stonehouse, Weston, Oswestry, Shropshire, SY10 9ES
☎ (01691) 676457
✉ info@stonehousebrewery.co.uk
🌐 stonehousebrewery.co.uk
Shop Mon-Fri 9am-5pm
Tours by arrangement

⊗ Stonehouse was established early in 2007 on a 15-barrel plant. The brewery is based in old chicken sheds and is next to the old Cambrian railway line, hence the beer names. 60 outlets are supplied direct, mainly in Wales, Shropshire and South Cheshire. Bottle-conditioned beers are available.

Station Bitter (OG 1041, ABV 3.9%)

Cambrian Gold (OG 1042, ABV 4.2%)

Wheeltappers (OG 1043, ABV 4.5%)

Off The Rails (OG 1048, ABV 4.8%)

Storm SIBA

Storm Brewing Co Ltd, 2 Waterside, Macclesfield, Cheshire, SK11 7HJ
☎ (01625) 431234
✉ thompsonhugh@talk21.com

Storm Brewing was founded in 1998 and operated from an old ICI boiler room until 2001 when the brewing operation moved to the current location, which until 1937 was a public house known as the Mechanics Arms. More than 60 outlets are supplied in Cheshire, Manchester and the Peak District. Seasonal beers: Summer Breeze (ABV 3.8%), Looks Like Rain Dear (ABV 4.8%, Xmas). Bottle-conditioned beers are also available.

Beauforts Ale (OG 1038, ABV 3.8%)
Golden brown, full-flavoured session bitter with a lingering hoppy taste.

Bitter Experience (OG 1040, ABV 4%)
A distinctive hop aroma draws you into this amber-coloured bitter. The palate has a mineral dryness that accentuates the crisp hop flavour and clean bitter finish.

Desert Storm (OG 1040, ABV 4%)
Amber-coloured beer with a smoky flavour of fruit and malt.

Twister (OG 1041, ABV 4%)
A light golden bitter with a smooth fruity hop aroma complemented by a subtle bitter aftertaste.

Bosley Cloud (OG 1041, ABV 4.1%) ◆
Dry, golden bitter with peppery hop notes throughout. Some initial sweetness and a mainly bitter aftertaste. Soft, well-balanced and quaffable.

Brainstorm (OG 1041, ABV 4.1%)
Light gold in colour and strong in citrus fruit flavours.

Ale Force (OG 1042, ABV 4.2%) ◆
Amber, smooth-tasting, complex beer that balances malt, hop and fruit on the taste, leading to a roasty, slightly sweet aftertaste.

Downpour (OG 1043, ABV 4.3%)
A combination of Pearl and lager malts produces this pale ale with a full, fruity flavour with a hint of apple and sightly hoppy aftertaste.

PGA (OG 1044, ABV 4.4%) ◆
Light, crisp, lager-style beer with a balance of malt, hops and fruit. Moderately bitter and slight dry aftertaste.

Tornado (OG 1044, ABV 4.4%) ◆
Fruity premium bitter with some graininess. Dry, satisfying finish.

Hurricane Hubert (OG 1045, ABV 4.5%)

A dark beer with a refreshing full, fruity hop aroma and a subtle bitter aftertaste.

Windgather (OG 1045, ABV 4.5%)
A gold-coloured beer with a distinctive crisp, fruity flavour right through to the aftertaste.

Silk of Amnesia (OG 1047, ABV 4.7%)
Smooth premium, easy-drinking bitter. Fruit and hops dominate throughout. Not too sweet, with a good lasting finish.

Storm Damage (OG 1047, ABV 4.7%)
A light-coloured, well-hopped and fruity beer balanced by a clean bitterness and smooth full palate.

Typhoon (OG 1050, ABV 5%)
Copper-coloured, smooth strong bitter. Roasty overtones and a hint of caramel and marzipan. Drinkable despite the gravity.

Stowey

Stowey Brewery Ltd, Old Cider House, 25 Castle Street, Nether Stowey, Somerset, TA5 1LN
☎ (01278) 732228
info@stoweybrewery.co.uk
stoweybrewery.co.uk
Tours by arrangement

Stowey was established in 2006, primarily to supply the owners' guesthouse and to provide beer to participants on 'real ale walks' run from the accommodation. 2007 saw the introduction of 'Brew your own Beer' breaks to guests. The brewery now supplies beer to two local pubs on a guest beer basis.

Nether Ending (OG 1044, ABV 4%)

Nether Underestimate a Blonde (OG 1044, ABV 4.2%)

Strands

Strands Brewery, Strands Hotel, Nether Wasdale, Cumbria, CA20 1ET
☎ (019467) 26237
info@strandshotel.com
strandshotel.com
Tours by arrangement

Strands began brewing in February 2007. The first beer produced was called Errmmm... as the owners couldn't think of a name for it.

Errmmm... (OG 1042, ABV 3.8%)

Corrsberg (ABV 4.1%)

T'Errmmm-inator (ABV 4.9%)

Strangford Lough

Strangford Lough Brewing Co, 22 Shore Road, Killyleagh, Downpatrick, Northern Ireland, BT30 9UE
☎ (028) 4482 1461
contact@slbc.ie
slbc.ie

Beers for the company are contract-brewed by an unknown brewery in England, though there are plans to build a plant in Northern Ireland. Bottle-conditioned beers: St Patrick's Best (ABV 3.8%), St Patrick's Gold (ABV 4.5%), St Patrick's Ale (ABV 6%), Barelegs Brew (ABV 4.5%), Legbiter (ABV 4.8%).

Strathaven

Strathaven Ales, Craigmill Brewery, Strathaven, ML10 6PB
☎ (01357) 520419
info@strathavenales.co.uk
strathavenales.co.uk
Shop Mon-Fri 9am-5pm (phone at weekend)
Tours by arrangement

Strathaven Ales is a 10-barrel brewery on the River Avon close to Strathaven and was converted from the remains of a 16th-century mill. The range is distributed throughout Scotland and the north of England. Seasonal beers: Duchess Anne (ABV 3.9%), Trumpeter (ABV 4.2%).

Clydesdale (OG 1038, ABV 3.8%)

Avondale (OG 1048, ABV 4%)

Old Mortality (OG 1046, ABV 4.2%)

Claverhouse (OG 1046, ABV 4.5%)

Stroud SIBA

Stroud Brewery Ltd, Unit 7, Phoenix Works, London Road, Thrupp, Stroud, Gloucestershire, GL5 2BU
☎ 07891 995878
Office: 141 Thrupp Lane, Thrupp, Stroud, Gloucestershire, GL5 2DQ
greg@stroudbrewery.co.uk
stroudbrewery.co.uk
Tours by arrangement

The brewery was established in 2005 with production commencing in June 2006 on a five-barrel plant. Around 50 outlets are supplied direct. Beers are locally themed and seasonal brews include Woolsack (ABV 5%) and Ding Dong (ABV 4.5%, Xmas). Three beers are regularly bottled.

Tom Long (OG 1039, ABV 3.8%)
An amber-coloured bitter with a spicy citrus aroma.

Red Coat (OG 1040, ABV 3.9%)
Ruby mild with a fruity bitterness.

Teasel (OG 1042, ABV 4.2%)
A classic best bitter with a dry, savoury finish.

Budding (OG 1045, ABV 4.5%)
A pale ale with a grassy bitterness, sweet malt and floral aroma.

Five Valleys (OG 1049, ABV 5%)
A traditional chestnut-coloured, rich and fruity strong ale.

Stumpy's

Stumpy's Brewery, Unit 6, Dean Farm, Whitwell Road, Whitwell, Isle of Wight, PO38 2AB
☎ (01983) 731731
☎ 07771 557378
info@stumpysbrewery.com
stumpysbrewery.com
Tours by arrangement

Stumpy's opened a five-barrel brewery in 2004 in Upper Swanmore in Hampshire. It relocated to the Isle of Wight in summer 2008, sharing premises with Yates' Brewery. Seasonal beer: Silent Night (ABV 5%, Oct-Feb).

Bottle-conditioned beers are also available (these account for about 75% of production).

Dog Daze (OG 1040, ABV 3.8%) ◆
A light, golden summer beer with a strong, malty aroma. Tastes rather thin and sweet and lacking in bitterness. A sweet, malty finish.

Hop a Doodle Doo (OG 1040, ABV 4%)

Hot Dog (OG 1045, ABV 4.5%)

Old Ginger (OG 1045, ABV 4.5%)

Old Stumpy (OG 1045, ABV 4.5%) ◆
Grassy best bitter, with a strong hoppy and fruity aroma. Some malt and bitterness in the flavour lead to a harsh finish.

Bo'sun's Call (OG 1050, ABV 5%)

Haven (OG 1050, ABV 5%)

Tumbledown (OG 1050, ABV 5%)

KB 1806 (OG 1070, ABV 7.2%)

Suddaby's SIBA

Suddaby's Ltd (Malton), Crown Hotel, 12 Wheelgate, Malton, North Yorkshire, YO17 7HP
☎ (01653) 692038
✉ enquiries@suddabys.co.uk
🌐 suddabys.co.uk

Suddabys no longer brew on site. The beers are contract brewed by Brown Cow (qv) and are only sold in bottled form in the beer & wine shop in Malton.

Sulwath SIBA

Sulwath Brewers Ltd, The Brewery, 209 King Street, Castle Douglas, Dumfries & Galloway, DG7 1DT
☎ (01556) 504525
✉ info@sulwathbrewers.co.uk
🌐 sulwathbrewers.co.uk
Tours daily at 1pm or by arrangement

☺ Sulwath started brewing in 1995. The beers are supplied to markets as far away as Devon in the south and Aberdeen in the north. The brewery has a fully licensed brewery tap and off sales open 10am-5pm Mon-Sat. Cask ales are sold to around 100 outlets and four wholesalers. Seasonal beers: Rein Beer (ABV 4.5%, Nov-Dec), Tam O'Shanter (ABV 4.1%, Jan-Feb), Happy Hooker (ABV 4%, Feb), Woozy Wabbit (ABV 5%, Mar-Apr), Hells Bells (ABV 4.5%, May-Jun), John Paul Jones (ABV 4%, Jul-Aug), Saltaire Cross (ABV 4.1%, Nov-Dec).

Cuil Hill (OG 1039, ABV 3.6%) ◆
Distinctively fruity session ale with malt and hop undertones. The taste is bittersweet with a long-lasting dry finish.

Black Galloway (OG 1046, ABV 4.4%)
A robust porter/stout that derives its colour from the abundance of Maris Otter barley and chocolate malts used in the brewing process.

Criffel (OG 1044, ABV 4.6%) ◆
Full-bodied beer with a distinctive bitterness. Fruit is to the fore of the taste with hop becoming increasingly dominant in the taste and finish.

Galloway Gold (OG 1049, ABV 5%) ◆
A cask-conditioned lager that will be too sweet for many despite being heavily hopped.

Knockendoch (OG 1047, ABV 5%) ◆
Dark, copper-coloured, reflecting a roast malt content, with bitterness from Challenger hops.

Solway Mist (ABV 5.5%)
A naturally cloudy wheat beer. Sweetish and fruity.

Summerskills SIBA

Summerskills Brewery, 15 Pomphlett Farm Industrial Estate, Broxton Drive, Billacombe, Plymouth, Devon, PL7 9BG
☎ (01752) 481283
✉ info@summerskills.co.uk
🌐 summerskills.co.uk

⊗ Originally established in a vineyard in 1983 at Bigbury-on-Sea, Summerskills moved to its present site in 1985 and has expanded since then. National distribution is carried out by wholesalers. 20 outlets are supplied by the brewery. Seasonal beers: Whistle Belly Vengeance (ABV 4.7%, Oct-Apr), Indiana's Bones (ABV 5.6%, Oct-Apr), Isambard Kingdom Brunel 1859 (ABV 4.7%, Apr-Oct). Bottle-conditioned beers are also available.

Cellar Vee (OG 1037, ABV 3.7%)

Hopscotch (OG 1042, ABV 4.1%)

Best Bitter (OG 1043, ABV 4.3%) ◆
A mid-brown beer, with plenty of malt and hops through the aroma, taste and finish. A good session beer.

Tamar (OG 1043, ABV 4.3%)
A tawny-coloured bitter with a fruity aroma and a hop taste and finish.

Menacing Dennis (OG 1045, ABV 4.5%)

Devon Dew (OG 1047, ABV 4.7%)

Summer Wine*

Summer Wine Brewery Ltd, Rock Cottage, 383 New Mill Road, Brockholes, Holmfirth, West Yorkshire, HD9 7AB
☎ (01484) 660597
✉ info@summerwinebrewery.co.uk
🌐 summerwinebrewery.co.uk

⊗ Summer Wine started brewing in 2006 in the cellar of the home of owner James Farran, using a 10-gallon kit with an emphasis on bottle-conditioned beers. The brewery upgraded to a half-barrel plant in 2007 and now produces cask ales for three local pubs. Further expansion is planned once bigger premises are found. Seasonal beers: Good Night Nick (ABV 4.2%, Dec), Elbow Grease (ABV 4.5%, May-Sep).

Aleshire (ABV 4.2%)

Rocker (ABV 5.2%)

Surrey Hills SIBA

Surrey Hills Brewery Ltd, Old Scotland Farm, Staple Lane, Shere, Guildford, Surrey, GU5 9TE
☎ (01483) 212812
✉ info@surreyhills.co.uk

🌐 surreyhills.co.uk
Open for beer sales Thu-Fri 12-2pm, 4-5pm; Sat 10am-12pm
Tours by arrangement

Surrey Hills started in 2005 and is based in an old milking parlour, hidden away down country lanes in the Surrey Hills. The beers are sold in around 40 local outlets —see website for up-to-date list. Seasonal beers (available for six months): Albury Ruby (ABV 4.6%, winter), Gilt Complex (ABV 4.6%, summer).

Hammer Mild (ABV 3.8%)

Ranmore Ale (ABV 3.8%)
A light session beer with bags of flavour. An earthy, hoppy nose leads into a citric grapefruit and hoppy taste and a clean, bitter finish.

Shere Drop (ABV 4.2%)
Hoppy with some balancing malt. There is a pleasant citric aroma and a noticeable fruitiness in the taste. The finish is dry, hoppy and bitter.

Suthwyk

Suthwyk Ales, Offwell Farm, Southwick, Fareham, Hampshire, PO17 6DX
☎ (02392) 325252
✉ mjbazeley@suthwykales.com
🌐 suthwykales.com/southwickbrewhouse.co.uk

Barley farmer Martin Bazeley does not brew himself. The beers are produced by Oakleaf Brewing (qv) in Gosport.

Bloomfields (ABV 3.8%)

Liberation (ABV 4.2%)

Skew Sunshine Ale (ABV 4.6%)

Palmerston's Folly (ABV 4.8%)

Sutton

See South Hams

Swan on the Green

Swan on the Green Brewery, West Peckham, Maidstone, Kent, ME18 5JW
☎ (01622) 812271
✉ info@swan-on-the-green.co.uk
🌐 swan-on-the-green.co.uk
Tours by arrangement

The brewery was established in 2000 to produce handcrafted beers. The beers are not filtered and no artificial ingredients are used. There are plans to expand the plant. One pub is owned and other outlets and beer festivals are occasionally supplied. Seasonal beers are brewed.

Fuggles Pale (OG 1037, ABV 3.6%)
A session bitter, traditionally hoppy, using local Fuggles hops.

Whooper (OG 1037, ABV 3.6%)
Straw coloured and lightly hopped with American Cascade for a subtle fruity aroma.

Trumpeter Best (OG 1041, ABV 4%)
A copper-coloured ale hopped with First Gold and Target.

Cygnet (OG 1048, ABV 4.2%)

Bewick (OG 1052, ABV 5.3%)
A heavyweight premium bitter hopped with Target for bite and softened with Kentish Goldings for aroma.

Swansea SIBA

Swansea Brewing Co, Joiners Arms, 50 Bishopston Road, Bishopston, Swansea, SA3 3EJ
☎ (01792) 232658/290197 (Office)

Office: 74 Hawthorne Avenue, Uplands, Swansea, SA2 0LY
✉ rorygowland@fsbdial.co.uk
Tours by arrangement

Opened in 1996, Swansea was the first commercial brewery in the area for almost 30 years and is the city's only brew-pub. It doubled its capacity within the first year and now produces four regular beers and occasional experimental ones. Four regular outlets are supplied along with other pubs in the South Wales area. Seasonal beers: St Teilo's Tipple (ABV 5.5%), Barland Strong (ABV 6%), Pwll Du XXXX (ABV 4.9%).

Deep Slade Dark (OG 1034, ABV 4%)

Bishopswood Bitter (OG 1038, ABV 4.3%)
A delicate aroma of hops and malt in this pale brown colour. The taste is a balanced mix of hops and malt with a growing hoppy bitterness ending in a lasting bitter finish.

Three Cliffs Gold (OG 1042, ABV 4.7%)
A golden beer with a hoppy and fruity aroma a hoppy taste with fruit and malt, and a quenching bitterness. The pleasant finish has a good hop flavour and bitterness.

Original Wood (OG 1046, ABV 5.2%)
A full-bodied, pale brown beer with an aroma of hops, fruit and malt. A complex blend of these flavours with a firm bitterness ends with increasing bitterness.

Swaton*

Swaton Brewery, North End Farm, Swaton, Sleaford, Lincolnshire, NG34 0JP
☎ (01529) 421241
✉ swatonbrewery@hotmail.co.uk
Tours by arrangement

Swaton commenced brewing in June 2007 on a five-barrel plant and is sited in the outbuildings of the owner's farm. It supplies beer festivals and local pubs. A visitor centre/cafe/shop is situated next to the brewery.

Happy Jack (OG 1040, ABV 4.2%)

Kiss Goodnight (OG 1041.8, ABV 4.5%)

Three Degrees (OG 1043.5, ABV 4.7%)

Taunton

Taunton Brewing Co Ltd, Unit 1F, Hillview Industrial Estate, West Bagbrough, Somerset, TA4 3EW
☎ (01823) 433999
✉ tauntonbrewingco@supanet.com
Tours by arrangement

⊗ Formerly Somerset Electric/Taunton Vale Brewery, established in 2003 in the cellar of the New Inn. Taunton Brewing Co took over in 2006, led by the former head brewer from Exmoor Ales, Colin Green. The brewery relocated in August 2007 and now uses a 10-barrel plant. 120 outlets are supplied. Seasonal beer: Taunton Tinsel (ABV 4.5%, Xmas).

Ale (OG 1039.8, ABV 3.8%)

Castle (OG 1043, ABV 4.2%)

Gold (OG 1045, ABV 4.5%)

Mayor (OG 1048.3, ABV 5%)

Timothy Taylor IFBB

Timothy Taylor & Co Ltd, Knowle Spring Brewery, Keighley, West Yorkshire, BD21 1AW
☎ (01535) 603139
✉ timothy-taylor.co.uk

Timothy Taylor is an independent family-owned company established in 1858. It moved to the site of the Knowle Spring in 1863. Its prize-winning ales, which use Pennine spring water, are served in all of the brewery's 28 pubs as well as more than 500 other outlets. In 2008 major investment took place in various parts of the brewery to help streamline production to cope with increasing sales.

Dark Mild (OG 1034, ABV 3.5%) ◆
Malt and caramel dominate the aroma and palate with hops and hints of fruit leading to a dry, bitter finish.

Golden Best (OG 1033, ABV 3.5%) ◆
A clean-tasting and refreshing, traditional pennine light mild. A little fruit in the nose increases to complement the delicate hoppy taste. Background malt throughout. A good session beer.

Best Bitter (OG 1038, ABV 4%) ◆
Hops and fruit combine well with a nutty malt character in this drinkable bitter. Bitterness increases down the glass and lingers in the aftertaste.

Landlord (OG 1042, ABV 4.3%) ◆
A hoppy, increasingly bitter finish complements the background malt and spicy, citrus character of this full-flavoured and well-balanced amber beer.

Ram Tam (OG 1043, ABV 4.3%) ◆
Caramel combines well with malt and hops to produce a well-balanced black beer with red hints and a coffee-coloured head.

Teignworthy SIBA

Teignworthy Brewery Ltd, The Maltings, Teignworthy, Newton Abbot, Devon, TQ12 4AA
☎ (01626) 332066
✉ sales@teignworthybreweryltd.co.uk
⊕ teignworthybrewery.com
Shop 10am-5pm weekdays at Tuckers Maltings
Tours available for trade customers only

Teignworthy Brewery was established in 1994 and is located in part of the historic Tuckers Maltings. The brewery is an 18-barrel plant and production is now up to 50 barrels a week, using malt from Tuckers. It supplies around 200 outlets in Devon and Somerset. A large range of seasonal ales is available: see website. Bottle-conditioned beers are also produced. Martha's Mild is suitable for vegans in bottle-conditioned form.

Reel Ale (OG 1039.5, ABV 4%) ◆
Clean, sharp-tasting bitter with lasting hoppiness; predominantly malty aroma.

Springtide (OG 1043.5, ABV 4.3%) ◆
An excellent, full and well-rounded, mid-brown beer with a dry, bitter taste and aftertaste.

Old Moggie (OG 1044.5, ABV 4.4%)
A golden, hoppy and fruity ale.

Beachcomber (OG 1045.5, ABV 4.5%) ◆
A pale brown beer with a light, refreshing fruit and hop nose, grapefruit taste and a dry, hoppy finish.

Teme Valley SIBA

Teme Valley Brewery, The Talbot, Bromyard Road, Knightwick, Worcester, WR6 5PH
☎ (01886) 821235
✉ enquiries@temevalleybrewery.co.uk
⊕ temevalleybrewery.co.uk
Tours by arrangement

Teme Valley Brewery opened in 1997. In 2005, new investment enabled the brewery to expand to a 10-barrel brew-length. It maintains strong ties with local hop farming, using only Worcestershire-grown hops. Some 30 outlets are supplied. Seasonal beers: see website. Bottle-conditioned beers are also available.

T'Other (OG 1035, ABV 3.5%) ◆
Refreshing amber offering an abundance of flavour in the fruity aroma, followed by a short, dry bitterness.

This (OG 1037, ABV 3.7%) ◆
Dark gold brew with a mellow array of flavours in a malty balance.

That (OG 1041, ABV 4.1%) ◆
A rich fruity nose and a wide range of hoppy and malty flavours in this copper-coloured best bitter.

Talbot Blond (OG 1042, ABV 4.4%)
A smooth, rich, pale beer.

Theakston

T&R Theakston Ltd, The Brewery, Masham, Ripon, North Yorkshire, HG4 4YD
☎ (01765) 680000
✉ info@theakstons.co.uk
⊕ theakstons.co.uk
Tours by arrangement

After 20 years under the control of first Matthew Brown and then Scottish & Newcastle, Theakstons returned to the independent sector in 2003 when the family bought back the company from S&N, and it is now controlled by four Theakston brothers. The brewery is one of the oldest in Yorkshire, built in 1875 by the brothers' great-grandfather, Thomas Theakston, the son of the company's founder. The Theakston's range, with the exception of Best Bitter, is brewed in Masham but as a result of restraints on capacity the company has contracted S&N to brew Best Bitter at John Smith's in Tadcaster. In 2004 a new fermentation room was added to provide additional flexibility and capacity, and further capacity was added in 2006. Seasonal beers: see website.

Traditional Mild (OG 1035, ABV 3.5%)
A rich and smooth mild ale with a creamy body and a rounded liquorice taste. Dark ruby/amber in colour, with a mix of malt and fruit on the nose, and a dry, hoppy aftertaste.

Best Bitter (ABV 3.8%)
A golden-coloured beer with a full flavour that lingers pleasantly on the palate. With a good bitter/sweet balance, this beer has a robust hop character, citrus and spicy.

Black Bull Bitter (OG 1037, ABV 3.9%)
A distinctively hoppy aroma leads to a bitter, hoppy taste with some fruitiness and a short bitter finish. Rather thin.

XB (OG 1044, ABV 4.5%)
A sweet-tasting bitter with background fruit and spicy hop. Some caramel character gives this ale a malty dominance.

Old Peculier (OG 1057, ABV 5.6%)
A full-bodied, dark brown, strong ale. Slightly malty but with hints of roast coffee and liquorice. A smooth caramel overlay and a complex fruitiness leads to a bitter chocolate finish.

Abraham Thompson

Abraham Thompson's Brewing Co, Flass Lane, Barrow-in-Furness, Cumbria, LA13 0AD
☎ 07708 191437
✉ abraham.thompson@btinternet.com

Abraham Thompson was set up in 2004 to return Barrow-brewed beers to local pubs. This was achieved in 2005 after an absence of more than 30 years following the demise of Case's Brewery in 1972. With a half-barrel plant, this nano-brewery has concentrated almost exclusively on dark beers, reflecting the tastes of the brewer. As a result of the small output, finding the beers outside the Low Furness area is difficult. The only frequent stockist is the Black Dog Inn between Dalton and Ireleth.

Dark Mild (ABV 3.5%)

Lickerish Stout (ABV 3.8%)
A black, full-bodied stout with heavy roast flavours and good bitterness.

Oatmeal Stout (ABV 4.5%)

Porter (ABV 4.8%)
A deep, dark porter with good body and a smooth chocolate finish.

Letargion (ABV 9%)
Black, bitter and heavily roast but still very drinkable. A meal in a glass.

John Thompson

John Thompson Inn & Brewery, Ingleby, Melbourne, Derbyshire, DE73 7HW
☎ (01332) 862469
✉ nick_w_thompson@yahoo.co.uk
johnthompsoninn.com
Tours by arrangement

John Thompson set up the brewery in 1977. The pub and brewery are now run by his son, Nick. Seasonal beers: Rich Porter (ABV 4.5%, winter), St Nicks (ABV 5%, Xmas).

JTS XXX (OG 1041, ABV 4.1%)

Gold (OG 1045, ABV 4.5%)

Thornbridge SIBA

Thornbridge Brewery, Thornbridge Hall, Ashford-in-the-Water, Bakewell, Derbyshire, DE45 1NZ
☎ (01629) 641000
✉ info@thornbridgebrewery.co.uk
thornbridgebrewery.co.uk
Tours by arrangement

The first Thornbridge craft beers were produced in 2005 in the 10-barrel brewery, housed in the grounds of Thornbridge Hall. 120 outlets are supplied direct. There are plans to expand the brewery to meet increasing demand and to install a bottling line. Three pubs are owned. Seasonal/occasional beers: Brother Rabbit (ABV 3.7%), Brock (ABV 4.1%, Sep-Mar), Hark (ABV 4.8%, Nov-Feb), McConnells (ABV 5%, Sep-Mar). Bottle-conditioned beers are also available.

Wild Swan (OG 1035, ABV 3.5%)
Extremely light bodied, pale gold beer with subtle lemon and spice aroma. Citrus notes continue in the taste, leading to a bitter aftertaste.

Lord Marples (OG 1041, ABV 4%)
An easy-drinking, copper-coloured, fruity session beer. Malty, with a citrus finish and long, bitter aftertaste.

Ashford (OG 1043, ABV 4.2%)
A brown ale with a floral hoppiness and delicate bitter finish.

Blackthorn Ale (OG 1044, ABV 4.4%)
Clear golden ale, with a slight aroma of floral hops. Nicely balanced flavours of hops, citrus and sweetness lead to a lingering fruit and hop aftertaste. Moreish, tasty and refreshing!

Jaywick (OG 1047, ABV 4.8%)
An American pale ale; golden in colour with honey, gooseberry and passionfruit on the nose. Medium-bodied with a malty, biscuity finish.

Kipling (OG 1050, ABV 5.2%)
Golden pale bitter with aromas of grapefruit and passion fruit. Intense fruit flavours continue throughout, leading to a long, bitter aftertaste.

Jaipur IPA (OG 1055, ABV 5.9%)
Complex, well-balanced IPA with a lovely blend of citrus and fruit flavours mixed with a slight sweetness and ending with a lingering, bitter finish. Hoppy and dangerously drinkable!

Halcyon (OG 1071, ABV 7.7%)

Rich fruit and hop character in the aroma. Chewy, juicy malts and intense hoppiness coming through in the mouth with a hint of tangerine and pear drops. Ends with well-balanced bitterness.

Saint Petersburg (Imperial Russian Stout) (OG 1073, ABV 7.7%) ◆
Full-bodied beer in the style of a Russian imperial stout. A combination of coffee, liquorice and roasted malt flavours gives way to a long bittersweet finish and aftertaste.

Three B's

Three B's Brewery, Laneside Works, Stockclough Lane, Feniscowles, Blackburn, Lancashire, BB2 5JR
☎ **(01254) 207686**
✉ **info@threebsbrewery.co.uk**
🌐 **threebsbrewery.co.uk**
Tours by arrangement

Robert Bell designed and began building his two-barrel brewery in 1998 and in 1999 he obtained premises in Blackburn to set up the equipment and complete the project. Now, after a move to larger premises, it is a 20-barrel brewery. 30 outlets are supplied. Seasonal beers: Easter Gold (ABV 4.5%), Fettler's Choice (ABV 4.2%, summer), Autumn Gold (ABV 4.5%), Santa's Skinful (ABV 4%, Xmas).

Stoker's Slake (OG 1036, ABV 3.6%) ◆
Lightly roasted coffee flavours are in the aroma and the initial taste. A well-rounded, dark brown mild with dried fruit flavours in the long finish.

Bobbin's Bitter (OG 1038, ABV 3.8%)
Warm aromas of malt, Goldings hops and nuts; a full, fruity flavour with a light dry finish.

Weavers Brew (OG 1040, ABV 4%)

Tackler's Tipple (OG 1043, ABV 4.3%)
A best bitter with full hop flavour, biscuit tones on the tongue and a deep, dry finish. A darker coloured ale with a fascinating blend of hops and dark malt.

Doff Cocker (OG 1045, ABV 4.5%) ◆
Yellow with a hoppy aroma and initial taste giving way to subtle malt notes and orchard fruit flavours. Crisp, dry finish.

Pinch Noggin (OG 1046, ABV 4.6%)
A luscious balance of malt, hops and fruit, with a lively, colourful spicy aroma of citrus fruit. A quenching golden beer.

Knocker Up (OG 1048, ABV 4.8%) ◆
A smooth, rich, creamy porter. The roast flavour is foremost without dominating and is balanced by fruit and hop notes.

Shuttle Ale (OG 1052, ABV 5.2%)
A strong pale ale, light in colour with a balanced malt and hop flavour, a Goldings hops aroma, a long dry finish and delicate fruit notes.

Three Castles SIBA

Three Castles Brewery Ltd, Unit 12, Salisbury Road Business Park, Pewsey, Wiltshire, SN9 5PZ
☎ **(01672) 564433**
✉ **sales@threecastlesbrewery.co.uk**
🌐 **threecastlesbrewery.co.uk**
Shop Mon-Fri 9am-4pm; Sat 9am-1pm
Tours by arrangement

Three Castles is an independent, family-run brewery, established in 2006. Its location in the Vale of Pewsey has inspired the names for its range of ales. The brewery has plans for expansion. Around 175 outlets are supplied. Seasonal beers: Holly Berry (ABV 4.4%, Xmas), Slay Belles (ABV 5.8%, Xmas). Bottle-conditioned beers are also available.

Barbury Castle (OG 1039, ABV 3.9%)
A balanced, easy-drinking pale ale with a hoppy, spicy palate.

Best Bitter (OG 1041, ABV 4.1%)

Vale Ale (OG 1043, ABV 4.3%)
Golden-coloured with a fruity palate and strong floral aroma.

Stoned (OG 1044, ABV 4.4%)

Castlewheat (ABV 4.5%)

Longbarrow (OG 1045, ABV 4.5%)
Copper-coloured with a spicy, nutty flavour and a hoppy aftertaste.

Knights Porter (OG 1046, ABV 4.6%)

Mad Spring Mild (OG 1047, ABV 4.7%)

Tanked Up (OG 1050, ABV 5%)
Copper-coloured strong ale.

Three Peaks

Three Peaks Brewery, 7 Craven Terrace, Settle, North Yorkshire, BD24 9DB
☎ **(01729) 822939**

Formed in 2006, Three Peaks is run by husband and wife team Colin and Susan Ashwell. The brewery is located in the cellar of their home. One beer is brewed at present on their 1.25-barrel plant but more are planned.

Pen-y-Ghent Bitter (OG 1040, ABV 3.8%)

Three Rivers

See 3 Rivers

Three Tuns SIBA

John Roberts Brewing Co Ltd t/a Three Tuns Brewery, 16 Market Square, Bishop's Castle, Shropshire, SY9 5BN
☎ **(01588) 638392**
✉ **tunsbrewery@aol.com**
🌐 **threetunsbrewery.co.uk**
Shop Mon-Fri 9am-5pm
Tours by arrangement

Brewing started on the site in 1642. In the 1970s the Three Tuns was one of only four brew-pubs left in the country. Nowadays the brewery and Three Tuns pub are separate businesses. Plans to increase the brew length are in progress. Around 125 outlets are supplied. Seasonal beers: see website.

Three8 / 1642 Bitter (OG 1042, ABV 3.8%)
A golden ale with a light, nutty maltiness and spicy bitterness.

XXX (OG 1046, ABV 4.3%)
A pale, sweetish bitter with a light hop aftertaste that has a honey finish.

Cleric's Cure (ABV 5%)
A light tan coloured ale with a malty sweetness. Strong and spicy with a floral bitterness.

Thwaites IFBB

Daniel Thwaites plc, Star Brewery, PO Box 50, Blackburn, Lancashire, BB1 5BU
☎ (01254) 686868
✉ marketing@thwaites.co.uk
thwaites.co.uk
Tours by arrangement

Established in 1807, Thwaites is still controlled by the Yerburgh family, decendents of the founder, Daniel Thwaites. The company owns around 400 pubs. Real ale isavailablein about 60% of these but Nutty Black is hard to find. Seasonal beers appear quarterly – see website for more information.

Nutty Black (OG 1036, ABV 3.3%)
A tasty traditional dark mild presenting a malty flavour with caramel notes and a slightly bitter finish.

Original (OG 1036, ABV 3.6%)
Hop driven, yet well-balanced amber session bitter. Hops continue through to the long finish.

Wainwright (OG 1042, ABV 4.1%)
A straw-coloured bitter with soft fruit flavours and a hint of malty sweetness.

Lancaster Bomber (OG 1044, ABV 4.4%)
Well-balanced, copper-coloured best bitter with firm malt flavours, a fruity background and a long, dry finish.

For Carlsberg:

Ansells Mild (OG 1035, ABV 3.4%)

Tigertops SIBA

Tigertops Brewery, 22 Oaks Street, Flanshaw, Wakefield, West Yorkshire, WF2 9LN
☎ (01229) 716238 / (01924) 897728
✉ tigertopsbrewery@hotmail.com

Tigertops was established in 1995 by Stuart Johnson and his wife Lynda. They own the brewery as well as running the Foxfield brew-pub in Cumbria (qv) but Tigertops is run on their behalf by Barry Smith. Five outlets are supplied. Seasonal beers: Billy Bock (ABV 7.9%, Nov-Feb), May Bock (ABV 6.2%, May-Jun).

Axeman's Block (OG 1036, ABV 3.6%)
A malty beer with a good hop finish.

Dark Wheat Mild (OG 1036, ABV 3.6%)
An unusual mild made primarily with wheat malt.

Thor Bitter (OG 1038, ABV 3.8%)
A light, hoppy bitter.

Charles Town Best Bitter (ABV 4%)

Blanche de Newland (OG 1044, ABV 4.5%)
A cloudy Belgian-style wheat beer.

Ginger Fix (OG 1044, ABV 4.6%)
A mid-amber ginger beer.

White Max (OG 1044, ABV 4.6%)
A light, German-style wheat beer.

Uber Weiss (OG 1046, ABV 4.8%)
A dark, German-style wheat beer.

Big Ginger (OG 1058, ABV 6%)
A strong, amber ginger beer.

Tindall EAB

Tindall Ales Brewery, Toad Lane, Seething, Norfolk, NR35 2EQ
☎ (01508) 483844
☎ 07795 113163
✉ greenangela5@aol.com
Shop Tue & Wed 9.30am-12.30pm
Tours by arrangement

Tindall Ales was established in 1998 and was situated on the edge of the medieval Tindall wood but moved to new premises in 2001. It is a family-run business and now only brews on a seasonal basis, meaning supply is limited. Bottle-conditioned beers are available.

Best Bitter (ABV 3.7%)

Mild (ABV 3.7%)

Alltime (ABV 4%)

Autumn (ABV 4%)

Ditchingham Dam (ABV 4.2%)

Seething Pint (ABV 4.3%)

Norfolk 'n' Good (ABV 4.6%)

Norwich Dragon (ABV 4.6%)

Honeydo (ABV 5%)

Tipples EAB

Tipples Brewery, Unit 6, Damgate Lane Industrial Estate, Acle, Norwich, Norfolk, NR13 3DJ
☎ (01493) 741007
✉ brewery@tipplesbrewery.com
tipplesbrewery.com

Tipples was established by Jason Tipple in 2004 on a six-barrel brew plant built by Porter Brewing Co. The brewery initially concentrated on the bottled market but cask ale production has since increased and there are plans for expansion on the existing site. Bottle-conditioned beers are available.

Longshore (OG 1036, ABV 3.6%)
Yellow hued with a soft, peachy aroma and creamy mouthfeel. The initial fruity apricot flavour quickly subsides to a long, dry bitterness.

Ginger (ABV 3.8%)
A spicy aroma introduces this well-balanced yellow-gold brew. Ginger dominates but does not overwhelm the supporting malty bitterness. Quick ginger nut finish.

Hanged Monk (ABV 4%)
A classic East Anglian mild. A well-rounded, malty aroma introduces a solid malty taste with an initial hoppy bite. Dark brown, as befits this style, the finish is mainly malt with a growing sweetness and roast influence.

Lady Evelyn (OG 1041, ABV 4.1%) ◆
Straw-coloured with a gentle citrus aroma that belies a clean hop bitterness in the initial taste. Lemon citrus background adds some depth to a light, undemanding summer ale.

Redhead (OG 1042, ABV 4.2%) ◆
A mix of hop and malt in the nose carries through to a first taste of bitter hoppiness and background malt. Bitterness continues to dominate the long finish as a grapefruit dryness creeps in.

Lady Hamilton (ABV 4.3%) ◆
Mid-brown with a caramel toffee nose. Sweet and full-bodied with a lingering malty finish. Some dryness can be detected towards the end.

Brewers Progress (ABV 4.6%)

Jacks' Revenge (ABV 5.8%) ◆
An explosion of malt, chocolate, roast and plum pudding fruitiness. Full-bodied with a deep red hue and a strong solid finish that develops into a vinous fruitiness.

Tipsy Toad

See Jersey

Tirril SIBA

Tirril Brewery Ltd, Red House, Long Marton, Appleby-in-Westmorland, Cumbria, CA16 6BN
☎ **(01768) 361846**
tirrilales.co.uk
Tours by arrangement

Tirril Brewery was established in 1999 in an abandoned toilet block behind the Queen's Head in Tirril. Since then it has relocated to the 1823 gothic brewing rooms at Brougham Hall and is now at the Red House Barn in Long Marton beneath the Pennines. Capacity has grown from 2.25 barrels to 20 barrels over the years. More than 50 outlets are supplied and one pub is owned. Seasonal beers: Graduate (ABV 4.6%, Dec), Balls Up (ABV 3.9%, summer).

John Bewsher's Best Bitter (OG 1038.5, ABV 3.8%)
A lightly-hopped, golden brown session beer, named after the landlord and brewer at the Queen's Head in the 1830s.

Brougham Ale (OG 1039, ABV 3.9%)
A gently hopped, amber bitter.

Charles Gough's Old Faithful (OG 1040, ABV 4%)
Pale gold, aromatic and well-hopped.

1823 (OG 1041, ABV 4.1%)
A full-bodied session bitter with a gentle bitterness.

Thomas Slee's Academy Ale (OG 1041.5, ABV 4.2%)
A dark, full-bodied, traditional rich and malty ale.

Red Barn Ale (OG 1043, ABV 4.4%)
A ruby red ale with a strong hop finish.

Titanic SIBA

Titanic Brewery Co Ltd, Unit 5, Callender Place, Burslem, Stoke-on-Trent, Staffordshire, ST6 1JL
☎ **(01782) 823447**
✉ **titanic@titanicbrewery.co.uk**
titanicbrewery.co.uk
Tours by arrangement

Founded in 1985, the brewery is named in honour of Captain Smith who hailed from the Potteries and had the misfortune to captain the Titanic. A monthly seasonal beer provides the opportunity to offer distinctive beers of many styles, each with a link to the liner. Titanic supplies 300 free trade outlets throughout the country. The brewery has three tied houses. Bottle-conditioned beer is also available.

Mild (OG 1036, ABV 3.5%) ◆
Sweet malt aroma with plumy fruit. Well balanced taste between plum jam sweetness and biscuity dryness leading to an increasing bitterness in the aftertaste.

Steerage (OG 1036, ABV 3.5%) ◆
Yellow bitter. Sweet aroma with hints of hops, gentle start developing bitterness. Well balanced for a light session beer with a long dry finish.

Lifeboat (OG 1040, ABV 4%) ◆
Tawny beer with a nutty aroma. Hoppy with touches of roast amongst fruit and a developing bitterness.

Anchor Bitter (OG 1042, ABV 4.1%) ◆
Golden best bitter. Sharp from the start, mouth-watering and spicy. Hoppy aroma and finish.

Iceberg (OG 1042, ABV 4.1%) ◆
Straw coloured brew with grassy and citrus aroma, extensive bitterness from the start. Refreshingly hoppy with a dry finish.

Stout (OG 1046, ABV 4.5%) ◆
Roasty toasty with tobacco, autumn bonfires, liquorice and chocolate but balanced perfectly with bitter, dry finish.

White Star (OG 1050, ABV 4.8%) ◆
Sharp and crisp and zesty like Pinot Grigio! Good hop bite and bitter finish. Yellow colour.

Captain Smith's Strong Ale (OG 1054, ABV 5.2%) ◆
Red with a hoppy aroma plus malt and a touch of sulphur. Fine balance of hop and caramel with roast and hints of malt and fruit. Sweet to start then a hoppy, bitter finish with a fruity layer.

Toll End

Toll End Brewery, c/o Waggon & Horses, 131 Toll End Road, Tipton, West Midlands, DY4 0ET
☎ **07903 725574**
Tours by arrangement

The four-barrel brewery opened in 2004. With the exception of Phoebe's Ale, named after the brewer's daughter, all brews commemorate local landmarks, events and people. Toll End is brewing to full capacity and produces around 300 gallons a week. Four outlets are supplied. Several specials are also brewed throughout the year.

William Perry (OG 1043, ABV 4.3%)

Phoebe's Ale/PA (OG 1044, ABV 4.4%)

Polly Stevens (OG 1044, ABV 4.4%)

Black Bridge (OG 1046, ABV 4.6%)

Tipton Pride (OG 1046, ABV 4.6%)

Power Station (OG 1049, ABV 4.9%)
Cask-conditioned lager.

Tollgate SIBA

Tollgate Brewery, Unit 8, Viking Business Centre, High Street, Woodville, Derbyshire, DE11 7EH
☎ (01283) 229194
✉ tollgatebrewery@tiscali.co.uk
Tours by arrangement

⊗ Tollgate, a six-barrel brewery that opened in 2005, is on the site of the old Brunt & Bucknall Brewery, which was bought and closed by Bass in 1927. More than 60 outlets are supplied. Seasonal beer: Woodville Winter Warmer (ABV 5.4%, Nov-Feb). Bottle-conditioned beers are also available.

Woodville Pale (OG 1042, ABV 4%)

Wooden Box Bitter (OG 1045, ABV 4.3%)

Red Star IPA (OG 1047, ABV 4.5%)

Tollgate Light/TGL (OG 1047, ABV 4.5%)

Billy's Best Bitter (OG 1048, ABV 4.6%)

Tomos Watkin

See under 'W'

Topsham & Exminster

See Exeter

Tower SIBA

Tower Brewery, Old Water Tower, Walsitch Maltings, Glensyl Way, Burton upon Trent, Staffordshire, DE14 1LX
☎ (01283) 530695
✉ towerbrewery@aol.com
Tours by arrangement

Tower was established in 2001 by John Mills, previously the brewer at Burton Bridge, in a converted derelict water tower of Thomas Salt's maltings. The conversion was given a Civic Society award for the restoration of a Historic Industrial Building in 2001. Tower has 20 regular outlets. Seasonal beers: Sundowner (ABV 4%, May-Aug), Spring Equinox (ABV 4.6%, Mar-May), Autumn Equinox (ABV 4.6%, Sep-Nov), Winter Spirit (ABV 5%).

Thomas Salt's Bitter (OG 1038, ABV 3.8%)

Bitter (OG 1042, ABV 4.2%) ◆
Gold coloured with a malty, caramel and hoppy aroma. A full hop and fruit taste with the fruit lingering. A bitter and astringent finish.

Malty Towers (OG 1044, ABV 4.4%) ◆
Yellow with a malty aroma and a hint of tobacco. Strong hops give a long, dry, bitter finish with pleasant astringency.

Pale Ale (OG 1048, ABV 4.8%)

Tower of Strength (OG 1076, ABV 7.6%)

For Castle Rock, Nottingham:

Sheriff's Tipple (OG 1035, ABV 3.5%)
A light-tawny session bitter with distinctive hop character.

For Hoskins Brothers, Leicester:

Hob Best Mild (ABV 3.5%)

Brigadier Bitter (ABV 3.6%)

Hob Bitter (ABV 4%)

White Dolphin (ABV 4%)

Tom Kelly's Stout (ABV 4.2%)

EXS (ABV 5%)

Ginger Tom (ABV 5.2%)

Old Navigation Ale (ABV 7%)

For Steamin' Billy Brewing Co (qv):

Country Bitter (OG 1036, ABV 3.6%)

Grand Prix Mild (OG 1036, ABV 3.6%)

Bitter (OG 1043, ABV 4.3%) ◆
Brown-coloured best bitter. Initial malt and hops aromas are superseded by fruit and hop taste and aftertaste, accompanied by a refreshing bitterness.

Skydiver (OG 1050, ABV 5%) ◆
Full-bodied, strong, mahogany-coloured beer in which an initial malty aroma is followed by a characteristic malty sweetness that is balanced by a hoppy bitterness.

Townes SIBA

Townes Brewery, Speedwell Inn, Lowgates, Staveley, Chesterfield, Derbyshire, S43 3TT
☎ (01246) 472252
✉ curly@townes48.wanadoo.co.uk
Tours by arrangement

⊗ Townes Brewery started in 1994 in an old bakery on the outskirts of Chesterfield using a five-barrel plant. It was the first brewery in the town for more than 40 years. In 1997, the Speedwell Inn at Staveley was bought and the plant was moved to the rear of the pub, becoming the first brew-pub in north Derbyshire in the 20th century. Seasonal beers: Stargazer (ABV 4.7%, Dec-Jan), Sunshine (ABV 3.7%, Jul-Aug). Bottle-conditioned beers are also available and are suitable for vegetarians and vegans.

Speedwell Bitter (OG 1039, ABV 3.9%) ◆
Well-balanced amber bitter with little aroma. Hints of caramel and hops lead to a bitterness developing in the long aftertaste.

Lowgate Light (OG 1041, ABV 4.1%)

Staveley Cross (OG 1043, ABV 4.3%) ◆
Amber-gold best bitter with a faint caramel aroma. Hoppy with bitterness present throughout, culminating in a very long, dry, slightly astringent aftertaste.

IPA (OG 1045, ABV 4.5%) ◆
Well-crafted flavoursome IPA of little aroma and a good bittersweet balanced taste. This leads to a lingering aftertaste, which is predominantly sweet with hoppy undertones.

Pynot Porter (ABV 4.5%) ◆
Classic red-brown porter with a faint malt and roast aroma. Roast malt flavours combine with vine fruit, becoming increasingly bitter towards the finish.

Staveleyan (OG 1049, ABV 4.9%)

Townhouse

Townhouse Brewery, Units 1-4, Townhouse Studios, Townhouse Farm, Alsager Road, Audley, Staffordshire, ST7 8JQ
☎ **07976 209437/07812 035143**
✉ **j.nixon2@btinternet.com**
Tours by arrangement

⊗ Townhouse was set up in 2002 with a 2.5-barrel plant. In 2004 the brewery scaled up to a five-barrels. Demand is growing rapidly and in early 2006 two additional fermenting vessels were added. Bottling is planned. Some 30 outlets are supplied.

Audley Bitter (OG 1038, ABV 3.8%)
A pale, well-balanced session bitter with a citrus hop character.

Flowerdew (OG 1039, ABV 4%) ◆
Golden with a wonderful floral aroma. Fabulous flavour of flowery hops delivering a hoppy bite and presenting a lingering taste of flowery citrus waves.

Dark Horse (OG 1042, ABV 4.3%)
A dark ruby ale with malt character and late hoppy finish.

A'dleyweisse (OG 1043, ABV 4.5%)
An English style wheat beer, full-bodied and golden with a strongly defined fruity hop character and a dry finish.

Audley Gold (OG 1043, ABV 4.5%) ◆
Straw colour with some hops on the aroma. An explosion of hops in the taste gives a perfect bitter effect, leaving a hoppy mouthfeel without too much astringency.

Barney's Stout (OG 1043, ABV 4.5%) ◆
Roast chocolate and toffee nose atop this black stout. Sweet start going bitter at the end, with roast throughout.

Armstrong Ale (OG 1045, ABV 4.8%)
A rich, fruity ruby red beer with a hoppy, dry finish.

Monument Ale (OG 1048, ABV 5%)
A copper-coloured, well-balanced strong ale with a pronounced malt character.

Traditional Scottish Ales

Traditional Scottish Ales Ltd, Unit 7c, Bandeath Industrial Estate, Stirling, FK7 7NP
☎ **(01786) 817000**
✉ **brewery@traditionalscottishales.com**
🌐 **traditionalscottishales.com**

A new company set up in 2005 to develop and market the Bridge of Allan, Stirling and Trossach's Craft Brewery products. The brewery is located in a former torpedo factory. A five-barrel plant is used for cask ales and a custom-built 20-barrel plant is dedicated to bottled products. More than 200 outlets are supplied. Bottle-conditioned beer is available. All bottled ales are suitable for vegetarians and vegans.

Stirling Bitter (OG 1039, ABV 3.7%)

Ben Nevis Organic (OG 1042, ABV 4%) ◆
A traditional Scottish 80/-, with a distinctive roast and caramel character. Bittersweet fruit throughout provides the sweetness typical of a Scottish Heavy.

Stirling Brig (OG 1042, ABV 4.1%)

Bannockburn Ale (OG 1044, ABV 4.2%)

Glencoe Wild Oat Stout Organic (OG 1048, ABV 4.5%) ◆
A sweetish stout, surprisingly not dark in colour. Plenty of malt and roast balanced by fruit and finished with a hint of hop.

William Wallace (OG 1050, ABV 4.8%)

Ginger Explosion (OG 1052, ABV 5%)

Lomond Gold Organic (OG 1054, ABV 5%) ◆
A malty, bittersweet golden ale with plenty of fruity hop character.

Red Mist (OG 1052, ABV 5%)
A raspberry beer.

1488 (OG 1075, ABV 7%)

For Trossach's Craft Brewery:

Waylade (OG 1040, ABV 3.9%)

LadeBack (OG 1048, ABV 4.5%)

LadeOut (OG 1055, ABV 5.1%)

Traquair SIBA

Traquair House Brewery, Traquair House, Innerleithen, Peeblesshire, EH44 6PW
☎ **(01896) 830323**
✉ **enquiries@traquair.co.uk**
🌐 **traquair.co.uk**
Shop Easter-Oct 12-5pm daily (Jun-Aug 10.30am-5pm)
Tours by arrangement

The 18th-century brewhouse is based in one of the wings of the 1,000-year-old Traquair House, Scotland's oldest inhabited house. The brewhouse was rediscovered by the 20th Laird, the late Peter Maxwell Stuart, in 1965. He began brewing again using all the original equipment, which remained intact, despite having lain idle for more than 100 years. The brewery has been run by Peter's daughter, Catherine Maxwell Stuart, since his death in 1990. The Maxwell Stuarts are members of the Stuart clan, and the main Bear Gates will remain shut until a Stuart returns to the throne. All the beers are oak-fermented and 60 per cent of production is exported. Seasonal beer: Stuart Ale (ABV 4.5%, summer).

Bear Ale (ABV 5%)

Traquair House Ale (ABV 7%)

Jacobite Ale (ABV 8%)

Tring SIBA

Tring Brewery Co Ltd, 81-82 Akeman Street, Tring, Hertfordshire, HP23 6AF
☎ **(01442) 890721**
✉ **info@tringbrewery.co.uk**

tringbrewery.co.uk
Shop 9am-5pm (12pm Sat, 6pm Wed-Fri); Closed Sun
Tours by arrangement (evenings only)

Founded in 1992, the Tring Brewery is based on a small industrial estate and brews 50 barrels a week. Most of the beers take their names from local myths and legends. In addition to the regular and seasonal ales, Tring brews a selection of monthly specials. There are plans to move the brewery to larger premises. Seasonal beers: Legless Lal's Winter Ale (ABV 4.5%), Royal Poacher (ABV 4.1%), Fanny Ebbs Summer Ale (ABV 3.9%), Huck-Me-Buck (ABV 4.4%), Santa's Little Helper (ABV 4.8%).

Side Pocket for a Toad (OG 1035, ABV 3.6%)
Citrus notes from American Cascade hops balanced with a floral aroma and a crisp, dry finish in a straw-coloured ale.

Brock Bitter (ABV 3.7%)
A light brown session ale with hints of sweetness and caramel, gentle bitterness and a floral aroma from Styrian hops.

Mansion Mild (ABV 3.7%)
Smooth and creamy dark ruby mild with a fruity palate and gentle late hop.

Blonde (OG 1039, ABV 4%)
A refreshing blonde beer with a fruity palate, balanced with a lingering hop aroma.

Ridgeway (OG 1039, ABV 4%)
Balanced malt and hop flavours with a dry, flowery hop aftertaste.

Jack O'Legs (OG 1041, ABV 4.2%)
A combination of four types of malt and two types of aroma hops provide a copper-coloured premium ale with full fruit and a distinctive hoppy bitterness.

Tea Kettle Stout (OG 1047, ABV 4.7%)
Rich and complex traditional stout with a hint of liquorice and moderate bitterness.

Colley's Dog (OG 1051, ABV 5.2%)
Dark but not over-rich, strong yet drinkable, this premium ale has a long dry finish with overtones of malt and walnuts.

Death or Glory (ABV 7.2%)
A strong, dark, aromatic barley wine.

Triple fff SIBA

Triple fff Brewing Co Ltd, Magpie Works, Station Approach, Four Marks, Alton, Hampshire, GU34 5HN
☎ (01420) 561422
sales-triplefbrewery@tiscali.co.uk
triplefff.com
Shop (ring for opening hours)
Tours by arrangement

The brewery was founded in 1997 with a five-barrel plant. Ever increasing demand has culminated in a £¾ million investment in a new 50-barrel plant. The brewery has two of its own outlets, the Railway Arms in Alton and the White Lion in Aldershot, as well as supplying over 200 other outlets. One or two seasonal beers are offered to complement the regular range. A newly refurbished shop, while supplying off sales, stocks an extensive range of beers from other local breweries.

Alton's Pride (ABV 3.8%)
Excellent clean tasting golden-brown session beer, full-bodied for its strength. A glorious aroma of floral hops. An initially malty flavour fades as citric notes and hoppiness take over leading to a lasting, hoppy, bitter finish.

Pressed Rat & Warthog (ABV 3.8%)
Complex hoppy and bitter mild not in the classic style but nevertheless delicious. Ruby in colour, a roast malt aroma with hints of blackcurrant and chocolate, lead to a well-balanced flavour with roast, fruit and malt vying with the hoppy bitterness and a dry, bitter finish.

Moondance (ABV 4.2%)
A pale brown-coloured best bitter, wonderfully hopped with an aromatic citrus hop nose, balanced by bitterness and a hint of sweetness in the mouth. Bitterness increases as the fruit declines, leading to a bittersweet finish.

Stairway (ABV 4.6%)
An aroma of pale and crystal malts introduces this pale brown beer with a flavour of summer fruits. Well-balanced with a dry, strong, hoppy finish. Predominantly bitter, but with some sweetness and malt.

Trossach's Craft

See Traditional Scottish Ales

Tryst

Tryst Brewery, Lorne Road, Larbert, Stirling, FK5 4AT
☎ (01324) 554000
johnmcgarva@tinyworld.co.uk
trystbrewery.co.uk
Shop Mon-Fri office hours; Sat am
Tours by arrangement

John McGarva, a member of Scottish Craft Brewers, started brewing in 2003 in an industrial unit near Larbert station. Around 30 outlets are supplied. Bottle-conditioned ales are available.

Brockville Dark (OG 1039, ABV 3.8%)

Brockville Pale (OG 1039, ABV 3.8%)

80/- (ABV 4%)

Buckled Wheel (OG 1043, ABV 4.2%)

Carronade IPA (OG 1043, ABV 4.2%)

Zetland Wheatbier (OG 1046, ABV 4.5%)

Tudor*

Tudor Brewery, Kings Arms, 29 Neville Street, Abergavenny, NP7 5AA
☎ 0871 529 2595
kingsarms-gastropub.co.uk

The Tudor Brewery was established in September 2007 in the Kings Arms pub in Abergavenny. It mostly produces beer for the pub.

Skirrid (ABV 4.2%)

Sugar Loaf (ABV 4.2%)

Tunnel SIBA

Tunnel Brewery Ltd, c/o Lord Nelson Inn, Birmingham Road, Ansley, Nuneaton, Warwickshire, CV10 9RX
☎ (02476) 394888
✉ info@tunnelbrewery.co.uk
🌐 tunnelbrewery.co.uk
Tours by arrangement

Bob Yates and Mike Walsh started brewing in 2005, taking the name from a rail tunnel that passes under the village. Pub and brewery are independent of one another but the beers are available in the pub as well as being supplied to more than 100 other outlets. Brewing more than doubled in 2008 and a new unit for storage and bottling has been established. Seasonal beers: see website. Bottle-conditioned beers are also available and are suitable for vegans.

Linda Lear Beer (OG 1038, ABV 3.7%)
A dark amber, fruity beer with a strong hop finish.

Let Battle Commence (OG 1038, ABV 3.8%)

Late Ott (OG 1040, ABV 4%)
Dark golden session bitter with a fruity nose and perfumed hop edge. The finish is dry and bitter.

Trade Winds (OG 1045, ABV 4.6%)
An aromatic, copper-coloured beer with an aroma of Cascade hops and a clean, crisp hint of citrus, followed by fruity malts and a dry finish full of scented hops.

Parish Ale (OG 1047, ABV 4.7%)
A reddish-amber, malty ale with a slight chocolate aroma enhanced by citrus notes. It becomes increasingly fruity as the English hops kick in. Smooth, gentle hop bitterness in the finish.

Shadow Weaver (OG 1046, ABV 4.7%)

Jean 'Cloudy' Van Damme (OG 1048, ABV 5%)

Stranger In The Mist (OG 1048, ABV 5%)

Nelson's Column (OG 1051, ABV 5.2%)
A ruby red, strong old English ale.

Boston Beer Party (OG 1056, ABV 5.6%)

Twickenham SIBA

Twickenham Fine Ales Ltd, Ryecroft Works, Edwin Road, Twickenham, Middlesex, TW2 6SP
☎ (020) 8241 1825
✉ info@twickenham-fine-ales.co.uk
🌐 twickenham-fine-ales.co.uk
Tours by arrangement

The 10-barrel brewery was set up in 2004 and was the first brewery in Twickenham since the 1920s. The brewery supplies around 200 pubs and clubs within five miles of the brewery and selected outlets in central London. It is looking to expand capacity in 2009. Seasonal/occasional beers: see website.

Sundancer (OG 1037, ABV 3.7%)
Lemon hops dominate the aroma and flavour of this yellow coloured beer. A dry bitterness, which is present in the taste, grows in the aftertaste.

Original (OG 1042, ABV 4.2%)
Malt is balanced by fruit on the nose, which follows through into the flavour and aftertaste where hops are also present. Traditionally brown in colour.

Naked Ladies (OG 1044, ABV 4.4%)
Gold in colour with strong, hoppy, bitter character. Citrus notes are noticeable throughout.

Pale Beauty (OG 1046, ABV 4.7%)
A pale gold beer with a pronounced fruity, citrus aroma and a dry, hoppy taste with an underpinning of juicy fruitiness.

Daisy Cutter (OG 1061, ABV 6.1%)
A golden-coloured, strong ale with a fruity, citrus nose and flavour.

Tydd Steam

Tydd Steam Brewery, Manor Barn, Kirkgate, Tydd Saint Giles, Cambridgeshire, PE13 5NE
☎ (01945) 871020
☎ 07932 726552
✉ tyddsteam@fsmail.net
Tours by arrangement

Tydd Steam opened in 2007 in a converted agricultural barn using a 5.5-barrel plant . The brewery is named after two farm steam engines which were formerly kept in the barn now used for brewing. The steam engines have now been moved to the Museum of Lincolnshire Life. 55 outlets are supplied direct. Seasonal beers: The Leveller (ABV 4.7%, winter), Yooligan (ABV 4.7%, Xmas).

Scoundrel (OG 1037, ABV 3.8%)

Swedish Blonde (OG 1038, ABV 4%)

Piston Bitter (OG 1042, ABV 4.4%)

Mother-in-Law (OG 1044, ABV 4.5%)

Piston Bob (OG 1044, ABV 4.6%)

Ufford

Ufford Ales Ltd, White Hart, Main Street, Ufford, Cambridgeshire, PE9 3BH
☎ (01780) 740250
✉ info@ufford-ales.co.uk
🌐 ufford-ales.co.uk
Tours by arrangement

Ufford Ales opened in February 2005. It supplies seven regular outlets in Lincolnshire and Cambridgeshire. Special beers are supplied to local festivals. Seasonal beers: Setting Sun (ABV 5.2%, summer), Snow Storm (ABV 5.6%, winter). Bottle-conditioned beer is also available.

White Hart (ABV 3.8%)

Idle Hour (OG 1040, ABV 3.9%)
Amber-gold bitter with a light malty aroma. The malt is supported in the mouth by a gentle hoppy bite as the bitterness grows.

Red Clover (ABV 4.5%)

Uley

Uley Brewery Ltd, The Old Brewery, 31 The Street, Uley, Gloucestershire, GL11 5TB
☎ (01453) 860120
✉ chas@uleybrewery.com
🌐 uleybrewery.com

Brewing at Uley began in 1833 as Price's Brewery. After a long gap, the premises were restored and Uley Brewery opened in 1985. It has its own spring water, which is used to mash in with Tucker's Maris Otter malt and boiled with Herefordshire hops. Uley serves 40-50 free trade outlets in the Cotswold area and is brewing to capacity. Seasonal beers: Reverend Janet (ABV 4.3%), Gilt Edge (ABV 4.5%).

Hogshead Cotswold Pale Ale (OG 1030, ABV 3.5%)
A pale-coloured, hoppy session bitter with a good hop aroma and a full flavour for its strength, ending in a bittersweet aftertaste.

Bitter (OG 1040, ABV 4%)
A copper-coloured beer with hops and fruit in the aroma and a malty, fruity taste, underscored by a hoppy bitterness. The finish is dry, with a balance of hops and malt.

Laurie Lee's Bitter (OG 1045, ABV 4.5%)
A copper-coloured, full-flavoured, hoppy bitter with some fruitiness and a smooth, long, balanced finish.

Old Ric (OG 1045, ABV 4.5%)
A full-flavoured, hoppy bitter with some fruitiness and a smooth, balanced finish. Distinctively copper-coloured, this is the house beer for the Old Spot Inn, Dursley.

Old Spot Prize Strong Ale (OG 1050, ABV 5%)
A distinctive full-bodied, red/brown ale with a fruity aroma, a malty, fruity taste, with a hoppy bitterness, and a strong, balanced aftertaste.

Pig's Ear Strong Beer (OG 1050, ABV 5%)
A pale-coloured beer, deceptively strong. Notably bitter in flavour, with a hoppy, fruity aroma and a bitter finish.

Ulverston

Ulverston Brewing Co, Diamond Buildings, Pennington Lane, Lindal in Furness, Cumbria, LA12 0LA
☎ (01229) 584280
☎ 07840 192022
✉ info.ubc@tiscali.co.uk
🌐 ulverstonbrewing.co.uk

The brewery went into production in 2006, the first beers to be brewed in Ulverston since the closure of Hartleys in 1991. It is situated in the old engine house of the long extinct Lindal Moor Mining Company. Most of the beers are named using a Laurel and Hardy theme after Ulverston's most famous son, Stan Laurel. Seasonal beers: UXB (ABV 4.2%), What the Dickens (ABV 4%, Nov).

Desert Son (ABV 3.8%)

Harvest Moon (OG 1039, ABV 3.9%)

Another Fine Mess (OG 1040, ABV 4%)

Laughing Gravy (OG 1040, ABV 4%)

Lonesome Pine (OG 1042, ABV 4.2%)

Stout Ollie (OG 1042, ABV 4.3%)

Bad Medicine (OG 1059, ABV 6.3%)

Uncle Stuarts

Uncle Stuarts Brewery, Antoma, Pack Lane, Lingwood, Norwich, Norfolk, NR13 4PD
☎ 07732 012112
✉ stuartsbrewery@aol.com
🌐 littlebeershop.co.uk
Tours by arrangement

The brewery started in 2002, selling bottle-conditioned beers and polypins direct to customers and by mail order. Since 2003, all the beers have also been available in nine-gallon casks. Seasonal beer: Xmas (ABV 7%).

North Norfolk Beauty (ABV 3.8%)

Pack Lane (OG 1038, ABV 4%)

Local Hero (ABV 4.7%)

Norwich Castle (ABV 5%)

Buckenham Woods (OG 1051, ABV 5.6%)
Spicy with more than a hint of raisin and sultana. Heavy aroma translates into a richly-flavoured ale with a surprisingly light and creamy mouthfeel.

Strumpshaw Fen (ABV 5.7%)

Norwich Cathedral (ABV 6.5%)

Union*

Union Brewery, Dartmoor Union, Fore Street, Holbeton, Devon, PL8 1NE
☎ (01752) 830288
✉ info@dartmoorunion.co.uk
🌐 dartmoorunion.co.uk
Union started brewing in 2007 on a three-barrel brew plant.

Pride (ABV 3.9%)

Jacks (ABV 4.5%)

Ushers

See Wadworth and Wychwood

Vale of Glamorgan

Vale of Glamorgan Brewery Ltd, Unit 8a, Atlantic Trading Estate, Barry, Vale of Glamorgan, CF63 3RF
☎ (01446) 730757
✉ info@vogbrewery.co.uk
🌐 vogbrewery.co.uk
Tours by arrangement (Max. 15 people)

Vale of Glamorgan Brewery started brewing in 2005 on a 10-barrel plant. More than 40 local outlets are supplied. Occasional beer: Oggy VoG (ABV 4%). Seasonal beers are brewed and bottle-conditioned beers are available.

Grog Y VoG (OG 1043, ABV 4.3%)

VoG Best (OG 1040, ABV 4.3%)

For Mochyn Du, Cardiff:

Cwrw'r Mochyn (ABV 4%)

Vale SIBA

Vale Brewery Co, Tramway Business Park, Luggershall Road, Brill, Buckinghamshire, HP18 9TY
☎ (01844) 239237
✉ info@valebrewery.co.uk
🌐 valebrewery.co.uk
Shop Mon-Fri 9am-5pm; Sat 9.30-11.30am
Tours by arrangement

Brothers Mark and Phil Stevens opened a purpose-built brewery in Haddenham in 1994. The plant expanded several times and to enable further growth moved to larger premises in the hilltop village of Brill in 2007. Four pubs are owned, including brewery tap the Hop Pole in Aylesbury, and around 250 local outlets are supplied. Seasonal beers: see website. Bottle-conditioned beers are also available and are suitable for vegetarians and vegans. Personalised bottling is also undertaken.

Best Bitter (OG 1036, ABV 3.7%)
This pale amber beer starts with a slight fruit aroma. This leads to a clean, bitter taste where hops and fruit dominate. The finish is long and bitter with a slight hop note.

Black Swan (OG 1038, ABV 3.9%)
A traditional ale, dark and smooth with a full roast flavour.

Wychart Ale (OG 1038, ABV 3.9%)
A full-flavoured beer with a finish of fruit and nut on the palate.

VPA/Vale Pale Ale (OG 1042, ABV 4.2%)
A dry, hoppy ale with a pronounced malt background.

Black Beauty Porter (OG 1043, ABV 4.3%)
A very dark ale, the initial aroma is malty. Roast malt dominates initially and is followed by a rich fruitiness, with some sweetness. The finish is increasingly hoppy and dry.

Edgar's Golden Ale (OG 1043, ABV 4.3%)
A golden, hoppy best bitter with some sweetness and a dry, bittersweet finish. An unpretentious and well-crafted beer.

Special (OG 1046, ABV 4.5%)

Grumpling Premium Ale (OG 1046, ABV 4.6%)

Gravitas (OG 1047, ABV 4.8%)
A strong ale packed with citrus flavours and rounded off by a dry, malty biscuit finish.

Valhalla

Valhalla Brewery, Shetland Refreshments Ltd, Baltasound, Unst, Shetland, ZE2 9DX
☎ (01957) 711658
✉ mail@valhallabrewery.co.uk
🌐 valhallabrewery.co.uk
Tours by arrangement

The brewery started production in 1997, set up by husband and wife team Sonny and Sylvia Priest. A bottling plant was installed in 1999 and work on a new brewhouse is proceeding. One outlet is supplied direct.

White Wife (OG 1038, ABV 3.8%)
Predominantly malty aroma with hop and fruit, which remain on the palate. The aftertaste is increasingly bitter.

Old Scatness (OG 1038, ABV 4%)
A light bitter, named after an archaeological dig at the south end of Shetland where early evidence of malting and brewing was found. One of the ingredients is an ancient strain of barley called Bere which used to be common in Shetland until the middle of the last century.

Simmer Dim (OG 1039, ABV 4%)
A light golden ale, named after the long Shetland twilight. The sulphur features do not mask the fruits and hops of this well-balanced beer.

Auld Rock (OG 1043, ABV 4.5%)
A full-bodied, dark Scottish-style best bitter, it has a rich malty nose but does not lack bitterness in the long dry finish.

Sjolmet Stout (OG 1048, ABV 5%)
Full of malt and roast barley, especially in the taste. Smooth, creamy, fruity finish, not as dry as some stouts.

Ventnor SIBA

Ventnor Brewery Ltd, 119 High Street, Ventnor, Isle of Wight, PO38 1LY
☎ (01983) 856161
✉ sales@ventnorbrewery.co.uk
🌐 ventnorbrewery.co.uk
Shop Mon-Fri 9am-5pm; Sat 10.30am-1pm

Beer has been brewed on the site since 1840. The beers today are still made with St Boniface natural spring water that flows through the brewery. Ventnor has a 10-barrel plant and supplies pub chains, wholesalers and supermarkets nationwide. Seasonal beers: see website. Bottle-conditioned beer is also available. Hygeia Organic Ale is suitable for vegetarians and vegans.

Golden Bitter (OG 1040, ABV 4%)
Creamy, light bitter with hints of honey and gorse persisting through to the aftertaste.

Sunfire (OG 1043, ABV 4.3%)
A generously and distinctively bittered amber beer that could be toned down if pulled through a sparkler.

Hippy High Ale (ABV 4.4%)
A light, hoppy beer brewed especially for Radio 1 DJ Rob Da Bank's first Bestival 2004 on the Isle of Wight.

Pistol Night (OG 1043, ABV 4.4%)
Deceptive light, flowery, hoppy bitter with scents and flavours of early spring that continue through to a pleasant and satisfying finish.

Oyster Stout (OG 1045, ABV 4.5%)
Rich, sugary, malty but watery dark brown beer.

Hygeia Organic Ale (OG 1046, ABV 4.6%)
A malty but refreshing beer.

Wight Spirit (OG 1050, ABV 5%)
Predominantly bitter, hoppy and fruity strong and very pale ale.

Sandrock Smoked Ale (OG 1056, ABV 5.6%)

A smoked beer created to commemorate the famous Sandrock Inn in Niton, tragically destroyed by fire in 1985. Brewed using peated malt and a combination of hops.

Verulam

See Alehouse

Village Brewer

See Hambleton

Wadworth IFBB

Wadworth & Co Ltd, Northgate Brewery, Devizes, Wiltshire, SN10 1JW
☎ (01380) 723361
✉ sales@wadworth.co.uk
🌐 wadworth.co.uk
Shop Mon-Fri 10am-4pm; Sat 10am-1pm
Tours by arrangement

A market town brewery set up in 1885 by Henry Wadworth, it is one of few remaining producers to sell beer locally in oak casks; the brewery still employs a cooper. Though solidly traditional, with its own dray horses, it continues to invest in the future and to expand, producing up to 2,000 barrels a week to supply a wide-ranging free trade, around 300 outlets in the south of England, as well as its own 259 pubs. All tied houses serve cask beer. Wadworth also has a 2.5-barrel micro-brewery used for brewing trials, speciality brews and the production of cask mild. A visitor centre has now opened offering tours of the brewery and cooperage. Seasonal beers: see website.

Henry's Original IPA (OG 1035, ABV 3.6%)
A light copper bitter with a balanced flavour and long-lasting biscuity aftertaste.

6X (OG 1041, ABV 4.3%) ◆
Copper-coloured ale with a malty and fruity nose, and some balancing hop character. The flavour is similar, with some bitterness and a lingering malty, but bitter finish.

JCB (OG 1046, ABV 4.7%)
An amber ale with a rich, malty body, complex hop character and a hint of tropical fruit in the aroma and taste. A barley sugar sweetness blends with nutty malt and hop bitterness before a dry, biscuity, bitter finish.

Wagtail

Wagtail Brewery, New Barn Farm, Wilby Warrens, Old Buckenham, Norfolk, NR17 1PF
☎ (01953) 887133
✉ wagtailbrewery@btinternet.com
🌐 wagtailbrewery.com
Shop Sat 10am-5pm

Wagtail brewery went into full-time production in 2006. There are plans to make it the first brewery to be turbine powered. All cask-conditioned beers are also available bottle conditioned and are suitable for vegetarians and vegans.

Best Bittern (OG 1040, ABV 4%)

Gold Rush (OG 1040, ABV 4%)

English Ale (OG 1042, ABV 4.2%)

Black Shuck (OG 1044, ABV 4.5%)

Hornblower (OG 1044, ABV 4.5%)

King Tut (OG 1044, ABV 4.5%)

Ruby Ale (OG 1044, ABV 4.5%)

Wapping

Wapping Beers Ltd, Baltic Fleet, 33a Wapping, Liverpool, Merseyside, L1 8DQ
☎ (0151) 707 2247 (Brewery) / (0151) 709 3116 (Pub)
✉ simon@wappingbeers.co.uk
🌐 wappingbeers.co.uk
Tours by arrangement

Wapping was established in 2002 using the kit from Passageway Brewery, in the cellar of the Baltic Fleet pub on the waterfront in Liverpool. The pub was refurbished in 2008 including expansion of the brewery. Around 20 new beers are produced each year, the best of which are added to the permanent beers list. Seasonal beers: Tabley Mild (ABV 3.6%, May), Winter Ale (ABV 6.5%, Dec-Jan). Bottle-conditioned beers are also available.

Bitter (OG 1036, ABV 3.6%)
Light, easy-drinking session beer with a good, bitter finish.

Bowsprit (OG 1036, ABV 3.6%) ◆
Dry, hoppy session beer with a satisfyingly dry, bitter aftertaste. Hint of fruitiness on the aroma.

Magnus 800 (OG 1037, ABV 3.7%)

Baltic Gold (OG 1039, ABV 3.9%) ◆
Hoppy golden ale with plenty of citrus hop flavour. Refreshing with good body and mouthfeel.

Blonde Wheat (OG 1045, ABV 4%)

Summer Ale (OG 1042, ABV 4.2%) ◆
Refreshing golden beer with floral hops dominating the nose and taste. Some fruit also on the aroma and in the taste. Good bitterness throughout, leading to a dry, bitter aftertaste.

Smoked Porter (OG 1050, ABV 5%)

Stout (OG 1050, ABV 5%) ◆
Classic dry roasty stout with strong bitterness balanced by fruit and hop flavours. The flavours follow through to a pleasantly dry finish.

Golden Promise IPA (OG 1052, ABV 5.5%)

Warcop

Warcop Country Ales, 9 Nellive Park, St Brides Wentlooge, Gwent, NP10 8SE
☎ (01633) 680058
✉ wiliam.picton@tesco.net
🌐 warcopales.com

A small brewery based in a converted milking parlour. Cask ales are also available bottle conditioned. The brewery has a portfolio of 28 beers which are made on a cyclical basis, with five to six beers normally in stock at any one time: see website for full range. Seasonal beers: see website.

Warrior

Warrior Brewing Co, 4 Old Matford House, Old Matford Lane, Alphington, Exeter, Devon, EX2 8XS
☎ (01392) 221451
✉ warrior@warrior.go-plus.net
🌐 jameswarrior.com

James and Jude Warrior started brewing in 2004. James has been a professional actor for more than 30 years and has to suspend brewing from time to time when he is called away to work in the theatre or appear before the cameras. The brewery has a five-barrel plant and supplies around 12 outlets. Seasonal beer: Custer's Last Stand (ABV 6.8%, Dec-Feb), Sitting Bull Stout (ABV 5%, Dec-Jan).

Golden Wolf (OG 1042, ABV 4%)
A pale golden beer with a biting, clean first taste and a refreshing, floral finish.

Tomahawk (OG 1042, ABV 4%)
A dry, refreshing bitter, full of flavour with a strong, lingering, hoppy taste.

Geronimo (OG 1049, ABV 4.9%)
Full-bodied with a robust and rounded malty flavour and a long, bittersweet finish.

Crazy Horse (OG 1049, ABV 5%)
A light, golden beer with a subtle blend of four different hops and a fresh, dry, distinctive taste.

Warwickshire

Warwickshire Beer Co Ltd, The Brewery, Queen Street, Cubbington, Warwickshire, CV32 7NA
☎ (01926) 450747
✉ info@warwickshirebeer.co.uk
🌐 warwickshirebeer.co.uk
Shop open most days inc. Sat am (please ring first)

Warwickshire is a six-barrel brewery operating in a former village bakery since 1998. Brewing takes place four times a week. The cask beers are available in 15-20 outlets as well as the brewery's four pubs. Bottle-conditioned beers are available.

Shakespeare's County (OG 1034, ABV 3.4%)
A very light session ale.

Best Bitter (OG 1039, ABV 3.9%)
A golden brown session bitter.

Lady Godiva (OG 1042, ABV 4.2%)
Blond, gentle, and full-bodied.

Churchyard Bob (OG 1049, ABV 4.9%)

Golden Bear (OG 1049, ABV 4.9%)
Golden in colour with well-balanced bitterness and spicy/fruity notes.

King Maker (OG 1055, ABV 5.5%)

Watermill

Watermill Brewing Co, Watermill Inn, Ings, Nr Windermere, Cumbria, LA8 9PY
☎ (01539) 821309
✉ info@lakelandpub.co.uk
🌐 lakelandpub.co.uk
Tours by arrangement

Watermill was established in 2006 in a purpose-built extension to the inn. The five-barrel plant and equipment were originally at the Hops Bar & Grill opposite Daytona International Speedway in Florida. The beers have a doggie theme; dogs are allowed in the main bar of the pub and usually get served with biscuits before their owners. The brewery was extended in 2008. Three local outlets are supplied as well as the pub itself.

Collie Wobbles (OG 1037.5, ABV 3.7%)
A pale gold bitter with a slight citrus taste. A good hop and malt balance gives way to a dry finish.

A Bit'er Ruff (OG 1041.5, ABV 4.1%)
Copper-coloured, balanced fruity beer with a lingering, bitter aftertaste.

Ruff Justice (OG 1041, ABV 4.2%)
A malty golden ale, well-balanced with caramel, light floral hops and a fresh, dry finish.

A Winters Tail (OG 1042, ABV 4.3%)
A warming, amber-coloured bitter, smooth in the mouth with a subtle hint of ginger and orange. Well-balanced with a small amount of pale chocolate malt.

Isle of Dogs (OG 1044, ABV 4.5%)
A golden bitter with a fresh, malty aroma and a distinctive citrus fruity flavour with an intense, dry aftertaste.

Wruff Night (OG 1047.5, ABV 5%)
Straw-coloured, sweet and fruity, uncomplicated beer with bitterness in a short-lived aftertaste.

Tomos Watkin SIBA

Hurns Brewing Co Ltd t/a Tomos Watkin, Unit 3, Alberto Road, Century Park, Valley Way, Swansea Enterprise Park, Swansea, SA6 8RP
☎ (01792) 797300
✉ phillparry@tomoswatkin.co.uk
🌐 hurns.co.uk
Shop Mon-Fri 9am-5pm
Tours by arrangement

Brewing started in 1995 in Llandeilo using a 10-barrel plant in converted garages. Tomos Watkin moved to bigger premises in Swansea in 2000 and the plant increased to a 50-barrel capacity. HBC Ltd was formed in 2002 when the Brewery was purchased from Tomos Watkin. Over 50% of production is now bottled beers (not bottle conditioned). More than 300 outlets are supplied. Seasonal beers: see website.

Cwrw Braf (OG 1038, ABV 3.7%)
A clean-drinking, amber-coloured ale with a light bitterness and gentle hop aroma.

Chwarae Teg (OG 1041, ABV 4.1%)
A golden ale with malty, nutty flavours.

Old Style Bitter/OSB (OG 1046, ABV 4.5%)
Amber-coloured with an inviting aroma of hops and malt. Full bodied; hops, fruit, malt and bitterness combine to give a balanced flavour continuing into the finish.

Aber Cwrw (ABV 4.7%)

An easy-drinking golden ale with a clean finish and balance.

Waveney

Waveney Brewing Co, Queen's Head, Station Road, Earsham, Norfolk, NR35 2TS
☎ **(01986) 892623**
✉ **lyndahamps@aol.com**

Established at the Queens Head in 2004, the five-barrel brewery produces three beers, regularly available at the pub along with free trade outlets. Occasional beers are brewed and there are plans to bottle beers. Seasonal beer: Raging Bullace (ABV 5.1%, Dec-Jan), Sugar Ray (ABV 4.4%, Mar-May).

East Coast Mild (OG 1037, ABV 3.8%)
A traditional mild with distinctive roast malt aroma and red-brown colouring. A sweet, plummy malt beginning quickly fades as a dry roasted bitterness begins to make its presence felt.

Lightweight (OG 1039, ABV 3.9%)
A gentle beer with a light but well-balanced hop and malt character. A light body is reflected in the quick, bitter finish. Golden hued with a distinctive strawberry and cream nose.

Great White Hope (OG 1047, ABV 4.8%)
A well-balanced golden brew with a dry, bitter character. Grapefruit in both aroma and taste gives depth and contrast. A long, slightly hoppy ending lingers on.

Wayland's

Wayland's Brewery, 6 Marley Close, Addlestone, Surrey, KT15 1AR
☎ **07956 531618**
✉ **mail@waylandsbrewery.co.uk**
🌐 **waylandsbrewery.co.uk**

Waylands is a small, independent, family-run company, established in summer 2007 on a 2.5-barrel plant. It expanded quickly to a five-barrel plant to meet local demand. 16 outlets are supplied direct. Seasonal beers: Martian Mild (ABV 3.7%, May), Hare Hill (ABV 4.5%), Olympic Gold (ABV 3.9%), Carolinas Pale Ale (ABV 4%), Marley's Ghost (ABV 5.2%, Xmas), Winter Warmer (ABV 4.6%), Dark Knight (ABV 4.2%).

Addled Ale (OG 1043, ABV 4.2%)
The pleasant estery aroma leads to a balanced taste where hops slightly dominate. This continues into the lingering aftertaste of this pale brown best bitter.

Blonde Belle (OG 1044, ABV 4.3%)
A pale golden-coloured ale with a mellow citrus flavour and a good hop character.

Surrey Special (ABV 4.8%)
A powerful, dark and complex ale with rich chocolate and roasted barley notes and a clean, bittersweet finish.

WC

WC Brewery, 3 Micklegate, Mickle Trafford, Chester, CH2 4TF
✉ **thegents@wcbrewery.com**
🌐 **wcbrewery.com**

Founded in 2003 by Ian Williams and Steve Carr, the WC Brewery is one of the smallest commercial breweries in the country. The Gents generally brew to order for local pubs and beer festivals. Seasonal beers: B'Day (ABV 3.8%, summer), Autumn's Platter (ABV 4.3%), Yellow Snow (ABV 5%, winter), Lift A Buttercup (ABV 4%, spring).

IP Ale (ABV 3.8%)
A pale beer, heavily hopped for extra bitterness and a lingering citrus finish.

Kami-Khasi (ABV 3.8%)
A pale and well-hopped bitter.

Golden Cascade (ABV 4%)
A light and refreshing bitter.

Gypsy's Kiss (ABV 4.1%)
A well-balanced pale ale with spicy citrus hop flavours.

Yank My Chain (ABV 4.5%)

SBD (ABV 5%)
A premium ale; rich, fruity and deceptively strong.

Wear Valley

Wear Valley Brewery, The Grand, South Church Road, Bishop Auckland, Co Durham, DL14 6DU
☎ **07810 751425**
✉ **wear-valley@wear-valley-brewery.co.uk**
🌐 **wear-valley-brewery.co.uk**
Tours by arrangement

The brewery was established in 2005 on a four-barrel plant situated at the rear of the Grand Hotel. It was opened by the Bishop of Durham and the first brew was named Bishop's Blessing in his honour. Most of the beers are locally themed. Around 20 outlets are supplied direct. Seasonal beers: Weardale Wheat (ABV 4.3%, Jun-Jul), Weardale Blonde (ABV 4%, Apr-May), Wear Wolf (ABV 4.3%, Oct), Hamsterley Gold (ABV 5%, Jun-Nov), Wear Three Kings (ABV 4.5%, Dec), Auckland Ale (ABV 4.3%, Sep-Oct), Death By Chocolate (ABV 4.6%, Jan-Mar). All beers are suitable for vegetarians and vegans.

Mild-ly Grand (OG 1035, ABV 3.5%)

Weardale Bitter (OG 1037, ABV 3.7%)

Auckland Glory (OG 1038, ABV 3.8%)

Blue Gentian (OG 1040, ABV 4%)

Tindale Tipple (OG 1040, ABV 4%)

Amos Ale (OG 1042, ABV 4.2%)

Eastgate (OG 1042, ABV 4.2%)

Hamsterley Dark Ale (OG 1042, ABV 4.2%)

Excalibur (OG 1045, ABV 4.5%)

Weatheroak

Weatheroak Brewery Ltd, Coach & Horses Inn, Weatheroak Hill, Alvechurch, Birmingham, West Midlands, B48 7EA
☎ **(0121) 445 4411 (eve)**
☎ **07798 773894 (day)**
✉ **dave@weatheroakales.co.uk**
🌐 **weatheroakales.co.uk**

Shop Fri & Sat 5.30-8.30pm

⊗ The brewery was set up in 1997 in an outhouse at the Coach & Horses. The first brew was produced in 1998. A real ale off-licence has been opened in nearby Alvechurch. Weatheroak supplies 40 outlets. Seasonal beers are brewed on a regular basis.

Light Oak (ABV 3.6%) ◈
This straw-coloured quaffing ale has lots of hoppy notes on the tongue and nose, and a fleetingly sweet aftertaste.

Ale (ABV 4.1%) ◈
The aroma is dominated by hops in this golden-coloured brew. Hops also feature in the mouth and there is a rapidly fading dry aftertaste.

Keystone Hops (ABV 5%) ◈
A golden yellow beer that is surprisingly easy to quaff given the strength. Fruity hops are the dominant flavour without the commonly associated astringency.

For Gate Hangs Well, Woodgate:

Scoop (ABV 3.7%)
A honey beer with a pleasing bitter flavour and slightly sweet aftertaste.

Duck and Cover (ABV 4.3%)

Weetwood

Weetwood Ales Ltd, Weetwood Grange, Weetwood, Tarporley, Cheshire, CW6 0NQ
☎ **(01829) 752377**
✉ **sales@weetwoodales.co.uk**
🌐 **weetwoodales.co.uk**

◎ The brewery was set up at an equestrian centre in 1993. In 1998, the five-barrel plant was replaced by a 10-barrel kit. Around 200 regular customers are supplied.

Best Bitter (OG 1038.5, ABV 3.8%) ◈
Pale brown beer with an assertive bitterness and a lingering dry finish. Despite initial sweetness, peppery hops dominate throughout.

Cheshire Cat (ABV 4%) ◈
Pale, dry bitter with a spritzy lemon zest and a grapy aroma. Hoppy aroma leads through to the initial taste before fruitiness takes over. Smooth creamy mouthfeel and a short, dry finish.

Eastgate Ale (OG 1043.5, ABV 4.2%) ◈
Well-balanced and refreshing clean amber beer. Citrus fruit flavours predominate in the taste and there is a short, dry aftertaste.

Old Dog Bitter (OG 1045, ABV 4.5%) ◈
Robust, well-balanced amber beer with a slightly fruity aroma. Rich malt and fruit flavours are balanced by bitterness. Some sweetness and a hint of sulphur on nose and taste.

Ambush Ale (OG 1047.5, ABV 4.8%) ◈
Full-bodied malty, premium bitter with initial sweetness balanced by bitterness and leading to a long-lasting dry finish. Blackberries and bitterness predominate alongside the hops.

Oasthouse Gold (OG 1050, ABV 5%) ◈
Straw-coloured, crisp, full-bodied and fruity golden ale with a good dry finish.

Wellington

See Crown

Wells & Young's

See New Nationals section

Welton's SIBA

Welton's Brewery, 1 Mulberry Trading Estate, Foundry Lane, Horsham, West Sussex, RH13 5PX
☎ **(01403) 242901/251873**
✉ **sales@weltons.co.uk**
🌐 **weltonsbeer.com**
Tours by arrangement

Ray Welton moved his brewery to a factory unit in Horsham in 2003, which has given him space to expand. Many different beers are brewed throughout the year. Around 400 outlets are supplied. Bottle-conditioned beers are available.

Pride 'n' Joy (ABV 2.8%) ◈
A light brown bitter with a slight malty and hoppy aroma. Fruity with a pleasant hoppiness and some sweetness in the flavour, leading to a short malty finish.

Horsham Bitter (ABV 3.8%)
Amber-coloured, bitter but with a huge aroma.

Old Cocky (OG 1043, ABV 4.3%)

Horsham Old (OG 1046, ABV 4.6%) ◈
Roast and toffee flavours predominate with some bitterness in this traditional old ale. Bittersweet with plenty of caramel and roast in a rather short finish.

Export Stout (ABV 4.7%)
Hints of burnt toast, balanced by good levels of hops with a long finish.

Old Harry (OG 1051, ABV 5.2%)

Wensleydale

Wensleydale Brewery Ltd, Manor Road, Bellerby, Leyburn, North Yorkshire, DL8 5QH
☎ **(01969) 622327**
✉ **info@wensleydalebrewery.com**
🌐 **wensleydalebrewery.com**
Tours by arrangement

⊗ Wensleydale Brewery (formerly Lidstone's) was set up in 2003 on a two-barrel plant in Yorkshire Dales National Park. A year later the brewery relocated to larger premises six miles away. Most beers are also available bottle conditioned. About 30 outlets are supplied.

Lidstone's Rowley Mild (OG 1037, ABV 3.2%) ◈
Chocolate and toffee aromas lead into what, for its strength, is an impressively rich and flavoursome taste. The finish is pleasantly bittersweet.

Forester's Session Bitter (OG 1038, ABV 3.7%) ◈
Intensely aromatic, straw-coloured ale offering a superb balance of malt and hops on the tongue.

Semer Water (OG 1041, ABV 4.1%)

Golden ale with a hint of banana on the nose. The taste is clean, crisp and hoppy, with grapefruit flavours also present.

Coverdale Gamekeeper (OG 1042, ABV 4.3%)
A light copper best bitter with a lingering aftertaste.

Aysgarth Falls (ABV 4.4%)
A thirst-quenching cloudy wheat beer with tart apple and banana fruit.

Black Dub Oat Stout (OG 1044, ABV 4.4%)
Black beer brimming with roasted chocolate taste and aroma.

Coverdale Poacher IPA (OG 1049, ABV 5%) ◆
Citrus flavours dominate both aroma and taste in this pale, smooth, refreshing beer; the aftertaste is quite dry.

Hardraw Force Strong Ale (ABV 5.6%)
A well-balanced premium ale with a fine malty, hoppy character.

Barley Wine (ABV 8.5%)
A rich, complex, strong ale with a lingering bittersweet aftertaste.

Wentworth SIBA

Wentworth Brewery Ltd, Power House, Gun Park, Wentworth, South Yorkshire, S62 7TF
☎ (01226) 747070
✉ info@wentworth-brewery.co.uk
🌐 wentworth-brewery.co.uk
Tours by arrangement

Brewing started at Wentworth in 1999. In 2006 custom-built brewing kit was installed, increasing production to 30 barrels a day. More than 300 outlets are supplied.

Imperial Ale (OG 1038, ABV 3.8%)
A tawny, bitter beer with a floral nose. There is a slight hint of sweetness on the aftertaste.

WPA (OG 1039.5, ABV 4%) ◆
An extremely well hopped IPA-style beer that leads to some astringency. A very bitter beer.

Best Bitter (OG 1040, ABV 4.1%) ◆
A hoppy, bitter beer with hints of citrus fruits. A bitter taste dominates the aftertaste.

Bumble Beer (OG 1043, ABV 4.3%) ▣
A pale golden beer, made with local honey, which gives it a unique and distinctive flavour throughout the year.

Black Zac (OG 1046, ABV 4.6%)
A mellow, dark ruby-red ale with chocolate and pale malts leading to a bitter taste, with a coffee finish.

Oatmeal Stout (OG 1050, ABV 4.8%) ◆
Black, smooth, with roast and chocolate malt and toffee overtones.

Rampant Gryphon (OG 1062, ABV 6.2%) ◆
A strong, well-balanced golden ale with hints of fruit and sweetness but which retains a hoppy character.

Wessex SIBA

CF Hobden t/a Wessex Brewery, Rye Hill Farm, Longbridge Deverill, Warminster, Wiltshire, BA12 7DE
☎ (01985) 844532
✉ wessexbrewery@tinyworld.co.uk
Tours by arrangement

⊗ The brewery went into production in 2001 as Hobden's Wessex Brewery and moved to a new building in 2004, at which time the name Wessex Brewery was adopted. 15 outlets are supplied by the brewery with all beers always available through wholesalers.

Naughty Ferret (OG 1037, ABV 3.5%)
A session bitter with full flavour. Tawny colour, spicy bitterness and citrus hop aroma.

Horningsham Pride (OG 1040, ABV 4%)
A pale, sweet, hoppy beer.

Crockerton Classic (OG 1041, ABV 4.1%)
A full-bodied, tawny, full-flavoured bitter; fruity and malty.

Kilmington Best (OG 1041, ABV 4.2%)
Sweet, hoppy bitter.

Deverill's Advocate (OG 1046, ABV 4.5%)

Warminster Warrior (OG 1045, ABV 4.5%)

Russian Stoat (OG 1080, ABV 9%)

West Berkshire SIBA

West Berkshire Brewery Co Ltd, Old Bakery, Yattendon, Thatcham, Berkshire, RG18 0UE
☎ (01635) 202968/202638
✉ info@wbbrew.co.uk
🌐 wbbrew.co.uk
Shop Mon-Fri 10am-4pm; Sat 10am-4pm
Tours by arrangement

The brewery, established in 1995, has since moved its main site to Yattendon. In 2006 the brewhouse was extended and a new plant installed, the original five-barrel plant at the Potkiln pub in Failsham has now closed. Around 100 outlets are supplied. One pub is owned, and the brewery hopes to acquire more to build a small estate. A monthly beer is also brewed – the beer names follow an annual theme.

Old Father Thames (OG 1038, ABV 3.4%)
A traditional pale ale with a full flavour despite its low strength.

Mr Chubb's Lunchtime Bitter (OG 1040, ABV 3.7%) ◆
A malty session bitter. A malty caramel note dominates aroma and taste and is accompanied by a nutty bittersweetness and a hoppy aroma.

Maggs' Magnificent Mild (OG 1041, ABV 3.8%) ◻ ▣ ◆
Silky, full-bodied dark mild with a creamy head. Roast malt aroma is joined in the taste by caramel, sweetness and mild, fruity hoppiness. Aftertaste of roast malt with balancing bitterness.

Good Old Boy (OG 1043, ABV 4%) ◆
Well-rounded, tawny bitter with malt and hops dominating throughout and a balancing bitterness in the taste and aftertaste.

Dr Hexter's Wedding Ale (OG 1044, ABV 4.1%) ◆
Fruit and hops dominate the aroma and are joined in the bittersweet taste by a hint of malt. The aftertaste has a pleasant bitter hoppiness.

Full Circle (OG 1047, ABV 4.5%) ◆
A golden ale with a pleasing aroma and taste of bitter hops with a hint of malt. The aftertaste is hoppy and bitter with a rounding note of malt.

Dr Hexter's Healer (OG 1052, ABV 5%) ◆
Amber strong bitter with malt, caramel and hops in the aroma. The taste is a balance of malt, caramel, fruit, hops and bittersweetness. Caramel, fruit and bitter-sweetness dominate the aftertaste.

West

West Brewery, Bar & Restaurant, Binnie Place, Glasgow Green, Glasgow, G40 1AW
☎ (0141) 550 0135
petra@westbeer.com
westbeer.com
Tours by arrangement
No real ale. West opened in 2006 and produces a full range of European-style beers. The brewery's copper-clad system, visible from the 300-seat bar and restaurant, is a fully-automated German one with an annual capacity of 1.5 million litres. Brewing is in strict accordance with the Reinheitsgebot, the German purity law, importing all malt, hops and yeast from Germany. Beers: Hefeweizen (ABV 4.9%); Munich-Style Helles (ABV 5%); St Mungo (ABV 4.9%); Helles Light (ABV 3.8%); Dunkel Hefeweizen (ABV 5.3%); Dunkel (ABV 4.9%).

Westbury

See Wessex

Westerham SIBA

Westerham Brewery Co Ltd, Grange Farm, Pootings Road, Crockham Hill, Edenbridge, Kent, TN8 6SA
☎ (01732) 864427
sales@westerhambrewery.co.uk
westerhambrewery.co.uk
Shop Mon-Fri 9am-5pm
Tours by arrangement (min 20 people, charge made)
The brewery was established in 2004 and restored a brewing tradition to Westerham that was lost when the Black Eagle Brewery was taken over by Ind Coope in 1959 and closed in 1965. Two of Black Eagle's yeast strains were deposited at the National Collection of Yeast Cultures and are used to recreate the true flavour of Westerham beers. The new brewery is based at the National Trust's Grange Farm in a former dairy and uses the same water supply as Black Eagle. Around 130 outlets are supplied in Kent, Surrey and Sussex. Seasonal beers: see website. Bottle-conditioned beers are also available.

Finchcocks Original (OG 1036.2, ABV 3.5%)

Black Eagle Special Pale Ale (OG 1038.5, ABV 3.8%)

Grasshopper Kentish Bitter (OG 1039, ABV 3.8%)

British Bulldog (OG 1043.5, ABV 4.3%)

William Wilberforce Freedom Ale (OG 1044, ABV 4.3%)

India Pale Ale (OG 1047, ABV 4.8%)

Special Bitter Ale 1965 (OG 1047.5, ABV 4.9%)

WF6

WF6 Brewing Co, c/o 21 Rose Farm Approach, Altofts, West Yorkshire, WF6 2RZ
☎ 07876 141336/07767 351611
r.d.turton@btinternet.com
wf6brewingcompany.co.uk
WF6 began brewing in 2004 with the brand name Birkwoods. The brewery is in a converted milking parlour. A custom-made five-barrel plant allows the brewery to produce a varying portfolio of seasonal beers, mostly at ABV 4.2%, that are supplied to distributors, pubs and festivals. Bottled beers are sold at farmers' markets. Brewing is currently suspended.

Whalebone

Whalebone Brewery, 163 Wincolmlee, Hull, East Yorkshire, HU2 0PA
☎ (01482) 226648
Tours by arrangement
The Whalebone pub, which dates from 1796, was bought by Hull CAMRA founding member Alex Craig in 2002. He opened the brewery the following year and his beers have names connected with the former whaling industry on the adjoining River Hull. Two or three outlets are supplied as well as the pub. Seasonal beers: Truelove Porter (ABV 4.7%), Joseph Allen (ABV 5%), Moby Dick (ABV 8%), Full Ship (ABV 8.4%).

Diana Mild (OG 1037, ABV 3.5%)

Neckoil Bitter (OG 1039, ABV 3.9%)

Wharfedale

See Dark Horse

Whim SIBA

Whim Ales Ltd, Whim Farm, Hartington, Derbyshire, SK17 0AX
☎ (01298) 84991

A brewery opened in 1993 in outbuildings at Whim Farm. Whim's beers are available in 50-70 outlets and the brewery's tied house, the Wilkes Head in Leek, Staffs. Some one-off brews are produced. Occasional/seasonal beers: Kaskade (ABV 4.3%, lager), Snow White (ABV 4.5%, wheat beer), Easter Special (ABV 4.8%), Stout Jenny (ABV 4.7%), Black Xmas (ABV 6.5%).

Arbor Light (OG 1035, ABV 3.6%)
Light-coloured bitter, sharp and clean with lots of hop character and a delicate light aroma.

Hartington Bitter (OG 1039, ABV 4%)
A light, golden-coloured, well-hopped session beer. A dry finish with a spicy, floral aroma.

Hartington IPA (OG 1045, ABV 4.5%)

Pale and light-coloured, smooth on the palate allowing malt to predominate. Slightly sweet finish combined with distinctive light hop bitterness. Well rounded.

White Horse

White Horse Brewery Co Ltd, 3 Ware Road, White Horse Business Park, Stanford-in-the-Vale, Oxfordshire, SN7 8NY
☎ (01367) 718700
🌐 whitehorsebrewery.com
Tours by arrangement

White Horse was founded on a modern industrial estate in 2004. The second-hand brewing plant was manufactured in Belgium and has a brew-length of 7.5 barrels. It uses the continental method of brewing with a lauter tun rather than an infusion mash tun. More than 150 outlets are supplied direct. Seasonal beers: Dragon Hill (ABV 4.2%, autumn), Flibbertigibbet (ABV 4.3%, summer), Saracen IPA (ABV 4.5%, spring), Giant (ABV 4.3%, winter), Rudolf The Red Nosed White Horse (ABV 4.8%, Xmas).

Oxfordshire Bitter (OG 1039, ABV 3.7%)
Golden bitter, well-hopped with a clean, fruity finish.

Village Idiot (OG 1044.5, ABV 4.1%)
A blonde ale with a complex hop aroma and taste.

Wayland Smithy (OG 1049, ABV 4.4%)
A red-brown ale with a nice biscuit flavour that is balanced with a spicy hop finish.

Black Horse Porter (OG 1052, ABV 5%)
Dark red porter with a chocolate character and a fruity/berry hop aroma and taste.

Guv'nor (OG 1066, ABV 6.5%)
A strong ale with a fruity finish.

For Turf Tavern, Oxford:

Summer Ale (OG 1042, ABV 4.1%)
A golden ale with a dry aftertaste.

Whitehaven*

Whitehaven Brewing Co Ltd, Croasdale Farm Barn, Ennerdale, Cleator, Cumbria, CA23 3AT
☎ (01946) 861755
🌐 twbcl.co.uk

The brewery was established in late 2007 on a 10-barrel plant.

Croasdale (ABV 3.4%)

Ennerdale (ABV 3.6%)

White Park*

White Park Brewery, Perry Hill Farm, Bourne End Road, Cranfield, Beds, MK43 0BA
☎ (01223) 911357
✉ info@whiteparkbrewery.co.uk
🌐 whiteparkbrewery.co.uk

White Park started brewing in late 2007 on a five-barrel plant.

First Flight (ABV 3.7%)

White Gold (ABV 3.8%)

Blonde (ABV 4%)

Cranfield Bitter (ABV 4.4%)

Nightjar (ABV 4.5%)

Whitewater

Whitewater Brewing Co, 40 Tullyframe Road, Kilkeel, Co Down, Northern Ireland, BT34 4RZ
☎ (028) 4176 9449
✉ bernard@whitewaterbrewing.co.uk
🌐 whitewaterbrewing.co.uk
Tours by arrangement

Set up in 1996, Whitewater is now the biggest brewery in Northern Ireland. The brewery has a 15-barrel brew length and produces 14 different ales and a real lager. Currently, Whitewater supplies 15 outlets and owns one pub, the White Horse, Saintfield, Co. Down. Seasonal beers: Solstice Pale (ABV 4%, summer), Nut Brown (ABV 4%, winter), Snake Drive (ABV 4.3%, spring), Sanity Claus (ABV 4.5%, Xmas), Bee's Endeavour (ABV 4.8%, autumn).

Mill Ale (OG 1038, ABV 3.7%)
A golden-coloured, light ale.

Blonde Lager (OG 1040, ABV 4%)

Glen Ale (OG 1043, ABV 4.2%)

Belfast Ale (OG 1046, ABV 4.5%)

White SIBA

White Brewing Co, 1066 Country Brewery, Pebsham Farm Industrial Estate, Pebsham Lane, Bexhill-on-Sea, East Sussex, TN40 2RZ
☎ (01424) 731066
✉ whitebrewing@fsbdial.co.uk
🌐 white-brewing.co.uk
Tours by arrangement

The brewery was founded in 1995 to serve local free trade outlets and some wholesalers. White has expanded production threefold with the addition of seasonal and occasional beers. Around 30 outlets are supplied. Seasonal beers: White Gold (ABV 4.9%, summer), Chilly Willy (ABV 5.1%, winter), Old White Christmas (ABV 4%). Bottle-conditioned beers are also available.

1066 Country Bitter (OG 1040, ABV 4%)
Amber-gold in colour, a light, sweetish beer with good malt and hop balance, and a bitter, refreshing finish.

Dark (OG 1040, ABV 4%)

Heart of Rother (ABV 4.5%)

Whitstable

Whitstable Brewery, Little Telpits Farm, Woodcock Lane, Grafty Green, Kent, ME17 2AY
☎ (01622) 851007
✉ whitstablebrewery@btconnect.com
🌐 whitstablebrewery.info
Tours by arrangement

Whitstable came about in 2003 when the Green family purchased the Swale and North Weald Brewery to supply their own outlets (a hotel and two restaurants) in Whitstable, and beer festival orders. In 2006 they opened a bar in East Quay selling their own beers and other micros. Seasonal beer: Kentish Reserve (ABV 5%, winter).

Native Bitter (OG 1037, ABV 3.7%)

East India Pale Ale (OG 1040, ABV 4.1%)
A light, refreshing pale ale with floral hop aroma and bitterness that give a well-balanced flavour.

Oyster Stout (OG 1047, ABV 4.5%)
Rich and dry with deep chocolate and mocha flavours.

Bohemium (OG 1044, ABV 4.9%)
Dry-hopped, cask-conditioned lager.

Wheat Beer (OG 1049, ABV 5%)

Raspberry Wheat (OG 1049, ABV 5.2%)

Whittington's SIBA

Whittington's Brewery, Three Choirs Vineyards Ltd, Newent, Gloucestershire, GL18 1LS
☎ (01531) 890555
✉ brewery@threechoirs.com
🌐 whittingtonbrewery.co.uk
Shop 9am-5pm daily (open later during summer)
Tours by arrangement (for a charge)

☺Whittington's started in 2003 using a purpose-built five-barrel plant producing 20 barrels a week. Dick Whittington came from nearby Gloucester, hence the name and feline theme. Around 80 outlets are supplied direct. Seasonal beers: Nine Lives (ABV 3.6%, Oct), Old Tom (ABV 3.9%, Mar-Apr), Summer Pale Ale (ABV 4%, May-Aug), Winters Tail (ABV 5.1%, Oct-Mar). Bottle-conditioned beer is also available.

Cats Whiskers (OG 1041, ABV 4.2%)

Why Not

Why Not Brewery, 17 Cavalier Close, Thorpe St Andrew, Norwich, Norfolk, NR7 0TE
☎ (01603) 300786
✉ colin@thewhynotbrewery.co.uk
🌐 thewhynotbrewery.co.uk

Why Not opened in 2006 with equipment located in a shed and custom-made by Brendan Moore of Iceni Brewery. The brewery can produce up to two barrels per brew. All beers are available in bottle-conditioned form and are occasionally put into casks to order.

Wally's Revenge (OG 1040, ABV 4%) ◆
An overtly bitter beer with a hoppy background. The bitterness holds on to the end as an increasing astringent dryness develops.

Roundhead Porter (OG 1045, ABV 4.5%)
A traditional old style London porter.

Cavalier Red (OG 1047, ABV 4.7%) ◆
Explosive fruity nose belies the gentleness of the taste. The summer fruit aroma dominates this red-gold brew. A sweet, fruity start disappears under a quick, bitter ending.

Norfolk Honey Ale (OG 1050, ABV 5%)
A golden beer with a honey nose. A definite hop edge leaves a honey aftertaste.

Chocolate Nutter (OG 1056, ABV 5.5%)

Wibblers*

Wibblers Brewery Ltd, c/o 11 Orchard Drive, Mayland, Essex, CM3 6EP
☎ (01621) 789003
☎ 07775 577982
✉ info@wibblers.com
🌐 wibblers.com

Wibblers was established commercially in August 2007 on a purpose-built 2.5-barrel plant. It also brews the now defunct Blanchfield Brewery beers. Special beers are brewed every month.

Quaffing Ale (OG 1035, ABV 3.5%)
Golden ale with light bitterness and a citrus aroma.

IPA Twist (OG 1036, ABV 3.6%)
Lightly hopped, dark golden in colour with a coriander twist.

Apprentice (OG 1039, ABV 3.9%)
Copper-brown ale with a pleasant hop finish.

Raging Bull (OG 1050, ABV 4.9%)
A special bitter with a malty flavour.

Stoat (OG 1050, ABV 4.9%)
A dry stout with coffee roasted bitterness, lightly hopped aroma with a higher bitterness to balance it out.

Wicked Hathern

Wicked Hathern Brewery Ltd, 17 Nixon Walk, East Leake, Leicestershire, LE12 6HL
☎ (01509) 559308
✉ sean.oneill@escapade-rs.com
🌐 wicked-hathern.co.uk

Opened in 2000, the brewery generally supplies beer on a guest basis to many local pubs and beer festivals, and brews commissioned beers for special occasions. All beers are available bottled from selected off licences (see website) and from Hathern Stores. Special cask beer is brewed for the Albion Inn, Loughborough, and special bottled beers for Hathern Stores and Alexander Wines in Earlsdon. The brewery itself is not currently operating and the beers are being produced by the Wicked Hathern brewers at Leek Brewery (qv). Seasonal beer: Gladstone Tidings (ABV 5.1%, Xmas).

Dobles' Dog (OG 1035, ABV 3.5%)
A full-bodied, stout-like dark mild with fruit and nut flavours on the palate. Gently bitter, malty finish with a lingering hint of roasted malts.

WHB/Wicked Hathern Bitter (OG 1038, ABV 3.8%)
A light-tasting session bitter with a dry palate and good hop aroma.

Cockfighter (OG 1043, ABV 4.2%)
A copper-coloured beer with an aroma of fruit, creamy malt and hop resins.

Hawthorn Gold (OG 1045, ABV 4.5%)
A pale golden ale with delicate malt and spicy hop in the aroma. The taste is hoppy and mostly bitter but with good malt support and body. Dry, malt and hops aftertaste.

Derby Porter (OG 1048, ABV 4.8%)

A deep ruby porter with a creamy nose of lightly smoky, chocolaty, nutty dark malts.

Soar Head (OG 1048, ABV 4.8%)
A dark ruby-coloured strong bitter with a cocktail of distinctive flavours.

Swift 'Un (OG 1048, ABV 4.8%)
A light-golden mellow beer with fruity overtones.

For Albion, Canal Bank, Loughborough:

Albion Special (OG 1041, ABV 4%)
A light, copper-coloured bitter with a nutty aroma and smoky malt taste, hops leading through.

Wickwar SIBA

Wickwar Brewing Co Ltd, Old Brewery, Station Road, Wickwar, Gloucestershire, GL12 8NB
☎ 0870 777 5671
bob@wickwarbrewing.co.uk
wickwarbrewing.co.uk
Shop Wed-Fri 9.30am-4.30pm; Sat 10am-12pm (Tel 01454 299592)
Tours by arrangement

Wickwar was established in 1990 in the cooper's shop of the former Arnold Perrett Brewery and since 2004 its home has been the original early 19th-century brewery. In addition to supplying beers to some 350 outlets in the vicinity of the brewery, Wickwar also supplies Coors, Scottish & Newcastle, Waverley TBS and Wetherspoon. Seasonal beers: see website. Bottle-conditioned beers are also available.

Coopers WPA (OG 1036.5, ABV 3.5%)
Golden-coloured, this well-balanced beer is light and refreshing, with hops, citrus fruit, apple/pear flavour and notable pale malt character. Bitter, dry finish.

Brand Oak Bitter (BOB) (OG 1039, ABV 4%)
Amber-coloured, this has a distinctive blend of hop, malt and apple/pear citrus fruits. The slightly sweet taste turns into a fine, dry bitterness, with a similar malty-lasting finish.

Cotswold Way (OG 1043, ABV 4.2%)
Amber-coloured, it has a pleasant aroma of pale malt, hop and fruit. Good dry bitterness in the taste with some sweetness. Similar though less sweet in the finish, with good hop content.

Rite Flanker (OG 1043, ABV 4.3%)
Amber in colour with a big malt taste and fruit notes and a hoppy finish.

IKB (OG 1045, ABV 4.5%)
A ruby-red ale with a complex hop aroma and flavour derived from the use of three hop varieties. Flowery but well balanced.

Old Arnold (OG 1047, ABV 4.8%)
A full-flavoured and well-balanced ale with malt, hops and cherry fruit throughout. Amber/pale brown, it is slightly sweet with a long-lasting, malty, dry, fruity and increasingly bitter finish.

Mr Perretts Traditional Stout (OG 1059, ABV 5.9%)
Aroma and taste of smoky chocolate malts and peppery hops. Dark fruits of black cherry and blackcurrant give hints of sweetness to the dry, quite bitter, slightly spicy, well-balanced taste.

Station Porter (OG 1062, ABV 6.1%)
This is a rich, smooth, dark ruby-brown ale. Starts with roast malt; coffee, chocolate and dark fruit then develops a complex, spicy, bittersweet taste and a long roast finish.

Williams SIBA

Williams Brothers Brewing Co/Heather Ale Ltd, New Alloa Brewery, Kelliebank, Alloa, FK10 1NT
☎ (01259) 725511
fraoch@heatherale.co.uk
heatherale.co.uk
Tours by arrangement

Bruce and Scott Williams started brewing Heather Ale in the West Highlands in 1993. A range of indigenous, historical ales were added over the following 10 years. The brothers now have their own 40-barrel brewery and bottling line and produce a range of hoppy beers under the Williams Bros banner as well as continuing with the range of historical ales. Around 30 outlets are supplied. Seasonal beers: Ebulum (ABV 6.5%, winter), Alba (ABV 7.5%, winter).

Gold (OG 1040, ABV 3.9%)

Fraoch Heather Ale (OG 1041, ABV 4.1%)
The unique taste of heather flowers is noticeable in this beer. A fine floral aroma and spicy taste give character to this drinkable speciality beer.

Black (OG 1042, ABV 4.2%)

Roisin-Tayberry (OG 1042, ABV 4.2%)

Red (OG 1045, ABV 4.5%)

Grozet (OG 1047, ABV 5%)

Joker (OG 1047, ABV 5%)

Willoughby*

Willoughby Brewing Co, Brockhampton Brewery, Whitbourne, Worcestershire, WR6 5SH
☎ 07974 371294

Willoughby began brewing in June 2008 on a six-barrel plant. Bottle-conditioned beers are planned.

Tried & Trusted (ABV 4.2%)

Willy's SIBA

Willy's Wine Bar Ltd, 17 High Cliff Road, Cleethorpes, Lincolnshire, DN35 8RQ
☎ (01472) 602145
Tours by arrangement

The brewery opened in 1989 to provide beer for its two pubs in Grimsby and Cleethorpes. It has a five-barrel plant with maximum capacity of 15 barrels a week. The brewery can be viewed at any time from pub or street.

Original Bitter (OG 1038, ABV 3.8%)
A light brown 'sea air' beer with a fruity, tangy hop on the nose and taste, giving a strong bitterness tempered by the underlying malt.

Burcom Bitter (OG 1044, ABV 4.2%)

Sometimes known as Mariner's Gold, although the beer is dark ruby in colour. It is a smooth and creamy brew with a sweet chocolate-bar maltiness, giving way to an increasingly bitter finish.

Last Resort (OG 1044, ABV 4.3%)

Weiss Buoy (OG 1045, ABV 4.5%)
A cloudy wheat beer.

Coxswains Special (OG 1050, ABV 4.9%)

Old Groyne (OG 1060, ABV 6.2%) ◈
An initial sweet banana fruitiness blends with malt to give a vanilla quality to the taste and slightly bitter aftertaste. A copper-coloured beer reminiscent of a Belgian ale.

Windie Goat

▤ Windie Goat Brewery, Failford Inn, Failford, South Ayrshire, KA5 5TF
☎ (01292) 540117
✉ enquiries@windiegoatbrewery.co.uk
🌐 windiegoatbrewery.co.uk

Established in 2006 in the old cellar of the Failford Inn, the brewery is named after an area of local woodland with the beer names derived from fishing pools in the River Ayr. Beer is supplied mainly to the inn and also to beer festivals on request. Further regular beers are planned.

Peden's Cove (ABV 3.5%)
A pale bitter, named after the area from where Alexander Peden preached.

Priest's Wheel (ABV 4.3%)
An amber ale with pale and crystal malt using three varieties of American hops.

The Dubh (ABV 4.6%)
A chocolate porter with a smooth, easy-drinking finish.

Windrush

See Burford

Windsor Castle

Windsor Castle Brewery Ltd t/a Sadler's Ales, 7 Stourbridge Road, Lye, Stourbridge, West Midlands, DY9 7DG
☎ (01384) 895230
✉ enquiries@windsorcastlebrewery.com
🌐 windsorcastlebrewery.com
Tours by arrangement

Thomas Alexander Sadler founded the original brewery in 1900 adjacent to the Windsor Castle Inn, Oldbury. Fourth generation brewers John and Chris Sadler re-opened the brewery in its new location in 2004. The brewery tap house was built and opened in 2006 next to the brewery. Around 250 outlets are supplied. An extensive range of bottle-conditioned beers are available as well as beer-based cheeses and condiments.

Jack's Ale (OG 1037, ABV 3.8%)
A very pale, hoppy bitter with a crisp and zesty lemon undertone.

Green Man (ABV 4%)
A smooth pale ale, brewed with lager hops.

Mild Ale (OG 1039, ABV 4%)
A Black Country dark mild with hints of chocolate and a dry finish.

Worcester Sorcerer (OG 1043, ABV 4.3%)
Brewed with English hops and barley with hints of mint and lemon, creating a floral aroma and crisp bitterness.

Mellow Yellow (OG 1045, ABV 4.5%)
A pale ale brewed with plenty of hop and honey.

Thin Ice (OG 1045, ABV 4.5%)
A pale ale. Bitter but with an orange and lemon finish.

IPA (OG 1048, ABV 4.8%)

Mud City Stout (OG 1066, ABV 6.6%)
Rich, full-bodied strong stout brewed with raw cocoa, fresh vanilla pods, oats, wheat and dark malts.

Winter's SIBA

Winter's Brewery, 8 Keelan Close, Norwich, Norfolk, NR6 6QZ
☎ (01603) 787820
✉ sales@wintersbrewery.com
🌐 wintersbrewery.com

David Winter, who had previous award-winning success as brewer for both Woodforde's and Chalk Hill breweries, decided to set up on his own in 2001. He purchased the brewing plant from the now defunct Scott's Brewery in Lowestoft. The local free trade is supplied.

Mild (OG 1036.5, ABV 3.6%) ◈
A solid malty mild with roast overtones and well-balanced, bittersweet undercurrent. A slightly coarse mouthfeel adds to the overall character of an olde time mild.

Bitter (OG 1039.5, ABV 3.8%) ◈
A well-balanced amber bitter. Hops and malt are balanced by a crisp citrus fruitiness. A pleasant hoppy nose with a hint of grapefruit. Long, sustained, dry, grapefruit finish.

Golden (ABV 4.1%) ◈
Just a hint of hops in the aroma. The initial taste combines a dry bitterness with a fruity apple buttress. The finish slowly subsides into a long, dry bitterness.

Revenge (OG 1047, ABV 4.7%) ◈
Blackcurrant notes give depth to the inherent maltiness of this pale brown beer. A bittersweet background becomes more pronounced as the fruitiness gently wanes.

Storm Force (OG 1053, ABV 5.3%) ◈
Rich and heavy with blackcurrant, sultanas and pepper vying with the more traditional malt and hop flavours. A long cloying finish loses both malt and hops.

Tempest (OG 1062, ABV 6.2%) ◈
Malt is foremost in both aroma and initial taste. A heavy fruitiness overwhelms the background hops and bitterness. The sweetness remains constant as the malt dwindles.

Wirksworth*

Wirksworth Brewery, 25 St John Street, Wirksworth, Derbyshire, DE4 4DR
☎ (01629) 824011
wirksworthbrewery.com

Wirksworth started brewing in autumn 2007 in a converted workshop on a 2.5-barrel plant. It was started as a retirement project by Jeff Green and supplies around 12 local Derbyshire pubs.

Cruckbeam (OG 1040, ABV 3.9%)

T'owd Man (OG 1050, ABV 4.9%)

Wissey Valley

Wissey Valley Brewery, Clover Club, Low Road, Wretton, Norfolk, PE33 9QN
☎ (01366) 500767
info@wisseyvalleybrewery.com
wisseyvalleybrewery.com
Tours by arrangement

The brewery was launched in 2002 as Captain Grumpy's and in 2003 moved to Stoke Ferry and was re-established as Wissey Valley. The brewery re-launched in 2006, moving to the neighbouring village of Wretton. Around 15 outlets are supplied direct as well as wholesalers and beer festivals. Bottle-conditioned beers are available.

Bitter (OG 1036, ABV 3.7%)

Missey Wissey Blackberry Ale (OG 1036, ABV 3.7%)

Old Grumpy Bitter (OG 1043, ABV 4.5%)

Walsingham Ale (OG 1043, ABV 4.5%)

Old Grumpy Porter (OG 1049, ABV 5%)

Tishtash Coriander Ale (OG 1047, ABV 5%)

Wizard SIBA

Wizard Ales, Unit 4, Lundy View, Mullacott Cross Industrial Estate, Ilfracombe, Devon, EX34 8PY
☎ (01271) 865350
mike@wizardales.co.uk
wizardales.co.uk
Tours by arrangement

Brewing started in 2003 on a 1.25-barrel plant, since upgraded to five-barrels. The brewery moved from Warwickshire to Devon in 2007. Around 20 local outlets are supplied. Seasonal beer: Bah Humbug (ABV 5.8%, Xmas).

Apprentice (OG 1038, ABV 3.6%)

Black Magic (OG 1040, ABV 4%)

One For The Toad (OG 1041, ABV 4%)

Mother in Law (OG 1043, ABV 4.2%)

Sorcerer (OG 1044, ABV 4.3%)

White Witch (OG 1045, ABV 4.5%)

Bullfrog (OG 1047, ABV 4.8%)

Druid's Fluid (OG 1048, ABV 5%)

Wold Top SIBA

Wold Top Brewery, Hunmanby Grange, Wold Newton, Driffield, East Yorkshire, YO25 3HS
☎ (01723) 892222
enquiries@woldtopbrewery.co.uk
woldtopbrewery.co.uk

Wold Top started brewing in 2003 and is an integral part of Hunmanby Grange, a family farm. It uses home-grown malting barley, chalk-filtered borehole water and some home-grown hops. Over 300 outlets are supplied. Seasonal beers: A4 Amber (ABV 4.4% spring & autumn), 5 Wold Rings (ABV 5%, Nov-Jan), Cracker Black (ABV 6%, Nov-Jan).

Wolds Way Pale Ale (OG 1036, ABV 3.6%)

Bitter (OG 1037, ABV 3.7%)

Falling Stone (OG 1041, ABV 4.2%)

Voluptuous Vicky (OG 1043, ABV 4.4%)

Mars Magic (OG 1044, ABV 4.6%)

Wold Gold (OG 1046, ABV 4.8%)

For Fine Ale Club, Colchester:

Against the Grain (OG 1046, ABV 4.5%)
Gluten-free beer.

Wolf

WBC (Norfolk) Ltd t/a The Wolf Brewery, Rookery Farm, Silver Street, Besthorpe, Attleborough, Norfolk, NR17 2LD
☎ (01953) 457775
info@wolfbrewery.com
wolfbrewery.com
Shop Mon-Fri 9am-5pm
Tours by arrangement

The brewery was founded by Wolfe Witham in 1996 using a 20-barrel plant. More than 200 outlets are supplied. Seasonal beers: see website.

Edith Cavell (ABV 3.7%)

Golden Jackal (OG 1039, ABV 3.7%)
A superbly balanced, easy-drinking beer with a lively hop and citrus dominated aroma. This leads into a tasty blend of hops and grapefruit that slowly dries out into a long, bitter finale.

Norfolk Lavender Honey (ABV 3.7%)

Wolf In Sheep's Clothing (OG 1039, ABV 3.7%)
A malty aroma with fruity undertones introduce this reddish-hued mild. Malt, with a bitter background that remains throughout, is the dominant flavour of this clean-tasting beer.

Bitter (OG 1041, ABV 3.9%)
Pale brown with a toffee malt aroma. The initial smoky malt flavour sits uneasily with the increasing bitterness that grows into a long, astringent finish.

Coyote Bitter (OG 1044, ABV 4.3%)
A well-balanced golden brew with a hop and citrus aroma. The dominant hoppy bitterness is countered by a malty, slightly sweet backdrop. Complex flavours continue to mix as the dry, bitter ending slowly fades.

Straw Dog (ABV 4.5%)

A smooth, subltly flavoured beer. An elderflower bouquet introduces a crisp citrus and hop taste that blends well with a soft, malty background. Initial bitterness slowly fades.

Granny Wouldn't Like It (OG 1049, ABV 4.8%) ◆
Red-brown with a pronounced malty bouquet. Bitterness increases throughout but is softened by a smoky malt background. Some roast notes and a gentle, fruity sweetness add depth.

Woild Moild (OG 1048, ABV 4.8%) ◆
Dark brown and creamy with overall roast-dominated flavour. Molasses and caramel add to the depth with more than a hint of sweetness also present. Finish somewhat more bitter and drier.

Wolverhampton & Dudley

See Marston's in the New Nationals section

Wonky Dog*

Wonky Dog Brewery, 34 New Street, Brightlingsea, Essex, CO7 0BZ
☎ (01206) 302185
✉ wonkydog@hotmail.co.uk
Tours by arrangement

⊗ Wonky Dog began brewing in spring 2007 on equipment from the Famous Railway Tavern Brewery. Local pubs and beer festivals are supplied.

Sunbeam (ABV 3.6%)

Whisky Galore (ABV 3.6%)

Tom Wood

See Highwood

Wooden Hand

Wooden Hand Brewery, Unit 3, Grampound Road Industrial Estate, Grampound Road, Truro, Cornwall, TR2 4TB
☎ (01726) 884596
✉ mel@woodenhand.co.uk
🌐 woodenhand.co.uk

⊗ Wooden Hand was founded in 2004 by Anglo-Swedish businessman Rolf Munding. The brewery is named after the Black Hand of John Carew of Penwarne, in the parish of Mevagissey – Carew lost his hand in fighting at the siege of Ostend in the reign of Elizabeth I. The brewery supplies around 50 outlets with a high percentage being sold further afield via wholesalers. A bottling line was installed in 2005, which also bottles for other breweries.

Pirates Gold (OG 1040.6, ABV 4%)
A slightly tart pale session bitter with hop aroma, light fruit yet malty underlying flavour and tangy fruit finish.

Cornish Buccaneer (OG 1043.6, ABV 4.3%)
A golden beer with full flavour hop character, good fruit and hop balance and a long, dry finish.

Black Pearl (OG 1050.6, ABV 4.5%)
A rich, nutty stout with good hop balance and dry chocolate finish.

Cornish Mutiny (OG 1048.6, ABV 4.8%)
Rich, full-bodied strong ale with distinctive full hop character. Slightly biscuity and complex flavour with full mouth finish.

Woodforde's SIBA

Woodforde's Norfolk Ales, Broadland Brewery, Woodbastwick, Norwich, Norfolk, NR13 6SW
☎ (01603) 720353
✉ info@woodfordes.co.uk
🌐 woodfordes.co.uk
Shop Mon-Fri 10.30am-4.30pm; Sat & Sun 11.30am-4.30pm (01603 722218)
Tours by arrangement (Tue & Thu evenings)

Founded in 1981 in Drayton, Woodforde's moved to Erpingham in 1982, and then moved again to a converted farm complex in Woodbastwick, with greatly increased production capacity, in 1989. A major expansion took place in 2001 to more than double production and included a new brewery shop and visitor centre. Woodforde's runs two tied houses with around 600 outlets supplied on a regular basis. Bottle-conditioned beers are available.

Mardler's (OG 1035, ABV 3.5%) ◆
The gentle malt signature of the aroma and first taste subsides slowly to be replaced by a mix of sweetness and roast. Smooth drinking with an underlying fruitiness.

Wherry (OG 1037.4, ABV 3.8%) ◆
Refreshingly hoppy with citrus overtones in both taste and aroma. The initial dry hoppiness is supported by a sweet lemony background that continues as the hops slowly subside.

Sundew Ale (OG 1039, ABV 4.1%)
A subtle golden beer, pale in colour and light on the palate with a distinct hoppy finish.

Nelson's Revenge (OG 1042.7, ABV 4.5%) ■ ◆
A rich, complex best bitter, with a beautiful mix of sweetness, malt, citrus, hop, and caramel, leading to an equally interesting long, satisfying finish. Copper-coloured with a smooth, warming mouthfeel.

Norfolk Nog (OG 1046.8, ABV 4.6%) ■ ◆
Well-balanced dark brown porter with a heavy roast malt character. Plenty of sweetness and caramel to add depth, countered by an underlying hoppy bitterness. Strong finish.

Admiral's Reserve (OG 1050, ABV 5%) ◆
Light tasting for its strength but well balanced throughout. Malt and caramel on the nose and initial flavour with a growing hop influence. Quick finish with a gentle bitterness.

Headcracker (OG 1065.7, ABV 7%) □ ◆
Surprisingly clean-tasting for a barley wine. A booming, plummy aroma buttressed with malt continues to become the dominant taste. A pleasant winey bitterness gives a counterpoint while a dry sultana plumminess provides a fitting finale.

Norfolk Nip (OG 1076, ABV 8.5%)

Dark mahogany in colour, this intensely flavoured beer has a stunning range of malts and hops enveloped by a warming balanced bitterness.

Woodlands SIBA

Woodlands Brewing Co, Unit 4-6, Creamery Industrial Estate, Station Road, Wrenbury, Cheshire, CW5 8EX
☎ (01270) 620101
✉ info@woodlandsbrewery.co.uk
🌐 woodlandsbrewery.co.uk
Shop 8am-5pm daily
Tours by arrangement

The brewery opened in 2004 with a five-barrel plant from the former Khean Brewery. The beers are brewed using water from a spring that surfaces on a nearby peat field at Woodlands Farm. There are plans to upgrade to a 10-barrel plant. 120 outlets are supplied including the brewery's first tied house, the Globe in Nantwich. Bottle-conditioned beers are available.

Mild (OG 1035, ABV 3.5%)

Drummer (OG 1039, ABV 3.9%) ◆
Clean, malty session bitter with lasting dry finish and increasing bitterness in the aftertaste.

Old Willow (OG 1041, ABV 4.1%)

Oak Beauty (OG 1042, ABV 4.2%) ◆
Malty, sweetish copper-coloured bitter with toffee and caramel flavours. Long-lasting and satisfying bitter finish.

IPA (OG 1043, ABV 4.3%) ◆
Pale, dry and very bitter beer with sharp initial tartness leading to a moderate fruitiness. Good citrus hop throughout but not strong enough for an IPA. Good dry aftertaste.

Bitter (OG 1044, ABV 4.4%)

Midnight Stout (OG 1044, ABV 4.4%) ◆
Classic creamy dry stout with roast flavours to the fore. Well-balanced with bitterness and good hops on the taste and a good dry, roasty aftertaste. Some sweetness.

Bees Knees (OG 1045, ABV 4.5%)

Redwood (ABV 4.9%)

Gold Brew (OG 1050, ABV 5%) ◆
Strong malty nose with fruit and sweetness balanced in the flavour. Hint of caramel and a dry finish.

Generals Tipple (OG 1055, ABV 5.5%)

Wood SIBA

Wood Brewery Ltd, Wistanstow, Craven Arms, Shropshire, SY7 8DG
☎ (01588) 672523
✉ mail@woodbrewery.co.uk
🌐 woodbrewery.co.uk
Tours by arrangement

The brewery opened in 1980 in buildings next to the Plough Inn, still the brewery's only tied house. Steady growth over the years included the acquisition of the Sam Powell Brewery and its beers in 1991. Production averages 70 barrels a week and around 200 outlets are supplied. Seasonal beers: see website. A monthly beer is also brewed.

Quaff (ABV 3.7%)
A pale and refreshing light bitter with a clean, hoppy finish.

Craven Ale (ABV 3.8%)
An attractively coloured beer with a pleasant hop aroma and a refreshing taste.

Parish Bitter (OG 1040, ABV 4%) ◆
A blend of malt and hops with a bitter aftertaste. Pale brown in colour.

Shropshire Lass (OG 1048, ABV 4.1%)
A golden ale with zesty bitterness.

Special Bitter (OG 1042, ABV 4.2%) ◆
A tawny brown bitter with malt, hops and some fruitiness.

Pot O' Gold (OG 1044, ABV 4.4%)

Shropshire Lad (OG 1045, ABV 4.5%)
A strong, well-rounded bitter, drawing flavour from a fine blend of selected English malted barley and Fuggles and Golding hops.

Old Sam (OG 1047, ABV 4.6%)
A dark copper ale with a ripe, rounded flavour and hop bitterness.

Wonderful (OG 1048, ABV 4.8%) ◆
A mid-brown, fruity beer, with a roast and malt taste.

Worfield

Worfield Brewing Co, All Nations Brewhouse, Coalport Road, Madeley, Shropshire, TF7 6DP
☎ (01746) 769606
✉ mike@worfieldbrew.fsbusiness.co.uk
🌐 worfieldbrewery.co.uk

Worfield began brewing in 1993 at the Davenport Arms and moved to Bridgnorth in 1998. Following the reopening of the All Nations in Madeley, the brewery produced Dabley Ale for the pub and in 2004 relocated to the All Nations. Around 200 outlets are supplied. Seasonal beers: Winter Classic (ABV 4.5%, Jan), Spring Classic (ABV 4.5%, Mar), Summer Classic (ABV 4.5%, Jun), Autumn Classic (ABV 4.5%), Ironfounders (ABV 4.6%), Bedlam Strong Bitter (ABV 5.2%), Redneck (ABV 5.5%, Xmas).

Coalport Dodger Mild (OG 1034, ABV 3.5%)

Dabley Ale (OG 1039, ABV 3.8%)

OBJ (OG 1043, ABV 4.2%) ◆
A light and sweet bitter; delicate flavour belies the strength.

Shropshire Pride (OG 1045, ABV 4.5%)

Dabley Gold (OG 1050, ABV 5%)

George Wright

George Wright Brewing Co, Unit 11, Diamond Business Park, Sandwash Close, Rainford, Merseyside, WA11 8LU
☎ (01744) 886686
✉ sales@georgewrightbrewing.co.uk
🌐 georgewrightbrewing.co.uk
Tours by arrangement

George Wright started production in 2003. The original 2.5-barrel plant was replaced by a five-barrel one, which has since been upgraded again to 25 barrels with production of 200 casks a week.

Black Swan (ABV 3.8%)
A dark, distinctive beer. Very creamy and full of malty flavour.

Drunken Duck (ABV 3.9%) ◆
Fruity gold-coloured bitter beer with good hop and a dry aftertaste. Some acidity.

Longboat (ABV 3.9%) ◆
Good hoppy bitter with grapefruit and an almost tart bitterness throughout. Some astringency in the aftertaste. Well-balanced, light and refreshing with a good mouthfeel and long, dry finish.

Pipe Dream (ABV 4.3%) ◆
Refreshing hoppy best bitter with a fruity nose and grapefruit to the fore in the taste. Lasting dry, bitter finish.

Pure Blonde (ABV 4.6%)
A premium blonde beer, very light in colour with a herbal nose, moreish floral taste and sweet finish.

Cheeky Pheasant (ABV 4.7%)

Roman Black (ABV 4.8%)

Blue Moon (ABV 4.9%) ◆
Easy-drinking strong, gold-coloured beer. Good malt/bitter balance and well hopped.

Wychwood

See Marston's in New Nationals section

Wye Valley SIBA

Wye Valley Brewery, Stoke Lacy, Herefordshire, HR7 4HG
☎ (01885) 490505
✉ sales@wyevalleybrewery.co.uk
🌐 wyevalleybrewery.co.uk
Shop Mon-Fri 10am-4pm
Tours by arrangement

Wye Valley was founded in 1985 in Canon Pyon, Herefordshire. The following year it moved to an old stable block behind the Barrels pub in Hereford and 2002 saw another move to the former Symond's Cider site at Stoke Lacy, upping capacity to brew 80 barrels a day. Growth and investment continue with the installation of a bottling line in autumn 2008 and plans for a new brewhouse in 2009. Bottle-conditioned beers are available.

Bitter (OG 1037, ABV 3.7%) ◆
A beer whose aroma gives little hint of the bitter hoppiness that follows right through to the aftertaste.

HPA (OG 1040, ABV 4%) ◆
A pale, hoppy, malty brew with a hint of sweetness before a dry finish.

Dorothy Goodbody's Golden Ale (OG 1042, ABV 4.2%)
A light, gold-coloured ale with a good hop character throughout.

Butty Bach (OG 1046, ABV 4.5%)
A burnished gold, full-bodied premium ale.

Dorothy Goodbody's Wholesome Stout (OG 1046, ABV 4.6%) ◆
A smooth and satisfying stout with a bitter edge to its roast flavours. The finish combines roast grain and malt.

Wylam SIBA

Wylam Brewery Ltd, South Houghton Farm, Heddon on the Wall, Northumberland, NE15 0EZ
☎ (01661) 853377
✉ admin@wylambrewery.co.uk
🌐 wylambrew.co.uk
Tours by arrangement

Wylam started in 2000 on a 4.5-barrel plant, which increased to nine barrels in 2002. New premises and brew plant (20 barrels) were installed on the same site in 2006. The brewery delivers to more than 200 local outlets and beers are available through wholesalers around the country. Seasonal beers: see website.

Bitter (OG 1039, ABV 3.8%) ◆
A refreshing, copper-coloured, hoppy bitter with a clean, bitter finish.

Hedonist (OG 1038, ABV 3.8%)

Gold Tankard (OG 1040, ABV 4%) ◆
Fresh, clean flavour, full of hops. This golden ale has a hint of citrus in the finish.

Magic (OG 1042, ABV 4.2%) ◆
Light, crisp and refreshing. Floral and spicy with a good bitter finish.

Whistle Stop (OG 1045, ABV 4.4%)

Northern Kite (OG 1046.5, ABV 4.5%)

Bohemia (OG 1046, ABV 4.6%) ◆
Tawny in colour with a heady bouquet of malt and hops, and a deep finish of fruit.

Haugh (OG 1046, ABV 4.6%) ◆
A smooth velvet porter packed with flavour. Roast malt and a slight fruitiness provide a satisfying beer with a smooth finish.

Landlords Choice (OG 1046, ABV 4.6%)
A single malt pale bitter.

Rocket (OG 1048, ABV 5%)
A copper-coloured strong bitter.

Wyre Piddle

Wyre Piddle Brewery Ltd, Highgrove Farm, Peopleton, Nr Pershore, Wiltshire, WR10 2LF
☎ (01905) 841853
✉ strongbow1@btopenworld.com
🌐 wyrepiddle.com

⊗ Wyre Piddle was established in 1992. The brewery relocated and upgraded its equipment in 1997 and moved to its current location in 2002, where it has continued to expand. The beers can be found in pubs throughout the UK and around 100 pubs are supplied directly in the Midlands. It also brews for Green Dragon, Malvern: Dragon's Downfall (ABV 3.9%). For Severn Valley Railway: Royal Piddle (ABV 4.2%) and for Inn Express: Usual (ABV 3.9%), Same Again (ABV 4.2%), Down the Hatch (ABV 4.8%). Seasonal beers: Piddle in the Sun (ABV 5.2%, summer), Yule Piddle (ABV 4.5%, Xmas).

Piddle in the Hole (OG 1039, ABV 3.9%) ◆
Copper-coloured and quite dry, with lots of hops and fruitiness throughout.

Piddle in the Dark (ABV 4.5%)
A rich ruby-red bitter with a smooth flavour.

Piddle in the Wind (ABV 4.5%) ◆
This drink has a superb mix of flavours. A hoppy nose continues through to a lasting aftertaste, making it a good, all-round beer.

Piddle in the Sun/Snow (ABV 5.2%) ◆
A dry, strong taste all the way through draws your attention to the balance between malt and hops in the brew. A glorious way to end an evening's drinking.

Yard of Ale*

Yard of Ale Brewing Company Ltd, Surtees Arms, Chilton Lane, Ferryhill, County Durham, DL17 0DH
☎ (01740) 655724
☎ 07828 712744
✉ surteesarms@btconnect.com
🌐 thesurteesarms.co.uk

Yard of Ale started brewing in April 2008 on a 2.5 barrel plant. Seasonal beers and bottle-conditioned ales are planned.

First Yard (ABV 3.8%)

Yates' SIBA

Yates' Brewery, The Inn at St Lawrence, Undercliff Drive, St Lawrence, Isle of Wight, PO38 1XG
☎ (01983) 731731

Office: Unit 6, Dean Farm, Whitwell Road, Whitwell, Ventnor, Isle of Wight, PO38 2AB
✉ info@yates-brewery.fsnet.co.uk
🌐 yates-brewery.co.uk
Tours by arrangement

Brewing started in 2000 on a five-barrel plant at the Inn at St Lawrence. Yates' now has 50 regular outlets. Seasonal beer: Yule B Sorry (ABV 5.5%, Xmas), Wight Winter (ABV 5%). Bottle-conditioned beers are also available.

Best Bitter (ABV 3.8%)
Initial sweetness is quickly balanced by subtle fruitiness and moderate hop bitterness. A full-flavoured beer with a bittersweet aftertaste.

Undercliff Experience (OG 1040, ABV 4.1%)
An amber ale with a bittersweet malt and hop taste with a dry, lemon edge that dominates the bitter finish.

Blonde Ale (OG 1045, ABV 4.5%)
A golden beer with a malty aroma, laced with floral, citrus hops. The taste is hoppy and bitter to start, with smooth malt support and light lemon notes. Dry, hoppy aftertaste.

Holy Joe (OG 1050, ABV 4.9%) ◆
Strongly bittered golden ale with pronounced spice and citrus character, and underlying light hint of malt.

Special Draught (OG 1056, ABV 5.5%) ◆
Easy-drinking strong, amber ale with pronounced tart bitterness and a refreshing bite in the aftertaste.

Yates

Yates Brewery Ltd, Ghyll Farm, Westnewton, Wigton, Cumbria, CA7 3NX
☎ (01697) 321081
✉ enquiry@yatesbrewery.co.uk
🌐 yatesbrewery.co.uk
Tours by arrangement

Cumbria's oldest micro-brewery, established in 1986. The brewery was bought in 1998 by Graeme and Caroline Baxter, who had previously owned High Force Brewery in Teesdale. Deliveries are mainly to its Cumbrian stronghold and the A69 corridor as far as Hexham. A brewhouse and reed bed effluent system have been added on the same site. Around 40 outlets are supplied. Seasonal beers: see website.

Bitter (OG 1035, ABV 3.7%) ◆
A well-balanced, full-bodied bitter, golden in colour with complex hop bitterness. Good aroma and distinctive flavour.

Fever Pitch (OG 1039, ABV 3.9%) ◆
Skilful use of lager malt and hops results in a pale beer with a light bitterness; melon fruit and a clean, refreshing finish.

Sun Goddess (OG 1042, ABV 4.2%) ◆
A complex honeyed beer, packed with tropical fruit.

Yeovil

Yeovil Ales Ltd, Unit 5, Bofors Park, Artillery Road, Lufton Trading Estate, Yeovil, Somerset, BA22 8YH
☎ (01935) 414888
✉ rob@yeovilales.com
🌐 yeovilales.com
Tours by arrangement

⊗ Yeovil Ales was established in 2006 with an 18-barrel plant. The brewery supplies free trade pubs throughout the South-west. Seasonal beers are brewed.

Glover's Glory (OG 1038, ABV 3.8%)

Star Gazer (OG 1039, ABV 4%)

Summerset (OG 1040, ABV 4.1%)

Yetman's

Yetman's Brewery, c/o 37 Norwich Road, Holt, Norfolk, NR25 6SA
☎ 07774 809016
✉ peter@yetmans.net
🌐 yetmans.net

⊗ A 2.5-barrel plant built by Moss Brew was installed in restored medieval barns in 2005. The brewery supplies local free trade outlets. Bottle-conditioned beers are available.

Red (OG 1036, ABV 3.8%)

Orange (OG 1040, ABV 4.2%) ◆
A distinctly malty beer in both taste and aroma. Copper coloured with a sustained bitter edge that becomes slightly astringent in the long finish.

Green (OG 1044, ABV 4.8%)

Yorkshire Dales

Yorkshire Dales Brewing Co Ltd, Seata Barn, Elm Hill, Askrigg, North Yorkshire, DL8 3HG
☎ (01969) 622027
☎ 07818 035592
✉ rob@yorkshiredalesbrewery.com
🌐 yorkshiredalesbrewery.com

Situated in the heart of the Yorkshire Dales, brewing started in 2005. Installation of a new five-barrel plant and additional fermenters at the converted milking parlour have increased capacity to 20 barrels a week. Over 100 pubs are supplied throughout the North of England. A monthly special is always available.

Butter Tubs (OG 1037, ABV 3.7%)
A pale golden beer with a dry bitterness complemented by strong citrus flavours and aroma.

Booze Moor (OG 1039, ABV 3.8%)
A pale ale with fruitiness throughout and a short, bitter finish.

Buckden Pike (OG 1040, ABV 3.9%)
A blonde beer with a crisp, fruity finish.

Herriot Country Ale (OG 1041, ABV 4%)
A straw-coloured pale ale with a good, hoppy flavour balance.

Nappa Scar Gold (OG 1041, ABV 4%)
A golden ale with citrus and peach flavours throughout.

Askrigg Ale (OG 1043, ABV 4.3%)
A pale golden ale with intense aroma that generates a crisp, dry flavour with a long, bitter finish.

Yorkshire Penny (OG 1046, ABV 4.5%)
Classic dry stout with rich liquorice and chocolate malt flavours.

York SIBA

York Brewery Co Ltd, 12 Toft Green, York, North Yorkshire, YO1 6JT
☎ (01904) 621162
✉ info@yorkbrew.co.uk
🌐 yorkbrew.co.uk
Shop Mon-Sat 12-6pm
Tours by arrangement (ring for daily tour times)

York started production in 1996, the first brewery in the city for 40 years. It has a visitor centre with bar and gift shop, and was designed as a show brewery, with a gallery above the 20-barrel plant and viewing panels to fermentation and conditioning rooms. The brewery owns several pubs and in 2006 additional space was acquired to increase production capacity. More than 400 outlets are supplied. Seasonal beers: see website.

Guzzler (OG 1036, ABV 3.6%)
Refreshing golden ale with dominant hop and fruit flavours developing throughout.

Stonewall (OG 1038, ABV 3.8%)
Balanced amber bitter where maltiness underlines strong hop and fruit aromas and flavours.

Decade (OG 1040, ABV 4.1%)
A light, hoppy beer with undertones of grapefruit in both aroma and palate.

Yorkshire Terrier (OG 1041, ABV 4.2%)
Refreshing and distinctive amber/gold brew where fruit and hops dominate the aroma and taste. Hoppy bitterness remains assertive in the aftertaste.

Centurion's Ghost Ale (OG 1051, ABV 5.4%)
Dark ruby in colour, full-tasting with mellow roast malt character balanced by light bitterness and autumn fruit flavours that linger into the aftertaste.

Young's

See Wells & Young's in New Nationals section

Zerodegrees SIBA

Blackheath: Zerodegrees Microbrewery, 29-31 Montpelier Vale, Blackheath, London, SE3 0TJ
☎ (020) 8852 5619

Bristol: Zerodegrees Microbrewery, 53 Colston Street, Bristol, BS1 5BA
☎ (0117) 925 2706

Reading: 9 Bridge Street, Reading, Berkshire, RG1 2LR
☎ (0118) 959 7959

Cardiff: 27 Westgate Street, Cardiff, CF10 1DD
✉ info@zerodegrees.co.uk
🌐 zerodegrees.co.uk
Tours by arrangement

Brewing started in 2000 in London and incorporates a state-of-the-art, computer-controlled German plant, producing unfiltered and unfined ales and lagers, served from tanks using air pressure (not CO2). Four pubs are owned. All beers are suitable for vegetarians and vegans. All branches of Zerodegrees follow the same concept of beers with natural ingredients. There are regular seasonal specials including fruit beers.

Fruit Beer (OG 1040, ABV 4%)
The type of fruit used varies during the year.

Wheat Ale (OG 1045, ABV 4.2%)
Refreshing wheat ale with spicy aroma; banana, vanilla and sweet flavours; dry, lasting finish.

Pale Ale (OG 1046, ABV 4.6%)
American-style IPA with complex fruit aroma and peach flavours. Clean bitter finish with long aftertaste.

Black Lager (OG 1048, ABV 4.8%)
Light, Eastern European-style black lager brewed with roasted malt. Refreshing coffee finish.

Pilsner (OG 1048, ABV 4.8%)
Clean-tasting refreshing Pilsner with a malty aroma and taste, accompanied by delicate bitterness and citrus fruits.

> Not all chemicals are bad. Without chemicals such as hydrogen and oxygen, for example, there would be no way to make water, a vital ingredient in beer.
> **Dave Barry**

R.I.P.

The following breweries have closed, gone out of business, suspended operations or merged with another company since the 2008 Guide was published:

Barefoot, Stannington, Northumberland
Blanchfields, Rochford, Essex
Bryn, Denbigh, NE Wales
Canavans, Liverpool, Merseyside
Carter's, Machen, Glamorgan
Cock & Hen, Fulham, London
Cuckoo, Hastings, East Sussex
Custom, Haywards Heath, West Sussex
Danelaw, Chellaston, Derbyshire
Dobbins & Jackson, Caerleon, Gwent
Doghouse, Scorrier, Cornwall
Dunkery, Exford, Somerset
Eagles Bush, Ham, Berkshire
Edale, Edale, Derbyshire
Eglesbrech, Falkirk, Scotland
Farmers Arms, Newton-in-Furness, Cumbria
Far North, Melvich, Scotland
Fellows, Morton & Clayton, Nottingham, Nottinghamshire
Frog & Parrot, Sheffield, South Yorkshire
Garton, Garton on the Wolds, East Yorkshire
Grand Union, Hayes, Middlesex
Juwards, Wellington, Somerset
Mash, London
Masters, Wellington, Somerset
Moorcock, Hawes, North Yorkshire
Nags Head, Abercych, Pembrokeshire
Owl, Oldham, Lancashire
Rosebridge, Wigan, Greater Manchester
Star, Steeple, Essex
Tarka, Yelland, Devon
Turkey, Keighley, West Yorkshire
Webbs, Cwm, Gwent
Weobley, Weobley, Herefordshire
Wharfedale, Skipton, North Yorkshire
White Star, Northam, Hampshire
Winchester, Southampton, Hampshire

Future breweries

The following new breweries have been notified to the Guide and will start to produce beer during 2008/2009. In a few cases, they were in production during the summer of 2008 but were too late for a full listing in the Guide:

Adur, Steyning, West Sussex
Birmingham, Nechells, Birmingham, West Midlands
Blackbeck, Egremont, Cumbria
Bollington, Bollington, Cheshire
Brew Company, Sheffield, South Yorkshire
Brewery at Dorking, Dorking, Surrey
Brockhampton, Whitbourne, Worcestershire
Buxton, Buxton, Derbyshire
Crown Inn, Little Staughton, Bedfordshire
Fifield Farm, Oxfordshire
Fox & Newt, Leeds, West Yorkshire
Full Moon Brewery, Henley Down, East Sussex
Leeming Waters, Oxenhope, West Yorkshire
Luckie Ales, Auchtermuchty, Kingdom of Fife, Scotland
Morrissey Fox, Marton Cum Grafton, North Yorkshire
Old Cross, Hertford, Hertfordshire
Old Farm, Whitebrook, Monmouthshire
Stringer, Ulverston, Cumbria
Thorne, Thorne, South Yorkshire
Trent Navigation, Nottingham, Nottinghamshire
White Hart, Weeley Heath, Essex

New nationals

The rapid growth of Greene King, Marston's and Wells & Young's since 2000 has given them the status of national breweries. Marston's is the new name for Wolverhampton & Dudley Breweries while Wells & Young's was formed when Young & Co of London closed its brewery in 2006 and all production was moved to Bedford. The new nationals do not match the size of the global brewers but they do reach most areas of Britain as a result of both their tied and free trade activities. Unlike the global producers or the old national brewers who disappeared in the 1990s, Greene King, Marston's and W&Y are committed to cask beer production. Greene King IPA is the biggest-selling standard cask beer in the country, closely followed by Young's Bitter, Marston's Pedigree now outsells Draught Bass in the premium sector, and Wells Bombardier is one of the fastest-growing premium cask brands. There is a down-side to this progress: in some parts of the country, the choice of real ale is often confined to the products of Greene King and Marston's, and their continued expansion, seen in the takeovers of Belhaven, Hardys & Hansons, Jennings, Refresh (Brakspear and Wychwood), Ringwood and Ridley's, is cause for concern for drinkers who cherish choice and diversity.

Greene King

Greene King plc, Westgate Brewery, Bury St Edmunds, Suffolk, IP33 1QT
☎ **(01284) 763222**
✉ **solutions@greeneking.co.uk**
🌐 **greeneking.co.uk**
Shop Mon-Sat 10am-5pm; Sun 12-4pm
Tours 11am, 2pm and evening by arrangement

⊗ Greene King has been brewing in the market town of Bury St Edmunds since 1799. In the 1990s it bought the brands of the former Morland and Ruddles breweries and has given a massive promotion to Old Speckled Hen, which in bottled form is now the biggest ale brand in Britain. As a result of buying the former Morland pub estate, the company acquired a major presence in the Thames Valley region. But it has not confined itself to East Anglia or the Home Counties. Its tenanted and managed pubs, which include Old English Inns and Hungry Horse, total more than 2,100 while the assiduous development of its free trade sales, totalling more than 3,000 outlets, means its beers can be found as far from its home base as Wales and the north of England. In 2005 Greene King bought and rapidly closed Ridley's of Essex. Also in 2005, the group bought Belhaven of Dunbar in Scotland. Belhaven has a large pub estate that has enabled Greene King to build sales north of border. In 2006 the group bought Hardys & Hansons in Nottingham, taking its pub estate to close to 3,000. Seasonal beers: Rumpus (ABV 4.5%, Jan), Prospect (ABV 4.1%, May), Triumph Ale (ABV 4.3%, May), Ale Fresco (ABV 4.3%, Jun), Tolly Original (ABV 3.8%, Aug), Ruddles Orchard (ABV 4.2%, Sep), Old Bob (ABV 5.1%, Sep), Firewall (ABV 4.5%, Nov). Bottle-conditioned beer: Hen's Tooth (ABV 6.5%).

XX Mild (OG 1035, ABV 3%)

H&H Mild (OG 1035, ABV 3.1%)

IPA (OG 1036, ABV 3.6%) ◆
Delightfully hoppy but thin beer with a surprisingly sweet and fruity finish. A good session beer if kept well.

Ruddles Best Bitter (OG 1037, ABV 3.7%) ◆
An amber/brown beer, strong on bitterness but with some initial sweetness, fruit and subtle, distinctive Bramling Cross hop. Dryness lingers in the aftertaste.

H&H Bitter (OG 1038, ABV 3.9%)

Morland Original Bitter (OG 1039, ABV 4%)

H&H Olde Trip (OG 1043, ABV 4.3%)

Ruddles County (OG 1048, ABV 4.3%) ◆
Sweet, malty and bitter, with a dry and bitter aftertaste.

Old Speckled Hen (OG 1045, ABV 4.5%) ◆
Smooth, malty and fruity, with a short finish.

Abbot Ale (OG 1049, ABV 5%)
A full-bodied, distinctive beer with a bittersweet aftertaste.

Belhaven

Belhaven Brewing Co, Spott Road, Dunbar, East Lothian, EH42 1RS
☎ **(01368) 862734**
✉ **info@belhaven.co.uk**
🌐 **belhaven.co.uk**
Shop open during tours
Tours by arrangement

⊛ Belhaven is located in Dunbar, some 30 miles east of Edinburgh on the East Lothian coast. The company claimed to be the oldest independent brewery in Scotland but it lost that independence when Greene King bought it. Belhaven owns 275 tied pubs and has around 2,500 direct free trade accounts. Seasonal beers: Fruit Beer (ABV 4.6%, Jul), Fruity Partridge (ABV 5.2%, Dec).

60/- Ale (OG 1030, ABV 2.9%) ◆
A fine but virtually unavailable example of a Scottish light. This bittersweet, reddish-brown beer is dominated by fruit and malt with a hint of roast and caramel, and increasing bitterness in the aftertaste.

70/- Ale (OG 1038, ABV 3.5%) ◆
This pale brown beer has malt and fruit and some hop throughout, and is increasingly bittersweet in the aftertaste.

Sandy Hunter's Traditional Ale (OG 1038, ABV 3.6%) ◆
A distinctive, medium-bodied beer. An aroma of malt and hops greets the nose. A hint of roast combines with the malt and hops to give a bittersweet taste and finish.

80/- Ale (OG 1040, ABV 4.2%)
One of the last remaining original Scottish 80 Shillings, with malt the predominant flavour characteristic, though it is balanced by hop and fruit. Those used to hops as the leaders in a beer's taste may find this complex ale disconcerting.

St Andrew's Ale (OG 1046, ABV 4.9%)
A bittersweet beer with lots of body. The malt, fruit and roast mingle throughout with hints of hop and caramel.

For Edinburgh Brewing Co (qv):

Edinburgh Pale Ale (ABV 3.4%)

For Maclay pub group (qv):

Signature (OG 1038, ABV 3.8%)
A pronounced malty note is followed by a digestive biscuit flavour. The beer has a late addition of Goldings and Styrian hops.

Kane's Amber Ale (ABV 4%)
A hoppy aroma gives way to a malty yet slightly bitter flavour.

Wallace IPA (ABV 4.5%)
A classic IPA in both colour and style, with a long, dry finish.

Golden Scotch Ale (ABV 5%)
Brewed to an original Maclay's recipe, the emphasis is firmly on malt.

Marston's

Marston's plc, Marston's House, Wolverhampton, West Midlands, WV1 4JT
☎ (01902) 711811
✉ enquiries@marstons.co.uk
🌐 wdb.co.uk

Marston's, formerly Wolverhampton & Dudley, has grown with spectacular speed in recent years. It became a 'super regional' in 1999 when it bought both Mansfield and Marston's breweries, though it quickly closed Mansfield. In 2005 it bought Jennings of Cockermouth and announced it would invest £250,000 in Cumbria to expand fermenting and cask racking capacity. In total, Marston's owns 2,537 pubs and supplies some 3,000 free trade pubs and clubs throughout the country. It no longer has a stake in Burtonwood Brewery (qv) but brews Burtonwood Bitter for the pub estate, which is owned by Marston's. It added a further 70 pubs in 2006 when it bought Celtic Inns for £43.6 million. In January 2007 it paid £155 million for the 158-strong Eldridge Pope pub estate. In July 2007 it bought Ringwood in Hampshire.

Banks's & Hanson's

Banks's Brewery, Park Brewery, Wolverhampton, West Midlands, WV1 4NY
Contact details as above

Banks's was formed in 1890 by the amalgamation of three local companies. Hanson's was acquired in 1943 but its Dudley brewery was closed in 1991. Hanson's beers are now brewed in Wolverhampton, though its pubs retain the Hanson's livery. Banks's Original, the biggest-selling brand, is a fine example of West Midlands mild ale but the name was changed to give it a more 'modern' image. Beers from the closed Mansfield Brewery are now brewed at Wolverhampton. Hanson's Mild has been discontinued.

Mansfield Dark Mild (OG 1035, ABV 3.5%)

Original (OG 1036, ABV 3.5%)
An amber-coloured, well-balanced, refreshing session beer.

Riding Bitter (OG 1035, ABV 3.6%)

Bitter (OG 1038, ABV 3.8%)
A pale brown bitter with a pleasant balance of hops and malt. Hops continue from the taste through to a bittersweet aftertaste.

Mansfield Cask Ale (OG 1038, ABV 3.9%)

For Burtonwood pub group:

Bitter (OG 1036.8, ABV 3.7%)
A well-balanced, refreshing, malty bitter, with a good hoppiness. Fairly dry aftertaste.

Brakspear

Brakspear Brewing Co, Eagle Maltings, The Crofts, Witney, Oxfordshire, OX28 4DP
☎ (01993) 890800
✉ info@brakspear-beers.co.uk
🌐 brakspear-beers.co.uk
Merchandise available online
Tours by arrangement

Brakspear, along with Wychwood (see below) was bought by Marston's in March 2007. Brakspear was originally based in Henley-on-Thames and is one of Britain's oldest breweries, founded before 1700 and run by the Brakspear family since 1779. In 2002, the brewery closed and became a pub company. Refresh UK, a company based in Witney and owners of Wychwood, bought the rights to the Brakspear brands and brewed them again from 2004 after moving the Henley equipment – including the famous 'double drop' fermenters – to Witney. NB Pubs that carry the Brakspear name belong to a separate company that has no connection with Brakspear Brewing Co, though the brewery does supply the pub company with beer. Bottle-conditioned beers are available.

Bitter (OG 1035, ABV 3.4%)
A classic copper-coloured pale ale with a big hop resins, juicy malt and orange fruit aroma, intense hop bitterness in the mouth and finish, and a firm maltiness and tangy fruitiness throughout.

Oxford Gold (OG 1040, ABV 4%)

Jennings

Jennings Bros plc, Castle Brewery, Cockermouth, Cumbria, CA13 9NE
☎ 0845 129 7185
🌐 jenningsbrewery.co.uk
Shop Mon-Fri 9am-5pm; Sat 10am-4pm; Sun 10am-4pm (Jul & Aug)
Tours daily (except Sun); 7 days a week Jul & Aug. Booking advised. Other tours by arrangement

◎Jennings Brewery was established as a family concern in 1828 in the village of Lorton. The company moved to its present location in

1874. Pure Lakeland water is still used for brewing, drawn from the brewery's own well, along with Maris Otter barley malt and Fuggles and Goldings hops. Regular specials reflect the Cumbrian heritage of Jennings and include Crag Rat (ABV 4.3%), Fish King (ABV 4.3%), Golden Host (ABV 4.3%), Tom Fool (4%).

Dark Mild (OG 1031, ABV 3.1%) ◆
A well-balanced, dark brown mild with a malty aroma, strong roast taste, not over-sweet, with some hops and a slightly bitter finish.

Bitter (OG 1035, ABV 3.5%) ◆
A malty beer with a good mouthfeel that combines with roast flavour and a hoppy finish.

Cumberland Ale (OG 1039, ABV 4%) ◆
A light, creamy, hoppy beer with a dry aftertaste.

Cocker Hoop (OG 1044, ABV 4.6%)
A rich, creamy, copper-coloured beer with raisiny maltiness balanced with a resiny hoppiness, with a developing bitterness towards the end.

Sneck Lifter (OG 1051, ABV 5.1%) ◆
A strong, dark brown ale with a complex balance of fruit, malt and roast flavours through to the finish.

Marston's

Marston, Thompson & Evershed, Marston's Brewery, Shobnall Road, Burton upon Trent, Staffordshire, DE14 2BW
☎ (01283) 531131
🌐 wdb.co.uk

Marston's has been brewing cask beer in Burton since 1834 and the current site is the home of the only working 'Burton Union' fermenters, housed in rooms known collectively as the 'Cathedral of Brewing'. Burton Unions were developed in the 19th century to cleanse the new pale ales of yeast. Only Pedigree is fermented in the unions but yeast from the system is used to ferment the other beers.

Burton Bitter (OG 1037, ABV 3.8%) ◆
Overwhelming sulphurous aroma supports a scattering of hops and fruit with an easy-drinking sweetness. The taste develops from the sweet middle to a satisfyingly hoppy finish.

Pedigree (OG 1043, ABV 4.5%) ◆
Sweet beer with a slight sulphur aroma. Has the hoppy but sweet finish of a short session beer.

Old Empire (OG 1057, ABV 5.7%) ◆
Sulphur dominates the aroma over malt. Malty and sweet to start but developing bitterness with fruit and a touch of sweetness. A balanced aftertaste of hops and fruit leads to a lingering bitterness.

For InBev UK:

Draught Bass (OG 1043, ABV 4.4%) ◆
Pale brown with a fruity aroma and a hint of hops. Hoppy but sweet taste with malt, then a lingering hoppy bitterness.

Ringwood

Ringwood Brewery Ltd, Christchurch Road, Ringwood, Hampshire, BH24 3AP
☎ (01425) 471177
✉ enquiries@ringwoodbrewery.co.uk
🌐 ringwoodbrewery.co.uk
Shop Mon-Fri 9.30am-5pm; Sat 9.30am-12pm
Tours by arrangement

Ringwood was bought in July 2007 by Marston's for £19 million. The group plans to increase production to 50,000 barrels a year. Some 750 outlets are supplied and seven pubs are owned. Seasonal beers: Boondoggle (ABV 4%, summer), Bold Forester (ABV 4.2%, spring), Huffkin (ABV 4.4%, autumn), XXXX Porter (ABV 4.7%, winter). Bottle-conditioned beers are also available.

Best Bitter (OG 1038, ABV 3.8%)
Fortyniner (OG 1049, ABV 4.9%)

Brewery organisations

There are three organisations mentioned in the Breweries section to which breweries can belong. The Independent Families Brewers of Britain (IFBB) represents around 35 regional companies still owned by families. As many regional breweries closed in the 1990s, the IFBB represents the interests of the survivors, staging events such as the annual Cask Beer Week to emphasise the important role played by the independent sector. The Society of Independent Brewers (SIBA) represents the growing number of small craft or micro brewers: some smaller regionals are also members. SIBA is an effective lobbying organisation and played a leading role in persuading the government to introduce Progressive Beer Duty. It has also campaigned to get large pub companies to take beers from smaller breweries and has had considerable success with Enterprise Inns, the biggest pubco. The East Anglian Brewers' Co-operative (EAB) was the brainchild of Brendan Moore at Iceni Brewery. Finding it impossible to get their beers into pub companies and faced by the giant power of Greene King in the region, the co-op makes bulk deliveries to the genuine free trade and also sells beer at farmers' markets and specialist beer shops. EAB also buys malt and hops in bulk for its members, thus reducing costs.

Old Thumper (OG 1055, ABV 5.6%)

Wychwood

Wychwood Brewery Ltd, Eagle Maltings, The Crofts, Witney, Oxfordshire, OX28 4DP
☎ (01993) 890800
✉ info@wychwood.co.uk
🌐 wychwood.co.uk
Shop Sat 2-6pm
Tours by arrangement

Wychwood Brewery is located on the fringes of the ancient medieval forest, the Wychwood. The brewery was founded in 1983 on a site dating back to the 1880s, which was once the original maltings for the town's brewery. A range of seasonal beers is produced, including Dog's Bollocks.

Hobgoblin (OG 1045, ABV 4.5%)
The beer was reduced in strength early in 2008 by the previous owner, Refresh UK.

Wells & Young's IFBB

Wells & Young's Brewing Co, Bedford Brewery, Havelock Street, Bedford, MK40 4LU
☎ (01234) 272766
✉ postmaster@wellsandyoungs.co.uk
🌐 wellsandyoungs.co.uk
Merchandise available online
Tours by arrangement

Wells & Young's was created in 2006 when Young's of Wandsworth, south London, announced it would close its brewery and transfer production to Bedford. The new company jointly owns the Bedford Brewery, which opened in 1976; the Wells family has been brewing in the town since 1876. Wells & Young's has a combined sales team that has expanded sales of such key brands as Wells Bombardier, the fastest-growing premium cask beer in Britain, and Young's Bitter, the fastest-growing standard cask bitter. Wells and Young's runs separate pub estates. In 2007, Scottish & Newcastle reached an agreement with W&Y to brew Courage beers at Bedford. A new company, Courage Brands Ltd, was created, with W&Y controlling 83% of the shares. The deal added a further 80,000 barrels a year at Bedford, taking volumes to more than 550,000-600,000 barrels and overtaking Greene King in size. The Courage beers are aimed primarily at the free trade. Some Wells' beers are now available in Young's pubs and vice-versa. Wells owns 250 pubs and 245 serve cask beer; Young's owns 215 pubs in London and the Home Counties. Seasonal beer: Young's Waggledance (ABV 4%). There are several occasional beers. Bottle-conditioned beers: Young's Bitter (ABV 4.5%). Young's Kew Gold (ABV 4.8%), Young's Special London Ale (ABV 6.4%).

Eagle IPA (OG 1035, ABV 3.6%) ◆
A refreshing, amber session bitter with pronounced citrus hop aroma and palate, faint malt in the mouth, and a lasting dry, bitter finish.

Young's Bitter (OG 1036, ABV 3.7%) ◆
Citrus hops on the nose linger into the palate where the bitterness grows, but the overall character of this pleasant bitter is balanced by maltiness that was not so noticeable in the Wandsworth version.

Wells Bombardier (OG 1042, ABV 4.3%) ◆
Gentle citrus hop is balanced by traces of malt in the mouth, and this pale brown best bitter ends with a lasting dryness. Sulphur often dominates the aroma, particularly with younger casks.

Young's Special (OG 1044, ABV 4.5%) ◆
A malty, slightly sweet pale brown beer with lemon fruitiness and a bitterness that lingers. Some hoppiness on the palate and aftertaste.

Young's Winter Warmer (OG 1055, ABV 5%) ◆
Dark roasted malt is noticeable throughout this smooth, sweetish, ruby-black-brown beer with raisin and caramel notes in both flavour and aftertaste. The aroma can be slightly perfumed.

For Courage Brands:
Courage Best Bitter (OG 1038.3, ABV 4%)

Courage Directors Bitter (OG 1045.5, ABV 4.8%)

SIBA Direct Delivery Scheme

In 2003 the Society of Independent Brewers (SIBA) launched a Direct Delivery Scheme (DDS) that enables its members to deliver beer to individual pubs rather than to the warehouses of pub companies. Before the scheme came into operation, small craft brewers could only sell beer to the national pubcos if they delivered beer to their depots. In one case, a brewer in Sheffield was told by Punch Taverns that the pubco would only take his beer if he delivered it to a warehouse in Liverpool and then returned to pick up the empty casks. In the time between delivery and pick-up, some of the beer would have been delivered by Punch to . . . Sheffield.

Now SIBA has struck agreements with Admiral Taverns, Edinburgh Woollen Mills, Enterprise Inns, New Century Inns, Orchard Pubs, and Punch, as well as off-licence chains Asda and Thresher to deliver direct to their pubs or shops. The scheme has been such a success that DDS is now a separate but wholly-owned subsidiary of SIBA. See www.siba.co.uk/dds

Global giants

Eight out of ten pints of beer brewed in Britain come from the international groups listed below. Most of these huge companies have little or no interest in cask beer. Increasingly, their real ale brands are produced for them by smaller regional brewers. The major change at the top of the industry was the takeover of Britain's biggest brewer, Scottish & Newcastle, by Carlsberg and Heineken in 2008. Carlsberg now controls S&N's interests in Russia and the Baltic and owns outright the Baltika breweries, along with Kronenbourg in France. Heineken now owns S&N's British interests including S&N Pub Enterprises, an estate of 1,170 pubs.

Anheuser-Busch UK

Anheuser-Busch UK, Thames Link House, 1 Church Road, Richmond, Surrey, TW9 2QW
☎ (020) 8332 2302

The company brews 'American' Budweiser at the Stag Brewery, Lower Richmond Road, Mortlake, London SW14 7ET, the former Watney's plant, which is now run as a joint operation with Scottish & Newcastle (qv). Budweiser in bottle, can and keg is brewed from rice (listed first on the label), malt and hops, with planks of wood – the famous beechwood chips – used to clarify the beer. Not to be confused with the classic Czech lager, Budweiser Budvar.

Carlsberg UK

Carlsberg Brewing Ltd, PO Box 142, The Brewery, Leeds, West Yorkshire, LS1 1QG
☎ (0113) 259 4594
carlsberg.co.uk/carlsberg.com

Tetley, the historic Leeds brewery with its open Yorkshire Square fermenters, now answers to the name of Carlsberg UK: Carlsberg-Tetley was unceremoniously dumped in 2004. A wholly-owned subsidiary of Carlsberg Breweries of Copenhagen, Denmark, Carlsberg is an international lager giant. In Britain its lagers are brewed at a dedicated plant in Northampton, while Tetley in Leeds produces ales and some Carlsberg products. Some 140,000 barrels are produced annually. Tetley's cask brands receive little or no promotional support outside Yorkshire, most advertising being reserved for the nitro-keg version of Tetley's Bitter.

Tetley's Dark Mild (OG 1031, ABV 3.2%) ◆
A reddish, mid-brown beer with a light malt and caramel aroma. A well-balanced taste of malt and caramel follows, with good bitterness and a satisfying finish.

Tetley's Mild (OG 1034, ABV 3.3%) ◆
A mid-brown beer with a light malt and caramel aroma. A well-balanced taste of malt and caramel follows, with good bitterness and a satisfying finish.

Ansells Best Bitter (OG 1035, ABV 3.7%)

Tetley's Cask Bitter (OG 1035, ABV 3.7%) ◆
A variable, amber-coloured light, dry bitter with a slight malt and hop aroma, leading to a moderate bitterness with a hint of fruit, ending with a dry and bitter finish.

Tetley's Imperial (ABV 4.3%)

Draught Burton Ale (OG 1047, ABV 4.8%) ◆
A beer with hops, fruit and malt present throughout, and a lingering complex aftertaste, but lacking some hoppiness compared to its Burton original. Carlsberg-Tetley also brews Greenalls Bitter (ABV 3.8%) for former Greenalls pubs supplied by wholesalers. Greenalls Mild has been discontinued.

Coors

Coors Brewers Ltd, 137 High Street, Burton upon Trent, Staffordshire, DE14 1JZ
☎ (01283) 511000
coorsbrewers.com

Coors of Colorado established itself in Europe in 2002 by buying part of the former Bass brewing empire, when Interbrew (now InBev) was instructed by the British government to divest itself of some of its interests in Bass. Coors owns several cask ale brands. It brews 110,000 barrels of cask beer a year (under licensing arrangements with other brewers) and also provides a further 50,000 barrels of cask beer from other breweries. In July 2008 Coors announced it was to launch two new cask beers: Red Shield (4.2%) and draught White Shield (5%). The beers will be brewed for Coors by Marston's. The bottled version of White Shield will be re-branded as 'Export White Shield'.

M&B Mild (OG 1034, ABV 3.2%)

Brewed for Coors by Everards:

Hancock's HB (OG 1038, ABV 3.6%) ◆
A pale brown, slightly malty beer whose initial sweetness is balanced by bitterness but lacks a noticeable finish. A consistent if inoffensive Welsh beer brewed for Coors by Brains.

Worthington's Bitter (OG 1038, ABV 3.6%)
A pale brown bitter of thin and unremarkable character.

M&B Brew XI (OG 1039.5, ABV 3.8%)
A sweet, malty beer with a hoppy, bitter aftertaste.

Worthington's White Shield (ABV 5.6%) ◆
Bottle-conditioned. Fruity aroma with malt touches. Fruity start with hops but the fruit lasts to a classic bitter finish.

Brewed under licence by Highgate Brewery, Walsall:

Stones Bitter (OG 1037, ABV 3.7%)

White Shield Brewery

White Shield Brewery, Horninglow Street, Burton-upon-Trent, Staffordshire, DE14 1YQ
☎ 0845 600 0598

Tours by arrangement

The White Shield Brewery – formerly the Museum Brewing Co – was based in the Museum of Brewing, and is part of Coors. Confusingly, while it brews White Shield, the beer is now a Coors brand (see above). The brewery opened in 1994 and recreated some of the older Bass beers that had been discontinued. In March 2008 Coors announced the visitor centre and museum, formerly the Bass Museum, would close at the end of June. The brewery continues to brew but production may be moved to another pilot plant within the Coors' complex, known as the Samuel Allsopp Brewery. Production is divided 50:50 between cask and bottled beers. Imperial Stout and No 1 Barley Wine are now brewed on an occasional basis and in bottle only, though draught versions are supplied to CAMRA festivals when supplies are available.

Worthington's St Modwen (OG 1038, ABV 4.2%) ◆
Hop and malt aroma. Delicate taste of hops and orange. Flowery citrus fruity finish.

Brewery Tap (OG 1042, ABV 4.5%)

Worthington E (OG 1044, ABV 4.8%)

Czar's Imperial Stout (OG 1078, ABV 8%) ◆
A library of tastes, from a full roast, liquorice beginning, dark toffee, brown sugar, molasses, Christmas pudding, rum, dark chocolate to name but a few. Fruit emerges, blackberry changing to blackcurrant jam, then liquorice root.

No 1 Barley Wine (OG 1105, ABV 10.5%) ◆
Unbelievably fruity! Thick and chewy, with fruit and sugar going in to an amazing complex of bitter, fruity tastes. Brewed in summer and fermented in casks for 12 months.

Guinness

Guinness closed its London brewery in 2005. All Guinness keg and bottled products on sale in Britain are now brewed in Dublin.

InBev UK

InBev UK Ltd, Porter Tun House, 500 Capability Green, Luton, Bedfordshire, LU1 3LS
☎ (01582) 391166
✉ name.surname@interbrew.co.uk
⊕ inbev.com

A wholly-owned subsidiary of InBev of Belgium and Brazil. Interbrew of Belgium became the world's biggest brewer in 2004 when it merged with Brazil's leading producer, Ambev, leapfrogging Anheuser-Busch in the production stakes. InBev bought Anheuser-Busch in July 2008. Its international name is now InBev and it is a major player in the European market with such lager brands as Stella Artois and Jupiler. It has some interest in ale brewing with the cask- and bottle-conditioned wheat beer, Hoegaarden, and the Abbey beer Leffe. It has a ruthless track record of closing plants and disposing of brands. In the summer of 2000 it bought both Bass's and Whitbread's brewing operations, giving it a 32 per cent market share. The British government told Interbrew to dispose of parts of the Bass brewing group, which were bought by Coors (qv). Draught Bass has declined to around 100,000 barrels a year: it once sold more than two million barrels a year, but was sidelined by the Bass empire. It is now brewed under licence by Marston's (see New Nationals section). Only 30 per cent of draught Boddingtons is now in cask form and this is brewed under licence by Hydes of Manchester (qv Independents section).

Scottish & Newcastle/Heineken

Scottish & Newcastle/Heineken, 2-4 Broadway Park, South Gyle Broadway, Edinburgh, EH12 9JZ
☎ (0131) 528 1000
⊕ scottish-newcastle.com (will be heinekeninternational.com)

Scottish & Newcastle/Heineken is Britain's biggest brewing group with close to 30 per cent of the market. At the time of going to press, it had not been decided whether the group would continue to be called S&N or would change to Heineken. Scottish & Newcastle was formed in 1960, a merger between Scottish Brewers (Younger and McEwan) and Newcastle Breweries. In 1995 it bought Courage from its Australian owners, Foster's. Since the merger that formed Scottish Courage, the group has rationalised by closing its breweries in Edinburgh, Newcastle, Nottingham, Halifax and the historic Courage (George's) Brewery in Bristol. The remaining beers were transferred to John Smith's in Tadcaster. It bought the financially stricken Bulmer's Cider group, which included the Beer Seller wholesalers, now part of WaverleyTBS. S&N/Heineken will continue to own Bulmer's. WaverleyTBS and the S&N pub estate. In 2003, S&N sold the Theakston's Brewery in Yorkshire back to the original family (see Theakston's entry in Independents section) but still brews some of the beers at John Smith's. In February 2004, S&N entered into an arrangement with the Caledonian brewery in Edinburgh that gave S&N a 30% stake in Caledonian and 100% control of the brewery's assets but in March 2008 S&N bought the whole of company, which is now a subsidiary of S&N/Heineken. S&N's sole Scottish cask beer, McEwan's 80/-, has been axed. The Courage brands are now brewed by Wells & Young's and owned by a new company, Courage Brands Ltd (see New Nationals section).

Berkshire

Berkshire Brewery, Imperial Way, Reading, Berkshire, RG2 0PN
☎ (0118) 922 2988

No cask beer. Due to close in 2010.

Caledonian

Caledonian Brewing Co Ltd, 42 Slateford Road, Edinburgh, EH11 1PH
☎ (0131) 337 1286
✉ info@caledonian-brewery.co.uk
⊕ caledonian-brewery.co.uk
Tours by arrangement

The brewery was founded by Lorimer & Clark in 1869 and was sold to Vaux of Sunderland in 1919. In 1987 the brewery was saved from closure by a management buy-out. The brewery site was purchased by S&N in 2004 and became a wholly-owned subsidiary of S&N/Heineken in 2008. A rolling programme of seasonal beers is produced. The Harviestoun Brewery (qv), which was a subsidiary of Caledonian, is now independent. The Caledonian beer range may change under new ownership.

Deuchars IPA (OG 1039, ABV 3.8%)

80 (OG 1042, ABV 4.1%)

XPA (ABV 4.3%)

Federation

Federation Brewery, Lancaster Road, Dunston, Gateshead, Tyne & Wear, NE11 9JR

The former co-operative brewery run by working men's clubs. S&N transferred production to Dunston when it closed its Tyneside plant in 2004 and bought Federation. 'Newcastle' Brown Ale is now brewed in Gateshead. No cask beer.

Royal

Royal Brewery, 201 Denmark Road, Manchester, M15 6LD

☎ (0161) 220 4371

Massive brewery in Manchester capable of producing 1.3 million barrels of beer a year. No cask beer.

John Smith's

John Smith's Brewery, Tadcaster, North Yorkshire, LS24 9SA

☎ (01937) 832091

scottish-newcastle.com (will be heinekeninternational.com)

Tours by arrangement

The brewery was built in 1879 by a relative of Samuel Smith (qv). John Smith's became part of the Courage group in 1970. Major expansion has taken place, with 11 new fermenting vessels installed. Traditional Yorkshire Square fermenters have been replaced by conical vessels.

John Smith's Bitter (OG 1035.8, ABV 3.8%) ◆
A copper-coloured beer, well-balanced but with no dominating features. It has a short hoppy finish.

For Theakston's of Masham (qv):

Theakston Best Bitter (OG 1038, ABV 3.8%)

Closure of the Bass Brewing Museum

At the end of June 2008, Coors closed its Visitor Centre in Burton-on-Trent, better known as the Bass Brewing Museum. The museum was created 27 years ago by Bass as a showcase for brewing in Burton, world-famous as the home of pale ale and India Pale Ale in the 19th century. It was taken over by Coors, when the American company bought the former Bass breweries early this century.

Coors said it costs £1 million year to maintain the centre and visitor numbers were falling – not surprising as it received no promotion locally or nationally. The closure led to uproar: the Burton Mail campaigned vigorously against Coor's plan, there was a march through the town and the local MP, Janet Dean, set up a steering group to see if the centre could be saved. Coors rapidly backtracked. The company said it would charge new owners just £1 a year rent, would make a one-off donation of £200,000 and an annual grant of £100,000. The steering group appointed a firm that specialises in saving museums to draw up a business plan for the site, with a view to turning it into a charitable trust that could apply for heritage lottery funding. As the Guide went to press, there was optimism that Britain's only national brewing museum could be saved.

The beers index

These beers refer to those in bold type in the breweries section (beers in regular production) and so therefore do not include seasonal, special or occasional beers that may be mentioned elsewhere in the text.

B

C

E

I

J

M

N

Q

R

S

T

U

V

W

Readers' recommendations

Suggestions for pubs to be included or excluded

All pubs are surveyed by local branches of the Campaign for Real Ale. If you would like to comment on a pub already featured, or on any you think should be featured, please fill in the form below (or copy it), and send it to the address indicated. Your views will be passed on to the branch concerned. Please mark your envelope with the county where the pub is, which will help us to direct the suggestion efficiently.

Pub name:

Address:

Reason for recommendation/criticism:

Pub name:

Address:

Reason for recommendation/criticism:

Pub name:

Address:

Reason for recommendation/criticism:

Your name and address:

Please send to: (Name of county) Section, Good Beer Guide,
230 Hatfield Road, St Albans, Hertfordshire AL1 4LW

Pub name:

Address:

Reason for recommendation/criticism:

Pub name:

Address:

Reason for recommendation/criticism:

Pub name:

Address:

Reason for recommendation/criticism:

Pub name:

Address:

Reason for recommendation/criticism:

Your name and address:

Please send to: (Name of county) Section, Good Beer Guide,
230 Hatfield Road, St Albans, Hertfordshire AL1 4LW

Pub name:

Address:

Reason for recommendation/criticism:

Pub name:

Address:

Reason for recommendation/criticism:

Pub name:

Address:

Reason for recommendation/criticism:

Pub name:

Address:

Reason for recommendation/criticism:

Your name and address:

Please send to: (Name of county) Section, Good Beer Guide,
230 Hatfield Road, St Albans, Hertfordshire AL1 4LW

Pub name:

Address:

Reason for recommendation/criticism:

Pub name:

Address:

Reason for recommendation/criticism:

Pub name:

Address:

Reason for recommendation/criticism:

Pub name:

Address:

Reason for recommendation/criticism:

Your name and address:

Please send to: (Name of county) Section, Good Beer Guide,
230 Hatfield Road, St Albans, Hertfordshire AL1 4LW

Pub name:

Address:

Reason for recommendation/criticism:

Pub name:

Address:

Reason for recommendation/criticism:

Pub name:

Address:

Reason for recommendation/criticism:

Pub name:

Address:

Reason for recommendation/criticism:

Your name and address:

Please send to: (Name of county) Section, Good Beer Guide,
230 Hatfield Road, St Albans, Hertfordshire AL1 4LW

Books for beer lovers

CAMRA Books, the publishing arm of the Campaign for Real Ale, is the leading publisher of books on beer and pubs. Key new titles include:

A Beer A Day

Jeff Evans

Written by leading beer writer Jeff Evans, *A Beer A Day* is a beer lover's almanac, crammed with beers from around the world to enjoy on every day and in every season, and celebrating beer's connections with history, sport, music, film and television. Why is 18 April a good day to seek out a bottle of Anchor's Liberty Ale? Which Fuller's beer best marks the date that the Grand National was first run? When would Brakspear's Triple go down a treat? Whether it is Christmas Eve, Midsummer's Day, Bonfire Night or just a wet Wednesday in the middle of October, *A Beer A Day* has just the beer for you to savour and enjoy.

£16.99 ISBN 978 1 85249 235 9

Good Beer Guide West Coast USA

Ben McFarland & Tom Sandham

Taking in the whole western seaboard of the USA, as well as Las Vegas, Alaska and Hawaii, this is a lively, comprehensive and entertaining tour that unveils some of the most exhilarating beers, breweries and bars on the planet. It is the definitive, totally independent guide to understanding and discovering the heart of America's thriving craft beer scene, and an essential companion for any beer drinker visiting West Coast America or seeking out American beer in the UK. Written with verve and insight by two respected young beer journalists, *Good Beer Guide West Coast USA* is a must – not just for those who find themselves on the West Coast, but for all discerning beer enthusiasts and barflies everywhere.

£14.99 ISBN 978 1 85249 244 1

Peak District Pub Walks

Bob Steel

A practical, pocket-sized travellers' guide to some of the best pubs and best walking in the Peak District, the book features 25 walks, as well as cycle routes and local attractions, helping you see the best of Britain's oldest national park while never straying too far from a decent pint. This book also explores some of the region's fascinating industrial heritage and has useful information about local transport and accommodation. Each route has been selected for its inspiring landscape, historic interest and beer – with the walks taking you on a tour of the best real-ale pubs the area has to offer.

£9.99 ISBN 978 1 85249 246 5

An Appetite for Ale

Fiona Beckett & Will Beckett

A beer and food revolution is underway in Britain and award-winning food writer Fiona Beckett and her publican son, Will, have joined forces to write the first cookbook to explore this exciting new food phenomenon that celebrates beer as a culinary tour-de-force. This collection of more than 100 simple and approachable recipes has been specially created to show